THE OXFORD HANDBOOK
OF CRIMINOLOGY

THE OXFORD HANDBOOK OF CRIMINOLOGY

SECOND EDITION

Edited by
MIKE MAGUIRE
ROD MORGAN
and
ROBERT REINER

OXFORD
UNIVERSITY PRESS

OXFORD
UNIVERSITY PRESS

Great Clarendon Street, Oxford OX2 6DP

Oxford University Press is a department of the University of Oxford.
It furthers the University's objective of excellence in research, scholarship,
and education by publishing worldwide in

Oxford New York

Athens Auckland Bangkok Bogotá Buenos Aires Calcutta
Cape Town Chennai Dar es Salaam Delhi Florence Hong Kong Istanbul
Karachi Kuala Lumpur Madrid Melbourne Mexico City Mumbai Nairobi
Paris São Paulo Shanghai Singapore Taipei Tokyo Toronto Warsaw

with associated companies in Berlin Ibadan

Oxford is a registered trade mark of Oxford University Press
in the UK and in certain other countries

Published in the United States
by Oxford University Press Inc., New York

British Library Cataloguing in Publication Data
Data available

Library of Congress Cataloging in Publication Data
Data available
ISBN 0-19-826297-3
ISBN 0-19-876485-5 (Pbk)

7 9 10 8 6

Printed in China

Preface

The first edition of *The Oxford Handbook of Criminology* was prepared in 1992–3 and published in 1994. The background to the enterprise was explained in the Introduction to the first edition and is expanded on in the Introduction which follows. Our editorial rationale has not changed. We wrote in 1994 that we hoped the *Handbook* would meet a teaching and research need. The sales of the first edition suggest that our hopes have not been disappointed. Our purpose with the second edition is the same as it was with the first, and is best summarized as follows.

First, we asked each of the thirty-one British scholars contributing to this collection of thirty-two original specially commissioned essays to provide a state-of-the-art map of their respective topics, drawing largely on British illustrative material. We asked them to draw on relevant theory and recent research, to point to policy developments and to highlight those aspects of current debate of which students and practitioners should be aware. We also asked them to provide a short guide to further reading and include comprehensive bibliographies so that students can follow up topics in greater detail.

Secondly, we selected contributors recognized for their research and scholarship, usually, though not always, in the topic areas about which we asked them to write. We have not stipulated the theoretical approach they should adopt, however, and we have approached scholars representing different perspectives. This is, as was the first edition, a collection of different voices. Our single ideal is that each author should review his or her respective literature, not intone any one vision.

Thirdly, we have tried to ensure that all the principal topics ordinarily included in criminology and criminology-related courses are covered. This was also our aim with the first edition, yet this collection differs from the first. This difference requires explanation.

The first edition proved to be a more complex task than we envisaged. In 1992–3 we approached several more potential authors than eventually contributed, and in the event not all the topics we wished to cover were covered. Some of the scholars we approached were unable to participate because of other commitments and we were not able always to find substitute authors. Moreover, because we gave our authors a relatively free hand regarding the manner in which they approached their subjects, the balance between chapters was not always as we anticipated. This inevitably led to some theoretical perspectives and substantive topics receiving less attention than they deserved. Coverage was not ideal, and this fact was reflected in the many comments received from colleagues or gleaned by our publishers.

The views collected from many of our readers coincided with our own, and this is reflected in the planning for the second edition, planning that has been made that much more easy by the familiarity that we as editors now have with our contributors, most of whom have not changed. The second edition incorporates two main changes. First, there is now a symposium of generally shorter essays covering theoretical issues of contemporary importance, an aspect of criminological study and research poorly represented in the first edition. Secondly, we have attempted to make the second edition more user-friendly, particularly for undergraduate students. The title pages now give a fuller indication of the topics covered, every chapter now incorporates an annotated guide to further reading, there is increased use of graphical illustrations in the text, and the general index is fuller.

Finally, the second edition is not merely revised; it is very up-to-date, the consequence of our authors' immersion in their subjects and the commitment of our publishers to publishing this text at a point in the year most convenient to our readers. Our authors all wrote their chapters during the winter of 1996–7. We delivered this text to Oxford University Press at the end of February 1997. The fact that it will be available to students six months later is a credit to everyone involved in the project at Oxford University Press. We would like to thank all our contributors for producing chapters of such a high standard while meeting such a demanding schedule.

MIKE MAGUIRE, ROD MORGAN, AND ROBERT REINER
March 1997

Contents

Notes on Contributors xiii

Introduction to Second Edition *Robert Reiner, Rod Morgan,*
 and Mike Maguire 1
 The Growth of Criminological Studies 1
 The Aims of the Oxford Handbook 3
 Theoretical and Methodological Considerations 3
 The Second Edition 5

Part I. General Theories of Crime and Control

Historical Development and Current Trends

1. Of Crimes and Criminals: The Development of Criminology
 in Britain *David Garland* 11
 The Contingency of the Criminological Present 11
 Orientations: A History of the Present 18
 Traditional Representations of Crime 21
 The Scientific Analysis of Crime in the Eighteenth and Early
  Nineteenth Centuries 23
 The Emergence of a Positive Science of the Criminal 30
 The Establishment of a Criminological Discipline in Britain 45

2. The History of Crime and Crime Control Institutions
 Clive Emsley 57
 The Extent of Crime 58
 The Offender 61
 The Police 65
 Prosecution and the Courts 74
 Punishment 76

3. Dumping the 'Hostages to Fortune'? The Politics of Law and
 Order in Post-War Britain *David Downes and Rod Morgan* 87
 British General Elections and 'Law and Order', 1945–1997 88
 Pressure-Group and Interest-Group Politics 112
 Matters of Scandal and Concern 121

4. Crime Statistics, Patterns, and Trends: Changing Perceptions
 and their Implications *Mike Maguire* 135
 Repainting the Canvas: The Production of New 'Knowledge'
  About Crime 135

Key Influences: The 'New Criminology', Victims, and the
    Situational Focus   143
The Official Picture   148
The Dark Figure Unmasked? The Advent of Crime Surveys   161
The 'Offender Population': Young, Male, and Poor?   172
Studies Other than Surveys   179

5. Media Made Criminality: The Representation of Crime
   in the Mass Media   *Robert Reiner*   189

Criminal Texts or Mental Chewing Gum? The Media and Crime Debate   189
The Content of Media Images of Crime   192
The Consequences of Media Images of Crime   210
The Causes of Media Representations of Crime   219

Core Analytical Perspectives

6. Sociological Theories of Crime   *Paul Rock*   233

Crime, Control, and Space   246
Radical Criminology   250
Functionalist Criminology   253
Signification   255

7. The Political Economy of Crime   *Ian Taylor*   265

The Business Cycle and Crime   266
The Political Economy of Inequality and Crime   272
The Costs of Crime and the Entry of Neo-Classical Economics   292
Crime and Free Market Society   297

8. Environmental Criminology   *Anthony E. Bottoms and Paul Wiles*   305

Environmental Criminology: A Brief History   307
Preliminary Methodological Issues   314
Explaining the Location of Offences   316
Explaining the Location of Offender Residence   330
The New Chicagoans   338
Bringing Together Explanations of Offence Locations and
    Offender Locations   342
Community Change and Crime   344
Crime and Late Modernity   349

9. Human Development and Criminal Careers   *David P. Farrington*   361

Conceptual and Methodological Issues   363
Development of Offending   367
Influences on Criminal Careers   382
Explaining the Development of Offending   395

Frontiers of Criminological Theory: A Symposium

10. Recent Social Theory and the Study of Crime and
    Punishment   *Richard Sparks*   409

Some Problems: Criminology as a 'Discipline' 410
Some Resources: Theory, Reflection, and Research 415
Some Big Issues: Action, Risk, Globalization 421
Social Theory, Criminology, and Politics 428

11. Criminology, Criminal Law, and Criminalization *Nicola Lacey* 437

The Relationship Between Criminology, Criminal Law, and Criminal
 Justice Studies 438
Criminal Law 440
What Can Criminology Bring to the Study of Criminal Law? 443
What Can Critical Criminal Law Bring to the Study of Criminology and
 Criminal Justice? 445
From Critical Criminal Law to Criminalization 448

12. Social Control *Barbara A. Hudson* 451

Defining Social Control 451
Criminology and the Control of Crime 452
The Sociology of Deviance and Control 453
From the Prison to the Community (and Back Again):
 Decarceration, Deinstitutionalization, and Transcarceration 460
Women and Social Control 464
Post-Social Control 465

13. Left Realist Criminology: Radical in its Analysis, Realist
in its Policy *Jock Young* 473

Being Realistic About Crime: The Critique of Left Idealism 474
Distancing From Crime: A Critique of Establishment Criminology 479
The Terrain of Change: Crime in an Age of Late Modernity 480
The Crisis of Aetiology and Penality 481
Left Realism: A Theoretical Synthesis 482
Being Tough on Crime Means Being Tough on Criminal Justice 491
Realist Strategies: Short-Term Gain, Long-Term Transformation 492

14. Censure, Crime, and State *Colin Sumner* 499

Hegemony Theory and the Social Censure of Crime 501
The Idea of the State and its Relation to the Hegemony Theory
 of the Social Censure of Crime 503

15. Feminism and Criminology *Loraine Gelsthorpe* 511

Setting the Scene for a Contemporary Review 511
The Intellectual Inheritance of Criminology 514
Feminism Within and Without Criminology: Feminist Assessments
 of the Interconnections Between Feminism and Criminology 516
Critical Reflections on Feminist Approaches to Criminology 525

16. Masculinities and Crimes *Tony Jefferson* 535

Orthodox Accounts and the 'Normal' Masculine Personality 536
The Social Break with Orthodoxy: Power and Multiple Masculinities 538

The Psycho-Analytic Break with Orthodoxy: Contradictory
  Subjectivities and the Social   539
Sexual Violence; Rape/Sexual Abuse/Murder   541
Youth Crime, Underclass Males, and Black Masculinity   549

17. Understanding Criminal Justice Comparatively   *David Nelken*   559

Approaches to Comparative Criminal Justice   561
Understanding the Control of Prosecution Discretion in Italy   565

Part II: Social Dimensions of Crime and Justice

18. Victims   *Lucia Zedner*   577

Classical Studies in Victimology   578
Mass Victimization Surveys   580
Local Crime Surveys   583
Fear of Crime   586
Impact of Victimization   590
The Victim Movement   595
Victims in the Criminal Justice System   597
Shifting Conceptions of Criminal Justice   602

19. Youth, Crime, and Justice   *Tim Newburn*   613

Images and Theories of 'Youth' and Deviance   614
Young People and Crime   626
Youth Justice   638

20. Mentally Disordered Offenders   *Jill Peay*   661

Mental Disorder and Offenders—A Case for Special Provision?   664
The Problem of Definition   666
Mentally Disordered Offender—A Minority Group?   669
Mental Disorder at Trial   679
Mental Disorder and Treatment   686
Protective Sentencing: Procedural Safeguards v. Treatment   692

21. Ethnic Origins, Crime, and Criminal Justice   *David J. Smith*   703

Conceptual Issues   705
Ethnic Minorities in Britain   707
Ethnic Minorities as Victims of Crime   711
Ethnic Minorities as Suspects and Offenders   720

22. Gender and Crime   *Frances Heidensohn*   761

The Prehistory of Gender and Crime   762
Women, Men, and Crime   764
Too Few to Count?   768
Domestic 'Secrets'   768
Women and Policing   769

Women and Sentencing 772
Gender Ratios and Gender Questions 773
Feminist Approaches to Criminology 773
Impact of Feminist Perspectives 775
Women and Crime 775
Women and Justice 778
Theorizing Women and Crime 784

Part III: Forms of Crime and Criminality

23. Criminal Collaboration: Youth Gangs, Subcultures,
    Professional Criminals, and Organized Crime *Dick Hobbs* 801

    Youth: Gangs and Subcultures 802
    British Studies 806
    Contemporary American Gang Research 813
    Professional Crime 815
    Organized Crime 822

24. Violent Crime *Michael Levi* 841

    The Risk of Violence 848
    Explaining Violence 859
    Dealing with Violent Crime 874

25. White-Collar Crime *David Nelken* 891

    Seven Types of Ambiguity 895
    The Ambivalent Response to White-Collar Crime 911

26. Drugs: Use, Crime, and Control *Nigel South* 925

    Legal Status and Properties of Drugs 925
    A Review of Post-War Trends in Drug Use 926
    The Control of Drugs: Britain and the Global Context 935
    Trends and Futures 950

Part IV: Criminal Justice Structures and Processes

27. Crime Prevention *Ken Pease* 963

    Crime Prevention Theory 965
    Primary Crime Prevention Research 969
    Focused Prevention: Hot Spots and Repeat Victimization 974
    Primary Crime Prevention: The Declining Years? 976
    The Re-Emergence of Community 980

28. Policing and the Police *Robert Reiner* 997

    Criminology and the Study of the Police 997
    The Development of Police Research 999

'Police' and 'Policing' 1003
Police Discretion: Its Nature, Operation, and Control 1008
Have the Police Got a Future? 1034

29. From Suspect to Trial   *Andrew Sanders* 1051
Models and Criminal Justice 1051
Police Decisions 'On the Street' 1054
Detention in the Police Station 1060
Prosecution and Diversion 1069
Pre-Trial Processes 1075
Reviewing Injustice 1080

30. Sentencing   *Andrew Ashworth* 1095
Sentencing and Politics 1095
Rationales for Sentencing 1096
The Mechanics of Sentencing 1102
Custodial Sentencing 1111
Non-Custodial Sentencing 1120
Sentencing Reform 1127

31. Imprisonment: Current Concerns and a Brief History
Since 1945   *Rod Morgan* 1137
The Emergence of the Modern Prison and the Use of Imprisonment 1141
The Mission: The Purpose of Imprisonment 1144
Who are the Prisoners? 1151
Organization, Privatization, and Accountability 1162
The Sociology of Prisons 1176
Future Prospects 1183

32. Community Penalties and the Probation Service   *George Mair* 1195
A Brief History of the Probation Service 1198
Community Penalties in 1995 1204
The Effectiveness of Community Penalties 1216

Index 1233

Notes on Contributors

MIKE MAGUIRE is Professor of Criminology and Criminal Justice at the University of Wales, Cardiff, having moved from the Oxford University Centre for Criminological Research in 1989. He has conducted major research projects and published in a wide variety of crime- and justice-related areas, writing principally on burglary, policing, prisons, victims, probation, and parole. His main publications include *Burglary in a Dwelling* (with Bennett, 1992), *Accountability and Prisons* (ed. with Morgan and Vagg, 1985), *The Effects of Crime and the Work of Victim Support Schemes* (with Corbett, 1987), *Victims of Crime: A New Deal?* (ed. with Pointing, 1988), *A Study of the Police Complaints System* (with Corbett, 1991), *The Conduct and Supervision of Criminal Investigations* (with Norris, 1992), *Prisons in Context* (ed. with King, 1994) and *Automatic Conditional Release: The First Two Years* (with Raynor, 1996). He has also published numerous papers in books and journals, in Britain and overseas. He is currently working on a book in the area of crime investigation, as well as a textbook on sentencing and the penal system, part of a series of which he is editor.

ROD MORGAN is Professor of Criminal Justice and Director of the Centre for Criminology and Criminal Justice in the Faculty of Law at the University of Bristol. He was an Assessor to the Woolf Inquiry into the disturbances at HM Prison Manchester and elsewhere in 1990 and has for many years acted as an expert advisor to Amnesty International and the Council of Europe on custodial conditions, conducting investigatory missions in many countries. Among his recent books are: *Coming to Terms with Policing* (ed. with Smith, 1989), *The Politics of Sentencing Reform* (ed. with Clarkson, 1995) and *The Future of Policing* (with Newburn, 1997). He has written on many aspects of criminal justice policy and is currently completing manuscripts on *Preventing Torture* (with Evans), *Crime Unlimited?* (a collection of essays edited with Carlen), and a new text on the prison system. His current research includes studies of: the prosecution of child abuse; the taking of victim statements and their use; and the incidence of violence in custodial settings.

ROBERT REINER is Professor of Criminology in the Law Department, London School of Economics, and Director of its Mannheim Centre for Criminology and Criminal Justice. He was formerly Reader in Criminology at the University of Bristol, and at Brunel University. He has a BA in Economics from Cambridge University (1967), an M.Sc. in Sociology (with Distinction) from the London School of Economics (1968), a Ph.D. in Sociology from

Bristol University (1976), and a Postgraduate Diploma in Law (with Distinction) from City University, London (1985).

He is author of *The Blue-Coated Worker* (Cambridge University Press, 1978), *The Politics of the Police* (Wheatsheaf, 1985; 2nd edn. 1992), *Chief Constables* (Oxford University Press, 1991), and editor of: (with M. Cross) *Beyond Law and Order* (Macmillan, 1991); (with S. Spencer) *Accountable Policing: Effectiveness, Empowerment and Equity* (London: Institute for Public Policy Research, 1993); (with M. Maguire and R. Morgan) *The Oxford Handbook of Criminology* (Oxford University Press, 1994), and *Policing Vols. I and II* (Aldershot: Dartmouth, 1996). He has published over 100 papers on policing and criminal justice topics. He is editor (with R. Morgan) of *Policing and Society: An International Journal of Research and Policy*, and was review editor of *The British Journal of Criminology* from 1987–95.

He was President of the British Society of Criminology from 1993–6. His present research is a study financed by the Economic and Social Research Council analysing changing media representations of crime and criminal justice since the Second World War.

ANDREW ASHWORTH is Vinerian Professor of English Law in the University of Oxford. He was Edmund-Davies Professor of Criminal Law and Criminal Justice from 1988 to 1997, having previously taught at the University of Manchester and at Worcester College, Oxford. He is an Associate of the Centre for Criminological Research, University of Oxford. He took his LLB at the London School of Economics (1968), followed by the BCL at Oxford University (1970) and a Ph.D. at Manchester University (1973). In 1993 he was awarded a Doctorate of Civil Law by Oxford University, and was elected a Fellow of the British Academy.

He has published journal articles and made contributions to books on a wide range of topics in criminal law and criminal justice. His books include *Principles of Criminal Law* (2nd edn., 1995), *Sentencing and Criminal Justice* (2nd edn., 1995), and *The Criminal Process: an Evaluative Study* (1994), and he co-edited (with Andrew von Hirsch) *Principled Sentencing* (1992). He has been editor of the *Criminal Law Review* since 1975, and general editor of the *Oxford Monographs on Criminal Law and Justice* since 1990. From 1989 to 1992 he was chairman of the Council of Europe's Select Committee on Sentencing.

ANTHONY BOTTOMS is Wolfson Professor of Criminology and Director of the Institute of Criminology at the University of Cambridge (1983–); he is also a Fellow of Fitzwilliam College, Cambridge. After graduating in Law at Oxford University, he was successively a student on the first post-graduate course in Criminology at the Cambridge Institute (1961–2), a direct-entrant probation officer, and a member of the Institute's research contract staff. In 1968, he was appointed as the first Lecturer in Criminology in the Faculty of Law, University of Sheffield; subsequently he became professor of

Criminology (1976–84) and Dean (1981–84) in the same Faculty. His interests within Criminology are wide-ranging, and he has written on topics as diverse as: the pre-trial process as viewed by defendants; social inquiry reports; the nature and effectiveness of community penalties; prisons; the sociology of punishment; dangerousness; urban crime and environmental criminology; and crime prevention. In 1996, he received the Sellin-Glueck Award of the American Society of Criminology for international contributions to criminology.

DAVID DOWNES is Professor of Social Administration at the London School of Economics. He has been a Senior Research Fellow at Nuffield College, Oxford, and an academic visitor at a number of universities in Europe and North America, including the University of Toronto, the University of California at Berkeley, the Free University of Amsterdam, and the University of Bologna. He has served on committees of the ESRC and NACRO and was editor of the *British Journal of Criminology*. He is the author, editor, and co-author of several works on delinquency, penal policy, and criminological theory. Among his more recent books is *Contrasts in Tolerance*, a study comparing British and Dutch penal policies.

CLIVE EMSLEY is Professor of History at the Open University. He was educated at the University of York and at Peterhouse, Cambridge. He has taught at the Open University since 1970, with temporary leaves at the University of Calgary, Alberta, Griffith University, Queensland, and the University of Paris VIII (St. Denis). Since 1995 he has been President of the International Association for the History of Crime and Criminal Justice.

His publications include *Policing and its Context 1750–1870* (1983), *Crime and Society in England 1750–1900* (2nd edn., 1996) and *The English Police. A Political and Social History* (2nd edn., 1996). He edited, with Louis A. Knafla, *Crime History and Histories of Crime, Studies in the Historiography of Crime and Criminal Justice in Modern History* (1996).

DAVID P. FARRINGTON is Professor of Psychological Criminology at Cambridge University, where he has been on the staff since 1969. His major research interest is in the longitudinal study of delinquency and crime, and he is Director of the Cambridge Study in Delinquent Development, a prospective longitudinal survey of over 400 London males from age 8 to age 40, funded by the Home Office. He is also co-Principal Investigator of the Pittsburgh Youth Survey, a prospective longitudinal study of over 1,500 Pittsburgh males from age 7 to age 20. In addition to nearly 200 published papers on criminological and psychological topics, he has published sixteen books, one of which (*Understanding and Controlling Crime*, (1986)) won the prize for distinguished scholarship of the American Sociological Association Criminology Section. He is President of the European Association of Psychology and Law, a member of the advisory boards of the US National Juvenile Court Data Archive and the Netherlands Institute for the Study of Criminality and Law Enforcement, joint editor of the Cambridge Criminology Series and of the journal *Criminal Behaviour and Mental Health*, and a member of the editorial boards of fourteen other journals. He has been Acting Director of the Cambridge Institute of Criminology, President of the British Society of Criminology, Chair of the Division of Criminological and Legal Psychology of the British Psychological Society, Vice-Chair of the US National Academy of Sciences Panel on Violence, a member of the US National Academy of Sciences Committee on Law and Justice, a member of the US National Academy of Sciences Panel on Criminal Career Research, and a member of the national Parole Board for England and Wales. He is a Fellow of the British Psychological Society and of the American Society of Criminology, and an Honorary Life Member of the British Society of Criminology and of the Division of Criminological and Legal Psychology of the British Psychological Society. He received BA, MA, and Ph.D. degrees in Psychology from Cambridge University, and the Sellin-Glueck Award of the American Society of Criminology for international contributions to criminology.

DAVID GARLAND is Professor of Law and Sociology at New York University. From 1979 until 1997, he taught in the Centre for Law and Society, Edinburgh University. He has an LLB (1997) and a Ph.D. (1984) from Edinburgh University, and an MA in Criminology (1978) from Sheffield University. In 1984/85 he was a Davis Fellow in the Department of History, Princeton University, and in 1988 he was a Visiting Professor in Boalt Law School at the University of California, Berkeley. He is the author of *Punishment and Welfare* (1985) and *Punishment and Modern Society* (1990) and the editor, with Peter Young, of *The Power to Punish* (1983), and with Antony Duff, of *A Reader on Punishment* (1995). He is a past member of the Editorial Board of the *British Journal of Criminology*, a Trustee of the Law and Society Association, and a Fellow of the Royal Society of Edinburgh.

LORAINE GELSTHORPE is a University Lecturer in Criminology at the Institute of Criminology University of Cambridge, and a Fellow of Pembroke College, Cambridge. She has a BA (Hons.) from Sussex University (1977) and an M.Phil. in Criminology (1979) and a Ph.D. in Criminology from Cambridge University (1984). Her books include *Women and Sexism and the Female Offender* (1989), *Feminist Perspective in Criminology* (1990, co-edited with Allison Morris), and *Minority Ethnic Groups in the Criminal Justice System* (edited in 1993). She is also co-author (with Mark Liddle) of three Home Office publications on inter-agency aspects of crime prevention (*Organisational Arrangements for the Delivery of Crime Prevention, Co-operation and Local Delivery, Issues for Action* (1994)), and has recently completed a Home Office research study on women and sentencing.

   Her current interests revolve around the concepts of discretion, discrimination, and social exclusion in criminal justice: race and gender issues in pre-sentence and psychiatric reports, women and ethnic minorities and criminal justice, and the detention of asylum seekers. At the same time, she continues to write on youth justice, and to reflect on aspects of qualitative research methodologies. She is editor of the British Society of Criminology *Newsletter* and a member of the *Howard Journal* and *Women and Criminal Justice* editorial boards.

FRANCES HEIDENSOHN is Professor of Social Policy at Goldsmiths' College, University of London. She is the author of *Women in Crime* (1996, 2nd edn.) and *Women in Control? The Role of Women in Law Enforcement* (1992), and co-editor with N. Rafter of *International Feminist Perspectives in Criminology* (1995).

DICK HOBBS is Reader in the Department of Sociology and Social Policy University of Durham. He is the author of *Doing the Business* (Oxford, 1988), for which he was awarded the 1989 Abrams Prize by the British Sociological Association, and *Bad Business* (Oxford, 1995). He has also edited books on research methods (with Tim May) and professional crime. He is interested in ethnography, various forms of deviant behaviour, and contemporary working-class culture.

BARBARA HUDSON is Reader in Criminology, Division of Sociology, University of Northumbria at Newcastle. She teaches and researches within the fields of criminology, penology, and sociology of law, with particular interests in the impact of penal strategies on the marginalized and disadvantaged. Publications include *Justice Through Punishment: A Critique of the 'Justice Model' of Corrections* (Macmillan, 1987); *Penal Policy and Social Justice* (Macmillan, 1993); *Racism and Criminology*, edited, with Dee Cook (Sage, 1993); *Understanding Justice: An Introduction to Ideas, Perspectives and Controversies in Modern Penal Theory* (Open University Press, 1996) and *Race, Crime and Justice*, edited (Dartmouth, 1996). Her current research concerns conflicts between logics of 'risk prevention' and 'justice' in penal strategies and the problem of how to do 'justice' to 'difference'.

TONY JEFFERSON is Professor of Criminology at Keele University. He originally trained as a teacher at Loughborough College of Education (Cert. Ed. 1968; B.Ed. 1969), and spent three years as a PE teacher and part-time youth worker before doing postgraduate work at the Centre for Contemporary Cultural Studies, University of Birmingham (1972–7) where he gained his MA in Cultural Studies (1974). Between 1977 and 1996 he was at the University of Sheffield, first as Research Fellow, then teaching criminology. He has researched and published widely on questions to do with youth subcultures, the media, policing, race and crime, anxiety and fear of crime, methodology, and masculinity. His publications include: *Resistance Through Rituals* (1976, edited with Stuart Hall), *Policing The Crisis* (1978, with Stuart Hall, Chas

Critcher, John Clarke, and Brian Roberts), *Controlling the Constable* (1984) and *Interpreting Policework* (1987, both with Roger Grimshaw, *Introducing Policework* (1988, with Mike Brogden and Sandra Walklate), and *The Case Against Paramilitary Policing* (1991).

NICOLA LACEY is Professor of Law at Birkbeck College, University of London. Before moving to this post in 1995, she was Fellow and Tutor in Law at New College, Oxford, and an Associate of the Centre for Criminological Research at the University of Oxford, having moved to Oxford from a lectureship at University College London in 1984. She graduated in law from University College London and took the BCL at the University of Oxford in 1981. She works in the fields of criminal law, criminal justice, and legal and social theory. Her publications include *State Punishment: Political Principles and Community Values* (Routledge, 1988); with Celia Wells and Dirk Meure, *Reconstructing Criminal Law* (Weidenfeld and Nicolson, 1990); with Elizabeth Frazer, *The Politics of Community: A Feminist Analysis of the Liberal-Communitarian Debate* (Harvester Wheatsheaf, 1993); and *Criminal Justice: A Reader* (Oxford University Press, 1994). She has published a wide range of articles on criminal law and criminal justice, and is currently working with Lucia Zedner on an ESRC funded project examining appeals to 'community' in criminal justice policy in Britain and Germany.

MICHAEL LEVI is Professor of Criminology at the University of Wales, Cardiff, where he moved after studies at Oxford, Cambridge, and Southampton. His major current research interests are white-collar and organized crime, policing the money trail, and jury decision-making in white-collar crime trials. In Wales, his major research activities have been on drugs and crime, assaults against the South Wales police, and the prevention of alcohol-related disorder in Newport. His books include *The Phantom Capitalists* (1981), *Regulating Fraud* (1987), *The Investigation, Prosecution and Trial of Serious Fraud* (1992), and *Money-Laundering in the UK* (1994). His book (with Andrew Pithouse), *Victims of White-Collar Crime*, will be published by Oxford University Press in early 1998, and he is preparing a book on *Global Responses to Money-Laundering*.

GEORGE MAIR is E. Rex Makin Professor of Criminal Justice at Liverpool John Moores University. He was previously a member of the Home Office Research and Planning Unit, latterly (1988–95) as Principal Research Officer responsible for research into community penalties. He has an MA (1973) from the University of Glasgow, an M.Sc. from the University of Strathclyde (1976), and received his Ph.D. from the London School of Economics (1987).

He is the author of many Home Office research reports, and has also written *Part Time Punishment?: The Origins and Development of Senior Attendance Centres* (1991), edited *Evaluating the Effectiveness of Community Penalties*

(1997), and co-edited with Tim Newburn *Working With Men* (1996). He is currently Executive Secretary of the British Society of Criminology.

DAVID NELKEN took a degree in History and Law and a doctorate in Criminology at Cambridge University. He then taught at Edinburgh University (1976–84) and University College London (1984–90) before moving to the University of Macerata in Italy where he is Distinguished Professor of Sociology and Head of Department. He is also Distinguished Research Professor of Law at Cardiff Law School and Honorary Visiting Professor of Law at University College London. He has held various visiting appointments: in 1966 he taught a course on comparative criminal justice as Pro-Seminar Visiting European Professor at the Boalt Hall Law School, University of California, Berkeley, and in 1998 will be teaching as Visiting Professor in the Department of Sociology, New York University.

David Nelken's work in criminology lies in the areas of social and legal theory, white-collar and organized crime, criminal justice and comparative criminology. He is active on the editorial boards of criminological, criminal law, socio-legal, and political science journals in Italy, the UK, and the USA— and is joint general editor of the *Dartmouth International Library of Criminology, Criminal Justice and Penology*. His book *The Limits of the Legal Process: A Study of Landlords, Law and Crime* (Academic Press, 1983), received the 1985 American Sociological Association (Criminology section) Distinguished Scholar Award. Recent publications include *The Futures of Criminology* (Sage, 1994); *The European Yearbook of Sociology of Law* (Giuffrè, 1994, with Alberto Febbrajo); *White-Collar Crime* (Dartmouth, 1994); *Globalisation, Legal Culture and Diversity* (Sage, 1995); *Law as Communication* (Dartmouth, 1996); *The Corruption of Politics and the Politics of Corruption* (Blackwell, 1996, with Mike Levi); *Comparing Legal Cultures* (Dartmouth, 1997); *Issues in Comparative Criminology* (Dartmouth, 1997, with Piers Beirne); and *The Centre-Left in Power: Italian Politics 1996* (Westview Press, 1997, with Roberto D'Alimonte).

Practical involvements include serving as a panel member in the *Children's Hearings* system in Edinburgh (1979–84), and acting as consultant to the *Secure Cities* research, policy and training programme of the Emilia-Romagna Regional government in Italy (1994–).

TIM NEWBURN is Head of Crime, Justice and Youth Studies at the Policy Studies Institute and Visiting Professor, Goldsmiths College, University of London. He has a B.Sc. (1980) and Ph.D. (1988) in Sociology, both from the University of Leicester. Among his books are: *Permission and Regulation: Law and Morals in Post-War Britain* (1992); *Persistent Young Offenders*, and *Young Offenders and the Media*, both with A. Hagell (1994); *Democracy and Policing*, with T. Jones and D. J. Smith (1994); *Just Boys Doing Business: Men, Masculinities and Crime*, edited with E. A. Stanko (1995); *Crime and Criminal Justice Policy* (1995); *Themes in Contemporary Policing*, edited with

W. Saulsbury and J. Mott (1996); *Working With Men*, edited with G. Mair (1996); *The Future of Policing*, with R. Morgan (1997); and *Private Security and Public Policing*, with T. Jones (1997). He is chair of the Southern Branch of the British Society of Criminology, the editor of *Policy Studies*, on the editorial board of *Criminal Justice Matters*, and general editor of the *Longman Criminology Series*.

KEN PEASE is Professor of Criminology at Manchester University. A psychologist by first training, he has been consultant to the United Nations Crime Branch on crime trends, to the United Nations Drug Control Programme on drug seizure data, and to various criminal justice agencies in the UK and elsewhere. He has been Visiting Professor of Psychiatry at the University of Saskatchewan. He has served as a member of the parole Board and is currently the only academic member of the National Board for Crime Prevention. He has published on a variety of criminal justice topics, his books including *Crime and Punishment: Interpreting the Data* (with Keith Bottomley, Open University Press, 1986), *Police Work* (with Peter Ainsworth, British Psychological Society, 1987), *Sentencing Reform: Guidance or Guidelines?* (with Martin Wasik, Manchester University Press, 1987) and *Criminal Justice Systems in Europe and North America* (with Kristina Hukkila, HEVNI, 1990). He is currently particularly interested in the phenomenon of repeated victimization of the same people.

JILL PEAY is a Senior Lecturer in Law at the LSE and an Associate Tenant at Doughty Street Chambers. She was formerly a Research Fellow at the Oxford Centre for Criminological Research, a Visiting Assistant Professor in Canada at the School of Criminology, Simon Fraser University, and a member of the Law Department at Brunel University. She has a Ph.D. in Psychology from Birmingham University (1980) and sat for six years on the Advisory Board of the International Academy of Law and Mental Health. She is the author of *Tribunals on Trial: A Study of Decision-Making under the Mental Health Act 1983* (Clarendon Press, 1989), co-author of *The Director of Public Prosecutions: Principles and Practices for the Crown Prosecutor* (Tavistock, 1987) and editor of *Inquiries after Homicide* (Duckworth, 1996). She is currently editing a book on Crime and Mental Disorder.

PAUL ROCK is Professor of Social Institutions at the London School of Economics. He was formerly Director of the School's Mannheim Centre for the Study of Criminology and Criminal Justice, editor of the *British Journal of Sociology* and review editor of the *British Journal of Criminology*. He obtained a B.Sc. from the LSE (1964) and a D.Phil. (1970) as a student at Nuffield College, Oxford. He has been a Visiting Professor at Princeton University (1974–5); the University of California, San Diego (1972); Simon Fraser University (1976); and the University of British Columbia (1976); a Visiting Scholar at the Programs Branch of the Ministry of the Solicitor General of

Canada (1981); and a Fellow of the Center for Advanced Study in the Behavioral Sciences, Stanford, California (1996).

He is author of *Making People Pay* (1973); *Deviant Behaviour* (1973); *The Making of Symbolic Interactionism* (1979); (with David Downes) *Understanding Deviance* (revised 2nd edn., 1995); *A View from the Shadows: The Ministry of the Solicitor General of Canada and the Justice for Victims of Crime Initiative* (1987); *Helping Victims of Crime: The Home Office and the Rise of Victim Support in England and Wales* (1990); *The Social World of an English Crown Court* (1993); and *Reconstructing a Women's Prison: The Holloway Redevelopment Project 1968–88* (1996). Jointly and singly, he has edited a comparable number of books. He has just completed a history of the origins and development of practical and political responses to the aftermath of homicide.

ANDREW SANDERS is Professor of Criminal Law and Criminology at the University of Bristol. He was formerly Deputy Director of the Centre for Criminological Research, University of Oxford, and a Fellow of Pembroke College. Prior to that he lectured at the University of Birmingham and Manchester Polytechnic (as it was then called). He has an LLB from the University of Warwick and a masters degree in Criminology from the University of Sheffield. He is a member of the Parole Board. He has co-authored (with Mike McConville and Roger Leng) *The Case for the Prosecution* (1991) and (with Richard Young) *Criminal Justice* (1994), and has edited *Prosecution in Common Law Jurisdictions* (1996). He has written extensively on police, prosecutions, criminal justice, and victims.

DAVID J. SMITH is Professor of Criminology at the University of Edinburgh. After graduating in Psychology and Philosophy at Oxford University in 1963, he worked for eight years as a market researcher, and joined the Board of a market research agency. In 1972, he started a new career in social research with Political and Economic Planning (PEP), which later merged with another independent institution to form the Policy Studies Institute (PSI). From 1978–94 he was Senior Fellow of the Policy Studies Institute and Head of Social Justice and Social Order Group. In 1988–9 he was Visiting Fellow of Lincoln College, Oxford.

He has carried out studies in three principal fields: ethnic and religious minorities, and related issues of equality and social justice; life course development and school effectiveness; and crime and criminal justice. Particular interests are policing, explaining crime trends, and life course development and criminal careers. His books include *Racial Disadvantage in Britain* (1977); *Police Effect: A Study of Multi-Racial Comprehensives* (1989); *Inequality in Northern Ireland* (1991); *Racial Justice at Work* (1991); *Democracy and Policing* (1994); and *Psychosocial Disorders in Young People: Time Trends and Their Causes* (1995, with Michael Rutter). He is currently planning a long-term study of youth transitions and crime in Edinburgh.

NIGEL SOUTH is Reader in the Department of Sociology and Director of the Health and Social Services Institute at the University of Essex. Recent books include (with V. Ruggiero) *Eurodrugs: Drug Use, Markets and Trafficking in Europe* (UCL, 1995) and (co-edited with C. Samson) *The Social Construction of Social Policy* (Macmillan, 1996). With R. Weiss he recently completed editing *Comparing Prison Systems: Toward a Comparative and International Penology* (Gordon and Breach) and he is currently co-editing (with V. Ruggiero and I. Taylor) *European Criminology: Crime and Social Order in Europe* (Routledge), and (with P. Beirne) *For a Green Criminology*, as a special issue of *Theoretical Criminology*.

RICHARD SPARKS teaches criminology at Keele University, having previously worked in The Open University and the University of Cambridge. In addition to his interests in theoretical criminology, he has written on a number of aspects of prisons and penal policy including regimes in long-term prisons; prison disorders; international comparisons in prison populations; and the politics of prison privatization. He is co-editor (with John Muncie) of *Imprisonment: European Perspectives* (Harvester Wheatsheaf, 1991) and co-author (with Tony Bottoms and Will Hay) of *Prisons and the Problem of Order* (Oxford University Press, 1996). He is also the author of *Television and the Drama of Crime* (Open University Press, 1992).

COLIN SUMNER is Professor of Law and Head of the Law School at the University of East London. For many years a Lecturer at the Institute of Criminology in Cambridge University, his main works include *Reading Ideologies* (1979) and *The Sociology of Deviance: an Obituary* (1994). He has taught the sociology of crime and deviance for over 20 years and has been a Visiting Professor at universities in Canada, Tanzania, Hong Kong, Spain, and Germany. He is co-editor of the journal *Theoretical Criminology*.

IAN TAYLOR is Professor of Sociology at the University of Salford in Greater Manchester. He has previously taught in the UK at the Universities of Sheffield and Glasgow, and, in Canada, at Carleton University in Ottawa, McMaster University in Hamilton, and the University of Alberta. He has also been a Visiting Professor at La Trobe University, Melbourne, Australia, and the University of Stockholm.

He is co-author, with Paul Walton and Jock Young, of *The New Criminology* (London: Routledge and Kegan Paul, 1973) and, with Karen Evans and Penny Fraser, of *A Tale of Two Cities: Global Change, Local Feeling and Everyday Life in the North of England; a study in Manchester and Sheffield* (London: Routledge, 1996), and author of *Law and Order: Arguments for Socialism* (London: Macmillan, 1981) and *Crime, Capitalism and Community* (Toronto: Butterworths, 1983). He has edited a number of collections of essays, including *Politics and Deviance* (with Laurie Taylor) (London: Penguin, 1973), *Critical Criminology* (with Paul Walton and Jock Young)

(London: Routledge and Kegan Paul, 1975), *The Social Effects of Free Market Policies* (Hemel Hempstead: Harvester Wheatsheaf, 1991), *Relocating Cultural Studies* (with Valda Blundell and John Shepherd) (London: Routledge, 1993), *Crime and Social Order in Europe* (with Vincenzo Ruggiero and Nigel South) (London: Routledge, 1998), and *Crime and Political Economy* (Aldershot: Dartmouth Press, 1998). His current research focuses on the relationships between crime and the post-Fordist transformation of the city, and also on firearms.

PAUL WILES is Professor of Criminology of the University of Sheffield. He was formerly Dean of the Faculty of Law (1990–5) and Director of the Centre for Criminological and Socio-Legal Studies (1985–9). Prior to working at Sheffield he was Research Fellow at the Institute of Criminology, University of Cambridge (1970–2); Lecturer in Sociology, London School of Economic and Political Science (1969–70); and Lecturer in Criminology, Department of Psychology, Sir John Cass College (1968–9).

During his career he has carried out research and written on both criminology and the sociology of law and teaches both criminology and jurisprudence. During the last five years his work has mainly been in criminology and he has completed research on public responses to and expectation of policing; on crime and other problems on industrial estates; on developing methods for local communities to plan targeted crime prevention; action research to develop and evaluate the role of police crime prevention officers; arson attacks against schools; on public awareness of drugs, drug taking, and prevention; on the development of alternative forms of policing; on the effects of design changes in public housing on crime; evaluating the crime reduction potential of the Youth Action Scheme. He is currently involved in evaluating phase two of the Safer Cities programme; in helping South Yorkshire Police developing GIS crime analysis; and helping the Sheffield criminal justice agencies develop an integrated information system. However, his central and long-term research interest continues to be on the spatial patterning of crime and the changes in those patterns in contemporary cities.

JOCK YOUNG is Professor of Criminology at Middlesex University, where he is the head of the Centre for Criminology. He graduated from the London School of Economics (B.Sc.) in 1965 and received his M.Sc. (1966) and Ph.D. (1972) from the same institution. Among his publications are: *The Drugtakers* (1971), *The New Criminology*, with I. Taylor and P. Walton (1973), *Critical Criminology*, edited with I. Taylor and P. Walton (1975), *Policing the Riots*, edited with D. Cowell (1982), *Confronting Crime*, edited with R. Matthews (1986), *Losing the Fight against Crime*, with R. Kinsey and J. Lea (1986), *The Islington Crime Survey*, with T. Jones and B. MacLean (1986), *Rethinking Criminology*, edited with R. Matthews (1992), *Issues in Realist Criminology*, edited with R. Matthews (1992), *What is to be Done about Law and Order?*, with J. Lea (1993), and *The New Criminology Revisited*, edited with P. Walton (1997).

Lucia Zedner is Fellow and Tutor in Law at Corpus Christi College, Oxford and an Associate of the Centre for Criminological Research, University of Oxford. She was formerly Lecturer in Law at the London School of Economics (1989–94) and before that a Prize Research Fellow at Nuffield College, Oxford (1987–9). She is a regular visitor to the Max Planck Institute for Foreign and International Criminal Law, Freiburg since holding a visiting fellowship there in 1993. She has a BA from the University of York (1982) and a D.Phil. from the University of Oxford (1988). She is a member of the editorial boards of the *British Journal of Criminology, The Howard Journal of Criminal Justice,* the *Law in Context* series, and the *Clarendon Studies in Criminology.* Her publications include *Women, Crime and Custody in Victorian England* (1991), with Jane Morgan *Child Victims: Crime, Impact and Criminal Justice* (1992), and many articles in the field of criminal justice.

Introduction to Second Edition

Robert Reiner, Rod Morgan, and Mike Maguire

THE GROWTH OF CRIMINOLOGICAL STUDIES

Criminals are highly productive people, as Karl Marx remarked ironically over a century ago (Marx, 1964: 375). We may debate the extent to which crime pays for its perpetrators, but there is a flourishing 'crime control industry' (Christie, 1993), which thrives as a result of 'respectable fears' (Pearson, 1983) about deviance. This includes the burgeoning apparatuses of social control, public and private, and the meta-enterprises which seek to portray the contours, consequences, and causes of crime, notably the mass media and official researchers and policy-makers. A small but rapidly growing corner of this field is the subject of this volume, academic criminology.

Like the recorded crime rate, the criminological enterprise—research and teaching—has grown apace in the last forty years as we described in our Introduction to the first edition of this *Handbook*. In the early 1950s, Hermann Mannheim at the London School of Economics, Leon Radzinowicz at Cambridge, and Max Grunhut at Oxford were almost lone pioneering figures teaching criminology in British universities. It was not until 1957 that the Home Office set up a Research Unit (see Croft, 1974; and the important Special Issue of the *British Journal of Criminology* on 'The History of British Criminology' edited by Paul Rock: 28:2, 1988). When the Cambridge Institute of Criminology was created with Home Office support and independent financial backing in 1959, it was the first postgraduate teaching and research centre of its kind. Prior to its formation remarkably little had been spent by any government on criminological research, as Lord Butler, the Home Secretary who provided much of the impetus for the establishment of the Cambridge Institute, was later to recall (see Butler, 1974: 3–6). Neither the University Grants Council nor the major trusts had shown much interest in supporting criminological research. At that time there were only two journals— the *British Journal of Delinquency* (forerunner of the *British Journal of Criminology*) and the *Howard Journal*—devoted to publishing articles of a criminological nature. There were virtually no undergraduate courses, which is not surprising because there was remarkably little research or theorizing on which teachers could draw. In the late 1950s lecturers preparing student reading lists had little difficulty incorporating most of the British official publications and independent research studies in which criminologists, whatever their substantive specialisms, might have an interest.

Today virtually no university social science faculty or law school is without a course which, either wholly or in part, encompasses the criminological terrain (though as we have noted in the first edition, they come with a wide range of titles and patterns). Taught postgraduate courses in the subject are proliferating apace, many of them directed at particular practitioner groups as well as geared to the teaching of research skills or advanced theory. Many universities now have research centres, some little more than letter-headings, but an increasing number with substantial personnel and resources, which carry criminology, socio-legal, policing, or criminal justice in their titles. The bi-annual British Criminology Conference, organized by the British Society of Criminology which is itself expanding rapidly, attracts the attendance of over 400 delegates, most of them lecturers or research officers in social science departments. Several other cognate professional associations are flourishing—for example, the Socio-Legal Studies Association, the Institute for the Study and Treatment of Delinquency, and the Howard League—which support publications, seminars, and conferences.

It is no longer possible, as once it was, for individuals to keep abreast of all this activity and output. Scores of research monographs and general texts of a criminological nature are published each year. At least a dozen British publishing houses carry a substantial list of criminology titles and many University centres have in-house monograph series. The *British Journal of Criminology* and the *Howard Journal* now compete with several other British-based academic journals in more specialized areas of criminology, such as the recently launched *Theoretical Criminology*, and journals on substantive areas like policing, victimology, and probation. In addition, most of the general social science and law journals regularly publish articles of a criminological character.

This explosion in academic activity is not surprising. The huge rise in recorded crime since the mid-1950s has led to considerable increases in the number of personnel employed in the various law and order services. This has led to an increased demand for persons with some criminological training, which has in turn fuelled pressure that there be more research conducted on criminological issues. Though academics are wont to complain about the level of financial support available for their work, the growth of funding for criminological research has been considerable. In the same way that the increase in recorded crime has outstripped the numbers of additional personnel employed by police forces, so research funding has almost certainly not kept pace with the huge increase in public spending on 'law and order' services generally (see Home Office, 1995). Nevertheless there has been a boom in criminological research. In addition to the substantial programme of work conducted within or funded by the Home Office, the Economic and Social Research Council (ESRC) has had a succession of programme initiatives directed wholly or partly at work of a criminological nature. Several of the major charitable foundations regularly fund research on aspects of crime and criminal justice and, in recent years, some local authorities and most criminal justice agencies have either set up their own research arms or contracted out work on aspects of crime or the performance of their own agencies. The recent ESRC initiative on *Crime and Social Order* attracted no fewer than 180 applications from individuals or groups wishing to compete for the £2.3 million the Council allocated. Moreover, though the Home Office has announced that reduced funds will in future be available for externally conducted research, the latest ESRC programme, on *Violence*, has been allocated more than £3 million and has attracted over 300 bids.

THE AIMS OF THE OXFORD HANDBOOK

As we remarked in the Introduction to the first edition, all three editors of this volume are long-serving members of British universities. Between us we have clocked up the better part of a century's experience of teaching and researching in areas which can broadly be called criminology. This has been in departments with several different primary disciplinary affiliations: sociology, social work and policy, law—even centres of criminology. Our teaching has been in a variety of institutional contexts: undergraduate and postgraduate degrees in social science, or in criminology/criminal justice or cognate titles, and to a variety of practitioner and professional groups. This book grows out of this varied and extensive experience.

We have long felt it a problem that there has been no single comprehensive textbook covering sufficient ground with enough depth to build a general criminology course around it. There are, to be sure, many excellent texts on most *specific* areas of crime and criminal justice, such as the criminal justice process, the penal system, policing, victims, gender, and race. There are also a number of well-established and stimulating texts on the theoretical development of criminology. However, reading lists for courses intending to cover theoretical and substantive issues have had to use a variety of different references (books and articles) for each topic. Reading lists have become dauntingly elephantine, and increasingly unfriendly to students of limited resources in time and money.

THEORETICAL AND METHODOLOGICAL CONSIDERATIONS

This was the gap we set out to fill. We aimed at producing a criminology handbook which would provide students with authoritative overviews of the major issues that most criminology courses cover, whether taught in schools of law or social science, to undergraduates, postgraduates, or practitioners. Because of the huge expansion of the field, and its increasing 'fragmentation' (Ericson and Carriere, 1994) in terms of substantive areas of specialization and epistemological, methodological, and political orientations, we decided immediately that we could not write such a text ourselves. Instead we sought to assemble a set of state-of-the-art papers covering the full range of issues addressed by criminology, and representing the diverse array of viewpoints in criminological discourse.

We explicitly eschewed adopting a single overall orientation or theoretical approach. We wanted to give readers access to the full array of issues and approaches found in contemporary criminological research and debate. We proceeded in what we regarded as a pragmatic way, identifying topics which feature most prominently in the courses we knew of, in criminology and socio-legal journals, and in publishers' lists. In the first edition this resulted in twenty-five separate chapters, organized into four broad sections: theoretical and historical perspectives; crime and causation; crime control and criminal justice; social dimensions of crime and justice. We tried to identify potential authors for these chapters who were both authorities on their subject and capable of clear, stimulating, well-organized exposition. We were in the event able to secure chapters from nearly all our first-choice authors, and the first edition certainly includes a large proportion of the best-known academic criminologists in Britain, writing on topics they are particular experts in.

We were aware as we worked on the first edition that this procedure had many pitfalls. Above all, for all our commitment to non-dogmatic inclusive-ness, a way of seeing is also always a way of not seeing (Burke, 1989). Editorial inclusion, however wide-ranging and non-partisan, always entails exclusion. One level of this is individual authorship. For most chapters several writers were obvious candidates. The chapters written by the editors themselves, for example, could have been offered to many outstanding authors in these areas. Choosing one author inevitably leaves out other equally or more worthy candidates, and was inevitably based as much as anything on the limits of our own circles of acquaintance.

A more serious issue is the impossibility of avoiding a limiting definition of the field. As we stated in our original introduction:

> there is no theoretical manifesto in these pages. We have not selected our authors according to some shared proselytising vision, nor have we sought to impose a common approach upon them . . . This is a collection of different voices, not a monolithic vision, though we intend it to be a comprehensive, state-of-the-art map of criminological analysis, research, and debate in Britain today.

Whilst this was our intention, it is in some ways disingenuous. As all who have gone beyond a simple positivism must acknowledge, selection has to be according to some underlying theoretical orientation, some definition of the boundaries of the art the state of which we seek to depict, and some criteria of qualifications for entry. Thankfully most of the reviews of the first edition were overwhelmingly positive, but the repeated fear of critics was that we were seeking to define and limit the field, to cut off debate and impose some sort of orthodoxy. This was certainly not our intention, but it has been alleged to be an effect, perhaps an inevitable effect, of launching an enterprise called *the* handbook of criminology.

Paradoxically we could only defend ourselves against this claim by having a clear theoretical standpoint, the truth of which we were convinced to the exclusion of other perspectives. We would then be in a position to develop arguments attempting to validate it. But we do not have such an absolutist conception of truth. Nor do we espouse a complete relativism about the limits of valid or useful criminological discourse. We strive to be as self-conscious and reflexively aware and critical as possible of our guiding assumptions and criteria (Nelken, 1994). Our aim is not to espouse a particular theoretical position but to provide a fair representation of the state of criminological research and debate in British Academia today. This is in effect a falsifiable empirical proposition rather than a theoretical or political agenda. The test of success is pragmatic: is the book recognized by the academic criminological community as a valid and useful resource for teaching and research? In these terms the reaction to the first edition suggests that our account was broadly acceptable, though with some arguments about excluded areas. These we have tried to incorporate in this revision.

THE SECOND EDITION

In addition to updating—itself a major exercise—the principal changes in this second edition are intended to rectify gaps and weaknesses which we became aware of as we reflected upon the enterprise in the light of reactions to the first edition. The coverage of substantive topics seemed broadly acceptable, and has for the most part been retained. There were three major issues we have tried to address: how to incorporate the frontiers of theoretical debate and controversy; how to avoid issues of social justice and discrimination from being marginalized; and how to clarify the contours and structure of the volume.

Giving attention to unsettled disputes and emerging frontier areas was problematic in a volume primarily designed to map the field. The latter undertaking clearly leans towards the established and settled core areas and approaches. We have attempted to deal with this issue by adding a number of new chapters exploring major theoretical controversies. Paul Rock's chapter provides a critical overview of the major sociological theories of crime in the established literature, in the light of current theoretical developments. We have also added a symposium section of eight new shorter chapters on some of the key frontiers of theoretical development and controversy. There is also a new chapter on the media and crime, an area on which research and debate have proliferated. To make room for these additions we have merged what in the first edition were two separate chapters on youth crime and juvenile justice.

We have also revised the structure of the volume to address the two other problems we felt were left by the first edition. As Jill Peay caustically but correctly pointed out in her chapter in the first edition, there was a striking quantitative imbalance of female to male authors (five women to twenty-one men), but the women were apparently ghettoized in a final section amorphously labelled 'social dimensions of crime'. The implication was that such matters as gender, juvenile justice, victims, and the mentally disordered were 'soft topics' and hence 'the women's lot'. We could only reply rather lamely that our chapters reflected the overall male–female ratio in criminology. We have not succeeded in rectifying the quantitative imbalance: this remains as low as six women to twenty-five men. However, we have tried to make issues of social justice and discrimination integral to the core sections. Two of the new chapters in the theoretical symposium are on gender issues, and the section on social dimensions of crime and justice becomes the pivotal link between the overtly theoretical first half of the volume and the more substantive consideration of specific areas of crime and criminal justice in the second.

We have also restructured the volume as a whole to make more explicit the parameters of criminological discourse as we see it currently. There are still four major sections: general theories of crime and control; social dimensions of crime and justice; forms of crime and criminality; and criminal justice structures and processes. The latter two sections comprise chapters reviewing substantive areas of crime and criminal justice. They are linked to the general theoretical perspectives by a section of chapters addressing the social structuring of crime, victimization, and criminal justice by the key social differences of gender, race, age, and mental disorder. The theoretical first section is itself sub-divided into a number of discrete areas: the historical development of crime, crime control institutions, criminology, and law-and-order politics and policy; representations of crime in criminal statistics, and the mass media; reviews of the core analytic perspectives which have dominated criminological explanation—sociology, political economy, ecology, and psychology; and the symposium on frontiers of theoretical controversy.

As with the first edition, this remains a project in progress. We hope it will be a useful volume for students, practitioners, and academics. However, it is our hypothesis about what best fits the current state of criminological discourse in Britain. As such it is falsifiable and corrigible, and will be further revised in the light of reaction from reviewers and readers.

REFERENCES

Burke, K. (1989), *On Symbols and Society*. Chicago, Ill.: Chicago University Press.

Butler, R. A. B. (1974), 'The Foundation of the Institute of Criminology in Cambridge', in R. Hood ed., *Crime, Criminology and Public Policy*. London: Heinemann.

Christie, N. (1993), *Crime Control As Industry*. London: Routledge.

Croft, J. (1978), *Research in Criminal Justice*. Home Office Research Study No 44. London: Home Office.

Ericson, R., and Carriere, K. (1994), 'The Fragmentation of Criminology', in

D. Nelken, ed., *The Futures of Criminology*, 89–109. London: Sage.

HOME OFFICE (1996), *Digest 3: Information on the Criminal Justice System in England and Wales*. London: Home Office Research and Statistics Department.

MARX, K. (1964), *Theories of Surplus Value, Part 1*. London: Lawrence and Wishart.

NELKEN, D. (1994), 'Reflexive Criminology?' in D. Nelken, ed., *The Futures of Criminology*, 7–42. London: Sage.

PEARSON, G. (1983), *Hooligans: A History of Respectable Fears*. London: Macmillan.

Rock, P., ed. (1988), *A History of British Criminology*. Oxford: Oxford University Press.

Part I

GENERAL THEORIES OF CRIME
AND CONTROL

1

Of Crimes and Criminals: The Development of Criminology in Britain

David Garland

INTRODUCTION: THE CONTINGENCY OF THE CRIMINOLOGICAL PRESENT

This essay presents an interpretation of the historical development of criminology in Britain. Any such history is inevitably a contentious undertaking, entailing theoretical choices and rhetorical purposes as well as the selection and arrangement of historical materials. Whether they acknowledge it or not, histories of the discipline necessarily come up against fundamental issues— What is 'criminology'? What are its central features? How are its conceptual and historical boundaries identified? In what institutional, political or cultural contexts should it be situated? It may therefore be useful to begin by outlining some of the theoretical assumptions which underpin the interpretation offered here.

I take criminology to be a specific genre of discourse and inquiry about crime—a genre which has developed in the modern period and which can be distinguished from other ways of talking and thinking about criminal conduct. Thus, for example, its claim to be an empirically grounded, scientific undertaking sets it apart from moral and legal discourses, while its focus upon crime differentiates it from other social scientific genres, such as the sociology of deviance and control, whose objects of study are broader and not defined by the criminal law. Since the middle years of this century, criminology has also been increasingly marked off from other discourses by the trappings of a distinctive disciplinary identity, with its own journals, professional associations, professorships and institutes. One of the central concerns of this essay will be to try to explain how such a discipline came to exist as an accredited specialism, supported by universities and governments alike.

My broad historical argument will be that modern criminology grew out

I am grateful to the following friends and colleagues for their help with this essay: Stanley Cohen, Mitchell Duneier, James B. Jacobs, Dorothy Nelkin, Robert Reiner, Paul Rock, and Peter Young. Research for this project was assisted by the Lindsay Bequest Fund of the Edinburgh University Law Faculty and by the New York University School of Law.

of the convergence of two quite separate enterprises—'the governmental project' and 'the Lombrosian project'—which together provided a social and an intellectual rationale for the subject. By talking about a 'governmental project' I mean to refer to the long series of empirical inquiries, which, since the eighteenth century, have sought to enhance the efficient and equitable administration of justice by charting the patterns of crime and monitoring the practice of police and prisons. This tradition of inquiry was eventually to become a major part of the criminological enterprise and to provide criminology with its central claim to social utility. The 'Lombrosian project', in contrast, refers to a form of inquiry which aims to develop an etiological, explanatory science, based on the premise that criminals can somehow be scientifically differentiated from non-criminals.[1] Although each of these projects has undergone important revisions during the twentieth century, and the situation of criminology has been significantly altered by its entry into the universities, I will suggest that the discipline continues to be structured by the sometimes competing, sometimes converging, claims of these two programmes. One pole of the discipline pulls its members towards an ambitious (and, I have argued elsewhere—Garland 1985*b*—deeply flawed) theoretical project seeking to build a science of causes. The other exerts the force of a more pragmatic, policy-orientated, administrative project, seeking to use science in the service of management and control. Criminologists have sometimes sought to overcome this tension by rejecting one project in favour of the other— either giving up the search for causes in favour of a direct policy orientation, or else disengaging from governmental concerns in the name of a pure (or a critical) science. However, the combination of the two seems essential to criminology's claim to be sufficiently useful and sufficiently scientific to merit the status of an accredited, state-sponsored, academic discipline.

The coming together of these two projects was by no means inevitable. The historical record suggests that it took several decades for officials to accept that the Lombrosian search for the causes of crime had any relevance to their administrative tasks, and, in fact, Lombroso's criminology had to be

---

[1] I use the concept of a 'project' here to characterize an emergent tradition of inquiry which, despite a degree of variation, shares a cluster of aims and objectives. The 'governmental' project refers to those inquiries which direct their attention to the problems of governing crime and criminals. Studies which fall within this tradition are not necessarily official, state-sponsored studies, although, from the nineteenth century onwards, the state came to dominate work of this kind. Nor are these inquiries necessarily focused upon state practices (such as criminal laws, police, prisons, etc.), since the governance of crime and criminals also occurs through 'private' institutions such as the family, boys' clubs, settlement houses, and so on. As I discuss later, the study of crime and criminal justice practices was not at first separate from a much broader concern with the rational goverance of the population in all its aspects. (On the concept of governmentality, see Foucault 1979; Burchell *et al.* 1991.) The 'Lombrosian' project refers to that tradition of inquiry, begun by Lombroso, which aims to differentiate the criminal individual from the non-criminal. By naming the etiological project in this way I wish to emphasize the continuity in scientific objective which runs from Lombroso to the present, rather than to suggest a continuity of method or of substantive analysis: most etiological studies of the twentieth century have de-emphasized the biological determinants which Lombroso took to be fundamental.

extensively modified before it could be of service to policy-makers and state authorities. Beyond that, the very idea of a science devoted to 'the criminal' seems in retrospect to have been something of an historical accident, originally prompted by a claim that was quickly discredited: namely, that 'the criminal type' was an identifiable anthropological entity. Were it not for the contingency of that intellectual event there might never have been any distinctive criminological science or any independent discipline. As an historical counterfactual, it is perfectly plausible to imagine that crime and criminals could have remained integral concerns of mainstream sociology and psychiatry and that 'criminological' research undertaken for government purposes could have developed without the need of a university specialism of that name. If this is so, and criminology has a contingent rather than a necessary place in the halls of science, then its history becomes all the more relevant to an understanding of the discipline.

In the light of the assumptions and arguments I have outlined here, history becomes essential to an understanding of the modern criminological enterprise. If we are to understand the central topics which criminology has marked out as its own, if we are to understand the discipline's relation to institutional practices and concerns, if we are to understand some of the key terms and conceptions which structure the discourse, then we will have to ask genealogical questions about the constitution of this science and examine the historical processes which led to the emergence of an accredited disciplinary specialism. Moreover, the kind of historical inquiry required is one which is sensitive to context and contingency, and to the relation between intellectual developments and the social practices out of which they emerge. If my claim is correct, and criminology is a product of the convergence of certain ideas and interests, in a particular institutional context, then its history cannot be treated, as it so often is, as the gradual unfolding of a science which was always destined to appear. Such is the prevalence of this kind of history that it may be worth discussing the shortcomings of received accounts, before going on to sketch an alternative approach.

Textbook Histories

Criminology's history is most often constructed in the form of a preface. It appears, usually in a few compressed and standardized pages, as the opening section of a book or article, introducing the reader to the subject and placing the author's text within a longer tradition. Sometimes the prefatory history has a job to do, providing the reader with enough historical understanding to appreciate the significance and provenance of the text that follows. At other times it is merely decorative, a routine flourish with little real purpose beyond getting started in a way that has come to be expected of authors. Ironically, this routine repetition of conventional historical wisdom can have an influence quite out of keeping with its value as scholarship. The telling and retelling of the standard historical tale is a most effective way of persuading the discipline's recruits that whatever else may be contested, this much, at least, can be taken for granted.

Occasionally, textbooks, research monographs, or critical studies make a feature of their historical introductions, offering a more extensive (and usually more tendentious) account of the subject's history, which acts as a kind of framing device for subsequent arguments.[2] On such occasions, history becomes a way of conducting theoretical debate by other means. The recovery of a lost theoretical tradition, the reinterpretation of the subject's early history, claims and counter-claims about the true 'founders' of the discipline, or critical summaries of previous patterns of thought, are all ways in which the subject's history gets drafted into current controversies and made to do duty for one side or the other.

The history of the discipline has, on a few occasions, formed the central subject-matter for a book or an article. Most of these excursions into historical criminology are minor attempts to attribute importance to a particular author whose influence upon the subject is felt to have been slighted,[3] but some historical writings have more ambitious intentions. Books such as Mannheim's *Pioneers in Criminology* (1960) or Radzinowicz's *Ideology and Crime* (1966)— both published by leading figures in the process of discipline-building—played an important role in shaping the contours and self-consciousness of the discipline, and sought to enhance its status by invoking a distinguished Enlightenment past and a progressive scientific mission. The recent collection entitled *The History of British Criminology* (Rock 1988*a*)—edited by one of the sociologists who helped remake British criminology in the 1960s and 1970s— professes similar discipline-forming ambitions, aiming to introduce new generations of criminologists to a revised history more in keeping with contemporary interests and understandings. It is not just the textbooks which have to be adjusted when a discipline changes; history must also be rewritten.

The received history of the discipline, often simplified into a tale of icons and demons (Beccaria, Lombroso, Burt, Radzinowicz . . .), a few key distinctions (classicism, positivism, radicalism . . .), and an overarching narrative in which ideological error is gradually displaced by the findings of science (e.g. the myth of the born criminal and its subsequent debunking), plays a small but significant role in shaping the horizons and reference points of contemporary criminology. A discipline's practitioners work with a sense of where their subject has come from and where it is going, which issues are settled and which are still live, who are the exemplars to imitate and who the anathemas to be avoided. Perhaps most importantly, the received history provides practitioners with a standard-issue kit of collective terms and shared values. Thus, for example, anyone who learned about the discipline's history from the textbooks of the 1970s would find it hard to identify with the methods and aspirations of 'positivism', even though this term was broad enough to include virtually

---

[2] See e.g. the historical introductions to the following: Taylor, Walton, and Young 1973; Morris 1957; Matza 1964.

[3] See e.g. Savitz *et al.* 1977; also Lyell 1913, Levin and Lindesmith 1937.

the whole discipline prior to the rise of 'labelling' theories and the associated anti-positivist critiques.[4]

The standard textbook account of criminology's history begins with the writings of criminal law reformers in the eighteenth century, particularly Beccaria, Bentham, Romilly, and Howard. These writers are said to have characterized the offender as a rational, free-willed actor, who engages in crime in a calculated, utilitarian way and is therefore responsive to deterrent, proportionate penalties of the kind that the reformers preferred. This 'classical school of criminology', as it is usually called, was subsequently challenged, in the late nineteenth century, by writers of the 'positivist school' (Lombroso, Ferri, and Garofalo are usually cited) who adopted a more empirical, scientific approach to the subject, and investigated 'the criminal' using the techniques of psychiatry, physical anthropology, anthropometry, and other new human sciences. The positivist school claimed to have discovered evidence of the existence of 'criminal types' whose behaviour was determined rather than chosen and for whom treatment rather than punishment was appropriate. Subsequent research refuted or modified most of the specific claims of Lombroso, and restored the credibility of some of the 'classicist' ideas he opposed, but the project of a scientific criminology had been founded, and this enterprise continues, in a more diverse and sophisticated way, today.

This standard textbook history is, of course, broadly accurate—it would be very surprising if it were not. But the broad sweep of its narrative and the resounding simplicity of its generic terms can be profoundly misleading if they are taken as real history, rather than as a kind of foundational myth, developed for heuristic rather than historical purposes.

Misleading Categories

A major defect of these histories is their uncritical use of key terms which then subsequently enter into standard criminological discourse in an equally unselfconscious way. The term 'classicism', to take an important example, is used as a generic term to denote the criminology of Beccaria and Bentham, and eighteenth-century thought more generally. It is also used, by extension, to describe modern theories which affirm the rationality and freedom of offenders' decision-making processes (see Roshier 1989). But, despite this conventional usage, it actually makes little sense to claim that these eighteenth-century thinkers possessed a 'criminology', given that they made no general distinction between the characteristics of criminals and non-criminals, and had no conception of research on crime and criminals as a distinctive form of inquiry. To use such a term to characterize eighteenth-century thought seriously

---

[4] See e.g. the discussions of 'positivism' in Taylor, Walton, and Young 1973 and in Matza 1964. The tradition of 'positivist criminology' has recently been re-evaluated and reaffirmed in the USA (see Gottfredson and Hirschi 1987), and in Britain, some of its sternest critics have modified their views and realigned themselves with some of its central concerns. For a discussion of the changing relationship between 'radical criminology' and 'positivism', see Young 1988.

misrepresents the character of these writings and forcibly assimilates them to a project that was not invented until a century later.

The notion that these various writers all maintained the same rational, free-will view of the offender is also a distortion, derived from the polemics of late nineteenth-century positivists rather than from a reading of the eighteenth-century texts. There are, for example, quite major differences between authors such as Bentham and Howard on the questions of human nature and freedom of choice; and Beccaria, as a good Lockean empiricist, viewed human character and conduct as shaped by sense impressions and habit as well as by free will and reason.[5] Other eighteenth-century writers on crime approached the question from a quite different perspective, stressing the social conditions which shaped individual conduct and using a deterministic language to describe the process of becoming criminal.[6] The notion of 'classicism' thus tends to dissolve under close scrutiny, deriving any coherence it has not from the facts of intellectual history but from the requirements of contemporary criminological teaching.

'Positivism' holds up little better as a descriptive term, although, unlike classicism, it at least has the merit of having been the self-description of a school of criminologists. The use of this word to describe the specific claims of Lombroso and his *scuola positiva* in the late nineteenth century (the born criminal, the constitutional and hereditary roots of criminal conduct, criminal types, etc.) and also to describe the huge and diverse range of criminological work which has been carried out within an empiricist framework (i.e. using 'theory-neutral' observation as a basis for inductive propositions, stressing measurement, objectivity, etc.) has been a source of great confusion in the discipline. Potted histories entrench this muddle whenever they talk indiscriminately about a 'positivist era' which stretched from the 1870s to the 1960s.

The Object of Inquiry

One of the most problematic issues to be addressed by any intellectual history is the question of criteria for inclusion and exclusion. If one is writing the history of criminology, what is to count as relevant? Where does the subject start and where does it stop? Textbook histories generally avoid the issue and simply begin with Beccaria, the arbitrariness of this decision being concealed by the fact that this is by now the traditional place to start. But one can see the problem much more clearly on those occasions when the intellectual history of criminology is the subject of a whole article or series of chapters. Thus, for instance, Israel Drapkin's essay in the *Encyclopedia of Crime and Justice* (Drapkin 1983)—like the more historically orientated textbooks by Bonger (1936) and Vold (1958)—seeks to provide a more serious, scholarly account of the subject's history. Drapkin traces criminology's intellectual

---

[5] On the differences between Howard and Bentham, see Ignatieff 1978. On Beccaria as a Lockean empiricist, see Zeman 1981.

[6] See the discussion of writers such as Henry Dagge and Mannasseh Dawes in Green 1985.

history back through the early modern period, the Middle Ages, and the classical period to the ancient world and 'prehistoric times'. The problem here is that the selection criteria are unargued and hopelessly broad. Criminology's history becomes the history of everything that has ever been said or thought or done in relation to law-breakers, and the links between this amorphous past and the particular present remain vague and unspecified. Worse still, the writings of ancient and medieval authors are ransacked in search of 'criminological' statements and arguments, as if they were addressing the same questions in the same ways as modern criminologists, and we are introduced to anachronistic creatures such as 'early modern criminology' and St Thomas Aquinas' analysis of 'criminogenic factors' (Drapkin 1983: 550).

This criminology-through-the-ages style of history is objectionable on a number of grounds. First of all, it distorts the meaning of earlier writers and conceals the fact that their statements are structured by assumptions and objectives—not to mention institutional contexts and cultural commitments—which are quite different from those of modern criminology.[7] Secondly, it gives the false impression that criminology is our modern response to a timeless and unchanging set of questions which previous thinkers have also pondered, though with notably less success. Criminology is seen as a science which was waiting to happen, the end point of a long process of inquiry which has only recently broken through to the status of true, scientific knowledge. This progressivist, presentist view of things fails to recognize that criminology is, in fact, a socially constructed and historically specific organization of knowledge and investigative procedures—a particular style of reasoning, representing, and intervening—which is grounded in a particular set of institutions and forms of life. It is a 'discipline', a regime of truth with its own special rules for deciding between truth and falsity, rather than the epitome of right thought and correct knowledge. To adopt this fallacious way of thinking about the discipline's history is to cut off from view the other 'problematizations' (as Foucault would call them) that the historical record reveals, and to forget that our own ways of constituting and perceiving 'crime' and 'deviance' are established conventions rather than unchallengeable truths. An important purpose of writing history is to help develop a consciousness of how conventions are made and remade over time, and thus promote a critical self-consciousness about our own questions and assumptions. The myth of an emergent criminology, progressing from ancient error to modern truth, does little to improve our understanding of the past or of the present.

My remarks up to now have been directed against criminology's history as told by criminologists to criminologists. But in recent years our historical understanding of the subject has been considerably advanced by the work of 'outsiders' who owe no allegiance to the discipline and whose work is driven by quite different historical and critical concerns. The writings of Michel Foucault (1977), Robert Nye (1984), Daniel Pick (1989), Martin Wiener (1990)

---

[7] The classic discussion of this problem in the history of ideas is contained in Skinner 1969.

and Marie-Christine Leps (1992) have, in their different ways, situated criminological discourse on a wider canvas, showing how this form of knowledge
was grounded in quite specific institutional practices, political movements, and
cultural settings. None of these authors provides an overall account of criminology's development, each one being concerned to understand the criminological ideas prevailing in a particular period or setting, rather than to produce
a genealogy of the discipline. But the analyses of these and other writers are
of great importance for the understanding of criminology's past and their work
adds breadth and depth to the somewhat narrower, diachronic account which
the present chapter sets out. Similarly valuable is the recent work done in the
newly developed field of the history of the human sciences by authors such as
Nikolas Rose (1988), Roger Smith (1988), Kurt Danziger (1990), and Ian
Hacking (1990). These writers have set out important methodological and
theoretical guidelines for work in this area—guidelines which I have tried to
follow in the present chapter. They have also developed cogent historical
analyses of disciplines such as psychology and statistics which are of great relevance for any account of criminology's development.[8]

ORIENTATIONS: A HISTORY OF THE PRESENT

I begin with the clear assumption that the phenomenon to be explained is a
present-day phenomenon—the modern discipline of criminology—and that my
task is to trace its historical conditions of emergence, identify the intellectual
resources and traditions upon which it drew, and give some account of the
process of its formation and development. This explicit concern to write a
history of the present acknowledges that our contemporary problems and
practices are quite distinct from those of the past; but equally, it recognizes
that our present arrangements were constructed out of materials and situations
which existed at earlier points in time. The present is continuous with the
past in some respects, and discontinuous in others. It is the historian's job to
identify the processes of transmutation which characterize change and, in
particular, the generation of those differences which constitute our modernity.

   Modern criminology, like any other academic specialism, consists of a body
of accredited and systematically transmitted forms of knowledge, approved
procedures and techniques of investigation, and a cluster of questions which
make up the subject's recognized research agendas. These intellectual materials
and activities are loosely organized by means of a 'discipline'—the standard
form of academic organization. The discipline establishes and enforces appropriate norms of evidence and argument, evaluates and communicates research
findings and other contributions to knowledge, fixes and revises the canon of

---

[8] The history of anthropology also contains many suggestive parallels with that of criminology;
see e.g. Darnell 1974.

theoretical and empirical knowledge, supervises the training of students, and distributes professional status and authority among accredited practitioners. These disciplinary functions are carried out, more or less effectively, by means of a variety of institutions—professional journals and associations, institutes and university departments, professional appointments, processes of peer review, letters of recommendation, training courses, textbooks, conferences, funding agencies, and so on—which make up the material infrastructure of the enterprise.[9] One has only to describe these taken-for-granted features explicitly to demonstrate that the modern discipline of criminology is indeed 'modern', and to pose the question of how such an institutional structure came to form itself around an intellectual specialism of this kind.

Modern criminology is a composite, eclectic, multidisciplinary enterprise. The subject is typically located in departments of law, sociology, or social policy—though there are now several independent centres of criminology in British universities—and training in criminology is normally at the post-graduate level, following on a first degree in a more basic field of study. In their research and teaching, criminologists draw upon a variety of other disciplines, most notably sociology, psychology, psychiatry, law, history, and anthropology—indeed, one of the major dynamics of modern criminology is the incessant raiding of other disciplines or ideologies for new ideas with which to pursue (and renew) the criminological project. They also address themselves to a wide range of research topics which somehow or other relate to crime and its control. Major areas of work include research on the incidence and distribution of criminal behaviour, inquiries about the causes or correlates of criminal conduct, clinical studies of individual delinquents and ethnographies of deviant groups, penological studies, victim studies, the monitoring and evaluation of criminal justice agencies, the prediction of future criminal conduct, the study of processes of social reaction, and historical work on changing patterns of crime and control. The list of 'central' topics is long and diverse, and each topic breaks down further into numerous sub-topics and specialisms. When one considers that these substantive areas have been approached using a variety of quantitative and qualitative methods, drawing upon the whole gamut of theoretical perspectives (psychoanalysis, functionalism, interactionism, ethnomethodology, Marxism, econometrics, systems theory, postmodernism, etc.) and ideological concerns (the implicit welfarism of most twentieth-century criminology, the radicalism of the 1970s, feminism, left realism, etc., etc.) it becomes apparent that modern criminology is highly differentiated in its theoretical, methodological, and empirical concerns.

The very diversity of the modern subject makes the question of its historical emergence and identity seem even more puzzling. How did this vast, eclectic bundle of disparate approaches, theories, and data come to acquire the status of a distinct academic specialism? At one level, the answer to this has already been set out above: the subject derives whatever coherence and unity it has

---

[9] On scientific disciplines and their development, see Lemaine *et al.* 1976.

from the exertions of its discipline-forming institutions. The danger of an exploding, unmanageable chaos of concerns is held in check by textbooks and teaching and a pattern of professional judgements which draw the subject together and establish its *de facto* boundaries. But this response begs a prior question, which is: Why has there emerged a discipline of this kind? What makes it possible and desirable to have a distinctive, specialist discipline of criminology in the first place? It seems to me that an answer to this question can be formulated if one has regard to the basic problem-structures or projects of inquiry which underlie these disparate investigations. My argument is, as suggested above, that criminology is structured around two basic projects—the governmental and the Lombrosian—and that the formation and convergence of these projects can be traced by studying the texts and statements which constitute criminology's historical archive. Criminology, in its modern form and in its historical development, is orientated towards a scientific goal but also towards an institutional field, towards a theoretical project but also towards an administrative task. Whatever fragile unity the discipline achieves emerges from the belief that these two projects are mutually supportive rather than incompatible, that etiological research can be made useful for administrative purposes, and that the findings of operational research further the ends of theoretical inquiry. Occasionally, criminologists lose this faith, and when they do, their arguments cast doubt on the very viability of the discipline.[10]

As with most 'human sciences', criminology has a long past but a short history.[11] Discourse about crime and punishment has existed, in one form or another, since ancient times, but it is only during the last 120 years that there has been a distinctive 'science of criminology', and only in the last fifty or sixty years has there been in Britain an established, independent discipline organized around that intellectual endeavour. My account of the emergence of the modern British discipline will be divided into four parts:

1. a brief discussion of what I will call 'traditional' representations of crime and criminals;
2. an outline of the empirical analyses that were brought to bear upon crime and criminal justice in the eighteenth and nineteenth centuries, and which began the tradition of inquiry which I call the governmental project;
3. an account of the emergence of a positive, specialist 'science of the criminal'—the Lombrosian project—in the late nineteenth century, both in continental Europe and in Britain;
4. an account of how these two projects converged in a way and to an extent which facilitated the formation of a criminological discipline in Britain in the middle years of the twentieth century.

---

[10] See e.g. the debates surrounding the development of a radical criminology which aimed to disengage from the policy goals of the state—a development which, for some writers, came to imply the dissolution of criminology as a discipline. See Bankowski *et al.* 1976, Hirst 1975. See also the recent reflections on the relationship between criminology and criminal justice policy by Petersilia 1991 and Bottoms 1987.

[11] For a theoretical discussion addressing this issue in the history of psychology, see Smith 1988.

This order of exposition implies a certain developmental pattern, and to some extent that seems appropriate. Criminological thought and practice have developed, at least in some respects, in a 'scientific' direction, and the analysis presented here is concerned precisely to chart this evolution and to reconstruct the events and developments which played a role in that transmutation. The chronology of events is constructed in order to show how our particular ways of organizing thought and research have come into existence. But it needs to be emphasized that no overall process of progressive development is being asserted here, and there are no exclusive boundaries neatly separating the thought of one period from the thought of another. Some residues of the 'traditional' ideas to be found in the seventeenth century still circulate today in the form of common-sense and moral argument. Forms of thought and inquiry which flourished in the eighteenth and early nineteenth centuries have been rediscovered in the late twentieth and adapted to serve contemporary purposes. Conversely, certain ideas and arguments which appeared progressive and persuasive to criminologists at the start of the present century have come to seem pseudo-scientific and faintly absurd.

Criminology's history is not one of steady progress and refinement, although whenever a framework of inquiry has endured for a long enough time, such refinements have taken place. Instead, it is a story of constant reformulation in response to shifting political pressures, changes in institutional and administrative arrangements, intellectual developments occurring in adjacent disciplines, and the changing ideological commitments of its practitioners. The very fact that a basic orientation of the discipline links it to a field of social problems and to administrative efforts to govern that field imparts a certain instability to the subject and constantly transforms its objects of study. As a discipline criminology is shaped only to a small extent by its own theoretical object and logic of inquiry. Its epistemological threshold is a low one, making it susceptible to pressures and interests generated elsewhere.

TRADITIONAL REPRESENTATIONS OF CRIME

Social rules and the violation of them are an intrinsic aspect of social organization, a part of the human condition. Discourse about crime and criminals— or sin, villainy, roguery, deviance, whatever the local idiom—is thus as old as human civilization itself. Wherever generalized frameworks developed for the representation and explanation of human conduct, whether as myths, cosmologies, theologies, metaphysical systems, or vernacular common sense— they generally entailed propositions about aberrant conduct and how it should be understood. As we have seen, some writers have taken this recurring concern with law-breakers as sufficient licence to talk about a 'criminology' which stretches back to the dawn of time. But rather than see such writings as proto-criminologies struggling to achieve a form which we have since perfected, it seems more appropriate to accept that there are a variety of ways in which crime can be problematized and put into discourse, and that 'criminology' is only one version among others. The propositions about crime and criminals which appear in the writings of ancient and medieval philosophers, the theologies of the Church of Rome and the Protestant Reform tradition, the mythico-magical cosmologies of the Middle Ages, and the legal thought of the early modern period were not aspiring criminologies, even though their subject-matter sometimes bears a resemblance to that which criminology seeks to explain. These broad resemblances begin to appear less compelling when one looks in detail at what the discourses involved and their implicit assumptions about the world. Entities such as fate and demons, original sin and human depravity, temptation, lust, and avarice are the products of mental frameworks and forms of life rather different from our own.[12]

The differences between these mentalities and our own can be quite instructive, pointing up some of the peculiarities of our accustomed ways of thinking about crime. It is significant, for example, that the major tradition of Western thought—Christianity, in all its variants—did not separate out the law-breaker as different or abnormal, but instead understood him or her as merely a manifestation of universal human depravity and the fallen, sinful state of all mankind.[13] 'There but for the grace of God go I' is an understanding of things quite alien to much of the criminology that was written in the late nineteenth and early twentieth centuries. In the same way, the explicitly moral and spiritual terms in which the Christian tradition discusses individual wrongdoing, the lack of reference to systematically controlled empirical evidence, the invocation of the Devil, or demons, or divine intervention to account for human action, and the appeal to scriptural authority as proof for propositions are all starkly contrastive reminders of the rather different rules governing modern criminological discourse.

But traditional accounts of crime—Christian and otherwise—are not entirely remote from modern thinking about the subject. Scattered around in the diverse literature of the early modern period, in criminal biographies and broadsheets, accounts of the Renaissance underworld, Tudor rogue pamphlets, Elizabethan dramas and Jacobean city comedies, the utopia of Thomas More and the novels of Daniel Defoe,[14] one can discover rudimentary versions of the etiological accounts which are used today to narrate the process of becoming deviant. Stories of how the offender fell in with bad company, became lax in his habits and was sorely tried by temptation, was sickly, or tainted by bad blood, or neglected by unloving parents, became too fond of drink or too idle to work, lost her reputation and found it hard to get employ-

---

[12] For a wide-ranging discussion, see Jean Delumeau's account (Delumeau 1990) of sin and fear in thirteenth- to eighteenth-century Europe.

[13] For developments of this point, see Zeman 1981; and also Faller 1987.

[14] On criminal biographies and broadsheets, see Faller 1987; Sharpe 1985. On crime and criminals in Tudor rogue pamphlets and Jacobean city comedies, see Curtis and Hale 1981. For descriptions of the Elizabethan underworld, see Judges 1930; Salgado 1972.

ment, was driven to despair by poverty or simply driven to crime by avarice and lust—these seem to provide the well-worn templates from which our modern theories of crime are struck, even if we insist upon a more neutral language with which to tell the tale, and think that a story's plausibility should be borne out by evidence as well as intuition.[15] Indeed, Faller's research (Faller 1987) suggests that what was lacking in these seventeenth- and eighteenth-century accounts was not secular or materialist explanations of the roots of crime, which were present in abundance alongside the spiritual explanations proffered by the church. What was lacking was a developed sense of differential etiology. Crime was seen as an omnipresent temptation to which all humankind was vulnerable, but when it became a question of why some succumbed and others resisted, the explanation trailed off into the unknowable, resorting to fate, or providence, or the will of God. When, in the late nineteenth century, the science of criminology emerged, one of its central concerns would be to address this issue of differentiation and subject it to empirical inquiry.

'Traditional' ways of thinking about crime did not disappear with the coming of the modern, scientific age, though they may nowadays be accorded a different status in the hierarchy of credibility. These older conceptions—based upon experience and ideology rather than systematic empirical inquiry—have not been altogether displaced by scientific criminologies, and we continue to acknowledge the force of moral, religious and 'common-sensical' ways of discussing crime. Expert, research-based knowledge about crime and criminals still competes with views of the subject which are not 'criminological' in their style of reasoning or their use of evidence. Judges, moralists, religious fundamentalists, and populist leader-writers still offer views on criminological subjects which are quite innocent of criminological science. Unlike physics or even economics, which have established a degree of monopoly over the right to speak authoritatively about their subjects, criminology operates in a culture which combines traditional and scientific modes of thought and action. Intuitive, 'instinctive', common-sense views about crime and criminals are still more persuasive to many—including many in positions of power and authority—than are the results of carefully executed empirical research.

THE SCIENTIFIC ANALYSIS OF CRIME IN THE EIGHTEENTH AND EARLY NINETEENTH CENTURIES

In most criminological histories, the true beginnings of modern criminological thought are seen in writings of the eighteenth and early nineteenth centuries.

---

[15] Matza (1969) analyses the recurring narratives of everyday discourse and shows how, in a slightly adapted form, these come to comprise the basic explanatory structures of contemporary criminological theory.

Radzinowicz's monumental *History* (1948) begins in 1750, as does his historical essay on *Ideology and Crime* (1966). Mannheim's earliest 'pioneer' is Beccaria, whose *Of Crimes and Punishments* first appeared in 1764. Even *The New Criminology* (Taylor, Walton, and Young 1973), the radical and immensely influential textbook of the 1970s, begins its account with Beccaria and 'the classical school of criminology'. There are good grounds for choosing to emphasize the role of these eighteenth-century writings in the formation of criminology, but, as I suggested earlier, the connections are not as straightforward as is usually assumed. I have already argued that the writings of Beccaria, Bentham, and the others did not constitute a criminology. But despite this, they did establish and develop some of the key elements and conditions necessary for the subsequent development of the subject in its modern form. They are quite properly a part of criminology's genealogy, having been a direct source for some of the subject's basic aims and characteristics, as well as having produced a stock of propositions and arguments which would feature prominently in the criminological discourse which developed in the twentieth century.

There are several genealogical strands which link certain eighteenth- and early nineteenth-century writers with the criminology which followed. Most importantly, Enlightenment writers such as Beccaria, Bentham, and Howard wrote secular, materialist analyses, emphasizing the importance of reason and experience and denigrating theological forms of reasoning. They viewed themselves as proceeding in a scientific manner and dealing objectively with an issue which had previously been dominated by irrational, superstitious beliefs and prejudices. Members of the *scuola positiva* would later disparage the 'classical school' for its 'unscientific' reliance upon speculative reasoning rather than observed facts, but this is not how these writers viewed themselves. Indeed, it was the 'classicists' who first established the claim that crime and its control could be studied in a neutral, scientific manner.

Another important connection between the literature of the reformers and the criminology that followed was that the reformers of the late eighteenth and early nineteenth centuries were writing about a set of legal institutions which were becoming (partly through those reformers' efforts) recognizably modern. The institutional concerns which animated the writings of Beccaria, Bentham, Howard, and the rest are, in an important sense, modern concerns— about the systematic arrangement of criminal laws and procedures in order to promote social policy goals; about the sentencing choices of magistrates; about the organization and conduct of professional police; about the design and purposes of prison regimes. The interest of these writers in the psychology of offending, the nature of criminal motivation, the possibilities of deterrence and reform, and the most appropriate way for state institutions to regulate individual conduct, are also questions which were to be become quite central to later criminology. These issues gripped the imagination of eighteenth-century thinkers because they lived in a world caught up in the dynamics of modernization. This was the period which saw the emergence of the centralized administrative state, a national economy and a population inceasingly subject to governance, an autonomous, secular legal system, the political relations of liberalism, and institutional enclosures like the prison and the asylum with their reformative, disciplinary regimes. The writings of Beccaria, Bentham, and Howard—like those of Benjamin Rush in America—were the first soundings of a modernist discourse about crime. As intellectual responses to the challenge of crime in a newly urbanized market society, they were addressing problems of a novel type, quite unknown in traditional social thought. This new social and institutional environment, modified in certain ways, also formed the background against which the science of criminology would subsequently emerge, and in that respect there is a broad continuity of reference which makes eighteenth-century discourse 'modern' in a way that earlier writing is not. (Indeed, it is precisely because the reformist discourse of Beccaria *et al.* and the scientific discourse of Lombroso share a common institutional context that they are able to be viewed as 'opposites'. Each one entails a programme for directing the modern field of criminal justice.)

If one widens the lens to look beyond Beccaria and Bentham to some of the other discourses on crime and criminals dating from this period, one can detect other lines of affiliation. Patrick Colquhoun and Henry Fielding, as well as a large number of Parliamentary and private committees of the late eighteenth and early nineteenth centuries, used empirical evidence to situate and measure the extent of various crime problems ('the late increase in robbers', the relation between 'indigence' and crime, 'the alarming increase in juvenile delinquency', the 'police of the metropolis', and so on).[16] As Leon Radzinowicz (1956), and, more recently, Robert Reiner (1988) have pointed out, these inquiries formed part of a wider 'science of police' which flourished in this period, concerned not just with crime or criminals, but with the regulation and maintenance of the whole population in the interest of economy, welfare, and good governance (see also Foucault 1979; Pasquino 1978). John Howard's investigation of the state of the prisons was undertaken as a work of charity and reform, but his methods were doggedly empirical, and his study laid much stress on measurement and systematic observation as a basis for its findings.[17] Howard's work in the 1770s sparked the beginnings of a line of empirical penological inquiry which, from the 1830s onwards, became an increasingly important element in the British criminological tradition.

By the middle years of the nineteenth century this 'scientific' style of reasoning about crime had become a distinctive feature of the emergent culture of amateur social science. The papers delivered by Rawson W. Rawson, Joseph Fletcher, and John Glyde to the Statistical Society of London used judicial statistics and census data to chart the distribution and demography of crime

---

[16] See Colquhoun 1797, 1800, 1806, 1814; Fielding 1751; and the discussion of the parliamentary and private committees of inquiry of this period in Radzinowicz 1956.

[17] See Howard 1973 [1777], 1973 [1789] and the discussion of his work in Ignatieff 1978.

and to match up crime rates with other social indices—just as A. M. Guerry
and Adolphe Quetelet had been doing in France and Belgium.[18] On the basis
of carefully calculated correlations, they drew conclusions about the moral and
social causes which influenced criminal conduct and presented their findings
as instances of the new statistical science and its social uses. Henry Mayhew,
writing in the middle years of the nineteenth century, was essentially a journalist
concerned with 'the social question' and the problem of the poor. But unlike
the moralists of a century earlier, his journalism was founded upon an empirical approach, using ethnographic and survey methods as well as life histories
and statistical data; and his analyses of *London Labour and the London Poor*
(1861–2) offered a series of empirically supported claims about the patterns
and causes of professional crime in the city.[19]

Another line of inquiry which flourished in this period, and whose advocates
would later be seen as progenitors of criminology, centred not upon the
population and its governance by a well-ordered state, but instead upon individuals and their ability (or lack of ability) to govern themselves. As early as
the 1760s and 1770s, Henry Dagge and Mannasseh Dawes argued that the
law's notions of a free-willed offender were often enough fictions in the face
of real social and psychological circumstances which limited choice and shaped
human conduct, and they drew upon the new materialist psychologies of the
time to explain how it was that causal processes could be acknowledged without entirely destroying the belief in man's free will (see Green 1985). Indeed,
both Thomas Zeman (1981) and Piers Beirne (1993) have recently shown that
Cesare Beccaria's account of human conduct is shaped not by metaphysical
assumptions about the freedom of the will, but instead by John Locke's
empiricist psychology and the new 'science of man' developed by the thinkers
of the Scottish Enlightenment.

During the nineteenth century this reconceptualization of human character
and conduct was taken up and developed in the field of medicine, especially
psychological medicine. The art of 'physiognomy'—which, it was claimed,
enabled its practitioners to judge character and disposition from the features
of the face and the external forms of the body—had been known since the
seventeenth century, but the essays of J. C. Lavater purported to give a
scientific foundation to this useful skill (Lavater 1792).[20] The craniometry and
phrenology of F. J. Gall and J. C. Spurzheim made similar claims in the early
nineteenth century, this time focusing upon the shape and contours of the

---

[18] See the discussion of the work of Rawson, Fletcher, and Glyde in Morris 1957. Beirne (1993)
provides detailed discussions of the work of Guerry and Quetelet and their place in the development of criminological thought.

[19] For a discussion of Mayhew's work and its relation to subsequent criminological analyses,
see Morris 1957.

[20] Richard Sennett (1977) provides an interesting account of various nineteenth-century efforts
to judge character by outward appearance and describes the cultural predicament which prompted
these concerns.

human skull as an external index of character.[21] By the 1830s physiognomy and phrenology had lost much of their scientific credibility and had become the obsession of a few enthusiastic publicists, but the quest to uncover the links between physical constitution and psychological character was continued in a different and more important line of research: the new science of psychiatry.

The emergence of a network of private asylums in the eighteenth century led to the development of a new quasi-medical specialism which was at first called alienism and subsequently came to be known as psychological medicine or psychiatry. The writings of asylum managers about their patients—about their conduct, the antecedents of their madness, and the forms of treatment to which they responded—formed the basis for a major tradition of scientific investigation, and one which would subsequently be an important source of criminological data and ideas.

Attempts to link psychological characteristics to physical constitutions formed an abiding concern of this new discipline, but equally significant for our purposes, is its intense focus upon the insane individual—a focus permitted and encouraged by the long-term confinement of asylum patients under the daily gaze of the alienist (see Porter 1987). The new psychiatry produced a huge scientific literature concerned with the description of different mental types, case histories and causal analyses of how their madness developed, and detailed accounts of how they responded to various forms of 'moral' and medical treatment. What was developing here was a new kind of empirical psychology, concentrating upon pathological cases and their rational management. And because many of these cases involved criminal conduct (whether of a minor or a serious kind) one of the offshoots of this enterprise was a developing diagnostic and prognostic literature claiming to give a scientific account of certain kinds of individual criminals. Particularly after the Lunacy Acts of the mid-nineteenth century, when the asylum network was expanded to house the country's poor as well as the well-to-do, the new psychiatric profession had more and more to say about conditions such as 'moral imbecility', 'degeneracy', and 'feeblemindedness' which were deemed to be prevalent among the populations dealt with by the poor-houses and the prisons. Consequently, when a science of the criminal began to develop in the last decades of the century, there already existed a tradition of work whose concerns ran in parallel with its own and from which it could draw a measure of support and encouragement. Indeed, for about fifty years after the publication of Lombroso's *L'Uomo Delinquente* (1876) the journals of the psychiatric profession were virtually the only ones in Britain which took a serious interest in Lombroso's project.

If one were reviewing all of the ideas and undertakings of the eighteenth and early nineteenth centuries that bore a resemblance to elements which later

---

[21] On phrenology and its links to subsequent criminological studies, see Savitz *et al.* 1977. More generally, see Cooter 1981.

appeared within the discipline of criminology, there would be other stories to tell. The various forms of charitable and social work with the poor, the societies for the care of discharged convicts, the management of workhouses, inquiries about the causes and extent of inebriety, investigations into the labour market, the employment and treatment of children, education, the housing of the poor, the settlement and boys' club movements, could all be identified as the roots of particular ingredients in the modern criminological mix. But one needs to recall that the ideas and forms of inquiry set out here did not add up to an early form of criminology for the simple reason that they did not 'add up' at all; nor could they until the later emergence of a form of inquiry centred upon the criminal, which drew together these various enterprises under the umbrella of a specialist criminological discipline. In their own time, they were discrete forms of knowledge, undertaken for a variety of different purposes, and forming elements within a variety of different discourses, none of which corresponds exactly with the criminological project that was sub-sequently formed. Beccaria, for example, developed his arguments about the reform of the criminal law within the broader context of a work on political economy. Colquhoun's writings about crime and police were, for him, one aspect of a treatise on government in which he addressed the changing prob-lems of governance thrown up by the emergence of urbanized market society and the baleful effects of trade and luxury upon the manners of the people. Physiognomists, phrenologists, and psychiatrists were attempting to under-stand the physical and mental roots of human conduct rather than to develop a particular knowledge of offenders and offending. Like the utilitarian psychology developed by Bentham, these were attempts to capture the springs of human action in general, not to single out the criminal for special and exclusive attention. None of these discourses was struggling to create a dis-tinctive criminological enterprise, though once such a subject was created, each formed a resource to be drawn upon, usually in a way which wrenched its insights about crime apart from the framework which originally produced them.

Certainly, if one looks back from the perspective of the present, one can glimpse the outlines of the governmental project and the Lombrosian project gradually taking shape in this period. Empirical studies of the police, of prisons, of crime rates and of the deterrent effects of criminal laws—the very stuff of criminology's governmental concerns—are already underway, conducted at first by amateurs but later by state officials utilizing the elementary tools of scientific method. However, these studies were not, at the time, viewed as distinct from other inquiries, into the market, morals, workhouses, or poverty. The broad concern animating all of these studies and more was a concern with governance and the use of empirical data and scientific methods to improve government's grip on the population. Only with the later professionalization and specialization of the various state agencies—and with the invention of 'criminology'—did the study of governance in criminal matters come to be viewed as distinct from the governance of the population in general. Similarly, one can see in the work of the nineteenth-century phrenologists and psychiatrists a concern to understand human conduct in scientific terms, to identify character types, and to trace the etiologies of pathological behaviours. But at this historical moment there was no focus upon the criminal as a special human type and no felt need for a specialism built around this entity. The splitting off of criminological studies, both in the administrative field and in the clinic, was a late nineteenth-century event which significantly changed the organization of subsequent thought and action.

Since the formation of criminology, its practitioners have repeatedly identified what they take to be their 'roots'—the various lines of descent which link their present practice to work done a century and more before. But this is perhaps the wrong way to look at things. A more accurate account might suggest that at the end of the nineteenth century the idea of a specialist criminological science emerged—centred, as it happens, on the figure of the 'criminal type'—and that, after a process of struggle, adaptation, and convergence, this subsequently led to the establishment, in a rather different form, of an independent criminological discipline. Since the discipline was characterized by an eclectic, multidisciplinary concern to pursue the crime problem in all its aspects, the subject is continually expanding to embrace all of the ways in which crime and criminals might be scientifically studied, and in so doing, it has constantly created new predecessors for itself. The connection between eighteenth- and twentieth-century discourse about crime is not a matter of tenacious traditions of thought which have survived continuously for 200 years. Rather, it is a matter of a certain broad similarity between forms of inquiry and institutional arrangements which prevailed in the eighteenth and the twentieth centuries, together with the tendency of the modern discipline to embrace everything that might be scientifically said about crime and criminals. Each time a new element is added to the criminological armoury—be it radical criminology, ecological surveys, or sociological theory—someone sooner or later discovers that eighteenth- and nineteenth-century writers were doing something similar, and that this new approach should therefore be considered a central feature of the criminological tradition, albeit one that was temporarily (and inexplicably) forgotten. But this recurring 'recovery of tradition' is perhaps better understood as a bid for intellectual respectability and disciplinary centrality than as a serious claim about the development of the subject. After all, the crucial requirement of a genealogy is continuity of descent, and it is precisely this continuity which is missing wherever 'traditions' have to be 'rediscovered'.

If this account is accurate, and if criminology is a specific organization of knowledge which first emerged in the late nineteenth century, then the key problem is to try to describe its particularity and to explain the historical transmutation which produced this new form of enterprise. It has to be shown how the project of a specialized science emerged out of some other project or set of projects, and how it marked itself off from what went before. It is to that task that I now turn.

THE EMERGENCE OF A POSITIVE SCIENCE OF THE CRIMINAL

From Criminal Anthropology to the Science of Criminology

The idea of a specialist science of the criminal was born out of the interaction of a specific intellectual endeavour and a certain social context. As is often the case, a transmutation was produced in the history of ideas when a particular set of ideas and inquiries was found to have relevance to a field which had previously been regarded as quite separate. Ironically enough, the scientific work which led Cesare Lombroso to found a specialist 'science of the criminal'—a key ingredient in the formation of the modern discipline of criminology—was not, in fact, criminological in any sense that we would recognize. Lombroso's criminal science grew, somewhat accidentally, out of an anthropological concern to study humanity and its natural varieties, using the methods of anthropometry and craniometry to measure the physical features of human subjects. Influenced by the physical anthropology of Paul Broca and a Darwinian concern with species and their evolution, Lombroso's study of Italian army recruits and asylum and prison inmates was an attempt to identify different racial types and to subject them to scientific scrutiny and categorization (see Gould 1981). By the 1870s, however, the science of 'racial anthropology', like the science of degeneracy developed by Morel, had begun to overlap with potent social concerns, as is shown by its identification of 'types' such as the genius, the epileptoid, and the insane which were patently derived from social policy interests rather than evolutionary processes. Thus, when Lombroso 'discovered' the 'criminal type' he was extending a line of research which was already well established, and actually restating, in a more vivid form, an observation that had already been made by psychiatrists such as Maudsley and prison doctors such as J. Bruce Thomson.

But if Lombroso's 'discovery' was old news, the significance he gave to it was altogether novel. For him, the apparent distinctiveness of the criminal type prompted an idea that no one had imagined before: the idea of a distinctive science of the criminal. His conception of the criminal as a naturally occurring entity—a fact of nature rather than a social or legal product—led Lombroso to the thought of a natural science which would focus upon this entity, trace its characteristics, its stigmata, its abnormalities, and eventually identify the causes which make one person a criminal and another a normal citizen. And the startling thing about this Lombrosian project for the scientific differentiation of the criminal individual was that, despite its dubious scientific credentials, it immediately met with a huge international response. In the twenty years following the appearance of *L'Uomo Delinquente* in 1876 this strange new science came to form the basis of a major international movement, manifesting itself in an outpouring of texts, the formation of new associations, international congresses, specialist journals, national schools of thought, and interested officials in virtually every European and American state. At the same time, Lombroso himself became something of a household name, featuring in the fiction of Tolstoy, Musil, Bram Stoker, and Conan Doyle as well as in countless journalistic essays and scientific reports.[22]

In the years immediately following the publication of Lombroso's sensational claims a group of talented disciples gathered around him and a journal, *La Scuola Positiva*, was founded to publicize the new research and its practical implications. But disciples such as Enrico Ferri and Raffaele Garofalo were not content merely to repeat the master's formulations, and even the early work of this Italian school showed a considerable diversity and eclecticism, widening out the analysis to examine the social and legal aspects of criminality as well as its 'anthropological' character. This process of differentiation within the research enterprise was amplified by the formation of rival schools of inquiry, notably the 'French School' which emphasized the sociological and environmental determinants of crime and played down the role of fixed constitutional attributes, and the 'German school' which included the study of criminalistics and the development of new forensic techniques and procedures. A series of highly publicized international congresses, beginning in 1883, aired these disputes at length, with much acrimony on all sides, and resulted in the modification of most of Lombroso's original claims, particularly on the subject of the 'born criminal' and the fatalistic implications this notion was seen to have for the treatment and reform of offenders.

What eventually emerged from this process—especially in the writings of important second-generation figures like Prins, Saleilles, and Von Hamel—was a scientific movement which was much more eclectic and much more 'practical' than the original criminal anthropology had been (see Garland 1985*a*). One indication of the process of revision and modification whereby Lombroso's original formulations were reworked into a more acceptable form was the adoption of the term 'criminology', which came into general use in the 1890s. The term was originally used not as an exact synonym for criminal anthropology but as a neutral generic term which avoided the partisanship implicit in the original term and others—such as 'criminal sociology', 'criminal biology', and 'criminal psychology'—which competed with it.

This new science of criminology, as it developed in the last decades of the nineteenth century, was characterized by a number of distinctive features.[23] It was an avowedly scientific approach to crime, concerned to develop a 'positive', factual knowledge of offenders, based upon observation, measurement, and inductive reasoning, and rejecting the speculative thinking about human character which had previously informed criminal justice practices. In keeping

[22] On the spread of the criminological movement at the end of the nineteenth century, see Garland 1985*a*; Nye 1984. On Lombroso in contemporary fiction, see Pick 1989; Gould 1981. On the development of criminal anthropology in the USA, see Rafter 1992. On the reception of Lombroso's work in Britain, see Radzinowicz and Hood 1986, which also provides the most detailed account of the indigenous traditions of thinking about crime in the nineteenth century.

[23] For an analysis of the science of criminology and its early development, see Garland 1985*b*.

with its Lombrosian origins, it focused its attentions upon the individual criminal, and in particular upon the characteristics which appeared to mark off criminals as in some way different from normal, law-abiding citizens. It assumed that scientific explanation amounted to causal explanation and therefore set itself the task of identifying the causes of crime, though it should be added that the notion of 'cause' was understood in a wide variety of ways, some of which were more 'determinist' than others, and the kinds of cause identified ranged from innate constitutional defects to more or less contingent social circumstances. Finally, it addressed itself to the investigation of a new, pathological phenomenon—'criminality'—which it deemed to be the source of criminal behaviour and which, in effect, became the subject's *raison d'être* and the target of its practical proposals.

This concern to produce a differential diagnosis of the individual criminal and the etiology of his or her offending behaviour was in turn linked to a definite programme of practical action, quite at odds with the legal principles which had previously underpinned criminal justice practice. The notion of the offender's free will was attacked as a metaphysical abstraction, as was the concept of legal responsibility. Uniformity of sentencing was viewed as a failure to differentiate between different types of offender, and the principle of proportionate, retrospective punishment was rejected in favour of a flexible system of penal sanctions adapted to the reformability or dangerousness of the specific individual. Criminal justice was to cease being a punitive, reactive system and was to become instead a scientifically informed apparatus for the prevention, treatment, and elimination of criminality. It was to be a system run by criminological experts, concerned to maximize social defence, individual reform, and measures of security rather than to uphold some outdated legalistic conception of justice.

That such a radical programme of research and reform could be developed and become influential is testimony to the extent to which the new criminology resonated with the concerns and preoccupations of the political and cultural milieux in which it emerged.[24] The popularity of Lombroso's work is probably explicable in terms of the extent to which his conception of the criminal type chimed with deep-rooted cultural prejudices and offered scientific respectability to middle class perceptions of 'criminal classes' forming in the growing cities (see Sennett 1977). But the viability of the criminological movement, and the fact that it so quickly became an international phenomenon, are indications that it was a programme of thought and action which successfully meshed with the social politics and institutional practices which were becoming established at the time. The increasing involvement of experts and scientists in the administration of social problems in the late nineteenth century, and the related development of statistical data as a resource for governing, is one background circumstance. So too is the developing concern on the part of governments,

---

[24] For a detailed account of the British cultural milieu in which the new criminological science took hold, see Wiener 1990.

Poor Law administrators, police, and local authorities to classify and differentiate the populations they dealt with, seeking to identify and separate out dangerous elements while shoring up the social attachments of the 'deserving poor' and the 'respectable' working classes. In this specific context, the criminological programme offered certain regulatory and legitimatory possibilities which made it attractive to late nineteenth-century governments and administrators.

The regulatory advantages of the new criminology lay in its rejection of the formal egalitarianism that had previously shaped the practices of criminal law and its enforcement. Against the principle that everyone should be treated equally, criminology offered to differentiate between constitutional and accidental criminality, thus identifying the real sources of social danger and marking out the contours of the criminal class in a scientific rather than a moralistic way. Criminology also promised to provide a more extensive and a more effective form of intervention and regulation. Concerned to diagnose an individual's level of dangerousness rather than to judge whether or not he or she had yet broken the law, criminology offered the prospect of a system of control in which official measures need not wait for an offence to occur, or be limited by any principle of proportionality. At the same time, this more interventionist system could also claim to be more humane, in so far as its rationale was the promotion of individual and social welfare and not merely the infliction of retributive punishment (see Garland 1985a; Wiener 1990).

Finally, as is by now well documented, the new criminology met with extensive interest and social support because it was closely linked to the new prisons which had, by the late nineteenth century, become a prominent feature of all Western societies. As Michel Foucault (1977) has shown, the disciplinary, reformative practices of the penitentiary prison acted as a practical 'surface of emergence' for the individualizing, differentiating discourse of criminology. What Lombroso invented was a science of individual differences; but the data and social arrangements necessary for the production of this science, as well as the practical context in which such a knowledge would be practically useful, were already inscribed in the architecture and regimes of the disciplinary prison. In the prison setting inmates were arranged in individual cells, and subjected to constant, individual surveillance for long periods of time, their behaviour and characteristics being continually monitored in order that disciplinary measures could be adjusted to deal with individual reactions and peculiarities. The systematic and differentiating knowledge of offenders to which this gave rise formed the basis for the new science of criminology, which slowly fed back into the practices of imprisonment, refining the prison's classifications and techniques, and enhancing the authorities' understanding of the individuals that were held in custody (see Garland 1985a). The widespread use of disciplinary imprisonment in late nineteenth-century Europe and America thus provided a ready-made setting through which criminology could emerge and establish itself as a useful form of knowledge. As Sir Evelyn Ruggles-Brise (1924) put it, *la science pénitentiaire* develops gradually into the science of the discovery of the causes of crime—the science of criminology'.[25] Lombroso's project was thus propelled not just by its own scientific logic but by a combination of institutional and cultural dynamics, a set of forces which were to sustain this form of inquiry long after Lombroso's own reputation was utterly destroyed.

The Development of Criminology in Britain

As was often pointed out at the time, British intellectuals and penal officials played very little part in the early development of this new criminological movement. Most of the relevant research and publication took place in Italy, France, and Germany, and the British were notable absentees at the international congresses held to debate the claims and counter-claims of the various schools. It was not until the Geneva Congress of Criminal Anthropology in 1896 that Britain first sent an official delegate—the prison inspector Major Arthur Griffiths—and Griffiths returned with a sceptical report (see Griffiths 1904) which confirmed the attitude of British officials to the claims of the new criminologists. Griffiths was later to write the first entry to appear on 'Criminology' in the *Encyclopaedia Britannica* (1910–11) in which he attacked the theory of criminal types, but went on to show a cautious interest in the penological ideas which were by then emerging from the movement.

The arm's-length attitude of the British penal establishment to the new criminology was something of a surprise to individual enthusiasts such as Havelock Ellis and William Douglas Morrison, both of whom did much to introduce continental ideas into this country. Ellis published a book entitled *The Criminal* in 1890 which was, in effect, a summary of the major ideas of criminal anthropology, and regularly reviewed foreign criminological publications for the *Journal of Mental Science* from 1890 to 1919; Morrison established and edited 'The Criminology Series' which published translations of works by Lombroso (1895), Ferri (1895) and Proal (1898), as well as publishing a number of his own works, including *Juvenile Offenders* (1896). One cause of this surprise was that many of the new criminologists, including Lombroso himself, pointed to earlier work published in Britain which appeared to contain the kinds of ideas which would later become central to the movement. Thus, in the 1860s the psychiatrist Henry Maudsley and the prison medical officer J. Bruce Thomson had written about 'the genuine criminal' and 'the criminal class', describing these individuals as 'morally insane', 'degenerate', 'defective in physical organisation . . . from hereditary causes' and 'incurable' in a way which appeared to be altogether 'Lombrosian' before Lombroso.[26]

---

[25] On the prison as a 'surface of emergence' for criminological knowledge, see Foucault 1977; also Garland 1992.

[26] Maudsley (1863: 73) refers to 'the criminal' as a 'fact in nature' and criminals as 'if not strictly a degenerate species, certainly . . . a degenerate variety of the species'. Thomson (1867: 341) states that 'all who have seen much of criminals agree that they have a singular family likeness or caste . . . Their physique is coarse and repulsive; their complexion dingy, almost atrabilious; their face, figure and mien, disagreeable. The women are painfully ugly; and the men look stolid, and many

But to describe Maudsley and Thomson as criminologists before the fact was misleading. Maudsley was engaged in a distinctively psychiatric endeavour (the development and application of typologies dealing with various mental disorders and pathologies) and Thomson's concern was to assess the impact of prison discipline upon the bodies and minds of prisoners (see Thomson 1867). Neither of them for a moment imagined that there was any justification for a distinctive scientific specialism centered upon the criminal. More importantly, during the 1870s and 1880s British medical and psychiatric opinion had shifted away from earlier attempts to characterize 'criminals' in such indiscriminating, pathological terms. From the 1870s onwards, prison doctors such as David Nicolson and John Baker set about redefining 'the morbid psychology of criminals', so as to differentiate a range of conditions rather than a single type. Nicolson (1878–9) emphasized that professional observation made it plain that only a minority of criminals were in any sense mentally abnormal, and he forcibly rejected any suggestion that offenders were generally 'incurable' or beyond the reach of prison reformation. During the same years, the nascent British psychiatric profession was learning that criminal courts would not tolerate psychiatric evidence which contradicted basic legal axioms about individual free will and responsibility, and it gradually developed a *modus vivendi* which aimed to minimize conflict between psychiatry and law. By the 1880s, leading figures of the new profession such as Needham, Hack Tuke, Nicolson, and Maudsley were taking pains to distance themselves from the embarrassing claims made by psychiatrists (Maudsley among them) in earlier years—claims which were now being taken up again by criminologists with their talk of 'born criminals', 'the criminal type', atavism, and so on (see Nicolson 1878–9; Maudsley 1889; Tuke 1889; Needham 1889; Baker 1892; Nicolson 1895; Garland 1988).

The relationship between the new continental movement and the studies of criminals carried out in Britain by prison doctors and psychiatrists is a complex one, and the assumption (made by Ellis and others) that the two were continuous is a simplification which glosses over important differences. Unlike Lombroso's anthropology, British psychiatry was not concerned to isolate discrete human 'types' and classify them by means of racial and constitutional differences. Instead, it was a therapeutically orientated practice based upon a system of classifying mental disorders which, like the disease model of nine-teenth-century medicine, discussed the condition separately from the individual in whom it might be manifested. Within the classification schemes of morbid psychology there was a variety of conditions which criminals were said to exhibit, including insanity, moral insanity, degeneracy, and feebleminded-ness (among others). But generally speaking, the criminal was not conceived of as a distinct psychological type.

of them brutal, indicating physical and moral deterioration. In fact there is a stamp on them in form and expression which seems to me the heritage of the class.' For a discussion of these debates, see Garland 1988; also Radzinowicz and Hood 1986.

More important than this theoretical difference was the way in which British psychiatry contrasted with Lombrosian anthropology in its practical commitments and its relationship to the institutions of criminal justice. In his early publications, Lombroso claimed that his ideas had great relevance for criminal law and penal policy, but, as his critics soon pointed out, he was not particularly well informed about the practical realities of crime and punishment.[27] In consequence, his penology was not just radical and at odds with current practices; it was also naïve and distorted, lacking a close familiarity with the normal range of offenders and the institutions that dealt with them. Lombroso's conception of the criminal type had emerged from the theoretical hypotheses of physical anthropology rather than extensive penological experience, and only gradually did he modify his views to bring them more into line with the way legal institutions worked. In contrast, the scientific thinking about the criminal which developed in British psychiatric and medico-legal circles was closely tied into professional tasks such as the giving of evidence before courts of law, or the decisions as to classification, diagnosis, and regimen which prison medical officers made daily. This practical experience was crucial in shaping the psychiatric approach to 'criminological' issues because it ensured that psychiatrists and prison doctors were well acquainted with the day-to-day realities of criminal justice and with the need to bring psychiatric propositions into line with the demands of courts and prison authorities.

The British tradition that was closest to the criminology developing on the continent was thus also somewhat hostile to it. The scientific studies conducted by British prison doctors and psychiatrists were, from an early stage, situated within an institutional framework which shaped their purposes and constrained their findings. In consequence, these studies were generally modest in their claims and respectful of the requirements of institutional regimes and legal principles. As far as most prison doctors and experienced psychiatrists were concerned, the majority of criminals were more or less normal individuals; only a minority required psychiatric treatment and this usually involved removing them from the penal system and putting them into institutions for the mentally ill or defective. And although the diagnostic and therapeutic claims of psychiatry changed over time, from an early stage there was a recognition that, for the majority of offenders, the normal processes of law and punishment should apply. Compared to the sweeping claims of criminal anthropology, the British medico-legal tradition was, by the 1890s, somewhat conservative, and generally dismissive of Lombrosian ideas. Senior psychiatric figures such as Maudsley and Conolly Norman referred publicly to the 'puerilities of criminal anthropology' and the 'lamentable extravagances' of the new theories (Norman 1895; Maudsley 1895). Sir Horatio Bryan Donkin, the first Medical

---

[27] See, for instance, the review by Arthur St John (1912) of Lombroso's work, in which he contrasts Lombroso's naïvety to the experienced practical understanding of a prison doctor such as James Devon.

Commissioner of Prisons, gave clear expression to the difference between the two traditions when he defined 'criminology', properly so-called, as the investigations undertaken by 'persons concerned in some way with the prison authorities who strive to discover just principles on which to base their work' and distinguished this from the newer 'doctrine and debate on the causation of crime' which he condemned as 'theories based on preconceived assumptions regardless of fact' (Donkin 1917).

So scientific research on individual criminals in Britain stemmed from a rather different root than did continental criminology, and inclined towards a more pragmatic, institutionalized approach to its subject. But, as I noted earlier, the international criminological movement tended to become more eclectic, more moderate, and more practical over time, gradually dissociating itself from extremist claims and adapting to the basic demands of the institutions it sought to influence. And as it became more respectable and more firmly established, the initial hostility of Britain's scientific and penological circles tended to fade. From the mid-1890s onwards, the English and Scottish Prison Commissions began to take an active interest in the movement, as did the leading psychiatric periodicals. Even the influential Gladstone Committee Report gave passing approval to the 'learned but conflicting theories' which have subjected 'crime, its causes, and treatment' to 'scientific inquiry' (Gladstone Committee 1895: 8). What seems gradually to have happened in Britain during the period leading up to the First World War is that 'criminology' ceased to be exclusively identified with its anthropological origins and instead became used as a general term to describe scientific research on the subject of crime and criminals. Grudgingly at first, but more and more frequently, prison officials, psychiatrists, and doctors began to refer to their researches as 'criminological', until this became the accepted name for a new scientific specialism. The irony is that, in Britain at least, criminology came to be recognized as an accredited scientific specialism only when it began to rid itself of the notion of the distinctive 'criminal type'—the very entity which had originally grounded the claim that a special science of the criminal was justified.

Most of the early British work which identified itself as criminological was actually a continuation of the older medico-legal tradition of prison research, now opened out to engage with an expanding criminological literature imported from Europe and North America. It is, for example, almost exclusively within the Reports of the Medical Commissioner of Prisons and of the various prison medical officers that one will find any official discussion of criminological science in the first few decades of this century, and most of the major scientific works on crime written in Britain before the 1930s were written by doctors with psychiatric training and positions within the prison service.[28] The first university lectures in 'criminology' delivered in Britain—

[28] See *inter alia* Sutherland 1908; Quinton 1910; Devon 1912; Smith 1922; Sullivan 1924; East 1927.

given at Birmingham by Maurice Hamblin Smith in 1921—were directed at postgraduate medical students within a course entitled 'Medical Aspects of Crime and Punishment', and long before Hermann Mannheim began teaching at the London School of Economics in 1935 there were courses on 'Crime and Insanity' offered at London University by senior prison medical officers such as Sullivan and East.[29] In the absence of any specialist periodicals devoted to criminology, criminological articles and reviews appeared chiefly in the *Journal of Mental Science, The British Journal of Medical Psychology*, and the *Transactions of the Medico-Legal Association* (from 1933 *The Medico-Legal and Criminological Review*), although the *Howard Journal* also carried some reviews, as did the *Sociological Review*.

The institutionally based, medico-legal criminology which predominated in Britain for much of the nineteenth century and the first half of the twentieth was, by its nature, an evolving, adaptive tradition. The criminological texts which it generated grew out of practical contexts which were forever changing, since institutions continually redefined their operations and took on new concerns, and also because new methods, theories, and techniques became available to the professionals who administered them. Many of the criminological texts written in the nineteenth century focused upon the problems of classifying particular offenders—as psychiatric rather than criminal cases, as morally insane, feebleminded, and so on—and of course these problems had a direct bearing upon the practices of penal institutions. As the penal system diversified in the early part of the twentieth century, developing specialist institutions for the inebriate, habitual offenders, the feebleminded, and for juveniles, and becoming more refined and differentiated in the classification of adult prisoners, the criminological literature similarly began to address itself to these new diagnostic and classificatory problems.[30] Thus, although this line of research came close to the concerns of the Lombrosian project in its focus upon individuals and their differential classification, it lacked the scientific ambition and theory-building concerns of the latter, being almost exclusively focused upon knowledge which was useful for administrative purposes.

In 1919, the emphasis upon individual character and specialized treatment prompted by the Gladstone Committee report—together with concerns about large numbers of shell-shocked and mentally disturbed men returning from the war—led the Birmingham Justices to establish a permanent scheme for the clinical examination of untried adult offenders. Previously such work had been done on an occasional, *ad hoc* basis, and depended upon the skill and interest of the local prison doctor. By appointing Hamblin Smith and W. A. Potts,

---

[29] According to his own account, Cyril Burt had regularly given lectures on juvenile delinquency at Liverpool University between 1906 and 1914, but these had occurred in the context of a psychology class rather than one devoted to 'criminology'. See Mannheim 1957.

[30] Works on alcoholism by W. C. Sullivan (1906), on recidivism by J. F. Sutherland (1908), and on the psychology of the criminal by M. Hamblin Smith (1922) and H. E. Field (1932) are significant examples of research derived from the developing penal-welfare complex.

both psychiatrically trained prison doctors, and charging them with these new duties, the Justices effectively created a new specialism of applied criminology. Before long, Potts and Hamblin Smith were adapting the standard mental tests for use in this area, publishing the results of their clinical studies, and writing extensively about the need for this kind of investigation and its implications for the treatment and prevention of crime. In *The Psychology of the Criminal* (1922*b*) and in a series of articles in the *Journal of Mental Science*, the *Howard Journal*, and elsewhere, Smith emphasized the importance of criminological study, though for him this meant the clinical examination of individual offenders for the purpose of assessment and diagnosis. As Britain's first authorized teacher of 'criminology', and as the first individual to use the title of 'criminologist', it is significant that Smith, like Donkin and Ruggles-Brise before him, rejected the search for 'general theories' in favour of the 'study of the individual'. It is also significant that the centres for criminological research and teaching which he proposed were envisaged as places where 'young medical graduates' would be trained to become expert in the medico-psychological examination and assessment of offenders (Smith 1922*a*).

Hamblin Smith was also one of the first criminological workers in Britain to profess an interest in psychoanalysis, which he used as a means to assess the personality of offenders, as well as a technique for treating the mental conflicts which, he claimed, lay behind the criminal act. In this respect Smith met with much official opposition, particularly from W. Norwood East; but there were others, outside the prisons establishment, who were more enthusiastic. In the winter of 1922–23 Dr Grace Pailthorpe assisted Smith in the psychoanalytic investigation of female offenders in Birmingham, and went on to complete a five-year study at Holloway, funded by a grant from the Medical Research Council. Her report (Pailthorpe 1932), which was completed by 1929, but held back by the MRC until 1932, claimed that crime was generally a symptom of mental conflict which might be psychoanalytically resolved. This radical approach met with some consternation in official circles (see East 1936: 319), but it excited the interest of a number of analysts and medical psychologists who formed a group to promote the Pailthorpe report and its approach. Out of their meetings emerged the Association for the Scientific Treatment of Criminals (1931), which, in 1932, became the Institute for the Scientific Treatment of Delinquency (ISTD) (see Glover 1960).

Most of the founder members of this group were involved in the new outpatient sector of psychiatric work, made possible by a developing network of private clinics, which included the Tavistock (1921) and the Maudsley (1923), the new child guidance centres, and, in 1933, the ISTD's own Psychopathic Clinic (which in 1937 was moved and renamed the Portman Clinic). This new field of practice gave rise to its own distinctive brand of criminological theory. The early publications of the ISTD emphasize the clinical exploration of individual personality, and in that sense are continuous with much previous work. But they also manifest a new preventative emphasis, which reflected the fact that the new clinics operated outside the formal penal system, and could deal with individuals before their disturbed conduct actually became criminal.[31] Eventually, the ISTD's emphasis upon psychoanalysis, and its open hostility to much official penal policy, ensured that it remained essentially an outsider body, operating at arm's length from the Home Office and the Prison Commission. This outsider status forms an important background to the later decision of the Home Office to establish a criminological institute at Cambridge, rather than under ISTD auspices in London, for although 'the formation of such a body was one of the original aims of the ISTD' (Glover 1960: 70), and the claims of the organization were canvassed to the Home Secretary in 1958, the Home Office appears not to have seriously considered such an option (see Radzinowicz 1988: 9).

Despite its subsequent neglect, the work of W. Norwood East, particularly *An Introduction to Forensic Psychiatry in the Criminal Courts* (1927) and *The Medical Aspects of Crime* (1936)—better represents the mainstream of British criminology in the 1920s and 1930s. East was a psychiatrically trained prison medical officer who became a leading figure in the 1930s as Medical Director on the Prison Commission and President of the Medico-Legal Society, and his views dominated official policy-making for a lengthy period. East was himself a proponent of a psychological approach to crime, but he considered its scope to be sharply delimited, and consistently warned against the dangers and absurdities of exaggerating its claims. Instead of theoretical speculation and scientific ambition he stressed the importance of 'day-to-day adminis-tration', and the practical impact of theoretical ideas. (Hence his criticism of deterministic ideas, which he thought promoted 'mental invalidism' instead of trying to build up a sense of social responsibility' (East 1931–2). In 1934 he established an extended experiment at Wormwood Scrubs prison, whereby those offenders deemed most likely to respond to psychological therapy—particularly sex offenders and arsonists—were subjected to a period of investi-gation and treatment. At the end of five years, East and Hubert's Report on *The Psychological Treatment of Crime* (1939) reaffirmed East's view that while 80 per cent of offenders were psychologically normal, and would respond to routine punishment, a minority might usefully be investigated and offered psychological treatment. The Report proposed a special institution to deal with such offenders—a proposal which was immediately accepted but not put into effect until the opening of Grendon Underwood prison in 1962. East and Hubert also recommended that this institution should function as a centre for

---

[31] As the editors of the *British Journal of Delinquency* put it in the first issue: 'The names of James Devon, Hamblin Smith, Norwood East and others bear witness to the honourable part played by Prison Medical Officers in the development of scientific criminology in this country. But the activities of the "institutional" criminologist have been rather overshadowed in recent years by the expansion of what might be called the "ambulant" approach to delinquency, i.e. the application of diagnostic and, where necessary or possible, therapeutic methods to early cases attending Delinquency Clinics, Child Guidance and Psychiatric Centres, etc., with or without probationary supervision. And to the extent that the Delinquency Clinic bridges the gap between the "non-delinquent" and the "recidivist", it is inevitable that the ambulant system should provide the most fruitful field for research into causes and methods of prevention' ('Editorial', *British Journal of Delinquency*, 1/1 (1950/1): 4).

criminological research, and it is significant that when a criminological centre is here proposed for the first time in an official report, it should be envisaged as part of a psychiatric institution, dealing only with a small minority of pathological offenders.

An important departure from this British tradition of clinically based psychiatric studies was *The English Convict: A Statistical Study*, published in 1913 by Dr Charles Goring under the auspices of the Home Office and the Prison Commission. This work was made possible by institutional routines, in so far as anthropometric methods were used in prisons for the identification of habitual offenders during the 1890s, and in fact one of its starting points was a desire to measure the impact of prison diet and labour upon the inmates' physiques. But the issues addressed by the final report went far beyond these institutional matters and engaged, for the first time in an official publication, with the theoretical claims of scientific criminology.

The analysis and tabulation of the vast quantity of data collected by the study was carried out in Karl Pearson's Biometrical Laboratory at the University of London—an unusual location for prison research but one which was well suited to the statistical and eugenic themes which dominated the final report. As its sponsors intended, the study gave a definitive refutation of the old Lombrosian claim that the criminal corresponded to a particular physical type, thus confirming the position which the British authorities had held all along. However, the significance of Goring's study went far beyond this negative and somewhat out-of-date finding. In fact, Goring's analysis began by *assuming* that there was no criminal type, and although it was not much noticed at the time, his study is chiefly notable for inventing a quite new way of differentiating criminals from non-criminals.

In the early part of the book, Goring set out extensive theoretical and methodological arguments which insisted that criminality should be viewed not as a qualitative difference of type, marked by anomaly and morbidity, but instead as a variant of normality, differentiated only by degree. Following the arguments of Manouvrier and Topinard, he pointed out that so-called criminal 'anomalies' are only 'more or less extreme degrees of character which in some degree are present in all men'. Moreover, he made it clear that his use of statistical method necessarily presupposed this idea of a criminal characteristic which is a common feature of all individuals, and he went on to name this hypothesized entity 'the criminal diathesis'. This conception of criminality as normal, rather than morbid or pathological, implied a new basis for criminological science, which Goring vigorously set forth. From now on, criminology could no longer depend on the clinical gaze of a Lombroso and its impressionistic identification of anomalies. (Goring had, in any case, provided a devastating critique of this 'anatomico-pathological method'.) Instead it must be a matter of large populations, careful measurement, and statistical analysis, demonstrating patterns of differentiation in the mass which would not be visible in the individual or to the naked eye.

Goring's own application of these methods purported to reveal a significant, but by no means universal, association between criminality and two heritable characteristics, namely low intelligence and poor physique, and suggested that 'family and other environmental conditions' were not closely associated with crime. From these findings he drew a series of practical, eugenic conclusions, declaring that 'crime will continue to exist as long as we allow criminals to propagate' and that government should therefore 'modify opportunity for crime by segregating the unfit' and 'regulate the reproduction of those constitutional qualities—feeblemindedness, inebriety, epilepsy, deficient social instinct, insanity, which conduce to the committing of crime' (Goring 1913). Here, as so often in subsequent studies, we see Lombroso's specific claims rejected, only to find that his basic assumptions and project are being reasserted in some new, revised form.

Although *The English Convict* had a considerable impact abroad, and especially in the USA, in Britain it received a much more muted response. On the one hand, Goring's attack had been centred upon theoretical positions which had little support in this country, other than from maverick outsiders such as Havelock Ellis. On the other, it appeared to have policy implications—particularly the possibility that inherited traits would render reformative prison regimes impotent—which were not altogether welcome in official circles. The Prison Commissioners, while supporting the study's publication as a Blue Book, refused to endorse its conclusions (see Garland 1985a), and Sir Bryan Donkin (1919) distanced himself from the book altogether, arguing that 'even correct generalisations . . . concerning criminals in the mass are not likely to be of much positive value in the study or treatment of individuals'. In much the same way W. C. Sullivan, the medical superintendent at Broadmoor, argued in *Crime and Insanity* (1924) that clinical rather than statistical methods were the only reliable means of obtaining useful, policy-relevant knowledge.

These exchanges are revealing because they show the extent to which British criminology up to this point was shaped by the interests and assumptions of official policy-makers and the institutions that they served. In the years before the First World War, the medico-legal assessment of individual offenders played an explicit role in the trial process and in the disposition of offenders after conviction, so the promised benefits of clinical research were readily apparent in a way that was not true of statistical studies. Later on, when criminal justice officials came to realize how they could use the results of actuarial calculations—in predicting response to treatment, deploying police resources, calculating crime rates, and so on—the balance of interest shifted the other way. Though he did not live to see it (having died in 1919), Goring's argument for the importance of statistical method and mass data in criminological research was the one which was ultimately most persuasive to the British authorities. By the end of the 1930s, the Prison Commission and the Home Office had each embarked upon large-scale, statistically based projects, subsequently published as East (1942) and Carr-Saunders *et al.* (1942), and this became a characteristic form of government-sponsored research in the years after 1945.

If East's work exemplified the mainstream British tradition of medico-psychiatric criminological research (with the ISTD's more radical clinical studies forming an important tributary), and Goring inaugurated a new stream of statistical studies, there was also another significant line of inquiry which influenced criminological work in the post-war period. This third stream is best represented by the eclectic, multifactorial, social-psychological research of Cyril Burt. When later criminologists such as Mannheim and Radzinowicz looked back upon their predecessors, they spent little time discussing the merits of *The English Convict* or *The Medical Aspects of Crime*. Instead, they invariably picked out Cyril Burt's 1925 study, *The Young Delinquent*, as the first major work of modern British criminology and as an exemplar for the discipline that they were helping to create.[32] Like most criminological texts in this period, *The Young Delinquent* emerged from a specific field of practice—it was not until the 1960s that research took off from an academic base—but in marked contrast to the work of East, Hamblin Smith, Sullivan, and co., this field of practice was outside the penal system, rather than central to it. In his post as educational psychologist to the London County Council, Burt was responsible for the psychological assessment and advice of London's school-child population, which involved him in examining thousand of individual problem cases, many of them behavioural as well as educational, and making recommendations for their treatment. Consequently, his criminological study was built upon a wider than usual population, dealing mostly with 'pre-delinquents' rather than convicted offenders, and it was not constrained by the narrowly penal concerns that affected most contemporary studies. Rather than inquire about specific classifications or distinctions, Burt was interested to specify all the possible sources of individual psychological difference, and thereby to identify the causal patterns which precipitate delinquency and non-delinquency.

The Young Delinquent was based upon the detailed clinical examination of 400 schoolchildren (a delinquent or quasi-delinquent group and a control group), using a battery of techniques which included biometric measurement, mental testing, temperament testing, and psychoanalytic and social inquiries, together with the most up-to-date statistical methods of factor analysis and correlation. Its findings were expansively eclectic, identifying some 170 causative factors which were in some way associated with delinquency, and showing, by way of narrative case histories, how each factor might typically operate. From his analysis, Burt concluded that certain factors, such as defective discipline, defective family relationships, and particular types of temperament, were highly correlated with delinquency, while the influence of other factors, such as poverty or low intelligence, while not altogether negligible, had been seriously overstated in the past. His major proposition was

[32] See Mannheim (1949: 11); also Radzinowicz (1961: 173–6): 'it may be said that modern criminological research in England dates only from Sir Cyril Burt's study of *The Young Delinquent*, first published in 1925. Its excellence in method and interpretation was at once recognized and it has stood the test of rapidly advancing knowledge.'

that delinquency was not the outcome of special factors operating only on delinquents, but was rather the result of a combination of factors—typically as many as nine or ten—operating at once upon a single individual. In consequence, the study of criminality must be, above all, multicausal in scope, while its treatment must be tailored to fit the needs of the individual case. The influence of Burt's work, and especially its eclectic, multifactorial search for the correlates of individual delinquency, was to become something of a hallmark of British criminology in the mid-twentieth century, though ironically enough (in view of Burt's modern reputation) his most immediate impact was to shift attention away from the purported intellectual deficiencies of delinquents towards questions of temperament and emotional balance.

The scientific criminology which developed in Britain between the 1890s and the Second World War was thus heavily dominated by a medico-psychological approach, focused upon the individual offender and tied into a correctionalist penal-welfare policy. Within this approach there were a number of important variants, and the enterprise was differently understood by different practitioners; but compared to the subject which exists today, criminology operated within rather narrow parameters. Sociological work, such as that developed by Durkheim in France at the turn of the century, or in Chicago in the 1920s and 1930s (which treated crime rates as social facts to be explained by sociological methods), was virtually absent. Instead the 'social dimension' of crime was conceived of as one factor among many others operating upon the individual— a good example of how the criminological project transforms the elements which it 'borrows' from other disciplines. Nor was the radicalism of foreign criminologists such as Enrico Ferri and Willem Bonger much in evidence here; indeed, if British criminology can be said to have developed radical analyses during this period, they were inspired by Freud rather than by Marx.[33]

The major topics of scientific interest were those thrown up as problems for the courts, the prison and the Borstal system—such as the mentally abnormal offender, recidivists, and especially juvenile delinquents—and the central purpose of scientific research was not the construction of explanatory theory but instead the more immediate end of aiding the policy-making process. The governmental project dominated, almost to the point of monopolization, and Lombroso's science of the criminal was taken up only in so far as it could be shown to be directly relevant to the governance of crime and criminals. Such a pragmatic, correctionalist orientation was, of course, hardly surprising when one recalls that the authors of pre-war criminological research in Britain were, virtually without exception, practitioners working in the state penal system or else in the network of clinics and hospitals which had grown up around it. In Britain, before the mid-1930s, criminology as a university-based, academic discipline simply did not exist.

---

[33] See for instance the works by Glover (1941, 1960), Aichhorn (1951), and Friedlander (1947).

THE ESTABLISHMENT OF A CRIMINOLOGICAL DISCIPLINE IN BRITAIN

The transformation of British criminology from a minor scientific specialism—the part-time activity of a few practitioners and enthusiasts—into an established academic discipline took place comparatively late, occurring some time between the mid-1930s and the early 1960s. Even then, it was by no means an inevitable or necessary development. Indeed, had it not been for the rise of Nazism in Germany, and the appointment of three distinguished European emigrés, Hermann Mannheim, Max Grunhut, and Leon Radzinowicz, to academic posts at elite British universities, British criminology might never have developed sufficient academic impetus to become an independent discipline. But however contingently, the process of discipline formation did take hold in the post-war period and its symbolic culmination occurred in October 1961 with the inauguration of a postgraduate course for the training of criminological researchers and teachers at the new Institute of Criminology at Cambridge. In the intervening years, the other concomitants of disciplinary status had gradually come into being, initially as the result of private initiatives, and then, in the late 1950s, with the support and funding of government.

Criminology teaching in the universities began to expand from the late 1930s onwards, catering to the needs of the fast-growing social work and probation professions and attracting a first generation of research students (such as John Spencer, Norval Morris, Tadeuz Grygier, and John Croft) who would go on to become important figures in the new discipline.[34] Cambridge University established a Department of Criminal Science in 1941, which sponsored research projects as well as a book series, and eventually formed the base upon which the Institute of Criminology was built. In 1950 Britain's first specialist criminology journal, the *British Journal of Delinquency* (renamed the *British Journal of Criminology* in 1960), was established as 'the official organ of the ISTD' and set about the task of moulding a coherent discipline out of the scores of small-scale research efforts dotted around the country. Editorials by Mannheim and his co-editors Edward Glover and Emmanuel Miller identified key aspects of an emerging research programme and the journal carried extensive discussions of methodology and data sources as well as acting as a kind of bulletin board through which researchers could keep abreast of activities in the expanding field. In 1953, the ISTD also established the

---

[34] According to the results of a survey carried out by Mannheim in the mid-1950s, twenty-one British universities claimed that criminology formed a part of their teaching curriculum, whether for undergraduate students or as a part of extension courses and diplomas taken by trainee social workers and probation officers (Mannheim 1957). From 1938 onwards, the ISTD was a centre for the University of London four-year Diploma Course in Social Studies, an evening course, of which the fourth year was devoted to criminology. Mannheim himself taught 'criminology as a separate subject in all its aspects' at the LSE from 1935 onwards.

Scientific Group for the Discussion of Delinquency Problems, which acted as a forum for discussion for several years until younger members of the group— some of them with newly created university posts in criminology—grew dissatisfied with the clinical and psychoanalytical emphasis of leading figures such as Glover and split off to found the more academically orientated British Society of Criminology. In 1956, Howard Jones published the first British criminology textbook, *Crime and the Penal System*, a work much influenced by the teachings of Mannheim at the LSE. In its emphasis upon penological issues and its assumption of a reforming, welfarist stance it encapsulated an important and continuing strand of British criminological culture. (Such was the pace of change in this, the discipline's take-off phase, that the third edition of the book, appearing only nine years later in 1965, was described by an otherwise sympathetic reviewer as 'sadly out of date' (Taylor 1968).)

The Criminal Justice Act of 1948 provided for the regular allocation of Treasury funds for the purposes of criminological research, but in the years that followed only a tiny annual budget was actually made available. However, the 1950s saw the emergence of an explicit and continuing commitment by the British government to support criminological research, both as an in-house activity and as a university-based specialism. This, in effect, marked the point of convergence between criminology as an administrative aid and criminology as a scientific undertaking—the consolidation of the governmental and Lombrosian projects—and it represents a key moment in the creation of a viable, independent discipline of criminology in Britain. This new and closer relationship beween government and criminological science not only endorsed criminology's claim to be a useful form of knowledge; it also gave official and financial backing to criminology's claim to scientific status and university recognition. Thus the Home Office proceeded to set up not just an infrastructure for policy-led research—which it did in 1957 with the opening of the Home Office Research Unit (see Lodge 1974)—but also an academic institute, the Cambridge Institute of Criminology, sited in a prestigious university, with the explicit task of undertaking scientific research and training recruits for the newly founded discipline of criminology (see Radzinowicz 1988). As the 1959 White Paper '*Penal Practice in a Changing Society*' announced, 'the institute should be able, as no existing agency is in a position to do, to survey with academic impartiality . . . the general problem of the criminal in society, its causes, and its solution.' (Home Office 1959).

This new-found compatibility between traditions which had often pulled in different directions had a number of sources. In part it was testimony to the degree to which the scientific strand of criminological research had modified its ambitions and adapted its terms to fit the institutional realities and policy concerns which so heavily influenced the marketplace of criminological ideas. In part it was attributable to the fact that research concerned to differentiate criminals from non-criminals, and especially those who would recidivate from those who would not, was thought to be important for the development of effective sentencing decisions (especially Borstal allocations) and decisions regarding early release. Thus, for example, the prediction research which claimed so much attention in the late 1950s could appear to satisfy both the needs of administration and the ends of science, in so far as these studies sought to identify offender characteristics which were highly correlated with subsequent offending. (In the event, the most effective prediction tables made little use of clinical information about the offender, and actually discredited to some extent the whole project of etiological research.) One might also suggest, however, that this convergence between the search for useful knowledge and the search for scientific truth was actually more apparent than real, because, in the event, the research agenda pursued by the Cambridge Institute, at least in the early years, was heavily influenced by immediate policy needs. Indeed, for the most part, it was scarcely distinguishable from the in-house research of the Home Office—a fact that did not go uncriticized at the time.

If the emergence of a criminological discipline was the coming together of traditions of inquiry that had once been more distinct, it was also, and more immediately, the achievement of a few key individuals, backed by an alliance of interested organizations. These discipline-builders had to struggle with all sorts of resistance, but their decisive advantage was that they acted in a context in which government ministers and officials had become receptive to the idea that policy-making could be enhanced by the availability of systematic research and trained expertise. The shrewd political skills and institution-building energies of Leon Radzinowicz were particularly important (not least in persuading the Wolfson Foundation to fund the British discipline's first chair and provide the Cambridge Institute with the resources to become one of the world's leading centres of criminological work),[35] as was the influential teaching of Hermann Mannheim and the proselytizing work that he and the other ISTD members conducted in academic and practical circles. Similarly, the impressive body of research publications produced by these authors and others such as Burt, Bowlby, Grunhut, Sprott, Mays, and Ferguson created a strong case for the value of criminology as an academic subject.

The practical and educational benefits to be derived from establishing institutes and university departments of criminology were also canvassed by a number of influential political figures and associations. Senior government officials such as Alexander Paterson, Sir Lionel Fox, Sir Alexander Maxwell, and Viscount Templewood made public declarations about the need for criminology; Margery Fry and George Benson MP made representations to the Home Office to this effect; and at various times the Howard League, the Magistrates' Association, the British Psychological Society, the National

---

[35] It is worth pointing out that the standard claim made by those who canvassed the British government to support the development of criminology—namely, that the UK was trailing far behind other countries in the pursuit of criminological research—was subsequently shown to be quite false. Radzinowicz's empirical survey of the state of criminology around the world suggested that, with the establishment of the Cambridge Institute and the Home Office Research Unit, British criminology probably enjoyed more official support than that of any other country, with the exception of the USA. See Radzinowicz 1961.

Association for Mental Health, the Royal Medico-Psychological Association, and the United Nations European Seminar on Crime all added their weight to the campaign to obtain government sponsorship and university recognition for the subject (see Radzinowicz 1988). In the event, criminology's most influential supporter was R. A. Butler, who as Home Secretary in the late 1950s took a personal interest in the development of the subject and was instrumental in extending government funding for criminological research, and in setting up the Cambridge Institute (see Butler 1974).

The government's interest in sponsoring the creation of a viable criminological enterprise was a combination of immediate penological concerns and broader conceptions of how the policy-making process ought to be organized. In the years immediately preceding the Second World War, a concern about increasing rates of juvenile offending prompted the Home Office to arrange a series of conferences and research projects in order to estimate the extent of the problem and identify its social and psychological roots. When, in the post-war years, the high wartime rates of delinquent behaviour failed to decline, the problem attracted extensive political and press attention and provided a compelling rationale for the promotion of criminological research. (It is note-worthy that henceforth, juvenile delinquency was to become a central topic in British criminology.) Similarly, the gradual development of a penal philosophy of 'treatment and training', centred upon the Borstal system and relying for its effectiveness upon accurate assessment and classification procedures, led to a growing demand for criminological knowledge and advice. More generally, the wartime experience of operational research and the utilization of expertise in the formation of strategy, together with the growing professionalization of administration and social work in the new welfare state, gradually convinced post-war governments of the value of research and expertise as a basis for social policy.[36] The same governmental mentality which looked to Beveridge and Keynes to solve the social and economic problems of the nation came to recognize criminology as a form of knowledge which should be integrated into the institutions of government. Criminology thus became an integral part of the process of 'social reconstruction', a small element in the post-war settlement which sought to secure stability and capitalist growth by means of welfare provision and social democratic management (see Mannheim 1946; Taylor 1981).

One might add that this tendency to appeal to expert, 'scientific' knowledge as a source of solutions to social and personal problems was increasingly apparent not just in government but also in the wider culture. As the prestige of the traditional moral and religious codes continued to wane, the new figure of the 'popular expert' began to appear more regularly on the radio and in the

[36] For a contemporary discussion of these developments see National Association for Mental Health 1949. Ten years later, Barbara Wootton's review of the social sciences and their role in policy-making was severely critical of criminology's achievements in this respect (Wootton 1959). For a retrospective account, see Wiles 1976.

press, teaching a mass audience how 'modern science' thought about age-old problems, including crime and delinquency.[37]

Once set in place, the component parts of the emergent discipline proceeded to establish the range of issues and research questions which was to characterize the subject. In hindsight, this research agenda is easily regarded as narrow and consensual, reflecting broad agreement about the importance of correctionalist aims and positivist methods and a traditional British bias against theoretical or sociological work (see Cohen 1981; Wiles 1976). However, there was actually a good deal of conflict and disagreement regarding the appropriate research agenda for the subject, and rather more diversity in intellectual style and policy orientation than the textbook histories have suggested. The major institutions in the newly created discipline—the Cambridge Institute and the Home Office Research Unit—were each, to differing degrees, tied into a framework of government-sponsored research which quickly assumed a distinctive pattern, although the Institute was home to other work as well, most notably Radzinowicz's monumental *History* (1948–86), and was careful to maintain its claim to academic independence. Neither organization concerned itself closely with the development of clinical studies of the causes of crime or with the task of theory-building, preferring instead to pursue knowledge which would be more readily obtained and more immediately accessible to the policy process. As Radzinowicz argued in 1961, 'the attempt to elucidate the causes of crime should be put aside' in favour of more modest, descriptive studies which indicate the kinds of factors and circumstances with which offending is associated. Using an interdisciplinary approach and a diversity of methods, research was to be focused upon 'descriptive, analytical accounts of the state of crime, of the various classes of offenders, of the enforcement of criminal law [and] of the effectiveness of various measures of penal treatment' (Radzinowicz 1961: 175).

This approach, well characterized by George Vold (1958) as 'administrative criminology', attracted harsh criticism at the time from those more attached to criminology's scientific and explanatory ambitions, particularly the psychoanalysts at the ISTD and the group of sociological criminologists that was forming around Mannheim at the LSE—just as it would later be criticized again in the 1970s, this time by a new generation of criminologists more attracted to critical and sociological theory. But to figures such as Radzinowicz, trying to establish a fledgling and still precarious discipline, the concern was to produce useful knowledge and produce it quickly, rather than risk the failure of a more ambitious programme of etiological research, a programme which, in any case, would depend on the production of a more accurate and wide-ranging description of criminal phenomena (Radzinowicz 1988).

This pragmatic vision of the criminological enterprise was echoed by the

---

[37] See the transcripts of the BBC radio series on the causes of crime in *The Listener* of 1929 and 1934, especially the broadcasts by Cyril Burt on 'The Psychology of the Bad Child' (6 February 1929) and on 'The Causes of Crime' (2 May, 1934).

1959 White Paper, which argued that etiological research 'is confronted with problems which are immense both in range and complexity', that 'there are no easy answers to these problems and progress is bound to be slow', and that consequently emphasis should be placed instead upon 'research into the use of various forms of treatment and the measurement of their results, since this is concerned with matters that can be analysed more precisely' (Home Office 1959: 5). The Home Office Research Unit began its work squarely within this newly constructed framework of science-for-government, using the methodologies of social science to measure and improve the effectiveness of penal treatments and trying to harness the concepts and classifications of academic criminology to the work of administering criminal justice institutions. Nor was it surprising that the paradigmatic study which shaped much of the unit's research in the first decade of its existence should be a prediction study— precisely the kind of work that formed a junction point between criminology's scientific and governmental concerns—and one, moreover, that focused on the Borstal, the British institution which more than any other embodied the correctionalist ideals of a scientific penology. The distinctive mixture of advanced statistical technique, correctively orientated classificatory concerns, and obvious policy relevance which characterized Mannheim and Wilkins' *Prediction Methods in Relation to Borstal Training* (1955) came to be the hallmark of the Research Unit's work throughout the 1950s and 1960s (see Clarke and Cornish 1983).

EPILOGUE

By the 1960s, then, one could say with confidence that a discipline of criminology had come into existence in Great Britain. Centred on the core institutions at Cambridge and London, but increasingly building a significant presence in universities and colleges throughout the country, the subject was well placed to benefit from the rapid expansion of higher education which occurred during this decade, and in the space of a few years criminology took on, rather suddenly, the character of a well-established discipline (see Rock 1988b). Indeed, such was the success of the new discipline in becoming a part of the academic scheme of things that many of its younger members seemed not to be aware of just how recently the battle for recognition had been won. Thus, in the critical writings which emerged in the late 1960s and 70s, in which a new generation of criminologists mounted a radical assault on all that had gone before, one gets the sense that what is being attacked is a very powerful criminological establishment, rather than a *parvenu* and somewhat precarious subject still in the process of constituting itself.[38]

---

[38] For examples of the radically self-critical criminology of this period, see Cohen 1971; Taylor and Taylor 1973; Taylor, Walton, and Young 1973; Taylor *et al.* (1975). In the context of these polemics—through which contemporary readers too often interpret the past—it is easy to forget

Gaining a secure place in the institutions of higher education had a major and unanticipated impact upon the discipline, so that no sooner had it become 'established' than it began to transform itself in significant ways. Many of the developments of the 1960s and 1970s—particularly the reassertion of theoretical ambition, the emergence of a strongly critical discourse, and a widespread dissatisfaction with criminology's relationship to correctionalist policies—are explicable in terms of a discipline adjusting to its new situation, pulled between the demands of policy relevance and the aspiration for academic credibility. Thus the discipline became not only more diversified, more specialized, more professional, and more self-critical in these years, it also became bitterly divided between those who sought to pursue the 'traditional' criminological agenda (in either its etiological or its administrative variant) and those associated with the National Deviancy Conference, founded at York in 1968, who were deeply critical of the medico-psychological assumptions, social democratic politics, and atheoretical pragmatism of what they termed 'positivist criminology' (see Cohen 1981; Wiles 1976; Young, this volume).

In those years, during which university funding seemed more secure than it would subsequently, and academic criminology momentarily enjoyed a degree of autonomy from government greater than at any time before or since, one of the repeated refrains of theoretical writing was that criminology had no epistemological warrant and that analytical considerations demanded that the discipline be dissolved into the broader concerns of sociology or social psychology. That such claims could be made, and made so forcefully, was a stark reminder of just how contingent was criminology's existence as a scientific subject. That they altogether failed to disturb the discipline and its continued expansion (see Rock, this volume) is perhaps a measure of the social and institutional forces which have come to underwrite the existence of British criminology.

Selected Further Reading

The history of criminology is probably too fissiparous and fragmented to be captured in a single text, however compendious, but two recent collections— *The Origins and Growth of Criminology*, edited by Piers Beirne (Dartmouth: Aldershot, 1994) and *The History of Criminology*, edited by Paul Rock (Dartmouth: Aldershot, 1994)—do a good job of suggesting the main lines of descent and development. Other worthwhile collections include Paul Rock (ed.) *A History of British Criminology* (Oxford: Oxford University Press, 1988) which features essays on the formation and contemporary character of the discipline; and the still useful *Pioneers in Criminology*, edited by H. Mannheim (London: Stevens, 1960) which, together with solid essays on the likes of

that criminological writings had never been wholly uncritical of official practices. Most British criminological work has been framed by an ameliorist, social democratic politics, often sharply critical of state policies. Opposition to the death penalty was, for instance, a central concern for many criminologists in the period up to the 1960s. On the complex relationship of criminological knowledge to state power, see Garland 1992.

Bentham, Lombroso, Durkheim, and Bonger, features essays on more peripheral figures such as Alexander Maconochie, Hans Gross, and Henry Maudsley.

Piers Bierne's *Inventing Criminology: Essays on the Rise of Homo Criminalis* (Albany: State University of New York Press, 1993) rescues Beccaria, Quetelet, Guerry, Tarde, and Goring from the condescension of textbook caricatures and explores each author's 'criminological' work in the context of their other writings and concerns. Despite decades of revisionist work of this kind, Leon Radzinowicz's essay *Ideology and Crime: A Study of Crime and its Social and Historical Context* (London: Heinemann, 1966) remains an illuminating introduction to the subject for undergraduates, and of course Radzinowicz's *History of the English Criminal Law and its Administration* in five volumes (vols. 1–4, London: Stevens; vol. 5, co-authored with Roger Hood, Oxford: Oxford University Press, 1986) is an indispensable source for anyone doing serious research in this field.

A number of studies follow the lead of Michel Foucault's classic work *Discipline and Punish* (London: Allen Lane, 1977) in analysing criminology as an apparatus of power/knowledge, linked into disciplinary and governmental institutions. Pasquale Pasquino's essay 'The Invention of Criminology: Birth of a Special Savior' (in G. Burchell, C. Gordon, and P. Miller (eds.) *The Foucault Effect: Studies in Governmentality* (London: Harvester Wheatsheaf, 1991), and my article 'The Criminal and his Science' (*British Journal of Criminology*, 25, (1985): 109–37), focus upon the emergence of the criminal delinquent as a new object of science and administration in nineteenth-century Europe, while my book *Punishment and Welfare: A History of Penal Strategies* (Aldershot: Gower, 1985) shows how a developing criminological discourse spiralled in and out of the penal-welfare institutions that emerged in Britain at the start of the 20th century. The Foucauldian account of criminology's history and its relation to power is reconsidered in my later article 'Criminological Knowledge and its Relation to Power: Foucault's Genealogy and Criminology Today' (*British Journal of Criminology*, 32/4, (1992): 403–22) which argues for a more differentiated account of power, of criminology, and of the various ways in which they relate to one another.

There are several useful accounts of the institutional history of criminology in Britain, often written by insiders who played a key part in the development of the subject. Radzinowicz's memoir *The Cambridge Institute of Criminology: Its Background and Scope* (London: HMSO, 1988) is a well-documented account of a formative moment in the academic discipline, as is the review of Home Office research, *Crime Control in Britain: A Review of Policy Research*, edited by R. V. G. Clarke and Derek B. Cornish (Albany: State University of New York, 1983). Stanley Cohen, himself an important 'insider' in a different strand of British criminology, offers a sociological analysis of post-war developments in 'Footprints on the Sand: A Further Report on Criminology and the Sociology of Deviance in Britain', in M. Fitzgerald, G. McLennan, and J. Pawson (eds.) *Crime and Society: Readings in History and Theory* (London: Routledge, 1981) and reflects upon the institutional and intellectual tensions that structured the field in the 1960s and 1970s. *The Sociology of Deviance: An Obituary* by Colin Sumner (Buckingham: Open University Press, 1994) is an extended essay on the history of 'the sociology of deviance', a form of analysis that bears an oblique and often critical relationship to criminology.

Finally, there are several works of social and intellectual history which, in their own way and for their own purposes, explore particular aspects of criminology's past. The most important of these are Daniel Pick's *Faces of Degeneration: A European Disorder, c.1848–c.1918* (Cambridge: Cambridge University Press, 1989), which situates Lombroso's work in the context of a history of the language of 'degeneration'; Robert Nye's *Crime, Madness and Politics in Modern France: The Medical Concept of National Decline* (Princeton: Princeton University Press, 1984), which develops a social history of the medical concept of deviance that played such a large role in the emergence of a scientific criminology; and Martin Wiener's *Reconstructing the Criminal: Culture, Law and Policy in England, 1830–1914* (Cambridge: Cambridge University Press, 1990), which traces the relationship between criminology, criminal policy, and broader cultural change.

REFERENCES

AICHHORN, A. (1951), *Wayward Youth*. London: Imago.

BAKER, J. (1892), 'Some Points Connected With Criminals', *Journal of Mental Science*, 38: 364.

BANKOWSKI, Z., MUNGHAM, G., and YOUNG, P. (1976), 'Radical Criminology or Radical Criminologist?', *Contemporary Crises*, 1/1: 37–51.

BECCARIA, C. (1963 [1764]), *Of Crimes and Punishments*. Indiana: Bobbs-Merill. First published in Italian as *Dei Delitti e Delle Pene*.

BEIRNE, P. (1998), *'Inventing Criminology: The Rise of 'Homo Criminalis'*. Albany, NY: State University of New York Press.

—— (1994), *The Origins and Growth of Criminology*. Dartmouth: Aldershot.

BONGER, W. (1936), *An Introduction to Criminology*. London: Methuen.

BOTTOMS, A. E. (1987), 'Reflections on the Criminological Enterprise', *Cambridge Law Journal*, 46/2: 240–63.

BURCHELL, G., GORDON, C., and MILLER, P., eds. (1991), *The Foucault Effect: Studies in Governmentality*. London: Harvester Wheatsheaf.

BURT, C. (1925), *The Young Delinquent*. London: University of London Press.

—— (1929), 'The Psychology of the Bad Child', *The Listener*, 6 February.

—— (1934), 'Causes of Crime', *The Listener*, 2 May.

BUTLER, R. A. (1974), 'The Foundation of the Institute of Criminology at Cambridge', in R. Hood, ed., *Crime, Criminology and Public Policy*. London: Heinemann.

CARR-SAUNDERS, A., MANNHEIM, H., and RHODES, E. C. (1942), *Young Offenders*. Cambridge: Cambridge University Press.

CLARKE, R. V. G. and CORNISH, D. B. (1983), *Crime Control in Britain: A Review of Research*. Albany, NY: State University of New York Press.

COHEN, S. (1981), 'Footprints in the Sand: A Further Report on Criminology and the Sociology of Deviance in Britain', in M. Fitzgerald, G. McClennan, and J. Pawson, eds., *Crime and Society*. London: Routledge.

COHEN, S., ed. (1971), *Images of Deviance*. Harmondsworth: Penguin.

COLQUHOUN, P. (1797), *Treatise on the Police of the Metropolis*, 4th edn. London: J. Mawman.

—— (1800), *Treatise on the Commerce and Police of the River Thames*. London: J. Mawman.

—— (1806), *Treatise on Indigence*. London: J. Mawman.

—— (1814), *Treatise on the Wealth, Power and Resources of the British Empire*. London: J. Mawman.

COOTER, R. (1981), 'Phrenology and British Alienists, 1825–1845', in A. Scull, ed., *Madhouses, Mad-Doctors and Madmen: The*

Social History of Psychiatry in the Victorian Era. London: Athlone Press.

CURTIS, T. C., and HALE, F. M. (1981), 'English Thinking about Crime, 1530–1620', in L. A. Knafla, ed., *Crime and Criminal Justice in Europe and Canada*. Waterloo Ontario: Wilfred Laurier University Press.

DANZIGER, K. (1990), *Constructing the Subject: The Historical Origins of Psychological Research*. Cambridge: Cambridge University Press.

DARNELL, R. (1974), *Readings in the History of Anthropology*. New York: Harper & Row.

DELUMEAU, J. (1990), *Sin and Fear: The Emergence of a Western Guilt Culture 13th–18th Centuries*. New York: St Martin's Press.

DEVON, J. (1912), *The Criminal and the Community*. London: John Lane.

DONKIN, Sir H. B. (1917), 'Notes on Mental Defect in Criminals', *Journal of Mental Science*, 63.

—— (1919), 'The Factors of Criminal Action', *Journal of Mental Science*, 65: 87–96.

DRAPKIN, I. (1983), 'Criminology: Intellectual History', in S. Kadish, ed., *Encyclopedia of Crime and Justice*, ii. 546–56. New York: Free Press.

EAST, W. NORWOOD (1927), *An Introduction to Forensic Psychiatry in the Criminal Courts*. London: J. A. Churchill.

—— (1931–2), 'Report of the Medical Commissioner', in *Report of the Commissioners of Prisons and Directors of Convict Prisons, 1930*,' PP 1931–2, Cmd 4151, xii.

—— (1936), *The Medical Aspects of Crime*. London: J. A. Churchill.

—— (1942), *The Adolescent Criminal: A Medico-Sociological Study of 4,000 Male Adolescents*. London: J. A. Churchill.

EAST, W. NORWOOD, and HUBERT, W. H. DE B. (1939), *Report on the Psychological Treatment of Crime*. London: HMSO.

ELLIS, H. (1890), *The Criminal*. London: Walter Scott.

FALLER, L. (1987), *Turned to Account: The Forms and Functions of Criminal Biography in Late Seventeenth and Early Eighteenth Century England*. Cambridge: Cambridge University Press.

FERRI, E. (1895), *Criminal Sociology*. London: Fisher Unwin.

FIELD, H. E. (1932), 'The Psychology of Crime: The Place of Psychology in the Treatment of Delinquents', *British Journal of Medical Psychology*, 12: 241–56.

FIELDING, H. (1988 [1751]), *An Enquiry into the Causes of the Late Increase of Robbers . . . and Other Related Writings*, ed. M. R. Zircar. Oxford: Oxford University Press.

FOUCAULT, M. (1977), *Discipline and Punish*. London: Allen Lane.

—— (1979), 'On Governmentality', *Ideology and Consciousness*, 6: 5–23.

FRIEDLANDER, K. (1947), *The Psychoanalytical Approach to Juvenile Delinquency*. London: Kegan Paul.

GARLAND, D. (1985a), *Punishment and Welfare*. Aldershot: Gower.

—— (1985b), 'The Criminal and his Science', *British Journal of Criminology*, 25/2: 109–37.

GARLAND, D. (1988), 'British Criminology before 1935', in P. Rock, ed., *A History of British Criminology*. Oxford: Oxford University Press.

—— (1992), 'Criminological Knowledge and its Relation to Power: Foucault's Genealogy and Criminology Today', *British Journal of Criminology*, 32/4: 403–22.

GLADSTONE COMMITTEE (1895), *Report of the Departmental Committee on Prisons*. PP 1895, lvi.

GLOVER, E. (1941), *The Diagnosis and Treatment of Delinquency*. London: ISTD.

—— (1960), *The Roots of Crime*. London: Imago.

GORING, C. (1913), *The English Convict: A Statistical Study*. London: HMSO.

GOTTFREDSON, M. R., and HIRSCHI, T., eds. (1987), *Positive Criminology*. Newsbury Park, Ca.: Sage.

GOULD, S. J. (1981), *The Mismeasure of Man*. New York: Norton.

GREEN, T. A. (1985), *Verdict According to Conscience: Perspectives on the English Trial Jury, 1200–1800*. Chicago: University of Chicago Press.

GRIFFITHS, A. G. F. (1904), *Fifty Years of Public Service*. London: Cassell.

—— (1910–11), 'Criminology', in *Encyclopaedia Britannica*, 11th edn. London: Encyclopaedia Britannica.

HACKING, I. (1990), *The Taming of Chance*. Cambridge: Cambridge University Press.

HIRST, P. Q. (1975), 'Marx and Engels on Law, Crime and Morality', in Taylor *et al.*, eds., *Critical Criminology*. London: Routledge and Kegan Paul.

HOME OFFICE (1959), *Penal Practice in a Changing Society: Aspects of Future Development*, Cmnd 645. London: HMSO.

HOWARD, J. (1973 [1777]), *The State of the Prisons in England and Wales*. Montclair, NJ: Paterson Smith. First published Warrington: W. Eyres.

—— (1973 [1789]), *An Account of the Principal Lazarettos of Europe*. Montclair, NJ: Paterson Smith. First published Warrington: W. Eyres.

IGNATIEFF, M. (1978), *A Just Measure of Pain: The Penitentiary and the Industrial Revolution*. London: Macmillan.

JONES, H. (1956), *Crime and the Penal System*. London: University Tutorial Press.

JUDGES, A. V., ed. (1930), *The Elizabethan Underworld*. London: Routledge (repr. 1965).

LAVATER, J. C. (1792), *Essays on Physiognomy, Designed to Promote the Knowledge and Love of Mankind*. London: J. Murray.

LEMAINE, G., MACLEOD, R., MULKAY, M., and WEINGERT, eds., (1976), *Perspectives on the Emergence of Scientific Disciplines*. Paris: Maison des Sciences de l'Homme.

LEPS, M.-C. (1992), *Apprehending the Criminal: The Production of Deviance in Nineteenth Century Discourse*. Durham, N.C.: Duke University Press.

LEVIN, Y., and LINDESMITH, A. (1937), 'English Ecology and Criminology of the Past Century', *Journal of Criminal Law, Criminology and Police Science*, 27/6: 801–16.

LODGE, T. S. (1974) 'The Founding of the Home Office Research Unit', in R. Hood, ed., *Crime, Criminology and Public Policy*. London: Heinemann.

LOMBROSO, C. (1876), *L'Uomo Delinquente*. Turin: Fratelli Bocca. (No English translation was ever published, but see G. Lombroso-Ferrero, *Criminal Man: According to the Classification of Cesare Lombroso*. New York: Putnam, 1911; repr. Montclair, NJ: Paterson Smith, 1972.

—— (1895), *The Female Offender*. London: Fisher Unwin.

LYELL, J. H. (1913), 'A Pioneer in Criminology: Notes on the Work of James Bruce Thomson of Perth', *Journal of Mental Science*, 59.

MANNHEIM, H. (1946), *Criminal Justice and Social Reconstruction*. Oxford: Oxford University Press.

—— (1949), Contribution to the Proceedings of the Conference, in National Association for Mental Health, *Why Delinquency? The Case for Operational Research*. London: NAMH.

—— (1957), 'Report on the Teaching of Criminology in the United Kingdom', in UNESCO, *The University Teaching of Social Sciences: Criminology*. Lausanne: UNESCO.

—— ed. (1960), *Pioneers in Criminology*. London: Stevens.

MANNHEIM, H., and WILKINS, L. (1955), *Prediction Methods in Relation to Borstal Training*. London: HMSO.

MATZA, D. (1964), *Delinquency and Drift*. New York: Wiley.

—— (1969), *Becoming Deviant*. Englewood Cliffs, NJ: Prentice-Hall.

MAUDSLEY, H. (1863), 'Review of A Prison Matron's *Female Life in Prison*', *Journal of Mental Science*, 9: 69.

—— (1889), 'Remarks on Crime and Criminals', *Journal of Mental Science*, 34: 159, 311.

—— (1895), 'Criminal Responsibility in Relation to Insanity', *Journal of Mental Science*, 41: 657.

MAYHEW, H. (1861–2), *London Labour and the London Poor*. London: Griffin, Bohn & Co.

MORRIS, T. (1957), *The Criminal Area*. London: Routledge and Kegan Paul.

MORRISON, W. D. (1896), *Juvenile Offenders*. London: Fisher Unwin.

NATIONAL ASSOCIATION FOR MENTAL HEALTH (1949), *Why Delinquency? The Case for Operational Research*. London: NAMH.

NEEDHAM, D. (1889), 'Comments on Maudsley's "Remarks on Crime and Criminals"', *Journal of Mental Science*, 34: 311.

NICOLSON, D. (1878–9), 'The Measure of Individual and Social Responsibility in Criminal Cases', *Journal of Mental Science*, 24: 1, 249.

—— (1895), 'Crime, Criminals and Criminal Lunatics: The Presidential Address to the Medico-Psychological Association', *Journal of Mental Science*, 41; 567.

NORMAN, D. C. (1895), 'Comments on Dr. Nicolson's Presidential Address', *Journal of Mental Science*, 41: 487.

NYE, R. (1984), *Crime, Madness and Politics in Modern France*. Princeton: Princeton University Press.

PAILTHORPE, G. W. (1932), *Studies in the Psychology of Delinquency*. London: HMSO.

PASQUINO, P. (1978), 'Theatrum Politicum: The Genealogy of Capital, Police, and the State of Prosperity', *Ideology and Consciousness*, 5: 41–54.

PETERSILIA, J. (1991), 'Policy Relevance and the Future of Criminology: The American Society of Criminology 1990 Presidential Address', *Criminology*, 29/1: 1–15.

PICK, D. (1989), *The Faces of Degeneration*. Cambridge: Cambridge University Press.

PORTER, R. (1987), *Mind-Forg'd Manacles: A History of Madness in England from the Restoration to the Regency*. Cambridge, Mass.: Harvard University Press.

PROAL, L. (1898), *Political Crime*. London: Fisher Unwin.

QUINTON, R. F. (1910), *Crime and Criminals 1876–1910*. London: Longmans, Green.

RADZINOWICZ, L. (1948–86), *A History of the English Criminal Law and its Administration, from 1750*, 5 vols. (Vol. 5 with R. Hood). London: Stevens.

RADZINOWICZ, L. (1961), *In Search of Criminology*. London: Heinemann.

—— (1966), *Ideology and Crime*. London: Stevens.

—— (1988), *The Cambridge Institute of Criminology: Its Background and Scope*. London: HMSO.

RAFTER, N. H. (1992), 'Criminal Anthropology in the United States', *Criminology*, 30/4: 525–45.

REINER, R. (1988), 'British Criminology and the State', in P. Rock, ed., *A History of British Criminology*. Oxford: Oxford University Press.

ROCK, P., ed. (1988*a*), *A History of British Criminology*. Oxford: Oxford University Press.

—— (1988*b*), 'The Present State of Criminology in Britain', in P. Rock, ed., *A History of British Criminology*. Oxford: Oxford University Press.

—— (1994), *The History of Criminology*. Dartmouth: Aldershot.

ROSE, N. (1988), 'Calculable Minds and Manageable Individuals', *The History of the Human Sciences*, 1/2: 179–200.

ROSHIER, B. (1989), *Controlling Crime: The Classical Perspective in Criminology*. Chicago: Lyceum Books.

RUGGLES-BRISE, Sir E. (1924), *Prison Reform at Home and Abroad: A Short History of the International Movement since the London Conference, 1872*. London: Macmillan.

SALGADO, G. (1972), *Cony-Catchers and Bawdy Baskets*. Harmondsworth: Penguin.

SAVITZ, L., TURNER, S. H., and DICKMAN, T. (1977), 'The Origin of Scientific Criminology: Franz Gall as the First Criminologist', in R. F. Meier, ed., *Theory in Criminology*. Beverley Hills: Sage.

SENNETT, R. (1977), *The Fall of Public Man*. London: Faber.

SHARPE, J. A. (1985), ' "Last Dying Speeches": Religion, Ideology and Public Execution in Seventeenth Century England', *Past and Present*, 107: 144–67.

SKINNER, Q. (1969), 'Meaning and Understanding in the History of Ideas', *History and Theory*,. 8/1: 3–53.

SMITH, M. H. (1922*a*), 'The Medical Examination of Delinquents', *Journal of Mental Science*, 68.

—— (1922*b*), *The Psychology of the Criminal*. London: Methuen.

SMITH, R. (1988), 'Does the History of Psychology have a Subject?', *The History of the Human Sciences*, 1/1: 147–78.

ST JOHN, A. (1912), 'Criminal Anthropology and Common Sense', *Sociological Review*, 5: 65–7.

SULLIVAN, W. C. (1906), *Alcoholism*. London: J. Nisbet.

—— (1924), *Crime and Insanity*. London: Edward Arnold.

SUTHERLAND, J. F. (1908), *Recidivism: Habitual Criminality and Habitual Petty Delinquency*. Edinburgh.

TAYLOR, I. (1981), *Law and Order: Arguments for Socialism*. London: Macmillan.

TAYLOR, I., and TAYLOR, L., eds. (1973), *Politics and Deviance: Papers from the National Deviancy Conference*. Harmondsworth: Penguin.

TAYLOR, I., WALTON, P., and YOUNG, J. (1973), *The New Criminology*. London: Routledge & Kegan Paul.

TAYLOR, I., WALTON, P., and YOUNG, J. eds. (1975), *Critical Criminology*. London: Routledge and Kegan Paul.

TAYLOR, R. S. (1968), 'Review of Jones' *Crime and the Penal System*, 3rd edn', *Howard Journal*, 12/3.

THOMSON, J. B. (1867), 'The Effects of the Present System of Prison Discipline on the Body and Mind', *Journal of Mental Science*, 12.

TUKE, H. (1889), 'Comments on Maudsley's "Remarks on Crime and Criminals" ', *Journal of Mental Science*, 34: 311.

VOLD, G. B. (1958), *Theoretical Criminology*. New York: Oxford University Press.

WIENER, M. (1990), *Reconstructing the Criminal: Culture, Law, and Policy in England, 1830–1914*. Cambridge: Cambridge University Press.

WILES, P. (1976), 'Introduction', in *The Sociology of Crime and Delinquency in Britain*, ii. Oxford: Martin Robertson.

WOOTTON, B. (1959), *Social Science and Social Pathology*. London: Allen and Unwin.

YOUNG, J. (1988), 'Radical Criminology in Britain: The Emergence of a Competing Paradigm', in P. Rock, ed., *A History of British Criminology*. Oxford: Oxford University Press.

ZEMAN, T. (1981), 'Order, Crime and Punishment: The American Criminological Tradition', Ph.D. thesis, University of California at Santa Cruz.

2

The History of Crime and Crime Control Institutions

Clive Emsley

Until the 1970s historians discussing developments in the area of crime control institutions in Britain tended to take a perspective formulated in Whig notions of progress and drawing on a positivist approach to crime and criminals. Crime tended to be seen as an absolute: it was largely understood in terms of theft and, to a lesser extent, violence; it was something perpetrated by 'criminals' on the law-abiding majority of the population. Improvements in the control mechanisms had been brought about by a progressive humanitarianism and the sensible, rational responses of reformers to abuses and inefficiences. Since the 1970s these perspectives and interpretations have been subjected to critical examination by a new generation of social historians. These historians began to work on court records in the hopes of penetrating the lives of the poor and socially disadvantaged; they have tended to concentrate on periods of social and economic upheaval such as the late sixteenth and early seventeenth centuries, or the years of industrialization and urbanization in the late eighteenth and early nineteenth centuries. The initial focus was on property crime, seen by some as a kind of 'protest' offence by the poor during periods of economic upheaval and privation. More recently, partly as a result of the interest in women's history and the recognition of the scale of domestic abuse in the past, the focus has shifted more to violent offences. All of these historians have sought to relate crime and the control of crime to specific economic, social, and political contexts; all have acknowledged that crime is something defined by the law, and that the law was changed and shaped by human institutions.

This chapter seeks to provide a synthesis of the recent research into the history of crime and its control in Britain from the late eighteenth century until the end of World War II. The period constitutes a long but nevertheless coherent unit, beginning with significant calls for reform in the system of punishment and for improvements in the policing of the metropolis, and ending with police and prisons poised for the major reorganizations of the 1960s and with crime beginning its dramatic post-World War II increase. The chapter begins with an assessement of the scale of crime across the period, followed by a discussion of the changes in the way that crime and the offender were perceived and understood by contemporaries and by subsequent historians. The focus then shifts to the solutions developed in response to these problems. A discussion of the origins of the police and their subsequent development is followed by a survey of the changes in the courts and the system of prosecution. The final section explores the different means deployed to remove the offender from society and to punish and/or reform him, or her. Of necessity, given the research which has been done, the main focus of the essay is England and Wales; unfortunately, as yet, there has been little detailed research into the developments within the independent Scottish legal system, while much of the work on Irish 'crime' has tended to concentrate on its manifestations within English cities.

THE EXTENT OF CRIME

Acknowledging that a crime is an action defined by the law which, if detected, will lead to some kind of sanction being employed against the perpetrator, enables the historian to draw some conclusions about a society's priorities and its attitudes towards social groups, individuals, and property. But the problem which commonly affects contemporaries, and which has much vexed the new generation of historians of crime, is estimating the scale of crime. There are no official statistics for crime in England before 1805. Historians of the eighteenth century and earlier have sought to construct figures from court records, particularly the indictment membranes for assizes and quarter sessions. Recognizing that such figures cannot give any precise picture of the incidence of crime, it has, nevertheless, been forcefully argued that they can give an idea of the pattern. In 1810 the government determined to start collecting criminal statistics annually; the first collection went back to 1805, but in the early years the statistics registered only committals. The system was refined during the first half of the nineteenth century notably with a reorganization into six main types of offence in 1834:

1. Offences against the person (ranging from homicide to assault);
2. Offences against property involving violence (robbery, burglary);
3. Offences against property without violence;
4. Malicious offences against property (arson, machine breaking, etc.);
5. Offences against the currency;
6. Miscellaneous offences (including riot, sedition, and treason).

Twenty-two years later an appendage to the County and Borough Police Act established the tripartite division of:

1. Indictable offences reported to the police;
2. Committals for trial both on indictment and before summary jurisdiction;
3. The number of persons convicted and imprisoned.

There has been considerable debate over the value of all of these different forms of statistics for historians. Some have maintained that because we cannot be sure why crimes were reported and prosecuted, and because of variations in recording practices across police jurisdictions, the figures are worthless for serious historical analysis (Tobias, 1972a: 18–25; Sindall, 1990: 16–28). Others, notably John Beattie, V. A. C. Gatrell, and David Philips, have insisted that careful use of the figures can permit the construction of useful, hypothetical graphs for the pattern of crime, and also enable conclusions to be drawn about the nature of crime and perceptions of criminality (Beattie, 1981; Gatrell, 1980; Philips, 1977). The kind of graph which emerges from the statistical studies for the period under review shows a steady increase in crime, particularly property crime, in the late eighteenth century, becoming much sharper from the first decade of the nineteenth century until about 1850 when the pattern levels out, except, most noticeably, for the offence of burglary. After World War I a steady, accelerating increase began again; it momentarily checked during World War II and the following decade, but then began to rise sharply once again. This pattern tends to make sense when deployed alongside other social data. The eighteenth-century increase coincides with major shifts in the economy, with population increase and with growing fears for the social order; the acceleration of the first part of the nineteenth century corresponds with the aggravation of these problems and new concerns generated by the example of the French Revolution and by the seemingly uncontrollable squalor of the new industrial cities. The question must remain whether these problems caused more crime *per se*, or whether they simply made people more sensitive to offences and prompted them to report and/or prosecute any crimes committed against them. The steady plateau of the second half of the nineteenth century coincides with what one historian dubbed the Victorian 'age of equipoise' (Burn, 1964); it was a period of confidence and faith in both the future and the idea of progress. Moreover, the growth of international markets and reductions in the price of food meant that problems in the home market were more easily off-set by both employers and employees than in the earlier years of the century; the necessity of stealing to survive consequently became less pressing as problems in primary production became less inter-related with production elsewhere in the economy. Burglary was one of the few offences which did not follow the general pattern in the second half of the nineteenth century. But the greater incidence of burglary itself may, in large measure, be a reflection of greater prosperity and the fact that ordinary people had more possessions in their homes. Both World Wars witnessed a slight reduction of crime in the judicial statistics; this could be explained by the fact that the police had a myriad of other tasks with which to contend and therefore relegated ordinary crime on their list of priorities; but also the needs of war shifted many of the young men often prone to committing criminal offences out of the country and subjected many of those that remained to new and stricter forms of control through the military. The steady increase of crime during the inter-war period might arguably reflect both the difficulties generated by the Depression and the

temptations offered by the first inklings of a consumer society; it was during
the inter-war years that motor vehicle ownership began to be widespread, and
that concerns began to be expressed about the way in which motor vehicle
offences were congesting the magistrates' courts.

But even if the statistical pattern makes some sense deployed against one set
of social criteria, caution remains necessary. The late eighteenth and early
nineteenth centuries, which witnessed a marked increase in the statistics of
crime, were also the key period for Britain becoming an urbanized society with
an economy rooted in industrial capitalism. Most contemporaries believed that
the burgeoning towns were much more prone to crime than the countryside;
however the evidence for this is difficult to come by. Of course there were
different opportunites for theft in the towns and the goods stolen could be very
different between town and country. But some poaching gangs were urban-
based and drew their members from the urban working class; while John
Glyde's study of crime in mid-nineteenth-century Suffolk concluded that while
one third of the county's inhabitants were urban dwellers they were responsible for only about a fifth of the crime (Glyde, 1856*a*: 146–7; Glyde, 1856*b*:
102–6). The inter-relationship between the growth of property crime and the
growth of capitalism was a popular area of analysis for the first serious
historians of crime, and it has been restated with particular verve by Peter
Linebaugh (Linebaugh, 1991). This work concentrated on the thefts of poor
men who were seen as resisting capitalism by their actions, and most of the
studies of the 'perks' taken by workers from the raw materials with which they
did their work reveal that the situation was far more complex than a simple
class-struggle model might suggest. There were times when the purchaser,
rather than the employer, was the victim of workplace fraud, and while
the employer might, in such circumstances, have had some concern for the
reputation of his business, this can scarcely be construed as an aspect of the
struggle between capital and labour. It is possible that many workers preferred
the steady wage which they earned under the capitalist system to a more
traditional form of payment part in kind and part in wage; the continuing
appropriation of goods, even in capitalizing textile industries, therefore is less
clearly a protest against new systems of payment and conditions of work.
Employers did not always prosecute the appropriation of perks. There
continued to be a variety of other sanctions which they could employ;
and occasionally they even took perks and fiddles into account when calculating pay rates (Davis, 1989; Emsley, 1996*a*: chapter 5; Randall, 1990).
Furthermore any simple equation that economic hardship prompted the
working class to crime is undermined by the fact that there does not appear
to have been anything other than a steady growth of offending during
the inter-war period in spite of the acute depression in many of the largest
and traditional centres of industrialization. A more profitable line of enquiry
delineating an inter-relationship between capitalism and crime has been the
exploration of the enormous scale of business and financial fraud during
the nineteenth and early twentieth centuries (Robb, 1992). This style of

offending netted profits for some far beyond the dreams of any non-fiction Bill Sikes.

Overall the statistics suggest that property crime was the most common form of offence. Court records reveal that most thefts involved objects of relatively little monetary value. In the eighteenth and early nineteenth centuries drying sheets were taken from washing lines or where they were stretched over hedges or fences; tools were stolen from fellow workmen; furniture, cutlery, plates, and mugs were taken from lodgings and inns. The proceeds of such thefts were often taken to a pawn shop, or the less salubrious 'dolly shop', and exchanged for a small amount of ready cash. In the long run the changes in the economy resulted in people having more disposable income, and as more people had more moveable property and as shops and warehouses had more goods for consumers, so the style of theft changed and the opportunities became greater. Yet, perhaps paradoxically, in spite of the growing opportunities for illicit appropriation in wealthy Victorian Britain, overall the statisitics of theft declined, and always very many of the victims were relatively poor people.

Statistically violence also declined over the same period. But the suggestion, largely based on figures for homicide, that there has been a general decline in interpersonal violence since the Tudor period has excited a lively debate (Cockburn, 1991; Sharpe, 1985; Stone, 1983 and 1985). The wife- and child-beater was increasingly demonized during the second half of the nineteenth century and was perceived as a phenomenon rooted in the poorest of the working class along with other vices. In the same period the growing delineation of the respectable standards expected from men in marriage pressed by both feminists and conservative moralists may have contributed to a diminution of overbearing and aggressive male behaviour. Yet assessing the scale of domestic abuse, especially when the construction of the idea of the family as a safe haven was at its peak and when the police were discouraged from involving themselves in private affairs, remains extremely difficult. Overall however, the evidence suggests that from the late eighteenth century at least, a high proportion of the victims of violence appear to have known their assailants or were related to them in some way; the major exception here was the police officer who, from the origins of the new police, was found in disproportionate numbers among assault victims (Gatrell, 1980).

THE OFFENDER

Yet whatever the statistics suggest about the predominance of petty theft and the scale of, and profits from, financial fraud, it was violent crime which frightened people and which newspaper editors knew sold their papers and vicariously enthralled their readers. The newspapers could contribute significantly to periodic scares by the way in which they chose to emphasize particularly horrific crimes either for the sake of sales, or for some crusading, legislative purpose. The image of Jack the Ripper is a good example of the former. There is no precise evidence that the appalling murders committed in Whitechapel towards the end of 1888 were all committed by the same individual; and while only the most pathetic women in one very small district of East London appear to have been at risk, the panic about the Ripper spread far and wide both geographically and socially. The garotting panic of 1862 provides an example of the press, and particularly the influential *Times*, building on concerns about offenders released on licence and manufacturing a scare from a few street robberies to encourage the passage of legislation authorizing harsh penalties against violent members of the 'criminal class' (Sindall, 1990). There has been no systematic survey of crime reporting in the press from the mid-eighteenth to the mid-twentieth centuries, but it is clear that even before the advent of cheap newspapers towards the end of the Victorian period, the reading public was being fed on cases of 'orrible murder and outrage perpetrated by members of a criminal class outside, and at war with, society.

The idea of a criminal subgroup was not new. Vagrants and beggars were perceived as such and consequently legislated against at least as far back as the Tudor and Stuart periods (Beier, 1985). The members of the criminal class portrayed in the writings of those interested in crime from the mid-eighteenth to the mid-nineteenth century had much in common with the Tudor 'sturdy beggar': they would not do an honest day's work because they sought a life of luxury and ease (Fielding, 1751: 169; Hanaway, 1772: 38; Colquhoun, 1796: 33). Yet events led to a significant shift in the perceptions of crime and criminality particularly in the first half of the nineteenth century. The wars against Revolutionary and Napoleonic France had severely limited access to foreign grain markets at a time when a series of bad harvests had led to food shortages, with resulting outbreaks of popular disorder and the need to increase poor rates. At the same time the war forced the propertied to dig deeper into their pockets for war taxes required by the national government, as well as for increased poor rates to assist the wives and children of poor men serving in the armed forces. For a variety of reasons the restoration of peace in 1815 did not bring an end to these escalating poor rates. The new national crime statistics, the first decade of which coincided with the last decade of the wars, while they only demonstrated an increase in committals and prosecutions, were taken as proof positive of a serious increase in crime. During the eighteenth century a crime was an individual action which the law sought to penalize; but against the background of the new statistics and resentment at increasing poor rates which a harsh reading of Malthusian theory deemed unnecessary, crime increasingly acquired a symbolic meaning as a kind of disease within society and a new stress was put on the pathological nature of the offender. By the 1840s the offender had become a member of the 'dangerous classes' lurking in the urban rookeries and slums; by the early 1860s the term the 'criminal classes' was rather more in vogue (Stevenson, 1983: 32 n.4).

Social commentators like Henry Mayhew and Angus Bethune Reach made forays into the rookeries of these so-called 'criminal classes'. The stigmatizing label, however, says more about these commentators and their readers than about the social group that they were studying, the individuals who committed crimes, or their motivation. Those labelled as the 'criminal class' were generally the poorest sections of the working class who eked out their existence in the uncertain casual labour market. Given their hard lives, their poor living conditions and inadequate diets, it is not surprising that members of this 'criminal class' often died young. With their poor diet and shabby clothing they also looked different from those in steady work; particularly they looked different from members of the growing middle class. The intrepid social invest-igators emphasized the differences by categorizing and describing the 'criminal classes' for their readers as if they were members of strange tribes in far-away lands; the physical differences suited well with Victorian notions that the face portrayed the character (Emsley 1996*a*: 68–75).

The 'criminals' of the 'criminal class' portrayed by Victorian commentators were essentially working class and male. Statistically offences by women were always very much fewer than those committed by men; moreover, the per-centage of women prosecuted in the principal courts from the late seventeenth through to the early twentieth century declined steadily. Single women living alone in towns and employed as domestic servants appear to have been more criminal than their sisters in the country; and while they were always far fewer than their male equivalents, their age of offending appears to have declined much more slowly. The explanation is probably to be found in the greater degree of family support and male protection available in the rural districts, but above all in the vulnerablity of women in the uncertain, casual labour situation of the town. This latter may also account for the fact that, while the proportion of female offenders before the courts was smaller than that of males, the percentage of female recidivists was higher; it appears to have been more difficult for a woman to shake off the stigma of prison than a man (Beattie, 1975; Feeley and Little, 1991; Zedner, 1991; King, 1996). For Victorian commentators, the female equivalent of the male criminal was the prostitute. Even sympathetic observers described the prostitute as entering her trade for the same kinds of reasons that men became criminals, notably idleness and the love of luxury; only very low on the list came the most probable spur to most prostitution, poverty. In her gaudy clothes and with her effrontery in propositioning potential clients, the archetypal prostitute was the antithesis of the ideal of Victorian womanhood. She also seemed much easier to apprehend than many male criminals. The notorious Contagious Diseases Acts passed in the middle of the nineteenth century, in an attempt to reduce the incidence of venereal disease in the armed forces, assumed that prostitutes were readily detectable, but inadvertently made thousands of ordinary working-class women the victims of officious and suspicious policemen (McHugh, 1980; Walkowitz, 1980).

The levelling out of the crime statistics, which implied a degree of success in the mechanisms of crime control, Social Darwinism, and the advent of social science led to a changing perception of the criminal classes as the century wore on. Criminals might still be described as those who shunned hard work and enjoyed the vagrant life, but they were also increasingly understood as individuals who turned to crime because of mental and physical, as well as moral, degeneracy: defects assumed to be passed on through heredity. Crime ceased to be seen as the work of a semi-organized criminal or dangerous class, and more that of, on the one hand, a small core of hardened professionals, and, on the other, a much larger group of socially and mentally inadequate individuals who generally indulged in petty offences. This perception led to increasingly careful categorization and separation as experts differentiated between the young and the habitual offender, the necessitous and the incorrigible, the opportunist and the professional (Wiener, 1990).

The judicial statistics commonly revealed a large number of young offenders; the mass of petty crime was always a young man's game. These offenders were rarely portrayed as part of the criminal class and, from the early nineteenth century at least, they were increasingly perceived as a group which needed to be protected both from immoral and uncaring parents and from hardened recidivists in prisons. Once the problem was identified a variety of expedients were tried either to reform the juvenile offender—industrial schools and reformatories—or to offer healthy alternatives—youth clubs and organizations—and thus prevention. The increase in juvenile offending during World War I, attributed by contemporaries to a weakening of parental control with fathers at the front and more mothers at work, prompted further attempts to foster such alternatives (Gillis, 1975; Margery, 1978; May, 1973; Bailey, 1987: 11).

Mayhew had categorized his criminals by their various crafts—possibly taking the argot verb for a particular offence and transforming it into a noun (Emsley, 1996a: 73). The garotting panic led some to assume that street robbers were professionals who specialized in a particular 'science of garotting' (Anon. 1863). By the early twentieth century criminal archetypes specializing in particular offences were commonly constructed in the press and by moral entrepreneurs: in the inter-war period there was the bag-snatcher, the motor bandit, and the razor gang; World War II saw the black-marketeer 'spiv'; in the aftermath of the war came the cosh-boy. Of course there were individuals who perpetrated each and every one of these offences, and, in the inter-war period it is possible to find something of an organized underworld involved in sexual vice, like the Messina family in London's Soho, and the gangs involved in gambling on the race tracks and at boxing matches, notably the Darby Sabini gang and the Brummagen Boys. This underworld could be vicious, but it generally fought amongst itself, as in the case of the Sheffield gang wars of the 1920s (Bean, 1981; Jenkins and Potter, 1988; Samuel, 1981). But even including these gangs, it is unlikely that more than a very few offenders were 'professionals' for whom crime was the principal source of income. The creation of the archetype often clouded the understanding of the offence, and the situation became particularly serious when policy was made with reference to the archetype rather than the problem; as was described above this problem arose with the enforcement of the Contagious Diseases Acts, and it was notable subsequently with the preparation of much anti-gambling legislation (Dixon, 1991: 37; Gatrell, 1990: 306–10; Pearson, 1983).

Since the eighteenth century at least politicians and jurists have always claimed that all Englishmen and women were equal before the law. This, it has been argued, was a trick in Hanoverian England which enabled the ruling, propertied elite, to run the country without a police force. The occasional example of an individual like Lord Ferrers, executed in 1760 for the murder of his steward, ensured the lower orders' faith in the law which, for most of the time, was concerned with reinforcing and upholding an unequal division of property (Hay, 1975). This argument has not gone unchallenged, and nineteenth-century governments became increasingly sensitive to accusations of class law. Yet the limited work which has been done on police practice and the sentencing policies of the courts suggests that the perception of stereotypes influenced both. Policemen, magistrates, and judges weighed up offenders according to their class, gender, and respectability and how they conformed with the accepted social mores; they then acted accordingly (Conley, 1991; Zedner, 1991). By the same token, while financial fraud was widespread—one estimate has it that as many as one sixth of the company promotions during the nineteenth century were fraudulent—the law was feeble in this area, the police were not geared up to pursuing such offenders, and such men who were convicted of major fraud were generally treated leniently in comparison with offenders from the 'criminal class' (Robb, 1992: chapter 7). It was always the quantity of petty crime and fears about violent crime which focused definitions, and treatment, of the offender.

THE POLICE

The traditional, Whig historians who studied the origins of the English police accepted fairly uncritically the notion that crime was increasing significantly at the end of the eighteenth and beginning of the nineteenth centuries. They also accepted, again uncritically, the claims of the early police reformers that the old system of parish constables and watchmen was totally inefficient and had quite outgrown its usefulness. The development of the new police, beginning with the creation of the Metropolitan Police in London in 1829, was therefore the logical solution of far-sighted men to a real and serious problem (Ascoli, 1979; Critchley, 1978; Reith, 1938 and 1943).

There were problems with the old system of policing. Some parish constables were inefficient; they were chosen in a variety of different ways from among the respectable members of local communities generally to serve for a year; few of them were professionals; and most of them had still to conduct their full-time trade or profession while they served. It is little wonder therefore that some men sought to avoid the office, and that others were reluctant to put their duties as constable before the needs of their trade and livelihood. Some town watchmen, who were recruited by local authorities and paid to patrol the streets after dark, were also inefficient. But while the constables and watchmen of Hanoverian England still await some detailed historical investigation, it is becoming increasingly clear that there were constables who took their role in the community seriously, that improvements were being made to the urban watches, and that, overall, the situation was by no means as bleak as has been traditionally portrayed.

The chief focus of concerns over crime and public order during the eighteenth century was London. It was the largest city in Europe comprising the cities of both London and Westminster, and spreading out into the counties of Middlesex, Surrey, and Kent. It was a booming commercial centre as well as the seat of government. Contemporaries viewed it with pride for its obvious prosperity; but they also viewed it with trepidation for its slums and for the temptations which its wealth appeared to provide for those who lived in those slums. The parish watches in the metropolis began to be reorganized and improved from early on in the century (Reynolds, 1991). Private thief-takers established themselves to investigate offences for victims; they took rewards from victims for the return of stolen property, and they also cashed in on the rewards offered by government for the apprehension leading to the conviction of offenders. Several unsavoury characters installed themselves in the entre-preneurial role of thief-taker organizing both the theft and the apprehension of the offender (Howson, 1970; Paley 1989*a*). Alongside these developments a new kind of magistrate—the trading justice—began to emerge in the metropolis and on its fringes. Trading justices have received almost as bad a press as the entrepreneurial thief-takers, yet they were by no means all bad and, sitting regularly in their offices, they provided a much-needed service for the increasing numbers who wanted legal problems solved quickly and easily and who were prepared to pay the justices' fees (Landau, 1984: 184–90). A marked step forward was made in the middle of the century when, under Henry Fielding and his blind half-brother Sir John Fielding, the magistrate's office in Bow Street became a model of how the trading justice might function. The Fieldings were supported by government money, which enabled them to keep their fees low; equally significant were their organization of half a dozen constables, the celebrated Bow Street thief-takers or 'Runners', and their experiment with night patrols organized to watch the main roads into the metropolis (Palmer, 1988: 78–9).

The Gordon Riots of 1780, when the variety of civil powers in the metro-polis showed themselves unable to cope with major disorder, prompted some to contemplate a centralized, professional system of policing. Indeed in 1785 such a body was proposed in a bill presented to Parliament. But the bill was poorly drafted, poorly presented, and provoked the fury of the powerful City of London which objected to having its authority over its own police replaced. The bill fell, though the system outlined in it was subsequently established in the city of Dublin. Seven years later a new bill was introduced to improve the policing of London, but rather than creating a centralized body of horse and foot answerable to government-appointed commissioners, this proposed only the creation of seven police offices along the lines of that in Bow Street. Each office was to be staffed by three stipendiary magistrates and six constables; the City of London was omitted from the proposal and continued with its own independent system. The Middlesex Justices Act successfully passed into law, and over the next thirty years government and private initiative built on the system. By 1828 the policing of London was in the hands of some 300 patrol-men working out of the Bow Street Office, about eighty men in the Thames River Police (originally established in 1798 by West India merchants), the twenty-four stipendiaries and their constables, the two City of London Marshals and their constables and patrol, and the dozens of parish constables and nightwatchmen of the individual metropolitan parishes (Palmer, 1988: 117–19, 143–7, 171–2; Rumbelow, 1971: 104–5). The effectiveness and honesty of these different policemen varied from district to district depending on what pay was available, what recruitment policies and what systems of supervision were enforced: some nightwatchmen were young and fit and worked relatively short beats which they got to know well and policed con-scientiously; and even the much-lauded Bow Street Police succumbed to the kinds of corruption present among the old thief-takers as a sucession of scandals in the aftermath of the Napoleonic wars revealed (Emsley, 1996a: 223 and 243, n.18).

The argument for sweeping aside such a motley system appeared a logical and forceful one to the traditional Whig historians of the police, especially since they accepted that most parish constables and watchmen were useless. Yet there were, to contemporaries, strong arguments for maintaining the system: there was concern that a centralized police was something peculiarly foreign, worst of all French, and that it would be a threat to liberty; there was even greater concern about central government encroaching on the rights of local government with a centrally directed police over which the localities would have no control. The police offices and the Bow Street patrols had been increasingly co-ordinated by the Home Office; but the Metropolitan Police, established in 1829, was a significant development in central government control.

The prime mover in the creation of the Metropolitan Police was the Home Secretary, Sir Robert Peel. He had first come to the Home Office in 1822 and during the mid-1820s he had embarked on a major rationalization of the criminal law; in Peel's mind police reform had always been central to his law reforms. He brought with him to the Home Office his experience of Ireland where he had served as Chief Secretary from 1812 to 1818 and where he had been instrumental in improving the police system. Manifestations of public disorder were different in the two countries. Ireland was overwhelmingly a peasant society; its Catholic minority was dominated by an Anglo-Irish gentry which was largely Protestant. In 1798 and again in 1803 there had been rebellions, and peasant guerrilla war continued to splutter on in the country-side. The magistracy was often reluctant to act in the face of disorder. Peel had created the Peace Preservation Force to help resolve these problems; one of his successors, Henry Goulburn, developed the force further in 1822 by legislation which established a French-style gendarmerie, the Irish Constabulary (Broeker, 1970; Palmer, 1988: 193–276). Peel remained in close touch with Goulburn throughout the latter's preparation of the Constabulary Bill, and while he recognized that the problems of the new industrial society in England were different, that magistrates were often active, that local authorities were jealous of their independence, and that there would be ferocious hostility to a French-style, military police, he nevertheless believed that some kind of national police system was desirable. Nor was he alone among the Tory cabinet in this belief. Concerns about public order were probably central in ministers' minds. While the duration and scale of the Gordon Riots had never been equalled, there had been sporadic disorders in the metropolis and in the provinces, both during and after the wars against Revolutionary and Napoleonic France. Yet it was not on the issue of maintaining public order that Peel chose to argue the need for a police, but on the problem of increasing crime; and it is possible that Peel's reforms of the criminal law, which made it easier to prosecute offenders and which reduced the amount of time lost by victim-prosecutors and their witnesses in the courts, had in themselves inflated the crime figures for the metropolis.

From the beginning in 1829 the constables of the new Metropolitan Police were informed that their first duty was the prevention of crime. It is arguable whether they were any more efficient at this than the more competent of the watches which preceded them, especially since they could be less numerous on the ground (Paley, 1989*b*: 114–17). But the new policemen did constitute a sizeable body which could be deployed across the metropolis to clear away street people and to suppress popular tumult. In their early years also Metropolitan Police officers and constables were commonly deployed in the provinces as a kind of national riot squad (Emsley, 1996*b*: 31, 42, 46, 54–6).

The Metropolitan Police provided a new model for consideration by those advocating police reform in the provinces. In the aftermath of the Napoleonic wars fear of disorder and of increasing crime was prompting a variety of developments in provincial policing. Some local Associations for the Prosecution of Felons organized private police, some towns improved their watches either through private Acts of Parliament or, after 1833, by taking advantage of the Lighting and Watching Act of that year. The Municipal Corporations Act of 1835 sought to establish uniformity among the chartered boroughs by requiring each elected municipality to appoint a watch committee, and each watch committee to appoint a police force. In 1829 the County of Cheshire established, by Act of Parliament, a constabulary of paid professionals whose task it was to supervise the existing parish constables and to liaise with the developing police in the towns of the county and its neighbours. Yet these reforms were generally found wanting by the Royal Commission on a Rural Constabulary which deliberated between 1836 and 1839; and it was the conclusions of that Royal Commission which have informed the Whig police histories.

Three men served on the Royal Commission: Colonel Charles Rowan, one of the first two commissioners of the Metropolitan Police; Charles Shaw-Lefevre, a Whig MP and country gentleman; and Edwin Chadwick, the dynamic Benthamite reformer who had earlier played a key role in drafting the Poor Law Commissioners' Report of 1834. Chadwick's enthusiasm for a centralized system was controlled by the other two commissioners, but it is clear that Chadwick was primarily responsible for drafting the Constabulary Commissioners' Report, and in so doing he underplayed the extent to which developments were taking place in the provinces and ignored the wishes of the majority of the magistrates in the different quarter sessions who were opposed to the kind of sweeping changes which he favoured (Brundage, 1986; Storch, 1989). The Whig government too was opposed to the extent of the changes proposed by the Commissioners' Report if for no other reason than that it recognized the impossibility of getting Parliament to agree to a national police force in which the control of local magistrates—then the unchallenged decision-makers for, and administrators of, the provinces through the medium of county quarter sessions—would be all but dispensed with. Instead the government introduced legislation which enabled county magistrates to establish county police forces if they so wished, with the Home Office playing only a distant supervisory role.

It is difficult fully to assess the extent to which the County Police legislation was adopted across England and Wales; twenty-four counties appear to have adopted it during the first two years of its existence; another eleven did so over the next fifteeen years, but nine of these seem to have appointed a constabulary for only parts of their jurisdiction (Foster, 1982: 19). The causes of adoption varied, as did assessments of the success of the new constabularies. In the early 1840s there was considerable agitation in several counties that the new forces be abolished, particularly because of their expense. In those counties which did not adopt the legislation there were new experiments to improve the existing system of parish constables, particularly by appointing professional superintending constables to oversee and organize their activities. Kent took the lead in these latter developments, yet when a parliamentary select committee investigated policing across the country in 1852 and 1853, no witnesses were called from that county.

The main fault with the superintending constables system seems to have been the way in which some magistrates sought to tie these policemen to petty sessions divisions and were jealous of requests that they be allowed to assist elsewhere in their county. By the early 1850s there was a dominant view in government circles that the county was the natural unit of local government, and Lord Palmerston, first as Home Secretary and then as Prime Minister, was keen to see a national system of county-based police forces, with only the larger towns maintaining their own independent police under watch committees. His initial ideas foundered on the hostility of the smaller boroughs, but in 1856 his Home Secretary, Sir George Grey, successfull negotiated the County and Borough Police Act through Parliament. This legislation made the creation of a police force obligatory on all counties of England and Wales and on all incorporated boroughs (even as late as this some small boroughs had not complied with the requirements of the Municipal Corporations Act). The Treasury was to pay one quarter of the pay and clothing costs of efficient forces, and 'efficiency' was to be assessed by three new Inspectors of Constabulary whose duty it was to inspect each force annually and report to Parliament.

The Metropolitan Police remained separate from the new legislation. It continued to be answerable, not to any representatives of local government, but to the Home Secretary, and the Metropolitan Police Commissioner himself made an annual report to Parliament. In the provinces, however, the system established by the 1856 Act largely survived for the next hundred years. Borough police forces were answerable to their watch committees; in some instances these committees took a close interest in the day-to-day operations of their men giving precise administrative and operational directives to their head constables. The chief constables of counties had more independence, since the police committees of quarter sessions met far less frequently than watch committees, and this infrequency of meeting continued after the magistrates' police committees were replaced, under the local government reorganization of 1888, by standing joint committees made up equally of magistrates and elected members of the new county councils.

Parallel with developments in England and Wales a similar system of policing emerged in Scotland. Towns were establishing their own forces by private legislation at the end of the eighteenth and beginning of the nineteenth centuries; the first public enactment came in 1833 with further legislation four-teen years later. At least twelve out of the twenty-eight Scottish counties had set up some form of force by 1839 when an Act authorized them to levy an additional Rogue Money assessment to create a constabulary. Lanarkshire was the only county of any significance which had not taken advantage of this legislation when an Act was passed in 1857 requiring the burghs and counties to establish police forces under terms similar to those of the earlier English and Welsh Act (Carson, 1984 and 1985; Carson and Idzikowska, 1989).

While the form of local control over the police established under the 1856 and 1857 Police Acts and the 1888 Local Government Act remained in place for the next hundred years, the reality of this control was gradually under-mined by the steady encroachment of the state. The Treasury grant to efficient provincial police forces was increased to half the cost of pay and clothing in 1874 specifically to give the Home Office a greater measure of control. But in general there was nothing conspiratorial in the steady encroachment of the state; rather it was the logical development of the increasing perception of policemen, by Home Office functionaries and by the police themselves, as the professionals and experts in the job of 'policing'. This prompted a succession of circulars and Acts of Parliament by which central government required specific administrative duties to be undertaken by the police without reference to their local police committees. More dramatic, and more noticeable in their impact on the links between senior police officers and civil servants, were the central government's concerns about managing national emergencies, notably strikes, subversion, and world wars. During the 1830s and 1840s squads of Metropolitan policemen had regularly been moved around the country to combat industrial disorder, agitation against the new Poor Law, Chartist demonstrations, and the Rebecca troubles in South Wales. But as time wore on the Home Office became increasingly reluctant to commit London policemen in this way, urging magistrates that they should establish their own police forces instead. As county forces developed there was some doubt about the extent to which they might be moved out of their jurisdiction to assist another force, though by the last quarter of the nineteenth century any such concerns were long gone and by the last decade of the century the Home Office was urging police forces to enter into mutual aid agreements. Few such agreements appear to have been made, and the strike wave before World War I witnessed an active Home Secretary, Winston Churchill, ordering both troops and police around the country to assist local forces against striking dockers, miners, and railwaymen. In Churchill's eyes, even where these were not national strikes (as in the case of the South Wales coal strike), they nevertheless threatened national security and supply, consequently they needed a national response. Churchill's more grandiose proposals for organizing police during strikes were defeated, and he himself moved from the Home Office in 1911, but the outbreak of war in 1914 brought a much greater linkage between central government and local police (Emsley, 1996*b*: 54–6, 68–9, and 112–19; Morgan, 1987: chapters 3 and 6; Weinberger, 1991: chapters 3 and 4).

The spy scares before the war had brought the provincial police forces into close contact with the embryonic sercret service. The war itself strengthened these developments as the police were ordered first to watch out for German spies and saboteurs, then for subversives who had taken German gold to undermine the war effort. The Russian Revolution produced a new kind of subversive in the minds of the authorities, the Bolshevik agitator, and fear of this creature lasted long after the war. A few chief constables, notably in South Wales, had major confrontations with their standing joint committees when they equated Labour Party membership and industrial unrest with Communism and Bolshevism; the Home Office backed the chief constables. Local police committees were bypassed by the Home Office as it prepared to confront widespread industrial unrest and communicated directly with chief constables. The Emergency Powers Act of 1920 was a key element in these changes enabling the Home Secretary to deploy up to 10 per cent of a police force outside its own jurisdiction, not necessarily for mutual aid (Emsley, 1996*b*: chapter 6; Weinberger, 1991: chapter 8).

Other developments, contemporaneous with the growing links between the police forces and the Home Office, also strengthened the idea of a single police service and undermined the local nature of the police. Towards the end of the nineteenth century the notion of policing as a skilled, professional trade, practised by men of similar origins with similar problems across the whole of the United Kingdom as well as in the Empire, began to emerge. These ideas were fostered by newspapers aimed at a police audience, and by campaigns to establish proper pension schemes and a weekly rest day. While both of these latter campaigns were successful there were many within the police forces who believed that a national police union would be the best means of ensuring a permanent voice for the rank and file in matters of pay, promotion, and discipline. The National Union of Police and Prison Officers was established in December 1913. The wartime pressures on the police, including longer hours and pay falling well below the level of inflation, encouraged recruitment to the union which, while not acknowledged by the authorities, fought a successful strike in London in August 1918 over pay and conditions. A second strike, a year later, involving Birmingham and Liverpool as well as London, was a disaster for the union. All the strikers were dismissed, and the union itself was banned, to be replaced by a Police Federation to which all men belonged up to and including the rank of inspector. The Federation was refused the right to strike. The Police Federation was among the recommendations of the commission appointed under Lord Desborough in the wake of the first police strike. Among the other proposals which it made, and which were accepted by the government, were that the pay and conditions of the police should be standardized and that half the total cost of the police, and not simply half the cost of pay and clothing, should be borne by the Treasury. Legal arguments, particularly Justice H. A. McCardie's controversial ruling in the case of *Fisher* v. *Oldham* in 1930 ([1930] 2 KB 364), tended further to undermine local authority over the police. Yet local independence remained sufficiently strong thoughout the inter-war years to check any hint of nationalization and, in particular, to prevent the forcible amalgamations of the smallest forces with their larger neighbours. It was the national emergency of World War II which provided the opportunity for central government to pass legislation enabling the Home Secretary to enforce amalgamations. The Labour government which came to power in 1945 was sufficiently impressed by the reports of the temporary wartime amalgamations to introduce legislation abolishing forty-five borough forces which, together with four voluntary amalgamations reduced the number of police forces in England and Wales to 131 by the end of 1947.

The argument for amalgamation and the abolition of the smaller forces was generally that such rationalization promoted efficiency. Yet police efficiency has always been notoriously difficult to estimate. The first Metropolitan Police constables were told that their principal task was the prevention of crime; and this instruction was taken up in the orders issued to the constables in provincial forces. The measurement of prevention is, of course, impossible; arrest statistics, however, are tangible. The new police were able to demonstrate their efficiency to watch committees, magistrates' police committees, and standing joint committees by arresting drunks, prostitutes, street sellers, and anyone else whose behaviour was offensive in a public place to Victorian perceptions of morality. Their presence may have had some impact on petty theft particularly in public places, and may, in consequence have contributed in some small measure to the levelling out of the crime statistics in the second half of the nineteenth century. Of course they did catch some offenders, but their methods were not particularly sophisticated. They appear to have accepted the notion of the criminal class and to have concentrated their efforts on containing stigmatized areas and the groups which lived in them; to paraphrase the explanation of one of the first commissioners of the Metropolitan Police to a parliamentary select committee, they guarded the elegant areas of St James by watching the slums of St Giles. Practices changed little in the first half of the twentieth century. The use of scientific and technological developments depended on the awareness and determination of a chief constable and what he was able to pursuade his police committee to purchase. But even when forces were equipped with radios, local pride and independence meant that they might not share frequencies. Detectives had been viewed with suspicion in the early nineteenth century as the man in plain clothes was feared as a spy; furthermore the early commissioners of the Metropolitan Police appear to have been wary of detective policemen since they were much more difficult to control and supervise than the uniformed constable patrolling a regular beat at a steady two-and-a-half miles an hour. A Home Office Committee was appointed in 1933 to investigate detective policing and, after deliberating for five years and investigating the situation elsewhere, particularly in North America, it concluded that England lagged far behind in training and the deployment of scientific aids. The committee's report led to significant developments in training, the exchange of information between forces, and the awareness of scientific aids; but the scale of the backwardness is demonstrated by the fact that even at the beginning of World War II some county forces, let alone the smallest borough forces, had no CID.

A lack of sophistication, however, was one of the main attributes of the image of the British Bobby as it developed during the nineteenth and early twentieth centuries. By the middle of the Victorian period at least he was perceived as solid and dependable; his ability to pull himself up by hard work and diligence from constable third class to superintendent or, in one of the smaller borough forces to head constable, made him, in the perception of the Victorian middle class, a working-class role-model in Samuel Smiles's self-help mould. At the same time the Bobby was seen as a mainstay of the British constitution which Victorians liked to think of as a model for the rest of the world; politicians, journalists, and senior policemen commonly reported the British police to be the best in the world. There were occasions when this image crumbled, and probably it was never particularly strong among the poorer sections of the working class. Furthermore as the ownership of private motor vehicles increased during the inter-war period, so, for the first time, the police were brought more and more into direct confrontation with 'respectable' members of society.

PROSECUTION AND THE COURTS

Just as policing increasingly became the preserve of experts and professionals from the mid-eighteenth century, so too did the system of prosecution and the activity within the courtroom. Throughout the eighteenth century the decision to prosecute an offender in England and Wales was generally taken by the victim, or by the victim's relations or friends. In Scotland, by the beginning of the century, the procurators-fiscal, subordinated to the Lord Advocate, had largely taken over the prosection of all serious crimes. But in England representatives of the central government rarely intervened; the occasional exceptions were coining cases commonly prosecuted by the Treasury Solicitor, and those few cases of treason or sedition which threatened the state and which were conducted by the Attorney General.

One of the problems in the English system was the expense; the prosecutor had to find fees and pay for a variety of legal documents. This appears often to have encouraged the victim to settle with the offender outside the courtroom; though compounding a felony with a monetary payment was itself an offence. The expense of prosecution also prompted men of property to organize themselves into subscription insurance clubs, known as Associations for the Prosecution of Felons, which met any prosecution costs that a member might incur (King, 1989; Philips, 1989). Legislation of 1752 authorized the payment of expenses to poor prosecutors in felony cases when the accused was convicted, and sixteen years later this payment was extended to all prosecutors. Peel's Criminal Justice Act of 1826 extended the provision to witnesses, and permitted such payment in some misdemeanour cases, notably assaults. These developments probably contributed to the increase in the number of prosecutors who came forward with charges, but well into the nineteenth century some victims still refused to prosecute, sometimes through fear, sometimes because of anxiety about the loss of time from work, or because the whole procedure seemed inconvenient. In the case of sexual offences, embarrassment, and the oppressive climate of Victorian morality which had little time for women who could not demonstrate their adherence to the expected norms of female behaviour, probably dissuaded many women from reporting, let alone prosecuting, an offence.

The Scottish system had its advocates in nineteenth-century England, but the idea of a public prosecutor was perceived as European, and French in particular; it was lumped together with political police and regarded as alien to English common law and constitutional traditions. However it is apparent that, as the nineteenth century wore on, the new police increasingly took on the role of prosecutor, though under the continuing official insistence that the English system was one of private prosecution. In the beginning the police assumption of this role was, at least in some instances, partly to uphold their own authority; but they also appear to have acted when no-one else came forward or because the victim was poor or a woman. The pattern of police involvement as prosecutors varied between the different force jurisdictions. Nevertheless by the last quarter of the nineteenth century prosecutors seem invariably to have been policemen, and the senior officers of municipal forces were often formally presenting cases to the courts much to the fury of another growing body of professionals—the lawyers (Emsley, 1996a: 190–3; Emsley, 1996b: 234–5; Hay, 1989: 36–47).

Criminal prosecutions were heard in three different kinds of court, each developing its distinctive style of practice between the mid-eighteenth and the mid-twentieth centuries. The most serious cases went before the county assize courts which generally met only twice a year, at Lent and in the Summer, until the early twentieth century. In London these cases were heard at the Old Bailey, more properly known as the Central Criminal Court after 1834; but the pressure of business in the metropolitan area meant that the courts here met far more frequently. County quarter sessions met four times a year and heard felony cases but, unlike the judges at the assizes, the magistrates of the county bench did not have the authority to hear capital offences. Less serious offences went before the summary jurisdiction of magistrates meeting in petty sessions. During the eighteenth century new legislation had permitted more and more cases to be heard summarily; the trend increased in the following century, particularly with the Juvenile Offenders Acts of 1847 and 1850, which empowered magistrates to try summarily any juvenile charged with simple larceny, the Criminal Justice Act of 1855, and the Prevention of Crime Act of 1879. These courts of petty sessions became more and more formal as the century progressed, and, in consequence of their growing workload and greater formality, the role of the quarter sessions declined. The formal petty sessions were increasingly known as police courts, something which concerned members of the legal profession and others, who were worried that this implied some linkage between the police and the courts.

In both the assize courts and the courts of quarter sessions, cases were heard before juries. However one of the most significant developments over the period was the way in which the jury shifted from being an active participant in a trial, with its members interrupting and asking questions, to becoming an audience whose task was simply to reach its verdict after watching the adversarial contest between professional lawyers. The process was gradual. It was not the result of any legislation or key legal rulings; rather it was the corollary of the growing authority of the legal profession. At the beginning of the eighteenth century it was rare for a man with legal training to prosecute, still less defend, in a run-of-the-mill criminal case. However by the 1730s prosecution counsel were appearing in increasing numbers, and defence counsel to a slightly lesser extent. It is not clear why the development occurred, especially since counsel increased the costs of a case markedly, but by the 1840s the lack of prosecuting counsel at an assize could provoke caustic comments from the presiding judge. Poor defendants had problems with this system; not only could they not give evidence on oath until after 1898, but there was not provision for legal aid until the Poor Prisoner's Defence Act of 1903. During the nineteenth century any defendent seeking a professional defence could get cheap counsel through the 'Dock Brief' system by which, for the fee of a guinea, he could obtain the services of a barrister without the mediation of a solicitor, but the services obtained in this way were rarely of much quality (Beattie, 1986: 352–62; Emsley, 1996a: 193–6).

The shift to summary jurisdiction may have speeded up the process between arrest, trial, and verdict, but it also brought anxieties. The legal profession complained about the impact on the fees, and consequently on the livelihood, of its members. More seriously, there was disquiet about the fact that an increase in summary trials meant a decrease in the number of defendants who had their cases heard before that keystone of the British constitution, the jury. The latter concern was compounded, first by the fear that magistrates, as men of property, might adjudicate in their own interest and, secondly, by the fact that so many magistrates were laymen with no formal training in the law. In a few instances some magistrates did hear cases when they themselves were involved; but such practice was frowned upon and always provoked critical comment. It was much more common for a magistrate to step down from the bench if he was involved in a case; but this, of course, did not always ensure an unbiased verdict since magistrates were appointed from the same social class. No government contemplated instituting the requirement of legal training for the men appointed as magistrates, it was simply accepted that they could take the advice of their clerks, who had legal training. Furthermore increasingly in the nineteenth century magistrates were bolstered by recorders, who were barristers, and by stipendiaries, who were also trained in the law. Indeed the pressure of business meant that the police courts in the cities came to be dominated by stipendiaries.

Tangentially it should be noted that the increasing shift to summary jurisdiction and the development of professional, bureaucratic police forces contributed to a significant change in the role of the magistrate. During the eighteenth century he (women were not eligible to serve until 1918) had an administrative as well as a judicial role. The former was reduced by the development of elected local government, in the boroughs by the Municipal Corporations Act 1835 and in the counties by the Local Government Act 1888. It was further reduced as the new police assumed more and more responsibility for making decisions in suppressing instances of disorder and riot.

PUNISHMENT

It used to be popular to think in terms of a steady amelioration in the punishment of offences from the notorious 'Bloody Code' of the eighteenth century, with over 200 capital statutes, to the final abolition of the death penalty in 1965, going hand in hand with a steady recognition of the need to reform the offender manifested by the development of the prison. Unfortunately historical processes have rarely moved in such a convenient linear fashion, and the changes in punishment and the reformation of offenders are no exceptions.

The number of capital statutes increased in the eighteenth century, but consolidation and codification were alien to the English legal tradition and consequently there were not 200 completely distinct offences for which persons could be executed; often separate statutes covered virtually the same offence but refered to a separate part of the country or tidied up an outstanding problem left over from an earlier law. Furthermore, even though the number of capital statutes increased, the number of executions declined over the century. Since the second half of the seventeenth century judges had been exercising their discretion to ensure that convicted offenders were not all executed. The Transportation Act of 1718, which authorized the sending of offenders to the American colonies, provided the best alternative means of avoiding execution and getting rid of offenders. As the eighteenth century wore on only those offences deemed to be the most aggravated were likely to be punished by death. This punishment was to be a terrible example to others. As a consequence, while sensibilities decreed that fewer should hang, the need for terrible examples, following concerns about violent crime in London in the middle of the century, led to the passage of the 1752 Murder Act which, in order to deter potential offenders, instructed that the bodies of convicted murderers be delivered to surgeons for dissection or, at the judge's discretion, be hanged in chains; furthermore, while there were usually two or three weeks between sentence and execution, under the Murder Act sentence was to be carried out the next day but one.

The shifting sensibilities which questioned the reliance on the death penalty seem to have been linked with developing arguments about the nature of God. The traditional view assumed links between God assessing sinners on the Day of Judgment and judges assessing offenders in the courts; as one cleric explained in 1739, there would be great 'confusion' in the state 'where men only stand in awe of them that can kill the body, and trouble not at the displeasure of that Almighty Being, who after he hath killed, hath power to cast into hell!'. However, increasingly during the eighteenth century, God, rather than being the God of wrath and vengeance, was understood as the benevolent Creator; He had never intended barbarous punishments and, consequently, far more appropriate than the gallows was the prison conducted on humane principles to encourage the offender's reformation (McGowen, 1988).

Prisons were not a new departure. From Tudor times petty offenders, vagrants, and prostitutes could have found themselves sentenced to a period in a Bridewell or House of Correction; and those awaiting trial on an indictment for felony were kept in prison, often for several months, awaiting trial. The use of imprisonment to punish simple felonies had been largely abandoned after the Transportation Act of 1718. Interest was revived during the 1760s and early 1770s, at least in part, because the combination of the occasional example on the gallows and transportation did not appear to be effectively deterring crime. The outbreak of the American War of Independence forced the issue; the courts might still sentence felons to transportation, but now there was nowhere that the sentence might be carried out. By the end of the 1780s the government had settled on the colony of New South Wales as its receptacle for felons; however by then moves for creating prisons where the offender might be reformed were already under way, partly through local initiative, but also with significant moves on the part of central government.

Pinpointing the reasons behind the growth of the prison has given rise to considerable debate. On one level there are the arguments which tie its development in with an interrelationship between forms of knowledge and the shifting strategies and institutions through which power is exercised; thus the prison becomes interlinked with the new expertise of medicine and psychiatry and with a new, enclosing, and restricting orientation to the body (Foucault, 1977). For others the emergence of the prison ties in with the needs of a new industrial order and its desire for a controllable, disciplined workforce (Ignatieff, 1978). On a more prosaic level there were obvious, practical difficulties which fostered change and reform. Typhus broke out in the crowded gaols made still more crowded by the temporary halt to transportation. The periodic baccanalia at Tyburn not only threatened order but also suggested that the traditional argument behind this kind of punishment, that it served to deter, was unconvincing; such suspicions fused with the changing view of God and the Enlightenment's perception of man as a rational being who could, through reason, be taught good behaviour. In 1767 Cesare Beccaria's *Dei Delitti e delle Pene*, already widely praised on the continent, appeared in English translation; it was warmly received for its criticisms of the barbaric punishments of the past and its exhortation to create a rational system within which punishment was certain and fitted the crime. Ten years later John Howard published his detailed and depressing account of *The State of the Prisons in England and Wales*. Rather than changing men's minds both of these books probably crystallized thoughts and ideas already in motion. In 1779 Parliament passed the Penitentiary Act providing for the construction of two prisons in the metropolis, one for 600 men and the other for 300 women who, instead of transportation, were to be reformed and taught the habits of industry. However financial retrenchment following the war against the American colonists and the enormous expense of the Revolutionary and Napoleonic wars slowed and constrained national developments along these lines. Millbank, the first national penitentiary, was not begun until 1812 and not opened until 1816.

The Revolutionary and Napoleonic wars compelled the government to take on the management of large numbers of prisoners. On the one hand there were the felons, held in increasing numbers on aged, dismasted warships known as the hulks because of the difficulties which war imposed on their shipment to Australia; on the other there were the large numbers of prisoners of war who had to be accomodated—the prison at Princeton on Dartmoor was opened in 1809 for 6,000 such. At the same time the chorus of demands for reform of the system of punishment became ever more shrill, driven by determined individuals like Sir Samuel Romilly, and by Evangelical reformist bodies such as, most notably, the Society for the Improvement of Prison Discipline and the Reformation of Juvenile Offenders which was established in 1815. Parliament, by no means the diehard reactionary institution it is sometimes portrayed as for this period, responded by reducing the number of capital statutes and by limiting the opportunities for graft and corruption among prison governors and their turnkeys. During the 1820s Peel successfully reformed and rationalized the criminal law; though whether this was the result of humanitarianism, or the desire to shore up a system cracking under the weight of increased prosecutions and convictions, remains a moot point (Gatrell, 1994). In 1833 a body of Criminal Law Commissioners was appointed to establish a rational system of punishment whereby punishment was to fit the crime; but their attempts foundered on the sheer complexity of the task.

Prison reform reached a climax in the 1830s with debates between the advocates of the separate system (wherein convicts were separated from each other in the belief that, in the quiet of their solitary cells, with their Bible, the exhortation of the chaplain, and their work at a hand crank, they would reach a realization of their wrongdoing and consequent repentence) and those of the silent system (wherein a strict discipline of silence would bring the prisoner to a similar recognition). The former, urged by William Crawford, a member of the Society for the Improvement of Prison Discipline, and by the Rev. Whitworth Russell, the chaplain of Millbank, who were both appointed to a new inspectorate of prisons in 1835, resulted in the opening of Pentonville in 1842. Pentonville was a bleak, dehumanizing establishment from which, in its early years, an annual toll of between five and fifteen of the 450 inmates were taken away to the asylum; and others sought escape through suicide. But while the separate and silent systems were experimented with in varying degrees across the country, the majority of prisons remained under the control of local authorities and developments here were constrained by local government finance and the pressures from rate-payers.

It was also during the 1830s that the number of offenders who were transported reached a peak of about 5,000 a year. There had always been debate about the effectiveness of transportation. During the eighteenth century there were a few who protested that, rather than punishing the offender, transportation gave him, or her, an undeserved opportunity to start a new life. By the early nineteenth century it was being alleged that some individuals were committing crimes deliberately so as to get themselves transported to a pleasant environment where the shortage of labour promised opportunity for profit and advancement. In reality the convict settlements in Australia could be harsh and cruel, yet the very fact that such allegations could be made in itself served to undermine the deterrence of the punishment. Furthermore as free settlers and the children of the convicts began to form the majority of citizens in the Australian colonies, so their opposition grew to the mother country foisting its dregs upon them. Dissatisfaction with transportation both in Britain and in the colonies brought about a steady reduction from the 1840s until, in 1857, it was abolished as a judicial sentence (though a handful of offenders continued to be sent to Western Australia until 1867).

The Annual Criminal Statistics reveal that, by the 1860s, over 90 per cent of those convicted of indictable offences were being sentenced to terms of imprisonment, and the gradual end of transportation confirmed the prison as the principal form of punishment. But the same period witnessed increasing fears about what to do with offenders once they were released from gaol. In many respects the popular asumptions about a separate 'criminal class' tended to undermine the notions of moral reformation which were central to prison policy during the second quarter of the century. Individuals stamped with the stigma of a prison term often found it difficult to find work, and this could be aggravated by the police marking them out as 'known offenders'. The Penal Servitude Act of 1853 attempted to address some of the problems. It extended sentences and toughened the discipline in prisons in lieu of transportation; it also formally introduced the ticket of leave system whereby convicts could be released on licence following good behaviour. A succession of acts followed seeking to fine-tune the system; but penal servitude, while it remained on the Statute Book until 1948, was never precisely defined, and the problems for the police in supervising those on tickets of leave, not to mention the threat which this supervision suspended over an ex-convict's head, were enormous.

It was popularly assumed that the garotting attacks of the 1850s and early 1860s were the work of members of the criminal class on tickets of leave. The panic prompted a further hardening of penal discipline with the 'Garotter's Act' of 1863; this also introduced flogging as a punishment for street robbery in addition to a prison term, and, like penal servitude, this provision remained on the Statute Book until 1948. The recommendations of a Lords Select Committee chaired by Lord Carnarvon, also in 1863, led to a further tightening of discipline within the national convict prisons; long-term prisoners sentenced to penal servitude now spent an initial nine months in solitary confinement in Millbank or Pentonville, before being moved to one of the public works prisons of Chatham, Dartmoor, Portland, or Portsmouth. The Scottish equivalent of these institutions was the General Prison in Perth, begun in 1840, opened in 1843, and completed in 1859. But in Scotland, as well as in England and Wales, the majority of gaols continued to be not these national institutions but smaller, local ones. Only in 1877 did legislation sweep away local management and, in consequence, begin to reduce the number of prisons. The Prisons Act of that year appointed prison commissioners, responsible to the Home Secretary, who were to superintend all prisons and submit annual reports to Parliament.

Centralization under the prison commissioners brought a uniform system of punishment across the country, which had been the aim of many reformers at least since the early nineteenth century; and punishment was now to be in private—not for the Victorians the public spectacle to deter potential offenders. Floggings and, after 1868, executions were to be carried out behind prison walls. But no sooner was the uniformity of punishment achieved than it began to be queried as the authorities sought to come to terms with the individuals who did not fit the criminal stereotype for whom the prison system had been designed, notably juveniles, women, and offenders from the higher social classes such as some of the Irish Nationalists and the gentlemen convicted of various forms of commercial fraud or embezzlement. At the same time the number of recidivists committed to prison was increasing, and while the decline of first offenders and the levelling out of the crime statistics suggested that the Victorian war against crime was a success, the recidivists were regarded as evidence of the prisons' overall failure to deter or to reform criminals. The problem became linked to the changing perception of professional criminals less as a 'class' and more as a small hard core bolstered by a much larger number of social inadequates who constituted that part of the population least able to cope with the pressures of modern life, especially modern urban life. This changing perception increasingly worked its way into sentencing policy and policy-making in general, notably with the report of the Gladstone Committee in 1895 and the direction pursued by the second chairman of the prison commissioners, Evelyn Ruggles-Brise. Alternatives were sought for incarceration, and, rather than seeking to eradicate the evil habits of a class, the treatment of offenders began to be geared, more and more, to what were perceived as the needs of particular individuals. Probation was introduced for first offenders in 1887 and was put on a more general footing twenty years later with social workers, in the form of probation officers, seeking to help the inadequate, petty criminal member of society to adjust to the community without being taken from that community. Borstals were developed for young offenders, and these particularly, but also in some degree the conventional prisons, were encouraged to employ what were, in contemporary parlance, scientific systems of therapeutics (Weiner, 1990: chapters 8 and 9).

The amelioration of the prison system during the inter-war period was gradual. The Victorian prison uniform with its broad arrows, the silence rule, and the punitive labour, were all mitigated in the 1920s. But the food and living conditions of prisoners remained poor and provoked a serious 'mutiny' among the inmates of Dartmoor in 1932. The policy of reducing incarceration and the search for alternatives were maintained, and the overall success of the system appeared to be underlined by the prison commissioners' ability to continue closing prisons but, at the same time, to maintain a surplus capacity. In 1951 the chairman could boast that it had only been necessary to build two institutions since the beginning of the century: Camp Hill on the Isle of Wight and Lowdham Grange Borstal (Fox, 1952: 98). In many respects the Criminal Justice Act of 1948, which swept away most of the severe vestiges of the Victorian system, was the climax of the shift towards rehabilitating individual offenders. It showed something of a liberal consensus between Labour and Conservative politicians, the penal reform lobby, and the professionals working in the system. The Act abolished corporal punishment; it provided preventive detention for the worst recidivist, but 'corrective training' for others; detention centres were created for young offenders who were felt to require something stiffer than probation but not as severe as Borstal; and attendance centres were established for a variety of petty offenders of all ages who could be required to attend in their free time and participate in a variety of activities not necessarily of their own choosing (Bailey, 1987: 302–5).

SHIFTS AND CONTEXTS

The 200 years surveyed here witnessed a shift from crime control mechanisms which were essentially local, personal and, since constables, thief-takers, justices, and gaolers took fees from clients and charges, entrepreneurial, to crime control institutions which were bureaucratic, largely impersonal, and increasingly centralized. This shift took place against the background of a move from a predominantly agrarian-based economy with a largely rural population, to an industrial, capitalist economy, with, from about 1850, a majority of people living in towns. The growing economy resulted in more moveable possessions owned by a greater variety of individuals, and this provided new and probably greater opportunities and temptations for theft; and while not necessarily accepting arguments about *anomie* leading to crime, the more complex, impersonal nature of towns probably also offered greater opportunities and temptations for crime. The question remains, however, what, if anything, was the relationship between economic and social change and the developing institutions of crime control?

Exploring the institutional developments in the light of the economic and social changes has been illuminating: clearly economic and social ideas influenced the understanding of offences and offenders; the growth of London and other big cities, together with fears about the new urban population, contributed to the creation of police forces; parallels can be detected between the nature of, and the supporters and advocates of, the prison, the new work-house, and the factory. Yet the development of crime control institutions has not been unique to liberal capitalist societies like Britain. Where Britain has been unique is in the perception of the state. During the nineteenth century, unlike the most influential and powerful of its continental neighbours, the British state acquired an aura of stability, success, and, above all, benevolence. It remains a moot point the extent to which this state acted in the interests of a new capitalist class; certainly businessmen as tax and ratepayers were often reluctant to provide the money for new police and prisons, and government, both central and local, often disappointed reformers by not raising the money necessary for their cherished projects. Yet the Victorian state and its successors did grow; and, in the name of greater efficiency and rationalization which, it was claimed, would benefit the population as a whole, it centralized. The people driving this growth, reformers, politicians, and civil servants, believed in progress and their own humanitarianism; the gradual amelioration of the penal system from the late nineteenth century, in itself, is an indication of the power of these beliefs. The same world view also influenced the first historians of these institutions and celebrated the police and prison systems as the achievements of a benificent, progressive state and society. A more cynical, more pessimistic age is also more critical of its institutions, and the contemporary historians of crime and crime control cannot so readily share an explanation for the changes they explore.

Selected Further Reading

The five volumes of Leon Radzinowicz, *A History of English Criminal Law and its Administration from 1750* (London: Stevens, 1948–86) is an invaluable reference work for the period, though students may find it a little daunting. Those looking for a gentler introduction to the subjects discussed above could usefully turn to the following:

J. M. Beattie, *Crime and the Courts in England 1660–1800*, Oxford: Clarendon Press, 1986. A scholarly but highly readable exploration of the way that English courts dealt with crime during the period of the Bloody Code. The main focus is on Surrey and Sussex.

Clive Emsley, *Crime and Society in England, 1750–1900*, 2nd. edn. London: Longman, 1996. A basic text, pulling together the recent research into the history of crime.

Clive Emsley, *The English Police: A Political and Social History*, 2nd. edn. London: Longman, 1996. A reassessment of the development of the English Police which draws on several largely unexplored provincial police archival collections as well as the better-known Parliamentary and Metropolitan Police records.

Douglas Hay and Francis Snyder, eds., *Policing and Prosecution in Britain 1750–1850*. Oxford: Clarendon Press, 1989. A collection of essays of consistently high quality discussing such issues as policing before the police and the social purposes and meanings of prosecution. The perspective is genuinely British, with essays on both Scotland and Ireland.

David J. V. Jones, *Crime and Policing in the Twentieth Century. The South Wales Experience*. Cardiff: University of Wales Press, 1996. The only historical study of twentiety-century crime and policy; it draws significantly, and most usefully, on the hitherto unused archives of the South Wales Police.

Martin J. Wiener, *Reconstructing the Criminal: Culture, Law and Policy in England 1830–1914*. Cambridge: Cambridge University Press, 1990. An important and illuminating assessment of how shifts in the concept of human nature shaped the development of criminal policy.

Lucia Zedner, *Women, Crime, and Custody in Victorian England*. Oxford: Clarendon Press, 1991. This excellent book has to be the starting point for any future historical work on women and crime in the modern period.

REFERENCES

ANON. (H. W. HOLLAND) (1863), 'The Science of Garrotting and Housebreaking', *Cornhill Magazine*, 7: 79–92.

ASCOLI, D. (1979), *The Queen's Peace: The Origins and Development of the Metropolitan Police 1829–1979*. London: Hamish Hamilton.

BAILEY, V., ed. (1981), *Policing and Punishment in Nineteenth–Century Britain*. London: Croom Helm.

—— (1987), *Delinquency and Citizenship: Reclaiming the Young Offender 1914–1918*, Oxford: Clarendon Press.

BEAN, J. P. (1981), *The Sheffield Gang Wars*. Sheffield: D and D Publications.

BEATTIE, J. M. (1975), 'The Criminality of Women', *Journal of Social History*, 8: 80–116.

—— (1981), 'Judicial Records and the Measurement of Crime in Eighteenth-Century England', in L. A. Knafla, ed., *Crime and Criminal Justice in Europe and Canada*, 127–45. Waterloo, Ontario: Wilfred Laurier University.

—— (1986), *Crime and the Courts in England 1660–1800*. Oxford: Clarendon Press.

BEIER, A. L. (1985), *Masterless Men: The Vagrancy Problem in Britain 1560–1640*. London: Methuen.

BROEKER, G. (1970), *Rural Disorder and Police Reform in Ireland, 1812–1836*. London: Routledge and Kegan Paul.

BRUNDAGE, A. (1986), 'Ministers, Magistrates and Reformers: The Genesis of the Rural Constabulary Act of 1839', *Parliamentary History: A Yearbook*, 5: 55–64.

BURN, W. L. (1964), *The Age of Equipoise: A Study of the Mid-Victorian Generation*. London: Allen and Unwin.

CARSON, W. G. (1984), 'Policing the Periphery: The Development of Scottish Policing 1795–1900', Part I, *Australian and New Zealand Journal of Criminology*, 17: 207–32.

—— (1985), 'Policing the Periphery: The Development of Scottish Policing 1795–1900', Part II, *Australian and New Zealand Journal of Criminology*, 18: 3–16.

—— and IDZIKOWSKA, H. (1989), 'The Social Production of Scottish Policing, 1795–1900', in D. Hay and F. Snyder, eds., *Policy and Prosecution in Britain, 1750–1850*, 267–97. Oxford: Clarendon Press.

COCKBURN, J. S. (1991), 'Patterns of Violence in English Society: Homicide in Kent 1560–1985', *Past and Present*, 131: 70–106.

COLQUHOUN, P. (1796), *A Treatise on the Police of the Metropolis*, 3rd. edn. London: C. Dilly.

CONLEY, C. A. (1991), *The Unwritten Law: Criminal Justice in Victorian Kent*. New York: Oxford University Press.

CRITCHLEY, T. A. (1978), *A History of Police in England and Wales*, 2nd. edn. London: Constable.

DAVIS, J. S. (1984), '"A Poor Man's System of Justice." The London Police Courts in the Second Half of the Nineteenth Century', *Historical Journal*, 27: 309–35.

—— (1989), 'Prosecutions and their Context: The Use of the Criminal Law in Later Nineteenth-Century London', in D. Hay and F. Snyder, eds., *Policing and Prosecution in Britain, 1750–1850*, 379–426. Oxford: Clarendon Press.

DE LACY, M. (1986), *Prison Reform in Lancashire, 1700–1850. A Study in Local Administration*. Manchester: Manchester University Press.

DIXON, D. (1991), *From Prohibition to Regulation: Bookmaking, Anti-Gambling and the Law*. Oxford: Clarendon Press.

EMSLEY, C. (1996a), *Crime and Society in England 1750–1900*, 2nd. edn. London: Longman.

—— (1996b), *The English Police: A Political and Social History*, 2nd. edn. London: Longman.

FEELEY, M. M., and LITTLE, D. H. (1991), 'The Vanishing Female: The Decline of Women in the Criminal Process, 1687–1912', *Law and Society Review*, 25: 719–57.

FIELDING, H. (1751), *An Enquiry into the Late Increase of Robbers*, London: A. Millar.

FORSYTHE, W. J. (1987), *The Reform of Prisons, 1830–1900*. London: Croom Helm.

—— (1991), *Penal Discipline, Reformatory Projects and the English Prison Commission, 1895–1939*. Exeter: University of Exeter Press.

FOSTER, D. (1982), *The Rural Constabulary Act 1839: National Legislation and the Problems of Enforcement*. London: Bedford Square Press/NCVO.

FOUCAULT, M. (1977), *Discipline and Punish: The Origins of the Prison*. London: Allen Lane.

FOX, Sir L. (1952), *The English Prison and Borstal Systems*. London: Routledge and Kegan Paul.

GATRELL, V. A. C. (1980), 'The Decline of Theft and Violence in Victorian and Edwardian England', in V. A. C. Gatrell, B. Lenman, and G. Parker, eds., *Crime and the Law: The Social History of Crime in Western Europe since 1500*, 238–370. London: Europa.

—— (1990), 'Crime, Authority and the Policeman State', in F. M. L. Thompson, ed., *The Cambridge Social History of Britain 1750–1950*, vol. 3: 243–310. Cambridge: Cambridge University Press.

—— (1994), *The Hanging Tree: Execution and the English People 1770–1868*. Oxford: Oxford University Press.

GILLIS, J. R. (1975), 'The Evolution of Juvenile Delinquency in England, 1890–1914', *Past and Present*, 67: 96–126.

GLYDE, J. (1856*a*), *Suffolk in the Nineteenth Century: Physical, Social, Moral, Religious and Industrial*. London.

—— (1856*b*), 'Localities of Crime in Suffolk', *Journal of the Statistical Society*, 19: 102–6.

HANAWAY, J. (1772), *Observations on the Causes of the Dissoluteness which Reigns among the Lower Classes of People: the Propensity of some to Petty Larceny: And the Danger of Gaming, Concubinage, and an Excessive Fondness for Amusement in High Life*. London: J. and F. Rivington.

HAY, D. (1975), 'Property, Authority and the Criminal Law', in D. Hay, P. Linebaugh, E. P. Thompson, *et al.*, *Albion's Fatal Tree: Crime and Society in Eighteenth-Century England*, 17–63. London: Allen Lane.

—— and SNYDER, F., eds. (1989), *Policing and Prosecution in Britian 1750–1850*. Oxford: Clarendon Press.

HOWSON, G. (1970), *Thief-taker General: The Rise and Fall of Jonathan Wild*. London: Hutchinson.

IGNATIEFF, M. (1978), *A Just Measure of Pain: The Penitentiary in the Industrial Revolution 1750–1850*. London: Macmillan.

INNES, J., and STYLES, J. (1986), 'The Crime Wave: Recent Writing on Crime and Criminal Justice in Eighteenth-Century England', *Journal of British Studies*, 25: 380–435.

JENKINS, P., and POTTER, G. W. (1988), 'Before the Krays: Organised Crime in London, 1920–1960', *Criminal Justice History: An International Annual*, 9: 209–30.

JONES, D. J. V. (1982), *Crime, Protest, Community and Police in Nineteenth-Century Britain*. London: Routledge and Kegan Paul.

—— (1992), *Crime in Nineteenth-Century Wales*. Cardiff: University of Wales Press.

KING, P. J. R. (1989), 'Prosecution Associations and their Impact in Eighteenth-Century Essex', in D. Hay and F. Snyder, eds., *Policing and Prosecution in Britain, 1750–1850*, 171–207. Oxford: Clarendon Press.

—— (1996), 'Female Offenders, Work and Life-cycle Change in Late-Eighteenth-Century London', *Continuity and Change*, 11: 61–90.

LANDAU, N. (1984), *The Justices of the Peace 1679–1760*. Berkeley, Cal.: University of California Press.

LINEBAUGH, P. (1991), *The London Hanged: Crime and Civil Society in the Eighteenth Century*. London: Allen Lane.

McCONVILLE, S. (1981), *A History of English Prison Administration, vol. 1, 1750–1877*. London: Routledge and Kegan Paul.

McGOWEN. R. (1988), 'The Changing Face of God's Justice: The Debates over Divine and Human Punishment in Eighteenth-Century England', *Criminal Justice History: An International Annual*, 9: 63–98..

McHUGH, P. (1980), *Prostitution and Victorian Social Reform*. London: Croom Helm.

MARGERY, S. (1978), 'The Invention of Juvenile Delinquency in Early Nineteenth-Century England', *Labour History*, 34: 11–27.

MAY, M, (1973), 'Innocence and Experience: The Evolution of Juvenile Deliquency in the Mid-Nineteenth Century', *Victorian Studies*, 17: 7–29.

MORGAN, J. (1987), *Conflict and Order: Labour Disputes in England and Wales 1900–1939*. Oxford: Clarendon Press.

PALEY, R. (1989*a*), 'Thief-takers in London in the Age of the McDaniel Gang, c.1745–1754', in D. Hay and F. Snyder, eds., *Policing and Prosecution in Britain, 1750–1850*, 301–41. Oxford: Clarendon Press.

—— (1989*b*), '"An Imperfect, Inadequate and Wretched System"? Policing London before Peel', *Criminal Justice History: An International Annual*, 10: 95–130.

PALMER, S. H. (1988), *Police and Protest in England and Ireland 1780–1850*. Cambridge: Cambridge University Press.

PEARSON, G. (1983), *Hooligan: A History of Respectable Fears*. London: Macmillan.

PHILIPS, D. (1977), *Crime and Authority in Victorian England: The Black Country 1835–1860*. London: Croom Helm.

—— (1989), 'Good Men to Associate and Bad Men to Conspire: Associations for the Prosecution of Felons in England, 1760–1860', in D. Hay and F. Snyder, eds., *Policing and Prosecution in Britain, 1750–1850*, 113–70. Oxford: Clarendon Press..

RADZINOWICZ, L. (1948–86), *A History of the English Criminal Law and its Administration from 1750*, 5 vols: 1 (1948) *The Movement for Reform*; 2 (1956) *The Clash between Private Initiative and Public Interest in the Enforcement of the Law*; 3 (1956) *Cross-Currents in the Movement for the Reform of the Police*; 4 (1968) *Grappling for Control*; 5 (with R. Hood) (1986) *The Emergence of Penal Policy in Victorian and Edwardian England*. London: Stevens and Sons.

RANDALL, A. J. (1990), ' "Peculiar Perquisites and Pernicious Practices": Embezzlement in the West of England Woollen Industry c.1750–1840', *International Review of Social History*, 35: 193–219.

REITH, C. (1938), *The Police Idea*. Oxford: Oxford University Press.

—— (1943), *British Police and the Democratic Ideal*. Oxford: Oxford University Press.

REYNOLDS, E. (1991), 'The Night Watch and Police Reform in London, 1720–1830', Ph.D. thesis, Cornell University.

ROBB, G. (1992), *White-Collar Crime in Modern England: Financial Fraud and Business Morality 1845–1929*. Cambridge: Cambridge University Press.

RUMBELOW, D. (1971), *I Spy Blue: The Police and Crime in the City of London from Elizabeth I to Victoria*. London: Macmillan.

SAMUEL, R. (1981), *East End Underworld: Chapters in the Life of Arthur Harding*. London: Routledge and Kegan Paul.

SHARPE, J. A. (1985), 'The History of Violence in England: Some Observations', *Past and Present*, 108: 206–15.

SINDALL, R. (1990), *Street Violence in the Nineteenth Century: Media Panic or Real Danger?* Leicester: Leicester University Press.

STEVENSON, S. J. (1983), 'The "Criminal Class" in the Mid-Victorian City: A Study of Policy Conducted with Special Reference to Those Made Subject to the Provisions of 34 & 35 Vict. c. 112 (1871) in Birmingham and East London in the Early Years of Registration and Supervision', D.Phil. thesis, University of Oxford.

STONE, L. (1983), 'Interpersonal Violence in English Society, 1300–1980', *Past and Present*, 101: 22–33.

—— (1985), 'A Rejoinder', *Past and Present*, 108: 216–24.

STORCH, R. D. (1989), 'Policing Rural Southern England before the Police: Opinion and Practice, 1830–1856', in D. Hay and F. Snyder, eds., *Policing and Prosecution in Britain, 1750–1850*, 211–66. Oxford: Clarendon Press.

TOBIAS, J. J. (1972a), *Crime and Society in the Nineteenth Century*. Harmondsworth: Penguin.

WALKOWITZ, J. R. (1980), *Prostitution and Victorian Society: Women, Class and the State*. Cambridge: Cambridge University Press.

WEINBERGER, B (1991), *Keeping the Peace? Policing Strikes in Britian 1906–1926*. Oxford: Berg.

WIENER, M. J. (1990), *Reconstructing the Criminal: Culture, Law and Policy in England, 1830–1914*. Cambridge: Cambridge University Press.

ZEDNER, L. (1991), *Women, Crime and Custody in Victorian England*. Oxford: Clarendon Press.

3

Dumping the 'Hostages to Fortune'? The Politics of Law and Order in Post-War Britain

David Downes and Rod Morgan

INTRODUCTION

For the purposes of this chapter we take the term 'the politics of law and order' to mean the public contestation of the dynamics of crime, disorder, and their control. The key players in this matrix are: the major political parties, in particular successive Home Secretaries and their ministerial and Opposition teams; senior civil servants who, despite their non-political role, bear crucial advisory responsibilities; pressure and interest groups in the criminal justice field; and the mass media. The private, off-stage, often confidential and even secretive processes of discussion, negotiation, and exchange, which provide the ingredients of public utterance and action, remain implicit rather than spelt out in what follows. Further, when we employ terms such as 'the Conservative Party' or 'the Labour Party' we do not mean to propagate the fallacy of misplaced concreteness: these terms are necessary abbreviations for the welter of possible responsibilities for actions and policies that may be the work of many thousands of individuals. Nor, in quoting the words of ministers or other politicians, do we assume that perfect comprehension can be achieved—if it ever can be—without much more detail about timing, context, multiple purposes, encoding and decoding artfulness, and much else. We assume that our readers will grasp that a limited purpose is pursued in making quotations and examples, namely, to demonstrate a point rather than to convey some total reality.

Compared with the contested party politics of the economy, foreign affairs, defence, health, housing, and education, those of 'law and order' are of remarkably recent origin: they emerged in the mid-1960s, but came decisively to the fore only with the 1979 election. This longstanding absence from party political discourse and contention is remarkable. Law and order are highly emotive and fundamentally political issues. Few topics can routinely arouse such passionate debate. That law and order were relatively insulated from the realm of party politics for so long testifies perhaps to the strength of belief that crime, like the weather, is beyond political influence; and that the operation of the law and criminal justice should be above it. This is not to deny that criminal law reform has long been regarded as the prerogative of Parliament. But once laws are enacted, the liberal doctrine of the separation of powers holds that their enforcement is the preserve of the police and the judiciary. Hence, bipartisanship has been the rule rather than the exception in the twentieth century on such matters as the response to crime, the nature of policing, sentencing policy, and so on. Even at the fringes of political life, few challenges were made to so profound a consensus.

The nature of and the reasons for the change from a broadly bipartisan to a sharply contested politics of law and order are central to our concerns in this chapter. But the prelude to that change was not without deep significance because the nature of the consensus itself was both complex and far from apolitical. This was, however, a politics more of nuance and inflection than of explicit difference. Also, the politics of law-breaking are not necessarily those of order-defiance (Elder, 1984), and the latter has a far more developed history, particularly in the realm of industrial conflict (Dixon and Fishwick, 1984). Friction over public order legislation and its enforcement has throughout the period been far more evident than that concerning straightforward criminality. It was the achievement of 'Thatcherism' to blur the difference between the two and even to fuse them symbolically to political effect. And the consequences of the change have been more than a simple matter of the major parties taking up starkly opposing stances across the range of relevant issues. Despite new, overt differences, a species of second-order consensus has emerged to replace former orthodoxies. Moreover, the politics of law and order are not confined to the party sphere. Extra-parliamentary processes have often been more vigorous than those within the confines of Westminster, and developments at local government level, or formulations by pressure groups and lobbies, have frequently been the stimulus for national attention. Finally, the eruption of particular scandals and concerns, via a rapidly changing media framework, have consistently proved catalysts for changing policies. In what follows, we shall address these topics in turn.

BRITISH GENERAL ELECTIONS AND 'LAW AND ORDER', 1945–1997

In 1945 Britain 'was a society both exhausted and exhilarated' (Morris, 1989: 13). The awesome task of post-war reconstruction led the three main parties to contend overwhelmingly about the priorities of rebuilding the economy and constructing the 'welfare state'. Despite fundamental ideological differences, out of this period was evolved a form of consensus, usually known as 'Butskellism',[1]

---

[1] 'Butskellism' was a word coined in the early 1950s to convey the similarity and continuity of economic policy between the outgoing Labour Chancellor of the Exchequer, Hugh Gaitskell, and the new Conservative Chancellor, R. A. Butler (see Marwick, 1990: chapter 6).

which set limits to the scope of political conflict. Full employment, core welfare rights in health, housing, income and maintenance, and education and economic growth based on Keynesian assumptions, were broadly accepted as shared goals, as was a mixed economy—though strong differences persisted over the nature of the mix. Crime and criminal justice were minor, taken-for-granted aspects of this consensus.

Our analysis of trends in the salience of 'law and order' as an issue in British politics is heavily reliant on manifestos for, and campaigning during, the relatively short (generally three-week) run-up to general elections. The method has obvious advantages. Such material provides a time series of supremely public character which has enabled political analysts to chart the changing complexion of party policies and their intended and actual appeal. The work of David Butler and his colleagues has furnished a thorough guide to the complexities and problems of interpretation. Against this view, it can be said that manifestos are formal exercises in party rhetoric which are little read and, as such, provide highly problematic guides to party thinking and influence. Such a view seems to us too dismissive. Manifestos are highly accessible documents and they play a major part in the process of democratic accountability. After elections they are constantly referred to by opponents of the government, and the notion of a mandate to pursue policies is heavily dependent on their prior legitimation by majority (or winning minority) vote by an electorate which has, in principle, had prior warning of party thinking and intentions. That electoral promises are far from sacrosanct does not alter the basis on which they rest: that voters have had the chance to assess the worth and credibility of party strategy.

In the first part of this section we describe and compare the way in which successive post-war manifestos and campaigns developed 'law and order' issues; we then attempt to discern the underlying reasons for the distinctive pattern that emerges.

The Post-War Manifestos and Campaigns

Not until 1959 did any party mention in a manifesto anything to do with topics of law and order, though in both 1955 and 1959 issues of legal aid and betting and gaming legislation were raised. In 1959, the new note struck by the Conservatives was simply 'to review the system of criminal justice and to undertake penal reforms which will lead offenders to abandon a life of crime. A scheme for compensating the victims of violent crime for personal injuries will be considered' (Conservative Party, 1959). In 1964, the Conservative manifesto extended its coverage to include: strengthening the police; the (abortive) Royal Commission on the Penal System; tougher measures against hooliganism; and supporting family ties to counteract delinquency. The Liberal Party implicitly attacked the inadequacy of the government's record by switching the emphasis on combating crime to prevention and rehabilitation (Liberal Party, 1964). Yet even in 1964, after thirteen years of continuous Conservative government, the Labour Party said nothing about law and order, or the government's record in the face of crime rates which had risen steeply since the mid-1950s. This self-denial was all the more noteworthy because in 1963, in the run-up to the coming election, Harold Wilson had convened a study group on crime and criminal justice under the chairmanship of Lord Longford. Though the group's report, *Crime—A Challenge To Us All*, became available only as Labour was taking up office in 1964, it was presumably known in advance that its members were 'breaking new ground' (Morris, 1989: 114), mainly on penal reform, the treatment of juveniles and capital punishment.

In 1966, however, after two years in government, the Labour Party for the first time devoted as much space to 'law and order' policy as the Conservatives. The preamble to its pledge to strengthen the police, reform juvenile justice, and modernize the prison system was implicitly critical of the Conservatives: 'For years Britain has been confronted by a rising crime rate, overcrowded prisons and many seriously undermanned police forces' (Labour Party, 1966). The Conservatives were also keen to 'beat the crime wave' in 1966, announcing policies which differed from Labour's only in that they favoured the formation of larger police forces and greater use of compensation orders by the courts. On one issue, however, they signalled a disagreement with Labour that was to persist for many years. Whereas the Labour reforms, drawing on the report of the Longford Committee, envisaged the end of juvenile courts and their powers, by contrast the Conservatives would 'preserve the juvenile courts and expand the methods available for dealing with the problems of young people' (Conservative Party, 1966). It should be stressed that, as previously, no party manifesto suggested that the level or form of crime was itself attributable to the politics of the party in government.

All that changed in 1970. In ways that mark this election rather than that of 1979 as the real watershed in the policies of 'law and order', all three major parties devoted more space than ever before in their manifestos to these issues. Moreover, the Conservatives, albeit in restrained fashion, argued that 'the Labour Government cannot entirely shrug off responsibility for the present situation'. The 'situation' was 'the serious rise in crime and violence' and increased fear of both (Conservative Party, 1970; for contemporary examinations of the nature of these problems see Downes, 1966; Cohen, 1972; Hall *et al.*, 1978). While the Conservatives laid this situation at the door of the Labour government, pointing to their having restricted 'police recruitment at a critical time' (a contentious argument, since full employment in the whole post-war period had bedeviled police pay levels and their effects on recruitment—see Bottoms and Stevenson, 1992), 1970 also saw them draw a clear connection between crime, protest, and disorders associated with industrial disputes. The law, the Conservative manifesto proclaimed, 'needs modernising and clarifying and needs to be made less slow and cumbersome, particularly for dealing with offences—forcible entry, obstruction and violent offences connected with public order—peculiar to the *age of demonstration and disruption*' (Conservative Party, 1970: 25, emphasis added). Against this thinly veiled linkage of issues of law-breaking and order-defiance that had hitherto been quite distinct in political discourse, Labour asserted its recognition that it was 'the first duty of government to protect the citizen, against violence, intimidation and crime', and undertook to prosecute vigorously . . . the fight against vandals and law breakers'. However Labour decried the breakdown of bipartisanship about crime: 'Nothing could be more cynical than the current attempts of our opponents to exploit for Party political ends the issue of crime and law enforcement' (Labour Party 1970). Indeed, the Labour manifesto sought to reassure the electorate that 'the streets of our cities are as safe today as those in any throughout the world. They must remain so' (*ibid.*: 26).

The chords struck in the 1970 election campaign persisted and grew more insistent in those of 1974 and 1979. In that of February 1974, the Conservative Party further increased the amount of space devoted to law and order issues in its manifesto, claiming some success during their period of office in reducing crime (the rate had barely risen between 1970 and 1973, though it was to soar in 1974). These 'encouraging signs' were attributed to the growth in police manpower, tougher penalties for offences involving firearms and vandalism, and the ability of the courts to impose compensation orders. More of the same types of measures were promised if the Party were re-elected (Conservative Party, 1974*a*). By contrast, the Labour Party, back in opposition, said nothing on law and order: it promised nothing and said nothing about the government's record (Labour Party, 1974*a*). The Liberal Party also said nothing though, continuing its well-established tradition, it advocated a Bill of Rights (Liberal Party, 1974).

The outcome of the February 1974 election—a narrow Labour victory with a hung Parliament in which the Labour government depended on Liberal support—led to a second election in October 1974. Once again the Labour Party said little about law and order and what it did say was couched in generalities and promised no specific measures (Labour Party, 1974*b*). By contrast the Conservative Party again devoted a substantial part of its manifesto to law and order issues. It vigorously pursued the approach of attacking the government's record, but with a significant difference. On this occasion, it was the government's integrity rather than its policies and priorities that was condemned. Following the traditional defence of the need for law and the protection it affords the weak against the strong, they continued: 'But recently the law has been under attack and these attacks have all too often been condoned and even endorsed by members and supporters of the present Government' (Conservative Party, 1974*b*). This veiled reference to the support given to the National Union of Mineworkers, in its successful deployment of mass picketing in 1973, by Labour MPs and key members of the then Shadow Cabinet, such as Tony Benn, gave the Conservative Party a crucial opening. The Clay Cross affair, in which the Labour government failed to prosecute Labour local councillors who had refused to increase rents in line with Conservative legislation during their period of office, was another lever to be deployed in prising apart the image of Labour and the wholehearted, not selective, support for the law without which there could be no freedom. A detailed array of specific policies were put forward in relation to policing, young offenders, and crime prevention, including the commitment to amend the Labour government's Children and Young Persons Act 1969, 'to deal more effectively with persistent juvenile offenders—for example, soccer hooligans— and the range of available institutions must be improved' (*ibid.*).

It is apparent, therefore, that by the mid-1970s it had been established that law and order issues could assume as much prominence in major party election manifestos as, for example, housing, transport, and urban renewal policy. However, while 'law and order' was not a question on which only the Conservatives pronounced, the manner in which the major parties dealt with the issues was increasingly different. The Conservatives were refashioning their traditional claim to be the natural party of government, representing the order of established authority (Honderich, 1990), a claim which had lost much credibility as a result of the Conservative defeats in the 1974 elections, following the huge loss of face involved in the miners' strike of 1973. By emphasizing respect for the law, the Conservatives—now under the leadership of Mrs Thatcher—were laying claim to a clear moral and practical ascendancy in this field. By contrast, Labour was experiencing difficulties in mounting a convincing counter-attack and, in the two 1974 elections, in effect ducked the issue. Since Labour nevertheless won those elections, that strategy seemingly paid off. The clear difficulty for Labour was the success with which the Conservatives were fusing the issues of law-breaking and order-defiance in the industrial relations field. Labour felt inhibited from unequivocally condemning disruptive and at times aggressive strike-related actions by its principal constituency, trade unionists. During the late 1970s, following the forced loan from the International Monetary Fund and especially during the strike-ridden 'Winter of Discontent'[2] of 1978–9, it seems probable that a number of anxieties symbolizing national decline came to be associated with Labour government: lack of economic competitiveness; fear of crime; fear of inner-city decay; fear of an explosion of black criminality; fears of youthful extremism (embodied in both the brief rise of the punks and far-right street demonstrations that culminated in the murder of Blair Peach at Southall[3]); and fears that the authorities could not cope with the array of problems thus presented. It was at this time that many an editorial was written on the 'ungovernability' of Britain. It was out of these ingredients that the major

---

[2] In autumn 1978, it was widely predicted that the Labour government, then with a much reduced majority, would call an election. It was not called. But a plethora of strikes ensued, notably in the health and other public services. The number of days lost from work rose above those recorded during the General Strike of 1926 (see Marwick, 1990: 261).

[3] On 23 April 1979 the National Front held a meeting at the Town Hall, Southall. It was a deliberate provocation to the predominantly Asian local community. An estimated 3,000 anti-National Front demonstrators gathered to protest, and approximately 4,000 police were drafted in to confront them. During the mêlée that ensued a white teacher, Blair Peach, was killed, possibly after having been struck by a member of the Metropolitan Police Special Patrol Group (see Marwick, 1990: 221).

differences between the parties on 'law and order' assumed their most polarized form in the 1979 election.

In 1979 the Labour government knew, because the Conservative Party had long signalled the fact, that its record in office was to be attacked on this front. In its manifesto, Labour devoted space to 'law and order' issues but dealt with them *within* the context of its objective of creating 'one nation' by eliminating the evils of inequality, poverty, and racial bigotry (Labour Party, 1979). It invoked the need to 'fight against crime and violence', protect citizens' rights and liberties, and continue to back the police more strongly than the Tories had done. Its focus was on attacking 'the social deprivation which allows crime to flourish'. Labour's 'law and order' policy was therefore implicitly to be found elsewhere in the manifesto, in its social and economic policies, though it gave such specific, if low-key, undertakings as to provide more law centres and extend legal aid and help for victims. By contrast, the Conservatives made restoring the 'rule of law', which they claimed that the Labour Party 'in government as in opposition . . . have undermined', one of their five major tasks; and they undertook to do so by implementing specific 'law and order' policies (Conservative Party, 1979). First, they would 'spend more on fighting crime even while we economise elsewhere'. Secondly, they would improve the pay and conditions of the police and, in particular, 'implement in full the recommendations of the Edmund-Davies Committee', which the Labour government had said it would implement in two stages rather than at once.[4] Thirdly, the police would be relieved of many non-crime-fighting duties. Fourthly, provision would be made for more effective sentencing, 'tough sentences . . . for violent criminals and thugs'; but also 'a wider variety of sentences' should be available for those offenders for whom 'long prison terms are not always the best deterrent'. Such measures would range from experiments with 'short, sharp shock' regimes in detention centres to making more compulsory attendance centres available 'for hooligans'. Finally, MPs would be given an early free vote on the restoration of capital punishment. Two other aspects of note were, first, in a substantial section on trade union reform, a proposal to revise the law on picketing to prevent 'violence, intimidation and obstruction'; and secondly, eight specific undertakings were given to achieve 'firm immigration control' which was said to be 'essential for racial harmony'. The 1979 Conservative manifesto brought 'law and order' to the fore as a major election issue and dispelled any lingering trace of bipartisan consensus.

By 1983, the party political battle over 'law and order' had been firmly joined. The Conservatives listed their achievements in office (all inputs as opposed to outputs) as: giving the police 'every possible backing'; revising police powers (in the Police and Criminal Evidence (PACE) Bill); giving the courts 'tougher and more flexible sentencing powers'; and embarking on a major

---

[4] The Edmund-Davies Committee of Inquiry (1978) had been set up by the Labour government primarily to advise on problems of low police recruitment and high wastage. The Committee recommended, *inter alia*, that police pay be increased and thereafter index-linked.

prison building programme (Conservative Party, 1983). Finally, broadening the scope of any 'law and order' discussion, and widening responsibility for it, they pronounced: 'Dealing with crimes, civil disobedience, violent demonstrations and pornography are not matters for the police alone. It is teachers and parents—and television producers too—who influence the moral standards of the next generation. There must be close co-operation and understanding between the police and the community they serve.'

The law and order issue was thus extended to embrace not only law violation and order-defiance, but also present and future morality.

Labour's 1983 manifesto (Labour Party, 1983) was the longest it had ever produced and twice as long as the Conservatives'. It devoted more space than ever before to law and order issues, spelling out a detailed programme of reform for reducing the prison population by non-custodial measures; for improving prison conditions, regimes, and prisoners' rights; and for enabling citizens to activate their rights under the law. Though stressing the need for support for the police, Labour pledged to repeal the PACE Act and replace it with a framework for police accountability which would 'protect the rights of individual suspects' and create elected police authorities.[5] Labour's programme made no reference to punishment, deterrence, or particular categories of heinous offenders. The policies they advocated were directly at variance with the existing and predicted programme of the Conservative administration. Otherwise, the Labour manifesto maintained the 'one nation' perspective and focused on 'healing the wounds' brought about by unemployment and cuts in public expenditure.

Both major parties displayed a greater realism and restraint in the 1987 election. The Labour Party manifesto (Labour Party, 1987) said nothing about the much amended Police and Criminal Evidence Act 1984, nor about the penal and criminal justice systems. Though elected police authorities figured once more as a pledge, police responsibility for 'all operational matters' was guaranteed. Social crime prevention schemes in the community were massively endorsed. However, for the first time in any but the most glancing way, the Labour Party shaped up to attack the Conservative 'law and order' record: 'eight years of rising crime, of greater insecurity on the streets and housing estates and in the home'. Labour attributed the continued steep rise in recorded crime directly to Conservative policies (though not necessarily those on 'law and order').

The Conservative manifesto (Conservative Party, 1987) was no more con-

---

[5] The first PACE Bill was widely held by the left (civil liberties groups and the Labour Party) significantly to increase police powers without providing adequate safeguards for suspects. Following the inner-city public disorders in St Pauls, Bristol, in 1980 and Brixton and elsewhere in 1981 (see Scarman Report, 1981), increased police use of paramilitary equipment and tactics, without that use having been sanctioned by public debate in either Westminster or police authority fora, led to major disputes between some police authorities and their chief constables. This in turn led to calls from the left for the full democratization of local police authorities and the empowerment of police authorities to determine general policy (see Christian, 1983; Spencer, 1985; Downes and Ward, 1986; Lustgarten, 1986; Reiner, 1992).

frontational than Labour's for the first time since law and order emerged as an electoral issue. Though making no concessions to the structural inequalities typically cited by Labour as producing crime, the Conservatives no longer implicitly claimed that their own policies would readily lead to lower crime rates or safer streets. Instead, responsibility for fighting crime was—in line with the 1983 manifesto—extended to 'all of us'; and the worsening crime rate was a problem 'not just in Britain but in most other societies too'. Its origins lie 'deep in society' (a rare reference to this hitherto taboo collectivity), though *not* in any form of social differentation such as wealth or income inequalities: rather, in poor parental support; in poor school discipline; and in the glamorization of violence and the attack on traditional values. The mobilization of communities to support the police by such schemes as Neighbourhood Watch, and tough measures against, *inter alia*, drug traffickers in the envisaged Criminal Justice Bill, betokened a persistently resolute stance against crime. Control of drug abuse and immigration—topics perhaps unfortunately discussed in adjacent sections of the manifesto—were priorities.

The Liberal/SDP Alliance produced the most radical law and order manifesto of 1987 (Liberal/SDP Alliance, 1987), after two elections in which the Liberals had adopted a position either compromising between Conservative and Labour (1979) or little different from the latter (1983). They advocated a Bill of Rights incorporating the European Convention of Human Rights; the establishment of local 'Crime Crisis Areas'; a Ministry of Justice; a strengthened Judicial Studies Board to lay down sentencing guidelines; a Royal Commission on Violence in the Media; and a requirement on local authorities to set up Crime Prevention Units.

The period immediately before the election of 1992 suggested the likely and lively engagement by the opposition parties with the government's record on law and order. The Labour Party produced a criminal justice policy document, *Seven Steps to Justice*, which represented its most ambitious thinking since the 1964 document *Crime—A Challenge to Us All* and seemed likely to provide much of the material for the law and order part of the Labour manifesto. The Conservative government produced a flurry of measures to tackle 'bail bandits' (Morgan and Jones, 1992), car theft, and 'hotting',[6] and teenage crime in general was addressed by 'work camps'. The Home Secretary, Kenneth Baker, termed Labour 'soft and flabby on crime'. His Shadow, Roy Hattersley, persistently called for more police strength (in part to neutralize that attack), and invoked social measures to stem the unprecedented rise in the crime rate. A sign that the Conservative Party may, for the first time, have been vulnerable on the law and order front was to be discerned in opinion poll findings that showed little difference between the two major parties on these issues. This presumably reflected two consecutive years, 1990 and 1991, during which recorded crime rose by an unprecedented and much-publicized 36 per cent. Whether or not

---

[6] The fashion for racing stolen cars around local estates. A related craze for 'ram-raiding', using stolen cars as battering rams for forcing entry into shops and even houses, also caused much concern during the period (see Webb and Laycock, 1992; Light *et al.*, 1993).

these rises were 'real', they are generally regarded as indicating gross trends (see Maguire, this volume). As such, they may be seen as 'real' in their political consequences.

In the event, somewhat anti-climactically, Labour chose to fight the 1992 election on a smaller front and fewer issues than any since 1945. Its manifesto (Labour Party, 1992) devoted only one half-column in a document of over twenty pages to law and order issues, focusing on crime prevention involving local authorities (who had been marginalized on this front by Conservative governments) and on implementing the Woolf Inquiry recommendations on prisons (see below). It was a recipe for reform that could have been culled from the eighteenth-century works of Henry Fielding and John Howard. By contrast, the Conservative document (Conservative Party, 1992) devoted five of its fifty pages to 'Freedom Under Law', siting crime prevention in 'communities', Neighbourhood Watch schemes, and community policing, without mention of local authorities; listing a number of modest reforms in each criminal justice field, and making the claim to have 'reversed the Labour Party's neglect of the prison service in the 1970s'. The Liberal Democratic Party's manifesto (1992) brought rising crime rates and soaring expenditure on police and prisons together in dramatic montage, listing reforms such as the creation of a Ministry of Justice as necessary for a more coherent policy-making process. The most striking feature of the campaign period, however, was Labour's disengagement from this whole terrain: even more strikingly than in 1983 and 1987, it was a clear case of 'the dog that did not bark'.

Election campaign analysis substantially bears out these trends. According to the Nuffield studies, 'law and order' topics (that is, if broad industrial relations issues are excluded) did not figure at all in the elections of 1945, 1950, 1951, 1955, and 1959. In their exhaustive scrutiny of election broadcasts, leaders' speeches, and press coverage, as well as constituency election addresses, there is not a single reference to a law and order topic—crime, policing, or immigration—by any of the three major parties (McCallum and Readman, 1946; Nicholas, 1951; Butler, 1952, 1956; Butler and Rose, 1960). Neither the 'race riots' in Nottingham and Notting Hill in 1958 nor the Street Offences Act of 1959 impinged on the 1959 election campaign. Even in that of 1964, with the notable exception of the campaign at Smethwick, where exploitation of the fear of immigration led to the defeat of Patrick Gordon Walker, Labour's Shadow foreign affairs spokesman, by Peter Griffith, who 'almost invariably linked immigration with violence, crime and disease', such issues were surprisingly marginal and all three party leaders were keen that it should remain so (Butler and King, 1965). Despite rising crime rates, and heavy media coverage of the youth cults of the day and the disturbances in which they regularly engaged, there was no attempt by the party leadership to exploit either law and order or immigration as an issue with which to attack the opposition.

'Law and order' emerged as a clear Conservative issue in 1966, more so in the campaigns than in the manifestos: 40 per cent of Conservative addresses mentioned crime, compared with none for Labour and only 2 per cent of

Liberal addresses (Butler and King, 1967). Yet immigration appears to have been less of an issue in 1966 than in 1964, perhaps due to Labour's acceptance, in a White Paper in August 1965, of the need for immigration control: only 11 per cent of Conservative addresses mentioned it compared to none among both Labour and Liberal addresses. It is not clear why such a high proportion of Conservative election addresses mentioned crime in 1966 when, according to the Nuffield studies, none had in any previous post-war election. However, the most plausible explanation is that substantial media coverage of youth cults and organized crime—1964–6 marked the climax of the notoriety of the Kray and Richardson gangland 'empires' (see Hobbs, this volume)—led to a groundswell of concern that was translatable into Conservative, though not Labour and Liberal, discourse.

Whatever the explanation for the party differences in 1966, they were amplified in 1970. In that year the Conservatives decided, for the first time, to attack the Labour government's 'law and order' record. There was incident enough on which the Conservatives could draw: 1968–9 saw, *inter alia*, the great 'permissive society' debate on homosexual and abortion law reform; the end of censorship by the Lord Chamberlain; the Paris and UK student demonstrations and occupations; the Rolling Stones drug furores; Enoch Powell's 'rivers of blood' speech against immigration (and for repatriation); anti-apartheid demonstrations (during the election campaign itself) against the South African rugby tour; and a spate of strikes which led to the abortive Labour government response of *In Place of Strife.*[7] It is not too surprising, therefore, that 'law and order' appears to have figured for the first time in the media coverage of an election. But the Nuffield analysis of constituency election addresses shows a clearly marked difference between the parties: 60 per cent of Conservative addresses compared to only 15 per cent of Labour mentioned law and order questions. 'Law and order' was now sixth in the Conservative 'top ten' of topics: it did not figure in the Labour top ten (Butler and Pinto-Duschinsky, 1971). The Conservatives won a handsome majority, an outcome hardly expected until, late in the campaign, opinion polls registered the decisive shifts.

The trend set in 1966 and 1970 continued in the two elections of February and October 1974. In that of February, the industrial relations crisis led the Conservatives to fight on a 'Who Governs?' front (Butler and Kavanagh, 1975*a*). When the narrow win by Labour left them without an overall majority, they went to the country again in October. Once more, 60 per cent of Conservative addresses mentioned 'law and order' compared to only 2 per cent of Labour and 7 per cent of Liberal. Although the Conservatives lost more heavily, Labour policies on immigration and defence were rated by polling

---

[7] *In Place of Strife* (Cmnd. 3888, 1969) was the White Paper discussion document aimed at curbing the trades unions' right to strike by proposing a commission to look at disputes; a secret ballot before a strike could be called; and a cooling-off period of up to two months between a strike threat and its implementation. Resistance from the trade unions led to the withdrawal of the proposals and, arguably, to Labour's unexpected defeat in the 1970 election.

respondents more negatively than those of the Conservatives (unfortunately, the parties' popularity on 'law and order' was not examined: see Butler and Kavanagh, 1975*b*).

It is apparent, therefore, that the seminal and much-analysed 1979 election represented the heightening of a trend in relation to 'law and order' issues which was already well established. In 1979, the Conservatives successfully promoted their positive public image on law and order, and all the evidence suggests that they did so to the great detriment of Labour. Nor was this lead simply a matter of the wounds inflicted on Labour by the 'Winter of Discontent' of 1978–9. 'Maintaining law and order' moved from sixth to fourth in the list of 'biggest failures of the present government' in the regular Gallup polls during 1975–8 (Butler and Kavanagh, 1980: 37–8). Across a range of policy issues tested by MORI polls between August 1978 and April 1979, *no* policy placed the Conservatives so far ahead of Labour as 'law and order': a thirty-point lead compared with eleven points for 'unemployment' and little difference for 'prices/inflation' and even 'industrial relations/strikes' (*ibid.*: 131). One third of Labour voters and almost half of Liberal voters expressing a clear preference on the issue thought that the Tories had a better 'law and order' policy than their own parties (*ibid.*: 163).

The salience of the 'law and order' issue for the Conservatives was heightened during the election period itself by a number of events and developments, such as the killing of a leading Conservative MP, Airey Neave, by an IRA bomb in the Palace of Westminster; the Southall Riot in the wake of a march by the National Front; and a number of statements by leading 'law and order' figures, such as Robert Mark, the then recently retired Commissioner of the Metropolitan Police, and Lord Denning, Master of the Rolls, asserting respectively that the unions enjoyed a Nazi Party-like immunity from the law and were 'almost above the law' (quoted in *ibid.*: 187). Press coverage, mostly in support of the Conservative Party, boosted the issue more than ever before. 'Law and order' emerged, not surprisingly, as a favourite topic in Conservative candidates' election addresses: an astonishing 87 per cent issued tough calls for action. By contrast, 66 per cent of Labour addresses were silent on the subject and those that did take it up argued that only social reform could tackle crime (*ibid.*: 297). Moreover, 35 per cent of Tory addresses mentioned the death penalty, compared to none among Labour (*ibid.*: 297). During the campaign, the Nuffield analysts conclude, the growth in Tory support on this issue was greater than for any other issue. 'Law and order' had become what political scientists term a 'valence issue'; that is, party and voters alike agree on the objectives, but doubt whether the party has the capacity to affect the issue. The voters of 1979 judged that the Tories put 'law and order' first, of which they overwhelmingly approved: they doubted whether Labour did so. Labour lost a substantial degree of its traditional working-class vote and got only half the trade unionists' vote. The Conservatives won a sizeable majority.

By 1983, law and order had begun to assume a less prominent role, but it remained a central card in a way in which, until the 1970s, it never had been.

No party could afford to cede this ground to the opposition, and all parties felt obliged to address it in some way during the campaign. By 1987, a kind of second-order consensus had been evolved whereby all parties asserted their support for the police and the need to increase their effectiveness; all parties agreed that crime prevention and victim support were priorities; and all parties accepted the logic of 'bifurcation' (Bottoms, 1977), according to which extended custodial sentences are appropriate for the most serious offenders, but an enhanced range of non-custodial measures for the less serious should be used. By 1987, 65 per cent of Labour, 74 per cent of Conservative, 74 per cent of Social Democrat, and 65 per cent of Liberal addresses mentioned the topic. Yet significant differences remained in the manner in which they dealt with an issue which all now felt obliged to discuss. Substantial minorities of Conservative addresses called for tougher sentences (30 per cent) or capital punishment (19 per cent), or claimed that Labour was anti-police (14 per cent). By contrast, Labour Party addresses talked of the crime which pervaded a divided society, a Britain divided by the Tories' social and economic policies. In 1987, the local election addresses comprehensively mirrored the presentational stances which, throughout the 1980s, had been developed in the national manifestos. It was a configuration that seemed likely to play a prominent role in the election of 1992. But in the event Labour chose to remain content with the neutralization of the issue, rather than its contestation, a strategy which arguably left the Conservative Party in a position of inert supremacy as the guardians of law and order. In spite of continued rising crime in the face of substantially increased expenditure on 'law and order' services, Labour made nothing of the topic during the 1992 campaign (Butler and Kavanagh, 1992; King, 1993). The opinion poll evidence suggested that the Conservatives still inspired greater confidence on this issue and six weeks before the election the Party capitalized on the fact by unveiling a poster depicting a policeman with one hand tied behind his back. The accompanying slogan was: 'Labour's soft on crime'.

Explaining the Trends: Images, Philosophies, and Constraints

Frank Parkin argued over two decades ago that the principal strength of the Conservative Party was its capacity to claim oneness with the bastions of traditional British sovereignty: the monarchy, the aristocracy, property, the armed forces, the ancient universities, the land, and the law (Parkin, 1967). The only countervailing force to this ruling-class ideology was that offered by the Labour Party as representative of the working-class labour movement and its trade union organization. Yet this constituency was always deviant with respect to the core values and most cherished allegiances of British traditionalism. The Labour Party could flourish only in direct relation to movement away from their sites, most typically in a single-occupation, one-class urban area like a mining town. Against the Tory Party's keystone value of what Macpherson (1962) termed 'possessive individualism', the Labour Party rests on an appeal to the alternative morality of redistributive social justice and community.

These ideological differences translated readily into quite distinct policy choices in the post-war period. The Conservative preference for owner-occupation in housing has contrasted sharply and successfully with Labour's emphasis on municipal rented accommodation. On the other hand, Labour's development of the National Health Service could still command such wide-spread support that the Conservatives strove to resist the claim that their policies amounted to privatization. In taxation, Labour supports progressive direct taxation of income and wealth; the Conservatives favour regressive indirect taxes on spending. The choices are fairly distinct. Yet issues of 'law and order' do not lend themselves to such clear-cut articulation along party lines. This asymmetry is not due to the absence of sharp differences between the parties in their *explanations* of the underlying causes of crime. For Conservatives, these inhere in the realms of individual pathology and/or lax authority whether imposed at parental or institutional level. For Labour, they derive far more from social and economic realities: inequality, deprivation, marginalization, and outright poverty. For Labour, the task of political persuasion is therefore to make connections between crime and public issues, such as trends in employment and welfare. For the Conservatives, the task is to *disconnect* them, to contest, indeed, the very act of making such connections as inimical to law and order maintenance (Downes, 1989a). In Conservative rhetoric, 'explanation' amounts to 'excuse', an equation Labour has failed to challenge at all effectively. Throughout the 1980s, Mrs Thatcher successfully deployed this philosophically unacceptable elision by using the rhetoric of moral outrage. Thus, her statement that rioting can never be 'justified by unemployment' (or poverty, or racism, or police malpractices) always overrode the logical objection—rarely voiced—that nevertheless such realities may help to explain it. Edged by such tactics into appearing to be 'soft' on crime, Labour reacted not by challenging the image but increasingly by claiming equal toughness to—if not greater toughness than—the Conservatives.

An attempt to resolve this impasse appeared in a speech given in February 1993 by Tony Blair, then Labour Shadow Home Secretary. Addressing public anger and unease following the abduction and murder in Liverpool of a two-year-old boy, James Bulger, Blair set out Labour's policy on law and order as being 'tough on crime, tough on the causes of crime'. As yet, in the run-up to the 1997 general election, it is the first part of this formula that has received most attention: the need to provide more secure places for serious juvenile offenders; the proposal that lengthy periods of imprisonment be available for breach of 'community safety orders' made on the testimony of police or local government officers against persons engaging in 'chronic anti-social behaviour'—nuisance, noise, and so on—not necessarily criminal or for which there may be insufficient evidence to bring a prosecution (von Hirsch *et al.*, 1995); and the endorsement of 'zero tolerance' policing on the fashionable New York model. It remains to be seen if and how the second part of the policy will be developed, but given the Labour Party's commitment not to increase personal taxation if elected, the prospects for any radical attack on the economic inequalities and social deprivations of contemporary Britain seem poor.

In the 1993–6 period, Labour produced a flurry of policy papers, several of which focused explicitly on the alleged causes of crime. *Tackling the Causes of Crime* (1996) linked crime, somewhat baldly, with problems of parenting, schools, and truancy, drugs and alcohol misuse, unemployment and recession, care in the community, homelessness and the youth service, and suggested forms of best practice at both local and national level to address them. Another paper, *Parenting* (1996), took the parent–child relationship to be the 'crucial factor' in youth crime and made extensive proposals for parental education and support. The main running, however, was made in terms of criticisms of the criminal justice system under the Conservatives, especially the falling conviction rate and delays in juvenile justice.[8]

These are all important issues, and Labour clearly feel they have fashioned a telling response to the Conservatives by focusing on flaws in the latter's chosen ground: the criminal justice system itself. The irony is that the Criminal Justice Act 1991 was the climax to a decade of policy-making which had reduced the proportionate use of imprisonment by use of enhanced community sanctions (in 1991–2, the prison population fell to 40,600 from a peak of 50,000 in 1988—see Morgan, this volume). At the same time, due largely to the economic background of deep and lasting recession, the crime rate rose by over 40 per cent. It was ideologically impossible, however, for the Conservatives to accept that link, so that after 1992 they resorted to the U-turn in penal policy associated with Michael Howard (see Ashworth and Morgan, this volume). The economy gradually recovered as a result of the forced devaluation of 1992, and with it the crime rate stabilized, despite the disarray of the criminal justice system. That Labour have focused so heavily on criminal justice rather than economic and social causes—though they have kept that ball in play—is a sign of their determination to wrest this ground from the traditional dominance of the Conservatives, even at the expense of fears that they are flirting with new forms of authoritarianism in the process.

It follows that party policies on law and order can be related only tenuously to their ideological foundations. Image—associations of ideas and mythology— lent the Conservatives weight as *the* party of 'law and order'. No warrant for this assumption can be found in any indicator of actual performance. If anything, the reverse holds true, since periods of Labour government have seen lower rises in the recorded crime rate, both relatively and absolutely, than have

---

[8] *Protecting our Communities* (1996) recommended Community Safety Orders and composite offences. *Breaking the Vicious Circle* (1996) proposed new treatment and testing programmes in relation to drug-related crimes. *Tackling Youth Crime: Reforming Youth Justice* (1996) urged, in particular, use of a Final Warning to replace cautioning. And *Honesty, Consistency and Progression in Sentencing* (1996) recommended, *inter alia*, a form of indeterminate sentencing for rapists, and argued for explicit progression in sentencing, i.e. opposing, without acknowledgement, the 'just deserts' principle of the 1991 Criminal Justice Act.

Conservative administrations (Downes and Young, 1987; Downes, 1989*b*; Young, 1992). Despite the similarity or even superiority of Labour by comparison with the Conservative record on law and order, Labour have nevertheless proved vulnerable on this front due to various hostages to fortune derived from their association with, and implicit need to defend, several key constituencies.

These hostages to fortune on the left are bound up integrally with the origins and continuing role of the Labour Party as the parliamentary voice of the trade unions, on the one hand, and as the major vehicle for progressive intellectuals of a non-Marxist, socialist persuasion, on the other. The uneasy alliance between the labour movement and intellectuals of both Fabian and the more left-wing *Tribune* group persuasions is the chief strand in the story of the Labour Party, each involving the party in a set of distinctive concerns on the 'law and order' front which have exposed it to accusations from the right of undermining the 'rule of law'. Paradoxically, though the right also bears hostages to fortune in distinct (though fewer) respects, these can be handled in ways that strengthen rather than weaken their association with the forces of law and order.

Trade Unions and Labour

The labour movement both launched and proved the main ballast of Labour Party history, but in the period 1978–85 arguably almost sank it. This is no place to essay analysis of the long and tangled history of the relationship between the Party and the movement. The major point is that the struggle to win basic labour rights, from assembly to picketing to the very process of unionization itself, of a kind now accepted as legitimate in all democratic states, entailed a great deal of order-defiance and law-violation. In the immediate post-war period, however, the dominance of the right wing within the labour movement lent it a new respectability. Two pivotal factors eventually led to the situation whereby, in the late 1970s and 1980s, trade unionism could be equated with hooliganism and violence.

First, the electoral, though not numerical, defeat of the Labour government under Attlee in 1951 ushered in a period during which Britain, unlike any other Western European country, enjoyed the fruits of post-war prosperity under a right-wing government. The association of ideas between Toryism and prosperity has proved lasting. Despite intervening periods in office, Labour appeared to be the party of the austerity years, with union links that could 'threaten' economic growth. By contrast, trade unions in Scandinavia and West Germany were seen as playing an essential part in the process of economic recovery and expansion.

Secondly, the peculiar nature of capitalist law in Britain (and the USA) places unique emphasis on the overriding priority to be accorded the rights of shareholders in company development. Again by contrast, such rights in West Germany, Japan, Scandinavian, and other industrial societies are tempered by the requirement to give far more consideration to two other entities: the community and the employees (see e.g., Dore, 1992, on Japan; Schneider-Lenné, 1992, on Germany). Rights, conditions, amenities, and wage levels which were granted relatively smoothly by a process of negotiated settlements in these countries were in Britain too often wrung from reluctant employers by protracted conflict involving strike action. The litany of protracted industrial conflict in Britain embraces manufacturing industries in historic decline as well as light industries in the ascendant after the Second World War. In the 1970s, the left in Britain came to associate success in industrial conflict with militancy, a strategic choice which heightened the linkages made by the right between the labour movement, violence, and lawlessness. The eventual climax to this sequence of events was the 'Winter of Discontent' of 1978–9 (see note 2 above), which led to the downfall of the Labour government and ushered in the Thatcherite era.

The unions at times colluded in the process. For example, the print unions presided over the notorious Fleet Street ghost worker scandal, whereby workers who were already relatively well paid also drew wages for non-existent employees (see Martin, 1981). Perhaps the most tragic instance was the misconduct of the National Union of Mineworkers in 1983 in embarking on a national strike without the legally prescribed ballot of members. This tactic split the miners' otherwise united front, legitimized the government's pursuit of the union's funds by sequestration, and neutralized the likelihood of open Labour Party support for the strike. These factors arguably led to the miners' defeat after eighteen months of bitter strike action, in which the union was hauled through the courts, hundreds of miners were unwarrantedly harassed or victimized by the police, and the strikers' cause was marred by occasional acts of outright criminality and, in one case, manslaughter. The fact that the dire predictions by the NUM leadership, under Arthur Scargill, of pit closures and mass redundancies have been cruelly vindicated by events, with a labour force of 220,000 in 1983 reduced to 41,000 in 1992, does not nullify the association of ideas between trade union militancy and law-violation that resulted.

The unexpected defeat of the Labour Party in the 1992 election was widely ascribed to the success with which the Conservatives and the right-wing tabloid press revived fears of the 'hostages to fortune'. 'Tax and spend' policies, renewed union powers, immigrants 'flooding' into the country, and even more unemployment featured heavily in the campaign (Linton, 1995). (Crime was largely absent from this catalogue, reflecting the previous three years' rise of over 40 per cent in the official crime rate.) The consequence is that Labour has since further redefined its relations with the trades unions, distancing itself from the militant wing and nurturing links with more 'responsible' leaders. In 1993 John Smith, then Party leader, succeeded in extending the franchise within the Party, giving majority voting rights to constituency members and MPs and reducing the block-voting powers of the unions, a tradition seen as inimical to the Party's claim to represent broad public interests. Under the present leader, Tony Blair, the Party Conference has voted to abolish Clause 4 of its constitution, which since 1920 had committed the Party, in principle if not in practice, to wholesale public ownership. Pre-strike secret ballots and the ban on secondary-picketing are to remain and the trade unions are no longer to sponsor MPs. And no commitment has been made to restoring to the public sector those industries and utilities privatized since 1979.

Fifteen years after the Conservatives' election [in 1979] the scope of labour reform exceeded even the wildest dreams of the New Right of the 1970s. There was no regulation of working time; no legally protected conditions for labour hired under fixed-term contracts; no minimum wage legislation; minimal employment protection; and employees had no legal right to representation at the workplace. The OECD, compiling a composite list of these measures, could, by the summer of 1994, rank Britain at zero—the lowest, apart from the US, in the industrialised world. (Hutton, 1995: 94)

Apart from the position of fixed-term contract labour, which the Conservatives would review, Labour is committed to restoring or strengthening all these rights, either by legislating or by joining the EU Social Chapter. In sum, the thrust of 'New Labour' has been to diminish union influence within the Party and to distance the Party further from any lingering association with union militancy, without losing union support or funding in the process. Even so, the right-wing tabloid press is reluctant to abandon so well-worn a hostage to fortune. 'Blair "all ready for sell-out"' (9 December) and 'Blair in "battle to death" with Unions' (27 December), were two headlines in the *Sun* on Labour–TUC relations at the end of 1996.

The New 'Underclass'?

The concept and formation of a new 'underclass' is vigorously contested (see e.g. Abercrombie and Ward, 1988; Dahrendorf, 1987; Macnicol, 1987; and, on the USA, Jencks and Peterson, 1991; Wilson, 1996). What is not disputed is that de-industrialization has fractured the links between steady manual work and the stable communities which it once sustained. Further, the official statistics attest to the fact that the least wealthy half of the population now holds a lower proportion of overall wealth than it did a decade ago and that income differentials between households have grown. The rich have become richer, the poor poorer. To the extent that there can be said to be an 'underclass', it comprises groups as diverse as impoverished single parents; discriminated-against minority groups; the long-term unemployed; the never-have-been-employed youth of the poorer housing estates; and, as ever, those who, as Henry Mayhew (1862) put it, 'will not work'. The old working class has decayed. High, endemic unemployment and non-employment rates have provided the tinder from which—from 1980 onwards—riots have been kindled by policing which may have been insensitive but was rarely outlandish: the real cause lies in the economic marginalization and political exclusion of disadvantaged youths in particular, whether black, white, or both (Lea and Young, 1984). Relations between 'underclass' and authority are inherently conflict-ridden at any time, since the lot of the socially excluded is to be under-protected and overcontrolled.

The key problem for the Labour Party is unfortunately much the same as that for sociologists; how to connect private troubles with public issues (Mills, 1959). When riots as vicious as that at the Broadwater Farm Estate in North London in 1985 flare up, and a police officer is hacked to death, the best way to make the connection is hardly to announce that 'the police got a good hiding'. This remark by Bernie Grant, the local black Labour MP for a constituency with a large black population, was perhaps the biggest single hostage to fortune handed to the Conservatives by a left-wing source. The 1987 Labour strategy on policing was watered down from a policy of local account-ability (strongly opposed by the police) to one of local consultation (little different from Conservative policy), due to fears that this and similar 'anti-police' remarks by left-wing sources would otherwise be quoted endlessly by the Conservatives in their campaigning: much the same backing-off process arguably occurred in 1992. However, Mr Grant did have a problem: how to supply a soundbite at the scene and under pressure which, by putting the events in context—that of racism, unemployment, and the oppressive policing resulting in the death of Mrs Groce, a West Indian mother of a black male suspect in a minor case of car theft, that had triggered the riot—did more than simply condemn the rioters. That he got it so resoundingly wrong in the event is in part a testimony to the massive difficulties in transcending sheer condemnation and moving on to explanation and constructive action. Given the constituencies involved, this was far more of a problem for Mr Grant and the Labour Party than for the Conservative government.

It is on this front that 'New Labour', and especially Jack Straw, Shadow Home Secretary in 1995–7, has moved most decisively to eliminate a potential 'hostage to fortune'. A series of policy announcements from 1994 onwards exorcised any trace of special pleading for socially disadvantaged offenders and even those guilty of no more than 'incivilities'. In 1995, Straw proposed a crackdown on 'squeegee merchants'—mostly youths who washed windscreens at traffic lights in return for small change, at times without clear consent from the 'captive' motorists. Shortly thereafter the Party published a consultation document *A Quiet Life* proposing that there be introduced a 'community safety order' for dealing with anti-social neighbours, the terms of which order outraged the civil liberties lobby. A further proposal was to enable local authorities to impose curfews on 10-year-olds out on the streets after 11 p.m. All these measures broke strikingly with 'Old Labour' thinking, which stressed broad social and economic measures and welfare support to control minor deviance. Straw's proposals also reflected enthusiasm for the apparent success of the policing methods of Bratton in New York. Indeed, the USA has been the role model for both Tory and Labour policy-makers in the 1990s, despite the fact that levels of homicide and violence in general remain several times higher than in Europe, a paradox explicable only in terms of the popularity of such 'tough on crime' policies with electorates.

It has, however, been by his broad acceptance of Michael Howard's U-turn on penal and sentencing policy that Jack Straw, Shadow Home Secretary, most clearly signalled his break with past Labour policy. The government's U-turn (see Ashworth and Morgan, this volume) was explicable as a response both to sharply rising crime rates and to the loss of the Conservative lead over Labour on 'law and order'. Howard clearly aimed to 'smoke Labour out' as a Party essentially 'soft on crime', by adopting a strong 'prison works' policy and by adopting a modified form of the 'three strikes and you're out' mandatory custodial sentencing policy embraced by President Clinton. Straw's decision to take a broadly bipartisan approach to such measures effectively neutralized this strategy, with seeming popular success: an ICM poll in August 1996 showed Labour to enjoy roughly double the support accorded the Conservatives on 'law and order' (*Guardian*, 7 August) without jeopardizing his position within the Party—his vote for the National Executive Committee by constituency members rose in autumn 1996. Moreover, in January 1997 Tony Blair, in an interview with the magazine for the homeless, *The Big Issue*, endorsed the 'zero tolerance' policing policy being pursued in the Kings Cross area of London, a policy which has reportedly involved sweeping the streets of homeless beggars. The fact that these much-publicized stances create fresh 'hostages to fortune' of a different kind post-electorally is clearly seen as a price worth paying to spike Conservative guns on this front. As a result, opposition to such measures has been displaced from the Labour Party to the Liberal Party, civil liberties and penal pressure groups, and the judiciary itself.

Though in their writings Labour leaders stress that their intolerance is focused on the causes of homelessness and other deprivations, their well-publicized public utterances emphasize first priority acceptance that public nuisance be cleared away and order restored. Such disorders have waxed as stable employment and the strength of the labour movement have waned. Working-class trade unionists demonstrate and take industrial action in pursuit of recognizable, collective ends, in ways—such as mass picketing—which may verge on or constitute law-violation under certain circumstances. Denied employment, the new 'underclass' is incapable of such organizational feats, though some remarkable examples of community action (see, for example, Campbell, 1993) give the lie to the view that the socially excluded are a 'new rabble' (Murray, 1994). However, riot and criminality may conceivably be interpreted as impoverished routes to these ends, but they are hardly recognizable or shared, and explanation in these terms all too easily sounds like special pleading. In short, the more the organized labour movement and the trade unions are pushed off the stage by endemic mass un- and non-employment, and by rapid technological change, the more the emergent underclass presents the Labour Party with a massive problem of translation. For example despite widespread and articulate opposition across the social spectrum, even the poll tax presented the Labour opposition with a particularly nasty version of the 'law and order' paradox, whereby the iniquitous character of the law would only be changed by strong public reaction, including non-compliance (since compliance would be taken by the government as confirming public acquiescence).[9] However, for the opposition to support non-compliance would have been denounced as inciting people to violate the law, an accusation that was indeed levelled against several Labour MPs who advocated it despite official Labour policy on the issue. Non-compliance would also have deprived Labour-controlled local authorities of essential income.

Civil Disobedience

Civil disobedience has been a substantial and generally honourable strand in the history of the Labour Party. The inter-war period was notable for such events as George Lansbury's imprisonment in 1921 for leading the non-payment of local precepts by Poplar Council in protest against the burden placed on local government to provide poor relief, the 1926 General Strike, and the 'hunger marches' of the 1930s Depression years, all of which were actively supported by Labour MPs (see Mowat, 1955). It might have been expected that, as Labour formed the government for seventeen of the post-war years, old habits would have died and indeed, for the first decade after the war, that seemed to be so. However, the Suez Crisis of 1956 revived the tradition, and the Campaign for Nuclear Disarmament, formed in the same year, founded the annual march to London from the first American forces' nuclear base at Aldermaston (see Taylor, 1988). Left-wing Labour MPs were prominent figures on these demonstrations which, although eminently peaceful, were increasingly drawn into association with extra-legal activities, such as the exposure by an Anarchist group on the 1961 march of the hitherto secret Regional Seats of Government bases. The formation of the Committee of 100 in 1961 brought a new repertoire to civil disobedience: the systematic violation of the law by leading and usually left-wing intellectuals to focus attention on the nuclear disarmament cause.

The Vietnam War from 1964 onwards provided the target for a rising crescendo of demonstrations which, with the rise of the student movement in the USA and its spread to Europe in the mid-1960s, added site occupations to the armoury of protest. Labour, which formed the government from 1964 to 1970, pursued a policy of damage-limitation with respect to the policing of such forms of protest. Media coverage of the October 1968 Grosvenor Square demonstration, however, lent a new imputation to reportage: the expectation that the potential for violence implicit in any mass movement would be realized. As Halloran *et al.* (1970) pointed out, the press greatly exaggerated such violence as did occur on that march.

[9] The so-called 'poll tax', or community charge, introduced by the Conservative government in 1988 to replace local authority rates, levied the same tax *per capita* regardless of income, wealth, or size of property. The only major exemptions concerned people on income support and students, who were charged 20 per cent of the tax.

After Grosvenor Square, and the student demonstrations in Paris in May 1968 which almost led to the collapse of the French government, the die was cast. No left-wing cause had street credibility without a march, demonstration, or occupation. The Clydebank occupation of 1972 firmly associated industrial militancy with key figures in the Labour Party following the much publicized conversion of Tony Benn to the merits of such direct action. The case of the 'Shrewsbury Three' in 1974 embodied the ease with which direct action by pickets could turn ugly and involve criminal prosecutions.[10] It was also in 1974 that the newly elected Labour government's Director of Public Prosecutions failed to prosecute Labour councillors in Bolsover who had refused to raise rents in accordance with the previous Conservative government's Rent Act. Another *cause célèbre* was the Grunwick strike and several months' long mass picket of 1976–7, which even right-of-centre Labour ministers such as Shirley Williams felt the need to attend, in solidarity with a workforce largely composed of Asian women who had been denied the right to unionize by their employer. The 1970s were characterized by a plethora of such events, the policing of which was frequently contentious and costly, and at times tragically counter-productive.

In the 1980s street protest turned sour. The symbolism had become devalued to the point where the absence of a demonstration or march against a measure was taken for popular compliance with it. The threshold for media coverage was raised to the point at which, unless a demonstration involved violence, little reportage could be expected. The poll tax riots of 1989–90 were the climax of these developments. By this juncture, however, the 'freedom of the streets' had been greatly constrained. Thereafter the strategy brought diminishing returns of publicity and, in the face of disruption and traffic congestion, of public support and interest. Bans on marches by the extreme right had been extended to all unless stringent criteria of stewardship and route-taking were met. In the 1992–6 period, civil disobedience was conducted on largely non-partisan lines on single-issue causes, such as the sustained opposition to new motorways (the Winchester and Newbury by-passes, the M11 link through Wanstead, etc.) and to the export of live animals. There was less call for Labour to take a position on these events; and fading memories of the halcyon days of civil disobedience tend to be associated with 'Old' rather than 'New' Labour.

If the increasing frequency and size of demonstrations heralded the eclipse of a Conservative government in 1974, their decreasing salience and vigour have marked the ascendancy of the neo-Conservative regimes since 1979. In so far as Labour is associated with both the decline and the unwanted side-effects of taking to the streets, its image as upholder of law and order is at risk. Only when the politics of the street are actively welcomed as a symbol of peaceable and healthy democracy is such a risk neutralized. Without them, the arena for the legitimate expression of views is greatly reduced.

---

[10] This *cause célèbre*, which involved sentences of imprisonment, arose out of a strike in the building industry and the use of 'flying pickets' (see Wallington, 1975).

Libertarian Criminal Law Reform

Though Labour Party history has been marked by a libertarian strand which has surfaced from time to time, the late 1960s witnessed a sustained programme of criminal law reform under a Labour government: the decriminalization of male homosexuality and abortion; the substantial relaxation of the censorship laws; the abolition of capital punishment; and the resolution of key problems threatening the legalization of casino gaming. The last of these stemmed from the sweeping legalization of gaming carried out by the Conservative government of Harold Macmillan in 1960 and 1963; a government which also decriminalized attempted suicide in 1963. It was left to a Labour Lord Chancellor, Gerald Gardiner, systematically to push the reform through, however. Two decades later, the entire period of liberalizing achievement by both Conservative and Labour was to be derided by the new right of Thatcher and Tebbit as the 'permissive society', having achieved nothing more than a slackening of authority and an unwanted release of baser passions. What was, by most standards, a major period of reform promoting greater tolerance and freedom of expression came to figure in the popular press and in rightwing ideology as the source of unprecedented rises in criminality in the 1980s.

What had been a relatively clear-cut battle between the 'progressive liberals'—who in the 1960s had migrated to the Labour Party to a much greater extent than before or since—and the forces of reaction, had in the 1980s become more complex, however. First, certain forms of backlash arose from unexpected quarters. For example, radical feminists, including such leading Labour MPs as Clare Short, and leading traditionalists, such as Mary Whitehouse, ranged themselves, albeit for different reasons, against pornography and the exploitation of women as exemplified on page three of the *Sun*. The porn merchants had made far narrower and more profitable use of the new-found liberties of expression of the 1960s than the exponents of liberalization had ever predicted. The average suburban newsagent carried a far greater spread of female nudity in the 1980s than the average Soho pornshop in the 1950s. Secondly, gay militancy had found forms of political expression which included material for primary schools. The resulting backlash included legal constraints such as section 28 of the Education Act 1988, which expressly forbade the inclusion of family imagery in school material other than that connoting the heterosexual nuclear family.

In sum, once basic freedoms had been won, the complications to which their extension gave rise tended to saddle Labour with the worst of both worlds, able neither to defend such developments as 'gay' schoolbooks nor to define where the line should be drawn afresh. Such defensiveness left such minorities as gays feeling betrayed, on the one hand, and the 'silent majority' feeling that Labour had allowed too much scope for deviant viewpoints, on the other. Conversely, Labour spokespersons who opposed such phenomena as the 'page three nude' could be castigated as killjoys. One notorious election-day ploy in the *Sun* (9 April 1992) was the substitution for the usual page three model of a stereotypically reverse image, a flabby parody of coquettishness. The caption read: 'Here's How Page 3 Will Look Under Kinnock.' Labour could be blamed for both the unwanted developments of libertarianism and the negative aspects of the selective backlash against them.

Since 1992 Labour has reacted more selectively to issues that might cause embarrassment on this front. First, by reverting strongly to its image as the Party of 'the family', Labour registered its disinclination to defend, let alone promote, the interests of such groups as single parents and gays, as actively as in the recent past. In 1996, for example, Labour abstained in the House of Commons vote to exclude homosexuals from the armed forces. Secondly, on issues such as the clauses in the 1996 Police Bill, which endorse phone-tapping and house searching on warrants issued by Home Office-appointed commissioners, with the role of the judiciary recast as a retrospective sample check, Labour's stance only belatedly changed from barely qualified active promotion to critical opposition. Labour has also abandoned its traditional opposition to the annual renewal of the Prevention of Terrorism Act. Thirdly, Labour has even ruled out debate within its ranks on certain sensitive issues. In 1996, for example, Clare Short, a Shadow cabinet member, was slapped down for expressing the view, following the proposal by some chief constables, that debate on the possible decriminalization of small-scale cannabis possession be reopened.

In the face of wide-ranging attacks on the potential for order-defiance and law-violation of several of its key constituencies Labour has reacted defensively, content to neutralize the appeal of the Conservatives wherever possible as *the* party of law and order, but backing away from outright contention on the issues involved. The scope for Labour to turn the tables on the Conservatives on these terms was limited by the simple 'rule of law' principle to which the latter adhered quite uncritically. Thus, the law-violations of the extreme right, or those endemic in the operations of the commercial-financial world of the City of London, or those emanating from flawed police procedures, could always be explained in terms of individual pathology, a 'few bad apples'. The kind of challenge to the very terms of the debate which Labour had mounted in some respects in the 1960s was increasingly foregone as anxieties about the electoral liabilities of the hostages to fortune rose.

By any objective standard, the period of Conservative government since 1979 has been a conspicuous failure in crime control terms. In spite of a host of crime prevention initiatives[11] and real increases in spending on the so-called 'law and order' services, increases greater than in any other branch of government expenditure—more police, better paid and with more powers; more courts with an increased range of penalties at their disposal; more prisons and more prisoners in them—the fear of crime has increased, there have been larger than normal rises in recorded crime, and a sequence of urban disturbances has

---

[11] These have included the development of Neighbourhood Watch and numerous other Watch schemes, the Safer Cities initiative, and the encouragement of multi-agency schemes of various types: see Pease, this volume.

occurred unprecedented in their ferocity this century. And yet, the polls suggest that until the early 1990s, the Conservative Party retained its supremacy as the party of 'law and order'. It managed to persuade a large section of the electorate that the rising tide of crime was not to be explained by the widened divide between rich and poor, the undermining of public goods and services, the emasculation of local government, and the lauding of competitive individualism to the detriment of collective responsibility. Rather, crime is to be ascribed to evil individuals or persons; generally young persons, subject to insufficient control by parents who have a duty to police their behaviour. Either way, criminals are to get their just deserts, punishment proportionate to their culpability and the harm they have caused. Explanatory references to structural forces—poverty, unemployment, discrimination, oppression, social and economic hopelessness, and alienation—are castigated as damaging to the ethos of personal responsibility on which the maintenance of law and order is said ultimately to depend. The question at stake is whether the hegemony of the philosophy of individual pathology, a philosophy closely allied to the paramountcy of the market in Conservative economic policy, can be sustained in the face of further increases in crime and disorder, and whether the Labour Party will continue to adopt a defensive law and order policy on the terrain that the Conservative Party has mapped out; or whether the tide will turn and the opposition successfully call into question the moral basis of the political economy which current law and order policies are designed to support.

In the event, the Labour Party chose to adopt an aggressive law and order policy on the very terrain mapped out by the Conservatives, refusing to be upstaged by the increasingly punitive policies of the Home Secretary, and even pre-empting certain ideas—curfews, the control of incivilities, and more rapid juvenile justice—overlooked by the government. Electronic tagging and mandatory sentencing were swallowed by Labour with barely a public hint of indigestion and the privatization of prisons, though initially opposed, seems now to be accepted. As a result, the mantle of opposition to such measures fell even more heavily on the Liberal Party, the liberal press, the Probation Service, the penal pressure groups and—at least in connection with mandatory sentencing and some aspects of prisoners' rights—the judiciary. The result appears to have been to neutralize Michael Howard's attempt to wrest back the image of the 'Party of law and order' to the Conservatives, though at considerable cost to Labour's credibility as the upholder of humane standards in criminal justice and penal policy.

In one respect, Labour was greatly aided by a change in Conservative fortunes from an unexpected quarter. In October 1992 Britain's exit was forced from the Exchange Rate Mechanism, at the cost of several billion pounds in a few days' attempt to prop up sterling, following a spate of financial scandals in the City of London. Given widespread unease about the moral 'state of the nation', the Prime Minister, John Major, attempted to reassert the government's standing by, *inter alia*, launching a 'Back to Basics' campaign on morality. This exercise backfired badly as the tabloid press homed in on the involvement in extra-marital affairs of several Conservative MPs, and a Minister, David Mellor. Over the next few years, Ministers were roundly criticized for their role in the earlier Thatcher administration's handling of arms sales to Iraq (by the Scott Report); two Conservatives MPs were accused of having taken 'cash for questions' in Parliament on behalf of lobby group interests (condemned by the Nolan Report, which set up new procedures for monitoring potential conflicts of interest); and the *Guardian* newspaper criticized a Minister of Defence, Jonathan Aitken, for allegedly accepting hospitality from Arab businessmen with arms trade connections. Several grisly murders, from that of James Bulger to the mass slaughter of sixteen school children and staff at Dunblane in Scotland, and the street killing of a London headmaster, Philip Lawrence, by a knife-wielding youth, led to a national debate. Though *some* aspects of the reactions could be defined as 'moral panic', the dignity and raw grief of the victims' closest kin commanded a respect which ensured a serious hearing for their campaign for a complete ban on the sale and ownership of handguns. The Labour and Liberal Parties were able to wrongfoot the government by supporting a total ban, whilst the Home Secretary was compelled by internal Party and interest group pressure to retain .22 weapons.

The result amounted to a moral inquest on an era in which the pursuit of economic salvation had visibly damaged social cohesion. It led to an institutional anxiety about incipient *anomie*: the breakdown of a recognizable moral order. The media were awash with debates, discussions, dialogues, and documentaries about every nuance of social pathology, from weapon control to the effects of media violence, though rarely in any decently informed, as distinct from sound-bite, fashion. For a time at least, the government appeared to have lost any convincing claim to integrity, competence, and expertise. For once, the Conservatives, accustomed to travelling lightly on the high moral ground of personal responsibility exercised in a social vacuum, and without the burden of 'hostages to fortune', were suddenly afflicted by a welter of illicit arms deals, hypocrisy in family affairs, serious frauds, and the antipathy of almost all branches of the criminal justice system to which they appealed for the 'rule of law'. In short 'sleaze' became the disease to which the Government seemed increasingly prone and, under these circumstances, the opposition parties could for once enjoy a certain *Schadenfreude*. It remains to be seen how far this issue can be turned to Labour's electoral advantage.

PRESSURE-GROUP AND INTEREST-GROUP POLITICS

As Bottoms and Stevenson (1992) argue, the fundamental variable in any assessment of 'What went wrong?' in post-war criminal justice policy and practice is the inexorable rise of the crime rate. From the mid-1950s onwards, this almost unbroken increase in crime of 5–6 per cent annually beggared explanation in terms of simple poverty and deprivation, as both were manifestly on the decline. With the rise in crime despite the rise in welfare and increasing prosperity came rises in criminological and pressure-group activity, attempts respectively to account for crime and to improve the nature of responses to it. The proliferation of pressure groups was not unique to the law and order field but was a trend in British politics as a whole in this period. Electoral behaviour was more capable of being altered by short-term single issues which could 'only with difficulty be forced within the straitjacket of the old, class-based, two-party system. A new political agenda centred on Europe, disarmament, the environment, quality of public and private services, and citizenship rights has already become well established in many countries of the European Community' (Gamble, 1990: 353).

Perhaps because law and order issues had never fitted that straitjacket to any marked extent, pressure groups in this field often bore pedigrees going back to before the Thatcher decade, though some—notably Inquest (founded 1981) and the Prison Reform Trust (founded 1982)—are of very recent origin. The oldest, the Howard League for Penal Reform, emerged in 1921 from the amalgamation of the original Howard Association, founded in 1866, and the more militant Penal Reform League, formed in the wake of the suffragette movement in 1907 (see Ryan, 1978). It has counterparts in many Commonwealth countries. Until the foundation of the National Association for the Care and Resettlement of Offenders (NACRO) in 1966, it had no real contenders in the field of penal reform. From the late 1960s, however, new pressure groups flourished: Radical Alternatives to Prison (RAP) in 1969; the Legal Action Group (LAG) in 1971; and, within the Labour Party, the Labour Campaign for Criminal Justice in 1978. JUSTICE had, however, preceded even NACRO: founded by Tom Sargent, it was a remarkably successful pressure group in its highly focused pursuit of legal reform. On occasion, alliances between two or more of these groups enhanced their effectiveness, as with the battle of the Howard League, JUSTICE and NACRO to expunge certain classes of ex-offender records in the Rehabilitation of Offenders Act 1974 (*ibid.*: 60–3).

The concept of the campaigning consortium was successfully adopted between 1978 and 1983 when New Approaches to Juvenile Crime—a grouping of NACRO and the principal social work and probation practitioner organizations, did much to generate the climate of opinion which led to the dramatic decline in the use of custody for juvenile offenders in the 1980s. The group used all the informational techniques which have made NACRO a force to be reckoned with: briefing papers and associated press releases were regularly produced; deputations to ministers were arranged; meetings with magistrates were held; and regular parliamentary briefings were organized. It was Lady Faithful, the group's organizer, who, against Government wishes, introduced amendments to the Bill which became the custody criteria for young offenders in the Criminal Justice Act 1982, section 1: this measure led to greatly reduced use of custody. Moreover, though cause and effect can never precisely be established, there seems little doubt that New Approaches to Juvenile Crime did much to counter the rhetoric of the early 1980s in support of the experimentally punitive 'short, sharp shock' regimes in detention centres—the courts used these centres less rather than more—and helped to lay the foundation whereby the DHSS funded more than 100 Intermediate Treatment programmes from 1983 onwards.

A more recent pressure grouping is the Penal Affairs Consortium, a lobbying collective which comprised thirteen organizations when it was formed in 1989 and which now comprises thirty-one, ranging from the Prison Governors' and the Prison Officers' Associations to NACRO, the Prison Reform Trust, the Howard League, and Liberty—a previously unthinkable combination. Some single-issue pressure groups, such as the National Campaign for the Abolition of the Death Penalty (1955), rise and fall as the issue around which they are built waxes and wanes. The extent of pressure group activity in 1990 can be gauged from the (by no means exhaustive) catalogue of such groups listed as having given evidence to the Woolf Inquiry into the prison disturbances of April that year. They ranged from the Aids and Prison Consortium Project to the Mental Health Foundation to Women in Prison and included some sixty-five groups in all, as well as professional associations, public service unions and ministries, and agencies of central and local government.

The sheer proliferation of such groups is striking, but less salient than the impressive professionalization of the major organizations in the field, particularly NACRO, the Prison Reform Trust, and the Howard League. Before 1970, the date assigned by Bailey (1987) to the final break-up of the post-war consensus on delinquency, pressure-group activity metaphorically sought to influence policy by a well-informed word in the ministerial ear. From that date, reformers increasingly began to beat on the ministerial door in a far more public, confrontational way, albeit one which was, if anything, even more highly informed. Douglas Hurd, Home Secretary from 1984 to 1988, remarked that such clamour was counter-productive. However, this metaphor should not be allowed to obscure the growth, especially in the 1980s, of myriad links between the Home Office and the pressure groups. In conferences, media debates, seminars, and the regular call for expert evidence on penal matters in particular, opportunities abounded for pressure groups to inform penal policy-making processes. None of these processes, either singly or in total, however, equalled the kind of unforced access that the Howard League enjoyed in its heyday of close informal as well as formal contact with the Home Office (see Ryan, 1978) or the strong role for criminological expertise provided by the Advisory Council on the Penal System (ACPS, 1966–80) and its predecessor the Advisory Council on the Treatment of Offenders (ACTO, 1944–64). The abolition of the ACPS in 1980 signalled the end of the inside track enjoyed by the more Establishment academic liberal reformers, adding to the scope for group activity. That inside track had, of course, carried the danger that research might uphold punitive measures, and inhibit strong contestation of government policy, as in the example of Max Grunhut's long gestation of a project which eventually reported in favour of detention centres, to the detriment of the Howard League's stance on the issue (Ryan, 1978: 83–4). Further, in its final years, the ACPS produced more and more lengthy reports—on *Young Adult Offenders* in 1974 and *Sentences of Imprisonment* in 1978—which attracted critical academic judgement as well as ministerial impatience (see Morgan, 1979). In the 1980s the government largely replaced advice from Royal Commissions and standing advisory bodies with official inquiries set up whenever a need was perceived.

It was this decline in government reliance on officially organized advice that stimulated the emergence of more professional pressure groups, most of them of recent origin and, even when beneficiaries of government funding—as NACRO has always been—more or less critical of government policy. The pressure groups have generally favoured: explanations of crime which stress social and economic inequality and individual vulnerability; use of social policy in general rather than criminal justice policy in particular to prevent or control crime; scepticism about the value of police powers and punitive methods (particularly imprisonment) as crime-control measures—indeed, they generally stress the discriminatory and unjust consequences of such methods for repressing already oppressed minorities (Ryan, 1978, 1983). Thus though there are substantial differences between these groups regarding their ideological commitments, constitutional form, access to policy-makers, and credibility with government, they have a good deal in common. They are generally perceived as left of centre, generally have allegiances with Liberal or Labour rather than Conservative politicians (though NACRO and the Prison Reform Trust are always careful to involve politicians of all parties on their councils), and tend, in spite of the consortia arrangements referred to above, also to have fragile relationships with the practitioner sectional groups, such as the Prison Officers' Association, the Police Federation, the Association of Chief Police Officers (ACPO), and the Magistrates' Association. The latter tend to adopt policies emphasizing the 'thin blue line' and the importance of their members' powers to safeguard the community from crime.

Given these dissonances, it is notable how much interchange occurred between the groups and the government in the 1980s. In other fields of social policy, such as education, where pressure groups of comparable expertise are largely lacking, ideologically driven changes since 1979 arguably met with less resistance, despite strong interest-group and practitioner unease or hostility. Given the immense imbalance of power between the groups and the Home Office, the latter could be said to have little to lose and much to gain from such contacts. The pressure groups provide positive feedback services for governments in furnishing early warnings of probable trouble, in canvassing feasible reforms, and in heightening the legitimacy of the governmental process itself. In a complex society, pressure-group and interest-group activities are the major avenues for active citizen participation in democratic decision-making. In the 1980s, pressure groups also fitted the ideological predispositions of the Thatcher administrations to accord client-based and consumerist agencies a better hearing, albeit at the expense of local government (which still harboured socialist residues) and the trade unions. Quangos and Royal Commissions were seen as stifling government and citizen initiative. The Woolf Inquiry of 1990 was a model of democratic participation by an informed citizenry (by comparison with, say, the average Royal Commission), holding seminars at which the views and evidence of different groups were debated rather than simply presented *seriatim*—though the views of prisoners were separately canvassed and, to that extent, somewhat devalued (Morgan, 1991; Sim, 1993). This consultative model was subsequently adopted by the Committee of Inquiry into Complaints about Ashworth Hospital in 1991–2, with similarly radical impact (Blom-Cooper Report 1992; see also Richardson, 1993).

Nevertheless, the huge imbalance of power remains a political reality. When 'pressured', the Home Office can brush aside any protest, as exemplified by the recent acceleration of prison privatization, a policy opposed vehemently by all the groups cited as well as the Prison Officers' and Prison Governors' Associations. The Conservative government in its drive to cut the cost of public services and expose them to the allegedly beneficial rigours of market competition has increasingly viewed the practitioner-representative organizations as little more than vested interests resisting any challenge to the inefficient monopolistic services within which they shelter. Thus the consultative instincts of senior judges, like Woolf, asked to undertake official inquiries, have seldom characterized ministerial policy initiatives. The early 1990s, for example, saw a series of initiatives regarding policing policy in which real consultation was lacking. Changes in the rank structure and proposals radically to alter the basis of police pay—changes recommended by the 1992 Sheehy Inquiry—and major amendments to the constitutional framework for the governance of the police—amendments first set out in the 1991 White Paper on *Police Reform* and implemented in the Police and Magistrates' Courts Act 1994—were taken speedily and *in spite of* the views of practitioners, local government associations, and the overwhelming majority of informed commentators.

The government's drive to effect change in law and order services in the face of practitioner opposition has prompted the Labour Party to move closer to the slighted practitioner organizations and distance themselves from the pressure groups whose liberal credentials and 'soft' image have themselves become hostages to fortune in the struggle for the political middle ground. As a consequence the pressure groups have not enjoyed the direct contacts and influence with the world of either Whitehall or Westminster in the 1990s which they achieved in the 1980s. To compensate for the deficit, the pressure groups have deployed their expertise in two respects: media influence and the appeal to comparative criminology.

Media influence is important to the pressure groups for the impact it may enable them to bring to bear on policy-making *and* for its sheer publicity value. The higher the profile the groups achieve the more members they may gain and the more they may be able to persuade public opinion to take note of the problems facing such unpopular groups as ex-offenders (see Schlesinger and

Tumber, 1992: 190–1). The Home Office and the police are not immune from pursuing the same strategy. Greater openness by police and prison staff is often inspired by the demand thus generated for more resources.

Comparative criminology has increasingly been used by the pressure groups to highlight the extent to which prisoners in Britain are both relatively more numerous than in virtually all other Western European countries and often held in worse conditions. The NACRO league table of numbers of prisoners per head of population (drawing on Council of Europe data) has been a feature of their briefings for the past decade. Analyses comparing Britain's current penal conditions unfavourably with those of the Netherlands (Tulkens, 1979; Downes, 1982, 1988). West Germany (Feest. 1988), the Netherlands, and Japan (Rutherford, 1984), and those of Britain in the recent past (King and McDermott, 1989, 1995) were drawn on by the pressure groups, as well as by criminologists in general, including those working within the Home Office Research and Planning Unit (Graham, 1988). The Woolf Inquiry (1991) broke new ground by interviewing British prisoners abroad, in Spain, the Netherlands, and West Germany, as well as drawing on comparative evidence for the second part of the Report. In 1989 Prison Reform International (PRI) was formed with, significantly, Vivien Stern, then Director of NACRO, as its Secretary General. PRI currently has an expanding membership drawn from almost fifty countries: the information pooled by that membership is providing an increasingly international backcloth to the shape of penal pressure-group politics in Britain.

The micro-politics of law and order are intimately bound up with the processes whereby the goals and agendas set by ministers are translated into policies and specific directives by civil servants. They are also creatively authored in key respects by senior civil servants, whose briefings and policy formulations have a distinct part to play in formal policy-making. As Rock (1990) has shown, policy formation within the Home Office is typically a matter of written argument developing creatively. For example, the 1991 Criminal Justice Act was the outcome of a lengthy, decade-long process of casting about for the most appropriate means of reducing the level of the prison population without either eroding the independence of the judiciary or offending the more reactionary wing of the Conservative Party. David Faulkner was a Deputy Under-Secretary at the Home Office from 1982, and for much of the decade he pursued that brief with the *imprimatur* of the Permanent Secretary, Sir Brian Cubbon. In the context of the demise of the rehabilitative policies that dominated the progressive field up to 1970, to be replaced by the 'just deserts' model pioneered in the USA (see e.g. American Friends Service committee 1971; von Hirsch, 1976; Martinson, 1974), Faulkner sought a compromise which would respect judicial independence and yet persuade sentencers to reduce their resort to imprisonment. The provision of *more* non-custodial measures had failed to achieve this effect in the 1970s. They had simply tended to be used as alternatives to *other* alternatives to custody. The major reason always given by sentencers for this result was that the existing alternatives were 'too soft'. Logically, tougher versions of existing community measures, especially probation, might succeed where the provision simply of extra alternatives had failed. That informed guesswork was incorporated, after much sounding and debate, in the 1991 Criminal Justice Act. In the event, core ingredients in the Act were soon reversed (by the Criminal Justice Act 1993, see Ashworth, this volume) but the legislation testified to the active working through of such measures by civil servants still stereotyped as passive bureaucrats. By their creation of a 'symbolic environment' (Edelman, 1971), by their active refinement of current issues, and by their deployment of arguments culled from gatherings as diverse as international conferences and informal discussion groups, it is possible, even in Britain, for senior civil servants such as Faulkner and, in an earlier period, Morrell (in connection with the Children and Young Persons Act 1970) to energize the field (see Rock, 1986, 1990; Bottoms, 1974; Rutherford, 1996; King and McDermott, 1995: chapter 1).

It would, however, be mistaken to assume that the benign hand of some concerned civil servant is always to be found behind major legislative and policy-making processes, or that policy initiatives are the outcome of an increasingly open and well-informed discussion between ministers and their advisers on the one hand and experts and practitioners working with a growing array of penal pressure groups on the other. Just as important, if not more commonplace, is the process of masterly inactivity or just plain drift. For example, analysis of the history of one penalty, the senior attendance centre order, has found little by way of cumulative rationality or systematic planning in its development (Mair, 1991). Other relevant processes at work can be found in the Select Committee stages of drafting legislation. The often painstaking scrutiny involved in this stage of a Bill's enactment can be the means for its profound amendment or effective termination by delay. For example, the Police and Criminal Evidence Act 1984 was a vastly different affair from the 1983 Bill which lapsed on the calling of the 1983 general election, after a clause-by-clause challenge to its composition by the opposition parties (see Ryan, 1983 for a searching analysis of parliamentary processes in this field). Such major transformations as a result of detailed parliamentary scrutiny are, however, increasingly the exception rather than the rule. Within four months of the implementation of the Criminal Justice Act 1991, the then Home Secretary, Kenneth Clarke, conceded, in the face of criticism from the judiciary and magistracy, that some of the detail within the legislation required amendment: critics argued that the Bill had received altogether too little parliamentary scrutiny.

Since 1993 and the advent of Michael Howard as Home Secretary, criminal justice policy-making has become dominated, to quite an unprecedented extent, by the politics of law and order. The lengthy process of gestation, consultation, and re-drafting which went with the decarceration policy of the 1980s was abruptly thrown into disarray by the 'Prison Works' U-turn of 1993. The Home Office has been turned away from the:

once standard processes of internal consultation, from committee meetings, briefings and circulating files, towards procedures that are more fragmentary, centrifugal and loosely bounded. Portions of criminal justice policy-making have become somewhat less cohesive, coherent, controlled and centralized as they come under the sway of devolution, 'contracting out', Next Steps Agencies and external consultants. . . . The newest modes of policy making are themselves the fruits of a new politics of populism, moralism and the market (Rock, 1995: 2).

The result is a prison population careering out of control, a penal estate seething with discontent and the resort to measures, such as the importation of a prison ship from the United States, which symbolizes desperate remedies.

By contrast, some policy innovations emerge out of the blue because of a minister's personal enthusiasm, or are the product of almost haphazardly won concessions granted during the committee stage of a bill, or are adopted following various lobbying by small groups of backbenchers, sometimes with the support of one or another of the Select Committees of the House of Commons. For example, section 58 of the Criminal Justice Act 1991, which provides for parents to be bound over if the court is satisfied that to do so would be desirable in the interests of preventing the commission of further offences by a young offender, would almost certainly not have been included in the Bill had it not been for the enthusiasm, against the tide of practitioner and pressure-group opinion, of John Patten, then a junior minister in the Home Office. Mr Patten originally proposed a much more drastic measure in order to ensure parental control of their children, a prophylactic he considered lacking. In March 1989 he proposed that it should be made a criminal offence for parents to fail to make reasonable efforts to prevent their children from committing offences. This proposition encountered considerable opposition and was dropped. The bind-over provision of section 58 was the barely acceptable substitute.

The enthusiasms of backbench MPs and peers may also carry the day, if they are backed by influential groups. We have already noted the example of Baroness Faithful backed by the Juvenile Justice lobby. A contrasting example is to be found in section 84 of the Criminal Justice Act 1991. This provides for the contracting out of the management of prisons and could in principle mean that every prison currently run by the Prison Service might be turned over to the private sector through the affirmative resolution procedure of section 84(5). This is an astonishing provision given that, as recently as 1987, the then Home Secretary, Douglas Hurd, informed the House of Commons that he did not 'think that there is a case, and I do not believe the House would accept that there is a case, for auctioning or privatising the prisons, or handing over the business of keeping prisoners safe to anyone other than government servants' (Hansard HC, 16 July 1987, vol. 119, col. 1299). The about-turn is explained by the fact that in 1986–7 the Select Committee on Home Affairs produced a brief report (1987) in which the majority of the Committee recommended that there should be experimentation on contracting out the management of prisons. By skilful lobbying (see Ryan and Ward, 1989, for background detail) various members persuaded a reluctant government to insert a clause providing for the contracting-out of remand prisons, a restrictive provision arrived at after consultation following a Green Paper on the question (Home Office, 1988). However, a backbench Conservative MP introduced an amendment to the Bill during the report stage, permitting the contracting-out of *any* existing or future prison, and the amendment was carried. Though the government maintained that it would not consider contracting out any prison other than the new remand prison at the Wolds, until that experiment had been carefully evaluated, the management of three more prisons was contracted out before any independent evaluation of the Wolds was commissioned and published (Bottomley *et al.*, 1997). The additions to section 84 are radically changing the shape of the penal system.

This discussion suggests, gratifyingly perhaps, that Parliament is frequently the site of innovatory discussion and intervention on aspects of criminal justice and penal policy. Unfortunately, many aspects of policy development receive remarkably little parliamentary scrutiny or debate. It needs to be emphasized that, because so much contemporary legislation (the Prison Act 1952, for example) is permissively diffuse, granting ministers and thus departments substantial discretionary powers, many important policy developments are preceded by virtually no public debate, Parliamentary or otherwise (see Richardson, 1993). Much policy is made by stealth or is announced as a *fait accompli,* challengeable only *ex post facto,* if it is challenged at all. For example, in 1983 the then Home Secretary, Leon Brittan, was able fundamentally to change parole policy without consulting either Parliament or the Parole Board and, in the event, his power to do so was upheld by the House of Lords following judicial review. In response to what he saw as growing public concern about the rise in violent crime, Mr Brittan announced in a speech to the Conservative Party Conference that he intended to use his discretion to ensure that certain classes of prisoners—serving sentences of five years or more for drug-trafficking or violence—would not get parole. Moreover, certain categories of murderer would in future serve at least twenty years. Needless to say, Mr Brittan's speech was well received by his immediate audience though it caused much controversy elsewhere, not least because some prisoners, already transferred to open prison conditions with the expectation that they would soon be released, fell foul of the new guidelines and were sent back to closed prisons. Two such prisoners challenged the new policy by way of judicial review but the House of Lords ruled, contrary to a first instance opinion, that since the Home Secretary had taken account of the relevant considerations of deterrence, retribution, and public confidence, he was under no obligation to consult even the Parole Board before making the changes *(Re Findlay* [1985] AC 318).

Policing provides a much broader example of the absence of parliamentary debate. Policing policy arguably underwent a sea-change in the early 1980s, with increased reliance on mutual aid between forces, sometimes under the direction of the National Reporting Centre (Spencer, 1985; Lustgarten, 1986); the deployment of new paramilitary equipment and techniques (Jefferson, 1990; Waddington, 1991); and the adoption of neighbourhood crime-prevention strategies (Bennett, 1990; Rosenbaum, 1988), without the benefit of research or public debate. Again, when police authorities sought to challenge some of these policies by judicial review, the High Court upheld the power of chief constables and the Home Secretary to make such far-reaching decisions. Or, to take a more recent example, the Criminal Justice Act 1991 incorporates no definition of a 'serious offence', yet on the court's interpretation of that term substantially hangs the future size and complexion of the prison population!

It is precisely because so much policy is made and implemented without adequate public debate of its implications that many analysts of criminal justice and penal policy insist that statutes should in future state more precisely what objectives agencies should pursue and what specific powers decision-makers should have, and provide for procedural rights for those citizens— suspects, prisoners, and mental hospital patients—caught up in the system (Richardson, 1993). Ideally, accountability should begin with Parliament and end with the day-to-day answerability of practitioners.

MATTERS OF SCANDAL AND CONCERN

The remaining variable is the unpredictable realm of scandal and concern. For all their pretensions, both parliamentary and extra-parliamentary groupings can be utterly outpaced by events which explode in such a way that unusual responses are called for by 'public opinion'—a phenomenon for which media attention is often taken to be the proxy. In the penal realm, for example, two types of events seemingly dwarf all others in their impact on the 'public': escapes and riots. The escapes of Ronald Biggs and George Blake in 1965–6, and the high security break-outs from Whitemoor and Parkhurst in 1994–5, radically changed the emphasis on security in the Prison Service. The rioting at Strangeways, Manchester, and other prisons in 1990 led to a major inquiry conducted by Lord Justice Woolf, the outcome of which appeared, initially, to set a new agenda for prisons but which the security lapses of 1994–5, combined with a rising prison population, have in turn knocked off course (see Morgan, this volume). In the realm of public order, the riots in Brixton (1981; see Scarman Report, 1981) and on the Broadwater Farm Estate (1985; see Gifford Report, 1986) far transcended other disturbances in their evocation of profound unease. Lord Scarman's Report on the events at Brixton led to the development of formal police community consultation (see Morgan, 1992). In 1993, in the wake of the horrific murder of two-year-old James Bulger by two juveniles, and a sustained police campaign regarding offences committed, particularly by juveniles, while on bail (see P. Morgan, 1992; Morgan and

Jones, 1992), custodial measures were introduced for serious juvenile offenders which contravened principles only just implemented in the Criminal Justice Act 1991 and which research suggested were ill-advised (see Newburn, this volume). Or, to take the most dramatic recent example, the massacre by Thomas Hamilton of schoolchildren and their teacher at Dunblane in 1996 stimulated the Government and Opposition literally to vie with each other over the extent to which gun control and, subsequently, control over other offensive weapons, should be tightened, a parliamentary competition still being played out as we write in January 1997.

However, not all scandals translate into calls for reform or change: for example, the so-called Moors Murders of the early 1960s, in which several children were fatal victims of sadistic sexual practices, were the source of heightened moral fears, but also of sheer bafflement. As Bottoms and Stevenson argue:

It is a fact well known to students of social policy that reforms of the system often take place not so much because of careful routine analysis by ministers and civil servants in the relevant Department of State, nor even because of a critique or exposé by an outside journalist or pressure group, but because one or more individual incident(s) occurs, drawing public attention to some underlying imperfections of policy in a dramatic way which seems to demand change. Very often an inquiry is set up after such incidents, and it is the report of the inquiry that sets the agenda for subsequent reforms; but the reforms would not have taken place without the public attention created by the original incident [1992: 23–4].

It is worth embellishing this point a little. Such incidents tend to generate change only when they discredit institutions so drastically and dramatically that their credibility and effectiveness—and, by extension, those of the government and the state—risk serious erosion unless changes are made. The damage is not simply symbolic, a matter of reputation and belief, though declining public confidence carries grave implications for the agencies of control and the caring professions. The authority of the modern state rests heavily on its claims to expertise (Giddens, 1984). Practical effects include the predictable increase in, for example, escape attempts in the wake of successful breakouts, and increasing dismissal rates in courts where juries no longer unquestioningly accept police evidence. As the latter point suggests, scandals can and should result in improved policy and practice. The abolition of capital punishment is arguably an example of 'things going right' in criminal justice and penal policy after a series of executions that caused public disquiet. Much hinges on the character of the response; and, we argue below, the trend has recently been towards specific and limited rather than wide-ranging and searching modes of inquiry. Nor are scandals randomly scattered throughout the system: the police and the prisons have produced far more than, for example, probation and after-care.

Prisons: From Mountbatten to Woolf to Learmont

The prison escapes of 1965–6 transformed the prison system. Until the mid-1960s, little was thought to be awry with the prison system, apart from its legacy of Victorian architecture and authoritarian regimes. R. A. Butler's famous White Paper, *Penal Practice in a Changing Society* (1959), seemed to have set the agenda for the next few decades. But the escapes made a 'public laughing-stock' of the Prison Department (Bottoms and Stevenson, 1992: 25) and the Labour Home Secretary, Roy Jenkins, felt that anxieties could be assuaged only by a rapid inquiry. This was conducted by Lord Mountbatten (1966) and resulted in a tough but perceptive report which discerned the major problem as a combination of insufficiently secure provision for the tiny minority of high-escape-risk prisoners and over-security for the great majority. The measures taken in the wake of the Mountbatten Report heightened security across the system, prioritized control and surveillance at the expense of other objectives (such as work, training, education, recreation, and better rights and conditions), and, in combination with the impact of adverse research findings, halted the spread of therapeutic regimes while leaving intact the differentiation between local and training prisons based upon that ideology (see King and Morgan, 1980, for a detailed inventory; also Morgan, this volume).

The growth of what Rutherford (1984) has termed 'high-cost squalor' in the penal system advanced most dramatically in the 1970s and 1980s, mainly because the new strategy was both labour-intensive and overly security-based. Conflicts between prisoners and staff, and staff and Prison Department officials, became endemic. The May Committee was appointed to resolve a pay dispute but widened its brief to look at the overall context. Its report (May Report, 1979) led to only one innovatory gain, an inspectorate independent of the Prison Department. The prisons continued to fester, conditions deteriorating on virtually all fronts (King and McDermott, 1989), locked into a logically endless drift borne of rising numbers and costs in a policy vacuum. When it came, however, the frequently predicted climax of two decades of often serious outbreaks of prison unrest took even informed observers by surprise in its scope and ferocity. Strangeways Prison, Manchester, the largest in the land, was completely taken over and gutted by its inmates, an occupation lasting three weeks that became a media event as prisoners humiliated the authorities by their rooftop defiance. One death, a host of injuries, and the terrorization of sex offenders occurred. Several other prisons erupted in a sequence of less sustained rioting.

The Woolf Inquiry into these disturbances broke new ground in several respects. It was completed in two stages: the first covered the disturbances, and addressed questions of responsibility and culpability; the second, with the then Chief Inspector of Prisons, Judge Stephen Tumim, examined the causes of so signal a system failure. This process enabled them to look in depth at the massive mismatch between needs and resources in the system; at the myriad ways in which containment fell far short of the humane; and at remedies in the short and longer terms (Woolf Report, 1991). Unusually, as mentioned above, evidence was gathered from prisoners at home and abroad. Uniquely, five public seminars were held at which specialists from government, the Prison Service, academic research, pressure groups, and other bodies debated key issues. The Report was widely acknowledged to have advanced the most comprehensive agenda for radical change in the penal system since the Gladstone Report of 1895. It pioneered a process for democratic account-ability and debate on urgent problems that should serve as a model for inquiries in all fields, not simply penal affairs.

Nevertheless, the Inquiry was debarred by its terms of reference from exploring one subject of utmost relevance to the topic, namely the judicial framework of sentencing policy. In one sense, the Prison Service is correct in stating that it cannot be held responsible for all aspects of its performance, since one key variable—that is, the number of prisoners it is called upon to contain—is largely beyond its control. That responsibility lies with the judiciary, and the prisons are under a statutory obligation to accept all those who are sent there by the courts. Unlike other institutions, and prisons in a few other countries such as the Netherlands, no legal limit is placed on the numbers any prison can be called upon to hold. Certified Normal Accommodation (CNA) is a formal baseline that is regularly exceeded. The power of the judiciary to stand aloof from the entire debate about penal policy is perhaps the most salient feature of the politics of law and order, since all agendas for reform must bow to their refusal to take part in any such process. This refusal, justified by the judicial elite in terms of the essential independence to embrace not simply their judgment of cases—where indeed it is vital—but the entire conspectus of sentencing trends and practices—where it is not—forces all other components of the criminal justice system to adjust to their often ill-co-ordinated actions. This feature of the system has led many to see better co-ordination as an end in itself—Woolf, for example, recommended the formation of the Criminal Justice Consultative Council (CJCC) and area fora, now in operation—the attainment of which will automatically bring improvement. But unless some agreed objective, such as a reduction in the numbers in prison, is laid down, this co-ordination is simply a means without an end. It is around these issues that the arguments for and against some version of a Sentencing Council have been made (Ashworth, 1983; Cavadino and Dignan, 1992: chapter 4), but the judiciary has so far largely insulated itself from the policy process. It is noteworthy that some commentators now see the CJCC, in which the judiciary has learnt to sit alongside key decision-makers from the other criminal justice agencies, as a vehicle for resuscitating the idea of a Sentencing Council (Ashworth and Hough 1996).

In September 1994 and January 1995 the Prison Service was again prey to security breaches—the escape of category A prisoners from Whitemoor and Parkhurst high security prisons—which led to high profile inquiries (Woodcock, 1994; Learmont, 1995), and, ultimately, to the sacking of the

Director-General (for details see Lewis, 1997). These events consolidated a trend already well established since the Home Secretary's pronouncement at the Conservative Party Conference in October 1993 that 'prison works' and that prison regimes should be 'austere'. The Woolf reformist agenda was effectively dislodged. The prison population rose steeply and continues to do so. The Woodcock and Learmont recommendations legitimated, on security grounds, the more punitive and restrictive climate in prisons. And Woolf's emphasis on justice in prisons was no longer mentioned. Talk of prisoners' rights gave way to a focus on incentives and privileges (for more detailed discussion, see Morgan, this volume).

Policing: Dixon to Robocop

The conventional wisdom about policing tends to the apocalyptic. Things have fallen apart since the Golden Age of policing in the 1950s, embodied in the folk hero, PC George Dixon, the linchpin of the community in the long-running TV serial *Dixon of Dock Green*. Nowadays, in Reiner's vivid contrast, the image of the police constable is more like *Robocop*, a barely human presence in a technological armour, holding a seething mob at bay with advanced weaponry (see Reiner on the police, this volume). The real story is more complex and less sensational. The Golden Age of policing was a myth based upon blind faith in authority and ignorance of actual police work at a time of relatively harmonious community relations. Declining public confidence in the police is due to rates of crime that have soared for social, economic, and cultural reasons that affect but hardly originate in policing; the exposure of forms of corruption that were customary rather than novel; and the growth of problems such as terrorism and drug trafficking which are unparalleled this century in their scale and viciousness. We are only now coming to grips with age-old problems that defy short-term solutions. The police are almost certainly now in a healthier state than before, but look worse because far more is known about their shortcomings, thanks to a mixture of fly-on-the-wall media exposure, scandals, research and the gradual move towards more stringent forms of both legal and political accountability (Morgan, 1996).

The three cases which came to dramatize public concerns about policing most vividly were those of the Guildford Four, the Maguire Seven, and the Birmingham Six. In all three cases, Irish suspects were convicted of causing explosions that killed multiple victims. Outrage as expressed through the media placed immense pressure on the police to get 'results'. Sentences of life imprisonment were accompanied by recommendations that at least twenty years be served in several cases. Fifteen to seventeen years later, after tireless campaigning, the verdicts were declared 'unsafe' and the prisoners freed. These and other cases of similar magnitude so eroded public confidence in the police and the courts, as shown by opinion polls, that a Royal Commission on Criminal Justice was appointed in 1991, the first Royal Commission for fourteen years, to inquire into the procedural issues involved and suggest remedies.

These cases exemplify the tendency for matters of notoriety to originate in taken-for-granted practices that are exposed as a result of unusual degrees of pressure or modes of scrutiny, rather than being exceptional instances of individual pathology—a 'few bad apples'. 'Constructing the suspect' by embellishing the evidence against him or her and ignoring countervailing evidence is standard police practice (McBarnet, 1981; McConnville, Leng, and Sanders, 1991). Once socialized into an occupational culture which affirms such practices as a necessary evil and a professional skill, designed ultimately to secure conviction in the ornate adversarial exchanges in open court, it is a small step for the police officer to fabricate evidence and 'lose' counter-evidence. The appeal of such procedures is the greatest when the suspect has 'previous' and is 'overdue' for conviction. The logic of methodical suspicion casts certain groups more readily into the suspect role than others. The moral economy of police work reinforces these images of deviance, certain groups being seen as 'slag', 'rubbish', and 'police property' (Reiner, 1992). If such variables as age, sex, ethnicity, demeanour, degrees of co-operativeness with the police, and the reputation of areas are consequential in routine offending, how much larger they loom when intense pressures for a 'result' are generated. Another example of unusual modes of inquiry bringing new focus to established practices was Roger Graef's 1982 TV documentary series on the Thames Valley police. The public outcry at the merciless grilling by officers of a female rape victim led to rapid changes in the procedures for the processing of similar cases. The impetus had also led to the heightened awareness and changing practices in cases of domestic violence (see Stanko, 1990; Dobash and Dobash, 1992; Levi in this volume).

Northern Ireland and its Impact

The context for the most notorious recent miscarriages of justice is of course the political quagmire of Northern Ireland and its ramifications for the control of terrorism in Britain. Since 1969, 'nearly 3,000 people have died because of political violence in Northern Ireland. The conflict has often spilled outside the borders of the region, leading to the deaths of approximately 200 people in Great Britain, the Republic of Ireland, and sites elsewhere in Europe, ranging from Gibraltar to Western Germany' (O'Leary and McGarry, 1993). Three thousand dead may seem a relatively small toll over two decades. 'However, scale matters. The population of Northern Ireland in the 1981 census . . . was estimated as 1,488,077. If the equivalent ratio of victims to population had been produced in Great Britain in the same period some 100,000 people would have died, and . . . in the USA . . . over 500,000, or about ten times the number of Americans killed in the Vietnam War' (*ibid.*: 2). Comparatively speaking, 'the death-toll in Northern Ireland alone made the UK absolutely the most violent liberal democracy during the same time-span' (*ibid.*: 4). Close to one in fifty of the population have suffered serious injuries over the period. The costs in law enforcement, paramilitary measures, compensation, and legal processes have been huge. One audit in 1985 estimated the annual direct costs of violence in Northern Ireland at £1,194 million *per annum* (*ibid.*: 22). The costs in terms of negative effects on public trust in British political institutions have been incalculable. The granting of strong emergency powers to the legal authorities under the regularly renewed Emergency Provisions Act in Northern Ireland and the Prevention of Terrorism Act throughout the UK has meant that departures from traditional English legal procedures have become normal in Northern Ireland and spill over into aspects of crime control in Britain (as, for example, in the short-lived 'control units' for recalcitrant prisoners in two English prisons in the 1970s, whose regimes paralleled forms of sensory deprivation used in Northern Ireland). 'Since 1973 no-jury single-judge courts have presided over cases arising from "scheduled offences", i.e. "terrorist offences", on the grounds that jury-trials are not safe from perverse verdicts or the intimidation of jurors and witnesses. Confessions are admissible as the sole basis for conviction on charges "of this kind"' (O'Leary and McGarry, 1993: 24). The rise and discrediting of 'super-grass' evidence in the 1980s (Greer, 1994); the abandonment of the 'right of silence' in 1988; the regular delay of several years in holding inquests on persons killed by the security forces (Amnesty International, 1978); and the violation of the European Convention on Human Rights on a number of fronts concerning interrogation and time held in custody; have all severely eroded the belief, both nationally and internationally, in the impartiality of British justice. They also provided the context within which routine police practices for constructing the suspect escalated into 'the greatest twentieth century crisis of confidence in the administration of justice in Great Britain' (*ibid.*). In the event the 1991–3 Royal Commission proved unequal to the task of tackling such deep-rooted problems.

Forms of Official Inquiry

The appointment of the Royal Commission (Runciman, 1993), and the unusually open and searching nature of the Woolf Inquiry, went against the grain of the trend, especially notable during the Thatcher years, increasingly to use the *ad hoc*, highly specific, departmental inquiry as a policy-making mechanism. Such inquiries were internal, as when HM Chief Inspector of Prisons was asked to consider the prison disturbances of 1986 (HMCIP, 1986); or external, conducted either by a committee, as in the case of the Prior Committee on prison discipline (Prior Report, 1985), or by an individual, usually a judge, as in the case of the Woolf Inquiry. The latter embrace both statutory inquiries, as in the cases of Lord Scarman's investigation of the Brixton disturbance in 1981 under section 32 of the Police Act 1964 (Scarman Report, 1981) or Sir Louis Blom Cooper's investigation of Ashworth Special Hospital 1991 under section 125 of the 'Mental Health Act 1988 (Blom-Cooper Report, 1992), and not statutory inquiries, as in the case of the Woolf Report.

Such inquiries may be resorted to for a variety of political reasons (see Morgan, 1991) but, unlike statutory or even non-statutory standing consultative bodies and Royal Commissions, they have the merit for ministers of being focused, relatively short-term, and manageable. Their terms of reference are precise and often, though not invariably, narrowly technical. By contrast, standing bodies, like the Advisory Council on the Penal System, are liable to take a robust view of their terms of reference; and Royal Commissions tend to be wide-ranging and long-lasting. Which mechanism is resorted to depends on the seriousness of the incident(s), the degree of loss of public confidence, and whether ministers have a clear objective, wish to distance themselves from a potentially unpopular solution, or play for time. What is clear is that straightforward assumptions about the political methodology likely to be adopted in relation to one mechanism or another can no longer be made. The Woolf and Blom-Cooper Inquiries were unusually open and consultative in their methods. It was widely anticipated that the 1992 Royal Commission on Criminal Justice would be the same, particularly since Sir John May's inquiry into the 'Guildford Four' miscarriage of justice (an inquiry eventually incorporated by the Royal Commission) had indicated his readiness to hold public seminars. In the event, the Royal Commission, though it took oral evidence in the usual manner and commissioned a good deal of research, was relatively orthodox: it held no seminars. The 1992 Sheehy Committee on police ranks, structure, and conditions of employment held one seminar, but under conditions of excessive secrecy (Sheehy Report, 1993). The 1990s have so far been characterized by a highly managerial and undemocratic strategy for developing 'law and order' policy. The second-order consensus alluded to above has proved short-lived.

CONCLUSIONS

The politics of law and order in the post-war period have been shaped by the nature of responses to the continuous rise in rates of recorded crime and to the unforeseen explosion of politically inspired terrorism and illicit drug trafficking. Three phases can be discerned in the party political sphere. First, until 1970 a consensus prevailed whose terms, heavily influenced by 'liberal progressive' ideology, implicitly rested on the non-partisan character of crime and on the merit of gradual shifts towards rehabilitative policies for its control. This consensus was not shared, other than for a range of juvenile offenders, by the judiciary who continued to adhere to broadly retributive and deterrent principles of sentencing, except for a small minority of clinically diagnosed mentally ill offenders. Governments of both left and right shared a strong reluctance to intrude into the judicial realm. The 1970 election was a watershed which, by 1979, had swept away the main supports of non-partisanship. The second phase, of sharp and growing contention between the parties for the 'law and order' terrain, saw the Conservative Party emerge relatively unscathed from Labour's tentative attempts to link rising crime with the social and economic effects of growing inequality and unemployment: the 'hostages to fortune' which the Labour Party, traditional attachments to the trade unions and to libertarian causes entail, initially led its leaders to seek to neutralize, rather than sharply contest, the Conservative hegemony on this issue. Since the 1992 Election a third phase appears to have begun. The Conservatives, bent on the further restructuring of public services to achieve cuts in public expenditure whilst simultaneously pursuing tough populist penal measures, have prejudiced their traditional support base with the judiciary, the police, and prison personnel. Meanwhile 'New Labour' has distanced itself from the trades unions, the penal pressure groups, and libertarian causes, particularly those entailing street protests. Labour has also been coy about opposing Conservative 'law and order' legislation. Indeed, Labour has on several occasions sought to out-tough Conservative legislative proposals. In the run-up to the 1997 general election the opinion poll evidence suggests that this populist strategy is paying off for Labour. The Party now enjoys greater public confidence regarding 'law and order' than do the Conservatives. Conservative hegemony on this issue appears to have been undermined and Labour's 'hostages to fortune' forgotten or receded.

Though the elements of a 'second-order consensus' remain in some respects—bifurcation, the need to reduce prison overcrowding, victim support, and crime prevention are all examples—the routes to those ends have often differed. The Labour Party, for example, has always placed greater emphasis on the role of local authorities as the linchpin of crime prevention initiatives of a social (rather than a purely situational) kind, and this continues (Labour Party, 1995). The Conservatives have stressed a host of alternative frameworks—Neighbourhood Watch, Safer Cities, and crime prevention through environmental design (see Clarke and Mayhew, 1980; Bottoms and Wiles, this volume)—which bypass local authorities rather than engage them in community crime prevention schemes: indeed, they have founded an independent organization, Crime Concern, to evangelize their approach. The stress on 'active citizenship' and the 'community' was evolved in the mid-1980s as a form of recognition by the government that reliance on the 'rule of law' alone was no longer serving as a credible strategy (Reiner and Cross, 1991). Crime rates and public disorder alike were reaching new heights. These new watchwords and strategies were intended to signify fresh thinking and active concern, on the one hand, and a refusal to countenance the role of social and economic variables, on the other. The irony is that the Home Office under the Conservatives has, since 1979, assembled a criminal justice and penal policy which, however unevenly, shares broad cross-party support. Yet the government struggled to put that policy into effect in a context rendered peculiarly unfavourable in crime control terms by the impact and character of their social and economic policies.

For the Labour Party the real Conservative enemy in crime-control terms is not the Home Office but the Treasury, the Department of Trade and Industry, and the ethos embodied in successive leaders (notably Mrs Thatcher) who deny the existence of 'society' and state that—as far as offenders are concerned— 'we should understand less and condemn more' (Mr Major in 1993). In other words, it is not so much that the Conservatives have tightened the screws on civil liberties and citizenship rights (apart from trades unions); in some ways they have even formally extended them. It is rather that they have effectively excluded far larger numbers of people from any conceivable activation of those rights—by doubling unemployment, quadrupling homelessness, increasing inequalities of wealth and income, and draining local authorities of both power and resources (see Stewart, 1992; Brake and Hale, 1992). The problem for the opposition parties has been that they have found it difficult to find ways of convincing the electorate that these connections exist and can be influenced by political decision-making in the medium to long term. The signs are that 'New Labour' has begun to persuade the electorate that a greater measure of equality of opportunity, a collective sense of social justice and the provision of good quality public services, is connected with the incidence of crime and the deepening sense of public insecurity that fuels fear of crime. But the Labour Party has had to sacrifice many of its traditional allegiances in order to build this platform of electoral credibility and it is not at all clear that the Labour Party, if elected in 1997, will pursue a markedly less punitive policy than that embarked on by the Conservatives in the first half of the 1990s.

Selected Further Reading

There have been few studies of the part played by 'law and order' in British political life. Philip Norton's *Law and Order and British Politics* (Aldershot: Gower, 1984) and Mike Brake and Chris Hale's *Public Order and Private Lives: The Politics of Law and Order* (London: Routledge, 1992), the latter a highly critical account of the Thatcher years, are exceptions. David Downes' edited collection, *Unravelling Criminal Justice* (Basingstoke: Macmillan, 1992), contains relevant essays, particularly those by Bottoms and Stevenson on the extent and difficulties of the liberal consensus, and McBarnet on the burgeoning field of tax avoidance and evasion. Roger Hood's collection, *Crime, Criminology and Public Policy: Essays in Honour of Leon Radzinowicz* (London: Heinemann, 1974), provides detailed scrutiny of the public policy issues of the mid-period, and Terence Morris' *Crime and Criminal Justice in Britain since 1945* (Oxford: Blackwell 1989) covers the entire period with shrewd political insight. Brendan O'Leary and John McGarry (*The Politics of Antagonism: Understanding Northern Ireland*, London: Athlone, 1993) are sure guides to the complexities of Northern Ireland, without which some key developments are lost. In *Beyond Law and Order: Criminal Justice Policy into the 1990s* (Basingstoke: Macmillan 1991) Robert Reiner and Malcolm Cross have collected a set of papers on most of the key aspects of criminal justice policy with their editorial chapter spelling out the political context. Finally,

Mick Ryan (*The Politics of Penal Reform*, London: Longman, 1983) is a political scientist in criminology who documents the micro-politics of penal reform in the wider political economy of Britain.

REFERENCES

ABERCROMBIE, N., and WARDE, S., eds. (1988), *Contemporary British Society*. Cambridge: Polity.

ADVISORY COUNCIL ON THE PENAL SYSTEM (1969), *The Regime for Long-term Prisoners in Conditions of Maximum Security*. London: HMSO.

AMERICAN FRIENDS SERVICE COMMITTEE (1971), *Struggle for Justice*. New York: Hill and Wang.

AMNESTY International (1978), *Report of an Amnesty International Mission to Northern Ireland*. London: International Secretariat, Amnesty International.

ASHWORTH, A. (1983), *Sentencing and Penal Policy*. London: Weidenfeld and Nicolson.

—— and HOUGH, M. (1996) 'Sentencing and the Climate of opinion', *Criminal Law Review*, 776.

BAILEY, V. (1987), *Delinquency and Citizenship: Reclaiming the Young Offender, 1914–1948*. Oxford: Clarendon Press.

BALL, A. B., HUFF, C. R., and LILLY, J. R. (1988), *House Arrest and Correctional Policy: Doing Time at Home*. Newbury Park, Cal.: Sage.

BENNETT, T. (1990), *Evaluating Neighbourhood Watch*. Farnborough: Gower.

BLOM-Cooper REPORT (1992), *Report of the Committee of Inquiry into Complaints about Ashworth Hospital*, Cm 2028. London: HMSO.

BOTTOMLEY, A. K., JAMES, A., CLARE, I., and LIEBLING, A. (1997), *Monitoring and Evaluation of Wolds Remand Prison*. Home Office Research and Planning Unit. London: Home Office.

BOTTOMS, A. E. (1974), 'On the Decriminalization of English Juvenile Courts', in R. Hood, ed., *Crime, Criminology, and Public Policy*. London: Heineman.

—— (1977), 'Reflections on the Renaissance of Dangerousness', *Howard Journal*, 16: 70–96.

—— and STEVENSON, S. (1992), 'What Went Wrong?: Criminal Justice Policy in England and Wales, 1945–70', in D. Downes, ed., *Unravelling Criminal Justice*. London: Macmillan.

BRAKE, M., and HALE, C. (1992), *Public Order and Private Lives.. The Politics of Law and Order*. London: Routledge.

BUTLER, D. (1952), *The British General Election of 1951*. London: Macmillan.

—— (1956), *The British General Election of 1955*. London: Macmillan.

—— and KAVANAGH, D. (1975a), *The British General Election of February 1974*. London: Macmillan.

—— and —— (1975b), *The British General Election of October 1974*. London: Macmillan.

—— and —— (1980), *The British General Election of 1979*. London: Macmillan.

—— and —— (1988), *The British General Election of 1987*. London: Macmillan.

—— and —— (1992), *The British General Election of 1992*. London: Macmillan.

—— and KING, A. (1965), *The British General Election of 1964*. London: Macmillan.

—— and —— (1967), *The British General Election of 1966*. London: Macmillan.

—— and PINTO-DUSCHINSKY, M. (1971), *The British General Election of 1970*. London: Macmillan.

—— and ROSE, R. (1960), *The British General Election of 1959*. London: Macmillan.

CAMPBELL, B. (1993), *Goliath: Britain's Dangerous Places*. London: Methuen.

CAVADINO, M., and DIGNAN, J. (1992), *The Penal System. An Introduction*. London: Sage.

CHRISTIAN, L. (1983), *Policing by Coercion*. London: GLC Police Support Unit.

CLARKE, R. V. G., and MAYHEW, P. (1980), *Designing Out Crime*. London: HMSO.

COHEN, S. (1972), *Folk Devils and Moral Panics*. London: MacGibbon and Kee.

CONSERVATIVE PARTY (1959), *The Next Five Years*. London: Conservative Party.

—— (1966), *Actions not Words*. London: Conservative Party.

—— (1970), *A Better Tomorrow*. London: Conservative Party.

—— (1974a), *Firm Action for a Fairer Britain*. London: Conservative Party.

—— (1974b), *Putting Britain First*. London: Conservative Party.

——(1979), *The Conservative Manifesto*. London: Conservative Party.

——(1983), *The Challenge of Our Times*. London: Conservative Party.

——(1987), *Our First Eight Years. The Next Moves Forward*. London: Conservative Party.

——(1992), *The Best Future for Britain*. London: Conservative Party.

CRAIG, F. W. S. (1975), *The British General Election Manifestos 1900–1974*. London: Macmillan.

DAHRENDORF, R. (1987), 'The Underclass and the Future of Great Britain', lecture delivered at Windsor Castle, 27 April.

DIXON, D., and FISHWICK, E. (1984), 'The Law and Order Debate in Historical Perspective', in P. Norton, ed., *Law and Order and British Politics*. Aldershot: Gower.

DOBASH, R. E., and DOBASH, R. D. (1992), *Women, Violence and Social Change*. London: Routledge.

DORE, R. P. (1992), *Japanese Capitalism, Anglo Saxon Capitalism: How will the Darwinian Contest Turn Out?* London: LSE Centre for Economic Performance Occasional Paper no. 4.

DOWNES, D. M. (1966), *The Delinquent Solution*. London: Routledge and Kegan Paul.

——(1982), 'The Origins and Consequences of Dutch Penal Policy since 1945: A Preliminary Analysis', *British Journal of Criminology*, 22: 325–62.

——(1988), *Contrasts in Tolerance. Post-War Penal Policy in the Netherlands and England and Wales*. Oxford: Clarendon Press.

——(1989a), 'Only Disconnect: Law and Order, Social Policy and the Community', in M. Bulmer, J. Lewis, and D. Piachaud, eds., *The Goals of Social Policy*. London: Unwin Hyman.

——(1989b), 'Thatcherite Values and Crime', *Samizdat*, May/June.

—— and WARD, T. (1986), *Democratic Policing*. London: Labour Campaign for Criminal Justice.

—— and YOUNG, J. (1987) 'A Criminal Failure', *New Society*, 13 May.

EDELMAN, M. (1971), *Politics as Symbolic Action*. Chicago, Ill.: Markham.

EDMUND-DAVIES REPORT (1978), *Report of the Committee of Inquiry on the Police*, Cmnd. 7283. London: HMSO.

ELDER, N. C. M. (1984), 'Conclusion', in P. Norton, ed., *Law and Order and British Politics*. Aldershot: Gower.

FEEST, J. (1988), *Reducing the Prison Population: Lessons from the West German Experience?* London: National Association for the Care and Resettlement of Offenders.

GAMBLE, A. (1990), 'The Thatcher Decade in Perspective', in P. Dunleavy, A. Gamble, and G. Peele, eds., *Developments in British Politics*, iii. London: Macmillan.

GIDDENS, A. (1984), *The Constitution of Society*. Cambridge: Polity.

GIFFORD REPORT (1986), *The Broadwater Farm Inquiry. Report of the Independent Inquiry into Disturbances of October 1985 at the Broadwater Farm Estate, Tottenham*. London: Karia Press.

GRAHAM, J. (1988), 'The Declining Prison Population in the Federal Republic of Germany', *Home Office Research and Planning Unit Research Bulletin*, 24: 47–52.

GREER, S. (1994), *Supergrasses*. Oxford: Oxford University Press.

HALL, S., CRITCHER, S., JEFFERSON, T., CLARKE, J., and ROBERTS, B. (1978), *Policing the Crisis: Mugging, the State, and Law and Order*. London: Macmillan.

HALLORAN, J. D., ELLIOTT, P., and MURDOCK, G. (1970), *Demonstrations and Communications*. Harmondsworth: Penguin.

HER MAJESTY'S CHIEF INSPECTOR OF PRISONS (1987), *Report of an Inquiry into the Disturbances in Prison Service Establishments in England between 29 April and 2 May*, HC 42. London: HMSO.

HOME AFFAIRS COMMITTEE (1987), *Fourth Report on Contract Provision of Prisons*. London: HMSO.

HOME OFFICE (1988), *Private Sector Involvement in the Remand System*, Cm 434. London: HMSO.

——(1993) *Police Reform*. Cm 2281, London: Home Office.

HONDERICH, T. (1990), *Conservatism*. London: Hamish Hamilton.

HUTTON, W. (1996), *The State We're In*. London: Vintage.

JEFFERSON, T. (1990), *The Case against Paramilitary Policing*. Milton Keynes: Open University Press.

JENCKS, C., and PETERSON, P. E., eds. (1991), *The Urban Underclass*. Washington, DC: Brookings Institution.

KING, A. (1993), *Britain at the Polls 1992*, New Jersey: Chatham House.

KING, R. D., and McDERMOTT, K. (1989), 'British Prisons 1970–97: The Ever-Deepening Crisis', *British Journal of Criminology*, 29/2: 107–28.

——(1995), *The State of Our Prisons*. Oxford: Clarendon.

—— and MORGAN, R. (1980), *The Future of the Prison System*. Farnborough: Gower.

LABOUR PARTY (1959), *Time for Decision*. London: Labour Party.

—— (1966), *Time for Decision*. London: Labour Party.

—— (1970), *Now Britain's Strong—Let's Make it Great to Live In*. London: Labour Party.

—— (1974a), *Let Us Work Together—Labour's Way Out of the Crisis*. London: Labour Party.

—— (1974b), *Britain Will Win with Labour*. London: Labour Party.

—— (1979), *The Labour Way is the Better Way*. London: Labour Party.

—— (1983), *New Hope for Britain*. London: Labour Party.

—— (1987), *Britain Will Win*. London: Labour Party.

—— (1992), *It's Time to Get Britain Working Again*. London: Labour Party.

—— (1995), *Safer Communities, Safer Britain*. London: Labour Party

LEA, J., and YOUNG, J. (1984), *What Is to Be Done About Law and Order?* Harmondsworth: Penguin.

LEARMONT REPORT (1995), *Review of Prison Service Security in England and Wales and the Escape from Parkhurst Prison on Tuesday 3rd January 1995*, Cm 3020. London: HMSO.

LEWIS, D. (1997), *Hidden Agenda*. London: Hamish Hamilton.

LIBERAL PARTY (1964), *Think for Yourself: Vote Liberal*. London: Liberal Party.

—— (1974), *Change the Face of Britain*. London: Liberal Party.

LIBERAL DEMOCRATIC PARTY (1992), *Changing Britain for Good*. London: Liberal Democratic Party.

LIBERAL/SDP ALLIANCE (1987), *Britain United: The Time Has Come*. London: Liberal/SDP Alliance.

LIGHT, R., NEE, C., and INGHAM, H. (1993), *Car Theft: The Offender's Perspective*, Home Office Research Study no. 130. London: HMSO.

LINTON, M. (1995), *Was it the Sun Wot Won It?*. Oxford: Nuffield College.

LUSTGARTEN, L. (1986), *The Government of the Police*. London: Sweet and Maxwell.

MCBARNET, D. (1981), *Conviction*. London: Macmillan.

MCCALLUM, R. B., and READMAN, A. (1946), *The British General Election of 1945*. Oxford: Oxford University Press.

MCCONVILLE, M, LENG, R., and SANDERS, A. (1993), *The Case for the Prosecution*. London: Routledge.

MACNICOL, J. (1987), 'In Pursuit of the Underclass', *Journal of Social Policy*, 293–318.

MACPHERSON, C. B. (1962), *The Political Theory of Possessive Individual*. Oxford: Oxford University Press.

MAIR, G. (1991), *Part-Time Punishment.. The Origins and Development of Attendance Centres*. London: HMSO.

—— and NEE, C. (1990), *Electronic Monitoring: The Trials and their Results*, Home Office Research Study no. 120. London: HMSO.

MARTIN, R. (1981), *New Technology and Industrial Relations in Fleet Street*. Oxford: Oxford University Press.

MARTINSON, R. (1974), 'What Works?— Questions and Answers about Prison Reform', *The Public Interest*, 35 (Spring): 22–54.

MARWICK, A. (1990), *British Society since 1945*. London: Penguin.

MAY REPORT (1979), *Report of the Committee of Inquiry into the United Kingdom Prison Services* (Chairman, Mr Justice May), Cmnd. 7673. London: HMSO.

MAYHEW, H. (1862), *Those That Will Not Work*, vol. 4 of *London Labour and the London Poor (1851–62)*. London: Griffin. Repr. ed. P. Quennell, *London's Underworld*, London: Spring Books, 1955.

MILLS, C. W. (1959), *The Sociological Imagination*. New York: Oxford University Press.

MORGAN, P. (1992), *Offending While on Bail: A Survey of Recent Studies*, Home Office Research and Planning Unit Paper no. 65. London: HMSO.

MORGAN, R. (1979), *Formulating Penal Policy: The Future of the Advisory Council on the Penal System*. London: National Association for the Care and Resettlement of Offenders.

—— (1991), 'Woolf. in Retrospect and Prospect', *Modern Law Review*, 54: 713–25.

—— (1992), 'Talking about Policing', in D. Downes, ed., *Unravelling Criminal Justice*. London: Macmillan.

—— (1996), 'Custody in the Police Station: How do England and Wales Measure Up in Europe', *Policy Studies*, 17: 55–72.

—— and JONES, S. (1992), 'Bail or Jail', in E. Stockdale and S. Casale, eds., *Criminal Justice under Stress*. London: Blackstone.

MORRIS, T. P. (1989), *Crime and Criminal Justice in Britain since 1945*. Oxford: Blackwell.

MOUNTBATTEN REPORT (1966), *Report of the Inquiry into Prison Escapes and Security by Admiral of the Fleet, the Earl Mountbatten of Burma*, Cmnd. 3175. London: HMSO.

David Downes and Rod Morgan

MOWAT, L. W. (1955), *Britain between the Wars, 1918–1940*. London: Methuen.

MURRAY, C. (1994), *Underclass: The Crisis Deepens*. London: Institute of Economic Affairs.

NICHOLAS, H. G. (1951), *The British General Election of 1950*. London: Macmillan.

O'LEARY, B., and MCGARRY, J. (1993), *The Politics of Antagonism: Understanding Northern Ireland*. London: Athlone.

PARKIN, F. (1967), 'Working-Class Conservatives: A Theory of Political Deviance', *British Journal of Sociology*, 18/3: 278–90.

PRIOR REPORT (1985), *Report of the Departmental Committee on the Prison Disciplinary System* (Chairman, Mr Peter Prior), Cmnd. 9641. London: HMSO.

REINER, R. (1992), *The Politics of the Police*, rev. edn. Brighton: Wheatsheaf.

—— and CROSS, M. (1991), 'Introduction', in R. Reiner and M. Cross, eds., *Beyond Law and Order: Criminal Justice Policy into the 1990s*. London: Macmillan.

RICHARDSON, G. (1993), *Law, Custody and Process: Prisoners and Patients*. London: Hamish Hamilton.

ROCK, P. (1986), *A View from the Shadows: The Ministry of the Solicitor General of Canada and the Justice for Victims of Crime Initiative*. Oxford: Clarendon Press.

—— (1995), 'The Opening Stages of Criminal Justice Policy Making', *British Journal of Criminology*, 35: 1–6.

ROSENBAUM, D. (1988), 'A Critical Eye on Neighbourhood Watch: Does it Reduce Crime and Fear?', in T. Hope and M. Shaw, eds., *Communities and Crime Reduction*. London: HMSO.

RUGGIERO, V. (1991), 'Public Opinion and Penal Reform in Britain', *Crime and Social Change*, 15: 37–50.

RUNCIMAN REPORT (1993), *Report of the Royal Commission on Criminal Justice*. Cm 2263, London: HMSO.

RUTHERFORD, A. (1984), *Prisons and the Process of Justice*. London: Heinemann.

—— (1996), *Transforming Criminal Policy*. Winchester: Waterside.

RYAN, M. (1978), *The Acceptable Pressure Group-Inequality in the Penal Lobby: A Case Study of the Howard League and PAP*. Farnborough: Saxon House.

—— (1983), *The Politics of Penal Reform*. London: Longman.

—— and WARD, T. (1989), *Privatization and the Penal System*. Milton Keynes: Open University Press.

SCARMAN REPORT (1981), *The Brixton Disorders 10–12 April 1981*. London: HMSO.

SCHLESINGER, P., and TUMBER, H. (1992), 'Crime and Criminal Justice in the Media', in D. Downes, ed., *Unravelling Criminal Justice*. London: Macmillan.

SCHNEIDER-LENNÉ, E. R. (1992), 'Corporate Control in Germany', *Oxford Review of Economic Policy*, 8: 11–23.

SHEEHY REPORT (1993) *Inquiry into Police Responsibilities and Rewards*. Cm 2280, London: HMSO.

SIM, J. (1993), 'Reforming the Penal Wasteland? A Critical Review of the Woolf Report', in E. Player and M. Jenkins, eds., *Prisons After Woolf*. London: Routledge.

SPENCER, S. (1985), *Called to Account*. London: National Council for Civil Liberties.

STANKO, E. A. (1990), *Everyday Violence*. London: Unwin Hyman.

STEWART, J. D. (1992), *Accountability to the Public*. London: European Police Forum.

TAYLOR, R. K. S. (1988), *Against the Bomb: the British Peace Movement 1958–1965*. Oxford: Clarendon Press.

TULKENS, H. (1979), *Some Developments in Penal Policy and Practice in Holland*. London: National Association for the Care and Resettlement of Offenders.

VON HIRSCH, A. (1976), *Doing Justice: The Choice of Punishments*. New York: Hill and Wang.

——, ASHWORTH, A., WASIK, A., SMITH, A., MORGAN, R., and GARDNER, J. (1995), 'Overtaking on the Right', *New Law Journal*, 145: 1501–16.

WADDINGTON, P. A. J. (1991), *The Strong Arm of the Law*. Oxford: Oxford University Press.

WALLINGTON, P. (1975), 'Criminal Conspiracy and Industrial Conflict', *Industrial Law Journal*, 4: 69–88.

WEBB, B., and LAYCOCK, G. (1992), *Tackling Car Crime: The Nature and Extent of the Problem*, Crime Prevention Unit Paper no. 32. London: Home Office.

WILSON, W. J. (1996) *When Work Disappears: The World of the New Urban Poor*. New York: Knopf.

WOODCOCK REPORT (1994), *Report of the Enquiry into the Escape of Six Prisoners from the Special Security Unit at Whitemoor Prison, Cambridgeshire, on Friday 9th September 1994*, Cm 2741. London: HMSO.

WOOLF REPORT (1991), *Prison Disturbances April 1990: Report of an Inquiry by the Rt Hon. Lord Justice Woolf (Parts I and II) and His Honour Judge Stephen Tumim (Part II)*, Cm 1456. London: HMSO.

YOUNG, J. (1992), 'The Rise in Crime in England and Wales 1979–1990'. Middlesex Polytechnic: Centre for Criminology.

4

Crime Statistics, Patterns, and Trends: Changing Perceptions and their Implications

Mike Maguire

At heart the extent of crime is a political as well as a behavioural matter . . . The figures for crime . . . are not 'hard facts' in the sense that this is true of the height and weight of physical bodies. They are moral not physical statistics. (Young 1988a: 175)

REPAINTING THE CANVAS: THE PRODUCTION OF NEW 'KNOWLEDGE' ABOUT CRIME

This chapter explores a number of interrelated questions regarding the state of our knowledge about 'crime levels', 'crime patterns', and 'crime trends'. These range from what may sound like (but are not) straightforward empirical and methodological questions, such as 'how much crime is there?', 'how is it changing?' and 'how do we find out?', to broader questions about the relationship between, on the one hand, the data which are collected and published about crime and, on the other, the perceptions, ideas, and theories which are formed about it.

A Changed Picture

There is no doubt that the picture of crime painted by such data in Britain in the 1990s is very different from the image which was presented to our predecessors in, say, the early 1950s by the information available at that time. Most obviously, it differs in terms of the number of criminal offences known to have taken place. The annual totals of offences officially recorded by the police and published in *Criminal Statistics* are now more than ten times greater (over five million, compared with around half a million).[1] Moreover, whereas earlier criminologists made only occasional, speculative reference to an

[1] The total number of notifiable offences recorded in 1996 was 5,033,800. Even when increased population is taken into account, the increase has been well over eightfold, from 1.1 offence per 100 population in 1950 to 9.5 per 100 in 1996.

unknown 'dark figure' of unrecorded crime, repeated investigation since 1982 by means of the British Crime Survey has demonstrated to a wide audience that only a minority of incidents which are recognized as 'crimes' by their 'victims' end up in the official statistics.

Equally important, the present picture presents considerably different *patterns* of crime. This is quite striking even among officially recorded offences: for example, crimes involving motor vehicles, relatively rare in the 1950s when there were few cars on the roads, now make up a quarter of the total;[2] offences of criminal damage, then an almost negligible category, now total over 950,000 per year (almost one fifth);[3] and crimes of violence against the person, although still one of the smaller categories, have greatly outgrown in number other important groups, such as sexual and fraudulent offences, which clearly exceeded them in the early 1950s.[4] It should also be remembered that, while the broad offence classifications used then and now in *Criminal Statistics* sound fairly similar ('larceny', 'receiving', 'breaking and entering' and 'frauds and false pretences' mutating into 'theft and handling stolen goods', 'burglary', and 'fraud and forgery'), the kinds of behaviour they cover are in some cases very different: for example, modern 'fraud' offences often involve cheque cards or computers, neither of which were there to be exploited in the 1950s. However, the difference in the overall picture of crime becomes even more dramatic if one looks beyond police statistics to the plethora of other sources of data which have become available over the intervening period. The sustained growth in officially recorded offences has been accompanied by a major growth in public, academic, media, and government attention to the subject of crime, and a corresponding increase in the resources devoted to finding out about it: not least through the establishment of a substantial research unit in the Home Office and the rapid expansion of criminology in universities.[5] As a consequence, more and more kinds of 'private' criminal activity which formerly lay largely hidden from public view—and which remain even now greatly under-represented in recorded crime figures—have

[2] Between 1950 and 1954, thefts of or from vehicles averaged under 45,000 per year, around 9 per cent of all recorded offences.

[3] Between 1950 and 1954, the average annual recorded total of 'malicious injuries to property' was just over 5,000.

[4] In 1996 (in round figures), recorded crimes of 'violence against the person' totalled 239,100, 'sexual offences' 31,200, and offences of fraud and forgery 135,900. Between 1950 and 1955, the average annual totals for the equivalent offences were roughly 6,900, 15,000, and 31,000, respectively. In 1996, crimes classified as violence against the person accounted for 4.7 per cent of all recorded crime; in 1950–4 they accounted for only 1.4 per cent. Particularly striking has been the increase in offences of wounding and assault (from 5,800 to 228,400).

Of course, many argue that robbery (where the figures have increased from 900 to 74,000) and rape (300 to 5,900), if not all sexual offences, should also be counted as violence against the person. *Criminal Statistics* now provides a global figure ('total violent crime'), which includes all the above.

[5] Over the period in question, academic criminology has developed from boasting merely a few lone scholars and only one research institute of any significance, to over 300 academics working countrywide (many in specialist 'Centres' attracting substantial research funds), and a flourishing market for publications. For useful accounts of the growth of post-war criminology, see Rock's (1988) edited Special Issue of the *British Journal of Criminology*.

not only become familiar subjects in television programmes and newspaper articles, but have been studied, described, and analysed in systematic fashion. Prominent among these are intra-household offences (such as domestic violence and child sex abuse), 'white collar' and corporate offences, and crimes between consenting parties (notably drug dealing), none of which attracted any sustained attention in the 1950s.

A third major difference lies in our perceptions of 'criminals'. In the early 1950s, offenders tended to be represented by experts, as well as by politicians and the media, almost as a breed set apart from the rest of society. Most criminological studies were based on samples of male prisoners, the bulk of whom were observed (a) to come from particularly deprived lower class backgrounds and (b) to exhibit a variety of serious social, psychological, or psychiatric 'problems'. 'Criminality' was thus widely regarded as something akin to a medical condition—caused by social or emotional deprivation or other faults in the offender's psyche, upbringing, or environment—which affected relatively small numbers of individuals and which required some form of 'treatment' to 'correct' it (see, for example, Bowlby, 1953).[6] However, it is now known from large-scale cohort studies that over one third of all males (though only 8 per cent of females) born in 1953 had acquired at least one criminal conviction for an indictable offence by the age of 31 (Home Office, 1989, 1993a).[7] Such findings, together with those of interview-based and ethnographic studies, have helped to bring about wider recognition that criminal behaviour is not a near-monopoly of poor and deprived young males. For example, child sex abuse (Baker and Duncan, 1985), domestic violence (Dobash and Dobash, 1992), football hooliganism (Murphy *et al.*, 1990), workplace theft (Ditton, 1977; Mars, 1982) and drug offences (Pearson, 1987) have all been shown to be committed by wide ranges of age groups and social classes—though, as will be discussed later, much less so by females than males. Publicity surrounding individual court cases has also played a part in this process: most obviously, a series of major frauds, some with direct financial consequences for large numbers of ordinary people (BCCI, Maxwell, Barlow Clowes, etc.) have demonstrated for all to see that criminals are to be found in 'suites' as well as on the streets (Levi and Pithouse, 1992).

None of this is to deny that there exist identifiable groups and individuals, many of them young males from deprived and disturbed backgrounds, who commit substantial numbers of the 'conventional' property offences like burglary, shoplifting, and theft from vehicles which make up the bulk of

---

[6] In the early 1950s, the Institute for the Study and Treatment of Delinquency was not only the only criminological centre in Britain, but published the main academic journal (The *British Journal of Delinquency*, later to become the *British Journal of Criminology*). The Institute was staffed mainly by people with a background in psychiatry or psychology (for a history, see Saville and Rumney, 1992).

[7] Cohort studies trace the progress of a given group of people over a long period of time, often from birth to maturity, collecting new data on them at regular intervals. The best known in criminology include cohorts followed by the Gluecks (1950) and by West and Farrington (e.g. 1969).

recorded crimes. Indeed, the authors of the above-mentioned cohort study of criminal careers (Home Office, 1993*a*) found that as many as 60 per cent of all court appearances made by males born in 1953 were attributable to just 7 per cent of the birth cohort, each convicted on four or more occasions.[8] Nor is it to deny that such persistent offenders, whose activities often seriously damage their own and their victims' lives, are worthy of special attention by criminologists, as well as by agents of the criminal justice and penal systems. However, what it should make us wary of are accounts and explanations which proceed as though virtually *all* crime were akin to predatory street crime or burglary, and *all* offenders were afflicted by social or psychological 'problems'.

In at least three important respects, then—dramatically higher totals of known offences, revelations of major 'new' kinds of criminal activity in previously unprobed areas of the social world, and recognition that many offenders are neither psychologically abnormal nor young males from the lower social classes—the phenomenon of crime appears very different to the informed observer in the 1990s from the way it did to his or her counterpart in the 1950s. (On a different tack, it is also worth flagging here a fourth difference—much greater awareness of the experience of crime from the *victim's* point of view—the importance of which will be discussed later.) Of course, the $64,000 question which remains is how much the differences reflect 'real' changes in forms and levels of criminal behaviour over this period and how much they are simply a function of new, improved or differently tuned channels of communication about what is happening 'out there'. No satisfactory answer to this could be expected without a wide-ranging search for relevant (and mainly obscure) historical evidence nor, equally importantly, without a thorough consideration of complex epistemological questions which underlie the differences between what have been called 'realist' and 'institutionalist' approaches to interpreting crime data (Biderman and Reiss, 1967; Bottomley and Coleman, 1981; Coleman and Moynihan, 1996). Such tasks are beyond the scope of this one chapter (though the latter issue will be addressed at a simple level). The more modest aim here is to examine the kinds of data on which our perceptions of the phenomenon of crime are built, outlining some of the main developments in criminology, as well as in other sources of information about crime, which have helped to transform and broaden these perceptions. A few general comments will also be made about the implications for academic criminology of a broad shift of focus which has accompanied the

---

[8] Put differently, this means that 21 per cent of those who had *any* court appearances, accounted for 60 per cent of the total appearances. It is also striking that, among males born in 1973, 40 per cent of all court appearances under the age of 17 were accounted for by offenders with four or more appearances (Home Office, 1993*a*:12). Taken together with the finding that a relatively small proportion (14 per cent) of the 1973 birth cohort had acquired any conviction before the age of 20, this seems to suggest at first sight that youth crime is increasingly concentrated among a relatively small number of prolific offenders, most other young people remaining free of offending. However, as the researchers point out, the change in the pattern may be largely explained by changes in police cautioning policy (*ibid.*: 4).

increased use of large-scale, quantitative methods of data collection: a shift from interest in the *offender* to interest in the *circumstances of the offence*.

Painting by Numbers?

The empirical data most often used by modern criminologists, as well as by policy-makers in the Home Office and elsewhere, derive from three main sources: statistical records routinely compiled by the police and criminal justice agencies; large-scale surveys (usually conducted or commissioned by government departments); and small-scale surveys and studies conducted by academic and other researchers.

With notable exceptions, the central feature of this raw material, and of the use made of it, is the predominance of *numbers* as a descriptive medium. Indeed, a salient feature of almost all modern forms of discourse about crime is the emphasis placed upon terms associated with its quantification and measurement: 'volume', 'extent', 'growth', 'prevalence', 'incidence', 'trends', and so on. In political and media debates, trends in aggregate crime figures are often put forward as evidence of failures or successes in criminal justice policy, or are treated as a sort of social barometer, supposedly indicative of, for example, declining standards of parenting or schooling. Among policy-makers, arguments for an initiative in response to a particular form of crime appear much stronger if accompanied by a convincing numerical represen-tation of 'the scale of the problem'. Criminologists, too, are well aware of the power of the 'language of figures', and even those primarily oriented towards qualitative research methods routinely produce quantitative data to reinforce and 'legitimate' their findings.

At the same time, it is important to note that, while numerical represen-tations of criminal behaviour (including movements or trends in regularly compiled statistics) have a considerable impact on our perceptions of the crime problem, these are by no means the only—nor necessarily the most influential—sources of information or insights about it. In fact, systematic data collection often *follows*, rather than generates, new insights and perspectives. Spectacular or shocking examples of forms of criminal behaviour hitherto considered relatively rare or of only marginal importance, may suddenly attract attention from the media and spark off a trawl for similar events, thus 'uncovering' (or, from another perspective, 'creating') a significant new 'crime problem'. Examples from Britain in the 1980s and early 1990s include the enormous boost in public, academic, and official attention to 'child sex abuse' produced by the Cleveland case (see, for example, Morgan, 1988), to 'corporate crime' by the Robert Maxwell pensions fraud, and to offending by children by the murder of James Bulger (for further discussion of the role of the media in such processes, see Reiner, chapter 5, this volume).

Changes in perception—and in the level of effort devoted to uncovering relevant information—may also be brought about partly through the per-sistence of interest groups who campaign or lobby to get a particular form of behaviour taken more seriously by the police and criminal justice system. This has happened in Britain in relation both to 'domestic violence' and to 'racial attacks'. In the former case, feminist writers and campaigners have done a great deal from the early 1970s onwards to raise awareness of the problem of violence by men against their partners. This has not only generated numerous surveys of the extent of such violence, but—by pressing police to arrest perpetrators, rather than simply noting something like 'domestic incident, advice given'—has had the effect of creating more official records of its incidence. Similarly, pressure from ethnic minority groups, and latterly from organizations such as Victim Support, led in the 1980s to police forces routinely recording and publishing data on the numbers and types of crimes in which there was thought to have been a racial motive.

Some writers—among the best known being Hall *et al.* (1978)—have claimed that a further source of new representations of the crime problem lies in the deliberate manufacture of specific 'crime waves' by governments (with assistance from the police and the media) during economic recessions, when their popularity is low and/or the legitimacy of the class-based social structure is weakened. Hall *et al.*'s main example was the 'mugging' scare in the early 1970s, which was created, they claimed, to focus public hostility upon, and justify greater social control over, the unemployed young black populations of inner cities. They pointed out that 'mugging' is a term which does not correspond to a legal offence category, and that the racially differentiated statistics issued by the Metropolitan Police department which fuelled the scare were highly unreliable (for further discussion, see Levi, this volume). Types of behaviour which government ministers have 'talked up' during the 1990s as meriting a stronger response—arguably exaggerating their prevalence and importance for political reasons—include 'benefit fraud', 'youth crime' (a vague, catch-all category, sometimes extended to anti-social behaviour by very young children), and actions involving trespass by 'squatters', 'travellers', 'rave' party-goers, and other socially marginalized groups.[9] No doubt similar arguments could be applied to such cases—though to what extent they represent cynical political plots and to what extent the driving forces have been public experiences and concerns, remains a matter for debate.

Whatever the source of the initial attention, if public and media interest in a particular form of activity reaches a sufficient level the result is likely to be some form of 'deviancy amplification' (Young, 1971) or 'moral panic' (the much-used term coined by Cohen (1973) in his study of social reaction to the emergence of 'mods and rockers'). In other words, as interest mounts,

---

[9] Not to be outdone, the opposition Labour Party attempted to improve its chances of election by denouncing the behaviour of 'squeegee merchants' (people who demand money for cleaning car windscreens at traffic lights) and 'aggressive beggars'. The government attack on socially marginalized groups was more than rhetorical, as legislation was passed to criminalize behaviour which had previously been covered only by civil law: the Criminal Justice and Public Order Act 1994 created the new criminal offence of 'aggravated trespass'. The Act also had the effect of criminalizing many of the activities of politically active groups such as road protesters and hunt saboteurs, with more obvious implications for civil liberties.

journalists discover and highlight new examples of the activity, heightened awareness of it among the public leads more people to report instances to the police (and perhaps more people to engage in it themselves), researchers begin to seek grants to investigate its 'scale' in a more systematic way, policy-makers ask agencies to keep new kinds of records, and politicians call for government action to respond to what is now judged to be a mounting problem. Such situations almost always involve a 'self-fulfilling prophecy' as the different elements of the process feed off each other, and it becomes extremely difficult to disentangle them in subsequent analyses of what happened—not least, to determine whether there ever was any 'real' increase in the relevant behaviour.

Fundamental Problems

The above examples serve as a useful introduction to some of the fundamental problems which are faced by anyone wishing to make general statements about the nature and extent of crime. They help, especially, to illustrate the point that the core object of study—'crime'—is, ultimately, a *social construct*. Looked at as an abstract formal category, it consists of a diverse set of behaviours which have in common (perhaps only) the fact that they are proscribed by the criminal law. The law, of course, changes over time, new offences being created and others being redefined or decriminalized, so that, even if we had god-like vision to spot every possible transgression, it would be difficult to make comparative statements about the 'level of crime' over a period of years (let alone comparing countries with different laws). More importantly, though, such statements would lack social meaning, which derives from the application in the real world of the label 'crime' or 'criminal' to specific incidents and people, *out of a much wider set of possible candidates for such a label*. This necessitates recognition by those involved in (or witnessing or hearing about) an incident, both that a crime has been committed and that this fact is of some significance to them or others. In most cases, too, for the event to have any publicly visible consequences requires its notification to the police and subsequent incorporation into official records as a specific criminal offence. Despite the apparently precise wording of legislation, such categorization is anything but mechanical and value-free: it is highly selective and value-laden, the product of complex social, political, and organizational processes.

One of the recurrent academic criticisms made of criminologists (particularly by sociologists) has been that they have tended to avoid serious consideration of these kinds of issues and their implications for the status of empirical knowledge in the subject. Partly because of the importance of government grants in the funding of research, it has been pointed out, the overall 'agenda' of criminology has always been heavily influenced, explicitly or implicitly, by the current (and often short-lived) preoccupations of legislators, policy-makers, and practitioners. Yet criminologists have often failed to acknowledge this or to take full account of the problematic nature of data, concepts, and categories which derive from official and institutional sources. Worse, some have claimed a spurious 'scientific' status for research and conclusions based solely upon such data: for example, treating samples of convicted offenders as though they were naturally occurring objects, the examination of which will reveal their inherent distinguishing properties (for one of the best-known and most extensive critiques of this 'positivist' tradition, see Taylor, Walton, and Young 1973; see also Garland, this volume). While—for reasons explained in the next section—such criticism is much less fair nowadays than in the past, it is still all too easy, especially for those engaged in government-funded research, to slip into unquestioning acceptance of policy-driven definitions and agendas.

There is still a tendency, too, to present the accumulation of data about unreported crime as the gradual unveiling of more and more of the 'complete picture', the 'true total' of criminal offences committed. However, if one takes seriously the argument that sequences of human activity become individually definable and quantifiable as 'crimes' only as the end product of a complex and constantly shifting array of interactive and interpretative social processes, the notion of a 'real', empirically discoverable total of offences becomes an absurdity.[10] A more appropriate metaphor for the production of criminological knowledge might be the constant repainting—by a motley army of artists with different styles and techniques—of a canvas of indeterminate size, each time highlighting new areas or depicting old areas in greater detail or different form.[11]

Finally, however, it is important to stress that awareness of the shaky foundations of criminological knowledge does not mean that one should abandon the collection and use of statistical data about crime. Certainly, it is important to recognize that, if presented in mechanical fashion without any deeper comprehension of their relationship to the reality they purport to represent, they can grossly distort the social meaning of events as understood by those experiencing or witnessing them. Ultimately, too, it is right to ask whether 'crime' (or any particular category of crime) is a phenomenon which can sensibly be described simply by adding up totals of diverse actions and incidents. On the other hand, *so long as their limitations are fully recognized*, crime-related statistics undoubtedly offer a valuable aid to understanding and explanation, as well as to the very necessary task of description. The key point to take from this preliminary discussion is that no conclusions should ever be drawn from any such data without a clear understanding of how they were compiled and what they represent.

[10] This view is not difficult to uphold if one is talking about 'all crime', or indeed about many specific classes of offence (for example, attempts to count 'assaults' involve subjective judgements about justification and intent, as well as level of injury—cf. Levi, this volume). However, it can be argued that some kinds of offence are so clear-cut, or are possible only in such limited circumstances, that there can be little argument about whether or not instances have occurred, and hence they can be quantified with some confidence: an extreme example might be the hijacking of aircraft.

[11] I am grateful to Clive Coleman and Jenny Moynihan (1996: 20–1) for improving my original metaphor by adding the notion of artists with different styles.

KEY INFLUENCES: THE 'NEW CRIMINOLOGY', VICTIMS, AND THE SITUATIONAL FOCUS

In order to gain a better understanding of how and why criminologists' ways of looking at crime—and of producing and interpreting information about it—have changed over the past fifty years, it is necessary first to make brief reference to three highly influential factors: the huge upheaval in the subject generated by 'deviancy theorists' and others in the late 1960s and early 1970s; the growing focus, during the 1980s, upon victims of crime; and the increased attention given in Home Office policy to crime prevention and opportunity reduction through alteration of the physical environment.

The Paradigm Shift in the 1970s

For much of the twentieth century, British criminology was dominated (though by no means monopolized—see Garland, this volume) by what has since been widely, and often disparagingly, referred to as the 'positivist' tradition.[12] Many criminologists were people with backgrounds in medicine or psychiatry, for whom the central goal was to understand and explain—and hence point the way to 'treatment' for—the 'criminality' of individual offenders. On the whole, their work was characterized by uncritical acceptance of narrow, conventional definitions of 'the crime problem'. Most were content to restrict their inquiries to officially defined offenders, focusing upon the predominantly male, lower-class 'recidivists' (repeat offenders) who provided the bread-and-butter work of the police and courts, and the majority of whom were convicted of a limited range of predatory property crimes such as burglary and petty theft. Some, as advocated by Sellin (1938), preferred to define their focus of inquiry according to social, rather than legal, categories of disapproved behaviour, using terms such as 'delinquency' or 'anti-social' or 'socially harmful' behaviour, rather than 'crime' (see, for example, Burt, 1944; Bowlby, 1953; West and Farrington, 1969). However, particularly during the 1950s and early 1960s as middle-class fears of the 'youth culture' increased, their attention was almost always directed at readily visible kinds of norm-violation, especially in cultural forms commonly displayed by working-class adolescents.[13] In either case, with the emphasis upon finding out what was 'wrong with' those who engaged in such activities, there was relatively little curiosity about other, more 'hidden' forms of crime, particularly those

---

[12] Positivism as a distinct, self-proclaimed 'school' is principally associated with the work of Italian scholars such as Ferri (1913) and Garofalo (1914), who had a major influence in the institutionalization of criminology in the USA in the early years of the 20th century.

[13] Many 'delinquency' studies included behaviour such as under-age smoking or drinking, 'horseplay' in groups on the street, truanting, and even rudeness to schoolteachers (see, for example, West and Farrington, 1969; Belson, 1968). Apart from general concern about 'rebelliousness', another reason for the concentration on youth was that this was regarded as one of the areas in which policy intervention was most likely to have an impact.

practised by more powerful social groups; and 'crime' itself continued to be treated essentially as an unproblematic concept.

However, since the late 1960s, when, galvanized by a new generation of scholars with a strong interest in sociological theory, the discipline began to burst out of its positivist strait-jacket, the task of understanding and explaining crime has been interpreted in a variety of new ways. The immediate impetus came from the work of American sociologists, including the influential 'labelling' theorists (e.g. Becker, 1963; Kitsuse, 1964), who popularized the argument that 'crime' (or 'deviance') was not an independently existing phenomenon, but simply a label attached for a variety of reasons to diverse forms of behaviour. In the words of Erikson (1964): 'Deviance is not a property inherent in certain forms of behaviour, it is a property conferred upon those forms by the audience which directly or indirectly witness them.' Their influence, mediated at first in Britain through the work of 'deviancy' theorists such as Rock (1973) and Cohen (1974), helped to initiate a broad shift in the focus of inquiry and level of explanation, away from 'the pathology of the criminal' towards 'the social construction of crime'—the social and political processes by which particular forms of activity and the actions of particular groups within society are (or are not) 'criminalized'. The way was thus opened to the growth of new academic schools such as interactionism, radical criminology, and socio-legal studies, which, though deeply split on many other grounds, shared this basic interest. Some writers engaged in macro-level analyses of the relationships between the interests of the ruling classes, the state and the shaping of 'crime' through the criminal law (see Taylor, Walton, and Young, 1975). Others, influenced by the work of other American sociologists such as Skolnick (1966), Cicourel (1968), and Manning (1977), conducted micro-level studies of the daily interactions through which legal and social rules are interpreted and deviant or criminal identities are created. This included exploration of systematic biases by the police and criminal justice system in the invocation and enforcement of legal rules (see Holdaway 1979; Bottomley and Coleman, 1981).

Among their many other influences, such approaches made virtually all criminologists distinctly more wary of accepting, as representations of an 'objective reality', the pictures of crime and criminals which are painted by official police and court records. These data, it became widely understood, created not just an *incomplete* picture of crime—through lacking the 'dark figure' of crimes not reported to the police—but a *systematically biased* picture of crime. Criminal statistics had to be analysed as the product, not of a neutral fact-collecting process, but of a record-keeping process which is geared first and foremost to organizational (primarily police) aims and needs. As such, they may tell us more about the organization producing them than about the 'reality' they are later taken to describe. In the words of Wiles (1971:188):

Criminal statistics are based on data collected not by agencies designed to collect information about crime, but agencies designed to enforce the law. The statistics which result are part of the attempt to achieve that goal. The nineteenth century political economists were right in seeing the collection of statistics by such agencies as part of the process of government, but the implication of this for the sociological study of crime is that statistics themselves must be explained, rather than that they provide data for the explanation.

This line of argument led some writers to conclude that there was no point in analysing crime figures for the purpose of finding out anything about the extent of any kind of illegal behaviour—if, indeed, it made any sense to speak of 'real' crime rates at all. For them, crime rates were simply 'indices of organisational processes' (Kitsuse and Cicourel, 1963) or 'an aspect of social organisation' (Black 1970), worthy of study only to help one understand the agency producing them.[14] This 'institutionalist', as opposed to 'realist', approach was also broadly the starting position adopted by Bottomley and Coleman (1981) in a major empirical study of crime-recording processes in police stations. However, although the study revealed a great deal about the influence of specific police interests, attitudes, and decisions in the creation of official statistics, the authors also reached the important conclusion that the decisions of many other people and agencies (notably personal and commercial victims, who between them initiate the vast majority of recorded crimes) had as much, if not more, to do with the overall 'shaping' of the figures.

This growing scepticism about the value of information from official sources had the further effect of raising criminologists' awareness of the rich potential of alternative sources of knowledge about crime, such as ethnographic or participant observation studies and data from agencies other than the police. Importantly, too, studies began to appear of previously neglected and largely hidden areas of 'deviant' and/or 'criminal' activity, such as drugtaking, workplace 'fiddles', corporate crime, domestic violence and sexual violence against women (examples being, respectively, Young, 1970; Ditton, 1977; Levi, 1981; Dobash and Dobash, 1979; Hanmer and Saunders, 1984).

The Perspective from the Victim

The search for new forms of knowledge generated a fertile period for British criminology in terms of theory and ideas, but it should be stressed that, with the emphasis upon understanding social processes rather than upon description or measurement, it did not immediately produce much new information in *statistical* form. On the contrary, there was a period when the climate in many parts of the discipline was distinctly *anti*-statistical, those who employed quantitative methodologies frequently being derided as 'mere empiricists'. In many cases, then, the new information acquired was qualitative (based, for example, on small numbers of detailed case studies) rather than quantitative.

---

[14] An alternative view was put forward by Taylor, Walton, and Young (1975), who argued that the statistics could be usefully analysed to reveal truths about the importance attached to various forms of property under a capitalist economy.

A marked change came about in the early to mid-1980s, fuelled to a large extent by a growth in attention to crime *victims*. This perspective, which had already been prominent for over ten years in the United States, rapidly began to affect the thinking of large numbers of British criminologists and policy-makers, informing debates about, *inter alia*, the relative rights of victims and offenders, policing policy, crime prevention, court processes, mediation, racial harassment, and male oppression of women (for overviews, see Zedner, this volume; Maguire and Pointing, 1988; Walklate, 1989; Heidensohn, 1989; Maguire, 1991; Davis *et al.*, 1997). More important for our purposes here, it has had the general effect of focusing attention much more upon the *offence* than the *offender*, including the production of large amounts of detailed information about where, when, how and against whom different types of crime are (or are likely to be) committed.

An early British example of a victim-focused study was Maguire and Bennett's work on residential burglary (Maguire 1982).[15] The researchers described it as a 'crime-specific' study: a detailed look at one particular form of crime, the circumstances under which it is committed, the motives and behaviour of those committing it, and the experiences of its victims. They mapped every burglary recorded by the police over various periods in three separate areas and conducted 'in-depth' interviews with as many of the victims as possible about the precise circumstances of the incident. A number of recurrent patterns were found, such as that burglaries tended to be clustered either in poorer housing areas or in more expensive properties close to main roads on the edges of towns; and that individual houses were more likely to be burgled if situated near road junctions or if they offered good cover (e.g. high hedges or fences) or access (e.g. rear or side alleys) to potential offenders. These patterns were tentatively explained in terms of interactions between, on the one hand, variations in the attractiveness of targets and in the risks and opportunities they offered and, on the other, the aims, thought processes and behaviour patterns of different types of offender (juvenile and adult, local and travelling, and so on). Findings of this kind, which also emerged from other studies of burglary in the United Kingdom (e.g. Winchester and Jackson, 1982; Bennett and Wright, 1984) and North America (Reppetto, 1974; Waller and Okihiro, 1978; Brantingham and Brantingham, 1975) contributed to a more general and growing theoretical interest in crime patterns as, for example, the product of 'opportunity' (Mayhew *et al.*, 1976) or as a by-product of 'routine activities' (Cohen and Felson, 1979). They also helped to stimulate attention to the decision-making processes of potential offenders in response to differential opportunities to steal, which later found theoretical expression

---

[15] Several North American studies, illustrating the value of attempting to understand crime through detailed information from or about victims, had been carried out considerably earlier. These include Von Hentig's (1948) classic, *The Criminal and his Victim*, Wolfgang's (1959) work on criminal homicide, and Amir's (1971) controversial study of forcible rape. Waller and Okihiro (1978) had also carried out a similar victim-oriented study of burglary in Canada.

in, among other approaches, 'rational choice theory' (Cornish and Clarke, 1986), as well as informing new approaches to crime prevention (see next section).

However, whatever their value in these respects, the obvious weakness of these burglary studies, as of most other crime-specific studies (e.g. Banton, 1985, on robbery), remained their reliance upon offences recorded by the police. Consequently, a far more influential factor in shifting criminological attention towards victims and the physical circumstances of offences—and in altering general perceptions about patterns of crime—was the investment of a substantial amount of government money, in 1982, in a method of gathering data nationwide on the incidence of *unrecorded* crime: the first British Crime Survey (BCS). Initially conceived primarily as a means of investigating the size of the 'dark figure', crime surveys (sometimes also called 'victim surveys') have developed into a flexible and rewarding research tool, gathering all kinds of details about the circumstances of offences, the relationships between offenders and victims, and the reactions of victims to what happened. It can plausibly be claimed that the BCS was the most significant development in British criminology during the 1980s, and its influence has remained strong through its repetition at regular intervals (the most recent, at the time of writing, being 1996). It will be discussed in more depth later in the chapter, together with comments on other kinds of crime survey.

New Thinking about Crime Prevention

Another factor in the shift of focus towards the offence, rather than the offender, was the growing disillusionment among influential policy-makers with the idea that crime can be controlled solely—or even principally—through the actions of the police and criminal justice system (cf. Brody, 1976; Clarke and Hough, 1984). Faced with the apparent failure of the police, courts and prisons to stem rising crime rates, the Home Office Research Unit, under the headship of Ronald Clarke, began a clear policy shift from the late 1970s towards research and initiatives in the area of crime prevention, in the sense of attempting to alter the physical environment, rather than the offender. This led eventually to the formation of a separate research unit, the Home Office Crime Prevention Unit.

The distinctive contribution of Home Office research during the early and mid-1980s was the development of 'situational crime prevention'. Eschewing any interest in what Clarke (1980) called 'dispositional' theories of crime (i.e. that certain people have a predisposition to offend and hence that the key to crime prevention lies in changing them), it set out to use detailed crime pattern analysis to pinpoint areas of the environment which could be altered in such a way as to make it less easy or less attractive for potential offenders to commit particular types of crime. The alteration might be through any of a variety of initiatives, including extra physical security, new design of buildings or vehicles, increased surveillance and the marking of property (for overviews and examples, see Clarke and Mayhew, 1980; Heal and Laycock, 1986; Pease, this volume).

This 'targeting' approach necessitated detailed knowledge about the prevalence, geographical and temporal patterning, as well as the physical 'mechanics', of particular offences, thus stimulating the Home Office to fund much more empirical research in these areas. At the same time, the already declining proportion of government funding which was granted for research into subjects connected with the psychology or social problems of individual offenders, shrank to virtually nil.

For these and other reasons, then—including a general expansion of interest in issues such as public sector accountability and managerial efficiency, which led to more research examining the data collection practices of crime-related agencies—criminology began to benefit from a rapidly growing storehouse of empirical data about the frequency, location, and physical circumstances of many kinds of criminal incidents. Since the beginning of the 1980s there have been, *inter alia*, a regularly repeated national crime survey, several substantial local crime surveys, various 'victimization' surveys of businesses, 'in-depth' interview studies of victims of specific types of offence, analyses of police message pads (as opposed to the traditional dependence on crime files) and trawls of data held by hospitals and other agencies to which people reveal 'crimes' they fail to report to the police. The most important of these will be discussed in some detail below. However, before commenting further about the explosion of new knowledge, it is time to take a closer look at the traditional sources of information and the basic picture of crime they produce.

THE OFFICIAL PICTURE

The key official publication in respect of crime figures is *Criminal Statistics*, the annual compilation of data derived from police and court records throughout England and Wales, which is collated and tabulated by the Home Office Research and Statistics Directorate.[16] Despite the caution with which they are now treated by criminologists and Home Office statisticians alike, and despite the increasingly high profile given in *Criminal Statistics* to comparative data from the British Crime Survey (see below), these statistics remain the primary 'barometer of crime' used by politicians and highlighted in the media. They are also—a use to which they are much better suited—influential in the resource and strategic planning of the Home Office and police forces. We now consider, briefly, how the police-generated statistics are constructed and what they

---

[16] Mention should also be made of the relatively new *Digest of Information on the Criminal Justice System* (Home Office, 1991, 1993*b*, 1995), which provides an excellent 'user friendly' summary of key statistics, using coloured graphs, bar charts, and pie charts, as well as of the half-yearly *Home Office Statistical Bulletin* (headed 'Notifiable Offences'), which publishes a brief summary of the latest six months' figures quite soon after they have been collected.

indicate about the total volume of crime, the relative frequencies of different offences, their geographical distribution, and broad trends over recent years. Later in the chapter, we shall also examine what the statistics based on court records appear to tell us about the characteristics of offenders.

Total Volume of Crime

The latest official figures available at the time of writing (Home Office, 1997) indicate that the total number of 'notifiable offences' recorded by the police in England and Wales in 1996 was just over five million.[17] Although this is the global figure referred to in most public debates about the extent of crime, it has to be emphasized that, *even as a record of criminal offences officially known to the authorities*, it is anything but complete. Notifiable offences are largely, though not fully, co-terminous with 'indictable' offences—i.e. those which may be tried in a Crown Court (Home Office, 1996*a*: 27).[18] This means that a large number of *summary* offences (i.e. those triable only in magistrates' courts) do not appear in the figures. No records are kept of the totals of such offences, although statistics are available on the numbers of people officially sanctioned for them. For example, in 1995, about 1.2 million people were convicted or formally cautioned for summary offences: a total, it is worth noting, well over double that of people convicted or cautioned for indictable offences.[19]

In addition, the 'official crime figures' do not include offences recorded by police forces for which the Home Office is not responsible, notably the British Transport Police, Ministry of Defence Police and UK Atomic Energy Authority Police, who between them record about 80,000 notifiable offences annually.[20] Nor, more significantly in terms of numbers, do they include numerous cases of tax and benefit fraud known to agencies such as Inland Revenue, Customs and Excise, and the Department of Social Security, which have investigative and prosecutional functions but which deal with the vast majority of cases by using their administrative powers to impose financial penalties (Levi, 1993). Again, such agencies keep internal records of the numbers of people dealt with in these ways, or of the total amounts of revenue saved, but not of the total numbers of 'offences' coming to their notice—a task which, given that a single offender may repeat the same kinds of fraud numerous times over a period, would require complex counting rules.

[17] Statistics on police-recorded crime are now issued every six months in summary form in Home Office *Statistical Bulletins*, less than three months in arrears. Detailed breakdowns are given in the annual *Criminal Statistics*, which take much longer to appear.

[18] 'Indictable' is used here as shorthand for offences which are either 'triable only on indictment' (i.e. in Crown Court) or 'triable either way' (i.e. in either Crown or Magistrates Court) under the 1977 Criminal Law Act.

[19] More than half of the summary offences were motoring offences, but even excluding these, more people were convicted or cautioned for summary offences (569,000) than for indictable offences (504,000) (Home Office, 1996*a*: 90).

[20] A number of these, in fact, overlap with offences recorded by the police, owing to joint operations or joint processing of cases. These agencies have published separate totals of notifiable offences since 1989.

It might be argued that, for practical purposes, it is perfectly adequate to judge the size and shape of 'the crime problem' by means of the notifiable offences recorded by the police, on the grounds that these embrace the most serious crimes, for which the vast majority of prison sentences are passed. However, they also include large numbers of incidents which it is difficult to claim are any more serious than many of the summary offences and the offences dealt with administratively, referred to above. For example, among the largest categories of notifiable offences, together making up around two-fifths of the total recorded, are theft from a vehicle, criminal damage, and theft from shops: most cases in these categories involve relatively small amounts of loss or damage. Again, attempts to commit notifiable offences are included, along with completed crimes. Meanwhile, not only do unprosecuted tax and benefit frauds often involve considerable sums of money, but among the uncounted (non-notifiable) summary offences are common assault, assault on a police officer, cruelty to children, driving after consuming alcohol, and indecent exposure, all of which include acts arguably more serious than many of the above-mentioned notifiable offences.

Changing views about the seriousness or otherwise of particular kinds of offence have led on occasion to changes in Home Office decisions about what to include in or exclude from the official crime totals. Most notably, prior to 1977, offences of criminal damage of £20 or less—which were not indictable—were not counted, but since that date they have been defined as notifiable and included. This decision immediately raised the 'total volume of crime' by about 7 per cent.[21]

In addition to the issue of which categories of offence are included, there are important questions to ask about how individual crimes are counted. Some kinds of offence tend to be repeated many times within a short period, to the extent that, though there may be several separate actions or people involved, they may be considered to form part of one concerted criminal incident. For example, a thief may go through twenty trouser pockets in a changing-room, or try the doors of a whole row of cars, or steal a cheque card and use it many times to obtain goods or cash. Equally, a large affray—for example, at a demonstration or a football match—may involve numerous assaults by many people on many others; or a man may assault his partner virtually every night for a period of months or years.

Prior to 1968, there was little consistency between police forces on how many offences to record when events of these kinds came to their notice. Following the recommendations of the Perks Committee in 1967, clearer 'counting rules' were established (Home Office, 1971), which tidied up some of the discrepancies between forces, but at the same time appear fairly arbitrary and, undoubtedly, understate the relative frequency of some offences.[22] The

[21] This is recognized in *Criminal Statistics* when comparisons are required between pre- and post-1977 figures, adjustments being made to the relevant tables. However, such comparisons are further complicated by the problem of inflation.

[22] These rules were revised again in 1980.

general rule is now that, if several offences are committed 'in one incident', only the most serious is counted: that is, unless violence is involved, in which case the rule is 'one offence for each victim'. There is also a broad (and by no means clear) guideline stating that only one offence will be counted in a 'continuous series of offences, where there is some special relationship, knowledge or position that exists between the offender and the person or property offended against which enables the offender to repeat the offence'. Thus, in the above examples, the changing room thief, the cheque fraudster, and the spouse abuser are likely to be credited with only one crime apiece, while the affray may produce quite a large number of offences. If the rule were changed, for example, to allow all cheque frauds to be counted separately, the overall 'official' picture of crime might look significantly different.

The illustrations we have looked at all demonstrate that statements about the 'total volume of crime' have to be hedged about with qualifications, even when they purport only to describe crimes officially known to state agencies: if different notification or counting rules were adopted (let alone new offences being created by legislation), the total could be raised or lowered significantly at a stroke.

However, the problems of police statistics are by no means restricted to formal questions of definition or rules of inclusion and exclusion. Not only do the figures (obviously) not include offences known to the public which fail to come to police notice, but a great deal of discretion remains in police hands about whether and how to record possible offences which do come to their notice. Reports from the public—which are the source of over 80 per cent of all recorded crimes (McCabe and Sutcliffe, 1978; Bottomley and Coleman, 1981)—may be disbelieved, or considered too trivial, or deemed not to constitute a criminal offence, with the result that they are either not recorded at all, or are officially 'no crimed' later. They may also be excluded ('cuffed') for less defensible reasons, such as to avoid work or to improve the overall clear-up rate (Bottomley and Coleman, 1981).[23] Calculations from crime survey data indicate that about 40 per cent of 'crimes' reported to the police do not end up in the official statistics, for good or bad reasons (Mayhew and Maung, 1992).

Equally, the numbers of offences 'discovered' by the police themselves—either in the course of patrols or observation, or through admissions by arrested offenders—are subject to all kinds of fluctuation. For example, planned operations against a particular type of offence will usually result in a considerable increase in arrests and the uncovering and recording of many new offences. This is particularly true of operations against 'victimless' crimes: for

---

[23] The more 'hopeless' cases, in terms of their potential for detection, that are omitted from the figures, the higher the proportion detected (the clear-up rate) is likely to be. If a division's or force's clear-up rate is exceptionally low, officers (especially those in the CID) can expect criticism from management as well as, in some cases the media. There is thus some incentive to 'massage' local crime statistics to avoid such criticism (for a first hand account of police behaviour in this respect: see Young, 1991).

example, a pop festival is almost guaranteed to generate a sudden dramatic boost in an area's recorded drug offences. Conversely, numbers may fall owing to a withdrawal of police interest in a particular type of crime, as in the late 1950s and early 1960s when, pending anticipated legislation to legalize homosexuality, most forces turned a blind eye to instances of 'indecency between males' and the recorded total of such offences declined to half the level previously regarded as 'normal' (Walker, 1971). The current rapid development of 'crime management' and 'proactive' policing systems based on the selective use of surveillance and informants to 'catch offenders in the act' (Audit Commission, 1993; Maguire and John 1996a, 1996b) is likely to have a significant impact upon the patterns of offences which come to light through police activity.

Types of Crime

Criminal Statistics currently lists the notifiable crimes recorded by the police under a total of sixty-four headings, each of them assigned a Home Office classification number (murder is no. 1, attempted murder no. 2, threat or conspiracy to murder no. 3, and so on). These are grouped under eight broader headings, namely 'offences of violence against the person', 'sexual offences', 'robbery', 'burglary', 'theft and handling stolen goods', 'fraud and forgery', 'criminal damage', and 'other notifiable offences'. Most of these groups contain a considerable variety of offences, in terms of both context and seriousness, but most are dominated numerically by just one or two. Thus the category 'violence against the person' includes offences as diverse as murder, causing death by reckless driving and concealment of birth, but over 90 per cent of its total is accounted for by what is referred to in the tables as 'other wounding etc.'—the largest category of which is offences of assault occasioning actual bodily harm (which tend to involve fists or feet rather than knives or other weapons). Similarly, 'sexual offences' range from rape to bigamy to indecency between males, but over half consist of indecent assault on a female. In other words, a relatively small number of offence categories play a major part in determining both the overall crime total and the size of each offence group in relation to the others. Moreover, trends in these dominant offence types tend to disguise countertrends in less prolific offences. Table 4.1 shows in simplified form the contributions of the main offence groups to the total number of offences recorded by the police in 1996. It also separates out 'autocrime' (the theft or unauthorized taking of, or theft from, motor vehicles) from other forms of theft.

If one looks at the figures as a whole, the picture of the 'crime problem' which emerges is one dominated by *property offences*, and above all by *theft associated with vehicles*. The 'theft and handling' group as a whole, with over 2,380,000 recorded offences, constitutes almost half of the sum total, with 'autocrime' alone accounting for 26 per cent. Burglary—primarily a property offence, though with the added (and often disturbing) element of trespass—

Table 4.1 Notifiable offences recorded by the police, 1996

	Number (to the nearest 1,000)	Per cent
Offence group		
Theft of/from vehicles	1,293,000	26
Other theft/handling	1,090,000	22
Burglary	1,164,000	23
Criminal damage	951,000	19
Violence (inc. robbery)	344,000	7
Fraud and forgery	136,000	3
Sexual offences	31,000	<1
Other	56,000	100
Total	5,034,000	100

Source: Adapted from *Notifiable Offences, England and Wales 1996*, Home Office Statistical Bulletin 3/97, London: Home Office, 1997.

makes up nearly another quarter of the total, and criminal damage almost one-fifth. The numbers of fraudulent, violent, and sexual offences appear very small in comparison.

The fact that offences against the person make up such a small proportion of all recorded crime has quite often been quoted in a reassuring tone, especially to support the argument that the popular media focus too strongly upon violence and distort its importance within the overall crime picture (see Reiner, this volume). However, the statistics can be misleading without an acknowledgement of the relative importance of violent offences judged by criteria other than sheer numbers: for example, in terms of public concern, the effects upon victims, or the number and length of prison sentences they attract. Sexual assaults, robberies, and woundings have been found to have a profound emotional impact on much higher proportions of victims than is the case with offences of theft (Maguire and Corbett, 1987). Fear of violence also severely restricts the social lives of many people (Maxfield, 1984; Young, Zedner, this volume). Strikingly, too, on any one day one cares to select, well over *40 per cent* of the total population of convicted prisoners will be found to be serving sentences for violent or sexual offences. By contrast, people sentenced for the much more common offences of theft, handling, fraud, and forgery (all of whom tend to attract considerably lighter sentences than violent offenders) together make up only about 12 per cent of the convicted prison population (Home Office, 1996*b*).[24]

Related comments can be made about fraud, where both the frequency and

[24] It should be noted that the proportion of violent offenders among *receptions* into prison (the other main statistic used to monitor trends in the use of imprisonment) is considerably lower: their prominence among the *population* reflects the disproportionate length of their sentences.

seriousness of offences known to the authorities are undoubtedly greater than the published police figures suggest. First, as explained earlier, the counting rules cause a great number of repetitive fraudulent acts, especially those involving cheque cards and false entries in accounts, to be recorded as only one or two 'sample' offences. Secondly, many fraudulent tax or benefit offences are dealt with administratively by the Inland Revenue, Customs and Excise, or Social Security departments, rather than as 'crimes'. Thirdly, if one measures the importance of property offences in terms of the value stolen, rather than the quantity of incidents, fraud comes out as of enormously greater significance than other categories. For example, Levi (1993) points out that the *minimum* criterion for cases to be accepted for investigation by the Serious Fraud Office is a fraud of £5 million, and that in April 1992 the Frauds Divisions of the Crown Prosecution Service were supervising cases involving nearly £4 billion. By contrast, the combined costs of the prolific offences of 'autocrime' and burglary for 1990 were estimated by the Association of British Insurers at under £1.3 billion. (Levi also points out that the alleged fraud in any one of several major cases—Barlow Clowes, Guinness, Maxwell, BCCI, Polly Peck—*alone* exceeded the total amount stolen in thefts and burglaries recorded by the police.)

This problem of minor offences 'counting' the same as major offences was recognized many years ago by Sellin and Wolfgang (1964), who devised a weighted index, based on the notional gravity of each recorded offence, which could be used to present an alternative picture of crime in any jurisdiction. This, they argued, would allow more realistic comparisons of the seriousness of the crime problem, either over time or in different cities, states, or countries. In brief, the authors attached a different score to each category of crime, based upon ratings of seriousness derived from interviews with random samples of the population. They were encouraged to discover a fair degree of agreement among raters, both about the order in which they placed offences and the degree of difference in 'seriousness' between them.

Various comparisons were carried out in the United States between changes in officially recorded crime rates and changes in 'crime rates' as measured by the Sellin-Wolfgang index. Some interesting results emerged—for example, Normandeau (1969) found some contrary trends in robbery in Philadelphia, as measured by the index and by the official Uniform Crime Rates—but at the end of the day, most criminologists abandoned it as both of dubious validity and dubious utility. Lesieur and Lehman (1975), for example, doubted whether seriousness is 'one kind of thing' that can be ordered along a scale as on a ruler, let alone whether adding up the scores would produce a total which had any meaning at all (see also Nettler, 1978). Such questions, of course, are also pertinent to debates about sentencing on the basis of 'just deserts'—whether it is possible to design 'fair' scales of punishment within which each type of crime is allocated a sentence deemed proportionate to its seriousness (for contrasting views, see Von Hirsch, 1986, and Hudson, 1987; for an overview, see Ashworth, this volume).

Finally, a long-standing criticism of the presentation of official statistics (see, e.g., McLintock and Avison, 1968) has been that they do not give a clear picture of the social or situational context of crimes. For example, 'robbery' includes actions as diverse as an organized bank raid, the theft at knifepoint of the contents of a shopkeeper's till, and a drunken attempt to snatch a handbag or necklace in the street. Knowing that 74,000 robberies were recorded in 1996, or that this represented an increase of 9 per cent over 1995, tells us very little about the events, nor whether different styles of robbery are declining or becoming more prevalent. Until recently, the only offences for which any attempt was made in *Criminal Statistics* to illustrate the context were homicide and offences involving firearms. Information is regularly provided in homicide cases about the age and sex of the victim, the relationship between the principal suspect and the victim, and the method of killing used. For example, in 1995 (as in most years) the highest victimization rate, expressed in terms of deaths per million population in each age group, was found among males under the age of one year (27 per million, against 14 per million overall); or, again, 41 per cent of female victims were killed by a current or former spouse, cohabitant, or lover, most commonly by means of strangulation or a sharp instrument (Home Office, 1996a:70–2).

A further step in the direction of providing 'context' has been taken in recent years, with experimental analysis of data (from a small number of forces) on offences of violence against the person. For example, assaults recorded in 1988 and 1989 were classified into 'street brawls' (the largest group among offences in which the victim was male), 'pub brawls', 'attacks on a public servant', and 'domestic violence' (the largest group for female victims). Again, analysis of assaults recorded in 1990–2 indicated that 52 per cent of violent attacks on women (but only 19 per cent of those on men) took place in their own or the offender's home. In addition, members of both sexes were several times more likely to be assaulted if they were between the ages of 16 and 24 than if they were over 40. While there are considerable doubts about the factual accuracy of these data (let alone the question of how much they reflect police decision-making and how much victim reporting), their publication in *Criminal Statistics* at least helps to draw wider attention to important questions about the relationships between gender, age, and violence (for further discussion of this topic, see the chapters by Heidensohn, Jefferson, and Levi, this volume).

Geographical Distribution

Criminal Statistics does not include detailed breakdowns of the distribution of recorded crime across the country, but basic figures are supplied separately for each of the forty-three police forces in England and Wales. Of course, some forces are much larger than others and in order to afford a ready means of comparison, crime rates are expressed for each in terms of numbers of recorded offences per 100,000 population. This is by no means a fully satisfactory way of compensating for the differences, as it takes no account of possible difference in the *compositions*, as opposed to the sizes, of the relevant populations. As Bottomley and Pease (1986: 11–12) point out in relation to changes in one area over time:

We should beware of easily reaching the conclusion that 'people commit crime, therefore more people can be expected to commit more crime' so that if the ratio between crime and population is unchanged then there can be nothing which requires an explanation. It can be seen at once that underlying such an assumption is an emergent theory about rates of offending, and possibly about rates of victimization, which leaves itself wide open to a series of supplementary questions such as whether all members of a population are equally 'at risk' of offending . . . what significance should be attached to the gender composition of the population . . . [and] given the change in the pattern of criminal opportunities, should one adjust for social changes like the number of cars registered.

It should also be noted that the rates provided may not reflect important differences between areas *within* forces. Nevertheless, they do offer some fairly consistent patterns. Table 4.2 shows the 'top ten' and 'bottom ten' police forces in 1995 in terms of recorded crime rates per 100,000 population. It is clear that most of those with the highest rates include major metropolitan and/or industrial areas within their boundaries, while those with the lowest rates are predominantly rural in character. One of the most interesting forces in this table is Nottinghamshire, which returned in 1995 the highest *per capita* crime rate in the country. This was not a new situation. Indeed, Nottinghamshire has long been an object of curiosity for its unexpectedly high crime rates and has been held up as a prime example of the potentially misleading nature of official statistics. Farrington and Dowds (1985) published a detailed study of police recording practices in the county, from which they concluded that its apparently huge crime rate relative to its neighbouring counties of Leicestershire and Staffordshire (which are socially not dissimilar to Nottinghamshire) was a function of (a) a much greater number and proportion of recorded crimes originating from admissions to the police (25 per cent, compared to 4 and 8 per cent in the other forces), (b) a greater number and proportion of recorded crimes involving property of little value (48 per cent valued at £10 or under, compared with 29 and 36 per cent) and (c) a somewhat higher 'true' crime rate, indicated by a public survey. The researchers stated:

It is reasonable to conclude that between two-thirds and three-quarters of the difference in crime rates . . . reflected differences in police reactions to crime, while the remaining one-third reflected differences in criminal behaviour.
   The research shows once again the difficulties of interpreting official statistics. Almost certainly, Nottinghamshire has never been the most criminal area in the country [Farrington and Dowds 1985: 70–1].

Interestingly, Nottinghamshire fell from its top place in the national table in 1981 to fifth place in 1982, a change which, Farrington and Dowds (*ibid.*) claimed 'is almost certainly attributable to changes in police policies for

Table 4.2 Notifiable offences per 100,000 population: selected police force areas, 1995

	Offences per 100,000 population
1. *The ten forces with the highest rates*	
Nottinghamshire	14,683
Humberside	14,434
Cleveland	14,232
West Yorkshire	13,495
Northumbria	13,466
Greater Manchester	12,723
West Midlands	12,105
South Yorkshire	11,819
South Wales	11,519
MPD (London)	11,029
2. *The ten forces with the lowest rates*	
Dyfed-Powys	4,110
Surrey	5,723
Suffolk	5,889
Wiltshire	6,200
North Wales	6,331
Hertfordshire	6,551
Essex	6,552
Devon & Cornwall	6,679
Norfolk	6,729
West Mercia	7,167

Adapted from Table 2.6, *Criminal Statistics England and Wales 1995*. London: HMSO (1996).

recording offences, which may have been caused partly by this research project'. The foregoing discussion provides us with two messages about the capacity of the official statistics to reflect patterns of crime across the country. On the one hand, they show considerable consistency in indicating differences in crime rates between the extremes of rural and metropolitan areas—differences one would expect according to most sociological theories of crime causation, as well as through ordinary experience. On the other hand, as the Nottinghamshire example shows, variations in recording practices can have such a great effect on the totals produced as to render 'face value' comparisons almost meaningless. This underlines once again the necessity to treat all police figures with caution, as well as the point that they can nevertheless yield valuable insights when one probes closely into the practices which generate them.

Trends

Although graphic references to the volume of offences (e.g. 'a burglary every 20 seconds') are not uncommon, the kinds of statistic most likely to feature in

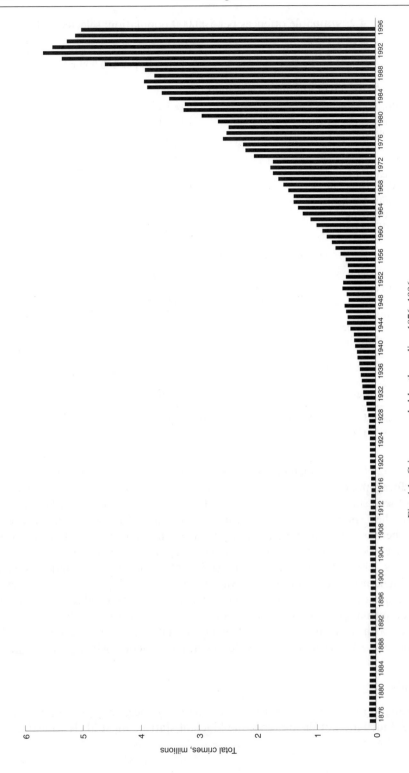

Fig. 4.1: Crimes recorded by the police, 1876–1996
Source: Home Office 1993(*b*) and *Criminal Statistics*.

newspaper headlines are those referring to apparent *trends* in recorded crime (e.g. 'burglary up 20 per cent'). In many cases, such figures refer only to a rise or fall relative to the previous year, or even previous quarter, paying no attention to the relationship between the latter and earlier years. Thus—even leaving aside the doubts about whether changes in recorded crime levels reflect real changes in criminal behaviour—they can be highly misleading in terms of longer term trends. Sometimes, too—a practice which, if used deliberately, is simply dishonest—commentators refer to a percentage fall or increase since a particular year, selecting as their baseline year one in which the official total had deviated significantly from the underlying trend. To take a concrete example, if one stated at the end of 1992 that, '[recorded] burglary has risen by 65 per cent since 1988', this would be factually correct, but it would be misleading not to point out that 1988 had produced one of the lowest recorded totals of burglary for many years and that, for example, the figure had risen by only 45 per cent since 1986.

Serious attempts to identify trends in recorded crime use figures produced at regular intervals over longer periods, and may represent the trend either in the form of a graph or through devices such as 'moving averages'. They also try to take account of changes in recording practice, such as allowing for the exclusion of minor offences of criminal damage prior to 1977, referred to above, as well as adjusting for legislative changes—the most important in the post-war years being the Theft Act 1968, which radically redefined a number of key offences including burglary (Maguire, 1982: 8–9).

As can be seen from Figure 4.1, the main features of trends in official crime statistics since their inception in 1876 have been a relatively unchanged picture until the 1930s, a clear rise up to and through the war (though tailing off a little in the early 1950s) then a sharp and sustained increase from the mid-1950s onwards. This saw a doubling of the figures within ten years (from roughly half a million crimes in 1955 to a million in 1964), another doubling over the next ten years, and yet another by 1990. The only sustained fall since the 1950s—albeit a very modest one—has occurred between 1993 and the time of writing (early 1997), and even this may be explained as a predictable 'correction' to the exceptionally large rises which were evident in 1990 and 1991 (see below).

It should be kept in mind that parallel long-term upward trends have been recorded in most other western democracies since the 1960s.[25] Indeed, it was from this time on that criminologists world-wide, hitherto used to fairly stable, if gradually increasing, crime rates, began to be faced for the first time with a phenomenon which laid down a serious challenge to most of the 'positivist' explanations of crime which had been put forward and gained broad acceptance during the 'quieter' years. Most of these, as mentioned earlier, postulated some form of pathology in individual offenders, caused

---

[25] An interesting exception was Switzerland, which produced such low crime rates that a distinguished American criminologist (Clinard, 1978) wrote a book attempting to explain why.

by some form of deprivation. How, it began to be asked, in a time of rising prosperity—which would, if anything, predict a *decrease* in crime according to such theories—could there be such an apparently massive increase in individuals with 'problems'?

Other features of the growth in recorded crime in England and Wales since 1969 (when the changes in definitions introduced by the 1968 Theft Act came into effect, making direct comparisons with earlier years problematic) include the following:

(i) The average annual rate of increase has been between 5 and 6 per cent. The upward slope (Fig 4.1) has been remarkably even, although there have been one or two major fluctuations, including a rise of 18 per cent in 1974. The late 1980s saw a period of slower growth, but this was followed by exceptionally sharp rises (of 17 and 16 per cent) in 1990 and 1991. These in turn were followed by modest falls (of 1 per cent, 5 per cent, 3 per cent, and 1 per cent) in 1993, 1994, 1995, and 1996. Some might argue that the falls were brought about by changes in policing and criminal justice policy, such as the spread of proactive methods of investigation or the government's advocacy of greater use of imprisonment. Others might see them almost as a natural correction after the 'blip' in 1990–2, crime totals reverting back to a level which kept them roughly in line with the long-term rate of increase. Alternatively, as will be discussed in the next section, both the 'blip' and the 'correction' may have had little basis in 'reality', being created largely by changes in the reporting behaviour of victims and the recording behaviour of the police.

(ii) The greatest *percentage* increase has been in offences of criminal damage: from about 13,000 in 1969 to over 950,000 in 1996—or to about 780,000, if offences of value £20 and below are excluded, as in 1969—a massive rise of over *6,000 per cent*. In *numerical* terms, as one would expect, the largest increases have been in various categories of theft, especially those involving vehicles. There were over two million more theft and handling offences recorded in 1996 than in 1969.

(iii) In recent years, the offences which have appeared to rise most sharply are rape and trafficking in controlled drugs, both of which exhibited average annual increases of over 10 per cent between 1985 and 1996. There appear to be special reasons, associated with police practice, in both cases: publicized improvements in the treatment of victims—and a greater willingness to believe them (Blair, 1985)—may have affected both reporting and recording behaviour in relation to rape, while more police and Customs resources have been put into operations against drug trafficking (which, of course, tends to be recorded only when arrests are made). All other major categories of crime have shown considerably lower long-term rates of increase, except for serious woundings (assaults which endanger life), which—unlike less serious violent offences—have increased at an average rate of 9 per cent a year. As, by dint of their seriousness and visibility, incidents which may merit this label are likely to become known to the police in a high proportion of cases (and hence to be less volatile than others in terms of reporting rates), such a sustained increase perhaps demands more attention and explanation than it has so far received from criminologists.

THE DARK FIGURE UNMASKED? THE ADVENT OF CRIME SURVEYS

As mentioned earlier, prior to the establishment of regular, large-scale crime surveys (in the United States in the 1970s and in the United Kingdom in the 1980s), criminologists used to spend a great deal of time debating whether the trends apparent in recorded crime reflected 'real' changes in levels of offending, or were primarily a function of changes in the propensity of the public to report crimes and/or of the police to record them. The extreme 'institutionalist' (as opposed to 'realist') view was that there was no such thing as an empirically measurable quantity of crime anyway. A more common view was that there *was* a real dark figure and that trends existed in the 'true' volume of crime, but that nothing could be deduced about this 'reality' from trends in recorded offences. In particular, great scepticism was expressed about the rapid rise in official crime figures since the 1960s—most of which, it was argued, could be accounted for by changes in reporting and recording behaviour. Explanations put forward included increases in the numbers of police officers (more people to uncover and record offences), the installation of telephones in more houses (thus making reporting easier), the spread of insurance (reporting being necessary to support a claim), reduced levels of public tolerance to violence, and the break-up of traditional communities (both the last making people more inclined to call in the police rather than 'sort the problem out themselves'). Finally, some suggested that crime figures were subject to deliberate manipulation for political reasons, either by the police (as a weapon in battles for more resources) or by political parties (e.g. to justify criminal justice policies or to divert attention from other social problems). One advocate of this view, the American criminologist, Hal Pepinsky, showed how significant increases in crime could be created simply by assiduously recording every trivial offence that comes to light: for example, he referred to one subdivision in a British city where almost half the year's 'increase in crime' had been produced by the police recording every admission by a single offender who frequently stole milk bottles from doorsteps.[26] On a wider scale, Selke and Pepinsky (1984) claimed that rises (and occasional falls) over time in crime figures in Indiana could be shown to coincide closely with shifts in the political needs of the party in power.

[26] This example comes from a small unpublished study he conducted while a Visiting Fellow at Balliol College, Oxford.

While few went as far as Pepinsky in doubting that *any* increases in criminal activity had been taking place, criminologists in the 1970s generally felt that the police figures had greatly exaggerated the *rate* of increase. (On occasion, too, this belief was echoed by politicians and civil servants, who found it a useful way of deflecting opposition criticism of the ineffectiveness of crime prevention policies.) Certainly, little academic attention was devoted to 'the rise in crime' as a genuine and pressing social problem. Yet by the early 1990s, public denials of its reality had largely disappeared, it having been broadly accepted by criminologists and policy-makers alike that certain forms of crime, at least, were now being committed much more frequently than in the past. This change was influenced by several factors, but perhaps most of all by the status and success achieved by crime surveys, to which we now turn. Other factors, such as the currency in the 1980s of 'left realist' ideas (see Matthews and Young, 1986; Young, this volume), will be referred to later.

National Surveys

In the mid-1960s, the first serious attempts were made to assess the extent of the 'dark figure' of crimes which were either not reported to the police or, having been reported, were not officially recorded by the police. Two substantial experimental surveys were conducted in the United States (Ennis, 1967; Bidermann and Reiss, 1967), wherein members of a random sample of households were asked whether anyone in the house had been the victim of a crime within the previous year and, if so, whether the matter had been reported to the police. A similar experiment was carried out in three areas of London in the early 1970s (Sparks, Genn, and Dodd, 1977).

In both countries, despite the many methodological problems identified by the researchers, governments were sufficiently persuaded of the value of such surveys to invest considerable sums of money in running them officially on a large scale. In the United States, the Department of Justice funded regular surveys at both a national and local level from 1972, and while the Home Office was slower off the mark, its crime surveys have moved rapidly into a position where they now rank alongside *Criminal Statistics* as a major source of data on crime and crime trends in Britain. Other European countries are rapidly following suit. Indeed, the notion of regular *international* crime surveys, building upon those undertaken by van Dijk *et al.* (1990) and Mayhew *et al.* (1993) is by no means an idle dream.

The *British Crime Survey* (BCS), undertaken by members of the Home Office Research and Planning Unit (now Research and Statistics Directorate), was first conducted in 1982, with further 'sweeps' (the radar metaphor consistently used by its authors) in 1984, 1988, 1992, 1994, and 1996. The main rationale for the survey—and, particularly, for its expensive repetition at regular intervals—is that, by asking samples of the public to describe crimes committed against them within a given recent period, the vagaries of crime reporting behaviour and police recording behaviour are neatly avoided, and the responses can be grossed up into a 'fuller' and hence, by implication, more 'valid' picture of crime and its trends in Britain.

To comment sensibly on the status of knowledge about crime derived from BCS, it is necessary to understand how its data are collected and compiled. The core findings of every survey are based on interviews with over 10,000 people aged 16 and over. For the first three surveys, these were members of households selected at random from the Electoral Register, but since 1992 the Postcode Address File (PAF) has been used as the sampling frame, it being argued that this produces a better representation of the population: the Electoral Register may significantly under-represent young people, the unemployed, ethnic minorities and those living in rented accommodation (Mayhew *et al.*, 1993: 149–51). The basic format of the part of the questionnaire which elicits information about crimes known to respondents, and the framework for presenting the figures, were established in the 1982 survey and have changed relatively little since.[27] Respondents are first asked whether 'you or anyone else now in your household' have been the victim of any of a series of crimes, each described to them in ordinary language, since 1 January of the previous year.[28] They are then asked whether 'you personally' have suffered any of a number of other offences. If any positive answers are received, interviewers complete a detailed 'Victim Form' for each incident (though if the respondent reports a number of similar events, these may treated as one 'series incident'—see below). The results of this exercise are analysed to produce estimated national totals of both 'household offences' and 'personal offences', based on calculations using, respectively, the total number of households and the total adult population of England and Wales.[29] The offence categories produced by the BCS are shown in Table 4.3. The first important point to note is that by no means all are coterminous with police categories. In fact, when making direct comparisons of 'official' and 'BCS' crime rates, only about two-thirds of the BCS-generated 'offences' can justifiably be used (Mayhew and Maung, 1992).[30] Vice versa, there are many categories of offence covered in the police-derived statistics which are not measured by the BCS. These include crimes against commercial or corporate victims (notably shop-lifting, burglary, and vandalism), fraud, motoring offences, and so-called 'victimless' crimes such as the possession of or dealing in drugs. The main BCS schedule also excludes offences against victims under 16 (though the 1992 'sweep' was designed to generate more information about these). And sexual offences, though asked

[27] However, the follow-up questionnaire, which asks questions of a more general nature, has been altered significantly on each 'sweep', while extra self-completion forms asking about people's own involvement in crime, and a form for interviewing a sub-sample of children aged 12–15, were introduced in 1992.

[28] The survey is usually conducted in January or February, which facilitates comparisons with the previous year's official crime figures.

[29] As the total interview sample deliberately includes an over-representation of households from denser urban areas (to maximize the chances of finding 'victims' to interview), the calculated victimization rates are weighted to take account of this.

[30] Those not directly comparable are 'common assaults', 'other household thefts', and 'other personal thefts'.

Table 4.3 Estimated totals of offences in England and Wales, 1995, as derived from the 1996 British Crime Survey and 1995 *Criminal Statistics*.

	BCS	(%)	Police	(%)
Comparable offence groups:				
Theft of/from vehicles	4,312,000	(23)	1,209,000	(23)
Vandalism private property	3,415,000	(18)	461,000	(9)
Burglary dwelling	1,754,000	(9)	644,000	(13)
Wounding	860,000	(4)	174,000	(3)
Robbery/theft from person	984,000	(5)	123,000	(2)
Bicycle theft	660,000	(3)	183,000	(4)
Subtotals	11,986,000	(63)	2,794,000	(55)
BCS offences not comparable with police data:				
Other household theft	2,266,000	(12)	***	***
Common assault	2,820,000	(15)	***	***
Other personal theft	2,075,000	(11)	***	***
Police-recorded offences not covered by/comparable with BCS:				
Burglary not dwelling	***	***	596,000	(12)
Vandalism public commercial property	***	***	453,000	(9)
Theft from a shop	***	***	276,000	(5)
Fraud and forgery	***	***	133,000	(3)
Theft of/from commercial vehicle	***	***	112,000	(2)
Other	***	***	736,000	(14)
Totals	19,147,000	(100)	5,100,000	(100)

Notes: All figures are rounded to the nearest 1,000. The 'comparable' police figures follow adjustments made by Mirrlees-Black *et al.* (1996), which include adding some offences recorded by the British Transport Police. These are not included in the overall police total, so the 'Other' figure in the 'non-comparable' section (736,000), which was arrived at by subtraction from this total, is a slight underestimate.
Sources: Mirrlees-Black *et al.* (1996) and *Criminal Statistics 1995*.

about, are reported to BCS interviewers so infrequently (for reasons discussed below) that no reliable estimates can be produced.

In other words, as their authors freely admit (see, for example, Hough and Mayhew, 1985: chapter 1) national surveys are much less successful in obtaining information about some types of incident than others. They do not produce an overall figure purporting to represent the 'total volume of crime', but concentrate instead upon selected categories of offence which are usually discussed individually or in sub-groups. The BCS, therefore, it cannot be too heavily stressed, provides an *alternative*, rather than a directly comparable overall picture of crime to that offered by police statistics: it is 'fuller' than the latter in some respects, but 'narrower' in others.

Let us look first at the areas where the two data sets do overlap and then at the BCS 'picture of crime' in the round. The authors of the initial BCS (Hough and Mayhew, 1983: 10) summarized the results of this exercise as follows :

Only for one category—thefts from motor vehicles—were the figures similar. For instance, the survey indicated twice as many burglaries as were recorded by the police; nearly five times as much wounding; twelve times as much theft from the person; and thirteen times as much vandalism (or criminal damage). . . . The overall ratio *for incidents which had been compared* was one in four [emphasis added].

It will be noted from the first section of Table 4.3 that, though the proportions have changed somewhat, the general thrust of this statement also holds for the results of the 1996 survey. In 1995, the total of notifiable offences recorded by the police in categories covered by the BCS was under three million, whereas the BCS produced evidence to suggest that nearly twelve million offences of these kinds had been committed in the same year.

As the authors rightly went on to point out, there is a strong temptation to interpret such figures as showing that there is 'four times as much crime' as the official records suggest: a trap into which many people have duly fallen. The problem lies in the wide variations between offences in terms of their reporting and (to a lesser extent) recording rates. These variations mean that the choice of offence groups to include in any comparison can significantly affect the overall ratio between the survey figures and the police figures. For example, if the comparison included survey data covering some of the offences in the final section of Table 4.3—let us say, estimates of instances of shoplifting or pilfering from work or cheque frauds, derived from surveys of employers or shopkeepers or bank employees—where the proportions which end up in police records are known to be tiny,[31] the overall 'dark figure' would emerge as a very much larger one. (In fact, the overall 'dark figure' estimated by Sparks *et al.* (1977) in their pioneering survey was one of *eleven* times the police figure, unlike the 'four times' estimate of the BCS. This is partly explained by the different spread of offences covered.) These remarks are highly pertinent to the difference between the 'image' of crime presented by the BCS and that presented by some local surveys, which will be discussed in the next section.

How, then, can we summarize the main picture of crime that has emerged from the British Crime Survey? First, the central message sent out by its authors during the initial passage of its results into the public domain was, in essence: the bad news is that there is a lot more crime than we thought, the good news is that most of it is petty. The emphasis upon 'the petty nature of most law-breaking' (Hough and Mayhew, 1983: 33) was designed to deflect a possible moral panic in reaction to the huge amount of 'new' crime revealed by the survey, but it also reflected the finding that unreported crimes generally involve much lower levels of financial loss, damage, and injury than those reported to the police.[32]

---

[31] See, e.g., Martin (1962) and Levi (1993).

[32] This message has been sent less loudly lately as the media and the public have become more used to the idea that there is a great deal of unrecorded crime. At the same time, the idea that 'minor' crime is of little importance has become less easy to sell to the public as the general level of tolerance for petty theft appears to have fallen significantly since the early 1990s.

Secondly, the BCS produces a picture of crime not wildly dissimilar in its broad 'shape' to that projected by police records: both sets of figures are dominated by 'autocrime' and both indicate low levels of violent offences in relation to property offences. Of course, as emphasized above, there are many kinds of offence (notably those against organizations as opposed to individuals, as well as 'victimless' crimes) which do not appear in the BCS figures at all, but most of these are either similar in nature to BCS crimes (e.g. burglary and criminal damage) or else constitute only small proportions of the totals of police-recorded crime. The main difference where directly comparable offences are concerned is that vandalism is more prominent among BCS offences than in the official statistics: it appears from the most recent survey that only about one in eight cases known to victims ends up in the police figures.

Thirdly, the series of 'sweeps' of the BCS, like most surveys in the United States, together suggest that, overall, increases in crime have been less steep than police figures suggest. Between 1981 and 1995, among the sub-set of offences which are comparable, the number of recorded crimes increased by 91 per cent, while those uncovered by the BCS rose by 83 per cent. Interestingly, the gap between the two rates of increase was much greater than this up to 1991 (from 1981 to 1991 the increases were 96 per cent and 49 per cent, respectively), but since then the BCS has indicated proportionately greater rises than the official figures. Indeed, between 1993 and 1995, for the first time the two sets of figures moved in different directions, the BCS indicating a *rise* in offences and the police figures a *fall*. In sum, as Figure 4.2 illustrates, the basic

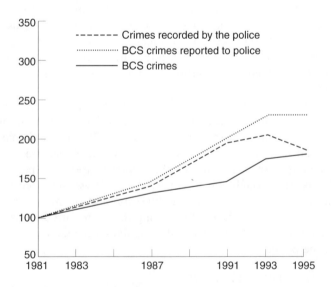

Fig. 4.2: Trends in comparable offences, *British Crime Survey* and crimes recorded by the police, 1981–95 (1981 = 100)

Source: Mirrlees-Black *et al.* 1996.

picture painted by the BCS is one of a fairly steady pattern of increase since the early 1980s, while police figures suggest a sharper rise followed by a fall.

As trends in crime are given so much prominence in the political and policy-making arenas, it is important to seek explanations of these differences. The long-term trend (of faster rises in official statistics than in BCS estimates) appears to be explained partly by increases in *'reporting rates'*—i.e. the proportion of offences known to victims which get reported to the police. Between 1981 and 1991, the BCS indicated a rise in reporting rates (among the sub-set of offences which are comparable with police figures) from 36 per cent to 50 per cent. Another equally important factor was an apparent increase in *'recording rates'*—i.e. the proportion of offences reported to the police which end up in the official records—in one particular type of offence: criminal damage ('vandalism'). While recording rates for most other offences fell slightly between 1981 and 1991, those for vandalism increased significantly, from 33 per cent to 56 per cent (Mayhew *et al.*, 1993: 116). As a result, while BCS estimates of the level of vandalism changed little over this period, the police figures *doubled*. As criminal damage constitutes quite an important category in both sets of figures, this factor alone distorted the overall picture to a significant extent. If it had been left out of the calculations entirely, 'BCS crime' and 'police crime' (in categories covered by the BCS) would have appeared in 1991 to be increasing at fairly similar rates.

Conversely, the apparent 'counter trends' between police and BCS figures which have appeared since 1991 seem to be explained mainly by a general fall in reporting rates (from 50 per cent to 46 per cent among all 'comparable' offences) and an even sharper fall in police recording rates, not just for vandalism but for all BCS offences (from 60 per cent to 50 per cent).

The above analysis has some important implications when considered alongside some of the political developments which took place in relation to crime in the early 1990s. It leads one to question very seriously whether *either* the dramatic increases in recorded crime between 1990 and 1992 (which helped to justify the equally dramatic switch in criminal justice policy and sentencing practice which has been evident since 1993) *or* the apparent fall in crime between 1993 and 1996 (which was trumpeted by the government as proof of the success of its tough new anti-crime strategies) ever 'really' happened. It also raises the question of *why* reporting and recording rates seem to have changed so much over such a short period of time. Mirrlees-Black *et al.* (1996: 25–6) suggest that the post-1991 fall in reporting rates may be due to demonstrable falls in the numbers of people covered by insurance, particularly in the poorer areas which are hardest hit by crime. However, they offer no explanation for the apparent falls in police recording rates (nor of the preceding *rise* in recording rates, especially for vandalism, between 1987 and 1991). One possibility is that, as argued by Hall *et al.* (1978) in relation to the disputed rise in 'mugging' in the early 1970s, and by Selke and Pepinsky (1984) in relation to fluctuations in crime rates in Indiana, certain 'political' factors were at work.

A case could be made, for example, that it suited supporters of a harder line on crime, including the police and some members of the government, first to raise the spectre of rapidly increasing 'lawlessness', hence justifying major increases in social control (as well as the repeal of the 'soft' Criminal Justice Act 1991), and then to be able to demonstrate that the 'medicine' was working and the 'crisis' was under control. However, there is no evidence of any deliberate manipulation of recording practices to support a crude conspiracy theory that the rise and fall was planned and manufactured. While 'political' factors in the broadest sense may well have played a part, it is likely that the reasons for the unusual fluctuations were vastly more complex, involving interactions between changes in policing, in insurance practice, in media attitudes and, indeed, in the public 'mood'.

Finally, it is important to remember that the BCS, perhaps even more so than the police figures, promotes a picture of crime in which certain modes of offending are prominent and others are systematically excluded or under-counted. The BCS picture is dominated above all by offences against private individuals and households which are *committed by strangers*, as it were 'out of the blue'. Most incidents reported to the survey consist of discrete incidents in which individuals suddenly and unexpectedly suffer the theft of or damage to a piece of their property, or an illegal entry into their house. Crime in this mode takes on an appearance in many ways akin to an accident, or an 'act of God'—an almost random event which can strike anyone at any time, but which is relatively rare in the life of any individual. This image was strengthened in the first BCS report by the calculation of the 'average risks' of falling victim to various types of offence:

a 'statistically average' person aged 16 or over can expect:

- a robbery once every five centuries (not attempts)
- an assault resulting in injury (even if slight) once every century
- a family car to be stolen or taken by joyriders once every 60 years
- a burglary in the home once every 40 years.

. . . These risks can be compared with the likelihood of encountering other sorts of mishaps: the chances of burglary are slightly less than the chances. . . . of a fire in the home; the chances a household runs of car theft are smaller than the chances . . . of having one of its members injured in a car accident [Hough and Mayhew, 1983: 15].

This manner of describing crime may correspond to many people's experience of it, especially among the middle classes. However, as will be discussed in the next section, it tends to leave out of the picture a number of very different kinds of experience. First of all, there are areas (in poor inner city districts, particularly) where even predatory, stranger-to-stranger offences like burglary are suffered by individuals far more often than the above figures suggest. Secondly, there are important kinds of criminal behaviour, inadequately measured by the BCS, which are closely tied up with *continuing relationships between 'offender' and 'victim'*. These include assaults resulting from disputes between neighbours, the battery of women by their partners, and the sexual and physical abuse of children. They also include the repeated threats and harassment from local gangs suffered in some areas by members of racial minorities and by other individuals who become targeted as 'different'.

Local Surveys and the Radical Critique

Concerns about the tendency of the BCS to distort 'real' experiences of crime—especially those of women, ethnic minorities, and the very poor—have been raised by several writers (see, for example, Matthews and Young, 1986; Stanko, 1988; Genn, 1988; Dobash and Dobash, 1992; Young, 1988 and this volume). They have also strongly influenced the design of a number of local crime surveys (e.g. Kinsey, 1984; Hanmer and Saunders, 1984; Jones *et al.*, 1986, 1987; Crawford *et al.*, 1990), funded mainly by local authorities, which have aimed to uncover areas of criminal behaviour not seriously touched by the BCS and, equally important, to examine and emphasize the extent to which victimization is *unequally distributed* among the population.

Some aspects of the distribution of risk were considered in the BCS from the start, but the main angle from which it was approached in the first report attracted a good deal of criticism. The main findings highlighted by the authors were that, for crimes of violence, males had higher victimization rates than females, and younger people higher than older; and that the risks were further related to lifestyle—for example, people who frequently went out drinking were more likely to be assaulted. From these findings they concluded, first, that offenders (or, at least, known offenders) and victims of violence shared several of the same social characteristics: the survey, wrote Hough and Mayhew (1983: 25), 'paints a . . . coherent picture of assault victims, in which the people they most resemble are their assailants'. And secondly that, this being the case, the fears of street violence expressed by both women and the elderly (which were much greater than those of young men) were to some extent out of proportion to the actual risks they faced. As will be discussed shortly, this latter point became a key target for some radical critiques of the BCS and the message it appeared to be sending out.

Other points from the first survey which received less attention included the finding that, where burglary was concerned, council properties were more vulnerable than owner-occupied dwellings (Hough and Mayhew, 1983, 1985). Results from the 1992 survey confirmed this in more detail, indicating that residents of 'the poorest council estates' faced a burglary risk 2.8 times the average and twelve times that of people living in agricultural areas (Mayhew *et al.*, 1993).[33] Similar patterns obtained for 'autocrime around the home' and robbery/theft from the person, though the greatest risk for the latter appeared to be in 'mixed inner metropolitan areas'. The 1988 survey paid particular attention to differential risk between racial groups. It was found that both

---

[33] Using the ACORN system of classification, the researchers assign every dwelling to one of 11 categories based on the demographic, housing, and employment characteristics of its immediate surrounding area (see Mayhew *et al.*, 1993: 173–6).

Afro-Caribbeans and Asians were more at risk than whites for many types of crime, the latter being particularly vulnerable to vandalism and robbery or street theft committed by strangers (Mayhew *et al.*, 1989).

Although these are all important findings, their impact has to some extent been diluted among the welter of other figures emerging from the surveys. By focusing chiefly upon inner city districts, local crime surveys have brought out much more vividly than the BCS the extent to which crime is concentrated in some small areas—predominantly those blighted by poverty—and, moreover, how particular forms of crime are suffered disproportionately by particular social groups within those areas. For example, the first Islington Crime Survey (Jones *et al.*, 1986) indicated that a third of all households had been touched by burglary, robbery, or sexual assault within the previous twelve months (a situation light years away from that of the notional 'statistically average' person referred to in the BCS). It also indicated that young, white females in the area were twenty-nine times more likely to be assaulted than white females over 45. As Young (1988*b*: 171) observes, such massive differences between subgroups illustrate 'the fallacy of talking of the problem of women as a whole, or of men, blacks, whites, youths, etc.' Rather, he insists, criminological analysis should 'start from the actual subgroups in which people live their lives.'

Writing in the same volume, two of the founders of the BCS (Mayhew and Hough, 1988) acknowledged that the increased attention given in later 'sweeps' of the BCS to the distribution of risk, was to some extent prompted by criticism of the superficial approach taken earlier on, and in particular of the handling of questions about the relationship between risk of victimization and fear of crime.[34] Much of this criticism was led by Jock Young and others broadly adhering to the 'left realist' school of criminology (cf. Matthews and Young, 1986; Young 1988*b*: 173–5 and this volume). They attacked in particular the inference, mentioned above, that fear of crime was in some senses 'irrational'[35] because both women and the elderly, who were less likely to be attacked, expressed greater fear than the young men who were 'objectively' at the greatest risk. Young (1988: 173–5) points out that such an approach, like the argument that fears are exaggerated because much crime is 'trivial' in terms of loss or injury, obscures the fact that what are 'objectively' similar events can have enormously different meanings and consequences for different people:

People differ greatly in their ability to withstand crime . . . The 'same' punch can mean totally different things in different circumstances . . . Violence, like all kinds of crime, is a social relationship. It is rarely random: it inevitably involves particular social meanings and occurs in particular hierarchies of power. Its impact, likewise, is predicated on the relationship within which it occurs . . . The relatively powerless situation of women—economically, socially and physically—makes them more unequal victims than men.

[34] A special analysis of BCS data on this topic (Maxfield, 1988) was also commissioned by the Home Office.
[35] In fairness to the authors of the BCS, it should be pointed out that they had anticipated several of the criticisms in qualifications to their original conclusions (which were anyway tentative), though these qualifications tended to be forgotten in the later controversy.

The other main strand of criticism concerned the extent to which some forms of crime still remained largely 'hidden' to the British Crime Survey, even though questions were asked which apparently covered them. Efforts to put this right were central to the design of the local crime surveys mentioned above. Perhaps the most significant aspect was the attention given to ways of obtaining more information about sexual and other assaults on women. These included less restrictive wording of questions and emphasis on sensitive approaches to these areas in the training and selection of interviewers. The results stand in considerable contrast to the BCS findings: in the Islington survey, for instance (Jones *et al.*, 1986), significantly higher levels of sexual assault were found, while over one-fifth of reported assaults were classified as 'domestic'—more than twice the BCS proportion. Moreover, questions were asked about incidents which would not necessarily be classified by the police as 'crime', but may be experienced as serious by victims, namely sexual and racial 'harassment'. It was found, for example, that over two-thirds of women under the age of 24 had been 'upset by harassment' in the previous twelve months.

A number of special surveys of women, mainly conducted by feminist writers, have also found high levels of actual or threatened sexual violence. For example, Hanmer and Saunders (1984) found that 59 per cent of 129 women surveyed in Leeds had suffered some form of threat, violence, or sexual harassment within the previous year, and Hall (1985) and Radford (1987) have produced even more startling figures. Among the most challenging of all was a survey by Painter (1991), based on a representative sample of over 1,000 married women, which suggested that 14 per cent had been raped by their husbands at some time during their marriage—over 40 per cent of them perceiving the incident as 'rape' at the time.[36]

Of course, there are major questions of definition to be tackled in relation to all the above findings, as well as to those of the BCS discussed earlier. Clearly, different surveys are 'measuring' different things. The large government-run surveys in Britain and elsewhere, while prepared to experiment, have broadly held on to the definitions of crime and the counting rules used by the police in compiling official statistics: this is to allow direct comparison and hence a convincing statement of the 'dark figure' and its fluctuations over time. The surveys carried out by academics have moved further away from official definitions of crime, towards alternative definitions favoured by their designers—which, the latter would claim, are also much closer to 'social reality' and the perceptions and priorities of ordinary people. Thus, for example, the 1992 BCS 'filter' question on sexual offences was simply 'Since 1st January 1991, have you been sexually interfered with, assaulted or attacked, either by someone you

[36] The question used was 'Have you ever had sex with your present husband (or previous husband) against your will, when you had clearly insisted that you did not want to and refused your consent?' This is a legal definition of rape, though despite court decisions which mean that a man can be convicted of raping his wife, it is unlikely that many police officers would arrest on allegations of refused consent by a wife living with her husband, without evidence of injury.

knew or by a stranger?', while most local surveys have used much broader definitions in their questions, including threats and 'pestering' behaviour.

Finally, a graphic illustration of the kinds of definitional and counting problems we have been discussing is provided by Genn (1988). Prompted by worries that the survey method leads to serious undercounting of certain types of crime, Genn revisited some of the female respondents to the pilot crime survey in which she was involved, all of whom had said they had been victimized many times. She gives an eye-opening account of the way that the lives of these women, in severely deprived areas of London, were blighted by frequent sexual and physical assaults, thefts, burglaries, and other forms of mistreatment, many of them from people with whom they had some sort of continuing relationship. Yet this kind of 'multiple victimization', she notes, is lost from view in most surveys, partly because—in order to create comparability with police recording practices—they tend to impose artificial limits (five, in the case of the BCS) upon the number of crimes that can be counted for any one victim, and partly because such victims may be less likely than others to respond to the survey or to admit their victimization to interviewers. (Similar comments could be made about other marginalized groups—the homeless, the mentally ill, those who drift from bed-sitter to bed-sitter, and so on—whose voice is not often heard in the large surveys. Such people may also be subject to exceptionally high levels of victimization.) At the same time, Genn raises fundamental questions, touched on earlier in this chapter, about how meaning-ful it is to 'count' certain crimes at all. She writes:

In asking respondents about their experiences of crime, victim surveys have tended to use an approach which Skogan has termed 'the events orientation': that which concep-tualises crime as *discrete incidents*. This . . . can be traced back to one of the original primary objectives of victim surveys: the estimation of the 'dark figure' of unrecorded crime for direct comparison with police statistics. In order to accomplish this, . . . infor-mation obtained from victims had to be accommodated within a rigid 'counting' frame of reference. *Although isolated incidents of burglary, car theft or stranger attacks may present few measurement problems, for certain categories of violent crime and for certain types of crime victim, the 'counting' procedure leads to difficulties. It is clear that violent victimization may often be better conceptualized as a process rather than as a series of discrete events.* This is most evident in cases of prolonged and habitual domestic violence, but there are also other situations in which violence, abuse and petty theft are an integral part of victims' day-to-day existence [1988: 91, emphasis added].

THE 'OFFENDER POPULATION': YOUNG, MALE, AND POOR?

Throughout this chapter we have looked at crime mainly from the point of view of those who experience it and of those who chart its incidence, the focus being upon how often, where, and against whom it is known and perceived to occur. Of course, what is glaringly absent from most of the discussion so far is information about the *perpetrators* of all these crimes. While it is important to conclude our account with some comments on this topic, these will be kept to a minimum, partly to avoid trespassing too much upon the territory of other authors in the volume, and partly because studies of offenders have become much rarer over the past two decades as criminologists' interests have leaned more towards victims, offence patterns, and the operations of the criminal justice agencies.

Just as the annual statistics compiled by the police produce an 'official' account of the extent of crime, to which victim surveys offer various alternative pictures, so the statistics compiled from court records (together with police cautioning records) produce a picture of all those officially held responsible for recorded offences, while various other studies and surveys—notably 'self-report studies'—have similarly provided alternative pictures of the offender population.

In looking at all those convicted of or cautioned for indictable offences in any given year, the first point to note is that their total is very much lower than the total of offences recorded. In 1995, for example, about 301,000 people were sentenced in court and a further 203,000 were cautioned—small figures compared with the recorded crime total of over five million offences. Some of these people, of course, were charged with more than one offence, or admitted others which were 'taken into consideration' by sentencers or simply 'written off' by the police. Even so, it remains true that, for the great majority of offences recorded by the police, nothing is officially known about those responsible. Of course, if one brings into the picture crimes which are not reported or recorded, the 'attrition rate' becomes even more striking. It can be calculated that under one in forty of the crimes identified by the BCS result in a conviction—a figure which drops to around one in eighty where 'vandalism' (at the level of notifiable offences of criminal damage) is concerned (Home Office, 1993*a*, 1995).

Such findings caused a considerable amount of political and media concern when they were first published, questions being asked about the effectiveness of the police and others in bringing offenders to justice. However, we are more interested here in their implications for our knowledge about offenders. Obviously, with such a large 'unknown', it cannot simply be assumed that the characteristics of 'offenders' as a whole can be inferred from those of adjudicated offenders—a central point which we shall return to in a moment. First, though, let us look at the official figures.

Among the half million or so offenders convicted or cautioned for indictable offences in 1995, 82 per cent were male, and 45 per cent were under the age of 21. The 'peak age' of offending—that is, the age at which people had the highest risk of acquiring a conviction or caution—stood at 18 for males and 15 for females (Home Office, 1996*a*).[37] It is also known from cohort studies

---

[37] The peak age for males has risen over the past few years from 15 to 18. Farrington and Burrows (1993) claim that this is due mainly to a significant fall in the number of boys under 16 cautioned or convicted for shop-lifting—itself largely explained by a growing tendency of the police to use alternative, informal ways of dealing with them (see also Home Office, 1996*a*:92).

using the Home Office Offenders Index that a high proportion of those convicted will have had a number of previous convictions: as noted earlier, it has been calculated that 60 per cent of all court appearances are accounted for by male offenders who have been convicted four or more times (Home Office, 1993*a*).

Another, more detailed, picture of adjudicated offenders—in this case, the sub-group thought to have offended seriously enough to warrant detention in a custodial institution—is provided by analysis of information held in prison records. The National Prison Survey (Walmsley *et al.*, 1992) provided a break-down of the social characteristics of 10 per cent of all male, and 20 per cent of all female, prisoners over the age of 17 held in custodial institutions in England and Wales in early 1991.[38] Like the sentenced and cautioned popu-lation, the prison population was shown to be predominantly young: excluding juveniles in both cases, 62 per cent of inmates were aged below 30, compared with 25 per cent of the general population. Males were even more strikingly over-represented, making up 96 per cent of all prisoners.

Disproportionate numbers of prisoners were also found to come from ethnic minorities: 15 per cent of male prisoners and as many as 23 per cent of female prisoners described themselves as black or Asian.[39] Where social class was concerned, 41 per cent of males had had unskilled or partly skilled jobs, compared with 18 per cent of the general population.

Other striking findings included the revelation that over a quarter of prisoners had at some time been in local authority care (compared with an estimated 2 per cent of the general population); 40 per cent of male prisoners had left school before the age of 16 (compared with 11 per cent of all British males); and 13 per cent had been 'of no fixed abode' before coming into prison (for further details, see Morgan, this volume).

Taken overall, these data clearly illustrate that the social characteristics of people who are arrested and processed by the criminal justice system—and particularly of offenders who are eventually sent to prison—present a very different pattern from that found in the general population. There are many more males, young people, black people, poor people, poorly educated people, and people with disturbed childhoods than one would find in a random sample.

Of course, as pointed out above, if only about 3 per cent of known crimes end in a conviction or caution, it is important to ask whether the other 97 per cent are likely to have been committed by a similarly skewed section of the population (or, indeed, by the very same people). This is the province of self-report studies—the technique by which samples of the population are asked in

[38] The survey included remand prisoners as well as those convicted, so was not, strictly speaking, a sub-group of all adjudicated offenders (a relatively small proportion will subsequently have been found not guilty).

[39] For a full discussion of the massive over-representation of black people in prisons in the USA and England and Wales, see Tonry (1994). Hood (1992) and Smith (this volume) provide more general discussions of the disproportionate black–white ratios, and the probable extent of racial bias, at each stage of the criminal justice process.

confidence whether they have committed crimes for which they have not been caught. On the one hand, these suggest that crime is committed by a much larger proportion of the population than is officially held responsible for it. On the other hand, survey respondents who have previously been in trouble with the law tend to admit to both *more serious* and *more frequent* offending behaviour than people who have never been convicted—which suggests that the criminal justice system 'gets it right' to some degree!

Depending upon the age, sex, and other social characteristics of those questioned, as well as upon the wording of the questions, self-report studies have generally found that between 40 and almost 100 per cent will admit to having committed at least one criminal offence during their lifetime. Most such studies have used samples of young males, often schoolchildren or students. For example, in one of the best early studies, Elmhorn (1965) found that 92 per cent of a random sample of teenage schoolboys in Stockholm admitted to at least one offence, while 53 per cent admitted to at least one 'serious' offence (roughly the equivalent of an indictable crime in Britain), principally theft. More recently, the first international self-report survey indicated that consistently high proportions of young people across a range of developed countries had committed at least one criminal offence (Junger-Tas *et al.*, 1994). Self-report studies of adults—particularly studies with a sound methodology—are rarer, although there are some useful data from a sample of 22–25-year olds which was included in the British version of the international survey, conducted by the Home Office (Graham and Bowling, 1995), as well as from the cohort used in the long-term studies of delinquency carried out by Cambridge University. Farrington (1989) reported that 96 per cent of the Cambridge cohort—which, it should be stressed, contains a higher than average proportion of working-class urban males—admitted to having committed at least one criminal offence by the age of 32. The Home Office survey found that nearly a third of 22–25 year old males (though only 4 per cent of females) admitted to committing a criminal offence *within the previous year* (Graham and Bowling, 1995: 25). Moreover, these figures exclude drug offences, which would have increased them considerably.

However, the authors of the above studies, like most other researchers in the field (e.g. Short and Nye, 1958; Christie *et al.*, 1965; Huizinga and Elliott, 1986; see also Farrington, 1973), found that much smaller proportions of respondents admitted to large numbers of offences, or *frequent* offending. Thus, for example, Graham and Bowling (1995) found that over a quarter of all offences admitted by 14–25-year-olds were committed by just 3 per cent of offenders. Equally, when one looks at the more *serious* offences, the numbers admitting to participation fall substantially.[40]

In sum, the general conclusion reached over twenty years ago by Hood and Sparks (1970: 51), after a summary of results of self-report studies from

---

[40] In the British self-report survey, for example, only 7 per cent of males aged 14–25 admitted to having committed, within the past year, any of a sub-set of the most serious offences asked about (car theft, bag snatching, burglary, robbery, fighting, arson, assault, and wounding).

several countries, seems to remain valid today: 'While it may be correct to say that to commit one or two delinquent acts is 'normal behaviour' for boys, to be involved in frequent criminal acts is apparently relatively rare.' An important qualification, however, is that self-report studies have generally covered a limited range of offences, chiefly the less serious forms of street crime. Many, too, have included vaguely defined 'delinquent' or 'anti-social' acts, such as 'defying parents' authority' or 'a fist fight with one other person' (Short and Nye, 1958), which would be unlikely to qualify as crimes if reported to the police. These features of their methodology have played a part in one of the most controversial issues surrounding the results of self-report studies, that of the social class of offenders.

The argument was started in earnest by the publication of Short and Nye's (1958) study, which indicated that middle-class boys were as likely as lower-class boys to be involved in delinquent acts, despite the fact that adjudicated offenders are predominantly working-class. This finding, supported by some (but contradicted by other) subsequent studies, suggested that there must be some major form of class bias in the processes of arrest and prosecution by which offenders come to official notice. A lively debate ensued over many years, focusing particularly on the reliability of the research methodologies employed. Questions were raised about the representativeness of the samples used, the suitability of the method of administering the questions (for example, self-completion questionnaires, as opposed to face-to-face interviews, may elicit a fuller response from middle-class than working-class people), the doubtful status as 'crime' of many of the acts asked about, the possibility of respondents telling lies and, indeed, the definition of 'lower class'—including the possible significance of differences between the urban and the rural working classes (for more detailed accounts of these problems and the related arguments, see Hood and Sparks, 1970; Braithwaite, 1979; Bottomley, 1979; Hindelang *et al.*, 1979, 1981; Bottomley and Pease, 1986; Coleman and Moynihan, 1996).

One of the most thorough reviews of the evidence has been that provided by Braithwaite (1979), who analysed forty-one self-report studies as well as over 250 other studies concerning the relationship between social class and crime. He concluded that, although the evidence was often contradictory and confusing, although police bias probably exaggerates the relative extent of working-class delinquency, and although self-report studies tend to exaggerate the relative extent of middle-class delinquency, the following statements may be made with some confidence:

1. Lower-class adults commit *those types of crime which are handled by the police* at a higher rate than middle-class adults.
2. Adults living in lower-class areas commit *those types of crime which are handled by the police* at a higher rate than adults who live in middle-class areas.
3. Lower-class juveniles commit crime at a higher rate than middle-class juveniles.
4. Juveniles living in lower-class areas commit crime at a higher rate than juveniles living in middle-class areas [Braithwaite, 1979: 62, emphasis added].

The most recent British contribution to the debate is the Home Office survey mentioned above, which confirmed the common finding—at least, among surveys based on self-completion questionnaires—of no significant association between social class and admissions to offending *as a whole*, but of a strong association, for both males and females, between social class and admissions of *more serious* offending (Graham and Bowling 1995: 33–5).

Of course, aside from lower class membership, statistical correlations have been claimed between many other social (as well as psychological and physical) factors and self-reported or officially defined offending. No more will be said here about the wide range of factors which are identified and discussed in depth by Farrington in this volume as distinguishing serious and persistent offenders from non-offenders or occasional minor offenders, except to reiterate the point (also emphasized by Braithwaite (1979) in relation to the social class of offenders) that the offences covered in the studies to which he refers are chiefly the common and visible predatory street offences like burglary and 'autocrime'—almost by definition the 'crimes of the poor'—rather than the more hidden kinds of crime which happen within the private space of the commercial world or within the household. Nor is there space here to do justice to debates about the complex and controversial issue of race and crime, which is tackled by Smith later in this volume. It will merely be noted in passing that perhaps the most interesting finding on this topic from a methodological (as well as sociological) point of view is that, despite the relatively high proportions of black people who are prosecuted and imprisoned, there tend to be few differences between black and white respondents in terms of offences admitted to self-report studies: to what extent this reflects 'reality' (and hence biases in the criminal justice system) and to what extent it arises from the unreliability of the self-report method, remains unclear.[41] However, we shall examine a little more closely what is perhaps the most interesting phenomenon of all to emerge from statistics on offenders, no matter what their source: *the overwhelming preponderance of males over females*.

This imbalance seems to be a universal feature of the criminal justice records of all modern countries, enduring over time, and confirmed by self-report studies and other research methods (Heidensohn, 1985 and this volume): it happens, for example, that the male–female ratio of convictions was almost precisely the same in 1892 as in 1992 (Home Office 1993c). Gender differences are also apparent when one looks at the types of offence for which males and females are convicted. For example, 66 per cent of all females convicted in England and Wales in 1994 had been charged with theft or handling stolen goods, compared with 39 per cent of males; on the other hand, convictions for

---

[41] For discussion and evidence on this issue, see Smith, this volume; Graham and Bowling (1995); and Hindelang *et al.*, (1981). The last study caused considerable debate through its finding that black males were three times less likely than white males to admit (to researchers) having committed offences which they were already 'known' (from official records) to have committed. This involved a technique known as a 'reverse record check', which is used to test the memory of survey respondents and/or their willingness to admit to crime.

burglary or drugs offences were relatively infrequent among all convictions of females (Home Office, 1995: 115).[42]

There has, it is true, been a very gradual upward trend since the 1960s in the proportion of females among those convicted or cautioned, as well as some small shifts in the pattern of female convictions which suggest greater involvement by women and girls in offences such as robbery and burglary—trends which gave rise to some controversy in the 1970s and early 1980s, around Adler's (1975) argument that the 'emancipation of women' was responsible for a greater number of women engaging in criminal activity, just as it had allowed women to engage in a wider range of legitimate economic and social activities. However, the rise in female cautions and convictions has not been strongly sustained: since the end of the 1970s, the female 'share' of officially defined offenders has fluctuated mainly between 16 and 17 per cent, rising to 18 per cent in the mid-1990s. (Moreover, several writers have commented, with regard to Adler's hypothesis, that the assumed 'female emancipation' is neither a proven phenomenon nor easily measurable—see, for example, Box, 1983.)

The argument that the official statistics grossly distort the 'true picture' and that a huge amount of female crime remains 'hidden', likewise finds little evidence to support it. Where 'traditional' property crime is concerned, the Home Office self-report survey found, for example, that males were, respectively, eight, six, and four times more likely than females to have committed burglary, car theft, and theft from vehicles (Graham and Bowling 1995: 13). Moreover, as Heidensohn (1989: 87) rightly points out:

There is little or no evidence of a vast shadowy underworld of female deviance hidden in our midst like the sewers below the city streets. As we have become increasingly aware in modern times, *quite the opposite is true.* There is a great deal of crime which is carefully hidden from the police, from families, friends and neighbours. Much of this takes the form of domestic violence, the abuse of children both physically and sexually, incest and marital rape. *The overwhelming majority of such cases involve men,* usually fathers and husbands injuring or abusing their wives and children [emphasis added].

Similar points can be made about another major area of crime which remains largely unrevealed by both police statistics and conventional crime surveys, that of corporate crime. As few women are in the high-level positions from which markets can be manipulated or business frauds perpetrated, it is safe to assume that this genre of crime, too, is overwhelmingly a male province.

To sum up, there now appears to be relatively little dispute about the broad validity of the general picture, as reflected in the official statistics, of the relative 'contribution' as offenders of males and females, but there is much more argument about the relative contributions of other major social groups, particularly black people and white people, and people from different social classes. Where the *persistent commission of common predatory street offences* is concerned, it is true, both 'official' and 'self-reported' offenders emerge with a broadly

---

[42] The equivalent proportions for burglary were 2 per cent compared with 11 per cent, and for indictable drugs offences they were 7 per cent compared with 15 per cent.

similar profile (partly, one may presume, because few persistent burglars or car thieves succeed in escaping conviction entirely). However, this does not alter the vital point that, just as victim surveys are vastly more effective in revealing 'hidden' instances of some kinds of crime than of others, so the perpetrators of different kinds of offence are not equally well 'revealed' through the medium of self-report studies. Thus, while respondents tend to be asked in great detail about the relatively visible kinds of anti-social activity which are associated with the court appearances of adolescents, they are not asked whether they have assaulted their partners or sexually abused their children, nor whether they have perpetrated a significant financial fraud. In many of the studies conducted, of course, there would have been little point in asking such questions, as the samples were drawn from groups of young males rather than being representative of the population as a whole. If a way could be found of overcoming the methodological and ethical problems of expanding self-report studies into such sensitive areas, the results might well support the indications from some (also methodologically problematic) victim surveys, that the perpetrators of intra-family violence and abuse are much more evenly distributed throughout the population (see, for example, Morgan, 1988; Morgan and Zedner, 1992; Dobash and Dobash, 1992; though for scepticism on this point, see Levi, this volume). And without doubt, they would confirm that the social class distribution of people involved in business fraud is skewed in a different direction from that of burglary and street robbery.

STUDIES OTHER THAN SURVEYS

Although the bulk of information relating to the 'crime picture' nationwide comes, by virtue of the vastly greater resources spent on gathering them, from data collected by the police and criminal justice agencies or by major government-run surveys rather than by individual criminologists, it is important to end this account with some (necessarily brief) mention of empirically based criminological studies which have not used survey methods and have been conducted only in a few local areas, yet have had a considerable influence on how we perceive crime.

At the extreme opposite end from national surveys are ethnographic or 'participant observation' studies of particular small groups or individuals. Most of these have been based upon groups of offenders, although a few have focused upon the lives of victims (especially women subjected to assault by men—see, for example, Counts *et al.*, 1992; Genn, 1988). Such studies do not use numbers at all, but try to convey the essence of their subjects' lifestyles, behaviour, and experiences by means of qualitative analysis, based on field notes acquired through close observation over a substantial period of time. Criminology has a long tradition in this kind of work, rooted in the 'Chicago' studies of the 1930s, which brought to life the dominant lifestyles, motivations, and *modi operandi* of, for example, the 'jack-roller' (Shaw, 1930) and the street corner gang (Thrasher, 1927: Whyte, 1955). However, apart from a strong period in the 1960s and early 1970s, this tradition has never really flourished in Britain, remaining largely a 'lone furrow' ploughed by a small number of talented ethnographers.

Even so, studies of this kind have produced important insights which have informed a great deal of other work, both theoretical and empirical. For example, path-breaking studies in the 1970s led to a greater understanding of the reality of 'joy-riding' in an inner city area (Parker, 1974), gang life in Glasgow (Patrick, 1973), and violence among female gangs (Campbell, 1981). More recently, Hobbs' (1988) ethnographic study conducted in the East End of London produced important insights about the influence upon both crime and policing of the unusual working-class entrepreneurial tradition in the area.

More common than purely ethnographic studies have been field research studies based on a catholic mixture of quantitative and qualitative methods, usually including face-to-face interviews with samples of offenders and/or victims using a semi-structured questionnaire. The samples may be drawn up primarily from official criminal justice records (like Maguire and Bennett's (1982) and Bennett and Wright's (1984) samples of 'burglars'), recruited from a variety of community schemes for offenders (as in Light's (1992) study of car thieves) or created via a 'snowballing' process of asking interviewees for introductions to potential new informants (as in Cromwell *et al.*'s (1991) study of burglars). While open to question about the 'representativeness' of their samples, such studies have usually carried more weight with policy-makers than have ethnographic studies, owing to the scope they give for producing statements of magnitude (e.g. '50 per cent of burglars interviewed said . . . '). At the same time, they have the advantage over large-scale surveys that they allow the researchers more scope to build up a rapport with those they interview, exploring matters in more depth and teasing out the subject's own understanding of events. Direct quotations from interviews can then be used to counterbalance any tendency of the figures and percentages to lose or distort the reality.

Studies of this kind have played a part in altering both criminologists' and policy-makers' perceptions of various kinds of crime. For example, Dobash and Dobash's (1979) study altered many people's notions of the scale and seriousness of domestic violence; Maguire and Bennett's (1982) research drew attention simultaneously to the relatively minor loss or damage suffered in most burglaries and the severe emotional impact that burglary has on many victims; and Pearson's (1987) work has helped to shift the perception of drug use as a swift and automatic path to addiction and dissolution, towards one of a culture in which at least *some* people can handle regular use over a long period while still leading an otherwise 'normal' life. Some of these studies have performed a 'myth-breaking' function, showing that the behaviour in question differs from what was commonly thought. Others have brought to people's attention areas of crime and victimization which had previously been largely ignored: examples include Ditton's (1977) examination of almost routine thefts by employees in all kinds of industries, Levi's (1981) work on long-firm fraud, and Morgan and Zedner's (1992) study of child victims. Further discussion of both ethnographic and field research studies can be found in Hobbs' chapter in this volume.

CONCLUDING COMMENTS

One of the central themes of this chapter has been the extent to which knowledge about 'crime' in all its manifestations has not only greatly expanded, but has shifted in focus over the last twenty or thirty years. A Rip Van Winkle-like criminologist waking up after, say, a forty-year sleep ready to resume his (he would almost certainly be male) task of 'explaining crime', would find himself confronted with a situation so foreign that he would find little in his theoretical toolbag with which to make sense of what he saw.

We have identified several major features of the changes he would have to come to terms with. First of all, instead of well under a million 'conventional' property and violent crimes, he would have to explain over 19 million (the BCS estimated total). Secondly, he would be confronted with evidence of widespread intra-familial crime, mainly sexual and physical abuse by men of women and children living with them. Thirdly, he would have to explain several massive corporate frauds and many other lesser forms of 'white collar crime'. Fourthly, he would have to explain an apparently major increase in international organized crime, much of it based on the smuggling and distribution of illegal drugs and the laundering of money from that trade (cf. Van Duyne, 1993). Fifthly, he would be pressed (probably for the first time) to take serious account of women in his studies—to ask why, for example, the sex distribution of victims and offenders is strongly skewed in many different types of crime. Finally, he would be confronted with ample evidence of the stark unpleasantness of crime from the point of view of the victim—and, moreover, the fact that a great deal of it is suffered by the poorest and most vulnerable members of society.

When one contemplates such a list (which is anything but complete), it quickly becomes clear why the traditional search for the 'criminologist's stone'—the 'cause(s) of crime'—has been largely abandoned. Contemporary criminologists are faced with a highly complex, diverse, information-rich, and rapidly changing field of activity, about which almost no generalizations can be made with any degree of confidence. The subject has of necessity seen more and more specialization, as individuals realize they cannot maintain expertise and keep abreast of new information across the growing range of topics it embraces. Not unnaturally, too, many have followed the lead of the most powerful institution in the field, the Home Office, in deciding to focus their attention firmly on 'the offence' (and the victim) rather than 'the offender': this is where the main investment in data collection has been put, most obviously in the case of the British Crime Survey, but also in lesser known surveys such as the Commercial Victimisation Survey (Mirrlees-Black and Ross, 1995). Increasingly, academics have taken advantage of the opportunity for secondary analysis of the growing body of BCS data: as each Survey has included questions on new areas, this offers rich pickings. Topics already explored include fear of crime, crime seriousness, crime and the elderly, risk of victimization, police–public contacts, the effects of victimization, and many more. Other academics have designed their own surveys to investigate new areas, including victims of fraud, crimes against business, and domestic violence.

Some criminologists with strong theoretical interests have tended to regard these general trends (the focus on offence patterns rather than offenders, and the value placed on surveys and statistics rather than qualitative data) as detrimental to the academic development of the discipline. Certainly, there is a danger that too much time is spent on descriptive analyses with short-term administrative goals, and the shortage of good observational and ethnographic studies is lamentable. On the other hand, it should be clearly recognized that a focus on patterns, trends, and the physical circumstances of crime can also be theoretically productive and raise many new and interesting questions. To take just a few examples, crime patterns have been examined and explained in terms of shifts in economic conditions (Field, 1990), unemployment (Box, 1987) housing (Smith, 1986) and 'routine activities' (Cohen and Felson, 1979), in each case yielding influential theoretical insights. At present, too, there is growing interest surrounding the concept of 'risk' (see Sparks, Hudson, this volume), which can be explored both empirically and theoretically, potentially to excellent advantage.

To conclude, this chapter has shown that, particularly since the advent of regular large-scale surveys, criminology has been acquiring a huge volume of new statistical data about crime. This can be seen as a positive benefit to the discipline, although at the same time there remain two dangers which have to be consciously avoided. One is that of forgetting the essentially shaky foundations of any knowledge about crime, and failing to treat measures of its 'volume', 'trends', 'distribution', and so on, with proper caution and a clear understanding of how the data were compiled and what they represent. The other danger is that of failing to realize the potential of the new knowledge in terms of the development of criminological theory. Undoubtedly, if only by dint of having to take account of so much more material, theoretical debate has become more disparate, and there is no strong consensus on the questions that should be tackled or how to tackle them. The 1980s saw increasing sophistication in data collection techniques and, in particular, important advances in knowledge about previously 'hidden' forms of crime. The challenge of the late 1990s and beyond seems to be to find new ways to make sense of it.

Selected Further Reading

The best recent British textbook on criminal statistics is *Understanding Crime Data*, by Clive Coleman and Jenny Moynihan (Open University Press, 1996). This covers in greater depth many of the issues discussed in this chapter, with the added advantage of a light and humorous touch which does not detract from the quality of the discussion. Despite their greater age, both *Understanding Crime Rates*, by Keith Bottomley and Clive Coleman (Farnborough: Saxon House, 1981) and *Crime and Punishment: Interpreting the Data* by Keith Bottomley and Ken Pease (Milton Keynes: Open University Press, 1986) remain high quality, illuminating books which include both theoretical and empirically based discussions of the status of crime data and the social processes which create them.

A useful edited book is Monica Walker's *Interpreting Crime Statistics* (Oxford: Oxford University Press, 1995), which has excellent chapters written by leading specialists on, *inter alia*, the design and interpretation of the British Crime Survey, homicide data, prison statistics, and the use of crime statistics for prediction.

Where official statistics are concerned, all students should make themselves familiar with the annual *Criminal Statistics*, prepared by the Home Office. The Home Office also publishes useful (and user-friendly) summaries of statistics from a variety of sources, especially in the frequent issues of the *Statistical Bulletin* and in the *Digest of Information on the Criminal Justice System in England and Wales*, which is issued about once every two years.

An enormous range of publications has been spawned by crime surveys, both local and national. For those interested in the methodology of such surveys, *Surveying Victims* by Richard Sparks *et al.* (Chichester: John Wiley, 1977) still repays attention, while probably the most influential local survey remains *The Islington Crime Survey: Crime, Victimization and Policing in Inner City London* by Trevor Jones *et al.* (Aldershot: Gower, 1986). By far the greatest output, of course, has emerged from the successive 'sweeps' of the British Crime Survey, each of which has generated interesting new material—not only through the raw results (the most recent being *The 1996 British Crime Survey*, by Catriona Mirrlees-Black *et al.*, 1996)—but in the many studies which have been derived from secondary analysis of the data. Most of these—or references to them—can be found in the sequentially numbered Home Office Research Series.

Finally, after a lean period of twenty or more years, important new self-report studies have begun to appear, notably the co-ordinated international survey (Junger-Tas *et al.*, 1994) and in particular its British version, of which a number of very interesting results are discussed by John Graham and Ben Bowling in *Young People and Crime* (Home Office Research Study No. 145, London: HMSO, 1995). Perhaps the best book on methodology in this area, however, remains that by Hindelang *et al.* (1981).

REFERENCES

ADLER, F. (1975), *Sisters in Crime*. New York: McGraw-Hill.

AMIR, M. (1971), *Patterns in Forcible Rape*. Chicago, Ill.: University of Chicago Press.

AUDIT COMMISSION (1993), *Tackling Crime Effectively*. London: Audit Commission.

BAKER, A., and DUNCAN, S. (1985), 'Child Sexual Abuse: A Study of Prevalence in Great Britain', *Child Abuse and Neglect*, 9: 457–67.

BANTON, M. (1985), *Investigating Robbery*. Aldershot: Gower.

BECKER, H. S. (1963), *Outsiders: Studies in the Sociology of Deviance*. London: Macmillan.

BELSON, W. A. (1968), 'The Extent of Stealing by London Boys and Some of its Origins', *The Advancement of Science*, 25: 171–84.

BENNETT, T., and WRIGHT, R. (1984), *Burglars on Burglary*. Aldershot: Gower.

BIDERMANN, A. D., and REISS, A. J. (1967), 'On Explaining the "Dark Figure" of Crime', *Annals of the American Academy of Politics and Social Science*, November.

BLACK, D. J. (1970), 'The Production of Crime Rates', *American Sociological Review*, 35: 4, 733–48.

BLAIR, I. (1985), *Investigating Rape: A New Approach for Police*. London: Croom Helm.

BOTTOMLEY, A. K. (1979), *Criminology in Focus*. London: Martin Robertson.

—— and COLEMAN, C. A. (1981), *Understanding Crime Rates*. Farnborough: Saxon House.

—— and PEASE, K. (1986), *Crime and Punishment: Interpreting the Data*. Milton Keynes: Open University Press.

BOWLBY, J. (1953), *Child Care and the Growth of Love*. Harmondsworth: Penguin Books.

BOX, S. (1983), *Power, Crime and Mystification*. London: Tavistock.

—— (1987), *Recession, Crime and Punishment*. London: Macmillan.

BRAITHWAITE, J. (1979), *Inequality, Crime and Public Policy*. London: Routledge and Kegan Paul.

BRANTINGHAM, P. J., and BRANTINGHAM, P. L. (1975), 'The spatial patterning of burglary', *Howard Journal*, 14, 2: 11–23.

BRODY, S. (1976), *The Effectiveness of Sentencing*, Home Office Research Study No 35. London: HMSO.

BURT, C. (1944), *The Young Delinquent*. London: University of London Press.

CAMPBELL, A. (1984), *The Girls in the Gang*. Oxford: Blackwell.

CHRISTIE, N. (1977), 'Conflicts as Property', *British Journal of Criminology*, 17, 1: 1–15.

—— ANDENAES, J., and SKIRBEKK, S. (1965), 'A Study of Self-reported Crime' in K. O. Christiansen, (ed., *Scandinavian Studies in Criminology*. London: Tavistock.

CICOUREL, A. V. (1968), *The Social Organization of Juvenile Justice*. New York: Wiley.

CLARKE, R. V. G. (1980), 'Situational Crime Prevention: Theory and Practice', *British Journal of Criminology*, 20: 136–47.

—— and HOUGH, M. (1984), *Crime and Police Effectiveness*. Home Office Research Study No 79. London: HMSO.

—— and MAYHEW, P., eds. (1980), *Designing Out Crime*. London: HMSO.

CLINARD, M. (1978), *Cities with Little Crime*. Cambridge: Cambridge University Press.

COHEN, S. (1974), 'Criminology and the Sociology of Deviance in Britain', in P. Rock and M. McIntosh, eds., *Deviance and Social Control*. London: Tavistock.

COHEN, L. E., and FELSON, M. (1979), 'Social Change and Crime Rate Trends: a Routine Activity Approach', *American Sociological Review*, 44: 588–608.

COLEMAN, C., and MOYNIHAN, J. (1996), *Understanding Crime Data*. Buckingham and Philadelphia, Penn.: Open University Press.

CORBETT, C., and MAGUIRE, M. (1988), 'The Value and Limitations of Victim Support Schemes' in M. Maguire and J. Pointing, eds., *Victims of Crime: A New Deal?* Milton Keynes: Open University Press.

CORNISH, D. B., and CLARKE, R. V. G. (1986), 'Situational Prevention, Displacement of Crime and Rational Choice Theory' in K. Heal and G. Laycock, eds., *Situational Crime Prevention: From Theory into Practice*. London: HMSO.

COUNTS, D, A., BROWN, J. K., and CAMPBELL, J. C. (1992), *Sanctions and Sanctuary: Cultural Perspectives in the Beating of Wives*. Oxford: Westview Press.

CRAWFORD, A., JONES, T., WOODHOUSE, T., and YOUNG, J. (1990), *Second Islington Crime Survey*. London: Middlesex Polytechnic.

CROMWELL, P. F., OLSON, A., and AVARY, D. W. (1991), *Breaking and Entering: An Ethnographic Analysis of Burglary*. Newbury Park, Cal.: Sage.

DAVIS, R., LURIGIO, A., and SKOGAN, W., eds. (1997), *Victims of Crime*. New York: Sage.

DITTON, J. (1977), *Part-time Crime*. London: Macmillan.

DOBASH, R. E., and DOBASH, R. P. (1979), *Violence against Wives*. London: Tavistock.
—— and —— (1992), *Women, Violence and Social Change*. London: Routledge.

ELMHORN, K. (1965), 'Study in Self-reported Delinquency Among School Children in Stockholm' in K. O. Christiansen., ed., *Scandinavian Studies in Criminology*. London: Tavistock.

ENNIS, P. (1967), *Criminal Victimization in the United States: A Report of the National Survey*. Washington, DC: US Government Office.

ERIKSON, K. T. (1964), 'Notes on the Sociology of Deviance' in H. S. Becker, ed., *The Other Side: Perspectives on Deviance*. New York: Free Press.

FARRINGTON, D. P. (1973), 'Self-reports of Deviant Behaviour: Predictive and Stable?', *Journal of Criminal Law and Criminology*, 64: 99–110.

—— (1989), 'Self-reported and Official Offending from Adolescence to Adulthood' in M. W. Klein, ed., *Cross-national Research in Self-reported Crime and Delinquency*. Dordrecht: Kluwer.

—— and BURROWS, J. N. (1993), 'Did Shoplifting Really Increase?', *British Journal of Criminology*, 33: 57–69.

—— and DOWDS, E. A. (1985), 'Disentangling Criminal Behaviour and Police Reaction' in D. P. Farrington and J. Gunn, eds., *Reaction to Crime: The Public, The Police, Courts and Prisons*. Chichester: John Wiley.

FERRI, E. (1913), *The Positive School of Criminology*. Chicago, Ill.: C. H. Kerr.

FIELD, S. (1990), *Trends in Crime and Their Interpretation: A Study of Recorded Crime in Post War England and Wales*. Home Office Research Study No. 119. London: HMSO.

GAROFALO, R. (1914), *Criminology*. Boston, Mass.: Little, Brown.

GENN, H. (1988), 'Multiple Victimization' in M. Maguire and J. Pointing, eds., *Victims of Crime: A New Deal?* Milton Keynes: Open University Press.

GOVERNMENT STATISTICAL SERVICE (1992), *Criminal Justice: Key Statistics in England and Wales 1991*. London: HMSO.

GRAHAM, J. G., and BOWLING, B. (1995), *Young People and Crime*. Home Office Research Study No. 145. London: HMSO.

HALL, R. (1985), *Ask Any Woman: A London Enquiry into Rape and Sexual Assault*. Bristol: Falling Wall Press.

HALL, S., CUTCHER, C., JEFFERSON, T., and ROBERTS, B. (1978), *Policing the Crisis*. London: Macmillan.

HANMER, J., and SAUNDERS, S. (1984), *Well-founded Fear*. London: Hutchinson.

HEAL, K., and LAYCOCK, G., eds. (1986), *Situational Crime Prevention: From Theory into Practice*. London: HMSO.

HEIDENSOHN, F. M. (1985), *Women and Crime*. London: Macmillan.

—— (1989), *Crime and Society*. London: Macmillan.

HINDELANG, M., HIRSCHI, T., and WEIS, J. (1979), 'Correlates of Delinquency: the Illusion of Discrepancy between Self-report and Official Measures', *American Sociological Review*, 44: 995–1014.

——, —— and —— (1981), *Measuring Delinquency*, Beverly Hills, Cal.: Sage.

HOBBS, R. (1988), *Doing the Business: Entrepreneurship, the Working Class and Detectives in the East End of London*. Oxford: Oxford University Press.

HOLDAWAY, S., ed. (1979), *The British Police*. London: Edward Arnold.

HOME OFFICE (1971), *Instructions for the Preparation of Statistics Relating to Crime*. London: HMSO.

—— (1989), *Criminal and Custodial Careers of those Born in 1953, 1958 and 1963*. Home Office Statistical Bulletin 32/89. London: Home Office.

—— (1991), *A Digest of Information on the Criminal Justice System*. London: Home Office Research and Statistics Department.

—— (1992), *Criminal Justice: Key Statistics in England and Wales 1990*. London: Government Statistical Service.

—— (1992a), *Gender in the Criminal Justice System*. London: Home Office.

—— (1992b), *Criminal Statistics, England and Wales 1991*. London: HMSO.

—— (1993), *Notifiable Offences, England and Wales, 1992*. Statistical Bulletin 9/93. London: Government Statistical Service.

—— (1993a), *Digest 2: Information on the Criminal Justice System in England and Wales*. London: Home Office Research and Statistics Department.

—— (1993b), *Criminal Justice Statistics 1882–1892*. Home Office Statistical Findings 1/93. London: Home Office Research and Statistics Department.

—— (1995), *Digest 3: Information on the Criminal Justice System in England and Wales*. London: Home Office Research and Statistics Department.

—— (1995a), *Criminal Statistics, England and Wales 1994*. London: HMSO.

—— (1996a), *Criminal Statistics, England and Wales 1995*. London: HMSO.

HOME OFFICE (1996*b*), *The Prison Population in 1995*. Home Office Statistical Bulletin, Issue 14/96. London: Home Office.

—— (1997), *Notifiable Offences, England and Wales, 1996*. Home Office Statistical Bulletin, Issue 3/97. London: Home Office.

HOOD, R. (1992), *Race and Sentencing: A Study in the Crown Court*. Oxford: Clarendon Press.

—— and SPARKS, R. (1970), *Key Issues in Criminology*. London: Weidenfeld and Nicolson.

HOUGH, J. M., and MAYHEW, P. (1983), *The British Crime Survey*. Home Office Research Study No. 76. London: HMSO.

—— and —— (1985), *Taking Account of Crime: Key Findings from the Second British Crime Survey*. Home Office Research Study No. 85. London: HMSO.

HUDSON, B. (1987), *Justice Through Punishment*. London: Macmillan Education.

HUIZINGA, D. and ELLIOTT, D. S. (1986), 'Reassessing the Reliability and Validity of Self-report Measures', *Journal of Quantitative Criminology*, 2: 293–327.

JONES, T., MACLEAN, B., and YOUNG, J. (1986), *The Islington Crime Survey: Crime, Victimization and Policing in Inner City London*. Aldershot: Gower.

—— LEA, J., and YOUNG, J. (1987), *Saving the Inner City: The First Report of the Broadwater Farm Survey*. London: Middlesex Polytechnic.

JUNGER-TAS, J., TERLOUW, G., and KLEIN, M. (1994), *Delinquent Behaviour Among Young People in the Western World: First Results of the International Self-Report Delinquency Study*. Amsterdam: Kugler.

KINSEY, R. (1984), *Merseyside Crime Survey: First Report*. Liverpool: Merseyside Metropolitan Council.

—— LEA, J., and YOUNG, J. (1986), *Losing the Fight Against Crime*. Oxford: Blackwell.

KITSUSE, J. I. (1964), 'Societal Reactions to Deviant Behavior: Problems of Theory and Method' in H. S. Becker, ed., *The Other Side: Perspectives on Deviance*. New York: Free Press.

—— and CICOUREL, A. V. (1963), 'A Note on the Uses of Official Statistics', *Social Problems* 11: 131–9.

LESIEUR, H. R., and LEHMAN, P. M. (1975), 'Remeasuring Delinquency: a Replication and Critique', *British Journal of Criminology*, 15: 69–80.

LEVI, M. (1981), *The Phantom Capitalists: The Organization and Control of Long-Firm Fraud*. London: Heinemann.

—— (1993), *The Investigation, Prosecution and Trial of Serious Fraud*. Research Report No. 14. London: Royal Commission on Criminal Justice.

—— and PITHOUSE, A. (1992), 'The Victims of Fraud', in D. Downes, ed., *Unravelling Criminal Justice*. Basingstoke: Macmillan.

LIGHT, R. (1993), *Car theft: The Offender's Perspective*. Home Office Research Study No. 130. London: HMSO.

MCCABE, S., and SUTCLIFFE, F. (1978), *Defining Crime: A Study of Police Decisions*. Oxford: Blackwell.

MCLINTOCK, F., and AVISON, N. H. (1968), *Crime in England and Wales*. London: Heinemann.

MAGUIRE, M. (1991), 'The Needs and Rights of Victims of Crime' in M. Tonry, ed., *Crime and Justice: a Review of Research*, 14: 363–433, Chicago, Ill.: University of Chicago Press.

—— in collaboration with BENNETT, T. (1982), *Burglary in a Dwelling: The Offence, the Offender and the Victim*. London: Heinemann Educational Books.

—— and CORBETT, C. (1987), *The Effects of Crime and the Work of Victims Support Schemes*. Aldershot: Gower.

—— and JOHN, T. (1996), *Intelligence, Surveillance and Informants: Integrated Approaches*. Police Research Group Crime and Prevention Series, Paper No. 64. London: Home Office.

—— and —— (1996*a*), 'Covert and Deceptive Policing in England and Wales: Issues in Regulation and Practice', *European Journal of Crime, Criminal Law and Criminal Justice*, 4: 316–34.

MANNING, P. (1977), *Police Work*. Cambridge, Mass.: MIT Press.

MARS, G. (1982), *Cheats at Work*. London: Allen and Unwin.

MARTIN, J. P. (1962), *Offenders as Employees*. London: Macmillan.

MATTHEWS, R., and YOUNG, J., eds. (1986), *Confronting Crime*. London: Sage.

MAUNG, N. A. (1995), 'Survey Design and Interpretation of the British Crime Survey', in M. Walker, ed., *Interpreting Crime Statistics*. Oxford: Oxford University Press.

MAXFIELD, M. G. (1984), *Fear of Crime in England and Wales*, Home Office Research Study No. 78, London: HMSO.

—— (1988), *Explaining Fear of Crime: Evidence from the 1984 British Crime Survey*. Home Office RPU Paper No. 43, London: HMSO.

MAYHEW, P., CLARKE, R. V. G., STURMAN, A., and HOUGH, J. M. (1976), *Crime as*

Opportunity. Home Office Research Study No. 34, London: HMSO.

—— ELLIOTT, D., and DOWDS, L. (1989), *The 1988 British Crime Survey*. Home Office Research Study No. 111, London: HMSO.

—— and HOUGH, J. M. (1988), 'The British Crime Survey: Origins and Impact' in M. Maguire and J. Pointing, eds., *Victims of Crime: A New Deal?* Milton Keynes: Open University Press.

—— and MAUNG, N. A. (1992), *Surveying Crime: Findings from the 1992 British Crime Survey*. Home Office Research and Statistics Department, Research Findings No. 2, London: HMSO.

——, —— and MIRRLEES-BLACK, C. (1993), *The 1992 British Crime Survey*. Home Office Research Study No. 132, London: HMSO.

MIRRLEES-BLACK, C., MAYHEW, P., and PERCY, A. (1996), *The 1996 British Crime Survey*. Home Office Statistical Bulletin, Issue 19/96. London: Home Office.

—— and ROSS, A. (1996), *Crime Against Retail Premises in 1993*. Home Office Research Findings No. 26, London: Home Office.

MORGAN, J. (1988), 'Children as Victims' in M. Maguire and J. Pointing, eds., *Victims of Crime: A New Deal?* Milton Keynes: Open University Press.

—— and ZEDNER, L. (1992), *Child Victims: Crime, Impact and Criminal Justice*. Oxford: Oxford University Press.

MURPHY, P., WILLIAMS, J., and DUNNING, E. (1990), *Football on Trial: Spectator Violence and Developments in the Football World*. London: Routledge.

NETTLER, G. (1978), *Explaining Crime*. New York: McGraw-Hill.

NORMANDEAU, A. (1969), 'Trends in Robbery as Reflected by Different Indexes', in T. Sellin and M. E. Wolfgang, eds., *Delinquency: Selected Studies*. New York: Wiley.

PAINTER, K. (1991), *Wife Rape, Marriage and the Law: Survey Report*. Manchester: Faculty of Economic and Social Science, University of Manchester.

PARKER, H. (1974), *View from the Boys; A Sociology of Downtown Adolescents*. Newton Abbot: David and Charles.

PATRICK, J. (1973), *A Glasgow Gang Observed*. London: Eyre Methuen.

PEARSON, G. (1987), *The New Heroin Users*. Oxford: Blackwell.

RADFORD, J. (1987), 'Policing Male Violence', in J. Hanmer and M. Maynard, eds., *Women, Violence and Social Control*. London: Macmillan.

REPPETTO, T. (1974), *Residential Crime*. Cambridge Mass.: Ballinger.

ROCK, P. (1973), *A Sociology of Deviance*. London: Hutchinson.

—— ed. (1988), 'The History of British Criminology', Special Issue of the *British Journal of Criminology*.

SAVILLE, E., and RUMNEY, D. (1992), *A History of the ISTD*. London: Institute for the Study and Treatment of Delinquency.

SELKE, W., and PEPINSKY, H. (1984), 'The Politics of Police Reporting in Indianapolis 1948–78' in W. J. Chambliss, ed., *Criminal Law in Action*. New York: Wiley.

SELLIN, T. (1938), *Culture, Conflict and Crime*. New York: Social Science Research Council.

—— and WOLFGANG, M. E. (1964), *The Measurement of Delinquency*. New York: Wiley.

SHAW, C. (1930), *The Jack Roller: A Delinquent Boy's Own Story*. Chicago: University of Chicago Press.

SHORT, J. F., and NYE, F. I. (1958), 'Extent of Unrecorded Juvenile Delinquency', *Journal of Criminal Law, Criminology and Police Science*, 49: 296–302.

SKOLNICK, J. H. (1966), *Justice Without Trial: Law Enforcement in Democratic Society*. New York: John Wiley.

SMITH, S. (1986), *Crime, Space and Society*. Cambridge: Cambridge University Press.

SPARKS, R., GENN, H., and DODD, D. (1977), *Surveying Victims*. Chichester: John Wiley.

STANKO, E. (1988), 'Hidden Violence against Women' in M. Maguire and J. Pointing, eds., *Victims of Crime: A New Deal?* Milton Keynes: Open University Press.

TAYLOR, I, WALTON, P., and YOUNG, J. (1975), *The New Criminology*. London: Routledge and Kegan Paul.

THRASHER, F. M. (1927), *The Gang*. Chicago, Ill.: Phoenix Press.

TONRY, M. (1994), 'Racial Disproportion in US Prisons' in R. King and M. Maguire, eds., *Prisons in Context*. Oxford: Oxford University Press.

VAN DIJK, J. J. M., MAYHEW, P., and KILLIAS, M. (1990), *Experiences of Crime Across the World: Key Findings of the 1989 International Crime Survey*. The Hague: Ministry of Justice.

VAN DUYNE, P. C. (1993), 'Organized Crime and Business Crime-enterprises in the Netherlands', *Crime, Law and Social Change* 19, March 1993: 103–42.

VON HENTIG, H. (1948), *The Criminal and his Victim*. New Haven, Conn.: Yale University Press.

VON HIRSCH, A. (1986), *Past or Future Crimes*. Manchester: Manchester University Press.

WALKER, M., ed. (1995), *Interpreting Crime Statistics*. Oxford: Oxford University Press.

WALKER, N. D. (1971), *Crimes, Courts and Figures: An Introduction to Criminal Statistics*. Harmondsworth: Penguin.

WALKLATE, S. (1989), *Victimology: The Victim and the Criminal Justice System*. London: Unwin Hyman.

WALLER, I., and OKIHIRO, N. (1978), *Burglary: the Victim and the Public*. Toronto: University of Toronto Press.

WALMSLEY, R., HOWARD, L., and WHITE, S. (1992), *The National Prison Survey 1991: Main Findings*. Home Office Research Study No. 128, London: HMSO.

WEST, D. J., and FARRINGTON, D. P. (1969), *Present Conduct and Future Delinquency*. London: Heinemann.

WHEELER, S. (1967), 'Criminal Statistics: A Reformulation of the Problem', *Journal of Criminal Law, Criminology and Police Science*, 58, 3: 317–24.

WHYTE, W. F. (1955), *Street Corner Society*. 2nd edn. Chicago, Ill.: University of Chicago Press.

WILES, P. N. P. (1971), 'Criminal Statistics and Sociological Explanations of Crime', in P. N. P. Wiles, ed., *The Sociology of Crime and Delinquency in Britain*. London: Martin Robertson.

WINCHESTER, S. and JACKSON, H. (1982), *Residential Burglary*. Home Office Research Study No. 74, London: HMSO.

WOLFGANG, M. (1959), *Patterns in Criminal Homicide*. Philadelphia, Penn.: University of Pennsylvania Press.

YOUNG, J. (1971), *The Drugtakers*. London: Paladin.

—— (1986), 'The Failure of Radical Criminology: The Need for Realism' in R. Matthews and J. Young, eds., *Confronting Crime*. London: Sage.

—— (1988*a*), 'Radical Criminology in Britain: The Emergence of a Competing Paradigm', *British Journal of Criminology*, 28, 2: 289–313.

—— (1988*b*), 'Risk of Crime and Fear of Crime: a Realist Critique of Survey-based Assumptions', in M. Maguire and J. Pointing, eds., *Victims of Crime: A New Deal?* Milton Keynes: Open University Press.

YOUNG, M. (1991), *An Inside Job*. Oxford: Clarendon Press.

5

Media Made Criminality: The Representation of Crime in the Mass Media

Robert Reiner

CRIMINAL TEXTS OR MENTAL CHEWING GUM?: THE MEDIA AND CRIME DEBATE

'We have got to tackle the question of excessive violence on our screens' declared Virginia Bottomley, the National Heritage Secretary, launching yet another 'crackdown' on TV violence (the *Guardian*, 11 December 1996: 5). This was just one recent episode in a very long-running saga. In that 'history of respectable fears' which Geoffrey Pearson has traced back through the last few centuries (Pearson, 1983), concern about the criminogenic consequences of the mass media is a perpetual refrain. 'The cinema is responsible for the increase in juvenile crime', claimed John Percival, Chief Constable of Wigan in 1916. He was giving 'evidence' to an enquiry by the so-called 'National Council for Morals', which was examining the sources of a supposed rise in juvenile crime (Mathews, 1994: 27). The same year a report representing all Chief Constables argued that 'The establishment of a central Government censor of cinematograph films is essential and will conduce to the reduction of juvenile crime in the country'(*ibid.*: 25).

'Twas ever thus. At the end of the eighteenth century, for example, the Middlesex magistrate Patrick Colquhoun, one of the architects of the modern British police, claimed that crime was rising because 'the morals and habits of the lower ranks in society are growing progressively worse' (Radzinowicz, 1956: 275). This was attributed to the erosion of positive cultural influences, such as religion, and the flourishing of malign forces. Amongst the latter Colquhoun singled out a supposed wave of bawdy ballad singers who went around entertaining in pubs. Unlike his present-day counterparts Colquhoun did not advocate censorship of these. Instead he urged the government to turn existing leisure pursuits to good effect. He wanted them to sponsor rival groups of ballad singers with wholesome and uplifting lyrics. He was confident that these eighteenth-century precursors of Sir Cliff Richard and Dame Vera Lynn would soon supplant their bawdy brethren in popular affection and influence.

Concern about media representations of crime is not confined to conservatives. A fundamental theme of the radical criminologies of the 1960s and 1970s was the power of mass media to foment fears about crime and disorder. The media manufactured the news (Cohen and Young, 1973), created moral panics about folk devils (Cohen, 1972), stigmatized outsiders (Becker, 1964), and amplified their deviance (Young, 1971), thus legitimating the drift to a law and order society (Hall, 1979) and a more authoritarian style of policing the crisis (Hall, *et al.*, 1978). Within the field of media studies the influential 'Cultural Indicators' project (launched in 1967 as part of the National Commission on the Causes and Prevention of Violence, cf. Signorielli and Morgan, 1990: 15) has sought to monitor the potentially damaging consequences of media representations of violence for democratic criminal justice and political institutions (Gerbner, 1995).

There are thus two polarized, critical perspectives about 'the crimes of mass media' (Ericson, 1995: p. xii). Each attributes great significance to media representations of crime, which are seen as essentially monolithic—a 'world at one with itself' (Hall, 1970). In their ideal-typical form they are polar opposites, sharing in common only their demonization of the media. The media-as-subversive tradition regards the media as a threat to law, order, and morality, whilst conversely the media-as-hegemonic approach sees the media as bolstering authoritarianism by cultivating exaggerated fears about criminality. Each has generated major research industries conducting empirical studies of media content, production, and effects.

Apart from these two apocalyptic approaches to media representations of crime two other general perspectives can also be distinguished. One is characteristic of those who have conducted detailed empirical studies of the production process or qualitative analyses of content. It is a view of the media as cultural cockpit, a site of ideological struggle. Whilst the competition for representation of different views is not conducted on a level playing field, such detailed studies reveal that many different groups and interests have access to the media (Ericson *et al.*, 1987, 1989, 1991; Ericson, 1991, 1995; Schlesinger *et al.*, 1991; Schlesinger and Tumber, 1992, 1993, 1994; Sparks, 1992). This perspective is critical of the functionalism and determinism it discerns in the view of the media as hegemonic, even though sharing its broadly critical politics. These conflicting interpretations of the role and operation of the media echo the general tension between structure and agency in sociological and criminological theories (Rock and Sparks, this volume).

A fourth perspective is that of the media-as-jester. This is the view that the media, or at any rate their representations of crime and violence, do not have significant effects at all. This is a view of many if not most workers in the media, especially those producing fictional entertainments, encapsulated in the legendary Goldwynism 'if you want to send a message, use Western Union'. In journalism it is a common contention of practitioners that news is more often the product of contingency than deliberation or planning. Cock-up prevails over conspiracy, and there is no systematic pattern to crime news or its significance (Murdock, 1982: 106–7). Nor should it be assumed that crime news is read or watched by the public in order to find out about crime, as a sort of informal criminology class. It has been argued persuasively that the interest of crime news stories derives from a variety of features which have nothing to do with the overt issue of crime. Instead they provide convenient vehicles for exploring common moral dilemmas (Katz, 1987; Dahlgren, 1988).

Because of the difficulties in rigorously establishing straightforward causal relationships between images and effects (which will be reviewed below) some researchers tacitly imply a similar position that media images of crime do not have coherent or significant implications. This often provokes the accusation that media researchers are blinkered by libertarian prejudices. As Melanie Phillips expressed this canard recently: 'for years, media academics have pooh-poohed any link between violence on screen and in real life' (the *Observer Review*, 8 December 1996: 2). She went on to denounce 'the cultural studies orthodoxy that media images have no direct influence on behaviour . . . such images merely provide "chewing gum for the eyes" '(*ibid.*). It is of course a non sequitur to move from the denial of a *direct* influence to the assertion of *no* influence, and Melanie Phillips' portrait of media studies 'orthodoxy' is a caricature. Nonetheless it does point uncomfortably to the way some libertarian opponents of censorship have interpreted the complexity and subtlety of the relationships between images and behaviour as a warrant for supposing there is none at all (in a manner analogous to Conservative ministers' jump from the assertion that unemployment is not straightforwardly related to crime to the claim that there is no link whatsoever).

In this chapter, I will review the broad contours of empirical research, theorization and policy debates about crime and the media. This will be organized in terms of three inter-related issues which have been the primary foci of research: the *content, consequences,* and *causes* of media representations of crime. Each has been the basis for a voluminous literature, mostly within a positivist paradigm, attempting to analyse separately the content, effects, and sources of media images of crime, primarily with a policy goal of controlling undesirable outcomes.

Although much of the research examines separately the content or the effects or the production of media images, these are phases of an intertwined process which can only be distinguished with some artificiality. Analysis of content always presupposes criteria of relevance in interpreting and coding aspects of communication, chosen because they are assumed to be related to some kind of presumptive effect. Creators of media products have in mind some anticipated audience responses, whatever their primary concerns— commercial, political, moral, or aesthetic. Any consequence of media images depends on how content is interpreted by different audience sections, and this often involves attempting to assess the meaning of the text intended by authors.

The organization of this chapter into the three main sections of causes, content, and consequence should be taken as a presentational convenience rather than an implication of hermetically sealed areas of concern. I will begin with a review of the literature on the content of representations of crime, which is the most voluminous, and usually implies particular positions about consequences and causes. I will then look at research attempting to assess the consequences of media images in terms of audience attitudes and behaviour, which has also been vast. Following this I will turn to the attempts to understand content by studying production processes. In the concluding section I will speculate about some future developments.

THE CONTENT OF MEDIA IMAGES OF CRIME

Problems of Content Analysis

Most analyses of the content of mass media have been within a positivist paradigm, quantitatively assessing patterns and trends in standard 'bits' of texts. As defined by one leading practitioner: 'content analysis is a method of studying and analyzing communications in a systematic, objective, and quantitative manner for the purpose of measuring certain message variables' (Dominick, 1978: 106). Whilst 'content analysis' so-called has been colonized by this positivist and quantitative approach, it may be distinguished from the more general project of the analysis of content. The claim made for content analysis of the traditional sort is that it 'provides for an objective and quantitative estimate of certain message attributes, hopefully free of the subjective bias of the reviewer' (*ibid.*: 106–7). Dominick goes on to concede that 'inferences about the effects of content on the audience are, strictly speaking, not possible when using only this methodology. More importantly, the findings of a particular content analysis are directly related to the definitions of the various content categories developed by the researcher. The validity of these definitions is an important consideration in the evaluation of any content analysis' (*ibid.*).

There are major problems with the claim that traditional content analysis is 'objective'. Whilst the categories used to quantify 'certain message attributes' may be free of 'subjective bias' they are neither randomly plucked out of thin air, nor do they miraculously reflect some singular structure of meaning objectively inherent in the texts analysed. They always embody some theoretical presuppositions of the researcher about criteria of significance. Moreover, whilst content analysis indeed cannot justify 'inferences about the effects of content on the audience', the categories selected for quantification often tacitly presuppose some theory about likely consequences. There would be little purpose in studying media texts (for anyone other than film or TV buffs) without a presupposition that the meanings conveyed by them have an impact on audience beliefs, values, or practices. The common tactic in content analyses (e.g. Gerbner, 1970; Gerbner *et al.*, 1980, 1984; Pandiani, 1978; Ditton and Duffy, 1983) of contrasting the pattern of media representations of crime and criminal justice with the 'real world' picture (supposedly conveyed by official statistics) is only of interest on the assumption that this 'distortion' leads to problematic consequences such as excessive fearfulness or support for vigilantism. Meticulously counting units of 'violence' is not a form of trainspotting for sadists but motivated by concern that exposure to these images carries risks such as copy-catting, desensitization, or heightened anxiety. Thus the 'objectivity' of traditional content analysis lies in the precision of the statistical manipulation of data, but these are generated through categories that necessarily presuppose some theory of meaning, usually about likely consequences (Gunter, 1985; Sparks, 1992: 79–80).

There is a further fundamental problem with traditional content analyses. They collate 'certain message attributes' according to characteristics set *a priori* by the observer. But what in the abstract may seem to be the 'same' image may have very different meanings within particular narrative genres and contexts of reception. How viewers interpret images of 'violence', for example, is not just a function of the amount of blood seen or screams heard. The same physical behaviour, for instance a shooting, means different things to any viewer depending on its placement in different genres, say whether it is news, a Western, a war film, or a contemporary cop show. It will be interpreted differently if the violence is perpetrated to or by a character constructed in the narrative as sympathetic. How audiences construe violence will vary according to their own position *vis-à-vis* the narrative characters, quite apart from any preferred reading intended by the creators or supposedly inscribed in the narrative. For example, the ride to the rescue of the 'heroic' Ku Klux Klan posse at the end of D. W. Griffith's 1915 epic *The Birth of a Nation* will have different meanings to a black audience in Harlem, a contemporary liberal audience in the Hampstead Everyman, or Southern whites in 1915.

This does not mean that analysis of content is impossible, or that quantification is necessarily misleading. Any reading of content, even an avowedly qualitative one, implies some quantification, contrasting observed behaviour with an implied norm, for example reading a character as 'brave' or 'strong'. Nor should the statistical manipulation of such categories be ruled out. The questions raised are about the claims of positivist content analysis to quantify in a value-free way aspects of a supposed objective structure in texts. They do not preclude numerical counts of features of texts. But these should be self-consciously seen as derived from the observer's frame of reference, according to explicit criteria. They need to be interpreted reflexively and tentatively as one possible reading. As such, they can yield valuable insights and raise interesting questions about the significance of trends and patterns in such data. There are several recent examples of such theoretically reflexive analyses of content, combining quantitative and qualitative methods (Ericson *et al.*, 1991; Schlesinger *et al.*, 1991; Sparks, 1992; Eaton, 1995). The project I am currently engaged on together with my colleagues Sonia Livingstone and Jessica Allen on *Discipline or Desubordination?: Changing Representations of Crime in the Media Since World War II* (funded by the ESRC as part of their 'Crime and

Social Order' initiative) includes a quantitative and qualitative historical study of images of crime in various media since 1945 (Reiner, 1996*a*), which is informed by a similar approach to analysis of content.

Content Analysis: A Review of Results

Having issued some health warnings about the methodological problems of content analyses, the next section will review their findings, with appropriate caution about what conclusions may be drawn. Most analyses of the content of media representations of crime have focused on news, print, and broadcast, although there are also some studies of fiction.

The fact/fiction boundary has always been particularly fluid in crime narratives. Crime and criminal justice have always been sources of popular spectacle and entertainment, even before the rise of the mass media (Foucault, 1975; Hay, 1975; Linebaugh, 1991; Gatrell, 1994). This gave rise to the genre of criminal biography and pre-execution confessions and apologias, of various degrees of authenticity, which flourished in the seventeenth and eighteenth centuries (Faller, 1987; Rawlings, 1992; Durston, 1997). Similar accounts continue to the present day, filling the 'true crime' shelves of bookshops (Rawlings, 1997), and they have been joined by the many volumes retelling the exploits of legendary detectives as if they were fictional sleuths (e.g. Fabian, 1950, 1954). On the side of overtly fictional crime narratives, ultra-realism (often a quasi-documentary style of presentation) has been common (using such devices as voice-overs giving precise dates and locations, and acknowledgements to the files of Scotland Yard and similar legendary police organizations as the source of stories).

The fact/fiction distinction has become even more fluid in recent times. There has been the growth of programming such as *Crimewatch* or Michael Winner's *True Crimes* which re-create actual cases. Fly-on-the-wall footage of actual incidents has proliferated: documentaries such as Roger Graef's pioneering 1981 Thames Valley Police series; newscasts of particular occurrences like the O. J. Simpson car chase, the video showing the beating of Rodney King, or the CCTV shots of Jamie Bulger being led away by his killers; live court reporting (as of the O. J. Simpson trial); and entertainment programming based on real cops in action. The media and criminal justice systems are increasingly penetrating each other (see Altheide, 1993; Schlesinger and Tumber, 1994), making a distinction between 'factual' and 'fictional' programming ever more tenuous. The implications will be explored further in the conclusions, but I will turn next to a consideration of the results of analyses of content.

Deviant News

Crime narratives and representations are, and have always been, a prominent part of the content of all mass media. Many studies have provided estimates of what proportion of media content consists of images of crime, sometimes comparing this across media, or over time.

The proportion of media content which is constituted by crime items clearly will depend on the definitions of 'crime' used. Probably the broadest approach is that taken by Richard Ericson and his colleagues in their penetrating study of newsmaking in Toronto (Ericson *et al.*, 1987, 1989, 1991). Their concern is 'social deviance and how journalists participate in defining and shaping it' (Ericson *et al.*, 1987: 3). Deviance is defined very broadly as 'the behaviour of a thing or person that strays from the normal. Here we are including as deviant not only serious forms of abnormal behaviour such as criminal acts, but also such behaviour as straying from organisational procedures and violations of common-sense knowledge' (*ibid.*: 4). When defined as broadly as this deviance is not a calculable part of news but its essence. 'Conceived in these broad terms, deviance is *the* defining characteristic of what journalists regard as newsworthy' (*ibid.*). Stories about crime in the narrower sense of violations of criminal law are a limited proportion of all news, albeit one which varies between outlets according to their medium (e.g. radio, TV, or print journalism) and market (e.g. 'quality' or 'popular' journalism).

Unsurprisingly, given the broad sweep of their concern, Ericson *et al.* arrive at one of the highest estimates of the proportion of news which is about 'deviance and control'. They calculate that 'the proportion of stories that were on topics of deviance and control' was 45.3 per cent in a quality newspaper; 47.5 per cent in a popular newspaper; 60.2 per cent on a quality television station; 47 per cent on a popular television station; 71.5 per cent on a quality radio station; and 64.2 per cent on a popular radio station (Ericson *et al.*, 1991: 239–42). Thus both medium and market influenced the proportion of news related to deviance.

Contrary to most other studies, 'quality' broadcasting outlets had more deviance stories than their downmarket counterparts. This was a consequence primarily of the broad definition of 'deviance and control' stories, including not only crime but 'violations of organisational procedures . . . and common-sense knowledge', as quoted above. The high proportion of such stories in the quality broadcasting media arises from 'their particular emphasis on deviance and control in public bureaucracies' (*ibid.*).

When the broad category of deviance is broken down into specific aspects, the findings of Ericson *et al.* become more in line with the generally perceived pattern. They adopt a broad concept of 'violence' in which ' "state violence" and "state terrorism" are conceptualised in the same way as various acts of violence by individual citizens' (*ibid.*: 244). Their concept includes not merely violent crimes but stories about policy debates to control the means of violence, or about 'harms to health and safety such as impaired driving, unsafe working environments, and unsafe living environments' (*ibid.*). This covers concerns which are more characteristic of 'quality' than 'popular' news outlets, but nonetheless Ericson *et al.* find that in each medium more attention is paid to violence by popular than quality journalism. Broadcast news gave more prominence to stories of violence than print (*ibid.*: 244–7).

Ericson *et al.* adopt an equally wide-ranging concept of 'economic' deviance.

This includes not only property crimes but 'questionable business practices . . . legal conflict over property . . . and social problems related to economic matters' (*ibid.*: 247). The 'quality' newspaper and radio station reported far more stories about economic deviance in this broad sense than their 'popular' counterparts. 'The reporting of economic *crimes* was rare in all news outlets. . . . Much more common in all news outlets were reports of violation of trust, with or without criminal aspects or criminal charges being laid' (*ibid.*). Consequently their data contradict the conventional findings of content analyses which 'criticised newspapers for their limited coverage of business crime' (Marsh, 1991: 73). Whilst Ericson *et al.* demonstrate that reports of corporate deviance feature prominently in the news, this does not necessarily undermine the more conventional conclusion that white-collar offending is obscured from public attention. Its reporting tends to be concentrated in 'quality' newspapers and is often restricted to specialist financial pages, sections or newspapers (Stephenson-Burton 1995: 137–44).

Ericson *et al.* also consider various other categories of deviance. 'Political' deviance includes improper 'actions by political authorities . . . actions by subjects in challenges to political authority . . . and violations of administrative procedures' (1991: 248). 'Ideological' deviance encompasses 'conflicts over political ideologies . . . cultural ideologies . . . and information control' (*ibid.*: 248–9). 'Diversionary' deviance refers to ' "morality" crimes' such as drugs, pornography or prostitution-related offences, or 'the regulation of leisure activities' (*ibid.*). Reporting of political and ideological deviance was generally more frequent and certainly no less common in 'quality' than 'popular' journalism, but 'diversionary' deviance featured more often in 'popular' outlets. Altogether Ericson *et al.* show that whilst the pattern of reporting varies in complex ways according to media and markets, deviance in a broad sense is the staple, defining feature of newsworthiness.

The Extent of Crime in the News

Most analyses of the content of media representations of crime have focused more narrowly on the legally defined category of crime, not the broad sociological concept of deviance adopted by Ericson *et al.* None the less estimates of the extent of crime stories vary considerably according to the precise definitions chosen. Some studies look only at stories about specific criminal incidents, but others include stories, articles, or editorials about the state of crime generally, about criminal justice, and about criminal-law violations related to political and social conflict, such as terrorism. The proportion of crime stories is a function of medium and market. It also exhibits variations between different times and places. 'Because of this variability, estimates of the proportion of total news that is devoted to crime coverage range from 5 to 25%' (Sacco, 1995: 142. Other useful reviews of this literature are Dominick, 1978; Garofalo, 1981; Marsh, 1991; Surette, 1992).

The lower estimates tend to come from earlier research such as a study by

Harris of three Minneapolis newspapers in 1890, 1904/5, and 1921, which found crime news accounted for about 4 per cent of total news space (Harris, 1932). A later study of 130 small and medium-sized US dailies between 1939 and 1950 found that on average 5 per cent of items dealt with major or minor crime (Swanson, 1955). An analysis of New York and Ohio papers found somewhat higher proportions of crime news (averaging 15 per cent in New York and 10 per cent in Ohio). There was a significant market variation: the *New York Times* devoted only 7 per cent of its space to crime compared to 28 per cent in the *Daily News* (Deutschmann, 1959).

The first study of crime news in Britain came to similar conclusions (Roshier, 1973). In the national papers studied the proportion of total news space devoted to crime varied according to market position. In September 1967 the percentage of crime news was 5.6 per cent in the *Daily Mirror*, 4.4 per cent in the *Daily Express*, 2.4 per cent in the *Daily Telegraph*. The *News of the World* gave crime much more prominence: 11 per cent of news space. There was no clear trend over time. In the dailies the proportion of crime news in 1967 was virtually the same as in 1938 (although it had been higher in 1955). The *News of the World* showed a similar U-shaped pattern: crime was 17.8 per cent of news in 1938, 29.1 per cent in 1955, and 11 per cent in 1967 (*ibid.*: 45).

More recent studies find higher proportions of crime-related items, in most media and markets. Graber studied crime news in 1976 in three national television networks, two local television news programmes, and three Chicago daily newspapers. She found that crime and justice topics accounted for 22 to 28 per cent of the items in the newspapers, 20 per cent of the topics on local television news, and 12 to 13 per cent on network television news (Graber, 1980: 24). The higher proportion of crime news is not necessarily a reflection of change over time, as she used a broader categorization of crime stories than earlier studies (including editorials, features, and letters to the editor, and items about criminal justice, or political crime, as well as reports of specific criminal incidents). In the United States a recent literature review of thirty-six content analyses of crime news conducted between 1960 and 1980 found considerable variation in the proportion of crime: from 1.61 per cent to 33.5 per cent (Marsh, 1991: 73).

In Britain more recent studies also find higher proportions of crime news than Roshier's average of 4 per cent for 1938–67 (Roshier, 1973). For example, a study of six Scottish newspapers in 1981 found that an average of 6.5 per cent of space was given to crime news (Ditton and Duffy, 1983: 161. See also Smith, 1984; Schlesinger *et al.*, 1991: 411–15). This rise was confirmed by a recent study comparing coverage of crime in ten national daily newspapers for four weeks from 19 June 1989 (Williams and Dickinson, 1993). 'On average, 12.7% of event-oriented news reports were about crime' (*ibid.*: 40). The proportion of space devoted to crime was greater the more 'downmarket' the newspaper. The smallest proportion of crime news was 5.1 per cent in the *Guardian*, the largest was 30.4 per cent in the *Sun* (*ibid.*: 41).

A recent study found that broadcast news in general devoted even more attention to crime reports than most newspapers (Cumberbatch *et al.*, 1995: 5–8). There were variations in the proportion of news items which concerned crime between different media operating in different markets. Independent Radio News carried the most crime news (over 21 per cent of all stories). Radio 1 also featured crime stories prominently, but Radios 2 and 4 carried fewer crime event stories (11 per cent), and Radio 5 the least (9 per cent). On television, crime stories were most prominent on Sky News (over 18 per cent) and ITN featured almost as many. BBC1 had fewer crime event pieces (11 per cent), but slightly more stories about crime in general and criminal justice (8 per cent). Crime news was more frequent than any other category for every medium at each market level (Cumberbatch *et al.*, 1995: 7).

Given that different studies work with vastly different concepts of crime, and have ranged over many different newspapers and places, it is not possible to conclude from a literature review whether there is a trend for a greater proportion of news to be about crime. Although later studies tend to find higher proportions of crime stories than earlier ones, they have also tended to adopt the broadest concepts of crime, so this may well be a result of the measurement procedures used rather than a reflection of change in the media. The one study which looked consistently at different years was Roshier's which found no clear pattern of change between 1938, 1955, and 1967.

The study I am conducting with Sonia Livingstone and Jessica Allen (Allen *et al.*, forthcoming) has collected data from the *Daily Mirror* and *The Times* on a consistent basis, examining a random sample of issues for each year between 1945 and 1991. We found an upward trend in the proportion of stories in both newspapers concerned with crime, although this was not straightforward and there were sharp cyclical fluctuations. In the *Daily Mirror* the average proportion of crime stories between 1945–51 was 9 per cent, whilst in *The Times* it was 7 per cent. Between 1985 and 1991 this had risen to 21 per cent in both papers. The percentage of crime stories overall, and *a fortiori* the proportion which is specifically about criminal activities as distinct from criminal justice is almost always slightly higher in the *Daily Mirror*. In both papers the proportion of stories about the criminal justice system, as distinct from the commission of criminal offences, has clearly increased since the Second World War. Criminal justice stories were on average 2 per cent of all stories in the *Daily Mirror* between 1945 and 1951, and 3 per cent in *The Times*. By 1985–1991 the average had increased to 6 per cent in the *Daily Mirror*, and 9 per cent in *The Times*. This is probably a reflection of the politicization of law and order policy in this period (cf. Downes and Morgan, this volume. We are conducting a detailed, qualitative analysis of a sample of stories which should shed further light on this issue, and on the overall trends).

In conclusion, estimates of the extent of news devoted to crime are highly sensitive to the varying definitions adopted by different researchers. It is also variable according to differences between media, markets, and over time.

Deviance and control in a broad sense are the very stuff of news. However, stories about the commission of particular offences are more common in 'popular' news outlets (although for official or corporate crime the reverse is true). The proportion of news devoted to crime, and even more so, the proportion about criminal justice, has increased over the last half-century.

The Pattern of Crime News

The main theme emphasized by content analyses has been the particular pattern of offences, victims, and offenders represented by the news. Much stress has been placed on the extent to which this pattern deviates from what is presented in official crime statistics (and, in some more recent studies, surveys of crime victims like the British Crime Survey). Official crime statistics and surveys are taken as representing the 'real' world of crime, usually without any acknowledgement at all of the many pitfalls in interpreting the meaning of such statistics (see Maguire in this volume; Reiner, 1996*b*).

Although many studies do recognize the problems of inferring effects on audiences from analyses of media content, there is usually an implicit assumption that the gap between media representations of crime and the reality supposedly disclosed by official statistics causes problems. Most commonly, the media are accused of exaggerating the risks of crime, presenting an image of the world which is 'scary' and 'mean' (Gerbner and Gross, 1976; Carlson, 1985). The fear of crime and the coping strategies to alleviate it, such as not venturing out at night, are said to be disproportionate to the actual risks, and thus unreasonable and problematic in themselves (see Sparks, 1992: chapter 1, for a cogent critique of the 'realist' conception of fear in such arguments). In addition the media over-emphasis on crime risks is claimed to increase political support for authoritarian solutions to a crisis of law and order which is largely the creation of media (mis-)representations (Hall *et al.*, 1978).

Whatever its consequences, crime news does exhibit remarkably similar patterns in studies conducted at many different times and places. From the earliest studies onwards analyses of news reports have found that crimes of violence are featured disproportionately compared to their incidence in official crime statistics or victim surveys. Indeed a general finding, emphasized originally in a pioneering study of Colorado newspapers, has been the lack of relationship between patterns and trends in crime news and crime statistics (Davis, 1952).

A recent paper reviewed thirty-six content analyses of crime news in the United States published between 1960 and 1988, and twenty studies in fourteen other countries between 1965 and 1987 (Marsh, 1991). All found an over-representation of violent and inter-personal crime, compared to official statistics, and an under-reporting of property offences. In America 'the ratio of violent-to-property crime stories appearing in the surveyed newspapers was 8 to 2; however, official statistics reflected a property-to-violent crime ratio of more than 9 to 1 during the survey period' (*ibid.*: 73). A similar pattern is found in the content analyses reviewed for other countries (*ibid.*: 74–6), including such British studies as Mawby and Brown, 1983 (84), Ditton and Duffy, 1983 (162–3), and Smith, 1984 (290–1).

British studies conducted in the 1990s continue to show the same pattern of over-representation of violent and inter-personal (especially sex) crimes. In some respects this tendency is increasing. Between 1951 and 1985 the number of rape trials increased nearly four times, from 119 to 450. In the same period, the number of rape cases reported in the press increased more than five times, from twenty-eight to 154. The percentage of rape cases reported in the press jumped from 23.5 in 1951 to 34.2 in 1985 (Soothill and Walby 1991: 20–2).

The proportion of news devoted to crime of different types and the prominence with which it is presented vary according to market and medium. In one month of 1989, 64.5 per cent of British newspaper crime stories dealt with personal violent crime, whilst the British Crime Survey found that only 6 per cent of crimes reported by victims were violent (Williams and Dickinson, 1993: 40). The percentage of stories dealing with crimes involving personal violence, and the salience they were given (as measured by where they appeared in the layout and the extent of pictures accompanying them) increased considerably the more downmarket the newspaper studied (*ibid.*: 40–3). Whilst on the one hand, the *Independent*, the *Guardian*, and *The Times* devoted 3–4 per cent of their news space to crimes of personal violence, this was over 19 per cent in the *Sun* and the *Star*. 'Middle-brow' papers like the *Daily Mail* or the *Daily Express* came closer to the tabloids (10–14 per cent) whilst the *Daily Telegraph* featured more violent crime than any other broadsheet (6 per cent: *ibid.*).

The pattern of offences reported varies according to medium as well as market. In Britain, the proportion of violent relative to other crimes reported in television news broadcasts is closer to the tabloid than quality or mid-market press, especially for local rather than national bulletins. A study of crime news in January–March 1987 found that the percentage of reports about non-sexual violence against the person in 'quality', 'mid-market', and 'tabloid' newspapers respectively was 24.7, 38.8, and 45.9. On national TV news it was 40 per cent, whilst on local bulletins violent crime stories were 63.2 per cent of all crime news. There was no significant difference between ITV and BBC1, but Channel 4 was more like the quality press (18.2 per cent: Schlesinger *et al.*, 1991: 412–15). Similar patterns are found for other offence categories: there are some 'market' differences between broadcast news channels, but on the whole the proportion of different offences portrayed on television news is closer to tabloid than broadsheet print journalism.

Violent crimes in general figure disproportionately in British broadcast news, although there are substantial variations according to medium and market. In one recent study, over 40 per cent of crime news items concerned death and murder on nearly all BBC Radio stations. On television, murder and death accounted for 53 per cent of all crime stories on Sky News, 42 per cent on ITN, and 38 per cent on BBC1 (Cumberbatch *et al.*, 1995: 25).

A further indirect consequence of the pattern of offences reported by news stories is an exaggeration of police success in clearing up crime (resulting largely from press reliance on police sources for stories). As summed up in a review of fifty-six content analyses in fifteen different countries between 1960 and 1988, 'the over-representation of violent crime stories was advantageous to the police . . . because the police are more successful in solving violent crimes than property crimes' (Marsh, 1991: 73).

There is a clear pattern to media portrayal of the characteristics of offenders and victims. Most studies find that offenders featuring in news reports are typically older and higher status offenders than those processed by the criminal justice system (Roshier, 1973: 45–6; Graber, 1980). This finding needs some qualification, however, in the light of the problems of official statistics. The profile of offenders dealt with by the criminal justice system is likely to be biased misleadingly towards lower status offenders. This is due to the high rate of 'attrition' of offences (especially white-collar ones), so that only a tiny minority of offenders are ever identified (cf. Maguire in this volume; Reiner, 1996*b*). In this respect the socio-economic characteristics of offenders in media stories may actually be closer to the—ultimately unknowable—'real' pattern than the official statistics which are based on the small proportion of offenders who are the losers of the criminal justice lottery. The over-representation of higher status offenders is more marked in reports of non-local crimes in the national press, than reports about crimes in the circulation area of a newspaper (Dussuyer, 1979; Garofalo, 1981: 324).

There is contradictory evidence about whether newspaper reports disproportionately feature ethnic minority offenders (Graber, 1980; Garofalo, 1981: 324; Marsh, 1991: 74; Sacco, 1995: 143). The one demographic characteristic of offenders which is overwhelmingly congruent in news stories and in all other data sources on crime is their gender: 'both crime statistics and crime news portray offending as predominantly a male activity' (Sacco, 1995: 143).

Studies assessing the profile of victims in news stories are fewer in number than analyses of the representation of offenders. However, they suggest similar patterns. News stories exaggerate the risks faced by higher status, white adults of becoming victims of crime (Cumberbatch and Beardsworth, 1976; Graber, 1980; Garofalo, 1981: 324; Mawby and Brown, 1983).

Another consistent finding of studies of content is the predominance of stories about criminal incidents, rather than analyses of crime patterns or the possible causes of crime. As summed up in one survey of the literature, 'crime stories in newspapers consist primarily of brief accounts of discrete events, with few details and little background material. There are very few attempts to discuss causes of or remedies for crime or to put the problem of crime into a larger perspective' (Garofalo, 1981: 325; Marsh, 1991: 76 draws similar conclusions from his literature review). Although an aspect of the more general event-orientation which is part of the 'eternal recurrence' of news (Rock, 1973), the 'mass media provide citizens with a public awareness of crime . . . based upon an information-rich and knowledge-poor foundation.

... Anyone interested in learning about crime from the mass media is treated to examples, incidents, and scandals but at such a level of description that it is impossible for them to develop an analytical comprehension of crime' (Sherizen, 1978: 204).

An important example of the concentration on events rather than exploration of underlying causes is the reporting of child sex abuse, which has systematically excluded issues of gender and focused primarily on the alleged excesses or failures of social workers in particular cases (Nava, 1988; Skidmore, 1995). Reporting of rape and other sex crimes is another area where issues of power and gender disappear in the fascination with the demonization of individual offenders or victims (Soothill and Walby, 1991; Lees, 1995).

The tendency to exclude analysis of broader structural processes or explanations is also evident in stories about political disorder (Halloran, Elliott, and Murdock, 1970; Hall, 1973: 232–43; Sumner, 1982; Tumber, 1982; Cottle, 1993). The portrayal of political conflict such as riot or terrorism is often in terms of sheer criminality, echoing the discourse of conservative politicians (Clarke and Taylor, 1980; Hillyard, 1982; Iyengar, 1991: 24–46). However, this varies according to different phases in the reporting of such conflicts (Wren-Lewis, 1981/2). After the initial reporting of events such as the 1981 Brixton Riots, which tends to be in terms of criminality, there is often a later phase of analysis of possible causes, especially if there is an official enquiry like Lord Scarman's (Murdock, 1982).

There are also variations between different media and markets. Print journalism, especially 'quality' newspapers and editorial pages, will often have more analysis, with radio news having the least, and television intermediate (Ericson *et al.*, 1991; Cumberbatch *et al.*, 1995: 7). Newspapers and quality broadcasting channels are also more likely to carry points of view critical of the actions of the authorities, giving some voice to those campaigning against officials. There has also been a tendency in recent years for critical and campaigning groups to gain access to the media, partly because of the sheer growth in the space for news in all outlets, partly because of the increasing politicization of law and order (Schlesinger and Tumber, 1994; Downes and Morgan, this volume). This is reflected in the increasing proportion of stories about criminal justice.

Although critical stories exposing wrongdoing by the police or other criminal justice officials are regularly published, and an aspect of the high news value attached to uncovering scandals amongst the powerful, this 'watchdog' function does not necessarily undermine the legitimacy of criminal justice institutions. Corruption and other police deviance stories have traditionally been framed within the 'one bad apple' framework, whereby the exposure of individual wrongdoing is interpreted as a testimony to the integrity of the system which dealt with it (Chibnall, 1977: chapter 5). As the volume of scandals has increased in recent years the 'one bad apple' story becomes harder to recycle. An alternative frame in which malpractice is often revealed within a damage limitation narrative is by presenting it as a story of institutional reform. This acknowledges the problems of previous practices but safeguards the legitimacy of the institution as one which is putting its house in order (Schlesinger and Tumber, 1994: chapter 7).

An earlier review of the literature about crime news concluded that 'it seems that a typical metropolitan paper probably devotes around 5–10% of its available space to crime news. Further, the type of crime most likely reported is individual crime accompanied by violence. Less than 5% of available space is devoted to covering the general issue of crime: its causes, remedies etc.' (Dominick, 1978: 108). This pattern remains recognizable, but there have been changes. The proportion of crime news is higher, and there is more about criminal justice. Whilst reports of violent *crime* still predominate, there are many stories about other types of deviance and control. More critical and analytic pieces have increased in frequency, especially in certain phases of disorders with a clear political dimension. Above all, every feature of the representation of crime in the news varies by media and market, and also shifts over time.

The Content of Crime Fiction

Studies of crime news have primarily used quantitative methods of content analysis, although some recent research has also used qualitative approaches. The analysis of crime fiction has been much more varied. Some social scientists have used quantitative content analysis methods to analyse crime fiction, primarily on television (Gerbner, 1970, 1972; Gerbner *et al.*, 1969, 1980, 1986; Dominick, 1978; Pandiani, 1978; Gunter, 1981, 1985; Carlson, 1985; Lichter *et al.*, 1991). More commonly, however, crime fiction—in print, the cinema, or on television—has been analysed using a variety of qualitative techniques and theoretical perspectives drawn from literary, film, and social theory, occasionally in combination with some quantification (McArthur, 1972; Shadoian, 1977; Rosow, 1978; Clarens, 1980 on gangster and crime movies; Haycraft, 1941; Watson, 1971; Symons, 1972; Cawelti, 1976; Palmer, 1978; Knight, 1980; Porter, 1981; Benstock, 1983; Most and Stowe, 1983; Mandel, 1984; Binyon, 1989; and Thompson, 1993; Clarke, 1996; on detective stories; Everson, 1972; Tuska, 1978; Meyers, 1981, 1989; Parrish and Pitts, 1990*a* on detective films and television shows; Reiner, 1978, 1981, 1992, 1994, 1996*a*; Park, 1978; Hurd, 1979; Kerr, 1981; Clarke, 1982, 1983, 1986, 1990; Dove, 1982; Dove and Bargainnier, 1986; Inciardi and Dee, 1987; Buxton, 1990; Parrish and Pitts, 1990*b*; Laing, 1991; Winston and Mellerski, 1992; Gitlin, 1994: chapters 11, 14; Sparks, 1992: chapter 6, 1993; Eaton, 1996 on police stories, films, and television shows; Nellis and Hale, 1982; Mason, 1996 on prison narratives).

As argued earlier, the fact/fiction distinction in crime narratives has always been rather tenuous, and is becoming more so. Indeed the genre of popular criminology, 'true crime' stories, has long been a staple form of infotainment, which has only recently begun to attract serious analysis (Peay, 1997;

Rawlings, 1997). It is hardly surprising, therefore, that the pattern of representation of crime in fictional stories, in all media, resembles the results of content analyses of crime news.

The Pattern of Crime Fiction

Respectable fears about waves of media crime are perennial, just as they are about crime waves in reality (Bell, 1960; Pearson, 1983. For some recent examples see Medved, 1992: chapter 12 and 'Watchdog Attacks ITV Over Glut of Crime Programmes', *The Times*, 25 April 1996: 6). However, whilst there have been important changes over time in *how* crime is represented in fictional narratives, crime stories have been a prominent part of most entertainment media, and there is little evidence of this increasing.

Stories of crime and detection have been staples of modern literature since the early days of the novel, as the works of Defoe, Fielding, and Dickens illustrate (Ousby, 1976; Durston, 1997). Detective story writers themselves (especially authors of the classic 'Golden Age' ratiocinative style mysteries) have been wont to trace their ancestry back as far as possible. Dorothy Sayers, for example, once wrote that: 'We find sporadic examples of it in Oriental folk-tales, in the Apocryphal Books of the Old Testament, in the play-scene in *Hamlet*; while Aristotle in his *Poetics* puts forward observations about dramatic plot-construction which are applicable today to the construction of a detective mystery' (Sayers, 1936: p. vii). In another anthology edited by her, 'the first four detective-stories in this book hail respectively from the Jewish Apocrypha, Herodotus, and the Aeneid' (Sayers 1928: 9). This was clearly an attempt to emphasize the 'snobbery' rather than the 'violence' of the classic detective story (Watson, 1971), as Sayers herself makes explicit in claiming that the 'criminological' element is secondary and almost incidental to the intellectual puzzle (Sayers, 1936: p. vii).

Whatever the truth of Sayers' claim there is no doubting the centrality of crime and detective stories in modern popular literature. As one contemporary crime novelist put it: 'One of the most consistently busy of Britain's home industries during the past fifty years has been the manufacture of crime fiction' (Watson, 1971: 13). The dominant style of crime fiction has varied between the classic puzzle mystery exemplified by Agatha Christie, the tougher private-eye stories pioneered by Dashiell Hammett and Raymond Chandler, the noirish thrillers and gangster stories of the *Black Mask* school, and the police procedurals of Ed McBain, Joseph Wambaugh, and others (an accessible history is Symons, 1972). Although each sub-genre is characteristic of a particular period—the classic mystery with the inter-war years, the private eye variant with the late 1930s and 1940s, the police procedural with the 1950s and 1960s—earlier styles remain popular, as witnessed by the perennial popularity of 'Golden Age' authors like Agatha Christie or Dorothy Sayers, and the early private-eye novels of Hammett and Chandler. New novels in these earlier traditions continue to proliferate (such as the classic puzzle mysteries of P. D.

James, Ruth Rendell, or Colin Dexter, and the Chandlersque private-eye stories of Ross McDonald, and more recently, Robert Parker, Jonathan Valin, and Roger Simon), even as new styles develop.

In the heyday of the 'Golden Age' detective story, the 1930s, crime novels were about 25 per cent of the popular fiction titles available through the W. H. Smith subscription library service (Watson, 1971: 31). The paperback revolution pioneered by Penguin in the late 1930s placed book-buying rather than book-borrowing within reach of a mass public. Crime fiction has consistently been a major factor in paperback sales.

Although it is impossible to give an exact figure, between a quarter and a third of total paperback output could probably be put into the category of 'thriller' of one kind or another. It is no exaggeration to say that, since 1945, at least 10,000 million copies of crime stories have been sold world-wide. English has been easily the top language, followed at a considerable distance by French, Spanish, German and Japanese: annual French sales top 30 million, annual German sales are put at 20–25 million, annual Japanese sales moved from some 14 million in the mid sixties to 20 million in the mid seventies [Mandel, 1984: 66–7].

The best-selling crime author has been Agatha Christie, with world sales well over 500 million, followed by such writers as Edgar Wallace, Simenon, Mickey Spillane, Ian Fleming, and Frederick Forsyth, all of whom have sold hundreds of millions of copies (*ibid.*).

Crime stories have also been a perennially prominent genre in the cinema, the dominant mass medium of the first half of the century (Solomon, 1976: chapters 4, 5; Clarens, 1980). As with its successors, television and video, it has perpetually been haunted by respectable fears about its portrayal of crime and violence (Sklar, 1975: chapter 10; Barker, 1984*a* and 1984*b*; Medved, 1992; Mathews, 1994; Miller, 1994). Whilst the way in which crime is represented in films has changed over time, it has not become more frequent. Together with Jessica Allen and Sonia Livingstone, I have analysed a random sample of 1,461 films released in British cinemas between 1945 and 1991, as part of our ESRC supported project, *Discipline or Desubordination?: Changing Media Representations of Crime Since the Second World War* (cf. Reiner, 1996*a*: 143–55 for details). We found that the proportion of crime films, and other films with significant crime content, has fluctuated cyclically since the Second World War. However, there is no long-term increase or decrease in crime films. Crime has been a significant concern of the cinema throughout: in most years around 20 per cent of all films in our sample are crime movies, and around half of all films have significant crime content.

Radio was the main broadcasting medium of the first half of the twentieth century. Stories about crime and law enforcement were a popular part of radio drama, in Britain and North America, although never as dominant as they subsequently became on television (Shale, 1996). In the United States it has been calculated that the proportion of evening radio programming taken up by crime stories was 4 per cent in 1932; 5 per cent in 1940; 14 per cent in 1948;

and 5 per cent in 1956, by which time there was significant competition from television (Dominick, 1978: 112–13).

Stories about crime and law enforcement have been prominent on television since it became the dominant broadcasting medium in the 1950s. In the early to mid-1950s the proportion of prime-time television devoted to shows about crime and law enforcement hovered just under 10 per cent (Dominick, 1978: 114). But by 1959 over one third of prime-time television was crime shows. Since then there have been cyclical fluctuations, but in most years at least 20 per cent of prime-time is given to crime shows, and in a few years nearly 40 per cent (*ibid.*).

Crime shows are just as much a staple of British television. As part of our previously cited ESRC study, Jessica Allen, Sonia Livingstone, and I have analysed the top-rated programmes from 1955 to 1991. During this period over seventy separate crime or law enforcement series have featured amongst the top twenty shows. In most years since 1955 around 25 per cent of the most popular television shows in Britain have been crime or police series. Whilst there are sharp cyclical fluctuations, there is no long-term trend.

Thus crime fiction, like crime news, is a prominent part of all types of mass medium, usually accounting for about 25 per cent of output. Whereas there was some tendency for the proportion of news space devoted to crime to increase in the last half-century, this was not true of fiction. Crime stories seem to have been a staple of popular entertainment throughout the modern period. Whilst concern about crime in fiction appears to have been a constant, there have been changes in *how* crime and criminal justice are represented, although the overall pattern is similar to that in news stories—and shows similar discrepancies from the picture conveyed by official crime statistics. The pattern of fictional representations of crime will be considered next.

Murder and other violent crimes feature predominantly in crime fiction, vastly more frequently than other offences which are far more common in official statistics. In our ESRC study Jessica Allen, Sonia Livingstone, and I analysed in detail the crime films which have done best at the British box office since the Second World War (Allen *et al.*, forthcoming). Murder was the primary crime (the McGuffin of the plot, in Hitchcock's terminology) in the overwhelming majority of films throughout the period. However, property offences provided the McGuffin in a significant minority of films up to the late 1960s, though seldom thereafter. Sexual and drug offences only begin to appear as central aspects of narratives after the late 1960s.

Up to the mid-1960s most films did not feature any crimes which were not directly related to the McGuffin. After that they begin to portray a world which is full of contextual crimes, unrelated to the central crime animating the narrative (to the point where characters like the eponymous *Dirty Harry* cannot go for a hamburger without coming across a bank robbery in progress). Up to the mid-1960s crime was represented usually as an abnormal, one-off intrusion into a stable order. Thereafter images of an all-pervasive, routinized threat of crime become more common. Linked to this is the increasing prevalence in films of police heroes: crime has become sufficiently routine to provide employment for a large bureaucracy, not just a diversion for enthusiastic amateurs at country house weekends.

Although murder has always been the most common central crime in movies, there is a clear trend to increasingly graphic representation of violence throughout the post-war period. Up to the early 1970s hardly any films in our sample showed more than a minor degree of pain or damage to the victim (beyond the fact of the murder itself!). Since then there has been an increasing number of films depicting severe suffering by victims, who are often represented as severely traumatized. There is an even more marked increase in the extent of violence shown in contextual crimes, as well as a growing frequency of violence not strictly necessary for the achievement of instrumental objectives (such as escaping arrest).

On television also, fictional narratives have always featured violent crimes far more prominently than other offences, and are focusing on them to an increasing extent. Studies of American television suggest that about 60 per cent of crime shown on prime-time shows consists of murder, assault or armed robbery (Dominick, 1973: 245; Garofalo, 1981: 326; Lichter *et al.*, 1991: 204; Sparks, 1992: 140).

A recent historical content analysis of 620 randomly selected prime-time TV shows broadcast between 1955 and 1986 demonstrated the growing preponderance of violent crime in television fiction (Lichter *et al.*, 1991: chapter 8). It found that 'television violence has far outstripped reality since the 1950s. In the first decade of our study, there were seven murders for every one hundred characters seen on the screen. This was more than 1,400 times the actual murder rate for the United States during the same time period' (*ibid.*: 185. The measure of 'reality' is taken to be the FBI *Uniform Crime Reports*. These suffer from the same limitations as other official crime statistics, but the murder figures are probably the least problematic).

Violent crimes apart from homicide also featured prominently.

Other violent crimes accounted for one crime in eight on TV during the decade 1955 to 1964. Violent crimes short of murder occurred at a rate of 40 for every 1,000 characters. At that time the real-world rate was only 2 in every 1,000 inhabitants. . . . During the second decade of our study, covering 1965 to 1975, crime rose both on TV and in the wider world. In the real world the rate for serious offences doubled to 25 for every 1,000 inhabitants, according to FBI statistics. Despite this increase in crime rates around the country, the television crime rate remained more than five times that of the real world, at 140 crimes per 1,000 characters. The FBI-calculated rate for violent crimes also doubled to 3 incidents per 1,000 inhabitants. The TV rate for violent crimes, at 114 incidents per 1,000 characters, was more than 30 times greater [Lichter *et al.*, 1991: 185–6].

The victimization studies which began in the late 1960s in the United States reveal far more crime of all kinds than the FBI statistics, but the 'television rate for violent crimes was still fifteen times higher than estimates from victimisation surveys' (*ibid.*).

In the third decade covered by Lichter *et al.*'s historical content analysis television and the world of statistically recorded crime converge slightly. On the one hand, broadcasting standards were altered in 1975 to create 'Family Viewing Time', which led to reduced levels of television violence.

The rate for serious crimes on television fell 3 percent to a 'low' of 110 crimes per 1,000 characters. The rate for violent crimes also dropped almost 3 percent, to 86 incidents in every 1,000 characters. . . . Thus, television and reality have moved closer together in terms of the overall crime rate, but television continues to present far more violent crimes than occur in real life [*ibid.*: 187].

The drop in the television violence rate was more than compensated for by the appearance of serious crimes which hitherto had hardly featured in genre crime fiction: prostitution and other organized vice such as pornography, and drug-related offences. On American television there was a fifteenfold increase in prostitution offences and a tenfold rise in drug-related crime between 1975 and 1985 (*ibid.*: 193, 201–3).

Ironically, in relation to property crime risks television has become safer than the world presented in official statistics. Between 1955–64 and 1975–84 the average annual rate for serious property offences in the United States increased from ten to fifty incidents per 1,000 people according to the FBI data. Victimization studies show the rate increasing from about 50 per 1,000 between 1965 and 1974 to 100 for every 1,000 inhabitants in 1975 to 1984. However, on television 'the rate for serious property crimes has remained steady at 20 incidents per 1,000 characters over the thirty years of our study' (*ibid.*: 191). Thus between 1955 and 1964 the television property crime rate exceeded the official statistics, but since then it has fallen far behind them, and *a fortiori* behind the picture presented by victimization surveys.

The portrayal of crime on television and other fiction presents it as predominantly violent, contrary to the picture in official statistics. Apart from statistical frequency, the *qualitative* character of crimes depicted in fiction is vastly different from the officially recorded pattern. Whilst most 'real' murders are extensions of brawls between young men, or domestic disputes, in fiction it is usually motivated by greed and calculation (Dominick, 1973: 250; Garofalo, 1981: 326–7; Reiner, 1996a: 153; Lichter *et al.*, 1991: 188). Rape is also presented in opposite ways in fiction and criminal justice statistics. In reality most reported rapes are perpetrated by intimates or acquaintances, not strangers (Barclay, 1995: 14). On television and other fiction, although rarely shown (and virtually never before the early 1960s) rape is usually committed by psychopathic strangers, and involves extreme brutality often torture and murder ('5% of the murders on TV result from rape' *ibid.*: 190).

Whilst crime fiction presents property crime less frequently than the reality suggested by crime statistics, the ones it portrays are far more serious than most recorded offences. Official statistics and victim surveys concur in calculating that the overwhelming majority of property crimes involve little or no loss or damage, and no physical threat or harm to the victim—indeed there is usually no contact at all with the perpetrator. In fiction, however, most property crimes involve tightly planned, high value, project thefts, and are frequently accompanied by violence (Garofalo 1981: 326; Lichter *et al.*, 1991: 192).

Related to the disproportionate emphasis on the most serious end of the crime spectrum is the portrayal of the demographic characteristics of offenders and victims presented by crime fiction. Offenders in fiction are primarily higher-status, white, middle-aged males (Pandiani, 1978: 442–7; Garofalo, 1981: 326; Lichter *et al.*, 1991: 197–200, 204). The social characteristics of victims are similar, although a higher proportion are female. Apart from gender, the demographic profile of offenders and victims in fiction is the polar opposite of criminal justice statistics (Pandiani, 1978; Garofalo, 1981; Lichter *et al.*, 1991; Barclay, 1995: chapters 2 and 3. See Sparks, 1992: 140–5, for a qualitative analysis).

A final important feature of fictional crime is the high clear-up rate. This is paralleled by crime news, but completely different from the picture presented by official statistics. In fiction the cops usually get their man (Dominick, 1973: 246; Garofalo, 1981: 327; Lichter *et al.*, 1991: chapter 9). Although crime fiction concentrates on the kind of serious violent crimes which do have the highest clear-up rates in reality, it has always exaggerated this considerably. In our sample of movies since 1945 (Reiner, 1996*a*), there was no film before 1952 in which criminals escaped capture, and hardly any up to the early 1970s. Thereafter, offenders get away with their crimes in an increasing number of films, albeit still a minority. Trends on television are similar, with the overwhelming majority of crimes cleared up by the police, but an increasing minority where they fail (Lichter *et al.*, 1991).

The police and criminal justice system are thus overwhelmingly portrayed in a positive light in popular fiction, as the successful protectors of victims against serious harm and violence. This continues to be so, although with increasing questioning of the inevitability of police success. This growing criticism of the police, within an overall positive image, is also represented in other aspects of crime fiction. Although the majority of police characters in films and television shows are represented as sympathetic, honest, and just, there is an increasing portrayal of police deviance. Corrupt, brutal, and discriminatory police officers have become more common since the mid-1960s in films (Reiner, 1996*a*) and television (Lichter *et al.*, 1991: chapter 9), as has acceptance of routine police violation of due process legal restraints (Dominick, 1978: 117; Garofalo, 1981: 327; Sparks, 1992: chapter 6).

The Media Representation of Crime: A Summary

The review of analyses of the content of media representations of crime suggests the following conclusions:

(i) News and fiction stories about crime are prominent in all media. Whilst there is evidence of increasing attention to crime in some parts of the media, overall this fascination has been constant throughout media history.

(ii) News and fiction concentrate overwhelmingly on serious violent crimes against individuals, albeit with some variation according to medium and market. The proportion of different crimes represented is the inverse of official statistics.

(iii) The demographic profile of offenders and victims in the media is older and higher status than those processed by the criminal justice system.

(iv) The risks of crime as portrayed by the media are both quantitatively and qualitatively more serious than the official statistically recorded picture, although the media underplay the current probabilities of victimization by property crimes.

(v) The media generally present a very positive image of the success and integrity of the police, and criminal justice more generally. However, in both news and fiction there is a clear trend to criticism of law enforcement, both in terms of its effectiveness and its justice and honesty. Whilst in the past the unbroken media picture was that *Crime Does Not Pay* (the title of a series of short films produced by MGM between 1935 and 1947), this is increasingly called into question in contemporary media news and fiction.

The next section will discuss the possible implications of this pattern of representation.

THE CONSEQUENCES OF MEDIA IMAGES OF CRIME

As discussed earlier, public and political concern about the relationship between crime and media has been animated by two polarized apocalyptic theories: the media as subversive, and the media as hegemonic. In addition, there have been those who wish to deny the media any significant role as other than harmless diversion—the media as jester; and the view of the media as cultural cockpit, a site of ideological contestation. In this section I will offer a brief overview and analysis of the huge research literature which attempts to identify and measure the effects of media images of crime. Much of the inspiration (and dollars) for empirical evaluations of media effects derives from the broader, apocalyptic concerns of subversion or hegemony. However, in practice research has sought to measure primarily two possible consequences of media images (which are not mutually exclusive): criminal behaviour (especially violence), and fear of crime.

The Media Connection: Offending Images and Criminal Conduct

There are many parallels between the heated debates concerning links between crime and the media and the equally vexed controversy about crime and unemployment. Those who wish to deny any connection whatsoever point to the equivocal results of empirical research, one-sidedly reading this as 'no causal links have been established', and concluding that research shows there is no relationship between crime and media images/unemployment. In considering the issue of possible effects of media on crime, I will follow the same broad approach as was taken by the late Stephen Box in his seminal study of the unemployment/crime connection (Box, 1987). I will first consider the way that the media feature in the most common social theories of crime, and then assess the empirical research evidence.

The Media and Criminological Theory

The media play at least a subordinate role in all the major theoretical perspectives attempting to understand crime and criminal justice (see Rock, this volume). To illustrate this I suggest that the various theories of crime can be assembled in a simple model. For a crime to occur there are several logically necessary preconditions, which can be identified as: labelling, motive, means, opportunity, and the absence of control. The media potentially play a part in each of these elements, and thus can feed into affecting fluctuating levels of crime in a variety of ways.

Labelling.   For an act to be 'criminal' (as distinct from harmful, immoral, anti-social, etc.) it has to be labelled as such. This involves the creation of a legal category. It also requires the perception of the act as criminal by citizens and/or law enforcement officers if it is to be recorded as a crime. The media are an important factor in both processes, and thus shape the boundaries and recorded volume of crime.

The role of the media in helping to develop new (and erode old) categories of crime has been emphasized in most of the classic studies of shifting boundaries of criminal law within the 'labelling' tradition. Howard Becker's seminal *Outsiders* analysed the emergence of the Marijuana Tax Act in the United States in 1937, emphasizing the use of the media as a tool of the Federal Bureau of Narcotics and its moral entrepreneurship in creating the new statute (Becker, 1963: chapter 7). Other famous examples are Stan Cohen's coinage of the influential concept of 'moral panic' in his study of the part played by the media together with the police in developing a spiral of respectable fear about clashes between 'mods' and 'rockers' (Cohen, 1972). Hall *et al.*'s wide-ranging analysis of the development of a moral panic about a supposed new type of robbery, 'mugging', emphasized the crucial part played by the media in stimulating public anxiety, and producing changes in policing and criminal justice practice which appeared to confirm the initial reports by processing more offenders: a self-fulfilling spiral of deviancy amplification (Hall *et al.*, 1978; see also Young, 1971).

Since these pioneering works many other studies have illustrated the crucial role of the media in shaping the boundaries of deviance and criminality, by creating new categories of offence, or changing perceptions and sensitivities, leading to fluctuations in apparent crime. For example, many accounts of the improved police treatment of rape victims during the 1980s highlight the key impetus to reform which was provided by Roger Graef's celebrated fly-on-the-wall documentary about the Thames Valley Police which sensitized public opinion to the frequently oppressive questioning of rape complainants (Zedner, this volume). One consequence, however, is a rise in the proportion of victims reporting rape, and an increase in the recorded rate. There are many other studies documenting media-created or amplified 'crime waves' and 'moral panics' (such as Fishman, 1981; Christensen, *et al.*, 1982; Best and Horiuchi, 1985; Nava, 1988; Altheide, 1993; Orcutt and Turner, 1993; Skidmore, 1995; Lees, 1995; Brownstein, 1995).

What all these studies illustrate is the significant contribution of the media to determining the apparent level of crime. Increases and (perhaps more rarely) decreases in recorded crime levels are often due in part to the deviance construction and amplifying activities of the media (Barak, 1994; Ferrell and Sanders, 1995).

Motive. A crime will not occur unless there is someone who is tempted, driven, or otherwise motivated to carry out the 'labelled' act. The media feature in many of the most commonly offered social and psychological theories of the formation of criminal dispositions. Probably the most influential sociological theory of how criminal motives are formed is Merton's version of *anomie* theory (Merton, 1938), echoes of which are found in such recent work as Lea and Young, 1984, and Dahrendorf, 1985. The media play a key role in these accounts of the formation of anomic strain generating pressures to offend. The media are pivotal in presenting for universal emulation images of affluent life-styles, which accentuate relative deprivation and generate pressures to acquire ever greater levels of material success regardless of the legitimacy of the means used.

Psychological theories of the formation of motives to commit offences also often feature media effects as part of the process. For example, various theories have claimed that the images of crime and violence presented by the media are a form of social learning, and may encourage crime by imitation or arousal effects, or erode internalized controls by disinhibition or desensitization through witnessing repeated representations of deviance (for discussions of these theories see Bailey, 1993; Carey, 1993; Wartella, 1995: 309–11; Livingstone, 1996: 308).

Means. It has often been alleged that the media act as an Open University of crime, spreading knowledge of criminal techniques. This is often claimed in relation to particular *causes célèbres* or horrific crimes (see for example some of the examples from the 1950s campaign against crime and horror comics: Barker, 1984). A notorious example was the allegation that the murderers of Jamie Bulger had been influenced by the video *Child's Play 3* in the manner in which they killed the unfortunate toddler (Morrison, 1997). A related line of argument is the 'copycat' theory of rioting (Tumber, 1982).

Opportunity. The media may increase opportunities to commit offences by contributing to the development of a consumerist ethos, in which the availability of tempting targets of theft proliferates. They can also alter 'routine activities' especially in relation to the use of leisure time, which structure opportunities for offending (Cohen and Felson, 1979). The domestic hardware and software of mass media use—TVs, videos, radios, CDs, personal computers, mobile phones—are the common currency of routine property crime, and their proliferation has been an important aspect of the spread of criminal opportunities.

Absence of controls. Given criminal labels, motivated potential offenders, with the means and opportunities to commit offences, crimes may still not occur if effective social controls are in place. These might be *external*—the deterrent threat of sanctions represented in the first place by the police; or *internal*—the still, small voice of conscience, what Eysenck has called the 'inner policeman'.

A regularly recurring theme of respectable anxieties about the criminogenic consequences of media representations of crime is that they erode the efficacy of both external and internal controls. They may lessen the efficacy of external controls by derogatory images of criminal justice, for example by ridiculing its agents, a key complaint at least since the days of Dogbery, resuscitated in this century by the popularity of comic images of the police, from the Keystone Cops onwards. Serious representations of criminal justice might undermine its legitimacy by becoming more critical, questioning for example the integrity and fairness, or the efficiency and effectiveness of the police. Negative representations of criminal justice could lessen public co-operation with the system, or potential offenders' perception of the probability of sanctions, with the consequence of increasing crime.

Probably the most frequently suggested line of causation between media representations and criminal behaviour is the allegation that the media undermine internalized controls, by regularly presenting sympathetic or glamorous images of offending. In academic form this is found in the psychological theories about disinhibition and desensitization, which were referred to in the section on the formation of motives (Wartella, 1995: 309–12 is a succinct summary and critique).

In sum, there are several possible links between media representations of crime and criminal behaviour which are theoretically possible, and frequently suggested in criminological literature and political debate. In the next section I will review some of the research evidence examining whether such a link can be demonstrated empirically.

Criminogenic Media? The Research Evidence

In a comprehensive review of the recent research literature, Sonia Livingstone remarked that 'since the 1920s thousands of studies of mass media effects have been conducted' (Livingstone, 1996: 306). She adds that even listing the references to research in the last decade would exhaust the space allocated to her article (some twenty pages). Several papers have appeared in the last few years providing general overviews of the evidence about media effects in relation to crime and violence (Bailey, 1993; Carey, 1993; Wartella, 1995; Livingstone, 1996).

The continuing availability of funding for this sort of research is, like second marriage, an indication of the triumph of hope over experience. For 'despite the volume of research, the debate about media effects—whether it can be shown empirically that specific mass media messages, typically those transmitted by television, have specific, often detrimental effects on the audiences who are exposed to them remains unresolved' (Livingstone 1996). Reviews of the literature regularly recycle the apotheosis of agnosticism represented by the conclusion of one major study from the 1960s: 'for some children, under some conditions, some television is harmful. For some children under the same conditions, or for the same children under other conditions, it may be beneficial. For most children, under most conditions, most television is probably neither particularly harmful nor particularly beneficial' (Schramm *et al.*, 1961: 11).

This meagre conclusion from the expenditure of countless research hours and dollars is primarily a testimony to the limitations of empirical social science (although it is often interpreted by conservative critics and libertarian or professionally interested defenders of media representations of crime and violence as a clean bill of health for such images). This is because the armoury of possible research techniques for assessing directly the effects of media images on crime is sparse, and suffers from evident and long-recognized limitations.

The primary technique used by such research has been some version of the classic experiment. The archetypal form of this is to show a group of subjects some media stimulus, say a film or TV programme or extract, and measure the response, in terms of behaviour or attitudes compared to before the experiment. In a characteristic example, children of 4 to 5 were shown a five minute film in the researcher's office, and then taken to a room with toys, and observed for twenty minutes through a one-way mirror (Bandura *et al.*, 1961, 1963). The children were randomly assigned to watch one of three films, enacting scenarios in which a boy who attacked another boy and some toys was depicted as either being rewarded, punished, or neither. The children (especially the boys) who saw the film with the boy rewarded for his attack by getting all the toys to play with were observed to carry out twice as much imitative aggression as the other groups, but no more non-imitative aggression.

This example shows all the problems of inferring conclusions about links between media and violence from laboratory-style experiments. Are the results a Hawthorn effect arising from the experimental situation itself? For instance were the more aggressive children who saw a film in which aggression was rewarded influenced by their perception that the experimenter approved of such behaviour? How far can results from one context of viewing be extrapolated to others? Do experimental results exaggerate the links in the everyday world by picking up short-term effects of media exposure which rapidly evaporate? Or do they underestimate the long-term cumulative effects of regular repeated exposures by measuring only one-off results? To some the artificiality of such experiments fatally compromises them (Cumberbatch, 1989). Others point out that 'laboratories' (or more typically researchers' offices or other convenient campus locations) are social situations 'whose particular dynamics and meanings must be considered . . . and generalisability depends on how far these same factors may occur or not in everyday life' (Livingstone, 1996: 310).

Given the huge number of such experimental studies (using different forms of stimuli and different types of measures of response, for different sorts of subjects, at many different times and places) it is hardly surprising that there are considerable variations in the extent of effect shown, if any. However, most studies do show *some* effect, and the few that conducted follow-ups over time found that whilst effects diminished over the fortnight or so after an experiment, they do not disappear (*ibid.*: 309–10). There are many suggestions in the experimental literature about the determinants of the degree of effect of media exposures, such as the extent of perceived realism of the representation, whether violence or deviance was seen as justified, punished, or rewarded, whether the viewers identified with the perpetrator, the variable vulnerability or susceptibility of the viewer, and so on (*ibid.*).

Typically, however, the effects of exposure to media stimuli in experimental situations are small. Interestingly, most of the research has looked at supposed negative effects of media, such as violence. The few studies which have examined the effect of 'prosocial' images, however, suggest that these are much larger (Hearold, 1986; Livingstone, 1996: 309). All of this has to be qualified, however, by the above caveats about how far such findings can be extrapolated to 'natural' contexts of viewing, and long-term effects in ordinary life (Wartella, 1995: 306).

Given the limitations of laboratory experiments, some studies have tried to assess the effects of media exposure in more or less 'natural' everyday situations. One method has been by looking at the introduction of some form of medium (usually television) in an area where it did not exist before. This was most frequently done in the 1950s when the spread of television ownership, first in the United States, then in the United Kingdom, provided the opportunity of a once-and-for-all natural experiment. One study of matched sets of thirty-four US cities in 1951 and 1955 found that larceny increased by about 5 per cent in the cities that gained access to television for the first time, compared to cities without TV or those that had been receiving it for some time (Hennigan *et al.*, 1952). However, British research in the same period does not find similar effects on deviance (Himmelweit *et al.*, 1958; Livingstone, 1996: 312–13). Since the virtually universal availability of television such natural experiments are seldom possible. One recent example found that children's verbal and physical aggression increased in a Northern Canadian town after television was introduced, compared to two towns with established television (Williams, 1986). Whilst such natural experiments do not suffer from the artificiality of their laboratory counterparts, they are of course less completely controlled: the possibility can never be ruled out that differences between experimental and control areas were due to factors other than television which changed at the same time.

The same issue arises in comparing the natural viewing habits of people who differ in their attitudes or behaviour concerning crime. Several studies have compared the viewing patterns of known offenders and (supposed) non-offenders. Some studies have concluded that more exposure to TV is related to greater aggressiveness (see Belson, 1978, and the other examples in Wartella, 1995: 307–9), others that the viewing preferences of delinquents are remarkably similar to the general pattern for their age (Hagell and Newburn, 1994). Neither conclusion is free from the possibility of other unmeasured factors explaining either the association or the lack of it.

Conclusion. A reading of any of the recent reviews of the research literature on possible links between media and criminal behaviour refutes the canard that libertarian wishful thinking has blinded researchers to the harm done by violent or deviant images. As one such survey found, 'distilling decades of laboratory, survey and field experimental studies, the current reviews conclude that there is a correlation between violence viewing and aggressive behaviour, a relationship that holds even when a variety of controls are imposed (for example age of subject, social class, education level, parental behaviour, attitudes towards aggression) and tends to hold across national boundaries' (Wartella, 1985: 306). However, the overall negative effects of media exposure seem to be small compared to other features in the social experience of offenders. Thus 'the question that remains is not whether media violence has an effect, but rather how important that effect has been, in comparison with other factors, in bringing about major social changes such as the postwar rise in crime' (*ibid.*: 312).

The problem with most of the effects debate and research is that it has often been directed at a rather implausible notion. What has been at issue is the will o' the wisp of a 'pure' media effect (analogous to the hunt for the snark of 'pure' discrimination in the literature on race and crime, cf. Smith, this volume). The implicit model behind much popular anxiety, which was imported into the research agenda (especially in earlier work), was of the media as an autonomous and all-powerful ideological hypodermic syringe, injecting ideas and values into a passive public of cultural dopes.

It is far more plausible that media images affect people, who are not passive recipients but active interpreters, in a complex process of interaction with other cultural and social practices. Changes in media representations do not come fully formed from another planet and produce changes in behaviour patterns *ex nihilo*. They are themselves likely to reflect on-going changes in social perceptions and practices. Changing media images will then be interpreted by different audience sections in various ways, which may reinforce or alter emerging social patterns. The relationship between developments in the media and in the wider society is a dialectical one. Whilst this makes the isolation and measurement of pure media effects chimerical, it certainly does not imply that media representations have no significant consequences.

As Sonia Livingstone concludes in her review of the effects research:

> Most media researchers believe that the media have significant effects, even though they are hard to demonstrate, and most would agree that the media make a significant contribution to the social construction of reality. The problem is to move beyond this platitude. . . . Part of the continued concern with media effects (aside from the occasional moral panics engendered around key issues) . . . is a concern with changing cultural understandings and practices. . . . The study of enculturation processes, which work over long time periods, and which are integral to rather than separate from other forms of social determination, would not ask how the media make us act or think, but rather how the media contribute to making us who we are [Livingstone, 1996: 31–2].

Most of the research on the consequences of media representations of crime has concerned their possible impact on offending. In the last thirty years, however, another policy and research issue has come to the fore: the impact of the media on public fear of crime, and the consequences of this. I will review this body of work in the next section.

The Media and the Fear of Crime

In recent years policy debates have focused increasingly on fear of crime as an issue potentially as serious as crime itself. Concern is not just about the unnecessary pain of excessive anxiety, nor even the damage done to trust and social relations by fear and the prevention strategies it encourages. In the 'cultivation analysis' tradition which George Gerbner and his associates have been developing for thirty years, media images of crime and violence are a threat to democracy.

> Fearful people are more dependent, more easily manipulated and controlled, more susceptible to deceptively simple, strong, tough measures and hard-line postures—both political and religious. They may accept and even welcome repression if it promises to relieve their insecurities and other anxieties. That is the deeper problem of violence-laden television [Signorielli, 1990: 102].

The essence of the 'cultivation analysis' developed by Gerbner and his colleagues is an on-going project of annual 'violence profiles': an elaborate content analysis of one week's prime-time television in an American city. When reel-world violence is compared to real-world crime as measured by official statistics it appears that the media images exaggerate the probability and severity of danger. This is said to 'cultivate' a misleading view of the world based on unnecessary anxiety about levels of risk from violent crime. The content analyses of programmes are the basis for construction of a set of 'television answers' to survey questions: the views about crime and violence which would be given by respondents 'if all we knew is what we saw' (Pandiani, 1978). The closeness of fit of actual survey respondents' answers to these questions is then analysed according to their pattern of television consumption. The general finding is that 'heavier' television viewing is associated with world-views closer to the 'television answer' (Carlson, 1985; Signorielli, 1990: 96–102). There has been extensive criticism of the empirical and theoretical validity of these claims (Sparks, 1992: chapter 4, is a penetrating and detailed review of these arguments).

The empirical debates have centred on three broad issues. How much of the association between measures of exposure to the media and of fearfulness survives the introduction of other control variables such as class, race, gender, place of residence, and actual experience of crime? (Doob and MacDonald, 1979; Gunter, 1987). Could any association between viewing and fearfulness result from the opposite causal process to that suggested by Gerbner and his associates: i.e. do more fearful viewers watch more TV rather than vice versa? More generally, it appears that 'cultivation' does not export well. British attempts to replicate the Gerbner findings have failed to do so, possibly because American television has a much higher violence profile (Wober, 1978). This means that 'the British *heavy* viewer may see less television violence than American *light* viewers' (Gunter, 1987: 250).

Gerbner and his colleagues have replied by various developments of their perspective, most significantly the concept of 'mainstreaming' (Gerbner *et al.*, 1980). This is the argument that television views are all-pervasive, constituting the cultural mainstream, and this dampens down the measurement of distinct effects. To a large extent 'cultivation' through heavy viewing reinforces wide-spread images in the dominant television-formed world-view. In order to rescue this plausible argument from untestability, subsequent research in the tradition has tried to measure mainstreaming by calculating the extent of 'the sharing of common outlooks among the heavy viewers in those demographic groups whose light viewers hold more divergent views' (Signorielli, 1990: 88).

Although the debate about the empirical validity of the cultivation hypothesis continues, there is evidence from other studies to confirm the plausible idea that exposure to media images is associated with fear of crime. A recent British study, for example, concluded after extensive multi-variate analysis that there was a significant relationship between reading newspapers with more emphasis on violent crime and measures of fearfulness expressed in a survey (Williams and Dickinson, 1993). This association survived control by a number of demographic variables, such as socio-economic status, gender, and age. However, this association was not found with behavioural concomitants of fear, such as going out after dark. Nor could the study rule out the possibility that fear led to heavier readership of newspapers with more crime, rather than vice versa. On the empirical issue, whilst it remains a reasonable hypothesis that much public fear of crime is created or accentuated by media exposure, the research evidence remains equivocal about the strength or even existence of such a causal relationship (Sacco, 1995: 151).

As with the research on media and criminal behaviour, much of this inconclusiveness is rooted in the theoretical limitations of positivist content analysis (Sparks, 1992: chapter 4). In Gerbner's violence profiles, for instance, items of violence are collated according to operational definitions used by observers, without reference to the narrative contexts within which they are embedded. As shown earlier, it remains the case that most narratives have conclusions in accordance with Miss Prism's celebrated definition of fiction: 'The good ended happily, and the bad unhappily'(Oscar Wilde, *Lady Windermere's Fan*, Act II). Although there is a trend towards the incorporation of more critical perspectives and greater ambivalence and ambiguity, most crime stories still have an underlying emphasis on just resolutions of conflict and violence (Zillman and Wakshlag, 1987). It is not obvious that exposure to high degrees of violence *en route* to a happy ending has a fear-enhancing effect. 'When suspenseful drama featuring victimisation is known to contain a satisfying resolution, apprehensive individuals should anticipate pleasure and enjoyment' (Wakshlag *et al.*, 1983: 238). Nor do counts of disembodied acts of violence distinguish between representations which are perceived as more or less 'realistic', and their differing impact.

Above all, quantitative assessments of the relationship between 'objectively' measured units of media content and survey responses cannot begin to understand the complex and dynamic inter-dependence of the differential experiences of crime, violence, and risk of different social groups and their subjective interpretations of the meaning of texts. The subtle intertwinings of differential social positions and life experiences with the reception of media texts is only beginning to be addressed by studies of content and interpretation using qualitative methods and ways of reading which are sensitive to the complexities of analysing meaning (Sparks, 1992; Schlesinger, Dobash *et al.*, 1992). As with the issue of the effects of media images on criminality, so too with fear, the issue is not whether media representations have consequences. Hardly anyone would deny this. The agenda is the unravelling of the complex inter-relationship of media content and other dimensions of social structure and experience in shaping offending behaviour and the fear of it.

Having examined the content and consequences of media representations of crime, the next section will consider the causes of these images. What processes and priorities produce the pattern of representation of crime?

THE CAUSES OF MEDIA REPRESENTATIONS OF CRIME

Crime stories are a prominent part of media output, whether news or entertainment. Within this there is a concentration of attention on serious violent and sexual offences, and on older, higher status victims and offenders. This has prompted two alternative apocalyptic interpretations: the media subvert authority by glamourizing and celebrating deviance; or the media reproduce a hegemonic ideology of law and order by spreading exaggerated fear of crime and an image of the authorities as vital for security. These polarized models both share an account of media institutions as publishing or broadcasting particular messages which suit the interests of those who control them. In both models commercial interests are a crucial part of the explanation. To conservative critics of the subversive character of mass culture, the problem is that commercialism drives the media to seek the lowest common denominator of taste and morality. Radical analyses of the media as reproducing dominant ideology point to the fact that media institutions are large business corporations, and are hardly likely to condemn the free market in which they flourish or the legal authorities that protect them.

Until recently accounts of the production of crime news were primarily based either on inferences drawn from content analyses and the political economy of the media (e.g. Hall *et al.*, 1978; Sherizen, 1978), or interviews with reporters and other creative personnel or the police (e.g. Chibnall, 1977; Fishman, 1981). It is only relatively recently that a number of studies based on observation of the news production process itself, and interviews with a wider range of sources, have been conducted (Ericson *et al.*, 1987, 1989, 1991; Schlesinger *et al.*, 1991, Schlesinger and Tumber, 1992, 1993, 1994; Skidmore, 1996).

Crime News as Hegemony in Action

Most of the earlier studies supported a version of the dominant ideology model. The immediate source of news content was the ideology of the reporter, personal and professional. However, a variety of organizational and professional imperatives exerted pressure for the production of news with the characteristics identified by content analyses. The sources of news production were seen as threefold:

The Political Ideology of the Press. The majority of newspapers have a more or less overtly C/conservative political ideology, and individual reporters are aware of this whatever their personal leanings. The broadcasting media, especially the BBC, are characterized by an ethic of political neutrality and professional objectivity in performing a public service of providing news information. In practice, however, this becomes a viewpoint which takes for granted certain broad beliefs and values, those of moderate, middle-of-the-road majority opinion—what Stuart Hall succinctly called a 'world at one with itself' (Hall, 1970). The master concepts of this world view include such notions as the 'national interest', the 'British way of life', and the 'democratic process' as epitomized by Westminster. In political or industrial conflict situations these are seen as threatened by 'mindless militants' manipulated by extremist minorities seeking 'anarchy' and subversion, with only the 'thin blue line' to save the day for law and order (Chibnall, 1977: 21). Political conflict is assimilated to routine crime as pathological conditions unrelated to wider social structures (Clarke and Taylor, 1980; Hillyard, 1982; Iyengar, 1991).

Traditional crime reporters explicitly saw it as their responsibility to present the police and the criminal justice system in as favourable a light as possible. In a study of crime reporters in the 1970s this was expressed thus by one: 'If I've got to come down on one side or the other, either the goodies or the baddies, then obviously I'd come down on the side of the goodies, in the interests of law and order' (Chibnall, 1977: 145). This of course did not mean that even the most pro-police crime reporter would not pursue stories of police mal-practice as assiduously as possible. But it did generate the tendency to present these within a 'one bad apple' framework (*ibid.*: chapter 5). However, the characteristics of crime reporting were more immediately the product of a professional sense of news values rather than any explicitly political ideology.

The Elements of 'Newsworthiness'. News content is generated and filtered primarily through reporters' sense of 'newsworthiness', what makes a good story that their audience wants to know about, rather than any overtly ideo-logical considerations. The core elements of this are immediacy, dramatization, personalization, titillation, and novelty (Chibnall, 1977: 22–45; Hall *et al.*, 1978; Ericson *et al.*, 1989). The value of novelty means that most news is about deviance in some form (Ericson *et al.*, 1987). The primacy of these news values explains the predoment emphasis on violent and sex offences, and the concentration on higher-status offenders and victims, especially celebrities. It also accounts for the tendency to avoid stories about crime in general or explanation of criminal trends and patterns.

These news values also encourage the presentation of political conflict in terms of individual pathology rather than ideological opposition. This was shown in a detailed study of the reporting of the 27 October 1968 anti-Vietnam War demonstration in Grosvenor Square (Halloran *et al.*, 1970). The media constructed their reporting around the issue of violence, crystallized in a photograph showing a policeman being held and kicked by demonstrators, which appeared prominently on most front pages the day after the event (Hall, 1973). The overall peacefulness of the occasion, let alone the broader issues of Vietnam, were subordinated to the emphasis on one dramatic but isolated incident of anti-police brutality. Most of the features of news reporting result not from ideology—political or professional—but are unintended consequences of a variety of structural and organizational imperatives of news-gathering.

Structural Determinants of News-Making. A variety of concrete organiz-ational pressures underlying news production have unintended consequences, bolstering the law-and-order stance of most crime reporting. For example, concentrating personnel at institutional settings like courts where newsworthy events can be expected to recur regularly is an economic use of reporting resources. But it has the unintended consequence of concentrating on cleared-up cases, creating a misleading sense of police effectiveness.

The need to produce reports to fit the time schedules of news production contributes to their event orientation, the concentration on specific crimes at the expense of analysis of causal processes or policies (Rock, 1973: 76–9). Considerations of personal safety and convenience lead cameramen covering riots typically to film from behind police lines, which unintentionally structures an image of the police as vulnerable 'us' threatened by menacing 'them' (Murdock, 1982: 108–9).

The police and criminal justice system control much of the information on which crime reporters rely, and this gives them a degree of power as essential accredited sources. The institutionalization of crime reporters as a specialist breed itself becomes a self-reinforcing cause of regular crime news. Crime reporters tend to develop a symbiotic relationship with the contacts and organizations they use regularly, especially the police (Chibnall, 1977: chapters 3 and 6). According to one influential account of news production, this means that such institutional sources as the police become the 'primary definers' of crime news, which tends to be filtered through their perspective. The structural dependence of reporters on their regular sources 'permits the institutional definers to establish the initial definition or *primary interpretation* of the topic in question. This interpretation then "commands the field" in all subsequent treatment and sets the terms of reference within which all further coverage of debate takes place' (Hall *et al.*, 1978: 58).

In sum, this account of news production within the hegemonic model sees news content as the largely unintended but determined consequence of structural processes. As one recent text summarizes it, 'journalists are not *necessarily* biased towards the powerful—but their bureaucratic organisation and cultural assumptions make them conduits of that power' (McNair, 1993: 48).

Crime News as Cultural Conflict

Recent more detailed observational and interview studies of the crime news production process qualify the deterministic implications of the hegemonic model (Ericson *et al.*, 1987, 1989, 1991; Schlesinger *et al.*, 1991, Schlesinger and Tumber, 1992, 1993, 1994; Skidmore, 1996). They do not overthrow its fundamental implications, however.

Ericson *et al.* confirm much of Chibnall's account of the structuring of news-gathering and presentation around a sense of news values, criteria leading to the selection of particular types of stories and perspectives. These constitute a 'vocabulary of precedents': not hard and fast rules but 'what previous exemplars tell them should be done in the present instance' (Ericson *et al.*, 1987: 348). This leaves room for flexibility and judgement; the newsroom is not charac-terized by normative consensus but negotiation and conflict between reporters, editors, and sources. News stories vary in character. Many are routine fillers, where a clearly established paradigm is followed, albeit with new names, dates, and details each time—although even here what usually makes a story news-worthy at all is some departure from expected norms, an element of freakish-ness or an opportunity to explore everyday moral dilemmas (Katz, 1987). But the big stories are ones where novelty is a high value, and there is more room for negotiation of angles and priorities.

There is always a tension between two contradictory pressures. The highest journalistic accolade is the 'scoop', reporting a high news value story which has not yet been reported. This exerts pressure to be ahead of the pack, to seek out sources which no rivals have yet found. However, the worst possible scenario is to miss important information which everybody else has. This generates a tendency to hunt in the pack, mining the same sources as rivals. The fear of failure usually prevails over the lure of the scoop, on minimax principles, which is why front pages tend to be so similar.

There are also systematic variations between news stories in different media and markets (Ericson *et al.*, 1991). This is partly because they have different variants of political and professional journalistic ideology according to patterns of ownership (state v. private, for example), and perceived audience (business or policy elites, other opinion leaders, liberal professionals, or a mass public seeking entertainment; local or national). These are interconnected with differences in technological resources, budgetary limitations, and the different 'grammars' of written and spoken language, still and moving pictures.

Observation also alerts analysts to the ever-present role of contingency and cock-ups (Ericson *et al.*, 1991: 93–4). 'We know that at the level of production news is more procedure-related than content-related' (*ibid.*), and procedures can be disrupted for all sorts of random reasons.

Detailed study reveals not only that there is more diversity, negotiation, and contingency within news organizations than the hegemony model implies, but also in the sources used. These range far beyond the accredited agencies of the formal criminal justice institutions (Schlesinger and Tumber, 1994). Groups critical of the establishment (such as penal reform or civil liberties groups) *are* given a voice, depending in part on their organizational and presentational skills, and their hold on interesting knowledge; and partly on medium and market differences. This is also a process which has gathered pace over time with the politicization of law and order (*ibid.* and Downes and Morgan, this volume). The news values of dramatization, personalization and titillation often lead to inputs from individual victims, offenders, witnesses, or their families and friends. The hegemonic model over-emphasizes the capacity of official viewpoints to monopolize the news.

Whilst more detailed analyses of news production in action do emphasize its contingency and fluidity compared to the determinism suggested by earlier accounts, they do not fundamentally change the picture of the role of crime news. Whilst news may be a competitive arena of conflicting viewpoints it is one which is culturally and structurally loaded (Schlesinger, 1989: 82). For all the fluidity and contingency which can be observed in the process of production, in the final analysis 'the news media are as much an agency of *policing* as the law-enforcement agencies whose activities and classifications are reported on' (Ericson *et al.*, 1991: 74). They reproduce order in the process of representing it.

Whilst there have been many studies of the production of crime news, there has been no comparable research on fiction. All we have are memoirs of writers, directors, and other creators of crime fiction, and fan-oriented biographies or accounts of the making of particular films or programmes. The only exception is one interview study of current Hollywood writers, directors, and producers of TV shows (Lichter *et al.*, 1991: Part IV). This suggests that today's Hollywood elite sees itself as having a mission. In essence they are an example of the 1960s radicals' long march through the institutions. Their ideology is a combination of acceptance of the economic and political institutions of America to which they owe their status and privileges, and the libertarian stance on issues of personal and sexual morality which they have carried since their youth. They feel a mission to put as much of this into their work as is compatible with the over-riding priority of keeping the audience ratings high and the networks happy. How this expressed ideology translates into actual creative and production practices has not been studied, however, in any research analogous to that on crime news.

CONCLUSION

The above review of research suggests that there has long been a complex interplay between media representations of crime, criminal behaviour, and criminal justice. With variations according to medium and market, the content of mass media news and entertainment is saturated with stories about crime. These disproportionately present the most serious and violent crimes, but strip these from any analytic framework: the emphasis is on crime as the product of individual choice and free-floating evil, diverting attention from any links to social structure or culture. Although there is strong evidence that media images can influence criminal behaviour, the effect is relatively small relative to other factors (Petley and Barker, 1997). The more significant role of media stories about crime is as part of the social control apparatus, reproducing as well as representing order. This works both through images which accentuate fear and thus support for law and order policies, and directly by presenting viewpoints which—though not monolithic—are loaded towards official perspectives.

The present trends indicate a growing symbiosis between media images, criminality, and criminal justice. This accentuates past patterns to an extent amounting to a qualitatively new stage. The always permeable borderline between purportedly factual and fictional narratives is eroding. A growing variety of criminal justice lobbies and pressure-groups seek to influence, and increasingly to construct, the news. For example, the Police Federation has for some years been using the formidable weapon of libel actions to constrain reporting of police deviance (*Observer*, 9 February 1997: 2).

The current stage of development reflects the impact of the more general features of 'postmodernity', such as the erosion of 'space-time distanciation' (Giddens, 1984; Thompson, 1995), on the relationship between media, crime, and criminal justice. The gap between criminal cases and their reporting in the media is narrowing, if not disappearing, and images have an ever-greater reciprocal feedback on criminality and criminal justice practice. (A vivid fictional treatment of the simultaneous implication of representations and reality with each other is Ben Elton's 1996 novel *Popcorn*.)

Increasing numbers of criminal justice events, such as the 1992 Los Angeles riots or the O. J. Simpson case, are broadcast around the world literally as they are happening. An ever-wider range of participants in the criminal justice process are not only seeking to influence representations but creating events specifically for the media (for example a press conference organized by a murder suspect to put her case: *Guardian*, 6 February 1997: 1). 'We live in a dramatised world' (Ericson, 1991: 235), where the media are increasingly participants in the processes they represent. Criminal justice agencies tailor their activities to public relations, how their activities will play on the news. Police investigate (sometimes instigate) all the crimes fit to print. Crimes and legal processes are not only immediately reflected in reporting, but increasingly created for news stories (Altheide, 1993, is a particularly vivid example of the incitement of offences by law enforcement agencies in order to have the successful investigation televised.)

This raises the spectre of 'a media spiral in which the representations of crime and the fear of crime precisely constitute . . . the hyperreal' (Osborne, 1996: 36). Certainly these developments vastly complicate the always vexed question of how images and narratives which are felt to be undesirable can be regulated or influenced. Perhaps hope lies precisely in the greater openness of the media to a diversity of inputs and influences (Ericson, 1991; Schlesinger and Tumber, 1994). Past experience, however, suggests the more pessimistic prediction that even though contemporary mass communications present 'an appreciably open terrain for struggles for justice' (Ericson 1991: 242), the dice are loaded in favour of dominant interests—even if they have to struggle harder for their hegemony.

Selected Further Reading

Richard Sparks' *Television and the Drama of Crime* (Milton Keynes: Open University Press, 1992) is a theoretically sophisticated critical review of content analyses of crime fiction, concentrating particularly on the issue of fear of crime. Classic studies of crime news are S. Cohen and J. Young, eds., *The Manufacture of News* (London: Constable, 1973); and S. Chibnall, *Law-and-Order News* (London: Tavistock, 1977). Two recent rigorous studies of the content and production of crime news are the trilogy by Richard Ericson, Patricia Baranek, and Janet Chan: *Visualising Deviance, Negotiating Control*, and *Representing Order* (Milton Keynes: Open University Press, 1987, 1989, and 1991 respectively), and Philip Schlesinger and Howard Tumber's *Reporting Crime* (Oxford: Oxford University Press, 1994). Useful reviews of the effects research are Ellen Wartella, 'Media and Problem Behaviours in

Young People', in M. Rutter and D. Smith, eds., *Psychosocial Disorders in Young People* (London: Wiley, 1995); and Sonia Livingstone, 'On the Continuing Problem of Media Effects', in J. Curran and M. Gurevitch, eds., *Mass Media and Society* (London: Arnold, 1996). Two invaluable recent collections of papers are R. Ericson, ed., *Crime and the Media* (Aldershot: Dartmouth, 1995); and D. Kidd-Hewitt and R. Osborne, eds., *Crime and the Media: The Post-Modern Spectacle* (London: Pluto, 1996).

REFERENCES

ALLEN, J., LIVINGSTONE, S., and REINER, R. (forthcoming), 'Discipline or Desubordination?: Changing Images of Crime in the Media Since the Second World War'. Report to the ESRC, not yet published.

ALTHEIDE, D. (1993), 'Electronic Media and State Control: The Case of Azscam', *The Sociological Quarterly* 34, 1: 53–69.

BAILEY, S. (1993), 'Fast Forward to Violence: Violent Visual Imaging and Serious Juvenile Crime', *Criminal Justice Matters*, 11 Spring: 6–7.

BANDURA, A., ROSS, D., and ROS, S. A. (1961), 'Transmission of Aggression Through Imitation of Aggressive Models', *Journal of Abnormal and Social Psychology*, 63, 3: 575–82.

BARAK, G., ed. (1994), *Media, Process, and the Social Construction of Crime*. New York: Garland.

BARCLAY, G. (1995) *Information on the Criminal Justice System in England and Wales: Digest 3*. London: Home Office.

BARKER, M. (1984a), *A Haunt of Fears*. London: Pluto.

—— (1984b), *The Video Nasties: Freedom and Censorship in the Media*. London: Pluto.

BECKER, H. (1964), *Outsiders*. New York: Free Press.

BELL, D. (1960), 'The Myth of Crime Waves', in *The End of Ideology*, 151–74. New York: Free Press.

BELSON, W. (1978), *Television Violence and the Adolescent Boy*. Westmead: Saxon House.

BENSTOCK, B., ed. (1983), *Essays on Detective Fiction*. London: Macmillan.

BEST, J., and HORIUCHI, G. T. (1985), 'The Razor Blade in the Apple: The Social Construction of Urban Legends', *Social Problems* 32, 5: 488–99.

BINYON, T. J. (1989), *Murder Will Out: The Detective in Fiction*. Oxford: Oxford University Press.

BOX, S. (1987), *Recession, Crime and Punishment*. London: Macmillan.

BROWNSTEIN, H. (1995), 'The Media and the Construction of Random Drug Violence', in J. Ferrell and C. R. Sanders, eds., *Cultural Criminology*, 45–65. Boston Mass.: Northeastern University Press.

BUXTON, D. (1990), *From The Avengers to Miami Vice: Form and Ideology in Television Series*. Manchester: Manchester University Press.

CAREY, S. (1993), 'Mass Media Violence and Aggressive Behaviour', *Criminal Justice Matters*, 11 Spring: 8–9.

CARLSON, J. M. (1985), *Prime-Time Law Enforcement: Crime Show Viewing and Attitudes to the Criminal Justice System*. New York: Praeger.

CAWELTI, J. G. (1976), *Adventure, Mystery and Romance*. Chicago: Chicago University Press.

CHIBNALL, S. (1977), *Law-and-Order News*. London: Tavistock.

CLARENS, C. (1980), *Crime Movies*. New York: Norton.

CLARKE, A. (1982), *Television Police Series and Law and Order* (Popular Culture Course Unit 22). Milton Keynes: Open University.

—— (1983), 'Holding the Blue Lamp: Television and the Police in Britain', *Crime and Social Justice*, 19: 44–51.

—— (1986), 'This is Not the Boy Scouts: Television Police Series and Definitions of Law and Order' in T. Bennett, C. Mercer, and J. Woollacott, eds., *Popular Culture and Social Relations*, 219–32. Milton Keynes: Open University Press.

—— (1992), ' "You're Nicked!" Television Police Series and the Fictional Representation of Law and Order', in D. Strinati and S. Wagg, eds., *Come On Down? Popular Media Culture in Post-War Britain*, 232–53. London: Routledge.

—— and TAYLOR, I. (1980), 'Vandals, Pickets and Muggers: Television Coverage of Law and Order in the 1979 Election', *Screen Education*, 36: 99–112.

CLARKE, J. (1996), 'Crime and Social Order: Interrogating the Detective Story' in J. Muncie and E. McLaughlin, eds., *The Problem of Crime*, 65–100. London: Sage.

COHEN, L., and FELSON, S. (1979), 'Social Change and Crime Rate Trends: A Routine Activities Approach', *American Sociological Review*, 44: 588–608.

COHEN, S. (1972), *Folk Devils and Moral Panics*. London: Paladin.

—— and YOUNG, J., eds. (1973), *The Manufacture of News*. London: Constable.

COTTLE, S. (1993), *TV News, Urban Conflict and the Inner City*. Leicester: Leicester University Press.

CUMBERBATCH, G. (1989), *A Measure of Uncertainty: The Effects of Mass Media*, Broadcasting Standards Council Research Monograph 1. London: John Libbey.

—— WOODS, S., and MAGUIRE, A. (1995), *Crime in the News: Television, Radio and Newspapers: A Report for BBC Broadcasting Research*. Birmingham: Aston University, Communications Research Group.

DAHLGREN, P. (1988), 'Crime News: The Fascination of the Mundane', *European Journal of Communication*, 3, 1: 189–206.

DAHRENDORF, R. (1985), *Law and Order*. London: Sweet and Maxwell.

DAVIS, J. (1952), 'Crime News in Colorado Newspapers', *American Journal of Sociology*, 57: 325–30.

DEUTSCHMANN, P. (1959), *News Page Content of Twelve Metropolitan Dailies*. Cincinnati, Ohio: Scripps-Howard Research Centre.

DITTON, J., and DUFFY, J.(1983), 'Bias in the Newspaper Reporting of Crime News', *British Journal of Criminology*, 23, 2: 159–65.

DOMINICK, J. (1978), 'Crime and Law Enforcement in the Mass Media', in C. Winick, ed., *Deviance and Mass Media*, 105–28. Beverly Hills, Cal.: Sage.

DOOB, A., and MACDONALD, G. (1979), 'Television Viewing and the Fear of Victimisation: Is the Relationship Causal?', *Journal of Personality and Social Psychology* 37, 1: 170–9.

DOVE, G. (1982), *The Police Procedural*. Bowling Green, Ohio: Bowling Green Popular Press.

—— and BARGAINNIER, E., eds. (1986), *Cops and Constables: American and British Fictional Policemen*. Bowling Green, Ohio: Bowling Green Popular Press.

DURSTON, G. (1997), *Moll Flanders: Analysis of 18th Century Criminal Biography*. Chichester: Barry Rose.

DUSSUYER, I. (1979) *Crime News: A Study of 40 Toronto Newspapers*. Toronto: University of Toronto Centre of Criminology.

EATON, M. (1995), 'A Fair Cop? Viewing the Effects of the Canteen Culture in *Prime Suspect* and *Between the Lines*', in D. Kidd-Hewitt and R. Osborne, eds., *Crime and the Media: The Post-Modern Spectacle*. London: Pluto.

ELTON, B. (1996) *Popcorn*. London: Simon and Schuster.

ERICSON, R. (1991), 'Mass Media, Crime, Law, and Justice'. *British Journal of Criminology* 31, 3: 219–49.

—— ed. (1995), *Crime and the Media*. Aldershot: Dartmouth.

—— BARANEK, P., and CHAN, J. (1987), *Visualising Deviance*. Milton Keynes: Open University Press.

—— —— and —— (1989), *Negotiating Control*. Milton Keynes: Open University Press.

—— —— and —— (1991), *Representing Order*. Milton Keynes: Open University Press.

EVERSON, W. (1972), *The Detective in Film*. New York: Citadel.

FABIAN, R. (1950), *Fabian of the Yard*. London: Naldrett.

—— (1954), *London After Dark*. London: Naldrett.

FALLER, L. (1987), *Turned to Account: The Forms and Functions of Criminal Biography in Late Seventeenth and Early Eighteenth Century England*. Cambridge: Cambridge University Press.

FERRELL, J., and SANDERS, C. R., eds. (1995), *Cultural Criminology*. Boston, Mass.: Northeastern University Press.

FISHMAN, M. (1981), 'Police News: Constructing An Image of Crime', *Urban Life*, 9, 4: 371–94.

FOUCAULT, M. (1977), *Discipline and Punish*. London: Penguin.

GAROFALO, J. (1981), 'Crime and the Mass Media: A Selective Review of Research', *Journal of Research in Crime and Delinquency*,18, 2: 319–50.

GATRELL, V. (1994), *The Hanging Tree: Execution and the English People 1770–1868*. Oxford: Oxford University Press.

GERBNER, G. (1970), 'Cultural Indicators: The Case of Violence in Television Drama', *Annals of the American Academy of Political and Social Science*, 338, 1: 69–81.

—— (1972), 'Violence in Television Drama: Trends and Symbolic Functions', in G. Comstock and E. Rubinstein, eds., *Television and Social Behaviour Vol. 1:*

Content and Control, 28–187. Washington, DC: US Government Printing Office.

—— (1995) 'Television Violence: The Power and the Peril', in G. Dines and J. Humez, eds., *Gender, Race and Class in the Media*, 547–57. Thousand Oaks, Cal.: Sage.

—— and GROSS, L. (1976), 'Living With Television: The Violence Profile', *Journal of Communication*, 26, 1: 173–99.

—— —— MORGAN, M., and SIGNORIELLI, N. (1980), 'The Mainstreaming of America: Violence Profile No 11', *Journal of Communication*, 30, 1: 19–29.

—— —— and —— (1984), 'Political Correlates of Television Viewing', *Public Opinion Quarterly*, 48, 2: 283–300.

—— —— —— and —— (1986) 'Living With Television: The Dynamics of the Cultivation Process', in J. Bryant and D. Zillman, eds., *Perspectives on Media Effects*, 17–40. Hillside, NJ: Lawrence Erlbaum.

GIDDENS, A. (1984), *The Constitution of Society*. Cambridge: Polity Press.

GITLIN, T. (1994), *Inside Prime Time*. Revised edn. London: Routledge.

GRABER, D. (1980), *Crime News and the Public*. New York: Praeger.

GUNTER, B. (1981), 'Measuring Television Violence: A Review and Suggestions for a New Analytic Perspective', *Current Psychological Research*, 1, 1: 91–112.

—— (1985), *Dimensions of Television Violence*. Aldershot: Gower.

HAGELL, A. and NEWBURN, T. (1994), *Young Offenders and the Media*. London: Policy Studies Institute.

HALL, S. (1970), 'A World At One With Itself', *New Society*, 18 June: 1056–8.

—— (1973), 'The Determination of News Photographs' in S. Cohen and J. Young, eds., *The Manufacture of News*, 226–43. London: Constable.

—— (1979), *Drifting Into A Law and Order Society*. London: Cobden Trust.

—— CRITCHLEY, C., JEFFERSON, T., CLARKE, J., and ROBERTS, B. (1978), *Policing the Crisis*. London: Macmillan.

HALLORAN, J., ELLIOTT, L., and MURDOCK, G. (1970), *Demonstrations and Communication*. London: Penguin.

HARRIS, F. (1932), *Presentation of Crime in Newspapers*. Minneapolis, Minn.: Minneapolis Sociological Press.

HAYCRAFT, H. (1941), *Murder For Pleasure*. New York: Appleton Century.

HAY, D. (1975), 'Property, Authority and the Criminal Law', in D. Hay, ed., *Albion's Fatal Tree*, 17–63. London: Penguin.

HEAROLD, S. (1986), 'A Synthesis of 1043 Effects of Television on Social Behaviour', in G. Comstock, ed., *Public Communications and Behaviour Vol. 1*, 65–133. New York: Academic Press.

HENNIGAN, K. M., DELROSARIO, M. L., HEATH, L., COOK, J. D., and CALDER, B. J. (1982), 'Impact of the Introduction of Television Crime in the United States: Empirical Findings and Theoretical Implications' *Journal of Personality and Social Psychology*, 42, 3: 461–77.

HILLYARD, P. (1982), 'The Media Coverage of Crime and Justice in Northern Ireland', in C. Sumner, ed., *Crime, Justice and the Mass Media*, 36–54. (Cropwood Papers 14) Cambridge: Institute of Criminology.

HIMMELWEIT, H., OPPENHEIM, A. N., and VINCE, P. (1958), *Television and the Child*. London: Oxford University Press.

HURD, G. (1979), 'The Television Presentation of the Police', in S. Holdaway, ed., *The British Police*. London: Edward Arnold.

INCIARDI, J., and DEE, J. L. (1987) 'From the Keystone Cops to Miami Vice: Images of Policing in American Popular Culture', *Journal of Popular Culture* 21, 2: 84–102.

IYENGAR, S. (1991), *Is Anyone Responsible? How Television Frames Political Issues*. Chicago, Ill.: Chicago University Press.

KATZ, J. (1987), 'What Makes Crime "News"?', *Media, Culture and Society*, 9, 1: 47–75.

KERR, P. (1981) 'Watching the Detectives: American Television Crime Series 1949–81', *Prime-Time*, 1, 1: 2–6.

KNIGHT, S. (1980), *Form and Ideology in Crime Fiction*. London: Macmillan.

LAING, S. (1991), 'Banging in Some Reality: The Original "Z-Cars"' in J. Corner, ed., *Popular Television in Britain: Studies in Cultural History*, 125–43. London: British Film Institute.

LEA, J., and YOUNG, J. (1984), *What is to Be Done About Law and Order?* London: Penguin.

LEES, S. (1995), 'Media Reporting of Rape: The 1993 British "Date Rape" Controversy', in D. Kidd-Hewitt and R. Osborne, eds., *Crime and the Media*, 107–30. London: Pluto.

LICHTER, S. R., LICHTER, L. S., and ROTHMAN, S. (1991), *Watching America*. New York: Prentice Hall.

LINEBAUGH, P. (1991), *The London Hanged: Crime and Civil Society in the Eighteenth Century*. London: Allen Lane.

LIVINGSTONE, S. (1996), 'On the Continuing Problem of Media Effects', in J. Curran and M. Gurevitch, eds., *Mass Media and Society*, 305–24. London: Arnold.

MANDEL, E. (1984), *Delightful Murder: A Social History of the Crime Story*. London: Pluto.

MARSH, H. L. (1991), 'A Comparative Analysis of Crime Coverage in Newspapers in the United States and Other Countries From 1960–1989: A Review of the Literature', *Journal of Criminal Justice*, 19, 1: 67–80.

MASON, P. (1996), 'Prime Time Punishment: The British Prison and Television', in D. Kidd-Hewitt and R. Osborne, eds., *Crime and the Media*, 185–205. London: Pluto.

MATHEWS, T. D. (1994), *Censored*. London: Chatto and Windus.

MAWBY, R., and BROWN, J.(1983), 'Newspaper Images of the Victim', *Victimology*, 9, 1: 82–94.

MCCARTHUR, C. (1972), *Underworld USA*. London: Secker and Warburg.

MCNAIR, B. (1993), *News And Journalism in the UK*. London: Routledge.

MEDVED, M. (1992), *Hollywood vs. America*. London: HarperCollins.

MERTON, R. (1938/1957), 'Social Structure and Anomie', *American Sociological Review*, 3: 672–82. Reprinted in R. Merton, *Social Theory and Social Structure*, Glencoe, Ill.: Free Press, 1957; revised edn., 1963.

MEYERS, R. (1981) *TV Detectives*. San Diego, Cal.: Barnes.

—— (1989), *Murder on the Air*. New York: The Mysterious Press.

MILLER, F. (1994), *Censored Hollywood: Sex, Sin and Violence on Screen*. Atlanta, Ga.: Turner.

MORRISON, B. (1997), *As If*. Cambridge: Granta.

MOST, G., and STOWE, W. (1983), *The Poetics of Murder*. New York: Harcourt, Brace and Jovanovich.

MURDOCK, G. (1982), 'Disorderly Images', in C. Sumner, ed., *Crime, Justice and the Mass Media*, 104–23. (Cropwood Papers 14), Cambridge: Institute of Criminology.

NAVA, M. (1988), 'Cleveland and the Press: Outrage and Anxiety in the Reporting of Child Sexual Abuse', *Feminist Review*, 28: 103–21.

NELLIS, M., and HALE, C. (1982), *The Prison Film*. London: Radical Alternatives to Prison.

ORCUTT, J. D., and TURNER, J. B. (1993), 'Shocking Numbers and Graphic Accounts: Quantified Images of Drug Problems in the Print Media', *Social Problems*, 40, 2: 190–206.

OSBORNE, R. (1996), 'Crime and the Media: From Media Studies to Post-modernism', in

D. Kidd-Hewitt and R. Osborne, eds., *Crime and the Media*, 25–48. London: Pluto.

OUSBY, I. (1976), *Bloodhounds of Heaven: The Detective in English Fiction From Godwin to Doyle*. Cambridge, Mass.: Harvard University Press.

PALMER, J. (1978), *Thrillers*. London: Edward Arnold.

PANDIANI, J. (1978), 'Crime Time TV: If All We Knew Is What We Saw . . . ', *Contemporary Crises*, 2: 437–58.

PARK, W. (1978), 'The Police State', *Journal of Popular Film*, VI, 3: 229–38.

PARRISH, R., and PITTS, M. (1990*a*), *The Great Detective Pictures*. Metuchen, NJ: Scarecrow.

—— and —— (1990*b*) *The Great Cop Pictures*. Metuchen, NJ: Scarecrow.

PEARSON, G. (1983), *Hooligan: A History of Respectable Fears*. London: Macmillan.

PEAY, J. (1997), 'The Power of the Popular', in J. Vagg and T. Newburn (eds.) *Emerging Themes in British Criminology*. Loughborough: British Society of Criminology.

PETLEY, J., and BARKER, M., eds. (1997), *Ill Effects: The Media/Violence Debate*. London: Routledge.

PORTER, B. (1981), *The Pursuit of Crime*. New Haven, Conn.: Yale University Press.

RADZINOWICZ, L. (1956), *A History of English Criminal Law*. Vols. 2/3. London: Stevens.

RAWLINGS, P. (1992), *Drunks, Whores, and Idle Apprentices: Criminal Biographies of the Eighteenth Century*. London: Routledge.

—— (1997), 'Crime Writers: Non-Fiction Crime Books', in J. Vagg and T. Newburn (eds.) *Emerging Themes in British Criminology*. Loughborough: British Society of Criminology.

REINER, R. (1978), 'The New Blue Films', *New Society*, 43, 808: 706–8.

—— (1981), 'Keystone to Kojak: The Hollywood Cop', in P. Davies and B. Neve, eds., *Politics, Society and Cinema in America*, 195–220. Manchester: Manchester University Press.

—— (1992), *The Politics of the Police*. Hemel Hempstead: Wheatsheaf.

—— (1994) 'The Dialectics of Dixon: The Changing Image of the TV Cop', in S. Becker and M. Stephens, eds., *Police Force, Police Service*, 11–32. London: Macmillan.

—— (1996*a*) 'Crime and Media' in H. Sasson and D. Diamond, eds., *LSE on Social Science*, 135–56. London: LSE Publishing.

—— (1996*b*) 'The Case of the Missing Crimes' in R. Levitas and W. Guy, eds.,

Interpreting Official Statistics, 185–205. London: Routledge.

ROCK, P. (1973), 'News As Eternal Recurrence' in S. Cohen and J. Young, (eds., *The Manufacture of News*, 64–70. London: Constable.

ROSHIER, B. (1973), 'The Selection of Crime News By the Press', in S. Cohen and J. Young, eds., *The Manufacture of News*, 40–51. London: Constable.

ROSOW, E. (1978), *Born to Lose*. New York: Oxford University Press.

SACCO, V. F. (1995), 'Media Constructions of Crime', *The Annals of the American Academy of Political and Social Science*, 539: 141–54.

SAYERS, D., ed. (1928), *Great Short Stories of Detection, Mystery and Horror*. London: Gollancz.

—— (ed. (1936), *Tales of Detection*. London: Dent.

SCHLESINGER, P., and TUMBER, H. (1992), 'Crime and Criminal Justice in the Media', in D. Downes, ed., *Unravelling Criminal Justice*, 184–203. London: Macmillan.

—— and —— (1993), 'Fighting the War Against Crime: Television, Police and Audience', *British Journal of Criminology*, 33, 1: 19–32.

—— and —— (1994), *Reporting Crime*. Oxford: Oxford University Press.

—— DOBASH, R., DOBASH, R., and WEAVER, C. (1992,) *Women Viewing Violence*. London: British Film Institute.

—— —— and MURDOCK, G. (1991), 'The Media Politics of Crime and Criminal Justice', *British Journal of Sociology*, 42, 3: 397–420.

SCHRAMM, W., LYLE, J. and PARKER, E. B. (1961), *Television in the Lives of Our Children*, Stanford, Cal.: Stanford University Press.

SHADOIAN, J. (1977), *Dreams and Dead Ends*. Cambridge, Mass.: MIT Press.

SHALE, S. (1996), 'Listening to the Law: Famous Trials on BBC Radio 1934–69', *Modern Law Review*, 59, 6: 813–44.

SHERIZEN, S. (1978), 'Social Creation of Crime News: All the News Fitted to Print', in C. Winick, ed., *Deviance and Mass Media*, 203–24. Beverly Hills, Cal.: Sage.

SIGNORIELLI, N. (1990), 'Television's Mean and Dangerous World: A Continuation of the Cultural Indicators Perspective', in N. Signorielli and M. Morgan, eds., *Cultivation Analysis: New Directions in Media Effects Research*, 85–106. Newbury Park: Sage.

—— and MORGAN, M., eds. (1990), *Cultivation Analysis: New Directions in Media Effects Research*. Newbury Park: Sage.

SKIDMORE, P. (1995), 'Telling Tales; Media Power, Ideology and the Reporting of Child Sexual Abuse in Britain', in D. Kidd-Hewitt and R. Osborne, eds., *Crime and the Media*, 78–106. London: Pluto.

SKLAR, R. (1975), *Movie-Made America*. New York: Vintage.

SMITH, S. (1984), 'Crime in the News', *British Journal of Criminology*, 24, 3: 289–95.

SOLOMONS, S. (1976), *Beyond Formula: American Film Genres*. New York: Harcourt, Brace, Jovanovich.

SOOTHILL, K., and WALBY, S. (1991), *Sex Crime in the News*. London: Routledge.

SPARKS, R. (1992), *Television and the Drama of Crime*. Buckingham: Open University Press.

—— (1993), 'Inspector Morse' in G. Brandt, ed., *British Television Drama in the 1980s*. Cambridge: Cambridge University Press.

STEPHENSON-BURTON, A. (1995), 'Through the Looking-Glass: Public Images of White Collar Crime', in D. Kidd-Hewitt and R. Osborne, eds., *Crime and the Media*, 131–63. London: Pluto.

SUMNER, C. (1982), '"Political Hooliganism" and "Rampaging Mobs": The National Press Coverage of the Toxteth "Riots"', in C. Sumner, ed., *Crime, Justice and the Mass Media*, 25–35. Cropwood Papers 14. Cambridge: Institute of Criminology.

SURETTE, R. (1992) *Media, Crime and Criminal Justice: Images and Realities*. Pacific Grove, Cal.: Brooks/Cole.

SWANSON, C. (1955), 'What They Read in 130 Daily Newspapers', *Journalism Quarterly*, 32, 4: 411–21.

SYMONS, J. (1972), *Bloody Murder*. London: Penguin.

THOMPSON, J. (1993), *Fiction, Crime and Empire: Clues to Modernity and Postmodernity*. Urbana, Ill.: University of Illinois Press.

THOMPSON, J. B. (1995), *The Media and Modernity: A Social Theory of the Media*. Cambridge: Polity Press.

TUMBER, H. (1982), *Television and the Riots*. London: British Film Institute.

TUSKA, J. (1978), *The Detective in Hollywood*. New York: Doubleday.

WAKSHLAG, J., VIAL, V., and TAMBORINI, R. (1983), 'Selecting Crime Drama and Apprehension About Crime', *Human Communication Research*, 10, 2: 227–42.

WARTELLA, E. (1995), 'Media and Problem Behaviours in Young People', in M. Rutter and D. Smith, eds., *Psychological Disorders in Young People*, 296–323. London: Wiley.

WATSON, C. (1971), *Snobbery With Violence: English Crime Stories and Their Audience*. London: Eyre Methuen.

WILLIAMS, P. and DICKINSON, J. (1993), 'Fear of Crime: Read All About It? The Relationship Between Newspaper Crime Reporting and Fear of Crime', *British Journal of Criminology*, 33, 1: 33–56.

WILLIAMS, T. M., ed. (1986), *The Impact of Television: A Natural Experiment in Three Communities*. New York: Academic Press.

WINSTON, R., and MELLERSI, N. (1992), *The Public Eye: Ideology and the Police Procedural*. London: Macmillan.

WOBER, M. (1978), 'Televised Violence and Paranoid Perception: The View From Great Britain', *Public Opinion Quarterly*, 42, 3: 315–21.

WREN-LEWIS, J.(1981/2), 'TV Coverage of the Riots' *Screen Education*, 40: 15–33.

YOUNG, J. (1971), *The Drug-Takers*. London: Paladin.

ZILLMAN, D., and WAKSHLAG, J. (1987), 'Fear of Victimisation and the Appeal of Crime Drama', in D. Zillman and J. Bryant, eds., *Selective Exposure to Communication*. Hillsdale, NJ: Erlbaum.

6

Sociological Theories of Crime

Paul Rock

INTRODUCTION

The Oxford English Dictionary defines sociology as 'the study of social organization and institutions and of collective behaviour and interaction, including the individual's relationship to the group'. That is a catholic definition which encompasses almost every situation in which individuals or groups can influence one another. Sociological theories of crime are themselves correspondingly catholic: they extend, for example, from descriptions of the smallest detail of street encounters between adolescents and the police to analyses of very large movements in nations' aggregate rates of crime over centuries, and it is sometimes difficult to determine where their boundaries should be drawn. As I shall show, it seems to some quite permissible to discuss big ideas about law, crime, and the state under the more general classification of criminology.

Theories are also intellectually eclectic. Sociological criminology has exchanged ideas with sociology proper since the beginning. After all, many criminologists are members of sociology departments and they are exposed to changes in intellectual fashion in their parent discipline. The result has been that almost every major theory in sociology has been fed in some form into criminology at some time, undergoing adaptation and editing in the process, and occasionally becoming very distant from its roots. Indeed, one of the distinctive properties of that process is that criminology can sometimes so extensively rework imported ideas that they will develop well beyond their original limits in sociology, becoming significant contributions to sociological theory in their own right. *Anomie*, the symbolic interactionist conception of the self and its others, and feminism are examples of arguments that have grown appreciably in scale and sophistication within the special environment of criminology.

And there is another form of intellectual eclecticism that characterizes criminology and, indeed, any field defined principally by its attention to an

Written at the Center for the Advanced Study of the Behavioral Sciences, Stanford, California. I am grateful for financial support provided by the National Science Foundation Grant SBR–9022192. I am also grateful to Stan Cohen, David Downes, Bridget Hutter, Gary Marx, and Robert Reiner for their comments on earlier drafts of this chapter.

empirical area. David Downes once called criminology a *rendez-vous* discipline: it is the study of *crime* that gives unity and order to the enterprise, not dogged adherence to any particular theory or social science. It is in the examination of *crime* that psychologists, statisticians, lawyers, economists, social anthropologists, sociologists, social policy analysts, and psychiatrists meet and call themselves criminologists and, in that encounter, their attachments to the conventions and boundaries of their parent disciplines may weaken. So it is that sociological criminologists have confronted arguments born and applied in other disciplines and, from time to time, they have domesticated them to cultivate new intellectual hybrids. Stan Cohen (1972) and Jock Young (1971) did so in the early 1970s, when they married the symbolic interactionism of Edwin Lemert (1951) and Howard Becker (1963) to the statistical theory of Leslie Wilkins (1964). So, too, as I shall show, sociological criminologists in the 1990s moulded and synthesized ideas taken variously from theories of risk, control, and social geography to make them distinctively their own.

Thus constituted, sociological criminology is at once marked by discontinuities and continuities. Its history may be represented as a staggered succession of tradings with different schools and disciplines which do not always sit well together. It is evident, for instance, that the feminist may entertain a conception of theory and the theorist very unlike that of the functionalist or rational choice theorist. Yet there are also unities of a kind. All competent criminologists may be presumed to have a working knowledge of the wide range of theory in their discipline; theory once mastered is seldom forgotten or neglected entirely, and there is a propensity for scholars overtly and covertly to weave disparate ideas together as problems and needs arise. Quite typical was an observation offered in the author's introduction to a work on the lives of urban street criminals in Seattle, Washington: 'I link . . . ethnographic data to criminological perspectives as a *bricoleur* seeking numerous sources of interpretation. Had I selected just one criminological perspective to complement these ethnographic data, the value of these firsthand accounts would be constrained' (1995: 5). Scholars thus tend frequently to be more utilitarian in practice than in principle, and, if there *is* an ensuing gap between a professed purity of theory and an active pragmatism of procedure, it may well be masked by the witting or unwitting obliteration of sources or the renaming of ideas. Seemingly distinct sociological theories are open to continual merging and blurring as the practical work of criminology unfolds.

There is no one royal way to lay out the sociology of crime: some have classified its component theories by their supposed political leanings (liberal, conservative, and radical, for instance); some by their attentiveness or inattentiveness to gender; some by their alleged metaphysical assumptions about the character of the social world (classical, positivist, 'social constructionist', and the like); some by their history; some by the great men and women who propounded them; and others, more prosaically, by schools of thought.

In an empirically driven sub-discipline where the boundaries between theories and parent disciplines are frequently frail and deceptive, where formally different theories often contend with the same problems in very much the same way, as useful a procedure as any is to identify and describe a number of broad families of theories that share some big idea or ideas in common. The organization of this chapter will therefore follow intellectual themes more closely than chronologies or hierarchies of thought in an attempt to convey some small part of the present preoccupations and environment of sociological criminology.

I shall take it that those themes, in their turn, seem quite commonly to take the form of different combinations of ideas about control, signification, and order. Crime, after all, is centrally bound up with the state's attempts to impose its will through law; with the meanings of those attempts to law-breaker, law-enforcer, observer, and victim; and with concomitant patterns of order and disorder. Criminologists differ about the weights and meanings that should be attached to those attributes: some, and control theorists in particular, would wish to be what Matza once called 'correctionalist', that is, to use knowledge about crime to suppress it. Others would look upon the exercise of control more critically. But they all feed off one another's ideas even if their practices and politics diverge. The attributes are visible features of the discipline's landscape, and I shall employ them to steer a a more or less straight route through Durkheimian and Mertonian theories of *anomie*; control theories; rational choice theory; routine activities theory; the work of the 'Chicago School'; studies of the relations between control and space, including Newman's 'defensible space', and more recent ideas of risk and the marshalling of dangerous populations; radical criminology; functionalist criminology; and 'labelling theory' and cultural and subcultural analyses of crime as meaningful behaviour. I shall take it that such a grand tour should take in most of the major landmarks which criminologists would now consider central to their field.

What this chapter cannot do, of course, is provide much context, history, criticism, and detail.[1] That would be impossible in a single short piece. I can hope at best to select only a few illustrative ideas that are of current or recent interest as well as discussing some of the older arguments that informed them.

Further, like any scheme of classification, this chapter will inevitably face problems of anomaly and overlap, not only internally but also with other chapters in the *Handbook*. If the study of crime cannot be severed from the analysis of control, the state, or gender, there will always be such problems at the boundaries. But the chapter should furnish the larger contours of a preliminary map of contemporary sociological theories of crime.

---

[1] Those features may be read elsewhere. For instance, David Downes and I have tried to supply them in our *Understanding Deviance* (1995).

Crime and Control

Anomie and the contradictions of social order

I shall begin by describing *anomie* theory, one of the most enduring and, for a while, hard-researched of all the ideas of criminological theory, and one that still persists in disguised form.

At heart, many theories take it that crime is a consequence of defective social regulation. People are said to deviate because the disciplines and authority of society are so flawed that they offer few restraints or moral direction. The idea is a very old one, antedating the emergence of sociology itself, but its formal birth into theory is linked indissolubly with *anomie* and the French sociologist, Émile Durkheim.

Durkheim awarded two rather different meanings to *anomie*, or normlessness. In *The Division of Labour in Society,* published in 1893, and in *Suicide,* published in 1897, he asserted that French society was in uneasy transition from one state of solidarity or integration to another. A society without an elaborate division of labour rested on what he called (perhaps misleadingly) the mechanical solidarity of people who not only reacted much alike to problems but also saw that everyone about them reacted alike to those problems, thereby lending objectivity, scale, and solidity to moral response, and bringing massive disapproval and repression to bear on the deviant. Such a social order was conceived to lie in the simpler past of pre-industrial society. The future of industrial society would be distinguished by a state of organic solidarity, the solidarity appropriate to a complex division of labour. People would then be allocated by merit and effort to very diverse positions, and they would not only recognize the legitimacy of the manner in which rewards were distributed, but also acknowledge the indispensability of what each did in his or her work for the other and for the common good. Organic solidarity would thus have controls peculiar to itself: 'Sheerly economic regulation is not enough . . . there should be moral regulation, moral rules which specify the rights and obligations of individuals in a given occupation in relation to those in other occupations' (Giddens 1972: 11). People might no longer think wholly in unison, their moral response might not be substantial and unanimous, but they should be able to compose their differences peaceably by means of a system of restitutive justice that made amends for losses suffered.

Durkheim's distinction between the two forms of solidarity and their accompanying modes of control was anthropologically suspect,[2] but it was in his analysis of the liminal state between them that criminologists were most interested. In that transition, where capitalism was thought to impose a 'forced division of labour', people acquiesced neither in the apportionment of rewards nor in the moral authority of the state. They were obliged to work and act

---

[2] The anthropology of deviance and control suggests that, in the main, 'simpler' societies are actually more restitutive in their disciplines and 'early modern' societies more repressive. See, for example, Llewellyn and Hoebel (1941) and Gluckman (1955).

in a society that enjoyed little legitimacy and that exercised an incomplete control over their desires. In such a setting, it was held, 'man's nature [was to be] eternally dissatisfied, constantly to advance, without relief or rest, towards an indefinite goal' (Durkheim, 1952: 256). Moral regulation was relatively deficient and people were correspondingly free to deviate. That is the first meaning Durkheim gave to *anomie*. His second will be visited on page 238.

Given another, distinctively American, complexion by Robert Merton, *anomie* became a socially-fostered state of discontent and deregulation that generated crime and deviance as part of the routine functioning of a society which promised much to everyone but actually denied them equal access to its attainment (Merton, 1938). People might have been motivated to achieve in the United States, but they confronted class, race, and other social differences that manifestly contradicted the myth of openness. It was not easy for a poor, inner-city adolescent to receive sponsorship for jobs, achieve academic success, or acquire capital. In a society where failure was interpreted as a sign of personal rather than social weakness, where failure led to guilt rather than to political anger, the pressure to succeed could be so powerful that it impelled people thus disadvantaged to bypass legitimate careers and take to illegitimate careers instead: 'the culture makes incompatible demands. . . . In this setting, a cardinal American virtue—"ambition"—promotes a cardinal American vice—"deviant behavior"' (Merton, 1957: 145).

Merton's *anomie* theory was to be modified progressively for some thirty years. In the work of Richard Cloward and Lloyd Ohlin, for example, his model was elaborated to include *illegitimate* routes to success. Their *Delinquency and Opportunity* (1960) described the consequences of young American men (in the 1950s and 1960s the criminological gaze was almost wholly on the doings of young American men) not only being pushed into crime by the difficulties of acquiring money and position in conventional ways, but also pulled by the lure of unconventional, criminal careers. There would be those who were offered an unorthodox path in professional or organized crime, and they could become thieves, robbers, or racketeers. There would be those for whom no path was available, and they could become members of conflict gangs. And there were those who failed to attain admission to either a law-abiding or a law-violating group, the 'double failures', who would, it was conjectured, give up and become drug-users and hustlers. Each of those modes of adaptation was, in effect, a way of life, supported by a system of meanings or a subculture, and Cloward and Ohlin provided one of the bridges between the structural and the interpretive models of crime which will be discussed at the end of this chapter.

In the work of Albert Cohen, *anomie* was to be synthesized with the Freudian idea of 'reaction formation' in an effort to explain the manifestly expressive and 'non-rational' nature of much delinquency. The prospect of failure was depicted as bringing about a major psychological rejection of what had formerly been sought, so that the once-aspiring working-class adolescent turned his back on the middle-class world that spurned him and adopted a style of behaviour that was its systematic inversion. The practical and utilitarian in middle-class life was transformed into non-utilitarian delinquency; respectability became malicious negativism; and the deferment of gratification became short-run hedonism. Again, in the work of David Downes, conducted in London in the early 1960s to explore how far beyond America *anomie* theory might be generalized, the ambitions of English adolescents were found to be so modulated by a stable and legitimated system of social stratification that working-class youth did not seem to undergo a taxing guilt or frustration in their failure to accomplish middle-class goals. They neither hankered after the middle class world nor repudiated it. Rather, their response was 'dissociation'. Where they *did* experience a strong dissatisfaction, however, was in their thwarted attempts to enjoy leisure, and their delinquencies were principally hedonistic, focused on drinking, fighting, and malicious damage to property, rather than instrumentally turned towards the accumulation of wealth. And that theme of the part played by the adolescent 'manufacture of excitement' was to be echoed repeatedly in the empirical and theoretical work of criminologists. Making 'something happen' in a world without significant cultural or material resources could easily bring about a drift into delinquency (see Matza, 1964; Corrigan, 1979; and Cusson, 1983).

Anomie and Social Disorganization

Durkheim's second reading of *anomie* touched on moral regulation that was not so much flawed as in a state of near collapse. People, he argued, are not endowed at birth with fixed appetites and ambitions. On the contrary, their purposes and aspirations are shaped by the generalized opinions and reactions of others, by a collective conscience, that can appear through social ritual and routine to be externally derived, solid, and objective. When society is disturbed by rapid change or major disorder, however, that semblance of solidity and objectivity can itself founder, and people may no longer find their ambitions subject to effective social discipline. It is hard to live outside the reassuring structures of social life, and the condition of *anomie* was experienced as a 'malady of infinite aspiration' that was accompanied by 'weariness', 'disillusionment', 'disturbance, agitation and discontent'. In extreme cases, Lukes observed, 'this condition would lead a man to commit suicide and homicide' (1967: 139).

Durkheim conceived such anomic deregulation to be a matter of crisis, innately unstable and short-lived. Disorganization could not be tolerated for very long before order of a sort would be restored. Indeed, sociologists are generally ill-disposed towards the term, believing that it connotes a want of understanding and perception on the part of the observer (see Whyte, 1942, and Anderson, 1976). They would hold that, even in Beirut, Bosnia, or Burundi at their most devastated, people were able to sustain a measure of organization within disorganization. Yet, on both the small and the large scale, there are clear examples of people living in conditions where informal control and co-operativeness are only vestigial; where formal control is either absent or erratic; where others are, or are seen to be, predatory and dangerous; where life is unpredictable; and where, as cause and consequence, there is little personal safety, much anxiety, and abundant crime. Take William Julius Wilson's description of life in the poorest areas of the American city: 'broken families, antisocial behavior, social networks that do not extend beyond the ghetto environment, and a lack of informal social control over the behavior and activities of children and adults in the neighborhood' (1996: p. xvi). On some housing estates in Paris, London (see Genn, 1988) and St Louis (Rainwater, 1970), social groupings have been portrayed as so lacking in cohesion that they enjoyed no shared trust, neighbour preyed on neighbour, and joint defensive action was virtually impossible.

Rampant *anomie* has been well documented (see Erikson, 1994). Consider Davis's half-prophetic description of MacArthur Park, one of the poorest areas of Los Angeles, as 'feral' and dangerous, 'a free-fire zone where crack dealers and streets gangs settle their scores with shotguns and Uzis' (1992: 6). Consider, too, Turnbull's description of the condition of the Ik of northern Uganda, a tribe that had been moved to a mountainous area after their traditional hunting grounds had been designated a national park. They could no longer live, co-operate, and work as they had done before; familiar patterns of social organization had become obsolete; and the Ik were portrayed as having become beset by 'acrimony, envy and suspicion' (1973: 239), 'excessive individualism, coupled with solitude and boredom' (*ibid.*: 238), and the victimization of the weak: 'without killing, it is difficult to get closer to disposal than by taking the food out of an old person's mouth, and this was primarily an adjacent-generation occupation, as were tripping and pushing off balance' (*ibid.*: 252).

A number of criminologists and others are beginning to prophesy a new apocalypse in which *anomie* will flourish on such a massive scale that entire societies will dissolve into chaos and lawlessness. There are parts of the world whose political structures are so radically disordered that it becomes difficult to talk about governments operating effectively within secure national boundaries at all. So it was that Kaplan wrote graphically about the road-warrior culture of Somalia, the anarchic implosion of criminal violence in the Ivory Coast, and Sierra Leone, which he depicted as a lawless state that had lost control over its cities at night, whose national army was a 'rabble', and which was reverting to tribalism. The future for many, he luridly predicted, would be a 'rundown, crowded planet of skinhead Cossacks and *juju* warriors, influenced by the worst refuse of Western pop culture and ancient tribal hatreds, and battling over scraps of overused earth in guerilla conflicts' (1994: 62–3). So, too, Martin van Creveld analysed what he called the ubiquitous growth of 'low-intensity conflict' waged by guerillas and terrorists who threatened the state's conventional monopoly of violence: 'Should present trends continue, then the kind of war that is based on the division between government, army, and people, seems to be on its way out. . . . A degree of violent activity that even as late as the 1960s would have been considered outrageous is now accepted as an inevitable hazard of modern life' (1991: 192, 194). If Kaplan and van Creveld are even partially gifted with foresight (and much of their argument is quite stark), the trends they foretell will be of major consequence to criminology. Without a viable state, legislature, laws, and law enforcement, without adequate state control over the distribution of violence, how can one write intelligently about a discrete realm of crime at all? Crime, after all, is dependent on a state's ability clearly to define, ratify, and execute the law. When the police of a state are massively and routinely corrupt (as they appear to be in Mexico[3]); when, for example, the Colombian president's aeroplane was found to be carrying large quantities of cocaine in September 1996 (see the *New York Times*, 22 September 1996); it is not difficult to acknowledge the disarray to which Stan Cohen pointed when he asked whether it was possible any longer to distinguish firmly between crime and politics. There has been, Cohen asserted, a widespread decline of the myth that the sovereign state can provide security, law, and order; a decline in the legitimacy of the state through corruption scandals; a growth of international crime and a rise of criminal states such as Chechnya; and, in Africa particularly, the emergence of barbarism, horror, and atrocity. In some settings, he remarked, 'lawlessness and crime have so destroyed the social fabric that the state itself has withdrawn' (1996: 9).

Control Theory

A second, large cluster of theories centres loosely around the contention that people seek to commit crime because it is profitable, useful, or enjoyable for them to do so, and that they will almost certainly break the law if they can. Even if that contention, with its covert imagery of feral man (and woman), is not strictly 'correct', control theorists would argue that it certainly points enquiry in a helpful direction. They are interested less in the fidelity of description than in its yield for policy intervention and prediction in concrete situations. Theirs is a theory of heuristics rather than of observational truths, and heuristics is thought to suggest that more will be learned by exploring a few, uncomplicated factors that seem to *prevent* people from offending than by investigating all the complicated motives, meanings, and antecedents of their actions. Travis Hirschi put the issue baldly, 'The question "Why do they do it?" is simply not the question the theory is designed to answer. The question is, "Why don't we do it?"' (1969: 34). Such a doctrine is a recognizably close neighbour of *anomie* theories in its focus on the regulation of potentially unbridled appetites, and, indeed, it is occasionally very difficult to distinguish one set of ideas from the other.

---

[3] See, for example, a report in the *New York Times*, 3 September 1996, of very substantial police involvement in extortion, kidnappings, thefts, and drug trafficking in Mexico.

Earlier variants of control theory, compiled in the 1960s and 1970s,[4] proceeded by drafting lists of the constraints which could check the would-be offender, an offender who, it was assumed for analytic purposes, could be you, me, or anyone. Thus, arguing against subcultural theory, and grounded in a Freudian conception of human impulses that required taming, Hirschi claimed that 'delinquent acts result when the individual's bond to society is weak or broken' (1969: 16). Four chief elements were held to induce people to comply with rules: attachment, commitment, involvement, and belief. Attachment reflected a person's sensitivity to the opinions of others; commitment flowed from a person's investment of time, energy, and reputation in conformity; involvement stemmed from a person's engrossment in conventional activity; and belief mirrored a person's conviction that he or she should obey legal rules. There is tautology and repetition in that formulation, but Hirschi nevertheless usefully directed the criminological mind towards answering his one big question, 'why *don't* we do it?'

Later, with Gottfredson, Hirschi developed control theory by turning to self-control and impulsivity. Crime, they claim, flows from low self-control: it provides a direct and simple gratification of desires that is attractive to those who cannot or will not postpone pleasure. In the main, it requires little skill or planning. It can be intrinsically enjoyable because it involves the exercise of cunning, agility, deception or power. It requires a lack of sympathy for the victim. But it does not provide medium- or long-term benefits equivalent to those that may flow from more orthodox careers. In short, it is, they say, likely to be committed by those who are 'impulsive, insensitive, physical. . . . Risk-taking, short-sighted, and non-verbal' (1990: 90).

David Matza would not have called himself a control theorist, but in his *Delinquency and Drift* he did effectively straddle theories of control, *anomie*, and signification, and he did portray delinquents and delinquency in a manner that control theorists would find compatible. It was indeed he who later wrote an eloquent case for what he called an appreciative criminology (see Matza, 1969). Delinquents are not very different from us, he argued. Most of the time they are conventional enough in belief and conduct, and it is difficult to predict who will conform and who will not. But there are occasions when the grip of control loosens, adolescents fatalistically experience themselves as if they were object and effect rather than as subject and cause, as if they were no longer morally responsible for their actions, and they will then find themselves released to drift in and out of delinquency. What aid that process of disengagement are widely circulating accounts or 'techniques of neutralization' (an idea that he had developed earlier with Gresham Sykes (Sykes and Matza, 1957)) which enable people methodically to counter the guilt and offset the censure they might experience when offending. Matza claimed that delinquents

---

[4] Control theory is, of course, again much older than criminology itself. It is as old as moralizing thought. But its first clear debut in criminology was in the work of Travis Hirschi and of Ruth Kornhauser, whose ideas were published very belatedly as *Social Sources of Delinquency: An Appraisal of Analytic Models* (1978).

could be fortified in their resolve by their ability to condemn their condemners (by asserting that police and judges were themselves corrupt and invalid critics, for instance); deny injury (by asserting that no significant harm was done); deny the victim (by asserting that the victim was of no consequence or deserved what happened); or appeal to higher loyalties (a noble motive could be cited for an ignoble deed).

Steven Box attempted to take analysis yet further by reconciling Hirschi's emphasis on social bonds with Matza's conception of drift. He compiled his own new alliterative list of variables that were held to affect control: secrecy (the delinquent's chances of concealment); skills (his mastery of knowledge and techniques needed for the deviant act); supply (his access to appropriate equipment); social support (the endorsement offered by peers and others); and symbolic support (the endorsement offered by accounts available in the wider culture) (1971: 150). The greater the access to requisite skills, secrecy, supplies, and social and symbolic support, the greater would be the likelihood of offending.

Perhaps one of the most telling and economical contributions to control theory was supplied by Harriet Wilson. Examining 'socially deprived' families in Birmingham, England, she was to conclude that what most sharply differentiated families with delinquent children from those with none was simply what she called the exercise of 'chaperonage' (1980). Parents who acted as chaperons effectively prevented their children from offending: they were so convinced that the neighbourhood in which they lived was dangerous and contaminating that they sought to protect them by keeping them indoors or under close supervision, escorting them to school, and prohibiting them from playing with others defined as undesirable.[5]

Control theory has also been applied with effect to the problem of gender differences in offending. Apart from age,[6] no other demographic feature at present so powerfully discriminates between offenders and non-offenders.[7] At one time, however, scant criminological attention was paid to female crime because there was so very little of it.[8] As Lemert once said, like Custer's men, criminologists rode to the sound of the guns, and there were few female guns indeed firing. By contrast, what made male offending appear so interesting was its sheer seriousness and scale.

However, when feminist criminologists and others began to ask Travis Hirschi's central question (without actually citing Hirschi himself), female offending became analytically transformed precisely *because* it was so rare. There was the new and intriguing riddle of the conforming woman, and the

---

[5] Her ideas are highly redolent of an earlier piece by Walter Reckless and others (1957).

[6] David Downes has reminded me how very little criminological work has been carried out on the crimes of the elderly. One exception is Stephens (1976).

[7] The differential has not been invariant over time. Until the early 1800s, women appeared to have represented a much larger proportion of the criminal population. See M. Feeley (1996).

[8] To be sure, gender was a key variable in the work of some of the early subcultural theorists such as Al Cohen, even if it was not pursued very far.

riddle was answered, in part, by reference to the effects of differentials in control. In particular, John Hagan and his colleagues put it that deviation as a form of fun and excitement was more commonly open to males than to females because daughters are more frequently subject to intense, continual, and diffuse family control in the private, domestic sphere. That control, by extension, not only removed girls from the purview of agents of formal social control, the criminal justice system, and the possibility of public identification as criminal. It also worked more effectively because it rested on the manipulation of emotional sanctions rather than the imposition of physical or custodial controls. Shaming strategies and the withdrawal of affection are seemingly more potent than fines, probation, or prison. It followed that the more firmly structured and hierarchical the family, the sharper the distinction drawn between male and female roles, the more women were confined to private space, the greater would be the disparity between rates of male and female offending (see Hagan *et al.*, 1979, 1985, and 1988). Pat Carlen gave that analysis yet another twist by reflecting that female criminals were most likely to emerge when domestic family controls were removed altogether, when what she called the 'gender deal' was broken, young women left home or were taken into care, and were thereby exposed to controls characteristically experienced by men (1988).[9] The answer to the 'crime problem', Frances Heidensohn once concluded, would have to lie in the feminization of control.

Rational Choice Theory

An increasingly important, but not indispensable, foundation for control theories is 'rational choice theory', a resuscitation of old utilitarian theories that preceded sociology and were once linked with Adam Smith, Jeremy Bentham, Cesare Beccaria, and James Mill. Rational choice theory has recently been re-introduced to criminology through the medium of a revived economics of crime,[10] and it brings with it the convenient fiction of economic man, a fiction which has an immediate affinity with the criminal man (or woman) of control theory. Economic man, deemed to be continually looking about him for opportunities, making amoral and asocial choices to maximize his personal utility, may not be an empirically grounded or well-authenticated entity, but, it is argued, he does help to simplify model-making, strip away what rational choice theorists conceive to be inessential theoretical and descriptive clutter,[11] and aim directly at what are conceived to be practically useful policy questions (see Clarke and Cornish, 1985). Economic man in his (or her) criminal guise does not have a past, complex motives, rich social life,

---

[9] That is not her only argument. She writes about what she calls the 'class deal' as well, and that is redolent of earlier work on the delinquent solution in the *anomie* tradition.

[10] For one very influential early article, see Becker (1968). For a more sophisticated example of work by economists, built in part on a critique of Becker, see Akerlof and Yellen (1994).

[11] Including, O'Malley (1992) would argue, issues of social justice and the social foundations of offending.

or, indeed, a recognizable social identity (a 'disposition' is how Ron Clarke would put it (1992)[12]). He or she does not need to have any of those attributes. He or she is very much like any one of us or, better still, like some Everyman who stands abstractly and plainly for all of us. He or she needs no such complexity because what weighs in control theory is the piecemeal analysis of discrete instances of disembodied offending behaviour in the settings in which they may take place (see introduction to Clarke and Felson, 1993).

In Ron Clarke's particularly influential formulation,[13] the rate of crime was held to vary in response to three broad configurations of factors. The first grouping revolved around increasing the effort Everyman would have to expend in committing a crime, and that entailed what was called 'target hardening' (by defending objects and people by shields and other devices); 'access control' (and that involved making it difficult for predators to approach targets); deflecting offenders (by encouraging them, for example, to act in a legitimate rather than an illegitimate manner through the provision of graffiti boards, litter bins, and spittoons); and 'controlling facilitators' (though gun control or checks on the sales of spray cans, for instance). The second revolved around increasing the risks of offending through the screening of people (by means of border searches, for example); formal surveillance by police, security guards, and others; surveillance by employees such as bus conductors, concierges, and janitors; and 'natural surveillance' (aided by lowering or removing obstacles such as hedges and shrubs, installing closed circuit television cameras, lighting the interiors of stores, and enhanced street lighting). The final grouping was 'reducing the rewards' of crime, itself composed of 'target removal' (using electronic transactions to reduce the number of cash payments, and thus the accumulation of cash in single places, for instance); property identification; removal of inducements (by the rapid cleaning of graffiti or repair of vandalized property); and rule setting (though income tax returns, customs declarations, and the like) (taken from Clarke, 1992: 13). A pursuit of those common-sense, sometimes indistinguishable but nevertheless practical ideas allowed research officers at the Home Office to undertake a long chain of illustrative studies, discovering, for example, that compact, old school buildings on small sites were a third as likely to be burgled as large, sprawling, modern buildings with their many points of access and weak possibilities of surveillance (see Hope, 1982); or that there was some twenty times as much malicious damage on the upper than on the lower decks of 'one man', double-decker buses whose drivers' powers of surveillance were confined to one level only (Mayhew *et al.*, 1976: 26).

None of those variables touched on conventional sociological questions

---

[12] Clarke's notion that disposition could be ignored was to be one of the chief planks of the *situational* crime prevention stance which he adopted. The specific situation and an ideal-typical, rational actor were all that were required for effective analysis, he claimed.

[13] Influential, not only because of its content, but also because Clarke himself was at one time the head of the Home Office Research Unit and his ideas were to lead to a substantial and sustained programme of research.

about who offenders might be, what they think, and how they act. They concentrated instead on the imagined impact of different forms of control on Everyman or Everywoman abroad in space, and from that it was but a short step to extend control theory to an analysis of the disciplines that are built into everyday social practices, on the one hand, and into the social uses of space, on the other.

Routine Activities Theory

Ron Clarke, the situational control theorist, and Marcus Felson, the theorist of crime and routine activities, agreed that they shared ideas in common (see Clarke and Felson, 1993). Clarke and his colleagues had asked what prevented specific criminal incidents from occurring in specific situations. Felson asked how such incidents originate or are checked in the routine activities of mundane social life (1994). Just as Clarke and others had emphasized how, for explanatory purposes, it was convenient to assume that offenders were little different from anyone else, so Felson and his colleagues argued that most criminals are unremarkable, unskilled, petty, and non-violent people much like us. Just as control theorists made use of a tacit version of original sin, so routine activities theory adopted a series of presuppositions about basic human frailty, the importance of temptation and provocation, and the part played by idleness ('We are all born weak, but . . . we are taught self-control', Felson claimed (1994: 20)).

The routine activities criminologist would argue that the analysis of predatory crime does not necessarily require weighty causes. Neither does it demand that the theorist commit the 'like-causes-like' fallacy which covertly insists that a 'pathological' phenomenon such as crime must be explained by a pathological condition such as alienation, poverty, family dysfunction, or oppression. Crime was taken to be embedded in the very architecture of every-day life. More precisely, it was to be found in the convergence in space of what were called motivated offenders, suitable targets, and capable guardians (see Cohen and Felson, 1979): being affected by such matters as the weight, value, incidence, and distribution of stealable goods (the growth in the quantity of portable, high-cost goods such as video-recorders will encourage more theft, for instance); the impact of motor cars (they aid rapid flight, permit the discreet transportation of objects, and give rise to a geographical dispersal of the population which dilutes surveillance); habits of leisure (adolescents now have larger swathes of empty time than did their predecessors, time in which they can get up to mischief); habits of work (when all members of a household are in employment, there will be no capable guardians to protect a home); habits of residence (single people are less effective guardians of property than are larger households); the growth of technology (telephones, for instance, amplify the public's ability to report crime); and so on. It is an uncomplicated enough theory but again, like its near neighbour, control theory, it does ask productive questions.

CRIME, CONTROL, AND SPACE

The Chicago School

Routine activities theory and control theory both talk about convergence in space, and space has always been analytically to the fore in criminology. Indeed, one of the earliest and most productive of the research traditions laid down in criminology was the social ecology and urban mapping practised by the sociology department of the University of Chicago in the 1920s and beyond (see Park, 1925; Thrasher, 1927; and Landesco, 1968).

As cities grow, it was held, so there would be a progressive and largely spontaneous differentiation of space, population, and function that concentrated different groupings in different areas. The main organizing structure was the zone, and the Chicago sociologists discerned five principal concentric zones shaping the city: the central business district at the very core; the 'zone in transition' about that centre; an area of stable working-class housing; middle-class housing; and outer suburbia.

The zone in transition was marked by the greatest volatility of its residents. It was an area of comparatively cheap rents, weak social control, internal social differentiation, and rapid physical change. It was to the zone in transition that new immigrant groupings most frequently came, and it was there that they settled into what were called 'natural areas', small communal enclaves that were relatively homogeneous in composition and culture.[14] Chicago sociologists plotted the incidence of social problems on to census maps of the city, and it was the zone in transition that was found repeatedly to house the largest proportions of the poor, the illegitimate, the illiterate, the mentally ill (see Faris and Dunham, 1939), juvenile delinquents (Shaw and McKay, 1942), and prostitutes (Reckless, 1933). The zone in transition was virtually co-extensive with what was then described as social pathology.[15] Not only were formal social controls held to be at their weakest there (the zone in transition was, as it were, socially dislocated from the formal institutions and main body of American society (see Whyte, 1942)); but informal social controls were checked by moral and social diversity, rapid population movement, and a lack of strong and pervasive local institutions: 'contacts are extended, heterogeneous groups mingle, neighborhoods disappear, and people, deprived of local and family ties, are forced to live under . . . loose, transient and impersonal relations' (Wirth, 1964: 236).

A number of the early Chicago sociologists united social ecology, the study of the patterns formed by groups living together in the same space, with the fieldwork methods of social anthropology, to explore the traditions, customs,

---

[14] Later critics, such as Suttles (1972), have questioned how natural or uniform those natural areas actually were.

[15] Of course, as later critics pointed out, some forms of social pathology, such as white collar crime, were to be found elsewhere. See Taylor, Walton, and Young, 1973.

and practices of the residents of natural areas.[16] They found that, whilst there may well have been a measure of social and moral dislocation between the zone in transition and the wider society, as well as within the zone in transition itself, those natural areas could also manifest a remarkable coherence and continuity of culture and behaviour that were reproduced from generation to generation and from immigrant group to immigrant group within the same terrain over time. Delinquency was, in effect, not disorganized at all, but a stable attribute of social life, an example of persistence in change: 'to a very great extent . . . traditions of delinquency are preserved and transmitted through the medium of social contact with the unsupervised play group and the more highly organized delinquent and criminal gangs' (Shaw and McKay, 1971: 260). Cultural transmission was to be the focus of the work pursued by a small group of second generation Chicago sociologists. Under the name of 'differential association', it was studied as a normal process of learning motives, skills, and meanings in the company of others who bore criminal traditions (see Sutherland and Cressey, 1955).

That urban research was to prepare a diverse legacy for criminology: the spatial analysis of crime; the study of subcultures (which I shall touch on below); the epidemiology of crime; crime as an interpretive practice (which I shall also touch on); and much else. Let me turn first to some examples of spatial analysis.

Control and Space: Beyond the Chicago School

The Chicago sociologists' preoccupation with the cultural and symbolic correlates of spatial congregations of people was to be steadily elaborated by criminologists. For instance, Wiles, Bottoms, and their colleagues, all originally working at the University of Sheffield, added two important observations. They argued first that, in a more tightly regulated Britain, social segregation did not emerge, as it were, organically with unplanned city growth, but with the intended and unintended consequences of policy decisions taken by local government departments responsible for housing a large proportion of the population in municipal accommodation.[17] Housing allocation was an indirect reflection of moral judgements about tenants that resulted, or were assumed to result, in the concentration of criminal populations (see Bottoms *et al.*, 1989). Further, and partly in accord with that argument, the reputations of natural areas themselves became a criminological issue: how was it that the moral meanings attached to space by residents and outsiders affected people's reputations, choices, and action? One's very address could become a constraining moral fact that affected not only how one would be treated by others in and about the criminal justice system (see Damer, 1974), but also how one

[16] It was Robert Park who first advocated that the modern city should be approached with a methodology once reserved for pre-literate peoples. See Park, 1915.

[17] That insight was originally conceived by Terence Morris (1958), and was later elaborated by Bottoms and Wiles.

would come to rate oneself as a potential deviant or conformist (see Gill, 1977).

Secondly, Bottoms and his colleagues argued, whilst the Chicago sociologists may have examined the geographical distribution of offenders, it was instructive also to scrutinize how offending itself could be plotted, because the two measures need not correspond (Baldwin and Bottoms, 1976). Offending has its maps. Indeed, it appears to be densely concentrated, clustered around offenders' homes, areas of work and recreation, and the pathways in between (Brantingham and Brantingham, 1981–2). So it was that, pursuing routine activities theory, Sherman and his colleagues surveyed all calls made to the police in Minneapolis in one year: and they discovered that only 3 per cent of all places produced 50 per cent of the calls; all robberies took place in only 2.2 per cent of places, all rapes in 1.2 per cent of places, and all car thefts in 2.7 per cent of places (Sherman *et al.*, 1989; see also Roncek and Maier, 1991).

Defensible Space

If offending has its maps, so does social control, and criminologists and others have become ever more interested in the fashion in which space, conduct, and control intersect. One forerunner was Jane Jacobs, who speculated about the relations between city landscapes and informal controls, arguing, for example, that dense, busy thoroughfares have many more 'eyes on the street' and opportunities for witness reporting and bystander intervention, than sterile pedestrian zones or streets without stores and other lures (Jacobs, 1965).

The idea of 'defensible space', in particular, has been borrowed from anthropology and architecture, coupled with the concept of surveillance, and put to work in analysing formal and informal responses to different kinds of terrain. 'Defensible space' itself leans on the psychological notion of 'territoriality', the sense of attachment and symbolic investment that people can acquire in space. Territoriality is held by some to be a human universal,[18] an imperative that leads people to wish to guard what is their own. Those who have a stake in a physical area, it is argued, will care for it, police it, and report strangers and others who have no apparent good purpose to be there.

What is quite critical is how space is marked out and bounded. The prime author of the idea of defensible space, Oscar Newman (1972), claimed that, other things being equal, what induces territorial sentiments is a clear demarcation between private and public areas, even if the demarcations are only token. The private will be protected in ways that the public is not, and the fault of many domestic and institutional buildings is that separations and segregations are not clearly enough inscribed in design. Alice Coleman and others took it that improvements to the physical structures of built space could then achieve a significant impact on crime: above all, she insisted on restrict-

---

[18] An idea challenged by defensible space theory's most robust critic, Bill Hillier (1973).

ing access to sites; reducing the interconnections between buildings; and emphasizing the distinction between public and private space and minimizing what Oscar Newman called 'confused space', the space that was neither one nor the other (Coleman, 1985, 1986). She has been roundly faulted, both methodologically[19] and analytically, for her neglect of dimensions other than the physical, but she and Newman have succeeded in introducing an analytic focus on the interrelations between space and informal control that was largely absent before. Only rarely have criminologists such as Shapland and Vagg enquired into the informal practices of people as they observe, interpret, and respond to the ambiguous, the deviant, and the non-deviant in the spaces around them (1988). It is Shapland and Vagg's contention that there is a continuous, active, and often informed process of surveillance transacted by people on the ground, a process which is so discreet that it has escaped much formal notice, and which meshes only haphazardly with the work of the police.

Crime, Powers, and Space

Surveillance has not always been construed as neutral or benign, and there are current debates about what its newest forms might portend (see Marx, 1996). Even its sponsors in government departments and criminal justice agencies have spoken informally about their anxiety that people are being encouraged to become unduly fearful of crime and retreat into private fastnesses. It began to be argued, especially by those who followed Michel Foucault, that a 'punitive city' was in the making, that, in Stan Cohen's words, there was 'a deeper penetration of social control into the social body' (1979: 356).

Some came to claim that there had been a move progressively not only to differentiate and elaborate the distribution of controls in space, but that there had also been a proliferating surveillance of dangerous areas, often conducted obliquely and with an increasingly advanced technology. Michel Foucault's (1977) dramatic simile of Jeremy Bentham's Panopticon[20] was to be put to massive use in criminology. Just as the Panopticon, or inspection house, was supposed to have permitted the unobserved observation of many malefactors around the bright, illuminated rim of a circular prison by the few guards in its obscured centre, just as the uncertainty of unobserved observation worked to make the controlled control themselves, so, Foucault and those who followed him wished to argue, modern society is coming to exemplify the perfection of the automatic exercise of power through generalized surveillance. The carceral society was a machine in which everyone was supposed to be caught: it relied on diffuse control through unseen monitoring and the individualization and 'interiorization' of control (Gordon 1972). Public space, it was said, was becoming exposed to ever more perfunctory, distant, and technologically driven policing by formal state agencies, whilst control in private and

[19] Again, most robustly, by Bill Hillier (1986).
[20] For the best description of the history of the Panopticon, see Semple, 1993.

semi-private space (the space of the shopping malls, university campus, and theme park) was itself becoming more dense, privatized, and widespread, placed in the private hands of security guards and store detectives, and reliant on a new electronic surveillance (Davis, 1992: 233).

What also underlies much of that vision is a new, complementary stress on the sociology of risk, a focus linked importantly with the work of Ulrich Beck (1992), which argues that people and groups are becoming significantly stratified by their exposure to risk and their power to neutralize harm. The rich can afford private protection, the poor cannot, and a new ecology emerges (Simon, 1987). Phrased only slightly differently, and merged with the newly burgeoning ideas about the pervasiveness of surveillance by machine and person (Gordon, 1986–7; Lyon, 1994), those theories of risk suggested that controls were being applied by state and private organizations, not on the basis of some moralistic conception of individual wrongdoing, but on a foundation of the identification, classification, and management of groups categorized by their perceived dangerousness (Feeley and Simon, 1992; Simon and Feeley, 1995). Groups were becoming ever more rigidly segregated in space: some, members of the new dangerous classes or under-class, being confined to prison, semi-freedom under surveillance, or parole in the community; others, the rich, retreating into their locked and gated communities, secure zones, and private spaces.

A paradigmatic case study has been supplied by Clifford Shearing and Philip Stenning's ethnography of Disney World as a 'private, quasi-feudal domain of control' (Shearing and Stenning, 1985: 347) that was comprehensively, discreetly, and adeptly controlled by employees, extensive surveillance, the encouragement of self-discipline, and the very arrangement of physical space.

In prophetic mood, again, criminologists have begun to identify new maps of city space bifurcated into a relatively uncontrolled 'badlands' occupied by the poor and highly controlled 'security bubbles' inhabited by the rich.[21]

RADICAL CRIMINOLOGY

So far, control has been treated without much direct allusion to the power, politics, and inequalities that are its bedfellows. There was to be a relatively short-lived but active challenge to such quiescence from the radical, new, or critical criminologies of the late 1960s and 1970s, criminologies that claimed their mandate in Marxism (Taylor, Walton, and Young 1973), anarchism (Kittrie, 1971, and Cohen, 1985) or populism (Quinney, 1970), and whose ambitions pointed to political activism or praxis (Mathiesen, 1972).

Crime control was said to be an oppressive and mystifying process that worked through legislation, law enforcement, and ideological stereotyping to

---

[21] A prime example is Bottoms and Wiles, 1996.

preserve unequal class relations (Chambliss, 1976, and Box, 1983). The radical political economy of crime sought chiefly to expose the hegemonic ideologies that masked the real nature of crime and repression in capitalist society. Most mundane crime, it was argued, was actually less politically or socially conse-quential than other social evils such as alienation, exploitation, or racism (Scraton, 1987). Much proletarian offending could be redefined as a form of redistributive class justice or as a sign of the possessive individualism which resided in the core values of capitalist society. Criminal justice itself was engineered to create visible crowds of working-class and black scapegoats who could attract the public gaze away from the more serious delicts of the rich and the more serious ills of a capitalism that was usually said to be in terminal crisis. If the working class reacted in hostile fashion to the crime in their midst, then they were, in effect, little more than the victims of a false consciousness which turned proletarian against proletarian, inflated the importance of petty problems, and concealed the true nature of bourgeois society. So construed, signification, the act of giving meaning, was either manipulative or miscon-ceived, a matter of giving and receiving incorrect and deformed interpretations or reality. Indeed, it was in the very nature of capitalist society that most people must be politically unenlightened about crime, control, and much else, and the task of the radical criminologist was to expose, denounce, and demystify.

It was concluded variously that crime was not a problem which the poor and their allies should actually address (there were more important matters for socialists to think about: Hirst, 1975); that the crime which *should* be analysed was the wrongdoing of the powerful (the wrong crimes and criminals were being observed: Chapman, 1967; Reiman, 1990) or that crime and its problems would shrivel into insignificance as a criminogenic capitalism gave way to the tolerant diversity of socialism (Taylor, Walton, and Young, 1973). The crime and criminals that chiefly warranted attention were those exceptional examples of law-breaking that seemed to represent an incipient revolt against the State, and they demanded cultivation as subjects of study, understanding, and possible politicization. Black prisoners, in particular, were sometimes depicted, and depicted themselves, as prisoners of class or race wars (Cleaver, 1969). Prisons were the point of greatest State repression, and prison riots a possible spearhead of revolution.

In its early guise, radical criminology withered somewhat under a quadruple-barrelled assault. In some places, and in America especially (where it had never been firmly implanted), it ran foul of university politics, and some depart-ments, such as the one at the University of California at Berkeley, were actually closed down. More often, radical criminology did not lend itself to the government-funded, policy-driven, 'soft money', empiricist research that came to dominate schools of criminology in North America in the 1970s and 1980s.

Second, was the effect of the publication of mass victim surveys in the 1970s and 1980s (Hough and Mayhew, 1983) which disclosed both the extent of working-class victimization and the manner in which it revolved around intra-class, rather than inter-class, criminality. It was evident that crime *was* a manifest problem for the poor, adding immeasurably to their burdens, and difficult to dismiss as an ideological distraction. Two prominent radical criminologists came frankly to concede that they had believed that 'property offences [were] directed solely against the bourgeoisie and that violence against the person [was] carried out by amateur Robin Hoods in the course of their righteous attempts to redistribute wealth. All of this [was], alas, untrue' (Lea and Young, 1984: 262).

Third was the critique launched from within the left by a new generation of feminist scholars who asserted that the victimization of women was no slight affair, and that rape, sexual assault, child abuse and domestic violence should be taken very seriously indeed (Smart, 1977). Not only had the female criminal been neglected, they said, but so had the female victim, and it would not do to wait until the revolution for matters to be put right. Once more, a number of radical criminologists gave ground. There had been, Jones, Maclean, and Young observed, 'a general tendency in radical thought to idealize their historical subject (in this case the working class) and to play down intra-group conflict, blemishes and social disorganization. But the power of the feminist case resulted in a sort of cognitive schizophrenia amongst radicals' (Jones *et al.*, 1986: 3). The revitalized criminology of women and 'left realism', the new reformist radical criminology, are both subjects of separate chapters in this handbook.

Fourthly, there was a critique launched belatedly from non-feminist criminologists who resisted the imperious claims of radical criminology (Downes and Rock, 1979; Inciardi, 1980). Marxist theories of crime, it was argued, lacked a comparative emphasis: they neglected crime in 'non-capitalist' and 'pre-capitalist' societies and crime in 'socialist' societies. There was a naïveté about the expectation that crime would wither away as the State itself disappeared after the revolution. There was an irresponsibility about radical arguments that 'reformism' would only strengthen the grip of the capitalist system.[22]

A number of radical and sceptical criminologists began to turn away from analyses of causation towards studies of social control (Cohen, 1985; Simon, 1993) and particularly the history of social control (see Scull, 1979). In Britain, criminologists such as Pat Carlen, Ian Young, and Jock Young prospered and, indeed, play a major role in affecting funding and publishing decisions. They are academically influential, and 'left realism', the revised radical criminology synthesized by Young and his colleagues, reviewed in another chapter in this handbook, remains a vibrant theory.

---

[22] That argument had been developed, for example, by Mathiesen (1974).

FUNCTIONALIST CRIMINOLOGY

Another, apparently dissimilar but substantially complementary, theory presented deviance and control as forces that worked discreetly to maintain social order. Functionalism was a theory of social systems or wholes, developed at the beginning of the twentieth century within a social anthropology grown tired of speculative accounts of the origins and evolution of societies which lacked the written history to support them, and dedicated to the scientific pursuit of intellectual problems. It was argued that the business of a social science necessitated moving enquiry beyond the reach of common sense or lay knowledge to an examination of the objective consequences of action that were visible only to the trained eye.[23]

There were three clear implications. First, what ordinary people thought they were doing could be very different from what they actually achieved. The functionalist was preoccupied only with objective results, and people's own accounts of action held little interest. Secondly, the functionalist looked at the impact made by institution upon institution, structure upon structure, in societies that were remarkable for their capacity to persist over time. Thirdly, those consequences, viewed as a totality, constituted a system whose parts were thought not only to affect one another and the whole, but which also affected them in return. To be sure, some institutions were relatively detached, but functionalists would have argued that the alternative proposition that social phenomena lack all influence upon one another, that there was no functional reciprocity between them, was conceptually insupportable. Systemic inter-relations were an analytic *a priori*, a matter of self-evidence so compelling that Kingsley Davis could argue that 'we are all functionalists now' (Davis, 1959).

There have been very few dedicated functionalist criminologists. Functionalists tend to deal with the properties of whole systems rather than with empirical fragments. But crime and deviance did supply a particularly intriguing laboratory for thought-experiments about social order. It was easy enough to contend that religion or education shaped social cohesion, but how much harder it would be to show that *crime* succeeded in doing so. After all, 'everyone knew' that crime undermined social structures. It followed that functionalists occasionally found it tempting to try to confound that knowledge by showing that, to the contrary, the seemingly recalcitrant case of crime could be shown scientifically to contribute to the working of the social system. From time to time, therefore, they wrote about crime to demonstrate the

[23] Delineating such a chasm between the intellectual and everyman is a commonplace feature of much social theorizing, and the theorizing of Marxists, functionalists, and psychoanalysts in particular. As Rorty argued, 'Plato developed the idea of . . . an intellectual by means of distinctions between knowledge and opinion, and between appearance and reality. Such distinctions conspire to produce the idea that rational inquiry should make visible a realm to which non-intellectuals have little access, and of whose existence they may be doubtful' (1991: 22).

potency of their theory. Only one functionalist, its grand master, Talcott Parsons, ever made the obvious, and therefore unsatisfying, point that crime could be what was called 'dysfunctional' or injurious to the social system as it was then constituted (Parsons, 1951). Everyone else asserted that crime actually worked mysteriously to support it.

The outcome was a somewhat miscellaneous collection of papers documenting the multiple functions of deviance. So it was that Kingsley Davis showed that prostitution shored up monogamy by providing an unemotional, impersonal, and unthreatening release for the sexual energy of the promiscuous married male (Davis 1937) (Mary McIntosh once wondered what the promiscuous married female was supposed to do about her sexual energy); Ned Polsky made much the same claim for pornography (Polsky 1967); Daniel Bell showed that racketeering provided 'queer ladders of success' and political and social stability in the New York dockside (1960); Émile Durkheim (1964) and George Herbert Mead (1918) contended that the formal rituals of trial and punishment enhanced social solidarity and consolidated moral boundaries; and, more complexly, Mary Douglas (1966), Kai Erikson (1966), Robert Scott (1972) and others argued that deviance offered social systems a dialectical tool for the clarification of threats, ambiguities, and anomalies in classification systems. The list could be extended, but all the arguments tended to one end: what appeared, on the surface, to undermine social order accomplished the very reverse. A sociological counterpart of the invisible hand transmuted deviance into a force for cohesion.

Functionalism was to be discarded by many criminologists in time: it smacked too much of teleology (the doctrine that effects act as causes); it defied rigorous empirical investigation; and, for some liberal and radical criminologists, it represented a form of Panglossian conservatism that championed the *status quo*. But its ghost lingers on. Any who would argue that, contrary to appearances, crime and deviance buttress social order; any who argue for the study of seamless systems; any who argue that the sociologist should mistrust people's own accounts of their actions; any who insist that social science is the study of unintended consequences; must share something of the functionalist's standpoint. *Anomie* theories that represented crime as the system-stabilizing, unintended consequence of strains in the social order are one example: deviance in that guise becomes the patterned adjustments that defuse an otherwise disruptive conflict and reconcile people to disadvantage (although, as I have argued, the theories can also envisage conditions in which crime becomes 'system-threatening'). Some versions of radical criminology provide another example. More than one criminologist has argued that crime, deviance, and control were necessary for the survival of capitalism (Stinchcombe, 1968). For instance, although they did not talk explicitly of '*function*', the neo-Marxists, Stuart Hall (1978), Frank Pearce (1976) and Jeffrey Reiman (1990), *were* recognizably functionalist in their treatment of the criminal justice system's production of visible and scapegoated roles for the proletarian criminal, roles that attracted public anxiety and outrage, deflected anger away from the State, and thereby emasculated political opposition. Consider, for example, Ferrell and Sanders's observation that 'The simplistic criminogenic models at the core of . . . constructed moral panics . . . deflect attention from larger and more complex political problems like economic and ethnic inequality, and the alienation of young people and creative workers from confining institutions' (1995: 10).

SIGNIFICATION

Labelling Theory

Perhaps the only other big idea outstanding is signification, the interpretive practices that order social life. There has been an enduring strain of analysis, linked most particularly to symbolic interactionism and phenomenology, which insists that people do not, and cannot, respond immediately, uncritically, and passively to the world 'as it is'. Rather they respond to their *ideas* of that world, and the business of sociology is to capture, understand, and reproduce those ideas; examine their interaction with one another; and analyse the processes and structures that generated them. Sociology becomes the study of people and practices as symbolic and symbolizing processes.

Central to that idea is reflectivity, the capacity of consciousness to translate itself into its own object. People are able to think about themselves, define themselves in various ways, toy with different identities, and project themselves imaginatively into any manner of contrived situation. They can view themselves vicariously by inferring the reactions of 'significant others', and, in so 'taking the role of the other', move symbolically to a distance outside themselves to inspect how they might appear. Elaborating action through 'significant gestures', the symbolic projection of acts and identities, they can anticipate the likely responses of others, and tailor their own prospective acts to accommodate them (Mead, 1934). In all this, social worlds are compacted symbolically into the phrasing of action, and the medium that makes that possible is language.

Language is held to objectify, stabilize, and extend meaning. Used conversationally in the anticipation of an act, it permits people to be both their own subject and object, speaker and thing spoken about, 'I' and 'me', opening up the mind to reflective action. Conferring names, it enables people to impart moral and social meanings to their own and others' motives (Mills, 1940; Scott and Lyman, 1970), intentions, and identities. It will matter a great deal if someone is defined as eccentric, erratic, or mad; a drinker, a drunk, or an alcoholic; a lovelorn admirer or a stalker. Consequences will flow from naming, consequences that affect not only how one regards oneself and one's position in the world, but also how one may be treated by others. Naming creates a self.

Transposed to the study of crime and deviance, symbolic interactionism and phenomenology gave prominence to the processes by which deviant acts are assembled and interpreted, judged and controlled, by subjects and others about them (Katz, 1988). A core pair of articles was Howard Becker's 'Becoming a Marihuana User' and 'Marihuana Use and Social Control' (1963), both of which described the patterned sequence of steps that could shape the experience, moral identity, and fate of one who began to smoke marihuana. Becoming a marihuana user was a tentative process, developing stage by stage, which required the user satisfactorily to learn, master, and interpret techniques, neutralize forbidding moral images of use and users, and succeed in disguising signs of use in the presence of those who might disapprove. It became paradigmatic.[24]

Deviance itself was to become more broadly likened to a moral career consisting of interlocking phases, each of which fed into the next; each of which presented different existential problems and opportunities; each of which was populated by different constellations of significant others; and each of which could distinctively mould the identity of the deviant. However, the process was also assumed to be contingent. Not every phase was inevitable or irreversible, and deviants could often elect to change direction. Luckenbill and Best provide a graphic description:

Riding escalators between floors may be an effective metaphor for respectable organizational careers, but it fails to capture the character of deviant careers. A more appropriate image is a walk in the woods. Here, some people take the pathways marked by their predecessors, while others strike out on their own. Some walk slowly, exploring before moving on, but others run, caught up in the action. Some have a desitination in mind and proceed purposively; others view the trip and enjoy it for its own sake. Even those intent on reaching a destination may stray from the path; they may try to shortcut or they may lose sight of familiar landmarks, get lost, and find it necessary to backtrack [1981: 201].

What punctuates such a career is acts of naming, the deployment of language to confer and fix the meanings of behaviour, and symbolic interactionism and phenomenology became known within criminology as 'labelling theory'. One of the most frequently cited of all passages in sociological criminology was Becker's dictum that 'deviance is not a quality of the act the person commits, but rather a consequence of the application by others of rules and sanctions to an "offender". The deviant is one to whom that label has successfully been applied; deviant behavior is behavior that people so label' (1963: 9).

Labelling itself is contingent. Many deviant acts are not witnessed and most are not reported. People may well be able to resist or modify deviant designations when attempts *are* made to apply them: after all, we are continually bombarded by attempts to label us and few succeed. But there are special occasions when the ability of the self to resist definition is circumscribed, and

---

[24] David Matza's *Becoming Deviant*, (1969), was, for example, presented as an extended treatise on the implications of those two papers.

most fateful of all may be an encounter with agents of the criminal justice system, because they work with the power and authority of the state. In such meetings, criminals and deviants are obliged to confront not only their own and others' possibly defensive, fleeting, and insubstantial reactions to what they have done, their 'primary deviation', but also contend publicly with the formal reactions of others, and their deviation can then become a response to responses, 'secondary deviation': 'When a person begins to employ his deviant behavior or a role based upon it as a means of defense, attack, or adjustment to the overt and covert problems created by the consequent societal reaction to him, his deviation is secondary' (Lemert, 1951: 76).

What is significant about secondary deviation is that it will be a symbolic synthesis of more than the meanings and activities of primary deviation. It will also incorporate the myths, professional knowledge, stereotypes, and working assumptions of police officers, judges, medical practitioners, prison officers, prisoners, policy-makers, and politicians. Drug-users (see Schur, 1963), mental patients, (Goffman, 1968; Scheff, 1966) homosexuals (Hooker, 1963) and others may be obliged to organize their significant gestures and character around the public symbols of their behaviour. Who they are and what they do may then be explained as much by the symbolic incorporation of a public response as by any set of original conditions. Control will be inscribed into the very fabric of a self.

What is also significant is that secondary deviation entails confrontations with new obstacles that foreclose future choice. Thus, Gary Marx has listed a number of the ironic consequences that can flow from forms of covert social control such as undercover policing and the work of *agents provocateurs*: they include generating a market for illegal goods; the provision of motives and meanings for illegal action; entrapping people in offences they might not other-wise have committed; the supply of false or misleading records; retaliatory action against informers, and the like (Marx, 1988: 126–7). Once publicly identified as a deviant, moreover, it becomes difficult for a person to slip back into the conventional world, and measures are being taken with increasing frequency to enlarge the visibility of the rule-breaker. In the United States, for instance, 'Megan's Law' makes it mandatory in certain jurisdictions for the names of sex offenders to be publicly advertised, possibly reducing risk but certainly freezing the criminal as a secondary deviant.

Culture and Subculture

Meanings and motives are not established and confirmed by the self in solitude. They are a social accomplishment, and criminology has paid sustained attention to signification as a collaborative, subcultural process. Subcultures themselves are taken to be exaggerations, accentuations, or editings of cultural themes prevalent in the wider society. Any social group which has permanence, closure, and common pursuits is likely to inherit or engender a subculture, but the criminologist's particular interest is in those subcultures that condone, promote, or otherwise make possible the commission of delinquent acts. A subculture was not conceived to be utterly distinct from the beliefs held by people at large. Nor was it necessarily oppositional. It was a *sub*culture, not a culture or a counterculture, and the analytic stress was on dependency rather than conflict or symbolic automony.[25]

The materials for subcultural theory were to be found across the broad range of criminology, and they could be combined in various proportions. *Anomie* theory supplied the supposition that social inequalities generate problems that may have delinquent solutions, and that those solutions, in their turn, could be shared and transmitted by people thrown together by their common disadvantage. Albert Cohen, the man who invented the phrase 'delinquent subculture', argued: 'The crucial condition for the emergence of new cultural forms is the existence, in effective interaction with one another, of a number of actors with similar problems of adjustment' (1957: 59). The social anthropology of the Chicago school, channelled for a while into differential association theory, supplied an emphasis upon the enduring cultural traditions shared by boys living, working, and playing together on the crowded streets of morally differentiated areas. Retaining the idea of a 'subculture of delinquency, David Matza and a number of control theorists pointed to the manner in which moral proscriptions could be neutralized by invoking commonly available extenuating accounts. 'Left realism' could be described as little more than early subcultural theory in a new guise. And symbolic interactionism supplied a focus on the negotiated, collective, and processual character of meaning. In all this, an argument ran that young men (it was almost always young men), growing up in the city, banded together in groups or 'near-groups' (Yablonsky, 1962) in the crowded public life of the streets, encountering common problems, exposed to common stereotypes and stigmas, are likely to form joint interpretations that are sporadically favourable to delinquency. Subcultural theory and research were to dominate explanations of delinquency until they exhausted themselves in the 1960s.[26]

Subcultural theory could also lend itself to amalgamation with radical criminology, and particularly that criminology which was preoccupied with the reproduction of class inequalities through the workings of ideology. In Britain, there was to be a renaissance of subcultural theory as a group of sociologists centred around Stuart Hall at the University of Birmingham gave special attention to the existential plight of young working-class men[27] about to enter the labour market. The prototype for that work was Phil Cohen's analysis of proletarian cultures in London: young men responded to the decline of

[25] The most rigorous early work that emphasized the important commonalities between delinquent subcultures and themes in the wider culture was Short and Strodbeck, 1967.

[26] Particularly important was to be David Matza's critique (1964) that subcultural theory was too robust in its assertions, that it exaggerated difference and over-predicted offending. His was to be an imagery of society that was more fluid, complex, and negotiated, and it found favour with many critics.

[27] Again, with the exception of the work of Angela McRobbie (McRobbie and Garber, 1976), the gaze was almost wholly on males.

community, loss of class cohesion, and economic insecurity by resurrecting in subcultural form an idealized and exaggerated version of working class masculinity that 'express[ed] and resolve[d], albeit "magically", the contradictions which remain hidden or unresolved in the parent culture' (1972: 23). Deviance became a form of symbolic resistance to tensions perceived through the mists of false consciousness. It was doomed to disappoint because it did not address the root causes of discontent, but it did offer a fleeting release. There was a contradiction within that version of subcultural theory because it was not easy to reconcile a structural Marxism which depicted adolescent culture as illusory with a commitment to understanding meaning (Willis, 1977). But it was a spirited and vivid revival of a theory that had gone into the doldrums in the 1960s, and it continues to influence theorizing (see Ferrell 1993). Indeed, interestingly, there are strong signs of a *rapprochement* between critical cultural studies and symbolic interactionism (see Becker and McCall, 1990).

CONCLUSION

Sociological theories of crime cluster together in groupings given a tenuous unity by a few big themes. What is uncertain, and what has always been uncertain, is how they may be expected to evolve in the future. Very few would have predicted the rapid demise of radical criminology, a brand of theorizing that once seemed so strong that it would sweep all before it, at least in large parts of Europe, Canada, and Australasia. Few would have predicted the resurgence of utilitarian theories of rational choice—they seemed to have been superseded forever by a sociology that pointed to the part played by social contexts in the shaping of meaning and action.

What may certainly be anticipated is a continuation of the semi-detached relations between criminology and its parent disciplines, and with sociology above all. The half-life of sociological theories is brief, often bound up with the duration of intellectual generations, and sociological theory is itself emergent, a compound of the familiar and the unfamiliar. It is to be assumed that there will always be something new out of sociology, and that criminology will almost always respond and innovate in its turn.

Other matters are also clear. First, criminology remains a substantively defined discipline, and it tends not to detain the great intellectual system-builders. Those who would be the sociological Newtons, the men and women who would explain the great clockwork of society, are often impatient with the limitations imposed by analysing the mere parts and fragments of larger totalities. Almost all the grand theorists have made something of a mark on criminology, but they, or their disciples, have rarely stayed long. Their concern is with the wider systemic properties of society, not the surface features of empirical areas. Thus the phenomenologist, Mike Phillipson, once remarked that '[we should] turn away from constitutive and arbitrary judgements of public rule breaking as deviance towards the concept of rule itself and the dialectical tension that ruling is a subject more central to the fundamental practice of sociology' (1974: 5). And Marxists (Bankowski *et al.*, 1977) and feminists (Smart, 1989) have said much the same about the relations between their theories and the sub-discipline of criminology.

Thirdly, criminology will probably persist in challenging economics as a contender for the title of the dismal science. Criminologists are not professionally optimistic. A prolonged exposure to the pain of crime, ever-rising rates of offending, frequent abuses of authority, misconceived policies and 'nothing' or very little appearing to work,[28] seems to have fostered a propensity amongst the larger thinkers to infuse their writing with gloom and to argue, in effect, that all is really not for the best in the best of all possible worlds. Stan Cohen once confessed that 'Most of us—consciously or not—probably hold a rather bleak view of social change. Things must be getting worse' (1979: 360). Prophecies of a criminological future will still be tinged at the margins with the iconography of Mad Max, Neuromancer, and Blade Runner.

Fourthly, there is the growing influence of government and government money in shaping criminological work. Policies and politics have conspired to make rational choice theory, the criminological anti-theory, particularly attractive to criminal justice agencies. Rational choice and control theories lay out a series of neat, inexpensive, small-scale, practicable, and non-controversial steps that may be taken to 'do something' about crime. Moreover, as theories that are tied to the apron strings of economics, they can borrow something of the powerful intellectual authority that economics wields in the social sciences.

Fifth is the persistence of a feminist influence. Crime is clearly gendered, the intellectual yield of analysing the connections between gender and crime has not yet been fully explored, and women are entering the body of sociological criminology in ever greater numbers (although, to be sure, some feminists, like Carol Smart, are also emigrating and absolute numbers remain small). Criminological feminisms and feminist criminologies (Gelsthorpe and Morris, 1988)[29] will undoubtedly sustain work on gender, control and deviance and, increasingly, on masculinity.[29]

Some role will continue to be played by the sociological criminology that attaches importance to the ethnographic study of signifying practices. Symbolic interactionism and phenomenology have supplied an enduring reminder of the importance of reflectivity; the symbolically mediated character of all social reality; and the sheer complexity, density, and intricacy of the social world. And, finally, one would hope that criminology will continue to contribute its own distinct analysis of the wider social world, an analysis that can take it beyond the confines of a tightly defined nexus of relations between

---

[28] 'Nothing works' is a phrase associated with Martinson (1974) and his review of the abundant failures of penal strategy.

[29] A recent special issue of *The British Journal of Criminology* focused precisely on the theme of 'Masculinities, Social Relations and Crime'. Special Issue, 1996. Vol. 36, No. 3.

criminals, legislators, lawyers, and enforcement agents. A criminology without a wider vision of social process would be deformed. A sociology without a conception of rule-breaking and control would be an odd discipline indeed.

Selected Further Reading

For a general introduction to sociological theories of crime and deviance, there are a few recent books which might be helpful: in particular D. Downes and P. Rock, *Understanding Deviance* (Oxford: Oxford University Press, 1995), and F. Heidensohn, *Crime and Society* (London: Macmillan, 1989). For phenomenological and labelling theories, see J. Douglas, *American Social Order* (New York: Free Press, 1971), and H. Becker, *Outsiders* (New York: Free Press, 1963); for critical and left realist criminology, see I. Taylor, P. Walton, and J. Young, *The New Criminology* (London: Routledge and Kegan Paul, 1973), and J. Lea and J. Young, *What is to be Done About Law and Order?* (London: Pluto Press, 1993); for 'routine activities' theory, see M. Felson, *Crime and Everyday Life* (Thousand Oaks, CA: Pine Forge, 1994); and for control theory, M. Gottfredson and T. Hirschi, *A General Theory of Crime* (Stanford, CA: Stanford University Press, 1990); T. Hirschi, *The Causes of Deliquency* (Berkeley, CA: University of California Press, 1969); and J. Wilson and R. Herrnstein, *Crime and Human Nature* (New York: Simon and Schuster, 1985).

REFERENCES

AKERLOF, G., and YELLEN, J. (1994), 'Gang Behavior, Law Enforcement, and Community Values', in H. Aaron *et al.*, eds., *Values and Public Policy*. Washington, DC: Brookings Institution.

ANDERSON, E. (1976), *A Place on the Corner*. Chicago, Ill.: University of Chicago Press.

BALDWIN, J., and BOTTOMS, A. (1976), *The Urban Criminal*. London: Tavistock.

BANKOWSKI, Z. *et al.* (1977), 'Radical Criminology or Radical Criminologist?', *Contemporary Crises*, 1.

BECK, U. (1992), *Risk Society*. London: Sage.

BECKER, G. (1968), 'Crime and Punishment: An Economic Approach', *The Journal of Political Economy*, 76.

BECKER, H. (1963), *Outsiders*. New York: Free Press.

—— and MCCALL, M. eds. (1990), *Symbolic Interaction and Cultural Studies*. Chicago: University of Chicago Press.

BELL, D. (1960), 'The Racket-Ridden Longshoremen', in D. Bell, *The End of Ideology*. New York: Collier.

BOTTOMS, A. *et al.* (1989), 'A Tale of Two Estates', in D. Downes, ed., *Crime and the City*. Macmillan: Basingstoke.

—— and WILES, P. (1996), 'Crime and Insecurity in the City', in C. Fijnaut *et al.*, eds., *Changes in Society, Crime and Criminal Justice in Europe*. The Hague: Kluwer.

BOX, S. (1971), *Deviance, Reality and Society*. London: Holt, Rinehart, and Winston.

—— (1983), *Power, Crime and Mystification*. London: Tavistock.

BRANTINGHAM, P., and BRANTINGHAM, P. (1981–2), 'Mobility, Notoriety, and Crime', *Journal of Environmental Systems*, 11 (1).

CARLEN, P. (1988), *Women, Crime and Poverty*. Milton Keynes: Open University Press.

CHAMBLISS, W. (1976), 'The State and Criminal Law', in W. Chambliss and M. Mankoff, eds., *Whose Law, What Order?* New York: Wiley.

CHAPMAN, D. (1967), *Sociology and the Stereotype of the Criminal*, London: Tavistock.

CLARKE, R. (1992), *Situational Crime Prevention*. New York, Harrow and Heston.

—— and CORNISH, D. (1985), 'Modeling Offenders' Decisions', in M. Tonry and N. Morris, eds., *Crime and Justice*, Vol. 6. Chicago, Ill.: University of Chicago Press.

CLARKE, R. and FELSON, M., eds. (1993), *Routine Activity and Rational Choice*. New Brunswick: Transaction.

CLEAVER, E. (1969), *Post-Prison Writings and Speeches*. London: Cape.

CLOWARD, R., and OHLIN, L. (1960), *Delinquency and Opportunity*. New York: Free Press.

COHEN, A. (1957), *Delinquent Boys*. New York: Free Press.

COHEN, L., and FELSON, M. (1979), 'Social Change and Crime Rate Trends', *American Sociological Review*, 44.

COHEN, P. (1972), 'Working-Class Youth Cultures in East London', *Working Papers in Cultural Studies*, Birmingham, 2.

COHEN, S., (1972), *Folk Devils and Moral Panics*. London: Paladin.

—— (1979), 'The Punitive City: Notes on the Dispersal of Social Control', *Contemporary Crises*, 3.

—— (1985), *Visions of Social Control*. Cambridge: Polity.

—— (1996), 'Crime and Politics: Spot the Difference', *British Journal of Sociology*, 47.

COLEMAN, A. (1985), *Utopia on Trial*. London: Hilary Shipman.

—— (1986), 'Dangerous Dreams', *Landscape Design*, 163.

CORRIGAN, P. (1979), *Schooling the Smash Street Kids*. London: Macmillan.

CUSSON, M. (1983), *Why Delinquency?* Toronto: University of Toronto Press.

DAMER, S. (1974), 'Wine Alley: The Sociology of a Dreadful Enclosure', *Sociological Review*, 22.

DAVIS, K. (1937), 'The Sociology of Prostitution', *American Sociological Review*, 2.

—— (1959), 'The Myth of Functional Analysis as a Special Method in Sociology and Anthropology', *American Sociological Review*, 24.

DAVIS, M. (1992), 'Beyond Blade Runner', *Open Magazine Pamphlet*, New Jersey.

—— (1992), *City of Quartz*. New York: Vintage.

DOUGLAS, M. (1966), *Purity and Danger*. London: Pelican.

DOWNES, D. (1966), *The Delinquent Solution*. London, Routledge and Kegan Paul.

—— and ROCK, P., eds. (1979), *Deviant Interpretations*. Oxford: Martin Robertson.

—— and —— (1995), *Understanding Deviance*. Oxford: Oxford University Press.

DURKHEIM, E. (1952), *Suicide*. London: Routledge and Kegan Paul.

—— (1964), *The Division of Labour in Society*. New York: Free Press.

ERIKSON, K. (1966), *Wayward Puritans*. New York: Wiley.

—— (1994), *A New Species of Trouble*. New York: Norton.

FARIS, R., and DUNHAM, H. (1939), *Mental Disorders in Urban Areas*, Chicago, Ill.: University of Chicago Press.

FEELEY, M. (1996), 'The Decline of Women in the Criminal Process', in *Criminal Justice History*, 15. Westport, Conn.: Greenwood Press.

—— and SIMON, J. (1992), 'The New Penology', *Criminology*, 30.

FELSON, M. (1994), *Crime and Everyday Life*. Thousand Oaks, Cal.: Pine Forge.

FERRELL, J. (1993), *Crimes of Style*. Boston, Mass.: Northeastern University Press.

—— and SANDERS, C. (1995), *Cultural Criminology*. Boston: Northeastern University Press.

FLEISHER, M. (1995), *Beggars and Thieves*. Madison, Wis.: University of Wisconsin Press.

FOUCAULT, M. (1977), *Discipline and Punish*. Harmondsworth: Penguin.

GELSTHORPE, L., and MORRIS, A. (1988), 'Feminism and Criminology in Britain', *British Journal of Criminology*, 28.

GENN, H. (1988), 'Multiple Victimisation' in M. Maguire and J. Pointing eds., *Victims of Crime: a New Deal?* Milton Keynes: Open University Press.

GIDDENS, A. (1972), *Emile Durkheim: Selected Writings*. Cambridge: Cambridge University Press

GILL, O. (1977), *Luke Street: Housing Policy, Conflict and the Creation of the Delinquent Area*. London: Macmillan.

GLUCKMAN, M. (1955), *The Judicial Process Among the Barotse of Northern Rhodesia*. Manchester: Manchester University Press.

GOFFMAN, E. (1968), *Asylums*. Harmondsworth: Penguin.

GORDON, C., ed. (1972), *Power/Knowledge*. Brighton: Harvester Press.

GORDON, D. (1986–7), 'The Electronic Panopticon', *Politics and Society*, 15.

GOTTFREDSON, M., and HIRSCHI, T. (1990), *A General Theory of Crime*. Stanford, Cal., Stanford University Press.

HAGAN, J., et al. (1979), 'The Sexual Stratification of Social Control', *British Journal of Sociology*, 30.

—— (1985), 'The Class Structure of Gender and Delinquency: Toward a Power-Control Theory of Common Delinquent Behavior', *American Journal of Sociology*, 90.

—— (1988), *Structural Criminology*. Cambridge: Polity Press.

HALL, S. et al. (1978), *Policing the Crisis*. London: Macmillan.

HILLIER, W. (1973), 'In Defence of Space', *RIBA Journal*, November.

—— (1986), 'City of Alice's Dreams', *Architecture Journal*, 9.

HIRSCHI, T. (1969), *The Causes of Delinquency*. Berkeley, Cal.: University of California Press.

HIRST, P. (1975), 'Marx and Engels on Law, Crime and Morality', in I. Taylor *et al.*, eds., *Critical Criminology*. London: Routledge and Kegan Paul.

HOOKER, E. (1963), 'Male Homosexuality', in N. Farberow ed., *Taboo Topics*. New York: Prentice-Hall.

HOPE, T. (1982), *Burglary in Schools*. London: Home Office.

HOUGH, M., and MAYHEW, P. (1983), *The British Crime Survey*. London: HMSO.

INCIARDI, J., ed. (1980), *Radical Criminology: The Coming Crises*. Beverly Hills, Cal.: Sage.

JACOBS, J. (1965), *The Death and Life of Great American Cities*. Harmondsworth: Penguin.

JONES, T. *et al.* (1986), *The Islington Crime Survey*. Aldershot: Gower.

KAPLAN, R. (1994), 'The Coming Anarchy', *The Atlantic Monthly*, February.

KATZ, J. (1988), *Seductions of Crime*. New York: Basic Books.

KITTRIE, N. (1971), *The Right to be Different*. Baltimore, Md.: Johns Hopkins Press.

KORNHAUSER, R. (1978), *Social Sources of Delinquency: An Appraisal of Analytic Models*. Chicago, Ill.: University of Chicago Press.

LANDESCO, J. (repr. 1968), *Organized Crime in Chicago*. Chicago, Ill.: University of Chicago Press.

LEA, J., and YOUNG, J. (1984), *What is to be Done about Law and Order?* London: Penguin Books.

LEMERT, E. (1951), *Social Pathology*. New York: McGraw-Hill.

LLEWELLYN, K. and HOEBEL, A. (1941), *The Cheyenne Way: Conflict and Case Law in Primitive Jurisprudence*. Norman, Okla.: University of Oklahoma Press.

LUCKENBILL, D., and BEST, J. (1981), 'Careers in Deviance and Respectability', *Social Problems*, 29.

LUKES, S. (1967), 'Alienation and Anomie', in P. Laslett and W. Runciman, eds., *Philosophy, Politics and Society*. Oxford: Blackwell.

LYON, D. (1994), *The Electronic Eye*. Cambridge: Polity Press.

MARTINSON, R. (1974), 'What Works? Questions and Answers about Penal Reform', *Public Interest*, 35.

MARX, G. (1988), *Under Cover*. Berkeley, Cal.: University of California Press.

MATHIESEN, T. (1974), *The Politics of Abolition*. London: Martin Robertson.

MATZA, D. (1964), *Delinquency and Drift*. New York: Wiley.

—— (1969), *Becoming Deviant*. Englewood Cliffs, NJ: Prentice-Hall.

MAYHEW, P., *et al.* (1976), *Crime as Opportunity*. London: Home Office.

MCROBBIE, A., and GARBER, J. (1976), 'Girls and Subcultures', in S. Hall and T. Jefferson eds., *Resistance through Ritual*. London: Hutchinson.

MEAD, G. (1918), 'The Psychology of Punitive Justice', *American Journal of Sociology*, 23.

—— (1934), *Mind Self and Society*. Chicago, Ill.: University of Chicago Press.

MERTON, R. (1938), 'Social Structure and Anomie', *American Sociological Review*, 3.

—— (1957), *Social Theory and Social Structure*. Glencoe, NY: Free Press.

MILLS, C. (1940), 'Situated Actions and Vocabularies of Motive', *American Sociological Review*, 5.

MORRIS, T. (1958), *The Criminal Area*. London: Routledge and Kegan Paul.

NEWMAN, O. (1972), *Defensible Space: People and Design in the Violent City*. London: Architectural Press.

O'MALLEY, P. (1992), 'Risk, Power and Crime Prevention', *Economy and Society*, 21.

PARK, R. (1915), 'The City: Suggestions for the Investigation of Human Behavior in the City Environment', *American Journal of Sociology*, 20.

—— (1925), 'Community Organization and Juvenile Delinquency', in R. Park and R. Burgess, eds., *The City*. Chicago, Ill.: University of Chicago Press.

PARSONS, T. (1951), *The Social System*. London: Routledge and Kegan Paul.

PEARCE, F. (1976), *Crimes of the Powerful*. London: Pluto.

PHILLIPSON, M. (1974), 'Thinking Out of Deviance', unpublished paper.

POLSKY, N. (1967), *Hustlers, Beats and Others*. Chicago, Ill.: Aldine.

QUINNEY, R. (1970), *The Social Reality of Crime*. Boston, Mass: Little Brown.

RAINWATER, L. (1970), *Behind Ghetto Walls*. Chicago, Ill.: Aldine.

RECKLESS, W. (1933), *Vice in Chicago*, Chicago, Ill.: University of Chicago Press.

—— *et al.* (1957), 'The Good Boy in a High Delinquency Area', *Journal of Criminal Law, Criminology, and Police Science*, 48.

REIMAN, J. (1990), *The Rich Get Richer and the Poor Get Prison*. New York: Macmillan.

Roncek, D., and Maier, P. (1991), 'Bars, Blocks, and Crimes Revisited: Linking the Theory of Routine Activities to the Empiricism of "Hot Spots"', *Criminology*, 29.

Rorty, R. (1991), *Objectivity, Relativism, and Truth*. Cambridge: Cambridge University Press.

Scheff, T. (1966), *Being Mentally Ill*. London: Weidenfeld and Nicolson.

Schur, E. (1963), *Narcotic Addiction in Britain and America*. London: Tavistock.

Scott, M., and Lyman, S. (1970), 'Accounts, Deviance and Social Order', in J. Douglas ed., *Deviance and Respectability*. New York: Basic Books.

Scott, R. (1972), 'A Proposed Framework for Analyzing Deviance as a Property of Social Order', in R. Scott and J. Douglas, eds., *Theoretical Perspectives on Deviance*. New York: Basic Books.

Scraton, P., ed. (1987), *Law, Order, and the Authoritarian State: Readings in Critical Criminology*, Milton Keynes: Open University Press.

Scull, A. (1979), *Museums of Madness: the Social Organization of Insanity in Nineteenth-century England*. New York: Allen Lane.

Semple, J. (1993), *Bentham's Prison: A Study of the Panopticon Penitentiary*. Oxford: Clarendon Press.

Shapland, J. and Vagg, J. (1988), *Policing by the Public*. Oxford: Clarendon Press.

Shaw, C., and McKay, H. (1942), *Juvenile Delinquency and Urban Areas*. Chicago: University of Chicago Press.

—— and —— (1971), 'Male Juvenile Delinquency and Group Behavior', in J. Short, ed., *The Social Fabric of the Metropolis*. Chicago, Ill.: University of Chicago Press.

Shearing, C., and Stenning, P. (1985), 'From the Panopticon to Disney World: The Development of Discipline', in A. Doob and E. Greenspan, eds., *Perspectives in Criminal Law*. Aurora: Canada Law Book.

Sherman, L., et al. (1989), 'Hot Spots of Predatory Crime: Routine Activities and the Criminology of Place', *Criminology*, 27.

Short, J., and Strodbeck, F. (1967), *Group Process and Gang Delinquency*. Chicago, Ill.: University of Chicago Press.

Simon, J. (1987), 'The Emergence of a Risk Society', *Socialist Review*.

—— (1993), *Poor Discipline: Parole and the Social Control of the Underclass*, Chicago: University of Chicago Press.

—— and —— (1995), 'True Crime: The New Penology and Public Discourse on Crime', in T. Blomberg and S. Cohen, eds., *Punishment and Social Control*. New York: Aldine de Gruyter.

Smart, C. (1977), *Women, Crime and Criminology*. London: Routledge and Kegan Paul.

—— (1989), *Feminism and the Power of Law*. London: Routledge.

Stephens, J. (1976), *Loners, Losers and Lovers*. Seattle, Wash.: University of Washington Press.

Stinchcombe, A. (1968), *Constructing Social Theories*. New York: Harcourt Brace and World.

Sutherland, E., and Cressey, D. (1955), *Principles of Criminology*, Chicago, Ill.: Lippincott.

Suttles, G. (1972), *The Social Construction of Communities*. Chicago, Ill.: University of Chicago Press.

Sykes, G., and Matza, D. (1957), 'Techniques of Neutralization', *American Sociological Review*, 22.

Taylor, I., Walton, P., and Young, J. (1973), *The New Criminology*. London: Routledge and Kegan Paul.

Thrasher, F. (1927), *The Gang*. Chicago, Ill.: University of Chicago Press.

Turnbull, C. (1973), *The Mountain People*. London: Paladin.

Van Creveld, M. (1991), *The Transformation of War*. New York: Free Press.

Whyte, W. (1942), *Street Corner Society*. Chicago, Ill.: University of Chicago Press.

Wilkins, L. (1964), *Social Deviance*. London: Tavistock.

Willis, P. (1977), *Learning to Labour*. Farnborough, Gower.

Wilson, H. (1980), 'Parental Supervision: A Neglected Aspect of Delinquency', *British Journal of Criminology*, 20.

Wilson, W. (1996), *When Work Disappears: The World of the New Urban Poor*. New York: Alfred Knopf.

Wirth, L. (1964), 'Culture Conflict and Misconduct', in *On Cities and Social Life*. Chicago, Ill.: University of Chicago Press..

Yablonsky, L. (1962), *The Violent Gang*. London: Pelican.

Young, J., (1971), *The Drugtakers*. London: Paladin.

7

The Political Economy of Crime

Ian Taylor

INTRODUCTION

Two hundred years ago, to talk or write of 'political economy' would have identified the speaker or writer as someone with a broad interest in issues of social and moral philosophy. It would have referenced a literature in which the term 'political economy' referred to, and investigated, the relationship between different forms of economic organization and the goal of the 'good society', the rights and duties of citizenship, and the question of individual and state obligation. In Scotland, these concerns were particularly forcefully addressed, by scholars like Adam Smith, David Hume, and Adam Ferguson; and, in continental Europe, by a wide variety of their contemporaries. By the late nineteenth century, sadly, much of what has been called 'classical political economy' had effectively been forgotten, as the rapid changes wrought by the rise of industrial society—in particular, the street violence and thieving of the 'dangerous classes'—presented established authority with a set of more pressing problems—including that of social control as such. So the triumph of a more pragmatic mode of social thought in the late nineteenth century (sometimes describing itself in the language of 'science' rather than morals)—challenged only by a few voices of conservative (e.g. Arnold, 1965 (1869)) or utopian (e.g. Ruskin, 1985 (1862)) persuasion—was also a triumph of a philosophically uninquisitive and narrow conception of the proper scope of 'political economy'. It was in the late nineteenth century, indeed, that economic thinking, under the influence of so-called marginalist economics, radically shifted focus—narrowing its interests to the essentially individualistic calculations involved in 'utility theory'—so re-defining the ambition of the discipline of economics and delimiting the so-called 'neo-classical' perspective (cf., *inter alia*, Caporaso and Levine, 1992).

In this chapter, my concern is to survey the literature of nineteenth- and twentieth-century criminology, and associated social scientific fields, in respect of the issue of 'political economy' and crime. What will very rapidly be apparent is that much of this literature works from within what was essentially a simplified and uncritical version of earlier forms of political-economic thinking. There are hosts of studies that purport simply to confirm, illustrate, or sometimes elaborate what George Vold in 1958 called 'the economic

determinist approach', namely, the proposition that economic life is fundamental and therefore the determining influence upon which all social and
cultural arrangements are made (Vold, 1958: 159–60). The primary concern of
this literature is to point up the causal relations between 'economic crisis', 'the
business cycle', or other *departures from normal economic conditions or
circumstances* and the outgrowth of crime. There is often very little curiosity,
in this pragmatic 'political economy' tradition, about the ways in which the
routine functioning of economies organized around the capital–labour relation
or around individual self-interest may in itself be a factor in crime. We shall
see later in this chapter, in our discussion of the 'costs of crime' literature, that
there is even less interest in these matters amongst the neo-classical economists
of the twentieth century. These larger issues *have* surfaced occasionally in the
broader literatures of social theory, most notably in the work of Merton (see
below), and they were once the subject of commentary by Marx himself, often
thought of as the original 'economic determinist', in a famous, ironic dis-
quisition on the productivity of crime under capitalism (Marx, 1969). One of
the themes in this survey on the issue of political economy and crime is the
need to retrieve the broader set of issues that are raised by social theory and
moral philosophy in any serious examination of these themes. This is particularly urgent a task at a historical moment like the present, given the rapid
transitions that are taking place from a world dominated by nation-
states pursuing essentially Keynesian economic policies to a deregulated
international 'free market economy', divided into competing economic
blocs.

Partly with this argument in view, but partly, also, for ease of reading
and consultation, this chapter is organized into four discrete, but connected,
sections, on (1) the business cycle and crime; (2) the political economy
of inequality and crime; (3) the costs of crime and the entry of neo-
classical economics; and finally (4) crime and free market societies. The
main concern is to provide an overview of a significant selection of the
literature, but there is also an argument, running throughout this chapter,
about the need to broaden out debate and to return to an earlier notion of
what constitutes a powerful, responsible consideration of the field of political
economy.

THE BUSINESS CYCLE AND CRIME

The earliest investigation of the relationship between economic conditions and
crime (nearly always acknowledged in criminological texts) is that by André-
Michel Guerry, in his *Statistique morale d'Angleterre comparée avec la
statistique morale de la France* (1833)—an examination of the first-ever set of
criminal statistics, released by the government of France in 1827. Guerry's
analysis (and that of Adolphe Quetelet, published in 1835) presented an

extremely detailed, statistically organized set of ecological maps of France, representing the rates of crime in relationship to geographical location and climate, levels of education, and occupation and employment. Quetelet's and Guerry's analyses were important for their suggestion that the relationships among economic activity, geographical location, and crime were reproduced over several years: there was, in other words, a law-like relation between economic and ecological factors and crime—a 'constancy of crime' under specific economic or other conditions.

The nineteenth-century proliferation of interest in the production of social and economic statistics also gave rise to a series of studies as to the relationship between 'the economic cycle' (which was now being understood, rather tentatively, as an inevitable aspect of industrial capitalist society) and rates of crime. An early study of court statistics in England and Wales during the 1840s by Whitworth Russell found a strong, positive relation between the general 'commercial and manufacturing distress' obtaining in 1842, in particular, and the number of prisoners appearing before the higher courts (Russell, 1847). A few years later, however, a study of committals to the House of Correction in Preston, Lancashire, over the period 1835–54 challenged this early attempt at a straightforward correlation between 'the business cycle' and crime rate. According to John Clay, the author of this particular study, 'economic hard times' may have added a few cases to the courts' workload, but 'good times' had produced a much more significant increase (Clay, 1855: 79). In Clay's view, the increase in summary convictions which occurred in the 1850s (subsequent to the travails of the 'hungry 1840s') was a function of 'the intemperance which high wages encourage among the ignorant and the sensual'.

The project of trying to demonstrate a strong statistical relationship between economic cycles and crime has been reasserted in scholarly work in criminology, as well as in popular political discussion, throughout the late nineteenth century and into the twentieth. One of the most influential studies, by Georg von Mayr (1867)—attempting to correlate the price of rye in Bavaria over the period 1835–61 and the numbers of offences against the person over the same period—concluded, with considerable authority, that 'for every half-penny increase in the price of rye there would be one theft per 100,000 persons, and for every drop in the price of rye there would be a corresponding decrease in the crime of theft' (von Mayr 1867, quoted at Vold, 1958: 167). Von Mayr's insistence on such a close, determinate relation between the price of a staple food commodity and crime helped to establish a piece of criminological received wisdom of the first half of the twentieth century— specifically, that the level of crime known to the police is an expression, more or less directly and straightforwardly, of the level of 'economic distress' in society (particularly in respect of the poorest sections of society).

In twentieth-century criminology, probably the best-known attempt at exploring the impact of the economic cycle on crime has been Georg Rusche and Otto Kirchheimer's examination of the relation between unemployment

and *imprisonment* (1939).[1] Rusche and Kirchheimer's analysis of these relationships in England, France, Germany, and Italy in the period between 1911 and
1928, and in Italy and Germany in the first years of fascism (1928–36), is
actually quite complex in its various conclusions, but the most usual interpretation of their overall argument is 'that prisons help to control the labour
supply by jettisoning inmates when labour is scarce and filling up when labour
is abundant' (Box and Hale, 1982: 21). Similar findings have been reported in
two separate studies of the relationship between unemployment and imprisonment in Canada (Greenberg, 1977; Kellough *et al.*, 1980) and by Jankovic
(1977) in an analysis of Californian imprisonment in the early 1970s. A further
study by Lessan (1991) uses American time-series data drawn from the period
1948–85 to examine the relationship between unemployment and imprisonment, with the addition of *inflation*, which is seen as a constraint on the state's

---

[1] Rusche and Kirchheimer's analysis has been subject to close critical examination in Box and
Hale (1982, 1985) and in a more extended fashion in Box (1987). Box and Hale concluded that
while 'the total population' under immediate sentence of imprisonment was 'sensitive to the level
of unemployment', the really important significance of the increase in unemployment in the 1930s
in Italy and Germany was that it was 'an *ideologically motivated* response to the perceived threat
of crime posed by the swelling population of economically marginalised persons' (Box and Hale,
1982: 22). According to this analysis, then, it is not that there is a direct relation between cycles
of unemployment and levels of imprisonment, explicable in terms of the dynamics of political
economy (the prison population never comprises more than a small minority of the unemployed:
it cannot directly 'take up' the reserve army of labour); it is rather that the cycles of the economy
are associated with shifts in the ideological mood consequent on what another analyst of these
issues, Dario Melossi, calls the 'political business cycle' (Melossi, 1985). The relationship between
economic cycles, crime, and punishment must be investigated as a topic *in social and political ideology*.
    It is worth noting here, also, a closely associated debate conducted by criminologists in the 1970s
with respect to the move taking place towards deinstitutionalization or decarceration of various
socially marginal populations, from the mentally ill to the pre-delinquent. A particularly important
text here is Andrew Scull (1977). Scull challenged the conventional, liberal account of this
pronounced move towards decarceration, with its emphasis on the newly developed capacities
of psychotropic drugs to control individuals in non-institutional settings and the associated
'humanist' critique of total institutions, by insisting that the most powerful explanation of
decarceration must be sought in the developing fiscal crisis of the capitalist state. A similar argument was later developed by Spitzer (1983) in an attempt to argue that capitalist political
economy involves the 'marginalization' of a significant fraction of the reserve army of labour, and
that the control of a certain proportion of the marginal population *within the community* is
necessary whenever the costs of incarceration become prohibitive. Later research findings
suggesting that control within the community can actually be as costly as institutional control
have, however, posed a challenge to explanations of control strategies that depend entirely on 'a
political economy'. In a more recently published piece, Spitzer argues that 'as it moves along its
twisted course, capitalism requires an *ever-changing* ensemble of strategies to meet new crises'
(Spitzer, 1983: 328, emphasis added).
    The move away from explanations of 'the logic of social control' based on *political economy* to
explanations based on a theoretical understanding of *ideologies of marginalization* is perhaps most
strongly developed in Jeffrey Reiman's *The Rich Get Richer and the Poor Get Prison* (1979). In
this powerful account of American penal policy and practice, Reiman's concern is to argue that
there is an ideological requirement that the enormous capital investment involved in prisons,
police, and other measures of crime control *must fail*—that they must sustain what he dubs 'a
pyrrhic defeat' because, in this failure, the criminal justice system thereby confirms the real seriousness of the danger which is posed by 'criminals', the fearful 'other' against which working
people and the propertied middle class alike can unite in common struggle.

ability to fund what Lessan calls 'placatory' measures: this study generally confirms the influence of unemployment on imprisonment, especially for males.

The theoretical argument embedded in Rusche and Kirchheimer is clear. It is not simply that capitalist economies experience continual cycles of boom and slump and that slumps tend to produce significant increases in crime: it is also, quite specifically, that capitalist economies systematically give rise to *or even require* instability in the employment chances of a section of the working population (a 'reserve army' of labour). When the business cycle throws this reserve army out of work, prisons fill up with unemployed workers attempting to maintain themselves through theft and other crime. In this respect, the political economy of capitalist societies is itself a determining factor in the cyclical production of crime and also the 'workload' of the criminal justice system itself. *Punishment and Social Structure* was first published in 1938. It could not have predicted the explosion of the prison populations that has been occurring in the majority of western societies in the 1980s and 1990s (with the prison population in the United States nearly tripling since the election of Ronald Reagan in 1981, and some 4.9 million American citizens (one out of every 189 men) under some form of correctional supervision at the end of 1994). There is no doubt, however, that Rusche and Kircheimer's analysis seems highly pertinent to the explanation of the 'explosion of penality' that has emerged in the context of deep crisis in the Fordist system of mass manu-facturing, and the return of mass unemployment in current post-Fordist cir-cumstances.

A criminological wisdom of this kind, focused on the close and essentially determinate relationship between crime, imprisonment, and economic distress, lies at the core of nearly all the Marxist criminological texts that emerged in North America (Platt and Takagi, 1969; Quinney, 1974) and in Europe (Melossi and Pavarini, 1981) in the 1970s. But an interest in the social effects of 'market failure' in otherwise healthy and dynamic capitalist societies has been at the heart of much social-democratic scholarship in the field—for exam-ple, in the 1970s, in the work of Harvey Brenner.

Harvey Brenner was widely known among sociologists of health and illness, epidemiologists, social work lobby groups, and others in the United States and in England for a number of published studies which purported to demonstrate the existence of a close causal relationship between unemployment and mortality and morbidity rates. His work was distinctive for its adoption of 'time series regression analysis', wherein the analyst 'lagged' the effects of unemployment over a period of years and thereby avoided the necessity of demonstrating the immediate, temporal coincidence of unemployment and its hypothesized effects. One of the most widely quoted of Brenner's findings in the United States was a study published in 1977, concluding that 'the 1.4 per cent rise in unemployment during 1970 [was] directly responsible for some 51,570 total deaths, including 1,740 additional homicides, 1,540 additional suicides, and for 5,520 additional state mental hospitalizations' (Brenner, 1977: 4).

Earlier, in evidence presented to the Joint Economic Committee of the US Congress, Brenner had argued that every 1 per cent increase in unemployment in that country had meant that 4.3 per cent more men and 2.3 per cent more women were introduced into state mental hospitals for the first time; that 4.1 per cent more people committed suicide; that 5.7 per cent more were murdered; and that 4 per cent more entered state prisons. In the next six years, in addition, 1.9 per cent would die from heart disease, cirrhosis of the liver, and other stress-related chronic ailments (Brenner, 1971). Research undertaken by Brenner in Liverpool in the late 1970s purported to demonstrate a similar type of causal relationship between income level and mortality, with every decline in income resulting in increased numbers of deaths, except in respect of homicide. The relationships identified by Brenner between level of parental income and infant mortality, on a one-year 'lag', and suicide, over two years, were significant, as was the relationship between unemployment in men over 40 and cirrhosis of the liver and cardiovascular mortality (Brenner, 1977). Brenner experienced greater difficulty in the attempts he made in his work (most of it done on American data) to relate unemployment specifically to crime and delinquency, since the official rates of both have tended to increase exponentially *throughout* the post-war period, irrespective of the stage of the economic cycle (Brenner, 1978). Brenner's overall analysis has, in any case, been subjected to significant critique, notably by Jon Stern, firstly on the issue of causal order (does unemployment produce illness or can the relationship work the other way round?) and, secondly, in respect of the warrantability of his choice of different lag periods (Stern, 1982). Eyer and other critics have also pointed specifically to the problems involved in using a three-year lag in attributing pathologies of health or social disorder to economic downturns (or unemployment) as distinct from the impending upturn of the business cycle, and the opportunities (and stresses and strains) associated with such an upturn (Eyer, 1977, 1981).[2]

Exactly these same issues of advancing a causal argument as distinct from offering merely correlational analysis—had been highlighted thirty years earlier in a well-known study, by Paul Wiers, of the fluctuating relationship between juvenile court cases and a variety of indices of economic conditions in Wayne County, Detroit, in the period between 1921 and 1943 (Wiers, 1945). In this particular study, Wiers found a particularly strong positive correlation between 'non-agricultural employment', department-store sales, gross national product, and industrial production, on the one hand, and the number of delinquent court cases, on the other. As George Vold was subsequently to observe, these results were in direct contradiction to von Mayr's famous study

[2] An earlier study which used econometric techniques to try to estimate the determinate relationships between unemployment and crime, focusing in particular on levels of police activity (Carr-Hill and Stern, 1979), has been widely quoted as suggesting that unemployment and crime are not related; but a later reanalysis of the data by Hakim (1982) 'confirms the association between crime and unemployment', suggesting that what Carr-Hill and Stern really analysed was 'the contribution of unemployment to explaining the number of police in each area' (Hakim, 1982: 452).

of 1867—suggesting, as they did, a strong positive relation between crime and economic *prosperity* rather than distress.

Attempts to relate economic conditions to crime rate gained popularity again in the late 1980s and early 1990s in both Britain and North America, consequent on the continuing and severe recessions in the economies of those two societies. Cantor and Lund's study of 1985 was notable for the argument it marshalled—against the established conventional wisdom within the litera-ture on the economics of crime—suggesting that 'unemployment' could act in some circumstances to *suppress* crime, in the sense of reducing the amount of criminal opportunity available. In areas of high unemployment, there are more people at home acting, in effect, as guardians of private property and private homes. In addition, they averred, unemployment can sometimes involve a number of domestic economies of scale (lower transport costs, savings on meals and subsistence, etc.) which offset the impact of wage loss. Over time, however—Cantor and Lund recognize—these compensations are likely to reduce in importance and to mitigate the economic effects of long-term unemployment. In this perspective, what economists call the 'suppressor effect' of unemployment was likely to be short term, and the negative consequences (in terms of personal dislocation and attraction into careers of property crime) to be visible only after a lag.

Allan and Steffensmeier's objective, in a study published in 1989, was to try and advance beyond straightforward analysis of the relationship between 'unemployment' and 'crime', as brute unqualified concepts, in order to examine whether the *quality* of work available in particular regions had an independent effect on levels of criminal activity in that locality. The theoretical focus of this work—important in all post-Fordist societies—was on what Allan and Steffesmeier call 'the labour market climate of a region' (1989: 110), and this was conceived by them as involving four different dimensions—*unemployment* itself (the proportion of the labour force without work but looking for work); *sub-unemployment* (the numbers and percentage of people without work for a lengthy period of time who have given up looking, i.e. those who are often identified as 'discouraged workers'); *low hours* (the percentage of the labour force employed only on a part-time basis by virtue of being unable to find full-time work) and *low wages* (the proportion of the labour force on sub-poverty level wages). From US census sources, Allan and Steffensmeier constructed two 100 per cent samples of males between 13 and 17 years of age and 18 and 24, identified their status on their four dimensions of unemployment, and then regressed these data against the four property crimes in the Uniform Crime Reports index (robbery, burglary, larceny, and auto theft). Their findings were, first, that full employment was, indeed, associated with low arrest rates, whilst 'unemployment', as a brute category, was generally associated with high arrest rates. But their analysis also suggested that poorly paid and part-time work, in the case of young adults (18–24-year-olds) tended to be associated with high arrest rates, but that this association did not hold in the case of the younger age group of adolescent males. Allan and Steffensmeier observe themselves that they were not surprised by this finding, since, they argued, most 'juveniles' in the labour market are only working on what they called a 'voluntary, part-time basis'.

In Britain, where there were 5.3 million offences known to the police in 1991 (compared to 2.4 million in 1979) and a record annual increase of 19 per cent in the twelve months to September 1991, a study by Simon Field suggested that the increases of the previous twelve years were most marked in respect of property crime (theft, burglary, and car crime) in the years where spending power decreased, and that in contrast the increases in crimes of violence (assault, armed robbery, and sex offences) were more marked in the years of relative economic boom. Field particularly noted a close correlation between economic boom, consumption of beer, and violent offences (Field, 1991). More recently, Eisner has released some early data on a large-scale investigation of the relationship between crime rates and economic conditions over ten-year time periods, as revealed in the available official statistics of seven different European societies, relating the growth rate in economic activity in those societies to crime (Eisner, 1996).

THE POLITICAL ECONOMY OF INEQUALITY AND CRIME

The last section was concerned with reviewing the criminological literature focusing on the determinate effects of the economic cycle on crime (and on incarceration) and dealing therefore with the relation between absolute levels of economic distress or deprivation and levels of crime and delinquency. There is also a distinct body of (usually quite specifically sociological) literature, which has been more interested in thinking about *inequalities in the distribution of economic return or economic well-being*, and the broad social effects of such inequalities, e.g. in respect of crime. In this approach it is not so much the 'volatility' of political economy which is at issue but the systematic or ongoing production of unequal opportunity and/or poverty.

Interest in the relationship between poverty, or 'absolute inequality', and crime predates the emergence of the discipline of criminology in the nineteenth century; it can be seen, for example, in the teaching of Christian leaders from St Paul through to Thomas More (1478–1535). In the late nineteenth century, there was widespread concern over the general consequences of poverty, in particular, on the prevalence of unruly begging, 'mendacity', and street crime—powerfully reflected, for example, in the urban commentaries of Henry Mayhew, the fiction of Charles Dickens and Charles Kingsley, and the utopian pamphleteering of late nineteenth-century critics of industrial capitalism like Edward Carpenter and John Ruskin.[3] Enrico Ferri (1856–1929), one of the

---

[3] For further discussion of the one criminological intervention made by the nineteenth-century utopian socialist Edward Carpenter, see Taylor (1991a).

founding fathers of the Italian *scuola positiva*, is remembered for his insistent emphasis in his *Criminal Sociology* on social and economic deprivation as one of the primary causes of crime, and for his advocacy of political action by the state to reduce deprivation and inequality as a policy measure made legitimate in terms of its effect on levels of crime.

Willem Bonger

In the first half of the twentieth century, probably the best-known criminological dissertation on the relation of deprivation and inequality to crime was that advanced by the Dutch Marxist criminologist, Willem Bonger (1876–1940). Along with many other socialist writers on crime and prison in the first half and middle of the twentieth century,[4] Bonger's search for the causes of crime in industrial capitalist society began with a serious attempt to understand not just the impact of the economic cycle but also workers' *routine* experience of insecurity within the capital–labour relationship. In the last years of the nineteenth century and early years of the twentieth century, wage labour was never secure. According to Bonger: 'The proletarian is never sure of his existence: like the sword of Damocles, unemployment is constantly hanging over his head' (1969 (1916): 49). In the periods of forced idleness which are imposed on workers, and also in economic downturns in the demoralizing work which is often required of workers during periods of employment, there is no real incentive for workers to develop any overall moral code or sense of collective social life and responsibility. The result is a spread of what Bonger calls 'egoistic' sentiments among workers, evidenced, on the one hand, in the carelessness of securely employed working people with respect to saving money, and also, on the other, the relative willingness of workers to engage in crime for material survival, particularly in response to periods of unemployment or penury.

Bonger's extended analysis of working-class 'egoism' in relation to a vast range of offence categories has been variously described in later literature as crude materialistic psychology or economic determinism. In fact, his analysis of offence types and offender behaviour was significantly more elaborate than either description would allow: his work is particularly noteworthy for the attention it gave to the routine subjection and inequality of women in early twentieth-century capitalist societies (and the powerful sense that patriarchal structures were very closely linked to the structures of capital), and also for the attention it gave to the relationship between the militarized character of capitalist states in the early twentieth century and the prevalence of violence in civil society even in periods of peace.

---

[4] A list of other socialist writers who wrote on crime as a function of poverty must also include, in England, Robert Blatchford, the editor of the *Clarion* newspaper, in his *Not Guilty: A Defence of the Bottom Dog* (1906); and, in the USA the IWW (International Workers of the World) leader Eugene Debs in his *Walls and Bars* (1927) and, of course, the Black Panther Party leader, George Jackson, in his famous polemic *Soledad Brother* (1970).

It is fair, however, for subsequent critics to see a certain kind of rigidity in Bonger's attempt to read off a single psychological predisposition from the experience of uncertainty, or absolute levels of poverty, experienced by working people caught up in the logic of capitalist political economy. And inasmuch as Bonger's work, like many other straightforwardly socialist accounts in its time, could be read as suggesting that the 'roots of crime' lay in some *absolute* level of deprivation or poverty, it was an account which lost power and influence when improved economic circumstances in the mid- to late 1930s failed to produce any radical reduction in the scale of the problem of crime. The instructive contrast, perhaps, is with the attempt made by Robert K. Merton, the American sociologist, writing in the 1930s, to try to explain the overall relation between the dynamic of an individual economy, the *culture* within which it is experienced, and the wide *variety of individual adaptations* which may arise.

Robert Merton

First published in 1938, but subsequently revised for inclusion in *Social Theory and Social Structure* (1957), Merton's classic essay on 'Social Structure and Anomie' advances an explanation of crime, delinquency, and other deviant individual adaptations based on the strains that were produced in mid-twentieth-century American society by the unequal distribution of legitimate means available to the population in general for the attainment of the dominant cultural goal of material success (Merton, 1963 (1938)).

For Merton, modifying the nineteenth-century work of Emile Durkheim, the key issue in explaining crime might be the existence of a condition of normlessness or *anomie*, particularly at times of economic downturn, when the opportunities for individual Americans to strive for, and attain, material success were blocked, as a result of the restriction of opportunities in the labour market and/or the opportunities for upward mobility through education. In this vision of *anomie*, the emphasis was not only on a *structure* of unequal opportunity—evident in the blockages placed before individuals in different class, ethnic, or other social positions; it was also on the strains produced in *individuals* at particular levels of the social formation who saw themselves as unable to achieve any share of the material wealth which had been so heavily prioritized as the dominant success goal of the society. It was not surprising to find widespread evidence, among social groups experiencing such a blockage of opportunity, of 'innovation' in respect of the means for achieving material success (theft, burglary, or other forms of property crime) or alternatively a 'retreatism' (for example, into drug abuse or vagrancy) on the part of those who had given up on the possibility of material success for themselves. The other adaptations to the mix of cultural goals and institutional opportunity structure confronting individuals identified by Merton (of 'conformity', 'ritualism', or 'rebellion') were understood by him to be heavily influenced by individuals' relationship to the political–economic *structure* of opportunity, though also to involve those individuals' interpretation of cultural pressures and demands.

The emphasis on the blockage of institutionalized means or on a 'political economy of unequal opportunity' is probably less important, however, in Merton's essay than his critical discussion of *the lack of moral regulation* of economic activity itself. In the early half of the twentieth century, there had emerged in America 'a heavy emphasis on wealth as a basic symbol of success without a corresponding emphasis upon the [legitimacy of the] avenues on which to march towards this goal' (Merton, 1963 (1938): 139). It was a culture in which 'money [had] been consecrated as value in itself, over and above its expenditure for articles of consumption or its use for the enhancement of power' (*ibid.*: 136).

The enormous value placed on money as a value itself without regard to the intrinsic value of the activity through which pecuniary success had been realized was accompanied by no obvious moral or legal qualification on such success: Al Capone was by no means an unwelcome guest in all social circles (especially at the baseball park) in 1930s Chicago. Americans of all back-grounds were, in effect, invited to pursue material success even by 'illegitimate means' without fear of social exclusion. For Merton, this essentially unregu-lated political economy was a significant source of crime and instability in the body of American society; and it was especially destabilizing because the lack of moral regulation meant that there could never be a settled sense of achieve-ment or accomplishment:

In the American Dream there is no final stopping point. The measure of 'monetary success' is conveniently indefinite and relative. At every income level . . . Americans want just about twenty-five per cent more (but of course this 'just a bit more' continues to operate once it is obtained). In this flux of shifting standards, there is no stable resting point, or rather, it is the point which manages to be 'just ahead' [Merton, 1963 (1938): 63].

In a society constructed around these dreams, then, there is a constant con-dition of unease and anxiety: a ceaseless striving for *more* income and/or material possessions as the only possible personal goal. This is a cultural condition which would tend to produce a radically egoistic individual, indif-ferent to the consequences of this individualistic pursuit of material success on others' material or personal and psychological security or their associated 'quality of life'.

The importance of Merton's essay and the advance it marked on Bonger's economic determinism and materialist psychology lies in the dynamic and contradictory capacity of the theory of *anomie* there developed to lay bare the links between the condition of a political economy and what Merton himself calls 'the cultural structure' of the broad society within which that economic activity was pursued, and then to produce a sociological account of some of the individual adaptations or effects (including crime) across the whole social formation. It was a classic essay not only in the sense that it offered a framework, derived from an understanding of the political economy of American capitalism at the time, within which to theorize systematically the overall effects of inequality within civil society, but also in making the links, specifically, between political economy, the dominant cultural goals of the society, unequal structures of opportunity, and patterns of crime.

Richard Cloward and Lloyd Ohlin

The most celebrated exposition of these links within the post-war American criminological literature is to be found in Richard Cloward and Lloyd Ohlin's *Delinquency and Opportunity: A Theory of Delinquent Gangs*, published in 1960. Cloward and Ohlin retained much of Merton's functionalist stress on the importance of universalistic cultural goals in ensuring the survival of a dynamic 'industrial society' in America, and, also like Merton, they were aware of the potentially disorderly consequences of structural blockages to individual achievement: 'If a cultural emphasis on unlimited success-goals tends to solve some problems in the industrial society, it also creates new ones. A pervasive feeling of position-discontent leads men to compete for higher status and so contributes to the survival of the industrial order, but it also produces acute pressure for deviant behaviour' (Cloward and Ohlin, 1960: 81–2).

Cloward and Ohlin go on to argue that the absence from particular neighbourhoods of legitimate opportunities for self-advancement (in the form of stable employment for high-school leavers, albeit of a low-paid kind, or, alternatively, the chance to go to college for the purpose of training or accreditation) creates the conditions for the emergence of delinquent youth subcultures. The precise shape and character of the subcultures emerging in particular neighbourhoods will be a function of the presence, or absence, in those neighbourhoods of stable 'illegitimate' criminal enterprises. Where such enterprises do exist, and involve significant numbers of the adult population, youthful delinquent activity will tend to be drawn towards, or be parasitic upon, such adult criminal enterprise (in the form, for example, of more or less organized theft or burglary). In such circumstances, recruitment into these youthful criminal subcultures might be the first stage of the recruitment of the young into a career of adult crime. In areas where such stable adult criminal enterprises do not exist, and opportunities for this kind of advancement are therefore blocked, young men will gravitate instead into the local 'fighting gang' or what Cloward and Ohlin call the 'conflict subculture'. Young men who fail to win acceptance in either a criminal or a conflict subculture will be drawn, as a result of this 'double failure', into drug use, alcohol abuse, or other forms of eventually self-destructive hedonism, in the context of what Cloward and Ohlin called the 'retreatist subculture'.

Cloward and Ohlin's analysis of delinquency has been subjected to extensive critical discussion in the subsequent criminological literature, both in North America and elsewhere. There is debate over whether the three models of delinquent subculture now have, or ever did have, any demonstrable empirical reference, and also over the model that is proposed by Cloward and Ohlin of the *sequence* through which young men are said to be recruited into the criminal, conflict, and retreatist subcultures. There has also been debate, especially among conservatively minded criminologists in the 1980s, over whether this model could still be said to apply to a free market society like the United States, in which the problems of the broad society are, it is argued, no longer those of blocked opportunity.[5] There has always been concern whether the Mertonian model adopted by Cloward and Ohlin could ever be transferred to societies (like Britain) where there is nothing like the dominant ideology of egalitarianism that characterizes the United States.[6] There have also been a host of other queries about the Cloward and Ohlin thesis, for example, in respect of the lack of interest shown in the dynamics of lower-class culture itself, the organization of the lower-class family, and problems at the level of schools in lower-class neighbourhoods. One of the best-known criticisms of Cloward and Ohlin (and also of other writers on subcultures in the 1960s) is of the complete lack of interest in that literature in issues of gender: women are present in the subcultural texts only in their role as mothers. The impact of the facts of political economy and the associated 'structures of opportunity' on adolescent girls in lower-class neighbourhoods is never a topic for discussion in this literature, and the result is that the idea of the masculine role *per se*, and the priorities that have traditionally been given in lower-class neighbourhoods in the United States as well as in Britain to young men getting jobs, are never problematized. For present purposes, the most important feature of Cloward and Ohlin's application of Merton to the analysis of youthful delinquency is the unambiguous emphasis they place on the influence of blocked opportunity of inequality of 'life chances' in the recruitment of young men into careers of delinquency and crime.

This connection was to be highly influential in the United States in the 1960s, especially in informing the inner-city job-creation programme, Mobilization for Youth; it also had some influence in Britain, notably in the Labour Party pamphlet of 1964, *Crime: A Challenge to Us All*, written by Lord Longford prior to the election of the 1964–70 Wilson government, although the argument in this pamphlet also exhibited concern, in a characteristically English Fabian fashion, about the pathological failure of working-class families to grasp what opportunities were presented to them for advancement

[5] For one attempt to revise Merton's typology of deviant adaptation with a view to understanding a social condition of 'unanticipated affluence' in the USA in the mid-20th century, and its differential social effects, especially 'at higher economic levels', see Simon and Gagnon (1976).

[6] Probably the most famous discussion of the inapplicability of American subcultural theory to the analysis of delinquency and youth subcultures in Britain is to be found in Clarke *et al.* (1978). The argument advanced is that the different youth subcultures emerging in post-war Britain were actually an attempt to resolve essentially unresolvable, brute facts of class and generational inequality experienced by every youthful cohort *in their imaginary lives* i.e. at the level, simply, of style. This is largely because, instead of there being a widespread experience of what Cloward and Ohlin call 'position-discontent' in Britain, there was a widespread sense of the *inevitability* of the rigid division of the society by class.

(Longford, 1964). Mobilization for Youth was to prove relatively short lived in the United States, encountering fairly quickly the resistance of private and public employers to the employment within their organizations of young people of low skill and inappropriate social or personal attributes (Jones, 1971). The English Fabian project of mobilizing ameliorist social work intervention into 'dysfunctional' or 'problem' working-class families ran up against the twin traditions within the English working class of insubordination towards authority, on the one hand, and a kind of inward-looking conservatism, on the other—traditions that quite accurately reflected working-class scepticism towards the possibility of fundamental change in their life possibilities.

The Political Economy of Post-war Youthful Unemployment

One other reason for the relatively short-lived interest in the United States in the Mobilization for Youth programme, with its Mertonian emphasis on tackling inequalities of opportunity for youth, may have been a recognition that these problems were not merely a matter of cultural prejudice or the uneven capacity of government agencies to help. What was beginning to become apparent to many observers in the United States in the late 1960s and early 1970s was that youth unemployment was taking on the character of an organic structural problem that was going to bedevil the American economy for the foreseeable future. In a classic analysis of the youth employment problem in the United States first published in 1970, John and Margaret Rowntree demonstrated that US unemployment had been concentrated among young people throughout the 1950s and 1960s and also that the unemployment figures for young people would have been even higher had it not been for the rapid expansion of the education system and the military. Between 1950 and 1965, there was an increase in enrolment of 3.68 million in schools and universities in the United States and an increase of 960,000 enrolments in the armed forces (Rowntree and Rowntree, 1970: 11). The overall impact on the pattern of employment of young people was considerable:

In 1950, only about 22.8 per cent of all men between the ages of 20 and 24 years were either in the armed forces or in schools; in 1965, the figure was 40 per cent . . . for men 18 to 24 years old, the data are even more impressive; of these 52.1 per cent, or more than half, were in school or college, the military or unemployed. . . . The figures for young women follow the same pattern: in 1950, 24.3 per cent of young women aged 18 and 19, and 4.5 per cent of women aged 20 to 24, were in school or college: by 1965 the figures had increased to 37.7 per cent and 11.8 per cent respectively [*ibid.*: 16].

The point which the Rowntrees wanted to emphasize, through this analysis of the American labour market between 1950 and 1965, was that 'if [young people] did venture outside army or school, they encountered unemployment rates two to five times the [national US] average' (*op. cit.*, 7).

Analysis of the American labour market in the later 1960s and early 1970s by Harry Braverman provided further evidence of the intensifying problem of structural unemployment—driven, in part, by the introduction of new labour-saving technology in the workplace and in part through the export of jobs by multinational corporations beyond the American borders (Braverman, 1974). One consequence of these changes was a significant 'de-skilling' of the American workforce, consequent on the replacement of workers in manu-facturing industry by machines and the rise of low-skill consumer industries. An increasingly obvious feature of the urban landscape and the broad labour market was the existence of a surplus population of unskilled and largely unemployable people, many of them young, and very many of them black. According to Braverman, this 'surplus population' of the 'de-skilled' was the contemporary form assumed by the famous 'reserve army of labour' discussed by writers like Rusche and Kirchheimer in the 1930s—an army of people whose insecure labour market position and insecure life chances were and are a function of the organization of industrial production according to the logic of capital.[7]

Phil Cohen: The Upward and Downward Options

Something of the same kind of argument is apparent in the account presented by Phil Cohen of the 'social effects' of the reconstruction of the British econ-omy during the post-war years (Cohen, 1972). Like Braverman, Cohen places particular emphasis on the effects of automation in the 1950s in replacing skilled workers with machines:

Craft industries . . . were the first to suffer; automated techniques replaced the traditional hand skills and their simple division of labour. Similarly the economics of scale provided for by the concentration of craft resources meant that the small scale family business was no longer a viable unit. Despite a long rearguard action many of the traditional industries . . . and many of the service and distributive trades . . . rapidly declined or were bought out [Cohen, 1972: 18].

The consequence, overall, was:

a gradual polarisation in the structure of the labour force—on the one side, the highly specialised, skilled and well-paid jobs associated with the new technology and the high growth sectors that employed them; on the other, the routine, dead end, low paid and unskilled jobs associated with the labour-intensive sectors, especially the service sectors [*ibid.*].

One effect of this development in the political economy of production was to accentuate and intensify the division that had always existed between the stable or 'respectable' sections of the working class (organized labour, the artisan class) and those who have variously been described as the disorgan-ized and residual, rough, sections of the working class. Specifically, the

---

[7] In 1988, a report by the Grant Commission in the USA confirmed that 'even during the economic expansion of the mid-1980s the social and economic position of younger Americans declined' (Hagan and Peterson, 1995: 2).

technological reorganization of work clearly identified what Cohen called an 'upward option' for some sections of the class, who were able to move up from the shop floor into office positions or minor research and development roles. But it also helped to redefine a large set of 'downward options' into residual, insecure, poorly paid jobs that offered little or no training or other opportunities for self-development or for a career. One key aspect of the 'downward option', from the mid-1960s onwards, was the widespread expectation of regular periods of unemployment.

Cohen clearly demonstrates how this reorganization of the post-war labour market was related to other aspects of working-class experience in Britain—in particular, in its effects on working-class neighbourhood and community. From the late 1950s onwards, large numbers of established working-class communities (of terraced housing built around the local corner store and public house), now identified in popular discussion as 'slums', were gradually broken up, and large proportions of the 'slum-dwellers' rehoused in large council estates or high-rise developments. The areas left behind drifted downwards, slipping into multiple occupation and a new role as 'transitional zones' for incoming immigrant populations. The newly created public housing developments had a chequered history, with the high-rise developments almost universally seen as complete failures in respect of creating or sustaining any sense of community, and some inner-city estates likewise. The belief that a sense of community and personal well-being could be constructed on estates or in high-rise buildings whose populations had rather unwillingly been uprooted from the neighbourhoods of their birth may have been a mistake. But perhaps equally crucially, this wholesale rehousing of the working class of Britain occurred against the background of the polarization of the labour market described by Cohen. Just as thousands of new jobs opened up for young people who had worked their way up to the 'upward options' described by Cohen, so also the 'downward' alternatives were increasingly apparent, in the decline in openings in manufacturing industry, in apprenticeships, and in other lower-level labour market opportunities. The official unemployment rate rose from 2.2 per cent in 1960 to 4.1 per cent in 1972 (Sinfield, 1981: 14). It may be no coincidence and some kind of support for the Mertonian emphasis on the relationship between crime and inequality that it was at just such a juncture that the annual criminal statistics started to show marked increases in the number of offences committed by young people. In 1968, for example, the increase in the number of offences known to the police in England and Wales was greater than any year since 1957, with the largest percentage increases in convictions occurring among 17–21-year-old males.

The Demise of Mass Manufacturing

The polarization of the labour market in the United States, Britain, and other western industrial societies that was produced by technological advances in the 1950s and 1960s was relatively insignificant, however, by comparison with the convulsions that occurred in the 1980s. Taking the official unemployment rate as the most immediate expression of these changes, there was a calamitous increase in unemployment in Britain. On official figures which quite notoriously have been subjected to a series of definitional changes, all of which have had the effect of deflating the overall official figure, unemployment increased from 4.1 per cent of the labour force in 1972 to 10.3 per cent in 1981. Official figures suggest that the highest level of unemployment in the 1980s in Britain was 12.4 per cent in 1983, declining to 6.8 per cent in 1990, returning to 11 per cent (three million) in 1992, and declining again to 8 per cent in 1996. At each of these moments of 'slump', the absolute numbers of unemployed people exceeded the totals at the previous low point. Economic commentators began to speak not only of 'the end of full employment' as a social and political project, but also of the fearful prospect of 'jobless growth'—i.e. a period of economic recovery that involves no *net* creation of new employment (Aronowitz and DiFazio, 1994). In Western Europe as a whole, in 1993, the annual average of unemployment was calculated officially at 11 per cent, in comparison to an average of only 1.6 per cent in the 1960s (Judt, 1996). Long-term unemployment (lasting over a year) was calculated at about one-third of the total of those still registering for work (*ibid.*).

Rehearsing some of the evidence about the increases in the size of the 'reserve army of labour' or unemployment from the 1960s to the present redirects attention to one of the themes of classical political economy: namely, the consequences of social exclusion in societies in which citizenship and individual worth and merit are in part a matter of 'work' and, indeed, employment. From this perspective, the explosive growth of recorded rates of crime is a measure, precisely, of the deep logic of exclusion unleashed by free market forces. This is, of course, an association which is challenged by philosophers of the right and by Conservative politicians, most famously by Prime Minister Margaret Thatcher, during the riots in England's inner cities in the summer of 1981, in her resounding declaration that 'unemployment was no excuse'. There may be some basis on which one could attribute moral blame to rioters; but we should not be blind to the truth that the riots of 1981, like those that followed on intermittently throughout the 1980s and early 1990s, occurred in areas of extraordinarily high unemployment (such as the north-east of England)—much of it spread over long periods of time. It is clear that unemployment in and of itself would not be a sufficient explanation of the occurrence of these riots (or, indeed, of the very high rates of theft, car crime, and assaults—the 'long slow riot of crime', as Jock Young has called it, which characterizes many of these areas): unemployment was just as high, on official measures, in many of these self-same areas in the 1920s without there being anything like the same rate of interpersonal and property crime reported to the police that was being reported in the 1980s and 1990s (Lea and Young, 1984: 90–3).

It is also true that the continuing outbreaks of crime and riot in America's ghetto areas, as well as in the inner cities of Britain, have been subject to an alternative cultural and sociological explanation, namely the theory of the underclass, particularly in the works of the American conservative commentator, Charles Murray (1990). Murray's approach is behavioural, in the sense that he wants to identify the emergence of a pathological type of behaviour and then explain that pathological behaviour in terms of its most immediate conditions of existence. For him, the source of much of the crime and dislocation in the inner city and the ghetto lies in the welfare policies that have been adopted by successive governments in Britain and the United States towards ghetto populations—policies, which have made it possible for deprived or disadvantaged people to survive outside the labour force. Such welfare policies have not provided the support for further initiative and personal development on the part of their clients (which may have been thought to be their original rationale). The argument instead is that these policies have encouraged a form of welfare state dependency in which the recipients of welfare remain content with their minimal conditions of life and do not take responsibility for improving on those conditions. But the second, associated alleged development, which gives cause for further concern, is the way in which young women in Britain, in such circumstances, knowingly become pregnant as a means of ensuring access to public housing, staying out of the labour market, and, in both the United States and Britain, obtaining state benefits over and above basic unemployment support. Murray points, for example, to the increase in illegitimate births in Britain from 10.6 per cent of all live births in 1979 to 25.6 per cent in 1988. The consequence of this, in Britain as in America, is a rather rapid increase in the number of single-parent female-headed households, with what Murray argues are disastrous effects in terms of the routine socialization of the children. The third element in Murray's definition of the underclass is its disproportionate involvement in crime, and especially violent crime. For Murray, the bulk of the 60 per cent increase in crimes of violence reported in the English criminal statistics between 1980 and 1988 was attributable to the activities of young men from the underclass, who, deprived of the dignity and the life-project of work in support of a family, tended to engage in other means of self-expression:

when large numbers of young men don't work, the communities around them break down, just as they break down when large numbers of young women have babies. The two phenomena are intimately related. Just as work is more important than merely making a living, getting married and raising a family are more than a way to pass the time. Supporting a family is a central means for a man to prove to himself that he is a 'mensch'. Men who do not support families find other ways to prove that they are men, which tend to take various destructive forms. As many have commented through the centuries, young males are essentially barbarians for whom marriage—meaning not just the wedding-vows, but the act of taking responsibility for a wife and children—is an indispensable civilising force [Murray, 1990: 22–3].

Murray's theses about the underclass in America and Britain have found many critics in both countries, not least because the policy sub-text of his writing is always the withdrawal of benefits from populations who are already officially in poverty in the context of recession and deindustrialization. Writers in Britain like Alan Walker accuse Murray of inventing an essentially ideological category (i.e. of lower-class people who are to be differentiated in terms of their conditioned behaviour from the rest of the working class—a resurrection of the Victorian distinction between the 'deserving' and 'undeserving' poor), for which there is no widespread evidence, and then ignoring the broad patterns of government policies that generate poverty among pensioners and the elderly, single parents in general, and the disabled. Curiously enough, however, Murray's earlier concern to recognize the differential responses of sections of the lower class in America (now translated to his work on the underclass in Britain) to the collapse of the industrial labour market and other developments in the 1980s do find some support in the work of the pioneering black scholar in America working on such issues, William Julius Wilson (1987). In contrast to many liberal scholars, Wilson squarely confronts the data on the disproportionate involvement of the black population of America in violent crime, and also recognizes the extraordinary increase in illegitimate births and in female-headed households in the black community in America. But where Murray would want to claim that these developments must be an expression of generous and self-defeating welfare programmes, especially for the single mother, Wilson shows that the real value of such benefits declined throughout the 1980s. Where liberal scholars have pointed to racism as an explanation of blacks' involvement in violent crime and other dysfunctional, anti-social behaviour, Wilson insists that such racism was far worse in earlier periods than it was in the 1980s. For Wilson, explanation of these contemporary phenomena of violent crime and 'labour force drop-out' among large sections of the black lower class in America must lie in an understanding of what he calls *historic discrimination*, a long-term systemic process of subordination and subjugation, as distinct from the immediate presenting symptoms involved in individual acts of discrimination or prejudice. To think that these long-term processes can have evolved without real structural effects in cutting whole sections of the black population off, over generations, from adequate training and education, and also imprisoning such people into tightly bounded ethnic ghettoes in which maladaptive individual behaviours were common, is merely naïve. Wilson points up not the 'culture of poverty' so beloved of earlier critics of the poor but rather a culture of exclusion and subordination which has had long-term, crippling cultural effects, which are not accessible to a quick policy fix, especially in competitive free market conditions. In Britain, throughout the 1980s and in the early 1990s, these processes of deindustrialization had quite extraordinarily sudden and fundamental effects. When measured in the same terms as it was before 1979 unemployment reached about four million in November 1992 (in contrast to the 'official' measure, resulting from over a dozen modifications since 1979, of 2.8 million), and adult male unemployment because firmly stuck at a level not seen since the 1930s (Hutton, 1992). On every available measure, inequality continued, until 1996,[8] to show ever-widening gaps between the richest and poorest sections of the society, and, in the meantime, levels of crime known to the police continued to escalate until 1993,[9] nearly doubling in the decade from 1981 to 1991. There were particularly steep increases in the numbers of attempted thefts reported to the police over this period (336 per cent) and in vehicle thefts. Burglaries increased by about 75 per cent, an increase apparent in British Crime Survey findings as well as in police statistics (Mayhew and Maung, 1992; see Maguire this volume, for a broad discussion of recent trends).

It matters enormously, in conditions of increasing economic polarization and crime, how analysts attempt to explain the relationship between these developments. Murray lays himself open to accusations of 'blaming the victim', particularly in his strictures on the problems posed by unmarried mothers in respect of the socialization they provide for their offspring and the overall character of 'family life' in such households. In complete contrast to Murray, however, analysis derived from political economy throws up an awareness of unemployment as a structural problem rather than a personal default, and also shows some understanding of the absolutely destructive effects that the acceleration of structural unemployment resulting from deindustrialization in the 1980s and 1990s have had on the lives of individuals and on communities in Europe and North America. It also recognizes that these destructive processes have been magnified, rather than modified, throughout the 1980s and 1990s by the dogged and unyielding pursuit by governments, especially in Britain and the United States, of free-market economic policies as a matter of faith, without any real care for the human consequences of this particular experiment in social engineering. The human effects of the free market experiment are clear and inescapable on the streets of Los Angeles and other parts of southern California (Currie, 1990*a*, 1990*b*) and in the 'Rust Belt' of the northern industrial cities of the United States (Henry and Brown, 1990).

These effects included all the well-known expressions of economic deprivation, from poor housing, ill-health, to interpersonal violence, but often in highly concentrated locations—most usually, the areas of settlement of different minority ethnic groups. So, for example, in New York City 70 per cent of blacks live in areas officially designated as areas of 'extreme poverty' (Sampson and Wilson, 1995: 41). This concentration of deprivation, as identified by Wilson and many other scholars, is reflected in similarly concentrated high rates of violent interpersonal crime and property crime. In the early 1990s, Afro-Americans accounted for 40–50 per cent of all homicides, forcible rapes,

---

[8] Figures released by HM Government in November 1996 suggested that 400,000 fewer people were living below the official poverty line in 1993–5 compared to 1992–3 (*Households below average income*, HMSO, 1996). However, it remained the case that the share of total income received by the poorest one-fifth of the population was still being measured, for 1993–5, at 6.8 per cent, compared to 9.8 per cent in 1979. 13.7 million people were still living below the official poverty line.

[9] The total number of offences recorded by the police in England and Wales declined from 5.3 million in 1993 to 4.9 million in 1995 (a decline of 8.1 per cent over two years). The comparable figure for 1981 was 2.8 million (*Criminal Statistics, England and Wales 1995* Cm *3421*).

armed robberies, and aggravated assaults in the United States (Hagan and Peterson, 1995: 19) but they were also much more frequently victimized by such crimes than were whites, by a factor of about 25 per cent (*ibid.*: 23). The 'life-time risk' of being murdered in the United States in the mid-1980s had already been measured at 1:21 for black American males as compared with 1:131 for whites (Sampson and Wilson, 1995: 37, quoting a US Justice Department study of 1985).[10]

Many of the older industrial areas of England, Scotland, and Wales, over the same period, began to be plagued by what would previously have been quite unknown levels of theft and burglary, car stealing, interpersonal violence, and also by a crippling sense of fear and insecurity, which cuts thousands of their residents off from the pleasures of the broader consumer society and the compensations of friendship and neighbourhood. So also, to repeat our earlier point, were they plagued by quite extraordinary levels of personal and family poverty, by poor physical health resulting from bad diet, and by the increasing levels of suicide and early death associated with loss of a personal sense of morale and self-regard. In Britain, as in the United States, an understanding of the pattern of crime is inextricably connected to an understanding of the political economy, not simply of unemployment, but more broadly of the new inequality characteristic of free market societies. Analysis is particularly urgent now into the *long-term* effects of this inequality and subordination in England, in respect of the unskilled working class in general, but, in particular, amongst young white working-class males left behind in the deindustrialization of the 1980s (the new 'poor whites') (cf. Taylor and Jamieson, 1996).[11]

There are a number of different accounts on offer as to the source and character of developments in Western economies in the 1980s and 1990s. Some accounts point to some continuities, rather than discontinuities, between present and earlier moments in the history of industrial society. Anthony Giddens (1991), for example, believes that we are experiencing a highly developed stage of capitalism, which he describes as High Modernity, in which there are many risks and dangers, but in which long-established patterns of conflict and accommodation still pertain. John Urry and Scott Lash (1987) point to what they call a 'disorganized capitalism', characterized by the growth of world markets, the emergence of a service class, a declining working class, and national wage bargaining, large monopolies overriding nation-state controls, diminution of class politics, increased cultural fragmentation and pluralism, decline

[10] For two graphic accounts of 'gang formation' and related aspects of youthful lifestyle in ethnic minority neighbourhoods in American cities with continuing high and long-term unemployment, see Jankowski 1991 and MacLeod (1988, 1993).

[11] According to Oliver James, the proportion of boys being raised in a lower-income family in England and Wales rose from 19 per cent in 1979 to 30 per cent in 1981 and has stayed at this level since then (James, 1995). For James, the increase in violence amongst young men after 1987—reported violence amongst 14–16-year-olds increasing from 6 to 13 per cent in 1993 is evidence of the existence of young children, especially young men, whose economic and moral horizons were mercilessly constrained by the grinding and continuing experience of poverty during the period of the Thatcher and Major governments.

of employment in extractive and manufacturing industries and regionally specialized industry, and a decline in plant size and industrial cities. For Lash and
Urry, there are all kinds of changes in the character of capitalism, but these
changes coexist, often rather uneasily, with established forms. In other
accounts, the emphasis is firmly on the radical character of the transformations
of the 1980s and 1990s. Stuart Hall, Ash Amin, and others speak of the move
towards specifically 'post-Fordist' methods of production and accumulation,
and the terminal decline of traditional plant-level industrial organization and
of whole economies organized around single industries (Hall and Jacques,
1990; Amin, 1994). Piore and Sabel (1984), two prominent American economists, argue in a highly influential analysis that the 1980s actually witnessed 'the
demise of mass production' as the engine of growth and capital accumulation.
In the developed world in general, they argue, domestic consumption of the
goods produced by manufacturing industry had begun to encounter limits in
the 1960s. By the mid-1970s, something over 90 per cent of all American
households had TV sets, refrigerators, toasters, washing machines, and
vacuum cleaners. Manufacturing industries began to move, with increasing
urgency, into world markets in search of customers; but, in the meantime,
there was a driving down of wage bills in Western economies through redundancies and other labour-saving measures. This process of deindustrialization
was accelerated by a set of precipitating circumstances, of which the two most
important were the abandonment of the Bretton Woods agreement in 1971 and
the oil crises of 1974 and 1979.

The Bretton Woods agreement had been struck at the end of the Second
World War, when the US government, confident about the future of the
American economy, agreed to underwrite a system of fixed exchange rates
among its European wartime allies, to provide a framework for economic
recovery from the war through trade. This system came to pose great strain on
the American economy in the 1960s and was abandoned. In its place has
emerged a much more uncertain situation, in which investors move money
around the world at enormous speed, in response to daily signals about the
health of particular companies or national economies. The power of unac-
countable and amorphous international financial forces is becoming far more
evident than the power of any national government, and the idea that individual governments can act effectively in terms of a purely national economic
policy (e.g. to reduce unemployment) increasingly problematic. It is a volatile
situation, and one in which the capacity of individual governments to engage
in effective projects of social reform or economic regeneration is limited and
having important effects at the level of popular morale ('Can't *they* [the gov-
ernment] do something about it?,' etc.).

The second set of precipitating circumstances producing the major transformation in international political economy were the so-called oil shocks of 1974
and 1979. The OPEC embargo of 1974, in particular, is seen as having shifted
the epicentre of economic expansion from the developed world to the oil-rich
countries of the developing world—the huge incomes which were then earned

by the OPEC countries are seen, by Piore and Sabel and many other commentators, as the primary reason for the vast expansion in the 'Eurodollar market'. Eurodollars are in effect a new kind of money—completely outside the control of any individual government—enmeshed in the vast network of international banks and financial institutions which have grown up as a result of the collapse of the fixed exchange-rate system.

The international economic situation which has developed through the 1980s is highly volatile and competitive, as major investors and financial institutions move enormous sums of money, sometimes in excess of any one nation's gross national product, around the international stock exchanges, which are now open twenty-four hours a day, at the slightest hint of a change in interest rates in a single jurisdiction or in the fortunes of particular corporations. In a world in which there is no secure store of value *all* players in the market, including national governments, are placed under pressure to take risks and to make increasingly rapid decisions in the search for competitive advantage. One of the most dramatic interpretations of developments in the 1990s, outlined by Edward Luttwak (erstwhile economics advisor to President Bush) suggests that 'capitalism' has now entered a 'turbo-charged' period, consequent on an irreversible globalization of competition for markets. This globalization may have irreversible and mostly undesirable effects in respect of the distribution of wealth and position between and within nation-states in the West (Luttwak, 1995). The position of most European societies may weaken with respect to the tiger-economies of South East Asia, and there will even be serious questions about the competitiveness of the American economy itself. Within each of these societies, there is likely to be a further and continuing intensification of patterns of inequality.

Individual multi-national corporations have adapted to the uncertainties of global markets by diversifying their sphere of operations (in respect of production and sales)—horizontally and vertically into different markets (the phenomenon of 'flexible accumulation')—but this is not an option that is always available to national governments. The deregulation of stock exchanges in individual countries in the early 1980s (in London, on 'Big Bang' day, 27 October 1986) is one means available to governments, given the globalized character of economic competition and accumulation activities, to attract the investment of overseas investors and financial institutions into their countries. So also is the resort to what must be identified as free-market policy by national governments within their own countries, rolling back the state's direct involvement in the kind of economic or social planning of the earlier post-war period, and rationalizing significantly the state's involvement in the provision of public goods in areas like health and welfare, transport, housing, and urban planning. It is important to note that, while the development of flexible accumulation strategies and the move towards twenty-four-hour stock exchange trading are international phenomena, the adoption of rigorously free market policies at the national level has been specific to Britain, in what is usually discussed as 'Thatcherism', and the United States, in respect of the decade of 'Reagonomics', culminating in November 1992 in the defeat of George Bush (see the discussion below of Elliott Currie's work on the connection between 'market society' and crime).

A coherent and contemporary political economy of crime must be able to make the connection between the 'liberalization' and internationalization of major speculative financial activity beginning in most Western capitalist societies in the early 1980s, and the sudden emergence of major frauds and other serious economic crimes that were thrust into public view, in short order, in the immediately ensuing period.

Crimes of the International Finance Market in the 1980s and 1990s

Probably the most widely publicized set of these economic and financial offences were those involving the offence of 'insider trading', particularly those cases in the United States involving sums of money beyond all previous experience. In May 1986, the Securities and Exchange Commission (SEC) accused Dennis Levine, a prominent US stockbroker, of making $12.6 million profit by trading on information gained (through espionage and bribes) from insiders in particular companies. In November of the same year, Ivan Boesky, another prominent broker, agreed to pay the SEC a penalty of $100 million to settle the charges of insider trading it was going to bring against him (in 1987 Boesky was sentenced to three years in prison). In September 1988 the SEC accused one of the top Wall Street firms of stockbrokers, Drexel Burnham Lambert, and one of its top executives, Michael Milken, of even more substantial insider trades as well as a variety of other stock-market manipulations, outright frauds, and other violations of federal securities laws, particularly in respect of the marketing of so-called 'junk bonds'; in December 1988 Drexel agreed to plead guilty to six felonies and settle the SEC charges by paying back $650 million. In November 1990 Michael Milken, having been indicted on ninety-eight charges of racketeering and securities fraud, was sentenced to ten years in prison (Stewart, 1991).

The scale of these insider trading frauds, in which individual investors were trading in monies equivalent to those of some national government departments, ensured that these American cases attracted international attention. But insider-trading cases were also common in many other Western societies. In France, in February 1989, Max Theret and Roger Patrice Pelat, business associates of President Mitterrand, were accused of using advance information on an American takeover bid of $1.26 billion to trade in shares of Pechiney-Triangle Industries. In Britain, on a rather smaller scale, Michael Collier, the chairman of Morgan Collier, was prosecuted in 1986 for making an instant profit of £15,000 on an insider trade, and the following year a Conservative MP, Keith Best, was similarly accused.

Another major activity in the international financial market receiving some public attention in this period was the activity of money laundering. The objectives of those involved in this activity are to shield money from tax within individual national jurisdictions, and also to disguise the origins or sources of the money as well as its ownership. The 1980s saw the proliferation throughout the world of a number of identifiable 'tax havens' or offshore banking systems for this purpose: the Cayman Islands, for example, which in 1964 had two banks, had by 1984 become the home of 360 foreign banks and 8,000 registered companies, and had more fax machines than any other country in the world (Blum, 1984: 22). Much of the money circulating through these havens is known to have originated from the international drug trade, but, even before the well-publicized collapse of the Bank of Credit and Commerce International in 1991, it was clear that these havens had been used for speculative accumulation by major banks and other legitimate financial institutions, including one of Italy's largest banks, the Banco Ambrosiano, which failed in 1984 as a result of such speculative activity (Santino, 1988). The scale of this laundering of 'hot money' through the international economy at the end of the 1980s was causing considerable concern among national governments: a Financial Action Task Force, set up by fifteen western governments in 1989, reported in April 1990 that some £43 billion was being laundered through the banking system, and feared for the stability of the system, particularly in respect of the smaller banking institutions (*Independent*, 12 April 1990).

The publicity given to insider trading and money laundering in the late 1980s (sometimes as a result of investigative journalism and sometimes as a result of 'whistle-blowing' by competitors of those involved in such activities) should not detract attention from the wide range of other fraudulent activities that began to be identified, in the same period, across a large number of financial fields. The problem of 'insurance fraud' by insurance salespeople as well as by claimants was an important developing field of economic crime in this period, as also were the problems of credit card, VAT, customs, and pension scheme fraud. There was also evidence of widespread fraudulent dealing in time-share holiday and retirement homes and a variety of other related activities in the financial services market, including the banks and other major financial institutions (cf. *inter alia* Levi, 1988). By the early 1990s, in Britain, a large number of voices were proclaiming that the system of 'self-regulation' that had been established in the Financial Services Act 1986 had palpably failed, and that a system of reregulation, like that which had been instituted even in the United States, was now required.[12] Further force was given to these arguments in 1995 after the collapse of Barings, Britain's largest brokerage house, consequent on the loss of £860 million as a result of the activities of one of its young 'futures traders', Mr Nick Leeson. These losses were built up over a three-year period, apparently unnoticed by Barings' own internal supervisors or the Bank of England's Board of Banking Supervision.

It should be obvious that a criminology of the international financial markets that grew up in the 1980s—and further developed in the 1990s—would look

---

[12] A first move in this direction, on the part of the new Labour Government elected in Britain in May 1997, was the unification of all the different agencies and systems of regulation under one unified authority, reporting to the Department of Trade and Industry.

very different from the political economy of crime that was drawn up by criminologists like Willem Bonger or sociologists like Robert Merton in the first half of the twentieth century. In the first instance, such a contemporary criminology would need to be focused on the powerful corporate institutions and individuals at the core of the major crimes in the new international markets, rather than, narrowly, on the street-corner delinquents or individual fraudsters who were the focus of earlier political-economic studies. But, secondly, it seems clear that the explanatory burden of such a political economy should focus on the broad structures of international economic development and corporate activity and the way in which the crimes of the period (money laundering, insider-trading, etc.) are a *systematic product*, in a key sense, of these newly competitive, international economic conditions as well as under-standing the cultural environment (stressing 'enterprise' and individualism above all other values) that has accompanied such economic developments in societies like the United States and Britain. In this sense, a political economy of contemporary market crime would want to advance beyond the essentially social-psychological approach adopted by the American student of 'white-collar crime', Edwin H. Sutherland, in his famous 1948 study of that name. And, thirdly, it should be apparent that any such political economy of crime in the contemporary market would have to be international in scope, like the activity it seeks to comprehend and/or control, and not be thought through, in the manner of most criminology of this century, in terms only of *national* policy and practice. It is quite clear, for example, that the control of money laundering in the 1990s can be achieved only through internationally co-ordi-nated activity that is capable of intruding into the activities of national banking systems and financial institutions. (For an extended review of many of the issues discussed in this section, see Nelken, this volume.)

The Political Economy of the International Drug Trade

To insist that any contemporary political economy of crime must focus on the large-scale processes of economic change, and on the powerfully placed insti-tutions that have been engaged in innovative forms of capital accumulation sometimes in breach of conventions, and legal and other regulations, that have been prized by national governments and some of their competitors is not, however, to suggest that these large-scale economic processes do not have major impact on the lives and practices of the lower class, the population that is the accustomed focus of more traditional criminology. It surely is no accident that the largest reported increases in crime, particularly those associated with the mushrooming problem of hard drugs, are reported in precisely those urban centres in North America and Europe that have suffered the greatest job losses as a result of what Piore and Sabel describe as 'the demise of manufacturing industry'. Mike Davis's (1988) account of the emergence of the gang wars and cocaine trade in Los Angeles, published some three years before the major Los Angeles riots of June 1992, clearly located the dislocation of the black community in that city as resulting from the 'sectoral deindustrialization' of southern California as a whole throughout the 1980s, with a wholesale 'hæmorrhaging' of high-wage industrial jobs, especially for young black men. The slow growth in the service sector, in the meantime, threw up employment disproportionately for young women; but blacks of both sexes continued to be excluded from those jobs thrown up in service outlets in the suburbs. With their opportunity for gainful employment in the legitimate business sector destroyed by deindustrialization and their search for alternatives obstructed by institutional racism, many young blacks began to innovate after the fashion of many more fortunately placed entrepreneurs in the 1980s and move into the lucrative business of the drug trade. The *opportunity* to enter this alternative form of productive employment arose as a result of the rerouting of the so-called 'cocaine trail' from Florida into California around 1984: and, with the development and dissemination of the techniques for distilling and cutting crack cocaine in so-called 'crack houses', the conditions of existence of the massive illegitimate business that is the southern California drug trade were laid. By 1988, the Los Angeles Attorney-General's Department was estimating that there was a 'hard-core gang' membership in Los Angeles of between 10,000 and 15,000, and gang-related killings in the city were running at one a day.

The importance of a political-economy approach to understanding the drug trade that emerged in American cities in the 1980s is underlined by the insight which such an approach also yields into the circumstances of the continuing production of the coca plant in countries like Colombia and Peru on the South American continent and Sri Lanka and Burma in south-east Asia. It is precisely these countries which have been disadvantaged in the new international global political economy—in part because they have not developed an indigenous industrial or financial commercial class, and now rely on whatever agricultural product they can produce, with minimal technology, and sell. The really powerful demand, and the highest market prices, are for drugs; and hence, despite all the attempts made by the US government to stem the production of the coca crop in Colombia and Peru (through defoliation raids and other measures), the international trade in such drugs continues to expand (McConohay and Kirk, 1988).

Explaining the conditions of existence of coca production, in South America, and the illegitimate business that organizes the distribution of cocaine and other drugs, especially in deindustrialized American cities, does not constitute an exhaustive explanation of drug-related crime. It is necessary also to explain the demand for such drugs (a demand which is not confined to desperate inner-city or ghetto areas). This explanatory challenge demands a critical understanding of cultural conditions in the deindustrialized, competitive, and individualistic labour market that has existed throughout much of America during the 1980s and which, by the early 1990s, was beginning to develop in Britain (cf. Taylor, 1992). Davis's account of the development of the drug trade in Los Angeles, later to be replicated by Elliott Currie in his interviews with 'delinquent youth' elsewhere in California (Currie, 1991), cannot be

transferred wholesale to the British situation. But there was considerable coverage in the local and national press in the 1990s of many inner-city areas in
Britain, in which individual incidents of crime, including shooting, were often
related to 'the drug trade'. The relationship between such drug-related violence
and other activities involved in the 'long, slow riot of crime' in Britain's inner
cities (car theft and 'joyriding' and 'ram-raiding', burglary, and assaults) may
take on a rather different form from that in the United States—not least
because the deprivation of the inner city, and also on problem council estates,
now extends deeply into a population of poor whites, unaccustomed to their
undeniable position as an underclass.

It is clear, however, that any adequate account of the international trade in
drugs, and its impact within individual societies, must take account of the
interpenetration of street-level criminal enterprise and organized crime, and
pay attention to the ways in which the international economic conditions of
the 1980s and 1990s have encouraged many legitimate businesses into
innovative or risky enterprise, some of it conducted 'offshore' through the new
international banking systems. One of the difficult tasks for any internationally
organized fraud squad in the late 1990s would be the identification of the
source or ownership of particular flows of 'hot money' it encounters moving
through the banking systems. The definitive analytical problem confronting a
political economy of the international drug trade in the 1990s might be that of
demonstrating the precise interconnectedness, in this sphere of social problems,
of the risk-taking enterprise of ostensibly legitimate brokers and traders, on
the one hand, and more recognizably illegitimate criminals, on the other. (For
further discussion of international drug markets, see South, this volume.)

THE COSTS OF CRIME AND THE ENTRY OF NEO-CLASSICAL ECONOMICS

Standing in complete contrast to the kind of political-economic analyses of
crime undertaken by critically minded social scientists discussed in the previous
section are the approaches to the analysis of crime adopted by economists
working within the neo-classical perspective. This approach first came to be
applied to crime in an influential fashion in the United States as in a famous
essay by the economist Gary Becker in 1968. Isaac Ehrlich (1973) subsequently
extended the economic approach to the study of punishment and deterrence,
and Kenneth Avio and Scott Clark (1976) reworked these studies using
Canadian economic and crime data.

Much of this early North American literature on the political economy of
crime is informed by a generalized political concern at the extraordinary costs
to the state (and, therefore, to taxpayers) of the continuing post-war expansion in the criminal justice system (provoked, according to a common-sense
view, by the rapid and accelerating increases in crime). The defining feature of

the literature is the use of the analytic techniques of neo-classical economics (and, specifically, econometrics) in the investigation of crime. The particular objective is to try to evaluate the *effectiveness* of particular forms of social control in the reduction of the incidence of humanly and economically costly crime. A large number of studies in this tradition try to measure the *differential* costs and benefits of different social control interventions on crime, and the cost of achieving a radical reduction—even to an outcome 'no crime'—of certain crimes. In the work of Lehtinen (1977), for instance, cost–benefit analysis is applied, more or less without qualification, to the disposition of convicted murderers in the United States; this analysis of the differential costs of long-term imprisonment versus execution results in firm support for the economic benefits of execution. This economic analysis of punishment began to find an echo among certain applied criminologists and social scientists in the 1980s. In Britain, the application of 'rational choice theory' was first undertaken by Derek Cornish and Ron Clarke, most notably in a monograph entitled *The Reasoning Criminal: Rational Choice Perspectives on Offending* (1986). The central argument advanced, quite straightforwardly, was that people engage in crime primarily because a good opportunity presents itself so to do. The situational decision to engage in an act of theft, for example, is taken in circumstances when people think the risk is worth taking that is, when the opportunity is clear and the chances of being observed and caught are small. This notion of the exercise of reasoned choice is a diluted version of the famous Benthamite calculus of human action being simultaneously deterred by pain and driven by pleasure. What Cornish and Clarke tried to do in *The Reasoning Criminal*, as well as in an earlier paper of 1985, to model the kinds of choices that people will make in different situations of opportunity, in relation to particular forms of crime.

The rational choice theorists have in common with early twentieth-century exponents of utilitarian economics—from whom their work derives—an indifference with respect to the larger questions of classical political economy discussed by Ferguson, Hume, and others in the eighteenth century, namely, the range of choices which are presented to people in respect of conformity and crime and the moral or social organization of the broad society (for example, in respect of equality of life chances). This indifference means that rational choice theorists effectively abstain from examining the ability of particular forms of economic organization to generate *productive work* or *paid employment* for the mass of citizens. Where neo-classical economists speak of the issue of unemployment, it is usually in an idealist rather than analytical fashion, that is to say, they bemoan the underdevelopment of the free market or of the enterprise culture (which has in some way been prevented from working its magic) as the self-evident source of the unemployment problem of the 1980s and 1990s (cf. *inter alia*, Pyle, 1983, 1993). So, for example, mass unemployment cannot be admitted as an empirical demonstration of the failure of free market arrangements (cf. Taylor, 1991*b*).

Rational choice theorists in criminology also seem largely indifferent, unlike the control theorists with whom they are sometimes confused (cf. Hirschi and Gottfredson, 1986) to the processes that might be thought to produce the personal quality of 'criminality' (or 'criminal propensity') in individuals or in particular neighbourhoods. The overwhelming interest of rational choice criminologists is in the *situations of opportunity* that can be analysed to arrive at the way in which they produce crime as an outcome. In fact, one of the first published studies in Britain making use of rational choice-type analysis was Cornish and Clarke's Home Office Research Unit study of the deterrent effects of steering-column locks in cars (Mayhew *et al.*, 1976). Subsequent work ranged widely across the newly established field of 'situational crime prevention', attempting to measure the consequences of different crime-prevention measures (for example, in the redesign of car parks, entrances to buildings in residential areas, lighting and security systems) on the level of crime. There has been a rediscovery of interest (inspired to some extent by the earlier work of Isaac Ehrlich) in the deterrent effects of punishment, and specifically the proposition that an increase in the level of sanction could have effects on the calculations engaged in by the offender at the key situational moment of opportunity (Silberman, 1976; Tittle, 1977, 1980).

In one subsequent study working within this overall framework, Piliavin *et al.* conducted a sophisticated empirical test in order to question this prop-osition. Their conclusion was that increases in sanctions do *not* feed through to potential offenders' perceptions, but they nonetheless argued that there was support for what they called 'the reward component of the rational choice model'—namely, the idea that when the rewards for engaging in a criminal act are significant, this will substantially outweigh most of the reasons for abstaining (Piliavin *et al.*, 1986). It surely is no surprise, given our earlier discussion of Merton, to find that young people in low-paid employment in the service industries or on welfare in the United States during the 1980s (the golden era of 'feel-good' Reaganomics, and the unleashing of free market policies in that country) were often persuaded that the rewards accruing from some forms of property crime were more compelling than the benefits which they were receiving from legitimate employment or the weekly welfare cheque. In another study conducted within the rational choice framework, Philip J. Cook (1986) suggested that the emphasis in that literature on 'target-hardening' was making many private homes and public buildings far less vulnerable to criminal attacks, and he wondered whether this might be having the effect on 'displacing' crime on to other targets. He speculated that the displacement effect might, in fact, be different for different types of offence, and that this needed detailed research. There is certainly evidence of this kind of displace-ment effect at work in studies of the policing of prostitution in both Britain and Canada. It is not so much that the reduction of opportunities in one place also reduces the overall prevalence of the offence behaviour; it is rather that the offending behaviour comes to be reorganized elsewhere in response to intrusive neighbourhood responses and intrusive policing (Lowman, 1989; Matthews, 1986).

Application of this kind of cost–benefit analysis to crime and to crime control is replete with methodological and theoretical problems,[13] not the least of which is the continuing lack of interest among utilitarian economists in models of human action other than those of the 'rational' Economic Man. Sociologists in general, and most sociologically informed criminologists, would see any such model as too one-dimensional and as far too inattentive to the symbolic and cultural dimensions of social life. Nevertheless, to note the interest in rational choice theory shown by such an influential social thinker as Anthony Giddens. For Giddens:

> situational interpretations of crime can quite easily be connected to the labelling approach, because they clarify one feature of criminality about which labelling theory is silent: why many people who are in no way 'abnormal' choose to engage in acts which they know could be followed by criminal sanctions [1989: 133].

Closely associated with this difficulty is the problem of the continuing insistence of economic analysts on extraordinarily restrictive and essentially quite ideological notions of 'social costs'—usually referring to the 'costs' of crime (or other socially problematic human activities) on propertied individuals or institutions within societies as currently and unequally constituted.[14] In the later 1980s, however, there was a perceptible shift in the debate around the social costs of crime and crime control. Both in the United States and in Britain, there was an increasingly widespread recognition that the extraordinary level of state investment in crime control was an ineffective kind of investment, inappropriate in a political culture in which all other forms of public expenditure were subject to increasingly stringent scrutiny.

In Britain these concerns were first voiced, ironically enough, by the so-called left realist school in respect of the declining efficiency of a police force which had been in receipt, from the early 1980s, of increasingly generous state support particularly as measured by the paltry clear-up rates in offences reported by the public (the consumer) to the police (the service-provider) (Kinsey *et al.*, 1986). In the United States, particular attention was paid to the continuing contradiction between the massive increase in the prison population that occurred in the 1980s, with 673,565 sentenced prisoners in state and federal institutions in June 1989, compared to 128,466 in 1974 (Greenberg, 1990: 40) and the continuing escalation in crimes of violence, robberies, and other disruptive and disorderly behaviours on American streets. Edwin Zedlewski, an economist based at the National Institute of Justice, published two studies (1985, 1987) arguing that these increases in numbers imprisoned were actually 'cost-effective'. But these studies were subsequently subjected to close critical examination by Greenberg, who showed that Zedlewski's computations of both costs and benefits were highly ideological (Greenberg, 1990). In particular, Zedlewski's computation of costs did not include any

[13] For discussion of some of the issues involved in cost–benefit analysis of the deterrent effects of punishment, especially in the work of Ehrlich (1973), see Beyleveld (1980).
[14] For discussion of the concept of social cost in the propagandist literature of free market economists from the mid-1970s to the present day, see Taylor (1991*b*).

measure of the costs of imprisonment to the imprisoned, and no normative argument is advanced to justify this exclusion. Nor is his computation of the benefits accruing to 'society' from imprisonment placed within any *comparative evaluation* of the benefits in terms of reduction in crime and in public anxieties, and an increased sense of well-being that might result from state expenditures in respect of health, education, transportation, or other areas of the 'public good'.

The cost of crime to the British state, though not at the level identified by Zedlewski for the United States in 1989 ($61.4 billion), is certainly of increasing significance. According to a Home Office Working Group reporting in 1988 (Home Office, 1988: 30–2), computation of the overall 'costs of crime' in the United Kingdom in the late 1980s would have had to include:

1. *Compensation to victims of crime*: £52,042,521 (excluding Northern Ireland), plus £7 million administrative costs of the Criminal Injuries Compensation Board.
2. *Policing*: overall cost of policing England and Wales in 1987: £3,500 million.
3. *Crown Prosecution Service*: £170 million for 1987–8.
4. *Legal aid in criminal cases*: £200 million in 1986–7.
5. *Criminal courts*: expenditure on Crown Court in 1986–7: £144 million; on magistrates' courts in 1986–7: £179 million.
6. *Probation service*: total costs of probation service in 1986–7 (in England and Wales only) £215 million.
7. *Prison service*: expenditure in 1986–7: £698 million (England and Wales).

The Home Office's figures, all from the late 1980s, do not claim to cover the overall cost to the state of crime (it does not include the cost of social workers), but, even on such an incomplete account (and recognizing that expenditure on policing may be seen as incurred for purposes other than the control of crime alone), it is apparent that the costs of these criminal justice institutions in England and Wales must be at least £5,000 million per year. It is unsurprising that analysts have begun to apply some version of cost-benefit analysis to these expenditures and, in particular, that social scientists with a critical interest in the larger issue of the public (rather than merely private) good have begun to ask whether these expenditures justify themselves—particularly in comparison to other imaginable patterns of expenditure of public monies in the interest of crime reduction in neighbourhoods and public territories and the creation of a sense of safety and civility in everyday public life.

Finally, attention should be drawn to some of the other issues that are usually ignored in the application of such an approach to crime and crime control. Probably most important of all is the absence of attention to the substantive social inequalities that are entailed in the routine operation of the political economies of Western free-market capitalist societies, inequalities that are more obvious in Britain in terms of class, and in the United States in terms of race, but inequalities (of opportunity and position) that are also quite fundamental and destructive in terms of gender. This inattention to substantive inequalities extends to a complete lack of curiosity on the part of cost-benefit analysts with respect to the inequalities that routinely structure the application of penal discipline and other measures of social control. In the United States, for example, recent figures have shown that one in four black men in the 20–29 age group is in prison, on probation, or on parole, compared to one in sixteen whites (Walker, 1991). In the mid-1990s, Afro-Americans had come to comprise one-third of all arrests and one half of all incarcerations in the United States (Hagan and Peterson, 1995: 16). In the United Kingdom, recent research has shown that entirely different assumptions inform the policing of tax evasion and other forms of fraud by the well off, on the one hand, and fraudulent supplementary benefit (welfare) claims by the poor, on the other (Cook, 1989*a*, 1989*b*). In 1987–8, for example, there were only 322 Inland Revenue prosecutions for tax fraud and evasion, compared with 9,847 prosecutions by the DHSS for supplementary benefit fraud (Cook, 1989*b*: 120). In 1982, according to a study by the National Association for the Care and Resettlement of Offenders, 268 'social security offenders' were imprisoned, compared to only thirty-two tax evaders (Cook, 1989*a*: 160), and subsequent analysis does not suggest any marked shift away from this differential application of punishment. The relationship between the everyday operation of these systems and the broad society's definition of itself as a democratic and just social formation is starkly posed. Although this is an issue which conventional proponents of cost-benefit analysis have almost entirely ignored, it is one which is attracting more attention as the routine costs of a repressive and expansive criminal justice system continue to escalate.

CRIME AND FREE MARKET SOCIETY

A key feature of neo-classical economic analysis of the costs and benefits of crime discussed in the last section is its continuing reification of 'the economy', separated off from the kinds of social and political relations which help to arrange and structure economic life, and the outcomes for individuals of particular patterns or economic activity that obtain in particular societies at particular times. That this kind of analysis is insensitive, in a descriptive and empirical sense, to broad historical change from the period of imperial or pioneer capitalism in the late nineteenth century, via the period of Keynesian or welfare state mixed economies in the mid-twentieth century (variously referred to as the period of compromise between capital and labour or the period of social reconstruction) to the contemporary period of deregulation and privatization (the 'free market experiment'). It also shows no interest in *evaluating*, in a theoretical, interrogatory, or morally curious fashion, the kinds of relationship that could be thought to exist between particular types of political economy and the character of social relations (including crime and the broader, connected question now very much on the agenda in most free market societies of the 'quality of life').

In an unpublished lecture originally given in London in November 1990,[15] the social democratic American criminologist, Elliott Currie, observed that post-war America was, in effect, a kind of 'natural laboratory' for examining the social effects of the freeing of market forces now under way in Europe, and he noted how the extraordinary triumphalist celebration of these free market policies within the United States during the 1980s had also been accompanied by quite frightening newspaper and television reports of crime on the 'ominous underside' of these policies (Currie, 1990a).[16] These stories could not fail to acknowledge the growth of poverty and homelessness (signified, in the United States, by the phenomenon of the 'bag lady', by sudden and rapid increases in preventable illnesses, by galloping inner-city drug abuse, and sharp rises in the 'already staggering levels of violent crime, which [had] long set [America] apart from every other advanced industrial nation' (Currie, 1990a: 3). Currie proceeded to argue that there was, indeed, a kind of causal relationship between the advent of 'market society' and the acceleration of violent crime, drug abuse, and other forms of social dislocation in America. This revolved around at least five 'links' or connections (Currie, 1990a: 10–20).

1. The promotion in market society of increased inequality and concentration economic depression.
2. The erosion by market society of the capacity of local communities for informal support, mutual provision, and effective supervision of the young.
3. Market society's promotion of crime via the stress and fragmentation it produces in the family.[17]
4. Market society's promotion of crime via its withdrawal of public provision of basic services from those it has already stripped of livelihoods, economic security, and community support.
5. Market society's promotion of crime via its magnification of a culture of Darwinian competition for status and resources and its encouragement of a level of consumption it cannot provide for everyone through legitimate channels.

[15] For a later and more extended development of this theme, see Currie's lecture to the 30th anniversary meeting of the National Association for the Care and Resettlement of Offenders (Currie, 1996).

[16] For two different elaborations of the social democratic critique of free market economies in the USA, see Currie (1990b) and Henry and Brown (1990).

[17] Currie's use of the term 'family' here (rather than household) should not identify him as an apologist for patriarchy, as his work as a whole is notably attentive to the particularly destructive effects on women of the pursuit of free market goals in the USA. In Britain, Pat Carlen has been at the forefront of the attempt to link the 'feminization of poverty' resulting from the Thatcher experiment with the increasing problems of women with respect to crime and the imposition of social control. The proportionate use of imprisonment for women has doubled in Britain in the last ten years and there is now a significant tendency fo women to be sent to prison for less serious offences than men (Carlen, 1988: 4).

Many of these links or connections are illustrated and, some would argue, confirmed in Mike Davis's (1990) extraordinary account (mentioned earlier) of the growth of gang violence and the drug trade in Los Angeles consequent on the deindustrialization of southern California in the early to mid-1980s. Many of them are also evident in the continuing acceleration of property crime and violence in many inner-city areas and council estates in Britain in the early 1990s. Elsewhere—in Sweden—Henrik Tham has begun the task of analysing the close relationship not between welfare dependency and crime but rather between the systematic withdrawal of welfare and the growth of crime, in a comparative analysis which also focuses on developments in Britain (Tham, 1997). The escalation of free markets can also find expression, of course, in the explosion in the number and variety of forms of fraud and market crime coming to public attention, as the Darwinian struggle for material self-aggrandisement that characterized the deregulation of the early to mid-1980s translates into a recessionary struggle for economic survival.

We cannot conclude, however, that the current explosion of property crime and violence in Britain, coincident as it undoubtedly has been with the free market experiment of the Thatcher and Major governments, is proof positive of a straightforward, law-like relation between the free market economy and something called crime. So, in the mid-1970s, conservatively minded criminologists like James Q. Wilson in the United States and Patricia Morgan in Britain anticipated the later work of Charles Murray in arguing that the key relationship was between the post-war development of a welfare state and of Keynesian intervention into the economy, on the one hand, and a generalized cultural condition of 'state dependency', on the other. They also argued that this form of dependency which Morgan, in particular, associated with 'social democracy' produced a kind of amoral self-interest in society, particularly in the so-called underclass (Wilson, 1975; Morgan, 1978). In this perspective there was also a causal relationship between the social democratic belief in state intervention *per se* as an answer to both economic and social problems, and the failure of parents and the state education system to provide appropriate moral socialization and education of the young. What neither Wilson nor Morgan may have anticipated were the extraordinary debacles involved in the deregulation of financial markets in the 1980s, from the Boesky affair in 1986 to the collapse of the Bank of Credit and Commerce International in 1991—all of them, presumably, the products of good families and effective 'socialization'—and the subsequent difficulties posed for proponents of the free-market economy themselves in addressing the issue of moral socialization 'by example'. Ironically enough, the advent of the free-market economy in North America and Britain in the 1980s, with its extraordinarily negative impact on the popular sense of justice and fairplay, on levels of economic equality as well on insecurity and stress in the workforce, may actually have undermined the credibility or appeal of material success as a personal goal within a market society. Amongst others, it may have created the conditions which have engendered an explosive growth of new forms of 'white-collar' enterprise crime, from complex insurance frauds, insider trading, to the international laundering of drug money.

These are large issues, but *contra* the assumptions of many practitioners of the tired discipline of applied economics, they are absolutely the stuff of a proper political economy, applied broadly to discussions of moral and social order. The investigation of these developments has been taken on as a responsibility of contemporary sociology, especially in continental Europe: there are pressing issues of causal explanation, as well as profound challenges in respect of moral argument, involved in understanding the rise, the consolidation and the current trajectory of free market political economies. They are issues of profound importance, too, for criminology in the late 1990s and beyond.

Selected Further Reading

Ash Amin (ed.) *Post-Fordism: a Reader*, Oxford: Basil Blackwell, 1994. Mike Davis *City of Quartz: Imagining the Future in Los Angeles*, London: Verso, 1990. Jay MacLeod *Ain't No Making It: Aspirations and Attainment in a Low Income Neighbourhood*, Boulder: Westview Press, 2nd edn., 1995. Vincenzo Ruggiero *Organised Crime in Europe: Offers that can't be refused*, Aldershot: Dartmouth, 1996.

REFERENCES

ALLAN, E. A., and STEFFENSMEIER, D. J. (1989), 'Youth Unemployment and Property Crime: Differential Effects of Job Availability and Job Quality on Juvenile and Youth Adult Arrest Rates', *American Sociological Review*, 50: 317–32.

ARNOLD, M. (1965 (1869)), *Culture and Anarchy*, ed. R. H. Super. Ann Arbor, Mich.: University of Michigan Press.

ARONOWITZ, S. and DiFAZIO, W. (1995), *The Jobless Future*. Minneapolis, Minn.: University of Minnesota.

AVIO, K., and CLARK, S. (1976), *Property Crime in Canada: An Econometric Study*. Toronto: University of Toronto Press.

BECKER, G. S. (1968), 'Crime and Punishment: An Economic Approach', *Journal of Political Economy*, 76: 169–217.

BEYLEVELD, D. (1980), *A Bibliography on General Deterrence Research*. Farnborough: Saxon House.

BLATCHFORD, R. (1906), *Not Guilty: A Defence of the Bottom Dog*. London: Clarion Press.

BLUM, R. H. (1984), *Offshore Haven Banks, Trusts and Companies: the Business of Crime in the Euromarket*. New York: Praeger.

BONGER, W. (1969 (1916)), *Criminality and Economic Conditions*. Bloomington, Ind.: Indiana University Press.

BOX, S. (1987), *Recession, Crime and Punishment*. London: Macmillan.

—— and HALE, C. (1982), 'Economic Crisis and the Rising Prisoner Population in England and Wales', *Crime and Social Justice*, 17: 20–35.

—— and —— (1985), 'Unemployment, Imprisonment and Prison Over-crowding', *Contemporary Crises*, 9: 209–28.

BRAVERMAN, H. (1974), *Labour and Monopoly Capital: The Degradation of Work in the Twentieth Century*. New York: Monthly Review Press.

BRENNER, H. (1971), *Time Series Analysis of Relationships Between Selected Economic and Social Indicators, vol. 1: Texts and Appendices*. Washington, DC: US Government Printing Office.

—— (1977), 'Health Costs and Benefits of Economic Policy', *International Journal of Health Services*, 7: 581–623.

—— (1978), 'Impact of Economic Indicators on Crime Indices', in *Unemployment and Crime*, hearing before the Subcommittee on the Judiciary, House of Representatives,

59th Congress, first and second sessions. Serial no. 47: 20–54.

CAPORASO, J. A., and LEVINE, D. P. (1992), *Theories of Political Economy*. Cambridge: Cambridge University Press.

CLARKE, J., CRICHTER, C., HALL, S., and JEFFERSON, T. (1978), 'Subcultures, Cultures and Class', in S. Hall and T. Jefferson, eds., *Resistance through Rituals*, 99–102. London: Hutchinson.

CARLEN, P. (1988), *Women, Crime and Poverty*. Milton Keynes: Open University Press.

—— (1989), 'Introduction', in P. Carlen and D. Cook, eds., *Paying for Crime*. Milton Keynes: Open University Press.

—— and Cook, D., eds. (1989), *Paying for Crime*. Milton Keynes: Open University Press.

CARR-HILL, R., and STERN, J. (1979), *Crime, the Police and Criminal Statistics*. New York: Academic Press.

CLARKE, R. V. G., and CORNISH, D. B. (1985), 'Modelling Offenders' Decisions: Framework for Research and Policy', in M. Tonry and N. Morris, eds., *Crime and Justice: An Annual Review of Research*, 147–86. Chicago, Ill.: University of Chicago Press.

CLAY, J. (1855), 'On the Effect of Good or Bad Times on Committals to Prison', *Journal of the Statistical Society of London*, 18: 74–9.

CLOWARD, R. E., and OHLIN, L. E. (1960), *Delinquency and Opportunity: A Theory of Delinquent Gangs*. New York: Free Press.

COHEN, P. (1972), 'Subcultural Conflict and Working Class Community'. *Working Papers in Cultural Studies*, 2: 5–52.

COOK, D. (1989a), *Rich Law, Poor Law: Different Responses to Tax and Supplementary Benefit Fraud*. Milton Keynes: Open University Press.

—— (1989b), 'Fiddling Tax and Benefits: Inculpating the Poor, Exculpating the Rich', in P. Carlen and D. Cook, eds., *Paying for Crime*, 109–27. Milton Keynes: Open University Press.

COOK, P. J. (1986), 'The Demand and Supply of Criminal Opportunities', in M. Tonry and N. Morriss, eds., *Crime and Justice: An Annual Review of Research*, vii, 1–27. Chicago, Ill.: University of Chicago Press.

CORNISH, D. B., and CLARKE, R. V. G. (1986), *The Reasoning Criminal: Rational Choice Perspectives on Offending*. New York: Springer-Verlag.

CURRIE, ELLIOTT (1990a), 'Crime and Free Market Society: Lessons from the United States', unpublished lecture given to international conference on 'Crime and Policing 1992: A Global Perspective', Islington, London, November.

—— (1990b), 'Heavy with Human Tears: Free Market Policy, Inequality and Social Provision in the United States', in Ian Taylor, ed., *The Social Effects of Free Market Policies*, 299–318. Hemel Hempstead: Harvester Wheatsheaf.

—— (1991), *Dope and Trouble: Portraits of Delinquent Youth*. New York: Pantheon.

—— (1996), *Is America Really Winning the War on Crime and Should Britain Follow its Example?* London: National Association for the Care and Resettlement of Offenders.

DAVIS, M. (1988), 'Nightmares in Los Angeles', *New Left Review* 170 (July/August): 37–60.

—— (1990), *City of Quartz: Excavating the Future in Los Angeles*. London: Verso.

DEBS, E. (1927), *Walls and Bars*. Chicago, Ill.: Socialist Party.

EHRLICH, I. (1973), 'Participation in Illegitimate Activities: A Theoretical and Empirical Investigation', *Journal of Political Economy*, 81: 531–67.

EISNER, M. (1995) 'Socio-Economic Modernization and Long-term Developments of Crime Theories and Empirical Evidence in Europe', paper presented to American Society of Criminology, Boston, 15–19 November.

EYER, J. (1977), 'Review of Mental Illness and the Economy', *International Journal of Health Services*, 6: 139–48.

—— (1981), 'Prosperity as a Cause of Death', *International Journal of Health Services*, 7: 125–50.

FIELD, S. (1991), *Trends in Crime and their Interpretation: A Study of Recorded Crime in Post-war England and Wales*, Home Office Research Study no. 119. London: HMSO.

GIDDENS, A. (1989), *Sociology*. Cambridge: Polity Press.

—— (1991), *Modernity and Self-Identity*. Cambridge: Polity.

GREENBERG, D. (1977), 'The Dynamics of Oscillatory Punishment Processes', *Journal of Criminal Law and Criminology*, 68: 643–51.

—— (1990), 'The Cost Benefit Analysis of Imprisonment', *Social Justice*, 17: 49–75.

GUERRY, A.-M. (1833), *Statistique morale d'Angleterre comparée avec la statistique morale de la France*. Paris.

HAGAN, J., and PETERSON, R., eds. (1995), *Crime and Inequality*. Stanford, Cal.: Stanford University Press.

HAKIM, C. (1982), 'The Social Consequences of High Unemployment', *Journal of Social Policy*, 11: 433–67.

HALL, S., and JACQUES, M., eds. (1990), *New*

Times: The Changing Face of Politics in the 1990s. London: Lawrence and Wishart.

HENRY, S. and BROWN, J. (1990), 'Something for Nothing: The Informal Outcomes of Free Market Policies', in Ian Taylor, ed., *The Social Effects of Free Market Policies*, 319–48. Hemel Hempstead: Harvester Wheatsheaf.

HIRSCHI, T., and GOTTFREDSON, M. (1986), 'The Distinction between Crime and Criminality', in T. F. Hartnagel and R. A. Silverman, eds., *Critique and Explanation: Essays in Honour of Gwynn Nettler*. New Brunswick, NJ: Transaction.

HOME OFFICE (1988), *Report of the Working Group on the Costs of Crime* (Standing Conference on Crime Prevention, 6 December). London: Home Office.

HUTTON, W. (1992), 'How Whitehall Cut the Dole Queues', *Guardian*, 11 November.

JACKSON, G. (1970), *Soledad Brother*. Harmondsworth: Penguin.

JAMES, O. (1995), *Juvenile Violence in a Winner Loser Culture*. London: Free Association Books.

JANKOVIC, I. (1977), 'Labour Market and Imprisonment', *Crime and Social Justice*, 9: 17–31.

JANKOWSKI, MARTIN SANCHEZ (1991) *Islands in the Street: Gangs and American Urban Society*. Berkeley, Cal.: University of California Press.

JONES, J. A. (1971), 'Federal Efforts to Solve Social Problems', in Ervin O. Smigel, ed., *Handbook on the Study of Social Problems*, 547–90. Chicago, Ill.: Rand McNally.

JUDT, T. (1996) 'Europe: The Grand Illusion' *New York Review of Books*, 42, 2: 6–9.

KELLOUGH, D. G., BRICKNEY, S. L., and GREENAWAY, W. K. (1980), 'The Politics of Incarceration: Manitoba 1918–1939', *Canadian Journal of Sociology*, 5: 253–71.

KINSEY, R., LEA, J., and YOUNG, J. (1986), *Losing the Fight against Crime*. Oxford: Blackwell.

LASH, S., and URRY, J. (1987), *The End of Organized Capitalism*. Cambridge: Polity.

LEA, J., and YOUNG, J. (1984), *What is to be Done about Law and Order?* London: Penguin.

LEHTINEN, M. (1977), 'The Value of Life: An Argument for the Death Penalty', *Crime and Delinquency*, 23: 237–52.

LESSAN, G. T. (1991), 'Micro-Economic Determinants of Penal Policy: Estimating the Unemployment and Inflation Influences on Imprisonment Rate Changes in the United States 1948–1985', *Crime, Law and Social Change*, 16: 177–98.

LEVI, M. (1988), *Regulating Fraud: White Collar Crime and the Criminal Process.*

London: Tavistock.

LONGFORD, F., ed. (1964), *Crime: A Challenge to Us All.* London: The Labour Party.

LOWMAN, J. (1989), *Street Prostitution: Assessing the Impact of the Law in Vancouver.* Ottawa: Department of Justice.

LUTTWAK, E. (1995), 'Turbo-charged Capitalism and its Consequences', *London Review of Books* (2 November): 6–8.

MACLEOD, J. (1987, 1995). *Ain't No Making It: Aspirations and Attainment in a Low Income Neighbourhood.* Boulder, Colo.: Westview Press.

McCONOHAY, M. J., and KIRK, R. (1988), 'Over There: America's Drug War Abroad', *Mother Jones*, 14, 2: 36–9.

MARX, K. (1969), 'The Apologist Conception for the Productivity of All Professions', in *Theories of Surplus Value*, 1, 387–8. Moscow: Foreign Languages Publishing House.

MATTHEWS, R. (1986), *Policing Prostitution: A Multi-Agency Approach.* Middlesex Polytechnic Centre for Criminology Paper No 1. London: Middlesex Polytechnic.

MAYHEW, P. M., CLARKE, R. V. G., STURMAN, A., and HOUGH, J. M. (1976), *Crime as Opportunity*, Home Office Research Paper No. 34. London: HMSO.

—— and MAUNG, N. A. (1992), *Surveying Crime: Findings from the 1992 Crime Survey.* London: Home Office Research and Statistics Department.

MAYR, G. VON (1867), *Statistik der Gerichtlichen Polizei im Königreiche Bayern und in einigen anderen Länderen.* Munich.

MELOSSI, D. (1985), 'Punishment and Social Action: Changing Vocabularies of Motive Within a Political Business Cycle', *Current Perspectives in Social Theory*, 6: 169–97.

—— and PAVARINI M. (1981) *The Prison and the Factory.* London: Macmillan (originally published in Italian as *Carcere e fabbrica. Bologna:* Società Editrice il Mulino, 1977).

MERTON, R. K. (1963 (1938)), 'Social Structure and Anomie', *American Sociological Review*, 3: 672–82; repr. in *Social Theory and Social Structure.* Glencoe: Free Press, 1957; rev. edn. 1963.

MORGAN, P. (1978), *Delinquent Fantasies.* London: Temple Smith.

MURRAY, C. (1990), *The Emerging British Underclass* (with responses by Frank Field, Joan C. Brown, Nicholas Deakin, and Alan Walker). London: IEA Health and Welfare Unit.

PILIAVIN, I., GARTNER, R., THORNTON, C., and MATSUEDA, R. L. (1986), 'Crime, Deterrence and Rational Choice', *American Sociological Review*, 51: 101–19.

PIORE, M., and SABEL, C. (1984), *The Second Industrial Divide*. New York: Basic Books

PLATT, T., and TAKAGI, P. (1968), *The Iron Fist and the Velvet Glove*. Berkeley, Cal.: Social Justice Associates.

PYLE, D. (1983), *The Economics of Crime and Law Enforcement*. London: Macmillan.

—— (1993) *Crime in Britain*. London: Social Market Forum Discussion Paper (May).

QUETELET, A. (1835), *Sur l'homme et le développement de ses facultés; essai de physique sociale*. Paris: Bachelier.

QUINNEY, R. (1974), *Critique of Legal Order: Crime Control in Capitalist Society*. Boston, Mass.: Little, Brown.

REIMAN, J. (1979), *The Rich get Richer and the Poor get Prison: Ideology, Class and Criminal Justice*. 2nd edn., 1984. New York: Wiley.

ROWNTREE, J., and ROWNTREE, M. (1970), 'The Political Economy of Youth', *Our Generation*, 6: 1–2; repr. in pamphlet form by the Radical Education Project, Ann Arbor, Mich.

RUSCHE, G., and KIRCHHEIMER, O. (1939), *Punishment and Social Structure*. New York: Russell and Russell.

RUSKIN, J. (1985 (1862)), *Unto this Last*, ed. Clive Wilmer. Harmondsworth: Penguin.

RUSSELL, W. (1847), Abstract of the 'Statistics of Crime in England and Wales from 1839 to 1843', *Journal of the Statistical Society of London*, 10: 38–61.

SAMPSON, R. J., and WILSON, W. J. (1995), 'Towards a Theory of Race, Crime and Urban Inequality' in J. Hagan and R. Peterson, eds., *Crime and Inequality*. Stanford, Cal.: Stanford University Press.

SANTINO, U. (1988), 'The Financial Mafia: The Illegal Accumulation of Wealth and the Financial-Industrial Complex', *Contemporary Crises*, 12, 3: 203–44.

SCULL, A. (1977), *Decarceration*. Englewood Cliffs, NJ: Prentice-Hall.

SELLIN, T. (1937), *Research Memorandum on Crime in the Depression*. Bulletin No. 27. New York: Social Science Research Council.

SILBERMAN, M. (1976), 'Towards a Theory of Criminal Deterrence', *American Sociological Review*, 41: 442–61.

SIMON, W., and GAGNON, J. H. (1976), 'The Anomie of Affluence: A Post-Mertonian Conception', *American Journal of Sociology*, 82, 2: 356–77.

SINFIELD, A. (1981), *What Unemployment Means*. Oxford: Martin Robertson.

—— (1992), 'The Impact of Unemployment upon Welfare', in Z. Ferge and J. E. Kolberg, eds., *Social Policy in a Changing Europe*. Frankfurt: Campus; Boulder, Col.: Westview Press.

SPITZER, S. (1975), 'Toward a Marxian Theory of Deviance', *Social Problems*, 22: 638–51.

—— (1983), 'The Rationalization of Crime Control in Capitalist Society', in. S. Cohen and A. Scull, eds., *Social Control and the State*, 312–34. Oxford: Martin Robertson.

STERN, J. (1982), 'Does Unemployment Really Kill?', *New Society*, 10 June: 421–2.

STEWART, J. B. (1991), *Den of Thieves*. New York: Simon and Schuster.

SUTHERLAND, E. H. (1948), *White Collar Crime*. New Haven, Conn.: Yale University Press.

TAYLOR, I. (1991*a*), 'A Social Role for the Prison: Edward Carpenter's "Prisons, Police and Punishment" (1905)', *International Journal of the Sociology of Law*, 19: 1–26.

—— (1991*b*), 'The Concept of Social Cost in Free Market Theory and the Social Costs of Free Market Policies', in Ian Taylor, ed., *The Social Effects of Free Market Policies*, 1–26. Hemel Hempstead: Harvester Wheatsheaf.

—— (1992), 'The International Drug Trade and Money-Laundering: Border Controls and Other Issues' *European Sociological Review*, 8, 2: 181–93.

—— and JAMIESON R. (1996) '"Proper Little Mesters": Nostalgia and Protest Masculinity in Deindustrialized Sheffield', in Sallie Westwood and John Williams, eds., *Imagining Cities*. London: Routledge.

THAM, H. (1997), 'Crime and the Welfare State; The Case of the United Kingdom and Sweden' in V. Ruggiero, N. South and I. Taylor, eds., *European Criminology: Crime and Social Order in Europe*. London: Routledge.

TITTLE, C. (1977), 'Sanctions, Fear and the Maintenance of Social Order', *Social Forces*, 55: 579–96.

—— (1980), *Sanctions and Social Deviance: The Question of Deterrence*. New York: Praeger.

VOLD, G. V. (1958), *Theoretical Criminology*. New York: Oxford University Press.

WALKER, M. (1991), 'Sentencing System Blights Land of the Free', *Guardian*, 19 June.

WIERS, P. (1945), 'Wartime Increase in Michigan Delinquency', *American Sociological Review*, 10: 515–23.

WILSON, J. Q. (1975), *Thinking about Crime*. New York: Basic Books.

WILSON, W. J. (1987), *The Truly Disadvantaged: The Inner City, the Underclass and Public Policy*. Chicago, Ill.: University of Chicago Press.

ZEDLEWSKI, E. W. (1985), 'When Have We Punished Enough?', *Public Administration Review*, 45: 771–9.

—— (1987), *Making Confinement Decisions*. Washington, DC: US Department of Justice.

8

Environmental Criminology

Anthony E. Bottoms and Paul Wiles

Environmental criminology[1] is the study of crime, criminality, and victimization as they relate, *first*, to particular *places*, and *secondly*, to the way that individuals and organizations shape their activities *spatially*, and in so doing are in turn influenced by *place-based* or *spatial* factors.[2]

Environmental criminology would be of little interest—either to scholars or those concerned with criminal policy—if the geographical distribution of offences, or of offender residence, were random. In fact this is (as we shall shortly see) very far from being the case. Indeed, in recent criminology there has been an increasing interest in the geographical 'hotspots' of crime and criminality which matches the parallel interest in other 'skews' in criminological data (for example, the fact that relatively few persistent offenders commit a very disproportionate proportion of all street crimes).[3]

The study of 'dangerous places' has a long and continuous history in the study of crime, from, for example, Henry Mayhew's (1862) famous ethnographic studies of the 'rookeries' of Victorian London, to Beatrix Campbell's (1993) feminist analysis—interestingly subtitled *Britain's Dangerous Places*—whose empirical focus was a group of council estates[4] (in Cardiff, Oxford, and Tyneside) that had experienced urban riots in 1991. Similarly, the study of the spatial patterning of crime and criminality can be traced back to the work of Adolphe Quetelet and André Michel Guerry in the first half of the nineteenth

---

[1] Other names sometimes given to this topic are 'the geography of crime', 'the ecology of crime', etc. The name is, of course, relatively unimportant, but in our view 'environmental criminology' is the best description of the field.

[2] 'Place' is not the same as 'space'. The former concept refers to a geographical location, with fairly definite boundaries, within which people may meet, engage in various activities, etc. 'Space' is a much broader concept, but environmental criminologists are interested in it because some social activities have become quite markedly *spatially differentiated* (e.g. the 'zoning' policies of some urban planners); on the other hand, modern transport and telecommunications allow for individuals (and organizations) to bridge spatial separation to a much greater extent than in previous generations.

[3] On this see the chapter by David Farrington, this volume

[4] For those unfamiliar with the British housing market, 'council estates' are areas in which tenants rent from the local political authority (a 'council'): i.e. they are a form of public housing. They reached their peak of importance around 1980, at which stage about a third of households in Great Britain were council tenants (and in some cities much more); hence this tenure form is much more extensive in Britain than in the United States (for a history and full account, see Merrett, 1979). Since 1980, various aspects of national government policy have led to a decline in the proportion of council tenants nationally.

century, and is now entering a new phase with the advent of (increasingly user-friendly) computerized mapping systems, which are coming into operational use in many police forces.[5]

It is no accident that environmental criminology was born in the nineteenth century, the century *par excellence* of industrialization and urbanization in most Western societies. The environmental conditions in the new urban and industrial areas both fascinated and appalled a number of observers as different as Charles Dickens (see Collins, 1962) and Frederick Engels (1842). Crime seemed, to many observers, to be integrally and obviously linked to these social developments. Yet with the benefit of hindsight, some caution is needed before reaching this conclusion. It certainly appears to be almost universally the case that, in any given country in a particular era, urban crime rates are higher than those in rural areas.[6] This fact is of great importance for criminological explanation (see e.g. Cressey, 1964: chapter 3; Braithwaite, 1989: chapter 3), and is a contrast that is customarily linked to sociological analyses of the greater segmentalization of daily life in cities as compared with villages (see e.g. the classic essay by Wirth, 1938). On the other hand, studies of actual historical developments in particular countries have by no means always shown a direct or simple temporal link between urbanization and crime (see e.g. Gillis, 1996), and in comparative studies of recent developments in crime, it is possible to point to a country such as Japan, which, in spite of rapid industrialization and urbanization, has nevertheless experienced a less rapid growth in crime than have most other advanced economies (see Government of Japan, 1996). These various considerations suggest, first, that urbanism is in some ways of central significance for criminology; yet, on the other hand, that urban social life can be differently organized in different countries (and in different locations in the same country), and that these differences are also of great importance criminologically.

---

[5] The real importance of this development for the future is not so much computerized mapping *per se*, but that this is based on digitized geo-coded data which means that Geographical Information Systems (GIS) will make geographical analysis of data very much easier than in the past. Even more interesting is that digital data are not necessarily subject to the same constraints of two dimensionality as traditional maps and (as we shall explain later) the future theoretical development of environmental criminology will depend on our ability to theorize and then analyse interactive effects between more than two dimensions—e.g. the effects of different population groups on offence rates in *both* time and space. Furthermore, GIS can act as the means of linking together any type of data which is capable of being geo-coded. Since publicly collected data increasingly have this capacity, then GIS will allow us to link a wide variety of data sets for analysis and so release 'added value' in analytical terms. This is a very exciting possibility since many public data (such as the official Criminal Statistics) are still constrained by design features which reflect the technology available to their Victorian originators.

[6] Lack of space means that the comparison between urban and rural areas will not be fully discussed. Criminological data of all kinds (police data, victimization surveys, self-report studies) consistently support the view that rates of crime and criminality in urban and rural communities are very different indeed. Yet, in any serious sense, this must be one of the most under-studied topics in criminology, and, curiously, even environmental criminologists have shown very little sustained interest in it. Urban sociologists have, quite rightly, pointed out that, in a sociological sense, modern societies are in effect entirely urbanized; yet paradoxically, despite this, the urban–rural distinction in crime and offender rates has remained very clear.

From what has been said so far, it will be apparent that, originally, the main source of interest underpinning the early development of environmental criminology was the creation of *modern societies*. As we shall see in more detail at the end of this chapter, however, a significant group of scholars now argue that the social transformations of the late twentieth century have already projected us from 'modern' to 'late modern' societies, a transformation that, it is said, may have as profound an influence on social life as the original arrival of industrialization and urbanization. We shall have to return to this thesis, and its criminological implications, after discussing the more orthodox literature of environmental criminology.

Traditionally, the two central concerns of environmental criminology have been *explaining the spatial distribution of offences* and *explaining the spatial distribution of offenders*. Hence, sections on these topics will form the core of this chapter. These central sections will, however, be preceded by an historical introduction and some methodological comments; and they will be followed by a brief discussion of the relationship between the areal distribution of offences and offenders. These 'static' analyses will then be supplemented by a review of studies of how social change can affect crime and criminality in particular areas. Finally, to conclude the chapter, some of the social transformations of 'late modernity' will be briefly described, and their consequences for criminology considered.[7]

ENVIRONMENTAL CRIMINOLOGY: A BRIEF HISTORY

In a chapter of this length there is not the space to discuss the nineteenth century precursors of environmental criminology.[8] However, because of its major subsequent influence, considerable attention must be paid to the criminological work carried out between the two world wars from within the Chicago School of Sociology (for general accounts of this group of sociologists, see Bulmer, 1984 and Kurtz, 1984).

The main Chicagoan criminological contribution came from Clifford Shaw and Henry McKay, whose *magnum opus* on juvenile delinquency in urban areas is still read, half a century on (Shaw and McKay, 1942). As well as making a theoretical contribution themselves—notably through the theory of 'social disorganisation' (see below)—Shaw and McKay's research heavily influenced much other criminological theory in the 1930s, notably Thorsten Sellin's (1938) 'culture conflict' theory and Edwin Sutherland's theory of

---

[7] The important but specialized topic of design and crime has had to be omitted for reasons of space Among the most important literature on design and crime, see Newman (1973), Poyner (1983), Coleman (1985, 1989), Poyner and Webb (1992), Taylor and Gottfredson (1986), and Department of the Environment (1997).

[8] On this nineteenth-century background see generally Morris, 1957: chapter 3; Radzinowicz, 1966: chapter 2; Tobias, 1972.

differential association (see Cressey, 1964). But Shaw and McKay's main contribution to criminology was empirical, and here their research embraced two very different styles, always seen by the authors as complementary. In the first place, they meticulously mapped the residences of juvenile delinquents, first of all in Chicago at different points in time, and then in other American cities. Secondly, they also tried, in the tradition of the Chicago School more generally, to stay close to the life of the people and the communities they were writing about, particularly by producing life histories of offenders and low life in the city[9] (see for example Shaw, 1930).

For present purposes, we can concentrate mainly on Shaw and McKay's mapping of delinquent residences. In developing this research, they drew upon the more general work in urban sociology of the Chicago School, notably that of Robert E. Park and Ernest W. Burgess, the dominant concept of which was 'human ecology'. Human ecology was seen as the study of the spatial and temporal relations of human beings as affected by the selective, distributive, and accommodative forces of the environment; the concept was derived, by analogy, from the botanical sub-discipline of plant ecology. Shaw and McKay drew only to a limited extent upon the most explicitly quasi-biological elements of Park's urban sociology (see Alihan, 1938: 83), but they made quite central use of Burgess's zonal theory of city development. According to this theory, the typical city could be conceptualized as consisting of five main concentric zones (see Figure 8.1), the innermost of which was described as the non-residential central business district (or 'loop'),[10] which was then circled by a 'zone in transition' where factories and poorer residences were intermingled, and finally by three residential zones of increasing affluence and social status. New immigrants, it was postulated, would move into the cheapest residential areas of the city (in the 'zone in transition') and then, as they became economically established, migrate outwards. This would be a continuous process, so that the 'zone in transition' would (as its name implies) have a high residential mobility rate and, by implication, a rather heterogeneous population. In the case of a rapidly expanding city, particular districts which had once been peripheral and affluent might become, in time, part of the zone in transition within the larger metropolis (see e.g. Rex and Moore, 1967, on Sparkbrook, Birmingham).

Applying this zonal model to their empirical data, Shaw and McKay made the following three central discoveries:[11]

> *First*, the rates of juvenile delinquency residence conformed to a regular spatial pattern. They were highest in the inner-city zones and tended to decline with distance from the centre of the city; and this was so not only in Chicago but in other cities as well (see Table 8.1).

---

[9] For a discussion of the importance of the life history method and its links to environmental criminology see Howard S. Becker's introduction to the 1966 edition of Shaw, 1930.

[10] So called because the business area in Chicago was within the inner loop of Chicago's elevated transit system—'the L'.

[11] This formulation draws on that of Finestone (1976: 25).

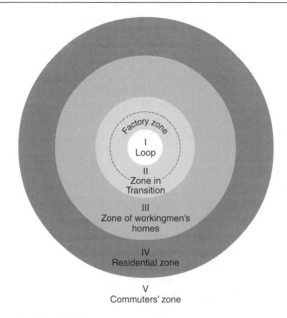

Fig. 8.1: E. W. Burgess's zone model of urban development
Source: Burgess (1925).

Table 8.1 Delinquency Residence Rates for the Concentric Zones of Seven American Cities, *c.*1930

	Zone 1	Zone 2	Zone 3	Zone 4	Zone 5
Chicago	10.3	7.3	4.4	3.3	–
Philadelphia	11.6	6.8	4.4	3.5	3.4
Richmond	19.7	12.2	6.4	–	–
Cleveland	18.3	10.2	7.8	7.0	5.1
Birmingham	14.1	6.9	6.4	–	–
Denver	9.4	7.1	4.2	3.7	3.2
Seattle	19.1	9.7	7.6	6.1	–

Source: Brantingham and Brantingham (1981: 14), collating data from various tables in Shaw and McKay (1931).

Secondly, the same spatial pattern was shown by many other indices of social problems in the city.

Thirdly, the spatial pattern of rates of delinquency showed considerable long-term stability, even though the nationality make-up of the population in the inner-city areas changed greatly from decade to decade (with successive waves of migration to American cities in the early twentieth century).

In seeking to explain these striking findings, Shaw and McKay focused especially upon the observed *cultural heterogeneity* and the *constant population movements* in the 'zone in transition'. As Robert Bursik (1986: 38) has pointed out, economic mobility lay at the heart of the process they described, but they did not posit a direct relationship between economic factors and rates of delinquency—rather, areas characterized by economic deprivation and physical deterioration were seen also as having population instability and cultural fragmentation, and it was these factors which especially influenced delinquency through a process which they called 'social disorganization' (although some later commentators have felt it could have been better described as 'lack of social organization'). This process, as seen by Shaw and McKay, was later well summarized by Finestone (1976: 28–9) in a passage that is worth quoting in full:

The same selective processes which made it relatively easy for the first generation of newcomers to the city to become aggregated in inner-city areas also permitted the location there of many illegitimate enterprises and deviant moral worlds. Such moral diversity within the inner-city areas meant that it was difficult if not impossible for immigrant communities to insulate themselves from illegitimate and criminal enterprises and influences. In the face of many centrifugal pulls, the traditional institutions, the family, the church, and the local community, became incapable of maintaining their solidarity. Their inability to organise effectively in defence of conventional values meant that they were unable to resist or limit the influence exercised upon their youth by the diverse value systems which became rooted in such areas. Continued high rates of delinquents in inner-city areas were a product of the joint operation of locational and cultural processes which maximised the moral diversity of population types at the same time as they weakened the collective efforts of conventional groups and institutions to protect their own integrity.'

Hence in Shaw and McKay's thinking, 'social disorganization exists in the first instance when the structure and culture of a community are incapable of implementing and expressing the values of its own residents' (Kornhauser, 1978: 63); and this was seen as strongly related to the genesis of juvenile delinquency because the community did not provide common and clear non-delinquent values and control.[12]

The subsequent history of the social disorganization concept is complex, and there have been a number of criticisms. Thus, many writers have argued that criminality might in certain circumstances stem from *organization* rather than disorganization, especially in areas with organized crime syndicates or well-entrenched criminal subcultures; those who take this view point out that just because actions are morally disapproved of, that does not mean that they are necessarily any less related to social organization, and not all groups share

---

[12] At various points in their writings, Shaw and McKay also speak of another and rather different theoretical approach to the explanation of criminality, namely that of *criminal subcultures*, linked to the *cultural transmission of delinquent values*. The precise relationship between these two varied theoretical strands of Shaw and McKay's work was not always made fully clear in their writings (see Kornhauser, 1978: chapter 3).

conventional value systems. Other critics have suggested that social disorganization theory pays insufficient attention to the distribution of power in society (see Snodgrass, 1976; cf. Bursik, 1986: 61); while yet others have suggested that the theory can be tautologous—that is, social disorganization theorists have sometimes used a single indicator (such as a delinquency rate) both as an example of disorganization and as an effect allegedly caused by disorganization. Finally, like a number of other early sociological theories of crime, it has been argued that social disorganization theory is over-deterministic and therefore over-predictive of crime (see e.g. Matza, 1964). Despite these various criticisms, the concept of social disorganization remains a live one in contemporary environmental criminology, and we will return to it later.

It is a measure of the standing and achievement of Shaw and McKay that, in the quarter-century immediately after the end of the Second World War, there were relatively few major new developments in environmental criminology, despite the publication of some significant individual research monographs (e.g. Lander, 1954; Morris, 1957). Moreover, throughout this period the relationship between crime and the urban environment was routinely referred to as 'the ecology of crime', so implicitly acknowledging the intellectual pre-eminence in the field of the Chicago School (interestingly, this nomenclature is not dead even today). But this post-war lack of challenge to the supremacy of the Chicago School was accompanied also by some loss of interest, among mainstream criminologists, in the spatial dimension of the study of crime. Accordingly, in 1965 a leading criminologist in Britain, Hermann Mannheim, commented in his major textbook that 'ecological theory . . . reached the peak of its popularity in the period between the two world wars, but has gradually retreated into the background in the decades after 1945' (Mannheim, 1965: 532).

But the 1970s were to see environmental criminology given fresh impetus; and in this respect two main developments were perhaps of particular importance.

The first of these might be described as the *rediscovery of the offence*. Shaw and McKay's work had been all about *areas of delinquent residence*, i.e. the areas where the juvenile delinquents lived. But these *high offender rate areas* (to adopt the usual technical term) are in fact not necessarily the same as *high offence rate areas* (i.e. areas with a high rate of offence commission), since offenders do not necessarily commit offences close to their homes (see further below). With few exceptions, most early work in environmental criminology (including that of Shaw and McKay) had shown very little systematic interest in offence locations.

Various different criminological developments combined to re-focus attention on *crimes* rather than *offenders* in the 1970s (see generally P. J. and P. L. Brantingham, 1981, Introduction). These included the first large-scale victim surveys (carried out in the USA in the late 1960s), and the early work of the Home Office Research Unit on 'crime as opportunity' (Mayhew *et al.*, 1976), leading in due course to the more sophisticated development of 'situational crime prevention' theory (see Clarke, 1995). Additionally, the early 1970s saw the publication of the influential work of the architect Oscar Newman (1973) and others on design and crime ('defensible space'); and C. Ray Jeffrey's (1971) wide ranging volume, *Crime Prevention through Environmental Design*. In the wake of these new strands of work, by 1981 Paul and Patricia Brantingham were able to open their influential edited book on environmental criminology with the following offence-centred paragraph—though apparently without realizing that their definition of 'environmental criminology' actually excluded most of Shaw and McKay's massive endeavours:[13]

A crime is a complex event. A crime occurs when four things are in concurrence: a law, an offender, a target, and a place. Without a law there is no crime. Without an offender, someone who breaks the law, there is no crime. Without some object, target, or victim, there is no crime. Without a place in time and space where the other three come together, there is no crime. These four elements—law, the offender, the target, and the place—can be characterized as the four dimensions of crime. Environmental criminology is the study of the fourth dimension of crime [P. J. and P. L. Brantingham, 1981: 7].

It will become apparent later in this chapter that this 'rediscovery of the offence' in environmental criminology has been of major importance in the field. Moreover, the careful synthesis of work on the explanation of *who commits offences* (offender-based theory) with work on the explanation of *where and why offences are committed* (offence-based theory) can be regarded as an issue of central significance in contemporary criminology (see further below).

The second major development of the 1970s came more in the field of explaining offender rates. Once again, it had its precursors. In his pioneering 1957 book, Terence Morris (1957) carried out an empirical study of Croydon, and showed that the areal rates of offender residence in that borough did not conform particularly well to the Chicago zonal hypothesis, not least because of the existence of high offender rate council estates located at a considerable distance from the urban centre (on council estates see note 4 above). Commenting on this point—a product, of course, of post-1920 British housing policy—Morris (1957: 130) shrewdly observed that:

where the provision of housing is not solely within the province of the market, and the local authority has stepped in to provide housing as a social amenity for a not inconsiderable proportion of the population, then the natural ecological processes of selection manifesting themselves in the cycle of 'invasion-dominance-succession' are likely to be severely modified by social policy, with strikingly different results.

All these points were to be confirmed and strengthened in work in the city of Sheffield, published in the 1970s (Baldwin and Bottoms 1976). Figure 8.2

---

[13] To be fair, in this source the Brantinghams (1981: 8) do refer to the 'movements that bring the offender and the target together at the same site', and to the question of 'how the fourth dimension of crime interacts with the other three dimensions'. It is nevertheless striking that their *definition* of environmental criminology does not embrace the study of the location of offender residence.

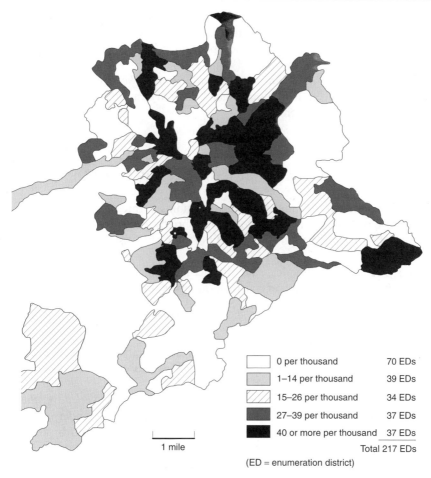

☐	0 per thousand	70 EDs
	1–14 per thousand	39 EDs
	15–26 per thousand	34 EDs
	27–39 per thousand	37 EDs
■	40 or more per thousand	37 EDs
		Total 217 EDs

1 mile

(ED = enumeration district)

Fig. 8.2: Areal distribution of adult male offender residences in Sheffield, 1966
Source: Baldwin and Bottoms (1976: 75).

illustrates the adult offender rates found in that city: while there is indeed
still something of a clustering of high offender rate areas around the central
business district, the data overall show 'no tidy zonal model . . . [rather], areas
with high and low offender residence rates were distributed throughout the city
in apparently haphazard fashion' (P. J. and P. L. Brantingham, 1984: 322). In
seeking to explain the offender rate patterns found, the Sheffield researchers
were drawn increasingly towards the exploration of the *direct and indirect
consequences of the operation of the housing market* (see for example Bottoms
and Wiles, 1986). As we shall see in later sections of this chapter, this emphasis
on housing markets has also been taken up by other researchers (some
influenced by the Sheffield research, and others working independently), and
has been found to be of particular significance when assessing change in

offender and offence rates in residential areas. These considerations have taken some researchers working on crime-related topics deep into analyses of the complex housing market contexts of particular local areas (see for example Taub *et al.*, 1984; Bottoms *et al.*, 1989).

The *rediscovery of the offence* and the *discovery of the significance of housing markets* have, between them, done much to revivify environmental criminology in the last quarter of a century.

PRELIMINARY METHODOLOGICAL ISSUES

Before we turn to substantive research findings, three key methodological issues in environmental criminology must briefly be addressed: they are the offence/offender distinction, the validity of official statistics, and the so-called 'ecological fallacy'.

The offence rate/offender rate distinction has already been highlighted above. It is an absolutely central issue in environmental criminology, as will quickly become apparent if one compares a map of offence locations in any given town with a map of offender residences in the same year (see, for example, Baldwin and Bottoms 1976: 58–79). Interestingly, however, research has shown that if one excludes areas such as the city centre and industrial districts, then there is a high (but not perfect) correlation between offender and offence rates in *residential* areas (Mawby, 1979).[14]

One should further note (see Bottoms and Wiles, 1986: Appendix) that, in any given geographical area, both the offence rate and the offender rate are in principle measurable both by official (police-recorded) data and by research-generated data seeking to improve upon official statistics (namely, victim surveys in respect of offence rates, and self-report studies in respect of offender rates). In practice, however, self-report studies carried out on an areal basis are rare. One should also be aware that there is an important distinction in principle between an *area offence rate* and an *area victimization rate*. The former measures all offences committed in an area, whether against businesses, individual residents, or individuals who are visiting the area; the latter measures all offences committed against a defined population (e.g. respondents to a household victim survey living in a particular residential district), *wherever those offences were committed.* Because of this conceptual difference, particular care must be taken in comparing total police-recorded offence rates for an area (which will be geographically bounded, but will include offences against businesses and individual visitors to the area) with overall rates generated from a household victim survey carried out in the same area (which will exclude crimes against businesses, and individual victims visiting the area, but will

---

[14] Unfortunately, some early research studies did not adequately appreciate the importance of the offence/offender rate distinction, with sometimes confusing results. For a discussion of such studies, see P. J. and P. L. Brantingham (1981:17).

include crimes committed against residents of the area when they have ventured outside the district, e.g. to the city centre or their place of work).

These considerations take us straight to the second methodological issue, that of the validity of official criminal statistics in relation to area-based data. There has been a lively and ongoing debate on this issue, with particular scepticism about the validity of official statistics being expressed during the heyday of labelling theory in the 1970s (for a useful historical overview of the debate, see Mawby, 1989). Commenting on this debate in a short space is difficult, but to begin with the uncontroversial, there is now little doubt that, on a large-area basis—for example as between different large counties—the message conveyed by official criminal statistics can be seriously misleading (see for example the study by Farrington and Dowds (1985) in Nottinghamshire and comparable counties), owing especially to different police investigative and recording practices in different administrative areas, and perhaps to differential levels of public reporting of crime to the police. On a smaller-area, within-city basis, however, as Mawby (1989) points out, there are two main grounds for believing that differential police-recorded offence and offender rates as between different areas might often express a basically true difference in crime or criminality levels:

> *First*, the results of victim surveys have consistently shown a higher crime victimization rate for inner-city areas and poor council estates, as compared with more affluent suburbs, exactly as shown in official police data (see for example the Merseyside crime survey (Kinsey, 1985) and the aggregated area-based results from different parts of England and Wales in the British Crime Survey (Hope and Hough, 1988, and Mayhew and Maung, 1992: Table 5). (Note, however, in respect of these results the previously mentioned distinction between victimization and offence rates.)
>
> *Secondly*, as part of the Sheffield project, a careful area-based analysis of the validity of official criminal statistics on offences and offenders in nine small areas was carried out by Mawby (1979) (see also Bottoms, Mawby, and Walker 1987, for a related victim survey). This showed 'no indication of area [offence and offender rate] differences being radically altered due to the different actions of the police (or indeed the public) in different areas' (Mawby, 1979: 182).

One must, however, be quite careful in interpreting the above results. On the one hand, the research cited certainly shows that differential official offence and offender rates in different small areas of cities *might* be valid indicators of real differences in crime/criminality levels. On the other hand, it is important not to overstate the results, nor to over-generalize from them. The Sheffield results, for example, largely concerned offences that were policed reactively rather than pro-actively, and different issues arise in respect of pro-actively policed offences such as prostitution (cf. Lowman, 1986). Moreover, P. J. and P. L. Brantingham's (1991: 4) somewhat grandiose claim that the Sheffield results appear 'to have established that official statistics are valid Euclidean indicators of area crime rate differences in that city, creating a working presumption that such might be the case in other places as well' unfortunately goes beyond the evidence of the Sheffield study.[15] The more modest truth is that official crime and offender data often seem to reflect real differences between sub-areas of cities, but that in any given case this cannot be taken for granted and must be investigated.

The third preliminary methodological issue to consider is the so-called 'ecological fallacy', discussed mathematically in a famous article by Robinson (1950). This fallacy, which was sometimes unfortunately evident in early studies in environmental criminology,[16] occurs where 'the assumption [is] made that the descriptive characteristics of *areas* having high proportions of offenders resident also [identify] . . . the *individuals* who are likely to commit crimes' (P. J. and P. L. Brantingham, 1981: 17). To take a simple example of the fallacy, in the 1960s various British research studies demonstrated that recorded crime rates were highest in areas with a relatively high rate of recent ethnic minority immigration (mostly from the Caribbean and the Indian sub-continent), but research also showed, at that time, that on an individual basis such immigrants had on the whole rather low offending rates (see Baldwin and Bottoms, 1976: 37–8, for references relating to this example). While Janson (1993) has recently argued that examples where ecological and corresponding individual correlations move in opposite directions are the exception rather than the rule, it is nevertheless clear that the wise researcher would do very well to seek to avoid the fallacy, in any instance where he/she has access primarily to area-based data (e.g. Census data) rather than individual data.

Having considered these three methodological issues, we can now turn to the substantive results of modern environmental criminology.

EXPLAINING THE LOCATION OF OFFENCES

We begin with the explanation of the location of offences. A preliminary problem here concerns how to measure areal offence rates, given that the use of the resident population as a denominator is often not very helpful (see Harries, 1981). To appreciate the force of this point, the reader might like to consider the obvious inappropriateness of using the resident population as a denominator for a study of, say, thefts of and from cars in commuter car-parks at semi-rural outer-city railway stations, drawing their passengers from a wide hinterland.

[15] This is most obvious in the 1980s follow-up study of one pair of areas (see Bottoms, Claytor, and Wiles, 1992); but even in the original 1970s small-area study, the ratio of survey-reported crime to officially recorded differences was substantially higher in a pair of high-rise council estates than in other comparable areas studied (see Bottoms, Mawby, and Walker, 1987: Table 5, row 4, and commentary at 138–9).

[16] See Baldwin (1979) for some examples of the ecological fallacy in early research studies.

Table 8.2 Per-Olof Wikström's suggestions for appropriate denominators in area studies of offence rates

Crime	Suggested best denominator	Chosen denominator
Family violence	No. of households	No. of households
Non-family violence and vandalism in residences	No. of residences	No. of residences
Violence in public	No. of meetings between people	Hectare
Vandalism in public	?	Hectare
Residential burglaries	No. of residences	No. of residences
Cellar/attic burglaries	No. of residences in multi-storey houses	No. of residences in multi-storey houses
Non-residential burglaries	No. of companies and public institutions	No. of people working in area
Thefts of and from cars	No. of cars	Hectare

Source: Wikström (1991: 196).

Wikström (1991), in a study of recorded offences in Stockholm, carefully considered the denominator problem for different kinds of offence. He distinguished between the 'suggested best denominator' for each offence, and the best practicable denominator within the data available for his own study (called 'the chosen denominator'). His choices in these two categories are shown in Table 8.2 and clearly illustrate the nature of the denominator problem, although readers should be aware that other choices could have been made.

Wikström's study provides one of the best illustrations of the way in which police recorded offences are locationally distributed in a major city. Previous research work in Sheffield (Baldwin and Bottoms, 1976) and elsewhere had shown that offences in general tend, in traditional cities, to be very much clustered around the city centre;[17] and the offence rates in Wikström's study (see Figure 8.3, (a), (b), and (c)) show this to be especially the case for violence in public, vandalism in public, and theft of and from cars. (Wikström does not present data concerning shoplifting or thefts from the person, but other research studies show that these offences also are particularly located in city centres.) However, it should be noted that there is nothing necessarily immutable about such patterns: for example, in cities that develop large shopping or entertainment complexes on peripheral sites, one would expect some corresponding modification of this traditional geographical pattern.

---

[17] In fact in Sheffield in 1966 24 per cent of recorded offences were committed within a half-mile radius of the centre of the city, though this area constituted less than 3 per cent of the total land area in the city (Baldwin and Bottoms, 1976: 57).

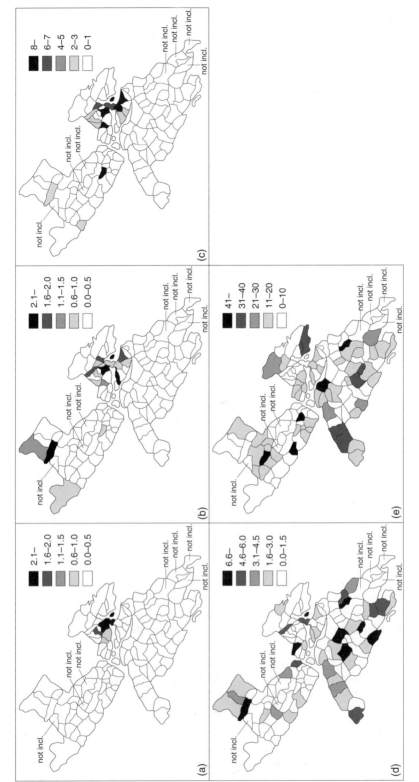

Fig. 8.3: Areal offence rates for selected types of crime, Stockholm, 1982: (a) violence in public per hectare; (b) vandalism in public per hectare; (c) thefts of and from cars per hectare; (d) family violence per 1,000 households; (e) residential burglaries per 1,000 residences

Source: Wikström (1991: 203–6).

Turning to offences in residential areas, the distributions of family violence and residential burglaries in Wikström's study are shown in Figure 8.3, (d) and (e). The highest rates of family violence were found in certain outer-city wards, and further analysis showed that there was a strong positive correlation (at an area level) between (i) an area's rates of recorded family violence and (ii) its score on a factor (derived from a factor analysis of social areas in Stockholm) which was labelled by Wikström as 'problem residential areas'[18] (Wikström, 1991: 226). Hence, and perhaps not surprisingly, police-recorded family violence was heavily concentrated in poorer public housing areas. A further inspection of the maps at Figure 8.3, (d) and (e), indicates however that the distribution of offences of residential burglary was substantially different from that of family violence, and additional analysis by Wikström (1991: 226–7) showed that residential burglaries in fact tended to occur in areas of high socio-economic status, and especially in districts where there were nearby high offender-rate areas. This finding, while not unique in the literature,[19] conflicts with the results of some other research studies, which suggest that rates of residential burglary are greatest in, or in areas close to, socially disadvantaged housing areas (for a summary, see Maguire and Bennett, 1982: 20–1). Possible reasons for these conflicting results will become apparent as the discussion proceeds.

Wikström's study fairly conclusively demonstrates, at any rate as regards crimes as measured by official data, *first* that there are marked geographical skews in the patterning of offence locations, and *secondly* that these can vary significantly by type of offence. This general message has been heavily reinforced, at a micro level of analysis, by research on so-called 'hotspots' of crime. For example, Lawrence Sherman *et al.* (1989) used 'police call data' for the city of Minneapolis for 1985–6, and found, *inter alia*, (i) that just 3.3 per cent of specific addresses or intersections in the city generated 50 per cent of crime-related calls to the police to which cars were despatched, and (ii) that there was considerable variation in the victimization rate (as measured by call data) of specific micro-locations even *within* high crime rate areas—that is, even high-crime areas have their relatively safe specific locations, as well as their 'hotspots' where the public are likely to be especially vulnerable.[20]

The above discussion of offence locations has been primarily descriptive. We need now to attempt to explain the variations discussed; and we will begin with the related concepts of opportunity and routine activities.

[18] This was derived from a factor analysis not including offence or offender data. The main loadings on the factor were: (i) positive loadings: percentage on public welfare assistance; immigrants (foreign citizens); non-profit housing; children with single working parents; and percentage blue-collar workers; (ii) negative loadings: old residences; mean income; flats in smaller houses; large residences; and percentage of people over 60 (Wikström, 1991: 123–4).

[19] See e.g. Baldwin and Bottoms (1976: 63), Winchester and Jackson (1982: 18–19). It should be pointed out that these studies, like Wikström's, are based on data recorded by the police, and it is likely that they proportionately overstate the number of high-value burglaries, since value is known to be related to the decision to report.

[20] See also Sherman's later discussion of 'hot spots' in Sherman (1995). For other similar work see Block and Block (1995), and for an excellent critical review Spelman (1995).

Opportunity Theory and Routine Activities Theory

As Clarke (1995) has shown in some detail, the concept of opportunity is a multifaceted one. In the context of environmental criminology, two aspects of opportunity are especially important (Bursik and Grasmick, 1993: 70). The first of these can be described as *target attractiveness*, a concept which includes both value (monetary and/or symbolic) and portability. In terms of the location of offences, the value of property can sometimes be of special importance, both as regards the general affluence of an area (see Wikström's data on residential burglary, above), and as regards the value of a particular target, by comparison with neighbouring potential targets. For example, in the British Crime Survey's analysis of car crime, it has been found that, within a given area, the cars of more affluent residents are more likely to be targeted.[21]

The second main dimension of opportunity might be described as *accessibility,* a concept that includes visibility, ease of physical access, and the absence of adequate surveillance. This dimension of opportunity is well illustrated from an analysis by a crime prevention team in Croydon of the risk rates for autocrime from different multi-storey car parks in the town centre (reported by Liddle and Bottoms; see table in Bottoms, 1994: 603). It was shown that the three short-stay car parks which were used primarily by shoppers (and which therefore had a constant stream of passers-by acting as a form of natural surveillance) had substantially lower crime rates than the long-stay car parks, primarily used by London commuters who would leave their cars all day in parks near the railway station where, in the nature of the case, there was much less coming and going by members of the public, as well as visibility and easy physical access.[22] Other (and similar) examples of the importance of accessibility and natural surveillance can also be found in the literature (see e.g. Clarke, 1983, or Mayhew *et al.*, 1976).

The 'opportunity' approach to the explanation of crime patterns, as outlined above, is very closely related to so-called 'routine activities theory', originally developed in an article by Cohen and Felson (1979) and subsequently elaborated mostly by Marcus Felson and others (see e.g. Felson, 1986, 1992, and 1995 and Eck, 1995). The central hypothesis of routine activities theory was originally stated as: 'the probability that a violation will occur at any specific time and place might be taken as a function of the convergence of likely offenders and suitable targets in the absence of capable guardians' (Cohen and Felson, 1979, 590).

However, of the three elements identified in the above quotation, routine

---

[21] Specifically, in thefts of and from cars from immediately around the house, 'consumerist' households were more likely to be victimized, even when area and type of residence were controlled for (see Mayhew *et al.*, 1993: 140–1). ('Consumerist' households were those owning three or more of five specified electronic consumer products).

[22] A complicating variable here was that each car on average stayed longer in the commuter car-park (= greater opportunity); however, even when the data were calculated as a 'rate per car park space' (in effect controlling for this difference), the commuter car parks had substantially higher autocrime rates

activities theory (as developed by its advocates) has in practice concentrated very heavily on the second and third (suitable targets and capable guardians).[23] That being so, the link with opportunity theory is self-evident; but there are nevertheless two features of the routine activities approach which develop and in a sense extend the straightforward concept of 'opportunity'. These features are as follows:

> *First*, there is a strong interest within routine activities theory in *the day-to-day activities of potential victims of crime, and of those potentially able to offer 'natural surveillance'*. There is therefore seen to be an interdependence between the varied social organization of daily life patterns (for example, in different decades, and/or in different places, and/or among different social groups in the same area) and the spatial-temporal structuring of illegal activities.
>
> *Secondly*, routine activities theory has an explicitly spatial dimension which, while implicitly present in simple opportunity theory, has not always been much developed by writers of that school. Routine activities theory, on the other hand, precisely because of its interest in the everyday lives of potential victims of crime and of potential 'natural guardians', specifically emphasizes 'the fundamental human ecological character of illegal acts as *events* which occur at specific locations in *space* and *time*, involving specific persons and/or objects'. (Cohen and Felson, 1979: 589, emphasis in original).

In sum, routine activities theory in effect embeds the concept of opportunity within the routine parameters of the day-to-day lives of ordinary people, and in doing so also emphasizes the spatial-temporal features of opportunity. For those interested in social theory, these features of Cohen and Felson's work present an intriguing parallel with Anthony Giddens's (1984) 'theory of structuration'—a major contemporary approach to some fundamental questions about the nature of human action in its relationship to social structures—since Giddens's theory also includes among its innovative features (i) a greater emphasis on routine daily social practices than is to be found in most social theory, and (ii) an unusual insistence (for a modern writer) that space-time issues lie at the heart of the concerns of social theory, and are not merely 'a particular type or "area" of social science which can be pursued or discarded at will' (Giddens 1984: 110).[24]

Once one begins—as in Cohen and Felson's approach—to link the opportunity concept to that of routine activities, then other relevant issues in

---

[23] See Cohen and Felson (1979: 589): 'Unlike many criminological enquiries, we do not examine why individuals or groups are inclined criminally, but rather we take criminal inclination as given and examine the manner in which the spatio-temporal organisation of social activities helps people to translate their criminal inclinations into action'. Felson has however subsequently considered the offender dimension to a limited extent: see e.g. Felson (1986).

[24] Interestingly, Felson has now developed his concept of 'guardianship' to include (a) the guardianship of targets, (b) the supervision of likely offenders by 'handlers', and (c) and supervision of places by 'managers', all of which can be studied spatially (Felson, 1995).

considering the spatial distribution of offences also begin to become apparent. One such issue is that of *self-policing*, as it affects potential offences against the person. Potential victims can respond to possible opportunities for them to be attacked by various kinds of 'avoidance' behaviour. Since there is clear empirical evidence of substantially greater harassment of women (especially younger women) in the public spaces of cities (see e.g. Anderson *et al.*, 1990: 23–4; Painter, 1992), it is hardly surprising that women especially are likely to engage in 'self-policing' activities of this kind as regards their use of public space (see e.g. Ramsay, 1989). Unfortunately, such routine self-policing activities might themselves have further social consequences of an unintended kind—hence Kate Painter (1992: 181) for example suggests that what she calls 'women's space evasion at night' might compound the fears of other women (who may see very few women using certain kinds of public space), and also perhaps help to undermine, by degrees, the overall quality of life in parts of the urban environment (see below on dynamic processes of social decline in specific neighbourhood contexts).

Taking all the evidence of this subsection together, there is not much doubt that the broad concept of 'opportunity' (understood here as incorporating the routine activities approach) powerfully influences crime locations. But is it the *only* relevant variable to be considered in explaining the spatial distribution of offences? A booklet published by the Home Office Crime Prevention Unit (Home Office, 1988: 15) a decade ago seemed to imply that it was:

Most crimes do not occur at random but tend to be concentrated in particular places or to occur at particular times of the day. This is a reflection of the fact that crime is most likely to occur where the opportunities for it are greatest. A housing estate renowned for the insecurity of its doors and windows, or a car park dimly lit and protected from public view will almost certainly attract the criminal. It is the link between opportunity and crime which explains the crime patterns revealed through . . . a crime profile [drawn from police crime data].

Unfortunately, the research literature suggests that matters are more complex than this. To begin to see why that is so, let us first consider an ethnographic study of convicted burglars in a Texas city (Cromwell *et al.*, 1991). These authors found, congruently with opportunity theory, that offenders weighed potential gains, levels of guardianship (e.g. signs of occupancy) and risks of detection at possible sites of residential burglary (see also Bennett and Wright 1984). Hence, it appeared that *active weighing of the opportunity factor at the potential crime site* was a significant factor in the ultimate decision whether or not to commit a particular crime. On the other hand, Cromwell *et al.* also found that there was individual variation in the degree of planning between burglars (see also Bennett and Wright, 1984);[25] complex interactive effects within groups of burglars; differences related to whether illicit drugs were used

---

[25] Note, however, that Cromwell and his colleagues used a different (and wider) definition of 'opportunistic' than did Bennett and Wright—see Cromwell *et al.*, 1991: 48.

by the offenders; and that interactions with fences could affect the decision processes.

Opportunity theory uses a rational model of decision-making, but all too often its exponents have assumed both that the form of rationality is instrumental and that the actual behaviour mirrors the model—as the above quotation from the Home Office Crime Prevention Unit illustrates. Cromwell *et al.*'s (1991) research suggests a less straightforward empirical reality, and this view has been strongly reinforced by the most recent research on burglars' decision-making, by Wright and Decker (1994), which shows that decisions to offend can be irrational, arational, or rational, and, when rational, are more likely to be affectually rather than instrumentally rational[26] and be driven by short-term, immediate emotional needs. Insofar as targets were instrumentally assessed for degree of risk, Wright and Decker found that because most crimes were committed to satisfy an immediate need (for money, drugs etc.)[27] this was more often based on existing routine knowledge rather than a calculated process of crime planning prior to the act.

The work of Cromwell *et al.*, and especially that of Wright and Decker, draws attention to the routine activities of *offenders*. As previously noted, that is a subject in which the proponents of 'routine activities theory' have normally shown rather little interest (see note 23); but, as we shall now see, others have considered the topic, not least in a spatial context—and with interesting results that can be used to complement the insights of the opportunity and routine activities theorists.

Offenders' Use of Space

It is a commonplace of criminological textbooks that much crime is committed close to offenders' homes, though, not surprisingly, that is more likely to be true for juvenile delinquents than for adult offenders (see e.g. Baldwin and Bottoms, 1976: chapter 3). However, while a number of so-called 'crime and distance' studies may be found in the literature,[28] empirically exploring the data on detected offenders' distance from home when committing offences, it can plausibly be argued that this issue is in fact rather less interesting than is the related question of *the relationship of the place of the offence to the offender's habitual use of space*. To put the matter in non-technical terms, perhaps it is really of little significance that offenders A and B are one mile

---

[26] 'Affectual' and 'instrumental' rationality are borrowed from Max Weber's terms *Wertrationalität* and *Zweckrationalität*. Weber, of course, long ago spelt out the difference between behaviour and action and the different kinds of rational action. He also was at pains to point out that models of rational action are ideal types against which empirical reality has to be compared and understood. See Weber, 1949 and 1968.

[27] Interestingly Wright and Decker point out that their work reveals more about the non-instrumental nature of a burglar's actions than earlier studies because they interviewed non-incarcerated subjects and they suggest that those in prison are more likely to rationalize the accounts of their previous actions.

[28] For a review of such studies see McIver, 1981, and Costanzo *et al.*, 1986.

from home, while offenders C and D are three miles from home when they commit offences in the city centre, which they all regularly frequent. On the other hand, the difference between a burglar who commits offences in an area he knows well and one who is prepared to search carefully for a suitable target in a completely unknown residential area, might be a subject of much greater criminological importance and interest.

In preliminary exploration of this issue, let us first note that there are some purely *opportunist* crimes, where a person responds 'there and then' to a set of attractive environmental cues[29] (e.g. a teenage boy calls at a friend's house, finds the back door open and £20 unguarded on the table); and also some *affectively spontaneous* crimes, where a person commits, say, an assault in the course of a sudden heated argument with an acquaintance. These offences, by definition, must occur in the place where the offender happens to be, as a result of his/her daily life-choices. More than a decade ago, however, Patricia and Paul Brantingham (1981) proposed, in a very interesting hypothetical paper, that the offender's daily life patterns might influence the location of offending behaviour even where the offender was engaging, to some degree, in a search pattern for a suitable target, having already decided in principle to commit an offence (as, perhaps, in burglary). All of us, it was argued by these authors, carry in our heads 'cognitive maps' of cities where we live. Some parts of the city we will know extremely well (e.g. the areas immediately around our home, near our workplace, and in the city centre where we go for shopping and entertainment purposes); and we will also tend to know well the roads linking these various areas. On the other hand, there will be some areas of the city which we hardly know at all, such as residential areas (away from main roads) in which we have no social acquaintances and nothing else to attract us. The Brantinghams innovatively postulated that most offenders will not commit offences in poorly known areas; hence offences, even 'search pattern' offences, were, they argued, most likely to occur where *criminal opportunities* intersected with *cognitively known areas*—a hypothesis schematically illustrated in Figure 8.4.

Whilst the degree of empirical testing of this hypothetical model has not been extensive, what evidence we have tends clearly to support it, at least for many crimes (see for example Rhodes and Conly, 1981; Brantingham and Brantingham, 1991: 1–5, 239–51; Figlio *et al.*, 1986: Part 2). To illustrate this, we may look briefly at two small-scale studies of burglars, both carried out in the United States.[30]

Rengert and Wasilchick (1985: chapter 3) carried out an interview study of imprisoned adult burglars from Delaware County, Philadelphia. Burglars' home residences tended to be located in the south of the county, while the high

---

[29] This uses Bennett and Wright's (1984) definition of 'opportunist': see note 25 above.

[30] It is also worth noting that the Brantinghams' model has been successfully used in police detective work in serial assault cases by reversing the logic of the model, and constructing an algorithm to proximate the offender's likely residential or other familiar area, hence narrowing down the number of possible suspects (see Rossmo, 1995).

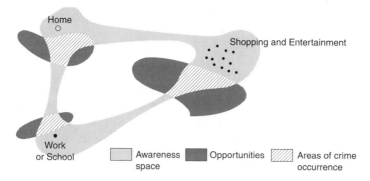

Fig. 8.4: The Brantinghams' hypothetical model of intersection of criminal opportunities with offender's cognitive awareness space

Source: Brantingham and Brantingham (1984: 362).

residential property values tended to lie in the north. Burglars were asked to rate each area of the county on a rating scale for familiarity: the results, not surprisingly, were that the areas near to offenders' homes were usually better known than other areas. When further asked for a scaled evaluation of each area of the county as a potential burglary site, the results were that the preferred areas for crime were generally not the burglars' home areas, but neither (with one exception in the north east of the county) were they the most affluent areas of the county. Interestingly, when these interview-based 'preferred' areas were compared with burglars' known offence locations (in their prior criminal records), there was a strong correlation, except that burglaries in the affluent north east area were very rare.

Hence, the adult recidivist burglars in this study tended to avoid the low-status areas of the south (because of poor target attractiveness and/or the higher probability of being caught in an area where they were well known), but they also avoided the unfamiliar affluent territory (with *good* burglary targets) to the north of the county.[31] Developing the analysis further, Rengert and Wasilchick obtained from their respondents details of their day-to-day journeys when not in prison (to their work, their usual recreational sites, etc.). They discovered that burglary sites were clustered very disproportionately in areas closest to the offenders' normal routes to work and recreation. By contrast, a very different directional pattern was observed for the few burglaries in the sample committed, not as a result of the offender's own search pattern, but because a secondary source (e.g. a fence) told the offender about an appropriate opportunity for crime. Overall, therefore, Rengert and Wasilchick's evidence can be seen clearly to support the hypotheses of the

[31] The following point, concerning the symbolic meaning of space, is also worth noting from this study: 'a cultural barrier to spatial movement [to the north of the county] seems to be West Chester Pike [a main road] . . . although the highway can be crossed easily, it seems to act as a perceptual dividing line between northern and southern parts of the county' (Rengert and Wasilchick, 1985: 62).

Brantinghams, while also showing that for some offences their propositions may be of little relevance.

An earlier study in Oklahoma City had found some similar results (Carter and Hill, 1979). Oklahoma City is a racially divided city, and neither black nor white offenders ventured much into residential areas predominantly lived in by the other ethnic group. Moreover, both groups of offenders committed offences predominantly in areas with which they were familiar, and where they felt comfortable ('ontologically secure', in sociological language). These facts, plus the fact that most blacks (offenders and non-offenders) in Oklahoma City had only a restricted familiarity with the city at large, explained 'the dense pattern of black [offenders'] crimes around their home neighborhoods' (Carter and Hill, 1979: 62). White offenders were (in general) familiar with more areas of the city, so their offences were more widely geographically spread.

Based on these findings, Carter and Hill (1979: 49) proposed an interesting distinction between 'strategic' and 'tactical' choices in search-pattern property crimes. 'Tactics' refer to 'short-term operational considerations for a specific crime', and may well be very strongly influenced by (rational) opportunity factors. However, these 'tactical' decisions, Carter and Hill suggest, will be taken only within a limited geographical framework already set by 'strategic' considerations. These 'strategic' considerations related especially to the issues of familiarity and ontological security referred to above and are thus more likely to be based on affective factors (e.g. 'areas towards which he has a favorable feeling': Carter and Hill, 1979: 49).

The offenders in Carter and Hill's study were much less able to articulate their 'strategic' than their 'tactical' choices, a point that is well illustrated in some conversational extracts printed by the authors (1979: 47–8).[32] These extracts strongly suggest that, to use the language of Giddens's structuration theory, offenders' broad choice of locations often seems to take place essentially in the realm of that *practical consciousness* which is so essential to the daily lives of all of us. 'Practical consciousness', in Giddens's terms, refers to the fact that human subjects largely act within a domain which cannot be expressed in terms such as 'motives' or 'reasons', but which 'consist of all the things which actors know tacitly about how to "go on" in the context of social life without being able to give them direct discursive expression' (Giddens, 1984: p. xxiii).[33] Wright and Decker's (1994) findings, discussed earlier, also point to the importance, for some aspects of the process of offending, of this reliance on pre-existing routine knowledge. These results and suggestions provide a plausible reason why so much offending takes place near offender's homes or other areas in which they routinely and regularly move.

---

[32] For example: 'they agreed that it is a lot of things, but no one thing in particular. One said, "you've got to look at the pros and cons of the situation". [But] what are they?—"I don't know . . . I just gotta feeling"' (Carter and Hill, 1979: 48).

[33] Hence, practical consciousness must be distinguished from 'discursive consciousness', which is 'what actors are able to say, or give expression to, about social conditions, including especially the conditions of their own action' (Giddens, 1984: 374).

Multiple Victimization

At this point, we must further complicate the emerging picture by drawing attention to a topic that has, until recently, been systematically neglected in criminological explanation, namely the issue of *multiple victimization*. This topic is covered more fully elsewhere in the present volume (see the chapter by Ken Pease), but for our purposes we need to note the following.

First, multiple victimization is not uncommon and the rate of multiple victimization varies by offence. For example, of those who reported being victimized in the 1996 British Crime Survey, 19 per cent of burglary victims had been victimized more than once; 28 per cent of car theft victims and 37 per cent of contact crime victims (Mirrlees-Black *et al.*, 1996—see also Farrell, 1995).

Secondly, even more interesting is that multiple victimization not only varies by offence type but its geographical distribution is also skewed. In particular multiple victimization is more common in high crime areas. Analysis by the Quantitative Criminology Group at Manchester University of the 1982 BCS data showed that 'the number of victimisations per victim rises markedly as area crime rates increase' (Trickett *et al.*, 1992) and, furthermore, between 1982 and 1988 the whole of the increased inequality in crime incidence as between different geographical areas in England and Wales was attributable to multiple victimization (Pease, 1993).

Thirdly, although multiple victimization is more common in high crime areas not everyone living in such areas is necessarily victimized, let alone multiply victimized.[34] This is because multiple victimization is also very unevenly distributed between individuals and households, and therefore geographically skewed even within high crime areas. In other words, the incidence of multiple victimization is geographically skewed at both the macro and micro levels. This skewed pattern mirrors, in a general sense, the skewed distribution of offence locations found by the hot spots analysis discussed earlier.

The Manchester Group's findings concerning the major contribution of multiple victimization to the increased cross-area crime inequalities of the 1980s inevitably directs attention to a macro level of analysis concerning possible relationships between crime trends and general social trends linked to studies in environmental criminology: a point to which we must return.

Wikström's Tentative Model for Explaining Offence Locations

So far, in this major section on explaining the location of offences, we have discussed opportunities, the routine activities of the general population, the

---

[34] For example, even in the worst decile areas of the country for property crimes, as measured in the 1988 British Crime Survey, 72 per cent of households had not been victimized even though the incident rate in such areas was 43 times higher than in the best decile areas (Farrell, 1995: Table A3).

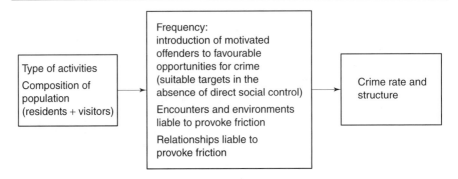

Fig. 8.5: Wikström's tentative model for explaining variations in crime rate and types of crime in the urban environment

Source: Wikström (1990: 24).

routine activities of offenders, and the role of multiple victimization. It is now time to try to draw some threads together, and seek to develop, if possible, some overall framework for understanding the way in which offences are geographically distributed.

Such a task was attempted by the Swedish criminologist Per-Olof Wikström (1990), as a prelude to a major study of crime in Stockholm. Wikström's 'tentative model', as he calls it, for the explanation of variations in crime rates and types of crime in the urban environment is set out in Figure 8.5.

This model begins (see left-hand box) by emphasizing basic *variations in land use* within the urban environment. This feature has two aspects: first, the types of activities which take place in the area (e.g. is the area predominantly residential or non-residential; if the latter, is it a shopping/industrial/leisure area, etc.); and secondly, the composition of the population at any given time (including here both residents and visitors). In drawing attention to these matters, Wikström also rightly emphasizes that particular areas may be the host to different kinds of activities (and/or populations) on different days of the week, or at different times of the day (cf. in this respect the difference between most city centres during weekday commercial hours, on weekday evenings, and on Friday and Saturday evenings).

Wikström's model then postulates that the *variations in land use* of the left-hand box will directly influence a number of criminologically relevant social interactions (see central box). The first of these is intended to embrace not only Cohen and Felson's emphasis on the routine activities of the general population, but also the Brantinghams' (1981) work on the cognitive spatial awareness of offenders (see Wikström, 1990: 21).

Wikström goes on to point out, however, that Cohen and Felson's concept of 'suitable targets' focuses principally upon theft and theft-related offences and upon instrumental personal crimes (e.g. robbery, stranger rape), and is less easily applied to expressive crimes (the majority of assaults or malicious

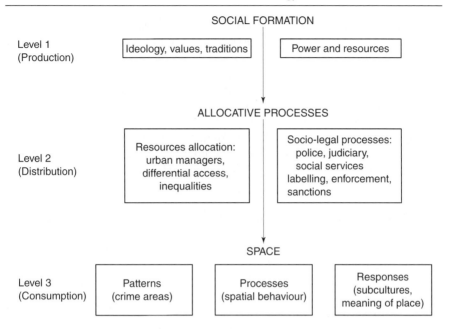

Fig. 8.6: David Herbert's conceptual framework for a geography of crime
Source: Herbert (1982: 26).

damage). Wikström therefore adds to the central box both 'encounters and environments liable to promote friction' and 'relationships liable to promote friction' (Wikström, 1990: 22–3). It hardly needs to be spelled out that the addition of these dimensions re-enforces the overall emphasis on routine activities within the explanation of offence location.

Wikström's 'tentative model' for explaining the location of offences is of very great interest and value. However, a number of points perhaps need to be made in elaboration and modification of the model.

In the first place, we should note that Wikström's model effectively begins with *variations in land use* in the city, taking this as essentially given. Wikström is well aware of the complexity of describing and analysing the diversity of sub-areas within a given urban environment (see Wikström, 1991: 181–4). Conceptually, however, it is perhaps worth taking this process a stage further by trying to set urban sub-areas within a wider sociological and geographical framework, in an attempt to explain more fully the types of activities and population composition found within specific areas (in other words, such a framework will ask questions logically prior to the matters raised in the left-hand box in Figure 8.5). A useful framework for this kind of exercise has been suggested by the geographer David Herbert (1982: 26)—see Figure 8.6. Whilst we would not wish to follow all of Herbert's specific concepts, his analysis very helpfully draws attention to the importance of three different levels of analysis.

First, there are the *macro-level material, political, and ideological factors* (of both political economy and ideology)—what Giddens (1984: 283) calls the 'structural principles' of a given society. Secondly, meso level *allocative processes*, within a given society, have considerable importance. Thirdly, both *spatial behaviour/processes* and the *meaning of place* are important at an individual or micro level—the latter being a specially significant issue, which has not always been given adequate attention by environmental criminologists. (Its significance derives from the fact that, to real-life actors, places are very often not just neutral locations for social interactions but may be, in symbolic terms, pregnant with meaning.) Additionally, Herbert's framework usefully emphasizes the intimate *interconnections* between the three levels that he specifies.

In short, therefore, to understand the land use variations in the left-hand box of Wikström's tentative model (Figure 8.5), we need a complex understanding of the interacting macro, meso, and micro social processes in society at large (see Figure 8.6).

We might perhaps add one further point. Wikström's model, as originally formulated, was essentially quantitative and factorial, and there is always the danger with such an approach that it underplays the more qualitative and processual aspects relevant to the subject (see also Bottoms and Wiles, 1992). The aggregate statistical patterns that the model seeks to portray are the result of perceptions and daily-life choices of individual actors within the city, and the way that these come together, and this raises the general (and very difficult) issue of how best to conceptualize the relationship between aggregate and individual dimensions of social reality in relation to crime (see generally Farrington *et al.*, 1993).[35] This relationship is, of course, an ongoing social process and a fully adequate model would need to pay fuller attention to the *changes* (as well as the continuities) in the use by social actors of different parts of the city.

With such modifications and developments, Wikström's outline model is of very considerable value in the explanation of offence locations.

EXPLAINING THE LOCATION OF OFFENDER RESIDENCE

We turn now to the problem of explaining the observed area distribution of offender residence.

As seen in an earlier section, traditionally this subject was heavily dominated by the conceptualizations of the Chicago School; and the explanations of the Chicago School were themselves strongly influenced by the facts of *stability over time* in the distribution of area offender rates, and (essentially) to the

---

[35] For an interesting paper on the methodological difficulties of integrating information from these different levels see Maltz (1995).

nature of land use in different zones of the city as an outcome of the operation of the market (Bursik, 1986: 61).

Post-World War II evidence, however, dealt a mortal blow to these under-pinning assumptions. As we saw earlier in this chapter (see Figure 8.2), offender rates in post-war British cities have borne little resemblance to the Chicagoan concentric ring pattern. Even in Chicago, careful analysis by Bursik (1986) has shown that the old areal regularities have broken down, and that while the areas of the city that underwent the most rapid social change generally experienced considerable increases in delinquency, nevertheless, there were some atypical areas where this relationship did not hold (see further Taub *et al.* (1984), discussed in a later section). Hence, while Shaw and McKay's social disorganization theory is still being supported and developed (see below), no-one would now defend—at least in any generalized fashion—the Chicago concentric ring theory and the formulation of urban process that went with it.

In order to see what might replace this approach, we shall look first at some statistical studies of the distribution of offender rates, and secondly at some more focused field research in local communities. Before turning to this evidence, however, let us consider how, in principle, area of residence and offender rates might be statistically related (this discussion develops that of Wikström, 1991: 130).

First, area of residence and offender rates might be related because more or less crime-prone individuals or groups are distributed (by the dynamics of the local housing market) to certain areas. In this kind of correlation, however, the social life of the area itself does not affect the criminality levels of the residents. To take an extreme example in order to make the point, there are some small council estates (or parts of estates) in British cities which are reserved for elderly tenants; obviously, one would expect such areas to have low offender rates, for reasons unconnected with social processes within the area.

Secondly, however, in principle *the social life of the area might itself influence criminal motivation*; and this possible influence is itself of two types. First, friendship patterns among local residents may lead to one being influenced by others to commit an offence. In such cases, it can be assumed (for the sake of argument) that the relevant social interactions would not have occurred had the offender lived elsewhere; but also that the transaction is a 'one-off' affair, not necessarily affecting the person's general way of living. Secondly, however, the social life of an area might have longer-term effects on a person's daily routines, social activities, thought processes, and even personality, such that his/her overall propensity to commit crime in certain situations is intrinsically affected. This kind of longer-term effect is obviously most likely to be mani-fested among young residents of an area, but the possibility of its occurring among older residents should not be ruled out.

In describing the first of the above possibilities, we referred to the operations of the local housing market as obviously relevant to the distribution of more or less crime-prone individuals to different areas. As we shall shortly see, one of our own central contentions is that the housing market is also the key to understanding the kinds of processes outlined in the second paragraph; but in order to see why this is so, we must examine some research studies.

Statistical Studies of Offender-rate Distribution

When the study of criminology at the University of Sheffield began, in the late 1960s, it was decided that it would be sensible to attempt, as a first major research project, a statistical study of recorded crime and offending in the city. Shortly before this project was begun, Rex and Moore (1967) had published an influential sociological analysis of Commonwealth migration to Birmingham, which emphasized how the detailed rules and social practices concerning access to particular kinds of housing were of *general* sociological importance in shaping the population composition of different geographical areas, and having significant subsequent effects on the kind of social community and social life developed in various districts. These observations seemed to the Sheffield researchers to be of some importance. Hence, in the statistical study of offender data and Census data that was then undertaken, it was decided to operationalize Rex and Moore's insights by classifying each Census enumeration district in terms of its predominant housing type, and then seeing whether these were of importance in 'explaining' (statistically) the offender rates of urban sub-areas, when population data were also considered. The answer proved to be emphatically in the affirmative (Baldwin and Bottoms, 1976: chapter 4). It was also found, however, that there were major variations in offender rates *within* the range of areas that shared a predominant housing type—for example, some council housing areas had very high offender rates, and some very low rates—and some preliminary more detailed exploration of the council sector revealed, *inter alia*, that there was no statistically significant relationship between the rate of tenant turnover on council estates and the offender rate (Baldwin and Bottoms 1976: 149–51, 169–71). These findings in general clearly suggested a potential importance for the housing market in explaining offender rates, but also (in the finding about residential mobility) indicated that one would have to look beyond the conceptualizations of the Chicago School—which, as we have seen, placed a special emphasis on residential mobility—if adequate sense were to be made of the data. This eventually led to more on-the-ground studies of particular areas in Sheffield, to be described in the next subsection.

Following on from the Sheffield statistical analysis of offender rates, Wikström (1991) conducted a similar analysis for Stockholm. He adopted a path model approach, hypothesizing that housing tenure variables would feed through to population composition variables, with the whole providing some statistical explanation of the varying offender rates in different districts. The final path model found that the housing type and social composition of areas explained about half the area variation in the total offender rates of different districts.

Wikström's statistical model itself is of some interest, *first* in seeming to confirm, from an overall analysis of offender rates in Stockholm, some of the messages of the Sheffield study; and *secondly* in showing—again like the Sheffield study—that the area offender rate is not by any means simply a reflection of the social class composition of the area. This last matter is of some general importance, since sceptics have not infrequently suggested that the study of high offender rate areas is simply the study of social class by another name.

Detailed Studies of Particular Areas

Whilst the statistical studies of offender rates on a whole-city basis (in Sheffield and Stockholm) seem to suggest that one must go beyond social class and social status in explaining differential offender rates, and seem further to suggest that the housing market is likely to be important in this respect, they are necessarily limited in their approach because they cannot address the qualitative aspects of social processes in particular areas.

Work in Sheffield subsequent to Baldwin and Bottoms's (1976) statistical analysis did, however, attempt this.[36] In particular, three pairs of small areas with contrasting offender rates were selected on the basis of the prior statistical analysis, with each pair being (in the mid-1970s) of a different housing type, as follows:

> *Pair 1: Low-rise council housing*
> Two adjacent areas, one with a high offender rate, one with a lower rate.
> *Pair 2: High-rise council dwellings*
> Two adjacent areas, one with a high offender rate, one with a lower rate.
> *Pair 3: Privately rented areas*
> Two non-adjacent areas, one with a high offender rate, one with a lower rate. The high-rate area was also, in the mid-1970s, Sheffield's principal prostitution area.

We will concentrate attention here on the first of these pairs, as it was in the mid-1970s (the following account draws principally upon Bottoms, Mawby, and Xanthos, 1989; for a follow-up study of the same areas in the 1980s see Bottoms, Claytor, and Wiles, 1992). Briefly, the original problem for explanation confronting the researchers was that these two small areas (population 2,500–3,000 each, and separated only by a main road), had (i) a 300 per cent difference in recorded offender rates, and a 350 per cent difference in recorded offence rates against individual residents and households, but (ii) no statistically significant differences at all on a set of key demographic variables (namely, sex; age; social class; ethnic origin; mean household size; percentage single; percentage male unemployment; age of termination of full-time education; and length of stay in current dwelling). Preliminary research (adult victim and

---

[36] For other detailed local British studies see e.g. Damer (1974); Herbert (1982: chapter 5, summarizing several of the author's studies in Cardiff); and Reynolds (1986).

juvenile self-report studies) established that the crime rate differences could not, for the most part, be regarded as artefactual. A further point of interest was that both areas had been built at approximately the same time (in the first quarter of the twentieth century), and both had, it seemed clear, begun as 'good', crime-free council areas. One of the estates (Stonewall) had retained this characteristic, but its neighbour (Gardenia) had 'tipped' sometime in the 1940s. Neither, however, was in any serious sense an 'area in transition'; rather, they were extremely settled, with 60 per cent of the adult residents in both areas having lived in their current dwelling for ten years or more.

The research team was unable to discover retrospectively exactly why Gardenia had tipped in the 1940s (though some speculative suggestions were made). But through detailed analysis of records in the local authority's housing department, plus ethnographic work in the areas, we were able to show that, once Gardenia had tipped, the local authority's rules of housing allocation had the unintended effects of maintaining the difference between the two areas,[37] and of ensuring that Gardenia attracted, as new tenants, predominantly (i) those in severe housing need, and (ii) those who had prior affective links with the area (relatives living on the estate etc.). To some extent, therefore, housing allocative processes were drawing to the two estates new residents with a differential propensity to offend (i.e. the first possible explanation for differential residential area offender rates discussed earlier). On the other hand, ethnographic work also showed that the second likely explanation also applied: the factors involved were very complex, and interactive, but included (in addition to the housing market context) certain physical geographical features; a mild criminal sub-culture in one part of the more criminal estate (Gardenia); the effects of the negative reputation of Gardenia on its residents and on potential residents; possibly a difference relating to the main schools serving the two areas; and some important differences in parental and peer socialization processes (see Bottoms, Mawby, and Xanthos, 1989: 67–75, especially 74).

Three points are of special importance about this case study. First, it must be re-emphasized that, in terms of social-class-related demographic variables, these two areas were almost identical; hence, the study presents a major obstacle to those who wish to argue that differential area offender rates are simply the product of macro-level aspects of social stratification, worked through to a local level. Secondly, very little in Shaw and McKay's conceptualization, nor that of later social disorganization theorists, helps one in explaining the difference between Gardenia and Stonewall, not least since neither area had high population turnover. And, thirdly, the researchers identified the operation of the local housing market as a key to understanding the areas; hence, this analysis reinforces David Herbert's (1982) emphasis, in his framework for a geography of crime, (see Figure 8.6) on meso-level

---

[37] Subsequently, however, there was some convergence between the two areas—but again this could be explained by housing market changes: see Bottoms, Claytor, and Wiles (1992).

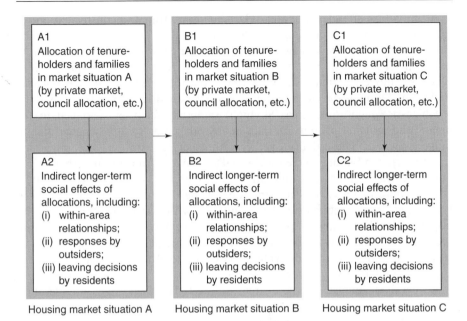

A1	B1	C1
Allocation of tenure-holders and families in market situation A (by private market, council allocation, etc.)	Allocation of tenure-holders and families in market situation B (by private market, council allocation, etc.)	Allocation of tenure-holders and families in market situation C (by private market, council allocation, etc.)
A2	B2	C2
Indirect longer-term social effects of allocations, including: (i) within-area relationships; (ii) responses by outsiders; (iii) leaving decisions by residents	Indirect longer-term social effects of allocations, including: (i) within-area relationships; (ii) responses by outsiders; (iii) leaving decisions by residents	Indirect longer-term social effects of allocations, including: (i) within-area relationships; (ii) responses by outsiders; (iii) leaving decisions by residents

Housing market situation A   Housing market situation B   Housing market situation C

Fig. 8.7: Diagrammatic representation of the relationship between the potential effects of the housing market and residential community crime careers

Source: Bottoms *et al.* (1992: 120).

allocative mechanisms in society as being important in relation to area differences in crime and offender rates.[38] The operation of the local housing market, however, does not work in a stand-alone fashion, nor only in relation to the population composition of an area. Rather, the Sheffield researchers stressed that the housing market could have crucial secondary social effects—in terms of, for example, the nature of the relationships which subsequently developed in an area, or responses by outsiders (including social control agents, potential residents, etc.). Subsequently, some of these effects might themselves have the potential to influence the housing market context of the area, e.g. by altering the area's perceived desirability, or perhaps escalating the number of residents wishing to leave. This complex interactive model is set out schematically in Figure 8.7 (taken from Bottoms, Claytor, and Wiles, 1992). It should be noted that the model has received strong implicit support from Hope and Foster's (1992) subsequent analysis of changes in criminality over time in another British council estate, but space precludes any detailed description of that study.

As previously noted, in the later stages of the Sheffield project, three pairs of areas (of contrasting housing types) were studied, with each pair having a

---

[38] It should be remembered (see earlier sec.) that local offence and offender rates tend to be positively correlated in *residential* districts.

high and a low offender rate area (Gardenia and Stonewall constituted one of the pairs). Without discussing the other areas in detail here, it is worth noting that the three high offender rate areas studied were (in the 1970s) very different in social terms. Both the other two high rate areas had higher proportions of recent move-ins than Gardenia (indicative of greater overall residential mobility). Alone of the three high rate areas, fewer than half of those living in the high-rise high-crime area (Skyhigh) said they felt they belonged to the area,[39] and a higher proportion than in any other area said they would like to move elsewhere. These data, together with other relevant evidence, suggested that residents in Skyhigh were substantially alienated from the area to a degree not shared in the other two high offender-rate areas. Meanwhile, the privately rented high-crime area was the only one of the three with substantial prostitution and drugs problems, and the only one with a sizeable ethnic minority population. These various points of difference between high offender-rate areas are of importance, because Chicago theorization would lead one to suppose that all high offender rate areas would tend to share broadly similar social characteristics, yet here were three that were very varied. Moreover, more detailed analysis of these areas showed that their high offender rate status, and the social and crime-type differences of each of them from the other two, could in every case be explained through the direct and indirect consequences of the housing market, as postulated in Figure 8.7. This further analysis, therefore, tends strongly to confirm the housing market approach as a key to an understanding of differential offender rates in different residential areas.[40]

Socialization Processes and Area Offender Rate Differences

One point in the preceding discussion now needs to be developed. When discussing Gardenia and Stonewall, it was noted that there were some important differences in peer and parental socialization processes as between the two estates. Since it is well known in the criminological literature that socialization processes can affect delinquency rates (the concentration here being upon parental socialization), it is not difficult to imagine some critics wishing to argue that much of the observed Gardenia–Stonewall area difference in criminality might be attributable to differential child socialization; the critics might then wish to pursue the case further by suggesting that the socialization difference was an *individual* effect, and hence that the extent to which there really were additional 'area contextual effects' in operation might be very doubtful (cf. Rutter and Giller, 1983: 204–6).

This line of argument is, however, in our view ultimately flawed, because it

---

[39] However, women respondents in the high-rate rented (prostitution) area also expressed alienation, to a degree similar to respondents of both sexes in Skyhigh.

[40] There is no published full comparative analysis of all three high-rate areas in the Sheffield study, but see Bottoms and Wiles (1986) for the nearest equivalent; see also Bottoms and Xanthos (1981) for a fuller account of Skyhigh (there called CFH).

fails to take account of the possibility that parental socialization processes might themselves be affected by area contextual characteristics. Yet exactly that possibility has been elaborated—in contradistinction to more traditional socialization theories—in Bronfenbrenner's (1979) so-called 'ecology of human development' frame of reference; and the Swedish criminologist Peter Martens (1990, 1993) has in recent years argued the case for the relevance of Bronfenbrenner's approach in criminological studies.

Bronfenbrenner particularly emphasizes that the child's development has to be seen in its *everyday context*; hence, he focuses less strongly than would some psychologists on purely psychological processes during the child's development, and more strongly on, as Martens (1993) puts it:

with *whom* the child *interacts* in day-to-day situations, the character of these inter-actions and in what ways persons outside the family can enhance or inhibit the quality of parent–child interaction. Hence, the focus is on . . . in Bronfenbrenner's own words, 'the actual environments in which human beings live and grow [Bronfenbrenner, 1979, p. xiv].

This 'actual environment' is then conceptualized in terms of a series of concentric circles (see Figure 8.8), in which the innermost represents the micro-level contexts in which the child is involved at any one time; the middle circle represents all those circumstances potentially having an indirect effect on these micro-level contexts (including parents' working status and conditions, local residential conditions, etc.); and the outer circle represents the macro-level context within which all this is set, and which obviously potentially affects the processes occurring in the middle circle. Among the consequences of all this, as Martens (1993) puts it, is that:

the success of parenting can depend on the support parents receive in their community in the form of social networks (relatives, neighbours, friends, etc.) or social services such as day nurseries and leisure centres. Parents living in a socially stable community have better outward conditions for their role than [other] parents.

At this point in the argument, one can begin to see some very interesting convergences between the way in which criminological understandings of *differential area offence rates* and of *differential area offender rates* have been developing. We saw in an earlier section that explanations of the location of offences now rely substantially, in various ways, on the concept of routine activities; but it was argued (via Herbert's framework) that such explanations needed to be set within a context of macro-social developments, and of meso-level allocative decisions by urban planners and others. As regards offender rates, it has been argued that the housing market (a crucial meso-level allocative mechanism) is of central importance, but that it has to be under-stood as operating in interaction with other social processes in the production of offender rates. Among those potential social processes is child socialization, and we have argued, via Bronfenbreuner and Martens, that child socialization should be seen not in purely psychological terms, but as influenced by the

Fig. 8.8: Schematic representation of relevant structures in an 'ecology of human development' socialization model

Source: Martens (1993), drawing on a Swedish article by K. Sandquist.

area context. In understanding that area context, however, not only are the everyday and routine activities of parents and others crucial to the child's socialization, but those processes themselves have to be set within meso-level and macro-level aspects of the organization of the wider society (Figure 8.8).

THE NEW CHICAGOANS

This chapter began with a fairly full explication of the work of Shaw and McKay, because it has remained a central reference point for much of the subsequent research. The city of Chicago has continued to be used as a vast laboratory for new generations of criminological researchers, and recently Robert Bursik and Harold Grasmick have laid claim to a re-flowering of the Chicago tradition of criminological explanation, and have given fresh prominence (within the context of contemporary criminology) to the study of high offender rate areas (Bursik and Grasmick, 1993).[41] Bursik and Grasmick present two main claims. They argue, first, that continuing research in Chicago (especially that by Bursik himself) supports Shaw and McKay's explanation of differential residential area offender rates: 'the most fully developed aspects of [Shaw and McKay's] model, which focused on the internal dynamics of local communities and the capacity of local residents to regulate the behavior of their fellow neighbors, continue to be significantly related to neighborhood variations in crime rates' (Bursik and Grasmick, 1993: p. x) But, secondly, Bursik and Grasmick argue that although Shaw and McKay saw the city as a set of inter-related neighbourhoods, they failed to take account of each neighbourhood's relations with the external world, and particularly the external world of politically organized social control. This lack, Bursik and Grasmick argue, can be corrected by linking social disorganization theory with control theory, as explicated by Ruth Kornhauser (1978):

this shortcoming of the social disorganisation perspective can be addressed by reformulating it within a broader systematic theory of community, which emphasises how neighborhood life is shaped by the structure of formal and informal networks of association. Not only is the orientation of a systematic model consistent with social disorganisation in its discussion of the regulatory capacities of networks embedded within the neighborhood, but it also formally addresses two aspects of community structure that Shaw and McKay virtually ignored: the networks amongst residents and local institutions, and the networks amongst local representatives of the neighborhood and external actors, institutions, and agencies [Bursik and Grasmick, 1993, p. x].

Bursik and Grasmick argue that much recent research provides empirical evidence for such a re-formulation, or what they refer to as the 'systemic theory of neighbourhood organisation'. Their systemic theory is that social control in neighbourhoods operates at three levels (following Hunter, 1985). The first is the *primary level* by which informal primary groups (such as families or friendship groups) socialize their members against deviance and sanction deviant acts. The second is the *parochial level* at which local networks and organizations (such as schools, businesses, or voluntary groups) exercise control. Finally, there is the *public level* at which agencies external to a neighbourhood either provide the resources to support primary and parochial level control (e.g. by adequately supporting schools or youth groups), or exercise external control, primarily by public policing. Basically, Bursik and Grasmick argue that the development and successful integration of these three levels of control takes time and can, therefore, only properly occur in neighbourhoods which are stable over time. Instability or, to use the concept of the original Chicago School, 'social disorganization' will, therefore, militate against the development of successful neighbourhood control over crime.

---

[41] Bursik and Grasmick are by no means the only criminological researchers who have been recently active in Chicago, as later secs. of this chap. will show. See also the very useful overview article by Sampson (1995).

Empirically testing this revised theory is difficult because, as we have seen earlier, it is not easy to construct measurable variables which instantiate social disorganization. Bursik and Grasmick reference various studies which they believe have successfully tested at least parts of their systemic theory of offender rates, but in particular they point to the re-analysis of the 1982 British Crime Survey data by Robert Sampson and Byron Groves (1989). Sampson and Groves used the BCS data set because, unlike its American equivalent, it provided sufficient respondents in small areas for analysis and survey data both about crime *and* about social behaviour and networks in areas. Their analysis demonstrates a link between their constructed measures of general area instability and intermediate community level behaviour (especially unsupervised groups of youths on the streets), which in turn are related to self-reported offending rates, and to victimization rates. Their conclusion is that:

our empirical analysis established that communities characterised by sparse friendship networks, unsupervised teenage peer groups, and low organizational participation had disproportionately high rates of crime and delinquency. Moreover, variations in these dimensions of community social disorganisation were shown to mediate in large part the effects of community structural characteristics (i.e. low socio-economic status, residential mobility, ethnic heterogeneity, and family disruption) in the manner predicted by our theoretical model. We have thus demonstrated that social-disorganisation theory has vitality and renewed relevance for explaining macro-level variations in crime rates [Sampson and Groves, 1989: 799].

Overall, however, Sampson and Groves are modest about their analysis and recognize both the problems of the data sets they used[42] and the sometimes modest degree of variance in crime explained by their model.[43] Nevertheless, their testing of the revised theory offers a possible explanation for variations in offender rates in demographically similar areas, as found in the Sheffield work, which is logically compatible with the role of housing markets in generating or sustaining such areal differences.

The revised theory certainly has a logical elegance—crime in neighbourhoods, it is argued, depends on a community's ability to organize control at three levels, and this depends on neighbourhood stability. Moreover, the theory overcomes some of the objections to the original theory of social disorganization by taking account of the political processes beyond the neighbourhood. However, we have seen how the Sheffield research identified a neighbourhood (Gardenia) which was residentially stable, and indeed scored

[42] Although, in fact, Sampson and Groves do not fully indicate the problems of the self-reported criminality measures in the 1982 British Crime Survey (the data most heavily relied on by Bursik and Gramsick in their overview of offender rate distributions). On these problems see Mayhew and Hough (1982), especially the following: 'from checks against CRO [Criminal Records Office] it emerged that less than half the people with criminal records were prepared to admit this to [BCS] interviewers. It must be recognized, therefore, that any estimates of the prevalence of offending based on the BCS [self-report] data are likely to be considerable underestimates' (*ibid.*: 26). It is also unlikely that the degree of under-reporting was even across areas.

[43] In particular, the R^2 values for the analysis of self-report offending were low: for personal violence, 0.06; and for property crime, 0.09.

well on some of the kind of measures which Sampson and Groves used to instantiate the capacity for social organization, and yet had high offender and victimization rates. This was an area whose life was organized around a mild criminal subculture, within which both youths and adults coped with their financially disadvantaged position by involvement in the black economy. This contra example raises two issues. First, it reintroduces a traditional objection to the theory of social disorganization discussed earlier, namely that the theory assumes a normative homogeneity across the society which may not exist, and Bursik and Grasmick (1993: 15) recognize that their theory does make such an assumption. However, the issue is not just whether such an assumption ought to be made, or even whether it is empirically valid. Their revised theory, as we have seen, recognizes the importance of political institutions outside the neighbourhood, but does not address the crucial question about normative homogeneity, in that context, namely, whether these institutions are necessarily regarded as legitimate within different neighbourhoods.[44] Secondly, empirically the apparent conflict between Sampson and Groves' analysis and the Sheffield example may simply be an artefact of the level of analysis.[45] In the end how well the revised theory explains variations in residential area crime rates is an empirical question, and as we write the New Chicagoans are conducting further research to test the theory.

The most recent empirical study of the black ghettos of Chicago by William Julius Wilson, however, suggests that a straightforward notion of 'social disorganization' does not adequately conceptualize the social processes in such neighbourhoods. Instead it is argued that:

what many impoverished and dangerous neighborhoods have in common is a relatively high degree of social integration (high levels of local neighboring while being relatively isolated from contacts in the broader mainstream society) and low levels of informal social control (feelings that they have little control over their immediate environment, including the environment's negative influence on their children). In such areas, not only are children at risk because of the lack of informal social controls, they are also disadvantaged because social interaction among neighbors tends to be confined to those whose skills, styles, orientations, and habits are not as conducive to positive social outcomes (academic success, pro-social behavior, etc.) as are those in more stable neighborhoods. . . . Despite being socially integrated, the residents of Chicago's ghetto neighborhoods shared a feeling that they had little informal social control over their

---

[44] Legitimation of a legal order is, of course, critical to its day-to-day functioning. For an empirical examination of the importance of legitimation for legal ordering see Tyler (1990).

[45] The Home Office's analysis of BCS crime rates in relation to constructed areas with common demographic characteristics (ACORN areas) masks the kind of variation in crime rates of areas with similar demographic structures found in Sheffield. The problem is that analysis at the national level homogenizes away local variations. This does not mean that the national level analysis is wrong—in this case that crime rates are related to demographic characteristics at a national level— but that within that general finding there is sufficient variation, such that at a more local level of analysis there is considerable variation in crime rates between areas with similar demographic characteristics. Similarly, Sampson and Groves' general finding may be correct, but there may still be areas at a local level of analysis which have high crime rates but do not fit their model of disorganization.

children in their environment. A primary reason is the absence of a strong organizational capacity or an institutional resource base that would provide an extra layer of social organization in their neighborhood [Wilson, 1996: 63–4].

This description is more complex and subtle than Bursick and Grasmick's theorization, and suggests that, instead of an area being characterized either by the presence or absence of 'social disorganization' *different types of social organization and disorganization can coexist in a neighbourhood*, some combinations of which may be conducive to different kinds of crime or lawlessness. This picture, in our view, fits much more closely to the evidence from the Sheffield research, and the existence of different types of high offender rate residential areas (see earlier discussion).

More generally, the New Chicagoans' revised theory, and its related empirical research, still uses the almost 'organic' notion of community of the original Chicago School. On this view, local communities and neighbourhoods are seen as at the heart of society, and in the normal case they will organize to control their members and to lever in support from politically organized institutions at the societal level. Communities which are unable to organize successfully will, on the other hand, fail to provide such control. This way of thinking about the centrality and naturalness of the local community has a long American ideological history, most recently articulated in 'communitarianism' (see e.g. Etzioni, 1993 and 1995).[46] However, such notions of community also hark back to more traditional forms of social organization and we will argue in the final section of this chapter that our social world may in fact be undergoing a radical transformation and, that being so, we need to consider how this may affect crime and criminality in local areas.[47]

BRINGING TOGETHER EXPLANATIONS OF OFFENCE LOCATIONS AND OFFENDER LOCATIONS

It cannot be claimed that environmental criminology has been particularly successful in integrating explanations of the location of offences and

---

[46] The desire to locate local communities as politically central also, of course, relates to American suspicions about over-centralized state power (originally reflecting their experience of the British state during colonialism) and the need to counterbalance the state with local power. For Europeans there are obvious, though rarely referenced, echoes of Durkheim's theory of order (Durkheim, 1984) and his political sociology (see Giddens, 1977).

[47] It is interesting that the most obvious low offender rate areas are middle class. Yet middle class areas are increasingly likely to reflect high occupational and geographical mobility which would seem, on the New Chicagoans' theorization, to undermine the stability needed for successful community defence against crime. However, the middle class tend to have the organizational skills to respond formally, rather than organically, to threats. In spite of high turnover they may none the less be successful in organizing formal parochial level institutions (e.g. the PTA or Scouts), and they can be especially good at using their organizational skills and political power to lever in the services of state institutions of social control and support, notably if their area is perceived to be under threat. For an interesting study of the moral order of a suburb see Baumgartner, 1988.

explanations of offender residence. At the time of the Chicago School, offender rates were emphasized to the virtual exclusion of offence rates; while more recent attention has been focused primarily on offence rates. Some environmental criminologists have, of course, considered both topics, especially when reviewing the field in general, but very few have paid serious attention to how one might best integrate explanations in the two sub-fields of study.

A recent general theory in criminology, by Gottfredson and Hirschi (1990) has, unusually, prioritized the integration of *offence explanations* and *offender explanations* as one of its major concerns. That feature of Gottfredson and Hirschi's work is one of its major strengths; but—unfortunately from an environmental criminologist's point of view—very little attention is paid, within the theory, to issues of crime and place. A main thrust of Gottfredson and Hirschi's approach to offence–offender integration is to treat classicism as the master-framework for the understanding of offence commission, and positivism as the master-framework for the understanding of the social production of offenders; and they further argue that these two frameworks are compatible. In a recent essay Bottoms (1993), has concurred wholeheartedly with the view that offence studies and offender studies need to be brought more closely together but has suggested that a more fruitful overarching theoretical approach than that suggested by Gottfredson and Hirschi might be found in Anthony Giddens's (1984) structuration theory. This framework has the following advantages:

(i) It provides an integrated ontological framework for social theory which, despite criticisms that may be made of it, nevertheless offers what has been described as 'the most systematic, interesting and sustained attempt so far found to develop an approach to social theory that transcends the dichotomies of determinism and voluntarianism, society and the individual, and object and subject' (Urry, 1986).

(ii) A central feature of structuration theory is to argue that 'the basic domain of study of the social sciences . . . is neither the experience of the individual actor, nor the existence of any form of societal totality, but *social practices ordered across space and time*' (Giddens, 1984: 2). Hence, both issues of *space* and the concept of *routines* are central to structuration theory in a way that is true of few other recent approaches to social theory; *prima facie*, therefore, the framework appears to offer much to environmental criminology, including the integration of offender and offence studies within an environmental context.

Space does not permit any further elaboration of these issues within the framework of this chapter, though it should be noted that some features of structuration theory have been introduced at appropriate earlier points in this chapter. The most important message of this subsection, however, is not specific to structuration theory: that message is simply to emphasize the general need for environmental criminology to provide a more adequately theorized integration of offender and offence location studies than it has usually achieved in the past.[48]

COMMUNITY CHANGE AND CRIME

So far in this chapter, area influences have been described in a somewhat static fashion, although the interactive model shown in Figure 8.7 contains within it the possibility of analysing dynamic changes in the housing market situations of particular areas, and the consequences of such changes.

In an important essay, Albert Reiss (1986) drew attention to the importance for criminology of changes in local communities, and he suggested that, analogously to the concept of the individual criminal career, one might speak in terms of local areas having 'community crime careers'. This is a concept that we have worked with in the context of the Sheffield study (see Bottoms and Wiles, 1986, 1992; Bottoms, Claytor, and Wiles, 1992); but, rather than use further Sheffield evidence here, let us consider the 'community crime career' idea using research studies from the United States, some based on studies of offenders and some on studies of offences.[49]

Schuerman and Kobrin (1986) carried out a statistical study of juvenile offender rates in different areas of Los Angeles for the period 1950–70. They found evidence for a three-stage process which appeared to underpin the emergence of particular districts as high offender rate areas over this period, and they were satisfied from the temporal patterning of the data that the causal influences were cumulative, and in the order specified. First, they argued, there were shifts in land use (for example, an increase in renting and decline in owner-occupation; and an increase in apartment dwellings). Secondly, there were changes in population-related features in areas (for example, a decline in total population size in the area; an increase, within the overall population, in the proportion of unrelated individuals; and an increase in residential mobility). Thirdly, there were changes in socio-economic status (more unskilled people; a higher proportion unemployed), and also in what Schuerman and Kobrin label, perhaps doubtfully,[50] 'subculture variables'

---

[48] For a further recent attempt at such integration see Bursik and Grasmick, 1993: chaps. 2 and 3. Essentially, these authors base their attempted integration upon the view that 'certain features of the routine activities model are very similar to those found in the social disorganisation framework, especially those pertaining to guardianship and systemic social control' (*ibid.*: 89).

[49] Although the studies use these two different measures one must remember that *in residential areas* they tend to be positively correlated.

[50] The authors admit that the census and administrative records to which they had access are not ideal for measuring this kind of variable, but nevertheless continue: 'the variables included such correlates of weakened social control as the ethnic composition of local populations, features of family organisation related to child neglect, and the kind of normative heterogeneity indicated by the presence of a population highly diverse in educational level. Variables indexing local subculture were drawn directly from these features' (Schuerman and Kobrin, 1986: 71–2). See also the earlier discussion of the work of Sampson and Groves, 1989.

(including an increase in the size of ethnic minority populations; and increased proportions of ethnic minority females working, and ethnic minority members with advanced education). Hence, overall, these authors concluded that 'Initial limited changes in land use induce a larger number of demographic changes, in turn fostering a still larger number of changes in the socio-economic features of the resident population . . . [and] ethnic, occupational and educational patterns representing shared adaptations to the set of background conditioning factors' (1986: 97). This proposed causal model, derived purely statistically from Census and offender data, of course fits extremely well with that postulated in the Sheffield study from more on-the-ground fieldwork experience (see Figure 8.7). But perhaps of even more interest in the Los Angeles research was a further finding, namely that it seemed to be:

the speed of structural change, rather than simply the fact of such change that initiates the transition of city neighborhoods from a low to a high-crime status. . . . [In particular] the high velocity of first-decade change primarily in socio-economic status and secondly in subculture that were highly related to the second-decade acceleration in the [offender] measure[51] [Schuerman and Kobrin, 1986: 97–98].

This emphasis on the speed of change raises particularly the issue of how areas 'tip' from low-crime to high-crime areas, sometimes quite speedily (as for example Gardenia seemed to do in Sheffield in the 1940s). This is an issue of some importance, not least since there is evidence from a variety of sources that tipping processes can often begin slowly and then rapidly accelerate.

One famous criminological theory relevant to tipping processes is the so-called 'broken windows' hypothesis of James Q. Wilson and George Kelling (1982). According to these authors, there is at least a strong likelihood that signs of disorder in an area—such as broken windows, housing abandonment, litter, and graffiti—will undermine the subtle and informal processes whereby communities normally maintain social control. For example, where signs of disorder are prevalent in an area, residents may shrink back into their own dwelling, and take no responsibility for what goes on in public spaces. Meanwhile, the increasing dilapidation of the public space means that it may become fair game for plunder and/or destruction, and may also act as an unintended invitation to those engaged in crime of a commercial or semi-commercial nature (drugs, prostitution, etc.) to come and 'trade' in the area.

The researcher who has been most active in seeking to investigate empirically the 'spiral of decay in American neighborhoods', as he calls it, is Wesley Skogan (1986, 1990). Skogan believes that the study of disorder is a vital, but very neglected, topic in criminology. He distinguishes between physical and social disorders (physical = abandoned or ill-kept buildings, broken streetlights, litter, vermin, etc.; social = public drinking, prostitution, sexual catcalling, etc.: Skogan, 1990: 4), but goes on to find that the two sorts of disorder are strongly correlated (*ibid.*: 51). Moreover, while 'disorder' might seem to be

---

[51] The word 'offender' has been substituted for the authors' original of 'crime', since they were working with offender data.

a concept much dependent on one's personal viewpoint, and therefore highly subjective, in fact the area in which survey respondents lived turned out to be much more important as a predictor of the number of disorders they reported than did any personal characteristics of the respondents. (Younger respondents did, however, perceive more disorders in the same areas than did older respondents, probably because they used public space more often.)

Skogan found, not surprisingly, that disorders tended to be highest in areas with low neighbourhood stability, poverty, and a high ethnic minority population. But the real interest of his research, for the purposes of this chapter, lies in his analysis of the consequences of disorder. Quite strong evidence of three impacts of disorder were found.

First, 'disorder undermines the mechanisms by which communities exercise control over local affairs' (Skogan, 1990: 65). On cross-sectional analyses, there was a negative relationship between the presence of disorder in an area and the extent to which residents were willing to help one another in a neighbourly way; and also in the extent to which residents engaged in simple crime-prevention activities such as property marking, or asking their neighbours to keep an eye on their home during an absence.

Secondly, 'disorder sparks concern about neighborhood safety, and perhaps even causes crime itself' (*ibid.*: 65). As we have seen, the evidence of Skogan's study was that disorder was statistically linked to areal poverty, ethnic minority residence, and social instability; not surprisingly, such areas tended also to have high crime rates. Disentangling the causal order of these variables is of course very difficult, especially in cross-sectional analyses, but a path model was presented based on thirty areas for which robbery victimization data were available, and it was suggested that 'there were no significant paths between those social and economic variables and neighborhood crime, except through disorder' (*ibid.*: 75). Skogan does not wish to overstate this conclusion, but believes it needs to be taken seriously, at least as a likely hypothesis for future research.

Thirdly, 'disorder undermines the stability of the housing market . . . [it] undercuts residential satisfaction, leads people to fear for the safety of their children, and encourages area residents to move away' (*ibid.*: 65). Drawing on work in the general field of urban sociology, Skogan suggests that selective out-migration from an area may be the most fundamental source of neighbourhood change. In the areas studied, there was a negative correlation between disorder and residents' degree of commitment to their area; moreover, this was related to moving intentions. Skogan goes on to note that these data probably underestimate the impact of disorder on local housing markets, since he had no data on perceptions of areas from anyone except area residents, and 'the stigma associated with high levels of visible disorder probably affects the perceptions and decisions of [potential in-migrants] as well' (*ibid.*: 84).

Overall, therefore, Skogan's research tends to support Wilson and Kelling's (1982) original 'broken windows' hypothesis. In the light of the Sheffield evidence, the fact that the housing market plays an important role within

Skogan's theorization is also of great interest. Unfortunately, Skogan makes no direct attempt to link his housing market variables to the crime variables; on the basis of Sheffield and Stockholm experience, the likelihood is that they are in fact related, in an interactive way. Finally, Skogan's emphasis on out-migration from areas as an engine of neighbourhood change is undoubtedly of great importance, and it links strongly both to Sheffield evidence and to an earlier Chicago study, to which we must now turn.

Richard Taub and his colleagues (1984) begin their book with the observation that, for many people, the relationship between crime (meaning here offence rates) and the deterioration of an area is obvious—crime causes deterioration. Their entire book is, however, in a sense an extended essay showing that this is an oversimplified conclusion. Three key points, from a very complex argument, are of special interest from the point of view of the environmental criminologist.

First, the authors conclude that crime levels are an issue in judging the quality of an area; however, these judgements are comparative rather than absolute. More importantly, the judgements made are a weighing up of an area's rewards and amenities against its disadvantages and lack of amenities, in which crime victimization levels are not necessarily the most important feature. In two areas of Chicago respondents from all ethnic groups (black, white, and hispanic) themselves judged the actual risk of crime to be above average, *yet were satisfied with the level of safety in the neighbourhood* (*ibid.*: 171–2).[52] One of these areas was the district where the University of Chicago is situated (Hyde Park-Kenwood). The University had spent its own funds and levered in federal and private funds for an area renewal programme. This involved, *inter alia*, (i) enforcing regulations against multi-occupation of certain dwellings, (ii) financially encouraging University staff to live in the area, (iii) setting up a large private security force, and (iv) establishing a fleet of buses, and emergency telephones at key points, to enhance feelings of personal safety. The net result of all this activity was an area which, despite being only 59 per cent white, was racially stable in population composition (no evidence of 'white flight'); and, a point of very great criminological interest, had rapidly appreciating property values despite a high crime rate.[53]

Secondly, Taub and his colleagues devote some attention to the ways in which individuals make decisions relevant to neighbourhood decline. They find some empirical evidence for a so-called 'threshold model' (akin to a 'domino process') in housing areas. In the present context, this threshold model might operate in the following way: early signs of deterioration will lead some residents to move away ('pioneers'); but some (e.g. the elderly) will not move

---

[52] In the majority of areas studied, of course, these two variables (risk of crime and satisfaction with level of safety) were negatively correlated.

[53] This finding probably does not disturb the conclusions from Skogan's study, since one might postulate that serious *disorder* (of the kind defined by Skogan) would almost certainly feature as a strong negative factor in most people's weighing of the advantages and disadvantages of an area.

whatever anyone else does ('conservatives'); while others in between these polar groups will in fact be influenced (often strongly so) by opinions and decisions of others in the area. Hence, if significant numbers try to move from the area this will influence others to do so.

The importance of this threshold model for present purposes is twofold. In the first place, it shows clearly how a 'tipping' process in an area can gather speed, and this re-emphasizes the importance of the 'velocity' dimension in Schuerman and Kobrin's results. Moreover, it shows, by implication, that once a tipping process is under way, there is very little that an individual can do to stop it, for an individual acting alone can have very little power to sway other individuals in an accelerating process of this kind. On the other hand, as Taub and his colleagues show, a corporate body can in fact influence the decisions of other individuals, and hence (in principle at least) halt a tipping process.[54] The University of Chicago seems to have achieved this in Hyde Park-Kenwood (at least as regards a tipping process into urban decline, and a racial tipping process; though, in this case, the crime rate remained high).

These considerations lead directly on to the *third* and last main point to be emphasized from Taub *et al.*'s research. In their closing chapter, they offer a threefold approach to the understanding of neighbourhood change: such change is, they suggest, always a product of the interaction between (i) ecological facts, (ii) individual decisions, and (iii) corporate decisions. 'Ecological facts' are defined as including (i) the potential employment base for neighbourhood residents, (ii) demographic pressures on the local housing market, (iii) the age and quality of the housing stock, and (iv) external amenities such as attractive physical locations (hills, lakes, etc.).[55] Taub *et al.* note that most previous theories of neighbourhood change have concentrated on ecological facts as the main explanatory variable, but they argue that this is an incomplete approach, as shown by some of their area case studies.

Finally, harking right back to the Chicago School, Taub *et al.* comment that, with hindsight, one can see only too clearly the central weakness of the urban model adopted:

because early sociological theories [did] not make a place for the decision rules of individual and corporate actors, [they led] to the too-simple view that the neighborhoods in a city are somewhat interchangeable parts of a single integrated urban system that operates according to univariate rules of evolution [Taub *et al.*, 1984: 186].

[54] 'Corporate' bodies in this context do not have to be businesses but can be any large organization with powerful local influence, be it business, charity, government (local or central), statutory agency, or a well organized local community group, the point being that effective corporate action of any kind alters the social dynamics in an area, and the confidence of individuals.

[55] This definition of 'ecological facts' is not wholly unproblematic from a sociological point of view, since it contains some physical features (hills, the nature of the housing stock), and some social-structural features such as the local employment base. However, it would not be difficult to create conceptual refinements which would deal with this difficulty, and the difficulty does not weaken the main thrust of Taub *et al.*'s argument.

Hence, ultimately, the study of community change and crime leads—just as did our following through of the implications of offence location studies and offender residence studies—to a linking together of micro, meso, and macro social processes. Nothing else will provide an adequate framework for explanation. In the study of change, however, because one's focus is more long-term, it is perhaps easier to see the macro-level and the overtly political processes in operation; hence it is particularly important to remember, when studying other and perhaps more static issues in environmental criminology, that these macro-level and political forces are always present, even if not very visible in a particular piece of local research. As we saw at the beginning of the section on offender residence, very much the same message has been embraced by the New Chicagoans.

CRIME AND LATE MODERNITY

So far this chapter has been concerned to summarize (with, we hope, a friendly but critical eye) the existing literature on environmental criminology. Now we turn to the future research agenda of environmental criminology. Our starting point is a recognition that the economically more advanced countries of the world are, in our view, at the present time undergoing some quite fundamental economic and social changes that will significantly affect the nature and patterning of crime. Environmental criminology needs to understand these transformations in order to explain crime in the future: to use the language we have been using so far, we need to understand these macro changes in order to offer explanations at the meso and micro level. The macro changes we are referring to are usually designated as the change from 'modernity' (basically, the social formations which emerged out of industrialization) to 'late modernity' or, alternatively, 'post-modernism'.[56] Many writers have discussed these changes, and whilst, as will by now have become apparent, we find Giddens's work particularly useful (see Giddens, 1990 and 1991), for present purposes we do not want to adopt a particular theoretical view but instead to concentrate on the empirical nature of the transformations.

Within the length of this chapter we can do no more than summarize those main areas of change which seem to us to have criminological implications, but for a fuller treatment see Bottoms and Wiles (1995).[57]

First, business and the flows of capital have become increasingly transnational and have created their own transnational orders. The ability of nation states to control this transnational capital and business is not very great,

---

[56] 'Post-modernism' in the hands of some writers has had methodological links with epistemological relativism, an intellectual position we reject, and so we would prefer 'late modernity' in order to focus on the empirical transformations presently taking place.

[57] For a general, historical account of how the processes of change can create new crime and social control patterns in a city see also Mike Davis's (1990) study of Los Angeles.

precisely because they do not operate solely within the territory of a nation state.[58] The result is that effective power is being increasingly either exercised at the transnational level or alternatively with the decline of state power at the local level,[59] leading to what is often described as the 'hollowing out' of power at the state level. Yet during modernity the nation state has been the prime location for the making of laws against crime and the control and policing of crime. If the state is being hollowed out in this way then the main definers of crime in the modern period will cede this power both upwards (to transnational capital and political organizations) and downwards (to local areas). We have already seen within Europe the EU taking such a role, and local campaigns and programmes against crime are increasingly common.

Secondly, manufacturing industry is now a declining proportion of total economic activity and business decisions are, as a consequence, less determined by the supply of raw materials for manufacture than by new considerations, such as the availability of highly skilled labour, or a pleasant environment to attract such labour. The wealth and prosperity of a city are thus no longer determined by its location relative to the physical resources of material production, and indeed nearness to such resources may result in environmental degradation which makes it less attractive to highly skilled labour. The result is that cities, or regions, can have very uneven and different economic development—for example, one of us works in a 'rustbelt' city (Sheffield) which is trying to overcome the problems of de-industrialization, and the other in a 'sunrise' city (Cambridge) which has developed new hi-tech industries. The economic structures, which (as we have seen) provide the macro framework for the routine activities which pattern crime, are therefore increasingly uneven and varied. On the one hand, declining traditional industries can leave environmentally blighted areas of cities, including residential areas originally built to provide labour for those industries, with high unemployment rates and having lost their most entrepreneurial residents. On the other hand, new information-based industries may flourish in semi-rural locations with 'homeworking' blurring the more traditional home/work divide.

Thirdly, recent technology means that neither time nor space is the fixed framework of our routines. Quite apart from 'virtual realities', we commonly shift time (by videoing television programmes to watch later), or space (by working on the move with mobile phones, computers etc.). The result can be

---

[58] Witness, for example, the British government's problems in dealing with recent sterling crises in which it had, in the end, to admit defeat at the hands of currency speculators and international capital markets. Nation states have attempted to respond by themselves trying to create supranational institutions for control, such as the European Union or the General Agreement on Tariffs and Trade. However, nation states, by their nature, find it difficult not to pursue their own narrow interests, and so such institutions are very much more difficult to create successfully than the transnational institutions of business and capital—witness the problems of the two examples just given.

[59] Not only has the state ceded power to the transnational level but some services must respond to increasingly differentiated local demands and the state is much less able to provide such services effectively than locally based institutions and organizations. Hence the state's ability to govern is being attacked from both above and below.

globalized cultures, no longer fixed in time or space, from which we can choose and indeed make a series of different choices. Television representations based on the culture of Australia or west coast America have taken on an autonomous existence and may be as 'real' to some British youth as anything else. Yet geographically localized cultures, in the sense of 'community' and spatially fixed institutions, such as churches and families, have been regarded by much criminological theory as the main defences against crime: hence the Chicagoans' concern with community 'disorganization' and crime.[60] Furthermore, a market culture of consumer choice depends on the financial ability of participants and may encourage crime by those who do not possess the (legitimate) resources to exercise such choice in the new global market place.

Fourthly, in our new social world we are increasingly dependent upon reflexively acquired social knowledge rather than tradition,[61] yet this new form of knowledge becomes ever more specialized and, in practice, forces us to take on trust the expertise of others, and the efficacy of abstract systems. For example, unless we are specially trained we have to trust the expertise of environmental scientists about, for example, radiation or pollution levels. The problem is that we are regularly presented with grounds for doubting whether we should grant such trust (it is not difficult to recall examples of environmental 'knowledge' being proved wrong) and so we increasingly suffer from insecurities which can compound each other into an overall and generalized sense of ontological insecurity. This ontological insecurity embraces everything, from the long-term sustainability of the planet to anxieties about day-to-day living. One response to doubts of the latter kind is the creation of 'security bubbles' deliberately designed to calm our insecurities and encourage our trust, many of which (such as women-only hotels, CCTV systems, gated residential estates, or well protected shopping malls) particularly focus on the insecurities associated with crime or disorder.

Fifthly, our new social world has developed new forms of social differentiation ranging from changes in gender roles to increasing economic polarization. From a criminological point of view these new forms change the context of the routine activities relating to crime (for example more working women can mean less occupied and guarded homes during the day: Cohen and Felson, 1979). Most importantly, increased economic polarization and the decline of traditional manufacturing industry, and the disappearance of many jobs through technological or other restructuring, have led to an apparently irreversible increase in the long-term unemployment of the unskilled. This has created an increasing social exclusion of some sub-groups of the population from effective participation in key areas of social life (ranging from jobs to

[60] Of course, this does not mean that local place-based community factors are no longer important in people's lives—they clearly are, but alongside the more globalized influences.

[61] In earlier societies, guides to action (from parents, company directors, or community leaders, etc.) tended to be based on maxims relating to *the past* ('tradition'): for example, 'we've always done things this way'. In contemporary societies, the reference-point is decreasingly the past, and increasingly the future ('let's have your projections for 2010'; 'let's do it this way, try it out and see if it works', etc.).

education and leisure facilities). Where particular groups experience multiple exclusion then the operation of the housing market may well concentrate them in particular residential areas (see Wiles, 1992). In the contemporary United States this has especially happened to poor blacks and produced the black ghettos of American rustbelt cities, such as Chicago or Detroit. The ghettos have alarmingly high offence and offender rates, and this has produced a generalized (although statistically largely misplaced) fear of the danger they may represent to the rest of the city, which mirrors the nineteenth century Victorian concerns about the dangerous classes (see Morris, 1994). An acrimonious debate has ensued about the reasons for such high ghetto crime rates. Both sides of the debate agree that in such areas social exclusion (especially from the labour market) goes together with distinct forms of neighbourhood culture and social organization, but they disagree about why this is the case and how it relates to crime. On the one hand, it has been argued that an 'underclass' has been created by poor, but welfare-dependent blacks being allowed to make irresponsible cultural choices not to support social institutions, such as two-parent families, which are capable of successfully socializing the young into non-criminal values and controlling any attempted deviance (see e.g. Murray, 1984). On the other hand, it has been argued that the culture and social organization of the ghetto and its crime is an adaptation by a people who have been systematically excluded and disadvantaged by the wider society (see Wilson, 1987 and 1996). The arguments from this American debate about the 'underclass' have since been borrowed to try and explain high crime and lawlessness in some British council estates (see Murray, 1990, 1994). More generally, the Canadian criminologist John Hagan (1994: chapter 3) has argued persuasively that the economic changes of late modernity, and especially growing economic polarization, have created the need for a 'new sociology of crime and disrepute' to replace some of the now less relevant sociologies of crime. Central to this new approach, Hagan argues, will be the study of the 'criminal costs of social inequality' (*ibid.*: 98).

These changes, of course, are not uniform either within, or between countries—indeed, that is one of the characteristics of late modernity. Nevertheless, they seem to affect all late modern societies to some degree. Future research in environmental criminology will to have to try and understand how these changes are affecting the distribution of crime in space and time. Clearly our cities, their surrounding hinterlands, and rural areas are being physically re-modelled by these processes, but this is happening in different ways in different places. The housing tenure map of Britain, for example, is being transformed, and we have already seen how important housing markets have been in environmental criminological explanations. The new housing markets will change crime patterns, but how is not yet clear: a shrinking public housing sector could produce increasing residualization of public housing and, at its most extreme, mirror the American problem of ghettos (see Wiles, 1992), but alternatively a more varied housing market could encourage a new social discipline, enforced by housing managers and the civil courts, which reduces residential area crime rates in at least some areas (cf. NACRO, 1996). The development of out-of-town shopping centres and leisure facilities is creating attractive new crime targets away from traditional city centres, but, because these are often legally privately owned places, they are more likely to be rigorously and privately policed though in an unobtrusive style that most of the public approve of (see Beck and Willis, 1995). The decline of time or space as a fixed framework for our lives could reduce the commitment to geographical neighbourhood and so reduce social control at the local level. On the other hand, these changes could mean that we learn successfully to base local control increasingly on the *public* rather than *parochial* level, or that residential areas become less important and parochial control is instead exercised in the locations where we choose to pursue our varied interests. Increasing social differentiation combined with the creation of security bubbles could lead to increased segregation and the exclusion of deviant or threatening groups (e.g. the exclusion of groups of young people from shopping malls) and the collapse of a public civic society into a series of private realms (e.g. private places with their own private police forces effectively enforcing their private law). Alternatively, increasing lifestyle choices may freely and spatially separate social groups with different interests (e.g. by lifestyle activities being provided at different places or in the same place at different times), and so reduce the potential for inter-group conflicts which produced crime in traditional city centres, especially at weekends.

We can be certain that changes in the geographical patterning of routine activities will alter the pattern of crime, but this will be modified by the differential use of social control, such as new technology (e.g. CCTV, flash card entry control, etc.) or manned security services. Since such changes in routine activities are most commonly the outcome of a large number of uncoordinated individual market decisions, the resulting changes in crime patterns will not be easy to predict. At the time of writing the consequences of the changes of late modernity for the patterns of crime in space and time are not clear—indeed, some evidence for all the above examples could be found. To some extent this is because we will have to await the results of new empirical research, but also because there is unlikely to be a single set of crime outcomes from the changes of late modernity. This is partly because (as already stressed) late modernity is itself an uneven process, although of itself that might simply suggest a limited number of different crime outcomes: for example, we could try to model the crime outcomes in 'rustbelt' cities compared to 'sunrise' cities. Some commentators seem to believe that is all that is involved; on this view, the forces of late modernity are global, and neither resistible nor manageable by political choices made by an increasingly weakened state. However, there is at present still clear evidence of national differences in the effects of late modern changes (see Lash and Urry, 1987), and also that broad historical differences, combined with very broad political choices as to the desired relationship between economic forms, individual freedom, and forms of social ordering can still produce very different social orders (compare, for example, contemporary Japan and the USA). Some of the alternative crime outcomes suggested above could therefore be influenced by these kinds of political choices, although the most important ones will increasingly be just as likely to be made at either the transnational or local level, as by the state.

The environmental criminology of the future will therefore need to continue to study crime patterns at local levels, but it will necessarily have to situate its explanations within a macro-level understanding of the emerging forces of late modernity. Some of the preoccupations of traditional environmental criminology will thus have to change—but there is every indication that this will remain an exciting and vibrant sub-specialization within criminological studies in the future.

Selected Further Reading

The two most accessible general introductions to the main themes of environmental criminology are P. J. and P. L. Brantingham, *Environmental Criminology* (revised edition), Prospect Heights, Ill.: Waveland Press, 1991, and P.-O. H. Wikström, *Urban Crime, Criminals and Victims: The Swedish Experience in an Anglo-American Comparative Perspective*, New York: Springer-Verlag, 1991. The first of these is an edited book, originally published in 1981 but revised in 1991, and still a good general introduction. The second is a more statistically orientated analysis of the Swedish experience in the light of the American and British literature. Wikström has written later material but this is a good general review.

For those wanting a brief review of the American literature a well written essay is R. J. Sampson, 'The Community' in J. Q. Wilson and J. Petersilia, eds., *Crime*, San Francisco, CA: Institute for Contemporary Studies, 1995. For those wanting a general review of a great deal of the American material, but with a bias towards fitting this into the new Chicagoans' thinking, the best book is R. J. Bursik and H. G. Grasmick, *Neighborhoods and Crime*, New York: Lexington, 1993.

For those interested in attempts to integrate research in environmental criminology with criminal careers research a good collection is D. P. Farrington, R. J. Sampson, and P.-O. H. Wikström, eds., *Integrating Individual and Ecological Aspects of Crime*, Stockholm: National Council for Crime Prevention, 1993.

Finally, for those interested in how environmental criminology might relate to general social theory and the changes of late modernity, they might try two of our recent essays: A. E. Bottoms and P. Wiles, 'Explanations of Crime and Place', in D. J. Evans, N. R. Fyfe, and D. T. Herbert, eds., *Crime, Policing and Place: Essays in Environmental Criminology*, London: Routledge, 1992, or 'Crime and Insecurity in the City', in C. Fijnaut, J. Goethals, T. Peters, and L. Walgrave, eds., *Changes in Society, Crime and Criminal Justice in Europe*, 2 vols., The Hague: Kluwer, 1995.

REFERENCES

ALIHAN, M. (1938), *Social Ecology*. New York: Columbia University Press.

ANDERSON, S., GROVE SMITH, C., KINSEY, R., and WOOD, J. (1990), *The Edinburgh Crime Survey: First Report*. Edinburgh: Scottish Office Central Research Unit Papers.

BALDWIN, J. (1979), 'Ecological and Areal Studies in Great Britain and the United States', in N. Morris and M. Tonry, eds., *Crime and Justice: An Annual Review of Research*, vol. 1. Chicago, Ill.: University of Chicago Press.

—— and BOTTOMS, A. E. (1976), *The Urban Criminal*. London: Tavistock.

BAUMGARTNER, M. P. (1988), *The Moral Order of a Suburb*. New York: Oxford University Press.

BECK, A., and WILLIS, A. (1995), *Crime and Security: Managing the Risk*. Leicester: Perpetuity Press.

BENNETT, T., and WRIGHT, R. (1984), *Burglars on Burglary*. Aldershot: Gower.

BLOCK, R. L. and BLOCK, C. R. (1995), 'Space, Place and Crime: Hot Spots Areas and Hot Places of Liquor-related Crime', in J. E. Eck and D. Weisburd, eds., *Crime and Place*. New York: Criminal Justice Press.

BOTTOMS, A. E. (1993), 'Recent Criminological and Social Theory and the Problem of Integrating Knowledge about Individual Criminal Acts and Careers and Areal Dimensions of Crime', in D. P. Farrington, R. J. Sampson, and P.-O. H. Wikström, eds., *Integrating Individual and Ecological Aspects of Crime*. Stockholm: National Council for Crime Prevention.

—— (1994), 'Environmental Criminology' in M. Maguire, R. Morgan, and R. Reiner, eds., *The Oxford Handbook of Criminology*. Oxford: Clarendon Press.

—— CLAYTOR, A. and WILES, P. (1992), 'Housing Markets and Residential Community Crime Careers: a Case Study from Sheffield', in D. J. Evans, N. R. Fyfe, and D. T. Herbert, eds., *Crime, Policing and Place: Essays in Environmental Criminology*. London: Routledge.

—— MAWBY, R. I., and WALKER, M. A. (1987), 'A Localised Crime Survey in Contrasting Areas of a City'. *British Journal of Criminology*, 27: 125–54.

—— —— and XANTHOS, P. (1989), 'A tale of two estates', in D. Downes, ed., *Crime and the City*. London: Macmillan.

—— and WILES, P. (1986), 'Housing Tenure and Residential Community Crime Careers in Britain', in A. J. Reiss and M. Tonry, eds., *Communities and Crime*. Chicago, Ill.: University of Chicago Press.

—— and —— (1992), 'Explanations of Crime and Place', in D. J. Evans, N. R. Fyfe, and D. T. Herbert, eds., *Crime, Policing and Place: Essays in Environmental Criminology*. London: Routledge.

—— and —— (1995), 'Crime and Insecurity in the City' in C. Fijnaut, J. Goethals, T. Peters, and L. Walgrave, eds., *Changes in Society, Crime and Criminal Justice in Europe*, 2 vols. The Hague: Kluwer.

—— and XANTHOS, P. (1981), 'Housing Policy and Crime in the British Public Sector', in P. J. Brantingham and P. L. Brantingham, eds., *Environmental Criminology*. Beverly Hills, California: Sage Publications.

BRAITHWAITE, J. (1989), *Crime, Shame and Reintegration*. Cambridge: Cambridge University Press.

BRANTINGHAM, P. J., and BRANTINGHAM, P. L. (1981a), *Environmental Criminology*. Beverly Hills, Cal.: Sage Publications.

—— and —— (1984), *Patterns in Crime*. New York: Macmillan.

—— and —— (1991), *Environmental Criminology* (revised edition). Prospect Heights, Ill.: Waveland Press.

BRANTINGHAM, P. L., and BRANTINGHAM, P. J., (1981), 'Notes on the Geometry of Crime', in P. J. Brantingham and P. L. Brantingham, eds., *Environmental Criminology*. Beverly Hills, Cal.: Sage Publications.

BRONFENBRENNER, U. (1979), *The Ecology of Human Development*. Cambridge, Mass.: Harvard University Press.

BULMER, M. (1984), *The Chicago School of Sociology*. Chicago, Ill.: University of Chicago Press.

BURGESS, E. W. (1925), 'The Growth of the City' in R. E. Park, E. W. Burgess, and R. D. McKenzie, eds., *The City*. Chicago: University of Chicago Press.

BURSIK, R. J. (1986), 'Ecological Stability and the Dynamics of Delinquency' in A. J. Reiss and M. Tonry, eds. *Communities and Crime*. Chicago, Ill.: University of Chicago Press.

—— and GRASMICK, H. G. (1993), *Neighborhoods and Crime*. New York: Lexington.

CAMPBELL, B (1993), *Goliath: Britain's Dangerous Places*. London: Methuen.

CARTER, R. L., and HILL, K. Q. (1979), *The Criminal's Image of the City*. New York: Pergammon Press.

CLARKE, R. V. G. (1995), 'Situational Crime

Prevention' in M. Tonry and D. Farrington, eds., *Building a Safer Society*. Chicago, Ill.: University of Chicago Press.

COHEN, L. E., and FELSON, M. (1979), 'Social Change and Crime Rate Trends: A Routine Activities Approach', *American Sociological Review*, 44: 588–608.

COLEMAN, A. (1985), *Utopia on Trial: Vision and Reality in Planned Housing*. London: Hilary Shipman.

—— (1989), 'Disposition and Situation: Two Sides of the Same Crime' in D. J. Evans and D. T. Herbert, eds., *The Geography of Crime*. London: Routledge.

COLLINS, P. (1962), *Dickens and Crime*. London: Macmillan.

COSTANZO, C. M., *et al.* (1986), 'Criminal Mobility and the Directional Component in Journeys to Crime', in R. Figlio *et al.*, eds., *Metropolitan Crime Patterns*. Monsey, NY: Criminal Justice Press.

CRESSEY, D. (1964), *Delinquency, Crime and Differential Association*. The Hague: Martinus Nijhoff.

CROMWELL, P. F., OLSON, J. N., and AVARY D'A. W. (1991), *Breaking and Entering: An Ethnographic Analysis of Burglary*. Newbury Park, California: Sage.

DAMER, S. (1974), 'Wine Alley: The Sociology of a Dreadful Enclosure', *Sociological Review*, 22: 221–48.

DAVIS, M. (1990), *City of Quartz: Excavating the Future of Los Angeles*. London: Vintage.

DEPARTMENT OF THE ENVIRONMENT (1997), *The Design Improvement Controlled Experiment: An Evaluation of the Impact, Costs and Benefits of Estate Remodelling*. London: Department of the Environment.

DURKHEIM, E (1984), *The Division of Labour in Society*. London: Macmillan.

ECK, J. E. (1995), 'A General Model of the Geography of Illicit Retail Marketplaces', in J. E. Eck and D. Weisburd, eds., *Crime and Place*. New York: Criminal Justice Press.

ENGELS, F. (1842), *The Condition of the Working Class in England*, in K. Marx and F. Engels (1970), *Selected Works*. Moscow: Progress Publishers.

ETZIONI, A (1993), *The Spirit of Community: The Reinvention of American Society*. New York: Simon & Schuster

—— (1995), *New Communitarian Thinking*. Charlottesville, Virginia: University of Virginia Press.

FARRELL, G. (1995), 'Preventing Repeat Victimisation', in M. Tonry and D. Farrington, eds., *Building a Safer Society*. Chicago, Ill.: Chicago University Press.

FARRINGTON, D. P., and DOWDS, E. A (1984), 'Disentangling Criminal Behaviour and Police Reaction' in D. P. Farrington and J. Gunn, eds., *Reactions to Crime*. Chichester: Wiley.

—— SAMPSON, R. J., and WIKSTRÖM, P.-O. H., eds. (1993), *Integrating Individual and Ecological Aspects of Crime*. Stockholm: National Council for Crime Prevention.

FELSON, M. (1986), 'Linking Criminal Choices, Routine Activities, Informal Control and Criminal Outcomes', in D. B. Cornish and R. V. G. Clarke, eds., *The Reasoning Criminal*. New York: Springer-Verlag.

—— (1992), 'Routine Activities and Crime Prevention', *Studies on Crime and Crime Prevention: Annual Review*, 1: 30–4.

—— (1995), 'Those Who Discourage Crime' in J. E. Eck and D. Weisburd, eds., *Crime and Place*. New York: Criminal Justice Press.

FIGLIO, R. M., HAKIM, S., and RENGERT, G. F., eds. (1986), *Metropolitan Crime Patterns*. Monsey, NY: Willow Tree Press.

FINESTONE, H. (1976), 'The Delinquent and Society: The Shaw and McKay Tradition', in J. F. Short, Jr., ed., *Delinquency, Crime and Society*. Chicago, Ill.: University of Chicago Press.

GIDDENS, A., ed. (1977), *Durkheim on Politics and the State*. London: Polity Press.

—— (1984), *The Constitution of Society*. Cambridge: Polity Press.

—— (1990), *The Consequences of Modernity*. Cambridge, Polity Press.

—— (1991), *Modernity and Self-Identity*. Cambridge: Polity Press.

GILLIS, A. R. (1996), 'Urbanisation, Socio-historical Context and Crime' in J. Hagan, A. R. Gillis, and D. Brownfield, *Criminological Controversies: A Methodological Primer*. Boulder, Colorado: Westview Press.

GOTTFREDSON, M. R., and HIRSCHI, T. (1990), *A General Theory of Crime*. Stanford, Cal.: Stanford University Press.

GOVERNMENT OF JAPAN (1996), *Summary of the White Paper on Crime*. Tokyo: Research and Training Institute, Ministry of Justice.

HAGAN, J. (1994), *Crime and Disrepute*. Thousand Oaks, Cal.: Pine Forge Press.

HARRIES, K. D. (1981), 'Alternative Denominators in Conventional Crime Rates', in P. J. Brantingham and P. L. Brantingham, eds., *Environmental Criminology*. Beverly Hills, Cal.: Sage Publications.

HERBERT, D. (1982), *The Geography of Urban Crime*. London: Longman.

HOME OFFICE, (1988), *The Five Towns Initiative: A Community Response to Crime Reduction*. London: Home Office.

HOPE, T., and FOSTER, J. (1992), 'Conflicting Forces: Changing the Dynamics of Crime and Community on a "Problem" Estate', *British Journal of Criminology*, 32: 488–504.

—— and HOUGH, M. (1988), 'Area, Crime and Incivility: a Profile from the British Crime Survey' in T. Hope and M. Shaw, eds., *Communities and Crime Reduction*. London: HMSO.

HUNTER, A. J. (1985), 'Private, Parochial and Public School Orders: The Problem of Crime and Incivilities in Urban Communities', in G. D. Suttles and M. N. Zald, eds., *The Challenge of Social Control: Citizenship and Institution Building in Urban Society*. Norwood NJ: Abex Publishing.

JANSON, C.-G. (1993), 'Ecological and Individual Approaches in the Study of Crime and Delinquency', in D. P. Farrington, R. J. Sampson, and P.-O. H. Wikström, eds, *Integrating Individual and Ecological Aspects of Crime*. Stockholm: National Council for Crime Prevention.

JEFFERY, C. R. (1971), *Crime Prevention Through Environmental Design*. Beverly Hills, Cal.: Sage Publications.

KINSEY, R. (1985), *Merseyside Crime Survey: First Report*. Liverpool: Merseyside County Council.

KORNHAUSER, R. R. (1978), *Social Sources of Delinquency*. Chicago, Ill.: University of Chicago Press.

KURTZ, L. R. (1984), *Evaluating Chicago Sociology*. Chicago, Ill.: University of Chicago Press.

LANDER, B. (1954), *Towards an Understanding of Juvenile Delinquency*. New York: Columbia University Press.

LASH, S., and URRY, J. (1987), *The End of Organized Capitalism*. Cambridge: Polity Press.

LOWMAN, J. (1986), 'Prostitution in Vancouver: Some Notes on the Genesis of a Social Problem', *Canadian Journal of Criminology*, 28: 1–16.

MAGUIRE, M., and BENNETT, T. (1982), *Burglary in a Dwelling*. London: Heinemann.

MALTZ, M (1995), 'Criminality in Space and Time: Life Course Analysis and the Micro-Ecology of Crime' in J. E. Eck and D. Weisburd, eds., *Crime and Place*. New York: Criminal Justice Press.

MANNHEIM, H. (1965), *Comparative Criminology*. London: Routledge and Kegan Paul.

MARTENS, P. L. (1990), 'Family, Neighbourhood and Socialization', in P.-O. H. Wikström, ed., *Crime and Measures Against Crime in The City*. Stockholm: National Council for Crime Prevention.

—— (1993), 'An Ecological Model of Socialisation in Explaining Offending' in D. P. Farrington, R. J. Sampson and P.-O. H. Wikström, eds., *Integrating Individual and Ecological Aspects of Crime*. Stockholm: National Council for Crime Prevention.

MATZA, D. (1964), *Delinquency and Drift*. New York: John Wiley.

MAWBY, R. I. (1979), *Policing the City*. Farnborough, Hants: Saxon House.

—— (1989), 'Policing and the Criminal Area', in D. J. Evans and D. T. Herbert, eds., *The Geography of Crime*. London: Routledge.

MAYHEW, H. (1862), *London Labour and the London Poor, vol. 4: Those That Will Not Work*. London: Griffin Bohn.

MAYHEW, P., and AYE MAUNG, N. (1992), *Surveying Crime: Findings from the 1992 British Crime Survey*. London: Home Office.

—— AYE MAUNG, N. and MIRRLEES-BLACK, C. (1993), *The 1992 British Crime Survey*. London: Home Office.

—— CLARKE, R. V. G., STURMAN, A., and HOUGH, J. M. (1976), *Crime as Opportunity*. Home Office Research Unit Study No. 34, London: HMSO.

—— and HOUGH, M. (1982), 'The British Crime Survey', *Home Office Research Bulletin*. No. 14, 24–7.

MCIVER, J. P. (1981), 'Criminal Mobility: A Review of Empirical Studies' in S. Hakin and G. Rengert, eds., *Crime Spillover*. Beverly Hills, Cal.: Sage.

MERRETT, S. (1979), *State Housing in Britain*. London: Routledge and Kegan Paul.

MIRRLEES-BLACK, C, MAYHEW, P., and PERCY, A (1996), *The 1996 British Crime Survey: England and Wales*. London: Home Office Statistical Bulletin 19/96.

MORRIS, L. (1994), *Dangerous Classes: The Underclass and Social Citizenship*. London: Routledge.

MORRIS, T. P. (1957), *The Criminal Area: A Study in Social Ecology*. London: Routledge and Kegan Paul.

MURRAY, C. (1984), *Losing Ground*. New York: Basic Books.

—— (1990), *The Emerging British Underclass*. London: Institute of Economic Affairs.

—— (1994), *Underclass: The Crisis Deepens*. London: IEA.

NACRO (1996), *Crime, Community and Change: Taking Action on the Kingsmeade Estate in Hackney*. London: NACRO.

NEWMAN, O. (1973), *Defensible Space*. London: Architectural Press.

PAINTER, K. (1992), 'Different Worlds: the Spatial, Temporal and Social Dimensions of

Female Victimization', in D. J. Evans, N. R. Fyfe, and D. T. Herbert, eds., *Crime and Policing: Essays in Environmental Criminology*. London: Routledge.

PEASE, K. (1993), 'Individual and Community Influences on Victimisation and their Implications for Crime Prevention', in D. P. Farrington, R. J. Sampson, and P.-O. H. Wikström, eds., *Integrating Individual and Ecological Aspects of Crime*. Stockholm: National Council for Crime Prevention.

POYNER, B. (1983), *Design Against Crime*. London: Butterworth.

—— and Webb, B. (1992), *Crime Free Housing*. Oxford: Butterworth Architecture.

RADZINOWICZ, L. (1966), *Ideology and Crime*. London: Heinemann.

RAMSAY, M. (1989), *Downtown Drinkers: The Perceptions and Fears of the Public in a City Centre*. Home Office Crime Prevention Unit Paper No. 19, London: Home Office.

REISS, A. J. (1986), 'Why are Communities Important in Understanding Crime?', in A. J. Reiss and M. Tonry, eds., *Communities and Crime*. Chicago, Ill.: University of Chicago Press.

RENGERT, G., and WASILCHICK, J. (1985), *Suburban Burglary*. Springfield, Ill.: Charles C. Thomas.

REX, J., and MOORE, R. (1967), *Race, Community and Conflict: A Study of Sparkbrook*. London: Oxford University Press.

REYNOLDS, F. (1986), *The Problem Housing Estate*. Aldershot: Gower.

RHODES, W. M., and CONLY, C. (1981), 'Crime and Mobility: an Empirical Study', in P. J. Brantingham and P. L. Brantingham, eds., *Environmental Criminology*. Beverly Hills, Cal.: Sage Publications.

ROBINSON, W. S. (1950), 'Ecological Correlations and the Behavior of Individuals', *American Sociological Review*, 15: 351–7.

ROSSMO, D. K. (1995), 'Place, Space and Police Investigations: Hunting Serial Violent Killers' in in J. E. Eck and D. Weisburd, eds., *Crime and Place*. New York: Criminal Justice Press.

RUTTER, M., and GILLER, H. (1983), *Juvenile Delinquency: Trends and Prospects*. Harmondsworth: Penguin Books.

SAMPSON, R. J. (1995), 'The Community' in J. Q. Wilson and J. Petersilia, eds., *Crime*. San Francisco, Cal.: Institute for Contemporary Studies.

—— and GROVES, W. B. (1989), 'Community Structure and Crime: Testing Social Disorganisation Theory', *American Journal of Sociology*, 94: 774–802.

SCHUERMAN, L., and KOBRIN, S. (1986), 'Com-

munity Careers in Crime' in A. J. Reiss and M. Tonry, eds., *Communities and Crime*. Chicago, Ill.: University of Chicago Press.

SELLIN, T. (1938), *Culture Conflict and Crime*. New York: Social Science Research Council.

SHAW, C. R. (1930) *The Jack Roller*. Chicago, Ill.: University of Chicago Press.

—— and MCKAY, H. D. (1931), *Social Factors in Juvenile Delinquency*. Washington, DC: Government Printing Office.

—— and —— (1942), *Juvenile Delinquency and Urban Areas*. Chicago, Ill.: University of Chicago Press.

SHERMAN, L. W. (1995), 'Hot Spots of Crime and Criminal Careers of Places', in J. E. Eck and D. Weisburd, eds., *Crime and Place*. New York: Criminal Justice Press.

—— GARTIN, P. R., and BUERGER, M. E. (1989), 'Hot Spots of Predatory Crime: Routine Activities and the Criminology of Place', *Criminology*, 27: 27–55.

SKOGAN, W. G. (1986), 'Fear of Crime and Neighborhood Change' in A. J. Reiss and M. Tonry, eds., *Communities and Crime*. Chicago, Ill.: University of Chicago Press.

—— (1990), *Disorder and Decline: Crime and the Spiral of Decay in American Neighborhoods*. New York: Free Press.

SNODGRASS, J. (1976), 'Clifford R. Shaw and Henry D. McKay: Chicago criminologists', *British Journal of Criminology*, 16: 1–19.

SPELMAN, W. (1995), 'Criminal Careers of Public Places', in J. E. Eck and D. Weisburd, eds., *Crime and Place*. New York: Criminal Justice Press.

TAUB, R., TAYLOR, D. G., and DUNHAM, J. D. (1984), *Paths of Neighborhood Change*. Chicago, Ill.: University of Chicago Press.

TAYLOR, R. B., and GOTTFREDSON, S. (1986), 'Environmental Design, Crime, and Prevention: An Examination of Community Dynamics', in A. J. Reiss and M. Tonry, eds., *Communities and Crime*. Chicago, Ill.: University of Chicago Press.

TOBIAS, J. J. (1972) *Urban Crime in Victorian England*. New York: Schocken Books.

TRICKETT, A., OSBORN, D. R., SEYMOUR, J., and PEASE, K. (1992), 'What is Different About High Crime Areas?', *British Journal of Criminology*, 32: 81–9.

TYLER, T. R. (1990), *Why People Obey the Law*. New Haven, Conn.: Yale University Press.

URRY, J. (1986), Book review of 'The Constitution of Society' by Anthony Giddens', *Sociological Review*, 34: 434–7.

WEBER, M. (1949), *The Methodology of the Social Sciences*. Trans. E. A. Shils and H. A. Finch. New York: Free Press.

—— (1968), *Economy and Society: An Outline of Interpretive Sociology*. 3 vols, ed. G. Roth and C. Wittich. New York: Bedminster Press.

WIKSTRÖM, P.-O. H (1990), 'Delinquency and the Urban Structure' in P.-O. H. Wikström, ed., *Crime and Measures Against Crime in The City*. Stockholm: National Council for Crime Prevention.

—— (1991), *Urban Crime, Criminals and Victims: The Swedish Experience in an Anglo-American Comparative Perspective*. New York: Springer-Verlag.

WILES, P. (1992), 'Ghettoization in Europe?', *European Journal on Criminal Policy and Research*, 1: 52–69.

WILSON, J. Q., and KELLING, G. (1982), 'Broken Windows', *The Atlantic Monthly* (March): 29–38.

WILSON, W. J. (1987), *The Truly Disadvantaged*. Chicago, Ill.: University Press.

—— (1996), *When Work Disappears: The World of the New Urban Poor*. New York: Alfred Knopf.

WINCHESTER, S., and JACKSON, H. (1982), *Residential Burglary*. Home Office Research Study No. 74, London: Home Office.

WIRTH, L. (1938), 'Urbanism as a Way of Life', *American Journal of Sociology*, 44: 1–24.

WRIGHT, R. T., and DECKER, S. H. (1994), *Burglars on the Job: Street Life and Residential Break-ins*. Boston, Mass.: Northeastern University Press.

9

Human Development and
Criminal Careers

David P. Farrington

The aim of this chapter is to review what is known about human development and criminal careers. A 'criminal career' is defined as the longitudinal sequence of offences committed by an individual offender. 'Offences' in this chapter are defined as the most common types of crimes that predominate in the official *Criminal Statistics*, including theft, burglary, robbery, violence, vandalism, and drug use. 'White collar' crime is not included here, because there has been little attempt as yet to study it from the perspective of human development and criminal careers.

A criminal career has a beginning (onset), an end (desistance), and a career length in between (duration). Only a certain proportion of the population (prevalence) has a criminal career and commits offences. During their careers, offenders commit offences at a certain rate (frequency) while they are at risk of offending in the community (e.g. not incarcerated or hospitalized). For offenders who commit several offences, it is possible to investigate how far they specialize in certain types of offences and how far the seriousness of their offending escalates over time.

The criminal career approach is essentially concerned with human development over time. However, criminal behaviour does not generally appear without warning; it is commonly preceded by childhood antisocial behaviour (such as bullying, lying, truanting, and cruelty to animals) and followed by adult anti-social behaviour (such as spouse assault, child abuse and neglect, excessive drinking, and sexual promiscuity). The word 'antisocial' of course involves a value judgement, but it seems likely that there would be general agreement among most members of Western democracies that these kinds of acts interfered with the smooth running of Western society.

In studying development, it is important to investigate developmental sequences over time, for example where one behaviour facilitates or acts as a kind of stepping stone to another. It is desirable to identify non-criminal behaviours that lead to criminal behaviours, and long-term developmental sequences including types of offending. For example, hyperactivity at age 2 may lead to cruelty to animals at 6, shoplifting at 10, burglary at 15, robbery at 20, and eventually spouse assault, child abuse and neglect, alcohol abuse, and employment and accommodation problems later on in life. Typically, a career of childhood anti-social behaviour leads to a criminal career, which often coincides with a career of teenage anti-social behaviour and leads to a career of adult anti-social behaviour. The criminal career is a legally defined subset of a longer-term and more wide-ranging anti-social career. A deeper understanding of the development of the criminal career requires a deeper understanding of the wider anti-social career.

It seems that offending is part of a larger syndrome of anti-social behaviour that arises in childhood and tends to persist into adulthood. There seems to be continuity over time, since the anti-social child tends to become the anti-social teenager and then the anti-social adult, just as the anti-social adult then tends to produce another anti-social child. However, the main focus of this chapter is on types of anti-social behaviour classified as criminal offences, rather than on other types classified for example as conduct disorder or anti-social personality disorder.

This chapter also reviews risk factors that influence the development of criminal careers. Fortunately or unfortunately, there is no shortage of factors that are significantly correlated with offending; indeed, literally thousands of variables differentiate significantly between official offenders and non-offenders and correlate significantly with reports of offending behaviour by teenagers and their peers, parents, and teachers. In this chapter, it is possible only briefly to review some of the most important risk factors for offending: individual difference factors such as high impulsivity and low intelligence, family influences such as poor child-rearing and criminal parents, socio-economic deprivation, school factors, and situational factors. Community influences are not reviewed because they are covered in the chapter on Environmental Criminology by Anthony Bottoms. Because of the chapter's focus on human development, unchanging variables such as sex and race are not reviewed.

The chapter ends with a brief review of the theoretical implications of research on human development and criminal careers. An attempt is made to propose a simple theory that accounts for as much of the complex reality as possible. The emphasis is on offending by males; most research on offending has concentrated on males, because they commit most of the serious predatory and violent offences. The review is limited to research carried out in the United Kingdom, the United States, and similar industrialized democracies.

Within a single chapter, it is obviously impossible to review everything that is known about the development of offending. I will be very selective in focusing on some of the more important and replicable findings obtained in some of the more methodologically adequate studies: especially longitudinal studies of large community samples. While most longitudinal surveys of offending focus primarily on lower-class and urban samples, some are based on large representative samples from the whole population (e.g. Wikström, 1987; Moffitt and Silva, 1988a; Fergusson *et al.*, 1993). Unfortunately, there is not space here to review the implications of research on human development and criminal careers for crime prevention and crime control (see Farrington, 1992a, 1994a, 1996c).

In studying human development, it is essential to carry out prospective longitudinal surveys. I will refer especially to knowledge gained in the Cambridge Study in Delinquent Development, which is a prospective longitudinal survey of over 400 London males from 8 to 32 (e.g. Farrington and West, 1990; Farrington, 1995*b*). Fortunately, results obtained in British longitudinal surveys of delinquency (e.g. Wadsworth, 1979: Kolvin *et al.*, 1990) are highly concordant with those obtained in comparable surveys in North America (e.g. McCord, 1979; Robins, 1979), the Scandinavian countries (e.g. Wikström, 1987; Pulkkinen, 1988) and New Zealand (e.g. Moffitt and Silva, 1988*a*; Fergusson *et al.*, 1993), and indeed with results obtained in British cross-sectional surveys (e.g. Hagell and Newburn, 1994; Boswell, 1995; Graham and Bowling, 1995). A systematic comparison of the Cambridge Study and the Pittsburgh Youth Study (Farrington and Loeber, forthcoming) showed numerous replicable predictors of delinquency over time and place, including impulsivity, attention problems, low school attainment, poor parental supervision, parental conflict, an antisocial parent, a young mother, large family size, low family income, and coming from a broken family.

CONCEPTUAL AND METHODOLOGICAL ISSUES

The Antisocial Syndrome

While the acts defined as offences are heterogeneous, it nevertheless makes sense to investigate the characteristics of offenders. This is because offenders are predominantly versatile rather than specialized (e.g. Klein, 1984; Farrington *et al.*, 1988*c*). In other words, people who commit one type of offence have a significant tendency also to commit other types. For example, 86 per cent of convicted violent offenders in the Cambridge Study also had convictions for non-violent offences (Farrington, 1991*b*).

Just as offenders tend to be versatile in their types of offending, they also tend to be versatile in their anti-social behaviour generally. In the Cambridge Study, delinquents tended to be troublesome and dishonest in their primary schools, tended to be aggressive and frequent liars at 12–14, and tended to be bullies at 14. By 18, delinquents tended to be antisocial in a wide variety of respects, including heavy drinking, heavy smoking, using prohibited drugs, and heavy gambling. In addition, they tended to be sexually promiscuous, often beginning sexual intercourse under 15, having several sexual partners by 18, and usually having unprotected intercourse (Farrington, 1992*d*).

As already mentioned, delinquency (which is dominated by crimes of dishonesty) seems to be only one element of a larger syndrome of anti-social behaviour which arises in childhood and usually persists into adulthood. In the Cambridge Study, a scale of 'antisocial tendency' was developed at 18, based on factors such as an unstable job record, heavy gambling, heavy smoking, drug use, drunk driving, sexual promiscuity, spending time hanging about on the street, anti-social group activity, violence, and anti-establishment attitudes (West and Farrington, 1977). The aim was to devise a scale that was not based on the types of acts (thefts and burglaries) that predominantly led to convictions, and it was found that the convicted males were usually anti-social in several other respects. For example, two-thirds (67 per cent) of those convicted up to 18 had four or more of these antisocial features at that age, compared with only 15 per cent of the unconvicted males.

More comprehensive scales of 'antisocial personality' were developed at ages 10, 14, 18, and 32, based on offending and on other types of anti-social behaviour (Farrington, 1991*a*). For example, the scale at age 14 included convictions, high self-reported delinquency, stealing outside home, regular smoking, having sexual intercourse, bullying, frequent lying, frequent disobedience, hostility to police, frequent truancy, daring, and poor concentration/restlessness. All these measures tended to be interrelated. However, the last two measures, of impulsivity, are arguably causes of anti-social behaviour rather than indicators of it. They were included for consistency with psychiatric criteria of anti-social personality disorder, but impulsivity will be reviewed as a risk factor for offending later in this chapter. It is often difficult to distinguish between causes, consequences and indicators of anti-social personality.

The Criminal Career Approach

The criminal career approach is not a criminological theory but a framework within which theories can be proposed and tested (see Blumstein *et al.*, 1986; Blumstein and Cohen, 1987). Dictionary definitions of the term 'career' specify two different concepts: a course or progress through life, or a way of making a living. The term is used in the first sense here. A 'criminal career' describes a sequence of offences committed during some part of an individual's life-time, with no necessary suggestion that offenders use their criminal activity as an important means of earning a living.

The criminal career approach emphasizes the need to investigate such questions as why people start offending (onset), why they continue offending (persistence), why offending becomes more frequent or more serious (escalation), and why people stop offending (desistance). The factors influencing onset may differ from those influencing other criminal career features such as persistence, escalation, and desistance, if only because the different processes occur at different ages. Indeed, in the Cambridge Study there was no relationship between factors influencing prevalence (official offenders versus non-offenders), those influencing early versus later onset, and those influencing desistance after age 21 (Farrington and Hawkins, 1991); and in the Pittsburgh Youth Study there was no relationship between factors influencing onset and those influencing escalation (Loeber *et al.*, 1991).

In order to understand the causes of offending, it is important to study developmental processes such as onset, persistence, escalation, and desistance.

However, it is also important not to restrict this study narrowly to offending, but also to study the onset, persistence, escalation, and desistance of other types of anti-social behaviour. Loeber and LeBlanc (1990) used many other concepts to describe developmental processes in anti-social careers, including acceleration and deceleration, diversification, switching, stabilization, and de-escalation. For example, 'retention' (escalating to serious acts while still committing trivial acts) was more common than 'innovation' (escalating and giving up trivial acts).

The criminal career approach is essentially concerned with human development over time. Most criminological theories focus on instantaneous or cross-sectional differences between official offenders and non-offenders or on cross-sectional correlates of the frequency or variety of self-reported offending. Furthermore, most criminological theories aim to explain offending when it is in full flow, in the teenage years. However, the criminal career approach focuses on within-individual changes over time and on the predictors of longitudinal processes such as onset and desistance, recognizing that the same person can be an active offender at one age and a non-offender at another. It also aims to explain the development of offending over all ages.

Criminal career research seeks to investigate whether aggregate career features are the same as or different from individual features (Blumstein *et al.*, 1988). For example, the age–crime curve over all individuals shows that the aggregate rate of offending increases to a peak in the teenage years and then decreases. The shape of this curve may reflect either changes in the prevalence of offenders at each age (the proportion of individuals who offend, out of the population) or changes in the frequency of offending (by those who are offenders at each age) or some combination of these. Most of the existing British and American evidence suggests that the aggregate peak age of offending primarily reflects variations in prevalence, and that individual offenders commit offences at a tolerably constant frequency during their criminal careers (Farrington, 1986a). On this model, a 30-year-old offender commits offences at roughly the same rate as an 18-year-old offender, although offenders are more prevalent in the population of 18-year-olds than in the population of 30-year-olds. Therefore, the flat age–crime distribution for individual offending frequency is quite different from the peaked distribution for prevalence and from the peaked aggregate age–crime curve.

Putting this point in a slightly different way, a key issue in criminal career research is to determine how far aggregate changes with age or during the course of a criminal career reflect changes within individual offenders as opposed to changes in the composition of the offending population. For example, juvenile offenders primarily commit their crimes with others, whereas adult offenders primarily commit their crimes alone (Reiss and Farrington, 1991; Tarling, 1993). Does this finding mean that offenders change their methods of offending as they get older, switching from co-offending to lone offending? Or does it mean that one population of co-offenders desists (drops out) and is replaced by a new population of lone offenders? The answer to this kind of question, which arises very frequently, has important theoretical and policy implications. Generally, the evidence suggests that changes occur within one population of offenders at different ages, rather than some offenders desisting and being replaced at later ages by a new population of offenders.

Similarly, criminal career researchers emphasize that different career features may be differently related to age. It has already been pointed out that prevalence peaks in the teenage years but that the individual offending frequency may not. Blumstein *et al.* (1982) found that the residual length of a criminal career (the time remaining up to the point of desistance) peaked between ages 30 and 40. While teenage offenders are quite prevalent in the teenage population, the average teenage offender does not commit offences at a particularly high frequency and tends to have only a relatively short criminal career remaining. In contrast, 30-year-old offenders are much less prevalent in the population of 30-year-olds, but the average 30-year-old offender tends to have a relatively long criminal career remaining. Looked at developmentally, 30-year-old offenders tend to be a subset of teenage offenders. Most teenage offenders desist from offending before age 30.

Definitions and Measurement

Anti-social behaviour covers a multitude of sins. It includes acts prohibited by the criminal law, such as theft, burglary, robbery, violence, vandalism, and drug use; as already mentioned, the definition of 'offending' in this chapter focuses on these types of acts. It also includes other clearly deviant acts such as bullying, reckless driving, heavy drinking, and sexual promiscuity, and more marginally or arguably deviant acts such as heavy smoking, heavy gambling, employment instability, and conflict with parents.

Offending is commonly measured using either official records of arrests or convictions or self-reports of offending. The advantages and disadvantages of official records and self-reports are to some extent complementary. In general, official records include the worst offenders and the worst offences, while self-reports include more of the normal range of delinquent activity. The worst offenders may be missing from samples interviewed in self-report studies (Cernkovich *et al.*, 1985). Self-reports have the advantage of including undetected offences, but the disadvantages of concealment and forgetting. By normally accepted psychometric criteria of validity, self-reports are valid (Huizinga and Elliott, 1986). For example, in the Pittsburgh Youth Study, the seriousness of self-reported delinquency predicted later court referrals (Farrington *et al.*, 1996a). However, predictive validity was enhanced by combining self-report, parent, and teacher information about offending.

The key issue is whether the same results are obtained with official records and self-reports. For example, if both methods show a link between parental supervision and delinquency, it is likely that supervision is related to delinquent behaviour (rather than to any biases in measurement). This chapter focuses on such replicable results. Generally, the worst offenders according to self-reports (taking account of frequency and seriousness) tend also to be the worst offenders according to official records (e.g. Farrington, 1973; Huizinga and Elliott, 1986). For example, in the Cambridge Study between ages 15 and 18, 11 per cent of the males admitted burglary, and 62 per cent of these males were convicted of burglary (West and Farrington, 1977). The predictors and correlates of official and self-reported burglary were very similar (Farrington, 1992c).

The results obtained in criminal career research depend on the methods of defining and measuring crime that are adopted. Most criminal career researchers focus on official records of arrests or convictions for relatively serious offences rather than on self-reports of relatively trivial infractions. Most criminal career results quoted in this chapter are based on arrests or convictions. With official records of relatively serious offences, the measured prevalence and frequency of offending are lower and the age of onset of offending is later. In principle, there is no reason why the criminal career approach could not be applied to self-reports of relatively trivial offences. In comparing official records and self-reports of the same behaviour, the underlying criminal career parameters (such as the individual offending frequency) might remain the same in each analysis, but the relationship between these parameters and the observed behaviour (e.g. convictions or self-reports) would vary.

Criminal career research requires exact information about the timing of offences. This is available in official records (e.g. of convictions), but not usually in self-reports. It would be convenient for criminal career researchers if offenders would keep a regular diary listing all their offences. The nearest approach to this is the type of calendar method used by Horney and Marshall (1991). Retrospective self-reports covering long periods of ten years or more are not accurate (see e.g. Yarrow *et al.*, 1970). In the Cambridge Study, in a systematic comparison of prospective repeated self-reports and long-term retrospective self-reports of offending by the same males, an average of 46 per cent of all offences admitted prospectively between ages 10 and 25 were denied retrospectively (in response to 'ever' questions) at 32 (Farrington, 1989c). The most frequent offenders are likely to have the greatest difficulty in providing valid retrospective self-reports of their offending careers, especially if they have low intelligence and are alcohol or drug abusers. Hence, prospective longitudinal data are needed.

DEVELOPMENT OF OFFENDING

Prevalence at Different Ages

One of the distinctive contributions of criminal career research has been to demonstrate the high cumulative prevalence of arrests and convictions of males (for a review, see Visher and Roth, 1986). In the Cambridge Study, 40 per cent of London males were convicted for criminal offences up to age 40, when these were restricted to offences normally recorded in the Criminal Record Office (Farrington, 1995a). In Newcastle-upon-Tyne, 31 per cent of males and 6 per cent of females were convicted of non-traffic offences up to age 32 (Kolvin et al., 1988). Similarly, a longitudinal follow-up of a 1953 English birth cohort in official records (Home Office Statistical Bulletin, 1995) found that 34 per cent of males and 9 per cent of females were convicted of non-traffic offences up to age 39.

Similar results have been obtained in other countries. In the Philadelphia cohort study, Wolfgang et al. (1987) showed that 47 per cent of males were arrested for non-traffic offences up to age 30, including 38 per cent of Caucasians and 69 per cent of African Americans. In Sweden, Stattin et al. (1989) discovered that 38 per cent of males and 7 per cent of females were officially registered for non-traffic offences by age 30. The curves showing the cumulative prevalence up to age 25 of offending by working-class males in London and Stockholm were remarkably similar (Farrington and Wikström, 1994).

The cumulative prevalence of self-reported offences is even higher. In the Cambridge Study, almost all of the males (96 per cent) had committed at least one of ten specified offences (including burglary, theft, assault, vandalism, and drug use) by the age of 32 (Farrington, 1989c). Many males commit minor acts, especially in their teenage years, that might, strictly speaking, be classified as offences. In order realistically to compare offenders and non-offenders, it is necessary to set a sufficiently high criterion for 'offending' (e.g. in terms of frequency, seriousness, duration, or in terms of arrests or convictions) so that the vast majority of the male population are not classified as offenders. Alternatively, more and less serious offenders could be compared.

An important focus of criminal career research is the relationship between age and crime. Generally, the 'point prevalence' of offending at each age increases to a peak in the teenage years and then declines. The age–crime curve obtained by following up a cohort of people over time (the same people at different ages) is often different from the cross-sectional curve seen in official statistics (which reflects different people at different ages; see Farrington, 1990a).

In the Cambridge Study, the peak age for the prevalence of convictions was 17 (Farrington, 1992b). The median age of conviction for most types of offences (burglary, robbery, theft of and from vehicles, shoplifting) was 17, while it was 20 for violence and 21 for fraud. Mean ages are typically higher than medians and modes (peaks), because of the skewed age–crime curve (Farrington, 1986a: 196). In national English data, the peak age varied from 14 for shoplifting to 20 for fraud/forgery and drug offences (Tarling, 1993). Similarly, in the Philadelphia cohort study of Wolfgang et al. (1987), the arrest rate increased to a peak at age 16 and then declined. In the Cambridge Study, the peak age of increase in the prevalence of offending was 14, while the peak age of decrease was 23. These times of maximum acceleration and deceleration in prevalence draw our attention to times in people's lives when important life events may be occurring that influence offending. They also indicate that the modal age of onset of offending is probably 14 and the modal age of desistance is probably 23.

Self-report studies also show that the most common types of offending decline from the teens to the twenties. In the Cambridge Study, the prevalence of burglary, shoplifting, theft of and from vehicles, theft from automatic machines, and vandalism all decreased from the teens to the twenties, but the same decreases were not seen for theft from work, assault, drug abuse, and fraud (Farrington, 1989c). For example, burglary (since the last interview) was admitted by 13 per cent at age 14, 11 per cent at 18, 5 per cent at 21, and 2 per cent at both 25 and 32. In their American National Youth Survey, Elliott *et al.* (1989) found that self-reports of the prevalence of offending increased from 11–13 to a peak at 15–17 and then decreased by 19–21.

Individual Offending Frequency

Since the pioneering research of Blumstein and Cohen (1979), much criminal career research has been concerned to estimate the individual offending frequency of active offenders during their criminal careers (for a review, see Cohen, 1986). For example, based on American research, Blumstein and Cohen concluded that the average active Index (more serious) offender committed about ten Index offences per year free, and that the individual offending frequency essentially did not vary with age. Furthermore, the average active Index offender accumulated about one arrest per year free.

In calculating the individual offending frequency and other criminal career parameters such as onset, duration, and desistance, a major problem is to estimate when careers really begin and when they really end. Tarling (1993: 53) assumed that careers began at the age of criminal responsibility and ended on the date of the last conviction. On this assumption, males in the 1953 birth cohort had a conviction rate of 0.5 per year (one every two years), while the corresponding figure for females was 0.3 per year (one every 3.3 years).

The British and American studies reviewed by Farrington (1986a) indicated that the individual offending frequency did not vary greatly with age or during criminal careers. However, Loeber and Snyder (1990) concluded that it increased during the juvenile years up to age 16, and Haapanen (1990) found that it decreased during the adult years. Furthermore, in the Stockholm Project Metropolitan, Wikström (1990) showed that frequency peaked at 15–17, and in retrospective self-report research with Nebraska prisoners Horney and Marshall (1991) concluded that it varied over time within individuals. Since there are several contrary studies indicating that frequency is stable with age (e.g. Home Office Statistical Bulletin, 1987; LeBlanc and Frechette, 1989), more research is clearly needed to establish the conditions under which it is relatively stable or varying with age.

If periods of acceleration or deceleration in the individual offending frequency could be identified, and if the predictors of acceleration or deceleration could be established (Farrington, 1987), these could have important implications for theory and policy. Barnett and Lofaso (1985) found that the best predictor of the future offending frequency in the Philadelphia cohort study was the past offending frequency.

There are many life events or conditions that might lead to an increase in the individual offending frequency. For example, using retrospective self-reports, Ball *et al.* (1981) found that Baltimore heroin addicts committed non-drug offences at a higher rate during periods of addiction than during periods when they were off opiates, suggesting that addiction caused an increase in offending. Using official records in the Cambridge Study, London males committed offences at a higher rate during periods of unemployment than during periods of employment (Farrington *et al.*, 1986*b*). This difference was restricted to offences involving material gain, suggesting that unemployment caused a lack of money, which in turn caused an increase in offending to obtain money. However, neither of these studies adequately disentangled differences in prevalence from differences in frequency.

The individual offending frequency cannot be estimated from aggregate data simply by dividing the number of offences at each age by the number of arrested or convicted persons at each age, because some persons who have embarked on a criminal career may not sustain an official record at a particular age. Barnett *et al.* (1987) tested several mathematical models of the criminal careers of the Cambridge Study males, restricting the analyses to persons with two or more convictions. They found that models assuming that all offenders had the same frequency of offending were inadequate. Hence, they assumed that there were two categories of offenders, 'frequents' and 'occasionals'. The data showed that both categories incurred convictions at a constant (but different) rate during their active criminal careers. Barnett *et al.* did not suggest that there were in reality only two categories of offenders, but rather that it was possible to fit the actual data with a simple model assuming only two categories.

The average 'street time' interval between each offence is the reciprocal of the individual offending frequency. Generally, this time interval decreases with each successive offence in a criminal career (e.g. Hamparian *et al.*, 1978; Tracy *et al.*, 1985). This decrease could mean either that the individual offending frequency was speeding up with each successive offence or that relatively low-frequency offenders were gradually dropping out of the offending population, so that this population was increasingly composed of high-frequency offenders at each successive offence transition. With the Philadelphia cohort data, Barnett and Lofaso (1985) concluded that offenders were not speeding up; offending frequencies stayed relatively constant over time, and the decreasing time intervals reflected a changing population of offenders.

Most prior studies of recidivism have used reconviction or no reconviction (or rearrest or no rearrest) within a short follow-up period of two or three years as the key dependent variable to be predicted. However, this is a rather insensitive measure. The individual offending frequency, and the associated (reciprocal) time intervals between offences, would be a more sensitive measure, and might give researchers a better chance of detecting the effect of sentencing or penal treatment on recidivism.

Onset

Criminal career research on onset using official records generally shows a peak age of onset between 13 and 16. For example, in the United States, Blumstein and Graddy (1982) showed that the age of onset curve for arrests of both white and non-white males peaked at age 15, and Stattin *et al.* (1989) also reported a peak age of 15 for males in a small Swedish city (Örebro). In the Swedish Project Metropolitan, Fry (1985) found that the peak ages of first arrest for Stockholm males and females were both at 13, while the peak age of onset for males in Finland was 16–17 (Pulkkinen, 1988). In the Cambridge Study, the peak age of onset was 14; 5 per cent of the males were first convicted at that age (Farrington, 1992*b*). The onset curves up to age 25 of working-class males in London and Stockholm were quite similar (Farrington and Wikström, 1994).

Rather than presenting the onset rate, taking all persons in a cohort still alive as the denominator, it might be better to present a 'hazard' rate. This relates the number of first offenders to the number of persons still at risk of a first offence, excluding those with a previous onset. In the Cambridge Study, the hazard rate showed a later peak than the onset rate at age 17; 6 per cent of the males still at risk were first convicted at that age (Farrington *et al.*, 1990*a*). Basically, the peak hazard rate was later and greater than the peak onset rate because of the decreasing number of males still at risk of a first conviction with increasing age (the denominator). McCord (1990) showed how hazard rates varied according to social background variables. In the Cambridge Study, the best childhood predictors of an early versus a later onset of offending were rarely spending leisure time with the father, high troublesomeness, authoritarian parents and high psychomotor impulsivity (Farrington and Hawkins, 1991).

In reality, and in a mathematical model, the true age of onset of offending will precede the age of the first conviction. By knowing the true individual offending frequency (which can be estimated from time intervals between offences), it is possible to estimate the true age of onset from the measured age of onset. For example, if the true individual offending frequency was two per year, and the measured age of onset (the first recorded offence) was at 13.0 years, the true age of onset would be at 12.5 years (since the average time to the first offence would be 0.5 years).

It would also be desirable to study sequences of onsets, to investigate how far the onset of one type of offence is followed by the onset of another type. The age of onset varies with different types of offences. In a study of Montreal delinquents, LeBlanc and Frechette (1989) discovered that shoplifting and vandalism tended to occur before adolescence (average age of onset 11), burglary and motor vehicle theft in adolescence (average onset 14–15), and sex offences and drug trafficking in the later teenage years (average onset 17–19). Judging from average ages of onset, the onset of shoplifting or vandalism might provide an early opportunity to detect future serious criminal offenders.

In the Cambridge Study, the average age of the first conviction was 17.5. The males first convicted at the earliest ages (10–13) tended to become the most persistent offenders, committing an average of 8.1 offences leading to convictions in an average criminal career lasting 9.9 years up to age 32 (Farrington, 1992b). Similarly, Farrington and Wikstrom (1994), using official records in Stockholm, and LeBlanc and Frechette (1989) in Montreal, using both self-reports and official records, showed that the duration of criminal careers decreased with increasing age of onset.

Clearly, an early age of onset foreshadows a long criminal career (see also Home Office Statistical Bulletin, 1987; Tracy and Kempf-Leonard, 1996). Whether it also foreshadows a high frequency of offending is less clear. Hamparian et al. (1978), in a study of violent juveniles in Ohio, reported that there was a (negative) linear relationship between the age of onset and the number of offences. Neglecting the possibility of desistance, this suggests that the offending frequency may be tolerably constant between onset and the 18th birthday. In agreement with this, Tarling (1993: 57) found no relationship between age of onset and the conviction rate. However, Tolan (1987) showed that the frequency of current self-reported offending was greatest for those with the earliest age of onset.

Aggregate results may hide different types of offenders. For example, Moffitt (1993) distinguished between 'life-course-persistent' offenders, who had an early onset and a long criminal career, and 'adolescence-limited' offenders, who started later and had a short criminal career. These groups were identified using conviction records in the Cambridge Study (Nagin et al., 1995). However, according to self-reports, the apparent reformation of the 'adolescence-limited' offenders was less than complete. At age 32, they continued to drink heavily, to use drugs, get into fights, and commit criminal acts.

It is important to establish why an early age of onset predicts a long criminal career and a large number of offences. Following Gottfredson and Hirschi (1986), one possibility is that an early age of onset is merely one symptom of a high criminal potential, which later shows itself in persistent and serious offending. On this theory, an early age of onset has no effect on underlying theoretical constructs. Another possibility is that an early age of onset in some way facilitates later offending, perhaps because of the reinforcing effects of successful early offending or the stigmatizing effects of convictions. In other words, an early onset may lead to a change in an underlying theoretical construct such as the probability of persistence. Nagin and Farrington (1992a) concluded that the inverse relationship between age of onset and persistence of offending in the Cambridge Study was entirely attributable to the persistence of a previously existing criminal potential, and that an early age of onset had no additional impact on persistence.

An onset offence of a particular type might predict a later frequent or serious criminal career. For example, the Home Office Statistical Bulletin (1987) showed that an onset offence of burglary or theft was particularly predictive of persistence in offending. This type of information might be useful in identifying at first arrest or conviction those at high risk of progressing into a persistent and serious criminal career.

Desistance

The true age of desistance from offending can be determined with certainty only after offenders die. In the Cambridge Study up to age 32, the average age of the last offence was 23.3, according to official records. Since the average age of the first offence was 17.5, the average length of the recorded criminal career was 5.8 years, with an average of 4.5 recorded convictions per offender during this time period (Farrington, 1992b).

In the Philadelphia cohort study, Wolfgang et al. (1972) showed how the probability of reoffending (persistence as opposed to desistance) increased after each successive offence. This probability was .54 after the first offence, .65 after the second, .72 after the third, and it reached an asymptote of .80 after six or more arrests. Assuming a probabilistic process with a probability p of persisting after each offence, and conversely a probability (1–p) of desisting, the expected number of future offences after any given offence is $p/(1-p)$, which at the asymptote (p = .80) is 4.

Several other researchers have replicated these results by showing the growth in the recidivism probability after each successive offence (see Blumstein et al., 1985; Tarling, 1993; Farrington and Wikström, 1994). For example, national English data for males born in 1953 shows that the probability of persistence increased from .45 after the first conviction to .83 after the seventh (Home Office Statistical Bulletin, 1995). The corresponding probabilities for females were from .22 to .78.

Barnett et al. (1987) proposed a more complex mathematical model for the Cambridge Study data, aiming to explain time intervals between convictions as well as recidivism probabilities. They distinguished 'frequents' and 'occasionals' who differed both in their rates of offending and in their probabilities of desisting after each conviction. The longitudinal sequences of convictions were fitted best by assuming persistence probabilities after each conviction of .90 for frequents and .67 for occasionals.

These models assume that desistance does or does not occur immediately after each conviction. Hence, an implicit assumption is that something connected with the conviction (e.g. the penalty) has an effect, with a certain probability. An alternative model is that, after onset, desistance occurs continuously as an annual process. With this assumption in the London data, the annual rate of desistance for the frequents (.11) was not significantly different from that of the occasionals (.14). It is difficult to distinguish between these alternative models on the basis of conviction sequences alone. However, they have very different theoretical and policy implications.

Barnett *et al.* (1989) also carried out a predictive test of their model with the Cambridge Study data. The model was developed on conviction data between the tenth and twenty-fifth birthdays and tested on reconviction data between the twenty-fifth and thirtieth birthdays. Generally, the model performed well, but it seemed necessary to assume that there was some intermittency (desisting and later restarting) in criminal careers. Some of the frequents ceased offending at an average age of 19 and then restarted after a period of seven to ten years with no convictions. It is important to establish why this restarting occurs. It may be connected to life changes such as losing a job or separating from a spouse.

Several projects have explicitly investigated why offenders desist. For example, in the Cambridge Study, getting married and moving out of London both fostered desistance (Osborn, 1980; West, 1982). Shover (1985) explicitly asked retrospective questions about desistance to older men who had given up offending. The main reasons advanced for desistance focused on the increasing costs of crime (long prison sentences), the importance of intimate relationships with women, increasing satisfaction with jobs, and becoming more mature, responsible, and settled with age. In the Gluecks' follow-up of 500 Boston delinquents, Sampson and Laub (1993) identified job stability and marital attachment in adulthood as crucial factors in desistance. Some policy implications of desistance research are that ex-offenders should be helped to settle down in stable marital relationships and in stable jobs, and helped to break away from their criminal associates.

Chronic Offenders

In the Philadelphia cohort study, Wolfgang *et al.* (1972) showed that 6 per cent of the males (18 per cent of the offenders) accounted for 52 per cent of all the juvenile arrests, and labelled these 6 per cent the 'chronic offenders'. The chronics accounted for even higher proportions of serious offences: 69 per cent of all aggravated assaults, 71 per cent of homicides, 73 per cent of forcible rapes, and 82 per cent of robberies. Frequency and seriousness of offending are generally related. Other researchers have largely replicated these results. For example, in the Cambridge Study, about 6 per cent of the males accounted for about half of all the convictions up to the age of 32 (Farrington and West, 1993). However, the offences of the chronic offenders were not more serious on average than those of the non-chronic offenders. The chronics committed more serious offences largely because they committed more offences.

In Stockholm, Wikström (1987) showed that only 1 per cent of Project Metropolitan cohort members (6 per cent of all offenders) accounted for half of all the crimes, while Pulkkinen (1988) in Finland found that 4 per cent of males and 1 per cent of females accounted for half of all the convictions. It is useful to quantify these disproportionalities using the Lorenz curve and the Gini coefficient (Fox and Tracy, 1988; Wikström, 1991: 29). The chronic offenders who account for a disproportionate number of all offences are clearly prime targets for crime prevention and control. However, a lot depends on how far they can be identified in advance.

Blumstein *et al.* (1985) pointed out that Wolfgang *et al.* (1972) identified the chronics retrospectively. Even if all the arrested boys were truly homogeneous in their underlying criminal potential, chance factors alone would result in some of them having more arrests and others having fewer. Because of these probabilistic processes, those with the most arrests—defined after the fact as the chronics—would account for a disproportionate fraction of the total number of arrests. For example, if an unbiased die was thrown thirty times and the five highest scores were added up, these would account for a dispro-portionate fraction of the total score obtained in all thirty throws (thirty out of 105, on average; 16.7 per cent of the throws accounting for 28.6 per cent of the total score).

The key question is how far the chronic offenders can be predicted in advance, and whether they differ prospectively from the non-chronic offenders in their individual offending frequency. Blumstein *et al.* (1985) investigated this in the Cambridge Study. They used a seven-point scale of variables measured at 8–10, reflecting child anti-social behaviour, family economic deprivation, convicted parents, low intelligence, and poor parental child-rearing behaviour. Of fifty-five boys scoring four or more, fifteen were chronic offenders (out of twenty-three chronics altogether), twenty-two others were convicted, and only eighteen were not convicted. Hence, it was concluded that most of the chronics could have been predicted in advance on the basis of information available at the age of 10. Similar conclusions were drawn in a later analysis (Farrington and West, 1993). It is true that only a minority of the high-scoring boys became chronics; however, as will be explained below, the remainder should not all be regarded as 'false positives' or mistakes in prediction.

Blumstein *et al.* (1985) developed a mathematical model in which all the London males were classified as 'innocents', 'desisters', or 'persisters'. The best fit to the recidivism probabilities in the survey was obtained by assuming that the probability of persisting after each conviction was .87 for persisters and .57 for desisters. The proportion of first offenders who were persisters was 28 per cent. Persisters and desisters differed in their *a priori* probabilities of persisting, not in their *a posteriori* number of convictions (as chronics did).

Interestingly, the number of predicted chronics among the offenders (thirty-seven 'high-risk' offenders scoring four or more on the seven-point scale) was similar to the hypothesized number of persisters (36.7) according to the math-ematical model. Furthermore, the individual process of dropping out of crime of the predicted chronics closely matched the aggregate drop-out process for persisters predicted by the mathematical model with parameters estimated from aggregate recidivism data. Hence, the high-risk offenders might be viewed as the identified persisters. According to the mathematical model, because of probabilistic processes, 18.3 of the 36.7 persisters $[36.7_x \, (.87)^5]$ should survive to have six or more convictions by the age of 25 (and hence be classified as 'chronics'). Actually, fifteen of the thirty-seven high-risk offenders became chronics. The mathematical model shows that it is inappropriate to view the other twenty-two offenders as 'false positives', because this concept reflects deterministic prediction.

Similarly, eight of the ninety-five low-risk offenders (scoring three or fewer) became chronics, compared with the probabilistic prediction of 5.7. The data were best fitted by assuming that 6.1 of the high-risk offenders were in fact desisters, while 6.1 of the low-risk offenders were in fact persisters. Hence, the true rate of false positives (i.e. incorrect identifications) was 6.1 out of thirty-seven (16 per cent) rather than twenty-two out of thirty-seven (59 per cent). It is important to partition apparent false positives into real mistakes in assignment to categories versus those who are predicted on a probabilistic model not to have the measured outcome. This also shows the important distinction between prospective predictions (e.g. high-risk offenders), true categories (e.g. persisters) and retrospectively measured outcomes (e.g. chronics).

Duration

There has been less research on the duration of criminal careers. Of course, the average duration increases with the length of the follow-up period. National figures for English males born in 1953 and followed up to age 39 showed that the average duration of criminal careers was 9.7 years (excluding one-time offenders, who had zero duration). The corresponding average duration for females was 5.6 years (Home Office Statistical Bulletin, 1995). Average career durations were similar in London and Stockholm (Farrington and Wikström, 1994).

As already mentioned, the boys first convicted at the earliest ages (10–13) in the Cambridge Study tended to be the most persistent offenders, with an average career length close to ten years up to age 32. Those first convicted at 10–11 had an average career length of 11.5 years (Farrington, 1992*b*). Over a quarter of all convicted males had criminal careers lasting longer than ten years. The average duration of criminal careers declined precipitously from age 16 (7.9 years) to age 17 (2.9 years), suggesting that those males first convicted as juveniles were much more persistent offenders than those first convicted as adults.

Barnett *et al.* (1987) estimated career lengths in the Cambridge Study up to the age of 25 using their mathematical model. On average, the frequents had a duration of 8.8 years and the occasionals had a duration of 7.4 years. (Both groups included only males with two or more convictions, in order to estimate time intervals between offences.) Hence, the frequents and occasionals did not differ much in their career lengths, although they differed considerably in their individual offending frequencies. Little is known about the predictors and correlates of lengths of criminal careers.

Another important concept is the residual length of a criminal career at any given point in time. Blumstein *et al.* (1982) used a life-table method to estimate residual career length and, as already mentioned, found that it increased to a peak between the ages of 30 and 40. One area where knowledge about residual career length is important is in estimating the incapacitative effects of imprisonment. If the average time served exceeds the residual career length, people would be imprisoned beyond the point at which they would have stopped offending anyway. Hence, valuable prison space might be wasted by incarcerating those who would in any case have desisted from offending.

Continuity

Generally, there is significant continuity between offending in one age range and offending in another. In the Cambridge Study, nearly three-quarters (73 per cent) of those convicted as juveniles at age 10–16 were reconvicted at age 17–24, in comparison with only 16 per cent of those not convicted as juveniles (Farrington, 1992b). Nearly half (45 per cent) of those convicted as juveniles were reconvicted at age 25–32, in comparison with only 8 per cent of those not convicted as juveniles. Furthermore, this continuity over time did not merely reflect continuity in police reaction to crime. For ten specified offences, the significant continuity between offending in one age range and offending in a later age range held for self-reports as well as official convictions (Farrington, 1989c).

Other studies (e.g. Hamparian *et al.*, 1985; McCord, 1991; Tracy and Kempf-Leonard, 1996) show similar continuity. For example, in Sweden, Stattin and Magnusson (1991) reported that nearly 70 per cent of males registered for crime before the age of 15 were registered again between ages 15 and 20, and nearly 60 per cent were registered between the ages of 21 and 29. Also, the number of juvenile offences is an effective predictor of the number of adult offences (Wolfgang *et al.*, 1987). There was considerable continuity in offending between the ages of 10 and 25 in both London and Stockholm (Farrington and Wikström, 1994).

It is not always realized that relative continuity is quite compatible with absolute change. In other words, the relative ordering of people on some underlying construct such as criminal potential can remain significantly stable over time, even though the absolute level of criminal potential declines on average for everyone. For example, in the Cambridge Study, the prevalence of self-reported offending declined significantly between the ages of 18 and 32, but there was a significant tendency for the worst offenders at 18 also to be the worst offenders at 32 (Farrington, 1990a).

There are two major alternative reasons for the continuity between past and future offending (Nagin and Farrington, 1992b). One is that it reflects a stable underlying construct such as criminal potential; this was termed the 'persistent heterogeneity' explanation. The second is that the commission of one crime leads to an increase in the probability of commission of future crimes, perhaps because of reinforcement or stigmatization; this was termed the 'state dependence' explanation. In predicting convictions during each age range in the Cambridge Study, the best model included age, low intelligence, daring, convicted parents, and poor child-rearing, but did not include prior convictions. Hence, prior convictions did not predict future convictions independently of background factors and age, so that the persistent heterogeneity explanation was supported. In other words, the continuity between past and future convictions reflected continuity in an underlying criminal potential.

Numerous studies also show that childhood conduct problems predict later offending and anti-social behaviour (e.g. Loeber and LeBlanc, 1990). Similarly, in the Cambridge Study there was evidence of continuity in anti-social behaviour from childhood to the teenage years. The anti-social personality scale at age 10 correlated .50 with the corresponding scale at age 14 and .38 with the scale at age 18 (Farrington, 1991*a*). In regard to specific types of anti-social behaviour, troublesomeness was the only factor measured at age 8–10 that significantly predicted bullying at both ages 14 and 18 (Farrington, 1993*a*). Again, troublesomeness at age 8–10 was the best predictor of chronic versus non-chronic offenders (Farrington and West, 1993) and of both truancy and aggression at age 12–14 in the secondary schools (Farrington, 1980, 1989*a*, 1996*a*).

There is also continuity in anti-social behaviour from the teenage to the adult years (Hodgins, 1994). In the Cambridge Study, a measure of adult social dysfunction was developed at age 32, based on (in the previous five years) convictions, self-reported offending, poor home conditions, poor cohabitation history, child problems, poor employment history, substance abuse, violence and poor mental health (a high score on the General Health Questionnaire; see Farrington *et al.*, 1988*a*, 1988*b*, and Farrington, 1989*b*). Similarly, a measure of anti-social personality was developed at the age of 32 which was comparable with the earlier anti-social personality measures. Anti-social personality at age 18 correlated .55 with anti-social personality at age 32 (Farrington, 1991*a*).

Expressing this another way, 60 per cent of the most anti-social quarter of males at age 18 were still in the most anti-social quarter fourteen years later at age 32. Bearing in mind the very great environmental changes between 18 and 32, as the males left their parental homes, went through a period of unstable living arrangements, and eventually settled down in marital homes, this consistency over time seems likely to reflect consistency in the individual's personality rather than consistency in the environment. It is often found that about half of any sample of anti-social children persist to become anti-social teenagers, and that about half of any sample of anti-social teenagers persist to become anti-social adults. Comparing the .55 correlation between ages 18 and 32 with the .38 correlation between ages 10 and 18, it is interesting that there was increasing stabilization of anti-social personality with age.

The continuity in anti-social personality does not mean that it is not desirable to study influences on criminal career features such as onset and desistance.

Unlike Gottfredson and Hirschi (1990), I would not argue that all criminal career features reflect only one underlying construct of criminal potential (low self-control). Also, the persistence of anti-social personality does not mean that there is no scope for change. The correlations between measures of anti-social personality at different ages (e.g. the .55 correlation between 18 and 32), and the fact that only about half of anti-social teenagers become anti-social adults, show that a great deal of relative change is occurring. This makes it possible to investigate factors that might encourage anti-social children to become less anti-social as they grow older, or that might foster early desistance.

There is specific as well as general continuity in anti-social behaviour from the teenage to the adult years. In the Cambridge Study, measures of absolute change and relative consistency were developed between ages 18 and 32 (Farrington, 1990a). For example, the prevalence of marijuana use declined significantly, from 29 per cent at age 18 to 19 per cent at age 32. However, there was a significant tendency for the users at age 18 also to be users at age 32 (44 per cent of users at age 18 were users at age 32, whereas only 8 per cent of non-users at age 18 were users at age 32). Other researchers (e.g. Ghodsian and Power, 1987) have also reported significant consistency in substance use between adolescence and adulthood.

In contrast, the prevalence of binge drinking and drunk driving increased significantly between ages 18 and 32, but there was again significant consistency over time; and the prevalence of heavy smoking did not change significantly between the ages of 18 and 32, and there was again significant consistency over time. Therefore, relative consistency could coexist with absolute increases, decreases, or constancy in anti-social behaviour in the Cambridge Study. In the Netherlands, Verhulst *et al.* (1990) also reported relative stability and absolute changes in childhood anti-social behaviour.

There is usually specific as well as general continuity in aggression and violence from the teenage to the adult years. Olweus (1979) reviewed sixteen surveys covering time periods up to 21 years, and reported an average stability coefficient (correlation) over time for male aggression of .68. Olweus and others (e.g. Cairns and Cairns, 1994) have argued that individual differences in aggression are almost as stable over time as individual differences in intelligence. Childhood and adolescent aggression is an important predictor of officially recorded violence in the adult years (Pulkkinen, 1987; Stattin and Magnusson, 1989).

In the Cambridge Study, aggression at age 16–18 was the best predictor of fighting at age 32 (Farrington, 1989a). Spouse assault at age 32 was significantly predicted by teacher-rated aggression at age 12–14, and by the anti-social personality measures at ages 14 and 18, but not (surprisingly) by aggression at age 18 (Farrington, 1994c). Bullying at 32 was specifically predicted by bullying at 14 and 18 independently of the continuity between aggression at 14 and 18 and aggression at 32 (Farrington, 1993a). Furthermore, a male's bullying at 14 and 18 predicted bullying by his child when he was 32, showing that there was intergenerational continuity in bullying. In their New York study, Eron and

Huesmann (1990) also found that a boy's aggression at age 8 predicted not only his aggression and spouse assault at age 30 but also the aggressiveness of his child.

Specialization and Escalation

In the Cambridge Study, offenders were predominantly versatile rather than specialized. About one-third of the convicted males up to age 32 (N = 50) were convicted of violence (assault, robbery or threatening behaviour). They committed a total of eighty-five violent offences (an average of 1.7 each), but they also committed 263 non-violent offences (an average of 5.3 each). Only seven of the fifty violent offenders had no convictions for non-violent offences (Farrington, 1991b). Other researchers (e.g. Hamparian et al., 1978; Snyder, 1988) have also found that the majority of recorded offences of violent offenders are non-violent. A model was tested that assumed that violent offences occurred at random in criminal careers (Farrington, 1991b). Since the data fitted this model, it was concluded that there was little indication that offenders specialized in violence. Furthermore, violent offenders and non-violent but persistent offenders were similar in childhood, adolescent, and adult features, as Capaldi and Patterson (1996) also found in the Oregon Youth Study. Hence, violent offenders are difficult to distinguish from frequent offenders.

Using criminal career data collected in the South East Prison Survey, Stander et al. (1989) investigated specialization using offence-to-offence transition matrices. Generally, these matrices did not change (were 'stationary') during the criminal career, and similar results were obtained by Tarling (1993: 129). Stander et al. studied whether the offending sequences could be viewed as a first order Markov chain (i.e. whether the probability of one offence following another was not influenced by the prior offending history), but concluded that they could not. While there was a great deal of generality in offending, there was some specialization superimposed on it. Stander et al. used the 'Forward Specialization Coefficient' (Farrington et al., 1988c) to quantify the degree of specialization. They found that sex offenders were the most specialized, and that specialization in fraud was especially marked for persistent offenders. Other criminal career research also suggests that there is a small degree of specificity superimposed on a great deal of generality or versatility in offending (Wolfgang et al., 1972; Kempf, 1987; Tracy et al., 1990). There is also some indication of increasing specialization (decreasing diversification) with age.

There has been less research on escalation, partly because of the prevailing belief in versatility and in the fact that different types of offences seem to be committed almost at random during criminal careers. In the Philadelphia cohort study, Tracy et al. (1990) found that the average seriousness of offences increased as offenders became older and with each successive offence. More information about escalation, and especially about the predictors of escalation, is needed.

Co-offending and Motives

Past criminal career research has mainly focused on prevalence, frequency, onset, desistance, duration, and specialization. However, there are many other features of offences that might be studied in criminal career research. These include whether a person commits an offence alone or with others; the location of the offence, and the distance travelled by offenders to commit it; motives for committing offences, including how far they are planned in advance; characteristics of victims; methods of committing crimes, including use of psychological or physical force; the offender's subjective probability of being caught by the police, convicted, and sentenced to imprisonment; and the offender's subjective utilities of the costs and benefits of offending. Except for the work of LeBlanc and Frechette (1989), there has been little research on these topics within the criminal career perspective, despite their potential relevance. I will focus on co-offending and motives here.

In the Cambridge Study, about half of all offences were committed with (usually one or two) others, and the incidence of co-offending was greatest for burglary and robbery (Reiss and Farrington, 1991). Co-offending declined steadily with age from 10 to 32. As already mentioned, this was not because co-offenders dropped out but because the males changed from co-offending in their teenage years to lone offending in their twenties. Males who committed their first offence with others tended to have a longer criminal career than those who committed their first offence alone, but this was largely because first offences with others tended to be committed at younger ages than first offences alone, and of course those with an early age of onset tended to have a longer criminal career. Transition matrices showed that there tended to be some consistency in co-offending or lone offending between one offence and the next.

Burglary, robbery, and theft from vehicles were especially likely to involve co-offenders. Generally, co-offenders were similar in age, sex, and race to the males themselves, and lived close to the males' homes and to the locations of the offences. However, the similarity between the males and their co-offenders, and their residential propinquity, decreased with age. Co-offending relationships tended not to persist for very long; rarely more than one year. About one-third of the most persistent offenders continually offended with less criminally experienced co-offenders, and hence appeared to be repeatedly recruiting others into a life of crime. Recruiting was especially common for burglary offences. (For a review of research on co-offending, see Reiss, 1988.)

The most common motives given for property offences (46 per cent of self-reported offences, 43 per cent of offences leading to convictions) were utilitarian, rational, or economic ones: offences were committed for material gain (West and Farrington, 1977). The next most common motives (31 per cent of self-reported offences, 22 per cent of conviction offences) might be termed hedonistic: offences were committed for excitement, for enjoyment, or to relieve boredom. In general, utilitarian motives predominated for most types of property offences such as burglary and theft, except that vandalism and motor vehicle theft ('joy-riding') were committed predominantly for hedonistic reasons, and shoplifting was partly utilitarian and partly hedonistic. Offences at younger ages (under 17) were relatively more likely to be committed for hedonistic reasons, while offences at older ages (17 or older) were relatively more likely to be committed for utilitarian reasons.

These results are similar to those reported by Petersilia *et al.* (1978) in a retrospective survey of about fifty armed robbers imprisoned in California. The main motives given for their crimes committed in the juvenile years were for thrills and because of peer influence, but the main motives given for their crimes committed in the adult years were to obtain money, for drugs or alcohol or to support themselves or their families. Similarly, LeBlanc (1996) in Montreal reported how utilitarian and hedonistic-impulsive motives changed during criminal careers. (For a review of research on motivation, see Farrington, 1993c.)

In the Cambridge Study, motives for aggressive acts (physical fights) were also investigated (Farrington *et al.*, 1982). The key dimension was whether the male fought alone or in a group. In individual fights, the male was usually provoked, became angry, and hit out in order to hurt his opponent and to discharge his own internal feelings of tension. In group fights, the male often said that he became involved in order to help a friend or because he was attacked, and rarely said that he was angry. The group fights were more serious, occurring in bars or streets, and they were more likely to involve weapons, produce injuries, and lead to police intervention. Fights often occurred when minor incidents escalated, because both sides wanted to demonstrate their toughness and masculinity and were unwilling to react in a conciliatory way. Similarly, Berkowitz (1978) interviewed convicted violent offenders and found that most incidents arose out of arguments and were angry outbursts intended primarily to hurt the victim; the second most frequent cause was a friend's need for assistance.

In the future, criminal career research should be expanded to study a wider range of career features, including immediate situational influences on criminal acts, locations of offences, addresses of offenders, and characteristics of victims.

INFLUENCES ON CRIMINAL CAREERS

Risk Factors

Risk factors are prior factors that increase the risk of occurrence of events such as the onset, frequency, persistence, or duration of offending. Longitudinal data are required to establish the ordering of risk factors and criminal career features. The focus in this chapter is on risk factors for the onset or prevalence of offending. Few studies have examined risk factors for persistence or duration. However, in the Cambridge Study, Farrington and Hawkins (1991) investigated factors that predicted whether convicted offenders before age 21 persisted or desisted between ages 21 and 32. The best independent predictors of persistence included the boy rarely spending leisure time with his father at age 11–12, low intelligence at age 8–10, employment instability at age 16, and heavy drinking at age 18. Indeed, nearly 90 per cent of the convicted males who were frequently unemployed and heavy drinkers as teenagers went on to be reconvicted after age 21.

It is also difficult to decide if any given risk factor is an indicator (symptom) or a possible cause of offending. The problems raised by impulsivity have already been mentioned. As other examples, are heavy drinking, truancy, unemployment, and divorce symptoms of an anti-social personality, or do they cause (an increase in) it? Similarly, to the extent that delinquency is a group activity, delinquents will almost inevitably have delinquent friends, and this result does not necessarily show that delinquent friends cause delinquency. Because of this problem, delinquent peers are not reviewed here as a possible risk factor for offending. It is important not to include a measure of the dependent variable as an independent variable in causal analyses, because this will lead to false (tautological) conclusions and an over-estimation of explanatory or predictive power (see e.g. Amdur, 1989).

It is not unreasonable to argue that some factors may be both indicative and causal. For example, long-term variations *between* individuals in anti-social tendency may be reflected in variations in alcohol consumption, just as short-term variations *within* individuals in alcohol consumption may cause more anti-social behaviour during the heavier drinking periods. The interpretation of other factors may be more clear-cut. For example, being exposed as a child to poor parental child-rearing techniques might cause anti-social tendency but would not be an indicator of it; and burgling a house might be an indicator of anti-social tendency but would be unlikely to cause it (although it might be argued that, when an anti-social act is successful in leading to positive reinforcement, this reinforcement causes an increase in the underlying anti-social tendency).

Cross-sectional studies make it impossible to distinguish between indicators and causes, since they can merely demonstrate correlations between high levels of one factor (e.g. unemployment) and high levels of another (e.g. offending). Longitudinal studies can show that offending is greater (within individuals) during some periods (e.g. of unemployment) than during other periods (e.g. of employment). Because within-individual studies have greater control over extraneous influences than between-individual studies, longitudinal studies can demonstrate that changes in unemployment within individuals cause offending with high internal validity in quasi-experimental analyses (Farrington, 1988*b*; Farrington *et al.*, 1986*b*). Longitudinal studies can also establish whether factors such as unemployment have the same or different effects on offending when they vary within or between individuals. Implications for prevention and treatment, which require changes within individuals, cannot necessarily be drawn from effects demonstrated only in between-individual (cross-sectional) research.

It is unfortunate that the static model of relationships between independent and dependent variables has dominated research and theories of offending. This model may have a veneer of plausibility in a cross-sectional study, at least if problems of causal order are neglected. However, it is not easily applied to longitudinal or criminal career data, where all presumed explanatory constructs and all measures of offending and criminal career features change continuously within individuals over different ages. Relationships between an explanatory factor in one age range and a measure of offending in another age range may vary a great deal according to the particular age ranges, and this needs to be systematically investigated by researchers.

It is also unfortunate that insufficient attention has been paid in the literature to protective factors as opposed to risk factors. Protective factors predict a low probability of offending, either in a total cohort or in a high-risk sample (Rutter, 1985; Farrington, 1994b). For example, Werner and Smith (1982, 1992) in Hawaii studied high-risk children who possessed a number of risk factors such as poverty, perinatal stress, family discord, and parental alcoholism. They found that the resilient children who did not display offending or anti-social behaviour as adults tended to have high intelligence and affectional ties with substitute parents.

The major risk factors for offending that are reviewed in this chapter are the individual difference factors of impulsivity and intelligence, and family, socio-economic, school, and situational factors. These factors often have additive, interactive or sequential effects, but I will consider them one by one.

Impulsivity

In the Cambridge Study, the boys nominated by teachers as lacking in concentration or restless, those nominated by parents, peers, or teachers as the most daring, and those who were the most impulsive on psychomotor tests all tended to be juvenile but not adult offenders (Farrington, 1992c). Later self-report questionnaire measures of impulsivity (including such items as 'I generally do and say things quickly without stopping to think') were related to both juvenile and adult offending. Daring, poor concentration, and restlessness were all related to both official and self-reported delinquency (Farrington, 1992d). Daring at age 8–10 was an important independent predictor of chronic offenders (Farrington and West, 1993) and of violence and spouse assault at age 32 (Farrington, 1989a, 1994c). Poor concentration or restlessness at age 8–10 was also an independent predictor of chronic offenders, and also of adult social dysfunction at age 32 (Farrington, 1993b).

Many other investigators have reported a link between the constellation of personality factors termed 'hyperactivity-impulsivity-attention deficit' or HIA (Loeber, 1987) and offending. For example, in a Swedish longitudinal survey,

Klinteberg *et al.* (1993) found that hyperactivity at 13 (rated by teachers) predicted violent offending up to the age of 26. Impulsivity was the best predictor of early onset offending in the Montreal longitudinal study (Tremblay *et al.*, 1994). Satterfield (1987) tracked HIA and matched control boys in Los Angeles between the ages of 9 and 17, and showed that six times as many of the HIA boys were arrested for serious offences. In the Cambridge Study, a combined measure of HIA at age 8–10 significantly predicted juvenile convictions independently of conduct problems at age 8–10 (Farrington *et al.*, 1990*b*). Lynam (1996) argued that children with both HIA and conduct problems were at greatest risk of chronic offending. In the most extensive research using eleven different impulsivity measures in the Pittsburgh Youth Study, White *et al.* (1994) found that behavioural impulsivity (e.g. restlessness) was more strongly related to delinquency than was cognitive impulsivity (e.g. poor planning), which was more closely linked to intelligence.

It has been suggested that HIA might be a behavioural consequence of a low level of physiological arousal. Offenders have a low level of arousal according to their low alpha (brain) waves on the EEG, or according to autonomic nervous system indicators such as heart rate, blood pressure, or skin conductance, or they show low autonomic reactivity (e.g. Venables and Raine, 1987; Raine, 1993). In the Cambridge Study, a low heart rate was significantly related to convictions for violence, self-reported violence, and teacher-reported violence, independently of all other explanatory variables (Farrington, forthcoming). In several regression analyses, the most important independent risk factors for violence were daring, poor concentration, and a low heart rate. Other researchers (e.g. Wadsworth, 1976; Raine *et al.*, 1990) have also identified a low heart rate as an important predictor and correlate of offending.

Low Intelligence

Low intelligence is an important predictor of offending, and it can be measured very early in life. For example, in a prospective longitudinal survey of about 120 Stockholm males, low intelligence measured at age 3 significantly predicted officially recorded offending up to age 30 (Stattin and Klackenberg-Larsson, 1993). Frequent offenders (with four or more offences) had an average IQ of eighty-eight at age 3, whereas non-offenders had an average IQ of 101. All of these results held up after controlling for social class. Also, in the Perry preschool project in Michigan, low intelligence at age 4 significantly predicted the number of arrests up to age 27 (Schweinhart *et al.*, 1993).

In the Cambridge Study, one-third of the boys scoring ninety or less on a non-verbal intelligence test (Raven's Progressive Matrices) at age 8–10 were convicted as juveniles, twice as many as among the remainder (Farrington, 1992*d*). Low non-verbal intelligence was highly correlated with low verbal intelligence (vocabulary, word comprehension, verbal reasoning) and with low school attainment at age 11, and all of these measures predicted juvenile convictions to much the same extent. In addition to their poor school performance, delinquents tended to be frequent truants, to leave school at the earliest possible age (which was then 15), and to take no school examinations.

Low non-verbal intelligence was especially characteristic of the juvenile recidivists (who had an average IQ of eighty-nine) and those first convicted at the earliest ages (10–13). Furthermore, low intelligence and attainment predicted self-reported delinquency almost as well as convictions (Farrington, 1992*d*), suggesting that the link between low intelligence and delinquency was not caused by the less intelligent boys having a greater probability of being caught. Also, measures of intelligence and attainment predicted measures of offending independently of other variables such as family income and family size (Farrington, 1990*b*). Similar results have been obtained in other projects (Wilson and Herrnstein, 1985; Moffitt and Silva, 1988*a*; Lynam *et al.*, 1993). Delinquents often do better on non-verbal performance tests, such as object assembly and block design, than on verbal tests (Walsh *et al.*, 1987), suggesting that they find it easier to deal with concrete objects than with abstract concepts.

Low intelligence and attainment predicted both juvenile and adult convictions (Farrington, 1992*c*). Low intelligence at age 8–10 was also an important independent predictor of spouse assault at age 32 (Farrington, 1994*c*). Low intelligence and attainment predicted aggression and bullying at age 14, and poor reading ability at age 18 was the best predictor of having a child bully at age 32 (Farrington, 1989*a*, 1993*a*). Also, low school attainment predicted chronic offenders (Farrington and West, 1993).

The key explanatory factor underlying the link between intelligence and delinquency is probably the ability to manipulate abstract concepts. People who are poor at this tend to do badly in intelligence tests such as the Matrices and in school attainment, and they also tend to commit offences, probably because of their poor ability to foresee the consequences of their offending and to appreciate the feelings of victims (i.e. their low empathy). Certain family backgrounds are less conducive than others to the development of abstract reasoning. For example, lower-class, poorer parents tend to talk in terms of the concrete rather than the abstract and tend to live for the present, with little thought for the future, as Cohen (1955: 96) pointed out many years ago. In some ways, it is difficult to distinguish a lack of concern for future consequences, which is a central feature of Wilson and Hernstein's (1985) theory, from the concept of impulsivity.

Modern research is studying not just intelligence but also detailed patterns of cognitive and neuro-psychological deficit. For example, in a New Zealand longitudinal study of over 1,000 children from birth to age 15, Moffitt and Silva (1988*b*) found that self-reported delinquency was related to verbal, memory and visual-motor integration deficits, independently of low social class and family adversity. Neuro-psychological research might lead to important advances in knowledge about the link between brain functioning and offending.

For example, the 'executive functions' of the brain, located in the frontal lobes, include sustaining attention and concentration, abstract reasoning and concept formation, anticipation and planning, self-monitoring of behaviour, and inhibition of inappropriate or impulsive behaviour (Moffitt, 1990). Deficits in these executive functions are conducive to low measured intelligence and to offending. Moffitt and Henry (1989) found deficits in these executive functions especially for delinquents who were both anti-social and hyperactive.

Supervision, Discipline, and Child Abuse

Loeber and Stouthamer-Loeber (1986) completed an exhaustive review of family factors as correlates and predictors of juvenile conduct problems and delinquency. They found that poor parental supervision or monitoring, erratic or harsh parental discipline, parental disharmony, parental rejection of the child, and low parental involvement with the child (as well as anti-social parents and large family size) were all important predictors.

In the Cambridge-Somerville study in Boston, McCord (1979) reported that poor parental supervision was the best predictor of both violent and property offenders. Parental aggressiveness (which included harsh discipline, shading into child abuse at the extreme) and parental conflict were significant precursors of violent offenders, while the mother's attitude (passive or rejecting) was a significant precursor of property offenders. Robins (1979), in her long-term follow-up studies in St Louis, also found that poor supervision and discipline were consistently related to later offending, and Shedler and Block (1990) in San Francisco reported that hostile and rejecting mothers when children were aged 5 predicted their frequent drug use at age 18.

Other studies also show the link between family factors and offending. In a Birmingham survey, Wilson (1980) concluded that poor parental supervision was the most important correlate of convictions, cautions, and self-reported delinquency. In their English national survey of juveniles aged 14–15 and their mothers, Riley and Shaw (1985) found that poor parental supervision was the most important correlate of self-reported delinquency for girls, and that it was the second most important for boys (after delinquent friends).

In the Cambridge Study, harsh or erratic parental discipline, cruel, passive, or neglecting parental attitude, poor supervision, and parental conflict, all measured at age 8, all predicted later juvenile convictions (West and Farrington, 1973). Poor parental child-rearing behaviour (a combination of discipline, attitude, and conflict), poor parental supervision, and low parental interest in education all predicted both convictions and self-reported delinquency (Farrington, 1992*d*). Poor parental child-rearing behaviour was related to early rather than later offending (Farrington, 1986*b*), and was not characteristic of those first convicted as adults (West and Farrington, 1977). Hence, poor parental child-rearing behaviour may be related to onset but not persistence. Poor parental supervision was related to both juvenile and adult convictions (Farrington, 1992*c*).

There seems to be significant intergenerational transmission of aggressive and violent behaviour from parents to children, as Widom (1989) found in a retrospective study of over 900 abused children in Indianapolis. Children who were physically abused up to age 11 were significantly likely to become violent offenders in the next fifteen years (Maxfield and Widom, 1996). Also, child sex abuse predicted later adult arrests for sex crimes in this survey (Widom and Ames, 1994). In the Cambridge Study, harsh discipline and attitude of parents when the boys were aged 8 predicted later violent as opposed to non-violent offenders up to age 21 (Farrington, 1978). More recent research (Farrington, 1991*b*) showed that harsh discipline and attitude predicted both violent and persistent offending up to age 32. The extensive review by Malinosky-Rummell and Hansen (1993) confirmed that being physically abused as a child predicted later violent and non-violent offending.

Broken Homes and Family Conflict

Broken homes and early separations are also risk factors for offending. In the Newcastle Thousand Family Study, Kolvin *et al.* (1990) reported that parental divorce or separation up to the age of 5 predicted later convictions up to the age of 33. McCord (1982) carried out an interesting study of the relationship between homes broken by loss of the natural father and later serious offending. She found that the prevalence of offending was high for boys reared in broken homes without affectionate mothers (62 per cent) and for those reared in united homes characterized by parental conflict (52 per cent), irrespective of whether they had affectionate mothers. The prevalence of offending was low for those reared in united homes without conflict (26 per cent) or in broken homes with affectionate mothers (22 per cent). These results suggest that it is not so much the broken home which is criminogenic as the parental conflict which causes it. Similarly, Fergusson *et al.* (1992) in the Christchurch (New Zealand) Child Development Study, found that parental separation before a child was 10 did not predict self-reported offending independently of parental conflict, which was the more important factor.

The importance of the cause of the broken home is also shown in the British national longitudinal survey of over 5,000 children born in one week of 1946 (Wadsworth, 1979). Boys from homes broken by divorce or separation had an increased likelihood of being convicted or officially cautioned up to the age of 21 in comparison with those from homes broken by death or from unbroken homes. Homes broken before the age of 5 were especially criminogenic, while homes broken after 10 were not. Remarriage (which happened more often after divorce or separation than after death) was also associated with an increased risk of offending. The meta-analysis by Wells and Rankin (1991) confirmed that broken homes were more strongly related to delinquency when they were caused by parental separation or divorce rather than by death.

In the Cambridge Study, both permanent and temporary (more than one month) separations before the age of 10 predicted convictions and self-reported delinquency, providing that they were not caused by death or hospitalization (Farrington, 1992*d*). However, homes broken at an early age (under 5) were not unusually criminogenic (West and Farrington, 1973). Separation before age 10 predicted both juvenile and adult convictions (Farrington, 1992*c*), and was an important independent predictor of adult social dysfunction and spouse assault at age 32 (Farrington, 1993*b*, 1994*c*).

In the Dunedin Study in New Zealand, single parent families dispro-portionally tended to have convicted sons; 28 per cent of violent offenders were from single parent families, compared with 17 per cent of non-violent offenders and 9 per cent of unconvicted boys (Henry *et al.*, 1996). Based on analyses of four surveys (including the Cambridge Study), Morash and Rucker (1989) concluded that the combination of teenage child-bearing and a single-parent female-headed household was especially conducive to the development of offending in children. Later analyses of the Cambridge Study showed that teenage child-bearing combined with a large number of children particularly predicted offending by the children (Nagin *et al.*, forthcoming).

Just as having parents who were in conflict with each other predicted a boy's delinquency in the Cambridge Study, convicted offenders at age 18 tended to be in conflict with their parents. Also, both juvenile and adult offenders tended to have a poor relationship with their wives or cohabitees at age 32, or had assaulted them, and they also tended to be divorced and/or separated from their children (Farrington, 1992*c*). However, getting married was one factor that led to a decrease in offending, just as becoming separated from a wife led to an increase (Farrington and West, 1995).

Convicted Parents

Criminal, anti-social, and alcoholic parents also tend to have delinquent sons, as Robins (1979) found. For example, in her follow-up of over 200 African-American males in St Louis (Robins *et al.*, 1975), arrested parents tended to have arrested children, and the juvenile records of the parents and children showed similar rates and types of offences. McCord (1977), in her thirty-year follow-up of about 250 treated boys in the Cambridge-Somerville study, reported that convicted fathers tended to have convicted sons. Whether there is a specific relationship in her study between types of convictions of parents and children is not clear. McCord found that 29 per cent of fathers convicted for violence had sons convicted for violence, in comparison with 12 per cent of other fathers, but this may reflect the general tendency for convicted fathers to have convicted sons rather than any specific tendency for violent fathers to have violent sons. Wilson (1987) in Birmingham also showed that convictions of parents predicted convictions and cautions of sons; more than twice as many sons of convicted parents were themselves convicted.

In the Cambridge Study, the concentration of offending in a small number of families was remarkable. Less than 6 per cent of the families were respon-sible for half of the criminal convictions of all members (fathers, mothers, sons, and daughters) of all 400 families (Farrington *et al.*, 1996*b*). Having a convicted mother, father, or brother by a boy's tenth birthday significantly predicted his own later convictions (West and Farrington, 1973). Furthermore, convicted parents and delinquent siblings predicted self-reported as well as official offending (Farrington, 1992*d*). Therefore, there is intergenerational continuity in offending.

Unlike most early precursors, a convicted parent was related less to offending of early onset (age 10–13) than to later offending (Farrington, 1986*b*). Also, a convicted parent predicted which juvenile offenders went on to become adult criminals and which recidivists at the age of 19 continued offending (West and Farrington, 1977). Hence, a convicted parent seemed to be a risk factor for persistence rather than onset. A convicted parent was the best predictor of spouse assault at age 32, and it was also an important independent predictor of chronic offenders, bullying at age 14, and adult social dysfunction at age 32 (Farrington, 1993*a*, 1993*b*, 1994*c*; Farrington and West, 1993).

These results are concordant with the psychological theory (e.g. Trasler, 1962) that criminal behaviour develops when the normal social learning process, based on rewards and punishments from parents, is disrupted by erratic discipline, poor supervision, parental disharmony, and unsuitable (antisocial or criminal) parental models. However, some part of the link between criminal parents and delinquent children may reflect genetic transmission (see e.g. Wilson and Herrnstein, 1985; Eysenck and Gudjonsson, 1989).

Socio-Economic Deprivation

Most delinquency theories assume that offenders disproportionally come from lower-class social backgrounds, and aim to explain why this is so. For example, Cohen (1955) proposed that lower-class boys found it hard to succeed according to the middle-class standards of the school, partly because lower-class parents tended not to teach their children to delay immediate gratification in favour of long-term goals. Consequently, lower-class boys joined delinquent subcultures by whose standards they could succeed. Cloward and Ohlin (1960) argued that lower-class children could not achieve universal goals of status and material wealth by legitimate means and consequently had to resort to illegitimate means.

Beginning with the pioneering self-report research of Short and Nye (1957), it was common in the United States to argue that low socio-economic status (SES) was related to official offending but not to self-reported offending, and hence that the official processing of offenders was biased against lower-class youth. However, many reviewers (e.g. Hindelang *et al.*, 1981; Thornberry and Farnworth, 1982) were unable to conclude that low SES was related to either self-reported or official offending. British studies have reported more consistent links between low social class and offending. In the British national survey, Douglas *et al.* (1966) showed that the prevalence of official juvenile delinquency in males varied considerably according to the occupational prestige and educational background of their parents, from 3 per cent in the highest category to 19 per cent in the lowest.

Numerous indicators of SES were measured in the Cambridge Study, both for the male's family of origin and for the male himself as an adult, including occupational prestige, family income, housing, employment instability, and family size. Most of the measures of occupational prestige (based on the Registrar General's scale) were not significantly related to offending. However, in a reversal of the American results, low SES of the family when the male was aged 8–10 significantly predicted his later self-reported but not his official delinquency (Farrington, 1992*d*).

More consistently, low family income, poor housing, and large family size predicted official and self-reported, juvenile and adult, offending. In the Cambridge Study, if a boy had four or more siblings by his tenth birthday, this doubled his risk of being convicted as a juvenile (West and Farrington, 1973). Large family size predicted self-reported delinquency as well as convictions (Farrington, 1979), and adult as well as juvenile convictions (Farrington, 1992*b*). Large family size was the most important independent predictor of convictions up to the age of 32 in a logistic regression analysis (Farrington, 1993*a*). Large family size at age 10 was also an important independent predictor of teenage violence, while low family income at age 8 was the best independent predictor of adult social dysfunction at age 32 (Farrington, 1989*a*, 1993*b*).

Many studies show that large families predict delinquency (Fischer, 1984). For example, in the National Survey of Health and Development, Wadsworth (1979) found that the percentage of boys who were officially delinquent increased from 9 per cent for families containing one child to 24 per cent for families containing four or more children. The Newsons in their Nottingham study also concluded that large family size was one of the most important predictors of offending (Newson *et al.*, 1993). A similar link between family size and anti-social behaviour was reported by Kolvin *et al.* (1988) in their follow-up of Newcastle children from birth to the age of 33, by Rutter *et al.* (1970) in the Isle of Wight survey, and by Ouston (1984) in the Inner London survey. The theoretical links between large family size and offending are not entirely clear. Family size could be classified as either a socio-economic or family factor. For example, the key underlying construct could be less attention given to each child or more overcrowded living conditions (Ferguson, 1952).

Socio-economic deprivation of parents is usually compared with offending by sons. However, when the sons grow up, their own socio-economic deprivation can be related to their own offending. In the Cambridge Study, official and self-reported delinquents tended to have unskilled manual jobs and an unstable job record at age 18. Just as an erratic work record of his father predicted the later offending of the Study male, an unstable job record of the male at age 18 was one of the best independent predictors of his convictions between the ages of 21 and 25 (Farrington, 1986*b*). Also, having an unskilled manual job at 18 was an important independent predictor of adult social dysfunction and anti-social personality at 32 (Farrington, 1993*b*, 1996*d*). Also, as already mentioned, the Study males were convicted at a higher rate when they were unemployed than when they were employed (Farrington *et al.*, 1986*b*), suggesting that unemployment in some way causes crime, and conversely that employment may lead to desistance from offending.

In recent years, there has been more interest in the idea of an emerging underclass in the United States and England than in low social class *per se*. For example, in England, Murray (1995) argued that life in lower-class communities was degenerating as illegitimacy rose, there was widespread drug and alcohol addiction, fewer marriages, more unemployment, more child neglect, more crime, and so on. He thought that new divisions were opening up in the lower half of the socio-economic distribution, as two-parent working class families increasingly left council estates, which became increasingly populated by an underclass predominantly consisting of single parent families. These ideas are somewhat controversial.

It seems clear that socio-economic deprivation is an important risk factor for offending. However, low family income, poor housing, and large family size are better measures and produce more reliable results than low occupational prestige. Poverty may have an effect on offending indirectly, through its effects on parenting factors such as supervision and discipline, as Sampson and Laub (1994) concluded.

School Factors

It is clear that the prevalence of offending varies dramatically between different secondary schools, as Power *et al.* (1967) showed more than twenty years ago in London. Characteristics of high delinquency-rate schools are well known (Graham, 1988). For example, such schools have high levels of distrust between teachers and students, low commitment to school by students, and uncertain and inconsistently enforced rules. However, what is far less clear is how much of the variation should be attributed to differences in school climates and practices, and how much to differences in the composition of the student body.

In the Cambridge Study, the effects of secondary schools on offending were investigated by following boys from their primary schools to their secondary schools (Farrington, 1972). The best primary school predictor of offending was the rating of troublesomeness at age 8–10 by peers and teachers. The secondary schools differed dramatically in their official offending rates, from one school with 20.9 court appearances per 100 boys per year to another where the corresponding figure was only 0.3. However, it was very noticeable that the most troublesome boys tended to go to the high delinquency schools, while the least troublesome boys tended to go to the low delinquency schools.

All the schools had overlapping catchment areas. The low delinquency rate secondary schools were over-subscribed, because parents who were most interested in their children's education, who tended to have high-achieving, well-behaved children, were very concerned that their children should go to these schools. Taking account of reports from primary schools, the head teachers of these secondary schools could pick and choose the best children out of all the applicants, leaving the high delinquency schools with lower-achieving, worse-behaved children. Hence, it was clear that most of the variation between schools in their delinquency rates could be explained by differences in their intakes of troublesome boys. The secondary schools themselves had only a very small effect on the boys' offending.

The most famous study of school effects on offending was also carried out in London, by Rutter *et al.* (1979). They studied twelve comprehensive schools, and again found big differences in official delinquency rates between them. High delinquency rate schools tended to have high truancy rates, low ability pupils, and low social class parents. However, the differences between the schools in delinquency rates could not be entirely explained by differences in the social class and verbal reasoning scores of the pupils at intake (age 11). Therefore, Rutter *et al.* argued that they must have been caused by some aspect of the schools themselves or by other, unmeasured factors.

In trying to discover which aspects of schools might be encouraging or inhibiting offending, Rutter *et al.* (1979) developed a measure of 'school process' based on school structure, organization, and functioning. This was related to school misbehaviour, academic achievement, and truancy independently of intake factors. However, it was not significantly related to delinquency independently of intake factors. Many aspects of the schools were not related to their delinquency rates: the age of the buildings, the number of students, the amount of space per student, the staff/student ratio, the academic emphasis (e.g. amount of homework or library use), the rate of turnover of teachers, the number of school outings, the care of the school buildings, and so on. The main school factors that were related to delinquency were a high amount of punishment and a low amount of praise given by teachers in class. However, it is difficult to know whether much punishment and little praise are causes or consequences of anti-social school behaviour, which in turn is probably linked to offending outside school.

The research of Rutter *et al.* (1979) does not show unambiguously that school factors influence offending. This is partly because of the small number of schools involved in the study (only nine containing boys), and partly because far more is known about individual-level risk factors for offending than about school-level risk factors. Because this was a pioneering study, important school-level risk factors may not have been measured. In order to advance knowledge about possible school effects on offending, longitudinal research is needed in which many factors are measured for primary school children, who are then followed up to a large number of secondary schools. This might make it possible convincingly to identify school factors that explained differences in offending rates independently of individual-level factors present at intake.

Situational Factors

It is plausible to suggest that criminal behaviour results from the interaction between an individual (with a certain degree of underlying anti-social tendency) and the environment (which provides criminal opportunities). Given the same environment, some individuals will be more likely to commit offences than others, and conversely the same individual will be more likely to commit offences in some environments than in others. Criminological research typically concentrates on either the development of criminal individuals or the occurrence of criminal events, but rarely on both.

As already mentioned, delinquents are predominantly versatile rather than specialized. Hence, in studying the development of criminal persons, it may not be necessary to develop a different theory for each different type of offender. In contrast, in trying to explain why offences occur, the situations are so diverse and specific to particular crimes that it probably is necessary to have different explanations for different types of offences.

The most popular theory of offending events suggests that they occur in response to specific opportunities, when their expected benefits (e.g. stolen property, peer approval) outweigh their expected costs (e.g. legal punishment, parental disapproval). For example, Clarke and Cornish (1985) outlined a theory of residential burglary which included such influencing factors as whether a house was occupied, whether it looked affluent, whether there were bushes to hide behind, whether there were nosy neighbours, whether the house had a burglar alarm, and whether it contained a dog. Several other researchers have also proposed that offending involves a rational decision in which expected benefits are weighed against expected costs (e.g. Farrington and Kidd, 1977; Cook, 1980). However, Trasler (1986) argued that rational choice theory may be more applicable to 'instrumental' property crimes than to 'expressive' crimes of violence or sex crimes.

While it is obvious that offences require opportunities, it is also probable that some individuals are more likely than others to seek out and create opportunities for offending and to select suitable victims. The 'routine activities' theory of Cohen and Felson (1979) attempted to explain how opportunities for crime arose and changed over time. They suggested that, for a predatory crime to occur, the minimum requirement was the convergence in time and place of a motivated offender and a suitable target, in the absence of a capable guardian. They argued that criminal opportunities varied with routine activities that provided for basic needs such as food and shelter. For example, the increasing number of working women, coupled with the increase in single-parent female-headed households, created increasing numbers of houses left unoccupied during the day, thus providing increasing opportunities for burglary.

In the Cambridge Study, as already mentioned, the most common motives given for offending were rational or utilitarian ones, suggesting that most property crimes were committed because the offenders wanted the items stolen

(West and Farrington, 1977). In addition, a number of cross-sectional surveys have shown that low estimates of the risk of being caught were correlated with high rates of self-reported offending (e.g. Erickson *et al.*, 1977). Unfortunately, the direction of causal influence is not clear in cross-sectional research, since committing delinquent acts may lead to lower estimates of the probability of detection as well as the reverse. Farrington and Knight (1980) carried out a number of studies, using experimental, survey, and observational methods, suggesting that stealing involved risky decision-making. Hence, it is plausible to suggest that opportunities for delinquency, the immediate costs and benefits of delinquency, and the probabilities of these outcomes, all influence whether people offend in any situation.

EXPLAINING THE DEVELOPMENT OF OFFENDING

In explaining the development of offending, a major problem is that most risk factors tend to coincide and tend to be inter-related. For example, adolescents living in physically deteriorated and socially disorganized neighbourhoods disproportionately tend also to come from families with poor parental supervision and erratic parental discipline and tend also to have high impulsivity and low intelligence. The concentration and co-occurrence of these kinds of adversities makes it difficult to establish their independent, interactive, and sequential influences on offending and anti-social behaviour. Hence, any theory of the development of offending is inevitably speculative in the present state of knowledge.

A first step is to establish which factors predict offending independently of other factors. In the Cambridge Study, it was generally true that each of six categories of variables (impulsivity, intelligence, parenting, criminal family, socio-economic deprivation, child anti-social behaviour) predicted offending independently of each other category (Farrington, 1990*b*). For example, the independent predictors of convictions between the ages of 10 and 20 included high daring, low school attainment, poor parental child rearing, a convicted parent, poor housing, and troublesomeness (Farrington and Hawkins, 1991). Hence, it might be concluded that impulsivity, low intelligence, poor parenting, a criminal family and socio-economic deprivation, despite their interrelations, all contribute independently to the development of delinquency. Any theory needs to give priority to explaining these results.

Some of the most important theories of delinquency have already been mentioned in this chapter. These include Cohen's (1955) status frustration–delinquent subculture theory, Cloward and Ohlin's (1960) opportunity–strain theory, Trasler's (1962) social learning theory, Wilson and Herrnstein's (1985) discounting future consequences theory, Clarke and Cornish's (1985) situational decision-making theory, and Gottfredson and Hirschi's (1990) self-control theory. The modern trend is to try to achieve increased explanatory power by integrating propositions derived from several earlier theories (e.g. Elliott *et al.*, 1985; Pearson and Weiner, 1985; Catalano and Hawkins, 1996). My own theory of male offending and anti-social behaviour (Farrington, 1986*b*, 1992*c*, 1996*b*) is also integrative, and it distinguishes explicitly between the development of anti-social tendency and the occurrence of anti-social acts. It is an explicit attempt to integrate developmental and situational theories. The theory suggests that offending is the end result of a four-stage process: energizing, directing, inhibiting, and decision-making.

The main long-term energising factors that ultimately lead to variations in anti-social tendency are desires for material goods, status among intimates, and excitement. The main short-term energizing factors that lead to variations in anti-social tendency are boredom, frustration, anger, and alcohol consumption. The desire for excitement may be greater among children from poorer families, perhaps because excitement is more highly valued by lower-class people than by middle-class ones, because poorer children think they lead more boring lives, or because poorer children are less able to postpone immediate gratification in favour of long-term goals (which could be linked to the emphasis in lower-class culture on the concrete and present as opposed to the abstract and future).

In the directing stage, these motivations produce an increase in anti-social tendency if socially disapproved methods of satisfying them are habitually chosen. The methods chosen depend on maturation and behavioural skills; for example, a 5-year-old would have difficulty stealing a car. Some people (e.g. children from poorer families) are less able to satisfy their desires for material goods, excitement, and social status by legal or socially approved methods, and so tend to choose illegal or socially disapproved methods. The relative inability of poorer children to achieve goals by legitimate methods could be because they tend to fail in school and tend to have erratic, low status employment histories. School failure in turn may often be a consequence of the unstimulating intellectual environment that lower-class parents tend to provide for their children, and their lack of emphasis on abstract concepts.

In the inhibiting stage, anti-social tendencies can be inhibited by internalized beliefs and attitudes that have been built up in a social learning process as a result of a history of rewards and punishments. The belief that offending is wrong, or a strong conscience, tends to be built up if parents are in favour of legal norms, if they exercise close supervision over their children, and if they punish socially disapproved behaviour using love-oriented discipline. Anti-social tendency can also be inhibited by empathy, which may develop as a result of parental warmth and loving relationships. The belief that offending is legitimate, and anti-establishment attitudes generally, tend to be built up if children have been exposed to attitudes and behaviour favouring offending (e.g. in a modelling process), especially by members of their family, by their friends, and in their communities.

In the decision-making stage, which specifies the interaction between the individual and the environment, whether a person with a certain degree of anti-social tendency commits an anti-social act in a given situation depends on opportunities, costs, and benefits, and on the subjective probabilities of the different outcomes. The costs and benefits include immediate situational factors such as the material goods that can be stolen and the likelihood and consequences of being caught by the police, as perceived by the individual. They also include social factors such as likely disapproval by parents or spouses, and encouragement or reinforcement from peers. In general, people tend to make rational decisions. However, more impulsive people are less likely to consider the possible consequences of their actions, especially consequences that are likely to be long delayed.

The consequences of offending may, as a result of a learning process, lead to changes in anti-social tendency or in the cost-benefit calculation. This is especially likely if the consequences are reinforcing (e.g. gaining material goods or peer approval) or punishing (e.g. legal sanctions or parental disapproval). Also, if the consequences involve labelling or stigmatizing the offender, this may make it more difficult for offenders to achieve their aims legally, and hence there may be an increase in anti-social tendency. In other words, events that occur after offending may lead to changes in energizing, directing, inhibiting or decision-making processes in a dynamic system.

Applying the theory to explain some of the results reviewed here, children from poorer families are likely to offend because they are less able to achieve their goals legally and because they value some goals (e.g. excitement) especially highly. Children with low intelligence are more likely to offend because they tend to fail in school and hence cannot achieve their goals legally. Impulsive children, and those with a poor ability to manipulate abstract concepts, are more likely to offend because they do not give sufficient consideration and weight to the possible consequences of offending. Children who are exposed to poor parental child-rearing behaviour, disharmony, or separation are likely to offend because they do not build up internal controls over socially disapproved behaviour, while children from criminal families and those with delinquent friends tend to build up anti-establishment attitudes and the belief that offending is justifiable. The whole process is self-perpetuating, in that poverty, low intelligence, and early school failure lead to truancy and a lack of educational qualifications, which in turn lead to low status jobs and periods of unemployment, both of which make it harder to achieve goals legitimately.

The onset of offending might be caused by increasing long-term motivation (an increasing need for material goods, status, and excitement), an increasing likelihood of choosing socially disapproved methods (possibly linked to a change in dominant social influences from parents to peers), increasing facilitating influences from peers, increasing opportunities (because of increasing freedom from parental control and increasing time spent with peers) or an increasing expected utility of offending (because of the greater importance of peer approval and lesser importance of parental disapproval). Desistance from offending could be linked to an increasing ability to satisfy desires by legal means (e.g. obtaining material goods through employment, obtaining sexual gratification through marriage), increasing inhibiting influences from spouses and cohabitees, decreasing opportunities (because of decreasing time spent with peers), and a decreasing expected utility of offending (because of the lesser importance of peer approval and the greater importance of disapproval from spouses and cohabitees).

The prevalence of offending may increase to a peak between the ages of 14 and 20 because boys (especially lower class school failures) have high impulsivity, high desires for excitement, material goods, and social status between these ages, little chance of achieving their desires legally, and little to lose (since legal penalties are lenient and their intimates—male peers—often approve of offending). In contrast, after the age of 20, desires become attenuated or more realistic, there is more possibility of achieving these more limited goals legally, and the costs of offending are greater (since legal penalties are harsher and their intimates — wives or girlfriends — disapprove of offending).

CONCLUSIONS

Research on criminal careers has greatly advanced knowledge about the prevalence, frequency, onset, persistence, and desistance of individual offending. For example, the peak age of offending in the teenage years primarily reflects a peak in prevalence; the individual offending frequency is relatively constant at different ages, and residual career length reaches a peak at age 30–40. The peak onset rate is at age 13–16, while the peak desistance rate is at age 21–25.

An early onset of offending predicts a long and serious criminal career, because of the persistence of an underlying criminal potential. In the Cambridge Study, more than a quarter of all convicted males had a recorded criminal career lasting more than ten years. A small group of chronic offenders account for a large proportion of the crime problem, and these chronics might have been identified with reasonable accuracy at the age of 10. Most offenders are versatile, but there is a small degree of specialization superimposed on a great deal of versatility. Co-offending and hedonistic motives decrease from the teens to the twenties, while lone offending and utilitarian motives increase.

The criminal career approach also has important implications for criminological theories: they should address developmental processes. The theory proposed here suggested that offending depended on energizing, directing, inhibiting, and decision-making processes. It aimed to explain the development of criminal potential and the occurrence of criminal acts. In addition to explaining between-individual differences in the prevalence or frequency of offending, theories should explain within-individual changes: why people start offending, why they continue or escalate their offending, and why they stop offending. For example, onset may depend primarily on poor parental child-rearing behaviour, persistence may depend on criminal parents and delinquent peers, and desistance may depend on settling down with spouses and cohabitees.

There are a number of ways in which criminal career research might be extended and improved. Existing research is largely based on official records of offending. Future projects are needed that obtain information about offending, including exact dates, by the self-report method in prospective longitudinal surveys. Existing research tends to group together all kinds of crimes, largely because of the versatility of offending, but future research should devote more attention to studying different kinds of crimes separately. This is more feasible with self-reports than with official records (because of the low prevalence and frequency of any given offence type in official records). Longitudinal researchers need to collect more information about immediate situational influences on criminal events and about a wider range of criminal career features. Existing research focuses mainly on males. More studies are needed that systematically compare different criminal career patterns of different categories of people (e.g. males versus females, lower class versus upper/middle class). Existing research focuses on individuals, but there could also be studies of the criminal careers of larger units, such as families, gangs, communities, and places.

Offending is one element of a larger syndrome of anti-social behaviour that arises in childhood and tends to persist into adulthood, with numerous different behavioural manifestations. However, while there is continuity over time in anti-social behaviour, changes are also occurring. It is commonly found that about half of a sample of anti-social children go on to become anti-social teenagers, and about half of anti-social teenagers go on to become anti-social adults. More research is needed on factors that vary within individuals and that predict these changes over time. Research is especially needed on changing behavioural manifestations and developmental sequences at different ages. More efforts should especially be made to identify factors that protect vulnerable children from developing into anti-social teenagers.

A great deal has been learned in the last twenty years, particularly from longitudinal surveys, about risk factors for offending and other types of anti-social behaviour. Offenders differ significantly from non-offenders in many respects, including impulsivity, intelligence, family background, and socio-economic deprivation. These differences may be present before, during, and after criminal careers. Since most is known about risk factors for prevalence and onset, research is needed on risk factors for frequency, duration, escalation, and desistance. While the precise causal chains that link these factors with anti-social behaviour, and the ways in which these factors have independent, interactive, or sequential effects, are not known, it is clear that individuals at risk can be identified with reasonable accuracy.

In order to advance knowledge about human development and criminal careers, a new generation of multiple-cohort longitudinal studies is needed (Farrington *et al.*, 1986*a*; Farrington, 1988*a*). For example, Tonry *et al.* (1991) recommended that seven cohorts should each be followed up for eight years, beginning during the pre-natal period (with a sample of pregnant women) and at ages 3, 6, 9, 12, 15, and 18. This study should advance knowledge about the development of offending and other types of anti-social behaviour from before birth up to the mid-twenties, covering the major periods of onset, persistence, and desistance of criminal careers. A similar project is currently being implemented in Chicago (Earls and Reiss, 1994).

One attraction of this design is that, by amalgamating data from adjacent cohorts, conclusions about twenty-five years of development could be drawn in a project taking only ten years from start to finish (including preparatory work, analysis, and writing up). Indeed, preliminary conclusions about development from before birth up to the age of 21 could be drawn in the first five years of the project. It is also important to include experimental interventions within longitudinal studies, to distinguish between causes and indicators, and to investigate the effects of prevention or treatment measures on criminal career features (Farrington, 1992e; Loeber and Farrington, 1994).

This chapter shows that much has been learned in the past twenty years about human development and criminal careers. With a major investment in new longitudinal studies, there can be considerable further advances in knowledge and theory, and consequent improvements in crime prevention and control. Because of the link between offending and numerous other social problems, any measure that succeeds in reducing offending will have benefits that go far beyond this. Any measure that reduces offending will probably also reduce alcohol abuse, drunk driving, drug abuse, sexual promiscuity, family violence, truancy, school failure, unemployment, marital disharmony, and divorce. It is clear that problem children tend to grow up into problem adults, and that problem adults tend to produce more problem children. Major efforts are urgently needed to advance knowledge about and reduce offending and anti-social behaviour.

Selected Further Reading

The classic volume on criminal career research is the report of the National Academy of Sciences Panel, *Criminal Careers and 'Career Criminals'* edited by A. Blumstein and colleagues in two volumes (Washington, DC: National Academy Press, 1986). The most interesting recent volume on this topic is *Analysing Offending: Data, Models and Interpretations* by R. Tarling (London: HMSO, 1993). This describes numerous sophisticated analyses of Home Office datasets. Turning to more developmental issues, the 100-page chapter by R. Loeber and M. LeBlanc ('Toward a Developmental Criminology' in *Crime and Justice*, vol. 12, Chicago, Ill.: University of Chicago Press, 1990) sets out many of the key ideas in detail. *Cross-National Longitudinal Research on Human Development and Criminal Behaviour*, edited by E. G. M. Weitekamp and H.-J. Kerner (Dordrecht: Kluwer, 1994) contains chapters by many of the leading researchers. For a general review of risk factors for offending, *The Psychology of Criminal Conduct* by R. Blackburn (Chichester: Wiley, 1993) can be confidently recommended as an excellent textbook. *Delinquency and Crime: Current Theories*, edited by J. D. Hawkins (Cambridge: Cambridge University Press, 1996) contains a selection of recent developmentally oriented criminological theories. The major policy implication of developmental criminology is developmental crime prevention, reviewed in a long chapter with this title by R. E. Tremblay and W. M. Craig in *Building a Safer Society: Strategic Approaches to Crime Prevention*, edited by M. Tonry and D. P. Farrington (Chicago, Ill.: University of Chicago Press, 1995). Finally, *Preventing Antisocial Behaviour*, edited by J. McCord and R. E. Tremblay (New York: Guilford Press, 1992) contains chapters by leading practitioners of developmental prevention.

REFERENCES

AMDUR, R. L. (1989), 'Testing Causal Models of Delinquency: A Methodological Critique', *Criminal Justice and Behaviour*, 16: 35–62.

BALL, J. C., ROSEN, L., FLUECK, J. A., and NURCO, D. N. (1981), 'The Criminality of Heroin Addicts: When Addicted and When Off Opiates', in J. A. Inciardi, ed., *The Drugs–Crime Connection*, 39–65, Beverly Hills, Cal.: Sage.

BARNETT, A., BLUMSTEIN, A., and FARRINGTON, D. P. (1987), 'Probabilistic Models of Youthful Criminal Careers', *Criminology*, 25: 83–107.

—— —— and —— (1989), 'A Prospective Test of a Criminal Career Model', *Criminology*, 27: 373–88.

—— and LOFASO, A. J. (1985), 'Selective Incapacitation and the Philadelphia Cohort Data', *Journal of Quantitative Criminology*, 1: 3–36.

BERKOWITZ, L. (1978), 'Is Criminal Violence Normative Behaviour? Hostile and Instrumental Aggression in Violent Incidents', *Journal of Research in Crime and Delinquency*, 15: 148–61.

BLUMSTEIN, A., and COHEN, J. (1979), 'Estimation of Individual Crime Rates from Arrest Records', *Journal of Criminal Law and Criminology*, 70: 561–85.

—— and —— (1987), 'Characterizing Criminal Careers', *Science*, 237: 985–91.

—— —— and FARRINGTON, D. P. (1988), 'Criminal Career Research: Its Value For Criminology', *Criminology*, 26: 1–35.

—— —— and HSIEH, P. (1982), *The Duration of Adult Criminal Careers*. Washington, DC: National Institute of Justice.

—— —— ROTH, J. A., and VISHER, C. A., eds. (1986), *Criminal Careers and 'Career Criminals'*. Washington, DC: National Academy Press.

—— FARRINGTON, D. P., and MOITRA, S. (1985), 'Delinquency Careers: Innocents, Desisters and Persisters', in M. Tonry and N. Morris, eds., *Crime and Justice*, vi, 187–219. Chicago, Ill.: University of Chicago Press.

—— and GRADDY, E. (1982), 'Prevalence and Recidivism in Index Arrests: A Feedback Model', *Law and Society Review*, 16, 265–90.

BOSWELL, G. (1995), *Violent Victims: The Prevalence of Abuse and Loss in the Lives of Section 53 Offenders*. London: The Prince's Trust.

CAIRNS, R .B., and CAIRNS, B. D. (1994), *Lifelines and Risks: Pathways of Youth in Our Time*. Cambridge: Cambridge University Press.

CAPALDI, D. M., and PATTERSON, G. R. (1996), 'Can Violent Offenders be Distinguished from Frequent Offenders? Prediction from Childhood to Adolescence', *Journal of Research in Crime and Delinquency*, 33: 206–31.

CATALANO, R. F., and HAWKINS, J. D. (1996), 'The social development model: A Theory of Antisocial Behaviour', in J. D. Hawkins, ed., *Delinquency and Crime: Current Theories*, 149–97. Cambridge: Cambridge University Press.

CERNKOVICH, S. A., GIORDANO, P. C., and PUGH, M. D. (1985), 'Chronic Offenders: The Missing Cases in Self-report Delinquency Research', *Journal of Criminal Law and Criminology*, 76: 705–32.

CLARKE, R. V., and CORNISH, D. B. (1985), 'Modelling Offenders' Decisions: A Framework for Research and Policy', in M. Tonry and N. Morris, eds., *Crime and Justice*, vi, 147–85. Chicago, Ill.: University of Chicago Press.

CLOWARD, R. A., and OHLIN, L. E. (1960), *Delinquency and Opportunity*. New York: Free Press.

COHEN, A. K. (1955), *Delinquent Boys: The Culture of the Gang*. Glencoe, Ill.: Free Press.

COHEN, J. (1986), 'Research on Criminal Careers: Individual Frequency Rates and Offence Seriousness', in A. Blumstein, J. Cohen, J. A. Roth and C. A. Visher, eds., *Criminal Careers and 'Career Criminals'*, i, 292–481. Washington, DC: National Academy Press.

COHEN, L. E., and FELSON, M. (1979), 'Social Change and Crime Trends: A Routine Activity Approach', *American Sociological Review*, 44: 588–608.

COOK, P. J. (1980), 'Research in Criminal Deterrence: Laying the Groundwork for the Second Decade', in M. Tonry and N. Morris, eds., *Crime and Justice*, ii, 211–68. Chicago, Ill.: University of Chicago Press.

DOUGLAS, J. W. B., ROSS, J. M., HAMMOND, W. A., and MULLIGAN, D. G. (1966), 'Delinquency and Social Class', *British Journal of Criminology*, 6: 294–302.

EARLS, F. J., and REISS, A. J. (1994), *Breaking the Cycle: Predicting and Preventing Crime*. Washington, DC: National Institute of Justice.

ELLIOTT, D. S., HUIZINGA, D., and AGETON, S. S. (1985), *Explaining Delinquency and Drug Use*. Beverly Hills, Cal.: Sage.

—— and MENARD, S. (1989), *Multiple Problem Youth: Delinquency, Substance Use and Mental Health Problems*. New York: Springer-Verlag.

ERICKSON, M., GIBBS, J. P., and JENSEN, G. F. (1977), 'The Deterrence Doctrine and the Perceived Certainty of Legal Punishment', *American Sociological Review*, 42: 305–317.

ERON, L. D., and HUESMANN, L. R. (1990), 'The Stability of Aggressive Behaviour—Even unto the Third Generation', in M. Lewis and S. M. Miller, eds., *Handbook of Developmental Psychopathology*, 147–56. New York: Plenum.

EYSENCK, H. J., and GUDJONSSON, G. H. (1989), *The Causes and Cures of Criminality*. New York: Plenum.

FARRINGTON, D. P. (1972), 'Delinquency Begins at Home', *New Society*, 21: 495–7.

—— (1973), 'Self-reports of Deviant Behaviour: Predictive and Stable?', *Journal of Criminal Law and Criminology*, 64: 99–110.

—— (1978), 'The Family Backgrounds of Aggressive Youths', in L. Hersov, M. Berger, and D. Shaffer, eds., *Aggression and Antisocial Behaviour in Childhood and Adolescence*, 73–93. Oxford: Pergamon.

—— (1979), 'Environmental Stress, Delinquent Behaviour, and Convictions', in I. G. Sarason and C. D. Spielberger, eds., *Stress and Anxiety*, vi, 93–107. Washington, DC: Hemisphere.

—— (1980), 'Truancy, Delinquency, the Home and the School', in L. Hersov and I. Berg, eds., *Out of School: Modern Perspectives in Truancy and School Refusal*, 49–63. Chichester: Wiley.

—— (1986a), 'Age and Crime', in M. Tonry and N. Morris, eds., *Crime and Justice*, vii, 189–250. Chicago, Ill.: University of Chicago Press.

—— (1986b), 'Stepping Stones to Adult Criminal Careers', in D. Olweus, J. Block, and M. R. Yarrow, eds., *Development of Antisocial and Prosocial Behaviour: Research, Theories and Issues*, 359–84. New York: Academic Press.

—— (1987), 'Predicting Individual Crime Rates', in D. M. Gottfredson and M. Tonry, eds., *Prediction and Classification: Criminal Justice Decision Making*, 53–101. Chicago, Ill.: University of Chicago Press.

—— (1988a), 'Advancing Knowledge about Delinquency and Crime: The Need for a Coordinated Programme of Longitudinal Research', *Behavioural Sciences and the Law*, 6: 307–31.

—— (1988b), 'Studying Changes Within Individuals: The Causes of Offending', in M. Rutter, ed., *Studies of Psychosocial Risk: The Power of Longitudinal Data*, 158–83. Cambridge: Cambridge University Press.

—— (1989a), 'Early Predictors of Adolescent Aggression and Adult Violence', *Violence and Victims*, 4: 79–100.

—— (1989b), 'Later Adult Life Outcomes of Offenders and Non-offenders', in M. Brambring, F. Losel, and H. Skowronek, eds., *Children at Risk: Assessment, Longitudinal Research, and Intervention*, 220–44. Berlin: De Gruyter.

—— (1989c), 'Self-reported and Official Offending from Adolescence to Adulthood', in M. W. Klein, ed., *Cross-national Research in Self-reported Crime and Delinquency*, 399–423. Dordrecht: Kluwer.

—— (1990a), 'Age, Period, Cohort, and Offending', in D. M. Gottfredson and

R. V. Clarke, eds., *Policy and Theory in Criminal Justice: Contributions in Honour of Leslie T. Wilkins*, 51–75. Aldershot: Avebury.

—— (1990*b*), 'Implications of Criminal Career Research for the Prevention of Offending', *Journal of Adolescence*, 13: 93–113.

—— (1991*a*), 'Antisocial Personality from Childhood to Adulthood', *The Psychologist*, 4: 389–394.

—— (1991*b*), 'Childhood Aggression and Adult Violence: Early Precursors and Later Life Outcomes', in D. J. Pepler and K. H. Rubin, eds., *The Development and Treatment of Childhood Aggression*, 5–29. Hillsdale, NJ: Erlbaum.

—— (1992*a*), 'Criminal Career Research: Lessons for Crime Prevention', *Studies on Crime and Crime Prevention*, 1: 7–29.

—— (1992*b*), 'Criminal Career Research in the United Kingdom', *British Journal of Criminology*, 32: 521–36.

—— (1992*c*), 'Explaining the Beginning, Progress and Ending of Antisocial Behaviour from Birth to Adulthood', in J. McCord, ed., *Facts, Frameworks and Forecasts: Advances in Criminological Theory*, iii, 253–86. New Brunswick, N.J.: Transaction.

—— (1992*d*), 'Juvenile Delinquency', in J. C. Coleman, ed., *The School Years*, 2nd edn., 123–63. London: Routledge.

—— (1992*e*), 'The Need for Longitudinal-experimental Research on Offending and Antisocial Behaviour', in J. McCord and R. E. Tremblay, eds., *Preventing Antisocial Behaviour: Interventions from Birth through Adolescence*, 353–76. New York: Guilford Press.

—— (1993*a*), 'Understanding and Preventing Bullying', in M. Tonry and N. Morris, eds., *Crime and Justice*, xvii, 381–458. Chicago, Ill.: University of Chicago Press.

—— (1993*b*), 'Childhood Origins of Teenage Antisocial Behaviour and Adult Social Dysfunction', *Journal of the Royal Society of Medicine*, 86: 13–17.

—— (1993*c*), 'Motivations for Conduct Disorder and Delinquency', *Development and Psychopathology*, 5: 225–241.

—— (1994*a*), 'Early Developmental Prevention of Juvenile Delinquency', *Criminal Behaviour and Mental Health*, 4: 209–27.

—— (1994*b*), 'Interactions between Individual and Contextual Factors in the Development of Offending', in R. K. Silbereisen and E. Todt, eds., *Adolescence in Context: The Interplay of Family, School, Peers and Work in Adjustment*, 366–89. New York: Springer-Verlag.

—— (1994*c*), 'Childhood, Adolescent and Adult Features of Violent Males', in L. R. Huesmann, ed., *Aggressive Behaviour: Current Perspectives*, 215–40. New York: Plenum.

—— (1995*a*), 'Crime and Physical Health: Illnesses, Injuries, Accidents and Offending in the Cambridge Study', *Criminal Behaviour and Mental Health*, 5: 261–78.

—— (1995*b*), 'The Development of Offending and Antisocial Behaviour from Childhood: Key Findings from the Cambridge Study in Delinquent Development', *Journal of Child Psychology and Psychiatry*, 36: 929–64.

—— (1996*a*), 'Later Life Outcomes of Truants in the Cambridge Study', in I. Berg and J. Nursten, eds., *Unwillingly to School*. 4th edn., 96–118. London: Gaskell.

—— (1996*b*), 'The Explanation and Prevention of Youthful Offending', in J. D. Hawkins, ed., *Delinquency and Crime: Current Theories*, 68–148). New York: Cambridge University Press.

—— (1996*c*), *Understanding and Preventing Youth Crime*. York: Joseph Rowntree Foundation.

—— (1996*d*), 'Psychosocial Influences on the Development of Antisocial Personality', in G. Davies, S. Lloyd-Bostock, M. McMurran, and C. Wilson, eds., *Psychology, Law and Criminal Justice: International Developments in Research and Practice*, 424–44. Berlin: de Gruyter.

—— (forthcoming), 'The Relationship between Low Resting Heart Rate and Violence', in A. Raine, D. P. Farrington, P. A. Brennan, and S. A. Mednick, eds., *Biosocial Bases of Violence*. New York: Plenum.

—— BARNES, G., and LAMBERT, S. (1996*b*), 'The Concentration of Offending in Families', *Legal and Criminological Psychology*, 1: 47–63.

—— BERKOWITZ, L., and WEST, D. J. (1982), 'Differences between Individual and Group Fights', *British Journal of Social Psychology*, 21: 323–33.

—— GALLAGHER, B., MORLEY, L., ST LEDGER, R. J., and WEST, D. J. (1986*b*), 'Unemployment, School Leaving, and Crime', *British Journal of Criminology*, 26: 335–56.

—— —— —— —— and —— (1988*a*), 'A 24-year Follow-up of Men from Vulnerable Backgrounds', in R. L. Jenkins and W. K. Brown, eds., *The Abandonment of Delinquent Behaviour*. 155–73. New York: Praeger.

—— —— —— —— and —— (1988*b*), 'Are There Any Successful Men from Criminogenic Backgrounds?, *Psychiatry*, 51: 116–30.

FARRINGTON, D. P. and HAWKINS, J. D. (1991), 'Predicting Participation, Early Onset, and Later Persistence in Officially Recorded Offending', *Criminal Behaviour and Mental Health*, 1: 1–33.

—— and KIDD, R. F. (1977), 'Is Financial Dishonesty a Rational Decision?, *British Journal of Social and Clinical Psychology*, 16: 139–146.

—— and KNIGHT, B. J. (1980), 'Four Studies of Stealing as a Risky Decision', in P. D. Lipsitt and B. D. Sales, eds., *New Directions in Psycholegal Research*, 26–50. New York: Van Nostrand Reinhold.

—— and LOEBER, R. (forthcoming), 'Trans-atlantic Replicability of Risk Factors in the Development of Delinquency', in P. Cohen, C. Slomkowski, and L. N. Robins, eds., *Where and When: The Influence of History and Geography on Aspects of Psychopathology*. Mahwah, NJ: Erlbaum.

—— —— ELLIOTT, D. S., HAWKINS, J. D., KANDEL, D. B., KLEIN, M. W., McCORD, J., ROWE, D. C., and TREMBLAY, R. E. (1990*a*), 'Advancing Knowledge about the Onset of Delinquency and Crime', in B. B. Lahey and A. E. Kazdin, eds., *Advances in Clinical Child Psychology*, xiii, 283–342. New York: Plenum.

—— —— STOUTHAMER-LOEBER, M. S., VAN KAMMEN, W., and SCHMIDT, L. (1996*a*), 'Self-reported Delinquency and a Combined Delinquency Seriousness Scale Based on Boys, Mothers and Teachers: Concurrent and Predictive Validity for African Americans and Caucasians', *Criminology*, 34: 493–517.

—— —— and VAN KAMMEN, W. B. (1990*b*), 'Long-term Criminal Outcomes of Hyperactivity-Impulsivity-Attention Deficit and Conduct Problems in Childhood', in L. N. Robins and M. Rutter, eds., *Straight and Devious Pathways from Childhood to Adulthood*, 62–81. Cambridge: Cambridge University Press.

—— OHLIN, L. E., and WILSON, J. Q. (1986*a*), *Understanding and Controlling Crime: Toward a New Research Strategy*. New York: Springer-Verlag.

—— SNYDER, H. N., and FINNEGAN, T. A. (1988*c*), 'Specialization in Juvenile Court Careers', *Criminology*, 26: 461–87.

—— and WEST, D. J. (1990), 'The Cambridge Study in Delinquent Development: A Long-term Follow-up of 411 London Males', in H.-J. Kerner and G. Kaiser, eds., *Criminality: Personality, Behaviour, Life History*, 115–38. Berlin: Springer-Verlag.

—— and —— (1993), 'Criminal, Penal and Life Histories of Chronic Offenders: Risk and Protective Factors and Early Identification', *Criminal Behaviour and Mental Health*, 3: 492–523.

—— and —— (1995), 'Effects of Marriage, Separation and Children on Offending by Adult Males', in J. Hagan, ed., *Current Perspectives on Aging and the Life Cycle. iv: Delinquency and Disrepute in the Life Course*, 249–81. Greenwich, Conn.: JAI Press.

—— and WIKSTRÖM, P.-O. H. (1994), 'Criminal Careers in London and Stockholm: A Cross-national Comparative Study', in E. G. M. Weitekamp and H.-J. Kerner, eds., *Cross-national Longitudinal Research on Human Development and Criminal Behaviour*, 65–89. Dordrecht: Kluwer.

FERGUSON, T. (1952), *The Young Delinquent in his Social Setting*. London: Oxford University Press.

FERGUSSON, D. M., HORWOOD, L. J., and LYNSKEY, M. T. (1992), 'Family Change, Parental Discord and Early Offending', *Journal of Child Psychology and Psychiatry*, 33: 1059–75.

—— —— and —— (1993), 'The Effects of Conduct Disorder and Attention Deficit in Middle Childhood on Offending and Scholastic Ability at Age 13', *Journal of Child Psychology and Psychiatry*, 34: 899–916.

FISCHER, D. G. (1984), 'Family Size and Delinquency', *Perceptual and Motor Skills*, 58: 527–34.

FOX, J. A., and TRACY, P. E. (1988), 'A Measure of Skewness in Offence Distributions', *Journal of Quantitative Criminology*, 4: 259–74.

FRY, L. J. (1985), 'Drug Abuse and Crime in a Swedish Birth Cohort', *British Journal of Criminology*, 25: 46–59.

GHODSIAN, M., and POWER, C. (1987), 'Alcohol Consumption between the Ages of 16 and 23 in Britain: A Longitudinal Study', *British Journal of Addiction*, 82: 175–80.

GOTTFREDSON, M., and HIRSCHI, T. (1986), 'The True Value of Lambda Would Appear to be Zero: An Essay on Career Criminals, Criminal Careers, Selective Incapacitation, Cohort Studies, and Related Topics', *Criminology*, 24: 213–33.

GOTTFREDSON, M., and HIRSCHI, T. (1990), *A General Theory of Crime*. Stanford, Cal.: Stanford University Press.

GRAHAM, J. (1988), *Schools, Disruptive Behaviour and Delinquency*. London: HMSO.

—— and BOWLING, B. (1995), *Young People and Crime*. London: HMSO.

HAAPANEN, R. A. (1990), *Selective Incapacitation and the Serious Offender*. New York: Springer-Verlag.

HAGELL, A., and NEWBURN, T. (1994), *Persistent Young Offenders*. London: Policy Studies Institute.

HAMPARIAN, D. M., DAVIS, J. M., JACOBSON, J. M., and McGRAW, R. E. (1985), *The Young Criminal Years of the Violent Few*. Washington, DC: Office of Juvenile Justice and Delinquency Prevention.

—— SCHUSTER, R., DINITZ, S., and CONRAD, J. P. (1978), *The Violent Few*. Lexington, Mass.: Heath.

HENRY, B., CASPI, A., MOFFITT, T. E., and SILVA, P. A. (1996), 'Temperamental and Familial Predictors of Violent and Non-violent Criminal Convictions: Age 3 to Age 18', *Developmental Psychology*, 32: 614–23.

HINDELANG, M. J., HIRSCHI, T., and WEIS, J. G. (1981), *Measuring Delinquency*. Beverly Hills, Cal.: Sage.

HODGINS, S. (1994), 'Status at Age 30 of Children with Conduct Problems', *Studies on Crime and Crime Prevention*, 3: 41–62.

HOME OFFICE STATISTICAL BULLETIN (1987), *Criminal Careers of Those Born in 1953: Persistent Offenders and Desistance*. London: Home Office.

—— (1995), *Criminal Careers of Those Born Between 1953 and 1973*. London: Home Office.

HORNEY, J., and MARSHALL, I. H. (1991), 'Measuring Lambda Through Self-reports'. *Criminology*, 29: 471–95.

HUIZINGA, D., and ELLIOTT, D. S. (1986), 'Reassessing the Reliability and Validity of Self-report Measures', *Journal of Quantitative Criminology*, 2: 293–327.

KEMPF, K. L. (1987), Specialization and the Criminal Career', *Criminology*, 25: 399–420.

KLEIN, M. W. (1984), 'Offence Specialization and Versatility among Juveniles', *British Journal of Criminology*, 24: 185–94.

KLINTEBERG, B. A., ANDERSSON, T., MAGNUSSON, D., and STATTIN, H. (1993), 'Hyperactive Behaviour in Childhood as Related to Subsequent Alcohol Problems and Violent Offending: A Longitudinal Study of Male Subjects', *Personality and Individual Differences*, 15: 381–8.

KOLVIN, I., MILLER, F. J. W., FLEETING, M., and KOLVIN, P. A. (1988), 'Social and Parenting Factors Affecting Criminal-offence Rates: Findings from the Newcastle Thousand Family Study (1947–1980)', *British Journal of Psychiatry*, 152: 80–90.

—— —— SCOTT, D. M., GATZANIS, S. R. M., and FLEETING, M. (1990), *Continuities of Deprivation? The Newcastle 1000 Family Study*. Aldershot: Avebury.

LEBLANC, M. (1996), 'Changing Patterns in the Perpetration of Offences over Time: Trajectories from Early Adolescence to the Early 30s', *Studies on Crime and Crime Prevention*, 5: 151–65.

—— and FRECHETTE, M. (1989), *Male Criminal Activity from Childhood Through Youth: Multi-level and Developmental Perspectives*. New York: Springer-Verlag.

LOEBER, R. (1987), 'Behavioural Precursors and Accelerators of Delinquency', in W. Buikhuisen and S. A. Mednick, eds., *Explaining Criminal Behaviour: Interdisciplinary Approaches*, 51–67. Leiden: Brill.

—— and FARRINGTON, D. P. (1994), 'Problems and Solutions in Longitudinal and Experimental Treatment Studies of Child Psychopathology and Delinquency', *Journal of Consulting and Clinical Psychology*, 62: 887–900.

—— and LeBlanc, M. (1990), 'Toward a Developmental Criminology', in M. Tonry and N. Morris, eds., *Crime and Justice*, xii, 375–473. Chicago, Ill.: University of Chicago Press.

—— and SNYDER, H. N. (1990), 'Rate of Offending in Juvenile Careers: Findings of Constancy and Change in Lambda', *Criminology*, 28: 97–109.

—— and STOUTHAMER-LOEBER, M. (1986), 'Family Factors as Correlates and Predictors of Juvenile Conduct Problems and Delinquency', in M. Tonry and N. Morris, eds., *Crime and Justice*, vii, 29–149. Chicago Ill.: University of Chicago Press.

—— —— VAN KAMMEN, W. B., and FARRINGTON, D. P. (1991), 'Initiation, Escalation and Desistance in Juvenile Offending and their Correlates', *Journal of Criminal Law and Criminology*, 82: 36–82.

LYNAM, D. (1996), 'Early Identification of Chronic Offenders: Who is the Fledgling Psychopath?', *Psychological Bulletin*, 120: 209–234.

—— MOFFITT, T., and STOUTHAMER-LOEBER, M. (1993), 'Explaining the Relation Between IQ and Delinquency: Class, Race, Test Motivation, School Failure or Self-control?', *Journal of Abnormal Psychology*, 102: 187–96.

MALINOSKY-RUMMELL, R., and HANSEN, D. J. (1993), 'Long-term Consequences of Childhood Physical Abuse', *Psychological Bulletin*, 114: 68–79.

MAXFIELD, M. G., and WIDOM, C. S. (1996), 'The Cycle of Violence Revisited 6 Years

Later', *Archives of Pediatrics and Adolescent Medicine*, 150: 390–5.

McCord, J. (1977), 'A Comparative Study of Two Generations of Native American', in R. F. Meier, ed., *Theory in Criminology*, 83–92. Beverly Hills, Cal.: Sage.

—— (1979), 'Some Child-rearing Antecedents of Criminal Behaviour in Adult Men', *Journal of Personality and Social Psychology*, 37: 1477–86.

—— (1982), 'A Longitudinal View of the Relationship Between Paternal Absence and Crime', in J. Gunn and D. P. Farrington, eds., *Abnormal Offenders, Delinquency, and the Criminal Justice System*, 113–28. Chichester: Wiley.

—— (1990), 'Crime in Moral and Social Contexts', *Criminology*, 28: 1–26.

—— (1991), 'Family Relationships, Juvenile Delinquency, and Adult Criminality', *Criminology*, 29: 397–417.

Moffitt, T. E. (1990), 'The Neuropsychology of Juvenile Delinquency: A Critical Review', in M. Tonry and N. Morris, eds., *Crime and Justice*, xii, 99–169. Chicago, Ill.: University of Chicago Press.

—— (1993), 'Adolescence-limited and Life-course-persistent Antisocial Behaviour: A Developmental Taxonomy', *Psychological Review*, 100: 674–701.

—— and Henry, B. (1989), 'Neuropsychological Assessment of Executive Functions in Self-reported Delinquents', *Development and Psychopathology*, 1: 105–18.

—— and Silva, P. A. (1988*a*), 'IQ and Delinquency: A Direct Test of the Differential Detection Hypothesis', *Journal of Abnormal Psychology*, 97: 330–3.

—— and —— (1988*b*), 'Neuropsychological Deficit and Self-reported Delinquency in an Unselected Birth Cohort', *Journal of the American Academy of Child and Adolescent Psychiatry*, 27: 233–40.

Morash, M. and Rucker, L. (1989), 'An Exploratory Study of the Connection of Mother's Age at Childbearing to her Children's Delinquency in Four Data Sets', *Crime and Delinquency*, 35: 45–93.

Murray, C. (1995), 'The Next British Revolution', *The Public Interest*, 118: 3–29.

Nagin, D. S., and Farrington, D. P. (1992*a*), 'The Onset and Persistence of Offending', *Criminology*, 30: 501–23.

—— and —— (1992*b*), 'The Stability of Criminal Potential from Childhood to Adulthood', *Criminology*, 30: 235–260.

—— —— and Moffitt, T. E. (1995), 'Life-course Trajectories of Different Types of Offenders', *Criminology*, 33: 111–39.

—— Pogarsky, G., and Farrington, D. P. (forthcoming), 'Adolescent Mothers and the Criminal Behaviour of their Children', *Law and Society Review*, 31.

Newson, J., Newson, E., and Adams, M. (1993), 'The Social Origins of Delinquency', *Criminal Behaviour and Mental Health*, 3: 19–29.

Olweus, D. (1979), 'Stability of Aggressive Reaction Patterns in Males: A Review', *Psychological Bulletin*, 86: 852–75.

Osborn, S. G. (1980), 'Moving Home, Leaving London, and Delinquent Trends', *British Journal of Criminology*, 20: 54–61.

Ouston, J. (1984), 'Delinquency, Family Background, and Educational Attainment', *British Journal of Criminology*, 24: 2–26.

Pearson, F. S., and Weiner, N. A. (1985), 'Toward an Integration of Criminological Theories', *Journal of Criminal Law and Criminology*, 76: 116–50.

Petersilia, J., Greenwood, P. W., and Lavin, M. (1978), *Criminal Careers of Habitual Felons*. Washington, DC: National Institute of Justice.

Power, M. J., Alderson, M. R., Phillipson, C. M., Shoenberg, E., and Morris, J. N. (1967), 'Delinquent Schools?', *New Society*, 10: 542–3.

Pulkkinen, L. (1987), 'Offensive and Defensive Aggression in Humans: A Longitudinal Perspective', *Aggressive Behaviour*, 13: 197–212.

—— (1988), 'Delinquent Development: Theoretical and Empirical Considerations', in M. Rutter, ed., *Studies of Psychosocial Risk: The Power of Longitudinal Data*, 184–199. Cambridge: Cambridge University Press.

Raine, A. (1993), *The Psychopathology of Crime: Criminal Behaviour as a Clinical Disorder*. San Diego: Academic Press.

—— Venables, P. H., and Williams, M. (1990), 'Relationships Between Central and Autonomic Measures of Arousal at Age 15 Years and Criminality at Age 24 years', *Archives of General Psychiatry*, 47: 1003–7.

Reiss, A. J. (1988), 'Co-offending and Criminal Careers', in M. Tonry and N. Morris, eds., *Crime and Justice*, x, 117–70. Chicago, Ill.: University of Chicago Press.

—— and Farrington, D. P. (1991), 'Advancing Knowledge about Co-offending: Results from a Prospective Longitudinal Survey of London Males', *Journal of Criminal Law and Criminology*, 82: 360–95.

RILEY, D., and SHAW, M. (1985), *Parental Supervision and Juvenile Delinquency*. London: HMSO.

ROBINS, L. N. (1979), 'Sturdy Childhood Predictors of Adult Outcomes: Replications from Longitudinal Studies', in J. E. Barrett, R. M. Rose, and G.L. Klerman, eds., *Stress and Mental Disorder*, 219–35. New York: Raven Press.

—— WEST, P. J., and HERJANIC, B. L. (1975), 'Arrests and Delinquency in Two Generations: A Study of Black Urban Families and their Children', *Journal of Child Psychology and Psychiatry*, 16: 125–40.

RUTTER, M. (1985), 'Resilience in the Face of Adversity: Protective Factors and Resistance to Psychiatric Disorder', *British Journal of Psychiatry*, 147: 598–611.

—— MAUGHAN, B., MORTIMORE, P., and OUSTON, J. (1979), *Fifteen Thousand Hours: Secondary Schools and their Effects on Children*. London: Open Books.

—— TIZARD, J., and WHITMORE, K. (1970), *Education, Health and Behaviour*. London: University of London Press.

SAMPSON, R. J., and LAUB, J. H. (1993), *Crime in the Making: Pathways and Turning Points through Life*. Cambridge, Mass.: Harvard University Press.

—— and —— (1994), 'Urban Poverty and the Family Context of Delinquency: A New Look at Structure and Process in a Classic Study', *Child Development*, 65: 523–40.

SATTERFIELD, J. H. (1987), 'Childhood Diagnostic and Neurophysiological Predictors of Teenage Arrest Rates: An 8-year Prospective Study', in S. A. Mednick, T. E. Moffitt, and S. A. Stack, eds., *The Causes of Crime: New Biological Approaches*, 146–67, Cambridge: Cambridge University Press.

SCHWEINHART, L. J., BARNES, H. V., and WEIKART, D. P. (1993), *Significant Benefits: The High/Scope Perry School Study Through Age 27*. Ypsilanti, Mich.: High/Scope.

SHEDLER, J., and BLOCK, J. (1990), 'Adolescent Drug Use and Psychological Health', *American Psychologist*, 45: 612–30.

SHORT, J. F., and NYE, F. I. (1957), 'Reported Behaviour as a Criterion of Deviant Behaviour', *Social Problems*, 5: 207–13.

SHOVER, N. (1985), *Aging Criminals*. Beverly Hills, Cal.: Sage.

SNYDER, H. N. (1988), *Court Careers of Juvenile Offenders*. Washington, DC: Office of Juvenile Justice and Delinquency Prevention.

STANDER, J., FARRINGTON, D. P., HILL, G., and ALTHAM, P. M. E. (1989), 'Markov Chain Analysis and Specialization in Criminal Careers', *British Journal of Criminology*, 29: 317–35.

STATTIN, H., and KLACKENBERG-LARSSON, I. (1993), 'Early Language and Intelligence Development and their Relationship to Future Criminal Behaviour', *Journal of Abnormal Psychology*, 102: 369–78.

—— and MAGNUSSON, D. (1989), 'The Role of Early Aggressive Behaviour in the Frequency, Seriousness and Types of Later Crime', *Journal of Consulting and Clinical Psychology*, 57: 710–18.

—— and —— (1991), 'Stability and Change in Criminal Behaviour up to Age 30', *British Journal of Criminology*, 31: 327–46.

—— —— and REICHEL, H. (1989), 'Criminal Activity at Different Ages: A Study Based on a Swedish Longitudinal Research Population', *British Journal of Criminology*, 29: 368–85.

TARLING, R. (1993), *Analysing Offending: Data, Models and Interpretations*. London: HMSO.

THORNBERRY, T. P., and FARNWORTH, M. (1982), 'Social Correlates of Criminal Involvement: Further Evidence on the Relationship Between Social Status and Criminal Behaviour', *American Sociological Review*, 47: 505–18.

TOLAN, P. H. (1987), 'Implications of Age of Onset for Delinquency Risk', *Journal of Abnormal Child Psychology*, 15: 47–65.

TONRY, M., OHLIN, L. E., and FARRINGTON, D. P. (1991), *Human Development and Criminal Behaviour: New Ways of Advancing Knowledge*. New York: Springer-Verlag.

TRACY, P. E., and KEMPF-LEONARD, K. (1996), *Continuity and Discontinuity in Criminal Careers*. New York: Plenum.

—— WOLFGANG, M. E., and FIGLIO, R. M. (1985), *Delinquency in Two Birth Cohorts*. Washington, DC: Office of Juvenile Justice and Delinquency Prevention.

—— —— and —— (1990), *Delinquency Careers in Two Birth Cohorts*. New York: Plenum.

TRASLER, G. B. (1962), *The Explanation of Criminality*. London: Routledge and Kegan Paul.

—— (1986), 'Situational Crime Control and Rational Choice: A Critique', in K. Heal and G. Laycock, eds., *Situational Crime Prevention: From Theory into Practice*, 17–24. London: HMSO.

TREMBLAY, R. E., PIHL, R. O., VITARO, F., and DOBKIN, P. L. (1994), 'Predicting Early Onset of Male Antisocial Behaviour from Preschool Behaviour', *Archives of General Psychiatry*, 51: 732–9.

VENABLES, P. H., and RAINE, A. (1987),
'Biological Theory', in B. J. McGurk, D. M.
Thornton, and M. Williams, eds., *Applying
Psychology to Imprisonment*, 3–27. London:
HMSO.

VERHULST, F. C., KOOT, H. M., and BERDEN,
G. F. M. G. (1990), 'Four-year Follow-up of
an Epidemiological Sample', *Journal of the
American Academy of Child and Adolescent
Psychiatry*, 29: 440–8.

VISHER, C. A., and ROTH, J. A. (1986),
'Participation in Criminal Careers', in
A. Blumstein, J. Cohen, J. A. Roth, and
C. A. Visher, eds., 'Criminal Careers and
"Career Criminals"', i, 211–91. Washington,
DC: National Academy Press.

WADSWORTH, M. E. J. (1976), 'Delinquency,
Pulse Rates, and Early Emotional
Deprivation', *British Journal of Criminology*,
16, 245–56.

—— (1979), *Roots of Delinquency: Infancy,
Adolescence and Crime*. London: Martin
Robertson.

WALSH, A., PETEE, T. A., and BEYER, J. A.
(1987), 'Intellectual Imbalance and Delinquency: Comparing High Verbal and High
Performance IQ Delinquents', *Criminal
Justice and Behaviour*, 14: 370–9.

WELLS, L. E., and RANKIN, J. H. (1991),
'Families and Delinquency: A Meta-analysis
of the Impact of Broken Homes', *Social
Problems*, 38: 71–93.

WERNER, E. E., and SMITH, R. S. (1982),
*Vulnerable but Invincible: A Longitudinal
Study of Resilient Children and Youth*. New
York: McGraw-Hill.

—— and —— (1992), *Overcoming the Odds:
High Risk Children from Birth to Adulthood*.
Ithaca, NY: Cornell University Press.

WEST, D. J. (1982), *Delinquency: Its Roots,
Careers and Prospects*. London: Heinemann.

—— and FARRINGTON, D. P. (1973), *Who
Becomes Delinquent?* London: Heinemann.

—— and —— (1977), *The Delinquent Way of
Life*. London: Heinemann.

WHITE, J. L., MOFFITT, T. E., CASPI, A.,
BARTUSCH, D. J., NEEDLES, D. J., and
STOUTHAMER-LOEBER, M. (1994), 'Measuring
Impulsivity and Examining its Relationship
to Delinquency', *Journal of Abnormal
Psychology*, 103: 192–205.

WIDOM, C. S. (1989), 'The Cycle of Violence',
Science, 244: 160–6.

—— and AMES, M. A. (1994), 'Criminal
Consequences of Childhood Sexual
Victimization', *Child Abuse and Neglect*, 18:
303–18.

WIKSTRÖM, P.-O. H. (1987), *Patterns of Crime
in a Birth Cohort*. Stockholm: University of
Stockholm Department of Sociology.

—— (1990), 'Age and Crime in a Stockholm
Cohort', *Journal of Quantitative Criminology*,
6: 61–84.

—— (1991), *Urban Crime, Criminals and
Victims: The Swedish Experience in an Anglo-
American Comparative Perspective*. New
York: Springer-Verlag.

WILSON, H. (1980), 'Parental Supervision: A
Neglected Aspect of Delinquency', *British
Journal of Criminology*, 20: 203–35.

—— (1987), 'Parental Supervision Re-
examined', *British Journal of Criminology*,
27: 275–301.

WILSON, J. Q., and HERRNSTEIN, R. J. (1985),
Crime and Human Nature. New York:
Simon and Schuster.

WOLFGANG, M. E., FIGLIO, R. M., and SELLIN,
T. (1972), *Delinquency in a Birth Cohort*.
Chicago, Ill.: University of Chicago Press.

—— THORNBERRY, T. P., and FIGLIO, R. M.
(1987), *From Boy to Man, from Delinquency
to Crime*. Chicago: University of Chicago
Press.

YARROW, M. R., CAMPBELL, J. D., and BURTON,
R. V. (1970), 'Recollections of Childhood: A
Study of the Retrospective Method', *Mono-
graphs of the Society for Research in Child
Development*, Serial No. 138, vol. 35
(No. 5).

10

Recent Social Theory and the Study of Crime and Punishment

Richard Sparks

INTRODUCTION

My aim in this chapter is to offer an accessible and very introductory account of some themes in recent social theory that are having, or may come to have (or in some cases in my own view *should* have), a bearing on the study of crime, criminal justice and penal systems. In such a short space it is impossible to give anything remotely approaching a full account of *any* of the various topics and positions in question—I can hope to say enough on each only to indicate why I view it as relevant and interesting and in the hope of stimulating readers to investigate further. Even so I have restricted the range of perspectives covered to the point where I can give a brief exposition of each, and develop at least the outline of a connected argument, rather than merely providing some sort of annotated reading list.

Exclusions are therefore unavoidable. Some of these are merely pragmatic: wherever possible I have avoided dealing at any length with issues that are addressed elsewhere in this volume, for instance. (This makes my chapter a strange one since it claims to be talking about crime and social theory without discussing in detail such central topics as feminism and criminology, theories of masculinity, the Marxist theory of the state or the literature inspired by Foucault on the 'governmentalization' of social regulation—see respectively Gelsthorpe, Jefferson, Sumner, and Hudson in this volume.) But it is also in the very nature of theoretical discussion that it selects and defines its objects, and reflects on ways of generating knowledge about them (and on the limits of such knowledge). In this sense *all* theoretical work, however large its scope and ambitions, remains partial and restricted in character—it manages (if at all) to place some sign-posts on the social landscape at the cost of acknowledging its own limits and conditions (cf. Mouzelis, 1995: 44). Bauman (1990: 12) (from whom more later) suggests that to 'theorize' about any topic of importance in the human sciences is to attempt to develop 'responsible speech' about it (in the senses at least of being accountable, methodical, and non-obvious). I hope to show that my selection of issues here is a responsible one—neither complete and definitive nor simply the result of the whimsical predilections of its author. It should also be made clear at the outset that this essay is *not* a review of *criminological* theories—that task arises elsewhere in this volume (see Rock and Hudson, amongst others) as well as in an increasing number of other texts (see for example the informative surveys in Muncie and McLaughlin, 1996*a*, 1996*b*; Muncie *et al.*, 1996; see also Morrison, 1995). Rather it is a glance down the other end of the telescope; it seeks to survey (if only in the briefest *tour d'horizon*) some of the larger domains of social and political thinking with which criminological concerns intersect. In what respects, I am asking, does looking at those intersections affect the way we view criminology's traditions or our assessment of its present state and future potentials?

The chapter goes like this: I shall begin by considering one or two aspects of criminology as 'a discipline' and its sometimes chary and ambivalent view of 'theory'. Then I sketch in some current positive views of the aims of social theory and its relation to substantive, including criminological, research. Next I go on briefly to raise several issues that have been much discussed in recent social theory (though not necessarily much within criminology to date). They are all issues which I take to be of potential interest to those who want to speak responsibly about the perplexities, tribulations, and predicaments of crime, criminal justice and the penal realm in the world that we inhabit. The issues in question are: (i) developments in the theory of action, especially in the work of Giddens and Bourdieu; (ii) some questions about 'risk' as an environment and constituent of social life; (iii) the notion of 'globalization' and its relation to the contemporary forms of social hierarchy, division, and exclusion. Finally I raise some open questions about criminology's understandings of politics and about some tendencies in political thought with which the social analysis of crime and punishment can or might fruitfully engage.

SOME PROBLEMS: CRIMINOLOGY AS A 'DISCIPLINE'

Social theory today is a multifarious array of activities, diverse in both methodological presuppositions and in substantive topics. There are few people alive (if any, and certainly not me) who can remotely claim to be conversant with all its main forms. Even the 'minor' field of criminology is pretty plural and sometimes shows a tendency to splinter into minute sub-specialisms. Unless one happens to have a special interest in this (in a 'sociology of sociology' spirit of curiosity) it can encourage a jaded, even cynical, reaction. It seems to encourage in some a nonchalant faddishness, a snapping-up of whatever is currently being sold hard in the theoretical supermarket. For others the same circumstance engenders an impatience with 'theory' altogether, and leads instead to a bluff, no-nonsense, crap-cutting resolve to get on with the criminology in a thorough, professional, policy-relevant way. In my view, the second reaction is not an uncommon one in criminology, for understandable reasons. Many criminologists (I am happy to say) have a quite strong sense of the practical and political dimensions of their 'dirty' subject, however differently they may interpret these. Many of us, to borrow Stones's (1996) useful terminology, aspire to be 'players' in rather than just 'floaters' over the fields we study. But although this outlook is in many ways more principled than the first, it is not necessarily more 'responsible' in Bauman's sense; and Pierre Bourdieu (a great social investigator by any standard) has some challenging things to say to both tendencies, as we shall shortly see. As Stones suggests, the 'players' may turn out to have much to learn from the 'floaters' and the 'dreamers' (cf. Christie, 1997).

To begin with some assertions which I shall hope to have defended in the course of this chapter: criminologists (by which I mean anyone seriously interested in the systematic study of any aspect of crime, criminal justice, and the penal realm) need social theory *because* they are enmeshed in an empirically complex, policy-relevant, politically contentious field and *not despite* these facts. Criminology cannot (and hence should not attempt to) 'police' its ever-porous boundaries with other disciplines; neither can it renew itself intellectually entirely from within (whatever 'within' might mean here). There is no more point in trying to legislate what may and may not be done under its name than there is in trying to disinvent 'it' because one fears or dislikes its suffix (whatever is apparently implied by its claim to be an -ology). There is however some point in asking how one goes about fulfilling the aspiration to do the best work one can, according to whatever canon of responsibility one is prepared to argue for, under the conditions that one encounters; and that is the spirit in which this essay sets off. That is, although this chapter takes a relaxed view of disciplinary boundaries and goes on some quite wide excursions away from what are generally taken to be the object-domains of much criminology, its aims are to seek out resources (albeit only a fraction of those that are out there) that may be constructively useful from the point of view of empirical enquiry. Even so, a further brief note on disciplinary boundaries may be in order.

To hold a catholic view of criminology and its relations with other fields of study in the human sciences is certainly not an argument for mere dilettantism or theoretical *laissez faire*. Neither is it to suggest that disciplinary distinctions have no *pragmatic* usefulness. Rather, it is to say that in a messy and irretrievably worldly activity like the study of crime and of systems of justice it is acutely necessary to reflect upon such question as: what is a topic of importance? what counts as evidence about it? what can and cannot be regarded as known? how best to write about it? what kinds of commitments and relationships does one contract in the course of such writing and with what ethical implications? what background assumptions are being made about individuals' actions *vis-à-vis* institutions and societies? or about understanding versus explanation as aims of enquiry, and hence about the observer's role and stance? or about the interpretation of texts like statutes, ordinances, newspaper editorials, and so on? (for a yet more extensive list of such questions see Nelken, 1994*a*). To take on such tasks does involve adopting an orientation of some kind towards existing traditions—orientations which may range from slavish replication to iconoclastic opposition. But whilst flourishing membership of 'a discipline' (as if presenting a badge of authority and expertise) may be rhetorically effective at times—dangerously so when it involves the domination of research agendas and individual careers—it is not in itself an argument.

Some writers have considered criminology's performance in these matters and despaired of it. For Alison Young (1996) it is a 'deadlocked discipline'. Carol Smart some years ago concluded that it was a hopeless case, unable to put seriously in question its own relations with the sources of social power and their definitions of its topics (for a more positive interpretation of the same issue see Garland, 1992). Smart famously writes:

The thing that criminology cannot do is deconstruct crime. It cannot locate rape or child sexual abuse in the domain of sexuality or theft in the domain of economic activity or drug use in the domain of health. To do so would be to abandon criminology to sociology . . . [Smart, 1990: 77].

But this is not the argument I want to pursue here. It is not that Smart's characterization of criminology has no basis. She is surely quite right in insisting that much (but all?) that is written in its name is unreflexive and theoretically limiting. But maybe Smart's conclusion only defers the problem. Is there anything here that intrinsically distinguishes the study of crime from the studies of, say, kinship or religion or medicine? If not then simply 'nesting' or subsuming one discipline within another may not help much. If there is (something special and problematic about crime), what is it? How would we go about studying *that*? Maybe we are again conflating disciplinary names with theoretical possibilities. To insist that 'criminology' *cannot* do or know certain things seems over-confident about knowing where its boundaries lie. Perhaps criminologists who display little interest in the larger world of social theory, and social theorists who dimiss criminology as a misconceived project, forever dominated by administrative definitions and pragmatic concerns, make parallel mistakes? Perhaps they are respectively defending a lost cause and attacking a straw figure? There is no way out of this impasse without further recourse to theory.

Jeffrey Alexander (1996) proposes an alternative way of thinking about the formation of disciplines in light of theoretical conditions that apply across the human sciences. He argues that for various well-known reasons energetic disagreement and the 'merging and straddling' of disciplinary perspectives (1996: 35) are endemic in the social studies. These reasons include the intrinsic connection between description and evaluation: 'The ideological implications of social science redound to the very descriptions of the objects of investigation themselves' (1996: 25). There is therefore little hope of disciplinary purity, nor of final consensus on major topics (those social scientists who think that such pristine conditions are accessible are described by Poggi as merely expressing their 'unrequited crush on the natural sciences' (1996: 45)). It follows, in Alexander's view, that 'The conditions which Kuhn identifies for paradigm crisis in the natural sciences are routine in the social' (1996: 24). The social sciences are inherently discursive and not just explanatory. They retain 'rational aspirations' but they also generalize, speculate, interpret, convince, persuade, intervene, and so on (1996: 26). These conditions both foster theoretical activity (because 'endemic disagreement makes the background assumptions of social science more explicit' (*ibid.*: 30)) and help to explain the formation of disciplines, traditions, and schools.

Disciplines, according to Alexander, give people ways of managing the inherent babble and confusion. They provide forums for discussion using shared vocabularies—they make possible the sort of fruitful disagreement in which at least the participants have a 'fair idea of what one another is talking about' (*ibid.*: 31). But because the idea of a discipline implies social organization as well as intellectual work, sometimes disciplines get captured by orthodoxies which suppress or marginalize heterodox perspectives. Then they tend to disguise or to forget the fact that the conflict of interpretations is endemic. Under such conditions of closure and mutual isolation the disciplines become obstacles to theoretical reflection and constraints on debate (see Garland, this volume).

Where does all this leave criminology? One answer is that it may not matter very much. The condition of criminology may be unsatisfactory in various ways but it is not in this respect particularly unusual; and in any case the past, present, or future *of the discipline* as such is in itself only of compelling interest to a rather small, quite eccentric group of people who call themselves criminologists. The domain of crime, criminal justice, and penality, however, is another and rather more important matter; and there are more substantial theoretical tasks at hand than merely beating the boundaries of the discipline once more (see Sumner, 1997: 131). The difficulties of criminology arise, amongst other reasons, because it has an intrinsically controversial and contested subject-matter, defined by the historically and culturally contingent boundaries of the criminal law. The topics it studies are embedded in complex institutional networks and cross-cut by competing interests and unequal distributions of power, influence, reputation and credibility. Consequently what happens 'inside' criminology itself is not immune from the effects of current distributions of power. Some of criminology's topics carry a heavy burden of emotional energy and psychic investment in such forms as anxiety, rage, humiliation, ambition, aspiration, resentment, hatred, contempt, and rejection (to say nothing of excitement, thrill, transgression, and escape); yet some styles of work try to clear these out of the way as if they merely obscured its 'real' subject-matter. The field that criminologists study includes a number of seemingly very purpose-rational organizations—but on closer inspection these seem also to contain important elements of symbolism: they are about managing problems but also, it appears, concerned with the demonstration of power and the projection of claims to legitimate authority. And surrounding the activities of these bodies there is unremitting and pervasive cultural activity—from the most earnest late-night radio discussion to the undisguised titillation of the airport bookshop.

There have been numerous attempts to comprehend the complexities implied here. Successively, students of crime and punishment have brought to bear perspectives influenced by symbolic interactionism (see Rock, this volume), Marxism (see Sumner, this volume); feminist theory (Naffine, 1996; and Gelsthorpe, this volume); the 'genealogical method' of Michel Foucault (1979) and other forms of historical sociology (Melossi and Pavarini, 1979; Garland, 1985). All of these and some others have seriously challenged the apparent fixity and obviousness of the boundaries of the criminal law and the inevitability of the actually existing apparatus of criminal justice, as well as the scientific pretensions of some previous criminologies. In these respects social theory is very far from unknown to criminology (and certainly not to the degree that is sometimes asserted). Indeed, once we query the boundaries drawn around criminology by some of its defenders and attackers alike, we might suggest that the contributions made by students of crime and punishment to the development of social theory has actually been rather greater than either party supposes—as the long and ultimately pointless debate over whether the contributions of Durkheim or Merton (or Foucault or Cohen) can properly be regarded as criminology ironically confirms.

Even so there remain further theoretical pastures to explore (and a few of these are briefly discussed in the remainder of this chapter). But more pressingly there are also new developments and configurations in the domain of crime and justice which would seem to call for novel theoretical work. These include (to give a very incomplete and off-the-cuff list) the effects of transnational and 'globalizing' tendencies in economic and cultural spheres on policing and crime; the delegation of former state functions to private contractors and the general extension of security industries, especially in the form of electronic surveillance; the intensifying effects of income-dispersion, residential segregation, and other forms of social exclusion on crime, policing, fear, and on the texture of urban life generally; the challenge of so redefining the boundaries of the discipline adequately to comprehend the phenomena of genocide, torture, systematic campaigns of rape and other crimes of the state, and many others. In many such cases the analytic challenges include comprehending the relations that exist between their *novelty* (new technologies, administrative systems, vocabularies) and their *archaisms* (the reassertion of antique moral distinctions; the redoubled emphasis on punishment, especially imprisonment) (on this see especially Garland, 1996).

Indeed, the intense politicization of crime and punishment in the United States, Great Britain, and some other states in recent years poses special problems for those who would prefer to continue with criminological business as usual and who engage with social theory only with great reluctance. For many such persons, used to working in what we may broadly call an 'enlightenment' mode, the world has changed in a rather drastic and unwelcome way. With only a hint of caricature, such a person may well have spent the greater part of a distinguished career holding fast to a *credo* which approximately ran: we are scientists; we accept public or charitable monies in order to do relevant research on important problems; we discover things; we make inferences from our findings and pass recommendations to the responsible authorities. It is not my aim to deride this position, so much as to suggest that its self-denying limitations lend it a rather tragic air now. Such a stance seems ever more implausible both in terms of its implied theory of knowledge and its grasp of policy and politics: and the realization that this is so seems apt to engender grief and indignation from some of those who have cleaved most conscientiously down the years to the hope of introducing some systemic rationality into, for instance, sentencing and other aspects of crime policy. Ironically, it may be those who least want to do 'theory' who now stand most in need of it—of a theory, say, of *why* their sage advice will go unheeded.

In other words, criminology navigates in the same deep and treacherous intellectual waters as the other social sciences and encounters all the same difficulties and dilemmas (about holism and individualism; explanation and understanding; certainty and indeterminism; involvement and detachment) as well as the special ones that flow from the peculiarities of its topics (historical contingency; proximity to the circuitry of political power; embeddedness in culture and capacity to arouse passion; restless and incessant change alongside a tendency towards archaism). In the face of these difficulties, I suspect, the greatest error that students of crime and justice can make is to attempt to shun rather than embrace them (cf. Ericson and Carriere, 1994). It is not just that seeking refuge in what C. Wright Mills called 'the lazy safety of specialization' (1959: 21) in fact exposes one to the danger of committing various kinds of conceptual solecism and category mistake; it is also that it suppresses what is basically most challenging and exciting about the enterprise. That is, it treats as a minor sub-specialism a set of concerns that in truth stand close to the heart of social theory's historic concerns with order, conflict, power, and the delineation of social boundaries, not to mention some of the most acute anxieties and indicative developments of our own times (see further Cohen, 1988, 1996).

SOME RESOURCES: THEORY, REFLECTION, AND RESEARCH

Introducing his succinct but deceptively dense review of issues in the philosophy of social science, Martin Hollis (1994) comments on the shocks sometimes delivered to accepted assumptions by external events, such as the European revolutions of 1989:

New regimes have replaced the old ones and, under the surface, old power groups have adapted and survived. So, even if some structural theories have bitten the dust, there is still a need to think about structures. Questions about structure and action have become more urgent and exciting . . . and they have been made harder by seeing what action can do. Abrupt reminders that social order is fragile call for renewed thought about collective freedom and the cement of social life [1994: 2].

These days, Hollis reckons, 'the realm of ideas is as unsettled as the map of nations' (*ibid.*: 5). Hollis is here pointing to the complex interlacing that exists between events in the realms of politics and economy and those in social thought. Nor is this just one-way traffic. Giddens has pioneered and popularized the inelegant but necessary notion of 'the double hermeneutic' (see for example, 1987: 18 amongst his many discussions of this term) to capture some intrinsic features of the social sciences' relations with the subjects of their studies—namely that they make interpretations of already interpreted practices, engaged in by concept-forming beings who may on occasion reappropriate the concepts devised by the social scientists for their own use. Hollis puts the same point more pithily. Social theories are, he says, 'tied to their own tails' (1994: 145); and he gives the example of the uses of concepts derived from Game Theory by Pentagon intellectuals in formulating the strategy of nuclear deterrence (which in turn became the paradigmatic example for some such theorists of a certain kind of 'non-cooperative equilibrium game'). Examples of this sort should seem commonplace to criminologists, many of whom (especially those who work in or close to government agencies or campaigning groups) spend their whole working lives engaged in such brokering. The question that is asked less often is just what this implies for the process of knowledge-production itself.

Some may find this off-putting rather than exciting. Certainly it would seem to pose some problems for a naïvely 'naturalistic' conception of the aims of the social sciences (i.e. one which sees them as directly similar to a traditional understanding of those of the natural sciences). Indeed the point may prove fatal to some of the conceptions of detached expertise and authority thereby implied. But the point is not made solely in a negative, cautionary spirit. For Giddens, the double hermeneutic is what makes the social sciences *possible* as well as making them difficult. It holds open the possibility of extending mutual knowledge and comprehension across boundaries of social difference—surely a pressing concern for criminology (see more broadly Calhoun, 1995; 1996). It raises some pointed issues about *how*, if, and when they do, the social sciences exert any influence on the nature and direction of institutional and cultural change, and about what it now means for those disciplines to aspire to be *critical* (points to which we return in the conclusion). Perhaps Mills (1959) was quite prescient when he argued that the development of sociological imagination was primarily a matter of cultivating a certain 'sensibility', one that under conditions of increasing social complexity and differentiation would come to be 'felt as a need'.

None of this, however, directly clarifies the relationship between social theory and the practice of social research. Let me briefly summarize four views on this. These views are distinct from but not necessarily antagonistic to each other, at least not in all respects. They are the conceptions of the uses of social theory held respectively by Runciman (1983), Mouzelis (1995), Bauman (1990) and Bourdieu (1993, 1996). What these rather different views have in common is that each is concerned to develop social theory in a way that is constructive for systematic social inquiry.

Runciman wants to defend a conception of social theory as science. It is a view regarded in some quarters nowadays as hopelessly naïve and old-fashioned. But Runciman is an exceptionally subtle and articulate advocate of this view. To qualify as science, Runciman argues, it is not necessary for the social sciences to attempt to expunge problems of meaning, ethics, and evaluation—indeed he insists that this cannot be done. It is only necessary that they (i) are pursued under some degree of methodological constraint which is different from, say, the creative arts; (ii) that they acknowledge the *possibility* of 'intersubjectively testable knowledge'; and (iii) that some such knowledge may be cumulative. That is, whatever their special complexities, the social sciences still in some sense aspire to 'discovery' (1983: 4–9). Unless we accept some such baseline, Runciman argues, we cannot rule anything out—for example the assertion that the First World War was initiated by the Belgian Army's invasion of Germany. What is distinctive about the social sciences, for Runciman, is that they inherently include *all four* of the elements of *reportage, explanation, description*, and *evaluation*. Each of these stages in accounts, in Runciman's view, involves a different sense of the term 'understanding', and each successive stage is more 'discretionary' for the observer (in the sense of being unamenable to contradiction or disproof). Reports are thus always constrained by evidence in a way that evaluations never can be (1983: 36–7). Like many significant social theorists, Runciman is concerned to abandon or transcend prevailing dualisms that he sees as inhibiting social inquiry—in his case those which draw an opposition between explanation and understanding and between science and evaluation.

There is a lot more, but this gives a flavour. Runciman's style is to defend a relatively orthodox view of the practice of social investigation but in a sophisticated and open way. One of the attractive features of his views is that, whilst holding to his conception of social theory as science, he emphasizes the difficulty and importance of writing good *descriptive* sociology (a much-derided and misunderstood endeavour). His is a conception of social theory that has its roots mostly in the classical writings of Max Weber (1864–1920). So Runciman's commitment to science would not cause him to dissent from Alexander's observations (1996: 27) that sociological debate is inherently 'underdetermined' by facts and characterized by unfinished theoretical discussion, and that these discussions are often very impassioned because 'they cut across the full range of non-empirical commitments that sustain competing points of view' (1996: 24). One could readily imagine that such a view would be attractive to many criminologists since it appears to reconcile a respect for 'the facts' with a tolerance of methodological and theoretical diversity and hence to offer some degree of reconciliation between criminology's quantitative/experimental and its interpretive/ethnographic traditions. When criminologists speak of seeking an 'integrated' or 'general' theory (as many do, especially in the United States) it is probably a notion of theory similar to this that they have (at least roughly) in mind.

Mouzelis views the role of theory in aiding the practice of research in the following way. Theory is a 'specialized subdiscipline' whose 'chief objective' is 'the critical assessment of existing conceptual tools and the construction of new ones':

> The *raison d'être* of such tools is, negatively, to solve puzzles that hinder open-ended, dialogic communication between social scientists; and, more positively, to facilitate the investigation of the social world via asking theoretically interesting questions, providing conceptual means for comparative work, moving from one level of analysis to another and so on [1995: 9].

Thus, although Mouzelis regards theory at least in part as a specialized activity he nevertheless views it as arising in the course of, and as looping back into, empirical inquiry. He thus indicates his distaste for 'theory' as 'substantive universal propositions . . . and contextless generalizations' (*ibid.*). Mouzelis borrows for this purpose Althusser's (1969) distinction between 'Generalities II' (theory as means/tool) and 'Generalities III' (theory as product). In short Mouzelis is anxious to defend a role for social theory which would prevent that theory descending into what Gregor McLennan pithily calls 'quite high level waffle' (1995: 121)—an accusation aimed with differing degrees of injustice at most ambitious system-builders from Parsons to Giddens and beyond. But McLennan is quite sharply critical of Mouzelis in this respect. In McLennan's view, attempts to circumscribe the roles for theory and to set apart 'theory' from 'speculation' in some degree unfit theory from getting to grips with the great transformations of our times (McLennan, 1995: 130). Notions such as a 'crisis of modernity' (for example, Wagner, 1994; 1996) cannot but be speculative in some degree: and as both McLennan (1995) and Stones (1996) point out these exclusions lead Mouzelis to rather conservative and peremptory dismissals of some of the most energetic developments in contemporary social thought, such as feminist theory and post-structuralism. Moreover, some issues that are discussed in a general way (such as Giddens's account of the 'duality' of agency and structure—see below) are not for that reason unconnected with feasible empirical research (e.g. Sparks *et al.*, 1996). Of course criminologists should know better than most what happens when we forbid speculation and philosophizing: we reify artificial disciplinary boudaries and fall prey to what Mills calls the 'illiberal practicality' of 'the bureaucratic ethos' (1959: 100). Yet Mouzelis is surely justified in wanting to sustain the reciprocal connection between theorizing and researching. It seems we still need some orientation on two issues with which we more or less began: namely, what is entailed in Bauman's notion of 'responsible speech', and what Bourdieu understands by his distinction between reflexive sociology (of which he is passionately in favour) and mere 'theoretical theory' (which he holds in very low regard).

For Bauman, as for Giddens, social theory and sociology are challenged in a special and productive fashion by their relations with common sense. They have no 'lofty equanimity' (and no particle accelerators) no automatic right to make authoritative pronouncements and have them believed (1990: 11). None of their topics and few of their concepts come 'clean and unused' (*ibid.*); indeed their prior meaningfulness is initially the condition of their intelligibility to the sociologist no less than to anyone else (see further O'Neill, 1995). However, Bauman distinguishes four pivotal differences between sociology and common sense. These are:

(i) Voluntary submission to rules of *responsible speech*, including procedural openness and awareness of competing positions. Bauman clearly intends that these be understood as rules that have ethical as well as technical force. They go to the questions of trustworthiness and seriousness (1990: 12).

(ii) The *size of field* exceeds that of our ordinary life-world. There is a concern to discover 'dependencies and interconnections' beyond those which can be 'scanned from the vantage point of an individual biography' (1990: 13).

(iii) There are explicit means of *making sense* of supra-individual interdependencies—'that toughest of realities which explains both our motives and the effects of their activation' (1990: 14).

(iv) The social sciences defamiliarize familiar things: they take things that are obvious and 'natural' and treat them as unexplained, perhaps puzzling, maybe quite arbitrary. Even in its 'armchair' form this is a key starting point. It is what Giddens (1989: 20) terms 'thinking oneself away' and Runciman the *technique du depaysement* (1983: 26).

The effect of such procedures, Bauman argues, is *anti-fixating*. They are in some measure devices for introducing flexibility into social relations and practices that have the appearance of fixity. Hence the social sciences often have, and in Bauman's view certainly should have, a tense and sometimes conflictual relationship with established power-holders.

It should by now be apparent that we have in some sense been moving down a scale of epistemological self-assurance—from Runciman's rather confident outlook on social theory as science (itself much more modest and modulated than some comparable statements of the 1950s or 1960s) to Bauman's rather quizzical and interrogative views. (There are much lower points on this scale, but we can postpone going down there for the time being.) Pierre Bourdieu's understanding of social theory combines aspects of each of these.

In a well-known interview Bourdieu (1996: 219) states trenchantly:

I never 'theorize', if by that you mean engage in the sort of conceptual gobbledygook that is good for textbooks and which by an extraordinary misconstrual of the logic of science, passes for theory in much of Anglo-American social science. I never set out to 'do theory' or 'construct a theory' . . . There is no doubt a theory in my work, or better, a set of thinking tools visible through the results they yield, but it is not built as such.

The word 'built' in this passage gives the game away. Bourdieu is contrasting his conception of theoretical work as an *activity* intimately involved in the practice of research with any idea of theory as an 'edifice'. Even so, it is striking to hear one of the world's leading 'social theorists' talk like this, and the point bears some expansion. Bourdieu says that what connects his various pieces of work is not 'a theory' but 'the logic of research, which is in my eyes inseparably empirical and theoretical'. He distinguishes this from 'theoretical theory' (an activity engaged in by 'epistemocrats'). Instead, he insists, theory is for him 'a program of perception and action . . . which is disclosed only in the empirical work which actualizes it. It is a temporary construct which takes shape for and by empirical work.' (1996: 220). In his view:

The summum of the art, in social science, is, in my eyes, to be capable of engaging in very high theoretical stakes by means of very precise and often very mundane empirical objects . . . or, what amounts to the same thing, to approach a major socially significant object in an unexpected manner [1996: 221].

However, there is not automatically any comfort here for an 'applied' and 'empirical' discipline like criminology. Bourdieu's dislike for 'theoretical theory' is plain enough ('society conversation and a subsitute for research'). But on the other hand the 'self-evident' significance of the topics of criminology is no guarantee of profundity: in Bourdieu's view the 'social or political significance of an object' does not in itself 'grant significance to the discourse that deals with it' (1996: 221). Bourdieu sets out some serious dangers for an under-theorized research programme (he does not mention criminology, but let us at least ask ourselves if the cap fits), principally that of practising some sort of '*half-science* which unknowingly accepts categories of perception directly borrowed from the social world' (1996: 224). These 'routine categories' are, in Bourdieu's view, 'naturalized preconstructions'. Not to reflect upon them is to 'leave one's own thought in an unthought state' (*impense*) and hence 'to condemn oneself to be nothing more than the instrument of what one claims to think' (1996: 226).

These views of Bourdieu's flow from his more general view that the power of established social categories depends in large degree on 'misrecognition' (*méconnaissance*) (an effect performed in his view by 'symbolic violence', a central term in his work but not one we have space to explore here, see Bourdieu, 1990; Bourdieu and Wacquant, 1992)—roughly speaking it means the capacity of the powerful to conceal the arbitrary and conditional nature of their definitions of social reality. Here we encounter a major reason why Bourdieu and others think it is so important that the social sciences be undertaken in a *reflexive* fashion, namely that the very 'categories of thought and instruments of analysis' that researchers deploy have otherwise unrecognized histories, implications, and effects. In criminology, as elsewhere, this speaks to the importance of social histories of the discipline and its understandings of its topics and problems (Garland, 1985) as well as to the 'anthropological moment' (Giddens, 1984: 284) facilitated by cross-cultural and comparative reflection (see especially Nelken, 1994*a*, 1994*b*; Melossi, 1994). Bourdieu's view that the path towards doing reflexive social research often begins with an experience of estrangement from one's academic environment, and even an intuitive sense of 'revolt' against dominant categories, also reminds us of some of the reasons why much of the most creative theoretical work in the social sciences today flows from feminism (e.g. Smith, 1988) (in criminology and legal studies now, for example, the task of expressly interrogating the category 'justice' is shouldered disproportionately by women: Hudson, 1996; Lacey, 1996; Daly, 1997).

We should be aware therefore that the reduced expectations of epistemological certainty or finality that many forms of social theory now entertain do not necessarily signal a diminished sense of the importance of social enquiry in sustaining careful, curious, and responsible communication (Stones, 1996). Indeed, of the views outlined above it is the more epistemologically circumspect positions of Bauman and Bourdieu which come closest to offering guidelines for grounded and contextual empirical work. If these views are no longer preferred from 'on high' (Layder, 1994) they remain culturally central, a point to which we return in conclusion. Bourdieu argues that reflexive sociology 'denaturalizes and thereby defatalizes the world' (1996: 222). That is, it deprives established categories and institutions of some part of their air of inevitability, whilst comprehending the weight of the powers and constraints that sustain them in being, and it is to this extent liberating. (As Pascal once said: 'The world overwhelms me, yet I understand it'.) There are few more 'natural' and 'fatal' categories than those of 'individual' and 'society', and it is to current developments in the understanding of each that we now turn.

SOME BIG ISSUES: ACTION, RISK, GLOBALIZATION

Here we note very briefly three major themes in social theory today: 'action', 'risk' and 'globalization'. They each have potentially far-reaching implications for the study of crime, punishment and social control.

Developments in the Theory of Action

Much current theoretical work records a sense of dissatisfaction with some traditional oppositions (or 'dualisms') in social thought. Primary here is the antique distinction between individual and society (along with its received social-theoretic counterpart the division between 'micro' and 'macro' levels of analysis: see Layder, 1994). Much social theory has accepted these distinctions and tried to cope with them in various ways. Some have radically prioritized *either* the 'micro' (e.g. Collins, 1981) *or* the 'macro' (Blau, 1977) dimension of analysis (and see generally Alexander *et al.*, 1987). Others have seen the issue as simply reflecting a necessary division of labour (Turner, 1988). Sometimes too this separation cross-cuts another one, namely that between 'subjectivist' (or 'interpretive') and 'objectivist' methods of inquiry. Yet others, however, such as Giddens (1984) and Bourdieu (1990), view the dualism itself as being fundamentally misconceived.

Giddens begins, as others have before him, from the question of how institutions, practices and cultures can continue to exist—how they 'stretch' across space and 'bite into' time. For Giddens this suggests not a 'dualism' but a 'duality'- the 'duality of structure'. In his view it is central that 'the structural properties of social systems are both medium and outcome of the practices they recursively organize' (1984: 25). In terms of the 'duality of structure' it is true *both* that 'structures are constituted through action' *and* that 'action is constituted structurally' (Giddens, 1976: 161). Hence the proper domain of study of the social sciences is the investigation of 'social practices ordered across space and time' (Giddens, 1984: 2).

In this way Giddens is able to sustain two propositions, both plausible in terms of our ordinary experience, but which have traditionally been seen as contradictory in much social thought. These are that social activity is 'always and everywhere the outcome of knowledgeable human agency', yet that such action is never unconstrained. Actions are preceded by 'unacknowledged conditions' and succeeded by an inherent inablility to anticipate or control all the possible consequences of acting (not least because other actors also act). Thus, whilst Giddens is at pains to emphasize that we are under virtually all circumstances agents (so that it is not proper to think of us *just* as the occupants of given roles, for example), nevertheless any situated actor confronts the structural properties of social systems as 'objective' or 'given': they cannot just be changed by an act of will (1984: 174–9; see also 1989: 258). Giddens summarizes his views on this point as follows:

The theory of structuration is not a series of generalizations about how far 'free action' is possible in respect of 'social constraint'. Rather it is an attempt to provide the conceptual means of analyzing the often delicate and subtle interlacings of reflexively organized action and institutional constraint [Giddens, 1991: 204].

A key criminological issue that arises here concerns the character of action within organizations and institutions (see especially Giddens, 1987: 164). Criminal justice agencies, especially the police and prisons, are both like and unlike other modern organizations. They share many of the same practices for maximizing control of system-reproduction—but they also retain 'direct control of the means of force'. Giddens introduces here the notion of the 'dialectic of control' in social systems: the actual state of affairs that prevails in any given social setting is the outcome of the influence upon one another of more and less powerful actors. Such 'dialectics' are of the essence of the topics that criminologists study, whether or not they theorize them in just these terms. Indeed, one line of objection to views such as those of Giddens is that they tend to over-stress the orderly and routine *reproduction* of practices (see e.g. Urry, 1991: 168), rather than those moments of resistance, innovation, or deviance at which the 'flow' of power becomes more clearly visible and evidently problematic (on the implications of this see further Sparks *et al.*, 1996: chapter 2).

Bourdieu's conception of practice has several features in common with Giddens's 'duality of structure'. Like Giddens, Bourdieu sees himself as being 'in double opposition' to an objectifying structural sociology and to a pre-social notion of the free individual: the former is incapable of comprehending agency, the latter of grasping the 'neccessity immanent in the social world' (1996: 215). Bourdieu employs the term *habitus* to designate his sense of the relation between the agent and a given 'field'. Bourdieu is concerned to show how we 'incorporate' the social—we become 'at home' within our own fields and not others—but we remain endlessly inventive. We are, so to speak, *fully social*, but not, as Wrong famously put it, 'over-socialized'.

Thus neither Giddens nor Bourdieu accept the old 'individual/society' polarity which pits the small yet already fully formed individual actor (a kind of 'mighty atom') against the big abstract-yet-overwhelming 'society'. For Giddens structures are 'reproduced practices'. Bourdieu abjures talk of 'society' altogether in favour of the language of *habitus* and *field*. These positions have an obvious bearing, it seems to me, in making explicit the conceptions of the agent that are generally implied within the various forms of social, including criminological, research.

There is, for example, an enormous theoretical task ahead in assessing the theoretical scope and plausibility of 'rational choice theory' (Clarke, 1995) and its cousin 'routine activities theory' (Felson, 1994; see also Pease, this volume). It does not at present seem very widely recognized by criminologists that such outlooks have their counterparts throughout the social sciences (but see Bueno de Mesquita and Cohen, 1995), some of them very ambitious in scope. For example, Elster (1989) is emphatic in arguing that the individual is the 'elementary unit' of social analysis and that rational choice assumptions can generate accounts of complex social phenomena—in other words to resolve the old macro–micro problem by plumping decisively for micro foundations. As such, rational choice theory is currently highly controversial in respect of such issues as its understanding of the agent (not least because it tends to treat the agent's rationally pursued preferences as given, rather than as part of what needs to be explained), its plausibility in real life as opposed to ideal-typical cases, its handling of 'emergent' phenomena like ethical norms and insti-tutional obligations, its very definition of rationality (see, for example, Hindess, 1988; Mouzelis, 1995: 28–40; Hollis, 1994: 133–41, 148–62). It could then be that rational choice and game-theoretic views were good at predicting outcomes under certain clearly defined conditions and that this made them pragmatically useful to some powerful people. But they might still be 'good' management consultancy yet poor candidates as social theory, maybe even, as

Bourdieu confrontationally puts it, 'well-founded illusions' (1996: 216)—that is, they have an unexamined (and in that sense uncritical) relationship with the political and intellectual contexts in which they happen to come to the fore. There would seem to remain some distance between the acting subject embedded in social practice (as Giddens or Bourdieu conceive of her or him) and the rationally deciding subject posited by game theory—or as Hollis puts it between *homo sociologicus* and *homo economicus*, even if we leave on one side for the moment the unthought sexism of these terms. In other words, we may need to know more about the agent's *wants and desires* (cf. Stones, 1996: 40) than rational choice theories generally promise to tell us; and we may also need to know more about the agent's *context* (their 'field' in Bourdieu's terms) than the particular 'game' that they happen to be playing here and now (cf. Stones, 1996: 98). One arena in which such distinctions are visible is in the conceptualization of *risk*.

Risk and Social Theory

There is an evident, indeed intrinsic, connection between the notions of rational choice and of risk. In rational-choice and game-theoretic perspectives it is always possible to state what a rational actor would do under defined conditions, so long as one also knows what her or his preferences are. He or she will maximize 'expected utilities' whilst minimizing risks. The rational actor always pursues the outcome that promises the greater expected utility. On the back of such simple assumptions many very complex game scenarios can be constructed.

Of course such well-defined conditions rarely obtain in their pure form. Even entirely rational actors are routinely involved in 'n-person' games, and they almost never have perfect information about risk. They face uncertainty as well as choice. And even a sociological neophyte may feel that there is something strange and illicit about bracketing questions of how actors *acquire* their preferences. As Mouzelis comments, when applied at the 'macro' level such perspectives may produce little more than 'the platitude that, as a rule, people choose the best means to realize their goals' (1995: 39). And, moreover, even such apparently simple and primordial entities as 'interests', let alone such tricky ideas as norms and rules, can be seen as socially constructed. Hollis perhaps speaks for many when he observes that no-one wants a completely rational agent for a neighbour (1994: 139).

Theorists of rational choice have many retorts to such jibes. One such is that the very purpose of an 'ideal-type' is to clarify why in reality both individual and collective behaviour so often departs from it—just how do real persons differ from fully rational ciphers? why is it so difficult to realize our interests even when we do single-mindedly pursue them? why do ostensibly rational decisions so often have perverse or self-defeating outcomes? and so on. Such concerns lead into two ways in which the notion of risk can be very fertile for social theory. These are, first, the social nature of *risk-perception* and, secondly, *risk-management* as an aspect of contemporary organizational and political life. We can discuss each of these only in the sketchiest way.

It is very often observed that ordinary conduct departs routinely from what, viewed from within the narrow confines of the theory of rational choice, would appear to be ideally rational. Some people accept or even actively pursue very risky lines of action: they smoke tobacco and abuse other dangerous drugs; drive cars too fast; spend all their money. But also they refuse to fly in perfectly safe aircraft; view harmless dogs with suspicion; spurn prime cuts of beef; keep all their money in low-interest accounts; and, notoriously, sometimes worry themselves sick over rare and exotic crimes. Are we simply in the presence here of individual differences, so that some people are always risk-takers while others are just 'life's worriers'? Even if so, many social theorists think that there is much more than this at stake.

Mary Douglas suggests that a risk is not a 'thing' but a way of thinking—not just the probability of an event 'but also the probable magnitude of its outcome, and everything depends on the value that is set on the outcome' (1992: 31). Douglas's 'cultural theory of risk' thus brings into special focus the way in which the identification of particular sources of threat and danger (and by extension whom we blame for them) refracts a given community's dispositions towards order and authority: 'There is no way of proceeding with analysing risk perception without typifying kinds of communities acccording to the support their members give to authority, commitment, boundaries and structure' (Douglas, 1992: 47). The presentiment of risk, therefore, is inherently political: it galvanizes action and prompts discourse. But studying the connections between risk, fear and blame can never be solely an activity of quantitatively cataloguing dangers and assorting responses to risk into boxes marked 'rational' and 'irrational' (Sparks, 1991).

In principle this suggests a daunting and exciting research agenda for criminologists, one that is being pursued now quite vigorously especially in relation to the vexed issue of the 'fear of crime' (Sparks, 1992; Girling *et al.*, 1997; Walklate, 1997; Jefferson and Hollway, 1997). Such an agenda would draw attention to the weight that attaches to the dangers of crime, and to some crimes rather than others, in the social and political conversations that go on in particular times and places—the social construction of their differential visibility (see further Pavarini, 1997). It also gives a clue about why amidst the proliferation of technical means of risk assessment in the administrative culture of modern societies (the generic 'probabilization' of which Hacking speaks (1991)) the social discourse of crime and punishment still 'falls into antique mode' (Douglas, 1992: 26) and refuses to shed 'its ancient moral freight' (*ibid.*: 35).

Douglas here nails a point about some of the complexities noted at the start of this chapter. Crime and punishment have consequences both for the very texture of personal life and for some embedded features of social organization. And they are janus-faced phenomena—they have both novel and archaic dimensions (cf. Garland, 1990). A number of social theorists have concluded that the identification and management of risks have become structuring principles of contemporary organizational and political life. Once they have been named and identified, risks demand responses from the responsible bodies even though it may exceed their powers substantially to control, let alone to abolish them. Thus for Beck (1992) as for Giddens (1990, 1991) thinking about danger *in terms of risk* is a pervasive feature of contemporary life. For Giddens we live in a world of 'manufactured uncertainty', and it is characteristic of such a 'risk-climate' that its institutions become *reflexive*—endlessly monitoring, adjusting and calculating their behaviour in the face of insatiable demands for information and pressures for accountability. For Beck: 'Risk may be defined as a systematic way of dealing with hazards and insecurities induced and introduced by modernization itself. Risks, as opposed to older dangers, are consequences which relate to the threatening force of modernization and to its globalization of doubt' (Beck, 1992: 21).

In Beck's view the 'risk society' is characterized by ambivalence: between faith in progress and nostalgia (or what Giddens elsewhere terms 'reactive traditionalism'); between demands for technical information and suspicion of experts and hence between authority and withdrawal of legitimacy; between local particularism and the utopic image of a world society; between indifference and hysteria. Nor does he doubt that such a society has authoritarian potentialities, arising in part from the accumulation of expert knowledge in the hands of elites (1992: 80) and partly on the formation of solidarities based in fear and given to scapegoating (1992: 75). Neither Giddens nor Beck has anything of note to say on crime and punishment as such—their focus lies primarily on the 'high-conqequence risks' of nuclear proliferation, environmental degradation, and so on. But analysts of crime and punishment have identified parallel developments in those arenas. Some of these focus on the novel reformulation of crime control in terms of risk management (see e.g. Feeley and Simon, 1992; Simon and Feeley, 1995; Simon, 1993; O'Malley, 1992; Ericson and Haggerty, 1997). Others stress the archaic persistence of displacement and scapegoating (Young, 1996). Still others emphasize the alignments that may occur between these in the pursuit of particular political projects (O'Malley, 1996; Garland, 1996; Sumner, 1997).

Globalization and the Problem of 'Place'

For writers like Beck and Giddens the key 'axes' of modernity are global in their effects. For Beck we are all 'living on the volcano'. For Giddens the 'risk-climate' of modernity is encompassing: 'no-one escapes'. Giddens elaborates:

Processes of change engendered by modernity are intrinsically connected to globalising influences, and the sheer sense of being caught up in massive waves of global transformation is perturbing. More important is the fact that such change is also intensive: increasingly it reaches through to the very grounds of individual activity and the constitution of the self . . . no one can easily defend a secure 'local life' set off from larger social systems and organizations [*ibid.*: 184].

For much recent social theory this is fundamental. It changes forever our sense of what it means to live 'here' as against there, of who 'we' are and of where we are 'at home' (Robertson, 1995). For some it means that the very language of discussion has to change. For some purposes at least it may no longer make sense to speak of 'a society' or 'a culture' in singular terms, as if national boundaries defined the influences on our lives (Lash and Urry, 1994). Rather we live in a world that is constantly being re-made by the global flows of capital and culture, with very uneven effects which tend to escape willed political control. Communications media are central to such arguments. They 'compress' time and distance (Thompson, 1996: 36), a capacity held by some to erode if not abolish the specificity of place (Meyrowitz, 1985).

Of course such arguments can be overdrawn. Certainly the economies and political systems of different nation-states continue to function differently in various respects. Neither have the distinctive features of linguistic, cultural, and legal traditions that generate, for example, divergent approaches to crime and penality abruptly been disinvented (Melossi, 1994). Can the 'globalization' perspective accommodate such criticisms? And what, in any case, does all this imply for the study of crime and punishment? I think the answers to these questions are 'yes, in part' and 'a great deal'.

First, it is not appropriate to equate globalization with homogenization, at least not in all respects. Rather, some commentators speak of 'divergent modernization', a process which produces not 'sameness' but rather many new 'particularizations' and 'hybridities' (Robertson, 1995). In this sense the contemporary world is more kaleidoscopic than it is uniform. It presents to us many shocks that arise from encountering difference (even in one 'place'); just as it may also give rise to 'despatialized commonalities' (similarities *not* based in 'place') (Thompson, 1996). Secondly, globalization certainly does not deliver unity at the levels of interest or outcome. In a globalizing economy it makes a fatal difference to one's life-chances *who* one is (in terms of one's skills and 'social capital') and *where one lives* (a 'sunrise zone' or 'rust-belt city', a 'gentrifying suburb', or an 'impacted ghetto'). In these respects the notoriously widening income-dispersions in many major economies, and the creation of structurally redundant populations within them, are key properties of capitalist globalization. There is little here of peace, love, and understanding; and criminologists can speak to these conditions in important ways if they choose to do so. Fourthly, that differing cultural and political traditions persist does not in itself discount the view that the nation-state has in some degree been 'hollowed-out' by the global economy and other supra-national involvements. If *that* is the picture, what briefly might some of its crimino-penal consequences be?

Criminologists interested in the geography and 'ecology' of urban crime have done much—though they have not always theorized their work in these terms—to render empirical accounts of the social impacts of macro-economic transformations. The differential 'urban fortunes' (Logan and Molotch, 1987) of late modernity are profoundly interlaced with the distribution of victimization-risks as they are with the entrenchment of 'suspect populations'. It is not just a matter of developing a microscopically detailed 'criminology of place' (Sherman *et al.*, 1989; Eck and Weisburd, 1996). It is also that these concerns speak directly to the spatial dynamics of inequality in the contemporary city, especially in the forms of 'white flight', 'ghettoization', and 'disrepute' and so on (see generally Skogan, 1990; Taub *et al.*, 1984; Hagan and Petersen, 1995; Hope, 1995). At 'the bad edge of postmodernity' in Los Angeles, Davis (1990, 1992) envisions a rigidly segregated metropolis, the aggressively policed bubbles of security of its affluent consumers sandwiched uneasily between the 'containment zone' at its core and its 'toxic rim'.

Furthermore, criminologists increasingly document the *transnational* character of crime and social control. This is partly a question of the cross-border flows of criminalized commodities (drugs, weapons, pornography, and so on) (Ruggiero, 1996). In part it also concerns the internationalization of control networks and the problems that arise thereby for received conceptions of accountability and democratic oversight (Sheptycki, 1995; Anderson *et al.*, 1995).

Finally, Garland (1996) has argued that the renewed politicization of penality in at least some nation-states is in some part a reaction against a perceived loss of state sovereignty. That is, in the face of routinely high volumes of crime (and we may add other structural constraints on the state's capacity to rule—to formulate its will and have it obeyed) the state turns to those levers of power over which it retains exclusive control (see also Pavarini, 1997). Amongst these the power to deliver punishment to offenders speaks with special eloquence and archaic resonance—it is Leviathan's ancient promise to its fearful and uneasy subjects. This seems an appropriate point at which to begin to conclude, since it reminds us that historically the problems of order and authority and the monopolization of legitimate violence have always provided the matrix in which social theory and crime intersect, and that this subject is, at its foundations, ineluctably political.

CONCLUSION: SOCIAL THEORY, CRIMINOLOGY, AND POLITICS

It is tempting at this point to admit defeat and stop. Even the very limited foray that I have undertaken here onto the terrain of contemporary social theory shows, if nothing else, that it is very slippery ground. It can hardly be otherwise: for social theory today confronts a restless, mobile, and unsettling world—one which, moreover never ceases to shock in its capacity for atrocious violence (unless, that is, we lose our capacity to be shocked). The accounts which Giddens, Beck, and others (including many whom I have not been able to mention) offer suggest a world in the throes of major transformations, with

no certain destination. Even the more restricted domain of crime and punishment (never in any case a comfortable place) seems to generate only troubling
and unfinished stories and permanent dilemmas. It seems wise to avoid the
neat gift-wrapping sometimes implied by the word 'conclusion'. Nevertheless,
I remain convinced that a criminology which does engage with the problems
of social theory is more reflexively aware of the possibilities and constraints
for knowledge and for practical intervention than one which does not, and that
it is to this extent less the victim of its circumstances (or, what is worse, the
unreflexive and uncomplaining servant of power). What kind of orientation
does this suggest? Here are just a few ideas.

One route that appeals to many commentators today is to suggest that the
culture and institutions that we encounter today have become post-modern.
There is a serious case for this terminology, though I cannot develop it properly
here (see Lyon, 1994; Docherty, 1993, amongst many). At a bare minimum the
term seems to convey the sense of an ending (of familiar and settled categories
losing their hold) and consequently of stepping into an uncertain and dis-
orienting future. In this respect it has an undeniable appeal. But the debate
itself is very messy and potentially disorients us further. Some people, such as
Giddens (1990) deny in a dismissive way that the notion of postmodernity is
useful at all, and waft it aside in one paragraph. For Giddens all the characteristics it claims to describe are aspects of modernity itself, albeit a 'late
modernity'. Others, like Foucault (quoted by Garland, 1995: 181), cannily
observe that it would be easier to say whether we were 'postmodern' if
only they felt they knew what modernity was. As Keane (1996: 44) affirms
modernity is itself 'a mosaic of contradictory tendencies'. Stephen Pfohl
reminds us that the term 'postmodern' itself is hardly new. C. Wright Mills
used it in 1959 in much the same spirit of perplexity as many do now (Pfohl,
1993: 26). Earlier uses have been noted. Even Zygmunt Bauman, for many
(including me) one of the wisest and most humane observers of the postmodern
scene, seems at one point to have given up the struggle over nomenclature.
'Perhaps' he says wryly, 'we live in a postmodern age, perhaps not' (Bauman,
1997: 79).

I am not sure that we need to decide on this question, and certainly no
attempt will be made to settle it here. But we do need ways of engaging with
the more perplexing aspects of the present. Even if we must leave on one side
some of the disputes over their wider referents (but see generally Kumar, 1997)
perhaps we might at least hazard some sketches of what modern and postmodern tendencies might look like in respect of crime, criminal justice, and
penality. Several questions present themselves. Are the changes currently
affecting the operation of the agencies of criminal justice of such a scale as to
constitute a qualitative transformation? For example, have those agencies been
revealed to be structurally incapable of addressing the problems that provide
their ostensible *raison d'être*? Or have the norms and rationales in terms of
which they conventionally claim authority themselves embarked upon a
terminal crisis of dissolution? Has the complexity of their operations or the

occult nature of their surveillance technologies reached such a point that any principle of democratic accountability has lost its purchase? What fate would await such a nostrum as 'policing by consent' in a setting where the very idea of normative consensus itself strains plausibility? What alternative modes of government, or citizens' strategies for protection, might then be in process of emergence? Would these be distinctively novel? Or might some of them turn out strangely to resemble *pre*-modern phenomena?

We need not expect simple or unequivocal, still less very optimistic, answers to these and other questions. Indeed, the very neatness of temporal succession implied in some uses of the terms 'modern' and 'post-modern' may itself be less than helpful (Garland, 1995), or at least subsidiary to the central task of documenting the transformations before us and the contexts of their emergence (Bauman, 1989). Recent theoretical work offers at least the following signposts.

First, some changes in the domain of criminal justice may be subtle rather than flagrant and they may tend to escape public visibility. For example, Feeley and Simon have suggested that criminal justice professionals in the United States have begun to change their ways of making sentencing and parole decisions, away from deliberations centred on desert and re-integration and towards prospective calculations of risk (Feeley and Simon, 1992). The effects of such changes may be profound (for example in stimulating the growth of prison populations) yet receive little public-political recognition or discussion.

Secondly, some of the most profound changes in the regulation of crime may well take place quite outside the formal system of criminal justice. They will concern instead the private consumption of security hardware and services, the development of new surveillance technologies (bar-coding, retinal scanning, cashless transactions, and so on). Such practices transfer the bulk of everyday crime-management away from the state and into the commercial market-place.

Thirdly, nevertheless the public consciousness of many contemporary societies remains marked by acute anxieties and often by nostalgic yearnings for imaginatively remembered landscapes of order and security; and crime and punishment remain vivid cultural preoccupations. Indeed, the very 'cultural sterility' (Simon and Feeley, 1995) of the technicist business of risk-management and its distance from inherited intuitions and 'sensibilities' (Garland, 1990) may itself exacerbate the intensity of demands for punishment and promote the state's recourse to 'symbolic display' (Garland, 1996), mediated through the 'virtual public square' of the television screen (Pavarini, 1997: 81) and the high degree of political theatre that inheres in some of our most characteristic current penal developments (see for example Simon, 1995, on the 'boot camp').

Even this fragmentary account seems sufficient to confirm that crime and crime control these days have a puzzling and ambiguous character, in that novelty and innovation tend to jostle side by side with archaic themes and tendencies and where the arcane language of 'managerialism' co-habits with 'populist punitiveness' (Bottoms, 1995). To me this suggests that the kinds of knowledge that criminologists need is by definition *cultural* and *political* as well as patiently empirical. We need to be able to grasp not just the technicalities of crime and crime control but also how they are taken up in everyday stories and images, as well as in the rhetorics of political campaigns. As John Keane writes:

It could even be said that those who live in the so-called democratic zone of peace are as much if not *more* troubled by violence than the majority of the world's population. The democratic zone of peace feels more violent because within its boundaries images and stories of violence move ever closer to citizens who otherwise live in peace, due to the risk calculations of insurance companies; the eagerness for publicity of policing authorities; campaigns to publicize violence and to mobilize the criminal process . . . ; and the development of a global system of communications . . . driven by the editorial maxim, 'if it bleeds, it leads' [Keane, 1996: 5].

Keane sees here a chronic sense of unease in the relationship between state and civil society, a tolerance of inequality that results in 'archipelagoes of incivility' (1996: 115), and a preference for purely privatized solutions that engender a 'scattering of violence' (1996: 147). One result is the degeneration of public discourse into either 'prepolitical pessimistic ontologies' (the language of born criminals and their violent natures) or the mere whimsy of 'utopian wishes' (1996: 142). Keane's language here may be somewhat florid for some tastes. But he correctly identifies, I think, the need to think about the problem of crime as part and parcel of our current current cultural and political condition. The reconstructions of criminological theory herein implied may or may not be post-modern but they are intrinsically *normative* as well as analytic and they cannot take place within narrow disciplinary parameters (Christie, 1997; Sumner, 1997; Bauman, 1997).

Finally, let us return to Giddens and his 'double hermeneutic'. For Giddens this means that the ideas used by social sceintists 'circulate in and out of the social world they are coined to analyse' (1987: 19). Sometimes we use the term 'participant-observation' to denote a special kind of fieldwork role. But on Giddens's account we are all in some sense participants as well as observers, and it is 'upon our capabilities for learning, in the world that is the legacy of modernity' that 'we predicate our futures'. In other words, it is not the purpose of reflexive social theory to leave us feeling baffled and disempowered. Rather it is to clarify the challenges to our understanding, and hence our points of possible intervention.

Selected Further Reading

Given that this chapter has touched upon many themes, albeit frustratingly briefly, it is difficult to cite a small number of readings that can properly be regarded as central. However, for a lucid review of current debates about the forms of social enquiry Martin Hollis's *The Philosophy of Social Science* (Hollis, 1994) is as good a starting-point as any. Hollis gives a useful account of the currently influential claims of rational choice theories. B. Hindess's

Choice, Rationality and Social Theory (Hindess, 1988) is a more extended critical account of the same theme. I have personally found the essays collected in Stephen Turner's *Social Theory and Sociology: the Classics and Beyond* (Turner, 1996) very helpful (this volume includes contributions by Alexander, Bourdieu, Calhoun, Wagner, and Wallerstein amongst others). In general the major social theorists provide the best introductions to their own work. In Giddens's case *The Constitution of Society* (Giddens, 1984) remains the central text, although *The Consequences of Modernity* (Giddens, 1990) offers a succinct statement of subsequent directions in his thinking. Bourdieu meanwhile has helpfully distilled his key ideas in *An Invitation to Reflexive Sociology* (Bourdieu and Wacquant, 1992) and *Sociology in Question* (Bourdieu, 1993).

The modernity/postmodernity duality is notoriously troubling and trouble-some, though the side-taking it seems to imply no longer seems as clear-cut (or as compulsory) as was the case until recently. Some help is at hand in the form of Krishan Kumar's *From Post-Industrial to Post-Modern Society* (Kumar, 1997) and especially Zygmunt Bauman's wise and compelling reflections in *Postmodernity and its Discontents* (Bauman, 1997).

Contrary to some opinions there is quite a lot of theoretically informed and provocative work going on in criminology and the sociology of deviance and social control. This is especially true of feminist theory (Naffine, 1996; Daly, 1997). Elsewhere, Wayne Morrison's *Theoretical Criminology* (Morrison, 1995) makes a bold and sustained attempt to confront some big issues. If pressed to identify two central theoretical problems for contemporary crim-inological enquiry I would nominate: (i) the debates surrounding the develop-ment of risk-management practices and the emergence of actuarial justice (Feeley and Simon, 1992; Simon and Feeley, 1995; O'Malley, 1996; Ericson and Haggerty, 1997) and (ii) the reappraisal of the character of social control and its relation to contemporary political orders in the recent work of David Garland (1996) and Colin Sumner (1997). In general the best advice to anyone wishing to stay abreast of current thinking is to keep their eye on the journals, especially *Social and Legal Studies*; *Crime, Law and Social Change*; *Theoretical Criminology*; and *The British Journal of Criminology*.

REFERENCES

ALEXANDER, J. (1996), 'The Centrality of the Classics', in S. P. Turner, ed., *Social Theory and Sociology: the Classics and Beyond.* Oxford: Blackwell.

—— GIESEN, B., MUNCH, R., and SMELSER, N., eds, *The Macro-Micro Link.* Berkeley, Cal.: University of California Press.

ALTHUSSER, L. (1969), *For Marx*, London: Allen Lane.

ANDERSON, M., DEN BOER, M., CULLEN, P.,

GILMORE, W., RAAB, C., and WALKER, N. (1995), *Policing the European Union.* Oxford University Press.

BAUMAN, Z. (1989), 'Hermeneutics and Modern Social Theory' in D. Held and J. Thompson, eds., *Social Theory of Modern Societies: Anthony Giddens and his Critics.* Cambridge: Cambridge University Press.

—— (1990), *Thinking Sociologically.* Oxford: Blackwell.

—— (1997), *Postmodernity and its Discontents*. Cambridge: Polity.

BECK, U. (1992), *Risk Society*. London: Sage.

BLAU, P. (1977), 'A Macrosociological Theory of Social Structure', *American Journal of Sociology*, 83: 26–54.

BOTTOMS, A. (1995), 'The Philosophy and Politics of Punishment and Sentencing', in C. Clarkson and R. Morgan, eds., *The Politics of Sentencing Reform*. Oxford University Press.

BOURDIEU, P. (1990), *The Logic of Practice*. Cambridge: Polity Press.

—— (1993), *Sociology in Question*. London: Sage.

—— (1996), 'Toward a Reflexive Sociology: a Workshop with Pierre Bourdieu' (with Loic Wacquant), in S. P. Turner, ed., *Social Theory and Sociology: the Classics and Beyond*. Oxford: Blackwell.

—— and WACQUANT, L. (1992), *An Invitation to Reflexive Sociology*. Cambridge: Polity Press.

BUENO DE MESQUITA, B., and COHEN, L. (1995), 'Game Theory and Crime', *Criminology*, 33, 4: 485–518.

CALHOUN, C. (1995), *Critical Social Theory: Culture, History and the Challenge of Difference*. Oxford: Blackwell.

—— (1996), 'Whose Classics? Which Readings? Interpretation and Cultural Difference in the Canonization of Sociological Theory', in S. Turner, ed., *Social Theory and Sociology*. Oxford: Blackwell.

CHRISTIE, N. (1997), 'Four Blocks against Insight: Notes on the Oversocialization of Criminologists', *Theoretical Criminology*, 1, 1: 13–23.

CLARKE, R. (1995), 'Situational Crime Prevention', in M. Tonry and D. Farrington, eds., *Crime and Justice: a Review of Research, vol 19*. Chicago, Ill.: University of Chicago Press.

COHEN, S. (1988), 'Against Criminology', in *Against Criminology*. London and New Brunswick: Transaction.

—— (1996), 'Crime and Politics: Spot the Difference', *British Journal of Sociology*, 47, 1: 1–21.

COLLINS, R. (1981), 'On the Micro Foundations of Macro-sociology', *American Journal of Sociology*, 86: 984–1014.

DALY, K. (1997), 'Different Ways of Conceptualizing Sex/Gender in Feminist Theory and their Implications for Criminology', *Theoretical Criminology*, 1, 1: 25–51.

DAVIS, M. (1990), *City of Quartz*. London: Verso.

—— (1992), *Beyond Blade Runner: Urban Control—the Ecology of Fear*. Westfield, NJ: Open Media, pamphlet 23.

DOCHERTY, T. (1993), *Postmodernism: A Reader*. Hemel Hempstead: Harvester Wheatsheaf.

DOUGLAS, M. (1992), *Risk and Blame*. London: Routledge.

ECK, J., and WEISBURD, D., eds. (1995), *Crime and Place*. Monsey, NY: Criminal Justice Press.

ELSTER, J. (1989), *The Cement of Society*. Cambridge: Cambridge University Press.

ERICSON, R., and CARRIERE, K. (1994), 'The Fragmentation of Criminology', in D. Nelken, ed., *The Futures of Criminology*, London: Sage.

—— and HAGGERTY, K. (1997), *Policing Risk Society*. Toronto: University of Toronto Press.

FEELEY, M., and SIMON, J. (1992), 'The New Penology', *Criminology*, 39, 4: 449–74.

FELSON, M. (1994), *Crime and Everyday Life*. Thousand Oaks, Cal.: Pine Forge Press.

GARLAND, D (1985), *Punishment and Welfare*. Aldershot: Gower.

—— (1990), *Punishment and Modern Society*. Oxford: Oxford University Press.

—— (1992), 'Criminological Knowledge and its Relation to Power: Foucault's Genealogy and Criminology Today', *British Journal of Criminology*, 32, 4: 403–22.

—— (1995), 'Penal Modernism and Postmodernism', in T. Blomberg and S. Cohen, eds., *Punishment and Social Control*, New York: Aldine de Gruyter.

—— (1996), 'The Limits of the Sovereign State: Strategies of Crime Control in Contemporary Society', *British Journal of Criminology*, 36, 4: 1–27.

GIDDENS, A. (1976), *New Rules of Sociological Method*. London: Hutchinson.

—— (1984), *The Constitution of Society*. Cambridge: Polity Press.

—— (1987), *Social Theory and Modern Sociology*. Cambridge: Polity Press.

—— (1990), *The Consequences of Modernity*. Cambridge: Polity Press.

—— (1991), *Modernity and Self-Identity*. Cambridge: Polity Press.

GIRLING, E., LOADER, I., and SPARKS, R. (1997), 'Crime and the Sense of One's Place: Globalization, Restructuring and Insecurity in an English Town', in N. South, V. Ruggiero, and I. Taylor, eds., *European Criminology*, London: Routledge.

HACKING, I. (1991), *The Taming of Chance*. Cambridge: Cambridge University Press.

HAGAN, J., and PETERSEN, R. (1995), *Crime and Inequality*. Stanford, Cal.: Stanford University Press.

HINDESS, B. (1988), *Choice, Rationality and Social Theory*. London: Unwin Hyman.

HOLLIS, M. (1994), *The Philosophy of Social Science: An Introduction*. Cambridge: Cambridge University Press.

HOPE, T. (1996), 'Inequality and the Future of Community Crime Prevention', in S. P. Lab, ed., *Crime Prevention at a Crossroads*. Cincinnati, Ohio: Anderson Publishing.

HUDSON, B. (1996), *Understanding Justice*. Buckingham: Open University Press.

KEANE, J. (1996), *Reflections on Violence*. London: Verso.

KUMAR, K. (1997), *From Post-Industrial to Post-Modern Society*. Oxford: Blackwell.

LACEY, N. (1996), 'Normative Reconstruction in Socio-legal Theory', *Social and Legal Studies*, 5, 2: 131–58.

LAYDER, D. (1994), *Understanding Social Theory*, London: Sage.

LOGAN, J. and MOLOTCH, H. (1987), *Urban Fortunes*. Berkeley, Cal.: University of California Press.

LYON, D. (1994), *Postmodernity*. Buckingham: Open University Press.

McLENNAN, G. (1995), 'After Postmodernism—Back to Sociological Theory?', *Sociology*, 29, 1: 117–32.

MELOSSI, D. (1994), 'The Economy of Illegalities; Normal Crimes, Elites and Social Control in Comparative Perspective', in D. Nelken, ed., *The Futures of Criminology*. London: Sage.

—— and PAVARINI, M. (1979), *The Prison and the Factory*. London: Macmillan.

MEYROWITZ, J. (1985), *No Sense of Place*. Oxford: Oxford University Press.

MILLS, C. WRIGHT (1959), *The Sociological Imagination*. Oxford: Oxford University Press.

MORRISON, W. (1995), *Theoretical Criminology*. London: Cavendish.

MOUZELIS, N. (1995), *Sociological Theory: What Went Wrong?*. London: Routledge.

MUNCIE, J. and McLAUGHLIN, E. (1996a), *The Problem of Crime*. London: Sage.

—— and —— (1996b), *Controlling Crime*. London: Sage.

—— —— and LANGAN, M. (1996), *Criminological Perspectives: A Reader*, London: Sage.

NAFFINE, N. (1996), *Feminism and Criminology*. London: Sage.

NELKEN, D. (1994a), 'Reflexive criminology?', in D. Nelken, ed., *The Futures of Criminology*. London: Sage.

—— (1994b), 'Whom Can You Trust?: The Future of Comparative Criminology', in D. Nelken, ed., *The Futures of Criminology*. London: Sage.

O'MALLEY, P. (1992), 'Risk, Power and Crime Prevention', *Economy and Society*, 21, 3: 252–75.

—— (1996), 'Risk and Responsibility', in A. Barry, T. Osborne and N. Rose, eds., *Foucault and Political Reason*. London: UCL Press.

O'NEILL, J. (1995), *The Poverty of Post-modernism*. London: Routledge.

PAVARINI, M. (1997), 'Controlling Social Panic: Questions and Answers about Security in Italy at the End of the Millenium', in R. Bergalli and C. Sumner, eds., *Social Control and Political Order*. London: Sage.

PFOHL, S. (1993), 'Twilight of the Parasites: Ultramodern Capital and the New World Order', *Social Problems*, 40, 2: 125–51.

POGGI, G. (1996), '*Lego quia inutile*: An Alternative Justification for the Classics', in S. P. Turner, ed., *Social Theory and Sociology: the Classics and Beyond*. Oxford: Blackwell.

ROBERTSON, R. (1995), 'Glocalization: Time-Space and Homogeneity-Heterogeneity', in M. Featherstone, S. Lash, and R. Robertson, eds. (1995), *Global Modernities*. London: Sage.

RUGGIERO, V. (1996), *Organized and Corporate Crime in Europe*. Aldershot: Dartmouth.

RUNCIMAN, W. G. (1983), *A Treatise on Social Theory. Volume I: The Methodology of Social Theory*. Cambridge: Cambridge University Press.

SHEPTYCKI, J. (1995), 'Transnational Policing and the Makings of a Postmodern State', *British Journal of Criminology*, 35, 4: 613–35.

SHERMAN, L., GARTIN, P., and BUERGER, M. (1989), 'Hot Spots of Predatory Crime: Routine Activities and the Criminology of Place', *Criminology*, 27, 1: 27–55.

SIMON, J. (1993), *Poor Discipline*. Chicago, Ill.: University of Chicago Press.

—— (1995), 'They Died with their Boots On: the Boot Camp and the Limits of Modernity', *Social Justice*, 22, 2: 25–48.

—— and FEELEY, M. (1995), 'True Crime: The New Penology and Public Discourse on Crime', in T. Blomberg and S. Cohen, eds., *Punishment and Social Control*. New York: Aldine de Gruyter.

SMART, C. (1990), 'Postmodern Woman Meets Atavistic Man' in L. Gelsthorpe and A. Morris, eds., *Feminist Perspectives in Criminology*. Buckingham: Open University Press.

SMITH, D. (1988), *The Everyday World as Problematic*. Milton Keynes: Open University Press.

SPARKS, R. (1992), *Television and the Drama of Crime*. Buckingham: Open University Press.

—— BOTTOMS, A. E., and HAY, W. (1996), *Prisons and the Problem of Order*. Oxford: Oxford University Press.

STONES, R. (1996), *Sociological Reasoning*. London: Macmillan.

SUMNER, C. (1997), 'The Decline of Social Control and the Rise of Vocabularies of Struggle', in R. Bergalli and C. Sumner, eds., *Social Control and Political Order*. London: Sage.

THOMPSON, J. (1996), *The Media and Modernity*. Cambridge: Polity Press.

TURNER, J. (1988), *A Theory of Social Interaction*. Cambridge: Polity Press.

WAGNER, P. (1994), *A Sociology of Modernity. Liberty and Discipline*. London: Routledge.

WAGNER, P. (1996), 'Crises of Modernity: Political Sociology in Historical Contexts', in S. P. Turner, ed., *Social Theory and Sociology: the Classics and Beyond*. Oxford: Blackwell.

WALKLATE, S. (1997), 'Risk and Criminal Victimization: A Modernist Dilemma', *British Journal of Criminology*, 37, 1: 35–45.

YOUNG, A. (1996), *Imagining Crime*. London: Sage.

11

Criminology, Criminal Law, and Criminalization

Nicola Lacey

To anyone other than a specialist, the proposition that the intellectual concerns of criminology are intimately connected with those of criminal law would probably seem obvious to the point of banality. Yet within the institutional construction of disciplines, such common sense is often effaced by the development of conceptual frameworks which illuminate particular aspects of a practical terrain whilst obscuring their links with others. This (in some ways productive) blindness is one to which lawyers are probably more prone than criminologists. Both the professional autonomy of legal practice and the technical nature of legal argumentation have lent themselves to the construction of relatively rigid disciplinary boundaries. By contrast, the status of criminology as a discrete discipline has always been a contested one, and criminological research is inevitably informed by the methods and insights of the social sciences in general—insights which continue to have a rather fragile position within legal scholarship (Garland in this volume; Nelken, 1987*b*; Sumner, 1994). It is nonetheless almost as rare to find a criminology course which concerns itself with the scope and nature of criminal law as it is to find a criminal law course which addresses criminological questions (Lacey, Wells, and Meure, 1990; Lacey, 1993, 1994).

In this chaper, I shall offer a tentative sketch of the relationship between criminal law, criminology, and criminal justice, and I shall then try to illustrate the links between criminal legal and criminological inquiry from two complementary perspectives. First, I shall ask what students of criminal law can learn from the study of criminology, examining some of the questions which a degree of criminological insight might prompt a criminal lawyer to ask. Secondly, I shall consider what criminologists can learn from criminal law scholarship. The main burden of my argument will be that an adequate grasp of the two fields may best be attained by conceptualizing them as interlocking spaces within a broader conceptual frame: that of 'criminalization' (Lacey, 1995*a*). The framework of criminalization, as I shall argue, keeps the close relationship of the criminal legal and criminological enterprises firmly in view,

I should like to express my thanks to Linsday Farmer, Lucia Zedner, and the editors of the *Handbook* for their thoughtful comments on an earlier draft of this chapter.

whilst avoiding a synthesis which would lose sight of their specificity. Such a framework is, moreover, implicit in some of the most intellectually persuasive recent contributions to criminal law scholarship. (Farmer, 1996*a* and *b*; Loveland, 1995; Norrie, 1993). In what follows, I shall assume that the reader is a student of criminology who may or may not have studied criminal law.

THE RELATIONSHIP BETWEEN CRIMINOLOGY, CRIMINAL LAW, AND CRIMINAL JUSTICE STUDIES

Within the academy in the United Kingdom, the study of the various social practices associated with 'criminal justice' is currently divided into three main blocks. These blocks are themselves marked by a combination of disciplinary tools and institutional objects. Broadly understood, criminology concerns itself with social and individual antecedents of crime and with the nature of crime as a social phenomenon: its disciplinary resources come mainly from sociology, social theory, psychology, and history. Criminologists raise a variety of questions about patterns of criminality and its social construction, along with their historical, economic, political, and social conditions of existence (see the chapters by Garland, Young, and Rock, this volume). Whilst, as Garland's contribution to this volume suggests, the dynamic social construction of crime gives reason for scepticism about criminology's discreteness as a discipline, it continues to hold a distinctive institutional position in the academy. Criminal law concerns itself with the substantive norms according to which individuals or groups are adjudged guilty or innocent. Contemporary criminal lawyers tend to be concerned not so much with the antecedents or overall patterns of these norms, but rather with their judicial interpretation in particular cases or sets of cases. They are also concerned with the doctrinal framework of 'general principles' within which that interpretive practice and—though more tenuously—legislative development purportedly proceed (Ashworth, 1995; Clarkson and Keating, 1995; Smith and Hogan, 1993; Williams, 1983). The rules of evidence and procedure which have an important bearing on the application and historical development of criminal law tend to find only a small place in criminal law courses, and are often dealt with in specialist, optional courses or relegated to interstitial treatment in criminal justice or legal methods courses. Criminal justice courses, which have a variety of legal, historical, sociological, and other foci, deal with institutional aspects of the criminal process such as policing, prosecution, plea bargaining, sentencing, and punishment, and with normative questions about the principles around which a criminal justice system worth the name ought to be organized (Ashworth, 1994; Lacey, 1994). The disciplinary balance of these courses depends on their context; criminal justice courses in law departments are often oriented towards procedural law, whilst those in sociology or criminology departments are more likely to focus on historical, sociological, or political issues. Within degree courses in law, only criminal law is regarded as a 'core' part of the curriculum.

Whilst the organization of research conforms less rigidly to the divisions between criminal law, criminal justice, and criminology, these categories nonetheless bear a close relationship to the different areas of expertise claimed by scholars within the field. This partitioning of the intellectual terrain is, it should be noted, both historically and culturally specific. To Continental European eyes, for example, the Anglo-American separation of criminal law and criminal procedure, and indeed of criminal law and sentencing, appears extraordinary (Cole *et al.*, 1987; Fletcher, 1978). And although a superficially similar tripartite division has characterized the British approach for much of this century, the rationale underlying the three branches of 'criminal science' of the 1920s and 1930s was rather different from that underlying today's division (Radzinowicz and Turner, 1945; Kenny, 1952: chapter 1, Part II).

What, then, is the significance of the contemporary partition between criminology, criminal law, and criminal justice? Even a brief sketch of the prevailing academic division of labour suffices to reveal that it is likely to repress certain important issues. Criminological insights about patterns of 'deviance' pose important questions about the working of criminal justice institutions such as police and courts. The practice of legal interpretation takes place within a particular social context and in relation to criminal laws which are themselves the product of a political process which is surely relevant to their application and enforcement. Practices of punishment take place against the background of prevailing concerns about patterns of criminality, about the vitality of social norms thought to be embodied in criminal law, and about the legitimacy of state power. Furthermore, the construction of the tripartite block itself is a porous one, given that criminal justice practices exist alongside and relate in an intimate, albeit complex way, to a variety of other—political, economic, moral, religious, educational, familial—normative and sanctioning practices (Lacey *et al.*, 1990: chapter 1).

Whilst it would clearly be impossible to address all criminal justice concerns within a single research project or course, there is a real risk that questions which transcend the prevailing boundaries marking off the three areas may be lost from view. For example, the relevance of the political context or of particular features of the criminal process to the development of legal doctrine in a series of appeal cases may be excluded from a criminal law course, whilst criminal justice or criminology courses may ignore the bearing of legal developments upon practices of prosecution and punishment. In short, a legitimate focus on the issues raised both within particular disciplines and in relation to particular institutional practices may serve to obscure broader questions about the assumptions on which those disciplines and practices are based. What are lawyers' implicit ideas about the nature of crime and of offenders? What assumptions do criminologists make about the nature of criminal law? And who, within the prevailing division of intellectual labour, is to study these important matters?

CRIMINAL LAW

Since the discreteness of both subject matter and disciplinary framework is probably most firmly established in relation to criminal law, I now want to focus on this area so as to examine the degree to which its pretensions to autonomy are justified. Of course, many criminal law scholars have concerned themselves with sociology and history and with questions about the criminal process: indeed, this socio-legal leaning has probably been more marked in criminal law than in other fields of legal scholarship over the last forty years (Hall, 1960; Packer, 1967). The objection to socio-legal approaches to criminal law has always been, however, that they underestimate or obscure the specificity of legal techniques and legal argumentation, reducing legal regulation to the exercise of political or economic power, and assuming legal decision-making to be explicable in terms of some crude set of personal, economic, or political causes. Furthermore, it may be argued that socio-legal scholars often ask the wrong kinds of questions about criminal law—questions which assume that law is to be judged in terms of its instrumental functions rather than its symbolic dimensions. These problems are probably best exemplified by American legal realism and Chicago-style law and economics, reductive approaches in which legal decision-making is explained, respectively, in terms of judicial actors' policy preferences and their concern to maximize economic efficiency (Farmer, 1995, 1996a; Nelken, 1987b). In the context of the debate about the proper balance between autonomy and openness in criminal law scholarship, the development over the last fifteen years of 'critical' approaches is worthy of particular attention (for a general review, see Nelken, 1987a; Norrie, 1992). For, as I shall now try to show, they promise to combine a focus on legal specificity without obscuring broader questions about the historical, political, and social conditions under which the apparently discrete and technical practices of modern criminal law flourish.

Early examples of critical criminal law scholarship, notably the work of Mark Kelman (1981), were closely associated with the American 'critical legal studies' movement. The movement embraces a group of scholars who seek to expose the 'politics of law' by means of a close examination of doctrinal principles and categories. Conventional criminal law scholars generally provide a brief resume of the moral/retributive, incapacitative, and deterrent aspects of criminal justice. They go on to give a terse statement of the competing concerns of fairness and social protection, due process, and crime control which are taken to inform the development and implementation of criminal law in liberal societies. From this point on, they take the idea of 'crimes' as given by acts of law-creation. In this way both political and criminological issues are quietly removed from the legal agenda. In contrast, critical criminal lawyers assume that the power and meaning of criminal laws depend on a more complex set of processes and underlying factors than the mere positing of prohibitory norms to be enforced according to a particular procedure.

Most obviously, they assume that the influences of political and economic power permeate the practice of doctrinal interpretation. Yet their view here is not the reductive, instrumental one of realism or the Chicago School; rather, critical criminal lawyers argue that judicial practice is shaped by tensions between competing values whose power infuses all social practices, and which cannot be reconciled by either legislative reform or feats of rationalizing interpretation.

The primary aim of early critical criminal law scholarship was to develop an internal or 'immanent' critique of the doctrinal framework within which different areas of law have been taken to be organized. Taking a close interest in the way in which criminal liability is *constructed* within legal discourse, critical scholars took as their focus the structure of 'general principles' which are usually taken to underpin criminal law in liberal societies. These included the aspirations of neutrality, objectivity, and determinacy of legal method which are associated with the rule of law, along with liberal ideals about the fair terms under which criminal punishment may be imposed upon an individual agent (Norrie, 1993). For example, Kelman's work scrutinized the basis of the 'mens rea' doctrine which purports to structure and justify the attribution of criminal responsibility to the free individual *via* the employment of standards of fault such as intent and recklessness. He showed that 'mens rea' veers in an unprincipled way between 'subjective' standards, in which attributions of responsibility depend on what the defendant actually intended or contemplated, and 'objective' standards, such as negligence, which impute to the defendant the state of mind of the 'reasonable man'. Following from this, Kelman emphasized the fact that criminal law doctrine evinces no consistent commitment to either a free-will or a determinist model of human behaviour (Kelman, 1981).

Furthermore, Kelman and others demonstrated the manipulability and indeterminacy of the generally accepted doctrinal framework according to which criminal liability is constructed in terms of three elements: 'actus reus' or conduct; 'mens rea' or fault; and defence (or, more accurately, its absence). For example, critical scholars pointed out that the issue of mistake could be conceptualized with equal doctrinal propriety as matter pertaining to the existence of the conduct or fault elements of a crime or to the existence of a defence (Lacey *et al.*, 1990: chapter 1). A person who assaults another person in the mistaken belief that that other person is in the process of committing an assault on a third party could, in other words, be regarded as having a defence, or as lacking the conduct or (in certain circumstances) mental elements of a crime. Since these conceptualizations sometimes affect the outcome of the legal analysis, this entails that doctrinal rules are not as determinate as the conventional theory of legal reasoning assumes. Moreover, critical analysis illustrated the fact that the outcome of legal reasoning is contingent upon factors such as the time frame within which the alleged offence was set. For example, whether or not a person is regarded as negligent, in the sense of having failed to reach a reasonable standard of care or awareness, may well depend on what range of conduct the court is able to examine. What appears an unreasonable lapse judged in itself may look more reasonable if evidence about its history can be admitted. Yet the influence of the framing process is not acknowledged within the doctrinal structure, which accordingly fails to regulate judicial interpretation in the way which is generally supposed.

The critical enterprise here is to hold criminal law up to scrutiny in terms of the standards which it professes to instantiate, and, in doing so, to reveal that, far from consisting in a clear, determinate set of norms, based on a coherent set of 'general principles', it rather exemplifies a contradictory and conflicting set of approaches which are obscured by the superficial coherence and determinacy of legal reasoning. By scrutinizing carefully the form which criminal legal reasoning takes, it becomes possible to reveal that practice as being not so much logical as ideological, and as serving the interests of a variety of powerful groups by representing criminal law as a technical and apolitical sphere of judgement (Norrie, 1993). An important part of this process is the (re)reading of cases, not merely as exercises in formal legal analysis, but also as texts whose rhetorical structure is at least as important as their superficial legal content (Goodrich, 1986). In this kind of reading, critical scholars emphasize the significant symbolic aspect of the power of criminal law, along with the implicit yet powerful images of wrongdoing and rightful conduct, normal and abnormal subjects, guilt and innocence which legal discourse draws upon and produces (Lacey, 1993).

The early critical focus on the intricacies of doctrinal rationalization and the exposure of conflicts which such rationalization obscures has, however, gradually been supplemented by a further set of questions suggested by the process of immanent critique. If critical criminal law was not to remain a set of observations about the apparent irrationality of legal doctrine, the question of the deeper logics underpinning legal discourse had to be addressed (Norrie, 1993). Hence questions about the broad socio-political conditions under which a particular doctrinal framework arises and 'works', and about the historical conditions of existence of particular doctrinal systems of classification (taken as 'given' within conventional scholarship) have begun to claim the attention of critical criminal law scholars (Norrie, 1993; Lacey, 1997).

This development, which might be conceptualized as 'external' critique, illuminates some important links between critical criminal law scholarship and socio-legal and sociological work on the criminal process. For as critical scholars have sought to understand the deeper political and historical logics underpinning the formal lack of logic of criminal law doctrine, and to grasp precisely how doctrinal ideology serves to obscure apparently obvious political questions about criminal law, new issues have begun to force themselves onto the critical agenda. These include questions about the ways in which a focus on certain portions of substantive criminal law, and a lack of attention to others, serves to perpetuate the myth of coherent 'general principles', and about the ways in which this selectivity relates to prevailing understandings of what constitutes 'real crime', the imperatives of 'law and order' politics and the deeper factors underpinning the governmental and judicial need to represent criminal law as just and as politically 'neutral'. They also include questions about the way in which a certain model of criminal procedure—that of trial by jury—plays a legitimating role which can only be maintained by diverting attention away from the exceptional nature of jury trials and the prevalence of lay justice, diversion from the criminal process and practices such as plea bargaining. Whilst earlier examples of critical criminal law scholarship were primarily concerned with the form of criminal legal reasoning, later examples have begun to examine the substantive patterns of criminal legislation and judicial interpretation, and the relationship between shifts in these frontiers of criminality and the broader social meaning of the practice of criminal justice (Loveland, 1995). Striking examples during the 1980s include the development of criminal law in the area of serious fraud (Weait, 1995) and the debate about homicide doctrine following a number of unsuccessful 'corporate manslaughter' prosecutions consequent upon incidents which would until recently have been regarded as fatal 'accidents' (Wells, 1993, 1995).

The full implications of internal critique, in other words, can only be realized once they are set in the context of a broader set of historical, political, and social questions about the conditions of existence and efficacy of particular doctrinal arrangements. These questions are not legal questions, nor do they detract from the importance of a specifically legal critique. What they do is to give that critique a far greater significance than it would otherwise have, both by relating it to a wider set of social-theoretic questions and by suggesting links with normative (typically philosophical) thinking about the conditions under which the criminal process might operate in less unjust, undemocratic, and oppressive ways. It is in this sense that critical criminal law scholarship has begun to open up a new agenda for cross-institutional and interdisciplinary study. This agenda, as I shall argue below, may best be understood within the framework of 'criminalization'.

WHAT CAN CRIMINOLOGY BRING TO THE STUDY OF CRIMINAL LAW?

It follows from what has been said in the last section that criminological thinking brings important insights to the study of criminal law. Since the specific practices of both legislation and legal interpretation take place within the context of broader social processes which shape not only the range and definition of criminal laws but also the particular subjects in relation to whom the courts apply their legal techniques, that context is an important factor in understanding the dynamics of legal interpretation. Ideas and principles which are central to criminal law doctrine and its broader accompanying framework, the ideal of the rule of law, begin to take on a different colour once we appreciate, as criminology helps us to do, the partiality and selectivity of their enforcement.

As an overtly coercive state practice within societies which think of themselves as liberal, criminal law confronts a serious challenge of legitimation. It seeks to meet this challenge by making a number of normative claims which relate both to the substance of legal norms and to the process through which they are enforced. In relation to the former, criminal law legitimates itself in two main ways. First, it does so by appealing to the objective, timeless normative status of the standards which it applies. Yet this poses problems of reconciliation with political manipulation of the frontiers of criminality by legislative changes and executive decisions which criminalize hitherto lawful activities or remove criminal sanctions from formerly prohibited conduct. Secondly, criminal law legitimates itself by appealing to the basis of its standards in common, shared understandings or commitments. This is difficult to reconcile with pervasive social conflict in relation to the existence or interpretation of particular criminal norms. Instructive contemporary examples include not only obvious disagreements about the propriety of criminalizing certain forms of sexual behaviour and commercial conduct but also dissensus about the proper standard of fault to be applied in the key offence of homicide (Lacey, 1993).

In relation to procedure and enforcement, criminal law legitimates itself as the fair and even-handed application of rules to subjects conceptualized in terms of their formal capacities for understanding and self-control. Yet how is this claim to be reconciled with the statistics on disparate patterns of enforcement along lines of race or ethnicity, gender, socio-economic status, age, place of residence (see the chapters by Nelken, Sanders, Heidensohn, and Smith in this volume)? Criminal law claims legitimacy by appealing to the detached and even-handed application of its standards to all who come before it. How is this claim to be reconciled with the pervasiveness of practices such as plea-bargaining, which are driven by the relative power relations of particular actors within the process and by managerialist concerns about the cost-efficient disposal of cases? Criminal law prides itself on its application of a standard of proof beyond reasonable doubt and on its tailoring of liability requirements to the particular individual before the court. How is this to be reconciled with extensive plea-bargaining or with the indeterminacy of 'mens rea' standards? Evidently, these legitimating strategies are heavily dependent on criminal law's capacity to sustain the aura of its separateness from the politics and practicalities of the criminal process. Many principles which are central to the 'common sense' of doctrinal criminal law come to look somewhat fragile as that separateness is eroded by a little knowledge of criminal justice. This realization itself propels the sorts of critical questions discussed above onto the consciousness of the criminal law scholar.

WHAT CAN CRITICAL CRIMINAL LAW BRING TO THE STUDY OF CRIMINOLOGY AND CRIMINAL JUSTICE?

The idea that criminological insight can sharpen the critical perspective of criminal lawyers will probably be accepted by anyone who has chosen to study criminology. The converse idea that criminologists or students of criminal justice ought to concern themselves with criminal law may be less intellectually digestible. For some students of criminology this has to do with a (not entirely unjustified) scepticism about the relative importance of law in determining social practices of labelling and punishment which are seen in broader sociological and political terms. For others it may have to do with a crude understanding of criminal law received from 'black-letter' positivist scholarship. The legal positivist approach views laws as the products of legislative or judicial decision, which operate straightforwardly as rules which are applied in a deductive way to cases coming before the courts. From a criminological perspective, legal positivism entails, once again, that the interesting questions are not legal ones but rather social and political ones having to do with the factors shaping the selection of cases coming before the courts and the influences upon legislative changes in the scope and contours of criminal prohibitions. This, however, is to miss out on the significance of law as an interpretive practice which plays a central role in the legitimation of the state's penal power. I shall suggest, therefore, that at least four aspects of critical criminal law scholarship are likely to generate important insights from a criminological point of view.

First, the critical criminal lawyer's focus on shifting boundaries of criminal law provides one important part of the broader criminal justice jigsaw. Whilst changes in the legislative content of criminal law are themselves highly significant as both political and legal events, the subsequent process of judicial interpretation is what shapes both the meaning and (to some degree) the social efficacy of new criminal laws. Judicial interpretations which, for example, render criminal laws very difficult to enforce will have both knock-on effects for future prosecution policy and implications for the symbolic meaning of the relevant law. An excellent example here is the law on incitement to racial hatred, whose strict interpretation has arguably rendered it virtually unenforceable and which is regarded by some as a *de facto* legitimation of racial abuse (Fitzpatrick, 1987). Long-standing aspects of the doctrinal framework of criminal law may facilitate or inhibit the movement of the boundaries of criminality in directions aspired to by political institutions and other groupings. One good example here is the inchoate move towards imposing criminal liability on corporations—a development which continues to be inhibited by the association of the 'mens rea' framework with the mental states of individual human agents (Wells, 1993). Another is the debate about how to administer the law of rape so as more even-handedly to recognize the sexual integrity of rape victims and defendants. This project is hindered by the doctrinal shape of the rape offence. Proof of rape turns on the victim's lack of consent—something which continues to be judged in relation to unduly broad evidence about the victim's (as opposed to the defendant's) sexual or other experience—and on a subjective standard of responsibility. This entails that even a grossly unreasonable mistake about the victim's consent can, in principle, exonerate the defendant—hence giving legal force to the defendant's (as opposed to the victim's) understanding of the encounter. These problems are reinforced by an adversarial court procedure in which the best defence strategy is almost invariably to attack the victim's character (Temkin, 1989; Smart, 1995).

Secondly, the critical criminal lawyer's focus on the specificities of legal reasoning sheds light on the ways in which power at one stage of the criminal process is both exercised and legitimated. Notwithstanding their relative infrequency, trial by jury and criminal appeals play a central role in the legitimation of the entire criminal process. A close appreciation of how these stages work—one which pays attention to the particularities of legal discourse—is therefore of central importance to any integrated understanding of criminal justice. For example, critical scholarship has generated important insights into the ways in which the power of law depends on the capacity of legal discourse to construct itself as generating 'truths' which are impervious to critical scrutiny from other perspectives (Smart, 1989). This in turn sheds light on processes by which other knowledges introduced as evidence in criminal trials—sociological or psychological knowledges, for example—are subtly invalidated or else modified in the course of 'translation' into the terms of legal discourse. A good example here is the slow and partial legal recognition of evidence about the effects of long-term violence in 'domestic' homicide cases. Whilst recent cases have begun to accept such evidence as relevant, its force is inevitably limited by the need to shape it to fit the conceptual straitjackets of legal defences such as provocation, self-defence, and diminished responsibility (Lacey, 1995b). For instance, there is a legal requirement that, to qualify as provocation or self-defence, a violent response must follow immediately upon provocative or threatening conduct. This has posed difficulties in several cases in which defendants (most of them women) who have been subject to 'domestic' violence kill their abusers, yet in which there is no immediate relation between the ultimate killing and a particular attack. The result is that defence lawyers have been forced to reconstruct the relevant evidence in psychiatric terms which accord with a diminished responsibility defence which misrepresents the defendant's position. Such transformations of non-legal knowledges in the legal process have generally been invisible to conventional legal analysis and have received only partial recognition and understanding in socio-legal scholarship.

This is not to imply a reductive, sociological reading of the criminal trial or the criminal appeal: nor is it, conversely, to deny the importance of interpretive questions about the meaning of the rituals and architecture of the trial as a public event. It is rather to assert that the images of subject and society, of guilt and innocence, of responsibility and non-responsibility, of the autonomy and independence of legal power, and of the objectivity and political neutrality of judgment which are produced within legal reasoning are discrete objects of criminal justice knowledge, and objects which can most fully be explicated by critical criminal lawyers. Whilst the ultimate direction of my argument is that these legal specificities have meanings which are systematically obscured by the structure of legal doctrine, these meanings cannot be grasped without a close analysis of those practices themselves, along with their historical development and place within particular professional institutions. Hence the critical criminal lawyer's approach of taking the doctrinal framework seriously in itself, but of simultaneously reading it as a clue to broader political factors, sheds light on matters of central concern to the criminologist. The alleged autonomy or 'closure' of legal reasoning has to be identified, and its *modus operandi* understood, before it can take its place as a phenomenon which may be interpreted within any general attempt to understand the nature of crime and the criminal process.

Thirdly, historical shifts in the patterns of 'general principles' which purportedly structure legal doctrine, and indeed in the degree of insistence on any such structure, are themselves significant from a criminological point of view. For example, the contemporary focus on 'mens rea' as the central doctrinal problem in legitimizing criminal liability is one which emerged only during the nineteenth century and which has reached its current predominance only in the second half of the twentieth century (Lacey, 1997). Before this, the organizing framework for doctrine was focused on the types of conduct proscribed rather than the basis on which individuals could fairly be held responsible for that conduct. The shift relates to a number of social developments of direct relevance to criminalization: a changing conception of the subject as an individual and of his or her relation to the polity and to government (Wiener, 1990); a shifting view of the legitimation problems posed by the criminal justice system (Norrie, 1993); a changing view of the role of criminal law as one form of social ordering among others, the latter driven by significant transformations in the shape and variety of criminal procedure over the last 150 years (Farmer, 1996*b*: chapter 3). Whilst these developments have been central to the social history of crime, their relationship with changes in the organizing framework of criminal law doctrine have been virtually ignored. Hence a promising avenue of inquiry into the general nature of crime and criminal justice has been closed off by the current organization of disciplines.

Finally, critical criminal law scholarship generates a finely tuned analysis of the shape of particular criminal laws and their interpretation over time. From a criminological or criminal justice point of view, it is all too easy to take 'criminal law' as a unitary, undifferentiated body of norms which are straightforwardly applied by the courts. Yet a close reading of cases and statutes reveals an enormous diversity among criminal laws: in terms of the style of their drafting; their scope; the construction of their subjects and objects; their assumptions about responsibility; their procedural requirements. Careful micro-level analysis of legal discourse illuminates assumptions about human nature, and about the status of various kinds of conduct, which structure legal reasoning, yet which may not appear on the face of legal arrangements. Good examples are the close feminist readings of criminal laws dealing with sexual offences, and with rape in particular (Temkin, 1989; Lacey *et al.*, 1990: chapter 5; Duncan, 1996; Zedner, 1995), which reveal a troubling set of assumptions about male and female sexuality and about the reliability of female witnesses. Similarly, the readings of criminal law's construction of homosexuality within queer legal theory (Moran, 1996) reveal a situation which is substantially at odds with the (relatively) liberal approach which appears on the surface of criminal laws. In a different field, critical readings of the property offences have generated a wealth of insights about their assumptions about honesty and propriety, their construction of the fragile lines between enterprise and dishonesty, and the ways in which this construction shifts as between different kinds of property offence (Lacey *et al.*, 1990: chapter 6; Hall, 1952). Such analysis of individual criminal laws or areas of criminal law generates an enormous amount of material which can illuminate the broad social meaning of criminalization. It also reveals a multi-directional process in which both legislature and courts are involved in reflecting, interpreting and shaping the social attitudes and norms upon which the efficacy and legitimacy of criminal justice depends.

FROM CRITICAL CRIMINAL LAW TO CRIMINALIZATION

My suggestion, then, is that criminology, broadly understood, and criminal law scholarship of a critical temper are complementary, albeit distinctive, tasks within the general intellectual enterprise of working towards an understanding of the diverse social practices associated with criminal justice. I have argued more fully elsewhere that the term 'criminalization' constitutes an appropriate conceptual framework within which to gather together the constellation of social practices which form the subject matter of criminology, criminal law, and criminal justice studies (Lacey, 1995*a*; see also Farmer, 1996*a*). Escaping the notion of crimes as 'given', the idea of criminalization captures the dynamic nature of the field as a set of interlocking practices in which the moments of 'defining' and 'responding to' crime can rarely be completely distinguished. It accommodates the full range of relevant institutions within which those practices take shape and the disciplines which might be brought to bear upon their analysis; it allows the instrumental and symbolic aspects of the field to be addressed, as well as encompassing empirical, interpretive, and normative projects. It embraces questions about offenders and victims, individuals and collectivities, state and society.

Within the framework of criminalization, we may therefore accommodate the relevant practices of a variety of social actors and institutions: citizens, the media, the police, prosecution agencies, courts, judges and lawyers, social workers, probation officers and those working in the penal and mental health systems, legislators, and key members of the executive. We are also able to acknowledge the relevance of a wide variety of disciplines to the analysis of these institutions: sociology, psychology, political science, economics, legal studies, moral and political philosophy, and anthropology, to name only the most obvious. This we can do without collapsing the study of criminalization into a chaotic mass which escapes rigorous analysis, and without falling prey to fantasies about the possibility of a unitary synthesis of different approaches. Doubtless the study of criminalization is less intellectually tidy than the all-encompassing 'theories of criminal justice' which have been academically fashionable since the 1960s (Hall, 1960; Packer, 1968; Gross, 1979). This seems an eminently worthwhile sacrifice for a field of scholarship which is sufficiently open to identify the intersecting issues which, as I argued earlier, are all too often lost from view in the prevailing division of labour within the field.

Selected Further Reading

Readers interested in the debate about 'critical criminal law' should consult the important early papers by Mark Kelman, 'Interpretive Construction in the Substantive Criminal Law' ((1981), *Stanford Law Review*, 33: 591) and David Nelken, 'Critical Criminal Law' ((1987) *Journal of Law and Society*, 14: 105). Alan Norrie's *Crime, Reason and History* (London: Butterworths, 1993) provides an extended application of critical method to criminal law, and pushes the critical approach forward by exploring the historical context in which criminal law doctrine has developed (see in particular chapter 1) and the relationship between criminal law doctrine and sentencing practice (see chapter 10). The interaction between the three fields distinguished in this chapter are studied more fully in N. Lacey, 'Contingency and Criminalisation', in I. Loveland (ed.), *Frontiers of Criminality* (London: Sweet and Maxwell, 1995). The relationship between questions of criminal law and those of criminal justice is explored in greater detail in N. Lacey, C. Wells, and D. Meure, *Reconstructing Criminal Law* (London: Butterworths, 1990), chapter 1. Lindsay Farmer's *Criminal Law, Tradition and Legal Order* (Cambridge: Cambridge University Press, 1996) provides another useful exposition of critical method in the criminal law field, and a fascinating case study of the interaction between national politics, criminal law, and criminal procedure in nineteenth-century Scotland: see in particular chapters 1 and 3.

REFERENCES

ASHWORTH, A. (1994), *The Criminal Process: An Evaluative Study*. Oxford: Oxford University Press.

—— (1995), *Principles of Criminal Law*, 2nd edn. Oxford: Clarendon Press.

CLARKSON, C., and KEATING, H. (1995), *Criminal Law: Text and Materials*, 3rd edn. London: Sweet and Maxwell.

COLE, G. F., FRANKOWSKI, S. J., and GERTZ, M. G., eds. (1987), *Criminal Justice Systems: A Comparative Survey*, 2nd edn. London: Sage.

DUNCAN, S. (1996), 'The Mirror Tells its Tale: Constructions of Gender in Criminal Law', in A. Bottomley, ed.., *Feminist Perspectives on the Foundational Subjects of Law*, 173. London: Cavendish.

FARMER, L. (1995), 'Bringing Cinderella to the Ball: Teaching Criminal Law in Context', *Modern Law Review*, 58: 756.

—— (1996a), 'The Obsession with Definition', *Social and Legal Studies*, 5: 57.

—— (1996b), *Criminal Law, Tradition and Legal Order: The Genius of Scots Law*. Cambridge: Cambridge University Press.

FITZPATRICK, P. (1987), 'Racism and the Innocence of Law', *Journal of Law and Society*, 14: 119.

FLETCHER, G. (1978), *Rethinking Criminal Law*. Boston, Mass., and Toronto: Little, Brown & Co.

GOODRICH, P. (1986), *Reading the Law*. Oxford: Blackwell.

GROSS, H. (1979), *A Theory of Criminal Justice*. Oxford: Oxford University Press.

HALL, J. (1952), *Theft, Law and Society*. New York: Bobbs-Merrill.

—— (1960), *General Principles of Criminal Law*, 2nd edn. Indianapolis, Ind. and New York: Bobbs-Merrill.

KELMAN, M. (1981), 'Interpretive Construction in the Substantive Criminal Law', *Stanford Law Review*, 33: 591.

KENNY, C. S. (1952), *Outlines of Criminal Law*, 16th edn., ed. J. W. C. Turner. Cambridge: Cambridge University Press.

LACEY, N. (1995a), 'Contingency and Criminalisation', in I. Loveland, ed., *Frontiers of Criminality*, chapter 1. London: Sweet and Maxwell.

—— (1995b), 'Feminist Legal Theory Beyond Neutrality,' *Current Legal Problems*, 1.

—— (1993), 'A Clear Concept of Intention: Elusive or Illusory', *Modern Law Review*, 56: 621.

—— (1994), 'Making Sense of Criminal Justice', in N. Lacey, ed., *Criminal Justice: A Reader*, 1. Oxford: Oxford University Press.

—— (1997), 'Contingency, Coherence and Conceptualism: Reflections on the Encounter between 'Critique' and 'Philosophy of the Criminal Law', in A. Duff, ed., *Philosophy and the Criminal Law*. Cambridge: Cambridge University Press.

—— WELLS, C., and MEURE, D. (1990), *Reconstructing Criminal Law: Critical Perspectives on Crime and the Criminal Process*. London: Butterworths.

LOVELAND, I. ed. (1995), *Frontiers of Criminality*. London: Sweet and Maxwell.

MORAN, L. (1996), *The Homosexual(ity) of Law*. London: Routledge.

NELKEN, D. (1987a), 'Critical Criminal Law', *Journal of Law and Society*, 14: 105.

—— (1987b), 'Criminal Law and Criminal Justice: Some Notes on their Irrelation', in I. Dennis, ed., *Criminal Law and Justice*, 139. London: Sweet and Maxwell.

NORRIE, A. (1992), 'Criminal Law', in I. Griggs Spall and P. Ireland, eds., *The Critical Lawyer's Handbook*, 76. London: Pluto Press.

—— (1993), *Crime, Reason and History*. London: Butterworths.

PACKER, H. (1968), *The Limits of the Criminal Sanction*. Stanford, Cal.: Stanford University Press.

RADZINOWICZ, L., and TURNER, J. W. C. (1945), 'The Meaning and Scope of Criminal Science', in L. Radzinowicz and J. W. C. Turner, *The Modern Approach to Criminal Law*. English Studies in Criminal Justice, iv. London: Macmillan.

SMART, C. (1989), *Feminism and the Power of Law*. London: Routledge.

—— (1995), *Law, Crime and Sexuality*. London: Sage.

SMITH, J. C., and HOGAN, B. (1996), *Criminal Law*, 8th edn. London: Butterworths.

SUMNER, C. (1994), *The Sociology of Deviance: An Obituary*. Buckingham: Open University Press.

TEMKIN, J. (1989), *Rape and the Legal Process*. London: Sweet and Maxwell.

WEAIT, M. (1995), 'The Serious Fraud Office: Nightmares (and Pipe Dreams) on Elm Street', in I. Loveland, ed., *Frontiers of Criminality*, chapter 4. London: Sweet and Maxwell.

WELLS, C. (1993), *Corporations and Criminal Responsibility*. Oxford: Clarendon Press.

—— (1995), 'Cry in the Dark: Corporate Manslaughter and Cultural Meaning', in I. Loveland, ed., *Criminality*, chapter 5. London: Sweet and Maxwell.

WIENER, M. (1990), *Reconstructing the Criminal: Culture, Law and Policy in England, 1830–1914*. Cambridge: Cambridge University Press.

WILLIAMS, G. (1983), *A Textbook of Criminal Law*, 2nd edn. London, Stevens.

ZEDNER, L. (1995), 'Regulating Sexual Offences within the Home', in I. Loveland, ed., *Frontiers of Criminality*, chapter 8. London: Sweet and Maxwell.

12

Social Control

Barbara A. Hudson

INTRODUCTION: DEFINING SOCIAL CONTROL

social control is one of those terms that appear in the sociological discourse without any corresponding everyday usage.

(Blomberg and Cohen, 1995: 4)

Social control is an important concept within sociology, arguably one of the most important. However, it has become one of those that sociologists have recourse to when all else fails; just about everything and anything has been seen in recent years as an instance of social control.

(Sumner, 1997: 1)[1]

This chapter will examine the body of criminological work which has analysed the nature of *social control* in modern society. Major themes to be covered are:

the relationship between crime and control;
the key characteristics of control strategies;
transformations in social control strategies;
the social control of women,

and a final section will look at emerging forms of control in late-modern or post-modern society. Key writers whose work will be discussed include Pat Carlen, Stanley Cohen, Michel Foucault, Edwin Lemert, Andrew Scull, and Jonathon Simon, and important concepts which will be introduced and explained include *decarceration, discipline, labelling, inclusionary and exclusionary controls, formal and informal controls, net-widening* and *surveillance*.

Social control was introduced into the sociological lexicon by one of the first prominent American sociologists, Edward A. Ross, in a paper written in 1896, and was then used as the title of the volume *Social Control* published in 1901. He used his new term to refer to all the processes which induce individuals to behave in conformity with the norms and values of their society: as well as criminal law, police, courts, and prisons, Ross's usage of the term includes religion, art, education, and public opinion (Coser, 1982: 13). This conception of social control thus encompasses the production of normal behaviour as well as the suppression of deviance. It also encompasses differing forms or

---

[1] I am grateful to Colin Sumner for sending me a pre-publication copy of this chapter.

techniques of control: educative/repressive; control through internalization of norms/control through external coercion.

On this formulation, social control really would include 'everything and any-thing' in social interaction, and might be rendered analytically meaningless because of its vagueness. It would be almost impossible to use for research because not only would its definition and theoretical standpoint vary, but so also would the range of phenomena, times, and societies to which it would be applicable (Chunn and Gavignan, 1988).

Criminology has generally adopted a more restricted definition of social control. It has followed those sociologies which define processes producing conforming, pro-social behaviour as 'socialization', differentiating them from 'social control', which then designates 'the repertoire of organized social responses to deviance'. (Blomberg and Cohen, 1995: 5). This definition allows for further differentiation into, for example, state-sponsored and non-state-sponsored responses to deviance; responses to crime and responses to other forms of deviance, such as mental illness or 'alternative lifestyles'; socially inclusive and socially exclusive strategies of control.

Ross's original wider meaning of control (including socialization processes as well as responses to deviance) remains important as contextual background for understanding strategies of control. Two of the most important strands in the 'criminology of control' have been investigations of the balance between conformity-producing and deviance-repressing modes of control, and of the ways in which both positive and negative dimensions of control are expressions of wider, cultural trends. The first of these themes is particularly prominent in work on the control of women; the second is dominant in the analysis of the development of modern penal systems.

CRIMINOLOGY AND THE CONTROL OF CRIME

Criminology is itself part of the apparatus of control in modern societies, as well as being concerned with the study of control. It is a body of knowledge developed to help the day-to-day work of police, courts, prison governors and medical officers, probation officers, social workers and forensic psychiatrists, as well as to inform legislators and policy-makers (Garland, 1985, 1988). Criminology is the stock-in-trade of criminal justice professionals: criminological knowledge is included in their training; it guides their deployment of resources; it assists their diagnoses, their classifications, their recommendations for rehabilitation or segregation.

Positive criminology has provided images of the offender—the 'delinquent' (Foucault, 1977) or *homo penalis* (Pasquino, 1991)—by constructing a repertoire of causal theories about the nature of the offender and the factors which might predispose him/her to crime. These theories have been used to develop the practices of reformist and rehabilitative control (Garland, 1985) that underpinned the development of prisons from the nineteenth century onwards, as well as the formation of institutions such as the probation service and juvenile justice agencies. Whilst the link between the production of criminological knowledge and being part of the apparatus of control might be most obvious in the case of positivist criminology, as Cohen (1988) points out, this link between criminology and the technologies of power predates the emergence of positivism. When the primary strategy of crime control was the devising of graduated schedules of penalties to provide predictable, proportionate punishments, penologists such as Beccaria in the eighteenth century proposed theories based on the construct of a free-willed offender, who would be deterred by the certainty of punishment. In the post-rehabilitation, post-positivist era of the late twentieth century, 'rational choice' theories of offenders have reappeared to underpin 'neoclassical' ideas of punishment. Most recently, in the 1990s, when control of crime is focused neither on understanding the offender nor on ensuring the fairness and predictability of punishments, but on the avoidance of victimization, criminology has duly obliged with the production of 'criminologies of everyday life' (Garland, 1996). In the latest criminologies, the primary object of knowledge is not the offender but the victim, whose lifestyle and routine activities may make her/him vulnerable to crime (Young, A., and Rush, 1994).

For Foucault, criminology has always been not only at the service of power, but part of the technologies of power; the pose of the detached intellectual discoverer of apolitical or even subversive knowledge is merely 'an elaborate alibi to justify the exercise of power' (Cohen, 1988: 5).

Much criminology, often referred to as mainstream or administrative criminology (Young, J., 1988, *inter alia*), contents itself with the unreflexive production of technicist information for legislators, criminal justice planners, and practitioners. Such literature, although part of the apparatus of social control, is not my concern here. More critical criminologies have sought to interrogate and understand the nature of control in modern societies, and it is this body of work which is discussed in what follows. Two themes in particular have been central to critical criminological interest in social control: the overall nature of control in modern liberal-democratic societies; and the relationship between formal structures for the control of crime and other social control processes.

THE SOCIOLOGY OF DEVIANCE AND CONTROL

Positivist criminology has always been preoccupied by the idea of social control—or often, with the lack of social control. The Chicago School of the 1920s, with its depiction of 'zones of transition', high-crime city areas between the central business district and the affluent inner suburbs, focuses on lack of control because of the absence of authority figures and role models, which comes about as the 'brightest and best' of the denizens of such areas move to better areas as they establish careers and families. This is a portrayal of delinquency-generating areas deficient in family and community controls which has direct descendants in contemporary 'underclass' theory (Murray, 1984, 1996) and policy prescriptions such as J. Q. Wilson's 'broken windows' hypothesis, now adopted as the 'zero tolerance' strategies of New York, apparently coming soon to England (Wilson and Kelling, 1982).

These explanations of high-crime areas sit alongside individual and cultural theories which attribute criminal propensities to various genetic or psychological traits, or to stereotyped ideas such as the spontaneous, expressive, anti-authoritarian culture of Afro-Caribbeans (Reiner, 1994; Wilson and Herrnstein, 1985). What these 'general theories of crime' have in common is that whatever the original conditions—biological, psychological, or socio-logical—the behavioural manifestation of these underlying factors which the different positivistic theories highlight is lack of control (Gottfredson and Hirschi, 1990). This concern with lack of control is hardly surprising: as Morrison points out, the idealized image of the 'normal' citizen of modernity is that of the controlled (both self- and socially controlled) individual (Morrison, 1995). Moreover if, as is often agreed, the production of order is the central problem of society and therefore the central concern of sociology, then the study of disorder—crime—must centre round the investigation of conditions which are conducive to the absence of control, and the discovery of remedies which might re-establish control and therefore reproduce order.

Until the 1960s, criminology's interest in control started and finished with the lack of control-leads-to-crime, causal sequence, and it was only with the emergence of 'labelling theory' that this simple formula was turned on its head. It was suggested that the converse might be true, that control might lead to crime. This reversal of traditional thinking was announced boldly by Edwin Lemert:

> Older sociology tended to rest heavily upon the idea that deviance leads to social control. I have come to believe that the reverse idea, i.e., social control leads to deviance, is equally tenable and the potentially richer premise for studying deviance in modern society [Lemert, 1967: p. v].

The work of Becker, Lemert, Cicourel, and others directed criminological attention away from an original deviant act which might arise from any number of causes and circumstances, and towards the processes by which the responses of social control agents could make it more, rather than less, likely that such an act would be repeated, that the one-off deviant might develop into the hard-core delinquent. These writers concentrated on the formation of deviant identity, the processes of social labelling, restriction of non-deviant opportunities, the consequences of labelling for self-perception, that make it likely that someone will drift further into, rather than out of, delinquency (Matza, 1964). Lemert's (1967) distinction between 'primary' and 'secondary' deviancy encapsulated the insights offered by 'labelling theory' about how social control processes might actually cause, rather than restrict, further delinquency: someone who acquires a criminal record, a delinquent reputation, becomes progressively less able to obtain legal employment, non-delinquent friends, as well as becoming progressively less able to think of themselves having any identity but that of a deviant. Becker's influential work, *Outsiders* (1963), introduced the idea of *criminalization* in his work on the history of marijuana taxation and legislation: the state might 'create' criminals by making certain activities illegal, for various reasons, which will propel those who pursue these activities into criminal networks, and will make them susceptible to the process of labelling and deviant identity-creation. These ideas are, of course, still put forward in debates about the desirability or otherwise of decriminalizing cannabis, ecstasy, and similar substances today. Becker also made an important distinction between the 'secret' deviant, and the labelled deviant: the person who commits an illegal act but is not apprehended and processed through the criminal justice system will not suffer the consequences of a criminal record and reputation, indeed can choose whether or not to reveal his/her deviancy, whether to enter a deviant subculture, or can keep the deviancy separate from the rest of her/his life. On the other hand, the person who is publicly labelled as deviant, even if innocent, will be a criminal in the eyes of the world, and will be dealt with as a criminal/deviant.

Goffman's work on mental illness showed the power of those with the authority to label, and demonstrated how once a classificatory label had been attached to someone, any resistance was taken as further demonstration of their deviancy (1959, 1963). For example, insisting on one's sanity in the face of a diagnosis of mental illness is taken to reveal lack of insight into one's conditions—denial, in today's terminology; in criminal justice, insistence on one's innocence means refusal of parole, because it is taken as demonstrating lack of remorse.

These ideas generated a body of work on the activities of control agents, displacing in influence within academic criminology the search for the causes or predisposing conditions of primary deviance. The activities of social workers, police officers, psychologists, and psychiatrists were investigated, with researchers' attention focusing on topics such as the way in which offenders and patients are constructed as difficult or deviant through practices of recording exceptional incidents—constructing case records from the time someone failed to keep an appointment, confessed to a further offence, rejected advice, rather than noting that several months of regular time-keeping, refraining from offending, taking medication, co-operating in therapy, had passed (Cicourel, 1968).

Labelling approaches succeeded in turning many of the most influential criminologists into 'new deviancy theorists' (Cohen, 1981), but they were themselves incorporated into the professional toolkit of criminal justice. Policies such as cautioning rather than prosecuting young and first offenders; 'gatekeeping' policies adopted by social workers and probation officers; the development of alternative-to-custody strategies were based on the insights of labelling theory. At each successive stage of criminal processing, such policies aimed to minimize the consolidation of delinquent lifestyles which would be brought about by offenders becoming further enmeshed in the criminal justice system.

The labelling, or *social reactions*, perspective on deviancy became the dominant stream of criminology as taught in sociology departments in the 1960s and 1970s, and influenced the education and practice of a generation of criminal justice professionals. It was subject to criticism, however, in particular that this labelling criminology concentrated on the activities of front-line agents of control, and that it was not situated in any wider theory of social control. Criminology was ripe, therefore, to embrace the so-called *revisionist* histories of social control which appeared in the 1970s, histories which situated the development of modern penal and wider control systems within the broader story of the emergence of modern capitalist, liberal society.

Durkheim, in his pioneering study of the production of order and cohesion in modern industrial society, had noted that, as societies become more advanced and complex, punishments become less severe. He cited imprisonment replacing death and mutilation as the sanction for most crimes, and argued that repressive forms of law, such as criminal law, tend to diminish, with conformity being secured more and more by restorative law, law concerned with complaints between individuals rather than crimes against the state/society (Durkheim, 1984). This was seen as a progressive 'humanization' of social control, partly due to the secularization of modern society consequent upon the Enlightenment's undermining of doctrines such as the divine right of kings, and its opening up of religious doctrines to contested interpretation and influence. It was also a consequence of the requirements of interdependence between people with different life experiences brought about by the division of labour, which Durkheim characterized as the movement from mechanical to organic solidarity. Crimes, seen as offences against fellow-citizens, lost their sacrilegious quality, and penalties merely had to state moral boundaries established by secular rather than divine power, and to restore imbalances of rights between humans rather than appeasing the gods.

In the 1960s and 1970s, however, a number of works appeared which challenged this 'progressive' story of social control becoming less repressive. Punishment and social control came to be seen as culturally consistent with other social forms, as serving the needs of political-economic power, and of being more sophisticated and effective, rather than necessarily more benign. The new histories of punishment began with Durkheim's observation of the rise in the use of imprisonment as punishment with modernization, but in answering the question 'why prison', they produced characterizations, not just of punishment, but of strategies of social control of which prison, and punishments generally, were just a part.

Pre-eminent amongst these new historians of punishment and control were Melossi and Pavarini (1981) and Foucault (1977). In their book *The Prison and the Factory*, Melossi and Pavarini started from the claim made earlier by

Rusche and Kirchheimer (1968), that in times of shortage—and therefore high value—of labour, punishments become more lenient, whereas in times of excess—and therefore low value—of labour, punishments become harsher and less constructive. Punishment is thus seen as a mechanism for regulation of the labour supply. This 'labour market' theory of punishment has been tested and adopted by other criminologists, notably Box and Hale (1982) and Jankovic (1977). They have used unemployment as their measure of over-supply of labour and imprisonment as their measure of penal severity, finding an association between high unemployment and rising use of imprisonment. (Of course the time period covered by Rusche and Kirchheimer, and Melossi and Pavarini, takes imprisonment as a measure of penal leniency, in place of death and mutilation, whereas more recently imprisonment is seen as severe in contrast to probation, community service, and other non-custodial penalties.) The general point is the same, however, that in times of labour shortage, more use will be made of sanctions which enable the criminal to return to, or join, the labour force, whereas in times of excess supply of labour, penalties will be such as to remove the offender from the labour market, for ever or for long periods. Penalties in times of high unemployment thus become not only more severe, but also less constructive, with more emphasis on simple containment, and less on education, training, and therapy. Although this simple link between labour markets and punishment has been contested, this work marked a decisive shift towards studying social control within an analytic framework of political economy.

Melossi and Pavarini extended the simple labour market hypothesis to argue that the essential link between the prison and the factory, the penal system and the work system, was *discipline*: the prison and the factory are disciplinary polarities, depending on discipline of time, place, and function. The factory depends on contractual discipline, whereas the prison inflicts coerced discipline; the factory utilizes the disciplined citizen, the prison produces the disciplined citizen: '[f]inally: "for the worker the factory is like a prison" (loss of liberty and subordination); "for the inmate the prison is like a factory" (work and discipline)' (Melossi and Pavarini, 1981: 188).

Foucault in *Discipline and Punish* also sees discipline as the fundamental principle of modern punishments. He opens the work by contrasting a public torture and execution in 1757, with a timetable and rules for a 'house for the reform of young prisoners', eighty years later. The first punishment is aimed primarily at demonstrating the absolute power of the sovereign over his subjects; the second demonstrates a new kind of 'governance', which utilizes sovereign power, new social science (including criminology), and techniques of observation and regulation to produce the docile, productive body needed by capitalist industrialism. Foucault's analysis of punishment is part of a wider analysis of power in modern society.

For Foucault and for Melossi and Pavarini, discipline is both object and mechanism of punishment; it is first and foremost a technology of power. Whilst Melossi and Pavarini see forms of punishment as reflective of other

social relations, Foucault sees the principles that he identifies as being characteristic of modern imprisonment, as being the principles of all social control.
Discipline, surveillance, the gaze of the expert and the administrator, are principles which he discovers in the *panopticon* prison of Jeremy Bentham, where
prisoners are kept in conditions of constant surveillance and constant purposive
and penitent activity. Bentham's design for the panopticon prison proposed a
central control circle, from which the guard could watch the prisoners on the
wings which radiated from it. Prisoners could not see the central circle, so
could never know at any particular moment whether they were being watched;
in order to escape further punishment for infraction of prison regulations they
would, therefore, assume that they were being watched, and would behave
properly at all times.

Discipline, in Foucault's account, thus becomes *dispersed*: from king to
government to official; from official to lower functionary. It also becomes
dispersed geographically: from the royal tower to the prison, to the local
prison, to the local probation centre or social work office. Punishment is
dispersed from the centre to what Foucault describes as 'tiny theatres of
punishment' dispersed throughout the realm; discipline is dispersed to the
extent that the boundaries between repressive discipline, informal discipline
(socialization), and self-discipline (internalization) dissolve.

These new theorists of punishment also incorporated other aspects of the
sociology of modernization, especially those which stressed the growth of
the power and functions of the state, and Weber's account of the progression
of bureaucratic-rationalization (Spitzer, 1983). Whilst they may differ in
emphasis, these revisionist accounts of the development of modern strategies
of control share many of the same concerns and assumptions:

scepticism about the professed aims, beliefs and intentions of the reformers; concern
with the analysis of power and its effects; curiosity about the relationships between
intentions and consequences; determination to locate the reform enterprise in the social,
economic and political contexts of the period. The problem of maintaining the
social order—in the case of crime, so obvious; in the case of mental illness less so, but
still traceable . . . becomes dominant [Cohen and Scull, 1983: 2].

Fuller, critical accounts of these social histories of control can be found in
Garland (1990), Howe (1994), and Hudson (1996), and space does not permit
more substantial discussion here. What is important for the relationship
between criminology and the wider sociology of social control is that these
histories of control established that modes of punishment reflected economic
relations; that they utilized the available knowledges and technologies of their
time; that there were continuities between the punishment of crime and the
control of other deviant populations. Punishment and other social control
processes were, on these accounts, part of the apparatus of a governance aimed
at producing a geographically stable, docile, workforce imbued with the
capitalist work ethic. They were conducted according to the rule-following
parameters of bureaucratic rationality, where power inheres in the office, not

the person; where the power attaching to any office, including the highest, is limited; where power is exercised for purposes and by means accorded legitimacy by the population.

That there are links between punishment and other modes of control is common ground between control theorists. Control of deviant populations such as the elderly, the mentally ill and handicapped, sufferers from contagious diseases, youthful delinquents, and adult criminals uses the same techniques and principles: diagnosis, labelling, segregation. Concepts such as *less eligibility* (Rusche, 1978; Melossi, 1985)—the idea that conditions inside an institution should be worse than anything the potential inmate is likely to encounter on the outside—were used to explain aspects of regimes in both prison and work-houses. Less eligibility is proposed as a deterrent to both crime and idleness, and acts as a limit to prison reform; it is also evident, for example, in current policy limiting housing benefit for the unemployed to the cost of a bed-sitting room or room in a shared house, not allowing for rent or mortgage payments for a whole house or flat.

Foucault described this continuum of productive and repressive control as *normalization.* He shows how, in medicine, in psychiatry, in sexuality, in criminality, knowledge and the procedures of control in which knowledge plays its part produce dichotomies of normality and deviance: the healthy and the sick, the sane and the insane, the pure and the perverted, the law-abiding and the criminal. These dichotomies then become characteristics of the rough and the respectable, the dangerous and the emperilled, the rational citizen and the irrational outsider, and the task modernity sets itself is to make the entire populace approximate to the standards of normality. Normalization will never be complete, which is why a crucial subdivision among the deviant is between the curable and the incurable, the corrigible and the incorrigible. Much of criminology, and the policies and practices of criminal justice and punishment, are concerned with this division: classification, leading to rehabilitation of the corrigible, lengthy, or permanent exclusion of the incorrigible.

Labelling theory, then, connected the study of crime with wider fields of deviance; 'revisionist penology' connected punishment with wider fields of control. What both achieved was a challenging of the idea that crime/deviance brings about punishment/control. Just as Lemert and his colleagues pointed to a link between control and further deviance, Foucault and the other control theorists pointed to a link between imprisonment and further offending: recidivism is for the sociology of punishment what secondary deviance is for the sociology of deviance. Commenting on the failure of the prison to reform offenders, Foucault suggests:

perhaps one should reverse the problem and ask oneself what is served by the failure of the prison; what is the use of these different phenomena that are continually being criticized; the maintenance of delinquency; the encouragement of recidivism, the trans-formation of the occasional offender into a habitual delinquent, the organization of a closed milieu of delinquency. . . . Penality would then appear to be a way of handling illegalities, of laying down the limits of tolerance, of giving free rein to some, of putting pressure on others, of excluding a particular section, of making another useful, of neutralizing certain individuals and of profiting from others. In short, penality does not simply 'check' illegalities; it differentiates them, it provides them with a general economy [Foucault, 1977: 262].

FROM THE PRISON TO THE COMMUNITY (AND BACK AGAIN): DECARCERATION, DEINSTITUTIONALIZATION, AND TRANSCARCERATION

Durkheim, Rusche, and Kirchheimer, Melossi and Pavarini, and Foucault were writing about the rise of imprisonment. They took as their subject the transformation of control from torture and execution to imprisonment; from the whim of individuals to the performance of scheduled procedures by state officials; from exclusion by death or banishment to inclusion through reform and rehabilitation. What was common to the control of different dimensions of deviance in the period of rapid industrialization in the late eighteenth and nineteenth centuries was the building of institutions to segregate and then to socialize recruits to the labour force and to isolate or normalize the deviant: schools, workhouses, and asylums were institutions which had much in common, both architecturally and socially, with prisons.

The period in which these works appeared and became influential in criminology, however, was a period in which the institutional response to deviance was subject to sustained critique, and during which total institutions appeared to be becoming less central to social control. Mental hospitals, for example, had begun to close following the 1959 Mental Health Act in England and Wales; the 1969 Children and Young Persons Act introduced supervision orders for young people, which was meant to lead to fewer young people being committed to children's homes for either delinquency or welfare reasons; community service and suspended sentences were introduced as alternatives to custody for offenders, and the use of probation was extended.

Three of the key writers on control in the era of decarceration are David Greenberg (1975, 1977), Andrew Scull (1977, 1983), and Stanley Cohen (1979, 1985). These authors have produced critiques of the move away from institutional corrections to community corrections that have used many of the ideas and theoretical perspectives of the historians of the prison-building era.

During the 1960s and early 1970s, community corrections such as work with adolescents designed to prevent the onset of delinquency (alternative schooling; neighbourhood projects in high-delinquency areas; placement of 'at risk' youngsters on social work caseloads; removal of children of single-parent, or supposedly inadequate, parents to children's homes; treatment of 'hyperactive' children with drugs and/or counselling, in much the same way that children are being diagnosed as having Attention Defecit Disorder and prescribed ritalin today) proliferated to general approval. Similarly, in the field of mental illness, it was taken as axiomatic that treatment in the community was preferable to treatment in hospital. To proponents of such policies, community corrections and treatments were regarded as incontrovertibly both more humane and more effective than institutional measures.

In a pioneering paper, David Greenberg (1975) challenged some of the assumptions behind community corrections, saying that they were not necessarily more humane, more effective, or less costly than institutional sanctions. Andrew Scull (1977) extended a similar analysis to the treatment of the mentally ill. Greenberg's amd Scull's thesis was that community treatment often amounted to malign neglect, with people left to fend for themselves, unsupported or inadequately supported in a rejecting, uncaring environment; receiving patchy, untested treatment/corrections; and that the move from the institution to the community might represent cost savings for the central state, which paid the costs of care in institutions, but represented additional costs to local authorities or voluntary agencies, who paid for community corrections and care. Only if central state institutions were closed down, and income transferred from central to local government, might there be cost savings. There was usually, it was pointed out, a trade-off between humanity, effectiveness, and cheapness: the provision of benign, effective community control and care is expensive.

Greenberg and Scull wrote in Marxist terms, restating the link between forms of control and the imperatives of the economy. They identified an apparent 'decarceration era' of the 1970s. What had occurred, they argued, was that the expanding demand for labour of the prosperous 1960s, which had encouraged the spread of rehabilitative sanctions designed to fit offenders and other deviants for the labour market, had encountered the fiscal crisis of the 1970s, triggered off by rises in world oil prices. As states were trying to rein back their public expenditure, recession led to mounting unemployment, so that the imperative of reducing money spent on deviant populations became stronger than the need to fit as many people as possible for the labour force.

A paradox of the decarceration period was that although there appeared to be a reduction in the incarceration of deviants, more and more people were being brought into the social control net. The paradox may have been more apparent than real: although the case for decarceration is supported by statistics for declining numbers of mentally ill patients institutionalized in hospitals at least in the USA and UK, evidence was much more equivocal in the case of incarceration of the criminal and delinquent (Hudson, 1984; Matthews, 1979; Scull, 1977). This apparent paradox has been explored most comprehensively by Cohen (1977, 1979, 1985), who demonstrated that the extension of community corrections seemed to fit Foucault's model of 'dispersed discipline'. Foucault had argued that the objective of the disciplinary control strategy that he depicted was:

to make of the punishment and repression of illegalities a regular function, coextensive with society; not to punish less, but to punish better; to punish with an attenuated severity perhaps, but in order to punish with more universality and necessity; to insert the power to punish more deeply into the social body [Foucault, 1977: 82].

Cohen documented the increasing number of people cautioned and convicted; he chronicled the strengthening of supervisory punishments; he observed the recruitment of friends, relatives, and neighbours into surveillance, the development of contracts and curfews. Phrases such as net-widening (more people subject to control); net-strengthening (sanctions such as probation and social work supervision having added requirements); blurring of the boundaries (between liberty and confinement, friend and controller) became part of the academic discourse of criminologists and the professional discourse of criminal justice practitioners. Prison came to be seen not just as a building but as a principle, the coercion of time and space (Hudson, 1984); a principle of disciplinary surveillance which could be most fully realized in the prison and the asylum, but which was present to varying degrees in most of the innovations of contemporary control. The probation office, the day hospital, the attendance centre, the clinic, are all places where offenders or patients are required to be for certain periods of time, and where they are assessed and observed.

Cohen also incorporated the ideas of the social historians of the rise of imprisonment that new strategies of control could not simply be interpreted as the putting into practice of humanitarian reforms. His (1985) analysis of the development of strengthened and widened control networks incorporated Rothman's (1980) idea that when the conscience of reformers met the convenience of administrators, convenience was usually the winner; that good intentions often had bad unintended consequences; that whatever appeared to be taking place by way of loosening and thinning the networks, the 'deeper structures' of control meant that whatever might seem to be happening in the direction of greater tolerance of diversity, normalization through the established mixture of socialization and repression would continue.

By the late 1980s, decarceration of the criminal seemed to be going into reverse, whilst deinstitutionalization of the mentally ill and of other 'problem populations' is still proceeding (children's homes and homes for the elderly continue to close, for example). Reformers and workers in the so-called caring professions, the very people who had been in the forefront of calls for the shift from institutional to community care in the 1950s and 1960s, began to complain of lack of institutional accommodation. Instead of following the same trajectories as the meta-analyses of control such as those of Cohen and Foucault had anticipated, the control of crime and of other forms of deviance seemed to be reversals of each other. In the case of crime and delinquency, the criticism of reformers and others today is that the mechanisms of community control have proliferated whilst the number of prisons and young offender institutions has also expanded; in the case of the mentally disordered, the criticism is that hospitals and asylums have closed, but have not been replaced by community care facilities (Hudson, 1993). Scull, in the first (1977) edition of his book *Decarceration* had expected the deinstitutionalizing trends of the care and control of mental illness to be followed by similar trends in the response to crime and delinquency; by the time of his revised edition (1984), he saw that this was not the case, that the response to these two forms of deviancy was diverging rather than converging.

Exploration of these different control trends, amounting to major revision of the decarceration thesis, is provided in a volume of essays which claims that what has been, and is, happening is not *de*carceration, but *trans*carceration (Lowman, Menzies, and Palys, 1987). Rather than moving from institutions to the community, the authors argue, people are experiencing an institutionally mobile deviant career. They are moving between jails/local prisons, half-way houses, sheltered accommodation, and in some cases on to federal penitentiaries/ dispersal prisons and/or to large state mental hospitals. Whether they are in an institution within the penal system or within the health/welfare system can vary not with their actual behaviour, but according to the exigencies of funding, to the relative strength and weakness of these sub-systems, and to ideological circumstances which render behaviour likely to be labelled as ill or criminal. Chapters in the collection thus comment on the 'criminalization' of mental illness and homelessness, as well as on the substitution of penal policy for social policy which has occurred in recent years (see also Hudson, 1993, chapter 3). Examples of shifts between penal and medical/welfare constructions of deviant behaviour in recent years include, importantly, the moves between responding to drug addiction as sickness, needing treatment and harm-reduction responses, or as crime, needing punitive responses. Much of the recent increase in prison populations in the USA is attributed to the 'war on drugs', a development which has particularly penalized black Americans (Tonry, 1995); similar policy shifts are taking place in England and Wales.

Understanding of changes in the balance between repressive and rehabilitative, coercive and socializing, exclusive and inclusive modes of control has been enhanced by the work of Stuart Hall (1980), Phil Scraton (1987), and others who have analysed the 'legitimation crisis' brought about by economic recession. If conformity cannot be secured by offering rewards to all or most of those who lead a law-abiding, orderly, and industrious life, then it must be obtained—and dissent and disorder discouraged—by increased repression. For this to be accepted by the majority of the population as legitimate, blame must be seen to be due to the deviants, rather than to the socio-economic system itself. The result of this has been described as 'authoritarian populism', whereby people who either fail to be economically successful by legitimate means, or who challenge the system, are constituted as 'suitable enemies' (Christie, 1986), worthy only of punishment and exclusion. Criminals, the homeless, strikers, refugees, and the unemployed are seen as forming an unemployable, crime-prone and crime-tolerant, feckless and dangerous underclass, from whom the respectable must be protected both economically and physically, as they walk the streets. Thus, even in times of economic hardship, increasing expenditure on punishment and other forms of repressive control is justified and even demanded.

WOMEN AND SOCIAL CONTROL

These histories and sociologies of control discussed above largely ignored the control of women. They are formulated in class terms—control of the working-class and the underclass or lumpenproletariat by the bourgeoisie or elite; in terms of power—control of the powerless by the powerful, but little, if any, attention is paid to gender. During the 1970s and 1980s, however, studies of the control of women have appeared which, had they been taken into account, would have greatly enriched the understanding of social control (Hudson, 1996).

Adrian Howe (1994), in her critique of the neglect of women by sociologists of punishment and control, says that most of the labour market studies have not considered the relationship between females, use of imprisonment, and economic recession. One of the few that has, she reports, finds that women's imprisonment, unlike that of men, declines during periods of economic recession. Howe suggests that this is because women's importance for keeping families together, and men under control, is more crucial than ever in times of economic hardship. This idea is consistent with findings that lenient treatment of women correlates with their presenting themselves as conventional women: good mothers (Farrington and Morris, 1983; Eaton, 1986). Howe's suggestion is also consistent with the widespread finding that the control of women is such as to uphold conventional gender and familial roles, as much as to penalize and control criminality (Carlen, 1983; Edwards, 1984).

Foucault's hypothesis of the disciplinary nature of control, and Cohen's refinement of the idea of the dispersal of discipline, have been challenged by, for example, Bottoms (1983), who argues that since the most common penalty for crime is the fine, it cannot be held that disciplinary forms are the most pervasive. Foucault's example of the disciplinary regime is taken from an institution for juveniles; many of Cohen's examples are also drawn from programmes for dealing with young offenders. Studies of the control of women also show the extensive use of normalizing strategies; for example Carlen's (1983, 1985) studies of women prisoners, Worrall's account (1990) of discursive constructions of female offending, show the operation of stereotypes of conventionality and techniques of normalization. The analysis developed by Foucault and Cohen would thus have been much enhanced, allowing for a more nuanced view of the limits and applications of disciplinary control, if its variable application to women and men had been considered (Hudson, 1996).

The control of women also illuminates the transcarceration thesis, as studies show the continuum of regulation of their lives through the penal system, the health/welfare system and informal social controls (Cain, 1989; Hutter and

Williams, 1981; Smart, 1995). Women are more readily assigned to the psychiatric realm than are men (Allen, 1987), whilst men—especially poor, black men—are more vulnerable to penalization without help or treatment (Carlen, 1993). Zedner (1991) has shown women 'disappearing' from criminal processes in the Victorian era—in the midst of the 'great incarceration'—to become the client group of the burgeoning social work and psychiatric professions. On the other hand in the 1990s, another period of increased incarceration, women's imprisonment is rising as fast as, and sometimes proportionately faster than, men's: these different trends need to be investigated if the dynamics of social control are to be properly analysed.

The importance of considering women alongside men in the sociology of control, is that it prompts understanding that gender, as well as class, is one of the principles underlying the distribution of power in society (MacKinnon, 1991). Exactly the same could be said of race: patterns of criminalization and penalization, studies of psychiatric labelling and participation in welfare programmes (Cook and Hudson, 1993), show that race, too, is a fundamental fissure around which power and control are deployed.

POST-SOCIAL CONTROL

From the mid-1980s onwards, criminology seemed to have retreated from concern with wider fields of deviancy and control, and once again to be focusing more exclusively on crime and punishment. The emergence of the 'left realist' paradigm, associated in England with the work of Jock Young (1986, 1987, 1988) and his colleagues and in America with the work of Elliott Currie and others (1985), is illustrative of this reconcentration in relation to the separation of crime from deviancy; Garland (1990) has produced a powerful analysis of punishment which, whilst paying appropriate regard to the wider context of control, foregrounds punishment as a discrete social institution. Whilst those who urged the restriction of the field to crime and punishment produced strong critiques of the control theorists, it can be held that the insights of feminist criminologists, especially, mean that crime and punishment cannot be understood without *transgressing* criminology into wider fields (Cain, 1989). Similarly, writers who are raising questions about the criminalization of the kinds of drugs taken most commonly by minority ethnic groups and the much more restrained campaign against other drugs (Tonry, 1985), as well as people who are investigating the expansion of penal policy to fill the void left by restriction of economic and social policy (Hall, 1980; Gamble, 1988) must look beyond the parameters of realist criminology (Hudson, 1993).

Social control is re-emerging as an important problem, not only because of these analytic requirements, but because of the appearance of new modes of control, which appear to dissolve some of the distinctions between coercive and non-coercive, penal and social, control. Closed-circuit television in city

centres; security patrols in shopping malls; strengthened asylum and immigration policies; expansion of electronic data collections, catch in the control
net the innocent as well as the guilty, and operate on distinctions such as
member/non-member, resident/non-resident, creditworthy or non creditworthy,
as much as on criminal/non-criminal. In the venues of late-twentieth century
England and America, the dress-code is as important as the criminal code
(Shearing and Stenning, 1985).

Much of the emerging analysis of these new modes of control is utilizing the
Foucauldian framework to ask whether the ubiquitousness of the electronic
eye denotes the arrival of the *panopticon society*, where social control is everywhere, and becomes so pervasive that the distinction between external control
and self-control disappears (Lyon, 1994; Poster, 1990). It would appear that
these developments signify further progress in the dispersal of discipline, but
that the essential project of the technologies of power identified by Foucault—
that of normalization—has been abandoned. The objective of the new strategies
of control is identification of the different and the dangerous in order to
exclude: from the club, from the apartment building, from the estate, from the
shopping mall, from the country.

These new control strategies have been described as forming an 'actuarial
regime', by Jonathan Simon. Changing people, which is difficult and expensive,
he says has been abandoned in favour of the simpler task of restricting people's
possibilities of movement and action, through exclusion from general and
particular locations and from opportunities to obtain goods and services, and
through their exclusion from participation in various activities:

Disciplinary practices focus on the distribution of behavior within a limited population.
. . . This distribution is around a norm, and power operates with the goal of closing
the gap, narrowing the deviation, and moving subjects towards uniformity. . . .
Actuarial practices seek instead to maximise the efficiency of the population as it
stands. Rather than seeking to change people ('normalize them', in Foucault's apt
phrase) an actuarial regime seeks to manage them in place [Simon, 1988: 773].

Actuarial techniques are most readily associated with the calculation of
insurance premiums, and it is claimed that new processes designed to control
risk—of crime, of accidents—are based on insurance principles. Insurance is
something that individuals take out individually, pooling risk with similarly
situated others, and the insurantial approach to crime is based on the principle
of *private prudentialism* (O'Malley, 1992), rather than on state strategies of
normalization.

Most of the new forms of control are operated by and on behalf of private
individuals and institutions, individually and in co-operation: cars, shops,
clubs, buildings, neighbourhoods. Terms like *state* and *social* have come to be
replaced by *individual* and *community* (Stenson, 1995). Following up arguments
made by Nikolas Rose (1996) and others about 'the death of the social',
O'Malley has argued that much control is now devolved to community groupings with shifting and overlapping membership, made up of individuals not

necessarily oriented to an ideal of community or society, but recognizing common interests for limited purposes (O'Malley, 1996).

This *post-social control*, based on individuals taking responsibility for their own safety (Garland, 1996) necessitates a rethinking of the concept and field of social control. The problematics of *the social* become at least as important as the problematics of *control* (Sumner, 1997). If 'social control' as it has been understood by criminology represents a fusion of European ideas of the state and the role of government, with American ideas of mass socialization in democratic societies (Melossi, 1990), then the various elements of the concept need to be substantially redefined.

New analyses of control in late modernity will need to reconsider the nature and function of the state, the community, and the individual, as well as the relationships between them (Garland, 1995, 1996; Lacey and Zedner, 1995; O'Malley, 1992; 1996). They will also need to decide whether or not the analytic frameworks developed to understand the nature of control in earlier stages of modernization are appropriate to investigations of control in late- or post-modernity. The evidence is that critical criminology's engagement with social control is meeting these new challenges: recent volumes such as those edited by Blomberg and Cohen (1995), Bergalli and Sumner (1997), and Nelken (1994) demonstrate the continuing vitality, richness, and importance of the study of social control.

Selected Further Reading

R. Bergalli and C. Sumner, eds., *Social Control and Political Order*, London: Sage, 1997.

D. Melossi, *The State of Social Control*, Cambridge: Polity Press, 1990.

These two books contain good accounts of the origins of the term 'social control' in American sociology, and the conflation of this American tradition which focuses on informal control, with the European tradition of political philosophy with its concentration on state power. Both books are concerned to reformulate the study of control to a field more appropriate to the contemporary era when governance is being dispersed from the state to the individual and the community.

T. G. Blomberg and S. Cohen, eds., *Punishment and Social Control: Essays in Honor of Sheldon L. Messinger*, New York: Aldine de Gruyter, 1995.

This volume also contains a range of essays reflecting the established concerns of social control theory. The essays by Jonathan Simon and Malcolm Feeley, Pat Carlen, and David Garland are particularly relevant to the issues of control in the post-modern era.

S. Cohen and A. Scull, eds., *Social Control and the State*, Oxford: Martin Robertson, 1983.

M. Foucault, *Discipline and Punish: the Birth of the Prison*, London: Allen Lane, 1977.

D. Melossi and M. Pavarini, *The Prison and the Factory: Origins of the Penitentiary System*, Basingstoke: Macmillan, 1981.

These are amongst the most important books of the 'revisionist' and 'political economy' body of literature on social control. Together they build the account of the links between capitalism and social control, the emergence of 'disciplinary' control and the spread of the control network, discussed in the chapter above.

S. Cohen, *Visions of Social Control: Crime, Punishment and Classification*, Cambridge: Polity Press, 1985.

J. Lowman, R. J. Menzies and T. S. Palys, eds., *Transcarceration: Essays in the Sociology of Social Control*, Aldershot: Gower, 1987.

A. Scull, *Decarceration: Community Treatment and the Deviant—A Radical View*, Englewood-Cliffs, NJ: Prentice-Hall, 1977 (revised edition 1984).

These books adopt fundamentally the same perspective as the books in the section above, but bring the insights of the 'revisionist' histories of social control to bear on developments in the mid-twentieth century. Cohen's analysis draws mainly on the ideas of Foucault; Scull's work is closer to the Marxist tradition of linking shifts in control to economic cycles.

D. Garland, *Punishment and Modern Society*, Oxford: Oxford University Press, 1990.

A. Howe, *Punish and Critique: Towards a Feminist Analysis of Penality*, London: Routledge, 1994.

B. A. Hudson, *Understanding Justice: An Introduction to Ideas, Perspectives and Controversies in Modern Penal Theory*, Buckingham: Open University Press, 1996, part two.

These three books provide full and critical accounts of the work on social control by Durkheim, Foucault, and Melossi and Pavarini. Garland argues for the necessity of incorporating the insights of Durkheim, Weber, and the political economy of writers such as Melossi and Pavarini alongside those of Foucault to provide a full account of punishment. He develops a strong synthesis of these different perspectives to demonstrate punishment as an expression of culture. Howe and Hudson both criticize the work of Foucault, Melossi and Pavarini, and the other 'revisionist historians' for their neglect of the social control of women. Howe pays particular attention to work on the control of women which has adopted a Foucauldian perspective; Hudson introduces feminist challenges to Marxist theory, and discusses feminist jurisprudence.

M. Cain, ed., *Growing Up Good: Policing the Behaviour of Girls in Europe*, London: Sage, 1989.

P. Carlen, *Women's Imprisonment: A Study in Social Control*, London: Routledge and Kegan Paul, 1983.

C. Smart, *Law, Crime and Sexuality: Essays in Feminism*, London: Sage, 1995.

These three books between them encompass most of the issues that have arisen in the study of the control of women. All are concerned with the control of women through constructions of feminity; through power imbalances between women and men; through issues of sexuality and motherhood. Cain's volume contains much on the control of young women; Carlen shows the circumstances and pressures that lead women to criminality, and the regimes they confront once they are imprisoned. Smart's collection of essays explores the control of women through civil as well as criminal law; discusses feminist constructions of masculinity; and engages with the challenges of postmodernism for the analysis of women and social control.

D. Garland, 'The Limits of the Sovereign State: Strategies of Crime Control in Contemporary Society', *British Journal of Criminology* (1996), 36, 4: 445–71.

D. Nelken, ed., *The Futures of Criminology*, London: Sage, 1994.

Along with the articles in the volume by *Blomberg and Cohen*, mentioned above, these works outline some of the most important issues and concepts emerging in the study of social control in the contemporary era, described by some as post-modern and by others, including Garland, as late-modern.

REFERENCES

ALLEN, H. (1987), *Justice Unbalanced: Gender, Psychiatry and Judicial Decisions*. Milton Keynes: Open University Press.

BECKER, H. (1963), *Outsiders: Studies in the Sociology of Deviance*. New York: Free Press.

BERGALLI, R., and SUMNER, C. (1997), eds., *Social Control and Political Order*. London: Sage.

BLOMBERG, T. G., and COHEN, C. (1995), eds., *Punishment and Social Control: Essays in Honor of Sheldon L. Messinger*. New York: Aldine de Gruyter.

BOTTOMS, A. (1983), 'Neglected Features of Contemporary Penal Systems', in D. Garland and P. Young, eds., *The Power to Punish*. London: Heinemann.

BOX, S., and HALE, C. (1982), 'Economic Crisis and the Rising Prisoner Population', *Crime and Social Justice*, 17: 20–35.

CAIN, M. (1989), ed., *Growing Up Good: Policing the Behaviour of Girls in Europe*. London: Sage.

CARLEN, P. (1983), *Women's Imprisonment: A Study in Social Control*. London: Routledge and Kegan Paul.

—— (1985), ed., *Criminal Women*. Cambridge: Polity Press.

—— (1993), 'Gender, Class, Racism and Criminal Justice', in G. Bridges and M. Myers, eds., *Inequality, Crime and Social Control*. Toronto: Westview.

CHRISTIE, N. (1986), 'Suitable enemies', in H. Bianchi and R. Van Swaaningen, eds., *Abolitionism: Towards a Non-Repressive Approach to Crime*. Amsterdam: Free University Press.

CHUNN, D. E., and GAVIGNAN, S. A. M. (1988), 'Social Control: Analytical Tool or Analytical

Quagmire', *Contemporary Crises*, 12, 2: 107–24.

CICOUREL, A. (1968), *The Social Organization of Juvenile Justice*. New York: Wiley.

COHEN, S. (1977), 'Prisons and the Future of Control Systems', in M. Fitzgerald *et al.*, eds., *Welfare in Action*. London: Routledge and Kegan Paul.

—— (1979), 'The Punitive City: Notes on the Dispersal of Social Control', *Contemporary Crises*, 3: 83–93.

—— (1981), 'Footprints in the Sand: A Further Report on Criminology and the Sociology of Deviance in Britain', in M. Fitzgerald, G. McLennan, and J. Pawson, eds., *Crime and Society: Readings in History and Theory*. London: Routledge and Kegan Paul.

—— (1985), *Visions of Social Control: Crime, Punishment and Classification*. Cambridge: Polity Press.

—— (1988), 'Criminology', in S. Cohen *Against Criminology*. New Brunswick, NJ: Transaction books.

—— and SCULL, A. (1983), eds., *Social Control and the State*. Oxford: Martin Robertson.

COOK, D., and HUDSON, B. (1993), eds., *Racism and Criminology*. London: Sage.

COSER, L. (1982), 'The Notion of Control in Sociological Theory', in Jack P. Gibbs, ed., *Social Control: Views from the Social Sciences*. Beverly Hills, Cal.: Sage.

CURRIE, E. (1985), *Confronting Crime: An American Challenge*. New York: Basic Books.

DURKHEIM, E. (1984), 'Two Laws of Penal Evolution', in S. Lukes and A. Scull, eds., *Durkheim and the Law*. Oxford: Basil Blackwell.

EATON, M. (1986), *Justice for Women? Family, Court and Social Control*. Milton Keynes: Open University Press.

EDWARDS, S. (1984), *Women on Trial*. Manchester: Manchester University Press.

FARRINGTON, D., and MORRIS, A. (1983), 'Sex, sentencing and reconviction', *British Journal of Criminology*, 23, 3: 229–48.

FOUCAULT, M. (1977), *Discipline and Punish: The Birth of the Prison*. London: Allen Lane.

GAMBLE, A. (1988), *The Free Economy and the Strong State: the Politics of Thatcherism*. Basingstoke: Macmillan.

GARLAND, D. (1985), *Punishment and Welfare: A History of Penal Strategies*. London: Gower.

—— (1988), 'British Criminology before 1935', *British Journal of Criminology*, 28, 2: 131–47.

—— (1990), *Punishment and Modern Society*. Oxford: Oxford University Press.

—— (1995), 'Penal Modernism and Postmodernism', in T. Blomberg and S. Cohen, eds., *Punishment and Social Control: Essays in Honor of Sheldon L. Messinger*. New York; Aldine de Gruyter.

—— (1996), 'The Limits of the Sovereign State: Strategies of Crime Control in Contemporary Society', *British Journal of Criminology*, 36, 4: 445–71.

GOFFMAN, E. (1959), 'The Moral Career of a Mental Patient', *Psychiatry*, 22: 2.

—— (1963), *Stigma*. Englewood Cliffs, NJ: Prentice-Hall.

GOTTFREDSON, D., and HIRSCHI, T. (1990), *A General Theory of Crime*. Stanford, Ca.: Stanford University Press.

GREENBERG, D. (1975), 'Problems in Community Corrections', *Issues in Criminology*, 19: 1–34.

—— (1977), ed., *Corrections and Punishment*. Beverly Hills: Sage.

HALL, S. (1980), *The Drift to a Law and Order Society*. London: Cobden Trust.

HOWE, A. (1994), *Punish and Critique: Towards a Feminist Analysis of Penality*. London: Routledge.

HUDSON, B. A. (1984), 'The Rising Use of Imprisonment: The Impact of "Decarceration" policies', *Critical Social Policy*, 11: 46–59.

—— (1993), *Penal Policy and Social Justice*. Basingstoke: Macmillan.

—— (1996), *Understanding Justice: An Introduction to Ideas, Perspectives and Controversies in Modern Penal Theory*. Buckingham: Open University Press.

HUTTER, B., and WILLIAMS, G. (1981), eds., *Controlling Women: The Normal and the Deviant*. London: Croom Helm.

JANKOVIC, I. (1977), 'Labour Market and Imprisonment', *Crime and Social Justice*, 8: 17–31.

LACEY, N., and ZEDNER, L. (1995), 'Locating the Appeal to Community in Contemporary Criminal Justice', *Journal of Law and Society*, 22, 3: 301–25.

LEMERT, E. (1967), *Human Deviance, Social Problems and Social Control*. Englewood Cliffs, NJ: Prentice-Hall.

LOWMAN, J., MENZIES, R. J., and PALYS, T. S. (1987), eds., *Transcarceration: Essays in the Sociology of Social Control*. Aldershot: Gower.

LYON, D. (1994), *The Electronic Eye: The Rise of the Surveillance Society*. Cambridge: Polity Press.

MACKINNON, C. A. (1989), *Toward a Feminist Theory of the State*. Cambridge, Mass.: Harvard University Press.

MATTHEWS, R. (1979), ' 'Decarceration' and the Fiscal Crisis', in B. Fine, R. Kinsey, J. Lea, S. Picciotto, and J. Young, eds., *Capitalism and the Rule of Law*. London: Hutchinson.

MATZA, D. (1964), *Delinquency and Drift*. New York: John Wiley.

MELOSSI, D. (1985), 'Punishment and Social Action: Changing Vocabularies of Motive within a Political Business Cycle', *Current Perspectives in Social Theory*, 6: 169–97.

—— (1990), *The State of Social Control*. Cambridge: Polity Press.

—— and PAVARINI, M. (1981), *The Prison and the Factory: Origins of the Penitentiary System*. Basingstoke: Macmillan.

MORRISON, W. (1995), *Theoretical Criminology: From Modernity to Postmodernism*. London: Cavendish Publishing.

MURRAY, C. (1984), *Losing Ground*, New York: Basic Books.

—— (1996), 'The Underclass' in J. Muncie, E. McLaughlin, and M. Langan, eds., *Criminological Perspectives: A Reader*. London: Sage/Open University Press.

NELKEN, D. (1994), ed., *The Futures of Criminology*. London: Sage.

O'MALLEY, P. (1992), 'Risk, Power and Crime Prevention', *Economy and Society*, 21: 252–75.

—— (1996), 'Post-Social Criminologies: Some Implications of Current Political Trends for Criminological Theory and Practice', *Current Issues in Criminal Justice*, 8: 26–38.

PASQUINO, E. B. (1991), 'Criminology: The Birth of a Special Knowlegde', in G. Burchell, C. Gordon and P. Miller, eds., *The Foucault Effect: Studies in Governmentality*. Chicago: University of Chicago Press.

POSTER, M. (1990), *The Mode of Information*. Cambridge: Polity Press.

REINER, R. (1993), 'Race, Crime and Justice: Models of Interpretation', in L. Gelsthorpe, ed., *Minority Ethnic Groups in the Criminal Justice System*. Cambridge: Institute of Criminology.

ROSE, N. (1996), 'The Death of the Social? Refiguring the Territory of Government', *Economy and Society*, 25, 3: 327–56.

ROTHMAN, D. (1980), *Conscience and Convenience: the Asylum and its Alternatives in Progressive America*. Boston: Little Brown.

RUSCHE, G. (1978), 'Labour Market and Penal Sanction: Thoughts on the Sociology of Punishment', *Crime and Social Justice*, 10: 2–8.

—— and KIRCHHEIMER, O. (1988), *Punishment and Social Structure*. New York: Russell and Russell.

SCRATON, P. (1987), ed, *Law, Order and the Authoritarian State*. Milton Keynes: Open University Press.

SCULL, A. (1977), *Decarceration: Community Treatment and the Deviant—A Radical View*. Englewood Cliffs, NJ: Prentice-Hall (rev. ed., 1984).

—— (1983), 'Community Corrections: Panacea, Progress or Pretence?', in D. Garland and P. Young, eds., *The Power to Punish*. London: Heinemann.

SHEARING, C. D., and STENNING, P. C. (1985), 'From the Panopticon to Disneyworld: The Development of Discipline', in A. N. Doob and E. L. Greenspan, eds., *Perspectives in Criminal Law*. Aurora, Ontario: Canada Law Books Inc.

SIMON, J. (1988), 'The Ideological Effects of Actuarial Practices', *Law and Society Review*, 22, 4: 772–800.

SMART, C. (1995), *Law, Crime and Sexuality: Essays in Feminism*. London: Sage.

SPITZER, S. (1983), 'The Rationalization of Crime Control in Capitalist Society', in S. Cohen and A. Scull, eds., *Social Control and the State*. Oxford: Martin Robertson.

Stenson, K. (1995), 'Communal Security as Government—the British Experience', in W. Hammerschick, I. Karazman-Moraewetz, and W. Stangl, eds., *Jahrbuch for Rechts und Kriminalsoziologie*. Baden-Baden: Nomos.

SUMNER, C. (1997), 'Social Control: the History and Politics of a Central Concept in Anglo-American Sociology', in R. Bergalli and C. Sumner, eds., *Social Control and Political Order*. London: Sage.

TONRY, M. (1995), *Malign Neglect: Race, Crime and Punishment in America*. New York: Oxford University Press.

WILSON, J. Q., and HERRNSTEIN, R. (1985), *Crime and Human Nature*, New York: Simon and Schuster.

—— and KELLING, G. (1982), 'Broken Windows: The Police and Neighbourhood Safety', *Atlantic Monthly*, March: 29–38.

WORRALL, A. (1990), *Offending Women: Female Offenders and the Criminal Justice System*. London: Routledge.

YOUNG, A., and RUSH, P. (1994), 'The Law of Victimage in Urbane Realism: Thinking Through Inscriptions of Violence', in D. Nelken, ed., *The Futures of Criminology*. London: Sage.

YOUNG, J. (1986), 'The Failure of Criminology: the Need for a Radical Realism', in R. Matthews and J. Young, eds., *Confronting Crime*. London: Sage.

—— (1987), 'The Tasks of a Realist Criminology', *Contemporary Crises*, 11: 337–56.

—— (1988), 'Radical Criminology in Britain: the Emergence of a Competing Paradigm', *British Journal of Criminology*, 28, 2: 289–313.

ZEDNER, L. (1991), *Women, Crime and Custody in Victorian England*. Oxford: Oxford University Press.

13

Left Realist Criminology: Radical in its Analysis, Realist in its Policy

Jock Young

Left realist criminology, as its name implies, is radical in its criminology and realistic in its appraisal of crime and its causes. Radical, in that crime is seen as an endemic product of the class and patriarchal nature of advanced industrial society. It is not a cosmetic criminology of an establishment sort which views crime as a blemish which, with suitable treatment, can be removed from the body of society which is, in itself, otherwise healthy and in little need of reconstruction. Rather it suggests that it is within the core institutions of society (its relationships of class and of gender) and its central values (such as competitive individualism and aggressive masculinity) that crime arises. Crime is not a product of abnormality but of the normal workings of the social order. Secondly, it is realistic in that it attempts to be faithful to the reality of crime. This involves several tasks: realistically appraising the problem of crime, deconstructing crime into its fundamental components (the square of crime), critically examining the nature of causality, being realistic about the possibilities of intervention, and, above all, fully understanding the changing social terrain in which we now live.

The particular political space in which left realism emerged was in the mid-1980s. The juxtaposition was the emergence of conservative ('neo-liberal') governments in many Western countries which pursued an overtly punishment-oriented approach to crime control and a liberal/social democratic opposition on the defensive. The right set out, quite consistently from their perspective, to generate market incentives in the work sphere and penal deterrence in the field of illegitimate behaviour. They actively pointed to the rise in the crime rate and entered vigorously into law and order campaigns on behalf of 'the silent majority', holding the offenders responsible and punishment the solution. The New Left position, which had its origins in the libertarianism of the 1960s, tended to resemble a mirror image of the right. That is it denied or downplayed the level of crime, portrayed the offender as victim of the system, and stressed a multi-culturalism of diversity and struggle where radicalism entailed the defence of the community against the incursions of the state, particularly the police and the criminal justice system. What was necessary was a criminology which could navigate between these two currents: which took crime seriously but which was radical in its analysis and policy (see Gitlin, 1995; Currie, 1992). Thus it was no accident that the first work in a realist vein appeared at approximately the same time. *What is to be Done About Law and Order?* (by John Lea and myself) came out in 1984; the Canadian, Brian MacLean, set up one of the first realist victimization studies in 1985, which was the same year that the distinguished American radical, Elliott Currie, produced *Confronting Crime*, to be followed in 1987 by William Julius Wilson's pathbreaking study, *The Truly Disadvantaged.*

Let us turn now to the fundamental components of realism, noting how it is clearly differentiated both from conservative policies and from those traditionally and currently associated with the left.

BEING REALISTIC ABOUT CRIME: THE CRITIQUE OF LEFT IDEALISM

The springboard for the emergence of realist criminology was the injunction to 'take crime seriously', an urgent recognition that crime was a real problem for a large section of the population, particularly women, the most vulnerable sections of the working class, and the ethnic minorities. It emerged as a critique of a predominant tendency in left wing and liberal commentaries which downplayed the problem of crime, talking about media instigated moral panics and irrational fears of crime. Such commentaries argued that public discourse about crime involved a displacement of the 'real' problems of the population (e.g. unemployment, exploitation, poverty) on crime as a potent symbol of social anxiety and enabled governments to legitimize their ever-increasing expenditure on law and order, often in fact directed at social unrest, at political and industrial militancy rather than crime itself. Crime control was, in fact, social control and the development of new policing and crime prevention techniques, such as the introduction of Neighbourhood Watch, CCTV, and even police domestic violence units, have been depicted in this light. Such left idealism (or what Elliott Currie calls 'progressive minimalism') has been frightened of entering the law and order debate for fear of adding to the prejudices of the population and whipping up public support for conservative crime control strategies. Though it originated in the 1960s, this minimalist view continues to dominate (Currie, 1992: 91).

Such a minimization of the effect of crime is combined with an idealization of reality, that is a denial of the level of pathology and dysfunction which occur amongst oppressed groups. Whereas generations of radicals in the past pointed to the way in which material conditions such as poverty caused massive problems on the level of the family and community, and, indeed, pointed to crime as an index of this, left idealists trenchantly reject such assertions as ethnocentric and even racist in their nature. A stark example of this was the resistance to the discussion of the dysfunctions occurring amongst black Americans in the ghettos so powerfully exposed in the writings of the prominent black scholar, William Julius Wilson:

Ghetto families were portrayed as resilient and capable of adapting creatively to an oppressive society. These revisionist arguments purporting to 'liberate' the social sciences from the influence of racism helped shift the focus of social scientists away from discussions of the consequences of racial isolation and economic class subordination to discussions of black achievement [1987: 6–9].

Yet, as Currie indicates, left idealism or minimalism continues to be a significant tendency in progressive commentary. It certainly did not disappear in the 1990s although far fewer commentators down-play the problem of crime to the degree that they did during the 'great denial' of the late 1960s and 1970s. (Young, 1991). What occurs is a familiar pattern where the focus is largely on the criminal justice system in a one-sided fashion, and crime itself is just a small bit player in the scenario. That is, a fully justified critique of criminal justice tends to proceed independently of the problem of crime which brought the response, however inadequate, into operation in the first place. Let me give two contemporary examples, Nils Christie's *Crime Control as Industry* (1993) and William Chambliss' two articles, 'Policing the Ghetto Underclass' (1994*a*) and 'Don't Confuse Me With Facts' (1994*b*). Christie's brilliant polemic is directed against the staggering rise in the use of imprisonment throughout the Western world. He hits the target well and I can but applaud him, *yet* his analysis is one-sided. Let me illustrate by examples from his book and from the articles of William Chambliss which, in part, derive from it:

1. *That the crime control industry is more of a problem than crime itself*
   Both are a problem, of course, and *both* must be acknowledged. The United States, for example, not only has a gargantuan prison population, it has an extremely high crime rate. For example, the chances of a young male dying from homicide in the United States is fifty-two times that of his British counterpart (Currie, 1996). It is vital that the problem of crime is constantly held in mind when discussing the crime control industry.

2. *That the prisons have expanded quite autonomously of the problem of crime*
   This seems to me to make the simple, yet frequent, mistake of assuming that, because there is obviously no linear relationship between rates of crime and rates of imprisonment, no relationship exists. Politicians and judges react in many ways at different times to the general rise in crime in the post-1960 period—sometimes, to decarcerate because of rising costs, sometimes to penalize more to increase deterrence, sometimes to bifurcate the offender population, and, thus, attempt to do both at the same time. It would be surprising if such variations in judgements could possibly result in a linear relationship, but that does not mean that the major motor of such changes is not the problem of crime. There is no doubt all sorts of relatively autonomous forces and interests propel the prison expansion, but to ignore crime is extraordinary; for in many ways

it is the crisis of crime which is the problem at base and the prison crisis which is an epiphenomenon (see Lowman, 1992: 158, n. 4).

3. *That the disproportionate number of blacks in prison is largely a product of the criminal justice system*

   In all countries of the Western world there is a disproportionate number of ethnic minority members in prison. This makes it easy to jump to the conclusion that this is largely due to prejudice at various levels of the criminal justice system. This assumes what John Lea and I have termed 'a democratic crime statistic', namely that the crime level of each section of the population is fairly equal and the disproportionality of the prison population is a product of judicial bias. Of course, this runs completely contrary to the fact that there is a high correlation between poverty and the sorts of crimes which are likely to result in imprisonment, and that certain ethnic minorities are much poorer than the general population. Bias, no doubt, exists within the criminal justice system, but differential crime rates must be brought into consideration (Lea and Young, 1993). To take the United States, for example, the disproportionate number of blacks in prison is a matter for general concern, but it must be constantly held in mind that the level of serious crime is also remarkably high. For instance, the homicide rate for blacks is 8.6 times that of whites in America, and it must be remembered that the vast majority of black homicides (94 per cent) are intra-racial (see Mann, 1993; DeKeseredy and Schwartz, 1996). Politicians such as Jesse Jackson regularly highlight the problem of black on black violence and consistently relate this to the poverty of the inner city. Elliott Currie (1996) notes that in 1992 in Philadelphia the rates of non-intentional serious injury amongst black men and women aged 20–29 were 175 per 1,000 per year and over a four year period a staggering 94 per cent of men of that age had been to a hospital emergency room at least once for some serious injury. No doubt there is bias in the crime statistics but, as Al Blumstein (1982) suggests, this goes both ways: the rates of blacks arrested for drugs is probably disproportionate where policing is proactive, but the rates of blacks arrested for violence is probably an underestimate, given that such violence is largely intra-racial and a biased police force will tend to be less responsive to a black complainant. Racism can lead to both over-representation and under-representation in the statistics.

4. *That if the war against drugs were to cease the predicament of the inner city dweller would dramatically improve*

   This argument runs that the war against drugs involves the criminalization of a large number of poor people (particularly ethnic minority members), that it encourages criminal gangs to enter the illegal economy of drug distribution, and that if the drugs were legal their effects would be relatively innocuous. Here again there is a half-truth in all this, but if taken too far any of these arguments leads to absurd positions and flaky politics (see Thompson, 1980: 149–80).

It should be pointed out that the crime rates in the inner cities would be high with or without drugs, that criminal gangs would not disappear with the end of the drugs war but merely enter other areas of profit (prostitution, extortion, gambling, etc.), and that the legal status of a drug, for example alcohol, scarcely reduces its role in precipitating violence. Furthermore, that the problem of drug use is often not so much the nature of the drug but the way in which drugs are consumed and the aims of consumption. Where, in situations of poverty and hopelessness, we have cultures of high risk-taking, the use of drugs to 'get out of your head' will continue whether legal or not, and so will the dangers. William Julius Wilson graphically describes the effects of drugs on the black community in his recent book, *When Work Disappears* (1996), but he does not make the mistake of divorcing drug use from economic predicament. Here again left idealism commits the fundamental mistake of seeing the problem of the most deprived part of the population as stemming largely from the state response to its predicament. Current crime control policies certainly make matters worse, but to lay too great emphasis on them ignores the structural problems of class and race which leave whole areas of the city idle and without hope. As Elliott Currie puts it:

the main thrust of liberal minimalism has been to portray fear and outrage about hard drugs as hysteria or manipulation; to argue that the real threat is not drugs themselves, but the war against drugs; and to downplay or reject evidence about the social and personal costs of hard-drug abuse, emphasising instead the horrendous costs of drug law enforcement. In so doing liberal minimalists have raised important issues. But, in the process, they have glossed over the drug problem itself [1992: 91–2].

5. *That the rise in imprisonment in the United States is a test case example of the irrationality of the penal response*
Because the crime rate in the United States has stabilized (or indeed perhaps decreased) over the last ten years yet the prison population has more than doubled, it is commonly argued that this clearly demonstrates the non-rational nature of the penal expansion. The stage is then set to look for other reasons which have caused the rise.

There are, in fact, many reasons directly concerned with the crime problem why American politicians and the judiciary might want to increase their rate of imprisonment, particularly if one of your dreams, like that of Newt Gingrich, was to bring the level of crime down to a European level. This is particularly true as the likelihood of imprisonment for serious offences had been declining in the United States over a considerable period (64 per cent between 1961 and 1971) (Wilson, 1975; Murray, 1997). Such a decline had occurred in many industrial countries (including England and Wales) and was presumably the result of the rapid increase in crime: namely that, although the prison capacity increased, it could never keep up with the increase in serious crime, so that, although the number of prisoners went up, the likelihood of going to prison decreased. One may disagree that increased imprisonment will cut crime rates significantly but many eminent criminologists hold views to the contrary. Incorrect it may be; irrational it is not, and there is no need, therefore, desperately to seek other reasons for the increase in the use of imprisonment (See Young, 1997c).

6. *That the concern about crime is a moral panic*
   The final part of the argument is to suggest that the reason for the increase in imprisonment is a moral panic about crime, created by conservative politicians, law enforcement agencies, and the mass media. Let us concentrate on the United States, for this is the *reductio ad absurdum* of this argument. Thus Bill Chambliss writes:

The creation of a moral panic over crime was brought about by a coalition of political, law enforcement and media interests that accounts for the growth of the crime industry. The media contributed its part to the creation of a moral panic and young black males particularly, and minorities generally, paid the price in the form of intensive police surveillance, imprisonment and institutionalized racism [1994a: 192].

In reality he notes earlier: 'Victim surveys show that it is very unlikely that anyone will be a victim of crime in any given year. . . . Indeed in a lifetime it is unlikely that most people will be the victim of a serious offence' (*Ibid.*: 184). And Tony Platt claims that in the United States 'a moral panic about crime and lawlessness is in full swing throughout the country' (1996: 3).

This is surely left idealism with a vengeance! To talk of moral panic about crime in the United States beggars the imagination and trivializes a concept which was introduced to contrast the panic about minor offences (e.g. cannabis or mods fighting on Brighton beaches) with real problems of crime (see Cohen, 1972; Young, 1971). I have already documented the appalling figures of violence within the African-American community, so high that a recent radical researcher writes that it is 'a form of black genocide, since the victim of homicide is most often another black person and the incidence of this crime is so pervasive' (Mann, 1993: 46). Are these writers really suggesting that there is a moral panic about black crime. And even the general homicide rate is staggeringly high: the number of homicides, for example, in Los Angeles with a population of 3.5 million, is greater than that of England and Wales with over fifty million inhabitants (Currie, 1996). Surely crime must be a major concern. Indeed, from a European perspective, how could such a level of violence be other than of great moral concern? And, indeed, the American public has consistently rated crime as a problem as have African Americans in particular. Yet the public are lambasted by these writers as if they were cultural dupes whose attitudes and opinions are a product of watching too much TV.

The above six beliefs, either singularly or as a package, form part of the conventional wisdom of liberal thinking about crime and the criminal justice system. At times they are part of a comprehensive structure of thought, at others merely items of belief, but their influence is continuing and substantial.

Thus we can see the characteristic syndrome of left idealism: great emphasis is placed on the criminal justice system as an autonomous agent which shapes and causes problems. Crime itself is played down, marginalized, and is not the focus of attention. Pathology and dysfunction within oppressed groups are minimized or denied. The causes of crime are either seen as obvious (e.g. poverty) or the product of criminal justice system intervention (e.g. the war on drugs) or, more radically, to be a chimera because crime is seen to have no reality itself other than the arbitrary definitions of criminal law (see Hulsman, 1986).

DISTANCING FROM CRIME: A CRITIQUE OF ESTABLISHMENT CRIMINOLOGY

Let us turn now to establishment criminology. Its key agenda is what might be termed *distancing*: that is to explain crime in a way which denies that there is any relationship with the core structure and values of society. The fault lies not in society, but in the individual who, because of some biological or psychological or social reason, has been rendered dysfunctional. The causes are numerous and sometimes accumulated willy nilly in a multi-factor 'theory', thus we can have genetics/low intelligence (Herrnstein and Murray, 1994), racial propensity (Rushton, 1995), genetics and inadequate child-rearing (Eysenck and Gudjonsson, 1989), inadequate single mothers (Murray, 1994), inadequate socialization in the first five years of life (Gottfredson and Hirschi, 1995), and all of these (Wilson and Herrnstein, 1985). Such propensities to commit crime are combined with opportunities to provide an 'integrated theory' which could be summed up as: differential human frailty confronting variable temptations gives rise to crime (Felson, 1994). Such a neo-positivism differs from the individualized positivism of the past: it freely acknowledges that crime is widespread, it grants free will but only in terms of the determining choices available, the criminal is more 'normal' than before but still the propensities of genetics and early childhood socialization create more or less vulnerability to crime. The actuarial criminal calculates the pluses or minuses of an action, just as in the legitimate market place, but some are more capable of rational calculation than others and some are more able to resist temptation. But above all the wider social structure of inequality and injustice is left out of the picture. In establishment criminology a simple materialism is propounded, but it is a materialism divorced from reality. Detached pieces of causality pirouette around a universe of isolated atoms: the family is blamed as if autonomous from the economy (see Currie, 1985), and each family separate from each other while a decline in morality is evoked as if it were a free-floating entity without any relationship to the market society.

Crime, furthermore, is a problem to be administered, to be dealt with by piecemeal interventions. This is a cosmetic criminology which views crime as a blemish on an otherwise trouble-free society. It thus reverses causality: crime causes problems for society rather than society causes the problem of crime. Thus, just as left idealism attempts to disconnect the criminal justice system from crime, establishment criminology attempts to disconnect crime from the wider society. In a sense neither is serious about crime: left idealism because it underplays crime as a problem, establishment criminology because, although often admitting the severity of the crime problem, it insists on regarding it as of superficial nature. Here, then, is the task of a radical realism: to make the proper connections between crime, the criminal justice system, and society: to be realistic in opposition to left idealism, to be radical in establishment criminology.

Let us turn, then, to the structure of society and to the widespread changes which have occurred over the recent period.

THE TERRAIN OF CHANGE: CRIME IN AN AGE OF LATE MODERNITY

The last third of the twentieth century has witnessed a remarkable transformation in the lives of citizens living in advanced industrial societies. The Golden Age of the post-war settlement with high employment, stable family structures, and consensual values underpinned by the safety net of the Welfare State has been replaced by a world of structural unemployment, economic precariousness, a systematic cutting of welfare provisions, and the growing instability of family life and interpersonal relations. And where there once was a consensus of value, there is now burgeoning pluralism and individualism (see Hobsbawm, 1994; Gitlin, 1995). A world of material and ontological security from cradle to grave is replaced by precariousness and uncertainty, and where social commentators of the 1950s and 1960s berated the complacency of a comfortable 'never had it so good' generation, those of today talk of a risk society where social change becomes the central dynamo of existence and where anything might happen. As Anthony Giddens put it: 'to live in the world produced by high modernity has the feeling of riding a juggernaut' (1991: 28; see also Beck, 1992; Berman, 1983).

Such a change has been brought about by market forces, which have systematically transformed the sphere both of production and consumption. This shift from Fordism to post-Fordism involves the unravelling of the world of work where the primary labour market of secure employment and 'safe' careers shrinks, the secondary labour market of short-term contracts, flexibility, and insecurity increases, as does the growth of an underclass of the structurally unemployed. It results, in Will Hutton's catch phrase, in a '40:30:30 society' (1995) where 40 per cent of the population is in tenured secure employment, 30 per cent in insecure employment, 30 per cent marginalized, idle, or working for poverty wages.

Secondly, the world of leisure is transformed from one of mass consumption to one where choice and preference are elevated to a major ideal and where the constant stress on immediacy, hedonism, and self-actualization has had a profound effect on late modern sensibilities (see Campbell, 1987; Featherstone, 1985). These changes both in work and leisure, characteristic of the late modern period, generate a situation of widespread relative deprivation and heightened individualism. Market forces generate a more unequal and less meritocratic society, market values encourage an ethos of every person for himself, together these create a combination which is severely crimogenic (see Young, 1998). Such a process is combined with a decline in the forces of informal social control, as communities are disintegrated by social mobility out of them and left to decay as capital finds more profitable areas to invest and develop. At the same time, families are stressed and fragmented by the decline in communities' systems of support, the reduction of state support, and the more diverse pressures of work (see Currie, 1997; Wilson, 1996). Thus, as the pressures which lead to crime increase, the forces which attempt to control it decrease.

Parallel to these processes which have produced crime and disorder in the late modern period, there has also been an increased diversity of value and debate about what is legitimate and illegitimate behaviour. The market forces which gave rise to a burgeoning individualism created a more diversified society, whereas the movement of population through immigration and the mass transit of people spurred on by business and tourism underscored this sense of diversity and pluralism. A criminology for the late twentieth century, therefore, needed to explain the rising levels of crime and disorder and be able to take on board the increasingly problematic nature of crime and deviance.

THE CRISIS OF ÆTIOLOGY AND PENALITY

A world, then, which in the immediate post-war period was characterized by relative stability in the spheres of work, the family and community, and extremely high living standards, was disturbed by the rise of crime and disorder. This was a world where there was a consensus stretching across a large section of informed opinion that the major cause of crime was impoverished social conditions (social positivism) and that crime was a minority phenomenon, which could be contained by the judicious intervention of the criminal justice system (neo-classicism). Anti-social conditions led to anti-social behaviour, political intervention, and economic reconstruction which improved conditions would, therefore, inevitably lead to a drop in the crime rate. Yet precisely the opposite happened. Slums were demolished, educational standards improved, full employment advanced, and welfare spending increased: the highest affluence in the history of humanity achieved, yet crime increased. In Britain, for example, between 1951 and 1971 the real disposable income per person increased by 64 per cent, whilst the crime rate more than doubled, with a rise of 172 per cent. Indeed, even *before* the recession of the 1980s, the crime rate began to rise, seemingly inexorably. Furthermore, the response of shoring up the criminal justice system, increasing the size of the police force and the capacity of the prisons, did not seem to work either. Vast sums were poured into the criminal justice system, yet not only did the crime rate continue to increase but the suspicion arose that the experience of imprisonment generated criminality and actually increased the volume of crime and, furthermore, that the police and the judiciary, by focusing on selected sections of population, actually increased the sense of injustice rather than decreased it. Thus the twin staples of modernity, progress through the enhancement of material conditions and progress through the rule of law, were challenged. There was, in short, a crisis of ætiology and of penality.

LEFT REALISM: A THEORETICAL SYNTHESIS

It was the palpable failure of the two main staples of criminological theory, neo-classicism and social positivism, which stretch back to the first foundations of Cesare Beccaria in the eighteenth century and Adolphe Quetelet in the early part of the nineteenth, which reverberated throughout the discipline. It is scarcely surprising, therefore, that the last third of the twentieth century witnessed the most extraordinarily fertile debate in criminology. Not only does the subject emerge as an interdisciplinary site of intense academic contest, it grows exponentially in its number of practitioners and students. It was out of this ferment that the strands which formed the future basis of realism, subcultural theory and labelling theory, emerged. Let us note at this stage the two key problems which needed explanation: first, the rise in crime despite affluence; secondly, the problematic nature of crime and the way in which the criminal justice system responded to it. That is, rule-breaking and rule-making: action and reaction.

The two major schools within sociology which were brought into play by sociologists in the late 1950s and early 1960s to help understand the rise of crime and the transformation of the criminal justice system were *anomie* theory and symbolic interactionism. The *anomie* theory of Robert K. Merton, itself closely influenced by Durkheim, was famously developed into subcultural theory by Albert Cohen, Richard Cloward, and Lloyd Ohlin. The symbolic interactionism of George Herbert Mead became popularized and rejuvenated by the ebullient work of Howard S. Becker, Edwin Lemert, Kai Erikson, and John Kitsuse. The first was concerned with the causes of crime, the relationship between the structure of society, and the second with the diversity of rules and the unintended consequences of their implementation. In short, with action and reaction. Indeed, the great contribution that labelling theory made to criminology and the study of deviance was the formula which every undergraduate studying the subject learns. Namely, that 'deviance is not a propensity *inherent* in any particular form of behaviour; it is a propensity *conferred* upon that behaviour by the people who come into direct or indirect contact with it' (Erikson, 1966: 6). That is the dyadic nature of crime and deviance, their double structure involving rule-breaking and rule-making. The two strands present themselves at the time (beginning of the 1960s) as oppositional. Indeed, labelling theory, the main contender against orthodoxy, came close to reversing the conventional wisdoms of causality by suggesting that social control gives rise to deviance rather than vice versa, and that, as most people have deviant natures, it is a question of many being called and few being chosen (see, e.g., Lemert, 1967: p. v; Becker, 1963: 26–7). But, as we have argued in *The New Criminology* (Taylor *et al.*, 1973), these positions are not either/or; in fact they are complementary. Subcultural theory is concerned with the causes of crime, labelling theory with the reaction against it; both are necessary for a fully social theory of crime; both fit together like pieces of a jigsaw puzzle. Further, subculture theory is about how people construct attempted solutions to problems confronted in their lives, whilst labelling theory (and the social constructionism which came after it) is about how people's lives are constructed from above by official labels, stereotypes, media, and legal discourses, etc. One is about construction up, the other construction down: the essential dyad of criminology; action and reaction, rule-breakers and rule-makers. To bring together these two processes is of great importance, yet there is very often a *partiality* of focus. It is commonplace, for example in social history, for radical scholars to focus on history from below whilst more traditional writers concentrate on history from above, when both dimensions are essential. People, after all, make their history, but they do not make it just as they please, but in circumstances, both material and ideational, which are directly encountered, given, and transmitted from the past.

To study crime and deviance, then, likewise requires us to understand human action and the reaction to it, but not merely as two unrelated items. That is the causes of crime on one side and the causes of the criminal justice system response on the other. For constructions up and construction down are not two independent factors in the explanatory process. Even on a causal level crime is scarcely a result of the one-off impact of forces which cause crime against those which seek to control it. For the two processes interact and shape each other. For example, as Mary McIntosh (1971) showed in her seminal article on the varieties of criminal organization; criminal groups become sophisticated in response to the security measures set against them, and the structure of such security becomes more elaborate in response to the sophistication of the criminal. Indeed, even the levels of violence used by both sides are determined by a process of interaction. But the reflexivity of offender and law enforcement towards each other is not merely limited to a calculation of risk and observation; crime and deviance, as David Matza so eloquently showed in *Becoming Deviant*, are enacted in the flux of not just physical power but of moral hegemony. The moral discourse of the offender is intimately shaped by the moral calumny which attaches to the offence and the excusing circumstances and vocabularies of motive, necessary to bring the actor to the edge of infraction, are a key to any explanation (and the same is true of the illegality of powerful groups, see Cohen, 1995).

The two strands, therefore, when taken together, contribute first of all the notion that crime is a dyad and, secondly, that the two elements of the dyad *cannot be studied separately* (see Young, 1977*b*). They are intimately and intricately involved in each other. Thus the whole basis of positivism, with its radical division of fact and value, is put at jeopardy. In particular, the belief that crime is a fact out there which can be studied separately and scientifically independently of its definition and that the definition does not transform and alter the subject matter. Instead, the definition is always contested, there is no scientific essence of what constitutes rape or murder, and the criminal justice system insistently 'contaminates' its object of attention by providing vocabularies of motive and self-concepts as to what constitutes a thief, a junkie, a hooligan, etc. But this is not all. This notion of an intimate dyad does not allow us to study the reaction against crime independently of crime itself. That is, the prison independently of crime, the discourse about prostitution separately from prostitution, the war against drugs autonomously from the drug problem. But this is precisely, as we have seen, what left idealism attempts and which the social constructionist school, of which it is part, explicitly attempts, namely, to bracket off the study of the formation of social problems from the study of social problems themselves and to focus on the former (see Kitsuse and Spector, 1973; Sumner, 1990, 1994).

The task of realism is, therefore, to bring these two major currents in sociology together. Their difference, as we have seen, is complementary, but it is also necessary to stress what they have in common. For both *anomie* theory and interaction are critical of positivism and both are radical in their analysis. Symbolic interactionism is, of course, a paramount critique of positivism, but what is frequently omitted in the various expositions of the *anomie* and subcultural schools is their own anti-positivist basis. Thus, Merton's pathbreaking article, 'Social Structure and Anomie' (1938), is explicitly a critique, first, of biological and, then, social positivism. Human consciousness and decision, the creation of value in a determinate world, are central to subcultural theory, as they are in labelling theory. Secondly, both are radical in that they root the problems of crime in the core structure and values of society and its institutions. *Anomie* theory is a critique of the system of distributive justice, labelling theory of criminal justice. Thus the causes of crime are seen, in *anomie* theory, to lie in the contradiction between the culture of meritocracy, which promises a dream of equal opportunity, and the class structure, which prevents it, whilst the reaction to crime is seen, in labelling theory, to violate the basic neo-classicist principles of liberal democracy. Instead of equality and fairness in the face of the law, we have the problem of *selectivity*: the offender is selected because of age, class, race, and gender, and punished disproportionally. Instead of a world of equality despite differences, we have one of inequality based on stereotype and difference. And thus, from each strand, we have the two ironies so graphically depicted by Matza (1967). The culture which aims to legitimize the system helps generate disorder, the law which aims to make tranquil the everyday transgressions within society seems to perpetuate and exacerbate the sense of injustice that caused crime in the first place. It is these two great traditions which realism seeks to bring together and to do so because they are complementary, because they have in common a rejection of positivism, because they are both radical in that they trace the source of crime and disorder to the core institutions of society, and, finally, because of their sense of irony and contradiction.

The Nature and Form of Crime

The central aim of left realism is to be faithful to the reality of crime: to the fact that all crimes must, of necessity, involve rules and rule breakers (i.e. criminal behaviour and reaction against it) and offenders and victims. That is, it should acknowledge the *form* of crime, the *social context* of crime, its trajectory through *time*, and its enactment in *space*. The problem with previous criminology, according to realism, is that it is partial. It has tended to focus on only part of the process of crime and not to encompass all of it. The focus was on the victim or on the offender, on the social reaction to crime, or on the criminal behaviour itself. Realism intends to bring together all aspects of the process: in this its approach emphasizes synthesis rather than a simple dismissal of opposing theories.

The form consists of two dyads, a *victim* and an *offender*, and of *actions* and *reactions*: of crime and its control. This deconstruction gives us four definitional elements of crime: a victim, an offender, formal control, and informal control.

Realism, then, points to a square of crime involving the interaction between police and other agencies of social control, the public, the offender and the victim. Crime rates are generated not merely by the interplay of these four factors, but as *social relationships* between each point on the square. It is the relationship between the police and the public which determines the efficacy of policing, the relationship between the victim and the offender which determines the impact of the crime, the relationship between the state and the offender which is a major factor in recidivism; it is the burgled public which creates the informal economy which sustains burglary, or the police who create, through illegalities, a moral climate which spur delinquents into crime. Lastly, the relationship between the four points of the square (offender,

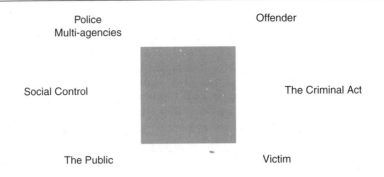

Police   Offender
Multi-agencies

Social Control   The Criminal Act

The Public   Victim

Fig. 13.1: The Square of Crime

victim, state agencies, and the public) varies with differing types of crime (see Lea, 1992).

Crime rates are a product, therefore, of changes in the number of possible offenders, the number of potential victims, and the changing levels of control exercised by the official agencies of control and the public. No explanation which does not embrace all these four factors can possibly explain crime rates. Let us focus, for the moment, quite simply on the relationship between social control in all its manifestations and the criminal act consisting of the dyad of victim and offender. That is on the criminal act and the reaction to it. If we examine changes over time, realists would point to these *necessarily* being a product of changes in criminal behaviour *and* changes in reactions to crime. Crime by its very nature is not a fixed objective thing: it varies with the definer. None of this makes it any the less 'real': for this is exactly what crime rates *really* are.

The Social Context of Crime

The social context consists of the immediate social interaction of these four elements and the setting of each of them within the *wider* social structure. Such an agenda was set out within *The New Criminology* (Taylor *et al.*, 1973), namely, that the immediate social origins of a deviant act should be set within its wider social context and that such an analysis should encompass both actors and reactors. Realism takes this a stage further, insisting, not only that actions of offenders and the agencies of the state must be understood in such a fashion, but that this must be extended to the informal system of social control (the public) and to victims (Young, 1996*b*).

The Temporal Aspect of Crime

The temporal aspect of crime is the past of each of the four elements of the square of crime and their impact on each other in the future. A realist approach sees the development of criminal behaviour over time. It breaks down this trajectory of offending into its component parts and notes how different agencies interact. Thus we can talk of the *background causes* of crime; the *moral context* of opting for criminal behaviour; the *situation of committing crime*; the *detection of crime*; the *response to the offender*; the *response to the victim*.

Criminal careers are built up by an interaction of the structural position the offender finds him- or herself in and the administrative responses to his or her various offences. Such moral careers are not confined to the offender. Other points of the square of crime change over time. Policing practices change in their interaction with offenders, the public's fear of crime in the city creates patterns of avoidance behaviour which consciously and unconsciously develop over time, victims—particularly repeated victims such as in domestic violence— change the pattern of their life as a consequence of such an interaction.

As an activity, crime involves a moral choice at a certain point in time in changing determinant circumstances. It has neither the totally determined quality beloved by positivism, nor the wilful display of rationality enshrined in classicist legal doctrine. It is a moral act, but one which must be constantly assessed within a determined social context. It is neither an act of determined pathology, nor an obvious response to desperate situations. It involves both social organization and disorganization. Realism eschews both the romanticism of left idealism which grants exaggerated levels of organization, and rationality to deviant behaviour and the desiccated scientism of positivist criminology which does just the reverse (see Wilson, 1987; Young, 1987; Matza, 1969).

The Spatial Dimension of Crime

The spatial dimension of crime is the material space in which this process enacts itself. All crime has a spatial dimension, and the geography of crime varies widely in terms of the specific crime, and just as specific crimes involve differing structures of relationships, they also involve particular structures in space. Therefore, left realism suggests that the control of crime must involve interventions at all points of the square of crime (e.g. through better policing, greater community involvement, protecting and empowering the victim, and dealing with the structural problems that cause offending). But it prioritizes intervention on the level of causes of crime over actions which take place *after* the crime has been committed (see Young and Matthews, 1992).

Causes of Crime

Realism sees a potent cause of criminal behaviour in *relative deprivation*. Crime can, therefore, occur anywhere in the social structure and at any period, affluent or otherwise—it is not dependent on absolute levels of deprivation or the level in the social structure of the offender (see Lea, 1992). Yet it is among the poor, particularly the lower working class and certain ethnic minorities, who are marginalized from the 'glittering prizes' of the wider society, that the push towards crime is greatest. To emphasize relative deprivation as a cause of crime is not to retreat into monocausality. There are many causes of crime. Even within the tradition of *anomie* theory, subcultural theorists have tended unduly to emphasize relative deprivation, the disjunction between aspirations and opportunities, over *anomie* as a lack of limits, a product of individualism. Moreover the *anomie* of the disadvantaged, which is largely concerned with relative deprivation, can be contrasted with the *anomie* of the advantaged, which is often a product of a limitless pursuit of money, status, and power (see Young, 1974; Simon and Gagnon, 1986; Taylor, 1990). The problem of the causes of crime is one which has perplexed criminologists and confused public opinion throughout the century. It is pertinent to point to three notions which inform the debate: absolute deprivation, total determinism, and mechanistic causation. All of these concepts are central to social democratic positivism and are fundamentally mistaken.

There is no evidence that absolute deprivation (e.g. unemployment, lack of schooling, poor housing, etc.) leads *automatically* to crime. Realist criminology points to relative deprivation in certain *conditions* as being the major cause of crime. That is, when people experience a level of unfairness in their allocation of resources and utilize individualistic means to attempt to right this condition. It is a reaction to the experience of injustice. Experienced injustice, coupled with an individualistic 'solution', can occur at different parts of society: like crime itself, it is certainly not a monopoly of the poor. Such individualistic responses of 'every man for himself' are particularly prevalent at certain times rather than others; it is the ascendent ethos of modern-day Britain, with its rising crime rate, and it is particularly prevalent in the United States, which has by far the highest crime rate of any advanced industrial society.

The notion that certain social conditions lead to crime is associated with the notion of total determinism. To say that poverty in the present period breeds crime is not to say that all poor people are criminals. On the contrary: most poor people are perfectly honest and many wealthy people commit crimes. Rather it is to say that the rate of crime is higher in certain parts of society in certain conditions. Crime, like any other form of behaviour, involves moral choice in certain restricting circumstances. It is not inevitable in any particular circumstances. That is why an ethos of individualism affects public morality and the incidence of crime. Conversely, crime is not merely a matter of moral choice, a wickedness distributed randomly throughout the world.

To say that crime is causal, therefore, is not to suggest a mechanistic notion of causation: as, for example, when we push a table—the table moves. Rather, because of the subjective element, certain circumstances facilitate increases in crime amongst parts of the population. Thus simple attempts to relate social factors such as unemployment to crime inevitably fail, however sophisticated the statistical techniques. Unemployment leads to discontent in those situations where people experience their circumstances as unjust, unnecessary, and, above all, *preventable*. Discontent leads to crime where individuals feel marginalized socially and politically. As we have seen, there are various, quite pronounced, reasons why such marginalization and relative deprivation has increased in the present period. Furthermore, we have a generation which has grown up used to Keynesian interventions in the economy, and which consequently sees unemployment, not as part of the natural order, but as a political product. Unemployment and relative impoverishment are experienced not as a fact of life, but as a failure of society and of government.

Mechanistic notions of crime causation assume an *immediate* causation. But it takes time for people to evaluate their predicaments and even longer for them to build up alternative solutions. Unemployment *now* does not relate to crime the day after tomorrow. Sub-cultures of youth, for example, build up and develop appraisals of their situation: they may not flourish until several years after the initial problem of unemployment. By the same token, the development of a hidden economy, including illegal activity, takes time to build up. Thus to correlate crime and unemployment at one moment of time obscures the fact that human evaluation and enterprise develop through *time*.

Finally, with regard to human constitution and crime, realism does not reject the fact of correlations between biology and crime, whether that involves body shape, hormone systems, size, or age. In rejecting biological reductionism, theories such as left idealism and labelling theory, throw the baby out with the bathwater and reject biology itself. It is a fact that larger, more powerful, people commit more violence than smaller people, that their male hormones correlate strongly with violence, that the well muscled are more of a threat than the plump and unfit. People do not, after all, cross the street at night to avoid old ladies. Thus realism argues that the causes of patriarchal violence against women or the machismo of lower-working-class youth are rooted in social situations, not biology, and that physical capacity to commit crime is merely an intervening variable.

The Problem of Specificity

Positivist criminology typically seeks generalizations which are independent of culture and social setting. Of course unemployment leads to crime, and it is self-evident that the recession has led to the rise in heroin use amongst young people, etc. But it is absurd to posit a mechanistic relationship between objective conditions and human behaviour. The fact of human reflexivity and consciousness does not generate simple linear relationships between, for example, levels of unemployment and crime or inequality and violence. Where linear relationships are to be found then they are more likely to be an artefact of the methods of measurement rather than a reflection of reality itself. Tendencies in a particular direction in a specified culture are another thing, but linear relationships abstracted from human meaning and social situation are a positivistic chimera. It is central to a realist position that objective conditions are interpreted through the specific sub-cultures of groups involved. This is the nature of human experience and social action. Generalization is possible, but only given specific cultural conditions and social understandings. Realism focuses on lived realities. It is concerned with the material problem which particular groups of people experience in terms of the major social axes of age, class, gender, and ethnicity and spatially within their locality (see DeKeseredy, 1997). It is these structural parameters which give rise to subcultures. Subcultures are problem-solving devices which constantly arise as people in specific groups attempt to solve the structural problems facing them. Crime is one form of subcultural adaptation which occurs where material circumstances block cultural aspirations and where non-criminal alternatives are absent or less attractive

The Impact of Crime

Realists are also critical of the alleged disjunction between fear of crime and risk of crime which forms such a background to conventional thinking about crime. Many of the glaring 'irrationalities' centre around the high fear of crime of women and of old people despite the low risk rates. The contrast is always made with the low fear of crime of young men, despite their having the supposedly highest risk rates of any social grouping. Realists point to the fundamental flaw of believing that there is an easy answer to what is a 'rational' level of fear of crime.

The realist method is not to look at the risk of crime in general. For general rates obscure by adding very low risk groups to groups with very high risks. Rather, the realist method delineates how crime is focused on certain geographical areas and certain groups within those areas, for example, blacks rather than whites, and poor people rather than rich. The most vulnerable in our society have the greatest risks of crime. But also the impact of crime on them is greater because of their lack of money and resources. Moreover, the people who suffer most from crime tend also to suffer most from other social problems (for example, physical and mental illness, bad housing, etc.). The effect of crime thus *compounds* other problems.

If we are to unravel the relationship between anxiety about crime and risk of crime we should, therefore, substitute impact rates for risk rates. We should note, also, that supposedly 'irrational' sectors of the community suffer from crimes which are 'invisible' to all but the most careful survey methods. Sexual crimes, domestic violence, and the harassment of women are cases in point: they generate much greater risk and impact rates than are usually presented (Mooney, 1993). Allowance must be made for the fact that supposedly low-risk groups such as women and the elderly are in part a function of their high level of avoidance tactics. What, for example, would the crime rate against women be if they acted like men in their levels of avoiding crime. Lastly, we must examine different tolerance levels to crimes such as violence. Why should women not have a greater intolerance of violence than men and hence a greater level of unease? Is not the low level of fear of crime by young males simply a product of their machismo values? (See Young, 1988.)

Attitudes to crime are more than a function of experience of crime, however, for some subgroups, fear of crime is, in part, a displacement of other forms of social unease (e.g. unemployment, racism, disquiet at the starkness of the built environment). Rather, anxiety about crime is one aspect of a particular sub-cultural position which includes different tolerance levels to social disorder, as well as a series of social anxieties, of which risk of crime is only one factor. 'Fear' of crime is, therefore, neither autonomous from, nor a simple reflex of, risk rates. What is certain, however, is that the major way of reducing fear of crime is to reduce the incidence of crime.

BEING TOUGH ON CRIME MEANS BEING TOUGH ON CRIMINAL JUSTICE

We must reject the notion of 'nothing works', the prevalent slogan of the 1980s; our problem is that we do not know exactly what works, for what offences, with regard to which offenders. The problem is both the level of explanation and the level of monitoring. We must stop asking what works and begin to look at how things work. And once we have set up interventions based on reasoned analysis rather than folk wisdom, we must halt the flood of badly maintained projects whose main theme is self-congratulation. If one-tenth of the projects which claimed success were half as successful as they claim, we would have 'solved' the crime problem. Part of our predicament is that the number of scientifically monitored interventions in crime control is surprisingly small, part that such monitoring is much more difficult than is usually supposed. There is a certain innocence about such interventions. Legislators expect that laws, once enacted, will both be satisfactorily implemented and, once implemented, effect these stated aims. Hallowed police practices, such as large-scale stop and search, are maintained in all their costly arbitrariness despite the fact that research shows 'yield' to be small and the resulting alien-ation of innocent individuals likely to be not merely ineffective but counter-productive (see Young, 1994). The problem is naïveté, rooted in common sense notions of obviousness. There is no reason to suppose that successful inter-vention in the social world is less difficult than in the natural world. Yet scientific interventions in the physical world are the result of a wealth of experiment and validation whilst the actual product, whether it be a bridge, aeroplane, or motor car, is a function of incessant research and development. Common sense did not create the space shuttle: why on earth should common sense dictate intervention in the much more complicated systems of social reality? It is this conception of *the social as simple* which beguiles the nature of criminal justice interventions and precludes adequate monitoring of effects. Furthermore, it is facile to assume a simple linear relationship between the quantity of an intervention and the amount of effect: for example, more police equal less crime or more punishment means greater deterrence. We must be aware of the declining marginal returns of any particular intervention and of the notion of 'too much' as well as 'too little'. For example, saturating an area like Brixton with police officers may start a riot and produce crime statistics greater than or equal to those of no policing whatsoever. We must look for the particular set of circumstances which produce effective policing. To do so requires us to examine what works, and, more importantly, to discover the causal *mechanisms* by which successful (and unsuccessful) policing occurs (Sayer, 1984).

Such an analysis indicates that it would be false to generalize from the present combination of effective, ineffective, and downright counterproductive parts of the criminal justice system. Some things work; some things do not work, some things possibly work in certain situations and not in others. None of this is to suggest that the criminal justice system is, or feasibly could be, the dominant mode of crime control. No manner of reform and change would achieve this. What it does suggest is that the present contribution of the criminal justice system could be raised but that to do so requires a more circumspect level of design and monitoring. Research, design, evaluation: all of these processes make sense, particularly if we take into account the vast sums we spend on the criminal justice system. But such vigorous examination must be matched by a determination to change practices and shift resources when something palpably does not work. Being tough on crime must include being tough on the criminal justice system.

For realism, the control of crime involves interventions on all levels: on the social causes of crime, on social control exercised by the community and the formal agencies, and on the situation of the victim. Social causation is given the highest priority. Formal agencies, such as the police, have a vital role, yet one which has been greatly exaggerated. It is not the 'Thin Blue Line', but the social bricks and mortar of civil society which are the major bulwark against crime. Good jobs with a discernable future, housing estates that tenants can be proud of, community facilities which enhance a sense of cohesion and belonging, a reduction in unfair income inequalities, all create a society which is more cohesive and less criminogenic.

REALIST STRATEGIES: SHORT-TERM GAIN, LONG-TERM TRANSFORMATION

Realism seeks both immediate intervention and long-term fundamental change. It is, first of all, a radical discipline which sets itself against an establishment criminology intent on standing in the way of change and which believes that crime is a mere hitch in the social system which can be corrected by disparate, unconnected, piecemeal measures. But it is also critical of that sort of radicalism which, believing that nothing much can be done short of fundamental transformations, focuses defensively on the inequities of the criminal justice system in a series of one-off campaigns. Vital as such activities are, it is necessary fully to enter the debate about law and order and to suggest immediate policies which will ameliorate the impact of crime and disorder upon wide sections of the population (Scharf, 1990; Hansson, 1995). This involves reform of the criminal justice system in terms of aims and effectiveness, but it is vital to note that immediate interventions in terms of social improvements may be just as effective in their impact.

Such immediate reforms cannot be seen as separate from the problem of long-term social change (Cohen, 1990). Indeed, such measures improve the morale of the community and thus facilitate the capacity for change. Moreover, they are unlikely to be successful if not couched in terms of long-term goals of social justice (Matthews, 1988; Lowman, 1992; Loader, 1997). For crime is about social justice gone wrong. Its solution is not order divorced from justice, but an order that springs out of a just society. We live in an era where there has been a widening division between those in secure employment and those who are insecure, a chasm between those in work and those who are structurally unemployed. The days of the inclusive society of full employment and secure careers are over. The meritocratic racetrack on which all are supposed to run and gain prizes proportionate to our effort has become more and more exposed for what it always was, a dream. The tracks separate out to a fast lane and a slow lane, with a substantial section of the population allocated to the role of spectators (the losers) watching the glittering prizes doled out to the successful (the winners). Relative deprivation abounds, matched by a rise in economic precariousness and insecurity. A rampant individualism, itself a spin-off of market values, adds to this and creates a society which is crimogenic, and self-destructive. Crime becomes a normality of life, incivilities part of the fabric of everyday existence. The problems are most pressing amongst the growing body of people excluded from full citizenship, but they occur at all reaches of society and indeed within the family, the basic building block of liberal democracy. The motor of disorder thus lies at the heart of the system in the inequalities of merit and reward, which grow more evident as we enter the twenty-first century, and in the values of individualism which break down the acceptance of the *status quo* which was necessary for it to function smoothly.

Establishment criminology eschews all talk of social injustice. Its first response is actuarial, its second nostalgic. Most immediately there arises a criminology which is about the management of risk (Feeley and Simon, 1994; van Swaaningen, 1997; Young, 1998). It is an actuarialism where the calculating criminal confronts the calculating public: the risk maker meets the risk taker, with no element of justice, indeed moral judgement, in the picture. As crime becomes a normal part of everyday life and the trouble-free management of the growing imprisoned population becomes more and more necessary, the task of the administrative criminologist becomes that of designing barriers, evaluating surveillance, and calculating the risk of disturbance—the protection of property, public space, and the management of prisons. A flourishing evaluation industry develops much of which is of little scientific validity, with few bothering to ask whether all the cost is worth it to maintain a system which is at basis fundamentally flawed. Establishment criminology evokes the unthinking order of the control theorists where basic values are drilled into the child from infancy, and morality is 'caught not taught' (Hirschi and Gottfredson, 1995). It attempts to revive the strong family (itself a prime site of crime and violence) where authority is unquestioned, and to rekindle a community which prioritizes order and certainty over justice and equality (Etzioni, 1993). These are lost causes: they are attempts to bolt nostalgia onto the fast changing world in which we find ourselves. Such nostalgia has, of course, attractions to politicians of both left and right (indeed their policies become increasingly indistinguishable) but there is no going back. 'For', as Marshall Berman evocatively puts it, 'our past, whatever it was, was a past in the process of disintegration; we yearn to grasp it, but it is baseless and elusive; we look back for something solid to lean on, only to find ourselves embracing ghosts' (1983: 333). Any realism worthy of its name must go with the rapid changes which late modernity brings upon us (Hofman, 1993; Lippens, 1994). We must argue for work, but we must not deceive ourselves that it will support the graduation-to-grave careers of yesteryear. We must argue for strong support for child rearing, but take note that the nuclear family for life is becoming a dwindling option. We must build strong communities but not expect them to resemble the soap operas we so avidly watch. If we are to construct a social democracy for the next century, we must use new building blocks. Work, family, and the community will all be transformed, yet the demand for citizenship and justice will be even greater. Only in this direction can we realistically talk of a programme which reduces crime and moves towards a social order which will be in the interests of the majority.

Selected Further Reading

An accessible introduction to realism is the fourth edition of M. Haralambos and M. Holborn, *Sociology: Themes and Perspectives* (London: Collins, 1995), ch. 7, followed by J. Lea and Jock Young, *What is to be Done About Law and Order?* (London: Pluto, 1993). A precise and interesting essay on taking crime seriously is Ian Taylor's *Law and Order: Arguments for Socialism* (London: Macmillan, 1981).

An American textbook which takes up a realist approach is W. DeKeseredy and M. Schwartz, *Contemporary Criminology* (Belmont, Cal.: Wadsworth, 1996) whilst an Australian text which has a good section on realism is R. White and F. Haines, *Crime and Criminology* (Melbourne: Oxford University Press, 1996).

The special edition of *Contemporary Crises Vol. 11* (1987) contains key essays; the international debate is dealt with in the two volumes edited by

Roger Matthews and Jock Young, *Rethinking Criminology and Issues in Realist Criminology* (London: Sage, 1992), supplemented by the Canadian volume by J. Lowman and B. MacLean, *Realist Criminology* (Toronto: University of Toronto Press).

Local survey work is epitomized in T. Jones, B. MacLean, and J. Young, *Islington Crime Survey* (Aldershot: Gower, 1986) and in the Belgian *Burt en Criminaliteit* (Brugge: Vanden Broele, 1992) by P. Hebberecht and H. Hofman. Recent specialist surveys include J. Mooney, *The Hidden Figure: Domestic Violence in North London* (Middlesex: Centre for Criminology, 1993) and F. Pearce, *Commercial and Conventional Crime* (Middlesex: Centre for Criminology, 1993).

Lastly, a useful comparative book on critical criminology is B. MacLean and D. Milanovic, *Thinking Critically About Crime* (Vancouver: Collective Press, 1997), and a collection of essays which places realism in the theoretical context of the movement into late modernity is P. Walton and J. Young (eds.), *The New Criminology Revisited* (London: Macmillan, 1997).

REFERENCES

AULD J., and DORN, N. (1986), 'Irregular Work, Irregular Pleasures', R. Matthews and J. Young, eds., *Confronting Crime*. London: Sage).

BECK, U. (1992), *Risk Society*. London: Sage.

BECKER, H. S. (1963), *Outsiders*. New York: Collier & Macmillan.

BERMAN, M. (1983), *All That Is Solid Melts Into Air*. London: Verso.

BLUMSTEIN, A. (1982), 'On Racial Disproportionality of the United States Prison Population', *Journal of Criminal Law and Criminology*, 33: 73–92

CAMPBELL, C. (1987), *The Romantic Ethic and the Spirit of Modern Consumerism*. Oxford: Blackwell.

CHAMBLISS, W. (1994a), 'Policing the Ghetto Underclass: The Politics of Law and Order Enforcement', *Social Problems*, 41, 2: 177–94.

—— (1994b), 'Don't Confuse Me With Facts— "Clinton Just Say No"', *New Left Review*, 204: 113–28.

CHRISTIE, N. (1993), *Crime Control as Industry*. London: Routledge.

COHEN, S. (1972), *Folk Devils and Moral Panics*. London: Paladin.

—— (1980), *Intellectual Scepticism and Political Commitment: The Case of Radical Criminology*. Amsterdam: University Press.

—— (1995), *Denial and Acknowledgement: The Impact of Information About Human Rights Violations*. Jerusalem: Center for Human Rights, Hebrew University.

CURRIE, D. H. (1992), 'Feminism and Realism in the Canadian Context', in J. Lowman and B. D. MacLean, eds., *Realist Criminology: Crime Control and Policing in the 1960s*. Toronto: University of Toronto Press.

CURRIE, E. (1985), *Confronting Crime: An American Challenge*. New York: Pantheon.

—— (1992), 'Retreatism, Minimalism, Realism: Three Styles of Reasoning on Crime and Drugs in the United States', in J. Lowman and B. D. MacLean, eds., *Realist Criminology: Crime Control and Policing in the 1990s*. Toronto: University of Toronto Press.

—— (1993), *Reckoning: Drugs, the Cities, and the American Future*. New York: Pantheon.

—— (1996), *Is America Really Winning the War on Crime and Should Britain Follow its Example*? London: NACRO.

—— (1997), 'Market Society and Social Disorder' in B. D. MacLean and D. Milanovic, eds., *Thinking Critically About Crime*. Vancouver: Collective Press.

DEKESEREDY, W. S. (1997), 'The Left Realist Perspective on Race, Class and Gender' in M. Schwartz and D. Milanovic, eds., *Race, Gender and Class in Criminology*. New York: Garland.

—— and SCHWARTZ, M. D. (1996), *Contemporary Criminology*. Belmont, Cal.: Wadsworth.

DOWNES, D. (1966), *The Delinquent Solution*. London: Routledge and Kegan Paul.

DUSTER, T. (1970), *The Legislation of Morality*. New York: The Free Press.

ERIKSON, K. (1966), *Wayward Puritans*. New York: Wiley.

ETZIONI, A. (1993), *The Spirit of Community*. New York: Crown Publishers.

EYSENCK, H., and GUDJONSSON, G. (1989), *The Causes and Cures of Criminality*. New York: Plenum Press.

FEATHERSTONE, M. (1985), 'Lifestyle and Consumer Culture', *Theory, Culture and Society* 4: 57–70.

FEELEY, M., and SIMON, J (1994), 'Actuarial Justice: The Emerging New Criminal Law', in D. Nelken, ed., *The Futures of Criminology*. London: Sage.

FERRELL, J., and SANDERS, C., eds. (1995), *Cultural Criminology*. Boston, Mass.: Northeastern University Press.

GIDDENS, A. (1991), *Modernity and Self-Identity*. Cambridge: Polity.

GITLIN, T. (1995), *The Twilight of Common Dreams*. New York: Henry Holt.

HANSSON, D. (1995), 'Agenda-ing Agenda: Feminism and the Engendering of Academic Criminology in South Africa' in N. Rafter and F. Heidensohn eds. *International Feminist Perspectives in Criminology*, 43. Milton Keynes: Open University Press.

HARVEY, D. (1989), *The Condition of Postmodernity*. Oxford: Blackwell.

HEBBERECHT, P., HOFMAN, H., PHILIPPETH, K., and COLLE, P. (1992), *Buurt en Criminaliteit*. Brugge: Vanden Broele.

HERRNSTEIN, R., and MURRAY, C. (1994), *The Bell Curve*. New York: The Free Press.

HOBSBAWM, E. (1994), *The Age of Extremes*. London: Michael Joseph.

HOFMAN, H. (1993), 'Some Stories of Crime Prevention', paper given to the Common Study Programme in Criminal Justice and Critical Criminology, University of Gent, 2 November.

HULSMAN, L. (1986), 'Critical Criminology and the Concept of Crime', in *Contemporary Crises* 10, 1: 63–80.

HUTTON, W (1995), *The State We're In*. London: Cape.

JONES, T., MACLEAN, B., and YOUNG, J. (1986), *The Islington Crime Survey*. London: Gower.

KINSEY, R., LEA, J., and YOUNG, J. (1986). *Losing the Fight Against Crime*. Oxford: Blackwell.

KITSUSE, J., and SPECTOR, M., (1973), 'Towards a Sociology of Social Problems', *Social Problems*, 20: 407–19.

LEA, J. (1992), 'The Analysis of Crime', in J. Young and R. Matthews, eds., *Rethinking Criminology: The Realist Debate*, London: Sage.

—— (1997), 'Post-Fordism and Criminality', in N. Jewson and S. MacGregor, eds., *Transforming the City*. London: Routledge.

—— and YOUNG, J. (1984), *What is to be Done About Law and Order?* Harmondsworth: Penguin.

—— and —— (1993), *What is to be Done about Law and Order?* 2nd edn. London: Pluto.

LEMERT, E. (1967). *Human Deviance, Social Problems and Social Control*. Englewood Cliffs, NJ: Prentice Hall.

LIDZ, C., and WALKER, A. (1980), *Heroin, Deviance and Morality*. Beverley Hills, Cal.: Sage.

LIPPENS, R. (1994), 'Critical Criminologies and the Reconstruction of Utopia. Some residual thoughts from the good old days', Erasmus Common Study Programme, Critical Criminology and the Criminal Justice System, University of Bari.

LOADER, I. (1997), 'Criminology and the Public Sphere: Arguments for Utopian Realism', in P. Walton and J. Young, eds., *The New Criminology Revisited*. London: Macmillan.

LOWMAN, J. (1992), 'Rediscovering Crime', in J. Young and R. Matthews, eds., *Rethinking Criminology*. London: Sage.

—— and MACLEAN, B. D., eds. (1992), *Realist Criminology: Crime Control and Policing in the 1990s*. Toronto: University of Toronto Press.

McINTOSH, M. (1971), 'Changes in the Organisation of Thieving', in S. Cohen, ed., *Images of Deviance*. London: Penguin.

MACLEAN, B. D. (1992), 'Introduction: the Origins of Left Realism', in B. D. MacLean and D Milanovic, eds, *New Directions in Critical Criminology*. Vancouver: Collective Press.

—— JONES, T., and YOUNG, J. (1985), *Preliminary Report on the Islington Crime Survey*. Middlesex University: Centre for Criminology.

MACLEAN, B. D., and MILANOVIC, D., eds. (1997), *Thinking Critically About Crime*. Vancouver: Collective Press.

MANN, C. R. (1993), *Unequal Justice: A Question of Color*. Bloomington, Ind.: Indiana University Press.

MATTHEWS, R. (1988), 'Review of *Confronting Crime*', *Contemporary Crisis*, 12: 81–3.

—— and YOUNG, J., eds. (1986), *Confronting Crime*. London: Sage.

—— and —— eds., (1992) *Issues in Realist Criminology*. London: Sage.

MATZA, D. (1969), *Becoming Deviant*. New Jersey: Prentice Hall.

MERTON, R. K. (1938), 'Social Structure and Anomie', *American Sociological Review*, 3: 672–82.

MOONEY, J, (1993), *The Hidden Figure: Domestic Violence in North London*. London: Middlesex University Centre for Criminology.

MURRAY, C. (1990), *The Emerging British Underclass*. London: Institute of Economic Affairs.

—— (1994), *Underclass: The Crisis Deepens*. London: Institute of Economic Affairs.

—— (1996), 'The Ruthless Truth: Prison Works', *Sunday Times*, 12 January, 2.

—— (1997), *Does Prison Work?*. London: Institute of Economic Affairs.

PEARCE, F. (1992), 'The Contribution of "Left Realism" to the Study of Commercial Crime', in J. Lowman and B. D. MacLean, eds, *Realist Criminology: Crime Control and Policing in the 1990s*. Toronto: University of Toronto Press.

PLATT, T. (1996), 'The Politics of Law and Order', *Social Justice*, 21, 3: 3–13.

RUGGIERO, V. (1992), 'Realist Criminology: A Critique', in J. Young and R. Matthews, eds., *Rethinking Criminology: The Realist Debate*. London: Sage.

RUSHTON, P. (1995) *Race, Evolution and Behavior*. New Jersey: Transaction.

SAYER, A, (1984), *Method in Social Science: A Realist Approach*. London: Hutchinson.

SCHARF, W. (1990), 'The Resurgence of Urban Street Gangs' in D. Hansson and D. Van Zyl Smit, eds. *Towards Justice? Crime and State Control in South Africa*. Cape Town: Oxford University Press.

SCHWARTZ, M. D., and DEKESEREDY, W. S. (1991), 'Left Realist Criminology: Strengths, Weaknesses and the Feminist Critique', *Crime, Law and Social Change*, 15: 51–72.

SIMON, W., and GAGNON, J. (1986), 'The Anomie of Affluence: A Post-Mertonian Concept', *American Sociological Review*, 82: 356–78.

SUMNER, C., ed. (1990), *Censure, Politics and Criminal Justice*. Milton Keynes: Open University Press.

—— (1994), *The Sociology of Deviance: An Obituary*. Milton Keynes: Open University Press.

TAYLOR, I., ed. (1990), *The Social Effects of Free Market Policies*. Hemel Hempstead: Harvester.

TAYLOR, I., WALTON, P., and YOUNG, J., (1973), *The New Criminology*. London: Routledge and Kegan Paul.

THOMPSON, E. (1980), 'The Secret State', in E. Thompson, *Writing by Candlelight*. London: Marlin.

TIERNEY, J. (1996), *Criminology: Theory and Context*. Hemel Hempstead: Prentice Hall.

VAN SWAANINGEN, R. (1997), *Critical Criminology: Visions from Europe*. London: Sage.

WILLIS, P. (1990), *Common Culture*. Milton Keynes: Open University Press.

WILSON, J. Q. (1985), *Thinking About Crime*. New York: Vintage Books.

—— and HERRNSTEIN, R. (1985). *Crime and Human Nature*. New York: Simon and Schuster.

WILSON, W. J. (1987). *The Truly Disadvantaged*. Chicago, Ill.: Chicago University Press.

—— (1996), *When Work Disappears*. New York: Knopf.

WOOLGAR, S., and PAWLUCH, D. (1984), 'Ontological Gerrymandering'. *Social Problems*, 32, 3: 214–27.

YOUNG, J. (1971), *The Drugtakers*. London: Paladin.

—— (1974), 'New Dimensions in Subcultural Theory', in J. Rex, ed., *Approaches to Sociology*, 160–86. London: Routledge and Kegan Paul.

—— (1986), 'The Failure of Criminology: the Need for a Radical Realism', in R. Matthews and J. Young, eds., *Confronting Crime*. London: Sage.

—— (1987), 'The Tasks of a Realist Criminology', *Contemporary Crises*, 2: 337–56.

—— (1988), 'Risk of Crime and Fear of Crime: The Politics of Victimization Studies', in M. Maguire and R. Pointing, eds., *Victims of Crime: A New Deal*, 164–74. Milton Keynes: Open University Press.

—— (1991), 'The Rising Demand for Law and Order and Our Maginot Lines of Defence Against Crime', in N. Abercrombie and A. Warde, eds., *Social Change in Contemporary Britain*. Cambridge: Polity.

—— (1992), 'Ten Points of Realism', in J. Young and R. Matthews, eds., *Rethinking Criminology*. London: Sage.

—— (1994), *Policing the Streets*. London: London Borough of Islington.

—— (1997a), 'Writing on the Cusp of Change: A New Criminology for an Age of Late Modernity', in P. Walton and J. Young, eds., *The New Criminology Revisited*. London: Macmillan.

—— (1997b), 'Breaking Windows: Situating The New Criminology', in P. Walton and J. Young, eds, *The New Criminology Revisited*. London: Macmillan.

—— (1997c), 'Charles Murray and the American Prison Experiment' in C. Murray

Does Prison Work? London: Institute of Economic Affairs.

—— (1997c), 'From Inclusive to Exclusive Society: Nightmares in the European Dream' in V. Ruggiero, N. South, and I. Taylor, eds., *European Criminology*. London: Routledge.

—— and Matthews, R (1992), 'Questioning Left Realism', in R. Matthews and J. Young, eds., *Issues in Realist Criminology*, 1–18. London: Sage.

—— and —— eds., (1992), *Rethinking Criminology: The Realist Debate*. London: Sage.

14

Censure, Crime, and State

Colin Sumner

Censure is a concept that stands independently of any particular concept of state or governance[1]. It denotes the practical process of disapproval and stigmatization which arises so frequently in situations of relational conflict. It also refers to the negative ideological formations which designate the practice, demeanour, or other manifestation of self or others as bad, unacceptable, criminal, wicked, mad, delinquent, and so forth. It is understood as both sign and practice; a negative occurrence which inhabits both formal and informal worlds, the spheres of the private and public, and the realms of the imagination and the 'world-out-there'. Censures have an 'in the air'-like quality, as items of culture or subculture, which is not synonymous with their institutionalization in law. They have a mental, spiritual, emotional, or psychological existence as the cuts, barriers, restrictions, guidelines, and controls which regulate our practice as individuals. The practice of censure is understood to be both individual and social: it can be idiosyncratic, personal, or untypical, yet it can also be collective, consensual, partial, and systematic.

I have designated the predominant censures of a society as social censures and taken them to be emotional-conceptual constructions largely framed within the ideological terrain of that society's hegemonic groups. Their sanctification by the state often takes the form of law, a composite political form of office, theatre, ritual, and violence, whose strategic political objective is sometimes simply to conquer and subordinate a population, territory, or space and sometimes, more complexly, to win the consent of already subjugated populations to a system or pattern of social institutions and practices. Social censures have therefore always been integral to the processes of state-formation, order-maintenance, or governance. To paraphrase and rewrite Foucault (1967: p. ix), they are the cuts which distinguish the expressed force of our rulers from that of the subordinate others: they define and denigrate the latter as a violence

---

[1] My own original formulations are to be found in Sumner (1976, 1981, 1982, and 1990a). Some development of the concept of social censure in relation to gender was made in Sumner (1990b), Gransee and Stammerman (1992), and Althoff and Leppelt (1995); in relation to hegemony and politics by Wing Lo (1992); in relation to punishment by Sumner (1995); in relation to social control in Bergalli and Sumner (1997); in relation to violence and culture in Sumner (1997), and in relation to criminological theory in general by Muncie and McLaughlin (1996) and Tierney (1996).

which is unlawful or criminal; they laud and legitimate the former as the necessary aggression of the social power in its quest for order and progress.

Social censures are thus not simply the negative ideological categories expressed in law but also the partisan judgements which positively constitute the very institutions of state and government as the legitimate force of the land. They are literally part of our constitution, whether that be the constitution of our institutions of state as mechanisms of societal organization or the constitution of our selves as the identities which drive our practices as individuals. For criminological research in the twentieth century to take so often the state's crime categories as adequate scientific definitions of human behaviour or social practice was, in effect, to elevate ideologically constructed, emotionally loaded, moral-political judgements to the status of rational universals which were supposedly free of passionate indignation and which allegedly did not vary with time, context, or culture. The fact that these categories sometimes resonate with our own identities as individuals partially constituted by those very same censures was to overlook completely the social and political processes which had forged, and continue to nurture, that mirror recognition. The whole basis of much of twentieth-century criminology from Lombroso onwards was thus flawed. Its scientific pretensions could be seen to be illusory: a castle of correlations founded on a bed of shifting sand. For so long in this century, the social fragility and historical contingency of the constitution of right and wrong has been protected by the institutions of state and the profession of criminology from the relentless tides of relational thinking.

At the end of this very same century, the moral absolutes of this state-propagated rational universalism seem so disfigured and shredded by the holocausts, hypocrisies, and corruptions of every amoral decade that we are witnessing the emergence of a new form of absolute: those doctrines which specify the present as the eternal form of being—fragmented, dislocated, abject, guilty, incoherent, and homeless—an absence that has no territory, no nation, no integrity, and thus no state or sciences of ethics. Many souls identify with the confused refugee: there can be no more 'moral panics' (Cohen, 1972); they are too alienated and embittered by the failure of their fathers and fatherlands to deliver the firmly located security and sense of place upon which they could found a morality to panic about. All they do is complain and censure in a 'culture of complaint' (see Hughes, 1993) unbounded by any territorially secure state and only partially orchestrated by global media, themselves seduced by their own cyberreal and most unvirtuous reality as the producers of daily spectacles of crime and deviance dislocated in time and space from any remaining indigenous communities and nation-states.

These ideas require further development. But they also demand a new reflection on what we supposed were the relations between the state and the social censure of crime. In this essay, I want to take the opportunity to advance further our understanding of those relations. I shall argue that social censures have a complex relation to the state but nevertheless that some conception of state is valuable to our understanding of how the sociality of social censures is constructed.

HEGEMONY THEORY AND THE SOCIAL CENSURE OF CRIME

Contrary to instrumentalist formulations of criminalization and crime categories, which portray the latter as an economic or political-strategic stick by which the state beats society into shape to create some kind of order, my earlier interpretations of social censures emphasized that they were ideological formations firmly lodged within the wider hegemonic cultures of dominant groups. Law and law enforcement were understood as concrete, practical manifestations of such social censures. Even when criminal law or criminalizations appeared to be very instrumental, and not at all imbricated within a struggle for ideological dominance, as in colonial social formations (see Sumner, 1982), it could easily be seen that, embedded within such legal texts and their operationalization, there were ideological concepts, and the concomitant emotions and rationality which gave them shape and which owed their existence to a culture that was at least hegemonic elsewhere. Hegemony theories of social censure thus emphasized that a will to dominate needed targets and targets needed selection, description, discrimination, and identification. The gun, the boot, and the whip needed pointing in the right direction, otherwise they were just random violence. Targets were understood as the products of ideological specifications, and the need to censure as crime was grasped as an ideologically and culturally structured emotional configuration. In short, even in the crudest forms of booty or colonial capitalism, instrumentalist conceptualizations were seen as lacking an important dimension of sociological analysis—the ideational and cultural.

It would be useful here to clarify this earlier claim about the hegemonic character of social censures.

- First, it would be a weak, albeit valid, claim if it only supposed that criminalization contained an ideational component. That ideological element had to be connected to a hegemonic project. It was essential to this analysis that the strategic imagination within the social censure of crime was ultimately rooted in a culture that was interested in legitimating and establishing in perpetuity its domination in a particular territory or had at least constructed its legitimating concepts and its desire for ideological (and not just military) hegemony in some previous struggle for power. So, for example, even the highly militaristic style of policing in British colonial Africa owed a huge debt, not only to the formation of that style within earlier colonial wars in Ireland, but also to the subsequent emergence of a symbolism and theory of permanent occupation of the minds of the colonized (see Ahire, 1991; Anderson and Killingray, 1991; also Fanon, 1967). We might also conjecture, along the same lines, that even the most physical pacification of females by males is a moment in a genealogy whose history includes the development and memory of the establishment of a hegemony over animals.

- Secondly, it would have been an overly strong claim if it had supposed that social censure occurred only within a struggle for the hearts and minds of a people. Plainly, in some historical contexts, there is no discernible concern to win consent to rule and, in those cases, social censure takes on a cold, pragmatic, instrumental, insensitive, or bureaucratic character. In South Africa of the 1950s and 1960s, or Thatcher's Britain, for example, the social censure of crime may have been rooted in a certain conservative, imperialist world-view forged in the heat of much earlier political struggles but it could not remotely be seen to have played any integrationist hegemonic role in relation to the whole population. Censure sometimes simply polarizes, divides, and alienates.

- Thirdly, the general claim that social censures had a hegemonic role never supposed that they were necessarily successful in promoting hegemony even where that may have been their clear objective. Active hegemonic struggles are always contests; some have been lost. Indeed, deploying social censures whose dynamic and impetus belonged to a bygone era, or which blatantly discriminated against large sections of the population in favour of the ruling groups, was a sure-fire recipe for ensuring opposition to the ruling culture. In such situations, counter-censures abound and can be active in the formation of alternative hegemonies. In these contexts, master-censures (see Sumner, 1990*b*) are often revealed as merely censures of the masters.

- Fourthly, sometimes it is necesary to recognize that a criminalizing censure was only aimed at, or could only have achieved, the support of certain sections of the population, and thus could only reinforce a very specific and limited hegemony. Indeed, it should not be forgotten that, even in the pure case with all other considerations cast aside, a social censure must always discriminate against, and possibly annoy, one or more sections of the population, namely its target group.

- Fifthly, it is vital never to forget that some social censures can be represented as universal moral rules or apolitical ethics because they really do command considerable assent from a majority of the population of a territory during a specific phase in a society's history. That is to say, they can be recognized and thus seen as reflections of an individual's own view of things—and thus as 'right'.

THE IDEA OF THE STATE AND ITS RELATION TO THE HEGEMONY THEORY OF THE SOCIAL CENSURE OF CRIME

Even with the above qualifications and clarifications, and even with a commitment to retaining a concept of hegemony (which retains its popularity despite all recent attempted deconstructions of the state concept), it may be that our time demands a reflection on the implications for the idea of state of the theory of social censures of crime as key features of hegemonic struggles—and of the implications of a transformed theory of state for a hegemony perspective on the social censures of crime.

The Idea of the State

Insofar as criminological theorizing in the 1970s used a theory of the state at all that theory was of the Marxist type. As Jessop observes (1990: 2), since that time there has been a decline of use of, and crisis within, Marxist state theory. This has coincided with the emergence or revival of a variety of approaches to politics or governance which draw little from any state theory of any kind. Jessop asserts that the reasons for the decline in Marxist state theory were to do with the crisis in Marxism and with the rise of alternative approaches concerned with feminism, ecology, single-issue politics, and so on, and that, nevertheless, there was a considerable revival of state theory at the end of the 1980s. Much of this literature is highly specialized and complex, whether deconstructionist in tenor or of the state-return type, and very little of it has impinged upon criminological thought, despite the fact that criminology is allegedly dealing with the very political phenomena of criminal justice systems and the social censure of crime. Therefore, I do not want even to attempt an exposition of either that or the earlier Marxist literature (see Jessop, 1990, for a comprehensive and authoritative review of debates in that area). That work needs to be done for the benefit of criminology at some stage soon, but for now it might be more useful to return to some basic points about the value of state theory and to summarize where contemporary state theory might be going.

At its simplest, the purpose of a theory of state is to talk about an important site of social power, and therefore it is of immense relevance to criminological theorizing given that the latter is concerned with such matters as the administration of criminal justice and the reasons for the emergence of particular criminal laws or penal strategies at particular points in a history. Those criminologies which excluded a theory of state tended to suppose that the state was too abstract a concept to be of use in its pragmatic analysis of penal systems or that all that really existed were government agencies and personnel unhampered by any co-ordination of policy and strategy, any relation to the economy or social divisions in general, or any overriding or underpinning tendency, albeit historically specific, towards the protection and furtherance of a particular type of social order and a particular set of social patterns and relationships. I have to say that I still find such an exclusion puzzling in its naïveté: it is extraordinarily difficult to see how the pattern of governmental activity and its relations with economy, culture, and social divisions could not be more visible to the criminological eye. It is not at all necessary to be a Conservative or a Marxist, nor to assert the power of capital, class, or whatever, to observe the fairly systematic patterning of the effects of the institutions of government and the recurrent major influences upon them. The concept of the state, in whatever type of social theorizing, did the job of summarizing the effects of a certain co-ordination of governmental powers and their constituent forces or influences. The common absence of such a concept, whether conservative, liberal, or Marxist, within criminology left it open to criticisms of empiricism, pragmatism, and collusion. All too often we were left with a history of bits and pieces of powerful action, or a sociology-free, amateurish, semi-social science which never questioned the roots or patterns of the behaviour of the society's most powerful institutions and some of its most powerful people. Of course, there have been many piecemeal critiques of particular laws, policies or cases in criminology but very little, until the development of critical criminology in the late 1960s, in the way of an analysis which connected the particular to the general. Consequently, some of our society's most violent or misery-creating tendencies remained free of a fundamental criticism of their recurrence and recalcitrance.

A concept of state then connects the particular case to the general movement. It connects the specific criminal law to the pattern of legislation in a history or genealogy. It connects the particular censures of crime to more generalized social relationships. It connects the micro-powers of individuals and institutions to the macro-powers of agencies and groups. It connects the singular criminal instance to the aggregate of criminalizations. Whichever conception of state is preferred, the job of the concept is to articulate the form of summation of social powers in a set of governmental institutions and to express the immediate basis of their effects on and in society. Of course, the state is an abstraction; a concept which articulates a number of institutions and practices—that is what abstractions do: they abstract from the particular to speak about the whole and the location of that whole within a universe of wholes. It need not be a totalizing concept which denies power to other sites in the society. Nor need it speak as if the state were an individual acting like a human being. Nor need it be tied to a theory of the primacy of class relations, or to a theory of the supremacy of the elite, or to a theory of the centrality of men, in the analysis of systems of political organization or domination. All of the above is reasonably elementary and has not yet registered in many forms of criminology.

The key problems with Marxist state theory at the end of the 1970s revolved around its connection to the theory of class exploitation as the central power-system in societies, and these problems had some negative effects upon critical criminology, weakening its capacity to link the censure of crime to general social patterns. These problems can be simplified as follows: (a) a too-frequent habit of talking of the state as if it were a human subject planning and doing things in a conscious, unified, purposive way; (b) a tendency to reduce the patterns of state practice to the supposed 'needs' of the economically dominant class, thus neglecting the effects and interventions of other social categories and divisions; (c) a tendency to assume that the state is not full of contradictions and conflicts, thus dismissing the important role of particular individuals or agencies; (d) an inclination to minimize the roles and effects of other forms of social power, as if the state dictated everything in society; (e) a frequent belief that the state had an overrriding historical function or goal and that everything its agents and agencies did was an expression of that function or goal; (f) a systematic neglect of the relationships between the state and the nation or national identity, and between the nation-state and the growing forces of international power (multinationals and international state agencies), thus being insufficiently able to analyse the increasing, concrete, decentring, and/or weakening of the state as a summation of national power; and (g) a stubborn disinclination to see any aspect or practice of state as a positive advancement of, or having potential for, democratic, ethical, popular, or legal restriction on more absolute, private, or narrower powers, the consequence of which was a minimization of the value of civil rights, human rights, corporate or socialized activities, and welfare provisions—which in turn led to a political quietism in relation to such questions as Thatcherism, the reunification of Germany, the transformations in South Africa, and the fall of communism in Eastern Europe. Nevertheless—and this needs much emphasis—none of the above represented a basis for throwing out a concept of state as such. The enthusiasm for stateless conceptions of the polity after 1980 was, on the one hand, a revelation of an anti-Marxism that was not innocent of class roots or political self-interest and, on the other hand, somewhat premature. The state is still with us and we still need to find the concepts to think it. Power is not now so dispersed, fragmented, and disjointed that we can celebrate an era of individual growth: it remains summarized and consummated at the summit, and that summit is not randomly constituted or random in its effects.

Advances in State Theory

Contrary to Dario Melossi (1990), I dislike the idea of returning to a Millsian conception of social control to resolve our difficulties with the concept of state (see my essays in Bergalli and Sumner, 1997)—however much one might revere Mills' work or recognize the immense significance of 1930s America for political thinking in the twentieth century (see Sumner, 1994, for an example of such respect). My rationalization for this antipathy, for present purposes, is that I cannot see a solid basis in our current constitution (in the double sense of constitution averred to earlier) for a resurrection of a democratic public built around shared vocabularies of motive, negotiable world-views or pluralistic procedures of debate in accessible media or political institutions. This constitution seems instead to be one which seems to preclude the politics which might be the basis for such a utopia. It is also one which constantly betrays Habermas's attempts to connect the idea of redeemable normative validity claims to some kind of democratic praxis in a community free of systematically distorted communication—I take Bernstein's commentary on these attempts, and those of writers like Benhabib, to be a strong and authoritative articulation of my own doubts (see Bernstein, 1995). Moreover, recourse to a rediscovered 'democratization' in Eastern Europe, as some kind of timely reminder of our loss of sense of democratic direction, is equally unsatisfactory—even in the heady days when Marxist theorizing of the state was a commonplace, our scorn for the communistic pretensions of the Stalinist East was frequently accompanied by a sense that it merely disclosed and disguised an undeveloped capitalism. So why should we now suppose that the current developments are 'democratizations' and not the manifestations of a 'corporate national populism which includes all its usual elements, from xenophobia to anti-Semitism' (Zizek, 1993: 200)? Our fascination with the disintegration of Eastern Communism is thus, as Zizek suggests, a symptom of our profound sense of the decay of Western democracy.

The clues to a way forward might rest in this instinctive disinclination to revive any existing theory of the current polity as the voluntary and sporadic, loose and contingent, disparate and fragmentary expression of a democratic society of individuals with a will to talk. As Zizek observes: 'A nation *exists* only as long as its specific *enjoyment* continues to be materialized in a set of social practices and transmitted through national myths that structure these practices' (1993: 202). In short, a strong sense of that grand old Marxian founding principle, which grounds social phenomena in social practices,[2] and their complex interrelation and effects, rather than over-bloated abstractions, seems a good guide through the uncertainty.

Following Poulantzas' work (well illustrated by Vogler (1990), and noting the connected critiques of state theory by Foucault and the Foucauldians (well exemplified by Garland (1985; 1990), and holding on to the idea of the foundational role of social practices, we could understand the state even today as an ensemble of practices and institutions which acts as the socially recognized summit and summation of a number of social powers themselves rooted in widespread social practices (for a fuller and more elaborated definition, see Jessop, 1990: 341). Without necessarily supposing any ultimate telos or logos, or any single motor (of class or gender) which might drive this ensemble, a conception of state can be formulated which, even in our times, has 'societalization' effects (see Jessop, 1990: 4). A non-essentialist, relational, concept of state is developed in Jessop's work, and for present purposes it is sufficient to note simply that, even using his work alone, we can see how the state can be

---

[2] Throughout, I shall be using this concept to refer to socially and ideologically structured purposive activities that have some generality within a field of social practices (see Sumner, 1979). It is both a relational conception, referring to internal and external structures of social activity, and also a conception of agency referring to the ideational component and effects of activities.

formulated in ways which provide extremely potent analytic tools. Combining a sense of the strategic-discursive-hegemonic character of the state with a grip of its intrinsic structural qualities and parameters, Jessop's work maintains the idea that political history is not just the particular but also the general—and in combination. The specifics of government can be emphasized at the same time as their structural-relational and hegemonic-discursive features—or as Garland has recently recognized, governmentality thinking needs combining with classical theories of the social (see Garland, 1997). Indeed, as Jessop points out, by combining the insights of both approaches one can deepen both: the micro-political analysis of power and the theories of the relative autonomy of hegemonic discourse, when combined with a relational analysis of condensed social power and its societalizing effects could even lead to the recognition that the state is not always in every historical period the 'crucial strategic terrain on which "macro-social" relations are codified and rendered coherent' (Jessop, 1990: 246). The state's role and its place in hegemonic struggle are always an historical issue which must be rooted in an anlysis of the configurations of practices, powers, and resistances of the day.

The State, the Social Censure of Crime, and Hegemony

If I can be permitted, for present purposes, to take it that the 'core of the state apparatus comprises a distinct ensemble of institutions and organizations whose socially accepted function is to define and enforce collectively binding decisions on the members of a society in the name of the common interest or general will' (Jessop, 1990: 341), we can see that state discourse and discourses about the state are very important to the constitution of the state itself and that the struggle for the definition of the common interest and general will is vital for the summative capacity of the state. Hegemonic projects are thus vital to secure the constitution of the state as a political and moral force, that is, as a force which can have effects within social practices (see, for example, Hall *et al.*, 1978). These projects tend to be attempts to address and resolve, in favour of the directive or ruling groups, ideological conflicts arising from deep tensions or antagonisms within the social relations which structure concrete economic, political, or cultural practices. If they are successful they give the state a certain power to create societal effects or, in other words, to codify, order, and regulate social practices in ways which are legitimized as societally or generally beneficial.

On this basis, it can easily be seen why the social censure of crime remains a vital part of the very constitution of the state and thus the political constitution of the society: the definition, identification, marginalization, and exclusion of practices which structurally challenge, oppose, obstruct, discomfort, or irritate the material or ideological foundations of the state, or, importantly, practices which offend groups of citizens whose support the state needs or wishes to cultivate, should, if handled with political sensitivity, not only reinforce the articulated *raison d'être* of the state but work constantly to define and redefine it. The crucial proviso to this conclusion is that these social censures must usually be spoken or written in the grammar of rational universalism not the angry rhetoric of group or individual self-interest. Censures are not just automatically social because they are predominant, their predominance rests in the state's ability to make sure these censures have societalizing effects. That is, the 'social' character of censures has to be constantly constructed, fought for, enforced, or massaged. Of course, the state does not have the sole capacity to make or disseminate censures with societalizing effects: the mass media also have considerable power today in this regard. However, I want to maintain that the enduring significance of the state is its precise ability to deploy censures with 'society-' or 'nation-' building effects, or societalizing effects. Indeed, I would argue that is in the very nature of the state that it has constructed and developed, over the centuries, special legitimizing properties for itself as *the* legitimator and enforcer of moral and political judgements, otherwise it would simply be another powerful ideological institution like the mass media. What gives the state its special power both coercively and ideologically is that historically it has won the social right to define the law of the land, and the procedures by which that law is created—and crucially to enforce that definition and procedure with violence legitimated as 'necessary force'. That is what many of the earlier historic struggles between church, parliament, judiciary, and monarchy have been all about. In the twenty-first century, that struggle may be replayed, but this time, perhaps, between the political executive and the global media.

In conclusion, if my argumentation is correct, social censures are not important simply because they are often sanctioned by the state as law; nor because they are predominant in a society. More subtly and profoundly, they are important because they are vital components of the constitution of the 'social' field of practices which defines and constructs the state itself as a crucial, and usually *the* crucial, site for the codification, integration, articulation, and enforcement of powers with societalizing effects. In short, there is a circle of relations between censure, the state, the law, and social practices. Albeit that this is a complex circle of interrelations, with many historical variations of form and content, censure is involved in the very definition of the state itself, marking it off from its enemies or friendly rivals; in the very definition of the law which defines and is expressed by the state; and in the constitution of the social practices which sustain the state or which challenge its authority and power. What makes censure 'social' is the capacity of particular sites of power to deploy it in ways which give it societalizing effects, and in that respect the state, whether it be national, local, or international, still plays an important role. To put it mildly, an analysis of criminalization which refuses to use a concept of state thus denies itself the full sociological capacity to speak of and compare the full range of sites of power which can legitimate particularistic censures as the social censures of crime and thus convert the practically rooted specific interest into a rational universal. Finally, of course, a statist analysis of power which does not grasp the significance of social censure in the constitution of the state itself, its hegemonic projects and its societalizing effects must always deny itself a sociological understanding of the moral-ideological and cultural character of politics.

Selected Further Reading

Chapter 2 of Sumner 1990*a* is probably the best way to start on the theory of social censures, and the argument there is well illustrated in Wing Lo (1992). Jessop's *State Theory* (1990) is an authoritative guide to many of the key debates within theories of the state over the last two decades, and Hall *et al.* (1978) demonstrate why, and how, many scholars got involved with hegemony theories in the analysis of crime. Tierney (1996) indicates the place of such theories in the history of criminology.

REFERENCES

AHIRE, P. T. (1991), *Imperial Policing: The Emergence and Role of the Police in Colonial Nigeria 1860–1960*. Milton Keynes: Open University Press.

ALTHOFF, M., and LEPPELT, M. (1995), *'Kriminalität'—eine diskursive Praxis.* Hamburg: LIT Verlag.

ANDERSON, D. M., and KILLINGRAY, D. (1991), *Policing the Empire*. Manchester: Manchester University Press.

BERGALLI, R., and SUMNER, C., eds. (1997), *Social Control and Political Order: European Perspectives at the End of the Century*. London: Sage.

BERNSTEIN, J. M. (1995), *Recovering Ethical Life*. London: Routledge.

COHEN, S. (1973), *Folk Devils and Moral Panics*. St Albans: Paladin.

FANON, F. (1967), *The Wretched of the Earth*. Harmondsworth: Penguin.

GARLAND, D. (1985), *Punishment and Welfare: A History of Penal Strategies*. Aldershot: Gower.

—— (1990), *Punishment and Modern Society*. Oxford: Clarendon Press.

—— (1997), '"Governmentality" and the Problem of Crime: Foucault, Criminology, Sociology', *Theoretical Criminology*, 1, 2: 173–213.

GRANSEE, C., and STAMMERMAN, U. (1992), *Kriminalität als Konstruktion von Wirklichkeit und die Kategorie Geschlecht: Versuch einer feministischen Perspektive*. Hamburg: Centaurus-Gerglasgesellschaft.

HALL, S., CRITCHER, C., JEFFERSON, T., CLARKE, J., and ROBERTS, B. (1978), *Policing the Crisis: Mugging, the State, and Law and Order*. London: Macmillan.

HUGHES, R. (1993), *Culture of Complaint*. London: Harvill.

JESSOP, B. (1990), *State Theory*. Cambridge: Polity.

MELOSSI, D. (1990). *The State of Social Control: A Sociological Study of Concepts of State and Social Control in the Making of Democracy*. Cambridge: Polity.

MUNCIE, J., and McLAUGHLIN, E., eds. (1996), *The Problem of Crime*. London: Sage.

SUMNER, C. S. (1976), 'Marxism and Deviancy Theory', in P. Wiles, ed., *The Sociology of Crime and Delinquency in Britain: Vol. 2: The New Criminologies*. London: Martin Robertson.

—— (1979), *Reading Ideologies*. London: Academic Press.

—— ed., (1982), *Crime, Justice and Underdevelopment*. London: Heinemann.

—— ed., (1990*a*), *Censure, Politics and Criminal Justice*. Milton Keynes: Open University Press.

—— (1990*b*), 'Foucault, Gender and the Censure of Deviance', in L. Gelsthorpe and A. Morris, eds., *Feminist Perspectives in Criminology*. Milton Keynes: Open University Press.

—— (1994), *The Sociology of Deviance: An Obituary*. Buckingham: Open University Press.

—— (1995), 'Censura, Cultura e Pena', *Dei Delitti e delle Pene*, iii, 127–36. In English: http://www.vel.ac.uk:80/faculties/socsci/law/csrps.html (University of East London,

School of Law, Research Publication Series, 1996, no. 2.

—— ed. (1997), *Violence, Culture and Censure.* London: Taylor and Francis.

TIERNEY, J. (1996), *Criminology: Theory and Context.* London: Harvester Wheatsheaf.

VOGLER, R. (1991), *Reading the Riot Act: The Magistracy, the Police and the Army in Civil Disorder.* Milton Keynes: Open University Press.

Wing Lo, T. (1992), *Corruption and Politics in Hong Kong and China.* Milton Keynes: Open University Press.

ZIZEK, S. (1993), *Tarrying with the Negative.* Durham: Duke University Press.

15

Feminism and Criminology

Loraine Gelsthorpe

INTRODUCTION: SETTING THE SCENE FOR A CONTEMPORARY REVIEW

Nearly ten years ago Allison Morris and I attempted to describe something of the relationship between feminism and criminology in Britain in the mid-1980s (Gelsthorpe and Morris, 1988). We recorded then that, despite some serious doubts whether a single feminist criminology could exist because it could not do justice to the differences and tensions that exist within the field, it was still possible to talk of feminist criminologies or, better still, of feminist perspectives in criminology. By this we meant that critical insights within different kinds of feminism could be used to transform and transgress both theory and the politics of research and action in criminology. In essence, we might say that feminists have been engaged in two main projects in relation to criminology: (i) a substantive and political project which has focused on the absence of a gender dimension in mainstream criminological theory, and on the need for equality and fairness in notions of justice and in the delivery of justice, and (ii) an epistemological and methodological project which has focused on the need to recognize forms of knowledge based on experience, and the need to use research methods sensitive to the task of eliciting an understanding of *women's experiences*. We were optimistic of change in criminology, if frustrated because of seemingly strong defences against feminist insights and research practices.

It strikes me now that it remains important to speak of different feminist perspectives, and perhaps too of different criminologies, for there is no one relationship, but a myriad of relationships between feminism and criminology; and the criminology of the 1970s which provided the context for the emergence of Carol Smart's 1976 text *Women, Crime and Criminology* (which possibly offers the first openly feminist critique of criminology in Britain) is not the criminology of the 1990s. The criminology of the 1990s seems much more diverse—and *possibly* diverse or open enough to accommodate some of the critical precepts of feminisms. At the same time, there are feminists who have made a strong case for abandoning criminology (Smart, 1990), and those who

I am grateful to Ruth Jamieson, Mark Fenwick, Sue Rex, Rod Morgan, and Mike Maguire for their helpful comments on an earlier draft of this chapter.

see fundamental incompatibilities (Stanko, 1993; Young, 1994) because of resistance to a feminist transformation of the discipline of criminology. In a percipient conclusion to her 1976 text Smart commented:

> Criminology and the sociology of deviance must become more than the study of men and crime if it is to play any significant part in the development of our understanding of crime, law and the criminal process and play any role in the transformation of existing social practices [Smart, 1976: 185].

Her concern was that criminology, even in its more radical form, would be 'unmoved' by feminist critiques. By 1990, she viewed criminology as the 'atavistic man' in intellectual endeavours, and wished to abandon it because she could not see what it had to offer feminism. But whereas the abandonment of criminology once seemed a logical response to criminological intransigence, I now believe that, given recent signs of critical thinking in criminology, there is good reason to pause before pursuing this option.

There have been several meaningful explorations of the relationship between feminism and criminology in the last ten years (Daly and Chesney-Lind, 1988; Gelsthorpe and Morris, 1990; Heidensohn, 1994; Young, 1994; Naffine, 1995; Rafter and Heidensohn, 1995, and Naffine, 1997). A key question which has perplexed some of these writers is whether the two key feminist projects I have mentioned make what might be described as the 'criminological project' untenable in and of itself. I mainly address the importance of the feminist epistemological and methodological project for criminology in this chapter (the second of the feminist projects mentioned above). Some of the broader issues relating to the first project which concern the impact of feminism on criminology are dealt with by Frances Heidensohn in this volume, and there is no space to rehearse them here.

So what is it about feminist work that might make criminological work untenable? When we speak of feminism, of course, we are speaking of something which is not obvious and which cannot be taken for granted (Delmar, 1986). In a powerful exposition of feminist thinking Rosemarie Tong (1989) illuminates some of the key differences between different feminist perspectives. Whilst her catalogue of feminisms and history of feminist thought is not the only one that might be produced (see Oakley, 1981, and Judith Evans, 1995, for example), Tong (1989) identifies and elaborates upon six main kinds of feminism:

> *Liberal feminism*—involving a commitment to reforms concerning equal civil rights and equality of opportunity and the recognition of women's rights in welfare, health, employment, and education;
> *Marxist feminism*—which aims to describe the material basis of women's oppression, and the relationship between the modes of production and women's status; and to apply theories of women and class to the role of the family.
> *Socialist feminism*—involving beliefs that women are treated as second-class citizens in patriarchal capitalism and that we need to transform

not only the ownership of the means of production, but also the social experience because the *roots* of women's oppression lie in the total economic system of capitalism.

Existential feminism—existentialism is a philosophical theory which argues that individuals are free and responsible agents able to transcend their social roles and determine their own development. Feminist existentialism is perhaps epitomized by Simone de Beauvoir's *The Second Sex* in which she argues that women are oppressed because they are 'Other' to man's 'Self', and that as 'Other' they are 'not man'. Man is taken to be the 'Self', the free, self-determining agent who defines his own existence, whilst woman remains the 'Other', the object, whose meaning is determined by what she is not.

Psycho-analytical feminism—psycho-analysis is a term invented by Freud (1897) to refer to his theory of the psyche and the methods and techniques he applied to understanding it. Whilst psycho-analysis has come under attack because of its seemingly inherent sexism (emphasizing biology over social relations and taking masculine characteristics as the norm), a feminist psycho-analysis has been developed to show how prevailing norms of gender are imposed and structure the human mind. Feminist psycho-analysis is sometimes referred to as gender theory.

Postmodern feminism—drawing on the general features of postmodernism as a major cultural phenomenon in the arts, architecture, philosophy, and economics which, *inter alia*, involve a rejection of the idea of single explanations or philosophies, feminist postmodernism involves opposition to essentialism (the belief that differences between men and women are innate—rather than socially/experientially constructed), and a belief in more plural kinds of knowledge. Some of the roots of postmodern feminism are found in the work of Simone de Beauvoir, whose critical exploration of women as the 'Other' has been turned on its head, so that the condition of 'Otherness' is celebrated in all its diverse forms. Emphasis on the positive side of 'Otherness' is a major theme in the associated deconstructionist approaches and in the celebration of a plurality of knowledges. The so-called rationality and objectivity of contemporary science also comes under attack in feminist postmodernism (Harding, 1986; Benhabib, 1992), and there are attempts to create fluid, open terms and language which more closely reflect women's experiences. There is a further dimension to feminist postmodernism here in the creation of a new language, *écriture feminine* (Cixous, 1976; Irigaray, 1977).

Postmodern feminism is perceived to have the most difficult relationship with the broad project of feminism (Tong, 1989; Nicholson, 1990), largely because of beliefs that feminism itself may be misconceived in assuming that it is possible to provide *overarching* explanations for women's oppression and identify steps towards its resolution. At the same time, it is arguable that feminist criminologists have at least been open to debates in this area and that this has been important in terms of developing the epistemological project that I have mentioned. I shall return to this point in due course.

Collectively, these different positions illustrate men's material interest in the domination of women and the different ways in which men construct a variety of institutional arrangements to sustain this domination, and argue for the case for the economy to be fully transformed. Also, there is the creation of concepts of 'womanculture' and alternative institutions, the reconstruction of reality from women's point of view and the exposure of a concealed masculine bias in the conceptual framework of much of traditional knowledge and false dualisms in traditional political theory. The aim has been to 'make visible the invisible' by bringing into focus the gender structure of society (Rowbotham, 1973; Mitchell, 1984; Mitchell and Oakley, 1986; Humm, 1992; 1995). Generally then, feminists have challenged the political, ontological, and epistemological assumptions that underlie patriarchal discourses as well as their theoretical contents, and have developed both an anti-sexist stance and a stance which involves the construction of alternative models, methods, procedures, and discourses, and so on.

Of course, such 'postage stamp' summaries do not do justice to the concepts and theories involved in feminisms, but I hope they are not misleading in outlining some of the key challenges to criminology. There are crucial, theoretical, conceptual and methodological distinctions within these feminist perspectives, and such ideas are not mutually exclusive (see, for example, Hirsch and Keller, 1990); different theorists might subscribe to different strands of thought within each group of theories. My intention is merely to create a broad impression of feminist claims and challenges. From this, it is possible to see how feminist approaches to criminology have been informed in a multiplicity of ways, and we can gain a broad impression of the direction of challenges to criminology and criminal justice.

THE INTELLECTUAL INHERITANCE OF CRIMINOLOGY

What does the intellectual endeavour involved in these feminisms mean for criminology? Large sections of the first and second volumes of the *Oxford Handbook* alone are testament to the dominant intellectual history of criminology alone, though it has been the subject of much debate and critique elsewhere too (Rock, 1988; Cohen, 1988; Garland, 1992, 1994; Young, 1994; Rock, 1994; Naffine, 1997, for example). What is beyond dispute, however, is that it was traditionally conceived as the scientific study of the causes of crime and that the 'scientific endeavour' involving 'methods, techniques or rules of procedure', more than substantive theory or perspective (Gottfredson and Hirschi, 1987: 10), is possibly 'healthier and more self-assured' than hitherto (Gottfredson and Hirschi, 1987: 18). The strident belief in an objective exter-

nal reality capable of measurement, and a fascination with causal and correlational factors—whether they be situational opportunities or low self-control
or relative deprivation—is reflected in the pages of new and old textbooks alike.

The essentials are that mainstream criminology has been dominated by a
persistent commitment to what Garland (1994) has described as 'the
Lombrosian project' and 'the governmental project'. What he means by the
Lombrosian project is a form of enquiry 'which aims to develop an etiological,
explanatory science, based on the premise that criminals can somehow be
scientifically differentiated from non-criminals' (Garland, 1994: 18)—essentially what is described as a 'science of causes'. The governmental project
involves a long series of empirical enquiries which 'have sought to enhance the
efficient and equitable administration of justice by charting the patterns of
crime and monitoring the practice of police and prisons' (1994: 18)—essentially
what might be described as 'conservative administrative criminology'. In examining developments in criminology, Naffine (1997) describes how the logic of
conventional 'scientific criminology' looms large and presses on even in the
1980s and 1990s.

There have been important intellectual/sociological starts along the way.
Sociological insights are evident in the history of the sociology of crime and
deviance, though women and 'gender' are absent from analyses (Millman,
1975; Smart, 1976; Scraton, 1990). And picking on one particular 'progressive'
criminology as an example, the 'New Criminology' (Taylor, Walton, and
Young, 1973) attempted to eschew the scientific orthodoxy and, instead,
illustrate how crime was socially constructed through the capacity of state
institutions to define and confer criminality on others. But they do this in an
'ungendered' way (Sumner, 1994; Naffine, 1997). In this progressive conception of events, crime is not simply an act, but a reflection of a political process.
The new criminologists had taken note of the new deviancy theorists' work on
social reaction (see, for example, Becker, 1963) seeing the application of a label
of deviance as part of a broader context of social, political, and cultural
relations. This meant grounding a transactional approach to deviancy in an
analysis of the political economy, class relations, and class practices. In developing an agenda for a social theory of deviance the new criminologists
connected the established influences of social interaction with a Marxist
perspective which prioritized structural relations. The development of critical
analysis subsequently involved a questioning of how certain acts become
'eligible' for regulation, selective law enforcement, and sentencing. But it is
argued that there is a total neglect of gender in this analysis.

Again, whilst left realist theoretical propositions give attention to the social
and political context of crime and crime control and, importantly, to victims,
it is argued that there is 'essentialism' in the thinking (see Brown and Hogg,
1992, and Carlen, 1992, for example) because of the partial or misconceived
recognition of gender (women's fear of crime is recognized, but not in a direct
way, for the fear of crime is generally a fear of men). As Jock Young (1994)
describes, left realism concerns a body of ideas which emerged in the 1980s as

a critique of existing criminological theory, and as a response to the pressing realities of crime. Left realism's analytical framework looks at the links between social order and social justice. At the same time, its critical stance involves the development of a whole raft of interventionist policies to deal with the realities of crime (incuding the experiences of victims). But this has been seen as inadequate when it comes to women's experiences. (Other criticisms are identified by contributors to Matthews and Young, 1992.) Overall, it has been argued that the left realists do no more than offer a sophisticated version of a scientific paradigm—a paradigm which is largely ungendered.

Equally, Foucauldian insights in criminology have been of crucial importance in directing attention to power and knowledge and the discursive practices of control. However, as Sumner (1990), for one, has pointed out, whilst Foucauldian thought addresses issues of discrimination, the deeper, structural condition of hegemonic masculinity is not addressed. The gendered character of disciplinary power has been ignored (Diamond and Quinby, 1988).

Despite these intellectual/sociological starts then, which offer important challenges to mainstream criminology and indicate some exciting critical insights, none has been adequate in conceptualizing gender; there has been no fundamental shift in gear to address feminists' questions about criminological knowledge. Feminist challenges to criminology have come from different directions—not always in forms that make the theoretical lineage clear, but in clear and unmistakable ways that question the epistemological basis and methodological processes of criminology.

FEMINISM WITHIN AND WITHOUT CRIMINOLOGY: FEMINIST ASSESSMENTS OF THE INTERCONNECTIONS BETWEEN FEMINISM AND CRIMINOLOGY

Whilst avoiding some of the internecine arguments about who or what is feminist (arguments which are all well rehearsed elsewhere—see Delmar, 1986; Morris, 1987; Daly and Chesney-Lind, 1988; Gelsthorpe and Morris, 1988, 1990, for example), we can identify a broad range of feminist work which questions criminology. Essentially, there is an early critique of criminological theory and of criminal justice practices (what I call 'the feminist political project') and then a more discursive questioning of the epistemological and methodological contours of the discipline (what I call 'the epistemological and methodological project').

The Early Critique

Drawing generally from the feminist positions outlined above, the feminist critique of criminology first developed with a comprehensive critique of the discipline. (This is not to undervalue the critical questions of criminologists such as Frances Heidensohn, writing in 1968, and those who came before—for example Smith, 1962, but simply to place emphasis on more avowedly feminist writings.) The early critique has been well rehearsed elsewhere (see, for example, Morris, 1987); suffice it to say here that it has frequently focused on two main themes of amnesia or neglect and distortion (Smart, 1976; Heidensohn, 1985). It is indisputable that women account for a very small proportion of all known offenders (cf. Greenwood, 1981) despite recently recorded increases (Home Office, 1995), and yet there has been relatively little attention given to women. The neglect of female criminality by a predominantly male profession of criminology is one of its determining features. The vast majority of studies of crime and delinquency prior to the 1980s were of male crime and male delinquency (Leonard, 1982; Scraton, 1990). The discipline was predominantly one of men studying other men. A second theme in the critique is that even when women were recognized, they were depicted in terms of stereotypes based on their supposed biological and psychological nature. Whilst the 'new criminology' challenged the assumptions of positivism in explaining male crime, it neglected to acknowledge how such assumptions remained most prevalent in academic and popular conceptions of female crime. Similarly, while analyses of class structure, state control, and the political nature of deviance gained credibility, the study of female crime remained rooted in notions of biological determinism and an uncritical attitude towards the dominant sexual stereotypes of women as passive, domestic, and maternal (Smart, 1976; cf. Brown, 1986). Tracing the continuance of sexist assumptions from Lombroso to Pollak and beyond, Smart examined how assumptions of the abnormality of female offenders came to dominate both theory and criminal justice policy—despite evidence of more critical thinking in relation to men and male crime. Eileen Leonard (1982) usefully summarized mainstream criminological theory by stating: 'Theories that are frequently hailed as explanations of human behaviour are, in fact, discussions of male behaviour and male criminality. . . . We cannot simply apply these theories to women, nor can we modify them with a brief addition or subtraction here and there' (1982: 181).

In essence, women were ignored or marginalized or distorted both in their deviancy and conformity and the exposure of criminology as the criminology of men marked the starting point of feminist attempts to find alternative modes of conceptualizing the social worlds of deviance and conformity, punishment, and control.

The focus of this general critique, however, has been regarded as limited, and some writers naïvely assumed that a remedy to criminological and criminal justice deficiencies could be sought by appropriating existing criminological theories and 'inserting' women, e.g. by discovering girl gangs (Velimesis, 1975) and considering females in relation to subcultural theory (McRobbie, 1980; Shacklady Smith, 1978). Rafter and Natalizia presented the message in a different way, suggesting that 'women only' studies should strive to produce a body of information as extensive as that which existed for men. In criminal justice practice there were strivings for 'equality' (that is, for women to be treated like men), though this early, undoubtedly unthinking and limited, liberal feminist position gradually came to be challenged by those who questioned the meaning and nature of equality (e.g. MacKinnon, 1987; Fudge, 1989; Smart, 1990). Some of these feminist claims and assertions do indeed now seem rather naïve, but the significance of the critique as a starting point for reflection and for changes in criminal justice practice should not be underestimated. Moreover, feminist contributions soon began to go well beyond a critique.

Dominant strands in the development of feminist perspectives in relation to criminology have included illuminations about discriminatory practices. To take just a handful of examples of this kind of empirical work, imprisoned women have been shown to be likely to experience the promotion and enforcement of a domestic role in penal regimes. Subject to petty and coercive systems of control, they are also more likely to be defined as in need of medical or psychological treatment, than as simply criminal (Morris, 1987; Carlen and Worrall, 1987; Dobash, Dobash and Gutteridge, 1986). The treatment of women in the courts suggests that the widely assumed concept of 'chivalry' may be misplaced, and that women who do not occupy the appropriate gender role may be seen by the court as 'doubly deviant' (see, for example, Edwards, 1984; Eaton, 1986; Gelsthorpe, 1989; Worrall, 1990). Another dominant strand has involved new ways of conceptualizing matters, the different ways in which conformity is produced for instance. Heidensohn (1985) concludes her review of women, crime, and criminal justice by arguing for a return to the sociology of gender and the use of insights from other studies of women's oppression. Such a redirection has helped expose the explicit *and* informal controls exercised over women—in the home and at work—and, above all, has focused on the rather peculiar notion of 'normal behaviour'. Smart and Smart, 1978; Hutter and Williams, 1981; Klein and Kress, 1976; and Allen, 1987; along with Cain (1989), have made apparent the correspondences between the policing of everyday life and policing through more formal mechanisms of social control. There has been a large body of empirical work drawing attention to female victims of crime and criminal justice processes (see, for example, Dobash and Dobash, 1992; Stanko, 1985, 1990; Walklate, 1989, 1992). Indeed, some of the focus on women and criminal justice developed from important feminist work in this area. And some writers have focused on women's role in social control (Zimmer, 1986; Jones, 1986; Heidensohn, 1989, 1992). Heidensohn (1992), for example, has given particular attention to gender and policing and the ways in which women police officers survive in a predominantly masculine occupation.

Transforming the Discipline?: Discursive Questionings of the Epistemological and Methodological Terrain of Criminology

In working towards a transformed discipline, we might say that feminist perspectives in criminology have moved through stages which resemble a 'Hegelian dialectic' of thesis, antithesis, and synthesis. To translate this into the language of feminism, these stages represent a critique of masculinist criminology, a deconstruction of mainstream portrayals of crime and criminality, and, finally, steps towards reconstructing adequate theoretical formulations. Clearly, the three stages do not necessarily follow sequentially throughout the discipline, but are recursive and ongoing. But the transformation (or need for a transformation) has been depicted in a number of different ways which are worth repeating here as illustration of the broad body of work which has outlined feminist challenges to criminology.

Kathleen Daly and Meda Chesney-Lind (1988) raise two key questions in relation to criminological theory: the first is whether theories generated to describe men's or boys' offending can apply to women and girls (what they call the 'generalizability problem'), and the second, why women commit less crime than men (what they term as the 'gender ratio problem'). In other words, they immediately express concern about '*gender*', the implication being that theories of crime must be able to take account of both men's and women's (criminal) behaviour, and that they must also be able to highlight factors which operate differently on men and women. But more than this, they draw attention to the crucial problematization of gender in different feminist perspectives—leading to a sophisticated notion of gender relations in which gender is seen not as a natural fact, but as 'a complex, historical, and cultural product; . . . related to, but not simply derived from, biological sex difference and reproductive capacities' (1988: 504). Thus complex gender codes are internalized in a myriad of ways to regulate behaviour. In other words, criminologists could learn a great deal from looking at feminist insights in relation to gender. Daly and Chesney-Lind also urge criminologists to read first-hand of women's experiences rather than rely on distorted received wisdom about women, for these accounts of experience have not only enriched feminist thought, but have become a central part of feminist analyses and epistemological reflections. There is encouragement for criminologists to reflect on the ethnocentricity inherent in mainstream criminological thinking too; the fact that questions are generally those of white, economically privileged men needs to be recognized. Finally, Daly and Chesney-Lind indicate the potentialities of points of congruence between feminist perspectives and other social and other political theories, and consequently between feminist theories and 'alternative to mainstream' theoretical trajectories in criminology (critical and Marxist criminologies, for example).

In *Feminist Perspectives in Criminology* (Gelsthorpe and Morris,1990) it was similarly noted that creative feminist contributions to criminology go well beyond critique. The contributors to this book both illustrate the hegemonic masculinity of most criminological work and clarify the foundations for future gender-concious work. To develop this latter point for a moment, particular attention is given to the ways in which feminist insights have changed the questions relating to violence against women. Whereas conventional theorists might focus on the pathological and structural aspects of violent individuals to explain their violence in particular situations, feminists have attempted to explain why men *as a group* generally direct their violence towards women. Similarly, whilst conventional writers might focus on the reasons why a woman might stay in an abusive relationship (perhaps signifying that there is something wrong with her), feminist writers might consider 'what factors inhibit women's opportunity to leave violent men?'. In this sense, the book is part of a reconstructive moment in criminology, though there are different views on the nature of the reconstruction. As previously indicated, there are some who have spelled out a wish to abandon criminology altogether, Carol Smart being one.

Carol Smart's distinctive contribution is to question whether the focus on female lawbreakers is a proper concern for feminism and whether a feminist criminology is theoretically possibly or politically desirable. She effectively draws attention to the rich and wide variety of feminist scholarship and contrasts it with the limited horizons of criminology. In focusing on the continuing 'marriage' of criminology to (unacknowledged) positivist paradigms and criminologists' pursuit of grand and totalizing theories she highlights criminology's isolation from some of the major theoretical and political questions which are engaging feminist scholarship elsewhere. Indeed, she suggests that feminist criminologists are risking something of a 'marginalised existence—marginal to both criminology and to feminism' (1990: 71) because of their continued engagement with the project of modernism—within which criminology is nurtured and sustained. Whilst feminists outside criminology are increasingly influenced by postmodern reappraisals of knowledge forms and scientific approaches to knowledge (indeed, are leading the way in such appraisals) and are thus questioning the notion of a universal reality (Fraser and Nicholson, 1988; Weedon, 1987; Harding, 1986, 1987) criminologists (and thus feminist criminologists) are perhaps stuck in the conventional mode of seeking 'the truth' through scientific, empirical endeavours—holding fast to the notion of referential finalities. Even the critical criminologies such as left realism, she argues, are flawed because the work is anchored within positivist paradigms. The work displays a belief that it is still possible objectively to uncover both the causes of and solutions to 'crime'. As Smart puts it, this begs questions whether an association with criminology is desirable:

for a long time, we have been asking 'what does feminism have to contribute to criminology (or sociology)?'. Feminism has been knocking at the door of established disciplines hoping to be let in on equal terms. These disciplines have largely looked down their noses (metaphorically speaking) and found feminism wanting. Feminism has been required to become more objective, more substantive, more scientific, more anything before a grudging entry could be granted. . . . It might be that criminology needs feminism more than the converse [1990: 83–84].

I shall return to this call for the abandonment of criminology in due course.

I want to turn now to the feminist epistemological and methodological project that I have foreshadowed. In the same volume (*Feminist Perspectives in Criminology*), Loraine Gelsthorpe, Liz Kelly, and Annie Hudson focus on the processes of knowledge production. Each author reflects on her research experiences and research methodologies—exploring some of the challenges presented by feminism and its core principles of relating research to practice; engaging with 'the researched'; recognizing their subjectivity in a non-hierarchical way; and using sensitive research methods which maximize opportunities to reflect more accurately the experiences of 'the researched'. Whilst ideas about feminist research practices have been the focus of much debate in recent years—a detailed, sophisticated, and reflexive debate in my view (Clegg, 1975; Stanley and Wise, 1983; Roberts, 1981; Cook and Fonow, 1986; Cain, 1986; Hammersley, Ramazanoglu, and Gelsthorpe, 1992) myths abound. For example, there is the oft-quoted and misunderstood phrase from sociologists Stanley and Wise that feminist research must be 'on, by and for women' (1983: 17), when attention to what they actually said indicates that they are *questioning* this. The phrase is certainly not the dictum that many have seen it to be, and in any case a number of feminist writers in criminology have contested this (Cain, 1986; Gelsthorpe and Morris, 1988; Gelsthorpe, 1990; Stanko, 1993). Close reading of the feminist discussions about research methods (Reinharz, 1979; Roberts, 1981; Bowles and Duelli Klein, 1983; Gelsthorpe, 1990, for example) ultimately reveal no fixed 'absolutes' beyond the need for sensitivity in the research task, for personal reflexivity—to reflect on the subjectivities of all involved, and commitment to make the research relevant to women.

Crucially, there is a focus on 'experience' in feminist research, but not in simplistic ways. The focus on women's 'experiences' (with feminist researchers' democratic insistence that women should be 'allowed to speak for themselves) has been used both to make women visible, and to link feminist ontology (that is, beliefs about the nature of the world) with feminist epistemology (that is, beliefs about what counts as appropriate knowledge). One might say, for example, that feminist beliefs about reality revolve around the idea that reality is constituted by various sets of structural constraints which subordinate and oppress women. Following on from this, appropriate knowledge is that which allows women to speak for themselves, rather than knowledge about men's worlds which so often presumes itself to be about women's worlds too. As Maureen Cain (1990a) puts it, strategies for the transformation of criminology involve reflexivity, deconstruction, and reconstruction and a clear focus on women and particularly women-only studies. This is not as a kind of corrective to traditional criminology which has excluded or marginalized women, but for 'women's unspeakable "experiences" to be captured, experienced, named and tamed' (Cain, 1990*a*: 9) without using men and their experiences as a yardstick against which women's experiences must be compared. Along with Smart (1990) Cain exhorts feminists to locate themselves outside the narrow boundaries of criminology. As she reflects:

Feminist criminology must explore the total lives of women, and there are no tools in existing criminological theory with which to do this. . . . Only by starting from outside, with the social construction of gender, or with women's experiences of their total lives, or with the structure of the domestic space, can we begin to make sense of what is going on. Feminist criminology must now start from outside [1990a: 10].

Thus Cain proposes a focus on the construction of gender, on discourses which lie beyond criminology, and on the sites which are relevant to women. The questions are about women, she emphasizes, not about crime. This is not to suggest that men are irrelevant to the task. Far from it, Cain's claims for serious consideration of gender do include men: 'We shall fall into essentialism if we exclude men from our analyses, even if we may wish to exclude them from much of our field research' (1990: 11). Similarly, she encourages us to learn from the world of women's political struggle:

we must record those forms of resistance to censure and policing which have been effective. This construction of an analytic dossier of women's political struggles, repression and resistance will have a moral function, will save us from continually having to reinvent the wheel, and will drive the creative political enterprise which has brought us this far [1990: 14].

This concern to place women's experiences, viewpoints, and struggles at the centre of projects has led to the development of what Sandra Harding (1987) has called 'feminist standpointism'. That is, a commitment to try and understand the world from the perspective of the socially subjugated—to see things through women's eyes. As Naffine (1997) helpfully outlines, citing Longino (1993), 'feminist standpointism' takes many forms, ranging 'from the romantic idea that women come, by nature or social experience, to be better equipped to know the world than are men to the more modest proposal that a social science adequate for women must proceed from a grasp of the forms of oppression women experience' (Longino, 1993: 201, cited in Naffine, 1997: 46). Whilst there are debates about the nature of women's 'shared' experience and women's different experiences, and about assumptions that women's realities are somehow 'more real' or produce 'better knowledge' than those discerned from traditional methodologies (Cain, 1986), there are no fixed views. Indeed, there is increasing recognition of ontological complexities which both justifies the focus on women's direct/first-hand 'experiences' and raises questions about the usefulness of standpointism. The implication that there is perhaps only 'one experience' or one standpoint is clearly very difficult. There has been a strong tendency to conflate women in feminist theory; different voices (standpoints) have sometimes assumed a false commonality, a false unity. In particular, race and class differences have been underplayed and the relational character of identity has been ignored. At the same time, the notion of 'feminist standpointism' has encouraged both theoretical and personal reflexivity in relation to knowledge and the processes of knowledge production through research and this can help overcome some of the problems of conventional methodologies associated with mainstream criminology.[1]

Of course, there are also methodological preferences within feminist research (for qualitative or quantitative analysis or whatever) but early dismissals of anything tainted with positivism have given way to critical reflections on the need to use research methods appropriate to the nature of the task (Eichler, 1980; Kelly, 1990). Feminist writers in criminology have indeed reflected long and hard on the research methodologies employed, but there is nothing to suggest that their ideas are fundamentally antithetical to those of criminologists, though they might urge criminologists in general to be more reflexive and to question the epistemological bases of knowledge. It would be hard to claim that some of the challenges to conventional research methodologies are distinctively and solely 'feminist' challenges, but it is clear that feminist writers have dared to reflect on the issues to a greater degree than a number of conventional criminologists, and in this way can lay claim to a concern with doing good research which is not automatically and unthinkingly driven by positivist paradigms and processes.

If we can characterize the first two main developments in feminist criminology as being *feminist empiricism* (as evidenced in the wide-ranging criminological research on women, crime, control, and justice to counter-balance the absence of women from conventional work), and *feminist standpointism* (drawing attention to the need to place women's experience at the centre of knowledge), the third might be described as *feminist deconstructionism* (Naffine, 1997) drawing on postmodern insights. Deconstructionism essentially involves the problematizing of language and concepts, with feminist writers in this field coming under the influence of key writers such as Foucault (1970, 1972) and Derrida (1978, 1981), and critical understandings of the constitution of perspective. This is very much a theme which is evident in the work of Alison Young (1994).

In counterpoising feminism and criminology Young (1994) outlines the mismatching of a dominant masculinist culture reflected in criminology along with the insouciant parochialism of criminological practitioners, and the aims of feminism consciously to revindicate representations of the feminine and women by and of women themselves. She argues that postmodern insights empower the feminist critic of criminology to 'resist the master-narratives' of criminology (1994: 71). 'Criminology', she suggests, 'as pre-eminent modernist

---

[1] Maureen Cain (1990*b*) develops the notion of standpointism using insights from philosophical realism (see Keat and Urry, 1975) to argue for a 'successor science' (a way of gaining both transitive and intransitive understandings of the world, and questioning those understandings at the same time) as an alternative to orthodox scientific values and research approaches, but there is not space to more than float her ideas here.

science, exists in continual suppression of Woman as unpresentable, as Other. Postmodernism, for a feminist critic, can expose this act of suppression and can work to reveal the organisation and self-representation of criminology in binary oppositions' (1994: 74). Giving examples of criminology's deployment of binary combinations (the 'normal' and the 'criminal', 'male' and 'female' criminals, for example, creating a criminological semantic rectangle), Young suggests that feminist interventions in criminology have hitherto been bound by such a rectangle, and that only a postmodern feminism can effect an escape from such constraints and analytical limitations. Naffine, however, identifies the feminist problem of working both within and without existing frames of reference and the limiting preoccupation with unravelling textual meaning, leaving untouched:

The economic, political and legal structures that help to keep . . . traditional meaning in place and make it appear natural and inevitable . . . alone it [deconstruction] is insufficient to undo the institutional systems that have been built upon, and that help to sustain, the economic and political power of men over women [1997: 89].

Naffine's own approach is to build on feminist insights thus gained to argue that we *can* challenge the constitution of meanings in criminological discourse *if* we recognize that meanings can change. In other words, instead of accepting the recalcitrance and intransigence of categories of meaning (woman, crime, rape and so on), we should realize the 'referential, relational and metaphorical nature of meaning' more fully (1997: 98). In this way, the fixed, negative categories and tight interpretations of meaning identified through deconstructionist approaches, can become fluid—changing their meaning. Naffine acknowledges that such a position bears testament to standpoint feminism (and to its ideas of conscious knowledge production from specific sites and experiences). (I would add that we can see traces of Giddensian thinking in this creative combination of deconstructionism and standpointism. In trying to move away from a natural science model for sociology and reconcile some elements of both the newer interpretative forms of sociology with the more traditional 'structural' forms (what he call 'institutional analysis') Giddens (1986) identifies a 'duality of structure'. That is, rather than recognizing two separate and opposed phenomena (structuralism—functionalism and the like on the one hand, and interpretation—subjectivity and the like on the other) we should recognize that social practices consist of both action and structure at the same time—structure is not 'external' to action; it is perhaps more 'internal' to the flow of action which constitutes the practices in question. In the same way, Naffine is promoting the concept of 'agency'—stemming from standpointism, to counteract some of the claims of feminist deconstructionists—and in this way is recognizing a 'duality' in the creation of knowledge). Thus Naffine (1997) is looking at some creative possibilities for effecting change in the epistemological assumptions that bind conventional criminology. As illustration, she looks at different ways in which understandings of the sexes (and thereby the logic of explanations) within the context of a major crime (the crime of rape) can be approached using insights of deconstructionism and feminist standpointism (1997: 98–119). In a further analysis of a particular genre of feminist crime fiction Naffine illustrates very clearly how images, meaning, and interpretation *can* change. The hard-boiled male detective as the central character in plots which involve women as vulnerable sexual sirens or sexual victims is transposed into something quite different—a female, often overtly feminine, expert who solves corporate crimes, not only crimes against women, and the offenders are very often ordinary men, like real killers. In this way stereotypical notions of powerful men, female victims, and glamorized sexual crimes are challenged—meanings and understandings are reshaped for us in fiction. Thus why not in real life too?

CRITICAL REFLECTIONS ON FEMINIST APPROACHES TO CRIMINOLOGY

Unsurprisingly, feminist work in criminology has drawn criticism. Leaving aside the rather fallacious, but significant inferences of some criminological writers that feminist work is somehow just ideological reasoning or irrelevant to criminological tasks (Bottomley and Pease, 1986; Walker, 1987), Marcia Rice (1990), for example, forcefully and rightly takes feminist writers to task because black women have been noticeably absent from discourse. Indeed, she argues that feminists have failed to notice that traditional machocentric criminology was constructed on *racist* and sexist ideologies, and that feminist work is equally ethnocentric.

Further, what Pat Carlen (1992) calls the 'theoreticist, libertarian, separatist and gender-centric tendencies' in feminist writings in general, and the strong 'abandon criminology' position of Carol Smart (1990) in particular, have come under attack. In a searching paper, which is part of a collection of papers appraising left realism, Pat Carlen (1992) identifies an unwillingness on the part of some feminists to link theoretical struggles with political struggles, because of assumptions that theoretical rigour and discourse will be subsumed or lost within engagement with politics and practice. (It is arguable that Smart is eminently 'engaged', in the field of law and politics and sexuality—outside criminology (Smart, 1995) , but Carlen's point is valid even if the direction in which it is offered is slightly awry). She also identifies a libertarian (and short-sighted) tendency in feminist thinking which is reflected in scepticism that involvement in criminal justice policy directed towards the reduction of crime cannot be one without an element of interference and 'social engineering'. I agree with her that this would be to abandon women caught up in the criminal justice system. Under the same heading of 'libertarian tendencies' Carlen focuses on what she believes to be mistaken feminist 'glorification' in 'allowing women to speak for themselves' (1992: 63), though whilst Carlen believes that feminists are suggesting this as a distinctly 'feminist' pursuit, and a pursuit which involves only women, it may be that this is merely identified and celebrated by feminists as 'good social science' and as a strategy which should be used with men too (Gelsthorpe, 1990; Cain, 1986).

Continuing in critical vein, Carlen suggests that the separatist tendency in feminist writings on crime and justice reflects a feminist reluctance (refusal?) to acknowledge theoretical advances in criminology so that theories continue to be hailed as 'malestream' or termed in some other cryptic, negative way. There is some validity in this claim I believe, and I shall return to it in the conclusion. A more obvious criticism relating to 'separatism', however, might be directed at ideas relating to the development of a feminist jurisprudence (MacKinnon, 1987; Smith, 1993; Olsen, 1995; Bottomley, 1996) because of the impracticability of the proposal, though Carlen suspends such criticism when it comes to her own agenda (see below).

The criticism of a 'gender-centric' tendency and the privileging of gender over race and class for example, in feminist approaches, undoubtedly hits hard. But recent debates begin to acknowledge this tendency in a constructive way (Hammersley, Ramazanoglu, and Gelsthorpe, 1992) and there is clear evidence that such issues are pressing within feminist approaches to criminology (Daly, 1994; Daly and Stephenson, 1995). This is a rather different criticism from the earlier comments of Rice (1990) and, more recently, Connell (1995) on the neglect of black perspectives. Whilst the privileging of gender is now commonly questioned, Rice and Connell both make the case for a specifically black feminist perspective within criminology. Rafter and Heidensohn (1995) present *International Feminist Perspectives* as a genuine attempt to deal with such issues by offering a multi-cultural collection of papers. But there is a difference between genuinely multi-cultural analysis and multi-cultural representations, as Daly (1994) has noted, and it is not clear that this point is dealt with.

Overall, Carlen suggests that feminists do not need to abandon criminology to employ the critical precepts of a deconstructionist approach and to work through some of the theoretical contradictions of knowledge and political strategy. Indeed, she outlines her own agenda for a feminist realist approach to criminology which involves the deconstruction and re-theorization of the problematic relation between 'women and crime' and justice for women. Carlen's academic agenda thus involves deconstruction of what is already known about women law-breakers via a 'bricolage' of concepts appropriated from a variety of theoretical discourses and research, the detailed empirical investigation of the different contexts (ideological, economic, political) in which women break the law, and their routes through various welfare and penal networks, and detailed investigation of the ideological discourses within which women's law-breaking is known. She also thinks there is scope for investigation of the utility of feminist jurisprudence along with more detailed analysis of social justice (1992: 65–6). Her political agenda, however, is conceptually broad in arguing that:

the aim should be to 'ensure that the penal system of female law-breakers does not increase their oppression as unconventional women, as black people and as poverty-stricken defendants still further; and to ensure that the penal regulation of law-breaking men is not such that it brutalises them and makes them behave even more violently or oppressively towards women in the future [1992: 66].

It is not clear that many feminist writers in criminology would fundamentally disagree with this.

So, despite criticisms of left realism for its positivistic, essentializing, deterministic, and popularizing tendencies, Carlen holds fast to left realism's critical attempts to overcome the 'impossibilism' of earlier critical criminologies and its political/practical focus. Whilst we cannot assume that feminists would wish to pin feminist perspectives in criminology to left realism, I do not believe that Pat Carlen is alone in being concerned that the abandonment of criminology could be seen as the abandonment of people to their fate in existing criminal justice practices. Indeed, if we can recognize a *political* project in criminology as well as a feminist political project, then it is surely worth sticking within criminology. I cannot see otherwise. Some of the moral and political dimensions of criminology are thoroughly defensible, even if certain epistemological assumptions are highly questionable. By all means, let us view the criminological tasks both within and without, but let us not cut off criminology's political nose to spite its face.

CONCLUSION

The Hallmarks of Feminism in the 1990s

The hallmarks of contemporary feminism and feminist approaches to criminology include a focus on *gender* as a central organizing principle for contemporary life, recognition of the importance of *power* in shaping social relations, a sensitivity to the way that the social *context* shapes human relations, recognition that all social reality must be understood as a *process*, and that research methods should take this into account. There is also political commitment to *social change* as a critical part of feminist scholarship and practice—hence a strong *political project*. Of crucial importance, too, is the *epistemological and methodological project*, the epistemological questioning and creative thinking about the production of knowledge and processes of knowledge production, and emphasis on personal and theoretical reflexivity. Some difficult issues remain unresolved in this of course, and, in my view, there is also scope for further development so that feminism embraces humanism without the humanistic paradigms so criticized by Foucault for example (Soper, 1990). In this way feminists could deal with the potential to close off and be self-referential. Also, whilst borrowed postmodern insights enhance the epistemological and methodological project by challenging and deconstructing the constitution of meaning in criminological discourse, I am not sure that there are useful postmodern insights regarding concrete practices and knowledges which could replace current ones. Postmodernists have very little to say about visions of justice, for example, and ways in which difference can be accommodated in notions of justice. This is vital to the broad feminist political project (Flax 1992). In sum, however, I would argue that there is an unmistakable openness in feminist thinking, and a willingness to engage with tough epistemological issues. Feminism has not escaped the epistemological crisis facing the social sciences; rather, it has embraced it and is working creatively within it.

The Hallmarks of Criminology in the 1990s

At the beginning of this chapter I claimed that the criminology of the 1990s is arguably more diverse (and plural) than the criminology of the 1970s and 1980s. But I sense that there is a qualitative difference in some of the criminologies of today too. Much of what we see is empiricist/positivist and tied to the Lombrosian and governmental projects (Garland, 1994), of course, but I also sense new ways of thinking about the social world in general and criminology in particular, and we need to acknowledge these advances. We can discern greater theoretical reflexivity than hitherto (Nelken, 1994; Morrison, 1994; Muncie, McLaughlin, and Langan, 1996; Henry and Milovanovic, 1996), a re-enchantment with the social—those very phenomena (emotions, intuition, personal experience, and mystical experience for example)—which were once outlawed by modernist projects—including criminology (Katz, 1988; Braithwaite, 1989; Garland, 1992, 1994) and an interest in intertextuality (Redhead, 1995; Stanley, 1996; Davis, 1990, for example). (Such stylistic innovations potentially have the same impact as Naffine's (1997) 'crime fictions' which turn on their head the meanings attached to crime, men and women, and so on.) Significantly, too, there is evidence that criminology is participating in the blurring of disciplinary boundaries (Ericson and Carriere, 1994) (a phenomenon which renders moves to abandon criminology as something of an empty gesture). Finally, we can discern an interest in 'alterity' (Nelken, 1994)—an interest in the significance of the 'other' and constitution of identity within modern intellectual and cultural life. Whilst these interests do not mirror feminist insights from empirical work, standpointism, and deconstructionism, and whilst I suspect that the heartlands of criminology remain untouched by feminism, there is something to encourage optimism. There is possibly scope to see more fluid/sensitive/gender aware criminologies on the horizon. The criminological project is in transition.

Overall, I believe that there is good reason to share Daly's (1994) notion of 'working within and against criminology' and to enjoin Naffine in her appeal to the ethical senses of criminologists to bring women (and other exiles) 'in from the cold' (1997: 153). As she says, 'We must let the exile bear witness' (1997: 153). Feminists have done much to question masculinist viewpoints of criminology, and to alter thinking. A *broad* reading of criminology suggests that there may now be a convergence of interests between feminism and criminology in some quarters, and thus scope for positive dialogue.

Selected Further Reading

The chief text which focuses on epistemological issues relating to feminism and criminology is: N. Naffine (1997), *feminism and criminology* (Cambridge: Polity Press). It offers an excellent synthesis of ideas relating to the relationship between feminism and criminology, providing both an intellectual history of criminology from a feminist viewpoint, and a more discursive discussion of feminist challenges to traditional scientific paradigms. Naffine's outline and assessment of feminist endeavours to break out of masculine standpoints and traditional scholarship and focuses on the contributions of empirical, standpoint, and deconstructionist feminism in particular. Having identified strengths and weaknesses in each of these feminist approaches to criminology, she shows (through the examples of rape and crime fiction) that changes in traditional paradigms *can* be achieved through a synthesis of ideas from standpointism and deconstructionism.

There are two edited collections which provide overviews of the relationship between feminism an criminology: the first is L. Gelsthorpe and A. Morris, eds. (1990), *Feminist Perspectives in Criminology* (Buckingham: Open University Press). This early collection of essays covers three broad areas: the feminist critique of criminology and its theoretical parameters, attempts to transform criminology through research methodologies, and the relationship between feminism, politics, and action. The second, and more recent, collection is N. H. Rafter and F. Heidensohn, eds. (1995), *International Feminist Perspectives in Criminology* (Buckingham: Open University Press). Contributors to this book describe the impact of feminism on criminology in countries ranging from the South—Australia and South Africa; Europe—Britain, Italy, Germany, Denmark, Norway and Finland, Poland and Eastern Europe; and North America. The book provides an overview of the different ways in which feminism has impacted on criminology in research, teaching, and policy (especially relating to crimes such as domestic violence and the abuse of children).

The area of feminist epistemology and methodology is vast, but the following provide a useful starting point for the interested reader: S. Harding, ed. (1987), *Feminism and Methodology* (Milton Keynes: Open University Press, and Bloomington, Ind.: Indiana University Press). Also, M. Fonow and J. Cook, eds. (1991), *Beyond Methodology* (Bloomingdon, Ind.: Indiana University Press), and K. Lennon and M. Whitford, eds. (1994), *Knowing the Difference. Feminist Perspectives in Epistemology* (London: Routledge). The contributors to these volumes explore the difference that adopting a feminist perspective can make in relation to traditional knowledge, but there are important subsidiary questions considered too, such as how are feminist perspectives themselves affected by difference.

REFERENCES

ALLEN, H. (1987), *Justice Unbalanced: Gender, Psychiatry and Judicial Decisions*. Milton Keynes: Open University Press.

BECKER, H. (1963), *Outsiders*. Glencoe, NY: Free Press.

BENHABIB, S. (1992), *Situating the Self: Gender, Community and Postmodernism in Contemporary Ethics*. Cambridge: Polity.

BOTTOMLEY, A., ed. (1996), *Feminist Perspectives on the Foundational Subjects of Law*. London: Cavendish Publishing.

BOTTOMLEY, K., and PEASE, K. (1986), *Crime and Punishment: Interpreting the Data*. Milton Keynes: Open University Press.

BOWLES, G., and DUELLI KLEIN, R., eds. (1983), *Theories of Women's Studies*. London: Routledge and Kegan Paul.

BRAITHWAITE, J. (1989), *Crime, Shame and Reintegration*. Cambridge: Cambridge University Press.

BROWN, B. (1986), 'Women and Crime: the Dark Figures of Criminology', *Economy and Society*, 15, 3: 355–402.

BROWN, D., and HOGG, R. (1992), 'Law and Order Politics, Left Realism and Radical Criminology: a View from Down Under', in R. Matthews and J. Young, eds., *Issues in Realist Criminology*. London: Sage.

CAIN, M. (1986), 'Realism, Feminism, Methodology, and Law', *International Journal of the Sociology of Law*, 14: 255–67.

—— ed. (1989), *Growing Up Good. Policing the Behaviour of Girls in Europe*. London: Sage.

—— (1990a), 'Towards Transgression: New Directions in Feminist Criminology', *International Journal of the Sociology of Law*, 18: 1–18.

—— (1990b), 'Realist Philosophy and Standpoint Epistemologies or Feminist Criminology as a Successor Science', in L. Gelsthorpe and A. Morris, eds., *Feminist Perspectives in Criminology*. Buckingham: Open University Press.

CARLEN, P. (1992), 'Criminal Women and Criminal Justice: The Limits to, and Potential of, Feminist and Left Realist Perspectives', in R. Matthews and J. Young, eds., *Issues in Realist Criminology*. London: Sage.

—— and WORRALL, A., eds. (1987), *Gender, Crime and Justice*. Milton Keynes: Open University Press.

CIXOUS, H. (1976), 'The Laugh of the Medusa', *Signs*, 1, 4: 875–93.

CLEGG, S. (1975), 'Feminist Methodology—Fact or Fiction?,' *Quality and Quantity*, 19: 83–97.

COHEN, S. (1988), *Against Criminology*. New Brunswick, NJ: Transaction Books.

CONNELL, P. (1995), 'Black, British and Beaten? Understanding Violence, Agency and Resistance'. Paper presented to the British Criminology Conference. (Loughborough).

COOK, J., and FONOW, M. (1986), 'Knowledge and Women's Interests: Issues of Epistemology and Methodology in Feminist Sociological Research', *Sociological Inquiry*, 56: 1–29.

DALY, K. (1994), 'Criminal Law and Justice System Practices as Racist, White and Racialised', *Washington and Lee Law Review*, 15, 2: 431–64.

—— and CHESNEY-LIND, M. (1988), 'Feminism and Criminology,' *Justice Quarterly*, 5, 4: 498–538.

—— and STEPHENSON, D. (1995), 'The "Dark Figure" of Criminology: Toward a Black and Multi-ethnic Feminist Agenda for Theory and Research', in N. H. Rafter and F. Heidensohn, eds., *International Feminist Perspectives in Criminology*. Buckingham: Open University Press.

DAVIS, M. (1990), *City of quartz: excavating the futures of Los Angeles*. London: Verso.

DELMAR, R. (1986), 'What is Feminism?' in J. Mitchell and A. Oakley, eds., *What is Feminism?* Oxford: Blackwell.

DERRIDA, J. (1978), *Writing and Difference*. Chicago, Ill.: Chicago University Press.

—— (1981), *Positions*. Chicago, Ill.: University of Chicago Press.

DIAMOND, I., and QUINBY, L., eds. (1988), *Feminism and Foucault*. Boston, Mass.: Northeastern University Press.

DOBASH, R. E., and DOBASH, R.P. (1992), *Women, Violence and Social Change*. London: Routledge.

—— —— and GUTTERIDGE, S. (1986), *The Imprisonment of Women*. Oxford: Blackwell.

EATON, M. (1986), *Justice for Women?* Milton Keynes: Open University Press.

EDWARDS, S. (1984), *Women on Trial*. Manchester: Manchester Universtiy Press.

EICHLER, M. (1980), *The Double Standard: A Feminist Critique of Feminist Social Science*. London: Croom Helm.

ERICSON, R., and CARRIERE, K. (1994), 'The Fragmentation of Criminology', in D. Nelken ed., *The Futures of Criminology*. London: Sage.

Evans, J. (1995), *Feminist Theory Today*. London: Sage.

Flax, J. (1992), 'Beyond Equality: Gender, Justice and Difference', in G. Bock and S. James, eds., *Beyond Equality and Difference*. London: Routledge.

Foucault, M. (1970), *The Order of Things: An Archæology of the Human Sciences*. London: Tavistock.

—— (1972), *The Archæology of Knowledge*. London: Tavistock.

Fraser, N., and Nicholson, L. (1988), 'Social Criticism Without Philosophy: An Encounter Between Feminism and Postmodernism', *British Journal of Law and Society*, 7: 215–41.

Fudge, J. (1989), 'The Effect of Entrenching a Bill of Rights upon Political Discourse: Feminist Demands and Sexual Violence in Canada', *International Journal of the Sociology of Law*, 17, 4: 445–63.

Garland, D. (1992), 'Criminological Knowledge and its Relation to Power: Foucault's Genealogy and Criminology Today', *British Journal of Criminology*, 32, 4: 403–22.

—— (1994), 'Of Crimes and Criminals: The Development of Criminology in Britain', in M. Maguire, R. Morgan, and R. Reiner, eds., *Oxford Handbook of Criminology*. Oxford: Clarendon Press.

Gelsthorpe, L. (1989), *Sexism and the female offender: an organizational analysis*. Aldershot: Gower.

—— (1990), 'Feminist Methodologies in Criminology: A New Approach or Old Wine in New Bottles?', in L. Gelsthorpe and A. Morris, eds., *Feminist Perspectives in Criminology*. Buckingham: Open University Press.

—— and Morris, A. (1988), 'Feminism and Criminology in Britain', *British Journal of Criminology*, 28, 2: 93–110.

—— and —— eds. (1990), *Feminist Perspectives in Criminology*. Buckingham: Open University Press.

Giddens, A. (1986), *The Constitution of Society. Outline of the Theory of Structuralism*. Cambridge: Polity.

Gottfredson, M., and Hirschi, T., eds., (1987), *Positive Criminology*. Newbury Park, Sage.

Greenwood, V. (1981), 'The Myth of Female Crime', in A. Morris and L. Gelsthorpe, eds., *Women and Crime*. Cambridge: Institute of Criminology.

Hammersley, M., Ramazanoglu, C., and

Gelsthorpe, L. (1992), 'Debate: Feminist Methodology, Reason and Empowerment', *Sociology*, 26, 2: 187–218.

Harding, S., ed. (1986), *The Science Question in Feminism*. Milton Keynes: Open University Press.

—— (1987), *Feminism and Methodology*. Milton Keynes: Open University Press.

Heidensohn, F. (1968), 'The Deviance of Women: A Critique and Enquiry', *British Journal of Sociology*, 19, 2: 160–75.

—— (1985), *Women and Crime*. London: Macmillan.

—— (1989), *Women and Policing in the USA*. London: Police Foundation.

—— (1992), *Women in Control? The Role of Women in Law Enforcement*. Oxford: Oxford University Press.

—— (1994), 'Gender and Crime,' in M. Maguire, R. Morgan, and R. Reiner, eds., *Oxford Handbook of Criminology*. Oxford: Clarendon Press

Henry, S., and Milovanovic, D. (1996), *Constitutive Criminology*. London: Sage.

Hirsch, M., and Keller, E., eds., (1990), *Conflicts in Feminism*. New York: Routledge.

Home Office (1995), *Criminal Statistics in England and Wales*. London: HMSO.

Humm, M., ed. (1992), *Feminisms: A Reader*. New York: Harvester Wheatsheaf.

—— (1995), *The Dictionary of Feminist Theory*. New York: Prentice Hall.

Hutter, B., and Williams, G., eds., (1981), *Controlling Women: The Normal and the Deviant*. London: Croom Helm in association with Oxford University Women's Studies Committee.

Irigaray, L. (1977), *Ce sexe qui n'en est pas un*. Paris: Editions de Minuit.

Jones, S. (1986), *Policewomen and Equality*. London: Macmillan.

Katz, J. (1988), *Seductions of crime: moral and sensual attractions in doing evil*. New York: Basic Books.

Keat, R., and Urry, J. (1975), *Social Theory as Science*. London: Routledge and Kegan Paul.

Kelly, L. (1990), 'Journeying in Reverse: Possibilities and Problems in Feminist Research on Sexual Violence,' in L. Gelsthorpe and A. Morris, eds., *Feminist Perspectives in Criminology*. Buckingham: Open University Press.

Klein, D., and Kress, J. (1976), 'Any Woman's Blues: a Critical Overview of Women, Crime and the Criminal Justice System', *Crime and Social Justice*, 5: 34–49.

LEONARD, E. (1982), *Women, Crime and Society: a Critique of Theoretical Criminology*. New York: Longman.

LONGINO, H. (1993), 'Feminist Standpoint Theory and the Problems of Knowledge', *Signs*, 19, 1: 201–12.

MACKINNON, C. (1987), *Feminism unmodified: discourses on life and law*. Cambridge, Mass: Harvard University Press.

MAGUIRE, M., MORGAN, R., and REINER, R., eds. (1994), *Oxford Handbook of Criminology*. Oxford: Clarendon Press.

MATTHEWS, R., and YOUNG, J. (1992), 'Questioning left realism', in R. Matthews and J. Young, eds., *Issues in Realist Criminology*. London: Sage.

MCROBBIE, A. (1980), 'Settling Accounts with Subcultures', in S. Hall and T. Jefferson, eds., *Resistance Through Rituals*. London: Hutchinson.

MILLMAN, M. (1975), 'She Did it All for Love: A Feminist View of the Sociology of Deviance', in M. Millman and R. M. Kanter, eds., *Another Voice: Feminist Perspectives on Social Life and Social Science*. New York: Anchor Books.

MITCHELL, J. (1984), *Women: The Longest Revolution*. London: Virago.

—— and OAKLEY, A. (1986), *What is Feminism?* Oxford: Blackwell.

MORRIS, A. (1987), *Women, Crime and Criminal Justice*. Oxford: Blackwell.

MORRISON, W. (1994), *Theoretical Criminology*. London: Cavendish Publishing.

MUNCIE, J., MCLAUGHLIN, E., and LANGAN, M., eds. (1996), *Criminological Perspectives. A Reader*. London: Sage, in association with the Open University.

NAFFINE, N., ed. (1995), *Gender, Crime and Feminism*. Dartmouth: Aldershot.

—— (1997), *feminism and criminology*. Cambridge: Polity Press.

NELKIN, D., ed. (1994), *The Futures of Criminology*. London: Sage.

NICHOLSON, L., ed., (1990), *Feminism/ Postmodernism*. New York: Routledge.

OAKLEY, A. (1981), *Subject Women*. Oxford: Martin Robertson.

OLSEN, F. (1995), *Feminist Legal Theory*. Aldershot: Dartmouth.

RAFTER, N. H., and HEIDENSOHN, F., eds. (1995), *International Feminist Perspectives in Criminology*. Buckingham: Open University Press.

REDHEAD, S. (1995), *Unpopular Cultures: The Birth of Law and Popular Culture*. Manchester: Manchester University Press.

REINHARZ, S. (1979), *On Becoming a Social Scientist: From Survey Research and Participant Observation to Experimental Analysis*. San Francisco, Cal.: Jossey-Bass.

RICE, M. (1990), 'Challenging Orthodoxies in Feminist Theory: A Black Feminist Critique,' in L. Gelsthorpe and A. Morris, eds., *Feminist Perspectives in Criminology*. Buckingham: Open University Press.

ROBERTS, H., ed. (1981), *Doing Feminist Research*. London: Routledge and Kegan Paul.

ROCK, P., ed. (1988), *A History of British Criminology*. Oxford: Oxford University Press.

—— (1994), 'The Social Organization of British Criminology', in M. Maguire, R. Morgan, and R. Reiner, eds., *Oxford Handbook of Criminology*. Oxford: Clarendon Press.

ROWBOTHAM, S. (1973), *Women's Consciousness, Man's World*. Harmondsworth: Penguin.

SCRATON, P. (1990), 'Scientific Knowledge or Masculine Discourses? Challenging Patriarchy in Criminology,' in L. Gelsthorpe and A. Morris, eds., *Feminist Perspectives in Criminology*. Buckingham: Open University Press.

SHACKLADY SMITH, L. (1978), 'Sexist Assumptions and Female Delinquency: An Empirical Investigation', in C. Smart and B. Smart, eds., *Women, Sexuality and Social Control*. London: Routledge and Kegan Paul.

SMART, C. (1976), *Women, Crime and Criminology*. London: Routledge and Kegan Paul.

—— (1990), 'Feminist Approaches to Criminology or Postmodern Woman Meets Atavistic Man', in L. Gelsthorpe and A. Morris, eds., *Feminist Perspectives in Criminology*. Buckingham: Open University Press.

—— (1995), *Law, crime and sexuality: essays on feminism*. London: Sage.

—— and SMART, B., eds. (1978), *Women, Sexuality and Social Control*. London: Routledge and Kegan Paul.

SMITH, A. (1962), *Women in Prison*. London: Stevens and Sons.

SMITH, P., ed. (1993), *Feminist Jurisprudence*. New York: Oxford University Press.

SOPER, K. (1990), 'Feminism, Humanism and Postmodernism', *Radical Philosophy*, 55: 11–17.

STANKO, E. (1985), *Intimate Intrusions: Women's Experience of Male Violence*. London: Virago.

—— (1990), *Danger Signals*. London: Pandora.

—— (1993), 'Feminist Criminology: An Oxymoron?' Paper presented to the British Criminology Conference, (Cardiff).

STANLEY, C. (1996), *Urban Excess and the Law: capital, culture and desire.* London: Cavendish Publishing.

STANLEY, L., and WISE, S. (1983), *Breaking Out: Feminist Consciousness and Feminist Research.* London: Routledge and Kegan Paul.

SUMNER, C. (1990), 'Foucault, Gender and the Censure of Deviance', in L. Gelsthorpe and A. Morris, eds., *Feminist Perspectives in Criminology.* Buckingham: Open University Press.

—— (1994), *The Sociology of Deviance: An Obituary.* Buckingham: Open University Press.

TAYLOR, I., WALTON, P., and YOUNG, J. (1973), *The New Criminology.* London: Routledge and Kegan Paul.

TONG, R. (1989), *Feminist Thought.* London: Unwin Hyman.

VELIMESIS, M. (1975), 'The Female Offender', *Crime and Delinquency Literature,* 7, 1: 94–112.

WALKER, N. (1987), *Crime and Criminology. A Critical Introduction.* Oxford: Oxford University Press.

WALKLATE, S. (1989), *Victimology.* London: Unwin Hyman.

—— (1992), 'Appreciating the Victim: Conventional, Realist or Critical Victimology?', in R. Matthews and J. Young, eds., *Issues in Realist Criminology.* London: Sage.

WEEDON, C. (1987), *Feminist Practice and Postructuralist Theory.* Oxford: Blackwell.

WORRALL, A. (1990), *Offending Women.* London: Routledge.

YOUNG, A. (1994), 'Feminism and the Body of Criminology', in D. Farrington and S. Walklate, eds., *Offenders and Victims: Theory and Policy.* London: British Society of Criminology and ISTD. British Criminology Conference Selected Papers, vol. 1.

YOUNG, J. (1994), 'Incessant Chatter: Recent Paradigms in Criminology', in M. Maguire, R. Morgan, and R. Reiner, eds., *Oxford Handbook of Criminology.* Oxford: Clarendon Press.

ZIMMER, L. (1986), *Women Guarding Men.* Chicago, Ill.: University of Chicago Press.

16

Masculinities and Crimes

Tony Jefferson

The great *unspoken* in the crime angst of the Eighties and Nineties was that it is a phenomenon of masculinity. Indeed crime is one of the cultures in which young men acquire the mantle of manhood [Campbell, 1993: 211].

What we notice shapes our understanding of anything. Take a (fictitious) newspaper report about two unemployed Afro-Caribbean teenage males 'mugging' (robbing) an elderly man at knife-point. Do we notice their youthfulness, their unemployed (hence poor) status, their racial origins, their use of violence, the 'mugging' label, how the item came to be regarded as newsworthy, or their 'maleness'? If we notice only their violence and/or their racial origins, our understanding will differ from one based on noticing, for example, their poverty and/or their newsworthiness. Until quite recently, their 'maleness' would have been so taken-for-granted, so unnoticed, as to be totally invisible; Campbell's great *unspoken*. Being unnoticed and unspoken it is unavailable to assist understanding; once noticed, it must change our understanding in some way. What follows is a brief progress report on some of the ways our understanding of crime has been disrupted as a result of some people (not all criminologists it must be said) noticing crime's 'maleness'.

This is not an easy topic to report on for two main reasons. First, masculinity (together with femininity) is both one of the most 'confused' concepts 'that occur in science' (Freud, quoted in Connell, 1995: 3) and, perhaps partly in consequence, highly contentious. Secondly, as everyone reading this should know, there is no single behaviour covered by the term 'crime', only a range of very different activities, from fiddling tax returns to genocide, only some of which, some of the time, attract the 'criminal' label. To meet these difficulties, I propose first to discuss major shifts in thinking about masculinity and then to take two broad categories of crime where thinking about masculinity has made some impact, namely, 'sexual violence' and 'youth crime', though obviously some crimes straddle categories. Space limitations require certain restrictions. I shall not discuss criminalization/criminal justice matters and shall confine myself to British empirical data, where possible. This restriction does not apply to theoretical and political developments beyond these shores. Far from it. Without these, this review would be seriously impoverished.

The first part of what follows leans on Connell's masterly introductory chapter to *Masculinities* (1995), adopted and adapted with a very broad brush. In this chapter he discusses the three strands—the psycho-analytic, the social psychological, and 'recent developments in anthropology, history and sociology' (*ibid.* 7)—that have, in their different ways, produced knowledge about masculinity in the twentieth century. However, in order to facilitate my later discussion of the relationship of these knowledges to the crime question, my schematic overview will be structured to emphasize the significant theoretical shifts. Thus, I start with what I call 'Orthodox Accounts and the "Normal" Masculine Personality'. Whether of the psycho-analytic or the social psychological kind, their central theoretical production has been that of a relatively fixed and unitary 'normal' masculine personality, the result of a successful oedipal resolution in its psycho-analytic variant, and of successful 'sex-role' learning in its social psychological one. The two subsequent shifts both post-date contemporary feminism. The first of these (Connell's 'recent developments . . . '), I call 'The Social Break with Orthodoxy: Power and Multiple Masculinities'. This is characterized theoretically by the concepts of multiple masculinities, power (since these masculinities are always structured in relations of domination/subordination), and an insistence on the social (or institutional) dimension to masculinities. The second shift is the moment of feminist and poststructuralist engagements with more recent and radical developments in psychoanalytic theorizing. I call this 'The Psychoanalytic Break with Orthodoxy: Contradictory Subjectivities and the Social'. The principal feature of this development is the (re)discovery and reworking of the fragile, contingent and contradictory character of masculinity (and femininity), without losing sight of the social.

ORTHODOX ACCOUNTS AND THE 'NORMAL' MASCULINE PERSONALITY

It was Freud who, as a turn-of-the-century Viennese physician struggling to make sense of his patients' troubled lives, first 'noticed' gender. Their diffi-culties in living a gendered existence were central to his clinical case-studies. These laid the basis for a new understanding very different from the taken-for-granted one where maleness was a 'natural' product of biological sex. Utilizing his revolutionary ideas about repression and the unconscious, and a variety of novel methods (dream analysis, free association, etc.) for symptomatically 'reading' what had been repressed, he came to see the importance of early parent–child relations, especially the tangled mixture of love and jealousy he found there, to the formation of sexuality and gender in adulthood. The crucial stage in this development he called the œdipal complex, the moment when, for boy children,[1] fear of the potentially castrating father wins out over desire for the mother. This leads, through internalization of his father's prohibitions (the moment of the formation of the super-ego), to identification with the masculine. This is also the moment when the cultural prohibitions of civilization win out over individual desire.

For Freud, this masculinity was built upon a constitutional bisexuality, and a complex mix of pre-œdipal desires and identifications. Hence, it was always multi-layered, consisting of masculine and feminine elements, conflict-ridden, and fragile. Moreover, this 'impure' basis made neurotics of us all. Freud saw no discontinuity between 'normal' and neurotic mental processes. But the history of mainstream psycho-analysis, in its pursuit of acceptance and respectability, was to be one of increasing conservatism, and a concomitant sanitization and simplification of its theory. Thus, by the mid-century, psycho-analytic orthodoxy effectively held that a successful resolution of the œdipal complex paved the way to mental health and the gender 'normality' of adult heterosexuality and marriage; by contrast, an unsuccessful resolution underlay various neuroses and assorted gender 'perversions', including homosexuality.

The social psychological equivalent of the 'normal', post-œdipal masculine personality of mainstream psycho-analysis is the 'normal' man of sex role theory. He is someone who has successfully learned his social script—the cultural norms and expectations of 'being a man' in our society: the male sex role. This idea emerged in the 1950s when 'sex difference' research—the myriad attempts from the 1890s on to measure 'scientifically' how men and women differ psychologically—met up with role theory, the efforts by social scientists from the 1930s to think how positions in social structures get reproduced. This conjunction produced the (now conventional) idea that the psychological differences between men and women (their 'sex differences') result from the learning of the cultural norms and behaviour appropriate to their sex—their 'sex role' (thus reproducing the social categories, men and women). Masculinity is thus the male sex role internalized.

Talcott Parsons saw the origins of the male and female sex roles in the functional requirements of small groups like the family for role differentiation. Thus he produced his influential distinction between 'instrumental' and 'expressive' roles, a distinction which remained within the realm of social explanations (Parsons and Bales, 1956).[2] 'Most often', however, as Connell reminds us, 'sex roles are seen as the cultural elaboration of biological sex differences' (1995: 22). In other words, there is at the heart of most sex role theory a depressing circularity: sex roles are derived from cultural norms which, in turn, are based in innate differences.

---

[1] Space does not permit the complementary sketching of the girl child's path; suffice it to say that this, more than anything, has alienated many feminists from the Freudian tradition.

[2] For a contemporary application of the Parsonian distinction between 'instrumental' and 'expressive' applied to thinking about gendered differences in aggression, see Anne Campbell (1993).

Ironically, the early sex difference research, conducted by the first generation of women admitted into North American research universities, found that psychological differences between the sexes are small or non-existent (a finding which echoes Freud's radical findings about the mixture of masculinity and femininity in all of us). But, somewhere along the way, this radical challenge to the doctrine of innate sex differences gets lost, despite the continuing failure in the welter of subsequent research to find many differences. Moreover, though the social nature of the theory allows for change, for new cultural norms to be transmitted, and for the possibility of role-conflict, in practice, and especially before the advent of contemporary feminism, the theory rests largely on highly static, conservative assumptions: that role-expectations are clearly defined, unproblematically internalized, and normative. Consequently, the personalities so produced contribute to the mental health and social stability of society. Mainstream sex role theory thus produces a social parallel to mainstream psycho-analysis: in both, conflict and contradiction are effectively erased, the continuity between normality and pathology is severed, and masculinity and femininity become polarized terms.

THE SOCIAL BREAK WITH ORTHODOXY: POWER AND MULTIPLE MASCULINITIES

Once male social scientists followed the lead of feminist historians, anthropologists, and sociologists in their gendered recasting of women's lives with complementary re-examinations of the lives of men *as men*, a number of important shifts occurred. Historical and anthropological evidence began to show something of the empirical *diversity* in masculinities, cross-culturally and in different historical time periods, though much of the work remains wedded theoretically to the idea of male sex roles. There has, however, also been a stronger focus on the *institutional sites*—labour market, the law, the state, colonialism, etc.—wherein cultural norms pointed up by role theory are embedded. This attention to the dynamic, changing nature of masculinities and to the institutional sites of such transformations has led to a recognition, by some, that masculinity is not simply an external role to be passively internalized, a mere product of socialization, but something constructed in the interactional and institutional struggles of everyday life, an achievement of *practice*. The idea of competing masculinities struggling within institutional settings, and within the broader class, race, and other social relations that constrain these, has rendered this work sensitive to power differences *between men*, as well as the more usual feminist focus on inequalities between men and women.

Diversity, institutions, practice, and power. Of course not all this new work manages to be properly sensitive to all these issues. Linking them up coherently in a single theoretical frame is hard enough, let alone putting them to work on concrete cases. Connell's (1987, 1995) own efforts in this regard are seminal: the centrality of practice and hence of historically constructed gender relations; a constraining, multi-structured field of gender relations comprising three interrelated but irreducible structures of labour, power, and cathexis (roughly, sexuality); the various levels—personality, gender regime (institutional), gender order (societal)—where the historical play of gender relations can be 'read'; and, most famously, his adaptation of Gramsci in coining the idea of hegemonic and subordinate masculinities to make sense of the relation between competing masculinities.[3]

What remains unclear in Connell's work, especially given his obvious interest in psychoanalysis (Connell, 1994), is why he puts an unspecified 'practice' in command? His short definition of masculinity regards it as 'simultaneously a place in gender relations, the practices through which men and women engage that place in gender, and the *effects* of those practices in bodily experience, personality and culture' (1995: 71, my emphasis). To my mind this Sartrean commitment to practice (Sartre was hostile to the psychoanalytic idea of unconscious motivations), of personality as constituted by the practices that collectively define a life, ignores another possibility; one that makes subjectivity and the role of the unconscious central, but without losing a grip on the social. *That* is the contribution of recent developments in psycho-analytic theorizing, to which I now turn.

THE PSYCHO-ANALYTIC BREAK WITH ORTHODOXY: CONTRADICTORY SUBJECTIVITIES AND THE SOCIAL

Ultimately the worth of psychoanalysis in understanding masculinity will depend on our ability to grasp the structuring of personality and the complexities of desire at the same time as the structuring of social relations, with their contradictions and dynamisms [Connell, 1995: 20–1].

Why I think Connell has not himself properly realized this aspect of his project has to do with his commitment to what some would now regard as a very modernist notion of structure, when much of the new, radical psycho-analytic theorizing is poststructuralist, and comes at the task heavily influenced by Foucault, discourse, and what has come to be known as the 'turn to language'. Now is not the time to enter the fray on the vexed question of the relation between discourse and the 'real' (see Jefferson, 1994), but the idea of social

---

[3] He has recently extended the notion of competing masculinities to include 'complicit' and 'marginalized'. The former refers to masculinities that benefit from hegemonic masculinity, hence are complicit with it, without practising the full hegemonic package; the latter to the way structures of class and race intersect with the gender order to produce an array of class- and race-specific masculinities. The masculinities of subordinated classes and races are always 'marginal' to the hegemonic masculinity of the dominant group (Connell, 1995: 79–81).

discourses offering up a range of subject positions (a reversal of Foucault's deterministic idea that discourses position subjects), seems to put the question of motivation/investment/identification/desire (call it what you will for the moment) back at the heart of the matter. How do subjects, for example, come to take up (desire/identify with) one (heterosexual) rather than another (homosexual) subject position within the competing discourses of masculinity? This route makes unavoidable a re-engagement with the split, contradictory subject of psychoanalysis, if Connell's 'practice' is to be fully understood. Where else are the complex and contradictory origins of desire, as Connell (1994) himself has so persuasively argued, taken seriously?

The figures who have been most influential in rendering this subject of psychoanalysis socially literate are Jaques Lacan, Melanie Klein, and other Object Relations theorists. Lacan's linguistically influenced revisions of traditional Freudian theory, principally his notion that it is the child's entry into the social world of language (and hence into Foucault's discursive realm) that founds the unconscious and self-identity, provide a significant opening towards a (non-reductive) social understanding of the psyche. The revisionist work of Melanie Klein and Object Relations theorists, especially their emphases on the importance of relational defence mechanisms (such as 'splitting' off unwanted 'bad' parts of the self and 'projecting' them into others, where they can be disowned) and on early 'object relating', laid a further basis for an understanding of the psyche which is simultaneously social (cf. Rustin, 1991, 1995). Chodorow's object relations-influenced account probably has been the most influential to date in theorizing about masculinity. A Professor of Sociology turned psychoanalyst, she has argued that the emotional dynamics underpinning the process of separation from the mother are different for girls and boys, leaving boys with *the* problem of masculinity, namely, how to relate, and girls with *the* problem of femininity, namely, how to separate (Chodorow, 1978). Its widespread appeal probably had more to do with its recognizable sociology than its psychoanalytic argument, a point she now seems to recognize since she has gone on to criticize this work for giving 'determinist primacy to social relations' (1989: 7; see also Chodorow, 1994). This also goes to show how difficult it is to work seriously with both personality and social relations 'simultaneously'. Nonetheless, in this area we have no other option.[4] Let us see now how my three models can help us understand shifts in approaches to the question of men, masculinities, and particular crimes.

---

[4] For a range of work addressing this issue, see Henriques, *et al.*, 1984; Hollway, 1989; Craib, 1987; Jefferson, 1994, 1996*a*, *b*, and *c*; 1997; Frosh, 1991, 1994: Elliott, 1992, 1996; Elliott and Frosh, eds., 1995; Jackson, 1990, 1995; Richards, 1990, 1994; Rustin, 1991, 1995; Wolfenstein, 1989; Kovel, 1981, 1988.

SEXUAL VIOLENCE: RAPE/SEXUAL ABUSE/MURDER

This cluster of crimes in which sex is somewhere implicated is undoubtedly the area where thinking about masculinity has impacted most, not surprisingly perhaps, given the importance of sexuality to constructions of masculinity. Indeed, it was the pathbreaking writings of American radical feminists on rape in the 1970s (Griffin, 1971; Brownmiller, 1976) which, being the first to notice and theorize the 'maleness' of rape, effectively kickstarted the whole current interest in theorizing the relationship between forms of masculinity and certain crimes. The connection with feminist politics, and its location outside criminology, are two enduring features of this work, as we shall see.

Amir's sociological findings based on convicted rapists in Philadelphia (Amir, 1967, 1971) had already begun to challenge the image of the rapist as psychopathic stranger, the 'monster' lurking in the bushes, that has traditionally dominated the common-sense discourse on rape. But its 'maleness' escaped him. Moreover, in characterizing 19 per cent of the rapes as 'victim-precipitated' (victim retracting consent after first agreeing, or not reacting strongly enough) he seemed to be blaming the female victim, thus provoking feminist ire. The feminist interventions finally despatched any notion that rape was an activity undertaken only by abnormal or pathological males, most impressively in Brownmiller's monumental historical and cross-cultural cataloguing of the ubiquity of rape. Further, these writings moved beyond the psychological and sociological characteristics of convicted rapists to connect rape to the (patriarchal) organization of society as a whole. In Brownmiller's case (1976: 17), rape was actually the *foundation* of 'the patriarchy'. Finally, and most controversially, *all* men were implicated. As Brownmiller provocatively put it, rape 'is nothing more or less than a conscious process of intimidation by which *all men* keep *all women* in a state of fear' (*ibid.* 15, emphases in original), an idea that produced the feminist slogan, 'all men are potential rapists'. From being a *criminal* act committed by a minority of *deviant* men, rape had become a key tactic in the social control of women and the reproduction of male dominance.

In terms of my three-stage model of theorizing masculinity, these early feminist writings straddle the first two stages. In linking masculinity to patriarchal social relations and thus emphasizing the centrality of power, these move beyond the narrow œdipal and sex-role frames characteristic of orthodox accounts of masculinity. In other ways, though, they fail to surmount orthodox thinking. Masculinity is conceptualized in the singular, effectively *the* ideology underpinning the range of practices and institutions that collectively constitute *the* all-embracing system of male domination that is patriarchal society. Secondly, the notion of how individual men come to acquire patriarchal, masculine values, whether these are seen as rooted in biology (as they were for Brownmiller) or (as became more common) culture, is, like sex-role theory, implicitly deterministic: Weber's 'iron cage'.

One interesting attempt to move beyond these limitations is contained in

Box (1983). In recognizing a number of differently motivated types of rape, ranging from the brutally 'sadistic' to the manipulative 'exploitation' rape,[5] and analysing these in relation to a multi-factorial model of causation involving economic inequality, the law, 'techniques of neutralization' as well as what he calls the 'masculine mystique', he takes an important step towards multiplicity without actually breaking with the notion of a singular 'culture of masculinity'. What he does suggest is that men's differential access to socio-economic resources, and different relationships to cultural stereotypes of masculinity, will affect whether, and how, they rape. Crucially, he took on the (lower) class bias of imprisoned rapists (largely convicted of 'anger' or 'domination' rapes), suggesting that masculine sex-role socialization in the contexts of socio-economic powerlessness and a 'subculture of violence' could begin to account for this class profile (an approach not dissimilar to Polk's more recent attempt (1994) to make sense of both the maleness and the class profile of homicide). Box also makes the important point that, for the sadistic rapist (the rarest category), the 'masculine mystique' factor is all-important. (This, as we shall see below, provides a point of connection with later work on serial killing.) Whereas radical feminism had all men down as 'potential' rapists, thus effectively answering the question of what function rape plays in a patriarchal society, Box was attempting to answer a more traditional criminological question, namely, which men actually become so.

James Messerschmidt's book, *Masculinities and Crime* (1993), offers the most sustained attempt yet by a criminologist to rethink this relationship away from the deterministic reductionism of early feminist theorizing, and thus breaks decisively with orthodox accounts. In so doing, he does for criminology what Connell has done for the study of masculinity more generally. From Giddens (1976, 1981) he takes the idea of a practice-based approach to social structure, and from Acker (1989) the notion that gender, race, and class relations are implicated simultaneously in any given practice. He combines these insights with Connell's (1987) concepts of a multiply structured field of gender relations and hegemonic and subordinated masculinities. Finally, he borrows from phenomenology the idea of the 'situational accomplishment' of gender (West and Zimmerman, 1987; Fenstermaker, West, and Zimmerman, 1991; Goffman, 1979). The result of this creative synthesis sees crime as a resource for the situational accomplishment of gender (1993: 79). It is a form of 'structured action', a way of 'doing gender', which simultaneously accomplishes (or 'does') class and race. Men's resources for accomplishing masculinity, as with those of Box's rapists, will vary, dependent on their positions within class, race, and gender relations. These differences will be reflected in the salience of particular crimes as masculinity-accomplishing resources. For those at the bottom of racial and class hierarchies, with consequently reduced opportunities for the accomplishment of hegemonic masculinity, crime can be particularly salient.

---

[5] For a similar typology of rapists, see Wyre (1986).

Having assembled this imaginative thesis, Messerschmidt proceeds to put it to work to explain a whole range of crimes, including those of the powerful. For present purposes, his analysis of the infamous Central Park 'wilding' rape case is crucial. This involved four teenage Afro-American youths brutally and repeatedly raping a white woman jogger, leaving her near to death, whilst jubilantly celebrating ('wilding') throughout. What Messerschmidt manages to demonstrate, with this difficult and politically sensitive example, is how such behaviour can be rendered meaningful by seeing it as a group resource for accomplishing masculinity in a context of class and race disadvantage where other such resources are pitifully few.

It is a brave attempt. It is certainly an advance on the early radical feminist explanations. What it singularly fails to do, however, is to problematize why these particular young men chose this particular form of 'wilding' behaviour to accomplish their masculinity when other similarly disadvantaged young Afro-American men, thankfully, do not. In other words, it is a purely socio-logical theory about which *groups* of men are more or less likely to get involved in particular sorts of crime; it has nothing to say about which *particular man or men* from any given group (usually only a minority) are likely to do so. This requires taking the psychic dimension of subjectivity seriously, especially its contradictoriness; not seeing the self, as Messerschmidt implicitly does, simply as unitary and rational, reflexively monitoring behaviour in the light of the responses of others (*ibid.* 77). This oversocialized, essentially Meadian version of the self (Mead, 1934), helps explain the fact that the examples given of 'doing gender', despite the theoretical importance of practice (doing), all end up explaining the reproduction, not the subversion, of gender/race/class. This emphasis on constraints rather than action explains the ultimately determin-istic feel to the analyses, and reveals the limits of a purely social break with orthodoxy.

Another study operating within a broadly similar theoretical framework, but linked to an idea from cultural anthropology that the core properties of hegemonic masculinity in patriarchal societies are 'procreation', 'provision', and 'protection' is that of Kersten (1996). In this, he attempts to explain contemporary (and puzzling) differences in rape rates between Australia, where rates are high, Japan, where they are low, and Germany, which has rates somewhere between the two. The high (and rising) rates in Australia are explained broadly in terms of the effects of the continent's 'deep social, cultural and economic crisis' on the traditional 'national masculinity' built on 'physical prowess and independence'. This, Kersten argues, affects both the newly marginalized, for whom crime, including rape, becomes (following Messerschmidt) a resource for accomplishing masculinity, and those attempting to live up to 'hegemonic masculinity'. In the latter case, the difficulties of rearing and providing for families heighten the salience of the purely protective dimension of 'good' masculinity, and, in consequence, 'the image of the rapist as stranger'. Thus, rising rape rates are connected to increases in rape behaviour *and* to heightened sensitivities, to underlying structural changes, and to their (differential) impact on competing masculinities. In Japan, by contrast, masculinity and assaultive behaviour are not mutually implicated, for a whole host of reasons—cultural, organizational, even architectural—that Kersten attempts to spell out. It is a valiant attempt to think masculinity onto the notoriously difficult terrain of comparative criminology; though, as with Messerschmidt, it remains locked into an exclusively social frame.

What was needed to transcend this 'purely social break' was a better sense of the complexities of men's experiences. One could argue that the return to (a socially literate) psycho-analysis within feminism, my third stage in thinking about masculinities, was prompted, ultimately, by some of the felt disjunctions between personal experience (which had always been a serious object of attention in feminism) and available feminist theory: for many women, for example, their love of and desire for particular men contradicted their theoretical understandings of men-in-general as oppressors, aggressors, potential rapists. Progress in turning a similar spotlight on men's experiences has been slight, but instructive.

Books recounting men's experiences of rape, as rapists, are rare. I know of two (Beneke, 1982; Levine and Koenig, eds., 1983).[6] Reading these, what is striking is the disjunction between how these men experienced themselves ('I had a kind of phobia about women, I just felt I wasn't good enough for them, like really inside'; 'women often made me feel inferior', Levine and Koenig, eds., 1983: 78, 84), and feminism's traditional depiction of the rapist as the personification of power. Here, Frosh's notion of the 'incoherence of the masculine state' (1994: 99) has telling, concrete purchase.

Where these ideas have been developed most is in two case-studies, both by feminists, one a Professor of English, the other a journalist, of the serial, sexual murderer, Peter Sutcliffe, the so-called 'Yorkshire Ripper' (Ward Jouve, 1988; Smith, 1989). The question of serial killing has generated a small publishing industry of its own. It may be useful, therefore, to outline the main strands, so as to distinguish clearly my own focus. There is the work on sadistic sexual murder of feminist writers like Cameron and Frazer (1987) and Caputi (1988), and, more generally on women killing, of Radford and Russell, (eds., 1992). In this work, the 'maleness' of the violence is certainly central, most thought-provokingly in Cameron and Frazer's idea that the 'common denominator' of sex-murderers is not misogyny, since not all their victims are women, but 'a shared construction of . . . masculinity' in which the 'quest for transcendence' is central (*ibid.* 166–7). However, because masculinity and patriarchy are conceptualized in the singular, theoretically speaking this work is a continuation (along with a whole range of other work on violence against women) of the

---

[6] I discount books like Scully's (1990). Though this purports to be a study of convicted rapists, the men's experiences are so heavily interpreted through a conventional sociological feminism that, whatever the men have to say is returned to them effectively (and unperceptively) reduced to 'justifications' and 'excuses' (*ibid.* 134). Similarly, descriptive studies of imprisoned rapists based partly on interview material (which are rare in this country) assist little (see Grubin and Gunn, 1990).

tradition inaugurated by the work of Brownmiller and Griffin on rape.[7] Then there is the emergent positivistic criminological literature responding to an apparently novel crime phenomenon (Levin and Fox, 1985; Holmes and DeBurger, 1988; Lester, 1995). Definitions, profiles, and typologies are central, based upon the careful assembling of what is known about killers' backgrounds, personalities, motives, methods, victims, and killing locations. Where the 'maleness' of the perpetrators is noticed, it is in a list of factors, conceptualized in the most orthodox terms: a failure to live up to sex-role norms (Levin and Fox, 1985: 53), for example. The understanding of Freud and the unconscious is risible (Holmes and De Burger, 1988: 98). The two final strands are the biographical accounts of particularly heinous killers written by journalists, which now constitute a whole sub-genre of biographical writing, and, what interests us here, certain feminist appropriations of these.

Once Peter Sutcliffe acquired his 'Yorkshire Ripper' tag, and thus became linked in the popular imagination to 'Jack the Ripper', the 'father' to the 'age of sex crime' (Caputi, 1987: 7), the interest of journalists (Beattie, 1981; Burn, 1984; Cross, 1981; Yallop, 1981; Smith, 1989) and academic feminists (Hollway, 1981; Bland, 1984; Ward Jouve, 1988) was assured—with the usual division of labour.[8] The former have done the leg work, attended the trial, conducted the interviews and produced detailed but essentially descriptive accounts of the case; the latter have offered their feminist-inspired theoretical re-readings. Only Smith, a feminist and a journalist who reported on the trial, manages both. Of the re-readings, it is the brilliant discussions of Sutcliffe's fragile and conflicted masculinity, in both Smith and Ward Jouve, that begins to develop the contours of an understanding of masculinity that is both socially literate and psychoanalytically complex.

Connell's notion, that it is in the 'detail of cases' that the deployment of psychoanalytic ideas will greatly assist our understanding of masculinity (Connell, 1995: 34), is superbly exemplified in these two accounts. They reach similar conclusions. Both tell the story of a boy who is painfully torn between the tough, masculine values of father, brother, and working-class neighbourhood, the mantle of masculinity required of him, and the quiet, gentle femininity of his beloved, long-suffering mother, with whom he strongly identified. They show something of the multiple ambivalences that this contradiction produced: the cruel cross-pressures of the socially required versus the psychically desired (but socially punished). And they outline many of the contingencies that, in repeatedly demonstrating his failure to live up to the social expectations of manliness, led him first to blame the feminine in himself, to hate part of himself, and then externalize that hatred and destroy women.

It was a grisly resolution. It was not inevitable. It was in some sense chosen.

---

[7] But see also, on pornography, Morgan, 1982; on sexual harassment, Farley, 1978; on terrorism, Morgan, 1989; on wife battering, Dobash and Dobash, 1979.

[8] Interestingly, in the writing of the book on the child murderer, Robert Black, the journalistic skills of Tim Tate are combined with the expertise of Ray Wyre, the founder of the Gracewell Clinic for sex offenders (Wyre and Tate, 1995).

But it is a resolution and a choice that displays a logic only within the detail of a life observed through a lens of masculinity which is simultaneously social and psychic, alert to the multiple contradictions within and between these dimensions, the anxieties and ambivalences these set up, and the compounding influence of contingencies. It is the strength of the accounts of both Smith and Ward Jouve that they do render Sutcliffe's life comprehensible, at least after a fashion. The fuller, journalistic accounts are drawn on, but transformed by the noticing of, and accounting for, a whole host of apparently inconsequential, overlooked details, thus rendering them theoretically meaningful.

This work has had little impact on the rape debate, which is still heavily influenced by radical feminism. Two decades on, discussions of the various violences against women are still effectively centred on unmasking the many visages of 'male power' (in the singular): for example, the (patriarchal) assumptions and practices in the conduct of rape investigations and trials which produce high 'attrition rates' and low rates of conviction (Adler, 1987; Chambers and Millar, 1983, 1986; Grace, Lloyd, and Smith, 1992; Lees and Gregory, 1995).[9] Some US feminists, however, have changed tack completely and rejected this orthodoxy as a form of 'victim-feminism' (Paglia, 1992; Roiphe, 1993). They regard its picture of woman-as-victim, passively powerless, as one that simply reinforces the conventional stereotype of the weak, helpless woman. These new 'power' (or 'post'?) feminist voices have emerged out of the complex sexual and racial politics on US campuses which engendered the debate about 'political correctness' (Dunant, 1994; Hollway and Jefferson, 1996a).[10] In particular, Paglia and Roiphe blame the growth of concern about campus 'date-rape' (Boumil, Friedman, and Taylor, 1993) on feminist extensions of the definition of rape (to include verbal as well as physical coercion, or any sex felt by the victim to be violating; see Roiphe, 1993: 68–70), and generally bemoan the denial of an active female sexuality in the dating scenario (Paglia, 1992: 49–74). Since both Paglia and Roiphe hail from the humanities and not the social sciences, and their purposes were primarily political, it is not surprising that they end up postulating a responsible, 'choosing' female subject, a simple inversion of radical feminism's passive victim of male power.[11]

But, in putting woman's sexuality back into the picture, by suggesting that she too is a sexual agent, it reconnected with a dimension that had become obscured by radical feminism's preoccupation with power. What was still absent was some more adequate theory of gendered subjectivity. It is this dimension that more recent work on particular date-rape cases is trying to develop (Jefferson, 1997; Hollway and Jefferson, 1996b),[12] using a theory of

---

[9] For the most theoretically interesting exception to this general rule, see Smart (1989, chapter 2).

[10] David Mamet's play and subsequent film, *Oleanna*, about a College Professor accused of sexual harassment and rape, and Michael Crichton's best-selling book, *Disclosure* (also made into a film) about a male victim of sexual harassment, are two popular manifestations of the debate.

[11] For a British journalist's view of the debate, see Grant, 1994.

[12] For an application of this approach to sexual harassment, see Hollway and Jefferson (1996a).

subjectivity derived from combining Foucault's notion of (social) discourses, together with various (psycho-analytically derived) concepts, such as anxiety and the defences of splitting and projection, in order to explain the discursive positions adopted (Jefferson, 1994; Hollway, 1989). Testing this approach on particular cases has involved deconstructions of existing journalistic accounts, highlighting those facts left unexplained, and reconstructions showing how sense can be made of ignored facts, once unconscious motivations and ambivalent feelings, and the anxieties and defensive splittings/projections these give rise to (for both parties) are recognized. The subjectivities that emerge from such analytical reconstructions turn out to be complexly and contradictorily gendered, a conclusion in line with Ward Jouve and Smith on the 'masculinity' of Sutcliffe.

A further instance of the fruitful rereading of journalistic accounts, one that is alert to the question of masculinity and the importance of addressing social and psychic dimensions, is Jackson's pamphlet on the James Bulger case (1995; see also Jefferson, 1996c). Its relevance here is that James' murder by two boys was preceded by a symbolic rape. It was a shocking and gruesome case, provoking widespread public revulsion and incomprehension, and, perhaps inevitably, much recourse to demonizing discourses. What the journalist David Smith does in his excellent book on the case (1995) is first remind us that killing by children is not new, then meticulously assemble the available evidence, and finally offer an explanation based on the unhappiness, mistreatment, and powerlessness that was characteristic of both boys' lives. He offers this explanation reluctantly, trusting initially that an explanation would emerge from the detail, thus nicely demonstrating the difference between the journalistic and the academic approach. What Jackson does is to take up the neglected issue of masculinity and show how the boys' lives could be understood as attempts to build up a more powerful sense of masculine identity, in the twin contexts of a powerlessness imposed by the frameworks that regulated them (family and school), and the 'idealised fantasy images of hypermasculine toughness, dominance and invulnerability' (*ibid.* 22) provided by the media and the male peer group, which exerted both a pull and a pressure. The resulting truancy, 'rape', and the killing of the toddler James are all read in this light, with the killing seen as an attempt to master their own anxieties and fears about their own babyishness by violently projecting them onto James, and destroying them there. Once again, the parallels with the Ward Jouve and Smith accounts of Sutcliffe at this point should be obvious.

One of the things the Bulger killing did was to reignite interest in the case of Mary Bell, the girl who was convicted of strangling two small children in 1968 when she was 11. Gitta Sereny's *The Case of Mary Bell*, first published in 1972, was republished in a new edition with a new preface and an appendix about the death of James Bulger (1995). Though Mary Bell was labelled a psychopath by two psychiatrists, thereby securing a conviction for manslaughter on the grounds of diminished responsibility, the similarity between her emotionally impoverished and rejecting background and her troublesome responses, and those of the two boy killers of James is striking. For Sereny, the emotional damage that all three children shared is the crucial feature, not their gender (which is never raised). Whether she is right or not, these cases suggest two things at least to bear in mind when thinking about masculinity. One is a reminder of the complex fluidity of gender formation, a point being developed most interestingly in the theoretical work of Jessica Benjamin (1990, 1995). How else explain Mary Bell's extremely 'masculine' fearlessness and inability to feel? This would seem to warn against pinning everything on gender difference and ignoring what we share by virtue of being human.[13] Secondly, if masculinity is used over-inclusively as an explanatory concept, the role of other significant factors may be obscured.

With these thoughts in mind, it might be in this spirit that we could usefully return to traditional criminological texts like West (1987) on sexual violence. There, the various portraits of rapists, pædophiles, etc., where weakness and inadequacy seem more in evidence than their social power as men, could surely benefit by more attention to the question of masculinity. On the other hand, his detailing of a variety of factors may alert us to the dangers of a too-inclusive use of the concept of masculinity (cf: Walklate, 1995: 180–1).

Lest this focus on individual cases serves to obscure the ultimate object of attention, in the Sutcliffe example a better understanding of the psychic under-pinnings of the gruesome social phenomenon, sadistic sexual murder, let me end this section by refocusing on the broadest possible meaning of the social, on what Bob Connell (1993) calls 'the big picture'. Take something like the rise of fascism in inter-war Germany which, with its genocidal outcome, ought to be of some interest to criminologists. So far as I know, no serious commentator has ever tried to deny fascism's complex social roots. But, in the wake of the Frankfurt school's efforts to understand the psychic underpinnings of its mass appeal, who would now deny the need also to understand the complexities of fascism's psychological roots? As Ehrenreich tellingly puts it, in her Foreword to the first volume of Theweleit's (1987) extraordinarily rich account of the fantasies of fascist Freikorpsmen, 'the problem [with sociological or marxist theories of fascism] . . . is that these theories have very little to tell us about what we ultimately need most to understand, and that is murder' (*ibid.* xi).

Understanding the roots of fascist violence is at the heart of Theweleit's work. Authority and the construction of the authoritarian personality were central to the Frankfurt school's understanding of fascism. For Theweleit (1987, 1989) it is the attraction of violence, and its origins in the construction of the particular masculinities of the men of the Freikorps, specifically their fear and hatred of the feminine, which is paramount. His work can thus be seen as a (very rich) case-study in masculinity. In attending to the connections between fantasy life and politics, it is sensitive to both psychic and social levels. The question Theweleit leaves open is how different was the psychic constel-

---

[13] Or inhuman. The recent conviction of Rosemary West for 10 murders, and the publication of Hindley's long letter to the *Guardian* (18 Dec. 1995), raise these issues very strongly.

lation of these men from that of other men. But, in the light of the present 'big picture', in which neither war, genocide, nor torture can be consigned safely to the historical past, it would seem madness to leave the question of masculine subjectivities out of account. As Benjamin and Rabinbach say in their Foreword to Theweleit's second volume:

no other work dives so deeply into the fantasies of violence, or into warfare itself as a symbolic system of desire . . . in this world of war the repudiation of one's own body, of femininity, becomes a psychic compulsion which associates masculinity with hardness, destruction, and self-denial [*ibid.*, p. xiii].

YOUTH CRIME, UNDERCLASS MALES, AND BLACK MASCULINITY

I want to end with a brief survey of thinking about young 'underclass' men with 'no future', ethnicity and crime, not only because there is relevant work being done here, but also because it is here in particular that we can witness the impact of key transformations in 'the big picture' on a range of subordinate and marginal masculinities across the developed world. But, first, a brief pre-history.

The idea of a connection between a life with 'no future' and crime is not new. Paul Goodman's passionate mid-1950s polemic, *Growing Up Absurd*, saw juvenile delinquency as 'the powerless struggling for life within . . . an unacceptable world' (1956: 197). He even saw this as a problem of 'manliness': 'If there is little interest, honour, or manliness in the working part of our way of life, can we hope for much in the leisure part?' (*ibid.* 235–6). But young men and manliness were assumed categories and not problematized. At around the same time, Albert Cohen (1955), the first of the subcultural theorists, did link male delinquent subcultures partly to anxiety about masculinity, but mostly to the 'status frustration' of growing up working-class in a world dominated by middle-class values (see Walklate, 1995: 166–7). It was only the class basis of youth subcultures that was subsequently taken up by British subcultural theorists and reworked using an admixture of marxist and semiotic concepts (Hall and Jefferson, eds., 1976). These were later to be roundly criticized for ignoring the gender dimension (McRobbie, 1980; Dorn and South, 1982). Paul Willis' classic, *Learning to Labour* (1977), was an early exception to the rule (of gender-blindness). He showed how working-class lads (willingly) take on hard, physical, working-class jobs, partly by rejecting the femininity associated with mental 'pen-pushing' labour (and hence the opportunity to 'get on' in class terms). But, despite Willis' important emphasis on practice, and the superb ethnography of his lads' school-based youth culture, the analytic categories of 'capitalism' and 'patriarchy' remained unidimensional, hence (now) problematic.

The issue of gender was not to resurface properly in the youth debate until the 1990s. When it did reappear, it was feminist writers who once again led the way, this time by drawing attention to the angry and destructive responses of 'underclass' males to their new social and economic marginalization (Campbell, 1991, 1993; Coward, 1994; but see also Jackson, 1992*a* and *b*; Jefferson, 1992). Written partly in response to the conservative 'take' on the underclass debate—that certain young men choose unemployment and crime because both are made easy for them (Murray, 1984, 1989, 1990)[14]—and partly as an attempt to understand the riots of 1991, Bea Campbell's journalistic foray into 'Britain's dangerous places', the new economic 'disaster areas', produced a compelling account of a subordinate masculinity in crisis.[15] Against the background of what she called the 'economic emergency' facing these areas, Campbell talked of how women translate their troubles and anger into 'strategies of survival and solidarity', how men court 'danger and destruction' (1993: 303). It works brilliantly as reportage, and at putting the issue of masculinity and crime on the criminological agenda. But, ultimately, the book succumbs to a kind of victim feminism, with its cast of fearful, long-suffering, somewhat idealized women, preyed upon by criminally predatory, somewhat pathologized young men, and the 'boys in blue' stuck uncomfortably in the middle of this contemporary war between the sexes.

Feminist academic and journalist Ros Coward also takes up this theme of the different responses of men and women to the economic destruction of their neighbourhoods, but adds a further twist, namely, the idea of the 'yob' as the 'classic scapegoat' left 'carrying the weight of masculinity which, for a variety of reasons, middle-class society finds increasingly unacceptable, and rhetorically dumps on the men of the lower class' (1994: 32). We might see this as a contemporary version of Stan Cohen's (1973) 'folk devils' argument, revitalized through the attention given to masculinity.

From within criminology, the late Mike Collison (1996), using interviews with young British male offenders, connected up notions of the 'risk society' and the importance of consumption in detailing how structurally excluded males ('reflexivity losers') accomplish masculinity in creating a street style of spectacular consumption, excessive drug use, and living life on the 'edge', in pursuit of a reputation for being 'mad.[16] Across the Atlantic, Bourgois (1995, 1996) has shown the effect of social and economic marginalization on young Puerto Rican male immigrants. Deprived of jobs and the ability to provide for a family—the culturally traditional avenue to patriarchal respect—their alternative 'search for respect' becomes centred on a misogynistic and parasitic life-style of crack dealing, sexual promiscuity, and interpersonal violence.

---

[14] For a broad overview of both the American and British debates, see Morris (1994); for a detailed, personal look at the US debate, see Auletta (1983); for an interesting and relevant thesis, see Dahrendorf (1985).

[15] What Connell now calls 'protest masculinity' (1995: 109–12).

[16] John Beynon's ESRC funded research on offenders, written up as *The Joy Generation* (1995; unpublished ESRC Report, ref. no R000233292), has a very similar feel.

All these accounts, journalistic or academic, are about the effects of the global restructuring of the economy on particular, subordinated, or marginalized masculinities. In terms of my three-stage model, these accounts are all at stage two: the world of 'power and multiple masculinities'. This is because, by focusing on the subordinate or marginalized masculinities of socially excluded youths, there is, implicitly anyway, a recognition of a dominant, countervailing, or mainstream masculinity. What would be needed to shift this sort of work into my stage three, where an interest in psychic as well as social dimensions is demanded, would be an analytic interest in particular cases to complement the sociological interest in the group. Until criminologists can believe that 'exceptional' cases can tell us something about the 'rule', indeed ought to be examined in order to alter our understanding of the rule, and need not entail (the much maligned) 'individualistic' explanations, progress will be slow.

Where this debate about subordinate or marginalized masculinities in crisis has proceeded furthest is in relation to the African-American male. It is at the heart of the debate about 'The Crisis of African American Gender Relations', recently featured in *Transition 66* (Summer, 1995). Though undoubtedly stimulated by the Thomas-Hill hearings (Morrison, ed., 1992) and the Tyson rape conviction (Shaw, 1993; Garrison and Roberts, 1994), this debate extends back at least to Wallace's brave critique of the macho politics of Black Power (1990; originally published in 1978).[17] In Britain, the race and crime debate has got itself bogged down trying to assess the degree to which Afro-Caribbean over-representation in official crime statistics can, or cannot, be attributed to discriminatory practices (see Smith's chapter in this volume). By contrast, the North American debate has had to recognize the role of masculinity much earlier. This has only partly to do with the massive over-representation of Afro-Americans in crime (and punishment) in the United States. More importantly, it has to do with the history of black–white relations since the abolition of slavery, the role of black males in the white imagination, and the response of young ('underclass') black men both to these white fantasies and to their continued (and worsening) social, economic, and political marginalization.

This tortured history has seen black males as the repressed other of the dominant (white) masculinity, a dialectic with a much longer history (see Hoch, 1979: chapter 3). But, in the context of a vicious and continuing history of racist violence and discrimination, the channels for achieving respect as a man have been both narrow and, in consequence, highly salient. Thus, the rise of the Afro-American athlete and entertainer, and 'cool' ghetto hustler, put bodily performance, sexuality, and toughness (the repressed other of 'civilized' white masculinity) at a premium—in line with restricted opportunities and prevailing mythologies.

The civil rights and black liberation movements of the 1960s may not have produced political emancipation, but they did produce a psychic shift (West, 1993: 18). This shift, in combination with the worsening plight of black

---

[17] But see Singh (1995) for an alternative assessment of the Black Panther party.

America (Wacquant, 1995), has fuelled black rage, which, having no legitimate outlets, gets turned inwards, creating both nihilism (West, 1993: chapter 1) and misogyny. This has to do with the limited availability of positive images for black men, and the emasculating effects of continuous and humiliating racism. Together, these made for the profoundly contradictory mix that is contemporary black macho: both an uplifting and unifying form of resistance to (hegemonic) white masculinity (the return of the repressed), *and*, in its misogyny and homophobia, a depressing source of community division (Wallace, 1990). The attempts to theorize all this specifically in relation to masculinity (Staples, 1989), and the problems of 'cool pose' (Majors, 1989; Majors and Billson, 1992) have largely relied on structural and/or sex-role theorizing (in a somewhat problematic combination with psycho-analytic theory in the case of Gibbs and Merighi, 1994) and, to that extent, remain limited. But, once the historical sensitivities of writers like Wallace (1990) and bell hooks (1992: chapter 6) are combined with the theoretical sophistication of Mac an Ghaill (1988; 1994*a* and *b*), an Irishman who has researched black masculinities in a British school informed by an awareness of the psychic dimension of masculinity, the current dominance of this theoretical model should be supplanted. My own work on Tyson (Jefferson, 1996*a* and *b*, 1997), a biographical case-study in the development of a particular form of black masculinity, is an attempt to shift the theoretical contours to include a psychic as well as a social dimension. That such life-history work can be undertaken without neglecting the social dimension is demonstrated wonderfully in Wolfenstein's monumental marxist/psycho-analytic account of the life of Malcolm X (1989). Perhaps one of the reasons this sort of approach has yet to be more widely adopted in relation to 'ordinary' crime—aside from the (misplaced) cultural hostility to psycho-analysis for (apparently) being interested only in individual cases—is that there is always more life material available in the case of major celebrities and other public figures (e.g. Malcolm X; Tyson). The petty thief and ordinary burglar rarely leave the kind of biographical traces necessary for this work. But a start could be made by returning to classic life-histories of ordinary crime, like Shaw's *The Jack Roller* (1930), to see what might be possible—or what future work of this kind might need to address. It seems to me that if any real progress on how gender/class/race/age issues intersect complexly will be achieved only when the contours of particular life-histories are mapped in relation to them.

CONCLUSION

Since this is very much 'work-in-progress', let me end by posing two crucial questions. One of the most original criminological texts of recent years, and one much cited in connection with the issue of masculinity and crime, is Katz's *Seductions of Crime* (1988). In it, he reverses the usual focus in criminology on background factors, and concentrates instead on 'those aspects in the fore-ground of criminality that make its various forms sensible, even sensually compelling, ways of being' (*ibid.* 3). It is constantly fascinating, insightful, and thought-provoking in its pursuit of 'the moral and sensual attractions in doing evil'. Yet, for all its concerns with the desirability of crime, it is (a) thoroughly sociological and (b) only fitfully concerned with the dimension of gender. When a psycho-analytic, gender-aware dimension is added, as it is, briefly, for example at the end of the chapter on 'Ways of the Badass', it adds little if any-thing to what has gone before. So this would seem to present two challenges to the thrust of my argument (both of which I have previously acknowledged). One is the extent to which a psycho-analytic dimension adds a *necessary* explanatory level. The second is the degree to which the question of mascu-linity aids our understanding. It might be a useful exercise for someone to go back to Katz with these two questions centrally in mind. Whatever the answers, my suspicion is that they will be both more contingent, given the vagaries of particular lives, and crime-specific than those of us interested in 'Theory' ideally would like.

Guide to Further Reading

The most comprehensive overview of the field of masculinity studies is to be found in Connell's *Masculinities* (1995, Polity). The most theoretically system-atic attempt to relate the concept of masculinity to the crime question is Messerschmidt's *Masculinities and Crime* (1993, Rowman and Littlefield). Walklate's introductory text, *Gender and Crime* (1995, Prentice Hall/Harvester Wheatsheaf), includes useful discussions of the recent debates on masculinity. The volume edited by Newburn and Stanko, entitled *Just Boys Doing Business? Men, Masculinities and Crime* (1994, Routledge), offers a range of attempts to think through the relationship between masculinities and crime and criminal justice issues, as does the Special Issue of the *British Journal of Criminology*, edited by Jefferson and Carlen (*Masculinities, Social Relations and Crime*, 36, 3, 1996). Finally, Campbell's journalistic account, *Goliath* (1993, Methuen), is a timely and readable attempt to use the notion of masculinity to understand the plight of young economically disadvantaged men growing up in Britain's contemporary urban wastelands.

REFERENCES

ACKER, J. (1989), 'The Problem with Patriarchy', *Sociology*, 23, 2: 235–40.

ADLER, A. (1987), *Rape on Trial*. London: Routledge & Kegan Paul.

AMIR, M. (1967), 'Victim Precipitated Forcible Rape', *Journal of Criminal Law, Criminology and Police Science*, 58: 493–502.

—— (1971), *Patterns in Forcible Rape*. Chicago, Ill.: University of Chicago Press.

AULETTA, K. (1983), *The Underclass*. New York: Vintage.

BEATTIE, J. (1981), *The Yorkshire Ripper Story*. London: Quartet/Daily Star.

BENEKE, T. (1982), *Men on Rape*. New York: St Martin's Press.

BENJAMIN, J. (1995), 'Sameness and Difference: Toward an 'Over-inclusive' Theory of Gender Development', in A. Elliott and S. Frosh, eds., *Psychoanalysis in Contexts*, 106–22. London: Routledge.

—— (1990), *The Bonds of Love: Psychoanalysis, Feminism and the Problem of Domination*. London: Virago.

BEYNON, J. (1995), *The Joy Generation*. Unpublished ESRC Report, ref. no R000233292.

BLAND, L. (1984), 'The Case of the Yorkshire Ripper: Mad, Bad, Beast or Male?', in P. Scraton and P. Gordon, eds., *Causes for Concern*, 184–209. Harmondsworth: Penguin.

BOUMIL, M. M., FRIEDMAN, J., and TAYLOR, B. E. (1993), *Date Rape: The Secret Epidemic*. Deerfield Beach, Fla.: Health Communications Inc.

BOURGOIS, P. (1996), 'In Search of Masculinity: Violence, Respect and Sexuality among Puerto Rican Crack Dealers in East Harlem', in T. Jefferson and P. Carlen, eds., *Masculinities, Social Relations and Crime*, Special Issue of *British Journal of Criminology*, 36, 3: 412–27.

—— (1995), *In Search of Respect: Selling Crack in El Barrio*. Cambridge: Cambridge University Press.

BOX, S. (1983), *Power, Crime and Mystification*. London: Tavistock.

BROWNMILLER, S. (1976), *Against Our Will: Men, Women and Rape*. Harmondsworth: Penguin.

BURN, G. (1984), *Somebody's Husband, Somebody's Son: The Story of Peter Sutcliffe*. London: Heinemann.

CAMERON, D., and FRAZER, E. (1987), *The Lust to Kill: A Feminist Investigation of Sexual Murder*. Cambridge: Polity.

CAMPBELL, A. (1993), *Out of Control: Men, Women and Aggression*. London: Pandora.

CAMPBELL, B. (1993), *Goliath: Britain's Dangerous Places*. London: Methuen.

—— (1991), 'Kings of the Road', *Marxism Today*, 20–23 December.

CAPUTI, J. (1988), *The Age of Sex Crime*. London: The Women's Press.

CHAMBERS, G., and MILLAR, A. (1983), *Investigating Sexual Assault*. Edinburgh: HMSO.

—— (1986), *Prosecuting Sexual Assault*. Edinburgh: HMSO.

CHODOROW, N. J. (1978), *The Reproduction of Mothering: Psychoanalysis and the Sociology of Gender*. Berkeley, Cal.: University of California Press.

—— (1989), *Feminism and Psychoanalytic Theory*. London: Yale University Press.

—— (1994), *Femininities, Masculinities, Sexualities: Freud and Beyond*. Lexington, Kentucky: The University Press of Kentucky.

COHEN, A. K. (1955), *Delinquent Boys*. New York: Free Press.

COHEN, S. (1973), *Folk Devils and Moral Panics*. London: Paladin.

COLLISON, M. (1996), 'In Search of The High Life: Drugs, Crime, Masculinity and Consumption', in T. Jefferson and P. Carlen, eds., *Masculinities, Social Relations and Crime*, Special Issue of *British Journal of Criminology*, 36. 3: 428–44.

CONNELL, R. W. (1987), *Gender and Power: Society, the Person and Sexual Politics*. Cambridge: Polity.

—— (1993), 'The Big Picture: Masculinities in Recent World History', *Theory and Society*, 22, 5: 599–623.

—— (1994), 'Psychoanalysis on Masculinity', in H. Brod and M. Kaufman, eds., *Theorizing Masculinities*, 11–38. London: Sage.

—— (1995), *Masculinities*. Cambridge: Polity.

COWARD, R. (1994), 'Whipping Boys', *Guardian Weekend*, 32–5, 3 September.

CRAIB, I. (1987), 'Masculinity and Male Dominance', *Sociological Review*, 34, 4: 721–43.

CRICHTON, M. (1994), *Disclosure*. London: Arrow.

CROSS, R. (1981), *The Yorkshire Ripper: The In-depth Study of a Mass Killer and His Methods*. London: Granada.

DAHRENDORF, R. (1985), *Law and Order*. London: Stevens and Sons.

DOBASH, R. E., and DOBASH, R. (1979), *Violence Against Wives: A Case Against Patriarchy*. New York: Free Press.

DORN, N., and SOUTH, N. (1982), *Of Males and Markets: A Critical Review of 'Youth Culture' Theory*. Research Paper 1, Centre for Occupational and Community Research. London: Middlesex Polytechnic.

DUNANT, S., ed. (1994), *The War of the Words: The Political Correctness Debate*. London: Virago.

ELLIOTT, A. (1992), *Social Theory and Psychoanalysis in Transition: Self and Society from Freud to Kristeva*. London: Routledge.

—— (1996), *Subject to Ourselves: Social Theory, Psychoanalysis and Postmodernity*. Cambridge: Polity.

—— and FROSH, S., eds. (1995), *Psychoanalysis in Contexts: Paths between Theory and Modern Culture*. London: Routledge.

FARLEY, L. (1978), *Sexual Shakedown: the Sexual Harassment of Women on the Job.* New York: McGraw-Hill.

FENSTERMAKER, S., WEST, C., and ZIMMERMAN, D. H. (1991), 'Gender Inequality: New Conceptual Terrain', in R. L. Blumberg, ed., *Gender, Family and Economy*, 289–307. Newbury Park, Cal.: Sage.

FROSH, S. (1991), *Identity Crisis: Modernity, Psychoanalysis and the Self.* London: Macmillan.

—— (1994), *Sexual Difference: Masculinity and Psychoanalysis.* London: Routledge.

GARRISON, J. G., and Roberts, R. (1994), *Heavy Justice: The State of Indiana v. Michael G. Tyson.* New York: Addison-Wesley.

GELSTHORPE, L. and MORRIS, A. (1990), 'Introduction: Transforming and Transgressing Criminology', in L. Gelsthorpe and A. Morris, eds., *Feminist Perspectives in Criminology*, 1–5. Milton Keynes: Open University Press.

GIBBS, J. T., and MERIGHI, J. R. (1994), 'Young Black Males: Marginality, Masculinity and Criminality', in T. Newburn and E. A. Stanko, eds., *Just Boys Doing Business?* 54–80. London: Routledge.

GIDDENS, A. (1976), *New Rules of Sociological Method.* London: Hutchinson.

—— (1981), 'Agency, Institution and Time-Space Analysis', in K. Knorr-Cetina and A. V. Cicourel, eds., *Advances in Social Theory and Methodology: Toward an Integration of Micro- and Macro-Sociologies*, 161–74. Boston, Mass: Routledge and Kegan Paul.

GOFFMAN, E. (1979), *Gender Advertisements.* New York: Harper and Row.

GOODMAN, P. (1956), *Growing Up Absurd.* New York: Vintage.

GRACE, S., LLOYD, C., and SMITH, L. J. F. (1992), *Rape: From Recording to Conviction.* Research and Planning Unit Paper 71. London: Home Office.

GRANT, L. (1994), 'Sex and the Single Student: The Story of Date Rape', in S. Dunant, ed., *The War of the Words*, 76–96. London: Virago.

GRIFFIN, S. (1971), 'Rape: The All American Crime', *Ramparts*, 26–35, September.

GRUBIN, D., and GUNN, J. (1990), *The Imprisoned Rapist and Rape.* London: Dept of Forensic Psychiatry, Institute of Psychiatry.

HALL, S., and JEFFERSON, T. eds. (1976), *Resistance through Rituals: Youth Subcultures in Post War Britain* London: Hutchinson.

HENRIQUES, J., HOLLWAY, W., URWIN, C.,

VENN, C., and WALKERDINE, V. (1984), *Changing the Subject: Psychology, Social Regulation and Subjectivity.* London: Methuen.

HOCH, P. (1979), *White Hero Black Beast: Racism, Sexism and the Mask of Masculinity.* London: Pluto.

HOLLWAY, W. (1981), ' "I Just Wanted to Kill a Woman." Why?: The Ripper and Male Sexuality', *Feminist Review*, 9, 33–40.

—— (1989), *Subjectivity and Method in Psychology: Gender, Meaning and Science.* London: Sage.

—— and JEFFERSON, T. (1996a), 'PC or not PC: Sexual Harassment and The Question of Ambivalence', *Human Relations*, 49, 3: 373–93.

—— and —— (1996b), ' "A Kiss is Just a Kiss": Date Rape, Gender and Contradictory Subjectivities'. Unpublished manuscript.

HOLMES, R. M., and DE BURGER, J. (1988), *Serial Murder.* London: Sage.

hooks, b. (1992), 'Reconstructing Black Masculinity', in b. hooks, *Black Looks: Race and Representation*, 87–113. Ontario, Canada: Between the Lines.

JACKSON, D. (1990), *Unmasking Masculinity: A Critical Autobiography.* London: Unwin Hyman.

—— (1992a), 'Riding for Joy', *Achilles Heel*, 13: 18–19; 37–8.

—— (1992b), 'The Silence of the Wolves', *Achilles Heel*, 13: 25–7.

—— (1995), *Destroying the Baby in Themselves: Why Did the Two Boys Kill James Bulger?* Nottingham: Mushroom Publications.

JEFFERSON, T. (1992), 'Wheelin' and Stealin' ', *Achilles Heel*, 13: 10–12.

—— (1994), 'Theorising Masculine Subjectivity', in T. Newburn and E. A. Stanko, eds., *Just Boys Doing Business? Men, Masculinities and Crime*, 10–31. London: Routledge.

—— (1996a), 'From "Little Fairy Boy" to "The Compleat Destroyer": Subjectivity and Transformation in The Biography of Mike Tyson', in M. Mac an Ghaill, ed., *Understanding Masculinities: Social Relations and Cultural Arenas*, 153–67 Buckingham: Open University Press.

—— (1996b), ' "Tougher Than The Rest": Mike Tyson and The Destructive Desires of Masculinity', *Arena Journal*, 6: 89–105.

—— (1996c), 'The James Bulger Case: A Review Essay' *British Journal of Criminology*, 36, 2: 319–23.

—— (1997), 'The Tyson Rape Trial: The Law, Feminism and Emotional "Truth" ', *Social and Legal Studies*, 6, 2: 281–301.

KATZ, J. (1988), *Seductions of Crime*. New York: Basic Books.

KERSTEN, J. (1996), 'Culture, Masculinities and Violence Against Women', in T. Jefferson and P. Carlen, eds., *Masculinities, Social Relations and Crime*, Special Issue of *British Journal of Criminology*, 36, 3: 381–95.

KOVEL, J. (1981), *The Age of Desire: Case Histories of a Radical Psychoanalyst*. New York: Basic Books.

—— (1988), *White Racism: A Psycho History*. London: Free Association Books.

LEES, S., and GREGORY, J. (1995), *Rape and Sexual Assault: A Study of Attrition*. London: Islington Council.

LESTER, D. (1995), *Serial Killers: The Insatiable Passion*. Philadelphia, Penn.: The Charles Press.

LEVIN, J., and FOX, J. A. (1985), *Mass Murder: America's Growing Menace*. New York: Plenum.

LEVINE, S., and KOENIG, J., eds. (1983), *Why Men Rape*. London: Stag.

MAC AN GHAILL, M. (1988), *Young, Gifted and Black: Student-Teacher Relations in the Schooling of Black Youth*. Milton Keynes: Open University Press.

—— (1994a), *The Making of Men: Masculinities, Sexualities and Schooling*. Buckingham: Open University Press.

—— (1994b), 'The Making of Black English Masculinities', in H. Brod and M. Kaufman, eds., *Theorizing Masculinities*, 183–99. London: Sage.

McROBBIE, A. (1980), 'Settling Accounts With Subcultures: A Feminist Critique', *Screen Education*, 39.

MAJORS, R. (1989), 'Cool Pose: The Proud Signature of Black Survival', in M. S. Kimmel and M. A. Messner, eds., *Men's Lives*, 83–7. New York: Macmillan.

—— and BILLSON, J. M. (1992), *Cool Pose: The Dilemmas of Black Manhood in America*. New York: Touchstone.

MEAD, G. H. (1934), *Mind, Self and Society*. Chicago, Ill.: University of Chicago Press.

MESSERSCHMIDT, J. (1993), *Masculinities and Crime*. Lanham, Md.: Rowman and Littlefield.

MORGAN, R. (1982), 'Theory and Practice: Pornography and Rape' in L. Lederer, ed., *Take Back the Night*, 125–40. London: Bantam.

—— (1989), *The Demon Lover*. London: Methuen.

MORRIS, L, (1994), *Dangerous Classes: The Underclass and Social Citizenship*. London: Routledge.

MORRISON, T., ed. (1992), *Race-ing Justice, Engendering Power: Essays on Anita Hill, Clarence Thomas and the Construction of Social Reality*. New York: Pantheon.

MURRAY, C. (1984), *Losing Ground*. New York: Basic Books

—— (1989), 'Underclass', *Sunday Times Magazine*, 22–46, 26 November.

—— (1990), *The Emerging British Underclass*. Choice in Welfare Series No. 2. London: Health and Welfare Unit, Institute of Economic Affairs.

PAGLIA, C. (1992), *Sex, Art, and American Culture*. New York: Vintage.

PARSONS, T., and BALES, R. F. (1956), *Family Socialization and Interaction Process*. London: Routledge and Kegan Paul.

POLK, K. (1994), *When Men Kill: Scenarios of Masculine Violence*. Cambridge: Cambridge University Press.

RADFORD, J., and RUSSELL, D. E. H. eds. (1992), *Femicide: The Politics of Women Killing*. Buckingham: Open University Press.

RICHARDS, B. (1990), 'Masculinity, Identification and Political Culture', in J. Hearn and D. Morgan, eds., *Men, Masculinities and Social Theory*, 160–9. London: Unwin Hyman

—— (1994), *Disciplines of Delight: The Psychoanalysis of Popular Culture*. London: Free Association Books.

ROIPHE, K. (1994), *The Morning After: Sex, Fear and Feminism on Campus*. New York: Little Brown & Co.

RUSTIN, M. (1991), *The Good Society and the Inner World: Psychoanalysis, Politics and Culture*. London: Verso.

—— (1995), 'Lacan, Klein and Politics: The Positive and Negative in Psychoanalytic Thought', in A. Elliott and S. Frosh, eds., *Psychoanalysis in Contexts: Paths between Theory and Modern Cultures*, 336–71. London: Routledge.

SCULLY, D. (1990), *Understanding Sexual Violence: A Study of Convicted Rapists*. Boston, Mass.: Unwin Hyman.

SERENY, G. (1972), *The Case of Mary Bell*. London: Arrow. Republished 1995, London: Pimlico.

SHAW, C. R. (1930), *The Jack Roller*. Chicago, Ill.: University of Chicago Press.

SHAW, M. (1993), *Down For The Count: The Shocking Truth Behind the Mike Tyson Rape Trial*. Campaign, Ill.: Sagamore.

SINGH, N. P. (1995), 'Black Liberation— the Theater of Nationality: The Black Panthers and "Undeveloped Country" of the Left', in C. E. Jones, ed., *The Black Panther Party Reconsidered: Reflections and*

Scholarship. Baltimore, Md.: Black Classic Press.

SMART, C. (1989), *Feminism and the Power of Law*. London: Routledge.

SMITH, D. J. (1995), *The Sleep of Reason: The James Bulger Case*. London: Arrow.

SMITH, J. (1989), 'There's Only One Yorkshire Ripper', in J. Smith, *Misogynies*, 117–51. London: Faber.

STAPLES, R. (1989), 'Masculinity and Race: The Dual Dilemma of Black Men', in M. S. Kimmel and M. A. Messner, eds., *Men's Lives*, 78–83. New York: Macmillan.

THEWELEIT, K. (1987), *Male Fantasies Volume 1: Women, Floods, Bodies, History*. Cambridge: Polity.

—— (1989), *Male Fantasies Volume 2: Male Bodies: Psychoanalysing the White Terror*. Cambridge: Polity.

TRANSITION (1995), 'Symposium: The Crisis of African American Gender Relations', *Transition*, 66, 5, 2: 91–175.

WACQUANT, J. D. (1995), 'The Ghetto, The State and The New Capitalist Economy', in P. Kasinitz, ed., *Metropolis: Centre and Symbol of Our Times*, 418–49. London: Macmillan.

WALKLATE, S. (1995), *Gender and Crime: An Introduction*. Hemel Hempstead: Prentice Hall/Harvester Wheatsheaf.

WALLACE, M. (1990), *Black Macho and the Myth of the Superwoman*. London: Verso.

WARD JOUVE, N. (1988), *'The Street-Cleaner': The Yorkshire Ripper Case on Trial*. London: Marion Boyars.

WEST, C. (1993), *Race Matters*. Boston, Mass.: Beacon Press.

WEST, D. (1987), *Sexual Crimes and Confrontations*. Aldershot: Gower.

WEST, C., and ZIMMERMAN, D. H. (1987), 'Doing Gender', *Gender and Society*, 1, 2: 125–51.

WILLIS, P. (1977) *Learning to Labour*. Farnborough: Saxon House.

WOLFENSTEIN, E. V. (1989), *The Victims of Democracy*. London: Free Association.

WYRE, R. (1986), *Women, Men and Rape*. Oxford: Perry Publications.

—— and TATE, T. (1995), *The Murder of Childhood: Inside The Mind of One of Britain's Most Notorious Child Murderers*. Harmondsworth: Penguin.

YALLOP, D. A. (1981), *Deliver Us From Evil*. London: Macdonald Futura.

17

Understanding Criminal Justice Comparatively

David Nelken

Current debates in criminology display increasing awareness of the need for comparative research. How far should we doubt the influence of inequality on crime in Britain just because this correlation does not hold true in some other countries? Can we introduce integrative forms of punishment here just because they seem to work well elsewhere? Should we be more concerned about the growth of transnational crime or the growth of transnational policing? But, despite its intellectual fascinations and possible practical benefits, there is still little methodological agreement on how best to approach the comparative study of crime and criminal justice (Nelken, 1994b). Given what is at stake the subject seems to merit more attention from theorists than it has so far received.

Comparative criminology is concerned with both crime and criminal justice, and indeed helps to show yet again how both need to be studied together. But, in keeping with the shift of attention within many national criminologies from crime to the workings of criminal justice, there is a similar growing interest in international comparisons of justice systems, and it is this sort of work that I want mainly to discuss here. Progress is certainly being made. A common but unsatisfactory way of trying to reach out to the experience of other systems used to be what could be called 'comparison by juxtaposition—'in Denmark we do this, what do you do in your country?' The resulting texts, whether produced by one or many hands, often had the merits of offering careful accounts of different systems of criminal justice in their legal, historical, and political settings but rarely brought into sharp focus what such comparisons were designed to achieve or even how we could be sure that like was being compared with like. But, increasingly, more ambitious attempts, from a variety of disciplinary starting points, are raising the level of methodological sophistication (see e.g. Heidensohn and Farrell, 1991; Heiland, Shelley, and Katoh, 1992; Hamilton and Sanders, 1992, Fennell, Harding, Jorg, Swart *et al.*, 1995; Fionda, 1995). There are even, finally, signs of the wider 'turn to interpretation' in the social sciences in the strategies being recommended for understanding criminal justice (Zedner 1995).

All this means that comparative work now has to face problems which go beyond the already serious technical, conceptual, and linguistic difficulties raised by the reliability of statistics, lack of appropriate data, meaning of terms, etc. Scholarly disagreements over the right approach to doing comparative criminology and criminal justice presently play themselves out with regard to a series of interconnected (though not necessarily isomorphic) choices between the search for explanation or for other forms of understanding, emphasizing similarities or differences, giving attention to the specificities of local culture or noting the effects of globalization, cultivating elegant theorizing or practical knowledge. Comparative criminal justice scholarship could even find itself, for better or worse, getting caught up in the increasingly heated postmodern debates over the viability of the Enlightenment project of building an explanatory social science. In other words, is the goal of comparative work to help further criminology's universalistic pretensions and provide a yardstick to measure how far they have been achieved? Or is it a prophylactic which protects us from such erroneous ambitions by showing us how claims about crime and criminal justice which purport to be universal actually take their sense and limits of applicability from the cultural context in which they are embedded?

Where do we go from here? A lot—everything?—depends on what our comparison is supposed to be achieving. And the still standard way of deciding this is to ask: are we trying to contribute to the development of explanatory social science, or to improve existing penal practice? Confusion, it is said, is caused by combining such different enterprises. The sociologist must be clear whether she is more interested in explanation or reform; only the first of these is properly termed comparative social science (see e.g. Feeley, 1997); 'the pull of the policy audience' only gets in the way of intellectual progress. Along the same lines, influential comparative sociologists recommend a division of labour in which the legal comparativist (with her strong interest in reform) stick to legal doctrine while the sociologist goes beyond this so as to explain the 'law in action' and other aspects of the 'legal infrastructure' which cannot be read out of legal texts (Blankenburg, 1997; Nelken, 1997*b*). My worry is that following these protocols too strictly can mean that social scientists lose touch with, rather than capture, those nuances of legal culture which bring the comparative exercise to life. What if effective comparison is as much a matter of good translation as of successful explanation? Can the social scientist afford to be quite so dismissive of the approach of comparative lawyers? Are legal rules really of interest to the sociologist only in terms of how far they are put into practice?

The aim of this piece is thus to challenge the standard starting points for comparative criminal justice by showing both that they oversimplify the methodological choices available and create false dichotomies between concerns which are not so easily separable. Even though the issues have wider application, for purposes of illustration I shall mainly be discussing comparative studies of prosecution discretion, referring especially to my ongoing research into the control of prosecution discretion in Italy.

APPROACHES TO COMPARATIVE CRIMINAL JUSTICE

There are, of course, important contrasts to be made between approaches to comparative work. We can, often we should, distinguish between research that sets out

(1) to test our theories of crime or social control (which we may call, for convenience, 'behavioural science')
(2) to show how crime and criminal justice are embedded within changing, local and international, historical and cultural contexts (which we will call, for simplicity, 'interpretivist')
(3) to classify and learn from the rules, ideals, and practice of criminal justice in other jurisdictions (which we can call 'legal comparativist').

But even amongst behavioural scientists there are different points of view about the role of comparative work. For some writers, taking the model of science seriously means that comparative work must show that cultural variability is as irrelevant to social laws as it is to physical laws. Gottfredson and Hirschi argue that failure to recognize this has meant that up until now 'cross national research has literally not known what it was looking for and its contributions have rightfully been more or less ignored' (Gottfredson and Hirschi, 1990: 179). Some of the most influential American explanations of crime, such as Merton's *anomie* theory and Cohen's sub-cultural theory of delinquency, seem almost deliberately ethnocentric in the sense that the explanation is designed to fit variables found in American society. For Gottfredson and Hirschi, however, the fact that Cohen's account of the frustrations of American lower-class children is hardly likely to be applicable to the genesis of delinquency in an African or Indian slum spells its doom. Rather than assume that every culture will have its own crime with its own unique causes which need to be sought in all their specificity, the object of criminological theorizing must be to transcend cultural diversity in order to arrive at genuine scientific statements (Gottfredson and Hirschi 1990: 172–3).

In this search for a universal criminology Gottfredson and Hirschi define crimes as 'acts of force or fraud undertaken in pursuit of self interest'. For them, different cultural settings cannot influence the causes of crime except by affecting the opportunities and the ease with which crimes can occur. They are therefore comforted by apparent cross-cultural consistency in correlations between crime involvement and age and sex differences, urban–rural differences, and indices of family stability. A similar approach is—or could be—followed by those scholars who seek to establish general laws about judicial institutions (though Gottfredson and Hirschi are happy just to *assume* that the criminal law has the universal task of reminding people both of their own long-term interests and those of other people). Shapiro's classic study of appeal courts, for example, sets out to demonstrate that higher courts always function primarily as agents of social control, whatever other political and legal differences may characterize the systems in which they are found, and whatever other legitimating ideologies they may themselves employ (Shapiro, 1981).

For most behavioural scientists, however, comparative work simply offers special opportunities to enlarge the range of variables to use in explanations of crime or criminal justice (Beirne and Nelken, 1997). For theories which link crime and industrialization, for example, it is strategically important to investigate apparent counter-instances such as Switzerland (Clinard, 1978) or Japan (Miyazawa, 1997) both so as to test existing hypotheses and uncover new ones. Likewise we can ask about variations in policing, courts, or prisons in terms of the patterns found in different cultures' historical periods. If the Dutch prison-rate could, at least until recently, be kept so much lower than that of other countries in Europe (Downes, 1988) this is important not only because it shows that there is no inevitable connection between crime rates and prison rates but also because it provokes us to look for the variables that explain the Dutch case.

Interpretavist approaches, on the other hand, question the starting points of such comparisons. Even the technical definition of crime varies between legal systems so that in Japan, for example, assaults that result in death are classified as assault, not murder; and in Greece the definition of rape includes lewdness, sodomy, seduction of a child, incest, prostitution, and procuring (Kalish, 1988). Less obviously, so does the stress put on responding to different sorts of behaviour as crime. In Germany or Italy the police and the mass media keep a remarkably low profile regarding most street crime or burglary, at least by British or American standards (Zedner, 1995; Nelken, 1996). Taking an extreme stand on the definition of crime as a cultural construction, however, could lead to a relativism by which criminological explanation would become irremediably ethnocentric (Beirne, 1983). This can be countered by the argument that if understanding 'the other' was really that difficult then even social science research into different social worlds at home would be impossible (Leavitt, 1990). And cultures are in any case rarely—and less and less—so sealed off from each other for them not to have some common language in which to express their concerns.

Far from being relativist the interpretavist approach actually presupposes the possibility of producing cross-cultural comparisons even if it seeks to display difference as much as similarity. This said, grasping the 'other' does require greater willingness to put assumptions in question the greater the cultural distance. Some of the most exciting current work in comparative criminal justice thus sets out to interpret what is distinctive in the practice and discourse of a given system of criminal justice by drawing an explicit or implicit contrast with another system, usually that of the scholar's culture of origin (Crawford, 1996; Melossi, 1996; Zedner, 1995; Nelken, forthcoming *b*). If the first approach uses culture (or deliberately simplified aspects of it) to explain variation in levels and types of crime and social control, this second approach seeks to use crime and criminal justice as an 'index' of culture. Rather than assume that all societies face similar problems—even if they solve them in somewhat different ways—the aim here is to bring out the importance of culture in shaping the definition both of the crime problem and the 'solutions' found for it (Nelken, 1996c). And a particular strength of this approach is the way it recognizes that data such as criminal or prosecution statistics used in behavioural science explanations are themselves cultural products whose interpretation requires considerable preliminary knowledge of the society concerned.

But the interpretative approach is not without its own problems (Nelken, 1995a). Care needs to be taken in assuming that a given feature of the practice or discourse of criminal justice indexes, or 'resonates' with, the rest of the culture. Cultural ideals and values of criminal justice do not necessarily reflect their wider diffusion in the culture. In many societies there is a wide gulf between legal and general culture, as where the criminal law purports to maintain principles of impersonal equality before the law in societies where clientilistic and other particularistic practices are widespread (Nelken 1991, 1992a, 1992b). A further difficulty is knowing who or what can speak for the culture (especially when matters are controversial). Very different results will be obtained by analysing texts, testing public attitudes, or relying on selected informants such as criminologists or public officials; and it is this last method which is relied on too much by both the interpretative and comparative law approaches.

Because the interpretative approach is so intensive it does not allow for large scale cross-cultural comparison: much therefore depends on which other system is taken as yardstick of comparison (and how this is to be justified). Taking criminal justice discourse in England as our starting point may reveal that France works with one model of 'mediation' whereas we have several (Crawford, 1997); on the other hand, if we compare ourselves with Germany, it seems to have several ideas of 'community' where we have just one (Lacey and Zedner, 1995, 1996). But what exactly is the significance of such findings? It is also not easy to get the balance right between identifying relatively enduring features of legal culture and acknowledging the way systems of criminal justice are influenced by developments beyond national borders. What are taken to be entrenched cultural practices in the realm of criminal justice can be overturned with remarkable rapidity (Downes, 1996). Different systems participate in common trends such as the attempt to construct a Fortress Europe (Ruggiero, Ryan, and Sim, 1995) or combat political corruption (Levi and Nelken, 1996); each responds in its own way to Europeanization, Americanization and globalization (Nelken, forthcoming a) but are also changed by such trends, or by the deliberate or constrained choice to adopt foreign models.

The third approach, that followed by comparativists, is particularly sensitive to the way processes of borrowing, imitation, or imposition help shape the details of the rules and procedures of criminal justice. Its historical classifications of systems in terms of families of law provide a corrective to explanations which start and finish with the nation-state. Another advantage lies in the way its language and concerns connect directly to those used by many of the legal actors themselves whose behaviour is being interpreted. It must be relevant to pay attention to rules and ideals to which actors are obliged at least to pay lip service and which they may well take as guides for much of the time. The evolution of legal discourse may also be better understood, even for sociological purposes, when related to its own forms rather than simply translated into sociological language (Nelken, 1995*b*). But the weaknesses of this approach, which are the converse of its strengths, come from its tendency to share rather than understand or criticize the self-understanding of the legal perspective. Because the terms it uses are legal and normative it will not capture much of what actors are trying to do, still less the influences of which actors are not aware.

Each of the three approaches to comparison—in its pure form—tends to be associated with a characteristic methodology—respectively (predictive) explanation, 'understanding by translation', and categorization–evaluation. But they rarely are found in their pure form. Sociologists—especially those interested in legal culture and ideology—need to know about law and legal procedures (and sometimes get them wrong); comparative lawyers often make sociologically questionable assumptions about what a system is trying to do and how it actually operates. The standard dichotomy between explanation and reform is therefore a crude way of distinguishing the search for universalistic scientific explanations from the concern for concrete understanding of the local and particular which is pursued by both the interpretative and comparative law approaches (Damaska, 1986). It could equally be argued that both behavioural science and interpretative approaches share an interest in different forms of explanation; conversely, comparative lawyers sometimes display a concern for universalizibility of a certain sort which puts them nearer the camp of the behaviourists, as when the comparative study of prosecution discretion is conducted in the light of a universalistic yardstick of the proper constitutional relationship between judge and prosecutor (Fionda, 1995). Key conceptual building blocks for comparing criminal justice, such as the term 'legal culture' (Nelken, 1995*a*, 1997*a*) figure in each of the three approaches, even if they are employed with meanings which both overlap and compete.

Debates within, as well as between, comparative law and sociological criminology turn on mixed questions of explanation and evaluation, so that it is not the choice of one or other of these aims which guarantees either insight or confusion (Nelken, 1983). Within the field of comparative law, Goldstein and Marcus, who reported that there was little America could learn from Europe in order to reform its pre-trial procedures, used sociological type arguments based on the attempt to see how the rules actually worked in practice (Goldstein and Marcus, 1977). But those who claimed that this understanding of Continental procedure was superficial were able to show how the very desire for generalizable explanation reinforced American ethnocentrism (Langbein and Weinberg, 1978). On the other hand Downes' sociological study of the role of prosecutors in keeping down prison rates in Holland (Downes, 1988) clearly had a practical purpose aimed at changing the situation in Britain but it was not (or at least not for that reason) unsuccessful in illuminating the Dutch situation. Much more thought therefore needs to be given to the relationship between explanation and cultural bias. A reflexive criminology (Nelken, 1994*a*) would seek to analyse this nexus with regards to *each* of the three approaches to comparative work we have so far distinguished.

UNDERSTANDING THE CONTROL OF PROSECUTION DISCRETION IN ITALY

But how can such different approaches be drawn together? The example I shall use is the constitutionally entrenched rule concerning mandatory prosecution in Italy, which purports to limit prosecution discretion so tightly that failure to prosecute is itself a ground for prosecution! This rule is of particular theoretical interest for present purposes, both because it seems to require a sociological impossibility (given the limits on prosecution resources), whilst at the same time—paradoxically—it can actually be shown to have helped Italian prosecutors achieve their remarkable recent success in driving from power the previously dominant class of governing politicians (Nelken, 1996*a*, 1996*b*). A better understanding of the criminal process in that country is also of some practical interest because its procedures represent, at least on paper, an extreme version of the 'legality principle' characteristic of many Continental European countries. This alternative method of controlling the rectitude of the pre-trial process, as compared to the safeguards employed in Anglo-American systems, has for many years been a central topic of enquiry for comparative law scholars of criminal justice (Goldstein and Marcus, 1977; Langbein and Weinreb, 1978), and it was recently looked into and once again rejected by the Royal commission on Criminal Justice in the United Kingdom (Leigh and Zedner, 1992).

But the aptness of this example for present purposes can best be seen from the way that talking about researching prosecution *discretion* in comparative perspective immediately draws the harsh criticism from some scholars that this could not possibly provide a sound basis for sociological work across cultures. As Johannes Feest put it, in commenting on a recent presentation of this research, 'if the term "discretion" is used in a technical-legal way then it is not translatable to begin with. But if it is used in a non-technical way then it has the disadvantage of being identical with a technical-juridical term of the English language which makes it confusing, at least to non English speakers' (Feest, 1996). His proposed solution—in keeping, I think, with the standard starting points I have mentioned—would be to look for a more universal socio-logical language for conducting such investigations, by talking about 'decision-making', or 'the power to define deviant conduct'; sociological terms such as 'social control' or 'total institutions' have proved their worth in the sociology of deviance, he argues, despite not being part of native language—or rather just for this very reason. Feest's argument rightly highlights the difficulties of doing comparative research into discretion, though the issue probably goes beyond the question of comparative methodology (thus some sociologists claim that any investigation of discretion is futile because official behaviour is socially rather than legally rule-governed; see Baumgartner, 1990). But I remain convinced that attempting to study prosecution *decision-making* whilst avoiding using the term *discretion* risks jettisoning the baby with the bath water. The problem is rather how best to examine each one in the light of the other.

How can we explain the mandatory rule of prosecution in Italy and what is there about it to explain? We could ask how the rule got to be what it is— noting for instance how it emerged in the immediate post-war period when it was unclear to the political parties who would be in command in the Ministry of Justice and whom the use of discretion might therefore favour. We might then also trace how later developments have taken Italy increasingly further from the patterns found in the rest of the Continental Europe (Guarnieri, 1993, 1997). But, above all, if we are interested in the explanation of variation in decision-making behaviour we will want to explore what prosecutors actually do in their everyday work, how this fits into the system as a whole—and how all this is affected, if at all, by the rule dealing with discretion.

One strategy we could follow would be to assume that all criminal justice systems of a certain complexity must face similar operational problems of coping with overload and efficient throughput of cases. Certainly, the Italian criminal justice system faces, it would appear, similar or even worse problems of coping than other comparable systems: the criminal law has enormous reach—it is expected to deal with many matters which in Anglo-American systems are dealt with by civil law or administrative bodies or even political machinery; in addition to ordinary crime the criminal courts are expected to process high levels of regulatory contraventions, fiscal crimes, administrative malpractice, white collar, and organized crimes. We might then argue that a function of legally permitted discretionary decision-making is that it makes it easier to manage these problems. For those systems, (or offices or individuals) where prosecution discretion is heavily restricted, on the other hand, we would expect to find flexibility coming from law-in-action 'functional equivalents' to discretion, both in the prosecutor's office and elsewhere in the system.

We can in fact identify numerous features of the Italian criminal process which do provide the chance to filter out cases or exercise priorities even in a regime of legally mandated prosecution. The threshold decision whether there is enough evidence to take a case to trial, or whether instead to opt for *archiavazzione*, does provide or require opportunity for exercise of choice. In practice, some heavy dossiers—the fruit of months or even years of prelimi- nary investigation—can end up simply being disposed of in this way (a recent example concerned *Gladio*—an allegedly illegal underground military organization created by the Italian secret service, with CIA finance. Though purportedly set up to repel external military invasion the claim made was that in fact it was secretly intended to deal with the threat that the Italian communist party might come legally to power). Like France and Germany, Italy too uses methods such as the Prosecutor fine to deal with less serious offences.

Decision-making in other parts of the criminal justice system is somehow much less controversial than the decision to prosecute. There is virtually no questioning of what Anglo-American writers call low-visibility operational police discretion, the (judicial) police are just presumed to be following the prosecutors' instructions or to be acting in an executive rather than judicial capacity. Post-sentence flexibility by reduction of punishment or sentence is introduced by the use of difficult-to-meet prescription periods, government amnesties, and the *condono*. More generally, the interpretation and application of rules of evidence both in pre-trial and sentencing decision-making in code-based systems without binding precedents provides considerable scope for interpretative disagreement. Another sort of flexibility is provided by competing and overlapping jurisdictions of types of law and courts, multiple supreme courts, and the three stages of trial. Little of this is labelled as discretion. But for the sociologist, it might be said, what counts is the way flexibility is built into the system rather than how it is labelled.

But we should be cautious not to go too far in searching for 'functional equivalents', as if every system is predestined to reach a certain level of efficiency. Even if we stay with functional language it is not easy to determine what is functional and for whom. Some left-wing prosecutors believe the courts are left dealing with an overload of low-level regulatory and fiscal contraventions so as to keep them from pursuing more politically sensitive matters. Likewise the apparently irrational distribution of courts around the country is explained mainly by political pressure not to lose the courthouse as a sign of local prestige. Even apparently minimal functional operating requirements are not met. Formalities and complicated division or overlapping of responsibilities help produce enormous delays for which Italy has been regularly condemned by the Court of Human Rights at Strasbourg: criminal cases can take up to ten years to go through all their stages; civil cases even longer; other administrative and other bureaucratic proceedings can take what the Italians call 'Biblical periods'. The language of functionalism may itself be misleading in so far as it presupposes a certain managerial vision of the purposes of a criminal justice system which is itself culturally variable.

The Italian criminal justice system then has some equivalents of discretionary decision-making, though not necessarily where they would be found in other systems, but they do not always serve the same function. Those who argue that the term discretion—unlike decision-making—does not have a common behavioural referent across cultures may well be right, but then it is exactly this variability which needs exploring. Research into discretion is not just about explaining variation in similar phenomena amongst different cultures but also about appreciating the variation in what each takes to be the phenomenon. The term is embedded in a specific political and cultural context, and its significance depends on excavating the role it plays in that context rather than just trying to extract its behavioural kernel in the actual decision-making behaviour of prosecutors. For example the lack of debate over police discretion in Italy may be explained less by functional requirements than the supposition that, in Continental Europe 'the idea of the administration of law belongs to a lower and more flexible order of things' (Goldstein and Marcus, 1977: 281).

In Anglo-American political and legal discourse discretion carries overtones of potentially unruly decision-making which needs to be exercised reasonably, and in the public interest; it can however be kept within bounds by mechanisms of accountability. In Italy, on the other hand, the term 'discretion' carries stronger overtones of inevitable arbitrariness, favouritism, and potential corruption. Acknowledging discretion is seen as abandoning the 'impersonal' ideal of the state and its 'rule of law' (Nelken 1991, 1992*a*, 1992*b*). It is only by adhering strictly to this vision that a bulwark can be maintained against the pressures of a strongly factionalized and personalized society where the 'public interest' has little meaning and where many fear that legalized discretion to prosecute would lead to impossible pressures being placed on decision-makers. In Holland, to take a contrasting example, prosecutors direct away from trial well over 50 per cent of the cases that come before them; here the use of the positively weighted term *beleid* (Blankenburg, 1994) reflects and underpins the faith in prosecutors' ability to use good judgement and act in ways which meet the public interest.

There is probably just enough overlap in meaning in the use of the term discretion for it to figure in comparative research concerned with the way the attempt to control legal decision-making reflects and helps constitute the trust-worthiness of the actors concerned (Bankowski and Nelken, 1981; Nelken, 1994*b*). But in each culture the meaning of (allowing) discretion is also coloured by its place in wider discourse. In Italy, for example, there are no exact linguistic (and conceptual) equivalents, for example, for terms like 'enforcement' or 'policy' or even 'criminal justice'; the Italian word for compromise carries pejorative overtones, and the word 'pragmatic' indicates lack of principle rather than the 'practical' British virtue of 'muddling through'.

But this does not prevent us from examining the way specific cultural definitions and debates about discretion interact with actual decision-making. Whilst patterns of behaviour cannot simply be deduced from normative (legal and cultural) rules, ignoring the contribution such rules make to shaping the context of action means that we easily slip up on the banana skin of presumed cultural similarity. The rule of mandatory prosecution may, from one angle, as Goldstein and Marcus argued, be regarded as something of a myth, (though if we want to understand a culture what could be more important than a myth?). But in fact the influence of the rule is certainly not limited to the level of the symbolic. The effect mandatory prosecution can have in everyday terms is well illustrated from a case which occurred in a small town in Central Italy. A man had separated from his first wife but the divorce had not finally been obtained (though apparently it was a matter of weeks rather than months). In the meantime the new companion, with whom he had been living since his separation, was diagnosed as having an incurable cancer, and to give her some comfort in the days before she died he decided that they should get married. This exposed him to a prosecution for bigamy—which duly took place. From the news report it was impossible to tell whether there could have been some special reason for prosecution, the case was presented simply as one resulting from the rule of mandatory prosecution.

Research which does not rely on newspaper reports also confirms that this rule can and does have effects at the everyday level—mainly by reinforcing bureaucratic formalism in the definition of the prosecutor's role. Obligatory prosecution goes hand-in-hand with other legal (and in-house) rules about having to deal with cases within set periods. Thus one lower court prosecutor I interviewed decided that she wanted to establish some priority in the thousands of cases on her desk, most of which involved minor contraventions. Rather than limit herself merely to legally classifying all the cases and passing them on down the line, she wanted to devote time to the careful preparation of witnesses and technical evidence in the more serious cases of manslaughter connected with unsafe working conditions and industrial pollution which she thought were otherwise likely to fail when they eventually came to trial some years later (perhaps in front of a not particularly well-informed lawyer serving as deputy judge). But the head of her office refused to allow this and threatened her with disciplinary proceedings or, worse, if she allowed any of the thousands of minor cases on her desk to become time-bound.

Yet the most remarkable consequence of the rule of mandatory prosecution is the way it can also (indirectly) help *increase* prosecutors' freedom to make crucial and sensitive decisions. In Italy, as in other Continental European countries, prosecutors are part of the judicial profession. But in Italy they can move rather more easily from one of these roles to the other, and they enjoy the same constitutional guarantees, the same automatic career progression, and the same self-governing body for matters of discipline. However, the outstanding feature of Italian prosecutors and prosecution offices, as compared to other civil law countries, is their autonomy from hierarchical bureaucratic control (Guarnieri, 1993, 1997). They are not subject to instructions from the Ministry of Justice and co-ordination of the different prosecution offices is rudimentary.

With autonomy comes the possibility—in the right circumstances—of exercising *much more* freedom of choice than would be found in an Anglo-American system. In the 1970s the so-called 'judges of assault' tried to use prosecution to improve worker safety and to attack pollution; in the 1990s the target of some prosecutors' offices, above all the Milan pool of *Mani Pulite* prosecuting judges, was political corruption. Because Italy is a society formally governed by innumerable laws, many of which are in fact unenforced or at least under-enforced, a strategy of prosecution starting from small cases, or easy-to-prove crimes (such as illegal financing of political parties or abuse of official duties), could be used, as in the recent *Tangentopoli* anti-corruption investigations to begin a process which led to the removal from power of many of those at the highest levels of society (Nelken, 1996*a*, 1996*b*). The rule of mandatory prosecution acted as no bar to such heavily loaded decisions, provided only that there was some minimal evidence of a crime having been committed. If anything, it provided a marvellous shield to protect prosecutors against important political and business defendants who would otherwise certainly have insisted that it was not in the public interest that their cases be proceeded with. Both for better and worse the existence of the rule makes it impossible to discuss the merits of prosecution decision-making as an exercise of 'policy-making' discretion (or perhaps we should say it helps disfavour such a way of approaching the problem).

For many observers *Tangentopoli* has magnificiently underlined the value of the rule of mandatory prosecution in Italy. But, for others, the events of past years only demonstrate how the rule helps conceal the too wide powers available to independent prosecutors. The fact that there is no way such momentous prosecution initiatives can be institutionally regulated by those outside the judiciary has for some time been a bane to those scholars (and politicians) critical of the present system, who argue that Italy should be brought more in line with other civil law countries (Di Federico, 1989; Nelken, 1992*b*). For them this means separating the careers of prosecutors and judges and returning the prosecutors to some form of effective central hierarchical control. In the meantime strenuous attempts are being made to change the prosecution process under the influence of the Anglo-American model. Although the rule of mandatory prosecution itself has not (yet) been touched, starting with the reforms of the new Code of Criminal Procedure of 1989, the possibility of greater flexibility has been introduced through alternatives to normal trial proceedings and schemes of plea bargaining, which are justified in part in the name of 'speed' and expediency. Things are changing slowly; some judges and, even more, many lawyers are uneasy about the new procedures. Those scholars who dislike these changes say that the trend towards embracing the Anglo-American pre-trial process, based as it is on confession and plea discounts, threatens the replacement of 'legality' by 'administration', conse-crating as ideal the type of pragmatic methods used by the anti-corruption prosecutors (behind the screen of mandatory prosecution) in a moment of political emergency.

The point of this chapter is not to argue that those who want to bring about a more equal society in Britain, or elsewhere, should immediately opt for the Italian rule of mandatory prosecution and its associated legal and political arrangements. Even the Italian system achieved the effects it did only during an exceptional period of political transition—though it is also fair to say that the judges played an important part in bringing about that transition (Nelken, 1996*a*). There is much to be learned, however, even for other societies, about the different possible meanings of prosecutorial constraint and prosecutorial independence which the events in Italy have thrown into relief. Beyond this, whether or not there are any practical implications to be drawn, even such a brief (and partial) examination of the Italian prosecution process should have shown the need to combine the different approaches to the study of criminal justice outlined earlier. This case-study suggests that it is above all the certainties buried in universalistic approaches to explanation, such as the claim that all systems find ways of relieving case-load pressures, or that criminal law must always serve the interests of the powerful, which may turn out to be cultural rather than scientific truisms. Understanding comes before as well as after explanation.

Selected Further Reading

The student of comparative criminal justice confronts a literature which is potentially unlimited and is far from consolidated. The three approaches indicated in the text borrow from works on law, sociology, history, economics, political science, and anthropology amongst others. A still important starting point for the attempt to theorize differences in criminal justice is Damaska (1988); interesting recent comparative studies include Downes (1988), and Hamilton and Saunders (1992); explorations of the concepts of legal culture will be found in the volumes edited by Nelken (1995*a*, 1997*a*, and forthcoming).

REFERENCES

BANKOWSKI, Z., and NELKEN, D. (1981), 'Discretion as a social problem', in M. Adler and S. Asquith, eds., *Discretion and Welfare*, 247–69. London: Heinmann.

BAUMGARTNER, M. P. (1992), 'The Myth of Discretion' in K. Hawkins, ed., *The Uses of Discretion*, 129–63. Oxford: Clarendon Press.

BEIRNE, P. (1983), 'Cultural Relativism and Comparative Criminology', *Contemporary Crises*, 7: 371–91.

—— and NELKEN, D., eds. (1997), *Issues in Comparative Criminology*. Aldershot: Dartmouth.

BLANKENBURG, E. (1994), *Dutch Legal Culture*. 2nd edn. Amsterdam: Kluwer.

—— (1997), 'Litigation Rates as Indicators of Legal Cultures', in D. Nelken, ed., *Comparing Legal Cultures*, 41–69. Aldershot: Dartmouth.

CLINARD, M. B. (1978), *Cities with Little Crime: the Case of Switzerland*. Cambridge: Cambridge University Press.

CRAWFORD, A. (1996), 'Victim/Offender Mediation and Appeals to Community in

Comparative Cultural Contexts: France and England and Wales', unpublished paper presented at the conference of the Law and Society Association, Glasgow, July.

DAMASKA, M. (1986), *The Faces of Justice and State Authority*. New Haven, Conn.: Yale University Press.

DI FEDERICO, G. (1991), 'Obbligatorietà dell'azione penale, coordinamento delle attività del pubblico ministero e loro rispondenza alle aspettative della comunità', *La Giustizia Penale*, 96: 148–171.

DOWNES, D. (1988), *Contrasts in Tolerance*. Oxford: Clarendon Press.

—— (1996) 'The Buckling of the Shields: Dutch Penal Policy 1985–1995', unpublished paper presented at the Onati Workshop on Comparing Legal Cultures, April.

FEELEY, M. (1997), 'Comparative Law for Criminologists: Comparing for What?', in D. Nelken, ed., *Comparing Legal Cultures*, 93–105. Aldershot: Dartmouth.

FEEST, J. (1996) Written comments on D. Nelken's paper, 'The Rule of Mandatory Prosecution in Italy and its relevance for

Comparative Criminal Justice', which was presented at the conference of the Law and Society Association, Glasgow, July.

FENNELL, P., HARDING, C., JORG, N., and SWART, B. (1995), *Criminal Justice in Europe: A Comparative Study*. Oxford: Clarendon Press.

FIONDA, J. (1995), *Public Prosecutors and Discretion: A Comparative Study*. Oxford: Clarendon.

GOLDSTEIN, A., and Marcus, M. (1977), 'The Myth of Judicial Supervision in Three Inquisitorial Systems: France, Italy and Germany', *Yale Law Journal* 87: 240.

GOTTFREDSON, M., and HIRSCHI, T. (1990), *A General Theory of crime*. Stanford, Cal.: Stanford University Press.

GUARNIERI, C. (1993), *Magistratura e Politica: pesi senza contrappesi*. Bologna: Il Mulino.

—— (1997), 'Prosecution in Two Civil Law Countries: France and Italy', in D. Nelken, ed., *Comparing Legal Cultures*, 183–95. Aldershot: Dartmouth.

HAMILTON, V. L., and Sanders, J. (1992), *Everyday Justice: Responsibility and the Individual in Japan and the United States*. New Haven, Conn.: Yale University Press.

HEILAND, H. G., SHELLEY, L. I., and KATOH, H., eds. (1992), *Crime and Control in Comparative Perspectives*. Berlin: de Gruyter.

HEIDENSOHN, F., and FARRELL, M. (1991), *Crime in Europe*. London: Routledge.

KALISH, C. (1988), *International Crime Rates*. Washington, DC: Bureau of Justice Statistics, US Department of Justice.

LACEY, N., and ZEDNER, L. (1996), 'Community in German Criminal Justice—A Significant Absence', unpublished paper presented at the conference of the Law and Society Association, Glasgow.

—— and —— (1995), 'Discourses of Community in Criminal Justice', *Journal of Law and Society*, 22 1: 301–20.

LANGBEIN, J., and WEINREB, L. (1978), 'Continental Criminal Procedure: Myth and Reality', *Yale Law Journal*, 87: 1549.

LEIGH, L., and ZEDNER, L. (1992), *Royal Commission on Criminal Justice: Research Study No.1*, London: HMSO.

LEVI, M., and Nelken, D., eds. (1995), *The Corruption of Politics and the Politics of Corruption*. Oxford: Blackwell.

LEAVITT, G. (1990), 'Relativism and Cross-Cultural Criminology', *Journal of Crime and Delinquency*, 27, 1: 5–29.

MELOSSI, D. (1996), 'The Radical Embeddedness of Social Control (or the Impossibility of Translation): Reflections Based on a Comparison of Social Control in Italian

and North American Culture', unpublished paper presented at the Onati International Institute for Sociology of Law, Spain.

MIYAZAWA, S. (1997), 'The Enigma of Japan as a Testing Ground for Cross Cultural Criminological Studies', in D. Nelken, ed., *Comparing Legal Cultures*, 195–215. Aldershot: Dartmouth.

NELKEN, D. (1981), 'The "Gap Problem" in the Sociology of Law: A Theoretical Review', *Windsor Yearbook of Access to Justice* 35–62.

—— (1991), 'Some Problems with the "Impersonal" Rule of Law in Italy', unpublished paper presented and distributed at the conference of Law and Society, Amsterdam, Holland, 28 June.

—— (1992*a*), 'The Rule of Law in Italy: a Comparative Approach', unpublished paper presented and distributed at the Colloquium on 'The Rule of Law in Western and Eastern Europe', Politics department, New York University, USA, April.

—— (1992*b*), 'Some Comments on the Relationship Between the Academic and Political Debates over Discretion in Italy', unpublished paper presented and distributed at the Conference of the International Political Science Association, Forli, Italy, July.

—— (1994*a*), 'Reflexive criminology', in D. Nelken, ed., *The Futures of Criminology*, 7–43. London: Sage.

—— (1994*b*), 'Whom Can You Trust? The Future of Comparative Criminology', in D. Nelken, ed., *The Futures of Criminology*, 220–44. London: Sage.

—— (1995*a*), 'Disclosing/Invoking Legal Culture', in D. Nelken, ed., *Legal Culture, Diversity and Globalisation*, special issue of *Social and Legal Studies*, 4, 4: 435–52.

—— (1995*b*), 'Can There be a Sociology of Legal Meaning?', in D. Nelken, ed., *Law as Communication*, 107–29. Aldershot: Dartmouth.

—— and LEVI, M. (1996), 'Introduction', in M. Levi and D. Nelken, eds., 'The Corruption of Politics and the Politics of Corruption', *Journal of Law and Society*, 23, 1: 1–18.

—— (1996*a*), 'The Judges and Corruption in Italy', in M. Levi and D. Nelken, eds., 'The Corruption of Politics and the Politics of Corruption', *Journal of Law and Society,* 23, 1: 95–113.

—— (1996*b*), 'Stopping the Judges', in M. Caciagli and D. Kertzer, eds., *Italian Politics: The Stalled Transition*, 186–204. Boulder, Colo.: Westview Press.

—— (1996c), 'Law without Order: A Letter from Italy', in V. Gessner, A. Hoeland, and C. Varga, eds., *European Legal Cultures*. Aldershot: Dartmouth.

—— (1997a) *Comparing Legal Cultures*. Aldershot: Dartmouth.

—— (1997b) 'Puzzling out Legal Culture: A Comment on Blankenburg', in D. Nelken, ed., *Comparing Legal Cultures*, 69–93. Aldershot: Dartmouth.

—— (forthcoming a), 'The Globalisation of Criminal Justice', in M. Freeman, ed., *Law at the Turn of the Century*. Oxford: Oxford University Press.

—— ed. (forthcoming b), *Contrasts in Criminal Justice*. Aldershot: Dartmouth.

RUGGIERO, V., RYAN, M., and SIM, J., eds. (1995), *Western European Penal Systems*. London: Sage.

SHAPIRO, M. (1981), *Courts*. Chicago, Ill.: Chicago University Press.

ZEDNER, L. (1995), 'In Pursuit of the Vernacular: Comparing Law and Order Discourse in Britain and Germany', in D. Nelken, ed., *Legal Culture, Diversity and Globalisation*, special issue of *Social and Legal Studies*, 4, 4: 517–35.

Part II

SOCIAL DIMENSIONS OF CRIME AND JUSTICE

18

Victims

Lucia Zedner

INTRODUCTION

Victims, once on the margins of criminological research, are now a central focus of academic research. Crime surveys, both national and local, and qualitative studies of the impact of crime, of victim needs and services have furnished a wealth of information which has permanently altered the criminological agenda. Academic research has been mirrored and encouraged by the growth of dynamic and influential groups set up to help victims and promote their interests. As a result, the victim has moved from being a 'forgotten actor' to key player in the criminal justice process. These changes have been fostered also by successive governments in their promotion of victims' interests and, increasingly, of victims' rights.

This chapter will examine the origins and genesis of studies in 'victimology' and the development of mass and local victim surveys. It will go on to examine research findings on the 'costs of crime': fear, constraints on lifestyles and mobility, and its impact on victims. The chapter will survey research on the harms suffered by victims, their consequent needs, together with the victim movement's response to these needs and provision of services. Finally, it will suggest that the growth of interest in victims has opened to question the very purpose of the criminal justice system and the place of victims within it. Mediation, reparation, and compensation are some of the more important manifestations of this change. Reorientation of the criminal justice process toward the victim connotes a shift in penological thinking which creates the possibility of challenging the prevailing paradigm of punishment and the chapter will conclude by examining the likelihood of this succeeding.

I would like to thank Paul Rock and the editors of the Handbook for their valuable comments and suggestions.

CLASSICAL STUDIES IN VICTIMOLOGY

Interest in victims has a long history. The term 'victimology' appears to have been coined first in 1949 by the American psychiatrist, Frederick Wertham, who called for 'a science of victimology' which would address itself to the sociology of the victim (Wertham, 1949). It is, however, the work of his contemporary Hans Von Hentig, *The Criminal and his Victim* (Hentig, 1948), which is now widely regarded as the seminal text in developing victim studies. Highly critical of the traditional offender-orientated nature of criminology, Von Hentig proposed a dynamic, interactionist approach which challenged the conception of the victim as passive actor. This focused simultaneously both on those characteristics of victims which might be said to have precipitated their suffering and on the relationship between victim and offender. He argued 'The law . . . makes a clear-cut distinction between the one who does and the one who suffers. Looking into the genesis of the situation, in a considerable number of cases, we meet a victim who consents tacitly, co-operates, conspires or provokes' (Von Hentig, 1948 quoted in Fattah, 1989: 44) By classifying victims into typologies based on psychological and social variables he suggested that certain individuals were 'victim-prone'.

Others took up these notions of victim-precipitation and victim-proneness. Mendelsohn, for example, sought to identify those characteristics which made some people more susceptible to victimization than others (Mendelsohn 1956). Drawing on explanations of accident causation, he attempted to quantify the victim's 'guilty contribution to the crime'. This approach went beyond the merely descriptive exercise of developing victim typologies to assign degrees of culpability. His classification reflects this moralistic approach, with categories ranging from the 'completely innocent' to the 'most guilty victim'. This form of 'victim blaming' was later to attract considerable criticism, but Mendelsohn's intent was less to exculpate the offender than to devise an explanatory model on which preventive programmes might be devised to reduce the extent and severity of victimization.

Not until Wolfgang's classic study *Patterns in Criminal Homicide* (1958) were Von Hentig's ideas subjected to systematic, empirical testing. Wolfgang defined victim-precipitated offences as those 'in which the victim is a direct, positive precipitator in the crime' (Wolfgang, 1958). Examining police records of 588 homicides in Philadelphia in the years 1948–52, he calculated that 26 per cent of known homicides resulted from victim-initiated resort to violence. The conclusion of his work, that some crime was victim-precipitated, inspired many subsequent studies replicating his approach (for example, by Amir, Hindelang, Gottfredson, and Garafalo). Whilst these studies were as much concerned with developing victim typologies as with identifying the extent and nature of victim precipitation, it is this latter aim, with its emotive connotations of victim-blaming that continues to attract criminological attention.

Perhaps the most controversial application of Wolfgang's model of victim precipitation is Amir's *Patterns of Forcible Rape* (1971). Amir analysed 646 forcible rapes recorded by the police in Philadelphia and concluded that 19 per cent were victim-precipitated. Amir's study provoked considerable disquiet and has been criticized both on methodological and ideological grounds. His definition of precipitation is broad and vague, encompassing all those instances in which 'the victim actually—or so it was interpreted by the offender—agreed to sexual relations but retracted . . . or did not resist strongly enough when the suggestion was made by the offender. The term also applies to cases in which the victim enters vulnerable situations charged sexually' (Amir, 1971: 262). This shift, from recognizing victim–offender interaction as a precipitating factor in crime to re-ascribing blame to the victim in rape cases, was heavily criticized by the newly emergent feminist movement. Methodological criticisms were also made. Since only a small proportion of rapes are reported (Temkin, 1987: 9), Amir's reliance on police records necessarily presents a very partial picture. Moreover, reports contained within police files are not unproblematic accounts: arguably they tell us as much about police attitudes to rape victims as they do about the aetiology of the crime. The chief difficulty with Amir's study (and others which followed its model) is that it conflates analysis of the dynamics of individual crimes with a more generalized re-attribution of responsibility to the victim. It moves from recognizing that risk of victimiz-ation is correlated with factors such as social background, time, and place to victim-blaming. In short, it seems to suggest 'that victims of assault have no one except themselves to blame if they deliberately walk in dark alleys after dark' (Anttila, 1974: 7).

More recently, Fattah has defended the hypothesis of victim-precipitation, arguing that in a rigorously pursued, value-free social science there is no reason why it should entail victim blaming. Although it has been used carelessly in the past, he argues, it is basically sound as an explanatory tool (Fattah, 1979 and 1991). Understood not as victim-precipitation but as the recognition that crime is a transaction in which both offender and victim play a role, such approaches might lead to a fuller understanding of crime. Unfortunately, how-ever, the tendency for victim-precipitation studies to lead to value-laden victim-blaming has undermined its potential explanatory power and attracted only criticism (Morris, 1987: 173–4; Walklate, 1989: 4–5). The narrow concen-tration of early victim studies on reassigning responsibility for crime offered few new, coherent theoretical insights (Rock, 1986: 72–3) and produced little by way of empirical findings other than that *some* victims bear *some* responsi-bility for *some* crimes (Miers, 1989: 15). As such it is perhaps not surprising that, throughout the 1960s and much of the 1970s, mainstream criminology remained firmly wedded to offender-orientated studies. More recently, 'radical' and 'critical' victimologists have consciously sought to challenge these strictures by engaging in analysis of the wider political, economic, and social context in which victimization should be understood, in political analysis of the rights of victims, and in cross-cultural analysis of the development of victims' move-ments (Mawby and Walklate, 1994).

MASS VICTIMIZATION SURVEYS

One of the most important factors in regenerating criminological interest in victims was the development of the victim survey. In America, in the 1960s, mass victimization surveys were designed to uncover the unreported 'dark figure' of crime. Pilot studies carried out on behalf of the US President's Crime Commission 1967 (Ennis, 1967; Reiss, 1967) were followed up by annual National Crime Surveys (NCS) carried out by the Bureau of Justice Statistics. The core findings of the annual NCS have been characterized as follows: 'that the bulk of events uncovered by the surveys are relatively trivial, that criminal victimization of the types measured is relatively rare, and that there is a large amount of repeat victimization' (Gottfredson, 1986: 251). Only as a consequence of later studies on the impact of victimization were these rather sanguine conclusions to be revised.

In Britain, the first major survey was carried out in London by Sparks, Genn, and Dodd (Sparks *et al.*, 1977). In addition to attempting to ascertain the extent and nature of unreported crime, it also asked questions about victims' perceptions of crime and attitudes to the criminal justice system. In so doing it may be said to have set the agenda for many subsequent surveys and smaller-scale, qualitative studies.

Nationally, crime surveys have been funded and administered by central government. The first British Crime Survey reported in 1983, drawing on a representative sample of over 10,000 people over the age of 15. Its main aim was to estimate the extent of crime independently of statistics recorded by the police. In addition it collected data on 'factors predisposing people to victimisation; the impact of crime on victims; fear of crime; victims' experiences of the police; other contacts with the police; and self-reported offending' (Mayhew and Hough, 1983). It has been replicated several times, reporting in 1985, 1989, 1992, 1994, and 1996 (Hough and Mayhew, 1985; Mayhew *et al.*, 1989; Mayhew and Maung, 1993; Mayhew *et al.*, 1994; Mirrlees-Black *et al.*, 1996). The first Scottish Crime Survey was carried out in 1983 (Chambers and Tombs, 1984). More recently, an ambitious cross-national crime survey was carried out using comparable surveys in fourteen countries (Van Dijk *et al.*, 1990) and further cross-national studies are presently in process (Koffman, 1996: 14). These new macro studies aim to quantify the true volume of victimization and to identify the social, economic, and demographic characteristics of the victim population. Their technique typically involves asking large samples of the population, nationally or in a given area, questions about crimes committed against them over a specified period—generally six months or a year. Non-household and non-personal offences (such as vandalism, shoplifting, and fraud) are excluded from BCS questionnaires. Information is collected about personal and property crimes committed (the time and place of the incident, its impact, whether or not it was reported to the police) and about the victims (their age, sex, race, social class, and their consequent attitudes and behaviour) (Crawford *et al.*, 1990: 2–3).

Perhaps their most significant finding is that, as anticipated, crimes reported to the police represent only a small fraction of those which occur. The first British Crime Survey revealed that around only one in four crimes of property loss and damage was recorded in the official statistics and around only one in five offences of violence. Successive BCSs combine to give a good picture of changing trends in crime. For example, the 1995 BCS found that thefts of household property had risen by about 50 per cent since 1981 and thefts of personal property by 31 per cent over the same period (Mirrlees-Black *et al.*, 1996: 20) The percentage of crimes reported to the police has also increased since the BCS began from 31 per cent in 1981 to 43 per cent in 1991, falling only slightly to 41 per cent in 1995 (Mirrlees-Black *et al.*, 1996: 16).

The 1995 BCS found that whilst the chance of being a victim of a minor offence was high, the risk of suffering a more serious offence was small (Mirrlees-Black *et al.*, 1996). Theft was the most common offence, and vehicle theft particularly so—over a third of all incidents revealed by the BCS involved theft of, or from, or criminal damage to, a vehicle (36 per cent). Burglaries, on the other hand, made up only 9 per cent of crimes, violent offences (wounding and robbery) made up 6 per cent, and common assaults another 15 per cent (Mirrlees-Black *et al.*, 1996: 13). To take one, much quoted, example from the 1989 BCS, the 'statistically average' adult can expect to have his home burgled once every thirty-seven years, or have the family car stolen once every fifty years. Whilst comforting to the general public, such figures are less than informative, since they gloss over major geographical, social, and economic differences. Risk of victimization generally is closely related to geographical area, and risk of personal victimization correlated with age, sex, and patterns of routine activity, such as going out in the evenings and alcohol consumption. For example, although over a quarter of vehicle owners suffered some form of crime against their vehicle, risk is closely related with living in the north, inner cities, flats and terraced houses, and young or 'better-off' households (Mirrlees-Black *et al.*, 1996: 45). More striking still are the correlates of burglary. The risk of being burgled was found to be much higher in inner city areas particularly in the north and in the Greater London area. Flats were at greater risk than houses, end of terrace than mid-terrace houses, and rented accommodation rather than owner-occupied homes. Households with lower levels of disposable income, with single-adult and with younger heads of households, and those without household insurance were all also at greater risk.

Crimes of violence also correlate closely with specific variables. Data from the 1988 BCS shows that robbery is twice as likely to occur to those under 45 than over and to men than women. Living in inner cities, especially in the West Midlands and London, and going out at night also increase the risk of victimization. Men make up the bulk of assault victims (80 per cent). Most at risk are those who are single, under 30 years old, drink heavily several evenings a week, and who assault others. Assaults were reported to occur most often in places of entertainment such as pubs and clubs, secondly in the workplace, and thirdly the home. However, such estimates do not take into account the likelihood that domestic assaults are under-reported even in crime surveys. That only 1 per cent of women and 0.3 per cent of men reported suffering domestic violence by a current or ex-partner in 1995 is almost certainly an underestimate (for reasons discussed below)(Mirrlees-Black *et al.*, 1996: 30).

For many types of crime, both Afro-Caribbeans and Asians tend to be more at risk than whites. In part this may be explained by the fact that they are overrepresented in social and age groups particularly prone to crime. Members of ethnic minority groups are disproportionately likely to be council tenants, or to live in younger households in socially disadvantaged areas. Pakistanis appeared to be most vulnerable to racially motivated crimes. They reported that nearly a third of all incidents had been racially motivated compared to 18 per cent of Indians and 14 per cent of Afro-Caribbeans (Fitzgerald and Hale, 1996: 2). Assaults, threats, and vandalism were those offences most often thought to be committed for racial reasons.

This new generation of victim surveys proved to be a valuable resource widely welcomed by criminologists: one which radically restructured the criminological agenda. Nonetheless, many methodological problems have been identified both by independent commentators and by the surveyors themselves. An initial difficulty lies in identifying a sample which is representative of the population. Past samples for the British Crime Surveys were drawn from the electoral register, a source known to under-represent ethnic minorities, the young, and the less socially stable—all groups particularly prone to victimization. Even amongst those actually approached, non-respondents may include disproportionate numbers of victims. Mindful of these methodological problems, since 1992 the BCS has drawn its sample from the Postcode Address File (a listing of all postal delivery points): a source likely to produce a more representative sample than the electoral register. All the surveys since 1988 also include an 'ethnic minority booster sample' to ensure a sample large enough to obtain statistically reliable findings.

As a measure of crime, victim surveys are also problematic in that they enumerate only those incidents for which individuals are able and willing to identify themselves as a victim. For this reason they tend to concentrate on physical and sexual assaults (though even these may not be readily revealed to an interviewer) and personal or household property crime. They necessarily ignore the entire gamut of corporate, environmental, and motoring offences. Nor can they easily uncover crimes against organizations, such as company fraud, shoplifting, or fare evasion (Hough and Mayhew, 1983: 3–4). Crimes in which the 'victim' is complicit, such as drug offences, gambling, and prostitution, are also unlikely to be revealed since this would entail confession to offences for which respondents may themselves face prosecution. Crimes where the victim and offender are known to each other are less likely to be reported to the interviewer, especially if the offender is a relative or a member of the household. In the case of domestic violence or sexual assault, the offender may even be present when the interview takes place. Even where he is not, the common assumption that 'real crime' is something that occurs only between strangers is likely to inhibit the revelation or recognition of much physical and sexual violence committed against women. As a consequence this 'hidden violence', as Stanko characterizes it (Stanko, 1988), is likely to be significantly undercounted in all but the most sensitive crime surveys. For example, the 1988 British Crime Survey revealed only fifteen cases of sexual assault amongst the 5,500 women surveyed (Mayhew *et al.*, 1989), a figure recognized by its authors and critics to be a gross underestimate.

The popular reporting of national crime surveys tends also to create a distorted picture of the distribution of crime. By ignoring geographic and social differentials, press reports have generally implied that the risk of victimization is uniformly low. Recent analysis of BCS data reveals that the uneven distribution of crime is explicable not by the numbers of those who are victims alone, but by the unequal concentration of repeat victimization on particular groups (Trickett *et al.*, 1995). Further distortion may result from the fact that educated, middle-class respondents appear better able to understand the questions posed and more willing to report offences to the interviewer. Further down the social scale, respondents may be so regularly exposed to crime that they fail to recognize activities as criminal or have difficulties in recalling all the offences perpetrated against them. Where the period under survey is more than a few months, problems of recall are likely to become especially marked. Victims may forget less serious incidents or may have difficulties in remembering whether a more distant occurrence fell within the specified time period.

LOCAL CRIME SURVEYS

Seeking to overcome some of the perceived inadequacies of the national surveys, local crime surveys have been carried out in Merseyside (1985), Islington (1986, 1990), Hammersmith and Fulham (1989), Edinburgh (1990), and Aberystwyth (1993). By focusing on particular localities these surveys attempted to pinpoint the higher levels of crime prevailing in socially deprived inner city areas; to highlight the disproportionate victimization of women, of members of ethnic minority groups, and of those lower down the social scale; and to set crime in its broader social context by including questions about racial and sexual harassment, drug abuse, and other forms of anti-social behaviour (Crawford *et al.*, 1990: 4). Questions about victims' encounters with the police have also been included to elicit public perceptions of police priorities and service delivery, and their opinions concerning the control and accountability of police forces. New questions also address the role of other agencies in responding to crime, for example local authority social services and housing departments and Victim Support schemes.

The nature and scope of these questions partly reflects a desire to establish the social context of victimization. More problematically, they are intended to create a database to be used in auditing police performance, allocating resources to combat particular crime problems, and developing policy initiatives. These policy-orientated goals arose partly from the fact that these 'second generation' crime surveys were funded mainly by radical local authorities committed to addressing problems faced by socially marginalized members of the communities they served. As Rock has commented, these local authorities were 'powerful patrons' whose pragmatic concern with problems of policy obliged those carrying out these local crime surveys to become 'the new administrative criminologists of the left' (Rock, 1988: 197).

Until recently, most local crime surveys focused on areas of dense population reflecting the presumption that crime is primarily an urban problem. However, growing recognition that some types of crime are highly prevalent in rural areas has led researchers to conduct rural crime surveys (Koffman, 1996: 89–114). The Aberystwyth Crime Survey (ACS) carried out in 1993 was a direct attempt to remedy the paucity of information about victimization in rural areas. It found that fear of crime in Aberystwyth was lower than that for Wales as a whole: 75 per cent of respondents felt very or fairly safe walking alone in their area after dark as compared to 57 per cent of Welsh respondents to the BCS (Koffman, 1996: 108). Levels of crime were also lower: just 1 per cent of ACS respondents had been victims of vehicle theft as opposed to over 5 per cent of Welsh BCS respondents, and ACS respondents suffered less than half the burglary rate of Wales as a whole. On the other hand, ACS respondents suffered much higher rates of vandalism and damage to vehicles: 19 per cent were victims as opposed to 15 per cent of Welsh BCS respondents (Koffman, 1996: 110).

In describing the trends and patterns of victimization, local surveys have documented the uneven distribution of risk: showing that certain age or social groups and particular residential areas are far more frequently subjected to crime than others. The Merseyside Crime Survey, for example, found that the incidence of burglary on Merseyside was three times higher than in the rest of England and Wales (Kinsey, 1984: 5). And the Second Islington Crime Survey found that 12 per cent of its respondents had been burgled compared to only 7 per cent of respondents to the British Crime Survey (Crawford *et al.*, 1990: 10). Curiously, whilst the BCS found a marked disparity between physical assaults against whites (5.5 per cent) and Afro-Caribbeans (9 per cent), the Second ICS found no appreciable difference between these groups (7 per cent and 6 per cent respectively). How one interprets such findings is open to doubt. It may be that Afro-Caribbeans in Islington are so exposed to violence that they tend to under-report assaults against them. Alternatively, it may be that the high concentration of ethnic minority populations in this Inner London borough levels out disparities in the victimization of whites and blacks. Such a possibility draws attention to the difficulties of comparing local studies of highly deprived, inner city areas with the findings of national surveys.

Local victimization surveys have shown themselves to be more sensitive than national surveys in revealing incidents of sexual assault. The first two British Crime Surveys revealed only one (unreported) case of attempted rape and seventeen and eighteen cases of sexual assault respectively in the 1983 and 1985 reports (Hough and Mayhew, 1983, 1985). In striking contrast, the first Islington Crime Survey estimated 1,200 cases of sexual assault in Islington during the period under review (Jones, 1986). Such disparities suggest major flaws in the wording of questions in the national survey and possibly also in the demeanour and approach of interviewers. Insensitivity in either sphere is unlikely to do much to uncover areas of 'hidden crime'. In displaying greater sensitivity both to local variation and to the feelings of victims themselves, this new generation of victim surveys has had greater success in revealing differential patterns of victimization and has prompted changes also to the BCS.

The notion of 'differential victimization' has been studied with reference not only to geographic, social, and economic variables but also to race and sex. We have seen, above, that women's personal experiences of crime may be less readily documented by mass victimization surveys. To rectify this, feminist researchers have carried out a number of studies of personal crimes against women (Dobash and Dobash 1980; Hanmer and Saunders, 1984; Hall, 1985; Stanko, 1988). Dobash and Dobash studied over 1,000 cases of domestic violence. Despite the gender-neutral character of this term, they found that over three-quarters of cases involved husbands assaulting their wives and only ten cases involved attacks on husbands by wives (Dobash and Dobash, 1979). They found that only 2 per cent of women reported the crime to the police, others preferring instead to seek help from friends or relatives. Recent research on domestic violence among ethnic minority communities has revealed that Pakistani women are particularly inhibited from reporting their plight because of cultural pressures, linguistic difficulties, lack of information, and fear of deportation (Choudry, 1996).

Sexual offences against women have also received increasing attention. One landmark study *Ask Any Woman* (Hall, 1985) carried out in London suggested that a third of respondents had been raped or sexually assaulted, though it has since been subject to methodological criticism. A study carried out in Leeds (Hanmer and Saunders, 1984) used a much broader definition of sexual violence and found that 59 per cent of women had been sexually assaulted at least once in the previous year, whilst Radford found that as many as 76 per cent of women had experienced some form of sexual violence over the previous year (Radford, 1987).

These surveys suggest levels of sexual crime against women far higher than those revealed by national victim surveys and infinitely higher than those indicated by police records. Hall, for example, found that only 8 per cent of those respondents claiming to have been raped and 18 per cent of those alleging sexual assault had reported their victimization to the police (Hall, 1980). Yet the considerable variation in the findings of these different surveys highlights a central difficulty in ascertaining the true extent and nature of sexual victim-ization (Morris, 1987: 165). The role of the media in creating and reinforcing stereotypes of what constitutes 'true' rape partly explains why victims whose experiences do not fit the prescribed pattern fail not only to report but even to recognize them as rape (Soothill and Walby, 1991). Prevailing assumptions about rape foster feelings of guilt and self-blame which also inhibit victims from reporting. As a consequence, the sensitivity of survey questions and in the approach and demeanour of the interviewer may dramatically alter response rates. A recent innovation is the use of computer-assisted personal interviewing (CAPI) in which interviewers use laptop computers to record responses. For particularly sensitive questions, the interviewer turns the computer around and allows the victim to key in his or her own response in confidence.

The example of rape victims may be seen to highlight wider problems inherent in victim surveys: not least the problem of how respondents come to perceive themselves as victims and why it is that some who have been the subject of a crime fail to recognize themselves as victims. Which offences remain in the memory of the respondent to be reported to the surveyor and which, and for what reasons, are simply forgotten? The conclusion by Reiss that 10 per cent of crimes reported to the police in the United States are not reported to those conducting victim surveys must make us wary of seeing the findings of victim surveys as in any way representing the 'true' figure of crime (Reiss, 1986).

In switching attention from offenders to victims, it could be argued that victim surveys did no more than suggest a new subject area for positivist criminology. Crime surveys have reconstituted our picture of crime and brought into question many prevailing assumptions about victimization. But the counting of crimes and detailed descriptions of victims could be said to do no more than provide a new measure of crime and a new set of portraits of offenders parallel to those previously drawn. Yet victim surveys have typically gone beyond the counting of unreported offences to ask questions about perceptions and reactions to crime. In so doing they provide the basis for the development of a new theoretical framework organized around questions about the attributes of crime victims, societal attitudes to crime, and the effects of crime on the community. Two areas in particular have caught the crimino-logical imagination: fear of crime amongst the public generally and the impact of crime upon those who are its victims.

FEAR OF CRIME

Interest in fear of crime originated in the United States in the 1960s during a period of race riots and growing urban violence. But it was the victim survey which, by providing data about the extent and severity of such fear, pinpointed an entirely new area for criminological enquiry (Maxfield, 1984; Garafalo, 1979; Skogan, 1986*a* and 1986*b*). Although clearly a corollary to interest in victimization, fear of crime is now recognized as a distinct social problem extending well beyond those who have actually been victimized to affect the lives of all those who perceive themselves to be at risk. Moreover, although fear of crime is closely related to levels of crime, and tends to increase as crime rises, it cannot be seen as a mere function of levels of criminal activity at any given time. This recognition of fear of crime as a distinct area of enquiry raises theoretical problems about what it is we mean by the term. To what exactly is it a reaction? What are its social correlates? Who is most vulnerable to fear, when, and why (Hale, 1996)? Ironically, the very carrying out of crime surveys may serve to increase sensitivity to the risks of crime. Situating questions about fear within a crime survey may consequently elicit higher levels of apparent anxiety than would otherwise be the case.

Generally, the term 'fear of crime' has been used to refer to perceived threats to personal safety rather than threats to property or more generalized perceptions of risk (Maxfield, 1984: 3). An immediate problem is how to control for variations in respondents' willingness to admit to such fears. Socialization alone is likely to make men less willing to admit to such feelings than women (Stanko and Hobdell, 1993). Another major methodological difficulty is how to phrase questions so as to identify the nature and level of this fear without distorting the data by importing other anxieties (Hale, 1996: 84–94). Questions in crime surveys typically ask 'How safe do you feel walking in your neighbourhood alone at night?' But, phrased in this way, such a question may also elicit answers relating to a given neighbourhood, fear of the dark, respondents' feelings of weakness, or other, non-crime-related, dangers. The construction of fear of crime may then be as closely related to feelings of power or vulnerability as it is to calculated perceptions of risk.

Crime surveys have produced problematic data that appear to show that levels of fear are far from closely correlated with actual risk (Hough, 1995). Young working-class men who spend a great deal of leisure time outside the home, particularly those who habitually visit pubs, may be most at risk but admit to very little fear, whereas women and the elderly commonly express profound anxiety despite lower levels of risk. The 1996 British Crime Survey found, for example, that 57 per cent of women, but only 12 per cent of men felt 'very unsafe' when alone after dark (Mirrlees-Black *et al.*, 1996: 53). Highlighting the weak correspondence between fear and risk, the BCS focused on the apparent irrationality of fears disproportionate to risk.

Suspicious that such findings are an administrative attempt to diminish the seriousness of crime as a social problem by discounting fear of crime as irrational, criminologists have examined the relationship between risk and fear (Young, 1988; Skogan, 1986*b*; Crawford *et al.*, 1990; Pain, 1995). The Islington Crime Survey asked respondents both about their fears and the 'probability of crime in the next year'. It found that although some people worry a good deal about crime, they appear to be well informed as to the likelihood of becoming a victim (Jones *et al.*, 1986: 9). The Second Islington Crime Survey went even further in attempting to identify the social structural causes of people's fear (Crawford *et al.*, 1990: 40). It sought to differentiate between fear of crime on the street, on public transport, and in the home, to develop gender-specific understanding, and to examine the ways in which personal behaviour determined and was itself affected by perceptions of risk.

If risk-assessment is not the sole determinant of fear, then other causal factors must be sought (Hale, 1996: 94–112). Fear of crime is primarily an urban phenomenon and may be seen as a reaction to 'local incivilities' such as poor street lighting, vandalism, boarded-up buildings, youths loitering on street corners, drunks, and other signals of a hostile environment (Crawford *et al.*, 1990: 82). Other correlates include perceptions of 'moral decline', anxiety among whites about the influx of racial minorities, or other changes to their neighbourhood (Skogan, 1986*b*: 138). This more diffuse sense of insecurity may be exacerbated by past personal experiences, by socialization, media portrayal of crime, or the perceived inadequacy of policing (Garafalo 1979: 82). Ironically, crime prevention efforts, whether by the police, Home Office literature, or media campaigns, may raise popular perceptions of risk and so stimulate increased fear. A recent controversial example is a government television advertisement which shows a pack of hyenas mauling a car in a lurid attempt to draw the public's attention to the dangers of leaving their vehicles unsecured.

Gender-specific analyses have been developed by feminist criminologists like Stanko (Stanko, 1985 and 1988) to explain women's greater fear of crime. First, since crimes against women, particularly sexual offences and assaults occurring within the home, are least susceptible to discovery or revelation, women may suffer far higher levels of victimization than are revealed even by crime surveys. The assumed 'irrationality' of women's fears, when judged against that level of risk known to the surveys, may be all too rational a reflection of 'hidden violence' (Stanko, 1988: 40). Secondly, merely counting offences takes no account of the differential impact of actual or potential violation. Women and the elderly may also be 'unequal victims' in that the physical, psychological, or economic costs of crime may be much greater for them than for other more robust or more affluent individuals (Crawford *et al.*, 1990: 70). The lower risks faced, if indeed they are lower, are more than offset by this greater vulnerability to the impact of crime. Racial harassment suffered by members of ethnic minority communities may involve incidents individually too 'minor' to be reported or recorded but which, when repeated over time, profoundly blight the lives of their victims (Cooper and Pomeyie, 1988). For those living in predominantly white communities, isolation may make them feel even more vulnerable.

Lifestyles and Mobility

These findings have led criminologists to consider the ways in which individuals' lifestyles are altered and life choices constrained by fear of crime. Several models of fear-related behaviour have been identified (see, for example, Skogan, 1986*a*). To the degree that they consider risks to be unacceptable, some individuals may withdraw from social life. Other people assess the costs and benefits of modifying their behaviour to achieve some reasonable level of risk and delimit their lifestyle accordingly. Yet here again behavioural responses are not tied solely or exactly to risk. The wealthy may be no more at risk, and in many situations are arguably less so, but they have the resources to take precautionary measures such as installing burglar alarms to their homes or taking taxis in preference to public transport.

A prime example is the development of Neighbourhood Watch schemes in settled 'affluent suburban areas, high-status non-family areas and in areas of modern family housing with higher incomes' (Mayhew *et al.*, 1989: 52), areas known to be less vulnerable to crime. The geographical spread of these schemes illustrates the way in which alleviating fear may be correlated to income rather than risk. One of the underlying purposes of Neighbourhood Watch is to enable communities to develop some sense of control over crime and so enjoy increased security and lower levels of fear. Interpreting the success of NW in this respect is complicated by the fact that those joining, often as a result of having been burgled in the past, tend to be more anxious initially than non-scheme members. Whilst it appears that members do enjoy feelings of being better protected as a result of their efforts (for example, installing home security devices) this does not seem to effect any marked diminution in levels of fear (Bennett, 1987). The 1988 BCS found that 60 per cent of NW members were 'very or fairly worried about being the victim of burglary' compared to only 55 per cent of non-members (Mayhew, 1989: 59). Since this does not appear to be explained solely by other fear-related factors (such as age, sex, perceptions of risk) it may be that anxiety is reinforced through the heightened sensitivity to danger brought about by belonging to NW schemes (Mayhew, 1989: 59–60).

The relationship between fear of crime and quality of life is also problematic. For example, fear may be an important factor in inhibiting mobility. Of respondents to the Second Islington Crime Survey nearly two-thirds gave fear of crime as a reason for not going out and 41 per cent gave it as a considerable part of the reason. However, other factors may also be at work, not least physical disabilities, financial restrictions, having nowhere to go, or preferring to stay at home in the evenings with friends or family (Crawford *et al.*, 1990: 59). The extent to which behaviour is limited by fear of crime varies considerably from avoiding certain places to never going out at night unaccompanied. Even those willing to go out at night alone report parking in well-lit areas, monitoring walking routes home, and developing strategies for avoiding or deflecting potential violations.

Both the BCS and the ICS found substantial differences in the impact of fear of crime on the lifestyles of men and women. The First Islington Crime Survey found that 36 per cent of women, compared to only 7 per cent of men, never went out after dark for fear of crime. Their avoidance behaviour, in the view of the authors of the ICS, 'limits their participation in public, to the extent of a virtual curfew' (Crawford *et al.*, 1990: 91). Significantly, however, the 1996 BCS found markedly lower levels: 11 per cent of women and 5 per cent of men said they never went out after dark but only 31 per cent of these women and 15 per cent of these men gave fear of crime as their reason for staying in (Mirrlees-Black *et al.*, 1996: 55).

The effects of crime and racial harassment against members of the ethnic minorities are often profound (Fitzgerald and Hale, 1996). Findings from the British Crime Survey suggest that while Asians are more likely to feel unsafe out alone after dark, Afro-Caribbeans feel safer than any other group alone on the street at night (Fitzgerald and Hale, 1996: 3). And yet the experience of Victim Support in responding to victims of racial harassment has revealed that 'many victim families end up living like prisoners in their homes or being forced to move away from a familiar environment; children are unsettled and both their education and social life suffer; women are scared to go about the normal tasks . . . and also feel insecure in their own homes' (Cooper and Pomeyie, 1988: 85).

IMPACT OF VICTIMIZATION

The earlier, large scale crime surveys tended to suggest that, in general, effects on victims were relatively mild and/or transitory. Sparks, Genn, and Dodd suggest that most victimization is no more than minimally disruptive since much crime consists of attempts, or results in little by way of loss or physical injury (Sparks *et al.*, 1977). The British Crime Surveys have each included questions about the impact of victimization and have concluded that relatively little harm was suffered by most respondents. The first BCS found that only 11 per cent were 'very much' affected and 17 per cent were 'quite a lot' affected at the time of the crime, by the time of the interview these had fallen to only 2 and 5 per cent respectively (Hough and Mayhew, 1985).

More recently, smaller scale, qualitative studies have suggested that victimization entails greater costs than the mass crime surveys had implied. Large scale studies have been criticized as unreliable guides to the impact of crime in that their respondents include very small numbers of serious crime victims and much larger populations of victims of petty infractions. As a consequence aggregate results 'tend to wash or attenuate the overall effect of crime' (Lurigio, 1987: 454). To rectify this tendency, qualitative research has focused on particular types of crime or specific victim groups. Studies have been carried out, for example, on burglary victims (Maguire, 1980; Maguire and Corbett,

1987), on victims of violence (Shapland *et al.*, 1985, Stanko, 1988), on rape victims (Burgess and Holstrom, 1974; Chambers and Millar, 1983) and on child victims (Finkelhor, 1979, 1986; Morgan and Zedner, 1992*a*). These studies, by concentrating on the more serious types of offence, have highlighted the acute stress and adverse physical, practical, or financial effects suffered by many victims.

Analysis of the impact of crime has been organized around types of impact and persistence of effects over time. Studies have shown that the vast majority of victims suffer in some way in the immediate aftermath of crime. Research by Lurigio in the United States found that most 'crime victims suffer from adverse, short-term psychological consequences as a result' (Lurigio, 1987: 464). In Britain, Maguire found that 83 per cent of the burglary victims in his study experienced strong reactions on discovering that their homes had been invaded, and that 65 per cent were still aware of some continuing impact on their lives four to ten weeks later (Maguire, 1982: 126–31). Perhaps surprisingly, Maguire found that, when asked about the worst aspect of burglary, only 32 per cent of victims spoke of loss or damage, while 41 per cent cited feelings of intrusion, and 19 per cent of emotional upset.

Personal crimes such as physical and sexual assault commonly entail longer term effects still. Shapland *et al.* studied 300 victims of assault, robbery, or rape. They found that 75 per cent of victims of violence were still mentioning some effect at the 'outcome interview' two and a half years after the offence (Shapland *et al.*, 1985: 98–9). Rape victims and victims of sexual abuse during childhood have been found to suffer persisting effects for many years afterwards (Burgess and Holstrom, 1974; Morgan and Zedner, 1992*a*: 44–5). Resick commented that rape victims experienced profound distress for several months after the crime and that 'many continue to experience problems with fear, anxiety, and interpersonal functioning for years after the event' (Resick, 1987: 474). Unsurprisingly, sexual assault victims seem to recover more slowly than victims of other types of crime suffering emotional disturbance, sleeping or eating disorders, feelings of insecurity or low self-esteem, or troubled relationships for months or even years after the event (Maguire and Corbett, 1987; Smith, 1989*a*; Kelly, 1988).

The types of effect victims are likely to suffer obviously vary according to the crime. Assaults may entail physical injury, shock, loss or damage to property, time off work, and financial losses (Shapland *et al.*, 1985: 97). The impact of burglary is more likely to be emotional (involving feelings of shock, insecurity, violation, etc.), financial, or practical (loss of property, disruption, mess, broken doors or windows) (Maguire, 1980). Child sexual abuse may inflict few visible or tangible injuries but is liable to induce profound feelings of 'fear, revulsion, shame and guilt' (Morris, 1987: 191). In the longer term child abuse victims may suffer impaired self-esteem, school learning problems, withdrawal and regressive behaviour (Finkelhor, 1986: 152–63). Whilst reactions are highly crime-specific, most studies suggest that some degree of psychological distress is the dominant reaction amongst crime victims. At its most severe, this distress has been formally recognized by psychologists as 'posttraumatic stress disorder'—a clinical condition whose symptoms include anxiety, depression, loss of control, guilt, sleep disturbance, and obsessive dwelling on the crime itself (Burgess and Holstrom, 1978; Jones *et al.*, 1987).

Recent studies have examined the differential impact of victimization, in order to understand why some victims are more severely affected than others by apparently similar crimes (British Journal of Criminology, 1995). Skogan identified a number of key factors in determining the differential impact of crime: isolation, resources, vulnerability, and previous experience (Skogan, 1986*b*: 140–3). Isolated people are not only more fearful of crime but are likely to suffer higher levels of stress when victimized. Thus those who live alone, with few friends or no close family, tend to feel the impact of crime more acutely than those who are well supported (Maguire, 1980). Criminal damage, theft, and burglary are all likely to place heavier burdens on those with fewer financial resources, particularly because these are the very groups least likely to be insured against such loss. Generalized feelings of vulnerability amongst groups such as women, ethnic minorities, and the elderly also appear to magnify the impact of crime. Lack of ability to resist or to defend oneself against an attacker may amplify pre-existing feelings of vulnerability. For children, a burglary of the family home may be a shocking invasion of the one place they perceived to be secure from the terrors of the world and may entail trauma quite out of proportion to the physical damage or loss of property incurred (Morgan and Zedner, 1992*a*: 63–4). Apart from feelings of vulnerability, actual physical weakness may result in victims suffering more serious injuries or taking longer to recover from assaults than those who are more robust (Garafalo, 1977). This said, the tendency to associate victimization with vulnerability tends to obscure the fact that men may also suffer as victims, as the expectations of masculinity inhibit them from expressing their reactions to victimization (Stanko and Hobdell, 1993).

The significance of previous experience is perhaps most difficult to calculate. A recent study suggests that 4 per cent of victims experience 44 per cent of all crimes (National Board for Crime Prevention, 1994). Multiple or series victimization appears to compound the impact suffered with each repeated occurrence and a minority of individuals are so repeatedly victimized that it becomes virtually impossible to distinguish the impact of discrete crimes from the generally impoverished quality of their life (Genn, 1988; Ellingworth *et al.*, 1995). Racial harassment is a good example here. The Commission for Racial Equality suggests racial harassment is 'widespread and persistent' in schools and colleges (CRE, 1988). For those who suffer continual 'name-calling and racial insults and abuse, graffiti . . . and racial violence varying from slapping, punching, jostling, and assault to maiming', the cumulative impact is far greater than any account of each individual incident would suggest (CRE, 1988: 7). Aside from previous crimes, other non-crime related life experiences may also be influential in determining the impact of crime. The death of a relative, divorce, separation, or other family trauma, illness, or pre-existing psychological problems may amplify or be amplified by the impact of crime.

Just as factors external to the crime may be relevant in determining its impact, so the consequences of crime extend beyond the incident itself. Considerable expenses may be incurred as a direct result of the crime for the replacement of uninsured property, for medical care, counselling, or funeral costs. Other expenses arising less directly may, nonetheless, be considerable. Some victims are driven to move house as a consequence of a traumatic burglary or to escape continuing attacks, harassment, or stalking. Some lose earnings or even risk their job after missing time from work for court attendances or due to crime-related illness or depression (Shapland, 1985: 104–5; Resick, 1987). Many crimes may place considerable stress on family relations. Domestic violence may lead to the break up of the family. The consequent dislocation affects not only those who are the direct victims but impinges also on those other members of the household who are its 'indirect victims'—most commonly the children (Morgan and Zedner, 1992*a*: 28–31).

The wider impact of crime on secondary or 'indirect' victims is increasingly recognized in the literature. The most obvious example is that of the families of murder victims (Black and Kaplan, 1988; Pynoos and Eth, 1984). Although they are not primary victims they suffer perhaps the most profound trauma of any crime victim. The trauma of sudden bereavement is often compounded by the viciousness of the attack or the senselessness of the killing. For those who witness homicide or other non-fatal assaults, feelings of shock or guilt for failing to intervene may be profound, and onlookers, too, may be victims (Victim Support, 1991; Pynoos and Eth, 1984). The mass of other less serious offences may also create 'indirect victims'. For example, over a third of the 400,000 households burgled every year include children who, though rarely recognized as victims, may be distressed or even traumatized as a result (Morgan and Zedner, 1992*a*). At its worst the impact of crime on those who are witnesses or obliged to live with its consequences may be such that they should properly be recognized as victims in their own right.

The impact of corporate or business crime upon its victims has only recently begun to receive proper recognition. Most victims of fraud are, by its very nature, unaware that they have been victimized at all or unwilling to recognize that they have been duped (Box, 1983: 17). Criminal negligence leading to workplace injuries and deaths is rarely recognized as crime. Large-scale incidents involving loss of life tend not to be popularly perceived of as crimes but as 'disasters'—witness Piper Alpha, Zeebruge, and Bhopal. Only with the intense media coverage of high-profile fraud cases such as those involving Barings Bank, BCCI, the Maxwell pension fund, and Guinness has attention been drawn to the plight of those who are their victims and the financial and emotional impact upon them (Levi and Pithouse, 1988, 1992, 1997).

Victims' Needs

The relationship between impact of crime and need is highly problematic. Those suffering the highest levels of harm or loss do not necessarily have correspondingly high needs. They may enjoy a supportive environment, be innately resilient, or otherwise able to overcome the effects of victimization. On the other hand, victims suffering objectively less serious crimes may require greater support if they are vulnerable or isolated. Criminological understanding of victims' needs is largely reliant on views expressed by victims themselves—a source which is necessarily problematic (Mawby, 1988: 132–3; Maguire, 1991: 403–6). Vocal, determined, or well-connected victims may do much to colour perceptions of need, ironically at the expense of those whose needs are greatest but whose very vulnerability or inability to ask for help ensures their silence. Educated, informed, and resourceful individuals are better placed to seek out help, be it practical assistance, information, or advice on future crime prevention. For these reasons, Shapland and her colleagues argue that needs as expressed by victims cannot be seen as 'objective' assessments (Shapland, 1985: 112).

Victims' expressions of need are determined in part by their cultural background, their expectations, and their knowledge of what services may be available to them. Those ignorant of the existence of available help may express only a diffuse, vague need for emotional support where others would specifically identify their desire for voluntary or professional counselling. The provision of services, too, plays a part in determining victims' needs. Expert-led innovations in the provision of support in turn drives victim expectations. Whilst researchers have attempted to identify, and even to calibrate, the needs of specific groups of victims (Shapland, 1985; Maguire and Corbett, 1987), the task must be a relativist one.

Whilst most attention has focused on the emotional impact and psychological needs, victims may also need practical help, information, and financial support. Practical needs tend to be short term and relatively easily satisfied. The mending of windows, replacement of keys, or broken locks following a burglary are obvious examples (Maguire, 1982). Longer-term practical help may be required following the most serious offences (Newburn, 1994): transportation to and from hospital for the treatment of injuries (Shapland et al., 1985), help with child-care following rape (Morgan and Zedner, 1992a), or refuge from domestic violence (Smith, 1989b). Provision of information for victims has also been identified as a major need. In the immediate aftermath of crime this may entail no more than advice on crime prevention, insurance, or compensation claims. But for more serious crimes, the progress of police investigations, prosecution decisions, and the dates and outcome of any trial are all likely to be a source of considerable interest and concern. Studies by Maguire and Corbett (1987), Shapland et al. (1985), and Newburn and Merry (1990) reveal the importance attached by victims to being kept informed of the progress of 'their case'. Largely as a result of these research findings, the Home

Office has made progressive attempts to improve the ways in which victims are kept informed by police and prosecutors (HO Circular 20/1988; Home Office 1990, 1996*b*) (of which more below).

THE VICTIM MOVEMENT

In the United States, a strongly rights-based victim movement emerged in the 1960s and 1970s. Largely conservative in outlook, often seeking a more punitive response to offenders, it was in some states associated with demands for the retention or re-introduction of the death penalty. Dissatisfied with the existing responses to victims, the movement demanded a reorientation of the criminal justice system to take account of the needs and the rights of victims. Although it has become more variegated, with some groups like 'Parents of Murdered Children' eschewing political involvement, many groups like 'Families and Friends of Murder Victims' engage in high profile political lobbying.

In Britain, the central organ of the victim movement, Victim Support (formerly the National Association of Victim Support Schemes, NAVSS) has a very different history. Beginning life as a local initiative in Bristol in 1974, Victim Support grew dramatically in the following decades (Rock, 1990). Its affiliated schemes now cover the entire country, calling on the services of some 12,000 volunteers who offer help to over a million victims a year (Home Office, 1996*a*: 33). Funding to Victim Support from the Home Office has risen from £5,000 in 1979–80 to over £11 million in 1996–7, an extraordinary increase at a time of financial retrenchment in other areas of public service.

Traditionally, Victim Support has maintained a relatively low-key political profile partly to maximize its pool of volunteers, of potential donors, and cross-party political support, and partly to preserve its charitable status. Where it sought legislative change, it avoided overt political lobbying, preferring to work behind the scenes to bring pressure to bear on issues such as services to victims by the police, compensation, and provision for the victim in court (Rock, 1990, 1991). In more recent years, however, Victim Support appears to have adopted a more overtly proactive role promoting rights for victims. Noting that 'offenders have clear rights in our system of justice but victims have no enforceable rights under the law', the Director of Victim Support, Helen Reeves, has demanded that victims should have the right to be heard, to be kept informed about the progress of 'their case', to provide information, to be protected by law enforcement agencies, to receive compensation and 'respect, recognition and support' (Victim Support, 1995). Whether so-called rights such as these can in practice be provided is debatable, and as such it is open to question whether use of the language of rights is misleading (Fenwick, 1995).

The main thrust of Victim Support's endeavour remains in the provision of services to individual victims at a local level. Given the considerable difficulty in identifying those most badly affected, the local schemes operate an 'outreach' service. This takes the form of 'crisis intervention' by volunteers contacting victims direct to offer a 'shoulder to cry on', practical services, and information. The means of contacting victims varies between letters, doorstep visits, or more rarely telephone calls. Maguire and Corbett found that whilst 90 per cent of those receiving unsolicited visits invited the caller in to talk, and half went on to discuss their feelings in depth or ask for practical help, only 7 per cent of those contacted by letter responded at all (Maguire and Corbett, 1987). Outreach is more expensive in terms of volunteers' time and scheme resources but its obvious advantages in sparing the victim from having to ask for help has made it the dominant model of Victim Support work.

Each local scheme operates under the guidance of a management committee; a central paid co-ordinator liaises with the police to collect details of victims on a daily basis, which are then distributed to a pool of volunteers who make contact and offers of help (Holtom and Raynor, 1988). Whilst this model forms the basis of Victim Support's organization, strong links with the community ensure considerable diversity of local policy and practice. Inner city urban schemes are fashioned by different crime patterns, social and economic problems, and political imperatives from their rural counterparts. The availability of volunteers also plays a part in determining the level of service a scheme is able to offer. Inner City areas with the highest crime rates lack an established middle-class community from which a pool of volunteers might be recruited. In rural areas, on the other hand, volunteers have to travel considerable distances to respond to victims in need. Although there is much variety of provision, levels of victim satisfaction with support when it is offered appears to be high.

In its early days, Victim Support focused mainly on 'conventional' victims of burglary, robbery, and theft, crimes generally committed by strangers. More recently, it has worked increasingly with the victims of sexual and violent crime, often committed by those known to them, and with the families of murder victims. Work with such victims inevitably tends to be of a very different nature from the general pattern of short-term 'crisis intervention', involving instead long-term support often by a pair of specially trained volunteers over months or even years.

Support for victims of domestic violence has largely been the preserve of the women's movement. The first women's 'refuge' was established at Chiswick by Erin Pizzey in 1972 for battered women. It was quickly emulated across the country as small, underfunded refuges proliferated, clearly fulfilling an unmet need in providing emergency accommodation for women fleeing from abusive partners. In the course of one year alone (1977–8), 11,400 women and 20,850 children were taken in by 150 refuges (Binney *et al.*, 1985). The refuge movement has maintained a precarious position, partly reliant on local authority funding yet often in conflict with conventional statutory services.

'Rape crisis' centres developed out of the same wave of re-emergent feminism in the 1970s, on a similar model to that of refuges. Rape crisis centres were first opened in London in 1976 and in Birmingham in 1979. By 1988 there were forty such centres in operation, offering emotional support, legal, and medical advice to women who have been sexually assaulted or raped (Anna T., 1988). With few funded posts, reliant mainly on the work of volunteers, rape crisis centres offer a twenty-four-hour telephone helpline and provide face-to-face counselling. Committed also to educating and informing the public about rape, these centres have been loathe to use the term 'victim'. Their objection rests on the grounds that 'using the word "victim" to describe women takes away our power and contributes to the idea that it is right and natural for men to "prey" on us' (London Rape Crisis Centre, 1984: ix). Replacing the term victim with 'survivor', rape crisis campaigners have deliberately differentiated their response from that of the rest of the victim movement (Kelly, 1988). Although based upon diverse feminist beliefs, the general commitment of rape crisis centres to radical feminism and their deep suspicion of police attitudes to rape has limited the interplay between their work and that of other voluntary and criminal justice agencies (Anna T., 1988).

A more recent development still is that of an array of new lobby groups seeking to promote victims' interests, such as the tiny pressure group 'Justice for Victims' campaigning on behalf of the families of homicide victims. Such groups tend to be more exigent in their promotion of victim's interests and rights and less mindful of the need to balance these against the rights of offenders. As such they represent a new and, in some cases, disturbing direction for the victim movement. Other groups such as the Suzy Lamplugh Trust, the Zito Trust which campaigns for victims of mentally disordered offenders, and SAMM (Support After Murder and Manslaughter) which primarily provides support after homicide focus on particular types of victim and tend to avoid making pronouncements about offenders.

Victim Support, women's refuges, rape crisis centres, and the newer victims' interest groups are far from enjoying coherence of outlook, organization, or method. The 'victim movement' is ideologically heterogeneous. Relations between the various agencies range from close co-operation to barely concealed hostility. As Van Dijk has observed from an international perspective, 'the movement's demands and achievements do not flow from a well-defined victimological theory, or in fact from any social theory at all' (Van Dijk, 1988). Despite, or perhaps because of, this heterogeneity, the combined impact of these endeavours has been enormous.

VICTIMS IN THE CRIMINAL JUSTICE SYSTEM

The role of the victim within the criminal justice system attracts increasing attention amongst criminologists and policy-makers alike. Without the co-operation of the victim in reporting crime, in furnishing evidence, in identifying the offender, and acting as a witness in court, most crime would remain unknown and unpunished. The reliance of the criminal justice system on the victim has proved to be a powerful bargaining tool for those seeking to further recognition of victims' needs and rights. This political impetus is important insofar as much of the criminological research into victims has been funded, promoted, and in many cases even instigated, by central or local government.

That victims became a focus for political concern may be related to the profound and growing sense of disillusionment across political parties with the ability of the criminal justice system to 'do anything' about crime. By contrast concern for the victim promised relatively easy, high public relations benefits (Rock, 1990). Across the political spectrum, those on the Left saw support and compensation to victims as a natural extension to national insurance, and as an important corollary to welfarism, whilst Conservative interest has been characterized as representing the softer face of the 'Law and Order lobby'. The financial backing given to Victim Support by Conservative governments since 1979 is consistent with their wider search for lost 'community' and promotion of 'active citizenship'. In 1990, the Home Office announced a 'Victim's Charter', which laid down the rights of victims, specifying how they were to be treated and what standards they had a right to expect, for example, information about the progress of their case, about trial dates, bail, and sentencing decisions (Home Office, 1990). Its message was reinforced by the publication of several other statements of standards of service for victims including the Crown Prosecution Service 'Statement on the Treatment of Victims and Witnesses' (1993) and the 'Court Users' Charter' (1994). In 1993 the Royal Commission on Criminal Justice made eleven recommendations specifically relating to victims, all of which were accepted by the government and subsequently implemented (Royal Commission on Criminal Justice, 1993). Taken together these recommendations seek to ensure that victims get better information about the progress of their case, that their views are obtained and considered, and that witnesses receive proper facilities and assistance in court. A Victim's Helpline set up in 1994 allows victims to contact prison authorities if they are concerned about unwanted contact from an offender or the arrangements for an offender's release. These developments were followed up in 1996 by a second 'Victim's Charter' (Home Office, 1996*b*) which sets twenty-seven standards of service which the various agencies of the criminal justice system are to deliver in four broad areas: provision of information to victims, taking victims' views into account, treating them with respect and sensitivity at court, and providing them with support. In common with all charters, however, the Victim's Charter has no legal status: its provisions encourage rather than bind and as such it is questionable whether it can be said to furnish 'rights' in any meaningful sense. Accordingly, it is perhaps better seen as a statement of intent rather than the provider of justiciable rights (Fenwick, 1995).

Pressure for the recognition of victims' rights has also been influential at the international level. In 1985, the General Assembly of the United Nations adopted a 'Declaration of the Basic Principles of Justice for Victims of Crime and Abuse of Power'. The Declaration lays down basic standards for the treatment of victims, including the right to information and fair treatment, consideration of their views, restitution and compensation, and the provision of victim services. The Council of Europe has also been active in this area, endorsing a 'Convention on State Compensation' for victims of violent crime in 1983 and making a series of recommendations on the role of victim in the criminal law and criminal process, on assistance to victims, and on crime prevention (Joutsen, 1987).

The political impetus to championing the rights of victims has played a major part in raising the profile of the victim. Research on victims' experiences of the criminal process has suggested that, at best, prosecution, conviction, and sentence may have a powerful cathartic effect in relieving victims' feelings of complicity and guilt (Adler, 1988: 140). Depending on the sanction meted out, victims may benefit from compensation for their losses and harms suffered, or enjoy feelings of increased security when a threatening offender is incarcerated. On the other hand, insensitive questioning by police, inadequate provision of information, delays, or unexplained decisions by the prosecution service to drop a case may each entail further suffering. At worst, the impact of the criminal process is tantamount to 'secondary victimization' (Maguire and Pointing, 1988: 11).

As the first point of contact with the criminal justice system, the police play an important role in shaping the victim's experience. The first British Crime Survey found that satisfaction with the police response was generally good, but that the young, particularly young males, tended to be more critical (Mayhew and Hough, 1983). Shapland and her colleagues modified this view by showing that whilst initial levels of satisfaction with the police were generally high, this tended to decline steadily as the case progressed (Shapland *et al.*, 1985: 83–9; see also Newburn and Merry, 1990). Dissatisfaction arose from police failure to keep victims informed, perceived inefficiency, unhelpfulness, or unfairness. Disillusionment was a product, therefore, of a growing feeling that 'the police did not care and were not doing anything' (Shapland *et al.*, 1985: 85). In a bid to respond to such criticisms, the Home Office now carries out regular surveys of public satisfaction with police services, each police force has issued a 'Statement of Policing Standards', and the Victim's Charter stipulates standards for police response to reports of crime by victims (Home Office, 1996*b*).

Particular efforts have been made to improve the police response to victims of sexual assault. Special interview suites in police stations, specially trained women officers, and joint interviewing with social workers in child abuse cases (Metropolitan Police and Bexley Social Services, 1987) are just a few of the innovations introduced in recent decades. Given these innovations, it is perhaps not surprising that victims of sexual assault appear to be more satisfied with the police than victims of physical assault or robbery (Shapland *et al.*, 1985: 87). For the mass of property crimes where a suspect is never located, there is often little more the police can do than inform the victim of the reasons for ceasing their enquiries (Newburn and Merry, 1990). However, in the case of more serious offences, victims look for sensitivity in the conduct of interviews, in the collecting of forensic evidence, in the handling of identification procedures, and for information about developments in the investigation.

In an attempt to ensure that victims are kept informed, both as a matter of routine and in response to personal enquiries, the Home Office has introduced a 'One Stop Shop' (OSS) initiative whereby the police become the single source of information to victims throughout the criminal process. Victims choosing to opt in to the OSS initiative are kept informed by the police about whether a suspect is cautioned or charged, whether the charge is altered, the date of any trial, the verdict, and sentence. Initially, the scheme applies only to crimes of domestic burglary, grievous bodily harm and attempted murder, robbery, sexual assault, criminal damage over £5,000, arson, and racially motivated offences. The scheme is a welcome move toward ensuring that the difficulties faced by victims in obtaining information from several different sources are overcome. This said, it is also open to criticism: many serious crimes (including domestic violence) have been excluded from the scheme and the police will be able only to inform victims of decisions made, not to offer any explanation of them.

Unlike jurisdictions such as France or Germany where victims have considerable rights to participate in the prosecution or to present civil claims within the criminal process (Jones, 1994; Kury *et al.*, 1994), in Britain victims have traditionally had little role other than as a source of evidence (Joutsen, 1994). In court, the victim is no more or less than a witness, and as such is placed in a position of vulnerability—at the mercy of questioning by defence counsel *and* prosecution alike. The predicament of victims called as witnesses is most starkly illustrated by the plight of rape victims and the extent to which they, quite as much as the defendant, are placed on trial (Temkin, 1987: 6–8; Soothill and Soothill, 1993). Other 'vulnerable' witnesses include children and those with learning difficulties. Recognition of their plight has led to innovations in court procedure and changes in the rules of evidence. In many courts where vulnerable witnesses are involved, judges may remove wigs and robes or come down from the bench; barristers too may derobe; quietly spoken victim/ witnesses may be provided with microphones; and provision has been made for the use of screens, of live video-links and pre-recorded video-taped interviews all intended to reduce the stress to victims (Morgan and Zedner, 1992*a*: 128–144 and 1992*b*; Spencer *et al.*, 1990). Unlike victim/witnesses in many US states, British witnesses do not enjoy representation by counsel or the protection of Victim/Witness Protection statutes. Recognition that victims are disempowered by the trial process has led to demands that they enjoy greater protections and have greater influence over its direction and outcome.

A more recent development still is the creation of 'The Witness Service'. Run by Victim Support and modelled on American victim-witness assistance programmes, it seeks to provide information and counsel to those called as witnesses in court. Established initially in 1990 with private funds in just seven

Crown Court centres, the pilot scheme proved so successful that the service has now been extended to all seventy-seven Crown Court centres in England and Wales and is funded by central government (though, as yet, it exists in only a minority of magistrates' courts). For witnesses obliged to wait in crowded, inhospitable areas often for interminable periods, the presence of Witness Service volunteers has been recognized as 'comforting and congenial, a symbolic end to their solitary and pariah status' (Rock, 1991). The Witness Service not only provides advice, information, and support to help witnesses through the stress of a court appearance, it works also to ensure the provision of better facilities, such as separate waiting areas for victims and their families and special provisions such as 'fast-tracking' of cases involving child witnesses (Parliamentary All Party Penal Affairs Group, 1996: 14)

In the United States the legal rights of victims have been greatly strengthened by the introduction of legislation passed by local and federal government in the past decade (Maguire, 1991: 379; Erez, 1994). The right to make 'victim impact statements' now exists in the majority of states. These are primarily used in setting the level of compensation but also inform sentencing decisions more generally. Even greater influence is accorded to 'victim statements of opinion' which allow the victim to indicate what sentence he or she would deem appropriate. Some states also require that victims be consulted prior to any plea-bargaining or decisions pertaining to parole.

In England demands for victims to have influence over prosecutorial discretion, the acceptance of a plea or the length of sentence have grown in recent years. Arguments in favour of increased victim participation in the criminal justice process include: recognition of their status as a party to the dispute (Christie, 1977); reduced risk of inflicting further psychological harm on the victim; greater victim co-operation and thereby the improved efficiency of the system; better information about harms suffered and thereby closer proportionality in sentencing (von Hirsch and Jareborg, 1991). Arguments against allowing victims a greater say include: the intrusion of private views into public decision-making; limitations on prosecutorial discretion; the danger that the victim's 'subjective' view undermines the court's objectivity; disparity in sentencing of similar cases depending on the resilience or punitiveness of the victim (Ashworth, 1993); and, finally, that to increase their involvement may entail further burdens on victims whilst raising their expectations unrealistically (Reeves, 1984; Parliamentary All Party Penal Affairs Group, 1996: 12). Lobbying to introduce victim statements has prevailed over these objections, and one recent review of the research claims that there is no evidence to support any of the predicted adverse effects (Erez, 1994: 17).

In 1995 a working group set up by the Director of Public Prosecutions to consider the place of the victim in the trial process recommended the introduction of victim statements on a pilot basis. These are intended to provide information concerning fears of further victimization; enable professionals to take victims' interests into account in respect of cautioning, charging, and bail decisions; inform the prosecutor of the wider circumstances of the case, of the effect of the crime on the victim, of the need for financial compensation, and of facts which refute misleading statements made by the defence in mitigation. In a pilot being conducted in six police force areas, two types of victim statement are being tested: one in which the statement is written by the victim in his or her own words and the other where it is taken by a police officer. In both cases, the provision of a statement by the victim is optional.

Other areas of innovation include the government's commitment to improving facilities for victim/witnesses called to court (Home Office, 1990), to reducing waiting times by improving listing systems, and to take the special needs of the victim into account in the construction of new court buildings, but progress in this final respect is necessarily slow.

SHIFTING CONCEPTIONS OF CRIMINAL JUSTICE

The proliferation of research about victims has raised larger questions about the very purpose of criminal justice and the place of the victim within it. Victim surveys have revealed that the public are not so punitive as had been expected and that many victims would welcome the opportunity to seek some reparation or even reconciliation in place of traditional punishment (Hough and Moxon, 1985). Those academics, policy-makers, and criminal justice professionals seeking a more positive paradigm than that of punishment have advocated various models of reparative justice reorientated towards the aims of mediation and restitution (Barnett, 1977; Braithwaite, 1990; Wright, 1982, 1991, 1995).

In its purest form, mediation seeks to provide a way of resolving disputes without recourse to the vagaries of the courts, allowing both parties to retain control and to voice their grievances under the supervision of a mediator, whether a trained professional or lay volunteer (Davis, 1992; Davis *et al.*, 1987; Marshall, 1991). The mediator makes no decisions and any resolution is reached by the mutual agreement of the two parties. In practice, mediation varies considerably from operating as a direct alternative to adjudication; through 'court-based' schemes taking referrals from the courts prior to sentencing as in South Yorkshire (see for example, Smith *et al.*, 1988); to meetings between victims and offenders already in custody as at Rochester Youth Custody Centre (Launay, 1985).

Mediation schemes were first introduced in Britain at the end of the 1970s. They have developed gradually, if slowly; by 1996 twenty-five initiatives were in operation, including fifteen fully fledged schemes bringing victims and offenders together on a one-to-one basis or in groups to hold regular discussions. Their aims are similarly various: from providing victims with tangible reparation and offenders with the hope of a reduced sentence; through providing a conduit for communication; to allowing both parties to understand one another better and, possibly, to resolve their conflict. A study by the Home

Office over two years (1985–7) found that in six schemes dealing with juveniles cautioned by the police, 57 per cent of all agreements involved some sort of explanation and apology, with just over 25 per cent involving material reparation (Marshall, 1991: 9). Although mediation has obvious attractions, sceptics have questioned whether it can really operate 'in the shadow of the court'. Victim Support has warned of the additional burdens, in terms of time, goodwill, and energy, it may place on the victim (Reeves, 1984). This said, Home Office research published in 1990 found that 80 per cent of victims and 86 per cent of offenders were satisfied by the process (Parliamentary All Party Penal Affairs Group, 1996: 15). Whilst mediation is proving successful in respect of crimes of low level seriousness, it is doubtful whether it could substitute for formal adjudication in the case of serious crime.

The paradigm of reparation rests on the recognition that crime is not only a wrong against society but often represents also a private wrong done by the offender to a specific victim. Historically, it is argued, the state has 'stolen' the dispute from the hands of victims and offenders, and, in so doing, has usurped the right of the victim to seek recompense for harms suffered (Christie, 1977; Ashworth, 1986; Wright, 1991: 1–9). Restorative theorists argue that compensating individual victims (but less often the wider community) should be the primary aim of the criminal justice system (Barnett, 1977; Wright, 1991; Davis, 1992). To quote Barnett, a leading proponent of restitution: 'Justice consists of the culpable offender making good the loss he has caused . . . Where we once saw an offense against society, we now see an offense against an individual' (Barnett, 1977: 287–8). This, it is claimed, would reduce reliance on negative, solely punitive disposals, and institute in their place positive attempts to rectify the specific harm caused by crime. Pure restitutionists, like Barnett, deny altogether the value of punishment and demand only that the offended party receive just compensation. In practice, pure restitution has nowhere overthrown the paradigm of punishment, and instead reparative principles are incorporated somewhat awkwardly into the existing punitive framework (Zedner, 1994; Dignan and Cavadino, 1996). The stigmatizing and deterrent qualities of punishment are retained, but alongside traditional punishments provision is made for compensation to identifiable victims.

Compensation is made through both the state-funded 'Criminal Injuries Compensation Scheme' and via compensation orders payable by the offender (Miers, 1991; Zedner, 1996). It is arguable that the initial impetus to these developments was largely negative, spurred on by the feeling that if punishment was failing to deter or to rehabilitate then at least some limited good might be achieved by compensating victims for the wrongs they have suffered. State-funded compensation was set up as early as 1964 in the form of the Criminal Injuries Compensation Scheme (CICS) which makes discretionary payments to victims of unlawful violence. It has been suggested that state-funded compensation is based on the premiss that the state is under an obligation to maintain law and order, the commission of crime may be said to result from a failure to fulfil that duty, and so compensation is payable accordingly (Council of Europe convention on 'Compensation for Victims of Violent Crime', 1983). In Britain, payments seem to be made on behalf of the community more as an expression of public sympathy than out of any clear sense of duty (Newburn, 1989). More cynically, it might be argued that compensation is paid partly in recognition of the state's reliance on the victim's co-operation in bringing offenders to justice. For the victim, engagement with the criminal justice process entails further costs: the time, energy, and stress of assisting the police with their investigation, and, for a few at least, the trauma of giving evidence as a witness in court. State-funded compensation may be said to represent 'payment' to victims for their co-operation in the criminal justice process (Barnett, 1977: 285) or compensation for the further costs or 'secondary victimization' suffered as in consequence.

Provision was made for CICS to be placed on a statutory footing by the Criminal Justice Act 1988, but the government appeared unwilling to take this step and, in 1993, attempted to make radical changes to the scheme without recourse to legislation (Home Office, 1993). These administrative changes were driven by recognition that the existing scheme could no longer be afforded and that stricter limits had to be placed both upon the costs of running the scheme and on awards paid out. This move was subsequently declared illegal by the House of Lords in an action brought by several trade union groups and other interested bodies (*R. v. Secretary of State for the Home Department, Ex parte Fire Brigades Union and others* [1995] 1 All ER 888 (CA), [1995] 2 All ER 244 (HL)). In response the Government passed the Criminal Injuries Compensation Act 1995 which repeals the provision in the Criminal Justice Act 1988 that compensation payments be based on common law principles and, in its place, introduces a new tariff scheme (Zedner, 1996: 188–9). The minimum award is set at £1,000 in order to exclude the numbers of small claims which were said to be creating backlogs in the processing of awards, though this effectively denies compensation to the mass of victims of minor assaults and robberies. The tariff then groups injuries of comparable severity into twenty-five bands, each receiving a standard fixed payment (from £1,000 to £250,000). For those who are incapacitated as a result of their injury for twenty-eight weeks or more a separate payment for loss of earnings (or potential earnings) and for the cost of any necessary special care is available. Though again this leaves those unable to work for periods of less than twenty-eight weeks without any compensation. Additional compensation payments are also payable in cases of fatal injury. Despite these few exceptions, it is clear that the single standard payment is intended to limit the steady growth in the cost of the CICS which under the old scheme was predicted to rise to £460 million by the year 2000, but which, under the new tariff scheme, is estimated to rise to £260 million. Significantly, the tariff scheme wholly ignores recommendations made by a Victim Support working party on compensation (Victim Support, 1993). It has further been criticized for unduly limiting maximum awards, for excluding any consideration of the complexities of individual cases, for failing to take full account of loss of earnings, and for removing parity between state compensation payments and civil awards (Zedner, 1996: 189). Compensation continues to be available only to victims of violence, though why they should be singled out for help denied to other victims remains a matter of debate (Ashworth, 1986; Duff 1987).

Although earlier provisions allowing the Board to take into account the victim's character and way of life have been abolished, the Board retains discretion to have regard to previous unspent criminal convictions, even those having no causal relation with the injury which is the subject of a claim. Where an applicant can be seen to have attracted assault through his own provocative conduct or where he has convictions for serious offences, however unconnected with the offence in question, then compensation will generally be withheld. It is less clear, however, why those who have committed a minor non-violent offence should be denied compensation when they are later violently assaulted.

The police play a significant role as 'gate-keepers' in deterring would-be recipients from applying, failing to inform those they consider inappropriate claimants about CICS, or giving information to the Board which calls into question the legitimacy of claims (Shapland *et al.*, 1985: chapter 7; Newburn and Merry, 1990). Without some strategy for ensuring that all victims are routinely informed of the existence of CICS, the police (and Victim Support schemes) may deprive victims of access to compensation. In contrast to this unregulated exclusion of 'undeserving victims', those who fulfil the stereotypical picture of a worthy or deserving recipient receive awards more readily than those who do not. Despite research evidence on the relative rarity of elderly women being violently robbed or assaulted, the 'poor, innocent little old lady' continues to represent the 'ideal victim' in the mind of the state (Newburn, 1989: 15; Christie, 1986).

Victim recourse to the Criminal Injuries Compensation Scheme has increased dramatically in recent years. The number of applications rose from 22,000 in 1979–80 to 65,977 in 1992–3 (Barclay, 1995: 17). The number of awards paid out by the Board for England and Wales over the same decade (excluding Scotland) rose more slowly from 17,500 to 36,638 in 1993. Whereas £109.3 million was paid out to victims in 1990–1, by 1994–5 this had risen to £175 million paid out to nearly 40,000 victims—a fourfold increase in compensation payments since 1978–9 (Home Office, 1996*a*: 33).

Compensation payable by the offender was introduced in the Criminal Justice Act 1972 which gave the courts powers to make an ancillary order for compensation in addition to the main penalty in cases where 'injury, loss, or damage' had resulted. The Criminal Justice Act 1982 made it possible for the first time to make a compensation order as the sole penalty. It also required that in cases where fines and compensation orders were given together, the payment of compensation should take priority over the fine. These developments signified a major shift in penological thinking, reflecting the growing importance attached to reparation over the more narrowly retributive aims of conventional punishment. The Criminal Justice Act 1988 furthered this shift by requiring courts to consider the making of a compensation order in every case of death, injury, loss, or damage and, where such an order was not given, imposed a duty on the court to give reasons for not doing so. It also extended the range of injuries eligible for compensation. These new requirements mean that if the court fails to make a compensation order it must furnish reasons.

Figures for the use of compensation orders suggest that the need for the criminal justice system to recognize and respond to the harms suffered by victims has firmly established itself in the minds of the courts. In 1994, 59 per cent of offenders sentenced in magistrates' courts for offences of violence, 32 per cent for burglary, 46 per cent for robbery, 38 per cent for fraud and forgery, and 56 per cent for criminal damage were ordered to pay compensation (Barclay, 1995: 16). Overall, 22 per cent of those sentenced for indictable offences in magistrates' courts were ordered to pay compensation. In Crown Courts the figure was much lower: only 9 per cent of those sentenced (partly due to the fact that compensation orders are not normally combined with custodial sentences). In 23 per cent of offences of violence, 6 per cent of burglary, 14 per cent of fraud and forgery, and 18 per cent of criminal damage a compensation order was made. This said, difficulties remain in determining what constitute reasonable grounds for failing to make an order. Where an order is made, problems arise in determining the degree of harm caused and, therefore, the level of compensation payable. In total, in 1994 97,000 compensation orders were made to a total value of £28 million (Home Office 1996a: 34). Around 80 per cent of compensation orders are paid in full within twelve months, not least because the courts have wide powers to enforce payment, including ultimately imprisonment. Nonetheless, the government is examining ways of improving the effectiveness of enforcement procedures.

The 1991 Criminal Justice Act contained a number of provisions which directly or indirectly fostered an even greater role for compensation. The maximum sum to be ordered by magistrates' courts was increased from £2,000 to £5,000 per offence so allowing for a much higher total sum to be awarded and, incidentally, encouraging the retention of a larger number of cases by magistrates' courts (Wasik and Taylor, 1991). Where offenders are social security claimants, payment of compensation can be deducted at source from income support. The attachment of compensation orders to suspended sentences is encouraged. Unhappily, the 1991 Act did not address the intended relationship between its primary commitment to just deserts (proportionality) and these significant moves toward reparative goals (Zedner, 1994: 230). The possibility of developing conceptions of crime-seriousness based on the assessment of harm to identifiable victims may provide a partial solution but as yet it is no more than a matter for academic debate (von Hirsch and Jareborg, 1991).

The problems entailed in reorientating the criminal justice system towards the victim in this way have not passed unobserved (Ashworth, 1986 and 1991; Duff, 1988; Miers, 1992). Objections to reparation focus primarily upon the argument that it has no penal character and that to secure reinstatement to the victim is no more than the enforcement of a civil liability. Reparation thus ignores the broader social dimension of crime: that it is not only the victim but also society that has been wronged. More pragmatically, it may lack the deterrent or punitive impact necessary to control crime. Moreover, to make reparation the sole aim of criminal justice would be effectively to decriminalize the mass of 'victimless' offences. Finally, Ashworth has argued that a reparative approach, by focusing on harm, fails to take sufficient account of the offender's culpability (Ashworth, 1986: 97).

Fundamental questions remain unresolved: should compensation be welcomed as a move towards a reparative system of criminal justice which seeks to place the victim on a equal footing with the offender? Or should reparation remain merely ancillary to the 'proper purpose' of punishment? How far are developments regarding compensation based on a coherent view of the rights and responsibilities of victim, offenders, and the state? Is it possible that victims' claims to justice have been overstated in recent years? And what are the implications of reparative models of justice for the mass of 'victimless' crimes?

CONCLUSION

Victims now attract an unprecedented level of interest, both as a subject of criminological enquiry and focus of criminal justice policy. Far from being simply a compartmentalized topic, victim research has impacted upon every aspect of criminological thinking and profoundly altered our picture of crime by uncovering a vast array of hidden offences, many against the most vulnerable members of society. Political pressure, too, has raised the victim's profile, ensuring recognition of victim needs and the importance of victim services. It has vastly expanded the role of compensation, provision of services, and information, and has allowed victims' interests to inform key decisions in the criminal justice process. At a time when the impulse to punish dominates, it remains doubtful whether reorientation towards the victim will in fact foster reintegrative or reparative ends. The danger is that concern for the victim may be used to justify the pursuit of punitivism in their name and the promotion of victims' interests over those of the offender.

Selected Further Reading

On the development of victimology from its early origins to the present day see Walklate (1989) *Victimology*, or Mawby and Walklate (1994) *Critical Victimology*. A good overview of the crime survey in all its forms is provided in Koffman (1996) *Crime Surveys and Victims of Crime*, whilst Mirrlees-Black *et al.* (1996) *The 1996 British Crime Survey* gives the latest findings from the BCS. A good survey of the literature on fear of crime and its impact is Hale (1996) 'Fear of Crime: A Review of the Literature' in the *International Review of Victimology*. For discussion of the impact of victimization and the needs of victims, the classic work is Shapland *et al.* (1985), *Victims and the Criminal Justice System*, which spawned later studies such as those by Maguire and Corbett (1987) and Morgan and Zedner (1992). On the development of services into a victim's movement see Rock (1990), *Helping Victims of Crime: The Home Office and the Rise of Victim Support in England and Wales*. The role of the victim in the criminal justice system is an area of lively debate. Classic texts are Barnett (1977), 'Restitution: A New Paradigm of Criminal Justice' in *Ethics* and Christie (1977), 'Conflicts as Property' in the *British Journal of Criminology*. More recent contributions include Wright, (1991) *Justice for Victims and Offenders*; Maguire (1991), 'The Needs and Rights of Victims of Crime', in Tonry (ed.), *Crime and Justice*; Joutsen (1994), 'Victim Participation in Proceedings and Sentencing in Europe' in the *International Review of Victimology*; and Zedner (1994), 'Reparation and Retribution: Are They Reconcilable?' in the *Modern Law Review*. Finally, two essential documents on the place of victims within the system are Victim Support (1995), *The Rights of Victims of Crime* and Home Office (1996), *Victim's Charter*.

REFERENCES

ADLER, Z. (1988), 'Prosecuting Child Sexual Abuse: A Challenge to the Status Quo', in M. Maguire and J. Pointing, eds., *Victims of Crime: A New Deal?* 138–46. Milton Keynes: Open University Press.

AMIR, M. (1971), *Patterns of Forcible Rape*. Chicago, Ill: University of Chicago Press.

ANDERSON, S., GROVE SMITH, C., KINSEY, R., and WOOD, J. (1990), *The Edinburgh Crime Survey: First Report*. Edinburgh: Scottish Office.

ANNA T. (1988), 'Feminist Responses to Sexual Abuse: The Work of the Birmingham Rape Crisis Centre', M. Maguire and J. Pointing, eds., *Victims of Crime: A New Deal?* Milton Keynes: Open University Press.

ANTTILA, I. (1974), 'Victimology: a New Territory in Criminology', *Scandinavian Studies in Criminology*, 5: 3–7.

ASHWORTH, A. (1986), 'Punishment and Compensation: Victims, Offenders and the State', *Oxford Journal of Legal Studies*, 6: 86–122.

—— (1992), *Sentencing and Criminal Justice*. London: Weidenfeld and Nicolson.

—— (1993), 'Victim Impact Statements and Sentencing', *Criminal Law Review*, 498–509.

BARCLAY, G., ed. (1991), *A Digest of Information on the Criminal Justice System*. London: Home Office.

—— ed. (1995), *A Digest of Information on the Criminal Justice System No. 3*. London: Home Office.

BARNETT, R. E. (1977), 'Restitution: A New Paradigm of Criminal Justice', *Ethics*, 87: 279–301.

BENNETT, T. (1987), *An Evaluation of Two Neighbourhood Watch Schemes in London*. Cambridge: Cambridge University Press.

BINNEY, V., HARKELL, G., and NIXON, J. (1985), 'Refuges and Housing for Battered Women', in J. Pahl, ed., *Private Violence and Public Policy*. London: Routledge and Kegan Paul.

BLACK, D., and KAPLAN, T. (1988), 'Father Kills Mother: Issues and Problems Encountered by a Child Psychiatric Team', *British Journal of Psychiatry*, 153: 624–30.

BOX, S., (1983), *Power, Crime and Mystification*. London: Routledge.

—— HALE, C., and ANDREWS, G. (1988), 'Explaining Fear of Crime', *British Journal of Criminology*, 28, no. 3: 340–56.

British Journal of Criminology (1995), 'Symposium on Repeat Victimization', 35, no. 3.

BURGESS, A. W., and HOLSTROM, L. L. (1974), *Rape: Victims of Crisis*. Bowie, Md.: Brady.

CHAMBERS, G., and MILLAR, A. (1983), *Investigating Sexual Assault*. Edinburgh: HMSO.

—— and TOMBS, J. (1984), *The British Crime Survey Scotland*. Edinburgh: Scottish Office.

CHOUDRY, S. (1996), 'Pakistani Women's Experience of Domestic Violence in Great Britain', *HORS Research Findings No. 43*. London: HMSO.

CHRISTIE, N. (1977), 'Conflicts as Property', *British Journal of Criminology*, 17: 1–15.

CLARKE, A. H., and LEWIS, M. J. (1982), 'Fear of Crime Among the Elderly', *British Journal of Criminology*, 22, no. 1: 49–62.

COMMISSION FOR RACIAL EQUALITY (1988), *Learning in Terror: A Survey of Racial Harassment in Schools and Colleges*. London: Commission for Racial Equality.

COOPER, J., and POMEYIE, J. (1988), 'Racial Attacks and Racial Harassment: Lessons from a Local Project', M. Maguire and J. Pointing, eds., *Victims of Crime: A New Deal?* Milton Keynes: Open University Press.

CORBETT, C., and HOBDELL, K. (1988), 'Volunteer-based Services to Rape Victims: Some Recent Developments', M. Maguire and J. Pointing, eds., *Victims of Crime: A New Deal?* Milton Keynes: Open University Press.

CRAWFORD, A., JONES, T., WOODHOUSE, T., and YOUNG, J. (1990), *Second Islington Crime Survey*. Middlesex: Middlesex Polytechnic.

—— —— —— and —— (1986), 'The Ideal Victim', in E. A. Fattah, ed., *From Crime Policy to Victim Policy*. London: Macmillan.

CROWN PROSECUTION SERVICE (1993), *Statement on the Treatment of Victims and Witnesses*. London: HMSO.

DAVIS, G. (1992), *Making Amends: Mediation and Reparation in Criminal Justice*. London: Routledge.

—— BOUCHERAT, J., and WATSON, D. (1987), *A Preliminary Study of Victim Offender Mediation and Reparation Schemes in England and Wales, Home Office RPU Paper 42*. London: HMSO.

DIGNAN, J., and CAVADINO, M. (1996), 'Towards a Framework for Conceptualising and Evaluating Models of Criminal Justice from a Victim's Perspective', *International Review of Victimology*, 4: 153–82.

DOBASH, R., and DOBASH, R. (1979), *Violence against Wives: A Case Against Patriarchy*. New York: Open Books.

—— (1984), 'The Nature and Antecedents of Violent Events', *British Journal of Criminology*, 24: 269–84.

—— (1992), *Women, Violence and Social Change*. London: Routledge.

DUFF, P. (1987), 'Criminal Injuries Compensation and "Violent" Crime', *Criminal Law Review*, 219–30.

—— (1988), 'The "Victim Movement" and Legal Reform', in M. Maguire and J. Pointing, eds., *Victims of Crime: A New Deal?* Milton Keynes: Open University Press.

ELLINGWORTH, D., FARRELL, G., and PEASE, K. (1995), 'A Victim is a Victim is a Victim?', *British Journal of Criminology*, 35, no. 3: 360–5.

ENNIS, P. H. (1967), *Criminal Victimization in the United States: A Report of a National Survey*. Washington, DC: US Department of Justice.

EREZ, E. (1994), 'Victim Participation in Sentencing: And the Debate Goes On . . . ', *International Review of Victimology*, 3: 17–32.

FATTAH, E. A. (1979), 'Some Recent Theoretical Developments in Victimology', *Victimology*, 4, 2: 198–213.

—— ed. (1986), *From Crime Policy to Victim Policy*. London: Macmillan.

—— (1989), 'Victims and Victimology: The Facts and the Rhetoric', *International Review of Victimology*, 1: 43–66.

—— (1991), *Understanding Criminal Victimization*. Scarborough, Ontario: Prentice-Hall.

FENWICK, H. (1995), 'Rights of Victims in the Criminal Justice System', *Criminal Law Review*, 843–53.

FINKELHOR, D. (1979), *Sexually Victimized Children*. New York: Free Press.

—— (1986), *A Sourcebook on Child Sexual Abuse*. New York: Sage.

FITZGERALD, M., and HALE, C. (1996), 'Ethnic Minorities Victimisation and Racial Harassment', *HO Research Study*. London: HMSO.

GARAFALO, J. (1979), 'Victimization and the Fear of Crime', *Journal of Research in Crime and Delinquency*, 16: 80–97.

GENN, H. (1988), 'Multiple Victimization', in M. Maguire and J. Pointing, eds., *Victims of Crime: A New Deal?* Milton Keynes: Open University Press.

GOTTFREDSON, M. R. (1984), *Victims of Crime: The Dimensions of Risk*. HORS No. 81. London: HMSO.

—— (1986), 'Substantive Contributions of Victimization Surveys', *Crime and Justice*, 7: 251–87.

HALE, C. (1996), 'Fear of Crime: A Review of the Literature', *International Review of Victimology*, 4: 79–150.

HALL, R. (1985), *Ask Any Woman*. Bristol: Falling Wall Press.

HANMER, J., and SAUNDERS, S. (1984), *Well Founded Fear*. London: Hutchison.

HINDELANG, M., GOTTFREDSON, M. R., and GARAFALO, J. (1978), *Victims of Personal*

Crime: An Empirical Foundation for a Theory of Personal Victimization. Cambridge, Mass.: Ballinger.

HOLTOM, C., and RAYNOR, P. (1988), 'Origins of Victims Support Philosophy and Practice', in M. Maguire and J. Pointing, eds., *Victims of Crime: A New Deal?* Milton Keynes: Open University Press.

HOME OFFICE (1990), *Victim's Charter: A Statement of the Rights of Victims.* London: HMSO.

—— (1993), *Compensating Victims of Violent Crime.* London: HMSO.

—— (1996*a*), *Protecting the Public: The Government's Strategy on Crime in England and Wales.* London: HMSO.

—— (1996*b*), *Victim's Charter.* London: HMSO.

HOUGH, M. (1995), 'Anxiety about Crime: Findings from the 1994 British Crime Survey', *HORS Research Findings No. 25.* London: HMSO.

—— and MAYHEW, P. (1983), *The British Crime Survey: First Report.* London: HMSO.

—— (1985), *Taking Account of Crime: Key Findings from the Second British Crime Survey.* London: HMSO.

—— and MOXON, D. (1985), 'Dealing with Offenders: Popular Opinion and the View of Victims', *The Howard Journal*, 24: 160–75.

JONES, D., Pickett, J., OATES, M. R., and BARBOR, P. (1987), *Understanding Child Abuse.* Basingstoke: Macmillan Education.

JONES, R. L. (1994), 'Victims of Crime in France', *Justice of the Peace*, 795–6.

JONES, T., MACLEAN, B., and YOUNG, J. (1986), *The Islington Crime Survey.* Aldershot: Gower.

JOUTSEN, M. (1987), *The Role of the Victim of Crime in European Criminal Justice Systems: A Crossnational Study of the Role of the Victim.* Helsinki: Heuni.

—— (1994), 'Victim Participation in Proceedings and Sentencing in Europe', *International Review of Victimology*, 3: 57–67.

KAISER, G., KURY, H., and ALBRECHT, H.-J. (1991), *Victims and Criminal Justice: Victimological Research: Stocktaking and Prospects.* Freiburg: Max Planck Institute.

KELLY, L. (1988), *Surviving Sexual Violence.* Oxford: Polity Press.

KINSEY, R. (1984), *Merseyside Crime Survey: First Report.* Liverpool: Merseyside County Council.

—— (1985), *Merseyside Crime and Police Surveys: Final Report.* Liverpool: Merseyside County Council.

KOFFMAN, L. (1996), *Crime Surveys and Victims of Crime.* Cardiff: University of Wales Press.

KURY, H., KAISER, M., and TESKE, R. (1994), 'The Position of the Victim in Criminal Procedure—Results of a German Study', *International Review of Victimology*, 3: 69–81.

LAUNAY, G. (1985), 'Bringing Victims and Offenders Together: A Comparison of Two Models', *The Howard Journal*, 24, 3: 200–12.

LEVI, M., and PITHOUSE, A. (1988), *The Victims of Fraud*, Report of the Economic and Social Research Council. London: ESRC.

—— (1992), 'The Victims of Fraud', in D. Downes, ed., *Unravelling Criminal Justice.* London: Macmillan.

—— (1997), *Victims of White-Collar Crime.* Oxford: Oxford University Press.

LURIGIO, A. J. (1987), 'Are All Victims Alike? The Adverse, Generalized, and Differential Impact of Crime', *Crime and Delinquency*, 33: 452–67.

—— SKOGAN, W. G., and DAVIS, R. C., eds. (1997), *Victims of Crime.* London: Sage.

MAGUIRE, M. (1980), 'The Impact of Burglary upon Victims', *British Journal of Criminology*, 20, no. 3: 261–75.

—— (1982), *Burglary in a Dwelling.* London: Heinemann.

—— (1985), 'Victims' Needs and Victims' Services', *Victimology*, 10: 539–59.

—— (1991), 'The Needs and Rights of Victims of Crime', in M. Tonry, ed., *Crime and Justice: A Review of Research*, 14: 363–433. Chicago, Ill.: Chicago University Press.

—— and CORBETT, C. (1987), *The Effects of Crime and the Work of Victim Support Schemes.* Aldershot: Gower.

MARSHALL, T. (1984), *Reparation, Conciliation and Mediation.* London: HMSO.

—— (1991), 'Victim–Offender Mediation', *HORS Research Bulletin No. 30*: 9–15. London: HMSO.

MAWBY, R. I., 'Victim's Needs or Victim's Rights: Alternative Approaches to Policy-making', in M. Maguire and J. Pointing, eds., *Victims of Crime: A New Deal?* Milton Keynes: Open University Press.

—— and GILL, M. L. (1987), *Crime Victims: Needs, Services, and the Voluntary Sector.* London: Tavistock.

—— and WALKLATE, S. (1994), *Critical Victimology.* London: Sage.

MAYHEW, P., and AYE MAUNG, N. (1992), 'Surveying Crime: Findings from the 1992 British Crime Survey', *HORS Research Findings No. 2.* London: HMSO.

—— and HOUGH, M. (1983), 'Note: The British

Crime Survey', *British Journal of Criminology*, 23: 394–5.

—— (1993), *The 1992 British Crime Survey*. London: HMSO.

—— ELLIOT, D., and DOWDS, L. (1989), *The 1988 British Crime Survey*. London: HMSO.

—— MIRRLEES-BLACK, C., and AYE MAUNG, N. 'Trends in Crime: Findings from the 1994 British Crime Survey' *HORS Research Findings No. 14*. London: HMSO.

MAXFIELD, M. G. (1984), *Fear of Crime in England and Wales*, HORS 78. London: HMSO.

—— (1988), *Explaining Fear of Crime: Evidence from the 1984 British Crime Survey*, HORPU Paper No. 43. London: HMSO.

MENDELSOHN, B. (1956), 'Une nouvelle branche de la science bio-psycho-sociale: Victimologie', *Revue internationale de criminologie et de police technique*, 10–31.

METROPOLITAN POLICE and BEXLEY SOCIAL SERVICES (1987), *Child Sexual Abuse: Joint Investigative Programme: Final Report*. London: HMSO.

MIERS, D. (1989a), 'Positivist Victimology: A Critique,' *International Review of Victimology*, 1: 3–22.

—— (1989b), 'The Criminal Justice Act 1988: The Compensation Provisions', *Criminal Law Review*, 32–42.

—— (1991), *Compensation for Criminal Injuries*. London: Butterworths.

—— (1992), 'The Responsibilities and the Rights of Victims of Crime', *Modern Law Review*, 55, no. 4: 482–505.

MIRRLEES-BLACK, C., MAYHEW, P., and PERCY, A. (1996), *The 1996 British Crime Survey*. London: HMSO.

MORGAN, J., and ZEDNER, L. (1992a), *Child Victims: Crime, Impact, and Criminal Justice*. Oxford: Oxford University Press.

—— (1992b), 'The Victim's Charter: A New Deal for Child Victims?', *The Howard Journal*, 294–307.

MORRIS, A. (1987), *Women, Crime and Criminal Justice*. Oxford: Blackwell.

NATIONAL ASSOCIATION OF VICTIM SUPPORT SCHEMES (1988), *The Victim in Court*. London: NAVSS.

NATIONAL BOARD FOR CRIME PREVENTION (1994), *Wise after the Event: Tackling Repeat Victimisation*. London: Home Office.

NEWBURN, T. (1989), *The Settlement of Claims at the Criminal Injuries Compensation Board*, HORS No. 112. London: HMSO.

—— (1994), 'The Long-term Needs of Victims of Crime: A Review of the Literature', *HORPU Paper No. 80*. London: HMSO.

—— and MERRY, S. (1990), *Keeping in Touch: Police–Victim Communication in Areas*, HORS No. 116. London: HMSO.

PAIN, R. H. (1995), 'Elderly Women and Fear of Violent Crime: The Least Likely Victims?', *British Journal of Criminology*, 35, no. 4: 584–98.

PARLIAMENTARY ALL PARTY PENAL AFFAIRS GROUP (1996), *Increasing the Rights of Victims of Crime*. London: Parliamentary Paper.

PIZZEY, E. (1974), *Scream Quietly or the Neighbours Will Hear*. London: IF Books.

PYNOOS, R. S., and ETH, S. (1984), 'The Child Witness to Homicide', *Journal of Social Issues*, 40, no. 2: 87–108.

RADFORD, J. (1987), 'Policing Male Violence', in J. Hanmer and M. Maynard, eds., *Women, Violence and Social Control*. London: Macmillan.

REEVES, H. (1984), 'The Victim and Reparation', *Probation Journal*, 31: 136–9.

REISS, ALBERT J. (1967), *Studies in Crime and Law Enforcement in Major Metropolitan Areas*. Washington, DC: US Department of Justice.

—— (1986), 'Official Statistics and Survey Statistics', in E. Fattah, *From Crime Policy to Victim Policy*. London: Macmillan.

RESICK, P. A. (1987), 'Psychological Effects of Victimization: Implications for the Criminal Justice System', *Crime and Delinquency*, 33, no. 4: 468–78.

ROCK, P. (1986), *A View from the Shadows*. Oxford: Oxford University Press.

—— (1988), 'The Present State of Criminology in Britain', *British Journal of Criminology*, 28, 2: 188–99.

—— (1990), *Helping Victims of Crime: The Home Office and the Rise of Victim Support in England and Wales*. Oxford: Oxford University Press.

—— (1991), 'The Victim in Court Project at the Crown Court at Wood Green', *The Howard Journal of Criminal Justice*, 30, 4: 301–10.

ROYAL COMMISSION ON CRIMINAL JUSTICE (1993), *Report*. London: HMSO.

SHAPLAND, J. (1984), 'Victims, The Criminal Justice System and Compensation', *British Journal of Criminology*, 24, 2: 131–49.

—— WILLMORE, J., and DUFF, P. (1985), *Victims and the Criminal Justice System*. Aldershot: Gower.

SKOGAN, W. G. (1986a), 'The Fear of Crime and its Behavioural Implications', in E. Fattah, ed., *From Crime Policy to Victim Policy*. London: Macmillan.

—— (1986b), 'The Impact of Victimization on Fear', *Crime and Delinquency*, 33: 135–54.

SMITH, D., BLAGG, H., and DERRICOURT, N. (1988), 'Mediation in South Yorkshire', *British Journal of Criminology*, 28, 3: 378–95.

SMITH, L. J. (1989*a*), *Concerns about Rape*, HORS No. 106. London: HMSO.

—— (1989*b*), *Domestic Violence: An Overview of the Literature*, HORS No. 107. London: HMSO.

SOOTHILL, K., and SOOTHILL, D. (1993), 'Prosecuting the Victim? A Study of the Reporting of Barristers' Comments in Rape Cases', *Howard Journal of Criminal Justice*, 32, no. 1: 12–24.

—— and WALBY, S. (1991), *Sex Crime in the News*. London: Routledge.

SPARKS, R., GENN, H., and DODD, D. J. (1977), *Surveying Victims*. London: Wiley.

SPENCER, J. (1990), *Children's Evidence in Legal Proceedings: An International Perspective*. Cambridge: University of Cambridge, Faculty of Law.

STANKO, E. A. (1985), *Intimate Intrusions*. London: Routledge and Kegan Paul.

—— (1988), 'Hidden Violence Against Women', in M. Maguire and J. Pointing, eds., *Victims of Crime: A New Deal?* Milton Keynes: Open University Press.

—— and HOBDELL, K. (1993), 'Assault on Men: Masculinity and Male Victimization', *British Journal of Criminology*, 33, no. 3: 400–15.

TEMKIN, J. (1987), *Rape and the Legal Process*. London: Sweet & Maxwell.

TRICKETT, A., ELLINGWORTH, D., HOPE, T., and PEASE, K. (1995), 'Crime Victimization in the Eighties', *British Journal of Criminology*, 35, no. 3: 343–59.

VAN DIJK, J. (1988), 'Ideological Trends within the Victims Movement: An International Perspective', in M. Maguire and J. Pointing, eds., *Victims of Crime: A New Deal?* Milton Keynes: Open University Press.

—— MAYHEW, P., and KILLIAS, M. (1990), *Experiences of Crime Across the World: Key Findings of the 1989 International Crime Survey*. Arnhem: Kluwer.

VICTIM SUPPORT, (1991), *Supporting Families of Murder Victims*. London: Victim Support.

—— (1993), *Compensation for Victims of Crime*. London: Victim Support.

—— (1995), *The Rights of Victims of Crime*. London: Victim Support.

VON HENTIG, H. (1948), *The Criminal and his Victim*. New Haven, Conn.: Yale University Press.

VON HIRSCH, A. and JAREBORG, N. (1991), 'Gauging Criminal Harm: A Living-Standard Analysis', *Oxford Journal of Legal Studies*, 11, 1: 1–38.

WALKLATE, S. (1989), *Victimology*. London: Unwin Hyman.

—— (1990), 'Researching Victims of Crime: Critical Victimology', *Social Justice*, 17, 2: 25–42.

WASIK, M., and TAYLOR, R. D. (1991), *Blackstone's Guide to the Criminal Justice Act 1991*. Oxford: Blackstone Press.

WERTHAM, F. (1949), *The Show of Violence*. New York: Vintage.

WOLFGANG, M. (1959), *Patterns in Criminal Homicide*. Philadelphia, Penn.: University of Pennsylvania Press.

WRIGHT, M. (1982), *Making Good*. London: Burnett.

—— (1991), *Justice for Victims and Offenders*. Buckingham: Open University Press.

—— (1995), 'Victims, Mediation and Criminal Justice', *Criminal Law Review*, 187–99.

YOUNG, J. (1988), 'Risk of Crime and Fear of Crime: A Realist Critique of Survey-based Assumptions', in M. Maguire and J. Pointing, eds., *Victims of Crime: A New Deal?* Milton Keynes: Open University Press.

ZEDNER, L. (1992), 'Sexual Offences', in S. Casale and E. Stockdale, eds., *Criminal Justice Under Stress*. London: Blackstone.

—— (1994), 'Reparation and Retribution: Are They Reconcilable?', *Modern Law Review*, 57: 228–50.

—— (1996), 'Reparation in Criminal Law', in A. Eser and S. Walther, eds., *Wiedergutmachung im Kriminalrecht: Internationale Perspektiven*, 109–227. Freiburg: Max Planck Institute.

19

Youth, Crime, and Justice

Tim Newburn

'Youth' is an elastic concept. It means different things, at different times, and in different places. This chapter is about those young people described, often in a very approximate manner, as teenagers, adolescents, or juveniles. More particularly, the focus of the chapter is upon those forms of anti-social behaviour often associated with juveniles; ranging from low-level forms of misbehaviour to more serious criminal offences.[1] The chapter is divided into three linked, though quite distinct, sections. The first looks at the different ways in which youthful deviance (whether or criminal or not) has been viewed and theorized. By contrast the second substantive section focuses more directly on empirical data on juvenile crime. Finally, the third section looks at the formal system for dealing with juvenile crime in England and Wales.[2]

The three sections of the chapter are organized around a series of inter-locking issues. The first part explores images of youth. It begins by looking at the emergence of our modern understanding of adolescence and of juvenile delinquency, and moves on to consider both the changing social circumstances of young people in post-war Britain and the ways in which youth cultures and subcultures have developed and been understood during this period. The study and analysis of subcultural styles, though providing significant insights into the changing meanings of youth and illustrating the low-level normality of much 'delinquency', provides only a very limited picture of juvenile crime. The second substantive section, therefore, looks at how much and what type of crime is committed by juveniles, and examines what we know about how this has changed. The section focuses on differences in offending patterns by young males and females, and by youth of different ethnic origins, looks at drug use by young people, and at the victimization of young people. It ends by looking at recent trends in levels of recorded juvenile crime and considers the relation-ship between them and changing practices within the criminal justice system. The final section in the chapter considers how the formal juvenile justice

I am grateful to Rob Allen, John Graham, Ann Hagell, Trevor Jones, Mike Maguire, and especially to Rod Morgan for commenting on initial drafts of this chapter.

[1] In this context 'juvenile' is legally defined as those people coming within the youth court age range, i.e. 10 and under 18.

[2] There is not the space here to discuss the very different systems that operate in Northern Ireland and Scotland. A full description of the philosophy and practice of the latter is contained in: A. Kelly (1996), *Introduction to the Scottish Children's Panel*. Winchester: Waterside Press.

system developed and, in particular, how it has changed in recent years. Rarely now does a month go by without a new initiative being announced for dealing with young offenders or for 'tackling' youth crime. Responses to juvenile crime, however, are rarely straightforward, for they are influenced not only by the view that such crime is particularly worrisome and problematic, but also by the belief that young people need to be treated differently from adults and should therefore be afforded special protection. This section considers the ways in which the philosophy and practice of juvenile justice have altered during the course of the last century, and what the major influences on such changes have been.

IMAGES AND THEORIES OF 'YOUTH' AND DEVIANCE

Geoffrey Pearson (1983, 1989, 1994) has repeatedly pointed out that all too often academic writing about the problems of youthful misbehaviour and of youth crime is ahistorical in character. He has been able to chart generalized complaints about 'juvenile delinquency' since at least pre-industrial seventeenth century 'Merrie' England. More distinctively 'modern' forms of complaint about juveniles began to appear during the urban and industrial revolutions of the early nineteenth century. Indeed, although youth cultures in Britain are generally thought of as a post-war phenomenon, they have been observable for far longer. The unhelpful, historical amnesia which tends to characterize the youth question means that 'youth cultures and youth crime assume the appearance of ever-increasing outrage and perpetual novelty' (Pearson, 1994: 1168). However, just as we must guard against the assumption that the problems of youth are a peculiarly post-war phenomenon so, having discovered parallels for our modern concerns as far back as the seventeenth century, we must not fall into the trap of thinking that it was ever thus. Both continuity and change are visible.

The Discovery of Adolescence

Below the age of 10 no child may be guilty of a criminal offence. Between the ages of 10 and 18, juvenile offenders are dealt with in what is now referred to as the 'youth court', distinguishable in style and approach from adult magistrates' courts which, together with the Crown Court, deal with offenders aged 18 or older. This system reflects, in crude terms, the distinctions made between three life stages: childhood, adolescence, and adulthood. However, just as the system itself is the product of a number of important historical forces, so the categories of childhood, adolescence, and adulthood are socially constructed and have their own history. The French historian Philippe Aries has argued that in the Middle Ages childhood was a considerably foreshortened period: 'Children were mixed with adults as soon as they were considered capable of doing without their mothers or nannies, not long after a tardy weaning (in other words at about the age of seven)' (Aries, 1973: 395). Society was divided by status which, generally speaking, was not age-related. In part this reflected the different demographic structure of society. Life expectancy at this time has been estimated as having been only 32, and almost half of the population would have been aged less than 20 (Stone, 1979). From the seventeenth century onward childhood was progressively extended and increasingly separated from adulthood. In Aries' view, it is only since that time that we have become preoccupied with the physical, moral, and sexual development of young people. As childhood as a separate category evolved, so there developed with it the idea that children were a responsibility—that they required protection—and, moreover, that children were creatures with the potential for good and evil, discipline being required to ensure that the former predominated over the latter (Anderson, 1980).

Furthermore, as these two phases in the life cycle were progressively separated and, through restrictions on work and the formalization of education, the transition between the two was extended, so the opportunity for the development of a further, intermediary phase increased. This we have come to refer to as 'adolescence'. For Aries (1973: 28): 'our society has passed from a period which was ignorant of adolescence to a period in which adolescence is the favourite age. We now want to come to it early and linger in it as long as possible'. Leaving aside the question whether he is right about the popularity of adolescence, it is clearly the case that adolescence has changed considerably during the course of this century and now continues for considerably longer than it did even fifty years ago (Coleman and Hendry, 1990). What brought this about? In part it was to do with the emergence and development of formal education in schools, and, linked with this, significant changes in the family. These changes in family structures were, it is argued, bound up with the development of market capitalism (Shorter, 1976) and the growth of individualism in philosophical, political, and religious thought (Stone, 1979). The end-product was the progressive isolation of the family changing it into the type of private, domestic unit we know today and, through the separation of work from domestic life, its transformation from a unit of production into a unit of consumption.

Though concerns about youth go back considerably further (Pinchbeck and Hewitt, 1969), it was in the nineteenth century that the distinctively modern adolescent started to appear. The Factory Acts limited working hours; compulsory education began to develop from the 1870s—albeit slowly—and urban working-class young people were developing what can perhaps be regarded as the first modern youth subcultures (Davis, 1990), such as the 'scuttlers' and 'peaky blinders' (Humphries, 1981; Pearson, 1993). Institutions were developed for delinquents and for those *at risk* of delinquency—the 'perishing classes'— and it was out of these that the modern juvenile justice system grew.

By the turn of the century, young people in the new cities and manufacturing towns were experiencing considerable economic independence, and leisure time was expanding. It was at this time that heightened concerns about delinquency and hooliganism emerged (Rook, 1899; Booth, 1902). Many aspects of popular culture were subject to 'fearful scrutiny' (Pearson, 1983) and 'a recognizable pattern of complaint was established: that young criminals were getting younger; that they were symptomatic of the breakdown of the family; that young people were becoming precociously independent' (Pearson, 1994: 1167). Adult fears concerned 'penny dreadful' comics, the behaviour of working-class holiday-makers at the seaside, the influence of the music halls and later the cinema, and 'gambling, drinking and the sometimes threatening and violent behaviour of local "roughs"' at football (Williams, 1991).

Perhaps the key representation of youth in the past century has been to see them as a 'problem'—either as its source, or as being 'at risk' (Griffin, 1993). The close association between 'youth' and 'crime' has remained generally undisturbed ever since and, in Pearson's (1983) thesis, it has been paralleled by a continual nostalgic yearning for a lost 'golden age' of tranquillity and calm. Social reproduction is the key in this. The future depends on the successful socialization and control of contemporary youth. Once this has been achieved, then previous generations that were the subject of respectable fears at the time can be viewed and presented in an altogether more favourable light. The continuity of concern about young people arises from such a cycle; the changing ways in which these concerns are articulated reflects the specific socio-economic circumstances of each period, and the differing ways in which 'youth' is conceptualized.

The 'discovery' of 'adolescence' (as understood as a physiological stage triggered by the onset of puberty) is generally associated with the American psychologist G. Stanley Hall. In his model, often referred to as a 'storm and stress' model, adolescence was conceived as a time of 'hormonal turmoil' (Griffin, 1993: 16), in which young people required freedom in order to fulfill their potential and control to instil discipline. Early theories of delinquency, such as that associated with Cyril Burt, owed much to Hall's work and shared elements of its biological determinism. Although theories of delinquency have broadened in their approach during the course of this century, the ways in which adolescence is conceived remain heavily influenced by the 'storm and stress' model. Nonetheless, even Burt's predominantly psychological theory of delinquency recognized the secondary influence of the social and cultural environment. Moreover, it appears that Burt's views were 'not held to be inconsistent with the belief in the causative role of unemployment and poverty' (Bailey, 1987: 15) which held sway in more radical political circles at the time. As a consequence, juvenile crime was generally perceived as resulting from deficient self-control, and control by others, particularly parents. Poor social conditions and inadequate opportunities for constructive use of leisure were also seen as problematic, and the response to the problem of 'delinquency' at this time was primarily via youth movements which sought to improve the leisure activities of working-class or, more particularly, 'rough' working-class, youth. Most of these were voluntary, often attached to churches. This conception of delinquency informed the philosophy and much of the practice of juvenile justice up to the Second World War and beyond.

Most official indicators of the level of juvenile crime suggested that it rose fairly steadily during the 1930s, and rose sharply, though with some ups and downs, during the war. War-time conditions—the black-out, high wages for youth labour, family disruption, the closure of schools and youth clubs—were blamed for much delinquency (Bailey, 1987). Indeed, family disruption or dysfunction is one of the few 'factors' that appears with regularity in much of the theorizing about delinquency, including psychoanalytic approaches (Schoenfeld, 1971), social control theories (Hirschi, 1969), and social learning theories (Feldman, 1977; see also Rock, this volume). With the end of the war and the advent of the welfare state, there was some expectation that crime would return to its pre-war levels. This proved not to be the case, though for the first decade or so the rate of increase in crime was not sharp. This was a time of broad political consensus (generally referred to as Butskellism—see the chapter by Downes and Morgan, this volume) and, after a period in which consumption was held back by rationing and wage-restraint, eventually also a time of optimism and increasing affluence.

Youth in Post-war Britain

The Butskellite programme of social reconstruction was aided and abetted by a vast army of scientists and professionals—planners, researchers, social workers, teachers—whose task was to support the state in its great endeavour. Considerable autonomy and power was often involved and, as will become clear in connection with the role of social workers in juvenile justice, this continued well into the 1960s. Part of this project of reconstruction was the creation and maintenance of a new social order. The causes of disorder were believed to lie in the consequences of the war and in the continuing inequalities of the post-war era, the solutions in successful economic management and the reduction of inequality. Of great concern were the effects of the war on the family and children. If anything, the family became even more central to the understanding of delinquency in the 1950s; such work involving the '"discovery" (and persistent rediscovery)' of the 'problem family' (Clarke, 1980: 73), together with the continuing influence of the work of Cyril Burt and John Bowlby, the ecological work of Mays, and the beginnings of community studies which identified the family as the 'central transmitting agency of social values and behaviour'.

'Youth' in post-war Britain appeared to transcend class. Although the sub-cultural styles that developed were, seemingly, distinctly class-based, there was wide concern over youth as a whole, and the development of phrases such as 'generation gap' gave expression to the feeling prevalent at the time that it was the differences between age groups as opposed to classes that were the more problematic. This received some support in sociological quarters from those who believed that traditional class divisions were being broken down by the affluence of the period (Goldthorpe *et al.*, 1969). Crucially, 'youth' were perceived to be one of the most striking indications of social change. For the moral entrepreneurs of the period, 'youth' was a problem; and 'a cornerstone in the construction of understandings, interpretations and quasi-explanations *about* the period' (Clarke *et al.*, 1976: 9).

The number of known juvenile offenders began to rise substantially from about 1955, as did public concern about youth in general. Young people were beginning to enjoy a degree of autonomy that was significantly greater than that of previous generations, and at the heart of this was their generally increasing affluence (Abrams, 1959; Pinto-Duschinsky, 1970). This led to the growth of increasingly spectacular youth styles based around the conspicuous consumption of 'leisure and pleasure' (Frith, 1983): the most spectacular off-shoot of what became known as 'mass culture' was the development of youth culture.

The first of the major post-war subcultures was the 'Teds'. The appearance of rock'n'roll in Britain lit the touch paper of respectable moral outrage (Gillett, 1983) and the quiff, 'Duck's Arse', long jackets with velvet collars, bootlace ties, drainpipe trousers, and suede shoes defined the style. Moral concern was focused in the main on the sporadic violence at rock'n'roll movies, on the occasional confrontations between rival groups of 'Teds', and on the so-called 'race riots' of the late 1950s. However, concerns about the general behaviour of young people in post-war British society focused on both sexual and criminal behaviour, and images of juvenile delinquency and more general-ized forms of rebellion or resistance were closely intertwined. It was not just violence associated with the 'Teds' therefore, but the blatant sexuality of what Melly (1972: 36) called 'screw and smash' music ('a contemporary incitement to arbitrary fucking and mindless vandalism'), which terrified older gener-ations. Though post-war thinking—influenced by Fabianism and positivism—looked for solutions in increasing prosperity, it seemed clear that 'consensus, affluence and consumerism had produced, not the pacification of worry and anxiety—their dissolution in the flux of money, goods and fashion—but their reverse: a profound, disquieting sense of moral unease' (Hall *et al.*, 1978: 233). The more liberal atmosphere of the 1960s, illustrated in the reform of the laws on obscenity, abortion, theatre censorship, capital punishment, divorce, and licensing, was counterbalanced, at least in part, by moral campaigns to check the 'permissive revolution' (Newburn, 1991).

A succession of white working-class subcultures followed in the wake of the Teds, and appeared with what seemed to be increasing speed. These included mods—of various sorts—whose style was 'sharp but neat and visually under-stated' (Hebdige, 1976: 88) and was broad enough to encompass sharp-suits, parkas, and the seemingly ubiquitous Vespa (Cohen, 1973). In opposition, sometimes literally, always stylistically, were the rockers. Similar to the Teds in that they originated from lower down the social scale than the mods (Barker and Little, 1964), they were unfashionable, unglamourous, and associated with leather, motor bikes, and an aggressive, often violent masculinity (Willis,

1978). Perhaps the most starkly aggressive of all subcultural styles were the skinheads who appeared in the late 1960s. Despite the fact that their appearance on the football terraces in large numbers was relatively brief—they were fairly quickly replaced by suedeheads and other variants on the style—they are lastingly associated with football hooliganism. The skinheads espoused traditional, even reactionary, values and, through their association with football violence and attacks on ethnic minorities and gays, quickly obtained folk devil status. Their racism, defence of territory, opposition to hippy values, their social origins (unskilled working class), and particular construction of style or 'bricolage' (Clarke, 1976*b*)—Doc Marten boots, cropped hair, braces—were interpreted by subcultural theorists as representing 'an attempt to recreate through the "mob" the traditional working class community' (Clarke, 1976*a*: 99).

Such subcultural theory grew out of a more generally functionalist sociology of delinquency whose origins lay in the Chicago School in the 1920s to 1940s. The pioneering work of Shaw and McKay (1942) focused on the spatial distribution of delinquency (levels of truancy and delinquency being found to vary greatly within the city of Chicago). Areas tended to retain high rates of delinquency despite often significant population change. Thrasher (1927) argued that adolescents in down-town Chicago had created a network of gangs with a distinctive culture as a response to the social disorganization of the slum. Following the Wall Street Crash and the Depression, however, it was argued that social disorganization had spread far beyond the inner-city, and from this it was a relatively small step to the suggestion that a form of generational consciousness was developing around a distinguishable youth culture, itself organized around leisure and consumption (Parsons, 1942). Sociology had long seen working-class adolescents' leisure as problematic, and understanding of differences in youth leisure activities, particularly in North American sociology, was closely linked with theories of crime and deviance (Roberts, 1983). Thus *anomie* theory, as articulated by Robert Merton (1938), saw deviance arising out of the 'strain' between culture and social structure. Where opportunity was more circumscribed than cultural ideology suggested, and where legitimate goals often could not be attained through legitimate means, deviant activity would often result. Such strain was felt to impact particularly heavily on the young. The concentration of such pressures resulted in the formation of deviant subcultures. As a variant on this thesis, Albert Cohen (1955) argued that, rather than being the product of strain resulting from thwarted economic opportunity, such subcultures represented an attempted solution to the problems experienced by adolescents in a class-based society. Cohen saw the delinquent subculture as a collective solution to exclusion from achieving middle-class success. The delinquent subculture develops behaviours which are 'negativistic, malicious and non-utilitarian' and committed to 'short run hedonism'. As a result of a process of 'reaction formation' the middle-class value system is inverted by the delinquent subculture. Closer to Merton than perhaps even Cohen was the theory put forward by Cloward and Ohlin (1960). They combined Merton's ideas of blocked social opportunities with Sutherland's (1939) theory of differential association—the particular focus being on why one form of deviance arises rather than another. What links all these subcultural approaches together is the opposition they posit between subcultures and the dominant or mainstream culture. The main critic of this position has been David Matza. He took the view that in some respects the values expressed by delinquents were but a variant of some of the values, such as excitement and toughness, present in the dominant culture (Matza and Sykes, 1961), and that, far from inverting dominant values, delinquents are committed to conventional morality and use 'techniques of neutralization' to justify their actions (Matza and Sykes, 1957).

Though the initial focus of *anomie* theory had been crime and delinquency, by the 1960s it was taking in entire youth cultures—these ranging from the conformist to the delinquent. It was not until the late 1960s that a distinctly British school of subcultural theory emerged. Its distinctiveness lay in taking traditional subcultural theory and locating it within cultural and historical time and place. In part this was a response to the perceived shortcomings of *anomie* theory—its tendency both to 'over-predict' delinquency and to ignore alternative options for adolescents—but also because the American legacy was viewed as being inapplicable to the British context in a number of ways (Downes and Rock, 1982). Downes (1966), in particular, argued that the type of gang culture so central to American theories was all but non-existent in Britain, that historically British social structure had a greater level of class consciousness, as well as a significantly different ethnic composition.

As British subcultural theory developed, so its focus moved gradually away from delinquency and increasingly towards leisure and style (the main exceptions being Patrick, 1973; Parker, 1974; and Gill, 1977). Parker's is a study of criminal subculture in which theft from cars provided a profitable adolescent interlude before the onset of a more respectable adult life or a more serious and long-term criminal career. Both his and Patrick's study—in which the focus was on the machismo of the 'hard man'—brought insights from labelling theory to bear on the study of subcultures. Parker's 'boys' used theft as a means of dealing with some of the problems they faced, dissociating themselves in part from the values of the dominant social order, and, like the delinquents in Downes' study, responded within the physical and material conditions which constrained their range of choice and freedom.

Subcultures emerged not just as a response to the problems of material conditions—their class circumstances, schooling, and so on. They were also taken to represent a symbolic critique of the dominant culture in which their 'style' was read as a form of resistance. Subcultures, at least from the viewpoint of the more radical commentators of the 1970s, were essentially oppositional rather than subordinate. It was this opposition, fundamentally, which gave rise to the kinds of societal reaction that Stan Cohen, utilizing interactionism, labelling theory, and the idea of deviancy amplification, first described as 'moral panics': wherein 'a condition, episode, person or group of persons emerges to become defined as a threat to societal values and interests' (1980: 9).

The most recurrent forms of moral panics in Britain since the war have been those surrounding youthful forms of deviance—from subcultural styles through football hooliganism to drug use. For their members, subcultures suggested solutions to material and socio-cultural problems, albeit that such solutions were symbolic. In a seminal essay on working-class youth culture, Phil Cohen (1972: 23) argued that the latent function of subculture was to:

express and resolve, albeit 'magically', the contradictions which appear in the parent culture. The succession of subcultures which this parent culture generated can thus be considered as variations on a central theme—the contradiction at an ideological level, between traditional working class puritanism and the new hedonism of consumption; at an economic level between being part of the socially mobile elite or the new lumpen proletariat.

The solution, however, is largely expressed through style rather than crime. The style of each subculture involves the creation of identities and images built upon objects appropriated from other cultures and eras. It was at this point that the vocabulary of cultural studies met various strands of the sociology of deviance. Discerning 'the hidden messages inscribed in code on the glossy surfaces of style, to trace them out as maps of meaning' (Hebdige, 1979: 18) became the key task.

Though the bulk of youthful styles in the 1960s were of working-class origin, the last years of the decade also saw the development of a middle-class counter-culture which, associated with both permissiveness and drug use, was guaranteed a hostile reaction from 'respectable' society. Brake (1985) argues that hippy culture in Britain was made up largely of students and ex-students and 'provided a moratorium for its members of approximately five years in which to consider one's identity and relationship to the world' (1985: 95). Drugs and sex were the foci of moral concern, and the late 1960s saw very significant increases in prosecutions for possession of marijuana and a concerted campaign of prosecutions against the underground press. The latter culminated in 1971 in the longest obscenity trial in British legal history, and the conviction of the editors of the magazine, *OZ* (later overturned on appeal), and the subsequent symbolic cutting of their hair to 'standard prison length' (Palmer, 1971; Newburn, 1991).

The dominant focus in British subcultural theory in the 1970s was on white, working-class male culture (Dorn and South, 1982). There were, at least in the earliest years of such writing, few attempts to understand either female delinquency or the styles associated with female subcultures, though the work of Angela McRobbie was both an early and a consistent exception (McRobbie and Garber, 1976; McRobbie, 1980, 1991). According to McRobbie and Garber (1976), because of their position within public and private worlds, girls tend to be pushed to the periphery of social activities and much 'girl culture' becomes a culture of the bedroom rather than the street (see also Frith 1983).

It is this, McRobbie (1980: 40) argues, that most subcultural theorists ignore:

in documenting the temporary flights of the Teds, Mods or Rockers, they fail to show that it is monstrously more difficult for women to escape (even temporarily) and that these symbolic flights have often been at the expense of women (especially mothers) and girls. The lads' . . . peer-group consciousness and pleasure frequently seem to hinge on a collective disregard for women and sexual exploitation of girls.

Subcultural theory had little to offer by way of explanation of the involvement of young women in criminal activity. In the 1980s, however, as the youth cultural scene went quiet, so the sociological students of style moved their focus away from youth and towards sexuality and ethnicity (McRobbie, 1994*a*).

By comparison with the 1960s, the early 1970s were a relatively quiet time on the youth subcultural front, though they did see the blossoming of Afro-Caribbean cultural resistance, in part associated with, and reinforced by, the mugging panic of the mid-1970s (Hall *et al.*, 1978). Up until this point there appears to have been no explicit association between black youth and crime, but, as Benyon (1986) argues, there has been a 'spiral of decline' in relationships between the police and black communities since. The association between black youth and crime became firmly established, and the 'view of the blacks as innately criminal, or at least more criminal than the white neighbours whose deprivation they share, which became "common sense" during the early 1970s, is crucial to the development of new definitions of the black problem and new types of racial language and reasoning' (Gilroy, 1987: 109). In subcultural terms, Hebdige (1987) argues that as the mood of some black British youth became more angry and bitter so the central messages of reggae and of Rastafarianism became increasingly relevant (see Cashmore, 1983).

In the late 1970s reggae also attracted punks 'who wished to give tangible form to their alienation' (Hebdige, 1979: 63). First visible around 1976, punk was visually and verbally violent, but less frequently physically so than was publicly portrayed (Savage, 1996). Moreover, with its links with Malcolm McLaren and Vivienne Westwood's King's Road shop, *Sex*, it incorporated a degree of commercialism which some commentators viewed as distinguishing it from previous, more 'authentic' subcultural styles (though for criticisms of this view see McRobbie, 1994*b*; Thornton, 1995). Punk attempted to undermine 'every relevant discourse' (Hebdige, 1979: 108). It used bin liners, safety pins, PVC, graffiti, ripped clothing, and bondage gear as a counterpoint to conventional dress style; and its music, dancing, band names, song titles, and language (Laing, 1985) provided further shock tactics to reinforce the sought-after outcast status. 'Things were never the same after punk' (McRobbie, 1994*b*: 159) and if hippies were a direct product of the permissive 1960s and early 1970s and punk was, in part, a reaction to hippy romanticism, then youth culture in the 1980s and after was profoundly shaped by the conservatism, economic depression and, more recently, the highly individualized consumerism of the times.

Youth at the *Fin de Siècle*

'Youth' is often both 'signifier' and 'embodiment' of significant social change (Pearson, 1994). Through the late 1970s and into the 1980s, social and economic conditions for many young people became dramatically tougher. The key defining features were unemployment and racism, and it was against this background that African-Caribbean cultural resistance burgeoned and that 'punk' appeared. From the late 1970s onward youth unemployment became a permanent feature of the social landscape: by the mid-1980s less than three-tenths of 16–17-year-olds had full time jobs (Roberts, 1995). In parallel with the precipitous decline in youth employment, especially full-time youth employment, and the withdrawal of entitlement to benefits for most 16–17-year-olds, there was also a significant expansion in the late 1980s of youth training schemes, though these have declined once more, and a massive rise in the numbers 'staying on' in education.[3] The major consequence of these structural changes was that, for those who eventually did find employment, the transition from 'school to work', or from dependent to independent living, was considerably extended. Together with the withdrawal or restriction of benefits (including those toward board and lodgings) the consequence has been to increase the general dependence of young people on their families—assuming there are families that are willing and able to support them.

Simultaneously, however, family patterns have been changing. The marriage rate (for first marriages) halved between 1971 and 1991 and the divorce rate more than doubled (Utting, 1995). Remarriages, where at least one partner is divorced, now account for over one third of all marriages and the rate of cohabitation has increased over the past twenty-five years from 6 per cent of couples before their wedding day to 60 per cent. Lone parenthood is increasingly common. Whereas in the early 1960s approximately one in twenty births occurred outside marriage, the figure was almost one in three by 1992, and the proportion of children brought up in lone parent families rose from 11 to 19 per cent between 1981 and 1992. In addition, it appears that inequality is once again on the increase. This is especially visible in family structures where 'there has been a shift towards double-income families, where both parents work but can spend less time with their children, and lone parenthood, with its associated vulnerabilities and stresses which also reflect on the children' (Joseph Rowntree Foundation, 1995). There is naturally much debate about the consequences of these changes in family structure. The available research evidence, however, suggests that children brought up in disadvantaged families where parental supervision is poor and discipline inconsistent are at greater risk of later offending. The developing gap between 'work rich' and 'work poor' families has meant that at least a proportion of young people face

---

[3] The activity status of 16–17-year-olds illustrates the changes. In 1985, 29 per cent of 16–17-year-olds were in a full-time job and 37 per cent in full-time education. By 1992, the respective figures were 13 per cent and 66 per cent.

considerable difficulties in negotiating the now extended transition into adult life (Wallace, 1987; Jones, 1995). Finally, there is a further, small group about whom relatively little is known. These young people, who are not in education (often having been excluded), training, or work—will disappear from the system altogether. For some this will be temporary; others may be 'permanently lost', and it is around these young people that many concerns about future criminal activity coalesce (Hagell and Newburn, 1994).

There are other recent trends which reinforce the picture of some of the harsher realities of being young in the late twentieth century. These include a significant rise in the 'psychosocial disorders' of youth (Rutter and Smith, 1995a) including: depressive disorders (Fombonne, 1995a), suicide rates (Diekstra et al., 1995), greatly expanded use of alcohol and illegal drugs (Silbereisen et al., 1995), and, though the data are somewhat equivocal, apparent increases in eating disorders (Fombonne, 1995b). In addition, there have been other 'lifestyle' changes such as the development of new patterns of youth leisure activities (which may or may not be acceptable, and may or may not be legal) and significant increases in youth homelessness (Anderson et al., 1993; Carlen, 1996). Explaining such trends is problematic, and Rutter and Smith (1995b: 784) conclude that:

the changing pattern of transitions in adolescence and early adult life may cause risks associated, for example, with a growth of youth culture, possible increasing isolation of adolescents from adults, greater financial dependence on parents that coincides with greater autonomy in other respects, earlier engagement in sexual relationships, a possible increase in psychosocial stressors, and increase in peer group influence and a greater number of breakdowns in cohabiting love relationships.

As the world of work has retreated as a realistic prospect for many so, it is argued, lifestyles dominated by consumption have occupied the foreground. This was reflected in youth culture in the 1980s which 'became more of an advertising medium than ever before; it was notable not for opposition, but for its role in selling everything from Levi 501 jeans to spot cream' (Redhead, 1990: 105). As a consequence much was made of the supposed 'end of youth culture'. Bottoms and Wiles (1994) suggest that one of the consequences of the increasing dominance of consumption is a gradual relocation of sources of trust in late modern society from groups or collectivities—kin, local community, religious group—to individualized relations. Given the importance of collective norms in limiting individual deviant actions, the criminogenic consequences of the relocation of trust are easy to see. Furthermore, they argue, this decline in traditional collectivities has impacted negatively on age-integrated leisure patterns and this, linked to globalization of aspects of youth culture and consumption, is likely both to reinforce age-specific activities and the boundaries between 'youth' and other social groups. Under such circumstances, 'respectable fears' about young people (Pearson, 1983) become exacerbated. The most recent and most consistent of respectable fears about youth concern drugs and drug use (Parker et al., 1995).

The late 1980s and 1990s saw the emergence of dance-based, drug-associated youth cultural styles, to which the acid house subculture and subsequent rave 'movement' or 'scene' were central. With its origins in Chicago House music and Euro-Pop (the Balearic Beat), acid house enjoyed a brief moment of approbation in the media, before its drug connections led to inevitable back-lash. Acid house parties and, more particularly, the use of ecstasy, were the focal point of moral campaigns. Such partying—or 'hedonism in hard times' (Redhead, 1993: 4)—was somewhat in contrast with the drabber youth culture of the late 1970s and early 1980s. Where 'punk had rejected such obvious pleasure a decade before . . . youth hedonism was now back, with a vengeance. A fortnight's holiday in the sun became packed into a single weekend—then the next weekend and the next' (McKay, 1996: 105).

Rave culture inspired considerable moral indignation—at least in the press—and was also subject to increasing legislative attention. Graham Bright MP, a well-known 'moral entrepreneur' associated with previous campaigns such as that against 'video nasties' (Newburn, 1991), introduced a Private Member's Bill further to restrict the holding of 'raves' or large-scale parties. The Entertainments (Increased Penalties) Act 1990 enabled courts to impose fines of up to £20,000 or prison sentences of up to six months for holding illegal parties. This was followed by the Criminal Justice and Public Order Act 1994 which contained provisions for dealing with raves, together with other forms of 'collective trespass' particularly those associated with 'new age travellers'. In late 1996 a Private Member's Bill—the Public Entertainments (Drug Misuse) Bill—was introduced, with Home Office support, which contained provisions giving local authorities powers to close down clubs where there is evidence of the sale and use of drugs. This arguably represents a significantly more repressive set of measures than most previous post-war youth cultures experienced. Moreover, as we will see in a later section of this chapter, this was part and parcel of a more authoritarian approach to juvenile offending and deviance in general.

I suggested towards the beginning of this chapter that one of the key rep-resentations of youth during the course of this century has been to see them as a 'problem'. Indeed, Pearson and others have illustrated the historical durability of such concerns about youth. Nonetheless, a distinctive conception of adolescence emerged in the mid- to late-nineteenth century, as did a more 'modern' concern about delinquency. In post-war Britain there emerged a more colourful or spectacular array of youth subcultures than had been visible before on the national stage. From the 1970s onwards, as structural circumstances changed and, more particularly, youth unemployment rose, youth cultures fragmented. This served further to reinforce the view that adolescence was a problematic period in the life-course, and that adolescents themselves were a problem. Though the specific nature of that problem varies by time and place, deviance, and, more particularly, delinquency or criminal activity have generally been central to it. It is this connection between young people and crime to which we turn next.

YOUNG PEOPLE AND CRIME

Though the activities of young people are both more visible and more closely policed than other age groups (Farrington and Burrows, 1993; Pearson, 1994; Loader, 1996) it is undeniably the case that a significant proportion of all crime is committed by young people (Hirschi and Gottfredson, 1983). This, in tandem with adult fears about youthful deviance, leads to young offenders occupying the 'dubiously privileged position', in changing guises, as society's number one folk devil (Muncie *et al.*, 1995). Though official statistics can only ever provide a crude estimate—low clear-up rates mean that only a minority of offences are ever linked to specific offenders—they nevertheless suggest that at least one quarter of all recorded crime is committed by 10–17-year-olds and that over two fifths is committed by those under 21 (Home Office, 1995*b*). Self-report studies confirm the by now largely accepted point that committing an offence in the teenage years is relatively common. Table 19.1 shows that over half of males and almost one third of females aged between 14 and 25 admit to committing one or more criminal offences at some point in their lives. At least one fifth of men will have a criminal conviction before the age of 20 (Home Office 1995*a*).

The relationship between age and crime has been the subject of considerable criminological analysis, and Smith (1995: 395), echoing Hirschi and Gottfredson, has suggested that 'probably the most important single fact about crime is that it is committed mainly by teenagers and young adults'. The main evidence for this lies in the rate of recorded offending attributed to offenders of particular ages—and this is generally reinforced by data collected from self-report studies. Thus, for example, in 1995 the number of known offenders per 100,000 males was 467 for those aged 10, 1,920 for those aged 12, 6,264 for those aged 15, and 8,376 for those aged 18, at which point the rate declines fairly quickly. Generally speaking the peak age of offending is higher for males than it is for females, currently 18 for males and 15 for females. Official statistics also suggest that the peak age of known male offending has increased; it was 14 years for males in 1971, 15 in 1980, had increased to 18 by 1990 and was still

Table 19.1 Cumulative participation (self-reported) of 14–25-year-olds in offending by sex

Offence group	Males	Females	All
	%	%	%
Property	49	28	39
Violence	28	10	19
Expressive	25	16	21
All offences	55	31	43

Source: Graham and Bowling (1995).

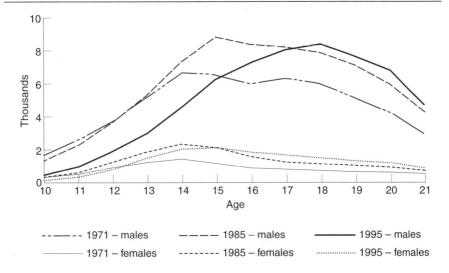

Fig. 19.1: Offenders found guilty or cautioned per 100,000 population by age
Source: *Criminal Statistics.*

18 at the time of the publication of the 1995 *Criminal Statistics* (see Figure 19.1).

The location of the peak age of offending in the mid- to late adolescent years has generally been taken as indicating that a significant proportion of young people will simply 'grow out of crime' (Rutherford, 1992). One recent self-report study (Graham and Bowling, 1995) though largely reinforcing what is already known from other sources about the peak ages of male and female offending, provides new evidence about the prevalence of offending for different age groups. The data show the peak age of offending for males to be 14 for 'expressive property offences', 16 for violent offences, 17 for serious offences, and 20 for drug offences. Among females, the peak age of offending is 15 for property, expressive, and serious offences, 16 for violent offences, and 17 for drug offences. Looking, however, at the proportions of males at different ages who admit to having committed various offences within a one-year period, Graham and Bowling (1995) found that expressive and violent offences were most prevalent among 14–17-year-olds, property offences (excluding fraud and theft from work) among 18–21-year-olds, and theft of motor vehicles among 22–25-year-olds. When fraud and theft from work were included within the property crime category, then 22–25-year-olds had the highest rate of offending. They (Graham and Bowling, 1995: 25) summarize these important findings in the following way:

Among males, the rate of participation in offending does not change dramatically between the ages of 14 and 25, but it does change markedly in character. Expressive behaviour directed against property—such as vandalism and arson—is most common in the mid-teens but all but ceases by the early twenties. Violent behaviour—ranging in seriousness from fighting to wounding—increases during the teenage years then drops off sharply in the twenties. Property offending remains relatively constant throughout this period, but as the most visible forms (such as shoplifting and burglary) decrease during the early twenties, less detectable forms of offending such as fraud and theft from work start to increase. Although most of those starting to commit fraud and theft from work during their late teens had switched from other offences, about 30 per cent were new offenders. For females, with the exception of drug offences, the prevalence of offending of all types drops off sharply after the mid-teens.

The somewhat different pictures of prevalence of offending suggested by self-report data and Criminal Statistics are not merely a product of different policing practices and the different methods by which the data were collected, they also potentially reflect Hindelang *et al.*'s (1979: 1009) claim that self-report instruments 'typically tap a domain of behaviour virtually outside the domain of official data'. Graham and Bowling (1995) suggest the difference is to be explained in part by the switch made by male offenders in their late teens/early twenties from relatively risky forms of property crime to much less visible and therefore detectable forms, and by a general deceleration in their offending. In short, the proportion of the young male population engaged in active offending does not decrease in early adulthood, but the nature of their offending changes as does its frequency.

Gender Ratio in Juvenile Offending

Though it is often youth in general that are viewed with concern, it is generally male youth that are seen as particularly problematic. Official statistics and self-report studies confirm the fact that offending is more widespread among males. The ratio of males to females convicted for all indictable offences by young offenders is 3.3:1.[4] For burglary, criminal damage, and drugs offences, however, the ratio is over 10:1. The relatively low overall ratio reflects the predominance of theft and handling stolen goods as the most common recorded offence type for both males and females. The ratio for the less serious summary offences is actually lower still, though this is largely explained by the inclusion of the offences of prostitution and TV licence evasion within this category.

Three points emerge from the data. First, there are significant differences in the offending ratio in relation to different offence types. Secondly, with the exception of drug offences, there is an overall narrowing of the gap between male and female offending rates. This is a relatively long-term historical trend (considerably longer than indicated by the table) and is also found in many other Western societies (Smith, 1995). Thirdly, despite this narrowing, there remains what appears to be a significant disparity in offending rates between men and women.

---

[4] Unless otherwise stated all statistics referred to are taken from *Criminal Statistics England and Wales, 1995*

Table 19.2 Ratio of male to female juvenile offenders found guilty or cautioned for indictable offences: England and Wales, 1980–1995

	1980	1985	1990	1995
Violence against the person	6.4	4.4	3.3	3.2
Burglary	22.3	21.6	13.8	16.5
Theft/handling stolen goods	5.8	2.8	2.9	2.1
Fraud and forgery	4.0	2.8	2.7	2.3
Criminal damage	15.0	16.0	9.8	10.5
Drug offences	–	–	7.7	11.6

Source: Criminal Statistics.

However, self-report studies suggest that the offending ratio between young men and women is probably considerably less extreme than might be suggested by the conviction statistics (Jensen and Eve, 1976; Hindelang *et al.*, 1979; also, Wilson and Herrnstein, 1985; Graham and Bowling, 1995). Both self-report data and official statistics show the male–female offending ratio to be related to offence seriousness and age. Thus, according to the Home Office self-report study, while the ratio for all offences is only 1.4:1 for 14–17-year-olds, it rises to 11.1:1 for 22–25-year-olds (Graham and Bowling, 1995). As far as seriousness is concerned, while the offending ratio for 14–17-year-old males and females for expressive offences is about 1:1 (that is, according to the self-report study, male and female offending rates appear to be about the same at this age for these offences), for violent offences it is approximately 1.8:1 (though this is still far lower than official statistics would suggest). Although there are important limitations to self-report methods (Box, 1981), nonetheless, they are now treated as reasonable indicators of actual behaviour (West and Farrington, 1977; Farrington, 1989; Hindelang *et al.*, 1981). What then are we to make of the apparently narrowing gap between male and female offending rates? Given the great changes that have taken place in (young) women's lives in recent decades one might expect this to be reflected, in part, in changed patterns of offending (Heidensohn, 1996). However, the possibility ought not to be discounted that part of the change being witnessed lies in the processing or treatment of female offenders by the criminal justice system (Morris and Gelsthorpe, 1981, though see Hedderman and Hough, 1996).

The Nature of Male and Female Offending

The predominance of property crime among those offences committed by young people is confirmed by official statistics. Juveniles, irrespective of age or sex, are most likely to be cautioned or convicted for theft and handling stolen goods. Burglary is the second most common source of cautions and convictions for male juvenile offenders (see Table 19.3).

Table 19.3 Percentage of young offenders found guilty at all courts or cautioned by type of offence, sex, and age group: England and Wales, 1995

	Males		Females	
	Aged 10 and under 14	Aged 14 and under 18	Aged 10 and under 14	Aged 14 and under 18
Violence against the person	8	11	7	12
Sexual offences	1	1	0	0
Burglary	17	16	3	4
Robbery	2	2	0	1
Theft and handling stolen goods	63	48	87	74
Fraud and forgery	1	2	1	3
Criminal damage	6	4	1	1
Drug offences	1	11	0	3
Other	1	5	0	2

Source: Criminal Statistics.

The pattern visible in Table 19.3 has been relatively stable for some time. Thus, for example, over the past ten years theft and handling stolen goods, followed by burglary and then violence against the person have, in that order, remained the most common offences for which male juvenile offenders are cautioned or convicted. The most serious offences are relatively uncommon. Thus, in the fifteen years between 1979 and 1994, 210 young people aged 17 or younger were convicted of murder (and over half of these were 17-year-olds), and a further 220 of manslaughter (Cavadino, 1996). There has, however, been a rise in recorded drugs offences since 1985 and a significant rise in the recorded rate of violence committed by juveniles since 1987. In his analysis of the official statistics, James (1995) shows that the prevalence of recorded violence against the person by juveniles increased slightly among 10–13-year-olds between 1980 and 1987 and declined slightly among 14–16-year-olds during the same period. Thereafter, a dramatic change appears to have taken place—though it is possible that this reflects changes in processing rather than actual behaviour. There was a 52 per cent increase in the recorded rate of violent offending among 10–13-year-olds between 1987 and 1993, and a 29 per cent increase in the rate for 14–16-year-olds in the same period; overall, an increase of approximately two-fifths in the rate of violent offending by juveniles. This may be compared with the prevalence rates for the most common juvenile offence category of theft and handling stolen goods where there was a decrease of almost two-fifths between 1987 and 1993. The juxtaposition of these two trends means that violent offences now account for a much larger proportion of recorded juvenile crime than was the case, for example, a decade ago. As a proportion of the overall number of juvenile cautions and convictions, violence against the person rose from 3 to 4 per cent for 10–13-year-olds between 1980 and 1987 and remained stable at 8 per cent for 14–16-year-olds. By 1993, violence against the person accounted for 9 per cent of cautions or convictions among the younger age category and for 13 per cent among the older age category. This rise is all the more startling, given the fact that, as we shall see, the number of known juvenile offenders declined markedly in the same period.

According to criminal statistics, violence by young females remains relatively rare. In 1980, 1,700 females aged 10–16 were cautioned or convicted for offences of violence against the person, this representing 5.4 per cent of all cautions and convictions for this age group. Since that time, the number of cautions or convictions for violent offences for female juveniles has been rising, and set against a background of the overall decline in the number of known juvenile offenders, violence also represents an increasing proportion of all offences for which young females are found guilty or cautioned. By 1991 2,700 females aged 10–16 were cautioned or convicted for offences of violence against the person, this representing 11.5 per cent of all cautions and convictions for the age group. In terms of participation rates, self-report data suggest that approximately 7 per cent of 14–17-year-old females will admit to having committed a violent offence within the previous year. With the self-reported peak age for such offending being 16 for males and females, the participation rate for violent offences then decreases fairly quickly, being 4 per cent for 18–21-year-olds and less than 1 per cent for 22–25-year-olds. Though the peak age for violent offending is the same for males and females, the participation rates are, predictably, higher for males of all age groups (Graham and Bowling, 1995).

Ethnic Minority Youth and Crime

A full discussion of ethnicity and youth crime is not within the scope of this chapter. However, discussion of such issues is not only important, but has frequently been contentious (cf. Fitzgerald, 1993; Smith, this volume). As was suggested in the first section of this chapter, it was not until the 1970s that there was any explicit association between black youth and crime. The increased concern arose partly as a result of the 'mugging panic' early in the decade, and other signs of poor or deteriorating relationships between the police and black youth. This was reinforced by the release of statistics by the Metropolitan Police suggesting that crime rates were particularly high among African-Caribbean youth in the capital. Other sources of data show black youth to be over-represented at all other stages of the criminal justice process: they are, for example, more likely to be prosecuted than are white youth, who are more likely to be cautioned (Landau and Nathan, 1983); they are more likely to be charged with offences which must be heard in the Crown Court (Audit Commission, 1996); and they are more likely to be remanded in, and sentenced to, custody (Smith, 1994). Much criminological discussion involves attempts to explain this over-representation of black youth in the criminal justice system. The debate revolves around the issue of whether it can be

Table 19.4 Cumulative participation (self-reported) in offending by ethnic origin

	White	Black	Indian	Pakistani	Bangladeshi
Property offences	39	38	25	24	12
Violent offences	19	25	13	18	7
Expressive offences	22	21	12	16	7
All offences	44	43	30	28	13

Source: Graham and Bowling (1995).

explained in part by higher rates of offending among black youth, or whether cumulative discrimination at all stages of the criminal justice process is the key (see Smith, this volume).

Given the now strong popular association between black youth and crime it is perhaps surprising how little rigorous, empirical research has been undertaken on this question. The most recent, and most useful, exception to this is the already mentioned Home Office self-report study, which included a booster sample of 808 young people from ethnic minorities (Graham and Bowling, 1995). The data from the study are striking, for they suggest that, in general, white and African-Caribbean youth have similar rates of participation in offending (see Table 19.4), though these are significantly higher than self-reported participation by South Asian youth. There is nevertheless significant variation between offence types. Thus, young white males are much more likely to be involved in fraud and theft from the workplace, whereas both African-Caribbean and Indian young people are more likely to steal from schools. White and Pakistani males are more like to be involved in vandalism than are African-Caribbean young men. The study also found that self-reported drug use was significantly higher among white youth than among ethnic minorities (see also Leitner *et al.*, 1993). 37 per cent of white young people admitted ever using drugs, only 24 per cent of African-Caribbeans did so, as did 20 per cent of Indian, 14 per cent of Bangladeshi, and 6 per cent of Pakistani young people.

Young People and Drug Use

There have been close associations between youth subcultures and illicit drug use since at least the hippy counter culture of the 1960s (Young, 1971). However, far from being perceived as problematic, 'during the 1960s and 1970s it was fashionable in social science and liberal circles to question whether the prevailing concern about drug use might not be an example of . . . "moral panic"' (Dorn and South, 1987: 2). This all changed in the late 1970s, and the years 1979–81 were the watershed during which 'the heroin habit' really began to take off and when, for the first time, its use became associated with the young unemployed (Pearson, 1987). The number of known addicts trebled between 1979 and 1983, and research in the late 1980s confirmed the impression of a significant spread of heroin use (Parker *et al.*, 1988). Public concern about increasing heroin use was followed by fears of a possible 'crack' epidemic though, in the main, the worst of these fears have not been realized. Research in the 1990s suggests that 'the picture now is one of continuing widespread availability of a great variety of drugs, use being shaped by familiar factors such as local supply, contexts of use, preferred styles of consumption and purpose or intent' (South, 1994: 399). Use is also partly distinguishable according to age. Parker *et al.* (1995) outline three contemporary drug arenas: the longer-term, injecting polydrug scene in which heroin, methadone, tranquilizers, and crack are dominant and which belongs largely to the 20–30 age group; the young adult scene (18–25-year-olds) which is dominated by cannabis and dance drugs (hallucinogens and stimulants); and there is the adolescent drug scene.

Data on the incidence and prevalence of drug use among young people are now available from a number of surveys (*inter alia*, Plant *et al.*, 1985; Balding, 1994; Measham *et al.*, 1994; Mott and Mirrlees-Black, 1995; Miller and Plant, 1996; Ramsay and Percy, 1996). Prevalence for 15–20-year-olds varies between 10 and 35 per cent in the national samples and 5 and 50 per cent in local samples. The surveys show cannabis to be the most popular drug, though use of LSD, amphetamines, and ecstasy has been on the increase since the late 1980s, as has polydrug use (Parker *et al.*, 1995). Drug use and age are clearly linked. Use of illicit drugs is rare in early teenage years, increases sharply in the mid-teens, and is generally shown to peak in the late teens or early twenties (Institute for the Study of Drug Dependence (ISDD), 1994).

The annual surveys conducted by Howard Parker and colleagues between 1991 and 1993 have been most influential (Measham *et al.*, 1994; Parker and Measham, 1994; Parker *et al.*, 1995). Conducted in schools in the North West of England, the surveys provide data on use of illicit drugs among samples of children aged approximately 14 in the first survey and 16 in the third. They have found that 59 per cent of respondents in the first year had been in situations where drugs had been available or offered, this figure rising to 71 per cent in the second survey and 76 per cent in the third year. Lifetime prevalence of drug trying ranged from 36 per cent when respondents were aged 14, to 51 per cent by the time they were 16 years old. The proportions saying they had used one or more illicit drug in the past year or the past month, though smaller, were still sizeable.

Research also shows drug use by young people to be on the increase. Mott and Mirrlees-Black (1995), for instance, note that the percentage of 16–19-year-olds reporting cannabis use more than doubled between 1983 and 1991. The late 1980s and early 1990s witnessed an increase in the use of dance drugs. Though this increase started from a relatively low baseline, by the mid-1990s dance drugs had become an important part of the youth drug scene (Measham *et al.*, 1993; Clements, 1993). This picture is reinforced by Parker *et al.*'s (1995)

Table 19.5 Lifetime prevalence of illicit drug trying

	Year One (1991) (Av. age 14)	Year Two (1992) (Av. age 15)	Year Three (1993) (Av. age 16)
Cannabis	32	42	45
Nitrites	14	22	23
LSD	13	25	24
Solvents	12	13	10
Magic Mushrooms	10	12	10
Amphetamine	10	16	18
MDMA (Ecstasy)	6	7	5
Cocaine	1	4	3
Tranquilisers	1	5	2
Heroin	0	3	1

Source: Parker *et al.* (1995: 14).

research. By the time of their final survey, 45 per cent of respondents admitted to having used cannabis and, in part reflecting the rise of the dance/rave scene, 24 per cent had used LSD, 18 per cent amphetamines, and 5 per cent ecstasy (see Table 19.5). As Shapiro (1997) has put it, the 'unique symbiosis' of key developments within popular music and the catalytic appearance of ecstasy have combined to bring about a significant spread in youthful drug use. Moreover, according to Parker *et al.* (1995), unlike the situation a decade previously, there were no longer any significant differences in the prevalence of illicit drug use by young men and women, though the authors recognize that in terms of the quantities, the frequency and the repertoire of drug use, gendered differences may still remain. Parker *et al.* (1995) conclude that the ways in which young people perceive and relate to illicit drugs is changing dramatically, and that adolescents in the 1990s now live in a world in which the availability of drugs is unexceptional, even 'a *normal* part of the leisure-pleasure landscape' (1995: 25; though for a critical review see Shiner and Newburn, 1997).

Young People, Victimization, and the Police

When the words 'youth' and 'crime' are linked, the picture in most minds will generally be of the young person as an offender. Given the frequency and prevalence of offending by young people this is not surprising. Young people, however, also frequently become victims of crime. Outside those studies which have focused specifically on child abuse and domestic violence, most criminological studies of victimization have paid scant attention to young people's experiences as victims of crime (though for some exceptions see Morgan and Zedner 1992; Anderson *et al.*, 1994; Aye Maung, 1995; Hartless *et al.*, 1995; Loader, 1996).

Whereas the first three British Crime Surveys focused on the experiences of those aged 16 or older, the fourth sweep included questions for 12–15-year-olds. The results are illuminating. They show that 12–15-year-old boys and girls are at least as much at risk of victimization as adults and, for some types of crime, more at risk than adults and older teenagers (Aye Maung, 1995). Within a period of little more than half a year one third of 12–15-year-olds recalled having been assaulted, almost a quarter had had property stolen and over one in twenty had experienced theft or attempted theft from the person. By contrast, less than one tenth of 16–19-year-olds had been assaulted (the figure was 1 per cent for 20–59-year-olds) and 6 per cent recalled having property stolen. The majority of assaults on 12–15-year-olds were found to have taken place at or near school, to have generally involved perpetrators of roughly the same age and, in the bulk of cases, not to have been deemed to be terribly serious incidents, though 10 per cent had left the victim feeling 'very frightened'. Incidents of 'harassment' followed a roughly similar pattern. African-Caribbeans generally faced higher risks than young people from other ethnic groups, paralleling the experience of victimization among adult groups (Office of National Statistics, 1996). Only about one in ten incidents were brought to the attention of the police, though the proportion rose to one in five of the more serious incidents experienced. By contrast one in three members of the sample said that they had had some form of contact with the police in the previous six to eight months. About one fifth had been stopped and 8 per cent said they had been searched, a higher rate than is the case for older age groups (Aye Maung, 1995). Juveniles were also less likely to be told why they were being stopped than were their elders. This, combined with the not infrequent experience for many of being 'moved on', contributed to the apparently paradoxical position in which young people feel both over-controlled and under-protected by the police (Anderson *et al.*, 1994; Aye Maung, 1995; Hartless *et al.*, 1995; Loader, 1996).

Despite the often-made assumption that young people are more likely to hold negative views of the police than older people, the 1992 British Crime Survey (BCS) found that 88 per cent of 12–15-year-olds agreed with the statement 'We need a police force in this country to keep law and order', and 63 per cent thought that the police did a very (10 per cent) or fairly (53 per cent) good job in their area. Less than one tenth said they felt the police did a very poor job. Paralleling the attitudes within the black adult population, the least favourable views of the police were held by young African-Caribbeans and, indeed, the views expressed by young people generally were found to correspond closely with the views expressed by the adults in the same households. The study was not able to explore such links in detail, but nevertheless concluded that 'how the police treat both young people *and* adults may well influence the attitudes the other group holds' (Aye Maung, 1995: 57). Though the police have made significant efforts in recent years actively to seek the views of young people and establish closer relationships with them, it is clear that young people continue to perceive that they are more likely to be responded to as a problem than to have their problems responded to.

Recent Trends in Youth Crime

For much of the last decade, as recorded crime has generally continued to increase, the patterns of offending by juveniles have departed dramatically from those of adults. Figure 19.2 shows the trends in the prevalence of recorded offending by male juveniles per 100,000 population between 1964 and 1995. Prevalence increased markedly from the mid-1960s to the mid-1970s, then stalled and dropped slightly in the second half of the 1970s before rising in the mid-1980s to approximately the level of ten years previously. The most significant decreases in the number of known juvenile offenders took place between 1985 and 1989, though the number continued to decline until 1993. In 1985 a total of 172,700 males and 40,700 females aged between 10 and 17 were cautioned for or convicted of indictable offences. By 1993, the respective figures had dropped to 100,200 for males and 29,300 for females. Within this general picture, the patterns for younger and older juveniles depart slightly. The prevalence of convictions of 10–13-year-olds has generally been in decline throughout the last thirty years, dropping from over 1,800 per 100,000 population in the early 1960s to just over 200 per 100,000 population in the early 1990s. The pattern for 14–16-year-olds is rather different, with the prevalence of convictions increasing steadily throughout the 1960s and 1970s, then falling throughout the 1980s and particularly sharply in the second half of the decade. In the mid-1980s approximately 60 per cent of the disposals for this age group were convictions, the other 40 per cent being made up of cautions. By 1993, this situation had reversed, with the proportion of convictions dropping to slightly under 38 per cent of the total. For both age groups the use of cautions increased throughout the period until the mid-1980s, and then began to drop. A similar pattern is visible in relation to young females. The prevalence of offending by both younger and older female age groups increased until approximately 1985, whereupon it began to drop, and continued to do so until 1989. The overall movement since that point has been upwards. There is a strong pattern here and Farrington (1992: 155) has noted that 'the sharp decreases in prevalence between 1985 and 1989 apply to convictions and cautions, males and females, and both age groups'.

The most thorough analysis of the downturn in recorded juvenile crime rates in the late 1980s is provided by Farrington (1992). Although he says that 'it is embarrassing to have to admit that there is little hard evidence either about true changes in juvenile delinquency in England and Wales or about the most likely explanations for any such changes' (1992: 161) he nonetheless concludes that 'the official figures probably reflect official reactions to delinquency more than juvenile misbehaviour' (1992: 155). He suggests that the reverse of the net-widening process that took place in the late 1960s and early 1970s occurred; that an increasing number of juveniles were given unrecorded warnings *rather* than recorded cautions. However, because the number of offenders dealt with informally are not recorded separately from cases when there is 'no further action', it is difficult to establish the impact of cautioning. Moreover, it is

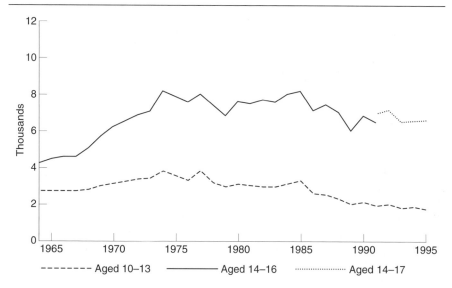

Fig. 19.2: Male offenders found guilty or cautioned for indictable offences per 100,000 population

Source: *Criminal Statistics.*

important to bear in mind that the use of informal warnings will tend to be at the very minor end of the offending scale. The Criminal Justice Act 1988 also had an impact through its reclassification of three types of offence—common assault, taking a motor vehicle without consent, and criminal damage over £400—from being triable in a Crown Court to being summary offences. Finally, both Allen (1991) and Farrington (1992) suggest that the introduction of the Crown Prosecution Service (the *Code for Crown Prosecutors* stresses the need to avoid the prosecution of juveniles wherever possible), the full implementation of the Police and Criminal Evidence Act (PACE), and the introduction of advanced disclosure of the prosecution case may also have had a significant impact in the mid-1980s, especially the major drop in the numbers sentenced between 1985 and 1986.

What of the possibility that offending itself was declining during the late 1980s? Farrington (1992) has considered the trends in burglary and shoplifting during the 1970s and 1980s. These are offences where juvenile offenders account for a significant proportion of offenders. The prevalence of burglary, he argues, remained relatively stable throughout the 1970s and early 1980s and the prevalence of shoplifting increased. In the second half of the 1980s the prevalence of both burglary and shoplifting declined sharply, and the fall of 69,900 in the number of juvenile offenders between 1984 and 1989 is almost entirely accounted for by a 46 per cent drop in the number of burglary offenders and a 48 per cent drop in theft offenders (Barclay and Turner, 1991). Farrington (1992), however, discounts the possibility that there can have been a *real* decline in burglary and shoplifting by juveniles during this period. The overall number of burglaries in England rose by over half between 1980 and 1987 (Farrington and Langan, 1992), and the numbers of shoplifters being apprehended appears to have remained fairly stable (Farrington and Burrows, 1993). Farrington (1992: 157) therefore concludes: 'Bearing in mind the very large increases in police-recorded crimes since 1985, it also seems likely that real juvenile offending has continued to increase since then, despite the decline in the official figures, *which is almost certainly an illusion caused by changes in police policies*' (emphasis added).

If Farrington is correct in his analysis that the fall in the number of known juvenile offenders does not reflect a *real* diminution in offending by juveniles: then it is to the operation of the criminal justice system that we must turn for an explanation. Doing so, however, is not to suggest that the rise and fall in numbers of known juvenile offenders are *merely* a product of the operation of the youth justice system, or that concerns about youth and crime are merely the product of labelling or moral panic. There are solid empirical reasons for the association between youth, particularly male youth, and crime. First, a significant proportion of recorded crime is committed by young offenders. Secondly, in whatever way it is measured, the peak age of offending is found to lie somewhere in mid- to late-adolescence. Finally, self-report studies confirm that offending is relatively common among young people. For almost 100 years now the focus of responsibility for responding to, or dealing with, that offending has been on the juvenile justice system. It is to the philosophy and practice of that system that we turn now.

YOUTH JUSTICE

The modern juvenile justice system emerged, as we have seen, in the same period as 'adolescence' and 'delinquency' were 'discovered'. Many of the social reformers in the nineteenth century who campaigned to protect children from danger and exploitation demanded that they should be removed from the 'adult' prison system and placed in privately managed, state-funded institutions. The Youthful Offenders Act 1854 provided the basis for reformatories (for the 'dangerous classes', i.e. delinquents) and legislation three years later established the industrial schools (for the 'perishing classes'). Although initially they were part of the educational system rather than the penal system, they housed children aged between 7 and 14 who had been convicted of vagrancy.

Juvenile courts began to emerge in various places around the turn of the century. They were not formally established until after the election of a reformist Liberal government in 1906 however. The Probation of Offenders Act 1907 provided a statutory basis for the probation service, and in 1908 the Children Act created the juvenile court. It also barred children under 14 from prison and restricted the imprisonment of 14–15-year-olds. The juvenile courts—special sittings of the magistrates' courts in the early years—were empowered to act in criminal cases and in cases of begging and vagrancy though they remained, in essence, criminal courts. Nonetheless, reflecting the changes that had taken place in the nineteenth century, the Act endorsed 'the conception of the child or juvenile as a special category' (Garland, 1985: 222). Moreover, by formalizing the use of reformatories and industrial schools the Act sought, according to the Lord Advocate, 'to treat these children not by way of punishing them—which is no remedy—but with a view to their reformation' (quoted in Garland, 1985: 222).

Also in 1908 'borstals' were created to cater for 16–21-year-olds (the 'juvenile-adult category') who 'by reason of his criminal habits and tendencies or associations with persons of such character, it is expedient that he should be subject to detention for such a term and such instruction and discipline as appears most conducive to his reformation and the repression of crime' (quoted in Garland, 1985). The welfare principle was further enshrined in the legislation—the Children and Young Persons Act 1993—which implemented the main recommendations of the Molony Committee (though it did not bar 16-year-olds from borstal as the committee had recommended). The Act prohibited capital punishment for those under 18, and reorganized the reformatory and industrial schools, bringing about the creation of 'approved schools' which provided juvenile offenders with education and training, and remand homes which kept remanded juveniles apart from adult prisoners. Between 1938 and 1945 recorded indictable offences rose by 69 per cent, and before long the prison population began to swell, and the increase in juvenile crime exposed the difficulties inherent in a system dependant on accommodation provided by charities and local authorities. A Criminal Justice Bill was introduced in 1947 which was based on recommendations made before the war which 'strongly emphasised the unwisdom of sending young persons to prison' (quoted in Bailey, 1987).

The 1948 Act placed a number of restrictions on the use of imprisonment and marked the beginning of a trend restricting the use of custody for juvenile offenders. It also introduced remand centres, attendance centres, support for probation hostels, and abolished corporal punishment. However, the Magistrates' Association renewed its demands for a new short-term custodial sentence and this was eventually accepted by the Government. The detention centre order introduced by the Act was intended to be a short unpleasant sentence which would combine hard work with the minimum of amusement— a sentence not unlike the 'short, sharp, shock' experiment of the early 1980s. In fact, detention centres were not provided until the 1950s, and even then their development was slow. Continuing concern about the 'welfare' of juveniles also found expression in the Children Act 1948. This sought to end the placement of neglected children in approved schools alongside offenders, and set up local authority children's departments with their own resources for residential care—'the first professional social work service exclusively for children' (Harris and Webb, 1987).

Levels of recorded crime rose in a generally sustained and sharp way from the mid-1950s on (see Maguire, this volume). For the first three decades of the period, the levels of recorded offences by juveniles followed a roughly similar pattern. Thus, there was an increase of approximately 98 per cent in the numbers of juvenile offenders per 100,000 population cautioned or convicted for indictable offences in the period 1961 to 1985. During the same period the number of offences recorded by the police increased by over 150 per cent. Windlesham (1993) has argued that from the early post-war period onwards 'the twin claws of the pincer that was to hold the development of penal policy fast in its grip were the remorseless increase in the incidence of crime, and the overcrowding in the prisons'.

Juvenile Justice Since the 1960s

The 1950s closed with the Ingleby Committee, which was set up in 1956. The major focus of the Committee's deliberations centred around the conflict that it felt existed between the *judicial* and *welfare* functions of the juvenile court. Though its major proposals, including raising the age of criminal responsibility to 14, did not become law—the Children and Young Persons Act 1963, by way of compromise, raised the age of criminal responsibility to 10—one author has argued that they were of considerable symbolic importance for later events (Bottoms, 1974). In 1965, a White Paper, *The Child, The Family and the Young Offender,* included proposals to establish family councils and family courts, and to abolish the juvenile courts. The White Paper was vehemently attacked by lawyers, magistrates, and probation officers. With its small parliamentary majority to protect, the Labour government withdrew the proposals (Clarke, 1980). Three years later, a second White Paper, *Children in Trouble,* was published and, after some relatively minor amendments, its central recommendations were incorporated in the Children and Young Persons Act 1969. The system of approved schools, and that of remand homes or remand centres for juveniles which existed alongside them, was abolished and replaced with community homes with residential and educational facilities. The juvenile court was retained. Care was preferred over criminal proceedings and the circumstances under which court proceedings were possible was narrowed. The intention was that the juvenile court should become a welfare-providing 'agency of last resort' (Rutter and Giller, 1983), referral only happening in those cases in which informal and voluntary agreement had not been reached between the local authority, the juvenile, and parents (Morris and McIsaac, 1978). It was also intended that detention centres and borstals for juveniles be phased out and replaced by a new form of intervention—intermediate treatment. 'This (though) was less a policy of decarceration than a reiteration of the traditional welfare abhorrence of the prison system' (Rutherford, 1986b).

For most of the century, and certainly for the whole of the post-war period up to 1970, there existed a consensus whose terms 'implicitly rested on the non-partisan character of crime and on the merits of gradual shifts towards rehabilitative policies for its control' (see Downes and Morgan, this volume). If the 1969 Children and Young Persons Act was the high point of 'welfarism', the general election of 1970 was the watershed for the previously existing political consensus, and perhaps for criminal justice generally (Bottoms and Stevenson, 1992). Indeed, as was suggested above, the period was one characterized by a lack of concensus and a turn towards authoritarianism (Hall *et al.*, 1978). The change of government which the general election brought about put paid to any possibility of full implementation of the 1969 Act, with the consequence that juvenile courts continued to function largely as they had before—criminal proceedings for 10–14s continued, powers in relation to 14–16-year-olds were not restricted, and the minimum age for qualification for a Borstal sentence was not increased. Perhaps most significantly, although care proceedings following commission of an offence were made possible, such powers were used exceedingly sparingly, and the number of custodial sentences rose from 3,000 in 1970 to over 7,000 in 1978 (Rutter and Giller, 1983; Cavadino and Dignan, 1992).

Against this background of rapidly increasing use of custody, it is worthwhile considering what full implementation of the 1969 Act would have meant. First, it would have abolished prosecution of any child under 14 for a criminal offence, with the exception of homicide. Secondly, it would have restricted civil care measures for that group as well. Thirdly, wherever possible, the assumption would have been that children would be dealt with outside court. Though 14–16-year-olds could have been prosecuted, non-criminal care proceedings would be available and the preferred alternative in most cases. For those prosecuted, there would have been two main disposals available—the care order and the supervision order—both of which would be supervised by social workers given considerable discretion (Bottoms, 1974). The intention was that the use of penal custody for offenders aged 14–16 should be phased out completely (Nellis, 1991). This added up to 'the most developed application of welfare principles to criminal justice ever seen in an English statute' (Bottoms and Stevenson, 1992: 36).

Partial implementation, and the consequences which flowed from that, led one group of commentators at the end of the decade to argue that the 'tragedy' of the 1969 Act was that people had 'been persistently led to believe that the juvenile criminal justice system has become softer and softer, while the reality has been that it has become harder and harder' (Thorpe *et al.*, 1980, quoted in Muncie, 1984). Though only partly implemented, the Act became the major scapegoat for the perceived ills of juvenile crime and juvenile justice in the 1970s—and the 'welfare' model it espoused was replaced by an expanding youth justice system in which the emphasis was increasingly on 'justice' or punishment. The Act was attacked from all sides (Harwin, 1982). Within three years of its implementation a sub-committee of the House of Commons Expenditure Committee had been set up to make recommendations for change. While accepting that there was a class of juvenile that required care and support rather than punishment, the Expenditure Committee nevertheless was much influenced by the view that there was also, as the Magistrates' Association put it in its evidence: 'a minority of tough sophisticated young criminals . . . [who] . . . prey on the community, at will, even after the courts have placed them in care. They deride the powerlessness of the courts to do anything effective' (quoted in Rutherford, 1986a). As a consequence the Committee argued that it was important to 'hasten the process in the case of certain offenders to deter others from embarking on criminal activities, to contain a hard core of persistent offenders, and to punish some offenders' (House of Commons Expenditure Committee, 1975, quoted in Morris and Giller, 1987). In response the government issued a White Paper (Home Office *et al.*, 1976) which was equally 'bifurcatory' in its approach. It recommended both a shift away from residential care and towards supervision and fostering, whilst also articulating considerable concern about what it believed to be the inadequate powers available for dealing with 'serious and persistent offenders' (Home Office *et al.*, 1976: paragraph 3). Bifurcation, or the 'twin-track approach' (Bottoms, 1977) is one in which the penalties are simultaneously increased for serious offenders and decreased for less serious offenders. The 1970s witnessed a doubling of the use of custody for juveniles with a concomitant decline in the use of community-based alternatives, whilst at the same time the use of cautions increased substantially.

Morris and Giller (1987) suggest that juvenile justice policy at the end of the 1970s 'bore little resemblance to that proposed in the 1969 Act'. Indeed, the *Conservative Manifesto* of 1979—the most avowedly 'law and order' manifesto in British political history—promised, among many other measures, to strengthen sentencing powers with respect to juveniles and young adults. The 1980 White Paper, *Young Offenders*, included proposals for the reintroduction of a limited number of detention centres with 'tougher' regimes—the so-called 'short, sharp, shock' treatment first mooted by William Whitelaw when Shadow Home Secretary (Harwin, 1982). This 'experiment' began in two centres—Send and New Hall—in 1980. The Home Secretary announced that life at the centres would 'be conducted at a brisk tempo. Much greater emphasis will be put on hard and constructive activities, on discipline and tidiness, on self-respect and respect for those in authority. . . . These will be no holiday camps and those who attend them will not ever want to go back' (quoted in Home Office, 1984). The experiments were quickly found to fail. The Home Office Young Offender Psychology Unit, which evaluated the initiatives, concluded: 'Apparently, the announcement of the policy did not affect crime rates generally: there was no interruption in trends in crime among young people generally, nor in the catchment areas of the two pilot project regimes especially' (Home Office, 1984). Despite this, Whitelaw's successor Leon Brittan remained steadfast in his public support of the new regimes and announced that they were to be extended to all detention centres (Muncie, 1990). 'The political damage was limited' suggests Windlesham (1993: 161), 'but it is hard to avoid the verdict that sound penal administration was made to serve the needs of a defective icon of political ideology'. The Thatcherite rhetoric remained tough: the streets were once again to be made safe, and the police were to be given new powers to sustain their fight against crime. However, the legislation emanating from the Home Office—at least as far as juveniles were concerned—contained countervailing tendencies. Thus, the Criminal Justice Act 1982 aimed to limit the use of custody for young offenders; it shortened the detention centre sentence and the end of borstals and indeterminate sentences was signalled with the new order for 'youth custody' (the institutions becoming known as Youth Custody Centres).

The 1980 White Paper and the 1982 Act jointly constituted a fairly fundamental attack on the welfarist principles that underpinned the Children and Young Persons Act. Gelsthorpe and Morris (1994: 972) have argued that they

represented a move away from treatment and lack of personal responsibility to notions of punishment and individual and parental responsibility. They also represented a move away from executive (social workers) to judicial decision-making, and from the belief in the 'child in need' to the 'juvenile criminal'—what Tutt (1981) called the 'rediscovery of the delinquent'.

It was against this background that the significant and sustained decline in recorded crime by young people took place in the latter half of the 1980s. The paradox is that 'the decade of "law and order" was also the decade of what has been called 'the successful revolution' in juvenile justice' (Rutherford, 1986*a*), and Lord Windlesham, himself a former Home Office minister, described this transformation as 'one of the most remarkable post-War achievements of deliberate legislative enactment' (Windlesham, 1993).

The Successful Revolution?

The 1980s have seen a revolution in the way the juvenile justice system operates in England and Wales. There are few areas of criminal justice practice of which we can be proud but this is an exception. . . . Many notions, which once seemed totally unrealistic, such as the abolition of juvenile imprisonment, are now viewed as achievable [Jones, 1989: p. i].

The reason that it was possible to make such a statement lay in the fall in the number of known juvenile offenders already described and in the declining number of 14–16-year-olds receiving custodial sentences. The number of male juveniles receiving custodial orders in England and Wales in 1988 was less than half that in 1984 and under 42 per cent of those in 1981 (see Figure 32.3 in Morgan, this volume), a decline in the use of custody not seen for other age groups. Nor was there a similar fall in the numbers of juveniles remanded in care or custody prior to sentence during the period in which the use of immediate custody for juveniles declined.

Several factors must be considered in explaining the remarkable fall in the use of custody for juveniles during the 1980s, and the decline in known juvenile offenders during the second half of that decade. First, there is demographic change. During the period 1981–88 there was approximately an 18 per cent drop in the population of 14–16-year-old males. This clearly had an impact on the overall numbers sentenced to immediate custody, but it does not explain the fall in the proportion of 14–16-year-old males sentenced to custody from 12 per cent in 1985 to 7 per cent in 1990.

Secondly, there were the provisions contained in the Criminal Justice Act 1982. The new powers it provided to magistrates to use the determinate sentence of youth custody (rather than commit to Crown Court with a recommendation for borstal training), and the reduction in the minimum length of the detention centre order it brought about, were widely thought to presage an increase in the prison population. However, the Act also contained restrictions on the use of custody and introduced a range of non-custodial penalties. Community service became available for 16-year-olds, though reservations were expressed about the appropriateness of the provision on the grounds that it might be used less as an alternative to custody and more as an alternative to other non-custodial penalties. Early indications, however, were that this was not the case and that the type of offender receiving community service was not dissimilar to that receiving custody. New requirements that could be added to supervision orders were also introduced, and Allen (1991) has argued that whilst it is far from conclusive, there is some evidence to suggest that supervision orders were used as an increasingly higher tariff option throughout the 1980s.

Thirdly, there was the increase in the 1980s of intensive intermediate treatment schemes. The term 'intermediate treatment' (IT) first appeared in the White Paper which preceded the Children and Young Persons' Act 1969 (Home Office, 1968). Originally IT was to be one possible requirement of a supervision order under the 1969 Act. However, because of the difficulties existing in juvenile justice in the early 1970s IT made little progress initially. A number of initiatives followed which aimed 'to relocate intermediate treatment at a higher point in the tariff' (Bottoms *et al.*, 1990), key amongst which was what later became known as 'systems management' or the 'new orthodoxy' (Jones, 1984). The decisive change followed the publication of a circular by the Department of Health and Social Security (as it then was) which stressed the importance of multi-agency approaches to the management of serious and persistent offenders and made available £15 million of seedcorn money to develop IT projects as alternatives to custody and care. 110 projects offering 3,389 places were set up by voluntary bodies in 62 local authority areas between 1983 and 1987 using this money (Allen, 1991). Though it is difficult to assess the impact of IT, the decline in the proportionate use of imprisonment for juveniles between 1985 and 1990 suggests that it did serve as an alternative to custody (though see Parker *et al.*, 1989).

Fourthly, there was diversion from court, the most important form of diversion in the period. This, as was shown in Farrington's (1992) analysis of crime trends in the period, appears to be key in understanding the significant decline in the number of juvenile offenders being formally processed in the latter half of the 1980s. Indeed, so successful was the general cautioning policy in relation to juveniles believed to be that, as early as 1988 in the Green Paper *Punishment, Custody and the Community*, the Home Office signalled its intention to transfer the lessons learnt in juvenile justice to policies in relation to offenders more generally, though it recognized that modifications would need to be made (Home Office, 1988: parahraphs 2.17–19). In emphasizing the reasons for seeking to restrict the use of custodial sentences for young offenders the Green Paper stated that 'most young offenders grow out of crime as they become more mature and responsible. They need encouragement and help to become law abiding. Even a short period of custody is quite likely to confirm them as criminals, particularly as they acquire new criminal skills from the more sophisticated offenders. They see themselves labelled as criminals and behave accordingly.' Diversion from custody and from court were emphasized and, consequently, cautioning continued to have a central role in this approach.

In the same period, two major new pieces of legislation affecting young offenders came into force. The Children Act 1989 finally removed all civil care proceedings from the juvenile court. The Criminal Justice Act 1991 changed the name of the juvenile court to the youth court and extended its jurisdiction to include 17-year-olds. The 1991 Act and subsequent Home Office Circular (30/1992) explaining the changes brought about by the legislation reminded sentencers of section 44 of the Children and Young Persons Act 1933, which states that 'all courts must have regard to the welfare of children and young people who appear before them'. The Act extended this consideration to 17-year-olds. The Act distinguished between 'children' aged 10 to 13 and 'young persons' aged 14 to 17. More recently, however, the Divisional Court ruled that the doctrine of *doli incapax* (the rebuttable presumption that children aged 10–13 are incapable of criminal intent) was no longer part of the criminal law. This was later overturned by the House of Lords (*C (A Minor)* v *DPP* [1996] 1 AC 1, HL). The legislation also gave magistrates new sentencing powers within the overall framework created by the 1991 Act (including unit fines, community sentences, and custody—see Mair this volume) along with a new scheme of post-custody supervision. The Act reduced the maximum term of detention in a YOI to twelve months, and brought 17-year-olds within the ambit of section 53 of the Children and Young Persons Act 1933 which gives the Crown Court the power to order longer terms of detention in respect of certain 'grave crimes'. Again reinforcing lessons learnt from developments in practice over the past decade, the 1991 Act signalled the importance of inter-agency and joint working by giving Chief Probation Officers and Directors of Social Services joint responsibility for making local arrangements ('action plans') for dealing with young offenders, and more generally for providing services to the youth court. Finally, the 1991 Act represents the final nail in the coffin of the 'welfare' model, but it further reinforced, though temporarily, the pre-eminence of the 'justice' model in juvenile justice.

The Rise of Populist Punitiveness

From 1991 onwards there was a noticeable change in the tenor of official concern about juvenile offending. Concerns were fuelled by several specific factors. The first was the well-publicized urban disturbances of 1991. Though different in scale, causes, and style from the inner city riots involving black and marginalized white youth in the early 1980s, the disturbances at Blackbird Leys (Oxford), Ely (Cardiff), and on the Meadowell estate in Tyneside focused attention on young men in large-scale violent confrontations with the police. In many cases, these were a consequence of attempts by the police to put a stop to the very public displays of 'joyriding' so popular with young men and with the journalists who increasingly turned up to record their activities (Campbell, 1993).

What these public disturbances did was allow long-standing concerns about young or very young offenders to be dusted down, distorted, sometimes exaggerated, and then served up in symbolic form via the mass media. Within much of the reporting of these events it was increasingly suggested that the greatest scourge of inner-city life was the young criminal who was so prolific in his activities that he, almost alone, was terrorizing local communities. Furthermore, it was then claimed, first by the police, but closely followed by politicians, that the police and the courts were powerless to deal with such offenders. The issue was taken up in a speech to the federated ranks of the Metropolitan Police in October 1992 by the then Home Secretary, Kenneth Clarke. A small number of children, he suggested:

are committing a large number of crimes. There is a case for increasing court powers to lock up, educate and train them for their own and everyone else's interest. We will certainly be taking a long hard look at the options which are available to the courts in dealing with serious offenders of this age. If court powers need to be strengthened or new institutions created, then they will be.

Clarke's speech was widely reported and stories of 'persistent juvenile offenders', as they were generally referred to, started to appear on a regular basis in the press. Thus, for example, the *Daily Mail* on 10 September 1992, under the headline, 'One-boy crime wave', began its story, 'He was only 11 when his life of crime began with the theft of chocolate bars from a corner shop . . . within two years he had become a one-boy crime wave'. The *Daily Express* (9 September 1992) summed up the police view with the headline, 'Mini-gangster is beyond our control'. The *Daily Star* (30 November 1992) following its report of a case involving an 11-year-old offender, headlined its editorial, 'We've got too soft', and went on: 'CHILDREN are supposed to be little innocents—not crooks in short trousers. But much of Britain is now facing a truly frightening explosion of kiddie crime. As we reveal today, too many youngsters are turning into hardened hoods almost as soon as they've climbed out of their prams'.

In the autumn of 1992, the House of Commons Home Affairs Committee

(HAC) announced an inquiry into issues affecting juvenile offenders and the particular problems of persistent offenders. The Committee received conflicting evidence about trends in juvenile crime and suggested that:

one possible explanation for the apparent discrepancy between ACPO's picture of greater juvenile offending and the decline in the number of juvenile offenders is a growth in the numbers of *persistent* offenders. . . . If there is a small but growing number of juvenile offenders responsible for many offences (some of which they may be convicted or cautioned for and some of which may go undetected) it is possible to reconcile the indisputable fact that the number (and rate, to a lesser extent) of known juvenile offenders has fallen over time with the more speculative assertion that the number of offences committed by juveniles has risen [HAC, 1993: paragraph 15].

Moreover, the majority of witnesses lent support to the suggestion that the most pressing problem was what the Committee described as 'persistent juvenile trouble makers'. It remains the case, however, that there are no British empirical data which can establish whether or not the number of persistent offenders has increased in recent years.

The Home Secretary, Kenneth Clarke, acted quickly. In March 1993, he announced that the government proposed to introduce legislation that would make a new disposal available to the courts. These 'secure training orders' were to be aimed at 'that comparatively small group of very persistent juvenile offenders whose repeated offending makes them a menace to the community' (*Hansard*, 2 March 1993, col. 139). The new order would apply to 12–15-year-olds (though this was later amended to 12–14-year-olds) who had been convicted of three imprisonable offences, and who had proved 'unwilling or unable to comply with the requirements of supervision in the community while on remand or under sentence'. The order was to be a custodial one and would be served in a 'secure training unit' which, he suggested, would provide 'high standards of care and discipline'. Regimes would include provision for education and training for inmates; after release individuals would be subject to 'rigorous, consistent and firmly delivered' supervision until their supervising social worker or probation officer felt that he or she was no longer a threat to society.

The public concern about juvenile crime which the Home Affairs Committee made reference to, and which had been stoked by the press, might not have reached the pitch it eventually did were it not for the tragic events of 12 February 1993 and their highly publicized aftermath. It was at approximately 3.30 that afternoon that 2-year-old James Bulger was abducted from the Strand shopping centre in Bootle, Liverpool. As time passed, and the young boy remained missing, the search spread and intensified. Enhanced still photographic images from the closed-circuit television cameras at the shopping centre were broadcast on national television. These showed James walking with, or being led by, one of two young people with whom witnesses had seen him leaving the shopping centre; pictures which appeared to convey both innocence and, because of what was then already suspected and later confirmed, something much more sinister. Eventually, two days later, James Bulger's battered body was found near a railway line in Liverpool, some two miles from the shopping centre. The abduction and murder of such a young child would always have had a significant public impact; in this case, however, the arrest and charging of two 10-year-old boys 'inspired a kind of national collective agony' (Young, 1996: 113), and provided the strongest possible evidence to an already worried public that something new and particularly malevolent was afoot.

The trial of the two youngsters accused of James Bulger's murder took place at Preston Crown Court in November 1993 amidst massive national and inter-national media interest. On the day after the verdict, 25 November, the *Daily Mail* carried twenty-four stories about the case, and a total of almost forty stories in the three days after the trial. The broadsheets gave it similar space: the *Guardian* including twenty-two articles and the *Daily Telegraph* twenty-three articles and two editorials (Franklin and Petley, 1996). The tone of most of the coverage—despite the age of the offenders—was harshly punitive. Though for some commentators the sheer horror of the crime made it inexplicable in any terms other than 'evil', within days of the end of the trial some of the 'usual suspects' were being rounded up to help explain how it could have happened. Somewhat unexpectedly, for there had been no mention during the trial, one of these was video films. In his summing-up the trial judge made reference to a film that, it was implied, one of the offenders, Jon Venables, might have watched. The judge said he felt that there ought to be an informed public debate about 'exposure to violent video films, including possibly *Childs Play 3*, which has some striking similarities to the manner of the attack on James Bulger' (*Guardian*, 27 November 1993). The response to this was swift. Questions were tabled in the House; David Alton MP put down an amendment to the Criminal Justice and Public Order Bill further to restrict access to video films; the Home Affairs Committee conducted an inquiry (HAC, 1994) and a group of academic psychologists came out firmly in favour of regulation (Newson, 1994).

Public discourse about the murder of James Bulger was particularly contra-dictory. On the one hand, for example, the police officer leading the murder inquiry reflected one fairly typical set of beliefs when he described the case as 'unique'. Though highly unusual the case clearly was by no means unique (Boswell, 1996). On the other hand, there was also the pervasive view—as frequently expressed in the media—that despite the highly unusual nature of the case, it somehow illustrated that there was something wrong with society generally, and youth crime and youth justice more particularly. Indeed, in some public/political discourse this most unusual and horrific of crimes became confused with the whole issue of persistent, yet less serious, offending. The Bulger case was the 'flashpoint' which ignited a new moral panic and led to further demonization of young people and, increasingly in the 1990s, also of lone mothers who were increasing in number and, in right-wing underclass theory (Murray, 1990), were perceived to be a key part of the 'problem'. With

politicians of all parties becoming increasingly punitive in their pronouncements, and the Labour Party's clichéd but resonant soundbite 'tough on crime,
tough on the causes of crime' apparently meeting with some success, the new
Home Secretary, Michael Howard, used his speech at the Conservative Party
conference to announce yet another new 'law and order' package. The choice
that Howard made in seeking to bolster his party's and his own fortunes was
to employ a strategy of 'populist punitiveness' (Bottoms, 1995).

The package of measures that Howard announced was punitive, involving a
reassertion of the central position of custody in a range of sanctions he
interpreted as having deterrence as their primary aim (see Ashworth, this
volume). Most famously, he announced that previous approaches which
involved attempts to limit prison numbers were henceforward to be eschewed.
The new package of measures would be likely to result in an increase in prison
numbers, an increase which he appeared to welcome:

I do not flinch from that. We shall no longer judge the success of our system of justice
by a fall in our prison population . . . Let us be clear. *Prison works.* It ensures that we
are protected from murderers, muggers and rapists—and it makes many who are
tempted to commit crime think twice [quoted in Gibson *et al.*, 1994: 83; emphasis
added].

The Criminal Justice and Public Order Act doubled the maximum sentence in
a young offenders' institution for 15–17-year-olds from one year to two. It
introduced the possibility that parents of young offenders could be bound over
to ensure that their children carried out their community sentences, and it
provided for the introduction of a new 'secure training order' for 12–14-year-
olds. The proposal was that five new secure training centres would be built,
each housing approximately forty inmates. The new sentences would be determinate, of a maximum of two years, half of which would be served in custody
and half under supervision in the community. There was widespread criticism
of, and resistance to, the new provisions for dealing with 12–14-year-olds.
Home Office-funded research cast doubt on the likely efficacy of such a policy
(Hagell and Newburn, 1994), the main voluntary organizations in the field
refused to consider becoming involved in the management of the new centres
(NACRO, 1994), and planning permission for the building of them was
consistently refused by local councils. Though it was originally anticipated that
the centres would be up and running in 1995, by the end of 1996 only one of
the five contracts had been let and building of the centre had yet to begin.

The resistance to secure training centres has, however, mainly come from
professionals working with young offenders, rather than opposition politicians.
By and large the secure training order met with relatively little political
hostility within Parliament. After the passage of the Act, the battle between
the Home Secretary and his Shadow for the law and order 'high ground'
escalated, a series of leaks from the Home Office announced numerous
proposed initiatives. In February 1995, a leaked Prison Service document
suggested that the government wished to introduce American-style 'boot camps'

for young offenders. Both the Director General of the Prison Service and the Home Secretary had visited America to inspect the high-impact incarceration programmes being run on Rikers Island and in other parts of the country. A report written by Prison Service officials after a visit to a number of US boot camps concluded that 'there is little point in devoting time and resources to considering an initiative which seems to have little to offer us'. More specifically, it said that:

there is no basis for this type of approach in terms of reducing offending, and its potential popular appeal would be undermined by the fact that we have tried this approach before with detention centres and abandoned it as a failure. . . . The question what advantage boot camps offer over detention centres is bound to be asked, and would not be easy to answer [quoted in Nathan, 1995].

Nonetheless, by August 1995 further leaks revealed that the government was to press ahead with the idea of boot camps—the first to be instituted at Thorn Cross near Warrington, though with a far more progressive regime than those associated with US boot camps. The same month, again via a leak, it became apparent that there had been correspondence between the Home Secretary and the Defence Secretary, Michael Portillo, exploring the possibility of using the Military Corrective Training Centre at Colchester for young offenders aged 18 and above. This was due to open in October 1996, but has been held up by legal problems and is due to open in early 1997. Nonetheless, the predictable consequence of such punitive rhetoric is visible in the increasing numbers of children and young people in prison establishments, and a projected rise of a further one third in the number of young males in custody by 2004 (Home Office, 1996*a*).

At the other end of the scale from custody, the cautioning system has also come in for increased scrutiny and criticism, and Home Office circular 18/1994 (Home Office, 1994) sought to place further limits on its use. The 1990 circular had stated that 'a previous conviction or caution should not rule out a subsequent one if other factors suggest it might be suitable'. At the launch of the new circular, the Home Secretary outlined the new approach. He said: 'From now on your first chance is your last chance. Criminals should know that they will be punished. Giving cautions to serious offenders, or to the same person time and again, sends the wrong message to criminals and the public' (quoted in Evans, 1994). Such a message is also contained in Labour Party proposals on the future of youth justice (Labour Party, 1996) where it is proposed that the formal caution be replaced by a 'Final Warning'. The name has clearly been chosen with care so as to preclude the possibility that such a measure might be used more than once for, as the Labour Party state categorically: 'Carrying on cautioning does not work and leads to a loss of public confidence' (1996: 9). Moreover, the Audit Commission (1996) has also recently lent its weight to arguments in favour of reform of the cautioning system, and, indeed, is critical of the youth justice system generally, characterizing it as expensive, inefficient, inconsistent, and ineffective. Additionally, however, the Audit

Commission has also added its voice to the growing roll-call of commentators (*inter alia*, Utting *et al.*, 1993; Farrington, 1996; Faulkner, 1996; Allen, 1997) calling for increased emphasis on 'criminality prevention' and, in particular, support for those interventions early in life which research suggests hold out the best hope for reducing youth crime (Farrington, this volume). The recently published Home Office Green Paper (Home Office, 1997) and supporting research evidence (Utting, 1997) reinforces this general message.

CONCLUSION

The primary focus of this chapter has been on 'adolescents' or 'juveniles'. This intermediary life-stage between childhood and full adulthood is generally thought of as a period characterized by problems and conflicts, partly because of the continuing dominance of the 'storm and stress' model. Not only is adolescence characterized by physiological and emotional difficulties or pressures, but young people appear to engage disproportionately in anti-social activities, including crime, in their adolescent years. For the majority there is a marked fall in criminal behaviour during early adult life, though a minority continue to persist in their offending 'careers'. In many ways, therefore, it has been the management of this 'problem population' until the point at which they 'grow up' which has been seen as the key task in controlling crime. In some respects, however, this appears to be becoming increasingly difficult.

There is evidence that 'growing up' is itself becoming more problematic. The transition from childhood to adulthood via adolescence has not only been elongated, but appears to have become more complicated. As youth unemployment has risen, and the period of full-time education has been extended, the move into full citizenship has been delayed for many, and completely stalled for some. In addition, there is evidence that those 'psychosocial disorders' which tend to rise or peak in the teenage years—suicide and suicidal behaviour, depression, eating disorders, and abuse of alcohol and psychoactive drugs (Rutter and Smith, 1995)—have been increasing markedly among young people since the Second World War. More centrally as far as this chapter is concerned, the level of crime committed by young people appears to have increased substantially over the past forty years. Though there was a significant decrease in the number of known juvenile offenders in the mid- to late-1980s, there is enough evidence of changed policing and prosecution practices to cast doubt on the decline in juvenile crime that this was taken by some to imply, and to suggest that juvenile crime most probably continued to increase during this period. What is less clear is whether increasing juvenile crime reflects an increase in the numbers of young offenders, an increase in the number of persistent offenders, an increase in the peak age of offending (i.e. greater numbers offending for longer), or some combination of these factors.

It appears from the most recent British self-report study (Graham and Bowling, 1995) that young men may not be 'growing out of crime' as early as was previously believed to be the case. This further reinforces concerns about the increasingly elongated and problematic nature of the 'transition' to responsible citizenship.

Broader structural and ideological forces have also been at work. Economic and social polarization has resulted in the increasing marginalization and exclusion of already disadvantaged social groups, and the last decade has been characterized by a 'mounting (and guilty) fear of a youth citizenry whose basic citizen rights to work, welfare and shelter have . . . suffered severe erosion' (Carlen, 1996: 53). The sustained and rampant economic individualism of the 1980s resulted in the gap between prosperous communities and poor communities widening still further (Green, 1994). Moreover, new patterns of marriage, divorce, and family formation transformed the social landscape, and a similar pattern of polarization has been taking place in relation to households, where the gap between 'work rich' and 'work poor' families has increased markedly (Joseph Rowntree Foundation, 1995). Without resorting to the pejorative language of 'underclass theory' (Murray, 1990) the implications of social exclusion for levels of crime, particularly among the young, are fairly clear.

The limitations of the formal criminal justice system in controlling crime are widely recognized. In many respects it is families, schools, neighbourhoods, and peer groups which constitute a much more powerful influence on young people as they grow up. However, it has been argued that these sources of informal social control have become decreasingly effective as inhibitors of crime, partly as a result of the 'disembedding processes of modernity' (Bottoms, 1995: 47). At a general level, the globalizing trends of the twentieth century have radically altered the nature of social relations, disembedding them from, in Giddens' (1990) terms, localized sources of trust—such as extended family, local neighbourhood, and church—and replacing these with individualized 'abstract systems' which tend to be less effective in informal social control terms (see Sparks, this volume). It is likely that these changes have played their part in increasing levels of crime, including youth crime, they may also have led to growing insecurity as traditional sources of trust have been undermined or replaced.

Thus we find ourselves in a period of rising crime and rising fear of crime, of increasing fiscal restraint and, though the worst of 'nothing works' pessimism may have passed, of a general absence of faith in the treatment paradigm. Though lip-service is occasionally paid to the wider questions of prevention (Labour Party, 1996), the response of politicians from both the main parties in these circumstances has generally been to embrace 'populist punitiveness'. Bottoms (1995) suggests three reasons for the attractiveness of such an approach. First, it is popular because of the belief that increased punitiveness may be effective in reducing crime through general deterrence and/or incapacitation. Secondly, because it is hoped that it will help foster a sense of moral consensus around issues where currently dissensus or moral pluralism exists. Thirdly, because politicians believe that it will be a vote-winner. 'The kinds of offences', he argues, 'most likely to be the subject of "populist punitiveness" stances are violent and sexual offences, on the one hand, and drugs on the other' (Bottoms, 1995: 40). It is arguably the case that the most likely 'subjects' of populist punitive discourses are, and have long been, young offenders. This certainly appears to hold true in the 1990s. Moreover, the 'disciplinary common-sense' (Hall, 1980) of the 1990s is largely bipartisan. The prevailing mood is one in which there is little political dissent from proposals to incarcerate ever-younger children, to introduce 'curfews', to introduce legislation to outlaw 'raves', to close clubs where drug-taking might occur, to institute new and harsher measures against squatters, new age travellers, the young homeless, the young unemployed, and actively to promote a 'zero tolerance' model of policing which is likely to target marginalized youth on the streets. The prospects for an immediate return to a more enlightened approach to juvenile justice look bleak.

Selected Further Reading

The liveliest introduction to the history of youth as a 'problem' is Geoffrey Pearson's *Hooligan: A History of Respectable Fears* (London: Macmillan, 1983). Little of what happened to young people in post-war Britain makes much sense without listening to the accompanying soundtrack. The best books on pop music are Nik Cohn's *Awopbopaloobop Alopbamboom* (London: Paladin, 1970), Charlie Gillett's *The Sound of the City* (London: Souvenir Press, 1983), and Jon Savage's *England's Dreaming: Sex Pistols and Punk Rock* (London: Faber and Faber, 1991). On subcultural styles, Dick Hebdige's *Subculture: The Meaning of Style* (London: Methuen, 1979) is still the one to pick up, though Ken Gelder and Sarah Thornton's *The Subcultures Reader* (London: Routledge, 1997) pulls together a mass of useful material. Anyone looking either for insight into the lives of young 'lads' or just an example of sociology as it should be written, should read Howard Parker's *View From the Boys* (London: David and Charles, 1974). On youth and crime the best overview, though now out of date, is Michael Rutter and Henri Giller's *Juvenile Delinquency: Trends and Perspectives* (Harmondsworth: Penguin, 1983—a fully revised edition is in production). There are a number of Home Office studies which provide useful data, particularly John Graham and Ben Bowling's *Young People and Crime*, and Natalie Aye Maung's *Young People, Victimisation and the Police* (both London: Home Office, 1995). Up-to-date and comprehensive reviews of the changing nature of youth justice are hard to come by. The most thorough introduction remains Allison Morris and Henri Giller's *Understanding Juvenile Justice* (Beckenham: Croom Helm, 1987); the Audit Commission's report, *Misspent Youth* (London: Audit Commission, 1996), is the most recent and sweeping critique.

REFERENCES

ABRAMS, M. (1959), *The Teenage Consumer*. London: Routledge and Kegan Paul.

ALLEN, R. (1991), 'Out of Jail: The Reduction in the Use of Penal Custody for Male Juveniles 1981–88', *Howard Journal of Criminal Justice*, 30, 1: 30–52.

—— (1997), *Children and Crime: Taking responsibility*. London: Institute for Public Policy Research.

ANDERSON, I., KEMP, P., and QUILGARS, D. (1993), *Single Homeless People*. London: HMSO.

ANDERSON, M. (1980), *Approaches to the History of the Western Family 1500–1914*. London: Macmillan.

ANDERSON, S., KINSEY, R., LOADER, I., and SMITH, C. (1994), *Cautionary Tales*. Aldershot: Avebury.

ARIES, P. (1973), *Centuries of Childhood*. Harmondsworth: Penguin.

AUDIT COMMISSION (1996), *Misspent Youth: Young People and Crime*. London: Audit Commission.

AYE MAUNG, N. (1995), *Young People, Victim-isation and the Police: British Crime Survey Findings on the Experiences and Attitudes of 12–15 Year Olds*. Home Office Research Study No. 140, London: HMSO.

BAILEY, V. (1987), *Delinquency and Citizenship: Reclaiming the Young Offender 1914–1948*. Oxford: Clarendon Press.

BALDING, J. (1994), *Young People and Illegal Drugs*. Exeter: Health Education Unit, University of Exeter.

BARCLAY, G., and TURNER, D. (1991), 'Recent Trends in Official Statistics on Juvenile Offending in England and Wales', in T. Booth, ed., *Juvenile Justice in the New Europe*. Sheffield: University of Sheffield.

BARKER, P., and LITTLE, A. (1964), 'The Margate Offenders—A Survey', *New Society*, 4, 96: 6–10.

BENYON, J. (1986), *A Tale of Failure: Race and Policing*. Policy Papers in Ethnic Relations No. 3, University of Warwick: Centre for Research in Ethnic Relations.

BOOTH, C. (1902), *Life and Labour of the People of London*. London: Macmillan.

BOSWELL, G. (1996), *Young and Dangerous: The Backgrounds and Careers of Section 53 Offenders*. Aldershot: Avebury.

BOTTOMLEY, A. K., and PEASE, K. (1986), *Crime and Punishment: Interpreting the Data*. Milton Keynes: Open University Press.

BOTTOMS, A. E. (1974), 'On the Decriminal-isation of the English Juvenile Courts', In R. Hood, ed., *Crime, Criminology and Public Policy*. London: Heinemann.

—— (1995), 'The Philosophy and Politics of Punishment and Sentencing', in C. M. V. Clarkson and R. Morgan, eds., *The Politics of Sentencing Reform*. Oxford: Oxford University Press.

—— BROWN, P., MCWILLIAMS, B., MCWILLIAMS, W., and NELLIS, M. (1990), *Intermediate Treatment and Juvenile Justice: Key Findings and Implications from a National Survey of Intermediate Treatment Policy and Practice*. London: HMSO.

—— and STEVENSON, S. (1992), 'What Went Wrong? Criminal Justice Policy in England and Wales 1945–1970', in D. Downes, ed., *Unravelling Criminal Justice*. Basingstoke: Macmillan.

—— and WILES, P. (1994), 'Crime and Insecurity in the City', paper presented at the Conference of the International Society of Criminology, Leuven, Belgium.

BOX, S. (1981), *Deviance, Reality and Society*. 2nd edn. London: Holt, Rinehart and Winston.

BRAKE, M. (1980), *The Sociology of Youth Culture and Youth Subcultures*. London: Routledge and Kegan Paul.

—— (1985), *Comparative Youth Culture*. London: Routledge.

CAMPBELL, B. (1993), *Goliath: Britain's Dangerous Places*. London: Methuen.

CARLEN, P. (1996), *Jigsaw: A Political Economy of Youth Homelessness*. Milton Keynes: Open University Press.

CASHMORE, E. (1983), *Rastaman: The Rastafarian Movement in England*. London: Unwin.

CAVADINO, M., and DIGNAN, J. (1992), *The Penal System: An Introduction*. London: Sage.

CAVADINO, P. (1996), 'Children Who Kill', *Young Minds Magazine*.

CLARKE, J. (1976a), 'The Skinheads and the Magical Recovery of Community', in S. Hall and T. Jefferson, eds., *Resistance Through Rituals*. London: Hutchison.

—— (1976b), 'Style', in S. Hall and T. Jefferson, eds., *Resistance Through Rituals*. London: Hutchison.

—— (1980), 'Social Democratic Delinquents and Fabian Families', in National Deviancy Conference, eds., *Permissiveness and Control:*

The Fate of Sixties Legislation. Basingstoke: Macmillan.

CLARKE, J., HALL, S., JEFFERSON, T., and ROBERTS, B. (1976), 'Subcultures, Cultures and Class: A Theoretical Overview', in S. Hall and T. Jefferson, eds., *Resistance Through Rituals: Youth Subcultures in Post-war Britain*. London: Hutchison.

—— and JEFFERSON, T. (1976), 'Working Class Youth Cultures', in G. Mungham and G. Pearson, eds., *Working Class Youth Culture*. London: Routledge and Kegan Paul.

CLEMENTS, I. (1993), 'Too Hot to Handle', *Druglink*, 8: 10–12.

CLOWARD, R. A., and OHLIN, L. E. (1960), *Delinquency and Opportunity: A Theory of Delinquent Gangs*. New York: Free Press.

COHEN, A. K. (1955), *Delinquent Boys: The Culture of the Gang*. New York: Free Press.

COHEN, P. (1972), 'Subcultural Conflict and Working Class Community', in S. Hall *et al.*, eds., *Culture, Media, Language*. London: Hutchison.

COHEN, S. (1980), *Folk Devils and Moral Panics*. London: Martin Robertson.

COLEMAN, J., and HENDRY, L. (1990), *The Nature of Adolescence*. London: Routledge.

DAVIS, J. (1990), *Youth and the Condition of Britain*. London: Athlone Press.

DIEKSTRA, R. F. W., KIENHORST, C. W. M., and DE WILDE, E. J. (1995), 'Suicide and Suicidal Behaviour Among Adolescents', in M. Rutter and D. J. Smith, eds., *Psychosocial Disorders in Young People: Time Trends and Their Correlates*. Chichester: Wiley.

DORN, N., and SOUTH, N. (1982), 'Of Males and Markets: A Critical Review of Youth Culture Theory', *Research Paper 1, Centre for Occupational and Community Research*. London: Middlesex Polytechnic.

—— and —— eds. (1987), *A Land Fit for Heroin? Drug Policies, Prevention and Practice*. Basingstoke: Macmillan.

DOWNES, D. (1996), *The Delinquent Solution*. London: Routledge and Kegan Paul.

—— and MORGAN, R. (1994), '"Hostages to Fortune"? The Politics of Law and Order in Post-war Britain', in M. Maguire, R. Morgan, and R. Reiner, eds., *The Oxford Handbook of Criminology*. Oxford: Oxford University Press.

—— and ROCK, P. (1982), *Understanding Deviance*. Oxford: Oxford University Press.

EVANS, R. (1994), 'Cautioning: Counting the Cost of Retrenchment', *Criminal Law Review*, 566–75.

FARRINGTON, D.P. (1977), 'The Effects of Public Labelling', *British Journal of Criminology*, 17, 112–25.

—— (1989), 'Self-reported and Official Offending from Adolescence to Adulthood', in M. W. Klein, ed., *Cross-National Research in Self-Reported Crime and Delinquency*. Dordrecht, Kluwer.

—— (1990), 'Age, Period, Cohort and Offending', in D. M. Gottfredson and R. V. Clarke, eds., *Policy and Theory in Criminal Justice: Contributions in honour of Leslie T. Wilkins*. Aldershot: Avebury.

—— (1992), 'Trends in English Juvenile Delinquency and their Explanation', *International Journal of Comparative and Applied Criminal Justice*, 16, 2: 151–63.

—— (1996), *Understanding and Preventing Youth Crime*. York: Joseph Rowntree Foundation.

—— and BENNETT, T. (1981), 'Police Cautioning of Juveniles in London, *British Journal of Criminology*, 21: 123–35.

—— and BURROWS, J. (1993), 'Did Shoplifting Really Decrease?', *British Journal of Criminology*, 33: 57–69.

—— and LANGAN, P.A. (1992), 'Changes in Crime and Punishment in England and America in the 1980s', *Justice Quarterly*, 9: 5–46.

—— OSBORN, S. G., and WEST, D. J. (1978), 'The Persistence of Labelling Effects', *British Journal of Criminology*, 18: 277–84.

FAULKNER, D. (1996), *Darkness and Light: Justice, Crime and Management for Today*. London: The Howard League.

FITZGERALD, M. (1993), *Ethnic Minorities and the Criminal Justice System*, Royal Commission on Criminal Justice Research Study No. 20. London: HMSO.

FOMBONNE, E. (1995a), 'Depressive Disorders: Time Trends and Possible Explanatory Mechanisms', in M. Rutter. and D. J. Smith, eds., *Psychosocial Disorders in Young People: Time Trends and their Correlates*. Chichester: Wiley.

—— (1995b), 'Eating Disorders: Time Trends and Possible Explanatory Mechanisms', in M. Rutter and D. J. Smith, eds., *Psychosocial Disorders in Young People: Time Trends and their Correlates*. Chichester: Wiley.

FRANKLIN, B., and PETLEY, J. (1996), 'Killing the Age of Innocence: Newspaper Reporting of the Death of James Bulger', in J. Pilcher and S. Wagg, eds., *Thatcher's Children: Politics, Childhood and Society in the 1980s and 1990s*. London: Falmer.

FRITH, S. (1983), *Sound Effects: Youth, Leisure and the Politics of Rock and Roll*. London: Constable.

GARLAND, D. (1985), *Punishment and Welfare: A History of Penal Strategies*. Aldershot: Gower.

GELSTHORPE, L. (1984), 'Girls and Juvenile Justice', *Youth and Policy*, II: 1–5.

—— and MORRIS, A. (1994), 'Juvenile Justice 1945–1992', in M. Maguire, R. Morgan, and R. Reiner, eds., *The Oxford Handbook of Criminology*. Oxford: Oxford University Press.

GIBSON, B., CAVADINO, P., RUTHERFORD, A., ASHWORTH, A., and HARDING, J. (1994), *Criminal Justice in Transition*. Winchester: Waterside Press.

GIDDENS, A. (1990), *The Consequences of Modernity*. Cambridge: Polity Press.

GILL, O. (1977), *Luke Street: Housing Policy, Conflict and the Creation of the Delinquent Area*. London: Macmillan.

GILLETT, C. (1983), *The Sound of the City*. London: Souvenir Press.

GILLIS, J. R. (1974), *Youth and History: Tradition and Change in European Age Relations, 1770–Present*. New York: Academic Press.

—— (1975), 'The Evolution of Juvenile Delinquency in England, 1880–1914', *Past and Present*, 67.

GILROY, P. (1987), *There Ain't No Black in the Union Jack*. London: Hutchinson.

GOLDTHORPE, J., LOCKWOOD, D., BECHOFER, F., and PLATT, J. (1969), *The Affluent Worker in the Class Structure*. Cambridge: Cambridge University Press.

GRAHAM, J., and MOXON, D. (1986), 'Some Trends in Juvenile Justice', *Home Office Research Bulletin*, 22: 10–13.

GREEN, A. (1994), *The Geography of Poverty*. Warwick: Institute of Emloyment Research.

GRIFFIN, C. (1993), *Representations of Youth: A Study of Youth and Adolescence in Britain and America*. Cambridge: Polity Press.

HAGELL, A., and NEWBURN, T. (1994), *Persistent Young Offenders*. London: Policy Studies Institute.

HALL, S. (1969), 'The Hippies: An American Moment', in J. Nagel, ed., *Student Power*. Merlin Press.

—— (1980), *Drifting into a Law and Order Society*. London: Cobden Trust.

—— CRITCHER, C., JEFFERSON, T., CLARKE, J., and ROBERTS, B. (1978), *Policing the Crisis. Mugging, the State and Law and Order*. London: Macmillan.

HARDING, C., HINES, B., IRELAND, R., and RAWLINGS, P. (1985), *Imprisonment in England and Wales: A Concise History*. Beckenham: Croom Helm.

HARRIS, R., and WEBB, D. (1987), *Welfare, Power and Juvenile Justice*. London: Tavistock.

HARTLESS, J., DITTON, J., NAIR, G., and PHILLIPS, S. (1995), 'More Sinned Against than Sinning: A Study of Young Teenagers' Experiences of Crime', *British Journal of Criminology*, 35: 114–33.

HARWIN, J. (1982), 'The Battle for the Delinquent', in C. Jones and J. Stevenson, eds., *The Yearbook of Social Policy in Britain, 1980–81*. London: Routledge and Kegan Paul.

HEBDIGE, D. (1976*a*), 'The Meaning of Mod', in S. Hall and T. Jefferson, eds., *Resistance Through Rituals*. London: Hutchison.

—— (1979), *Subculture: The Meaning of Style*. London: Metheun.

—— (1987), *Cut'n'Mix: Culture, Identity and Caribbean Music*. London: Methuen.

HEDDERMAN, C., and HOUGH, M. (1994), 'Does the Criminal Justice System Treat Men and Women Differently?', *Home Office Research and Statistics Department Research Findings No. 10*. London: Home Office.

HEIDENSOHN, F. (1996), *Women and Crime*. Basingstoke: Macmillan.

HINDELANG, M. J., HIRSCHI, T., and WEIS, J. G. (1979), 'Correlates of Delinquency: the Illusion of Discrepancy between Self-report and Official Measures', *American Sociological Review*, 44: 995–1014.

HIRSCHI, T. (1969), *Causes of Delinquency*. Berkeley, Cal.: University of California Press.

—— and GOTTFREDSON, M. (1983), 'Age and the Explanation of Crime', *American Journal of Sociology*, 89: 552–84.

HOME AFFAIRS COMMITTEE (1993), *Juvenile Offenders*. Sixth Report. London: HMSO.

—— (1994), *Video Violence and Young Offenders*. Fourth Report. London: HMSO.

HOME OFFICE (1965), *The Child, The Family and the Young Offender*. Cmnd. 2742. London: HMSO.

—— (1968), *Children in Trouble*. Cmnd. 3601. London: HMSO.

—— (1980), *Young Offenders*. Cmnd. 8045. London: HMSO.

—— (1984), *Cautioning by the Police: A Consultative Document*. London: Home Office.

—— (1984), *Tougher Regimes in Detention Centres: Report of an Evaluation by the Young Offender Psychology Unit*. London: HMSO.

—— (1985), *The Cautioning of Offenders*. Circular 14/1985. London: Home Office.

—— (1988), *Punishment, Custody and the Community*. Cm 424. London: HMSO.

—— (1990), *The Cautioning of Offenders*. Circular 59/1990. London: Home Office.

—— (1994), *The Cautioning of Offenders*. Circular 18/1994. London: Home Office.

—— (1995*a*), *Criminal Careers of Those Born between 1953 and 1973*. Home Office Statistical Bulletin 14/95. London: Home Office Research and Statistics Department.

—— (1995*b*), *Digest 3: Information on the Criminal Justice System in England and Wales*. London: Home Office Research and Statistics Department.

—— (1996), *Projections of Long-term Trends in the Prison Population to 2004*. Home Office Statistical Bulletin 4/96, London: Home Office Research and Statistics Department.

—— (1997), *Preventing Children Offending: A Consultation Document*. Cm 3566. London: Home Office.

HOME OFFICE et al. (1976), *Children and Young Persons Act 1969: Observations on the Eleventh Report of the Expenditure Committee*. Cmnd 6494. London: HMSO.

HUMPHRIES, S. (1981), *Hooligans or Rebels? An Oral History of Working Class Childhood and Youth, 1889–1939*. Oxford: Basil Blackwell.

INSTITUTE FOR THE STUDY OF DRUG DEPENDENCE (ISDD) (1994), *Drug Misuse in Britain 1994*. London: ISDD.

JAMES, O. (1995), *Juvenile Violence in a Winner–Loser Culture*. London: Free Association Books.

JEFFERSON, T. (1976), 'Cultural Responses of the Teds', in S. Hall and T. Jefferson, eds., *Resistance Through Rituals*. London: Hutchison.

JENSEN, G. F., and EVE, R. (1976), 'Sex Differences in Delinquency: An Examination of Popular and Sociological Explanations', *Criminology*, 13: 427–48.

JONES, D. (1989), 'The Successful Revolution', *Community Care*, 30 March, pp. i–ii.

JONES, G. (1995), *Family Support for Young People*. London: Family Policy Studies Centre.

JONES, R. (1984), 'Questioning the New Orthodoxy', *Community Care*, 11 October: 26–9.

JOSEPH ROWNTREE FOUNDATION (1995), *Income and Wealth: Report of the JRF Inquiry Group*. York: Joseph Rowntree Foundation.

LABOUR PARTY (1996), *Tackling Youth Crime: Reforming Youth Justice*. London: Labour Party.

LAING, D. (1985), *One Chord Wonders: Power and Meaning in Punk Rock*. Milton Keynes: Open University Press.

LAYCOCK, G., and TARLING, R. (1985), 'Police Force Cautioning: Policy and Practice', *Howard Journal of Criminal Justice*, 24, 2: 81–92.

LOADER, I. (1996), *Youth, Policing and Democracy*. Basingstoke: Macmillan.

McKAY, G. (1996), *Senseless Acts of Beauty: Cultures of Resistance Since the Sixties*. London: Verso.

McROBBIE, A. (1980), 'Settling Accounts with Subcultures: A Feminist Critique', *Screen Education*, 39: 37–49.

—— (1991), *Feminism and Youth Culture: From 'Jackie' to 'Just Seventeen'*. London: Macmillan.

—— (1994*a*), 'A Cultural Sociology of Youth', in A. McRobbie, *Postmodernism and Popular Culture*. London: Routledge.

—— (1994*b*), 'Shut Up and Dance: Youth Culture and the Changing Modes of Femininity', in A. McRobbie, *Postmodernism and Popular Culture*. London: Routledge.

—— and GARBER, J. (1976), 'Girls and Subcultures: An Exploration', in S. Hall and T. Jefferson, eds., *Resistance Through Rituals*. London: Hutchison.

MAGUIRE, M. (1994), 'Crime Statistics, Patterns and Trends: Changing Perceptions and their Implications', in M. Maguire, R. Morgan, and R. Reiner, eds., *The Oxford Handbook of Criminology*. Oxford: Oxford University Press.

MANNHEIM, H., and WILKINS, L. (1955), *Prediction Methods in Relation to Borstal Training*. Home Office Study in the Causes of Delinquency and the Treatment of Offenders, No. 1. London: Home Office.

MATZA, D., and SYKES, G. (1957), 'Techniques of Neutralization', *American Sociological Review*, 22: 664–70.

—— and —— (1961), 'Juvenile Delinquency and Subterranean Values', *American Sociological Review*, 26: 712–19.

MAY, M. (1973), 'Innocence and Experience: the Evolution of the Concept of Juvenile Delinquency in the Mid-nineteenth Century', *Victorian Studies*, 17: 1.

MAYHEW, H. (1861), *London Labour and London Poor*. London: Griffin, Bohn and Co.

MEASHAM, F., NEWCOMBE, R., and PARKER, H. (1993), 'The Post-heroin Generation', *Druglink*, May/June: 16–17.

—— (1994), 'The Normalization of Recreational Drug Use amongst Young People in North-West England', *British Journal of Sociology*, 45, 2: 287–312.

MELLY, G. (1972), *Revolt into Style*. Harmondsworth: Penguin.

MERTON, R. (1938), 'Social Structure and Anomie', *American Socioligical Review*, 3: 672–82.

MILLER, P. McC., and PLANT, M. (1996), 'Drinking, Smoking and Illicit Drug Use among 15 and 16 Year Olds in the United Kingdom', *British Medical Journal*, 17 August: 313, 394–7.

MILLER, W. B. (1958), 'Lower Class Culture as a Generating Milieu of Gang Delinquency', *Journal of Social Issues*, 15, 1: 5–19.

MORGAN, J., and ZEDNER, L. (1992), *Child Victims: Crime, Impact and Criminal Justice*. Oxford: Oxford University Press.

MORRIS, A., and GELSTHORPE, L. (1981), 'False Clues and Female Crime', in A. Morris and L. Gelsthorpe, eds., *Women and Crime*, Cropwood Series No. 13, Cambridge: University of Cambridge.

—— and GILLER, H. (1987), *Understanding Juvenile Justice*. Beckenham: Croom Helm.

—— and McISAAC, M. (1978), *Juvenile Justice?* London: Heinemann.

MUNCIE, J. (1984), *The Trouble with Kids Today*. London: Hutchison.

—— (1990), 'Failure Never Matters: Detention Centres and the Politics of Deterrence', *Critical Social Policy*: 53–66.

—— COVENTRY, G., and WALTERS, R. (1995), 'The Politics of Youth Crime Prevention: Developments in Australia and England and Wales', in L. Noaks, M. Levi, and M. Maguire, eds., *Issues in Contemporary Criminology*. Cardiff: University of Wales Press.

MURDOCK, G., and McCRON, R. (1976), 'Consciousness of Class and Consciousness of Generation', in S. Hall and T. Jefferson, eds., *Resistance Through Rituals: Youth Subcultures in Post-war Britain*. London: Hutchison.

MURRAY, C. (1990), *The Emerging Underclass*. London: Institute of Economic Affairs.

NATHAN, S. (1995), *Boot Camps: Return of the Short, Sharp Shock*. London: Prison Reform Trust.

NELLIS, M. (1991), 'The Last Days of "Juvenile" Justice?', in P. Carter, T. Jeffs, and M. Smith, eds., *Social Work and Social Welfare Yearbook 3*. Milton Keynes: Open University Press.

NEWBURN, T. (1991), *Permission and Regulation: Law and Morals in Post-war Britain*. London: Routledge.

NEWSON, E. (1994), *Video Violence and the Protection of Children*. Nottingham: University of Nottingham.

OFFICE OF NATIONAL STATISTICS (1996), *Social Focus on Ethnic Minorities*. London: HMSO.

PALMER, T. (1971), *The Trials of OZ*. London: Blond and Briggs.

PARKER, H. (1974), *View From The Boys*. London: David and Charles.

—— MEASHAM, F., and ALDRIDGE, J. (1995), *Drug Futures: Changing Patterns of Drug Use amongst English Youth*. London: ISDD.

—— NEWCOMBE, R., and BAKX, K. (1988), *Living With Heroin: The Impact of Drugs 'Epidemic' on an English Community*. Milton Keynes: Open University Press.

—— SUMNER, M., and JARVIS, G. (1989), *Unmasking the Magistrates: The 'Custody or Not' Decision in Sentencing Young Offenders*. Milton Keynes: Open University Press.

PARLIAMENTARY ALL-PARTY PENAL AFFAIRS GROUP (1981), *Young Offenders: A Strategy for the Future*. Chichester: Barry Rose.

PARSONS, T. (1942), 'Age and Sex in the Social Structure of the United States', *American Sociological Review*, 7: 604–16.

PATRICK, J. (1973), *A Glasgow Gang Observed*. London: Methuen.

PEARSON, G. (1983), *Hooligan: A History of Respectable Fears*. Basingstoke: Macmillan.

—— (1987), 'Social Deprivation, Unemployment and Patterns of Heroin Use', in N. Dorn and N. South, eds., *A Land Fit for Heroin? Drug Policies, Prevention and Practice*. Basingstoke: Macmillan.

—— (1989), ' "A Jekyll in the Classroom, a Hyde in the Street": Queen Victoria's Hooligans', in D. Downes, ed., *Crime in the City: Essays in Honour of John Barron Mays*. London: Macmillan.

—— (1994), 'Youth, Crime and Society', in M. Maguire, R. Morgan, and R. Reiner, eds., *The Oxford Handbook of Criminology*. Oxford: Oxford University Press.

PINCHBECK, I., and HEWITT, M. (1969), *Children in English Society*. London: Routledge and Kegan Paul.

PINTO-DUSCHINSKY, M. (1970), 'Bread and Circuses? The Conservatives in Power 1951–64', in V. Bogdonor and R. Skidelsky, eds., *The Age of Affluence*. London: Macmillan.

PLANT, M., PECK, D., and SAMUEL, E. (1985), *Alcohol, Drugs and School Leavers*. London: Tavistock.

RADZINOWICZ, L., and HOOD, R. (1990), *The Emergence of Penal Policy in Victorian and Edwardian England*. Oxford: Clarendon Press.

RAMSAY, M., and PERCY, A. (1996), *Drug Misuse Declared: Results of the 1994 British*

Crime Survey. Home Office Research Study 151, London: Home Office.

REDHEAD, S. (1990), *The End of the Century Party: Youth and Pop Towards 2000*. Manchester: Manchester University Press.

—— (1993), 'The End of the End-of-the-century Party', in S. Redhead, ed., *Rave Off*. Avebury: Aldershot.

ROBERTS, K. (1983), *Youth and Leisure*. London: George Allen and Unwin.

—— (1995), *Youth and Employment in Modern Britain*. Oxford: Oxford University Press.

ROOK, C. (1899), *The Hooligan Nights*. London: Grant Richards.

ROYAL COMMISSION ON CRIMINAL PROCEDURE (1981), *Report*. London: HMSO.

RUTHERFORD, A. (1986a), *Growing Out of Crime: Society and Young People in Trouble*. Harmondsworth: Penguin.

—— (1986b), *Prisons and the Process of Justice*. Oxford: Oxford University Press.

—— (1992), *Growing Out of Crime: The New Era*. Winchester: Waterside Press.

RUTTER, M., and GILLER, H. (1983), *Juvenile Delinquency: Trends and Perspectives*. Harmondsworth: Penguin.

—— and SMITH, D. J. (1995a), *Psychosocial Disorders in Young People: Time Trends and their Correlates*. Chichester: Wiley.

—— and —— (1995b), 'Towards Causal Explanations of Time Trends in Psychosocial Disorders of Youth', in M. Rutter and D. J. Smith, eds., *Psychosocial Disorders in Young People: Time Trends and their Correlates*. Chichester: Wiley.

SAVAGE, J. (1996), *Time Travel, From the Sex Pistols to Nirvana: Pop, Media and Sexuality 1977–1996*. London: Chatto and Windus.

SCHOENFELD, C. G. (1971), 'A Psychoanalytic Theory of Juvenile Delinquency', *Crime and Delinquency*, 17: 479–80.

SHAPIRO, H. (forthcoming), 'Dances with Drugs: Pop Music, Drugs and Youth Culture', in N. South, ed., *Drugs: Cultures, Controls and Everyday Life*. London: Sage.

SHAW, C. R., and MCKAY, H. (1942), *Juvenile Delinquency and Urban Areas*. Chicago, Ill.: University of Chicago Press.

SHINER, M., and NEWBURN, T. (1997), 'Definitely, Maybe Not? The Normalization of Recreational Drug Use Amongst Young People', *Sociology*, summer.

SHORTER, E. (1976), *The Making of the Modern Family*. London: Collins.

SILBEREISEN, R. K., ROBINS, L., and RUTTER, M. (1995), 'Secular Trends in Substance Use: Concepts and Data on the Impact of Social Change', in M. Rutter and D. J. Smith, eds., *Psychosocial Disorders in Young People:*

Time Trends and their Correlates. Chichester: Wiley.

SMITH, D. JAMES (1994), *The Sleep of Reason: The James Bulger Case*. London: Century.

SMITH, D. JOHN (1995), 'Youth Crime and Conduct Disorders', in M. Rutter and D. J. Smith, eds., *Psychosocial Disorders in Young People: Time Trends and their Correlates*. Chichester: Wiley.

SOUTH, N. (1994), 'Drugs and Crime', in M. Maguire, R. Morgan, and R. Reiner, eds., *The Oxford Handbook of Criminology*. Oxford: Oxford University Press.

STONE, L. (1979), *The Family, Sex and Marriage in England 1500–1800*. Harmondsworth: Penguin.

THORNTON, S. (1995), *Club Cultures: Music, Media and Subcultural Capital*. Oxford: Polity Press.

THRASHER, F. (1927), *The Gang*. Chicago, Ill.: University of Chicago Press.

TUTT, N. (1981), 'A Decade of Policy', *British Journal of Criminology*, 21: 246–56.

—— and GILLER, H. (1983), 'Police Cautioning of Juveniles: The Practice of Diversity', *Criminal Law Review*: 587–95.

UTTING, D. (1995), *Family and Parenthood: Supporting Families, Preventing Breakdown*. York: Joseph Rowntree Foundation.

—— (1997), *Reducing Criminality Among Young People: A Sample of Relevant Programmes in the United Kingdom*. London: Home Office.

—— BRIGHT, J., and HENDERSON, C. (1993), *Crime and the Family*. London: Family Policy Studies Centre.

WALKER, M. A., ed. (1995), *Interpreting Criminal Statistics*. Oxford: Clarendon Press.

WALLACE, C. (1987), *For Richer, For Poorer: Growing Up In and Out of Work*. London: Tavistock.

WEST, D. J., and FARRINGTON, D. P. (1977), *The Delinquent Way of Life*. London: Heinemann.

WILKINSON, C., and EVANS, R. (1990), 'Police Cautioning of Juveniles: The Impact of Home Office Circular 14/1985', *Criminal Law Review*: 165–76.

WILLIAMS, J. (1991), 'Having an Away Day: English Football Spectators and the Hooligan Debate', in J. Williams and S. Wagg, eds., *British Football and Social Change: Getting into Europe*. Leicester: Leicester University Press.

WILLIS, P. (1978), *Profane Culture*. London: Routledge and Kegan Paul.

WILLMOTT, P. (1966), *Adolescent Boys of East London*. London: Routledge and Kegan Paul.

WILSON, J. Q., and HERRNSTEIN, R. (1985), *Crime and Human Nature*. New York: Simon and Schuster.

WINDELSHAM, LORD (1993), *Responses to Crime (vol. 2),: Penal Policy in the Making*. Oxford: Oxford University Press.

YOUNG, A. (1996), *Imagining Crime: Textual Outlaws and Criminal Conversations*. London: Sage.

20

Mentally Disordered Offenders

Jill Peay

Current policy remains disarmingly straightforward. 'Mentally disordered offenders should, wherever appropriate, receive care and treatment from health and personal social services rather than in custodial care' (Reed Report, 1991, Community Advisory Group: para. 2.1). It mirrors a humanitarian view widely held since the introduction of the Mental Health Act 1959 and underlined by the Butler Report; namely that 'In making a hospital order the court is placing the patient in the hands of the doctors, foregoing (sic) any question of punishment and relinquishing from then onwards its own controls over them' (1975: para. 14.8).

Where mentally disordered people offend, punishment and protection are not overriding criteria, nor even necessarily relevant ones. Diversion and treatment are paramount. Or are they? A contrary view, reflecting the darker side of public conceptions of the mentally disordered offender, was captured by Rubin (1972: 398): 'certain mental disorders [are] characterized by some kind of confused, bizarre, agitated, threatening, frightened, panicked, paranoid or impulsive behaviour. That and the view that impulse (i.e. ideation) and action are interchangeable support the belief that all mental disorder must of necessity lead to inappropriate, anti-social or dangerous actions'.

This view finds expression in the arrangements for discretionary life sentences for offenders of an 'unstable' character (*R. v. Hodgson* (1967) 52 Cr. App. R 113) who are in a 'mental state which makes them dangerous to the life or limb of members of the public' (*R. v. Wilkinson* (1983) 5 Cr. App. R (S) 105 at 109). It emerges also in the *Report on Mentally Disturbed Offenders in the Prison System* (Home Office/DHSS, 1987) where it was noted, in the context of transferring prisoners to hospital for treatment, that 'the response to the needs of individual mentally disturbed offenders has to take account of the legitimate expectation of the public that government agencies will take appropriate measures for its protection' (Home Office/DHSS, 1987: para. 3.6). It is also evident in the arrangements under the Criminal Justice Act 1991; although proportionality in sentencing is the leading principle, with sentences being 'calculated on the basis of what the person deserves for the offence committed, and not lengthened for any supposed deterrent or rehabilitative reasons' (Ashworth, 1992: 229), there is a limited—but important—exception for violent and sexual offences where it is 'necessary to protect the public from serious harm' (section 2(2)(b). Indeed, section 28(4)(a) arguably has the potential to exclude mentally disordered offenders from being tied into the Act's central proportionality principle. Finally, the provisions of Section 2 of the Crime (Sentences) Act 1997 (see Ashworth, this volume) for mandatory life sentences for a second serious offence will seemingly trump the court's discretion to impose certain kinds of therapeutic disposals on offenders found to be disordered at the point of sentence, thereby challenging at one stroke forty years of consistent jurisprudential thinking. Such legislative proposals are highly contentious and at odds with considered legal and psychiatric opinion (Eastman, 1997).

It is paradoxical that, on the one hand, calls for diverting the mentally disordered offender from the damaging effects of the criminal justice system grow louder, demanding ever earlier diversion; yet, on the other hand, there appears to be a growing distrust of therapeutic disposals for those offenders who find themselves at the end of the criminal justice process. The recent airing of a new power for the courts to combine a prison sentence with an immediate direction that an offender be sent to hospital (Home Office/Department of Health, 1996) and its subsequent inclusion in the Crime (Sentences) Bill 1996, despite widespread condemnation by the professions, illustrates a growing desire to maintain penal control over mentally disordered offenders. Such a desire is, of course, only one manifestation of a wider trend (see Ashworth in this volume) but it may also be fuelled by concern about re-offending by former psychiatric patients. These concerns have been magnified by the recent spate of high-profile inquiries into homicides committed by those who have had contact with the specialist mental health services; since the publication of the *NHS Executive Guidance* (Department of Health, 1994) these 'Inquiries after Homicide' are now mandatory (Peay, 1996; Sheppard, 1996). It is particularly galling to those involved in treating the mentally disordered that such concerns persist despite repeated demonstrations that 'Re-offending rates are in fact no higher than for any other class of offender' (Murray, 1989: p. iii) and the knowledge that when psychiatric patients kill, they are much more likely to kill themselves than others (Sims, 1996).

Much of the confusion arises because of the tensions inherent across both the continuum of ordered–disordered behaviour and that of law-abiding—law-breaking behaviour. In essence, our responses to those we deem 'mentally disordered offenders' are complex. Notions of care/treatment are seen as peculiarly appropriate for the seriously disordered, provided this does not also arise in conjunction with offending of a worrying nature. Similarly, notions of protection/punishment are traditionally confined to serious offenders, again assuming an absence of obvious disorder. Yet these tensions are confounded where it is argued (or denied) that disorder and offending exist side-by-side in one individual, or, more confusingly still, interact. The questions posed by the handling of those mentally disordered offenders isolated as meriting 'special' provision, whichever limb of the bifurcated policy (special care or special control) is adopted, cannot be answered readily. Moreover, 'special' provision all too easily manifests itself in special discrimination (Campbell and Heginbotham, 1991).

The conflict is primarily between welfarism and legalism. Gostin (1986: p. v) distinguishes the two approaches thus: legalism occurs 'where the law is used to wrap the patient in a network of substantive and procedural protections against unjustified loss of liberty and compulsory treatment'; whereas welfarism occurs where 'legal safeguards are replaced with professional discretion which is seen as allowing speedy access to treatment and care, unencumbered by a panoply of bureaucracy and procedures'.

Gostin argues that the Mental Health Act 1983, which encompasses both the mentally disordered non-offender and the mentally disordered offender, achieves a balance between the two principles, retaining welfarism as established by the 1959 Act, but enhancing safeguards for patients' rights in such areas as treatment without consent (the Act established the Mental Health Act Commission) and continued detention of offender patients (Mental Health Review Tribunals—MHRTs—acquired the power to discharge restricted patients). This balance is arguably least satisfactory when resolving the dilemmas posed by mentally disordered offenders. For example, the ruling in *R.* v. *Merseyside MHRT and Another. ex p. K* ([1990] 1 All ER 694 (CA)) that a restricted patient was not entitled to an absolute discharge, even though there was no evidence of current mental disorder, on the basis that there was a liability to relapse, illustrates a philosophy for mentally disordered offenders of 'once ill, always ill'. This philosophy is strikingly at odds with a criminal justice approach that strives to deal with offenders on the basis of what they have done, rather than who they are. In turn, it impels the criminal justice system to focus on the ideology of a just measure of punishment, in the recognition that offending behaviour may be no more than an adopted response to an environment which may or may not change, independent of any individual measure of pain. In stark contrast, mental health professionals are arguably more interested in the enduring features of individuals, placing the individual at the centre of the problem and thereby providing the justification for treatment.

It is evident that a chapter devoted to 'mentally disordered offenders' cannot be the focus for the discussion of the needs of some single, easily identifiable group. This chapter will do little more than chart a path through muddied waters, muddying them further as it passes. Although learned texts may seek to confine the mentally disordered to a single chapter and the law may, in isolated places, achieve a coherent strategy, neither confinement nor coherence is evident where an overview is attempted. The mentally disordered are not a class and the law, practitioners, policy-makers, and the caring professions will mix and match philosophies in response to the problems created by *individual* offender-patients. Accordingly, notions of justice, treatment, and, indeed, the very existence of a group of 'disordered offenders' will harry this chapter.

The chapter is divided into seven sections. The first examines the concept of mentally disordered offenders: do such offenders constitute an isolated category meriting special provision, or do the issues this 'group' raise have wider implications for the study of criminology? The second addresses the problem of definition: what do the various stages of the criminal justice process include or exclude from the gamut of definitions applying to the 'mentally disordered offender'? Thirdly, are mentally disordered offenders a minority group? What is their incidence, what impact do they have on the criminal justice system, what are the mechanisms for diverting offenders outwith the penal system, and to what extent do such offenders nonetheless remain intertwined with conventional custodial populations? Fourthly, mental disorder at trial. Section five examines the fundamental justification for separate provision—treatment—looking particularly at a key problematic group, namely psychopathic offenders, who straddle the ordered–disordered offending continuum. The sixth section tackles some hidden agendas—bifurcation, detention for protective purposes, due process at discharge/release and the seventh formulates some conclusions.

MENTAL DISORDER AND OFFENDERS—A CASE FOR SPECIAL PROVISION?

Confronting the topic of 'mentally disordered offenders' demands painful examination of a number of key areas. This text is not atypical in treating the mentally disordered as an isolated topic, isolated together with gender, race, youth, and victims. Yet three of these reflect absolute characteristics of an offender, whilst victimology is a comparatively new field. However, all these topics have perhaps a common theme; namely, being 'inconvenient' for a criminology imbued with male, adult, mentally healthy, formerly non-victimized values. It is my intention in this chapter to demonstrate that the lessons to be learnt from how we deal conceptually, practically, and in principle with those deemed 'mentally disordered offenders' have as much to say about topics regarded as central to, or ranging across, the scope of criminology as they have to say about 'marginal' groups. Thus, mentally disordered offenders should not be seen as a Cinderella area.

To argue for the existence of a discrete group of mentally disordered offenders, presupposes a category of mentally ordered offenders. This does not deny the mental element in most crimes, but merely assumes some to be rational and some unacceptable. As Lord Devlin noted with reference to the insanity defence

it is reason which makes a man responsible to the law, reason and reason alone. It is reason which gives him sovereignty over animate and inanimate things. It is what distinguishes him from the animals, which emotional disorder does not; it is what makes him man; it is what makes him subject to the law. So it is fitting that nothing other than a defect of reason should give complete absolution [Smith and Hogan, 1988: 200].

But such a clear-cut division is problematic. In the area of so-called normal offending, defences are frequently advanced or mitigation constructed which draw on elements of 'diminished responsibility', 'unthinking' behaviour, or merely a response to extreme social stress. Concepts of limited rationality will be familiar to criminologists. Yet few of these offenders would wish for the special treatment which may follow a finding of 'defect of reason'. Why not? Is it a recognition of the punishing aspects of such treatment? Or a desire not to be stigmatized along with the helplessly mad? Or merely that some level of disordered thinking should alleviate punishment, if not excuse it altogether?

'Complete absolution' is clearly a legal nicety. Mentally disordered offenders find themselves confined in hospitals, prisons, therapeutic regimes within prisons, and, most notably, within the remand population. The disorders offenders present at court create opportunities at defence and mitigation, but lead to problems thereafter for those into whose care or custody they are sent. Mentally disordered offenders exist in one shape or form across the entire criminal justice system, and 'disorder' may be found to a greater or lesser extent—partly dependent on the incentives for its construction—throughout offending populations.

Accordingly, one theme which runs through this chapter concerns a plea that the component parts of the concept be disaggregated: mentally disordered offenders are first and foremost people; whether they may have offended or whether they may be disordered will be matters for individual resolution. Prioritization of one aspect (the mentally disordered element) of an individual's make-up readily leads to neglect of other, perhaps more pertinent, aspects. As the Reed Committee (1992) recognized, mentally disordered people may have other needs which are arguably as important in respect of their special status within the criminal justice system. As the Committee's earlier Report (1991: Overview, para. 7.ii) details, such categories may include: black and ethnic minority group members; women; the elderly; children and adolescents; sex offenders; substance misusers; people with personality (or psychopathic) disorders; or sensory disabilities; or brain damage; or learning disabilities (the new term for mental handicap); and, arguably, the homeless. There is no pure form of mentally disordered offender. To assume that there is would be both to mislead and to negate the transparent and frequently reiterated need for flexibility within the mental health and criminal justice agencies; a flexibility which is required not only in respect of the movement of people between available resources, but also in the conceptualization of 'mentally disordered offending'. Without it, the gap between expectations and provision cannot be bridged.

THE PROBLEM OF DEFINITION

Hoggett (1996: 97) admirably details the interactions between the mentally disordered offender and the criminal justice system at all of its stages noting that 'the fact that a person who is alleged to have committed a criminal offence may be mentally disordered can affect the normal processes of the law at several points'. These crisis points are sketched below. No attempt is made to replicate the detail of Hoggett's analysis, but some key themes emerge which reflect how an individual's mental state may affect prosecution, conviction, disposal, treatment, and release.

'Mental disorder' is itself problematic; indeed, it is a term of acute terminological inexactitude. Definitions of mental disorder act like a concertina, expanding and contracting in order to accommodate different client groups with little or no coherence. Their mismatch frequently results in uncertainties and anomalies. For example, the presence of a disorder of a particular form may be sufficient for compulsory admission to hospital, but its absence in the same form may be insufficient to bring that period of detention to an end. Such grey areas dog the entire field.

In order to illustrate the effects of this concertina, it is necessary to go into the statutory provisions in some detail. Those familiar with, and those who do not wish to become confused by, this legal exposition could readily move on to the next section.

The Mental Health Act 1983, section 1(2), defines mental disorder as 'mental illness, arrested or incomplete development of mind, psychopathic disorder *and any other disorder or disability of mind'* (emphasis added), and provides further definitions of severe mental impairment, mental impairment, and psychopathic disorder. There is no definition of mental illness despite this being one of the key classifications under the Act. Psychopathic disorder is defined as 'a persistent disorder or disability of mind (whether or not including significant impairment of intelligence) which results in abnormally aggressive or seriously irresponsible conduct on the part of the person concerned'; regrettably this definition neither corresponds with psychiatric definitions of personality disorder nor absolves itself of a tautological association with behaviour likely to be criminalized. The problems posed by psychopathic disorder are discussed further below, but it is worth noting here that forensic psychiatrists have been and remain deeply divided about whether psychopathic disorder should even be in the Mental Health Act: Cope's (1993) survey of forensic psychiatrists found 53 per cent in favour and 47 per cent against. The 1983 Act does make clear that a person may not be dealt with under the Act as suffering from mental disorder 'by reason only of promiscuity or other immoral conduct, sexual deviancy or dependence on alcohol or drugs'. Section (1)(3) thus serves to count out from treatment under the Mental Health Act many of those in prison deemed by psychiatrists to be mentally disordered (see Gunn *et al.*, 1991 below).

In addition to the catch-nearly-all phrase emphasized above, the 1983 Act may be conceived as having a dual hierarchy of mental disorder. The first tier encompasses mental illness and severe mental impairment. The second, psychopathic disorder and mental impairment. To invoke many of the sections of the 1983 Act in respect of this second tier (e.g. a hospital order under section 37; transfer from prison to hospital under section 47) it is necessary to satisfy an additional criterion that medical treatment in hospital be 'likely to alleviate or prevent a deterioration' of the individual's condition. Notably, this treatability requirement does not always have to be satisfied; for example, MHRTs determining whether or not to discharge a patient under section 72 only have to 'have regard' to it and may refuse to discharge a patient even though the patient's 'treatability' would not be sufficient to justify admission (*R. v. Cannons Park MHRT ex p. A.* [1994] 2 All ER 659 (CA)). Such flexibility confuses the role of clinicians and gaolers.

Some alleged offenders may be diverted into hospital, with a civil admission constituting a real alternative to involvement with the criminal justice system. For admission under either section 2 (for assessment—twenty-eight days' duration) or section 4 (cases of emergency—seventy-two hours' duration) the presence of *mental disorder* 'of a nature or degree which warrants detention of the patient in hospital' is sufficient. Similarly, section 136 (mentally disordered persons in a public place—removal to a place of safety) requires the person to appear to a constable to be suffering from mental disorder and to be in immediate need of care or control. All of these sections are accordingly broadly inclusive. Under section 3 (admission for treatment—six months' duration) the criteria are somewhat narrower; the patient must be suffering from one of the four categories above *and*, in the case of psychopathic disorder or mental impairment, the treatability criterion must be satisfied.

For hospital orders, a therapeutic post-conviction order, the criteria in respect of the definition of mental disorder are the same as in section 3 above, but the court must also be of the opinion under section 37(2)(b) 'having regard to all the circumstances including the nature of the offence and the character and antecedents of the offender, and to other available methods of dealing with him, that the most suitable method of disposing of the case is by means of an order under this section'. This makes medical evidence favouring a therapeutic disposal a necessary prerequisite, but not necessarily determinative. The courts may choose to punish or protect in the face of medical evidence, even given the additional option of attaching a restriction order under section 41 where 'necessary for the protection of the public from serious harm'. Indeed, *R. v. Birch* (1989) 90 Cr. App. R 78 makes clear that a restriction order can be made by the courts even where there is medical evidence that the offender is not regarded as dangerous. A 'hospital order with restrictions' attaches limits to psychiatrists' control over the subsequent release of the patient and, with the exception of the MHRT's power to discharge, places all control over the movements of the restriction order patient with the Home Secretary. In 1995 there were a total of 649 hospital orders under section 37(1) and (3) and 203 restriction orders (Kershaw and Renshaw, 1996). Many, if not most, 'disordered' offenders do not receive the therapeutic 'hospital order' disposal, even though their culpability may be mitigated, if not absolved, by their mental state (see Ashworth and Gostin, 1984; Verdun-Jones, 1989).

Remand to hospital for treatment under section 36 requires mental illness or severe mental impairment, but curiously precludes those charged with murder; whilst section 35 remand to hospital for reports and section 38 interim hospital orders may be satisfied by the broader classifications of mental illness, severe mental impairment, mental impairment, or psychopathic disorder—with no treatability criterion. Notably, the Crime (Sentences) Act 1997 seeks to extend the period of the interim hospital order from six to twelve months— presumably with a view to ensuring confident predictions about therapeutic outcomes can be made by the courts before ordering a therapeutic disposal.

For transfer from prison to hospital under section 47, for those serving sentences of imprisonment, there must be mental illness, severe mental impairment, mental impairment, or psychopathic disorder (with the latter two satisfying the treatability criterion). But for other prisoners, for example remand prisoners, their transfer under section 48 demands both the first-tier classifications of mental illness or severe mental impairment *and* that the prisoner be in 'urgent need' of medical treatment in hospital. Other routes into psychiatric care may follow a finding of 'unfit to plead' (a legal test: see below) or where mental disorder provides a defence, for example not guilty by reason of insanity, or a partial defence, for example manslaughter by reason of diminished responsibility. Although not greatly used, both insanity verdicts and findings of 'unfit to plead' heavily feature offenders with diagnoses of schizophrenia, perhaps conforming best with lay notions of mental illness.

Within the prison system, an equally mixed population presents itself. The Reed Report (1991, Prison Advisory Group: para. 2.1) recognizes three groups of disordered offenders. First, those meeting the four narrow classifications under the 1983 Act and needing in-patient treatment. Secondly, those falling within the International Classification of Diseases (WHO, 1978) but not meeting Mental Health Act criteria or requiring in-patient treatment, and thirdly, those 'who ask for the help of the caring agencies within the prison system'. Quite where alcohol and drug abuse falls is not clear. However, the Reed Report glossary (1991: Overview) specifies the mentally disordered offender as someone 'who has broken the law. In identifying broad service needs this term is sometimes loosely used to include mentally disordered people who are alleged to have broken the law.' Even this definition is less helpful than it seems; it would exclude those deemed not guilty by reason of insanity and is unclear whether it applies only to the most recently caught and convicted or whether the label constitutes a life-long attribution.

Finally, the Reed Report (1991, Community Advisory Group: para. 1.6) recognizes three categories of mentally disordered offenders: alleged offenders for diversion into the health and social services and away from the criminal justice system; mentally disordered offenders discharged or diverted from hospital or prison; and non-offenders in the community who are vulnerable and may need assistance to prevent their offending. The third category would permit intervention for non-offenders predicted as likely to offend. In an era when notions of early intervention to prevent future offending (whether on the basis of social disadvantage or diagnostic category—the latest being 'attention deficit hyperactivity disorder' amongst children) are rife, it is a definitional problem worth resolving. Moreover, where one recent study has shown particularly high levels of psychiatric disorder—including a prevalence of 28 per cent for conduct disorder—amongst adolescents in the care system (McCann *et al.*, 1996), it is a problem of some urgency.

Yet mental disorder is *not* a once-and-for-all classification—some disorders can come and go, and frequently do so at inconvenient points in an offender's history. Criminal justice agencies must be sufficiently flexible to accommodate such individuals' needs, in much the same way as hospitals should be sufficiently secure to accommodate those whose intermittently violent behaviour makes them unattractive to a wholly open local hospital. To deal with individuals either as offenders or as mentally disordered or, perhaps worst of all, as mentally disordered offenders, may negate both the right to treatment and the nascent right to a proportional measure of punishment (see below). Too often paternalistic assumptions about the 'mental disorder' element, and protective-predictive ones about the offending element, leave prisoner-patients with more than their 'just' deserts.

In terms of an individual's treatment needs, the facilities available, the desire and reluctance of the caring professions to treat, their ability to enforce treatment and to continue to detain, no one set of rules apply. So there is unlikely to be any one easy solution.

MENTALLY DISORDERED OFFENDERS—A MINORITY GROUP?

This question may be addressed from a number of perspectives. First, there is the contribution mentally disordered offenders make to the totality of offending. Secondly, the impact they have upon the criminal justice system, and, thirdly, the contribution they make to custodial populations. Parallels here may be made with the arguments about race and offending. Mental disorder may correlate with certain kinds of offending, but is rarely causative; yet there is a progressive concentration in the criminal justice system of those suffering from mental disorder (Gunn *et al.*, 1991; OPCS, 1986). Quite why this should be is not clear. However, with only 2 per cent of offences resulting in conviction and sentence, the scope for selective inclusion of visible offenders is obvious; combining notions of inept offending with the range of views held by the relevant 'gatekeepers' as to the needs of this problematic group will undoubtedly contribute to a highly skewed criminal justice 'output'. Earlier in the process it is difficult to disentangle the impact of various policies and diversion schemes; on the one hand they serve to filter offenders away from the formal process whilst on the other, their net widening effect cannot be discounted. It is, however, important to note that surveys of incidence at the earliest stages will be an under-representation as the police, the CPS, and the courts are likely to identify those with the most obvious symptomatology, whilst surveys of custodial populations will include those whose disorders have been exacerbated, or brought about, by the process of prosecution and punishment. Again, the tension between a desire to obtain treatment for the 'deserving' mentally disordered offender, protective concerns where that desire may be frustrated, and the tendency of imprisonment to make 'bad people worse' (Home Office, 1990: para. 2.7), plays itself out amongst a shifting population.

Although the arguments are complex the policy is clear. Wherever possible mentally disordered offenders are to be cared for and treated by health and social services rather than in the criminal justice system. Yet the numbers of disordered offenders still to be found within that system who could benefit under alternative regimes belies the policy. Home Office Circular No 66/90, *Provision for Mentally Disordered Offenders*, attempted to address this anomaly: first, by drawing attention to those legal powers relevant to the mentally disordered; secondly, by reinforcing the desirability of making best use of resources; and, thirdly, by ensuring that the mentally disordered are not prosecuted where this is not required by the public interest. Where prosecution is necessary Circular 66/90 stressed the importance of finding non-penal disposals wherever appropriate. Yet, however effective diversion schemes become, there will always be offenders with mental disorders in the penal system, either because of late onset of the disorder, or where the nature of the offending/disorder makes a penal disposal inevitable. Such offenders are supposedly not to be denied access to treatment. Provision exists either for treatment within prison (on a voluntary basis),[1] or for transfer within or outwith the prison system.

So, crudely put, the issues become those of numbers, identification, diversion, integration with custodial populations, and transfer to therapeutic regimes. At the start of the process, one is looking for a needle in a haystack; at the end, at remand populations being 'swamped' by those with unmet mental heath needs.

Numbers

The best epidemiological evidence from the United States indicates that major mental disorder accounts for at most 3 per cent of the violence in American

---

[1] Even offenders certified as transferable under the 1983 Act cannot be treated on a compulsory basis under its provisions while still in prison.

society (Monahan, 1992). However, the contribution that the mentally disordered make to the totality of offending would be almost impossible to estimate; like juvenile offenders, their offences are frequently highly visible, petty, and repeated. As Burney and Pearson (1995) observe, the great majority of mentally disordered offenders are to be found not on psychiatric wards but in local facilities supported by health, housing, and social services. Properly resourcing these facilities could have a major preventive impact (see also Barham and Hayward, 1995). It is paradoxical, therefore, as Burney and Pearson (1995: 309) conclude, that 'a court appearance may be the only way that their needs will become apparent'; yet that very involvement with the criminal justice system may constitute the reason why community services are denied to these individuals.

Developments in the mental health field have also mirrored those for 'normal' offenders, with greater reliance being placed on control by and punishment in the community. The introduction of supervision registers, requiring the identification of those at risk of committing serious violence or suicide or of serious self-neglect, was quickly overtaken by the Mental Health (Patients in the Community) Act 1995. This provides supervised after-care for patients who have been detained under the 1983 Act and includes powers to require the patient to live at a specific address, to attend for medical treatment, and, most controversially, to convey patients to the appropriate places, including back to hospital. As Gunn (1996) points out, the supervision register proved highly controversial and was regarded as unnecessary in the context of pre-existing detailed care programmes. The jury remains out on the 1995 Act.[2]

It is also paradoxical that the shift to community care, combined with the lack of reality of that care and support, brings more mentally disordered people into contact with the criminal justice system (NACRO, 1993). Homelessness, the co-morbidity of alcohol, drug, and mental health problems, and the associated stress can all induce incidents leading to criminal charges. Burney and Pearson's (1995) report on the Islington Mentally Disordered Offenders Project details how, although there may be only a small number in need of psychiatric hospitalization, there is a larger number of repeat petty offenders, and a third amorphous group of those sad and difficult people, where it is not clear whether or what type of intervention might be appropriate. Diversion accordingly becomes something of a logistical nightmare. Ideally, the problem requires the relevant personnel to be alive to the problem groups, having access to specialized services and permeability between service providers.

---

[2] In essence, the debate has concerned the need to balance care and control. Doing so in the community is arguably more fraught than in an institutional setting. The ever popular psychiatric probation orders attempt such a balance but, like guardianship orders, they lack any element of compulsory treatment. In the context of a power under the 1995 Act to take patients to hospital, where compulsory treatment can be administered, the controversial 'community treatment order' (Fennell, 1992) may have become otiose without ever being realized.

Identification

A study of 2,721 people detained at seven London police stations (Robertson *et al.*, 1995) found thirty-seven people to be actively mentally ill and twenty to be possibly unwell. A further eighteen people were brought to the police station as in need of care and control in a place of safety (section 136 Mental Health Act 1983) during the period of observation. The disposal of the thirty-seven suggested a degree of bifurcation; they were four times as likely to be released without further action as other detainees, but slightly more likely to be charged where persistence or violence was involved. Even though this vulnerable group made up only 2 per cent of those passing through the seven police stations, the researchers noted that a small number were still interviewed without an appropriate adult being present; it is a worrying finding that even with Home Office researchers on site, the mentally unwell can still slip through the safety net of the appropriate adult system.[3]

Similarly, Palmer and Hart's (1996) study in South Yorkshire also questioned the effectiveness of safeguards in the Police and Criminal Evidence Act 1984 for mentally disordered and mentally handicapped suspects. Relevant personnel lacked detailed knowledge of the provisions and had difficulties in identifying for whom the safeguards were intended, leading to inconsistent implementation. The lack of specialist mental health training amongst police surgeons and the lack of training *per se* amongst 'appropriate adults' further undermined the safeguards' effectiveness. Palmer and Hart's observation that the police were good at identifying those with overt symptoms, but less so with others (despite what were the best of intentions) supports Gudjonsson *et al.*'s (1993) assertion that the police were good at spotting schizophrenia but poor at clinical depression.

This 1993 study also detailed the risk of vulnerable individuals making false confessions. Laing (1995), reviewing the development of psychiatric assessment schemes at police stations, highlighted the vital role that solicitors have in identifying such vulnerable people. Whether the likelihood of false confessions has increased with the new requirements in sections 34–36 of the Criminal Justice and Public Order Act 1994 (namely, to warn suspects that the failure to provide explanations may be held against them in court) is another reason why all parties at police stations need to be alive to the special needs of the mentally vulnerable. Without this, Fennell (1994: 70) anticipates 'a further sorry procession through the Court of Appeal of miscarriages involving false or unreliable confessions by this vulnerable group'.

Under PACE, the presence *or suspicion* of mental disorder, as defined in the Mental Health Act 1983, should trigger all of the protections and additional rights to which the mentally vulnerable are entitled, including the right to have an appropriate adult present during questioning (Code C). Since psychopathic

---

[3] Gudjonsson *et al.* (1993) found with a sample of 156 suspects a significantly higher level of disorder; namely in 7 per cent of cases. A further 3 per cent were classified as mentally handicapped.

disorder falls within this definition, it would be interesting to know how frequently the police's definition of a 'psychopath' (a common enough epithet) impels them to adhere to these special protections. This may be another area where the mismatch between different agencies' expectations for, and definitions of, 'the mentally disordered' impedes the full protection to which that group is entitled in law. Thus, where custody officers equate the presence of mental disorder with abnormal behaviour (see e.g. Palmer and Hart, 1996) they will be most likely to miss disorders such as depression and 'psychopathy'.[4] A failure to identify either the obscure or the obvious may contribute both to the risk of wrongful conviction and the failure properly to divert vulnerable individuals to the services they require.

Court Assessment and Diversion Schemes

The burgeoning number of practical initiatives to divert mentally disordered offenders from the formal process (Blumenthal and Wesseley, 1992, identified forty-eight schemes with thirty-four more being planned; Department of Health, 1995, estimates 100 plus operating) might suggest that there is 'an invisible army of the mad tramping daily through our courts'. Burney and Pearson's (1995) on-going evaluation of a court-based diversion scheme in an Inner London magistrates' court would suggest otherwise. Although there is a large number of potential diversion points there is a relatively tiny number of mentally disordered offenders in need of services passing through at any one point.

Although the schemes take many forms, they share the innovative and proactive approach of getting psychiatrist, CPS, mentally disordered alleged offender, and sentencer together at court. They aim to prevent offenders being remanded in custody for reports merely because they do not enjoy stable community ties or because of the absence of bail hostels;[5] ultimately, disposal into a custodial setting should be avoided where a therapeutic one would be more appropriate.

In addition to the various diversion schemes there are also formal powers under the 1983 Act to divert offenders into the hospital system. Sections 35 and 36 permitted remand to hospital for reports and treatment respectively; section 38 initiated interim hospital orders—to avoid the difficulty that could arise out of the 'once and for all' disposal to hospital under a section 37 hospital order. The interim order permits the court to 'hedge its bets'.

---

[4] This, in turn, would support the contention that psychopathic disorder is a label attached not in order to assist offenders but subsequently to justify a more punitive or protective approach.

[5] The Reed Report (1991, Prison Advisory Group) recommended that magistrates' use of their powers to send an accused to prison solely for medical reports (regarded as wrong in principle and an unjustifiable use of the prison system) should be reviewed. Limiting these powers might result in an increase in magistrates' use of section 35, although clearly not all offenders would fit the required Mental Health Act classifications, nor would sufficiently secure provisions necessarily be available.

Although a punitive order should not follow where an offender responds to treatment under section 38 and is returned to court for sentence, a punitive approach may be adopted where it becomes apparent that no 'cure' is possible.

However, Fennell (1991) notes that none of these orders has been frequently used; in stark contrast, 5,569 psychiatric reports were carried out by prison medical officers following remand in 1989. Indeed, Dell *et al.*'s (1991) work on remand prisoners asserted that courts remand in custody essentially for psychiatric and social reasons, rather than for reasons of public safety or the seriousness of offence—as the denial of bail implies. Yet, as Fennell notes (1991: 338) if all those offenders currently remanded to prison were sent to hospital, it would result in a 30–35 per cent increase in the numbers of compulsory admissions to hospitals.

Should the mentally disordered be exempt from prosecution altogether? The Reed Report (1991, Community Advisory Group: para. 2.25) notes: 'comprehensive and reliable information about the suspect's mental condition' should be available so that the CPS may consider the desirability of proceeding against a person who is mentally disordered. But this is not without its problems. Some commentators believe that those with mental handicap should be prosecuted and held responsible where responsibility exists (Carson, 1989). Indeed, the *Code for Crown Prosecutors* already requires the CPS to consider a defendant's mental condition, yet disorder *per se* is not regarded as a sufficient basis for not proceeding. Home Office Circular 66/90, paralleling the *Code*, also distinguishes in paragraph 6 those forms of mental disorder made worse by the institution of proceedings and those which come about by reason of instituting proceedings. Finally, Robertson (1988) suggests that the presence of disorder may make prosecution more likely where a guilty plea is anticipated. Hence, in the decision to prosecute, the presence of mental disorder may act as a mitigating factor and pre-empt action or it may act as an incentive to proceedings being taken. The public interest in ensuring that the offence will not be repeated needs to be weighed against that of the welfare of person in question.

Problems of due process also dog the diversion arena. Does the earlier involvement of psychiatrists inevitably favour welfarism over legalism? Are alleged offenders being made offers they cannot refuse? And, as Fennell notes (1991: 336–7), assuming an offender is prepared to be diverted 'hospital authorities and local authorities have considerable discretion as to whether to accept responsibility for that person. If he is a persistent petty offender, or is potentially disruptive, he is unlikely to be afforded priority status in the queue for scarce resources.' With the drop at district level in in-patient beds for the adult mentally ill from around 150,000 in the 1950s to approximately 63,000 in the early 1990s, and a reluctance by some to see offender-patients integrated with 'non-offenders', diversion and community care may have real limits to their ability to absorb all those whom the courts might wish so to allocate.

Prison Populations

In discussing remands to hospital while awaiting trial, Hoggett (1996: 108) provocatively asks whether it is worse to languish in hospital without trial or prison without treatment; this question has real force, given the extent of mental disorder within the prison population. Examination of this (i) details the range of disorders recognized by psychiatrists amongst an offending population; (ii) underlines the 'irrelevance' to many of these offenders of their mental disorder (since it has not resulted in their being subject to special provisions); and (iii) re-emphasizes the central point that offenders with mental disorder are not some minority group of only marginal concern to the criminal justice system.

Research by Gunn *et al.* (1991) entailed a survey of *sentenced* prisoners in England using a 5 per cent sample of men serving six months or more: 1,365 adults and 404 young offenders agreed to take part. 37 per cent had disorders diagnosed by the psychiatric survey team. Their diagnoses went far wider than Mental Health Act classifications, to include, for example, drug and alcohol abuse; notably however, 2 per cent of the population was diagnosed as suffering from psychosis; and 3 per cent of the population was thought to be in need of transfer to hospital where drugs could be administered on a compulsory basis, victimization by other prisoners avoided, and unpredictable violence or incidents of self-harm be better controlled. As the authors argued (1991: 338):

By extrapolation the sentenced prison population includes over 700 men with psychosis and around 1,100 who would warrant transfer to hospital for psychiatric treatment. Provision of secure treatment facilities, particularly long term medium secure units, needs to be improved. Services for people with personality, sexual and substance misuse disorders should be developed both in prisons and the health service.

The psychiatric survey approach has now been extended to the *remand* population (Brooke *et al.*, 1996). Given the numbers of individuals remanded to prison for psychiatric reports it is only to be expected that this population would show a higher incidence of mental disorder (Dell *et al.*, 1991). However, Brooke *et al.* have found an incidence of 63 per cent, with 5 per cent of the remand population suffering from psychosis.

Are these figures shocking in absolute terms? Arguably yes. First, because the problem is in no sense new or surprising. The survey reported in 1991 was, in effect, a re-run of a survey conducted in 1972 (Gunn *et al.*, 1978) of the South East prison population. This earlier study found 31 per cent with psychiatric disorders, of whom 2 per cent were psychotic. This high level of disorder (in its broadest sense) but 'low' level of psychosis (the latter comparable with that in the community) is a common finding of such surveys.[6]

---

[6] The Home Office/DHSS (1987) found 4.8 per cent of the sentenced male population serving over six months to be suffering from mental disorder within the terms of the Mental Health Act. Prins (1990: 249) cites 14,228 prisoners referred to prison psychiatrists for the year ending March 1986.

Secondly, because of the incidence of suicide in prison. Over half of the 242 prisoners who committed suicide between 1980–9 were on remand (Fennell, 1991: 340) whilst one third of prison suicides have a history of mental disturbance (Dooley, 1990). And, thirdly, a prison population rising above 56,000 in 1996 would, by extrapolation, mean some 1,960 prisoners in need of transfer to hospital; yet, the available total of secure beds stood in 1996 at around 1,700 Special Hospital beds and 1,200 NHS medium secure places (Department of Health, 1995). Not only do these figures fall short of the 2,000 places deemed necessary by the Interim Report of the Butler Committee in 1974, but they fall manifestly short of the latent demand in the prison population.[7] There simply are not enough secure beds. In turn, the bed shortage goes against notions that mentally disordered offenders should be dealt with outwith custodial care, and in conditions of no greater security than is justified by the degree of danger they present to themselves and others (Department of Health, 1995).

However, considering the number and variety of hurdles that mentally disordered offenders have to jump in order *not* to be diverted from the prison population, an incidence of 37 per cent suggests a number of additional hypotheses. First, these filters may fail either effectively to identify or, if identified, to divert these offenders into the hospital system. For example, Birmingham *et al.* (1996: 1523), in observing that fewer than a quarter of diagnosable mentally disordered remand prisoners were identified as such on initial screening at reception by the prison medical service, note 'In a busy remand prison abnormal behaviour is often tolerated or perceived as a discipline problem and dealt with punitively, while the "quietly mad" are ignored.' Moreover, treatment in hospital for some types of offender is simply not a probable outcome; difficult or violent behaviour will often discount a therapeutic disposal. Thus, the courts perceive a need for a psychiatric referral, but this ultimately is not matched by those providing the services, who define their role in a more limited way (Dell *et al.*, 1991). Where the courts cannot force doctors to accept patients for treatment, prison sweeps up.

Secondly, the incidence of 37 per cent may be substantially accounted for by the tautological relationship between personality disorder/drug/alcohol and sexual problems, and offending behaviour (over 30 per cent of the sample appeared in these groups, with over one in three of these being thought to require further assessment or transfer to hospital or to a therapeutic community like Grendon Prison). This would both make the absolute numbers of mentally disordered offenders higher than the incidence of mental disorder in the community and contribute to the prison population where disagreements among doctors about treatability and the lack of suitable facilities for those suffering from personality disorder and sexual deviation result in resort to prison by default. Of course, the mismatch between the narrow criteria for

---

[7] The Reed Report (1991: Overview, para. 22) identified the required provision of medium secure beds, designed for patients who are too ill for prison but insufficiently ill for special hospitals, at 1,500. By the end of 1995 there were 1,246 restricted patients in the special hospitals, and 1,236 in other hospitals (Kershaw and Renshaw 1996).

Mental Health Act disposal at the point of sentence and the subsequent broad clinical diagnosis of disorder will have further exacerbated these figures.

Or perhaps the reality is as Shapland (1991: 2) notes: '[w]e shall always have mentally disordered offenders in what we are currently calling the penal system not because of lack of facilities, but because of intrinsic contradictions in our ideas about mental disorder and its relation to offending'. Although the sentencing of mentally disordered offenders is predicated on notions of diversion and treatment, there has always been the possibility of recourse to a penal disposal where there are elements of culpability (or predicted dangerousness) which require punishment (or control) as most recently espoused in *R. v. Birch* above. Indeed, even where doctors are willing and able to treat an offender, the courts may still insist upon a penal sentence (see *Mortimer*, below).

The prospects for reform of offenders following such disposals are recognized as bleak (Home Office, 1990: para. 2.7). 'For most offenders, imprisonment has to be justified in terms of public protection, denunciation and retribution. Otherwise it can be an expensive way of making bad people worse.'

Transfer to Hospital

The development of mental disorder *after* imprisonment, together with a persistent failure to identify all those needing treatment at an earlier stage, makes necessary some transfer mechanism. Transfer from prison to hospital, with or without a restriction direction, has a history plagued with problems. Again the basic premiss is difficult to contest, namely that detention in prison is inappropriate for those whose mental disorder is sufficiently serious to justify transfer to hospital; yet the figures suggested that transfer was consistently under-used (Grounds, 1991). Difficulties moving patients on from the special hospitals clearly results in fewer beds being available for transferred prisoners. Moreover, since offender-patients tend to remain in conditions of greater than necessary security for longer than is justifiable, and neither RSUs, local hospitals, nor the local authority can be made to accept a patient even if it is agreed that he or she is ready to proceed to a less secure environment, any log-jam effect is enhanced.[8] Problems with remission to prison where a patient is untreatable,[9] or is mentally ill and, having responded to medication in hospital, is predicted as being likely to refuse to continue with treatment in a prison environment where no compulsion can be used, can create further difficulties. Clearly, a policy of flexible transfer will succeed only where the psychiatric system is geared to meet increased demand: in the context of an under-provision of secure facilities, this looks unlikely.

[8] Since the Home Secretary has the power to direct the admission of a prisoner *without* the agreement of the hospital managers, it makes the argument in favour of retaining clinicians' agreement under section 37(4) look less compelling.

[9] Although patients are transferred back from hospital to prison, the numbers are small by comparison. In 1995 134 patients were returned to prison, whilst 725 went in the opposite direction (Kershaw and Renshaw, 1996).

Yet, recent statistics (Kershaw and Renshaw, 1996) show a significant and arguably welcome increase in the numbers of prisoners transferred from prison to hospital.[10] For sentenced prisoners, there has been a threefold increase in the numbers transferred during the five years prior to 1995, whilst for unsentenced prisoners, there has been a massive increase, with thirty-eight prisoners transferred in 1985 and 474 in 1995. However, do the increased numbers suggest greater flexibility in the use of transfer provisions *per se* or a growing reluctance by the courts to use therapeutic disposals in the first instance?

Two aspects of transfer are noteworthy. First, as Grounds (1990) argues, transfer may be motivated as much by a desire to protect the public as by a wish to insure that the patient receives the care needed. Yet, as he details (1991: 67) the purpose of the legislation 'is not preventative detention beyond sentence, but the enabling of hospital treatment during sentence'; that particular groups, for example Afro-Caribbeans, are over-represented amongst section 47 transfers may rightly result in their feeling aggrieved about potential mis-use of the legislation. Grounds also noted the trend during the period 1960–83 towards later transfer; indeed, during the last decade of the operation of the Act, a third of transfers to Broadmoor were made in the last month before the prisoner's earliest date of release and one in eight in the final week.

Secondly, transferred patients are in a disadvantageous position. As Grounds (1990) argues in his study at Broadmoor, prior to the 1959 Act detention continued only up to the expiry of sentence; thereafter, such patients had to be discharged or sent to county asylums for further treatment. After 1959 they could be detained on a notional hospital order *after* their prison sentence expired. And they enjoyed fewer safeguards than patients admitted under civil provisions. Although there was recourse to review by a MHRT, this is an inadequate safeguard where the test to be applied does not equate to that for a new admission. Hence, the late transfers which troubled the Butler Committee (1975: para. 3.42) as being only 'almost entirely theoretical' were, as noted scathingly by Grounds, clearly there in practice. These concerns become all the more pertinent in an era when the use of hospital direction orders (a sentence of imprisonment with a direction that the offender be admitted to hospital) have found their way into the Crime (Sentences) Act 1997 (Chiswick, 1996). As Eastman (1996: 490) fears, these orders could prove attractive to a judiciary favouring concepts of 'punishment and public protection'; should they subsequently be extended from those suffering from psychopathic disorder to those with mental illness or mental impairment he anticipates an 'avalanche effect' (*ibid.*: 492).

As Fennell (1991: 333) concludes his thorough review of diversion of mentally disordered offenders from custody (writing prior to the Reed Report) 'it is likely that, despite current policies of diversion, significant numbers of mentally disordered offenders will remain in prisons, and therefore there is an

---

[10] Indeed, increases in the numbers of transferred prisoners substantially account for the marked increase in the 'restricted' hospital population (Kershaw and Renshaw, 1996).

urgent need to consider how a humane and therapeutic psychiatric service might be provided within the prison system'. And here is the nub of the problem; if mentally disordered offenders cannot be neatly packaged and swept into the caring system, some means of offering effective 'treatment' (if not compulsory treatment, anathema to psychiatrists) within prison will have to be considered. But, if treatment is provided for the mentally disordered offender, why not to other offenders? They make up 63 per cent of the sentenced population; are they any less deserving of the opportunity for change?

Hence, the possible resurgence of a treatment movement within criminology; although its genesis may derive equally well from disillusionment with just deserts and humane containment for what is evidently a 'damaged' population, the presence and extent of mentally disordered offenders in the prison population constitutes a compelling force. Although the view was ominously expressed (Home Office, 1991: para. 1.28) that 'offenders are not given sentences of imprisonment by the courts for the purposes of ensuring their rehabilitation', attempts to reform specific groups remain on the agenda; their implications and rationale demand examination.

MENTAL DISORDER AT TRIAL

At trial the impact of the mentally disordered offender's mental state lacks any coherence. This is attributable to a number of factors. First, the law's ambivalent attitude towards those whom it would wish to hold responsible/culpable for their actions but for whom punishment is manifestly inappropriate. Eastman (1992: 1549) notes, for example, the difficulty the law has in distinguishing between revenge killings and valid defences and striking a balance between principles 'broad enough to allow "in" to a defence specific case types where it is just so to do, whilst ruling "out" cases where it would be unjust to determine reduced or absent culpability'. Secondly, the criminal law has a wholly inconsistent approach to the relevance of mental disorder when determining what standard of behaviour ought to be met. For example, mental disorder is irrelevant for the objective application of Caldwell recklessness (see *Elliot* v. *C (a minor)* [1983] 1 WLR 939), but is relevant to the second objective limb of the test in duress (*Bowen* [1996] Crim. LR 577 (CA)) and may be relevant to the second objective limb in provocation where the provocation goes to the mental 'disorder'.[11] Thirdly, although the fluctuating conflict between the disciplines of psychiatry and law has resulted in law largely winning the battle over the grounds for conviction, psychiatry has been

---

[11] Judgments from the Privy Council in *Luc* ([1996] 3 WLR 45) and the Court of Appeal in, for example, *Thornton* ([1996] 1 WLR 1174) and *Ahluwalia* ([1992] 4 All ER 889) cannot readily be reconciled, with the former holding that the provocation must relate to the mental 'disorder' and the Court of Appeal cases seemingly being prepared to permit a more generous application.

welcomed by the criminal justice system in influencing the scope for and nature of disposal (Johnstone, 1996). Moreover, it is evident that psychiatric and psychological evidence 'is increasingly prevalent and influential in criminal proceedings' (Roberts, 1996). This reflects the paradoxical reliance on a defendant's mental state where it might avoid culpability or mitigate sentence, but an avoidance of such 'labels' where it might increase the likelihood of 'undesirable' sentences. Finally, it is a battle ground whose perimeters and parameters have changed; the mandatory life sentence following a conviction for murder has had a significant impact on the evolution of the excusatory defences of diminished responsibility and provocation (with mental disorder being central to the former but peripheral to the latter), whilst diminished responsibility has also served to plug some of the gaps in the too narrowly drawn M'Naghten criteria. Similarly, the relationship between provocation and self-defence serves to illustrate how conceptual notions of the responsible man can exclude women (through the inapplicability of the provocation test within traditional male/female interactions), leaving women to be pathologized through resort to diminished responsibility.

Meanwhile, some leavening of the selectivity of provocation has occurred with the partial recognition of two concepts necessary for 'battered woman syndrome'; namely, cumulative provocation and the relegation of a time delay from a legal bar to a defence of provocation, to one where it is simply evidence of whether self-control was in fact lost suddenly (Nicolson and Sanghvi, 1993). The pathologizing of female criminal behaviour has been one adaptation to 'gender blindness' in law (Koe, 1992). Maier-Katkin (1991) and Wilczynski (1991) illustrate the phenomenon not only with respect to statutory provision (e.g. infanticide) but also in the way in which defences, technically equally open to both men and women, are employed with various degrees of success in cases of spousal homicide or filicide. The interaction of mental disorder, law, and the trial processes is thus a complex and fascinating area; its continuing evolution will merely be touched upon here for illustrative purposes in respect of four topics; unfit to plead (disorder at the point of trial), not guilty by reason of insanity (those 'M'Naghten Mad' at the time of the offence), infanticide (an exceptional charge for women), and diminished responsibility (a qualified defence to murder).

Arguably, all four of these areas represent crisis points for legal theory in that the consequences of a full application of the law would or did constitute intolerable outcomes for 'needy' individuals, attributable directly to the court's lack of discretion. Importation of psychiatric reasoning and the construction of concepts of responsibility have enabled offenders to be dealt with primarily on the basis of their medical condition rather than on the basis of their criminal behaviour. Hence, treatment for who they are, not for what they have done. Of course, the danger is that once deference to psychiatric notions is permitted, welfarism need no longer be tempered by legalism and outcomes which challenge notions of justice can arise. Hence, psychiatry's role in managing and controlling offenders efficiently may even legitimize forms or length of confinement which could not be justified in purely legal-punitive terms.

Major statutory reform occurred with the introduction of the Criminal Procedure (Insanity and Unfitness to Plead) Act 1991 (hereafter the '1991 Act'). Dissatisfaction about the arrangements under the Criminal Procedure (Insanity) Act 1964 for the 'insane' and 'unfit' had been longstanding. It arose primarily out of the mandatory disposal which followed such findings (namely, indefinite confinement in a mental hospital); and counsel would not infrequently advise clients to avoid such outcomes by pleading guilty to offences they may not have committed or about which counsel could not be confident of securing a jury acquittal. Although the Mental Health Act 1983 improved the theoretical position of these patients—in that they were entitled to be discharged by MHRTs where the presence of continuing disorder could not be established—use of the provisions remained minimal (Mackay, 1991). Given that the purpose of both unfitness findings and the insanity verdict is to protect vulnerable individuals and excuse defendants not fully responsible for their crimes from punishment, their under-usage was an indictment of the law. Although the grounds for such determinations under the 1991 Act remain the same, the consequences that follow have changed radically, with the 1991 Act increasing the court's disposal options to include:

— an admission order (equivalent to a hospital order)
— an admission order with restrictions (which may be indefinite or of fixed length)
— guardianship
— a supervision and treatment order
— absolute discharge

However, for findings arising in respect of murder charges, the disposal remains mandatory; namely, the equivalent of a hospital order with indefinite restrictions.

It is still too early to assess whether the 1991 Act has enhanced use of the 'unfit' and 'insanity' provisions, although the indications are that the insanity verdict remains deeply unpopular.[12] Of course, if the Crime (Sentences) Act 1997 with its mandatory sentencing provisions were to be implemented, it is likely that there would be a significant shift in the use of these orders, as a means of avoiding 'relevant' convictions.

---

[12] The Act came into force on 1 January 1992. Kershaw and Renshaw (1996) cite the numbers of restriction orders arising out of the 'unfit' and 'insanity' provisions, indicating little usage. However, these figures are misleading since they do not include the 'other disposals' permissible since the 1991 Act; indeed, the figures do not now appear to be collected in any consistent form. A computer run provided by the Home Office (Morgan-Rowe, 10 December 1996, personal communication) of *Crown Court* disposals has 'unfit' figures rising to 26 and 'insanity' to 12 for 1995. Professor Mackay, who is conducting research for the ESRC, has attempted to track the disposals' use nationally. He has indicated that 'unfit' provisions may have increased into the region of 40 per year, but 'insanity' verdicts remain barely in double figures (personal communication 11 December 1996), confirming the improbability of the latter being much used in the magistrates' courts (see below).

Unfit to Plead

'Unfit to plead' provisions attempt to protect individuals from the ordeal of trial if their mental state might cause that trial to be unfair. The Criminal Procedure (Insanity) Act 1964 did not provide any specific test of unfitness, nor could it simply be equated with certifiability for the legal criteria did not 'fit neatly with any diagnostic criteria' (Chiswick, 1990: 174). Eastman (1990) argued that psychiatrists constructed an interpretation out of the legal criteria for fitness (*R.* v. *Pritchard* (1836) 7 C & P 303); namely, that the defendant 'can plead to the indictment, be of sufficient intellect to comprehend the proceedings so as to make a proper defence, know that he might challenge any one of the jurors to whom he may object and comprehend the details of the evidence'. The mandatory disposal under the 1964 Act notably led to a significant psychiatric distortion towards such findings of fitness, with the result that many were in practice tried when unfit, and many more when not maximally fit.

Between 1979 and 1989 only 229 unfitness findings were recorded, with the numbers consistently declining, reaching a mere eleven in 1989 (Mackay, 1991). Grubin (1991), conducting a similar survey, found over 50 per cent of unfitness cases had a primary diagnosis of schizophrenia with a further 23 per cent being mentally handicapped or brain damaged; over a third of the total alleged offences were of a mild or nuisance level. Disposal in Mackay's (1991) sample was primarily to local hospitals or RSUs. 30 per cent of the sample was remitted for trial during the research period—with 11 per cent ultimately being found not guilty. At the time of the survey, forty patients had been discharged, whilst many others remained in hospital, their legal cases unresolved. Concerns about this, together with the decline in use of the plea and the inflexibility of the disposal despite the triviality of the cases, were powerful reasons for change.

The 1991 Act requires unfitness to be determined by jury on the evidence of two or more doctors, one of whom is approved. If found unfit, then the trial will not proceed. However, a (new) jury will then consider on the basis of such evidence adduced by the prosecution and by a person appointed by the court to put the case for the defence whether the accused did the act or made the omission charged. During this 'trial of the facts' there will be no examination of the accused's intention. If the jury is satisfied that the *actus reus* is not made out, then the accused will be acquitted. If made out, and the accused remains unfit, then the court will have access to the increased range of disposals. The provisions accordingly do not allow for the legal issues to remain in limbo; accused persons found to be unfit will either be acquitted and walk away from the court or be found to have done the act or made the omission charged and be liable to 'therapeutic' intervention.[13]

---

[13] Difficulties nonetheless remain, as illustrated by the case of Szymon Serafinowicz, the first person (not) to be tried under the War Crimes Act 1991. Committed on murder charges,

Not Guilty by Reason of Insanity

For a verdict of not guilty by reason of insanity it must be established that the accused falls within the ambit of the M'Naghten Rules, their essence being that the accused:

at the time of the committing of the act . . . was labouring under such a defect of reason, from disease of the mind, as not to know the nature and quality of the act he was doing, or, if he did know it, that he did not know he was doing what was wrong [*M'Naghten's Case* (1843) 10 Cl. & F 200 at 210].

The Rules provide a legal test of responsibility for the mentally disordered. Insanity in the medical sense is not sufficient for the defence, although mental disorder *per se* at the point of the act alleged to constitute a crime is clearly a prerequisite.

Although the insanity defence was rarely used (Dell, 1983) and regarded by some as 'obsolete' (Smith and Hogan, 1988: 185), Mackay's (1990) research provided a new perspective. Looking at cases over a fourteen-year period up to 1988, his research revealed that the verdict occurred primarily not in murder cases, but in other non-fatal offences against the person of an unprovoked nature. Schizophrenia was overwhelmingly the commonest diagnosis (51 per cent sample). Curiously, given legal scholars' preference for the first limb of M'Naghten (did not know the nature or quality of the act), in well over half of the sample the second limb of the test (did not know that it was wrong) accounted for the verdicts. This may, of course, be partly attributable to the failure to distinguish between lack of knowledge of legal wrong (as required by law) and lack of knowledge of moral wrong (frequently a better fit with the facts of the sample). But, as Mackay notes (1990: 251) 'the general impression gained . . . was that the wrongness issue was being treated in a liberal fashion by all concerned, rather than in the strict manner regularly depicted by legal commentators' (see e.g. Dell, 1983; Verdun-Jones, 1989).

Equally contrary to widely held beliefs, of the forty-nine special verdicts, two accused were immediately released by the courts, one successfully appealed against the special verdict, and of the remaining the majority went not to special hospitals but to local hospitals or RSUs. For the last group, the disposal was clearly *not* the psychiatric equivalent of a life sentence with ten (of twenty-six) patients being discharged within nine months. For the special hospital patients, periods of detention were longer, with 50 per cent not having been discharged by 1991 and 50 per cent being detained for periods of up to nine years. Given that fear of disposal was thought to be the main reason for non-use of the insanity verdict, such anxieties may have been misplaced or exaggerated. Yet, the figures of six or fewer insanity verdicts a year were a cause for genuine concern, suggesting that a number of offenders who *might*

Serafinowicz was found unfit to plead by a jury who heard conflicting evidence as to his dementia before his trial commenced. Rather than moving to a 'trial of the facts', the Attorney General entered a plea of *nolle prosequi* permanently staying the proceedings.

have benefited from the 'not guilty' verdict were being deterred by the perceived consequences of this course of action, and had opted for guilty verdicts instead.

Under the 1991 Act a verdict of not guilty by reason of insanity will require evidence from two or more medical practitioners (one approved in the field of mental disorder). After initial confusion, the courts have now clarified that the insanity defence applies both in the Crown Crown Court and as a defence in summary trials (*R.* v. *Horseferry Road Magistrates' Court, ex p. K* [1996] 3 All ER 733).

Infanticide

The Infanticide Act 1938 created a special category of offence under section 1(1) where a woman causes the death of her child of under twelve months when her mind was: 'disturbed by reason of not having fully recovered from the effect of giving birth to the child or by reason of the effect of lactation consequent upon the birth of the child'.

The provision enables the court to avoid the mandatory life sentence for murder and impose whatever penalty it thinks fit. Given that the homicide rate among children under the age of one year is greater than that of any other age group, it is curious that only twenty-seven homicides of children were classified as infanticide during the period 1982–9; manslaughter on grounds of diminished responsibility was the most common outcome in cases of child homicide (Wilczynski and Morris, 1993). Since the defence of diminished responsibility encompasses a wider group of victims, including those over twelve months and the children of others, this is not wholly surprising. However, a charge of infanticide can provide a defence where a mother kills in circumstances of extreme stress arising out of, for example, poverty, social deprivation, failure of bonding, or otherwise being unable to cope with a new baby; such circumstances would not readily fall within the defence of diminished responsibility. Moreover, as there is no requirement for causality on a charge of infanticide between a woman's distressed condition and her actions in taking life (Maier-Katkin and Ogle, 1993) it provides considerable scope for a psychiatric defence. Although such usage may come dangerously close to making 'adverse social conditions a defence to child killing' (Smith and Hogan, 1988: 363) the Criminal Law Revision Committee (1984: paras. 103–6) wished to ratify this approach by extending the offence to cover stresses caused by 'circumstances consequent to the birth'. As Hoggett (1996: 114) questions, should such stresses amount to an excuse, and if so, why should they not apply to fathers as well, or to others provoked to kill by intolerable circumstances, currently falling outside the ambit of provocation?[14]

---

[14] In *R.* v. *Doughty* ((1986) 83 Cr. App. R 319) the Court of Appeal held that a defence of provocation by a man based on a baby's persistent crying could properly be left to the jury.

Diminished Responsibility

The Homicide Act 1957, section 2(1), enabled a defendant to be found not guilty of murder, but guilty of manslaughter by reason of diminished responsibility where the defendant could establish:

he was suffering from such abnormality of mind (whether arising from a condition of arrested or retarded development of mind or any inherent causes or induced by disease or injury) as substantially impaired his mental responsibility for his acts and omissions in doing or being a party to the killing.

The abnormality test, 'a state of mind so different from that of ordinary human beings that the reasonable man would term it abnormal' (Lord Parker CJ in *R.* v. *Byrne* [1960] 2 QB 396 at 403), is sufficiently wide to include a gamut of disordered states—even if transient. It includes the failure to resist an impulse where, although the ability to resist was present, it was substantially less than that of an ordinary man and the offender could not, or could not without substantial difficulty, have resisted. Arguably, it provides a psychiatrist's charter at trial; similarly, the substantial responsibility test implies it is possible to have degrees of responsibility. And if there can be lesser degrees of responsibility, why should the defence be confined to murder?

The defence of diminished responsibility, and the peculiar reliance on it by women who kill, should not be seen in isolation from the 'alternative' defences of provocation and self-defence. Broadly, the qualified defences of diminished responsibility and provocation are regarded in law as excuses—with the focus being on the actor—whilst self-defence is a justification and focuses on the act; where successful it provides a complete defence. Yet women in England and Wales make more use of 'psychiatric defences' such as diminished responsibility, whilst men resort to self-defence (and increasingly in the USA, women as well—Raeder, 1992; Wells, 1994) or lack of intent to kill. The upshot is that women are more likely to receive psychiatric disposals and men penal sentences. Hence 'men are bad and normal, women are mad and abnormal' (Wilczynski, 1991). Pathologizing women via infanticide, diminished responsibility and arguably provocation, rather than utilizing self-defence—which leaves an offender with a normal response to abnormal circumstances rather than an abnormal response to common circumstances (giving birth/woman battering)—may help to explain why women are grossly outnumbered by men in the prison population, but are only outnumbered by men in the special hospitals at about a rate of 8:1.[15] Hence, gender rather than mental disorder may be the pre-eminent factor in determining special treatment; or as Nicolson and Sanghvi argued (1993: 735) successful defences for battered women are dependent on their conforming to a 'socially constructed image of femininity, continuing the tendency whereby the character of women killers, rather than their actions, are placed on trial'. Departure from the normal principles of

---

[15] Patients detained on restriction orders (Kershaw and Renshaw, 1996).

criminal law presently pathologizes women's behaviour, when a better solution might be to abolish the mandatory life sentence for murder; or for women to make more imaginative use of an 'honest but unreasonable mistake' in respect of the circumstances in which they resort to self-defence. Currently, practice requires the distortion of concepts to accommodate legal solutions.

MENTAL DISORDER AND TREATMENT

Treatment is the fundamental justification for separate provision for mentally disordered people who have committed offences. But it is not readily clear what is meant by treatment or what treatment is attempting to alter—the 'underlying disorder', the offending behaviour, or the link, if any, between the two? And if it is the likelihood of criminal behaviour *per se*, the justification for treatment will not be confined to a 'mentally disordered' sub-group of offenders. Accordingly, an examination of this relationship and any resultant failure to establish causality might undermine the whole basis for treatment. This leads into the final section on protection. Here, the argument is turned on its head; where mental disorder provides a basis, not for a therapeutic disposal, but for a lengthier custodial disposal than would be proportionate to the seriousness of the offence. Should there then be a compensatory right to treatment for their disorder? At present, no such right exists.

For one particularly problematic group, those with 'psychopathic disorder', attempts to rationalize the law have stemmed not from concerns about treatment, justice, or due process, but explicitly from anxiety about re-offending by those 'prematurely' released from the hospital system. Although an earlier legislative attempt to extend control over these offenders by, if necessary, prolonging their detention fell by the wayside (Peay, 1988), this occurred partly out of a recognition that the proposals might have led to not more control but less. It is ironic that the provisions in the Crime (Sentences) Act 1997 in respect of 'psycopathic offenders', namely the introduction of a hospital direction order, will result in *only* those psycopathically disordered offenders who satisfy the 'treatability criterion' being eligible for the new order. Yet, it is the psychopathically disordered about whom forensic psychiatrists are so sharply divided in their willingness to offer treatment (Cope 1993).

---

[16] A sentence of imprisonment which permits the offender to be sent directly to hospital. These proposals stemmed from a specialist working group (Reed, 1994) and were the subject of a consultation document (Home Office/Department of Health, 1996). Despite being roundly condemned by practitioners, the proposals have found their way into the Crime (Sentences) Act in a corrupted form (namely, to be applicable only to those psychopaths deemed treatable).

What is the Relationship between Mental Disorder and Offending
Behaviour?

As Prins (1990) has amply demonstrated, the relationship between mental
abnormality and criminality is an uncertain one. Prins summarizes the
principal psychiatric classifications of disorder and illustrates the forms of
offending which may be more (or less) likely to be associated with them,
concluding (1990: 256) 'Most psychiatric disorders are only very occasionally
associated with criminality'. Prins also illustrates well the difficulties of establishing cause and effect in this troubled area: 'we are trying to make connections
between very different phenomena, and these phenomena are the subject of
much debate concerning both substance and definition' (*ibid.*: 247).

Another emphasis in the literature concerns the relationship between mental
disorder and *violence* (Monahan, 1992; Wesseley and Taylor, 1991). The overwhelming correlates of violence are male gender, youth, lower socio-economic
class, and the use/abuse of alcohol or drugs, and not the diagnosis of major
mental disorder. Indeed, there has been resistance to the idea that mental
disorder may be a risk factor for the occurrence of violence; Monahan and
Steadman (1983) question the logic of why those with paranoid delusions
should be any more or less likely to attack their tormentors than those who
are in fact being tormented. However, the ground has been shifting (Monahan
and Steadman, 1994) and may shift further; it remains regrettably too early to
report with any confidence what may be coming out of the major MacArthur
risk assessment study (Monahan, 1996). On the one hand, there are data to
indicate that lack of control and associated violent behaviour may be a
prerogative of the *currently actively psychotic* (Swanson *et al.*, 1990; Link,
Andrews, and Cullen, 1992). On the other hand, whilst there is a weak association between mental illness and violence in the community, that association
is significantly enhanced in the context of a 'substance abuse disorder'; moreover, mental disorders 'in sharp contrast to alcohol and drug abuse—account
for a minuscule proportion of the violence that afflicts American society'
(Monahan, 1997).

In contrast, merely weighing the contribution of Bluglass and Bowden's
Principles and Practice of Forensic Psychiatry (1990) might lead one to conclude
that there is no form of *criminal* behaviour without a psychiatric element, with
chapters on everything from Amok to Sexual Asphyxia (regrettably, nothing
on Zealotry). It provides a comprehensive state of the art review. Equally, two
new journals—*Criminal Behaviour and Mental Health* and *The Journal of
Forensic Psychiatry*—have also focused in their assorted ways on the relationship between mental ill health and criminal behaviour. I could not do justice
to this body of knowledge. I merely wish to make a couple of observations pertinent to this path of medicalized explanations.

First, offence categories amongst 'disordered offenders' mirror those of
'normal' populations, with the only differences being that the disordered populations are slightly less likely to be convicted of offences of violence and

slightly more likely to have committed property offences.[17] Images of axe-wielding maniacs are based on highly visible and intuitively attractive evidence, but are not statistically replicable.[18]

Secondly, the suggestion that many of the offending population have themselves been offended against constitutes another form of medicalized explanation of their behaviour (Gunn, 1992); undoubtedly the level of disorder and disadvantage amongst the prison population testifies to the inadequacies of the average confined offending population, but it is, in essence, an index of social failure, not criminogenic predispositions. Although the study of personality development/disorder, including abuse, may help us to understand crime in some individuals, can correlation and causation be so readily disentangled (Player, 1992)? How can it be determined what the relevance of the victimization was to the individual, if observations are based on psychiatric contact with those who have offended, or offended and volunteered themselves as 'damaged'—seeking some psychiatric explanation for their behaviour? Offenders are, after all, only too willing to have their behaviour treated as something 'uncontrollable'. As inconvenient as this interpretation may be for criminologists seeking to avoid discriminatory treatment for the 'mentally disordered', offenders are prepared to be perceived as victims, even if they show a greater reluctance to be labelled as 'mentally disordered'. The scene is set; offenders desire to accommodate and incorporate psychiatric explanations of their behaviour; victimization in one form or another—like the mother–child relationship—is a common, if not universal, experience; psychiatrists are peculiarly reliant on what their clients tell them; offending is widespread. All of the ingredients are present to permit a re-structuring of experiences as explanations or excuses.

Or is the victim/offending relationship merely coincidental? The danger is twofold. Once criminologists start down this path it is hard to see where it ends. Are not all offences equally open to medicalization? Even seemingly comprehensible property offences may, especially where trivial items are involved, require some less readily accessible explanation than mere acquisitiveness. Secondly, a medicalized explanation precedes a medicalized solution. But if treatment is adopted and then fails, is the next step to throw away the key?

Psychopathic Disorder

There is likely to be some association between disorders of personality and criminality, since the legal definition of psychopathic disorder under the 1983 Act includes the element that the disorder has resulted in 'abnormally

---

[17] Although property offences include robbery which requires the use or threat of violence. In practice, many robbery charges only involve a minimal level of violence (Genders, 1991).

[18] Even the remand population (manifestly the most 'disordered' sub-sample: Taylor and Gunn, 1984) exhibits strikingly high suicide levels (Dooley, 1990) and not violence against others. Of 64 prison suicides in 1996, 36 were on remand.

aggressive or seriously irresponsible conduct'. In essence, it is a legal category defined by persistently violent behaviour. The 'criminal' behaviour attracts attention to the offender, who may subsequently be diverted into care.[19] This, in turn, creates therapeutic and conceptual difficulties for a psychiatric profession employing clinical concepts of personality disorder (Grounds, 1987). Confusion seems endemic. Some argue that the label 'psychopathic disorder' adds nothing to an understanding of the condition—and indeed, doubt the very existence of an underlying medical condition. Others judge the label to be 'little more than a moral judgement masquerading as a clinical diagnosis' (Prins 1991: 119, citing Blackburn), whilst some recognize a disorder, but doubt whether any psychiatric intervention could be successful. Yet others argue that an attempt should be made to continue to treat selected psychopathic offenders since the 'sheer range of psychopathology makes it more appropriate . . . to think of the psychopathic disorders rather than a single entity' (Coid, 1989: 755).

Despite the confusion 'some working concept of psychopathy is necessary for the use of those involved in this field' (Prins, 1991: 124), even if a mere definition does not ensure consistent application, classification, or identification of treatment needs. Roth's definition (1990: 449) is noteworthy:

It comprises forms of egotism, immaturity, aggressiveness, low frustration tolerance and inability to learn from experience that places the individual at high risk of clashing with any community that depends upon co-operation and individual responsibility of its members for its continued existence. It has a characteristic sex distribution, age of onset, family history of similar symptoms and disorders and family constellations and influences that show a large measure of consistency in their course and outcome . . . One purpose of describing psychopathic personalities in longitudinal as well as cross-sectional perspective is to intervene in the early formative years . . . The treatments so far discovered achieve a relatively low rate of success. This does not justify abrogating responsibility for the care of psychopathic individuals.

It is also important to stress that people suffering from 'psychopathic disorder' rarely find themselves subject to civil commitment, which would be expected if the disorder were genuinely problematic for the individual. Perhaps the 'mythical' personality type—ruthless, cold, uncaring, and egocentric—actually benefits the entrepreneur.

Psychiatrists find themselves in a dilemma. The era of psychiatric optimism which preceded the 1959 Act has been replaced, particularly in respect of the treatment of aberrant behaviour, by an era of psychiatric pessimism. Psychiatrists are increasingly wary of being asked to 'treat' psychopathic offenders, when that treatment can more readily be characterized as detention and control. Hospital as prison. Nonetheless, psychopathic disorder remains

---

[19] The admission figures for 1996 of offenders suffering from psychopathic disorder given a restriction order indicate the infrequency with which the provisions are used (21 orders or 10 per cent of admissions). Yet the numbers recalled in 1995 after receiving a conditional discharge (17 per cent of all recalls) suggests the relative vulnerability of this group (Kershaw and Renshaw, 1996).

one of the four key organizing categories within the 1983 Act, even if as moderated by the 'treatability' test. The profession is expected to offer treatment only to those it can realistically hope to help; the untreatable, even if clearly disordered, receive penal disposals—with the probability of a determinate sentence, the likelihood of release without 'treatment', and the possibility of subsequent re-offending. Paradoxically, psychiatrists have found themselves criticized both for a failure to provide control and containment, and for failing to offer treatment to those who subsequently re-offend; a reviled position paralleling that of social workers.

Here is the difficulty. What is it that treatment is designed to alter; underlying pathology or re-offending rates? Equally, the profession is unable to say with any confidence how long treatment will take, what the nature and extent of it must be, what outcome is likely, whether the treatment will work or whether—on completion—it has worked.[20] It takes a brave and eminent psychiatrist to argue that the profession ought to be in the business of risk prediction and management (Gunn, 1996).

Treatment in Prison

Prison is an inappropriate location for patients with psychotic disorders. The inability to impose medication, together with the damning acceptance in *Knight* v. *The Home Office* ([1990] 3 All ER 237) that there may be 'circumstances in which the standard of care falls below that which would be expected in a psychiatric hospital without the prison authority being negligent' make this unarguable. But, what about the potential in prison for the treatment of other mentally disordered offenders?

Efforts to provide treatment for sex offenders in prison is one burgeoning area (see Reed Report, 1992, Report of the Official Working Group on Services for People with Special Needs: Discussion Paper 4). However, it is a movement whose implications go beyond this specialist group. The Woolf Report (1991) urged that the treatment of sex offenders could be used as a paradigm for specialist provision for offenders with drug or alcohol problems or, for example, for those who have problems with anger management. As Sampson (1994: 201) observes, 'The sex offender initiative is a test of the potential for the prison system to adapt to the individual needs of a group of prisoners and to move from simple containment to the more ambitious process of addressing the reasons why individuals are in prison at all'. Problematically however, one test of success is to be that of sexual recidivism; yet, there is a paucity of clinical evidence that treatment reduces re-offending (Player, 1992).

---

[20] See, for example, the Kirkman case (West Midlands RHA, 1991). Following 17 years of treatment in both a special hospital and RSU, a programme of carefully structured release, a stable relationship, and psychiatric endorsement of his release, Kirkman killed a woman on his first day following discharge. He had touched her leg whilst assisting her with some repairs, panicked, and stabbed her. He subsequently committed suicide whilst on remand.

Moreover, to use recidivism as a measure of success runs curiously counter to the ethos established at Grendon (psychiatric) Prison which specializes in dealing with, amongst other groups, sex offenders.[21] Genders and Player (1995), who conducted a major study of the therapeutic regime at Grendon, note Woolf's (1991) distinction between prison for reformative treatment and the new rehabilitative approach, making prisoners address their offending behaviour as a means of preparing them for release. The environment is demanding yet promotes individual responsibility and prevents 'a creeping and all-pervading dependency by prisoners on the prison authority' (Woolf, 1991: para. 14.13). Genders and Player observe that Grendon perceives crime as neither exclusively a function of personal pathology nor as structurally caused; it directs therapy not primarily towards the prevention of crime, but as a means of promoting the welfare of each inmate proffering an individual resolution via relief of the pain and distress of its prisoners. If offending is reduced that is a welcome by-product, but it is neither the primary focus of treatment nor the index by which treatment is judged.

Genders and Player chart the stages of an inmate's therapeutic career, a 'career' which takes some eighteen months in Grendon to complete, and argue that any assessment of subsequent reconviction should be measured only against those who have passed through all stages of this career. When such an approach is adopted (Cullen, 1993) there are some limited but encouraging data to suggest that those rated 'successes' in therapy at Grendon have lower reconviction rates. All sorts of caveats need to be made about the validity of such data (Genders and Player, 1995: 184–6); moreover, the authors remain cautious about the theoretical basis for a link between progress in therapy and future criminality. Is there any logical reason why such a link should exist? Any progress at Grendon represents only a small part of the prison experience; any change Grendon facilitates may have little or no bearing on an individual's subsequent social situation or structural position in society. Notably, Gunn and Robertson's (1987) study had found *no* significant differences in reconviction rates in respect of either frequency or severity of offending for Grendon releases with a matched control group. Grendon's 'successes', as Genders and Player point out, may alter their behaviour only in respect of how they deal with problems, which may or may not have led them into criminal difficulties in the past. That may, in itself, be a sufficient justification for the treatment endeavour, but it should not be confused with questions of re-offending. Nor, as Player (1992) cautions, where the emphasis is on the unobtainable 'quick fix', should the risk of a shift towards more draconian methods of control be ignored.

---

[21] Grendon has few discipline problems with what is a highly problematic population and accordingly works well as a form of control. As Genders and Player (1995) point out, the knowledge, by all concerned, that the rest of the prison system provides a very different form of containment underpins Grendon's success.

This minefield may be crudely summarized;

(i) 'treatment' may mean many different things—ranging from the administration of anti-psychotic medication to the acquisition of social survival
skills;

(ii) if the relationship between the disorder and the offending behaviour is not
primarily causal, there is less justification for excusing from punishment—
the 'mad and bad' theory—and offenders should remain entitled to protection of their rights as offenders, whilst not being denied access to
treatment;

(iii) even if there is some causal element, there is no reason why punishment
for the partially responsible (and hence, partially guilty) should not be
combined with treatment, where requested;

(iv) successful treatment for a disorder may have no bearing on future criminality; mentally disordered offenders should be accorded proportionality
in the length of confinement; release should not be determined on the
basis of predictions of future offending (in the way it plays no part in
release from a determinate sentence);

(v) as Campbell and Heginbotham (1991: 135) argue, where an offender is
treatable and there is some causal connection between the disorder and
their offending behaviour, then there may be less (or no) justification for
continued detention after treatment;

(vi) the conflict between jurisprudential logic, which may sanction punishment
and treatment for the 'culpable' mentally disordered offender, and
decades of a humanitarian response endorsing a common sense preference
for treatment rather than punishment, ought to be reversed in favour of
the former only where treatment can be demonstrated to be wholly
inappropriate.

PROTECTIVE SENTENCING: PROCEDURAL
SAFEGUARDS V. TREATMENT

Mentally disordered offenders, like all offenders, are overwhelmingly not
dangerous; but some are. Arguments favouring limited special measures have
their attractions, if only to deal with that small but worrying group about
whom unsubstantiable fears of future offending abound; but their *quid pro quo*
is that the preventive rationale should be tempered by procedural safeguards.
Similarly, the arguments for bifurcation in the field of mentally disordered
offenders are inherently appealing, where diversion into humanitarian care
protects offenders from damaging penal sentences. Yet the implications of
these two propositions under our existing arrangements are that the route into
confinement will affect both whether and what type of treatment will be given
and the route out of confinement.

Concepts of dangerousness and its alleged association with mental disorder pepper the academic literature and the rhetoric of sentencing. Here is not the place for a review of that literature (Floud and Young, 1981; Radzinowicz and Hood, 1981; Peay, 1982; Bottoms and Brownsword, 1983; Prins, 1986; Wood, 1988). Suffice it to say that academics and policy-makers have been fiercely divided on both predictive grounds—will it work?—and on questions of rights—should it be allowed to work? In essence, the argument embodies the distinction between statistical and legal-clinical decision-making; crudely put, the difference between risk factors associated with groups of people who have common characteristics (much of the risk prediction literature is of this nature) and the determination of whether any one individual within that group will be amongst those where risk is realized (the kinds of decisions faced by courts, MHRTs, discretionary lifer panels, and clinicians).

Notions that offenders may be entitled to a proportional measure of punishment have been challenged by Walker (1996: 7), who argues that there may be no such 'right' where offenders have forfeited the presumption of being harmless because they have previously attempted or caused harm to others. In these circumstances precautionary sentencing may be justifiable. But how is such precautionary sentencing to be limited? And are mentally disordered offenders at greater risk of imposition of such a sentence? Dworkin (1977) described the restraint and treatment of the 'dangerously insane' as an insult to their rights to dignity and liberty—an infringement that could *only* be justified, not where crime reduction might result, but where the danger posed was 'vivid'. Bottoms and Brownsword (1983: 21) unpacked the concept of vivid danger into its elements of seriousness, temporality (that is frequency and immediacy), and certainty. Certainty was pivotal to precautionary sentencing, but even a high probability of future offending should become relevant only if the behaviour anticipated involved causing or attempting 'very serious violence'. Thus, the right to a proportional measure of punishment would yield a *'prima facie* right to release for the prisoner at the end of his normal term', and this would apply—in the absence of *'vivid* danger'—equally to the alleged 'dangerous offender'. But at this point theory and practice diverge.

The leading principle of the Criminal Justice Act 1991 is that custodial sentences should be commensurate with the seriousness of the offence. However, this principle is subject to a number of exceptions. Most notable is section 2(2)(b) which permits courts to sentence 'where the offence is a violent or sexual offence, for such longer term (not exceeding that maximum) as in the opinion of the court is necessary to protect the public from serious harm from the offender'. The operation of section 2(2)(b) has been discussed elsewhere (Ashworth, this volume; Von Hirsch and Ashworth, 1996) but the manner in which it bites on mentally disordered offenders is critical. Under the Act medical reports are normally required where the court is considering passing a custodial sentence and the offender is or appears to be mentally disordered (section 4(I)). In *Fawcett* ((1995) 16 C. App. R (S) 55) the Court of Appeal held 'if the danger is due to a mental or personality problem, the sentencing court should . . . *always* call for a medical report before passing sentence under s.2(2)(b), in order *to exclude a medical disposal'* (emphasis added).[22] Garland J outlined the factors which would assume prominence in qualifying for a longer than normal sentence; they included irrational acts, unusual obsessions or delusions, a lack of remorse or unwillingness to accept medication, and any inability on the part of the offender to appreciate the consequences of his or her actions—all factors arguably more likely to be associated with those suffering from mental disorder. Moreover, and perhaps most worryingly, Garland J noted that 'the fact that the defendant does have previous convictions need not necessarily itself be a qualifying factor, particularly where there is a mixture of minor offending, and some personality disorder, or other mental abnormalities'. Again, those with mental vulnerabilities seem to be peculiarly singled out as posing a risk.

Solomka (1996) has detailed how these provisions can lead to psychiatrists' reports, written for the decision concerning the appropriateness of a thera-peutic disposal (the alternative being a fixed proportionate custodial sentence), being used to justify a longer than normal sentence. In his study of the first thirty-five Court of Appeal decisions under section 2(2)(b) he notes that twenty-two of them involved psychiatric evidence. Clearly, the potential for 'ratcheting-up' exists. The appearance of mental disorder (lay notions) leads to a psychiatric report which, where it does not recommend a therapeutic disposal, is likely to have made reference to a series of signs and symptoms which sentencers find worrying, leading to a longer than normal sentence where offenders neither acquire special rights to treatment nor to any of the (limited) procedural safeguards enjoyed by discretionary life sentence prisoners.

Conceding the principle of preventive sentencing can create a number of further difficulties. First, protective imperatives can infect the way in which decisions are made about the release of even non-offenders amongst the detained psychiatric population; fears of future offending can lead to inappro-priate denial of release (Peay, 1989: 184). They can also lead to inappropriate transfer (Grounds, 1990) and to offender-patients being detained in hospital for periods commensurate with their offence rather than on the basis of assessed recovery from their disorders (Dell and Robertson, 1988).

There is also evidence (*Mortimer* [1996] Crim.L.R. 836) that the Court of Appeal has been prepared to uphold a sentence of disproportionate length not falling within section 2(2)(b) where there was psychiatric evidence that the appellant had a persistent compulsion to kill his wife and children. As attractive as the decision may appear on pragmatic-safety grounds, where the legislative framework does not permit this, it is another manifestation of unjust dealings with the 'mentally disordered alleged dangerous would be offender'. Finally, in *Fleming* ((1995) 14 Cr. App. R (S) 151) the Court of Appeal upheld

---

[22] Fawcett, sentenced to imprisonment, suffered from a personality disorder 'approaching psychopathic disorder'; her condition was thought to be unlikely to change.

a life sentence on a chronic paranoid schizophrenic, despite the availability of a bed in a special hospital, and despite existing authority (*Howell* (1985) 7 Cr. App. R (S) 360) to the effect that judges should not sentence offenders to imprisonment to avoid decisions about their release falling subsequently into the hands of an MHRT.[23] Protective confinement appears to be self-justifying and highly infectious.

There have, however, been some chinks in this litany of disadvantage. Paralleling the way lawyers were sufficiently concerned about the position of restricted patients under the Mental Health Act 1959 (resulting ultimately in the case of *X* v. *UK* ((1981) 4 EHRR 181) and the substantial enhancement of patient safeguards under the 1983 Act), unease about the position of discretionary life prisoners—another group whose mental state has affected their sentence—has resulted in this group gaining enhanced review procedures. The discretionary life sentenced population make up approximately one fifth of the total lifer population—the rest being mandatory life sentences. For the one in five due process will rule.

Following reluctantly from the ECHR decisions in *Weeks* v. *UK* ((1988) 10 EHRR 293) and *Thynne, Wilson and Gunnell* v. *UK* ((1991) 13 EHRR 666) (see Richardson, 1991)[24] the government extended the powers of the Parole Board under the Criminal Justice Act 1991, so that in future it will take the final decision about release in discretionary life sentence cases. The Board under section 34 will have to be satisfied 'that it is no longer necessary for the protection of the public that the prisoner should be confined'.

Spelling out the involvement of predictions of dangerousness is a first step in ensuring that such predictions are made with due regard to the rights of an offender not to be unjustifiably detained. A second necessary step is to ensure procedural fairness; the position of discretionary lifers has been somewhat improved to place them on the same footing as restricted patients applying to MHRTs. In this respect, all the problems which bedevil tribunals are likely to be replicated (Peay, 1989).[25] The burden of proof militates against release—how can an offender prove that he is safe when in conditions of security? Moreover, having improved the position of the discretionary lifer, disparities emerge with the mandatory life sentence and for those on long determinate

[23] This course in *Fleming* was distinguished from *Howell* on the basis that Fleming had been previously discharged from hospital and had gone on, some years later, to kill.

[24] Weeks' life sentence was imposed for purposes of social protection because of his mental instability and potential dangerousness. Denial of regular access to a body which had the power to release him breached Article 5(4) of the European Convention on Human Rights: 'Everyone who is deprived of his liberty by arrest or detention shall be entitled to take proceedings by which the lawfulness of his detention shall be decided speedily by court and his release ordered if the detention is not lawful'. In *Thynne, Wilson and Gunnell* v. *UK* the ECHR made plain that *Weeks* was of general application to all discretionary life-sentence prisoners detained on the basis of mental disorder and dangerousness; at some point in a life sentence the punitive element would expire, leaving detention on the grounds of continued dangerousness the sole criterion. The Court argued that this must change over time; accordingly a mechanism for review must exist.

[25] What, for example, will be the position of those who continue to protest their innocence, where admissions of guilt are used as an index of assessing future risk to the public?

sentences. There is evidence that the progress made in response to the position of the mentally disordered offender will influence these groups too, in favour of greater procedural fairness; the House of Lords in *Doody* ([1993] 3 All ER 92), having had regard to the 'enhanced' position of discretionary lifers, concluded that mandatory lifers should enjoy a series of rights including the right to know the minimum time to be served as recommended by the trial judge. Moreover, whilst the Secretary of State was entitled to depart from the judge's advice, prisoners were to be given reasons for any departure from the judges' recommendation together with a right to make submissions.

Welfarism and legalism may strain in different directions. Protectionism and due process may do likewise. But it appears that back-door protectionism is to be repeatedly challenged by up-front due process, a movement deriving from the so-called mentally disordered offender, but potentially extendable to all.

CONCLUSIONS

If the basic premise of this chapter is accepted, namely that mentally disordered offenders are not, and should not be treated as an isolated category, the conclusions that follow are of broader significance.

First, effort should be devoted to developing a pluralistic model of the criminal justice system. This has been discussed in detail elsewhere (Peay, 1993). Piecemeal tinkering may provide solutions for the problems posed by specific offenders; it is insufficient as a basis for addressing problems across the ordered–disordered offending continuum.

Secondly, if the mentally disordered cannot effectively be identified and marginalized, diversion and transfer can never be the solution. Resource allocation needs to be across the board, not in respect of a limited number of beds for potentially difficult offender-patients.

Thirdly, and stemming from this, it is unrealistic to confine treatment to hospital settings. Lord Justice Woolf (Woolf Report, 1991) and a former Chief Inspector of Prisons (Tumim, 1990) have both stressed the need to provide psychiatric services in prison equal to those in mental hospitals. The Reed Report (1991: Overview, para. 20) recommends contracting in a full mental health care service from the NHS. Whether, as in the United States (Miller, 1992), due process safeguards for the mentally disordered will be closely followed by the right to treatment in prison, and its more problematic flip side, compulsory treatment in prison, are open questions. What is clear, is the need to think more carefully about the circumstances under which treatment will be offered, to whom, and what the consequences will be where it is deemed unsuccessful or inappropriate. Currently, the statutory framework includes preventing 'a deterioration' under the 1983 Act's treatability criterion; yet prisons have a recognized deteriorative impact. Logically, if ludicrously, this should make it impossible for clinicians to deny treatment to the psychopathically disordered. A pluralistic model would require the same limitations on intervention for all offenders and, arguably, that of proportionality could constitute a sound foundation for greater fairness between offenders.

Fourthly, the justifications are many for singling out subsections of 'disordered offenders' for special treatment. But special treatment can readily become special control; to be seduced by the notion that risk can be managed through the containment of identifiable individuals is to allow discriminatory treatment for that group, whilst failing to tackle the roots of the problem. It is a false dawn.

Finally, the failure to agree on a definition of what constitutes a mentally disordered offender, or to apply it consistently even if criteria could be agreed, is likely to result in there being a mismatch of expectations amongst the various personnel and agencies dealing with such offenders. As Watson and Grounds (1993) have observed, greater liaison combined with overcoming the boundaries between different parts of the criminal justice and health agencies will be insufficient all the time the discrepancy in expectations remains. Pursuing a pluralistic model may go some way to addressing these fundamental problems.

Selected Further Reading

Of the references cited below, chapter 5 in Hoggett (1996) provides an excellent overview of the technicalities of the law relating to mentally disordered offenders, whilst the Reed Report, in all of its assorted parts, provides a comprehensive review of the state of play in the early 1990s, setting the parameters of policy development for the decade. Burney and Pearson (1995) is a thoughtful analysis of diversion, drawing on original data, whilst the studies by Gunn *et al.* (1991) and Brooke *et al.* (1996) detail the prevalence of mental disorder in the convicted and remand populations respectively. Monahan (1992) remains one of the best analyses of the problematic relationship between violence and mental disorder. Finally, for a critical review of the likely developments in the field of sentencing mentally disordered offenders, see Eastman (1996).

REFERENCES

ASHWORTH, A. (1992), 'Face the 1991 Act' (editorial), *Criminal Law Review*, 229–31.

—— and GOSTIN, L. (1984), 'Mentally Disordered Offenders and the Sentencing Process', *Criminal Law Review*, 195–212.

BARHAM, P., and HAYWARD, R. (1995), *Relocating Madness from the Mental Patient to the Person*. London: Free Association Books.

BIRMINGHAM, L., MASON, D., and GRUBIN, D. (1996), 'Prevalence of Mental Disorder in Remand Prisoners: Consecutive Case Study', *British Medical Journal*, 313: 1521–4.

BLUGLASS, R., and BOWDEN, P., eds. (1990), *Principles and Practice of Forensic Psychiatry*. Edinburgh: Churchill Livingstone.

BLUMENTHAL, S., and WESSELY, S. (1992), 'The Extent of Local Arrangements for the Diversion of the Mentally Abnormal Offender from Custody', Report submitted to the Department of Health from the

Institute of Psychiatry and King's College Hospital Medical School, London.

BOTTOMS, A., and BROWNSWORD, R. (1983), 'Dangerousness and Rights' in J. W. Hinton, ed., *Dangerousness: Problems of Assessment and Prediction*. London: Allen and Unwin.

BROOKE, D., TAYLOR, C., GUNN, J., and MADEN, A. (1996), 'Point Prevalence of Mental Disorder in Unconvicted Male Prisoners in England and Wales', *British Medical Journal*, 313: 1524–7.

BURNEY, E., and PEARSON, G. (1995), 'Mentally Disordered Offenders: Finding a Focus for Diversion', *The Howard Journal*, 34: 291–313.

BUTLER, LORD (1974), *Interim Report of the Committee on Mentally Abnormal Offenders*, Cmnd. 5698. London: HMSO.

—— (1975), *Report of the Committee on Mentally Abnormal Offenders*, Cmnd. 6244. London: HMSO.

CAMPBELL, T., and HEGINBOTHAM, C. (1991), *Mental Illness: Prejudice, Discrimination and the Law*. Aldershot: Dartmouth.

CARSON, D. (1989), 'Prosecuting People with Mental Handicaps', *Criminal Law Review*, 87.

CHISWICK, D. (1990), 'Fitness to Stand Trial and Plead, Mutism and Deafness', in R. Bluglass and P. Bowden, eds., *Principles and Practice of Forensic Psychiatry*. Edinburgh: Churchill Livingstone.

—— (1996), 'Sentencing Mentally Disordered Offenders. A New Law to "Protect the Public" will Block Beds in Secure Units', *British Medical Journal*, 313: 1497–8.

COID, J. (1989), 'Psychopathic Disorders', *Current Opinion in Psychiatry*, 2: 750–6.

COPE, R. (1993), 'A Survey of Forensic Psychiatrists' Views on Psychopathic Disorder', *Journal of Forensic Psychiatry*, 4: 215–35.

CRIMINAL LAW REVISION COMMITTEE (1984), 15th Report: *Sexual Offences*, Cmnd. 9213. London: HMSO.

CULLEN, E. (1993), 'The Grendon Reconviction Study Part 1', *Prison Service Journal*, 90: 35–7.

DELL, S. (1983), 'Wanted: An Insanity Defence that can be Used', *Criminal Law Review*, 431.

—— and ROBERTSON, G. (1988), *Sentenced to Hospital: Offenders in Broadmoor*. Maudsley Monographs 32. London: Institute of Psychiatry.

—— GROUNDS, A., JAMES, K., and ROBERTSON, G. (1991), *Mentally Disordered Remanded Prisoners: Report to the Home Office* (unpublished).

DEPARTMENT OF HEALTH (1994), *Guidance on the Discharge of Mentally Disordered People and their Continuing Care in the Community*. NHS Executive HSG(94)27 and LASSL(94)4, 10 May 1994.

—— (1995), 'Mentally Disordered Offenders (Including Implementation of the "Reed" Review—Current Initiatives and Issues)'. Produced for Legal Action Group and Doughty Street Chambers conference, London, 21 October.

DOOLEY, E. (1990), 'Prison Suicide in England and Wales, 1972–87', *British Journal of Psychiatry*, 156: 40–5.

DWORKIN, R. (1977), *Taking Rights Seriously*. London: Duckworth.

EASTMAN, N. (1990), 'Unfit to Plead: The Test of being "Under Disability"'. Paper presented to Law Society's Mental Health Sub-Committee Conference, London, 8 June.

—— (1992), 'Abused Women and Legal Excuses', *New Law Journal*, 142: 1549–50.

—— (1996), 'Hybrid Orders: An Analysis of their Likely Effects on Sentencing Practice and on Forensic Psychiatric Practice and Services', *Journal of Forensic Psychiatry*, 7: 481–94.

—— (1997), 'Hybrid Justice: Proposals for the Mentally Disordered in the Crime (Sentences) Bill, the Ethical, Legal and Financial Implications', *Psychiatric Bulletin*, 21, 3: 129–31.

FENNELL, P. (1991), 'Diversion of Mentally Disordered Offenders from Custody', *Criminal Law Review*, 333–48.

—— (1992), 'Balancing Care and Control: Guardianship, Community Treatment Orders and Patient Safeguards', *International Journal of Law and Psychiatry*, 15: 205–35.

—— (1994), 'Mentally Disordered Suspects in the Criminal Justice System', *Journal of Law and Society*, 21: 57–71.

FLOUD, J., and YOUNG, W. (1981), *Dangerousness and Criminal Justice*. London: Heinemann.

GENDERS, E. (1991), 'Types of Violent Crime'. Report to the Home Office. Oxford: Centre for Criminological Research, University of Oxford.

—— and PLAYER, E. (1995), *Grendon: A Study of a Therapeutic Prison*. Oxford: Clarendon Press.

GOSTIN, L. (1986), *Mental Health Services—Law and Practice*. London: Shaw and Sons.

GROUNDS, A. (1987), 'Detection of "Psychopathic Disorder Patients" in Special Hospitals: Critical Issues', *British Journal of Psychiatry*, 151, 474–8.

—— (1990), 'Transfers of Sentenced Prisoners

to Hospital', *Criminal Law Review*, 544–51.

—— (1991), 'The Transfer of Sentenced Prisoners to Hospital 1960–1983' *British Journal of Criminology*, 31/1: 54–71.

GRUBIN, D. H. (1991), 'Unfit to Plead in England and Wales 1976–1988: A Survey', *British Journal of Psychiatry*, 158: 540–8.

GUDJONSSON, G., CLARE, I., RUTTER, S., and PEARSE, J. (1993), *Persons at Risk During Interview in Police Custody: The Identification of Vulnerabilities*. RCCJ Research Study no. 12.

GUNN, J. (1992), 'Psychiatry and Criminology—a Reconciliation', Paper presented to the British Society of Criminology, AGM, London, 29 January.

—— (1996), 'The Management and Discharge of Violent Patients', in N. Walker, ed., *Dangerous People*. London: Blackstone Press.

—— MADEN, A., and SWINTON, M. (1991), 'Treatment Needs of Prisoners with Psychiatric Disorders', *British Medical Journal*, 303: 338–341.

—— and ROBERTSON, G. (1987), 'A Ten Year Follow-up of Men Discharged from Grendon Prison', *British Journal of Psychiatry*, 151: 674–8.

—— DELL, S., and WAY C (1978), *Psychiatric Aspects of Imprisonment*. London: Academic Press.

HOGGETT, B. (1996), *Mental Health Law*, 4th edn. London: Sweet and Maxwell.

HOME OFFICE (1990), *Crime, Justice and Protecting the Public*, Cm 965. London: HMSO.

—— (1991), *Custody, Care and Justice*. London: HMSO.

—— DEPARTMENT OF HEALTH AND SOCIAL SECURITY (1987), *Report of the Interdepartmental Working Group of Home Office and DHSS Officials on Mentally Disturbed Offenders in the Prison System in England and Wales*. London: Home Office/DHSS.

—— DEPARTMENT OF HEALTH (1996), *Mentally Disordered Offenders—Sentencing and Discharge Arrangements*. A discussion paper on a proposed new power for the courts.

JOHNSTONE, G. (1996), 'From Experts in Responsibility to Advisers on Punishment: The Role of Psychiatrists in Penal Matters', Studies in Law, University of Hull: Law School.

KERSHAW, C., and RENSHAW, G. (1996), *Statistics of Mentally Disordered Offenders England and Wales 1995*. Home Office Statistical Bulletin, Research Statistics Directorate, Issue 20/96.

KOE, H. (1992), 'Domestic Violence, Gender Blindness and Concepts of Criminal Responsibility', Paper presented at Brunel University, Uxbridge, 2 March.

LAING, J. (1995), 'The Mentally Disordered Suspect at the Police Station', *Criminal Law Review*, 371–81.

LINK, B., ANDREWS, H., and CULLEN, F. (1992), 'The Violent and Illegal Behaviour of Mental Patients Compared to Community Controls', *American Sociological Review*, 57: 275–92.

MACKAY, R. D. (1990), 'Fact and Fiction about the Insanity Defence', *Criminal Law Review*, 247–55.

—— (1991), 'The Decline of Disability in Relation to the Trial', *Criminal Law Review*, 87–97.

McCANN, J. B., JAMES, A., WILSON, S., and DUNN, G. (1996), 'Prevalence of Psychiatric Disorders in Young People in the Care System', *British Medical Journal*, 313, 1529–30

MAIER-KATKIN, D. (1991), 'Postpartum Psychosis, Infanticide and the Law', *Crime, Law and Social Change*, 15, 2: 109–124.

—— and OGLE, R. (1993), 'A Rationale for Infanticide Laws', *Criminal Law Review*, 903–14.

MILLER, R. D. (1992), 'Economic Factors Leading to Diversion of the Mentally Disordered from the Civil to the Criminal Commitment Systems', *International Journal of Law and Psychiatry*, 15: 1–12.

MONAHAN, J. (1992), 'Mental Disorder and Violent Behaviour. Perceptions and Evidence' *American Psychologist*, 47: 511–521.

—— (1996), 'The MacArthur Violence Risk Assessment Study', An executive summary of the research of the working group (Steadman, H., Robbins, P., Monahan, J., Appelbaum, P., Grisso, T., Mulvey, E., and Roth, L.). Proceedings of the MacArthur Foundation Research Network Violence, Competence and Coercion: The Pivotal Issues in Mental Health Law Oxford, Wadham College, 3–4 July.

—— (1997), 'Clinical and Actuarial Predictions of Violence', in D. Faigman, D. Kaye, M. Saks, and J. Sanders, eds., *West's Companion to Scientific Evidence*. St Paul Minn.: West Publishing Company.

—— and STEADMAN, H. (1983), 'Crime and Mental Disorder: An Epidemiological Approach', in M. Tonry and N. Morris, eds., *Crime and Justice: An Annual Review of Research*, vol. 4, 145–89. Chicago, Ill.: University of Chicago Press.

—— and —— eds. (1994), *Violence and Mental Disorder: Developments in Risk Assessment*. Chicago, Ill.: University of Chicago Press.

MURRAY, D. J. (1989), 'Review of Research on Re-offending of Mentally Disordered Offenders', *Research and Planning Unit Paper 55*. London: Home Office.

NACRO (1993), *Mentally Disordered Offenders and Community Care*, Mental Health Advisory Committee Policy Paper no. 1. London: NACRO Publications.

NICOLSON, D., and SANGHVI, R. (1993), 'Battered Women and Provocation: The Implications of R v Ahluwalia', *Criminal Law Review*, 728–38.

OPCS (1986), *Morbidity Statistics from General Practice: Third National Study 1981–82*. London: HMSO.

PALMER, C., and HART, M. (1996), *A PACE in the Right Direction?* Institute for the Study of the Legal Profession, Faculty of Law, University of Sheffield.

PEAY, J. (1982), 'Dangerousness—Ascription or Description?' in P. Feldman ed., *Developments in the Study of Criminal Behaviour. Volume 2: Violence*. Chichester: Wiley.

—— (1988), 'Offenders Suffering from Psychopathic Disorder: The Rise and Demise of a Consultation Document', *British Journal of Criminology*, 28: 67–81.

—— (1989), *Tribunals on Trial: A Study of Decision-Making Under the Mental Health Act 1983*. Oxford: Clarendon Press.

—— (1993), 'A Criminological Perspective' in W. Watson and A. Grounds, eds., *Mentally Disordered Offenders in an Era of Community Care*. Cambridge: Cambridge University Press.

—— ed. (1996), *Inquiries after Homicide*. London: Duckworth.

PLAYER, E. (1992), 'Treatment for Sex Offenders: A Cautionary Note'. *Prison Service Journal*, 85: 2–9.

PRINS, H. (1986), *Dangerous Behaviour, the Law and Mental Disorder*. London: Tavistock.

—— (1990), 'Mental Abnormality and Criminality—an Uncertain Relationship', *Medicine, Science and Law*, 30/3: 247–58.

—— (1991), 'Is Psychopathic Disorder a Useful Clinical Concept? A Perspective from England and Wales', *International Journal of Offender Therapy and Comparative Criminology*, 35/2: 119–25.

RADZINOWICZ, L., and HOOD, R. (1981), 'A Dangerous Direction for Sentencing Reform', *Criminal Law Review*, 756–61.

RAEDER, M. (1992), 'Evidentiary Procedural and Substantive Ramifications of Premenstrual Syndrome and Battered Women Syndrome', Paper presented to Reform of Evidence—a conference of the Society for the Reform of Criminal Law, Vancouver, August 1992.

REED REPORT (1991), *Review of Health and Social Services for Mentally Disordered Offenders and Others Requiring Similar Services*. London: Department of Health/Home Office.

—— (1992), *Review of Health and Social Services for Mentally Disordered Offenders and Others Requiring Similar Services*. London: Department of Health/Home Office.

REED, J. (1994), *Report of the Department of Health and Home Office Working Group on Psychopathic Disorder*. London: Department of Health/Home Office.

RICHARDSON, G. (1991), 'Discretionary Life Sentences and the European Convention on Human Rights', *Public Law*, 34–40.

ROBERTS, P. (1996), 'Will you Stand Up in Court? On the Admissibility of Psychiatric and Psychological Evidence', *Journal of Forensic Psychiatry*, 7: 63–78.

ROBERTSON, G. (1988), 'Arrest patterns among mentally disordered offenders', *British Journal of Psychiatry*, 153: 313–16.

—— PEARSON, R., and GIBB, R. (1995), *The Mentally Disordered and the Police. Research Findings no. 21*, London: Home Office Research and Statistics Department.

ROTH, M. (1990), 'Psychopathic (Sociopathic), Personality', in R. Bluglass and P. Bowden, eds., *Principles and Practice of Forensic Psychiatry*. Edinburgh: Churchill Livingstone.

RUBIN, D. (1972), 'Predictions of Dangerousness in Mentally Ill Criminals', *Archives of General Psychiatry*, 27: 397–407.

SAMPSON, A. (1994), 'The Future for Sex Offenders in Prison', in E. Player and M. Jenkins, eds., *Prisons after Woolf: Reform through Riot*. London: Routledge.

SHAPLAND, J. (1991), 'Where Do We Put Them? Coping with Mentally Disordered Offenders'. Paper presented to the British Criminology Conference, York, July.

SHEPPARD, D. (1996), *Learning the Lessons. Mental Health Inquiry Reports Published in England and Wales Between 1969–1996 and Their Recommendations for Improving Practice*. 2nd edn. London: Zito Trust.

SIMS, A. (1996), *Report of the Confidential Inquiry into Homicides and Suicides by Mentally Ill People*. London: Royal College of Psychiatrists.

SMITH, J. C., and HOGAN, B. (1988), *Criminal Law*. 6th edn. London: Butterworths.

SOLOMKA, B. (1996), 'The Role of Psychiatric Evidence in Passing "Longer than Normal" sentences', *Journal of Forensic Psychiatry*, 7: 239–55.

Swanson, J., Holzer, C., Ganju, V., and Jono, R. (1990), 'Violence and Psychiatric Disorder in the Community: Evidence from the Epidemiological Catchment Area Surveys', *Hospital and Community Psychiatry*, 41, 761–770.

Taylor, P., and Gunn, J. (1984), 'Violence and Psychosis. I. Risk of Violence Among Psychotic Men', *British Medical Journal*, 288: 1945–9.

Tumim, S. (1990), Report of a Review by Her Majesty's Chief Inspector of Prisons for England and Wales, *Suicide and Self Harm in Prison Service Establishments in England and Wales*, Cm. 1383, London: HMSO.

Verdun-Jones, S. (1989), 'Sentencing the Partly Mad and Partly Bad: The Case of the Hospital Order in England and Wales', *International Journal of Law and Psychiatry*, 12: 1–27.

Von Hirsch, A., and Ashworth, A. (1996), 'Protective Sentencing under Section 2(2)(b): The Criteria for Dangerousness', *Criminal Law Review*, 175–83.

Walker, N., ed. (1996), *Dangerous People*. London: Blackstone Press.

Watson, W., and Grounds, A., eds. (1993), *Mentally Disordered Offenders in an Era of Community Care*. Cambridge: Cambridge University Press

Wells, C. (1994), 'Battered Woman Syndrome and Defences to Homicide: Where Now?', *Legal Studies*, 14: 266–76.

Wessely, S., and Taylor, P. (1991), 'Madness and Crime: Criminology versus Psychiatry', *Criminal Behaviour and Mental Health*, 1: 193–228.

West Midlands Regional Health Authority (1991), *Report of the Panel of Inquiry Appointed to Investigate the Case of Kim Kirkman*.

World Health Organization (1978), *Mental Disorders: Glossary and Guide to their Classification in accordance with the Ninth Revision of the International Classification of Diseases, Injuries and Causes of Death*. Geneva: WHO.

Wilczynski, A. (1991), *Images of Parents who Kill their Children*. Paper presented to the British Criminology Conference, York, July.

—— and Morris, A. (1993), 'Parents who Kill their Children', *Criminal Law Review*, 31–6.

Wood, D. (1988), 'Dangerous Offenders, and the Morality of Protective Sentencing', *Criminal Law Review*, 424–33.

Woolf, Lord Justice (1991), *Prison Disturbances April 1990*, Report of an Inquiry by the Rt. Hon. Lord Justice Woolf (Parts I and II), and His Honour Judge Stephen Tumim (Part II). Cm 1456, London: HMSO.

21

Ethnic Origins, Crime, and Criminal Justice

David J. Smith

In many different countries certain specific ethnic groups are far more often caught in the net of criminal justice than others. It is striking that the particular ethnic groups having elevated rates of official offending can be completely different from one country to another (Tonry, 1997). In England and Wales, it is black people, whose families originally came from the Caribbean from the late 1940s onwards, who are likely to be criminalized (see below).

Is this because the criminal justice system treats black people unfairly, or because black people are more likely than others to offend? Since there is a strong incentive for the various actors to invest heavily in one or other of these explanations, the issue has become highly contentious. In seeking to address the question in a serious way, we come up against difficult conceptual issues, as well as a deficit of useful information.

The central conceptual problem is to decide what constitutes fairness in this context. It would clearly be unfair for a police officer to stop and search someone because he was black, or for a court to give someone a stiffer sentence for the same reason. That would be to use race or ethnic group as a criterion for decision-making, to the detriment of an ethnic minority. It would be akin to direct discrimination against a black person applying for a job or seeking to rent accommodation, which has been unlawful in Britain under the Race Relations Acts since 1968. However, the difficult problems concern decision making that is apparently blind to race or ethnicity, but in practice tends to work to the disadvantage of black people. For example, black suspects may tend to be remanded in custody (rather than granted bail) because a higher proportion are judged to have an unstable family background; and convicted black offenders may tend to be given long sentences because a higher proportion have pleaded not guilty. There is no widely agreed method for deciding which criteria, among those having an uneven impact on different ethnic groups, are nevertheless legitimate.

There should be a way of settling the question, because the law, at least in its rhetoric, seeks to impose a universal framework which, among other things, determines what behaviour is lawful and what criminal. Whenever we ask the question whether crime rates vary between ethnic groups we are appealing to a universal framework of this kind. The model works best in a homogeneous society. It tends to break down to the extent that there are diverse groups that differ in their perceptions and definitions of deviance, in the methods they use to control it, and in their readiness to appeal to the formal legal process; or where decision-making rules or enforcement methods have an uneven impact on these diverse groups.

Especially in the case of the post-colonial countries, a further dimension of the problem is the close connection between the law and the concept of the nation. The majority group has a unique connection with the moral, religious, and cultural tradition that shaped the legal system. At the same time adherence to the law 'symbolizes the imagined community of the nation and expresses the fundamental unity and equality of its citizens' (Gilroy, 1987: 74). Yet neither the law nor the corresponding sense of identity grew out of a tradition that included the present ethnic minorities. It may be argued, therefore, that the rules and processes according to which they are judged to be criminal spring from a tradition which, far from being universal, belongs exclusively to the dominant group.

Against this, it may be said that the rule of law is part of the enterprise of nation-building. The project, which will never be finally accomplished, is to establish the law as a universal framework that is equally the property of all citizens. One objective of this chapter is to assess how far this has yet been accomplished, at least in the case of ethnic minorities.

From a review of the fragmentary evidence available, a further objective is to judge how far the elevated official offending rate of black people is a consequence of bias, impartial application of rules or criteria that work to the disadvantage of black people, or an elevated actual rate of offending. If the effects of apparently neutral criteria turn out to be an important part of the explanation, then deciding which of these criteria are justifiable becomes a central issue. Some of the problems that arise in trying to resolve this issue will be discussed. Finally, the chapter will rehearse some possible explanations of an elevated rate of actual offending among black people. Although the evidence for England and Wales is too thin at present to rule out any of these theories, it is enough to make some of them seem more plausible than others.

The chapter is organized in five main sections. The first deals with conceptual issues, while the second provides background information about ethnic minorities in Britain to support the later account of their interactions with the criminal justice system. The third section summarizes what is known about rates of victimization among different ethnic groups, and about racially motivated crime and racial harassment. The fourth section considers ethnic minorities as suspects and offenders. The final section sets out the main conclusions and rehearses possible explanations.

CONCEPTUAL ISSUES

The central question to be addressed is how close the criminal justice system comes to constituting a universal framework within which all ethnic groups are treated equally. There is room for considerable discussion about what is meant by equal treatment in this context. It certainly cannot mean that everyone should be treated the same. Obviously, the guilty, and not the innocent, should be punished, and people should be punished more or less severely depending on the seriousness of the offence. Slightly less obviously, someone with a long record of past offending should be punished more severely than someone convicted for the first time. Possibly, although this is more controversial, a person with a stable family life and a steady job should be given a community-based sanction, whereas a person without those supports should be sent to prison. In other words treating people equally must mean that people in like circumstances and categories in relevant respects should be treated equally.

It is common ground that ethnic group should not itself be a criterion that determines how people are treated. But which *other* criteria are relevant and legitimate? And how far, if at all, should their *impact* on different ethnic groups be taken into account? At one extreme there is the view that equal treatment means the impartial application of existing rules and principles regardless of their impact on different ethnic groups. If, on that view, more black than white people are committed to prison because more black people are judged to lack a stable family or a steady job, that does not constitute unequal treatment. At the other extreme, there is the view that any policies, rules, or procedures that have the effect of punishing a higher proportion of one ethnic group than another are unjust, and that law and policy should be adjusted so as to achieve equal outcomes (say, in terms of proportion imprisoned) for different ethnic groups, and also for different social classes.

It is difficult to defend either of these extreme views. Ensuring that equal proportions of different social groups are punished has never been seen as an objective of the criminal justice system, and does not seem a valid interpretation of the ideal of equality before the law. Few would accept the idea that either enforcement or the decisions of the courts should have the aim of achieving equal punishment of different social groups. That would imply unequal treatment of individuals who had committed similar offences and had comparable records. Whenever there was an increase in offending within a particular social group, the system would have to respond by reducing penalties for offenders within that group.

On the other hand, the view that any uneven impact on different ethnic groups should be disregarded seems equally questionable. Apparently neutral rules or criteria may work to the disadvantage of a particular ethnic group, yet perhaps they could be changed without the sacrifice of any fundamental principle. For example, many police forces will not caution juveniles (instead of setting in train a prosecution) if they are known to have committed two or more previous offences. In an area where police law enforcement tends to target black youths (for example, through drugs raids on Reggae clubs) a rule of this kind works to the disadvantage of black people, and, arguably, amounts to treating them unequally. The rule could be relaxed without sacrificing any fundamental principle: after all, police cautions are already given to juveniles who are known to have committed previous offences.

This analysis suggests that equality of treatment within the criminal justice system cannot be interpreted as equality of outcome (say, the same proportion of different ethnic groups committed to prison). Nor can it be interpreted as merely the neutral application of existing rules and criteria, whatever their effect. Instead, it is necessary to adopt an intermediate position. The legitimacy and suitability of existing rules and criteria must be critically reviewed in the light of their impact on different ethnic groups.

These polar views about what constitutes equal treatment are similar to the two opposing models of justice implied in discussion of anti-discrimination law. McCrudden, Smith, and Brown (1991) describe them as the *individual justice model* and the *group justice model* of legislation against race and sex discrimination. The aims of these polar models of anti-discrimination legislation conflict in important ways, and the actual legislation represents a compromise between them. The Race Relations Act 1976 and the Sex Discrimination Act 1975 incorporate elements of the group justice model through the concept of *indirect discrimination*: the use of a condition or requirement which is such that a considerably smaller proportion of one than of another group can comply with it, which is to the other's detriment, and where the person using the condition or requirement cannot show it to be justified. The concept of indirect discrimination belongs within the group justice model because it is concerned with the outcomes for groups resulting from the application of some rule or principle. However, conflict with the individual justice model is minimized by the qualification that criteria working to the disadvantage of a particular ethnic group may always be used as long as they can be justified. The statute did not enlarge on what would constitute a justification. In many cases, the condition or requirement is presented as a test of performance or ability. For example, where job applicants are required to take an aptitude test on which members of an ethnic minority tend to score lower than whites, the point at issue is whether the test is a valid and appropriate measure of performance in the job: if it is, then its use is justifiable (and non-discriminatory) even though it works to the disadvantage of the ethnic minority.

At present the decisions at certain key stages of the criminal justice process do not fall within the provisions of the anti-discrimination legislation, although there have been calls for this to be changed (Commission for Racial Equality, 1991). If the scope of the legislation were to be extended to criminal justice, this would highlight the problem of deciding whether particular criteria that work to the disadvantage of an ethnic minority can be justified. On the surface, decision-making criteria within the criminal justice system are often analogous to aptitude tests. For example, a police officer might adopt the practice of stopping and searching any group of two or more young men with long hair and earrings walking on the streets after midnight. This might be justifiable in terms of results, in the sense that young men of this description are often found to be in possession of illicit drugs. Again, wherever a suspect was cheeky or unco-operative, a police officer might decide to arrest and charge him with some offence or other. This also might be justifiable in terms of results, in the sense that cheeky or unco-operative suspects usually end up being convicted of some offence. Yet these examples, of course, illustrate that decision-making criteria within the criminal justice system, unlike employee selection criteria, can seldom be justified purely in terms of results. In the first example, it may be granted that long-haired youths with earrings out after midnight are more likely to be in possession of illicit drugs than pensioners at noon, but invasion of a person's liberty is justified, under English law, only if there is a specific reason to suspect that he has committed an offence. In the second example, the police officer's use of the criterion of cheekiness and lack of co-operation is self-validating, because he or she is in a position to construct the arrest and in most cases to ensure a successful prosecution. Similarly, those who plead guilty are nearly always found guilty, but that does not show that the guilty plea is proof of guilt. Within criminal justice there is no independent test of the results achieved by using a criterion, so that some justification other than results is required.

This chapter does not tackle the problem of how to determine whether rules or criteria that work to the disadvantage of an ethnic minority are justifiable. The more limited aim is to show whether the uneven impact of neutrally applied rules accounts in large or small part for the over-representation of black people in English prisons, and to provide illustrations of the rules in question.

ETHNIC MINORITIES IN BRITAIN

According to the 1991 census, which for the first time included a question on ethnic origin, 5.5 per cent of the population of Britain belonged to an ethnic minority group at that time. Among these, three broad groups can be identified: black people, who were 1.6 per cent of the population, among which 0.9 per cent originated from the Caribbean; South Asians, who were 2.7 per cent, among whom 1.5 per cent originated from India, 0.9 per cent from Pakistan, and 0.3 per cent from Bangladesh; and other minorities, which accounted for 1.2 per cent, among whom 0.3 per cent were of Chinese origin, while 0.4 per cent were other Asians.

Ethnic minorities have a distinctly younger age structure than the majority white population. For example, all ethnic minorities accounted at the census date for 6.9 per cent of the population aged 16–24, compared with 5.5 per cent of all age groups, and 2.7 per cent of those aged 45 and over. Because most crime is committed by males up to the age of 30, it is important to take account of the unusual age structure of the ethnic minority groups when evaluating their recorded crime rates.

The ethnic minorities counted in these statistics are those which are perceived by the majority to be physically distinct, and which are visually identifiable. The vast majority of these people are either themselves migrants, or descendants of people who migrated to Britain since the Second World War. The earliest wave of migration, which was from the Caribbean, got under way in the early 1950s, but most of the inflow happened more recently.

It was the Race Relations Act 1968 which first made it unlawful to discriminate on grounds of race, colour, or ethnic or national origins, in the provision of goods, facilities, and services. A pioneering research project carried out in 1966–7, before the Act was passed, which used a combination of field experiments and surveys, showed that racial discrimination 'ranged from the massive to the substantial' (Daniel, 1968). In this study, the findings from three complementary methods of research converged in a particularly powerful way. First, Daniel carried out the first major sample survey of ethnic minorities in six English towns that were already centres of immigrant settlement. Respondents were asked for their general views on the extent of racial discrimination, but also about any personal experience of it. Secondly, Daniel developed a series of controlled experiments to test the extent of racial discrimination in natural situations. For example, where respondents had claimed personal experience of racial discrimination on applying for a job, testers belonging to various ethnic groups were sent to apply for a job currently on offer at the same firm. Thirdly, Daniel conducted interviews with people in a position to discriminate, such as the owners or managers of firms and the staff of local authority housing departments, and in some cases confronted them with evidence from a controlled test of their own organization that showed discrimination had occurred.

Neither the field experiments nor the interviews with discriminators showed any difference in the extent or nature of discrimination against specific groups, as long as these were considered to be racially distinct from the majority. The study demonstrated that perceived 'colour' was the important factor, by including a Turkish Cypriot actor in the experiments. Discrimination against the Turkish Cypriot was substantially lower than against the Afro-Caribbean, Indian, or Pakistani, but there was no difference in the level of discrimination against these last three groups.

The Indian and Pakistani respondents in the survey were much less likely than the Afro-Caribbeans to say they had encountered discrimination, but Daniel showed that this was because of the different survival strategies adopted by South Asians compared with Afro-Caribbeans in Britain. Afro-Caribbeans, expecting more of British people, adopted a more outgoing style of life: they were likely to apply for a job at a firm they had never heard of, or apply cold to rent accommodation. South Asians looked for job opportunities through their established social networks, and from the beginning made extraordinary efforts to buy rather than rent accommodation. Daniel's experiments showed that the level of discrimination against members of the two groups was the same, where they put themselves in the same situation. But in real life, the Afro-Caribbeans placed themselves in situations in which they might face discrimination more often than South Asians. They were therefore more likely to encounter face-to-face the hostility and rejection that South Asians tended to avoid. Hence, levels of discrimination against South Asians and Afro-Caribbeans in comparable situations were the same, but personal experience of discrimination, and awareness of it, was substantially greater among Afro-Caribbeans. Subsequent research in the 1970s (Smith, 1977) and 1980s (Brown, 1984; Brown and Gay, 1986) confirmed that the initial pattern continued. Jowell and Prescott-Clarke (1970) pioneered the method of correspondence testing for job discrimination in recruitment to employment, which was then used again in several subsequent studies (Smith, 1977; Brown and Gay, 1986). Correspondence tests, like personal and telephone tests, have always shown the same level of discrimination against Afro-Caribbeans and South Asians.

In the 1960s, the migrants were largely concentrated in unskilled and semi-skilled manual jobs in the main conurbations and the textile towns of Lancashire and Yorkshire. Initially, a large proportion of South Asians had little English, and even today a substantial minority (around 20 per cent) do not speak English well. The South Asian population was always diverse, with a substantial minority of highly educated people together with a larger proportion having little or no education. From 1969 onwards the migration of Asians from East Africa swelled the number who were well educated and who had experience of managing businesses. More recently, migration from Bangladesh has introduced a group of generally poor Asians with little education. By contrast, Afro-Caribbeans were always a more homogeneous population in social, economic, and cultural terms. Very few were uneducated, but few had higher education qualifications obtained in the West Indies. From the beginning, a high proportion of the men were skilled manual workers, and that remains the case today.

The process of development for ethnic minorities from the 1960s to the present time has been one of increasing differentiation (Jones, 1993; Modood *et al.*, 1997). There are increasing differences between specific minority groups, and also between members of each particular group. People of African Asian and Indian origin now have a profile similar to that of white people in terms of educational qualifications and job levels. On the other hand, the Muslim groups (principally those of Pakistani and Bangladeshi origin) are at a substantial disadvantage in terms of job levels, rate of unemployment, educational and job qualifications, income, and standard of living (Jones, 1993; Modood *et al.*, 1997). Afro-Caribbeans occupy an intermediate position. In cultural terms, the specific ethnic minorities have always been more different from each other than each group is from the white majority. What they had in common was the racial discrimination and hostility displayed by white people and institutions.

The different groups adopted entirely different strategies. Thirty years later, the original cultural differences, and the differences in human and financial capital, have proved far more influential than the hostility and discrimination directed at all groups perceived to be racially distinct (Modood *et al.*, 1997). As a result, the socio-economic positions of the specific minority groups are drawing further apart.

The sequence of field experiments suggests that there was a substantial decline in racial discrimination following the Race Relations Act 1968, but that discrimination nevertheless continued at a fairly high level (Smith, 1977). No further declines in the level have been recorded since 1974, although the latest experiments were carried out in 1986. These showed that about 40 per cent of South Asian and Afro-Caribbean job applicants were refused an interview where a similarly qualified white applicant was offered one (Brown and Gay, 1986).

It is clear that concern about high crime rates among Afro-Caribbeans is relatively recent. In a report published in 1972, the Home Affairs Committee of the House of Commons on Race Relations and Immigration expressed some disquiet about difficult relations between the police and young Afro-Caribbeans, but on the whole tended towards the view that Afro-Caribbeans were less criminal than whites; certainly, two chief constables put forward that view in their evidence to the Committee (Home Affairs Committee, 1972). The years between 1972 and 1976 'saw the definition of blacks as a low crime group turned round 180 degrees' (Gilroy, 1987: 92). Giving evidence to the Home Affairs Select Committee in the 1975–6 session, the Metropolitan Police made it clear that they considered crime rates were high among Afro-Caribbeans, and also complained about anti-police campaigning by black activist groups (House of Commons, 1976: 182). As Gilroy (1987) has pointed out, this swing in official opinion was probably the result of a series of high-profile confrontations between the police and Afro-Caribbeans.

In the context of disturbances such as these, the Metropolitan Police provided statistical evidence in its 1976 submission to the Home Affairs Committee to support the proposition that there was a specific crime problem among ethnic minorities. These statistics were confined to street offences, in which black people were most often involved. From this point onwards, public discussion of the threat of rising crime was linked with discussion of racial conflict and with the perceived problem of street crime among Afro-Caribbeans. These offences were usually labelled 'mugging' even though they included a high proportion of handbag snatches without the use or threat of violence. It has been argued that the growing public and police perception of black people as criminal was closely connected with the conception of 'mugging' and its promotion in the media as a typically black crime (Hall *et al.*, 1978).

In the 1980s, relations between black (Afro-Caribbean) people and the police were at the forefront of public consciousness. There were a considerable number of disturbances expressing hostility by black people towards the police during the 1980s, most notably the riots in 1981 in Brixton and several other urban areas. These disturbances led to various official and unofficial reports, of which the Scarman report on the Brixton Disorders (Scarman, 1981) was by far the most influential. In the space of ten years, therefore, there was a swing from muted official concern about relations between Afro-Caribbeans and the police, together with an official view that ethnic minorities tended to be law-abiding, to anti-police riots in which black people played the major part, and an official view that there was a black crime problem.

Throughout the period, it was Afro-Caribbeans, and not South Asians, who were highlighted in public discussion of crime and disorder. The famous conflicts in the 1970s revolved around Afro-Caribbean clubs and cultural events such as the Notting Hill Carnival. The anti-police riots of the 1980s took place in areas of Afro-Caribbean concentration (such as St Paul's in Bristol, Brixton in south London, and Moss Side in Manchester); although white people as well as Afro-Caribbeans took part, there is little evidence that South Asians were involved. Many South Asian shopkeepers were victims in the 1985 riots in the Lozells and Handsworth areas of Birmingham.

Survey results and experiments on racial discrimination have consistently shown that prejudice and hostility among the public at large are just as great against South Asians as against Afro-Caribbeans (Daniel, 1968; Rose *et al.*, 1969; Jowell and Prescott-Clarke, 1972; Smith, 1977; Brown, 1984; Brown and Gay, 1986). Nevertheless, it is only Afro-Caribbeans, and not South Asians, who have become associated in public debate and in the public mind with predatory crime.

In the 1990s, the Muslim groups (originating from India as well as from Pakistan and Bangladesh) have become more active, assertive, and politically organized as a consequence of the Rushdie affair (Modood, 1990). This development has been associated with the growth of specifically anti-Muslim prejudice (Modood, 1994). There are some early indications that debate in the mass media may come to focus on Muslim involvement in crime. A race relations specialist employed within government has argued that a rise in Muslim involvement in crime is to be expected (FitzGerald, 1995) but no convincing evidence has yet emerged to show that this is already happening.

ETHNIC MINORITIES AS VICTIMS OF CRIME

Racial harassment and racially motivated crime have been an issue in British public debate since the Notting Hill Race Riots of 1958. Except where racial hatred was involved, however, there has been little interest over most of this period in criminal victimization of ethnic minorities, and far more interest in offending by black people and in conflicts between black people and the police. One consequence of this unbalanced debate is that little is known about the links between victimization and offending among ethnic minorities. These matters are inherently difficult to research in Britain, where specific ethnic minorities form such small proportions of the population. In general, there are no official statistics based on police records that show the race or ethnic group of the victim, or of the offender according to the victim, and none about persons arrested. The main sources of information are the British Crime Surveys (BCS) of 1988 and 1992, and fragmentary statistics for London on crimes recorded by the police. These are for selected years up to the mid-1980s. They provide very limited data on intra-racial offending for two kinds of offence; and they use an obviously inadequate classification of the race or ethnic group of the offender.

Rates of Victimization

The BCS 1988 showed that rates of victimization were distinctly higher among both Afro-Caribbeans and South Asians than among white people, both for household crimes and for personal crimes (Mayhew, Elliott, and Dowds 1989; see also Maguire, and Zedner, both this volume). More recently, these findings have been confirmed by an analysis of the combined samples from the 1988 and 1992 BCS (see Table 21.1). Compared with white people, Afro-Caribbeans had a high rate of victimization in the case of burglary, vehicle theft, bicycle theft, assault, and robbery. Among South Asians, the high rates of victimization were for household vandalism, burglary, damage to vehicles, threats, and robbery or theft from the person.

Both the earlier (Mayhew, Elliott, and Dowds, 1989) and the later (FitzGerald and Hale, 1996) reports set out the results of multivariate analyses designed to show whether the difference in victimization between ethnic minorities and

Table 21.1 Victimization rates by ethnic group (British Crime Survey 1988 and 1992)

| | Percentage reporting victimization | | |
	White	Afro-Caribbean	Asian
Household vandalism	4.3	3.5	**6.2
Burglary with loss	3.0	**6.7	**4.6
Vehicle crime (owners)			
Vandalism	9.1	10.0	**11.6
All thefts	19.1	**27.3	21.0
Bicycle theft (owners)	5.0	**9.1	4.7
Other household theft	6.8	5.7	5.8
All household offences	30.8	**34.8	**36.2
Assaults	3.4	**5.9	4.0
Threats	2.5	3.3	**4.5
Robbery/theft from person	1.3	**3.2	**3.1
Other personal thefts	3.9	4.5	3.1
All personal offences	9.7	**13.9	**13.0

* Significantly different from whites at the 10 per cent level.
* Significantly different from whites at the 5 per cent level.
Source: FitzGerald and Hale 1996, table 2.1.

whites could be explained by known factors. For example, ethnic minorities might have a higher rate of victimization because they are more likely than whites to be unemployed, on low incomes, living in council housing, or in an inner city area with a high crime rate. Of course, this would not show that the high rate of victimization among ethnic minorities is of no consequence—it would not explain it away—but it might throw light on the causal mechanisms. The more recent analysis (FitzGerald and Hale, 1996) took account of sex, age, occupation of head of household, unemployment, tenure, marital status, educational level, household income, whether in an inner city area, and whether in a high crime area.[1] Five different models analysed the risks of victimization for a particular offence (assault, threats, robbery, burglary, and household vandalism). In broad terms, the difference in rate of victimization between ethnic minorities and whites became less or in some cases disappeared once these factors were taken into account.

In part, these differences arise because ethnic minorities tend to live in inner city areas, and in high crime neighbourhoods.[2] Thus, 69 per cent of Afro-Caribbeans, and 44 per cent of South Asians in the BCS sample were in inner city areas, compared with only 16 per cent of whites. Again, 62 per cent of Afro-Caribbeans, and 55 per cent of South Asians were in high-risk neighbourhoods, compared with only 11 per cent of whites (FitzGerald and Hale, 1996: calculated from table 1.3). In the case of threats, robbery, and burglary, victimization risks were shown to be higher in inner city areas than elsewhere in the context of the multivariate model; and for robbery, burglary, and household vandalism, victimization was shown to be greater in high crime than in other neighbourhoods.

In general, risks of victimization were found to decline with age, so that the relative youth of the ethnic minority population partly explained their high rate of victimization. However, in the case of assault and threats, the risk of victimization did not decline with age among the ethnic minorities to the same extent as among the general population. Risks of victimization were consistently higher among those in rented than in owned accommodation, which partly explained high victimization risks among Afro-Caribbeans, who were more likely to be in rented accommodation than other groups. The risks of threats and burglary were higher among middle-class than working-class people (indexed by whether the head of household was in a manual occupation); also, the risk of assault was higher among middle-class than working-class Afro-Caribbeans. However, these class differences do not help to explain the high overall risk of victimization among ethnic minorities (who are concentrated in the working class, which is less at risk).

[1] The models shown in FitzGerald and Hale (1996) seem more illuminating than those shown in the earlier report (Mayhew, Elliott, and Dowds, 1989). For comments on the earlier models, see Smith (1984).

[2] High-crime neighbourhoods were defined by means of the ACORN classification, which is based on very small areas (census enumeration districts containing 150 households on average) and makes use of census data. For further information, see Mayhew, Elliott, and Dowds (1989), App. G.

In the context of these models, the rate of victimization among Afro-Caribbeans was elevated (i.e. significantly higher than among whites) only in the case of burglary. Among Pakistanis, the rate of victimization was not elevated for any of the five offences. Among Indians, the rate of victimization remained elevated in the context of the models for robbery, burglary, and household vandalism. The risk of assault was actually found to be lower among each of the three ethnic minority groups than among whites in the context of the multivariate models. However, as mentioned above, the risk of assault did not decline with age among the ethnic minorities in the same way as among whites. Broadly speaking, these findings suggest that in large part, ethnic minorities have a higher risk of victimization than whites because of their area of residence or pattern of daily activities: factors that might be understood in terms of routine activity theory (Cohen and Felson, 1979) and environmental criminology (see Bottoms and Wiles, this volume). In large part, therefore, it seems that the elevated rate of victimization is not directly connected with racial hostility. On the other hand, some features of the findings, such as the unusual relationship between assault victimization and age among ethnic minorities, cannot be explained by environmental or routine activity theory, and suggest that racial hostility may also play a part.

In the case of Afro-Caribbeans, the relatively high level of victimization is connected with the relatively high crime rate. Much crime is committed near to where the offender lives (see Bottoms and Wiles, this volume), and either on people the offender knows or on others in similar circumstances (for example, belonging to the same social class or ethnic group). It is interesting, for example, that victimization is particularly high among offenders (Smith, 1983a). Hence, it is not surprising that black-on-black crime accounts for a substantial proportion of the victimization of black people (see Figure 21.1). A serious limitation of these findings from the British Crime Survey (BCS) is that they relate only to the minority of cases[3] where the victim could describe the offender. This inflates the proportion of black offenders, because black people are more likely to commit offences involving personal contact, such as robbery and theft from the person, than ones that do not, such as burglary (see below). It is nevertheless striking that 44 per cent of offences on Afro-Caribbeans were committed by black people, according to the victims, bearing in mind that black people account for only 1.6 per cent of the population. The proportion of white victims who said the offender was black was much lower, at 8 per cent.

The extent to which crime is intra-racial probably varies widely according to the type of offence. The published BCS findings do not throw light on this, and small sample sizes may make it difficult or impossible to do so. Some fragmentary data are, however, available for crimes recorded by the police in London in 1984 and 1985. A reworking of some of these data for 1985 is shown

---

[3] Across all offences, the proportion of victims who could say something about the offender was 38% (FitzGerald and Hale, 1996: calculated from table 3.4), but this proportion was highest for assaults and threats (98%) and robbery (65%).

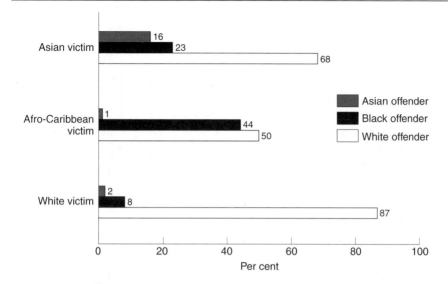

Fig. 21.1: Race or ethnic group of victim and offender (British Crime Survey 1988 and 1992)
Source: FitzGerald and Hale, 1996, Table 2.2.

Note: The figure (like the original table) is based on cases where the victim could say something about the offender. It shows whether all or some of the offenders were white, black, and Asian, so the same incident can appear in more than one category.

in Table 21.2. Two categories of offence are shown: assaults, and robbery and other violent theft. These two offences may have been chosen because the personal contact they involve means that the victim often gets a look at the offender. As set out in a later section, they are offences for which the black offending rate tends to be high. Confining the analysis to cases where the victim could describe the offender, 60 per cent of black victims of assault, and 75 per cent of black victims of robbery and violent theft, said their assailant had been non-white. In the case of assaults, there was a large difference between black and white victims in this respect: only 26 per cent of white victims of assault said their assailant had been non-white. In the case of robbery and other violent theft, however, the proportion who said their assailant had been black was almost as high among white as among black victims (66 per cent compared with 75 per cent).

From these highly incomplete findings, it is clear that the high rate of victimization of black people is explained at least in part by their high rate of offending. However, some aspects of the high rate of black victimization are unlikely to be explained by black offending. For example, burglary victimization with loss was twice as high among Afro-Caribbean as among white households (see Table 21.1), yet burglary is an offence that is probably not particularly high among black people (see later section). The high rate of victimization of South Asians, of course, cannot be explained by intra-racial offending, since offending levels are certainly no higher among South Asians

Table 21.2 Race or ethnic group of assailants and victims: London, 1985

| | Victim's appearance | | | | | | | |
| | All victims | | White European | | Afro-Caribbean | | Asian | |
Assailant's appearance	Per cent of all	Per cent excluding 'not known'	Per cent of all	Per cent excluding 'not known'	Per cent of all	Per cent excluding 'not known'	Per cent of all	Per cent excluding 'not known'
Assaults:								
White	37	63	40	69	17	28	27	51
Non-white	18	31	15	26	37	60	23	42
Mixed	3	6	3	5	7	11	4	7
Not known	41		42		39		46	
Robbery:*								
White	20	24	21	25	14	16	18	20
Non-white	56	67	55	66	64	75	60	69
Mixed	8	10	8	9	7	9	9	11
Not known	16		17		15		13	

Source: Home Office (1989a), Table 3.

Note: Under each victim group, the first column shows percentage distributions including 'not known' data; the second shows recalculated percentage distributions omitting 'not known' data. Classifications used for victims and assailants do not match. For example, 'non-white' in the assailant classification presumably includes 'black-skinned' and 'Asian' in the victim classification. Three categories in the victim classification ('dark European', 'other', and 'unrecorded') have been left out of the above table, but these cases are included in the total column above. This table is recalculated from the original, which showed rounded percentages: it therefore involves some approximation.

*Also includes 'other violent theft'.

than among whites. In small part, it may possibly be explained by black-on-Asian offending (see Figure 21.1).

Victims and the Police

When offences are grouped broadly, analysis of the BCS of 1988 and 1992 has shown little difference between ethnic groups in the proportion of victims who reported the incident to the police (FitzGerald and Hale, 1996: table 3.3a). The Policy Studies Institute London survey in 1981 similarly found no significant differences between ethnic groups in the proportion of victims who reported incidents to the police (Smith, 1983a: 76). A more detailed analysis of offences reveals certain differences, however. Pakistanis, although twice as likely as whites to be the targets of serious threats, were less than half as likely to report them to the police. Also, Afro-Caribbeans were less likely than whites to report robbery or theft from the person to the police (FitzGerald and Hale, 1996: table 3.3b).[4]

The BCS 1988 found that satisfaction after reporting to the police was lower among ethnic minorities than among white people (Mayhew, Elliott, and Dowds, 1989), and analysis of the BCS 1992 showed that this difference remained when the effect of other factors was taken into account in the context of a multivariate model (Mayhew, Aye Maung, and Mirrlees-Black, 1993). This finding was confirmed by analysis of the combined samples from the 1988 and 1992 BCS. The difference is not large, however. The proportion dissatisfied with the police response was 46 per cent among South Asians and 40 per cent among Afro-Caribbeans, compared with 33 per cent among whites (FitzGerald and Hale, 1996: table 3.7).

The 1981 London survey also showed lower levels of satisfaction among ethnic minorities than among whites. In marked contrast to the BCS, however, the 1981 London survey showed that the police appeared to have been more active and successful where the victim was Afro-Caribbean than white. 'Where the victim was a West Indian, the police were more likely to take some action, to make a full investigation, to move quickly and to catch the offender than where the victim was white or Asian' (Smith, 1983a: 84). Possibly this contrast arises because the PSI survey asked more concrete and factual questions than the BCS, so that the BCS findings reflect general anti-police attitudes among ethnic minorities (especially Afro-Caribbeans) rather than police actions in the particular case (FitzGerald and Hale, 1996: 37).

In the BCS 1988, respondents were asked whether they had taken action about incidents they had observed in the past five years. Over 10 per cent in each case had observed instances of shoplifting, vandalism, and 'serious fights',

[4] This could be because personal theft or robbery of black people is often committed by black people, and because 'mugging' has become the symbol of black crime (FitzGerald and Hale, 1996: Table 3.4). Against this, however, Afro-Caribbeans were equally likely to report offences against them by black and white people; but sample sizes are too small to show whether this applies to thefts and robberies from the person specifically.

while a few (3 per cent) had observed theft from parked cars. The proportion who had reported such incidents to the police ranged from around one-quarter (for stealing from cars and vandalism) to around one-tenth (for shoplifting and serious fights). The proportion who had reported such incidents to the police did not vary between ethnic groups (Skogan, 1990: 48).

Racially Motivated Crime and Harassment

We have seen that the elevated rate of victimization among ethnic minorities arises, to some extent, because these minorities fall into demographic groups that are at higher than average risk, and because they tend to live in areas where victimization risks are relatively high. However, another reason is that ethnic minorities are the objects of some racially motivated crimes. They may also be the victims of a pattern of repeated incidents motivated by racial hostility, where many of these events on their own do not constitute crimes, although some crimes may occur in the sequence, so that the cumulative effect is alarming and imposes severe constraints on a person's freedom and ability to live a full life. Racial harassment is the term that is used to describe a pattern of repeated incidents of this kind.

Genn (1988) and Bowling (1993) have pointed out that victim surveys have not been designed to describe patterns which develop over time. Instead, they have aimed to count discrete incidents, using definitions parallel to those applied by the courts. This is most appropriate for crimes such as car theft or burglary, where most incidents *are* discrete from the viewpoint of the victim. It is least appropriate for crimes which take place within a continuing relationship (family violence, incest) or within a restricted social setting (the school, the workplace, the street).

A further difficulty in studying racially motivated crime or racial harassment is establishing racial motivation. One approach is to accept the victim's view; another is for an observer to make a judgement based on a description of the facts. Definitions used vary in the emphasis given to these two types of criterion, and in other detailed ways, so that it is often difficult to compare the results from different studies.

Although racial attacks and harassment, on any reasonable definition, are ancient phenomena, they have 'arrived relatively late on the political policy agenda and thence onto the agenda of various statutory agencies' (FitzGerald, 1989). The first major report on the subject, *Blood on the Streets*, was published by Bethnal Green and Stepney Trades Council in 1978. Since then there has been an official report by the Home Office (1981) based on statistics of incidents recorded by the police; a report by the House of Commons Home Affairs Committee (1986), which has also recently initiated a further inquiry; and two reports by an Inter-Departmental Group set up to consider racial attacks (Home Office, 1989c, 1991). National statistics on racial incidents recorded by the police have been regularly reported in Hansard. National survey-based statistics were first generated by the third PSI survey of racial minorities carried out in 1982 (Brown, 1984). More comprehensive information has become available recently from the British Crime Surveys of 1988 and 1992 (Mayhew, Elliott, and Dowds, 1989; FitzGerald and Hale, 1996) and from the fourth PSI survey of ethnic minorities carried out in 1994 (Virdee, 1997).

Police records are virtually useless as a measure of the amount of racially motivated crime, because most of these incidents are not reported to the police, and because incidents that the victim regards as racially motivated are often not recorded as such by the police (Virdee, 1997: 262). In an analysis of the PSI 1982 survey of ethnic minorities, Brown (1984: 260, table 134) identified assaults where there was a probable racial motive from studying victims' detailed descriptions of the incidents. On the most restrictive definition (counting assaults only where the motive was plainly racist) the survey showed an incidence of racial attacks around ten times higher than revealed by the statistics derived from police records and published by the Home Office (1981). Police statistics have shown large rises in racially motivated crime since the mid-1980s, but, as Virdee (1997) has pointed out, this could reflect an increase in rates of reporting or recording, and does not reliably demonstrate an actual increase in the level of harassment.

In the BCS (1988 and 1992 combined), 24 per cent of offences reported by South Asians and 14 per cent of those reported by Afro-Caribbeans were racially motivated in the respondent's view. Types of incident most often seen as racially motivated were assaults and threats, and also household vandalism in the case of South Asians. These surveys showed only a slight increase between 1987 and 1991, in marked contrast with the police statistics, which showed a large increase (FitzGerald and Hale, 1996: table 2.3a).

PSI's 1994 survey asked about three types of incident (attacks, damage to property, and insults) in the past twelve months where the victim thought there was a racist motivation. Looking at the results for ethnic minorities combined (Caribbeans, South Asians, and Chinese) it found that 1 per cent had been racially attacked, 2 per cent had been victims of racially motivated damage to property, and 12 per cent had been racially insulted. These results suggest that over a quarter of a million people had been subject to some form of racial harassment over a twelve-month period, as compared with the 10,000 incidents recorded by the police. There were some fairly small differences in experience of racial insults between specific minority groups, but no significant differences in the case of racial attacks and damage to property. Men, and people aged 16–44, were more likely to be victims of racial harassment than women, and those aged 45 or more. Racial harassment was a considerably greater hazard for ethnic minorities living in a predominantly white neighbourhood than for those living in a neighbourhood with a substantial ethnic minority population. This suggests that black or Asian neighbourhoods have protective value for the ethnic minorities living in them (Virdee, 1997).

The PSI findings confirm other sources in showing that racial harassment tends to be a process involving a sequence of incidents, rather than an isolated event. In fact, three-fifths of those subject to racial harassment in the past twelve months had experienced more than one incident, and 22 per cent had experienced five or more. In two-thirds of cases, there was more than one offender. Offenders were predominantly male and young, but one-third of them were thought to be aged 30 or over (Virdee, 1997).

Local surveys, like the PSI survey, have generally tried to cover low-level harassment as well as criminal offences. They tend to suggest that racial harassment, on a broad definition, is a problem affecting a high proportion of South Asians and Afro-Caribbeans (London Borough of Newham, 1986; Saulsbury and Bowling, 1991). In a study of an East London housing estate, Sampson and Phillips (1992) found over a period of six months an average of four and a half attacks against each of thirty Bengali families, although seven families were not attacked, while six families were attacked twelve or more times. A sequence of incidents recorded for one family was: stones thrown and chased; threatened and prevented from entering flat; punched and verbal abuse; attempted robbery; chased by gang of youths; common assault.

Taken together, these findings suggest that there is a substantial risk of racial harassment for members of ethnic minority groups in England and Wales, although only about one in seven of Afro-Caribbean and South Asian people are conscious of having changed or restricted their pattern of life in response (Virdee, 1997: 285). Racially motivated crime also accounts for about one-fifth of crime victimization of ethnic minorities, and therefore helps to explain their elevated rate of victimization.

ETHNIC MINORITIES AS SUSPECTS AND OFFENDERS

The criminal justice process can be regarded as a sequence of decisions starting with behaviour that someone considers to be deviant or offensive, and ending with the punishment of an offender. A number of choices are available at every stage. Most of these result in the matter being dropped or resolved or in action being taken by methods other than criminal justice process. Hence the number of remaining cases successively diminishes from one stage to the next. In principle, bias against ethnic minorities could occur at any of these stages. These potential biases might best be studied by means of a longitudinal study following individuals through several stages, but no research of that kind has yet been attempted. Nevertheless, some useful conclusions can be drawn from considering each stage separately.

In summarizing the research results, it would be neat to start at the beginning of the sequence and move towards the end. However, the ethnic composition of the prison population must be examined first, because it provides striking evidence of something that needs to be explained.

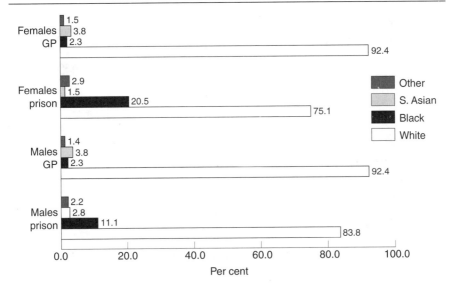

Fig. 21.2: Prison compared with general population: England and Wales, 1994

Source: Prison Statistics England and Wales 1994 (prison population); Labour Force Survey, 1995 (general population).

The comparison is with the general population (GP) aged 15–39.

The Prison Population

Statistics of the prison population by ethnic group were first published for 1985 and have been published annually since. These counts of the population on a specific date reflect both the number admitted to prison and the length of their sentences. From 1993, a new classification by ethnic origin was introduced, congruent with that used in the census and in the Labour Force Survey. From the same date, the nationality of prisoners was also shown in the published statistics. Nationality can be used as an indication of place of residence: it is reasonable to assume that the majority of foreign nationals in prison were not resident in Britain at the time of the offence. In many cases, the offences (such as drug running) probably involved travelling between the country of origin and Britain.

Figure 21.2 compares the prison population in 1994 with the general population aged 15–39.[5] The most striking feature is the over-representation of the black groups (people of West Indian, Guyanese, and African origin) among the prison population. These groups were 11.1 per cent of the male prison population, compared with 2.3 per cent of the general population aged 15–39. Females were only a small proportion—3.7 per cent—of the prison population, but the black groups accounted for an astonishing 20.4 per cent of this small

---

[5] The National Prison Survey showed that 84% of the prison population in 1991 consisted of people aged 17–39 (Walmsley, Howard, and White, 1992: 9, Table 1), making it appropriate to compare the prison population with the general population within this age band.

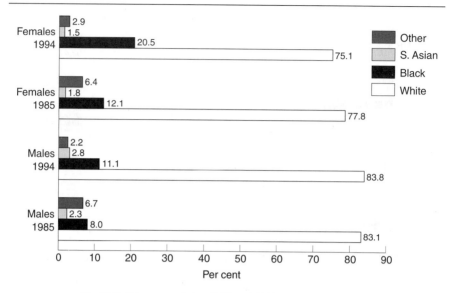

Fig. 21.3: Prison population 1985 and 1994: England and Wales
Source: Prison Statistics England and Wales, 1994.

female prison population, compared with 2.3 per cent of the general population aged 15–39. Whereas black people were heavily over-represented among the prison population, South Asians (people of Indian, Pakistani, and Bangladeshi origin) were under-represented in prison, especially in the case of females. The other groups (including those of Chinese, Arab, and mixed origin) were over-represented among the prison population, but this is hard to interpret, since this category is so heterogeneous.

There was some increase between 1985 and 1994 in the proportion of prisoners belonging to the black groups (see Figure 21.3). This increase was particularly marked in the case of females, possibly reflecting an increase in the number of drugs 'mules' arrested (see below). The black groups accounted for a rather larger proportion of prisoners on remand than of sentenced adults but for a smaller proportion of sentenced young offenders (see Figure 21.4).

As has been pointed out by Home Office statisticians (1996) and by FitzGerald and Marshall (1996), information on prisoners' nationality, available from 1993, gives some indication of the number of prisoners who were not resident in Britain prior to conviction or remand in custody. A substantial proportion of ethnic minority prisoners were foreign nationals, and the proportion was higher—over half—among female than among male prisoners (see Figure 21.5). To a considerable extent, the high representation of certain ethnic minority groups in prison arises because of the arrest of foreign 'mules' caught bringing drugs into Britain (Green, 1991). A more appropriate comparison between the prison population and the general population is one that takes account of nationality (see Figure 21.6). Among the male prison

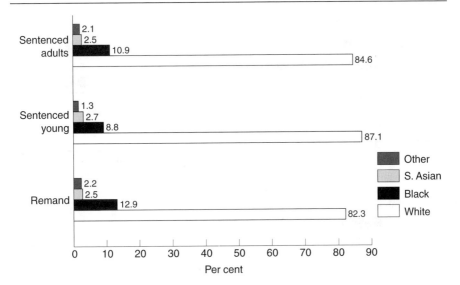

Fig. 21.4: Prison population 1994 by type of prisoner: England and Wales, males
Source: Prison Statistics England and Wales, 1994.

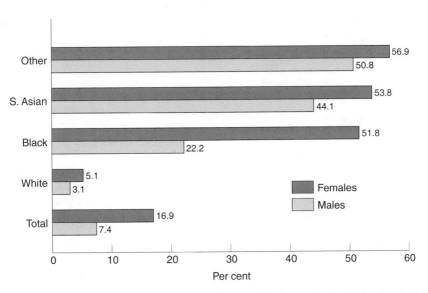

Fig. 21.5: Percentage of the prison population who were foreign nationals: England and Wales 1994
Source: Prison Statistics England and Wales, 1994.

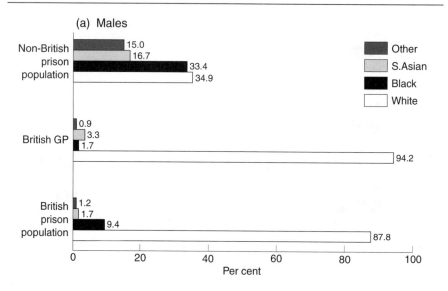

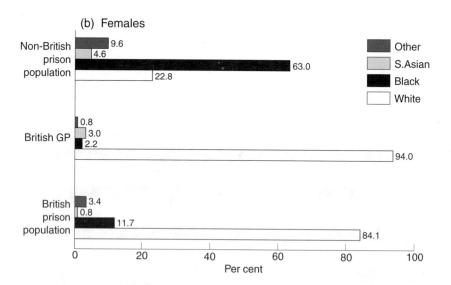

Fig. 21.6: Ethnic group and nationality of the prison population: England and Wales, 1994

Source: Prison Statistics England and Wales 1994 (prison population); Labour Force Survey 1995 (general population).

The comparison is with the general population (GP) of British nationality aged 15–39.

population of British nationality, 9.4 per cent were black in 1994, compared with 1.7 per cent of the general population of British nationality aged 15–39. Among females, too, there was a similar, sharp contrast. These findings show that the high representation of black people in prison arises partly because of the imprisonment of foreigners, but that when the comparison is confined to people of British nationality, black people remain heavily over-represented in the prison population.

This can be demonstrated more clearly by calculating the rate of imprisonment per head of population in the relevant age groups (see Figure 21.7). Confining our attention to British nationals, the rate of imprisonment was six times as high among black people as among white people, in the case of both men and women. The rate of imprisonment of South Asians was considerably lower than that of white people: about half in the case of men and one-third in the case of women. Figure 21.8 shows that the overall rate of imprisonment for South Asian men masks differences between the more specific groups. Among Pakistani men, the rate of imprisonment was about the same as among whites, whereas it was substantially lower among Indian and Bangladeshi men.

For prisoners under sentence (72 per cent of the total) the published statistics show the type of offence they committed according to ethnic group and nationality. Confining our attention to British nationals, these statistics have been used to calculate rates of imprisonment per head of population in the relevant age group, according to offence and ethnic group (see Figure 21.9). For all offences, the rate of imprisonment of South Asian males is the same as for whites, or lower; it is particularly low for theft and handling, burglary, and sexual offences other than rape. For all offences except sexual offences other than rape, the rate of imprisonment of black men is several times higher than for whites. As shown more clearly in Figure 21.10, these contrasts are much stronger for three types of offences—drugs, robbery, and rape—than for the others. For example, the rate of imprisonment for drugs offences was 10.8 times as high among black as among white men. These statistics exclude foreign nationals, so they probably cannot be explained by arrests of 'mules'.

In summary, these prison statistics show that by the end of the criminal justice process, black people (Afro-Caribbeans and black Africans) were far more likely to be undergoing the most severe penalty available—a prison sentence—than white people. Equally striking, they show that South Asians were less likely to be in prison than white people: in more detail, the rate of imprisonment among Indians and Bangladeshis was much lower than among whites, whereas among Pakistanis it was about the same. Finally, they show that the contrast in rates of imprisonment varied substantially according to the type of offence. The evidence about the outcome of the criminal justice process at the final stage therefore strongly raises the question whether black people are equally treated. Answering that question is much more difficult, but the pattern of results within the prison statistics themselves already gives some purchase.

First, it is highly significant that rates of imprisonment are no higher among South Asians than among white people. As set out earlier, racial discrimination

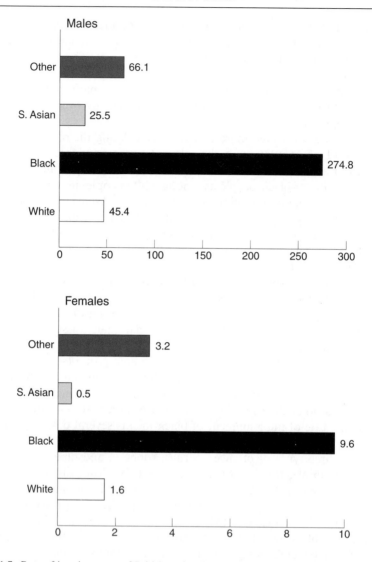

Fig. 21.7: Rate of imprisonment of British nationals: England and Wales, 1994

Source: Prison Statistics England and Wales 1994; Labour Force Survey 1995.

The figure is confined to people with British nationality. It shows the rate of imprisonment per 10,000 people of British nationality aged 15–39.

against South Asians, for example in employment and housing, is just as prevalent as against Afro-Caribbeans (Daniel, 1968; Smith, 1977; Brown and Gay, 1986). Other manifestations of hostility, such as racial attacks, are also at least as common against South Asians as against Afro-Caribbeans (Home Office, 1981; Brown, 1984; Mayhew, Elliott and Dowds, 1989). It follows that any generalized notion of 'racism' is incapable of explaining the high rate of

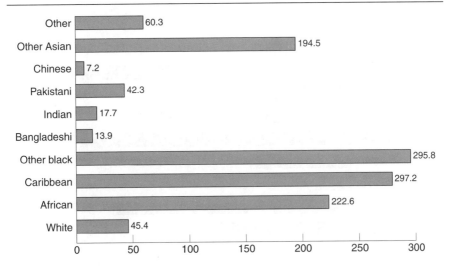

Fig. 21.8: Rate of imprisonment among British males by detailed ethnic group: England and Wales, 1994

Source: Prison Statistics England and Wales 1994; Labour Force Survey 1995.

The figure is confined to males of British nationality. It shows the rate of imprisonment per 10,000 people aged 15–39.

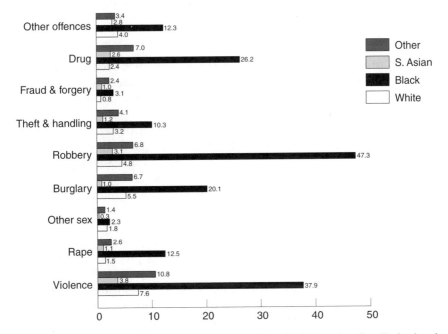

Fig. 21.9: Rate of imprisonment by type of offence, males of British nationality: England and Wales, 1994

Source: Prison Statistics England and Wales 1994; Labour Force Survey 1995.
The figure is confined to men of British nationality. It shows rates of imprisonment per 10,000 aged 15–39.

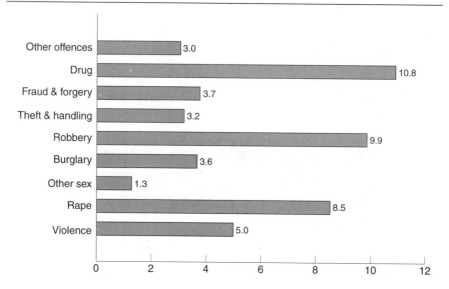

Fig. 21.10: Ratio between rate of imprisonment of black and white British men, by type of offence: England and Wales, 1994

Source: Prison Statistics England and Wales 1994; Labour Force Survey 1995.

The figure shows the ratio between the bars for black and white men shown in Fig. 21.9. For example, in the case of drugs offences, the rate of imprisonment of British black men was 10.8 times as high as for British white men.

imprisonment of Afro-Caribbeans. Some commentators, such as Reiner (1989, 1993) and Hudson (1993) have not discussed this fundamental point. Others, such as Jefferson (1993), have recognized its importance but have argued that hostile racial stereotypes of South Asians and black people are distinct. On this view, black people, but not South Asians, are stereotyped as 'the criminal other', and that specific stereotype leads to their criminalization. What remains to be explained, however, is why racial hostility towards South Asians, which is certainly just as strong, and expresses itself in discrimination and racial attacks, should not result in the criminalization of that group as well.

Secondly, it is also potentially important that the contrast in rates of imprisonment between black and white people varies according to the type of offence. If the over-representation of black people among prisoners is the result of bias at various stages of the criminal justice process, then the contrast in rates of imprisonment between black and white people should be greatest for offences whose detection depends on proactive investigation and the use of discretion; the contrast should be least for offences where victims generally do not know the ethnic group of the offender, and where the authorities have to decide whether to investigate before they know the ethnic group of the offender (Wilbanks, 1987: 65). In fact, some of the main features of the observed pattern do fit the theory that black people end up in prison because of selective reporting of offences and discretionary law enforcement. The high rate of imprisonment of black people for drugs offences is particularly telling. Arrests for drugs offences notoriously arise from the exercise of police discretion, and it is easy for police and customs officers to target law enforcement in this field at a particular ethnic group. The relatively low rate of imprisonment of black people for burglary may also fit the theory. Householders do not know the ethnic group of the burglar when they decide to report a burglary to the police; and police action against burglary tends to be untargeted and ineffective. However, prosecutions for burglary sometimes arise out of stop and search activity, which is known to target black people (as set out in a later section), and from questioning known offenders, which could in principle be targeted on black people. Thus interpretation of the pattern is based on rather vague assumptions at present, and more detailed information is needed before firm conclusions can be drawn.

Self-reported Offending

As part of an international research project, the Home Office carried out a national survey of young people aged 14–25 between November 1992 and January 1993. The sampling strategy allowed for over-representation of ethnic minorities (before re-weighting) and produced subsamples of about 200 black people and 500 South Asians within a total sample of around 2,500. The core of the study was a battery of (normally self-completed) questions about the respondent's own offending and use of illicit drugs. The questioning covered two expressive property offences, fifteen acquisitive property offences, and five violent offences, together with use of thirteen mostly illicit drugs. There were no significant differences in patterns of self-reported offending between black and white respondents, either in terms of lifetime participation in the three types of offence, or in terms of frequency over the past twelve months. Self-reported offending was considerably lower among each of the three South Asian groups (those of Indian, Pakistani, and Bangladeshi origin) than among white or black respondents. Self-reported use of drugs was considerably lower among all four ethnic minority groups than among white respondents. For individual drugs, these differences were statistically significant in the case of cannabis, LSD, amphetamines, magic mushrooms, and glue or gas (Graham and Bowling, 1996).

The findings for young black people contradict evidence from other sources such as victims' reports (see below), which suggest that the rate of offending is considerably higher among black than among white people. Although the self-report method has been widely used by psychologists and criminologists to study patterns of offending and conduct disorders in young people, there has never been good evidence to show that it is an adequate basis for making quantitative estimates. Farrington (1973) demonstrated that self-reports had some validity, in the sense that the extent of self-reported offending is related to the acquisition of an official criminal record. He was also able to show in the context of a longitudinal study that self-reported offending to some extent predicts the later acquisition of a criminal record (so the correlation does not arise merely because those who are caught thereby become more likely to admit to their offending). However, he also showed that self-report measures, although having some validity, are rather unreliable. For example, many respondents denied having committed offences which they claimed to have committed at an earlier interview.

There is evidence from American studies of systematic differences between ethnic groups in the extent to which people conceal or exaggerate their offending (see Sampson and Lauritsen, 1997). Junger (1989) found large systematic biases of this kind in a study of young people in the Netherlands, although her conclusions were contested by Bowling (1990). More generally, differences between all groups (for example, between males and females) tend to be much smaller in self-report studies than indicated by any other method.

There are obviously serious sampling problems in carrying out self-report studies. Individuals leading unconventional lives, particularly those who carry out a large number of offences, are unlikely to be included in these surveys for a variety of reasons. A substantial proportion of frequent offenders will be living in some kind of institution at any given time, and will therefore be excluded from a survey.

There is clearly a major conflict between the findings of Graham and Bowling's self-report study and the other sources considered in later sections. Most importantly, the self-report results conflict with victims' descriptions of offenders (see the next section below). The most likely explanation is that there are systematic differences between ethnic groups in the way they answer questions on self-reported offending. Although this conclusion is supported by much research in the USA, and some in the Netherlands, it is not yet supported by research carried out in Britain.

Victims' Reports

So far the analysis has established that the final outcome of the criminal justice process is a very high rate of imprisonment of black people (but *not* South Asians). The next step is to return to the beginning of the process, and to consider the limited evidence on how the disparity arises at each successive stage.

Apart from drugs and traffic offences, the bulk of offences processed by the police and the courts first come to notice as a result of victims' reports. It is possible that because of racial hostility or fear white victims are more strongly motivated to report an incident to the police if they think the offender was black. The problem for such a theory is that because racial hostility is directed just as much against South Asians as against black people, this should also lead to an elevated rate of reported offences by South Asians. It is important to weigh this against any evidence on the other side of the question.

Victim survey data show that in only about 35–40 per cent of cases can the victim say something about the offender (Smith, 1983*a*: 71; FitzGerald and Hale, 1996: table 3.4). In the remaining 60 per cent of cases, the victim's decision to report the incident cannot be racially biased, because he or she did not know the ethnic group of the offender. This substantially reduces the scope for the victim's reporting behaviour to have an influence.

Among offenders who *are* described by victims, there is a substantial over-representation of black people. The PSI survey of Londoners carried out in 1981 found that people described as 'black' were represented among offenders about four times as strongly as among the general population, whereas South Asians were substantially under-represented among offenders described by victims (Smith, 1983*a*: 73). The findings of the BCS of 1988 and 1992 are broadly in agreement (see Figure 21.1): 8 per cent of offenders described by white victims were 'black', while 2 per cent were Asian, whereas black people accounted for about 2 per cent of the young male population, and South Asians for about 4 per cent (see 'GP' in Figure 21.3).[6]

Police data are available for London in 1984 and 1985 for two kinds of offence (assaults, and robbery or other violent theft: see Table 21.2). Confining the analysis to cases where the victim could describe the offender, 31 per cent of assailants were non-white in the case of assaults, and 67 per cent in the case of robbery and other violent thefts. These statistics are difficult to interpret because of the vagueness of the term 'non-white'. The proportion of offenders described by victims as 'non-white' was extraordinarily high in the case of robbery and other violent theft.

A combined analysis of the 1982, 1984, and 1988 BCS data showed little difference in the proportion of incidents of personal violence reported to the police according to whether the offender was described as white or non-white (Shah and Pease, 1992). Shah and Pease (1992: 198–9, Table 6) also showed that recalled incidents involving a white offender were no more recent than those involving a black offender, which argues against differential recall according to the ethnic group of the offender.

Three points emerge from this analysis of evidence about the first stage of the criminal justice process. First, if victims are more likely to report incidents to the police where the offender is perceived to be black, this can have an influence in no more than 40 per cent of cases involving individual victims, for in the remaining cases the victim cannot describe the offender. Secondly, black people are heavily over-represented among offenders described by victims before the criminal justice process begins. Thirdly, there is little or no difference in the proportion of incidents reported to the police according to whether the offender is perceived to be black. These findings suggest that differential reporting to the police is not a significant factor leading to the criminalization of black people, and that much of the difference in rate of criminalization between black and white people arises at the earliest possible stage: when the offence is observed, and before it is reported.

---

[6] These comparisons are, however, distorted by the fact that the proportion of victims who can describe the offender varies widely according to the offence; and some direct contact offences (such as robbery and theft from the person) are ones in which black people specialize. Nevertheless, even if offences are considered individually, victims' reports show substantial over-representation of black offenders.

Police Stops

Among those offenders who are processed by the criminal justice system, a considerable proportion are drawn into the net through the exercise of discretionary powers by the police, particularly stop and search. Thus, a survey of London police officers carried out in 1982 showed that 23 per cent of arrests arose from a stop (Smith, 1983*b*: 81, Table V.3). The proportion of arrests arising from a stop was particularly high for driving offences (64 per cent), taking and driving away a vehicle, or vehicle theft (47 per cent), and drugs offences (39 per cent) (Smith, 1983*b*: 87, Table V.6). At that time, most of the stop and search powers were not consolidated within national legislation, although a variety of local powers existed. Consequently, police practice on stops may have varied widely between different parts of the country, and the use of stop and search was probably greater in London than in most other places. Since the Police and Criminal Evidence Act 1984 (PACE) came into force, police throughout England and Wales have had authority to stop persons or vehicles on the reasonable suspicion that they would find stolen goods or prohibited articles, and to carry out searches of vehicles and persons stopped. Other legislation also gives police authority to stop and search for other reasons, for example to look for controlled drugs. Hence, it seems likely that a substantial proportion of arrests now result from stops throughout the country. Clearly the over-representation of black people at later stages in the process could in principle arise partly because the police use their discretion to stop a larger proportion of black people than of other ethnic groups.

Pattern

A survey carried out in three parts of Manchester in 1980 found no significant difference between Afro-Caribbeans and whites in terms of the proportion who had been 'stopped, searched or arrested' within the last year, or in the number of times this had happened (Tuck and Southgate, 1981). These data do not distinguish between stops and arrests, and because of the rather small sample sizes, the 1.43:1 ratio between the 10 per cent of Afro-Caribbeans and the 7 per cent of white people who were 'stopped, searched, or arrested' does not reach statistical significance. This survey covered a single police division which extended over parts of five wards and had a population of 33,000. Other studies, which have all covered larger and more heterogeneous areas, have found differences in stop rates between black and white people. Willis (1981), who analysed stops recorded at four police stations, found that these were two to three times as high for black people as for the general population.[7] The PSI survey of Londoners carried out in 1981 found that the proportion stopped in the previous twelve months was 24 per cent for Afro-Caribbeans, 17 per cent for whites, and 7 per cent for South Asians. Also, among those who had been stopped at all, Afro-Caribbeans had on average been stopped twice as often as white people. The stop rate among young males aged 15–24 was found to be

---

[7] She estimated that about half of the stops actually carried out were recorded.

very high. Within this group, 66 per cent of the Afro-Caribbeans had been stopped an average number of 4.1 times in twelve months, while 44 per cent of the whites had been stopped an average number of 2.6 times (Smith, 1983*a*: 96–100). In an observational study carried out in 1986–7 in three police divisions (two in London and one in Surrey), Norris *et al.* (1992) found that black people accounted for 28 per cent of persons stopped by the police, compared with 10 per cent of the local population. Among males aged up to 35, they calculated that the stop rate per 100 population was about thirty-three for blacks, compared with about ten for whites.[8] National data are available from the British Crime Survey 1988, which was carried out well after national stop powers were consolidated in PACE. Within the fourteen-month reference period, 15 per cent of white people, 20 per cent of Afro-Caribbeans, and 14 per cent of South Asians said they had been stopped by the police. The difference in stop rate between Afro-Caribbeans and white people or South Asians remained after taking account of a range of socio-demographic variables (Skogan, 1990: 28). An analysis of the 1992 BCS used a wider definition of 'stops', including, as well as traffic and pedestrian stops, orders to show documents or give a statement, and other police-initiated contacts in which respondents were under suspicion. On this basis, 36 per cent of Afro-Caribbean respondents had been 'stopped' during the reference period, compared with 22 per cent of whites and the same proportion of Asians (Skogan, 1994).

Jefferson (1988) and Walker (1987) have suggested that the study of parts of Manchester (Tuck and Southgate, 1981) failed to find a difference between Afro-Caribbean and white people in stop rates because it was carried out in a relatively small and homogeneous area. They believe that what is being observed in the BCS and the PSI London survey is differences in policing practice between types of area: for example, higher stop rates in disadvantaged urban settings where concentrations of Afro-Caribbeans tend to be high. Jefferson (1993) has suggested in particular that the style of policing is more a response to the social and housing composition of the area than to the ethnic group of potential suspects. Whatever the merits of this argument in general terms, it is not needed to explain the Tuck and Southgate findings. These do not relate to stops alone, and as Skogan has pointed out (1990: 53) they do not necessarily indicate a different ratio between the rate of police-initiated encounters among Afro-Caribbean and white people from that shown by the BCS: the sample size in the Tuck and Southgate study was simply too small to demonstrate a contrast of the order shown by the BCS.

In a later article, Jefferson, Walker, and Seneviratne (1993) used police records of stops and searches to compare parts of Leeds where ethnic minorities accounted for more versus less than 10 per cent of the population.[9]

---

[8] Because the same individuals are often stopped repeatedly, this does not equate with the proportion of the population who were stopped.

[9] The Police and Criminal Evidence Act 1984 requires the police to make a record where a member of the public is stopped *and* searched, and these are the records used by Jefferson *et al.* The earlier survey findings referred to stops as a whole, a far more inclusive category.

They found that in areas of *low* ethnic concentration, the stop rate was *higher* for black than for white or South Asian people, whereas in areas of *high* ethnic concentration, the stop rate was *lower* for black than for white or South Asian people. However, the 1981 PSI survey of Londoners showed no difference in stop rates (all stops, regardless of whether there was a search) among either Afro-Caribbeans or South Asians according to the concentration of ethnic minorities in the local area, defined as a census enumeration district, which contains 150 households on average. Also, the survey showed no difference in stop rates among white people according to the concentration of ethnic minorities in the ward where they lived (unpublished data available from the author on request).

From a survey carried out as part of the Leeds study within census enumeration districts having a high concentration (10 per cent or more) of ethnic minorities, Jefferson and Walker (1992, 1993) found that the stop rate (in 1987) was *lower* among black and South Asian people than among white people living nearby. They interpreted this result as showing that the stop rate is determined by the social characteristics of the areas rather than the ethnic group of the individual. It is more likely, however, that the finding reflects the unusual characteristics of those white people who live in areas of high ethnic concentration. For example, Jefferson and Walker's own results show that a high proportion of this particular white population lives in rented accommodation and is transient, characteristics associated with police targeting.

On balance, there is a consistent body of evidence to show that Afro-Caribbeans are more likely to be stopped than white people or South Asians. There is some conflict of evidence about how marked these differences are, but they are much smaller than the differences in rates of imprisonment. They probably do make some contribution to explaining the high rate of imprisonment of Afro-Caribbeans, but they can only explain a small part of it. That is not only because the ethnic differences in stop rates are relatively small, but also because this kind of policing generates less than one-quarter of arrests.

Decision

Given that black people (but *not* South Asians) are more likely to be stopped by police than white people, the question that arises is how police officers take these decisions, and whether they amount to unequal treatment of black people. As Skogan (1990: 32) has pointed out, the most important factor here is that the vast majority of stops do not produce an arrest or prosecution. The BCS 1988 showed that of those stopped on foot, only 4 per cent reported being arrested, and 3 per cent were prosecuted. The comparable figures for those involved in traffic stops were 1 per cent arrested and 10 per cent prosecuted—the prosecutions being mainly fixed penalty and vehicle defect notices (Skogan, 1990: 32). The low 'strike rate' is confirmed by local surveys in Merseyside (Kinsey, 1985) and London (Smith, 1983a), and by earlier national estimates from police records (Willis, 1983). The implication of the low 'strike rate' is that the exercise of this kind of police power is highly discretionary. The law requires in principle that the police officer should have 'reasonable suspicion' to justify stopping or searching someone, but in practice this criterion is extremely weak, and largely unenforceable.

The question whether the relatively high stop rate for black people amounts to unequal treatment is therefore very hard to answer. The PSI survey of Londoners found that the proportion of stops leading to an arrest or to an offence being reported was the same for Afro-Caribbeans and white people (Smith, 1983*a*: 116). In their observational study, Norris *et al.* (1992) found that the police took 'formal action' in 40 per cent of cases following a stop of a black person, compared with 31 per cent of cases where the person was white, a difference that was not statistically significant. At one level these findings show that the higher stop rate of Afro-Caribbeans is 'justified by results', which may suggest that it does not amount to unequal treatment. As pointed out under the first heading in this chapter, however, decisions made within the criminal justice system tend to be self-validating. Decisions at later stages may be influenced by a need to justify a decision taken earlier. It remains possible that the police, having stopped a higher proportion of black than of white people, then work harder to find offences with which to charge the black suspects.

Observational research casts some further light on this. On the basis of extensive observations of policing in London, including 129 stops, Smith and Gray (1983: 233) concluded that 'from the way that police officers talk about stops . . . it is clear that the question of what their legal powers may be does not enter into their decision-making except in the case of rare individuals'. Where there was no specific reason for making the stop (connected with the person's behaviour or appearance) police officers were nevertheless applying criteria which they associated with the chance of getting a 'result'. The researchers gained the impression that whether the person was black was one of these criteria, but that other criteria were more important.

The observational study by Norris *et al.* (1992) is the only one to cast light on the question whether police decisions are influenced by the demeanour of black and white people. In all, Norris and colleagues, working in two police divisions in London and one in Surrey, observed 213 police stops which involved 319 people. A higher proportion of blacks than of whites (56 compared with 42 per cent) were stopped on general suspicion rather than tangible evidence.[10] There was no difference between white and black persons with regard to whether they were calm versus agitated, or civil versus antagonistic. A significantly higher proportion of white than of black persons stopped appeared to be under the influence of alcohol (20 per cent compared with 8 per cent at the time of the stop). Police demeanour towards the person stopped was rated as 'negative' in a higher proportion of cases where the person was white than where he or she was black (27 per cent compared with

---

[10] This difference is significant at better than the 5% level of confidence (calculated by the present author from Norris *et al.*'s published results).

10 per cent at the time of the stop). These findings speak strongly against the theory that the high stop rate of black people is caused by their hostile behaviour towards the police. They suggest, instead, that stops of black people are rather more likely to be speculative than stops of white people.

The 1988 BCS found that once stopped, Afro-Caribbeans were substantially more likely to be searched than white people or South Asians (Skogan, 1990: 34). In the case of traffic stops, this difference remained significant after controlling for the effects of a number of factors including past arrests within a multivariate model.

Police Behaviour

The 1988 BCS found that Afro-Caribbeans who had been stopped were much more likely than white people or South Asians to think the police had been impolite (Skogan, 1990: 36). People were more critical of police behaviour if the stop led to some sanction (such as arrest or a reported offence), but this did not explain the difference between Afro-Caribbeans and white people. Respondents were more likely to think the police had been polite where a reason was given for the stop, a finding which replicates the 1981 London survey (Smith, 1983a). Again, this did not explain the difference between Afro-Caribbean and white people.

The 1981 London survey found little or no difference between ethnic groups in the proportion who said the police explained the reason for the stop (Smith 1983a: 107–9). A smaller proportion of Afro-Caribbeans than of white people or South Asians thought the police were polite, and that they behaved in a fair and reasonable manner, but these differences were not striking (Smith, 1983a: 112).

Smith (1983a) conducted an intensive analysis of the relationship between critical views of the police (the belief that they fabricate evidence, use unnecessary violence, etc.) and patterns of contact with them. This showed a strong correlation between the amount of contact (of any kind) and critical views, although a later analysis (unpublished) showed that service contacts, primarily as a victim of crime, were associated with negative views only if those specific contacts were negatively evaluated. Within this general framework, stops tended to dominate the picture as (mildly) adversarial contacts that were very large in quantity and associated with critical views of the police. In a survey of parts of Leeds, Jefferson and Walker (1993) also found a relationship between the number of times stopped and critical views. From these findings it is likely that the large-scale practice of stop and search, and the disproportionate stopping of Afro-Caribbeans, has been among the causes of hostility between Afro-Caribbeans and the police. However, both the Leeds and London studies show that the relatively high level of criticism of the police among Afro-Caribbeans compared with white people cannot be wholly explained by their personal encounters with the police (see Smith, 1991, for further discussion of this point on the basis of the London findings).

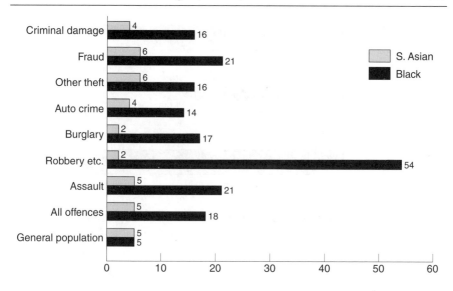

Fig. 21.11: Percentage of persons arrested who were black and South Asian: London, 1987

Source: Home Office 1989*a*, Table 4.

1. The figure includes persons arrested in London for notifiable offences that were followed by further action (caution, referral to juvenile bureau, charge).
2. The general population figures are estimates for 1984–6 of the black and South Asian population of London aged 10 and over as a percentage of the total population aged 10 and over.
3. 'Robbery etc.' includes 'theft from the person' except for pickpocketing, which is included under 'other theft'.

Arrests

No national statistics are available on the ethnic group of persons arrested, but data are available for London (the Metropolitan Police District) for certain years, starting in 1975.[11] Figure 21.11 summarizes the results for 1987. Black people formed a much higher proportion of those arrested than of the general population, whereas South Asians formed exactly the same proportion of the two groups, and this pattern had been broadly the same from 1975 onwards. The proportion of those arrested who were black varied little according to the offence, except that it was extraordinarily high for robbery (54 per cent in 1987).

For certain offences between 1975 and 1985, the Metropolitan Police also recorded the ethnic origin of the offender from the victim's description. For these offences, there is a fairly close correspondence between the proportion of offenders described as non-white by victims and the proportion of people arrested who were non-white (see Figure 21.12). The statistics cover only a few specific offences, and they may well be influenced by police recording practices.

[11] These statistics cover arrests for notifiable offences (that excludes minor including most traffic offences) that were followed by further action (caution, referral to juvenile bureau, or charge).

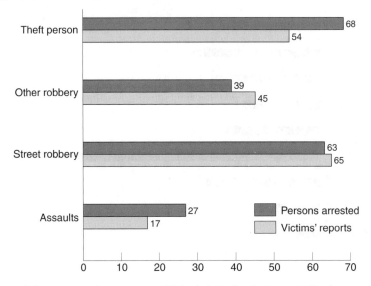

Fig. 21.12: Percentage who were non-white: victims' descriptions of offenders compared with police records of persons arrested, London, 1985

Source: Home Office 1989*a*.

1. For victims' reports, the figure shows the percentage who were 'non-white', whereas for arrests it shows the percentage who were 'black or Asian'.
2. For victims' reports, the percentages are based on cases where the victim could describe the offender. They otherwise cover all recorded offences in the categories shown.

None the less, they suggest that there was little or no tendency for police arrests, given a reported offence, to target black people.

Disregarding the victims' descriptions of offenders, the London statistics show such a large difference in arrest rates *per head of population* between black and white people that an explanation substantially in terms of biased policing is implausible. For example, using the 1983 London statistics, Walker (1987) calculated that if the actual rate of burglary by black and white offenders were the same, then the arrest statistics would imply that black burglars had four and a half times the chance of being arrested compared with white burglars; in the case of robbery the difference would be fourteen to one.

On any reasonable assessment, therefore, the London statistics reflect a much higher rate of offending among black than white people. They do not resolve the issue as to whether there is bias in policing practice. The comparison between victims' reports and arrest statistics (Figure 21.12) tends to suggest that the overall effect of any such bias is fairly small, but this evidence is fragmentary.

Walker (1992) analysed the arrest rates of males aged 11–35 in six police sub-divisions within Leeds during a six-month period in 1987, when police recorded whether people arrested were white, black, or Asian. Like other elements within this research programme, this analysis compares white and black people living in the same very small areas (census enumeration districts (EDs), containing 150 households on average). In the high ethnic concentration EDs (those with more than 10 per cent 'non-white households'), the arrest rate for black people was lower than for white people, while in the lower-concentration EDs the arrest rate was higher for black than for white people. This mirrors the pattern shown for stops (see earlier section). As before, the likely explanation is that white people in areas of high ethnic concentration are an unusual and high-crime group. In the city as a whole, the arrest rate was more than twice as high for black as for white people.

In the PSI London survey respondents who said they had been arrested were asked about their treatment under arrest by the police. A substantial minority had serious criticisms to make, including specific allegations of gross misconduct in many cases. However, Afro-Caribbeans were no more likely than white people to think they had been badly treated or to make serious allegations of this kind.

Decision to Prosecute

Unfortunately, evidence on the flow of cases from arrest to prosecution is fragmentary. It is here that longitudinal studies are particularly needed, but they have not yet been carried out. In principle it is entirely possible that following an arrest[12] ethnic minorities are more likely than white people to be prosecuted. However, the available evidence suggests that if there is a bias of this kind, its effects overall are small. This can be shown by comparing persons arrested in London in 1985 with persons proceeded against for indictable offences at magistrates' courts in 1984 and 1985. As can be seen from Figure 21.13, this comparison shows no appreciable difference between the ethnic composition of these two groups, which suggests that ethnic group was not a factor in determining whether arrested persons would be prosecuted.

However, discussion of bias in the flow from arrest to prosecution has tended to concentrate on juveniles, because official policy in the field of juvenile justice has encouraged alternatives to prosecution and discretionary decision-making, which may make bias more likely. Certainly, in the United States, the evidence that black people are at a disadvantage within the criminal justice process is much stronger for juveniles than for adults (Sampson and Lauritsen, 1997). Juveniles account for only about 10 per cent of the cases that come to court, so the general picture, as reflected in the London statistics (Figure 21.13) is dominated by adults. Detailed research on cautioning of juveniles—based on data that are now about twenty years old—suggests that young black

---

[12] A large number of prosecutions—nearly all for minor, especially traffic, offences —originate from the police reporting an offence, followed by a summons, without the suspect ever being arrested. However, in the vast majority of cases involving more serious (notifiable) offences, the criminal process is started by an arrest, so the analysis here concentrates on the path from arrest to prosecution.

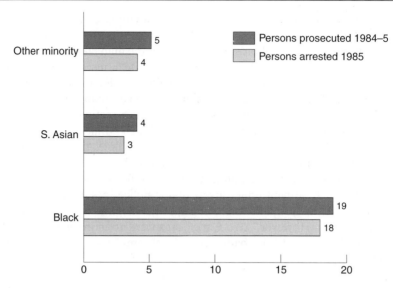

Fig. 21.13: Persons arrested compared with persons prosecuted, London 1984–5: percentages belonging to ethnic minority groups

Source for arrests: Home Office 1989*a*, Table 4.
Source for prosecutions: Home Office 1989*b*, Table 1.

offenders may have been substantially more likely to be prosecuted than young white offenders. Even though this has little impact on the numbers of black people prosecuted overall (because most of these are adults), the results for juveniles may have wider significance, if interactions with the police and courts during youth are an important influence on the development of an adult criminal career.

The Commission for Racial Equality (1992) summarized the early results of ethnic monitoring in five police forces of the processing of juvenile suspects. In four of the five areas, a considerably higher proportion of Afro-Caribbean than of white juvenile suspects were prosecuted. From certain limited analyses reported, it seems likely that the difference in treatment between ethnic groups may be explained by the proportion denying the offence (there is evidence that this is higher for Afro-Caribbeans than for whites), the proportion having previous convictions (higher among Afro-Caribbeans than whites in some areas), and the proportion already on bail or warrant or still subject to conditional discharge (apparently higher among Afro-Caribbeans than whites in the West Midlands).

A few more detailed studies have been reported of the police processing of juvenile suspects, but even the most recent of these (Landau and Nathan, 1983) uses data that are now nearly twenty years old. The processing of juvenile offenders has changed substantially over the last twenty years, so there is no knowledge, based on systematic research, of the operation of current policies and practices. Landau (1981) and Landau and Nathan (1983) examined police decisions on juvenile suspects made during the last quarter of 1978 in five police divisions in London. At that time there was a two-stage procedure. At Stage A, the police either charged immediately (19.6 per cent of cases) or referred the case to the juvenile bureau (80.4 per cent). At Stage B, the bureau either decided to charge after all (37.9 per cent), to caution (36.3 per cent), or to take 'no further action' (6.2 per cent). The analyses compared black (Afro-Caribbean and black African) juveniles with whites; South Asians, and other ethnic groups, were excluded. At the first stage, a substantially higher pro-portion of black than of white juveniles were immediately charged, and this applied to every type of offence except auto crime. In the context of a multi-variate model including age, sex, offence, area (two boroughs included in each of three areas), and previous offences, there remained a substantial difference in the probability of immediate charge between black and white juveniles. As Walker (1987) has pointed out, the analysis did not take account of social class. At the second stage, the minority (6.2 per cent) for whom no further action was taken were unaccountably excluded. Among the remainder, 53.7 per cent of the whites, compared with 39.7 per cent of the blacks, were cautioned. A substantial difference remained between black and white juveniles in the probability of being cautioned in the context of a logistic regression model including the following independent variables: previous criminal record; offence; ethnic group; whether a 'latch-key child', that is, according to the official record, left on their own without parental control on a regular basis; age; area (three groups of two boroughs). Sex and tenure of accommodation (a proxy for social class) were also investigated, but were only weakly related to whether the juvenile was cautioned or charged, and were not included in the final model. The probability of a caution was higher for white than for black juveniles for all six types of offence except 'traffic and other'.

Making use of a distinction developed by Weber (1954), the variables included in Landau and Nathan's analysis can be sorted into three groups: criteria of formal justice (the offence, previous criminal record); criteria of substantive justice (age, whether a latch-key child); and illegitimate criteria (sex, ethnic group, tenure, area). The analysis shows that variables of all three types have an important influence on the outcome, but previous criminal record (a criterion of formal justice) has the strongest effect.

The use of the illegitimate criteria clearly amounts to direct discrimination. The substantive criteria work to the disadvantage of black youths, but whether they indirectly discriminate depends on whether it is justifiable to use them, as discussed under the first heading in this chapter. Landau and Nathan (1983: 147) thought it was not justifiable, and that the system should revert to empha-sizing criteria of formal justice. The problem with this approach is that in juvenile justice systems throughout Europe and North America, the attempt to divert young people from court is associated with discretionary decision-making that takes account of the support networks surrounding the young person.

From Landau and Nathan's results it looks as though direct discrimination was considerably more important than the use of apparently neutral criteria as a cause of the difference in cautioning rate between black and white juveniles. Their model suggests that large differences between black and white children in the probability of cautioning remain when family background factors are held constant.[13] It follows that abandoning the criterion of parental control would not make much difference.

In short, there is clear evidence that a higher proportion of Afro-Caribbean than of white juvenile suspects were prosecuted from studies of data now nearly twenty years old, but no evidence about current practice. This seems to have occurred mainly because of direct discrimination, but also because of the application of intelligible criteria which may or may not be justifiable but which work to the disadvantage of Afro-Caribbeans. Nevertheless, from the limited information available, there seems to be little ethnic bias overall in the flow from arrest to prosecution. The results for juveniles, although important in themselves, have little effect on the general picture, because juveniles account for only about 10 per cent of persons prosecuted.

The Courts

The process prior to sentencing

Any tendency for ethnic minorities to be tried in Crown Courts rather than magistrates' courts could lead to a relatively high rate of imprisonment for those groups. It is well established that black defendants are, in fact, more likely than white defendants to be tried in Crown Courts. Statistics have been published for London in 1984 and 1985 covering prosecutions for indictable offences. As shown in Figure 21.14, the proportion of males committed for trial at the Crown Court was considerably higher among blacks and South Asians than among whites. Also, a higher proportion of black females than of white females were committed for trial at the Crown Court, although this did not apply to South Asians (Home Office, 1989*b*: Table 4). This general pattern has been confirmed by two further studies in London and Leeds (Walker, 1988, 1989; Brown and Hullin, 1992).

The tendency for black defendants to be tried at Crown Courts may arise partly because of the distribution of offences: for example, a relatively high proportion of black defendants are charged with robbery, and a high proportion of robbery cases (over 80 per cent) are tried at Crown Courts. However, this is not the main explanation, since the difference remains within broad offence types, with the exception of robbery, where it is reversed (see Figure 21.14). This anomalous finding for robbery is significant, since it has been argued (Blom-Cooper and Drabble, 1982) that black people tend to be

---

[13] e.g., among latch-key children aged 10–14 in area 2 who were accused of crimes of violence, the probability of being cautioned was 0.663 for white children compared with 0.271 for black children (Landau and Nathan, 1983: Table 4).

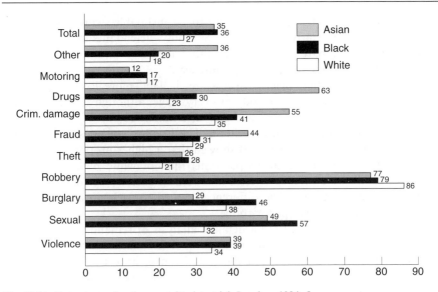

Fig. 21.14: Percentage of males committed to trial, London, 1984–5

Source: Home Office 1989*b*, Table 3. The chart shows the percentage of those proceeded against at magistrates courts for indictable offences who were committed for trial. Violence = violence against the person; sexual = sexual offences; theft = theft and handling; fraud = fraud and forgery.

charged with robbery in circumstances where a white person would be charged with theft. That would mean that robbery offences tend to be less serious in the case of black than white defendants, which would explain why a smaller proportion of these cases against black people go to the Crown Court.

It seems that although black defendants are more likely than whites to end up in Crown Court, this is not the result of their own decisions. Among cases going to Crown Court, the proportion that *have* to be tried there (because the offence is indictable only) is higher for black male than for white male defendants (Hood, 1992: 51, Table 5; Walker, 1989: 359, Table 8). Hood's study of cases heard at five Crown Courts in the West Midlands in 1989 showed that the proportion of defendants *electing* for trial at the Crown Court was no higher for black males (8 per cent) than for whites (11 per cent). A study of cases heard by magistrates' courts in Leeds in 1989 confirmed the West Midlands pattern; it showed that a higher proportion of Afro-Caribbean than of white defendants were committed for trial at the Crown Court, but this reflected the pattern of committals by magistrates, and not the choices of defendants (Brown and Hullin, 1992: 51).

At each stage following arrest and charge, the suspect may be either remanded in custody or released on bail pending the next hearing. Whether ethnic minority defendants are more likely than white defendants to be remanded in custody at any stage is important for two reasons. First, imprisonment before trial is serious in itself, so that a higher likelihood of imprisonment before trial, if not shown to be justifiable, would be unequal treatment of a particularly serious kind. Secondly, defendants in prison find it more difficult to prepare a defence than those at liberty, and there is evidence (Hood, 1992) that they receive stiffer sentences.

There is evidence that black suspects are, in fact, more likely than white suspects to be remanded in custody at every stage, although it is not known whether this is a consequence of direct discrimination, or of the impartial application of apparently neutral criteria. The London statistics for 1984 and 1985 (Home Office, 1989*b*: Table 3) showed that a higher proportion of black (9 per cent) and South Asian (8 per cent) than of white men (5 per cent) accused of indictable offences were committed in custody by magistrates for trial at the Crown Court. The difference applied to each group of offences considered separately, except for robbery.

Walker (1989) has conducted a detailed analysis of remands at every stage for her database of London cases in 1983 involving males aged 17–25. In the case of both police remands and remands by magistrates at some stage, a higher proportion of black than of white defendants were remanded in custody. For example, of those remanded by magistrates before trial for indictable-only offences, 53 per cent of the black men aged 17–20 were remanded in custody at some point, compared with 41 per cent of the whites; in the case of those aged 21–25 the comparable figures were 61 per cent for black men and 48 per cent for white men (Walker, 1989: 363, Table 14). In the case of police remands, these differences were smaller. There is no information from Walker's study about how these decisions were made by police and magistrates. These officials may have been using apparently neutral criteria that work to the disadvantage of black suspects, but nothing is known about the criteria used, or about their precise effects.

The police were much more likely to remand in custody than magistrates, but allowing for that difference of policy, there was a high degree of consistency between police and magistrates: for example, very few defendants bailed by police were later remanded in custody or given a custodial sentence by magistrates. Walker argued that police decisions about black and white defendants could be justified in the sense that they tended to predict later decisions by magistrates. As discussed under the first heading in this chapter, however, decisions within criminal process cannot be convincingly validated in this way. Decisions at different stages may be consistent, but consistently discriminatory.

From Hood's (1992) findings, a considerably higher proportion of the black (23 per cent) than of the white male defendants (11 per cent) pleaded not guilty at trial at the Crown Court. This confirms earlier indications from Walker's (1989) data for London. There is also some information about the rate of acquittal according to ethnic group for the two largest areas of ethnic minority settlement (London and the West Midlands). It suggests that ethnic minorities were, if anything, more likely to be acquitted than white defendants, although the overall difference was small. The London statistics showed little or no difference overall in the rate of acquittal between ethnic groups either at the magistrates' courts or at the Crown Courts (Home Office, 1989*b*: Tables 5 and 6). There were, however, some differences in acquittal rates for certain indictable offences. The most striking of these was that among males tried at the Crown Court for criminal damage, 44 per cent of blacks, 38 per cent of South Asians, but only 27 per cent of whites were acquitted. Similarly, Walker's findings for males aged 17–25 prosecuted in London in 1983 showed little or no difference overall in acquittal rates between ethnic groups (Walker, 1989). However, her findings for boys aged 14–16 showed a higher rate of acquittal for blacks than for whites both at the magistrates' courts and at the Crown Courts (Walker, 1988: 448, Table 6). For both courts combined, 15.3 per cent of young black defendants were acquitted completely, compared with 9.5 per cent of whites, and 10.9 per cent of South Asians.

Hood's study of cases at five West Midlands Crown Courts in 1989 provided some information about acquittal rates. Among male defendants at the five courts combined, the acquittal rates were 9.1 per cent for whites, 11.1 per cent for blacks, and 16.7 per cent for South Asians and others (Hood, 1992: calculated from Table 1, p. 32). However, there was considerable variation between the five courts. At one of them (Dudley) the acquittal rate was higher among whites than among blacks, whereas at three courts acquittal rates were considerably higher among blacks than among whites.

On one interpretation, the fact that the acquittal rate is only slightly higher for black than for white defendants argues against the hypothesis of a massive bias against blacks at earlier stages. If many black people were brought to trial because of bias, then the presumably weak cases against them ought to be dismissed. On the opposite interpretation, however, massive bias at earlier stages might be complemented by additional efforts to construct cases against black suspects, and by further bias against them at the trial, leading to roughly similar acquittal rates for whites and blacks. On the available evidence, it is not possible to choose between these interpretations. Hence the pattern of acquittals does not point unequivocally at bias or its absence, but it fits most easily with the hypothesis that there is no massive bias at earlier stages.

Sentencing

London statistics on prosecutions for indictable offences in 1984 and 1985 (Home Office, 1989*b*) show that there was no significant difference between sentences imposed in magistrates' courts on white and black offenders, but that South Asians and members of other ethnic minority groups were much more likely than whites or blacks to be fined and less likely to be given a custodial sentence. At the Crown Court, however, 57 per cent of black offenders were given immediate custody, compared with 51 per cent of whites, 50 per cent of South Asians, and 49 per cent of other ethnic groups. The high figure for blacks was due to the higher proportion given youth custody (19 per cent of blacks compared with 11 per cent of whites). Analysis by age of the offender

and offence group (the only other information available in these official statistics) explains a part of these differences, but considerable variation between
ethnic groups in the use of custody remains within offence groups for each age
group considered separately.

One feature of the results was that black men were far more likely than white
men to be given custodial sentences for sexual offences. This is partly because
a higher proportion of these sexual offences were rapes where the offender was
black (24 per cent) than where he was white (3 per cent). However, as already
observed, the converse pattern exists in the case of robbery (robberies committed by white men are more serious: Blom-Cooper and Drabble, 1982), yet
black men were still more likely than white men to receive immediate custody
for robbery. For the most part, the difference in sentences imposed on black
and white men cannot be explained by the offence, as far as that is known from
the official statistics.

Among those receiving sentences of immediate custody at the magistrates'
courts, there was no difference in average sentence length between ethnic
groups. At the Crown Court, South Asians received considerably longer
custodial sentences, on average, than whites. Also, young black males (aged
17–20) received longer custodial sentences than young white males, although
there was no similar difference among those aged 21 or more. The Home Office
suggested that 'the longer sentence length for Asians reflect[s] the high
proportion of drug trafficking offenders' (1989*b*: paragraph 24). A separate
table showed that among those convicted of drugs offences, the specific offence
was drug trafficking for 64 per cent of Asians compared with 17 per cent of
whites and 27 per cent of blacks (*ibid.*: Table 18).

From the limited information available in these statistics, it is not possible
to tell whether the sentences imposed reflect equal or unequal treatment of
different ethnic groups. A number of studies have pursued this question
(McConville and Baldwin, 1982; Crow and Cove, 1984; Mair, 1986; Moxon,
1988; Voakes and Fowler, 1989; Hudson, 1989; Brown and Hullin, 1992;
Hood, 1992). However, as Hood (1992) has convincingly argued, the earlier
studies had serious limitations which for the most part prevent any definite
conclusions being drawn from them on the central question under consideration. Hood's study of sentencing in five Crown Courts in the West Midlands
collected far more extensive information than the others about the cases and
offenders, and used far more powerful analytic methods, so it is at present the
best available source. Its main limitation (but also a strength in analytic terms)
is that it did not cover sentencing by the magistrates' courts. Some up-to-date
information about that is, however, available from Brown and Hullin's study
in Leeds.

There were 2,884 sentenced male offenders in Hood's sample. Over the five
Crown Courts covered by the study, 56.6 per cent of the blacks were sentenced
to custody, compared with 48.4 per cent of the whites, and 39.6 per cent of the
Asians. However, there were substantial variations both between individual
courts and between individual judges in the relative sentences they imposed on

blacks and whites. Differences in the use of custody between ethnic groups were found to be greatest where the judges' discretion was greatest, that is for offences at a middling level of seriousness. In fact, for each type of offence examined, there was no such difference for the most serious offences or for the least serious ones. This finding parallels the results of American studies (Sampson and Lauritsen, 1997).

All of the differences between ethnic groups occurred among those aged 21 or over: there was no difference for young offenders. Also, there was no difference in custody rate between black and white offenders in employment: the differences were confined to those who were unemployed. This happened because 'being unemployed was a factor significantly correlated with receiving a custodial sentence if the defendant was black but not if he was white or Asian' (Hood, 1992: 86). A higher proportion of the black male defendants pleaded not guilty than of the whites (23 compared with 11 per cent), and a not guilty plea was associated overall with an increased probability of custody. Because of the detailed pattern of the relationships, the difference in pleas between ethnic groups did not help to explain the difference in the use of custody, but it did help to explain the length of custodial sentences. An important factor associated with the use of custody for blacks was that they were more likely to be remanded in custody at the time they were sentenced. This could not be wholly explained by variables known to be legally relevant to the bail/custody decision.

Among adult males given custodial sentences, these sentences tended to be considerably longer for South Asians and blacks than for whites. This was partly because South Asians and blacks were more likely to plead not guilty than whites, and because of the detailed characteristics of their case and prior record, summed up as the seriousness of the offence. Those pleading not guilty were given considerably longer sentences on average. Among those who pleaded guilty, there was little difference in length of sentence between ethnic groups after controlling for the seriousness of the offence. Among those who pleaded not guilty, however, sentences were considerably longer for blacks and Asians than for whites after allowing for the seriousness of the offence.

Multivariate analyses were carried out to show whether a difference in sentencing according to ethnic group remained after allowing for the forms of legal process used (e.g. mode of trial), details of the offence (e.g. seriousness), and the offender's prior criminal record. After allowing for a wide range of such factors, it was found that the probability of custody remained 5 per cent higher for black than for white men, whereas it remained 5 per cent lower for South Asian men. The raw difference in use of custody between ethnic groups was reduced after taking account of these variables, but it did not disappear. The remaining difference between black and white men was significant at the 93 per cent level of confidence.

The plea as a criterion influencing the sentence is an important example of an apparently neutral criterion that works to the disadvantage of black people. It is important because it raises difficult conceptual issues in a particularly acute form. On the one hand it is argued that the discount for a guilty plea is what makes a fair system of criminal justice a practical possibility. Without it, the number of full trials would grow to unmanageable proportions. This would lead to under-funding, a decline in the quality of decision-making, and increased inequality between defendants according to their resources. On the other side, it is argued that black people are hostile to mainstream institutions in part because they believe the conditions of their lives are shaped by racial bias. Refusal to plead guilty is therefore a consequence of past experience of racial bias. So if the tariff is higher for those pleading not guilty, the effect is that black people are being punished more severely than others because they have been subject to racial bias and hostility in the past. Without explaining just how he would evaluate the balance between these conflicting arguments, Hood concluded that '[t]here is clearly a need to consider the implications of the policy which favours so strongly those who plead guilty, when ethnic minorities are less willing to let the prosecution go unchallenged' (1992: 191).

Hood estimated that in the West Midlands, 24.4 per cent of the male prison population was black, compared with 3.8 per cent of the resident population, a ratio of 6.4:1[14] He estimated that 70 per cent of this difference was accounted for by the number appearing for sentence, taking account of all stages prior to sentence, but not the profile of offences; 10 per cent 'by the more serious nature of the offences and other legally relevant characteristics of the charges on which black defendants were convicted' (1992: 130); 7 per cent by greater use of custody than expected (after taking account of legally relevant variables); and 13 per cent 'by lengthier sentences, which appears to be entirely due to a greater propensity to plead not guilty, and to the lengthier sentences for those who did so' (1992: 130). These findings imply that 80 per cent of the difference emerged from stages prior to the Crown Court, although 'decisions at all these stages . . . might be affected by racial factors' (Hood, 1992: 130). The 13 per cent of the difference that relates to lengthier sentences for black males arose in its entirety from the higher tariffs attaching to not guilty pleas. The remaining 7 per cent of the difference related to greater than expected use of custodial sentences, and cannot, therefore, be explained by legally relevant variables. It might be attributable to direct discrimination, or alternatively to legally relevant variables not captured by the study.

No study comparable to Hood's (which covered only Crown Courts) has been carried out of race and sentencing in magistrates' courts. As mentioned above, London statistics for 1984 and 1985 (Home Office, 1989b) showed no difference in sentences imposed on black and white offenders, although those imposed on South Asians were less severe. A recent study by Brown and Hullin (1992) of sentencing in magistrates' courts in Leeds found no significant difference overall in sentences imposed according to ethnic group. The information collected by this study was relatively limited, and the analysis was not

---

[14] The comparison is a rough one, because not all persons in prison in the West Midlands are drawn from the resident population of the region.

sufficient to address the question whether discrimination had occurred. However, together with the London statistics, these findings do suggest that the extent of any racial discrimination in sentencing is considerably less in the magistrates' than in the Crown Courts.

DISCUSSION

For whatever reason, black people (but not South Asians) are more likely to become entangled with the web of criminal justice than white people. The central task of this chapter is to consider how far this has happened because of bias, impartial application of criteria that work to the disadvantage of black people, or an elevated actual rate of offending.

If there is evidence of racial or ethnic bias in criminal justice, we need to consider why this bias is against black people but not South Asians, who have been equally subject to discrimination in other spheres. Where black people are placed at a disadvantage through the application of apparently neutral criteria, there is a need to review these criteria in the light of their consequences for ethnic minorities, and to consider whether it is justifiable to go on using them. If there is evidence of higher actual rates of offending among black people than among other ethnic groups, then the next step is to explain why this is so, and in particular to consider the links between any bias in law enforcement and criminal process and the criminalization of the black minority.

Main Findings

First, ethnic minorities—both black people and South Asians—are found to be at higher risk of crime victimization than white people. This difference arises partly because the socio-demographic profile of ethnic minorities tends to increase their risk of victimization, but some difference remains after controlling for the effect of these variables. The elevated risk of victimization is also connected with characteristics of the neighbourhoods where ethnic minorities live. A third factor is that a substantial minority of offences on black people (and to a lesser extent on South Asians) are committed by black people, who probably have an elevated level of offending (see below). However, black-on-black crime is only a small part of the explanation of high black victimization because black people are such a small proportion of the population.

Secondly, at the end of the criminal justice process, black people (Afro-Caribbeans and black Africans) are about six times as likely to be in prison as white people or South Asians.

Thirdly, the pattern of offences for which black people were arrested and imprisoned is consistent with the theory that they tend to be the targets of proactive law enforcement. Also, there is some evidence of bias against black people at various stages: in the targeting of police enforcement; the decision to prosecute juveniles; and sentencing by the Crown Courts. None of this evidence, however, is entirely clear-cut. It can be argued, for example, that the high police stop rate of black people is 'justified' by results (reported offences, arrests, and prosecutions). With regard to decisions to prosecute juveniles, the relevant studies are out of date, and probably did not include all of the relevant variables. With regard to sentencing, the leading study (Hood, 1992) did suggest some racial bias, but its measured effects were rather small, especially when compared with the effects of other variables.

Fourthly, at various points, black people are placed at a disadvantage by the application of apparently neutral criteria. The clearest examples are the influence of social background factors on the decision to prosecute rather than caution a juvenile (black children are less likely to have the stable family background that makes cautioning more likely); the influence of social background factors on sentencing; and the lower sentencing tariff for suspects who plead not guilty. The relationship between guilty plea and sentence accounts for a substantial part (perhaps around 15 per cent) of the difference in rate of imprisonment between black and white people.

Fifthly, although some bias against black people has been demonstrated at several stages, and although some apparently neutral criteria have been shown to work to the disadvantage of black people, the magnitude of these effects seems small compared with the stark contrast in rates of arrest and imprisonment between black and white people. A possible theory is that the stark contrast is mainly or entirely caused by cumulative bias and the use of criteria that work to the disadvantage of black people at each different stage of the criminal justice process. That theory has recently received support from the results of a study of young people aged 14–25 (Graham and Bowling, 1996) which showed no difference in rates of self-reported offending between black and white youths. However, those findings do not seem convincing in the light of sampling problems, the inherent limitations of the self-report method in terms of validity and reliability, and the evidence that the truthfulness of self-reports may be systematically related to ethnic group (Junger, 1989, but see also Bowling, 1990). There is a considerable weight of evidence that contradicts the findings of the self-report study, and suggests instead that the stark contrast in rates of imprisonment cannot be mainly the cumulative result of the operations of criminal justice process at each stage.

- The cumulative effects theory would predict a steady increase in the proportion of black people among suspects and offenders from the earliest to the latest stage of the process. In fact, the proportion of black people is about the same among suspects as described by victims, persons arrested, and the prison population.
- Arising directly from the first point, it is impossible to account for the high representation of black people at early stages (for example, according to victims' reports) in terms of bias.

- Even at stages where bias has been demonstrated, its potential impact is fairly limited. For example, proactive law enforcement does target black people to some extent: but most clear-ups do not result from proactive law enforcement, and most proactive law enforcement cannot be targeted on black people. Hence the total effect of this bias must be modest, especially in relation to the stark differences in rates of arrest and imprisonment between black and white people. To take another example, black juveniles are considerably more likely to be prosecuted rather than cautioned compared with comparable white juveniles, but there is no evidence of a similar difference in the case of adult offenders, who account for 90 per cent of the cases coming before the courts. Hence, the bias in cautioning of juveniles, though important, has only a small significance as an explanation of the difference in rates of imprisonment between black and white people.
- Although proactive law enforcement targeted on black people can help to explain the arrest rates for certain offences (notably, robbery) it cannot for others (such as burglary) for which proactive law enforcement cannot for the most part be targeted on black people and is in any case singularly ineffective.
- Contrary to what has been stated by some commentators (for example, Reiner, 1989, 1993) it is not the case that bias has been demonstrated at every stage of the process. Most notably, black people are, if anything, more likely to be acquitted than white people. There is not a steady accumulation of bias from one stage to the next.
- The acquittal rate is only slightly higher among black than white defendants. This is difficult to reconcile with the hypothesis of massive bias against black people at earlier stages, which should lead to the cases against them being relatively weak. Although not conclusive in itself, this argument carries some weight in the context of the rest of the evidence.

A fair assessment of the limited evidence is that although some bias against black people has been demonstrated at several stages of the process, and although some decision-making criteria clearly work to the disadvantage of black people, in large part the difference in rate of arrest and imprisonment between black and white people arises from a difference in the rate of offending.

Fifthly, South Asians—collectively the largest part of the ethnic minority population—are not over-represented among offenders described by victims, persons arrested, or the prison population. No bias has been demonstrated against them at any stage, and at various points they tend to be favoured compared to white or black people. In other contexts, South Asians are just as much subject to racial hostility and discrimination as black people. The bias against black people that has been demonstrated within the criminal justice system is therefore different from that existing in other contexts such as employment. It is not adequately described as part of a generalized 'racism'. More plausibly it springs from a perception of black people specifically, as distinct from other ethnic minorities, as a threat to law and order. However exaggerated, those perceptions are not unconnected with reality, since crime rates are higher than average among black people, but they also help to shape that reality, since racial hostility and discrimination will through a sequence of interactions cause black crime rates to rise still further.

Returning to the broad perspective established at the beginning of this chapter, the process of gaining acceptance for a single, universal standard of law applicable equally to all ethnic groups seems in some ways to be well advanced. Ethnic group is by no means the most important characteristic influencing rates of offending or victimization, or the way people interact with the police, the probation service, or the courts. Sex and age are far more important predictors, and social class is probably more important, too. Although Afro-Caribbeans are considerably more hostile to the police than white people or Asians, the contrast between age groups is much starker. The ethnic minorities do not reject the criminal justice system or deny its legitimacy. As victims of crime, or as bystanders, they are just as likely as white people to report matters to the police.

On the other hand, it cannot be claimed that law enforcement and criminal process have the same impact on black and white people. In the past, claims of unequal treatment have tended to be exaggerated, and hence to lack credibility. There is evidence that law enforcement targets black people, and there is some evidence of bias at various stages of criminal process. Probably more important than bias is the effect of apparently neutral criteria which nevertheless work to the disadvantage of black people. Yet these effects seem much too small to account for the stark difference in rates of imprisonment between black and white people. In large part, this difference probably reflects a difference in rates of offending.

Explaining Bias

To the extent that there is bias in law enforcement and criminal process, there is a need to explain why this is directed against black people and not against South Asians. A part of the background to any explanation is that criminalization is the result of a sequence of interactions between black people and the authorities. Thus, high crime rates among black people may possibly be explained partly in terms of labelling and deviance amplification, and racial prejudice among the authorities may have had a role in initiating and maintaining such a system of interaction. It may be impossible to answer the question 'Which came first?' A widely shared official view of the early 1970s that people originating from the West Indies were a law-abiding community changed within three or four years to an equally widespread official view that black crime was a particular threat. It has been argued that this was a cultural shift (Hall *et al.*, 1978), yet it could alternatively have been caused by rising crime rates among the second generation of young people whose parents had migrated from the West Indies.

Bias against black people specifically in law enforcement and criminal justice process seems like the counterpart to a growing tendency from the late 1970s onwards for young black people to define their identity in opposition to the central structures of authority in British society, most notably the police. From the Notting Hill Carnival of 1978 onwards, there has been a succession of anti-police riots or uprisings, in which black people have always played a central role. Survey research shows that young black people are generally very hostile to the police, and considerably more so than young white people (Smith, 1983*a*; Skogan, 1990). Yet, surprisingly, the evidence from observational studies of police–black encounters does not support this kind of explanation (Smith and Gray, 1983; Norris *et al.*, 1992). The collective hostility of the police and black people towards each other does not seem to be expressed at the micro level of individual encounters.

The outgoing survival strategy adopted by black people in Britain contrasts with the culturally enclosed strategy of South Asians (Daniel, 1968; Smith, 1977). White people were just as much inclined to discriminate against South Asians as against black people, but black people were far more likely to encounter discrimination because they were more likely, for example, to apply for a job cold, whereas South Asians would be more likely to seek out opportunities through relatives and friends. One consequence of these different approaches to surviving in Britain may be that white people have formed very different notions of the black and South Asian communities. They are more likely to feel the need to control the behaviour of black than that of South Asian people, because the behaviour of South Asians tends to be hidden from them.

Reviewing Decision-making Criteria

Black people are placed at a substantial disadvantage because guilty pleas attract a higher sentencing tariff. They also suffer from the use of factors such as stable family background in making decisions for example about cautioning versus prosecution, especially of juveniles. As set out under the first heading in this chapter, the question which decision-making criteria are justifiable or legitimate raises deep and difficult problems in the philosophy of law, which are outside the scope of this chapter. Nevertheless, three simple conclusions do emerge from the present analysis.

First, it seems important that decision-making criteria should be reviewed in the light of their consequences for different groups, including racial or ethnic ones. However particular criteria are to be justified in detail, at a minimum their effects on racial or ethnic groups should be taken into consideration. The reason for taking this view is that membership of an ethnic group is an important source of personal identity. The use of a criterion that has an adverse impact on a whole ethnic group will be seen as an attack on that group, unless the reasons for adopting it are compelling.

Secondly, these decision-making criteria cannot be validated internally by the results they produce within criminal process. For example, the criteria used by the police when deciding who to stop and search cannot be validated by pointing to the results (such as offences reported, arrests, or prosecutions); police decisions to refuse bail cannot be validated by the later decisions of magistrates to refuse bail to the same suspects; and the system of offering inducements to plead guilty cannot be validated by showing that nearly all of those who plead guilty are convicted. The reason is that the later outcomes are not independent of the earlier decisions, but flow from them and are partly shaped by them; hence they cannot alone justify them. The most that can be said is that outcomes need to be taken into consideration when evaluating decision-making procedures.

Thirdly, it is, unfortunately, not likely that disadvantage to ethnic minorities from the application of apparently neutral criteria can be altogether avoided by changing the criteria. The reason is that the unavoidable element of discretion in the application of the criteria will remain. The best example here is the decision about whether to caution or charge juvenile suspects. A system for diverting juvenile offenders from the courts is likely to be advantageous to a relatively high-offending group, such as black people. On the face of it, such a system (particularly if operated by the police) is bound to involve a large amount of discretion, subject to minimal oversight and review. This allows scope for direct racial discrimination. The obvious response is to require greater use of formal criteria. Any criteria that fit with the underlying principles of cautioning are, however, likely to work to the disadvantage of a high offending group, such as black people. That means either adopting inappropriate criteria that have an equal impact on different ethnic groups, which would undermine support for cautioning, or reverting to a more discretionary approach. This illustrates the substantial practical problems that arise in seeking to improve decision-making procedures.

Explaining Black Offending

It seems likely that the two main findings of this review are linked: that is, discrimination against black minorities interacts with high rates of offending by those same groups. Crime arises from a sequence of interactions. It seems likely that in certain sequences racial hostility on one side and antagonism to authority on the other become mutually reinforcing. Within this sequence of interactions, actual rates of offending among black people begin to rise; this rise in turn causes an increase in racial hostility and discrimination. It can well be imagined that the interaction between racial stereotypes, discrimination, antagonism to authority, and actual rates of offending among black people, produces a cycle of deviance amplification. These effects would be magnified by the large-scale conflicts between black people and the police that became so salient over the past fifteen years and acquired intense significance for young black people (Small, 1983).

Despite the claims that some have made, researchers have not demonstrated that there is a steady cumulation of discrimination through each stage of the criminal justice process. However, a more relevant perspective would be the life cycle of the individual. For the young black male, there may be a cumulation of interactions which greatly increase the likelihood of entanglement with criminal process and subsequent criminality.

It will also be important to consider broader causes of crime. Black people tend to live in areas of social stress, where crime rates among all ethnic groups are high; they have a much higher rate of unemployment overall than white people, and a lower standard of living, and a higher proportion of them are in poverty (Modood *et al.*, 1997). However, certain other racial minority groups—South Asian Muslims, in particular—are more disadvantaged in these respects than black people, yet have much lower crime rates. It would be fruitful to focus on this striking difference in future research.

It would be wrong to assume that these contrasts are a permanent feature of the social scene. Concern about crime among black people did not appear until the mid-1970s, although it is difficult to say whether there was an actual increase in the black crime rate around that time. Recent research (Modood *et al.*, 1997) has shown some improvement in the conditions of life of black people in Britain over the ten years up to 1990. There is currently a striking increase in the number of black people going into higher education. Along with such changes, it is entirely possible that the proportion of young black people who are criminalized will decrease. It is also, unfortunately, possible that the crime rate will rise among South Asian Muslims who arrived in Britain more recently than migrants from the West Indies, and who currently suffer greater social and economic disadvantages (FitzGerald, 1995).

Nevertheless, the difference in rate of imprisonment between black and South Asian people is so striking that it can hardly be explained by differences in economic hardship or in the timing of the migration. What the difference may possibly indicate is that the outgoing and integrative strategy initially adopted by migrants from the Caribbean was met by rejection leading to conflict, which the more separatist and inward-looking strategy of South Asians tended to avoid. Of course these broad generalizations greatly oversimplify the great range of adaptations made by different groups over more than one generation, but they may contain a kernel of truth.

Selected Further Reading

A brief discussion of the topics treated in more detail here is provided by R. Reiner, 'Race, Crime and Justice: Models of Interpretation', in L. Gelsthorpe and W. McWilliams, eds., *Minority Ethnic Groups and the Criminal Justice System*. Cambridge: Institute of Criminology, Cropwood Conference Series No. 21, 1993. An indispensable and up-to-date source of information and comment for a range of developed countries is *Ethnicity, Crime and Immigration: Comparative and Cross-National Perspectives*, which forms volume 21 of M. Tonry, ed., *Crime and Justice: A Review of Research*. Chicago, Ill.: University of Chicago Press, 1997. Strongly recommended as a stimulus for serious thought about the issues is W. Wilbanks, *The Myth of a Racist Criminal Justice System*. Monterey, Cal.: Brooks/Cole, 1987, which sets out to argue the case that racial disparity in US prisons reflects a disparity in rates of offending. M. Tonry, *Malign Neglect: Race, Crime and Punishment in America* places this American debate in a broader perspective (New York: Oxford University Press, 1995). The best British study of racial bias in criminal justice is R. Hood, *Race and Sentencing*. Oxford: Oxford University Press, 1992. This uses a wealth of information and refined statistical procedures to examine sentencing by Crown Courts in the Midlands. On bias in cautioning of juveniles, the study by S. F. Landau and G. Nathan, although dated, remains important ('Selecting Delinquents for Cautioning in the London Metropolitan Area', *British Journal of Criminology*, 23, 2: 128–49, 1983). In this field, the largest volume of work has been on the police. The most important studies are D. J. Smith and J. Gray, *Police and People in London: The PSI Report*. Aldershot: Gower, 1985; W. Skogan, *The Police and the Public in England and Wales: A British Crime Survey Report*. Home Office Research Study no. 117. London: HMSO, and C. Norris, N. Fielding, C. Kemp, and J. Fielding, 'Black and Blue: An Analysis of the Influence of Race on Being Stopped by the Police', *British Journal of Sociology* 43, 3: 207–24, 1992.

REFERENCES

BETHNAL GREEN AND STEPNEY TRADES COUNCIL (1978), *Blood on the Streets*. London: Bethnal Green and Stepney Trades Council.

BLOM-COOPER, L., and DRABBLE, L. (1982), 'Police Perception of Crime: Brixton and the Operational Response', *British Journal of Criminology*, 22: 184–7.

BOWLING, B. (1990), 'Conceptual and Methodological Problems in Measuring "Race" Differences in Delinquency: A Reply to Marianne Junger', *British Journal of Criminology*, 30: 483–92.

—— (1993), 'Racist Harassment and the Process of Victimization: Conceptual and Methodological Implications for the Local Crime Survey', in J. Lowman and B. D. MacLean, eds., *Realist Criminology: Crime and Policing in the 1990s*. Vancouver: Collective Press.

BROWN, C. (1984), *Black and White Britain: The Third PSI Survey*. London: Heinemann.

—— and GAY, P. (1986), *Racial Discrimination: 17 Years After the Act*. London: Policy Studies Institute.

BROWN, I., and HULLIN, R. (1992), 'A Study of Sentencing in the Leeds Magistrates' Courts:

The Treatment of Ethnic Minority and White Offenders', *British Journal of Criminology*, 32, 1: 41–53.

COHEN, L. E., and FELSON, M. (1979), 'Social Change and Crime Rate Trends: A Routine Activities Approach', *American Sociological Review*, 44: 588–608.

COMMISSION FOR RACIAL EQUALITY (1985), *Review of the Race Relations Act 1976: Proposals for Change*. London: Commission for Racial Equality.

—— (1991), *Review of the Race Relations Act*. London: Commission for Racial Equality.

—— (1992), *Cautions v. Prosecutions: Ethnic Monitoring of Juveniles by Seven Police Forces*. London: Commission for Racial Equality.

CROW, I., and COVE, J. (1984), 'Ethnic Minorities and the Courts', *Criminal Law Review*, 413–17.

DANIEL, W. W. (1968), *Racial Discrimination in England*. Harmondsworth: Penguin.

EQUAL OPPORTUNITIES REVIEW (1987), *Law Reports* 15 September–October: 36–7.

FARRINGTON, D. P. (1973), 'Self-Reports of Deviant Behaviour: Predictive and Stable?',

Journal of Criminal Law and Criminology, 64: 99–110.

FITZGERALD, M. (1989), 'Legal Approaches to Racial Harassment in Council Housing: The Case for Reassessment', *New Community*, 16, 1: 93–105.

—— (1995), '"Race" and Crime: The Facts', paper presented at the British Society of Criminology biennial conference, Loughborough, July.

—— and HALE, C. (1996), *Ethnic Minorities: Victimisation and Racial Harassment: Findings from the 1988 and 1992 British Crime Surveys.* Home Office Research Study No 154. London: Home Office.

—— and MARSHALL, P. (1996), 'Ethnic Minorities in British Prisons: Some Research Implications', in R. Matthews and P. Francis, eds., *Prisons 2000: An International Perspective on the Current State and Future of Imprisonment*, 139–62. London: Macmillan.

GENN, H. (1988), 'Multiple Victimization', in M. Maguire and J. Ponting, eds., *Victims of Crime: A New Deal?* Milton Keynes: Open University Press.

GILROY, P. (1987), *There Ain't No Black in the Union Jack: The Cultural Politics of Race and Nation.* London: Hutchinson.

GRAHAM, J., and BOWLING, B. (1996), *Young People and Crime.* Research Study No. 145. London: Home Office Research and Statistics Department.

HALL, S., CRITCHER, C., CLARKE, J., JEFFERSON, T., and ROBERTS, B. (1978), *Policing the Crisis.* London: Macmillan.

HOME OFFICE (1981), *Racial Attacks: Report of a Home Office Study.* London: Home Office.

—— (1992), *Statistical Bulletin, 20/82.* London: Home Office.

—— (1989a), *Crime Statistics for the Metropolitan Police District by Ethnic Group, 1987: Victims, Suspects and Those Arrested.* Home Office Statistical Bulletin 5/89. London: Home Office.

—— (1989b), *The Ethnic Group of Those Proceeded Against or Sentenced by the Courts in the Metropolitan Police District in 1984 and 1985.* Home Office Statistical Bulletin 6/89. London: Home Office.

—— (1989c), *The Response to Racial Attacks and Harassment: Guidance for the Statutory Agencies: Report of the Inter-Departmental Racial Attacks Group.* London: Home Office.

—— (1991), *The Response to Racial Attacks: Sustaining the Momentum: The Second Report of the Inter-Departmental Racial Attacks Group.* London: Home Office.

—— (1996), *Prison Statistics England and Wales 1994.* Cm 3087. London: HMSO.

HOOD, R. (1992), *Race and Sentencing.* Oxford: Clarendon Press.

HOUSE OF COMMONS HOME AFFAIRS COMMITTEE (1986), *Racial Attacks and Harassment.* Session 1985–86, HC 409. London: HMSO.

HOUSE OF COMMONS SELECT COMMITTEE ON RACE RELATIONS AND IMMIGRATION (1972), *Police/Immigrant Relations.* HC 71. London: HMSO.

—— (1976), *The West Indian Community.* HC 180. London: HMSO.

HUDSON, B. A. (1989), 'Discrimination and Disparity: The Influence of Race on Sentencing', *New Community*, 16, 1: 23–34.

—— (1993), 'Penal Policy and Racial Justice', in L. Gelsthorpe and W. McWilliam, eds., *Minority Ethnic Groups and the Criminal Justice System.* Cambridge: University of Cambridge Institute of Criminology.

JEFFERSON, T. (1988), 'Race, Crime and Policing: Empirical, Theoretical and Methodological Issues', *International Journal of the Sociology of Law*, 16: 521–39.

—— (1993), 'The Racism of Criminalization: Policing and the Reproduction of the Criminal Other', in L. Gelsthorpe and W. McWilliam, eds., *Minority Ethnic Groups and the Criminal Justice System.* Cambridge: University of Cambridge Institute of Criminology.

—— and WALKER, M. A. (1992), 'Ethnic Minorities in the Criminal Justice System', *Criminal Law Review*, 83–95.

—— and —— (1993), 'Attitudes to the Police of the Ethnic Minorities in a Provincial City', *British Journal of Criminology*, 33, 2: 251–66.

—— —— and —— SENEVIRATNE, M. (1992), 'Ethnic Minorities, Crime and Criminal Justice: A Study in a Provincial City', in D. Downes, ed., *Unravelling Criminal Justice.* London: Macmillan.

JONES, T. (1993), *Britain's Ethnic Minorities.* London: Policy Studies Institute.

—— MacLEAN, B., and YOUNG, J. (1986), *The Islington Crime Survey: Crime, Victimization and Policing in Inner-City London.* Aldershot: Gower.

JOWELL, R., and PRESCOTT-CLARKE, P. (1970), 'Racial Discrimination and White-collar Workers in Britain', *Race*, 9: 397–417.

JUNGER, M. (1989), 'Discrepancies Between Police and Self-Report Data for Dutch Racial Minorities', *British Journal of Criminology*, 29: 273–84.

KINSEY, R. (1985), *Final Report of the Merseyside Crime and Police Surveys.* Liverpool: Merseyside County Council.

LANDAU, S. (1981), 'Juveniles and the Police', *British Journal of Criminology*, 21, 1: 27–46.

—— and NATHAN, G. (1983), 'Selecting Delinquents for Cautioning in the London Metropolitan Area', *British Journal of Criminology*, 23, 2: 128–49.

LONDON BOROUGH OF NEWHAM (1987), *Report of a Survey of Crime and Racial Harassment in Newham*. London: London Borough of Newham.

MAIR, G. (1986), 'Ethnic Minorities, Probation and the Magistrates' Courts', *British Journal of Criminology*, 26, 2: 147–55.

MAYHEW, P., ELLIOTT, D., and DOWDS, L. (1989), *The 1988 British Crime Survey*. Home Office Research Study No. 111. London: HMSO.

McCONVILLE, M., and BALDWIN, J. (1982), 'The Influence of Race on Sentencing in England', *Criminal Law Review*, 652–8.

McCRUDDEN, C., SMITH, D. J., and BROWN, C. (1991), *Racial Justice at Work: The Enforcement of the 1976 Race Relations Act in Employment*. London: Policy Studies Institute.

MAYHEW, P., AYE MAUNG, N., and MIRRLEES-BLACK, C. (1993), *The 1992 British Crime Survey*. Research Findings No. 9. London: Home Office.

MODOOD, T. (1990), 'British Asian Muslims and the Rushdie Affair', *Political Quarterly*, 61, 2: 143–60. Reproduced in J. Donald and A. Rattansi, eds., *'Race', Culture and Difference*, 260–7. London: Sage, 1992.

—— (1994), *Racial Equality: Colour, Culture and Citizenship*. London: Runnymede Trust and Trentham Books.

—— BERTHOUD, R., LAKEY, J., NAZROO, J., SMITH, P., VIRDEE, S., and BEISHON, S. (1997), *Ethnic Minorities in Britain: Diversity and Disadvantage*. London: Policy Studies Institute.

MOXON, D. (1988), *Sentencing Practice in the Crown Court*. Home Office Research Study No. 102. London: HMSO.

NORRIS, C., FIELDING, N., KEMP, C., and FIELDING, J. (1992), 'Black and Blue: An Analysis of the Influence of Race on Being Stopped by the Police', *British Journal of Sociology*, 43, 3: 207–24.

REINER, R. (1989), 'Race and Criminal Justice', *New Community*, 16, 1: 5–22.

—— (1993), 'Race, Crime and Justice: Models of Interpretation', in L. Gelsthorpe and W. McWilliam, eds., *Minority Ethnic Groups and the Criminal Justice System*. Cambridge: University of Cambridge Institute of Criminology.

ROSE, E. J. B., DEAKIN, N., ABRAMS, M., JACKSON, V., PESTON, M., VANAGS, A. H., COHEN, A., GAITSKELL, J., and WARD, P. (1969), *Colour and Citizenship*. London: Oxford University Press.

SAMPSON, A., and PHILLIPS, C. (1992), *Multiple Victimisation: Racial Attacks on an East London Estate*. Police Research Group, Crime Prevention Unit Series, Paper No. 36. London: HMSO.

SAMPSON, R. J., and LAURITSEN, J. L. (1997), 'Criminal Behavior, Criminal Justice: On Racial and Ethnic Disparities in the United States', in M. Tonry, ed., *Ethnicity, Crime and Immigration: Comparative and Cross-National Perspectives*. Chicago, Ill.: University of Chicago Press.

SAULSBURY, W., and BOWLING, B. (1991), *The Multi-Agency Approach in Practice: the North Plaistow Racial Harassment Project*. Research and Planning Unit Paper No. 64. London: HMSO.

SCARMAN, LORD (1981), *The Brixton Disorders 10–12 April 1981: Report of an Inquiry by the Rt. Hon. the Lord Scarman, OBE*. Cmnd. 8427. London: HMSO.

SHAH, R., and PEASE, K. (1992), 'Crime, Race and Reporting to the Police', *The Howard Journal*, 31, 3: 192–9.

SKOGAN, W. (1990), *The Police and Public in England and Wales: A British Crime Survey Report*. Home Office Research Study No. 117. London: HMSO.

SMALL, S. (1983), *Police and People in London: II A Group of Young Black People*. London: Policy Studies Institute.

SMITH, D. J. (1977), *Racial Disadvantage in Britain*. Harmondsworth: Penguin Books.

—— (1983a), *Police and People in London: I A Survey of Londoners*. London: Policy Studies Institute.

—— (1983b), *Police and People in London: II A Survey of Police Officers*. London: Policy Studies Institute.

—— (1991), 'Police and Racial Minorities', *Policing and Society*, 2: 1–15.

—— and GRAY, J. (1983), *Police and People in London: IV The Police in Action*. London: Policy Studies Institute.

—— (1994), 'Race, Crime and Criminal Justice', in M. Maguire, R. Morgan, and R. Reiner (eds.), *The Oxford Handbook of Criminology* (1st edn.). Oxford: Clarendon Press.

STEVENS, P., and WILLIS, C. (1979), *Race, Crime and Arrests*. Home Office Research Study No. 58. London: HMSO.

TONRY, M. (1997), 'Ethnicity, Crime and Immigration', in M. Tonry, ed., *Ethnicity,*

Crime and Immigration: Comparative and Cross-National Perspectives. Chicago, Ill.: University of Chicago Press.

TUCK, M., and SOUTHGATE, P. (1981), *Ethnic Minorities, Crime and Policing: A Survey of the Experiences of West Indians and Whites.* Home Office Research Study No. 70. London: HMSO.

VIRDEE, S. (1997), 'Racial Management', in T. Modood *et al., Ethnic Minorities in Britain: Diversity and Disadvantage.* London: Policy Studies Institute.

VOAKES, R., and FOWLER, Q. (1989), *Sentencing Race and Social Inquiry Reports.* Bradford: West Yorkshire Probation Service.

WALKER, M. A. (1987), 'Interpreting Race and Crime Statistics', *Journal of the Royal Statistical Society,* A 150, Part 1: 39–56.

—— (1988), 'The Court Disposal of Young Males, by Race, in London in 1983', *British Journal of Criminology,* 28, 4: 441–59.

—— (1989), 'The Court Disposal and Remands of White. Afro-Caribbean, and Asian Men London, 1983', *British Journal of Criminology,* 29, 4: 353–67.

—— (1992), 'Arrest Rates and Ethnic Minorities: A Study in a Provincial City', *Journal of the Royal Statistical Society,* 155, Part 2: 259–72.

WALMSLEY, R., HOWARD, L., and WHITE, S. (1992), *The National Prison Survey 1991: Main Findings.* Home Office Research Study No. 128. London: HMSO.

WEBER, M. (1954), *Max Weber on Law in Economy and Society.* Edited by M. Rheinstein. Cambridge, Mass.: Harvard University Press.

WILBANKS, W. (1987), *The Myth of a Racist Criminal Justice System.* Monterey, Cal.: Brooks/Cole.

WILLIS, C. F. (1983), *The Use, Effectiveness and Impact of Police Stop and Search Powers.* Home Office Research and Planning Unit Paper No. 15. London: Home Office.

22

Gender and Crime

Frances Heidensohn

Any account of the connections between gender and crime must begin by confronting a paradox; this is that while these links have long been known to take distinctive forms wherever crime has been systematically recorded, their significance was ignored and marginalized throughout much of the history of criminology. In the latter part of the twentieth century, however, this situation was transformed; from being a criminological Cinderella this topic became the focus of a great deal of attention and the source of some of the major developments in the field. In order to cover this subject, then, it is important to explain its prehistory and standing as well as addressing the extensive material which appeared in the modern period of high fertility.

First it is necessary to clarify the terms being used and to outline the main aspects of the subject which will be covered in this chapter. *Longman's Dictionary* (1984) defines gender simply as 'sex', but for social scientists 'sex' and 'gender' are usually differentiated. 'Sex' is commonly used to describe the innate biological characteristics of humans, their femaleness or maleness. 'Gender' on the other hand, covers the social characteristics and usages associated with one sex or the other. Since such roles and customs can vary and be modified it follows that 'masculine' and 'feminine', the terms applied to the respective genders, are much more flexible than 'female' and 'male'. It is possible, for example, to describe a woman's clothing as 'masculine' or a man as having a 'feminine sensibility'. (Biological sex can, of course, be altered too, but this usually requires drastic surgical and pharmaceutical intervention as well as presenting the individual concerned with vast social and legal challenges to surmount.)

Of course the definition of what is a woman (or a man) is by no means always straightforward (Edwards, 1984). Once one considers the meaning of gender roles to individuals and groups, the situation becomes very complex. It has been increasingly recognized, for instance, that differences between the experiences of ethnic groups may be as great as those between men and women (Arnold, 1990; Chigwada, 1991). In this chapter I try as far as possible to acknowledge such differences where they matter, as well as noting and analysing the important similarities between categories and persons.

In practice, most social enquiry is concerned with issues both of sex and of gender, although the second term is used more often because it covers both aspects of innate and acquired characteristics and the interaction between them and society. In the case of crime there is an elision made between the two forms of categorization which has considerable salience for the study of this field. For as long as systematic records of crime have been kept the sex of offenders has been noted. Indeed sex has sometimes had significance as a legal category in relation to criminal acts. While criminal law broadly applies equally to women and to men, there have been, and still are, some exceptions. Male homosexual acts have at certain times been defined as criminal in most western countries, while lesbian acts have not. Criminal codes often treat prostitute activities of males and females differently. Under English common law women charged with felony committed in the presence of their husbands (except murder and treason) could rely on the presumption that they acted under compulsion (Mannheim, 1965: 691–3) until this was abolished in 1925.

Primarily, noting the sex of offenders was necessary for routine purposes in the criminal justice system, especially once segregation was practised in prisons (Smith, 1962; Zedner, 1991). Obviously, only the sex of known offenders can be registered, and thus data on this topic are subject to even more limitations than those considered in general elsewhere in this volume (see Maguire and Smith, this volume). Despite these reservations, certain trends and patterns in female criminality as compared with male have long been observed. In summary these are:

(a) that women commit a small share of all crimes;
(b) that their crimes are fewer, less serious, more rarely professional and less likely to be repeated;
(c) in consequence, women are represented in very small numbers in penal establishments.

The attentive reader will see at once that I have moved from discussing the question of sex and gender to a focus on *women*, or women compared with men. This shift reflects what has happened historically in the history of criminology, although, as I shall argue later in this chapter, masculine gender and its relation to crime became an area of increasing interest in the late twentieth century. There is a marked contrast between this situation and that which obtained during what can be described as the prehistory of this subject. As I have already suggested, a grasp of this history is important in understanding more recent developments.

THE PREHISTORY OF GENDER AND CRIME

It has often been asserted that the subject of women and crime suffered from criminological neglect until the late twentieth century. While this statement is broadly true, it does need some qualification. Female criminality was *relatively* neglected and was treated in certain very specific ways.

Accounts of female criminality published during the nineteenth century and the earlier twentieth century can be usefully divided into two groups: practical criminologies and essays at theory which were frequently characterized by their psychological or biological reductionism. By practical criminologies I mean that range of mainly Victorian studies which dwelt on women's social and moral position and especially their vulnerability to 'falling' into crime and deviance. They were written by prison chaplains (Horsley, 1887), doctors (Acton, 1857), journalists (Mayhew, 1861), lawyers (Pike, 1876), and amateur social scientists concerned with 'denouncing casinos and dancing saloons as sources of female corruption' (cited in Zedner, 1991: 61). As Zedner points out, many of these descriptions locate the origins of female crime in the same sources as those of male: variously poor urban conditions and moral weakness (*ibid.*). Most, however, she notes, regarded women as more vulnerable because their 'purity', and hence their whole moral being could be at risk.

Later in the nineteenth century, women criminals became, as did their male conterparts, the subjects of enquiry of positivist criminology. Lombroso and Ferrero's *The Female Offender* (1895) is the best known example of this trend and the only one generally cited. Their study does deal, albeit crudely, with both the sex crime ratio and 'generalizability' (see below) problems. In the case of the latter, they failed to find the numbers of 'born female criminals' marked by physical, atavistic traits which they had anticipated. They argued that all women were less evolved than men, and thus closer to primitive types, but also that natural selection had bred out the criminal tendencies among women, since more 'masculine' women did not find sexual partners. Most of the flaws in positivism, and the inadequacies of Lombroso's methods, are represented in this work.

It is however, notable for several features. First, it has frequently been used to represent psychological and bio-determinist theories of female crime. Secondly, it survived and was cited as a convincing commentary on female criminality (Mannheim, 1965) long after comparable work on males had been rejected (Heidensohn, 1985), and has, it has been argued, cast a long shadow over women's penal treatment (Dobash *et al.*, 1986). Both of the key problems of gender and crime are tackled in *La Donna Delinquente* (*The Female Offender*), but it is characteristic of so much of this literature and other, related, types that such issues are not discussed in studies of male offenders. Another feature of Lombroso's work was that, as modern scholarship had demonstrated, it was a contribution to a range of complex debates about criminality and social control in late nineteenth century and early twentieth century Europe (Beirne, 1988; Garland, 1985*a*) in which Lombroso was subject to serious challenge. What is fascinating is that, while the force of some of these criticisms had been overestimated (see, for instance, Beirne's appraisal of *The English Convict* as unsuccessful, 1988), evaluations of Lombroso and Ferrero have been much more neglected. Frances Kellor, an American sociologist, conducted comparative studies which did not substantiate Lombroso's findings, and indeed showed social and environmental factors to be much more important.

The consequence of this was a scenario reminiscent of *Sleeping Beauty*. Whereas the rest of the criminological world moved on from positivism, embracing in particular a series of sociological theories of crime and deviance, female crime was cut off from most of this as though by thickets of thorn (Smart, 1977; Leonard, 1982). Those few studies which did appear in the first half of the twentieth century seem very isolated and lack a base. Pollak's treatise (1951) I have characterized (1985) as curiously outside and unrelated to all the fervour of work of the time on 'strain' theory and sub-cultures. It exists in an ahistoric limbo in which women, as domestic servants and full-time housewives, commit *more* crime than men, but keep this hidden through devious means and by exploiting men's innate chivalry. This relative neglect and isolation in research on female crime was a major target of criticism for the many, and many varieties of feminist criminologists, who were to transform work on this subject in the late twentieth century. Their primary focus was on women and crime, and thus their central theme is that in ignoring women's experiences of crime as both perpetrator and victim the subject was impoverished (Smart, 1977; Heidensohn, 1968, 1985). Implicitly however, this criticism also extends to the limitations of all studies of crime which do not address questions of gender. In order to demonstrate how central these questions are we shall now look in detail at evidence and analysis of the configurations of gender in three areas: crime, criminal justice, and punishment. Given the emphases in past and recent studies in these areas, the main focus will be on women, but comparisons will also be made between women and men and the importance of gender to each topic will also be addressed.

WOMEN, MEN, AND CRIME

'Women commit much less crime than men do' is a statement that has achieved the status of a truth universally acknowledged. Closer examination leads, however, to some qualification. On most comparisons, the differences are remarkable, robust, and, as we shall see, appear to be valid. The overall female share of recorded crime appears to be fairly stable: in England and Wales in 1984, 84 per cent of known offenders were male, and in 1995 the figure was 82 per cent (Barclay, 1995, and Home Office, 1996). Of the population born in 1953 34 per cent of men, but only 8 per cent of women had a conviction for an indictable or other serious offence by the age of 40 (see Figure 22.1).

Remarkably similar figures for the female proportion of arrests are shown in one US survey (Poe-Yamagata and Butts, 1996) (Table 22.1). The authors of this study emphasize the shift in the gender ratio over the period, although this is of three percentage points. Yet in another review, of a much longer time period, Steffensmeier concludes that, for 'trends in female crime: it's still a

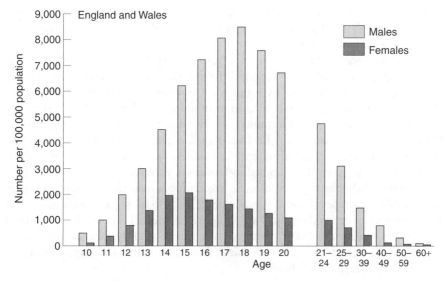

Fig. 22.1: Persons found guilty of, or cautioned for, indictable offences per 100,000 population by age group, 1995

Table 22.1 Female proportion of juvenile and adult arrests, 1983, 1988, and 1993

	Female proportion of arrests of persons under age 18			Female proportion of arrests of persons under age 18		
Most serious offence	1983	1988	1993	1983	1988	1993
*All Arrests**	21%	22%	24%	16%	17%	19%
Violent Crime Index	11	11	13	11	11	13
Murder/non-negligent manslaughter	11	7	6	14	13	10
Forcible rape	1	2	2	0	1	1
Robbery	7	7	9	8	9	9
Aggravated assault	16	15	18	13	13	15
Property Crime Index	20	20	24	24	26	27
Burglary	7	7	10	7	9	10
Larceny-theft	27	26	31	31	32	33
Motor vehicle theft	11	10	14	8	10	10
Arson	10	10	12	14	16	17
Weapons offence	6	7	8	8	8	8
Drug abuse offence	16	12	11	14	16	17

*Includes offences not detailed below.

Data Sources: Federal Bureau of Investigation, *Crime in the United States 1983*, *Crime in the United States 1988*, and *Crime in the United States 1993*.

man's world' and that 'overall, the pattern of change was similar for both sexes', although he does note increases in women's share of larceny, fraud, drug offences, and assault (1995).

Such differences seem to be common across a variety of nations and cultures. In surveying material on Europe, I found that 'crime is still an activity over-whelmingly dominated by men in all European countries. In France in 1986 . . . of persons . . . dealt with in criminal proceedings 81.27% were male and 18.73% female . . . in Germany . . . 79.5% were male and 20.5% female'. Similar, or lower shares, can be found in the Netherlands and Scandinavia (Heidensohn, 1991). This apparently consistent pattern has led some commentators to suggest that women offenders are 'only 10% of the trouble'. Considering different types of offence and changes over time, a more complex and qualified picture emerges. Women contribute to all types of offending, but their share varies considerably. Taking figures of violent offenders for England and Wales during the 1980s, women's share rose slightly from 9 per cent in 1979 to 11.2 per cent in 1989 (Home Office, 1990). In other types of crime, there is considerable variation.

Arguments about whether female crime was rising at a faster rate than male and that thus the female share was going up have been a highly contended criminological issue since the 1970s. Indeed, this is one of the few topics to do with women and crime to excite widespread attention. (Heidensohn, 1989: chapter 5). The issue was first raised by Freda Adler (and in a more modified form by Rita Simon) who argued

(a) that female crime rates had been rising more rapidly in the late 1960s and early 1970s;
(b) women offenders were changing their patterns of offending to more 'masculine' styles, becoming more aggressive and violent and that this was
(c) due to the growth of the modern women's movement (1975 and 1975). 'Liberation', in short, 'causes crime'.

These contentions have been much discussed and analysed. Two aspects of the thesis need to be distinguished: that of rising female crime rates and that of the influence of feminism. On the first, no very clear picture emerges and, given what we know of the limitations of such data (see Maguire, this volume) great caution is necessary. Smart, for instance, taking long time-series for England and Wales, finds that female crime rates were already rising at a faster rate than male long before the advent of the modern women's movement (1979), although Austin is critical of some of her interpretation (1981). Austin has also argued that male and female crime rates will eventually converge (1993). Smart pointed out, too, the dangers to which interpretations of figures on female criminality are *additionally* subject: because numbers are so small they are highly susceptible to shifts in policing, recording, and other policies. Further, measuring percentage changes may give an exaggerated view—an increase from five to ten cases is 100 per cent.

Authors who tried to define and measure female emancipation and to test its relationship with crime experienced difficulty and were scarcely convincing (Box and Hale, 1983*b*). They found little plausible linkage. Critics of this view have argued that a theory of marginalization or impoverishment would be more plausible (Chapman, 1980; Carlen, 1990).

Modern historical work on crime has experienced a renaissance and studies of women offenders have been one offshoot of this. They enrich, and also complicate, the patterns of crime we are trying to unravel. Writing of Britain in the eighteenth century, Mclynn says that 'Only 12 per cent of the accused in the home counties in 1782–7 were female' (1989: 128). Nonetheless, Feeley and Little (1991), taking a sample of Old Bailey cases tried between 1687 and 1912, found 45 per cent of defendants were women. Others have pointed out, none the less, that women participated in food riots in the premodern period (Beattie, 1975). Figures for these, and earlier, periods need to be treated with even more circumspection than those from today. In particular, they record such phenomena as 'The Criminal Classes'; Zedner notes that:

Overall there was a considerable decline in those designated as the 'criminal classes'. Over the period 1860–90 they fell by more than half. The number of women fell at roughly the same rate as men, remaining at around a fifth of the total in this category over the period [Zedner, 1991: 20].

She concludes that this relatively low rate was due to the exclusion of prostitutes, vagrants, and tramps. In terms of convictions, Zedner notes 'overall, women's crimes made up a steady 17% of all summary convictions' (1991: 34), with drunkenness, assault, and larceny the commonest types of offences. In contrast to the steady state in summary jurisdiction 'over the second half of the nineteenth century, women formed a declining proportion of those proceded against by indictment . . . (from 27% of the total in 1867 to only 19% by 1890)' (1991: 36). Zedner's detailed work on nineteenth century data confirms on the whole the 'modest share' view of female as compared with male. She also notes some reporting of a decline in convictions of women for serious offences by the end of the century (1992: 23).

Other writers have asserted that women's share of criminality declined relatively in certain modern periods (Mannheim, 1965; Feest, 1985). Boritch and Hagan (1990), taking the period 1850 to 1950 in Toronto, document such a trend and claim that this was due to the success of moral entrepreneurs of the first wave of feminism who provided diversion from criminality and stigma through non-punitive interventions in women's lives. Jones also records a fall in female crime, 'The mid Victorian years witnessed a concerted campaign against the crime and violence associated with "women of the streets" and a sustained fall in reported female attacks on property and persons, especially by the very young' (1982: 7). Most historians are both more cautious or rely either on changed practices of recording, controlling, and classifying crime and misdemeanours (Walkowitz, 1980), 'chivalry' arguments (Mclynn, 1989), views about the changed nature of femininity in Victorian Britain (Zedner, 1991) or combinations of all three.

TOO FEW TO COUNT?

Women's low share of recorded crime can be substantiated, with certain reservations. While for decades, as I pointed out above, this finding proved to be of little interest to criminologists, this situation changed in the 1970s and considerable efforts were expended in searching for the hidden iceberg of female crime. Pollak had, of course, already (1950) insisted that hidden female crime far exceeded revealed and concealed male crime, but he did not evince any new sources of material, relying instead on assertions about thefts by domestic servants. Several modern writers have sought to demonstrate a similar point, albeit less dramatically, by using self report studies, 'bystander' or observer accounts, or victim surveys (Smith and Visher, 1980; Gold, 1970; Mawby, 1980; Pratt, 1980; Burney, 1990; Hindelang, 1979; and see Box, 1983 for a review). While many of these researchers did find 'hidden' female crime, they also found hidden male crime too and do not suggest that the ratios derived from official data should be reversed.

DOMESTIC 'SECRETS'

Our understanding of other features of the gender ratio has not, in any case remained static. The subject of victimization, and the contributions of feminists amongst others, to its 'discovery' are covered elsewhere in this volume. It is important to note how the focus on the 'private' harms perpetrated within the home in domestic violence, physical, and sexual abuse of children alters the gender ratio adversely for men, since they are largely, though not exclusively the offenders in such crimes. While measures of incidence are shadowy, victim surveys do suggest that there are low reporting rates for such offences and yet a high rate of distress (Jones *et al.*, 1986; Hamner and Saunders, 1984; Stanko, 1990). Serious sexual crimes such as rape also have low reporting rates because of women's fear of shame and of police and court procedures (see Maguire, Reiner, and Zedner, this volume). Some attempts have been made to redress the gender 'imbalance' in such private and personal crimes. Dobash and Dobash (1991: 258ff.) review family violence research in the United States which seeks to show that there is an equivalence in violence between spouses with husbands more likely to be victims than wives. The Dobashes also review what they call 'violence-against-women research' and conclude that empirical studies conclusively support an asymmetric view which further imbalances the gender ratio.

Two Home Office studies published together provide useful counterpoints on domestic violence. Mirlees-Black (1995) considers the complexities of its incidence, noting the 1992 British Crime Survey (BCS) estimate of 'one in ten women who have lived with a partner have at some time experienced physical violence'. Bush and Hood-Williams describe an ethnographic study of a London housing estate where 'domestic violence . . . may even be seen as part of ordinary life. The climate of acceptance ensures that few will seek the assistance of statutory agencies and that those who do will first have to overcome the conviction that they brought the violence on themselves' (1995: 11).

Other related topics have also been considered in this way. Child sexual abuse by women, including mothers, has been the subject of some concern (Kidscape, 1992) even though the proportion of women carrying out such acts is still acknowledged to be very small. Research on abuse of children in the home by the British National Society for the Prevention of Cruelty to Children (Creighton and Noyes, 1989) is significant in that their data enable comparisons to be made of the relative risks to which children are exposed with parents, step-parents etc. This study, based on some 8,274 children on NSPCC registers, indicates the *suspected* abusers. In the period covered (1983–7) natural mothers were implicated in 33 per cent and natural fathers in 29 per cent of the physical injury cases. When the figures were adjusted to take account of which parent the child lived with then the natural fathers were implicated in 61 per cent and mothers in 36 per cent of cases. Moreover, these figures, as the authors point out, make no allowance for time spent with children, and especially not of time alone with them. Such findings, based as they are on observations and not on police evidence or court verdicts, may be even less robust than official crime records. Whether they record assumptions rather than acts, there is perhaps some significance in their consistency with all the other material noted in this section.

WOMEN AND POLICING

The nature and tasks of modern policing have been much discussed both in academic and public debate (Reiner, 1985; Reiner and Shapland, 1987; and see Reiner, this volume). In particular, the culture of police agencies and the impact this has on their activities have been anatomized as based on macho values, stressing aggression, sexism, racism, and giving status to serious crime work (Smith and Gray, 1983; Young, 1991). There are differing views on how far attitudes derived from such values affect police in their work with citizens (Smith and Gray, 1983). What is not in doubt is that many researchers, and representatives of minority groups and, increasingly, the general public, have become critical of police behaviour towards citizens and suspects. The police themselves have recognized this and have tried to alter policies and procedures in response.

Police operate within a very considerable range of discretion, processing only a proportion of incidents and citizens through to a full criminal charge (and being limited at that stage by the Crown Prosecution Service). How women fare in such encounters is another considerably contested area and one on which it is much harder to reach conclusions than on criminal behaviour. No record exists of *all* police–public encounters. However, there are significant sex differences in reported contacts. Thus in the Policy Studies Institute survey of policing in London, more men than women (63 per cent to 51 per cent) had had recent contacts with the police. Class and race complicated the issue: 87 per cent of unemployed men, but only 16 per cent of Asian women, reported direct encounters. Surveys do show that frequent contact with the police lowers the esteem in which they are held and this may help to explain women's slightly greater support for police. It is particularly their treatment of *men* from ethnic minorities (including the Irish) that has been linked to the cop culture discussed above.

Women, it has been argued by many writers, benefit from the values the canteen culture gives rise to (Morris, 1987: 80–1). They are seen as in need of protection, not punishment, and accorded the respect of chivalry. Indeed this view was long adduced in explanation of lower rates of recorded female crime (Mannheim, 1965). More recent work suggests a more complex picture in which 'demeanour' (Piliavin and Briar, 1964) is a key factor in determining police reactions as well as seriousness and recidivism (Harris, 1992).

Gender appears to be only one factor in determining police decisions: 'to be older, apologetic and "respectable" is as advantageous for men as for women and gender is only one of many variables to consider in the complex process of police arresting behaviour' (Harris, 1992: 95). However, there does not appear to be a neatly constructed demonology from least to most deviant, cross-tabulated by sex, demeanour, and aggression. If there were, as Visher noted (1983: 19), then violent women offenders would be at one extreme, yet they do not seem so to feature (and see Allen, 1987).

The opposite view to the 'police as knights-in-shining-armour' has been advocated from a growing number of sources in the 1980s and 1990s. These fall broadly into two groupings: those who have examined police treatment of women and girls as *victims*, especially of domestic violence and sexual crimes, and those who have encountered the police as members of 'deviant' groups such as political protestors, and members of sexual and other minorities.

Female victimization is discussed in detail elsewhere in this book (Zedner, this volume), as are the reported attitudes and practices of the police and other agencies, and the changes, or attempted changes, in procedures made in response to widespread criticism. Several writers suggest that police officers transfer their low evaluation of women as victims to women as offenders and respond to them as women and thus as inferior (Jones, 1987; and see Dunhill, 1989, for a selection). The louder 'voices' which many women have sought to express as a result of modern feminism have given graphic details of some experiences (e.g. Peckham, 1985; Reynolds, 1991).

Evidence, in short, on this topic is patchy, and conclusions necessarily tentative. It is clear from criminal statistics that cautioning is used more heavily for female than male offenders. Yet this seems to be mainly based on the less serious and less frequent nature of female offending.

Several groups of deviant women have reported particularly repressive treatment by the police and accused them of especially harsh treatment. Prostitutes have long complained, and more recently campaigned, as have others on their behalf, about such treatment. The nineteenth century Contagious Disease Acts, and the opposition organized against them (Petrie, 1971) have been followed by a series of such groupings in the twentieth century (see below). Høigard and Finstad, in their study (1992) of street prostitution in Norway, describe the women's fear of police brutality, sexual advances, and their failure to offer protection against dangerous clients. McLeod outlines a somewhat different pattern in Britain. Harassment and entrapment were reported, but also a degree of accommodation (1982: 106).

While street prostitutes are one, untypical group of women who have frequent contact with the police, the converse is true of the other deviant women who make complaints about how the police have treated them. The militant suffragettes were among the first political protestors to object to police manhandling of them, a tradition carried on by the Greenham Common women and other demonstrators (Strachey, 1978; A. Young, 1991). What distinguishes these accounts from those of men is that they often allege sexual abuse and humiliation. These are still more marked in the episodes recounted by lesbian, Irish, and black women (e.g. Natzler, O'Shea, Heaven, and Mars, 1989). Organizations which monitor such policing grew in the 1970s and 1980s, but were affected by cuts in aid to voluntary organizations (GLC, 1985). While such stories are harrowing without systematic monitoring, it is impossible to tell how typical they are, or how gender specific. Many accounts have parallels in the histories of male offenders, although sexual abuse and humiliation are usually reserved for homosexual men.

Most discussions of these issue are based on the sexist notion that all police officers are male and the stereotyped one that 'the police' are a unified body with common aims and procedures. Growing numbers of women entered the police in the late twentieth century, an average of 10 per cent in the United States, with up to 20 per cent in some cities. In Britain 14 per cent of all officers were women, with 25 per cent of recruits being female (Heidensohn, 1992). Women's entry into policing in both countries was promoted in the late nineteenth century and early twentieth century precisely to provide protection to female and juvenile offenders and victims, which it was felt they did not receive from an all-male force (Carrier, 1988; Feinman, 1986). For more than fifty years, until integration in the 1970s, small numbers of female officers worked in this fashion in both systems.

Both the pioneer policewomen of the early days and present-day officers report extensive harassment and abuse by their male colleagues (Heidensohn, 1992). Young has (Heidensohn, 1994*a*) given an extensive account of such attitudes and behaviour in a British force (1991). A series of studies (Anderson *et al.*, 1993; Brown and Heidensohn, 1996) document widespread harassment of female officers by their male colleagues in Britain and many other countries. Reports of scandals have also focussed public attention on these issues (Halford, 1993).

Very little work has been done to demonstrate whether female officers treat female offenders in distinctive ways (see Heidensohn, 1985 and 1992, for reviews). Carey (1977) found no differences. Some studies report women as being more punitive towards their own sex (Worrall, 1990). But women in law enforcement agencies handle all their cases within a male-dominated system. They may either be more censorious or feel the need to appear so (see Heidensohn, 1992, for one such episode).

There are further questions, raised increasingly in more thoughtful analyses, to do both with variations within groups and systems and with standards and perceptions of fairness and appropriateness. As I have suggested elsewhere (1985, 1987), women are policed by the same agencies and using the same laws as men are. Some, however, perceive and protest about their treatment in distinctive ways. Partly this seems to be due to their experience of much greater levels of informal social control 'outwith' the formal agencies. Husbands, partners, families, social workers, the church, can all be seen as giving particular attention to assuring the conformity of women (Heidensohn, 1985). Gender is, in short, a variable of some significance in debates about policing. Primarily this is because official policing has been seen as an extremely masculine occupation, reserved for men. As a result, women's experience of it may be more or less harsh, appropriate or inappropriate, largely, though not entirely, depending on how far this situation has been remedied. Because it was long assumed, in Britain especially, that gender-based policing was normal, its failures in this and other respects have been tackled only late in the twentieth century.

WOMEN AND SENTENCING

We have already observed that gender has its greatest impact on recorded patterns of offending. With some important exceptions it is the differences which this gives rise to which are reflected in sentencing patterns. Most notably, the numbers of women in prison are small at any one time (about 1,800—2,000 during the 1990s). Moreover, they form a very small percentage of the total population which is overwhelmingly male: the ratio is around 30:1. However, the numbers of women sentenced to immediate imprisonment grew faster than comparable figures for males for much of the 1980s, although there was a fall for both from 1987–90. Many women in prison are there as untried or unsentenced prisoners, and it has been argued, since many of the former are not subsequently imprisoned, that women are subject to 'punitive remands' (Heidensohn, 1985). Whereas nearly 20 per cent of males convicted of indictable offences go to prison, only 5 per cent of females do so.

Courts appear to use the full range of the tarriff less for women than for men despite their apparent suitability for diversionary or alternative sentences (Moxon, 1988). About one fifth of adult female offenders are the subject of probation orders, very few receive community service orders, and the use of fines declined during the 1980s, while discharges were used more widely. Alternatives to women's imprisonment have been developed at the local level (Carlen, 1990) but have not yet led to its abolition.

At first sight, then, gender might not seem to be a key variable in sentencing. Rather women's low levels of offending, mainly property-related and non-violent crimes could be seen as the basis for their treatment. However, as I shall discuss below, arguments both about chivalry afforded to women and about their being, under some circumstances, more punitively dealt with, have been discussed in modern academic and popular debate (Kennedy, 1992). It is certainly true that females fit awkwardly, if at all, into most parts of the criminal justice system and present puzzles and problems to it. Typically perhaps, the Home Office volumes, *Criminal Statistics* (1992 etc.), give far less detail and no graphics on the sentencing of women.

GENDER RATIOS AND GENDER QUESTIONS

The gender ratio problem, according to Daly and Chesney-Lind, leads to the following queries: 'Why are women less likely than men to be involved in crime? Conversely, why are men more crime-prone than women? What explains gender differences in rates of arrest and in variable types of criminal activity?' (1988: 515). They express some scepticism about finding answers to such questions given the limitations of existing data and juxtapose what they call gender ratio scholarship to work on generalizability, that is on questions of theory. 'Do theories of men's crime apply to women? Can the logic of such theories be modified to include women?' (1988: 514). They insist that both need to be 'bracketed' together (1988: 519). How have explanations of male and female criminality developed and how far in practice have answers to these questions been found?

FEMINIST APPROACHES TO CRIMINOLOGY

I have already suggested that there was a prehistory to the study of this field. Its modern cultivation can be said to have started in the late 1960s as one of the by-products of modern second wave feminism. Definitions of feminism abound (Mitchell and Oakley, 1986; Stanley and Wise, 1984) and will not be rehearsed here. Being 'woman-centred' and stressing the importance of gender in social structures and relations are at least two key components. As far as criminology is concerned, there are, if anything, greater problems. Gelsthorpe and Morris (1988) seek to define a canon of work which has certain core features, although in a later account they suggest a diversity of perspectives (1990) while Smart doubts either the possibility or validity of such an enterprise (1981, 1990). I am sceptical about an 'add and stir' approach, simply mixing feminism into criminology, I do recognize that there have been considerable contributions made by scholars who would accept a feminist label to the field and that this may be one way of defining it (1985, 1989).

Precise demarcations may elude us. Of the changes in assumptions, above all in this part of the subject, and of the massive contribution to the literature, there can be no question. Scholars from other perspectives began to write much more extensively about gender at the very end of the twentieth century. In particular, major mainstream texts notably started to include gender as a key theme (Braithwaite, 1989; Hagan, 1989). What is striking, however, is that they were doing so *in response* to the criticisms raised by feminists and also to the sheer volume and range of work which they had produced. I therefore make no apology for starting with these perspectives and will include other contributions within that framework.

PIONEERING

It is useful, if arbitrary, to divide feminist criminological studies into two phases: of pioneering and consolidation. The pioneers defined the agenda for the study of gender, which remains broadly unaltered. Consolidation has seen a range of studies produced in response to that agenda. It is now possible to suggest what the future might possibly hold too.

In articles published in the late 1960s, Marie Andrée Bertrand (1969) and I (1968) drew attention to the neglect of women in the study of crime and to the stereotyped distortions which were imposed by those few authors who did address this topic on their female subjects. There was a widespread tendency, for example, to sexualize all female deviance and to ignore any rational or purposive part of it. It was the gender ratio problem which provided the stimulus for these critiques: 'the patterns . . . of male and of female deviance were long ago observed, . . . nevertheless, the focus of research has been very much away from this particular area' (Heidensohn, 1968: 160–1). It was this lack which was emphasized in all the early pioneer work. More precisely perhaps, two aspects were stressed: 'Orthodox, control-oriented criminology . . . has virtually ignored the existence of female offenders . . . . An important consequence of this lack of development has been the total neglect of any critical analysis of the common-sense perceptions of female criminality inform- ing classical . . . and contemporary studies' (Smart, 1977: 3). In short, *absence* from the literature and/or *distortion* of their experiences when present were the accusations levelled at criminologists.

Successive studies from this phase filled out this picture. Leonard (1982) examined major theorists in detail showing how their ideas failed to deal with the gender gap and urged that women might be fitted back in again. Milman (1982) analysed in depth the appreciative stance of labelling theorists such as Howard Becker (1963). Central to Becker's approach was to take the perspective of the deviant as social critic, yet in discussing jazz musicians' wives it was the men's view point alone which he quoted.

IMPACT OF FEMINIST PERSPECTIVES

Reviewing British criminological research of the past decade Jefferson and Shapland declared 'feminism was *the* growth area in criminology . . . and now has a very powerful presence in the field . . . . However . . . one can argue that *despite* the massive growth about women, crime, law and criminal justice . . . the experience of women remained marginal to the *criminological* enterprise' (1994: 282). This judgement provides one challenging summary of the impact of feminist work on criminology. The body of this work is now so great that readers should refer to summaries and the extensive bibliographies and reviews they offer (Gelsthorpe and Morris, 1990; Rafter and Heidensohn, 1995; Heidensohn, 1996). Here I shall outline developments under three major headings:

1. *Women and crime*
   In what ways gender affects criminal activity.
2. *Women and justice*
   How women (as compared with men) experience the criminal justice and penal systems.
3. *Key concepts*
   The concepts and approaches which have been developed to provide theories of the relationships of gender to crime and criminology.

WOMEN AND CRIME

In the 1970s Smart (1977) suggested that women's crimes had been ignored because they did not constitute a major social problem. She was concerned about the consequences of possible exposure, fearful of what I later called the Falklands factor, the dire consequences of moving from the periphery to the centre of world attention. Many aspects of female offending have been studied since then. Female criminals have found their own voices (Carlen, 1985; Reynolds, 1991) or observers have presented the perspectives of women who murder their husbands (Browne, 1987), who are prostitutes (McLeod,

1982; Miller, 1986), are members of violent gangs (Campbell, 1981 and 1984), take crack cocaine (Maher, 1990), or are involved in other serious forms of offending (Daly, 1991). Many of these studies are characterized by giving offending women a voice, and are small-scale and ethnographic in approach. Several large-scale studies of female offenders have been conducted in the United States, notably on homicide (Jurik and Russ, 1990; Davies, 1996). Three characteristics are attributed to female offending in these studies. They suggest that women do act with a sense of agency, if sometimes a distinctive one, that their offences constitute purposive action. Finally they contribute to the (re)discovery of female iniquity.

Agency

Much of the 'prehistoric' work on women cited above stressed the irrational nature of their actions. Their behaviour was determined by their physiology or their instincts. Such ideas have not been absent from more modern debate, for example in relation to the effects of menstruation (Dalton, 1980), although caution is expressed now (Vanezis, 1991). In contrast, the majority of modern studies have emphasized how rational and purposive were the women offenders whom they studied.

Carlen, for example, in a series of ethnographic studies of convicted women in the United Kingdom has shown how they are caught in two constricting structures, the gender bind and the class bind, and yet how their choosing to offend and the type of offence was often made on the basis of carefully weighed consideration. 'Property crime was *chosen* because certain types (e.g. shoplifting and cheque fraud) were seen to be so "easy" and because women, most women expressed inhibitions about engaging in prostitution' (1988: 34). She does stress also the variety of the offending patterns and the short-term nature of their rewards (1988: 45). Such emphasis is found in other kinds of deviant activities too. Many social researchers have sought to challenge the view of drug users as 'dope fiends', helpless addicts, hooked after one shot or smoke and at the mercy of evil pushers (Pearson, 1987; MacGregor, 1989). While women drug users have been studied far less often the same notion of at least initial choice, occurs. 'In analysing the career of the woman addict, I found her career is inverted and that is the essence of its social attraction' (Rosenbaum, 1981: 11). Maher using her field research amongst young crack-cocaine users in New York, is highly critical of the official response which defines pregnant women who use crack as irresponsible and criminal (1990). She argues that (a) many of them manage their lives well and (b) deliver healthy infants in most cases.

In a somewhat similar way, Mcleod (1982) and Miller (1986) suggest that prostitution is one kind of reasonable, if restricted and ultimately destructive, choice made by some women whose other options are very restricted. Even grave violence, such as homicide, has been depicted as the 'last option' when no others exist in battering relations, when, it is argued 'Women . . . are extremely knowledgeable about the patterns of violence in their relationships' (Browne, 1987: 184). Such views are supported by several appraisals of historical material on violence perpetuated by women which shows that they were, even in the eighteenth and nineteenth centuries able to make skilful use of conventions about femininity to obtain leniency (McLynn, 1989; Hartmann, 1984; Jones, 1991; Heidensohn, 1991).

Contributions from all these sources suggested the development of what Daly has termed the 'leading scenario' for a typical entry for women into a career of petty crime. In this 'scenario' women whose lives are constrained by poverty and poor education 'choose' petty crime. Daly herself, however, has argued that it is possible to find a variety of 'pathways' to criminality for women. She records major routes to crime which are distinctive for women.

Street women
Harmed and harming women
Battered women
Drug connected women
Other [Daly, 1994: 47–8].

The first three of these pathways Daly found paralleled in the lives of male offenders, but they also included a significant category she labelled 'costs and excesses of masculinity' (1994: 67–8).

The (Re)discovery of Iniquity

The study of female offenders has undergone various phases since the 1960s. During one of these far more attention was devoted to women as victims than as perpetrators of crime. This was true at both an academic level (Stanko, 1984, 1990; Hammer and Saunders, 1984; Dobash and Dobash, 1979, 1992) and also at a practical, policy level where refuges for victims of domestic violence were set up (Pizzey, 1974), rape crisis centres founded (Anna T, 1988), and helplines for victims of sexual abuse instituted (Parton, 1992). For many, this remains the most important contribution which modern feminism has made to criminology and criminal justice (Lupton and Gillespie, 1994). It is credited by Young with being a key factor in the shaping of left realism (1986).

Crucial although this development was (it is explored more fully by Zedner elsewhere in this volume), it did mean in effect that offending by women was much less a focus of enquiry. In the late 1980s and 1990s, however, this changed and the range and variety of female crime were explored rather more fully, especially violence committed by them. Partly this was again stimulated by a confrontation with older debates which were re-emerging in new forms. The notion of the especially evil women, the 'witch' of mythology, had stalked the texts of earlier writers such as Lombroso and Ferrero and Pollak. Adler and Simon had put forward the notion of a new, ruthless female criminal. The new factors lay in the approach taken, for example, by the American 'family violence' school, which argued (Dobash and Dobash, 1992) contrary to the arguments of many researchers in the field of domestic violence that as many women abused their husbands or partners as did the latter their wives and partners. Several notable court cases also focused on aspects of female offending, including the trial of a female serial killer and a notorious child death in New York which raised questions about women's acceptance of, or collusion in, the abuse of children (Johnson, 1991). The prominence of child abuse and child sexual abuse cases also led, as Parton points out (1992), to a focus on family interaction and the roles played by mothers in such cases. Several thorough journalistic studies covered women's involvement in international terrorism (Macdonald, 1991), and homicide (Jones, 1991; Reynolds, 1991), while a spate of books appeared covering aspects of female violence (Lloyd, 1993; Krista, 1993). For the most part, these did not attempt to theorize women's participation in violence, although one approach did suggest that gender roles in the use of legitimate violence were important in understanding women's low share of such actions (Heidensohn, 1992*a*).

WOMEN AND JUSTICE

Much modern research on women and crime is marked by its engagement with debates from the past. This is nowhere more true than in relation to women's experiences of the criminal justice and penal systems. One old and commonly held view of why women's crime rates were so low was that the police, the courts, and other agencies extended 'chivalry' towards them. As a result they were protected from the full rigours of the law (Mannheim, 1965). Of course, we have already seen that the sex crime ratio differential is related more to a smaller 'pool' on which agencies may draw. Nevertheless, discussions have focused around this topic and a series of concepts which modify the notion of chivalry have been advanced and discussed. These include the notions of double deviance and double jeopardy, of stigma, and of the importance of formal and informal controls in the lives of women.

Chivalry

Several authors have reviewed and/or researched the respective treatment of women and men by the courts. Smith (1988) reviewing the British literature was unable to come to a clear-cut conclusion about whether men and women were treated in different ways by the courts, although the proposal of systematic chivalric bias is supported by Allen's study (1987), which showed violent women offenders receiving more sympathetic and individualized justice for serious crimes for which men got no comparable understanding. Other British researchers have found a more complex pattern in which courts appear to have somewhat conventional and stereotyped views of gender roles which they then reinforce with conviction and sentencing. Farrington and Morris (1983) found that apparent court leniency towards women was due to their lesser criminal records, while Eaton (1986) noted that men *and* women conforming to conventional roles were better treated than those such as homosexuals or single mothers. She stresses that gender expectations differed and that women were supposed to take much more responsibility for home-making and for domestic morality. Carlen (1983) also found Scottish sheriffs distinguishing between 'good' and 'bad' mothers and being prepared to sentence them accordingly. Worrall (1990) discerned a still more complex situation in which various agents and agencies contrived to play down and almost to 'lose' female offenders in the system.

In the United States, Daly (1989) found that it was children and the family, rather than women themselves, who were the focus of chivalry, or 'judicial paternalism', as the courts seek to support and conserve the fabric of society. In marked contrast, Player, in studying crime in an inner city area, found that black women were more likely to be stopped and questioned than white women were and that the police had different perceptions of them (1989). Daly, using a sample of matched pairs, in a study of New Haven felony court concluded that men and women were not sentenced differently for like crimes (1994: 259).

Double Deviance and Double Jeopardy and Stigma

Women's low share of recorded criminality is so well-known that it has significant consequences for those women who do offend. They are seen to have transgressed not only social norms but gender norms as well. As a result they may well, especially when informal sanctions are taken into account, feel that they are doubly punished. Carlen (1983, 1985) notes the prevalence of informal punishment of women by their partners. Several observers have stressed that concern over the anomalous position of deviant women leads to excessive zeal in their treatment, in remands in custody for reports and more medicalized interventions (Heidensohn, 1981; Edwards, 1984). Such approaches are particularly marked towards young girls whose minor sexual misdemeanours seem to be consistently more harshly handled than those of boys (Chesney-Lind, Parker *et al.*, 1981; Webb, 1984; Cain, 1989, and see the chapter on juveniles in this book). Such bias is not, as Gelsthorpe emphasizes (1989: 147), the sole determining factor in the way young people are handled by agencies. Other variables, such as organizational features, were important as well. Much evidence has accumulated to suggest that women suffer especially from the stigma associated with deviance. I have discussed the negative and positive forces that affect this (1996).

Much of the sense of injustice felt by women who come before the courts stems from their perceptions of such agencies as male-dominated and unsympathetic to them (Heidensohn, 1986; Scutt, 1981). Such feelings have been much increased by the greater publicity now given to crimes, especially violent crimes against women and what are often perceived as inappropriate reactions to them (Edwards, 1989). Such reactions are by no means consistent; they vary by age, ethnic background, and social class, and whether a woman has herself been a victim (Schlesinger *et al.*, 1992). What research does make clear is the considerable effect victimization can have on women's world views (Stanko, 1990; Walklate, 1990). Such was the concern about public reaction to these issues that the Home Office published a research paper reviewing evidence on the claim 'that the criminal justice system in England and Wales routinely discriminates against women' concluding 'that the weight of evidence is against this claim' (Hedderman and Hough, 1994: 1). The authors do not specify who makes these claims and outline some of the complexities in such 'disparity' studies. These problems are helpfully discussed in a review of gender bias studies by Steffensmeier *et al.* who conclude that factors other than gender influence court decisions (1993: 435). Farnworth and Teske in a California court study also insist on an interactive approach, noting the importance of age and race and gender differences and their interaction (1995: 41).

Too Few to Count in a Cinderella Service

Prison and prisonation studies of institutions for men were started much earlier than similar work on women (Sykes, 1956; Cressey, 1961). However, once the first studies had been completed in the United States in the 1960s (Ward and Kassebaum, 1966; Giallombardo, 1966) this is one area in which there was something of a catching-up exercise. Those pioneer studies insisted that the penal life of women was distinctive: largely because of their small numbers and restricted provision, female felons in the United States felt the pains of imprisonment, the loss of family and home, more acutely and there-fore set up alternative sexual relationships with one another (Ward and Kassebaum, 1966) or formed 'pseudo-families' to replace their missing kin. Subsequent research has focused on a series of critical issues:

(a) Are women 'too few to count' in the prison system?
(b) do regimes for women have special characteristics?
(c) do women respond differently to imprisonment?

Women, as the discussion above makes clear, are almost too few to count in the prison system. In England and Wales they constitute under 2,000 of pris-oners at any one time out of some 50,000. Ratios in other countries are similar (Pollock-Byrne, 1990). There tend to be two models of provision in the west. In federal systems such as Canada (Shaw, 1991) and Germany (Heidensohn, 1991) women tend to be incarcerated in small, scattered units. They lack basic facilities, such as for education and work. In central systems, such as France and the United Kingdom, they are concentrated in larger units and are often remote from family and friends (Cario, 1985; Heidensohn, 1991). The United States manages to combine both sets of disadvantages with federal peni-tentiaries too far away for women to sustain relationships with their children and local correctional facilities which suffer from being overcrowded and inadequate.

Prison for Women

Historically, women have usually been subject to broadly the same prison system as men (Forsythe, 1994), but with distinctive variations introduced from time to time. Welfare objectives have sometimes been to the fore, especially in the nineteenth century and in relation to women in moral danger. Rafter has catalogued the history of one such institution in the United States and noted how the lofty intentions of its founders led it to becoming additionally repressive of its female inmates who were infantilized by middle-class maternalism (1983, 1985).

Zedner describes the parallel history of two schemes in Britain primarily designed for women. Like the Massachusetts example, these had aims which were thought especially appropriate for women: diversion from the penal system, care and welfare of offenders, and providing them with moral protection. In the first programme from 1898–1914 a number of inebriate reformatories for habitual female drunkards were founded. The official assumption was 'that the female inebriate was the greatest problem and must therefore, be the main focus of their work' (Zedner, 1991: 233) and their purpose 'quite simply, to create of the enfeebled and degraded drunk a model of healthy, domesticated femininity' (1991: 237). In consequence a special system was set up with much emphasis on fresh air, clean living, and close supervision. The experiment failed.

Having defined the female inebriate primarily as a moral offender, reformatories operated on the promise that, by providing a sufficiently propitious environment and benign moral influences her cure could be achieved. Finding, instead, women resiliently resistant to the intentions of the regime, or so feeble-minded as to be irredeemable, the very momentum of the endeavour collapsed [Zedner, 1991: 263].

This initiative was followed by another in which assumptions about female deviance had changed and centred on a switch to 'feeble mindedness' as a prime cause of female crime and deviance and indeed, wider social evils (Simmons, 1978). Again, women, because of their reproductive role, were the especial focus of such policies, in which containment was emphasized (Zedner, 1991: 296). It was the undermining of its key assumptions which damaged this approach irreparably, although not before many women had been institutionalized to protect society and themselves.

As Zedner points out, such case histories are highly instructive. They show that when women are the subjects of special penal treatment it frequently results in the development of benevolently repressive regimes for them which emphasize dependency and traditional femininity and fail to provide the skills which could aid rehabilitation. Secondly, such programmes tend to be determined by assumed characteristics and needs of women, rather than well-explored evidence. Such cases are not merely found in the past. The rebuilding of Holloway Prison for women in Britain during the 1970s was based on views about women offenders being physically or mentally sick or both, and thus needing a therapeutic environment. The case was not proven and the design of the prison proved unsatisfactory and controversial (Radical Alternatives to Prison, 1969; Heidensohn, 1975). Ironically, it was its lack of adequate psychiatric facilities for treating disturbed women which was the focus of most concern (Carlen, 1985; Padel and Stevenson, 1988). Paul Rock's detailed reconstruction of the politics behind the new Holloway provides unparalleled insight into this topic (Rock, 1996).

Research in women's prisons in Britain in the 1980s and 1990s stressed both the distresses and discomforts common to men and women and certain features largely suffered by the latter. Women in prison are still less likely to receive good education, training, and job opportunities and more likely to have to carry out domestic tasks. This is, however, part of a wider policy which tends to define criminal women as doubly deviant, needing additional pressures to conform and be rehabilitated (Carlen, 1983; Dobash and Dobash, 1986). Petty modifications, no uniforms, better decor, soften the contours of the women's system but do not alter its basic shape. Despite all these factors, Eaton has presented women's survival strategies after imprisonment, noting their skill and resourcefulness (1993).

Women's Responses to Imprisonment

The literature on responses to imprisonment is vast and, unsurprisingly, dominated by studies of men. There are, to oversimplify, two major areas of interest: prisonization, and inmate subcultures. By the first is meant how far prisoners become adapted to their prisons and thus unable to cope with the outside world (Sykes, 1956). The earliest sociological studies (Sykes, 1956; Irwin and Cressey, 1962) observed that (male) prisons in the United States were notable for the prevalence of inmate subcultures. These were characterized by distinctive slang or argot and by a range of role types, such as Schrag's 'square johns, right guys, cons and outlaws' (1961). Two kinds of explanation are offered for this phenomenon. Sykes' 'pains of imprisonment' argument (1958) was that prisoners responded to the losses they felt in prison—of liberty, security, privacy, sex, etc.—by setting up compensating structures and roles. Irwin and Cressey (1962) on the other hand favour external influences as causative, insisting that prisoners bring their (pre)prison criminal values with them.

Much research on prisons for women in the United States has used the now rather aged features of such studies to explore women's reactions. Some important sex differences are found in responses to imprisonment, especially in subcultures. As noted above, studies in the 1960s noted the salience of sexual and emotional relations in female correctional establishments. Several studies found women's commitment to inmate codes to be less than men's (Tittle, 1969; Kruttschmitt, 1981). In Scotland, Carlen (1983) found little evidence of inmate solidarity or indeed the presence of subcultures. One of the paradoxical conclusions of a review of research on female subcultures is that they are weaker and more diffuse than male (Pollock-Byrne, 1990), yet, certainly in Britain, women perceive the pains of imprisonment as sharper and react with much greater vehemence against them (Heidensohn, 1975 and 1980; Casale 1989; Mandaraka-Sheppard, 1986; Carlen, 1985). A higher proportion of women are charged with disciplinary offences, doses of tranquilizers prescribed are higher, and there is a significant incidence of self-mutilation.

However, as Pollock-Byrne points out, the US subculture studies should be read with two caveats. They all use comparisons with males as a baseline, assuming, for instance, that men and women experience the same deprivations when inside. Secondly, there is more evidence that in establishments for both sexes there have been considerable changes which have altered subcultural patterns. Race is one very important one (Shaw *et al.*, 1990; Arnold, 1991). Another is the closer ties developed with communities which have lessened inmate isolation. Clark and Brudin (1990) for instance report, as two inmate participants, on a programme for AIDS/HIV education at a New York State prison which broke down many conventional barriers.

Reviewing the considerable body of work on women's experiences in prison and indeed on the whole of the criminal justice system reveals diversity, complexity, and, sometimes, contradiction. While there are common features of women's contribution to crime they have, it seems, less in common in how they experience society's reaction to it. Black women in the United States, native women in Canada and Australia all experience distinctive forms of penality from white women. Within such categories, too, class 'normality' and family situation may all also play a part. One of the pioneer projects of feminist criminology was to seek theoretical explanations which would help in understanding female criminality. Decades on from that era it is important to recast the original questions but no less vital to consider the answers, as we shall do in the next section.

Concepts and Continuing the Critique

The title of my first contribution to this field was 'The Deviance of Women: A *Critique* and an *Enquiry*' (1968, emphasis added). My enquiry concerned the lack of interest in sex differences in recorded criminality and in female deviance in itself, my critique was of the limitations of existing explanations of these two matters. These two points still serve as useful guides for considering the considerable range of conceptual studies which have appeared since then. There is now, when one enquires of bibliographies and data bases, much to consider of an explanatory kind. However, it is still vital to engage in a dialogue with mainstream criminology, especially about the assimilation of ideas about gender.

This area has been, as I trust all I have already written about it has indicated, one of the most fruitful and dynamic in the whole of criminology. It is not, then, surprising that its theoretical development has proceeded through considerable challenge and debate. In the section that follows I shall outline, in summary, some of the key contributions and also indicate how they are part of a continuing debate. As in all such debates, there has never been full, clear discussion of every issue; there is no great masterscript covering all roles and perspectives.

THEORIZING WOMEN AND CRIME

One summary of work in feminist criminology divided its conceptual concerns into the *gender gap* and the *generalizability* problem. Some theorists have attempted to deal with these issues; however, the most significant work of feminist theorists is to be found in *explanations of female criminality*. Partly however, because of problems in developing such approaches and also because of wider difficulties and developments there is another, and growing, category of criminological *feminist sceptics* who proffer no answers but ask further and profounder questions.

The Gender Gap and Generalizability

We have already noted the main contributors to theories about the gender gap: the so-called 'liberation causes crime' theorists (Adler, 1975; Simon, 1975) and the consequent debates about their views. This approach is one of the few perspectives on female crime to have been subjected to thorough empirical testing, to have been disproved (Box, 1983; Box and Hale, 1983; Austin, 1981; Smart, 1979; Steffensmeier, 1980). Strictly speaking the 'liberation hypothesis' was not a single coherent theory; indeed Adler and Simon differ in key aspects of their approaches, although both see increased equality for women as a key variable in causing their patterns of criminal behaviour.

However, Adler contended that the battle to emancipate women had been won by the mid-1970s, and thus male and female behaviour were converging, with females resembling males more and more by becoming aggressive and violent. Simon, on the other hand, suggested an opposite situation and outcome. Women's opportunities had not yet expanded very much; when they did so, their violence would diminish and their property crimes increase with their growing opportunities. Both approaches fail when tested because they do not fit statistical trends, because criminal women are amongst those least likely to be affected by feminism (and those most affected by it, middle-class white women, are the least likely to be criminal), and because criminal women tend to score highly on 'femininity' scores whereas 'masculine' scoring women are less delinquent (Naffine, 1987). These ideas are not supported, then, by the evidence. 'Yet ironically it is around this theme that a considerable debate has focused, putting female criminality into mainstream discussion' (Heidensohn, 1989: 95).

Much of the initial critique of criminology's failure to address the issues of gender and of women was directed at the limits of conventional theories. They could not for the most part account for the gender gap and broke down when applied to women as well as men, usually because they overpredicted female crime. Some critics went on to suggest that some criminological theories could be applied to women with success if only they were developed or modified (Leonard, 1982; Morris, 1987). Indeed this was a criticism Greenwood (1980) made of feminist criminologists: that they merely wished to add women back in. In practice it is hard to find examples of this, although Smith and Paternoster (1987) have suggested that 'gender-neutral' theories of delinquency should be developed and try to do this in a study of marijuana use. They take factors from classic theories of male delinquency and conclude 'factors that influence participation decisions and the frequency of marijuana use are similar for males and females' (1987: 156).

This does not, however, explain the differences in recorded or self-reported narcotic offences. Nor does it explain why many other researchers find gender-specific theories important in just such areas (Auld *et al.*, 1986; Rosenbaum, 1981).

Gender Theories

In the early days of work on women Carol Smart issued a warning: 'In the movement towards developing a feminist perspective a critique of sexism is vital, but in itself a critique alone cannot constitute a new theoretical approach. . . . In particular more research is needed in the area of women and crime' (1977: 183). This has in fact turned out to be the agenda for most of those who have contributed to this field. Once more it will be helpful to adopt a taxonomy within which we can group the work we are reviewing. This would include studies of patriarchy, of social and economic marginalization, of control, and finally there is a group of feminosceptics who have focused particularly on epistemological issues.

Patriarchy

Patriarchy is simply the rule of fathers, but defining it and using it as a concept has not proved at all simple for feminists, who have none the less used it frequently. Many writers have tried to define and refine it (Mitchell and Oakley, 1986; Walby, 1989) and subjected it to rigorous criticisms (Pollert, 1996). Quite often it appears to signify the rule of men or the power of men, and especially the use of these against women. On the whole patriarchy, or male power, are not used very much as direct explanations of female crime. The concept is employed nevertheless in at least two important ways: to explain women's experience of the criminal justice system, and the gendered nature of much criminal victimization, especially from violence and abuse within the home.

Indeed, it is from concern about women's treatment as victims in the processes of the criminal justice system and their experience of 'family law' that much of the evidence comes which has led, as Dobash and Dobash put it to 'some feminist activists and scholars (arguing) that it is impossible to use the law and legal apparatus to confront patriarchal domination and oppression when the language and procedures of these social processes and institutions are saturated with patriarchal beliefs and structures, (1992: 147). Victims and victimization are topics covered fully elsewhere in this volume. It is only the elision of the issues which I wish to discuss here. Susan Edwards, whose earlier work did emphasize sexist aspects of criminal justice (1981 and 1984) puts this view forcefully:

A consideration of patriarchy has been central to an understanding of sex/gender division within the law . . . the criminal justice process . . . and policing . . . it is the precise juncture of bourgeois and male interest which constitutes the corner-stone of women's experience and corresponding oppression. In everyday experience women's need for protection, women's voice as victims of crime, as criminal offenders and as victims of the law has been totally eclipsed [1989: 13].

Carol Smart (1989) has gone furthest in arguing that 'it is important to think of non-legal strategies and to discourage a resort to law as if it holds the key to unlock women's oppression' (1989: 5). Boldly she concludes:

a main purpose of this book has been to construct a warning to feminism to avoid the siren call of law. But of equal importance has been the attempt to acknowledge the power of feminism to construct an alternative reality to the version which is manifested in legal discourse [1989: 160].

Howe has extended Smart's discussion and insisted on its relationship with Carlen's apparently more pragmatic approach (1994: 213–15 and *passim*). In the 1980s there was widespread discussion of the work of Carol Gilligan (1982, 1987) who argued that men and women differ in approaches to moral questions, with men stressing 'justice' as an independent concept while women focus more on a relational notion of caring.

I used Gilligan's dichotomy as the basis of an ideal-type model of two types of justice system: the *Portia*, rational, judicial, and masculine, and the *Persephone*, relational, informal, and feminine, and explored what the effects of using such an alternative system might be. The conclusion was that such approaches had been adopted at certain times and had not always been beneficial (1986). Daly, in a review of this and other applications of Gilligan's difference discourse, disagrees with this approach and concludes

in canvassing feminist scholarship for ways to rethink the problem of justice for men and women accused of crime, I find little guidance. . . . I would like to see a feminist conception of criminal justice which maintains a focus on women's lives and on redressing harms to women, but which does not ignore those men who have been crippled by patriarchal, class and race relations [1989].

These comments could serve us the basis for the whole of this series of perspectives. What these studies amount to is a sophisticated critique of the administration of justice and the structures in which it operates. Clearly, there are certain gender-specific forms of discrimination rife within it. However, as Gelsthorpe (1989: 137–45) goes to great lengths to point out, it is impossible to try and demonstrate the existence of a conspiracy behind such practices. It is even more difficult to relate them, ætiologically to women's crime, since although women can be shown to be more socially and economically oppressed than men, their experience of the system as perpetrators, rather than victims, is far less. Where links can be made is through social construction theories which actually deconstruct the meanings of concepts such as rape (Rafter, 1990) or, as in Zedner's work quoted above, those of 'inebriation' and 'feeble mindedness' as applied to women. As Zedner's studies show, redefinitions of female deviance can diminish their apparent deviance or increase it (1991). This is not, of course, solely due to the operation of the criminal justice system. On the contrary, many other features of the Zeitgeist contribute: culture, values, changes in medical science. Politics and the media have also played crucial roles in such developments, as Young, for example, shows in her analysis of the media reactions to the women protesters at the Greenham Common Airbase in Britain in the 1980s. She argues that the criminal justice system and the media rely on each other's definition of deviance (1990).

This set of approaches informs much writing on women and crime. It leads us to question some of the most basic assumptions about law, justice, and punishment in our society and to raise queries about unstated 'patriarchal' values. However, it is also then essential to question all the other implicit parts of the system and we are likely, as Daly points out, to need to raise at least as many points about what happens to men, especially if they are young, poor, and come from minorities as we do about women.

Marginalization

Economic explanations of criminal behaviour go back at least as far as Bonger and, albeit implicitly, to Marx as well (Taylor *et al.*, 1975). More recently, critical criminologists insisted on the criminogenic capacities of capitalist societies (*ibid.*). *Critical Criminology* omits all consideration of gender, yet this is surely a crucial test for such theories since women are generally poorer than men in most, especially capitalist, societies and have suffered more in modern recessions (Millar and Glendinning, 1989). Some writers researching female crime have put forward a variation of such approaches in arguing that deviant women are an especially marginalized group.

Part of the purpose of proposing this perspective is to counteract the liberation hypothesis discussed earlier. Chapman (1980) stressed that the rise in female property crime was due to women's poverty, and especially to the problems of single mothers, a growing proportion of the poor. In an empirical study Jurik (1983) found support for such findings. A series of studies undertaken by Carlen in Britain elaborate on this theme (Carlen, 1983, 1985, 1988). She concludes:

the analyses presented here claim only to indicate that, under certain, relatively rare *combinations* of otherwise general economic and ideological conditions, some women are more likely than not to choose to break the law and/or be imprisoned. Such analyses do *not* assume or imply that the women involved have no choice [1988: 162, original emphasis].

Recent work from Europe (Pitch, 1995; Platek, 1995) and elsewhere (Hansson, 1995) suggests parallel concerns and has also focused much more fully on women of colour (e.g. the special edition of *Women and Criminal Justice*, 1995). Obviously, as Carlen suggests, poverty can be an important factor in the choice of women's criminal careers. It then often reinforces such choices by limiting others. Yet, as Daly showed in her study cited above, other factors, such as abuse in childhood and marriage or relationships with men with associations with drugs, are also important. None of these offender-based, somewhat positivist approaches can answer certain important queries, however, namely are the situations of those not convicted of crimes necessarily different? In short do these explanations fulfil necessary and sufficient conditions of theorizing; or have they, perhaps, not addressed the right questions?

Control and Conformity

A quite different approach has been adopted by a number of other writers who have sought to understand female criminality. So called 'control theory' was developed originally by Hirschi and his colleagues (1969) who sought to explain delinquency by the failure of social bonding processes. The emphasis shifted from deviance and what caused it to conformity and what impaired it. Hirschi's work has been much criticized, notably for its weak theoretical base, although it appears to have empirical support from large survey studies (see Downes and Rock, 1988, for a review).

In various modified forms, control theories have been applied to women because 'an examination of female criminality and unofficial deviance suggests that we need to move away from studying infractions and look at conformity instead, because the most striking thing about female behaviour . . . is how notably conformist to social mores women are' (Heidensohn, 1996: 11). In the same book I suggested that women were subject to a series of pressures and rewards to conform to which men were not. Informal sanctions discourage women and girls from straying far from proper behaviour: parents will disapprove or impose sanctions, as will gossip, ill-repute, and male companions. Fear of crime, harassment, and stigma all aid this process. A range of other commitments—to children, family, community, etc.—occupy women much more fully than they do men. Finally, public images and culture encourage daring deviance in men, but suggest that deviant women are punished (1996: chapters 5 and 9). Hagan and colleagues have also offered gender-specific versions of their general control theory, arguing that girls are much more subject to controls within the family than are boys (1979). Extensive empirical testing of various related hypotheses produced somewhat inconclusive results. Hagan found more informal control of girls, more formal of boys, in his Canadian study, and some predictive value for his hypothesis. Others found, however, that while greater social bonds among girls (and women) explained some of the sex crime ratio differences, they did not do so fully (Smith, 1979; Mawby, 1980; Shover *et al.*, 1980). Further, some of the differences were not in the expected direction. Thus girls who were 'masculine' in their identification in the last study were *less* delinquent than indeterminate or 'feminine' girls (Norland *et al.*, 1981).

These approaches do at least try and account for the gender gap and to present a generalizable theory of a kind, even though it seems only to have limited explanatory power, since the operation of the bonds is not fully theorized. (Although Hagan does attempt this in another text, 1990.) Naffine is especially critical of such approaches because they depict females as essentially passive (1987: 68–70) whereas male delinquency is glorified as active and defiant. She misses, I think, the rising tide of comment on women's own contribution to social control, especially of their own sex. In *Women and Crime* I discussed it at some length, noting women's higher investment in conformity and stability. More recently a spate of studies have focused on women's role as social control agents both historically (Carrier, 1988; Boritch and Hagan, 1990; Daly, 1988) and in modern times (Zimmer, 1986; Martin, 1980 and 1989; Jones, 1986; Heidensohn, 1989 and 1992). In a complex analysis, Worrall has suggested that women offenders do act within the criminal justice system to alter their own fates, although they are able to do so only because, as women, they confront *two* systems of social control.

They are effectively offered a contract which promises to minimize the consequences of their criminality by rehabilitating them within the dominant discourses of feminity (that is, domesticity, sexuality and pathology). Despite these programmes of feminization, such women it is argued, attempt to resist such construction by exploiting the contradictions of official discourses [1990: 163].

Almost all the empirical testing of control theories has been conducted with juvenile subjects. Measures of delinquency often include relatively minor infractions such as truancy and under-age drinking. This does limit the value of such studies where adults and more serious crimes are concerned. Gender-specific social control is, nevertheless, a widely cited component of most efforts to discuss women and crime. There is also clearly scope within such an approach to ask about many further issues: the control of males, for instance, or the role of women in control.

In reviewing theories of female criminality advanced in recent times, Pollock Byrne makes a succinct if gloomy point. 'Unfortunately feminist criminology has not offered any comprehensive theory to supplement those it has criticized' (1990: 25). It is hard to disagree with this. Despite a considerable body of work in the field, theoretical crocks of gold have still failed to appear. What has developed is a much more sustained and sophisticated critique and several important conceptual contributions which still have some scope in application. For the most part, the debate is still with older and existing theories and with the development of second-order constructs. This does not merely reflect poverty of imagination, indeed it is truer to say that something of an epistemological crisis has affected social science and feminism and studies of crime are implicated. There are, however, pitfalls in these approaches, as I have argued in a review of my own research experiences with 'deviant' women (1994*b*).

Feminist Sceptics

Much modern feminist debate in social science has focused on methodological issues. How should women be studied? What is feminist analysis? Numbers of articles and books have sought to respond to these questions and several scholars have particularly applied the answers to the study of gender and crime. These debates are complex, subtle, and sometimes arcane, and are beyond the scope of these chapters. What I do wish to do is to draw attention to the proposals made by several scholars who have tackled the epistemological crisis. What characterizes them all, to some degree, is their scepticism about either the past of this field or its future. Smart (1990) mounts the most devastating attack on criminology 'It is very hard to see what criminology has to offer feminism' (*ibid.*: 84). This contrasts with what she sees as the value and influence of feminist post-modernism on analyses of women's experiences (1990: 83). It is also in contrast to other possible approaches such as feminist empiricism and what is termed 'standpointism' (Harding, 1986). The latter is based in experience and on the argument that only a shared perspective with the subject gives research adequate insight and knowledge. Smart favours the deconstruction of everything, insisting that no meanings should be taken for granted.

Cain in the same volume tries also to describe what she calls the 'successor science' and lays down criteria for its operation (1990: 125–40). Somewhat confusingly, she calls her approach 'realism'.

Rafter (1990) also advocates a ruthless deconstruction of all laws, concepts, etc. as does Bertrand (1992). Once again, the source of this continuing critique is outside criminology, although in these examples it is debates within feminism itself which have fuelled these developments. *La lutte continue*, no doubt, without resolution of the issues, although these developments suggest yet further room for growth and dynamism as advocated by Klein in her spirited call for new approaches to justice (1995).

CONCLUSIONS

Alice in Wonderland and *Through the Looking Glass*

An intelligent enquirer who has followed the growth of this topic during the late twentieth century may feel that she has moved from the world of *Alice in Wonderland* to that of *Through the Looking Glass*. It is possible to construe all the modern work on women and crime as a great heap of glistening treasure. There is diversity, great range, rich material. It is possible to find the answers to many questions. There are still many puzzles and absurdities, but it is even possible to use key concepts to explain the studied world. Yet one of the main lessons which recurs throughout all the texts, articles, and reports is simple yet stunning in its implications. That is that Alice should be in the other strange place, through the glass where everything is reversed or upside down.

Then it becomes clear that we have to ask different questions. Not what makes women's crime rates so low, but why are men's so high? Such questions are being asked in a few places (Kersten, 1991; Newburn and Stanko, 1993), but they are the crucial ones, intellectually and politically. There is already a new *policy* agenda for law and order which highlights the gendered nature of much personal crime: domestic violence, rape, child abuse etc. It is in the impact of such studies that its effect should be found.

There has been a significant shift in the study of crime because of feminist perspectives on it. New ideas have been developed. The most important contribution of all, however, was to see the centrality of gender to crime and to press for that. We know a vast amount about women and crime viewed through the prism of gender. Research on masculinity and crime is a fast-developing area (Messerchmidt, 1993 and 1995; Newburn and Stanko, 1994; Jefferson and Carlen, 1996) and is likely to provide some very challenging ideas to both criminology and to feminist perspectives on crime. As Nelken has suggested, it is with just such a reflexive synthesis that the futures of criminology are likely to be preoccupied (1994).

Selected Further Reading

On women and crime F. M. Heidensohn, *Women and Crime* (1996) is now an updated second edition and remains the standard work. For historical perspectives on imprisonment, see L. Zedner, *Women, Crime and Custody in Victorian England* (1991), Oxford University Press, and her 'Wayward Sisters' in N. Morris and D. J. Rothman, eds. (1995), Oxford University Press, and on the USA, N. Rafter, *Partial Justice*, Transaction, 1992. On prison, P. Carlen, *Women's Imprisonment*, Routledge and Kegan Paul, 1983, and R. P. Dobash and S. Gutteridge, *The Imprisonment of Women*, Oxford, Blackwell, 1986, while M. Eaton, *Women after Prison*, Open University Press, 1992, cover other aspects. Relevant selections of readings can be found in L. Gelsthorpe and Morris, eds., *Feminist Perspectives in Criminology* (1990), N. Rafter and

F. M. Heidensohn, eds., *International Feminist Perspectives in Criminology* (1995) (both Open University Press), and T. Newburn and E. A. Stanko, eds., *Just Boys Doing Business?* 1994, Routledge. On gender and criminal justice professions, refer to S. E. Martin and N. Jurik, *Doing Gender, Doing Justice*, 1995 Sage, and F. M. Heidensohn *Women in Control? The Role of Women in Law Enforcement*, 1992, Oxford.

REFERENCES

ACTON, W. (1857), *Prostitution: Considered in its Moral, Social and Sanitary Aspects in London and Other Large Cities and Garrison Towns*. London: Frank Cass.

ADLER, I. (1975), *Sisters in Crime*. New York: McGraw Hill.

ALLEN, HILARY (1987), *Justice Unbalanced*. Milton Keynes: Open University Press.

ANDERSON, R., BROWN, J. and CAMPBELL, E. (1993), *Aspects of Sex Discrimination Within the Police Service in England and Wales*. London: Home Office.

ANNA, T. (1988), 'Feminist Responses to Sexual Abuse: The Work of the Birmingham Rape Crisis Centre', in M. Maguire and J. Pointing, eds., *Victims of Crime*. Milton Keynes: Open University Press.

ARNOLD, R. (1990), 'Processes of Victimization and Criminalization of Black Women', *Social Justice*, 17, 3: 153–66.

AULD, J., DORN, N., and SOUTH, N. (1986), 'Irregular Work, Irregular Pleasures: Heroin in the 1980s', in R. Matthews and J. Young, eds., *Confronting Crime*. London: Sage.

AUSTIN, R. L. (1981), 'Liberation and Female Criminality in England and Wales'. *British Journal of Criminology*, 21, 4: 371–4.

—— (1993), 'Recent Trends in Official Male and Female Crime Rates: The Convergence Controversy', *Journal of Criminal Justice*, 21: 447–66.

BARCLAY, G. C., ed. (1995), *Digest 3, Information on the Criminal Justice System in England and Wales*. Home Office. London: HMSO.

BEATTIE, J. M. (1975), 'The Criminality of Women in Eighteenth Century England', *Journal of Social History*.

BECKER, H. S. (1963), *Outsiders: Studies in the Sociology of Deviance*. London: Macmillan.

BEIRNE, P. (1988), 'Heredity versus Environment', *British Journal of Criminology*, 28, 3: 315–39.

BERTRAND, M. A. (1969), 'Self-Image and

Delinquency: A Contribution to the Study of Female Criminality and Women's Image', *Acta Criminologica*.

—— (1991), 'Advances in Feminist Epistemology in the Field of Social Control', paper delivered to the *American Society of Criminology*.

BORITCH H., and HAGAN, J. (1990), 'A Century of Crime in Toronto: Gender, Class, and Patterns of Social Control, 1859 to 1955', *Criminology*, 20, 4: 567–99.

BOX, S. (1981), *Deviance, Reality and Society*. London: Holt, Rinehart and Winston.

—— (1983), *Power, Crime and Mystification*. London: Tavistock.

—— and HALE, C. (1983), 'Liberation and Female Criminality in England and Wales', *British Journal of Criminology*, 23, 1: 35–49.

BRAITHWAITE, J. (1989), *Crime, Shame and Reintegration*. Cambridge: Cambridge University Press.

BROWN, J., and HEIDENSOHN, F. (1996), 'Exclusion Orders', *Policing Today*, 20–24.

BROWNE, A. (1987), *When Battered Women Kill*. London: Collier Macmillan.

BUCKLE, A., and FARRINGTON, D. (1984), 'An Observational Study of Shoplifting', *British Journal of Criminology*, 24, 1: 63–73.

BURNEY, E. (1990), *Putting Street Crime in its Place*. London: Centre for Inner City Studies, Goldsmiths' College.

CAIN, M., ed. (1990*a*), *Growing up Good*. London: Sage.

—— (1990*b*), 'Realist Philosophy and Standpoint Epistemologies or Feminist Criminology as a Successor Science', in L. Gelsthorpe and A. Morris, eds., *Feminist Perspectives in Criminology*. Buckingham: Open University Press.

CAMPBELL, A. (1981), *Girl Delinquents*. Oxford: Basil Blackwell.

—— (1984), *The Girls in the Gang*. Oxford: Blackwell.

CAREY, K. (1977), 'Police Attitudes to Women

Offenders', paper presented to British Sociological Association Conference.

CARIO, R. (1985), 'La Criminalité des Femmes: Approche Differentielle', Université de Pau et des Pays de l'Adur thesis for Dr d'Etat.

CARLEN, P. (1983), *Women's Imprisonment*. London: Routledge and Kegan Paul.

—— (1985), *Criminal Women*. Oxford: Polity Press.

—— (1988), *Women, Crime and Poverty*. Milton Keynes: Open University Press.

—— (1990), *Alternatives to Women's Imprisonment*. Milton Keynes: Open University Press.

—— and WORRALL, A., eds. (1987), *Gender, Crime and Justice*. Milton Keynes: Open University Press.

CARRIER, J. (1988), *The Campaign for the Employment of Women as Police Officers*. Aldershot: Avebury/Gower.

CASALE, S. (1989), *Women Inside. The Experience of Women Remand Prisoners in Holloway*. London: Civil Liberties Trust.

CHAPMAN, J. (1980), *Economic Realities and the Female Offender*. Lexington: Lexington Books.

CHESNEY-LIND, M. (1986), 'Women and Crime: the Female Offender', *Signs*, 12, 1: 78–96.

CHIGWADA, R., 'The Policing of Black Women', in E. Cashmore and E. McLaughlin, eds., *Out of Order*. London: Routledge.

CLARKE, J., and BOUDIN, K. (1990), 'Community of Women Organize Themselves to Cope with the AIDS Crisis: A Case Study from Bedford Hills Correctional Facility', *Social Justice*, 17, 2: 90–109.

COHEN, A. K. (1955), *Delinquent Boys*. London: Free Press.

COHEN, S., and SCULL, A., eds. (1983), *Social Control and the State*. Oxford: Blackwell.

CREIGHTON. S. J., and NOYES, P. (1989), *Child Abuse Trends in England and Wales 1983–1987*. London: NSPCC.

CRESSEY, D. R., ed. (1961), *The Prison*. New York: Holt, Rinehart and Winston.

DALTON, K. (1980), 'Cyclical Criminal Acts in the Premenstrual Syndrome', *Lancet*, 2: 1070–1.

DALY, K. (1988), 'The Social Control of Sexuality: A Case Study of the Criminalization of Prostitution in the Progressive Era', *Research in Law, Deviance and Social Control*, 9: 171–206.

—— (1989*a*), 'Rethinking Judicial Paternalism: Gender, Work-Family Relations and Sentencing, *Gender and Society*, 3, 1: 9–36.

—— (1989*b*), 'Criminal Justice Ideologies and Practices in Different Voices: Some Feminist Questions About Justice', *International Journal of the Sociology of Law*, 17: 1–18.

—— (1990), 'Reflections on Feminist Legal Thought', *Social Justice*, 17, 3: 7–24.

—— (1994), *Gender, Crime and Punishment*. New Haven, Conn.: Yale University Press.

—— and CHESNEY-LIND, M. (1988), 'Feminism and Criminology', *Justice Quarterly*, 5, 4: 498–538.

DAVIES, K. (1996), 'Masculinity or Marginality? Structural Correlates of Female Perpetrated Intimate Partner Homicide', paper delivered at the American Society of Criminology Meetings.

DOBASH, R. E. and DOBASH, R. P. (1979), *Violence Against Wives*. London: Open Books.

—— —— (1992), *Women, Violence and Social Change*. London: Routledge.

—— —— and GUTTERIDGE, S. (1986), *The Imprisonment of Women*. Oxford: Blackwell.

DOWNES, D. M., and ROCK, P. E. (1988), *Understanding Deviance*. 2nd edn. Oxford: Oxford University Press.

DUNHILL, C., ed. (1989), *The Boys in Blue. Women's Challenge to the Police*. London: Virago.

EATON, M. (1986), *Justice for Women?* Milton Keynes: Open University Press.

—— (1993), *Women After Prison*. Buckingham: Open University Press.

EDWARDS, S. M. (1984), *Women on Trial*. Manchester: Manchester University Press.

EDWARDS, S. (1989), *Policing 'Domestic' Violence*. London: Sage.

EINSELE, H. (1981), 'Female Criminality in the Federal Republic of Germany', Strasbourg: Council of Europe.

FARNWORTH, M. and TESKE, R. (1995), 'Gender Differences in Felony Court Processing: Three Hypotheses of Disparity', *Women and Criminal Justice*, 6, 2: 23–44.

FARRINGTON, D. (1981), 'The Prevalence of Convictions', *British Journal of Criminology*, 21, 2: 173–5.

—— and MORRIS, A. M. (1983), 'Sex, Sentencing and Reconviction', *British Journal of Criminology*, 23, 3: 229–48.

FEELEY, M., and LITTLE, D. (1991), 'The Vanishing Female: The Decline of Women in the Criminal Process, 1687–1912', *Law & Society Review*, 25, 4: 719–57.

FEEST, J. (1985), 'Frauenkriminalität' in G. Kaiser *et al.*, eds. (1985), *Kleines Kriminologisches Wörterbuch*. Müller. (Heidelberg, 1985).

FEINMAN, C. (1986), *Women in the Criminal Justice System*. New York: Praeger.

FIGUERIA-McDONOUGH, J. (1984), 'Feminism and Delinquency', *British Journal of Criminology*, 24, 4: 325–42.

GARLAND, D. (1985), *Punishment and Welfare*. Aldershot: Gower.

GELSTHORPE, L. (1989), *Sexism and the Female Offender*. Aldershot: Gower.

—— and MORRIS, A. (1988), 'Feminism and Criminology in Britain', *British Journal of Criminology*, 28, 2: 223–40.

—— and —— eds. (1990), *Feminist Perspectives in Criminology*. Buckingham: Open University Press.

GENDERS, E. and PLAYER, E. (1986), 'Women's Imprisonment. The Effects of Youth Custody', *British Journal of Criminology*, 26, 4: 357–71.

GIALLOMBARDO, R. (1966), *Society of Women: A Study of a Woman's Prison*. New York/London: Wiley.

—— (1974), *The Social World of Imprisoned Girls*. New York: Wiley and Sons.

GILLIGAN, C. (1982), *In a Different Voice*. Cambridge, Mass.: Harvard University Press.

—— (1987), 'Moral Orientation and Moral Development', in E. Kittay and D. Meyers, eds., *Women and Moral Theory*. NJ: Rowman and Littlefield.

GLENNERSTER, H. (1995), *British Social Policy Since 1945*. Oxford: Blackwell.

GOLD, M. (1970), *Delinquent Behaviour in an American City*. Belmont: Brooks Cole.

GREATER LONDON COUNCIL (1985), *Breaking the Silence*. London: GLC Women's Equality Group.

GREEN, P. (1991), *Drug Couriers*. London: Howard League for Penal Reform.

GREENWOOD, V. (1981), 'The Myth of Female Crime', in A. Morris and L. Gelsthorpe, eds., *Women and Crime*. Cambridge: Cropwood Conference Series No. 13.

HAGAN, J. (1987), *Modern Criminology: Crime, Criminal Behaviour and Its Control*. New York: McGraw-Hill.

—— SIMPSON, J. H., and GILLIS, A. R. (1979), 'The Sexual Stratification of Social Control: A Gender-based Perspective on Crime and Delinquency', *British Journal of Sociology*, 30.

HALFORD, A. (1993), *No Way Up the Greasy Pole*. London: Constable.

HANMER, J., and SAUNDERS, S. (1984), *Well-founded Fear*. London: Hutchinson.

HANSSON, DESIREE (1995), 'Agenda-ing Gender: Feminism and the Engendering of Academic Criminology in South Africa', in N. Rafter and F. M. Heidensohn, eds., *Engendering Criminology: The Transformation of a Social Science*. Buckingham: Open University Press.

HARDING, S. (1986), *The Science Question in Feminism*. Ithaca, NY: Cornell University Press.

HARRIS, R. (1992), *Crime, Criminal Justice and the Probation Service*. London: Routledge.

HARTMAN, M. (1977), *Victorian Murderesses*. London: Robson Books.

HARVEY, L., and PEASE, K. (1987) 'The Lifetime Prevalence of Custodial Sentences', *British Journal of Criminology*, 27, 3: 311–15.

HEDDERMAN, C. and HOUGH, M. (1994), 'Does the Criminal Justice System Treat Men and Women Differently?' Home Office Research Findings, No. 10. London: HMSO.

HEIDENSOHN, F. M. (1968), 'The Deviance of Women: A Critique and an Enquiry' in *British Journal of Sociology*, 19, 2: 160–75.

—— (1970), 'Sex, Crime and Society', in G. A. Harrison, ed., *Biosocial Aspects of Sex*. Oxford: Blackwell.

—— (1975), 'The Imprisonment of Females', in S. McConville, ed., *The Use of Imprisonment*. London: Routledge and Kegan Paul.

—— (1981), 'Women and the Penal System', in A. Morris and L. Gelsthorpe, eds., *Women and Crime*. Cambridge: Cropwood Conference Series No. 13.

—— (1985), *Women and Crime*. London: Macmillan, and New York: New York University Press.

—— (1986), 'Models of Justice: Portia or Persephone? Some Thoughts on Equality, Fairness and Gender in the Field of Criminal Justice', *International Journal of Sociology of Law*, 14.

—— (1989a), *Crime and Society*. Basingstoke: Macmillan.

—— (1989b), *Women in Policing in the USA*. London: Police Foundation.

—— (1991), 'Women and Crime in Europe', in F. Heidensohn and M. Farrell, eds., *Crime in Europe*. London: Routledge.

—— (1992a), 'Danger, Diversion or a New Dimension?', paper delivered at Seminar on Women and Violence at University of Montreal, Quebec.

—— (1992b), *Women in Control? The Role of Women in Law Enforcement*. Oxford: Oxford University Press.

—— (1994a), ' "We Can Handle It Out Here". Women Officers in Britain and the USA and the Policing of Public Order', *Policing and Society*, 4, 4: 293–303.

—— (1994b), 'From Being to Knowing. Some Reflections on the Study of Gender in Contemporary Society', *Women and Criminal Justice*, 6, 1: 13–37.

—— (1995), 'Feminist Perspectives and their Impact on Criminology and Criminal Justice in Britain', in Hahn N. Rafter and F. Heidensohn, (eds., *International Feminist Perspectives in Criminology*. Buckingham: Open University Press

—— (1996), *Women and Crime*. 2nd edn. Basingstoke: Macmillan.

HINDELANG, M. (1979), 'Sex Differences in Criminal Activity', *Social Problems*, 27.

HIRSCHI, T. (1969), *Causes of Delinquency*. Berkeley, Cal: University of California Press.

HØIGÅRD, C. and FINSTAD, L. (1992), *Backstreets Prostitution, Money and Love*. Oxford: Polity.

—— and SNARE, A. (1983), *Kvinners Skyld*. Oslo: Bakgater.

HOME OFFICE (1996), *Criminal Statistics England and Wales 1995*. Cmnd. 3421. London: HMSO.

HOOD-WILLIAMS, J. and BUSH, T. (1995), 'Domestic Violence on a London Housing Estate', in C. Byron, ed., *Home Office Research Bulletin*, No. 37.

HORSLEY, J. W. (1887), *Jottings from Jail: Notes and Papers on Prison Matters*. London: T. Fisher Unwin.

HOWE, A. (1994), *Punish and Critique Towards a Feminist Analysis of Penality*. London: Routledge.

IRWIN, J. and CRESSEY, D. (1962), 'Thieves, Convicts and the Inmate Culture', *Social Problems*, 10, 3: 145–7.

JEFFERSON, T. and CARLEN, P., eds. (1996), 'Masculinities, Social Relations and Crime', *British Journal of Criminology*, 36, 3. Special Issue.

—— and SHAPLAND, J. (1994), 'Criminal Justice and the Production of Order and Control: Criminological Research in the UK in the 1980s'. *British Journal of Criminology*, 34, 3: 265–90.

JOHNSON, J. (1991), *What Lisa Knew*. London: Bloomsbury.

JONES, D. (1982), *Crime, Protest, Community and Police in Nineteenth Century Britain*. London: Routledge.

JONES, S. (1986), *Policewomen and Equality*. London: Macmillan.

—— (1987), 'Women's Experience of Crime and Policing', discussion paper (mimeo), Centre for the Study of Community and Race Relations. Brunel University.

JONES, T., MACLEAN, B., and YOUNG, J. (1986), *The Islington Crime Survey*. Aldershot: Gower.

JURIK, N. (1983), 'The Economics of Female Recidivism', *Criminology*, 21, 4: 3–12.

—— and GREGWARE, P. (1992), 'A Method for

Murder: The Study of Homicides by Women', *Perspectives on Social Problems*, 4: 179–201.

KELLOR, F. (1900*a*), 'Psychological and Environmental Study of Women Criminals', *American Journal of Sociology*, 5: 527–43.

—— (1900*b*), 'Criminal Sociology: Criminality Among Women', *Arena*, 23: 516–24.

KENNEDY, H. (1992), *Eve was Framed*. London: Chatto and Windus.

KERSTEN, J. (1989), 'The Institutional Control of Girls and Boys', in M. Cain, ed., *Growing Up Good*. London: Sage.

—— (1991), 'A Cross-Cultural Debate of Crime and its Causes in Australia, Germany and Japan, paper presented to Australian and New Zealand Criminology Conference, Melbourne, Australia.

KLEIN, D. (1973), 'The Ætiology of Female Crime: A Review of the Literature', *Issues in Criminology*, 3: 3–30.

—— (1995), 'Gender's Prism: Toward a Feminist Criminology', in N. Rafter and F. Heidensohn, eds., *Engendering Criminology: The Transformation of a Social Science*. Milton Keynes: Open University Press.

KRISTA, A. (1993), *Women and Violence*. London: Harper Collins.

KRUTTSCHITT, C. (1981), 'Prison Codes, Inmate Solidarity and Women: A Re-examination', in M. Warren, ed., *Comparing Female and Male Offenders*. Newbury Park: Sage.

LEONARD, E. B. (1982), *A Critique of Criminology Theory: Women, Crime and Society*. New York and London: Longman.

LLOYD, A. (1993), *Women and Violence*. Harmondsworth, Penguin.

LOMBROSO, C., and FERRERO, W. (1895), *The Female Offender*, with an introduction by W. D. Morrison. London: T. Fisher Unwin.

LONGMAN'S ENGLISH DICTIONARY (1984). London: Longman

LUPTON, C., and GILLESPIE, T., eds. (1994), *Working with Violence*. Baskingstoke: Macmillan.

MACDONALD, E. (1991), *Shoot the Women First*. London: Fourth Estate.

MACGREGOR, S., ed. (1989), *Drugs and British Society*. London: Routledge.

MCLEOD, E. (1982) *Women Working: Prostitution Now*. London: Croom Helm.

MCLYNN, F. (1989), *Crime and Punishment in the Eighteenth Century*. Oxford: Oxford University Press.

MAHER, L. (1990), 'Criminalizing Pregnancy— The Downside of a Kinder, Gentler Nation?', *Social Justice*, 17, 3: 111–35.

MANDARAKA-SHEPPARD, A. (1986), *The Dynamics of Aggression in Women's Prisons in England*. Aldershot: Gower.

MANNHEINN, H. (1965), *Comparative Criminology*. London: Routledge Kegan Paul.

MARTIN, S. E. (1980), *Breaking and Entering*. Berkeley, Cal.: University of California Press.

—— (1990), *On the Move—The Status of Women in Policing*. Washington, DC: Police Foundation.

MATTHEWS, R. and YOUNG, J., eds. (1986), *Confronting Crime*. London: Sage.

MAWBY, R. (1980), 'Sex and Crime: The Results of a Self-Report Study', *British Journal of Sociology*, 31, 4: 525.

MAYHEW, H. (1861), *London Labour and London Poor*. Vols. I–IV. London: Griffin (repr. London: Spring Books, 1962).

MILLAR, J. and GLENDINNING, C. (1989), 'Gender and Poverty', *Journal of Social Policy*, 18, 3: 363–83.

MILLER, E. (1986), *Street Woman*. Philadelphia, Penn.: Temple.

MILLMAN, M. (1982), 'Images of Deviant Men and Women', in M. Evans, ed., *The Woman Question*. London: Fontana.

MIRLEES-BLACK, C. (1995), 'Estimating the Extent of Domestic Violence: Findings from the 1992 BCS', in C. Byron, ed., *Home Office Research Bulletin. No. 37*. London: HMSO.

MITCHELL, J., and OAKLEY, A., (eds. (1986), *What is Feminism?* Oxford: Basil Blackwell.

MORRIS, A. (1987), *Women, Crime and Criminal Justice*. Oxford: Basil Blackwell.

—— and GELSTHORPE, L. eds., (1981), *Women and Crime*. Cambridge: Cropwood Conference Series No. 13.

MOXON, D. (1988), *Sentencing Practice in the Crown Court*. Home Office Research Study No. 103. London: HMSO.

MUKHERJEE, S. K., and SCUTT, J. A. (1981), *Women and Crime*. Australian Institute of Criminology/George Allen and Unwin.

NAFFINE, N. (1987), *Female Crime*. Sydney: Allen and Unwin.

NATZLER, C., O'Shea, M., Heaven, O., and Mars, M. (1989), all in C. Dunhill, ed., *The Boys in Blue Women's Challenge to the Police*. London: Virago.

NELKEN, D., ed. (1994), *The Futures of Criminology*. London: Sage.

NEWBURN, T., and Stanko, E., eds. (1994), *Just Boys Doing Business: Masculinity and Crime*. London: Routledge.

NORLAND, S., WESSEL, R. C., and SHOVER, N. (1981), 'Masculinity and Delinquency', *Criminology*, 19, 3: 421.

PADEL, V., and STEVENSON, P., eds. (1988), *Insiders: Women's Experience of Prison*.

London: Virago.

PAHL, J. (1978), *A Refuge for Battered Women: A Study of the Role of a Women's Centre*. London: HMSO.

PARKER, H., CASBURN, M., and TURNBULL D. (1981), *Receiving Juvenile Justice*. Oxford: Basil Blackwell.

PARTON, N. (1991), *Governing the Family*. Basingstoke: Macmillan.

PEARSON, G. (1987), *The New Heroin Users*. Oxford: Blackwell.

PETRIE, G. (1971), *A Singular Iniquity—The Campaigns of Josephine Butler*. London: Macmillan.

PIKE, L. (1876), *A History of Crime in England*. London: Smith Elder.

PILIAVIN, I., and BRIAR, S. (1964), 'Police Encounters with Juveniles'. *American Journal of Sociology*, 70: 206.

PITCH, T. (1995), 'Feminist Politics, Crime, Law, and Order in Italy', in N. H. Rafter and F. Heidensohn, eds., *International Feminist Perspectives in Criminology*. Buckingham: Open University Press.

PIZZEY, E. (1973), *Scream Quietly or the Neighbours Will Hear*. Harmondsworth: Penguin.

PLATEK, MONIKA (1995), 'What It's Like For Women: Criminology in Poland and Eastern Europe', in N. Rafter, and F. M. Heidensohn, eds.) *Engendering Criminology: The Transformation of a Social Science*. Buckingham: Open University Press.

PLAYER, E. (1989), 'Women and Crime in the City', in D. Downes, ed., *Crime in the City*. London: Macmillan.

POE-YAMAGATA, E., and BUTTS, J. (1996), *Female Offenders in the Juvenile Justice System*. Rockville, Md.: US Department of Justice.

Pollak, O. (1950), *The Criminality of Women*. New York: A. S. Barnes/Perpetua.

POLLERT, A. (1996), 'Gender and Class Revisited; or the Poverty of "Patriarchy"', *Sociology*, 304: 639–59.

POLLOCK-BYRNE, J. (1990), *Women, Prison and Crime*. Belmont, Cal.: Wadsworth.

RADICAL ALTERNATIVES TO PRISON, *Alternatives to Holloway*. London: Christian Action Publications.

RAFTER, HAHN N. (1983, 1985), 'Chastizing the Unchaste: Social Control Functions of a Women's Reformatory 1894–31', in S. Cohen and A. Scull, eds., *Social Control and the State*. Oxford: Blackwell.

—— (1990), 'The Social Construction of Crime and Crime Control', *Journal of Research in Crime and Delinquency*, 27, 4: 376–89.

—— and HEIDENSOHN, F., eds. (1995), *International Feminist Perspectives in Criminology*. Buckingham: Open University Press.

REINER, R., and SHAPLAND, J., eds. (1987), 'Introduction: Why Police?', *British Journal of Criminology* (Special Issue on Policing in Britain), 27, 1: 1–4.

REYNOLDS, A. (1991), *Tight Rope*. London: Sidgwick and Jackson.

ROCK, P. E. (1996), *Reconstructing a Women's Prison*. Oxford: Clarendon Press.

ROSENBAUM, M. (1981), *Women on Heroin*. New Brunswick, NJ: Rutgers University Press.

SCHLESINGER, P., DOBASH, R. E., and DOBASH, R. P. (1992), *Women Viewing Violence*. London: British Film Institute.

SCHRAG, C. (1961), 'A Preliminary Criminal Typology', *Pacific Sociological Review*, 4, 2: 11

SCUTT, J. A. (1981), 'Sexism in Criminal Law', in S. K. Mukherjee and J. A. Scutt, *Women and Crime*. London: Allen and Unwin.

SHAW, M. (1991), *The Federal Female Offender*. Ottawa: Solicitor General of Canada, No. 1991–3.

SHAW, R., ed. (1991), *Prisoners' Children: What are the Issues?* London: Routledge.

SIMMONS, H. G. (1978), 'Explaining Social Policy: The English Mental Deficiency Act of 1913', *Journal of Social History*, 11, 3.

SIMON, R. J. (1975), *Women and Crime*. Toronto/London: Lexington.

SMART, C. (1977), *Women, Crime and Criminology*. London: Routledge Kegan Paul.

SMART, C. (1977), 'The New Female Criminal: Reality or Myth?', *British Journal of Criminology*, 19, 1: 50–1.

—— (1989, *Feminism and the Power of Law*. London: Routledge.

SMART, C. (1990), 'Feminist Approaches to Criminology or Post-modern Woman Meets Atavistic Man', in L. Gelsthorpe and A. Morris, eds., *Feminist Perspectives in Criminology*. Buckingham: Open University Press..

SMITH, A. D. (1962), *Women in Prison*. (Library of Criminology). London: Stevens and Sons.

SMITH, D. A. (1979), 'Sex and Deviance: An Assessment of Major Sociological Variables', *Sociological Quarterly*, 20: 183.

—— and VISHER, A. C. (1980), 'Sex and Involvement in Deviance/Crime: A Quantitative Review of the Empirical Literature', *American Sociology Review*, 45: 691–701.

SMITH, D. and GRAY, J. (1983), *Police and People in London*. Vols. I–IV. London: Policy Studies Institute.

—— and PATERNOSTER, R. (1987), 'The Gender Gap in Theories of Deviance: Issues and Evidence', *Journal of Research on Crime and Delinquency*, 24: 140–72.

SMITH, L. J. F. (1988), 'Images of Women—Decision-Making in Courts', in A. Morris and C. Wilkinson, eds., *Women and the Penal System*. Cropwood Conference Series. Institute of Criminology.

STANG DAHL, T. (1987), *Women's Law: An Introduction to Feminist Jurisprudence*. Oxford: Oxford University Press.

STANKO, E. (1984), *Intimate Intrusions*. London: Routledge Kegan Paul.

—— (1990), *Everyday Violence*. London: Pandora.

—— (1993), *Men and Crime*. Buckingham: Open University Press.

STANLEY, L. and WISE, S. (1983), *Breaking Out*. London: Routledge Kegan Paul.

STEEL, BRENT S., and LOVRICH, N. P. (1987), 'Equality and Efficiency Trade-offs in Affirmative Action: Real or Imagined? the Case of Feminine in Policing', *Social Science Journal*, 24, 1.

STEFFENSMEIER, D. J. (1978), 'Crime and the Contemporary Woman: An Analysis of Changing Levels of Female Property Crime, 1960–75', *Social Forces*, 57.

—— (1980), 'Assessing the Impact of the Women's Movement on Sex-Based Differences in the Handling of Adult Criminal Defendants'. *Crime and Delinquency*, 26: 344–57.

—— (1995), 'Trends in Female Crime: It's Still a Man's World', in B. Raffel Price and N. J. Sokoloff, eds., *The Criminal Justice System and Women*. New York: McGraw-Hill.

—— KRAMER, J., and STREIFEL, C. (1993), 'Gender and Imprisonment Decisions', *Criminology*, 30, 3: 411–46.

STRACHEY, R. (1978), *The Cause*. London: Virago.

SYKES, G. (1956), *Society of Captives*. Princeton, NJ: Princeton University Press.

TAYLOR, I., WALTON, P., and YOUNG, J. (1973), *The New Criminology*. London: Routledge Kegan Paul.

—— —— and YOUNG, J. (1975), *Critical Criminology*. London: Routledge Kegan Paul.

THOMAS, W. I. (1923), *The Unadjusted Girl*. Boston, Mass.: Little, Brown.

TITTLE, C. (1969), 'Inmate Organization: Sex Differentiation and the Influence of Criminal Sub Cultures', *American Sociology Review*, 34: 492–505.

US DEPARTMENT OF JUSTICE and FEDERAL BUREAU OF INVESTIGATION (1984ff.), *Uniform Crime Reports*. Washington DC.

VANEZIS, P. (1991), 'Women, Violent Crime and the Menstrual Cycle: A Review', *Medicine, Science and the Law*, 31, 1: 11–14.

VISHER, C. A. (1983), 'Gender, Police Arrest Decisions and Notions of Chivalry', *Criminology*. 21: 5–28.

WALBY, S. (1989), 'Theorising Patriarchy', *Sociology*, 23, 2: 213–34.

WALKER, R. (1985), 'Racial Minority and Female Employment in Policing', *Crime and Delinquency*. 31, 4: 555–72.

WALKLATE, S. (1989), *Victimology*. London: Unwin Hyman.

WALKOWITZ, J. (1980), *Prostitution and Victorian Society*. Cambridge: Cambridge University Press.

WARD, D. A., and KASSEBAUM, G. G. (1965), *Women's Prison*. London: Weidenfeld.

WEBB, D. (1984), 'More on Gender and Justice: Girl Offenders on Supervision', *Sociology*, 18: 367–81.

WOMEN'S NATIONAL COMMISSION (1991), *Women and Prison*. London: Cabinet Office.

WOMEN AND CRIMINAL JUSTICE (1995), Special Issue on Women's Culture and the Criminal Justice System. 7, 1.

WORRALL, A. (1990), *Offending Women*. London: Routledge.

YOUNG, A. (1990), *Femininity in Dissent*. London: Routledge.

YOUNG, J. (1986), 'The Failure of Criminology: The Need for a Radical Realism', in R. Matthews and J. Young, *Confronting Crime*. London: Sage..

YOUNG, M. (1991), *An Inside Job*. Oxford: Oxford University Press.

ZEDNER, L. (1991), *Women, Crime and Custody in Victorian England*. Oxford: Oxford University Press.

ZIMMER, L. (1986), *Women Guarding Men*. Chicago, Ill.: University of Chicago Press.

Part III

FORMS OF CRIME AND CRIMINALITY

23

Criminal Collaboration: Youth Gangs, Subcultures, Professional Criminals, and Organized Crime

Dick Hobbs

The aim of writing is to create coherence. The risk is that coherence will be imposed on an actual disorder and a forgery thus produced [Matza 1969: 1].

That outlaw shit ain't in the economic mainstream [Doctorow, 1989: 126].

Collectivities of criminals are bound to attract the attention of law enforcement agencies, the media, and the general public. As a threat to the social, economic, and political order, groups of criminals are more capable of impacting than solitary villains, and as metaphors of collective transgression, the gang, mob, firm, outfit, or organization carry implicit essences of consolidated deviant intent, which are intensified by the potential of communal action. These confederations contain elements of interaction that enable individuals to collaborate, and the purpose of this chapter is to examine these interactions, and the principles around which they are organized.

The range of organizational and structural variations on this admittedly ambiguous theme is immense. Its scope covers haphazard temporary collaborations between individuals, through youthful subcultural experimentations, via a range of youth gangs featuring wide variations in hierarchical emphasis. It also covers affiliations of professional career criminals, some of whom work within confederations of long-standing crime groups, that present a rather ambiguous threat to the contemporary political and economic order. Of all the problems that litter this wide-ranging mutant of a chapter, the issue of definition threatens to kill off both description and debate. What will become clear is that strict legalistic definitions are little more than convenient templates for criminal justice operatives, while the irony lies in the fact that so much of the relevant data are derived from criminal justice agencies (Manning. 1989). Although some of these problems of definition will be addressed in the relevant sections, it is important to emphasize that the common thread that runs through this chapter is the organization of deviance or, more specifically the social, economic, and interactive principles around which deviant collaborations are organized.

The chapter is organized into three sections; youth gangs and subcultures, professional crime, and organized crime. Each section will contain reviews of the relevant literature and attempt to chart historical changes and trends, both in the social science literature and in criminal collaborations themselves. The emphasis of the chapter is on the influence of the political economy upon successive generations of criminal collaborations, their origins, *modus operandi*, and the principles around which they are organized. The rapidly changing character of the political economy ensures that many of the traditional theoretical props upon which social scientists have framed their work are no longer reliable tools in either identifying or investigating late modern criminal collaborations. Consequently such an approach makes it possible to question the validity of this conventional three-part distinction, and suggests that the political economy of post traditional society has sufficiently blurred these categories so as to render them little more than convenient indicators of the division of academic labour.

Any form of co-offending requires a degree of collaboration which, even at its most mundane level, indicates organization, and co-offending, as Reiss and Farrington (1991) have shown, features in approximately half of all offences. Further, the significance of co-offending is indicated in their finding that men whose first offence involved others tended to have longer criminal careers than solitary criminals, and that they tended to share not only gender, but also age and neighbourhood, as well as living in homes that shared close proximity to the site of offences. These similarities between offenders were found to decline as they became older, and consequently there is a youth-specific commonality of territorial and gender-specific deviance which requires some attention. This tendency for delinquency to manifest itself as a group activity (see also Shaw and McKay, 1931; Gold, 1970; Reiss, 1986) leads us to the first of a trio of devices around which deviant action is organized.

YOUTH: GANGS AND SUBCULTURES

Everybody was wild, and I wanted to be with the wild crowd, because I liked it. I didn't want to be a nerd, or nothing like that. I figured it was wise, so being wild became a habit. I used to get into trouble and do atrocities [Bourgois, 1995: 194].

This first section is broadly concerned with the various devices around which youth are organized. These feature the various agglomerations of youth, for instance the gang, and the near group; more subtle manifestations based around group expressions of personal limitations and frustrations in the form of subcultures; and the organization of youthful deviance around stylistic devices. Following this largely historical trawl through the literature, I will look at some of the contemporary work on gangs.

Gangs

As Geoffrey Pearson clearly indicates, deviant youth have always managed to attract a disproportionate amount of fear and ire from the rest of society. As long ago as the 1600s named gangs of young men ' . . . found amusement in breaking windows, demolishing taverns, assaulting the watch' (Pearson, 1983: 188). However, their activities have been subject to much speculation and not a little ambiguous analysis. Henry Mayhew's ventures into Victoria's meaner streets verifies that the children of the urban poor were especially problematic and in need of control, and with the spectre of a continental-style uprising of what Mary Carpenter, in a foretaste of late twentieth century underclass terror, called the 'perishing' and 'dangerous' classes ever present, a process of categorization and exclusion, underpinned by the segmentation of the work-force according to age, gender, race, and, most importantly, economic viability, accelerated throughout the nineteenth century (Stedman Jones, 1971). Despite the apparent global reality of youth gangs (Oschlies, 1979; Spergel, 1995: chapter 1), the relevant academic literature is predominantly American, and although the first academic usage of 'gang' is credited to Sheldon (1898), the earliest definition of a gang is provided by Puffer (1912: 7) as 'one of the three primary groups . . . the family, the neighbourhood, and the play group', the gang representing the play group. This seemingly anomalous emphasis on the gang as a play group is reiterated in Thrasher's seminal *The Gang* (1927), which has proved an enduring influence upon subsequent generations of scholars. Yet predating Thrasher by a number of years Riis (1892, 1902), estab-lished gangs as alternative agencies of socialization for young immigrants for whom mainstream economic integration was problematic (cf. Asbury, 1928).

However, Thrasher's monumental study constituted the first serious attempt at documenting, comprehending, and indeed enumerating a phenomenon that was to emerge as a staple social problem of urban society. Operating within a social ecology framework, Thrasher identified an astonishing 1,313 youth gangs operating within Chicago's 'poverty belt'. Lacking methodological or theoretical cohesion, Thrasher was unforthcoming regarding certain aspects of his methodology (see Short, 1963), although we do know that he utilized census and court data, observations, personal documents, and interviews. The fact that Thrasher included virtually every youthful working-class street collabor-ation, from loose-knit groups of drug users and institutionalized sports clubs to violent groups of street pirates, is somewhat bemusing, yet it is the quali-tative data with their descriptions of everyday gang activity that have impacted upon subsequent generations of writers. Thrasher's definition of a gang emphasizes the role of conflict in integrating collective behaviour with the development of a tradition, structure, espirit de corps, solidarity, morale, group awareness and attachment to local territory (*ibid.*: 46).

Running like a thread through Thrasher's work is the notion that gangs occupy spaces or interstices between sections of the urban fabric. Thrasher's

work resembles that of Shaw and McKay (1942), in that it locates gang delinquency within 'delinquency areas' of the city, which are also slum neighbourhoods typified by multiple examples of social breakdown and disorganization,[1]
which in turn was filtered through the experiences of successive waves of immigrants (Park *et al.*, 1925). Thrasher stressed the disorganization of immigrant
communities as providing the major dynamic for youth gangs, which are manifestations of 'the disorganisation incident to cultural conflict among diverse
nations and races gathered together in one place and themselves in contact
with a civilisation foreign and largely inimical to them' (Thrasher, 1927: 154).
Black gangs made up only 7.16 per cent of Thrasher's sample (*ibid.*: 130), and
conflict existed mainly between gangs of white immigrants, with blacks seen as
fair game for all groups (*ibid.*: 139–40). As we will see in later sections, the
notion of deviant structures being interstitial, filling the void created by urban
disorganization, is an enduring theme of studies of deviant collaborations. This
is the crucial proposition of Thrasher's work, which is reinforced by Shaw and
McKay's (1942) thesis that delinquency is organized around working-class
territorial imperatives, which are themselves defined by the experiences of low
income, poor housing, and poor health. The gang is a refuge: the interstitial
character of the non-gang world, which includes the (disorganized) family,
cannot provide for the needs of working class youth (Tannenbaum, 1939). As
Yablonsky has noted, these studies stress a delinquent career that begins as
a form of play that brings the youth into conflict with the community (in
particular the family) which has failed to incorporate the youth. The gang
becomes an alternative family where criminal careers are nurtured, and
towards which the sanctions of legitimate society are focused, thereby creating
a delinquent hierarchical structure within which the youth can formulate
criminal associations and progress (Yablonsky, 1962: 147–8).

At this stage it can be observed that lacking an all-encompassing definition
(Ball and Curry, 1995),[2] the terms gang and delinquency have blurred into one
rather awkward area of delinquent youth organization, and the term gang
often retains its viability basically as a bridging concept (Finestone, 1976: 45).
In many ways Yablonsky's 'near-group' deals with this problem of organizational definition by emphasizing ways in which formations of delinquent
youth possesses a chameleon-like quality, in that they are in a state of constant
flux. He goes on to locate three types of near group, 'social', which is self-
explanatory, 'delinquent', who are organized specifically around delinquent
action, and 'violent', those groups providing violent gratification. Yablonsky
located the gang midway between mobs which are characterized by anonymity
and spontaneity, and gangs which were organized around shared functions and
goals (Yablonsky, 1959, 1962).

---

[1] For a critique of social disorganization theory, see Anthony Bottoms, this volume.

[2] Indeed after a perusal of the vast literature available it is difficult to disagree with Ball and
Curry's contention that many definitions of gangs are little more than 'veiled expressions of
bourgeois disapproval' (1995: 227).

The loose-knit flexibility of Yablonsky's 'near group' certainly brings us closer to engagement with subcultural studies which were orientated towards situating a range of delinquent collaborations within the context of broader societal shapes and shifts, and most importantly within the parent community. In one of the most influential sociological studies Whyte (1943) offers a view of the gang that notionaly supports the early Chicago studies, but progresses to emphasize even further the importance of communal action. By utilizing a classical methodology, Whyte describes structural arrangements that are co-operative and highly supportive, whose longevity is rooted within the community as opposed to its conflictual relations with it. The corner boys of Boston thrived within a structured environment of mutual obligations, which yet again questions the validity of presumptive theorizing based upon disorganization. Suttles (1968) reinforced the thesis regarding an informal organization whose primary function is to protect the 'defended neighbourhood', by stressing the evolution of street-corner cultures that feature community specific, essentially functional attributes that are an essential part of the local community. The street gang is made up of youths who are, 'hardly the unruly and unreachable youths that we are led to expect. . . . The street corner groups not only make their members known to the remainder of the neighbourhood, but create a network of personal acquaintances that augment those already in existence' (Suttles, 1968: 172–3). The notion of gangs being crucial to the local social order is central to the ethnographic work of Whyte and Suttles, and in their loose-knit informality emphasize a local order within which agglomerations of youth thrive more in harmony than in conflict with their locale. These studies stress collaborations somewhat less structured, yet more explicitly functional, than the early studies, and are not concerned with youth as a problem, succeeding via exemplary ethnographic work in retaining the vitality and energy of youth gangs that was first expressed by Thrasher.

Subcultures

As Bordua (1961) has noted, while the early gang studies tended to stress the hedonistic fun gained from gang membership, subcultural theories of delinquent action, which were inspired by Cohen's seminal work (1955) are typified in terms of the strains and anxieties emanating from a harsh social environment. (See Katz, 1988, for a masterful reminder of the hedonism that lies at the root of much deviance.) Cohen's work was, in turn, a response to Robert Merton's (1938) contention that deviance (the term deviance and not crime holds special significance here) results from the strain induced by American society's failure to live up to the promise of universal access to upward social mobility, which in turn is exemplified by material success. The disjuncture between cultural goals and structural means led to strain and subsequently deviant adaptations that were essentially anomic. Albert Cohen regarded status frustration as providing the motive for youths forming sub-cultures, identifying the sub-culture, or more specifically the gang, as providing a solution to the problem of status frustration. Because working-class kids are disadvantaged in a school system which is founded on middle-class values, this leads to failure, loss of self esteem, and resentment.

According to Cohen, this failure will result in guilt and shame; the youth is 'on the market for a solution' (1955: 119). Cohen suggests that the solution is the formation of a gang that shares a contempt for, and denies any attachment to, middle-class standards. The subsequent attitude is manifested as 'non-utilitarian, malicious, negativistic behaviour, directed primarily at property'. Merton's stress upon monetary gain was regarded as inappropriate, the subculture in the form of the gang was for Cohen an alternative social form that displayed its contempt for the 'American dream', by engaging in essentially non-utilitarian activities such as vandalism, truancy, and violence.

Cloward and Ohlin (1960) were considerably closer to Merton's theoretical formulation, stressing blocked access to monetary success, and identifying a high degree of gang specialization, taking any one of three forms: criminal—whose prime concern is crimes against property, where local opportunities existed for recruitment into adult criminal groups; conflict—fighting gangs, e.g. *West Side Story*, were regarded as forming when recruitment into these criminal groups was not a possibility; retreatist, involving drug taking, alienation, and a general withdrawal from society which is inspired by the youth's double failure to succeed in either legitimate or illegitimate spheres. Matza and Sykes contested this notion of alienation, claiming that delinquents were not isolated, but had picked up and emphasized particular values of the dominant culture, namely 'subterranean values of leisure' (1961: 717–18). The delinquent sub-culture was merely a stretched version of the values of hedonistic consumption which counterpoint the ethos of productive work within the dominant value system. Delinquency therefore should be analysed as a cultural annexe of the adult world, and the delinquent as a reflection or caricature of normative society.

The problem of youth gangs and subcultures was not restricted to the United States, and the notion of youth as a reflection of societal trends was most clearly noted by Hoggart's identification of the corrosive influence of America on British cultural life (1957). Teenage *Angst* was commodified, and the global marketing of delinquency, which specifically targeted working-class youth (Abrams, 1959), inspired a new interest in the 'youth problem' (Bradley, 1992: 12–14; Gillet, 1983: 254–7; Hebdige, 1988: 54–6; Street, 1992: 304).

BRITISH STUDIES

boys aged between fifteen and twenty, with drape suits, picture ties and an American slouch [Hoggart, 1957: 203].

Youth and the Parent Culture

Downes's explicitly English study (1966) found that because of early socialization in school, working-class youth accept dull routine tasks at work, and
that the world of work seldom disappoints. Downes found no evidence that
working-class delinquents were status frustrated, as implied by Cohen, nor
were they alienated, as proposed by Cloward and Ohlin. Both propositions
require the adolescent to have internalized middle-class norms, requiring a
gap to exist between aspiration and achievement (*ibid.*: 109). By accepting
the prospect of low occupational status, the 'corner boy' is released from the
pressure of upward mobility and, as Downes has noted, in accepting the status
imposed by school and work, and neither aspiring to middle-class norms nor
refuting their legitimacy, notions of status frustration and alienation were not
applicable. Downes discovered the existence of what he calls 'street corner
groups', rather than the gangs of the American inner city as described by
Cloward and Ohlin.

Downes' criticisms of Matza and Sykes are centred around the Americans'
claim that delinquency is a phenomenon that is classless, in the sense that it is
equally distributed throughout society. Downes describes this thesis as
'perverse', running counter to the considerable evidence indicating that there
is a powerful relationship between social class and deviant activity. In
analysing Matza and Sykes's thesis concerning leisure, we come to the essence
of Downes' argument. The process that Downes describes is one of dissociation.
The youth recognizes that work offers a mere wage in exchange for his labour,
and he dissociates himself from middle-class oriented aims and practices, both
educational and occupational. It must be stressed that this process constitutes
neither frustration, nor alienation, as the aspirations of the working-class youth
conform to his allotted station both at school and at work. Consequently the
more debasing, boring, or repetitive the job, the more dissociated the youth
will become, and the more he will try to recoup in the sphere of leisure the
freedom, achievement, autonomy, and excitement that are unavailable at work.

Taking the concept of dissociation as given, it is essential that we should
look at the relationship between the delinquent sub-culture and the parent-
culture. Mays (1954) in his study of Liverpool, located delinquency as a social
tradition that is part of the youth's essential adjustment to the subcultural
context of underprivileged neighbourhoods. Howard Parker, in his Liverpool
study (1974), found that working-class youths take over traditional practices,
behind which lie traditional values. Integral to this process of cultural transmission is an awareness of the limitations and restraints imposed by the job
market with its poor pay, poor conditions, and lay offs. 'The boys' were born
into a structured, clearly defined delinquent territory, and, like Downes'
London study, Parker found that delinquency was tied up with the local job
market. The boys were preoccupied with leisure goals, as were the local adults.
Indeed this is hardly surprising as the adolescents and adults of the
'Roundhouse Estate', where the study was situated, shared most of the basic

structural constraints and social inequalities. Consequently, their world views are consistent and in harmony much more than they are in opposition, involving 'an accommodation to a particular structural situation, rather than a rejection of dominant values and lifestyles'. The suggestion here is that membership of working-class subcultures demonstrates an essential sense of continuity with the parent culture.

'The essential continuity between the adolescent and adult male worlds' has also been noted by Gill (1977: 94). Gill found that tension and aggression between adolescent and adult males was rare, in other words that there was no generation gap. The corner boys of 'Casey's Corner' had inherited a delinquent tradition which, in turn, had originated as a result of a specific housing policy (*ibid.*: 117). For the Luke St. kids unemployment was a norm that had to be accepted (*ibid.*: 110), and if work was found, it would be monotonous, badly paid, and uncongenial. The solution was dissociation as detailed by Downes, and a subcultural tradition of wildness, ranging from petty theft to riotous behaviour, but most commonly consisting of 'hanging about', a youthful pastime that has been noted by virtually every observer of delinquent subcultures (cf. Klein, 1971; Short and Strodbeck, 1965).

Indeed, the British experience can by typified by Gibbens and Ahrenfeldt that, 'Gangs are always present in the next district or they existed last year, never here and now' (1966: 83), and is best summarized by Cohen as 'Loose collectivities or crowds within which there was occasionally some more structured grouping, based on territorial loyalty' (1973: 128).

Patrick's study therefore is an exceptional study of an exceptional area. Patrick gives an insider's account of fighting gangs based on territory, a network of area-oriented violent action that conforms in many ways to Thrasher's structured gang, with its leadership and defined roles. However, the loose membership and image of the group as a collectivity based on spontaneous violence are indicative of Yablonsky's 'violent gang'. Patrick observed that 'The Glasgow juvenile gang has little internal cohesion of its own; it exists to oppose others' (1973: 89) and is a long-standing Glaswegian institution (*ibid.*: 154). Patrick has noted that the gangs are centred around the old housing areas, and that the long traditions of the gang can be matched with a convergence of traditional socio-economic deprivation that is unmatched elsewhere in Britain (*ibid.*: 118). An interlocking network of inequality had produced an enduring gang subculture hinging on dissociation at an early age from middle-class norms, and survival in a climate of socio-economic hardship that has narrowed the possibilities for action. Patrick's work is echoed in the Chicago study of Short and Strodbeck (1965), in the manner in which gangs are located as communal solutions to threats. Yet ironically, given the common perception of gangs as an essentially American phenomenon, unlike the Chicago counterparts, the Glasgow gang retained something approaching permeability across generations, thus affording Patrick's Glaswegians some marked similarities with the quasi-institutions of late twentieth-century streetlife found in the studies of Moore (1978, 1991), and Hagedorn (1988).

These British studies with their emphasis upon the essential continuity between the parent culture and youth culture, echo Miller's thesis that, in manifesting itself as a one-sex peer group, the delinquent subculture is a variant of traditional working-class culture, and that delinquents are merely more involved with the 'focal concerns' of the adult parent culture: trouble, toughness, smartness, and excitement (Miller, 1958). These studies are also quite remarkable for the manner in which they situate communal youth deviance within a context of work, as opposed certainly to contemporary American studies that locate the common experience of unemployment as significant in the formation and continuity of gangs.

Style

The Centre for Contemporary Cultural Studies (CCCS) at Birmingham University produced in the 1970s a highly innovative series of studies that focused on the manner in which sub-cultural forms emerged as methodologies of resistance. Post-war youth cultures are seen in terms of their relationship to the class structure, and their subsequent actions as attempts to solve contradictions within the parent culture (Hall and Jefferson, 1976).

Phil Cohen's comparatively short essay (1972) identified three factors that underpin all traditional working-class communities. These factors are:

1. The extended kinship structure;
2. The ecology of the neighbourhood;
3. The structure of the local economy.

Economic change and the subsequent destruction of the local culture produced contradictions within the working-class family, and subcultures represent ways of trying to retrieve some of the socially cohesive elements destroyed in the parent culture, that are linked to an explanation of the options facing the respectable working class. At an ideological level there is, for the respectable working class, a contradiction between traditional working-class puritanism and what Cohen calls the 'new hedonism of consumption'. At an economic level the contradiction lies between the socially mobile elite and the new *lumpen*, or in terms of the work developed by the CCCS (cf. Hebdige, 1979; Clarke, 1976) between mod and skinhead.

The mod movement of the early to mid-1960s was an attempt to explore the upward option available to working-class youth, and the essence of the mod style lay in the ability to re-define previously acceptable commodities, and re-locate their meanings. For instance, the innocuous motor-scooter, sharp suits, pills: the basis of the style was in the appropriation and reorganization of subjective elements of the objective world that would otherwise restrict action.

The skinhead subculture is regarded as being an attempt to explore the 'lumpen option'. The skinhead has attempted to recreate traditional working-class community, and in doing so exaggerates working-class norms to a point that they become a middle-class caricature of the working man. The skinhead's sense of territory is probably also more exaggerated than any comparable group, and, as Taylor (1971) pointed out in the case of football 'ends', this is an attempt to retrieve some control of what was once an integral part of working-class life, the end providing an arena for territorial protection (see also Daniel and Maguire, 1972). Collective solidarity is also apparent in the predilection for racist violence which is explained in terms of reactions against the evaporation of traditional working-class life.[3] The emphasis upon symbolism that is prevalent within the Birmingham School, and especially in the work of Hebdige and Clark, has been heavily criticized by a number of writers on the grounds of its romantic emphasis upon resistance, ignoring instances when the style is essentially conservative and supportive: neither reworked or reassembled, but appropriated intact from dominant commercial culture (Cohen, 1980: 12; see Hobbs, 1988: chapter 6 for a further discussion of the mod and skinhead subcultures).

The frequently cited ethnography of Willis (1977) offers a view of subcultural resistance that, although it emanates from youth, is adapted to the workplace via school. For Willis the rules of resistance are learnt by low-achieving boys at school, where they are subjected to disciplinary factors that ideally prepare youth for life on the 'shop floor' of the local factory. The somewhat dated industrial context of Willis's work should not detract from the centrality of his thesis that the state, in the form of the educational system, is culpable for creating forms of youthful resistance which are often functional to the requirements of capitalism; notably the reinforcement of a traditional form of masculinity that makes the transformation from the world of school to the world of work relatively seamless (Corrigan, 1976, 1979).

That the subcultural cannot be romanticized to the level of a solution is to state the obvious. Therefore, that stylistic invention, even in the form of 'subordinate cultures' (Willis, 1978), is no answer to the combined effects of poor housing, inadequate education, and badly paid dead-end jobs or unemployment, is hardly a revelation. The subcultural solution is an imaginary one. Given the absence of a structured alternative such as the American style gang, British youth are unable to alleviate the stupefying boredom and lowly status that are the facts of both their working and non-working days. The subcultural response should be seen as an attempt to mark out the world territorially and linguistically, so as to construct specific, concrete, and identifiable social formations that serve as collective responses to the enacted environment of their material experience.

Like much of the work emanating from the CCCS, McRobbie concentrates upon the oppositional as opposed to the illegal and, in her work on the culture of femininity, highlights the method by which young working-class women construct an essentially insubordinate anti-school subculture. McRobbie's

---

[3] The skinhead style always had close associations with right-wing political movements, and in recent years the style has come to represent in explicit terms fascistic tendencies in a number of countries that are experiencing rapid social change (Spergel, 1995: chapter 1).

work takes us from 'the street', and into the domestic realm (McRobbie and Garber, 1976), creating a set of solutions within the bedroom-based teeny bopper subculture, that are every bit as 'magical' as that of the spectacular solutions of the masculine equivalent. Also, as McRobbie (1978) points out, the anti-school element of the female subculture, which is expressed via impertinence, is as crucial in preparing women for the realities of the labour market as are Willis's lads pre-shop floor collaborations. Although some American-based material on women in gangs will be briefly addressed below, it is vital to stress that, despite rises in female delinquency, the ethos around which it is organized remains elusive (Cowie *et al.*, 1968), and with few exceptions, the distinctiveness of youthful female deviant organization remains largely invisible in British studies. Similarly race, although not ignored by British writers, is afforded little attention, often presented in terms of the heroic status of black stylistic devices in relation to white working-class youths scanning of possible options (Hebdige, 1979).

Race

In contrast to the United States (see below), black youth culture does not feature predominantly in the British literature and tends to be presented in terms of its relationship to the police, as a social problem, rather than as an entity in its own right; a courtesy afforded to white youth, whose every stylistic nuance was pored over by academics. Black youth do, however, feature in a number of British studies that highlight the very specific contradictions faced by non-white populations. Rastafarianism in Britain is located by Cashmore (1979) as predominantly a religious, as opposed to subcultural form, and there have been a number of critiques of social policy decisions involving all arms of the state, and the police in particular, who have, as Solomos (1988) has indicated, contributed considerably to creating a context within which black youth action should be understood (Hall *et al.*, 1976; Cashmore and Troyna, 1982; Keith, 1993). The hustling culture described by Pryce in his study of Bristol, conforms to the classic, essentially disorganized response to racism and poverty; a reproduction of urban Caribbean culture, emphasizing a form of strain theory which identifies crime as a form of rebellious self-expression, carried out in the context of racially defined leisure and occupational opportunities (see Valentine, 1978; Robins, 1992).

From the British perspective then, youth subcultures, while they must be studied within the context of the parent culture, are only rational entities when viewed in the broader context of the overall relationship in which they exist with the dominant class. When viewed from this standpoint, subcultural action can be seen to be not only illusory, but also, as Robins and Cohen (1978) have noted, negative and self-destructive. They are usually manifested as essentially loose-knit stylistic devices, operating within the boundaries of class-specific locations, whose functions are largely recreational and allegedly symbolic, incorporating elements of both resistance and incorporation. However, styles and subcultures are not gangs, they do not constitute social structures. Yet in the United States, gang research has adapted to social change, and continued to flourish around the accepted wisdom that within that culture structures based upon law violation (Short and Strodtbeck, 1965), communality, chrono-logical age, territoriality, organizational differentiation (Miller, 1975), race, and gender exist as an alternative social, and increasingly economic, entity.

Females and Gangs

Despite male dominance of delinquent gangs, female participation in gang action is a long-established phenomenon (Asbury, 1927), although the form of this participation is generally presented as peripheral, as sexual auxiliaries or minor accomplices to the mainstream activities of male gang members (Short and Strodtbeck, 1965; Patrick, 1973). The theoretical implications are that the strain that is so heroically represented by the male gang, will be expressed by female working-class youth via promiscuous sexuality. Conversely, female gang members could exhibit explicitly 'male' characteristics of a violent propensity (Cohen and Robins, 1978), they were, as Campbell indicates, 'either tomboys or sex objects' (1990: 167).

The reproduction of normative gender roles within both girl gangs and male-dominated gangs, within which women operate at the periphery, is an outstanding feature of many studies (Quicker, 1983; Campbell, 1984), estab-lishing violence in particular as an essentially ambivalent feature of a social form which both contradicts and enforces normative images of working-class femininity (Horowitz, 1983). As for why young women do not show the same tendency as young men to engage in gang activity, Thrasher, who located only six gangs of his massive sample as female, identified a lack of aggression and the relative intensity of the supervision of young women as opposed to their male peers, is contradicted by Campbell's seminal ethnographic work, which indicated a traditional and familiar willingness to defend turf, albeit with marginally less terminal potential than their male counterparts (1984), to which they have evolved as established auxiliaries (Miller, 1975). Parallels with the non-gang world are clear, yet given the single parenthood and welfare dependency that constitutes their futures, 'The attraction of the gang is no mystery in the context of the isolation and poverty that is awaiting them' (1990: 182).

In many ways this quote from Campbell describes contemporary American work on gangs. Within modern American gang research, there remains the time-honoured unresolved debate concerning definition, and contemporary debates would seem to confirm much of what some of the earlier writers had sought to establish, that a single model of *the* gang does not exist; rather, gangs come in a wide variety of forms. A recognition of the changing condition of the parent class is a major innovation of recent studies of gangs (Hagedorn, 1988), as is an emphasis upon violent and other explicitly criminal character-istics (Klein and Maxson, 1989).

CONTEMPORARY AMERICAN GANG RESEARCH

Since the 1970s, gangs have established themselves as a major social problem whose activities have altered in accord with shifts in the fortunes of the nation's urban economies. As for the extent of the problem, Miller estimates that 83 per cent of America's largest cities had gangs, along with 27 per cent of cities with a population of 100,000 or more, and 13 per cent of cities with populations of 10,000 or more (Miller, 1982). Similar findings were reported by Needle and Stapleton (1983). More recent work supports the thesis that the larger conurbations are more prone to gang formation (Curry *et al.*, 1994), although ethnographic work in compact social settings indicates that they are also likely to produce their own gangs (Hagedorn, 1988; Vigil, 1988). It would appear that the harder researchers look, the bigger the gang problem becomes (Institute for Law and Justice, 1994), for eliciting numerical data on a subject that is ill-defined and dominated by law enforcement agencies which will often have an interest in inflating the phenomenon can be a problematic exercise (see Spergel, 1994: 26–42; Hagedorn, 1990: 240–59, for interesting discussions of the validity of different methods of gang research).

Modern gang researchers have explicitly located race as a major feature of youth gangs, which highlights the manner in which ground-breaking studies such as Thrasher's took race for granted, by placing the emphasis on immigration and the subsequent process of culturation. For instance Moore's (1978) work stresses the way in which, excluded from the mainstream of economic life, informal Chicano culture is supported by prison gang culture (cf. Camp and Camp, 1985) to form neighbourhood gangs that were territorially based, segregated by age, and were violent and drug-orientated. Moore's later work (1991) further emphasized the role of the broader political economy in changing the function of the gang, making it a form of alternative neighbourhood government in the absence of legitimate institutions.

Central to the theme of change that is so apparent in these new gang studies, and accompanying the emphasis on race, is the location of gangs within an urban underclass (Hagedorn, 1988; Vigil, 1988; Moore, 1991). The term underclass was initially expressed by Wilson as a predominantly non-white urban American problem (Wilson, 1987), claiming that economic changes within urban America have produced transformations in class structure that effectively exclude those at society's rump. The British debate has been largely dominated by Murray's (1990) 'moral turpitude' (Westergaard, 1992) use of the term, and is fiercely contested in the British context (cf. McNichol, 1993, Mann, 1992) where it has been drained of both its liberal roots and its empirical grounding (cf. Levitas, 1996). However, common to both countries is the perception of a working-class mutation, no longer active in the workforce, violent, and dependant on welfare. The notion of such a monster emerging from the swamp of late twentieth-century capitalism wearing a reversed baseball cap, intent on apparently ignoring the Mertonian concept of upward mobility upon which

American society is grounded, constitutes rather more of a threat in the United States than in Britain, where such a myth has hardly been a central societal prop.

Enterprise (1)

However, such fears may be unfounded, for there has in these new studies been a marked shift towards understanding gangs in terms of the adoption of market prerogatives within traditional territorial frameworks. The destruction of established territories that were based upon racially defined working-class neighbourhoods is associated with a decline in traditional male employment; the drugs trade offers an alternative sphere of enterprise, and the structure of the gang is an ideal adaptive device for entrepreneurial engagement. As a consequence violent conflict is as likely to be market, as opposed to turf, driven. This is crucial as it locates gangs not, as in the classical sense described by Thrasher, as interstitial, but as part of mainstream economic and social life.

However, in the post-industrial age the notion of territory becomes more problematic, for in the light of the destruction of those traditional working-class areas that formed the basis for gang affiliation, gangs, despite having become quasi-institutions (Fagen, 1990; Moore, 1991), would appear to be relying upon increasingly artificial or symbolic territorial boundaries (Katz, 1988: 146), although localized variations are, in the form of community and neighbourhood variables (Skolnick *et al.*, 1993), central to the process of deindustrialization and globalization (Robertson, 1995). Gang activity does appear to be an increasingly rational activity (Sanchez-Janowski, 1991), and for contemporary youths suffering 'multiple marginality' (Vigil, 1988), the gang offers opportunities to redefine the youth problem in terms of entrepreneurial imperialism via the drugs trade (Taylor, 1990). Most crucially the mainstream presumption of upward mobility has been eroded (Hagedorn. 1988), and as the shift from the formal to the informal economy is compounded, and traditional forms of working-class organization are made redundant, gangs can represent one of the few traditional strategies that retain the potential to adapt to the market, and are elevated to the forefront of the practical consciousness of youth, and to the cutting edge of entrepreneurial strategy (see Davis, 1990: chapter 5). This emulation of organized crime has led Hagedorn (1990) to pose some crucial questions that can only be answered by future generations of researchers. Is this entrepreneurial shift typical? Are there different types of gang-related economic organizations? Do these new gangs resemble contemporary small businesses with a high rate of failure and their employees working part-time for less than subsistence wages? And do these new gangs have any non-economic functions? (Hagedorn, 1990: 243).

Empirical evidence for this shift varies, some researchers reporting well-organized drug distribution operations (Skolnick, 1990; Taylor, 1990; Padilla, 1992), while others question this portrayal (Waldorf and Lauderback, 1993), and the issue of local variations on collaborative criminal strategies is central to the overall thesis of this chapter. The point is that entrepreneurial trends in inner city life have led to the formation of strategies that should not to be regarded as totally separate from the influences of mainstream society. For the demands of the American dream, according to Horowitz (1983), also implicitly mandate an affiliation to competing demands of 'honor', which within the gang, with its emphasis upon character and self respect, constitutes a subcultural solution. Such a mandate allows for diversity (Fagen, 1989), and trends that are driven by the political economy can be located within a historical context, for gangs based upon entrepreneurship as a central ethos (Padilla, 1993), show close similarities with the street gangs of the early part of the twentieth century, who on developing rudimentary organizational structures based upon race, class, and territory, evolved via the Volstead Act into America's principal organized crime groups (Lacey, 1991: chapter 3; Stuart, 1985: chapters 2, 3, 4; Ianni, 1972). Nearly eighty years on, old and new youth gangs, both acquisitive and non-acquisitive, can be seen as rational attempts at discovering solutions to, and acquiring insulation from, their economic, ethnic, and class marginality via the construction of identity around a form of 'local patriotism' (Sanchez-Jankowski, 1991: 99) that has essentially ambiguous symbiotic relationships with its host communities.

Summary

To summarize, the early gang studies charted the emergence of youth gangs from poor disorganized urban neighbourhoods. Arranged around race and territorial imperatives, American theories of status frustration and alienation resulted in subcultural theories organized around strain and conflict. British studies questioned the application of American research to British society, and suggested that delinquent groups are organized around dissociation, locating delinquent subcultures within the broader parent culture, and stressed the inherited quality of the problems to which delinquent subcultures are a response, perceiving the emergence of subcultures as an attempt to solve ideological and economic contradictions within the parent culture. Contemporary American studies locate gangs as a segment of a racialized urban underclass, and stress variation, diversity, and flexibility.

PROFESSIONAL CRIME

What your supposed to do is act like a fuckin' professional. A psychopath is not a professional. You can't work with a psychopath, 'cause ya don't know what those sick assholes are gonna do next [Tarrantino 1994: 24–6].

Having discussed the various possibilities to emerge from youthful collaborations, this section is concerned with rational, specialized, and successful unambiguously acquisitive activity. It will look at the classical works on

professional crime, and the debate surrounding their subcultural interpretations; the ethical frameworks that provide some alleviation of the ambiguity
that is implicit in professional crime; the illusory non-instrumental character
that informs much professional criminal activity; and finally the impact of the
broader political economy.

Lifeworlds and Subcultures

Sutherland's *The Professional Thief* (1937) is a landmark in criminological
research. In his case study of Chic Conwell, Sutherland introduces readers to
a concept of criminality, not as an all-encompassing monolith defined and
identified by legal criteria, but as a fragment of criminal activity that is to be
understood as a separate behaviour system (see Hollingshead, 1939). Ignoring
legal *Diktats* and concentrating upon cultural disposition, Sutherland offers a
direct challenge to the dominant Chicagoan explanation of crime as being the
result of social disorganization (see also Landesco, 1968). What Sutherland
discovered was a well-established behaviour system, located within relatively
cohesive groups that shared the following characteristics; technical skill, consensus via a shared ideology, differential association, status, and organization.

While support for this model is to be found in subsequent empirical work
(Maurer, 1955), the volatile nature of the market place has created a context
within which Sutherland's concept of professional crime is contested. Lemert
(1958) for instance regards the cheque forger as a loner with few skills, while
the President's Commission (1966), stresses the importance of 'hustlers' who
are adaptable, engaging in a wide range of criminal activity, and lacking a
shared consensus with other hustlers, therefore calling to question the notion
of a cohesive behaviour system as suggested by Sutherland.

Einstadter (1969), who considered the subcultural possibilities that can
emerge when a group of specialists share a commitment, further explored
Sutherland's theory. Although he discovered consistency of practice and a
measure of ideological coherence, Einstadter found that armed robbers did not
rely upon a system of tutelage, or maintain relationships with quasi-legitimate
agents such as 'fences' with one foot in the straight world. On the other hand,
Shover (1973) has clearly established that the burglar comes closer to
Sutherland's classic analysis than the cheque forger and the armed robber, and
proposes that it is the exigencies of burglary that necessitate the creation of
networks of dependency, rather than non-instrumental cultural bonding based
upon common occupational status. Further, although Shover acknowledges
that these networks will continue to evolve due to changes in policing, security,
and technology, it is apparent that burglary could never become totally defunct
in the manner of, for example, safe-blowing (Chambliss, 1972; Letkemann,
1973; Hobbs 1995*a*), or indeed alter as drastically as cheque forgery (Lemert,
1958).

For most professional thieves links with the legitimate world are crucial, and
it is important to broaden the scope of any analysis to include what Mack

and Kerner (1975) have called 'background operators'. For instance, the dealer in stolen goods is pivotal to the competent and efficient functioning of any professional thief, and Walsh (1977), Walsh and Chappell (1974), Steffensmeier (1986), Klockars (1974), Maguire and Bennett (1982: chapter 4), Wright and Decker (1994: chapter 6) all situate the trade in stolen goods within a milieu dominated by the mores of mainstream economic activity. Mack and Kerner claim that the high status of the front line operator is illusory, and that the organization behind the front-liners warrants greater attention. Over two decades on, Mack and Kerner's observations deserve to be taken seriously, for professional criminal networks, like other sub-systems of organized capitalism, are increasingly typified by profound and complex relations that will be marked by local, regional, national, and international characteristics and, as in the case of youth gangs, they may manifest themselves at street level as marginal and essentially disorganized.

Wright and Decker (1994) locate burglary, not within an amorphous market place, nor within the structured social relations of a sub-culture. Their emphasis lies with the generating milieu of 'streetlife'. Although only a few of their sample of burglars actually regarded themselves as burglars, a significant number possessed the kind of specialized exclusive knowledge that is not acquired by non-criminals, by specialist police personnel, or by convicted non-property offenders. (Logie, Wright, and Decker, 1992).

Letkemann (1973), who uses the term 'rounder' to describe the all-purpose adaptive criminal, also stresses that a commitment to making a living from crime provides the best criterion for differentiating between professional and non-professional offenders. The all-purpose non-specialist 'rounder' or 'hustler' (Holzman, 1983; Polsky, 1964, 1971; Roebuck and Johnson, 1962) is ideally suited to a criminal milieu dominated by the concept of the market, with a labour force fragmented into flexible coalitions of similarly disposed individuals. The temporary nature of these coalitions is ensured by the unpredictable nature of market forces and by the advantages to be gained from an ever-changing work place and *modus operandi* (Hobbs 1995a).

Skill (Inciardi, 1976), craft (Mcintosh, 1971), and competence (Shover, 1973), are the everyday methodologies inherent in the committal of crime as work (Letkemann, 1973), and the question of what constitutes a competent performance is central to Luckenbill's (1981) study of armed robbery. The central problem for the robber is how to gain and maintain the compliance of victims, and Luckenbill perceives robbery as a series of transactions managed by the robber, involving his victims in the accomplishment of four interrelated tasks. On establishing his presence with the victim, the interaction is transformed into 'the robbery frame', the goods are transferred to the robber, and finally the robber leaves the scene.

Goffman (1952) provides an in-depth exploration of the maintenance of compliance in the case of confidence tricksters, where the victim's acceptance of failure is regarded as vital for the successful completion of a crime. Goffman, concentrating upon the relationship between the confidence trickster and his victim or 'mark', regards the skilful manipulation of the victim as central to the stage-management of the ongoing crime drama. Yet, unlike Luckenbill's study, Goffman presents the con-game as an allegorical comment upon everyday interactions, for the mark has invested in an interaction that promises profit rather than loss. As a consequence the management of failure is more crucial than in the case of armed robbery, and the importance of the victim's rationalizations brings this aspect of professional crime closer to processes found in legitimate projects.

In his study of the world of the professional killer, Levi (1981) utilized frame analysis to discover that professional murderers, unlike professional thieves, are able, by virtue of the exclusivity of their specialism, to establish a rarefied niche within the labour market. By dehumanizing and reframing the victim as a target, and by receiving monetary reward for his services, the professional murderer avoids self-stigmatization, and enhances the status of murderer to that of a rational market operative, thereby commercializing impersonal violence and commodifying death .

Ethics

Claims have been made that professional crime is organized around an ethical code of practice, upon which the identity and solidarity of professional criminals are formulated (see for instance Maurer, 1955). Inviting parallels with legitimate professional communities, and drawing heavily upon Sutherland's notion of a coherent group possessing 'a complex of abilities and skills, just as do physicians, lawyers or bricklayers' (1937: 197), the notion of an unwritten code providing a framework for a sharply delineated association of professional criminals is a highly pervasive concept. Professional criminals are keen on the notion of such a code, for, as in the legitimate world, there is a noticeable tendency to hark back to a golden age of predictability, stoicism, honour, and reliability (Shover, 1973: 512). Aged villains in particular are predisposed to nostalgia, yearning for stability and a mythical age when justice, or at least informal justice, served as a structural prop for their criminal activity that stands in stark relief to the amorphous nature of contemporary crime (see Kray, 1991; Lambrianou, 1992; Campbell, 1991: chapter 6; Fraser, 1994).

Applying a code of ethics to an activity that is marked by chaotic, apparently incoherent, interludes (Reuter, 1984) and littered with violent episodes has been called into question (Hobbs, 1995a, 1997), as professional criminals are overwhelmingly ambivalent to any coherent ethical framework (Ball *et al.*, 1978; Jennings *et al.*, 1991; Short, 1992). However, the notion of a distinct and homogeneous environment of professional crime enables contemporary professional criminals to inject a sense of retrospective order into their manic lifeworlds. This underworld fantasy is constituted by the incessant recurrence of sacred myths related to traditional strategies and iconic individuals, and functions to preserve a highly significant illusion of the perpetuation of an expert system (Hobbs, 1997, 1995a). By blending their experiences of the enacted environments of contemporary crime markets with this sense of 'retrospective unity' (Bauman, 1992: 138), an imaginary community that leans heavily upon an invented tradition (Anderson, 1983; Hobsbawm, 1983) is created.

The most coherent claim for a self-contained code of professional criminal ethics linked to professional criminals is to be found in studies of prison subcultures. Both Irwin (1970) and Irwin and Cressey (1962) stress that the most crucial aspect in determining an inmate's adaptation to prison is the culture that he brings with him to the institution. Further, the culture of the professional criminal is most easily adapted to prison regimes, for the identity is one that carries currency—in particular qualities of 'rightness', 'solidness', 'honesty', 'responsibility', and 'loyalty', both inside and outside the context of institutional confinement. Former identities are enhanced, and the professional's commitment to a criminal identity is an important component to an individual's adaptation to incarceration, verifying prison as an authentic and central element of criminal culture (Irwin and Cressey, 1962; see also Cohen and Taylor, 1972: chapter 7; McVicar, 1982; Fraser, 1994; Mason, 1994; Foreman, 1996).

However, for those readers for whom the world of prison may seem some way removed from the enacted environment of professional crime (Solway and Waters, 1977: 163), the code of professional criminal ethics is little more than a rhetorical device that has evolved to retain some sense of exclusive order in the face of a rapidly changing environment and ever-fluctuating personnel (Taylor, 1984: 76). As the President's Commission states, 'The shifting, transitory pattern of most professional criminals working relationships was found to be accompanied by the absence of any strong ethical codes' (President's Commission, 1967: 98).

Hedonism

The life world of the professional criminal is not prone to 'sub-systems of purposive rational action' (Habermas, 1984), and is perfectly illustrated by the essentially narcissistic drive implicit in a 'life lived without a safety net' (Pileggi, 1987: 39). First-hand accounts of 'life as party' (Shover and Honaker, 1991), confirm the centrality of 'earning and burning money' (Katz, 1988: 215) as a way of confirming the professional criminal's commitment to an identity defined by conspicuous consumption, and funded by crime (Hohimer, 1981: 19; Wideman, 1985: 131; Taylor, 1983: 14). It is important to understand the cultures that are carved out to sustain professional crime, for such an understanding indicates that there is not some vast gulf between instrumental and non-instrumental crime (see Anderson *et al.*, 1989). For what becomes apparent is that the market place can create environments that will enable simultaneous entrepreneurial and hedonistic engagement. This apparent ambiguity is a powerful tool of all professional criminals, and is a crucial device in structuring the identities of those practitioners engaging with leisure markets, for whom the ambivalence between hedonism and 'pure' economic engagement can seal the instrumental properties of professional criminality within identifiable networks of deviant action. The fragmented narratives that make up the personnel rosters of these networks serve as contingencies for markets that generate fragmentation, and produce a far more potent marketing arrangement that is hamstrung neither by arcane practices and their attendant folk memories, nor by the tribal sensibilities of previous eras. As Bauman has noted, 'The more secure the fragmentation, the more desultory and less controllable the resulting chaos' (1993: 13).

Given the emphasis on non-specialization that is located above in the work of the President's Commission, Letkemann, Holzman, and Polsky, and the refutation of the relevance of underworld scenarios to contemporary crime, it is evident that an exploration of the broader social maelstrom of which professional criminals are but a segment could be a profitable exercise. Entrepreneurship is now the primary ideological buttress of contemporary society, acknowledging the overt quest for wealth acquisition by both legitimate and illegitimate interests (cf. Burrows, 1991; Heelas and Morris, 1992). There is now an ambiguous frisson to the term professional criminal that is entirely appropriate in a post-traditional order that has made obsolete class-based notions of structural and ideological constraint (Pakulski and Waters, 1996).

Mack (1964) situated professional crime within a conventional class-orientated sub-culture, focusing upon the role of the traditional class base from which most 'full-time miscreants' emerge, and indicating the role of contemporaneous notions of competence in maintaining networks of professional crime. However, the era that Mack was describing did not feature the drug trade as a significant, let alone dominant, practice and crime was a relatively simplistic category. The exclusivity of the professional criminal's milieu has been permanently breached by enterprise culture. Consequently although normative commerce provides the most crucial clues to understanding 'full time miscreants' (Mack, 1964), the cultural origins of professional criminals are no longer exclusively proletarian.

Enterprise (2)

The crucial ambiguity between notions of criminal and legal commercial activity is ideally illustrated by the drugs trade (Langer, 1977; Dorn and South, 1990; Williams, 1989). Drug dealing offers unparalleled scope and variety to those who seek to explore entrepreneurial frontiers. However, the drugs trade does not constitute a static homogenous economic sphere. Dunlap *et al.* (1994) and Bourgois (1995) both stress that there is more to be gleaned from the market place than economic viability, and the explicit absence of enabling 'underworlds' has created criminal formations that owe more to the everyday tribulations of running a small business than to the contingencies of traditional professional crime (cf. Hobbs, 1995*a*: chapter 9; Ruggiero, 1996).

Mirroring the fragmentation of the legitimate economy (Lash and Urry, 1987; Piore and Sabel, 1984) and subsequent changes in the workforce, women are more likely to become involved in serious criminality (Taylor, 1993). Fagen, highlighting the declining status of young men, has located female involvement in the cocaine economy as indicative of crucial alterations to the social controls that had prevailed in poor urban neighbourhoods, which in turn relate to changes in the structural circumstances of women living in these neighbourhoods (Fagen, 1994: 186). The contingencies of cocaine markets were seen as relatively open to women who are able to achieve a degree of status traditionally denied by the exigencies of street networks (Taylor, 1993). This emergent body of work indicates that the heavily gendered world of professional crime may be showing signs of remodelling according to the host culture's template (cf. Ruggiero and South, 1995: 138–41).

It is extremely problematic to attempt to formulate criminal typifications within the context of a contemporary market place that, despite its domination by a single commodity, drugs, remains as fragmented by class, race, and gender as the so-called legitimate economic sphere (Ruggeiro, 1993; Adler and Adler, 1983). Further, such fragmentation will have a major impact upon the continuity of illegal enterprise, for successful illegal entrepreneurs will seek to invest in legal enterprises, and the lack of suitable opportunities within ghetto cultures (Ruggiero, 1993), compared to those of elite markets (Adler and Adler, 1983), is a serious stumbling block to consistent growth, and diminishes the possibility of skill, consensus, shared ideology, and, crucially, organization being allowed to acquire maturity.

Crimes that were previously central to the concept of professional status, for example armed robbery, have become haphazard, essentially amateur excursions (Morrison and O'Donnell, 1994; Walsh, 1986: chapter 3), performed with minimal planning and base levels of competence. Only 11 per cent of Walsh's sample of robbers provided a self-description of thief or robber (Walsh, 1986: 57). However, enterprise culture has spawned a highly flexible practitioner, skilled and culturally resourced for multiple entrepreneurial engagements, committed not to a subculture, but to financial gain; his practice is marked by the competent manipulation of markets and the maximization of profit.

Despite the traditional schooling in rough places of many professional criminals (Wideman, 1985; Gibbs and Shelley, 1982; Pruis and Irini, 1980), the cultures that nurture professional crime now feature variations that reflect the range of activities that constitute the expert exploration of new markets (Levi, 1987: p. xix; Dorn *et al.*, 1992: 31–62). Yet the term professional crime is far from obsolete (Cressey, 1972: 45). For the fluidity of contemporary opportunity structures merely mirrors the shifts that characterize modern societies, which in turn constitute fresh opportunities. Once we retune our perceptions of contemporary markets we can focus upon professionals, 'as fluid sets of mobile marauders in the urban landscape alert to institutional weakness in both legitimate and illegitimate spheres' (Block, 1983: 245).

Summary

A distinct subcultural analysis of professional crime has gradually given way
to an understanding that located the organization of professional crime around
the characteristics of a specific criminal act, and the presumption of a common
class base shared by its practitioners. As the socio-economic context within
which crime is framed has altered, so the blurring of legitimate and illegitimate
economies has produced a form of professional crime that is organized around
normative commercial practice, and in particular entrepreneurship.

ORGANIZED CRIME

You know what's wrong with the world today? People aren't true to any one
philosophy. They pick and choose among all different ones. They choose loyalty when
it suits them. They choose independence when it suits them. They choose change
when it suits them. They do exactly as they please, and they can always find a way to
justify what they're doing, they can make it seem like, no matter what, they're being
true to some morality or other. But you can't just pick up little pieces of the package.
You go with the whole program, or it doesn't mean a thing [Joe 'Piney' Armone, in
O'Brien and Kurins, 1991: 276].

The socio-economic context that is identified above retains if anything even
greater cogence for reading organized crime. Seeking out a definition of a
complex, ever-mutating range of phenomena is not the purpose of this section;
indeed, as Kelly (1986) has pointed out, such an exercise is neither possible nor
desirable. Although definitional disputes abound in this area, the review of the
literature undertaken by Albanese shines some light upon the problem. The
result is

there is great consensus . . . that organised crime functions as a continuing enterprise
that rationally works to make a profit through illicit activities, and that it insures its
existence through the use of threats or force and through corruption of public officials
to maintain a degree of immunity from law enforcement . . . organised crime tends to
be restricted to those legal goods and services that are in great public demand through
monopoly control of an illicit market [Albanese, 1996: 3; cf. Hagen, 1983; Maltz, 1976,
1985, 1990].

The purpose of this section is to discuss the broad area of organized crime and
its close relations, illicit enterprise and serious crime, via some of the central
debates and themes to be gleaned from the relevant literature, namely, the historical role of organized crime in relation to the state and urban development;
two brief strands noting the marked emphasis on ethnicity that many writers
have adopted in order to understand organized crime; and finally, as in the
previous two sections, the political economy's impact upon the practice of
organized crime, and the seamless nature of its relationship with the legitimate

socio-economic order. The focus will be upon organized crime in the United States, for that is the origin of both the bulk of the available literature, and some of the more abrasive debates. Although other cultures will be referred to, it is entirely appropriate within the context of a chapter stressing the economically driven nature of criminal cultures that the twentieth century's most potent economic force should be its prime focus of attention.

Pirates and Gangsters

Although there are historical studies on this phenomenon in abundance, the origins of sociological concerns with organized crime are located, yet again, in Chicago. Yet, the theoretical drift of many of the historical studies suggests a few interesting themes that are later picked up by some contemporary writers, for, as Browning and Gerrassi (1980) indicate, the state's ambiguous relationship to organized crime has initiated some of its most significant examples. The establishment and maintenance of British colonies was, in Elizabethan times, largely the prerogative of state-sponsored pirates, their licence to plunder was exploited to the full, and, as in the modern world, their success was rewarded by legitimation and an entrée into polite society (Sherry, 1986). As commercial cultures emerged as the bedrock of pre-industrial Britain, piracy came to be seen as a threat to the comportment of legitimate trade, but not before it had succeeded in forming corrupt alliances with government officials (Rankin, 1969). The emergence of America as an exporting economy in its own right led to the withdrawal of the supporting structures, havens, and above all the markets upon which piracy relied (Karraker, 1953), and by the end of the eighteenth century's second decade piracy as an ongoing concern was dead.

By the time Landesco's study of Chicago was originally published in 1927 this pattern of market exploitation, violence, incorporation, and institutional legitimation had succeeded in repeating itself many times over during the exploration of natural resources and subsequent establishment of the industrial and commercial empires upon which modern America was founded. The fortunes of the Astors (corruption, extortion, violence, fraud: cf. Myers, 1936; Loth, 1938), the Vanderbilts (political insurrection, violence: cf. Andrews, 1941; Loth, 1938), the Rockefellers (corruption, violence: Lloyd, 1963), Henry Ford (violence: Sinclair, 1962), and other seminal figures of American, indeed global, capitalism were established via dubious practices and outright criminality (see Block and Chambliss, 1981; Abadinsky, 1990: 59–74). As Daniel Bell points out:

the foundation for many a distinguished older American fortune was laid by sharp practices and morally reprehensible methods. The pioneers of American capitalism were not graduated from Harvard's School of Business Administration. The early settlers and founding fathers, as well as those who 'won the west' and built up cattle, mining and other fortunes, often did so by shady speculations and not an inconsiderable amount of violence [Bell, 1953: 152].

Coupled with the corruption of urban American politics, with its violence, graft, and vote rigging (Werner, 1928; Hofstadter, 1956; McCaffrey, 1976), this was the environment that existed long before the term organized crime, a 'new label for old phenomenon' (Woodiwiss, 1987: 8), entered common usage. Organized crime was a catch-all term for both the established villainy of the new urban centres and the innovative configurations of street gangs who were so ideally situated to exploit the opportunities offered by prohibition (Thrasher, 1927: 281–92). Landesco (1968), who first published his study of Chicago in 1929, although not as crucial a figure to the study of organized crime as Thrasher is to gangs or Sutherland is to professional crime, has provided a crucial groundbreaking study that situates organized crime in Chicago as central to the indigenous socio-political landscape. Out of print within the year, and not reprinted for forty years, Landesco locates organized crime as a local phenomenon that is a mirror of the world of legitimate business. Like Thrasher the social disorganization of poor working-class areas was regarded by Landesco as the key to understanding organized crime, and, like Thrasher, Landesco was keen to highlight the functional role that community-based criminality played, including providing rare successful role models for the poor.

Prohibition, which lasted from 1920 to 1933, was a turning point in American crime (for a comprehensive review of the politics of prohibition and its repeal, see Kyvig, 1985). Vast profits emanated from this unpopular law which prohibited the manufacture, transportation, sale, and importation of intoxicating liquor. The era was a criminogenic free-for-all with up-and-coming Jewish and Italian street criminals, thieves, and pimps, conflicting and colluding with Irish and Polish crime groups (Haller, 1974; Block, 1983: 130–41), not forgetting well-established political forces (Asbury, 1950). For as Landesco pointed out, political corruption was, in the context of American cities, endemic and central to the functioning of organized criminality. The repeal of the Volstead Act witnessed the penetration of organized crime into every orifice and alcove of American economic life (Kobler, 1971; Woodiwiss, 1993) and, as Haller notes, criminals had had to familiarize themselves with banking, insurance, business takeovers, the chemical and cosmetic industries, transport, shipping, the copper, corn, and sugar markets, as well as bottling and labelling industries (1985: 142). Meanwhile others extended their criminal activities further afield (Haller, 1985: 152; Bell, 1953: 136–42; Pillegi, 1995) into gambling, and 'The old clear line between underworld and upperworld became vague and easily crossed' (Fox, 1989: 51).

Ethnic Succession

Ethnicity has traditionally been regarded as the principal dynamic that drives organized crime (Woodiwiss, 1993), and the notion of outside forces polluting an otherwise pristine environment remains an enduring method of locating responsibility for modes of criminality that are perceived as especially menacing. In American society there was little significant academic concern with organized crime after Landesco, as journalists and Hollywood were left to mythologize the exploits of Capone and Luciano *et al.* unhampered by reality, the rise of the gangster being presented as a trajectory that reflected the hopes and aspirations of a nation founded on the principle of upward mobility (Warshow, 1948; Bell, 1953).

Bell considered crime to be an essential component of American society, 'A Queer Ladder of Social Mobility' (1964), that is essentially functional in offering an alternative mode of upward mobility to ethnic groups who found more traditional paths blocked by the rigid stratification of conventional society. This essentially romantic version of the social evolution of American culture is afforded considerable credibility by Ianni's (1972) ethnography of the 'Lupollo' crime family. According to Ianni, 'The Irish came first, and early Irish gangsters started the climb up the ladder . . . the Irish won wealth power and respectability . . . In organised crime the Irish were succeeded by the Jews . . . The Jews quickly moved on up the ladder into the world of business, a more legitimate means of economic and social mobility. The Italians came last' (Ianni, 1972: 49). 'At their first entrance into this society, immigrants and their children grasp at the immediate means of acquiring what the New World has to offer. As they are acculturated, their crimes become more American and in time merge into the area of marginal legitimate business practice' (*ibid.*: 61).[4] The thesis leans heavily upon a version of strain theory as briefly discussed above in the section on gangs and sub-cultures (cf. Kelly, 1986: 23), and Ianni, in a later work, indicated that new ethnic groups are usurping the Italians, who, having achieved economic success in both criminal and legitimate fields, moved on to create fresh opportunities for Blacks and Puerto Ricans, the city's new immigrant groups. 'We shall witness over the next decade the systematic development of what is now a scattered and loosely organised pattern of emerging black control in organised crime into the Black Mafia' (Ianni, 1974: 12). The origins of these 'modern' organized crime groups, according to Ianni, are formed, like the Irish, Jews, and Italians before them, from street-corner youth gangs as a form of self- and turf-protection (1972: 54).

Lupsha (1981, 1983) casts doubt upon the notion of ethnic succession, pointing out that despite an improvement in their economic status, Italians, 'while withdrawing from street and direct front line operations' (1981: 5) remain prominent in organized crime, and goes on to cast doubt upon strain theory as a credible explanation, claiming that involvement in organized crime is a 'rational choice, rooted in one perverse aspect of our values, namely, that only "suckers" work, and that in our society, one is at liberty to take "suckers"

---

[4] The basic premise of Ianni's work is not supported by Haller (1970), who in an analysis of the ethnic origin of Chicago's principal organized crime figures, found that the Italians and the Irish were running almost neck and neck with 30% and 29% respectively, while the Jews tailed behind with 20%. This contradicts Ianni who claimed that 'The Italians did not get a leg up on organised crime until the late 1930s' (Ianni, 1972: 49). Although six pages later this process of upward mobility is brought forward to the late 1920s.

and seek easy money' (1981: 22). Further, the succession thesis is contradicted by both the multi-ethnic networks described by Block (1983) and the continued presence of Irish individuals and groups such as the Westies in contemporary organized crime (Pillegi, 1987: 96–106; Cummings and Volkman, 1992: 127–9, 200–4; President's Commission, 1986). The notion of ethnic succession does however have its roots in attempts to understand crime as an essential part of socio-economic life, and not as a separate entity operating beyond the boundaries of normative human endeavour. Its acceptance, particularly by the entertainment industry, owes much to its familiarity as a marketable myth, portraying capitalism as a dynamic 'natural' process. Then there was the Kefauver Commission.

Alien Conspiracy

In 1950 Senator Estes Kefauver chaired the Special Senate Committee to Investigate Organized Crime in the United States, and brought the subject 'into the great expanded political arena that was one of the consequences of World War II' (Block, 1983: 123). Essentially Kefauver condensed essentially localized community-based organized crimes into Organized Crime, replacing violence and corruption with a national conspiracy (Block, 1983: 123) run by 'a sinister criminal organisation known as the Mafia operating throughout the country . . . a direct descendant of a criminal organisation of the same name originating in the island of Sicily' (US Senate, 1951: 2). What amounted to an assumption of the Mafia's existence (Albini, 1971: 210), built upon America's obsession with conspiracy (Smith, 1975) and post-war fear of subversion (Block, 1983). The committee decided that organized crime was 'the expression of a moral conspiracy aimed at the vitals of American life' (Block, 1983: 123). Law-enforcement witnesses provided unsubstantiated allegations and failed to provide sufficient evidence for a nationwide hierarchical ethnic conspiracy (Moore, 1974). However, the model that subsequently developed claimed that organized crime had been imported via Italian immigrants, who had brought with them membership of traditional secret criminal societies such as the Mafia and the Camorra. While the resurrection of Mafia demonology, which had largely lain dormant during the maelstrom of prohibition, has been proven to be exaggerated and highly simplified (Blok, 1974; Smith, 1971, 1975, 1980), a meeting featuring a number of organized crime figures in Appalachin in 1957 (Bonanno, 1983; Salerno and Tompkins, 1969) reinforced the public's growing belief that 'forces outside of mainstream American culture are at work which seek to pervert an otherwise morally sound, industrious, and democratic people' (Potter 1994: 10).

The alien conspiracy theory, fed both the public's voracious appetite for conspiracy set in the context of Hollywood gangster scenarios, and law enforcement agencies' need to confirm their assumptions and seek out criminal hierarchies that mirror the organizational hierarchies of policing (Reuter, 1986). As Chambliss points out 'the law enforcement system maximises its visible effectiveness by creating and supporting a shadow government that manages the rackets' (1978: 92). In the absence of any evidence, the concept received an enormous boost in 1963 when Joseph Valachi appeared before a Senate sub-committee declaring, to the amazement of organized crime investigators, the existence of the Cosa Nostra, and described a bloody feud in 1931, the Castellammarese War, which after up to sixty deaths, succeeded in reconciling competing crime groups and created the 'new' Mafia (Cressey, 1967; Turkus and Feder, 1951; Maas, 1968). The significance, and indeed the very existence, of the Castellammarese War has since been successfully contested by Block (1978, 1983: chapter 1; cf. Nelli, 1976; Inciardi *et al.*, 1977: 100). The existence of a highly structured criminal organization called La Cosa Nostra (a term that nobody had heard before Valachi's testimony) proved a godsend for government officials seeking a hook upon which to hang Kefauver and Apalachin. To describe Valachi's testimony as flawed is something of an understatement (Hawkins, 1969; Block, 1978, 1983), yet it remained the sole evidence of the existence of a national criminal conspiracy:

During the years following his revelations, the great majority of published books, articles and news items that have attempted to describe the structure of organised crime in America clearly reveal a heavy reliance on Valachi . . . Not infrequently it would appear, he either withheld facts that should have been known to him or deliberately lied [Peterson, 1983: 425; cf. Potter, 1994: 31–4].

It is during this era that Donald Cressey emerged as the most influential academic concerned with organized crime. As a member of the 1967 Presidential Task Force, Cressey put meat on the bones of Valachi's testimony, and described a strict Italian/American bureaucratic hierarchy of organized criminality that exhibited many of the structural features of legitimate corporate enterprise. Cressey's claim that the twenty-four families of the American Mafia were controlled by a Commission made up of the leaders of the most powerful families (Cressey, 1969: pp. x–xi) suggests an alternative government controlling a national criminal conspiracy that seeks to monopolize criminal opportunities (Schelling, 1976) and constitutes a serious threat to democratic structures by the corruption of public officials (Cressey, 1967, 1969; cf. O'Brien and Kurins, 1991, for a more recent law-enforcement-orientated view of the day-to-day workings of the Commission). Cressey's stress on the importance of the Castellammarese War as a defining moment for organized crime is lifted almost in its entirety from Valachi's statement (Cressey, 1969: chapter 3), while, as Block indicates, Cressey's portrayal of organized crime, and in particular the division of labour and the function of violence as exemplified by the role of the enforcer (*ibid.*: 164–7), bear close comparison with the work of Turkus and Feder (1951). Cressey's work has not stood the test of time, at best it constitutes an over elaboration founded on myth (Morris and Hawkins, 1970; Smith, 1975). His interpretation of evidence, particularly wire taps, indicates a considerable strain to load the data into the mould of a national criminal conspiracy (Hawkins, 1969), and a leap in faith regarding the competence and effectiveness of police agencies to collect and analyse relevant materials (Reuter and Rubinstein, 1978: 69–71). Most importantly however, Cressey's formalistic overview (Reuter 1994: 100–1), stressing an extraordinarily high degree of efficiency (Anderson, 1979: 33), while it may fit the perceptions of police managers, is contradicted by the majority of empirical studies that have subsequently emerged which stress flexibility and the ability to adapt (Lupsha, 1981), multiple relationships driven by the quest for personal gain (Albini, 1971: 288), inter-ethnic co-operation (Block, 1983: chapter 2), and a non-monopolistic, essentially fragmented market place (Reuter, 1984; Reuter and Rubinstein, 1978).

Given the absence of any causal link between ethnicity and organized crime, ethnicity can at best be regarded as a variable 'that becomes significant only when it is found in combination with a host of other variables that seek to explain the complex puzzle of organised criminal involvement' (Albini, 1988: 347–8). Indeed to stress ethnicity to the extent of the exclusion of other variables shrouds many distinguishing marks of the enacted environments of contemporary socio-economic life. When viewed from a perspective that regards organized crime, not as separate, exclusive, and essentially removed from normative civil society, but as one of its central props (Chambliss, 1978), what emerges is a loose system of power relationships (Albini, 1971) that interacts seamlessly with both upper and underworlds.

Enterprise (3)

As we can see from the brief discussion of the Volstead Act above, conditions were created for the transformation of legal markets into illegal markets and the rapid evolution of powerful criminal enterprises, while hardly affecting either the demand for alcohol or its method of production (Lodhi and Vaz, 1980). Once the benchmark of legitimacy is passed by the dynamics of the market, a context is created within which the illicit entrepreneur can thrive (Smith, 1980). 'Where the old neighbourhood and the new market place intersect, profit can be accrued, with neither the risk of confrontation nor the nurturing comfort inherent in the old "underworld"' (Hobbs, 1997). The spheres of opportunity that are created are essentially malleable and, unlike those manifested in the old underworld, are not located in fixed terrain (Chaney, 1994: 149), but within both local and global networks, the conformations of which are ambiguous, engaging with ongoing criminal opportunities which often constitute variations upon themes that have been established by the precedents of indigenous markets. The notion of a 'spectrum of enterprise' (Smith, 1980) enables an understanding of crime in terms of economic activity, as opposed to some 'evil empire'. The overwhelming weight of evidence regarding organized crime groups indicates that they can be located within a socio-economic terrain that is essentially unremarkable, yet they remain marginally distinct 'in respect of their dynamism, the degree to which they undercut traditional habits and customs, and their global impact' (Giddens, 1991: 1).

As legitimate markets have globalized, accelerating the disintegration of traditional cultures, so global drug markets have contributed to the erosion of traditional criminal territories and their criminal progeny. The dialectic between the local and the global (Giddens, 1990: 64; 1991: 22) typifies the entire spectrum of enterprise and the resultant enacted environment, where intricate relations between global and local spaces are negotiated (Robins, 1991), is too elaborate and disparate for the notion of a criminal underworld to carry any contemporary weight (Hobbs, 1995*a*, 1997). Smith's spectrum (which was based on the now dated Bureau of the Budget, Standard Industrial Classification) should now be realigned to take globalization into account, for local organized crime has now mutated into forms of enterprise that should be regarded as indigenous renditions of global markets. This new environment is where; 'the business of crime is planned, contacts are made, some crimes are carried out, the fruits of crime are often enjoyed, and the methodologies for the integration of organised criminals into civil society are established' (Block, 1991: 15).

It should be stressed that to highlight the role of globalization is not the same as making a claim for 'transnational organized crime'. The devastation of sovereign boundaries and the superfluity of Cold War histories have led to an increased concern with transnational organized crime (see Labrousse and Wallon, 1993; Williams, 1993; Sterling, 1994; Calvi, 1993), yet the term trans-national is inappropriate and essentially misleading in referring to organized crime, for it is a term that is normally assigned to cross-border activity involv-ing the explicit exclusion of the state (Hobsbawm, 1994). The relationship between the state and organized crime however is sufficiently ambiguous (Woodiwiss, 1993; Pearce, 1976; Bullington and Block, 1990) to render the term 'transnational organized crime' at best problematic, as it effectively shrouds the involvement of the state in utilizing criminality for a variety of ends, but particularly as an alternative means of implementing foreign policy. The utility of the term should be regarded within the context of moral panics that have emerged as a response to the disintegration of the Eastern bloc and found a home within the budget wars of declining western states (cf. Naylor, 1995).

The ambiguous nature of the relationship between organized crime and the state is clearly indicated by Rawlinson (1996), who, in using Russian organized crime as an exemplar, makes a case for a four-part model to be applied to this relationship. These four stages suggest that when the state is stable, organized crime operates outside the legitimate socio-political system. The second stage is reached when the dominant system has weakened, and is forced to negotiate with organized crime to 'acquire from illegal sources that which cannot be gained legitimately' (*ibid.*: 29). The third stage indicates the penetration of organized crime into legitimate structures, while the final stage indicates the role of organized crime as the major power-holder, no longer needing to 'negotiate on the terms favoured by the dominant system' (Rawlinson, 1996: 32).

It is important to note that Rawlinson's model is as particular to Russia as, for instance, those of Arlacchi (1986) or Hess (1973) are to the political histories of Italy. Indeed the Italian model of regional isolation, socio-cultural disorganization and the development of alternative localized hierarchies (Hess, 1973), which in turn evolve via their negotiations with different political regimes and markets (cf. Lewis, 1964; Duggan, 1989; Ruggiero, 1996), highlights that, despite the undeniable ability of contemporary organized crime groups to operate across national boundaries and the subsequent response by police agencies world-wide (Sheptycki, 1995), organized crime remains an essentially local phenomenon grounded in highly specific historical practices and relationships. Even the Sicilian Mafia is as Arlacchi indicates, restricted by the traditionalism and territoriality that constitute the very roots of its power. In short the Mafia's relationship with the state is not as problematic as its relationships with other Mafia groups, where coercive power rather than negotiation will be the deciding factor. In turn these market confrontations will be dominated by rules of engagement dictated by traditional territorial values rather than market prerogatives (Arlacchi, 1986: chapter 6). As Hobsbawm ruefully notes, 'A man may be a social bandit on his native mountains, a mere robber on the plains' (1972: 18).

This is not to deny the fact that recent changes in both business practice and the status of the nation-state are responsible for the infiltration of organized crime into legitimate state structures. Rather, we should view organized crime as a cultural phenomenon rather than as a police problem; the local and particular manifestation of criminal collaborations, territorially rooted in multiple indicators of disadvantage, sensitive to markets yet informed by precedent. When articulated within local trading networks (Dorn *et al.*, 1992: 3–59; cf. Piore and Sabel, 1984), the commercial viability of organized crime can be retained by continually realigning in the context of global markets (Giddens, 1991: 21–2; cf. Hobbs, 1995*a*: chapter 5). As indicated by Robertson (1992, 1995), globalization has intensified the viability of locality as a context for a distinct social order and, as Hobbs (1997), and Ruggiero (1995) argue, the organization of criminal labour mirrors trends in the organization of legitimate labour. Local criminal organization was always deeply entrenched in the cultures of the urban working class, and de-industrialization and the consequent fragmentation of traditional communities have resulted in their transformation into disordered mutations of traditional proletarian culture (Hobbs, 1995*a*). Transactions within the new criminal market, in common with its legitimate counterpart, are within networks of small flexible firms featuring short-term contracts and lack of tenure, and, as Potter explains, these networks are 'flexible, adaptive networks that readily expand and contract to deal with the uncertainties of the criminal enterprise' (1994: 12; cf. Albini, 1971; Haller, 1971; Reuter, 1984). Organized crime is, to paraphrase Latour, 'Local at all points', constituting 'continuous paths that lead from the local to the global, from the circumstantial to the universal, from the contingent to the necessary' (Latour, 1993: 117).

CONCLUSION

And the first thing you learn is there are no ordinary rules of the night and day, there are just different kinds of light, granules of degree, and so no reason to have more or less to do in one than in another. The blackest quietest hour was only a kind of light [Doctorow 1990 : 73–4).

The forms of consumption and circulation that dominate contemporary socio-economic life are direct consequences of the emergence of the market place as the dominant dynamic (Soja, 1989), and to engage with any analysis that remains harnessed to the trappings of traditional cultures and subcultures (Horne and Hall, 1995) is pointless. Crime, when viewed as central to the everyday rhythms of late twentieth century society, has inherited and adapted many of its formal and informal precepts and practices from legitimate economic spheres (Block, 1983: chapter 2). This is not therefore a 'culturally constituted world' (McCracken, 1988), material success is crucial and depend-ant upon competent performance within the constraints of the dynamics of local class histories that have been realigned in negotiation with global markets. Youthful inhabitants of the ever-changing ecology of the late twentieth century have retained their tribal sensibilities while proving highly professional operatives in the world of organized crime (Williams, 1989). While the time-honoured youthful activities of 'hanging around' are as firmly entrenched as ever, and the negotiation of, and engagement with, racial intolerance remain part of the enacted environment of youth, instrumental action in the light of collapsed inner city economies has taken on a new significance. It is no longer merely a case of the most promising material from juvenile gangs being recruited into professional and organized crime. Apprenticeships into adult deviant groups are no longer necessary; the youth group itself can now evolve into something more substantial (Williams, 1989: 14–61). Engagements with these new markets offer upward mobility (Bourgois, 1995), a trajectory away from the 'ecological communities' and their signature deviant coalitions (Burgess, 1929; cf. Thrasher, 1927; Landesco, 1929; Morris, 1957: chapters 2, 4, 11), which are in turn as influential upon contemporary structures of crim-inality as they were in the writings of Mayhew (1861) and Booth (1889).

The translation of what are often ancient territorial priorities into market prerogatives is reflected in the world of professional criminals, their traditional skills and crafts going the way of their legitimate proletarian counterparts in exchange for commercial competence. The dilution and eventual disappear-ance of the legitimate employment market redefines criminal coalitions, not in terms of gangs, sub-cultures, specializations, or hierarchical structures, but in the context of the new decentered, unpredictable trading economies created by the harsh post-industrial thrust that has laid waste to traditional communities 'emptied out' of marketable labour and traditional forms of governance (Wilson, 1987; cf. Ruggiero and South, 1995: chapter 6).

New networks of criminal entrepreneurs, some with ancient affiliations, have no need to limit themselves to the parameters of specific neighbourhoods, and operate across locales defined by opportunity. As Bauman has indicated, 'Cultural authorities turn themselves into market forces, become commodities, compete with other commodities, legitimize their value through the selling capacity they attain' (1992: 52). It is entirely rational, and according to the logic of the market, natural, for deviant coalitions to adopt entrepreneurial strategies, thereby adapting to the perpetual renegotiations that regulate relations between both individuals and groups (Giddens, 1979: 65–6), and reproduce themselves in the form of constantly mutating social systems of culturally indeterminable origins, and multifarious economic destinations (Hobbs, 1995a).

Fraud and the drug trade represent generic criminal engagements with the market place that clearly indicate the merging of 'upper and underworld' (Levi, 1987: 194). Structural changes to the market place, such as the deregulation of the London Stock Exchange in 1986, and key technological innovations, particularly in the field of communications (Levi, 1987: 3), have created an environment that enables criminals to attack information or money when and where it is most vulnerable in a similar way that the cosh, motor car, shotgun, the thermic lance, and readily available explosives had enhanced the practice of previous generations of thieves (cf. McIntosh, 1971, 1975). The adaptability and capacity to mutate that are inherent in contemporary crime call into question convenient academic categories such as gangs, professional, organized, and white collar. Further, the evolution of commercial practices that focus upon a serious crime community who, 'embedded in a matrix of legality' (Block, 1996), can penetrate to the very heart of an increasingly irrelevant nation state, questions the continued spotlight being continuously trained on the lower orders. We have yet to even begin to theorize this phenomenon, the vocabulary of criminology remaining conveniently retarded.

Selected Further Reading

The work of Thrasher (1927, 1963), Sutherland (1937), and Landesco (1929, 1968), are the classic readings in their respective fields. These Chicagoan studies provide the framework upon which subsequent investigations will inevitably be based. In a similar vein, Whyte's (1943) seminal ethnography, and Cohen (1955), Cloward and Ohlin (1960), and Downes (1966), establish and explore the sub-cultural tradition. Phil Cohen's study locates subcultures within the local political economy, and the powerful body of work of contemporary American gang studies can be explored in the work of Horowitz (1983), and Hagedorn (1988), Williams (1989), Padilla (1993), and Bourgois (1995).

Einstadter (1969), Shover (1973), and Lemert (1958) (all reprinted in Hobbs: 1995b) provide critiques of Sutherland while presenting vibrant renditions of professional crime, and Hobbs (1995a) has attempted to place the concept of professional crime within a contemporary context. Both Dunlap *et al.* (1994), and Adler and Adler (1983) indicate the ambiguity of the term professional crime In organized crime. Bell (1964), Cressey (1972), and Ianni (1972) have proved to be hugely influential, while Lupsha (1983), Albini (1971), Haller (1971), and Reuter (1984) suggest, from the standpoint of their respective disciplines, alternative perspectives. Blok (1974), Arlacchi (1986), and Ruggiero (1996) provide a European perspective. The ethnography of Chambliss (1978) and Potter's excellent study (1994) situate organized crime as a segment of the political economy, while useful examples of Block's hugely influential body of work can be found in his collection of papers and essays (1994).

REFERENCES

ABADINSKY, H. (1990), *Organised Crime*. 3rd edn. Chicago, Ill.: Nelson Hall.

ABRAMS, M. (1959), *The Teenage Consumer*. London: Routledge and Kegan Paul.

ADLER, P., and ADLER, P. (1983), 'Shifts and Oscillations in Deviant Careers: The Case of Upper Level Drug Dealers and Smugglers', *Social Problems*, 31: 195–207.

ALBANESE, J. (1996), *Organised Crime in America*. 3rd edn. Cincinnati, Ohio: Anderson.

ALBINI, J. L. (1971), *The American Mafia: Genesis of a Legend*. New York: Appleton-Century-Crofts.

—— (1988), 'Donald Cressey's Contributions to the Study of Organized Crime: An Evaluation', *Crime and Delinquency*, 34, 3: 338–54.

ANDERSON, A. (1979), *The Business of Organised Crime*, Stanford, Cal.: Hoover Institute Press.

ANDERSON, B. (1983), *Imagined Communities*. London: Verso.

ANDERSON, R. J., HUGHES, J. A., and SHARROCK, W. W. (1989), *Working for Profit: The Social Organisation of Calculation in an Entrepreneurial Firm*. Aldershot: Avebury.

ARLACCHI, P. (1986), *Mafia Business: The Mafia Ethic and the Spirit of Capitalism*. London: Verso.

ASBURY, H. (1927), *The Gangs of New York*. New York: Capricorn.

—— (1950), *The Great Illusion: An Informal History of Prohibition*, Garden City, NY: Doubleday.

BALL, J., CHESTER, L., and PERROTT, R. (1978), *Cops and Robbers*. London: Andre Deutsch.

BALL, R., and CURRY, D. (1995), 'The Logic of Definition in Criminology: Purposes and Methods for Defining "Gangs"', *Criminology*, 33, 2: 225–45.

BAUMAN, Z. (1992), *Intimations of Modernity*. London: Routledge.

—— (1993), *Modernity and Ambivalence*. Cambridge: Polity.

BELL, D. (1953), 'Crime as an American Way of Life', *The Antioch Review*, 13: 131–54.

—— (1961), *The End of Ideology*. London: Free Press/Collier-Macmillan.

—— (1963), 'The Myth of the Cosa Nostra', *The New Leader*, 461 26: 12–15.

BENNETT, T., and WRIGHT, R. (1984), *Burglars on Burglary*. Aldershot: Gower.

BLOCK, A. (1978), 'History and the Study of Organized Crime', *Urban Life* 6 (Jan.): 455–74.

—— (1983), *East Side–West Side: Organizing Crime in New York, 1930–1950*. Newark, NJ: Transaction.

—— (1991), *The Business of Crime*, Boulder, Col.: Westview Press.

—— (1994), *Space Time and Organised Crime*. New Brunswick, NJ: Transaction.

—— (1996), *Oil, Gas, Diamonds, Gold and Organised Crime*, paper presented to the ASC Annual meeting, Chicago, Ill.

—— and CHAMBLISS, W. J. (1981), *Organizing Crime*. New York: Elsevier.

BLOK, A. (1974), *The Mafia of a Sicilian Village*. New York: Harper.

BONNANO, J. (1983), *A Man of Honor: The Autobiography of Joseph Bonnano*. New York: Simon and Schuster.

BOOTH, C. (1889), *Labour and Life of the People*. London: Williams and Norgate.

BORDUA, D. (1961), 'Delinquent Subcultures: Sociological Interpretations of Gang Delinquency', *Annals of the American Academy of Political and Social Science*, 338: 120–36.

BOURGOIS, P. (1995), *In Search of Respect*. Cambridge: Cambridge University Press.

BRADLEY, D. (1992), *Understanding Rock 'n' Roll: Popular Music in Britain 1955–1964*. Buckingham: Open University Press.

BROWNING, F., and GERASSI, J. (1980), *The American Way of Crime*. New York: G. P. Putnam and Sons.

BULLINGTON, B., and BLOCK, A. A. (1990), 'A Trojan Horse: Anti-Communism and the War on Drugs', *Contemporary Crises*, 14: 39–55.

BURROWS, R., ed., (1991), *Deciphering the Enterprise Culture*. London: Routledge.

CALVI, F. (1993), *Het Europa van de Peetvaders. De Mafia Verovert een Continent*. Leuven: Kritak Balans.

CAMP, G., and CAMP, C. G. (1985), *Prison Gangs: Their Extent, Nature, and Impact on Prisons*, Washington, DC: US Department of Justice.

CAMPBELL, A. (1984), *The Girls in the Gang*. New York: Basil Blackwell.

—— (1990), 'Female Participation in Gangs', in C. R. Huff, ed., *Gangs in America*, 163–82. Newbury Park: Sage.

CAMPBELL, D. (1991), *That was Business, This is Personal*. London: Mandarin.

CASHMORE, E. (1979), *Rastaman*. London: Allen and Unwin.

—— and TROYNA, B., eds. (1982), *Black Youth in Crisis*. London: Allen and Unwin.

CHAMBLISS, W. J. (1972), *Box Man*. New York: Harper and Row.

—— (1978), *On the Take*. Bloomington, Ind.: Indiana University Press.

CHANEY, D. (1994), *The Cultural Turn*. London: Routledge.

CLARKE, J. (1976), 'The Skinheads and the Magical Recovery of Community', in S. Hall and T. Jefferson, eds., *Resistance through Rituals*. London: Hutchinson.

—— *et al.* (1976), 'Subcultures, Cultures and Class: A Theoretical Overview' in S. Hall and A. Jefferson, eds., *Resistance Through Rituals; Youth Subcultures in post-War Britain*. London: Hutchinson University Library.

CLOWARD, R. A., and OHLIN, L. E. (1960), *Delinquency and Opportunity: A Theory of Delinquent Gangs*. New York: Free Press.

COHEN, A. K. (1955), *Delinquent Boys: The Culture of the Gang*, Glencoe, Ill.: Free Press.

COHEN, P. (1972), 'Subcultural Conflict and Working Class Community', *Working Papers in Cultural Studies, No. 2*, Centre for Contemporary Studies, University of Birmingham.

COHEN, S. (1973), *Folk Devils and Moral Panics*. London: Paladin.

—— (1980), *Folk Devils and Moral Panics*. 2nd revised edn. London: Martin Robertson.

—— and TAYLOR, L. (1972), *Psychological Survival*. Harmondsworth: Penguin.

CORRIGAN, P. (1976), 'Doing Nothing', in S. Hall and T. Jefferson, eds., *Resistance through Rituals*. London: Hutchinson.

—— (1979), *Schooling the Smash Street Kids*. London: Macmillan.

COWIE, J., COWIE, B., and SLATER, E. (1968), *Delinquency in Girls*. London: Heinemann.

CRESSEY, D. R. (1967), 'The Functions and Structure of Criminal Syndicates', in *Task Force Report: Organized Crime*, President's Commission on Law Enforcement and the Administration of Justice. 25–60. Washington, DC: US Government Printing Office.

—— (1969), *Theft of the Nation: The Structure and Operations of Organized Crime in America*. New York: Harper and Row.

—— (1972), *Criminal Organisation*. London: Heinemann.

CUMMINGS, J., and VOLKMAN, E. (1992), *Mobster*. London: Warner.

CURRY, G. D., and SPERGEL, I. A. (1988), 'Gang Homicide, Delinquency and Community', *Criminology*, 26, 3: 381–405.

—— BALL, R. A., and FOX, R. J. (1991), *Gang Crime and Law Enforcement Record Keeping*. Washington, DC: National Institute of Justice.

DANIEL, S., and McGUIRE, P., eds. (1972), *The Paint House—Words from an East End Gang*. Harmondsworth: Penguin.

DAVIS, M. (1990), *City of Quartz*. London: Verso.

DOCTOROW, E. L. (1989), *Billy Bathgate*. London: Picador.

DORN, N., MARJI, K., and SOUTH, N. (1992), *Traffickers*. London: Routledge.

—— and SOUTH, N. (1990), 'Drug Markets and Enforcement', *British Journal of Criminology*, 30, 2: 171–88.

DOWNES, D. (1966), *The Delinquent Solution: A Study in Subcultural Theory*. London: Routledge and Kegan Paul.

DUGGAN, C. (1989), *Fascism and the Mafia*. New Haven, Conn.: Yale University Press.

DUNLAP, E., JOHNSON, B., and MANWAR, A. (1994), 'A Successful Female Crack Dealer: Case Study of a Deviant Career', *Deviant Behaviour*, 15: 1–25.

EINSTADTER, W. J. (1969), 'The Social Organisation of Armed Robbery', *Social Problems*, 17: 64–83.

ERICKSON, M. L., and JENSEN, G. F. (1977), 'Delinquency is Still Group Behavior: Toward Revitalizing the Group Premise in the Sociology of Deviance', *Journal of Criminal Law and Criminology*, 68, 2: 262–73.

FAGAN, J. (1989), 'The Social Organization of Drug Use and Drug Dealing among Urban Gangs', *Criminology*, 27, 4: 633–69.

—— (1990), 'Social Processes of Delinquency and Drug Use Among Urban Gangs', in C. R. Huff, ed., *Gangs in America*. 183–219. Newbury Park: Sage.

—— (1994), 'Women and Drugs Revisited: Female Participation in the Cocaine Economy', *The Journal of Drug Issues*, 24, 2: 179–225.

FINESTONE, H. (1976), *Victims of Change— Juvenile Delinquents in American Society*. Westport, Conn.: Greenwood Press.

FOREMAN, F. (1996), *Respect*. London: Century.

FOX, S. (1989), *Blood and Power: Organized Crime in 20th Century America*. New York: William Morrow.

FRASER, F. (1994), *Mad Frank*. London: Little Brown.

GIBBENS, T., and AHRENFELDT, R., eds., *Cultural Factors in Delinquency*. London: Tavistock.

GIBBS, J. S., and SHELLEY, P. L. (1982), 'Life in the Fast Lane: A Retrospective View by Commercial Thieves', *Journal of Research in Crime and Delinquency*, 19: 299–330.

GIDDENS, A. (1979), *Central Problems in Social Theory*. London: Macmillan.

—— (1990), *The Consequences of Modernity*. Cambridge: Polity Press.

—— (1991), *Modernity and Self-Identity*. Cambridge: Polity Press.

GILL, O. (1977), *Luke Street: Housing Policy, Conflict and the Creation of the Delinquent Area*. London: Macmillan.

GILLET, C. (1983), *The Sound of the City: The Rise of Rock and Roll*. 2nd edn. London: Souvenir Press.

GOFFMAN, E. (1952), 'On Cooling the Mark Out: Some Aspects of Adaptation to Failure', *Psychiatry*, 15: 451–63.

GOLD, M. (1970), *Delinquent Behaviour in an American City*. Belmont Cal.: Brooks/Cole.

HABERMAS, J. (1984), *The Theory of Communicative Action*, Vol. 1. London: Heinemann.

HAGAN, F. (1983), 'The Organized Crime Continuum: A Further Specification of a New Conceptual Model', *Criminal Justice Review*, 8: 52–7.

HAGEDORN, J. (1988), *People and Folks: Gangs, Crime and the Underclass in a Rustbelt City*. Chicago, Ill.: Lake View.

—— (1990), 'Back in the Field Again: Gang Research in the Nineties', in C. R. Huff, ed.,

Gangs in America, 240–62. Newbury Park: Sage.

—— (1994), 'Homeboys, Dope Fiends, Legits and New Jacks', *Criminology*, 32: 197–219.

HALL, S. and JEFFERSON, T., eds., (1976), *Resistance through Rituals*. London: Hutchinson.

HALLER, M. (1971), 'Organized Crime in Urban Society: Chicago in the Twentieth Century', *Journal of Social History*, 5: 210–34.

—— (1985), 'Bootleggers as Businessmen: From City Slums to City Builders', in D. Kyvig, ed., *Law, Alcohol, and Order: Perspectives on National Prohibition*. 139–57. Westport, Conn.: Greenwood.

—— (1990), 'Illegal Enterprise: A Theoretical and Historical Interpretation', *Criminology*, 28, 2: 207–35.

HAWKINS, G. (1969), 'God and the Mafia', *The Public Interest*, 14: 24–51.

HEBDIGE, D. (1979), *Subculture: The Meaning of Style*. London: Methuen.

—— (1988), *Hiding in the Light: On Images and Things*. London: Routledge.

HEELAS, P., and MORRIS, P., eds. (1992), *The Values of the Enterprise Culture*. London: Routledge.

HESS, H. (1973), *Mafia and Mafiosi: The Structure of Power*. Lexington, Mass.: D. C. Heath.

HOBBS, D. (1988), *Doing the Business: Entrepreneurship, Detectives and the Working Class in the East End of London*. Oxford: Clarendon Press.

—— (1995), *Bad Business*. Oxford: Oxford University Press.

—— (1995b), *Professional Criminals*. Aldershot: Dartmouth.

—— (1997), 'Professional Crime: Change Continuity and the Enduring Myth of the Underworld', *Sociology*, 31, 1: 57–72.

HOBSBAWM, E. (1972), *Bandits*. London: Pelican.

—— (1983), 'Introduction: Inventing Traditions' in E. Hobsbawm and T. Ranger, *The Invention of Tradition*. 1–15. Cambridge: Cambridge University Press.

—— (1994), *The Age of Extremes*. Harmondsworth: Penguin.

HOFSTADTER, R. (1956), *The Age of Reform: From Bryan to F.D.R.* New York: Knopf.

HOGGART, R. (1957), *The Uses of Literacy*. London: Chatto and Windus.

HOLLINGSHEAD, A. B. N. (1939), 'Behaviour Systems as a Field for Research', *American Journal of Sociology*, 4: 816–22.

HOLZMAN, H. R. (1983), 'The Serious Habitual Property Offender as Moonlighter: An Empirical Study of Labour Force

Participation Among Robbers and Burglars', *Journal of Criminal Law and Criminology*, 73: 1774–92.

HORNE, R., and HALL, S. (1995), 'Anelpis: A Preliminary Expedition into a World Without Hope or Potential', *Parallex*, 1: 81–92.

HOROWITZ, R. (1983), *Honor and the American Dream: Culture and Identity in a Chicano Community*, New Brunswick, NJ: Rutgers University Press.

—— (1987), 'Community Tolerance of Gang Violence', *Social Problems*, 34: 437–50.

HUNT, G., RIEGEL, S., MORALES, T., and WALDORF, D. (1993), 'Changes in Prison Culture. Prison Gangs and the Case of the "Pepsi Generation"', *Social Problems*, 40, 3: 398–409.

IANNI, F. A. J. (1972), *A Family Business: Kinship and Social Control in Organized Crime*. New York: Russell Sage Foundation.

—— (1974), *Black Mafia: Ethnic Succession in Organized Crime*. New York: Simon and Schuster.

INCIARDI, J. (1976), 'The Pickpocket and his Victim', *Victimology*, 1: 141–9.

—— (1984), 'Professional Theft' in R. Meier, ed., *Major Forms of Crime*. Beverly Hills, Cal.: Sage.

—— BLOCK, A. A., and HALLOWELL, L. A. (1977), *Historical Approaches to Crime*. Beverly Hills, Cal.: Sage.

INSTITUTE for LAW and JUSTICE (1994), *Gang Prosecution in the United States*. National Institute of Justice, Office of Justice Programs. US Department of Justice, August.

IRWIN, J. (1970), *The Felon*. Englewood Cliffs, NJ: Prentice Hall.

—— and CRESSEY, D. (1962), 'Thieves, Convicts and the Inmate Culture', *Social Problems*, 10: 142–55.

JENNINGS, A., LASHMAR, P., and SIMSON, V. (1991), *Scotland Yard's Cocaine Connection*. London: Arrow.

KARRAKER, C. (1953), *Piracy was a Business*. Rindge, NH: Richard R. Smith

KATZ, J. (1988), *Seductions of Crime*. New York: Basic Books.

KELLY, R. (1986), *Organized Crime: A Global Perspective*. Totowan, NJ: Rowman and Littlefield.

KLEIN, M. W. (1971), *Street Gangs and Street Workers*. Englewood Cliffs, NJ: Prentice-Hall.

—— and MAXSON, C. L. (1989), 'Street Gang Violence', in N. A. Wetner and M. E. Wolfgang, eds., *Violent Crime, Violent Criminals*. Newbury Park, Cal.: Sage.

—— —— and CUNNINGHAM, L. C. (1991),

'"Crack", Street Gangs, and Violence', *Criminology*, 29: 623–50.

KLOCKARS, C. (1975), *The Professional Fence*. London: Tavistock.

KOBLER, J. (1971), *Capone: The Life and World of Al Capone*. Greenwich, Conn.: Fawcett.

KRAY, R. (1991), *Born Fighter*. London: Arrow.

KYVIG, D. (1979), *Repealing National Prohibition*, Chicago, Ill.: University of Chicago Press.

LABROUSSE, A., and WALLON, A., eds. (1993), *La Planète des Drogues*. Paris: Seuil.

LACEY, R. (1991), *Little Man*. New York: Little Brown.

LAMBRIANOU, T. (1992), *Inside the Firm*. London: Pan.

LANDESCO, J. (1968), *Organised Crime in Chicago*. 2nd edn. Chicago, Ill.: University of Chicago Press.

LANGER, J. (1977), 'Drug Entrepreneurs and Dealing Culture', *Social Problems*, 24: 377–86.

LASH, S., and URRY, J. (1987), *The End of Organised Capitalism*. Cambridge: Polity Press.

LATOUR, B. (1993), *We Have Never Been Modern*. London: Harvester Wheatsheaf.

LEMERT, E. (1958), 'The Behaviour of the Systematic Check Forger', *Social Problems*, 6: 141–9.

LETKEMANN, P. (1973), *Crime as Work*. New Jersey: Prentice Hall.

LEVI, K. (1981), 'Becoming a Hit Man: Neutralisation in a Very Deviant Career', *Urban Life*, 10: 47–63.

LEVI, M. (1987), *Regulating Fraud*. London: Tavistock.

—— (1991), 'Developments in Business Crime Control in Europe', in F. Heidensohn and M. Farrell, eds., *Crime in Europe*. London: Routledge.

LEVITAS, R. (1996), 'The Concept of Social Exclusion and the New Durkheimian Hegemony', *Critical Social Policy*, 16, 1: 1–20.

LEWIS, N. (1964), *The Honoured Society*. New York: Putnam's.

LLOYD, H. D. (1963), *Wealth Against Commonwealth*, ed. by T. C. Cochran, Englewood Cliffs, NJ: Prentice-Hall.

LODHI, A., and VAZ, E. (1980), 'Crime: A Form of Market Transaction', *Canadian Journal of Criminology*, 22, 2: 141–50.

LOGIE, R., WRIGHT, R., and DECKER, S. (1992), 'Recognition Memory Performance and Residential Burglary', *Applied Cognitive Psychology*, 6: 109.

LOTH, D. (1938), *Public Plunder: A History of*

Graft in America. New York: Carrick and Evans.

LUCKENBILL, D. (1981), 'Generating Compliance: The Case of Robbery', *Urban Life,* 10: 25–46.

LUPSHA, P. A. (1981), 'Individual Choice, Material Culture, and Organized Crime', *Criminology,* 19: 3–24.

—— (1983), 'Networks Versus Networking: Analysis of an Organized Crime Group', in G. P. Waldo, ed., *Career Criminals.* 59–87. Beverly Hills, Cal.: Sage.

MAAS, P. (1968), *The Valachi Papers.* New York: Putnam's.

MACK, J. (1964), 'Full-time Miscreants, Delinquent Neighbourhoods and Criminal Networks', *British Journal of Sociology,* 15: 38–53.

—— and KERNER, H. J. (1975), *The Crime Industry.* Lexington, Mass.: Saxon House, Lexington Books.

MAGUIRE, M., and BENNETT, T. (1982), *Burglary in a Dwelling.* London: Heinemann.

MALTZ, M. (1976), 'On Defining "Organized Crime" ', *Crime and Delinquency,* 22: 338–46.

—— (1985), 'Towards Defining Organized Crime', in H. Alexander and G. Caiden, eds., *The Politics and Economics of Organized Crime,* Lexington, Mass.: D. C. Heath.

—— (1990), *Measuring the Effectiveness of Organized Crime Control Efforts,* Chicago, Ill.: Office of International Criminal Justice, University of Illinois.

MANN, K. (1991), *The Making of an English 'Underclass'?* Milton Keynes: Open University Press.

MANNING, P. K. (1989), 'On the Phenomenology of violence', *Criminologist,* 14, 4: 1–22.

MASON, E. (1994), *Inside Story.* London: Pan.

MATZA, D. (1964), *Delinquency and Drift.* New York: Wiley.

—— (1969), *Becoming Deviant,* Englewood Cliffs, NJ: Prentice Hall.

—— and SYKES, G. (1961), 'Juvenile Delinquency and Subterranean Values', *American Sociological Review,* 26: 712–19.

MAURER, D. W. (1955), *The Whizz Mob.* New Haven, Conn.: College and University Press.

MAYHEW, H. (1861), *London Labour and the London Poor.* 4 Vols. Facsimile edn. 1968. London: Dover.

MAYS, J. B. (1954), *Growing Up in the City: A Study of Juvenile Delinquency in an Urban Neighbourhood.* Liverpool: Liverpool University Press.

McCAFFREY, L. J. (1976), *The Irish Diaspora in America.* Bloomington, Ind.: Indiana University Press.

McCRACKEN, G (1988), *Culture and Consumption.* Bloomington, Ind.: Indiana University Press.

McINTOSH, M. (1971), 'Changes in the Organisation of Thieving', in S. Cohen, ed., *Images of Deviance.* Harmondsworth: Penguin.

—— (1975), *The Organisation of Crime.* London: Macmillan.

McROBBIE, A. (1978), 'Working Class Girls and the Culture of Femininity', in Women's Studies Group, Centre for Contemporary Cultural Studies, *Women Take Issue: Aspects of Women's Subordination.* London: Hutchinson.

—— and GARBER, J. (1976), 'Girls and Subcultures: An Exploration', in S. Hall and T. Jefferson, eds., *Resistance through Rituals,* London: Hutchinson.

McVICAR, J. (1979), *McVicar By Himself.* London: Arrow.

MERTON, R. K. (1938), 'Social Structure and Anomie', *American Sociological Review,* 3, 5: 672–82.

MILLER, W. B. (1958), 'Lower Class Culture as a Generating Milieu of Gang Delinquency', *Journal of Social Issues,* 14: 5–19.

—— (1975), *Violence by Youth Gangs and Youth Groups as a Crime Problem in Major American Cities.* Report to the National Institute for Juvenile Justice and Delinquency Prevention. Washington, DC: Office of Juvenile Justice and Delinquency Prevention.

—— (1982), *Crime by Youth Gangs and Youth Groups in the United States,* report prepared for the National Youth Gang Survey. Washington, DC: Office of Juvenile Justice and Delinquency Prevention.

MOORE, J. W. (1978), *Homeboys: Gangs, Drugs, and Prison in the Barrios of Los Angeles.* Philadelphia, Penn.: Temple University Press.

—— (1988), 'Changing Chicano Gangs: Acculturation, Generational Change, Evolution of Deviance or Emerging Underclass?' in J. H. Johnson, Jr. and M. L. Oliver, eds., *Proceedings of the Conference on Comparative Ethnicity.* Los Angeles, Cal.: Institute for Social Science Research, UCLA.

—— (1991), *Going Down to the Barrio: Homeboys and Homegirls in Change.* Philadelphia, Penn.: Temple University Press.

MOORE, W. H. (1974), *Kefauver and the Politics of Crime.* Columbus Miss.: University of Missouri Press.

MORRIS, N., and HAWKINS, G. (1970), *The Honest Politician's Guide to Crime Control.* Chicago, Ill.: University of Chicago Press.

MORRIS, T. P. (1957), *The Criminal Area.* London: Routledge and Kegan Paul.

MORRISON, S., and O'DONNELL, I. (1994), 'Armed Robbery: A Study in London', *Occasional Paper No. 15.* Oxford: Oxford Centre For Criminological Research.

MURRAY, C. (1990), *The Emerging British Underclass.* London: Institute of Economic Affairs.

MYERS, G. (1936), *History of Great American Fortunes.* New York: Modern Library.

NAYLOR, R. T. (1995), 'From Cold War to Crime War', *Transnational Organised Crime,* 1, 4: 37–56.

NEEDLE, J. A., and STAPLETON, W. V. (1983), *Police Handling of Youth Gangs.* Washington, DC: US Department of Justice, Office of Juvenile Justice and Delinquency Prevention, National Institute for Juvenile Justice and Delinquency Prevention.

NELLI, H. S. (1976), *The Business of Crime.* New York: Oxford University Press.

O'BRIEN, J. and KURINS, A. (1991), *Boss of Bosses.* New York: Simon and Schuster.

OSCHLIES, W. (1979), *Juvenile Delinquency in Eastern Europe: Interpretations, Dynamics, Facts.* Cologne: Boehlau Verlag.

PADILLA, F. (1992), *The Gang as an American Enterprise.* New Brunswick, NJ: Rutgers University Press.

PAKULSKI, J. and WALTERS, M. (1996), *The Death of Class.* London: Sage.

PARK, R., BURGESS, E., and McKENZIE, R. (1925), *The City.* Chicago, Ill.: University of Chicago Press.

PARKER, H. J. (1974), *View from the Boys, A Sociology of Down Town Adolescents.* Newton Abbott: David and Charles.

PATRICK, J. (1973), *A Glasgow Gang Observed.* London: Eyre Methuen.

PEARCE, F. (1976), *Crimes of the Powerful.* London: Pluto.

PEARSON, G. (1983), *Hooligan: A History of Respectable Fears.* London: Macmillan.

PETERSON, V. (1983), *The Mob: 200 Years of Organized Crime in New York.* Ottawa, Ill.: Green Hill.

PILEGGI, N. (1987), *Wise Guy.* London: Corgi.

—— (1995), *Casino.* New York: Simon and Schuster.

PIORE, M. and SABEL, C. (1984), *The Second Industrial Divide.* New York: Basic Books.

POLSKY, N. (1964), 'The Hustler', *Social Problems,* 12: 3–15.

—— (1971), *Hustlers, Beats and Others.* 2nd edn. Harmondsworth: Pelican.

POTTER, G. W. (1994), *Criminal Organisations.* Prospect Heights, Ill.: Waveland Press.

PRESIDENT'S COMMISSION ON LAW ENFORCEMENT AND ADMINISTRATION of JUSTICE (1967), Task Force Report, chapter 7, 'Professional Crime'. Washington, DC: US Government Printing Office.

PRYCE, K. (1979), *Endless Pressure: A Study of West Indian Lifestyles in Britain.* Harmondsworth: Penguin.

PUFFER, J. A. (1912), *The Boy and His Gang.* Boston, Mass.: Houghton Mifflin.

QUICKER, J. C. (1983), *Homegirls.* San Pedro, Cal.: International Universities Press.

RANKIN, H. (1969), *The Golden Age of Piracy.* New York: Holt, Rinehart and Winston.

RAWLINSON, P. (1996), 'Russian Organised Crime: A Brief History', *Transnational Organised Crime,* 2, 2/3: 28–52.

REUTER, P. (1984), *Disorganised Crime.* Cambridge, Mass.: MIT Press.

—— (1986), 'Methodological and Institutional Problems in Organized Crime Research', paper prepared for the conference on Critical Issues in Organized Crime Control. Washington, DC: Rand Corporation.

—— (1987), *Racketeering in Legitimate Industries: A Study in the Economics of Intimidation.* Santa Monica, Cal.: Rand Corporation

—— (1994), 'Research on American Organised Crime', in R. Kelly, Ko-lin Chin and R. Schatzberg, eds., *Handbook of Organized Crime in the United States.* 91–120. Westport: Greenwood Press.

—— and RUBINSTEIN, J. B. (1978), 'Fact, Fancy, and Organized Crime', *The Public Interest,* 53: 45–68.

RIIS, J. A. (1892, *The Children of the Poor.* New York: Arne Press (reprinted 1971).

ROBERTSON, R. (1992), 'Globality and Modernity', *Theory Culture and Society,* 9, 2: 25–44.

—— (1995), 'Glocalisation: Time-Space and Homogeneity-Heterogeneity' in M. Featherstone, S. Lash, and R. Robertson, eds., *Global Modernities.* London: Sage.

ROBINS, D. (1992), *Tarnished Vision: Crime and Conflicts in the Inner City.* Oxford: Oxford University Press.

—— and COHEN, P. (1978), *Knuckle Sandwich: Growing Up in the Working-Class City.* Harmondsworth: Penguin.

ROBINS, K. (1991), 'Tradition and Translation: National Culture in its Global Context', in J. Corner and S. Harvey, S., eds., *Enterprise and Heritage.* London: Routledge.

ROEBUCK, J., and JOHNSON, R. (1962), 'The Jack of All Trades Offender', *Crime and Delinquency,* 8: 172–81.

RUGGIERO, V. (1993), 'Brixton, London: A Drug Culture without a Drug Economy?',

International Journal of Drug Policy, 4, 2: 83–90.

—— (1995), 'Drug Economics: A Fordist Model of Criminal Capital', *Capital and Class*, 55: 131–50.

—— (1996), *Organised and Corporate Crime in Europe*. Hants: Dartmouth.

—— and SOUTH, N. (1995), *Eurodrugs*. London: UCL Press.

—— and —— (forthcoming), 'The Late Modern City as a Bazaar', *British Journal of Sociology*.

SALERNO, R., and TOMPKINS, J. S. (1969), *The Crime Confederation*. Garden City, NY: Doubleday.

SANCHEZ-JANKOWSKI, M. (1990), *Islands in the Street: Gangs in American Urban Society*. Berkeley, Cal.: University of California Press.

SCHELLING, T. (1976), 'What is the Business of Organized Crime?', in F. Ianni and E. Ruess-Ianni, eds., *The Crime Society—Organized Crime and Corruption in America*. 69–82. New York: Times-Mirror.

SHAW, C. R. and McKAY, H. D. (1931), *Social Factors in Juvenile Delinquency*. Washington, DC: US Government Printing Office.

—— and McKAY, H. D. (1942), *Juvenile Delinquency and Urban Areas*. Chicago, Ill.: University of Chicago Press.

SHEPTYCKI, J. (1995), 'Transnational Policing and the Makings of a Postmodern State', *British Journal of Criminology*, 35, 4: 613–35.

SHERRY, F. (1986), *Raiders and Rebels*. New York: Hearst Marine Books.

SHORT, J. F., and STRODTBECK, F. (1965), *Group Process and Gang Delinquency*, Chicago, Ill.: University of Chicago Press.

—— (1963), Introduction to 1963 abridged version of F. Thrasher, *The Gang*, (1927): pp. xv–liii, Chicago, Ill.: University of Chicago Press.

SHORT, M. (1992), *Lundy*. London: Grafton.

SHOVER, N. (1973), 'The Social Organisation of Burglary', *Social Problems*, 20: 499–514.

—— and HONAKER, D. (1991), 'The Socially Bounded Decision Making of Persistent Property Offenders', *The Howard Journal*, 31: 276–93.

SINCLAIR, A. (1962), *The Era of Excess: A Social History of Prohibition Movement*, Boston, Mass.: Little, Brown.

SKOLNICK, J. H. (1990), 'The Social Structure of Street Drug Dealing', *American Journal of Police*, 9: 1–41.

—— BLUTHENTHAL, R., and CORREL, T. (1993), 'Gang Organisation and Migration', in S. Cummings and D. Monti, eds., *Gangs*. New York: SUNY.

—— CORREL, T., NAVARRO, E., and RABB, R. (1988), *The Social Structure of Street Drug Dealing*. Sacramento, Cal.: Office of the Attorney General of the State of California.

SMITH, D. C. JR. (1971), 'Some Things that May be More Important to Understand about Organized Crime than Cosa Nostra', *University of Florida Law Review*, 24: 1–30.

—— (1975), *The Mafia Mystique*. New York: Basic Books.

—— (1980), 'Paragons, Pariahs, and Pirates: A Spectrum-Based Theory of Enterprise', *Crime and Delinquency*, 26: 358–86.

SOJA, E. W. (1989), *Postmodern Geographies*. London: Verso.

SOLOMOS, J. (1988), *Black Youth, Racism and the State: The Politics of Ideology and Policy*. Cambridge: Cambridge University Press.

SOLWAY, I., and WATERS, J. (1977), 'Working the Corner: The Ethics and Legality of Ethnographic Fieldwork Among Active Heroin Addicts', in R. S. Weppner, ed., *Street Ethnography*. Beverly Hills, Cal.: Sage.

SPERGAL, I. (1995), *The Youth Gang Problem*. New York: Oxford University Press.

STEDMAN-JONES, G. (1971), *Outcast London*. Oxford: Oxford University Press.

STEFFENSMEIER, D. J. (1986), *The Fence: In the Shadow of Two Worlds*. Totowa, NJ: Rowman and Littlefield.

STERLING, C. (1994), *Crime Without Frontiers*. London: Little Brown.

STREET, J. (1992), 'Shock Waves: The Authoritative Response to Popular Music', in D. Strinati and S. Wagg, eds., *Come on Down? Popular Media Culture in Post-war Britain*. London: Routledge.

STUART, M. (1985), *Gangster*. London: W. H. Allen.

SUTHERLAND, E. (1937), *The Professional Thief*. Chicago, Ill.: University of Chicago Press.

SUTTLES, G. D. (1968), *The Social Order of the Slum*. Chicago, Ill.: University of Chicago Press.

SYKES, G. (1958), *The Society of Captives*. Princeton, NJ: Princeton University Press.

TANNENBAUM, F. (1939), *Crime and the Community*. New York. Columbia University Press.

TARRANTINO, Q. (1994), *Reservoir Dogs*. London: Faber.

TAYLOR, A. (1993), *Women Drug Users: An Ethnography of a Female Injecting Community*. Oxford: Clarendon Press.

TAYLOR, C. S. (1990), *Dangerous Society*. East Lansing, Mich.: Michigan State University Press.

TAYLOR, I. (1971), 'Soccer Consciousness and Soccer Hooliganism', in S. Cohen, ed., *Images of Deviance*. Harmondsworth: Penguin.

TAYLOR, L. (1983), 'Ducking and Diving', *New Society*, 6 January, 13–15.

—— (1984), *In the Underworld*. Oxford: Blackwell.

THRASHER, F. (1927), *The Gang*. Chicago, Ill.: University of Chicago Press.

TURKUS, B., and FEDER, S. (1951), *Murder, Inc.: The Story of the Syndicate*. New York: Farrar, Straus, and Young.

UNITED STATES SENATE (1951), *Special Committee to Investigate Organized Crime in Interstate Commerce*, New York: Didier.

VALENTINE, B. (1978), *Hustling and Other Hard Work: Life Styles in the Ghetto*. New York: Free Press.

VIGIL, J. D. (1988), *Barrio Gangs: Street Life and Identity in Southern California*. Austin, Tex.: University of Texas Press.

WALDORF, D., and LAUDERBACK, D. (1993), *Gang Drug Sales in San Francisco: Organized or Freelance?* Alameda, Cal.: Institute for Scientific Analysis.

WALSH, D. (1986), *Heavy Business*. London: Routledge.

WALSH, M. E. (1977), *The Fence*. Westport, Conn.: Greenwood Press.

WALSH, M., and CHAPPELL, D. (1974), 'Operational Parameters in the Stolen Property System', *Journal of Criminal Justice*, 2: 113–29.

WARSHOW, R. (1948), 'The Gangster as Tragic Hero', *The Partisan Review*: 240–4.

WERNER, M. R. (1928), *Tammany Hall*. Garden City, NY: Doubleday, Doran.

WESTERGAARD, J. (1992), 'About and Beyond the "Underclass"', *Sociology*, 26, 4: 575–87.

WHYTE, W. F. (1943), *Street Corner Society, The Social Organisation of a Chicago Slum*. Chicago, Ill.: University of Chicago Press.

WIDEMAN, J. E. (1985), *Brothers and Keepers*. New York: Penguin.

WILLIAMS, P. (1993), 'Transnational Criminal Organisations and National Security', *Survival*, 36: 96–113.

—— and SAVONA, E., eds. (1995), 'The United Nations and Transnational Organised Crime', *Transnational Organised Crime*, 1, 3.

WILLIAMS, T. (1989), *The Cocaine Kids*. Reading, Mass.: Addison-Wesley.

WILLIS, P. (1977), *Learning to Labour: How Working Class Kids Get Working Class Jobs*. London: Saxon House.

—— (1978), *Profane Culture*. London: Routledge and Kegan Paul.

WILSON, W. J. (1987), *The Truly Disadvantaged*. Chicago, Ill.: University of Chicago Press.

WOODIWISS, M. (1987), 'Capone to Kefauver: Organized Crime in America', *History Today*, 37: 8–15.

—— (1993), 'Crime's Global Reach', in F. Pearce and M. Woodiwiss, *Global Crime Connections*. 1–31. London: Macmillan.

WRIGHT, R., and DECKER, S. (1994), *Burglars on the Job*. Boston, Mass.: North Eastern University Press.

YABLONSKY, L. (1959), 'The Gang as a Near-group', *Social Problems*, 7: 108–17.

—— (1962), *The Violent Gang*. New York: Macmillan.

24

Violent Crime

Michael Levi

INTRODUCTION

This chapter is concerned principally with how much violent crime of various kinds, including sexual violence, there is (focused mainly on England and Wales but also including some comparative dimension), the extent to which such crimes have been rising, and how violent crimes can best be explained. This necessitates first a careful look at the ways in which violent crime can be conceptualized and defined, what social attitudes to violence consist of, then an examination of the risks faced by different groups of the population for different sorts of violence, and finally an assessment of how criminologists, psychologists, and sociologists have sought to account for the causes of and social reactions to 'violence'. The implications of these data for the control of violence will then be reviewed.

What Constitutes Violent Crime and How is Our Conception of 'the Problem of Violence' Generated?

What we place into the category of 'violent crime' makes a big difference to the range of behaviour we have to explain. The official criminal statistics of violent crime consist of legal categories such as homicide, grievous bodily harm, wounding, or actual bodily harm ('notifiable offences'). Supposedly less serious crimes such as common assault—which includes, via the use of discretion and Crown Prosecution Service charging standards, much domestic and street violence, and assaults against the police—are triable only at magistrates' courts and are excluded from the main statistics, thereby reducing the apparent level of 'violent crime', although some idea of their dimensions can be obtained both from victimization surveys and from court statistics on the number of people convicted of and cautioned for them. But one could be more imaginative and include deaths and injuries from reckless behaviour (itself a flexible term):

    1. on the roads (e.g. in 1995, 3,621 people were killed on the roads.[1]
       Even looking at criminal justice data, omitted from the Home Office

---

[1] A fall of 30% from 5,165 in 1985. I am grateful to the Office of National Statistics for these data.

classification of homicides are the 284 offenders convicted in 1995 of causing death by reckless or careless driving, with their own cars or with stolen
cars).

2. following breaches of health and safety regulations in factories and mines,
   or on offshore oil rigs and car ferries, or from *e coli* or other microbio-
   logical diseases resulting from breaches of the public health legislation.[2]

The latter might be included on the grounds that though employers hardly ever
intend workers or consumers to be hurt, harms commonly result from paying
'piece-work' which encourages workers to take risks with their own welfare,
from disregard (or, more ideologically and tautologically, 'insufficient regard')
of the health risks of products, or from economies such as employing poor
English speakers and untrained staff in roles such as maritime work where life
and environmental preservation represent a real but infrequent risk. In that
sense, they are not mere accidents but the result of a *process* of profit-
maximizing self-centredness by corporations which define as acceptable the
levels of risk they (rationally or not) expect or who do not even consider that
others are being put at risk.

We could also move into the violent crime category sexual violence—rape
and indecent assaults upon both sexes—which, alongside consensual sex
involving a female under 16 or a male under 18, is classified as a 'sexual' rather
than 'violent' crime in the criminal statistics. After that, there is more scope
for moral entrepreneurship: what about acts such as racial or sexual harassment that induce the *fear* of violence without necessarily hitting someone?
These include obscene telephone calls, received by 8 per cent of women in
1991; threatening calls, received by 1 per cent (Buck *et al.*, 1995); and even
indecent exposure, described by an interviewee in one research study as 'rape
from afar' (Beck, 1995)? What about the activities of the 'Nashville
Footstomper', a man convicted of assault in 1977 for stamping on the toes of
twenty-four women? Did he somehow misinterpret the drive to stamp out
violent crime?

For reasons of space, and despite the high rate of robbery in some inner city
areas,[3] I intend to spend little time on 'instrumental' violence where financial
gain is the motive. This is despite the facts that:

---

[2] In 1989, people in Britain had a 100 times greater chance of being killed in the oil and gas
industry, and a 12 times greater chance of being killed in the coal mining industry than they did
from homicide (Royal Society, 1992). I appreciate that this does little to reassure victims of
homicide, but we ought to be clearer about such probabilities if we are interested in saving lives.
Likewise, the understandable focus on dangerous driving by car 'thieves' should not blind us to
the fact that vastly more people are killed and injured by those driving their own cars (whatever
the ratio of sound to dangerous driving by car thieves and car owners *of comparable ages* respectively). If avoidable deaths in the course of heavy industrial work have dropped markedly, largely
due to the reduction of economic activity, serious illnesses from food poisoning has risen seven-
fold in the past decade, reaching over 84,000 in 1996, allegedly resulting from 'strict liability'
violations of food regulations to save money (*Guardian*, 7 March 1997).

[3] Including those of shopkeepers, reported by Hibberd (1993) as affecting 1 in 6 Midlands and
1 in 4 London small shops in one year. During 1995–6, 4 out of every 100 retail outlets surveyed
experienced a robbery or till snatch (British Retail Consortium, 1997).

1. many robbers also obtain a 'high' from the violence or threats they employ (Katz, 1988);
2. some inner-city violence is motivated by territorial narcotics goals (Blumstein, 1996; though for a sceptical perspective, see Brownstein, 1996),[4] and
3. a reputation for violence *can be* economically functional in obtaining 'consent' from persons blackmailed and to earn money as an arbiter of disputes between criminals or, where civil and/or criminal law is deemed unsatisfactory, as an arbiter of disputes between *non*-criminals: see, for example, the analysis of the Mafia by Reuter (1983) and Gambetta (1994).[5] Indeed, where reputation is strong enough, one may have no need actually to employ violence, at least until fearless and violent competitors (such as Chechen, Colombian, or Russian gangs) come along.

I intend also to devote little attention to collective violence, though the presence of 'significant others' can act as a key trigger to the individual 'propensity' to behave aggressively.[6] Instead, I will focus upon the risks of non-domestic 'sexual' and 'non-sexual' (in form) violence among different groups, in the contexts of their domestic, workplace, and leisure activities, and the value of conventional explanations of violent crime in accounting for this.

Attitudes to Violence

As a society, we are obsessed with violent crime, particularly murder. (For an intriguing essay into our perceptions of evil, see Masters, 1997.) Contrary to initial preconceptions on the part of conflict theorists, the results of serious-ness surveys in the West tend to show a high degree of consensus among peo-ple of different social classes in their ratings of the relative seriousness of property and violent offences (Levi and Jones, 1985; O'Connell and Whelan, 1996). There are variations by age, older people generally rating crimes more seriously. Contrary to 'subculture of violence' theory (Wolfgang and Ferracuti, 1967), people of colour are no more tolerant of violence than are whites, though British research found that people of Afro-Caribbean origin were more tolerant than whites of violence between people who were acquainted, which in reality is the majority of assaults (Sparks, Genn, and Dodd, 1977; Hough and Mayhew, 1985). Analysing the 1984 British Crime Survey, Pease (1988) found almost perfect concord between people of different ages, sexes, and socio-economic groupings, including their views on the seriousness of sex

---

[4] The fall in the US homicide rate in the mid-1990s is partly attributable to the fall in the use of crack cocaine, though this may be due more to 'crack-heads' using guns to get funds to buy drugs than to inter-dealer wars. But there is an obvious escalation when some carry guns, making others easy prey unless they follow suit.

[5] Conversely, however, I will be including 'violence in the workplace', even though the savings in failing to ensure safe working conditions could be said to constitute a financial motive.

[6] The mere fact that some people behave violently while others do not is not itself evidence of differential 'inner propensities' to violence: it can simply reflect different situational pressures, some of which—policing, housing, and family relationships, for example—may be consistent over time. See Waddington (1992) for an overview of collective violence.

crimes. Nor did it make any difference whether or not they had been victims of crime. However despite the well-tested methodology of such surveys, there may be socio-economic and gendered differences in what people *mean* by such ratings, particularly where justifiability and excusability are involved. For example, prior attitudes as well as the way that interactions are represented in court will influence whether a sexual assault is a 'real rape' (Adler, 1987; Lees, 1997).

Culture shapes the conditions under which we attribute responsibility and blame to individuals whose acts result in harmful consequences, even though there may be high agreement within and between different cultures and over time. In mediated form, it also has its effect on criminal law: thus, the Law Lords, later supported by the European Court of Human Rights, decided that it was not a violation of human rights but rather violent crime even when adults consented beforehand to severe sado-masochistic sexual acts.[7] The law defines 'provocation' in homicide as requiring a *sudden and temporary* loss of self-control by the killer, though many feminists argue that the experience of being long-term abused by some women who kill ought to be construed as excusable provocation.[8] By contrast with cross-gender partner violence, where assumptions about 'provocation' abound,[9] violence in public places may be misleadingly stereotyped as being a conflict between a guilty offender and an innocent victim, especially where there is an age or status difference, rather than—as discussed later—an escalating interactive process (Toch, 1972; Athens, 1980). Labels such as 'war criminals' and 'genocide' are usually applied against those out of power—though Serbia may be a rare exception. Equally, those who commit 'crimes of obedience' (Kelman and Hamilton, 1989) define themselves *and are commonly defined in their culture* as 'loyal' rather than as being 'violent conspirators in a process of genocide', such as the murder of some 800,000 Tutsis in Rwanda during the 1990s—more than the total UK homicides in the past two centuries—let alone the millions killed in the Nazi Holocaust itself. How did so many Rwandans and Germans manage 'not to notice' that this genocide was going on, and thus avoid being, in their own eyes, blameworthy? A socio-biologist might argue that not noticing represents a personal survival-enhancing factor, while psychoanalysts and sociologists

---

[7] See the 'Spanner' case, *R* v. *Brown (Anthony) and others* [1994] 1 AC 212, later upheld in Europe in *Laskey* v. *UK*, European Court of Human Rights, (*The Times*, Law Report, 20 February 1997).

[8] See *Thornton* [1982] Crim. LR 54, *Ahluwalia* [1983] Crim. LR 63, where the courts have ruled that delayed reaction to abuse makes the defence of provocation less plausible but not unarguable. The 'overcontrolled' males in Megargee's (1966) typology likewise are slow-burning 'explosives', so this phenomenon is not gender-specific though it may account for a larger proportion of killings by women. Historically the law, judges, and jurors have been more sympathetic to men who claim that sexual jealousy made them lose control than to women who kill in 'lukewarm blood': but what level of irritation is acceptable to lead us to deem killings or woundings to be excusably provoked? Should the test of provocation be 'objectively' behavioural or in the mind of the killer? If the latter, particularly, how do we test the claim?

[9] Including where race trumps gender, as in the acquittal of African American football star O. J. Simpson of murdering his blonde wife, where post-trial jury interviews revealed that black American women on the jury felt that his wife was a 'bitch' who deserved the prior beatings she had received (though they believed that Simpson had not killed her) (personal communication).

from the 'Frankfurt school' might stress the impact of authoritarian child-rearing with its stress on social conformity, plus the learned hatred of particular categories of (non)person, as causes of genocide.

Why does our conception of violent 'crime' take the form that it does? There are no ultimately satisfactory answers to this question, since the accounts below are insufficiently grounded in historical *process* to demonstrate why things turned out that way, and, moreover, historical processes themselves are not wholly determinate. Hall *et al.* (1978) and subsequent *marxisant* writers argue that intensified stories about 'mugging' during the 1970s formed part of a combined police and media attempt to associate 'the crime problem' with 'young blacks', with the objective of justifying police repression in the interests of capitalist control; others might eschew the broad ideological *rationale* as over-theorized, but might accept that there were and/or are now conscious and/or unconscious alliances between police (to justify inner city police operations) and crime reporters (to use cheap, voyeuristic programmes which appeal to, and exacerbate, the underlying fears of the public in order to increase newspaper sales and viewing figures). (For a good review of the politics of crime journalism, see Schlesinger and Tumber, 1994.) Moreover, the struggle for control of the working class (and 'ethnic') areas of the city, if necessary by violent means (Holdaway, 1983), is as important to police morale and culture as it is to organized criminals who seek immunity from police intervention. By contrast, in a different context of health and safety 'violence', Pearce and Tombs (1992) argue that the reason this is not treated as 'real' violence is that corporate control over the political economy leads to its being marginalized in the interests of profit maximization. However, other devotees of corporate manslaughter prosecutions such as Wells (1993) accept that there is something qualitatively different about unintended but reckless harms, even though the way we construct notions of 'reckless' and 'negligent' rather than malevolent is learned. (Similar arguments could be applied to reckless and careless driving, though without the economic motivation for ignoring safety issues.[10]) This intentionality issue is one which is central to many reactions to crime, including harmful driving: it could be argued that we over-inculpate street violence and under-inculpate economic and motoring 'violence'. Finally, in relation to violence against women, critics point up the benefits to patriarchal control of the mythology that women are somehow responsible for provoking male aggression (Dobash and Dobash, 1992).

Cohen (1981, originally 1971) deployed the phrase 'moral panic' to point up the way in which campaigning groups amplified some social problems, using the media to whip up anxieties.[11] Moral entrepreneurship on violence issues is not restricted to the political right: feminists have tried to redress the traditional

[10] Except inasmuch as fast driving can be encouraged by advertising of cars in order to sell more.

[11] A neglected feature of Cohen's work is that the initial fear of crime had a genuine basis in experience: indeed, there is a serious conceptual problem in whether we can ever discredit fears as 'irrational' and—if we can discredit some such fears—on how we can do so consistently. See also Young (1988).

media and police neglect of violence against women and to shift the focus away from victim culpability in sex crime cases: with more success in the police than with prosecutors or in the courts (Lees, 1997). The development of 'racial/racist assaults' as a social problem in Britain has been analysed thoughtfully by Bowling (1993).

But the tabloid media remain obsessed by allegedly *new* (or newly rising) crimes such as 'rural violence' (often mistaking commuter dormitory towns and villages for rural areas—see Tuck, 1989), violence in schools (especially by outsiders against children, or by pupils against teachers), female violence, and violence against children. Thus, it is the *rate of change* (or *perceived* rate of change) rather than absolute levels that are exciting to them, though sometimes, tabloid newspapers such as the *Daily Mail* can *de*-amplify such panics, as they did over satanic abuse scares in the early 1990s.[12] Against Conservative government policy, the media have generally supported weapons-control policies, such as, in 1996, the ban on handguns (following the killing of children at a primary school in Dunblane, Scotland) and on 'combat knives' (after the stabbing of headmaster Phillip Lawrence). The hundreds of millions of pounds spent compensating gun-owners and gun vendors would have produced a better violence-reducing yield in another setting, yet the imperative to do something about dramatic, newsworthy crimes privileges such actions compared with the constant drip of male-on-male street violence and male-on-female domestic violence, neither of which is 'new' or technologically soluble enough to merit campaigns. To the extent that the media drive political and policing responses—though the media usually claim that they merely *reflect* 'public opinion'—such coverage is consequential in practical terms (see Reiner's 'media-mode crime' in this volume).

As Sparks, Genn, and Dodd (1977) observed, fear of crime may act as a surrogate for all sorts of disparate psychological and social phenomena: fear of getting old, poor health, social change, declining community, job insecurity, etc.[13] Support for the relationship between fear of crime (especially violence) and fear of social change can be found in Dowds and Ahrendt (1996). Instead of asking why do women and the elderly fear crime 'irrationally', why do we not ask why young men are so 'irrational' as to disregard the risks they face? However, neat though such an inversion is, such an approach to risk ignores the superior salience of the positive motivation to do the things that would have to be foregone to reduce the incidence of violence—companionship, heavy drinking, and the chance of finding a sexual partner, for example[14]—or,

---

[12] It is arguable that the campaign of the *Daily Mail* and *Mail on Sunday* represented a defence of family autonomy against the state and its hated bureaucratic front-line, the social worker. But the demystification remains valid nonetheless.

[13] These also fuel racist attitudes, which have longer histories.

[14] I prefer the term 'incidence' rather than 'risk' here, because, properly examined, the risk of street victimization should be a proportion of the occasions on which people go out: it is entirely possible that over-60s have a higher rate than young people of being mugged as a proportion of the times they go out, even though the proportion of over-60s who are mugged is much lower than the proportion of young people mugged.

in the case of prostitutes, money and the avoidance of beating by 'their' pimp.[15] In general, people are more fearful about risks over which they feel they have no control: an example is the greater concern about being killed or injured in public transport accidents than when driving (even taking into account the effect of seeing larger numbers injured or killed in public transport than in private motoring accidents). This would make more understandable the preoccupation of the public (as well as the media) with out-of-the-blue sexual or non-sexual attacks by strangers, even though the number of assaults by acquaintances is much higher[16] (see, for a good empirical review of anxiety about crime, Hough, 1995).

Measuring Violence: Some Preliminary Comments

Although individual cases can serve just as well—the killing of Jamie Bulger or the school massacre at Dunblane—crime statistics are a major battleground on which media, official, and local concern can be mobilized. For example initially, the US National Study of the Incidence and Severity of Child Abuse and Neglect used an operational definition of 'child maltreatment' that did not specify how much harm was required before a case counted as maltreatment, and 30 per cent of all children were classed as victims. When a minimum degree of demonstrable harm was specified, the proportion dropped to *1* per cent (Burgdorf and Eldred, 1978)! If the latter percentage had been reported initially, would child abuse have become such a major social issue? Gil (1975: 347) states that child abuse is 'inflicted gaps or deficits between circumstances of living which would facilitate the optimum development of children, to which they should be entitled, and to their actual circumstances, irrespective of the sources or agents of the deficit'. By that criterion, the amount of child abuse would be vast, even if we could agree on what constituted 'the optimum development of children', which seems unlikely. Popular discussion of 'violence against children' often reviews the age range 0–17 as if it were a homogeneous category, all being technically juveniles. This is dramatically powerful but analytically unhelpful, since the lifestyle patterns of relatively independent teenagers are enormously different from those of parentally dependent under-5s.

[15] This is complicated by the threat from those who have pimps if they *do* stop work.

[16] This does not mean automatically that the *risk* of being attacked by an acquaintance is higher. As a proportion of the number of times that one is *plausibly* at risk of being attacked, the ratio of attacks to opportunities may be higher for strangers than for acquaintances. In practice, operationalizing the concept of 'opportunities' here is far from easy, given the bizarre sorts of circumstances that can trigger sexual attacks. For example, if going shopping counts as an 'assault opportunity' for every stranger one passes, the chance of being attacked per 'person opportunity' falls to an extremely low level, even if a high proportion of women who lead an active night life are assaulted.

THE RISK OF VIOLENCE

The reaction to data among students is typically to turn over the pages until they reach the interesting stuff. To paraphrase the Nazi propagandist Goebbels, 'whenever I hear the phrase "criminal statistics" I reach for my revolver'. However, the crime figures *are* important to illuminate:

1. contemporary debates (for example among feminists) about who are the typical *sufferers* from violence, especially multiple victimization;
2. *explanations* of violence. For example, the frequency of violence and its social distribution, and their stability over time and place, tell us a great deal about the relative plausibility of biological/personality-based explanations for violent behaviour, on the one hand, or subcultural/cultural explanations, on the other. This, in turn, helps us to assess the justifications offered by politicians and the media for their policies, for though policies driven by popular appeal and/or retributivism may need no validation by research evidence, we can only hope that rationality imposes *some* constraints, at least on populist 'law'n'order' movements outside the United States (see Downes and Morgan, this volume.)

Is violence getting worse, as the media constantly suggest? Victims seldom feel better or worse because they would have stood a greater or lesser chance of being beaten up or raped a year earlier. Nevertheless, the theme of social deterioration is an important one in general explanations, particularly since it is often asserted that 'in the good old days', when 'we had the death penalty and corporal punishment', there was less violent crime. In fact, the homicide rate today is roughly half what it was in the mid-seventeenth century, though the pattern of homicide is very different, being much more intra-familial now than then (Nuttall, personal communication). Gatrell (1980) has shown that the Victorian era did witness a significant fall in the level of violent crime (at least outside the home), and Gurr's review (1990) points to large American and English fluctuations within a general decline attributable to the 'civilising process'.

Whether measured by official statistics or victimization surveys (which commenced only in 1981 in England and Wales), there seems little doubt that there has been a substantial increase in violent crime during the 1980s and 1990s in England and Wales, let alone since the tranquil 1950s. For example, the recorded victimization rate for rape more than trebled between 1984 and 1995, from 6 to 19 per 100,000 population (though with small numbers and changing police methods for this offence, this *could* be merely the result of a greater proportion of rapes being recorded). The recorded victimization rate for violence against the person increased during the period 1984–94 from 348 to 477 per 100,000 population for males, and from 119 to 271 per 100,000 for females, and has been rising since. (Note that the numerical as well as percentage increases were greater for women than for men.) British Crime

Survey data suggest that since 1981 domestic violence has risen to 3.4 times its original level (though it fell in 1993–5); that acquaintance violence has more than doubled; that stranger violence has risen 12 per cent; and that 'mugging'—robbery and theft from the person—has risen by 54 per cent, mostly since 1991 (Mirrlees-Black *et al.*, 1996). Thus, despite media amplification of 'new trends' such as rural or female gang violence, or violence by the very young, the public have reason to be more fearful, although the *degree* of their fear may be made worse by their over-estimates of the chances of being assaulted, especially outside the home.

Perceptions of riskiness involve much more than merely the estimated fatalities or injuries in some unit of time: they involve an activity's voluntariness, its personal controllability, and its familiarity, in ways not captured by the models traditionally used in mathematical risk assessment (Royal Society, 1992: 91). In making collective risk assessments on behalf of 'society' (for example over police resource allocation, including policies over racial harassment, domestic violence, and investigations of 'accidents' at work), policy-makers implicitly or explicitly weight the opinions of particular individuals or groups about which crimes are serious and which should be dealt with through the criminal process. One study discovered that Americans only slightly under-estimated the risk of homicide and, taken in the context of other judgements, it was noted that the grossest over-estimates of fatality tended to be vivid or easily imaginable causes of death (Lichtenstein *et al.*, 1978). More generally, Tversky and Kahneman (1973) (see also Kahneman and Tversky, 1982) suggest that the easier it is to recall or imagine an event, the more likely we are to judge that it is risky or happens frequently. This perceptual process applies not only to crime victims but also to police and parole decision-takers, whether dealing with violence or any other type of crime. Mass-media reportage serves as a substitute for direct experience—though research shows that people typically are active interpreters rather than passive consumers of what they see—and it is in this context that the impact of violence in the media must be considered. Thus, because (at the risk of tautology) dramatic crimes are more memorable, we are more frightened of them (and less frightened of more frequent but *less* dramatic crimes) than we need to be.

Calculating 'real' risks depends on knowledge of crime, and victimization surveys (see Maguire and Zedner, this volume) are the best measures we have. However, they cannot tell us about homicides. The average chances of being murdered are highest under the age of 1 and between 16 and 29, reflecting child abuse and then 'honour contests', mostly between males. Those under 1 year old have the highest homicide risk of any age group in England and Wales: twenty-seven deaths per million children in 1995—the lowest total since 1989—but because there are relatively few children of that age, the *number* killed was 'only' eighteen.[17] Runaways and elderly people with known heart conditions

[17] The rate drops to 8 per million for 1–4-year-olds; 6 per million for 5–15-year-olds; and rises to 20 per million—the second highest risk—for those aged 16–29; 17 to those aged 30–49; 12 to those aged 50–69; and 7 for those aged 70 or more. Some socio-biologists would account for the

may be murdered without being known to the police: neither Dennis Nilsen's homosexual drifter victims (Masters, 1985) nor the women sexually assaulted and then murdered by Fred and Rosemary West in Gloucester during the 1980s and 1990s had been classified as murder victims until their fortuitous discovery. (The problems are greater still in many Third World countries, where thousands permanently simply disappear, sometimes—as in Latin America—murdered by paramiliatary 'death squads'.)

As regards the risk of non-fatal violence, the British Crime Survey (hereafter BCS) indicates that more than one in eight people aged 16–29; one in 100 people aged 60 or over; and one in twenty-five people aged 30–59 were victims of violence in 1995 (Mirrlees-Black *et al.*, 1996). Those who live in the inner city have a third greater risk than the average of being attacked, while those who live in Greater London or the West Midlands have twice the risk of those who live in the East Midlands or East Anglia. As regards ethnicity, one in thirty-three white Britons and Indian Britons were assaulted, compared with one in twenty Pakistani and one in seventeen Afro-Caribbean Britons. As regards robbery/theft from the person, one in 100 white, one in fifty Pakistani, and one in thirty-three Afro-Caribbean Britons and Indian Britons were 'mugged' in 1995. When one looks at threats—a category of crime that is often under-valued[18]—Asians are much more at risk than other groups, and were also much more likely to see these threats as being racially motivated (Fitzgerald and Hale, 1996; see also Maung and Mirrlees-Black, 1994). Some of these 'threats' would come from the police, who in turn would see most of their responses as a professional approach to dealing with 'the crime problem'.

Gender

Possibly because women are rightly seen as more unambigous 'victims' of violence than are men, particularly *young* working class men, the 'problematic' to be explained has sometimes focused more on male violence against women rather than male violence *per se* (Dobash and Dobash, 1992). Although there are—as far as is known—more male than female *victims* of violence, there are probably marginally more female than male victims of *repeat* violence, especially of frequently repeated violence.[19] Yet the *direction* of 'domestic violence' is not as clear-cut as may be thought by readers. Research findings

---

vulnerability of the very young in terms of it being more sensible to reject offspring before rather than after much economic and emotional investment has been made in them; others might have a more situational explanation, as we shall examine later. In most respects these are parallel accounts at different levels.

[18] A dramatic personal memory occurred in my childhood when my father, an extermination camp survivor, came down one morning to find a swastika painted on our doorstep. No violence or threat needed to be 'offered'. Stalking, 'heavy breathing', or other telephonic threats to women can have a similar effect (Buck *et al.*, 1994), *a fortiori* when they appear to be systematic and personalized.

[19] The 1995 BCS (Mirrlees-Black *et al.*, 1996: 64, Table A4.1) does not break down repeat victimization data by gender, but combining the data with Table A4.2, one may deduce that the

by Straus and Gelles (1990) in the United States based on two large national surveys exclusively on violence in the home appear to reveal first, as many male as female victims, and secondly, that men are more likely than women to be victims of severe violence by their partner (a 'fact' unsupported by English homicide and BCS data). This research has been criticized (Dobash and Dobash, 1992: chapter 9; Dobash *et al.*, 1992) because it may reduce help for women[20] and for failing to take account of:

1. the greater damage that men cause women than women cause men; and
2. the alleged difference between women's violence, which is provoked by genuine male threats, and men's violence, which is based on their power-control fantasies rather than on women's threats or 'unreasonable' taunting (Dobash *et al.*, 1992; Archer, 1994).

Not only are female homicide victims in the United States twice as likely as male victims to be killed by an intimate partner (in the years to 1995), but also females experienced seven times as many incidents of non-fatal violence by an intimate as did males in the 1992–3 national crime survey (Craven, 1996). British Crime Survey data suggest that most British domestic violence also is male on female (Mirrlees-Black, 1995; Mirrlees-Black *et al.*, 1996; and previous BCS reports). Though the dynamics of female-on-male violence remain under-explored, it appears that these criticisms of Straus and Gelles have substance. However, the differences also may reflect a combination of different measures—aggression versus violent crime—and different national patterns of gendered behaviour.

In 1995, just under a third of all homicide victims (in the Home Office definition of that term) were female, a falling percentage reflecting the static risks for women compared with a rising trend in homicides against men by former friends, acquaintances, and strangers. The lowest ratio of male to female victims in the age group 16–70 was 2.3 to one (per population). Consequently, the fact that only 8 per cent of homicides of males compared with 41 per cent of females were by spouses, lovers, and cohabitants (past and present) is misleading: because of the higher homicide rates against men, there were 2.44 females for every one male victim of 'partner homicide' in 1995. The age distribution of victims would suggest that the low risks of homicide (though not of sexual violence) outside do not simply reflect women being 'protected' by patriarchy from going out, but rather that women of any age seldom get involved as *direct participants* in 'honour contests' (to use the felicitous phrase of Polk, 1994, in his excellent account of masculinity and homicide). This should be seen in conjunction with data from crime surveys about violent crimes, since—serial killers, contract/profit-oriented killers, and

larger *numbers* of disproportionately inter-male acquaintance and stranger violence counter-balance the larger *percentage* of disproportionately female domestic violence victims who are assaulted three or more times.

[20] Though there is no reason in principle why provisions for women should depend on the rate of male victimization, and if there were not also good methodological criticisms, such policy consequences would be technically irrelevant.

haters apart—the distinction between many homicides and less lethal acts is one of interaction and consequence rather than initial motivation. Felson and Messner (1996) argue that in the United States, lone assailants sometimes kill people to avoid retaliation (then or later) or criminal prosecution: in this sense, homicide is a tactic rather than being either fortuitous or planned.

The 1995 British Crime Survey (BCS) (Mirrlees-Black *et al.*, 1996) found that overall, 6.7 per cent of men and 3.8 per cent of women had been victims of one or more 'contact crimes'—note the softened phrase compared with 'violent crimes'—in 1995. Expressed differently, one might note that in one year alone, one in fifteen men and one in twenty-six women were victims of violence: an average rise of almost 50 per cent since the 1988 BCS (for which, see Mayhew *et al.*, 1989). Men under 30 are three times as likely as women of the same age to be violently assaulted by a stranger or an acquaintance (largely in post-drinking brawls or 'honour contests'), but in 1995, 1 per cent of women reported having been hit once or more by a current or ex-partner, compared with 0.3 per cent of men (Mirrlees-Black *et al.*, 1996: 30). This is only an annual figure—not a lifetime experience one—nor does it include repeat victimization, which may be more common and more intensive against women than against men *in the home*. (Though we cannot assume that the findings of Dobash and Dobash, 1979, in Scotland that there was one recorded for every ninety-nine assaults against women in their police sample applies to female victims generally over time, especially since the policing environment has changed to make earlier intervention more likely.) The impact data are not broken down by gender, but domestic violence reported to the BCS interviewers was less likely than other violence categories to involve a weapon, though it was typically more severe in physical impact than were muggings or attacks by strangers or acquaintances (Mirrlees-Black *et al.*, 1996: Table A4.6): psychological impact was not measured (see also Hood-Williams and Bush, 1995).

The 1992 BCS found that *in their lifetimes*, 8 per cent of women had experienced some physical violence that did not require medical attention; 2 per cent of women had experienced some physical violence leading to occasional medical attention; and 1 per cent had had frequent medical attention.[21] Reviewing the methodology of the above data, Mirrlees-Black (1995) admits that the BCS does not measure domestic violence very accurately, ignoring, for example, women in refuges, though they anyway might not turn up in the sample. Nevertheless, in my view, even allowing for this, the BCS data suggest that *in England and Wales as a whole*, *actual* violence in the home is *not* a common experience for a large *proportion* of women. Furthermore, even assuming that a substantial proportion of the assaults on men are a reaction to threats or perceived threats by them, men do not always escape unscathed. So there

---

[21] The 18–29 age group was no different on the more physically serious injuries, but 14 per cent of them had experienced physical violence that did *not* (in their view) require medical attention: whether this means that there are inter-generational differences or that they simply remembered better is unknown.

is little evidence that *taking England and Wales as a whole*, 'cultures of masculinity' are routinely manifested in physical violence towards women, whatever their intended or unintended effect on women, assaulted or not assaulted, may be. Of course, these data do not measure threats or expectations of harm should women be 'disobedient', so they underestimate the power of patriarchy.

Finally, there are likely to be regional variations in levels of violence against women, as on men, reflecting demographic differences. For example, Mooney (1993) revealed that 10 per cent of North London women (of whom four fifths were injured) had experienced violence from their partners during 1992, and that 5 per cent of women had had a bone broken during their lifetime as a result of this. (The 'lifetime prevalence rate' of marital violence was over a quarter in this study, which did not examine female on male violence.)

Sexual Violence

The term 'sexual violence' has expanded from a rape or unwanted physical 'fondling' of someone to whom the suspect was not married, to rape in marriage,[22] child sexual abuse, and—in the view of some—'sexual harassment', i.e. behaviour and language by men which makes women feel uncomfortable. Key questions include (a) how far we should push the test of *women's perceptions* as against the more conventional criminal law test of *men's awareness* of sexual intimidation; and (b) how far should one aggregate different levels of victimization into the generic term 'sexual violence'. It is clearly right to complain that forced anal sex or vaginal sex using objects other than a penis are not legally 'rape' but are extremely serious:[23] but are unwanted sexual propositions or even being 'touched up' 'the same sort of thing' as rape, even though the attitude set of the males involved may be similar to those committing rape? (If the 'touching up' were part of a persistent pattern, for example at work, the seriousness would increase markedly. And for some women, even one 'grope' *is* as serious as rape.)

In England and Wales, there were 4,986 recorded rapes on women and 150 recorded rapes on men (an offence introduced by the Criminal Justice and Public Order Act 1994), plus a further 16,784 indecent assaults on women and 3,150 on men: these figures have almost doubled in the last decade. If these data reflected the amount of sexual offending—which they do not—it would mean that roughly one in 1,000 women were sexually assaulted in 1995, slightly higher than the average for 1990–4 (Watson, 1996). Going beyond recorded

---

[22] After more than two centuries in which men could not be convicted of raping their wives—though in law they could have been convicted of indecent assault and non-sexual violent crimes—the English courts finally held that husbands were liable to conviction, the old common law being declared to be 'a fiction which had become anachronistic and offensive': see *R.* v. *C (Rape: Marital Exemption)* [1991] 1 All ER 755; and *R.* v. *R* [1991] 2 WLR 1065, affirmed by the House of Lords [1991] 3 WLR 767.

[23] They have always been prosecutable as wounding and grievous bodily harm, though there are no data on actual prosecutions for this.

crime, victimization survey data on sexual violence for the United Kingdom are poor in quality, and are no longer measured by the BCS, since earlier surveys had so few reported. The survey of 1,007 married women in the United Kingdom by Painter (1991) revealed that 14 per cent of women had been raped by their husbands at some time during their marriage, 3 per cent of them six times or more. Mooney's (1993) study in North London concluded that 6 per cent of women had been forced to have sex—2.4 per cent by violence—with their partners during the previous twelve months.[24]

Estimates of rape in the United States are much higher. This does *not*, however, mean that the United Kingdom would have those rates if only our research was better. Americans have generally much higher rates for most violent crimes, and in 1980 the *per capita* recorded rape rate in the United States was eighteen times that in England and Wales (West, 1983). Johnson (1980) suggested that almost a third of girls then aged 12 would suffer a violent sexual attack (including from their partners) in their lifetime, while Russell (1984)'s survey in San Francisco estimated this proportion at almost half, noting also that 14 per cent of women who had ever been married reported that their husband or ex-husband had raped them.

Comparative Data on Violent Crime

Societies vary enormously in their rape rates, matrifocal ones tending to have low rates (Sanday, 1981; Scully, 1990; White and Sorensen, 1992). *Recorded* rape statistics for 1990 show that the rape rate in England was 130 per million; in France, 81.8 per million; in India, 7.65 per million; in Italy, 22.8 per million; in Russia, 89 per million; in South Africa, 630 per million; and the United States, 600 per million. This may tell us more about cultural variations in the reporting and recording of rape than it does about rape itself, though one does not have to accept the general approach of 'rational choice' theorists to accept that rape is more likely where the victim will feel too stigmatized or expects to be disbelieved if she (or, especially in inter-gay assaults, he) complains.

As for comparative data on homicide, let us note that in Rio de Janeiro, during 1993, there were 4,253 *recorded* homicides: more than twice the number in New York City, and six times the number in the whole of England and Wales that year. Looking at rates per 100,000 population, Australia scores two; the United States scores around nine; Guatemala sixty-three; and, in Europe, Germany 1.1 and the United Kingdom 1.2 (slightly up from 1.0 a decade ago). Below are some homicide rates (including murder, manslaughter, and infanticide, but excluding attempts) for European capitals, undistorted by

---

[24] As in other contrasts between local and national surveys, the local ones are often more insightful because they give us a sense of place (Genn, 1988; Young, 1988), but also have the potential to mislead because there is no reason to suppose that they are typical of culturally diverse areas. Major metropolitan inner city areas are very different from other areas sampled in the BCS Acorn housing types in other spheres of criminal risk, so there is no non-axiomatic reason to suppose that gender violence levels will be the same elsewhere.

the raw figures—in which London and Amsterdam are easily the highest figures—which fail to reflect their population.[25] Note the stability of homicide rates, except for Stockholm (due to changes in recording practice) and Belfast, where changes in homicide rates (within the range eighteen to fifty-eight numerically) reflect the ebb and flow of political violence. Except for violence in the drugs trade—which gives Amsterdam extra problems—there is modest but intriguing variation within Europe which is hard to explain by religious, ethnic or other demographic criteria.

Table 24.1 Homicide rates per 100,000 in selected European cities

City	1990	1991	1992	1993	1994
London	2.5	2.5	2.4	2.2	2.3
Belfast	5.7	18.5	14.0	14.0	10.2
Edinburgh	2.7	1.8	2.1	2.5	2.0
Dublin	1.1	1.2	2.1	0.8	1.3
Amsterdam	8.2	3.7	7.1	6.9	8.4
Berlin	–	2.7	3.2	4.4	3.9
Brussels	–	3.4	3.5	3.1	3.7
Lisbon	–	4.0	4.8	4.5	5.6
Rome	2.9	2.1	1.6	1.5	1.6
Stockholm	3.7	3.4	3.8	5.4	–

The International Crime Surveys (ICS) show the following data on crimes against the person (from van Dijk and Mayhew, 1993):

Table 24.2 Percentage victimized during a 12-month period

Country	Sexual assaults	Assaults	Assaults with force
Belgium (88 + 91)	0.6	1.9	0.7
England & Wales (88 + 91)	0.3	2.8	1.1
Finland (88 + 91)	0.5	3.5	1.7
France (88)	0.6	2.0	1.5
West Germany (88)	1.7	3.1	1.9
Italy (91)	1.0	0.8	0.4
Netherlands (88 + 91)	0.9	3.7	2.0
Northern Ireland (88)	0.4	1.8	1.1
Norway (88)	0.6	3.0	1.6
Poland (91)	2.0	4.2	1.9
Scotland (88)	0.8	1.8	1.1
Spain (88)	0.7	3.1	1.6
Sweden (91)	0.8	2.7	1.4
Switzerland (88)	0.0	1.2	0.7

[25] I am grateful to Gordon Barclay at the Home Office for the data below.

The (forthcoming) 1996 survey shows that over a five-year period, England and Wales had the highest non-sexual assault rates (including threats), though the UK was lowest for sexual assaults. Rates almost everywhere were rising, but among advanced industrial nations, the least violent were Switzerland, Italy, and Japan—which had the lowest of all—illustrating:

1. that you can have a low crime rate and various styles of capitalism, from highly individualistic to corporatist, provided that you have close family relationships as well as relative affluence; and
2. that, in the case of Switzerland, you can have very low homicide and assault rates at the same time as commonly available guns for the 'citizen army' (Killias, 1993), showing the importance of culture as well as opportunity factors in the aetiology of violence (Cook and Moore, 1995).

Social Class

There is surprisingly little material on social class and risk, largely because official statistics on recorded crime or offenders are not collected on that basis. Victimization survey data do yield important information on victims and where, as is often the case, victims know the offenders, they are *capable*, if the questions are asked, of revealing the social background of offenders too. However, they are not free from problems of differential social class interpretation of physical acts as 'violent' ones (see also Maguire, this volume). It is common for studies of violence against women and against children to observe that violence is no respecter of social class and is spread throughout society. This is true but misleading, for it tells us nothing about variations in the *proportions* of different social groups who become victims or, for that matter, offenders. There is also fierce debate among feminists about the salience of class and ethnicity, as contrasted with gender alone, to violence. Social class is inferred only indirectly by housing type, but the evidence from the British Crime Surveys indicates significant social-class differences in vulnerability to other forms of violence, including to being 'mugged': thus, council tenants are a third more likely, and private renters three quarters more likely, to become victims of violence than those who live in their own homes[26] (Mirrlees-Black *et al.*, 1996: Table 4.1). There are strong social-class differences in rape by husbands (Painter, 1991). In the United States, survey data suggest that rates of child abuse are 40 per cent higher in blue-collar than in white-collar families, and are 62 per cent higher among the very poor (Straus, Gelles, and Steinmetz, 1980). Likewise, with violence outside the family, where social class differences are greater than for family violence (Weis, 1989). Most violence is intra-class and intra-race, partly reflecting lifestyles in where males engage in honour contests or domestic oppression.

Homicide offers the most valid *recorded* crime data set for ascertaining the social class of victims, but there are no systematic English studies. However,

---

[26] Though perhaps paradoxically, the higher the household income (to the surprisingly low £20,000 per year cut-off point), the higher the prevalence of violence.

almost all major 'child abuse' deaths involve working-class children. Both Australian (National Committee, 1990; Polk, 1994) and American (Green and Wakefield, 1979) studies indicate that homicide victims come disproportionately from the lower social classes and since most homicides—*a fortiori* the 'family killings'—are 'cleared up' and are intra-class, it seems evident that the poor are most likely to be injured and killed, whether by violence (including terrorism) as conventionally defined or by injury at work.[27]

Age

The 'lifestyle' approach to victimization relates risk to the patterns of living in which people engage (see Pease, this volume). Young people are more at risk of becoming victims of any form of violence except spouse abuse, and this is related to the general patterns of life they lead, including the kinds of group drinking and quarrels in public places they get into (Tuck, 1989). The 1992 BCS included a special sample of 12–15-year-olds, and found that over six to eight months, a third said that they had been assaulted at least once (though only 7 per cent considered that they had been victims of 'violent crime'); and a fifth had property stolen when away from home. Additionally, over a fifth had been harassed, which was seldom defined by them as crime. The main offenders were people they knew, often in or around school. This 7 per cent compared with assault rates of 9 per cent for 16–19-year-olds and 1 per cent for 20–59-year-olds in the 1992 BCS (Maung, 1995). A survey of 11–15-year-olds in Edinburgh found that half the young people surveyed had been victims of an assault, 'threatening behaviour', or theft from the person over the previous nine months; the proportion who had been 'touched up' or had been 'flashed at' was higher for girls than for boys, varying from 14 per cent for 11–12-year-old boys (declining thereafter) to 17 per cent for 11–12-year-old girls and 30 per cent of 14–15-year-old girls. Only 14 per cent of assaults, 8 per cent of threatening behaviour, 16 per cent of thefts from the person were reported to the police, and only slightly higher percentages of sexual crimes were reported to other adults, let alone to the police (Anderson *et al.*, 1990). In the United States, 12–19-year-olds were estimated to have suffered 1.8 million crimes annually: roughly twice the rate of the adult population, though those 16–19-year-olds were far more likely to be victims of rape, robbery, and assault than were those aged 12–15 (National Crime Survey, 1986). The older the victims were, the more likely they were to be attacked by strangers and to suffer serious injuries.

Occupation

In research, though far less so in theoretical analyses of masculinities, which neglect it (Archer, 1994: Jefferson, this volume) increasing attention is being

---

[27] The latter is close to being a tautology: only those in consumer complaints departments would be likely to become victims of assault, for white-collar staff would seldom work on scaffolding, chop materials in workshops, etc.

paid to the risks of violence among different occupational groups while at work, excepting the sort of 'corporate violence' risks discussed earlier. It is not always conceptually clear whether the best way of looking at these risks is in relation to the numbers of people doing a particular job or the numbers of the people with whom they have to deal: rates per prisoner are relatively easy to calculate, but for police it is far harder. The 1988 British Crime Survey informs us (Mayhew *et al.*, 1989: 32) that 16.8 per cent of male workers aged 16–30 and 17 per cent of male workers aged 31–45 had experienced verbal abuse by the public over the previous fourteen months, and that occupations with a three times or more than average risk of violence included not only the police but also welfare workers, nurses, female office managers, and 'entertainment managers' such as publicans and 'bouncers'.[28] No comparable data are available from the later surveys, but one can estimate from the 1995 data that about 10 per cent of attacks on men and a smaller percentage of attacks on women were at work. The 1996 Retail Crime Costs Survey—which over-samples the large firms—found that 9,000 staff were victims of physical violence, and 167,000 were subjected to threats of violence and verbal abuse (British Retail Consortium, 1997).

Looking at the 'caring and controlling professions', an earlier study by Rowett (1986) had shown that one in ten social workers were assaulted each year: in inner city areas, the proportion was one in four, though residential social workers were more at risk than their community colleagues (see also Norris, 1990.) In 1993, there were 2,667 *reported* cases of violence against staff in male prisons: a ratio of six per 100 *inmates* (Ditchfield and Harries, 1996). The average risk of assaults against police officers—estimated by successive *Police Review* surveys at one in seven in 1988—differs only modestly from the average risks for men in the active police age group: in 1988, almost one in three males aged 16–24 and over one in twenty males aged 25–39 were assaulted (Mayhew *et al.*, 1989), though possibly with less severity than the police. As in other areas of violence, such physical risk data understate the impact of implicit and explicit threats.

Finally, some comments are appropriate about the 'corporate death and injury rates' in different occupations. Seventeen police and no prison officers were killed on duty in England and Wales in the period 1986–95—seven of them with firearms—an average of one per 100,000 annually. (A further eighty-three officers were injured by firearms in the period 1988–95.) Partly because of the Piper Alpha explosion, by far the highest risk of death per 100,000 employees was oil and gas extraction, with 87.3 deaths annually per 100,000 over the period 1986–92. The construction industry ranked fifth per 100,000, but had the largest *number* of fatalities. Coal mining, followed by the railways, had the highest injury rates. The fact that the police and prison officers are paid more than they would otherwise get to take the risk of violence may only be

---

[28] Except for office managers, the same categories had a 3-times greater than average risk of being threatened at work. Teachers, whose risk of assault was no greater than average, were 3 times as likely as the average to have been threatened at work.

an intriguing consequence of the perception that they alone are seen as 'victims of occupational violence' as well as of their social role: but given these occupational death rates, why do most of us see their work as more dangerous and 'violent' than that of miners and building workers or, for that matter, social workers?

EXPLAINING VIOLENCE

The conceptual issue of 'what acts count as violence' does not cause too many difficulties for criminologists in practice *because they usually ignore it*. Almost all the literature on explaining violent crime focuses exclusively on the 'conventional' areas of violence, sometimes—but by no means always—including rape. Interestingly, where criminologists seek to go beyond this, as Kempe and Kempe (1978) did in their text *Child Abuse*, they seldom attempt any genuine theoretical integration: what we are offered is a series of *types* of child abuse without a very clear idea of the ways in which the same explanation will or will not do for all.[29] Similar difficulties arise in the case of rape and even homicide. One can put a positive gloss on this and argue that this simply reflects the absence of coherence in causation and assault dynamics. Some people have a frankly psychotic or psychopathic view of the world and their relationship with it, and it is appropriate to take as the object of explanation 'why are these people so different?' Other violent offenders are closer to normal behaviour for their gender and age, and the appropriate focus is on social learning, situational interaction, cognitive processing, and opportunity factors. Feminist literature attempts the greatest level of theorizing violence across the board: thus Campbell's classic (if empirically flawed in places) study *Goliath* gives us an impassioned analysis of the loss of meaning in *men*'s lives, which can account for their violence against each other as well as against women (Campbell, 1993; see, further, Jefferson, this volume). However, feminist scholarship often neglects (i) those areas of corporate 'violence' which do not have female victims, and (ii) violence for gain such as robbery (though see Newburn and Stanko, 1994).

Given the enormous heterogeneity of forms of violence discussed earlier in this chapter, is it plausible that any one theory or theoretical paradigm can account for all these manifestations, or even serve as a common thread in all of them? As in the other areas of crime discussed in this volume, there is disagreement over what sort of explanation we are looking for. An explanation of why this person did that crime in a particular place and time? (The criminologist's *whatsortofpersondunnit*?) Literature on serial killers and rapists tends to take this form, seldom exploring whether and/or why there are variations

---

[29] We are also treated to an attempt to apply the evocative term 'violence' to emotional hurt, without any clarification of the outer limits of unjustifiable distress: children may cause as well as receive emotional hurt, a complication which is readily ignored or trivialized.

over time and between cultures in the frequency of the phenomenon, or even
the psychopathology of suspects except inasmuch as it helps to narrow down
the range of plausible suspects. (For a good review in this genre, see Holmes
and Holmes, 1996, though even *before* reading the *Oxford Handbook*, many
students should be able to improve on their theoretical literature review! For
a deeply sceptical view of the social construction of serial homicide, see
Jenkins, 1994.) No better illustration of social obsession with gruesome
celebrity can be found than the trials of the African-American athlete O. J.
Simpson (Barak, 1996) and the trial of Fred and Rosemary West, the 'butchers
of Gloucester'. On the other hand, although the most gruesome murderers and
rapists may draw comfort from their caricatured degradation of women or
men (or certain perceived 'sorts of women or men'), it makes little sense to
regard them as anything approaching 'normal' representatives of chauvinism:
their behaviour fortunately is too rare to be seen in this light.

Alternatively, are we searching for an explanation of different *rates* of
violence in different geographical areas or different countries? Or for different
rates of victimization, by occupation, age, ethnicity, and gender (as discussed
earlier); locations; weather; motivation? Different sorts of answers are required
for different levels of explanation, which partly explains why attention has
been paid to such a variety of factors as autonomic nervous systems, circulating hormones (such as testosterone and corticosterone), food metabolisation,
electro-encephalogram readings, social and economic status (absolute or by level
of social inequality), gender, ethnicity, media coverage, and level of 'victim-
precipitation' (i.e. the role of the victim in 'provoking' the violent incident).[30]
One of the persistent difficulties with many approaches to explaining violence
(and, for that matter, victimization risks) is that though they may lay down
social indicators or 'marker variables'—some of which illuminate the dynamics
of the phenomenon—they seldom generate anything close to a causal account
which makes sense of *non*-violence as well as of violence. The accounts that
come closest to helping us understand why this person committed that crime
on that particular occasion are retrospective reviews: but the psychosexual
conflicts which they reveal are much more common than violent behaviour,
even if one takes into account opportunity variables. Those who write about
violence understandably reflect their background disciplines, and although
they mostly formally acknowledge that heredity, personality, family conflicts,
cultural (including gendered), and situational factors all influence violent
behaviour, it is the *relative* salience of these variables that produces a clear
divide. I shall attempt to do justice to this multiplicity of perspectives, but

---

[30] Attribution theorists have shown female victim deserts to be such an integral part of the
patriarchal culture that such defensiveness by feminists is appropriate. Nevertheless, it is questionable whether female violence against partners is always justifiable: the phrase 'protective reaction
violence' is uncomfortably close to the justification given by the former US government for the
bombing of Kampuchea! Victim-precipitation can apply to workplace injuries, for example, the
link between the *machismo* of refusing to wear safety clothing and an enhanced risk of injury
among manual workers, though piece-work payment systems also increase risk.

given space constraints, I shall reflect my biases by concentrating on the social interactionist and socio-cultural explanations, whilst acknowledging that these too *over*predict levels of violence. Hence the importance of the data on the incidence and prevalence of violence which are presented in the first part of this review.

Some features of social organization are not reflected in any of these macro-cosmic accounts but nevertheless appear to be significant in accounting for violence. Gartner (1990) has conducted some cross-national research in developed countries to see what factors best account for variation in homicide rates. She concludes that more micro-level research is required but observes (*ibid.*: 102) that

Nations with greater material deprivation, more cultural heterogeneity, more family dissolution, higher female labor force participation, and greater exposure to official violence generally have higher homicide rates. . . . A disproportionate number of teens and young adults was not associated with higher homicide rates for any age group, among these 18 nations. . . . Female labor force participation may influence homicide by raising the motivations for female and child homicide, rather than by weakening controls.

Braithwaite (1989) focuses likewise on economic inequality as a primary pre-dictor of homicide rates, and this is implicated in the connections made between imperilled 'masculinities' and violence (Polk, 1994; and Jefferson, this volume). Links between unemployment and criminality are stronger for property crime than for violent crime (see Field, 1990), but more sophisticated sociological accounts might separate out the unemployed into those who are psychologically integrated into 'straight society' and those who see themselves as part of an 'underclass' (and are policed as if they were).

Biology and Violence

Most work on the biology of violence concentrates on the physiology of the brain and how, under certain circumstances, it can lead to loss of self-control (Moir and Jessell, 1995). Violence has also been associated with endogenous and exogenous physiological factors such as eating chocolate (Lester, 1991), the menstrual cycle (Fishbein, 1992), testosterone (Archer, 1990), and the weather (Cheatwood, 1995). It is fairly easy to make fun of the *general* value of the impact, for example, of chocolate on suicide and homicide (Lester, 1991)—is the chocolate lobby to rival the gun lobby in preventing its prohib-ition?—but for some individuals, particular physiological triggers may apply under rare combinations of conditions that one may discover only after the violent incident. Brownmiller (1975) is one of the few feminists to argue that rape is the result of *biological drives* rather than being learned masculinity which is functional for male hegemony. The natural selection hypothesis that rape is a historical adaptation which substitutes for lawful access to repro-ductive mates is difficult to falsify, but many rapists do in fact enjoy access to

consenting (or at least uncomplaining) females, and their generalized aggressiveness to people and to property suggests that 'the selfish gene' is not
restricted to the desire to reproduce genetically. Classic methods such as twin
studies of demonstrating inheritability of violent tendencies (Brennan *et al.*,
1995; Mednick *et al.*, 1987; Rowe, 1990) can hardly account for changes in
violent crime rates in the same society over time, nor the frequency of violence
among those who *sometimes* behave violently, whatever other methodological
problems they may have. Similar problems face those who would explain
violence in terms of brain disorders or the metabolization of glucose (Eronen,
1995; Moir and Jessell, 1995; Raine, 1993*a*, 1993*b*, 1994, 1995). However, such
difficulties in explaining the *in*frequency of violent crime among 'the violent'
also apply to sociological and social psychological/cognitive accounts, so they
are not unique to biology and crime.

Even given a conventional view of what constitutes 'violent crime'—i.e.
excludes genocide, war crimes, and corporate violence—controversy rages
about the role of genetic factors. Wilson and Herrnstein (1985), Brennan *et al.*
(1995), and Herrnstein (1995) argue that they *are* important and that even the
possession of an extra Y (male) chromosome is associated with violence. Some
people behave violently for a long time in a variety of settings: although the
manifestations of aggression vary, a child who is top of the distribution for
aggression at age 8 is likely to be near the top twenty years later. Psychological
research has tended to focus upon the role of 'temperament', whose origin is
obscure but which seems to be a relatively stable phenomenon. Children who
are extremely inhibited or uninhibited at 21 months are likely to be similarly
classified at age 7.5. Farrington (1989) has argued that when they are children,
violent offenders tend to be high on hyperactivity-impulsivity-attention deficit,
tend to be restless and lacking in concentration, lack empathy (the ability to
identify with others' feelings), and find it difficult to defer gratification. This
may look like a caricature of the 'feckless poor' but is an *intra*-class discrimi-
nator of aggression levels (see further, Farrington, this volume).

However, there are socio-biological approaches which are more dynamic
and therefore can accommodate changing violence rates. Burgess and Draper
(1989) examine family violence in evolutionary terms, arguing that under
certain conditions, child maltreatment has a benefit in helping the fittest survive:
moreover hostility towards stepchildren, for example, may be explicable in
terms of our being prepared to act in a more hostile way towards people who
share none of our genes,[31] while greater rates of violence against poor and
'physically challenged' children are understandable in relation to competition
for scarce resources and optimizing future individual reproductive potential.[32]
(They explicitly state, however, that violence may currently be maladaptive.)

---

[31] One might add that most so-called 'family violence' is committed by intimates who do not
share the genes of their victims but rather are relatives by marriage.

[32] Natural selection arguments take into account epidemiological data but, like most functionalist explanations, tend towards the tautological. Selection operates at the level of the individual
person or even the individual gene, rather than in terms of 'reproducing the population': the latter

The analysis of homicide by Wilson and Daly (1988, 1994) explores the evolutionary dimensions, including gender ones, which are understandable in terms of male attitudes of ownership of women, which have arisen from different evolutionary selection pressures on men and women which favour male risk-taking and female risk-avoidance. They stress that homicide predominantly occurs between individuals who are not related genetically, and that even when mothers kill, they normally are young ones who kill when they have a lot of time left to reproduce. Quite apart from the presence of alternative explanations, such as poverty and lack of social support for *some* young mothers, their theory requires the killers to believe that they will not be held accountable, since it is difficult to conceive further children while in most prisons. However, this is not to do justice to the general sophistication of their approach. For example, Daly and Wilson observe (1988: 128), partly caricaturing the stress on victim-offender interactions by Wolfgang (1958):

A seemingly minor affront is not merely a 'stimulus' to action, isolated in time and space. It must be understood within a larger social context of reputation, face, relative social status, and enduring relationships. Men are known by their fellows as 'the sort who can be pushed around' or 'the sort who won't take any shit', as guys whose girlfriends you can chat up with impunity or guys you don't want to mess with. In most social milieus, a man's reputation depends in part upon the maintenance of a credible threat of violence.

The difference between sociobiologists such as they and social interactionists lies more in their breadth of perspective and analysis of the *origins* of attitudes than in the situated accounts of behaviour. We may see that although *some* biologists and especially physionomists may be trapped in a static framework which obviously cannot account for the enormous variations in the extent of violence across societies and over time, the more sophisticated do take such variability into account, even though their analysis of the reasons behind such changes may be functionalist and teleological rather than genuine explanations.

Psycho-analytical and Clinical Psychology Approaches to Violence

For decades, psycho-analytical explanations of violence (and crime in general) have been subjected to hostile criticisms from positivists on the grounds that they are 'not science', and from feminists and sociologists on the grounds that they individualize and internalize influences on behaviour. It is true that the predictive abilities of such explanations are poor, and that the pseudo-analytical categorizations are often more like lists than conceptually coherent constructs. Guttmacher (1973) tells us that the average murderer was free of any psychopathology or mental illness, but possessed a defective conscience,

is simply an aggregated consequence of individual selections. One problem posed for natural selection theory is the high prevalence of unrecorded incest. Another problem is how to account for variations in violence such as the alleged increase in attacks upon 'disabled' people in Germany during the 1990s.

caused *inter alia* by emotional deprivation and inadequate nurturing, and goes on to provide an unilluminating list of other 'types'. Likewise, psychopathy is a rag-bag concept into which is often dumped anyone who does not change behaviour after punishments that would deter most of us.

On the other hand, as Jefferson also acknowledges (this volume), some killers and rapists are obviously very disturbed and traumatized, as well as committing acts of such vileness that there is clearly something very 'wrong' with their mental 'make-up' (see Malmquist, 1995, for a more thoughtful psychiatrist's approach to explaining violence). Gresswell and Hollin (1994) have provided a more helpful typology of multiple murderers, breaking motivation into four areas:

1. Visionary killers, who suffer from delusional beliefs about particular victims;
2. Missionary killers, who have decided to rid society of certain types of people (such as prostitutes);
3. Hedonistic or lust killers, who seek to remove the memory of humiliation by projecting rage onto their victims (found also by Hale, 1994); and
4. Power and control killers, who use killing as a form of domination.

However, Brown (1991) argues that following stress, serial killers develop a taste for killing which relieves anxieties and is positively reinforced by the dissolution of anxiety, rather like other forms of addiction. These approaches are not incompatible, but they reflect the different approaches of psychiatrists and psychologists to cognitive processes.

There remains a great deal of dispute over the role of sexual abuse in childhood as a factor in such behaviour, not least because of the bitter debate over whether 'false memory syndrome' exists (Pendergrast, 1997), but one would have to be a strange individual to deny the relevance of relationships with parents and other family/authority figures in forming attitudes and behaviour. Illuminating as it is to explore offenders' feelings when they commit crime (Katz, 1988), the origin of those feelings may be explored, albeit often unfalsifiably, by psychiatrists.

Sociocultural and Social Psychological Explanations of Violence

I have grouped these together because although they spring from different academic traditions—sociology and social psychology—they are mutually consistent, the former being oriented towards culture, social structure, and stratification (Wolfgang, 1958; Wolfgang and Ferracuti, 1967; Curtis, 1975; Scully, 1990), the latter towards the more immediate cognitive and interpersonal dynamics that 'produce' the violent behaviour (Toch, 1969; Frude, 1989, 1994).

One of the earliest comprehensive attempts to explain violence was the 'subculture of violence' (Wolfgang and Ferracuti, 1967). While not providing an account of why the supposed subculture developed in the first place, they revealed that many acts of violence arise from incidents that are trivial in origin—insult, curse, or a jostle—whose significance is blown out of all proportion in poor neighbourhoods where self-esteem is low. A more micro-sociological successor to their approach is the 'lifestyle' theoretical paradigm, based on victimization survey research, which shows that offenders and victims of street violence not only belong to the same social, age, and gender groups—for example, schoolchildren (Maung, 1995) and two thirds of those who attacked 16–24-year-olds were in the same age group (Davidoff and Greenhorn, 1991)—but also that victims are likely to have criminal records not dissimilar to assailants. (One of the important consequences of this is that under current legal interpretations (Miers, 1997: chapter 7) unless the Criminal Injuries Compensation Authority deems it inappropriate, such victims are likely to be denied state compensation on the grounds either of their conduct at the time or their prior criminal convictions, however blameless their behaviour on this occasion.)

Curtis (1975) later developed the 'subculture of violence' approach to account for the higher incidence of black than of white violence, arguing *inter alia* that black people were expected to have a lower 'boiling point' and that their identities were much more fragile precisely because of the racism and economic discrimination in the wider society: a point developed also by Blau and Blau (1982) and by Currie (1985).

Feminist critics express concern that the focus on social stratification evades the central issue about violent crime, which is that it is committed primarily by *men*.[33] Feminist theories of male violence against women stress the social construction of masculinity, violence, and sexuality in patriarchal society whose object is to reproduce and maintain their relative status and authority over women (Hanmer *et al.*, 1989; Scully, 1990; Dobash *et al.*, 1992; Newburn and Stanko, 1994; Jefferson, this volume). Wife-beating, for example, is seen as an interactive process in which—even discounting the effects of rosy retro-spection on early stages of relationships—the women started out feeling loved and interpreted male possessive behaviour as a gesture of commitment: only later did this sense of possession escalate into paranoid violence at the least threat to his control or 'patriarchal rights' (Dobash and Dobash, 1979). However, such accounts are unsatisfactory in illuminating variations in violence against women (and men) over time or in different societies, and the shift to the more fluid 'masculinities' is an attempt to deal with the issue of variation, whatever difficulties still remain in accounting for the gendered changes (Morgan, 1987; Newburn and Stanko, 1994; Jefferson, this volume). Feminists are far from agreed upon the role of race and class, as contrasted with gender, in violent crime (Hanmer, Radford, and Stanko, 1989), though Campbell and Muncer (1994), who argue that male and female aggression styles are distinct, stress the importance of social status. However, though race and class factors

---

[33] About 90% of English killers are male, roughly half of whom were aged 18–29 at the time of their conviction.

are more pronounced in non-family than in spousal or parent–child violence, the data cited earlier indicate that theories based solely on gender seriously overpredict levels of violent crime both within and between societies.

Whether or not men are biologically more aggressive than women, the level and manifestation of *machismo* are culturally variable. Thus Strong (1995), writing about the conditions of Colombian society that enabled major drugs traffickers such as Pablo Escobar to develop their power bases, discusses the role of the *sicarios*: young men on motorcycles who are willing to assassinate anyone for a few dollars, simply to prove themselves in a country where 'reputation' is crucial both for dignity and sexual display (and, where the object of attention fails to be impressed, can create sufficient anger to result in rape). This, plus 'turf wars', was why the homicide rate doubled between 1970 and 1980. Between 1980 and 1986, the homicide rate in the city of Medellin alone quadrupled to 2,000 killings. In Colombia, as in many Latin American countries, male ego insecurity is prevalent and leads to large numbers of 'honour contests' (Polk, 1994). Compared with Colombia, British representations of *machismo* thankfully are tame. As Strong (1995: 157) puts it, echoing Campbell's (1993) journalistic account of the male British underclass: 'The *sicarios* were characterized by their adoration for their mothers, their religious superstition and their relentless consumerism. In a world in which fathers were mostly dead, drunk, unemployed or simply absent, it was around the mothers that households hinged.'

Accounting for Rape

Explanations of rape are predominantly sociocultural and social interactionist, arguing that rape reflects more general attitudes by men towards women in any particular society and that a substantial proportion of rapes arise from misinterpreted (to male advantage unless convicted) and unreciprocated seductions (Sanday, 1981; Sorensen and White, 1992; Scully, 1990; White and Sorensen, 1992). Felson (1993) argues that while most rapists *prefer* non-coercive strategies to obtain sex, subjectively defined sexual deprivation is their primary motivation, and rapists have high levels of both marital and extramarital intercourse. Whether with women or (in prison) with men, they regard others as being there for their sexual gratification. These accounts are *social* psychological, but the role of individual psychopathology (or grossly mis-read 'sexual scripts') is important in some cases of 'blitz rapes' where there is no real interaction beforehand between offender and victim (see West, 1983). It would be a caricature to assert that this is anything other than an awful parody of the bifurcation by men into 'good girls' and 'bad girls' that is more commonplace, since there is no evidence that a substantial proportion of men regard a woman merely walking in the street as parading her sexuality. In *some* societies, rape is directed towards women who display most independence (Sanday, 1981), thereby attracting the functionalist 'explanation' that its purpose is to keep all women subjugated (Brownmiller, 1975). In Britain and the United States it is primarily young males attacking young females of similar background and ethnicity: almost two thirds of rape victims and almost half of indecent assault victims knew their attackers previously, and two thirds of rapes and half the indecent assaults took place at the home of the victim or suspect (Smith, 1989; Watson, 1996).[34] Unless women are the target group for subjugation on the part of those males who have few economic goods to exchange for (relative) monogamy or by wealthy men who do not fear the criminal law or for their social reputation, such a distribution of victims is hard to explain in terms of *collective* male interests.[35] There is insufficient detail to test whether or not these are 'date rapes', but the data support the argument that the explanation for sexual violence must be sought in male misperceptions of females' attitudes towards them and/or in their beliefs that if they 'go too far' in such situations, the consequences will not be very serious (see Chappell, 1989).

Rape is often part of a general tendency to use violence (Pollard, 1994). Rapists may subscribe to rape mythology that if they continue despite female protestations, the women will enjoy the experience: to admit otherwise is to admit to themselves that they are unattractive, a conclusion that is all the more humiliating if one of their friends has had sex (or *claimed* to have had sex) with the woman. Herein may lie the true significance of Amir's (1970) controversial finding that a large percentage of rape victims had a 'bad reputation': men might find it harder to retreat from sex under those circumstances, as well as (incorrectly) feeling that there was no 'real harm' in indulging themselves with a 'spoiled female'. As for Amir's (1970) finding that 70 per cent of rapes are planned, this has been misused to illustrate premeditation: his definition of 'planned rape' is that it occurs when the offender rapes the victim in a place other than where they first met. So if a man met a woman in a bar, and went to either of their homes in the hope of voluntary sex, but raped her when she did not consent, this would constitute 'planned rape' on his definition. Yet although many men are careless about women's feelings, there seems more reason to suppose that most rapes are unplanned but potentiated by 'cultures of masculinity'.

Based on interviews with American rapists, Scully (1990: 91) observes that rapists have nothing in their background to predict rape specifically but rather are typical of non-white-collar felons. From the perspective of the rapists, almost no act—however brutal—is a 'real' rape and almost no man is a rapist.

---

[34] I have counted 'no suspect' and 'unrecorded' as not acquainted, since one presumes that if people have gone to the trouble of getting a sexual assault recorded, they would want to see an offender they could identify punished.

[35] Natural selection theorists would regard it as nonsensical to suggest that there could be a gene which generated behaviour which benefited a group as a whole. The high proportion of young females as victims, 'explained' by some socio-biologists as an attempt to maximize offenders' reproduction—though given female contraception, a more maladaptive response today—also owes much to their more active night life. Older women go out less, having responsibility for child-care under current gender roles. The situational opportunity factors are omitted from most socio-biological accounts (e.g. see Thornhill and Thornhill, 1992).

The key to justifying violence to others (and to themselves) is to make what was in fact rape appear ambivalent in terms of consent. Those who denied their rapes were prone to believe, or at least to assert, that women found them particularly desirable. Admitters, on the other hand, were much more aware of the emotional impact and took satisfaction in the belief that their victims felt powerless, humiliated or degraded. Neither group felt guilt or shame during or after the rape, nor did either group members feel empathy for their victims at the time. Indeed, the desire to dominate a woman is also a major component of rapists' sexual fantasies.

In short, at the risk of producing precisely the sort of list for which I criticized Guttmacher, rape can arise:

1. as a means of revenge and punishment;
2. as an afterthought or a bonus that they add to a burglary or robbery, as 'another thing to take';
3. as a male bonding activity in groups (especially in the aftermath of war, to their subjects' 'womenfolk'); and
4. to make a fantasy come true to control and dominate impersonally (Scully, 1990: 166).

The question why most men who have chauvinistic attitudes and could rape do *not* do so remains unresolved by any of the research literature. One could hypothesize that non-rapists fear more than rapists for their social reputations, for the expected future feelings of the prospective victim, or for the direct and indirect socio-economic consequences of arrest and conviction: but these concepts lack analytical specificity.

The Culture of Masculinity and Violence against Authority Figures

Comments from senior officers and politicians, and media reports of violent incidents, sometimes depict violent outcomes as the result of interactive social processes, but they normally have little difficulty in blaming the public (or rather, some 'hooligan' section of the public which is hostile to the police). By contrast, in the specific area of violence in which police are hurt, early American research by Toch (1969) observed that many police victims of assault become so because they are personally insecure and wish to prove to themselves and others that they are Real Men by daring others to defy them. (In societies such as the United States with ready recourse to fatal weapons, such Desperately Seeking Challenges can be a dangerous thing to do.) This explanatory approach is also generalized to other contexts, such as inmate–inmate and inmate–officer violence in prison (Toch, 1979: 272–3):

The term 'brawling' is used advisedly, because, as this man sees it, his conflicts with officers are 'fights'. In other words, they are disputes which are settled physically, as disputes must be settled among men. This view is partially shared and reinforced by the officers, who repeatedly describe in vivid detail the wrestling holds they deploy to neutralize the man. . . . The man is said to have 'communication problems' and these are reciprocal. . . . The central issue often appears to be that the man feels himself treated like a child, and that his version of *machismo* holds that no man must be ordered about by another man, and that it is demeaning and insulting to be told to do things, particularly when you have explained why you do not wish to do them or would have explained if you could have.

The issue of the man's reactions to uniforms does not necessarily enter the equation because the man sees encounters between himself and officers as personal, and perceives custodial instructions as originating in whims and expressions of disdain or disrespect. When the man feels disdained or disrespected in this way he reacts at the first available opportunity, which makes his behaviour unpredictable, because his reaction does not necessarily coincide with the move that originates the offense to which he reacts.

Similar reactions to other authority figures—such as teachers or employers— among the de-subordinated might be expected, with similarly polarized interpretations of the *justifiability* of the demands by authority figures. To many people, including journalists, all such challenges are indicators of cultural disturbance and psychopathy (see Farrington, this volume), but to others, they indicate a desire for personal autonomy which is being invaded by the powerful.

A focus upon the police as a traditional subculture of masculinity would follow the lines of a general or force or area or shift police subculture in which aggressive policing was encouraged or, at least, was not actively *dis*couraged. Adherents to this 'Dirty Harry' subculture believe—along with detectives who 'strengthen' evidence against those they 'know' to be guilty—that unless they act firmly, 'things will get out of hand', and they must especially clamp down on 'known troublemakers' in their area who set a bad example to others by demonstrating 'contempt of cop'. How do they know who the troublemakers are? Every police officer who joins an area has these individuals or families pointed out to him by supervisors either in the police station or out on the beat. Other prime candidates are young 'ethnics', bikers, and other potential 'rowdies'. An alternative view is that in the great majority of cases of assault on police, members of the public who may be more generally anti-social and anti-authority become the worse for wear on drink and, fortified by the low penalties attached to attacks (principally a small fine) as well as by the (lower than in 'the old days') expected (low) probability of bystander intervention on behalf of the police, indulge in untrammeled violence which is generally unprovoked by any misconduct on the part of the police. In the minds of the beleaguered officers, the large amount of low-level verbal abuse and hostility to their presence in some licensed premises and city centres late at night makes it necessary to intervene to stop the area turning into a 'no-go' one. Whether or not police and public are right in believing that there is less respect for the police nowadays and that society is getting more violent, these beliefs impinge upon police anxieties about loss of control and can result in 'heavy-handed policing', particularly if:

1. their supervisory and senior officers encourage 'active' policing, and
2. the section of the public they are dealing with are seen as 'criminal' and/or 'anti-police' types who belong to a 'subculture of violence'.

It is tempting to explain the rise in assaults against the police since the tranquil early 1950s in terms of the greater ease with which modern communications enable a police officer to get to the scene of the 'disturbance' while it is still in its upswing: a view with which some older police officers concur. However, this is to ignore the high assault rates in the period 1850–1927, when communications were also slow.

To the extent that assaults against the police *have* been increasing in recent years, this may also be because police legitimacy in the eyes of the public has diminished—which the police acknowledge has happened but do not usually attribute to a general deterioration in *police* behaviour—and/or because the police have become less skillful in the handling of relations with the public (see Which, 1990; Skogan, 1990; Reiner, 1992). The process of desubordination to authority is a generalized feature which is implicated in assaults against a variety of personnel—police, prison officers, social workers, teachers—all of whom pose a threat to the desire for autonomy. This may be extended to others who threaten or are expected, reasonably or unreasonably, to threaten in the future the self-gratification of the offender. Looked at in this way, what may look like individual paranoia may be understood to have some socio-cultural roots.

More generally, however, interviews with assailants and observation of police work support Toch's (1969) view that the way the police approach the public—such as appearing to pick on them; making them face humiliation in front of their friends or their girlfriends to whom they wish to present a *machismo* image;[36] or standing physically very close, thereby (a) winding them up psychologically, and (b) bringing themselves within ready head-butting range, is an important dimension to understanding assaults against the police (Christopher *et al.*, 1989). Whatever the pleasure that individual officers obtain from violence (Katz, 1988) changes in the nature of 'cop culture' or 'prison officer culture', as well as in officers' *perceptions* of being assaulted or killed themselves may account for variations in violence by police and prison officers. Also relevant is Bernard's (1990) conclusion that a subculture of angry aggression arises under conditions when serious social disadvantage is combined with individual social isolation.[37] Peer activity routines, once established, are likely to account for the immense social class and status group and gender variations in the prevalence of different forms of violence. The virtual abolition of opportunities for traditional unskilled labouring work has reduced the incentives for conformity, but those unacquainted with the role of socializa-

[36] Research suggests that those who are convicted of assault against the police predominantly have friends present with them who believe that such behaviour is justified (Christopher, Noaks, and Levi, 1989).

[37] See also Shepherd (1990) for similar conclusions reached from an interesting survey of hospital casualty admissions in Bristol.

tion and ongoing social controls might be surprised that violence (and crime for gain) among the underclass is so low, rather than that it is so high.

Let us now turn to what research indicates about individual involvement in violence.

Individual-level Accounts of Violence

Psychological approaches to explaining individual-level violence have moved from the relatively crude frustration-aggression approach (later refined to suggest that frustration raises arousal which may be interpreted as anger), through social learning theory (Bandura, 1973) in which aggression is learned vicariously through watching (though this too has been criticized for over-interpretation of play as aggression), to more cognitive and behavioural theories. Huessman and Eron (1989) argue that aggressive behaviour is largely controlled by programmes or 'scripts' about what events are likely to occur, how the person should react to the events, and what will result. These 'scripts' have been learned during the child's early development and are retrieved from memory on the appropriate environmental cues. Children are likely to be influenced by parents' own cognitive processes, so people who are 'paranoid' and view the world as hostile reinforce the child's scripts. (People may learn 'rape scripts' in a like manner.) Such individual-level accounts emphasize the interactive nature of much violent behaviour, although the behavioural cues which 'trigger' the violent conduct may vary not only with the general cognitive state of that person but also with the drugs, including alcohol and tranquil-lizers, that s/he has consumed. In research on non-sexual child abuse, for example, Frude (1989) notes that the child's behaviour may influence the aggression levels of the parent(s) and may also provide a less responsive feed-back to parental discipline methods, though the negative attitudes of parents towards their children, as well as factors such as social isolation, poverty, etc. were salient to the risk of abuse. In his later exploration of marital violence, Frude (1994) reiterates the importance of interaction, stressing the salience of:

1. relationship dissatisfaction, which leads to more negative evaluation of the partner's behaviour and to anger;
2. the couple's power relationship, which can be exacerbated when the male has fewer resources than the female (Straus and Gelles, 1990); and
3. the couple's conflict style. Violence is particularly common in relation-ships which have high 'ambient conflict', involving frequent rows and the absence of inhibitions in attacking the self-esteem of their partner.

The worse the self-esteem of the partner, the more likely it is that anger aggression will be generated in the process, and even the most ('objectively') mild behaviour can lead to violence, especially around sex and money.

Toch (1969) has usefully distinguished several types of violent offender: the 'self-image demonstrator', who uses violence to demonstrate toughness which he believes will be admired by his peers; the 'self-image defender', who tends to feel easily slighted or disparaged and will react to defend his ego; and the 'reputation defender', who acts as a member of a group to defend the values of the group when s/he believes them to be threatened. They all involve various methods of coping with fragile self-concepts: this may be class or status-group linked, in so far as those who are used to commanding social resources and respect may be less prone than poor whites or people of colour to having their self-images undermined. On the other hand, some high-status people expect respect and may react aggressively—for example, by firing staff or 'freezing' partners—when contradicted or thwarted: whether this ever comes to be defined as 'violence' or 'violent crime' depends upon what they do and how they do it.

There is much popular belief in the intergenerational aspect of child physical and sexual abuse, but even if the great majority of 'child abusers' were abused children, it would be possible that only a tiny proportion of abused children grew up to abuse their children. Many abusing parents misperceive their children's culpability and treat the baby as if it were an adult who 'made a mess' *deliberately* (Frude, 1989): however, some children are objectively more difficult to handle, cry more, and give less affection, thereby making a cycle of escalating violence more probable. Situational opportunity variables are also salient to baby battering: modern nuclear families are far more isolated than extended families found in many Third World countries, where parents are seldom alone in the house. (Different considerations apply to physical punishment of older children, who are considered in many cultures, in extended or in nuclear families, to be properly blameworthy and 'reformable' by being beaten. Systematic incest patterns also are found in extended families.)

Are violent offenders specialists? Because of the distortions generated by non-reporting and non-prosecution of family violence (and injuries in the workplace), criminal career data based on official statistics are prone to specific distortions. American research suggests that violent offenders have longer criminal careers and are less likely to stop in the early stage of their offending than are property criminals (Blumstein *et al.*, 1986). Nearly all London offenders studied by Farrington were convicted of non-violent as well as violent crimes, and only a quarter of their crimes were violent. Essentially, although 70 per cent of violent offenders are convicted of only one violent offence, they are frequent general offenders who appear to turn to violence after property crime. In London, the majority of juvenile violent offenders did go on to commit adult violent offences (and those who did not committed *non*-violent offences as adults). Home Office (1989) data on the prospective and retrospective criminal careers of rapists suggest similar generalized offending. Of those convicted of rape in 1985, 55 per cent had previous convictions for theft and 43 per cent for burglary.[38] Though many of these offences will have been against men, just under half the offenders had previous convictions for

---

[38] No statistics are kept, but in the UK, unlike the US, burglary-rape is rare.

one or more offences involving violence—a third of them for sexual offences, but only 3 per cent had rape convictions.

However, since the majority of offenders were not convicted of more than one violent offence, ideas such as 'careers of violence' are not very useful, at least outside the family context and, it is suggested, among some *extra*-familial pædophiles. Even within the family violence context, it is far from clear what proportion of men who have hit their wives do so again, let alone escalate the level of violence. Fagan's (1989) review of the cessation of family violence notes that three quarters of spouse abusers stop after legal sanctions are taken against them, but for how long they stop is uncertain, since the follow-up periods are not long. The shorter the time and less severe the battering, the more likely people are to stop beating (although it should be noted that in their replication of their original study, Sherman and Smith (1992), observe that this effect is found only for 'respectable' batterers.) These findings of low recidivism for violence (see also Farrington, this volume) have, or ought to have, important implications for those who believe in 'incapacitating the violent offender'.

Situational Factors and Violence: the Role of 'Substance Abuse'

Finally, readers should be aware of one factor that is relevant to both cultural and biological/pharmacological accounts of violence. Most people know others who behave much more aggressively when they have been drinking heavily or, more rarely, while under the influence of illegal drugs such as amphetamines or steroids. Though some violent offenders report (to this author) that they choose to get 'tanked up' with alcohol to put themselves in an appropriate mood for the fight they desire anyway, i.e. it is an enjoyment enhancer as well as disinhibitor, heavy drinking permeates almost every venue in which violence occurs.[39] However, it is very rare for such people to be violent every time that they consume those substances, so it cannot be said, for example, that the drink is a sufficient or even necessary explanation of their violence, even if one disregards powerful cross-cultural evidence that the relationship between substance use and aggression depends upon social norms and expectations (Collins, 1989; Fagan, 1990). Notwithstanding this, the opportunities for certain types of interaction offered by heavy alcohol use, combined with fragile self-respect of a kind that anyway would be threatened by a male or his female companion being 'looked at in a particular way' even when sober, implicate alcohol in the process of becoming violent.

Adolescents who drink or use drugs are more likely than those who do not to commit violent acts, though this may simply reflect the risk-taking mental set of those who also have their first sexual experiences early (Herrnstein, 1995). Likewise, there is a positive correlation between (a) the severity and frequency of violent delinquency, and (b) the seriousness and frequency of

---

[39] As Prof. Al Reiss observed to me (over a drink or two), when discussing the causes of violence: 'the explanation is booze, booze, booze'.

drug-taking (Fagan, 1990). American research indicates a positive relationship between alcohol use and violence, both against wives (Frieze and Browne, 1989) and generally. British research indicates a strong relationship between crimes of violence and beer consumption (Field, 1990), though this may be an artefact of street violence occurring where young people cluster and become embroiled in disputes when they leave drinking places (Tuck, 1989; Ramsay, 1996). Drinking and drug-taking can be indulged in as trauma-less fun, but although some offenders are part of a peer culture in which 'handling it' without aggression is expected, frequent 'poly-substance abusers' tend to be people with low self-esteem who find it difficult to confront problems in relationships. Common accompaniments are violence to self and to others, as well as generalized aggression. Collins (1989) observes that individuals with alcohol disorders frequently have other personality disorders, including crippling anxiety or sudden changes in relationships and mood.

As regards illicit substances, except in so far as there may be 'commercial' violence resulting from a desire to dominate drugs distribution or extort money from sellers, there is no evidence that the *pharmacological* effect of cannabis, hallucinogens, or opiates makes people violent: if anything, the reverse is true. There is a more plausible link between violence and amphetamines and solvents but, as with alcohol, demonstrating the causal link is confounded by the intervening personality variables. A thoughtful overview by Fagan concludes (1990: 299) that:

intoxication affects cognitive processes that shape and interpret perceptions of both one's own physiology (i.e. expectancy) and the associated behavioral response. The cognitive processes themselves are influenced by cultural and situational factors that determine the norms, beliefs, and sanctions regarding behaviors following intoxication. . . . Propensity toward aggression reflects explanations regarding the use of personal power to resolve perceived conflicts.

DEALING WITH VIOLENT CRIME

It is not my objective here to set out a normative account for how 'we' should deal with the large range of offences grouped artificially as 'violent crime', but some brief comments on the implications of theory and data for strategies of control are appropriate.[40] Clearly, there are major differences in modes of control, depending on whether one believes in punishing wrongdoing because it is retributively just or whether one is seeking primarily to reduce future violence. Many people *believe* that severe penalties will achieve both objectives, but the evidence for this is scant. As regards retribution, it may be pointed out that in the area of corporate 'violence' at work and 'risky motoring', retri-

---

[40] I shall deal with only some aspects of the prevention of violence: see Farrell (1992) and Pease, this volume.

butivism has *never* been practised as a dominant response: a socially equitable approach to retributivism would require a massive expansion of resources in prosecuting corporate crime, but Braithwaite and Pettit (1990) argue that this would lead to less rather than more safety. As regards reducing the rate of violent crime, it seems evident that some major socio-economic and cultural changes need to occur: the question is how we get from here to there.

There is evidence to suggest that a focus upon multiple victims is a sensible as well as humane approach to crime reduction. As regards domestic violence, initial research in the United States suggested that irrespective of subsequent action, a routine arrest policy might have a preventive effect on repeat offenders. However, replications of that research have found that, whether measured by victim interviews or by official statistics, arrest had no overall effect on reducing repeat violence. Indeed, possibly because it made them more angry at their partners, arrests *increased* recidivism among unemployed and unmarried people with a low stake in conformity, though it reduced it among the married and employed. (See, *inter alia*, Sherman and Smith, 1992.) The research suggests that legal controls depend upon a bedrock of commitment to informal control rather than being an effective substitute for it.

At the level of penal policy, violent crime has long been at the forefront of debate, being used as a superficially coherent category to justify severe sanctions on all principles of punishment, the dominant principle being that which yields the greatest severity. For example where, as for most 'domestic murderers', the expected reoffending rate is extremely low and there is little to suggest either an individual or general deterrent point in severe punishment, denunciatory and retributivist principles—sometimes allied with assertions about general deterrent 'needs'—are used to 'justify' not letting offenders out at the earliest possible date. (Though such offenders typically are released earlier than others.) Where the expected reoffending rate is higher, incapacitative principles are added to this list, particularly where retributive grounds alone would not be sufficient to keep someone in custody. In British terms, this reached its apotheosis (or nadir) with the 'two strikes and you're out' proposals for mandatory imprisonment for burglars and violent offenders in the Crime (Sentencing) Bill 1997—albeit diluted in the subsequent Act. Even under the now repealed limiting retributivist provisions of the Criminal Justice Act 1991, special rules applied to sexual and violent crime, which enabled sentencers lawfully to take into account expected future harm as well as past harm. However, by the late 1990s, the emphasis had shifted to a politically popular 'principle' of public protection irrespective of cost and general impact on crime levels.

Despite the rhetoric of seriousness with which violent crime is surrounded, the fine is actually the most common sentence for violence, even for offences such as assaulting the police which might have been expected to attract magisterial wrath. However, bifurcation has meant that the more serious types of violence have attracted very tough sentences, so that by 1996 a third of the entire prison population, and four fifths of the *long-term* prison population were there for violence (including rape). Their *conviction* rate may have been declining (Lees, 1997)—almost half were acquitted in 1995—but 90 per cent of convicted rapists were sentenced to immediate custody, and the average (and median) sentence was over six years in 1995. Eighteen offenders were sentenced to two years' imprisonment or less.[41] Whether many offences of rape and violence other than for financial gain are really deterrable by long sentences is questionable: the main 'justification' is retribution—given huge impact of the offence on victims—and, more questionably, public protection.

Treatment for Violence against Women

In the case of domestic violence, there is evidence that re-education programmes can make a difference, at least in the short term, to behaviour as well as to attitudes. Thus, only 33 per cent of men participating in one such Scottish programme had committed another violent act against their partners in twelve months, compared to 75 per cent who were dealt with by other sanctions. Further, only 7 per cent participating in the programmes, compared with 37 per cent of men punished in other ways, initiated five or more violent incidents during the follow up period (Dobash *et al.*, 1996. See also Dobash and Dobash, 1992). Treatment programmes for sex offenders have been very poorly provided for until recently, though they are now widespread (Barker and Morgan, 1993). In the past, claims for effectiveness by entrepreneurs have been largely unsubstantiated (West, 1983). However, there is some evidence that community-based treatment programmes can further reduce reoffending rates as well as changing attitudes towards offending: a two-year follow-up showed that (a) 4.5 per cent were reconvicted of sex offences, compared with 9 per cent for a probation sample; and (b) those in charge of programmes were fairly accurate in diagnosing who had benefited most from treatment (Beech *et al.*, 1996; Hedderman and Sugg, 1996).

Incapacitating the Violent Offender

Most of the sentencing debate has been over what do about serious violence (excluding serious corporate and motoring 'violence'), where—at least among academics, who seem more troubled than politicians about justifications for punishment—arguments rage about whether 'dangerous offending' can be predicted and what accuracy of prediction would justify keeping people in custody to prevent future crimes (Floud and Young, 1981; Haapanen, 1990).

---

[41] In 1990, the median sentence for rape was also 6 years. Whereas in 1984, 30% of convicted rapists received sentences of 5 years or longer, by 1987, following the guideline judgement *R.* v. *Billam* [1986] 1 WLR 349, the proportion receiving such sentences rose to 80% in 1987. In *Attorney-General's Reference (No. 7 of 1989)* (1990) 12 Cr.App.R (S) 1, a man convicted of the rape of his former cohabitee had a 2-year sentence increased to 4½ years. Armed bank robbers would expect to get longer sentences, and retributivists might find this to be wrong, though on pure deterrence grounds, the difference might be defensible. Box (1983) and others are technically correct in asserting that most rapists do not go to prison, but only in the grossly misleading tautological sense that unconvicted offenders do not receive custodial sentences.

Morris and Miller (1985: 15–16) note that 'with the best possible predictions of violent behavior we can expect to make one true positive prediction of violence to the person for every two false positive predictions', but go on to observe that a group of three people, one of whom will soon commit an act of serious violence, is a very dangerous group indeed. To cause problems for the most liberal of consciences, we have only to consider what we would do about someone who had 'only' committed an assault but warned us that he would kill us personally if he had the chance. Dangerousness is a probabilistic condition, not an event, and even if the person does not turn out to injure someone, s/he may remain 'dangerous' to some degree. (It is helpful to think of dangerousness/non-dangerousness as a spectrum of risk rather than as a binary concept.)

Morris and Miller (1985: 21) observe that the:

societal decision, the moral decision, is not whether to place the burden of avoiding the risk on the false positives, but how to balance the risk of harm to society and the certain intrusion on the liberty of each member of the preventively detained group. At some level of predicted harms from the group, the intrusions on each individual's liberty may be justified.

We seldom have the opportunity of discovering what those incapacitated would have done had they been released, thereby making it difficult to test the validity of our expectancy rates. Morris and Miller argue that it is proper to take the dangerousness of the group into account in sentencing provided that no individual is sentenced to longer than s/he otherwise would have deserved and that individuals are properly allocated to the groups estimated as dangerous. But if we are to inject any rationality other than popularity into the process at all, what does the evidence tell us about re-offending and the impact of incapacitation? One relevant factor here is the proportion of the population who account for different sorts of crime. This can change over time: the rate of violent offending by the cohort born in 1958 in Philadelphia exceeded that of the 1945 Philadelphia cohort by a factor of 3:1 for homicide, 1.7:1 for rape; and 2:1 for aggravated assault and burglary, and they were *more* likely than the 1945 cohort to be violent recidivists (Tracy, Wolfgang, and Figlio, 1990: 276, 281). The 7.5 per cent of the 1958 cohort described as 'chronic offenders' accounted for 61 per cent of the homicides, 75 per cent of the rapes, 73 per cent the robberies, 65 per cent of the aggravated assaults: the 1945 'chronics' had committed an even higher proportion of *cleared up* violent crimes, presumably because violence was more widespread among the later group. But offending may be less concentrated and less repetitive in Britain, where other features of underclass desperation are milder.

Rape

British research since Radzinowicz (1957) consistently shows that sex offenders re-offend (or are reconvicted) less than many other 'types' of criminal. Of rapists convicted in 1951, 6 per cent were reconvicted of sex crimes by 1973, though those who did reoffend were just as dangerous a decade after their conviction as they had been earlier (Soothill, Jack, and Gibbens, 1976). Of 264 people convicted of rape in 1972, 4.5 per cent had been reconvicted of rape by 1985 (Home Office, 1989), and a review of Offenders Index data found that within five years of their first such conviction, 10 per cent of sexual offenders were reconvicted of a further sexual offence (Marshall, 1997).[42] Of those aged 30 or over discharged from prison in 1992 for rape and other serious offences, none without convictions prior to their recent offence and only one per cent with prior convictions were reconvicted within two years (Kershaw *et al.*, 1997a: 6). 16 per cent of patients released after restriction under the Mental Health Act or Criminal Procedure (Insanity) Acts were reconvicted for some offence within two years (Kershaw *et al.*, 1977b: 6). The proportion of *all* restricted patients who were released and were reconvicted within two years was 13 per cent for both sexual offences and other types of violence. So there, too, among those let out, the risks are modest compared with general reoffending rates.

In contemporary British sexual culture, and despite longer sentences,[43] the rate of *re*offending may be higher among those convicted today than it was among the 1951 and 1972 rape cohorts: but there is no evidence yet that it actually is higher, and certainly not that it is as high as it is among American sex offenders, up to a third of whom commit further rapes after release.

Some of the rapists in the reconviction studies—like any other set of offenders—are likely to have committed other, unreported crimes against women or, because the prosecution was not allowed to tell the jury of their prior sexual convictions, may have escaped conviction or even prosecution for rapes they had 'in fact' committed. But given the police predilection for 'rounding up the usual suspects' in serious offences like rape which have a high police priority once recorded, their unconvicted recidivism would have to be enormous to bring the rape reoffending rate up to as far as one quarter. Home Office (1989) data indicate that 'only' 3 per cent of those convicted of rape in 1985 had previous convictions for rape, so even if they were incapacitated, this alone would have little impact upon the total volume of rape unless there were also a general deterrent effect.

Homicide

How likely are killers to reoffend? To some extent, data are artificial here, because only the expected best risks are let out in any numbers in any one year.

---

[42] Over a quarter were reconvicted for violence within 5 years of discharge, 1 in 5 for theft and 1 in 6 for burglary: this supports the view that rape is part of a general profile of aggression, not all of it towards women. Altogether, 1 in 3 convicted of rape were reconvicted for *some* offence within 2 years and 54% within 5 years of discharge. Even these percentages are lower than for offenders generally.

[43] If Sherman and Smith's (1992) finding that arresting those without major social ties for domestic violence *increased* their hostility applies also to rape, the rise in reoffending might be partly *because* of longer sentences.

But of the 1,145 persons convicted between 1972 and 1990 who were released on licence from a life sentence for homicide, 3 per cent were reconvicted of a grave offence—i.e. one with a *maximum* of life imprisonment—within five years, and 1 per cent within two years. Within five years of release, 19 per cent were reconvicted of less serious offences: those without prior convictions before their imprisonment were only half as likely to be reconvicted afterwards (Kershaw *et al.*, 1997*a*: 11). So this suggests that the 'right offenders' are being let out, even though there may be a huge proportion of killers who, on public safety grounds alone, could be released earlier without substantial risk.

As regards the effect on the homicide rate of incapacitating killers, it is salient that fewer than 2 per cent of those convicted for homicide had previous convictions for killing: this does not, of course, reflect the *inherent* unlikelihood of homicides to reoffend—for more might have killed again if they had been released earlier—but the number of 'repeat killers' constituted 0.03 per cent of the number of released killers at liberty altogether. Those who killed strangers were much more likely than those who killed acquaintances to have been convicted of some form of crime before, and they were twice as likely as those who killed a family member to have been convicted before. Whether family killers would be more likely to have previous convictions if their *previous* involvements in 'domestic' violence had been prosecuted is unknown, but their 43 per cent previous conviction rate is not far above the norm for males. Offenders convicted of section 2 (diminished responsibility) manslaughter within the family had the *lowest* percentage of prior convictions (28 per cent), which actually is lower than the average for the male population at large. (We should note that 7 per cent of the male population have convictions for violence by age 31.) Of those convicted of homicide, only one in six had previous convictions for offences of violence against the person, sexual offences, or robbery, so unless there is a general deterrent effect as well as an incapacitative one, the homicide rate would be reduced by 'only' one sixth even if one kept out of circulation every convicted violent offender. (Though among those with six or more previous convictions, 75 per cent had at least one prior conviction for violence.) Out of the 4,688 people convicted of homicide in the period 1986–95, thirty-six had previously been convicted of homicide (Criminal Statistics, 1996). We have no way of knowing what the repeat homicide rate would look like if killers were released sooner, but these data are a clear indication that homicide is not easy to deter or prevent by means of incapacitation or long prison sentences for violent crime.

What does the reoffending rate have to be to justify general incapacitation for violent crime? This is a political (and financial) question, but in anything approaching a rational world, information about risks ought to be relevant to it. There remains the possibility of refining categories of violent offender so that we can discover which 'sorts of people' are most likely to become serial rapists or killers (Canter and Heritage, 1990), but the claims made for offender profiling far outstrip their actual predictive value, particularly in the United Kingdom where sufficiently detailed information on offenders has not been kept (Davies and Dale, 1996). With the possible exception of men who have sex with young boys *outside* their families, who appear (from self-reports in the United States) to be the most recidivistic among any set of violent and/or sex offenders (Abel *et al.*, 1987), this is true *a fortiori* of the selective incapacitation of particular individuals within these categories of violence. It is generally agreed that the diagnosis of *individuals* as 'dangerous' by clinicians has very little basis (Brody and Tarling, 1981), though Monahan and Steadman (1994) argue that judgments *can* be improved and refined: a serious problem also for the theory of parole decisions as individualized rehabilitation judgements.

More generally, the dilemmas in what we decide to do about violence or any other type of crime depend on how painful our interventions are to those who have offended or whom we predict will become offenders. There are far fewer objections to crime reduction strategies if our predictions lead us to improve the quality of life and job prospects in inner cities, and/or to provide better lighting and transport for residents and potential victims, than if they lead us to play 'electronic tag' with those who might go out at night and commit offences, or to keep relatively minor offenders in prison for lengthy periods in case they commit further offences. Those involved in parole and sentencing decisions, particularly politicians, are usually much more afraid of being blamed for letting out someone who reoffends than they are of keeping some-one inside whom no-one will ever know would *not* have reoffended. That is the personal and political reality which underlies the continuing popularity of incapacitation for violent crime.

CONCLUSIONS

Few of the accounts of violent crime examined in this review are mutually exclusive, though they may have been competing for theoretical and ideological primacy as models of how we should go about the task of explanation and over what the most serious forms of violence are. I have stressed, perhaps *ad nauseam*, the enormous variation within that all too often simplified term, 'violent crime'. Much of the criminological progress during the 1980s and 1990s has been in refining our understanding of the risks of crime for different groups and the way that this relates to their lifestyles. Fuelled by feminist research and campaigns for action, fear of crime and the impact of crime on victims (see Zedner, this volume) have been major growth areas.

By contrast with this focus on 'the victim', the causes of violence have received comparatively little criminological attention. This is not simply because victims are easier to get to, both physically and mentally, than are offenders and because the discovery of the victim has been a major area of criminal policy interest. It partly reflects also the greater theoretical simplicity of generating interesting facts about patterns of victimization than of explaining fundamentally why violence happens where and when it does, and not in other places at other times. 'The ethos of masculinity' is one analytical thread that runs through much of the ætiological discussion—see also Jefferson, this volume—and as Polk (1994) argues, when overlaid with social class, it helps to account not just for 'typical' homicides but also for homicides for predatory gain and, one might add, for many sexual crimes too. But though the ever more subtly operationalized concept of *machismo* may be theoretically coherent, it is far from being theoretically complete, and its over-socialization component requires us to find other methods of accounting for, first, the non-violence of all males most of the time, and secondly, the non-violence of the majority of adult working-class and middle-class males all of the time. The personal and cultural dynamics of what constitutes a challenge 'requiring' a violent response have been explored, and have been accounted for largely in terms of sophisticated social learning theory, including expectancy theory. Although it seems inappropriate to dignify with the *sobriquet* 'rational' the decision to head-butt a complete stranger because 'I didn't like the way he looked' and, in some cases, to do this fairly regularly to other strangers, much apparently 'mindless' violent behaviour is understandable in the context of the emotional needs of offenders for respect, which may have its psychodynamic roots in miserable (and/or misogynistic) family relationships but may also often have (to him, beneficial) consequences for that person's status and control within the family and/or peer group. Violence is more functional to those who practise it in poor neighbourhoods than in middle-class ones, where self-control is valued and aggression is more likely to be channelled into business competition (which may have unintended or uncared about consequences for worker, consumer, or environmental unsafety). Moreover, although there is a custodial compromise in prison and even on the streets which enables much aggressive display to go unpunished, those who are not deemed to be part of the 'dangerous classes' may enjoy their rugby or rowing club 'binges'; while in review articles such as this, the punier among the academicians parody delinquent gang members by 'trashing' the analytic abilities of their rivals, or fight for their friends' academic reputations. Each group has its own culturally approved outlets for aggression.[44]

Outside a war-time or quasi-war-time context of ethnic or national oppression,[45] serial killers or rapists cannot properly be described as 'normal' personalities, though before being arrested, they may not be identified by workmates or families as 'weirdos' (or as any more weird than many non-serial rapists or killers). Few of even the most hardened chauvinists or 'rape myth subscribers' would seek to justify such serial violence in peace time, and

---

[44] Though personally, I would rather receive a bad academic review, however unmerited, than have my face smashed in.

[45] Examples include the alleged rapes of thousands of Muslim women by Serbs during the fight over Bosnia in 1992–3 (see Brownmiller, 1975, on earlier wars). The complex of motives include the desire to humiliate and demoralize the enemy; the desire to increase one's own and group reproduction rate by inseminating 'the enemy's womenfolk'—pregnant women appear deliberately to have been spared from being raped (*Independent*, 8 February 1993); and the heightened erotic sense that, among males, sometimes accompanies total power.

offenders receive almost no cultural support, since their behaviour lacks any remotely plausible pretence of ambiguity. Without a climate in which sexual anxieties and 'double standard' expectations of women were prevalent, there would be far fewer cases in which women became the 'appropriate' victims of delusions of power and humiliation. But the fact that most known violence occurs between young working-class males suggests that violence has both expressive and instrumental functions in status competition between males, as well as having the intended or unintended value of 'keeping women in their place'.

We have learned a great deal in recent decades about patterns of violent behaviour and the factors that influence them, such as social class, ethnicity, and gender. The learning from role models on screen and in (ever more fractured) families and neighbourhoods about how to respond to tensions, plus differences in individual temperament and life circumstance, play a major part in accounting for variations in rates of violence. Retrospective accounts by killers and rapists help us to make sense of 'why it happened'. However *why*— outside learned and/or biological gender variations—people, even sometimes those from the same family and brought up apparently similarly, turn out to have different temperaments and cognitive sets remains mysterious. Becker (1973), in an attempt to mitigate attacks on the idea that the labelling of people as 'criminals' intensified their involvement in crime, observed that he had not really meant to put forward a 'theory', merely a 'perspective' in which he would 'illuminate things formerly obscure'. This introductory overview has posed more questions than it has answered, but I am less apologetic than was Becker for these theoretical inadequacies: violent crime is a subject which is usually accompanied by more heat than light, and the specification of areas of uncertainty is worthwhile in itself. If this discussion of the causes of violent crime is ultimately unsatisfying, much of the reason lies in the inherent difficulty of teasing out the interaction between the myriad influences on human aggression and its specific outlet in violent crimes of different kinds. Whether ultimately it will be possible to resolve these difficulties is a subject for a much larger analytical project.

Selected Further Reading

For general theoretical approaches to violent crime across the board, good sources are
J. Archer (ed.), *Male Violence*, London: Routledge; T. Bernard, 'Angry Aggression among the "truly disadvantaged"' (1990), *Criminology*, 28, 1: 73–93; T. Jefferson and P. Carlen (eds.), *Masculinities, Social Relations and Crime*, Special Issue of British Journal of Criminology (1996), 36, 2, with articles by Jefferson and Kersten; the Journal of Social Issues (1992) Special Issue on comparative violence; J. Monahan and H. Steadman, *Violence and Mental Disorder: Developments in Risk Assessment*, Chicago: Chicago University Press, 1994; T. Newburn and B. Stanko (eds.), *Just Boys Doing*

Business, London: Routledge, 1994; K. Polk, *Men who Kill*, Cambridge: Cambridge University Press, 1994; and N. Weiner and M. Wolfgang (eds.), *Pathways to Criminal Violence*, Newbury Park, Cal.: Sage, 1979.

For a slightly idiosyncratic, less 'academic' analysis of homicide, see B. Masters, *The Evil That Men Do*, London: Black Swan, 1997.

For violence against children and women inside the home—which I am not seeing as a homogeneous category—see R. E. and R. D. Dobash, *Women, Violence, and Social Change*, London: Routledge, 1992; R. E. and R. D. Dobash, M. Daly, and M. Wilson, 'The Myth of Sexual Symmetry in Marital Violence', *Social Problems* (1992), 39, 1: 71–91; L. Ohlin and M. Tonry (eds.), *Family Violence*, Chicago: University of Chicago Press; and L. Sherman and D. Smith, 'Crime, Punishment, and Stake in Conformity: Legal and Informal Control of Domestic Violence', *American Sociological Review*, 57, 680–90 (1992).

For literature on sexual violence, see R. Felson, 'Sexual Coercion: A Social Interactionist Approach', in R. Felson and J. Tedeschi (eds.), *Aggression and Violence: Social Interactionist Perspectives*, Washington, DC: American Psychological Association, 1993; and D. Scully, *Understanding Sexual Violence*, London: HarperCollins, 1990.

For a review of serial violence, see R. and S. Holmes, *Profiling Violent Crimes: an Investigative Tool*, Thousand Oaks, Cal.: Sage (1996).

REFERENCES

ABEL, G., BECKER, J., MITTELMAN, M., CUNNINGHAM-RATHNER, J., ROULEAU, J.-L., and MURPHY, W. (1987), 'Self-reported Sex Crime of Non-incarcerated Paraphiliacs', *Journal of Interpersonal Violence*, 2, 6: 3–25.

ADLER, Z. (1987), *Rape on Trial*. London: Routledge.

AMIR, M. (1971), *Patterns of Forcible Rape*. Chicago, Ill.: University of Chicago Press.

ANDERSON, S., KINSEY, R., LOADER, I., and SMITH, C. (1990), *Cautionary Tales: a Study of Young People and Crime in Edinburgh*. Edinburgh: Centre for Criminology.

ARCHER, J. (1990), 'The Influence of Testosterone on Human Aggression', *British Journal of Psychology*, 82: 1–28.

—— (1994), 'Violence Between Men', in J. Archer, ed., *Male Violence*. London: Routledge.

ASHWORTH, A. (1992), *Sentencing and Criminal Justice*. London: Weidenfeld and Nicolson.

ATHENS, L. (1980), *Violent Criminal Acts and Actors*. London: Routledge.

BANDURA, A. (1973), *Aggression: A Social Learning Analysis*. Englewood Cliffs, NJ: Prentice-Hall.

BARAK, G., ed. (1996), *Representing O.J.: Murder, Criminal Justice and Mass Culture*. New York: Harrow and Heston.

BARKER, M., and MORGAN, R. (1993), *Sex Offenders: A Framework for the Evaluation of Community-Based Treatment*. London: Home Office.

BECK, R. (1995), *Rape from Afar*. Paper presented at British Criminology Conference, Loughborough.

BECKER, H. (1973), *Labelling Theory Reconsidered*. New York: Free Press.

BEECH, A., FISHER, D., BECKETT, R., and FORDHAM, A. (1996), 'Treating Sex Offenders in the Community', *Home Office Research Bulletin*, 38: 21–6.

BERGMAN, D. (1991), *Deaths at Work: Accidents or Corporate Crime*. London: Workers' Educational Association.

BERNARD, T. (1990), 'Angry Aggression Among the "Truly Disadvantaged"', *Criminology*, 28, 1: 73–93.

BLAU, J., and BLAU, P. (1982), 'The Cost of Inequality: Metropolitan Structure and Violent Crime', *American Sociological Review*, 47: 114–29.

BLUMSTEIN, A. (1996), 'Youth Violence, Guns, and Illicit Drugs Markets', *National Institute of Justice Research Preview*. Washington, DC: US Department of Justice.

BLUMSTEIN, A., COHEN, J., ROTH, J. and VISHER, C. (1986), *Criminal Careers and 'Career Criminals'*. Washington, DC: National Academy Press.

BOWLING, B. (1993), 'Racial Harassment and the Process of Victimisation: Conceptual and Methodological Implications for the Local Crime Survey', *British Journal of Criminology*, 33: 231–50.

BOX, S. (1983), *Power, Crime, and Mystification*. London: Tavistock.

BRAITHWAITE, J. (1989), *Crime, Shame, and Reintegration*. Cambridge: Cambridge University Press.

—— and BRAITHWAITE, V. (1980), 'The Effects of Income Inequality and Social Democracy on Homicide', *British Journal of Criminology*, 20: 45–53.

—— and Pettit, P. (1990), *Not Just Deserts: a Republican Theory of Criminal Justice*. Oxford: Oxford University Press.

BRENNAN, P., MEDNICK, S., and VOLAVKA, J. (1995), 'Biomedical Factors in Crime', in J. Wilson and J. Petersilia, eds., *Crime*. San Francisco, Cal.: ICS Press.

BRITISH RETAIL CONSORTIUM (1997), *Retail Crime Costs Survey*. London: British Retail Consortium.

BRODY, S., and TARLING, R. (1981), *Taking Offenders out of Circulation*. London: HMSO.

BROWN, J. (1991), 'The Psychopathology of Serial Sexual Homicide: A Review of the Possibilities', *American Journal of Forensic Psychiatry*, 12: 13–21.

BROWNMILLER, S. (1975), *Against Our Will*. Harmondsworth: Penguin.

BROWNSTEIN, H. (1996), *The Rise and Fall of a Violent Crime Wave: Crack Cocaine and the Social Construction of a Crime Problem*. New York: Harrow and Heston.

BUCK, W., CHATTERTON, M., and PEASE, K. (1995), *Obscene, Threatening and Other Troublesome Telephone Calls to Women in England and Wales, 1982–1992*. Research and Planning Unit Paper 92. London: Home Office.

BURGDORF, K., and ELDRED, C. (1978), *System of Operational Definitions*. Rockville, Md.: Westat.

BURGESS, R., and DRAPER, P. (1989), 'The Explanation of Family Violence: the Role of Biological, Behavioral, and Cultural Selection', in L. Ohlin and M. Tonry, eds., *Family Violence*. Chicago, Ill.: University of Chicago Press.

CAMPBELL, A., and MUNCER, S. (1994), 'Men and the Meaning of Violence', in J. Archer, ed., *Male Violence*. London: Routledge.

CAMPBELL, B. (1993), *Goliath*. London: Methuen.

CANTER, D., and HERITAGE, R. (1990), 'A Multivariate Model of Sexual Offence Behaviour: Developments in "Offender Profiling". 1', *Journal of Forensic Psychiatry*, 1: 185–6.

CHAPPELL, D. (1989), 'Sexual Criminal Violence', in N. Wiener and M. Wolfgang, eds., *Pathways to Criminal Violence*. Newbury Park, Cal.: Sage.

—— GEIS, G., SCHAFER, S., and SIEGEL, L. (1977), 'A Comparative Study of Forcible Rape Offenses Known to the Police in Boston and Los Angeles', in D. Chappell, R. Geis, and G. Geis, eds., *Forcible Rape*. New York: Columbia University Press.

CHEATWOOD, D. (1995), 'The Effects of the Weather on Homicide', *Journal of Quantitative Criminology*, 11: 51–70.

CHRISTIE, N. (1981), *Limits to Pain*. Oxford: Martin Robertson.

CHRISTOPHER, S., NOAKS, L., and LEVI, M. (1989), *Assaults upon the Police: The Assailant's Perspective*. London: Home Office, unpublished.

COHEN, S. (1981), *Folk Devils and Moral Panics*, 2nd edn., London: Paladin.

COLLINS, J. (1989), 'Alcohol and Interpersonal Violence: Less than Meets the Eye', in N. Weiner and M. Wolfgang, eds., *Pathways to Criminal Violence*. Newbury Park, Cal.: Sage.

COOK, P., and MOORE, M. (1995), 'Gun Control', in J. Wilson and J. Petersilia, eds., *Crime*. San Francisco, Cal.: ICS Press.

CRAVEN, D. (1996), *Female Victims of Violent Crime: Select Findings*. Washington, DC: US Department of Justice.

CURRIE, E. (1985), *Confronting Crime: An American Challenge*. New York: Pantheon Books.

CURTIS, L. (1975), *Violence, Race and Culture*. Lexington, Mass.: Lexington Books.

DALY, M., and WILSON, M. (1988), *Homicide*. New York: de Gruyter.

—— and —— (1994), 'Evolutionary Psychology of Male Violence', in J. Archer, ed., *Male Violence*. London: Routledge.

DAVIDOFF, L., and DOWDS, L. (1989), 'Recent Trends in Crimes of Violence Against the Person in England and Wales', *Home Office Research Bulletin*, 27: 11–17.

—— and GREENHORN, M. (1991), 'Violent Crime in England and Wales'. Paper presented at the British Criminology Conference, York.

DAVIES, A. and DALE, A. (1996), 'Locating the Stranger Rapist', *Medicine, Science and the Law*, 36: 146–56.

DITCHFIELD, J., and HARRIES, R. (1996), 'Assaults on Staff in Male Local Prisons and Remand Centres', *Home Office Research Bulletin*, 38: 15–20.

DOBASH, R. E., and DOBASH, R. D. (1979), *Violence against Wives*. New York: Free Press.

—— and —— (1992), *Women, Violence, and Social Change*. London: Routledge.

—— —— DALY, M., and WILSON, M. (1992), 'The Myth of Sexual Symmetry in Marital Violence', *Social Problems*, 39, 1: 71–91.

DOWDS, L., and AHRENDT, D. (1996), 'Fear of Crime', in R. Jowell *et al.*, eds., *British Social Attitutudes: the 12th Report*. Aldershot: Dartmouth.

DIJK, J. VAN, and MAYHEW, P. (1993), 'Criminal Victimisation in the Industrialised World: Key Findings from the 1988 and 1992 International Crime Surveys', in A. del Frate, U. Zvekic, and J. van Dijk, eds., *Understanding Crime: Experiences of Crime and Crime Control*. Rome: UNICRI.

ERONEN, M. (1995), 'Mental Disorders and Homicidal Behavior in Female Subjects', *American Journal of Psychiatry*, 152: 1216–18.

FAGAN, J. (1989), 'Cessation of Family Violence: Deterrence and Disuasion', in L. Ohlin and M. Tonry, eds., *Family Violence*. Chicago, Ill.: University of Chicago Press.

—— (1990), 'Intoxication and Aggression', in M. Tonry and J. Wilson, (eds., *Drugs and Crime*. Chicago, Ill.: University of Chicago Press.

FARRELL, G. (1992), 'Multiple Victimisation: Its Extent and Significance', *International Review of Victimology*, 2: 85–102.

FARRINGTON, D. (1989), 'Early Predictors of Adolescent Aggression and Adult Violence', *Violence and Victims*, 4: 307–31.

—— (1991), 'Childhood Aggression and Adult Violence: Early Precursors and Later Life Outcomes', in D. Pepler and K. Rubin, eds., *The Development and Treatment of Childhood Aggression*. Hillsdale, NJ: Erlbaum.

—— and DOWDS, E. (1985), 'Disentangling Criminal Behaviour and Police Reaction', in D. Farrington and J. Gunn. eds., *Reactions to Crime: The Public, the Police, Courts and Prisons*. Chichester: John Wiley.

—— and LANGAN, P. (1992), 'Changes in Crime and Punishment in England and America in the 1980s', *Justice Quarterly*, 9, 1: 5–31.

FELSON, R. (1993), 'Sexual Coercion: a Social Interactionist Approach', in R. Felson and J. Tedeschi, eds., *Aggression and Violence: Social Interactionist Perspectives*. Washington, DC: American Psychological Association.

—— and MESSNER, S. (1996), 'To Kill or Not to Kill? Lethal Outcomes in Injurious Attacks', *Criminology*, 34: 519–45.

FIELD, S. (1990), *Trends in Crime and Their Interpretation*. London: HMSO.

FISHBEIN, D. (1992), 'The Psychobiology of Female Aggression', *Criminal Justice and Behaviour*, 19: 99–126.

FISCHHOFF, B. (1989), 'Risk: A Guide to Controversy', Appendix C in *Improving Risk Communication*. Washington, DC: National Academy Press.

FITZGERALD, M., and HALE, C. (1996), *Ethnic Minorities, Victimisation and Racial Harassment*. Home Office Study No. 154. London: Home Office.

FLOUD, J., and YOUNG, W. (1981), *Dangerousness and Criminal Justice*. London: Heinemann.

FRIEZE, I., and BROWNE, A. (1989), 'Violence in Marriage', in L. Ohlin and M. Tonry, eds., *Family Violence*. Chicago, Ill.: University of Chicago Press.

FRUDE, N. (1989), 'The Physical Abuse of Children', in K. Howells and C. Hollin, eds., *Clinical Approaches to Violence*. Chichester: John Wiley.

—— (1994), 'Marital Violence: An Interactional Perspective', in J. Archer, ed., *Male Violence*. London: Routledge.

GAMBETTA, D. (1994), *The Sicilian Mafia*. Cambridge, Mass.: Harvard University Press.

GAROFALO, J. (1987), 'Reassessing the Lifestyle Model of Personal Victimisation', in M. Gottfredson and T. Hirschi, eds., *Positive Criminology*. London: Sage.

GARTNER, R. (1990), 'The Victims of Homicide', *American Sociological Review*, 55, 1: 92–107.

GATRELL, V. (1980), 'The Decline of Theft and Violence in Victorian and Edwardian England', in V. Gatrell, B. Lenmna, and G. Parker, eds., *Crime and the Law: the Social History of Crime in Western Europe since 1500*. London: Europa Publications Ltd.

—— (1990), 'Crime, Authority, and the Policeman-State, 1750–1950', in F. Thompson, ed., *The Cambridge Social History of Britain, 1750–1950*. Cambridge: Cambridge University Press.

GENN, H. (1988), 'Multiple Victimisation', in M. Maguire and J. Pointing, eds., *Victims of Crime: a New Deal?* Milton Keynes: Open University Press.

GIL, D. (1975), 'Child Abuse', *American Journal of Orthopsychiatry*, 45, 3: 345–56.

GREENE, E., and WAKEFIELD, R. (1979), 'Patterns of Middle and Upper Class Homicide', *Journal of Criminal Law and Criminology*, 70, 2: 172–81.

GRESSWELL, D., and HOLLIN, C. (1994), 'Multiple Murder: a Review', *British Journal of Criminology*, 34: 1–29.

GURR, T. (1990), 'Historical Trends in Violent Crime: a Critical Review of the Evidence', in N. Wiener, M. Zahn, and R. Sagi, eds., *Violence: Patterns, Causes, Public Policy.* San Diego, Cal.: Harcourt Brace Jovanovich.

HAAPANEN, R. (1990), *Selective Incapacitation and the Serious Offender.* New York: Springer-Verlag.

HALE, R. (1994), 'The Role of Humiliation and Embarrassment in Serial Murder', *Psychology*, 31: 17–23.

HANMER, J., RADFORD, J., and STANKO, E. (1989), *Women, Policing, and Male Violence: An International Perspective*, London: Routledge.

HEALTH and SAFETY COMMISSION (1992), *Annual Report, 1991/92.* London: HMSO.

HEALTH and SAFETY EXECUTIVE (1988), *The Tolerability of Risk from Nuclear Power Stations.* London: HMSO.

HERRNSTEIN, R. (1995), 'Criminogenic Traits', in J. Wilson and J. Petersilia, eds., *Crime.* San Francisco, Cal.: ICS Press.

HIBBERD, M. (1993), *Violent Crime in Small Shops.* London: Police Foundation.

HOLDAWAY, S. (1983), *Inside the British Police.* Oxford: Basil Blackwell.

HOLMES, R., and HOLMES, S. (1996), *Profiling Violent Crimes: an Investigative Tool.* Thousand Oaks, Cal.: Sage.

HOME OFFICE (1989), *Statistics on Offences of Rape 1977–1987.* Statistical Bulletin 4/89. London: Home Office.

HOUGH, M. (1995), *Anxiety about Crime: Findings from the 1994 British Crime Survey.* Research Study No. 147, London: Home Office.

—— and MAYHEW, P. (1985), *Taking Account of Crime: Key Findings from the 1984 British Crime Survey.* London: HMSO.

HUESSMAN, L., and ERON, L. (1989), 'Individual Differences and the Trait of Aggression', *European Journal of Personality*, 3: 95–106.

JENKINS, P. (1994), *Using Murder: The Social Construction of Serial Homicide.* New York: de Gruyter.

JOHNSON, A. (1980), 'On the Prevalence of Rape in the United States', *Signs*, 6: 136–46.

JONES, S., and LEVI, M. (1987), 'Law and Order and the Causes of Crime: Some Police and Public Perspectives', *Howard Journal of Criminal Justice*, 26, 1: 1–14.

KAHNEMANN, D., SLOVIC, P., and TVERSKY, A. (1982), *Judgment under Uncertainty: Heuristics and Biases.* Cambridge: Cambridge University Press.

KATZ, J. (1988), *The Seductions of Crime: The Moral and Sensual Attractions of Doing Evil.* New York: Basic Books.

KEMPE, R., and KEMPE, C. (1978), *Child Abuse.* London: Fontana.

KERSHAW, C., DOWDESWELL, P. and GOODMAN, J. (1997a), *Life Licensees—Reconvictions and Recalls by the End of 1995: England and Wales.* London: Home Office.

—— —— and —— (1997b), *Restricted Patients —Reconvictions and Recalls by the End of 1995: England and Wales.* London: Home Office.

KILLIAS, M. (1993), 'Gun Ownership, Suicide and Homicide: An International Perspective', in A. del Frate, U. Zvekic, and J. van Dijk, eds., *Understanding Crime: Experiences of Crime and Crime Control.* Rome: UNICRI.

LESTER, D. (1991), 'National Consumption of Chocolate and Rates of Personal Violence (Suicide and Homicide)', *Journal of Orthomolecular Medicine*, 6: 81–2.

LEES, S. (1997), *Carnal Knowledge: Rape on Trial.* London: Penguin.

LEVI, M., and JONES, S. (1985), 'Public and Police Perceptions of Crime Seriousness in England and Wales', *British Journal of Criminology*, 25, 3: 234–50.

—— and PITHOUSE, A. (1992), 'Victims of Fraud' in D. Downes, ed., *Criminal Justice.* London: Macmillan.

LICHTENSTEIN, S., SLOVIC, P., FISCHHOFF, B., LAYMAN, M., and COMBS, B. (1978), 'Judged Frequency of Lethal Events', *Journal of Experimental Psychology (Human Learning and Memory)*, 4: 551–78.

McINTOSH, M. (1975), *The Organisation of Crime.* London: Macmillan.

MALMQUIST, C. (1995), *Homicide: a Psychiatric Perspective.* Washington, DC: American Psychiatric Press, Inc.

MARSHALL, P. (1997), 'The Prevalence of Convictions for Sexual Offending', Research Findings No. 55. London: Home Office.

MASTERS, B. (1986), *Killing for Company.* London: Jonathan Cape.

—— (1997), *The Evil That Men Do*. London: Black Swan.

MAUNG, N (1995), *Young People, Victimisation and the Police*. Research Study No. 140. London: Home Office.

—— and MIRRLEES-BLACK, C. (1994), *Racially Motivated Crime: A British Crime Survey Analysis*. Research and Planning Unit Paper 82. London: Home Office.

MAYHEW, P., ELLIOTT, D., and DOWDS, L. (1989), *The 1988 British Crime Survey*. London: HMSO.

MEGARGEE, E. (1983), 'Undercontrolled and Overcontrolled Personality Types in Extreme Antisocial Aggression', *Psychological Monographs*, 80 (3, whole No. 611).

MESSNER, S., and GOLDEN, R. (1992), 'Racial Inequality and Racially Disaggregated Homicide Rates: An Assessment of Alternative Theoretical Explanations', *Criminology*, 30, 3: 421–37.

MIERS, D. (1997), *State Compensation for Criminal Injuries*. London: Blackstone Press.

MIETHE, T. (1984), 'Types of Consensus in Public Evaluations of Crime: An Illustration of Strategies for Measuring "Consensus"', *Journal of Criminal Law and Criminology*, 75, 2: 459–73.

MIRRLEES-BLACK, C. (1995), 'Estimating the Extent of Domestic Violence: Findings from the 1992 BCS', *Home Office Research Bulletin*, 37: 1–10.

—— MAYHEW, P., and PERCY, A. (1996), *The 1996 British Crime Survey: England and Wales*. London: Home Office.

MOONEY, J. (1993), *The Hidden Figure: Domestic Violence in North London*. London: Islington Council.

MOIR, A., and JESSEL, D. (1995), *A Mind to Crime: The Controversial Links between the Mind and Criminal Behaviour*. London: Michael Joseph.

MONAHAN, J., and STEADMAN, H. (1994), *Violence and Mental Disorder: Developments in Risk Assessment*. Chicago, Ill.: Chicago University Press.

MORGAN, D. (1987), 'Masculinity and Violence', in J. Hanmer and M. Maynard, eds., *Women, Violence, and Social Control*. London: Macmillan.

MORRIS, N., and MILLER, M. (1985), 'Predictions of Dangerousness', in M. Tonry and N. Morris, eds., *Crime and Justice*, vi. Chicago, Ill.: Chicago University Press.

NATIONAL COMMITTEE (1990), *Violence: Directions for Australia*. Canberra: Australian Institute of Criminology.

NATIONAL CRIME SURVEY (1986), *Teenage Victims: A National Crime Survey Report*. Washington: Government Printing Office.

NEWBURN, T., and STANKO, B., eds. (1994), *Just Boys Doing Business*. London: Routledge.

NICHOLLS, T. (1991), 'Industrial Injuries in British Manufacturing Industry and Cyclical Effects: Continuities and Discontinuities in Industrial Injury Research', *Sociological Review*, 39, 1: 131–9.

NORRIS, D. (1990), *Violence against Social Workers—The Implications for Practice*. London: Jessica Kingsley.

O'CONNELL, M., and WHELAN, A. (1996), 'Taking Wrongs Seriously: Public Perceptions of Crime Seriousness', *British Journal of Criminology*, 36, 2: 299–318.

PAINTER, K. (1991), *Wife Rape, Marriage and the Law*. Manchester: Manchester University.

PEARCE, F., and TOMBS, S. (1992), 'Realism and Corporate Crime', in R. Matthews and J. Young, eds., *Issues in Realist Criminology*. London: Sage.

PEARSON, G. (1983), *Hooligan*. London: Macmillan.

—— SAMPSON, A., BLAGG, H., STUBBS, P., and SMITH, D. (1989), 'Policing Racism', in R. Morgan and D. Smith, eds., *Coming to Terms with Policing*. London: Routledge.

PEASE, K. (1988), *Crime Seriousness: Findings from the British Crime Survey*. London: Home Office Research and Planning Unit.

PENDERGRAST, M. (1997), *Victims of Memory*. London: HarperCollins.

POLK, K. (1994), *Men who Kill*. Cambridge: Cambridge University Press.

POLLARD, P. (1994), ''Sexual Violence Against Women: Characteristics of Typical Perpetrators', in J. Archer, ed., *Male Violence*. London: Routledge.

RADZINOWICZ, L., ed. (1957), *Sexual Offences*. London: Macmillan.

RAINE, A. (1993*a*), *The Psychopathology of Crime: Criminal Behaviour as a Clinical Disorder*. London: Academic Press.

—— (1993*b*), 'Features of Borderline Personality and Violence', *Journal of Clinical Psychology*, 49: 277–81.

—— BUCHSBAUM, M., STANLEY, J., and LOTTENBERG, S. (1994), 'Selective Reductions in Prefrontal Glucose Metabolism in Murderers', *Biological Psychiatry*, 36: 365–73.

—— and STODDARD, J. (1995), 'Glucose Metabolism in Murders: Response', *Biological Psychiatry*, 38, 342–3.

RAMSAY, M. (1996), 'The Relationship between Alcohol and Crime', *Home Office Research Bulletin*, 38: 37–44.

REINER, R. (1992), *The Politics of the Police*. 2nd edn. Hemel Hempstead: Wheatsheaf.

REUTER, P. (1983), *Disorganized Crime*. Cambridge, Mass: MIT Press.

ROWETT, C. (1986), *Violence in the Context of Local Authority Social Work*. Cambridge: Institute of Criminology.

ROYAL COMMISSION (1929), *Report*. Royal Commission on the Police. London: HMSO.

ROYAL SOCIETY (1992), *Risk: Analysis, Perception, Management*. London: The Royal Society.

RUSSELL, D. (1984), *Sexual Exploitation*. Beverly Hills, Cal.: Sage.

SANDAY, P. (1981), 'The Socio-cultural Context of Rape: A Cross-cultural Study', *Journal of Social Issues*, 37, 4: 5–27.

SCHRAGER, L., and SHORT, J., (1980), 'How Serious a Crime? Perceptions of Organizational and Common Crimes', in G. Geis and E. Stotland, eds., *White-Collar Crime: Theory and Research*. Beverly Hills, Cal.: Sage.

SCULLY, D. (1990), *Understanding Sexual Violence*. London: HarperCollins.

SHEPHERD, J. (1990), 'Violent Crime in Bristol: An Accident and Emergency Department Perspective', *British Journal of Criminology*, 30, 3: 289–305.

SHERMAN, L., and SMITH, D. (1992), 'Crime, Punishment, and Stake in Conformity: Legal and Informal Control of Domestic Violence', *American Sociological Review*, 57: 680–90.

SKOGAN, W. (1990), *The Police and Public in England and Wales: A British Crime Survey Report*. London: HMSO.

SMITH, L. (1989), *Concerns about Rape*. London: HMSO.

SOOTHILL, K., JACK, A., and GIBBENS, T. (1976), 'Rape: A 22 year Cohort Study', *Medicine, Science, and the Law*, 16, 1: 62–9.

SORENSEN, S., and WHITE, J. (1992), 'Adult Sexual Assault: Overview of Research', *Journal of Social Issues*, 48: 1–8.

SPARKS, R. (1980), 'Crime and Punishment', unpublished paper presented at American Society of Criminology Conference, San Francisco, Cal..

—— GENN, H., and DODD, D. (1977), *Surveying Victims*. Chichester: John Wiley.

STANKO, B. (1990), *Everyday Violence*. London: Unwin Hyman.

STRAUS, M. and GELLES, R. (1990), 'How Violent are American Families? Estimates from the National Family Violence Survey and Other Studies', in M. Straus and R. Gelles, eds., *Physical Violence in American Families*. New Brunswick, NJ: Transaction.

—— —— and STEINMETZ, S. (1980), *Behind Closed Doors*. New York: Anchor Press.

STRONG, S. (1995), *Whitewash: Pablo Escobar and the Cocaine Wars*. London: Pan.

THORNHILL, R., and THORNHILL, N. (1992), 'The Evolutionary Psychology of Men's Coercive Sexuality', *Behavioural and Brain Sciences*, 15: 363–421.

TOCH, H. (1969), *Violent Men*. Harmondsworth: Penguin.

—— (1979), 'Perspectives on the Offender', in H. Toch, ed., *Psychology of Crime and Criminal Justice*. London: Holt, Rinehart and Winston.

TOMBS, S. (1992), 'Safety, Statistics, and Business Cycles: A Response to Nichols', *The Sociological Review*, 40, 1: 132–45.

TRACY, P., WOLFGANG, M., and FIGLIO, R. (1990), *Delinquency Careers in Two Birth Cohorts*. New York: Plenum Press.

TUCK, M. (1989), *Drinking and Disorder: A Study of Non-Metropolitan Violence*. London: HMSO.

TVERSKY, A., and KAHNEMANN, D. (1973), 'Availability: a Heuristic for Judging Frequency and Probability', *Cognitive Psychology*, 4: 207–32.

VLEK, C. and STALLEN, P. (1981), 'Judging Risks and Benefits in the Small and in the Large', *Organizational Behaviour and Human Performance*, 28: 235–71.

VON HIRSCH, A. (1986), *Past or Future Crimes*. Manchester: Manchester University Press.

WADDINGTON, D. (1992), *Contemporary Issues in Public Disorder*. London: Routledge.

WALKLATE, S. (1990), *Victimology*. London: Unwin Hyman.

WALMSLEY, R. (1986), *Personal Violence*. London: HMSO.

WATSON, L. (1996), *Victims of Violent Crime Recorded by the Police England and Wales, 1990–1994*. London: Home Office.

WEIS, J. (1989), 'Family Violence Research Methodology and Design', in L. Ohlin and M. Tonry, eds., *Family Violence*. Chicago, Ill.: University of Chicago Press.

WELLS, C. (1993), *Corporations and Criminal Responsibility*. Oxford: Oxford University Press.

WEST, D. (1983), *Sexual Crimes and Confrontations*. Aldershot: Gower.

WHICH (1990), 'The Police', *Which?*, May, 258–61.

WHITE, J., and SORENSEN, S. (1992), 'A Socio-cultural View of Sexual Assault: From Discrepancy to Diversity', *Journal of Social Issues*, 48: 187–95.

WILSON, J., and HERRNSTEIN, R. (1985), *Crime*

and Human Nature. New York: Simon and Schuster.

WILSON, M. and DALY, M. (1992), 'Who Kills Whom in Spouse Killings: On the Exceptional Sex Ratio of Spousal Homicides in the United States', *Criminology*, 30, 2: 189–214.

WOLFGANG, M. (1958), *Patterns in Criminal Homicide*. Philadelphia, Penn.: University of Pennsylvania Press.

—— and Ferracuti, F. (1967), *The Subculture of Violence*. London: Tavistock.

YOUNG, J. (1988), 'Risk of Crime and Fear of Crime: A Realist Critique of Survey-based Assumptions', in M. Maguire and J. Pointing, eds., *Victims of Crime: a New Deal?* Milton Keynes: Open University Press.

25

White-Collar Crime

David Nelken

INTRODUCTION

In April 1992 Carlo de Benedetti, chairman of Olivetti and architect of its recent growth as one of Italy's major corporations, rang his head office from Switzerland to ask how Olivetti's shares were doing. He was not pleased to be told that they had gone down in value. 'Is this because of a general fall in prices on the Milan exchange' he asked. 'No', came the reply, 'it is because you have just been sentenced to 6 years prison for your role in the Banca Ambrosiano crash of 1982.'

This story exemplifies what is typically conjured up by a certain idea of white-collar crime. Successful business or professional people are apparently caught out in serious offences, sometimes for behaviour which they did not expect to be treated as criminal, and for which it is difficult to secure a conviction. The Jekyll and Hyde contradiction between respectability and crime raises questions which are unlike those posed by other types of criminal behaviour. Why do they do it when they have so much to lose? How representative are they or their practices of other businessmen or business life in general? How likely are they to be caught? Is there one law for the rich and another for the poor?

One of the biggest difficulties in approaching this subject is to find a way of putting the dramatic and newsworthy cases of business misbehaviour in some sort of context and proportion. Study of the distribution and frequency of white-collar crimes is made problematic by the fact (not in itself unimportant) that, especially in the common law countries where the concept was first formulated, most white-collar crimes are not included in the official statistics which serve as the basis for debates about 'the crime problem'. The usual difficulties of interpreting the statistics of crime are greatly magnified here (Levi, 1985). Falling back on the information recorded by specialized enforcement agencies (often not even made public) serves mainly as a source for describing methods of control rather than the misbehaviour being controlled. Nor can it be assumed that there is any uniformity in the meaning of data obtained in this way. A few agencies are reactive, and depend on complaints; others are proactive but the level of enforcement is restricted by limited resources (in Britain factories are inspected for safety offences on average once every four years). Much regulation is geared to using prosecution as a last resort—thus the number of prosecuted offenders says little about the theoretical level of crime; conversely, the number of visits or warnings cannot be used as an index of the incidence of deliberate law-breaking. There is a danger of double counting where the same behaviour is dealt with by different agencies or where one firm has more sub-units than another. This also creates problems about defining recidivism—which were ignored by Sutherland in his pioneering study (Sutherland, 1949). There are problems of classifying the date and location of some of these offences (a factor which often helps secure their immunity). Shifts in legislative mandates, and in the number, expertise, politics, and motivation of enforcers, make a treacherous basis for studies of changes in offending patterns over time. Finally, supplementing official statistics with victim reports is difficult because the victims are often unaware of their victimization; and even where this is not the case, as in organizations subject to fraud, there is often unwillingness to admit to vulnerability (see Levi and Pithouse, 1997).

These difficulties mean that discussions of the subject in textbooks are forced to rely unduly on newspaper reports or on the activities of crusading journalists (see e.g. Coleman, 1985). Obtaining information in this way complicates the task of assessing the accuracy, frequency, or representativeness of the cases reported. Newspapers, or those who feed them their stories, initiate crime-control campaigns for reasons which may have little to do with the long-term trend in the misbehaviour at issue. It is therefore hard to tell, for example, whether business or financial crimes are increasing or are just more newsworthy, or to decide if change is the result of an increase in a given kind of misbehaviour or more the consequence of a trend towards the use of formal and legal, rather than informal, means to deal with it.

Despite these problems there have been some useful studies, drawing on agency records to survey the rate of corporate offending (Clinard and Yeager, 1980), or court records to establish the type of offenders normally apprehended for what the authors call 'middle-class crimes' (Weisburd *et al.*, 1991). What we know about white-collar crime also comes from interviews with enforcers as well as observation of their work (e.g. Carson, 1970; Hawkins, 1984; Hutter, 1988; and cf. Nelken, 1991); interviews with businessmen (e.g. Lane, 1953; Braithwaite, 1984); biographies of and retrospective accounts by offenders (e.g. Geis, 1968); participant observation in offending organizations (e.g. Nelken, 1983: chapter 2); experimental techniques such as those used by consumer organizations (Green, 1990: chapter 2), as well as other sources (and for useful methodological hints on researching these type of offences see Levi, 1985).

Although most of the literature on white-collar crime is American, major contributions have been made by other English-language scholars such as Braithwaite, Carson, and Levi. The equivalent term for white-collar crime is also widely found in other languages, and even used in foreign court proceedings. There are also interesting contributions, sometimes in foreign languages, which could serve as a useful starting-point for comparative research (e.g. Tiedemann, 1974; Cosson, 1978; Magnusson, 1985; Clarke, 1990*b*; Delmas-Marty, 1990; Zigler, 1990; Van Duyne, 1993; Passas and Nelken, 1993; Savelsberg, 1994). But, despite the similarities of modern industrialized economies, there are important differences in general and legal culture which affect the response to white-collar crime and which have not yet been sufficiently explored (see Nelken, 1994; Levi and Nelken, 1996). In civil law countries such as Italy there are few of the special enforcement agencies used to deal with occupational offences found, for example, in America, Britain, and Australia. Instead, normal police forces, often spearheaded by specialized financial police, conduct investigations of safety or pollution cases, and businessmen or politicians with white collars regularly see the inside of prisons (though few seem to stay there for long). American outrage over business misbehaviour may be connected to what Wright-Mills (1963/1943) saw as the small-town values of American social reformers, as well as to a peculiar, American, love-hate relationship with big businesses (are they the ultimate proof of capitalist success or a threat to the market and to the individual?). In countries with a strong Catholic heritage the respectability attached to capitalist profit-making may be less secure than in Protestant countries (Ruggiero, 1996).

Much of the literature on white-collar crime continues to be concerned to demonstrate the seriousness and diffuseness of such offending, and to show that its costs and damages dwarf those of conventional, or ordinary, crime. Colossal fines and settlements are imposed in cases of some financial crimes, for example, Michael Milken, the junk bond king, paid over US$650 million dollars in court-ordered restitution even before sentence. The collapse of the savings and loan institutions (similar to what in Britain are described as Building Societies) in the United States in the late 1980s may end up costing a trillion dollars, many times the cost of the Marshall Plan or the Korean war; but the real impact is blunted because the costs are to be covered by a US government fifty-year loan (Pontell and Calavita, 1993; Zimring and Hawkins, 1993). Contrary to what is supposed by some definitions (e.g. Edelhertz, 1970) there is also no reason to exclude violence and death from the province of white-collar crime. There are a number of case-studies which document this, even without going into more controversial calculations of the overall number of fatal accidents or diseases occurring at work which could have been prevented and prosecuted (Box, 1983: 28 ff; Hills, 1988; Slapper, 1991). Carson's study of the loss of life in the exploration for oil in the North Sea (confirmed by later events such as the blowing up of the Piper Alpha oil rig in 1988 with the loss of 168 lives), for instance, showed that many lives could have been saved with rudimentary attention to safety considerations (Carson, 1982). The devastating consequences of the nuclear disaster at Chernobyl, the chemical explosion at Bhopal, the suffering caused by the sale of the drug thalidomide, or the contraceptive known as the Dalkon shield, are other well-known examples.

Despite all this evidence, white-collar crimes are still subjected to very different interpretations. It might seem odd that sociologists familiar with

Durkheim's argument that society considers dangerous those behaviours it responds to as criminal, rather than the other way round, should keep trying to prove that white-collar crime is really criminal simply because it causes great harm. The answer must be that they hope in this way to influence the social definition of such conduct. Debates over the causes and control of white-collar crime do connect to different political evaluations of the misdeeds of business or capitalism (thus it is interesting to note how political conservatives tend to favour structural explanations of business malpractice rather than peronal guilt—thus changing places with liberals in comparison with their positions on ordinary crime (Zimring and Hawkins, 1993). But they should not be simply reduced to this and can reflect more specific disagreements over the nature of these forms of behaviour.

This is well demonstrated if we compare the different lessons drawn from roughly similar materials even by authors who do not otherwise seem to disagree much politically. We can take as an example two recent overviews by writers who offer sharply contrasting assessments of the subject, though neither seeks to cast doubt on the normal operations of capitalist forms of production and organization. Green's *Occupational Crime* (1990) is a comprehensive American textbook devoted to systematizing the now voluminous data on white-collar crime and its control. It uses the same categories of criminological analysis and explanation which serve for other types of crime. White-collar crime is seen as even more criminal than ordinary crime, even if at the same time it is more likely to escape control; as Geis argues in his foreword, 'occupational crime is without a doubt more dangerous, both in physical and in fiscal terms, than street crime' (Geis, 1990: p. xv). Considerable attention is therefore devoted to discovering more effective ways of bringing criminal penalties to bear on this type of conduct. On the other hand, Clarke's *Business Crime* (1990), though considering much the same data, is largely devoted to showing the differences between these sorts of offences and those more usually handled as crimes. For Clarke:

Business crime, however, in the sense in which it is used here, covers a much wider range of misconduct, which may be none the less damaging and otherwise undesirable, resulting from duress, incompetence, negligence, lack of training, lack of clarity in the rules, opportunism, technical infraction, or sheer muddle-headedness, rather than calculated deceit motivated by greed [Clarke, 1990a: 16].

It follows that such crime should not be handled in the same way as ordinary crime:

Pursuing business crime as fraud, through criminal prosecution, though appropriate for a minority of cases, is irrelevant and impossible for the majority. Furthermore if criminal prosecution is pursued as the sole or even the principal means of control, it will fail to achieve anything more than public hysteria and expense, and the jailing of a few of the less lucky and competent villains [Clarke, 1990a: 16].

SEVEN TYPES OF AMBIGUITY

Why is there still so much disagreement over white-collar crime? As with the equivocal designs produced by Gestalt psychologists, do we find it difficult to see 'the criminal' and 'the respectable person' in one and the same figure? Following Aubert (1952) I shall argue that ambiguity about the nature of white-collar crime and the best way of responding to it, forms an essential key to the topic and can be used to provide insights into this type of crime as well as the 'ordinary' crime with which it is contrasted. As the subject has become more established scholars have either tended to abandon Aubert's insight or to concentrate on only one or two of the sources of ambiguity which will be considered here. They also tend to divide somewhat dogmatically into those, on the one hand, who point to the ambiguous features of white-collar crime so as to explain and justify special treatment for this misbehaviour and those, on the other, who claim that ambiguity is a socially constructed smoke-screen which ought to be dispelled. In this chapter I do not purport to settle the question of how far the features which supposedly make white-collar crime more ambiguous than ordinary crime are (merely) socially constructed. I shall, however, try to do something to clarify the uncertainties produced by the literature itself by offering a critical review both of those arguments which assert that ambiguity is intrinsic to the misbehaviour itself and of those which attempt to prove that white-collar crime is 'essentially' the same as ordinary crime but is transformed by the social reaction to it.

To provide a common thread to the following overview of what has been written about the definition, causes, and responses to white-collar crime I shall seek to illustrate seven different sources of ambiguity which surround this topic. (I use the term ambiguity loosely to embrace the various forms of equivocalness, uncertainty, and ambivalence referred to in and produced by discussions of the characteristics of white-collar crime.) The first ambiguities which I shall consider arise in trying to define what is meant by white-collar crime. The ambiguous way the concept is used in the criminological literature means that it is not clear what range of crimes is being referred to. From the outset, Sutherland's concept has also been criticized for seeking to apply the crime label to behaviours whose definition as crime is legally or sociologically controversial. The second set of ambiguities belongs more to discussions of the causes of white-collar crime. Whilst many scholars try to apply the usual criminological frameworks of explanation to this kind of offending, others have used the topic precisely so as to place these schemes in doubt. Ambiguity also surrounds discussions of the commission of these offences. Thus some writers stress the point that this type of offending behaviour takes place in a more respectable context than most other crimes, and that it is the product of more ambiguous intentions than is the case for ordinary crime. The third set of ambiguities derives from the regulation and handling of white-collar crime. White-collar crimes are often controlled in a different, and more ambivalent, way than ordinary crime, and it is controversial how far this reflects, reinforces, or even creates its ambiguity. The uncertain status of these crimes may also be seen to reflect a process of transition and social change in which the public is not yet ready for more outright criminalization of these behaviours. It is also argued that control of these offences is hampered by problems of competing values and social costs which do not arise in repressing ordinary crime.

I shall be taking these various ambiguities one by one, partly for purposes of exposition and partly because there are important differences amongst the sources and types of ambiguity. Taken as a whole, however, many of these ambiguities are mutually reinforcing, and thus help shape the perceived character of white-collar crimes as a social phenomenon. If, for example, different and predominantly administrative methods of enforcement are used in dealing with white-collar, as opposed to ordinary, crime, this will shape public opinion concerning their relative seriousness. But, at the same time, such (alleged) differences in public attitudes also serve as justifications offered by legislators and regulators for their different treatment of white-collar crimes. On the other hand, any given source of ambiguity may have implications under a number of different headings. For example, the fact that white-collar crimes generally take place in private settings represents a special feature of their causation which may facilitate their commission. This also serves as an impediment to normal policing methods which helps explain the use of other forces and forms of enforcement. Finally, the importance of respecting 'privacy' as a value also figures as an argument in policy debates over the appropriateness or otherwise of strengthening controls.

White-Collar Crime as a Contested Concept

1. If Sutherland merited a Nobel prize, as Mannheim thought, for pioneering this field of study, he certainly did not deserve it for the clarity or serviceableness of his definition. What, if anything, is there in common between the marketing of unsafe pharmaceuticals, the practice of insider trading, 'long-firm' fraud, computer crime, bank embezzlement, and fiddling at work? Though Sutherland claimed to be interested in reforming criminological theory, rather than changing society, the appeal of this topic, particularly through the 1970s and 1980s, was unquestionably linked to its progressive connotations and its implicit accusations of bias in the making and enforcing of criminal law (Yeager, 1991: chapter 1). The apparent success of the label in finding public acceptance, while lacking a clear or agreed referent, may testify less to its coherence than to its capacity to name a supposed threat (as with the term 'mugging'). Not all examples of white-collar crime are ambiguous (e.g. embezzlement), just as not all ambiguous deviance is white-collar crime. But considerable disagreement over the range of misbehaviour referred to, as well as doubts about the coherence of those behaviours it does include, makes the category as a whole rather ambiguous. And, peculiarly enough, those white-

collar offences whose criminal character seems most unambiguous—such as bank embezzlement or (on some definitions) credit card fraud—are the ones least likely to illustrate the theoretical or policy-relevant features of white-collar crime in which Sutherland and his successors have been most interested.

We will not deal here with the intrinsic difficulties built into Sutherland's definition of white-collar crime as a crime committed by 'a person of high status in the course of his occupation' (1949: 9), which were discussed in the first edition of this handbook at 361–3. But it is important to recognize that the problem of definition cannot just be put aside in order to get on with more interesting matters because the solution found for this problem ultimately determines the findings of any investigation. This is seen clearly in the recent attempt, by Weisburd *et al.* (1991), to put to the test the assumed relationship between white-collar crime and the class background of those convicted for such crimes. Their findings (Weisburd, 1991: 184 ff.) are that 'contrary to the portrait generally presented we find a world of offending and offenders that is very close to the everyday lives of typical Americans'. The majority of offenders 'do not necessitate nor do their defences rely upon elite social status'. The authors argue that small frauds are as normal a part of business context as street crimes are in poor communities and conclude that 'the people we studied are the core American criminals whose ranks will grow as society becomes more middle class, as credit cards and credentialling grows, and television continues to hammer home the message of consumption'. The study is of great value in showing us that common crime and white-collar crime lie on a continuum and in proposing (inductively) a new category of offending intermediate between common and corporate crime. But the definition of white-collar crime used in this work, based as it was on criminal convictions rather than administrative proceedings, and biased towards smaller-scale frauds (the crimes they selected included securities fraud and antitrust violations, bribery, embezzlement, mail fraud, tax fraud, false claims and accounting, and credit fraud) was almost bound to produce the picture of middle-class crime which the authors describe.

If some ambiguity is created by the way the category of white-collar crime seems to merge into relatively humdrum crimes of the middle classes there is also uncertainty at the opposite extreme about where to draw the line between white-collar crime and organized crime. As predicted in the first edition, the overlap between these types of enterprise crime has become an important new focus of research (though one already anticipated in the theory of illegal enterprises put forward by Smith and others in the 1980s). Ruggiero, for example, claims that Sutherland created an unsatisfactory distinction between these two types of criminal behaviour (leaving only gangsters in the category of organized crime) which has wrongly been taken over by later criminologists. This approach to white-collar crime can also be seen as a way of relegitimating ordinary business behaviour by stressing that only some such behaviour should be considered criminal (Ruggiero, 1996: 45). For Ruggiero, white-collar/organized crime should be seen as a normal rather than pathological aspect of business life, and its causes should be sought in wealth and power rather than greed as such. Organized crime, he argues, once we get away from ethnic streotypes, involves the same flexible consumer-oriented behaviour which characterizes all successful business behaviour. Offering a wealth of examples of business-type crimes Ruggiero argues that both white-collar and organized criminals use similar techniques, share the same illegal know-how, and the same values—even if perpetrators come from different backgrounds. Their crimes are performed in or by organized structures, thrive on collusion, and normally enjoy the connivance of administrators and legislators (Ruggeiro, 1996).

In part we may be witnessing real changes in the phenomena pointed to by these different criminological labels. In the first place, business crime may be taking on some of the characteristics of organized crime. As Reichman observes 'insider trading as practiced in the 1980's is a form of crime that combines elements of the traditional categories of occupational and organizational crime' (Reichman, 1992: 56). Likewise, traditional organized crime groups, such as the Mafia or the Camorra in Italy, or the Chinese or Taiwanese Triads, have become increasingly capitalistic in orientation and ethos (see e. g. Arlachi, 1985; or Gambetta's theis of the Mafia as an industry of private protection: Gambetta, 1994). In post-Communist countries which are without a recent history of capitalist markets it may be indeed be artificial to draw a line between business and organized crime. More broadly, globalization may be leading to similar forms of structural integration of legitimate and illegitimate business activities, making regular collaboration between business and organized criminals both more possible and more necessary (Nelken, forthcoming).

On the other hand, this thesis should not be pushed too far. Claims concerning a symbiotic relationship between ordinary business, white-collar crime and organized crime *presuppose* important differences rather than total overlap. Organized crime groups are able to gain legitimacy, respectability, protection, access, expertise, suppliers, customers, investment opportunities, or various other advantages from such relationships, and these benefits would be attenuated if the differences were to disappear. Both white-collar crime and organized crime cover such a continuum of activities that there will clearly be some that fall outside any attempt to categorize them together (think, on the one hand, of a small food shop breaking hygiene regulations and, on the other, of a classical protection racket based on territorial domination). What is certainly true is that the distinction between these types of crime will vary according to the type of crime and the structure of the industry under consideration.

By common agreement Sutherland's definition is not considered a helpful starting point for doing research into white-collar crime. Apart from its internal contradictions (are we dealing with crimes committed for or against organizations?), changes in class structure, forms of business activity, organizational forms and cultural valuations all threaten to undermine its empirical coherence. But what other definitions can be found which do not simply rely on selecting the most appropriate-seeming crimes from the official criminal statistics? One common inductive strategy is to start from the data produced by the non-police administrative agencies generally entrusted with dealing with business offences (especially in common law countries). This was the source of data used in the comprehensive Clinard and Yeager study which focused on various Federal regulatory bodies (Clinard and Yeager, 1980). Non-police agencies in Britain include the Post Office, British Transport Police, Customs, water authorities, local government, Ministry of Agriculture, etc. (see Royal Commission, 1980). But though these agencies may have some enforcement practices in common it would be quite wrong to describe all the type of offenders they prosecute as white-collar criminals. Another strategy is to seek to develop typologies of different kinds of crime which fit under the general heading of white-collar crime. The difficulty here is that the categories thus created are still likely to end up as containers for somewhat disparate behaviours. Green (1990) distinguishes organizational occupational crime, state authority occupational crime, professional occupational crime, etc. But these headings cannot pretend to be either theoretically defined or even coherent classifications of types of crime. The offences considered as state crime range from bribe-taking to genocide; whilst the chapter on individual occupational crime—which is admitted to be a 'catch-all' category—includes behaviour as different as employee theft and securities crimes. The drawbacks to inductivism are evident in the artificial distinctions which lead Green to discuss the crimes committed by bribe-givers in a different chapter from those of bribe-takers. Nonetheless, the range of crimes brought under the rubric of the white-collar crime concept continues to grow: Friedrichs (1996) devotes chapters to state corporate crime, enterprise crime, contrepreneurial crime, avocational crime, finance crime, and techno crime.

There are also a variety of attempts to rethink Sutherland's concept in a more deductive fashion. Some of these are deliberately modest, such as Clarke's extended definition of business crime in terms of its distinguishing features (Clarke 1990*a*: chapter 3). In the rest of the book Clarke seeks to illustrate the applicability of his definition to a series of different areas of misbehaviour (and justifies a refusal to develop typologies partly on the somewhat odd grounds that opting for any one typological scheme would exclude another which might be more appropriate for other purposes). Despite the richness of his descriptions his approach can be criticized for already building in as part of his definition of business crime those controversial features of the social response which are less geared to prosecution than in the case of ordinary crime. It is also unclear why the book is entitled *Business Crime* when the thrust of the argument is intended to undermine this label.

Of greater value are the more ambitious efforts aimed at finding a key theoretical variable which could produce a coherent focus for further research. Recent examples (which go beyond the somewhat unimaginative 'crimes of the powerful', 'crimes of the upperworld', or 'elite crimes') include Shapiro's focus on the increasing need to trust agents and the consequent exposure to various forms of abuse of such trust in which agents subordinate the interests of their principals to their own gain (Shapiro, 1989). Coleman and others stress the importance of the growth of organizational actors in what has been called the 'assymetric society' (Gross, 1980; Coleman, 1992). These approaches may include more or less than the offences that Sutherland covered; Shapiro's proposal, for example, seems to be derived from her previous empirical research interests in securities frauds and would not be applicable, say, to pollution crimes; its focus on agents also lets principals off the hook. But they promise to be theoretically more productive than Sutherland's concept.

2. If there are basic uncertainties about what is being referred to when talking of white-collar crime there are also long-standing doubts whether or not all the misbehaviours discussed under this rubric can be considered to count as crime. Most of the continuing controversy, as well as the stimulus, generated by this topic, is due to the fact that it appears to straddle the crucial boundary between criminal and non-criminal behaviour. Since this is a well-aired problem, and the debates can be found in all the Readers on this subject (e.g. Geis, 1968), I will confine myself to drawing out their relevance to the issue of ambiguity. Many scholars have argued that the (mis)behaviours discussed by Sutherland or his followers do not always satisfy the legal criteria for crime; some even go so far as to insist on the necessity for a penal conviction at court (e.g. Tappan, 1947). It is, admittedly, ironic that Sutherland himself was unable to publish the names of the companies, whose administrative violations he described in his book, because of his publisher's fears that he would then be exposed to claims of libel for describing them as criminal (this was only remedied in the uncut version published much later; Sutherland, 1983). Restricting attention to those crimes found in the ordinary criminal statistics, however, too easily robs the term of all its sense. The results of following such a definition make it possible to argue that white-collar crime is an otiose category and that white-collar criminals, like all ordinary criminals, are young, feckless, and unsuccessful (see Hirschi and Gottfredson, 1987, 1989, and the criticism by Steffensmeier, 1989).

Others have made virtually the opposite attack, complaining that many white-collar crimes are merely technically criminal and are not socially considered on a par with ordinary crimes; hence they do not satisfy the requirements of a sociological definition of crime (see e.g. Burgess, 1950, criticizing Hartung, 1950). Whilst this is a more acute criticism it tends to assume the unchanging circularity of social definitions and underestimates the potential for change (a process in which criminology can play a part).

The fact that such opposite criticisms can be raised is confirmation of the ambiguity of this concept—which is also reflected in the use of descriptions such as 'regulatory crimes' or *mala prohibita*. Sutherland, and many later scholars, chose to include in their definition of white-collar crime not only misbehaviours with criminal penalties, but also those which carried only civil or administrative sanctions. This was done precisely so as not to beg the question whether the choice of these generally lighter sanctions was justified (or only a sign of the power of the offenders involved). But it is only a small (if significant) step from this to argue for the inclusion in the category of white-collar crime of other types of harmful business behaviour which have succeeded (through much the same political and economic pressures) in avoiding being subject to any sanctions at all.

Must we use law to draw the line? One of the contributions made by the topic of white-collar crime to criminology lies in this very difficulty of assimilating all that Sutherland was getting at without breaking the boundaries of the discipline. Should the definition of crime adopted for sociological purposes be the same as that of the law? What are the dangers of tying criminology to a starting point defined by another discipline? If we allow the political process to define what counts as crime is this a politically conservative choice? Is it just good tactics—a way to avoid alienating the 'liberals' (as Box, 1983, argues)? It is now assumed that we must refer to the law because otherwise it would be impossible to decide who is to define (business) deviance (Coleman, 1987). But this was exactly the decision that the labelling perspective tried to force criminologists to face. The topic of white-collar crime thus illustrates the possibility of divergence between legal, social, and political definitions of criminality—but in so doing it reminds us of the artificiality of all definitions of crime.

Explaining the Causes of White-Collar Crime

3. Can white-collar crime be explained using the normal frameworks of criminological explanation? Certainly, more needs to be done in studying 'the how'—the *modus operandi*—rather than just the 'why' of such misbehaviour (Levi, 1985). In addition, the closeness of class backgrounds of many criminologists to these offenders may make it difficult to gain the correct distance from which their behaviour could be seen as sufficiently puzzling. A leading theoretical textbook assures us 'The question of why white-collar offenders behave the way they do can be answered in a relatively straightforward way; they want to make a profit' (Vold and Bernard, 1986: 338). But this is perilously close to accounting for bank robbery in terms of the money to be gained from such activity. The question remains why most businessmen apparently channel their profit-making activities in other ways. Because of the political distaste felt for 'crimes of the powerful' there are also almost no attempts to 'appreciate' the point of view of such criminals.

More generally, the continuing problem of *what* exactly needs to be explained continues to confuse the search for causes. Is white-collar crime conventional or unconventional behaviour for those who commit it? Why is so much effort put into keeping criminal activities secret even from other members of the same organization (Hirschi and Gottfredson, 1987)? Where the explanatory approach adopted is to look for the individual motivations of what is taken to be clearly criminal behaviour, white-collar crime becomes just another test of standard theories of crime causation. Its novelty, if any, is tied to the emergence of new opportunities, for new groups, to commit old offences—for example through the use of computers to carry out frauds. Where, instead, the issue becomes the criminogenic properties of business, of capitalism, or organizational behaviour in general, then the normative fabric of everyday business life seems placed in doubt and the actual evidence of white-collar crime seems to fall far short of what would be predicted.

These difficulties have not discouraged a series of attempts to explain the causes of white-collar crime, and there are even a number of good reviews of such work (see e.g. Braithwaite, 1985, who concludes, however, that 'only banal generalisations are possible', or Coleman, 1987, who furnishes a (banal?) synthesis of existing work in terms of opportunity and motivation theory). I shall comment on explanations concerned with the whole area of white-collar crime. But, as already noted, the search for causes may be limited to typologies of crime, such as crimes by professional people, or even to specific offences. And, obviously, where the topic is theoretically reformulated this will affect what needs to be explained. For Shapiro, for example, the study of white-collar crime belongs to the wider study of the maintenance and abuse of trust (see also Nelken, 1994; Friedrichs, 1996). Attention should focus on the rising need to rely on agents and the consequent increased exposure to the risks of their malpractices. Trust is required insofar as it is difficult to tell when agents are putting their self interests above those of their principals, especially as they tend to be the 'repeat players', and to act at a distance, but efforts to limit their discretion are self-defeating To understand causation there therefore needs to be 'the marriage of a systematic understanding of the distribution of structural opportunities for trust abuse with an understanding of the conditions under which individual or organisational fiduciaries seize or ignore these illicit opportunities' (Shapiro, 1989: 353).

The concept of white-collar crime was certainly not invented in order to provide comfort for standard approaches to causation in criminology. Sutherland hoped to use these misbehaviours as ammunition against the reigning tendency to explain crime in terms of individual or social pathology. By ridiculing the idea that businesses or businessmen could be said to misbehave because of their difficult childhoods he intended to reform criminological theory and show that only his theory of 'differential association' could account for all forms of criminal behaviour. There is ample evidence of the diffusion of definitions favourable to white-collar forms of lawbreaking in business circles, whether these are based on loyalty to the firm, the alleged requirements of business life, or dislike of government regulation. But Sutherland's theory is nevertheless now regarded as flawed and superficial, and the search for a universal theory of crime has lost its attractions. Ironically, those who are most committed to the subject of white-collar crime are now under attack by criminologists who argue that there is no need for this special category of criminal behaviour precisely because it gets in the way of general explanations of the crime phenomenon (Hirschi and Gottfredson, 1987; Gottfredson and Hirschi, 1990: chapter 9).

Both proponents of 'strain' and of 'control' theories have tried to make sense of white-collar crime. Whatever his original focus may have been, most strain theories find their inspiration in Merton's concept of *anomie* which is applied to corporate crime in particular. White-collar crimes can be seen, for example, as an 'innovative' response on the part of businesses (or particular roles such as middle management) to the strain of conforming to cultural prescriptions to maintain profits even in difficult circumstances (Passas, 1990). The strain may be located in the business environment as such, in particular industries, or in particular firms. For example, the conditions under which the major car manufacturers in the United States constrain their car dealers to operate, is such as to pressure them to cut corners if they want to survive economically (Leonard and Weber, 1970); other situations may facilitate rather than directly coerce criminal solutions (Needleman and Needleman, 1979).

Control theories are premised on the initial question, why don't we all commit crimes when the temptations are so strong? The reply given is that most of us, the generally law-abiding, have too much invested in relationships and in legitimate society. The best way to rob a bank may indeed be to own one—or work in one—but, we assume, most of those in this position do not do so. This approach is a weak candidate for explaining white-collar crime because it finds it difficult to account for how middle-class criminals (and even most of those who find themselves in a position to embezzle) ever achieved their social positions in the first place. It also needs to show why they would be willing to risk their investment (Wheeler, 1992). One argument that could be suggested could be based on the idea of 'over-investment'. The finding of Weisburd and his colleagues in their sample of middle-class criminals was that 'many of our offenders have the material goods associated with successful people but may barely be holding their financial selves together' (Weisburd *et al.*, 1991: 65). This could be interpreted as meaning that such offenders are, if anything, so strongly tied to social expectations and obligations that they are willing to offend to maintain their position! (and so *anomie* and control theories meet up). In any case a number of more particular ingredients of control theory are regularly recycled in explaining white-collar crime; these include the importance placed on the neutralization of social controls through the use of justifications learned within or outside the company. Typical theoretical syntheses in textbooks dealing with white-collar crime draw, on the one hand, both on the 'strain' elements of capitalist competition and striving for business or individual success, and, on the other hand, on the large possible variety of such 'techniques of neutralisation' (see e.g. Box, 1983; Coleman, 1987; Green, 1990).

The labelling approach has, strangely, been comparatively neglected in the study of white-collar crime. One reason for this could be that criminologists here line up with those doing the labelling (see Katz, 1980; Yeager, 1991: chapter 1). There is of course the apparent paradox that it is the 'insiders' rather than the 'outsiders' who are being labelled—but the paradox normally disappears once the details of who is really affected become clearer. In any case, few would now want to deny the importance of legislative or other battles over the labelling of business misbehaviour. The perspective would seem peculiarly relevant given the relative recency of many laws regulating business, the sharp swings between political projects of regulation and deregulation, and the divergent views of different groups on the appropriateness of criminalization. Attention has recently turned to the success of techniques of 'non-labelling' or 'de-labelling' in diluting or avoiding the imposition of the criminal label, for example, in shaping the (mis)behaviour involved in some tax-avoidance schemes (McBarnet, 1991). However, my earlier study of the social construction of landlord crime (Nelken, 1983) remains one of the few works to have examined the process of labelling and de-labelling in the same area of business misbehaviour (though see also now Cook, 1989). I showed that those actually apprehended for landlord crime were small immigrant landlords involved in disputes with their tenants (for similar findings for other white-collar crimes see Hutter, 1988; Croal, 1989). With some effort it was possible to portray their self-help methods as criminal, but the malpractices characteristic of large business landlords stayed immune to criminalization because of their similarity to ordinary business behaviour—a 'limit' of the legal process which was, paradoxically, concealed by actually exaggerating the capacity of law to control such behaviour (Nelken, 1983).

The attempt to explain white-collar crime within the 'normal science' approaches used in criminology shows itself not only in theories of causation but also in the positivist search for the peculiar characteristics associated with offenders and offences and the methodology appropriate to this task. Sutherland (1949, 1983) himself was keen to show the widespread nature of white-collar offences. He examined infringements of rules governing fair labour practices, by General Motors and others, violations of rules against the restraint of trade, especially common in the major companies in the film industry, infringements of patents, and misrepresentation in advertising involving household names such as Bayer aspirin, Quaker Oats, Carnation milk, Phillips' milk of magnesia, Hoover vacuum cleaners, and Encyclopaedia Britannica. He particularly stressed the duration of some offences and the 'recidivism' of some of the companies concerned.

Clinard and Yeager (1980), in the most wide-ranging documentary study of corporate crime to date, examined all the federal administrative, civil, and criminal actions initiated in 1975 and 1976 by twenty-five federal agencies against 582 of America's largest corporations. The violations they examined were divided into non-compliance with agency regulations; environmental pollution; financial crimes, such as illegal payments or tax offences; labour discrimination, including unsafe working practices; manufacturing offences, such as the distribution of unsafe products; and unfair trading practices, including price-fixing arrangements. Going beyond Sutherland, they tried to control comparisons for the time available to commit offences and the different size of the companies they investigated. They found that three fifths of their sample had had charges brought against them in those years. Whilst 13 per cent of the companies accounted for just over half the violations, large, medium, and small companies were all well represented amongst the violators. Where Sutherland had found the film, mercantile, and railroad industries particularly engaged in violations, Clinard and Yeager found their black sheep in the oil, pharmaceutical, and motor vehicle industries, which all had more than their proportional share of violations. The oil industry, for example, was involved in three fifths of all serious violations, with twenty-two of twenty-eight oil refining firms guilty of at least one violation in the period under consideration; car manufacturers were responsible in all for one sixth of all the violations discovered and a third of the manufacturing violations overall; pharmaceutical manufacturers accounted for one-tenth of all violations and all seventeen companies were found to have committed at least one violation.

Some of Clinard and Yeager's findings were artefacts which resulted from using data which depended on the vagaries of regulatory regimes: the higher offending rates of diversified firms, for example, may simply mean that thay were more exposed to different regulatory agencies (though the firms concerned may also have faced problems in maintaining oversight of their different operations). Their investigation produced some statistical support for the proposition that violations increased as financial performance became poorer; this was particularly marked for environmental and labour offences. On the other hand, firms with higher than average growth rates were more likely to have engaged in manufacturing violations. The authors admitted that the causal variables on which they concentrated—size, growth rate, diversification, and market power and resources had only limited predictive power. Even the more confident of their claims concerning crime rates and economic performance have now been questioned in the later literature (Braithwaite, 1985). Their study was unable to allow for the complicating factor of why and when agencies choose to uncover violations, and has been criticized for taking agency records as the measure of corporate crime and for failing to see such behaviour as endemic to capitalism (Young, 1981).

A central debate amongst scholars of white-collar crime in fact concerns the extent to which corporate and business crime should be seen as an inevitable consequence of capitalism. Box (1983), in a Marxist-influenced application of Merton, argues that corporations are criminogenic, because if legal means are blocked they will resort to illegal means to maintain or increase profitability. As and when necessary, they will use techniques aimed at competitors (e.g. industrial espionage or price fixing), at consumers (e.g. fraud or misleading advertising), or at the public at large (e.g. environmental pollution). Those recruited to work in corporations learn to justify such behaviour on the grounds that 'business is business' (cf. Pearce, 1976). This is particularly true for those who rise to the top and who then have a disproportionate influence over the ethos of their firms (although they generally take care not to be directly involved or informed of the illegal activities made necessary by their drive for profit). For those who subscribe to this theory businessmen comply with the law insofar as they see it enforced strictly (thereby denying competitive advantage to those who would break it). Where there are few effective controls, as in the Third World, capitalism shows its true face, selling unsafe products, paying low wages and exploiting the complaisance of poor and corrupt governments and regulators.

On the other hand, a number of attempts have been made to question the idea that capitalism as such is criminogenic. If Merton's *anomie* theory is to be pressed this far it is at least necessary to go on to discuss the alternative, non-criminal modes of responding to 'strain', and (what Merton did not do) offer an explanation of when and why each mode is chosen. The argument appears to predict too much crime and makes it difficult to explain the relative stability of economic trade within and between nations, given the large number of economic transactions, the many opportunities for committing business crimes, the large gains to be made, and the relative unlikelihood of punishment. This theory also has difficulty in accounting for improvements in safety and increases in the quality of goods under capitalism. If it is somewhat over-simplified to argue that only a small proportion of businessmen are 'bad apples', it is not much more convincing to assume that all businesses act as 'amoral calculators' and would choose to offend but for the availability of serious sanctions (Pearce and Tombs, 1990, 1991). The desire to continue in business, to maintain self-respect and the goodwill of fellow businessmen go a long way to explaining reluctance to seize opportunities for a once-only wind-fall. Trading competitors (as well as organized consumer groups) can serve as a control on illicit behaviour for their own reasons. Law-abidingness can often be definitely in the competitive interests of companies. Braithwaite (1985) illustrates how American pharmaceutical companies able to obtain Federal Drug Administration authorization for their products are in this way guaranteed lucrative markets in countries which cannot afford their own expensive drug-testing facilities. It could be said that the clear evidence of exploitation and the sale of dangerous goods in Third World countries reflects an anomalous situation and is at least partly the result of the freedom of manœuvre of powerful multi-national companies who are not exposed to sufficient competition.

Marxist theory in any case has no need to assume that all business crime will be tolerated. Many forms of business misbehaviour made into crimes may reflect changing forms of capitalism or inter-class conflict. At any given period, some corporate crimes, such as anti-trust offences, will not be in the interest of capitalism as a whole, so it is important to distinguish what is in the interests of capitalism from what suits particular capitalists. Even if the latter may succeed in blocking legislation or effective enforcement, at least in the short term, this does not prove that it is capitalism as such which requires the continuation of specific forms of misbehaviour. Moreover, capitalism is a set of practices and not just an important set of social actors. Practices may remain free from effective control even if the group concerned is not particularly economically powerful. Thus the relative immunity from control of abuses of the Rent Acts committed by private business landlords in Britain has been attributed less to their importance within the social structure and more to objective difficulties in controlling their behaviour without affecting normal commercial transactions (Nelken, 1983). When professional criminals succeed in getting away with serious forms of business-related crime such as 'long-firm' fraud, it is implausible to say that this is in the interest of any capitalist group (Levi, 1985).

Without underestimating the fruitfulness of hypotheses based on the capacity of capitalism to generate business crime, it is prudent to add that all organizations can be criminogenic insofar as they tend to reward achievement even at the expense of the outer environment (Kramer, 1992). This would help explain why public organizations such as the army, the police, or government bureaucracies also generate crime and corruption (these behaviours are increasingly being included in textbooks on white-collar crime). Likewise the far from positive record of the former communist regimes in matters of worker safety, environmental pollution, or corruption cannot be blamed on the pressures of competition. Even in capitalist societies it is often the absence of market pressures which explains some types of business misbehaviours such as the ease with which government subsidy programmes are diverted to improper uses.

4. We have seen so far that there are, on the one hand, doubts about how far the same explanations will work for white-collar crime as for ordinary crime and, on the other hand, risks of over-explanation in accounts which relate it too closely to ordinary business behaviour. For some commentators, however, the central issue to pose concerns the extent to which white-collar crimes come about in similar ways to other criminal behaviour. Clarke's book on business crime, for example, argues strongly that these misbehaviours are typically 'less criminal' in their inception and motivation than much ordinary crime (Clarke, 1990*a*). Whereas many textbook presentations of white-collar crime simply list a variety of dangerous behaviours in a way which emphasizes their harmful consequences and implies that these are incurred deliberately or at least recklessly, Clarke attempts to recover their sense by putting them back into their everyday business context.

For Clarke there are a series of factors which distinguish the commission of business crimes. Their location in the midst of ordinary business and occupational activity both facilitates their achievement and helps prevent their detection by colleagues and superiors as well as outside authorities. As compared to ordinary crimes such as burglary, the perpetrator has every justification to be present at the scene of the crime. Indeed Clarke claims that, unlike ordinary crimes where a crucial clue is present at the scene, with white-collar crimes the problem is rather to discover whether there has been an offence rather than to identify the culprit. Police or regulatory agencies are reluctant to enter private settings without invitation and are often not called upon even where an offence has been committed. White-collar crimes are frequently what we could call 'complainantless crimes' and those who suffer the consequences of them cannot be relied upon to act as a reliable source of criminal intelligence. Clients of professionals are often unable to assess their performance—this is why they need to turn to them in the first place. Workers may simply be unaware of the risks to which they have been exposed; consumers will often not appreciate what they have lost; competitors will be unaware of collusive practices. The behaviour which constitutes white-collar crime is often indistinguishable on its surface from normal legal behaviour. For example, for fraud to succeed, it must obviously succeed in mimicking the appearance of legitimate transactions, and it is not unusual for those guilty of this crime to remain undetected for years or even a lifetime. Unlike all except 'victimless crimes' the involvement of the victim is apparently voluntary (though sometimes the result of the lure of easy money).

A further claim concerning the supposed distinctiveness of white-collar crime is virtually true by definition. The criminal aspects of the business or occupational activities under consideration are often *secondary* or *collateral* features, both in priority and in the succession of events, of an undertaking pursued for other, legitimate, purposes. Criminal consequences, such as damage to the health of workers or to the environment, often come about either as a result of omissions, or because of financial pressures or unanticipated opportunities for gain; they are not inherent to the economic activity as such. Such criminality is difficult to recognize (in time) because of the narrow and constantly changing line between acceptable and unacceptable business behaviour. Even such essential features of outrightly crooked schemes as the deliberate withholding of payment to creditors may exist as practices in the legitimate world of business—for example as a desperate manœuvre by small businesses trying to survive on tight margins, or as a more cynical use of market strength by large enterprises exploiting the dependence on their patronage of small contractors. This makes it difficult for all concerned—creditors, regulators, and others—to tell whether, or at what point, the intention permanently to avoid payment was formed.

Ambiguity surrounds not only the goals of the activity in the midst of which white-collar crime is encountered but also, it is argued, the degree of intentionality involved. There are certainly notorious cases of cold-blooded calculation such as the way Ford went ahead with its dangerous design for the Ford rear engine because it estimated that the potential payment of damages would be less than the cost of recalling the cars (Dowie, 1988), or the manner in which P & O disregarded repeated requests for the installation of bow warning-lights to improve safety on their on–off ferries. But, it is argued, these are the exceptions (and even these cases did not end in criminal convictions). More commonly it is difficult to distinguish malevolence from incompetence and, as Clarke insists, in business and professional life, we are often more concerned about the harmful effects of the latter. A professional is specifically valued for her competence rather than for her honesty as such (which is perhaps taken for granted); in large organizations and bureaucracies there is considerable scope for laziness or disinterest which may have tragic consequences. These points, it is said, are less true of ordinary crime.

On the other hand, many scholars would insist that these aspects of the setting and commission of white-collar crimes mainly point to problems of detection and do not negate the essential similarities between these and ordinary crimes. Businesses involved in offending behaviour often do their best to organize so as to minimize the costs of their infractions (concealing compromising knowledge from directors, 'appointing vice presidents responsible for going to jail', etc.). Conversely, there are also occasions where enforcement against ordinary crime has to overcome similar difficulties of categorization. The difficulty of identifying the 'really' criminal cases is not unique to white-collar crime. The definition of 'dishonesty' in the English law of theft, for example, leaves it to the jury to decide whether the behaviour at issue demonstrates the requisite level of criminal intent in terms of what ordinary people would consider stealing: the business world would probably be capable of answering a similar question. Many ordinary crimes, such as assault, also fall on a continuum that runs from accidental to deliberate, but we do not let this place the appropriateness of criminal sanctions in doubt. Indeed we take trouble to hold individuals responsible for the consequences of their assaults even when this exceeds their intention or even their foresight (see *R. v. Le Brun* [1991] 3 WLR 653, CA (Criminal Division), for a recent example). Much also depends on the 'time-frame' adopted for identifying the commission of an offence. For example, the conduct that causes a serious breach of health or safety standards may have been unintended at the time of the accident but deliberate when the choice was made not to install up-to-date costly measures of prevention (Kelman, 1981). Philosophical studies of when we choose to describe an action as voluntary or not assert that (because of the difficulty of defining what is meant by 'will') this is itself a way of indicating our evaluation of the actions in question rather than simply a description.

Like so much concerning the social definition of white-collar crime the question of intention therefore easily lends itself to social construction. Much ambiguity or, conversely, the provision of a cover of ostensible legality, is a contingent product of social processing. Thus accountants and barristers may use their professional skills to help businesses construct tax-avoidance schemes which must then appear as anything but deliberate attempts to evade tax (McBarnet, 1991). Even if a case reaches trial, defence lawyers work hard to redefine the misconduct as not having been deliberate (Mann, 1985). White-collar criminals may even find they have allies in the redefinition of their behaviour in those trying their misbehaviour. In the course of research into deviance by professionals I made a study of the (confidential) proceedings of English family practitioner tribunals, which deal with cases where dentists and other professionals are alleged not to have complied with their National Health contracts. Here everything is done to avoid the impression that potentially criminal behaviour is at issue even though in cases where misconduct is proved fixed withholdings from payment serve the function of fines. In one case, for example, a dentist admitted to 'fraud', in deliberately claiming for more work than he had done, only to find the tribunal members pleading with him to retract his admission (and claim inadvertence) so that they could retain jurisdiction.

Whilst it is debatable how far the ambiguous aspects alleged to characterize the commission of white-collar crime are intrinsic features restricted to this type of misbehaviour, there are certainly some important cases where criminals deliberately exploit the appearance of legitimate business. In fact the overlap between white-collar crime and more clear-cut kinds of crime, such as organized crime, has so far been relatively neglected in comparison to the attention given to the boundary between white-collar crime and ordinary business behaviour. Professional or organized criminals may *create* ambiguity by fostering the impression of genuine business enterprises, if necessary by trading normally for an initial period. At other times they may penetrate legitimate companies, especially when these have fallen on hard times, and use them to launch purely criminal activities such as 'long-firm' frauds (Levi, 1981). Organized criminal businesses may seek to monopolize the market for legitimate goods and services, such as public construction projects or waste-processing, beating their competitors with their lower marginal costs and using violence or corruption against competitors or those with the power to award lucrative contracts, as with Camorra enterprises in the Campania area of Italy and the activities of many of the cosche of the New Mafia (Arlachi, 1985). The division of labour between legitimate and illegitimate business, by contrast, can also represent an attempt to disguise the criminal presuppositions of legal enterprises. Legitimate business may call upon the service of criminals for particular operations such as loan repayment, money laundering, or tax evasion (Block, 1991: chapters 5 and 6). They may also take indirect advantage of the operations of international criminals—for example major electrical companies apparently find it financially profitable to buy and resell (at the expense of other wholesalers) examples of their own products illegally smuggled on to the market (Van Duyne, 1993). Legal enterprise may rely on organized criminals to supply a disciplined workforce, as in the New York construction industry (New York State Organized Crime Task Force, 1988), or to get rid of industrial waste-products in illegal ways so as to reduce their external costs of production (Szasz, 1986). With the growth of concern about the environment and the explosion of new regulatory crimes in this and other areas (cf. Sgubbi, 1990), we may predict a considerable increase in this sort of collaboration. Conversely, organized criminals may call upon legitimate businesses, such as printers or supermarkets, in developing major frauds such as those against the EEC agricultural subsidy programmes (Passas and Nelken, 1993); such symbiosis is also essential for the purpose of recycling money earned in illegal activities. The steady growth in international and transnational trading— and the changing face of national and economic borders in Europe—is also leading to an increase in different types of criminals seeking to profit from the opportunities these changes offer them (Passas and Nelken, 1993; Van Duyne, 1993). Current research on white-collar crime is increasingly concerned with exploring the relationship between legal, semi-legal, and illegal economic activities. This normally requires giving attention to the comparative dimension because the relationships between businessmen, professionals, and organized criminals vary in different countries and because many of these crimes have an international dimension which exploits differences between national legal systems (Nelken, forthcoming). Appreciation of the political and economic structures conducive to such operations requires the criminologist to be open to concepts pioneered in disciplines other than sociology, including ideas about clientilism in political science, legal and illegal monopolies in economics, and risk analysis in accounting and management science.

THE AMBIVALENT RESPONSE TO WHITE-COLLAR CRIME

5. As the above discussion will have already illustrated, there are various ways in which the control of white-collar crime can also play a part in its causation. Government and business may share similar imperatives which coincide to favour offending. Carson's description of the importance of 'speed' in the calculations of both the Treasury and the oil companies in the exploitation of North Sea oil, and the consequent sacrifice of ordinary safety standards, is an extreme example of such objective coincidence of interests (Carson, 1981). The Bank of England may be caught between its duties as regulator of the banking system and its desire not to compromise the credibility of one of the major clearing banks (*Economist*, 1992). But, even where government and offenders are clearly opposed, weak regulatory regimes or moves towards deregulation may provide an incentive to offending. One common strategy which leads to increased crime is the combination of removing legal or informal constraints on a business sector with the simultaneous resort to (new) criminal penalties to be avalable as a last resort. Complex and changing regulatory regimes, especially those involving government payment schemes, may in themselves provide the opportunity for crime (Vaughan, 1983; Passas and Nelken, 1993).

The methods adopted in responding to white-collar crime play a particularly important part in shaping this type of behaviour inasmuch as the difficulty of relying on complainants means that the accent must be put on prevention and proactive enforcement. In this way our information about these types of misbehaviour often tells us more about the theories and priorities of the controllers than anything else (for example the belief that small firms are more likely than large ones to bend the rules will inevitably find confirmation in the statistics of violations discovered).

But the main issue which needs to be discussed under this heading is the charge that the different enforcement methods used to respond to white-collar as compared to ordinary crime reinforces their ambiguous status and indirectly contributes to their causation. Is the difference in handling the cause or consequence of the distinctiveness of white-collar crime? Many scholars stress the fact that white-collar crimes are difficult to detect and control. It is difficult to prove intention when dealing with decisions taken within an organization (and legal thinking has not yet caught up with the importance of organizations), trials are long and expensive, juries have problems in under-standing the evidence in complex fraud cases; professional advisers acting for businessmen can delay or defeat prosecution. Extra powers for obtaining evidence given to the Department of Trade inspectors or the recently established Serious Fraud Office go only some of the way to dealing with these difficulties, as the spectacular collapse of the recent Blue Arrow prosecutions, amongst others, demonstrates. A premium is therefore placed on achieving compliance without the need for prosecution (although this is used as a threat, the need to resort to it is seen as failure). It is considered still better to rely on self-regulation by an industry or by the business itself. But reliance on self-policing can easily lead to conflicts of interest. For example, banks find themselves both potential participators in money laundering but also required to detect and deter it (Levi, 1991*a*, 1991*b*).

Some scholars (such as Clarke, 1990*a*, but here his views are more widely shared) argue that the way white-collar crimes are handled reflects the special circumstances of these offences. It makes sense to use compliance in the regulation of occupations because the offender can easily be found at his or her place of occupation and it is feasible to put repeated pressure on him or her. Violations of safety or pollution standards are difficult and costly to conceal. Even the apparently self-defeating practice of giving advance warning of inspection visits does not therefore lead to concealment of offending. The difficulty in other business offences, Clarke argues, is to identify the com-mission of an offence rather than find the offender. But even here offenders in organizations do tend to leave a 'paper trail' of their actions.

Different interpretations of the nature of white-collar crime lead to corre-sponding views concerning the best way to handle it. Clarke argues that an approach based on criminal prosecution is inappropriate for all but a few cases of business crime, because complainants are mainly interested in recompense and only go to the police if all else fails; the criminal process polarizes the parties, involves delay, carries risks of failure, and, above all, does nothing to secure future improvement in the relevant working practices. Existing enforce-ment practices make more sense; suggestions for improvement should be based mainly on trying to internalize better methods of control within businesses themselves rather than increase prosecution (Stone, 1975, is a classic discussion of this theme). But the opposite point of view is also well supported. Green summarizes an extensive American literature which offers various proposals for improving the effectiveness of prosecution against white-collar crimes (Green, 1990: chapter 8; see also Groves and Newman, 1986). The assumption behind much of this work is that business behaviour is in fact particularly well suited to the application of deterrent criminal sanctions. Offences (it is alleged) are strictly instrumental and offenders have much to lose from prosecution; prison, if only it were to be used regularly, would be more potent than for ordi-nary criminals. The main problem in current practice is that of producing a level of fines sufficient actually to deter business. Solutions such as stock dilution, equity fining, ceding shares to the state, may all work, but in cases where there has been physical injury may give the wrong message that everything can ultimately be paid for. Informal and formally initiated negative publicity is unlikely to put a firm out of business, but can and does have collateral effects and may help produce beneficial procedural changes within firms (Fisse and Braithwaite, 1985). Green's discussion is thin on the questions which are central for Clarke concerning the possible counter-productive effects of using the normal criminal process for white-collar crime. On the other hand, many of Clarke's arguments against the use of prosecution could also be made regarding ordinary crime—certainly the victim usually gains little from from the criminal process and seems rather used by the system to serve its own ends.

For many observers the difficulties of controlling white-collar crime, and the need to rely on compliance techniques, should rather be attributed to a lack of political will to provide the resources necessary for a full-blown prosecution approach. In Britain proportionally few policemen are assigned to the fraud squad, the prestige of such assignements is low and term of service short (Levi, 1987). For the United States Calavita and Pontell argue that the savings and loans crash was partly due to the lack of trained thrift examiners and the overloaded FBI agents directed to clear up the scandal (Calavita and Pontell, 1992). Even the famous and feared American Securities and Exchange Commission, according to Shapiro, is forced to choose between detection or enforcement and uses the criminal sanction in only around 11 per cent of its cases (Shapiro, 1984).

The actual combination of objective difficulties and political priorities in decisions over prosecution is often concealed by ideologically loaded communication. Much white-collar crime is subject to regulation under the heading of strict liability by which, in theory, even unintentional offending can be held criminally culpable. Criminal law textbooks and philosophic writers discuss whether or not this is justified by the difficulty of proving intention in complex modern industrial processes. However, investigations of the 'logic in use' of the inspectorates responsible (at least in common law countries) for some of the most important areas of social regulation, such as those concerning worker safety or environmental pollution, tell a different story. In practice, apart from cases in which accidents have taken place, breaches of rules will normally be sanctioned only if both *mens rea*—and even recidivism—have been shown by a refusal to correct matters pointed out by the inspector in warning visits and letters (Carson, 1970; Hawkins, 1984, Hawkins and Thomas, 1984; Hutter, 1988). The inspectors involved in such enforcement activity refuse to see themselves as 'industrial policemen' and see their role rather as one geared to advising and cajoling the majority of fundamentally law-abiding businessmen. One consequence (perhaps even an intended one, see Carson, 1974, 1980) of this difference between theory and practice is that the imposition of strict liability reduces the stigma associated with these offences so as to reinforce the impression that they represent behaviour which is merely *mala prohibita* rather than *mala in se*. Enforcement techniques which concentrate on consequences rather than intentions by collapsing the distinction between incompetence and deliberateness thus often end up diluting rather than extending criminal stigma.

Difficulties of enforcement may be exaggerated to conceal other decisions (or 'non-decisions') about responding to criminal behaviour by economically influential groups. In an important later study Carson argued convincingly that the causes of accidents on North Sea oil rigs were little different from those which lead to accidents in factories or construction (Carson, 1981). The claim that the high level of injuries was due to the difficulty of regulating activities operating 'at the frontiers of technology' at hitherto untried depths of oil exploration at sea was not supported by his careful examination of the relevant case-records. The crucial issue was the fact that the responsibility for ensuring compliance with the normal standards of safety had not been assigned to the factory inspectors of the Health and Safety inspectorate (here being seen in more heroic light than in Carson's earlier work) but to the Department of Energy. But, since this was also the body responsible for encouraging oil exploration to proceed as fast as possible in the interests of the British balance of payments, there was an inevitable conflict of interests in which the interests of the weakest groups were sacrificed.

Since Sutherland the subject of white-collar crime has also been the focus of attempts to prove that the rich and powerful are treated more favourably by the criminal justice system. Some caveats should be entered here. The main basis for the relative immunity of businessmen in the criminal process (at least in Anglo-American jurisdictions) derives from political choices regarding which behaviour to make criminal in the first place and, only to a lesser extent, from the way their offences are categorized. Those effectively criminalized for business-related offences tend to be small businessmen, quite often from immigrant backgrounds (Nelken, 1983; Croal, 1989). It is a mistake to confuse the macro (legislative) and micro (enforcement) logics which keep criminality and respectability apart. Many of those working in the criminal justice system would actually be interested (and have an interest in) successful prosecutions of 'the powerful'. Thus apparently ineffective legislative outcomes are often best studied as a product of 'coherence without conspiracy' (Nelken, 1983). This does not mean, of course, that there cannot also be more explicit cases of prejudice, and there have rightly been many attacks on alleged bias and injustice in the handling of white-collar crimes, from enforcement to trial and beyond. As with most accusations of bias, however, the difficulty is ensuring that like is being compared with like.

A recent debate over the alleged leniency involved in using 'compliance' methods for dealing with white-collar regulatory offences is that between Pearce and Tombs, on the one hand, and Hawkins on the other (Pearce and Tombs, 1990, 1991; Hawkins, 1990, 1991). But although the argument represented opposing positions which are quite widely shared, it did not take matters much further. Pearce and Tombs began by criticizing Hawkins',and other recent descriptions of the compliance approach, for giving the appearance of being persuaded by the 'logic in use' of those whose enforcement strategy they described. In this way, it was alleged, they (indirectly) confirmed an unfair *status quo* instead of supporting the adoption of stricter methods which could reduce the level of harm caused by such offences. Hawkins fiercely challenged this as a misreading of the role of interpretive sociology (which was not directed towards policy evaluation), but then went on to endorse the compliance strategy in general terms without necessarily agreeing with all its tactics or the level of severity of the sanctions applied. For their part, Pearce and Tombs recommended that prosecution should begin at an earlier stage, they favoured the imposition of (low) fines rather than simply warning notices and wanted there to be more use of other sanctions such as the withdrawal of licences. In his reply, Hawkins pointed out that very few of the violations noted in routine proactive enforcement do eventually turn out to be the cause of serious harm, and that it is not possible to predict which will do so.

Unless Pearce and Tombs really want to cut back sharply on enforcement discretion their proposals are unlikely to produce much change in current practice. And to insist on legal action each time a violation is revealed, as was tried for a time by the American mines authority, tends to be counter-productive in terms of alienating the goodwill of those being regulated. It also risks producing a political backlash leading to deregulation, as happened in the case of this agency. As this summary suggests, this and similar debates fail to make progress mainly because the policy arguments of Hawkins and others like him assume as givens exactly those political realities which their critics would like to see changed. A valuable study which points this moral is Cook's comparison of the harsh response to those suspected of social security fraud with that meeted out to those engaged in tax frauds of very similar kinds (Cook, 1989). The very different treatment received by each group relates less to the practical possibilities of enforcement (more or less the same), or to fears of counter-productive effects from tougher penalties, but rather follows from a set of associated beliefs about the relative worth and importance of main-taining the goodwill of each set of offenders.

Some of the most fruitful proposals for strengthening the control of white-collar crime, which acknowledge the force of both sides of this debate, are presently being developed by Braithwaite on the basis of his research into the successes and failures of regulation in very different industries and businesses, such as drug manufacturing, coal mining, and nursing homes. He suggests that businesses (beyond a certain size) should be obliged by government to write a set of rules tailored to the unique contingencies of their firm. These rules should be submitted for comment and amendment to interest groups including citizen groups. Firms should have their own internal compliance units with statutory responsibility on the director to report cases of violation, and the function of government inspectors would be to audit, and if necessary sanction, the performance of this unit (see e.g. Braithwaite, 1995).

It might be thought that the study of bias in the prosecution and trial of white-collar crimes should be more straightforward than an evalution of the justificiability of its special style of enforcement; but even here there is no consensus. Analysis of the penalties meeted out for serious frauds in Britain as compared to other types of crime certainly suggests that these are the crimes which are the most rewarding (Levi, 1991c). Shapiro, in her study of securities offenders in the United States detected a tendency for higher status offenders to be less likely to receive criminal penalties instead of being dealt with by admnistrative and civil measures (Shapiro, 1984, 1989). But in their more comprehensive American study Weisburd *et al.* (even after double-checking) found that higher status offenders were more likely to get prison (Weisburd *et al.*, 1991: 7). In their earlier study Wheeler *et al.*, using a sample of pre-1980 American social enquiry reports and case files, showed that penalties for white-collar crimes depended on the normal criteria for other crimes: prior record, seriousness of crime, degree of involvement of offender, the nature and harm to the victim, etc., though there was also some limited evidence of judges identifying with the offender more than in cases of ordinary crimes, especially if the latter involve personal violence (Wheeler, 1988). They left it open whether the judges were merely reproducing (unconsciously or deliberately) the biases of the wider population.

Instead of demanding that white-collar criminals be treated like ordinary criminals, we could argue the reverse (though this is rarely done). Why not apply the methods used for dealing with businessmen and professionals to ordinary criminals? Much of what purports to be regulation or self-regulation of white-collar crime is bogus or ineffectual and deserves to be attacked as such. But there is also much to be learned from the variety of forms of regulation and self-regulation designed to reduce violations without criminalizing the offender. Even if it would probably be impossible to model the handling of ordinary crime too closely on that used for businessmen the differences are not as great as made out. All non-police agencies—even when not dealing with powerful offenders—put the emphasis on recovering money rather than securing convictions (Royal Commission on Criminal Procedure, 1980). The problem of apprehending and maintaining pressure on ordinary criminals is not as great as it seems: the police do know just where to lay their hands on juvenile delinquents—and quite a few other criminal suspects.

In a sense compliance does already get used with ordinary criminals (Pearce and Tombs mention police control of prostitution and gambling as an example of compliance, but they use this to show the danger of collusion and corruption in the use of such methods). The role of social work and diversion (before trial) and probation or other techniques of rehabilitation (after conviction) is similar. And the choice between co-operation or compulsion is repeatedly offered to ordinary criminals from the stage of pleading guilty to obtaining parole. A crucial difference, however, is that it is usually necessary for an offender accused of ordinary crime to suffer the stigma of a conviction before consideration is given to compliance, whereas the opposite is true for business offenders handled in this way. The temptation is to believe that, beyond a certain point, enforcement against ordinary crime is geared precisely to maximizing stigma even at the expense of effectiveness. Pearce and Tombs do seem correct in tracing the difference in approach to the (untested) assumption that businessmen are basically disposed to respond to a compliance approach (whereas ordinary criminals are presumed to require punishment)—though they prefer the equally untested assumption that businessmen should be dealt with as 'amoral calculators'. The evidence, at least from interviews, is that managers say that they do not, for the most part, think in deterrence terms, because only unethical managers are seen to respond to deterrence. Reputable managers 'cut corners' to try to save the company, they may bend, but do not violate, the rules and do not act for personal gain. But those interviewed do concede that this process can get out of control, and that it is difficult to be ethical when not running at a profit (Simpson, 1992; Yeager, 1995). It is reasonable to conclude that practical considerations regarding effective enforcement provide insufficient justification for the extent of the present contrast between methods used for ordinary and business crimes. A considerable merit of Braithwaite's long-standing search for an effective as well as just approach to the control of all types of crime—what he calls 'reintegrative shaming' (Braithwaite, 1989, 1995)—is that it builds in a series of attempts at compliance as a prelude to prosecution.

6. Whatever the reasons or justifications for the methods used to control white-collar crime, the ambivalence of the social response to this sort of behaviour is also related to wider social factors which have both objective and subjective dimensions. For Aubert (as well as for writers such as E. A Ross, who anticipated Sutherland's ideas on this topic) the ambiguity of white-collar crimes reflected the objective fact that they were the index of important transitions in social structure. A good example of this phenomenon is the practice of 'insider trading' on the stock exchange and in other financial institutions, which has recently come to be penalized in Britain (but is still not criminal in all European countries). Even now practioners can have difficulty in drawing the line between legal and illegal conduct (a problem exploited by defence lawyers) and can justify as good business the competetitive testing of the limits of legality (Reichman, 1992). As Clarke argues,

It would have perplexed leading members of these institutions up to the end of the 1950's to be told that they were doing anything reprehensible in acting on such information. It was precisely because of the access to such information that one was part of the City, and one was part of the City in the clear expectation of making a considerable amount of money [Clarke, 1990a:162].

The crime of insider trading therefore nicely symbolizes the change from a time when there were only 'insiders' (see also Stanley, 1992).

Ambiguity thus results from a situation in which previously legal behaviour has only recently been redefined, and it is exacerbated when the boundaries are changed in ways which are to some extent outside the control of the community being regulated. But we could extend Aubert's analysis by saying that social and legal definitions of crime may be out of joint, either because public attitudes have not caught up with the legal recognition of important economic and social changes or because the law has not yet recognized the seriousness of behaviour which causes public concern (in both cases these processes will be mediated by interest and pressure groups). As a further complication we should note that economic and legal definitions will not always coincide (insider trading is still seen as economically useful by some economists). Conversely, at any given time there will be some practices which are quite legal but of dubious economic value, a current example being corporate raiding so as to bid up the price of a business and sell on at a profit. It is therefore not always easy to tell when the time has arrived at which certain business practices have lost all economic justification.

In a stimulating recent paper Calavita and Pontell discuss the economic justifications of the types of practices which were the subject of financial scandals and prosecutions during and after the period of Reaganite relaxation of economic controls in the 1980s (Calavita and Pontell, 1992). This period saw the breaking down of barriers between banks and other financial institutions and a great increase in the scale and internationalization of financial transactions. Drawing on the idea of the French economist Allais, they argue that much of what is produced in what he calls the 'casino economy' is of illusory economic benefit. If, for example, it takes only 12 billion dollars of commercial trade to generate 400 billion dollars of foreign-exchange transactions, the opportunities for manipulating money are far in excess of the goods to which they correspond. The system is kept going only by trust in the backing of these transactions, but an excess of confidence can equally bring about disaster if it allows the production of 'junk bonds' or helps sustain unsound financial institutions. They point to various characteristic abuses of this period, such as corporate takeovers, currency trading, and futures trading, 'land flips', 'daisy chains', and other forms of property speculation, and the switching of loans to confuse auditors regarding actual assets. Emblematic for them was the accumulation of enormous uncollectable loans relying on federal deposit insurance in the massive 'savings and loans' scandal.

Calavita and Pontell may none the less be wrong in thinking that all the practices from which these scandals arose (which they associate with finance capital as opposed to industrial capital) can be controlled severely without risk to jobs or to economically sound activities. Much of what they describe, shorn of obvious abuses (and it should be noted that the savings and loans fiasco was as much the result of too generous government guarantees to bank investors, as it was of speculation and financial mismanagement), may point to changes in what makes economic sense in a world where the costs of production increasingly favour countries other than the United States and Western Europe. They themselves may be relying on an outdated model of industrial capitalism as the only proper conception of a functioning economy. This said, much white-collar and financial crime grows out of the opportunities to exploit objective changes in organizational forms of business trading (particularly marked in a period of increasing global competition) in ways which the law—

especially national laws—is slow to deal with or incapable of catching in time (see e.g. Pearce and Snider, 1995; Tombs, 1995).

A more subjective source of ambivalence in the social response to white-collar crime is the assumption that there is less public concern about these behaviours, and therefore less support for severe sanctions, than is the case with more familiar street crimes—especially those involving violence (though this may be the result of existing methods of control). A series of studies have therefore sought to demonstrate that the public in fact ranks examples of these crimes quite severely as compared to ordinary crimes (see e.g. Cullen *et al.*, 1983; Green, 1990: 47–57). Harsh attitudes towards such conduct, going well beyond the penalties actually meeted out, can be documented in cases of culpable disasters caused by white-collar offenders (Calavita *et al.*, 1991). On the other hand, some recent attempts to measure public attitudes to white-collar crime do reveal greater leniency in public attitudes (see e.g. Goff and Nason-Clarke, 1989). Much depends on the way questions about different crimes are phrased and the extent to which effort is made to refer to the possible side-effects of the use of certain sanctions. But, even if it were to be shown that there was greater public ambivalence towards white-collar crimes than ordinary crimes, writers such as Box would only regard this a further challenge 'to sensitize people to not seeing processes in which they are victimised as disasters or accidents' (Box, 1983: 233).

7. Many of the sources of ambiguity discussed so far can also be related to the value conflicts and policy dilemmas so often cited as explaining, and even justifying, a cautious response to white-collar crime. The regulation of white-collar crime has been seen as the locus of a number of different awkward policy choices. Risk-taking is said to be the motor of the capitalist economy, but someone has to pay the price of the inevitable failures. The pursuit of greater health and safety has costs in terms of national and international competitiveness and jobs, and this explains (justifies?) the acceptance of no more than a 'reasonable' level of safety or pollution. In many areas of business crime enforcers are obliged to choose between going for punishment (and stigmatiz-ation), or else achieving compliance or maximizing the amount of revenue recovered. Other dilemmas are more particular. If we are worried about money laundering, does this mean that we want to see banks become a crucial part of the justice system? What about the rights to privacy and confidentiality? (Levi, 1991*a*, 1991*b*).

But we should not be too quick to assume that such *post hoc* philosophical dilemmas or justifications are the actual movers of political action. To explain the actual social weight given to these conflicting values we also need to provide a sociology of public policy choices. Starting from a Marxist perspective, Snider, for example, examines the dialectic between the state, business interests, pressure groups, public opinion, etc., in an attempt to explain the contrasting fate of different types of regulation (Snider, 1991, but see also the more hopeful analysis by Braithwaite, 1995). She argues that the resistance to effec-tive implementation of legislation concerning health and safety at work is explicable in terms of the fact that these laws are not in the interest of business itself (except where they can be used by large businesses to beat off the competition of smaller firms). Industry tends—with the collusion of the state—to balance the safety of workers against the increased costs of production. The victims of these crimes are diffuse, though not as diffuse as the victims of crimes against the environment. Antitrust legislation has more success because the state is interested in bringing down its costs as a major purchaser from the private sector, and at least parts of the business world are in favour of such laws. On the other hand the monopolies and cartels which already control many major markets provide firm resistance and, of less importance, unions may be ambivalent because of the threat to jobs which could follow the break-up of large conglomerations. Insider trading and stock market fraud, she claims, should encounter least resistance (as the success of the American Securities and Exchange Commission supposedly illustrates) because here the interests of the state and business coincide. Business needs to be able to raise money on the stock market and government does not want to have to bail out defrauded investors. We will be reminded of the social determination of these policy dilemmas if we accept that the control of ordinary crime may also have a number of negative side-effects, on the offender, his family, and the community, which tend to be ignored when the crucial criterion of policy choice is reduced to the need to continue business as usual.

The potential of criminology to contribute to shaping public policy concerning the best way to regulate white-collar crime is likely to increase in importance—but it is unlikely to be univocal in its recommendations. There will also always be a need for denouncing the 'crimes of the powerful' and their many illegal (as well as semi-legal and legal) ways of causing harm. But practical experience as well as theoretical considerations would suggest that there are severe difficulties in using the criminal law to control the groups most powerful within a given society (quite apart from the danger that tougher measures may have counter-productive effects for their victims). It is extremely difficult to get laws passed which represent a real threat to current economic interests and, even when such laws exist, when it comes to enforcement the choice may lie between stigmatization without effective regulation or regulation without stigmatization. On the other hand, as we have seen, it is too easily taken for granted that treating white-collar crime as crime, or fitting it into the usual paradigm of criminological explanation, goes hand in hand with a belief in the appropriateness of actually using criminal sanctions to reduce the behaviour; this is one reason why the argument over ambiguities has tended to get pulled one way or the other, depending on the practical conclusions the analyst wanted to draw. Yet there are many precedents for criminological explanations which do not indicate the individual offender as the key causal factor or the appropriate point of intervention (e.g. blocked opportunity theories of juvenile delinquency). Most of those who offer explanations which refer to capitalism or other structural factors of ordinary business life do, as it happens, also want to criminalize the offender (see e.g. Box, 1983). But, as Cohen has argued, a focus on crime in organizations needs to avoid seeking to assign blame in identifying the important links relevant to organizational outcomes (Cohen, 1977). Whether it is right for law to attach criminal penalties to certain behaviours, and to seek to enforce such penalties when this misses the underlying causes of such behaviour, is a question which goes beyond the scope of criminology. But it is certainly not a question confined to white-collar crimes nor irrelevant to many more ordinary ones.

Selected Further Reading

An essential starting point for studying what was originally meant by the label of white-collar crime remains Edwin H. Sutherland, *White-collar Crime: The Uncut Version*, New Haven, Conn.: Yale University Press, 1983. Useful overviews of the field include Steven Box, *Power, Crime and Mystification*, London: Tavistock, 1983; Michael Clarke, *Business Crime: Its Nature and Control*, Oxford: Polity Press, 1990; Hazel Croal, *White-collar Crime*, Milton Keynes: Open University Press, 1994; David Nelken, ed., *White-collar Crime*, Aldershot: Dartmouth, 1994; and David O. Friedrichs, *Trusted Criminals: White-collar Criminals in Contemporary Society*, Belmont: Wadsworth, 1996. More detailed case-studies can be sampled in Kip Schlegel and David Weisburd, eds., *White-Collar Crime Reconsidered*, Boston, Mass.: Northeastern University Press, 1992 and Michael Tonry and Albert Reiss, Jnr., eds., *Beyond the Law: Crime in Complex Organizations*, Chicago, Ill.: University of Chicago Press, 1993.

On the response to the sort of white-collar crime which gets dealt with by the ordinary courts in Britain the best work is that by Mike Levi, *Regulating Fraud*, London: Tavistock, 1987, and Mike Levi and Andrew Pithouse, *Victims of White-collar Crime*, Oxford: Oxford University Press, 1997. An original approach to the increasingly important problem of the overlap between white-collar and organized crime is Vincenzo Ruggiero, *Organised Crime and Corporate Crime in Europe*, Aldershot; Dartmouth, 1996.

REFERENCES

ARLACHI, P. (1985), *Mafia Business*. Oxford: Oxford University Press.

AUBERT, V. (1952), 'White-collar Crime and Social Structure', *American Journal of Sociology*, 58: 263–71.

BLOCK, A. (1991), *Perspectives on Organising Crime*. Boston: Mass./London: Kluwer.

BOX, S. (1983), *Power, Crime and Mystification*. London: Tavistock.

BRAITHWAITE, J. (1984), *Corporate Crime in the Pharmaceutical Industry*. London: Routledge Kegan Paul.

—— (1985), 'White-collar Crime', *Annual Review of Sociology*, 11: 1–25.

—— (1989), *Crime, Shame and Integration*. Cambridge: Cambridge University Press.

—— (1995), 'Corporate Crime and Republican Criminological Praxis', in F. Pearce and J. Snider, eds., *Corporate Crime*. 48–72. Toronto: University of Toronto Press.

BURGESS, E. (1950), 'Comment to Hartung', *American Journal of Sociology*, 56: 25–34.

CALAVITA, K., *et al.* (1991), 'Dam Disasters and Durkheim', *International Journal of the Sociology of Law*, 19: 407–27.

—— and PONTELL, H. (1992), 'The Savings and Loans Crisis, in M. Erdmann and R. Lundman, eds., *Corporate and Governmental Deviance*. Oxford: Oxford University Press.

CARSON, W. G. (1970), 'White-collar Crime and the Enforcement of Factory Legislation', *British Journal of Criminology*, 10: 383–98.

CARSON, W. G. (1974), 'Symbolic and Instrumental Dimensions of Early Factory Legislation', in R. Hood, ed., *Crime, Criminology and Public Policy*. 107–38. London: Heinemann.

—— (1980), 'The Institutionalisation of Ambiguity: The Early British Factory Acts', in G. Geis and E. Stotland, eds., *White-collar Crime: Theory and Research*. 142–73. London and New York: Sage.

—— (1981), *The Other Price of Britain's Oil*. Oxford: Martin Robertson.

COHEN, A. K. (1977), 'The Concept of Criminal Organisation' *British Journal of Criminology*, 18: 97–111.

CLARKE, M (1990a), *Business Crime: Its Nature and Control*. Oxford: Polity Press.

—— (1990b), 'The Control of Insurance Fraud: A Comparative View', *British Journal of Criminology*, 30.

CLINARD, M., and YEAGER, P. (1980), *Corporate Crime*. New York: Free Press.

COLEMAN J. W. (1985), *The Criminal Elite: The Sociology of White-collar Crime*. New York: St Martins Press.

—— (1987), 'Toward an Integrated Theory of White-collar Crime', *American Journal of Sociology*, 93, 2: 406–39.

—— (1992), 'The Assymetric Society', in M. Erdmann and R. Lundman, eds., *Corporate and Governmental Deviance*. 95. Oxford: Oxford University Press.

COOK, D. (1989), *Rich Law, Poor Law*. Milton Keynes: Open University Press.

COSSON, J. (1978), *Les Industriels de la Fraude Fiscale*. Paris: Editions du Seuil.

CROAL, H. (1989), 'Who is the White-collar Criminal?', *British Journal of Criminology*, 29: 157–74.

CULLEN, F., *et al.* (1983), 'Public Support for Punishing White-collar Criminals', *Journal of Criminal Justice*, 11: 481–93.

DELMAS-MARTY, M. (1990), *Droit Pénal des Affaires*. 2 vols. Paris: Presses Universitaires de France.

DOWIE, M. (1988), 'Pinto Madness', in Stuart L. Hills, ed., *Corporate Violence: Injury and Death for Profit*. Totowa, NJ: Rowman and Littlefield.

ECONOMIST (1992), 'The Blue Arrow Affair', 7 March: 23.

EDELHERTZ, H. (1970), *The Nature, Impact and Prosecution of White-collar Crime*. Washington, DC: US Government Printing Press.

FISSE, B., and BRATHWAITE, J. (1985), *The Impact of Publicity on Corporate Offenders*. Albany, NY: State University of New York Press.

GAMBETTA, D. (1994), *The Sicilian Mafia: An Industry of Private Protection*. Oxford: Oxford University Press.

GEIS, G. (1968), 'The Heavy Electrical Equipment Anti-trust Cases of 1961', in G. Geis, ed., *White-Collar Crime*. New York: Atherton Press.

—— (1990), 'Foreword', in G. S. Green, *Occupational Crime*. Chicago, Ill.: Nelson Hall.

GOFF C., and NASON-CLARKE, N. (1989), 'The Seriousness of Crime in Fredericton New Brunswick: Perceptions toward White-collar Crime', *Canadian Journal of Criminology*, 31: 19–34.

GOTTFREDSON, M., and HIRSCHI, T. (1990), *A General Theory of Crime*. Stanford, Cal.: Stanford University Press.

GREEN, G. S. (1990), *Occupational Crime*. Chicago, Ill.: Nelson Hall.

GROSS, E. (1980), 'Organisational Structure and Organisational Crime', in G. Geis and E. Stotland, eds., *White-Collar Crime: Theory and Research*. New York: Sage.

GROVES, W. B., and Newman, G., eds. (1986), *Punishment and Privilege*. Albany, NY: Harrow and Heston.

HARTUNG, F. (1950), 'White-collar Offences in the Wholesale Meat Industry in Detroit', *American Journal of Sociology*, 56: 25–34.

HAWKINS, K. (1984), *Environment and Enforcement: Regulation and the Social Definition of Pollution*. Oxford: Clarendon Press.

—— (1990), 'Compliance Strategy, Prosecution Policy and Aunt Sally: A Comment on Pearce and Tombs', *British Journal of Criminology*, 30: 444–66.

—— (1991), 'Enforcing Regulation: More of the Same from Pearce and Tombs', *British Journal of Criminology*, 31: 427–30.

—— and THOMAS, J. M., eds. (1984), *Enforcing Regulation*. Kluwer Nijhoff.

HILLS, S. L., ed. (1988), *Corporate Violence: Injury and Death for Profit*. Totowa, NJ: Rowman and Littlefield.

HIRSCHI, T., and GOTTFREDSON, M. (1987),

'Causes of White-collar Crime', *Criminology*, 25: 949–74.

— and GOTTFREDSON, M. (1989), 'The Significance of White-collar Crime for a General Theory of Crime', *Criminology*, 27: 359–72.

HUTTER, B. (1988), *The Reasonable Arm of the Law?* Oxford: Clarendon Press.

KATZ, J. (1980), 'The Social Movement Against White-collar Crime', *Criminology Review Yearbook*, 161–84.

KELMAN, S. (1981), 'Substantive Interpretation in the Criminal Law', *Stanford Law Review*, 33: 591–67.

KRAMER, R. C. (1992), 'The Space Shuttle Challenger Explosion: A Case Study of State-Corporate Crime', in K. Schlegel and D. Weisburd, *White-collar Crime Reconsidered*. 214–43. Northeastern University Press

LANE, R. 1953 'Why Businessmen Violate the Law', *Journal of Criminal Law, Criminology and Police Science*, 44: 151–65.

LEONARD, W. N., and WEBER, M. G. (1970), 'Automakers and Dealers; A Study of Criminogenic Market Forces', *Law and Society Review*, 4: 407–24.

LEVI, M. (1981), *The Phantom Capitalists*. London: Gower Press.

— (1985), 'A Criminological and Sociological Approach to Theories of and Research into Economic Crime', in D. Magnuson, ed., *Economic Crime-Programs for Future Research*. Report No. 18. 32–72. Stockholm: National Council for Crime Prevention, Sweden.

— (1987), *Regulating Fraud*. London: Tavistock.

— (1991a), 'Pecunia Non Olet; Cleansing the Money Launderers from the Temple', in *Crime, Law and Social Change*, 16: 217–302.

— (1991b), Regulating Money Laundering', *British Journal of Criminology*, 31: 109–25.

— (1991c), 'Fraudulent Justice? Sentencing the Business Criminal', in P. Carlen and D. Cook, eds., *Paying for Crime*. 86–108. Milton Keynes: Open University Press.

— and NELKEN, D., eds. (1996), *The Corruption of Politics and the Politics of Corruption*, special issue of the *Journal of Law and Society*, 23: 1.

— and PITHOUSE, A. (1997), *Victims of White-collar Crime*. Oxford: Oxford University Press.

MCBARNET, D. (1991), 'Whiter than White-collar Crime: Tax, Fraud Insurance and the Management of Stigma', *British Journal of Sociology*, 42: 323–44.

MAGNUSSON, D., ed. (1985), *Economic Crime—Programs for Future Research*. Report No. 18. Stockholm: National Council for Crime Prevention.

MANN, M. (1985), *Defending White-collar Crime*. New Haven, Conn.: Yale University Press.

MILLS, C. WRIGHT (1963/1943), 'The Professional Ideology of Social Pathologists', in C. Wright-Mills, *Power Politics and People*. 525–52. New York: Oxford University Press.

NEEDLEMAN, M. L., and NEEDLEMAN, C. (1979), 'Organizational Crime: Two Models of Crimogenisis', *Sociological Quarterly*, 20: 517–28.

NELKEN, D. (1983), *The Limits of the Legal Process: A Study of Landlords, Law and Crime*. London: Academic Press.

— (1991), 'Why Punish?', *Modern Law Review*, 53: 829–34.

— (1994), 'Whom Can you Trust? The Future of Comparative Criminology', in D. Nelken, ed., *The Futures of Criminology*. 220–44. London: Sage.

— (forthcoming), 'The Globalisation of Criminal Justice', in M. Freeman, ed., *Law at the Turn of the Century*. Oxford: Oxford University Press.

NEW YORK STATE ORGANIZED CRIME TASK FORCE (1988), *Corruption and Racketeering in the New York City Construction Industry*. New York: Cornell University Press.

PASSAS, N. (1990), 'Anomie and Corporate Deviance', *Contemporary Crises*, 14: 157–78.

— and NELKEN, D. (1993), 'The Thin Line between Legitimate and Criminal Enterprises: Subsidy Frauds in the European Community', *Crime, Law and Social Change*, 19: 223–43.

PEARCE, F. (1976), *Crimes of the Powerful: Marxism, Crime and Deviance*. London: Pluto.

— and SNIDER, L. (1995), 'Regulating Capitalism', in F. Pearce and L. Snider, eds., *Corporate Crime*. 19–48. Toronto: University of Toronto Press.

— and — (1990), 'Ideology, Hegemony and Empiricism: Compliance Theories of Regulation', *British Journal of Criminology*, 30: 423–43.

— and — (1991), 'Policing Corporate "Skid Rows"', *British Journal of Criminology*, 31: 415–26.

PONTELL, H. N., and CALAVITA, K. (1993), 'The Savings and Loan Industry', in M. Tonry, and A. Reiss, Jnr. eds. *Beyond the Law: Crime in Complex Organizations*. 203–47. Chicago, Ill., University of Chicago Press.

REICHMAN, N. (1992), 'Moving Backstage: Uncovering the Role of Compliance

Practices in Shaping Regulatory Practices', in K. Schlegel, and D. Weisburd, *White-collar Crime Reconsidered*. 244–68. Chicago, Ill.: Northeastern University Press.

RUGGIERO, V. (1996), *Organised Crime and Corporate Crime in Europe*. Aldershot: Dartmouth.

ROYAL COMMISION on CRIMINAL PROCEDURE (1980), *Prosecutions by Private Individuals and Non-Police Agencies*. Research Study No. 10. London: HMSO.

SAVELSBERG, J. (1994), *Constructing White-collar Crime: Rationalities, Communication, Power*. Philadelphia, Penn.: University of Pennsylvania Press.

SGUBBI, F. (1990), *Il Reato Come Rischio Sociale*. Bologna: Il Mulino.

SHAPIRO, S. (1984), *Wayward Capitalists*. New Haven, Conn.: Yale University Press.

—— (1989), 'Collaring the Crime, Not the Criminal: Reconsidering "White-Collar Crime"', *American Sociological Review*, 55: 346–65.

SIMPSON, S. S. (1992), 'Corporate Crime Deterrence and Corporate Control Policies Views from the Inside', in K. Schlegel and D. Weisburd, *White-collar Crime Reconsidered*. 289–308. Boston, Mass.: Northeastern University Press.

SLAPPER, G. (1991), *Corporate Manslaughter: An Examination of Prosecutorial Policy*. LLM dissertation, University College, London.

SMITH, D. J., Jr. (1980), 'Paragons, Pariahs and Pirates: A Spectrum-based Theory of Enterprise', *Crime and Delinquency*, 26: 358–86.

SNIDER, L. (1991), 'The Regulatory Dance: Understanding Reform Processes in Corporate Crime', *International Journal of the Sociology of Law*, 19: 209–36.

STANLEY, C. (1992), 'Serious Money: Legitimation of Deviancy in the Financial Markets', *International Journal of the Sociology of Law*, 20: 43–60.

STEFFENSMEIER, D. (1989), 'On the Causes of White-collar Crime: An Assessment of Hirschi and Gottfredson's Claims', *Criminology*, 27 : 345–58.

STONE, C. (1975), *Where the Law Ends: The Social Control of Corporate Behaviour*. New York: Harper and Row.

SUTHERLAND, E. H. (1949), *White-collar Crime*. New York: Holt Rinehart and Winston.

—— (1983), *White-collar Crime: The Uncut Version*. New Haven, Conn.: Yale University Press.

SZASZ, D. (1986), 'Corporations, Organised Crime and the Disposal of Hazardous

Waste: An Examination of the Making of a Criminogenic Regulatory Structure', *Criminology*, 24: 1–27.

TAPPAN, P. (1947), 'Who is the Criminal?', *American Sociological Review*, 12: 96–102.

TIEDEMANN, K. (1974), 'Kriminologische und Kriminalistische Aspekte der Subventionserchteichung', in H. Schafer, ed., *Grundlagen der Kriminalistik, 13/1: Wirtschaftskriminalität, Weissen-Kragen Kriminalität*. Hamburg: Steinton.

TOMBS, S. (1995), 'Corporate Crime and New Organizational forms', in F. Pearce and L. Snider, eds., *Corporate Crime*. 132–47. Toronto: University of Toronto Press:.

VAN DUYNE, P. (1993), 'Organised Crime and Business Crime Enterprises in the Netherlands', *Crime, Law and Social Change*, 19: 103–43.

VAUGHAN, D. E. (1983), *Controlling Unlawful Organizational Behaviour*. Chicago, Ill.: University of Chicago Press.

VOLD, G., and BERNARD, T. (1986), *Theoretical Criminology*. 3d edn. Oxford: Oxford University Press.

WEISBURD, D., WHEELER, S., WARING, E., and BODE, N. (1991), *Crimes of the Middle Classes: White-collar Offenders in the Federal Courts*. New Haven, Conn. and London: Yale University Press.

WHEELER S. (1992), 'The Problem of White-collar Crime Motivation', in K. Schlegel and D. Weisburd, *White-collar Crime Reconsidered*. 108–24. Boston, Mass.: Northeastern University Press.

—— MANN. K., and SARAT, A. (1988), *Sitting in Judgement: The Sentencing of White-collar Crimes*. New Haven, Conn.: Yale University Press.

YEAGER, P. C. (1991), *The Limits of Law: The Public Regulation of Private Pollution*. Cambridge: Cambridge University Press.

—— (1995), 'Management, Morality and Law, Organizational Forms and Ethical Deliberations', in F. Pearce and L. Snider, eds., *Corporate Crime*. 147–68. Toronto: University of Toronto Press.

YOUNG, T. R. (1981), 'Corporate Crime: A Critique of the Clinard Report', *Contemporary Crises*, 5: 323–36.

ZIGLER, J. (1990), *La Suisse Lave Plus Blanc*. Amsterdam: Uitgeverij Balanss.

ZIMRING, F., and HAWKINS, G. (1993), 'Crime, Justice and the Savings and Loans Crisis', in M. Tonry, and A. Reiss, Jnr. eds., *Beyond the Law: Crime in Complex Organizations*. 247–92. Chicago, Ill.: University of Chicago Press.

26

Drugs: Use, Crime, and Control

Nigel South

The next government should give this whole issue far higher priority as an international problem that can only, as things stand, finance the expansion of organised crime; corrupt officialdom; boost money laundering; and increase drug related crime [Downes, 1997: 11].

The earlier version of this chapter opened with a different quotation, remarking on the surprising lack of British criminological work on drugs and alcohol then available. This deficiency has been greatly remedied in the intervening period. This chapter updates the earlier review. The focus is on the British experience,[1] with some reference to the international literature.

The structure of the chapter is as follows: 'Legal Status and Properties of Drugs'; 'A Review of Post-war Trends in Drug Use'; 'The Control of Drugs in Britain (and Internationally)'; 'Drugs, Alcohol, and Crime'. The 'Conclusion' identifies a number of trends and notes some key issues for the 'drugs debate' at the end of the century.

LEGAL STATUS AND PROPERTIES OF DRUGS

This chapter is principally concerned with *illegal* drugs, that is those designated illegal for purposes of possession or use or trade according to various domestic laws and international agreements and treaties (Bruun *et al.*, 1975). In Britain the classification of illegal drugs is a tiered system reflecting official perceptions of their relative harmfulness. Thus Class A includes heroin and other strong opiates, cocaine, LSD, and Ecstasy (MDMA); Class B includes cannabis, amphetamines and barbiturates and Class C tranquillizers, some mild stimulants, and now Anabolic Steroids. Maximum penalties are highest for Class A, lowest for Class C.

---

[1] It should be noted that here, and generally throughout the literature, reference to Britain or the United Kingdom, still tends to mean England and Scotland. The lack of substantial work on Wales and Northern Ireland persists, though the Institute for the Study of Drug Dependence (ISDD) (1994: 100–1) notes several recent surveys on drug-prevalence and some related crime. Murray (1994) discusses available data on drugs in Northern Ireland.

Various texts describe the properties and effects of illegal and legal drugs, the most accessible, authoritative review being the Institute for the Study of Drug Dependence's (ISDD's) *Drug Abuse Briefing* (1996*a*). In terms of general effects, drugs such as alcohol, barbiturates, tranquillizers, and heroin have a depressant effect on the nervous system, whilst caffeine, amphetamines, cocaine, and tobacco are stimulants. Cannabis, LSD, and Ecstasy distort perception, cannabis having a relaxing effect, LSD producing hallucinogenic effects, while Ecstasy and similar drugs may produce restlessness and mild visual distortions. However, actual behaviour and subjective experience will be strongly shaped by other influences, such as culture, context, and expectations, and, of course, relative purity versus adulteration of drugs.

A REVIEW OF POST-WAR TRENDS IN DRUG USE

In this section I shall review information on the prevalence and incidence of post-war drug use, then discuss variations relating to social categories (age, etc.), and, finally, debates concerning 'drugs and social deprivation'.

We should first emphasize that legal drugs are also sources of numerous problems. Prescribed and 'over the counter' (OTC) drugs may lead to misuse or dependency. The number of tranquillizer prescriptions issued has been declining since 1979; nonetheless estimates of patients with problems with these drugs have ranged between 250,000 and 1.25 million, and their mass marketing ensures a level of availability which inevitably leads to seepage of such drugs into the illegal market.

Undoubtedly, the Royal College of Psychiatrists (1986, 1987) was correct to call *alcohol* 'Our Favourite Drug' (Bunton, 1990). According to Alcohol Concern (1991: 8):

UK alcohol consumption reached a post-war peak of 7.7 litres per head of total population in 1979, falling by more than 10% to 6.9 litres per head in 1982 but with a strong recovery to 7.4 litres in 1988. . . . Overall alcohol consumption is . . . twice as high as in the mid 1950s, but still much lower than in the 18th and 19th centuries.

In the mid-1990s alcohol is more widely available through commercial outlets than ever, and despite legal restrictions around 60 per cent of young people between 13 and 17 are likely to have bought alcohol from a pub or off-licence (ISDD, 1996*a*: 40). Unsurprisingly, there has recently been an increase in specialist concern about alcohol use and young people (Royal College of Physicians, 1995), with particular attention being focused on new designer drinks, such as very strong 'white' ciders, and fruit flavoured alcoholic drinks ('alco-pops') (McKeganey *et al.*, 1996).

By contrast with deaths caused by illicit drugs—a few hundred per year (see ISDD, 1996*b*)—mortality associated with alcohol is considerably higher, with estimates ranging from 5,163 to 40,000 (Alcohol Concern, 1991: 4–6). Tobacco has only relatively recently faced widespread social disapproval: in Britain about 32 per cent of people over 16 smoke tobacco, and Action for Smoking and Health (ASH) estimates tobacco related deaths as around 110,000 per year. (ISDD, 1996*b*).

However, such comparison is not straightforward support for the view that illegal drugs should be decriminalized because 'they cause less harm than legal drugs'. The point is that legal drugs are widely available, illegal drugs are not; the health related consequences of widespread availability of presently illegal drugs are not known. Furthermore, the legality of some drugs does not mean that they do not contribute to 'legal harms', i.e. crime. Alcohol, for example, contributes to crimes of violence and social disturbance, drink and driving offences (including manslaughter deaths); whilst both alcohol and tobacco, despite their legal status, are commodities which (more than ever) attract smuggling activity to profit from avoidance of taxation, as well as hijacking and theft.

A Short History of Drug Use Trends since the Second World War

In this section, I am concerned with the post-war period. I shall outline features of nineteenth-century drugs and alcohol use, and the related origins of medical, moral, and legal reactions in the later section on 'Controls'.

During the Second World War, illegal drug use attracted little attention. Trafficking routes were obviously disrupted world-wide, and in the United States, where heroin and opium had been a pre-war source of concern, supply was diminished. Interestingly, amphetamine achieved unusual, if limited, approval in the war—and again later in the Vietnam conflict—being used by servicemen and flyers to relieve fatigue and anxiety.

The 1950s

During the early 1950s in Britain, both drug availability and official activity in this sphere were minimal. However, by the late-1950s an 'emerging drug sub-culture' seemed to be detectable in the West End of London, associated with one particular supplier (Spear, 1969: 254), and bohemian and jazz cultures were associated with some drug use (MacInnes, 1985; Spear, 1969; Tyler, 1995: 169–70, 315–16). The availability of cannabis and of heroin, albeit in limited circles, was sufficient to move the Ministry of Health to bring together in 1958 an Inter-Departmental Committee on Drug Addiction under Sir Russell Brain. The Committee reported in 1961. Meanwhile in the United States, resurgence of popular concern (and legislative response) was rather more evident—as reflected in 'popular accounts' of the new youth fashions of the 1950s and a purported 'link' between rock and roll, the mixing of black and white youth, communism and drugs (Inciardi, 1986: 103–4).

The 1960s

Examining trends for the late 1950s, the 1961 Brain Committee reported that drug supply was 'almost negligible' and Britain was deemed to have no drug problem worth speaking of (Ministry of Health, 1961: 9). Policy was a continuing success. However, as Spear (1975) has observed, the 1960 addict statistics were not completed in time for the Committee to consider them, and, in fact, the number of addicts known to the Home Office was rising (Mott, 1991: 78); and it continued to rise—from a 1960 figure of 454 to 753 by 1964 (*ibid.*: 79). Whilst these were extremely modest rises compared to developments in the 1980s, they suggested a new source of addicts had appeared who were not in touch with the medical services—new and younger British users, as well as a group of Canadian heroin addicts who had arrived in London in the late 1950s. The period of the 1960s is now culturally enshrined as one of artistic and political protest, anti-establishment sentiments, and an embrace of alternative cultures. Drug use (particularly cannabis, amphetamine, and heroin) increased among youthful groups drawn from the middle- and working-class mainstream. The Brain Committee was re-convened in 1964 to report on changes occurring and its recommendations, produced in 1965, were to have a major impact upon the British response to serious drug use (Mott, 1991: 78–9; Pearson, 1991: 176–8).

In September 1967, quantities of 'Chinese' heroin were seized by the Metropolitan Police (Mott, 1991: 82), whilst around this time, several doctors had started prescribing methedrine ampoules (methylamphetamine) on a large scale, and this had fed a growing illicit market (*ibid.*; Leach, 1991). For many official, medical, and media observers the irresponsible prescribing of opiate-type drugs by a small minority of either gullible, or profit-motivated, private practitioners was at the heart of a changing West-End drug scene (Ruggiero and South, 1995: 19–23). Elsewhere, for others, cannabis and psychedelic drugs 'fitted' (Young, 1971; Willis, 1978) with the style, values, and music of the hippy counter-culture (Auld, 1981), but it should also be remembered that for most youth, the intoxicant most widely used was alcohol.

From the 1970s to the 1980s

Between 1973 and 1977, only 4,607 new 'addicts' came to official notice (Giggs, 1991: 153). With regard to use of opiates then, much of the 1970s presented a picture of relative stability, low rate of growth, and localized concentration, predominantly in the London area. By the tail of the decade however, there were signs of change, and the 1980s presented a profoundly different picture.

During the late 1970s, new sources of heroin were noted. Contrary to official perceptions that increasing availability was once again a sign of seepage from generous prescribing onto an illegal market (DHSS, 1984), in fact a whole new era was opening. Political shifts in the Golden Crescent region of South West Asia (Iran, Pakistan, and Afghanistan) had opened new supply routes, while

Iranian exiles had converted capital into heroin after the downfall of the Shah and imported it to Britain. Cheap, high-purity heroin was becoming readily available and with a tighter prescribing policy adopted by the new Drug Dependency Units (DDUs; see below), and police success in dealing with the supply of Chinese heroin, the new sources of availability stimulated the market (Mott, 1991: 85). Of crucial importance for the spreading popularity of heroin use in the next few years was that the new heroin imports could be *smoked*, the prepared drug being heated and the smoke being inhaled ('Chasing the dragon'), snorted, or sniffed (Auld *et al.*, 1986). These methods overcame the deep psychological barrier that use of the needle for injecting posed to many; suddenly use of the most fascinating drug of all was more accessible and the mode of administration familiar and 'ordinary' (Mott, 1991: 85–6). For some, familiarity with sniffing amphetamine or cocaine made the move from 'one white powder to another'—heroin, seem easy (Hartnoll *et al.*, 1984). 'Scoring smack' (Lewis *et al.*, 1985) was not difficult in the new drug markets; further it was of higher purity and cheaper in real terms than it had been four to five years before (Mott, 1991: 87–8). For the period 1981 to 1985, Home Office notifications of 'new addicts' came to 21,030 (Giggs, 1991: 153) and their spatial distribution around the country represented such an unanticipated spread that many commentators adopted an 'epidemic' analogy (for a critical view of this analogy see Young, 1987: 426–8).

Ditton and Speirits (1982) were among the first to note and discuss this 'new wave' of heroin addiction in areas beyond London, in this case the Glasgow metropolitan area. Taylor (1993) updated the local picture with a particularly useful emphasis upon the drug using patterns of women. Work in Edinburgh was carried out against a background of extremely high rates of HIV transmission between drug injectors and partners (Robertson, 1987), and together with that of Parker *et al.* (1988) examining trends in the Wirral, Merseyside, confirmed a picture of the very rapid spread of heroin use, *at least in some areas* (Donoghoe *et al.*, 1987; Giggs, 1991; Pearson *et al.*, 1986). Based on the breadth of available data (from national statistics, e.g. 'notifications' of addicts to the Home Office, as well as local surveys), ISDD (1990: 9) suggested that 'using a multiplier of five, it can be estimated that between 74,000 and 112,000 people in the UK were dependent on opiates at some time in 1989'.

The late 1980s also saw considerable official and popular concern over 'crack'. This was prompted by alarmist warnings from a visiting representative of the US Drug Enforcement Administration. For the end of the 1980s data suggested that use of 'crack' in Britain appeared to be quite limited (Shapiro, 1989). Despite a rise in numbers of seizures of crack, from thirty in 1988 to 350 in 1990, 'these were still less than a fifth of all cocaine seizures and netted less than a kilo of the drug' (Shapiro, 1991: 40).

Overall, at the end of the 1980s, heroin remained important, cocaine was increasing in availability but still of *relatively* minor concern, and the market was dominated by cannabis and amphetamine (ISDD, 1990: 9). However, in 1988 Acid House music had already heralded a whole new wave of dance-drug culture, bringing with it the return of LSD and new acquaintance with MDMA/Ecstasy (Shapiro, 1997).

The 1990s and into the twenty-first Century

By the early 1990s, Britain had developed what remains a 'poly drug' culture. Of course, mixing drugs, purposeful selection for different effects and/or use of alternatives to the preferred 'drug of choice' in time of scarcity, were not new phenomena. What seems new is the integration into young people's drug cultures of an approach to available drugs as a hedonistic smorgasbord. Here, there is use of a variety of illegal and legal drugs (Davis and Ditton, 1990); young people 'pick 'n' mix' (Parker and Measham, 1994); there is subcultural and commercial cross-over of 'labelling', e.g. Parker *et al.* (1996: 24–5) point out that one of the top selling strong ciders popular among their sample is called 'White Diamond', one of the more popular ecstasy brand names is 'Diamond White'; and so on. No longer is drug culture supposedly hidden away in a *sub*-culture; now it is argued that it is part of mainstream culture, and the question is 'how much of the popular open ground can drugs colonize?'. The Ecstasy dance-culture has proved distinctive, not least in being a culture of relatively 'ordinary' people whose 'deviance' rests in being enthusiasts of dance and particular dance-drugs. The results of the large survey of cohorts of 14–16-year-olds in North-West England by Parker *et al.* (*ibid.*) suggest that a pattern of 'normalization' of drug use is under way within the lifestyles and attitudes of those surveyed. Others (Shiner and Newburn, 1996; forthcoming) find this a contentious and exaggerated conclusion. This emerging debate about 'normalization' or otherwise is one of tremendous significance, not least in its implications for drug-laws and the planning and providing of services.

In the late 1980s and at the start of the 1990s, heroin availability was still high, but there were some signs and predictions that its use was in decline. However heroin use has seen a significant resurgence, with record seizures in 1995 having no discernible effect on street price, and the drug now appealing to three 'new' types of users: 'crack users who have self-medicated with heroin; young socially deprived users (the "new scag kids"); and graduates from the dance scene' (Shapiro, 1996: 8–9).

Furthermore, despite HIV/AIDS concerns (*British Journal of Addiction*, 1992), (now somewhat de-emphasized in policy and practice), injection is still a major mode of administration. Amphetamine and other drugs long administered intravenously remain popular, whilst certain prescription drugs and preparations for pain relief or travel sickness can be prepared from pill form for injection, with attendant serious health problems (Gilman, Traynor, and Pearson, 1990).

The broad picture for the early-1990s remains applicable to the mid-late 1990s: one of continuing widespread availability of a great variety of drugs, use being shaped by familiar factors such as local supply (Fraser and George, 1988; George and Fraser, 1989; Giggs, 1991: 171), peer-group fashion and influence (Parker *et al.*, 1996; Shiner and Newburn, 1996), contexts of use (Auld, 1981; Becker, 1963; Zinberg, 1984), preferred styles of consumption (Auld *et al.*, 1986; Pearson, 1987*a*), and purpose or intent e.g. sociability, 'retreatism', 'energy' supply, and so on (Pearson, 1992*a*); on most of these points see Parker *et al.* (1996) and Shiner and Newburn (1996).

Some recent research has reported on drug use trends between the early and mid-points of the decade. Miller and Plant (1996) report on a 1995 study with a sample of 7,722 school pupils aged 15 and 16 finding 'Almost all . . . had drunk alcohol, . . . 42.3% had at some time used illicit drugs, mainly cannabis. 43% of boys and 38% of girls had tried cannabis. . . . Levels of drug use . . . were higher in Scotland than in England, Wales or Northern Ireland' (*ibid.*: 394); 'for all types of drug experimentation, there seems to have been a large rise since 1989' (*ibid.*: 397). As Hough (1996: 10) reports: 'The British Crime Survey (Mott and Mirlees-Black, 1995) and the Four Cities Survey (Leitner *et al.*, 1993) suggest that around a third of people between 16 and 30 have taken illegal drugs at some time in their lives.' For Parker *at al.* (1996) the 'unequivocal' conclusion was that 'for young people growing up in urban North-West England during the 1990s, exposure to drugs is the norm' (but see comments above).

Most crack or cocaine users in Britain would seem to be poly-drug users (Shapiro, 1991: 42; Mirza *et al.*, 1991; Ditton and Hammersley, 1996), not using excessively and not developing heavy dependence (*Druglink*, 1992*a*: 6). Evidence is mixed about the degree to which crack or cocaine is becoming a favoured drug among African-Caribbean users (Shapiro, 1991: 42). As would be expected, it is major metropolitan centres that report concentrations of cocaine use; enforcement and treatment statistics probably underestimate the amount of cocaine and crack available on the market, but there are no clear indications that use is likely to increase dramatically in the foreseeable future (*ibid.*: 44). Other drugs of recent concern include Ketamine, (Druglink, 1992*b*: 6), and GHB (colloquially, 'GBH'; see also ISDD, 1996*c*)

Of methodological interest is that, since the mid–late 1980s and through the 1990s, data have been provided by both sophisticated surveys (variously large-scale, longitudinal, comparative), and detailed locality studies (the most authoritative digest and commentary on national, regional, and local studies is ISDD, 1994). The latter have increasingly adopted a more comprehensive, 'multi-agency' approach, drawing together information from the statutory and non-statutory agencies as well as street-level, family, and community respondents (Drug Indicators Project, 1985; for the 1990s, see the series of papers from the Home Office Drugs Prevention Initiative, e.g. Duke *et al.*, 1996; Shiner and Newburn, 1996).

Social Divisions and Drug Use: Class, Gender, Ethnicity, Age, and Sexuality

While perhaps more abundant than in the past, our available data must nonetheless be treated with caution.

Class: historically, illegal drug use has always crossed class boundaries. During the early years of the century, and into the 1920s, drug users ranged from medical professionals, who had abused their access to opiates and other drugs, through 'therapeutic addicts' of different class backgrounds, who had become dependent during the course of pain-killing treatment with opiate-type drugs, through working-class users of opiate-based patent medicines, to recreational users of illegal drugs. The latter were relatively few in number but included those on the bohemian fringes of high society; opium smokers were found in Limehouse, East London, whilst, across the city, in the West End some young, white male criminals and female prostitutes were using cocaine recreationally (Parssinen, 1983: 216–17; Kohn, 1992). However, while there was some considerable concern over drugs in this period (Kohn, 1992), evidence suggests that the extent of use was limited.

Apart from some sensationalist journalism of the 1950s concerned with cannabis as a 'social menace', linked to immigrant black culture and threatening to the white *status quo* (Tyler, 1995: 169–70), it was the 1960s that represented the next significant period of class and drug use change. Alarm over the (modest) rise in availability of opiate drugs in the West End of London was in part related to the emergence of a new type of user—young and working class. Middle-class youth also used heroin but were particularly associated with images of a counter-culture: the 'hippy' life-style and drugs such as cannabis and LSD. By the 1970s, drug use clearly cut across all social classes. None the less, social class remains an important variable as regards patterns of use. Leitner *et al.* (1993) found, roughly speaking, that members of high social-class groups are the more likely to encounter and try drugs, but that members of lower-class groups who become users show patterns of use that are more dangerous, in terms of frequency, and mode, of use.

Gender: studies of women and drug use (illegal or legal) remain relatively, but less, rare than previously (see Ettorre, 1992; Ettorre and Riska, 1995; Maher, 1995; Taylor, 1993; Erickson and Watson, 1990; Henderson, 1990; McConville, 1991; Rosenbaum, 1981*a*, 1981*b*; South, 1994: 400–1). Research has shown a lower prevalence of problem drug use for women than men, except in relation to tranquillizers, though the gap may be evening out somewhat in some circumstances (Giggs, 1991:166). It is no longer true that drug *use* is predominantly male to the extent that it has been, although drug *dealing* probably remains so, and there are familiar social prejudices operating against women in the drugs economy which explain this (Ruggiero and South, 1995: 138–41; Taylor, 1993). Similarly, a familiar pattern of an unequal burden of care falls upon female partners or relatives (principally mothers) of male heroin (or other heavy drug) users (Auld *et al.*, 1986).

Ethnicity: drug use within ethnic minorities has received even less research attention than drug use by women. The 'Four Cities' (Leitner *et al.*, 1993) study and data from the 1992 British Crime Survey (BCS) (Mott and Mirrlees-Black, 1995) suggest similar proportions of white and African-Caribbean drug use in the population (including cannabis), but whites were more likely to have used amphetamine or hallucinogens. Asian drug use remains low generally (one in ten Asians reported drug use), however suggestions from the street as well as the BCS are that heroin use is increasing among Asian youth, and Webster (1996) found some increased use of cannabis and other drugs in a small sample of Asian youth. Tyler (1995: 203, 212–14) reports on relationships between black populations and localized drug cultures, whether involving heroin or crack-cocaine. Pryce (1979) discussed cannabis in the context of African-Caribbean youth and street culture, and Oswald (1982) provided a very useful account of the significance of 'ganja' for Rastafarian youth and some of the cultural reasons for its use among other young blacks. Possession of cannabis by black youth and police 'stop and search' tactics were a background factor in several instances of inner-city unrest in the 1980s (Pearson, 1991) and the manufacture and sale of 'crack' have been associated by the police and media with illegal Jamaican immigrants involved in 'Yardie' gangs (Tyler, 1995: 214–25). Whatever the (questionable) extent of such an association, in terms of *use* in the African-Caribbean community, cannabis is the favoured and most widely used drug. Research in Lewisham by Mirza *et al.* (1991) suggested some cocaine use in the black community, very little amphetamine use, and that heroin and other opiates account for only about 20 per cent of main drug use. Indeed, amidst the growth of heroin use in Britain in the 1980s, one striking feature was the relative absence of black users.

Prison and probation service statistics suggest that a high proportion of ethnic minority individuals (compared to the white population) have come to the attention of the criminal justice system for drug-related reasons. However, while such statistics tell us something about, for example, police arrests of black and other minorities for possessing, and the high number of court cases involving cannabis, they tell us little or nothing about actual patterns of drug use. One reason that we know so little about such use is because the counselling and advice services which provide information about street level use among white clients simply do not seem to attract minority clients. Only recently have research and service initiatives attempted to understand why this should be so (Awiah *et al.*, 1992; but see also *Druglink*, 1992c: 5; Black Drug Workers Forum, 1996–). Ruggiero and South (1995: 116–19) have described the situation of blacks in the drug-dealing economy as mirroring their secondary and exploited status in the legitimate economy, but also pointed to both the practical research problems and 'political correctness' which have inhibited further criminological research in this area, problems which have not hampered or been detrimental to the rich history of research on drug problems and minorities in the United States (e.g. Trimble *et al.*, 1992).

Age: use of illegal drugs is largely confined to the young. However, it should be remembered that in the nineteenth century, presently illegal drugs were used by or administered to a wide age-range (from infancy to senility), and in the late twentieth century one characteristic of the drug scene is that it also embraces a wide age-range of different kinds of drug users: from those who were twenty-something in the 1960s and are now fifty-something, to those who are in their teens today. None the less, with fluctuations over time and in different areas, the majority of drug users can be described as young, relatively few being over 35, with this being consistent regardless of class or gender. Limited data relating to ethnicity means no firm conclusions can be drawn on this point, but cannabis use by some African-Caribbean smokers is not tied to white cultural associations with youth (Oswald, 1982).

In terms of endeavour to chart drug-using 'careers', a preoccupation of many studies has been the question 'when did drug (legal and illegal) use start'? Evidence suggests that teen (and early teen) years are significant (Parker *et al.*, 1996; Swadi, 1988). Most studies suggest that, for most young people, experimentation (and little more) with illegal drugs involves cannabis, amphetamine, and other Class B drugs, and from the early 1990s onward, occasional to regular use of Ecstasy and LSD (Class A). A clear portrait of dance-drug 'career-use' is obviously unavailable at such an early stage, although very high-profile ecstasy-related deaths (sixty between 1989 and 1996), have meant the demonization of the drug in the eyes of the media and authority (Shapiro, 1998). Nonetheless, in the careers of most drug users, 'escalation' to 'harder' drugs and long-term continuation of use are confined to a minority.

Sexuality: male gay culture: in 1996, *Gay Times* (1996: 17–37) produced a survey of 685 gay men, over half of whom use drugs, one in six taking Ecstasy weekly and, interestingly, 20 per cent using cocaine regularly, particularly as part of the clubland scene; 33 per cent used *both* Ecstasy and amphetamine, reflecting a multi-drug culture. I know of no comparable survey concerned with lesbian drug cultures.

Debates about the Correlation between Drug Use and Social Deprivation

Various studies in the 1980s undertook an examination of hypothesized links between drug use and socio-economic conditions. Peck and Plant (1986) found significant and positive correlations between average annual unemployment statistics, cautions, and convictions for drug offences, and notifications of users in treatment between 1970 and 1984. Pearson *et al.*'s (1986) study in the North of England found that areas with a high concentration of use frequently exhibited very high rates of unemployment, single-parent families, limited mobility, and other indices of social disadvantage. In a decade in which debates about the construction of an 'underclass' have raged even more fiercely (Lister, 1996), it is also important to note Pearson's (1987*b*) elaboration on this finding, that multiple deprivation and drug misuse may be mutually reinforcing in an area that is already socially deprived, contributing to a downward spiral of the social and economic 'reputation' of the area, availability of amenities, credit-availability and so on. The 'Four City' (Leitner *et al.*, 1993) study incorporated 'booster group' samples from measurably deprived areas but did not find *significantly* higher rates of use compared to the main ('non-deprived') samples. While there may be some correlation between drug use and high rates of deprivation, this may also be an inverse relationship, where localities with high indices of deprivation nonetheless have *low* rates of use; similarly, there are socially advantaged, middle-class areas with *high* rates of drug use. The explanatory variable proposed here, and one which probably has fairly universal validity, is that of availability. Where supply and distribution conduits are well developed, then class and other social factors may have diminished significance in predicting onset and spread of use. This would seem to be the case in relation to the recent dance-drug culture.

THE CONTROL OF DRUGS: BRITAIN AND THE GLOBAL CONTEXT

During the nineteenth century, opiate preparations were commonly marketed and widely used throughout Europe and North America (Berridge and Edwards, 1987; Musto, 1973). On both sides of the Atlantic, opiate-based medicines and tonics were used as an analgesic, as a sedative, a febrifuge, a remedy for cholera, and as children's 'quieteners'. Apart from such therapeutic use, reports between the 1830s and 1860s describe the *recreational* use of opiates in factory districts, seaports, and the Fenlands (Parssinen, 1983: 212) and the literature of the period indicates experimentation and familiarity with the drug in literary and bohemian circles (Berridge and Edwards, 1987: 49–61). The question of *control* was, however, emerging.

The Industrial Revolution and other social developments promoted interest in the subject of 'public health', particularly in relation to the fitness of the urban working class. In this context, the use of opiates gave rise to some concern (although use of opiates for pleasure and pain-relief among the middle class apparently received less disapproval and attention at this point, Berridge and Edwards, 1987: 97–112, 49–61). A different provocation of public discussion about opiates was their common use as a means of sedating children— a practice which led to many cases of children dying of opium poisoning (Parssinen, 1983: 207; Pearson, 1991: 170). Additionally, from around the 1870s onward, sensational accounts of Chinese 'Opium Dens' in the Limehouse area of London's East End provided a sinister stereotype of corruption and alien culture to associate with opium use, along with ideas of Oriental conspiracy and 'clandestine organization' (Kohn, 1992: 18–20).

The hypocrisy of such sentiments lies, of course, in the great efforts that Britain herself had put into developing the nineteenth-century international opium trade, exporting the drug from India to China (Berridge and Edwards, 1987) and even engaging in two wars (1839–42 and 1856–8) to secure the future of the trade, when China sought to reduce its opium importation and associated problem of rising addiction.

In light of this connection, it is perhaps less surprising to find that domestic control over opiate use in Britain remained limited. Nonetheless, in the latter half of the century, moral opposition to opium use and Britain's opium trade was growing. Further, there was a shift in perception of opium use from seeing it as an indulgence or habit, as in the first part of the nineteenth century, to viewing it as a 'problem', classifiable in various ways by the new medical discourses (Berridge, 1979). Medical practitioners attempted to bring the treatment and control of those dependent upon opium within the provisions of the 1888 Inebriates Act which applied to the voluntary detention of 'habitual drunkards'. In this particular endeavour to extend professional power they failed. Pharmacists had fared better, with the 1868 Pharmacy Act removing morphine and opium derivatives from the shelves of general stores and giving their profession the monopoly of dispensing, a system eventually extended to patent medicines by the 1908 Poisons and Pharmacy Act (Pearson, 1991: 171). Modest restrictions on supply developed but control of *use* remained unaddressed by legislation. 'Insanity', certified to be the result of addiction, could lead to institutionalization and the 1890 Lunacy Act was sometimes applied, but only with the passing of the 1913 Mental Deficiency Act did legislation embrace 'any sedative, narcotic or stimulant drug' within the definition of an 'intoxicant', and thereby allow for the detention of 'moral imbeciles' in asylums or under the guardianship of another (Pearson, 1991: 171).

As well as 'medical entrepreneurs', 'moral crusaders' were also active in seeking the introduction of new control measures. In 1874, the Society for the Suppression of the Opium Trade was formed, largely supported by Quaker campaigners, and in time drawing Parliamentary support from the Radical wing of the Liberal party (Berridge and Edwards, 1987: 176–80). In terms of political developments, the Report of the Royal Commission on Opium, published in 1895, has been widely regarded as something of a 'whitewash' (*ibid.*: 186–7), but the important *economic* development was that, even as moral and political debates waxed and waned, by the early 1880s the 'signs of decline in the importance of opium as an Indian revenue item were already visible' and 'by 1885, China was probably producing just as much opium as she imported. . . . In the 1890s, exports of Indian opium began to decline absolutely as well as relatively' (*ibid.*: 178). By 1906, it was neither an act of great moral conviction nor one incurring great financial loss for a new Liberal Government to commit Britain to phasing out opium exports from India to China.

By the early years of the twentieth century a polarity had emerged between the medical view of drug use as addictive or a 'disease', and a moral view of it as a vice to be controlled by law and punishment (Berridge, 1979; Smart, 1984). However, the concerns about vice that finally introduced the first real penal response to drug use in Britain arose, not as a result of peace-time lobbying, but in the context of war-time emergency. During the early years of the First World War, press and public were aroused by threats to the troops posed by prostitution and cocaine! (Kohn, 1992: 23–66). Similarly, concern about the productivity of war workers in the factories prompted calls for restriction of alcohol availability. Therefore, in 1916, Regulation 40 B of the

Defence of the Realm Act (DORA), made possession of cocaine or opium a criminal offence except for professionals such as doctors, or where supplied on prescription (Kohn, 1992: 44; Spear, 1994: 4). DORA Regulations also introduced the licensing laws (Dorn, 1983: 64–5) restricting opening times of public houses and regulating alcohol sales (relaxed only in the 1980s). Of course, it is the latter measure which had the greatest long-term impact, but with regard to the cocaine 'threat', legal control was now exercised and unauthorized possession was criminalized. A significant step had been taken and the role of the Home Office was brought to centre stage in the control of drugs (Tyler, 1995: 312–13; Pearson, 1991: 172; Berridge, 1978: 293).

Subsequently, various influences such as the United States' push for Prohibitionist policies, its increasing ability to set the agenda for drug control (but not alcohol control, which members of the League of Nations had no interest in), and the peculiar *de facto* ratification of the 1912 Hague Convention on Opium through ratification of the post-war Versailles Treaty (Article 295) (Bruun *et al.*, 1975: 12), encouraged further government legislation in the form of the Dangerous Drugs Acts of 1920 and 1923. These made possession of opiates and cocaine illegal except where prescribed by a doctor. The Home Secretary gained powers to regulate the manufacture, distribution, and legitimate sale of these drugs and policing practice and public perception reflected the new status of illegal drugs as a criminal matter (Parssinen, 1983: 217; Pearson, 1991: 172).

Control in relation to alcohol went in the opposite direction however. DORA regulations were at first ignored and then lifted, and as Steele (1986: 7) puts it, 'The Licensing Act of 1921 set the seal upon a movement which continues to this day. . . . The 1961 Act matched with the 1964 elimination of retail price maintenance provided a drink entrepreneurs charter. Outlets of all kinds could, and did, multiply.'[2]

The 'British System'

Following DORA and then the 1920 Act, the new Ministry of Health had vied with the Home Office for authority over the formulation of subsequent regulations. For a few years, the Home Office made 'consistent attempts to impose a policy completely penal in direction' (Berridge, 1984: 23). The response from the Ministry of Health and medical lobby was the 1924 Rolleston Committee, generally cited as the origin of the 'British system' of response to drugs. Chaired by Sir Humphrey Rolleston, President of the Royal College of Physicians, the 1926 Report of the Departmental Committee on Morphine and Heroin Addiction aimed to define the circumstances in which prescription was appropriate and the precautions to be taken to avoid the possibility of abuse (Ministry of Health, 1926: 2; Tyler, 1995: 313–14; Pearson,

---

[2] On the history of alcohol control policy see Bunton, 1991; Dorn, 1983; Williams and Brake, 1980; and Central Policy Review Staff, 1979 (denied publication in Britain).

1991: 173; Spear, 1994: 5). Hence, the Committee offered recommendations allowing for prescription of heroin and morphine to enable gradual withdrawal, or to 'maintain' a regulated supply to those judged unable to break their dependence or those whose lives would otherwise suffer serious disruption.

Given the influential view that this development represents a profoundly different path from that taken by the United States, it is important to make two points. First, the view that Rolleston held of addicts was resolutely that they were 'middle class, middle aged, often from the medical profession and invariably an abuser of morphine. About five hundred such individuals existed nation-wide, and rather than representing a threat they were to be pitied' (Tyler, 1995: 313); only as 'an afterthought' was passing consideration given to the existence of working-class use of opiate-based patent medicines (*ibid.*).

Secondly, the contention that it was the nature of the British response which avoided the creation of the criminal activity associated with the US experience can be challenged by looking at when such criminality actually emerged in the United States. As Parssinen (1983: 219) suggests

Although the Harrison Act (of 1914) probably strengthened the connections between narcotics addiction and the urban underworld, these connections were firmly in place long before 1914. The increasingly hard-line American enforcement and treatment policy during the 1920s was less cause than effect of the emerging criminal-addict [see also Inciardi, 1986: 16–17].

In other words, in terms of numbers of drug users, and the drugs-crime relationship, the British and US experiences were divergent already, ahead of the passing and subsequent interpretation of legislation.[3]

In Britain the drugs issue was receding in significance even as the Rolleston Committee deliberated: medical and recreational addiction was in decline. Press and public fascination persisted and sensational stories still made news (Kohn, 1992), but generally such subcultures of use as had existed were fragile, and scarcity, related expense, and law enforcement efforts deterred both users and suppliers of cocaine and opiates. As Parssinen (1983: 220) argues, 'in Britain as in America, drug policy was less a cause than it was the effect of the addict population. Put simply, narcotic drug maintenance was accepted in Britain in the 1920s because the addict population was small, elderly and dying off.'

Recent writers (Smart, 1984; Pearson, 1991; Dorn and South, 1994; Kohn, 1992) agree that apparently dominant medical discourses of the time were in fact shadowed and influenced by strong moral and penal positions. Nonetheless, one reason for a general acceptance of the success of 'Rolleston'

---

[3] How the 1914 Harrison Act was interpreted in its application is important. Initially set out as a taxation and regulatory code rather than a penal measure aimed at users, it was the influence of the US Treasury and decisions of the Supreme Court that changed the nature of the Act, contributing to the conditions necessary for expansion of the illegal drug market (Inciardi, 1986: 14–15)

is that, through the 1930s to the late 1950s, Britain did indeed experience no serious problems with illegal drugs. As Berridge and Edwards (1987: 254) observe, however, the contrast in this period between the American and British experience had rather less to do with the triumph of the Rolleston philosophy than with the 'enormously different social conditions in the cities of the two countries—different patterns of poverty, urban decay, ethnic underprivilege and entrenched criminal organization'.

Despite such domestic calm, Britain has been signatory to a long, and continuing, string of control measures throughout the century. As Bean (1974: 35) noted, the political momentum of international control initiatives meant that, between 1920 and 1964, all of the significant drugs legislation passed in Britain was less a response to any real domestic problem and more the result of willingness to meet national obligations set by international treaties (Ruggiero and South, 1995: 99–101). The 1960s, however, brought a change to this reassuring assessment of the domestic scene. Nationally as well as internationally, drugs were a new social problem, associated with new challenges to society. In March of 1961 in New York, the UN Single Convention on Narcotic Drugs was signed, drawing together provisions of nine previous treaties signed between 1912 (Hague Convention) and 1953 and extending control to cover the plants, poppy, coca, and cannabis. The UN International Narcotics Control Board was established the same year to monitor the working of the Convention.

Back in London, with evidence of new patterns of drug availability, the Brain Committee was reconvened. Amphetamine was a new problem (pep pills and purple hearts were associated with new youth cultures) and new legislation—the 1964 Drugs (Prevention of Misuse) Act and accompanying regulations—were introduced to control possession, production, and supply. This Act also introduced aspects of the Single Convention into British law and a 1966 modification added LSD to its provisions for control. In 1965 the Dangerous Drugs Act ratified the Single Convention and the Brain Committee published its new report. This was to lead to major legislation in the form of the Dangerous Drugs Act of 1967. Prescribing was to continue, but general medical practitioners were to be more tightly controlled by regulations and were to 'notify' to the Home Office new addicts not previously in treatment. The aim was to intervene to prevent seepage of prescribed opiates (and similar drugs) into the illicit market. Specialist Drug Dependency Units or 'clinics' were opened from 1968, initially in and around London, as the centres of expertise in the treatment of addiction. Henceforth, only their doctors could prescribe heroin and cocaine; however, General Practitioners were not barred from prescribing other drugs (such as methadone and diconal) for treatment and some GPs have played a significant role in working with users (Glanz and Taylor, 1986) although the majority of GPs have resisted involvement (Advisory Council on Misuse of Drugs (ACMD), 1989).

In practice, the new clinics sought to break client dependence on street drugs by prescribing injectable (soon changed to oral) methadone as a 'substitute' drug, without the same attractions and thought suitable for planned detoxification and cessation of prescribing, or 'maintenance'. Thus medical *management* of addiction was endorsed, within a framework which also placed doctors in a role with responsibility for *regulating* supply and *controlling* the spread of dependence (Pearson, 1991: 178–81).

Debates aired around the dichotomies of 'soft' and 'hard' drugs, and 'users' and 'dealers', during the 1960s were reflected in the 1971 Misuse of Drugs Act which made an important distinction between possession offences and supply offences. Drug users could be characterized as sad and weak types, corrupted by drug dealers who were very bad types; the former needed counselling or treatment; the latter deserved the harshest punishment. Hence, despite the perceived liberalism of many legislative developments in these 'permissive' years, drugs received rather conservative treatment: even a call by the respectable Advisory Council on Drug Dependence (Wootton Committee, 1968) for liberalization of the law relating to cannabis was dismissively rejected (Young, 1971: 198–201). In Europe in 1971, the Pompidou Group was established to exchange information on drug problems, and at the UN a Convention on Psychotropic Substances included drugs not covered by the Single Convention (such as amphetamine, LSD).

The recent status of drug control as a 'war' on drugs can perhaps be traced to the mobilization in the United States of public and official sentiment against drugs by President Nixon (Inciardi, 1986: 117–18). In the early 1970s crime was ranked as pre-eminent among the urban problems of the United States, with drugs close behind, although we might also note that drug related corruption in police services also caused some alarm in these same years and prompted inquiries in London and New York. In the 1980s President Reagan launched a new (or renewed) 'war on drugs' and the coincidence of the conservative politics of the President and the new British Prime Minister, Mrs Thatcher, set the tone for the rhetoric—but, thankfully, not all of the practice—of drug control in that decade.

Drugs in Britain in the 1980s became a political and politicized issue (Stimson, 1987), yet one which attracted a political consensus which (generally) persists (Berridge, 1991: 179). Such consensus enabled the government to take the earlier proposals of the Hodgson Committee (convened by the Howard League in 1980, reporting in 1984) to make provision for the recovery of the profits of crime, jettison its liberal recommendations relating to sentencing, and introduce the far reaching Drug Trafficking Offences Act (DTOA) of 1986 (Dorn *et al.*, 1992: chapter 10; Dorn and South, 1991). Overall, while tough enforcement priorities led the government's agenda, nonetheless, the tradition of compromise was maintained in criminal justice, health, and social policy responses (Dorn and South, 1994; Collison, 1993: 383; Henham, 1994: 224–5). The government's 'strategy document', *Tackling Drug Misuse* (first published 1985), proposed five fronts for action largely organized around enforcement, but including prevention and treatment.

In the mid-1990s, the government has introduced a new set of 'drugs strategies', one each for England, Scotland, Wales, and Northern Ireland, and with some regional variation in emphasis. The England strategy, 'Tackling Drugs Together' (1995) adopts a community crime-prevention emphasis, forming multi-agency Drug Action Teams to promote local initiatives. 'Drugs in Scotland: Meeting the Challenge' (1994) is more clearly a document with a harm-minimization slant (Ashton, 1994, 1995*a*); these have been followed by 'Forward Together: A Strategy to Combat Drug and Alcohol Misuse in Wales' (1996) and 'Drug Misuse in Northern Ireland' (1995).Yet already there have been pessimistic forecasts about what such strategies may or may not achieve; for example, Ashton's (1995*b*) recent prognosis regarding the English strategy suggests that by the time of the strategy review in 1998, treatment and prevention are unlikely to have proven themselves a great success, funding will be as inadequate as ever, and drug use will have continued to rise despite the new 'co-ordination structures'. All of this will:

leave a choice of declaring the policy a success because without it things would have been worse, a failure because the tide has not been turned, or a promising venture in need of adjustment or a greater impetus. Like the proverbial decision over whether the glass is half full, this choice will be determined as much by what the decision-makers want to see as by any scientific calculation [Ashton, 1995: 6].

Law Enforcement and Criminal Justice

In 1973 a Central Drugs and Illegal Immigration Unit had been established at Scotland Yard, becoming the Central Drugs Intelligence Unit in 1974, with a brief to serve the United Kingdom, though remaining part of the Metropolitan Police. The National Drugs Intelligence Unit (NDIU) superceded this in 1985, providing a joint police and customs services' 'clearing house' for the collation and networking of information. (Dorn *et al.*, 1992: 152–8; 1991). Throughout the country the Regional Crime Squads established seventeen specialist drugs wings to help them undertake investigations that crossed local police force boundaries. These developments reflected the recommendations of the Association of Chief Police Officers' (ACPO's) Broome Committee report (reprinted in Dorn *et al.*, 1992). Internationally, co-operation was highlighted, customs liaison officers were posted abroad and Britain's encouragement of drug crop-substitution or eradication programmes and rural development projects was given a higher profile. In 1992 the new National Criminal Intelligence Service became operational, drawing together various police intelligence databases, including the NDIU (on drugs law enforcement see Collison, 1995; Wright *et al.*, 1993; Dorn *et al.*, 1992; 1991) An early attempt to provide an economic appraisal of the cost-effectiveness of expenditure on drugs-related police and customs enforcement argued that such a task is seriously hampered by the inadequacy of the empirical data available (British Journal of Addiction, 1989); this probably remains true, although the advent of perform-ance indicators and other measures of 'success' are supposed to have facilitated auditing of criminal justice effectiveness (e.g. Chatterton *et al.*, 1995). The roles of the Crown Prosecution Service and the Probation service are discussed in Hough (1996: 23–5).

Enforcement Statistics

Possibly, one way of measuring the 'impact' of enforcement is by looking at the detection of drugs—reflected, it is presumed, in annual seizure statistics. This is, of course, a partial measure, but one which government, enforcement agencies, and media place great emphasis upon. Years of high seizure are greeted as either (a) a sign of the increased success of enforcement efforts and/or (b) a reflection of an increasing incoming tide of drugs that requires investment of yet further enforcement resources to stem it. Whichever view is taken, seizure statistics should be treated with caution: just one or two seizures of very large amounts can inflate the figures unrepresentatively; correspondingly, low seizure figures do not mean low importation or distribution, for several large consignments may have avoided enforcement agencies' attention. Generally, customs and the police (in most countries) are unlikely to feel able to claim much more than a 10 per cent interception rate (Stimson, 1987: 49–50).

Law enforcement statistics, then, are subject to severe limitations. They can reflect only detection, seizures, and convictions; drugs offences are rarely reported in the same way as robberies or assault (ISDD, 1990: 15). At street level of enforcement, various police forces and strategy commentators have supported the idea of 'low level policing' aimed at disrupting street markets (Lee, 1996) and diverting users from criminalization to counselling and treatment (Gilman and Pearson, 1991). This is a development encouraged by recent policy recommendations (ACMD, 1991, 1994) and can incorporate the now-widespread use of 'referral cards' or leaflets giving details of helping agencies, which police can hand out when cautioning or in other less formal encounters (Hough, 1996: 21–3). The rise of increased use of cautions and of referral to drugs agencies is of great significance because, as Henham (1994: 231) therefore observes:

The dominant trend in simple possession cases is towards release with a caution, thus reflecting a trend towards general relaxation of penalties for soft drug use in European countries; . . . It is apparent that *de facto* de-criminalisation of soft drug use and possession has occurred in certain European countries without necessitating deliberate sentencing policy changes.

It should be emphasized, of course, that as these developments are *not* the result of centrally directed deliberate policy change, they are patchy: employed in relation to some drugs (e.g. cannabis, heroin) but not others (cocaine offences do not usually receive a caution: Collison, 1994*a*: 28). Similarly some police force areas (e.g. Merseyside, parts of London) have been more willing to pursue cautioning and referral schemes than others.

Sentencing

Data on national sentencing trends have not been the subject of much scrutiny. Dorn *et al.* (1992: chapter 10) discuss the rising trend in penalties, noting their expressive and symbolic function as well as how their escalation runs counter to any policy goals aimed at reducing use of custody. Briefly, this escalation has developed as follows. In 1972, i.e. before the 1971 Misuse of Drugs Act (MDA) had come into effect, sentences were frequently of between six months and two years. By 1976 when the MDA had been in operation for three years, the numbers of persons receiving a prison sentence had approximately doubled by comparison with 1972, and of these the majority received sentences of between six months and three years. From 1983 onwards, the courts could refer to the Lord Chief Justice's guidelines (from *R.* v. *Aramah* [1983] CLR 371–3) which suggested a raised tariff, subsequently amended upward as a result of *R.* v. *Bilinski* [1987] CLR 783 (Dorn *et al.*, 1992: 185–6). In practice, sentences of ten years or more have become common; the 1985 Controlled Drugs (Penalties) Act raised the maximum penalty for trafficking in Class A drugs from fourteen years to life imprisonment; and with the implementation of the 1986 DTOA, such sentences may also include asset confiscation (Dorn and South, 1991; Levi, 1991). So far seizure of assets has not proved as efficacious a tool as hoped: early evidence suggests that, while the number of confiscation orders and the amounts forfeited have been rising (respectively, from 203 and £1.2 million in 1987 to 1,000 or so and £10.1 million at the beginning of the 1990s (Collison, 1994*a*: 36)), so too have the scale and profits of the drugs economy

The trend in increasing penalties has continued into the 1990s: the 1991 Criminal Justice Act introducing further penalties for trafficking; the 1993 Criminal Justice Act extending confiscation orders (Thomas, 1994); and broad provisions of the 1994 Criminal Justice and Public Order Act affecting drug users, ravers, prisoners, and other groups. Increases in fines for possession or supply of certain drugs will lead to an inability to pay, and further imprisonment of more drug users for fine defaulting, and the former Home Secretary had proposed minimum seven year sentences for repeat drug dealers. Sentencing guidelines for the courts have already been amended post-*Bilinski*, by the Court of Appeal which further argued that where quantities of drugs are involved, sentencing should be based more on weight and purity rather than, as in the past, value at street level which had simply meant that if availability increased and the street price fell, then the appropriate sentence on the tariff would also 'fall' (i.e. increase in drugs on the street, meant decrease in sentence in the court). Provisions of the DTOA and subsequent legislation have had to respond to various amendments but into the 1990s, the working principles and spirit of the original act remain in force through the 1994 Drug Trafficking Act.

Home Office data on 'offenders dealt with' (Home Office, 1991) show a consistent rise in the number of persons 'found guilty, cautioned or dealt with by compounding for drugs offences' between 1986 and 1990. The pattern is not the same for all drugs offences, e.g. heroin declines; cocaine, LSD, cannabis all rise (ISDD, 1991). But, overall, for 'all drugs', the trend is upwards. In 1992, over 65 per cent of the UK drug offender population were aged below 24 years, and 90 per cent were male (ISDD, 1994: 6). 'Unlawful possession' is far and away the most frequent offence dealt with.

Conclusions about the impact of sentencing are difficult to draw; referring to heroin users, Mott (1989: 32) observes that 'there has been very little research specifically aimed at investigating the effect of court sentences, or of different types of sentence, on the subsequent drug using and criminal behaviour of heroin users. What there is suggests that sentences of imprisonment may have little effect'. Except, that is, that more than ever it must be appreciated that prison is not an effective environment for reducing commitment to a drug-using lifestyle. Drugs are widely available in prisons, and the sharing of injecting equipment makes risk of HIV/AIDS, or forms of hepatitis, a serious problem (ACMD, 1993). Drug testing seems to be encouraging a shift to drugs that are harder to detect, which includes a shift from cannabis to opiates.

Drugs, Alcohol, and Crime

Drugs and Crime

The illegality of certain drugs obviously makes their possession, supply, or preparation and manufacture an offence (McBride and McCoy, 1982: 145). But evidently the debate about the drugs/crime relationship is wider than this.

Typically, drug-related crime is non-violent and acquisitive, involving theft, shoplifting, forgery, or burglary (Chaiken and Chaiken, 1991) or prostitution (Plant, 1990). More serious drug-related crimes of violence, murder, large-scale trafficking, and money laundering occur and may be increasing in Britain— although by comparison with the United States they remain relatively infrequent (on the United States see various essays in Weisheit, 1990; Tonry and Wilson, 1990). In Britain today, as Hough (1996: 1) observes:

the costs sustained by victims of drug-related crime are substantial: crimes committed by dependent heroin users alone may involve losses of between £58 million and £864 million annually. The costs to the criminal justice system of dealing with drug misusers are similarly substantial: if drug-related crime absorbed 5 per cent of criminal justice resources, this would cost about £500 million.

Recent research on drug-crime careers of crack-cocaine and heroin users (Parker and Bottomley, 1996) suggests individual crack-cocaine users may be spending £20,000 per year, and dependent heroin users £10,000 per year, deriving their income largely from acquisitive crime, although benefits and legal work income also contributed. Other work (Collison, 1994*b*; Parker, 1996) has noted a greater hedonistic attachment to a consumption-oriented lifestyle among young users, and that petty crime is routinely engaged in for support.

Studies have largely focused on heroin and crime, tending to exclude more casual, recreational drug use (McBride and McCoy 1982: 143; but see Mott, 1985; Greenberg, 1976), and, since the 1980s on dealing/trafficking and crime. It remains important to remember that the majority of studies on 'drugs and crime' concern '*men*, drugs and crime'. Generally, as in criminology more broadly, drugs research has neglected research on women (Ruggiero and South, 1995: 138–41). A rough division may be made in the literature between studies suggesting that 'criminal lifestyles may facilitate involvement with drugs' and those suggesting that 'dependence on drugs then leads to criminal activity to pay for further drug use'.

'Involvement in Criminal Activity Leads to Drug Use'

Some studies (Mott and Taylor, 1974) provide evidence that a high proportion of heroin users were already involved in delinquent or criminal activities before they started using heroin or other drugs. McBride and McCoy (1982: 145) note that 'Eldridge (1952) argued that because heroin use was illegal, and the source and distribution of heroin was part of a criminal underworld . . . few non-criminal innocents were seduced into the initiation of heroin use'. Thus the argument would be that: (a) involvement in deviant/criminal-oriented sub-cultures or groups would be likely to lead a person to encounter the availability of drugs sold within that culture; (b) such a person would have a deviant lifestyle which would accommodate deviant drug use with relative ease; and (c) whilst money from criminal activity might then pay for the drugs, it was not drug addiction or use which led to the perpetration of crime.

Work in this vein follows the classic New York study by Preble and Casey (1969), which emphasized that it is the activity and lifestyle surrounding drug use, as much as drug taking itself, which is attractive to users. As described in this tradition of ethnographic and ecological perspectives, the hustling, enter-prising, dynamic life of the street user is quite the opposite of the stereotyped portrayal of the dazed and dozing junkie. In Scotland, studies by Hammersley and colleagues challenged the view that heroin use is a direct causal determi-nant of criminal activity (Hammersley *et al.*, 1989): although the two are related, use of other drugs is also related to crime (an obvious but often neglected point) and furthermore, it is a prior history of criminality that is the more important determinant of crime frequency. Thus, considering teenage drug users' involvement in crime, they observe that 'explanations of delin-quency are likely to be more relevant . . . than explanations invoking "drug addiction"' (Hammersley *et al.*, 1990: 1592). Importantly, Hammersley *et al.* found that moderate heroin users were not significantly more criminal than cannabis/alcohol users.

'Involvement in Drug Use Causes Crime'

Of course, other studies argue that there *is* a *causal* link, and 'drug use (particularly heroin) causes crime' (Chaiken and Chaiken, 1990: 204). Some crimes seem to have a clear relationship with drug use. In the early 1980s (and in the 1960s to a lesser extent) there was concern about break-ins to pharmacies with stocks of controlled drugs (Mott, 1986). Jarvis and Parker (1989) found that the criminal convictions of one group of heroin users doubled after they started using heroin regularly and concluded that 'addiction leads to acquisitive crime'.

The simple resolution of this debate is to agree with Nurco *et al.* (1985: 101) who sensibly suggested that 'the long and continuing controversy over whether narcotic addicts commit crimes primarily to support their habits or whether addiction is merely one more manifestation of a deviant and criminal life-style seems pointless in view of the fact that addicts cannot be regarded as a homogeneous group'. Hough (1996: 10–18) provides useful, further review of 'drugs and crime' studies.

Drugs, Crime and Drug Markets

Diversity and sophistication of organization is evident in drug markets, albeit that the British market is best characterized in terms of 'disorganized crime' rather than an image of 'Mafia' and 'Mr Bigs' (Ruggiero and South, 1995; Dorn *et al.*, 1992; Reuter, 1983). Use of violence and of firearms by traffickers has reportedly been rising (O'Connor, 1995), and money laundering has developed in various ways (Levi, 1991; South, 1992). Most studies of drug markets have concerned heroin and/or cannabis; local crack and cocaine markets are discussed in Bean and Pearson (1992); Ruggiero and South (1995: 118–19); Miles (1994). For some participants involved in large-scale trafficking/dealing, high rates of profit are achievable, although for users engaging in small-scale dealing and non-drug crimes then the returns per crime are probably small and the total *per annum* quite modest.

The picture of drug markets as fragmented, with a diversity of participants from highly successful entrepreneurs (Hobbs, 1995) to petty-criminal users and dealers, often caught within the criminal justice system (Ruggiero and South, 1995), has certain strategic implications. Advisably, enforcement efforts should employ intelligence sources to target the specific vulnerabilities of the different participants in drug markets. Of course, drug trafficking is a global phenomenon, and while it may not be characterized by monopolistic control it does involve criminal cartels and conspiracies, which in turn may involve 'legitimate' actors such as state security agencies and corporations (Chambliss, 1989; McCoy *et al.*, 1972; Levi, 1991: 301).

Treatment, Rehabilitation, Drugs, and Crime

The issue of *treatment* of drug users by the medical system raises several key criminological questions, e.g. what kinds of treatment are most efficacious in (a) reducing reliance on the illegal market for drug supply, and (b) reducing related criminal activity engaged in to generate funds for purchasing drugs? Unfortunately, as Jarvis and Parker (1990: 29) have remarked 'evidence of the efficacy of medical treatment, whatever form it might take, is neither plentiful nor conclusive'. Hough (1996: 26–46, 51) provides a very thorough review of treatment under probation and court orders, in therapeutic communities and prison settings, and of a substantial sample of evaluations.

One key underlying assumption of the practice of 'maintaining' drug users on methadone or other substitutes (or even heroin and cocaine) has been that this will remove the need to resort to criminal activity and erode the profitability of an illegal market in drugs (Mott, 1989: 32). Some significant studies (e.g. Weipert *et al.*, 1979; Bennett and Wright, 1986) reported maintenance having little clear impact on criminal activity. One careful and important study (Hartnoll *et al.*, 1980) compared the effect of prescribing injectable heroin versus oral methadone on users' criminal activity and, with various qualifications, concluded that there was no indication of 'a clear overall superiority of either (treatment) approach' in terms of achieving abstinence or of reducing illicit drug use and associated criminal activity (Mott, 1989: 32). Of course, drug users in treatment are the minority: during the 1970s, moves toward a more disciplinary style of managing drug-user patients meant less chance of a prescription for heroin and instead methadone maintenance, or detoxification with reducing doses. These options were and are unattractive to many users, discouraging take up of treatment by some and encouraging drop out by others. However, there is evidence that 'flexible' drug treatment programmes *can* retain patients *and* reduce criminal activity (Jarvis and Parker, 1990: 32). If studies clearly and unequivocally showed that treatment results in decline in criminal activity, then the case for *compulsory* treatment (Johnson, 1989) would, no doubt, be put forward more frequently and with more force. However the evidence does not provide such certainty. Jarvis and Parker (1990) noted that many users felt they were 'growing out of drugs' or were weary of 'hassle' from the police, hence the reasons they were receiving treatment, and the success of treatment outcomes (measured as less likelihood of using illicit sources of drugs or committing offences) may have less to do with treatment *per se* and more to do with personal biography and situation. On the other hand, Hough (1996: 47) argues the evidence suggests that *at the very least*, 'coerced treatment appears to be no less effective than voluntary treatment', that the criminal justice system could administer such regimes, and that 'drug testing provides a technology to make this coercion meaningful'. Hough does however note both ethical (*ibid.*: 3) and motivational (*ibid.*: 48, 50–1) problems that would arise in relation to coerced treatment programmes.

In summary, studies are by no means unanimous in their conclusions about the impact of treatment upon crime behaviour. A number suggest that unrealistic goals and unattractive abstinence orientations will lead to client drop-out, possibly increased involvement in crime, and a 'chaotic' lifestyle (Hartnoll *et al.*, 1980; Pearson, 1991). Other approaches suggest tailored therapeutic programmes can be effective, and that methadone treatment can help reduce acquisitive crime rates in areas of heroin-based drug markets (Parker and Kirby, 1996), although the new poly-drugs scenes are unlikely to respond to such programmes. Broadly, Hough's (1996) exhaustive review is interestingly optimistic and positive about the prospects for effective interventions and impacts.

A key concept for practice that emerged in the 1980s became the standard practice philosophy for the 1990s—this is harm minimization. Arguably not a new idea and familiar in relation to alcohol misuse ('Don't Drink and Drive!') the concept was developed further in relation to illegal drugs and concerns about HIV transmission, the aim being to reduce legal, social, and financial, as well as health, harms. Harm minimization first received 'official' endorsement in the pre-AIDS, 1984 ACMD *Prevention* report. This report concluded that policy and practice should be developed to (a) reduce the risk of initial drug misuse, and (b) reduce the harm associated with misuse. Although now somewhat de-emphasized, it was most evidently HIV/AIDS and the considerable impact this had on British drug policy that substantially influenced practice. ACMD (1988, 1989) reports on AIDS provided the legitimation for a whole new wave of developments, including syringe exchange schemes to draw injecting users into contact with services, supply clean injecting equipment and provide harm-minimization advice (for a broad review of the sex, HIV, and drugs issues, see Donoghoe, 1992). A major contribution to the success of such initiatives has been changes in policies adopted by the police service in many areas.

Alcohol and Crime

Since the 1960s, road accidents and deaths related to drinking and driving have attracted increasing attention from the police and various community groups. This higher profile and tougher penalties and enforcement seem to have had an impact, and fatalities and serious injuries attributable to drinking and driving fell significantly between 1979 and 1989 (Alcohol Concern, 1991: 24–6). However groups such as Alcohol Concern argue that much public education still needs to be done; there have been calls to reduce the 'drink-drive limit' further and, in many areas, the police regularly mount high-profile anti-drink-driving campaigns.

During the 1980s, concern and discussion grew about the health problems and social harm caused by alcohol, and particularly its use by young people (British Medical Association, 1986; Royal College of Psychiatrists, 1986; Mott, 1990). A recurrent theme has been the extent to which alcohol consumption is responsible for certain forms of criminal behaviour (Russell, 1993). This has been a concern of long-term, follow-up studies examining criminal careers and drinking careers. These suggest that 'criminality and alcohol abuse tend to run in parallel, as both have their peak incidence in young adults and tend to diminish with age. Those who continue with heavy drinking and petty crime into mid-life tend to become habitual drunkenness offenders' (d'Orban, 1991: 298). The latter have, at various times, been a source of moral, medical, and penal concern since the nineteenth century and in turn faced fines, prison or treatment programmes in various forms (Johnstone, 1996: 33–100, provides a valuable history of medical and penal approaches to 'the inebriate').

Of course, concerns about the relationship between alcohol and crime are not new. According to Lombroso:

Alcohol . . . is a cause of crime, first because many commit crime in order to obtain drinks, further, because men sometimes seek in drink the courage necessary to commit crime, or an excuse for their misdeeds; again, because it is by the aid of drink that young men are drawn into crime; and because the drink shop is the place for meeting of accomplices, where they not only plan their crimes but squander their gains . . . it appears that alcoholism occurred oftenest in the case of those charged with assaults, sexual offences, and insurrections. Next came assassinations and homicide; and in the last rank those imprisoned for arson and theft, that is to say, crime against property [Lombroso, 1911/1968: 95–6].

As Collins (1982: p. xvi) observes, dominant opinions about the role of alcohol in criminal behaviour have probably changed little, more research may have been done but its sophistication has not necessarily improved greatly, and the prisoners that Lombroso interviewed for his research have been followed by later generations of prisoners, asked similar questions, despite greater awareness of the problems inherent in generalizing from such respondent groups. Conclusive findings seem elusive however: Collins (*ibid.*: 289) writes, 'The consistency and strength of the alcohol-crime empirical association is sufficient to justify the inference that alcohol is *sometimes* causally implicated in the occurrence of serious crime. Questions of *how* alcohol exerts its crimi-nogenic influence have not been satisfactorily answered' (emphasis added). More recently, Light (1994: 55–8) concurs that there has been an 'assumed link' between alcohol and crime, but all we can really conclude is that 'alcohol does not *directly* cause crime, but that it may be implicated indirectly.' (*ibid.*: 63).

D'Orban (1991: 296) observes that 'studies of offences of violence show that the majority of the offenders, the victims or both, had consumed alcohol prior to their offence'. Other commentators note that whatever the alcohol *consump-tion* levels of the offenders (be it higher or lower than average), consideration of their drinking 'must be related to *specific* criminal incidents' (emphasis added) (Mott, 1990: 25; Murphy, 1983; Myers, 1982). McMurran and Hollin (1989) looked at the drinking habits of 100 English young offenders and found that where drinking and delinquency are 'functionally related, the drinking can be an antecedent to the commission of the delinquent act, or it can be a conse-quence of the crime' and 'the same degree of involvement between drinking and delinquency was evident for younger and older offenders' (*ibid.*: 386). Ramsay (1996) explores the question (inspired by research interest in illegal drug use and criminality) whether acquisitive crime is perpetrated to buy alcohol, again with some uncertainty about any causal connection; he also explores strategies aimed at reducing alcohol-related violence.

As with illegal drug consumption, *belief* about how alcohol is 'supposed' to affect behaviour, *coupled* with the influences of immediate social context and wider culture, are as important for the behavioural outcome as the amount of alcohol consumed (Mott, 1990: 25; Royal College of Psychiatrists, 1986; Pearson, 1992*a*). The Cambridge Study on Delinquent Development (West and Farrington, 1977; Mott, 1990: 25) described offenders who reported heavy drinking and engaging in fights as 'less socially restrained, more hedonistic, more impulsive, more reckless, and more aggressive than their non-delinquent peers. They smoked more, they drank more, they gambled more. They had a faster lifestyle, they went out more, they visited bars, discotheques and went to parties more often' (Mott, 1990). Recent studies of young offenders (Parker, 1996; Collison, 1996) suggest that alcohol and drugs have become even more central to a 'consumption-oriented' lifestyle, and that this lifestyle is funded by persistent petty crime. Data from the British Crime Survey have found that young men who have been drinking heavily are more likely than moderate drinkers to: (i) become involved in minor violent offences, and (ii) be victims of some crime of violence (Mott, 1990: 25–6). Evidence from a number of studies associates disorderly conduct offences with recent alcohol consumption, the location of violent or disorderly conduct offences to be in or near licensed premises in 20–30 per cent of cases, the timing of such offences to be likely to follow the end of licensing hours, and to occur on a Friday or Saturday night and involve young men (Mott, 1990: 26). Similar findings resulted from investigation of the wave of 'lager lout' outbreaks of disorderly conduct which police and media reported as a serious problem in the normally quiet towns and villages of rural England (Tuck, 1989). Masculinity, alcohol, and violence are a complex relationship deserving further attention (Tomsen, 1997; Light, 1994: 63, 66). Brain (1986) examines (among other matters) 'the recurrent media claim that alcohol causes a percentage of the aggression we see in our everyday lives' and observes that 'the question "Does alcohol cause aggression" is . . . grossly over-simplistic' (*ibid.*: p. ii). Socialization and cultural expectations, stereotypes and labelling, circumstances and significant others, all play their part in shaping people's identities as 'aggressive' and as 'drinkers' (Borrill and Stevens, 1993). Such definitions change across time and cultures (Levine, 1983; Coid, 1986) and are also strongly influenced by positive and negative images of alcohol use in entertainment media and alcohol advertising.

CONCLUSIONS: TRENDS AND FUTURES

Theory

The sociological and criminological literature continue to draw on *anomie*, subculture, and labelling theories. Ruggiero and South (1995: 200–4) question whether these approaches are applicable in the European context at the end of the twentieth century. A number of classic studies representative of different theoretical traditions are reprinted in South (1995: volume 1) while Hough (1996: 8) very usefully summarizes non-sociological explanatory models of drug dependence ('moral', 'disease', 'behavioural') as well as three sociological models: 'coping' (drug use to cope with deprivation); 'structure' (drug use as 'work' and part of a meaningful lifestyle); and 'status' (drug use provides status within the subculture, and is a positive rather than negative life-situation).

Enforcement

European fora and other international bodies continue to place enforcement high on their agendas, although a recent European Union study of legislation and judicial practice in Member States has noted discrepancies between countries and urged more effective co-ordination (Leroy, 1992). Cross-border and globalized law-enforcement are now part of the 'war on drugs'. Drug-related anti-terrorism and anti-money-laundering strategies and agreements continue to develop.

Domestically we are seeing the further development of intelligence gathering and processing capabilities, now involving the Security Service. The National Criminal Intelligence Service (NCIS) is to be partnered by a new National Crime Squad, providing it with an operational arm, while a new customs investigation department has further strengthened the enforcement establishment aimed at drugs. Support for 'low-level policing' generally remains positive, although as Hough (1996: 20) notes this is also a costly strategy, both organizationally and in social terms. 'Embedding' this approach in proper community policing may be the way forward. Overall, enforcement and other drug-control policies must confront the likelihood that the 'war on drugs' is not one that can be won. If drug markets cannot be eradicated, then perhaps we should be asking 'what kind of drug markets are *least* undesirable?' and trying to shape them in that direction (Dorn and South, 1990).

Policy and Practice

Domestically, sentencing follows the harsh pattern the law enables. However, it is encouraging that the development of a pragmatic harm-minimization, referral, and diversion, response has been taken up by various police and probation services (Bild, 1992). It is to be hoped that despite problems that are well recognized genuinely multi-agency initiatives can take forward more imaginative and less 'punishment-obsessed' programmes of intervention and diversion for drug users. Recommendations in the ACMD (1991, 1994) 'criminal justice' reports are steps in this direction. Despite the slide of AIDS/HIV down the agenda of social concern, drug- and alcohol-related health issues must still be appreciated as having serious implications for the criminal justice system.

Futures

Policy and practice preoccupation with heroin, crack-cocaine, and now Ecstasy, LSD, and amphetamine-type drugs should not exclude consideration of other drug use. Cannabis is the key drug in the enforcement statistics, yet argued to be relatively harmless compared to traditionally designated 'dangerous drugs' (ACMD, 1982; Ashton and Shapiro, 1982: 9–10), and in the mid-1990s is clearly a recreational drug of choice for a significant population (Mott and Mirrlees-Black, 1995). Hence in Britain and Europe more widely, the question whether it justifies the enforcement resources expended upon it suggests that debates about legalization or decriminalization of cannabis use will continue, perhaps fuelled by pressures for recognition of the drug's therapeutic value in alleviating some painful conditions. The debate about overall decriminaliz-ation or legalization of drugs may gather further momentum in the late 1990s and beyond. Proponents (Nadelman, 1989; Stevenson, 1991; Graham, 1991; Release, 1992) argue that the costly, counter-productive and unsuccessful efforts of law enforcement as a response to drug use suggest legalization is a wiser alternative. It is suggested that availability would not mean unacceptable rises in use and that taxation of legal supply would provide funds for edu-cational, health, and counselling responses. Regulation would ensure purity levels, and hence reduce health hazards caused by adulterants, and legal avail-ability would remove the profit motive that drives the criminal market. Opponents (Inciardi and McBride, 1989; Wilson, 1990) argue that legalization *would* increase use, thereby increasing serious costs to society. More 'middle-road' commentators suggest that the impact of legalization and commercial-ization on third-world producer countries could be highly negative (Dorn, 1992) and that the frequently cited example of *de facto* decriminalization of cannabis—the Netherlands—is actually a case of a policy aimed at preserving 'market separation', keeping cannabis supply distinct from supply of drugs with an 'unacceptable risk' (*ibid.*: 111) Note however that the Netherlands' cannabis policy has undergone a degree of restrictive re-thinking recently (Horstink-Von Meyenfeldt, 1996: 103–4).

Despite criticisms of the 'treatment/enforcement' bifurcation of British domestic policy as largely mythical (Henham, 1994: 224–5), the early British tradition, promoted by the Rolleston report, did provide a crucial and symbolic foundation for subsequent innovations. By contrast, the former government's 'new' drug strategies do not seem to offer coherence, or the likelihood of deliv-ering a better deal for drug users, or fewer drug problems for society. The final word here should rest with the late Bing Spear, who did so much to shape British drugs policy in a positive direction. As Spear (1995: 13) recently argued—what we really need is 'a fundamental rethink', instead 'all we get from our current political masters is rhetoric' and 'glossy government publi-cations'.

Selected Further Reading

General: various classic and important recent articles are reprinted in N. South (ed.), *Drugs, Crime and Criminal Justice* (volumes 1 and 2; Aldershot: Dartmouth, 1995); see also the reprinted selection in R. Coomber (ed.), *Drugs and Drug Use in Society: A Critical Reader* (Dartford: Greenwich University Press). Early classic texts are: H. Becker, *Outsiders* (Glencoe: Free Press, 1963); and J. Young, *The Drugtakers* (London: Paladin, 1971). A good, very readable 'overview' is A. Tyler, *Street Drugs* (London: Hodder and Stoughton, revised edition, 1995). On gender, see E. Ettorre, *Women and Substance Use* (London: Macmillan, 1992); on services and practice developments, see J. Strang and M. Gossop (eds.), *Responding to Drug Misuse: The British System* (Oxford: Oxford University Press, 1993).

On History: V. Berridge and G. Edwards, *Opium and the People* (New Haven, Conn.: Yale University Press, 1987); D. Courtwright, *Dark Paradise: Opiate Addiction in America before 1940* (Cambridge, Mass.: Harvard University Press, 1982); M. Kohn, *Dope Girls: The Birth of the British Drug Underground* (London: Lawrence and Wishart, 1992).

On Drugs, Drug Markets and Crime: N. South (ed.), as above, volume 2; M. Tonry and J. Q. Wilson (eds.), *Drugs and Crime* (Chicago, Ill.: Chicago University Press, 1991); V. Ruggiero and N. South, *Eurodrugs: Drug Use, Markets and Trafficking in Europe* (London: UCL Press, 1995); N. Dorn, K. Murji, and N. South, *Traffickers: Drug Markets and Law Enforcement* (London: Routledge, 1992); M. Collison, *Police, Drugs and Community* (London: Free Association, 1995).

On Drugs, Criminal Justice and Policy: M. Hough, *Drugs Misuse and the Criminal Justice System: A Review of the Literature* (London: Home Office, Drugs Prevention Initiative, paper 15); N. Dorn, J. Jepsen, and E. Savona (eds.), *European Drug Policies and Enforcement* (London: Macmillan, 1996); concerning arguments for and against legalization of drugs, see R. Stevenson (and rejoinder from P. Reuter, M. Farrell, and J. Strang), in *Winning the War on Drugs: To Legalise or Not?* (London: Institute for Economic Affairs, Hobart paper 124).

On Alcohol and Crime-Related Problems: on penal policy and 'the inebriate', G. Johnstone, *Medical Concepts and Penal Policy* (London: Cavendish, 1996); J. Collins (ed.), *Drinking and Crime* (London: Tavistock, 1982).

On Drugs and AIDS/HIV: *British Journal of Addiction* (special issue), 1992, 87: 3; J. Strang and G. Stimson (eds.), *AIDS and Drug Misuse* (London: Routledge, 1991).

REFERENCES

ACMD (ADVISORY COUNCIL ON MISUSE OF DRUGS) (1984), *Prevention*. London: HMSO.
—— (1988), *AIDS and Drug Misuse, Part 1*. London: HMSO.
—— (1989), *AIDS and Drug Misuse, Part 2*. London: HMSO.
—— (1991), *Drug Misuse and the Criminal Justice System, Part 1*. London: HMSO.
—— (1993), *AIDS and Drug Misuse—An Update*. London: HMSO.
—— (1994), *Drug Misuse and the Criminal Justice System, Part 2*. London: HMSO.
ALCOHOL CONCERN, (1991), *Warning: Alcohol Can Damage Your Health*. London: Alcohol Concern.
ASHTON, M. (1994), 'New Drug Strategies for England and Scotland', *Druglink*, November/December: 6–7.
—— (1995*a*), 'Strategic Progress Uneven across UK', *Druglink*, 10, 4: 5.
—— (1995*b*), 'English National Strategy goes Live', *Druglink*, 10, 4: 6.
—— and SHAPIRO, H, (1982), 'Cannabis Stalemate, Part 1, Cannabis and Health', *Druglink*, Winter: 8–10.
AULD, J. (1981), *Marijuana Use and Social Control*. London: Academic Press.
—— DORN, N., and SOUTH, N. (1986), 'Irregular Work, Irregular Pleasures: Heroin in the 1980s', in R. Matthews and J. Young, eds., *Confronting Crime*. London: Sage.
AWIAH, J., BUTT, S., DORN, N., PEARSON, G., and PATEL, K. (1992), *Race, Gender and Drug Services*. London: Institute for the Study of Drug Dependence.
BEAN, P. (1974), *The Social Control of Drugs*. Oxford: Martin Robertson.
—— and PEARSON, Y. (1992), 'Cocaine and Crack in Nottingham 1989/90 and 1991/92', in J. Mott, ed., *Crack and Cocaine in England and Wales*. 20–32. London: Home Office.
BECKER, H. (1963), *Outsiders: Studies in the Sociology of Deviance*. Glencoe, NY: Free Press.
BENNETT, T., and WRIGHT, R. (1986), 'The Impact of Prescribing on the Crimes of Opioid Users', *British Journal of Addiction*, 81: 533–9.
BERRIDGE, V. (1978), 'War Conditions and Narcotics Control: The Passing of the Defence of the Realm Act Regulation 40 B', *Journal of Social Policy*, 7, 3: 285–304.
—— (1979), 'Morality and Medical Science: Concepts of Narcotic Addiction in Britain, 1820–1926', *Annals of Science*, 36: 67–85.

—— (1984), 'Drugs and Social Policy: The Establishment of Drug Control in Britain, 1900–1930', *British Journal of Addiction*, 79: 1.
—— and EDWARDS, G. (1981), *Opium and the People: Opiate Use in 19th Century England*. 2nd edn. New Haven, Conn.: Yale University Press.
BILD, M. (1992), 'Probation, Harm Reduction and Drug Services', *Druglink*, 7, 2: 10–12.
BLACK DRUG WORKERS FORUM, (1996–), bi-monthly newsletter inserts in *Druglink*, London: Institute for the Study of Drug Dependence.
BORRILL, J, and STEVENS, D. (1993), 'Understanding Human Violence: The Implications of Social Structure, Gender, Social Perception and Alcohol', *Criminal Behaviour and Mental Health*, 3: 129–41.
BRAIN, P., ed. (1986), *Alcohol and Aggression*. London: Croom Helm.
BRITISH JOURNAL of ADDICTION, (1989), 'Economic Aspects of Illicit Drug Problems' (A. Wagstaff and A. Maynard on 'Economic Aspects of the Illicit Drug Market and Drug Enforcement Policies in the United Kingdom: Summary of Report', followed by Commentaries), *British Journal of Addiction*, 84: 461–75.
—— (1992), 'Special Issue: AIDS, Drug Misuse and the Research Agenda', *British Journal of Addiction*, 87, 3.
BRITISH MEDICAL ASSOCIATION (1986), *Young People and Alcohol*. London: British Medical Association.
BRUUN, K., PAN, L., and REXED, I. (1975), *The Gentlemen's Club: International Control of Drugs and Alcohol*. Chicago, Ill.: University of Chicago Press.
BUNTON, R., (1990), 'Regulating our Favourite Drug', in P. Abbot and G. Payne, eds., *New Directions in the Sociology of Health*. London: Falmer.
CENTRAL POLICY REVIEW STAFF (1979), *Alcohol Policies*. London: Cabinet Office, unpublished. Reprinted and published as *Alcohol Policies in the United Kingdom*, (1982). Stockholm: Sociologiska Institutionen, Stockholm Universitet.
CHAIKEN, J., and CHAIKEN, M, (1990), 'Drugs and Predatory Crime', in M. Tonry and J. Wilson, J., eds., *Drugs and Crime* (Crime and Justice vol. 13). Chicago, Ill.: University of Chicago Press.
CHAMBLISS, W. (1989), 'State Organised Crime', *Criminology*, 27, 2: 183–208.

CHATTERTON, M., GIBSON, G., GILMAN, M., GODFREY, C., SUTTON, M., and WRIGHT, A. (1995), *Performance Indicators for Local Anti-Drug Strategies: A Preliminary Analysis*. London: Home Office, Police Research Group.

COID, J. (1986), 'Socio-Cultural Factors in Alcohol-related Aggression' in P. Brain, ed., *Alcohol and Aggression*. London: Croom Helm.

COLLINS, J., ed. (1982), *Drinking and Crime: Perspectives on the Relationships between Alcohol Consumption and Criminal Behaviour*. London: Tavistock.

COLLISON, M. (1993), 'Punishing Drugs: Criminal Justice and Drug Use', *British Journal of Criminology*, 33, 3: 382–99.

—— (1994a) 'Drug Crime, Drug Problems and Criminal Justice: Sentencing Trends and Enforcement Targets', *Howard Journal of Criminal Justice*, 33, 1: 25–40.

—— (1994b) 'Drug Offenders and Criminal Justice: Careers, Compulsion, Commitment and Penalty', *Crime, Law and Social Change*, 21: 49–71.

—— (1995) *Police, Drugs and Community*. London: Free Association.

—— (1996) 'In Search of the High Life: Drugs, Crime, Masculinity and Consumption', *British Journal of Criminology*, 36, 3: 428–44.

DEPARTMENT of HEALTH and SOCIAL SECURITY (DHSS) (1984), *Medical Working Group on Drug Dependence: Guidelines on Good Clinical Practice in the Treatment of Drug Misuse*. London: DHSS.

DAVIS, J., and DITTON, J. (1990), 'The 1990s: Decade of the Stimulants?', *British Journal of Addiction*, 85: 811–13.

DITTON, J., and HAMMERSLEY, R., eds. (1996), *A Very Greedy Drug: Cocaine in Context*. Reading: Harwood.

—— and SPEIRITS, K. (1982), 'The New Wave of Heroin Addiction in Britain', *Sociology*, 16, 4: 595–8.

DONOGHOE, M. (1992), 'Sex, HIV and the Injecting Drug User', *British Journal of Addiction*, 87: 405–16.

—— DORN, N., JAMES, C., JONES, S., RIBBENS, J., and SOUTH, N. (1987), 'How Families and Communities Respond to Heroin', in N. Dorn and N. South, eds., *A Land Fit for Heroin?: Drug Policies, Prevention and Practice*. London: Macmillan.

D'ORBAN, P. (1991), 'The Crimes Connection: Alcohol', in I. Glass, ed., *The International Handbook of Addiction Behaviour*. London: Routledge.

DORN, N. (1983), *Alcohol, Youth and the State:*

Drinking Practices, Controls and Health Education. London: Croom Helm.

—— (1992), 'Clarifying Policy Options on Drug Trafficking: Harm Minimization is Distinct from Legalization', in E. Buning *et al.*, eds. *Reduction of Drug Related Harm*. London: Routledge.

—— HENDERSON, S., and SOUTH, N. (eds.) (1992), *AIDS: Women, Drugs and Social Care*. London: Falmer Press.

—— MURJI, K., and SOUTH, N. (1991), 'Mirroring the Market?: Police Reorganisation and Effectiveness Against Drug Trafficking', in R. Reiner and M. Cross, eds., *Beyond Law and Order*. London: Macmillan.

—— —— and —— (1992), *Traffickers: Drug Markets and Law Enforcement*. London: Routledge.

—— and SOUTH, N., eds. (1987), *A Land Fit for Heroin?: Drug Policies, Prevention and Practice*. London: Macmillan.

—— and —— (1990), 'Drug Markets and Law Enforcement', *British Journal of Criminology*, 30: 171–88.

—— and —— (1991), 'Profits and Penalties: New Trends in Legislation and Law Enforcement Concerning Illegal Drugs', in D. Whynes and P. Bean, eds., *Policing and Prescribing: The British System of Drug Control*. London: Macmillan.

—— and —— (1994), 'The Power Behind Practice: Drug Control and Harm Minimisation in the Inter-Agency and Criminal Law Contexts', in J. Strang and M. Gossop, eds., *Heroin Addiction and Drug Policy: The British System*. Oxford: Oxford Medical..

DOWNES, D. (1997), 'What the Next Government Should Do about Crime', *Howard Journal of Criminal Justice*, 36, 1: 1–13.

DRUG INDICATORS PROJECT. (1985), *Drug Problems: Assessing Local Needs*. London: Drug Indicators Project, Birkbeck College, University of London.

DRUGLINK (1991). 'Law Reform Group Rejects Decriminalisation', *Druglink*, 6, 1: 5.

—— (1992a), 'Low Dependence and Use Typical of British Cocaine/Crack Users', *Druglink*, 7, 3: 6.

—— (1992b), 'Ketamine Supplements Ecstasy at the Rave', *Druglink*, 7, 3: 6.

—— (1992c), 'Ethnic Minorities "Not Underrepresented" Says Report', *Druglink*, 7, 5: 5.

DUKE, K., MACGREGOR, S., and SMITH, L. (1996), *Activating Local Networks: A Comparison of two Community Development Approaches to Drug Prevention*, Drugs Prevention Initiative Paper 10. London: Home Office.

ELDRIDGE, W. (1952), *Narcotics and the Law*. New York: American Bar Foundation.

ERICKSON, P., and WATSON, V. (1990), 'Women, Illicit Drugs and Crime', in L. Kozlowski, *et al.*, eds., *Research Advances in Alcohol and Drug Problems*, volume 10, 251–72. New York/London: Plenum Press.

ETTORRE, E. (1992), *Women and Substance Use*. London: Macmillan.

—— and RISKA, E. (1995), *Gendered Moods: Psychotropics and Society*. London: Routledge.

FELDMAN, H. (1968), 'Ideological Supports to Becoming and Remaining a Heroin Addict', *Journal of Health and Social Behaviour*, 9, June: 131–9.

FRASER, A., and GEORGE, M. (1988), 'Changing Trends in Drug Use: An Initial Follow-up of a Local Heroin Using Community', *British Journal of Addiction*, 83, 6: 655–63.

GAY TIMES. (1996), 'Drugs and Us: The Ostrich Mentality', *Gay Times*, September: 17–37.

GEORGE, M., and FRASER, A. (1989), 'Changing Trends in Drug Use: A Second Follow-up of a Local Heroin Using Community', *British Journal of Addiction*, 84, 12: 1,461–6.

GILMAN, M., and PEARSON, G. (1991), 'Lifestyles and Law Enforcement', in D. Whynes and P. Bean, eds., *Policing and Prescribing: The British System of Drug Control*. London: Macmillan.

—— TRAYNOR, P., and PEARSON, G. (1990), 'The Limits of Intervention: Cyclizine Misuse', *Druglink*, 5, 3: 12–13.

GIGGS, J. (1991), 'The Epidemiology of Contemporary Drug Abuse', in D. Whynes and P. Bean, eds., *Policing and Prescribing: The British System of Drug Control*. London: Macmillan.

GLANZ, A., and TAYLOR, C. (1986), 'Findings of a National Survey of the Role of General Practitioners in the Treatment of Opiate Misuse: Extent of Contact with Opiate Misusers', *British Medical Journal*, 293: 427–30.

GRAHAM, G. (1991), 'Criminalisation and Control', in D. Whynes and P. Bean, eds., *Policing and Prescribing: The British System of Drug Control*. London: Macmillan.

GREENBERG, S. (1976), 'The Relationship between Crime and Amphetamine Abuse: An Empirical Review of the Literature', *Contemporary Drug Problems*, Summer, 5, 2: 101–30.

HAMMERSLEY, R., FORSYTH, A., and LAVELLE, T. (1990), 'The Criminality of New Drug Users in Glasgow', *British Journal of Addiction*, 85: 1583–94.

—— —— MORRISON, V,. and DAVIES, J. (1989),

'The Relationship between Crime and Opioid Use', *British Journal of Addiction*, 84: 1029–44.

HARTNOLL, R., LEWIS, R., and BRYER, S. (1984), 'Recent Trends in Drug Use in Britain', *Druglink*, 19: 22–4.

—— MITCHESON, M., BATTERSBY, A., BROWN, G., ELLIS, M., FLEMING, P., and HEDLEY, N. (1980) 'Evaluation of Heroin Maintenance in Controlled Trial', *Archives of General Psychiatry*, 37: 877–84.

HENDERSON, S., ed. (1990), *Women, Drugs, HIV: Practical Issues*. London: Institute for the Study of Drug Dependence.

HENHAM, R. (1994), 'Criminal Justice and Sentencing Policy for Drug Offenders', *International Journal of the Sociology of Law*, 22: 223–38

HOBBS, D. (1988), *Doing the Business: Entrepreneurship, the Working Class and Detectives in the East End of London*. Oxford: Clarendon.

—— (1995) *Bad Business: Professional Crime in Britain*. Oxford: Oxford University Press.

HOME AFFAIRS COMMITTEE (1985), *Misuse of Hard Drugs: Interim Report*. London: HMSO.

HOME OFFICE (1991), *Statistics of the Misuse of Drugs: Seizures and Offenders Dealt with, United Kingdom, 1990*. London: Home Office (Statistical Bulletin, 19/91, September).

HORSTINK-VON MEYENFELDT, L. (1996) 'The Netherlands: Tightening Up of the Cafes Policy', in N. Dorn, J. Jepsen and E. Savona, eds., *European Drug Policies and Enforcement*. London: Macmillan.

HOUGH, M, (1996), *Drugs Misuse and the Criminal Justice System: A Review of the Literature*. London: Home Office, Drugs Prevention Initiative.

INCIARDI, J. (1986), *The War on Drugs: Heroin, Cocaine and Public Policy*. Palo Alto, Cal.: Mayfield.

—— and McBride, D. (1989), 'Legalisation: A High Risk Alternative in the War on Drugs', *American Behavioural Scientist*, 32, 3: 259–89.

INSTITUTE FOR THE STUDY OF DRUG DEPENDENCE (ISDD) (1990), *Drug Misuse in Britain: National Audit of Drug Misuse Statistics*. London: Institute for the Study of Drug Dependence.

—— ed. (1991), *Drug Misuse in Britain: National Audit of Drug Misuse Statistics*. London: Institute for the Study of Drug Dependence.

—— (1994), *Drug Misuse in Britain, 1994*. London: Institute for the Study of Drug Dependence.

—— (1996a) *Drug Abuse Briefing*. 6th edn.

London: Institute for the Study of Drug Dependence.

—— (1996*b*) 'Drug Deaths', Factsheet. London: Institute for the Study of Drug Dependence.

—— (1996*c*), 'New Drugs Update', *Druglink*, 11: 3.

JARVIS, G., and PARKER, H, (1989), 'Young Heroin Users and Crime', *British Journal of Criminology*, 29: 175–85.

—— and —— (1990), 'Can Medical Treatment Reduce Crime Amongst Young Heroin Users?', *Home Office Research Bulletin* (Research and Statistics Department), 28: 29–32.

JOHNSON, B. (1989), 'Crime and Compulsory Treatment', *Druglink*, 4, 3: 12–13.

JOHNSTONE, G. (1996), *Medical Concepts and Penal Policy*. London: Cavendish.

KOHN, M. (1992), *Dope Girls: The Birth of the British Drug Underground*. London: Lawrence and Wishart.

LEACH, K. (1991), 'The Junkies' Doctors and the London Drug Scene in the 1960s: Some Remembered Fragments', in D. Whynes and P. Bean, *Policing and Prescribing: The British System of Drug Control*. 35–59. London: Macmillan.

LEE, M. (1996) 'London: "Community Damage Limitation" Through Policing?' in N. Dorn, J. Jepsen and E. Savona, eds., *European Drug Policies and Enforcement*. London: Macmillan.

LEITNER, M., SHAPLAND, J., and WILES, P. (1993) *Drug Usage and Drugs Prevention*. London: Home Office.

LEROY, B. (1992), 'The EC of 12 and the Drug Demand', *Drug and Alcohol Dependence*, 29: 269–81.

LEVI, M, (1991), '*Pecunia Non Olet*: Cleansing the Money-launderers from the Temple', *Crime, Law and Social Change*, 16: 217–302.

LEVINE, H, (1983), 'The Good Creature of God and the Demon Rum: Colonial American and 19th Century Ideas About Alcohol, Crime and Accidents', in R. Room and G. Collins, eds., *Alcohol and Disinhibition: Nature and Meaning of the Link*. 347–73. Rockville, Mld.: National Institute on Alcohol Abuse and Alcoholism,

LEWIS, R., HARTNOL, R., BRYER, S., DAVIAUD, E., and MITCHESON, M. (1985), 'Scoring Smack: The Illicit Heroin Market in London, 1980–83', *British Journal of Addiction*, 80: 281–90.

LIGHT, R. (1994), 'Questioning the Link Between Alcohol and Crime', in E. Stanko, ed., *Perspectives on Violence*. London: Quartet.

LISTER, R. (1996), *Charles Murray and the Underclass: The Developing Debate*. London: Institute of Economic Affairs and *Sunday Times*.

LOMBROSO, C. (1968), *Crime: Its Causes and Remedies*. Montclair, NJ.: Patterson Smith, originally published 1911.

MACINNES, C. (1985), *City of Spades*. London: Alison and Busby.

MAHER, L. (1995), 'In the name of Love: Women and Initiation to Illicit Drugs' in R. Dobash, R. Dobash, and L. Noaks, eds., *Gender and Crime*. Cardiff: University of Wales Press.

McBRIDE, D., and McCOY, C. (1982), 'Crime and Drugs: The Issues and Literature', *Journal of Drug Issues*, Spring: 137–51.

McCONVILLE, B. (1991), *Women Under the Influence: Alcohol and its Impact*. London: Grafton.

McMURRAN, M., and HOLLIN, C. (1989), 'Drinking and Delinquency', *British Journal of Criminology*, 29, 4: 386–93.

McKEGANEY, N., FORSYTH, A., BARNARD, M., and HAY, G. (1996), 'Designer Drinks and Drunkenness Amongst a Sample of Scottish Schoolchildren', *British Medical Journal*, 313: 401.

MILES, R. (1994), 'Cocaine Markets and Enforcement in Britain', in E. Savona, N. Dorn, and T. Ellis, eds., *Cocaine Markets and Law Enforcement*. Rome: UNICRI.

MILLER, P., and PLANT, M. (1996), 'Drinking, Smoking and Illicit Drug Use Among 15 and 16 Year Olds in the United Kingdom', *British Medical Journal*, 313: 394–7.

MINISTRY of HEALTH. (1926), *Report of the Departmental Committee on Morphine and Heroin Addiction*. London: HMSO.

—— (1961), *Drug Addiction: Report of the Interdepartmental Committee*. London: HMSO.

MIRZA, H., PEARSON, G., and PHILLIPS, S. (1991), *Drugs, People and Services in Lewisham*, (Final Report of the Drug Information Project). London: Goldsmiths College.

MOTT, J. (1985), 'Self-reported Cannabis Use in Great Britain in 1981', *British Journal of Addiction*, 80: 37–43.

—— (1986), 'Opioid Use and Burglary', *British Journal of Addiction*, 81: 671–7.

—— (1989), 'Reducing Heroin Related Crime', *Home Office Research Unit Bulletin*, 26: 30–3.

—— (1990), 'Young People, Alcohol and Crime', *Home Office Research Bulletin* (Research and Statistics Department), 28: 24–8.

MOTT, J. (1991), 'Crime and Heroin Use', in D. Whynes and P. Bean, P, eds., *Policing and Prescribing: The British System of Drug Control*. London: Macmillan.

—— and MIRRLEES-BLACK, C. (1995), *Self-Reported Drug Misuse in England and Wales: Findings from the 1992 British Crime Survey*. London: Home Office.

—— and TAYLOR, M. (1974), *Delinquency Amongst Opiate Users*, Home Office Research Study No. 23. London: HMSO.

MURPHY, D, (1983), 'Alcohol and Crime', *Home Office Research and Planning Unit Research Bulletin*, 15: 8–11.

MURRAY, M, (1994), 'Use of Illegal Drugs in Northern Ireland', in J. Strang and M. Gossop, eds., *Heroin Addiction and Drug Policy: The British System*. Oxford: Oxford Medical.

MYERS, T, (1982), 'Alcohol and Violent Crime Re-examined', *British Journal of Addiction*, 77: 399–414.

NADELMAN, E. (1989), 'Drug Prohibition in the United States: Costs, Consequences and Alternatives', *Science*, 245: 939–47

NURCO, D., BALL, J., SHAFFER, J., and HANLON, T. (1985), 'The Criminality of Narcotic Addicts', *The Journal of Nervous and Mental Disease*, 173, 2: 94–102.

O'CONNOR, K. (1995), 'Drugs with Menace', *The Metropolitan Journal*, 14, July: 7.

OSWALD, P. (1982), 'The Healing Herb?', *Youth in Society*, July, 68: 21–2.

PARKER, H. (1996), 'Alcohol, Persistent Young Offenders and Criminological Cul-de-sacs', *British Journal of Criminology*, 36, 2: 282–99.

—— BAKX, K., and NEWCOMBE, R. (1988), *Living with Heroin: The Impact of a Drugs 'Epidemic' on an English Community*. Milton Keynes: Open University Press.

—— and BOTTOMLEY, T. (1996), *Crack Cocaine and Drugs-Crime Careers*. London: Home Office, Research and Statistics Directorate, Paper 34.

—— and KIRBY, P. (1996), *Methadone Maintenance and Crime Reduction on Merseyside*. London: Home Office, Police Research Group.

—— and MEASHAM, F. (1994), 'Pick 'n' Mix: Changing Patterns of Illicit Drug Use amongst 1990s Adolescents', *Drugs: Education, Prevention and Policy*, 1, 1: 5–14.

—— —— and ALDRIDGE, J. (1996), *Drugs Futures: Changing Patterns of Drug Use Amongst English Youth*. London: Institute for the Study of Drug Dependence.

—— and NEWCOMBE, R, (1987), 'Heroin Use and Acquisitive Crime in an English Community', *British Journal of Sociology*, 3: 331–50.

PARSSINEN, T, (1983) *Secret Passions, Secret Remedies: Narcotic Drugs in British Society, 1820–1930*. Manchester: Manchester University Press.

PEARSON, G, (1987a) *The New Heroin Users*. Oxford: Basil Blackwell.

—— (1987b), 'Social Deprivation, Unemployment and Patterns of Heroin Use', in N. Dorn and N. South, eds., *A Land Fit for Heroin?: Drug Policies, Prevention and Practice*. London: Macmillan.

—— (1991), 'Drug Control Policies in Britain', in M. Tonry and J. Q. Wilson, eds., *Drugs and the Criminal Justice System* (Crime and Justice, 14): 167–227.

—— (1992a) 'The Role of Culture in the Drug Question', in G. Edwards, M. Lader and C. Drummond, eds., *The Nature of Alcohol and Drug Related Problems*. Oxford: Oxford University Press.

—— (1992b), 'Drugs and Criminal Justice: A Harm Reduction Perspective', in E. Buning, E. Drucker, P. O'Hare, and R. Newcombe, eds., *Reduction of Drug Related Harm*, London: Routledge.

—— GILMAN, M., and McIVER, S. (1986), *Young People and Heroin: An Examination of Heroin Use in the North of England*. London: Health Education Council; Aldershot: Gower/Avebury (1987).

PECK, D., and PLANT, M. (1986), 'Unemployment and Illegal Drug Use: Concordant Evidence from a Prospective Study and National Trends', *British Medical Journal*, 293: 929–32.

PLANT, M., ed. (1990), *AIDS, Drugs and Prostitution*. London: Routledge.

PREBLE, E., and CASEY, J. (1969), 'Taking Care of Business: The Heroin User's Life on the Street', *International Journal of the Addictions*, 4, 1: 1–24.

PRYCE, K. (1979), *Endless Pressure: A Study of West Indian Lifestyles in Bristol*. Harmondsworth: Penguin.

RAMSAY, M. (1996), 'The Relationship Between Alcohol and Crime', *Home Office Research and Statistics Directorate Research Bulletin*, 38: 37–44.

RELEASE (1992), *A Release White Paper on Reform of the Drug Laws*. London: Release.

REUTER, P. (1983), *Disorganised Crime: Illegal Markets and the Mafia*. Cambridge. Mass.: MIT Press.

ROBERTSON, J. (1987), *Heroin, AIDS and Society*. London: Hodder and Stoughton.

ROSENBAUM, M. (1981a), *Women on Heroin*.

New Brunswick, NJ: Rutgers University Press.

—— (1981*b*), 'Sex Roles among Deviants: The Woman Addict', *International Journal of the Addictions*, 16: 859–77.

ROYAL COLLEGE of PHYSICIANS and BRITISH PÆDIATRIC ASSOCIATION (1995), *Alcohol and the Young*. London: Royal College of Physicians.

ROYAL COLLEGE of PSYCHIATRISTS (1986), *Alcohol: Our Favourite Drug*. London: Tavistock.

—— (1987), *Drug Scenes: A Report on Drugs and Drug Dependence by the Royal College of Psychiatrists*. London: Gaskell.

RUGGIERO, V., and SOUTH, N. (1995), *Eurodrugs: Drug Use, Markets and Trafficking in Europe*. London: UCL.

RUSSELL, J. (1993), *Alcohol and Crime*. London: Mental Health Foundation.

SHAPIRO, H. (1989), *Crack: A Briefing*, London: Institute for the Study of Drug Dependence.

—— (1991), 'Contemporary Cocaine Use in Britain', in Institute for the Study of Drug Dependence, ed., *Drug Misuse in Britain*. London: Institute for the Study of Drug Dependence.

—— (1996), 'Heroin in the '90's: From A to B', *Druglink*, 11, 3: 8–9.

—— (1998), 'Dances with Drugs', in N. South, ed., *Drugs: Cultures, Controls and Everyday Life*. London: Sage.

SHINER, M., and NEWBURN, T. (1996) *Young People, Drugs and Peer Education*. London: Home Office, Drugs Prevention Initiative.

—— and —— (forthcoming) ' "It's not normal!": Drug Use by Young People', *Sociology*.

SMART, C. (1984), 'Social Policy and Drug Addiction: A Critical Study of Policy Development', *British Journal of Addiction*, 79: 31–9.

SOUTH, N. (1992), 'Moving Murky Money: Drug Trafficking, Law Enforcement and the Pursuit of Criminal Profits', in D. Farrington and S. Walklate, eds., *Offenders and Victims: Theory and Policy*. 167–93, London: British Society of Criminology.

—— (1994), 'Drugs: Control, Crime and Criminological Studies', in M. Maguire, R. Morgan and R. Reiner, eds., *The Oxford Handbook of Criminology*. 1st edn. Oxford: Oxford University Press.

—— ed. (1995), *Drugs, Crime and Criminal Justice*. Vol. 1. Aldershot: Dartmouth.

SPEAR, B. (1969), 'The Growth of Heroin Addiction in the UK', *British Journal of Addiction*, 64: 245–55.

—— (1975), 'The British Experience', *The John Marshall Journal of Practice and Procedure*, 9: 67–98.

SPEAR, B. (1995), 'A personal account', *Druglink*, 10, 5: 12–13.

STEEL, D. (1986), 'Alcohol and Drugs: Unsuitable Attachment?', *Druglink*, 1, 3: 7.

STEVENSON, R. (1991), 'The Economics of Drug Policy', in D. Whynes and P. Bean, eds., *Policing and Prescribing: The British System of Drug Control*. London: Macmillan.

STIMSON, G. (1987), 'The War on Heroin: British Policy and the International Trade in Illicit Drugs', in N. Dorn and N. South, eds., *A Land Fit for Heroin?: Drug Policies, Prevention and Practice*. London: Macmillan.

STRANG, J., and STIMSON, G., eds. (1991), *AIDS and Drug Misuse*. London: Routledge.

SWADI, H. (1988), 'Drug and Substance Abuse among 3,333 London Adolescents', *British Journal of Addiction*, 83: 935–42.

TAYLOR, A. (1993) *Women Drug Users*. Oxford: Clarendon Press.

TOMSEN, S. (1997), 'A Top Night: Social Protest, Masculinity and the Culture of Drinking Violence', *British Journal of Criminology*, 37, 1: 90–102.

TONRY, M., and WILSON, J. (1990), *Drugs and Crime*, (Crime and Justice, 13). Chicago, Ill.: University of Chicago Press.

TRIMBLE, J., BOLEK, C., and NIEMCRYK, S. (1992), *Ethnic and Multicultural Drug Abuse*. New York: Howarth.

TUCK, M. (1989) *Drinking and Disorder: A Study of Non-Metropolitan Violence*, Home Office Research Study No. 108. London: HMSO.

WEBSTER, C. (1996), 'Asian Young People and Drug Use', *Criminal Justice Matters*, 24: 11–12.

WEIPERT, G., D'ORBAN, P., and BEWLEY, T. (1979), 'Delinquency by Opiate Addicts Treated at Two London Clinics', *British Journal of Psychiatry*, 134: 14–23.

WEISHEIT, R., ed. (1990), *Drugs, Crime and the Criminal Justice System*. Cincinatti, Ohio: Anderson Publishing Co.

WEST, D., and FARRINGTON, D. (1977), *The Delinquent Way of Life*. London: Heinemann.

WHYNES, D., and BEAN, P. (1991), *Policing and Prescribing: The British System of Drug Control*. London: Macmillan.

WILLIAMS, P., and BRAKE, T. (1980), *Drink in Great Britain, 1900–1979*. London: Edsel.

WILLIS, P. (1978), *Profane Culture*. London: Routledge.

WILSON, J. (1990), 'Drugs and Crime', in M. Tonry and J. Q. Wilson, eds., *Drugs and Crime* (Crime and Justice vol. 13). Chicago, Ill.: University of Chicago Press.

WRIGHT, A., WAYMONT, A., and GREGORY, F. (1993) *Drugs Squads: Drugs Law Enforcement and Intelligence in England and Wales*. London: Police Foundation.

WOOTTON COMMITTEE (1968), *Cannabis: Report by the Advisory Committee on Drug Dependence*. London: HMSO.

YOUNG, J. (1971), *The Drugtakers: The Social Meaning of Drug Use*. London: Paladin.

—— (1987). 'Deviance', in P. Worsley, ed., *The New Introducing Sociology*. London: Penguin.

ZINBERG, N. (1984), *Drug, Set and Setting: The Basis for Controlled Intoxicant Use*. New Haven, Conn.: Yale University Press.

Part IV

CRIMINAL JUSTICE STRUCTURES AND PROCESSES

27

Crime Prevention

Ken Pease

Behaviour becomes a crime when the state enacts sanctions against it. Government then takes on a role in identifying and dealing with its perpetrators. Criminal law sets out the circumstances in which behaviour is to be deemed a crime, and the penalties which may be applied to those committing it. Generally, crimes are those actions whose nature is thought so socially disturbing as to require state involvement. Murder is a crime in all countries. Singing out of tune is not. The scope of criminal law changes in rough accordance with public concerns. Restrictions on certain breeds of dog and certain calibres of firearm exemplify recent extensions of criminal law in the United Kingdom, and (rather longer ago) the decriminalization of sexual acts between consenting adult males in private represented a retreat of criminal law from behaviour no longer deemed to justify state interference.

We should constantly remind ourselves that, in crime, we have a set of actions or omissions united only in their proscription by law. This is important when thinking about crime prevention for three reasons:

1. Since crime consists of diverse behaviour, we should not look for universality in techniques of prevention.
2. Because an action is a crime, this does not mean that the best way to control it is through the police and the courts. The behaviour itself must be understood, to determine where change could best be brought about.
3. The scope of the criminal law is morally problematic. A society in which more crime is prevented is not necessarily a more pleasant society. The burdens and restrictions imposed on people to prevent crime must be balanced against the harm caused by the crime prevented.

Crime prevention involves the disruption of mechanisms which cause crime events (modified from Ekblom, 1994). How to disrupt them is the central question. Three broad perspectives on crime causation can be distinguished. They concentrate on structure, psyche, and circumstance respectively (the three S's, at least if you say them aloud). *Structural* views take prevention to be achievable only by economic and social change. These views are most common among criminologists with a background in sociology, and are also found among practitioners within criminal justice. More common are views of crime as a product of the human *psyche*, so that the greatest prevention possibilities lie in changing established or potential offenders by control or reform. These views are reflected in the rhetoric of offender change favoured by many sentencers and politicians. The revival of offender change as fashionable penology seems to be under way (see Gendreau and Ross, 1987; McGuire, 1994). The third perspective on crime control is that it may be achieved by quite modest adjustments in *circumstance*, i.e. the social and physical settings in which crime occurs. This tradition is of much more recent origin within criminology (although see Garland, 1996, and Bottoms and Wiles, this volume). It has generated a large amount of research and evaluation.

The structural approach to crime prevention takes the debate straight into politics (see, for example, Hutton, 1996). Crime prevention is defensible as a free-standing discipline only when minimum standards of social justice are perceived to apply. Could crime prevention be ethically neutral in regimes and at times like pre-Mandela South Africa, where social injustice was enshrined in criminal law? Many *current* regimes also fail the test of minimum standards of social justice. In such regimes, crime prevention by means other than legal reform seems tasteless. How fair do social arrangements have to be before primary crime prevention becomes appropriate? Should one prevent shop theft when the alternative for the thief is to starve? When the alternative is undernourishment? When the alternative is a non-ideal diet? On the other hand, crime causes much distress, often to those also disadvantaged in other ways. To insist on a totally fair society before crime prevention is deployed is to leave people unnecessarily vulnerable to harm and loss. Such issues have seldom been addressed within the crime prevention literature, but they do have implications for its practice. There is currently extensive debate about how individual rights and obligations must be balanced in ensuring citizen safety and happiness, with liberal and communitarian philosophers debating these issues (see Conway, 1995, and Hughes, 1996*a*, for introductions to the debate and its policy ramifications). The growing body of scholarship about how crime prevention politics translates and uses concepts of community is a fascinating one. It deals with why crime prevention takes the form it does, how crime control relates to issues of governance, and in particular how invoking the community in the service of crime control reflects and reinforces wider social changes. These are topics of fundamental importance. Witnessing how simple problem-solving approaches get drowned in a sea of funding problems, political rhetoric appealing to (particular) communities, defensiveness about community safety priorities among practitioners, played out against changing patterns of social and trust relationships in late modern societies, makes it clear that understanding the technology of crime prevention is less difficult than understanding its organizational context. A chapter of equal length to this one could be written for the *Handbook* detailing these problems. However, understanding what is possible by simple means of crime prevention seems the essential first step. If no-one knows what simple crime prevention can do, there is no benchmark against which to understand the political, social, and economic reasons why it fails to make simple changes. Fortunately for the reader, there is a good literature on these points. The work of Crawford, 1994; 1995;

Crawford and Jones, 1995), Gilling (1993, 1994*a*, 1994*b*; 1996) Hughes (1994; 1996*a*, 1996*b*) Liddle and Gelsthorpe (1994*a*, 1994*b*, 1994*c*) and Stenson (1991, 1993) are particularly helpful because of their personal involvement in the complexities of crime prevention practice. Bottoms and Wiles (1996) offer a unique and persuasive attempt to locate these trends within general social theory. The number of *recent* references here confirms that this is an area of intense activity.

Setting aside these issues for the limited purposes of this chapter leaves crime prevention by changing psyche or circumstance as the alternative approaches. These approaches have been classified by Brantingham and Faust (1976). *Primary prevention* reduces crime opportunities without reference to criminals or potential criminals. *Secondary prevention* seeks to change people, typically those at high risk of embarking upon a criminal career, before they do so. *Tertiary prevention* is focused upon the truncation of the criminal career, in length, seriousness, or frequency of offending. It deals with the 'treatment' of known offenders. The Brantingham and Faust classification was later refined by Van Dijk and De Waard (1991).

Primary, secondary, and tertiary prevention take place in parallel in the United Kingdom, and in other Western countries known to the writer. The police lead in primary prevention; youth services assume leadership in secondary prevention; the prison and probation services have led in tertiary prevention. The growth in multi-agency approaches to crime prevention and the appointment of community safety officers by local authorities have blurred these borders. Many people engaged in local crime prevention have little idea of the differences between them (see Buck, 1997). This chapter will be devoted to primary crime prevention. Those interested in secondary and tertiary prevention are directed to the Farrington, Ashworth, and Mair chapters in this volume. Primary and secondary prevention are not alternatives. Their integration has been discussed by Farrington (1995).

CRIME PREVENTION THEORY

Theories of crime are also theories of crime prevention. They differ in the scale of change necessary to achieve that end (for accounts of relevant theories see Kornhauser, 1978; Lilly *et al.*, 1989; Garland, 1990). They also vary in their selection of what needs to be understood. One approach takes the motivated offender, another the crime event, as the thing to be explained. Primary crime prevention is underpinned by theories of the crime event. Three theories of central interest here are the lifestyle approach of Hindelang *et al.* (1978), the routine activities theory of Cohen and Felson (1979), and the rational choice position of Cornish and Clarke (1986). In addition, the problem-oriented policing (POP) perspective of Herman Goldstein (1990) sits well with the concerns of primary crime prevention. The crime prevention taxonomy of

Clarke (1995) will also be described, as an important conceptual tool. These five approaches will be dealt with in outline. Their essential common feature is that *crime is conceived as a by-product of the way we conduct our everyday lives*. Owning many goods of high value and low volume, we suffer theft. Having active age-segregated social lives in anonymous city areas increases the number of incidents of friction which we can expect. Because the causes of crime are rooted in the details of life, crime control is also focused upon everyday life, rather than diverted into a separate system of blame and punishment.

Routine Activity Theory

Routine activity theory began as an explanation of predatory crime, but was extended to cover other crime types. It holds that three elements must converge in time and space for a crime to occur. These are a motivated offender, a suitable victim, and the absence of a capable guardian. As routine activity patterns disperse people away from their families and households, offenders will find targets lacking capable guardians. The decline of conventional communities weakens the informal social controls which supply capable guardianship. Economic changes increase suitable targets. Suitable targets can be thought of through variables summarized in the acronym VIVA, namely Value, Inertia, Volume, and Access. Low volume, high value goods to which not everyone has access and which can be easily moved are ideal targets for property crime. Marcus Felson's advice to crime researchers and theorists (1986) makes clear why the theory appeals to advocates of primary crime prevention:

Count television sets, monitor their portability, check their location. Examine travel patterns away from home; numbers of persons moving about with family, friends or strangers; adolescent activities with peers and parents; automobilization of youth; shopping patterns, parking patterns and so forth. Check household composition, housing types and patterns of occupancy of buildings and of ties among occupants. Look at hourly patterns of activity and where people are on the map. Check parental position vis-a-vis their own children and patterns of recognition among neighbours. Like physics and physiology, criminogenesis derives from a movement of physically bounded and identifiable entities about the physical world—movements that can be tracked according to map, clock, and calendar, and that from time to time assemble or disperse the four minimal elements in the web of informal crime control [Felson, 1986: 127–8].

An account of Marcus Felson's theory, together with its implications, are to found in Felson (1993).

Lifestyle Theory

The lifestyle approach (Hindelang *et al.*, 1978), considered variations in rates of personal victimization. Lifestyle incorporates routine activities, both locational and leisure. These determine one's likelihood of personal victimization by reference to the people with whom one associates and to whom one is exposed.

Themes of research inspired by lifestyle theory have included differences in rates of victimization by age, sex, and ethnicity, and the usually high correspondence between the demographic characteristics of victims and offenders (e.g. Singer, 1981). Lifestyle theory was modified by Garofalo (1987) to incorporate *direct* effects of social structure upon victimization, recognizing that people may be forced to live in places which they would not choose, and whose hazards they experience independently of their lifestyle. Garofalo also inserts reactions to crime, target attractiveness, and individual differences as determinants of victimization risks.

One way of deciding whether theories are really different is to see if, when both make predictions about the same thing, those predictions differ. The theories in question here have generally not met 'head-on' because of differences in the kinds of data their proponents typically use. In the writer's view, the theories are not distinguishable from their predictions. In the future, someone may be ingenious enough to devise a way of making the theories generate predictions which differ. Alternatively, the theories may be consolidated into a single 'lifestyle routines' theory. Most likely, a consolidated theory will go forward under the routine activities title.

Rational Choice Theory

This theory begins with an assumption that offenders seek to benefit themselves by their criminal behaviour. This entails making decisions and choices, however rudimentary their rationality might be, being constrained by limits of time, ability, and the availability of relevant information (Clarke and Cornish, 1985). Because offences differ very widely in their 'choice-structuring properties', the focus for Cornish and Clarke is upon the immediate context of a crime. One effect of the Clarke and Cornish approach has been to interview offenders about what shaped their immediate behaviour. This enterprise, reviewed by Ekblom (1991*a*) has proven remarkably fruitful in generating crime prevention ideas (see e.g. Maguire, 1982; Bennett and Wright, 1984; Nee and Taylor, 1988; Taylor and Nee, 1988), and in understanding the way in which the structuring of offender choice will shape patterns of crime displacement (see Cornish and Clarke 1988*a*, 1988*b*).

While the Clarke and Cornish formulation deals both with the initial decision to become involved in crime and with the decision to commit a particular crime in a particular context, its influence has tended to be greater in the second than in the first application. This second arm of the Clarke and Cornish approach complements lifestyle and routine activities theory by its injection of a consideration of how routine activities and lifestyle work at the point of offender choice. It has been criticized as being more applicable to crime for gain than other crime (Trasler, 1986, 1993). The consolidation of rational choice with routine activities theory is already under way (Clarke and Felson, 1993).

Problem-Oriented Policing

An innovation of the last decade which reinforces primary crime prevention is the problem-oriented policing (POP) movement inspired by Herman Goldstein (see Goldstein, 1990). POP seeks to replace the call for service with the problem as the basic unit of police work.

In handling incidents, police officers usually deal with the most obvious, superficial manifestations of a deeper problem—not the problem itself. They may stop a fight but not get involved in the factors that contributed to it. They may disperse a group of unruly juveniles but not feel under any obligation to inquire into what brought the youths together in the first instance. They may investigate a crime but stop short of exploring the factors that may have contributed to its commission, except as these are relevant to identifying the offender. In handling incidents, police are generally expected to deal with the disruptive, intolerable effects of a problem. That requires a response quite different from what might be involved in dealing with the underlying conditions or problem. Clearly, some officers go further, dealing with the problem itself. But most policing is limited to ameliorating the overt, offensive symptoms of a problem. To go beyond that is considered extra [Goldstein, 1990: 33].

POP thus focuses on the crime event and analyses its immediate determinants. These determinants will fall into the categories identified by the three theories described above. The growth in influence enjoyed by POP in North America (and latterly the United Kingdom, see Leigh *et al.*, 1996) may stimulate primary crime prevention.

The Clarke Taxonomy of Primary Prevention

From time to time, Ron Clarke modifies his taxonomy of crime prevention. The version reproduced here as Table 27.1 is summarized from Clarke (1995). It can be thought of as the repertoire of primary (situational) prevention. Two common misconceptions dispelled by the taxonomy are that:

1. Primary prevention equates with physical target hardening;
2. Physical and social methods of prevention are separable.

It will be seen from Table 27.1 that only one of the twelve alternatives involves target hardening. Many methods are directly or indirectly social. Natural surveillance is obviously directly social, and access control by badge only works when someone is prepared to act on someone else's lack of a badge. Table 27.1 illustrates that primary crime prevention is not synonymous with physical prevention, still less with target hardening. It is concerned with the immediate situation in which the crime may take place, and how that can be manipulated, either socially or physically (but see Gilling, 1994*b*, for a sceptical view about the incorporation of physical and social elements in the same problem solving process).

Table 27.1 The twelve techniques of primary prevention

Increasing the Effort	Increasing the Risks	Reducing the Reward
Target Hardening	*Entry/exit Screening*	*Target Removal*
Steering Locks	Baggage Screening	Phonecard
Bandit Screens	Merchandise Tags	Removable Car Radio
Access Control	*Formal Surveillance*	*Identifying Property*
Entryphones	Security Guards	Property Marking
ID Badges	Speed Cameras	Vehicle Licensing
Deflecting Offenders	*Employee Surveillance*	*Removing Inducements*
Pub Location	Park Attendants	Graffiti Cleaning
Cul-de-sacs	CCTV	Rapid Repair
Controlling Means	*Natural Surveillance*	*Rule Setting*
Gun Control	Street Lighting	Hotel Registration
Credit Card Photo	Defensible Space	Tenancy Agreements

PRIMARY CRIME PREVENTION RESEARCH

Having identified the theories and perspectives which inform primary crime prevention, its foundation in research should be described. Almost all well-conceived and properly implemented primary prevention projects achieve at least some success in crime control (see Poyner and Webb, 1993). Research attention to primary crime prevention in the United Kingdom can be dated as beginning in 1976. (For a review of British research and policy, see Bottoms, 1990.) The event was the publication of *Crime as Opportunity* (Mayhew *et al.*, 1976), inspired by patterns of suicide. When toxic town gas was replaced by natural gas, the suicide method of preference, gas poisoning, ceased to be available. The *total* number of suicides decreased. This meant that many people to whom the favoured method was denied chose not to kill themselves. A similar thing happened when US vehicle regulations on catalytic conversion were introduced, since a hosepipe from the exhaust into the car's interior does not kill the occupants when a catalytic converter is fitted to the vehicle (see Clarke and Mayhew, 1988, for an account of both effects). If reduction in suicide could be effected by removing opportunities to kill oneself, could not some reduction in burglary or cheque fraud be effected by removing opportunities to commit these crimes? The *Crime as Opportunity* report included research on the prevention of car theft by the introduction of steering-column locks (Mayhew *et al.*, 1976, 1979; Webb, 1994). The compulsory fitting of steering-column locks to all cars in West Germany led to a reduction in the theft of cars, sustained over at least a decade. The compulsory fitting of steering-column locks to all *new* cars in the United Kingdom led to a reduction in the proportion of stolen cars which were new. Other work by the same group in the Home Office Research Unit and elsewhere quickly followed.

Primary Prevention Successes

Some of the post-1976 successes that have been achieved by primary prevention
were serendipitous, like the effects on motorcycle crime of the legal requirement for motorcycle riders to wear helmets (Van Straelen, 1978; Mayhew,
1991). More were deliberate. In the aggregate, the scale and variety of successful crime prevention enterprise is impressive. A selection of these achievements
will be presented. Since the first edition of this Handbook, many more have
been published. The chapter could have been taken up simply listing them.
What follows is merely a selection.

    Some crime on underground stations was prevented by the introduction of
closed-circuit television cameras (Burrows, 1979), as was bus vandalism
(Poyner, 1988, 1991), and shop theft (Van Straelen, 1978). Cheque fraud was
reduced to less than a fifth of its previous level by incorporating a photograph
on cheque guarantee cards (Knutsson and Kuhlhorn, 1981, 1992). Fraud by
inserting items other than coins into parking meters was reduced by making
the last item inserted visible to passers-by (Decker, 1972, 1991). Simple precautions reduced types of shop theft (Ekblom, 1986). Electronic article
surveillance reduces shop theft by 35 to 75 per cent (DiLonardo, 1996). Ink
tags (used on garments, where tampering releases ink onto the garment) are
deemed even more successful in comparable retail environments (DiLonardo
and Clarke, 1996). In a study comparing approaches to shop theft, tagging
achieved a lasting decrease, store redesign a temporary reduction, which was
wearing off after six weeks. Uniformed guards achieved no reduction
(Farrington *et al.*, 1993). Well-publicized domestic property marking substantially reduced the incidence of burglary (Laycock, 1985). Obscene telephone
calls were deterred by allowing the display of calling numbers on victims'
phones (Clarke, 1991) and publicized call-tracing (Buck *et al.*, 1995). Security
screens protect employees from robbery, whether in banks (Clarke *et al.*, 1991),
Post Offices (Ekblom, 1987, 1991*b*), buses (Poyner *et al.*, 1988), or, more
ambiguously, building societies (Austin, 1988). Markus (1984) has demonstrated
the effect of target-hardening upon thefts from public telephone kiosks, a
finding replicated by Challinger (1991). Laycock (1984) showed that target-
hardening reduced burglary of chemists' shops. In a recently published evaluation
of a raft of domestic burglary prevention programmes (Ekblom, Law, and
Sutton, 1996) simple target hardening had an effect which was costed. Poyner
(1991) showed the effect of formal and informal surveillance upon rates of
theft from parked cars. The pooling of street information to inform policing
of a shipyard parking area was also effective in reducing thefts from cars (Eck
and Spelman 1988, 1991). Diverse programmes have achieved reductions in
levels of fare evasion (DesChamps *et al.*, 1991; Van Andel, 1989, 1991). Webb
and Laycock (1992*a*) implicate publicity and management in achieving crime
reduction in one part of the London Underground. Smith and Burrows (1986)
documented the effects of simple changes in management procedure on frauds
in a hospital and on the prevention of abuses of car import regulations. The

American Bar Association (1986) assessed the effects of a raft of measures upon drunk driving. Crime against schools in Wigan was reduced by modest situational measures, with immense cost savings (Bridgeman, 1996).

Closed Circuit Television (CCTV)

The reason for discussing CCTV here is not because it has enjoyed uniform success in preventing crime, nor that it offers a uniquely hi-tech approach to crime prevention. It is because it currently enjoys a vogue in the United Kingdom (Groombridge and Murji, 1994). Home Secretary Howard wrote in 1996, 'I am absolutely convinced that CCTV has a major part to play in helping to detect and reduce crimes and to convict criminals' (Home Office, 1996). The bulk of Home Office expenditure on crime prevention now goes on CCTV for public places (Koch, 1996). Most, but not all, evaluations suggest a reduction in crime in areas covered by cameras (Poyner, 1988, 1991; Tilley, 1993; Brown, 1995; Short and Ditton, 1996; Durham, 1996). Reductions of between 14 per cent and 100 per cent have been claimed. A useful review of these successes is offered by Horne (1996). In principle, CCTV should prevent crime at locations within its range. The reason for qualifying one's enthusiasm for this technology is not that it will fail to prevent crime, but that its technological and operational base is currently precarious. Purchase of equipment by businesses is typically cost-driven (Hearnden, 1996), and often technically deficient or inappropriate equipment is bought. Nick Ross notes (personal communication) that some three quarters of CCTV tapes sent to his *Crimewatch* programme are too poor in quality to allow recognition of offenders. As for open street surveillance by CCTV, its long-term effects will depend upon the competence and acumen of those employed to monitor screens. Studies of CCTV control rooms, yet to be published, raise concerns on this score. Finally, surveillance of people in the streets, and the possible sale of tapes as entertainment for profit, make CCTV one of the more contentious avenues of primary prevention. Discussions of prevention often have the CCTV camera as an implicit underlying image of surveillance and intrusion (Davies, 1996). While its potential should be exploited, CCTV should not drive debates about primary crime prevention.

Risk Analyses

The studies above reported the effects of primary crime prevention. A related product of the same research tradition has been a set of crime risk analyses. Such studies direct attention to attributes of people or things associated with their victimization, and hence require opportunity-reducing measures to be taken. They can be regarded as the necessary analysis preceding primary crime prevention. An early study of Manchester buses identified those parts of the interior which were most prone to criminal damage. This led the bus company to use vandal-proof materials in the most vulnerable seats (Sturman, 1976,

1980). Hauber (1978) noted those characteristics of public transport systems associated with high levels of fare evasion. Hope (1980, 1982, 1986) listed features of school design strongly linked to the probability of burglary victimization. Small, old, and compact schools were least crime-prone. Crime risks vary by model and attributes of car (Southall and Ekblom, 1985, Burrows and Heal, 1979, 1980; Houghton, 1992; Clarke and Harris, 1992), type of house (Winchester and Jackson, 1982), and location and surveillability of phone kiosks (Mayhew *et al.*, 1979, 1980). The pre-payment coin meter for gas and electricity was shown to be criminogenic (Hill, 1986). As with bus vandalism, the research led to a swift withdrawal of these meters by fuel companies. Hunter and Jeffery (1991) distinguished convenience stores according to their robbery-proneness, and LaVigne (1994) showed factors associated with motorists who drive off from petrol stations without paying. Ekblom and Simon (1988) analysed patterns of crime and racial harassment in Asian-run shops, and Burrows (1988, 1991) rehearsed methods for the prevention of retail crime through analysis. Phillips and Cochrane (1988) described a crime-analytic approach to controlling crime and nuisance in a shopping centre, as did Smith (1987) in relation to crime in hospitals. Webb and Laycock (1992*b*) described the changing balance between recovered and unrecovered stolen cars, with the implications for prevention. Ekblom (1988) set out techniques of crime analysis which make for the identification of patterns, a process developed by Berry and Carter (1992). In fraud prevention, Levi (1988) spelled out a prevention strategy, and Levi *et al.* (1991) generated a very detailed set of technological and other solutions to cheque and credit card fraud. This last study well illustrates the dynamic of primary crime prevention, with changes in technology evoking changes in criminal method, which in turn evoke changes in technology (see also Walsh, 1994). The implementation of many of the measures which Levi recommended was linked to a decline in the fraud losses of the card companies (see Webb, 1996). Masuda (1996) shows that a decline in such fraud can be achieved by instant verification of a card-holder's identity. Risk analyses have been carried out for many non-obvious crimes. For instance, such analyses have been conducted for ransom kidnappings in Sardinia (Marongiu and Clarke, 1993), drink driving (Homel, 1993), violence in pubs and clubs (Homel and Clark, 1994), and political violence (Taylor, 1993).

Architectural and Environmental Design

Crime prevention through environmental design, usually referred to as CPTED, has attracted enough attention to be considered separately. This approach has resulted in police forces in the United Kingdom creating specialist posts of architectural liaison officers, who offer advice on the design of buildings and public areas to make them less likely to attract crime and disorder (see Johnson *et al.*, 1993). A criticism has been that housing, shopping areas, schools, and the like were designed in ways that a moment's thought would have shown to be criminogenic, but such thought was never given until the work had been done and the crime started.

Architectural determinism was pioneered by Jane Jacobs (1961) and C. Ray Jeffery (1971). Its most famous exponent was Oscar Newman (1972, 1976), whose term 'defensible space' is the verbal tag by which thinking of this kind is best known. Recent British interest in such work is spearheaded by Coleman (1985). It was last comprehensively reviewed by Bannister (1991). CPTED takes physical features of the built environment to be criminogenic. Its exponents vary in the proportion of any differences in rates of crime which are attributed to design and social factors.

Newman's four critical features were

1. *territoriality*: the subdivision of places into 'zones of influence' to discourage outsiders and to encourage residents to defend their areas;
2. *surveillance*: the design of buildings to allow easy observation of territorial areas;
3. *image*: the design of buildings to avoid stigma in low-cost or public housing;
4. *environment*: the juxtaposition of public housing with safe zones.

Despite the criticisms of the Newman approach (reviewed by Mayhew, 1979), it remains an attractive way of thinking about prevention, because it offers advice on what to do about crime, which can be and has been put into practice. Rubenstein *et al.* (1980) identified the design approaches employed to make space more defensible as follows:

(a) improving external lighting;
(b) reducing opportunities for offender concealment;
(c) reducing unassigned open spaces;
(d) locating outdoor activities in sight of windows;
(e) increasing designated walkways;
(f) increasing pedestrian activity.

Newman's earlier work has been heavily criticized on the basis of its unjustified generality (Mawby, 1977) and its neglect of the role of social factors, both directly and in mediating the effects of architectural features (Merry, 1981; Smith, 1986, 1987; Taylor *et al.*, 1980). In his later writings (e.g. Newman and Franck, 1982) Newman acknowledges that resident characteristics are stronger predictors of crime levels than are design features. Defensible space notions have not fared especially well in the face of research evidence (Reppetto, 1974; Waller and Okihiro, 1978). Alice Coleman's (1985) forceful advocacy of the strong architectural determination of crime levels came at a time when the literature was suggesting a more complex picture. Furthermore, Coleman's eccentric use of statistical analysis leads her to unjustified conclusions (Smith, 1986). The debate has been heated. Some features of the built environment are criminogenic and some criminocclusive (see, for example, Winchester and Jackson, 1982; Poyner, 1983; Bentvelsen and Van der Zon, 1987). The danger of the heat in this debate is that the relevance of simple measures in design will be neglected.

Fierce controversy has surrounded the effects of street lighting upon crime and fear levels. North American research shows conflicting findings (Fleming and Burrows, 1986), and British research less effect on crime levels than on fear of crime (Ramsey, 1991). This is also the pattern suggested by the largest single British study (Atkins *et al.*, 1991). Other research (Painter, 1988, 1989*a*, 1989*b*, 1991) suggests more substantial effects on crime rates in a more restricted area. The differences may indicate that lighting enhancement for crime prevention purposes should be restricted to extremely localized problem sites rather than be installed generally. What is needed is more very specific bespoke lighting solutions in small areas, probably in conjunction with other approaches (as in Griswold, 1984), rather than uprating over a wide area. This is consistent with the most recent review of the literature, which contends:

street lighting can reduce crime and disorder when focused on badly lit, mixed use, pedestrian transit routes, in localised trouble spots where offender and target convergence is predictable, visibility is poor, and surveillance restricted. In short, the results from these projects may be indicative of the conditional circumstances in which street lighting can be effective [Painter, 1996: 333].

FOCUSED PREVENTION: HOT SPOTS AND REPEAT VICTIMIZATION

Primary crime prevention is often successful, and in many ways (like the design of new products, buildings, and ways of doing things) can be incorporated at little or no extra cost. There remains the issue of where and when to implement crime prevention measures. Fortunately for this purpose (although dreadful for the people concerned), crime is concentrated on particular areas, and on particular places and people within them. At the area level, this concentration creates crime hot spots (see Sherman *et al.*, 1989, Sherman, 1995; and Bottoms, this volume). At the level of the individual place or person, it is known as repeat victimization. Farrell (1995) provides a review, and Bridgeman and Sampson (1994) offer a practitioner's guide.

Repeat victimization sometimes exists almost by definition, as in domestic violence, embezzlement (where the employer–employee relationship is a necessary condition of the offence), and many kinds of fraud, including computer and cheque fraud. For these offences, it is self-evident that the prevention of repeat victimization would prevent most crime of the type. This is equally true of commercial burglaries (Mirrlees-Black and Ross, 1995), where, for instance, 2 per cent of manufacturers accounted for a quarter of the burglaries. The same pattern is found for domestic burglaries (Polvi *et al.*, 1990), racial attacks (Sampson and Phillips, 1992), and serious property crimes against schools (Burquest *et al.*, 1992). The same studies show there to be a marked reduction in the rate of repeats over short periods of time after a first victimization. The practical significance of this is that, given that the period of elevated risk is quite short, temporary precautions can be taken. The prevention of *repeat* victimization may prove to be a cost-efficient strategy of crime prevention generally. In England and Wales, the prevention of repeats is to be a police performance indicator. There are a number of advantages to using prior victimization as a way of prioritizing crime prevention:

1. Because it is based on examination of the individual circumstances of a crime, it will tend to involve the appropriate measures, social and physical, for the prevention of repeat victimization.
2. Preventing repeat victimization protects the most vulnerable social groups, without having to identify those groups, which can be socially divisive. Having been victimized already represents the least contentious basis for the claim to be given crime prevention attention.
3. Repeat victimization is highest, both absolutely and proportionately, in the most crime-ridden areas (Trickett *et al.*, 1992), which are also the areas that suffer the most serious crime (Pease 1988). The prevention of repeat victimization thus *automatically* directs attention to the areas which need it most, rather than areas with influential citizens (Harvey *et al.*, 1988).
4. The rate of victimization offers a realistic scheduling for crime prevention. Preventing repeat victimization is a way of 'drip-feeding' crime prevention. That is to say, because victimization occurs at a constant or slightly rising rate, the effort expended is roughly constant.
5. A high rate of victimization would tend to convert attention to repeat victimization into a community initiative, with the advantage over conventional community approaches of being rooted in real events suffered by citizens.

Besides its usefulness in scheduling crime prevention, work on repeat victimization also serves to highlight the way in which the crime problem is depicted in official data. The conventional measure is of crime incidents per citizen. This is made up of two elements: the number of people victimized, and the number of times each victim is victimized. Looking at property crime, it seems that some 3–4 per cent of households suffer some 40 per cent of the victimizations (Ellingworth *et al.*, 1995). The figures vary by year and crime type, and some exaggeration by chronic victims is possible. However, the data are very similar to unpublished work in both Sweden and the United States. The conventional way of presenting crime rates disguises this concentration of victimization on the small minority. The separation of prevalence and concentration is important in understanding crime at the small area level too, as Hope (1995) showed in his work in Hull. It is also crucial in clarifying how crime prevention is working. In an unpublished evaluation of an initiative against domestic violence, Graham Farrell and Alistair Buckley showed that, measured in terms of calls to the police, numbers of victims (prevalence) increased, but the number of calls from each victim (concentration) went down. These two changes offset each other, and the total number of calls remained roughly the same. If the initiative had been measured by total calls, it would have looked like a failure. In fact, the pattern is exactly what would have been hoped for in a successful programme. Most victims of domestic violence do not report their victimization. When police service improves, more report, so prevalence increases. Since at least some get the help they need to prevent the violence continuing, the number of calls per victim goes down. This highlights the need to separate prevalence and concentration in measuring crime.

Repeat victimization thus has profound implications for criminology. In the present context, it is simply argued to be probably the most effective way of deploying resources on crime prevention (see Anderson *et al.*, 1995). It also brings the functions of victim support and crime prevention closer together. Those who need victim support are, it turns out, those in most urgent need of crime prevention help (see Pease and Laycock, 1996).

PRIMARY CRIME PREVENTION: THE DECLINING YEARS?

Given its frequent success, and incorporation into current policy (Garland, 1996), why has primary crime prevention not permeated our thinking more fully? There is a schizoid feeling about it. On the one hand there is a literature enumerating prevention techniques, largely directed at the private sector's techniques of self-protection, in which there seems little or no obligation to demonstrate prevention success. The sense of the techniques is deemed self-evident. The most comprehensive example of this is Lawrence Fennelly's *Handbook of Loss Prevention and Crime Prevention*, which has now gone into its third edition (Fennelly, 1996). This excellent reference book assumes the efficacy of situational prevention and does not feel the need to cite rigorously evaluated success. The Fennelly volume will be the primary reference source of security managers charged with protecting their organizations against crime. To them, the effectiveness of primary prevention is not at issue.

In contrast to the Fennelly self-confidence, criminologists and police crime prevention officers face inertia and scepticism about claims of efficacy when attempting to make crime prevention a feature of public policy. Before going on to explore the contrast between public- and private-sector prevention, the problems typically encountered by advocates of primary crime prevention will be rehearsed and commented upon. In brief, they are:

1. The claims of crime displacement, whereby crime is moved around rather than prevented, haunts the subject. If total, displacement could be held to render primary crime prevention useless.
2. The lack of imagination which characterizes the public sector in its attempts to translate crime prevention policy into practice.
3. The dominance in local authorities of those who find primary prevention unappealing.

Crime Displacement: Conventional Views

There is little point in the policy-maker investing resources and effort into situational [crime] prevention if by doing so he merely shuffles crime from one area to the next but never reduces it. For this reason, the possibility of displacing crime by preventive intervention is a crucial issue for the policy-maker [Heal and Laycock, 1986: 123].

This 'crime shuffling' is what is *conventionally* meant by displacement. Displacement can induce a 'paralyzing extreme case pessimism' (Cornish and Clarke, 1986: 3). This is because of the practical limitations upon the measurement of displacement. One can show complete displacement to have occurred, but one can never show complete displacement not to have occurred. The prudent researcher of domestic burglary prevention will examine rates of the same offence in areas contiguous to a project area, to see whether crimes prevented in the project area have simply moved outside it. She may even look at the rate of the offence more generally in the police force area of interest. It is less likely that she will look at other property offences in contiguous areas, still less in the police force area as a whole. The probability that she will look still wider is effectively zero, since she is operating within a budget. Even if money were unlimited but displacement were to diverse offences and places, the effect would disappear into the normal variation in crime rates. Thus if some burglars turn to robberies close to home, some to robberies far from home, some to cheque fraud, some to drug-dealing, and so on, even total displacement would be undetectable. Total displacement is always something with which the extreme case pessimist can taunt the researcher, and never something that can be gainsaid. Whatever the truth, the sceptic can always add 'Ah but . . . '.

In the above, the *conventionality* of the definition of displacement was stressed. The best-known classification of displacement was devised by Reppetto (1976) and is set out below as modified form by Hakim and Rengert (1981). The classification is:

> temporal: committing the intended crime at a different time;
> spatial: committing the intended crime to the planned type of target in another place;
> tactical: committing the intended crime using a different method; and
> crime type/functional: committing a different type of crime from that intended.

Perpetrator displacement is a category added by Barr and Pease (1990). This occurs where a crime opportunity is so compelling that even if one person passes it up, others are available to take their place (as in stealing by finding, or drug supply).

There is an obvious overlap of these categories. For instance, spatial displacement must always be temporal displacement too. No one can be in two places at once! That apart, they strike the writer as an extraordinarily unimaginative categorization of the circumstances under which offenders change their minds, or have circumstances change their minds for them. This is not a criticism of Reppetto, who laid the foundation, but of those of us who came after and failed to develop the classification. Some space will be devoted to such a development, since it is of crucial importance for the assessment of crime prevention programmes.

Crime Displacement or Crime Deflection?

Perhaps the most fundamental flaw in the literature on crime displacement is its failure to consider how crime patterns arise. Before crime gets displaced, it must get placed. Why is the pattern of crime as it is? In England and Wales, the 10 per cent of parliamentary constituencies with the highest crime incidence suffer thirty-five times the amount of crime as the 10 per cent with the lowest incidence, and the patterns can be more extreme depending on areal unit and crime type chosen (Trickett *et al.*, 1992, 1995). These patterns do not emerge by chance, but are a function of both attractive and repulsive forces. Traditionally, displacement has been seen as a process of repulsion, whereby an initiative leads crime to go elsewhere. Stenzel (1977) noted that developments in an area can attract as well as repel crime, a point developed by Barron (1991*a*, 1991*b*), and by Block and Block (1995). The analogy of a force field in which repulsion and attraction interact should be the starting point for understanding crime (dis)placement. The neglect of Stenzel's point for so long illustrates how one-dimensional the perception of crime displacement has been. Crime is where it is because of the balance of effort and advantage for the offender currently built in to social and physical arrangements. There are two things which may happen when a crime is prevented. It may re-emerge as another crime (displacement). It may also prevent other crimes indirectly (the free-rider, or diffusion of benefits effect). If an offender does not know which places or people are protected and which are not, he or she may generalize from the decision not to commit crime against protected targets to decide not to commit crimes against other targets nearby. In this way the benefits of prevention are diffused. Research shows that the free-rider effect can be substantial (see e.g. Miethe, 1991; Clarke, 1991; Hesseling, 1995). The fact that displacement has been long debated, and that diffusion of benefits has been so neglected suggests that displacement is dominant not because it reflects a real attempt to understand crime flux, but because it serves as a convenient excuse for doing nothing ('Why bother? It will only get displaced').

A second crucial flaw in considering displacement has been to judge the movement of crime from one setting to another as necessarily a failure. This is mistaken. Barr and Pease (1990, 1991) preferred the word 'deflection' over 'displacement'. Deflection may be a success. Displacement is never referred to as a success. Crime deflection is benign when the deflected crime causes less harm and misery than the original crime. It is also benign when there are good reasons for concentrating crime in particular locations. An obvious instance is prostitution. A distinct red-light area in cities away from residential areas offers the possibility of avoidance. Clearly located areas for drug-dealing offer similar, albeit more contentious, benefits. In short, the view that all displacement/deflection is bad and that all patterns of crime are equally desirable is naïve. Displacement/deflection should be seen as a tool of policy rather than as an unmitigated evil.

None of the above should be taken to concede that displacement really is total. The most recent review suggests that it is not (Hesseling, 1995). There are good reasons for believing that review. Crimes are often closely distributed around an offender's home (Forrester *et al.*, 1988), or around a particular purpose (like theft of a means of transport; see Mayhew *et al.*, 1979), or around a particular criminal method, and this plausibly reduces the type and location of crime which should be scrutinized for displacement effects. Where that has been done, displacement has been shown to be far from total.

Prevention in Practice

The examples of successful crime prevention cited earlier were intelligently conceived and implemented. However, perfect implementation by government and local practitioners cannot be relied upon. There are probably fundamental political reasons for this, and many of the references to the relevant debate were listed earlier in the chapter. In what follows, the discussion primarily concerns perceptions of how crime prevention should work and competence in its implementation, but there is a blurred boundary between these concerns and the wider political themes alluded to earlier. Let us take the Home Office as an example. Several steps have been taken to improve the status of primary prevention over the last few years. For example, the publications from the Police Research Group of the Home Office disseminate good practice. The Crime Prevention Centre, which trains police officers as crime prevention officers, has been moved from portable buildings behind Staffordshire Police Headquarters to more prestigious premises in North Yorkshire. However, government expenditure on crime prevention represents only 3 per cent of expenditure on crime and criminal justice matters (Barclay, 1995). Within specifically Home Office expenditure on crime prevention, some 78 per cent goes on CCTV schemes (Koch, 1996). The way the money is dispensed is interesting. Local authorities are invited to submit proposals for appropriate CCTV schemes. They are not asked to submit proposals for maximally effective local schemes for prevention. In other words, whatever the crime problem, 78 per cent of the answer is assumed by Home Office ministers to lie in CCTV.

The bank robber Willie Sutton, when asked why he robbed banks, is alleged to have replied 'Because that's where they keep the money'. If one asks a local authority why it bids for a CCTV system, the same answer applies. The emphasis on CCTV invites local agencies to be cynical, to get money in, and spend it in ways which are of greatest local use and which can be reconciled to Home Office requirements for report. The process whereby local politics and expedience shape expenditure on crime is well documented (Gilling 1994*a*,

1994*b*; Buck 1997). In short, *good* primary prevention requires a clear crime focus, an objective analysis of the presenting problem, and a choice of means from among those available. What is *actually* happening is that, by its patterns of expenditure, the Home Office demonstrates the marginality of crime prevention; by the way it makes money available, it by-passes the necessary analysis, and once the money hits the maelstrom of local politics, expenditure is a matter more of need and expedience than crime control.

THE RE-EMERGENCE OF COMMUNITY

Social disorganization has long been deemed a factor in determining levels of crime (see Shaw and McKay, 1942), but the focus of the earlier tradition lay with the supply of motivated offenders rather than of criminal opportunities. Alongside the classic crime-as-opportunity studies collected in *Designing Out Crime* (Clarke and Mayhew, 1980) was a study by Sheena Wilson whose significance lay, *inter alia*, in identifying child density as a determinant of levels of vandalism, thereby implicating the policy of housing departments in the allocation of families to dwellings. This role has also been emphasized in a series of studies performed in Sheffield by Tony Bottoms, Paul Wiles, and their colleagues (see Bottoms *et al.*, 1989; Bottoms and Wiles 1991*a*, 1991*b*). They contend: in order to understand and explain rates of offending, it is vital to consider who lives where; how they came to live there; what kind of social life the residents have created; how outsiders (including official agencies) react to them; and why they remain in the areas and have not moved (paraphrased from Bottoms and Wiles, 1991*a*: 122).

The renewed emphasis on social factors in crime prevention has taken many forms. Hope and Shaw (1988) criticize some applications of primary crime prevention as suggesting that a community is under attack from without, rather than the more usual circumstance of being predated upon from within. King (1989) emphasizes the role of social crime prevention through local democracy, and contrasts the French approach, which incorporates such an emphasis, with the individualistic approach to crime prevention '*à la* Thatcher', and the latter's associated emphasis on opportunity reduction. Bottoms and Wiles (1991*b*) regard the neglect of people dynamics as a fault of Anglo-American criminology in general rather than of the United Kingdom in Thatcher's thrall.

Perhaps the most trenchant critique of a primary prevention tradition is offered by Currie (1988). He distinguishes two conflicting visions of what community crime prevention is. The two phases differ fundamentally in their conception of a community. Phase 2 emphasizes 'those more tangible structures and institutions that underlie and shape community attitudes' (1988: 281), and is less concerned with the offender as a focus of intervention. Perhaps most fundamentally, Phase 2 thinking differs in considering the place of crime in the scale of priorities for communities. Phase 1 thinkers, says Currie, envision the community exerting its moral authority over bad people who seem to appear from nowhere, and who will surely take over if we do not wave the wand of traditional values at them—through tough policing, among other means. (*ibid.*: 282) He contends that at its worst, Phase 1 thinking:

can slide into a kind of nostalgic voluntarism that exhorts shattered communities to pull themselves up by their own bootstraps, without help—and without money . . . Phase 1 is no longer very impressive as a strategy against serious crime. . . . The over-selling of Phase 1 ideas has tangible and disturbing consequences: it diverts resources away from other things we might do, while offering facile but easily dashed hopes that quick solutions will stop crime [*ibid.*: 284].

Phase 2, by contrast, is more complicated in its understanding of crime and how communities might combat it. But 'it is also far more promising, especially as a strategy for preventing *serious* crime, not merely reducing fear or taming neighbourhood incivilities. It is also, it is suggested, far more attuned to deeper and more fruitful criminological traditions' (*ibid.*: 282).

Extended consideration has been given here to the Currie critique for two reasons: First, I am unsure of what constitutes a Phase 2 approach, other than its complexity and its location of the crime problem alongside other social problems. Secondly, it seems to me that Currie caricatures the kinds of research done under Phase 1 traditions. Not all crime takes place in the kinds of shattered community whose image he evokes. There are many ways and places in which simple measures can be fruitful. Thirdly, even in shattered communities, simple measures may represent a kind of toehold on order through which a nucleus of community organization may be formed. In change programmes the first step should usually be the one most easily implemented, so that some experience of success may form the core of more ambitious efforts at change.

Whatever one may feel about the change, the *Zeitgeist* of crime prevention has recently moved away from the situational towards the complex and communal, and this has influenced and been reflected in the organizational arrangements for crime prevention activity. The Morgan Report (1991) advocates a statutory responsibility upon local authorities for 'community safety', and this will probably be realized in modified form, after the change of government in the United Kingdom in 1997. The loosening of crime prevention to become community safety, and the backgrounds of those now being recruited as community safety officers probably means a de-emphasis of primary prevention in favour of secondary and tertiary prevention. This may be hastened by the popularity of *zero tolerance* programmes imported from the United States, and inspired by a work of Wilson and Kelling (1982). This asserts that disorder actually spawns serious crime, as unchecked rule-breaking escalates into something worse. The new popularity of that orientation, some sixteen years after its first appearance in print, says that something is happening in the political arena which merits explanation.

The trend away from primary prevention can be illustrated by the experience of the Safer Cities programme in Great Britain (Standing Committee on Crime Prevention, 1991). This programme, launched in 1988, set out to reduce crime, to lessen the fear of crime, and to create safer cities within which economic enterprise and community life could flourish. In was launched in 1988 and was wound up in 1995. The programme emphasized situational measures, some two-thirds of expenditure being on such measures. The programme enjoyed early success in reducing domestic burglary (Ekblom *et al.*, 1996). However, as time went on, there was a clear gravitation away from primary prevention and towards offender-oriented schemes, both in England and Wales and also in Scotland (Carnie, 1995; Sutton, 1996), summarized as Table 27.2.

Table 27.2 Proportion of money spent on particular scheme types by year

	89/90	90/91	91/92	92/93
Offender	14	21	25	30
Situational	73	70	63	55
Other	13	8	12	15

Modified from Sutton (1996).

This shows that despite the success of a programme directed largely towards primary prevention, co-ordinators moved away from the approach. Sutton cites many reasons for this. One local co-ordinator said that 'it was felt that target-hardening simply led to displacement' (Sutton, 1996: 19). Another identified the change as resulting from the easing of Home Office direction, implying that the natural instincts of the co-ordinators could take over. 'Where the move towards implementing more offender-oriented schemes was mentioned by coordinators, it was mainly in terms of the coordinators' development into "more rounded crime prevention professionals", "seeing the wider picture" and tackling crime problems with a broader brush' (Sutton, 1996: 20; see also Laycock and Tilley, 1995). 'This is a strikingly thought-provoking result, given that the situational measures adopted were subsequently found to have been cost-effective in reducing burglary' (Sutton, 1996: 20).

Who knows whether the drift is a function of the discipline background of those involved, the local political and organizational pressures to which they were subjected, the necessary empirical research underpinning which some co-ordinators felt unable to deliver, or a general perceived *heartlessness* of primary prevention? It is now clear, however, that there is a dynamic in implementation which worked against primary prevention in the Safer Cities context, and which may be general. That it occurred in the face of the success of the situational measures is both fascinating and depressing.

Prospects for Primary Prevention: Motives, Implications, and Political Will

To repeat the plot so far, primary crime prevention directs attention to the crime event, not the criminal actor. Much research has shown well-implemented primary crime prevention to be typically successful in reducing crime. This is fully reflected in private-sector self-protection, where security measures and risk management proliferate. It is not so in public policy. The conventional criticisms of primary crime prevention in the public sector have been discussed, and some reasons offered for this. However, the greatest relevant difference is the motive for crime prevention. If a company makes security decisions, it does so having estimated that they will benefit the company itself. In the public sector, this is not so. For present purposes, the public sector is defined as having three components:

1. The actions of public bodies to ensure the safety of themselves and citizens;
2. The actions of citizens towards the protection of themselves and others;
3. The actions of private providers of goods and services towards the protection of those using the goods and services in question.

Can we assume the wish to prevent crime in the above contexts? There is a chasm between possibility and achievement which means that the answer is either no, or that the wish takes a position subordinate to other purposes. Alternatively, the domains of policy are so segmented that action in one segment is taken with indifference to its crime consequences in another. Some twelve years ago, I was driving home from a Young Offenders' Institution when two news items on the car radio illustrated the latter point. At the time, the favourite car for thieves was the Ford Cortina, because of its good performance and risible security. Many young car thieves were sent to detention centres. The two news items were:

1. The announcement of record profits for the Ford Motor Company;
2. The opening of two strict-regime detention centres, intended more effectively to reform or deter those detained.

The link between the news items was that many of those who would be sent to those detention centres would be young car thieves. The cars they took would disproportionately be Ford Cortinas. This was an instance in which the failure to provide adequate security in the Cortina cost money and distress through the criminal justice process. What is more, the commercial choice which had visited the costs of police, court, and detention on the public purse had contributed, through low expenditure on car security, to record profits for the Ford Company. Levi *et al.*'s comment is central: 'We are acutely aware that if—as in pollution control—the "externalities" of costs to the public were taken into account, the costing of crime prevention in *every* sphere would take a different form' (1991: 1). Because public provision so effectively cushions corporate and insured crime victims from the costs of crime, and because national and local government are so segmented, even massively successful crime prevention measures cannot be guaranteed implementation. The spectacular reduction in cheque fraud after the incorporation of a photograph on cheque cards in Sweden (see above) has not led to such a measure being taken in the United Kingdom. There is no doubt a threshold of cost above which simple crime prevention will come into play, but that threshold is massively above the point at which the crime represents a significant *social* problem. An interesting case study is offered by Mueller and Adler. They observe that, as transatlantic passenger traffic by sea gave way to the aeroplane, an epidemic of losses of ocean liners occurred, most of them old and marginally maintained.

It is clear to us that most of the losses were avoidable. . . . Some vessels were over-insured at the time of loss. In several cases, the operators were or had been in the process of bankruptcy, or the vessel was declared to be unprofitable. . . . Above all, there were the six liners en route to the ship breakers for scrap, some of whom sank close to their final destination. We have been unable to ascertain whether the insurance value of a ship destined for the breakers is greater than her scrap value [1991: 105].

The same authors had identified a similar phenomenon when obsolete cargo ships sank in large numbers after the advent of ship containerization (Mueller and Adler, 1985). Put generally, the crime prevention motive interlocks with other motives, and usually occupies a subsidiary role. Carter writes:

Ideally when deciding how much to spend on loss prevention the individual should allow for social costs and benefits but, as in other private economic decisions, he will normally be concerned only with items which affect his own pocket. At present after a theft the individual incurs only a little part of the cost of apprehending, convicting and punishing the thief (for example the cost of appearing in court); but neither does he receive a tax or rate rebate for taking precautions which are expected to reduce his demand on public services [1974: 32].

Field and Hope (1990) apply a simple economic model to the decision-making of individual households, and find that at the individual level, the optimal amount of crime prevention installed is sub-optimal at the community level. The under-provision of crime prevention is no mystery. It is a function of economic rationality given the incentives and disincentives which tax, time, and insurance impose upon the individual. This personal calculus is potentially modifiable by the operation of the insurance market, and the way in which the insurance market works merits some attention. The unit of account for the police (and the victim) is the crime. The unit of account for the insurance industry is the pound sterling (Pease and Litton, 1984). Insurers are concerned with making an overall profit on a class of business. They are thus not interested in risky small-premium business because the anticipated cost of processing claims is too high (Fenn, 1986). Thus, for whole areas, household insurance is effectively unavailable. These will by definition be the areas in greatest need of incentives towards crime prevention. Within areas in which insurance is available, the pressure to prevent crime will be exerted in proportion to the size of the possible loss. Insurance incentives to prevent crime are exerted upon places where large losses are possible, that is, places which are numerically trivial when one counts crimes rather than pounds. There is a mismatch between where crime is and where insurance exerts its pressure to prevent crime. A side-effect of this is that insurance is given in those sectors of the market where there is most to gain by insurance fraud, as in the loss of passenger ships described earlier. No one knows the proportion of all property crime which is created by insurance (but see Litton, 1990, 1996).

The exclusion of crimes against the person from the consideration of incentives derives from the fact that most research and evaluation from a primary prevention perspective has *relatively* neglected crimes of violence, except in so far as this is attempted through the protection of place, as in lighting studies. Three reasons may be put forward for this:

1. People move, places do not. Victims of violence cannot easily be protected across places.
2. The expenditure of crime prevention energy has been moulded by the individual and corporate economic concerns of victims. Although violent crimes are acknowledged as more serious than crimes against property, economic interests and pressure on the police do shape crime prevention effort (Harvey *et al.*, 1988).
3. Much violence occurs between intimates (Smith, 1989; Stanko, 1990). Crime prevention has typically been characterized as protecting victims against external dangers (Hope and Shaw, 1988).

Sometimes, reasons for non-implementation cannot be dignified even by economic interest. Personal rivalries and ideological differences can subvert crime prevention efforts. They 'can increase social conflicts and provide a site for power struggles to be played out. Negotiating an agreement between conflicting groups is . . . often essential for the implementation of a crime prevention strategy' (Sampson, 1991: 30). A local authority housing department's wish for quiet estates is in tension with its wish to have a ready location for problem families. A school may have its wish not to have its equipment stolen offset by the knowledge that new equipment would work better. Individual victims, particularly if insured, may not feel compelled to prevent their own victimization.

In short, insufficient attention has been given to the *pressure* on people to prevent crime. This is sometimes very meagre, sometimes absent. The scope of simple situational measures of crime prevention must be measured against what is truly intended, not against the standard of that to which lip service is paid. In the most thoroughgoing analysis of this issue to date, Laycock and Tilley (1995) distinguish:

1. Legislative mandates, effective 'when directed at the manufacturers of goods that are particularly vulnerable to crime' (*ibid.*: 542).
2. Exhortation, for instance in the award scheme 'Secured by Design' given to house builders who meet police-approved security specifications.
3. Publicity, of questionable efficacy in most circumstances.

To this can be added the changes in financial incentives; for example local taxation serves to make small businesses less likely to take crime prevention measures, and insurance does the same for private citizens and businesses. A thorough review of fiscal pressures towards and against crime prevention seems timely.

Perhaps because a real economic motive to prevent crime is currently lacking, failures of implementation often intrude, and these have yielded some tragi-comedy. Implementation problems are reviewed by Hope (1985). Hope and Murphy (1983) describe many instances of implementation failure. A sensible and well-considered scheme of target-hardening directed at schools failed because the anti-climb paint used was applied too thinly—true to the traditions of painters but useless for the anti-climb purpose; replacing tarmac underneath windows by greenery got as far as breaking up the tarmac; replacing frequently broken windows by a proprietary material much more difficult to break was thwarted by the reluctance of local authority employees to store the new material; finally, the overtime offered to caretakers at the most heavily victimized schools provoked resentment among their colleagues at other schools who did not have the same opportunity for making extra cash, so the patrols were discontinued. In another project (Barker *et al.*, 1992) a new sports area, upon completion, went overnight from being deemed so vulnerable that it required security patrols during the night to being regarded as capable of fending for itself without any oversight. Stories like these do not make one sanguine about the status which the implementation of crime prevention would be afforded were it to come directly under local authority control. If implementation failure really is the result of the lack of a motive to act, its effects are doubly pernicious. First, it makes things fail which could have succeeded. Secondly, it creates a dynamic whereby earlier avoidable failures provide a reason for not trying again. Failures to prevent crime have to be ascribed to theory or implementation failure. If ascribed to theory failure, the implication is that no conceivable implementation of that kind could prove successful. If ascribed to implementation breakdown, the theoretical basis lives, to be reincarnated in more effective forms. The danger is that implementation failure is interpreted as theory failure, which closes off an avenue of possible application.

A second response to apparent failure is the myopic reproduction of the technique over time and place, unchanged by the lessons of research. This may be not because of what the research reveals, but because of how it is translated into media presentations and popular consciousness. Consider Neighbourhood Watch. The British evaluative research on the topic was scrupulous in choosing the best schemes for evaluation (Bennett, 1987, 1990, 1991) and arguing that the appropriate next steps concerned the dynamics of how Neighbourhood Watch was supposed to work. In effect, Bennett concluded that implementation failure had occurred. Nonetheless, reactions to the research were less thoughtful than the research itself. Its unthinking opponents persuade themselves that theory failure has been demonstrated. Its proponents continue to advocate it, despite the obvious implementation failures which descriptive research reveals, and the variety of forms which it can take (Husain and Bright, 1990).

Futures in Crime Prevention

It seems absurd to be optimistic about crime prevention. Yet primary prevention is often possible and sometimes easy. There have been major successes, which have not been implemented widely. This is attributable to the absence of an adequate motivation to do so. The scale of successful property crime prevention effort now is probably as great as could realistically be expected in the absence of inducements to change that scale. If primary crime prevention is to assume greater generality, it must research more fully into crimes of violence and crimes between intimates. This is beginning to occur for bullying and child sexual abuse. One way of moving in this direction involves the closer integration of victim support and conventional crime prevention. Another relatively neglected area is that of victimless crime, drug use in particular. While some secondary and tertiary prevention programmes could be characterized as demand reduction, it will probably always be the case that less preventive effort will be directed towards crimes without victims.

Evidence that many of those carrying out primary prevention work become disenchanted with it cannot be ignored. The liberal-communitarian debate and the undeniable complexities surrounding the political uses and rhetoric of community safety will be pre-eminent in scholarship and practice. For all its success, primary crime prevention may fall further out of fashion, to be replaced by secondary and tertiary measures whose efficacy is much less impressive, and which carry with them the baggage of blame and punishment. Primary prevention will, however, remain the practice of choice in the private sector and among affluent households where the benefits of crime reduction fall to those investing in it.

Selected Further Reading

Felson, M. (1993),*Crime and Everyday Life*. London: Pine Forge.
This book explains why crime rises and falls, and suggests ways in which changes may affect the trends. It is clear and enjoyable to read.

Felson, M., and Clarke, R. V.(1996), *Business and Crime Prevention*. Monsey, NY: Criminal Justice Press.
This offers insights into how new technology and other changing ways of doing business are reflected in crime patterns. This volume is one of a series published by the Criminal Justice Press, most under the sole or joint editorship of R. V. Clarke, which detail innovations in prevention. All are worth reading.

Fennelly, L. J. (1996), *Handbook of Loss Prevention and Crime Prevention*, 3rd edn. Boston: Butterworth-Heinemann.

This is the book for a security manager tasked with preventing loss through crime suffered by the organization. It shows how the field is seen when the need to prevent crime against a particular target is taken as read.

Tonry, M. and Farrington, D. P. (1995), *Building a Safer Society: Strategic Approaches to Crime Prevention.* Chicago, Ill.: University of Chicago Press.
This volume is a collection of readings which range widely across the topic. It includes chapters on community crime prevention, situational crime prevention, preventing substance abuse, preventing repeat victimization, among others. When written it was probably the definitive academic source for the study of crime prevention.

REFERENCES

AMERICAN BAR ASSOCIATION (1986), *Drunk Driving Laws and Enforcement: An Assessment of Effectiveness.* Washington, DC: American Bar Association.

ANDERSON, D., CHENERY, S., and PEASE, K. (1995), *Biting Back: Tackling Repeat Burglary and Car Crime.* Crime Detection and Prevention Paper No. 58. London: Home Office.

ATKINS, S., HUSAIN, S., and STOREY, A. (1991), *The Influence of Street Lighting on Crime and Fear of Crime,* Crime Prevention Unit Paper No. 28. London: Home Office.

AUSTIN, C. (1988), *The Prevention of Robbery at Building Society Branches,* Crime Prevention Unit Paper No. 14. London: Home Office.

BANNISTER, J. (1991), *The Impact of Environmental Design upon the Incidence and Type of Crime,* Central Research Unit Paper. Edinburgh: Scottish Office.

BARCLAY, G. (1995), *Information on the Criminal Justice System in England and Wales.* London: Home Office.

BARKER, M., PEASE, K., and WEBB, B. (1992), *Community Service and Crime Prevention: The Cheadle Heath Project,* Crime Prevention Unit Paper No. 39. London: Home Office.

BARR, R., and PEASE, K. (1990), 'Crime Placement, Displacement and Deflection', in N. Morris and M. Tonry, eds., *Crime and Justice: A Review of Research,* vol. 12. Chicago, Ill.: University of Chicago Press.

—— and —— (1991), 'A Place for Every Crime and Every Crime in its Place: An Alternative Perspective on Crime Displacement', in D. J.

Evans, N. R. Fyfe, and D. T. Herbert, eds., *Crime, Policing and Place: Essays in Environmental Criminology.* London: Routledge.

BARRON, J. M. (1991*a*), *Shuffling Crime Around: Offender Responses to Preventive Action,* unpublished MA thesis, University of Manchester.

—— (1991*b*), 'Repulsive and Attractive Displacement', paper presented to the American Society of Criminology, San Francisco.

BENNETT, T. (1987), *An Evaluation of Two Neighbourhood Watch Schemes in London,* report to the Home Office. Cambridge: Cambridge University Institute of Criminology.

—— (1990), *Evaluating Neighbourhood Watch.* Aldershot: Gower.

—— (1991), 'Themes and Variations in Neighbourhood Watch', in D. J. Evans, N. R. Fyfe and D. T. Herbert, eds., *Crime, Policing and Place: Essays in Environmental Criminology.* London: Routledge.

—— and WRIGHT, R. (1984), *Burglars on Burglary: Prevention and the Offender.* Farnborough: Gower.

BENTVELSEN, T., and VAN DER ZON, F. (1987), *Petty Crime in High Rise Buildings Developed after the Second World War.* Delft: Delft University Press.

BERRY, G., and CARTER, M. (1992), *Assessing Crime Prevention Initiatives: The First Steps,* Crime Prevention Unit Paper No. 31. London: Home Office.

BLOCK, R. L., and BLOCK, C. B. (1995) 'Space, Place and Crime: Hot Spot Areas and Hot Places of Liquor-Related Crime', in J. E. Eck and D. Weisburd, eds., *Crime and Place.* Monsey, NY: Willow Tree Press.

BOTTOMS, A. E. (1990), 'Crime Prevention Facing the 1990s', *Policing and Society*, 1: 3–22.

—— MAWBY, R. I., and XANTHOS, P. (1989), 'A Tale of Two Estates', in D. Downes, ed., *Crime and the City*. London: Macmillan.

—— and WILES, P. (1991*a*), 'Housing Markets and Residential Community Crime Careers', in D. J. Evans, N. R. Fyfe, and D. T. Herbert, eds., *Crime, Policing and Place: Essays in Environmental Criminology*. London: Routledge.

—— and —— (1991*b*), 'Explanations of Crime and Place', in D. J. Evans, N. R. Fyfe, and D. T. Herbert, eds., *Crime, Policing and Place: Essays in Environmental Criminology*. London: Routledge.

—— and —— (1996), 'Understanding Crime Prevention in Late Modern Societies', in T. Bennett, ed., *Preventing Crime and Disorder*. Cambridge: Institute of Criminology.

BRANTINGHAM, P. J., and FAUST, F. L. (1976), 'A Conceptual Model of Crime Prevention', *Crime and Delinquency*, 22: 130–46.

BRIDGEMAN, C. (1996), *Crime Risk Management: Making It Work?* Crime Detection and Prevention Paper No. 70. London: Home Office.

—— and SAMPSON, A. (1994), *Wise After the Event: Tackling Repeat Victimisation*. London: Home Office.

BROWN, B. (1995), *Closed Circuit Television in Town Centres: Three Case Studies*. Crime Detection and Prevention Paper No. 68. London: Home Office.

BUCK, W. (1997), *Crime Prevention on Merseyside*, unpublished Ph.D. thesis, Manchester University.

—— CHATTERTON, M., and PEASE, K. (1995), 'The Prevention of Obscene, Threatening and Other Nuisance Telephone Calls: A Call-Tracing System', *Security Journal*, 6: 171–5.

BURQUEST, R., FARRELL, G., and PEASE, K. (1992), 'Lessons from Schools', *Policing*, 8: 148–55.

BURROWS, J. N. (1979), 'Closed Circuit Television and Crime on the London Underground', in P. Mayhew, R. V. Clarke, J. N. Burrows, J. M. Hough, and S. W. C. Winchester, eds., *Crime in Public View*, Home Office Research Study No. 49. London: HMSO. Reproduced in R. V. Clarke and P. M. Mayhew, eds., *Designing Out Crime*. London: HMSO, 1980.

—— (1988), *Retail Crime: Prevention through Crime Analysis*, Crime Prevention Unit Paper No. 11. London: Home Office.

—— (1991), *Making Crime Prevention Pay: Initiatives from Business*, Crime Prevention Unit Paper No. 27. London: Home Office.

—— and HEAL, K. (1979), 'Police Car Security Campaigns', in J. Burrows, P. Ekblom, and K. Heal, eds., *Crime Prevention and the Police*. Home Office Research Study No. 55. London: HMSO. Reproduced in R. V. Clarke and P. M. Mayhew, eds., *Designing Out Crime*. London: HMSO, 1980.

CARNIE, J. K. (1995), *The Safer Cities Programme in Scotland; Overview Report*. Edinburgh: Scottish Office Central Research Unit.

CARTER, R. L. (1974), *Theft in the Market*, Hobart Paper No. 60. London: Institute of Economic Affairs.

CHALLINGER, D. (1991), 'Less Telephone Vandalism: How Did It Happen?', *Security Journal*, 2: 111–19. Reproduced in R. V. Clarke, ed., *Situational Crime Prevention: Successful Case Studies*. New York: Harrow and Heston, 1991.

CLARKE, R. V. (1991), 'Deterring Obscene Phone Callers: The New Jersey Experience', in R. V. Clarke, ed., *Situational Crime Prevention: Successful Case Studies*. New York: Harrow and Heston.

—— (1995) ,'Situational Crime Prevention', in M. Tonry and D. P. Farrington, eds., *Building a Safer Society*. Crime and Justice vol. 19. Chicago, Ill.: University of Chicago Press.

—— and FELSON M., eds. (1993), *Routine Activity and Rational Choice*. London: Transaction.

—— FIELD, S., and McGRATH, G. (1991), 'Target Hardening of Banks in Australia and Displacement of Robberies', *Security Journal*, 2: 84–90.

—— and HARRIS, P. M. (1992), 'Auto Theft and its Prevention', in M. Tonry, ed., *Crime and Justice 16*. Chicago, Ill.: University of Chicago Press.

—— and MAYHEW, P. M., eds. (1980), *Designing Out Crime*. London: HMSO.

—— and —— (1988), 'The British Gas Suicide Story and its Criminological Implications', in N. Morris and M. Tonry, eds., *Crime and Justice: An Annual Review of Research*, vol. 10. Chicago, Ill.: University of Chicago Press.

COHEN, L. E., and FELSON, M. (1979), 'Social Change and Crime Rate Trends: A Routine Activity Approach', *American Sociological Review*, 44: 588–608.

COLEMAN, A. (1985), *Utopia on Trial*. London: Hilary Shipman.

CONWAY, D. (1995), *Classical Liberalism: The Unvanquished Ideal*. New York: St Martins Press.

CORNISH, D. B., and CLARKE, R. V., eds. (1986), *The Reasoning Criminal: Rational Choice Perspectives on Offending*. New York: Springer-Verlag.

—— and —— (1988*a*), 'Understanding Crime Displacement: An Application of Rational Choice Theory', *Criminology*, 7: 933–47.

—— and —— (1988*b*), 'Crime Specialization, Crime Displacement and Rational Choice Theory', in H. Wegener, F. Losel, and J. Haisch, eds., *Criminal Behaviour and the Justice System: Psychological Perspectives*. New York: Springer-Verlag.

CRAWFORD A. (1994), 'The Partnership Approach to Community Crime Prevention: Corporatism at the Local Level?' *Social and Legal Studies*, 3: 497–519.

—— (1995), 'Appeals to Community and Crime Prevention', *Crime, Law and Social Change*, 22: 97–126.

—— and JONES, M. (1995) 'Inter-agency Co-operation and Community-based Crime Prevention', *British Journal of Criminology*, 35: 17–33.

CURRIE, E. (1988), 'Two Visions of Community Crime Prevention', in T. Hope and M. Shaw, eds., *Communities and Crime Reduction*. London: HMSO.

DAVIES, S. G. (1996), 'The Case Against: CCTV Should Not Be Introduced', *International Journal of Risk, Security and Crime Prevention*, 1: 327–31.

DECKER, J. F. (1972), 'Curbside Deterrence: An Analysis of the Effect of a Slug Rejectory Device, Coin View Window and Warning Labels on Slug Usage in New York City Parking Meters', *Criminology*, 9: 127–42.

—— (1991) 'Curbside Deterrence'. In R. V. Clarke, ed., *Situational Crime Prevention: Successful Case Studies*. New York: Harrow and Heston 1992.

DESCHAMPS, S., BRANTINGHAM, P. L., and BRANTINGHAM, P. J. (1991), 'The British Columbia Transit Fare Evasion Audit', *Security Journal*, 2: 211–18. Reproduced in R. V. Clarke, ed., *Situational Crime Prevention: Successful Case Studies*. New York: Harrow and Heston.

DILONARDO R. L. (1996), 'Defining and Measuring the Economic Benefit of Electronic Article Surveillance', *Security Journal*, 7: 3–9.

—— and CLARKE, R. V. (1996), 'Reducing the Rewards of Shoplifting: An Evaluation of Ink Tags', *Security Journal*, 7: 11–14.

DURHAM, P. (1996), 'Why CCTV? A Cure Looking for an Illness', in Home Office, *CCTV: Looking Out For You*. London: Home Office.

ECK, J., and SPELMAN, W. (1988), *Problem Solving: Problem Oriented Policing in Newport*. Washington, DC: Police Executive Research Forum/National Institute of Justice.

—— and —— (1991), 'Thefts from Vehicles in Shipyard Parking Lots', in R. V. Clarke, ed., *Situational Crime Prevention: Successful Case Studies*. New York: Harrow and Heston.

EKBLOM, P. (1986), *The Prevention of Shop Theft: An Approach Through Crime Analysis*, Home Office Crime Prevention Paper No. 5. London: Home Office.

—— (1987), *Preventing Robbery at Sub-Post Offices*, Home Office Crime Prevention Paper No. 9. London: Home Office.

—— (1988), *Getting the Best out of Crime Analysis*, Home Office Crime Prevention Unit Paper No. 10. London: Home Office.

—— (1991*a*), 'Talking to Offenders: Practical Lessons for Local Crime Prevention', in O. Nello, ed., *Urban Crime: Statistical Approaches and Analyses*. Barcelona: Institut d'Estudies Metropolitans de Barcelona.

—— (1991*b*), 'Preventing Post Office Robberies in London: Effects and Side Effects', in R. V. Clarke, ed., *Situational Crime Prevention: Successful Case Studies*. New York: Harrow and Heston.

—— (1994), 'Proximal Circumstances: A Mechanism-Based Classification of Crime Prevention', in R. V .Clarke, ed., *Crime Prevention Studies 2*. Monsey, NY: Willow Tree Press.

—— and SIMON, F. (1988), *Crime and Racial Harrassment in Asian-Run Small Shops: The Scope for Prevention*, Crime Prevention Unit Paper No. 15. London: Home Office.

—— LAW, H., and SUTTON, M. (1996), *Domestic Burglary Schemes in the Safer Cities Programme*, Research Findings 42. London: Home Office Research and Statistics Directorate.

ELLINGWORTH, D., FARRELL, G., and PEASE, K. (1995), 'A Victim is a Victim is a Victim: Chronic Victimisation in Four Sweeps of the British Crime Survey', *British Journal of Criminology*, 35: 360–5.

FARRELL, G. (1995), 'Preventing Repeat Victimisation', in M. Tonry and D. P. Farrington, eds., *Building a Safer Society. Crime and Justice 19*. Chicago, Ill.: University of Chicago Press.

FARRINGTON, D. P., BOWEN, S., BUCKLE, A., BURNS-HOWELL, T., BURROWS, J., and

SPEED, M. (1993), 'An Experiment on the Prevention of Shoplifting', in R. V. Clarke, ed., *Crime Prevention Studies 1*. Monsey, NY: Willow Tree Press.

FELSON, M. (1986), 'Linking Criminal Choices, Routine Activities, Informal Control and Criminal Outcomes', in D. B. Cornish and R. V. Clarke, eds., *The Reasoning Criminal: Rational Choice Perspectives on Offending*. New York: Springer-Verlag.

—— (1993), *Crime and Everyday Life*. London: Pine Forge.

FENN, P. (1986), 'Insurance against Theft: A Market Contribution to Crime Prevention', in *Crime UK: An Economic and Policy Audit*. Oxford: Hermitage.

FENNELLY, L. J. (1996), *Handbook of Loss Prevention and Crime Prevention*, 3rd edn. Boston, Mass.: Butterworth-Heinemann.

FIELD, S., and HOPE, T. (1990), 'Economics, the Consumer and Crime Prevention', in R. Morgan, ed., *Policing Organised Crime and Crime Prevention: British Criminology Conference 1989*. Vol. 4. Bristol: Bristol Centre for Criminal Justice.

FLEMING, R., and BURROWS, J. (1986), 'The Case for Lighting as a Means of Preventing Crime', *Home Office Research Bulletin*, 22: 14–17.

FORRESTER, D. P., CHATTERTON, M. R., and PEASE, K. (1988), *The Kirkholt Burglary Prevention Demonstration Project*, Crime Prevention Unit Paper No. 13. London: Home Office.

GARLAND, D. (1990), *Punishment and Social Theory*. Oxford: Clarendon.

—— (1996), 'The Limits of the Sovereign State: Strategies of Crime Control in Contemporary Society', *British Journal of Criminology*, 36: 445–71.

GAROFALO, J. (1987), 'Reassessing the Lifestyle Model of Personal Victimisation', in M. R. Gottfredson and T. Hirschi, eds., *Positive Criminology*. London: Sage.

GENDREAU, P., and ROSS, R. R. (1987), 'Revivification of Rehabilitation: Evidence from the 1980s', *Justice Quarterly*, 4: 349–407.

GILLING, D. (1993), 'Crime Prevention Discourses and the Multi-agency Approach', *International Journal of the Sociology of Law'* 21: 145–57.

—— (1994a), 'Multi-agency Crime Prevention: Some Barriers to Implementation', *Howard Journal*, 33: 109–26.

—— (1994b), 'Multi-Agency Crime Prevention in Britain: The Problem of Combining Situational and Social Strategies', in R. V. Clarke, ed., *Crime Prevention Studies 2*. Monsey, NY: Willow Tree Press.

—— (1996) 'Policing, Crime Prevention and Partnerships', in F. Leishman, ed., *Core Issues in Policing*. London: Longman.

GOLDSTEIN, H. (1990), *Problem-Oriented Policing*. New York: McGraw-Hill.

GRISWOLD, D. B. (1984), 'Crime Prevention and Commercial Burglary: A Time Series Analysis', *Journal of Criminal Justice*, 12: 493–501.

GROOMBRIDGE, N., and MURJI, K. (1994), *Obscured by Cameras? CCTV and Policing*. Criminal Justice Matters No. 17. Autumn. London: Institute for the Study and Treatment of Delinquency.

HAKIM, S., and RENGERT, G. F. (1981), *Crime Spillover*. Beverly Hills, Cal.: Sage.

HARVEY, L., GRIMSHAW, P., and PEASE, K. (1988), 'The Work of Crime Prevention Officers', in R. Morgan and D. J. Smith, eds., *Coming to Terms with Policing*. London: Routledge.

HAUBER, A. R. (1978), 'Fraud and Public Transport', *Research Bulletin*, no. 2. The Hague: Research and Documentation Centre, Netherlands Ministry of Justice.

HEAL, K., and LAYCOCK, G. K. (1986), *Situational Crime Prevention: From Theory into Practice*. London: HMSO.

HEARNDEN, K. (1996) 'Small Businesses Approach to Managing CCTV to Combat Crime', *International Journal of Risk, Security and Crime Prevention* 1: 19–31.

HESSELING R. B. P. (1994), 'Displacement: A Review of the Empirical Literature'. In R. V. Clarke, ed., *Crime Prevention Studies 2*. Monsey, NY: Willow Tree Press.

HILL, N. (1986), *Pre-Payment Coin Meters: A Target for Burglary*, Crime Prevention Unit Paper No. 6. London: Home Office.

HINDELANG, M. J., GOTTFREDSON, M. R., and GAROFALO, J. (1978), *Victims of Personal Crime: An Empirical Foundation for a Theory of Personal Victimisation*. Cambridge, Mass.: Ballinger.

HOMEL R. (1993), Drivers Who Drink and Rational Choice: Random Breath Testing and the Process of Deterrence'. In R. V. Clarke and M. Felson, eds., *Routine Activity and Rational Choice*. London: Transaction.

—— and CLARK, J. (1994),'The Prediction and Prevention of Violence in Pubs and Clubs', in R. V. Clarke, ed., *Crime Prevention Studies 3*. Monsey, NY: Willow Tree.

HOME OFFICE, *CCTV: Looking Out For You*. London: Home Office.

HOPE, T. J. (1980), 'Four Approaches to the Prevention of Property Crime in Schools', *Oxford Review of Education*, 6: 231–40.

HOPE, T. J. (1982), *Burglary in Schools: The Prospects for Prevention*, Home Office Research and Planning Paper No. 2. London: Home Office.

—— (1985), *Implementing Crime Prevention Measures*, Home Office Research Study No. 86. London: HMSO.

—— (1986), 'School Design and Burglary', in K. Heal and G. K. Laycock, eds., *Situational Crime Prevention: From Theory into Practice*. London: HMSO.

—— (1995), 'The Flux of Victimisation', *British Journal of Criminology*, 35: 327–42.

—— and MURPHY, D. (1983), 'Problems of Implementing Crime Prevention: The Experience of a Demonstration Project', *Howard Journal*, 22: 38–50.

—— and SHAW, M. (1988), 'Community Approaches to Reducing Crime', in T. Hope and M. Shaw, eds., *Communities and Crime Reduction*. London: HMSO.

—— and —— eds. (1988), *Communities and Crime Reduction*. London: HMSO.

HOUGHTON, G. (1992), *Car Theft in England and Wales: The Home Office Car Theft Index*, Crime Prevention Unit Paper No. 33. London: Home Office.

HORNE C. J. (1996), 'The Case For: CCTV Should Be Introduced', *International Journal of Risk, Security and Crime Prevention*, 1: 317–26.

HUGHES, G. (1994) 'Talking Cop Shop: A Case-study of Police Community Consultative Groups in Transition', *Policing and Society* 4: 253–70.

—— (1996a), 'Communitarianism and Law and Order', *Critical Social Policy*, 49: 17–41.

—— (1996b) 'Strategies of Multi-Agency Crime Prevention and Community Safety in Contemporary Britain', *Studies on Crime and Crime Prevention*, 5: 221–44.

HUNTER, R. D., and JEFFERY, C. R. (1991), 'Environmental Crime Prevention: An Analysis of Convenience Store Robberies', *Security Journal*, 2: 78–83.

HUSAIN, S., and BRIGHT, J. (1990), *Neighbourhood Watch and the Police*. Swindon: Crime Concern.

HUTTON, W. (1996), *The State We're In*. Revd. edn. London: Vantage.

JACOBS, J. (1961), *Death and Life of Great American Cities*. New York: Random House.

JEFFERY, C. R. (1971), *Crime Prevention through Environmental Design*. London: Sage.

JOHNSON V., SHAPLAND, J., and WILES, P. (1993), '*Developing Police Crime Prevention Managemant and Organisational Change*.

Crime Prevention Unit Paper 41. London: Home Office.

KING, M. (1989), 'Social Crime Prevention à la Thatcher', *Howard Journal*, 28: 291–312.

KNUTSSON, J., and KUHLHORN, E. (1981), 'Macro-measures against Crime: The Example of Check Forgeries', *Information Bulletin, no. 1*. Stockholm: Swedish National Council for Crime Prevention. Reproduced in R. V. Clarke, ed., *Situational Crime Prevention: Successful Case Studies*. New York: Harrow and Heston, 1992.

KOCH B. (1996), 'National Crime Prevention Policy in England and Wales 1979–1995'. Unpublished D.Phil. thesis. Cambridge: Institute of Criminology.

KORNHAUSER, R. (1978), *Social Sources of Delinquency*. Chicago, Ill.: University of Chicago Press.

LAVIGNE N. (1994), 'Gasoline Drive-Offs: Designing a Less Convenient Environment', in R. V. Clarke, ed., *Crime Prevention Studies 2*. Monsey, NY: Willow Tree Press.

LAYCOCK, G. K. (1984), *Reducing Burglary: A Study of Chemists' Shops*, Crime Prevention Unit Paper No. 1. London: Home Office.

—— (1985), *Property Marking: A Deterrent to Domestic Burglary?*, Home Office Crime Prevention Unit Paper No. 3. London: Home Office. Reproduced in K. Heal and G. K. Laycock, eds., *Situational Crime Prevention: From Theory into Practice*. London: HMSO, 1986.

—— and TILLEY, N. (1995), 'Implementing Crime Prevention', in M. Tonry and D. P. Farrington, eds., *Building a Safer Society. Crime and Justice 19*. Chicago, Ill.: University of Chicago Press.

LEIGH, A., READ, T., and TILLEY, N. (1996), *Problem-Oriented Policing: Brit Pop*, Crime Detection and Prevention Paper 75. London: Home Office.

LEVI, M. (1988), *The Prevention of Fraud*, Crime Prevention Unit Paper No. 17. London: Home Office.

—— BISSELL, P., and RICHARDSON, T. (1991), *The Prevention of Cheque and Credit Card Fraud*, Crime Prevention Unit Paper No. 26. London: Home Office.

LIDDLE, M., and GELSTHORPE, L. (1994a) *Inter-agency Crime Agency: Organising Local Delivery*. Crime Prevention Paper No. 52. London: Home Office.

—— and —— (1994b) *Crime Prevention and Inter-agency Cooperation*. Crime Prevention Paper No. 53 London: Home Office.

—— and —— (1994c) *Inter-agency Crime Prevention: Further Issues*. Crime Prevention Paper No. 54. London: Home Office.

LILLY, J. R., CULLEN, F. T., and BALL, R. A. (1989), *Criminological Theory: Context and Consequences*. London: Sage.

LITTON, R. A. (1990), *Crime and Crime Prevention for Insurance Practice*. Aldershot: Avebury.

—— (1996), 'Does Insurance Cause Crime?', *International Journal of Risk, Security and Crime Prevention*, 1: 63–6.

MAGUIRE, M. (1982), *Burglary in a Dwelling*. London: Routledge.

McGUIRE, J. (1995), *What Works: Reducing Reoffending*. Chichester: Wiley.

MARKUS, C. L. (1984), 'British Telecom Experience in Payphone Management', in C. Levy-Leboyer, ed., *Vandalism Behaviour and Motivations*. Amsterdam: Elsevier-North-Holland.

MARONGIU, P., and CLARKE, R. V. (1993), 'Ransom Kidnapping in Sardinia: Subcultural Theory and Rational Choice', in R. V. Clarke and M. Felson, eds., *Routine Activity and Rational Choice*. London: Transaction.

MASUDA, B. (1996), 'An Alternative Approach to the Credit Card Fraud Problem', *Security Journal*, 7: 15–21.

MAWBY, R. I. (1977), 'Defensible Space: A Theoretical and Empirical Appraisal', *Urban Studies*, 14: 169–79.

MAYHEW, P. M. (1979), 'Defensible Space: The Current Status of a Crime Prevention Theory', *Howard Journal*, 18: 150–9.

—— (1991), 'Displacement and Vehicle Theft: An Attempt to Reconcile Some Recent Contradictory Evidence', *Security Journal*, 2: 233–9.

—— CLARKE, R. V., and HOUGH, J. M. (1976), 'Steering Column Locks and Car Theft', in P. M. Mayhew, R. V. Clarke, A. Sturman, and J. M. Hough, eds., *Crime as Opportunity*, Home Office Research Study No. 34. London: HMSO.

—— —— —— and WINCHESTER, S. W. C. (1979), 'Natural Surveillance and Vandalism to Telephone Kiosks', in P. M. Mayhew, R. V. Clarke, J. N. Burrows, J. M. Hough, and S. W. C. Winchester, eds., *Crime in Public View*, Home Office Research Study No. 49. London: HMSO.

—— —— —— and —— (1980), 'Natural Surveillance and Vandalism to Telephone Kiosks', in R. V. Clarke and P. M. Mayhew, eds., *Designing Out Crime*. London: HMSO.

—— —— STURMAN, A., and HOUGH, J. M. (1976), *Crime as Opportunity*, Home Office Research Study No. 34. London: HMSO.

MERRY, S. E. (1981), 'Defensible Space Undefended: Social Factors in Crime Control through Environmental Design', *Urban Affairs Quarterly*, 16: 397–422.

MIETHE, T. D. (1991), 'Citizen-Based Crime Control Activity and Victimisation Risks: An Examination of Displacement and Free Rider Effects', *Criminology*, 29: 419–40.

MIRRLEES-BLACK C., and ROSS A. (1995), *Crime Against Retail and Manufacturing Premises: Findings from the 1994 Commercial Victimisation Survey*, Home Office Research Study No. 146. London: HMSO.

MORGAN REPORT (1991), *Safer Communities: The Local Delivery of Crime Prevention through the Partnership Approach*. London: Home Office.

MUELLER, G. O. W., and ADLER, F. (1985), *Outlaws of the Ocean—The Complete Book of Contemporary Crime on the High Seas*. New York: Hearst Marine.

—— and —— (1991), 'When Passenger Rates Go Down—So Do Passenger Liners: An Inquiry into the Opportunity of Sinking Wisely', *Security Journal*, 2: 102–7.

NEE, C., and TAYLOR, M. (1988), 'Residential Burglary in the Republic of Ireland: A Situational Perspective', *British Journal of Criminology*, 27: 103–18.

NEWMAN, O. (1972), *Defensible Space: Crime Prevention through Urban Design*. London: Architectural Press.

—— (1976), *Design Guidelines for Achieving Defensible Space*, National Institute of Law Enforcement and Criminal Justice. Washington, DC: US Government Printing Service.

—— and FRANCK, K. A. (1982), 'The Effects of Building Size on Personal Crime and Fear of Crime', *Population and Environment*, 5: 203–20.

PAINTER, K. (1988), *Lighting and Crime Prevention: The Edmonton Project*. London: Middlesex Polytechnic Centre for Criminology.

—— (1989a), *Lighting and Crime Prevention for Community Safety: The Tower Hamlets Study*. London: Middlesex Polytechnic Centre for Criminology.

—— (1989b), *Crime Prevention and Public Lighting with Special Focus on Women and Elderly People*. London: Middlesex Polytechnic Centre for Criminology.

—— (1991), *An Evaluation of Public Lighting as a Crime Prevention Strategy with Special Focus on Women and Elderly People*. Manchester: University of Manchester Faculty of Economics and Social Studies.

PAINTER, K. (1996),'Street Lighting, Crime and Fear of Crime', in T. Bennett, ed., *Preventing Crime and Disorder*. Cambridge: Institute of Criminology.

PEASE, K. (1988), *Judgements of Offence Seriousness: Evidence for the 1984 British Crime Survey*, Research and Planning Unit Paper No. 44. London: Home Office.

—— and LAYCOCK, G. (1996), *Reducing the Heat on Hot Victims*. Washington, DC: Bureau of Justice Statistics.

—— and LITTON, R. (1984), 'Crime Prevention: Practice and Motivation', in D. J. Muller, D. E. Blackman, and A. J. Chapman, eds., *Psychology and Law*. Chichester: Wiley.

PHILLIPS, S., and COCHRANE, R. (1988), *Crime and Nuisance in the Shopping Centre: A Case Study in Crime Prevention*, Crime Prevention Unit Paper No. 16. London: Home Office.

POLVI, N., LOOMAN, N., HUMPHRIES, C., and PEASE, K. (1990), 'Repeat Break-and-Enter Victimisation: Time Course and Crime Prevention Opportunity', *Journal of Police Science* 17: 8–11.

POYNER, B. (1983), *Design against Crime: Beyond Defensible Space*. London: Butterworth.

—— (1988), 'Video Cameras and Bus Vandalism', *Security Administration*, 11: 44–51. Reproduced in R. V. Clarke, ed., *Situational Crime Prevention: Successful Case Studies*. New York: Harrow and Heston, 1991.

—— (1991), 'Situational Crime Prevention in Two Parking Facilities', *Security Journal*, 2: 96–101. Reproduced in R. V. Clarke, ed., *Situational Crime Prevention: Successful Case Studies*. New York: Harrow and Heston.

—— WARNE, C., WEBB, B., WOODALL, R., and MEAKIN, R. (1988), *Preventing Violence to Staff*. London: HMSO.

—— and WEBB, B. (1993) 'What Works in Crime Prevention', in R. V. Clarke, ed., *Crime Prevention Studies 1*. Monsey, NY: Criminal Justice Press.

RAMSEY, M. N. (1991), *The Effect of Better Street Lighting on Crime and Fear: A Review*, Crime Prevention Unit Paper No. 29. London: Home Office.

REPPETTO, T. A. (1974), *Residential Crime*. Cambridge, Mass.: Ballinger.

—— (1976), 'Crime Prevention and the Displacement Phenomenon', *Crime and Delinquency*, 22: 166–77.

RUBENSTEIN, H., MURRAY, C., MOTOYAMA, T., ROUSE, W. V., and TITUS, R. M. (1980), *The Link between Crime and the Built Environment: The Current State of Knowledge*. Washington, DC: National Institute of Justice.

SAMPSON, A. (1991), *Lessons from a Victim Support Crime Prevention Project*, Crime Prevention Unit Paper No. 25. London: Home Office.

—— and PHILLIPS, C. (1992), *Multiple Victimisation: Racial Attacks on an East London Estate*, Crime Prevention Unit Paper No. 36. London: Home Offfice.

SHAW, C. R., and MACKAY, H. D. (1942), *Juvenile Delinquency and Urban Areas*. Chicago, Ill.: University of Chicago Press.

SHERMAN, L. W. (1995), 'Hot Spots of Crime and Criminal Careers of Places', in J. E. Eck and D. Weisburd, eds., *Crime and Place*. Monsey, NY: Willow Tree Press.

—— GARTIN, P., and BUERGER, M. E. (1989), 'Hot Spots of Predatory Crime: Routine Activities and the Criminology of Place', *Criminology*, 27: 27–55.

SHORT E., and DITTON J. (1996), *Does Closed Circuit Television Prevent Crime? An Evaluation of the Use of CCTV Surveillance Cameras in Airdrie Town Centre*. Edinburgh: Scottish Office.

SINGER, S. (1981), 'Homogeneous Victim–Offender Populations: A Review and some Research Implications', *Journal of Criminal Law and Criminology*, 72: 779–88.

SMITH, L. J. F. (1987), *Crime in Hospitals: Diagnosis and Prevention*, Crime Prevention Unit Paper No. 7. London: Home Office.

—— (1989), *Domestic Violence*, Home Office Research Study No. 104. London: HMSO.

—— and BURROWS, J. (1986) 'Nobbling the Fraudsters: Crime Prevention through Administrative Change', *Howard Journal*, 25: 13–24.

SMITH, S. J. (1986), 'Utopia on Trial: Vision and Reality in Planned Housing', *Urban Studies*, 23: 244–6.

—— (1987), 'Design Against Crime? Beyond the Rhetoric of Residential Crime Prevention', *Journal of Property Management*, 5: 146–50.

SOUTHALL, D., and EKBLOM, P. (1985), *Designing for Crime Security: Towards a Crime-Free Car*, Crime Prevention Unit Paper No. 4. London: Home Office.

STANDING COMMITTEE ON CRIME PREVENTION (1991), *Safer Communities: The Local Delivery of Crime Prevention through the Partnership Approach*. London: Home Office.

STANKO, E. A. (1990), 'When Precaution is Normal: A Feminist Critique of Crime Prevention', in L. Gelsthorpe and A. Morris, eds., *Feminist Perspectives in Criminology*. Milton Keynes: Open University Press.

STENSON, K. (1991), 'Making Sense of Crime Control', in K. Stenson and D. Cowell, *The Politics of Crime Control*. London: Sage.

—— (1993) 'Community Policing as a Government Technology', *Economy and Society* 22: 373–89.

—— and COWELL, D. (1991) *The Politics of Crime Control*. London: Sage.

STENZEL, W. W. (1977), *Saint Louis High Impact Crime Displacement Study*, paper given at the National Conference on Criminal Justice, February.

STURMAN, A. (1976), 'Damage on Buses: The Effects of Supervision', in P. M. Mayhew, R. V. Clarke, A. Sturman, and J. M. Hough, eds., *Crime as Opportunity*, Home Office Research Study No. 34. London: HMSO.

—— (1980), 'Damage on Buses: The Effects of Supervision', in R. V. Clarke and P. Mayhew, eds., *Designing Out Crime*. London: HMSO.

SUTTON, M. (1996), *Implementing Crime Prevention Schemes in a Multi-Agency Setting: Aspects of Process in the Safer Cities Programme*. Home Office Research Study 160. London: HMSO.

TAYLOR, M. (1993), 'Rational Choice, Behaviour Analysis and Political Violence', in R. V. Clarke and M. Felson, eds., *Routine Activity and Rational Choice*. London: Transaction.

—— and NEE, C. (1988), 'The Role of Cues in Simulated Residential Burglary', *British Journal of Criminology*, 28: 14–26.

—— GOTTFREDSON, S., and BROWER, S. (1980), 'The Defensibility of Defensible Space', in T. Hirschi and M. Gottfredson, eds., *Understanding Crime*. London: Sage.

TILLEY, N. (1993) *Understanding Car Parks, Crime and CCTV: Evaluation Lessons from Safer Cities*. Crime Prevention Unit Paper 42. London: Home Office.

TRASLER, G. (1986), 'Situational Crime Control and Rational Choice: A Critique', in K. Heal and G. K. Laycock, eds., *Situational Crime Prevention: From Theory into Practice*. London: HMSO.

—— (1993), 'Conscience, Opportunity, Rational Choice, and Crime', in R. V. Clarke and M. Felson, eds., *Advances in Criminological Theory*. New Brunswick: Transaction.

TRICKETT, T. A., ELLINGWORTH, D., HOPE T., and PEASE, K. (1995), 'Crime Victimisation in the Eighties: Changes in Area and Regional Inequality', *British Journal of Criminology*, 35: 343–59.

—— SEYMOUR, J., OSBORN, D., and PEASE, K. (1992), 'What Is Different about High Crime Areas?', *British Journal of Criminology*, 2: 81–90.

VAN ANDEL, H. (1989), 'Crime Prevention that Works: The Case of Public Transport in the Netherlands', *British Journal of Criminology*, 29: 47–56.

—— (1991), 'The Care of Public Transport in the Netherlands', in R. V. Clarke, ed., *Situational Crime Prevention: Successful Case Studies*. New York: Harrow and Heston.

VAN DIJK, J. J. M., and DE WAARD, J. (1991), 'A Two-dimensional Typology of Crime Prevention Projects: With a Bibliography', *Criminal Justice Abstracts*, 23: 483–503.

VAN STRAELEN, F. W. M. (1978), 'Prevention and Technology', in J. Brown, ed., *Cranfield Papers*. London: Peel Press.

WALLER, I., and OKIHIRO, N. (1978), *Burglary: The Victim and the Public*. Toronto: University of Toronto Press.

WALSH, D. (1994), 'The Obsolescence of Crime Forms', in R. V. Clarke, ed., *Crime Prevention Studies 2*. Monsey, NY: Willow Tree Press

WEBB, B. (1994) 'Steering Column Locks and Motor Vehicle Theft: Evidence from Three Countries', in R. V. Clarke, ed., *Crime Prevention Studies 2*. Monsey, NY: Willow Tree Press.

—— (1996) 'Preventing Plastic Card Fraud in the UK', *Security Journal*, 7: 23–5.

—— and LAYCOCK, G. K. (1992a), *Reducing Crime on the London Underground: An Evaluation of Three Pilot Projects*, Crime Prevention Unit Paper No. 30. London: Home Office.

—— (1992b), *Tackling Car Crime: The Nature and Extent of the Problem*, Crime Prevention Unit Paper No. 32. London: Home Office.

WILSON, J. Q., and KELLING, G. (1982) 'Broken Windows', *The Atlantic Monthly*, March, 29–38.

WILSON, S. (1980), 'Vandalism and Defensible Space on London Housing Estates', in R. V. Clarke and P. Mayhew, eds., *Designing Out Crime*. London: HMSO.

WINCHESTER, S., and JACKSON, H. (1982), *Residential Burglary: The Limits of Prevention*, Home Office Research Study No. 74. London: HMSO.

28

Policing and the Police

Robert Reiner

INTRODUCTION: CRIMINOLOGY AND THE STUDY OF THE POLICE

In popular culture cops and robbers are a conceptual couple, the former perennially chasing the latter. In criminology until relatively recently this was not the case. For most of its history criminology has focused on robbers and assorted miscreants, but the activities of cops and other agents of the criminal justice process were outside its purview. The legal and criminal justice systems were taken for granted—though they were responsible for making the laws the breaking of which was the theoretical hunting ground of criminology, and corralled the captive law-breakers who were the raw material for much criminological research.

Prior to the rise of the positivist interpretation of criminology (which coined the name for the new discipline in the late nineteenth century), there had flourished a variety of competing disourses about crime, criminals, and control (Garland, this volume). In these 'proto-criminologies' the criminal justice system was at the centre of analytic and policy concern. The so-called 'classical' school associated pre-eminently with Beccaria (Vold and Bernard, 1985: chapter 1; Roshier, 1989; Morrison, 1994) was concerned primarily with constructing a rational and efficient system of criminal law and justice.

At much the same time in the late eighteenth and early nineteenth centuries, there flourished a vigorous branch of political economy known as the 'science of police' (Pasquino, 1980; Reiner, 1988). This saw as its problematic the understanding of crime and disorder and the development of appropriate policies for its prevention and control. Its leading British exponent was Patrick Colquhoun, a Middlesex magistrate and architect of the first professional police force in Great Britain (the 1800 Thames River Police). Although Colquhoun is best known today as one of the precursors of Peel's Metropolitan Police, 'police' in the modern meaning of people in blue uniforms figured as only a relatively small part of his project.

The term 'police' was used then in a much broader way to connote the whole craft of governing a social order by economic, social, and cultural policy (Rawlings, 1995). The police in our contemporary sense were seen as merely a small part of the whole business of domestic government and regulation, all of which was relevant for the understanding and control of crime and disorder. This perspective was one widely shared by the leading political economists of the day, from Adam Smith (Smith, 1763) to Bentham. Colquhoun himself wrote several works on political economy, such as *The Treatise on Indigence*, in addition to his better remembered and more directly influential *Treatise on the Police of the Metropolis* (cf. Radzinowicz, 1956).

The positivist 'science of criminology' in the late nineteenth century largely eclipsed this earlier concern with the functioning of criminal law and justice. The problematic became the explanation of 'criminality', initially seen as a non-social defect of specific individuals (Garland, 1985). Even sociological theories of crime did not remove the blinkers which excluded the functioning of policing and the criminal justice process from the intellectual province of criminology. There were, to be sure, lively debates about how criminology should interpret the concept of crime. Was it satisfactory merely to take over legalistic definitions, or was it necessary to develop more sociologically coherent and theoretically adequate concepts (cf. Nelken's discussion in this volume of 'White-collar crime as a contested concept')? But the functioning of the police and other criminal justice institutions was not part of the research or theoretical concerns of criminologists.[1]

During the early 1960s an epistemological break occurred in the criminological enterprise, under the broad banner of 'labelling theory', which paved the way for new forms of radical and critical criminology (Taylor, Walton, and Young, 1973: chapters 5–9; 1975; Downes and Rock, 1988: chapters 7, 8, 10; Morrison, 1995; Garland, Rock, Sparks, Sumner, and Young, this volume). The essential departure of the new approaches was to make problematic, intellectually as well as politically, the structure and functioning of criminal justice agencies, rather than the people they labelled as offenders.(The key references are Becker, 1964; Lemert, 1967.) Deviants were not special cases, objects of the criminological gaze because of their peculiar pathologies. They were human actors whose subjectivities were to be appreciated, not just corrected (Matza, 1964, 1969).

The other side of the picture was that the behaviour and practices of criminal justice agents were not to be taken for granted as an automatic professional response to pathological deviance. They had to be understood as interacting with deviants in ways that structured the phenomena of apparent criminality, and were themselves analytically and politically problematic (Becker, 1968). This intellectual conjuncture brought the police onto the research agendas of criminologists.

In this chapter the development and findings of police research over the last thirty years will be reviewed. The next section will explore the origins and growth of research on the police. The third section of the chapter will address

---

[1] The flourishing of penology as the empirical study of modes of punishing and/or treating offenders after sentence is not really an exception to this. It is the application of the premise of positivist criminology (that criminality has causes which can be understood) to the development of ameliorative techniques for curing or removing these causes.

the fundamental but frequently overlooked questions: what is policing and who are the police? The fourth section will argue that the central concept underlying police research has been *discretion*, the recognition that the police do not automatically translate law into policing practice. Research on police work and organization will be reviewed in terms of three aspects of discretion: (1) what patterns are implicit in its exercise, and what are its social consequences? (2) how can these patterns be explained? (3) how can the operation of police discretion be controlled? Finally, in the concluding section of the chapter possible future trends in policing will be considered.

THE DEVELOPMENT OF POLICE RESEARCH

Police Research in the United States

Systematic research on the police developed at roughly the same time, the early 1960s, on both sides of the Atlantic.[2] In the United States the key motor driving early police research was concern with civil rights, then the dominant domestic political issues. It was recognized that police practice often departed from legal standards, and could result in abuse of rights and discrimination. The response of politicians and the judiciary was to seek to close the gap by more tightly prescribing the requirements of due process of law (notably through the landmark Supreme Court decisions in *Miranda*, 384 US 436, 865 S. Ct. 1602, 16 L Ed. 2d 694 (1966), and other cases which collectively mounted a 'due process revolution' (Graham, 1970)).

The intellectual response by researchers in criminal law and criminology was to analyse the sources of police deviation from the rule of law, offering a more solid basis for the practical efforts to close the gap (Goldstein, 1960; Goldstein, 1963; La Fave, 1962, 1965; Davis, 1969, 1975; Reiner, 1996*a* vol. II, Part I). Sociological research examined how the police role, organization, culture, personality, and socialization structured deviation from due process values (Stinchcombe, 1963; Skolnick, 1966; Bittner, 1967*a* and 1967*b*; Bordua, 1967; Niederhoffer, 1967; Bayley and Mendelsohn, 1968; Wilson, 1968).

Within criminology, the 1960s were the heyday of 'labelling theory'. This generated numerous studies of how the organizational and cultural biases of the police produced or amplified deviance by focusing on targets which reflected police stereotypes (Piliavin and Briar, 1964; Werthman and Piliavin, 1967). The culmination of this early phase of US police research was the large-scale observational study mounted by Reiss and Black for the 1967 Presidential Commission on Law Enforcement, a product of the urban riots (Reiss, 1968, 1971; Black, 1970, 1972; Black and Reiss, 1970).

[2] There had been one influential sociological study of the police conducted earlier, by William Westley for his Ph.D in the late 1940s. This was published as a book only in 1970, although two papers published in the 1950s were an important reference for the 1960s researchers in both Britain and the USA (Westley, 1953, 1956, 1970).

The Presidential Commission was the precipitant of a profound alteration in the character and direction of police research in the United States after the late 1960s, reflecting broader political shifts. In 1968 'law and order' displaced 'civil rights' as the key domestic political issue (Harris, 1970). The debate about policing moved away from concern about police deviation from legality to more technical and managerial questions about police effectiveness in controlling crime and disorder. The Presidential Commission set up the Law Enforcement Assistance Administration, which poured money into projects aimed at boosting police efficiency, and research evaluating and developing these (Goulden, 1970; Platt and Cooper, 1974).

This resulted in a lucrative police research industry, largely outside academia, although increasingly important as a source of financial support for research by academics as well. The theoretical and civil libertarian impulses which had given birth to police research were largely eclipsed by the huge growth of policy-oriented, managerial work (Rumbaut and Bittner, 1979). However, the earlier traditions of small-scale and detailed observational research survived, as did some critical work, and efforts to develop a theoretical understanding of policing. (Bittner, 1970, 1974; Manning, 1970, 1977; Van Maanen, 1973, 1974; Manning and Van Maanen, 1978; Bernstein *et al.* 1974—a rare example of a Marxist analysis of the American police).

In the 1980s the increasing influence of ideas of 'community policing' resulted in something of a synthesis of these approaches. Instead of police efficiency and legal and community accountability being seen as contradictory concerns, police leaders, policy-makers, and researchers have argued they are inextricably interdependent (Skolnick and Bayley, 1986, 1988; Greene and Mastrofski, 1988; Trojanowicz and Bucqueroux, 1990; Moore, 1992; Skolnick and Fyfe, 1993; Bayley, 1994; Fielding, 1996).

Police Research in the United Kingdom

The sources of British police research were a combination of changes in the politics of law and order, theoretical developments in criminology and sociology, and the shifting institutional context of social science research. The growth of police research in Britain clearly reflects the trends in the politics of law and order which have occurred in the post-war period (Reiner, 1989*b*).

The 1950s were the heyday of cross-party consensus on law and order, as on other social issues (Downes and Morgan, this volume). The British police were routinely referred to as role models for the world (Gorer, 1955). The pedestal on which they stood is illustrated by the popularity of the TV series *Dixon of Dock Green*, which encapsulated the cosy stereotype of the British bobby (Clarke, 1983; Sparks, 1992: 26–9). The few books written about the police were within the same celebratory mode.

In the late 1950s a series of scandals aroused increasing public concern about the police. By 1959 this had reached a pitch where the Home Secretary was forced to establish a Royal Commission to look at the role, organization, and accountability of the police (Critchley, 1978: 270–4; Bottoms and Stevenson, 1990, 1992: 25–7). This was the most sweeping official review of the structure and functioning of the police since they were initially established in their modern form early in the nineteenth century (Royal Commission, 1962).

The earliest sociological research on the police in Britain developed in this context. The first empirical study of policing in Britain, Michael Banton's *The Policeman in the Community*, was published in 1964 (Banton, 1964). Banton was well aware of the mood of increasing questioning of the police, but he played down such concerns. Unlike much subsequent police research, Banton's study was inspired by scholarly questions of sociological theory rather than more immediate issues of policy or politics (Holdaway, 1989).

Banton's pathbreaking study was responsible for many ideas and approaches which have been repeatedly returned to.[3] It initiated what became the central research strategy of most subsequent work, detailed participant observation. Its account of the police role as primarily consisting of non-law enforcement 'peace-keeping' tasks has been echoed and developed in much subsequent work in Britain and around the world (Cumming *et al.* 1964; Martin and Wilson, 1969; Punch, 1979; Waddington, 1993; Bayley, 1994; Becker and Stephens, 1994). The peace-keeping role of the police arose as much from the tendency for the police to 'under-enforce' the law by exercising their discretion not to arrest as from the inherent character of the public's demand for police services.

The exercise of discretion was informed primarily by the values embedded in the informal culture of the police themselves. Banton's analysis of police culture identified characteristics which have been replicated in many subsequent studies, notably police suspiciousness, internal solidarity and social isolation (Skolnick, 1966: chapter 3; Reiner, 1992a: chapter 3; Skolnick and Fyfe, 1993: chapter 5).

Banton's key analytic theme, the dependence of formal on informal social control, has often been re-emphasized (Shapland and Vagg, 1988; Morgan and Newburn, 1997), shorn of the encumbrance of functionalist social theory within which Banton embedded it. Despite eschewing any concerns with scandal or muck-raking, Banton was acutely aware that there were severe threats to the comparatively benign and consensual mode of policing he described. He anticipated that the British police might lose their sacred aura, and had to construct a new basis for legitimation of their authority.[4]

---

[3] Banton's work influenced the development of American as well as British studies of the police. This was partly because, unlike most later research, it was comparative in approach. Banton's influence is apparent on such classic American police studies as Skolnick, 1966; Wilson, 1968; Bayley and Mendelsohn, 1968; Reiss, 1971; and Manning, 1977. The latter is also one of the few pieces of research to incorporate study of more than one country, albeit reversing Banton's trans-Atlantic trajectory in being an American scholar's analysis of British as well as American policing.

[4] In the optimistic scientist mood of the mid-1960s Banton sees more sociology in police training as a possible tool for this. If only PC Dixon had read some Durkheim he might never have turned into Dirty Harry!

These themes were developed by a number of young British researchers in the early 1970s whose work provided a firm anchorage for analysis of the rules and meanings constituting police occupational culture.[5] The key theme was the charting of what industrial sociologists might call the *informal organization* of police work, echoing the importance in early American research of the discovery of discretion. Observation found that the backstage life of the police—apparently the acme of a bureaucratic, rule-bound organization, disciplined to discipline others—was in fact a fluid world, seething with tensions, spontaneity, and deviance. Ingeniously varied interpretations of the 'Ways and Means Act' structured patterns of deviation of the 'law in action' from the 'law in the books'. Police organization was a 'mock bureaucracy' (Gouldner, 1954), the quasi-militaristic drill and discipline of the station masking the discretion and deviance of the streets.

This research was inspired by scholarly rather than practical concerns, but its political and policy implications were fairly evident. Holdaway sums it up in his representative collection of essays: 'One of the basic themes running through this book . . . is that the lower ranks of the police service control their own work situation and such control may well shield highly questionable practices' (Holdaway, 1979: 12).

As the 1970s drew to a close the political implications of policing and police research were prominent, reflecting a growing politicization of all aspects of national life. 'Law and order' became a central political issue, and an important ingredient of the Conservative victory in the 1979 General Election (see Downes and Morgan this volume). The police themselves were becoming an overt pressure group on the political stage (Reiner, 1978*a*: 268–9; 1980).

This politicization of policing was reflected in the emergence of two new strands of research. In the academic world overtly critical or Marxist work on the police proliferated. One strand was historical analysis of the role of the police in relation to class conflict (e.g. Storch, 1975, 1976; Cohen, 1979). Another key theme was the need to enhance police accountability (Brogden, 1977, 1981; Hain, 1979, 1980; Cowell *et al.*, 1982; Jefferson and Grimshaw, 1984). Others offered general accounts of policing as a means of state control (Bunyan, 1976; Hall *et al.*, 1978; Scraton, 1985). Some of the first-generation sociological researchers published more critical theoretical and political analyses (Cain, 1977, 1979; Reiner, 1978*b* and 1978*c*).

The other new strand of police research in the late 1970s was policy-oriented research commissioned by government bodies or even the police themselves. A variety of official bodies began to stimulate an ever-widening stream of research directed towards answering problems of policing policy (Reiner, 1989*b*, 1992*c*).

[5] The main examples are Cain, 1973; Chatterton, 1976, 1979, 1983; Holdaway, 1977, 1979, 1983; Manning, 1977, 1979—a leading American sociologist's analysis of Anglo-American policing; Reiner, 1978*a*; Punch, 1979*b*, 1985—observational studies of the Dutch police by a British sociologist. The influence of Banton on the development of police research has recently been underlined by Chatterton, 1995; Holdaway, 1995; and Reiner, 1995 in a collection to mark his retirement.

Despite their origins such studies are far from uniformly managerialist in style or conclusions. For example, one of the first pieces of independent research commissioned by a police force was the celebrated study of policing in London conducted for the Metropolitan Police (Met) by the Policy Studies Institute (Smith *et al.*, 1983). This produced a warts-and-all portrait which was significant in building up a head of steam for police reform initiatives. Many studies by the Home Office Research and Planning Unit or the Police Foundation (an independent charity established in 1980 to promote police research) have questioned central assumptions of policy and practice. Much research in the early and mid-1980s was sponsored by radical Labour local authorities, notably the Merseyside and Islington Crime Surveys (Kinsey *et al.*, 1986; Jones *et al.*, 1986).

Official policy-oriented research is thus not necessarily uncritical or managerialist. None the less there was a significant trend during the 1980s for policy-oriented research to eclipse theoretical or critical work. Some theoretically inspired work continued, and much policy-oriented work continues to be informed by liberal or even radical values, but the fastest growth areas are in managerialist studies of immediate policy relevance. This is now often conducted by the police themselves, or by government agencies with responsibilities for policing (Brown, 1996).

Before reviewing the findings of police research, the next section will consider the conceptual issues who are the police and what is policing?

'POLICE' AND 'POLICING'

Most research rests on a taken for granted notion of the police (Cain, 1979). The police are assumed to be a state agency mainly patrolling public places in blue uniforms, with a broad mandate of crime control, order maintenance, and service functions. They are supplemented by non-uniformed departments concerned primarily with the investigation and processing of criminal offences and sundry administrative tasks.

Understanding the nature of *policing*, especially over a broader span of space and time, requires some conceptual deconstruction of this assumed idea of *the police*. Modern societies are characterized by what can be termed 'police fetishism': the ideological assumption that the police are a functional prerequisite of social order, the thin blue line defending against chaos.[6] In fact many societies have existed without a formal police force of any kind, and certainly without the present model. The contribution of the police to the

---

[6] An amusing exemplification of this is Morrison's analysis of the picture of the police in children's stories. Enid Blyton's *Mr Plod and Little Noddy*, for instance, describes the consternation in Toytown when PC Plod is put out of action for a while by an injury. 'Who is going to protect us against robbers?', wail the anxious inhabitants. It is inconceivable that order can be protected (until Noddy agrees to deputize for Mr Plod: cf. Morrison, 1984). Similar conceptions

control of crime and maintenance of order today is debatable, as studies of police effectiveness imply (Reiner, 1992*a*: 146–56; Bayley, 1994). The problematic nature of the present notion of the police is increasingly evident, because contemporary societies are characterized by a process of fragmentation of the police function (cf. the Conclusion below).

It is important to distinguish between the ideas of 'police' and 'policing'. The 'police' are a particular kind of institution, whilst 'policing' implies a set of processes with specific social functions. 'Police' are not found in every society, but 'policing' is arguably a universal requirement of any social order, which may be carried out by a variety of different processes and institutional arrangements.

The idea of policing is an aspect of the more general concept of social control. Social control is itself a complex and much debated notion (cf. Hudson this volume; Cohen and Scull, 1983; and Zedner, 1993). In some sociological theories social control is seen broadly as everything that contributes to the reproduction of social order. This makes the concept all-encompassing, including all aspects of the formation of a culture and the socialization of the individuals who are its bearers. An example of this broad usage is Park and Burgess's classic sociology textbook, which declared that 'All social problems turn out finally to be problems of social control' (Park and Burgess, 1924: 785). Therefore social control should be 'the central fact and the central problem of sociology' (*ibid.*: 42).

The problem with this broad concept of social control is its amorphousness. It fails to distinguish the specificity of social control as a sub-category of all social processes. This is that they are essentially negative, intended to prevent or react to threats to social order. As Cohen acerbically expressed it, the broader usage is 'a Mickey Mouse concept', and the term should be restricted to refer to 'the organised ways in which society responds to behaviour and people it regards as deviant, problematic, worrying, threatening, troublesome or undesirable' (Cohen, 1985: 1–2).

In either its broad or its more specific interpretations the idea of social control may be regarded positively or negatively, according to whether a consensus or conflict model of society is espoused. In conservative versions of functionalist sociology (especially during the heyday of Parsonian functionalism in the 1950s), social control was seen as the necessary bulwark of the consensus underpinning social order. Ensuring adequate control mechanisms against deviance or disintegration was a functional prerequisite of any viable society, although especially problematic in rapidly changing modern societies. Accomplishing adequate social control was seen as 'the major problem of our time' (Landis, 1956).

The development of labelling theory and subsequent radical criminologies

of the necessity of the police underpin the widespread fears about police strikes, which are seen as inevitably producing disorder, a perception fuelled by horror stories about Boston in 1918, Liverpool in 1919, and Montreal in 1969. In fact numerous police strikes have occurred with little apparent effect on lawlessness (Ayres and Wheelen, 1977; Reiner, 1978: 5–6).

changed the evaluation of social control institutions. Far from being seen as a necessary protection against deviance, social control came to be regarded as producing deviance through the effects of labelling and stigmatization. Social control agents were seen as oppressors to be questioned and opposed (Becker, 1967). More structuralist or Marxist versions of critical criminology saw these simple reversals of moral blame as merely making social control agents 'fallguys' for the wider structure of power and privilege (Gouldner, 1968; McBarnet, 1979).

The concept of policing is closely related to that of social control, and is subject to the same variations in usage and interpretation. Indeed a recent dictionary definition identifies policing as 'the function of maintaining social control in society' (Wilson, 1993). However, as with the broad usage of social control, this wide definition of policing carries the danger of amorphousness. It misses the specificity of the idea of policing as a particular aspect of social control processes. Thus *punishment* is clearly an aspect of social control, but is usually regarded as something which should be kept separate from policing, even though any police intervention may be experienced as punitive by those who are policed. The police may in fact often exercise forms of kerbside punishment—the Rodney King case in Los Angeles being a notorious recent example—but this is seen as scandalous in terms of a liberal democracy's values of legality (Skolnick and Fyfe, 1993). Policing is not coterminous with social control but a specific phase or aspect of it.

The concept of policing connotes efforts to provide security through surveillance and the threat of sanctioning (Spitzer, 1987; Shearing, 1992). Policing is the set of activities *directed* at preserving the security of a particular social order (although the effectiveness of any form of policing is a moot point). Policing does not encompass all activities intended to produce order. It excludes *post hoc* punishment, as well as activities intended to create the conditions of social order (for example socialization, measures to secure family stability, encouragement of religion, or other forms of internalized ethical controls).

The specificity of policing as a sub-set of control processes is the creation of systems of surveillance coupled with the threat of sanctions for discovered deviance (immediately or by initiating penal processes). The most familiar such system is the one denoted by the modern sense of police: regular uniform patrol of public space coupled with *post hoc* investigation of reported or discovered crime or disorder.

Policing may be carried out by a diverse array of people and techniques, of which the modern idea of police is only one (Spitzer and Scull 1980). Policing may be done by professionals employed by the state in an organization with an omnibus policing mandate—the archetypal modern idea of *the* police—or by state agencies with primarily other purposes (like the Atomic Energy Authority Police, Parks Constabularies, the British Transport Police and other 'hybrid' policing bodies cf. Johnston, 1992: chapter 6). Police may be professionals employed by specialist private policing firms (contract security) or security personnel hired by an organization whose main business is something else (in-house security cf. Shearing and Stenning, 1981; South, 1988). Policing functions may be performed by citizens in a voluntary capacity within state police organizations (like the Special Constabulary: cf. Leon, 1989; Gill and Mawby, 1990), in association with the state police (like Neighbourhood Watch schemes: Bennett, 1990; McConville and Shepherd, 1992), or in completely volunteer bodies (like the Guardian Angels, and the many vigilante bodies which have flourished at many times and places: Johnston, 1996a). Policing functions may be carried out by state bodies with other prime functions, like the Army in Northern Ireland, or by employees (state or private) as an adjunct of their main job (like concierges or shop assistants who also guard against theft). Policing may be carried out by technology, like security cameras or listening devices (although these can of course only be used in association with human operators at some point). These policing strategies are proliferating today (Newburn and Jones, 1997), even though it is only the state agency with the omnibus mandate which is still popularly understood by the label *the* police.

Until modern times policing functions were primarily carried out as a by-product of other social relationships and by citizen 'volunteers' or private employees. Anthropological studies show that many pre-literate societies have existed without any formalized system of social control or policing. A well-known study of fifty-one pre-industrial societies found a relationship between legal evolution and societal complexity (Schwartz and Miller, 1964). *Police*, in the sense of a 'specialized armed force used partially or wholly for norm enforcement', were found in only twenty of the fifty-one societies (*ibid.*: 161). Police appear 'only in association with a substantial degree of division of labour' (*ibid.*: 166), and are usually preceded by other elements of a specialized legal and governmental system like money, mediation, and damages.

Specialized policing institutions emerge only in relatively complex societies. They are not, however, a straightforward reflex of a burgeoning division of labour, as the Durkheimian undertones of Schwartz and Miller's analysis imply. Whilst policing may originate in collective and communal processes of social control, specialized police forces develop hand-in-hand with the development of social inequality and hierarchy. They are means for the emergence and protection of more centralized and dominant state systems (Spitzer, 1975).

A valuable recent review of the anthropological literature concludes that the development of specialized police 'is linked to economic specialisation and differential access to resources that occur in the transition from a kinship- to a class-dominated society' (Robinson and Scaglion, 1987: 109, 199; Robinson *et al.*, 1994). During this transition communal policing forms are converted in incremental stages to state-dominated ones, which begin to function as agents of class control in addition to more general social control. The complex and contradictory function of contemporary police, as simultaneously embodying the quest for general and stratified order—'parking tickets' as well as 'class repression' (Marenin, 1983)—is thus inscribed in their birth process.

British police ideology has rested upon the idea of a fundamental distinction between its model of community based policing and an alien, 'Continental', state-controlled system (Mawby, 1991, 1992). Conventional histories of the British police attempt to trace a direct lineage between ancient tribal forms of collective self-policing and the contemporary Bobby (Lee, 1901). The consequence of this populist pedigree is supposed to be a uniquely popular police force (Reith, 1956).

Such claims have been characterized aptly as 'ideology as history' (Robinson, 1979). It is true that many European systems of police did develop more overtly as instruments of state control (Chapman, 1970). Revisionist histories, however, have emphasized the relationship between modern police development and the shifting structures of class and state in Britain as well as the United States and other common law systems (Silver, 1967; Storch, 1975, 1976; Miller, 1977; Brogden, 1982; Emsley, 1983, 1991, this volume; Scraton, 1985; Reiner 1992*a*: chapters 1 and 2). The supposedly benign 'British' model was in any case for home consumption only. A more militaristic and coercive model was from the outset exported to colonial situations (Brogden, 1987; Palmer, 1988; Brogden and Shearing, 1993).

Although contemporary patterns of police vary considerably in detail, they have tended to converge increasingly around fundamentally similar organizational and cultural lines, without the qualitative distinctions of the kind implied in traditional British police ideology (Mawby, 1991, 1992; Bayley, 1985; Brodeur, 1995). This is facilitated by the emergence of a new international of technocratic police experts who are responsible for the diffusion of fashions in police thinking around the globe.

It is problematic to define contemporary police mainly in terms of their supposed function (Klockars, 1985). As Bittner has emphasized, the police are called upon routinely to perform a bewildering miscellany of tasks, from traffic control to terrorism (Bittner, 1970, 1974). The uniting feature of police work is not a particular social function, whether it be crime control, social service, order maintenance or political repression. Rather it is that all demands on the police involve 'something that ought not to be happening and about which someone had better do something *now!*' (Bittner, 1974: 30). In other words, policing tasks arise in emergency situations, usually with an element of social conflict.

The police may invoke their legal powers to handle the situation, but more commonly they resort to a variety of ways and means to keep the peace without initiating legal proceedings[7] (Bittner, 1967; Kemp, Norris, and Fielding,

---

[7] The police are also not usually regarded as responsible for all elements of keeping the peace. Their task is the emergency response to threats of disorder, not the creation of its preconditions (although this has been implied in some very broad conceptions of community policing: cf. Alderson, 1979). Waddington expresses the point well: 'The police are the social equivalent of the AA or RAC patrolmen, who intervene when things go unpredictably wrong and secure a provisional solution' (Waddington 1983: 34). In terms of this analogy, they are neither service-station mechanics nor car makers nor road builders. However, like the AA they may legitimately advise on policies for which their work experience may be relevant as well as co-operating with other agencies to prevent future problems.

1992). None the less, underlying all their tactics for peace-keeping is their bottom-line power to wield legal sanctions, ultimately the use of legitimate force. 'A benign bobby . . . still brings to the situation a uniform, a truncheon, and a battery of resource charges . . . which can be employed when appeasement fails and fists start flying' (Punch, 1979a: 116).

The distinctiveness of the police lies not in their performance of a specific social function but in being the specialist repositories for the state's monopolization of legitimate force (Bittner, 1974: 35). This should not be construed to imply that all policing is about the use of force. On the contrary, 'good' policing has often been seen as the craft of handling trouble without resort to coercion, usually by skilful verbal tactics (Muir, 1977; Chatterton, 1983; Bayley and Bittner, 1984; Kemp, Norris and Fielding, 1992).

To sum up, 'policing' is an aspect of social control processes involving surveillance and sanctions intended to ensure the security of the social order. The order in question may be based on consensus, or conflict and oppression, or an ambiguous amalgam of the two, which is usually the case in modern societies.

Whilst policing may be universal, the 'police' as a specialized body of people given the primary responsibility for legitimate force to safeguard security is a feature only of relatively complex societies. The police have developed as 'domestic missionaries' in the endeavours of modern, centralized states to propagate and protect a dominant conception of peace and propriety (Storch, 1976).

This is not to say, however, that they have been mere tools of the state faithfully carrying out tasks determined from above. A considerable extent of police discretion is inevitable, above all because of the nature of police work as dispersed surveillance. The next two sections will analyse the concept of discretion and its functioning, which has been a key intellectual underpinning of police research.

POLICE DISCRETION: ITS NATURE, OPERATION, AND CONTROL

Many jurisdictions have denied the legitimacy of police discretion. Some continue to do so, especially outside the common law tradition. In the United States many states have had full enforcement statutes, requiring the police to initiate criminal proceedings whenever there was evidence of an offence (Allen, 1984; Williams, 1984).

The starting point for empirical research on the police in the United States in the early 1960s was the recognition that the police did not and could not enforce the law fully. Discretion was inevitable because the volume of incidents that could be regarded as breaches of the law would always outstrip police capacity to process them. Choices about priorities were inescapable. Discretion was also inevitable as a matter of logic: translating general rules of law into enforcement decisions in particular fact situations could not be mechanistic and automatic. It required interpretation of the meaning of the rules, with an inherently subjective element. Discretion could also be desirable. It avoided the oppressiveness of invoking the full panoply of criminal law to deal with incidents not commonly regarded as warranting this.

The difficulty was that discretion opened the way for disparity and discrimination in legal decision-making. If police organizations did not operate mechanistically, automatically enforcing the rules laid down by legislatures and courts—if the 'law in action' deviated from the 'law in the books' (in the terminology of American legal realism)—it became important to understand the operation of the law in practice. This could be done only by empirical research on the reality of police work, to understand its dynamics, and be able to regulate undesirable practices.

In Britain the reality and desirability of police discretion had never been denied completely (Reiner and Leigh, 1992). None the less there was an air of scandalous revelation when the early British sociological studies of the police emphasized its extent. The theme of these studies is encapsulated in the title of an article summing up the early British and American work, 'The Police Can Choose' (Lambert, 1969).

The recognition that the police did not adhere mechanistically to the rule of law raised the prospect of discrimination and other malpractices. The answer to this, however, could not be the traditional response to revelations of police wrongdoing: slap on new rules, or enforce existing ones more rigorously. The research showed that police discretion was exceptionally hard to control. The dispersed character of routine uniformed or plain-clothes police work gave it 'low visibility' from the point of view of police management or any outside regulatory bodies (Goldstein, 1960). This was particularly true of decisions *not* to invoke the law, which might never be reviewed by anyone at all apart from the operational police officer, who was in effect a 'streetcorner politician' (Muir, 1977). The street cops determined the policies in practice of the whole organization.

Because of the low visibility of everyday police work, 'the police department has the special property . . . that within it discretion increases as one moves down the hierarchy' (Wilson, 1968: 7). For many years research concentrated on the dynamics of rank-and-file policing. Supervisory and senior management levels were almost completely neglected. The gap between 'street' and 'management' cops was emphasized (Ianni and Ianni, 1983), and the real action was supposed to emanate from the cultural imperatives of the former.

In the late 1970s a structuralist critique of this position developed, inspired mainly by the work of Doreen McBarnet (McBarnet, 1978, 1979, 1981; Ericson, 1981, 1982; Shearing, 1981*a*, 1981*b*; Brogden, 1982, 1983; Grimshaw and Jefferson, 1987). This argued that the almost complete rule scepticism of the early sociology of the police, implying the virtual irrelevance of formal law and policy, made the street cops 'the "fall-guys" of the legal system taking the blame for any injustices' (McBarnet, 1981: 156). Although some degree of discretion was inevitable, the British law took an unnecessarily permissive stance to police powers, which could be regulated more tightly. The principles of the rule of law should be embodied in a set of specific legal rules specifying the legitimate limits of police practice in a clear, unambiguous, and strictly enforced way. By framing the powers of the police in elastic and vague rules 'the judicial and political elites' effectively condoned police deviation.

McBarnet's argument paved the way for more detailed studies of the interaction between legal rules and police practice ('blue-letter law': cf. Reiner and Leigh, 1992), as well as studies of the supervisory and management ranks of the police (Currie, 1986; Chatterton, 1987; Grimshaw and Jefferson, 1987: Part IV; Reiner, 1991). In the ensuing sections we will review the results of research on the pattern of exercise of police discretion, its consequences, causation, and control.

The Operation of Police Discretion

Police discretion has often been lauded as not only inevitable but wise and desirable. The central premise of the policing philosophy advocated by Lord Scarman in his Report on the 1981 Brixton disorders (Scarman, 1981)—which has become the conventional wisdom of the police elite (Reiner, 1991: chapter 6)—was that public tranquillity should have a greater priority than law enforcement if the two conflicted. Discretion, 'the art of suiting action to particular circumstances', was the better part of police valour.

The problem is that research on police practice has shown that police discretion is not an equal opportunity phenomenon. Some groups are much more likely than others to be at the receiving end of the exercise of police powers. A general pattern of benign under-enforcement of the law disguises the often oppressive use of police powers against unpopular, uninfluential, and hence powerless, minorities. Such groups have been described graphically as 'police property' (Cray, 1972; Lee, 1981: 53–4). The social powerlessness which makes them prey to police harassment also allows the police to neglect their victimization by crime. They tend to be over-policed and under-protected.

The main grist to the mill of routine policing is the social residuum at the base of the social hierarchy (Brogden, Jefferson, and Walklate, 1988: chapter 6). Those who are stopped and searched or questioned in the street, arrested, detained in the police station, charged, and prosecuted are disproportionately young men who are unemployed or casually employed, and from discriminated-against ethnic minorities. The police themselves recognize that their main business involves such groups, and their mental social maps delineate them by a variety of derogatory epithets: 'assholes' (Van Maanen, 1978), 'pukes' (Ericson, 1982), 'scum', 'slag' (Smith *et al.*, 1983: vol. IV, 164–5), 'prigs' (Young, 1991). In turn public attitude surveys show that such groups have the most negative views of the police (Smith *et al.*, 1983: vol. I, 314–15, vol. IV,

162–8; Jones and Levi, 1983; Hough and Mayhew, 1983, 1985; Kinsey, 1984; Jones *et al.*, 1986; Crawford *et al.*, 1990; Skogan, 1990, 1996).

The basic organization and mandate of the police in an industrial society tend to generate this practical concentration on policing what has currently come to be known as the underclass (Dahrendorf, 1985: 98–107). Most police resources are devoted to uniformed patrol of public space (over 65 per cent according to Tarling, 1988: 5). It has long been recognized that the institution of privacy has a class dimension (Stinchcombe, 1963). The lower the social class of people, the more their social lives take place in public space, and the more likely they are to come to the attention of the police for infractions. People are not usually arrested for being drunk and disorderly in their living rooms, but they may be if their living room is the street. Detective work—the next most important concentration of police resources (about 15 per cent according to Tarling, 1988)—largely involves processing those handed over by uniform patrol. Even when it does not, detectives' clientele is still largely the same police property group of 'rubbish' or 'toe-rags' (Maguire and Norris, 1992: 9–11) whose comparative lack of the rights conferred by the institutions of privacy exposes them more easily to detection.

The end result is that most of those handled by the police are from the 'police property' groups. The overwhelming majority of people arrested and detained at police stations are economically and socially marginal. One study of prisoners in custody found that over half (55 per cent) were unemployed. Most of the rest (a third overall) were in manual working-class jobs, predominantly unskilled ones. Only 6 per cent of the sample had non-manual occupations, and of these only one-third (i.e. 2 per cent overall) were in professional or managerial occupations. Most detainees were young (59 per cent under 25), 87 per cent were men, and 12 per cent were black (Morgan, Reiner, and McKenzie, 1990). The weight of adversarial policing falls disproportionately on young men in the lowest socio-economic groups.

Racial Discrimination

Numerous studies have shown that the police disproportionately exercise their powers against black people (Jefferson, 1988; Reiner, 1989, 1993; Smith, this volume). This has been well documented with respect to stop and search in the street (Willis, 1983, Smith *et al.*, 1983; Jones *et al.*, 1986; Crawford *et al.*, 1990; Skogan 1990); arrest (Stevens and Willis, 1989; Smith *et al.*, 1983; Jefferson and Walker, 1992), and the decision to prosecute (Landau, 1981; Cain and Sadigh, 1982; Landau and Nathan, 1983). The evidence that black people are disproportionately at the receiving end of police powers is overwhelming. What remains contested is the extent to which this is due to more black offending or to discrimination by the police because of individual or institutionalized racism. The politically charged nature of this debate has often been reflected in the adoption of polarized either/or positions. However, the evidence suggests that a complex interaction between police discrimination and social pressures generating disproportionate offending by young black people is the most plausible interpretation of the current pattern (Reiner, 1989, 1993; Smith, this volume).

It is also widely documented that ethnic minorities are disproportionately victimized by crime of all kinds, often due to racist motives, and that they perceive the police response as frequently inadequately sympathetic or effective. These problems are related to the issue of racial discrimination within the police force in the treatment of ethnic minority officers (Holdaway, 1991, 1996). The evidence on race and policing will not be reviewed here in further detail, as it is discussed thoroughly in Smith's chapter in this volume.

Gender and Policing

The issue of sex discrimination in policing has also been a vexed one in recent years. A fundamental difference between the debates about race and sex discrimination in policing is that, whereas black people are disproportionately at the receiving end of police powers, the opposite is true of women. The very small proportion of female suspects or offenders at every stage of the process is probably the most consistent pattern in criminal justice. Feminist criminologists have rightly underlined the maleness of the overwhelming majority of processed offenders as perhaps the most important though usually overlooked feature of crime (see Heidensohn's discussion, this volume).

It does not follow, however, that the police do not deal with women suspects or potential suspects in discriminatory ways. It has plausibly been suggested that police officers tend to regard women with a conventional imagery bifurcating them into either 'whores' or 'wives' (Heidensohn, 1985: 58; Brogden, Jefferson, and Walklate, 1988: 119–20). A consequence could be that the low rate of formal processing of women as suspects masks a complex web of discrimination. Some women may escape suspicion because of 'chivalry' placing them outside the frame of likely offenders in the stereotypes of investigating officers (Visher, 1983; Morris, 1987: 80–1). Yet others, such as teenage girls behaving in sexually precocious or deviant ways, or prostitutes, may be dealt with by the police at a lower threshold of entry into the system because they violate the officers' codes of acceptable behaviour, or may be seen paternalistically as in need of 'protection' from themselves (Brogden, Jefferson, and Walklate, 1988; Dunhill, 1989). As Heidensohn concludes in her chapter in this volume, 'evidence on this topic is patchy, and conclusions necessarily tentative'.

There is much clearer evidence of discrimination at the expense of women in their treatment by the police as victims (Walklate, 1996). Calls to domestic disturbances have always been a significant part of the police workload, but notoriously have tended to be treated by officers without recourse to criminal proceedings even where evidence of assault is present (Dobash and Dobash, 1979; Stanko, 1984). 'Domestics' are seen as messy, unproductive, and not 'real' police work in traditional cop culture (Reiner, 1978: 177, 214–15, 244–5;

Young, 1991: 315–16). This issue has become highly charged in the last two decades, and around the world police forces have attempted to improve their response to domestic assaults, with debatable results (Edwards, 1989; Hanmer, Radford, and Stanko, 1989; Sheptycki, 1991, 1993; Dobash and Dobash, 1992; Sherman, 1992). There has also been much concern about insensitive or even hostile treatment of rape victims, an issue dramatically highlighted a decade ago by a celebrated episode of Roger Graef's TV documentary on the Thames Valley Police which filmed a very disturbing interrogation of a rape victim (BBC 1, 18 January 1982). Despite considerable improvements since then (Blair, 1985; Temkin, 1987: 158–62), the treatment of rape victims by police remains problematic (Hanmer, Radford, and Stanko, 1989).

It is also clear from a growing volume of evidence that women are discriminated against as police officers, in terms of career prospects as well as harassment in the job. Until less than twenty years ago discrimination within police forces was open and institutionalized in the existence of separate departments carrying out radically different functions. This itself followed from widespread resistance within (and outside) the force to the initial recruitment of policewomen in the early decades of this century (Carrier, 1988). Since the Sex Discrimination Act 1975 women have been formally integrated into the same units as male officers. Nonetheless the continuation of discrimination has been documented by numerous studies (Bryant *et al.*, 1985; Jones, 1986, 1987; Graef, 1989: chapter 6; Young, 1991: chapter 4; Heidensohn, 1992; Walklate, 1992, 1996; Brown *et al.*, 1993).

The issue of harassment and discrimination against women in the force was vividly highlighted by the much publicized action brought by the former Assistant Chief Constable of Merseyside, Alison Halford, alleging discrimination against her in her attempts to be promoted (Halford, 1993). Since then one woman chief constable has been appointed (Pauline Clare in Lancashire), and several others have achieved assistant chief constable rank.

Many commentators have argued that the unequal employment and promotion of policewomen is not only important as an issue of justice, but to dilute the machismo element in police culture which has been seen as an important source of abuse. As Heidensohn's chapter in this volume makes clear, however, this argument is not firmly founded on research evidence that women officers police differently from their male colleagues, though it remains plausible (see also Heidensohn, 1992).

Police Discretion and the Rule of Law

The evidence of discrimination itself shows that policing practice routinely departs from the principles of the rule of law. This is supported more generally by research evidence about the extent to which the police exceed their legal powers. In a liberal democracy the police are subject to a tension between the values of crime control and due process (in terms of the distinction introduced in Packer, 1968; see also Sanders, this volume). When subject to pressure to produce results in terms of effective law enforcement the police will frequently cut corners in the procedures demanded by the principles of legality[8] (Skolnick, 1966).

The space for this deviation between police practice and the rule of law is created by the low visibility of routine police work, behind the 'blue curtain' of secrecy in cop culture (Stoddard, 1968). This allows police officers considerable scope for the construction of *post hoc* accounts of their actions which are glossed in legally acceptable terms even though these bear scant relationship to the real grounds for their decisions (Manning, 1977, 1979; Chatterton, 1979, 1983; Ericson, 1981, 1982; Holdaway, 1983). Observational studies have documented time and again that the decision-making process of police officers on the streets is not governed by the terms of legal discourse, even though these appear as a presentational justification in subsequent reports and paper-work.

The celebrated Policy Studies Institute research on policing London expressed the issue well in terms of a distinction between three sets of rules: 'working', 'inhibitory', and 'presentational' (Smith *et al.*, 1983: vol. IV, 169–72). 'Working' rules are those which underpin police practice. These derive from the informal culture of the police and bear a problematic relationship to official police policy and legal rules. 'Inhibitory' rules are formal ones which are effectively sanctioned and therefore influence practice even if they are not accepted as legitimate by the rank-and-file. 'Presentational' rules are those rules which have no bearing on police practice, but which nonetheless provide the terms in which after-the-event accounts must be oficially couched.

Since the 1980s there has been a thoroughgoing attempt to revamp police powers and legal procedures in Britain. Partly this has purported to construct a regime of safeguards to inhibit more effectively any deviation from the rule of law. The main landmark has been the Police and Criminal Evidence Act 1984, and the on-going process of continuous assessment it generated (Zander, 1991; Reiner, 1992: chapter 6; Sanders, this volume). In addition, senior police officers and the HM Inspectorate of Constabulary have in recent years attempted to respond to a perceived decline in public confidence due to serious miscarriage of justice scandals by attempting to implement a cultural change in police forces, making them accept an ethical commitment to professional procedures (Williamson, 1996). The extent to which these strategies have succeeded will be reviewed in the section on control of discretion below. The reform attempts themselves testify to the widespread deviation from the rule of law which has characterized policing, under the euphemism of 'noble cause corruption' (in the words of Sir Paul Condon). Policing has reflected social power and reproduced social divisions rather than impartial justice. In the following section we will look at explanations of this pattern of operation of police discretion.

---

[8] This is the precipitating factor leading to most miscarriages of justice, such as the Guildford Four, the Birmingham Six, and the Tottenham Three and other cases (Woffinden, 1989; Rozenberg, 1992).

The Explanation of Police Discretion

Three broad approaches to explaining why police discretion operates as it does can be distinguished. These are *individualistic, cultural,* and *structural* accounts.

Individualistic Explanations

Many concerns about police work, such as impatience with legal restraints, race, and sex discrimination, have been attributed to the idea that a peculiar kind of person, with an authoritarian personality, is drawn to police work. As the distinguished radical barrister (and now judge) Stephen Sedley put it 'the uniformed mind . . . tends frequently to be a mind for which authority has its special attraction, to which the helmet and the truncheon have a particular appeal' (Sedley, 1985: 9).

A formidable body of research has been conducted to ascertain whether police work does attract people with distinctive personalities, in particular authoritarianism. It is clear from many studies, conducted in different parts of the world, that police officers tend to have a particular constellation of attitudes which has been described as a 'police personality' (Balch, 1972). The characteristics of this are in many respects similar to the psychological model of authoritarianism. What is debatable is whether this 'personality' results from pre-existing individual peculiarities of police officers, or whether it is the product of collective adjustment to the shared predicament of doing police work, a 'working personality' (Skolnick, 1966: chapter 6).

This issue can only be resolved by comparing the characteristics of police recruits with socially similar control groups. Much research attempting this has been conducted in the United States and Britain. One highly influential British study did conclude that police recruits were more authoritarian than civilian control groups (Colman and Gorman, 1982). The findings of this research had been sent to Lord Scarman during his enquiry into the 1981 Brixton disorders and informed his analysis, which attributed such problems as racial discrimination to the failings of particular police officers rather than the institution. However, Colman and Gorman's study has been subject to extensive criticism on methodological grounds, especially because of the unrepresentative control groups used (Waddington, 1982). Some other studies have also found disproportionate authoritarianism amongst police recruits (Brogden *et al.*, 1988: 14–15, cites examples).

Most research, however, does not support the view that police recruits are more authoritarian than comparable civilian samples (McNamara, 1967: 163–252; Niederhoffer, 1967: 103–52; Bayley and Mendelsohn, 1968: 14–30; Skolnick, 1969: 252; Cochrane and Butler, 1980; Brown and Willis, 1985). Studies of the socialization of police recruits suggest the typical pattern is that after a temporary liberalizing effect of initial training (Brown and Willis, 1985; Fielding, 1988), exposure to practical policing develops in officers a distinctive constellation of values and perspectives, akin to authoritarianism. This is better understood as a cultural adaptation to the exigencies of police work than as the unfolding of a set of basic personality traits (Brogden *et al.*, 1988: chapter 2; Reiner, 1992: chapter 3).

Cultural Explanations

The impact of the informal culture of the rank-and-file is the most common explanation of police working practices found in the research literature. The first systematic formulation of this perspective was in Jerome Skolnick's seminal study of the work of detectives in California (Skolnick, 1966: chapter 3). Synthesizing the findings of his own research and those of earlier studies, Skolnick argued that certain common tensions and problems were inherently associated with the police task in liberal democracies. These generated a shared sub-culture amongst the police rank-and-file which facilitated the resolution of these difficulties. The police in a liberal democracy are faced with a basic dilemma: they are under pressure to achieve results in the form of law enforcement, but the rule of law restricts the methods they can use. They are also visible embodiments of social authority, which exposes to them to perennial danger from those recalcitrant to authority, and creates tensions in all their social relationships. These inescapable elements of the police lot—authority, danger, pressure to achieve results without violating due process of law—give rise to a common cultural reaction: a set of informal rules, rites, and recipes for coping.

Skolnick identified three main aspects of cop culture, and subsequent studies have amplified these and suggested other features (Reiner, 1992: chapter 3). The core characteristics of the police culture which Skolnick emphasized were suspiciousness, internal solidarity coupled with social isolation, and conservatism.

Suspiciousness is a common police attitude because it arises from the pressure to achieve results in the form of detection of offenders. It also results from the police concern with danger; people and places are constantly scrutinized to ascertain whether they present risks to the officer. Suspiciousness may also be deliberately cultivated as an aspect of police training, but fundamentally it is a way of coping with the pressures of the job. Although it is an inevitable aspect of policing, suspiciousness raises many problems. The tendency rapidly to assess whether people encountered may be offenders or dangerous makes the police prone to operate with prejudiced stereotypes of potential 'villains' and 'troublemakers'. This is an important source of the discriminatory exercise of discretion.

Internal solidarity and *social isolation* are mutually reinforcing. Solidarity is knitted from the intense experience of confronting shared dangers and pressures, the need to be able to rely on colleagues in a tight spot, and the bonding from having done so. Isolation is the product of organizational aspects of the work such as the shift system, the need to maintain social distance in order not to compromise authority, and the wariness with which members of the public interact with authority figures. Police solidarity and isolation are problematic even if inevitable. Solidarity can become a device for shielding wrong-doing. Social isolation can exacerbate the unrealistic or prejudiced stereotypes underlying discrimination.

Conservatism in a moral and social rather than political sense is inherently related to the core police function of symbolizing and safeguarding authority. Charged with upholding the law and preserving public peace the police are likely to have an elective affinity for conservatism. Embracing change and empathizing with deviance are wont to generate a degree of cognitive dissonance in police officers. This is not to say that police officers can never be liberal in their sympathies and perspective, but it is unlikely to be the norm.

Political conservatism is less universal a feature of police culture, although it is certainly much more common than radicalism. Police officers have generally inclined to the Right in their politics (Reiner, 1992: 191–4). This is subject to a countervailing tendency which has been apparent in some circumstances. The police are generally recruited from working-class origins, and often have backgrounds in the labour movement (Reiner, 1978*a*: 140, 149–50; Reiner, 1991: chapter 4, 183–5). It has indeed been cogently argued that the formation of modern police organizations involved a complex process of *de-radicalization* in which police officers were culturally torn away from their labour roots and sympathies (Robinson, 1978).

Their own position as employees has generated conflicts and pressures which have resulted in most countries in the formation of police unions or similar representative associations (Reiner, 1978). These have often been distant from, even hostile to, the general trade union and labour movements. At certain conjunctures their interests have coalesced, however, for example in the period immediately following the First World War in both Britain and the United States. The Police Federation in England and Wales during the 1970s and 1980s became increasingly identified with the Conservative Party, playing a significant part in the Tories' successful capture of the law-and-order mantle in the 1979 General Election. However, in recent years a variety of tensions have developed between the Conservative government and the police, primarily due to the increasing rigour with which policies to restrict public expenditure have begun to bite on the police (Rawlings, 1989). The result has been an ever more evident *rapprochement* between the Police Federation and the Labour Party and concurrent alienation between the Tories and the police. Despite the contradictory character of police politics, their culture undoubtedly remains predominantly conservative in a broad sense, and this is under-pinned by the nature of the police role.

Skolnick's sketch of police culture has been developed in several ways by subsequent analysts. Numerous studies have emphasized the important traits of *racism* and *machismo* as frequently encountered aspects of the police outlook, already adverted to by Skolnick in his account of police conservatism (Holdaway, 1983; Smith *et al.*, 1983; Graef, 1989; Young, 1991).

Others have emphasized the degree to which police officers have a strong sense of commitment to the values of what they see as 'real' policing—fighting crime and catching criminals. Thus the pressure to produce results does not arise only from outside moral panics about law and order. Police officers often seem to have a sense of *mission* concerning their work, regarding it almost as a sacred duty, although this may be hidden behind a surface veneer of cynicism and resentment at obstacles inhibiting 'real' police work (Manning, 1977; Reiner, 1992: 111–14). They are eager for action to achieve the ends of crime-fighting (Holdaway, 1977, 1983). This connects back to the machismo element in police culture and is an important ingredient in discrimination against women within the force and the lack of seriousness with which crimes against women in the domestic context have often been regarded (Young, 1991; Heidensohn, 1992, and in this volume).

Researchers since Skolnick have not only amplified his account of the central characteristics of the core police culture. There has also been significant analysis of the structured variations in culture both within and between police forces.

Cultural Variations Within Forces

The rank structure and division of labour give rise to structured permutations of police culture within police organizations. There are also variations due to age, gender, ethnic group, educational and social background, as well as individual personality. Police culture is certainly not monolithic, and officers exhibit its characteristics to varying degrees.

The most obvious cultural gulf is between the street level and the management ranks. The latter have supervisory and disciplinary powers over the former. As the arbiters of the career prospects of the rank-and-file the management strata clearly have potentially conflicting interests and perspectives on a number of issues. This is accentuated when (as was the case in British county forces until the Second World War) there is lateral entry of senior ranks and they come from more privileged social and educational backgrounds (Reiner, 1991: chapter 2).

The divergent interests of different ranks are reflected in their organization into different representative associations (in Britain the Police Federation for ranks up to chief inspector, with more senior officers belonging to the Superintendents' Association or the Association of Chief Police Officers). Senior ranks are mainly concerned with administration, and with presenting a public face of acceptable standards of conduct to external audiences, rather than the direct delivery of a service. Senior officers will often be in an adversarial role vis-à-vis the rank-and-file, especially if scandals break out and complaints need investigation.

The rank-and-file often hold derogatory images of the managerial levels as parasitic pen-pushers rather than 'real' police. Many studies here and abroad have emphasized this gulf between the cultures of 'street cops' and 'management cops' (Ianni and Ianni, 1983; Punch, 1983). It clearly introduces an important qualification into the picture of a solidary police culture.

Nonetheless it is important not to lose sight of the common interests which unite all ranks in the police force. They share a stake in the status, reputation, and resources of the organization. When these are under threat there is a coalescence of interest and action. Thus since 1989 there has been a series of unprecedented common initiatives between the British police staff associations, concerned to counter a perceived decline in the public standing of the police and hostile government proposals for reorganization on a more 'business-like' basis.

Even the normal cultural gulf between street and management cops may be analysed as something of a cynical, Faustian bargain. It allows management cops to do their business of presenting acceptable glosses of police practice to influential public audiences whilst being shielded from the more sordid aspects of street policing. Only when the 'wheel comes off' in a scandal does a token show of conflict between ranks occur.

In addition to the structured source of culture conflict based on the hierarchy of rank, the organizational division of labour produces systematic differences in the subculture associated with specialisms. The most hallowed is the perennial rivalry between uniform and detective branches. Each has a characteristic ideology which emphasizes the greater importance of its own role and an associated negative image of the other. Thus uniform branches will often stress the bedrock nature of their role in the organization, and that contrary to public impressions they actually apprehend the majority of offenders (Maguire and Norris, 1993). The CID will be resented for taking over cases for court processing after the hard work of capture has already been accomplished, grabbing the glamour and the glory. For their part detectives pride themselves on being at the heart of 'real' policing, dealing with crime and criminals, in particular the more serious cases (Hobbs, 1988: chapters 4, 8). They will look down on the more humdrum peace-keeping service and low-level crime work of the patrol branches, and castigate those stuck there as plodding and dull 'woodentops'. In turn, both operational patrol and CID officers will have negative images of administrative personnel or specialists in branches like training or community relations who are perceived as removed altogether from 'real' police work.

There are also differences in outlook and style amongst groups of patrol officers at constable level, who constitute the majority of police officers. Several studies in different parts of the world and at different times have documented these. What is striking is the similarity of the types of subculture which have been depicted, even though these are referred to by different names in different studies (Reiner, 1992*a*: 129–33). Four types of variation of the basic police culture have been pinpointed: a peace-keeper, a law-enforcer, an alienated cynic, and a managerially inclined professional. Essentially these correspond to different career aspirations and trajectories, based on variations in educational and social background as well as individual personality.

Peace-keepers are those who are committed to and fulfilled in the diverse jobs performed by patrol officers. They do not respond to trouble inevitably in terms of law enforcement. In Lord Scarman's terms they attach greater priority to maintaining public tranquillity than enforcing the law at all costs. They are as keen on the service role of the police as their control functions, although they neglect neither. *Law-enforcers* see 'real' policing as the control of crime and criminals. Service work and tasks like domestic disputes, which are not easily assimilated into the perspective of cops *v.* villains, are disdained as tiresome distractions, 'rubbish'. The street cops should be left free to pursue villainy as they know best, but are hampered by outside do-gooders and their own bosses, the management cops, who are over sensitive to legal niceties at the expense of substantive justice. *Alienated cynics* are officers who have become frustrated with failure in the job and are disenchanted with it altogether. They are merely serving out time until retirement pension requirements have been fulfilled, and they attempt to avoid work wherever possible. In police argot these are referred to as 'uniform-carriers' or 'coat-hangers', wearing the uniform but not pursuing its purposes. Uniform-carriers seldom start that way. Usually they have become disillusioned by failure: either personal failure to be promoted or transferred to a desired specialism; or failure in a job, for example the acquittal of suspects the officer has invested effort in apprehending and 'knows' to be guilty. *Managerial professionals* are rank-and-file officers ambitious for promotion. In a form of anticipatory socialization they already exhibit attitudes associated with management rather than street cops. They see the virtue of all arrangements and policies ordained from on high and refrain from the general canteen chatter at the expense of the 'bosses'. If frustrated in his ambitions this type of constable is prime material for the uniform-carrying coterie. But for the moment he apes what are seen as the requisite attitudes of high rank and responsibility.[9]

Cultural Variations Between Forces

The extent of features of police culture such as suspiciousness, solidarity, social isolation and conservatism, can vary over time and between places. It depends upon the particular social and political contexts in which forces operate, and may be affected by deliberate management policies.

The first study to concentrate on the analysis of differences in the styles of whole police organizations was James Q. Wilson's *Varieties of Police Behaviour* (1968). This distinguished between three departmental cultures found in Wilson's comparative research on eight forces in the United States, which he called the watchman, legalistic, and service styles. These were related to departmental policy choices, but particular styles were only possible in conducive social and political contexts.

[9] Senior officers are not themselves a monolithic group, although they may be perceived that way—as a faceless bunch of bureaucrats—by those they command. A variety of perspectives and styles can be found amongst them too, generated by variations in their working situations, career patterns, and individual personalities (Reiner, 1991: chapter 12).

The *watchman* style emphasized order maintenance rather than law enforcement, and reflected the typical patrol officer's perspective writ large. Patrol officers had wide discretion in how they handled their beats. Professionalization and bureaucratization were hardly developed. The *legalistic* style emphasized universalistic and impartial law enforcement with officers allowed no legitimate discretion over how rules and standards should be applied. The organization was highly bureaucratic and professional. The *service* style emphasized the provision of helpful services to citizens. The favoured reaction to deviance was the formal caution, not the (often benign) neglect of the watchman approach, nor the automatic prosecution associated with the legalistic style. Public relations and community involvement were emphasized.

Each style was rooted in particular social and political preconditions. Legalistic departments had usually displaced watchman ones after a corruption scandal which brought in a reforming city administration. Alternatively they arose as a reflection of shifts in the balance of city power, favouring stable business groups with an interest in rational, universalistic authority as a framework for long-run planning. Paradoxically, argued Wilson, legalistic departments were most often accused of racial discrimination, despite the emphasis on impartial law enforcement. Their concern with law enforcement as a priority led to the adoption of more aggressive patrol tactics in inner-city areas which black residents perceived as harassment. The service style was possible only in middle-class suburban communities with a strong consensus on values and life-styles.

Subsequent comparative studies of different forces have also demonstrated a range of variations in culture. A study of seventeen US cities in the late 1960s found that there was considerable variation in the extent to which their police practices were oriented to 'law and order' or 'civil rights' values. These were not explicable by differences in the individual demographic characteristics of the police officers: they were features of the departmental culture as a whole. To some extent the researchers found that the 'civil rights' approach was more common in areas where there was less conflict, and the police had more opportunity for non-enforcement related interaction with citizens. However, the main factor appears to have been the ideologies of the police chief and the mayor (who usually was responsible for the chief's appointment). The more sympathetic these were to black people and their perspectives, the more policing practice was oriented to 'civil rights' rather than 'law and order'. This suggests that policing styles can be significantly affected by political elites.

A number of British studies have also pinpointed cultural variations between forces. Cain's pioneering research demonstrated that there were significant differences in the cultures of a rural and a city force (Cain, 1973). The rural police were strongly integrated into their communities, but the city officers were more alienated from their publics and identified with each other. This difference between rural and urban police cultures has been a recurring theme of subsequent research, and clearly is a function of differing policing problems (Shapland and Vagg, 1988; Shapland and Hobbs, 1989; Young, 1993).

Another study compared Devon and Cornwall with Greater Manchester when their forces were led by two chief constables whose perspectives characterised the opposite poles of policing philosophy, John Alderson and James Anderton. It suggested that the rural/urban cultural difference may be accentuated by force policy (Jones and Levi, 1983). Public ratings of the police in Devon and Cornwall were generally more favourable than Greater Manchester, and police in the former also had a more accurate perception of public views than in the letter, suggesting a closer relationship. However, this was not the product of a simple rural/urban difference. Plymouth had the lowest public satisfaction with the police in the Devon and Cornwall force area, suggesting that it is indeed harder to cultivate positive police–public relations in urban contexts. However, relations with the public appeared better than those found in relatively small country towns within the Greater Manchester force area, indicating that the overall culture of the force was also a significant factor.

An ethnographic study comparing two inner-city London police stations suggested that management *can* achieve discernible cultural change even in unpropitious circumstances (Foster, 1989). In one station substantial changes in style and practice were introduced successfully, altering the culture in the direction intended by the Scarman Report with its philosophy of 'community policing'. The reason for the successful change was solid commitment and support of the entire management hierarchy. In the other station the managerial and supervisory ranks were divided, and the attempt to introduce similar changes was frustrated by the resilience of the traditional police culture. A similar conclusion, suggesting the possibilities of reform even in tough city areas is offered by a study of six innovative police chiefs in the United States in the 1980s who re-oriented their departments towards a community policing culture (Skolnick and Bayley, 1986).

The overall conclusion implied by the studies of variations in police culture is that although there are certain common tendencies which are generated by the basic features of police work in any contemporary industrial society, the strength and style of their expression can differ. This is partly because of differences in social and political context, partly because of different management philosophies. Police culture is not monolithic and invariant, but responsive to the social structure and official policy which may mould it. This suggests that even though accounts of police culture may be descriptively true, explanations of police practice have to be rooted at a more fundamental structural level. It is this which determines police culture itself, and hence policing practice.

Structural Explanations

Structural explanations supplement rather than supplant cultural accounts. The major analyses of police culture do not represent this as a freestanding phenomenon into which successive generations of police are socialized as so many passive cultural dopes. The culture is generated and sustained by the problems and tensions of the police role, structured by legal and social pressures and exigencies.

The culturally supported values and beliefs of police officers are an important element in explaining their practices, but not the whole story. These values and beliefs are translated into action in concrete situations where other pressures have also to be taken account of. These include those rules of law and police policy which are effectively enforced and become inhibitory rules on police practice whatever the officers think of them in their hearts (Smith *et al.*, 1983: vol. IV, 169–72). For example, officers who are racially prejudiced may nonetheless be restrained from acting in overtly discriminatory ways by clear and effectively sanctioned rules barring this (*ibid.*: chapter 4). The police may be resentful of some of the safeguards for suspects introduced by the 1984 Police and Criminal Evidence Act, but none the less will implement them to the extent that they are formulated in ways which can be and are effectively sanctioned by supervisors and/or the courts (Morgan *et al.*, 1990). It is also clear that the content of police culture is not unchanging or impenetrable: struggles for the hearts and minds of the rank-and-file may achieve at least a limited degree of success.

Thus cultural accounts must be grounded in structural analysis of the police role. They must also consider the context in which police work is carried out, to ascertain what countervailing pressures inhibit the straightforward translation of police values into operational practice.

Police work is structured by the core mandate and organization of the police. The modern police are primarily organized for the regular uniform patrol of public space, coupled with *post hoc* investigation of reported or discovered crime or disorder. Police practice is fundamentally structured by the legal and social institution of privacy (Stinchcombe, 1963), which is socially patterned by class and gender. Certain people are more likely to lead their lives in public space than others: young men from socially and economically marginal groups, who have restricted access to private areas for either work or leisure. In our racially discriminatory social structures these groups are also disproportionately black. It is these groups which become 'police property', and disproportionately subject to coercive police powers.

There is an isomorphism between the structure of social power and the mapping of the population as potential trouble and hence suspicious in police culture (Norris, 1989; Reiner, 1992*a*: 117–21). This is because police culture is a 'subterranean process in the maintenance of power' (Shearing, 1981). Police culture is complexly structured by the place the police occupy in the social order and not an independent variable determining police practice (Ericson, 1982; Jefferson, 1988; Brogden *et al.*, 1988: chapter 3; Holdaway, 1989; Fielding, 1989; Reiner, 1992*a*: chapter 3). The racism, sexism, impatience with legal formality, and other characteristics of police culture which have alarmed liberal critics are not simply manifestations of pathological authoritarian personalities, excessive exposure to the *Sun*, or a self-sustaining canteen cowboy ethos. Such factors may over-determine the character of police culture.

But the basic determinant is the role the police are assigned in the social order: moral street-sweeping. Their control powers are primarily directed against the young, male, disproportionately black, economically marginal, street population which threatens the tranquillity of public space as defined by dominant groups. Police prejudices are more a product than a cause of the differential use of police powers, which is a result of the socially structured nature of the police mandate (Manning, 1971). The next section will consider how (if at all) this might be controlled.

The Control of Police Discretion

The formal control of police discretion in this country is limited by the common law doctrine generally referred to as constabulary independence. As stated in its strongest form by Lord Denning this holds that a

constable . . . is not the servant of anyone, save of the law itself. No Minister of the Crown can tell him that he must, or must not, keep observation on this place or that; or that he must, or must not, prosecute this man or that one. Nor can any police authority tell him so. The responsibility for law enforcement lies on him. He is answerable to the law alone [*R.* v. *Metropolitan Police Commissioner, ex p. Blackburn* [1968] 2 QB 136].[10]

The doctrine appears to give police officers in Britain a strong measure of legitimate discretion, by contrast with jurisdictions where there is an ideal of full enforcement (Williams, 1984*a* and 1984*b*; Linnan, 1984). The contrast is doubtless greater in jurisprudential theory than social practice, as the police inevitably exercise a degree of *de facto* discretion even when full enforcement statutes purport to operate.

There are a variety of mechanisms by which police decision-making and discretion may be influenced. Two levels of decision-making can be distinguished in this regard: decisions taken by *individual* officers in the course of routine police work on a case-by-case basis; and general *policy* decisions about organizational matters and about how whole classes of cases should be dealt with.

These two levels are not hermetically sealed categories. The policy in practice of a police force is the sum of myriad discretionary decisions by officers in individual incidents, which are problematically related to formal policy. On the other hand, all policy decisions have some effect on the structuring of individual discretion—even if it is only the need for street cops to find ways of covering up practices divergent from the principles espoused by management cops.

---

[10] It should be noted that these oft-cited words of Lord Denning are strictly speaking *obiter dicta*. There has been general agreement in the critical literature with Laurence Lustgarten's corrosive analysis that 'seldom have so many errors of law and logic been compressed into one paragraph' (Lustgarten, 1986: 64). None the less, the doctrine of constabulary independence is now so firmly embedded that the judiciary is unlikely to abandon it easily.

Individual Accountability

There are two principal channels for holding individual officers to account for alleged wrong-doing: the courts and the complaints process.

Legal accountability. In traditional police ideology this is the main mechanism of police accountability in Britain (Mark, 1977: 56). Individual officers are accountable to the courts for the way they exercise their powers. Statute and common law provide powers to the police to accomplish their duties, but set limits on their legitimate use. The statutory powers of the police in the investigation of offences are largely consolidated in the Police and Criminal Evidence Act 1984 (PACE), and in the arena of public disorder in the Public Order Act 1986. (For details of these Acts see respectively Zander, 1991, and Smith, 1987.)

One avenue of redress for individuals who believe they have been subject to a wrongful exercise of police powers has always been a civil action in tort against the particular constable. Until recently this was seldom a practical possibility. The costs of the action were prohibitive. In addition, police authorities were not vicariously liable at common law for the torts of constables. Since most police officers have limited personal means there was no financial incentive to sue. This has been altered by the extension of legal aid, coupled with the Police Act 1964, which did expose police authorities to vicarious liability for the wrongful actions of constables. This has made it much more worthwhile for people to take civil actions against the police for wrongful use of their powers. The substantial growth of civil actions against the police has also been spurred by lack of confidence in the complaints system. Substantial damages have sometimes beeen awarded to successful litigants (Clayton and Tomlinson, 1987). However, the main channel of legal control over policing is by the routine safeguards over the exercise of police powers which have been developed by statute and case law.

PACE attempts for the first time to develop a comprehensive set of safeguards for suspects,[11] in the context of extended and rationalized powers for the investigation of offences. This is intended to achieve the 'fundamental balance' between adequate police powers and safeguards over their exercise which was the axiom of the 1981 Royal Commission on Criminal Procedure (RCCP) Report. PACE was the Report's legislative culmination (albeit only after an exceptionally tortuous Parliamentary passage).

The exercise of any of the powers which PACE accords the police is governed

[11] Prior to PACE there was limited protection for suspects afforded by the Judges' Rules, a set of non-statutory administrative directions laying down procedures for questioning and taking statements originally formulated in 1912. These were much less detailed and rigorous than the Codes of Practice issued under PACE, and lacked the status derived from having a statutory underpinning. It was found by the 1977 Fisher Report into the *Confait* case that the rules had little effect on the normal practices of the police. This was the immediate trigger for the establishment of the Royal Commission on Criminal Procedure which reported in 1981. The recommendations of the Royal Commission ultimately culminated in PACE albeit with some considerable amendment (Leigh, 1986).

by requirements which are set out partly in the Act itself, partly in the Codes of Practice which accompany it. These Codes specify detailed procedures for the police to follow concerning stop and search; search and seizure; detention and questioning of suspects; identification parades; and tape-recording of interviews. Revised Codes, incorporating the fruits of experience, are supposed to be issued from time to time, the first of which came into effect on 1 April 1991 (Zander, 1991: 60).

The RCCPs sought to overcome the perennial problem of the low visibility of routine police work primarily by requiring that each exercise of a police power had to be recorded with reasons, as nearly contemporaneously as possible. PACE and the accompanying Codes of Practice rely heavily on this. For example, section 1 extends powers to stop and search for stolen goods and a number of other prohibited articles. However these must be justified by 'reasonable suspicion', and the fact of and reasons for the search be recorded as soon as possible and made available to the suspect. The safeguards are underpinned by section 67 of PACE which makes failure to comply with them a disciplinary offence. PACE also makes breaches of the Codes admissible as evidence in any criminal or civil proceedings, and gives judges a broad discretion to exclude evidence gathered in ways which would render the proceedings as a whole unfair (section 78). In addition, PACE includes sections purporting to enhance police accountability more generally, for example through the complaints process and by community consultation.

During its protracted Parliamentary passage critics of PACE were particularly vexed about its reliance on internal police recording and discipline, and the largely discretionary role given the courts in overseeing the procedures. Since the Act came into operation, however, criticism has come primarily from the police who have complained regularly that the record-keeping and other procedural requirements hamper effective investigation. There has been an extensive programme of research evaluating the impact of PACE on police practice.[12]

Some studies emphasize the extent to which it remains the case that suspects fail to be accorded what are supposed to be their rights. They argue that the Act does not fundamentally erode the structural advantage which the police have in the investigation process, especially after a suspect is in police custody (Sanders, this volume). Others have suggested that the new procedures have made substantial changes in the treatment of suspects, even if there remains much scope for improvement. For example, the majority of suspects do not receive legal advice before being interviewed, despite the police being required to inform them of their rights. However, all studies concur in the finding that there has been a considerable increase in the proportion who do see a solicitor. When the revised Codes of Practice added the requirement that suspects must

---

[12] The main studies are Maguire, 1988; Brown, 1989; Irving and Mackenzie, 1989; Sanders *et al.*, 1989; Morgan *et al.*, 1990; Dixon *et al.*, 1990; Bottomley *et al.*, 1991; McConville *et al.*, 1991; Brown *et al.*, 1992. The overall debate and findings are summarized in Reiner, 1992*a*: chapter 6, and Reiner and Leigh, 1992.

also be informed that legal advice is available free of charge the proportion taking it up increased further (Brown *et al.*, 1992). It also appears to be the case that the courts in general have been more vigorous in excluding evidence gathered in violation of PACE procedures than they were under the old Judges' Rules (Feldman, 1990).

When the government was forced to establish the Royal Commission on Criminal Justice in 1991 in the wake of the successful appeal by the Birmingham Six (and the other *causes célèbres* which came to light in the late 1980s), it was hoped by civil libertarians that the protection of suspects would be boosted even further. In the event its recommendations on police powers and safeguards (Royal Commission, 1993) amounted only to detailed foot-notes to PACE, 'an almost endless list of recommendations for administrative, piecemeal changes, many of which have been ignored' (Rose, 1996: 16).

The government has adopted these in a one-sided way. Most of the recommended new powers, such as those to take samples for DNA analysis, were incorporated into the Criminal Justice and Public Order Act 1994. On the other hand the Act introduces the right for the prosecution to comment adversely on a suspect's exercise of the right to silence in police interviews, with a corresponding change in the caution given beforehand (Williamson, 1996: 33). This overturns the recommendations of the Royal Commissions both on Criminal Procedure (1981) and Criminal Justice (1993), which had seen the right to silence as a cornerstone safeguard for suspects. The clear legislative trend at present is for extensions of police powers without corresponding safeguards, as in the controversial Police Bill introduced into Parliament in December 1996 which considerably extends powers of surveillance inside private homes. The impact on police and judicial practice has yet to be seen.

On balance it appears that the regime of safeguards established in recent years has had some impact on police practice, inhibiting gross violations of suspects' rights. However, much of the change is doubtless presentational rather than substantive. The pressures on the police to achieve results have intensified and, as Sanders emphasizes in his chapter in this volume, they inevitably have an adversarial role and hold the balance of power in relation to suspects. Whilst malpractice may be reduced by strict safeguards coupled with measures to expose backstage areas of policing, legal accountability is inevitably limited by the low visibility and high discretion of police work.

The Complaints Process. A statutory procedure for handling complaints against the police was first established by the Police Act 1964. The process relied entirely on police investigation and adjudication. The only independent element occurred in cases raising the possibility of criminal proceedings against an officer, when the papers were sent to the Director of Public Prosecutions (DPP). For many years there was growing criticism of the absence of any independent element in handling complaints against the police.

The Police Act 1976 established an independent Police Complaints Board (PCB) which reviewed the police investigation papers. Although opposed by most police opinion the system failed to command public confidence. Critics pointed to the impeccably Establishment character of PCB members, and to its complete lack of independent *investigative* powers. Reliant as it was on the case-file already constructed by the police it is hardly surprising that the PCB almost never overturned the internal police decision not to bring charges.

In the early 1980s as policing became embroiled in ever greater controversy, support for the idea of a completely independent complaints system grew. The 1981 conversion of the Police Federation to the view that this was necessary for public confidence showed how it had become a widespread orthodoxy. An element of independence in the investigation as well as adjudication of complaints was achieved finally by PACE in 1984.[13] This replaced the PCB by the Police Complaints Authority (PCA). The PCA took over the adjudicatory powers of the PCB, but also acquired powers to supervise some police investigations. It is required to do so for complaints alleging death or serious injury caused by police, and empowered to do so in any other case where it is considered it to be in the public interest by the PCA or Home Secretary.

A major study evaluating the PCA suggests that it can operate effectively in its supervisory role, although resource constraints normally prevent more than token supervision (Maguire and Corbett, 1991). However the same research—as well as other studies—shows that the system fails to command confidence amongst complainants, the police or the public at large (*ibid.*; Brown, 1987). It seems clear that only a fully independent system could command widespread confidence, although chief constables remain convinced it would be less effective in reality (Reiner, 1991: 286–300). Experience in other countries shows that independent systems can operate well, although without necessarily sustaining more complaints than internal procedures, and consequently not satisfying critical opinion any better (McMahon and Ericson, 1984; Loveday, 1988; Goldsmith, 1991).

The complaints process offers a possible avenue of redress for people wronged by the police, but it is doubtful whether it could ever function effectively enough to be a significant control over police discretion. No matter who does the investigating, complaints against the police are hard to sustain because of the low visibility of most encounters. This turns most cases into a head-on collision of testimony in which the complained against police officer usually has the advantage.

Policy Accountability

The discretion of the rank-and-file police officer is structured (although not determined) by the management style and policies developed by the chief officer in a force. What avenues are there for the public accountability of these policy decisions?

The present formal structure of police governance in England and Wales is

---

[13] PACE introduced another important innovation in the complaints process. It established a system for the informal resolution of minor complaints, subject to the consent of complainant and police officer. This relieves the formal system of the pressure of having to investigate these cases, and also appears to achieve a higher level of complainant satisfaction (Corbett, 1991).

set out primarily in the Police Act 1964 (which largely implemented the recommendations of the 1962 Report of the Royal Commission on the Police) and the Police and Magistrates' Court Act 1994, which were consolidated as the Police Act 1996. The 1964 Act enshrined the so-called 'tripartite' system of accountability for the (currently forty-one) provincial forces in England and Wales, comprising local police authorities, the home secretary, and chief constables.

The two London forces differ from this pattern. The Metropolitan Police have since 1829 had the Home Secretary as their police authority. Although the establishment of a local police authority for London was promised in 1993, the only change thus far has been the appointment of an unelected quango, the Metropolitan Police Committee, to advise the Home Secretary. The City of London force is accountable to the Common Council of the City of London (the Aldermen and Mayor), as well as the Home Secretary.

The 1964 Police Act divided accountability for provincial policing between chief constables, responsible for 'direction and control' of their forces; local police authorities, with the duty of 'maintenance of an adequate and efficient police force for the area' (section 4); and the Home Secretary, who was expected to use a variety of powers to further the efficiency of policing throughout the country. Under the 1964 Act police authorities consisted two-thirds of elected local councillors, and one-third of JPs (who are selected by the Lord Chancellor).

There has been vigorous debate about what the 1964 Act's provisions really meant (Marshall, 1965, 1978; Lustgarten, 1986; Reiner, 1991: chapter 2). Until the late 1970s this dispute involved academic and other commentators rather than the parties in the system. It seemed to be accepted that the role of the police authority was to be a sounding-board for the professional expert, the chief constable (Brogden, 1977). Police authorities might exercise some influence over broad policy matters such as how the budget should be spent, but even on this, and certainly on 'operational' issues, they were generally content to accept the chief's guidance. The Home Secretary's formidable powers remained dormant.

This cosy consensus was shattered by the increasing politicization of policing issues in the late 1970s (Reiner, 1992*a*: chapter 2). In 1981 radical Labour councils were elected in most large cities, and the metropolitan police authorities which they controlled began to try and influence policing policy in a number of controversial areas, notably public-order tactics in the urban disorders of that year (and later the 1984–5 miners' strike and the 1985 disorders). Highly publicized conflicts occurred in several large cities between the chief constable and the police authority, notably in Greater Manchester (McLaughlin, 1990) and Merseyside (Loveday, 1985). In London the Greater London Council (GLC) led a vigorous campaign to establish a local police authority for the capital, and its police committee was an important monitoring body covering Met policy carefully and critically despite lacking any statutory powers.

The clashes underlined the impotence of local police authorities under the tripartite system. Under the Police Act 1964 in cases of dispute the Home Secretary acted as arbiter. Invariably Home Secretaries supported the chief constables against police authority attempts to influence what chiefs described as 'operational' matters. To maintain the myth of local accountability the Home Office encouraged the proliferation of police–community consultative committees. These lack any power, and have been widely assessed as 'talking-shops' which legitimate rather than challenge local police dominance over police authorities (Morgan, 1989, 1992).

In the late 1980s the almost complete powerlessness of the local authority leg of the tripartite structure was highlighted by developments in statute and case law. The Local Government Act 1985 abolished the metropolitan author-ities, replacing them with Joint Boards which proved much more pliant to police leadership (Loveday, 1991). In an important case in 1988 the Northumbria Police Authority sought a judicial review of the decision by the Home Secretary providing plastic bullets for riot-control training in local forces where the police authority refused to sanction their purchase by the chief constable. The Court of Appeal rejected the Authority's case, holding that both under the 1964 Police Act and under the Royal Prerogative the Home Secretary had a duty to do what he felt necessary for preserving the Queen's Peace, on advice from the chief constable and the HM Inspectorate of Constabulary. This entitled the Home Secretary to over-ride the police authority's views (*R*. v. *Secretary of State for the Home Department, ex p. Northumbria Police Authority* [1988] WLR 590).

The tripartite structure became increasingly unbalanced. Local police auth-orities enjoyed only such influence as the other two parties, the chief constable and the Home Secretary, deemed it wise to accord it. Most chief constables, however, accepted policies emanating from the Home Office as binding, even though they were formally merely advisory (Reiner, 1991: chapter 11). This was not only because the Home Secretary controls most of the purse strings. The Home Secretary also controls the various career aspirations chief constables may entertain, such as appointment as an HM Inspector of Constabulary, or a knighthood or peerage.

The centralizing trend has become more apparent still as a result of the recent reforms of the structure of police governance. Originally announced by Kenneth Clarke in March 1993, and published by Michael Howard in June 1993 in the White Paper, *Police Reform*, these culminated in the Police and Magistrates' Courts Act 1994 (which received its Royal Assent in July after a conflict-ridden passage). The Police Act 1996 (which received Royal Assent on 22 May) consolidates the Police Act 1964, the Police and Criminal Evidence Act 1984, Part IX, and the Police and Magistrates' Courts Act 1994 into the currently definitive statutory statement of the structure of police governance.

The most controversial changes are to the structure of police authorities. Section 4 of the 1996 Act limits the normal size of police authorities to seven-teen (although the Home Secretary has discretion to increase this under section 2). This uniform size, regardless of the area or population covered, itself signifies a departure from the conception of police authorities as primarily *representative* local bodies. The specified functions of police authorities are subtly altered from the 1964 Act's section 4 formulation, 'maintenance of an adequate and efficient' force. Section 6 of the 1996 Act changes this to 'efficient and effective'. The precise scope of this responsibility remains as gnomic as in the 1964 version, but the symbolism is obvious. The prime motif of the new-fangled police authorities is that they are to be 'businesslike' bodies, the local watchdogs of the managerialist, value-for-money, private enterprise ethos which the government has tried to inject into the whole public sector (Leishman, Loveday, and Savage, 1996: chapters 1 and 3).

The democratically elected councillor component of police authorities has been reduced from two-thirds to just over a half (nine out of the normal total of seventeen members: *Police Act 1996*, Schedule 2, paragraph 1 (1) (a)). Three members are magistrates (i.e. just under one-sixth instead of one-third: paragraph 1 (1) (b)).

The remaining five members are appointed under the complex and arcane procedures detailed in Schedule 3 to the 1996 Act. The rationale running through the fourteen sections and umpteen sub-sections of the mind-numbingly labyrynthine selection game seems to be to allow the Home Secretary as many bites at the cherry as possible, without simply letting him or her choose. The original version of the Bill did indeed do precisely this, but so overtly centralizing a measure drew the wrath of a number of former Conservative Home Secretaries in the House of Lords, who staged a revolt against this aspect of the legislation. Hence the smokescreen of the tortuous process in the final version of the Act. The Home Secretary appoints one of the three-member selection panel, the police authority itself appoints another, and the two members thus selected appoint the third member. They then nominate four times as many people as the number of vacancies on the authority to the Home Secretary, applying criteria specified by the Home Secretary, and the Home Secretary short-lists half of them. If the selection panel nominate fewer people than twice the number of vacancies to be filled, the Home Secretary makes up the shortfall. This brief summary of the arrangements cannot do justice to their cumbersome complexity—but it does show how the Home Secretary remains the linchpin of the process.

The Chair of the authority is chosen by the members themselves. This was another concession resulting from the House of Lords revolt agains the clear centralizing thrust of the Bill. It was originally planned that the Chair would be chosen by the Home Secretary. Overall the final version of the Act leaves police authorities with a slight preponderance of elected members, but this is a fig-leaf to hide the centralization which was nakedly apparent in the Bill as originally presented to Parliament.

The intention is to make police authorities more 'businesslike', but the business they will be doing is that of central government rather than the local electorate. Police authorities have new duties to issue an annual policing plan for their area (Police Act 1996, section 8) and local policing objectives (section 7). The chief constable has the same general function of 'direction and control' of the force as in the 1964 Act, but this must be exercised with regard to the local policing plan and objectives which the authority draws up in liaison with him (section 10). This is an empowerment of the authority compared to the 1964 Act, but it largely has to act as a conduit for the Home Secretary's priorities. The Home Secretary decides the codes of practice for police authorities (section 39), sets national objectives and performance targets which local plans must incorporate (sections 37 and 38), determines the central government grant to police forces which covers most of their expenditure according to formulae which are at his discretion (section 46), and can direct police authorities about the minimum amount of their budgetary contribution (section 41) and any other matters (section 40).

Although it seems clear that overall the Police and Magistrates' Courts Act 'substantially shifts the balance of power away from local government towards central government' (Leishman, Cope, and Starie, 1996: 21), it has been officially represented by the government itself as doing precisely the opposite. This claim is based on the relaxation of the detailed controls which used to exist on precisely how chief officers spent their budgets. In future chief constables will be free to allocate their budgets in whatever way they feel is best suited to carry out the policing plan. The White Paper on *Police Reform* (Home Office, 1993) anticipates explicitly that chief officers will pay attention to the advice of the Audit Commission and the Inspectorate of Constabulary. These bodies have been encouraging devolution of decision-making to Basic Command Units in forces on the model of schemes like Sector Policing in the Met (Dixon and Stanko, 1993). It is widely assumed that the pursuit of nationally determined performance targets will paradoxically drive chief officers to devolve a considerable measure of responsibility to local commanders (Hough, 1996: 66–8).

This new independence may prove somewhat illusory, when the changes in police governance are considered in the context of the other elements of the government's police reform package. The Sheehy Inquiry into Police Responsibilities and Rewards, which reported in the same week of June 1993 as the *Police Reform* White Paper (Sheehy Report, 1993), recommended that all police officers should be appointed on short-term contracts and subject to performance-related pay (PRP). The criteria for successful performance and the assessment of whether these have been satisfied would be governed by the Home Secretary via the new police authorities (which on the White Paper's plan would be controlled by central government appointees).

This would have constituted a formidably centralized system of control over policing. Without abandoning the constabulary independence doctrine in any formal way, the Home Secretary would colour the use of discretion by constables by setting and assessing the criteria for performance which will determine pay and job security. The police would no longer be accountable in the gentlemanly 'explanatory and co-operative' style which (in Geoffrey

Marshall's words) characterized the impact of the 1964 Police Act (Marshall, 1978). Nor would they be subject to the 'subordinate and obedient' style of accountability to democratically elected local authorities which was demanded by the Act's radical critics. Instead they would be subject to a new market-style discipline which can be called 'calculative and contractual' (Reiner and Spencer, 1993). Whilst not concerned directly with the details of policing as the other modes of accountability purported to be it could penetrate the parts of policing which they could not reach, the day-to-day operation of discretion. This would be by attaching offers which could not be refused to the attainment of the targets specified in policing plans.

The clear centralization apparent in the original version of the reforms has not materialized (Loveday, 1995). The Police and Magistrates' Courts Act reached the statute book in considerably modified form because of Peer pressure exercised mainly by Conservative former Home Secretaries. The toughest aspects of Sheehy's recommendations were defeated by a storm of opposition from police representative associations. The watered-down versions of these measures which has resulted leaves a lot open to detailed argument and development. As Newburn and Jones show, 'the nexus of control is a complicated one, and how it works in practice will, like the previous arrangements, be heavily dependent on how the relevant parties choose to use their powers' (Newburn and Jones, 1996: 125).

There are likely to be all sorts of unintended consequences of the changes, rebounding on the reforms' framers (Reiner, 1996b). The new independent members of police authorities, for example, may well confound the expectations of both advocates and opponents of the legislation. Given their local concerns about the quality of service delivery they could well align themselves with elected police authority members and chief police officers against the central government on such matters as the effect of tight centrally set budgets.

Whatever the impact of the measures in practice, there has certainly been a profound transformation in the formal organization of police governance in the years since 1994. There has been as much criticism of the style in which these changes have been carried out as their substance. Unlike previous major changes in police accountability there was no Royal Commission (as many commentators advocated). The reforms emanated from internal Home Office enquiries with minimal outside consultation. Although the measures were predicated on a clear, contentious conceptualization of the police role as being primarily 'catching criminals' (as paragraph 2.2 of the White Paper, *Police Reform*, specifies) there was no public debate about this narrowing of the traditional police mandate. In theory and practice this had hitherto been seen as encompassing a much broader spectrum of concerns, including crime prevention and management, order maintenance and peace-keeping, emergency and other services (Reiner, 1994; Bayley, 1994).[14] The narrow emphasis on

---

[14] In 1993 the Home Office established an internal Review of Police Core and Ancillary Tasks, to ascertain which jobs the police could hive off as being ancillary to their newly defined core of 'catching criminals', as defined by the White Paper. Although widely feared to be the harbinger

crime detection, now pushed to the forefront by the government's White Paper, had hitherto been seen by most official enquiries, notably the Scarman Report of 1981, as a deformation of rank-and-file police culture to be rebutted by management as much as possible not actively promoted by policy and performance targets.

One very welcome response to the absence of public debate was the establishment in 1994 by the Policy Studies Institute and the Police Foundation of an Independent Inquiry into *The Role and Responsibilities of the Police*, chaired by Sir John Cassels (Newburn and Morgan, 1994). This reported in 1996 (Police Foundation/Policy Studies Institute, 1996) and also published a useful volume of essays collating the expert evidence produced for the inquiry (Saulsbury, Mott, and Newburn 1996).

The Report endorsed the statement of the policing mission enshrined in 1991 in the police service's Statement of Common Purposes and Values (Police Foundation/Policy Studies Institute, 1996: paragraph 1.4). This encompassed upholding the law, crime prevention and detection, keeping the peace, and assisting the community: the broad conception of the police role advocated by the community policing philosophy of Lord Scarman, John Alderson, and others, which has become the dominant view of police leaders (Reiner, 1991: chapter 6).

The Independent Inquiry, like the majority of the 'policing policy network' (Leishman, Cope, and Starie, 1996: 17–20) apart from the Home Secretary, recognizes the inherent limitations on the police capacity to control crime which has been revealed by research (including that of the Home Office itself). It also emphasizes the undoubted need for the police to be managed and targeted as efficiently and effectively as possible. This involves both enhancing accountability of the police to public concerns and priorities *and* public debate about policing to sensitize the public to the limitations of police capacity to resolve the problems of crime, disorder and insecurity. This limitation arises only in small part from mismanagement or misdirection of the police. It is primarily due to the deep roots of policing problems in wider social, political-economic, and cultural processes (Bayley, 1994).

CONCLUSION: HAVE THE POLICE GOT A FUTURE?

British policing is facing momentous changes, as the previous section has already indicated. The architect of these changes, former Home Secretary Kenneth Clarke, claimed that they amounted to the most profound reorganization since Sir Robert Peel's original establishment of the Metropolitan Police

---

of widespread contracting-out and privatization, in the event the Posen Report (Home Office, 1995) was unable to find many tasks which could be designated as ancillary beyond escorting wide loads on highways (Reiner, 1994; Jones and Newburn, 1996: 107).

in 1829. Granted some political licence for this hyperbole, there can be no doubt that the police have experienced themselves as in deep crisis in recent years. They are facing great upheavals, only partly as a result of the government's reorganization. This conclusion will attempt to analyse their predicament, and hazard a glance at the future. Although the concentration will be on the British police, the underlying pressures to which they are subject are found in other jurisdictions too.

One interpretation of the particularity of the crisis in British policing is indeed that they are undergoing a normalization process. Having been in certain respects very different from police forces, either in Europe or in the rest of the common law world (Bayley, 1985; Mawby, 1991; Brodeur, 1995), there is now something of a convergence in organization and style. Facing similar domestic crime problems, and indeed confronting a common problem of growing international crime, police forces are adapting in similar ways, and this is facilitated by a direct diffusion of ideas and innovations through conferences, exchanges, and increasing collaboration (Anderson, 1989; Dorn, South, and Murji, 1991; McLaughlin, 1992; Anderson and den Boer, 1992; Walker, 1993; Sheptycki 1995; Anderson *et al.*, 1996).

The modern British police were established during the first half of the nineteenth century against widespread opposition across the social and political spectrum (Emsley, 1991, and this volume; Reiner, 1992*a*: chapter 1). As a way of overcoming this, the architects of the British police tradition (Peel, and the first two Metropolitan Commissioners, Rowan and Mayne) strove to construct a distinctive organizational style and image for the police (Miller, 1977; Emsley, 1991; Reiner, 1992*a*: chapter 2). This emphasized the idea of the police as an essentially civilian body, minimally armed, relying primarily on the same legal powers to deal with crime as all citizens shared, strictly subject to the rule of law, insulated from governmental control, and drawn from a representative range of working-class backgrounds to facilitate popular identification. An influential official inquiry by the police staff associations succinctly summarized this conception: 'traditional British policing is relatively low in numbers, low on power, and high on accountability; . . . it is undertaken with public consent' (*Operational Policing Review*, 1990: 4).

This image of British policing did not develop because of some peculiar affinity of British culture for civic values, as some more conservative historians have suggested. In colonial situations (including Ireland) British policing developed on an overtly militaristic model (Brogden, 1987; Palmer, 1988). The pacific image of the British bobby was a myth deliberately constructed in order to defuse the virulent opposition which existed to the very idea of police in early nineteenth-century Britain. That it succeeded owed at least as much to the long-term process of greater social integration and consensus over the century between the 1850s and the 1950s as to any actions of the police themselves.

By the mid-1950s, however, the police had negotiated a huge degree of public support. This is attested to by the evidence of surveys and much contemporary documentation, indicating a high degree of popular trust, even affection, for the police. The police stood as symbols of the nation. Behind this facade there is much evidence from oral histories and memoirs that in the 'Golden Age' of consent to policing, the treatment of the 'police property' groups at the base of the social hierarchy was rough, ready, and uninhibited by notions of legality or justice (Mark, 1978: chapters 2–4; Cohen, 1979; White, 1990; Brogden, 1991; Young, 1991). None the less the high regard the population in general accorded the police in Britain was unparalleled in the experience of any other country.

In the last thirty years the process of growing acceptance of the police in Britain has been reversed. A number of changes have plunged them into acute controversy and conflict: corruption and miscarriage of justice scandals; accusations of race and sex discrimination; increasing public disorder and the militarization of police tactics (Jefferson, 1990; Waddington, 1991, 1994; Waddington, 1992, 1996; McKenzie, 1996); rising crime and an apparently declining police ability to deal with it; decreasing public accountability as forces have grown larger, more centralized, and more reliant on technology (Reiner, 1992a: chapter 2). In recent years the leadership of police forces has recognized this problem and tried to introduce reforms to deal with it. They have sought to professionalize management standards, improve training, streamline working procedures, and become more open to the public through consultation of various kinds. They have tried to re-orient the culture of policing around an explicit mission of service and ethos of consumerism (*ibid.*: chapter 7; Rose, 1996: chapter 6).

None of this self-engineered change has been sufficient to satisfy the government. As discussed above, since 1993 it has launched a restructuring of police organization and accountability intended to make policing more 'businesslike' according to standards set by central government. The police feel under attack as never before, and all the staff associations have strongly condemned the government's plans. The political alignments over policing appear to have turned full circle from the days when law and order was seen as a clear Tory issue, and the police were the pets of the Thatcher government.

The political space for this government confrontation with the police comes from the erosion of public support (although this has bottomed out in the 1990s, probably in response to the quality of service initiatives: cf. Skogan, 1996; Bucke, 1996). The police are widely perceived as guilty of systematic malpractice as well as falling down on the job, despite generous treatment in terms of pay and conditions compared to other public services throughout the 1980s.[15] This perception is largely exaggerated: malpractice was certainly prevalent in the past as well, though more readily covered up. Although police resources have increased, they have been outstripped by the growing demands placed upon the police. Between 1981 and 1994 the total number of police

---

[15] This certainly seems to be the government view and a motive for the reforms: cf. Rose 1996: 330.

officers in England and Wales rose by just under 6 per cent, from about 120,000 to 127,358, and the number of civilian staff rose by 31 per cent to nearly 51,000 (Barclay *et al.*, 1995: 62). However, recorded crime increased by 111 per cent between 1981 and 1993 (*ibid.*: 1), emergency (999) calls to the police by 72 per cent, and the number of vehicles on the road by 38 per cent (*Your Police: The Facts,* Association of Chief Police Officers, 1993: 3). Clearly the growth in police personnel has nowhere near kept pace with the increased demand for police services. Whether justified or not, however, there has clearly been a decline in public confidence in the police, even though this remains robust compared to many other public institutions (Skogan, 1996; Bucke, 1996).

The prospects for reversing this decline by the government's new 'business-like' approach are dim. Their strategy rests upon a fundamental misconception of policing, which, whilst common, has for many years been called into question by research. The premise underlying current initiatives is that if properly organized policing can have a significant impact on crime levels, deterring crime in the first place by uniform patrol, and detecting criminals efficiently after the event if crimes do occur. This can be referred to as the rational deterrent model of policing.

By this standard it certainly seems at first sight that the police in Britain are far less efficient and effective than they used to be, despite large increases in resources. In the period since the Second World War recorded crime levels have increased inexorably. In 1950 the police recorded about 500,000 offences, but by 1995 this had increased to over five million. Whilst this may be due in part to increases in reporting by the public and recording by the police, the evidence of victim surveys (notably the Home Office British Crime Surveys) suggests that there has also been a substantial increase in victimization (an 83 per cent since 1981 according to the 1995 BCS: cf. Bottomley and Pease, 1986; Mayhew and Aye Maung, 1992; Reiner, 1996c; Maguire, this volume). The proportion of these crimes which are cleared up by the police has fallen dramatically over the same period, from nearly 50 per cent to 26 per cent in 1994 (Barclay *et. al.*, 1995: 26). Whilst the clear-up rate is a notoriously inadequate measure of police performance (Audit Commission, 1990, 1993) the decline in it has been politically damaging for the police, and exposed them to the government's current policing initiatives.

There is, however, a substantial body of research evidence, much of it emanating from the Home Office Research and Planning Unit, suggesting that policing resources and tactics have at best a tenuous relationship to levels of crime or the clear-up rate (Clarke and Hough, 1980, 1984; Reiner, 1992a: 146–56; Bayley, 1994; Morgan and Newburn, 1997). Innovative strategies may have some impact in particular situations but not on the overall levels of crime (Reiner, 1992a: 153–6; Sherman, 1992b; Bayley, 1994; Morgan and Newburn, 1997). The police should be seen primarily as managers of crime and keepers of the peace; they are not realistically a vehicle for reducing crime substantially. Crime is the product of deeper social forces, largely beyond the ambit of any policing tactics, and the clear-up rate is a function of crime levels and other aspects of workload rather than police efficiency.

Underlying the many specific causes of controversy over policing, such as malpractice, militarization, or apparently declining effectiveness, there is a deeper and more fundamental change in contemporary society, often labelled as 'postmodernity' (Reiner, 1992*b*). We saw earlier that the rise of a specific organization specializing in policing functions coincides with the development of modern nation states, and is an aspect of the process by which they sought to gain centralized control over a particular territory. This was particularly true of the British case where bureaucratic police organizations came into being comparatively late by European standards and coincided with the historical trajectory towards greater social integration after the initial impact of the Industrial Revolution. The British police have always been unique on a comparative scale for concentrating in the same organization a variety of policing functions—crime prevention, detection, peace-keeping, public order maintenance, and the preservation of state security, which in other countries are divided between separate bodies. In all societies the symbolic functions of the police are at least as important as their direct instrumental effectiveness in dealing with crime and disorder. This is particularly true in Britain, where the police came to stand—together with the Monarchy whose Peace they are sworn to protect—as symbols of consensual and legitimate order.

The position of the police as an organization symbolizing national unity and order is threatened fundamentally by the advent of those social changes labelled as 'postmodernity'. The term has been used by social theorists from a variety of perspectives to refer to a complex set of cultural, social, and economic developments which are seen as fundamentally transforming the modern world into a new kind of social order. The most common theme of these analyses is the sense of fragmentation and pluralism. Whereas accounts of modernization reflect a Whig notion of unilinear progress, the postmodernist perspective calls into question any 'grand narrative' of historical development (Lyotard, 1984).

Postmodern culture lacks any central reference point or conception of the good life (Harvey, 1989; Jameson, 1992). The role of intellectuals is no longer to be 'legislators' mapping brave new worlds of progress but 'interpreters' of a pluralistic mosaic of lifestyles none of which can trump the others in legitimacy (Bauman, 1987). Consumerism becomes the driving force of action, the 'pleasure principle' displacing the Puritan asceticism and discipline which was the cultural foundation of modern industrialism (*ibid.*).

The social structure of postmodernity follows the same dynamic of fragmentation, dis-organization, pluralism, and de-centring (Giddens, 1990). As one of its leading theorists puts it: 'The postmodern order is split into a multitude of contexts of action and forms of authority. . . . The nation state declines in importance and the cohesive totality is replaced by a multiplicity of sites of social reproduction' (Giddens, 1992). Economic changes have transformed the economic and social framework, dispersing the centralized 'Fordist' production systems of modern times (Hall and Jacques, 1989), and polarizing the class structure into what is often referred to as the 'two thirds, one-third society' (Therborn, 1989; Hutton, 1996; Hills, 1996).

Whilst the majority participate, albeit very unevenly and insecurely, in unprecedented levels of consumption, a substantial and growing 'underclass' is permanently and hopelessly excluded (Dahrendorf, 1985: chapter 3; Galbraith, 1992). Certainly with the political dominance of free-market economic policies there is no prospect at all of their incorporation into the general social order. In other words, the 'police property' group is far larger than ever before, and more fundamentally alienated. This economic fragmentation interacts with a long and complex process of cultural diversification, declining deference, erosion of moral absolutes, 'desubordination' (Miliband, 1978) and growing 'anomia' (Dahrendorf, 1985: chapter 2) to create a more turbulent, disorderly social world.

In this context, the British conception of the police as a body with an omnibus mandate, symbolizing order and harmony, becomes increasingly anachronistic. The British police are likely to move more towards the international pattern of specialist national units for serious crime, terrorism, public order, large-scale fraud, and other national or international problems. Local police providing services to particular communities will remain, but with sharp differences between 'service'-style organizations in stable suburban areas, and 'watchman' bodies with the rump duties of the present police, keeping the lid on underclass symbolic locations.

For those in society who can afford it, provision of security will be increasingly privatized, either in residential areas or the 'mass private property' where more and more middle-class leisure and work takes place (Shearing and Stenning, 1983, 1984, 1987; South, 1988; Hoogenboom, 1991; Rawlings, 1991; Johnston, 1991, 1992, 1993, 1996*b*; Shearing, 1992, 1996; Jones and Newburn, 1995; Newburn and Jones, 1997). Specialized human policing in any form, however, will become a smaller part of an array of impersonal control processes built into the environment, technological control and surveillance devices, and the guarding and self-policing activities of ordinary citizens (Bottoms and Wiles, 1996; Pease, 1996). *The* police will be replaced by a more varied assortment of bodies with policing functions, and a more diffuse array of policing processes: 'pick'n'mix' policing for a postmodern age (Reiner, 1996*b*). Police officers can no longer be totems symbolizing a cohesive social order which no longer exists. They will have to perform specific pragmatic functions of crime management and emergency peace-keeping in an effective and just way, or forfeit popular and political support.

Selected Further Reading

Standard texts synthesizing research and debates on policing are R. Reiner, *The Politics of the Police*, 2nd edn. Hemel Hempstead: Wheatsheaf, 1992; M. Brogden, T. Jefferson and S. Walklate, *Introducing Policework*. London: Unwin Hyman, 1988; S. Uglow, *Policing Liberal Society*. Oxford: Oxford

University Press, 1988; M. Stephens, *Policing: The Critical Issues*. Hemel Hempstead: Wheatsheaf, 1988; and N. Fielding, *The Police and Social Conflict*. London: Athlone, 1991.

Excellent assessments of current policing issues are D. Bayley, *Police for the Future*. New York: Oxford University Press, 1994; R. Morgan and T. Newburn, *The Future of Policing*. Oxford: Oxford University Press, 1997; F. Leishman, B. Loveday, and S. Savage, eds., *Core Issues in Policing*. London: Longman, 1996. A comprehensive collection of classic and recent articles is R. Reiner, ed., *Policing Vols. I and II*. Aldershot: Dartmouth, 1996.

REFERENCES

ALDERSON, J. (1979), *Policing Freedom*. Plymouth: Macdonald and Evans.

ALLEN, R., ed. (1984), 'Discretion in Law Enforcement', Special Issue of *Law and Contemporary Problems*, 47: 4.

ANDERSON, M. (1989), *Policing the World*. Oxford: Oxford University Press.

—— and DEN BOER, M., eds. (1992), *European Police Co-operation*. University of Edinburgh: Department of Politics.

—— —— CULLEN, P., GILMORE, W., RAAB, C., and Walker, N. (1995), *Policing the European Union: Theory, Law and Practice*. Oxford: Oxford University Press.

AUDIT COMMISSION (1993), *Helping With Enquiries*. London: HMSO.

AYRES, R., and WHEELEN, T. (1977), *Collective Bargaining in the Public Sector*. Gaithersburg, Md.: International Association of Chiefs of Police.

BALCH, R. W. (1972), 'The Police Personality: Fact or Fiction?', *Journal of Criminal Law, Criminology and Police Science*, 63, 1: 106–19.

BANTON, M. (1964), *The Policeman in the Community*. London: Tavistock.

—— (1971), 'The Sociology of the Police', *Police Journal*, 44, 3: 227–43.

—— (1973), 'The Sociology of the Police II', *Police Journal*, 46, 4: 341–62.

—— (1975), 'The Sociology of the Police III', *Police Journal*, 48, 4: 299–315.

BARCLAY, G. C., TAVARES, C., and PROUT, A. (1995), *Digest 3: Information on the Criminal Justice System in England and Wales*. London: Home Office Research and Statistics Department.

BAUMAN, Z. (1987), *Legislators and Interpreters: Modernity,Postmodernity and Intellectuals*. Cambridge: Polity Press.

BAYLEY, D. (1985), *Patterns of Policing*. New Brunswick, NJ: Rutgers University Press.

—— (1994), *Police for the Future*. New York: Oxford University Press.

—— and BITTNER, E. (1984), 'Learning the Skills of Policing', *Law and Contemporary Problems*, 47, 4: 35–60.

—— and MENDELSOHN, H. (1968), *Minorities and the Police*. New York: Free Press.

BECKER, H. (1964), *Outsiders*. New York: Free Press.

—— (1967), 'Whose Side Are We On?', *Social Problems*, 14, 3: 239–47.

BECKER, S., and STEPHENS, M., eds. (1994), *Police Force, Police Service*. London: Macmillan.

BENNETT, T. (1990), *Evaluating Neighbourhood Watch*. Aldershot: Gower.

BERNSTEIN, S., PLATT, T., FRAPPIER, G., RAY, G., SCHAUFFLER, R., TRUJILLO, L., COOPER, L., CURRIE, E., and HARRING, S. (1982), *The Iron Fist and the Velvet Glove: An Analysis of the U.S. Police*. 3rd edn. Berkeley, Cal.: Center for Research on Criminal Justice.

BITTNER, E. (1967a), 'The Police on Skid Row: A Study in Peace-keeping', *American Sociological Review*, 32, 5: 699–715.

—— (1967b), 'Police Discretion in the Emergency Apprehension of Mentally Ill Persons', *Social Problems*, 14, 3: 278–92.

—— (1970), *The Functions of the Police in Modern Society*. Chevy Chase: National Institute of Mental Health.

—— (1974), 'Florence Nightingale in Pursuit of Willie Sutton: A Theory of the Police', in H. Jacob, ed., *The Potential for Reform of Criminal Justice*. Beverly Hills, Cal.: Sage.

BLACK, D. (1970), 'Production of Crime Rates', *American Sociological Review*, 35: 733–48.

—— (1971), 'The Social Organisation of Arrest', *Stanford Law Review*, 23: 1087–111.

—— and REISS, A. (1967), 'Patterns of Behaviour in Police and Citizen Transactions', in US President's Commission on Law Enforcement and the Administration of Justice, *Studies in Crime and Law Enforcement in Major Metropolitan Areas.* Field Surveys III: 2. Washington, DC: US Government Printing Office.

—— and —— (1970), 'Police Control of Juveniles', *American Sociological Review* 35: 63–77.

BLAIR, I. (1985), *Investigating Rape: A New Approach for Police.* London: Croom Helm.

BORDUA, D., ed. (1967), *The Police: Six Sociological Essays.* New York: Wiley.

BOTTOMLEY, A. K., COLEMAN, C., DIXON, D., GILL, M., and WALL, D. (1991), *The Impact of PACE: Policing in a Northern Force.* University of Hull: Centre for Criminology and Criminal Justice.

BOTTOMS, A. E., and STEVENSON, S. (1990), 'The Politics of the Police 1958–1970', in R. Morgan, ed., *Policing, Organised Crime and Crime Prevention* (British Criminology Conference Papers 4). Bristol University: Centre for Criminal Justice.

—— and WILES, P. (1996), 'Crime and Policing in a Changing Social Context', in W. Saulsbury, J. Mott, and T. Newburn, eds., *Themes in Contemporary Policing.* London: Police Foundation/Policy Studies Institute.

BRODEUR, J.-P., ed. (1995), *Comparisons in Policing: An International Perspective.* Aldershot: Avebury.

BROGDEN, A., and BROGDEN, M. (1984), 'From Henry VIII to Liverpool 8: The Unity of Police Street Powers', *International Journal of the Sociology of Law*, 12, 1: 37–58.

BROGDEN, M. (1977), 'A Police Authority: The Denial of Conflict', *Sociological Review*, 25, 2: 325–49.

—— (1982), *The Police: Autonomy and Consent.* London: Academic Press.

—— (1983), 'The Myth of Policing By Consent', *Police Review*, 22 April.

—— (1987), 'The Emergence of the Police: The Colonial Dimension', *British Journal of Criminology*, 27, 1: 4–14.

—— (1991), *On the Mersey Beat: An Oral History of Policing Liverpool Between the Wars.* Oxford: Oxford University Press.

—— JEFFERSON, T., and WALKLATE, S. (1988), *Introducing Policework.* London: Unwin.

—— and SHEARING, C. (1993), *Policing for a New South Africa.* London: Routledge.

BROWN, D. (1987), *The Police Complaints Procedure: A Survey of Complainants' Views.* London: HMSO.

—— (1989), *Detention at the Police Station Under the Police and Criminal Evidence Act 1984.* London: HMSO.

—— ELLIS, T., and LARCOMBE, K. (1992), *Changing the Code: Police Detention Under the Revised PACE Codes of Practice.* London: HMSO.

BROWN, J. (1996), 'Police Research: Some Critical Issues', in F. Leishman, B. Loveday, and S. Savage, eds., *Core Issues in Policing.* London: Longman.

—— MAIDMENT, A., and BULL, R. (1993), 'Appropriate Skill-Task Matching or Gender Bias in Deployment of Male and Female Officers?', *Policing and Society*, 3: 121–36.

BROWN, L., and WILLIS, A. (1985), 'Authoritarianism in British Police Recruits: Importation, Socialisation or Myth?', *Journal of Occupational Psychology*, 58, 1: 97–108.

BRYANT, L., DUNKERLEY, D., and KELLAND, G. (1985), 'One of the Boys', *Policing*, 1, 4: 236–44.

BUCKE, T. (1996), *Policing and the Public: Findings From the 1994 British Crime Survey.* Research Findings No. 28. London: Home Office.

BUNYAN, T. (1976), *The Political Police in Britain.* London: Quartet.

CAIN, M. (1971), 'On the Beat: Interactions and Relations in Rural and Urban Police Forces', in S. Cohen, ed., *Images of Deviance.* Harmondsworth: Penguin.

—— (1973), *Society and the Policeman's Role.* London: Routledge.

—— (1977), 'An Ironical Departure: The Dilemma of Contemporary Policing', in K. Jones, ed., *Yearbook of Social Policy in Britain.* London: Routledge.

—— (1979), 'Trends in the Sociology of Police Work', *International Journal of Sociology of Law*, 7, 2: 143–67.

—— and SADIGH, S. (1982), 'Racism, the Police and Community Policing', *Journal of Law and Society*, 9, 1: 87–102.

CARRIER, J. (1988), *The Campaign For the Employment of Women As Police Officers.* Aldershot: Avebury.

CHAPMAN, D. (1970), *Police State.* London: Macmillan.

CHATTERTON, M. (1976), 'Police in Social Control', in J. King, ed., *Control Without Custody.* Cambridge University: Institute of Criminology.

—— (1979), 'The Supervision of Patrol Work Under the Fixed Points System', in S. Holdaway, ed., *The British Police.* London: Edward Arnold.

CHATTERTON, M. (1983), 'Police Work and Assault Charges', in M. Punch, ed., *Control in the Police Organisation*. Cambridge, Mass.: MIT Press.

—— (1987), 'Assessing Police Effectiveness', *British Journal of Criminology*, 27, 1: 80–6.

—— (1995), 'The Cultural Craft of Policing—Its Past and Future Relevance', *Policing and Society*, 5, 2: 97–108.

CLARKE, A. (1983), 'Holding the Blue Lamp: Television and the Police in Britain', *Crime and Social Justice*, 19: 44–51.

CLARKE, R., and HOUGH, M., eds (1980), *The Effectiveness of Policing*. Farnborough: Gower.

—— and —— (1984), *Crime and Police Effectiveness*. London: Home Office Research Unit.

CLAYTON, R., and TOMLINSON, H. (1987), *Civil Actions Against the Police*. London: Sweet and Maxwell.

COCHRANE, R., and BUTLER, A. J. (1980), 'The Values of Police Officers, Recruits and Civilians in England', *Journal of Police Science and Administration*, 8, 8: 205–11.

COHEN, P. (1979), 'Policing the Working Class City', in B. Fine, R. Kinsey, J. Lea, S. Picciotto, and J. Young, eds., *Capitalism and the Rule of Law*. London: Hutchinson.

COHEN, S. (1972), *Folk Devils and Moral Panics*. London: Paladin.

—— (1985), *Visions of Social Control*. Cambridge: Polity.

—— and SCULL, A., eds. (1983), *Social Control and the State*. Oxford: Martin Robertson.

COLMAN, A., and GORMAN, L. (1982), 'Conservatism, Dogmatism and Authoritarianism Amongst British Police Officers', *Sociology*, 16, 1: 1–11.

CORBETT, C. (1991), 'Complaints Against the Police: The New Procedure of Informal Resolution', *Policing and Society*, 2, 1: 47–60.

COWELL, D., JONES, T., and YOUNG, J., eds. (1982), *Policing the Riots*. London: Junction Books.

CRAWFORD, A., JONES, T., WOODHOUSE, T., and YOUNG, J. (1990), *The Second Islington Crime Survey*. London: Middlesex Polytechnic Centre for Criminology.

CRAY, E. (1972), *The Enemy in the Streets*. New York: Anchor.

CRITCHER, C., and WADDINGTON, D., eds. (1996), *Policing Public Order: Theoretical and Practical Issues*. Aldershot: Avebury.

CRITCHLEY, T. A. (1967, 2nd edn. 1978), *A History of Police in England and Wales*. London: Constable.

CUMMING, E., CUMMING, I., and EDELL, L. (1964), 'The Policeman As Philosopher, Guide and Friend', *Social Problems*, 12, 3: 276–86.

CURRIE, C. (1986), 'Divisional Command', *Policing*, 2, 4: 318–24.

DAHRENDORF, R. (1985), *Law and Order*. London: Sweet and Maxwell.

DAVIS, K. C. (1969), *Discretionary Justice*. Urbana, Ill.: University of Illinois.

—— (1975), *Police Discretion*. St Paul, Minn.: West Publishing.

DIXON, B., and STANKO, E. A. (1993), *Serving the People: Sector Policing and Police Accountability*. London: Islington Council.

DIXON, D., BOTTOMLEY, A. K., COLEMAN, C. A., GILL, M., and WALL, D. (1990), 'Safeguarding the Rights of Suspects in Police Custody', *Policing and Society*, 1, 2: 115–40.

DOBASH, R., and DOBASH, R. (1979), *Violence Against Wives*. London: Open Books.

—— and —— (1992), *Women, Violence and Social Change*. London: Routledge.

DORN, N., SOUTH, N., and MURJI, K. (1991), 'Mirroring the Market? Police Reorganisation and Effectiveness Against Drug Trafficking', in R. Reiner and M. Cross, eds., *Beyond Law and Order*. London: Macmillan.

DOWNES, D., and ROCK, P. (1988), *Understanding Deviance*. Oxford: Oxford University Press.

DUNHILL, C., ed. (1989), *The Boys in Blue: Women's Challenge to Policing*. London: Virago.

EDWARDS, S. (1989), *Policing 'Domestic' Violence*. London: Sage.

EMSLEY, C. (1983), *Policing and Its Context 1750–1870*. London: Macmillan.

—— (1991), *The English Police: A Political and Social History*. Hemel Hempstead: Wheatsheaf.

ERICSON, R. (1981), *Making Crime: A Study of Detective Work*. Toronto: Butterworth.

—— (1982), *Reproducing Order: A Study of Police Patrol Work*. Toronto: University of Toronto Press.

FELDMAN, D. (1990), 'Regulating Treatment of Suspects in Police Stations: Judicial Interpretation of Detention Provisions in the Police and Criminal Evidence Act 1984', *Criminal Law Review*: 452–571.

FIELDING, N. (1988), *Joining Forces*. London: Routledge.

—— (1989), 'Police Culture and Police Practice', in M. Weatheritt, ed., *Police Research: Some Future Prospects*. Aldershot: Avebury.

FOSTER, J. (1989), 'Two Stations: An Ethnographic Analysis of Policing in the Inner City', in D. Downes, ed., *Crime and the City*. London: Macmillan.

GALBRAITH, J. K. (1992), *The Culture of Contentment*. London: Sinclair-Stevenson.

GARLAND, D. (1985), *Punishment and Welfare: A History of Penal Strategies*. Aldershot: Gower.

GIDDENS, A. (1990), *The Consequence of Modernity*. Cambridge: Polity Press.

—— (1992), 'Uprooted Signposts At Century's End', *The Higher*, 17 January: 21–2.

GILL, M., and MAWBY, R. (1990), *A Special Constable*. Aldershot: Avebury.

GOLDSMITH, A., ed. (1991), *Complaints Against the Police: The Trend To External Review*. Oxford: Oxford University Press.

GOLDSTEIN, H. (1964), 'Police Discretion: The Ideal vs. the Real', *Public Administration Review*, 23: 140–8.

GOLDSTEIN, J. (1960), 'Police Discretion Not To Invoke the Criminal Process: Low Visibility Decisions in the Administration of Justice', *Yale Law Journal*, 69: 543–94.

GORER, G. (1955), *Exploring English Character*. London: Cresset.

GOULDEN, J. (1970), 'The Cops Hit the Jackpot', *The Nation*, 23 November: 520–33.

GOULDNER, A. (1954), *Patterns of Industrial Bureacracy*. London: Routledge.

—— (1978), 'The Sociologist As Partisan', *The American Sociologist*, May: 103–16.

GRAEF, R. (1989), *Talking Blues*. London: Collins.

GRAHAM, F. (1970), *The Due Process Revolution: The Warren Court's Impact on Criminal Law*. Rochelle Park, NJ: Hayden Book Co.

GREENE, J., and MASTROFSKI, S., eds. (1988), *Community Policing: Rhetoric or Reality?* New York: Praeger.

GRIMSHAW, R., and JEFFERSON, T. (1987), *Interpreting Policework*. London: Unwin.

HAIN, P., ed. (1979), *Policing the Police*. London: Calder.

—— (1980), *Policing the Police 2*. London: Calder.

HALFORD, A. (1993), *No Way Up the Greasy Pole*. London: Constable.

HALL, S., CRITCHER, C., JEFFERSON, T., CLARKE, J., and ROBERTS, B. (1978), *Policing the Crisis*. London: Macmillan.

—— and JACQUES, M., eds. (1989), *New Times: The Changing Face of Politics in the 1990s*. London: Lawrence and Wishart.

HANMER, J., RADFORD, J., and STANKO, E. A., eds. (1989), *Women, Policing and Male Violence*. London: Routledge.

HARRIS, R. (1970), *Justice: The Crisis of Law, Order and Freedom in America*. London: Bodley Head.

HARVEY, D. (1989), *The Condition of Postmodernity: An Inquiry Into the Origins of Cultural Change*. Oxford: Blackwell.

HEIDENSOHN, F. (1985), *Women and Crime*. London: Macmillan.

—— (1992), *Women in Control? The Role of Women in Law Enforcement*. Oxford: Oxford University Press.

HILLS, J. (1996), 'The Bridge that Failed: The Changing Distribution of Income and Wealth in the UK', in H. Sasson and D. Diamond, eds., *LSE on Social Science*. London: London School of Economics.

HOBBS, D. (1988), *Doing the Business: Entrepreneurship, The Working Class and Detectives in the East End of London*. Oxford: Oxford University Press.

HOLDAWAY, S. (1977), 'Changes in Urban Policing', *British Journal of Sociology*, 28, 2: 119–37.

—— ed. (1979), *The British Police*. London: Edward Arnold.

—— (1983), *Inside the British Police*. Oxford: Blackwell.

—— (1979), 'Discovering Structure: Studies of the British Police Occupational Culture', in M. Weatheritt, ed., *Police Research: Some Future Prospects*. Aldershot: Avebury.

—— (1991), *Recruiting A Multi-Ethnic Police Force*. London: HMSO.

—— (1995), 'Culture, Race and Policy: Some Themes of the Sociology of the Police', *Policing and Society*, 5, 2: 109–21.

HOOGENBOOM, B. (1991), 'Grey Policing: A Theoretical Framework', *Policing and Society*, 2, 1: 17–30.

HOUGH, M. (1996), 'The Police Patrol Function: What Research Can Tell Us', in W. Saulsbury, J. Mott, and T. Newburn, eds., *Themes in Contemporary Policing*. London: Police Foundation/Policy Studies Institute.

—— and MAYHEW, P. (1983), *The British Crime Survey*. London: HMSO.

—— and —— (1985), *Taking Account of Crime: Key Findings From the Second British Crime Survey*. London: HMSO.

HUTTON, W. (1996), *The State We're In*. London: Vintage.

IANNI, E. R., and IANNI, F. (1983), 'Street Cops and Management Cops: The Two Cultures of Policing', in M. Punch, ed., *Control in the Police Organisation*. Cambridge, Mass.: MIT Press.

IRVING, B., and McKENZIE, I. (1989), *Police Interrogation*. London: Police Foundation.

JAMESON, F. (1992), *Postmodernism: Or the Cultural Logic of Late Capitalism?* London: Verso.

JEFFERSON, T. (1988), 'Race, Crime and Policing: Empirical, Theoretical and Methodological Issues', *International Journal of the Sociology of Law*, 16, 4: 521–39.

—— (1990), *The Case Against Paramilitary Policing*. Milton Keynes: Open University Press.

—— and GRIMSHAW, R. (1984), *Controlling the Constable*. London: Muller.

—— and WALKER, M. (1992), 'Ethnic Minorities in the Criminal Justice System', *Criminal Law Review*: 83–96.

—— —— and SENEVIRATNE, M. (1992), 'Ethnic Minorities, Crime and Criminal Justice: A Study in a Provincial City', in D. Downes, ed., *Unravelling Criminal Justice*. London: Macmillan.

JOHNSTON, L. (1991), 'Privatisation and the Police Function: From "New Police" to "New Policing"', in R. Reiner and M. Cross, eds., *Beyond Law and Order*. London: Macmillan.

—— (1992), *The Rebirth of Private Policing*. London: Routledge.

—— (1993), 'Privatisation and Protection: Spatial and Sectoral Ideologies in British Policing and Crime Prevention', *Modern Law Review*, 56: 771–92.

—— (1996a), 'What is Vigilantism?', *British Journal of Criminology*, 36, 2: 220–36.

—— (1996b), 'Policing Diversity: the Impact of the Public-Private Complex in Policing', in F. Leishman, B. Loveday, and S. Savage, eds., *Core Issues in Policing*. London: Longman.

JONES, S. (1986), 'Caught in the Act', *Policing*, 2, 2: 129–40.

—— (1987), *Policewomen and Equality*. London: Macmillan.

—— and LEVI, M. (1983), 'The Police and the Majority: The Neglect of the Obvious', *Police Journal*, 56, 4: 351–64.

JONES, T., McLEAN, B., and YOUNG, J. (1986), *The Islington Crime Survey*. Aldershot: Gower.

—— and NEWBURN, T. (1995), 'How Big is the Private Security Sector?', *Policing and Society*, 5: 221–32.

—— —— and SMITH, D. (1994), *Democracy and Policing*, London: Policy Studies Institute.

KEMP, C., NORRIS, C., and FIELDING, N. (1992), *Negotiating Nothing: Police Decision-Making in Disputes*. Aldershot: Avebury.

KINSEY, R. (1984), *The Merseyside Crime Survey*. Liverpool: Merseyside County Council.

—— LEA, J., and YOUNG, J. (1986), *Losing The Fight Against Crime*. Oxford: Blackwell.

KLOCKARS, C. (1985), *The Idea of Police*. Beverly Hills, Cal.: Sage.

LA FAVE, W. (1962), 'The Police and Non-Enforcement of the Criminal Law', *Wisconsin Law Review*: 104–37 and 179–239.

—— (1965), *Arrest: The Decision To Take A Suspect Into Custody*. Boston, Mass.: Little, Brown.

LAMBERT, J. (1969), 'The Police Can Choose', *New Society*, 14, 364: 430–2.

—— (1970), *Crime, Police and Race Relations*. Oxford: Oxford University Press.

LANDAU, S. (1981), 'Juveniles and the Police', *British Journal of Criminology*, 21, 1: 27–46.

—— and NATHAN, G. (1983), 'Selecting Delinquents For Cautioning in the London Metropolitan Area', *British Journal of Criminology*, 23, 2: 128–49.

LANDIS, P. A. (1956), *Social Control: Social Organisation and Disorganisation in Process*. Chicago, Ill.: Chicago University Press.

LEE, J. A. (1981), 'Some Structural Aspects of Police Deviance in Relations With Minority Groups', in C. Shearing, ed., *Organisational Police Deviance*. Toronto: Butterworth.

LEE, M. (1901), *A History of Police in England*. London: Methuen.

LEIGH, L. (1986), 'Some Observations on the Parliamentary History of the Police and Criminal Evidence Act 1984', in C. Harlow, ed., *Public Law and Politics*. London: Sweet and Maxwell.

LEISHMAN, F., COPE, S., and STARIE, P. (1996), 'Reinventing and Restructuring: Towards a "New Policing Order"' in F. Leishman, B. Loveday, and S. Savage, eds., *Core Issues in Policing*. London: Longman.

—— LOVEDAY, B., and SAVAGE, S., eds. (1996), *Core Issues in Policing*. London: Longman.

LEMERT, E. (1967), *Human Deviance, Social Problems and Social Control*. New York: Prentice Hall.

LEON, C. (1989), 'The Special Constabulary', *Policing*, 5, 4: 265–86.

LINNAN, D. K. (1984), 'Police Discretion in a Continental European Administrative State: The Police of Baden-Wurttemberg in the Federal Republic of Germany', *Law and Contemporary Problems*, 47, 4: 185–224.

LOADER, I. (1996), *Youth, Policing and Democracy*. Basingstoke: Macmillan.

LOVEDAY, B. (1985), *The Role and Effectiveness of the Merseyside Police Committee*, Liverpool: Merseyside County Council.

—— (1988), 'Police Complaints in the USA', *Policing*, 4, 3: 172–93.

—— (1991), 'The New Police Authorities', *Policing and Society*, 1, 3: 193–212.

—— (1995), 'Contemporary Challenges to Police Management in England and Wales. Developing Strategies for Effective Service

Delivery', *Policing and Society*, 5, 4: 281–302..

LUSTGARTEN, L. (1986), *The Governance of the Police*. London: Sweet and Maxwell.

LYOTARD, J.-F. (1984), *The Postmodern Condition*. Manchester: Manchester University Press.

McBARNET, D. (1978), 'The Police and the State', in G. Littlejohn, B. Smart, J. Wakeford, and N. Yuval-Davis, eds., *Power and the State*. London: Croom Helm.

—— (1979), 'Arrest: The Legal Context of Policing', in S. Holdaway, ed., *The British Police* London: Edward Arnold.

—— (1981), *Conviction*. London: Macmillan.

McCONVILLE, M., SANDERS, A., and LENG, R. (1991), *The Case for the Prosecution: Police Suspects and the Construction of Criminality*. London: Routledge.

—— and SHEPHERD, D. (1992), *Watching Police, Watching Communities*. London: Routledge.

McLAUGHLIN, E. (1990), *Community, Policing and Accountability: A Case Study of Manchester 1981–1988*, Ph.D Thesis, Faculty of Law: University of Sheffield.

—— (1992), 'The Democratic Deficit: European Unity and the Accountability of the British Police', *British Journal of Criminology*, 32, 4: 473–87.

McMAHON, M., and ERICSON, R. (1984), *Policing Reform*. University of Toronto: Centre of Criminology.

McMANUS, M. (1995), *From Fate to Choice: Private Bobbies, Public Beats*. Avebury: Ashgate Publishing Co.

McNAMARA, J. (1967), 'Uncertainties in Police Work: The Relevance of Police Recruits' Backgrounds and Training', in D. Bordua, ed., *The Police*, New York: Wiley.

MAGUIRE, M. (1988), 'Effects of the "PACE" Provisions on Detention and Questioning', *British Journal of Criminology*, 28, 1: 19–43.

—— and CORBETT, C. (1991), *A Study of the Police Complaints System*. London: HMSO.

—— and NORRIS, C. (1992), *The Conduct and Supervision of Criminal Investigations*. London: HMSO.

MANNING, P. (1970), 'The Police: Mandate, Strategies and Appearances', in J. D. Douglas, ed., *Crime and Justice in American Society*. Indianapolis, Ind.: Bobbs-Merrill.

—— (1977), *Police Work: The Social Organisation of Policing*. Cambridge, Mass: MIT Press.

—— (1979), 'The Social Control of Police Work', in S. Holdaway, ed., *The British Police*. London: Edward Arnold.

MARENIN, O. (1983), 'Parking Tickets and Class Repression: The Concept of Policing in Critical Theories of Criminal Justice', *Contemporary Crises*, 6, 2: 241–66.

MARK, R. (1977), *Policing A Perplexed Society*. London: Allen and Unwin.

—— (1978), *In the Office of Constable*. London: Collins.

MARSHALL, G. (1965), *Police and Government*. London: Methuen.

—— (1978), 'Police Accountability Revisited', in D. Butler and A. H. Halsey, eds., *Policy and Politics*. London: Macmillan.

MARTIN, J. P. and WILSON, G. (1969), *The Police: A Study in Manpower*. London: Heinemann.

MATZA, D. (1964), *Delinquency and Drift*. New York: Wiley.

—— (1969), *Becoming Deviant*. Englewood Cliffs, NJ: Prentice Hall.

MAWBY, R. (1991), *Comparative Policing Issues*. London: Unwin.

—— (1992), 'Comparative Police Systems: Searching For a Continental Model . . . ', in K. Bottomley, T. Fowles, and R. Reiner, eds., *Criminal Justice: Theory and Practice*. London: Institute for the Study and Treatment of Delinquency/British Society of Criminology.

MILIBAND, R. (1978), 'A State of Desubordination', *British Journal of Sociology*, 29, 4: 399–409.

MILLER, W. (1977), *Cops and Bobbies*. Chicago, Ill.: Chicago University Press.

MIRRLEES-BLACK, C., MAYHEW, P., and PERCY, A. (1996), *The 1996 British Crime Survey*. London: Home Office Research and Statistics Directorate.

MOORE, M. (1992), 'Problem-Solving and Community Policing', in M. Tonry and N. Morris, eds., *Modern Policing*. Chicago, Ill.: Chicago University Press.

MORGAN, R. (1989), 'Policing By Consent: Legitimating the Doctrine', in R. Morgan and D. Smith, eds., *Coming to Terms With Policing*. London: Routledge.

—— (1992), 'Talking About Policing', in D. Downes, ed., *Unravelling Criminal Justice*. London: Macmillan.

—— McKENZIE, I., and REINER, R. (1990), *Police Powers and Policy: A Study of Custody Officers*, unpublished Final Report to the Economic and Social Research Council.

—— and NEWBURN, T. (1997), *The Future of Policing*. Oxford: Oxford University Press.

MORRIS, A. (1987), *Women, Crime and Criminal Justice*. Oxford: Blackwell.

MORRISON, C. (1984), 'Why PC Plod Should Come Off the Beat', *Guardian*, 30 July: 8.

MORRISON, W. (1995), *Theoretical Criminology*. London: Cavendish.

MUIR, W. K. (1977), *The Police: Streetcorner Politicians*. Chicago, Ill.: Chicago University Press.

NEWBURN, T., and JONES, T. (1997), *Private Security and Public Policing*. Oxford: Oxford University Press.

—— and MORGAN, R. (1994), 'A New Agenda for the Old Bill', *Policing*, 10, 3: 143–50.

NIEDERHOFFER, A. (1967), *Behind the Shield*. New York: Doubleday.

NORRIS, C. (1989), 'Avoiding Trouble: The Police Officer's Perception of Encounters With the Public', in M. Weatheritt, ed., *Police Research: Some Future Prospects*. Aldershot: Avebury.

PALMER, S. H. (1988), *Police and Protest in England and Ireland 1780–1850*. Cambridge: Cambridge University Press.

PARK, R., and BURGESS, E. (1929), *Introduction to the Science of Sociology*. Chicago, Ill.: Chicago University Press.

PASQUINO, P. (1978), 'Theatrum Politicum: The Genealogy of Capital—Police and the State of Prosperity', *Ideology and Consciousness*, 4: 41–54.

PEASE, K. (1996), 'Opportunities for Crime Prevention: The Need for Incentives', in W. Saulsbury, J. Mott, and T. Newburn, eds., *Themes in Contemporary Policing*. London: Police Foundation/Policy Studies Institute.

PILIAVIN, I., and BRIAR, S. (1964), 'Police Encounters With Juveniles', *American Journal of Sociology*, 70, 2: 206–14.

PLATT, A., and COOPER, L., eds. (1974), *Policing America*. Chicago, Ill.: University of Chicago Press.

POLICE FOUNDATION/POLICY STUDIES INSTITUTE (1996), *The Role and Responsibilities of the Police: Report of an Independent Inquiry*. London: Police Foundation/Policy Studies Institute.

PUNCH, M. (1979*a*), 'The Secret Social Service', in S. Holdaway, ed., *The British Police*. London: Edward Arnold.

—— (1979*b*), *Policing the Inner City*. London: Macmillan.

—— (1983), 'Officers and Men', in M. Punch, ed., *Control in the Police Organisation*. Cambridge, Mass.: MIT Press.

—— (1985), *Conduct Unbecoming: The Social Construction of Police Deviance and Control*. London: Tavistock.

—— and NAYLOR, T. (1973), 'The Police: A Social Service', *New Society*, 24, 554: 358–61.

RADZINOWICZ, L. (1948–68), *A History of English Criminal Law Vols. 1–4*. London: Stevens.

RAWLINGS, P. (1991), 'Creeping Privatisation? The Police, the Conservative Government and Policing in the Late 1980s', in R. Reiner and M. Cross, eds., *Beyond Law and Order*. London: Macmillan.

—— (1995), 'The Idea of Policing: a History', *Policing and Society*, 5: 129–49.

REINER, R. (1978*a*), *The Blue-Coated Worker*. Cambridge: Cambridge University Press.

—— (1978*b*), 'The Police, Class and Politics', *Marxism Today*, 22: 69–80.

—— (1978*c*), 'The Police in the Class Structure', *British Journal of Law and Society*, 5, 2: 166–84.

—— (1988), 'British Criminology and the State', *British Journal of Criminology*, 29, 1: 138–58.

—— (1989*a*), 'Race and Criminal Justice', *New Community*, 16, 1: 5–22.

—— (1989*b*), 'The Politics of Police Research', in M. Weatheritt, ed., *Police Research: Some Future Prospects*. Aldershot: Avebury.

—— (1991), *Chief Constables*. Oxford: Oxford University Press.

—— (1992*a*), *The Politics of the Police*. 2nd edn. Hemel Hempstead: Wheatsheaf.

—— (1992*b*), 'Policing A Postmodern Society', *Modern Law Review*, 55, 6: 71–781.

—— (1992*c*), 'Police Research in the United Kingdom: A Critical Review', in N. Morris and M. Tonry, eds., *Modern Policing*. Chicago, Ill.: Chicago University Press.

—— (1993), 'Race, Crime and Justice: Models of Interpretation', in L. Gelsthorpe and B. McWilliam, eds., *Minority Ethnic Groups and the Criminal Justice System*. Cambridge University: Institute of Criminology.

—— (1994), 'What Should the Police Be Doing?', *Policing*, 10, 3: 151–7.

—— (1995), 'From Sacred to Profane: The Thirty Years War of the British Police', *Policing and Society*, 5, 2: 121–8.

—— ed. (1996*a*), *Policing Vols. I and II*. Aldershot: Dartmouth.

—— (1996*b*), 'Have the Police Got A Future?', in C. Critcher and D. Waddington, eds., *Policing Public Order: Theoretical and Practical Issues*, 261–7. Aldershot: Avebury.

—— (1996*c*), 'The Case of the Missing Crimes', in R. Levitas and W. Guy, eds., *Interpreting Official Statistics*, 185–205. London: Routledge.

—— and LEIGH, L. (1994), 'Police Power', in C. McCrudden and G. Chambers, eds., *Individual Rights and the Law in Britain*, 69–108. Oxford: Oxford University Press.

—— and SPENCER, S., eds. (1993), *Accountable*

Policing: Effectiveness, Empowerment and Equity. London: Institute for Public Policy Research.

REISS, A. J. (1971), *The Police and the Public.* New Haven, Conn.: Yale University Press.

REITH, C. (1956), *A New Study of Police History.* London: Oliver and Boyd.

ROBINSON, C. C., SCAGLION, R., and OLIVERO, J. M. (1994), *Police in Contradiction: The Evolution of the Police Function in Society.* Westport, Conn.: Greenwood.

ROBINSON, C. D. (1978), 'The Deradicalisation of the Policeman', *Crime and Delinquency*, 24, 2: 129–51.

—— (1979), 'Ideology As History' *Police Studies*, 2, 2: 35–49.

—— and SCAGLION, R. (1987), 'The Origin and Evolution of the Police Function in Society', *Law and Society Review*, 21, 1: 109–53.

ROCK, P., and COHEN, S. (1970), 'The Teddy Boy', in V. Bogdanor and R. Skidelsky, eds., *The Age of Affluence 1951–1964.* London: Macmillan.

ROSE, D. (1996), *In the Name of the Law: The Collapse of Criminal Justice.* London: Jonathan Cape.

ROSHIER, R. (1989), *Controlling Crime.* Milton Keynes: Open University Press.

ROYAL COMMISSION ON CRIMINAL JUSTICE (1993), *Report.* Cm 2263. London: HMSO.

ROYAL COMMISSION ON THE POLICE (1962), *Final Report.* Cmnd. 1728. London: HMSO.

ROZENBERG, J. (1992), 'Miscarriages of Justice', in E. Stockdale and S. Casale, eds., *Criminal Justice Under Stress.* London: Blackstone.

RUMBAUT, R. G. and BITTNER, E. (1979), 'Changing Conceptions of the Police Role: A Sociological Review', in N. Morris and M. Tonry, eds., *Crime and Justice 1.* Chicago, Ill.: Chicago University Press.

SANDERS, A., BRIDGES, L., MULVANEY, A., and CROZIER, B. (1989), *Advice and Assistance at Police Stations and the 24-Hour Duty Solicitor Scheme.* London: Lord Chancellor's Department.

SAULSBURY, W., MOTT, J., and NEWBURN, T., eds. (1996), *Themes in Contemporary Policing.* London: Police Foundation/Policy Studies Institute.

SCARMAN, LORD (1981), *The Brixton Disorders.* Cmnd. 8427. London: HMSO.

SCHWARTZ, R. D., and MILLER, J. C. (1964), 'Legal Evolution and Societal Complexity', *American Journal of Sociology*, 70, 1: 159–69.

SCRATON, P. (1985), *The State of the Police.* London: Pluto.

SEDLEY, S. (1985), 'The Uniformed Mind', in J. Baxter and L. Koffman, eds., *The Police:*

The Constitution and the Community. London: Professional Books.

SHAPLAND, J., and HOBBS, R. (1989), 'Policing on the Ground', in R. Morgan and D. Smith, eds., *Coming To Terms with Policing.* London: Routledge.

—— and VAGG, J. (1988), *Policing By the Public.* London: Routledge.

SHEARING, C. (1981a), 'Subterranean Processes in the Maintenance of Power', *Canadian Review of Sociology and Anthropology*, 18, 3: 283–98.

—— ed. (1981b), *Organisational Police Deviance.* Toronto: Butterworth.

—— (1984), *Dial-A-Cop: A Study of Police Mobilisation.* Toronto: University of Toronto: Centre of Criminology.

—— (1992), 'The Relation Between Public and Private Policing', in M. Tonry and N. Morris, eds., *Modern Policing.* Chicago, Ill.: Chicago University Press.

—— (1996), 'Public and Private Policing', in W. Saulsbury, J. Mott, and T. Newburn, eds., *Themes in Contemporary Policing.* London: Police Foundation/Policy Studies Institute.

—— and STENNING, P. (1983), 'Private Security: Implications for Social Control', *Social Problems*, 30, 5: 493–506.

—— and —— (1984), 'From the Panopticon to Disney World', in A. N. Doob and E. L. Greenspan, eds., *Perspectives in Criminal Law: Essays in Honour of John Ll. J. Edwards.* Toronto: Canada Law Book Co.

—— and —— eds. (1987), *Private Policing.* Beverly Hills, Cal.: Sage.

SHEPTYCKI, J. (1991), 'Innovations in the Policing of Domestic Violence in London, England', *Policing and Society*, 2, 2: 117–37.

—— (1993), *Innovations in Policing Domestic Violence.* Aldershot: Avebury.

—— (1995), 'Transnational Policing and the Makings of a Postmodern State', *British Journal of Criminology*, 35, 4: 613–35.

SHERMAN, L. (1992a), *Policing Domestic Violence: Experiments and Policy Dilemmas.* New York: Free Press.

—— (1992b), 'Police and Crime Control', in M. Tonry and N. Morris, eds., *Modern Policing.* Chicago, Ill.: Chicago University Press.

SILVER, A. (1967), 'The Demand For Order in Civil Society', in D. Bordua, ed., *The Police.* New York: Wiley.

SKOGAN, W. (1990), *The Police and Public in England and Wales: A British Crime Survey Report.* London: HMSO.

—— (1996), 'Public Opinion and the Police', in W. Saulsbury, J. Mott, and T. Newburn, eds., *Themes in Contemporary Policing.*

London: Police Foundation/Policy Studies Institute.

SKOLNICK, J. (1966), *Justice Without Trial*. New York: Wiley.

—— (1969), *The Politics of Protest*. New York: Bantam.

—— and BAYLEY, D. (1986), *The New Blue Line*. New York: Free Press.

—— and —— (1988), *Community Policing: Issues and Practices Around the World*. Washington, DC: National Institute of Justice.

—— and —— (1993), *Above the Law: Police and the Excessive Use of Force*. New York: Free Press.

SMITH, A. (1763), *Lectures on Jurisprudence*. Reprinted, Oxford: Oxford University Press, 1978.

SMITH, A. T. H. (1987), *Offences Against Public Order*. London: Sweet and Maxwell.

SMITH, D., GRAY, J., and SMALL, S. (1983), *Police and People in London Vols. 1–4*. London: Policy Studies Institute.

SOUTH, N. (1988), *Policing For Profit*. London: Sage.

SPARKS, R. (1992), *Television and the Drama of Crime*. Milton Keynes: Open University Press.

SPITZER, S. (1975), 'Punishment and Social Organisation: A Study of Durkheim's Theory of Evolution', *Law and Society Review*, 9, 4: 613–37.

—— (1987), 'Security and Control in Capitalist Societies: The Fetishism of Security and the Secret Thereof', in J. Lowman, R. J. Menzies, and T. S. Palys, eds., *Transcarceration: Essays in the Theory of Social Control*. Aldershot: Gower.

—— and SCULL, A. (1977), 'Social Control in Historical Perspective', in D. Greenberg, ed., *Corrections and Punishment*. Beverly Hills, Cal.: Sage.

ST. JOHNSTON, E. (1978), *One Policeman's Story*. Chichester: Barry Rose.

STANKO, E. A. (1985), *Intimate Intrusions: Women's Experience of Male Violence*. London: Routledge.

STEVENS, P., and WILLIS, C. (1989), *Race, Crime and Arrests*. London: HMSO.

STINCHCOMBE, A. (1963), 'Institutions of Privacy in the Determination of Police Administrative Practice', *American Journal of Sociology*, 69, 2: 150–60.

STODDARD, E. (1968), 'The Informal Code of Police Deviancy: A Group Approach to Blue-Coat Crime', *Journal of Criminal Law, Criminology and Police Science*, 59, 2: 201–13.

STORCH, R. (1975), 'The Plague of Blue Locusts: Police reform and Popular Resistance in Northern England 1840–1857', *International Review of Social History*, 20, 1: 61–90.

—— (1976), 'The Policeman as Domestic Missionary', *Journal of Social History*, 9, 4: 481–509.

TARLING, R. (1988), *Police Work and Manpower Allocation*. Research and Planning Unit Paper 47. London: Home Office.

TAYLOR, I., WALTON, P., and YOUNG, J. (1973), *The New Criminology*. London: Routledge.

TEMKIN, J. (1987), *Rape and the Legal Process*. London: Sweet and Maxwell.

THERBORN, G. (1989), 'The Two-Thirds, One-Third Society', in S. Hall and M. Jacques, eds., *New Times*. London: Lawrence and Wishart.

TROJANOWICZ, R., and BUCQUEROUX, B. (1990), *Community Policing*. Cincinnati, Ohio: Anderson Publishing.

VAN MAANEN, J.(1973), 'Observations on the Making of Policemen', *Human Organisation*, 32, 4: 407–18.

—— (1974), 'Working the Street', in H. Jacob, ed., *The Potential for Reform of Criminal Justice*. Beverly Hills, Cal.: Sage.

VINCENT, C. E. HOWARD (1893), *The Police Code and General Manual of the Criminal Law for the British Empire*. London: Francis Edwards and Simkin.

VISHER, C. (1983), 'Gender, Police Arrest Decisions and Notions of Chivalry', *Criminology*, 21, 1: 5–28.

VOLD, G., and BERNARD, T. (1985), *Theoretical Criminology*. 3rd edn. New York: Oxford University Press.

WADDINGTON, D. (1992), *Contemporary Issues in Public Disorder*. London: Routledge.

WADDINGTON, P. A. J. (1982), 'Conservatism, Dogmatism and Authoritarianism in the Police: A Comment', *Sociology*, 16, 4: 592–4.

—— (1983), 'Beware the Community Trap', *Police*, March: 34.

—— (1991), *The Strong Arm of the Law*. Oxford: Oxford University Press.

—— (1993), *Calling the Police*. Aldershot: Avebury.

—— (1994), *Liberty and Order: Policing Public Order in a Capital City*. London: UCL Press.

WALKER, N. (1993), 'The International Dimension', in R. Reiner and S. Spencer, eds., *Accountable Policing: Effectiveness, Empowerment and Equity*. London: Institute for Public Policy Research.

WALKLATE, S. (1992), 'Jack and Jill Join Up At Sun Hill: Public Images of Police Officers', *Policing and Society*, 2, 3: 219–32.

—— (1996), 'Equal Opportunities and the Future of Policing' in F. Leishman, B. Loveday, and S. Savage, eds., *Core Issues in Policing*. London: Longman.

WERTHMAN, C., and PILIAVIN, I. (1967), 'Gang Members and the Police', in D. Bordua, ed., *The Police*. New York: Wiley.

WESTLEY, W. (1953), 'Violence and the Police', *American Journal of Sociology*, 59, 1: 34–41.

—— (1956), 'Secrecy and the Police', *Social Forces*, 34, 2: 254–7.

—— (1970), *Violence and the Police*. Cambridge, Mass.: MIT Press.

WHITE, J. (1990), *The Worst Street in London*. London: Routledge.

WILLIAMS, G. (1984a), *The Law and Politics of Police Discretion*. Westport, Conn.: Greenwood Press.

—— (1984b), 'Police Rulemaking Revisited: Some New Thoughts On An Old Problem', *Law and Contemporary Problems*, 47, 4: 123–84.

WILLIAMSON, T. (1996), 'Police Investigation: the Changing Criminal Justice Context', in F. Leishman, B. Loveday, and S. Savage, eds., *Core Issues in Policing*. London: Longman.

WILLIS, C. (1983), *The Use, Effectiveness and Impact of Police Stop and Search Powers.* Research and Planning Unit Paper 15. London: Home Office.

WILSON, C. (1993), 'Police', in W. Outhwaite, T. Bottomore, E. Gellner, R. Nisbet, and A. Touraine, eds., *The Blackwell Dictionary of Twentieth-Century Social Thought*. Oxford: Blackwell.

WILSON, J. Q. (1968), *Varieties of Police Behaviour*. Cambridge, Mass.: Harvard University Press.

WOFFINDEN, B. (1989), *Miscarriages of Justice*. London: Coronet.

YOUNG, J. (1971), 'The Role of the Police As Amplifiers of Deviancy', in S. Cohen, ed., *Images of Deviance*. London: Penguin.

YOUNG, M. (1991), *An Inside Job*. Oxford: Oxford University Press.

—— (1993), *In the Sticks: An Anthropologist in a Shire Force*. Oxford: Oxford University Press.

ZANDER, M. (1991), *The Police and Criminal Evidence Act 1984*. 2nd edn. London: Sweet and Maxwell.

ZEDNER, L. (1993), 'Social Control', in W. Outhwaite, T. Bottomore, E. Gellner, R. Nisbet, and A. Touraine, eds., *The Blackwell Dictionary of Twentieth-Century Social Thought*. Oxford: Blackwell.

29

From Suspect to Trial

Andrew Sanders

MODELS OF CRIMINAL JUSTICE

The principles underlying different criminal justice systems vary according to history, culture, and ideology. The adversary principle is an important characteristic of the English system and of other common law systems such as those of Australia, Canada, and the United States. This principle is often characterized as embodying the search for 'proof' rather than 'truth' (Damaska, 1973). The search for 'truth' is usually said to be embodied in 'civil law' systems (such as the French), which are 'inquisitorial'. It would be nice if 'proof' and 'truth' were synonymous and sought with equal vigour, as one of Britain's leading Chief Constables has advocated (Pollard, 1996), but examination of the 'due process' and 'crime control' models developed by Packer (1968) will show that this is unrealistic.

'Due process' values prioritize civil liberties in order to secure the maximal acquittal of the innocent, risking acquittal of some guilty people. 'Crime control' values prioritize the conviction of the guilty, risking the conviction of some (fewer) innocents and infringement of the liberties of some citizens to achieve the system's goals. Due-process-based systems tightly control the actions and effects of crime-control agencies, while crime-control-based systems, with their concern for convictions, do not. A pure crime-control system would prioritize the search for truth by adversarial law enforcement agencies at literally all costs. Police officers who 'knew' that someone is guilty would either have this knowledge accepted as proof by a court or would be allowed to seek proof of it by any means. Put in this way, of course, the need for controls in a crime-control system becomes clear. Objective proof is needed, and law enforcement methods must be limited by humanitarian or libertarian standards even at the cost of knowledge. However, a pure due-process system would prioritize proof and controls at literally all costs. Guilty verdicts would be allowed only on proof beyond literally all doubt, and law enforcement officials would need objective evidence before interfering with any civil liberties, however slight. And so we see the criminal justice system dilemma. Absolute proof, and completely innocuous methods of securing it, cannot be insisted upon. But to insist on uncontrolled discretion in the way the truth is sought is equally unacceptable. No system can correspond exactly with either model (as no system is entirely adversarial or entirely inquisitorial), but in most systems the values of one or the other model appear to predominate.

As soon as the police challenge any individual whom they have any reason to suspect, an adversarial relationship is formed. In Britain, this triggers due-process protections, such as the caution against self-incrimination and the requirement of 'reasonable' suspicion for the exercise of coercive powers. On arrest the suspect is generally taken to a police station and detained. This triggers further due-process protections such as a right of access to lawyers and others as civil liberties are further eroded by lengthy detention, interrogation, search of the suspect's home, fingerprinting, and so forth. In order to charge, further evidence is required and further protections are provided: the Crown Prosecution Service (CPS) to vet the case and legal aid to prepare a defence. In order to convict there must be yet more evidence. So, due-process require-ments become more stringent at each stage, in parallel with the increased coerciveness of suspicion, accusation, and trial. Suspects may be believed to be guilty by the police, and may indeed be guilty 'in truth'. But in the absence of sufficient evidence (i.e. sufficient proof) due process requires that they be exonerated. At the final stage proof need not be absolute, but only 'beyond reasonable doubt'. Legal guilt and actual guilt are therefore not synonymous. Even in a due process system there will occasionally be legally guilty persons who are not 'actually' guilty, and many actually guilty persons who are not legally guilty. This means that all systems will produce some cases like the infamous 'miscarriage' cases of the last twenty years: the Birmingham Six, Guildford Four, Bridgewater Four, West Midlands Police Serious Crime Squad cases, and so forth. Whether or not these are evidence of system failure depends on how often they occur, why they occur, and whether there are adequate systems of review and appeal.

In crime-control systems it might be thought that there would be more legally guilty persons who are not actually guilty, but fewer actually guilty persons who are not legally guilty. Crime-control advocates argue, though, that crime-control systems rely on professional experts (usually the police) to identify and secure evidence from suspects. Crime control is therefore more efficient not merely at identifying the guilty, but also at identifying the innocent (Walkley, 1987: 5). More guilty verdicts could mean more actually guilty people being found guilty and fewer actually innocent people so found. However, this assumes that professional expertise really is that good; that the police can be trusted to find, rather than to manufacture, the evidence (and indeed that such a distinction between discovery and manufacture can be sustained); and that the overriding goal of the police will always be the discovery of the truth as distinct from, for instance, gathering criminal intelligence, clearing the streets, defending themselves, or simply putting away known troublemakers.

This chapter will question these assumptions and, in so doing, will show that *both* due-process *and* crime-control ideologies—like adversarial and inquisi-torial systems—are concerned to discover the 'truth'. It will also show that criminal justice processes have other, less obvious, goals. One difference between the different models lies in their methods of discovery of the truth and their degrees of success. Doubts about, for instance, the way each side in the adversarial trial guards 'its' evidence lead critics to argue for more 'transparency' in the pursuit of truth (Pollard, 1996), while doubts about the impartiality of inquisitorial systems reveal different ways in which the truth can be obscured (Zander, 1991; Sprack, 1992; Trouille, 1994). Similarly, doubts about police efficiency and propriety on the part of advocates of due process lead them to argue for the process of legal proof; while advocates of crime control argue that court processes and legal protections obstruct truth discovery.

Despite the clarification provided by Packer's models, their value is limited. 'Truth', for example, is not, and should not be, the only yardstick by which to evaluate a system. Ashworth argues that justice and fairness are also crucial. He tries to give concrete expression to these slippery concepts by developing a framework of ethical principles derived from the European Convention on Human Rights (Ashworth, 1994, 1996). Despite the acclaim which this approach has received from some (e.g. Morgan, 1996*a*) it creates as many problems as it solves. For example, Ashworth's principles include rights for victims ('to respect' and 'to compensation') which are major lacunae in Packer's models. However, no guidance is provided on how to reconcile these rights with those of suspects and defendants when conflicts occur. Other rights are reformulations of key due-process principles. Many of them are vague, such as 'to be treated fairly and without discrimination' and 'reasonable grounds for arrest and detention'. Those which are precise, such as the 'right of innocent persons not to be convicted', are not absolute, but may be undercut by the kinds of considerations one finds—although Ashworth and Morgan do not acknowledge this—in the crime-control model. The limitations of the Packer models are not, therefore, solved by Ashworth's human rights approach. Its main value is to specify standards by which to evaluate our present system. Sanders and Young (1994*b*) conducted a similar exercise, examining how far the law governing pre-trial decision-making met the standards imposed by the concept of the Rule of Law, and concluded that most of it fell a long way short. This chapter will concentrate on the social processes of criminal justice rather than its legal framework, but it is significant that much crime control-oriented decision-making is consistent with the law, rather than contrary to it (McConville *et al.*, 1991).

Another promising framework is that of social integration and exclusion. Faulkner (1996) characterizes the 'exclusion' approach as one whereby 'Crime is to be prevented by efficiency of detection, certainty of conviction and severity of punishment. . . . "Criminals" are to be seen as an "enemy" to be defeated and humiliated, in a "war" in which the police are seen as the "front line".' He contrasts this with Locke's view, that 'the end of law is not to abolish or restrain but to preserve and enlarge freedom'. On this inclusionary approach, 'Authority will not be respected if it is simply imposed: it has to be accountable and it has to be legitimate. . . . Solutions to the problem of crime have to be sought by inclusion within the community itself' (*ibid.*: 6). The integration/ exclusion model needs to be fleshed out and its applicability to criminal justice will then need to be evaluated. On the face of it, though, it offers more than any of the other models, for the inclusion approach combines the comprehensiveness of the human rights model with a clear sense of purpose.

POLICE DECISIONS 'ON THE STREET'

The due process origins of our system can be seen in the fact that, in the first decades after the establishment of the police, sufficient evidence to prosecute was needed before street powers could be exercised. Stop-and-search powers did not exist, and arrest was restricted to 'the apprehending or restraining of one's person in order to be forthcoming to answer an alleged or suspected crime' (Blackstone, 1830: 289): arrested persons were to be taken directly before the magistrates, who decided whether to prosecute. In theory, then, police investigation had to take place *before* arrest, although in reality many people used to be held by the police without formal arrest (supposedly 'helping the police with their enquiries'). Arrests are now often made to *facilitate* investigation, bringing the formal rules into line with a crime-control reality. The current legal position is now somewhere between the crime-control and due-process polarities. Both stop-and-search and arrest without judicial warrant are allowed for most 'normal' crimes (theft, burglary, serious assaults, sexual offences, drugs offences, public order offences, possession of offensive weapons, etc.), and the police are periodically given more powers for more offences. The Police and Criminal Evidence Act (PACE), in 1984, provided the first nation-wide stop-and-search powers. They were extended in relation to certain types of knife by the Criminal Justice Act 1988, extended further by the Criminal Justice and Public Order Act in 1994, and extended yet again in the Prevention of Terrorism (Additional Powers) Act 1996. The police must have 'reasonable suspicion' in order to exercise either power. The Code of Practice on stop-and-search issued by the Home Office under the authority of PACE states that 'there must be some objective basis' for the suspicion (paragraph 1.6), which 'can never be supported on the basis of personal factors alone' (paragraph 1.7). The 'objective' factors envisaged (which apply equally to arrest) include 'information received', someone 'acting covertly or warily', and someone 'carrying a certain type of article at an unusual time or in a place' where there have been relevant crimes recently (paragraph 1.6) (see generally Sanders and Young, 1994*a*: 2 and 3).

Discretion

Discretion is at the root of criminal justice practice. Police officers necessarily exercise discretion in deciding whether to stop and search and arrest. Some people look less 'suspicious' than others, and multitudes of actual or likely offences have to be prioritized. Minor offenders (prostitutes, unlicensed street traders, and so forth) are often simply ignored (Smith and Gray, 1983). Arrest is less frequent than formal action even for relatively serious violence (Clarkson *et al.*,1994; Hoyle, 1997). Similarly, when officers are able to be proactive (as compared to their usual reactive mode) they have to use discretion about the offences or offenders in which to invest scarce time. Discretion is also created as a consequence of the way offences are defined. Most offences require *mens rea* (a 'guilty mind') which, broadly, amounts to intent. Thus breaking someone's leg by tripping them up would be a crime if done deliberately, but not if done accidentally. A police officer could make an arrest if she reasonably suspected the former, but not if she suspected the latter. However, since intent is so difficult to assess, officers have ample scope to arrest or not according to their preference. So, stop-and-search and arrest decisions are constrained only loosely by law: the powers themselves, based on reasonable suspicion, are ill-defined and subjective, the offences for which the powers are exercised are similarly ill-defined, and the police set their own priorities.

If discretion is not structured primarily by law is it exercised arbitrarily or is it structured by something else? Research on policing suggests four levels at which discretion is structured. First, there are general policing goals. To say that a prime function of the police is to maintain order, control crime, and catch criminals may be trite, but it identifies a fundamental conflict between policing goals and the due-process model. In so far as that model is an obstacle course it can only get in the way of policing goals. To expect the police to abide by due process standards voluntarily—without coercion through 'inhibitory' rules—is therefore unrealistic. The second level is force policy. In the United States, in particular, this can vary considerably from locality to locality (Meehan, 1993). Walmsley (1978) analysed arrest and prosecution figures for homosexuality offences before and after the 1967 Sexual Offences Act (which partially legalized adult male homosexuality). Arrests were considerably higher after the Act than before. This was despite the fact that, assuming no change in the level of homosexual activity, the level of homosexual offences must have gone down as a result of the legal changes. It is likely that police forces were reluctant to arrest and prosecute while the law was the subject of debate, but no longer felt constrained under the new law. Then there is 'cop culture' (see Chan, 1996; Reiner, this volume). Its elements of sexism and racism, and its stereotyping of people and groups of certain types (on 'rough' estates, with certain lifestyles, etc.) affect the way officers view society. Take the Code of Practice's reference to 'wary' actions and what is normal for certain 'times and places'. How one views these matters depends on one's culture and individual officers' own ways of mediating that culture. The final level, then, is that of the individual. Police officers are not representative of the population. They tend to be from social strata 'C1' and 'C2', to be more conservative than the average, and to be white and male. The homogeneity of this group, coupled with police training and socialization processes, enables 'cop culture' to be easily reproduced.

Patterns of Bias and Police Working Rules

Research has found that the weak constraints imposed on discretion by law allow considerable scope for bias in policing. Prior to the implementation of PACE in the mid-1980s study after study produced similar findings (e.g. Stevens and Willis, 1979; Tuck and Southgate, 1981; Field and Southgate, 1982; Smith and Gray, 1983; Willis, 1983). Smith and Gray, for example, found that there was no 'reasonable suspicion' in one third of all stops which they observed, and Willis found that stop and search was often based on the suspects' 'movements'. 'This category', Willis remarked, 'covered stops on grounds which police officers find it hard to specify.' This would be consistent with the crime-control model if officers relied on intangible but reliable 'instinct' or 'experience', but the arrest rate (which was generally low at perhaps 10 per cent of all stops) was particularly low in the 'movements' cases. However, as stop-and-search is useful for intelligence-gathering (Brogden 1985; McConville *et al.*, 1991), a low arrest rate is not inconsistent with crime-control goals. It certainly appears that due-process standards, even the minimal requirements of 'reasonable suspicion', were rarely adhered to. These findings are, of course, consistent with research in the United States (see, for instance, Piliavin and Briar, 1964; and, generally, Reiner, 1992), which has similar rules on stop-and-search and arrest. Stops were often based on classic stereotypes leading to patterns of bias on lines of class, gender, and race (discussed by Reiner and by Smith, from a different perspective, this volume).

The introduction of PACE in the mid-1990s was intended to make some difference. For although PACE gives more, not less, power to the police, it also incorporates more controls than operated hitherto. These include requirements to tell suspects why they are being arrested or stop-searched and to make records of the incident. However, stop-and-search and arrest decisions are of intrinsically low visibility (Goldstein, 1960). Thus written records can be constructed after the event (McConville *et al.*, 1991: chapter 5). No longer are stops recorded as 'movements', but the reason for stops could be unchanged. As one officer put it to McConville *et al.* (1991), he would stop a suspect 'instinctively and then think about how he would satisfy a disinterested third party' (field notes). This suggests that the Code has altered the way officers *account* for their exercise of discretion, but not the way they *actually* exercise it. Accounts of incidents can correspond as much with legal expectations as with the reality of the incidents (Scott and Lyman, 1968; Ericson, 1981). Moreover, few stops are recorded at all. But this is only a breach of PACE if PACE powers are actually exercised (that is, if the stop is not consensual) and if there is a search or arrest (Sanders and Young, 1994*a*: chapter 2). Predictably, research has not found the control and accountability mechanisms in PACE to be effective. Norris *et al.* (1992) observed 272 stops in one London borough, of which 28 per cent were of black people despite only 10 per cent of the local population being black. The effect is continued at the arrest stage: black people constituted 16 per cent of all Metropolitan Police arrests in 1987, but comprised only 5 per cent of the capital's population (Home Office, 1988). In Leeds in 1987, 6 per cent of arrests were of black people, who comprised just 3 per cent of the population (Jefferson and Walker, 1992). Black people, Brown concluded in a review of PACE research, are more likely to be stopped than white people or Asians, more likely to be repeatedly stopped, more likely (if stopped) to be searched, and more likely to be arrested (1997: chapters 2 and 4; see also NACRO, 1997). How far race in itself leads to this disproportionate attention from the police and how far it stems from other socio-demographic factors (namely, class, gender, and location) is not known. It may be that crime is disproportionately prevalent among young black males, but this is a crime-control justification which should not be accepted without evidence. As it happens, although more stops lead to more arrests, the proportion of stops which lead to arrest decreases as the number of stops rises. This predictable consequence of the crime-control approach can be observed in most years since 1986 as the number of stops has increased fivefold since 1986 yet the proportion leading to arrest declined from 17 per cent in 1984 to 12 per cent in 1986 (see Sanders and Young, 1994*a*: chapter 2; Brown, 1997: chapter 2). In other words, it is rare for police suspicions to be borne out by evidence on which to base an arrest.

McConville *et al.* (1991) identify several 'working rules' which structure police decision-making. The first is 'previous' (i.e. being known to the police). Sometimes this 'bureaucratic' mode of suspicion (Matza, 1969) is sufficient on its own. As an arresting officer told McConville *et al.*: 'When you get to know an area, and see a villain about at 2.00 a.m. in the morning, you will always stop him to see what he is about' (1991: 24). The second concerns disorder and police authority. Dealing with disorder is a prime police task. Although Shapland and Vagg (1988) found that the police do not usually arrest when they intervene in disorderly incidents, arrests are usual if the disorder does not cease even when it is trivial and only the police are involved (Brown *et al.*, 1994). This is in part because of the challenge thereby presented to police authority, even if no specific charge fits the facts. Hoyle (1997) found the same in relation to domestic violence incidents. Other working rules include consideration of types of victims and their wishes, 'information received', and workload. But perhaps the most important working rule is 'suspiciousness'. This entails the suspect 'being in the right place at the right time', or being 'out of the ordinary' or 'unco-operative', or keeping the wrong company, or its being 'just a matter of instinct' on the officer's part, 'something undefinable' (all these phrases are from officers quoted in McConville *et al.*, 1991: 26–8). This is Matza's (1969) other main mode of investigation.

Both pre- and post-PACE research (Willis, 1983; McConville *et al.*, 1991, respectively) found that police officers could not say precisely what made them suspicious, illustrating the continuity of police behaviour pre- and post-PACE.

This is encapsulated in the principle of 'incongruity' (Dixon *et al.*, 1989), and is precisely the kind of consideration against which the Code of Practice (referred to above) cautions the police in its attempt to identify 'objective' factors which would satisfy a third party. One form of incongruity is the presence of individuals of one ethnic group in an area predominantly made up of other ethnic groups. Black people are disproportionately stopped and arrested in these circumstances (Jefferson and Walker, 1992) primarily when they are incongruous, i.e. not in 'their own' areas. This accords with the more radical literature on social control and police (e.g. Brogden, 1985; Scraton, 1987) and is consistent with 'crime control' models in their broadest formulations.

Dixon *et al.* (1989) argue that non-adherence to due-process standards is not so much wilful failure by police officers as the failure of due-process standards to meet the reality of policing. Policing is about the creative use of experience in crime control. The development, and diminution, of suspicion is a dynamic process. It cannot, they argue, be reduced to compartmentalized legalistic steps dependent on precisely measured levels of evidence. The police police as best they can, reducing legal restraints to merely presentational significance. The effect of PACE on the operation of discretion is clearly limited. Police working rules gel with cop culture stressing the importance of 'facing down' challenges to authority, investigating the incongruous, picking on 'known criminals', and so forth far more than with PACE. This is not to say that, under certain conditions, changes in formal rules are completely ineffective. Hoyle's (1997) study of domestic violence assessed the impact of a Home Office Circular which encouraged arrest wherever there was evidence of an offence. Arrests rose significantly as a result, although not to the extent that full adherence to the Circular would have produced. The perception by 'cop culture' of domestic assaults as 'rubbish' can, it seems, be overcome, albeit not entirely. As Chan (1996) argues, police culture is not independent of societal pressures and legal rules. Whether or not, and the way in which, practices and rules correspond is always an empirical matter. So, Hoyle found that, in the enthusiasm of police officers to at least partially operationalize this new policy, many arrests took place on inadequate evidence: a classic example of legal rules being overridden by non-legal concerns.

Stop-search and Arrest: Inclusionary or Exclusionary?

Arrests usually follow information from, and complaints by, victims or witnesses (Shapland and Vagg, 1988; Reiss, 1971; Zander, 1979; Steer, 1980; McConville and Baldwin, 1981). If few arrests are proactive, does discretion, and the patterns of bias which are reflected by it, play only a minor part in determining the shape of the official suspect population? Do claims that stereotyping and the 'mode of suspicion' structure the suspect population really 'not stand the test of empirical examination'? (Steer, 1980: 126). McConville *et al.* (1991) argue that most of the studies cited above are based on indictable offences, missing out the summary offences (such as public order, prostitution, drunkenness, etc.) in which police initiative is more pronounced. Also, the issue is less who is influenced by stereotyping as whether the initiator, whoever he or she is, is so influenced. Store detectives stereotype (Cameron, 1964; Murphy, 1986), and doubtless 'ordinary' members of the public do too. Further, citizen initiation rarely takes the form of citizen arrest. More usually it is simply the transmission of information to the police. That information has to be sifted, evaluated, and acted upon (or not) by the police. In one American study only two-thirds of citizen complaints were taken seriously by the police (Black, 1970). McConville *et al.* (1991: 2) provide several examples where, even when the police did act upon complaints (for instance, by an ex-lodger and by a restaurateur), the way in which they acted, whether or not to arrest, was decided according to the working rules discussed earlier, and Sanders *et al.* (1997) provide further examples. In other words, police discretion and the exercise of judgement are still operative even when arrests are citizen-initiated. The same is true of information from informants, on which the police increasingly depend (Maguire and Norris, 1992; Norris, 1995). Information from the public is one resource among many which the police use in exercising discretion on the street according to their own priorities, and so the community is harnessed by the police in an inclusionary way, but only where doing so is consistent with police working rules.

The increased formal powers of stop-search and arrest given to the police in the 1980s and 1990s, together with the ability of the police to stop-search and arrest largely when they want to on the basis of broad intangible suspicion, have led to the increased use of this intrusive activity throughout the late 1980s and 1990s. The more stops that are done, the more arrests there are, which is more intrusive still. Other new laws, such as section 5 of the Public Order Act 1986, provide arrest powers for trivial offences which the police use extensively to bolster their authority (Brown *et al.*, 1994). Young males, especially from poor and minority sections of the community, bear the brunt of all this power (Meehan, 1993; Brown, 1997: chapters 2 and 4). They feel—with some justification—discriminated against, and the consequent social unrest creates a vicious spiral of yet more policing and more unrest (Scarman, 1981; Keith, 1993; NACRO, 1997). The police use arrest powers to stamp their authority on challengers, often without any intention of prosecuting (Singh, 1993; Choongh, 1997). The poor and underprivileged are treated dismissively as part of, and in order to emphasize, their exclusion from normal standards of protection (Young, 1991).

These developments lead Sanders and Young (1994*b*) to argue that the Rule of Law is undermined in two ways. First there are no effective controls on the use of these powers. Secondly, putting people with little power in the same formal legal position as the police, in that stops may be carried out 'consensually', treats unequals as equals. This gives the powerful (i.e. the police) more power still, and it does not provide substantive equality. This is consistent with the argument that the power of the police to arrest for breach of the peace could be a breach of the European Convention on Human Rights (Nicolson and Reid, 1996), although the uncertainty with which the claim is made should serve as a warning about the limited value of the human rights framework.

DETENTION IN THE POLICE STATION

We have already noted that only in relatively recent years has the law moved in a crime-control direction by allowing interference in the liberty of the citizen in the absence of sufficient evidence to prosecute. This movement was initially unplanned, *ad hoc*, and imprecise, giving rise to legal 'fudges' like 'helping police with their enquiries'. The Royal Commission on Criminal Procedure (RCCP) (1981) was therefore urged, on the one hand, to prohibit pre-charge detention (the due-process position) and on the other to extend it (the crime-control position). The Royal Commission decided that pre-charge detention should be reduced, and allowed only when it was 'necessary': 'We do seek to alter the practice whereby the inevitable sequence on the creation of reasonable suspicion is arrest, followed by being taken to the station' (*ibid.*: paragraph 3.75). In this and other ways the Royal Commission attempted to satisfy both due-process and crime-control lobbies. The Royal Commission on Criminal Justice (RCCJ) (1993) also claimed that it balanced due process and crime control, although it avoided these terms, and many critics argue that it was actually captured by the 'crime control' lobby (McConville and Bridges, 1994; Field and Thomas, 1994; Young and Sanders, 1994). Although some of its proposals were acted upon, the RCCJ did not attempt to re-think criminal justice in the way that even the RCCP did. It therefore did not change the shape of the system significantly. This is more remarkable than it sounds, for the RCCJ was established because of a series of miscarriages of justice which came to light in the late 1980s. If, as many argue, miscarriages occur because of crime-control processes in both the pre- and post-PACE eras, this will be recognized as culpable complacency which fails to address the underlying problems.

Detention without Charge

In line with the Royal Commission's recommendations, PACE provides that anyone at a police station should either be free to leave at will or be under arrest (section 29). If the latter, there are clear time limits on how long a suspect can be held: normally twenty-four hours, but in exceptional cases up to thirty-six hours, or even ninety-six hours with the leave of the magistrates (sections 41–44). On arrest, all suspects, except in exceptional cases, should be taken directly to a police station (section 30). It is then for the 'custody officer' (the old station sergeant, with an enhanced role and training) to decide whether or not the suspect should be detained. There are only two grounds for detention: in order to charge the suspect, or, where there is insufficient evidence to charge, in order to secure that extra evidence. But this is allowed only where detention is *necessary* for that purpose (section 37), and only for as long as it is necessary; senior officers are supposed periodically to review detention to ascertain this.

The aims of these provisions should be clear. Being either arrested or free to go was designed to eliminate the travesty of 'helping the police with their enquiries'. Clear time limits were designed to ensure that both suspects and police knew what their respective rights and powers were, and to ensure that suspects were not intimidated by the prospect of indefinite detention. And immediate transit to a police station where a custody officer then becomes responsible for the suspect (and then, only when detention is 'necessary'), was designed to ensure that suspects did not remain in the hands of officers who might mistreat them.

These powers, and the limits on them, are an attempt to balance due process and crime control. The concept of 'balance' has been attacked by Ashworth (1996), and we can see why. For example, 'independent' custody officers have to complete 'custody sheets' on all suspects which record the particulars of their detention, and so forth. Yet, like records of stop-and-search, this written 'evidence' of the encounter (providing objective evidence of what happened, to protect suspects against police fabrications) is written by the police against whom this is supposed to be a protection! Custody records and stop-and-search records suffer the same inevitable problems (McConville *et al.*, 1991: chapter 5; Sanders and Bridges, 1990). It is not surprising to find that many of the RCCP's hopes have not been fulfilled: 'helping with enquiries' has not been eliminated, detention is hardly ever refused, and detention is continued for as long as investigating officers wish (subject to the time limits in PACE) by custody officers in the same routinized way that it is authorized in the first place (McKenzie *et al.*, 1990; McConville *et al.*, 1991; Dixon *et al.*, 1990).

Access to Legal Advice

The most striking due-process provision of PACE is the provision, in sections 58–59, of free legal advice to all suspects who request it. Information about this unambiguous right has to be provided by the custody officer to the suspect. Advice may be delayed in exceptional cases but not denied outright. Custody records state whether or not suspects were informed of their rights, whether or not suspects requested advice, and what (if anything) happened then. Request rates have now risen to around 38 per cent and actual advice rates to around 33 per cent (Brown, 1997: chapter 6). This is a massive increase over the pre-PACE situation, but it is still lower than one might have expected. Why should nearly two out of three people reject an entirely free service? Why do over one out of ten requests fail?

The research, the most recent being conducted by Brown *et al.* (1992) and McConville *et al.* (1994), is summarized by Sanders and Young (1994*a*: 124–46) and by Brown (1997: 6). First, some suspects do not request advice because they are not informed (wholly or partly) of their rights. Secondly, some suspects' requests are denied, ignored, or simply not acted upon. Sanders and Bridges (1990) estimated that in some 10.5 per cent of cases *which the police knew the researchers were observing* the police actually broke the law (the Code of Practice made under the authority of PACE). Custody records recorded some of these malpractices but failed to record the majority, under-lining the point made in relation to the recording of reasons for stop-and-search and detention: records made by the police are inevitably a feeble safeguard for suspects against the police. Thirdly, the police often use 'ploys' to attempt to dissuade suspects from seeking advice and to persuade them to cancel their requests. These ploys ranged from the incomprehensible reading of rights to scare stories, such as 'You'll have to wait in the cells until the solicitor gets here'.

The problem does not lie wholly with the police. Many suspects have negative attitudes towards solicitors, which is not surprising, given their level of service. Advice is frequently provided by telephone, rather than in person, in many cases solicitors do not attend interrogations, and when they do they are usually passive. Legal aid lawyers have a generally non-adversarial stance and take their lead from the police. They routinely allow the police to use intimidatory tactics, such that in one notorious case the suspect's lawyer had not objected to intimidation which the Court of Appeal condemned without hesitation (this was the Cardiff Three case, discussed by Sanders and Young, 1994*a*: 4). Sometimes defence lawyers are actually sought by the police to put their case to recalcitrant suspects! McConville *et al.* (1994: 8) found one firm, which specialized in criminal work, advising—over the telephone—'Tell the truth, son, you won't go far wrong on that advice.' The net result is that the possibility of help from a solicitor is one thing among many which a suspect weighs up when he is detained. As we shall see, it is not always in the best interests of suspects to accept this help, if such it is, if there are any costs attached to it. Even the RCCJ condemned the general standard of police station advice. Although its approach was regarded by many as inadequate (see the contributions by Bridges, Cape, and Hodgson in McConville and Bridges, 1994) the response from the regulatory agencies does not even go as far as the RCCJ recommended (Sanders, 1996a).

Police Interrogation

Interrogation has assumed ever greater importance in police investigation over the years. Nearly half of all detained suspects are now interrogated (Leng, 1992: 2). In part this is because, as we have seen, investigation now usually takes place after, rather than before, arrest. It is also a product of the *mens rea* requirements of substantive criminal law. It is usually necessary to prove that the suspect intended the offences or was reckless. Since these are features of the suspect's mental state the best evidence is his or her confession (Sanders, 1987; McConville *et al.*, 1991: 4; Evans, 1992). Even when other ways of securing evidence are available, interrogation often serves as a 'short cut' and produces information about other offences and other offenders (Softley, 1980). The due-process insistence on the prosecution proving its own case originally prohibited non-consensual interrogation, but this changed in 1912 when the Judges' Rules first allowed interrogation before charge. Confessions were invalid if secured 'involuntarily' or 'oppressively', but the 1981 RCCP, based on Irving's (1980) research, questioned how meaningful it was to talk of confessions given under conditions of involuntary detention being 'voluntary'. The PACE Code of Practice on Detention and Questioning sets out basic standards for interrogation (the provision of proper heating, ventilation, breaks, access to solicitors and others, and so forth), but also states that a police officer is 'entitled to question any person from whom he thinks useful information can be obtained. . . . A person's declaration that he is unwilling to reply does not alter this requirement' (Note 1B). So, police officers may attempt to persuade suspects to change their minds and to hold them, subject to the time limits, for as long as that takes. Given the importance attached by most suspects to the shortest detention possible (Brown *et al.*, 1992), and recent changes to the right of silence (see below) the pressures on suspects to speak are considerable.

How is evidence of guilt secured? First there are those many suspects who simply and speedily acquiesce, against whom there would often be plenty of evidence anyway (Irving and McKenzie, 1989; Moston *et al.*, 1992). Secondly, many suspects are susceptible to 'deals' (confessions in exchange for favours or reduced charges): 'They always want to deal. When they're arrested they're immediately in the game of damage limitation' (CID officer, quoted by Maguire and Norris, 1992: 5). Then there are those who are intimidated by their situation by being held against their will in 'police territory' where the environment is deliberately denuded of psychological supports (Driver, 1968; Holdaway, 1983; Walkley, 1987), by being in fear of spending the night in the cells (Sanders *et al.*, 1989), or by the employment of any number of 'tactics' against them (Irving, 1980; Irving and McKenzie, 1989; Softley, 1980; Evans, 1992; McConville *et al.*, 1994). Such tactics include offering inducements such as bail, claiming that there is overwhelming evidence against the suspect, using custodial conditions such as return to the cells, and so forth. If a tactic does not work in the initial interrogation, twenty-four hours (or more) allows time for further interrogation. Evans (1992: 49) found a strong statistical association between the use of tactics and confessions.

Extreme tactics are now unacceptable in formal interrogations since they are tape recorded. This gives rise to a fourth way of securing confession: through informal interrogation. The extent of this is controversial but its existence is not. Informal interrogation occurs on the way to the police station (the 'scenic route': McConville and Morrell, 1983; Evans and Ferguson, 1991; Maguire and Norris, 1992: 5); before and after formal interrogations (Sanders and Bridges, 1990; McConville *et al.*, 1991: 4, 7; McConville, 1992); and in the cells under the guise of 'welfare visits' (Dixon *et al.*, 1990). A classic instance is discussed by Leng (1992): a suspect having been silent throughout two interviews, the third opened with the officer stating, 'You have intimated that you wish to tell me about the matters which I have spoken to you about earlier.' Custody records are supposed to record the precise times at which interviews begin and end, but this does not prevent officers having 'a little chat to get things straight before I switch on the tape' (Evans and Ferguson, 1991; see also Evans, 1992: 36; McConville, 1992). It is precisely on confessions allegedly made 'informally' (but not repeated 'formally') that so many appeals have turned, especially in the West Midlands Police Serious Crime Squad investigation (Kaye, 1991). To the extent that 'tactics' are now used less frequently in formal interrogations than they were before PACE, it is likely that they are now simply being used more under 'low visibility' conditions (Maguire and Norris, 1992). Research by Brown *et al.* (1992) and Moston and Stephenson (1993), although methodologically flawed (Sanders and Young, 1994*a*: 178–9) found that officers admitted to a considerable amount of informal interviewing. The low visibility of informal interviews provides the opportunity to officers to 'gild the lily' (Holdaway, 1983). As one officer told Maguire and Norris (1992: 46–7), there was nothing to prevent him from distorting the contents of informal conversations 'if I was dishonest'.

Coercion may occur too, in both informal and formal interrogations. This is inevitable under English law, for the job of the police interrogator is to elicit answers even from suspects who have declared a refusal to provide answers: in other words, to change their minds. Tactics are designed to do this, and not all tactics are of the 'carrot' variety: 'Sometimes it's necessary to shout at people . . . you have to keep up the pressure' (detective, quoted by McConville *et al.*, 1991: 4). Even interrogation practices which would be innocuous to most people are coercive to vulnerable people (Gudjonsson and MacKeith, 1982; Littlechild, 1995). Procedures for identifying, and making allowances for, vulnerable people in police custody are inadequate (Laing, 1995; Palmer, 1996). And even supposedly non-vulnerable people often make 'coerced-passive' confessions (McConville *et al.*, 1991: 4) as a result of leading questions (defended by Walkley, 1987) and legal-closure questions (Irving, 1985). Thus suspects get trapped into accepting they have 'stolen' when they in fact would put it in a different, exculpatory, way (see also Sanders *et al.*, 1989: 7; Evans, 1992).

Finally, there are false confessions. Just as not all 'informal' confessions are manufactured, not all manufactured confessions are false. On the other hand, false confessions can arise in the most controlled circumstances, although the less regulated the interrogation, the more likely they are to occur. Gudjonsson and MacKeith (1988) discuss various types of false confession arising from coercion, but coercion is not always necessary. Questioning taking the form of a supported direct accusation (i.e. an accusation with details of the crime itself) can lead to internalization by suggestible suspects whose subsequent 'confessions' will contain only the details provided by the police themselves (Moston, 1992). While vulnerable suspects figure particularly among cases of false confession (Littlechild, 1995), many people who are apparently robust are vulnerable to police tactics and the sheer fear of being cut off and confined for a period of time beyond one's own control. As one of the authors of a false confession in the 'Kerry Babies' case put it, 'I didn't think my mind was my own' (O'Mahony, 1992). Whilst false confessions arising from disorientation are doubtless very rare, falsity can be a matter of interpretation and degree. McConville *et al.* argue that interrogation is a process of construction whereby facts are made and not discovered. An example is given by Maguire and Norris (1992: 4), who report a CID sergeant saying that he had been taught, whenever he found people carrying knives to induce them to say they were for their own protection. This, unknown to the suspect, constitutes admission of the crime of carrying an 'offensive weapon'. This type of confession, with elements of falsity arising from the process of case construction, is doubtless far more common than 'false confessions', yet equally likely to lead to wrongful convictions.

While the police do not seek false (or even coerced) confessions, McConville *et al.* argue that their adversarial role inevitably leads to the crime-control value that this is a price worth paying. This view contrasts with that of Moston (1992), who argues that police failure to verify confessions and avoid leading questions is simply a matter of technical competence, a failure of training, and the decision to adopt adversarial styles. Inquisitorial styles, going under labels such as 'investigative interviewing' or 'ethical interviewing' are advocated, by the Home Office and the police as well as by academics such as Moston. These new interview styles have received some attention in the literature (see e.g. Williamson and Cherryman and Bull in Leishman *et al.*, 1996). However, there has not yet been any research on the use and impact of these new interview styles (Brown, 1997: chapter 7). Solutions such as these, along with technical solutions, such as better training or video recording (Baldwin, 1991), imply a bureaucratic explanation for false confessions and coercion. They presuppose that due process is achievable in interrogation. McConville *et al.* argue that the search for 'better' or more 'objective' interrogation is naïve, because the job of the police is to build a case, not to identify verifiable facts. Miscarriages of justice arising from coercion and false confessions would be more effectively reduced by preventing confession evidence forming the sole basis of convictions and by providing the defence with the same resources as are provided to the prosecution than by trying to change interrogation practices.

The Right of Silence

Over half of all suspects who are interrogated either confess or make incriminating statements to the police (see, for instance, Softley, 1980; Sanders *et al.*, 1989; and Evans, 1992). We have seen that the police have various methods of securing confessions, but these do not always work, and they work with varying success according to a wide range of factors, in particular, offence severity, prior legal advice, and strength of evidence (Moston *et al.*, 1992). Evans (1992) also found age and criminal record to be significant. From the due-process point of view high confession rates are surprising. From the crime-control viewpoint the question is why the police should be impeded by suspects' silence.

Whether silence does impede the police turns principally on three things: what, precisely, 'silence' means in this context; what the association is between silence and outcome; and in what ways the police are obstructed by silence.[1] Few suspects in the post-PACE studies exercise absolute silence (Willis *et al.*, 1988: 2–4 per cent; Sanders *et al.*, 1989: 2.8 per cent; Moston *et al.*, 1993: 8 per cent; McConville and Hodgson, 1992: 2.5 per cent). However, some suspects (a further 5.3 per cent in Sanders *et al.*) simply make flat denials, while others answer some questions and not others (11–15 per cent in Irving and McKenzie, 1989; and a further 8 per cent in Moston *et al.*, 1993), and some suspects are silent at the start but then answer questions later (or vice versa). So studies which simply count the number of interviews in which questions were not answered at some point can be misleading: 12.3–23 per cent of interviews in the Home Office Working Group studies (Home Office, 1989) were so identified.[2] Leng (1992), re-analysing McConville *et al.*'s (1991) data and taking these points into account, found a 'true' silence rate of 4.5 per cent. However, he found that in only a small percentage of 'no further actions' or acquittals was silence exercised, and that these negative outcomes rarely seemed to be a product of silence. Moston and Williamson (1990) also found little association between silence and charge, plea, or verdict (see also Moston, 1992). Leng found that 'ambush' defences, in particular, were rare. When they were used, they were unsuccessful. When genuine ambush defences were mounted (in between 1.7 and 5.1 per cent of all contested trials) they were unsuccessful. Most acquittals were the result of unanticipated, but not *unanticipatable*, defences, for sometimes they were exculpatory statements to which the police would not listen in interrogation.

The RCCJ examined this evidence, concluding that the right to silence should be retained, as abolition would benefit the police in few cases, and would put pressure on innocent people instead of experienced criminals. Despite this, the government changed the law in line with the changes it had already made in Northern Ireland. The Criminal Justice and Public Order Act 1994 now provides that, when someone relies in court on a fact which s/he could have been reasonably expected to mention when questioned by the police, the court can draw an adverse inference from this silence. Similarly, courts can draw adverse inferences from failures to answer questions in court. Exactly what inferences a court should draw from silence is a matter of debate (Dennis, 1995; Jackson, 1995; Pattenden, 1995). Munday comments that,

---

[1] There are, of course, arguments of principle, both for and against the right, which do not turn on empirical matters. See Greer (1990) and Easton (1991). The RCCJ was not concerned with matters of principle, which made it easier for the government to ignore its recommendations that it remain.

[2] See Leng (1992) for a penetrating analysis of these 'counting' problems in which he suggests that Moston *et al.* (1992) and the Home Office Working Group overestimate the 'true' rate of silence by about 28 per cent.

although the Northern Ireland provisions passed their first test in the European Court of Human Rights, the Court 'expand[s] its repertoire of human rights concepts with bewildering rapidity' (1996: 385). This illustrates one of the problems with a human rights framework such as advocated by Ashworth and by Morgan, but it also suggests that both the legal and the political future of these provisions is uncertain.

A Sea Change in the Nature of Detention?

Rather than leading to less pre-charge detention, the RCCP's scheme (enacted in PACE) has led to more. The formalisation of pre-charge procedures was intended to protect suspects, and it may do so to some extent. But its unintended consequence has been to lead to more arrests (fewer suspects being held in limbo), more police station interrogation (instead of interviews at home), and the rushing (in some cases) of the charging process to beat the time limits. Despite PACE, detention can still be lengthy and intimidating, access to lawyers can be obstructed and is often of little value, and the police have learnt to substitute psychological pressure for physical pressure. On the broader impact of PACE on policing, researchers have reached different conclusions. As part of a critique of *The Case for the Prosecution* (McConville *et al.*, 1991) Dixon divides criminal justice researchers into two main camps: the 'sea change theorists' who argue that PACE has significantly obstructed the police and enhanced protections for suspects; and 'new left pessimists', such as myself, who argue that the changes are largely cosmetic. Dixon places his own work between these camps, arguing that whether legal rules change police practices 'depends on what kind of rules and what kind of culture, what kind of reform and when' (1992: 536). This seems to me to be an indisputable sociological truth with which few researchers would disagree, but it does not resolve the argument about the significance of the changes.[3] It seems that PACE, like any other new law, has changed practices, but largely by *shifting* the unwanted behaviour instead of eradicating or even reducing it. Thus there is little violence now, but there is more use of other tactics and pressures, and confessions purportedly given in 'informal' interrogations are still admissible. The PACE framework is similar to the post-*Miranda* approach in the United States, where interrogation has similarly shifted from physical to psychological strategies. As Leo puts it, 'The law has also empowered the police to create more specialised and seemingly more effective interrogation strategies . . . they can lie, they can cajole, and they can manipulate.' (1994: 116). The new rules and constraints which are implicitly relied upon by Dixon are access to lawyers, tape recording of interrogation, custody records, and the general supervisory role of the custody officer. As we have seen—and as Dixon (1991) partially acknowledges himself—these developments hardly represent a 'sea change' in policing.

---

[3] The specific controversy about *The Case for the Prosecution* is discussed at length elsewhere. See the articles by McConville and Sanders, Leng, Dixon, Morgan, and Reiner in Noaks *et al.*, eds., 1995.

Sanders and Young (1994*b*) argue that PACE only appears to provide a 'balance' between due process and crime control because we now unquestioningly accept the right of the police to use coercive powers. But why, they ask, do suspects not want to wait for a lawyer, for instance, to come to the station? Why are so many people so vulnerable that PACE has to establish elaborate codes and protections? Why do suspects 'voluntarily' answer police questions? Only because they are in the police station against their will in the first place. So, for example, most suspects do want lawyers, but the desire to get out of the station quickly is stronger (Brown *et al.*, 1992). It is police power that makes suspects make this choice. And why is police station legal work so poor so often? Again, largely because the police have the power to create the forces that so shape it. Solicitors send unqualified staff, give telephone advice, or miss interrogations largely because of all the time they would otherwise waste. But it is the police who control the time-frame (Sanders, 1996*a*). And the legal 'trading' which undermines adversarialism is forced onto lawyers—who, it has to be admitted, usually need little persuading—because the police are in control. Once the police are given the right to detain, the rule of law is jeopardized, due process is made unviable, and human rights norms are tested to their limit. Thus, Sanders and Young argue, PACE does not merely 'balance' rights and powers poorly, but, in providing the right to detain in such broad circumstances, it cedes most practical power to the police. The 'sea change', if there has been one, has been in favour of the police, even to the extent of compromising the right of silence, without the help of the 1994 legislation.

Why do we put up with this? Sanders and Young argue that it is because it is not 'we' who bear the brunt of these powers. Most people who are stopped, searched, arrested, detained, and interrogated are young working-class men, especially in ethnic minorities. The treatment they are given is frequently humiliating—and deliberately so (Young, 1991; Singh, 1993). Opinion-formers, lawyers, and legislators, on the other hand (older middle-class men in the main), are very rarely subjected to these exclusionary processes. It is true that over one third of men will have been convicted of at least one non-motoring offence before they reach the age of 40, which means that many more than this will have been stopped, arrested, and/or reported for motoring offences. But the way in which police power is exercised and its frequency are as important as outcome (Tyler, 1990), and this bears down far more heavily on the poor than on the wealthy. Of course some middle-class people are roughly treated and some poor people are not. But the contrast between the integrated and the excluded is as striking in the field of criminal justice as in other fields of social policy. Arguably, major advances in liberty are only ever secured in the United Kingdom when the middle classes are threatened. If so, we can expect this divided society to manifest these exclusionary processes for a long time to come.

PROSECUTION AND DIVERSION

When the police were first established they gradually took over responsibility for prosecution in the absence of any specific or exclusive prosecution powers or controls over their discretion. As arrest turned into a tool for (rather than the culmination of) investigation, pre-charge detention arose and the police developed various non-prosecution dispositions. There are now well over a million police prosecutions per year, but around one in four suspects are released from pre-charge detention with no further action (NFA), and many suspects are cautioned. In fact, as many juveniles are cautioned as are prosecuted. Many other agencies also prosecute. These include the Inland Revenue (IR), Department of Social Security (DSS), Health and Safety Inspectorate, Customs and Excise, and so forth. Although these agencies follow a diversity of policies and procedures (Lidstone *et al.*, 1980; Sanders, 1996*b*: Part IV) they all share a propensity not to prosecute. The DSS is the most prosecution-minded of the non-police agencies. The DSS mounted 8,090 prosecutions in 1986–7, compared to the IR's 459 in the same year (Cook, 1989: 7), despite the far greater number of tax offences. These agencies caution far more often than they prosecute, and NFA even more often than that (Sanders, 1985*a*), although they do attempt to secure compliance with the law and/or secure financial compensation through informal negotiation. Whether their approach is so different from that of the police because the offences with which they deal are viewed differently by 'society', or whether the causal effect is in the other direction, is not clear (see Nelken, this volume). However, it is clear that even the treatment of people who are unlawfully killed is completely different: non-police agencies virtually never ask the police to consider prosecuting for manslaughter in circumstances where this would be viable and, arguably, desirable (Slapper, 1993). Thus arrest does not necessarily lead to prosecution, prosecution need not be the normal response to suspected crime, and the specific charge prosecuted is an entirely discretionary matter (see generally Sanders, 1996*b*).

No Further Action

Comparison of the results of research by, for instance, Steer (1980: Table 4) with that of McConville *et al.* (1991) indicates a rise in the NFA rate over the years, especially since the introduction of PACE. This is consistent with the 'new left pessimist' argument that PACE reflects and reproduces a 'crime-control' trend. Police officers decide both whether to arrest and whether to charge, and they make release decisions themselves on the basis of their own criteria and on evidence collected and evaluated by themselves. Sifting is in the hands of the professionals. Procedural due process may be satisfied by different evidential thresholds for arrest and charge, but we have seen that the threshold for arrest can fall short of substantive due process. The increasing level of NFAs lends weight to this view.

McConville *et al.* (1991: 6) found that many arrests were a result of pressure from the public. If the police arrested reluctantly the outcome was often NFA, usually after consultation with the victim, regardless of the strength of evidence. Other reasons for NFA in cases where the police did find (or could have found) evidence include the doing of 'deals' with suspects, especially informants. And just as prosecution is sometimes used to protect the police against allegations of malpractice (Wilcox, 1972) so in some circumstances NFA prevents the airing in public of events about which the police prefer to keep quiet (McConville *et al.*, 1991: 111). Some NFAs, of course, are simply cases in which the police would have liked to prosecute had they had more evidence. The obstacle here is rarely physical or legal, but simply one of resources. The police rarely seek evidence other than from eye witnesses, the victim, and the suspect himself. They could often investigate further but choose not to (Leng, 1992). Cases are a product of police work, and so the absence of a case is also a police product. On the other hand, many NFAs are a product of purely speculative arrests (McConville *et al.*, 1991: 2). Often the police accept that the suspect did not commit the offence or that there is no evidence: for instance, where the police 'trawl' local people with relevant previous convictions simply to eliminate them from a major rape enquiry; where suspects are arrested so that they can be held pending their questioning as witnesses; and where *all* inhabitants of, and visitors to, a building where there has been a drugs raid are arrested, even though the building consists of several self-contained flats (Leng, 1992).

Further, arrest and detention is not always geared to prosecution. If the police arrest in furtherance of the 'assertion of authority' working rule, for instance, the arrestee may be detained in order to be humbled. The exercise of power is sometimes an end in itself. It is sometimes used to terrorize sections of the population such as the Irish (Hillyard, 1993). NFAs would have been anticipated even at the moment of arrest. In these types of case, and in many of those discussed earlier, no due-process standards, substantive or procedural, are adhered to. The working rules discussed earlier are the motor driving police dispositions.

Police Diversion

Although the ratio of prosecutions to cautions is about 4:1, this reflects a massive increase in the cautioning of both adults and juveniles since the 1970s. The Royal Commission on Criminal Procedure (1981: Table 23.4) noted considerable variations in cautioning rates among police forces that could not be explained solely by offence variations (Sanders, 1985*b*). As with arrest policies, police forces had their own cautioning policies. The Home Office responded in 1985 with new guidelines which established clearer criteria for prosecution and caution: offence seriousness, previous convictions, dramatic mitigating circumstances, wishes of the victim, and so forth. However, both inter-force and intra-force disparity continued (Wilkinson and Evans, 1990), because of the procedural arrangements for prosecution and caution (discussed below) and the guidelines themselves. The latter are vague (how serious an offence or record? what kinds of personal circumstance should be taken into account?), manipulable (the police themselves sometimes influence the wishes of victims), and non-prioritized (are victims' wishes, suspect's circumstances, or offence seriousness to predominate?). New guidelines were produced in 1990 and again in 1994, but their impact is not likely to be significant, except that the latest change aims to reverse the trend of increasing cautions (Evans, 1994). Diversion is none the less encouraged in many cases which would once have been prosecuted, because it is cheaper than prosecution and because it avoids stigmatizing offenders. Drawing on labelling theory (e.g. Becker, 1963), it is now generally accepted that prosecution and punishment can exaggerate criminal self-identity. The 1990 caution guidelines exhort cautioning as 'reducing the risk that [offenders] will re-offend' (Home Office, 1990: paragraph 5). Thus 'courts should only be used as a last resort, particularly for juveniles and young adults' (*ibid.*: paragraph 7).[4]

The cost-reduction and stigma-avoidance objectives would be undermined if cautions were used in cases which would not otherwise be prosecuted. The guidelines therefore warn, first, against 'net-widening' (*ibid.*: paragraph 3). This occurs when cautions are used as alternatives to NFA rather than to pros-ecution, although it is difficult to assess how widespread this is (Ditchfield, 1976; Morris *et al.*, 1980; Cohen, 1985; Pratt, 1986; Duff, 1993). Secondly, pre-conditions for caution (HO, 1990: annex B, paragraph 2) are set out: that there is sufficient evidence to prosecute and that the suspect admits the offence and accepts the caution. Both Steer (1970) and Sanders (1988*a*) found that the preconditions (which predated the 1985 guidelines) were often ignored. Indeed, some suspects were cautioned precisely *because* there was insufficient evidence to prosecute! McConville *et al.* (1991: chapter 7), and Evans and Ferguson (1991) found that little had changed in more recent years. Over 20 per cent of the juveniles cautioned in the latter study, for instance, made no clear admission. The low-visibility nature of caution decisions also enables the police to use cautions as bargaining tools with suspects who would normally be prosecuted (McConville *et al.*, 1991: 6).

Both on the street and in the station, rules have little effect on police behaviour unless they are both enforceable and enforced (neither applying to cautioning) or coincide with police working rules. These controls often do not coincide, for cautioning can serve crime control objectives. Cohen's original (1985) 'net widening' thesis was that less obviously coercive measures (the whole spectrum of 'community' policing and 'community' dispositions) were developing in order to exercise more control over the suspect population. The police want

---

[4] The rise in juvenile cautioning has been so great that more juveniles are now cautioned than are prosecuted. For discussion see Lee (1995) and Newburn in this volume.

to have on record suspects who are not prosecuted, and for these purposes legalistic questions of evidence and admission are trivial distractions. On this argument due process is subordinated to crime control in the practice of cautioning. Similarly, ostensibly cautionable cases are often prosecuted where this serves policing objectives; and the interests of the victim whether opposed to those of the suspect or not are also sometimes subordinated to those of the police (Hoyle, 1997; Sanders *et al.*, 1997).

The patterns of bias identified in street policing (race, class, and so forth) may also be evident in prosecution and diversion decisions. This has certainly appeared to be so with juvenile decisions (Evans, 1992; Fitzgerald, 1993; Lee, 1995), and may be true with adults too (Sanders, 1985*a*). But the greater class bias is between police-enforced and other crime. Despite variations in the use of police cautioning the overwhelming pattern is, in adult cases, the use of prosecution instead of caution. Both the police and other types of agency have near-absolute discretion. The police (dealing with mainly working-class crime) use it one way, while most other agencies (dealing with mainly middle-class crime) use it in another. It is difficult to see how this can be justified in terms of offence seriousness, previous criminality, and so forth (Sanders, 1985*a*; Cook, 1989), except, perhaps, in terms of a narrowly defined 'efficiency' (Hutter, 1988). Efficiency, of course, is the crux of the crime-control ideology. Thus the dispositions of both police and non-police agencies serve to further the different working rules of those different agencies. And the stigmatizing and exclusionary process of prosecution is used routinely against the poor but rarely against the wealthy.

Police Charging

In most cases the police now decide, following arrest, whether or not to charge. The usual threshold used to be a *prima facie* case. This, the RCCP believed, led to many acquittals, and it recommended the more stringent criterion of 'a reasonable prospect of conviction'. Sanders (1985*b*) certainly found that weak evidence often led to acquittal, but also found that by no means all cases even passed the *prima facie* threshold. More recently, McConville *et al.* (1991: chapter 6) found the same in relation to the new threshold, as did research done for the RCCJ (Block *et al.*, 1993). McConville *et al.* (1991) argue that the police continue to follow their working rules when making charge decisions, and follow American and English writers (such as Bittner, 1967; and Chatterton, 1976) in arguing that the charge, like stop-and-search, arrest, interrogation, and caution is a resource for the police as much as it is an end in itself. Decisions to charge cases which are weak and to fail to charge cases which are strong are inconsistent and incomprehensible only in terms of the official guidelines. They are perfectly rational in terms of police working rules. This increases the acquittal rate, but convictions are only one dimension on the crime-control scale. Acquisition of information (through interrogation which is then justified by charge), assertion of authority, protection of an officer against whom a complaint is expected are all reasons which McConville *et al.* (1991) found officers gave for charging with little or no regard for the rules. One might add to the list, contrary to McConville *et al.*'s expectations, the charging of suspected offenders against vulnerable victims (Sanders *et al.*, 1997).

Unlike cautions, which are usually decided by inspectors or more senior officers, charges are a matter for the arresting officer and custody officer. Very rarely do custody officers caution or NFA when the arresting officer wants a prosecution, or vice versa, for custody officers are inevitably in a weak position in inquiring into evidential strength. If they try to evaluate arresting officers' evidence they have only one source of information on which to draw (apart from the suspect): that same arresting officer. McConville *et al.* are the only researchers to have looked at custody officers' charge decisions since Chatterton's (1976) early work, which reached similar conclusions about charge sergeants. These conclusions are that, as one custody officer put it, 'I would go along with what the arresting officers have to say'. As an arresting officer said: 'Perhaps by the book. . . . "The custody officer will decide" sort of thing, but in practice it's different. He trusts your judgement' (McConville *et al.*, 1991: 119–20). Cop culture prevents the suspect from rising high on the hierarchy of credibility: 'I accept that [the officer's] got no cause to be telling lies and the other chap has' (McConville *et al.*, 1991: 119). Arresting officers can, in other words, 'construct' their cases to achieve the results they want, and may even 'gild the lily' in the process (Ericson, 1981; Holdaway, 1983). Case construction involves selection, interpretation, and creation of facts. Cases are constructed deliberately to appear strong, in accordance with adversarial principles (McBarnet, 1981). Since the system is concerned more with legal truth than with actual truth, the police are also more concerned with the former, sometimes 'creating' facts which bear little relation to any reality which the suspect might recognize (Kaye, 1991; Maguire and Norris, 1992). Again, this is simply a continuation of processes revealed in study of interrogation and other policing practices. It follows that, just as officers can secure cautions when NFA would be more in keeping with the rules, so they can secure charges when cautions would be more appropriate (and vice versa). The same factors apply with juveniles, despite relatively sophisticated juvenile liaison arrangements: many juveniles are still charged immediately, and even multi-agency juvenile bureaux still rely on police constructions (Evans and Ferguson, 1991).

The Crown Prosecution Service

The RCCP realized that, left to their own devices, the police would not consistently apply the guidelines on evidential sufficiency and cautioning. To secure consistency, and to counterbalance extra police powers, it recommended establishing the Crown Prosecution Service (CPS). Apart from organizational and accountability matters with which we shall not be concerned here (on which see [1986] *Criminal Law Review*), the government followed the Royal

Commission's recommendations in the Prosecution of Offences Act 1985 and built the CPS around the pre-existing system. The police continue to charge, summons, caution, and NFA as before. Once charged or summonsed, though, the accused becomes the responsibility of the CPS, which decides whether to continue the prosecution. The CPS is headed by the Director of Public Prosecutions (DPP), whose office had previously been responsible for national prosecutions of particular importance and for the prosecution of police officers. The Code for Crown Prosecutors provides guidance on prosecution decisions in almost identical terms to those discussed before on evidential sufficiency and cautionability, so that poor police decisions can be corrected by the CPS.

McConville *et al.* (1991) found, from research in three police-force areas, that the CPS rarely dropped cases which were evidentially weak, and that when they did so this was usually on the initiative of the police and/or only after several court appearances. There were three main reasons for this: policy (the furtherance of police working rules, shared by both prosecutors and police officers); the chance of a freak conviction (because verdicts are so hard to predict); and guilty pleas (just because a case is evidentially weak it does not follow that the defendant will contest the case; weak cases are continued in the often correct expectation of a guilty plea). If the CPS is passive in relation to weak cases where case failure is a measure of institutional efficiency, it is not surprising to discover that it is even more passive in relation to cautionable cases. McConville *et al.* (1991) found no cautionable cases at all being dropped on grounds of cautionability alone, despite many similar cases being cautioned by the police. Again, where police working rules point to prosecution, the CPS is reluctant to stop the case (Gelsthorpe and Giller, 1990). In more recent years there has been a significant rise in discontinuances, both on evidential and 'public interest' grounds, although the former outnumber the latter by two to one (Crisp and Moxon, 1994). However, many 'public interest' discontinuances are of trivial cases, and are made on cost grounds. That there is scope for far more diversion by the CPS has been confirmed by Crisp *et al.* (1994), who found that cases which went through experimental 'Public Interest Case Assessment' (PICA) schemes were far more likely to be discontinued than normal. Despite this, many cases which were assessed as cautionable were not discontinued and yet received nominal penalties. McConville *et al.*'s argument that the police and CPS insist on prosecuting when they have extraneous reasons for so doing would appear to hold firm. Similarly, the findings of Cretney and Davis (1996) and Sanders *et al.* (1997) that the police and CPS prosecute weak cases with victims of domestic violence and with vulnerable victims because they believe in the guilt of the suspect despite the probability that problems concerning the victims' testimony will lead to acquittal, supports this argument in relation to the evidential strength issue.

The CPS is in a structurally weak position to carry out its ostensible aims primarily because of police case construction. The CPS reviews the quality of police cases on the basis of evidence provided solely by the police. This is like the problem of written records, where those who are being evaluated write their own reports. Cases being prosecuted are usually presented as prosecutable; the facts to support this are selected, and those which do not are ignored, hidden, or undermined. Thus weaknesses or cautionable factors, whether known by the police or not, often emerge only in or after trial (Leng, 1992). This situation is exacerbated when the CPS relies on police summaries, which are very selective indeed (Baldwin and Bedward, 1991). Moodie and Tombs (1982) and Duff (1997) in Scotland (Duff in relation to psychiatric cases), and Gelsthorpe and Giller (1990) in England cite prosecutors who agree that the police present them only with what seems relevant to them as prosecutors (as distinct from neutral intermediaries). Similarly, when the police seek advice from the CPS, they can obtain the advice they want by carefully selecting the information they present (Sanders *et al.*, 1997). This is why PICA schemes, which present prosecutors with information from non-police sources, lead to increased numbers of discontinuances.

Attempts to resolve problems of due process and disparity in cautioning by using the CPS suffer another structural problem. Although cautionable cases which are prosecuted are in theory reviewable by the CPS, prosecutable (and NFA-able) cases which are cautioned are not. If the police decide to caution the case ends with them. However able or willing the CPS may be to deal with cases which should be cautioned, they cannot deal with cases which should *not* have been cautioned. This means that disparity will continue, and the violations of due process inherent in police cautioning procedures remain untouched by the CPS. That the CPS is primarily a police prosecution agency is hardly surprising in an adversarial system, but it does suggest that suspects cannot rely on the CPS, as presently constituted, to protect them. Prosecutors could become adequate reviewers of either evidence or public interest only if placed in an entirely different structural relationship with the police. This would require fundamental changes in the adversarial system, and might even then be unsuccessful, if such impressionistic evidence as we have of continental systems is anything to go by (Leigh and Zedner, 1992; Field, 1994).

PRE-TRIAL PROCESSES

Police Bail

After charge, the custody officer decides whether to release on bail or to hold the suspect in custody pending the next magistrates' court hearing (usually the next morning). Section 38 of PACE allows detention only if the suspect's real name and address cannot be ascertained, if he is unlikely to appear in court to answer the charge, if he is likely to interfere with witnesses or further police investigations, or if he is likely to commit further significant crimes. Most of these provisions require the custody officer to predict what might happen if the suspect were released. However, the custody officer has to rely on what the investigating officers say, and what little may be known about the suspect's previous record of appearing in court, offending on bail, and so forth. Also, suspects cannot prove that they would not have done something wrong had they been given the opportunity to do it. Thus decisions are taken quickly on the basis of inadequate information; although decisions are taken by independent officers to protect suspects from partisanship most of the information used will come from the very officers against whom protection is provided; and assessment of the quality of decision-making is almost impossible. So the initial bail/custody decision is entirely for the police, without real accountability.

This gives the police a powerful bargaining tool in interrogation. Although they should not offer 'inducements' (of which bail is one), this is a recognized interrogation 'tactic' (Irving, 1980): 'They [the police] said if I cough I'll get bail; if not then I'll be in court tomorrow' (McConville and Hodgson, 1992: 79). The opportunity for informal 'chats' discussed above ensures that such negotiations need never take place in front of tape recorders or solicitors, and most suspects know or think they know that they can make deals on these lines. For bail bargaining is 'all part of the relationship' (detective, quoted in McConville *et al.*, 1991: 63). The building of relationships is a vital working rule, and, like other working rules, cannot simply be legislated away (Maguire and Norris, 1992). The value of bail as currency is enhanced by the fear of being held overnight. The power (and apparent power) of the police to deny bail is enhanced by the failure of many solicitors to attend the station and, when they do, to stay long. Implicit bargaining over bail leading to 'voluntary' confessions is part of the differential power relationship between officer and suspect which leads suspects 'voluntarily' to agree to many similar things like stop-and-search, attendance at the station, search of premises, and so forth. It is another example of what Sanders and Young (1994*b*) characterize as the treating of unequals as equal in order to produce an appearance of due process and the rule of law while subverting these ideals in reality.

Court Bail

Defendants who are granted police bail are not thereafter remanded in custody unless circumstances change. When defendants are not granted police bail, court bail may or may not be opposed by the police (through the CPS), and may or may not be requested by the defendant (usually through a solicitor). The CPS do not always oppose bail when the police ask them to, though when they do not they almost invariably ask for conditions to be attached to bail (Morgan, 1996*b*). Not surprisingly, magistrates usually reach the same conclusions as the police and CPS, for they consider similar criteria and similar information (Simon and Weatheritt, 1984; Hucklesby, 1996). However, a magistrate, like a custody officer, has 'to come to a decision on the basis of probabilities and not certainties' (Hailsham, quoted in Zander, 1988: 241). This gives scope for the exercise of discretion and judgement, leading to disparity between different courts (Hucklesby, 1996; Paterson and Whitaker, 1994 and 1995). Overall, about 11–13 per cent of magistrates' cases are denied bail each year. Of the cases which are committed to the Crown Court, some 19–22 per cent are denied bail (Morgan and Jones, 1992). Most hearings seem to take less than ten minutes (Doherty and East, 1985). This shocked Lord Woolf (1991), and reflects the limited information which is usually provided (Hucklesby, 1996). When information from more diverse sources is presented, bail is less frequently opposed by the CPS and more frequently granted. Bail information schemes, organized by local probation services, lead to the release of higher proportions of defendants than normal, demonstrating the partial (i.e. adversarial) approach of the police and the over-cautious approach of many courts. Mair and Lloyd (1996), in an appraisal of bail information schemes, estimate that by 1996 these schemes covered over 190 magistrates' courts and thirty-eight prison establishments. As with diversion from prosecution, these schemes show the potential in the CPS for more independence if independent information is provided to it.

A suspect's being remanded in custody can obstruct defence work (including preparation of bail applications). Thus defendants remanded in custody are, all other things being equal, more likely to be convicted and, if convicted, to be given custodial sentences than those given bail. But since not all defendants remanded in custody are convicted and given custodial sentences, some defendants who are legally innocent are held in custody, and some whose offence or circumstances do not warrant custodial sentences, are also held in custody before sentence. Thus in 1992, 39 per cent of defendants in custody in the magistrates' courts received non-custodial penalties, and a further 21 per cent were acquitted (Morgan, 1996*b*). On the other hand, 10–17 per cent of all persons released on bail commit further offences while at liberty (Morgan and Jones, 1992). Clearly magistrates have inadequate information on which to make confident decisions, yet the stakes are high. Offending on bail is undesirable; yet so, in a supposedly due-process-based system, is pre-trial imprisonment of some seven to ten weeks when so many remanded defendants are not subsequently jailed. Magistrates seem to cope by over-using conditions when they do grant bail (Hucklesby, 1994), and by developing an 'unquestioning culture' whereby information from the CPS is seen as factual but information from the defence is seen as partial. Magistrates even sometimes refer to prosecutors as 'our solicitor' (Hucklesby, 1996: 218–19, 224).

Guilty Pleas

The overwhelming majority of defendants—around 70 per cent in the Crown Court and 90 per cent in the magistrates' courts—plead guilty (Ashworth, 1994). As McBarnet (1981) says, this is surprising in a system where one is presumed innocent until proved to be guilty. Why do so many defendants give up their right to put the prosecution to proof? The extensive American literature provides explanations ranging from bureaucratic to conflict models (see, for instance, McConville and Mirsky, 1988, 1992, 1995). This wide range of perspectives, together with the non-adversarial attitudes, practices, and organizational modes of modern lawyers, was explored earlier in this chapter. The nature of the legal profession, both its solicitor branch (McConville *et al.*, 1994; Mulcahy, 1994) and the Bar (Baldwin and McConville, 1977; Morison and Leith, 1992) is crucially important, although Sanders and Young (1994*a* and 1994*b*) argue that it is the wider system and wider society that shapes legal attitudes and practices. What is beyond doubt is that, in both the United Kingdom and United States, police and prosecutorial pre-trial practices are geared in large part to securing guilty pleas. Confessions are particularly important, for it is difficult for suspects to contest, in court, the guilt which they admitted to the police earlier. Confessions, then, guarantee guilty pleas in all cases except those in which the suspect can convince a court (note the shift in the onus of proof) that the confession was obtained unlawfully or is otherwise unreliable. For as long as the law permits conviction on the basis of uncorroborated confession alone (which is not allowed in France) the police will inevitably seek confessions without corroboration. The potential for police law-breaking (to secure confessions) and for false confessions (unverified by corroborative evidence but produced under pressure) is clear.

Defendants are encouraged to plead guilty through bargaining. Explicit plea bargaining over sentence with the judge is not permitted (Curran, 1991). However, courts are now urged by the Criminal Justice and Public Order Act (section 48) to 'take into account' guilty pleas, which they had done in practice for many years anyway. The 'sentence discount' is around 25–30 per cent, and plea sometimes determines not just the length, but also the type, of sentence (see the case of *Bird*, discussed by Curran, 1991). However, since no offences other than murder have fixed sentences in Britain, the difference between reducing sentence for a guilty plea and raising it for a not guilty plea is largely presentational. Bargaining also takes place over the seriousness of the charge and over venue, for cases which are kept in the lower courts are generally sentenced more lightly (Sanders and Young, 1994*a*: 6 and 7). Many magistrates courts have pre-trial reviews which aim, among other things, to promote plea bargaining (Brownlee *et al.*, 1994).

We have seen that defence lawyers often fail to attend interrogations, sending to suspects the due process message that it is the court, not police questioning, which is important (Sanders *et al.*, 1989). However, this facilitates crime-control practices at the police station, and hence confessions, leaving little for the defence lawyer to do in court other than to mitigate on a guilty plea and to bargain. By failing to be adversarial in the police station, defence lawyers often deny their clients the opportunity to be adversarial in court. Defence lawyers frequently make commitments on behalf of their clients. Baldwin, in a study of pre-trial reviews, claimed that none of the bargaining he observed 'could fairly be described as improper' (1985: 97), which is surprising in view of his earlier findings (with McConville) to the contrary (Baldwin and McConville, 1977). In fact Baldwin shows that defence lawyers frequently provide information to the prosecution which they need not, agree not to press their case when it might succeed, and agree to 'lean on' or 'pressure' their clients or 'beat them over the head'. This is the message of other recent English research too (e.g. McConville *et al.*, 1991, 1994). The result is a remarkably high guilty plea rate, achieved with the co-operation of the legal defence community. What is regarded by Baldwin (1985: 85) as 'not standing on their rights' is in fact the defence failure to insist on due process. The crime-control structure of arrest, interrogation, and prosecution practices is concealed and legitimated by the defence community. Inevitably, some innocent people plead guilty: over 10 per cent of guilty pleaders in the Crown Court claim to be innocent, in a similar number of cases the CPS believe there would have been a reasonable chance of acquittal, and in around half of these cases—some 1,400 each year—claims of innocence are believed by their barristers (Zander and Henderson, 1993).

We have seen that many defendants are jailed wrongly under the bail system and that many people are convicted wrongly under the guilty plea system. Police power in relation to bail creates a powerful bargaining tool. The more likely one is to be innocent the more powerful are the pressures to plead guilty—one will be more fearful of custody, hence more likely to confess in exchange for bail, and weak cases are given greater sentence discounts than are strong cases. The RCCJ accepted the risk of the innocent sometimes pleading guilty because of 'the benefits to the system . . . of encouraging those who are in fact guilty to plead guilty' (1993; 111), although it underestimated the risks on scandalously thin grounds (McConville and Mirsky, 1994). Moreover, the production of confessions and guilty pleas hides the absence of legal grounds in many cases for arrest, detention, and prosecution; this encourages 'fishing expeditions' by the police which impact not only on the legally guilty (whether factually so or not) but also on those held without charge (or prosecuted and acquitted) who should never have been deprived of their liberty without reasonable suspicion in the first place (McBarnet, 1981; McConville *et al.*, 1991; McConville and Mirsky, 1992). Finally, the system has discriminatory effects: since black defendants contest their cases more often than do white defendants they get heavier sentences (Hood, 1992). We have seen assembly-line justice: the sacrifice of innocent people and less serious offenders in order to deal severely with the others, the placing of sifting in the hands of the police, and greater deference given by magistrates to prosecutors than defence lawyers. These are all classic hallmarks of Packer's crime-control model, although of course there are due-process elements in the process too. Ashworth (1994) argues that the human rights perspective is applicable to bail and plea-bargaining. But that model gives little sense of the integrated way in which all these processes work together with a common purpose and it is inherently vague. No human rights perspective can completely outlaw either plea bargaining (although legislation can, and it has done in Alaska: Carns and Kruse, 1991) or remands in custody. The worst excesses of English and American law and practice are probably contrary to the European Convention, and human rights-based systems do use pre-trial custody far less than do Anglo-American models (see Padfield, 1993, for instance, in relation to Canada). But the argument is still one of a matter of degree, which takes us little further than the earlier statement that these processes embody both due process and crime control values.

REVIEWING INJUSTICE

Criminal justice systems, like any human systems, need reviewing mechanisms, for some degree of fallibility is inevitable. There are four types of mechanisms: preventive, punitive, compensatory, and restitutionary. They can operate in relation to two types of injustice: abuse of power and wrongful conviction. Preventive mechanisms were envisaged by the RCCP as a necessary counter-weight to the extra powers it wished to grant to the police and which became PACE. They include custody officer reviews of detention, and the review function of the CPS. We have seen that these are of little value in this respect. The jury could be seen as a review mechanism of more importance because of its independence. Thus juries sometimes acquit on grounds of 'equity' (i.e. in the face of strict legal rules) because they believe that the police or state have behaved oppressively (Enright and Morton, 1990). But we should not exaggerate the role of the jury. As we have seen, enormous efforts are made to avoid jury trial, by securing trials in magistrates courts and/or guilty pleas. Little more than 1 per cent of defendants are tried by jury in the United Kingdom, and even in these cases the judge is enormously influential (Sanders and Young, 1994a). And while juries sometimes prevent wrongful conviction they cannot prevent any of the many abuses of power documented earlier—such as stop/search, detention, and remand in custody—although the existence of the jury may sometimes act as a deterrent against oppressive behaviour. Many people who suffer abuse of power are deemed to be legally innocent by the police and sifted out before trial, obstructing the opportunity to expose injustice to and through the jury.

The other main preventive mechanism in respect of wrongful convictions is the exclusion in court of unlawfully obtained evidence. Only unreliable or oppressively obtained confession evidence is automatically excluded. Trial courts may hear unfairly obtained evidence, e.g. from unlawful stops, police-car interrogations, and after denial of access at their discretion. The working rules used by courts to decide what to allow are difficult to determine. Although the courts exclude more evidence now than was the case before PACE, and do so more often than critics expected, in many cases where the right to legal advice is obstructed the decision to allow the evidence is upheld (Birch, 1989; Feldman, 1990; Sanders, 1990). Neither courts nor Parliament adopt the American 'fruit of the forbidden tree' doctrine which is the hallmark of due process. Instead the emphasis is on the probative value of evidence, however it was obtained (up to a point): the crime-control doctrine. Like jury trials, the exclusion of evidence can help only the minority of defendants who contest their cases. However, there is a punitive element here too. In so far as evidence is *sometimes* excluded because it was obtained unfairly or oppressively, the police are being punished in a roundabout way for their abuse of power, especially if an acquittal results. It is arguable that the most powerful influence on police interrogation practices, making them adopt less overtly intimidatory, is the trend towards exclusion of evidence (Sanders and Young, 1994*a*).

There are three other punitive mechanisms available, all concerned with the abuse of power rather than with wrongful convictions. The first is the complaints and discipline procedure. Despite the introduction of the Police Complaints Authority (PCA) in 1985, very few complaints are substantiated. In 1993, a typical year, only 750 complaints were substantiated—7.2 per cent of the complaints which were investigated, but only 2.1 per cent of those initially made (Home Office, 1994). The difference in these figures is because of withdrawn complaints, something which often happens because of police pressure (Maguire and Corbett, 1991). There are three possible explanations for the low level of substantiation: that most complaints are unjustified; that most police investigations (and PCA scrutiny) are biased; and that evidence of malpractice cannot be obtained in most cases. The first two explanations are doubtless partially true. Regarding bias, the discrediting process discussed by Box and Russell (1975) in relation to the pre-PCA system is unaffected by changes in the structure of supervision, for all complaints are still investigated by the police themselves. Even the Police Complaints Board (PCB), which was replaced by the PCA, was aware of this problem. It commented that some officers say of some complainants (particularly in assault cases) that 'his previous record makes his evidence unreliable . . . it would be helpful if such conclusions were not preconceived but the result of the investigation' (1980: paragraphs 59–62). The PCA is in the same position as is the CPS *vis-à-vis* investigating police officers. Rather than reinvestigate, the PCA simply peruses a carefully constructed document. The discomfort felt by the PCB (and now the PCA) rarely allowed it to reverse negative findings, for, like the CPS, it receives information from the police alone. This will inevitably be incomplete or worse. 60 per cent of officers interviewed by Maguire and Corbett 'admitted the existence of something like a "code of silence" among junior officers' (1991: 71). Complaints have been unsuccessful in some of the most notorious miscarriage cases, such as *Confait*, in which malpractices were revealed only some years after the event (Sanders and Young, 1994*a*). Most complainants interviewed by Maguire and Corbett thought 'that the PCA was on the side of the police' (1991: 176). Since even the Metropolitan Police Commissioner has acknowledged how little faith the public in general has in the PCA (*Guardian*, 25 April 1988), who is to say that they are wrong? Even the Lord Chief Justice once called for 'dynamite' be put under the PCA (*Guardian*, 15 December 1993), although it is not clear whether he sought movement on its part or complete destruction.

The complaints system fails all due-process tests (openness, not allowing officials to be judges in their own cause, giving all parties a fair hearing, and so forth) and fails to deter the police from crime-control practices in general and law-breaking in particular, as even the RCCJ acknowledged. Like the rest of the system, black and working-class people seem to bear the brunt of its failings. This should be surprising only if we see complaints as the products of pathological 'bad apples'. If they are on the contrary regarded as normal reflections of policing practice (Goldsmith, 1991), both the behaviour complained of and the closing of ranks preventing a high proportion of substantiation are to be expected (Irving and Dunnigham, 1993). Moreover, as in other contexts, officers do not see the 'black letter' of the law as the dividing line between acceptable and unacceptable behaviour. As Maguire (1992) notes, police investigators probably do not consciously try to exonerate officers who 'overstep the mark', but 'the mark' is not a clear or unchanging line. It depends on the circumstances at the time, the police working rules being pursued, and the characteristics of the complainant.

It is not surprising to find that many people are deterred from complaining, and instead prosecute or sue the police. Prosecutions are rare for obvious reasons, not least because few types of police malpractice are actually criminal; however, prosecutions were brought (unsuccessfully) against some of the officers in the Birmingham Six case. Prosecutions are occasionally initiated by the DPP following invocation of the complaints procedure, but this happened in only twenty-three cases in 1993 (Home Office, 1994). Punitive damages can be awarded in civil actions, and juries are becomingly increasingly outraged at police behaviour. In a notable case in 1996 (some four years after being punched, kicked, racially abused, and illegally detained for ninety minutes) Kenneth Hsu was awarded £220,000 in punitive damages. Significantly, and typically, the officers remain unpunished and undisciplined. Traditionally, juries have free rein on such matters. In February 1997, though, the Metropolitan Police successfully persuaded the Court of Appeal to establish guidelines for damages for police malpractice. The Court stated that the maximum sum that could be awarded for abuse of police power was £50,000, and that Hsu's damages amounted to £35,000. This was on the grounds that the main purpose of a civil action is to award compensation (*Guardian*, 20 February 1997). Whilst true, this position—like so many legal positions— is unreal: it ignores the unavailability of any other effective punitive mechanism, and it tries to put a price on the effects of police brutality. Actions are expensive, lengthy, and difficult to win, but civil actions have nonetheless increased in number throughout the 1980s and 1990s, indicating the inadequacy of the other available remedies. It is estimated that the police, nationwide, could be paying £300 million a year in damages by 2005 (*ibid.*) Wrongful arrest and false imprisonment are traditional actions in tort, but there are no new torts or crimes. Thus the 'right' to a lawyer is not a real right, for there is no court action available to enforce it or to seek compensation for its denial. The same is true of most unlawful interrogation (Sanders, 1988*b*), the caution guidelines, and the Code for Crown Prosecutors. It seems that it is more important to protect property, reputation, and tranquillity than it is to protect the civil liberties of 'police property'. Unlike the complaints system, court-based remedies are open and complainant-driven, as distinct from being police-driven, but their disadvantages render them equally ineffective in preventing or punishing miscarriages of justice.

The final review mechanism is restitutionary, i.e. returning suspects and defendants to the position they were in before being abused or wrongfully convicted. Of course, this is impossible in relation to the abuse of power, but wrongful convictions can be overturned by the Court of Appeal. Again, though, this channel is blocked to the majority that plead guilty unless the plea was not made freely. As with police powers, a formalistic notion of 'free will' is adopted by the courts which ignores the real-life pressures to plea bargain. Of not guilty pleaders in the magistrates courts, about 8 per cent appeal against conviction, of whom fewer than one third succeed. Only about 4 per cent of not guilty pleaders in the Crown Court manage to appeal, of whom fewer than half succeed (Sanders and Young, 1994*a*). These figures reflect the enormous obstacles put in the way of defendants who want to appeal. As Malleson observes, 'The appeal process can be likened to an obstacle race: only the determined, strong, and well-prepared will reach the end—and they are likely to be found in the higher reaches of the offence and sentence scale' (1991: 328). Initial appeals were unsuccessful in all the celebrated miscarriages of justice of the last twenty years such as the Birmingham Six, whose convictions were eventually overturned after several attempts by the 'C3' section of the Home Office to get the Court of Appeal to look at the case again. Very restrictive rules are adopted by the Home Office and the Court to keep such cases to a minimum, which even the RCCJ criticised, and which no doubt contributed to so many of these wrongly convicted people spending so long in prison. The Court of Appeal justifies these rules by claiming deference to the jury, but it is quite happy to interfere with jury verdicts in respect of the quantum of damages for victims of police malpractice. New evidence is usually needed to appeal successfully, but without money, extra legal aid, or dedicated lawyers—all rarely sighted in the British and American criminal justice systems—this is very difficult to obtain. C3 sometimes asks the police to re-investigate, but these investigations suffer the same faults as complaints investigations. Dedicated lawyers and relatives, with meagre resources, have a far better track record of turning up persuasive new evidence than do police inquiries, although much of the credit for the quashing of the convictions of the Guildford Four should go to a Detective Inspector in a Home Office-ordered police inquiry (Rozenberg, 1992). C3 is now being replaced by a new body, the Criminal Cases Review Authority, some four years after the RCCJ recommended it. However, this body will suffer the same structural flaws as the PCA, so not too much should be expected of it (Thornton, 1993), and the Court of Appeal will remain a hurdle (Malleson, 1995; Schiff and Nobles, 1996). As Nobles *et al.* argue, we need 'a Court of Last Resort with personnel drawn from outside the legal profession' (1993: 19). The chances of this happening cannot be high.

CONCLUSION

Criminal justice continually evolves in response to new ideas, new pressures, and new scandals. No system corresponds exactly with any one model, and there are always gaps between rhetoric, rules, and reality. Criminal justice rhetoric is a response to public and party pressures; rules are designed for, rather more than by, the agencies operating them; and reality represents those agencies' attempts to steer a course between those rules and their own priorities. Thus we have seen a largely due-process-based rhetoric, rules which (often incoherently) combine both crime control and due process, and a largely crime-control reality. Inquisitorial faith in the crime-control-based fact-finding ability of the police and the CPS can be found alongside adversarial justification of their construction of cases to be as legally strong as possible without pursuing exculpatory lines of investigation. Even in court the presumption of innocence is compromised by the erosion of the right of silence, the guilty plea system, and bail systems whereby most decisions are made on the basis of police information. Due process requires legal representation, but crime-control processes (in the station and through guilty pleas) thrive because legal representatives do not challenge them.

The law appears to exert little moral force on the police, for there is a gap between many legal rules and the working rules of the police. If the rules were enforced rigorously (and it should not be assumed that is possible, even through improved complaints systems or an exclusionary rule) it is not clear whether crime would be less well controlled. It depends on how successful the police (and associated agencies) are in establishing actual guilt and innocence. The infamous miscarriages of justice of the last twenty years raise serious doubts about this, as do the less dramatic findings of research on unsuccessful stops, NFAs in the police station, and the failure of cases in court. Just because due process is a suspect-orientated way of establishing 'truth' it does not follow that it is a less effective one. As it is, law-breaking by the police and lesser failures of due process are tolerated by a system which fails to punish and deter the police or to compensate most victims of those practices. It is argued by critics of 'new left pessimists' such as myself that changes to legal rules can radically change police practices rather than simply do so at the margin. Critics point to an apparent effect of PACE on changes in interrogations, leading to 'ethical interviewing', less informal interviewing, fewer confessions, and a drop in convictions. There is as yet no hard evidence on this, but early indications do suggest that there is some truth in this. However, the effect is, first, seen in the speedy response of government to erode the right of silence, thus returning to the police their eroded interrogation power; and, secondly, to displace crime-control activity to another part of the system. One example is an explosion in the use of informants which is even less controllable and of less visibility than interrogation (Norris, 1995; Audit Commission, 1996). Another example is that—in a Bill which is likely to become law in 1997—the police are given discretion to withhold material from the defence which would previously have had to be disclosed, and they are given powers electronically to eavesdrop on suspects (*Guardian*, 13 January 1997). The police constantly find new ways of securing traditional objectives, and when they need the help of authority, late twentieth-century judges and governments are rarely found wanting.

Whether the crime-control reality of criminal justice is primarily a product of bureaucratic pressures or societal structures remains an open question, but the results are clear. Patterns of bias on the street particularly concerning class and race are reproduced throughout the system, so that in the prisons black and working-class people in particular are grossly over-represented. Cynicism about criminal justice abounds. The complaints system lacks credibility. Police rule-breaking is not regarded as deviant. The police discipline 'toe rags' without judicial authority or oversight. Lawyers treat their clients with disdain. As labelling theory insists, criminals are best regarded merely as the legally guilty. Suspects are not a subset of the wider criminal population; rather, criminals are a subset of the wider (official) suspect population. How closely this relates to the 'actually guilty' population must remain a matter of speculation, but any close relationship could well be coincidental. For I would argue that the criminal justice system is not primarily geared to detecting and punishing criminal activity. It—and its modern arm, the police—has always been at least as concerned with high-level politics and low-level disorder: that is, with the control of the less powerful. It follows that, contrary to the rhetoric of the crime-control model, the interests of victims (especially less powerful victims) are furthered where this fits in with broader working rules, but not necessarily otherwise. This is certainly the implication of Gregory and Lees' (1996) research, which found a high attrition rate in sexual assault cases (on the treatment of victims in general by the criminal justice system: see Zedner, this volume). The social integration and exclusion approach should, in future, help us to understand these processes more than any other model, for according to this approach the system prioritizes authority and control over the less powerful above justice, the Rule of Law, and the interests of victims—for victims can be the victims of exclusionary practices as much as of criminal practices.

Prospects for change depend in part on one's view of the reasons for the failure of criminal justice to live up to its rhetoric. Bureaucratic explanations, which focus on the values of particular institutions, produce more optimistic scenarios than do societal ones. The former influenced the 1981 Royal Commission and led to the PACE Act. They also depend on the impact of changes to criminal justice processes, about which we know too little. There has been an explosion of criminal justice research in the last twenty years, but most of it is 'top-down', trying to solve the system's problems; very little has been 'bottom-up', asking what it feels like for suspects and defendants. Research should pay more attention to the experiences of suspects, to the lessons to be drawn from Northern Ireland, and to the linking of theoretical, policy, and empirical questions (Hudson, 1993; Sanders, 1997) for when it has done (notable examples are those of Hillyard, 1993; Singh, 1993; Choongh, 1997) the results are illuminating, if unsurprising to new left pessimists.

Only rarely is the fundamental question 'why prosecute?' asked in relation to the police. As Davis and Cretney (1996) and Hoyle (1997) observe, the highlighting of domestic violence as a serious social problem has led the police and CPS—contrary to the expectations of this 'new left pessimist' at any rate—to take it seriously by prosecuting more readily. But for many of these victims, and many others, prosecution is no solution. It often does too much and too little: in many cases it does too much by stigmatizing the offender and driving a wedge between him and the victim; and it does too little to protect the victim from re-offending. In other cases it does too much by putting the victim through the ordeal of the court process and too little by allowing a plea bargain, discontinuance, or acquittal which minimizes the harm done to the victim. For victims and defendants alike (in cases of many types, not just domestic violence) a reintegrative approach would be more effective and less alienating than the punitive dichotomous approach embodied in prosecution. Since victims are generally less punitive than the tabloid media would have us believe, this might be widely welcomed. So there is scope for the development of cautioning schemes and more extensive restorative 'caution-plus' initiatives. But restorative schemes remain in their infancy, and traditional police cautioning is sometimes used in a far from 'welfarist' way. Lee (1995) describes many cautioning processes as 'degradation ceremonies', her accounts of which sound similar to the accounts of the humiliation of 'toe rags' in the custody room provided by Singh (1993) and the non-prosecution processes of the DSS (Cook, 1989). We do not know how typical are Lee's findings, or those of Singh, because too few people care about how suspects and defendants are treated to fund the research which would enable us to find out.

My argument is that prosecution processes and many diversionary processes are exclusionary. The question 'why prosecute?' is a question that could only be asked from an inclusionary perspective. The question is at least implicitly asked in one sphere of criminal justice: 'white-collar' law enforcement. Here, inclusionary policies are adopted by non-police agencies. They avoid prosecution and the other trappings of crime control such as arrest, detention, oppressive interrogation, and so forth. Instead they use techniques of 'compliance'. It is hardly credible that these differences are the product of bureaucratic pressures or accident. Present practice reflects processes of inclusion for 'white collar criminals' and processes of exclusion for the poor, deprived, and powerless. This is a society in which some of the most damaging criminals are treated in the most humane ways while those who are society's victims are treated as society's enemies so that, in time, they live up to their labels.

Selected Further Reading

There are now several texts on criminal justice, many of which cover sentencing and penal policy as well as the earlier stages discussed in this chapter. Most take either a 'legal' or a 'social policy' approach. Two texts which integrate legal and sociological material, and which do not discuss sentencing and penal policy, are A. Ashworth, *The Criminal Process* (Oxford: Oxford University Press, 1994) and A. Sanders and R. Young, *Criminal Justice* (London: Butterworths, 1994). These books, new editions of which are expected in 1988, utilize contrasting theoretical frameworks: Ashworth has a human rights approach, while Sanders and Young use Packer's crime-control and due-process models. A different perspective is provided by G. Stephenson, *The Psychology of Criminal Justice* (Oxford: Blackwell, 1992). For a detailed legal treatment see K. Lidstone and C. Palmer, *The Investigation of Crime—A Guide to Police Powers* (2nd edn., London: Butterworths, 1996).

Among the edited collections, N. Lacey, ed., *Criminal Justice* (Oxford: Oxford University Press, 1994) provides a very broad selection of previously published articles and book extracts. C. Walker and K. Starmer, eds., *Justice in Error* (London: Blackstone, 1993) take miscarriages of justice as their theme. All the chapters are written for the volume but summarize the salient issues arising from the main stages of the pre-trial and trial process. A new edition is expected in 1997. R. Young and D. Wall's *Access to Criminal Justice* (London: Blackstone, 1996) also contains specially written chapters, but they are focused on legal aid and the legal profession. Several of the titles in the International Library of Criminology and Penology (Aldershot: Dartmouth), such as R. Reiner, *Policing*, D. Nelken, *White Collar Crime*, and A. Sanders, *Prosecutions,* have useful collections of reprinted journal articles.

The Royal Commission on Criminal Justice, which reported in 1993, came in for a considerable amount of critical scrutiny. Two edited collections are by M. McConville and L. Bridges, eds., *Criminal Justice in Crisis* (Aldershot: Edward Elgar, 1994) and S. Field and P. Thomas, eds., *Justice and Efficiency?* (Oxford: Blackwell, 1994). The twenty-two research studies commissioned by the Commission are summarized in a Special Edition of the *Home Office Research Bulletin* (No. 35, 1994).

Among the monographs in this area of work, D. McBarnet, *Conviction* (London: Macmillan, 1981) is still well worth reading for its analysis of the relationship between legal rules and the reality of the criminal justice system. M. McConville, A. Sanders, and R. Leng, *The Case for the Prosecution* (London: Routledge, 1991) is a critical examination of the working of PACE and the CPS which has provoked considerable academic debate. A different interpretation is provided by D. Brown in *PACE Ten Years On: A Review of the Research* (London: Home Office, 1997). Lawyers receive critical scrutiny from J. Morison and P. Leith, *The Barrister's World* (Buckingham: Open University Press, 1992) and M. McConville, J. Hodgson, L. Bridges, and A. Pavlovic, *Standing Accused* (Oxford: Oxford University Press, 1994). New books which are bound to attract attention when they are published in 1997 or 1998 are C. Hoyle, *Policing Domestic Violence: The Role of the Victim* (Oxford: Oxford University Press) and S. Choongh, *Inside the Nick: Policing and Social Discipline* (Oxford: Oxford University Press). Provocative treatments of the subject from a journalist and a feminist respectively are provided by D. Rose, *In the Name of the Law* (London: Jonathan Cape, 1996) and H. Kennedy, *Eve was Framed* (London: Chatto and Windus, 1992).

REFERENCES

ASHWORTH, A (1994), *The Criminal Process.* Oxford: Oxford University Press.

—— (1996), 'Crime, Community and Creeping Consequentialism', *Criminal Law Review,* 220.

AUDIT COMMISSION (1996), *Detecting a Change—Progress in Tackling Crime.* London: Audit Commission.

BALDWIN, J. (1985), *Pre-Trial Criminal Justice.* Oxford: Blackwell.

—— (1991), 'Videotaping in Police Stations', *New Law Journal,* 141: 1512–16.

—— and BEDWARD, J. (1991), 'Summarizing Tape Recordings of Police Interviewing', *Criminal Law Review,* 671–9.

—— and McCONVILLE, M. (1977), *Negotiated Justice.* Oxford: Martin Robertson.

BECKER, H. (1963), *Outsiders: Studies in the Sociology of Deviance.* New York: Free Press.

BIRCH, D. (1989), 'The Pace Hots Up: Confessions and Confusions under the 1984 Act', *Criminal Law Review,* 95–116.

BITTNER, E. (1967), 'The Police on Skid-Row: A Study of Peace-keeping', *American Sociological Review,* 32: 699–715.

BLACK, D. (1970), 'Production of Crime Rates', *American Sociological Review,* 35: 733–48.

BLACKSTONE, W. (1830), *Commentaries.* London: Macmillan.

BLOCK, B., CORBETT, C., and PEAY, J. (1993), *Ordered and Directed Acquittals in the Crown Court.* London: HMSO.

BOX, S., and RUSSELL, K., (1975), 'The Politics of Discreditability: Disarming Complaints Against the Police', *Sociological Review,* 23: 315–46.

BROGDEN, M., (1985), 'Stopping the People: Crime Control versus Social Control', in J. Baxter and L. Koffman, eds., *Police: The Constitution and the Community.* Abingdon: Professional Books.

BROWNLEE, I., MULCAHY, A., and WALKER, C.

(1994), 'Pre-trial Reviews, Court Efficiency and Justice', *Howard Journal,* 33: 109.

BROWN, D (1997), *PACE Ten Years On: A Review of the Research.* Home Office Research Study No. 155. London: HMSO.

—— and ELLIS, T. (1994), *Policing Low Level Disorder.* Home Office Research Study No. 135. London: HMSO.

—— —— and LARCOMBE, K. (1992), 'Changing the Code: Police Detention under the Revised PACE Codes of Practice', Home Office Research Study No. 129. London: HMSO.

CAMERON, M. (1964), *The Booster and the Snitch.* New York: Free Press.

CARNS, T., and KRUSE, C., 'A Re-evaluation of Alaska's Plea Bagaining Ban', *Alaska Law Review,* 8: 27.

CHAN, J (1996), 'Changing Police Culture', *British Journal of Criminology,* 36: 109.

CHATTERTON, N. (1976), 'Police in Social Control', in J. King, ed., *Control without Custody.* Cambridge: Institute of Criminology.

CHOONGH, S. (1997), *Inside the Nick: Policing and Social Discipline.* Oxford: Oxford University Press.

CLARKSON, C., CRETNEY, A., DAVIES, G., and SHEPHERD, J. (1994), 'Criminalising Assault', *British Journal of Criminology,* 34: 15.

COHEN, S. (1985), *Visions of Social Control.* Cambridge: Cambridge University Press.

COOK, D. (1989), *Rich Law, Poor Law.* Milton Keynes: Open University Press.

Criminal Law Review (1986), special issue on 'The New Prosecution Arrangements', 1–44.

CRETNEY, A., and DAVIS, G (1996), 'Prosecuting Domestic Assault', *Criminal Law Review,* 162.

CRISP, D, and MOXON, D (1994), *Case Screening by the Crown Prosecution Service.* Home Office Research Study No. 137. London: HMSO.

—— WHITTAKER, C., and HARIS, J. (1994),

Public Interest Case Assessment Schemes. Home Office Research Study No. 138. London: HMSO.

CURRAN, P. (1991), 'Discussions in the Judge's Private Room', *Criminal Law Review*, 79–86.

DENNIS, I. (1995), 'The CJPO 1994: The Evidence Provisions', *Criminal Law Review*, 4.

DAMASKA, E. (1973), 'Evidentiary Barriers to Conviction and Two Models of Criminal Procedure: A Comparative Study', *University of Pennsylvania Law Review*, 121: 506–89.

DITCHFIELD, J. (1976), *Police Cautioning*. Home Office Research Study No. 37. London: HMSO.

DIXON, D. (1991), 'Common Sense, Legal Advice, and the Right of Silence', *Public Law*, 233–54.

—— (1992), 'Legal Regulation and Policing Practice', *Social and Legal Studies*, 1: 515.

—— BOTTOMLEY, A., COLEMAN, C., GILL, M., and WALL, D. (1989), 'Reality and Rules in the Construction and Regulation of Police Suspicion', *International Journal of the Sociology of Law*, 17: 185–206.

—— (1990), 'Safeguarding the Rights of Suspects in Police Custody', *Policing and Society*, 1: 115–40.

DOHERTY, M., and EAST, R. (1985), 'Bail Decisions in Magistrates' Courts', *British Journal of Criminology*, 25: 251–66.

DOWNES, D., and ROCK, P. (1988), *Understanding Deviance*. Oxford: Oxford University Press.

DRIVER, P. (1968), 'Confessions and the Social Psychology of Coercion', *Harvard Law Review*, 82: 42–61.

DUFF, P. (1993), 'The Prosecutor Fine and Social Control', *British Journal of Criminology*, 33: 481.

—— (1997), ' Diversion from Prosecution into Psychiatric Care', *British Journal of Criminology*, 37: 15.

EASTON, S. (1991), *The Right to Silence*. Aldershot: Avebury.

ENRIGHT, S., and MORTON, J. (1990), *Taking Liberties*. London: Weidenfield.

ERICSON, R. (1981), *Making Crime*. London: Butterworths.

EVANS, R. (1991), 'Police Cautioning and the Young Adult Offender', *Criminal Law Review*, 598–609.

—— (1992), 'The Conduct of Police Interviews with Juveniles', Royal Commission on Criminal Justice, Research Study No. 8. London: HMSO.

—— (1994), 'Cautioning: Counting the Cost of Retrenchment', *Criminal Law Review*, 566.

—— and FERGUSON, T. (1991), *Comparing Different Juvenile Cautioning Systems in One Police Force*. London: Home Office, unpublished report.

FAULKENER, D. (1996), *Darkness and Light*. London: Howard League.

FELDMAN, D. (1990), 'Regulating Treatment of Suspects in Police Stations', *Criminal Law Review*, 452–71.

FIELD, S. (1994), 'Judicial Supervision and the Pre-Trial Process', in S. Field and P. Thomas, eds., *Justice and Efficiency?* Oxford: Blackwell.

—— and SOUTHGATE, P. (1982), *Public Disorder*. Home Office Research Study No. 72. London: HMSO.

—— and THOMAS, P., eds. (1994), *Justice and Efficiency?* Oxford: Blackwell.

FITZGERALD, M. (1993), 'Ethnic Minorities and the Criminal Justice System', Royal Commission on Criminal Justice, Research Study No. 20. London: HMSO.

GELSTHORPE, L., and GILLER, H. (1990), 'More Justice for Juveniles: Does More Mean Better?', *Criminal Law Review*, 153–64.

GOLDSMITH, A., ed. (1991), *Complaints against the Police: A Comparative Study*. Oxford: Oxford University Press.

GOLDSTEIN, J. (1960), 'Police Discretion not to Invoke the Criminal Process: Low Visibility Decisions in the Administration of Justice', *Yale Law Journal*, 69: 543.

GREER, S. (1990), 'The Right to Silence: A Review of the Current Debate', *Modern Law Review*, 53: 709–30.

GREGORY, J., and LEES, S. (1996), 'Attrition in Rape and Sexual Assault Cases' *British Journal of Criminology*, 36: 1.

GUDJONSSON, G., and MACKEITH, J. (1982), 'False Confessions', in A. Trankell, ed., *Reconstructing the Past*. Deventer: Kluwer.

—— and —— (1988), 'Retracted Confessions: Legal, Psychological and Psychiatric Aspects', *Medicine, Science, and the Law*, 28: 187–94.

HILLYARD, P. (1993), *Suspect Community*. London: Pluto.

HOLDAWAY, S. (1983), *Inside the British Police*. Oxford: Blackwell.

HOME OFFICE (1988), *Criminal Statistics*. London: HMSO.

—— (1989), *Report of the Working Group on the Right of Silence*. London: Home Office, unpublished report.

—— (1990), *The Cautioning of Offenders*. Circular No. 59/1990. London: Home Office.

—— (1994), *Police Complaints and Discipline*. Home Office Statistical Bulletin 13/94. London: HMSO.

HOOD, R. (1992), *Race and Sentencing*. Oxford: Oxford University Press.

HOYLE, C. (1997), *Policing Domestic Violence: The Role of the Victim*. Oxford: Oxford University Press.

HUCKLESBY, A. (1994), 'The Use and Abuse of Conditional Bail' *Howard Journal*, 33: 258.

—— (1996), 'Bail or Jail', *Journal of Law and Society*, 23: 213.

HUDSON, B. (1993), *Racism and Criminology*. London: Sage.

HUTTER, B. (1988), *The Reasonable Arm of the Law? The Law Enforcement Procedures of Environmental Health Officers*. Oxford: Oxford University Press.

IRVING, B. (1980), *Police Interrogation: A Study of Current Practice*. London: HMSO.

—— (1985), 'Research Into Policy Won't Go', in E. Alves and J. Shapland, eds., *Legislation for Policing Today: The PACE Act*. Leicester: Leicester University Press.

—— and DUNNINGHAN C., 'Human Factors in the Quality Control of CID Investigations', Royal Commission on Criminal Justice, Research Study No. 21. London: HMSO.

—— (1989), *Police Interrogation: The Effects of the PACE Act*. London: Police Foundation.

JACKSON, J. (1995), 'Interpreting the Silence Provisions', *Criminal Law Review*, 587.

JEFFERSON, T., and WALKER, M. (1992), 'Ethnic Minorities in the Criminal Justice System', *Criminal Law Review*, 83–95.

KAYE, T. (1991), *Unsafe and Unsatisfactory*. London: Civil Liberties Trust.

KEITH, M. (1993), *Race, Riots and Policing*. London: UCL Press.

LAING, J. (1995), 'The Mentally Disordered Suspect at the Police Station', *Criminal Law Review*, 371.

LEE, M. (1995), 'Pre-court Diversion and Youth Justice', in L. Noaks, ed. (1995), *Contemporary Issues in Criminology*. Cardiff: University of Wales Press.

LEIGH, L., and ZEDNER, L. (1992), *A Report on the Administration of Criminal Justice in the Pre-Trial Phase in France and Germany*. RCCJ Research Study No. 1. London: HMSO.

LEISHMAN, F., LOVEDAY, B., and SAVAGE, S. (1996), *Core Issues in Policing*. London and New York: Longman.

LENG, R. (1992), 'The Right to Silence in Police Interrogation', RCCJ Research Study No. 10. London: HMSO.

LEO, R. (1994), 'Police Interrogation and Social Control', *Social and Legal Studies*, 3: 93.

LIDSTONE, K., HOGG, R., and SUTCLIFFE, F. (1980), *Prosecution by Private Individuals and Non-Police Agencies*. London: HMSO.

LITTLECHILD, B. (1995), 'Re-assessing the Role of the Appropriate Adult', *Criminal Law Review*, 540.

MALLESON, K. (1991), 'Miscarriages of Justice and the Accessibility of the Court of Appeal', *Criminal Law Review*, 323.

—— (1995), 'The Criminal Cases Review Commission', *Criminal Law Review*, 929.

McBARNET, D. (1981), *Conviction*. London: Macmillan.

McCONVILLE, M. (1992), 'Videotaping Interrogations: Police Behaviour on and off Camera', *Criminal Law Review*, 522–48.

—— and BALDWIN, J. (1981), *Courts, Prosecution, and Conviction*. Oxford: Oxford University Press.

—— and BRIDGES, L., eds. (1994), *Criminal Justice in Crisis*. Aldershot: Edward Elgar.

—— HODGSON, J., BRIDGES, L., and PAVLOVIC, A. (1994), *Standing Accused*. Oxford: Oxford University Press.

—— and HODGSON, J. (1992), 'Custodial Legal Advice and the Right to Silence', RCCJ Research Study No. 16. London: HMSO.

—— and MIRSKY, C. (1988), 'The State, the Legal Profession, and the Defence of the Poor', *Journal of Law and Society*, 15: 342–60.

—— and —— (1992), 'What's in the Closet: The Plea Bargaining Skeletons', *New Law Journal*, 142: 1373–81.

—— and —— (1994), 'Re-defining and Structuring Guilt in Systemic Terms', in M. McConville and L. Bridges, eds. (1994), *Criminal Justice in Crisis*. Aldershot: Edward Elgar.

—— and —— (1995), ' The Rise of Guilty Pleas', *Journal of Law and Society*, 22: 443.

—— and MORRELL, P. (1983), 'Recording and Interrogation: Have the Police Got it Taped?', *Criminal Law Review*, 158–62.

—— SANDERS, A., and LENG, R. (1991), *The Case for the Prosecution*. London: Routledge.

—— and SHEPHERD, D. (1992), *Watching Police, Watching Communities*. London: Routledge.

McKENZIE, I., MORGAN, R., and REINER, R. (1990), 'Helping the Police with their Enquiries', *Criminal Law Review*, 22–33.

—— —— and —— (1992), 'Complaints against the Police: Where Now?', unpublished paper.

MAGUIRE, M., and CORBETT, C. (1991), *A Study of the Police Complaints System*. London: HMSO.

—— and NORRIS, C. (1992), *The Conduct and Supervision of Criminal Investigations*, RCCJ Research Study No. 5. London: HMSO.

MAIR, G., and LLOYD, C. (1996), 'Policy and Progress in the Development of Bail Schemes in England and Wales', in F. Paterson, ed., *Understanding Bail in Britain*. London: HMSO.

MATZA, D. (1969), *Becoming Deviant*. New York: Prentice-Hall.

MEEHAN, A. (1993), 'Internal Police Records and the Control of Juveniles', *British Journal of Criminology*, 33: 504.

MOODIE, S., and TOMBS, J. (1982), *Prosecution in the Public Interest*. Edinburgh: Edinburgh University Press.

MORGAN, P. (1996b), 'Bail in England and Wales: Understanding the Operation of Bail', in F. Paterson, ed., *Understanding Bail in Britain*. London: HMSO.

MORGAN, R. (1996a), 'The Rule is the Process and the Process is the Punishment', *Modern Law Review*, 59: 306.

—— and JONES, P. (1992), 'Bail or Jail?', in S. Casale and E. Stockdale, eds., *Criminal Justice under Stress*. London: Blackstone.

MORISON, J., and LEITH, P. (1992), *The Barrister's World*. Oxford: Oxford University Press.

MOSTON, S. (1992), 'Police Questioning Techniques in Tape Recorded Interviews with Criminal Suspects', *Policing and Society*, 3.

—— and STEPHENSON, G. (1993), 'The Questioning and Interviewing of Suspects outside the Police Station', Royal Commission on Criminal Justice, Research Study No. 22. London: HMSO.

—— —— and WILLIAMSON, T. (1992), 'The Effects of Case Characteristics on Suspect Behaviour during Police Questioning', *British Journal of Criminology*, 32: 23–40.

—— —— and —— (1993), 'The Incidence, Antecedents and Consequences of the Use of the Right to Silence during Police Questioning', *Criminal Behaviour and Mental Health*, 3: 30–47.

—— and WILLIAMSON, T. (1990), 'The Extent of Silence in Police Interviews', in S. Greer and R. Morgan, eds., *The Right to Silence*, Centre for Criminal Justice, Bristol: University of Bristol.

MULCAHY, A. (1994), 'The Justifications of Justice', *British Journal of Criminology*, 34: 411.

MUNDAY, R. (1996), 'Inferences from Silence and European Human Rights Law', *Criminal Law Review*, 370.

MURPHY, D. (1986), *Customers and Thieves*. Farnborough: Gower.

NACRO (National Association for the Care and Resettlement of Offenders) (1997), *The Tottenham Experiment*. London: NACRO.

NICOLSON, D., and REID, K. (1996), 'Arrest for Breach of the Peace and the European Convention on Human Rights', *Criminal Law Review*, 764.

NOAKS, L., ed. (1995), *Contemporary Issues in Criminology*. Cardiff: University of Wales Press.

NOBLES, R., SCHIFF, D., and SHALDON, N. (1993), 'The Inevitability of Crisis in Criminal Appeals', *International Journal of the Sociology of Law*, 21: 1.

NORRIS, C. (1995), 'Practice, Problems and Policy: Management Isues in the Police Use of Informers. Unpublished paper.

—— et al. (1992), 'Black and Blue: an Analysis of the Influence of Race on Being Stopped by the Police', *British Journal of Sociology*, 43: 207.

O'MAHONEY, P. (1992), 'The Kerry Babies Case: Towards a Social Psychological Analysis', *Irish Journal of Psychology*, 13: 223.

PACKER, H. (1968), *The Limits of the Criminal Sanction*. Stanford, Cal.: Stanford University Press.

PADFIELD, N. (1993), 'The Right to Bail a Canadian Perspective', *Criminal Law Review*, 510.

PALMER, C. (1996), 'Still Vulnerable After All These Years' *Criminal Law Review*, 633.

PATTENDEN, R. (1995), 'Inferences from Silence', *Criminal Law Review*, 602.

PATERSON, F., ed. (1996), *Understanding Bail in Britain*. London: HMSO.

—— and WHITAKER, C. (1994), *Operating Bail*. Edinburgh: HMSO.

—— and —— (1995), 'Criminal Justice Cultures: Negotiating Bail and Remand', in L. Noaks, ed. (1995), *Contemporary Issues in Criminology*. Cardiff: University of Wales Press.

PILIAVIN, I., and BRIAR, S. (1964), 'Police Encounters with Juveniles', *American Journal of Sociology*, 70: 206–14.

POLLARD, C. (1996), 'Public Safety, Accountability and the Courts', *Criminal Law Review*, 152.

POLICE COMPLAINTS BOARD (1980), *Triennial Report*. London: HMSO.

PRATT, J. (1986), 'Diversion from the Juvenile Court', *British Journal of Criminology*, 26: 212–33.

REINER, R. (1992), *The Politics of the Police*. 2nd edn. Brighton: Wheatsheaf.

REISS, A. (1971), *The Police and the Public*. New Haven, Conn.: Yale University Press.

ROSENBURG, J. (1992), 'Miscarriages of Justice', in S. Casale and R. Stockdale, eds., *Criminal Justice under Stress*. London: Blackstone.

ROYAL COMMISSION ON CRIMINAL JUSTICE (1993), *Report*. London: HMSO.

ROYAL COMMISSION ON CRIMINAL PROCEDURE (1981), *Report*. London: HMSO.

SANDERS, A. (1985*a*), 'Class Bias in Prosecutions', *Howard Journal of Criminal Justice*, 24: 176–99.

—— (1985*b*), 'Prosecution Decisions and the Attorney-General's Guidelines', *Criminal Law Review*, 4–19.

—— (1987), 'Constructing the Case for the Prosecution', *Journal of Law and Society*, 14: 229–53.

—— (1988*a*), 'The Limits to Diversion from Prosecution', *British Journal of Criminology*, 28: 513–32.

—— (1988*b*), 'Rights, Remedies and the PACE Act', *Criminal Law Review*, 802–12.

—— (1990), 'Access to Legal Advice and s. 78 PACE', *Law Society Gazette*, 31 October: 17–23.

—— (1996*a*), 'Access to Justice in the Police Station', in R. Young, and D. Wall, *Access to Criminal Justice*. London: Blackstone.

—— ed. (1996*b*), *Prosecutions in Common Law Jurisdictions*. Aldershot: Dartmouth.

—— (1997), 'Criminal Justice', in P. Thomas, ed., *Reviewing Socio-Legal Studies*. Aldershot: Dartmouth.

—— and BRIDGES, L. (1990), 'Access to Legal Advice and Police Malpractice', *Criminal Law Review*, 494–509.

—— —— MULVANEY, A., and CROZIER, G. (1989), *Advice and Assistance at Police Stations and the 24 Hour Duty Solicitor Scheme*. London: Lord Chancellor's Department.

—— and YOUNG, R. (1994*a*), *Criminal Justice*. London: Butterworths.

—— and —— (1994*b*), 'The Rule of Law, Due Process and Pre-trial Criminal Justice' *Current Legal Problems*, 47: 125.

—— CREATON, J., BIRD, S., and WEBER, L. (1997), *Victims with Learning Disabilities: Negotiating the Criminal Justice System*. Oxford: Centre for Criminological Research, Occasional Paper No. 17.

SCARMAN, LORD (1981), *The Scarman Report: The Brixton Disorders*. London: HMSO.

SHIFF, D., and NOBLES, R. (1996), 'The Criminal Appeals Act 1995', *Modern Law Review*, 59: 573.

SCOTT, M., and LYMAN, S. (1968), 'Accounts', *American Sociological Review*, 33: 46–62.

SCRATON, P., ed. (1987), *Law, Order, and the Authoritarian State*. Milton Keynes: Open University Press.

SHAPLAND, J., and VAGG, J. (1988), *Policing by the Public*. London: Routledge.

SKOGAN, W. (1990), *The Police and Public in England and Wales*. Home Office Research Study No. 117. London: HMSO,.

SIMON, F., and WEATHERITT, M. (1984), *The Use of Bail and Custody by London Magistrates' Courts*. London: HMSO.

SINGH, S. (1993), 'Understanding the Long Term Relationship Between Police and Policed', in M. McConville and L. Bridges, eds. (1994), *Criminal Justice in Crisis*. Aldershot: Edward Elgar.

SMITH, D., and GRAY, J. (1983), *Police and People in London*. Aldershot: Gower.

SLAPPER, G. (1993), 'Corporate Manslaughter', *Social and Legal Studies*, 2: 423.

SOFTLEY, P. (1980), *Police Interrogation: An Observational Study in Four Police Stations*. London: HMSO.

SPRACK, J. (1992), 'The Trial Process', in E. Stockdale and S. Casale, eds., *Criminal Justice Under Stress*. London: Blackstone.

STEER, J. (1980), *Uncovering Crime: The Police Role*. London: HMSO.

STEVENS, P., and WILLIS, C. (1979), *Race, Crime, and Arrests*. Home Office Research Study No. 58. London: HMSO.

—— and —— (1981), *Ethnic Minorities and Complaints against the Police*. London: Home Office.

THORNTON, P. (1993), 'Miscarriages of Justice: A Lost Opportunity', *Criminal Law Review*, 926.

TROUILLE, H. (1994), 'A Look at French Criminal Procedure' *Criminal Law Review*, 735.

TUCK, M., and SOUTHGATE, P. (1981), *Ethnic Minorities, Crime and Policing*. Home Office Research Study 70. London: HMSO.

TYLER, R. T. (1990), *Why Do People Obey the Law?* New Haven, Conn., and London: Yale University Press.

WALKLEY, J. (1987), *Police Interrogation*. Police Review. London: HMSO.

WALMSLEY, R. (1978), 'Indecency between Males and the Sexual Offences Act 1967', *Criminal Law Review*, 400–7.

WILCOX, A. (1972), *The Decision to Prosecute*. London: Butterworths.

WILKINSON, C., and EVANS, R. (1990), 'Police Cautioning of Juveniles: The Impact of Home Office Circular 14/1985', *Criminal Law Review*, 165–76.

WILLIS, C. (1983), *The Use, Effectiveness, and Impact of Police Stop and Search Powers*. Research and Planning Unit Paper No. 15. London: Home Office.

—— (1988), *The Tape Recording of Police Interviews with Suspects*. Home Office Research Study 97. London: HMSO.

WOOLF, LORD JUSTICE (1991), 'Prison Disturbances April 1990', Report of an Inquiry by The Rt. Hon. Lord Justice Woolf (Parts I and II) and His Honour Judge Stephen Tumim (Part II), Cm 1456. London: HMSO.

YOUNG M. (1991), *An Inside Job*. Oxford: Oxford University Press.

YOUNG, R., and SANDERS, A. (1994), ' The RCCJ: A confidence trick?', *Oxford Journal of Legal Studies*, 14: 435.

ZANDER, M. (1979), 'The Investigation of Crime: A Study of Cases Tried in the Old Bailey', *Criminal Law Review*, 203–19.

—— (1988), *Cases and Materials on the English Legal System*. London: Weidenfeld.

—— (1991), 'What the Annual Statistics Tell Us about Pleas and Acquittals', *Criminal Law Review*, 252–8.

—— and HENDERSON, P. (1993), 'Crown Court Study', Royal Commission on Criminal Justice, Research Study No. 19. London: HMSO.

30

Sentencing

Andrew Ashworth

The passing of a sentence on an offender is probably the most public face of the criminal justice system. This chapter discusses several aspects of sentencing policy, law, and practice. It begins by noting the increasing politicization of sentencing policy, a trend which threatens to marginalize principled and empirically based arguments. Such an approach is rejected here. The chapter goes on to examine the various rationales for sentencing. It then discusses the procedural aspects of sentencing in England and Wales, and goes into some details of custodial sentencing and non-custodial sentencing. It concludes by considering future directions for sentencing policy.

SENTENCING AND POLITICS

The introduction, by the Crime (Sentences) Act 1997, of mandatory and minimum sentences marks the culmination of a trend towards the increased politicization of sentencing policy. As Downes and Morgan show (this volume), the bipartisan approach to criminal policy was eroded in the late 1970s. The 1979 general election was won partly on a 'law and order' ticket. In the late 1980s, however, as the then government became more assured of its position, the opportunity was taken (under Douglas Hurd as Home Secretary) to create policies aimed at greater consistency and rationality in sentencing. When the Criminal Justice Act 1991 became law, there was little opposition in Parliament to its principal thrust, and no significant adverse comment in the newspapers (Windlesham, 1993). The judges and some magistrates, however, objected to the fettering of the discretion they had previously enjoyed, objections which gained some strength from the abysmal drafting of parts of the 1991 Act. Their campaign was soon taken up more widely, and in 1993, a year of heightened media interest in law and order, the then Home Secretary Kenneth Clarke announced the abandonment of unit fines and changes in the provisions on sentencing repeat offenders and multiple offenders. That year saw not only the passing of the Criminal Justice Act 1993, which raised various maximum sentences too, but also the appointment of Michael Howard as Home Secretary, and his widely reported twenty-seven-point plan on law and order. In 1994 came the Criminal Justice and Public Order Act, with a cocktail of measures such as curtailment of the right of silence and tougher sentences for young offenders, including the provisions for secure training centres for persistent offenders aged 12, 13, or 14 (see Windlesham, 1996, for a detailed contemporary history). A populist sentencing policy soon came to be thought politically advantageous for both major parties, with Howard leading the way and challenging the opposition to disagree, at peril of being called 'soft on crime'. This punishment auction reached its zenith in the White Paper *Protecting the Public* (1996), which proposed a mandatory life sentence for the second serious sexual or violent crime, and mandatory minimum sentences for repeat drug offenders and repeat burglars. The proposals were roundly condemned as ill-conceived by the then Lord Chief Justice, Lord Taylor, and other leading judges. Although the government made some significant late concessions to the judicial critics, the Crime (Sentences) Act 1997 largely embodies this populist policy.

RATIONALES FOR SENTENCING

The events of recent years can only sharpen interest in examining the justifications for sentencing in general and for particular sentencing policies. When a court passes sentence, it authorizes the use of state coercion against a person for committing an offence. The sanction may take the form of some deprivation, restriction, or positive obligation. Deprivations and obligations are fairly widespread in social contexts—e.g. duties to pay taxes, to complete various forms, etc. But when imposed as a sentence, there is the added element of condemnation, labelling, or censure of the offender for what has been done. In view of the direct personal and indirect social effects this can have, it calls for justification.

Much writing about the rationales of sentencing has focused on one or more particular justifications. In order to unravel punishment as a social institution, however, and to understand the tensions inherent in any given 'system', there is benefit in identifying the main thrusts of the several approaches. Among the issues to be considered are the behavioural and the political premises of each approach, its empirical claims, and its practical influence.

Desert or Retributive Theories

Retributive theories of punishment have a long history, including the writings of Kant and Hegel. In their modern guise as the desert approach, they came to prominence in the 1970s, to some extent propelled by the alleged excesses and failures of rehabilitative ideals (von Hirsch, 1976; Bottoms and Preston, 1980). Punishment is justified as the morally appropriate response to crime: those who commit offences deserve punishment, it is claimed, and the amount of punishment should be proportionate to the degree of wrongdoing. The justification for the institution of punishment also incorporates the consequentialist element of needing to deter crime: without the restraining effect of a system of state punishment, anarchy might well ensue (see von Hirsch, 1993; Duff, 1986). The behavioural premise of desert is that individuals are responsible and predominantly rational decision-makers. The political premise is that all individuals are entitled to equal respect and dignity: an offender deserves punishment, but does not forfeit all rights on conviction, and has a right not to be punished disproportionately to the crime committed.

Proportionality is the key concept in desert theory. Cardinal proportionality is concerned with the magnitude of the penalty, requiring that it not be out of proportion to the gravity of the conduct: five years' imprisonment for shoplifting would clearly breach that, as would a small penalty for a very serious offence. Social conventions and cultural traditions tend to determine the 'anchoring points' of the punishment scale, i.e. the contrasting levels at which sentences are set in different national or historical contexts (cf. Downes, 1988, on the Netherlands and England at that time; Graham, 1990, on Germany), although these conventions can change for various reasons. Ordinal proportionality concerns the ranking of the relative seriousness of different offences. In practice, much depends here on the evaluation of conduct, especially by sentencers, and on social assumptions about traditional or 'real' crime (e.g. street crime) compared with new types of offence (e.g. commercial fraud, pollution). In theory, ordinal proportionality requires the creation of a scale of values which can be used to assess the gravity of each type of offence: culpability, together with aggravating and mitigating factors, must then be assimilated into the scale. This task, which is vital to any approach in which proportionality plays a part, makes considerable demands on theory (see von Hirsch and Jareborg, 1991; Ashworth 1995: chapter 4).

Deterrence Theories

Deterrence theories regard the prevention of further offences through a deterrent strategy as the rationale for punishing. As an exercise of state power, sentencing can be justified only by its consequences. The quantum of the sentence depends on the type of deterrent theory. There is little modern literature on individual deterrence, which sees the deterrence of further offences by the particular offender as the measure of punishment. A first offender may require little or no punishment. A recidivist might be thought to require an escalation of penalties. The seriousness of the offence becomes less important than the prevention of repetition. Traces of this approach can certainly be detected in the treatment of persistent offenders in modern sentencing practice, especially in the tougher sentences for repeat offenders in the 1997 Act.

More attention has been devoted to general deterrence, which involves calculating the penalty on the basis of what might be expected to deter others from committing a similar offence. Major utilitarian writers such as Bentham

(1789; cf. Walker, 1991) and economic theorists such as Posner (1985) develop the notion of setting penalties at levels sufficient to outweigh the likely benefits of offending. The behavioural premise is that of responsible and predominantly rational, calculating individuals—a premise that criminologists may call into question. The political premise is that the greatest good of the greatest number represents the supreme value, and that the individual counts only for one: it may therefore be justifiable to punish one person severely in order to deter others effectively, thereby overriding the claims of proportionality. Satisfactory empirical evidence of the effect of deterrent sentencing on individual behaviour is difficult to obtain. The conditions must be such that non-offending can safely be ascribed to the deterrent effect of the legal penalty rather than to any of the other myriad influences on people's conduct, such as the perceived risk of detection, the opinions of significant others, etc. (Beyleveld, 1980; cf. Walker, 1991). Few research findings meet that criterion, and those that do provide support for general deterrent sentencing only in a few types of situation (see Zimring and Hawkins, 1973; Beyleveld, 1979; Riley, 1985; Harding, 1990).

Rehabilitative Sentencing

Sentencing aimed at the reformation of the offender's lawbreaking tendencies has a lengthy history, being evident in the early days of probation and of borstal institutions. The rationale here is to prevent further offending by the individual through the strategy of rehabilitation, which may involve individual casework, therapy, counselling, intervention in the family, etc. Still a leading rationale in many European countries, it reached its zenith in the United States in the 1960s and then declined spectacularly in the 1970s. Research by Martinson was widely represented as demonstrating that treatment programmes usually failed, swamping the more qualified judgement in an English survey by Brody and in the National Academy of Sciences report in the United States (Martinson *et al.*, 1974; Brody, 1975; National Academy of Sciences, 1979). In terms of effectiveness, the true position is probably (as with deterrence) that certain rehabilitative programmes are likely to work for some types of offender in some circumstances. A humanitarian desire to provide help for those with obvious behavioural problems has ensured that various treatment programmes continue to be developed: some authors argue that rehabilitative theory was discarded prematurely (cf. Hudson, 1987, with von Hirsch and Ashworth 1992: chapter 1), and strong claims are still made for the rehabilitative efficacy of certain programmes (McGuire, 1995).

The behavioural premise of rehabilitative theory is that some or many criminal offences are to a significant extent determined by social pressures, psychological difficulties, or other problems which impinge on individuals. The links with positivist criminology are strong. The political premise is that offenders are seen as unable to cope and in need of help from experts, and therefore (perhaps) as less than fully responsible individuals. The rehabilitative approach indicates that sentences should be tailored to the needs of the particular offenders: insofar as this needs-based approach places no limits on the extent of the intervention, it conflicts with proportionality and with the notion of a right not to be punished disproportionately. Its focus instead is upon the processes of diagnosis and treatment by trained professionals. In practical terms the pre-sentence report, formerly the social enquiry report, is an essential element in the pursuit of this approach to sentencing.

Incapacitative Sentencing

The incapacitative approach is to identify offenders or groups of offenders who are likely to do such harm in the future that special protective measures (usually in the form of lengthy incarceration) should be taken against them. The discretionary sentence of life imprisonment has been used increasingly for this purpose, and the Criminal Justice Act 1991 authorized courts to go beyond proportionate sentences and to impose 'public protection' sentences for violent and sexual offenders who are considered likely to do serious harm (von Hirsch and Ashworth, 1996). There also appears to be an element of incapacitative reasoning behind the mandatory sentences of life imprisonment for second serious sexual or violent offences contained in the Crime (Sentences) Act 1997. That Act may also be said to aim at the selective incapacitation of repeat domestic burglars and class A drug traffickers, by means of minimum sentences (cf. Blumstein *et al.*, 1986, for an analysis of the US experience of selective incapacitation).

The incapacitative approach has no behavioural premise. It is neither linked with any particular causes of offending nor dependent on changing the behaviour of offenders: it looks chiefly to the protection of potential victims. The political premise is often presented as utilitarian, justifying incapacitation by reference to the greater aggregate social benefit. It is sometimes said that in these cases the rights of potential victims are being preferred to the rights of the offenders. This notion of a conflict of rights attracted some discussion in the Floud report, which also found that predictions of 'dangerousness' tended to be wrong more often than not (Floud and Young, 1981); rather different analyses of the conflict of rights can be found in Bottoms and Brownsword (1982) and Wood (1988). The repeatedly confirmed fallibility of predictive judgements (e.g. Brody and Tarling, 1981; Monahan, 1996) calls into question the justification for any lengthening of sentences on grounds of public protection, and yet the political pressure to have some form(s) of incapacitative sentence available to the courts has been felt in most countries. If this is the reality of penal politics, then there is surely a strong case for procedural safeguards to ensure that the predictive judgements are open to thorough challenge. The Criminal Justice Act 1991 is defective in this respect, not even insisting on expert medical opinion, and the Crimes (Sentences) Act 1997 assumes a high risk of serious harm without requiring any evidence.

Restorative and Reparative Theories

These are not theories of punishment. Rather, their argument is that sentences should move away from punishment of the offender towards restitution and reparation, aimed at restoring the harm done to the victim and to the community (see Zedner, this volume, and references). Most restorative theories would therefore envisage less resort to custody, with onerous community-based sanctions requiring offenders to work in order to compensate victims. They may also support victim–offender mediation, and counselling for offenders to reintegrate them into the community. Such theories are often based on a behavioural premise similar to rehabilitation, but their political premise is that just compensation for victims should be recognized as more important than notions of just punishment on behalf of the state.

Legal systems based on a restorative rationale are rare, although many (including UK systems) allow courts to order offenders to pay compensation to victims. Two recent restorative initiatives are noteworthy. One is the development, in New Zealand and Australia, of Family Group Conferences whereby young offenders come with their families to meet the victim and victim's family and also community representatives, to discuss an appropriate response to the offence (Morris, Maxwell, and Robertson, 1993). This approach has links with Braithwaite's goal of 'reintegrative shaming' (Braithwaite, 1989), and it is significant that they include community representatives as well as members of the victim's family. A second and more widespread initiative, although some may doubt that it is 'restorative', is to allow victims to submit a 'victim impact statement' to the court, detailing the effects of the crime from their point of view. In line with the Victim's Charter, experiments with the provision of victim impact statement to prosecutors began in some parts of England in 1996. In some countries a VIS may also include the victim's opinion on the appropriate sentence, a development which raises deep questions about crimes as public and/or private wrongs (see Ashworth, 1993).

Social Theories

There has been a resurgence of writings which emphasize the social and political context of sentencing (see Duff and Garland, 1995: chapter 1). Important in this respect are Garland's (1990) analysis of the theoretical underpinnings of historical trends in punishment, and Hudson's arguments (1987, 1993) in favour of a shift towards a more supportive social policy as the principal response to the problem of crime. Those who have been influenced by H. L. A. Hart's distinction (1968) between the general justifying aim of punishment (in his view, utilitarian or deterrent) and the principles for distribution of punishment (in his view, retribution or desert) should consider the challenge to this dichotomy in Lacey's work (1988). She argues that both these issues raise questions of individual autonomy and of collective welfare and that, rather than denying it, we should address this conflict and strive to ensure that neither value is sacrificed entirely at either stage. In developing this view she explores the political values involved in state punishment and argues for a clearer view of the social function of punishing.

The political philosophy underlying the work of Braithwaite and Pettit (1990) is what they term republicanism, at the heart of which lies the concept of dominion. Its essence is liberty, not in the sense of simple freedom from constraint by others, but more in the form of a status of guaranteed protection from certain kinds of interference, based on a political compromise in which each citizen has participated. This leads them to propose that sentences should increase the dominion of victims with the least loss of dominion to the offenders punished. Since dominion lays emphasis on reassuring citizens about the prospect of liberty, it might require long preventive sentences based on deterrence or incapacitation. They gesture towards (vague) upper limits on severity, but not lower limits, and their view is that the censuring function of the criminal justice system can and should so far as possible be fulfilled by means other than punishment. There is thus no recognition of an individual's right not to be punished more than is proportionate to the seriousness of the crime: all depends on what will advance overall dominion, which might happen to be more or less in any individual case than the 'deserved' punishment (cf. von Hirsch and Ashworth, 1993; Pettit and Braithwaite, 1993).

Appraising the Rationales

One of the aims of the Criminal Justice Act 1991 was to depart from the previous vagueness over sentencing aims—the 'cafeteria' system of sentencing—and to promote some clarity. Desert was installed as the primary rationale, except for the relatively rare cases where the conditions for imposing an incapacitative sentence for 'public protection' were met. Deterrence was not to be used to justify a disproportionately severe sentence. Rehabilitative considerations became important when choosing among community orders of a similar severity, and also serve as a justification for probation orders and supervision after early release from custody. Compensation orders have priority over fines and not over custody. This legal framework was hardly conflict-free, but it established some parameters. Within a couple of months of the 1991 Act coming into force the Lord Chief Justice reinstated general deterrence as an aim in certain cases (*Cunningham* (1993) 96 Cr. App. R 422); a few months later began the government's retreat from the 1991 Act, so that deterrence and incapacitation are now prominent in the Criminal Justice and Public Order Act 1994 and the Crime (Sentences) Act 1997.

These developments make clear the socio-political basis for much sentencing policy. The above summary of several rationales, necessarily brief and omitting much of their richness, has referred to the behavioural and theoretical bases of each one. Criminologists have also tended to evaluate the approaches in terms of their effectiveness, and doubts were expressed earlier about the efficacy of strategies of individual deterrence, general deterrence, rehabilitation, and incapacitation. In respect of the last two it may be possible to refine techniques for identifying suitable targets, but it is also important to note that the object of discussion is *marginal* preventive effects. Thus a sentencing system based on desert is likely to deter and incapacitate to a certain degree, and so the proponents of deterrent or incapacitative theories must seek to justify the search for extra increments of prevention, by reference to evidence of likely success and the types of measure which must be adopted in order to achieve that success. It is here that concrete evidence is wanting (cf. Walker and Padfield, 1996: chapters 7, 22).

Even if there were satisfactory evidence of efficacy, however, there remain issues about the rights involved in punishment—notably, those of victims and of offenders. The victim's right to receive compensation from the offender is surely undoubted, but in what circumstances should it give way to the offender's interest in not being utterly impoverished for months or years to come? Should victims be allowed to express an opinion on sentence to the court, or would this be unfair in subjecting offenders to the varying dispositions (vindictive, sympathetic) of different victims? What rights should be accorded to offenders? Deterrence theory seems to regard individual offenders as mere units in the overall calculation of social benefit; incapacitative theory overrides the right not to be punished more than is proportionate to the offence in certain situations, the definition of which is contentious; and rehabilitative theory has often failed to recognize any such general right, especially when invoked in support of indeterminate sentences. It may therefore be seen as a strength of desert theory that it limits punishment to what is proportionate, and proposes criteria for determining proportionality. Some limits on state power out of respect for the rights of the offender are proposed in the republicanism of Braithwaite and Pettit (1990) and the communitarianism of Lacey (1988), although neither book works out the detailed implications.

The choice of one or more rationales for punishment has no necessary connection with the level of punitiveness in a sentencing system. The argument that desert theory leads to harsh penalties is not sustainable on an international comparison (von Hirsch, 1993: chapter 10). Indeed, many desert theorists have argued for lower levels of penalty. Recent events in England and Wales show the government appealing to deterrent and incapacitative rationales in support of its tough, populist approach, but in reality many politicians are less concerned with the actual results of the proposed policies than with their vote-winning potential. Rarely can the socio-political context of sentencing policy have been so manifest.

THE MECHANICS OF SENTENCING

In this part of the chapter some basic elements of the law and practice of sentencing are set out. The various stages of a criminal case are discussed, together with the procedures which surround the sentencing stage itself.

The Selection of Cases for Sentence

It is a commonplace that the courts pass sentence for only a small proportion of the crimes committed in any one year. According to the British Crime Survey, only some 47 per cent of offences committed are reported.[1] Police recording practices reduce that figure, so that only 27 per cent of all offences are recorded as such. Since only one-fifth of these offences are 'cleared up' (i.e. traced to an offender) by the police, the figure is further reduced to a mere 5 per cent of offences committed. By no means all those offences which are cleared up result in the taking of official action, perhaps because the suspected offender is too young, perhaps because the evidence is not sufficiently strong. This reduces to 3 per cent of all crimes the numbers proceeded with (Home Office, 1995: 25). Overall about one-third of offenders are cautioned rather than prosecuted: that leaves 2 per cent of all offences in any one year which result in convictions and court sentences (see further Maguire, this volume). This is not to suggest that sentencing is unimportant, for it may be thought to have a social or symbolic importance considerably in excess of the small proportion of crimes dealt with. But it does suggest the need for caution in assessing the crime-preventive effects of sentencing. Those theoretical rationales which look to the social consequences of sentencing may overestimate its potential for altering general patterns of behaviour.

The selection of cases for sentence is not merely a quantitative filtering process. There are also various filters of a qualitative kind, some formal, some informal. The role of the regulatory agencies is significant: the Health and Safety Executive, the Alkali Inspectorate, and the various pollution inspectorates do not record all breaches of the law as crimes (see e.g. Hawkins and Thomas, 1984; Hutter, 1988). These and other agencies, such as the Inland Revenue and the Customs and Excise, also have various means of enforcing compliance without resort to prosecution, such as warning notices or the 'compounding' of evaded tax and duty (Sanders, 1985). For those offences reported to the police, decisions are formally regulated by National Standards.[2] The low visibility of crucial decisions (whether to warn an offender informally, or to take no further action, or to administer a formal caution, or to prosecute) leaves the police with ample leeway to advance their own working priorities above the concerns of the formal guidelines (see Sanders, this volume). Where the police decide to prosecute, the Crown Prosecution Service has the power to drop the case if the evidence is insufficiently strong or if it is not in the

---

[1] Mayhew *et al.* (1994); note that their figures relate only to certain categories of offence, although most of the common offences are included.

[2] These are now to be found in Home Office Circular no. 14/1994, which was designed to reduce the use of cautioning. However the cautioning rate for indictable offences, which rose from 33% in 1990 to 41% in 1993, fell back only to 40% in 1995.

public interest to proceed. The Code for Crown Prosecutors (3rd edn., 1994) contains guidance on this decision and on choice of charge, which may in turn determine the level of court at which the case is heard (see below). At the stage of plea the true extent of negotiated justice is not known, but there is no shortage of empirical evidence that negotiation is a familiar part of justice in magistrates' courts (Baldwin, 1985) and in the Crown Court (Riley and Vennard, 1988). Indeed, the Royal Commission on Criminal Justice (1993) recommended a system whereby defendants could canvass the judge about the likely sentence before deciding on their plea.

In summary, therefore, the offences for which the courts have to pass sentence are both quantitatively and qualitatively different from what might be described as the social reality of crime. The courts see only a small percentage of cases. Even if it may be assumed that these are generally the more serious offences, how they are presented in court may be shaped as much by the working practices and priorities of the police, prosecutors and defence lawyers as by any objective conception of 'the facts of the case' (see also Sanders, this volume).

Crown Court and Magistrates' Courts

Of the two levels of criminal court in England and Wales, the Crown Court deals with the more serious cases and the magistrates' courts with the less serious. The Crown Court sits as a trial court with judge and jury. However, some two-thirds of Crown Court cases involve a guilty plea, and these are dealt with by judge alone, since juries have no part in sentencing. The most serious Crown Court cases are taken by a High Court judge on circuit, but the majority of cases are taken by a Circuit Judge (full-time) or by a Recorder or Assistant Recorder (part-time). The magistrates' courts are organized on a local basis: there are some 30,000 lay magistrates in England and Wales, and they usually sit in benches of three, advised by a justices' clerk. Typically a lay magistrate will sit in court one day a fortnight. There are also some sixty or more full-time stipendiary magistrates, together with some who sit part-time. Stipendiaries are professionally qualified full-time appointees, and are mostly assigned to metropolitan areas, where they tend to take the longer or more difficult cases.

What determines whether a case is heard in a magistrates' court or in the Crown Court? English law has three categories of offence. Indictable-only offences are the most serious group, and may only be dealt with in the Crown Court. Summary-only offences are the least serious group, and may only be dealt with in the magistrates' courts. Between them lies the category of offences triable either way. These are offences of intermediate gravity, which will generally be tried in magistrates' courts unless either the defendant elects to be committed for Crown Court trial (an absolute right, which accounts for some three-fifths of committals to the Crown Court), or the magistrates decide that the case should be committed to the Crown Court (two-fifths of cases). During the 1980s the magistrates' courts tended to commit an ever-increasing proportion of defendants to the Crown Court for trial, but the provisions of the Criminal Justice Act 1988 were designed to transfer some business away from the Crown Court and appear to have achieved that effect. Although it is widely believed that magistrates' courts are more prosecution-minded (Riley and Vennard, 1988; Hedderman and Moxon, 1992), magistrates' courts are limited in their sentencing to six months' custody, or twelve months' on two or more convictions, and their sentences are comparatively much lower than those in the Crown Court.[3] Under the Criminal Procedure and Investigations Act 1996 there is to be a new procedure whereby defendants intending to plead guilty to either-way offences may, in certain circumstances, opt to be sentenced in the magistrates' court.

Hand in hand with this continued transfer of business from Crown Court to magistrates' courts has been a movement to relieve magistrates' courts of many traffic cases by enabling the police to issue fixed penalty notices. Thus in 1995 some 84,000 defendants were tried in the Crown Court, some 1.93 million people were prosecuted in the magistrates' courts, and a further seven million fixed penalty notices were issued.

Maximum Sentences

Apart from a few common law offences which have no fixed maximum (e.g. manslaughter, conspiracy to outrage public decency), Parliament has generally provided the maximum sentence for each offence. Much statutory consolidation of criminal offences was completed in the mid-nineteenth century, and there have been several reforms of the criminal law in the last thirty years. Apart from that, maxima have been set at different times, in different social circumstances, and without any overall plan. Indeed, the statutory maxima set in the nineteenth century were much influenced by the traditional periods of transportation (Thomas, 1978; Radzinowicz and Hood, 1985: chapter 15). Many had hoped that the Advisory Council on the Penal System would be able to improve the coherence of the system, but in its 1978 report on *Sentences of Imprisonment: A Review of Maximum Penalties* it declined to revise the various statutory maxima, regarding the task as too controversial.[4]

Parliament continues to alter maximum sentences in a piecemeal way: for example, the Criminal Justice Act 1993 doubled the maxima for causing death by dangerous driving and causing death by careless driving whilst intoxicated to ten years, whilst leaving untouched the five-year maximum for causing death by aggravated vehicle-taking. These new maxima have had an impact on practical sentencing levels (see *Attorney-General's References Nos. 14 and 24 of*

---

[3] Comparing two matched samples, Hedderman and Moxon (1992: 37) found that the Crown Court used custody three times as often and that the sentences were, on average, two and a half times as long.

[4] It did, however, recommend the adoption of lower 'normal maxima', based on past practice, with a power to exceed them in exceptional cases. For discussion, see Radzinowciz and Hood (1978).

1993 (1994) 15 Cr. App. R (S) 640), whereas the reduction of the maximum sentence for theft from ten to seven years in the 1991 Act has had no discernible effect.

The Range of Available Sentences

Beneath the maximum penalty for the offence, the court usually has a wide discretion to choose among alternatives. In England and Wales the range of alternatives is wider than in most other jurisdictions, but before they are considered two general points should be noted. First, the tradition is to create maximum penalties in terms of either a period of custody or an amount or level of fine: no offences have been assigned probation or community service as the maximum penalty. Secondly, since the mid-1960s there has been a tendency to enact broadly defined offences with relatively high maximum penalties: for example, in England and Wales there is a single offence of theft with a maximum of seven years' imprisonment, whereas in many other European countries there are grades of theft with separate maxima. The English approach leaves sentencers with much greater discretion (see Thomas, 1974).

At the lowest level, the range of available sentences begins with absolute and conditional discharges, and binding over. Fines come next, and a compensation order should be considered in every case involving death, injury, loss, or damage. What are termed 'community sentences' by the Criminal Justice Act 1991 include probation orders, community service orders, combination orders (part probation, part community service), and curfew orders. Then come suspended sentences of imprisonment, and imprisonment itself. For offenders under the age of 21, the custodial sentence takes the form of detention in a young offender institution; suspended sentences are unavailable; and attendance centre orders can be made. All these forms of sentence are discussed further below. There are separate orders for young offenders and for mentally disordered offenders.

Discretion in Sentencing

Alleged inconsistencies in sentencing have been a frequent cause for concern. This might seem an obvious consequence of the expanse of discretion left by fairly high maximum penalties and the wide range of available sentences. But there is a paradox here. Many sentencers seem to place more emphasis on the restrictions on 'their' discretion than on the choices that remain. Judges have been critical of the various limits which Parliament places on their powers, and of the duties imposed upon them. Courts are now under an obligation to consider making a compensation order in every case of death, injury, loss, or damage; and in drug trafficking cases a court is required to follow the prescribed statutory procedure for confiscation of the offender's assets (cf. Thomas, 1995). Even before some of these restrictions were imposed in the late 1980s, judges expressed themselves as having little choice in the sentences they passed: 'the least possible sentence I can pass . . . ', 'I have no alternative but to . . . ' (Oxford Pilot Study, 1984: 53–4). To some extent this terminology may reflect the constraints imposed by Court of Appeal decisions, but it is more likely that it reflects self-generated constraints which stem from the attitudes and beliefs of the sentencer.

The paradox is that, despite these feelings of constraint, the sentencer's discretion is considerable in legal terms. The Criminal Justice Act 1991 sought to impose a new structure and new restrictions, but it left considerable room for judicial discretion in the length of custodial sentences, in the decision to impose custody or not, and among the various community orders. Moxon's study of 2,000 cases yielded a model which is claimed to predict 80 per cent of Crown Court sentences, giving rise to the suggestion that 'differences between individual judges' did not have 'a particularly big impact on the *overall* pattern of sentences' (Moxon, 1988: 64, emphasis in original). Magistrates' courts have upper limits on their powers, but otherwise the choice among alternatives is little affected by Court of Appeal decisions (of which few are relevant). Just as Hood (1962) showed that some benches are 'probation-minded' and others are not, so Tarling (1979) demonstrated that among the thirty courts he surveyed the use of probation varied between 1 and 12 per cent, suspended sentences between 4 and 16 per cent, fines between 46 and 76 per cent, and so on. Significant elements of these variations remained after account had been taken of the different 'mix' of offences coming before the courts (Tarling *et al.*, 1985). As Hood found in his study of motoring cases (1972), membership of a particular bench tends to be a major determinant of a magistrate's approach to sentencing. The influence of magistrates' clerks, who generally undertake the initial training of new magistrates, may be considerable (Darbyshire, 1984). In the last few years the Magistrates' Association's *Sentencing Guidelines* (now 1997) have been used quite widely, but there remains considerable variation. Research shows that, in relation to the imposition of fines, some 55 per cent of areas follow the Magistrates' Association's guidelines, a further 28 per cent use them with significant modifications, and some 17 per cent proceed on a different basis (Charman *et al.*, 1966). Thus to some extent the power of local traditions or certain justices' clerks continues to be felt.

Whilst discretion is important to enable sentencers to take account of the wide and varying range of factors that might be relevant, it does leave decision-making open to irrelevant influences (see Galligan, 1986; Hawkins, 1992). For example, Hood's 1992 study has shown that at some courts black offenders are significantly more likely to receive custody than similarly situated white offenders. Farrington and Morris (1983) have shown, as have other studies, that the apparent leniency of sentences on women may conceal a trend of severity against a minority of female offenders who appear to lack 'respect-ability' and 'domesticity'. Judges tend to argue strongly against any curtailment of 'their' discretion—an argument raised loudly against the mandatory and minimum sentences in the Crime (Sentences) Act 1997—but rarely acknowledge the risks of discrimination, individual idiosyncrasy, and other irrelevant influences which accompany discretion that is not well structured or well monitored.

Information about the Offence

Courts depend for their information on what they hear or what they are told. Since over 90 per cent of cases in magistrates' courts and around two-thirds of cases in the Crown Court are pleas of guilty, the information is usually constructed for the court by the prosecutor or others. The main source of information about the offence is likely to be the statement of facts which the prosecutor reads out. It will usually have been compiled by the police, and the way in which it describes or omits certain factors may reflect a particular view of the offence, or perhaps a 'charge-bargain' struck with the police (see Sanders, this volume; McConville *et al.*, 1991: chapter 7). Sometimes the statement of facts may have been reconstructed, wholly or in part, by the prosecuting lawyer as a result of a change of plea or other negotiations: in *Beswick* ([1996] Crim. LR 62) it was held that the judge can require a 'Newton hearing' (see below) if not satisfied that the facts as stated are true. In addition to the prosecution statement of facts, the court may gather further information about the offence from the defence plea in mitigation, and perhaps from a pre-sentence report (formerly, social enquiry report). Any account of 'the facts' is likely to be selective, determined to some extent by the compiler's preconceptions. It is likely that judges and magistrates will be influenced by the selections made by those who inform them, as well as by their own preconceptions.

The prosecution's account of the facts may be disputed by the defence. In a trial there is usually an opportunity to resolve these matters, but this is not always so: some facts relevant to sentencing are irrelevant to criminal guilt. The greatest difficulty arises where the defendant pleads guilty, but only on the basis of a more favourable version of the facts than the prosecution presents. The courts have developed a procedure for resolving most such issues by means of a pre-sentence hearing, known as a 'Newton hearing' (after the leading case of *Newton* (1982) 4 Cr. App. R (S) 388), at which evidence is presented and witnesses may be heard. There is now a wealth of case law on the situations in which a 'Newton hearing' is necessary and on the procedures to be followed, but there remains a need for an authoritative commitment to the same evidentiary protections for the defendant as apply at the trial itself (Wasik, 1985*b*; Ashworth, 1995: chapter 12). The outcome can have a considerable effect on the length of a custodial sentence, and proper safeguards should therefore be introduced.

Information about the Offender

The court may obtain information about the offender from at least five sources—the police antecedents statement, the defence plea in mitigation, a pre-sentence report, a medical report, and the offender's own appearance in court.

The contents of the *police antecedents statement* are regulated by a Practice Direction from the Lord Chief Justice [1966] 2 All ER 929. The principal element is information about previous convictions, but there may also be reference to age, education, employment, and domestic circumstances (see Shapland, 1981: 123–30). The purpose of a *defence plea in mitigation* is to show the offender and offence in the best light. In practice, it appears that a realistic recognition of any aggravating factors may improve the credibility of what is said in mitigation (Shapland, 1981: chapter 5). Judges have tended to trust the factual basis of pleas in mitigation more than pre-sentence reports, particularly because the latter may be prepared some weeks before the trial (Oxford Pilot Study, 1984: 43–5).

The purpose of a *pre-sentence report* under the Criminal Justice Act 1991 is to assist the sentencer by providing information and analysis of offence, offender, and related matters. The form of the reports is now regulated by National Standards (Home Office, 1995): the offence analysis should 'assist the court's understanding of why the offender committed this offence at this time', referring to the context of the offence, the impact on the victim, and the offender's attitude. The report should give personal and social information which provides 'a balanced picture of the offender, spelling out both strengths and weaknesses'. There should be 'a concise statement of the report writer's professional judgment of the risk of re-offending and the risk of harm to the public' presented by the offender. The report may conclude with 'a proposal inviting the court to consider the merits' of a particular programme, within the framework of a community sentence.

A *medical report* is relatively rare, but a court may decide to call for one and section 4 of the Criminal Justice Act 1991 requires a court to obtain one before passing a custodial sentence if the defendant is or appears to be mentally disordered (see further Peay, this volume). The impact of *the offender's own appearance* and demeanour in court is difficult to gauge, but judges recognize that they take account of it and tend to feel that sentencing would be even more difficult if they did not see the offender in person (Cooke, 1987: 58; Oxford Pilot Study, 1984: chapter 3). This fifth source of influence serves to demonstrate that the impact of the reports, etc., received by a court may be mediated by the attitudes of the sentencer (Shapland, 1987).

Representations on Sentence

Some of what is said by an advocate making a defence plea in mitigation will bear directly on the sentence. Although the tendency has been for advocates only rarely to mention Court of Appeal decisions or even particular forms of sentence, the Court of Appeal has occasionally urged counsel to be more explicit and to cite relevant decisions (e.g. *Ozair Ahmed* (1994) 15 Cr. App. R (S) 286). Both practitioners and senior judges are divided on this, but if the rule of law is to exert its proper effect on sentencing decisions there is a need for more citation of precedents. It is clear, however, that counsel has a duty to prevent the judge from passing an unlawful sentence (e.g. *Hartrey* [1993] Crim. LR 230), by drawing the judge's attention to the relevant authority.

The English tradition is that the prosecutor plays no part in sentencing, in the sense that no sentence is 'asked for' or recommended. It is sometimes assumed that such a practice would lead to higher sentences, although this has not been the outcome in the Netherlands, where prosecutors recommend sentences and judges rarely exceed the recommendation (van Duyne, 1987: 144–5). As already mentioned, in some areas of the country there are experiments with victim impact statements (Victim's Charter, 1996), which are submitted to the prosecutor, not directly to the court.

Appeals against Sentence

A person who is sentenced in a magistrates' court may appeal to the Crown Court. The appeal is usually heard by a judge sitting with two magistrates, and it takes the form of a re-hearing. The Crown Court is then empowered to pass any sentence which the magistrates' court could have imposed, whether more severe or more lenient than the original sentence. The possibility of a more severe sentence tends to discourage appeals. Fewer than 1 per cent of offenders appeal, mostly those who have been sentenced to custody.[5] Where there is a disputed point of law, the defendant may appeal to the Divisional Court by means of case stated or for judicial review.[6]

A person sentenced in the Crown Court may appeal to the Court of Appeal (Criminal Division) on a point of law. Otherwise an offender may apply for leave to appeal against sentence to the Court of Appeal. Applications for leave to appeal are parcelled out to individual High Court judges: little is known about how these decisions are made. If an offender is granted leave to appeal, the Court will hear submissions, usually from defence counsel only, and increasingly including reference to other decided cases. The Court may substitute any sentence which is not more severe than the original sentence. The Court hears appeals from about 7 per cent of defendants sentenced in the Crown Court, about one quarter of which succeed.[7]

There is no prosecution appeal against sentence in England and Wales. Such appeals exist in several other European and Commonwealth countries, but the closest approximation in English law is the power of the Attorney General to refer to the Court of Appeal cases in which the sentence is thought to be unduly lenient. The power, introduced by the Criminal Justice Act 1988, is now exercised in some fifty cases per year. The Court of Appeal may increase the sentence if it is found to have been outside the normal range for the offence, and in a majority of referred cases it has increased the sentence (Shute,

[5] Criminal Statistics 1989, Table 6.7.
[6] See Wasik (1984).
[7] Criminal Statistics 1989, Table 6.7.

1994). These decisions undoubtedly contribute to the corpus of sentencing guidance for lower courts.

English Sentencing Procedures

From this brief review, three main themes emerge. First, it is evident that other actors, apart from judges and magistrates, exert considerable influence on the sentencing process. Not only do the police and prosecutors select and shape the cases which come to court, but they (together with probation officers and defence lawyers) provide the courts with information which they have selected and constructed. There may also be suggestions, implicit or sometimes explicit, as to sentence. Secondly, what courts may receive in terms of information about the offence and the offender, and representations on sentence, is governed mostly by court practice and judicial decisions. Apart from pre-sentence reports, there is little legislative intervention in the field. The judges themselves have developed 'Newton hearings'. They could equally develop or modify other practices. And thirdly, there are several points at which the approach or attitude of the sentencer may be influential. Thus, despite the growth of legislation on sentencing, there remains considerable room for different approaches to be taken by particular judges or particular benches of magistrates. More research and analysis of the decision-making of sentencers is needed, to discover to what extent legal or other factors actually determine judicial sentencing.

CUSTODIAL SENTENCING

The Evolution of a 'Tariff'

Maximum sentences are generally high, and English law has long had only one mandatory minimum sentence,[8] although the effect of the Crime (Sentences) Act 1997 is to add one, possibly three, more. Most day-to-day sentencing practices are little affected by legislative constraints. For Crown Court sentencing some normal ranges or starting points have developed, often termed 'the going rate' by judges and 'the tariff' by others. Historically the idea of 'normal' sentences can be traced back at least as far as the 'Memorandum of Normal Punishments' drawn up by Lord Alverstone, the Lord Chief Justice, in 1901 (Thomas, 1978; Radzinowicz and Hood, 1985: 755–8). Since 1907 the Court of Criminal Appeal, and since 1966 its successor the Court of Appeal (Criminal Division), has adjusted and altered aspects of the tariff. Increased reporting of Court of Appeal decisions on sentencing has assisted the concretization of sentencing principles, and the publication of the first edition

---

[8] 12 months' disqualification from driving on conviction for drunk driving.

of Dr David Thomas's *Principles of Sentencing* (1970) was a landmark in the development of a common law of sentencing. In the last fifteen years it has become normal practice for Court of Appeal judgments to refer to previous decisions.

It remains true, however, that the bulk of Court of Appeal decisions deal with fairly severe and long sentences, whilst relatively few decisions have a direct bearing on day-to-day sentencing in the Crown Court for the majority of offences, which tend to be thefts, burglaries, deceptions, and handling stolen goods. Here, the 'going rate' stems largely from court practice. There appears to be less sense of a 'going rate' for offences which attract non-custodial sentences. In the magistrates' courts, as we have seen, the Magistrates' Association has taken the initiative in developing its own sentencing guidelines, in an effort to fill the vacuum created by the lack of guidance from other quarters.

Whether the Court of Appeal can fulfill both the role of deciding appeals in individual cases and the task of providing guidance for the lower courts remains open to question. The latter task surely requires a body with the time and experience to consider the whole range of crimes in relation to the available sentences, criminal justice practices and criminological knowledge. It is a policy function, for which a small number of senior judges working through long lists of cases might not be the most appropriate agency: see the final section of this chapter.

Statutory Restrictions on Custodial Sentences

Section 1(4) of the Criminal Justice Act 1982 introduced restrictions on custodial sentences for offenders under 21 which were amended in 1988 and remained in force until 1992. For the first time, they required courts to justify their custodial sentences on grounds of either the seriousness of the offence, the protection of the public, or a history of failure to respond to non-custodial sentences. The 1980s saw a spectacular decline in the use of custody for juveniles (7,900 in 1981 to 1,500 in 1991) and some decline for young adults, and the statutory restrictions on custody were regarded as one contributory factor.

The Criminal Justice Act 1991 extended legislative restrictions on custody to offenders of all ages. The scheme is as follows. A court may not impose a custodial sentence unless the case satisfies the custody threshold in section 1(2). The court must satisfy itself that the offence was so serious that only a custodial sentence can be justified. This may be seen as an application of the 'desert' or proportionality principle, combined with a policy of restraint in the use of custody. The application of the section and the development of work-able criteria were left to the Court of Appeal, but the response has been disappointing. The Court's first statement after the implementation of the 1991 Act was that an offence satisfies the custody threshold in section 1(2) if it 'would make right-thinking members of the public, knowing all the facts, feel that justice had not been done by the passing of any sentence other than a custodial one' (*Cox* (1993) 96 Cr. App. R 452 at 455). The Court has subsequently held that this test was satisfied in a case of obtaining goods valued at £35 by deception (*Keogh* (1994) 15 Cr. App. R (S) 279), in a case of theft of £17 by a ticket clerk (*McCormick* (1995) 16 Cr. App. R (S) 134), and in many other cases in which the policy of using custody restrictively was neither followed nor even mentioned. In effect, the courts have failed to carry out the responsibility bestowed upon them by Parliament in section 1(2)(a), the Court of Appeal having declined to develop criteria to guide lower courts at the crucial custody borderline (see further Ashworth and von Hirsch, 1997).

Two provisions in the 1991 Act were changed within months of their introduction. The courts were very critical of the 'two offence rule' introduced by the 1991 Act: it applied whenever a court was sentencing an offender for several offences, and permitted the court to consider only the combined seriousness of any two of those offences when deciding on the type of penalty (e.g. prison, community sentence) that was deserved. The Criminal Justice Act 1993 swept away this restriction. Judges, magistrates, and others were also critical of section 29 of the 1991 Act. Its effect was frequently mis-stated as 'courts are not allowed to take account of previous convictions', whereas it was intended to reflect the common law principle that a good record may mitigate while a bad record should not lead to a disproportionate sentence. The Criminal Justice Act 1993 replaces section 29 with a provision allowing courts to take account of any previous convictions of an offender or any failure of his to respond to previous sentences, when 'considering the seriousness of the offence'. There has been no authoritative interpretation of the new provision by the Court of Appeal (cf. Wasik and von Hirsch, 1994). The policy behind both these repealed sections of the 1991 Act was to restrain courts from imposing substantial sentences on people who commit a number of minor offences. Too little was heard of this policy in the early 1990s, when attention was focused on the abysmal drafting of the 1991 Act. Even less has been heard of it since, and it seems possible that the 1993 changes contributed to the huge rise in the custodial population in the mid-1990s.

If a case fails to satisfy the custody threshold, taking account of the relevant aggravating and mitigating factors (see below), a non-custodial sentence should be given. If, however, it satisfies section 1(2), the duration of the custodial sentence is governed by section 2(2). Chiefly, this means that the length of sentence should be 'commensurate with the seriousness of the offence'. It was always likely that the courts would interpret this as confirming the 'tariff' or 'going rate' (see below), but it was startling to find Lord Taylor, the Lord Chief Justice, declaring that the new law does allow courts to take account of deterrence. He stated that the phrase 'commensurate with the seriousness of the offence' must mean 'commensurate with the punishment and deterrence that the offence requires' (*Cunningham* (1993) 96 Cr. App. R 422 at 425). Since the 1990 White Paper had stated that desert and proportionality should be the primary touchstone of sentencing, and had criticized deterrence as a largely inappropriate principle (Home Office, 1990: para. 2.8), this was an extraordinary interpretation. Although Lord Taylor did accept that an 'exemplary sentence' on a particular offender would be unlawful, this judgment amounted to a defiant statement of 'business as usual' by the judiciary.

Proportionality and the Court of Appeal

The courts may be said to operate a kind of 'tariff' when calculating the length of custodial sentences. A conventional 'going rate' for many offences has developed over the years, shaped and assisted by judgments of the Court of Appeal. The logic of the upper echelons of the tariff was considered by Lord Justice Lawton in his judgment in *Turner* ((1975) 61 Cr. App. R 67 at 89–91). He started from the assumption that it would be absurd if an offender could receive longer sentences for armed robbery than for murder itself. So he estimated the number of years that a murderer without mitigating circumstances could expect to spend in prison, and then ranged the sentences for other serious offences just beneath that. He took the period for the murderer as fifteen years in prison, equivalent to a determinate sentence of twenty-two years (less the one-third remission which obtained in 1975). Just beneath this notional twenty-two years he placed a number of 'wholly abnormal' offences, such as political kidnapping and bomb attacks. He then held that armed robbery should be placed at the next level down, yielding around eighteen years for the two offences in that case. This scheme continues to apply more or less to the upper end of the 'tariff', but the lower reaches are less well settled.

The Court of Appeal's greatest achievement in exercising its policy function has been the formulation of 'guideline judgments'. Lord Lane, the Lord Chief Justice in the 1980s, would occasionally take a particular case and, rather than giving a judgment on the facts alone, would construct a judgment dealing with sentencing for all the main varieties of that particular crime. The first of these was in the case of *Aramah* ((1982) 4 Cr. App. R (S) 407), where guidance was given on sentencing levels for the whole gamut of drugs offences, from large-scale trafficking down to possession of small amounts for individual use. This judgment was subsequently readapted (in *Aroyewumi* (1995) 16 Cr. App. R (S) 211) so that its guidance is calibrated according to weight and purity level rather than estimates of 'street value', and parallel guidance for 'ecstasy' cases was given in *Warren and Beeley* ([1996] 1 Cr. App. R (S) 233). A much-discussed guideline judgment is that in *Billam* ((1986) 8 Cr. App. R (S) 48) on rape. The Lord Chief Justice established two starting points, of five years and eight years imprisonment, according to the presence or absence of certain factors. He went on to enumerate eight aggravating factors, three mitigating factors, and certain factors which courts should not take into account. The judgment has subsequently been extended to deal with cases of rape of a wife or former partner (in *W* (1993) 14 Cr. App. R (S) 256). Although the *Billam* guideline judgment is technically quite well developed, it says little about the relative effect to be given to the various aggravating factors it enumerates, a failure which impairs its contribution to sentencing consistency (see Ranyard, Hebenton, and Pease, 1994).

Guideline judgments are intended by the Lord Chief Justice to be binding on judges and magistrates, and it seems that they are so regarded. This method of guidance seems to have caused less judicial opposition than the systems in certain American states (see section below on 'International Patterns in Sentencing Reform'), probably because it has been developed *by* judges *for* judges, and because the guidance is in the familiar narrative form of a judgment. Lord Chief Justices have used it both to supply guidance for relatively unusual crimes (e.g. mortgage frauds in *Stevens* (1993) 14 Cr. App. R (S) 372), and to alter sentencing levels where they are thought to be too low (e.g. serious road traffic offences in *Boswell* (1984) 6 Cr. App. R (S) 257) or too high (e.g. social security frauds in *Stewart* (1987) 9 Cr. App. R (S) 135).

One advantage of guideline judgments is that they cover most manifestations of a particular crime at once, and produce more coherence than a series of separate judgments in different cases. Another advantage is that judges appear to respect them. There are, however, three major disadvantages in the way they have been used in this country. First, around twenty such judgments have been delivered, without any explicit linking of the separate punishment scales they establish. For example, are the rape guidelines set at the right level, compared with the guidelines for mortgage fraud or robbery? Proportionality issues of this kind must be addressed. Secondly, relatively few such judgments have been delivered, covering only a small number of crimes. There is no evidence of a judicial willingness to formulate guideline judgments for the offences which occupy most of the time of sentencers, e.g. theft, burglary, deception, and handling stolen goods. When the opportunity to give detailed guidance on burglary of dwellings was presented to Lord Lane in 1990, he largely avoided the issue: *Mussell* ((1990) 12 Cr. App. R (S) 607). Unless crimes such as burglary are made the subject of sentencing guidelines, the judiciary will continue to be open to the criticism that its guideline judgments are only peripherally relevant to everyday practice, and also open to politicians' charges that burglary sentencing is in need of legislative intervention. Thirdly, it must be questioned whether the Court of Appeal is the right body, given its restricted time, its restricted membership, and its restricted perspectives, to formulate general guidance of this kind.

Aggravation and Mitigation

When courts are determining the seriousness of an offence, they should have regard to its aggravating and mitigating features. Moxon found that custody is significantly more likely in Crown Court cases where the victim is elderly, or the offender is a ringleader, or the offence was planned, or a weapon was used

(Moxon, 1988: 9), and there are Court of Appeal judgments supporting all these aggravating factors (see Ashworth, 1995: chapter 5.3). Among the mitigating factors recognized by the courts are various forms of reduced culpability (e.g. mental disturbance, financial pressures) and a good previous record. Section 28 of the 1991 Act goes further and permits courts to 'take account of any such matters as, in the opinion of the court, are relevant in mitigation of sentence'. This allows courts to continue giving effect to various factors that have no bearing on the offence or the offender's culpability—the collateral impact of the sentence on others, an act of heroism by the offender, the payment of compensation to the victim, or the giving of information to the police about other offenders (Ashworth, 1995: chapter 5.5).

Perhaps the most substantial mitigating factor is the plea of guilty, which can earn a discount of up to one-third off the sentence: *Buffrey* ((1993) 14 Cr. App. R (S) 511). Parliament confirmed the importance of this discount in section 48 of the Criminal Justice and Public Order Act 1994 as part of its strategy to persuade more defendants to plead guilty at an earlier stage (rather than on the morning of the trial, which wastes resources and inconveniences victims and witnesses). Section 48 makes it clear that courts should give a graduated discount, according to the stage at which the guilty plea was entered. The Magistrates' Association's *Sentencing Guidelines* state: 'for a timely guilty plea allow a discount of about a third'. Substantial discounts place enormous pressure on defendants to forego the right to trial which goes with the presumption of innocence. Where defendants are advised that the discount may make the difference between a custodial and a non-custodial sentence, the risk of innocent people pleading guilty is particularly high.

The 'Public Protection' Exception

Although the scheme of the 1991 Act is based on sentencing according to the seriousness of the offence, the Act creates one exception to the proportionality principle. Where a court is dealing with a sexual or violent offender, section 2(2)(b) permits it to impose a longer than proportionate sentence (though within the statutory maximum) if that is 'necessary to protect the public from serious harm from the offender'. The Act defines the key terms, but does not require a court to consider a psychiatric report before imposing such a sentence. In the many cases it has considered, the Court of Appeal has developed some guidance on how this power should be exercised. It has quashed several longer than proportionate sentences, but on other occasions has upheld such sentences on rather speculative reasoning (see von Hirsch and Ashworth, 1996; and Peay, this volume). Many commentators saw this provision in the 1991 Act as a necessary political counterweight to other sections which sought to reduce the use of custody. As we have seen, in the mid-1990s the use of custody has increased substantially across the board.

Custodial Sentences and Executive Release

One aspect of sentencing which is open to much public misunderstanding is the meaning of custodial sentences in terms of the time served. The system has changed several times in the last two decades, and seems likely to change again. Before the Criminal Justice Act 1991, the general principle was that every prisoner would have one-third deducted ('remission') from the sentence on starting a custodial sentence. From 1968, release on parole for part or all of the middle one-third of the sentence became possible too. The government made several changes to the effects of remission and parole during the 1980s, and the Carlisle Committee (1988) responded to judicial disquiet by proposing a new system.

This was implemented, more or less, by the Criminal Justice Act 1991. Remission was abolished. Parole was replaced by two systems of early release. All those serving terms of under four years are conditionally released after one-half, subject to serving the unexpired balance if they are convicted of another offence which was committed during the second half of the full sentence. Additionally, those serving between one and four years are subject to supervision on licence until the three-quarters point in their sentence. A system of discretionary conditional release was introduced for those serving four years and over, who may be so released after one-half of their sentence. Those not considered suitable for discretionary release are conditionally released after two-thirds of their sentence, and are then subject to supervision until the three-quarters point.

One result of the 1991 Act is that every part of a custodial sentence counts for something. Conditional release means that the possibility of return to custody remains until the last day of the sentence pronounced in court. Moreover, all those serving longer than one year receive some supervision on release. These merits of the post-1991 system seemed lost on the previous government, however, and the Crime (Sentences) Act 1997 is set to abolish the entire system in favour of what has been termed 'honesty in sentencing'. This does not, however, mean that prisoners will serve the whole period announced in court. The Act provides that prisoners serving sentences of two months and under three years may be awarded up to six 'early release days' per month for good behaviour. Prisoners serving sentences of three years or longer become eligible for release, on a recommendation of the Parole Board, after serving five-sixths of the sentence. All prisoners sentenced to twelve months or longer will be released under supervision, which will continue for at least three months.

One effect of these changes would be that, if judges did not alter their sentencing practices by revising the tariff downwards, offenders would serve longer in prison than under the existing law. This was not the intention, and therefore Section 26 of the Crime (Sentences) Act 1997 provides that courts should impose a term equal to two-thirds of the sentence which would have been passed before the Act. Although intended to avoid the covert lengthening of sentences, this provision risks exposing the judiciary to ridicule in the popular press, as they impose what appear to be lower sentences. The sentencing system appears likely to be subjected to more ill-informed criticism, as a result of a change which has not been supported by good arguments and which fails to live up to its claim of 'honesty'.

Mandatory Sentences

The centrepiece of the Crime (Sentences) Act 1997 is the introduction of three new mandatory and minimum sentences. Despite strong and well-reasoned criticisms of the mandatory sentence for murder (see Windlesham, 1993: chapter 7; Windlesham, 1996: chapter 9), the Act will introduce a mandatory sentence of life imprisonment for a second serious sexual or violent conviction. Strong doubts have been expressed whether this provision will be as conducive to public safety as the government claims (Hood and Shute, 1996). The only leeway left to the courts is to impose a different sentence if there are 'exceptional circumstances', a restrictive phrase which is unlikely to allow much scope to judges.

In its original form the 1997 Act was also drafted so as to include two mandatory minimum sentences. A third class A drug-trafficking conviction was to lead to a mandatory minimum sentence of seven years' imprisonment. A third conviction for domestic burglary was to lead to a mandatory minimum sentence of three years' imprisonment. Many offenders falling within these categories would receive longer sentences in any event, but the injustice of courts having to impose such sentences in some inappropriate cases (and the tradition of judicial discretion) led to strong opposition in the House of Lords. In the last days of the Parliamentary session the government was forced to make concessions, with the result that these two minimum sentences do not have to be imposed in cases where it would be 'unjust in all the circumstances' to do so—much less restrictive than the 'exceptional circumstances' formula. Hence the seven- and three-year sentences are referred to here as minimum sentences, as distinct from mandatory minimum sentences.

Several objections to mandatory minimum sentences were influential in bringing about this loosening of the legislative formula. First, the evidence from the United States suggests that they have no significant effects on crime rates. This is hardly surprising if the clear-up rate for offences is so low as to give a good chance of avoiding detection, as the Lord Chief Justice pointed out (Taylor, 1996). Secondly, they sometimes result in the imposition of clearly inappropriate and unjust sentences. Thirdly, this potential for injustice tends to lead prosecutors and judges to find ways of circumventing the mandatory provisions. Fourthly, where the mandatory provisions cannot be avoided, defendants are likely to plead not guilty in large numbers: in the US federal system, trial rates are two-and-a-half times higher for offences with mandatory minima (Tonry, 1996: chapter 5). Fifthly, the introduction of mandatory minima may have the effect of driving up, or distorting, relative sentence levels for other offences. Some judges opposed these changes on the ground that they undermine judicial independence, but this is unconvincing.

There is no constitutional reason why Parliament should not legislate on sentencing. A stronger argument is that the crime-preventive claims made for mandatory minima are simply unsubstantiated, and that the public are being deceived rather than protected.

Review of Policy and Practice

The Crime (Sentences) Act 1997 came after three years of sustained campaigning by Michael Howard, then Home Secretary, for tougher sentences. Spurred on by loud enthusiasm from the tabloid press, he began by promoting a new custodial sentence for young offenders, the secure training centres for repeat offenders aged 12, 13, and 14 (Criminal Justice and Public Order Act 1994, part I). He continued to repeat the phrase 'prison works', and in 1995 foreshadowed the introduction of mandatory minimum sentences. The mass media, especially certain newspapers, continued to campaign for higher sentences. Following the change of government in May 1997 it is unclear to what extent the various parts of the Crime (Sentences) Act will be implemented. The Labour Party failed to oppose many of its provisions. Now in government, it must decide which sections (if any) to bring into force.

It is also significant that, since early 1993, the courts have increased their use of custodial sentences—by imposing custody in a higher proportion of cases, and for longer—with relatively little encouragement from the legislature. Three changes in the 1993 Act (doubling the maxima for causing death on the roads, and removing restrictions when dealing with multiple offenders or repeat offenders) may have had some effect, but this can hardly account for a rise from 40,000 in December 1992 to 60,000 in April 1997 (for further analysis of imprisonment rates and international comparisons, see Morgan, this volume). The steep upward trend was also apparent in the proportionate use of custody: from 4.8 per cent (1992) to 8.8 per cent (1995) in magistrates' courts, and from 44.3 per cent (1992) to 55.7 per cent (1995) in the Crown Court. In the main the judiciary and the magistracy appear to have been responding to what they regard as the climate of opinion in society, fuelled largely by political and media rhetoric rather than by carefully constructed opinion surveys (cf. Hough, 1996; Ashworth and Hough, 1996).

While it may thus be said that significant numbers of politicians, sentencers, and the media appear to agree on the desirability of increased resort to imprisonment, this alliance breaks down when it comes to the question of method. Most judges categorically reject the need for mandatory sentences of any kind, and call for trust to be reposed in their discretion to impose the appropriate sentence for each individual case. No doubt this view is reinforced by the remnants of untenable views about the independence of the judiciary. It is also supported by Lord Taylor's argument that the deterrent assumptions behind the 1997 Act cannot be sustained (Taylor, 1996). But one should not overlook the judiciary's own failings in respect of sentencing policy—their determination to resist the 1991 Act so far as possible, manifested by Lord Taylor's extraordinary decision in *Cunningham* (discussed above); the Court of Appeal's failure to give a clear lead on the interpretation of section 1(2)(a) on the custody threshold; the reluctance of successive Lord Chief Justices to formulate guidelines on the most frequent offences in everyday practice, such as theft, deception, burglary, and handling stolen goods; and the unwillingness of the judiciary to allow independent research into the working philosophies of Crown Court sentencers (cf. Oxford Pilot Study, 1984). The judiciary was right to oppose the Crime (Sentences) Act 1997. But it should have been opposed on the right grounds, and without distracting attention away from the need to put the judicial house in order too.

NON-CUSTODIAL SENTENCING

Thus far the focus has been on custodial sentencing, chiefly in the Crown Court. But the figures for 1995 show that, combining the numbers in magistrates' courts and the Crown Court, over 80 per cent of indictable offenders were dealt with by non-custodial sentences.

The scheme of the Criminal Justice Act 1991 is that the different forms of sentence should be regarded as a kind of pyramid, with courts requiring good reasons to move up from one stage to the next. At the lowest level come absolute and conditional discharges. At the next level come fines. Then a court may take the step up to a community sentence only if it is satisfied that the offence is serious enough to warrant this. And the step from community sentence to custody should be taken, as we saw above, only if the court is of the opinion that the offence is so serious that only a custodial sentence can be justified. In addition to this general framework, there are the Magistrates' Association's *Sentencing Guidelines*, revised in 1997, which offer guidance to magistrates on sentencing for certain frequent offences. These guidelines have no legal standing, but they represent an effort by the magistracy to foster consistency by developing guidance and patterns of reasoning. Importantly, they deal with common offences such as theft, deception, handling, and burglary— the very offences on which the Court of Appeal has failed to give guidance.

Discharges

The least order a court can make on conviction is an absolute discharge.[9] Such orders are usually reserved for cases of very low culpability, or where the offender is ill, or where the court thinks the prosecution should not have been

[9] Powers of Criminal Courts Act 1973, sections 7 and 13, substituted by Criminal Justice Act 1991, Schedule 1.

Table 30.1 Males aged 21 and over sentenced for indictable offences: percentage use of different sentences

	1975	1980	1985	1990	1995
Discharge	9	7	9	13	15
Fine	55	52	43	43	34
Probation	6	5	7	7	11
Community Service	1	4	7	7	11
Combination Order	–	–	–	–	3
Suspended Imprisonment	13	12	12	10	1
Immediate Imprisonment	16	17	19	17	24
Total numbers sentenced	170,000	200,300	211,700	188,400	178,400

Table 30.2 Females aged 21 and over sentenced for indictable offences: percentage use of different sentences

	1975	1980	1985	1990	1995
Discharge	21	18	23	32	30
Fine	58	53	41	32	26
Probation	13	15	18	18	20
Community Service	0	2	3	4	7
Combination Order	–	–	–	–	3
Suspended Imprisonment	5	7	8	8	2
Immediate Imprisonment	3	4	7	6	10
Total numbers sentenced	39,600	43,300	38,400	30,500	26,800

brought (Wasik, 1985*a*). A conviction followed by a discharge does not rank as a conviction for any other purposes. The same applies to a conditional discharge: however, the condition is that the offender is not convicted of another offence within a specified period (up to three years), and if there is such a conviction, the offender is liable also to be re-sentenced for the original crime. Conditional discharges are quite widely used, amounting to some 15 per cent of adult male indictable offenders in 1995 and 30 per cent of adult female indictable offenders. Their use has increased considerably in the last twenty years, as the above tables demonstrate, possibly because of the decline in fining. Courts also have various powers to 'bind over' offenders, an order much used in some courts and little used in others.

Fines

Although the fine remains the most-used sentence, even for indictable offences, it has declined significantly in proportionate use in recent years—from 55 per cent in 1975 to 34 per cent in 1995 for adult males, and from 58 per cent to

26 per cent for adult females. This spectacular decline may be associated with the growth of unemployment in the 1980s, with courts being reluctant to fine unemployed offenders or feeling it inappropriate to fine them small amounts. The 'displacement' appears to have been partly to more demanding sentences, such as community sentences, and partly to discharges.

In an attempt to revive the use of the fine and to increase its fairness, the 1991 Act introduced 'unit fines' into magistrates' courts. In essence the court had to calculate the fine by assessing the seriousness of the offence on a scale from one to fifty units and then, in a separate enquiry, determine the offender's 'weekly disposable income' so as to decide how much the offender should pay per unit. Prior to the introduction of the Act there had been experiments in four courts, suggesting that magistrates welcomed the new approach, that fines were perceived as fairer, and that fewer offenders were sent to prison in default of payment (Moxon *et al.*, 1991). However, the statutory scheme introduced far higher maximum amounts per unit than the experiments. The higher fines then attracted the attention of the mass media, which insisted on relating the fines to the offence rather than to the varying means of offenders. Despite this gross misunderstanding of the purpose of unit fines—to equalize the impact of fines on people of different means—the government responded to the ensuing clamour by abolishing the entire system of unit fines in the Criminal Justice Act 1993, returning to the broad principle that courts should take account of the financial circumstances of each offender. Despite the smooth operation of unit fines in other European countries, it was apparently decided not to amend the statutory scheme so as to bring it closer to the successful experiments. The courts are now relatively unfettered by legal requirements in calculating the amounts of fines. The impact of the legislative change was immediate: in the last quarter of 1992 the average fine for unemployed offenders in magistrates courts was £66, whereas by the last quarter of 1993 it had risen to £78; at the end of 1992 the average fine for employed offenders was £233, whereas by the end of 1993 it had declined to £158 (Home Office, 1994).

A survey in 1996 found that whilst 83 per cent of areas use the Magistrates' Association guidelines, or a modified version of them, some 17 per cent of areas use a form of unit fine. The research also found that courts using unit fines were more consistent and that they made clearer distinctions in fine levels according to the incomes of offenders, whereas other courts often made little distinction between those on low and medium incomes (Charman *et al.*, 1996). These findings confirm the prediction that, in the absence of unit fines, a general statutory exhortation to take account of the means of offenders has insufficient effect.

Since 1990 the number of offenders committed to prison in default of payment of fines has begun to rise again, after a fall in the 1980s, and in 1994 the figure reached almost 24,000. In principle it is wrong that someone whose offence was adjudged only serious enough for a fine should then be sent to prison, a result avoided by several other European systems. It is therefore encouraging to see that the Crime (Sentences) Act 1997 contains provisions which will make available to courts two alternatives to the use of custody for fine defaulters—short community service orders and curfew orders (with the further alternative of an attendance centre order if the offender is under 25). However, the 1997 Act stopped short of legislating to require courts to give reasons for not trying certain default measures before others, thereby allowing considerable local variations to persist.

Compensation Orders

Although there were miscellaneous powers beforehand, the present compensation order was introduced in 1972. In 1982 courts were allowed to use it as the sole order in a case, and courts were required to give priority to a compensation order over a fine if the offender has limited means. The 1988 Criminal Justice Act requires a court to consider making a compensation order in every case involving death, injury, loss, or damage, or to give reasons if it decides not to make an order. This was effective in increasing the frequency of orders. In 1995 compensation orders were most frequently made in magistrates' courts in cases of violence (57 per cent), criminal damage (55 per cent), and fraud and forgery (36 per cent). In the Crown Court the proportionate use of compensation orders was lower, presumably because of the much higher imprisonment rate. Again, the three leading types of offence were violence (20 per cent), criminal damage (16 per cent), and fraud and forgery (14 per cent).

The contribution of compensation orders to greater justice for victims is important, but possibly more at a symbolic level than in terms of actual recompense for large numbers of victims (see further Zedner, this volume). To some extent this is because compensatory principles inevitably come into conflict with other sentencing principles: for example, although compensation orders have priority over fines, the amount of a compensation order must still be reduced so as to be within the means of the offender. To some extent it is simply that few victims have the opportunity of receiving money from this source, because the offender must be detected, prosecuted, convicted, and in funds before a court can make a compensation order. The rise in police cautioning in recent years may have contributed to an overall decline in the total number of compensation orders made (even though they are made in a higher proportion of cases coming before the courts): in 1983 some 128,000 orders were made, but by 1993 the number had fallen to 96,000. Some police forces operate 'caution plus' schemes which make compensation a condition of cautioning, but it is questionable if this approach is the best for victims.

Community Sentences

In the 1980s and before, sentences such as probation and community service were officially described as alternatives to custody. This terminology did not assist in persuading courts to use them instead of custody, largely because they were not believed to be true alternatives. The 1990 White Paper proposed that the terminology be replaced by references to punishment in the community, emphasizing its demanding nature and the restrictions on liberty involved. The 1991 Act gave effect to this scheme by using the term 'community sentence'. The four forms of community order for adult offenders are probation, community service, combination orders, and curfew orders. A court should not impose any such order unless satisfied that the offence is serious enough to warrant it: this is intended to convey the greater severity of community sentences as compared with discharges and fines. If the court decides that the case is serious enough, it should ensure that the community order or orders are (a) the most suitable for the offender, and (b) impose restrictions on liberty which are commensurate with the seriousness of the offence: Criminal Justice Act 1991, section 6. This scheme is designed to bring the proportionality principle into non-custodial sentencing, whilst allowing some room for choices (e.g. between probation and community service) which reflect the perceived needs of the offender.[10] In most such cases a 'pre-sentence report' (see above) will have been prepared by the probation service to 'assist' the court.

The theory and practice of community sentences are discussed by Mair, this volume, and so only a brief outline of the legal framework will be given here. A probation order may be for between six months and three years. The basic order requires supervision by a probation officer, and the obligations are set out in National Standards. Five additional requirements are available to courts: residence, specified activities, attendance at a probation centre, mental treatment, or treatment for drug or alcohol dependency. Between 1990 and 1995 the use of probation orders increased from 8 to 11 per cent for adult males, and from 18 to 20 per cent for adult females. Some three-quarters of orders are completely satisfactorily.

A community service order may be for between forty and 240 hours, requiring the performance of unpaid work during leisure hours. Again, the National Standards set out various obligations. Between 1990 and 1995 the use of community service orders increased from 7 to 11 per cent for adult males, and from 4 to 7 per cent for adult females. Some three-quarters of orders are completed satisfactorily.

Combination orders are introduced by the 1991 Act. They may consist of forty to 100 hours' community service combined with one to three years of probation, with or without additional requirements. The 1990 White Paper envisaged that they would be used for persistent non-serious property offenders, in cases where custody might otherwise be considered. In the event, most combination orders have been imposed by magistrates' courts (some 11,600 in 1995, compared with 2,900 in the Crown Court).

A curfew order is intended to restrict an offender's movements for between two and twelve hours per day for up to six months. The 1991 Act provides for a curfew order to be combined with electronic monitoring in areas where the

---

[10] The proposals by Wasik and von Hirsch (1988) were influential; for a different approach, see Morris and Tonry (1990).

mechanism is available. An experiment with electronic monitoring in 1990 was not a conspicuous success (Mair and Nee, 1990) and yet, despite the formidable objections of principle to 'tagging' (von Hirsch, 1993: chapter 9), the government decided in 1995 to press ahead with the experimental implementation of curfew orders with electronic monitoring in three parts of the country. It seems that courts are still fairly reluctant to use the measure, but the former government's ideological commitment to electronic monitoring gave rise in November 1996 to a further proposal for their use, this time to deal with troublesome young offenders aged 10 and upwards.

In relation to young offenders, there are two more forms of community sentence that are available: the supervision order, which may be regarded as a 'junior' alternative to the probation order for less mature youngsters; and the attendance centre order, which is available for offenders aged 14 to 20. For further discussion, see Newburn, this volume.

Suspended Sentences

A sentence of imprisonment of two years or less may be suspended for a period of up to two years. If the offender is convicted of another offence committed during the operational period, the court must activate the suspended sentence in addition to the sentence for the new crime, unless it is 'unjust to do so'. Suspended sentences did not succeed in lowering the prison population following their introduction in 1967. Research showed that courts sometimes defied the law by imposing suspended sentences when immediate imprisonment would not be justifiable, and by imposing longer sentences when suspending (Bottoms, 1981; Moxon, 1988: 34–8). Although the suspended sentence is meant to be the most severe of non-custodial measures, it seems that many courts and offenders regard it as a 'let-off'. Suspended sentences were abolished for offenders under 21 in 1982, and abolition has clearly been contemplated for adults. The 1991 Act retains them in restricted form: a court may impose a suspended sentence only if immediate custody is justified and if there are 'exceptional circumstances' in favour of suspension. The Court of Appeal has confirmed that the term 'exceptional' must be interpreted restrictively, although it has wavered occasionally (Campbell, 1995), and the figures show that suspended sentences are now passed much less frequently: in the Crown Court, they declined from 10 per cent of adult male indictable sentences in 1990 to only 1 per cent in 1995, and from 8 to 2 per cent for adult female offenders. If a court does suspend, it must consider adding a fine or compensation order, to give the sentence an immediate sting: Criminal Justice Act 1991, section 5.

Review of Policy and Practice

To what extent has the new concept of 'punishment in the community', reinforced by the framework in the 1991 Act, succeeded in expanding the numbers dealt with non-custodially and reducing the numbers sentenced to custody? If one compares the figures for 1990 and 1995, the proportionate use of community sentences has increased in magistrates' courts from 20 to 28 per cent, and in the Crown Court from 25 to 30 per cent. However, in the same period the proportionate use of immediate custody has increased in magistrates' courts from 4.4 to 8.8 per cent, and in the Crown Court from 43 to 56 per cent. It seems to follow that, if the rise in community sentences has not been at the expense of custodial sentences, it must have been at the expense of lesser measures. Thus one finds that fines in magistrates' courts have declined from 50 to 37 per cent in this period, and fines in the Crown Court from 7 to 3 per cent. As Tables 30.1 and 30.2 show, these trends can also be discerned over a twenty-year period. The emasculation of the suspended sentence by the 1991 Act will also have contributed to the recent rise in both custody and community sentences, although it is not clear in what proportions.

As has happened on many occasions in the past, when new non-custodial measures have been introduced in the hope that some offenders will be diverted from custody, the result appears to have been a form of net-widening, with the new non-custodial measures being applied to offenders who would previously have received a lesser form of sentence. To some extent this demonstrates some of the difficulties of ensuring that sentencing practice follows the intended penal policy. In relation to community sentences and other non-custodial measures, the Court of Appeal makes hardly any contribution in terms of guidance, and so the legislation stands virtually alone.

However, there may be some force in an alternative explanation. In the last decade there has been a significant rise in the proportionate use of police cautions for indictable offences, both for adult males (from 7 per cent in 1985 to 26 per cent in 1995) and for adult females (from 19 to 44 per cent). This is one reason why the total numbers sentenced for indictable offences has declined in recent years, as Tables 30.1 and 30.2 show. The higher cautioning rate should mean that many less serious offenders who would have been sentenced in the 1980s do not now come to court at all. The ones that do come to court are the most serious, and it would hardly be surprising if a higher proportion of severe sentences (imprisonment, community sentences) resulted. As Tables 30.1 and 30.2 demonstrate, this analysis is not a complete fit, since the rise in the proportionate use of discharges since 1985 goes against it (if minor offenders are being cautioned, there ought to be fewer discharges). But, in other respects, this argument may have some explanatory force, in addition to net-widening and to the rising tide of punitiveness in recent years.

Since these changes have occurred at a time when the community sentences were made tougher and more demanding, some of Stanley Cohen's warnings have become more rather than less pertinent. His 1979 warnings of increased social control through net-widening, blurring, and the thinning of the mesh were questioned by Bottoms (1983), who showed that it was the fine rather than surveillance-based measures which increased in the 1970s. But the 1980s saw the decline of the fine and the rise of custody, community service, and probation. Cohen's thesis was thus rekindled (Cohen, 1985), and the 1991 Act's reliance on punishment in the community—even to the extent of legislating for electronic surveillance—establishes its continued relevance. On one view this is the inevitable price for any element of progress in a society whose political system is much affected by punitive lobbies: the greater use of non-custodial sanctions can only be bought by making them tougher, and also perhaps by continuing to imprison certain groups of offenders for extremely long periods.

SENTENCING REFORM

Judicial Independence

For many years it has been argued that the fundamental constitutional principle of judicial independence makes it wrong for Parliament to 'interfere' with the sentencing discretion of the judiciary. However, the deceptive ambiguity of this argument was rightly denounced in the 1990 White Paper (Home Office, 1990a: para. 2.1; see further Munro, 1992; Ashworth, 1995: chapter 2): there is a difference between an impartial judiciary, which is fundamental, and a prohibition of legislation on sentencing, which is unfounded. However, the latter argument has been revived by some judges in their criticisms of the mandatory and minimum sentences in the Crime (Sentences) Act 1997. Lord Taylor did not take this approach in his widely-publicized lecture criticizing the proposed mandatory minimum sentences (Taylor, 1996): he recognized that there was no constitutional objection to the government's proposals, and instead sought to attack them as unwise and unworkable.

The Training of Sentencers

The Judicial Studies Board organizes seminars for newly appointed judges and refresher courses for other judges. The seminars tend to involve lectures on recent developments in legislation and in Court of Appeal decisions, and group discussions of particular issues (Judicial Studies Board, 1995). The Board itself includes judges, civil servants, magistrates, and academics. The Board exercises a general superintendence over the training of magistrates through its Magisterial Committee, but it remains the case that most training of magistrates is undertaken locally. This practice may tend to confirm local bench traditions and the preferences of the local liaison judge and of the justices' clerk, who will usually lead the training.

Seminars and training days often succeed in bringing to light the current concerns of sentencers. Whether they conduce to consistency in sentencing depends partly on the amount of legislative and judicial guidance that is available—which, for many everyday sentencing decisions, is not great—and partly on the attitudes to sentencing which they foster.[11]

Structuring Discretion

While there are powerful objections to mandatory and mandatory minimum sentences, on the ground that they curtail sentencing discretion and produce unfairness by requiring courts to treat different cases as if they were alike, there is a strong case for structuring the discretion of the courts in order to achieve certain goals. The 1991 Act attempted to do this by means of a framework of legislative restrictions. The government expressed the hope that the Court of Appeal would give further guidance to structure practical sentencing (Home Office, 1990*a*: para. 2.17), but it has failed to do so in two major spheres— 'seriousness' questions at the custody threshold, and sentencing for run-of-the-mill offences against the Theft Acts. The Magistrates' Association has tried to remedy the deficiency by issuing guidelines for the magistrates' courts, but, as we have seen, these have no legal force and are not followed in some areas. To what extent local courts adopt these guidelines depends largely on the key actors mentioned above, local liaison judges, and justices' clerks. Training cannot be expected to produce the consistency of approach unless there is sufficient guidance on practical sentencing issues which has been authoritatively agreed. The prospects of providing that in the present system, with so much local autonomy, seem slender.

The large tracts of everyday Crown Court sentencing which are hardly touched by Court of Appeal guidance remain problematic. Unstructured discretion allows in the personal preferences of the judge, and if the concept of the 'rule of law' has any stable meaning, it must exclude such preferences. While the English system does now have a leading principle—proportionality or 'desert'—the key concept of seriousness will remain open to diverse interpretations unless the Court of Appeal addresses itself to the formulation of guidance which covers the bulk of sentencing decisions, i.e. crimes such as theft, deception, burglary, and handling stolen goods.

International Patterns in Sentencing Reform

Recent years have seen major sentencing reforms in several countries, and reform proposals in many others (for discussion, see Clarkson and Morgan, 1995). Most attention has been focused on the various 'guideline systems' in the United States. Minnesota, Oregon, and other states have introduced guidelines which indicate sentence ranges according to the type of offence and the criminal history of the offender, and which attempt to shape sentencing practice in certain ways. Usually there is a permanent Sentencing Commission to monitor practice, and often there is appellate review to determine the

---

[11] Cf. Bond and Lemon (1981).

propriety of judicial departures from the guidelines (cf. von Hirsch, 1995 with Frase, 1995; Tonry, 1996). Since 1987 there have been guidelines for federal sentencing, issued by the US Sentencing Commission, which also monitors practice. These guidelines are inherently more complex, and also have to incorporate several mandatory minimum sentences introduced by Congress. Critics point to the absence of clear rationales, the difficulties of applying them, their subservience to previous practice and their lack of concern for rising prison populations (Doob, 1995; Tonry, 1996). However, the creation and extension of mandatory minimum penalties for certain crimes seems to be a greater political concern than the shortcomings of the federal sentencing guidelines (Windlesham, 1996: Part III).

Closer to the approach taken in the English reforms of 1991 are the systems introduced in Finland in 1976 and in Sweden in 1989. The Swedish statute states the aims and principles of sentencing, requiring the court to assess the 'penal value' (i.e. seriousness) of the offence and giving guidance on aggravating and mitigating factors. It leaves the courts to interpret and apply the rules to particular cases, and provides for appellate review (Jareborg, 1995).

In Australia there have been some sentencing reforms in New South Wales, with various strategies to alter the way in which sentences are calculated, and also the introduction of a computerized sentencing information system for use by judges. In Victoria the Sentencing Act 1991 introduced a fairly comprehensive rationalization of sentencing, including a 'truth in sentencing' provision which required judges to adjust their sentences downwards to ensure that the abolition of remission did not result in longer effective sentences. Two years and a change of government later, however, Victoria also experienced 'law and order' legislation which raised sentences for serious sexual and violent offenders (Freiberg, 1995).

Further Reform in England and Wales

The Criminal Justice Act 1991 represented a technical advance in certain ways (compare Wasik, 1993, with Thomas, 1995). It introduced a primary rationale for English sentencing (desert), and clarified the extent to which other 'aims' such as public protection, rehabilitation, and deterrence should play a part. It also introduced a framework of legislative restrictions on the use of custodial and community sentences. The Act furthered 'truth in sentencing' by reforming parole and remission so as to ensure that all parts of a custodial sentence count for something.

In two of its aims, greater consistency in sentencing and wider use of community sentences in place of short custodial sentences, it has not been a success. Four reasons for this seem to emerge clearly. First, the Act was unwelcome to influential sections (possibly a majority) of the judiciary. Many judges were fundamentally unhappy about legislative attempts to impose any kind of framework on sentencing, and believe that maximum discretion is the best way forward. Secondly, they were strengthened in this belief by obscure and inept drafting of the statute, as a result of which clear policies were sometimes turned into mysteries. Thirdly, the Act left considerable discretion to the courts within the legislative framework, but the government's expressed hope that the Court of Appeal would 'fill in the gaps' with detailed guidance was not fulfilled. The Lord Chief Justice began, in *Cunningham* ((1993) 15 Cr. App. R (S) 444), by misinterpreting the key phrase 'commensurate with the seriousness of the offence'; and he quickly followed this by applying a manifestly vacuous test, 'the opinion of right-thinking people', to the key provision on the custody threshold in *Cox* ((1993) 15 Cr. App. R (S) 458). And fourthly, within months of the implementation of the 1991 Act, the mass media and politicians became in the grip of a moral panic about law and order, which was then turned into government policy when Michael Howard became Home Secretary in 1993. The 1991 Act could not be expected to withstand that, and similar events in Victoria and other jurisdictions around the same time bear out the political spirit of the 1990s, termed 'populist punitiveness' and compellingly analysed by Bottoms (1995).

However, aside from the political battle over mandatory and minimum sentences, there remain wider and persistent questions about the structuring of sentencing. How can more and better guidance on the sentencing of ordinary crimes be produced and promulgated? Is the Court of Appeal the most suitable body for this task? Senior judges may have considerable experience of the most serious offences, but do they know enough about the 'ordinary' crimes which constitute the bulk of Crown Court and magistrates' court sentencing? Circuit judges do now sit in the Court of Appeal from time to time, but there is no evidence that they have contributed significantly to the Court's policy-making function. Even if the judges in the Court of Appeal have the knowledge, do they have a sufficiently wide perspective for the policy-making function which this undoubtedly is—determining the relative severity of community orders, deciding whether particular orders are 'commensurate' with the seriousness of the offence, guiding others on the custody threshold? In the unlikely event that this breadth of experience can be claimed, do they have the time and resources to fashion sufficient guidance for all lower courts, whilst also operating as an appellate court? Questions of this kind have prompted calls for the creation of a sentencing council, containing sentencers of all levels and other criminal justice professionals, to formulate detailed and practical guidance (Ashworth, 1983; Justice, 1990). Such a council would not follow the American model of devising a guideline system, but would rather build on the best of English traditions in forms of guidance (e.g. narrative guideline judgments). The 1990 White Paper re-affirmed faith in the Court of Appeal and Judicial Studies Board to 'contribute to the development of coherent sentencing practice' (Home Office, 1990a: para. 2.20). The analysis above suggests that this faith was misplaced, and so the arguments for a sentencing council should be reconsidered. Whether the Criminal Justice Consultative Committee, with its wide range of criminal justice professionals, could provide the nucleus of a sentencing council should be examined.

The issue of consistency in sentencing ranges wide, as the recommendations of the Council of Europe (1993) make clear. Whatever the mechanism chosen in a particular country, there are various common themes—clarity of rationales for sentencing, penalty structures, the use of previous convictions, giving reasons, and sentencing studies, information, and research—which require a more principled approach, as the Council of Europe report points out. Thus, in this country, the general principles of sentencing relating to previous convictions and multiple offenders need to be reconsidered and then articulated further: there has been a succession of cryptic and unsatisfactory legislative provisions, none of which has set out the full range of principles that ought to be applied, which are scattered through Court of Appeal decisions. Other aggravating and mitigating factors would benefit from clear restatements, whether in legislation or in some other form. Moreover, as argued in the earlier parts of this chapter, sentencing should not be regarded as an isolated and all-important function: it is substantially conditioned by decisions taken earlier in the criminal process, where clear and well-considered policies should also be devised and enforced, as was confirmed by the research of Hood (1992) on race and sentencing (see Smith, this volume). A clear legislative statement on equality before the law, instead of the oblique reference in section 95 of the Criminal Justice Act 1991, might have both symbolic and instrumental value. There is also, as the Council of Europe emphasized, a need for further research into the impact of rules and principles upon practical sentencing, for too often in criminological research it has been found that practices do not conform to the declared policies. A simple comparison of the amount and findings of research into the police (see Reiner, chapter 28, this volume) with those of research into sentencers shows the poverty of information on how the system actually works.

Selected Further Reading

Among the considerable literature on sentencing and related issues, a dozen books might be selected for further reading. An excellent overview of the sociology of punishment may be found in David Garland, *Punishment in Modern Society* (Oxford: Oxford University Press, 1990). Wider readings on rationales for sentencing may be found in A. von Hirsch and A. Ashworth (eds.), *Principled Sentencing* (Boston, Mass.: Northeastern University Press, 1992) and in R. A. Duff and D. Garland (eds.), *A Reader on Punishment* (Oxford: Oxford University Press, 1994). Two influential recent monographs on sentencing theory are Nicola Lacey's *State Punishment* (London: Routledge, 1988) and Andrew von Hirsch's *Censure and Sanctions* (Oxford: Oxford University Press, 1993).

Three current texts can be recommended for further details on sentencing law and practice: Martin Wasik, *Emmins on Sentencing* (2nd edn., London: Blackstone Press, 1993); Andrew Ashworth, *Sentencing and Criminal Justice* (2nd edn., London: Butterworths, 1995); and Nigel Walker and Nicola

Padfield, *Sentencing: Theory, Law and Practice* (2nd edn., London: Butterworths, 1996).

Wider discussions of sentencing, from both empirical and normative points of view, may be found in D. Pennington and S. Lloyd-Bostock (eds.), *The Psychology of Sentencing* (Oxford: Oxford Centre for Socio-Legal Studies, 1987). Large-scale empirical studies are reported in David Moxon, *Sentencing Practice in the Crown Court* (Home Office Research Study No. 103, London: HMSO, 1988) and by Roger Hood, *Race and Sentencing* (Oxford: Oxford University Press, 1992). Stimulating discussions of sentencing reform in national and international contexts may be found in K. Pease and M. Wasik (eds.), *Sentencing Reform: Guidance or Guidelines?* (Manchester: Manchester University Press, 1987) and in C. Clarkson and R. Morgan (eds.), *The Politics of Sentencing Reform* (Oxford: Oxford University Press, 1995).

REFERENCES

ADVISORY COUNCIL ON THE PENAL SYSTEM (1978), *Sentences of Imprisonment: a Review of Maximum Penalties.* London: HMSO.

ASHWORTH, A. (1983), *Sentencing and Penal Policy.* London: Weidenfeld and Nicolson.

—— (1993), 'Victim Impact Statements and Sentencing', *Criminal Law Review*, 498–509.

—— (1995), *Sentencing and Criminal Justice.* 2nd edn. London: Butterworths.

—— and HOUGH, M. (1996), 'Sentencing and the Climate of Opinion', *Criminal Law Review*, 776–87.

—— and VON HIRSCH, A. (1997), 'Recognizing Elephants: the Problem of the Custody Threshold', *Criminal Law Review*, 187.

BALDWIN, J. (1985), *Pre-Trial Justice in Magistrates' Courts.* Oxford: Oxford University Press.

BENTHAM, J. (1948), *Principles of Morals and Legislation.* Oxford: Blackwell.

BEYLEVELD, D. (1979), 'Deterrence Research as a Basis for Deterrence Policies', *Howard Journal*, 18: 135–49.

—— (1980). *A Bibliography of General Deterrence.* New York: Saxon House.

BLUMSTEIN, A., COHEN, J., ROTH, J., and VISHER, C. (1986), *Criminal Careers and Career Criminals.* Washington, DC: National Academy Press.

BOND, R. A., and LEMON, N. (1979). 'Changes in Magistrates' Attitudes during the First Year on the Bench', in D. Farrington, K. Hawkins, and S. Lloyd-Bostock, eds.,

Psychology, Law and Legal Processes. London: Macmillan.

BOTTOMS, A. E. (1981). 'The Suspended Sentence in England, 1967–78', *British Journal of Criminology*, 21: 1–26.

—— (1983), 'Neglected Features of Contemporary Penal Systems', in D. Garland and P. Young, eds., *The Power to Punish*, 166–202. London: Heinemann.

—— (1995), 'The Philosophy and Politics of Punishment and Sentencing', in C. Clarkson and R. Morgan eds., *The Politics of Sentencing Reform.* Oxford: Oxford University Press.

—— and BROWNSWORD, R. (1982), 'The Dangerousness Debate after the Floud Report', *British Journal of Criminology*, 22: 229.

—— and PRESTON, R. H., eds. (1980), *The Coming Penal Crisis.* Edinburgh: Scottish Academic Press.

BRAITHWAITE, J. (1989), *Crime, Shame and Reintegration.* Cambridge: Cambridge University Press.

—— and PETTIT, P. (1990), *Not Just Deserts.* Oxford: Oxford University Press.

BRODY, S. R. (1975), *The Effectiveness of Sentencing*, Home Office Research Study no. 35. London: HMSO.

—— and TARLING, R. (1981), *Taking Offenders out of Circulation*, Home Office Research Study no. 64. London: HMSO.

CAMPBELL, J. Q. (1995), 'A Sentencer's Lament on the Imminent Death of the Suspended Sentence', *Criminal Law Review*, 293–5.

CARLISLE, LORD (1988), *The Parole System in England and Wales*, Report of the Review Committee. London: HMSO.

CLARKSON, C., and MORGAN, R., eds., (1995), *The Politics of Sentencing Reform*. Oxford: Oxford University Press.

COHEN, S. (1979), 'The Punitive City', *Contemporary Crises*, 3: 339–63.

—— (1985), *Visions of Social Control*. New York: Plenum.

COOKE, R. K. (1987), 'The Practical Problems of the Sentencer', in D. Pennington and S. Lloyd-Bostock, eds., *The Psychology of Sentencing*. Oxford: Centre for Socio-Legal Studies.

COUNCIL OF EUROPE (1993), *Consistency in Sentencing*, Recommendation No. R(92) 17. Strasbourg: Council of Europe Press.

CROWN PROSECUTION SERVICE (1994), *Code for Crown Prosecutors*. 3rd edn. London: Crown Prosecution Service.

DARBYSHIRE, P. (1984), *The Magistrates' Clerk*. Chichester: Barry Rose.

DOOB, A. (1995), 'The United States Sentencing Commission Guidelines: If You Don't Know Where You are Going, You Might not Get There', in C. Clarkson and R. Morgan, eds., *The Politics of Sentencing Reform*. Oxford: Oxford University Press.

DOWNES, D. (1988), *Contrasts in Tolerance.* Oxford: Oxford University Press.

DUFF, R. A. (1986), *Trials and Punishments*. Cambridge: Cambridge University Press.

DUFF, A., and GARLAND, D., eds., (1994), *A Reader on Punishment*. Oxford: Oxford University Press.

FARRINGTON, D., and MORRIS, A. (1983), 'Sex, Sentencing and Reconvictions', *British Journal of Criminology*, 23: 229–48.

FLOUD, J., and YOUNG, W. (1981), *Dangerousness and Criminal Justice*. London: Heinemann.

FRASE, R. (1995), 'Sentencing Guidelines in Minnesota and other American States: a Progress Report', in C. Clarkson and R. Morgan, eds., *The Politics of Sentencing Reform*. Oxford: Oxford University Press.

FREIBERG, A. (1995), 'Sentencing Reform in Victoria: A Case-Study', in C. Clarkson and R. Morgan, eds., *The Politics of Sentencing Reform*. Oxford: Oxford University Press.

GALLIGAN, D. (1986), *Discretionary Powers*. Oxford: Oxford University Press.

GARLAND, D. (1990), *Punishment and Modern Society*. Oxford: Oxford University Press.

GRAHAM, D. (1990), 'Decarceration in the Federal Republic of Germany', *British Journal of Criminology*, 30: 150–70

HARDING, R. (1990), 'Rational Choice Gun Use in Armed Robbery', *Criminal Law Forum*, 1: 427.

HART, H. L. A. (1968), *Punishment and Responsibility*. Oxford: Oxford University Press.

HAWKINS, K., ed. (1992), *Discretion*. Oxford: Oxford University Press.

—— and THOMAS, J., eds. (1984), *Enforcing Regulation*. Boston: Kluwer-Nijhoff.

HEDDERMAN, C., and MOXON, D. (1992), *Magistrates' Court or Crown Court? Mode of Trial Decisions and Sentencing*, Home Office Research Study No. 125. London: HMSO.

HOME OFFICE (1990), *Crime, Justice and Protecting the Public*. London: HMSO.

—— (1994), *Monitoring of the Criminal Justice Acts 1991–1993—Results from a Special Data Collection Exercise*, Statistical Bulletin 20/94. London: Home Office.

—— (1995a), *Digest 3: Information on the Criminal Justice System in England and Wales*. London: Home Office.

—— (1995b), *National Standards for the Probation Service*, 2nd edn. London: Home Office.

—— (1996), *Protecting the Public*. London: HMSO.

HOOD, R. (1962), *Sentencing in Magistrates' Courts*. London: Tavistock.

—— (1972), *Sentencing the Motoring Offender*. London: Heinemann.

—— (1992), *Race and Sentencing*. Oxford: Oxford University Press.

—— and SHUTE, S. (1996), 'Protecting the Public: Automatic Life Sentences, Parole and High Risk Offenders', *Criminal Law Review*, 788–800.

HOUGH, M. (1996), 'People Talking about Punishment', *Howard Journal of Criminal Justice*, 191.

HUDSON, B. (1987), *Justice through Punishment: a Critique of the Justice Model of Corrections*. London: Macmillan.

HUTTER, B. (1988), *The Reasonable Arm of the Law*. Oxford: Oxford University Press.

JAREBORG, N. (1995), 'The Swedish Sentencing Reform', in C. Clarkson and R. Morgan, eds., *The Politics of Sentencing Reform*. Oxford: Oxford University Press.

JUDICIAL STUDIES BOARD (1995), *Report, 1992–95*. London: HMSO.

JUSTICE (1990), *Sentencing: the Way Forward*. London: Justice.

LACEY, N. (1988), *State Punishment*. London: Routledge.

McCONVILLE, M., SANDERS, A., and LENG, R. (1991), *The Case for the Prosecution*. London: Routledge.

MAGISTRATES' ASSOCIATION (1997), *Sentencing Guidelines*. London: the Magistrates' Association.

MAIR, G., and NEE, C. (1990), *Electronic Monitoring: the Trials and their Results*, Home Office Research Study no. 120. London: HMSO.

MARTINSON, R., LIPTON, D., and WILKS, J. (1974), 'What Works? Questions and Answers about Prison Reform', *Public Interest*, 35: 22–54

MAYHEW, P., MAUNG, N. A., and MIRRLEES-BLACK, C. (1993), *The 1992 British Crime Survey*, Home Office Research Study no. 132. London: HMSO.

McGUIRE, J., ed. (1995), *What Works?* London: Sage.

MONAHAN, J. (1996), *Mental Illness and Violent Crime*. Washington, DC: National Institute of Justice.

MORRIS, A., MAXWELL, G. M., and ROBERTSON, G. P. (1993), 'Giving Victims a Voice: a New Zealand Experiment', *Howard Journal of Criminal Justice*, 32: 304.

MOXON, D. (1988), *Sentencing Practice in the Crown Court*, Home Office Research Study no. 103. London: HMSO.

—— SUTTON, M., and HEDDERMAN, C. (1991), *Unit Fines: Experiments in Four Courts*. London: Home Office.

MUNRO, C. (1992), 'Judicial Independence and Judicial Functions', in C. Munro and M. Wasik, eds., *Sentencing, Judicial Discretion and Judicial Training*. London: Sweet & Maxwell.

NATIONAL ACADEMY OF SCIENCES (1978), *Deterrence and Incapacitation: Estimating the Effects of Criminal Sanctions on Crime Rates*. Washington, DC: National Academy of Sciences.

OXFORD PILOT STUDY (1984), *Sentencing in the Crown Court*, by A. Ashworth, E. Genders, G. Mansfield, J. Peay, and E. Player. Oxford: Centre for Criminological Research.

PENNINGTON, D., and LLOYD-BOSTOCK, S., eds. (1987), *The Psychology of Sentencing*. Oxford: Centre for Socio-Legal Studies.

PETTIT, P., and BRAITHWAITE, J. (1993), 'Not Just Deserts, Even In Sentencing', *Current Issues in Criminal Justice*, 4: 225–39.

POSNER, R. (1985), 'An Economic Theory of the Criminal Law', *Columbia Law Review*, 85: 1193–231.

RADZINOWICZ, SIR LEON, and HOOD, R. (1978), 'A Dangerous Direction for Sentencing Reform', *Criminal Law Review*, 713–24.

—— and —— (1986), *The Emergence of Penal Policy in Victorian and Edwardian England*. London: Stevens.

RANYARD, R., HEBENTON, B., and PEASE, K. (1994), 'An Analysis of a Guideline Case as applied to the Offence of Rape', *Howard Journal of Criminal Justice*, 33: 203.

RILEY, D. (1985), 'Drinking Drivers: The Limits to Deterrence', *Howard Journal of Criminal Justice*, 24: 241–56.

—— and VENNARD, J. (1988), *Triable-Either-Way Cases: Crown Court or Magistrates' Court*, Home Office Research Study no. 98. London: HMSO.

ROYAL COMMISSION ON CRIMINAL JUSTICE (1993), *Report* (chair: Lord Runciman). London: HMSO.

SANDERS, A. (1985), 'Class Bias in Prosecutions', *Howard Journal*, 24: 176–99.

SHAPLAND, J. (1981), *Between Conviction and Sentence*. London: Routledge.

—— (1987), 'Who Controls Sentencing? Influences on the Sentencer', in D. Pennington and S. Lloyd-Bostock, *The Psychology of Sentencing*. Oxford: Centre for Socio-Legal Studies

SHUTE, S. (1994), 'Prosecution Appeals against Sentence: The First Five Years', *Modern Law Review*, 57: 745.

TARLING, R. (1979), *Sentencing Practice in Magistrates' Courts*, Home Office Research Study no. 56. London: HMSO.

TAYLOR, LORD (1996), 'Continuity and Change in the Criminal Law', *King's College Law Journal*, 1.

THOMAS, D. A. (1970), *Principles of Sentencing*. London: Heinemann.

—— (1974), 'The Control of Discretion in the Administration of Criminal Justice', in R. Hood, ed., *Crime, Criminology and Public Policy*. London: Heinemann.

—— (1978), *The Penal Equation*. Cambridge: Institute of Criminology.

—— (1995), 'Sentencing Reform: England and Wales', in C. Clarkson and R. Morgan, eds., *The Politics of Sentencing Reform*. Oxford: Oxford University Press.

TONRY, M. (1996), *Sentencing Matters*. New York: Oxford University Press.

VAN DUYNE, P. (1987), 'Simple Decision-Making', in D. Pennington and S. Lloyd-Bostock, *The Psychology of Sentencing*. Oxford: Centre for Socio-Legal Studies.

VICTIM'S CHARTER (1996). 2nd edn. London: Home Office.

VON HIRSCH, A. (1976), *Doing Justice*. New York: Hill and Wang.

—— (1993), *Censure and Sanctions*. Oxford: Oxford University Press.

—— (1995), 'Proportionality and Parsimony in American Sentencing Guidelines: The Minnesota and Oregon Standards', in C.

Clarkson and R. Morgan, eds., *The Politics of Sentencing Reform*. Oxford: Oxford University Press.

—— and Ashworth, A., eds. (1992) *Principled Sentencing*. Boston, Mass.: Northeastern University Press.

—— and —— (1993), 'Desert and the Three Rs', *Current Issues in Criminal Justice*, 5: 9–12.

—— and —— (1996), 'Protective Sentencing under Section 2(2)(b): the Criteria for Dangerousness', *Criminal Law Review*, 175–83.

—— and Jareborg, N. (1991), 'Gauging Criminal Harm: a Living Standard Analysis', *Oxford Journal of Legal Studies*, 11: 1–38.

Walker, N. (1991), *Why Punish?* Oxford: Oxford University Press

—— and Padfield, N. (1996), *Sentencing: Theory, Law and Practice*, 2nd edn. London: Butterworths.

Wasik, M. (1985a), 'The Grant of an Absolute Discharge', *Oxford Journal of Legal Studies*, 5: 211.

—— (1985b), 'Rules of Evidence at the Sentencing Stage', *Current Legal Problems*, 38: 187–210.

—— (1993), 'A Fresh Look at Sentencing Aims', in E. Stockdale and S. Casale, eds., *Criminal Justice under Stress*. London: Blackstone Press.

—— and von Hirsch, A. (1994), 'Section 29 Revisited: Previous Convictions and Sentencing', *Criminal Law Review*, 409.

Windlesham, Lord (1993), *Responses to Crime: Volume 2*. Oxford: Oxford University Press.

—— (1996), *Responses to Crime: Volume 3*. Oxford: Oxford University Press.

Wood, D. (1988), 'Dangerous Offenders and the Morality of Protective Sentencing', *Criminal Law Review*, 424–33.

Zimring, F., and Hawkins, G. (1973), *Deterrence: the Legal Threat in Crime Control*. Chicago, Ill.: University of Chicago Press.

31

Imprisonment: Current Concerns and a Brief History since 1945

Rod Morgan

In March 1996 the Conservative Government set out its future strategy for dealing with crime in a White Paper, *Protecting the Public* (Home Office, 1996*a*). The government announced it intended pursuing policies which would significantly increase the prison population and proclaimed that 'prison works', a statement first made by Michael Howard, then Home Secretary, at the Conservative Party Conference in October 1993. The assertion reversed much of the thinking which had informed the Criminal Justice Act 1991. The 1991 Act was premised on the objective of greater parsimony by the courts in their use of imprisonment. During the period 1990–3, when the Criminal Justice Act 1991 was being debated, passed, and implemented, the average daily prison population in England and Wales (Scotland and Northern Ireland have separate prison systems) stabilized at around 45,000, a figure not much higher than a decade previously. By December 1992, shortly after the Act came into force, the population had fallen to 40,600, the lowest figure for many years. But by early 1997, as a result of the reversal of several important provisions in the 1991 Act by the Criminal Justice Act 1993 (see Ashworth, this volume) and the encouragement provided by ministerial rhetoric, the number of prisoners had risen to over 59,000. According to the Director General of the Prison Service our prisons will probably be required to accommodate more than 65,000 prisoners by the time this text is published and, according to the government's own modest estimates, the latest proposals for sentencing reform—the Crime (Sentences) Bill 1996—will, if implemented, add a further 10,800 to the number of offenders in custody (*ibid.*: para. 13.8). These developments represent a surge in the prison population, a surge both actual and predicted, which is unprecedented this century.

The growth in prison numbers is being matched by a huge expansion in prison places, though whether the latter will keep pace with the former remains to be seen. During the period 1945–85 the prison system was dogged by escalating overcrowding. It was on average 0.5 per cent overcrowded in the 1950s, and 5.4, 8.5, and 10–15 per cent overcrowded in the 1960s, 1970s, and 1980s respectively. In the 1980s, however, there began the largest prison building programme since the nineteenth century. Between 1980 and 1996 twenty-one new prisons were opened, providing 11,285 additional places. A further 7,500 places were created by developing existing prisons, though this was partially offset by some loss of accommodation as a result of the extensive programme of refurbishment undertaken in older institutions. The building programme will continue, and needs to if serious overcrowding is now to be avoided. No matter how one measures overcrowding, the total number of prison places and prisoners came briefly into equilibrium during 1993, though the spare capacity never proved sufficient to eliminate overcrowding in every prison. By Spring 1994, however, system overcrowding had returned and now looks set to continue well into the twenty-first century. This in spite of the government's latest proposals that a substantial new programme of prison building take place, a programme which, if implemented, will provide a further 17,000 prison places by 2011–12, 70,000 places overall. This represents an increase of one third on the 53,000 places currently provided.

This massive expansion is going to cost a great deal of money, though it is unclear what the implications will be for unit costs per prisoner. We currently spend about £1.5 billion *per annum* on prisons. This translates into about £550 per week, or £28,350 *per annum*, per prisoner.[1] About 100,000 individuals are committed annually to the 138 separate prisons and young offender establishments currently provided. Approximately 41,000 full-time equivalent staff, about 25,000 of them uniformed prison officers,[2] are employed to make sure they stay there, an overall prisoner to staff ratio of 1.4:1.

All this is a far cry from the situation fifty years ago. In 1946 there were about forty prisons, approximately 15,000 prisoners and around 2,000 staff, a prisoner staff ratio of 7.5:1 (Home Office, 1947). It is true that the big Victorian prisons which still form the hub of the system today would be recognizable to a prisoner from that period. But only just. The external layouts and galleried wings remain much the same. But the grounds have been in-filled with modern gate-lodges, visiting centres, education blocks, workshops, gymnasia, and new accommodation wings. Practically all the cells are now equipped with lavatories and sinks so that slopping-out has gone. Pastel colours have replaced drab painted walls of green, cream, and brown and fitted cell furniture is gradually displacing the stark iron beds and meagre lockers of the past. Moreover the majority of prisoners are now accommodated in modern purpose-built prisons constructed since the 1950s on green-field sites, many of them replacing the converted houses and war-time camps that were taken over for use as prisons in the immediate post-war period.

---

[1] These figues are significantly greater than those selected by the Prison Service for its Key Performance Indicator on expenditure. The latter, KPI 8, is based not on cost per prisoner, nor yet available prisoner place, but 'Baseline CNA' which conveniently understates total costs per prisoner (Prison Service, 1996*a*: 25. For a detailed discussion see King and McDermott, 1995: 304–14).

[2] The Prison Service no longer includes in its published reports information about how many staff are employed. Information received by the author from Prison Service HQ states that in November 1996 39,707 staff were employed, 37,675 in establishments and 2,032 in Headquarters. These figures do not include the staff employed in contracted-out institutions.

At the same time the social character of prison life has changed in subtle ways that can scarcely be characterized as progress. There are no longer rows of convicts hand-sewing mailbags in silence. The flogging triangles and bread and water dietary punishments have been abolished. The shabby ill-fitting serge uniforms of grey and brown have been phased out. But though prisoners now have more creature comforts, may use the telephone and can see their families more often in more civilized environments, these gains have to be set against new psychological pressures and insecurities that almost certainly have not diminished the pains of imprisonment and which for some prisoners prove unbearable.

Most contemporary prisoners are in custody for far longer than their predecessors. The average time spent in custody awaiting trial has grown enormously. And though custodial sentences were used proportionately more often by the courts in the 1940s, the sentences were typically short compared to now. In 1945 approximately 80 per cent of offenders sentenced to immediate imprisonment were serving six months or less, life sentences were rare, and prisoners serving determinate sentences over ten years almost unknown. Of the daily average sentenced population fewer than 20 per cent were serving eighteen months or more. Today the number serving a life sentence, or a determinate sentence of over ten years, is such that at any one time there are nearly 5,000 of them in custody.

Prisoners today are subject to security measures unknown or scarcely developed half a century ago—prison perimeters made virtually impenetrable by multiple high-tech barriers, landings and stairwells draped with wire mesh, CCTV, electronic locking systems, intensive staff surveillance, strip searches, and random compulsory drug testing. Moreover, there was no overcrowding in the 1940s and the amount of time many prisoners now spend out of their cells is modest compared to that which was taken for granted in most training prisons thirty years ago. Some communal activities—like eating in dining halls, for example—are now considered too risky an arrangement to be generally viable.

Though these matters are difficult to assess it seems certain that prisons have become less orderly and safe. Concerted acts of prisoner indiscipline used to be rare (Fox, 1952: 160) and staff industrial action unheard of. In recent years prison disturbances have become commonplace and managing prison officers became for a period a more difficult task for prison administrators than managing prisoners. The 1970s and 1980s witnessed a litany of serious industrial disputes and prisoner disorders leading to two major inquiries—the May Committee in 1978–9 and the judicial inquiry conducted by Lord Justice Woolf in 1990–1—the reports of which have become landmarks for analysts of prisons policy. Fear has become a significant feature of much prison life (King and McDermott, 1995: chapter 3). By the early 1990s it had become evident that both hard and soft drugs were freely available in many prisons, with all the violent and intimidating consequences that invariably stems from that habit and trade (HMCIP, 1995: 5–7; Seddon, 1996). More than 3,000 prisoners are segregated for their own protection, either under Rule 43 or in the twenty-four vulnerable prisoner units (VPUs) scattered around the country. The number of recorded assaults on both staff and prisoners has greatly increased and in the most recent year for which statistics are available, sixty-five prisoners—an all-time record—committed suicide (Prison Service, 1996*b*: 53).

The result is that prisons are seldom out of the news and dominate ministerial in-trays. Prisons are: costly; overcrowded, in spite of the huge prison building programme; a constant management headache; a conspicuous failure in terms of the subsequent behaviour of those committed to them (almost three quarters of all young offenders and approaching half of all adults are reconvicted within two years of release (Home Office, 1996*b*: chapter 10)); and of marginal value in terms of public protection, because so small a proportion of those responsible for offences are caught, convicted, and imprisoned (see Home Office, 1995: 25). All of which means that there is perennial debate about the purpose and value of imprisonment. What constitutes a sensible rate of imprisonment? Though international comparisons are fraught with difficulty (Pease, 1994), all three British jurisdictions rely on the use of imprisonment to an extent greater than most other countries in Western Europe. In 1996 about 108 persons were incarcerated per 100,000 population in England, compared (according to 1993 figures) to eighty-six in France, eighty-one in Germany, seventy-two in Belgium and fifty-one in the Netherlands (Home Office, 1996*b*: Table 1.14). There are other countries with far higher incarceration rates—the USA, China, and most countries in Eastern Europe, for example—but these countries have markedly different crime rates, histories, or political cultures. They do not make comfortable penal bedfellows.

Should we, as some politicians and judges argue, be relatively unconcerned about the size of our prison population and focus rather on the serious crime against which the courts have a duty to protect the public by locking up more offenders for longer? And if locking up more offenders means that conditions in prisons are less than ideal—'austere' as Michael Howard thinks they should be—should we conclude that this is no more than prisoners deserve? Or does the prison, as others argue, reflect a punitively British obsession, an expensive anachronism, and a largely chimerical crime control device, the use of which we could significantly reduce without risk to anyone? Should we regard poor prison conditions as a bar to our claims to be civilized and a misuse of state power against vulnerable and disadvantaged minorities? What after all should prisons be like: dark deterrent statements of the consequences of committing crime; training camps in citizenship; or protective therapeutic communities for damaged and sometimes dangerous offenders?

We cannot examine all these issues in this chapter. Rather, the aim is to examine six questions. What are the social forces associated with the use of imprisonment? What are the purposes of imprisonment and what objectives should prison administrators set themselves? What is the character of the prison population and how is it changing? How are prisons organized and made accountable, including those the management of which has been privatized? How do the dynamics of prison life—that is, the sociology of the prison— affect objectives? And how might prisons change in the near future? The discussion will focus largely on the situation in Britain. However, prisons, like other social institutions, operate in an increasingly international stream of policy development and are particularly influenced by our closer ties with Europe (see Sim, Ruggiero, and Ryan, 1995). Some references will therefore be made to initiatives and analysis from elsewhere.

THE EMERGENCE OF THE MODERN PRISON AND THE USE OF IMPRISONMENT

Prisons, as mere places of confinement, have existed since time immemorial. Yet prisons as we know them today—places to which offenders are sent as a punishment, there also to be worked on and changed—are a feature of modernity, a product of the industrial age. The modern prison emerged slowly in Northern Europe from the sixteenth century onwards, but it was not until the late eighteenth and early nineteenth centuries that the idea came to fruition. The gaols that John Howard travelled up and down the country visiting and laboriously recording in the 1770s were mostly small and seldom purpose-built. They were rooms in ancient fortresses or city gateways, stables behind the keeper's house, or cellars within town halls. Only in the major cities were there prisons built for the purpose, and here their inhabitants were typically herded together, little subject to regulation save in the exploitative interests of their custodians (Howard, 1784). When opened in 1842, only a little over half a century later, Pentonville Prison, dubbed the 'Model Prison' and still in use today, represented the scale of the transformation: over 500 identical cells in each of which a prisoner was separately to live in silence according to a routine meticulously regulated by a uniformed staff employed by the state. The modern prison, and its institutional counterpart—the work-house for the indigent poor, the asylum for the insane, the reformatory for wayward youth, and the penitentiary for fallen women—reflected what Foucault (1967: chapter 2) has termed 'the great confinement' and emerged alongside the factory. They were social and architectural counterparts. In the factories labour was rationalized for the purposes of more efficient production. In the new institutions of confinement those unproductive sections of the labour force were differentiated, segregated, and disciplined. John Howard's proposals for the better regulation of the insanitary and morally corrupting gaols of the eighteenth century were the corollary of the managerial revolution being wrought in Richard Arkwright's mill at Cromford and Josiah Wedgewood's factory at Etruria. Over each of their model buildings, both actually and metaphorically, was placed a clock according to the hands of which everything was now done (McGowan, 1995).

Prisons have historically had three uses: custodial, coercive, and punitive. Though imprisonment was used from medieval times as a punishment, it was generally for minor offences (Pugh, 1968). Its primary legal function was custodial or coercive. Accused persons held awaiting 'gaol delivery' (the arrival of travelling courts) or following conviction pending execution of sentence, generally an assault on the body or death, carried out in a public place. To this was later added imprisonment pending transportation to the colonies. The coercive function of imprisonment was almost entirely for civil debt and, at the time of John Howard's travels, accounted for half the persons he found in custody. The modern prison emerged as its function changed from being primarily custodial-coercive to punitive—a transformation dramatically illustrated in the opening pages of Foucault's seminal study *Discipline and Punish: The Birth of the Prison* (1977), where the grotesquely brutal execution of a regicide in 1757 Paris is juxtaposed with the clockwork precision of a totally regulated daily regime at a Paris reformatory half a century later. For Foucault the modern prison, with its mechanisms of total surveillance, represented a new a form of knowledge and power, irrespective of the interests that power served. Between 1750 and 1850, throughout most of Europe, imprisonment became the principal punishment for serious crime—*carceral* rather than *corporal* punishment, addressing the soul (or the mind) rather than the body (or the outward reputation)—judicial torture was formally abolished (Peters, 1984), and the death penalty, henceforth carried out within prisons rather than in public, was reserved for only the most heinous crimes (Spierenburg, 1984).

During the nineteenth century this transformation was mostly represented as a vital sub-plot in the Whig version of history as progress: the triumph of reason over superstition, civilization over barbarism. John Howard, Elizabeth Fry, and other penal reformers were depicted in hagiographic terms, saviours during the Enlightenment whose efforts ushered in humanity. Some Victorian observers, for example Charles Dickens, had their doubts, discovering in the reformed prisons new torments systematically imposed in the name of the people (Collins, 1962; see also Mayhew and Binny, 1862), a phenomenon which in the twentieth century became devastatingly apparent with the rise of the totalitarian state, the re-emergence of torture, and the mass incarcerations of the concentration camps, gulags, and resocialization centres.

Attention naturally turned to the origins of those mechanisms which twentieth-century states were manifestly using to oppress their citizens. Rusche and Kirchheimer (1968), pioneering Marxist theorists in the realm of penal studies whose work in the 1930s only became widely known when republished, argued that it was not punishment that needed to be explained but specific and concrete *forms of punishment*. Particular penalties, they argued, could be linked to particular modes of production and labour market conditions. When labour was cheap and plentiful, penalties were careless of human life and health. When labour became more valuable the penal system responded to the economic imperatives of the day: transportation was developed to serve the interests of imperialism; the Houses of Correction were designed to make productive use of the recalcitrant poor; and 'less eligibility', the utilitarian doctrine that convicted prisoners are less morally deserving than the least well-off persons enjoying their freedom in the community, and should therefore not enjoy a life-style and facilities superior or equal to those enjoyed outside the prisons and workhouses, was an ancillary discipline for the labour market beyond the walls (see also Melossi and Pavarini, 1981). In a similar vein it has since been argued that the proportionate use of imprisonment has declined in most jurisdictions with the growth of the welfare state and onset of fiscal crisis (Scull, 1977). Why keep large numbers of offenders expensively incarcerated if less eligibility can be assured through carefully graduated transfer payments from which deductions can easily be made?

Rusche and Kirchheimer's economic determinism was crude, and their analysis did not exactly fit the facts, but their work stimulated a wealth of scholarship such that today there is a rich historical penal policy literature on which students may draw. A more nuanced account has emerged of historical and contemporary 'penality', that is, our ideas about and practices of imprisonment (Garland and Young, 1983). The eighteenth-century penal reformers were nearly all motivated by religious faith, pursuing what they perceived to be a humanitarian mission. There *was* a growing revulsion against public corporal and capital punishment which, the evidence suggests, was also counter-productive in that it often served to inflame rather than subdue the mob. Imprisonment comprised both a vivid and subtle symbolic message. The reformed prisons, monolithically built in rusticated stone, generally sited in the new working-class districts of the expanding urban centres, represented the growing power of the state. Whereas the transaction between the public executioner and the hapless offender appeared personal and, because often botched, frequently seemed arbitrary, the mysterious prison represented impersonal regularity, orderliness, and certainty. In the age of liberty it was particularly apt that those who breached the social contract should lose their freedom. Prison sentences were meted out, proportionate to the gravity of the offence and were served, at least in theory, in a perfectly regulated environment where, the regimen emphasized, all were stripped of their external identities and treated equally (see Ignatieff, 1978; McConville, 1981).

The multi-faceted appeal of the prison and imprisonment, then and now, emphasizes that imprisonment, like punishment generally, needs to be understood from a variety of angles, as: a technical means to an end; a coercive relationship; an instrument of class domination; a form of power; and an expression of collective moral feeling ritually expressed (for reviews of the sociological literature, see Garland, 1990; Cavadino and Dignan, 1992). To the extent that imprisonment serves different social functions this suggests that attempts to change the degree to which imprisonment is used are unlikely to succeed simply by proclaiming the utilitarian shortcomings of the enterprise.

What is clear is that all developed societies, whatever their ideological pretensions, employ imprisonment as their principal penalty for serious crime.

Yet the rate at which imprisonment is used varies greatly over time and between jurisdictions (Rutherford, 1984; Christie, 1993). Practically everybody, be they politicians, the police, prosecutors, and sentencers, claims to support the use of imprisonment only as a last resort when no other measure will suffice and maintains that this is the basis of their decision-making. Yet the collective outcome of their decision-making varies greatly and the evidence suggests that these variations cannot fully be explained by: crime rates; changing fashions in the philosophy of punishment; demographic factors; levels of economic activity; or public-policy considerations. Though factors subsumed by these headings—unemployment or the supply of prison places, for example—have undoubtedly influenced the rate of imprisonment in some countries in some periods (Zimring and Hawkins, 1991), the use of imprisonment is a complex issue explained by variable contextual factors (for example, see Downes, 1988 and 1997, for examinations of penal policy in the Netherlands). The rate of imprisonment is not determined by factors beyond government control. It is ultimately a matter of political choice. Do we wish in Britain to march in step with the United States which has a rate of imprisonment almost six times that of our own? Or, rather, do we wish to identify with our neighbours in North West Europe, most of whom have incarceration rates half to two-thirds our own?

THE MISSION: THE PURPOSE OF IMPRISONMENT

Legal Purposes

The most fundamental way of answering the question: what are prisons for?; is to distinguish the legal uses which we have already identified: custody, coercion, and punishment.

Suspects refused bail and detained before trial, or convicted but not yet sentenced (generally awaiting medical or pre-sentence reports), are held in custody for no other reason than to ensure that the course of justice proceeds to its conclusion and that the public, victims, witnesses, and sometimes suspects themselves, are protected against the likelihood of harm in the interim. Moreover, a small number of non-criminal prisoners—those held under the Immigration Act, for example—are held in prisons pending completion of inquiries or execution of an administrative decision. There is no justification for holding such prisoners in conditions more oppressive than is warranted by the fact of custody itself: either they are not eligible for punishment (the unconvicted are subject to the presumption of innocence) or, if convicted, the court has not yet determined that loss of liberty is the appropriate sentence.

Offenders held coercively—nowadays almost entirely fine defaulters—are kept in prison for as long as they fail to comply with a court order that they pay a financial penalty or some other payment enforced by the court. As soon as they meet their obligations in the community, or once the custodial period in lieu of payment is served, they are released. In this case the prison, in the form of both the loss of liberty itself and possibly also conditions in custody, is being used in an attempt to pressurize the offender into conforming.

Finally, there are persons held punitively—nowadays the great majority—as a sanction for offences of which they stand convicted. Since the abolition of the death penalty in 1965 imprisonment has been the most serious penalty the courts can impose in Britain. In fact it has been the principal penalty for serious crime ever since the decline of corporal punishments and the phasing out of transportation in the eighteenth and nineteenth centuries respectively (Radzinowicz and Hood, 1990). The punishment of imprisonment for sentenced prisoners might comprise both loss of liberty and harsh living conditions in the name of 'less elibility' or deterrence. Today prison administrators generally disavow such purposes, reiterating Paterson's famous dictum that offenders are sent to prison 'as a punishment, not for punishment' (Ruck, 1951: 23). However, it is difficult to square conditions and practices in many prisons with this disavowal and 'less eligibility' remains a potent political, if not adminis- trative, imperative (Garland, 1990), an imperative given a new spur by Michael Howard's stipulation that prison conditions be 'austere' (Sparks, 1996). Further, it seems clear that remand prisoners, in spite of the presumption of innocence, tend, both in Britain and elsewhere, to be viewed by prison staff as sentenced prisoners in waiting (Fox, 1952: 286): their living conditions are generally among the worst to be found in the system (King and Morgan, 1976; Morgan, 1993).

This raises an important issue. A distinction needs to be drawn between the reasoning which leads sentencers to send offenders to prison and the objectives pursued by those who manage prisons. Ideally the two should be consistent and spring from the same principles. But they are not the same, and hitherto sentencers have generally not been required to spell out the rationale for their decisions. Whatever justifications sentencers have for using imprisonment (see Ashworth, this volume), prison administrators have practically to manage prisons with regard to the welfare of staff as well as prisoners. Their main point of reference is the Prison Rules (SI 1964, no. 388), the first two of which enjoin the encouragement of 'good and useful lives', the promotion of 'self- respect', and the development of 'personal responsibility'. This formula came in for a good deal of criticism in the 1970s. The criticism was prompted partly by loss of confidence in rehabilitative thinking, stemming from empirical evidence that rehabilitative programmes were largely ineffective (Lipton *et al.*, 1975; Brody, 1976) and the observation that the rehabilitative perspective had led to considerable discretionary powers being granted to executive agencies, the exercise of which contravened the rules of procedural justice (American Friends Service Committee, 1971; Morris, 1974; Hudson, 1996: Part 1).

Treatment and Training v. Humane Containment

In Britain it was argued that the treatment and training paradigm adopted by
the Prison Department in fulfilment of Prison Rule 1 was dangerous, not least
because it was appealing; it suggested that prisons, despite all the indications
to the contrary, were positive establishments fulfilling a noble purpose (King
and Morgan, 1980: chapter 1). If imprisonment could be justified on the
ground that it could make prisoners less likely to offend, then sentencers were
more likely to be deluded into using imprisonment for this purpose. On this
basis longer and indeterminate sentences had been argued for in preference to
short and determinate sentences, so that the authorities would have time to do
their remedial work and offenders could be released when treatment or
training had successfully been undertaken (this was part of the rationale for
introducing parole—see Maguire, 1992). Thus, argued King and Morgan,
treatment and training militated against a more parsimonious use of custody
within a 'justice' rights-based framework. According to this view the aims of
sentencers and prison managers, though analytically separable, cross-fertilize.

In their critique of Rule 1, which they spelt out in evidence to the May
Committee, King and Morgan claimed that 'treatment and training' was a
rhetorical doctrine that had never squared with the reality of prison life. Rule
1 was so vague that it had never been operationalized. It was inspired by
aspirations incapable of fulfilment, something that prison staff had always
known. Moreover, it quite arbitrarily excluded remand and trial prisoners
from view. Far better, they argued, to try to turn the concept of 'humane
containment'—the term coined by the Prison Department to describe the little
they offered in local prisons—into a reality.

For King and Morgan the term 'humane containment' was preferable to
'treatment and training' because it was practical and prosaic: 'because [it] may
fail to fire the imagination', so it might 'prevent the excesses of the past' (1980:
38). They argued that, properly—rather than cynically—considered, 'humane
containment' was consistent with a 'justice model', and should embrace three
major principles: *minimum use of custody*—'Imprisonment should be used only
as a last resort . . . [and] for the minimum length of time consistent with
public safety'; *minimum use of security*—'Prisoners should be subject to only
that degree of security necessary to safeguard the public against any realistic
threat'; and *normalization*—'As far as resources allow, and consistent with the
constraints of secure custody, the same standards which govern the life of
offenders in the community should be held to apply to offenders in prison'
(*ibid.*: 34–7). King and Morgan further argued for a new set of Prison Rules
and a comprehensive review of the instructions issued to governors on the
interpretation of the Prison Rules. Policy objectives needed to be spelt out: it
was necessary 'to specify the standards against which they are to be measured,
and the strategies to be used for achieving them' (*ibid.*: 30).

King and Morgan's arguments did not convince the May Committee, who
thought they had 'much force' but:

there is a danger that it may throw out the good with the unattainable . . . 'humane containment' suffers from the fatal defect that it is a means without an end . . . it can only result in making prisons into human warehouses—for inmates and staff. It is not . . . a fit rule for hopeful life or responsible management . . . mere 'secure and humane containment' is not enough. Prison staff cannot be asked to operate in a moral vacuum and the absence of real objectives can in the end lead only to the routine brutalization of all the participants [May Report, 1979: paras. 4.24 and 4.28].

Nevertheless, the Committee agreed 'that the rhetoric of "treatment and training" has had its day' (*ibid.*: para. 4.27). They proposed that Rule I be replaced by a statement of 'positive custody' in which the purpose of detention of convicted prisoners 'shall be to keep them in custody which is both secure and yet positive', the duty of the authorities being to 'create an environment which can assist [prisoners] to respond and contribute to society as positively as possible', to 'preserve and promote . . . self respect', minimize security and the harmful effects of custody, and prepare prisoners for release (*ibid.*: para. 4.26).

In response, King and Morgan trenchantly dismissed the May Committee formulation. 'Positive custody', they maintained, had 'no real meaning': it was more concerned with the 'generation of hope than . . . the generation of objectives' and was therefore as rhetorical as 'treatment and training' (King and Morgan, 1980: 29). It did not cover unconvicted prisoners. It imposed no 'obligations on the prison authorities' and conferred 'no rights on prisoners. Indeed it would always be open to the authorities to justify any activity by intentions rather than results' (*ibid.*). 'What the May Committee appeared not to recognise is that prisons have sometimes been *inhuman warehouses*' (*ibid.*: 25). This retort has undoubtedly carried the weight of critical opinion since 1980. The May Committee formula has not been officially adopted and the penal pressure groups and most academic commentators have weighed in on the side of positive rights for prisoners (Richardson, 1985), and timetables for the introduction of legally enforceable minimum standards for prison conditions (Casale, 1984; Maguire *et al.*, 1985, part two; Casale and Plotnikoff, 1989). Nevertheless, King and Morgan were unable to rescue the slogan 'humane containment' from its original Prison Department cynical application to the local prisons which were increasingly deprived of resources and pro- grammes and in which nothing positive was happening. This led Ian Dunbar, then a Prison Department Regional Director, to conclude:

Although [humane containment focuses on prison life] more directly and exclusively than does the treatment model . . . in practice it has led to even greater disillusionment. At least the treatment model gave the service something to believe in and some hope. Humane containment has led to the cynicism of human warehousing [Dunbar 1985: 7].

Likewise Vivien Stern, then Director of the National Association for the Care and Resettlement of Offenders (NACRO), was worried by the 'moral vacuum' argument. 'Treatment and training' had had its day, but neither 'positive custody' nor prisoners' rights and enforceable standards had been adopted; and the management-orientated *Statement of Tasks* adopted by the Prisons Board in 1984 (reprinted in Train, 1985) seemed insufficient. The list of 'tasks' were all 'about the means, but not about the ends. Such a moral vacuum soon fills up with cynicism and defeatism' (Stern, 1987: 229). The problem, Bottoms argued, was that 'humane containment' was too barren a concept; it was present- rather than future-orientated, it failed to motivate staff, it invested no hope in the enterprise, it was 'ontologically insufficient' (Bottoms, 1990).

In fact, as the appearance of a *Statement of Tasks* made clear, the Prisons Board, in the absence of any political prompting to amend the statutory framework, adopted a formula which owed more to the requirements of the government's Financial Management Initiative (FMI) than to the penal debate. The FMI required of all public-sector services a statement of objectives, means for measuring performance, and devolution to managers of control over those resources which determine their capacity to set and attain objectives (Prime Minister, 1982). In the Prison Department, as in other government departments, the emphasis was on the three Es—Economy, Efficiency, and Effectiveness—performance indicators, and the rest of the FMI baggage-train. Thus the preamble to the *Statement of Tasks* was narrowly technical—'to use with maximum efficiency the resources of staff, money, building and plant made available . . . in order to fulfill . . . the relevant provisions of the law'. There then followed a bald statement of what was legally required: delivering the untried and unsentenced to court; keeping everyone in secure custody providing prisoners with 'as full a life as is consistent with the facts of custody, in particular . . . the physical necessities of life'—health-care work, education, exercise, opportunity to practice religion, etc.; and enabling prisoners 'to retain links with the community and where possible assist them to prepare for their return to it' (*ibid.*).

This statement was what the FMI required; but, like 'humane containment', it was not inspirational. Further, it provided no rights and laid down no standards. Yet ironically it set in train the management initiatives and information systems for which King and Morgan had argued. It did not answer the question: what are prisons for? But it did begin to focus attention on the question: what services are being delivered to prisoners? The inevitable result was that as more sophisticated data began to emerge about how little was being delivered, and at what cost, so the debate eventually returned to broader purposes and how staff could be persuaded to change what was being delivered. The catalyst that got the debate going again was trouble, this time in the shape of the disorders at Strangeways Prison, Manchester, and other prisons in April 1990. Lord Justice Woolf embarked on a wide-ranging inquiry which made 'identifying the task of the Prison Service' a central question (Woolf Report, 1991; Morgan, 1991).

The Woolf Inquiry

Some commentators have found Woolf's discussion of the purposes of imprisonment disappointing. He provided no review of the debate as it had developed. Further, contrary to most current opinion, Woolf found merit in the May Committee's statement of 'positive custody' and, with two caveats, endorsed the Prison Service's current Statement of Purpose which is displayed outside all establishments: 'Her Majesty's Prison Service serves the public by keeping in custody those convicted by the courts. Our duty is to look after them with humanity and to help them lead law abiding and useful lives in custody and after release.' Woolf's two caveats were vital, however. First, he was critical of the absence of any reference to justice. Secondly, he did not agree that the Statement adequately covered the unconvicted and unsentenced (1991, paras. 10.16–64).

Woolf's use of the term justice was arguably too broad (see Morgan, 1992*a*), but it tied together sentencing and prisons policy. Woolf maintained that when the Prison Service says it 'serves the public' it does so by more than simply keeping in custody those committed by the courts. It does so best by furthering the objectives of the criminal justice system, namely, by preventing crime. That means at the very least by: looking after prisoners with humanity; safeguarding prisoners' 'civil rights which are not taken away expressly or by necessary implication' (*Raymond* v. *Honey* 1982, 759, quoted in Woolf, 1991: para. 10.22); minimizing 'the negative effects of imprisonment which make re-offending more likely'; requiring 'the offender to confront and take responsibility for the wrong doing which resulted in his . . . imprisonment'; providing the 'prisoner with an opportunity to obtain skills which will make it easier to obtain and keep employment and enable him to maintain his family and community contacts'; ensuring 'that life in prisons . . . [is] as close to life outside as the demands of imprisonment permit'; and seeing 'that the prisoner is properly prepared for his return to society' (para. 10.29). Woolf stated that this did not mean 'a return to what came to be known as the treatment model' (para. 10.34). Imprisonment is not justified for reformative purposes, nor is 'being a criminal . . . a creative condition'. However, 'we regard it as part of the Prison Service's role to ensure . . . that a prisoner . . . should have an opportunity of training', for if prisoners are released 'in an embittered and disaffected state' then the criminal justice objective of preventing re-offending is undone (paras. 14.8–9). Thus:

If the Prison Service contains [the] prisoner in conditions which are inhumane or degrading . . . then a punishment of imprisonment which was justly imposed will result in injustice . . . it is the Prison Service's duty to look after prisoners with humanity. If it fulfils this duty, the Prison Service is partly achieving what the Court must be taken to have intended when it passed a sentence of imprisonmen [paragraph 10.19].

Woolf assumed that Paterson's dictum was no longer penological rhetoric but had come into its own as a statement of what sentencers use prisons for. In this he was endorsing a 1984 Prison Department view: 'Imprisonment itself . . . is the punishment inflicted by law and no further available hardship should be imposed on a prisoner except by way of formal disciplinary action' (Home Office, 1984: para. 108).

But how valid is Woolf's assumption that sentencers intend the punishment of imprisonment to comprise loss of liberty alone?

In 1991 his assumption seemed reasonable. The various official statements that preceded the introduction of the Criminal Justice Act 1991 incorporated three ingredients that reinforced the Prison Service's *Statement of Purpose*. First, the use of custody is not justified by the aim of making offenders in some sense better. If that is the object then it is more likely to be accomplished by the offender remaining in the community (Home Office, 1990: para. 2.7; Home Office, 1991: para. 1.28). Secondly, though deterrence in the general educative sense of the term continued to command support, the idea of deterrence in its more individualistic calculative sense had lost credibility (1991: para. 2.8). It was no longer believed that making prison conditions more unpleasant would better persuade prisoners to desist from re-offending or dissuade potential offenders from committing crime. Further, what the Home Office refers to as the 'attrition rate'—the statistically low likelihood that particular categories of offenders will have their offences reported and will be apprehended, prosecuted, convicted, and sentenced to a penalty of a given type (see Home Office, 1995: 25)—made much deterrence theory implausible. Combined with the generally pessimistic assessments of the 'incapacitative' impact of imprisonment (Brody and Tarling, 1980; Zimring and Hawkins, 1995), this suggested that the public is made only very marginally more safe from crime by more offenders being put in prison or kept there longer. Thus, thirdly, current sentencing theory (as set out in sections 1 and 2 of the Criminal Justice Act 1991) is that the primary objective for sentencing is denunciation of and retribution for crime, supplemented in certain circumstances by the need for public protection. The penalty of imprisonment is simply loss of liberty.

In 1991 the government implicitly claimed, therefore, to be committed to Paterson's dictum and maintained that though imprisonment could not be *justified* by the prospect of improving offenders, nevertheless the Prison Service must 'do everything it can, consistent with maintaining a person's loss of liberty, to help make imprisonment a positive and constructive experience' (Home Office, 1990: para. 2.9). Woolf's accusation of injustice, then, most appropriately applied to the manifest failure of the Prison Service universally to provide prison regimes consistent with the new realism in sentencing.

Woolf's achievement was to bring together terms hitherto considered incompatible, and in 1991 there seemed a real prospect of forging an alliance between 'new realism' in sentencing theory and a 'neo-rehabilitative' approach to prisons administration, with justice as the underlying leitmotif. The state, Woolf implicitly argued, had a duty to *facilitate* rather than *coerce* treatment or training (Morris, 1974), and prisoners should be able legitimately to expect—possibly establish a right to—facilities whereby they could address whatever personal shortcomings and social disadvantages were associated with their offending. This is what Rotman has described as a rights model of rehabilitation, 'humanistic and liberty-centred' as opposed to 'authoritarian and paternalistic' (Rotman, 1986). The model emphasizes the view that the legal rights that prisoners retain as citizens generate feelings of dignity and self-worth, that prisoners are legally responsible individuals and must be treated accordingly, that the state has a duty to ensure that prisons are not destructive environments, and that potentially self-improving facilities and programmes are not provided at the discretion of the administration to be downgraded whenever it is administratively convenient or judged ineffective. In all of these respects Woolf, by placing justice at the heart of his analysis and recommendations, sought to restore the legitimacy of the penal enterprise (see Sparks, 1994).

In 1997, however, Woolf's vision has all but evaporated and his assumptions about sentencing seem questionable. There has been a U-turn in government policy. In a political climate in which the major political parties are vying with each other to sound tough on crime (see Downes and Morgan, this volume), a form of penal populism (Bottoms, 1995) involving greater resort to imprisonment is being pursued which flies in the face of the available evidence about effective crime control.

WHO ARE THE PRISONERS?

Prisoners are overwhelmingly young, male, socially and economically disadvantaged, repetitive property offenders. In most respects British prison populations reflect the character of prisoner populations in other advanced industrialized democratic jurisdictions. If the primary function of the police is to sweep the streets of the most readily identifiable (and thus vulnerable) offenders, then the function of the prison system is repeatedly to contain them. Prisons have accurately been described as 'penal dustbins'. Prisoners from socially privileged backgrounds attract disproportionate media attention largely because of their rarity. Prisons—their occupants, staff, and culture—are a feature and hazard of working-class or 'underclass' life. Only governors have traditionally been 'gentlemen', and invariably their reminiscences betray their identification with that strange animal, the 'toff' prisoner thrust into an alien underclass world (see Priestley, 1989: 40; Blake, 1927: chapter 6; Clayton, 1958: chapter 8).

The Growth in the Long-term Prison Population

We must distinguish prison 'receptions' and the 'average daily population' (ADP). Most custodial experiences are surprisingly transitory. If all categories of prisoner are included then the overwhelming majority are in prison for a matter of days, weeks, or months rather than years, even if, for some, the experience is repeated. Remand prisoners are on average in custody for less than two months. If sentenced prisoners—those prisoners in prison the longest—are considered alone, then, when early release provisions are taken into account, over 80 per cent are released within twelve months of receipt.[3] The ADP figures tell a different story, however. Long-term prisoners dominate prisons both numerically and, more importantly, culturally. Of the sentenced male adult ADP, 46 per cent are serving sentences of more than four years. Many of them are in prison for years, some, possibly, for the rest of their lives.

The contrast between prison receptions and the ADP is becoming more marked. In a prescient article Bottoms described a policy whereby attempts are made to distinguish 'ordinary', 'mundane', or 'non-threatening' offenders from 'serious', 'exceptional', and 'dangerous' offenders (Bottoms, 1977). He termed this process bifurcation, the function of which is to reassure the public by locking up the latter for longer while increasingly catering for the former by means of 'community penalties'. The Criminal Justice Act 1991, section 2(6) explicitly provides for bifurcation: violent or sexual offenders are singled out as candidates eligible for custodial sentences longer than their 'just deserts' if there is need to protect the public from serious harm. The Crime (Sentences) Bill 1996 goes further. It provides for mandatory life sentences for persons convicted of a second serious violent or sexual offence.

Bifurcation has been pursued at several decision-making levels and its impact is reflected in the changing character of the prison population. In spite of the increase in recorded crime, the number of prisoners received annually has declined, though that downward trend has been reversed since 1992. There has been a dramatic increase in the number of prisoners received with very long sentences. In 1965, the year that the death penalty was abolished, eighty-eight prisoners were received with sentences of ten years or more, including life: the figure rose to 210, 313, and 556 in 1975, 1985, and 1995 respectively. By contrast, both the number and proportion of prisoners received with sentences of less than twelve months has declined, though this trend has also been reversed in the 1990s.

The increase in the number of long-term prison receptions, and the increased length of those long-term sentences,[4] has been matched by an increase in the proportion of sentences actually served in prison. In 1985 the average time served by life-sentence prisoners released on licence was 10.7 years. In 1995 the average duration was 13.8 years. Both murderers (for whom the life sentence is mandatory) and discretionary life-sentence prisoners are now generally required to remain longer in prison before being conditionally released. More-over, bifurcation has characterized executive release policy across the whole range of sentences. The shorter the sentence, the smaller the proportion of the

---

[3] All figures, unless stated otherwise, are taken from the annual prison statistics, the most recent of which was published in August 1996 (Home Office, 1996*b*). For a more comprehensive review of prison statistics see Morgan (1995).

[4] Statutorily defined as one of four years or more: Criminal Justice Act 1991, s. 33.

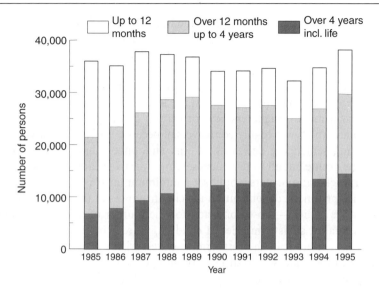

Fig. 31.1: Male sentenced population by length of sentence 1985–95
Source: Home Office, 1996*b*: Fig. 1.6.

sentence the prisoner has been required to serve in prison (see Home Office, 1996: Table 4.13).

This bifurcation in sentencing and executive release policy has transformed the character of the ADP. Long-term prisoners now preoccupy prison administrators because long-term prisoners dominate life in most training prisons (see Figure 31.1). In the mid-1960s, when security considerations first came to the fore in prisons administration, 11 per cent of the sentenced ADP (young and adult, male and female) were serving sentences of four years or more, including life. The proportion rose to 14, 23, and 42 per cent in 1975, 1985, and 1995 respectively. The actual numbers tell the story even more dramatically. In 1965 there were approximately 3,600 prisoners serving sentences of four years or more including life.[5] By 1995 there were almost as many prisoners serving life sentences alone (3,307) and almost five times as many (17,040) serving sentences of four years or more, including life.

Part of the explanation for the population trends described above lies in the introduction in 1967 of parole (superimposed on an existing policy which had been in existence since 1940 of one-third automatic remission for good conduct on all determinate sentences) and its development since. After a cautious beginning, when parole was seen very much as a privilege to be earned by prisoners who had reached a 'recognisable peak in their training' (Home Office, 1965), executive release was gradually liberalized (see Carlisle Report, 1988; Maguire,

---

[5] The figure is approximate because the numerical band then used in the annual statistics was 'over three years'.

1992). Following initiatives by two Home Secretaries, Roy Jenkins in 1974 and Leon Brittan in 1983, an increasing proportion of short- and medium-sentence prisoners received parole almost routinely. Indeed, after 1987 all prisoners serving sentences of twelve months or less were automatically released without assessment at the half-way point in their sentences. In the case of Leon Brittan's initiative, however, this liberalization at the lower end of the sentence range was balanced by a much tougher policy for certain categories of longer-term prisoner, a policy which was highly controversial because it effectively involved ministers making sentencing decisions. It was announced that: parole would not normally be granted at all to prisoners serving over five years for violent offences or drug-trafficking; ministers would set a minimum tariff period to be served by life-sentence prisoners, dependent on the circumstances of their offence; and special categories of lifer—those convicted for the murder of police or prison officers, the sexual or sadistic murder of children, murder by firearms in the course of robbery, or murder in the furtherance of terrorism—would not normally be released until they had served at least twenty years.

The policy of ministers setting a minimum tariff period to 'meet the interests of deterrence and retribution' was modified in 1987 in the case of discretionary life sentences (following *R.* v. *Secretary of State for the Home Department, ex p. Handscombe* (1991), *The Times*, 4 March) such that the recommendations of the judiciary were strictly adhered to. In the case of mandatory life sentences for murder, however, ministers, typically junior ministers, continued to determine the tariff to be served and, as evidence given to a House of Lords Select Committee showed, ministers typically altered upwards the tariffs recommended by trial judges and the Lord Chief Justice (House of Lords, 1989). Since 1994 (following *R.* v. *Secretary of State for the Home Department, ex p. Doody* (1994) 1 AC 531, HL) mandatory lifers have had the right to know: the minimum period the judge thought they should serve; any alteration in the tariff set; the reasons for all such decisions; and to make representations. It has become apparent that sometimes ministers have increased the tariff recommended by the judge by as much as ten years (Creighton and King, 1996: chapter 10). Even when the tariff has been served, lifers may not be released on the basis that they present a continued risk to the public or, most controversially, to maintain public confidence in the criminal justice system. In what is undoubtedly the most famous case where this consideration arises—that of Myra Hindley—it arguably amounts to sentencing by the tabloid press. Michael Howard has announced that he will never authorize Hindley's release, and that of a handful of other convicted murderers. His decision is not binding on his successors, but it will undoubtedly make their decisions more difficult in a tough 'law and order' climate.

The Brittan rules proved highly controversial. They removed discretion from the Parole Board, involved ministers rather than judges deciding what certain sentences should be, and exacerbated the less than consistent gulf between sentences passed and sentences served. The policy also had consequences for control in prisons: it did terrible damage to the morale of both staff and prisoners, as prisoners brought back from open prisons (to which they had been transferred with the expectation of early release) and long-termers now felt they had little to lose. In 1987–8 the parole system was thoroughly reviewed by the Carlisle Committee, whose recommendations were, with certain important exceptions, adopted and incorporated in the Criminal Justice Act 1991. The current system provides for: automatic conditional release at the half-way point of sentences under four years; Parole Board responsibility for release decisions for prisoners serving determinate sentences of between four and seven years, the threshold for release being the half-way point in sentences, with conditional release up to the three-quarter point; and continued involvement of the Home Secretary in release decisions of sentences of seven years or more, though the Brittan rules have been abolished (for an evaluation of the new automatic conditional release system see Maguire *et al.*, 1996).

If the Crime (Sentences) Bill 1996 is enacted then parole, though not release on licence of life sentence prisoners, will be abolished and replaced by modest earned early release decided by prison staff. This measure, combined with the increasing imposition of very long sentences, will perpetuate the build-up of the long-term prison population. It follows that the Prison Service has to cater to the needs of the majority of committals, for whom the experience of custody is transitory, within a prison system which, on a day-to-day basis, has to accommodate prisoners of whom an ever increasing number must regard the prison as their home. There is inevitably a tension between the needs of the two groups.

Gendered Prisons and the Growth in the Number of Women Prisoners

Prisoners are overwhelmingly male—94.1 per cent of all receptions and 96.2 per cent of the ADP. Moreover, since it has long been the policy for women to be housed in institutions used exclusively for women (though some remand prisons accommodate males and females in separate wings), and because, until relatively recently, prison officers were employed exclusively to work with prisoners of the same sex, prisons are heavily gendered institutions. This has influenced the differential regimes thought appropriate for male and female prisoners, the nature of the relationships between prisoners and staff, the character of the activities provided, the relative use of drugs, disciplinary measures, and so on (for accounts of the history of women's imprisonment see Dobash, Dobash, and Gutteridge, 1986; Zedner, 1994, 1995). The tendency has been to label women prisoners as mad or sad rather than bad and the activities organized for them have been geared to the roles of mother and homemaker rather than the labour market (Carlen, 1983). Thus the only major local prison to have been rebuilt this century—Holloway, the largest prison for women—was redesigned to operate on medically oriented therapeutic lines (Rock, 1996), an approach considered particularly appropriate for women, but marginalized for men, as evidenced by the failure to replicate the experimental therapeutic prison at Grendon Underwood (Genders and Player, 1994).

The female prison population is in several respects different from that of the male population. It is not clear that women, all other things being equal, are more likely to receive a custodial sentence, but the differences between the men and women in custody do raise important questions of justice. First, 25 per cent of the female ADP comprises remands compared to 22.2 per cent for men. This is in spite of the fact that the average remand period for women is significantly shorter than for men (forty-three compared to fifty-six days in 1995). The principal explanation for the disparity is that a far lower proportion of female than male custodial remands—34 compared to 47 per cent—do not subsequently receive a custodial sentence, a situation that prompts the question whether many of them need have been remanded in custody. Sentenced women prisoners also differ from men. They are typically: older (a lower proportion of both receptions and ADP are under 21); serving shorter sentences (23.5 compared to 16.8 per cent of the sentenced ADP serving sentences of one year or less); less recidivist (a much higher proportion having no previous convictions, and a much lower proportion having many convictions); and less likely to have committed offences of violence (14 compared to 21.5 per cent of receptions). Some writers, notably Carlen (1990; Carlen and Tchaikovsky, 1996), argue that these differences in the male and female prison populations mean that the imprisonment of women is *different* from that of men and indicate that, despite the relatively small number of women in prison, there is a powerful case for there being substantially fewer. In fact the opposite is occurring. At the time of writing there are approximately 2,500 women in prison, a 56 per cent increase on the average number in 1990 compared to a 26 per cent increase in the number of men.

Ethnicity, Nationality, and Imprisonment

The Prison Service has for many years monitored more closely the ethnic composition of the population with which it deals than possibly any other public service. 17 per cent of male prisoners and 24 per cent of female prisoners are members of ethnic minorities, two-thirds of them Afro-Caribbean. This substantial over-representation of the ethnic minorities in the population generally has prompted a good deal of research (see Smith, this volume). As Tonry (1994) has argued, the true scale of the issue is revealed only when incarceration rates are computed for racially disaggregated populations, a method the Home Office has adopted in its most recent set of *Prison Statistics*. This shows that if foreign nationals and children under 16 years are excluded from the analysis, black residents are imprisoned at 7.8 times the rate of white residents—a difference greater than in the USA—whereas persons of South Asian origin are incarcerated at 0.77 the white rate. Further, within these groups there are significant differences, Africans being incarcerated at a rate much higher than Caribbeans, and people of Pakistani origin being incarcerated at a rate two or three times as high as Bangladeshis and Indians respectively (see Figure 31.2).

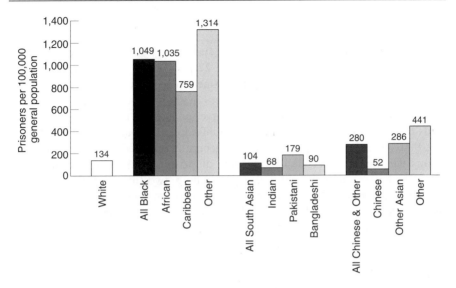

Fig. 31.2: Incarceration rates* by ethnic group, 30 June 1995
Source: Home Office: 1996*b*: Fig. 9.8.
*British nationals, excluding children under 16 years

The latest data on the ethnicity of prisoners enable the reasons for the over-representation of minorities to be examined in a more focused manner. Nationality is one factor. Just over 4,000 prisoners, or 8 per cent of the prison population now comprise foreign nationals, a rising tide noted throughout Europe (Tomashevski, 1994). A significant proportion of these foreign prisoners are not normally resident in Britain. Whereas only 3 per cent of white prisoners are foreign, the proportions of black, South Asian, and Chinese prisoners is 24, 42, and 50 per cent respectively. Moreover a significantly higher proportion of women prisoners are foreign (16 per cent) than are male prisoners (8 per cent), and almost two-thirds of these foreign women are Afro-Caribbean, a large proportion of them sentenced for drugs offences. This is the consequence of the well-publicized problem of women being apprehended at ports of entry as drug 'mules' (Green, 1991). Another factor is the relative youth of the ethnic minorities compared to the white population: thus the over-representation is greatest among young adult prisoners. Finally, the ethnic minorities are most over-represented among the remand population—a feature which has attracted much critical attention (see Hood, 1992; Fitzgerald and Marshall, 1996)—and among sentenced prisoners their offence and sentence profile is different from the white population. Within all the ethnic minority groups, male and female, foreign nationals and British, the proportion of drug offenders is significantly higher than that of whites. Drug offences, particularly trafficking, attract longer than average sentences, and this explains part of the general over-representation.

The Young but Ageing Prison Population

Imprisonment is experienced largely by the young. In 1995, 34 per cent of remand and unsentenced receptions, and 27 per cent of sentenced receptions, were under 21 years of age. Of adult prisoners received under sentence, 60 per cent were under 30 years of age. Prisoners in their 20s dominate life in most prisons. This is unsurprising. Though crime, or at least the sort of crime that leads to conviction, is largely the activity of adolescents and young adults, the fact that sentences of imprisonment are generally imposed on repeat offenders means we should expect the modal age of prisoners to be higher than that of convicted criminals generally. Approaching two-thirds of the offenders sentenced to immediate custody have three or more previous convictions and over a quarter have eleven or more. The modal age of sentenced male prisoners is 26, though that for women is significantly higher, at 33 years.

Yet the prison population is ageing. First, the number of young prisoners has been reduced in recent years, and though this trend has been marginally reversed in the 1990s, it has not greatly affected the long-term trend. The period since 1945 has seen several custodial sentences for prisoners under 21—immediate imprisonment, borstal training, detention in a detention centre, and youth custody—but all were replaced by detention in a young offender institution by the Criminal Justice Act 1988, for which sentence the minimum age was raised in 1991 from 14 to 15 years. It follows that the only sensible way to consider the use of custody for young offenders is to aggregate all sentences for persons under 21 years. The results of this exercise are depicted in Figure 31.3. Though the number of young offender receptions has risen since 1993, thereby tracking the upward trend in the use of custody for adults, nevertheless the number of offenders under 21 sentenced to an immediate custodial sentence remains half of that in the early 1980s and is now at about the same level it was thirty years ago.

The number of juveniles held on remand has also risen in the last year or two, though remanding in custody of 14-year-old boys ceased in 1992. The government has said it is committed to ending remands in prison of 15- and 16-year-old boys (girls of this age are already excluded), a commitment prompted by the furore over the suicide of two 15-year-old boys in local prisons in 1990 and 1991. Since then any sense of urgency appears to have evaporated. In 1995 thirty-four 15-year-old boys and 104 16-year-old boys were remanded in custody in 1995, respectively two and three times as many as in 1991. It seems likely that further tragedies will arise before social services departments are made wholly responsible for the pre-trial custody of juveniles.

At the other end of the scale, the number of middle-aged and even elderly prisoners has grown. Though the population of adults in their early 20s received under sentence has increased, younger prisoners tend to have shorter sentences. The consequence is the overall ageing of the ADP. In 1985 almost half the sentenced ADP was under 25 years and approximately 12 per cent was aged 40 years or more; in 1995 the proportions were one-third and 18 per cent.

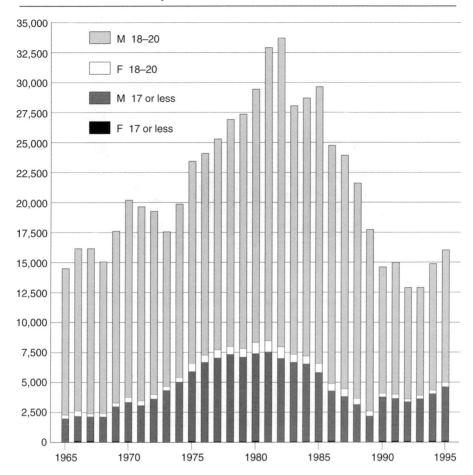

Fig. 31.3: Males and females under 21 received serving immediate custodial sentences

There are now over 600 prisoners at any one time over 60 years of age, many of them serving long sentences.

A More Intractable Prison Population?

It is difficult to evaluate the extent to which prisoners are more intractable today than once they were, the contention generally advanced by prison staff. As the proportionate use of imprisonment has risen since 1992 the Prison Service has been called upon to deal with a core of more difficult prisoners *and* larger numbers of less sophisticated repeat offenders. The proportion of sentenced receptions who have been convicted of crimes of violence (including sexual offences and robbery) is, at 21 per cent, the same as it was ten years

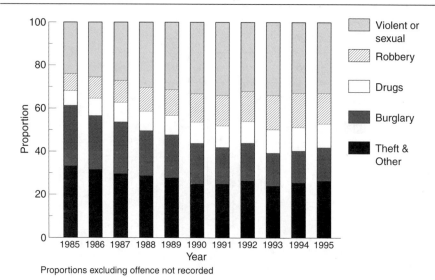

Fig. 31.4: Sentenced population by type of offence, 30 June 1985–95
Source: Home Office, 1996*b*: Fig. 1.5.

ago. Moreover the limited data available suggest that the prison population is
not more recidivist today. Indeed the proportion of sentenced prisoners with
no previous convictions appeared to be greater in 1995 than it was in 1985,
and the proportion with many previous convictions smaller (see Home Office,
1996*b*: table 4.9, compared to Home Office, 1986: table 4.3). However, because
sentences are now longer—particularly those for violent offences—and parole
is less readily given for longer sentences, a substantially higher proportion of
the sentenced ADP has been convicted of offences of violence—44 per cent in
1995, compared to 31 per cent in 1985 (see Figure 31.4). There has also been
a gradual build-up of prisoners—those convicted of drug-related offences, for
example—who fall outside the definition of violent offenders, but many of
whom may be more inured to violence.

Furthermore, the fact that so many prisoners have little or no prospect of
early release, and are subject to ever tighter control and security, is likely to
heighten tension. Certainly major prison disturbances are now more common.
And, to the extent that prisoner disciplinary proceedings reflect the incidence
of prisoners' offences (which they may not) or are an index of stability (which
arguably they are), then the number of offences against the Prison Rules
punished per head of population has risen in recent years, and the increase has
been in every type of establishment, except those for women, where offence
levels were already relatively high (Home Office 1996*d*: table 2). These indices
are not straightforwardly related, however. Burglars, for example, are the most
prolific offenders against the prison disciplinary code and they are typically
serving short- or medium-term sentences: as a group they commit twice as

many offences in prison as do prisoners convicted for violent or drug-related offences (*ibid.*: Chart 3).

Prisoners' Socio-economic Character and Personal Relationships

The prison population is socially and economically disadvantaged relative to the population generally. A survey of prisoners conducted on behalf of the Home Office (Walmsley *et al.*, 1992)[6] shows that, in addition to their ethnic characteristics discussed above, prisoners are disproportionately working class (83 per cent of male prisoners are from manual, partly skilled, or unskilled groups, compared to 55 per cent of the population generally) and exhibit telling indicators of social stress. An implausibly high proportion, 23 per cent, reports having been in local authority care below the age of 16. For prisoners under 21 the figure is 38 per cent. This compares with approximately 2 per cent for the population generally. Though this self-reported experience of care may be inaccurate, it probably reflects the extent of prisoners' contact with social services when children. There is also evidence of fragility in prisoners' family relationships. A much higher proportion of prisoners than one would expect from their age profile and social background were cohabiting, and many fewer were married at the time of their incarceration compared to the population at large. At the time of interview the differences were greater still, suggesting the breakdown of relationships as a result of imprisonment. Further, though a high proportion of prisoners had dependent children living with them prior to imprisonment (32 per cent of males and 47 per cent of females) a significant proportion said their children were being looked after by their ex-spouse or ex-partner (27 per cent of men and 19 per cent of women with children) and, in the case of women, the majority (52 per cent) said their children were being looked after by relatives or were in care with foster parents (12 per cent). The survey did not investigate why so many prisoners were taken into care when children, but the evidence suggests that many children of prisoners are destined to suffer the same disadvantageous start in life (see Shaw, 1992).

Many prisoners have generally precarious toeholds on life outside prison. 13 per cent had no permanent residence prior to their incarceration (they were roofless, or living in a hostel or some other temporary accommodation), and of those who had a permanent residence and were not living with their partners, two-thirds were living in rented accommodation, nowadays very much a minority form of tenure. Prisoners are no better placed in the employment market. 43 per cent said that they left school before the age of 16 (compared to 11 per cent of the population generally), and of the remainder very few continued education beyond 16. 43 per cent had no educational qualification whatsoever (many of these prisoners are functionally illiterate) and only 8 per cent had qualifications beyond 'O' level. A third were unemployed before their

---

[6] For earlier partial surveys of the prison population see Banks and Fairhead, 1976; Fairhead, 1981; Mott, 1985.

imprisonment, two-fifths of those under 25: almost three times as many as one would expect to find in the population generally.

Prisoners' Mental Health

The mental health of prisoners has been a perennial cause for concern. In 1991 the most comprehensive survey of the mental health of the sentenced population yet undertaken (Gunn *et al.*, 1991) estimated that of adult male and females 2.1 and 1.1 per cent respectively were suffering from psychoses; 5.8 and 15.5 per cent from neuroses; 8.8 and 16.1 per cent from personality disorders; and 1.0 and 2.6 from organic disorders. Moreover, almost a quarter of all males and approaching one-third of all females were regular substance abusers or were substance-dependent. Thus, though the incidence of serious psychiatric illness of disorder is small—the data suggest that there are approximately 700 sentenced prisoners suffering psychotic illness in the system at any one time— it appears that approximately two-fifths of all males and two-thirds of all females have pronounced psychiatric or behavioural problems. The remand population exhibits more acute problems (Lart, 1997) not least because many psychotic or mentally handicapped prisoners are remanded in custody not because of the seriousness of their alleged offences, but because of their need for social or psychiatric help, 'an inefficient, ineffective and inhumane way of securing psychiatric assessment and treatment' (Dell *et al.*, 1991: 423).

In conclusion, prisoners are drawn disproportionately from groups that are socially and economically marginal to the life of the community, though it is not clear to what extent their marginality preceded or followed their typically repeated convictions. What is certain is that imprisonment is not likely to enhance their life chances. Further, the personal inadequacy of many prisoners compounds the vulnerability which is a general characteristic of prison life and makes it essential that we turn to an age-old question: *quis custodies custodiet*? Who guards the guards?

ORGANIZATION, PRIVATIZATION, AND ACCOUNTABILITY

Prisoners and prisons combine features inherently controversial. Prisoners stand condemned legally, are judged deficient morally, and are of little account politically. They are drawn disproportionately from the ranks of the powerless. Prisons are relatively 'total institutions' (Goffmann, 1969). Since the essence of imprisonment is loss of liberty, it is all too easy for prison systems to adopt secretive and restrictive policies, ostensibly in fulfilment of their mandate. When prisoners protest, their pleas are often not heard or, when heard, not listened to. Winston Churchill was surely correct when he maintained, in a much-quoted passage, that 'the mood and temper of the public in regard to the treatment of crime and criminals is one of the most unfailing tests of the civilisation of any country' (*HC Debates*, col. 1354, 20 July 1910). It follows that the accountability of a prison system is an acid test of its acceptability: to ensure that prisoners are not ill-treated, we have to know what is done to them in our collective name.

Expenditure on prisons since 1979 has risen by more in real terms than that of almost any other central government service. Yet, in spite of the massive building programme and the greatly improved staff-prisoner ratio, the evidence suggests that until recently the delivery of services to prisoners either had not improved or had deteriorated (Morgan, 1983; King and McDermott, 1995). The litany of prison disturbances was immensely costly and their analysis suggested that the bad conditions in which prisoners lived, and the injustices to which they were subject, were a prime cause. It was partly because the prison budget appeared to be a bottomless pit, and partly because the government was in any case committed to greater competition in the provision of public services, that what Douglas Hurd, when Home Secretary, initially considered unthinkable became thinkable: provision was made to contract out the management of prisons (Ryan and Ward, 1989). The Criminal Justice Act 1991, section 84, provides for the management of any prison to be contracted out to any agency the Secretary of State thinks appropriate. In April 1992 a new purpose-built prison for remand prisoners, the Wolds, opened under the management of Group 4 Security: there are now four prisons under private management, operated by three different companies, and more are planned. Prison escort services have also been contracted out to commercial security companies. Moreover, in April 1993, the Prison Service became an agency outside the Home Office. These developments have had significant implications for the running and accountability of prisons, though not always in the manner predicted.

From 1877, when they were brought wholly under central government control, until the Wolds Prison opened in 1992, prisons in England were the sole undivided financial and administrative responsibility of the Home Secretary, until 1962 via the Prison Commission, and subsequently by the Prison Department, a department within the Home Office (renamed the Prison Service in the mid-1980s). The Prison Service was reorganized in 1990. The 138 institutions are now grouped into twelve geographical areas (except for the five dispersal prisons which constitute a special area of responsibility), each headed by an area manager. The supreme executive body is the Prisons Board, chaired by the Director General who is accountable to the Secretary of State, who is in turn answerable to Parliament. When Mr Derek Lewis, a man with no previous experience of prisons, was recruited from the commercial world in 1992 to head the new Prison Service Agency, it was hoped that the day-to-day operation, as opposed to the strategic direction, of the Service would be made more efficient and placed at arm's length from the Home Secretary. The latter has so far proved not to be. In 1995 Mr Lewis was sacked by the Home Secretary in the wake of the break-outs from Whitemoor and Parkhurst. Though the report from the subsequent inquiry demonstrated the extent of day-to-day interference by the Minister, the inquiry team failed, or was unwilling, to make the connection between this factor and the management ills and low morale of the Service (Learmont Report, 1995).

The Legal Framework

The administration of prisons is governed by the Prison Act 1952. The Act lays down the general duties of the prison authorities; provides for personnel; defines what a prison is; and, most importantly, empowers the Minister to make rules for the management of prisons. Such rules are exercisable by statutory instrument. The current rules date from 1964 (SI No. 388, as amended) and elaborate on issues covered in the Act. They state the purpose of prisons, describe aspects of prison regimes (e.g. exercise, cells, privileges) and decision-making (e.g. parole, early release); cover staff and prisoner disciplinary procedures; and define the duties of prison boards of visitors (for a detailed discussion of the Rules see Loucks and Plotnikoff, 1993).

The Prison Service is required to produce an annual report for the Minister to lay before Parliament, and this is supplemented by the annual prison and prison disciplinary statistics produced by the Home Office (Home Office, 1996*b*, 1996*c*). Since becoming an agency the Service has also published an annual *Corporate Plan* (Prison Service, 1996) which sets out the Service's aims and 'key performance indicators' (KPIs). This has not proved to be quite the benefit for public accountability which might have been expected. Though data are now collected and annually reported which relate to the Service's KPIs— the number of hours prisoners spend out of their cells engaged in 'purposeful activities', for example—the published data are few and are presented as national aggregates. It is still not possible, therefore, to learn what is happening in particular establishments, a defect which an ex-prisoner has sought to remedy by independently producing a *Prisoners' Handbook* (Leech, 1995). Moreover, the Prison Service's annual report has become progressively briefer, more glossy, and less informative about aspects of administration which used to be reported. Information is no longer provided, for example, about the number and type of staff employed, the distribution of prescribed drugs (see Sim, 1990: chapter 5), the types of work or training in which prisoners are engaged, or the number of prisoners in each security category.

The absence of detailed data on the quality of prison regimes would arguably not matter were the Prison Rules to lay down specific conditions and facilities to which prisoners were entitled. But they seldom do. The Rules are ungenerous in their provisions, are usually not specific, and, even when specific, generally grant prison managers extensive discretion whether facilities will be provided and access assured (Richardson, 1993*a*). Moreover, the courts have held that breaches of the Prison Rules do not provide the basis for an action for breach of statutory duty and do not vest prisoners with any special rights (*Hague* v. *Deputy Governor of Parkhurst Prison* [1991] 3 All ER 733, confirming *Arbon* v. *Anderson* [1943] KB 252). Moreover, actions for false imprisonment are not available to prisoners challenging the conditions of their otherwise lawful custody (*Hague*, above, confirming *Williams* v. *The Home Office (no 2)* [1981] 1 All ER 1211). Though there is a well-established principle that the prison authorities owe a duty of care to prisoners (*Ellis* v. *Home Office* [1953] 2 QB 135), and though prisoners have been paid compensation (see Creighton and King, 1996: chapter 3), it is agreed that actions based on generally bad custodial conditions are unlikely to succeed (Feldman, 1993). When challenged, governors or the Home Office inevitably claim they are doing their best in difficult circumstances and liability for negligence is unlikely to be found in the face of such submissions. There is another route, namely judicial review, by which legal intervention may be sought. This approach has enjoyed some success in relation to the making of some decisions by the prison authorities, but the courts have maintained a largely 'hands-off' posture in relation to prison conditions.

The Prison Estate

Many British prisons provide imaginative prisoner programmes delivered by committed staff in physical settings and relaxed atmospheres which are arguably in the first rank of any prison system in Europe and a good deal better than many (for an overview of European prison systems see Van Zyl Smit and Dunkel, 1991). Most prisons are now modern, uncrowded, have good facilities, and are not prone to major disorder. There is a dark side, however. Some prisons are old and ill-resourced. Until recently many of them were insanitary and grossly overcrowded. In 1980 the then Director General of the Prison Department described the prison conditions in some of the institutions for which he was responsible as an 'affront to civilised society' (Home Office, 1981*a*: 2). These were the 'bricks of shame' about which Stern (1987), quoting Oscar Wilde's Ballad of Reading Gaol', wrote. How were these bricks laid down and allowed to remain?

There are two main types of institutions. First, the local prisons and remand centres whose primary task is to receive prisoners from and deliver prisoners to the courts and to assess and allocate those serving sentences sufficiently long for it to be thought sensible that they be allocated. Secondly, there are the prisons to which sentenced prisoners are allocated, the young offender institutions (YOIs) and, for adults, the training prisons. YOIs and training prisons are further subdivided into closed and open institutions. In fact these subdivisions reflect a prisoner security classification and the level of security which institutions are able to provide. All prisoners are security classified A, B, C, or D according to a basic scheme adopted in 1966 on the recommendation of Lord Mountbatten, following his investigation of notorious breaches of security (Mountbatten Report, 1966). Category A prisoners, whom Mountbatten envisaged would comprise no more than 120, but now comprise 7–800 (Learmont Report, 1995: para. 5.3), are those 'whose escape would constitute a danger to the public, the police or the security of the state'. Category D prisoners are those suitable for open conditions, that is, those who may be trusted not to abscond. Category B and C prisoners are those required to be held in closed conditions providing more or less security. Trial and remand prisoners are, with the exception of a few provisionally categorized as A, all assumed to be Category B. It follows that local prisons and remand centres which, broadly speaking, cater for anyone committed by the courts, are essentially Category B establishments, though in most local prisons some specially strengthened cells and areas are set aside for a few Category A prisoners.

The allocation of sentenced Category A prisoners has been the subject of long-running controversy (King and Elliott, 1977; King and Morgan, 1980). Mountbatten recommended that they be confined to a single purpose-built fortress, but on the recommendation of the Radzinowicz Committee (ACPS, 1968), it was decided that they should be dispersed among a few high-security prisons, the majority of whose occupants would be Category B or even C. In fact Category A prisoners have never been wholly accommodated in the so-called 'dispersal prisons'—pre-existing high-security units were retained and others developed—and the dispersal policy has been subtly modified so that there is now less dispersal than Radzinowicz envisaged (Home Office, 1984; Prison Service, 1991). There are currently five Category A dispersal prisons.

It is increasingly common for institutions to have multiple functions (e.g. male prisons to have a small unit for females, adult prisons to have a wing for young prisoners, training prisons to include a small section for remand prisoners). This is an important development which, in the light of Woolf's recommendation that there be developed 'community prisons' (1991: paras. 11.49–11.68), is likely to become more common. It has become more difficult, therefore, to delineate the numbers and characteristics of different types of institutions. Moreover, it is a feature of penal institutions that their titles and functions change rather more frequently than their facilities and culture.

At the time of writing there are thirty-seven predominantly local prisons for males (of which three contain small units for women) and two training prisons that have small units for remand prisoners. There are eighteen remand centres for remands under 21 years of age, the majority of which are part of a local prison or YOI complex. There are sixty-seven male training prisons, five of which are high-security dispersal prisons and twelve of which are open prisons. There are twenty-two YOIs—the number has been significantly reduced in recent years in response to the declining number of young prisoners—of which four are open. Finally, there are sixteen prisons that wholly, partly, or occasionally accommodate women, though the hub of the women's system, Holloway Prison in London, is a multi-functional local prison which accommodates between a quarter and a fifth of the total female prison population (Casale, 1989; Rock, 1996). Prisons for women are also open or closed.

About these 138 institutions it is possible to generalize as follows. A quarter of the estate—thirty-five institutions—comprises Victorian, generally radial, institutions. Most of these prisons fulfill a role similar to that they had over a century ago. Most are local prisons in major cities or county towns, formerly city or county gaols. One or two—like Dartmoor and Parkhurst—occupy isolated sites, a legacy of their former role as government centres for convicts awaiting transportation. They are now training prisons, with a regional or national role. Many of the open prisons and YOIs are former military camps, residential institutions, or country houses, but most now incorporate more recently added accommodation blocks. Thus the majority of prisons, more than three-fifths, are entirely or mostly purpose-built since the 1950s. Only two prisons were built in the first half of the twentieth century.

The Prison Estate and 'Treatment and Training'

This pattern of capital investment reflects the Prison Service's historical commitment to treatment and training. Until the 1990s nearly all the new building went into the 'training' sector for adults or youths. The training establishments also got the lion's share of other resources and were largely protected from overcrowding, which was concentrated, as a matter of policy, in the local establishments. Here, in treatment and training terms, nothing much was expected to happen. In the local prisons were concentrated the prisoners excluded from the noble mission: the untried and unsentenced, legally ineligible for treatment and training; prisoners serving short sentences, for whom there was said to be insufficient time to achieve anything; and the seriously recalcitrant, judged to be beyond the training pale. Over time the local prisons became the dumping grounds for many of those prisoners with whom the training prisons could not cope, those administratively segregated or 'inappropriately allocated' (see Woolf Report, 1991: paras. 12.221–263).

The official explanation for crowding the local prisons was that Victorian prisons, with their large cells, could be crowded to a degree that modern prison cells could not. There was some truth in this, and one or two of the older radial training prisons were allowed to become crowded when system crowding was at its height. But this explanation was belied by the fact that the modern purpose-built remand centres, with small cells, were also crowded. Concentrating crowding in remand establishments was managerially convenient. It prejudiced the noble mission least and it was assumed—a reasonable assumption prior to the disturbances in 1986 (several of which occurred in remand establishments—see HMCIP, 1987*b*)—that remand prisoners would accept the disgraceful conditions in which they were often housed in a way that medium- and long-term sentenced prisoners would not. In the 1970s and early 1980s most of the disturbances occurred in high-security long-term prisons. And the attention of most untried prisoners *is* focused largely on their cases and prospects. They are oriented to life beyond the walls and, it used to be thought, are therefore least likely to protest about their living conditions.

The consequence was that those prisoners who on any criterion should have been given the least oppressive conditions—the untried subject to the presumption of innocence—typically experienced the most impoverished regimes

(King and Morgan, 1976; Casale and Plotnikoff, 1990; Morgan, 1993*a*) and vice versa. These were the conditions that were 'an affront to a civilised society' and in report after report the Chief Inspector of Prisons chronicled: the 'degrading' and 'insanitary' accommodation; the slopping-out procedures; the 'enforced idleness'; the prolonged daily cellular confinement; the miserable visiting rooms; and the general absence of facilities (for particularly graphic examples see HMCIP, 1988, 1990, 1993).[7] About the untried there was general agreement. They were the 'forgotten people' (HMCIP, 1989; para. 4.30), held in 'completely insupportable' conditions (House of Commons Home Affairs Committee, 1981: para. 54), 'the worst . . . the prison system has to offer' (Stern, 1987: 33). Most damningly, the Council of Europe Committee for the Prevention of Torture (the CPT; for an account see Morgan and Evans, 1994), concluded in 1990 that conditions in Brixton, Leeds, and Wandsworth prisons—all three Victorian local prisons—amounted to 'inhuman and degrading' treatment (Council of Europe, 1991). The phrase could not have been used lightly: it suggested that the conditions might be held to breach Article 3 of the European Convention for the Protection of Fundamental Human Rights. It was certainly difficult to see that the conditions complied with Prison Rules 1 and 2, with their references to the encouragement of useful lives, self-respect, and a sense of personal responsibility.

Minimum or Aspirational Standards

Critical opinion arguably became monomaniacally obsessed with the bad physical conditions—particularly 'slopping out'—in local prisons in the 1980s. But this is unsurprising. The building programme further improved conditions in the training prison sector, with the consequence that the state of the local prisons was thrown into ever starker relief. There seemed to be no limit to crowding, and as the rising system capacity was soaked up by the rise in the prison population, so the prospect of an end to overcrowding in the local prisons looked like a mirage. The majority of persons who experienced imprisonment never saw anything but their local prison (Sparks, 1971), and the courts maintained their hands-off policy regarding prisoners' general quality of life. Raising basic standards in local prisons became the litmus test for radical change. The penal pressure groups and prison staff associations unanimously pressed for the adoption of a code of minimum living standards which, set alongside a clearly delineated timetable for implementation, would in the end be incorporated in a new set of Prison Rules and made legally enforceable (Casale, 1984; Gostin and Staunton, 1985; Casale and Plotnikoff, 1989, 1990).

[7] Among earlier detailed descriptions of prison life are several research studies (Morris and Morris, 1963; Emery, 1970; Sparks, 1971; Bottoms and McClintock, 1973; King and Morgan, 1976; King and Elliot, 1977; Jones and Cornes, 1977; Carlen, 1983), some excellent prisoner, though regrettably no good staff, autobiographical accounts (Benney, 1948; Norman, 1958; Curtis, 1973; Caird, 1974; Boyle, 1977, 1984; Peckham, 1985), and a few anthologies of prison writings or interviews (Parker, 1970, 1973; Priestley, 1989; Padel and Stevenson, 1988; Casale, 1989).

In his analysis of the background to the 1990 prison disturbances Woolf focused on the intolerable conditions in which many prisoners, particularly remand prisoners, were living. His response to the standards debate was very different from that of Lord Godard who had held that 'it would be fatal to all discipline in prisons if governors and warders had to perform their duty with the fear of an action before their eyes if they in any way deviated from the rules' (*Arbon* v. *Anderson* [1943] KB 252), or Lord Denning, who held that 'if the courts were to entertain actions by disgruntled prisoners, the governor's life would be made intolerable' (*Becker* v. *Home Office* [1972] 2 QB 407). Woolf did not favour excessive judicial intervention in prison life, certainly nothing approaching the extraordinary litigiousness of the US system (Jacobs, 1980; Morgan and Bronstein, 1985), which is nowhere replicated in Europe (Van Zyl Smit and Dunkel, 1991). But he was nevertheless keen to extend the modest degree of judicial intervention which the domestic and European courts have undertaken in recent years (particularly in relation to disciplinary proceedings and prisoners' access to the courts and lawyers).[8]

In order that living conditions be addressed Woolf favoured an interlocking hierarchy of 'contracts' or 'compacts'—between the Chief Executive of the Service and the Minister, between area managers and governors, between governors and officers, and between governors and prisoners—setting out resources and facilities to be provided for a stated prison population. This would permit, in the case of prisoners, 'legitimate expectations' to be generated (Woolf Report, 1991: para. 12.129), which 'could provide a platform for an application for judicial review' were those expectations unreasonably not met (*ibid.*: para. 12.123). The contracts should not be drawn up in such a way that they would give prisoners private rights leading to awards of damages if breached. But the contracts might lead, Woolf hoped, to the promulgation of aspirational standards, to a system of accrediting prisons for having achieved those standards (as happens in the USA) and, eventually, to the incorporation of those standards in a new set of Prison Rules. Furthermore, Woolf recommended that prisoners be given reasons, in writing if they reasonably request it, 'for any decision which materially and adversely affects them' (*ibid.*: paras. 14.300, 14.307).

[8] In 1975 the Court of Appeal held that prisoners were not entitled to legal representation at disciplinary hearings (*Fraser v. Mudge* [1975] 3 All ER 1036). Likewise in 1978 the Divisional Court held that disciplinary hearings were not subject to judicial review (*R.* v. *Board of Visitors of Hull Prison ex p. St Germain* [1978] 2 WLR 598). The decision was overturned by the Court of Appeal (*R.* v. *Board of Visitors of Hull Prison ex p. St Germain* [1979] All ER 701), thereby opening up the prospect that this and other cases be decided by the courts on their merits. Five years later it was held (*R.* v. *Secretary of State ex p. Tarrant and another* [1984] 1 All ER 799) that though prisoners were not entitled to legal representation, Boards had a discretion to grant it (see Fitzgerald, 1985; Prior Report, 1985; Richardson, 1993*a*).

Apart from disciplinary hearings, judicial intervention has had most practical effect with regard to prisoners' correspondence and access to the courts, both areas of direct interest to the legal profession. Initial headway was made at the European Court of Human Rights (ECHR). The case of *Silver* v. *UK* ((1983) 5 ECHR 347) led to significant changes in the system of censorship, for example (for detailed discussion of reported cases and their impact see Feldman, 1993, Richardson, 1993*a*).

Woolf's recommendations would, if implemented, have represented a significant advance on the position, which still prevails, in which prisoners can be and are transferred in large numbers, without explanation, to prisons relatively distant from their homes as part of a normal 'training' allocation, better to distribute prisoner numbers within the prison estate, or as an administrative control measure. Prisoners still have no entitlement to be given reasons for either their initial or subsequent security classification. These decisions critically affect the quality of prisoners' lives. Moreover, several of the structural recommendations which framed Woolf's concern to protect basic living standards were rejected or sidelined. His proposal that there be introduced a prison rule that no prison hold more prisoners than 3 per cent above its CNA, except temporarily, or following the laying by the Minister of an authorizing certificate before both Houses of Parliament (*ibid.*: paras. 11.141–11.142) was rejected (Home Office, 1991: para. 6.13). His suggestion that remand prisoners not be automatically categorized as B was rejected (Home Office, 1991: para. 520), and his proposal that the proportion of prisoners in high-security categories be reduced—a recommendation made repeatedly by those who have reviewed the working of the security classification system (see King and Morgan, 1980: chapter 3; Prison Department, 1981; Morgan, 1983; Home Office, 1984; HMCIP, 1984; Scottish Prison Service, 1990; Hadfield and Lakes, 1991) was ignored. Finally, his recommendation that clusters of 'community prisons' be developed so that prisoners be able better to maintain their community ties (Woolf Report, 1991: paras. 11.49–11.68), though accepted in principle, was made all but impossible by the dramatic growth in the prison population and the need to find places for them. Indeed further disturbances, like that at Wymott in September 1993, were directly attributable to inappropriate allocation policies stemming from precisely these population pressures (HMCIP, 1993*b*).

The Prison Service did not ignore the standards debate. But the steps taken were modest and they were in a direction different from that for which the penal pressure groups had asked. In response to Woolf the Service undertook to develop a 'model regime' for local prisons and remand centres, 'taking particular account of the needs for unconvicted prisoners' (Home Office, 1991: para. 7.16). This undertaking was fulfilled in the following year (Prison Service, 1992*b*) and in 1994 the Service adopted national *Operating Standards* that all establishments would 'aim to meet over time' (Prison Service, 1994). The standards are 'not prisoner entitlements', however. On the contrary their enjoyment is 'conditional upon prisoners complying with the obligations placed upon them', obligations which have since been spelt out in a 'national framework for incentives and earned privileges' (Prison Service, 1996*b*: 26–7). Core 'earnable privileges' have been established—including 'extra or improved' visits, eligibility to participate in enhanced earning schemes, and time out of cell for association—with every prison being expected to develop prisoner 'compacts' according to which prisoners may enjoy 'basic', 'standard', or 'enhanced' levels of privilege depending on their compliance. This is the framework which the government now proposes, in the Crime (Sentences) Bill, to use so that prisoners be able to 'earn' their early release.

Woolf's 'contracts' have subtly been turned, as some commentators warned was likely (Casale, 1993), into mechanisms for exerting greater paternalistic control *over* prisoners rather than establishing minimum standards and rights for *their* protection. Judicial review to enforce prisoners' legitimate expectations'—a 'notoriously flexible' doctrine (Richardson, 1993*b*)—now seems a fragile and remote means for securing prisoners' redress against any general decline in custodial standards. Prisoners may individually complain about any unjust allocation of privileges, but this is no safeguard against any decline in overall standards consequent to a rising population and cuts in the prison budget. In 1996, after several years of reported improvement, the Prison Service recorded a decline in the average hours per prisoner in 'purposeful' activity and the proportion of prisoners held in establishments which unlock prisoners for more than twelve hours on weekdays (Prison Service, 1996*a*: 15).

Inspection and Complaints

Part of the case for establishing a code of standards for prisoners' living conditions is that the effectiveness of all grievance-ventilation and accountability mechanisms depends on there being a rudder by which overseers can steer. The ability to be accountable *to* someone depends on knowing what one is accountable *for*.

Every prison in England and Wales is served by a board of visitors, a body of lay volunteers, currently appointed by the Secretary of State, and the last vestigial link with the days when most prisons were administered by local government. Until April 1992 the boards had three functions: inspecting the state of the prison; hearing prisoner grievances; and undertaking disciplinary hearings of more serious charges. The third function was long held by critics to be incompatible with the first and second and the principal reason why the boards' 'watchdog' role was so poorly developed (Martin, 1975; Justice, 1983; Maguire and Vagg, 1984; Prior Report, 1985). This criticism, plus evidence that there remained major shortcomings in the quality of justice dispensed by boards, in spite of procedural improvements following the decision in 1979 that board disciplinary hearings are subject to judicial review (Light and Mattfield, 1988; Morgan and Jones, 1991), led to the recommendation that boards no longer be involved in disciplinary proceedings (Woolf Report, 1991: paras. 14.363–435).[9] Boards of visitors were relieved of their disciplinary

---

[9] Prior to April 1992 there were in effect three levels at which offences committed in prison could be dealt with. If they were relatively minor they were dealt with by governors whose powers of punishment were limited to 28 days' loss of remission: 95 per cent of cases were dealt with by governors. If they were more serious they could be committed to the Board of Visitors, whose powers were limited to 120 days' loss of remission (prior to 1986 there was no limit to the amount of remission that boards could remove in the case of grave offences). In the case of serious offences against the prison disciplinary code (Prison Rule 47) that were also *prima facie* criminal offences, the prison authorities could refer the matter to the police who might in turn refer it to the Crown

function, and the close identification with local management to which their disciplinary role was said to lead. But it is not clear that boards have become more willing publicly to criticize conditions or staff (boards, with some commendable exceptions, have repeatedly been accused of failing to act decisively during prison disturbances to protect prisoners from staff reprisals—see Home Office, 1977; Thomas and Pooley, 1980; Martin, 1980; Woolf Report, 1991: paras. 8.124–8.126), nor that their credibility with prisoners has improved (Worrall, 1995).

There has been a prisons inspectorate, outwith the Prison Service, though part of the Home Office, since 1981. The establishment of HMCIP was recommended by the May Committee (1979: 92–6) and represents that Committee's only lasting achievement (for an account of HMCIP's early development see Morgan, 1985). Prior to 1981 the prisons inspectorate was part of the management of the Prison Department and its reports were confidential. Today the Inspectorate's reports are published and, under the leadership of successive Chief Inspectors (notably Judge Steven Tumim 1987–95), HMCIP has established a reputation for independence and robust criticism. HMCIP is charged with reporting to the Minister 'on the treatment of prisoners and conditions in prison' (Prison Act 1952, section 5a(3)), and does so by conducting regular inspections of prisons; undertaking occasional thematic reviews of aspects of policy; and investigating major incidents. The Chief Inspector's critiques have invariably attracted publicity, but they have sometimes lacked policy bite because it is not always clear by what standards he concludes that provisions are 'impoverished', 'degrading', 'unacceptable', and so on. On the occasions when his criteria and solutions have been made precise, as in his unequivocal denunciation of 'slopping out' (HMCIP, 1989, and as co-author of Part II of the Woolf Report, 1991: para. 11.105), the impact has been considerable.

It was partly lack of precision, and thus accountability, which robbed the prisoner complaints system of credibility with prisoners and which, *inter alia*, led Woolf to conclude that there was an absence of justice in prisons. Prisoners have always been able to complain about any aspect of their custody to their board of visitors, to their governor, or to the Secretary of State by way of petition. But the system lacked the straightforwardness, expedition, effectiveness, and independence which Woolf argued any satisfactory grievance ventilation system should have (Woolf Report, 1991: para. 14.309). Changes were already in train when Woolf was conducting his inquiry. In 1990, following a series of reports (Ditchfield and Austin, 1986; HMCIP, 1987a; Home Office, 1989), a new integrated grievance system was introduced, designed, *inter alia*, to reduce the delays which characterized previous arrangements. Prisoners are now expected to complain first to unit managers or the duty

---

Prosecution Service with a view to prosecution. In April 1992 the middle tier was removed, meaning that the maximum punishment which could be imposed in internal proceedings was reduced from 120 to 28 days' loss of remission, which, with the abolition of remission with the implementation in October 1992 of the Criminal Justice Act 1991, became 28 days' deferred release.

governor or to the board of visitors, with the option, if they are dissatisfied with the outcome, of taking the matter further to the area manager. At all levels time limits for replies have been introduced and replies must be reasoned and in writing. Prisoners may still take up their complaints externally (to an MP or to the 'ombudsman', or by seeking judicial review in the domestic or European courts), but these relatively time-consuming avenues are likely to be considered appropriate only for more serious complaints of particular types.

Woolf welcomed the new system but, like previous commentators, considered there should be an independent 'complaints adjudicator' at the apex of the system (*ibid.*: paras. 14.326–362). This independent element has since been introduced in the form of a Prisons Ombudsman, the first of whom was appointed and began receiving complaints in 1994. No evaluation of the new complaints system has yet been conducted, though HMCIP reports suggest that the time limits are often breached. Like HMCIP the first Prisons Ombudsman, Sir Peter Woodhead, has proved to be both independent and assertive. In his first two reports he has fully described the obstacles he has had to confront, and they have been many. His office, and terms of reference, is not spelt out in statute and the ministerial documents that describe his brief contained ambiguities and lacunae (Prison Ombudsman, 1996: paras. 2.1–2.25). However, he is not restricted, as his title implies, to matters of maladministration. He may consider the merits of decisions, including disciplinary awards and the clinical judgements of prison doctors, and his remit covers both state-run and contracted-out prisons.

In about a quarter of all cases the Prison Ombudsman has failed to meet the target set for him of providing a substantive answer to complaints within eight weeks of receipt. But he has explained why this is so, and the reasons lend substance to the rumours that the Ombudsman has upset both the Home Secretary and the Prison Service. He was initially not given staff sufficient to cope with the number of complaints received. There have been numerous delays by the Service in providing him with the documents which form the basis of the bulk of his investigations. And there have been repeated disputes over his powers and access to information, disputes about which the Ombudsman has not been afraid to go public. Moreover, though the majority of complaints received in his first eighteen months of operation were found to be ineligible, of those that were eligible and fully investigated 44 per cent were upheld. It seems clear, as the Ombudsman sardonically observes, that 'the initial Prison Service consideration of complaints is not based on the same criteria as mine' (*ibid.*: para. 6.33).

Privatization

Privatization, or more accurately contracting out,[10] has been by far the most controversial prisons development of the 1990s (for general reviews of

---

[10] Contracting out is not synonymous with privatization. Both the management of prisons and the delivery of services within state-managed prisons could be contracted out to non-commercial

competing arguments see Logan, 1990 and Shichor, 1995). The privatized management of prisons has been vigorously opposed in principle on the ground that the administration of state punishment is fundamentally a state responsibility and because it is wrong to derive financial profit from the deliberate infliction of pain by the state. A pragmatic long-term objection is that the growth of privatized prisons represents an investment stake by the shrinking military-industrial complex in the burgeoning crime-control complex, an investment which will create a vested interest in the expanded use of imprisonment. The huge growth of the prison population in the United States, which currently stands at 1.6 million or 600 per 1,000 population, is generally taken as the spectre to which privatization is leading or might lead (Christie, 1994; Donziger, 1995). Most of the argument about privatization has concerned day-to-day accountability, however.

The Criminal Justice Act 1991, the terms of which have since been extended to all prisons, including those in Scotland, provides that for every contracted-out prison a 'controller', a Crown Servant, is appointed to oversee the running of the prison and ensure compliance with the Prison Rules and the specific terms of the contract. The 'prison custody officers' and the 'director' appointed by the contractor must be approved, and though they have the power to search prisoners and their visitors they do not have formal disciplinary powers. These are vested in the controller, who in practice is a governor-grade employee of the Prison Service with an office within the contracted-out prison. Thus, it is argued by the government and some commentators, contracted-out prisons are *more accountable* than state-run prisons. The state has in no sense relinquished its responsibilities. And in addition to the general legal framework, the contract is a backdoor means of delivering the higher standards which cannot be enforced in state-run establishments. Moreover, the contracting out of particular services within prisons—employment, education, and training, the provision of food, laundry, and medical services, and so on—arguably represents the normalization of prison regimes for which many critics have long pressed. Whether privatization reflects the demise of the rehabilitative ideal, and acceptance that prisoners can as easily be warehoused by the private sector as the state (Beyens and Snacken, 1996: 241), or, rather, a means, through the contract, of breathing life back into the rehabilitative ideal (Taylor and Pease, 1989) is contested and remains to be seen.

The deeply felt antagonisms over privatization—not least among the prison staff associations who have vigorously opposed it, but from whose senior ranks the security industry has easily recruited its directors—has stimulated a process of disinformation and selective reporting which has made objective appraisal difficult. The government pursued privatization primarily to tackle restrictive staff practices, and thus high costs, in a state-run system not noted for its innovative or effective management. By this test the success of the

agencies such as local government or the major charities. To date, however, contracts have been awarded almost entirely to commercial providers, notably the leading security companies.

initiative does not rest only on the relative unit costs of contracted-out compared to state-run institutions—costs that for various reasons are not comparable—but rather in the degree to which practices in state-run prisons are transformed by the threat of privatization and the need to tender against contractor-competitors. What is clear is that, after some early difficulties, the small contracted-out sector is setting some high standards—the Chief Inspector's report on Doncaster Prison, managed by Premier Prison Services, refers to several aspects of its performance as 'impressive' or 'outstanding' (HMCIP, 1996*b*)—though not necessarily higher than those achieved in equivalent state-run prisons (Bottomley *et al.*, 1997; James *et al.*, 1997).

This raises the question whether privatization involves an increasingly segmented prison system with higher or lower standards prevailing in different institutions depending on whether they are local or training, state-run or contracted-out (Morgan, 1993*b*). There is also the ancillary question whether the state service is to be left with responsibility for the high-security and more intractable, and thus most costly, sectors of the system.

Special Units

The Prison Service has become preoccupied (as have other systems in Europe—see Van Zyl Smit and Dunkel, 1991; Muncie and Sparks, 1991) with the containment and control of a relatively small but growing number of long-term and allegedly 'dangerous' or 'disruptive' prisoners (see Bottoms and Light, 1987). Thirty years ago there was no talk of dangerous prisoners and no maximum-security accommodation in the system. Now there are almost 3,000 places in the dispersal prisons and the network of special security and special (control) units (SSUs and SUs), of which there are currently three each. The terminology represents an important distinction. Prisoners who are a *security* risk are not necessarily a *control* problem. Indeed, though the two occasionally overlap, quite the contrary. Many prisoners who have the personal capacity and external organization backing to escape from relatively secure prisons—international drugs racketeers, for example—are often model prisoners (though according to Laycock (1983: 33) over 70 per cent of terrorists are considered by staff to be involved in subversive activity). Conversely, some prisoners, including many of the 3,300 sex offenders, would be judged to present a profound danger to the public were they to escape yet are themselves at risk within the prison community. They must be segregated or held in the VPUs.

The proliferation of special prisoner statuses and units poses problems for procedural and substantive justice. It also complicates the question of standards and upsets the balance of incentives and discentives for good behaviour (Home Office, 1984). Model prisoners may, in King and Elliot's phrase (1977), be held in an 'electronic coffin' if considered a security threat (for reviews of the history and operation of the SSUs, see Walmesley, 1989, and Bottomley and Hay, 1991) or suffer an impoverished regime in segregation if they are repeatedly attacked by fellow prisoners (Priestley, 1981; Prison Reform Trust, 1990). Conversely, some special units may absorb such disproportionate resources, afford so many privileges, and gain such a prestigious reputation that the envy and opposition of the service is excited because it is said that the occupants are being rewarded for their bad behaviour.[11] How to create conditions within which security and order can be achieved with respect to long-term and difficult prisoners, yet establish a ladder of opportunity whereby those prisoners will wish to be recategorized and transferred to less secure conditions, is the single most difficult management issue confronting the Prison Service (Home Office, 1984; Dunbar, 1985; Scottish Prison Service, 1990). Before considering how the English Prison Service is addressing that issue, and what the future shape of the system is likely to be, we need first to consider the social dynamics of prison life.

THE SOCIOLOGY OF PRISONS

Prisons represent the power of the state ultimately to coerce, and order within prisons may in the last resort rest on the use of force by staff. Yet disorder is not the norm of prison life. Order in prisons, as in any other social setting, is negotiated (McDermott and King, 1988). The negotiation is not between equals; yet order within prisons is for the most part achieved with the consent, albeit the grudging consent, of prisoners who invariably far outnumber the prison officers who guard them. Disturbances may have become a perennial feature of the British penal landscape, but most prisons are orderly most of the time. By the same token, the 110,000 offences against the prison disciplinary code that are punished each year belie the fact that staff and prisoners generally coexist harmoniously: frictions are for the most part resolved through more subtle accommodations or the use of what the Prison Officers' Association once described honestly as the 'alternative disciplinary system' (1984: 2). These assertions prompt the question of what counts as order within prisons and whose standpoint prevails.

The sociological literature on prisons points to the existence of a prison culture—a set of attitudes and a way of doing things—in which both prisoners and prison officers have roles. This literature is largely American and mostly based on studies of long-term prisoners in relatively high-security prisons. It is questionable, therefore, to what extent that literature applies to Britain or all prisons within Britain. Few social scientists have been permitted to set up their

---

[11] The most famous example of the marginalization of a special unit concerned the Barlinnie prison Special Unit, Glasgow (see Boyle, 1977, 1984; Coyle, 1987; Cooke, 1989). In England Grendon Underwood prison, a prison which provides a psychiatrically orientated therapeutic regime which has not been replicated elsewhere, has to some extent suffered the same process (see Genders and Player, 1994).

anthropological huts on British prison landings,[12] and though a good deal can be learnt about life in prison from the autobiographical accounts of prisoners, few prisoners have written analytically about the minutiae of daily life.[13] Prison staff, retired or serving, have contributed even less to the literature.[14] To the extent that prisons exhibit a specific culture there has been a long-standing debate whether it is of primarily indigenous or imported origin. The indigenous approach is represented by Sykes's classic account of the *Society of Captives* (1958) and Goffmann's seminal discussion of *Asylums* (1968). Both writers stress the distinctiveness of prison life (Sykes specifically and Goffmann generally) in relation to 'total institutions'—prisons, psychiatric hospitals, detention camps, and so on—because of their encompassing character, relatively shut off as prisoners are from the world at large. Within this tradition the prison has been seen as a more or less closed social system in which it is the task of one group of persons, the prison officers, to manage or process another group, the prisoners. Sykes's focus is on the 'pains of imprisonment'— the various deprivations that living in prisons involves—while Goffmann's stress is on the dynamics of mortification—the transformation of the self—that results from entering a 'people-processing' institution. In both accounts the prisoner is described as being under psychological assault, with the usual supports for and expressions of personal identity—possessions, control over personal appearance, autonomy of movement, personal privacy and security, and so on—being greatly diminished. Prisoners may develop individualistic responses to these stresses, responses ranging from escape attempts or playing the role of the barrack-room lawyer to psychological withdrawal or intensive auto-didacticism. However, for Sykes the distinctive aspect of the prison culture—largely, though not entirely, its emphasis on prisoner solidarity against staff—represents a functional response to these social and psychological assaults: a means by which the rejected can reject their rejectors (McCorkle and Korn, 1954) and thus maintain a degree of self-esteem. According to this view, the more that prisoners adopt a cohesive stance, the more the pains of imprisonment can be mitigated for everyone.

---

[12] Major exceptions include the Morrises (Morris and Morris, 1963), King and colleagues (King and Morgan, 1976; King and Elliott, 1977; King and McDermott, 1989, 1992); Carlen (1983) and Bottoms and colleagues (Bottoms and McClintock, 1973; Sparks *et al.*, 1997). Though not allowed to set up their hut on a landing, Cohen and Taylor (1972) gathered rich material on long-term prisoners' experience of custody by running an educational class within a prison.

[13] Recent British exceptions have been Caird (1974), Boyle (1977, 1984), and Peckham (1985). There is of course a rich international literature of prison writings, of which the most important recent example is Serge (1970).

[14] As far as I am aware the only British prison governor or officer, retired or serving, who has written about his experience since Miller (1976) and Cronin (1967) is Coyle (1994): neither of the first two of these accounts, or indeed those of predecessors (see Priestley, 1989, for an anthology), is particularly analytical or repays attention, except in ways the authors probably did not intend. By contrast, several well-known American contributions to the sociology of prison literature have come from persons with direct involvement in prisons administration: Clemmer (1940) was a senior prisons administrator; Morris (1974) was appointed a 'special master' by a court to oversee the implementation of an order relating to a prison; and, most recently, Dilulio (1987), a former warden, has reflected generally on the business of *Governing Prisons*.

This process represents a paradox. Some of the relative deprivations of prison life are the result of staff attempts to maintain external security and internal order. Yet to some extent the pains of imprisonment stimulate a solidaristic counter-culture subversive of official objectives. Thus the apparently total power of staff is compromised by their need to reach an accommodation with their charges in order that routine tasks be accomplished. In this way, whatever purposes prisons officially pursue—treatment and training, rehabilitation, deterrence, and so on—are in practice undermined by the daily reality of the negotiated settlements which take place between officers and prisoners. This suggests that in reality prisons are unlikely to be about the pursuit of noble missions: they are ultimately more about practical survival in settings which, because inherently coercive, have extreme potential for instability and disorder.

The problem with indigenous accounts of prison culture is that they fail to provide any ready explanation of change other than the sort of minor shifts from crisis to equilibrium which might occur within a closed system. For example, indigenous accounts do not explain the more fundamental changes in operational policy and prisoner response which have taken place in British prisons since 1945 or, more dramatically, which occurred in American prison systems in the wake of the black civil rights movement in the 1960s. Thus, by contrast, importation theorists stress the connection between relationships within prisons and those outside—for example, changes in political expectations, the legitimacy of authority, and legal culture (see Jacobs' (1977) classic study of *Stateville* Prison, Illinois). Importationists also highlight the degree to which the cultural norms to which prisoners subscribe, and the individual roles they adopt in prison, are extensions of subcultures of which they are a part, or roles that they occupied, before being incarcerated (Irwin and Cressey, 1962; Irwin, 1970). According to this approach the prison culture is not peculiar to prison at all: it is both a microcosm of the wider society and a sort of career continuation of the criminal culture of the streets from which a high proportion of prisoners are drawn. Thus Irwin and Cressey identify a 'thief subculture' outside prison which stresses group loyalty and toughness. To the extent that there is group solidarity between *some* prisoners within prison, then this 'convict' or 'prisoner' subculture is both an extension of that street culture *and* an adaption in response to the contingencies of life inside.

Today the indigenous and importationist perspectives are generally seen as complementary (Jacobs, 1979). Moreover, whatever is to be learnt from the American literature, British prisons are unlikely to exhibit the same cultural patterns as have been found in the USA. There has hitherto not, for example, been sophisticated organized crime in Britain on the scale found in the USA; nor, with one or two notable exceptions in particular cities, have criminal street gangs regularly employing life-threatening violence been a prominent feature of British crime, and thus their influence has not been greatly felt in prisons. Further, maximum-security prisons of the kind which are widely employed for the mainstream prison population in some US states (Texas, for example: see

Martin and Ekland-Olson, 1987) have only recently become part of the English system, and even today only a minority of the prison population is housed in such conditions. Finally, though British society is riven by deeply engrained class differences and, since the mass immigration from the Caribbean and the Indian subcontinent in the period since 1945, racial divides, Britain is nevertheless culturally a relatively homogeneous society. There are not the deep cleavages which in the USA have historically separated the African-American from the white population and in more recent times, the Hispanic from the English-speaking community. These cleavages have fatally dominated parts of the American prison scene (Colvin, 1992) to an extent largely undreamt-of in Britain and, indeed, most of Western Europe. Not surprisingly, therefore, Mathieson's (1965) classic study of a Norwegian prison failed to reveal much in the way of prisoner solidarity. On the contrary, prisoners were relatively weak and isolated: they were vulnerable to the discretionary favours which the staff were in a position to distribute.

The British 'sociology of prisons' literature has emphasized the complexity and varied quality of prison communities: researchers, critical of stereotypical portrayals of staff and prisoners, have argued that both groups adapt to the particular circumstances in which they find themselves. Total institutions may be characterized by social relations and 'ways of doing things' that are different from those prevailing in the world outside, but prisons nevertheless differ a good deal along all the regime dimensions that Goffmann provisionally identified (see Jones and Cornes, 1977: chapter 4; King and McDermott, 1989). Further, it is clear that the regimes which different groups of prisoners experience differ considerably within prisons (King and Morgan, 1976; chapter 3): this is evident also from many of the institutional reports of HMCIP. Thus, while prisoners' responses to custody may owe much to their previous institutional and criminal careers, they are also shaped by the length of their sentences (see e.g. Sapsford, 1983, on life-sentence prisoners), the physical restrictions to which they are subject (see Cohen and Taylor, 1972, on a high-security unit), and whatever opportunities and facilities (or lack of them) are provided (King and Elliot, 1977; Sparks, Bottoms, and Hay, 1996).

It is also evident from the dismally limited literature on prison staff that the background characteristics of prison officers have changed a good deal in recent years, as have their working conditions. Officers now, as in the past, generally join the Service in their late 20s or 30s, after a spell in other occupations. But whereas the majority used to be recruited from the regular armed forces (Morris and Morris, 1963: chapter 4; Jones and Cornes, 1977: chapter 7), this is seldom the case today. Thirty years ago few prison officers had any educational qualifications. Today the indelibly working-class culture of the majority, shaped now by previous experience of manual and clerical work rather than military discipline, is blended with a sizeable minority of recruits with 'A' levels or degrees (26 per cent in 1985—see Marsh *et al.*, 1985: table 3.6) seeking advancement within an integrated career structure. Moreover, the simple world of the 'gentleman' governors and prison 'screws' of the 1940s and

1950s has been complicated by the employment of women in all institutions and at all levels, and the importation of specialists who, in the 1960s and 1970s at least, took on the majority of the plum 'treatment and training' tasks— education, social work, and the various therapies with which the Service flirted (Thomas, 1972: chapter 9). It should always be remembered that prison officers typically spend a far higher proportion of their lives in prison than do their charges. They also have a culture, shaped by their previous experience and the increasingly complicated managerial context within which they operate. The living conditions of prisoners are the working conditions of prison officers.

In criminal career terms, indigenous and importationist factors may reinforce each other. Clemmer (1940), a pioneer American analyst of the prison community, wrote of the process of 'prisonization', the gradual destructive socialization of prisoners into the norms of prison life which make it difficult for them successfully to adapt to a law-abiding life outside, thereby possibly deepening criminality. The idea of prisonization, which most researchers have rejected on the ground that it posits too mechanical and linear a process, bears a close resemblance to the idea of institutionalization, a syndrome which analysts of closed mental hospitals have employed to describe the adjustment, with pathological consequences, of patients to stultifying regimes (see Barton, 1959). Most of the prison studies identify a minority of prisoners whose reaction to custody is one of extreme social withdrawal or retreatism, though they appear to be in a minority (see Morris and Morris, 1963: 173–4). However, there are abundant references to prisoners knowing how to 'do time' passively 'behind their doors', typically 'old lags' imprisoned on many previous occasions and resistant to more open regimes and extended association (see Morris and Morris, 1963: 172–3; King and Elliott, 1977: 241–4). These recidivist prisoners could well be said to be 'institutionalized' or 'prisonized' within a penal tradition which was still the norm when the Morrises undertook their study of Pentonville in the 1960s, and which lives on in the local prisons where most short-sentence prisoners continue to do their time today.

To the extent that there is a prisoner culture it is plausible to see it as the product of utilitarian responses which different groups of prisoners, depending on their background, reputation, offence, and length of sentence, make to the pressures and opportunities arising out of captivity. There may be an informal code of not 'grassing' to staff, but there is also as much rivalry and hatred in prisons as there is comradeship (Morris and Morris, 1963: 168). Moreover, there are plenty of ways in which prisoners can and do inform staff about those prisoners whose behaviour they may wish to control, either for reasons of power play or simply to prevent a breakdown in the orderliness which most prisoners and staff have a vested interest in preserving. All the British studies emphasize with Sykes that one of the worst aspects of prison life is having to live with other prisoners. This may be because fellow prisoners are 'dirty in their personal habits, socially unpleasant or guilty of crimes which other prisoners regard as revolting' (Morris and Morris, 1963: 168–9); or because of a lack of privacy within a highly restricted physical space (Cohen and Taylor, 1972: 80–1); or because of the discomforting strategies which colleagues adopt to cope with whatever time they have to serve (King and Elliott, 1977: chapter 8); or for reasons of racial prejudice (Genders and Player, 1989).

Clearly there are moral and power hierarchies within prison communities. One of the reasons why most prisoners are keen that order, however tenuous, should be maintained (and, as a collary, do not wish to get involved in any incident if it erupts) is that major disturbances provide opportunities to settle scores and confirm moral hierarchies (see Woolf 1991, section 3). It is doubtful that British prisoner communities can be simply characterized in class analogy terms in which the gangsters constitute a ruling class and the sex offenders (or 'nonces') a lumpenproletariat (Genders and Player, 1994): the categories 'gangster' and 'sex offender' are themselves problematic and subject to subtle qualifications relating to the nature of a prisoner's original offence and the reputation he or she establishes within prison (Cohen and Taylor, 1972: chapter 3). Nevertheless, it is clear that certain categories of sex offenders, particularly those who have committed offences against children, are generally preyed on and anathematized, and that established professional criminals who have experienced prison before, who are generally older and are doing longer than average sentences, tend within training prisons to be the 'top men' (King and Elliot, 1977: 254–6). However, social prominence within the prison community is a complex matter. Whereas Irwin's professional Californian thieves were allegedly orientated to the outside world, King and Elliot's 'top men' had as few outside contacts as their 'retreatists'. Nor were they heavily involved in the prisoner culture of barter in contraband goods and power cliques. On the contrary, their reputation enabled them to secure good positions (attractive cell locations and valued jobs) and non-interference from prisoners and staff alike, so that they were able to 'do their own bird' in relative peace and security. The prisoners prominent in 'jailing' activities—regarded by the 'top men' as 'hotheads', 'tearaways', and 'Borstal boys'—were on the whole younger, shorter-sentence prisoners whose criminal careers were disorganized (*ibid.*: 250–2).

It follows that power structures within prisons vary a good deal according to the nature of the prison (there has, for example, been virtually no research attention given to the predatory behaviour which, according to HMCIP, dominates some young offender and low-security adult institutions—see HMCIP, 1992*a*, 1992*b* for two recent examples) and depend less on a rigid class structure and rather more on a fluid pattern of competing groups based on ethnic and regional affinities as well as prior friendships and 'business' interests (Sparks, Bottoms, and Hay, 1996: chapter 5). There is not one prisoner world, but many (Rock, 1996: 39–41) and it is a shifting world, constantly being renegotiated. This conclusion makes comprehensible the fact that attempts at predicting where trouble will occur and who will spark it off, or participate in incidents once they have started, have borne little fruit. Ditchfield's review (1990) of the literature on disturbances and control in prisons found little evidence that the likelihood of incidents could straight-forwardly be related to such factors as overcrowding, architectural design, or prisoner facilities, though changes, both positive and negative, likely to destabilize power structures and relationships seemed to increase the likelihood of disorder (see also Adams, 1992: chapters 5–7). Moreover, attempts by prison psychologists to identify prisoners likely to be control problems, or to find common features among those prisoners identified by governors as control problems and transferred to special units, have not been conspicuously successful (see Williams and Longley, 1987; and a critical review by King and McDermott, 1990). Nor, despite references by senior prison administrators to disorder-prone 'toxic mixes' in their reviews of some recent prison disorders (see HMCIP, 1987*b*, on disturbances at Wymott and Northeye in 1986; also Ditchfield, 1990: chapter 4), was the Woolf Inquiry able to identify a pattern among the prisoners prominent in the 1990 disturbances. There was, as Woolf concluded, 'no single cause of the riots and no simple solution or action which will prevent rioting' (1991: para. 9.23), nor was there any basis on which prisoners could be categorized for 'control' as opposed to 'security' purposes (*ibid.*: paras. 9.43–9.50). The fact 'that a prisoner who creates control problems in one prison, may behave with complete propriety in another' (*ibid.*: para. 9.48) suggested to Woolf that more attention needed to be paid to the quality of relationships between prisoners and staff, to the nature of regimes, to procedural justice, and to day-to-day fairness (*ibid.*: section 9).

This is in line with what analysts of the prison community have long main-tained: namely, that 'order' and 'control' are not synonymous (Young, 1987). Given his broader insight it is unfortunate, therefore, that Woolf employed 'control' rather than 'order' in his troika of objectives—'security', 'control' , and 'justice'—to be kept in balance (*ibid.*: paras. 9.19–9.23; for commentary, see Morgan, 1992*a*). For whereas control measures may be designed to achieve order, they tend often to produce the reverse outcome. This is the essence of King and McDermott's (1990) critical analysis of the use of transfers to control 'troublesome' prisoners and Sparks *et al.*'s (1996) comparison of staff-prisoner dynamics in two dispersal prisons.

There are three lessons to be drawn from this research. First, though there are undoubtedly a few prisoners whose response to most penal situations is so disruptive or aggressive—the extreme case being prisoners who have killed within prison—that they must for a time be placed in special units, attention needs most to be paid to trouble-generating *situations* and *procedures* rather than to the relatively illusive 'disruptive' population. Removal of 'troublesome' prisoners is seldom a solution. Such labelled prisoners often go on to confirm their labels (Boyle's autobiographical accounts (1977, 1984) are object lessons in this process) and the situation within which their troublesome behaviour was first identified typically generates further trouble. Secondly, and following logically from the first, it is the regime experienced by the 'mainstream' popu-lation which has crucially to be got right. It is within mainstream situations that trouble sporadically occurs and the proliferation of special units disrupts the ladder of incentives and disincentives on which the stability and fairness of the whole system ultimately rests. Thirdly, positive relationships between prisoners and basic grade prison officers are critical to the quality of prisoners' lives. This suggests, to take the crime-preventative analogy adopted by Sparks *et al.* (1996), that benefits are likely to flow from adopting a 'social' rather than 'situational' control strategy, in effect what Dunbar (1985) termed 'dynamic security'. This involves devising 'active' regimes for prisoners in which prison officers are positively involved *with* prisoners in the delivery of programmes, services, and facilities between which prisoners may exercise a degree of responsible choice. It is not without significance that the same lessons are implicit in the developing literature on suicide prevention in prison (Lloyd, 1990). There are a few prisoners who recognizably feel so suicidal that they can be identified and focused measures taken to prevent them taking their own lives (Prison Service, 1992*a*; Liebling, 1992). The latter should not involve segregation in an environment within which suicide is made physically imposs- ible: by definition, 'strip cells' of the sort that used regularly to be employed can only deepen the slough of despond. More importantly, a high proportion of prison suicides are not predictable: they occur more or less randomly within the mainstream population. The solution is to enhance the quality of life for *all* prisoners in an attempt to mitigate the pressures which give rise to suicidal tendencies (HMCIP, 1990*b*). This focus on general prison standards was central to the Woolf Report.

FUTURE PROSPECTS

Over two decades the British prison services have perennially been said by commentators to be in crisis (see, for example, Evans, 1980; Shaw, 1992)—a crisis of order, of legitimacy, of staff morale. Use of the word crisis represents dramatic licence. The British prison services fulfill their intrinsically difficult mandate relatively efficiently most of the time, and they do so in a manner which is publicly a good deal more accountable than most systems in Europe (Morgan, 1993). They are remarkably free from corruption. In spite of the high security lapses of 1994–5 the number of escapes by prisoners who pose a genuine threat to the public is small and declining (Prison Service, 1996*a*: 11–12). Following the disturbances in 1990 there had, by the end of 1996, been only one major subsequent disturbance—that at Wymott in 1993. And though there is of course violence, and fear of violence, in British prisons, no prisoner has been killed in a British prison, by either staff or fellow prisoners, for over ten years (King and McDermott, 1995: chapter 3) and no officer has died while on duty at the hands of prisoners in recent memory. Moreover, the material conditions in which most prisoners now live are undoubtedly better in 1997 than for many years. There is only modest overcrowding, the indignities of slopping out are largely a thing of the past and most prisoners are able today to receive visits more frequently in accommodation more pleasant than ever previously known. These improvements in prisoners' living conditions have been matched by improved industrial relations and staff working conditions. The long overtime hours worked until the 1980s have gone and staff turnover is low and declining (Prison Service, 1996*a*: 27).

Yet though our prisons can by no stretch of the imagination be said to be in crisis—on the verge of breakdown—their problems are many and the gains of recent years are at grave risk of being lost. The recent massive surge in the prison population, a surge which no reputable commentator has been able to justify in terms of public protection, threatens the stability of the system. The background to the surge, and the mechanics of its production, are discussed in Ashworth and Downes and Morgan, this volume. It has politically been talked into being—the rhetoric of 'prison works'—and engineered by judicial decisions taken without crime preventive justification. Space does not permit analysis of how the prison population could without prejudice to public safety be reduced, but at various points in this chapter indications have been given. The recent growth in the number of juvenile prisoners who, it is generally agreed, should not be held in prison. The large number of mentally disordered prisoners who similarly do not belong. The explosion in the number of women prisoners the characteristics of whom suggest that many need not have been confined.

There are other categories of potential population reduction on which we have not touched. The more than 20,000 fine defaulters imprisoned each year, offenders for whom imprisonment was originally not considered by the courts to be appropriate, the revenue from whose fines has been lost and huge expense incurred instead when, arguably, more cost-effective enforcement methods could have been applied. The gradual increase in the remand population—now 22 per cent of ADP—for many of whom custody could arguably have been avoided or, just as importantly, shortened. Initiatives have been taken to reduce the remand population (Morgan and Jones, 1993), but they need to be pursued with greater energy.

The core questions, however, relate to the threshold at which the courts determine that imprisonment is proportionately appropriate a punishment and the average duration of custodial sentences. The evidence does not support the contention that the increasing duration of sentences, sentences both passed and served, is better safeguarding the public from becoming victims of crime. Sentencing tariffs need systematically to be formulated which recognize that fact and avoid the waste of public funds and human liberty which Ashworth's 'rising tide of punitiveness in recent years, involves (see Ashworth, this volume). The size of our prison population is neither determined by, nor determines, the level of crime. It is very largely a symbolic gesture politically decided. It could be substantially smaller, as it is elsewhere in Europe in countries with crime patterns similar to our own. If the political will is not summoned to restrain the current surge in the prison population then prison system overcrowding will persist and possibly grow, living and working conditions in prisons will almost certainly be reduced, and tensions will inevitably rise. It is worth recalling what the then Director General of the Prison Service said in his oral evidence to the Woolf inquiry:

The life and work of the Prison Service have, for the last twenty years, been distorted by the problem of overcrowding. That single factor has dominated pressure on staff, and as a consequence has soured industrial relations. It has skewed managerial effort . . . away from positive developments. The removal of overcrowding is . . . an indispensable pre-condition of sustained and universal improvement in prison conditions.[15]

Overcrowding, however, is not the only factor which threatens the gains of recent years. Prisons policy has been knocked off course by scandal, in this case the escapes of high security prisoners from Whitemoor and Parkhurst Prisons in September 1994 and January 1995, and the subsequent official inquiry reports (for review symposia see *Howard Journal*, 1996, and *Cropwood Report*, 1997). It is not yet clear whether the most fundamental of the recommendations of the Woodcock (1994) and Learmont (1995) Reports are to be acted on—those for new 'supermax' prisons and a revision of the prisoner security classification system. However, both reports have already exercised sufficient influence seriously to increase the 'depth' of imprisonment—levels of security, surveillance, and restriction, lack of autonomy, and so on—to which many prisoners, particularly long-term high-security prisoners, are now subject. To what extent King and Morgan's 'minimum security' principle is being breached is a question about which there will legitimately be argument. But minimizing the risk of breaches of security appears currently to be given such primacy that preventing crime—the objective which Woolf insisted should be common to all criminal justice agencies, and which in a prison context necessarily involves investment of trust and the taking of some risk—seems in many respects to have been lost sight of. Woolf saw 'security', 'control', and 'justice' as complementary and symbiotic components in acceptable prison regimes, each of which must be given their 'due weight' (*ibid.*: para. 3.32). Learmont makes no reference to justice and sees 'care' and 'custody' as conflicting elements. Giving them their due weight results in 'confusion' (*ibid.*: para. 3.31 and 3.35), which is why, in Learmont's opinion, custody must be the Prison Service's 'primary purpose' (*ibid.*: para. 3.40).

This view appears currently to be prevailing. To the extent that it continues to prevail, it represents a change of direction for the Prison Service away from the balance which is essential to the proper purpose of prison regimes, namely crime prevention. Some prisoners *are* dangerous and their escape needs *absolutely* to be prevented. The vast majority of prisoners, however, are not dangerous and their custody is transitory. It makes no sense to deny them opportunities for home leave and other situations of trust—all of which opportunities have been severely cut back in the 1990s—which, very shortly, when

---

[15] Evidence of Mr Chris Train: transcript of Seminar D, Day 6, Lord Justice Woolf's Inquiry into Prison Disturbances, City University, 22 October 1990: 5

they gain their total freedom, we will expect them to exercise in a responsible law-abiding manner. It is a short-sighted policy which owes more to the political convenience of ministers than sensible criminal justice policy.

The increasing security quotient in prisons is also immensely costly. It costs two and a half times as much to keep a prisoner in a dispersal prison as in an open prison (Prison Service, 1996c: Table D). It follows that the implementation of the Learmont recommendations—proportionately more prisoners in higher security accommodation, more impenetrable prison perimeters, more searching of buildings, prisoners, and prison visitors, and so on—means necessarily, in the context of general cutbacks in public expenditure, spending less on prisoner programmes and facilities. This is the backcloth to the downturn in prisoner 'purposeful activity' recorded by the Prison Service (1996a: 15) and the regular press reports of reductions in prison education, offence-related programmes, social work provision, and so on, developments about which the new Chief Inspector of Prisons, Sir David Ramsbotham, has outspokenly expressed concern. The Learmont recommendations are being implemented during a period when the government's drive for economies is being applied to the Prison Service with unprecedented rigour. The Service is being required to achieve cuts in unit costs of 13.5 per cent over three years. The consequence is reduced facilities for prisoners and less liberal regimes. The situation, the Chief Inspector maintains, is 'very serious': financial cuts, combined with rising overcrowding, 'is doing real damage to all the progress that has been made over the past 4–5 years' (HMCIP, 1996: 2–3).

Equally damaging, however, is the confusion which once again reigns within the Prison Service about priorities and future direction. The U-turn in government policy represented by the retreat from the central tenets of the Criminal Justice Act 1991 by the Criminal Justice Act 1993 has been paralleled with regard to prisons by the publicly stated acceptance of the Learmont recommendations in 1995, and the sacking of the Director General, Mr Derek Lewis, when, only four years earlier, the Woolf Report had been welcomed and widely seen as setting the reformist agenda for the next millennium.

The fundamental nature of these U-turns can scarcely be overstated. A greatly increased prison population is now being *planned* as a matter of stated government *policy* (Home Office, 1996: chapter 13): there is no longer any pretence that a larger population might be the consequence, largely beyond government control, of a changing pattern of crime or the independent decisions of the courts. As we have seen, imprisonment is officially said now to be an effective deterrent, a proposition disavowed in government policy statements preceding the 1991 Act and contradicted by Home Office research reviews (Brody, 1976). Less eligibility and what is effectively punishment *within* prisons is back with a vengeance in the form of 'austere' regimes, a notion which the Service was forced to acknowledge, for example, by abandoning its plans electrically to wire all cells so that prisoners could plug in all those appliances— radio, TV, computers, and so on—which in the late twentieth century most citizens take for granted and which are so essential a part of communication and education as well as entertainment. Finally, the gradual move towards prisoners' rights and the delivery of basic standards has been cast aside in favour of 'earned privileges' with prison officers handing out good marks for prisoner compliance. The paternalism of 'treatment and training' has returned, but without any guarantee that training or basic standards will be provided. If this approach is extended to the award of 'earned' early release, as the government proposes in the Crime (Sentences) Bill 1996 (Home Office, 1996: para. 9.1), it is difficult to envisage that it will be done with the justice—both due process and fairness—which Woolf thought was lacking in so many staff decisions affecting the quality of prisoners' lives, and on which he insisted. Whatever rhetoric is deployed, it is highly unlikely that the subjective day-to-day appraisals of prison officers, decisions which might result in part or all of the final fifth of sentences not being served, will be perceived by offenders as 'honesty in sentencing', and that peace will be preserved. Nor, when we know that the quantity and quality of prisoners' relationships with their families is one of the best predictors of future offending (Ditchfield, 1994), is it good sense that extra or better quality visits be earned. Certainly we know that prisoners generally value their visits above almost all else. But should prisoners' partners and children be deprived of contact, and long-term relationships possibly prejudiced, in order that prison staff be given an additional control carrot?

In conclusion, then, the British prison services are on the cusp of change, buffeted, in spite of agency status, by ministerial interference in aspects of operational policy, the result of the increasingly populist politics of 'law and order' policy. Senior prison administrators are uncertain where their priorities lie and whether the resources allocated to them will suffice to cope with the increasing demands made on the Service. And all this is occurring with the maximum glare of publicity. It seems highly improbable that this combination of difficult circumstances will be survived without further troubles.

Selected Further Reading

Discussions of imprisonment ideally take place within the broader context of the debate on the philosophy and sociology of punishment: Nigel Walker's *Why Punish?* (Oxford: Oxford University Press, 1991) is an excellent introduction to the former and David Garland's *Punishment and Modern Society* (Oxford: Oxford University Press, 1990) provides a masterly overview of the major theorists who have explored the latter.

The current organization of imprisonment is heavily influenced by past practice. Michael Ignatieff's *A Just Measure of Pain* (London: Macmillan, 1978) provides an inspirational account of the emergence of imprisonment as the principal penalty for serious crime at the end of the eighteenth and beginning of the nineteenth centuries, and Sir Leon Radzinowicz and Roger Hood's *The Emergence of Penal Policy in Victorian and Edwardian England* (Oxford: Clarendon Press, 1990) and Sean McConville's *A History of English Prison Administration* (London: Routledge, 1981) provide scholarly accounts of the development of imprisonment. *The Oxford History of the Prison* (edited by Norval Morris and David Rothman, New York: Oxford University Press, 1996) comprises a fine collection of essays by leading historians on the international origins and use of imprisonment.

As far as the contemporary use and organization of imprisonment is concerned, there is no substitute for becoming familiar with the annual report of the Prison Service on the *Work* of the Service and the Home Office Research and Statistics Department's annual volume of *Prison Statistics*. There is no comprehensive up-to-date academic text on the organization of prisons in the UK, though Michael Cavadino and James Dignan's *The Penal System: An Introduction* (London: Sage, 1992) and Roy King and Kathleen McDermott's *The State of Our Prisons* (Oxford: Clarendon, 1995) provide accessible and critical accounts of aspects of the system. The latter usefully devotes a chapter to each of the Prison Service's key aims in turn. Equally surprising is the absence of a British text reviewing the sociology of prisons literature, though the topic is introduced in several of the research monographs cited in this chapter, notably Richard Sparks, Tony Bottoms, and Will Hay's *Prisons and the Problem of Order* (Oxford: Clarendon, 1996). The *Report* of the Woolf Inquiry into the 1990 riots is essential reading for anyone interested in the reformist agenda, though it is an unwieldy text not made easy to digest by the inexcusable absence of an index.

Imprisonment is ultimately an experience which only those who have been incarcerated can adequately relate. Victor Serge's *Men in Prison* (London: Gollancz, 1970), Rod Caird's *A Good and Useful Life* (London: Hart-Davies, 1977), Jimmy Boyle's *A Sense of Freedom* (London: Canongate, 1977) and Audrey Peckham's *A Woman in Custody* (London: Fontana, 1985) are among the best contemporary accounts.

REFERENCES

ADAMS, R. (1992), *Prison Riots in Britain and the USA.* New York: St Martins Press.

ADVISORY COUNCIL ON THE PENAL SYSTEM (1968), *The Regime for Long-Term Prisoners in Conditions of Maximum Security* (Radzinowicz Report). London: HMSO.

AMERICAN FRIENDS SERVICE COMMITTEE (1971), *Struggle for Justice: A Report on Crime and Punishment in America.* New York: Hill and Wang

BANKS, C., and FAIRHEAD, S. (1976), *The Petty Short-Term Prisoner.* Chichester: Howard League and Barry Rose.

BARTON, R. (1959), *Institutional Neurosis.* Bristol: John Wright.

BENNEY, M. (1948), *Gaol Delivery.* London: Longmans Green.

BEYENS, K., and SNACKEN, S. (1996), 'Prison Privatization: An International Perspective', in R. Matthews and P. Francis, eds., *Prisons 2000: An International Perspective on the Current State of and Future of Imprisonment.* Basingstoke: Macmillan.

BLAKE, W. (1927), *QUOD.* London: Hodder and Stoughton.

BOTTOMLEY, A. K., and HAY, W. eds. (1991), *Special Units for Difficult Prisoners.* Hull: Centre for Criminology and Criminal Justice.

—— JAMES, A., CLARE, E., and LIEBLING, A. (1997), *Monitoring and Evaluation of Wolds Remand Prison,* Home Office Research and Planning Unit. London: Home Office.

BOTTOMLEY, K. (1995), *CRC Special Units: A*

General Assessment. London: Home Office Research and Planning Unit.

BOTTOMS, A. E. (1977), 'Reflections on the Renaissance of Dangerousness', *Howard Journal*, 16/2: 70–6.

—— (1990), 'The Aims of Imprisonment', in *Justice, Guilt and Forgiveness in the Penal System*, Edinburgh University Centre for Theology and Public Issues Paper no. 18., Edinburgh.

—— (1995), 'The Philosophy and Politics of Punishment and Sentencing', in C. Clarkson and R. Morgan, eds., *The Politics of Sentencing Reform.* Oxford: Oxford University Press.

—— and LIGHT, R. (1987), *Problems of Long-Term Imprisonment.* Aldershot: Gower.

—— and McCLINTOCK, F. H. (1973), *Criminals Coming of Age.* London: Heinemann.

BOYLE, J. (1977), *A Sense of Freedom.* Edinburgh: Canongate.

—— (1984), *The Pain of Confinement: Prison Diaries.* Edinburgh: Canongate.

BRODY, S. (1976), *The Effectiveness of Sentencing*, Home Office Research Study no. 35. London: HMSO.

—— and TARLING, R. (1980), *Taking Offenders out of Circulation*, Home Office Research Study no. 64. London: HMSO.

CAIRD, R. (1974), *A Good and Useful Life.* London: Hart-Davis.

CARLEN, P. (1983), *Women's Imprisonment.* London: Routledge.

—— (1990), *Alternatives to Women's Imprisonment.* Milton Keynes: Open University Press

—— and TCHAIKOVSKY, C. (1996), 'Women's Imprisonment in England and Wales at the End of the Twentieth Century, Realities and Utopias', in R. Matthews and P. Francis, eds., *Prisons 2000: An International Perspective on the Current State and Future of Imprisonment.* Basingstoke: Macmillan.

CARLISLE REPORT (1988), *The Parole System in England and Wales: Report of the Review Committee* (Carlisle Report), Cm 532. London: HMSO.

CASALE, S. (1984), *Minimum Standards for Prison Establishments.* London: NACRO.

—— (1989), *Women Inside: The Experience of Women Remand Prisoners in Holloway.* London: Civil Liberties Trust.

—— (1993) 'Conditions and Standards', in E. Player and M. Jenkins, eds., *Prisons After Woolf: Reform through Riot.* London: Routledge.

—— and PLOTNIKOFF, J. (1989), *Minimum Standards for Prisons: A Programme of Change.* London: NACRO.

—— (1990), *Regimes for Remand Prisoners.* London: Prison Reform Trust.

CAVADINO, M., and DIGNAN, J. (1992), *The Penal System: An Introduction.* London: Sage.

CHRISTIE, N. (1994), *Crime Control as Industry: Towards Gulags, Western Style.* London: Routledge.

CLAYTON, G. F. (1958), *The Wall is Strong: The Life of a Prison Governor.* London: John Long.

CLEMMER, D. (1940), *The Prison Community.* New York: Holt, Rinehart, and Winston.

COHEN, S., and TAYLOR, L. (1972), *Psychological Survival.* Harmondsworth: Penguin.

COLLINS, P. (1962), *Dickens and Crime.* Basingstoke: Macmillan.

COLVIN, M. (1992), *The Penitentiary in Crisis: from Accommodation to Riot in New Mexico.* Albany, NY: State University of New York Press.

COOKE, D. J. (1989), 'Containing Violent Prisoners: An Analysis of the Barlinnie Special Unit', *British Journal of Criminology*, 29, 1: 129–43.

COUNCIL OF EUROPE (1991), *Report to the United Kingdom Government on the Visit to the United Kingdom Carried Out by the European Committee for the Prevention of Torture and Inhuman or Degrading Treatment or Punishment from 29 June 1990 to 10 August 1990.* Strasbourg: Council of Europe.

COYLE, A. (1987), 'The Scottish Experience with Small Units', in A. E. Bottoms and R. Light, eds., *Problems of Long-Term Imprisonment.* Aldershot: Gower.

—— (1994), *The Prisons We Deserve.* London: HarperCollins.

CREIGHTON, S., and KING, V. (1996), *Prisoners and the Law.* London: Butterworths.

CRONIN, H. (1967), *The Screw Turns.* London: Longman.

CURTIS, D. (1973), *Dartmoor to Cambridge.* London: Hodder and Stoughton.

DELL, S., GROUNDS, A., JAMES, K., and ROBERTSON, G. (1991), *Mentally Disordered Remanded Prisoners: Report to the Home Office.* Cambridge: University of Cambridge.

DILULIO, J. (1987), *Governing Prisons: A Comparative Study of Correctional Management.* New York: Free Press.

DITCHFIELD, J. (1990), *Control in Prisons: A Review of the Literature*, Home Office Research Study no. 118. London: HMSO.

—— (1994) 'Family Ties and Recidivism', in *Research Bulletin*, 36. London: Home Office Research and Planning Department.

DITCHFIELD, J., and AUSTIN, C. (1986), *Grievance Procedures in Prison*, Home Office Research Study no. 91. London: HMSO.

DOBASH, R., DOBASH, R., and GUTTERIDGE, S. (1986), *The Imprisonment of Women*. Oxford: Blackwell.

DONZIGER, S. R. (1995), *The Real War on Crime: the Report of the National Criminal Justice Commmission*. New York: Harper Collins.

DOWNES, D. (1988), *Contrasts in Tolerance: Post-War Penal Policy in the Netherlands and England and Wales*. Oxford: Oxford University Press.

—— (1997), 'The Buckling of the Shields: Dutch Penal Policy 1985–1995', in N. South and R. Weiss, eds., *International Prison Systems*. Reading: Gordon and Breach.

DUNBAR, I. (1985), *A Sense of Direction*. London: Prison Service.

EMERY, F. E. (1970), *Freedom and Justice within Walls: The British Prison Experiment*. London: Tavistock.

EVANS, P. (1980) *Prison Crisis*. London: Allen and Unwin.

FAIRHEAD, S. (1981), *Persistent Petty Offenders*, Home Office Research Study no. 66. London: HMSO.

FELDMAN, D. (1993), *Civil Liberties and Human Rights in England and Wales*. Oxford: Oxford University Press.

FITZGERALD, E. (1985), 'Prison Discipline and the Courts', in M. Maguire, J.Vagg, and R. Morgan, eds., *Accountability and Prisons: Opening Up a Closed World*. London: Tavistock.

FITZGERALD, M., and MARSHALL, P. (1996), 'Ethnic Minorities in British Prisons: Some Research Implications', in R. Matthews and P. Francis, eds., *Prisons 2000: An International Perspective on the Current State and Future of Imprisonment*. Basingstoke: Macmillan.

FOUCAULT, M. (1967), *Madness and Civilisation*. London: Tavistock.

—— (1977), *Discipline and Punish: The Birth of the Prison*. London: Allen Lane.

FOX, L. (1952), *The English Prison and Borstal System*. London: Routledge.

GARLAND, D. (1990), *Punishment and Modern Society: A Study in Social Theory*. Oxford: Oxford University Press.

—— and YOUNG, P. (1983), 'Towards a Social Analysis of Penality', in D. Garland and P. Young, eds., *The Power to Punish*. London: Heinmann.

GENDERS, E., and PLAYER, E. (1989), *Race Relations in Prison*. Oxford: Clarendon Press.

—— (1994), *Grendon: A Study of a Therapeutic Prison*. Oxford: Clarendon Press.

GOFFMANN, E. (1968), 'The Characteristics of Total Institutions', in *Asylums*. Harmondsworth: Penguin.

GOSTIN, L., and STAUNTON, M. (1985), 'The Case for Prison Standards: Conditions of Confinement, Segregation and Medical Treatment', in M. Maguire, J. Vagg, and R. Morgan, eds., *Accountability and Prisons: Opening Up a Closed World*. London: Tavistock.

GREEN, P. (1991), *Drug Couriers*. London: Prison Reform Trust.

GUNN, J., MADEN, A., and SWINTON, M. (1991), *Mentally Disordered Prisoners*. London: Institute of Psychiatry.

HADFIELD, R., and LAKES, G. H. (1991), *Summary Report of an Audit of Custody Arrangements for Category A Prisoners and of an Inquiry in DOC I Divison*. London: Home Office/Prison Service.

HER MAJESTY'S CHIEF INSPECTOR OF PRISONS (1984), *Prisoner Categorisation Procedures*. London: Home Office.

—— (1987a), *A Review of Prisoners' Complaints*. London: Home Office.

—— (1987b), *Report of an Inquiry into the Disturbances in Prison Service Establishments in England between 29 April and 2 May 1986*, HC 42. London: HMSO.

—— (1988), *HM Remand Centre Risley*. London: Home Office.

—— (1989), *Prison Sanitation*. London: Home Office.

—— (1990a), *HM Prison Brixton*. London: Home Office.

—— (1990b), *Suicide and Self-Harm in Prison Service Establishments in England and Wales*, Cm 1383. London: HMSO.

—— (1990c), *HM Prison Leeds*. London: Home Office.

—— (1992a), *YOI Feltham*. London: Home Office.

—— (1992b), *HM Prison Acklington*. London: Home Office.

—— (1993a), *HM Prison Cardiff*. London: Home Office.

—— (1993b), *Report of an Inquiry into the Disturbance at HM Prison Wymott on 6 September 1993*, Cm 2371. London: HMSO.

—— (1996a), *Annual Report, April 1995–March 1996*. London: HMSO.

HOOD, R. (1992), *Race and Sentencing: A Study in the Crown Court*. Oxford: Clarendon Press.

HOME OFFICE (1947), *Report of the Commissioners of Prison and Directors of Convict Prisons for the Year 1946*, Cmd. 7271. London: HMSO.

—— (1965), *The Adult Offender*, Cmnd. 2852. London: HMSO.

—— (1977), *Report on Inquiry into the Cause and Circumstances of the Events at HM Prison Hull 31 August to 3 September 1976* (the Fowler Report). London: HMSO.

—— (1981), *Annual Report of the Work of the Prison Department 1980*, Cmnd. 8228. London: HMSO.

—— (1984), *Managing the Long-Term Prison System: The Report of the Control Review Committee*. London: HMSO.

—— (1986), *Prison Statistics England and Wales 1985*, Cm 210. London: HMSO.

—— (1989), *An Improved System of Grievance Procedures for Prisoners' Complaints and Requests: Report of a Working Group*. London: Home Office.

—— (1990), *Crime, Justice and Protecting the Public*, Cmnd. 965. London: HMSO.

—— (1991), *Custody, Care and Justice: The Way Ahead for the Prison Service in England and Wales*, Cmnd. 1647. London: HMSO.

—— (1995), *Digest 3: Information on the Criminal Justice System in England and Wales*. London: Home Office.

—— (1996a), *Protecting the Public: The Government's Strategy on Crime in England and Wales*, Cm 3190. London: Home Office.

—— (1996b), *Prison Statistics England and Wales 1995*, Cm. 3087. London: Home Office.

—— (1996c), *Statistics of Offences against Prison Discipline and Punishments England and Wales 1995*, Cm 3316. London: HMSO.

HOUSE OF COMMONS HOME AFFAIRS COMMITTEE (1981), *The Prison Service*, vol. 1, HC 412, 1980/1. London: HMSO.

HOUSE OF LORDS (1989), *Report of the Select Committee on Murder and Life Imprisonment*, HL 78, 1988/9. London: HMSO.

HOWARD, J. (1784) *The State of the Prisons in England and Wales with Preliminary Observations, and an Account of some Foreign Prisons and Hospitals*, 3rd edn. Warrington: n.p.

HUDSON, B. (1996), *Understanding Justice: An Introduction to Ideas, Perspectives and Controversies in Modern Penal Theory*. Buckingham: Open University Press.

IGNATIEFF, M. (1978), *A Just Measure of Pain*. London: Macmillan.

IRWIN, J. (1970), *The Felon*. Eaglewood Cliffs, NJ: Prentice-Hall.

—— and CRESSEY, D. (1962), 'Thieves, Convicts and the Inmate Culture', *Social Problems*, 10/92: 145–55.

JACOBS, J. (1977), *Stateville: The Penitentiary in Mass Society*. Chicago, Ill.: University of Chicago Press.

—— (1979), 'Race Relations and the Prisoner Sub-Culture', in N. Morris and M. Tonry, eds., *Crime and Justice: An Annual Review of Research*, vol. 1. Chicago, Ill.: University of Chicago Press.

—— (1980), 'The Prisoners' Rights Movement and its Impacts, 1960–1980', in N. Morris and M. Tonry, eds., *Crime and Justice: An Annual Review of Research*, vol. 2. Chicago, Ill.: University of Chicago Press.

JAMES, A. L., BOTTOMLEY, A. K., CLARE, E., and LIEBLING, A. (1997), *Privatizing Prisons: Rhetoric and Reality*. London: Sage.

JONES, H., and CORNES, P. (1977), *Open Prisons*. London: Routledge.

JUSTICE (1983), *Justice in Prisons*. London: Justice.

KING, R. D., and ELLIOTT, K. (1977), *Albany: Birth of a Prison—End of an Era*. London: Routledge.

—— and MCDERMOTT, K. (1989), 'British Prisons 1970–1987: The Ever-Deepening Crisis', *British Journal of Criminology*, 29: 107–28.

—— and —— (1990), 'My Geranium is Subversive: Some Notes on the Management of Trouble in Prisons', *British Journal of Sociology*, 41: 445–71.

—— and —— (1995), *The State of Our Prisons*. Oxford: Clarendon Press.

—— and MORGAN, R. (1976), *A Taste of Prison: Custodial Conditions for Trial and Remand Prisoners*. London: Routledge.

—— and —— (1980), *The Future of the Prison System*. Aldershot: Gower.

LART, R. (1997) *Crossing Boundaries: Accessing Community Mental Health Services for Prisoners on Release*. Bristol: Policy Press.

LAYCOCK, G. (1983), 'Highly Dangerous Offenders', *Home Office Research Bulletin*, no. 15: 32–5.

LEARMONT REPORT (1995), *Review of Prison Service Security in England and Wales and the Escape from Parkhurst Prison on Tuesday 3rd January 1995*. Cm. 3020. London: HMSO.

LEECH, M. (1995), *The Prisoner's Handbook*. Oxford: Oxford University Press.

LIEBLING, A. (1992), *Suicides in Prison*. London: Routledge.

LIGHT, R., and MATTFIELD, K. (1988), 'Prison Disciplinary Hearings: The Failure of Reform', *Howard Journal*, 27: 266–82.

LIPTON, D., MARTINSON, R., and WILKS, J. (1975), *The Effectiveness of Correctional Treatment*. New York: Praeger.

LLOYD, C. (1990), *Suicide and Self-Injury in Prison: A Literature Review*, Home Office Research Study no. 115. London: HMSO.

LOGAN, C. H. (1990), *Private Prisons: Pros and Cons*. New York: Oxford University Press.

LOUCKS, N., and PLOTNIKOFF, J. (1993), *Prison Rules: A Working Guide*. London: Prison Reform Trust.

MCCONVILLE, S. (1981), *A History of English Prison Administration*, vol. 1: 1750–1877. London: Routledge.

MCCORKLE, L., and KORN, R. (1954), 'Resocialisation within the Walls', *Annals of the American Academy of Political and Social Science*, 293: 88–98.

MAGUIRE, M. (1992), 'Parole', in E. Stockdale and C. Casale, eds., *Criminal Justice under Stress*. London: Blackstone.

—— PERROUD, B., and RAYNOR, P. (1996), *Automatic Conditional Release: The First Two Years*, Home Office Research Studies 156. London: Home Office.

—— PINTER, F., and COLLIS, C. (1984), 'Dangerousness and the Tariff: The Decision-making Process in Release from Life Sentences', *British Journal of Criminlogy*, 24: 250–68.

—— VAGG, J., and MORGAN, R., eds. (1985), *Accountability and Prisons: Opening Up a Closed World*. London: Tavistock.

MCGOWAN, R. (1995) 'The Well-Ordered Prison: England 1780–1865', in N. Morris and D. Rothman, eds., *The Oxford History of the Prison*. New York: Oxford University Press.

MARSH, A., DOBBS, J., MONT, J., and WHITE, A. (1985), *Staff Attitudes in the Prison Service*. London: HMSO.

MARTIN, J. (1975), *Boards of Visitors of Penal Institutions* (the Jellico Report). Chicester: Barry Rose.

MARTIN, S. J., and EKLAND-OLSON, S. (1987), *Texas Prisons: The Walls Came Tumbling Down*. Austin, Texas: Texas Monthly Press.

MATHIESON, T. (1965), *The Defences of the Weak*. London: Tavistock.

MAY COMMITTEE (1979), *Report of the Committee of Inquiry into the United Kingdom Prison Services*, Cmnd. 7673. London: HMSO.

MAYHEW, H., and BINNY, J. (1862) *The Criminal Prisons of London and Scenes of Prison Life*. London: Charles Griffin.

MELOSSI, D., and PAVARINI, M. (1981) *The Prison and the Factory: The Origins of the Penitentiary*. Basingstoke: Macmillan.

MILLER, A. (1976), *Inside, Outside*. London: Queensgate.

MORGAN, R. (1983), 'How Resources are Used in the Prison System', in *A Prison System for the '80s and Beyond: The Noel Buxton Lectures 1982–3*, 21–42. London: NACRO.

—— (1985), 'Her Majesty's Inspectorate of Prisons', in M. Maguire, J. Vagg, and R. Morgan, eds., *Accountability and Prisons: Opening Up a Closed World*, 106–23. London: Tavistock.

—— (1991), 'Woolf: In Retrospect and Prospect', *Modern Law Review*, 54: 713–25.

—— (1992), 'Following Woolf: The Prospects for Prisons Policy', *Journal of Law and Society*, 19: 231–50.

—— (1993a), 'An Awkward Anomaly: Remand Prisoners' in E. Player and M. Jenkins, eds., *Prisons After Woolf: Reform through Riot*. London: Routledge.

—— (1993b) 'Prisons Accountability Revisited', *Public Law*, 314–32.

—— (1995) 'Prison', in M. Walker ed., *Interpreting Crime Statistics*. Oxford: Clarendon Press.

—— and BRONSTEIN, A. (1985), 'Prisoners and the Courts: The US Experience', in M. Maguire, J. Vagg, and R. Morgan, eds., *Accountability and Prisons: Opening Up a Closed World*, 264–80. London: Tavistock.

—— and EVANS, M. (1994), 'Inspecting Prisons: The View from Strasbourg', in R. D. King and M. Maguire, eds., *Prisons in Context*. Oxford: Clarendon Press.

—— and JONES, H. (1991), 'Prison Discipline: The Case for Implementing Woolf', *British Journal of Criminology*, 31: 280–91.

—— and JONES, S. (1992), 'Bail or Jail?', in E. Stockdale and S. Casale, eds., *Criminal Justice Under Stress*. London: Blackstone.

MORRIS, N. (1974), *The Future of Imprisonment*. Chicago, Ill.: University of Chicago Press.

MORRIS, T., and MORRIS, P. (1963), *Pentonville: A Sociological Study of an English Prison*. London: Routledge.

MOTT, J. (1985), *Adult Prisons and Prisoners in England and Wales 1970–1982: A Review of the Findings of Social Research*, Home Office Research Study no. 84. London: HMSO.

MOUNTBATTEN REPORT (1966), *Report of the Inquiry into Prison Escapes and Security*, Cmnd. 3175. London: HMSO.

MUNCIE, J., and SPARKS, R. (1991), 'Expansion and Contraction in European Penal Systems', in J. Muncie and R. Sparks, eds., *Imprisonment: European Perspectives*. London: Harvester Wheatsheaf.

NORMAN, F. (1958), *Bang to Rights*. London: Secker and Warburg.

PADEL, U., and STEVENSON, P. (1988), *Insiders: Women's Experience of Prison*. London: Virago.

PARKER, T. (1970), *The Frying Pan*. London: Hutchinson.

—— (1973), *The Man Inside*, London: Michael Joseph.

PEASE, K. (1994), 'Cross-national Imprisonment Rates: Limitations of Method and Possible Conclusions', in R. D. King and M. Maguire, eds., *Prisons in Context*. Oxford: Clarendon Press.

PECKHAM, A. (1985), *A Woman in Custody*. London: Fontana.

PETERS, E. (1985), *Torture*. New York: Blackwell.

PRIESTLEY, P. (1981), *Community of Scapegoats*. Oxford: Pergamon Press.

—— (1989), *Jail Journeys: The English Prison Experience 1918–1980*. London: Routledge.

PRIME MINISTER (1982), *Efficiency and Effectiveness in the Civil Service*. London: HMSO.

PRIOR REPORT (1985), *Report on the Departmental Committee on the Prison Disciplinary System*. London: HMSO.

PRISON DEPARTMENT (1981), *Report of the Working Party on Categorisation*, P5 Division. London: Prison Department.

PRISON OFFICERS' ASSOCIATION (1984), *The Prison Disciplinary System: Submissions to the Home Office Departmental Committee on the Prison Disciplinary System*. London: Prison Officers' Association.

PRISON SERVICE (1991), *The Control Review Committee 1984: Implementation of the Committee's Recommendations*, Directorate of Custody. London: Home Office/Prison Service.

—— (1992a), *Caring for Prisoners at Risk of Suicide and Self-Injury: The Way Forward*. London: Prison Service.

—— (1992b), *Model Regime for Local Prisons and Remand Centres*. London: Prison Service.

—— (1994), *Operating Standards*. London: Prison Service.

—— (1996a), *Corporate Plan 1996–9*. London: Prison Service.

—— (1996b), *Prison Service: Annual Report and Accounts April 1994—March 1995*. London: Prison Service.

PUGH, R. B. (1970), *Imprisonment in Mediaeval England*. Cambridge: Cambridge University Press.

RADZINOWICZ, L., and HOOD, R. (1990), *The Emergence of Penal Policy in Victorian and Edwardian England*. Oxford: Clarendon Press.

RICHARDSON, G. (1985), 'The Case of Prisoners' Rights', in M. Maguire, J. Vagg, and R. Morgan, eds., *Accountability and Prisons:*

Opening Up a Closed World, 46–60. London: Tavistock.

—— (1993a), *Law, Custody and Process: Prisoners and Patients*. London: Hodder and Stoughton.

—— (1993b), 'From Rights to Expectations', in E. Player and M. Jenkins, eds., *Prisons After Woolf*. London: Routledge.

ROCK, P. (1996), *Reconstructing a Women's Prison: The Holloway Redevelopment Project*. Oxford: Clarendon Press.

ROTMAN, E. (1986), 'Do Criminal Offenders Have a Constitutional Right to Rehabilitation?', *Journal of Criminal Law and Criminology*, 1023–68.

RUCK, S. K., ed. (1951), *Paterson on Prisons: Prisoners and Patients*. London: Hodder and Stoughton.

RUSCHE, G., and KIRCHHEIMER, O. (1939), *Punishment and Social Structure*. New York: Columbia University Press.

RUTHERFORD, A. (1984), *Prisons and the Process of Justice*. Oxford: Oxford University Press.

RYAN, M., and WARD, T. (1989), *Privatisation and the Penal System: The American Experience and the Debate in Britain*. Milton Keynes: Open University Press.

SAMPSON, A. (1990), *Sex Offenders in Prison*. London: Prison Reform Trust.

SAPSFORD, R. (1983), *Life Sentence Prisoners*. Milton Keynes: Open University Press.

SCOTTISH PRISON SERVICE (1990), *Opportunity and Responsibility*. Edinburgh: Scottish Prison Service.

SCULL, A. (1977), *Decarceration: Community Treatment and the Deviant*. Englewood Cliffs, NJ: Prentice-Hall.

SEDDON, T. (1996), 'Drug Control in Prisons', *Howard Journal*, 35: 327–35.

SERGE, V. (1970), *Men in Prison*. London: Gollancz.

SHAW, R., ed. (1992), *Prisoners' Children: What are the Issues?* London: Routledge.

SHAW, S. (1992), 'Prisons', in E. Stockdale and S. Casale, eds., *Criminal Justice Under Stress*. London: Blackstone.

SHICHOR, D. (1995), *Punishment for Profit: Private Prisons—Public Concerns*. Thousand Oaks, Ca.: Sage.

SIM, J. (1990), *Medical Power in Prisons: The Prison Medical Service in England 1774–1989*. Buckingham: Open University Press.

—— RUGGIERO, V., and RYAN, M. (1995), 'Punishment in Europe: Perceptions and Commonalities', in V. Ruggiero, M. Ryan, and J. Sim, eds., *Western European Penal Systems: A Critical Analysis*. London: Sage.

SPARKS, R. F. (1971), *Local Prisons: The Crisis in the English Penal System*. London: Heinemann.

SPARKS, R. (1994), 'Can Prisons be Legitimate? Penal Politics, Privatization, and the Timeliness of an Old Idea', in R. D. King and M. Maguire, eds., *Prisons in Context*. Oxford: Clarendon Press.

—— (1996), 'Penal "Austerity": The Doctrine of Less Eligility Reborn?', in R. Matthews and P. Francis, eds., *Prisons 2000: An International Perspective on the Current State and Future of Imprisonment*. Macmillan: Basingstoke.

—— BOTTOMS, A. E., and HAY, W. (1996), *Prisons and the Problem of Order*. Oxford: Clarendon Press.

SPIERENBERG, P. (1984), *The Spectacle of Suffering: Executions and the Evolution of Repression, from a Preindustrial Metropolis to the European Experience*. Cambridge: Cambridge University Press.

STERN, V. (1987), *Bricks of Shame: Britain's Prisons*. Harmondsworth: Penguin.

SYKES, G. (1958), *The Society of Captives*. Princeton, NJ: Princeton University Press.

TAYLOR, M., and PEASE, K. (1989), 'Private Prisons and Penal Purpose', in R. Matthews, ed., *Privatising Criminal Justice*. London: Sage.

THOMAS, J. E. (1972), *The English Prison Officer since 1850*. London: Routledge.

—— and POOLEY, R. (1980), *The Exploding Prison*. London: Junction Books.

TOMASHEVSKI, K. (1994), *Foreigners in Prison*. Helsinki: European Institute for Crime Prevention and Control.

TONRY, M. (1994), 'Racial Disproportion in US Prisons', in R. D. King and M. Maguire, eds., *Prisons in Context*. Oxford: Clarendon Press.

TRAIN, C. (1985), 'Management Accountability in the Prison Service', in M. Maguire, J. Vagg, and R. Morgan, eds., *Accountability and Prisons: Opening Up a Closed World*, 177–86. London: Tavistock.

VAN ZYL SMIT, D., and DUNKEL, F., eds., (1991), *Imprisonment Today and Tomorrow: International Perspective on Prisoners' Rights and Prison Conditions*. Deventer: Kluwer.

WALMSLEY, R., HOWARD, L., and WHITE S. (1992), *The National Prison Survey 1991: Main Findings*, Home Office Research Study no. 128. London: HMSO.

WILLIAMS, M., and LONGLEY, D. (1987), 'Identifying Control—Problem Prisoners in Dispersal Prisons', in A. E. Bottoms and R. Light, eds., *Problems of Long-Term Imprisonment*. Aldershot: Gower.

WOODCOCK REPORT (1994), *Report of the Enquiry into the Escape of Six Prisoners from the Special Security Unit at Whitemoor Prison, Cambridgeshire, on Friday 9th September 1994*. Cm 2741. London: HMSO.

WOOLF REPORT (1991), *Prison Disturbances April 1990: Report of an Inquiry by the Rt. Hon. Lord Justice Woolf (part I and II) and His Honour Judge Stephen Tumim (Part II)*, Cm 1456. London: HMSO.

WORRAL, A. (1994), *Have You Got a Minute?* London: Prison Reform Trust.

YOUNG, P. (1987), 'The Concept of Social Control and its Relevance to the Prisons Debate', in A. E. Bottoms and R. Light, eds., *Problems of Long-Term Imprisonment*, 97–114. Aldershot: Gower.

ZEDNER, L. (1994), *Women, Crime and Custody in Victorian England*. Oxford: Clarendon Press.

—— (1995), 'Wayward Sisters', in N. Morris and D. Rothman, eds., *The Oxford History of the Prison*. New York: Oxford University Press.

ZIMRING, F. E., and HAWKINS, G. (1991), *The Scale of Imprisonment*. Chicago, Ill.: Chicago University Press.

—— (1995), *Incapacitation*. New York: Oxford University Press.

32

Community Penalties and the Probation Service

George Mair

INTRODUCTION

The idea of 'community penalties' is a relatively new one in the United Kingdom.[1] Prior to the 1991 Criminal Justice Act, probation and community service were spoken of as specific court disposals and there was no official term which included the various sentences that were served in the community. The most commonly used term was probably non-custodial disposals, but this had two related drawbacks: first, it suggested that custody was the 'natural' penalty, and second it had a somewhat apologetic tone implying that real punishment was not part of the deal. With the introduction of the 1991 Act, however, came the new terminology and with it an expanded role for the probation service in England and Wales. For a brief moment, it indeed looked as if the probation service might well take its place 'centre-stage' in the criminal justice process—a position which all probation officers would probably have agreed was entirely appropriate. The probation service by 1991 was involved in virtually all aspects of that process: in decisions regarding bail, in providing information to sentencers via pre-sentence reports, in organizing and running two major sentences (the probation order and the community service order), and in work with prisoners both during and after custody.

That the probation service occupies such a key position in the criminal justice process is something of a well-kept secret. The image of probation officers is not highly developed in the way that images of the police, sentencers, and prison officers are.[2] Members of these agencies are frequently demonized and praised by the media, while members of the probation service remain back-stage quietly getting on with their work. The problem with this is that

---

[1] Although the fine and other financial penalties can be seen as community penalties, in this chapter the term is used to describe those sentences which are organized and administered by the probation service, as well as attendance centre orders and curfew orders. In Scotland, there is no probation service as such, although probation and community service orders (as well as a pre-decessor of the combination order) are run by local authority social work departments.

[2] The image problem was recognized by the Association of Chief Officers of Probation (ACOP) in the early 1990s, when proposals were put forward to carry out research into public perceptions of the probation service. In the event, some work was carried out, but the results have never been published.

probation officers all too often have seemed to be isolated from the other criminal justice agencies and somewhat smug and complacent about what they do and how they do it. There is a tendency to hide behind 'social work values' which are rarely, if ever, expressed;[3] for example, probation officers often claim to treat offenders with respect and humanity, recognizing their dignity as individuals, but why such admirable sentiments are claimed as social work values, and precisely how they are translated into work with offenders to reduce their offending remains unclear. Probation officers have basked in being the decent, caring face of the criminal justice system for many years; the police, prosecutors, sentencers, and prison officers do the dirty work while probation officers 'help' people. I am not aware of any research on the topic, but my impression is that a comparative analysis of studies of the police, prosecutors, sentencers, prison officers, and probation officers would show far more adverse criticism of the other agencies than of the probation service.

In fact, the probation service had scarcely reached 'centre-stage' before it was moved backstage again. Within months of the implementation of the 1991 Act, key parts of the legislation had been changed and a much more overtly punitive stance began to be talked up from the Home Office (the arrival of Michael Howard as Home Secretary in 1993 was a critical moment for penal policy). Of particular relevance to the probation service were proposals in the Green Paper, *Strengthening Punishment in the Community* (Home Office, 1995*a*; even the title is significant), such as that the courts would have more discretion to decide upon the content of community penalties, and the removal of the requirement that offenders consent to a community sentence; a review of probation training arrangements (Dews and Watts, 1994) which proposed scrapping the requirement for probation officers to possess a social work qualification (the CQSW/Dip.SW) and ending the national training scheme; and the increased accountability demanded by the government in terms of National Standards (Home Office, 1992, 1995*b*) and performance indicators (Home Office, 1996*a*). Such changes—proposed and actual—threatened to change the very nature of probation work. And the pressure on the probation service was increased further with the sea-change in penal policy by which diverting offenders from custodial sentences ceased to be an unofficial objective, and the idea that 'prison works' legitimated sending offenders to custody for crimes which previously would have received a community penalty.

But although community penalties and the probation service remain in the background, they cannot be marginalized. In 1995 almost 130,000 offenders were sentenced to community penalties by the courts compared to 79,000 who were sentenced to immediate custody (Home Office, *Criminal Statistics*). Thus, while prison may be a key symbol of punishment, numerically far fewer

---

[3] Interestingly, one Chief Probation Officer has recently come to the same conclusion: 'Probation officers are very prone to talk about values, without carefully defining what that means' (Roberts, 1996: 8).

offenders are sent to prison than receive community penalties (and, of course, it should not be forgotten that fines remain the most popular sentence with around one million imposed in 1995). The situation is the same in the United States where in 1995 around 1.5 million offenders were serving custodial sentences (Bureau of Justice Statistics, 1996*a*)—a fact which seems to be fairly well known—whereas in 1994 around three million adults were on probation (Bureau of Justice Statistics, 1996*b*)—a fact which seems to be not nearly so well known (although it may be that it is conveniently forgotten or ignored). Probation services not only deal with more offenders than prisons, they do so with fewer staff and a considerably lower budget: at the end of 1994 a total of 16,400 staff were employed by the probation service in England and Wales (Home Office, *Probation Statistics*), while the prison service had 38,800 staff (March 1995 figures; Home Office, 1995*c*); expenditure on probation in 1993–4 was £488 million, while for prisons it was £1,510 million (Home Office, 1995*c*). Importantly, too, in terms of reconviction rates—traditionally seen as the bottom-line in terms of the effectiveness of court sentences—prisons are no more effective than community penalties (for a more detailed discussion of effectiveness, see below).

In sum, in relation to other criminal justice agencies, the significance of the probation service and community penalties is often under-estimated (by researchers as well as by the general public), yet by virtue of the number of offenders supervised, its costs, and its central position at the very heart of the criminal justice process the probation service occupies a vital role. Indeed, a full understanding of penal policy and practice is impossible without taking account of developments in community penalties in recent years.

This chapter will discuss the significance of community penalties in England and Wales (using Scottish material where appropriate), concentrating on those penalties which are available for those aged 17–18 and above. The first section will look at the history of community penalties in the twentieth century, high-lighting the key changes which have taken place. Secondly, an account will be given of the major community penalties which are available in the United Kingdom concentrating upon how they are used, changes in their use, and what such changes might mean. The third section will focus on what, in many ways, is *the* key issue for community penalties at present—that of effectiveness. The various meanings of effectiveness will be discussed, as will the political pressure to demonstrate effectiveness; current debates about the resurgence of rehabilitation, the death of 'Nothing Works', and the role of meta-analysis will also be considered. In the final section, the future of community penalties will be contemplated, using the material which has been discussed in the preceding sections.[4]

---

[4] The legal framework for community penalties is described by Andrew Ashworth, this volume. For a discussion of the statistics available on community penalties see Hine (1995), although she only considers trends up to 1991.

A BRIEF HISTORY OF THE PROBATION SERVICE

The history of community penalties is, for all intents and purposes, the history of the probation service. It would scarcely be an exaggeration to state that without the existence of a probation service there would be no community penalties; only the attendance centre order, which has existed as a court sentence since the 1948 Criminal Justice Act (although it has had little impact except upon juveniles), and the curfew order (which has existed officially since the 1991 Act, but has been tested in only three areas, and remains at the time of writing available in only these three areas) are not organized and run by the probation service.

Various histories of the probation service and its role have been written, although these have tended to follow a somewhat old-fashioned conception of history (Bochel, 1976; Haxby, 1978; Jarvis, 1972), relying on simple chronological accounts which have described what happened without detailed analysis and explanation. Even these accounts, if read carefully, suggest that the emergence of the probation service was not a neat affair characterized by consensus. However, community penalties desperately require a revisionist history of their emergence which takes full account of the socio-political background against which they appeared. The work of Michael Ignatieff (1978) with regard to the origins of the penitentiary in England, of Anthony Platt (1969) on the origins and development of the child-saving movement in the United States, of David Rothman (1980) on the development of Progressive penal policies in the first half of the century in the United States, and of David Garland (1985) on the emergence of the 'penal-welfare' strategy in Britain around the turn of the century, all provide a potential framework for such a study and hooks upon which it could hang. There are hints about how such a project might look in some of the work of McWilliams (1983, 1985, 1986, 1987) and in an interesting article by Young (1976), but serious historical work on a broad scale remains a glaring gap in the literature. Lacking such work, and given the limited space of this essay, it would be unwise to embark upon anything more than a straightforward (and inevitably simplified) account of the evolution of the probation service.

It is generally agreed that precursors of probation include the practice of Warwickshire magistrates in the 1820s who would commit young offenders into the care of suitable and willing employers; and the development and systematization of this approach by Matthew Davenport Hill in Birmingham in the middle of the century (Bochel, 1976: 4–5). But other developments in the second half of the nineteenth century are critical for an understanding of how the probation service emerged and developed—principally, as McWilliams (1983) has shown, the jurisdiction of the magistrates' courts was extended, and there was what could almost be described as a moral panic about the extent of drunkenness and drink-related offences. As a result of the latter, two Church of England Temperance Society officers were appointed to work in a handful of London Police Courts in 1876. Finally, there was the 'Massachusetts scheme', probably the first systematic example of probation supervision, which had begun in that US state in 1869 and was seen as highly successful (Radzinowicz and Hood, 1986: 635–6).

In 1887 the Probation of First Offenders Act was passed, introducing the concept of probation officially for the first time. Courts were enabled to release first offenders on probation—having taken account of the characteristics and background of the offender and the offence. In practice, the power was used only patchily partly because there were no powers of supervision. Twenty years later, with the Probation of Offenders Act 1907 a recognizable form of probation was implemented, although the appointment of probation officers remained a matter for the discretion of the courts. Even at this early stage of the history of probation, key tasks and issues can be identified which are still significant today. The objective of probation supervision was the moral reformation of the offender and the prevention of crime. The consent of the offender was necessary for a probation order to be made. Probation officers could make enquiries into the characteristics and background of those charged with offences. They were very much local officials who were officers of the court and they could carry out:

Regular visits . . . to those put on probation, with inquiries about their behaviour, mode of life, and employment. . . . In the case of children there should also be visits to the school and inquiries of the Head Teacher as to the child's attendance and progress. Adults were to be helped to find suitable employment and young men put in touch with clubs and other healthy recreation . . . the officer . . . should not give money or help in kind except in very exceptional circumstances . . . [he] should not be used to collect instalments of fines [Radzinowicz and Hood, 1986: 644].

Various conditions could be inserted in the probation order including prohibiting the offender from associating with thieves, and requiring abstention from intoxicating liquor if the offence was drink-related.

While the 1907 Act did not satisfactorily resolve all of the issues facing the new disposal, it set probation on its way and in general terms development continued slowly, quietly and fairly steadily for the next forty years. The number of offenders placed on probation grew, as did the number of probation officers, which led, inexorably, to a more bureaucratic structure and the introduction of Principal Probation Officers. The National Association of Probation Officers was formed in 1912. Debates about the abilities of probation officers who were officials of the Church of England Temperance Society led to proposals for the training of probation officers. In 1925 the Criminal Justice Act made it mandatory for every Petty Sessional Division to have a probation officer attached to it. And the 'religious, missionary ideal' began to be superceded by the rise of the 'scientific, diagnostic ideal' (McWilliams, 1985: 261)—which, of course, had implications for training.

The 1948 Criminal Justice Act repealed and replaced the 1907 Probation of Offenders Act, and extended the work of the probation service to include prison after-care; the minimum period for a probation order was fixed at twelve months (this was reduced to six months in 1982). Also in the Act—just—were attendance centres (Mair, 1991) which became the first non-custodial sentence to be introduced since the probation order, although the centres only catered for those aged 12–20 with a maximum number of hours of attendance of twelve, and so could not be said to offer any real competition to the probation order (the maximum number of hours of attendance at senior attendance centres is now 36).

The most significant factors, however, in the post-war development of community penalties were the massive rise in recorded crime and the ensuing growth in the prison population which began in the mid-1950s and led to serious prison overcrowding. This latter development in particular set the agenda for what became known as 'alternatives to custody' for the best part of thirty years. The Morison Committee (Home Office, 1962) was set up partly to reassure the public that the probation service was capable of dealing with offenders effectively (one of its recommendations was that after-care should become an integral part of the work of the probation service). The 1967 Criminal Justice Act extended the after-care responsibilities of probation officers with the introduction of parole, and formalized the title of the service as 'probation and after-care'. The 1972 Criminal Justice Act introduced the community service order (perhaps the most important community penalty in the second half of the century), and experimental day training centres, both of which were expected to act to divert offenders from custody. Thus, by the mid-1970s, the idea of keeping offenders out of prison was widely accepted by politicians, academics, sentencers, and probation practitioners as a major objective of the work of the probation service; although it should be added that very different reasons might have been offered for pursuing this—moral (locking offenders up was morally wrong), humanitarian (custody damaged the lives of offenders as well as their families), financial (prison is very expensive), or political cynicism (keeping offenders out of prison helped to reduce overcrowding and therefore the risk of prison riots and bad publicity).

At the same time as diversion from custody became a probation service aim, the 'rehabilitative ideal' which had lain behind both the 'missionary ideal' and the 'scientific diagnostic ideal', was in trouble. Probation had been in existence for some sixty years or more but had not proved conclusively its effectiveness in terms of rehabilitation. The much-quoted (although possibly rarely read in full) article by Robert Martinson, 'What Works? Questions and Answers about Prison Reform' (1974), was widely seen as the death-knell for rehabilitation, although a close reading of the article suggests that the picture presented by Martinson was rather more complex than is commonly perceived (Mair, 1995a). A 'British version' of Martinson was published two years later (Brody, 1976), and this again showed a much more complex situation than could be covered by the simplistic formula of 'Nothing Works' (which, it should be noted, was never stated by Martinson). Perhaps most significantly, Brody's study was published immediately prior to another Home Office study which set out the results of the IMPACT (Intensive Matched Probation and After-Care Treatment) experiment (Folkard *et al.*, 1976). The IMPACT study was the result of a major piece of research (although the report itself was less than forty pages in length) and it would seem that expectations were high that it would demonstrate once and for all the effectiveness of social work supervision of offenders. But not only were the times not propitious—by 1976 'Nothing Works' had assumed a dominant role—but IMPACT found very little evidence of anything at all (although efforts have been made to reassess IMPACT's findings, e.g. Roberts, 1990; and Thornton, 1987, it is still seen as a failure).[5]

Together, the demise of rehabilitation and the pressure on the penal system caused by prison overcrowding led to the era of diversion from custody. This period lasted approximately from the mid-1970s to 1990 and produced a crop of books which focused on this aspect of the work of the probation service (Pointing, 1986; Stanley and Baginsky, 1984; Vass, 1990). Perhaps more importantly, it was during this period that questions began to be raised about the nature of the social control exercised over offenders (Cohen and Scull, 1983; Cohen, 1985), and on whether diversionary policies led to 'net widening', that is more offenders being processed as a result of diversion rather than fewer (Cohen, 1985, seems to have been responsible for starting this hare; see McMahon, 1990, for a sceptical look at the evidence).

Diversion from custody, however, was always compromised by the vagueness of this objective in official policy terms. The so-called 'penal crisis' which dominated the 1970s and 1980s (see Bottoms and Preston, 1980) led to many government initiatives to reduce the size of the prison population, but this was done obliquely rather than directly. Thus new disposals such as community service and day centres (introduced in place of day training centres in the 1982 Criminal Justice Act) were to be used for imprisonable offences, but this was certainly not the same as stating clearly that they should be used for those offenders who were prison-bound. It may be expecting too much of any government to admit that it cannot control prison overcrowding and therefore, by implication, crime itself, but the official stance towards 'alternatives to custody' cannot have helped community penalties to achieve their unofficial objective. In any event, this new role for non-custodial disposals was not uncomplicated, as the assumption seemed to be that the cause of prison over-crowding was simply sending too many non-serious offenders to prison. Reducing the prison population might have taken a variety of forms—encouraging sentencers to pass shorter sentences, making more use of bail rather than remands in custody (and the probation service has become heavily involved in bail information schemes: see Lloyd, 1992), stopping the practice of sending fine defaulters to prison, as well as using probation and community service for the less serious prison-bound offenders—but such careful targeting

---

[5] It should be noted that it is by no means clear that probation officers themselves lost faith in rehabilitation; no research was ever carried out to discover whether this was the case and, as McWilliams (1987: 114) notes: 'In the post-diagnostic era the probation service has not actually lost its sense of mission'.

of the problem was not commonplace (for a study carried out during the early 1980s which tried various approaches to cut the prison population in one English county see Smith *et al.*, 1984; Mair, 1985). The use of non-custodial sentences alone to reduce the prison population was bound to fail, and it did.

The result, of course, was that by the early 1980s—with a Thatcherite government in power making loud noises about law and order but also the need for financial stringency—a case could be made for the probation service being a fairly ineffective organization. It had failed at rehabilitation; it had failed at reducing the prison population (which had, in effect, replaced rehabilitation as the aim of probation work); and it was committed to 'soft' social work values which meant that offenders who deserved punishment received help instead.

In April 1984, a *Statement of National Objectives and Priorities* (SNOP; Home Office, 1984) for the probation service was published. As its title suggests, this document set out a list of prioritized objectives for the probation service. Although not quite as earth-shaking as at first thought (many probation officers seemed to see it as representing the end of probation as they knew it, but subsequent events were to render it relatively innocuous), SNOP was a 'watershed for the probation service, as it signalled a clear return by the Home Office to a more interventionist stance with regard to the service' (Mair, 1996: 30). The objective of diverting offenders from custody remained high, but behind SNOP one can see the beginnings of government pressure for the probation service to be more accountable, more aware of how its resources were used, and more managerial—issues which were to take on increasing importance in the 1990s.

Probation services responded to SNOP by setting their local objectives (see Lloyd, 1986) which demonstrated that there were considerable variations amongst areas in how they proposed to prioritize their work. SNOP was the first of a flurry of Green Papers (Home Office, 1988*a*, 1990*a*, 1995*a*), White Papers (Home Office, 1990*b*, 1996*b*), Blue Papers (Home Office, 1991*a*, 1991*b*), and even a 'Peppermint' paper (Home Office, 1990*c*), which focused to a greater or lesser extent on the work of the probation service and community penalties. Attempts continue to make the service more financially accountable, though this has proved difficult (see Humphrey, 1991). National standards for community penalties were introduced (first for community service in 1989) in 1992 and subsequently revised and made more rigorous without any systematic investigation of their impact (Home Office, 1995*b*). Three-year plans began to be prepared annually by the Home Office for the probation service (the first appearing in 1993) and these included performance indicators; and probation services began to be subjected to cash limits (Field and Hough, 1993).

Initially, such initiatives were certainly viewed with some apprehension by probation officers, although the major role which was being carved out for community penalties under the 1991 Criminal Justice Act tended to hold such worries in abeyance. The Act was possibly the most significant criminal justice legislation since the 1948 Criminal Justice Act. A more coherent approach to sentencing was introduced based on a 'just deserts' framework focused on the seriousness of the offence, which meant that the idea of diversion from custody was banished. In line with this, a graduated system of disposals was devised: with the unit fine system offering a more equitable approach to financial penalties; and custody and community penalties becoming, in effect, the same kind of sanction—both provided punishment, one in the community and the other outside it. This blurring of the edges between custodial and community penalties continued with a new approach to the early release of prisoners, whereby automatic conditional release was envisaged as a scheme where part of the sentence was served in custody and the remainder in the community. The probation order ceased to be imposed *instead* of a sentence and became a sentence of the court. And a new sentence was introduced—the combination order, which combined probation and community service. While the Act was controversial and sentencers in particular were quite unhappy about it, probation officers tended to welcome it and looked forward to its early teething problems being resolved (Mair and May, 1995).

Within months of its implementation, however, key facets of the Act had been dismantled, and with the arrival of Michael Howard in the Home Office in 1993 more serious worries developed. The review of probation training (Dews and Watts, 1994) could find little hard evidence that there were major problems with the training of probation officers, but nevertheless concluded that there *were* such problems and recommended radical change. Cash limits, which had originally been reasonably generous in order to allay probation fears, began to squeeze budgets which had lost the promise of growth at the start of the decade. And probation officers agonized about their response to the introduction of curfew orders and failed to be named as responsible officers for such cases (staff at Securicor and Geografix, the two organizations running the 1995–6 trials were given the task), thereby losing the chance to influence the new sentence.

Ninety years on from its official beginnings, the probation service is in a rather odd situation. On the one hand, the practical tasks associated with probation work remain very much as they were in 1907 (see above), yet many changes have taken place in offenders, offences, the structure of society, and theories of crime and how to deal with it. Thus the air of benevolent, Victorian do-gooding which hangs around probation work does not seem particularly appropriate for late twentieth-century offenders. On the other hand, there have been considerable changes in what might be termed the superstructure of the probation service. There has been a remarkable growth in groupwork at the expense of one-to-one casework and an increase in specialist activities (Boswell *et al.*, 1993), though there is no evidence that such developments have been planned in any rational way (see Mair, 1995*b*). More community penalties have been introduced—although the rationale for introducing new sentences is rarely clear—and the probation service has taken on more responsibilities (bail information schemes, work with victims, mediation, etc.). Community penalties have become more controlling and probation officers have become more accountable (though not without a struggle—see Humphrey *et al.*, 1993; May, 1991); and the tradition of professional autonomy and discretion has been constrained, though not eroded completely. Centralization and managerialism have hit the probation service (and the other criminal justice agencies), and privatization is a constant threat (Clarke *et al.*, 1994; Statham and Whitehead, 1992). Just how far these superstructural changes have changed the nature of probation work remains a matter for debate.

Various statements have been made which have tried to encapsulate neatly the changes which have taken place in the probation service:

The history of the probation service . . . is one which saw a loosely grouped organis-ation of practitioners, with high personal autonomy, confidence and clear purpose in a rehabilitative mission, adopt a significant managerial structure . . . and a dominant focus on court sentencing levels as a standard against which to measure performance [Humphrey *et al.*, 1993: 1].

The probation service's orientation has moved from a theologically to a psychiatrically driven discourse and then to what has been termed a post-psychiatric paradigm based less on therapy than on system involvement and offender management [Harris, 1994: 34].

And McWilliams argues for a development from saving souls through a diagnostic era to a period of pragmatism characterized by three schools of thought—'the managerial, the radical and the personalist' (McWilliams, 1987). My own preference, if one has to indulge in trying to formulate a simple description to sum up ninety years of the history of the application of com-munity penalties by the probation service would be a move from rehabilitation to diversion to punishment in the community.

Perhaps the most significant recent development is a revival of faith in rehabilitation, which has resulted in a variety of conferences and several books (McGuire, 1995; Palmer, 1992, 1994). This phenomenon will be discussed in more detail below in the section on effectiveness, but while this resurgence of the idea that treatment works seems to have led to increased optimism among probation officers, it is based upon fairly flimsy foundations, and it will be interesting to see if it can be sustained in the cold light of good research.

COMMUNITY PENALTIES IN 1995

The Probation Order

One major change which has taken place in the use of community penalties in the past forty-five years has been that the probation order—the only significant such disposal in 1950—has lost the great number of juveniles it once dealt with. In 1950 more than two-thirds of male offenders sentenced to probation for indictable offences were under the age of 18 (16,071 out of a total of

23,141), and this was the case for 38 per cent of female offenders so sentenced (1,715 out of a total of 4,478). Over the next twenty years the proportion of juveniles sentenced to probation orders decreased until, by 1971, with the implementation of the Children and Young Persons Act 1969, probation orders could no longer be made on offenders under the age of 17 (see Haxby, 1978: 301–14). Supervision orders became the sentence for juveniles and these tended to be the business of local authority social work departments. With the benefit of hindsight, it is possible to claim that losing juveniles was the first step in the probation service's journey to becoming a fully fledged criminal justice agency without the baggage of social work values (a journey which, it should be added, is not yet—and may never be—completed).

Simply in terms of the number of orders made, the probation order appears to be alive and well, if not actually thriving, as Table 32.1 shows.

Table 32.1 Offenders sentenced for indictable offences by type of sentence 1973–95 (thousands)*

Sentence	1973	1983	1991	1993	1994	1995
Probation	23.8	34.0	34.3	30.7	34.8	32.9
C.S.O.	–	31.4	29.5	32.8	32.9	30.5
Combination order	–	–	–	6.1	8.1	8.9
Fine	173.6	199.3	118.7	102.9	98.2	89.4
Discharge	43.2	58.7	64.7	66.1	63.7	57.3
Custody	41.2	69.8	48.9	46.6	53.0	60.0
Suspended sentence	20.8	29.8	21.1	2.7	2.4	2.5
Other	35.9	38.9	18.8	18.8	20.5	20.5
Total No.	338.5	461.9	336.0	306.7	313.6	302.0

Source: Home Office, *Criminal Statistics.*
  * Discharge includes absolute and conditional discharges; custody includes detention centre, borstal, and youth custody; and other includes supervision orders, attendance centre orders, care orders (the bulk of these three being made on juveniles), partly suspended sentences of imprisonment, and any other sentences passed.

After a considerable increase in the *number* of orders made between 1973 and 1983, the situation seems to have stabilized with relatively minor fluctuations in the 1990s. Proportionately, however, the picture is rather different; in 1973 and in 1983 probation orders made up 7 per cent of disposals, whereas in the 1990s, despite worries about the end of probation (as a result of the introduction of the combination order, of the redefinition of the community service order as a *punishment* rather than reparation to the community, of the introduction of the curfew order), the order has increased its market share to around 11 per cent. But this is in respect of indictable offences and the picture with regard to the less serious summary offences is rather different (the distinction between indictable and summary offences is explained in Maguire, this volume; see also Coleman and Moynihan, 1996: 23–45).

Table 32.2 Offenders sentenced to probation for indictable offences by type of offence 1977–95 (per cent)

Offence	1977	1983	1991	1995
Violence	6.5	6.7	9.6	9.4
Sexual	3.4	2.6	2.3	2.4
Robbery	0.4	0.3	0.5	0.6
Burglary	18.2	17.3	22.1	16.1
Theft/handling	58.7	56.7	45.8	44.7
Fraud/forgery	7.8	8.2	7.0	7.6
Criminal damage	2.6	2.9	4.3	4.3
Drugs offences	–	–	3.8	7.0
Motoring	0.4	2.3	1.1	1.5
Other	2.2	3.2	3.5	6.1
Total Number (thousands)	23.0	34.0	34.3	32.9

Source: Home Office, *Criminal Statistics*.

In 1973, around 5,000 probation orders were made for summary offences and this figure remained the same ten years later. By 1991, however, over 13,000 offenders were sentenced to probation for summary offences, a figure which had increased to 16,500 by 1995. Thus, in proportional terms, summary offences accounted for 17 per cent of probation orders in 1973 but for one-third in 1995. Such growth is very much a double-edged sword: growth in the number of probation orders made is a good thing from the probation service point of view (it demonstrates the order is popular and may lead to increases in budgets); however, growth in the use of the order for summary offences may not be so desirable. The probation order has long had a reputation (rightly or wrongly) as a 'soft option' which is appropriate only for relatively minor offences (its origins are important here). The probation service has, of course, tried to combat such a perception by emphasizing that probation is an appro-priate sentence for many so-called 'serious' offences. The increased use of probation for summary offences, where almost nine out of ten sentences are fines, can only reinforce the idea that the probation order is not a feasible option where serious offenders are concerned; a continuation of this trend would—in the long run—marginalize the order.[6]

Table 32.2 shows the offences of those who have been sentenced to probation orders over the last twenty years. It is worth noting that, while the probation order continues to be used for those offences we might consider to be particu-larly serious (the first four in the table), it is increasingly used for the more minor offences (where there is less risk to the public) in the lower half of the table. There has been a considerable drop in its use for offences of theft/

[6] To a considerable extent, the increased growth in respect of summary offences has been as a result of the reclassification of some triable either way offences as summary, but this does not invalidate the argument.

handling and—since 1991—a decrease in its use for burglary.[7] Like the increased use of probation for summary offences, these are developments which may not bode well for the future.

While there are signs that the probation order is moving down-tariff by being used more often for offenders who pose little risk to the public, it is—paradoxically—at the same time being used more often in the Crown Court. In 1983, 18 per cent of probation orders made for indictable offences were passed in the Crown Court; by 1991 the proportion had increased to 28 per cent and in 1995 stood at one-quarter. One way for the probation order to be taken seriously as a sentence is for it to be used in the Crown Court, and it will be important for probation staff to try to ensure that this foothold is consolidated. There is an associated development which should be noted at this point, and that is the increased use of probation for those offenders with a previous record of custody: in 1981 around 24 per cent of those commencing probation orders had previously served a custodial sentence, while by 1994 the comparable figure was 42 per cent (provisional figures for 1995 show 41 per cent). Conversely, the proportion with no previous convictions has decreased over the same period (see Home Office, *Probation Statistics*). These two developments are difficult, at first sight, to reconcile with the tendency for the probation order to move down-tariff with regard to the offences it is used for.

The key to the increased usage of probation in the Crown Court and for those with experience of custody is the rise of the probation order *with added requirements*. Table 32.3 shows the percentage of offenders commencing probation supervision with additional requirements between 1981 and 1994 (both the 1982 and 1991 Criminal Justice Acts introduced significant new requirements).

In 1981, almost nine out of ten probation orders had no additional requirements; by 1994 this was the case for only three-quarters of probation orders. Indeed, in 1994 more than one in ten orders had a requirement to participate in specified activities added to the basic order. Additional requirements give an image of greater control over an offender and would appear to be popular with sentencers, who may be willing to make use of probation with additional requirements for offenders who would be considered too dangerous for an ordinary probation order. If someone is attending a probation centre, participating in a specified activity, or residing in a probation hostel, the impression is given that the offender is under greater surveillance than a normal probation order can offer.

Specified activities have overtaken probation centres (previously known as day centres) as the most popular additional requirement. In the mid-1980s, it looked as if day centres might be the future for probation (Mair, 1988), but their popularity declined. Specified activities offer the chance to focus explicitly

---

[7] The rise in the use of probation for burglary between 1983 and 1991 is at least partly attributable to the 1988 Green Paper (Home Office, 1988a) and its associated *Tackling Offending* initiative (Home Office, 1988b), both of which urged the use of community sentences—especially forms of intensive probation—for burglaries which were not of the most serious.

Table 32.3 Offenders commencing probation supervision by type of additional requirement 1981–94 (percentage)*

Type of additional requirement	1981	1985	1990	1994
Non-residential mental treatment	3.4	2.3	1.8	0.9
Residential mental treatment	0.8	0.5	0.3	0.1
Residence in approved probation hostel	3.6	3.2	2.3	1.3
Residence in other institution	0.5	0.5	0.6	0.3
Other residential requirement	0.8	0.6	0.8	0.7
Probation centre	1.0	4.3	6.6	5.7
Report to specified person at specified place	–	0.1	1.6	1.5
Participate in specified activities	–	2.0	9.0	13.5
Mental treatment by/under qualified medical person	–	–	–	0.6
Residential drugs/alcohol treatment	–	–	–	0.6
Non-residential drugs/alcohol treatment	–	–	–	1.2
Drugs/alcohol by/under qualified medical person	–	–	–	0.8
Extended requirements for sex offenders	–	–	–	0.1
Other requirements	3.2	2.3	3.1	2.1
No additional requirement	87.5	85.2	75.9	73.2
Total Number	35,850	41,750	46,282	49,119

Source: Home Office, *Probation Statistics*.
* As a result of counting procedures, figures do not add to the total.

on a problem whereas a probation centre uses a more scattershot approach; with the pressures of cash limits biting more deeply, the more expensive probation centres (which required a building and offered a variety of activities) are giving way to the better targeted specified activities requirements which may offer better value for money.

Finally, and briefly, what are the characteristics of those offenders who are sentenced to probation in terms of age and gender? The proportion of women on probation has declined: in 1981, one-third of probation orders were made on female offenders, but by 1994 this figure had dropped to 18 per cent. This is an interesting development as probation has traditionally been seen as the natural home for female offenders. Two points are worth making. First, this may be a sign that the political emphasis that probation is not there to help people who have social problems and who happen to have offended has taken root in the service and the courts. And secondly, it raises the question of what is happening to female offenders—one part of the answer may be that they are increasingly being sentenced to imprisonment for what appear to be trivial offences.

The age of those being sentenced to probation orders is also changing, with the order being used less for young offenders aged 17–20: in 1981 two-fifths of those commencing probation orders were in this age group, whereas by 1994 only one-quarter were. This trend is partly a result of demography, but may also be due to the increasing demonization of young offenders by the media (with the encouragement of government) which has led to tougher sentences for such offenders.

It is difficult to discern any clear trends in the recent history of the probation order. If anything, there seems to be a form of bifurcation occurring with moves towards the order being used for serious offences on the one hand (signalled by the growth in Crown Court usage, and increasing use for those with previous experience of custody), and for more minor offences on the other (marked by the considerable growth in the use of probation for summary offences). This schizophrenic approach to the probation order may be due to the conflicting messages about the order which have emanated from government in recent years: probation as a demanding penalty which can be used for offenders who pose a risk to the community; and probation as not being tough enough and needing to become more punitive before it can be used for serious offenders. It is possible that we are witnessing the slow demise of the straight probation order, and what this may mean for the probation service will be discussed in the final section of the paper.

The Community Service Order

Community service was introduced in the 1972 Criminal Justice Act as a result of a recommendation made by the Advisory Council on the Penal System (ACPS, 1970; for detailed accounts of the development of community service orders see Pease, 1985; Vass, 1984; Whitfield and Scott, 1993; Young, 1979). The Advisory Council had been given the task of considering 'what changes and additions might be made in the existing range of non-custodial penalties, disabilities, and other requirements which may be imposed on offenders' (ACPS, 1970: 1), as a result of increasing prison overcrowding. The ACPS report argued that community service could fulfil various penological objectives: it would involve reparation to the community, it could act as an alternative to a custodial sentence, it could provide punishment, and it could rehabilitate.[8] This philosophical confusion about what community service was for (could it possibly do everything its supporters claimed), has been both a help and a hindrance since its beginnings.

There can be little doubt that when the first community service schemes were introduced, they were intended by government to provide an alternative to custodial sentences. This, however, did not stop some probation services treating community service as a sentence in its own right and using it simply as an alternative to another non-custodial sentence (Pease *et al.*, 1975). The reparative element seemed to take precedence over the punitive or the directly rehabilitative; indeed, little was heard of community service as *punishment* until

---

[8] Baroness Wootton, who chaired the sub-committee of ACPS which prepared the report, later admitted to being 'slightly ashamed' of the way community service was designed to appeal to all shades of penal opinion (Wootton, 1978: 128).

the 1990s, when this concept was forced back onto the agenda of community sentences (although there has been no coherent discussion about the precise place of punishment in community sentences, and it is hard to escape the conclusion that it has by no means been fully assimilated by probation officers).

Community service was first introduced in six probation areas as an experiment at the start of 1973; without taking note of the results of the research which Pease and his colleagues were undertaking (Pease *et al.*, 1975; Pease, 1983) the experiment was extended to all probation areas from 1974 onwards. In 1974 1,000 offenders were sentenced to community service for indictable offences; by 1980 this figure had grown to 19,500 (Home Office, *Criminal Statistics*). As Table 32.1 (above) shows, by 1983 almost as many community service orders were being made as probation orders (and this for a sentence which was scarcely ten years old), although numbers declined somewhat as the 1980s advanced. The reasons for this decline probably lie, to a certain extent, in the diversity of practice which research uncovered in the operation of community service. McIvor (1992: 5–6) makes the point well:

The lack of agreement among sentencers and among probation staff concerning the appropriate use of community service remained unresolved (see, for example, Vass, 1984). The use of community service orders varied from area to area (Young, 1979) as did the types of work that offenders on community service were required to perform, with schemes differing widely in their relative use of agency, group and 'fallback' placements (Fletcher, 1983; B. McWilliams, 1980; Read, 1980). Schemes likewise differed in the manner in which absences from placements were categorised (as acceptable or not) and in the way in which the requirements of orders were enforced (B. McWilliams, 1980; Young, 1979). Vass (1984) documented the 'creative' recording of hours worked and the reluctance of community service staff to return offenders to court who were in breach of their requirements . . .

Indeed, early in the history of community service an attempt was made by Ken Pease to inject more consistency into the sentence by arguing that orders of less than 100 hours should be imposed where the sentence was *not* an alternative to custody and that an order of 240 hours should be the equivalent of at least twelve months custody (Pease, 1978*a*; for further contributions to this debate see Pease, 1978*b*; Trewartha, 1978; Willis, 1978; and Vass, 1986). In the late 1980s, a study carried out for the Home Office found considerable differences in the operation and organization of community service (Thomas, Hine, and Nugent, 1990). Such a range of documented disparities had serious implications for equity of treatment among offenders, and it is not surprising that the first set of National Standards introduced in 1989 were for community service (for a brief discussion of their impact see Lloyd, 1990). The decline in the number of community service orders has stopped, although, like the probation order, there have been fluctuations in the last few years. In terms of orders made as a proportion of all sentences for indictable offences, community service's market share has grown from almost 3 per cent in 1978 to almost 7 per cent in 1983; by 1995 it was 10 per cent.

Table 32.4 Offenders sentenced to community service for indictable offences by type of offence 1977–95 (per cent)

Offence	1977	1983	1991	1995
Violence	7.8	8.6	13.2	14.1
Sexual	–	0.3	0.3	0.3
Robbery	1.0	0.3	1.0	0.6
Burglary	26.4	25.2	25.1	14.8
Theft/handling	52.0	46.2	38.0	37.7
Fraud/forgery	3.9	6.0	7.4	9.5
Criminal damage	2.0	2.5	2.7	2.3
Drugs offences	–	–	3.4	7.2
Motoring	3.9	8.6	2.4	3.6
Other	2.0	1.9	6.1	9.5
Total Number (thousands)	10.2	31.4	29.5	30.5

Source: Home Office, *Criminal Statistics.*

With regard to summary offences, the picture is similar to that for probation. Throughout most of the 1980s around 10 per cent of community service orders were made for summary offences; by 1991 it was 31 per cent (reclassification of offences is again responsible to some extent for this); and by 1995 37 per cent. For a court sentence which was originally seen as closer to custody than a probation order, almost two out of five community service offenders are now sentenced for summary offences—a higher proportion than is the case for probation.

What about the types of offences for which community service is used? Table 32.4 sets out the picture for the last twenty years. In its early days, half of the community service orders made for indictable offences were for theft/ handling and one-quarter for burglary; by 1995 just over one-third of orders were made for theft/handling and 15 per cent for burglary (it is interesting to compare this table with Table 32.2 which shows the offences for which probation orders were made—on the face of it, both sentences look as if they are used for very similar offenders). Like the growth in the use of community service for summary offences, this decrease in use for theft and burglary is a worrying tendency for the probation service. On the other hand, following the trend for the probation order, there has been an increase in the proportion of community service orders made for indictable offences at the Crown Court: in 1983 26 per cent of community service orders were passed at the Crown Court; by 1991 this had grown to 37 per cent and in 1995 the figure stood at 33 per cent.

If the community service order is to be taken seriously as a major community penalty it must be used for offenders who pose some degree of risk to the community, and one measure of this is the proportion of offenders who received community service orders who had a previous record of custody. In this light, the signs are not good: in 1981 40 per cent of those who commenced a community service order had previously served a custodial sentence; by 1991 this figure had dropped to 34 per cent; and by 1994 it stood at only 29 per cent (provisional information for 1995 shows a further decrease to 27 per cent). This decline, of course, has occurred as the probation order has been increasingly used for those who have served a sentence of imprisonment.[9]

Community service has tended to be seen as a sentence which is not particularly appropriate for female offenders (it can involve heavy labour, and arrangements might be required for child-care). Although the proportion of probation orders made on females has dropped, probation remains a popular sentence for women. In 1981, almost 6 per cent of those commencing community service were female; ten years later, in 1991, the same proportion applied, while in 1994 it had risen slightly to 7 per cent. This may have something to do with greater efforts on the part of probation officers to make opportunities for community service for female offenders; although it may also signal the changing image of community service as punitive, and an increasingly tough approach to the sentencing of women.

Community service, like the probation order, is being used less for younger offenders: in 1985 half of those commencing community service orders were under 21 (community service was extended to 16-year-olds in 1983), whereas by 1994 this proportion had dropped to a quarter.

The picture for community service appears rather more troubling than that for the probation order. Apart from its increased usage in the Crown Court (and this has dropped slightly since 1991), the rapid growth and development which characterized its first ten years have not been sustained. It may well be difficult to keep a community sentence at a high-tariff level over time (for example, some probation day centres found themselves moving down-tariff despite their best efforts: see Mair, 1988), but community service seems to have slipped down-tariff quite dramatically. The wide-ranging appeal, which was seen as a positive advantage of community service at the start of its life, may have become a handicap; a sentence which was once primarily seen as reparative is now viewed officially as a punitive measure (although how far this perception is shared by sentencers and probation officers is another matter). And what has been referred to as 'the most promising new penal disposal of the post-war period, arguably of the century' looks as if it may be sliding inexorably towards the 'penalization' future described by Pease 15 years ago (Pease, 1981: 49).[10]

---

[9] It is worth noting that the length of both probation and community service orders has decreased consistently over the past decade.

[10] McWilliams and Pease (1980) set out four 'cameos' which offered possible futures for the community service order: bureaucratization, probationization, penalization, and standardization. One can see evidence of all of these in the community service of the 1990s. Pease (1981: 46) has described penalization as follows: 'If the philosophy of those imposing community service became more punitive, the tasks would lose the idealism of personal service to those in need and become more explicitly work-gang oriented. Offenders would be "processed" through their orders in ways that would require the least possible labour. . . . Little attention would be given to providing

The Combination Order

The new kid on the block is the combination order which, as the name suggests, is an amalgam of the probation order and the community service order. It is perhaps surprising that such an obvious combination had not been introduced earlier (it has been available in Scotland since the late 1970s, but has not been the subject of research), but the redefinition of community service as punishment meant that the mixture of social work help and dealing with offending behaviour as well as administering punishment with a dash of reparation must have looked irresistible on paper. Whether adding 2+2 in this manner did give an answer of 4 remains unclear however. The implication of the 1990 White Paper, *Crime, Justice and Protecting the Public* (Home Office 1990*b*), was that the combination order represented a fairly demanding sentence and would be used for offenders who might have been imprisoned. But even on paper, a short combination order of twelve months probation and sixty hours community service compared to a lengthy order of twenty-four months probation, 100 hours of community service and a requirement to attend a probation centre looked as if they could apply to offenders at very different points on the spectrum of seriousness.

As Table 32.1 (above) shows, the combination order has taken off quickly since it was introduced in October 1992. In 1995 almost 9,000 offenders were sentenced to the order for indictable offences—around 3 per cent of all sentences for indictable offences. Interestingly, however, for a sentence which was touted as appropriate for serious offenders, another 5,700 combination orders were made for summary offences; in other words, almost 40 per cent of combination orders were made for less serious offences—a higher proportion than for either probation orders or community service orders.

It is too early to detect any real trends in the way combination orders are used, but Table 32.5 shows the offences for which the order was used between 1993 and 1995.

A glance at this table suggests immediately a possible reason for the drop in the use of probation and community service for offences of burglary—almost one-quarter of combination orders were made for burglary. But apart from this, there is little evidence that the new order is being used for very different offences compared to the probation and community service orders (cf. Tables 32.2 and 32.4).

The first version of the National Standards suggested that the combination order should be used primarily in the Crown Court (Home Office, 1992), a reflection of the official view that this was a serious sentence, pitched further up-tariff than probation or community service—a view shared by the probation service which had campaigned to restrict the order to the Crown Court. In fact,

work that is challenging to the worker or beneficial to the recipient. Schemes could be staffed by relatively untrained, and hence cheaper, staff. . . . Offenders proving refractory in such an environment would be quickly returned to court, with no thought given to providing alternative work placements.'

Table 32.5 Offenders sentenced to the combination order for indictable offences by type of offence (per cent)

Offence	1993	1994	1995
Violence	14.7	14.8	13.5
Sexual	–	1.2	–
Robbery	1.6	1.2	1.1
Burglary	27.8	24.7	22.5
Theft/handling	32.8	34.6	33.7
Fraud/forgery	6.5	7.4	7.9
Criminal damage	3.3	3.7	3.3
Drugs offences	4.9	6.2	7.9
Motoring	3.3	2.4	3.3
Other	4.9	4.9	6.7
Total Number (thousands)	6.1	8.1	8.9

Source: Home Office, *Criminal Statistics*.

the opposite has happened—the majority of combination orders have been made in the magistrates' courts. In 1995, more than two-thirds of orders made for indictable offences were made by magistrates—a rather similar proportion to probation or community service. This seems to have been partly due to magistrates seeing the new order as the answer to their prayers, and partly due to reluctance on the part of probation services to market the order carefully to magistrates (Mair *et al.*, 1997). The new edition of the National Standards (Home Office, 1995*b*) omitted the reference to the Crown Court as being the home for the combination order, and it will be interesting to see if the order becomes used more often there.

In terms of its usage for those with a previous record of custody, the combination order is surprisingly close to the probation order; provisional figures for 1995 show 42 per cent of combination orders being used for such offenders—very close to the probation figure of 41 per cent. It is also worth noting that the new order is used proportionately more often than either probation or community service for offenders under the age of 21.

To summarize, while it is still early days for the combination order, it has certainly made a good start in terms of the number of orders made. It is, however, difficult to escape the conclusion that the new order has increased the controlling and demanding nature of community penalties generally, without making any impact upon the number of offenders sentenced to custody.

Curfew Orders and Attendance Centre Orders

In terms of the number of orders made, these two sentences play a minimal role. It is difficult to find out how many offenders are sentenced to attend a *senior* attendance centre as data are provided for attendance centres generally and junior centres are far more common than senior ones. There are fewer than thirty senior attendance centres in England and Wales and they deal with around 1,000 offenders a year. As for curfew orders (provision for which was included in the 1991 Criminal Justice Act), they have yet to be introduced on a national basis and have just completed a trial period in three areas of the country. The real significance of these two sentences, however, lies in the fact that they are community penalties which are not run by the probation service, and, as such, they may offer a vision of the future.

Senior attendance centres have languished on the margins of court sentences since the first one opened in 1958. With their inclusion in the 1948 Criminal Justice Act, they became the first new non-custodial sentence since the probation order but their development has been slow and they are still not available to all courts. They are run by the police on behalf of the Home Office and usually open for three hours every second Saturday afternoon, with a regime of physical training, first aid, woodwork, car maintenance, etc. Various reasons may be adduced for the low levels of interest in the centres, but the lack of probation involvement is probably the key. The probation service has shown that it can develop a sentence which it was ambivalent about (the community service order), and it is possible that if the service had been given responsibility for senior attendance centres they would not have languished as they have (for a full account of the development and practice of senior attendance centres see Mair, 1991).

Curfew orders with electronic monitoring have yet to begin their career as a full-scale sentence in this country (although electronic monitoring of offenders is in use in the United States, Canada, Sweden, Australia, Israel, the Netherlands, Singapore). The Home Office research into the 1994–5 trials (Mair and Mortimer, 1996) suggested that the sentence was feasible in practical terms (the equipment worked, the staff coped, the organization functioned adequately) but questioned how many offenders it might be used for. It took a great deal of hard work to encourage the courts in the three areas to sentence the numbers they did (eighty-three in total in the first twelve months) and many more offenders would be required to render the sentence cost-effective on a national basis. Probation service apprehensions about the sentence undoubtedly had something to do with the low numbers being sentenced to curfew orders. Generally, electronic monitoring is not viewed positively by probation officers in the United Kingdom. Since the first trials of electronic monitoring in this country in 1989–90 probation officers have not been keen to get involved with it, seeing 'tagging' as demeaning and an infringement of civil liberties. By the end of the latest trials, however, it looked as if probation officers were willing to think again—albeit reluctantly, having realized that the sentence was probably here to stay. Probation involvement is also necess-ary to help those offenders on curfew orders to cope with any difficulties encountered; during the trials, the staff of the organizations responsible for electronic monitoring carried out this task, although it was not part of their job, and if they had been working at full capacity it would not have been possible.

As provider of pre-sentence reports (PSRs) to the courts, the probation service holds the key to community penalties and, as such, can influence the use of a sentence.[11] If probation officers do not like a sentence (because it is run by the police, or involves a purely punitive approach) they will be unlikely to propose it as a feasible option in a PSR, which means that the sentence will be starved of offenders; a situation which has been noted in respect of senior attendance centres and curfew orders—see Mair, 1991; Mair and Mortimer, 1996. Thus, for community penalties to be successful, they would seem to need the positive involvement of the probation service (or some other agency which would have responsibility for them) as a basic minimum.

THE EFFECTIVENESS OF COMMUNITY PENALTIES

What is perhaps most surprising about the current obsession with how effective community penalties are, is that it has taken so long to become a major issue. Criminal justice agencies generally, like so many state organizations, seemed to be immune from the kind of questions which ordinary businesses would have to consider every day. This is not to argue that criminal justice can, or should, be treated as a business, but its precise status remains unclear and thus renders such issues as effectiveness much more problematic than they might be. Despite the reverberations which followed the publication—and mis-interpretation—of the work of Robert Martinson and his colleagues in the United States and Stephen Brody in the United Kingdom (Brody, 1976; Lipton *et al.*, 1975; Martinson, 1974) that in terms of reconviction rates 'Nothing Works', questions about effectiveness remained a minor preoccupation of the probation service. Rather more effort was put into trying to demonstrate that community penalties could act as an alternative to custody (though this aim was not accepted by all probation officers), but effectiveness was still a back-ground issue. It was only the arrival of the Thatcher government in 1979 which led to the cold winds of business ideology and practices entering the debate about community penalties (as well as the work of the other criminal justice agencies).

Since 1979 effectiveness has become a—and, increasingly, *the*—key factor in the debate about community penalties. The problem is, however, pinning down what effectiveness means, and this presupposes a degree of clarity about

---

[11] Precisely how much influence a PSR has on a sentencer is unclear. Bottoms and McWilliams (1986: 254) sum up the situation as follows: 'report writers can and do have an influence upon sentencers, though probably only in a minority of cases; however, that influence can apparently be both away from *and towards* custodial sentences' (emphasis in original). But if a sentence is consistently not mentioned in PSRs, it is quite possible that sentencers—particularly magistrates— will forget it exists.

the aims and objectives of community penalties. But while such clarity would be an advantage in assessing how effective a community penalty was, it would have the disadvantage of providing a ready-made rod with which to chastise the probation service (or the government) if effectiveness was not achieved. Thus, in the 1996–9 *Three-Year Plan for the Probation Service* the following 'responsibilities' are set out (Home Office, 1996*a*: 1):

- [to] provide the courts with advice and information on offenders to assist with sentencing decisions
- implement community sentences passed by the courts
- design, provide, and promote effective programmes for supervising offenders safely in the community
- assist prisoners, before and after release, to lead law-abiding lives
- help communities prevent crime and reduce its effects on victims
- provide information to the courts on the best interests of children in family disputes
- work in partnership with other bodies and services in using the most constructive methods of dealing with offenders and defendants

To operationalize these vague and ambiguous 'responsibilities' in order that they might be evaluated in terms of practical effectiveness would be a difficult task. To take just one responsibility at random (and how a responsibility relates to an aim or objective is unclear), it could be easily claimed that to 'implement community sentences passed by the courts' successfully all that the probation service would have to do would be to allocate offenders to the sentence. Just how much that says about effectiveness is open to question. More confusing is the fact that the 1994–7 *Plan* identified seven operational and four management goals, while the 1995–8 version reduced these to three, each of which had a list of means for achieving the goal, desirable developments which might be pursued, and objectives to be attained (the same three goals remain in the 1996–9 *Plan*). There are also 'priorities' for the service which are set by the Home Secretary for the planning period, but which changed between the 1995–8 *Plan* and that for 1996–9. Thus the probation service has responsibilities, goals, means for achieving these, desirable developments (whatever their status is), objectives, and priorities. Effectiveness remains obscure behind such a smoke-screen. And the water is further muddied by the fact that in the National Standards, each of the three main community penalties is provided with aims. The probation order's purpose is defined (Home Office, 1995*b*: 17) as:

- securing the rehabilitation of the offender
- protecting the public from harm from the offender, or
- preventing the offender from committing further offences.

The community service order's purpose is 'to prevent further offending by re-integrating the offender into the community' (Home Office, 1995*b*: 34), while the aim of the combination order consists of—as might be expected—

the purposes of probation and community service added together. And finally, in this flurry of possible factors which might measure the effectiveness of community penalties, the Probation Inspectorate's programme of Quality and Effectiveness inspections should not be forgotten (although in the interests of clarity, forgetting these inspections might be sensible).

But despite—or because of—the confusion about what the aims and objectives (or goals and responsibilities) of the probation order (or the various community penalties) might be, questions about effectiveness will not go away. Initially, the pressure came from government which was trying to square the circle of cutting costs and improving law and order (see Morgan and Downes, this volume), but with budgetary constraints, decreasing numbers of offenders, increased tasks and more authoritative voices asking about effectiveness (e.g. the Audit Commission in its 1989 report *The Probation Service: Promoting Value for Money*), probation services themselves have begun to take seriously the question of just how effective their work is.

The problem, as has been identified above, remains the definition of effectiveness. The usual measure has been reconviction rates, and there has been increasing interest in using these as a measure of effectiveness by the Home Office. It is surely no coincidence that while the 1991 *Probation Statistics* contained nothing at all about reconviction rates, the 1992 volume had a separate chapter of eight pages on the topic and by 1993 this had grown to twenty-two pages. In general, however, reconviction studies have been few and far between for community penalties and have tended to ignore the complexities and limitations of reconviction rates as a clear and simple measure of anything (see Home Office, 1983, 1986, 1993; Phillpotts and Lancucki, 1979). Building on the critiques begun by people such as Brody (1976), Michael Maltz (1984) began seriously to alert researchers to the problems associated with reconviction rates, and, more recently, Lloyd and his colleagues have listed a series of limitations of reconviction rates (Lloyd *et al.*, 1994: 3–10):

- they do not take account of all of the aims of sentencing
- a wide range of definitions have been used to measure reconvictions
- reconvictions do not measure reoffending
- what is a 'correct' follow-up period?
- when do you start counting reconvictions?
- how should one take account of the time-lag between offence and conviction?
- all reconvictions are not of equal severity
- it is difficult to compare the reconviction rates for different sentences
- how can the effects of policing and prosecution practice be accounted for?
- adequate and accessible data-bases have been (and continue to be) a problem
- interpreting reconviction rates is complex

These limitations certainly do not rule out the use of reconviction rates as a measure of effectiveness, but they do emphasize that rates of reconviction are *not* 'neutral, technical . . . unproblematic and easily understood' (Lloyd *et al.*, 1994: 3). A simplistic reliance upon recidivism as the sole criterion for judging the success or failure of a sentence is one of the two major failures in the work of Robert Martinson, who remains so closely associated with the idea that in terms of the effective rehabilitation of offenders 'Nothing Works' (Martinson, 1974). The second failing in Martinson's work is a blindness towards issues of context and implementation:

Martinson's study also fails to account for *how* a programme's success is influenced by the particular manner in which it is operated and organized. This is not surprising, since the primary studies themselves generally fail to address these issues. At most, researchers spend a paragraph or a page describing a programme; we are rarely given the full rationale for why it exists. Researchers only occasionally study how programmes are planned, how they are put into practice, and how and why they change over time. Yet these matters are crucial to determining the success or failure of a project. For example, if a large number of the projects Martinson considered were poorly planned, badly implemented, starved of resources, or were administered by untrained and uncommitted staff with a high turnover rate—would it be any surprise to find the programmes had failed? [Mair, 1995*a*: 459].

Despite convincing demonstrations about how the 'Nothing Works' credo came to be established as a result of media attention (Palmer, 1978), despite swift responses purporting to show that some forms of 'treatment' did, in fact 'work' (Gendreau and Ross, 1979), and despite the fact that Martinson's original article was equivocal and cautious to say the least, 'Nothing Works' rapidly became accepted from the mid-1970s onwards as the paradigm within which research into corrections generally—and community penalties in particular—was located. Any debate about 'Nothing Works' followed the lines defined by Martinson: take a sample of studies, review them, and claim they show Nothing/Something Works (even with the advent of meta-analysis, discussed below, this path has been followed, see Whitehead and Lab, 1989; Andrews *et al.*, 1990*a*; Lab and Whitehead, 1990; Andrews *et al.*, 1990*b*).[12]

In fact, if we put to one side the more extreme meaning of 'Nothing Works', the most recent and most detailed comparative reconviction study suggests that there is indeed little difference in the reconviction rates of the four main penalties. Lloyd and his colleagues (1994) compared the actual reconviction rates (taking account of pseudo-reconvictions[13] which led to a drop in the raw reconviction rate for each disposal) of prison, straight probation orders,

---

[12] Opponents of 'Nothing Works' like to claim that Martinson recanted his views shortly before his death, although modified might be a more appropriate term (Martinson, 1979). There has even been some debate about this (see Doob and Brodeur, 1989; Gendreau, 1989).

[13] Lloyd *et al.* (1994: 41) define pseudo-reconvictions as 'those reconvictions recorded in a follow-up period that were actually for offences committed prior to the start of the follow-up'. For a discussion of the potential effects of pseudo-reconvictions on reconviction rates: see Lloyd *et al.*, *ibid.*: 7.

Table 32.6 Predicted and actual reconviction rates for four disposal groups, 1987

Sentence group	Actual % reconvicted	Predicted % reconvicted	Total Number
Probation	43	45	2,448
CSOs	49	52	2,394
4A/4B	63	60	3,354
Prison	54	53	9,615

Source: Lloyd *et al.*, 1994.

probation orders with 4A/4B requirements, and community service orders with their predicted rates.[14] Table 32.6 sets out the results of their work.

While a case might be made for community penalties being more effective than custody, on the grounds that for both probation and community service the actual reconviction rate was lower than that predicted, two points should be borne in mind: first, that the least effective penalty was probation with a 4A/4B requirement and, secondly, that the difference between actual and predicted rates for all sentences was small and possibly subject to sampling error. As the authors note 'A more cautious and more sustainable conclusion is that there is little to choose between these sentencing options in terms of their impact on reoffending—whether the impact is construed as deterrent or rehabilitative' (Lloyd *et al.*, 1994: 51). Indeed, it may be worth emphasizing that one conclusion which is certainly not sustainable is that prison is more effective than community penalties in terms of reconviction rates.

The study confirmed what previous studies had suggested—that the key correlates of reconviction were age, sex, offence, and criminal history. The sentence itself has little effect. But this is to consider disposals in the aggregate, and there is evidence that when individual examples of the same sentence are examined differences in reconviction rates appear: Mair and Nee (1992) found that while the overall reconviction rate for a sample of probation day centres was 63 per cent, half a dozen centres had rates in excess of 75 per cent, while four had rates of less than 50 per cent; similarly, the reconviction study of community service carried out by Pease *et al.* (1977) showed an overall reconviction rate of 44 per cent, with one scheme producing a disappointing rate of

[14] Court disposals vary widely according to the age, sex, criminal history, and offences of offenders sentenced to them, and these factors are closely associated with reconviction. In order to take account of these differences, a risk of reconviction score was calculated for each individual in the sample using a logistic regression model. The average score for all individuals was calculated to provide a predicted risk of reconviction for each disposal group. If the actual reconviction rate is lower than that predicted then it is possible to claim that the sentence has had a positive effect on reconviction; if the actual rate is higher than that predicted, then the sentence has had a negative effect (see Lloyd *et al.*, 1994). 4A and 4B requirements are probation day centres and specified activities requirements respectively (the 4A/4B terminology was used prior to the 1991 Criminal Justice Act); they are used for more serious offenders than straight probation orders.

66 per cent while another achieved 39 per cent. A great deal more work will be required to uncover the differences *within* sentences (such as the method of implementation, the detailed regime adopted, the quality of staff, etc.) which might contribute to such a range of reconviction rates.

Looking at reconviction rates from a simple yes/no approach, where any reconviction equals failure and no reconviction equals success, is not enough. Besides comparing predicted and actual reconviction rates and examining the rates associated with individual examples of sentences (which is often bedevilled by small numbers), it is useful to examine such matters as the time taken to reconviction, the seriousness of the reconviction offence, and the frequency of reconviction. If, for example, an offender is reconvicted but the offence is less serious than the original offence, or if the time taken to reconviction is considerably longer than the gap between prior convictions, or if only two offences are recorded in the twenty-four-month follow-up period whereas in the previous twenty-four months fifteen offences had been recorded, then it would seem sensible to claim that—despite the fact that a reconviction had been recorded—some form of effective intervention may have occurred (for some examples of studies which look at these facets of reconviction rates: see Lloyd *et al.*, 1994; Mair and Nee, 1992; Roberts, 1989).

While reconviction rates may be used in a more sophisticated fashion and with more concern for their limitations, this does not necessarily make them the sole criterion for judging the effectiveness of community penalties. One of the most significant developments for such penalties in the past decade has been the renaissance of rehabilitation and the so-called death of 'Nothing Works' which is based almost entirely on evidence of recidivism from meta-analytic studies (for discussions of meta-analysis see Glass *et al.*, 1981; Rosenthal, 1991; Wolf, 1986). Glass (1976: 3, emphasis in original) has defined meta-analysis as follows:

Primary analysis is the original analysis of data in a research study. . . . *Secondary analysis* is the re-analysis of data for the purpose of answering the original research question with better statistical techniques, or answering new questions with old data. . . . *Meta-analysis* refers to the analysis of analyses . . . the statistical analysis of a large collection of analysis results from individual studies for the purpose of integrating the findings.

Meta-analysis has been assumed by many probation officers to prove definitively that 'treatment' or 'rehabilitation' works, and that community penalties are, therefore, effective but matters are not (as might be expected) quite as simple as this.

In the first place, only a handful of meta-analyses concerning community penalties generally have been carried out and these have concentrated on juvenile delinquents in the United States (Andrews *et al.*, 1990*a*; Lipsey, 1992; Garrett, 1985; Gottschalk *et al.*, 1987; Whitehead and Lab, 1989), which may not be especially relevant to the kinds of offenders sentenced to community penalties in the United Kingdom. The meta-analyses continue to rely heavily on studies carried out in the 1950s and 1960s, and lessons which might have worked then may well not be helpful in the changed circumstances of the 1990s. There are statistical questions around meta-analysis which its criminal justice practitioners tend to ignore (Copas, 1995). Detailed examination of meta-analysis can uncover issues which raise questions about the claims of effectiveness which are made.[15] Taking as an example Lipsey's (1992) study, partly as a result of its ambition (it covers more than 400 studies) and partly because Lipsey sets out very clearly the categories for the variables studied:

For the primary delinquency measure (which is not always recidivism) half of the follow-up studies have follow-up periods of less than six months. Almost half of the studies were coded as having low treatment integrity (43.8 per cent), and approximately 75 per cent were either low or moderate on this rating (79.5 per cent). Twenty per cent of the studies covered institutionalized juveniles and 50 per cent covered non-juvenile justice interventions. Almost two-thirds of the programmes were less than two years old, which raises questions about the lasting impact of an initially enthusiastic response to a program. Finally, one- quarter of the programs were administered by criminal justice personnel, one-quarter by mental health personnel, and 20 per cent by lay persons [Mair, 1995a: 461–2].

The claims made by those who have carried out meta-analyses have, on the whole, tended to be cautious but many practitioners have seen the results of meta-analysis as the answer to their prayers and have taken them at their face value. There has been an almost evangelical movement amongst many probation officers on behalf of cognitive behavioural approaches (based on the work of Robert Ross: see Ross and Fabiano, 1985; Ross *et al.*, 1988) which meta-analysis is assumed to have endorsed as *the* effective treatment modality. As with such movements, however, other probation officers are vehemently opposed to this approach and it will be interesting to see how this debate is resolved (if it ever is).

The claims made on behalf of meta-analysis go too far. Principles for effective programmes are set out, and these are said to have originated from meta-analysis, but they are not always the same principles even when expounded by the same author; for example Andrews and his colleagues (1990a) set out three principles which should be taken into account, while by 1995 these have been expanded first to four, and then to sixteen (Andrews, 1995). The important point to remember is that meta-analysis cannot demonstrate the truth of such claims, as the primary sources used say very little about such issues as treatment integrity or the use of structured programmes. Meta-analysis may suggest that treatment works in the general sense of having an overall positive effect on recidivism, but it cannot tell us precisely

---

[15] It should be noted that all the meta-analyses cited—with one possible exception—conclude that rehabilitative treatment has a positive impact upon recidivism. The exception is the study by Whitehead and Lab (1989: 291), where the authors claim that 'correctional treatment has little effect on recidivism', but they do not calculate an overall effect size. Losel (1993), however, did calculate an effect size for this meta-analysis and found it to be positive.

what treatment should be used, when, for how long, with which offenders, within which programmes, etc. But if meta-analysis is not the Holy Grail for community penalties it does offer ways forward; as Losel (1995: 103) suggests 'It is more the case that [meta-analyses] form a guide for a new generation of studies on theoretically well founded offender treatment and its evaluation.'

Apart from making better use of reconviction analyses and being cautious about how the 'results' of meta-analysis are utilized, how might the effectiveness issue be developed further in relation to community penalties? One way forward is to use a variety of measures of success; as a community penalty has various objectives, then various measures will be required to assess its level of success or failure (and different measures may be needed for different sentences). Such criteria as reconviction rates, diversion from custody, cost effectiveness, sentencer satisfaction, offender satisfaction, evidence of changed attitudes on the part of offenders might all be considered. So too might such factors as successful completions, and evidence of assistance with the problems/ needs presented by offenders which are likely to be associated with offending. Indeed, it should be emphasized that efforts to expand the criteria used to measure effectiveness have occurred and continue, with differing degrees of interest and success. Diversion from custody was a key measure of effectiveness for community service (McIvor, 1990; Pease *et al.*, 1977) and for probation day centres (Mair, 1988; Vass and Weston, 1990). Cost effectiveness studies are still under-developed, despite the pioneering work of Stephen Shaw (1980), and more recent attention by Martin Knapp and his colleagues (Knapp *et al.*, 1990, 1992; Knapp and Netten, 1997). Sentencer satisfaction with the work of the probation service is now monitored by the Home Office (May, 1995) and individual probation areas are increasingly trying to do this. The views of offenders have been studied (Bailey and Ward, 1992; Ditton and Ford, 1994; Fielding, 1986; Mair and May, 1997) and again, individual probation services are moving along these lines (see Beaumont and Mistry, 1996). Instruments have been designed to measure offenders' change in attitude over the course of a community sentence (*e.g.* the CRIME–PICS scale developed by Frude *et al.*, 1994). Completion rates are complicated by how community penalties are enforced and how breach practice is carried out, and despite the introduction of National Standards there is still widespread variation in enforcement (Ellis *et al.*, 1996; Maguire *et al.*, 1996). And while it is difficult to measure how effectively the problems/needs of offenders are dealt with, recent research on need assessment scales suggests that this could become easier to do in future (Aubrey and Hough, 1997).

Such measures of outcome on their own, however, will not supply easy answers to questions about the effectiveness of community penalties. The measures themselves may have to be prioritized and/or combined to give a composite score. And without studying the context of community penalties, any measures of effectiveness would be interpreted in a vacuum and, as such, not particularly helpful. Process as well as outcome evaluations will be necessary.[16] All of this requires time and money, neither of which is thick on the ground at any time, and especially now when Home Office funding for research is being cut and quick and simple answers are increasingly demanded. Despite the difficulties, some studies have been carried out which approximate to the ideal just outlined (Bottoms *et al.*, 1990, 1993, 1994; McIvor, 1992; Mair *et al.*, 1994; Raynor, 1988) and it is to be hoped that such work will continue (the evaluation by Raynor and his colleagues of the STOP programme in Mid-Glamorgan looks particularly promising: Lucas *et al.*, 1992; Raynor and Vanstone, 1994*a*, 1994*b*).

The confidence that the 'Nothing Works' dragon has finally been slain has engendered considerable optimism amongst those who work in community penalties. But even those who evince most confidence (McGuire and Priestley, 1995; Underdown, 1995) admit that more work is needed. A great deal of research has been carried out into various community penalties in the past few years (*e.g.* on dealing with sex offenders in the community—Barker and Morgan, 1993; Beckett *et al.*, 1994; on probation motor projects—Martin and Webster, 1994; on dealing with drug-misusing offenders—Nee and Sibbitt, 1993; Sibbitt, 1996; on the combination order—Mair *et al.*, 1997; on the work of probation services in developing employment opportunities—Downes, 1993; Roberts *et al.*, 1996), as well as into other aspects of the work of the probation service (e.g. pre-sentence reports—Gelsthorpe *et al.*, 1992; the automatic conditional release scheme—Maguire *et al.*, 1996; enforcement and breach—Ellis *et al.*, 1996; the assessment and allocation process—Burnett 1996), yet a sustained and coherent approach to effectiveness is still lacking. It may be difficult to reach agreement amongst probation staff about what constitutes effectiveness for community penalties, as the work of Humphrey and Pease (1992, 1993) and May (1991) has suggested. And, as has been noted previously, there are many competing definitions of effectiveness. But effectiveness remains the most significant issue facing community penalties, and the need to demonstrate effectiveness is more important than ever.

CONCLUSIONS

The foregoing discussion of community penalties and the probation service suggests a situation which, if not quite a crisis, has the potential to become such in the near future. Community penalties are an easy target for a government which is blatantly utilizing a harsh penal discourse in an effort to win popular support; and given the present state of penal politics (February 1997), it seems unlikely that the pressure on the probation service will be eased signifi-

---

[16] 'A process evaluation will show how an initiative was devised in the first place and the reasons for this; it will show how it was put into practice and whether or not this differed from the blueprint; it will investigate developments over time and attempt to demonstrate why subsequent changes took place.' (Mair *et al.*, 1994: 8).

cantly by any change of government. Thus, budgetary constraints, together with demands to demonstrate effectiveness and accountability and to provide rigorous penalties in the community, are likely to continue. These are issues which the probation service will have to continue to grapple with; indeed, it is a struggle which is, ultimately, unwinnable as government can keep tightening the regulations and changing the rules.

Community penalties themselves seem to exist in a state of some confusion. They have, within thirty years or so, been justified primarily on the grounds of rehabilitation, then as offering diversion from custody, and they are currently expected to provide punishment in the community—although it remains unclear what this means in practice (on the ground, rehabilitation is staging a major comeback). But they are also, as has been shown, slipping down-tariff in terms of the kinds of offenders they are dealing with, and this could have serious consequences in terms of marginalization. In addition, there is some evidence to suggest that the three main community penalties—the probation order, the community service order, and the combination order—may be competing for similar offenders, which raises the question whether these three penalties can be differentiated from each other adequately and, if not, whether all three penalties are necessary.

It seems to me not entirely fanciful to envisage the straight probation order withering away into a backwater used only for minor offences, community service losing any sense of reparation and becoming purely and simply punitive, and the combination order and probation with added requirements becoming exclusively exercises in surveillance and control. If this were to happen, the whole nature of probation work would change, and probation officers would, at best, become case managers—as has happened to a great extent in America. This possibility creeps closer with the changes in training, the potential extension nationally of the curfew order, and the requirement that probation services spend 5 per cent of their revenue expenditure on partnership projects with outside agencies.

Ironically, one bright light on the horizon for community penalties is the continuing rise in the prison population. It seems unlikely that prisons can be built fast enough (or enough holiday camps or prison ships be found) to accommodate offenders if the present rate of custodial sentencing continues. Community penalties may, therefore, revert to their recent task of providing alternatives to custody, which would ensure their survival in terms of the number of offenders dealt with, but would mean yet another change in direction. And for how long would such a change hold, and how would it appeal to probation officers?

Community penalties and the probation service as a whole are drifting directionless. David Garland has recently argued that 'the crime control agencies of the state have begun to represent themselves in ways which suggest a more modest, and more self-contained remit' (Garland, 1996: 459), and this may pose particularly acute problems for the probation service. While there have been many academic efforts at carving out a role for the probation service in the past twenty years, from the Bottoms and McWilliams 'Non-Treatment Paradigm' which was very much a response to the idea that 'Nothing Works' (Bottoms and McWilliams, 1979), to the recent debate in the *Howard Journal* between Mike Nellis, Adrian James, and Jon Spencer (Nellis, 1995*a*, 1995*b*; James, 1995; Spencer, 1995; see also Shaw and Haines, 1989), none have become accepted as dominant. Home Office views of community penalties are characterized by constant shifts which too often seem to be dependent upon political whim. Community penalties and the probation service are too important to be left like this; they badly need an agreed direction for the future and some stability to pursue this. Otherwise, the full potential of community penalties to provide effective sentences will never be achieved.

Selected Further Reading

There is no single text which covers adequately the topic of community penalties and the probation service. Historical accounts of the origins and development of the probation service are generally fairly ancient themselves, though it is worth reading Dorothy Bochel's *Probation and After-Care* (Edinburgh: Scottish Academic Press, 1976) which provides a fairly literal account from the 1887 Probation of First Offenders Act to the 1972 Criminal Justice Act. David Haxby's *Probation: A Changing Service* (London: Constable, 1978) is a useful analysis of developments in probation from the Morison Committee in 1962 up to 1975, as well as an argument for the service to become a 'Community Correctional Service'. There is no critical introduction to what the probation service does: a straightforward, descriptive account is provided by Anthony Osler in his *Introduction to the Probation Service* (Winchester: Waterside Press, 1995). Astonishingly, there is nothing which can be recommended on the probation order, as this sentence remains under-researched. For community service, Gill McIvor's *Sentenced to Serve* (Aldershot: Avebury, 1992) provides an excellent account of the most detailed research carried out into this penalty; more general accounts of community service can be found in Ken Pease's essay 'Community Service Orders' which is to be found in Tonry and Morris' edited volume, *Crime and Justice: An Annual Review of Research Volume 6* (Chicago, Ill.: University of Chicago Press, 1985), and in the collection edited by Dick Whitfield and David Scott, *Paying Back: Twenty Years of Community Service* (Winchester: Waterside Press, 1993). Debates around the issue of effectiveness are covered reasonably thoroughly (though not definitively) in two edited collections: James McGuire's *What Works: Reducing Reoffending* (Chichester: John Wiley, 1995), and George Mair's *Evaluating the Effectiveness of Community Penalties* (Aldershot: Avebury, 1997). Finally, some books which together capture many of the issues facing community penalties in the 1990s and all of which are worth reading: *Probation: Politics, Policy and Practice* (Buckingham: Open University Press, 1991) by Tim May; *Crime, Criminal Justice and the Probation Service* (London: Routledge, 1992) by Robert Harris; *Managing the Probation*

Service: Issues for the 1990s (Harlow: Longman, 1992) edited by Roger Statham and Philip Whitehead; *Effective Probation Practice* (London: Macmillan, 1994) by Peter Raynor, David Smith, and Maurice Vanstone; and *Working with Offenders* (London: Jessica Kingsley, 1996) edited by Gill McIvor.

REFERENCES

ADVISORY COUNCIL ON THE PENAL SYSTEM, (1970), *Non-Custodial and Semi-Custodial Penalties*. London: HMSO.

ANDREWS, D. A. (1995), 'The Psychology of Criminal Conduct and Effective Treatment', in J. McGuire, ed., *What Works: Reducing Reoffending*. Chichester: John Wiley.

—— ZINGER, I., HOGE, R., BONTA, J., and GENDREAU, P. (1990a), 'Does Correctional Treatment Work? A Clinically Relevant and Psychologically Informed Meta-Analysis', *Criminology*, 28: 369–404.

—— —— —— and —— (1990b), 'A Human Science Approach or More Punishment and Pessimism: A Rejoinder to Lab and Whitehead', *Criminology*, 28: 417–29.

AUBREY, R., and HOUGH, M. (1997), *Assessing Offenders' Needs: Assessment Scales for the Probation Service*. Home Office Research Study No. 166. London: Home Office.

AUDIT COMMISSION (1989), *The Probation Service: Promoting Value for Money*. London: HMSO.

BAILEY, R., and WARD, D. (1992), *Probation Supervision: Attitudes to Formalised Helping*. Belfast: Probation Board for Northern Ireland.

BARKER, M., and MORGAN, R. (1993), *Sex Offenders: A Framework for the Evaluation of Community-Based Treatment*. London: Home Office.

BEAUMONT, B., and MISTRY, T. (1996), ' "Doing a Good Job Under Duress" ', *Probation Journal*, 43: 200–4.

BECKETT, R., BEECH, A., FISHER, D., and FORDHAM, A. S. (1994), *Community-Based Treatment for Sex Offenders: An Evaluation of Seven Treatment Programmes*. London: Home Office.

BOCHEL, D. (1976), *Probation and After-Care: Its Development in England and Wales*. Edinburgh: Scottish Academic Press.

BOSWELL, G., DAVIES, M., and WRIGHT, A. (1993), *Contemporary Probation Practice*. Aldershot: Gower.

BOTTOMS, A. E., BENNETT, T., KRARUP, H.,

McWILLIAMS, B., O'MAHONEY, D., and ROSE, G. (1994), *Community Penalties for Young Offenders: Part B—The Individual Outcome Study*. Cambridge: University of Cambridge Institute of Criminology.

—— BROWN, P., McWILLIAMS, B., McWILLIAMS, W., NELLIS, M., in collaboration with PRATT, J. (1990), *Intermediate Treatment and Juvenile Justice*. London: HMSO.

—— HAINES, K., and NELLIS, M. (1993), *Community Penalties for Young Offenders: Part A—The Processual Study*. Cambridge: University of Cambridge Institute of Criminology.

—— and McWILLIAMS, W. (1979), 'A Non-Treatment Paradigm for Probation Practice', *British Journal of Social Work*, 9: 159–202.

—— and —— (1986), 'Social Enquiry Reports Twenty-Five Years after the Streatfeild Report', in P. Bean and D. Whynes, eds., *Barbara Wootton: Social Science and Public Policy—Essays in her Honour*. London: Tavistock.

—— and PRESTON, R. H., eds. (1980), *The Coming Penal Crisis: A Criminological and Theological Exploration*. Edinburgh: Scottish Academic Press.

BRODY, S. (1976), *The Effectiveness of Sentencing: A Review of the Literature*, Home Office Research Study No. 35. London: HMSO.

BUREAU OF JUSTICE STATISTICS (1996a), *Prison and Jail Inmates, 1995*. Washington, DC: US Department of Justice.

—— (1996b), *Correctional Populations in the United States, 1994*. Washington, DC: US Department of Justice.

BURNETT, R. (1996), *Fitting Supervision to Offenders: Assessment and Allocation Decisions in the Probation Service*, Home Office Research Study No. 153. London: Home Office.

COHEN, S. (1985), *Visions of Social Control: Crime, Punishment and Classification*. Cambridge: Polity Press.

COHEN, S. and SCULL, A., eds. (1983), *Social Control and the State: Historical and Comparative Essays*. Oxford: Martin Robertson.

COLEMAN, C., and MOYNIHAN, J. (1996), *Understanding Crime Data: Haunted by the Dark Figure*. Buckingham: Open University Press.

COPAS, J. (1995), *Some Comments on Meta-Analysis*. Department of Statistics, University of Warwick.

DEWS, V., and WATTS, J. (1994), *Review of Probation Officer Recruitment and Training*. London: Home Office.

DITTON, J., and FORD, R. (1994), *The Reality of Probation: A Formal Ethnography of Process and Practice*. Aldershot: Avebury.

DOOB, A. N., and BRODEUR, J.-P. (1989), 'Rehabilitating the Debate on Rehabilitation', *Canadian Journal of Criminology*, 31: 179–92.

DOWNES, D. (1993), *Employment Opportunities for Offenders*. London: Home Office.

ELLIS, T., HEDDERMAN, C., and MORTIMER, E. (1996), *Enforcing Community Sentences*, Home Office Research Study No. 158. London: Home Office.

FIELD, S., and HOUGH, M. (1993), *Cash-Limiting the Probation Service: A Case Study in Resource Allocation*, Research and Planning Unit Paper 77. London: Home Office.

FIELDING, N. (1986), *Probation Practice: Client Support under Social Control*. Aldershot: Gower.

FLETCHER, A. E. (1983), *Organisational Diversity in Community Service*. Manchester: Department of Social Administration, University of Manchester.

FOLKARD, M. S., SMITH, D. E., and SMITH, D. D. (1976), *IMPACT: Volume 2 The Results of the Experiment*, Home Office Research Study No. 36. London: HMSO.

FRUDE, N., HONESS, T., and MAGUIRE, M. (1994), *CRIME-PICS II*. Cardiff: Michael & Associates.

GARLAND, D. (1985), *Punishment and Welfare: A History of Penal Strategies*. Aldershot: Gower.

—— (1996), 'The Limits of the Sovereign State: Strategies of Crime Control in Contemporary Society', *British Journal of Criminology*, 36: 445–71.

GARRETT, C. (1985), 'Effects of Residential Treatment on Adjudicated Delinquents', *Journal of Research in Crime and Delinquency*, 22: 287–308.

GELSTHORPE, L. R., RAYNOR, P., and TISI, A. (1992), *Quality Assurance in Pre-Sentence Reports*. Report to the Home Office

Research and Planning Unit. Cambridge: University of Cambridge Institute of Criminology.

GENDREAU, P. (1989), 'Programs that do not Work: A Brief Comment on Brodeur and Doob', *Canadian Journal of Criminology*, 31: 193–5.

—— and ROSS, R. R. (1979), 'Effectiveness of Correctional Treatment: Bibliotherapy for Cynics', *Crime and Delinquency*, 25: 463–89.

GLASS, G. (1976), 'Primary, Secondary and Meta-Analysis of Research', *Educational Researcher*, 5: 3–8.

—— McGAW, B., and SMITH, M. L. (1981), *Meta-Analysis in Social Research*. Newbury Park, Cal.: Sage.

GOTTSCHALK, R., DAVIDSON, W., GENSHEIMER, L., and MAYER, J. (1987), 'Community-Based Interventions', in H. Quay, ed., *Handbook of Juvenile Delinquency*, New York: Wiley.

HARRIS, R. (1994), 'Continuity and Change: Probation and Politics in Contemporary Britain', *International Journal of Offender Therapy and Comparative Criminology*, 38: 33–45.

HAXBY, D. (1978), *Probation: A Changing Service*. London: Constable.

HINE, J. (1995), 'Community Sentences and the Work of the Probation Service', in M. Walker, ed., *Interpreting Crime Statistics*. Oxford: Clarendon Press.

HOME OFFICE (annual), *Criminal Statistics England and Wales*. London: HMSO.

—— (annual), *Probation Statistics England and Wales*. London: Home Office.

—— (1962), *Report of the Departmental Committee on the Probation Service*, Cmnd. 1650. London: HMSO.

—— (1983), *Statistical Bulletin 18/83—Reconvictions of Those given Community Service Orders*. London: Home Office.

—— (1984), *Probation Service in England and Wales: Statement of National Objectives and Priorities*. London: Home Office.

—— (1986), *Statistical Bulletin 34/86—Reconvictions of Those given Probation Orders*. London: Home Office.

—— (1988a), *Punishment, Custody and the Community*, Cm 424. London: HMSO.

—— (1988b), *Tackling Offending: An Action Plan*. London: Home Office.

—— (1990a), *Supervision and Punishment in the Community*, Cm 966. London: HMSO.

—— (1990b), *Crime, Justice and Protecting the Public*, Cm 965. London: HMSO.

—— (1990c), *Partnership in Dealing with Offenders in the Community: A Discussion Paper*. London: Home Office.

—— (1991*a*), *Organising Supervision and Punishment in the Community: A Decision Document*. London: Home Office.

—— (1991*b*), *Partnership in Dealing with Offenders in the Community: A Decision Document*. London: Home Office.

—— (1992), *National Standards for the Supervision of Offenders in the Community*. London: Home Office.

—— (1993), *Statistical Bulletin 18/93—Reconvictions of those given Probation and Community Service Orders in 1987*. London: Home Office.

—— (1995*a*), *Strengthening Punishment in the Community: a Consultation Document*, Cm 2780. London: HMSO.

—— (1995*b*), *National Standards for the Supervision of Offenders in the Community*. London: Home Office.

—— (1995*c*), *Digest 3: Information on the Criminal Justice System in England and Wales*. London: Home Office.

—— (1996*a*), *The Probation Service: Three Year Plan for the Probation Service 1996–1999*. London: Home Office.

—— (1996*b*), *Protecting the Public*. Cm 3190. London: HMSO.

HUMPHREY, C. (1991), 'Calling on the Experts: The Financial Management Initiative (FMI), Private Sector Management Consultants and the Probation Service', *Howard Journal*, 30: 1–18.

—— and PEASE, K. (1992), 'Effectiveness Measurement in the Probation Service: A View from the Troops', *Howard Journal*, 31: 31–52.

—— —— and CARTER, P. (1993), *Changing Notions of Accountability in the Probation Service*. London: Institute of Chartered Accountants.

IGNATIEFF, M. (1978), *A Just Measure of Pain: The Penitentiary in the Industrial Revolution 1750–1850*. London: Macmillan.

JAMES, A. (1995), 'Probation Values for the 1990s—and Beyond?', *Howard Journal*, 34: 326–43.

JARVIS, F. V. (1972), *Advise, Assist and Befriend: A History of the Probation and After-Care Service*. London: National Association of Probation Officers.

KNAPP, M., and NETTEN, A. (1997), 'The Cost Effectiveness of Community Penalties: Principles, Tools and Examples', in G. Mair, ed., *Evaluating the Effectiveness of Community Penalties*. Aldershot: Avebury.

—— ROBERTSON, E., and MCIVOR, G. (1992), 'The Comparative Costs of Community Service and Custody in Scotland', *Howard Journal*, 31: 8–30.

—— THOMAS, N., and HINE, J. (1990), *The Economics of Community Service Orders: A Study of Costs in Five English Areas*. Personal Social Services Research Unit, University of Kent at Canterbury.

LAB, S. P., and WHITEHEAD, J. T. (1990), 'From "Nothing Works" to "The Appropriate Works": The Latest Stop on the Search for the Secular Grail', *Criminology*, 28: 405–16.

LIPSEY, M. (1992), 'Juvenile Delinquency Treatment: A Meta-Analytic Inquiry into the Variability of Effects', in T. D. Cook *et al.*, eds., *Meta-Analysis for Explanation: A Casebook*. New York: Russell Sage Foundation.

LIPTON, D., MARTINSON, R., and WILKS, J. (1975), *Effectiveness of Correctional Treatment: A Survey of Treatment Evaluation Studies*. Springfield, Mass.: Praeger.

LLOYD, C. (1986), *Response to SNOP*. Cambridge: Institute of Criminology.

—— (1990), 'National Standards for Community Service: The First Two Years of Operation', *Home Office Research Bulletin*, 31: 16–21.

—— (1992), *Bail Information Schemes: Practice and Effect*, Research and Planning Unit Paper 69. London: Home Office.

—— MAIR, G., and HOUGH, M. (1994), *Explaining Reconviction Rates: A Critical Analysis*, Home Office Research Study No. 136. London: HMSO.

LOSEL, F. (1993), 'The Effectiveness of Treatment in Institutional and Community Settings', *Criminal Behaviour and Mental Health*, 3: 416–37.

—— (1995), 'The Efficacy of Correctional Treatment: A Review and Synthesis of Meta-Evaluations', in J. McGuire, ed., *What Works: Reducing Reoffending*. Chichester: John Wiley.

LUCAS, J., RAYNOR, P., and VANSTONE, M. (1992), *Straight Thinking on Probation One Year On*. Bridgend: Mid-Glamorgan Probation Service.

MCGUIRE, J., ed. (1995), *What Works: Reducing Reoffending*. Chichester: John Wiley.

—— and PRIESTLEY, P. (1995), 'Reviewing "What Works": Past, Present and Future', in J. McGuire, ed. *What Works: Reducing Reoffending*. Chichester: John Wiley.

MCIVOR, G. (1990), 'Community Service and Custody in Scotland', *Howard Journal*, 29: 101–13.

—— (1992), *Sentenced to Serve: The Operation and Impact of Community Service by Offenders*. Aldershot: Avebury.

McLaughlin, E., and Muncie, J. (1994) 'Managing the Criminal Justice System', in J. Clarke, A. Cochrane, and E. McLaughlin, eds., *Managing Social Policy*. London: Sage.

McMahon, M. (1990), '"Net-Widening": Vagaries in the Use of a Concept', *British Journal of Criminology*, 30: 121–49.

McWilliams, B. (1980), *Community Service Orders: Discretion and the Prosecution of Breach Proceedings*. Manchester: Department of Social Administration, University of Manchester.

McWilliams, W. (1983), 'The Mission to the English Police Courts 1876–1936', *Howard Journal*, 22: 129–47.

—— (1985), 'The Mission Transformed: Professionalisation of Probation between the Wars', *Howard Journal*, 24: 257–74.

—— (1986), 'The English Probation System and the Diagnostic Ideal', *Howard Journal*, 25: 241–60.

—— (1987), 'Probation, Pragmatism and Policy', *Howard Journal*, 26: 97–121.

Maguire, M., Perroud, B., and Raynor, P. (1996), *Automatic Conditional Release: The First Two Years*, Home Office Research Study No. 156. London: Home Office.

Mair, G. (1985), 'Working Together? The "System" in Action', in D. Moxon, ed., *Managing Criminal Justice*. London: HMSO.

—— (1988), *Probation Day Centres*, Home Office Research Study No. 100. London: HMSO.

—— (1991), *Part Time Punishment? The Origins and Development of Senior Attendance Centres*. London: HMSO.

—— (1995a), 'Evaluating the Impact of Community Penalties', *University of Chicago Law School Roundtable*, 2: 455–74.

—— (1995b), 'Specialist Activities in Probation: "Confusion Worse Confounded"?', in L. Noaks, M. Levi, and M. Maguire, eds., *Contemporary Issues in Criminology*. Cardiff: University of Wales Press.

—— (1996), 'Developments in Probation in England and Wales 1984–1993', in G. McIvor, ed., *Working With Offenders*. London: Jessica Kingsley.

—— Crisp, D., Sibbitt, R., and Harris, J. (1997), *The Combination Order*. Unpublished report to the Home Office.

—— Lloyd, C., Nee, C., and Sibbitt, R. (1994), *Intensive Probation in England and Wales: An Evaluation*, Home Office Research Study No. 133. London: HMSO.

—— and May, C. (1995), *Practitioners' Views of the Criminal Justice Act: A Survey of Criminal Justice Agencies*, Research and Planning Unit Paper 91. London: Home Office.

—— and May, C. (1997), *Offenders on Probation*, Home Office Research Study No. 167. London: Home Office.

—— and Mortimer, E. (1996), *Curfew Orders with Electronic Monitoring*, Home Office Research Study No. 163. London: Home Office.

—— and Nee, C. (1992), 'Day Centre Reconviction Rates', *British Journal of Criminology*, 32: 329–39.

Maltz, M. (1984), *Recidivism*. London: Academic Press.

Martin, J. P., and Webster, D. (1994), *Probation Motor Projects in England and Wales*. London: Home Office.

Martinson, R. (1974), 'What Works? Questions and Answers about Prison Reform', *Public Interest*, 35: 22–54.

Martinson, R. (1979), 'New Findings, New Views: A Note of Caution Regarding Sentencing Reform', *Hofstra Law Review*, 7: 243–58.

May, C. (1995), *Measuring the Satisfaction of Courts with the Probation Service*, Home Office Research Study No. 144. London: Home Office.

May, T. (1991), *Probation: Politics, Policy and Practice*. Buckingham: Open University Press.

Nee, C., and Sibbitt, R. (1993), *The Probation Response to Drug Misuse*, Research and Planning Unit Paper 78. London: Home Office.

Nellis, M. (1995a), 'Probation Values for the 1990s', *Howard Journal*, 34: 19–44.

—— (1995b), 'The "Third Way" for Probation: A Reply to Spencer and James', *Howard Journal*, 34: 350–3.

Palmer, T. (1978), *Correctional Intervention and Research: Current Issues and Future Prospects*. Lexington, Mass.: D. C. Heath and Co.

—— (1992), *The Re-Emergence of Correctional Intervention*. Newbury Park, Cal.: Sage.

—— (1994), *A Profile of Correctional Effectiveness and New Directions for Research*. Albany, NY: State University of New York Press.

Pease, K. (1978a), 'Community Service and the Tariff', *Criminal Law Review*: 269–75.

—— (1978b), 'Community Service and the Tariff: A Reply', *Criminal Law Review*: 546–9.

—— (1981), *Community Service Orders: A First Decade of Promise*. London: Howard League.

—— (1983), 'Penal Innovations', in J. Lishman, ed., *Social Work with Adult Offenders*. Aberdeen: University of Aberdeen Press.

—— (1985), 'Community Service Orders', in M. Tonry and N. Morris, eds., *Crime and Justice: An Annual Review of Research Volume 6*. Chicago, Ill.: University of Chicago Press.

—— BILLINGHAM, S., and EARNSHAW, I. (1977), *Community Service Assessed in 1976*, Home Office Research Study No. 39. London: HMSO.

—— DURKIN, P., EARNSHAW, I., PAYNE, D., and THORPE, J. (1975), *Community Service Orders*, Home Office Research Study No. 29. London: HMSO.

—— and MCWILLIAMS, W. (1980), 'The Future of Community Service', in K. Pease and W. McWilliams, eds., *Community Service by Order*. Edinburgh: Scottish Academic Press.

PHILLPOTTS, G. J. O., and LANCUCKI, L. B. (1979), *Previous Convictions, Sentence and Reconviction*, Home Office Research Study No. 53. London: HMSO.

PLATT, A. M. (1969), *The Child Savers: The Invention of Delinquency*. London: University of Chicago Press.

POINTING, J., ed. (1986), *Alternatives to Custody*. Oxford: Basil Blackwell.

RAYNOR, P. (1988), *Probation as an Alternative to Custody*. Aldershot: Avebury.

—— and VANSTONE, M. (1994*a*), *Straight Thinking on Probation: Third Interim Evaluation Report: Reconvictions Within 12 Months*. Bridgend: Mid-Glamorgan Probation Service.

—— and —— (1994*b*), 'Probation Practice, Effectiveness and the Non-Treatment Paradigm', *British Journal of Social Work*, 24: 387–404.

RADZINOWICZ, L., and HOOD, R. (1986), *A History of English Criminal Law and its Administration from 1750: Volume 5—The Emergence of Penal Policy*. London: Stevens and Sons.

READ, G. (1980), 'Area Differences in Community Service Operation', in K. Pease and W. McWilliams, eds., *Community Service by Order*. Edinburgh: Scottish Academic Press.

ROBERTS, C. (1989), *Young Offender Project: First Evaluation Report*. Worcester: Hereford and Worcester Probation Service.

—— (1990), 'Nothing Works Re-Assessed: The Effectiveness of Forms of Probation Supervision on Subsequent Criminal Careers', paper presented to the ACOP Finance and Resources Group. Blackpool.

ROBERTS, J. (1996), 'Roles and Identity', paper presented at the Probation Studies Unit Colloquium 'The Probation Service—

Responding to Change'. University of Oxford, 16–17 December.

ROBERTS, K., BARTON, A., BUCHANAN, J., and GOLDSON, B. (1997), *Evaluation of a Home Office Initiative to Help Offenders into Employment*. London: Home Office.

ROSENTHAL, R. (1991), *Meta-Analytic Procedures for Social Research*. Newbury Park, Cal.: Sage.

ROSS, R. R., and FABIANO, E. A. (1985), *Time to Think: A Cognitive Model of Delinquency Prevention and Offender Rehabilitation*. Johnson City, Tenn.: Institute of Social Sciences and Arts.

—— —— and EWLES, C. D. (1988), 'Reasoning and Rehabilitation', *International Journal of Offender Therapy and Comparative Criminology*, 32: 29–35.

ROTHMAN, D. J. (1980), *Conscience and Convenience: The Asylum and its Alternatives in Progressive America*. Boston, Mass.: Little, Brown and Co.

SHAW, R., and HAINES, K., eds. (1989), *The Criminal Justice System: A Central Role for the Probation Service*. Cambridge: University of Cambridge Institute of Criminology.

SIBBITT, R. (1996), *The ILPS Methadone Prescribing Project*, Home Office Research Study No. 148. London: Home Office.

SMITH, D., SHEPPARD, B., MAIR, G., and WILLIAMS, K. (1984), *Reducing the Prison Population*, Research and Planning Unit Paper 23. London: Home Office.

SPENCER, J. (1995), 'A Response to Mike Nellis: Probation Values for the 1990s', *Howard Journal*, 34: 344–9.

STANLEY, S., and BAGINSKY, M. (1984), *Alternatives to Prison: An Examination of Non-Custodial Sentencing of Offenders*. London: Peter Owen.

STATHAM, R., and WHITEHEAD, P., eds. (1992), *Managing the Probation Service: Issues for the 1990s*. Harlow: Longman.

SHAW, S. (1980), *Paying the Penalty: An Analysis of the Cost of Penal Sanctions*. London: NACRO.

THOMAS, N., HINE, J., and NUGENT, M. (1990), *Study of Community Service Orders: Summary Report*. Birmingham: Department of Social Policy and Social Work, University of Birmingham.

THORNTON, D. M. (1987), 'Treatment Effects on Recidivism', in B. J. McGurk, D. M. Thornton, and M. Williams, eds., *Applying Psychology to Imprisonment: Theory and Practice*. London: HMSO.

TREWARTHA, R. (1978), 'Community Service and the Tariff: A Further Comment', *Criminal Law Review*, September: 544–6.

UNDERDOWN, A. (1995), *Effectiveness of Community Supervision: Performance and Potential*. Manchester: Greater Manchester Probation Service.

VASS, A. A. (1984), *Sentenced to Labour: Close Encounters with a Prison Substitute*. St Ives: Venus Academica.

—— (1986), 'Community Service: Areas of Concern and Suggestions for Change', *Howard Journal*, 25: 100–11.

—— (1990), *Alternatives to Prison: Punishment, Custody and the Community*. London: Sage.

—— and WESTON, A. (1990), 'Probation Day Centres as an Alternative to Custody: A "Trojan Horse" Examined', *British Journal of Criminology*, 29: 255–72.

WHITEHEAD, J. T., and LAB, S. P. (1989), 'A Meta-Analysis of Juvenile Correctional Treatment', *Journal of Research in Crime and Delinquency*, 26: 276–95.

WHITFIELD, D., and SCOTT, D., eds. (1993), *Paying Back: Twenty Years of Community Service*. Winchester: Waterside Press.

WILLIS, A. (1978), 'Community Service and the Tariff: A Critical Comment', *Criminal Law Review*: 540–4.

WOLF, F. M. (1986), *Meta-Analysis: Quantitative Methods for Research Synthesis*. Newbury Park, Cal.: Sage.

WOOTTON, B. (1978), *Crime and Penal Policy: Reflections on Fifty Years Experience*. London: Allen and Unwin.

YOUNG, P. (1976), 'A Sociological Analysis of the Early History of Probation', *British Journal of Law and Society*, 3: 44–58.

YOUNG, W. (1979), *Community Service Orders*.

Index

Aberystwyth Crime Survey 584
abortion 109
absolute discharge 1120–1
abuse *see* child abuse; sexual abuse
abuse of power 1080
  arrest powers 1059–60
  review mechanisms:
    complaints and discipline procedure
    1081–2; prosecution/litigation 1082;
    unlawfully obtained evidence, exclusion
    of 1080–1
  stop-and-search powers, 1059
acid house sub-culture 625, 929–30
Acker, J. 542
acquittal rates, ethnic minorities and 744–5,
  751
Action for Smoking and Health 927
active citizenship 129, 598
actual guilt:
  legal guilt, and 1052
Adler, F. 178, 766, 784, 984
administrative criminology 49, 493–4
adolescence 625, 651
  discovery of 614–17
advice *see* legal advice
Advisory Council on Drug Dependence 940
Advisory Council on the Penal System
  (ACPS) 114, 115, 128, 1105, 1209
Advisory Council on the Treatment of
  Offenders (ACTO) 114
affectively spontaneous crimes 324
Afro-American males 551–2
Afro-Caribbeans:
  crime, involvement in 710–11
    imprisonment rates 725–8; juvenile crime
    631
  cultural resistance 622, 623
  education 709
  fear of crime 590
  police, relations with 710–11
  proportion of British population 707
  racial discrimination:
    personal experiences of 708–9
  victimization 635
    rates of 712, 714; risk of 582, 584, 713
  see also ethnic minorities
age:
  community service 1212
  crime and 626–7
    desistance from offending 373–4; onset
    of offending 371–3; peak age of

offending 398, 627, 638; prevalence at
  different ages 367–9
criminal responsibility, of 640
drug use and 633, 933–4
probation orders, offenders sentenced to
  1208–9
risk of violence and 857
Ahrendt, D. 846
Ahrenfeldt, R. 808
Aitken, Jonathan 112
Alcohol Concern 948
alcohol use 926, 927; *see also* drugs
  crime, relationship to 948–50
Alderson, John 1022, 1034
Alexander, Jeffrey 412–13, 417
alienism 27
Alkali Inspectorate 1103
Allan, E. A. 271–2
Allen, H. 778
Allen, Jessica 193, 205, 206
Allen, R. 637, 644
Althusser, L. 418
Alton, David 648
American capitalism 823
American dream, 275 806
Amin, Ash 286
Amir, M. 146, 541, 579, 867
Anderton, James 1022
Andrews, D. A. 1222
anomie theory 254, 258, 482–3, 484–5, 561,
  619, 620, 903, 906
  contradictions of social order and 236–8
  social disorganization and 238–40
anti-discrimination legislation:
  models of justice 706
  racial discrimination 708
anti-social behaviour 361–2, 399, 482
  continuity in 378
  definitions and measurement 366–7
anti-social personality 364
  continuity in 378–9
anti-social syndrome 363–4
anti-social tendency 363–4
  variations in 396
appeals:
  conviction, against 1083–4
  sentence, against 1110
approved schools 639, 640
Aquinas, St Thomas 17
architectural design, crime prevention through
  972–4

area offence rate 314
area victimization rate 314
Aries, Philippe 614–15
Arkwright, Richard 1141
Arlacchi, P. 830
armed robbery 817, 821
arrest 1054
  breach of the peace, for 1059–60
  detention without charge 1060–1
  due process protections 1052, 1060
  no further action (NFA) 1069–70
  police decision-making 1058–9
    bias, patterns of 1056–7; discretion 1055,
    1058, 1059
  powers of police, absence of controls on
    1059–60
  rates:
    ethnic groups 737–9, 750; females 764–5
Ashton, M. 941
Ashworth, A. 607, 1053, 1061, 1067, 1184
Asians:
  South Asians, risk of victimization 582
  see also ethnic minories
assaults, 155; *see also* sexual violence; violent
  crime
Association for the Scientific Treatment of
  Criminals 39
Association of British Insurers 154
Association of Chief Police Officers (ACPO)
  115, 1018
Associations for the Prosecution of Felons 74
attacks on a public servant 155
attendance centre orders 1125, 1198, 1200,
  1214–15
Aubert, V. 895, 917
Audit Commission 650–1
Austin, R. L. 766
Australia:
  sentencing reforms 1129
  transportation to 78, 79–80
authoritarian populism 463
autocrime 136, 152, 154, 169
  joy-riding 180, 646
Avio, Kenneth 292

Back to Basics campaign 111–12
bail:
  bargaining over 1076
  court bail 1076–7
  information schemes 1077
  police bail 1075–6
Bailey, V. 114
Baker, John 35
Baker, Kenneth 95
Baldwin, J. 333, 1078–9
Ball, J. C. 370
Banco Ambrosiano 289
Bank of Credit and Commerce International,
  289, 299
Bank of England 289

Bannister, J. 973
Banton, Michael 1001
Barings Bank 289
Barlinnie Prison Special Unit 1176 n.
Barnett, A. 370, 373, 374, 376
Barnett, R. E. 603
Barr, R. 977, 978
Barron, J. M. 978
battered woman syndrome 680, 685
Bauman, Z. 417, 418, 419, 429, 820, 832
BBC 198, 200
Bean, P. 939, 946
Beattie, John 59
Beccaria, C. 15, 16, 24, 25, 26, 28, 78, 482
Beck, U. 250, 426
Becker, Gary 292
Becker, H. 211, 234, 256, 308 n., 454, 455,
  483, 775, 882
behavioural science 561–2
Beirne, P. 26, 763
Bell, D. 254, 823, 825
Bell, Mary 547–8
Beneke, T. 544
Benjamin, J. 548, 549
Benn, Tony 91, 108
Bennett, T. 146, 180, 817, 986
Benson, George 47
Bentham, J. 15, 16, 24, 25, 28, 249, 458,
  1097–8
Benyon, J. 622
Bergalli, R. 467
Berkowitz, L. 382
Bernard, T. 870
Bernstein, J. M. 506
Berridge, V. 939
Bertrand, M. A. 774, 790
Best, J. 256
Best, Keith 288
Beveridge, William Henry 48
bias:
  gender bias 779, 780 *see also* sex discrimi-
    nation
  policing and 1056–8, 1072
  racial bias 749–53 *see also* racial discrimi-
    nation
Biggs, Ronald 121
Bill of Rights 95
biology:
  crime and 31, 489
  violence and 861–3
Birmingham School 809, 810
Birmingham Six 125, 1027, 1052, 1082,
  1083
Bittner, E. 1007
Black, D. 999
black liberation movement 551
Black Mafia 825
black people:
  acquittal rates 744–5
  Britain, in 707

crime and 283, 284–5, 476, 478, 703
  explaining black offending 754–5;
    juvenile crime 622, 631–2
  drug trade and 290–1
  imprisonment rates 725–9
  masculinity, concepts of in youth crime
    549–52
  remand in custody 743–4
  sentencing 745–9
  victimization, rates of 712–17
  youth culture 811–12
  see also Afro-Caribbeans; ethnic minorities
Black Power 551
Blair, Tony 100, 104, 106
Blake, George 121
Blau, J. 865
Block, A. 826, 827
Block, C. B. 978
Block, R. L. 978
Blom-Cooper, L. 127, 128, 746
Blomberg, T. G. 467
Bluglass, R. 687
Blumstein, A. 366, 369, 371, 375, 377, 476
Boesky, Ivan 288, 299
Bonger, W. 16, 44, 273–4, 275, 289, 787
Bordua, D. 805
Boritch, H. 767
born criminal 31
borstals 81, 639, 640
Bottomley, A. K. 145, 156
Bottomley, Virginia 189
Bottoms, A. E. 112, 122, 247, 248, 333, 343,
    349, 464, 624, 693, 965, 980, 1099,
    1126, 1148, 1152, 1216, 1226
Bourdieu, P. 411, 417, 419–21, 422, 423–4
Bourgois, P. 550, 820
Bow Street Police 67
Bow Street Runners 66
Bowden, P. 687
Bowlby, John 617
Bowling, B. 175, 627–8, 718
Box, S. 242, 268 n., 457, 542, 905, 919, 1081
Brain Committee 927, 928, 939
Braithwaite, J. 176, 861, 875, 902, 906, 915,
    917, 919, 1100, 1101, 1102
Brake, M. 621
Brantingham, Paul and Patricia 312–13, 324,
    328
Brantingham, P.J. 965
Braverman, Harry 279
breach of the peace, power to arrest for
    1059–60
Brennan, P. 862
Brenner, Harvey 269–70
Bretton Woods Agreement 286
Bridgeman, C. 974
Bridges, L. 1061–2
Bridgewater Four 1052
Bright, Graham 625
Britain, drug-related violence in 291–2

British Crime Surveys 136, 147, 162–1, 169,
    171, 182, 200, 580, 581, 583
  impact of victimization 590
  young victims 635
British Criminology Conference 2
British general elections, law and order
    policies in *see* law and order
British Journal of Criminology 1, 2, 45
British Journal of Delinquency 1, 45
British Journal of Medical Psychology 38
British Psychological Society 47
British Society of Criminology 2, 46
British Transport Police 149
Brittan, Leon 120, 642, 1154–5
Brixton riots (1981) 121, 127, 202, 710–11,
    1010
broadcasting:
  crime fiction 205–6, 207–8
  crime news 198, 200, 202; *see also* media
    representations of crime
  TV violence 189
Broadwater Farm riots (1985) 105, 121
Broca, Paul 30
Brody, S. 1098, 1200, 1216, 1218
broken homes 388–9
Bronfenbrenner, U. 337
Broome Committee 941
Brown, C. 706
Brown, D. 1061, 1064
Brown, I. 748
Brown, J. 864
Browning, F. 823
Brownmiller, S. 541, 545, 861
Brownsword, R. 693, 1099
Brummagen Boys 64
Buckley, Alistair 975
Bulger, James 100, 112, 121, 139, 194, 212,
    547, 647–9, 847
Burgess, E. 308, 1004
Burgess, R. 862
burglary 152–3, 154, 817
  trends in 637–8
Burney, E. 671, 673
Burrows, J. 173, 970
Bursik, R. J. 310, 331, 338–40, 342, 344 n.
Burt, Cyril 43–4, 616
Bush, George (US President) 288
Bush, T. 769
business crime *see* white-collar crime
business cycle
  crime rate and 266–72
Butler, David 89
Butler, Lord 1
Butler, R. A. 48, 88 n., 123
Butler Report 661, 678
Butskellism 88–9, 617

Cain, M. 521–2, 523 n., 790, 1021
Calavita, K. 913, 918
California, drug trade in 290–1

Cambridge Institute of Criminology 1, 46, 47, 48, 49
Cambridge Study in Delinquent Development 363, 364, 367, 368, 369, 371, 372, 373, 374, 376, 377, 378, 379, 380, 950
Cambridge University 40
  Department of Criminal Science 45
Cameron, D. 544
Camorra 898, 910
Camp Hill prison 81
Campaign for Nuclear Disarmament 107
Campbell, A. 865
Campbell, B. 305, 550, 866
Campbell, D. 812
Capaldi, D. M. 380
capital statutes 77, 79
capitalism:
  crime and 60, 269, 285–6
    white-collar crime 905–6
  High Modernity 285
Capone, Al 275, 825
Caputi, J. 544
Cardiff Three case 1062
Carey, K. 772
Carlen, P. 243, 252, 298 n., 464, 525–7, 779, 782–3, 788, 1156
Carlisle Committee 1155
Carnarvon, Lord 80
Carpenter, Edward 272
Carpenter, Mary 803
Carr-Hill, R. 270 n.
Carr-Saunders, A. 42
Carson, W. G. 893, 911, 914
Carter, R. L. 326, 984
Casey, J. 945
Cashmore, E. 811
Cassels, Sir John 1034
causes of crime 561
  anomie theory 485
  distancing from crime 479–80
  left realism 487–489
  unemployment 488–9
  white-collar crime 895, 901–11
cautioning 1071–2, 1086, 1126
Cayman Islands 289
CCTV (closed circuit television) 971, 979
censure *see* social censure
Central Criminal Court 75
Central Drugs and Illegal Immigration Unit 941
Central Drugs Intelligence Unit 941
Centre for Contemporary Cultural Studies (Birmingham University) 809, 810
Certified Normal Accommodation 123
Chadwick, Edwin 69
Chambliss, W. 475, 826–7
Chan, J. 1058
Chandler, Raymond 204
Chapman, J. 787–8
Chappell, D. 817

charges 1072–3
  case construction 1073
  pre-charge procedures, formalization of 1060, 1067
Chatterton, N. 1073
Chernobyl 893
Chesney-Lind, M. 519, 773
Chibnall, S. 222
Chicago House music 625
Chicago School 246–7, 258, 307, 308, 311, 330–1, 338, 342, 348, 441, 453–4, 619
  New Chicagoans 338–42, 349
Chicago studies 179
child abuse 769, 778, 847
  intergenerational aspect 872
  sexual abuse 139, 388, 778
    impact on victims 591; media reporting of 202; violent behaviour caused by 864
childhood 614–15, 651
  anti-social behaviour 361–2
  transition to adulthood 651; *see also* adolescence
children:
  killing by 547–8
  killing of 684
  see also parents
Children and Young Persons Act (1969) 640, 641
Christchurch (New Zealand) Child Development Study 388
Christie, Agatha 204, 205
Christie, Nils 475
chronic offenders 374–6, 398
Church of England Temperance Society 1198, 1199
Churchill, Winston 71, 1162
Cicourel, A. 144, 454
CID 1019
cinema, crime films and 205, 206–7
civil disobedience 107–8
Clark, Scott 292
Clarke, Kenneth 118, 646, 647, 1030, 1034, 1095
Clarke, M. 894, 899, 907, 912, 913, 917
Clarke, Ron 147, 244, 245, 293, 968
Clarke, R. V. 294, 320, 394, 395, 965, 966, 967
class *see* criminal class; social class; underclass
classical school of criminology 15, 16, 24, 997
Clay, John 267
Clay Cross affair 91
Clemmer, D. 1177 n., 1180
Clinard, M. 898, 904–5
Clinton, Bill (US President) 106
closed circuit television (CCTV) 971
  emphasis on 979
Cloward, R. A. 237, 276–8, 395, 483, 619–20, 806, 807
Clydebank occupation 108

co-offending 381–2, 398
Code for Crown Prosecutors 637, 674,
    1104
cohabitation 623
Cohen, Albert 237, 258, 386, 390, 395, 483,
    549, 619, 805–6, 921
  subcultural theory 561
Cohen, C. 467
Cohen, J. 369
Cohen, L. E. 321, 328, 394, 965
Cohen, P. 258, 279–80, 621, 809, 811
Cohen, Stan 140, 211, 234, 240, 249, 260, 453,
    460, 462–3, 464, 550, 620, 808, 845,
    1004, 1071, 1126–7
cohort studies 137 n., 138
Coleman, A. 248–9, 973
Coleman, C. A. 145
Coleman, J. W. 900, 902
Collier, Michael 288
Collins, J. 874, 949
Collison, Mike 550
Colombia 291, 866
Colquhoun, P. 25, 28, 189, 997
combination orders 1124, 1203, 1213–14
  purpose, 1217–18
Commercial Victimization Survey 182
Commission for Racial Equality 592, 740
Committee of Inquiry into Complaints about
    Ashworth Hospital 116
community care 671
community change, crime and 344–9
community corrections 460–1
community crime career 344
community crime prevention 129, 980–7
community homes 640
community penalties *see* community sentences
community prisons 1166
community sentences 1123–5, 1126, 1195,
    1196–7, 1203; *see also* probation
      orders; probation service
  alternatives to custody 1225
  attendance centre orders 1214–15
  combination orders 1213–14
  community service orders 1209–12
  curfew orders 1214–16
  effectiveness 1216–24
    meta-analysis 1221–3; reconviction rates
      1218–21
  justification 1225
  probation orders 1204–9
  research 1224
community service 1123, 1124, 1209–12
  age factors 1212
  gender factors 1212
  purpose 1217
  statistics 1211
  summary offences 1211
comparative criminal justice 559–73
  approaches to 561–5
    behavioural science 561–2; interpretivist

561, 562–3; legal comparativist 561,
    563–4
  Italy, prosecution discretion in 565–71
comparative criminology 559–60
comparativist approach 561, 563–4
compensation 603–4, 1100, 1101, 1102
  access to 605
  costs 296
  Criminal Injuries Compensation Scheme
    603–5
  offender, payable by 605–6
compensation orders 605–6, 1123
complaints system 1081–2
  prisoner complaints 1172–3
computerized mapping 306
conditional discharges 1121
conditional release 1117
confessions 1063
  coercion 1064
  false 1064–5
  guilty pleas and 1078
  informal 1064
  police tactics and 1063
confidence tricksters 817–18
conflict sub-culture 276
Connell, Bob 548
Connell, P. 526
Connell, R. W. 536, 537, 539, 542, 545
consequences of offending 397
Conservative Party 598, 649
  Back to Basics campaign 111–12
  law and order policies 108, 111, 129–30, 642
    ideologies 99–102; post-war manifestos
      89–99, 642
  Police Federation and 1017
  Protecting the Public (White Paper, 1996)
    1137
constabulary independence 1024, 1032
Contagious Diseases Acts 63
contracted-out prisons 1173–4
control of crime:
  criminology and 452–3
  see also social control
control theory 240–3
  white-collar crime 903
  women, application to 788–9
convictions:
  appeals against 1083
  see also wrongful convictions
Cook, D. 915
Cook, Philip J. 294
cop culture *see* police culture
Cope, R. 666
Corbett, C. 594, 596, 1081
Cornish, D. B. 293, 294, 394, 395, 965, 967
corporal punishment, abolition of 81
corporate crime 139, 178
corporate deviance 196
corporate fraud 181
Cosa Nostra 827

cost–benefit analysis 293–296
costs of crime 292–7
  United Kingdom 296
  United States 296
Council of Europe:
  Committee for the Prevention of Torture
    1168
  Convention on State Compensation 599
county police 69, 71
court bail 1076–7
Court of Appeal 1083
  appeals against sentences 1110
  sentencing, guideline judgments and
    1114–15
court procedure, vulnerable witnesses and 600
Court Users' Charter 598
Coward, Ros 550
Coyle, A. 1177 n.
CPS *see* Crown Prosecution Service
CPTED (Crime Prevention Through
    Environmental Design) 972–4
Crawford, William 79
Cressey, D. 782, 819, 827–8, 1178
Cretney, A. 1074, 1086
crime 141
  attitudes to 490–1; *see also* fear of crime
  being tough on 491–2
  business cycle and 266–72
  causes of *see* causes of crime
  costs of 292–7
  definitions 561, 562
  extent of 58–61; *see also* crime statistics
    new knowledge 135–42
  fear of *see* fear of crime
  financial *see* financial offences
  free market society and 297–300
  inequality and 272–92
  late modernity and 349–54
  left realism 485–6
    impact of crime and 490–1
  media images *see* media representations of
    crime
  organized *see* organized crime
  political economy of *see* political economy
    of crime
  professional *see* professional crime
  social class and 176–7, 178
  social context of 486
  spatial dimension 487
  temporal aspect 486–7
  theories of 211–13; *see also* sociological
    theories of crime
  traditional representations of 21–3
  types of 152–5
  unemployment and 266–72
Crime, Justice and Protecting the Public
    (White Paper, 1990) 1213
Crime Concern 129
crime control mechanisms
  historical development 57–83

  see also police; prosecution; punishment
crime control systems 1051, 1052–3, 1054,
    1072, 1079, 1084, 1085
crime deflection 978
crime displacement 977–9
  classification 977–8
crime fiction 31, 194, 224
  content of 203–4
  pattern of 204–9
    cinema 205, 206–7; radio 205–6;
      television 206, 207–8
  police and criminal justice system
    portrayal of 209
crime level 141
crime narratives 194
crime news 196–9; *see also* media representa-
    tions of crime
  broadcast news 198, 200, 202
  cultural conflict and 222–4
  pattern of 199–203
  political ideology of the press 220–2
  structural determinants of news-making
    221–2
  violent crime, reporting of 199–200
crime patterns, 136; *see also* crime statistics;
    crime surveys
  opportunity theory 320–3
  routine activities theory 320–3
crime prevention 294, 652, 963–95
  architectural and environmental design
    147–8, 972–4
  closed circuit television (CCTV) 971
  community crime prevention 980–7
  expenditure 979–80
    under-provision 984
  fear of crime and 588
  focused prevention: hot spots 974–5; repeat
    victimization 974–6
  futures in 987
  insurance 984–5
  motive 983–4
  new thinking 147–8
  political will 983
  practice 979–80
  pressure to prevent crime 985
  primary prevention 147, 965, 968–74
    crime displacement, claims of 976, 977–9;
      critiques of 976, 980–1; moves away
      from 982; post-1976 successes 970–1;
      prospects for 983–7; research 147,
      969–74; risk analyses 971–2; techniques
      of 968–9
  removal of opportunities 969
  Safer Cities programme 982
  secondary prevention 965
  situational 147
  structural approach 963–4
  target-hardening 148, 968, 970, 986
  tertiary prevention 965
  theories 965–6

lifestyle theory 966–7; problem-oriented policing 968; rational choice theory 967; routine activity theory 966
Crime Prevention Centre 979
crime risks 490
　media over-emphasis on 199
crime statistics 135–6, 144–5
　changed picture 135–9, 181
　fundamental problems 141–2
　geographical distribution 155–7
　New Criminology 143–8
　offender population 172–9
　official picture 148–61
　prison population 174
　sources 139
　studies other than surveys 179–81
　total volume of crime 149–52
　trends 157–61
　types of crime 152–5
　validity of 315
　violent crime 854–6
crime surveys 161–72, 586
　cross-national 580
　fear of crime 586–8
　international surveys 162
　local surveys 169–72, 583–6
　methodological problems 582
　national 580–1
　national surveys 162–9
　rural 584
crime trends 157–61; *see also* crime surveys
crime waves 140
Crimewatch 194
criminal anthropology 30, 31, 34, 36
criminal behaviour:
　criminal career approach, *see* criminal careers
　economic explanations 787
　media and 211–17
　see also anti-social behaviour
Criminal Behaviour and Mental Health 687
criminal biology 31
criminal careers 487
　age and crime 367–9
　anti-social syndrome 363–4
　approach 364–6
　broken homes and family conflict 388–9
　chronic offenders 374–6, 398
　co-offending and motives 381–2
　continuity 377–80
　convicted parents 389–90
　definition 361
　desistance from offending 373–4
　development of offending 367–82
　explanation of 395–8
　duration 376–7
　family size and 391
　future research 399
　human development and 361–401
　　definitions and measurement 366–7

impulsivity 384–5
individual offending frequency 369–71
influences on 382–4
intelligence level 385–7
onset 371–3
risk factors 362, 382–4
school factors 392–3
situational factors 394–5
socio-economic deprivation 390
specialization and escalation 380
supervision, discipline and child abuse 387–8
Criminal Cases Review Authority 1083
criminal class 34, 62–3, 80
criminal collaboration 801–2; *see also* organized crime; professional crime; youth gangs; youth sub-culture
Criminal Injuries Compensation Scheme (CICS) 603–4
　access to 605
　criticisms of 604–5
　exclusion from 605
　minimum award 604
　police, role of 605
　tariff scheme 604
　victim recourse to 605
criminal justice:
　adversarial principle 1051, 1053
　bail *see* bail
　comparative research 559–73; *see also* comparative criminal justice
　complaints and discipline procedure 1081–2, 1085
　crime-control systems 1051, 1052–3, 1079, 1084, 1085
　decision-making criteria, ethnic minorities and 706–7
　due process systems 1051–2, 1084 *see also* due process
　ethnic minorities and 705–7; *see also* ethnic minorities; racial bias 749–53
　exclusionary processes 1053, 1058–60, 1068
　human rights approach 1053, 1067
　inclusionary approach 1053–4
　justice and fairness 1053
　models of 1051–4
　'new left pessimists' 1067, 1084, 1086
　police custody 1060–8; *see also* police custody
　police decision-making 1054–60
　　bias, patterns of 1056–8, 1072; discretion 1054–6; stop-search and arrest 1058–60; working rules 1057–8, 1084
　pre-charge procedures, formalization of 1060, 1067
　pre-trial processes 1075–80
　probation *see* probation orders; probation service
　proof, search for 1051, 1052
　prosecution *see* prosecution

criminal justice (*cont.*):
  reparative justice 603–7
  research 1085–6
  reviewing injustice 1080–4; *see also*
    reviewing mechanisms
  'sea change theorists' 1067
  sentencing *see* sentencing
  shifting conceptions of 602–7
  silence, right to 1065–7
  social integration approach 1053
  studies in 438
    criminal law's contribution to 445–8;
      criminology and criminal law and
      438–9
  truth, search for 1051, 1052, 1053
  victims:
    rights of 1053
    role of 597–602
Criminal Justice Consultative Council (CJCC)
  123
criminal law 438, 440–3, 561
  criminology and criminal justice and 438–9
    contribution to study of 445–8
  study of 443–4
Criminal Law Commissioners 79
criminal negligence 593
criminal psychology 31
criminal responsibility, age of 640
criminal science, emergence of 30–44
criminal sociology 31
Criminal Statistics 135, 136, 148, 149 n., 150,
  152, 155
criminal sub-cultures 276, 310 n.
criminal subgroup 62
criminal type 30, 41
criminality 32, 41–2
criminalization 448–9
criminals *see* criminal careers; criminal class;
  criminality; offenders
criminology 12, 259–60, 438
  comparative 559–60
  control of crime and 452–3
  criminal law and criminal justice studies:
    contribution to 443–4; relationship
    between 438–9
  development in Britain 34–44
  discipline of 45–50, 410–15, 437
  environmental *see* environmental criminol-
    ogy
  establishment criminology 493–494
    critique of 479–80
  feminism and *see* feminist criminology
  functionalist 253–5
  hallmarks of, in 1990s 528–9
  historical development in Britain *see*
    historical development of criminology
  intellectual inheritance of 514–16
  left realism *see* left realism
  modern discipline 18–21
  New Criminology 143–8, 515

  policing, study of 997–9
  positivist tradition 30–34, 143–4
  sociological theories *see* sociological
    theories of crime
  studies in:
    criminal law's contribution to 445–8;
      funding for research 46; growth of 1–3
  theories:
    media and 211–17
  university departments 45, 47, 50
  victim's perspective 145–7
Crisp, D. 1074
critical criminology 787
Croft, John 45
Cromwell, P. F. 322, 323
Crown Court 1104–5
  appeals against sentences 1110
  combination orders 1213
  ethnic minorities tried in 742–5
  expenditure on 296
  probation orders 1207
Crown Prosecution Service 637, 1052,
  1073–5, 1103
  bail, opposition to 1076, 1077
  expenditure on 296
  Statement on the Treatment of Victims and
    Witnesses 598
Cubbon, Sir Brian 117
Cultural Indicators project 190
cultural practices 562–3
curfew orders 1124–5, 1198, 1203, 1214–16
  electronic monitoring 1215
Currie, E. 288, 298, 465, 474, 475, 476, 980–1
Curtis, L. 865
custodial sentencing 1111–20; *see also*
  imprisonment; sentencing
custody *see* police custody; prisons; remand in
  custody
custody officers 1060, 1061
Customs and Excise 149, 1069, 1103

Dagge, Henry 26
Daily Express 197, 200, 646
Daily Mail 200, 646, 648, 846
Daily Mirror 197
Daily News 197
Daily Star 646
Daily Telegraph 197, 200, 648
Daly, K. 519, 526, 528–9, 773, 777, 779, 788
Daly, M. 863
dangerous places 305
Daniel, S. 810
Daniel, W. W. 708
Danziger, Kurt 18
Darby Sabini gang 64
Dartmoor Prison 81
date-rape 546, 867
Davis, G. 1074, 1086
Davis, K. 253, 254
Davis, M. 239, 290, 291, 299, 349 n., 428

Dawes, Mannaseh 26
day centres 1207, 1223
de Beauvoir, Simone 513
de Benedetti, Carlo 891
death penalty, abolition of 76, 77
decarceration 460–4
decision-making:
  ethnic minorities, decision to prosecute 739–42, 750
    reviewing criteria 753–4
  police 1054–60
Decker, S. 323, 326, 817
defence lawyers:
  failure to attend interrogations 1062, 1078
  failure to insist on due process 1079
  guilty plea rates and 1078–9
  level of service 1062, 1078
defence plea in mitigation 1109
defensible space 248–9, 312, 973
Defoe, Daniel 22
deindustrialization 280–8
deinstitutionalization 460–1, 462–3
delinquency 310, 363, 549, 614, 618, 807
  anti-social tendency 363–4
  community corrections 460–1
  delinquent residence 308–10, 311
  impulsivity 384–5
  political economy and 276–8
  risk factors 383
  spatial distribution 619
  study of 143 n.
  The Young Delinquent (1925) 43–4
  theories of 616–17
    sociological theories 241, 247
    sub-cultural theory 561
  youth and deviance, images and theories of 614–25
  youth sub-culture 619–20
Dell, S. 674
Denning, Lord 98, 1024
Department of Social Security 149, 1069
Depression 619
deprivation 487–8
Derrida, J. 523
Desborough, Lord 72
desert theory 1096–7, 1102
  proportionality 1097
desistance from offending 373–4, 397–8
detention *see* police custody; imprisonment; prisons
detention centres 82, 639, 640
deterrence theories 1097–8, 1101
development of offending 367–82
  explanation of 395–8
  individual offending frequency 369–71
  prevalence at different ages 367–9
deviancy 144, 483
  amplification 140
  sociology of deviance 453–40, 566

youth and deviance, images and theories of 614–25
deviant news 194–6
deviant sub-cultures 619
Devlin, Lord 664–5
Dexter, Colin 205
Dickens, Charles 272, 306, 1142
Digest of Information on the Criminal Justice System 148 n.
Dilulio, J. 1177 n.
diminished responsibility 547, 665, 685–6
discharges 1120–1
discipline 457–8, 464, 466
discretion:
  comparative research 565–6
  decision-making 568
    Italy 566–8
  police 1054–6 *see also* police discretion
  prosecution:
    mandatory prosecution rule in Italy 565–71
  sentencing 1106–8
discretionary release 1117
discrimination *see* racial discrimination; sex discrimination
Disney World 250
disorder 345–6
  consequences of 346
dissociation 807–8
distancing from crime 479–80
Ditchfield, J. 1181–2
Ditton, J. 181, 929
diversionary deviance 196
Divisional Court 1110
divorce rate 623
Dixon, D. 1058, 1067
Dixon of Dock Green (TV serial) 125
Dobash, R. D. and R. E. 180, 768, 786, 852
Dodd, D. 580, 590, 846
doli incapax 645
domestic violence 140, 155, 446, 582, 585, 768–9, 777–8, 849, 851, 852, 873, 1086
  dealing with 875
    treatment for violence against women 876
  distribution of offences 319
  explanations for violence 862
  police attitudes to 1012–13, 1058
  victim support 596
  women's refuges 596, 597
Dominick, J. 192
Donkin, Sir Horatio Bryan 36–7, 39, 42
D'Orban, P. 949
Douglas, J. W. B. 390
Douglas, Mary 254, 425–6
Dowds, E. A. 156, 315
Dowds, L. 846
Downes, D. 234, 238, 564–5, 620, 807
Downes, D. and Morgan, R. 1095
Drabble, L. 746
Draper, P. 862

Drapkin, Israel 16–17
drugs:
  acid house parties 625
  classification of illegal drugs 925
  control of 935–50
    British system 937–41; criminal justice
      941–4; Drug Action Teams 941; Drug
      Dependency Units 939–40; drugs
      strategies 940–1; enforcement statistics
      942; futures 952; historical aspects
      935–7; intelligence gathering 951; law
      enforcement 941–4, 951; opiate use
      935–6; sentencing 951; war against
      drugs 476–7, 940, 951
  crime, relationship with 944–50
    alcohol 948–50; criminal involvement
      leading to drug use 945; drug markets
      946; drug use causing crime 945–6;
      gender factors 945; international drug
      trade 290–2; treatment and rehabilita-
      tion, impact of 946–8
  detection 942
  legal drugs 926–7
  legalization 476
  trade in 820–1, 829, 832; female involve-
    ment 821; opium trade 935–936;
    trafficking 946; youth gangs and 814
  treatment of drug users 946–9
    harm minimization 948
  trends 950–2
    enforcement 951; policy and practice
      951; theory 950–1
  use 621, 624–5, 925–59
    1950s 927; 1960s 928; 1970s–1980s 928–30;
      1990s 930–1; age and 633, 933–4;
      alcohol 926; class and 932; crime and
      945–6; decriminalization of cannabis use
      952; ecstasy 625; ethnicity and 932–3;
      explanations of violence and 873–4;
      gender and 932; heroin habit 632–4;
      post-war trends, review of 926–35;
      sexuality and 934; social deprivation and
      934–5; social divisions and 931–4;
      tobacco 927; young people 632–4
  violence and 873–4
due process 1051–3, 1054, 1084
  access to legal advice 1061
  cautioning 1071–2
  defence failure to insist on 1079
  detention without charge 1060, 1061
  non-adherence to 1058; police interrogation
    1063, 1065
  policing goals and 1055
  pre-charge procedures 1060
  reality of policing and 1058
  reasonable suspicion, requirement of 1052
  self-incrimination, caution against 1052
Duff, P. 1075
Dunblane school massacre (1996) 112, 122,
  846, 847

Dunedin Study 389
Dunlap, E. 820
Durkheim, Émile 44, 254, 274, 414, 456, 482,
  894
  anomie theory 236–7, 238
Dworkin, R. 693

early release 1117
East, W. Norwood 39, 40, 42, 43
Eastman, N. 678, 679, 682
Eaton, M. 779
ecological facts 348
ecological fallacy 316
ecology of crime *see* environmental crimino-
  logy
Economic and Social Research Council
  (ESRC) 2
  Crime and Social Order initiative 3
  Violence programme 3
economic cycle, crime rate and 266–72
economic deviance 195–6
economic distress 267
economics *see* political economy of crime
ecstasy 625
Edmund-Davies Committee of Inquiry (1978)
  93
education:
  school factors in offending 392–3
  system 811
Edwards, G. 939
Edwards, Susan 786
Ehrlich, Isaac 292, 294
Einstadter, W. J. 816
Eisner, M. 272
Ekblom, P. 967, 972
Eldridge, W. 945
electronic monitoring 1124–5, 1215
Elliot, K. 1175, 1181
Elliott, D. S. 369
Ellis, Havelock 34, 42
Elmhorn, K. 175
Elster, J. 423
Encyclopaedia Britannica 34
Engels, Friedrich 306
enterprise culture 820–1
environmental criminology 305–59
  community change and crime 344–9
  future research agenda 349
  history of 307–14
  late modernity 349–54
  location of offences 316–30
  location of offender residence 330–2
  methodological issues 314–16
    area-based data 314–15, 316; ecological
      fallacy 316; official crime statistics,
      validity of 315
  new Chicagoans 338–42
  offence locations and offender locations,
    bringing together of 342–4
  offenders' use of space 323–6

environmental design:
  crime prevention through 972–4
  street lighting 974
equal treatment:
  ethnic minorities and 705–6
  see also inequality; racial discrimination; sex
    discrimination
Ericson, R. 195–6, 222
Erikson, K. 144, 254, 483
Eron, L. 379–80, 871
escalation 380
Escobar, Pablo 866
establishment criminology:
  critique of 479–80
  left realism and 492–4
ethics, professional criminal 818–19
ethnic minorities 703–59; *see also* Afro-
    Caribbeans; Asians; black people
  age structure 707–9
  bias against 749–53; *see also* racial
    discrimination
  Britain, in, 707–11
  crime, involvement in 710–11
    juvenile crime 631–2
  domestic violence 585
  drug use and 932–3
  education 709
  equality of treatment:
    criminal jusice system 705–6
  prison population 476, 1156–7
  process of development:
    differences between groups 709–10
  racial discrimination 710, 711
    anti-discrimination legislation 706, 708;
      personal experiences of 708–9; police
      discretion 1012
  racial harassment 588
    effect on mobility 590
  risk of victimization 582, 584
  suspects and offenders, as 720–49
    acquittals 744–5; arrest rates 737–9, 750;
      bias 749–53; courts 742–9; decision to
      prosecute 739–42, 750; explaining
      black offending 754–5; imprisonment
      rates 725–9, 749; police behaviour
      736–7; police stops 731–7; pre-
      sentencing processes 742–5; prison
      population 721–9; remand in custody
      743–4; reviewing decision-making
      criteria 753–4; self-reported offending
      729–30; sentencing 745–9; victims'
      reports 730–1
  victims of crime, as 711–20
    intra-racial crime 714–15; police,
      satisfaction with 717–18; racial
      harassment 718–20; racially-motivated
      crime 718–20; rates of victimization
      712–17; risk of victimization 582, 584,
      713, 749
ethnographic studies 179

Euro-Pop 625
Eurodollars 287
European Convention of Human Rights 1053
Evans, R. 1063, 1071
evidence:
  unlawfully obtained evidence, exclusion of
    1080–1
Exchange Rate Mechanism 111
exclusionary processes 1053, 1058–10, 1068,
    1086
existential feminism 513
extent of crime 58–61
  fundamental problems 141–2
  see also crime statistics
Eyer, J. 270

Fagan, I. 873, 874
Fagan, J. 821
Faithful, Lady 113, 119
Faller, L. 23
false confessions 1064–5
family conflict 388–9; *see also* domestic
    violence
Family Group Conferences 1100
family patterns, changes in 623
family size, criminal careers and 391
Farnworth, M. 780
Farrell, G. 974, 975
Farrington, D. 156, 173, 175, 315, 369, 372,
    383, 395, 636, 637–8, 644, 729, 779,
    802, 862, 872, 1107
fascism 548
Fattah, E. A. 579
Faulkner, D. 117, 1053
Faust, F. L. 965
FBI, 207
fear of crime 199, 490, 491, 586–8, 845 n.,
    846–7
  causal factors 588
  crime prevention efforts and 588
  lifestyles and mobility, effect on 589–90
  media and 217–19
  Neighbourhood Watch schemes and 589
  quality of life and 589
  risk and 587–8
  urban phenomenon 588
  women 588, 590
Feder, S. 827
Feeley, M. 430, 767
Feest, Johannes 565–6
Felson, M. 245, 321, 321 n., 328, 394, 965,
    966
Felson, R. 852, 866
females *see* women
feminism 766, 865
  criminology and 511–33; *see also* feminist
    criminology
  assessments of interconnections 516–25
  existential 513
  liberal 512

feminism (*cont.*):
  Marxist 512
  postmodern 513–14
  psychoanalytical 513
  socialist 512–13
feminist criminology 260, 511–33, 773–4
  critical reflections on 525–7
  feminist critique of criminology 516–25
  hallmarks of 527–8
  impact of, 775
  intellectual inheritance of criminology
    514–16
  pioneering 774–5
  types of feminism 512–13
feminist deconstructionism 523
feminist empiricism 523
feminist standpointism 523
Fennell, P. 672, 674, 678
Fennelly, Lawrence 976
Ferguson, Adam 265
Ferguson, T. 1071
Fergusson, D. M. 388
Ferrell, J. 255
Ferrero, W. 763, 777
Ferrers, Lord 65
Ferri, E. 15, 31, 34, 44, 272–3
Field, Frank 283
Field, S. 272, 984
Fielding, Henry 25, 66
Fielding, Sir John 66
Financial Action Task Force 289
Financial Management Initiative 1148
financial market, crimes in 288–90
financial offences 299; *see also* white-collar
    crime
  insider trading 288
  insurance fraud 289
  international financial market crimes
    288–90
  money laundering 288–9
fines 1121–3, 1197, 1203
Finestone, H. 310
Finland, sentencing reforms 1129
firearms offences 155
FitzGerald, M. 722
Fleming, Ian 205
Fletcher, Joseph 25
flogging 80
Floud report 1099
football hooliganism 619, 621
Forsyth, Frederick 205
Foster, J. 335
Foucault, M. 17, 33, 249, 429, 452, 453,
    456–8, 459–60, 461–2, 464, 466, 499,
    506, 516, 523, 540, 547, 1141, 1142
Fox, Sir Lionel 47
Frankfurt School 845
fraud 65, 153–4, 299, 832
  insider trading 288
  insurance fraud 289

money laundering 288–9
  prosecutions for 297
  victims of 593
Frazer, E. 544
Frechette, M. 372, 381
free market policies, crime and 284, 287–8,
    294, 297–300
French Revolution 59
French School 31
Freud, S. 536, 537, 545
Frosh, S. 544
Frude, N. 871
Fry, Elizabeth 1142
Fry, Margery 47
functionalist criminology 253–5

Gaitskell, Hugh 88 n.
Gall, F. J. 26
Gambetta, D. 843, 898
gangs *see* youth gangs
gangsters 823–4
Garber, J. 621
Gardiner, Gerald 109
Garland, D. 31, 33, 35, 42, 428, 438, 458,
    465, 506, 507, 515, 1100, 1198, 1225
Garofalo, Raffaele 15, 31, 967
garotting 80
Gartner, R. 861
Gatrell, V. 59, 848
gay men, drug use and 934
gay militancy 109
Geis, G. 894
Gelles, R. 851
Gelsthorpe, L. 519–20, 521, 643, 774, 779, 787
gender:
  community service 1212
  crime and 761–797
    feminist approaches to criminology
      773–5; gender ratios and gender
      questions 773; male crime *see* male
      crime; masculinity; prehistory of
      762–764; women, men and crime
      764–7; women and crime 775–8,
      784–90; *see also* women
  domestic secrets 768–7
  drug use and 932
  juvenile offending 628–9
  meaning of gender 761
  offenders 177–8
  policing and 1012–13
  probation orders, offenders sentenced to
    1208
  women and justice 778
    chivalry 778–9; concepts 783–4; double
      deviance 779–80; gender bias 779, 780;
      imprisonment 780–3; women's prisons
      781–2
  women and policing 769–72
  women and sentencing 772–3
gender gap 785

Genders, E. 691
General Strike (1926) 92 n., 107
generation gap 617
genetics, violence and 862
Geneva Congress of Criminal Anthropology 34
Genn, H. 172, 580, 590, 718, 846
genocide 844–5
Geographical Information Systems 306 n.
geography of crime *see* environmental criminology
Gerassi, J. 823
Gerbner, George 217, 218, 219
German School 31
ghetto populations 282, 283, 352
Gibbens, T. 808, 877–8
Gibbs, J. T. 552
Giddens, Anthony 285, 295, 321, 326, 330, 343, 349, 416, 418, 419, 422–3, 426, 429, 431, 480, 524, 542
Gill, O. 808
Gilligan, Carol 786
Gilroy, P. 710
Gingrich, Newt 477
girl culture 621
Gladio 566–7
Gladstone Committee report 37, 38, 81, 123
globalization 652
    organized crime 829, 830
    'place', problem of 426–8
Glover, E. 39, 45, 46
Glyde, John 25, 60
Godard, Lord 1169
Goffman, E. 455, 817–18, 1177
Goldstein, A. 564, 568
Goldstein, Herman 965, 968
Goodman, Paul 549
Gordon Riots (1780) 66, 68
Goring, Dr Charles 41–3
Gostin, L. 663
Gottfredson, M. 241, 343, 372, 395, 561, 626
Goulburn, Henry 68
Gould, S. J. 30
governmental project 13, 515
Graber, D. 197
Graddy, E. 371
Graef, Roger 126, 194, 212, 1013
Graham, J. G. 175, 627–8
Grant, Bernie 105
Grasmick, H. 338–40, 342, 344 n.
Gray, J. 735, 1056
Greater London Council 1029
Greece:
    rape, definition of 562
Green, G. S. 894, 899, 912–13
Greenberg, D. 295, 460, 461
Greenham Common women 771, 787
Greenwood, V. 785
Gregory, J. 1085
Grendon Underwood Prison 40, 691, 1176 n.

Gresswell, D. 864
Grey, Sir George 69
Griffin, S. 545
Griffith, D. W. 193
Griffith, Peter 96
Griffiths, Major Arthur 34
Groce, Mrs 105
Grosvenor Square demonstration (1968) 107
Grounds, A. 678
Group 4 Security 1163
group fights 382
Groves, Byron 340–1
Grubin, D. H. 682
Grunhut, Max 1, 45, 114
Grygier, Tadeuz 45
Guardian 112, 197, 200, 648
Gudjonsson, G. 1064
Guerry, A. M. 26, 266–7, 305–6
Guildford Four 125, 1052, 1083
guilt:
    evidence of, securing 1063
    legal guilt and actual guilt 1052
guilty pleas 1077–80, 1116
    confessions and 1078
    free will 1083
    plea bargaining 1078
    sentence discounts 1078, 1079
    wrongful convictions 1079
Gunn, J. 671, 675, 691
Gurr, T. 848

Haapanen, R. A. 369
Habermas, J. 506
Hacking, Ian 18
Hagan, J. 243, 352, 767, 789
Hagedorn, J. 808, 814
Hakim, S. 977
Hale, C. 268 n., 457
Halford, Alison 1013
Hall, G Stanley 616
Hall, R. 171, 585, 845
Hall, S. 140, 167, 211, 220, 254, 258, 286, 463
Haller, M. 824, 825 n.
Hamilton, Thomas 122
Hammersley, R. 945
Hammett, Dashiel 204
Hamparian, D. M. 372
handguns, ban on 846
Hanmer, J. 171, 585
Hansen, D. J. 388
Harding, Sandra 522
Harris, F. 197
Hart, H. L. A. 1100
Hart, M. 672
Hattersley, Roy 95
Hauber, A. R. 972
Hawkins, J. D. 383
Hawkins, K. 914–15
Health and Safety Executive 1103
Health and Safety Inspectorate 1069

health and safety regulations, breaches of 842
Hebdige, D. 622, 810
hedonism 819–20
Heidensohn, F. 243, 517, 518, 526, 1012, 1013
Henry, B. 387
Herbert, David 329–30, 334–5
heroin use 632–3
Herrnstein, R. 386, 395, 862
Hess, H. 830
high-crime areas 453–4
Hill, K. Q. 326
Hill, Matthew Davenport 1198
Hindelang, M. 177 n., 628, 965
Hindley, Myra 1154
Hirschi, T. 240, 241, 242, 343, 372, 395, 561,
    626, 788
historic discrimination 283
historical development of criminology 11–21
    British criminology 34–44
    classical school 15–16
    criminological discipline, establishment of
        45–50
    criminology-through-the-ages 16–17
    governmental project 12, 515
    labelling theory 144
    Lombrosian project 12–13, 30–34, 515
    misleading categories 15–16
    modern criminology 11–12, 18–21
    New Criminology 143–8
    new thinking about crime prevention 147–8
    object of inquiry 16–18
    positivist school 15, 16, 30–4
    science of the criminal, emergence of 30–4
    scientific analysis of crime in 18th and early
        19th centuries 23–9
    textbook histories 13–15, 16
    traditional representations of crime 21–3
    victims, growth in attention to 145–7
history of crime and crime control 57–86
    extent of crime 58–61
    offender 61–5
    police 65–73
    prosecution and the courts 74–6
    punishment 76–82
    shifts and contexts 82–3
HIV/AIDS 948, 951
HMCIP 1172, 1173
Hobbs, D. 830
Hobbs, R. 180
Hodgson Committee 940
Hoggart, R. 806
Hoggett, B. 666, 675, 684
Hollin, C. 864, 949
Hollis, M. 415–16, 424
Holloway Prison 782, 1155, 1166
Holmes, R. 860
Holmes, S. 860
Holzman, H. R. 820
Home Office:
    C3 section 1083

Crime Prevention Unit 147
    Research and Statistics Directorate 148
    Research Unit 46, 49, 50, 147
    Young Offender Psychology Unit 642
Home Office Statistical Bulletin 148 n.
homicide 155; *see also* murder; violent crime
    children 684
    comparative data 854–5
    dealing with 878–80
    diminished responsibility, defence of 685–6
    explanations for violence 863, 864, 866
    incapacitating killers, effect of 879
    motivation 864
    provocation 844
    reoffending 878–9
    risk of 849–50, 851
        gender factors 851; social class and 856
homosexuality:
    decriminalization 109
    drug use and gay men 934
    gay militancy 109
Hood, R. 175, 743, 744, 745, 746, 747, 748,
    1107, 1131
Hood-Williams, J. 769
Hope, T. 335, 972, 975, 980, 984, 986
Horne, C. J. 971
Horney, J. 367, 369
Horowitz, R. 815
hot spots 319, 974–975
hotting 95
Hough, M. 944, 948, 951
housing market 313–14, 331–2, 333–4
Howard, John 15, 16, 24, 25, 78, 1141,
    1142
Howard, Michael, 101, 106, 111, 118, 649,
    971, 1030, 1095–6, 1119, 1137, 1140,
    1145, 1154, 1196, 1203
Howard Association 113
Howard Journal 1, 2, 38, 39
Howard League 2, 47, 113, 114, 115
Howe, A. 458, 464
Hoyle, C. 1057, 1058, 1086
Hsu, Kenneth 1082
Hubert, W. H. de B. 40
Hudson, Annie 521
Hudson, B. 458, 1100
Huesmann, L. R. 379–80
Huessman, L. 871
Hullin, R. 748
human development:
    criminal careers and 361–401; *see also*
        criminal careers
    conceptual and methodological issues
        363–367; criminal career approach
        364–6, 398; definitions and measure-
        ment 366–7
    development of offending 367–82
human ecology 308
humane containment 1146
Hume, David 265

Hurd, Douglas 114, 119, 1095, 1163
Hutton, Will 481

Ianni, F. A. J. 825
ideological deviance 196
Ignatieff, Michael 1198
illegal drugs *see* drugs
illegitimate births 282, 283
IMPACT (Intensive Matched Probation and After-Care Treatment) 1201
impact of crime:
  left realism 490–1
  secondary victims 593
  victims, on 590–3
  victims' needs and 594–5
imprisonment 460, 462; *see also* prisoners; prisons
  aggravation and mitigation 1115–16
  conditional release 1117
  current concerns 1137–93
  discretionary release 1117
  early release 1117
  ethnicity and 1156–7
  executive release 1117–18, 1153
  government policy 1186
  guideline judgments 1114–15
  historical use 1142–4
  mandatory sentences 1118–19, 1154
  pains of 1177, 1178
  proportionality 1114–15
  'public protection' exception 1116
  purposes of:
    debate on 1140; legal purposes 1144–5; treatment and training *v.* humane containment 1146–8; Woolf Inquiry 1149–51
  rates of:
    ethnic minorities 725–9, 749, 750; rise in use 475, 477
  review of policy and practice 1119–20
  statutory restrictions 1112–14
  'tariff' 1114, 1154, 1184
    evolution of 1111–12
  time spent in custody 1139
  'two offence rule' 1113
  unemployment and 267–9
  women 780–3
  young people 638, 639
impulsivity 384–5
incapacitative sentencing 1099, 1101
incitement to racial hatred 445
indecent exposure 842
The Independent 200
Independent Radio News 198
indictable-only offences 1104
indirect discrimination 706
indirect victims 593
individual-level violence, explanations of 871–3
individual offending frequency 369–71

industrial conflict 102–4
  Winter of Discontent (1978–9) 92, 98, 103
industrial schools 639
inequality:
  crime and 272–292, 296–7
  family structures 623
infanticide 684, 685
injustice, mechanisms for the review of 1080–4
Inland Revenue 149, 1069, 1103
inner cities, crime in 476–7
innocence, presumption of 1084
Inquest 113
insanity, 27; *see also* mentally disordered offenders; mentally ill
insider trading 288, 898, 917
Institute for the Scientific Treatment of Delinquency (ISTD) 39–40, 43, 45–6, 47, 49
Institute for the Study and Treatment of Delinquency 2, 137 n.
Institute for the Study of Drug Dependence 926
institutionalization 1180
instrumental violence 842–3
insurance fraud 289
intellectual inheritance of criminology 514–16
intelligence level and crime 385–7, 397
Intensive Matched Probation and After-Care Treatment (IMPACT) 1201
inter-familial crime 181
interest groups 112–21
intermediate treatment (IT) 644
international drug trade 290–2
international financial market crimes (1980s and 1990s) 288–90
interpretative approach 561, 562–3
interrogation by police *see* police interrogation
intra-racial crime 714–15
Ireland:
  Irish Constabulary 68
  Peace Preservation Force 67–8
Irish nationalists 81
Irish Republican Army (IRA) 98
Irving, B. 1063
Irwin, J. 782, 819, 1178, 1181
Islington Crime Surveys 170, 171, 584, 587–8, 589, 590
Islington Mentally Disordered Offenders Project 671
ISTD *see* Institute for the Scientific Treatment of Delinquency
Italy:
  criminal justice system:
    delays 567; discretionary decision-making 566–8; mandatory prosecution rule 565–71; police discretion 567, 568; post-sentence flexibility 567
  Tangentopoli anti-corruption investigations 570
ITN 198, 200

Jack, A. 877–8
Jack the Ripper 62
Jackson, D. 547
Jackson, Jesse 476
Jacobs, Jane 248, 973
James, O. 285 n., 630
James, P. D. 204–5
Jankovic, I. 457
Janson, C.-G. 316
Japan, assault in 562
Jefferson, T. 733, 734, 736, 775, 864
Jeffrey, C. Ray 312, 973
Jenkins, Roy 123, 1154
Jessop, B. 503, 507
Jones, Howard 46
Jones, T. 1033
Journal of Forensic Psychiatry 687
Journal of Mental Science 34, 38, 39
Jowell, R. 709
joy-riding 180, 646
Judges' Rules 1025 n., 1063
judicial bias 476
judicial interpretation 445
Judicial Studies Board 1127
juries 75, 1080
JUSTICE 113
Justice for Victims 597
juvenile court 614, 638–9, 640, 641
    change of name to youth court 645
juvenile crime 617, 626–38; *see also* delin-
        quency, juvenile
    Afro-Caribbean youth 631
    black masculinity 551–3
    ethnicity and 631–2
    increase in 639, 640, 651–2
    male and female offending 629–31
    New Approaches to Juvenile Crime 113–14
    peak age of offending 627–8
    recent trends 636–8
    underclass males 549–53
    violent offending 630–1
juvenile justice 638–45
    1960s, since 640–3
    approved schools 639, 640
    bifurcation 642
    borstals 639, 640
    cautioning system 650–1
    Children and Young Persons Act (1969)
        640, 641
    community homes 640
    Criminal Justice Act 1991 645
    custody 113, 639, 641, 643
        fall in use of 643–4; reassertion of
            central position of 649; restrictions on
            use of custodial sentences 645;
            revolution in 643–5
    detention centres 639, 640
    ethnic minorities 739–42
    imprisonment 638, 639
    intermediate treatment schemes 644

non-custodial penalties 644
populist punitiveness, rise of 646–51, 652–3
post-custody supervision 645
reformatories and industrial schools 639
secure training centres 649
secure training orders 647, 649
supervision orders 644
US-style boot camps 649–50
youth court 645
juvenile offenders 64, 121–22, 616, 618
    decline in numbers 643–5
    gender ratio 628–9
    increase in numbers of 640
    persistent offenders 646, 647
juvenile victims 634–5

Kahneman, D. 849
Kaplan, R. 239, 240
Katz, J. 552
Keane, J. 429, 431
Kefauver Commission 826
Kelling, G. 345, 346, 981
Kellor, Frances 763
Kelly, Liz 521
Kelly, R. 822
Kelman, Mark 440, 441
Kempe, C. 859
Kempe, R. 859
Kerner, H. J. 816–17
Kersten, J. 543, 544
Keynes, J. M. 48
King, M. 980
King, R. 194, 1005, 1146, 1147, 1175, 1181,
        1182, 1185
Kingsley, Charles 272
Kircheimer, O. 267–9, 279, 456–7, 1142–3
Kitsuse, John 483
Klein, D. 790
Klein, Melanie 540
Klinteberg, B. A. 385
Knapp, Martin 1223
Knight, B. J. 395
Kobrin, S. 344–5, 348
Koenig, J. 544
Kolvin, I. 388, 391
Kornhauser, Ruth 339

labelling theory 144, 255–7, 455, 456, 459,
        485, 998, 999, 1004
    media, role of 211
    white-collar crime 903–4
Labour Campaign for Criminal Justice 113
labour market, polarization of 279–80
Labour Party 277, 649
    law and order policies 105, 108, 110, 111,
        129–30
        ideologies 99–102
        post-war manifestos 89–99
    Parenting (1996) 101
    Police Federation and 1017

Tackling the Causes of Crime (1996) 101
  trade unions and 102–4
Lacan, Jacques 540
Lacey, N. 1100, 1102
Laing, J. 672
Lambert, Drexel Burnham 288
Landau, S. 741–2
Landesco, J. 824, 825
Lansbury, George 107
large families 391
Lash, Scott 285–6
late modernity 480–1
Latour, B. 830
Laub, J. H. 374
Lavater, J. C. 26
LaVigne, N. 972
law and order, politics of 87–131
  British general elections (1945–97) 88–112
  civil disobedience 107–8
  explaining the trends 99–102
  libertarian criminal law reform 109–12
  new 'underclass' 104–7
  Northern Ireland and its impact 125–7
  official inquiry, forms of 127–8
  policing 125–6
  post-war manifestos and campaigns 89–99
  pressure-group and interest-group politics
    112–21
  prisons 123–5
  scandal and concern, matters of 121–8
Law and Order Lobby 598
law enforcement:
  drugs 941–4, 951
    enforcement statistics 942; sentencing 943–4
  racial bias 749–53
Lawrence, P. 112, 846
Laycock, G. K. 970, 985
Lea, J. 212, 476
Learmont Report 1185, 1186
LeBlanc, M. 365, 372, 381
Lee, M. 1086
Lees, S. 1085
Leeson, Nick 289
left idealism 474–9
left realism 252, 258, 295, 465, 473, 482–97,
    515–16
  aetiology and penality, crisis of 481–2
  causes of crime 487–9
  impact of crime 490–1
  interventions 491–2
  late modernity 480–1
  nature and form of crime 485–6
  short-term gain, long-term transformation
    492–4
  social context of crime 486
  spatial dimension of crime 487
  specificity, problem of 489–90
  temporal aspect of crime 486–7
  theoretical synthesis 482–91
Legal Action Group 113

legal advice
  access to 1061–2
  level of service 1062, 1068, 1078
    failure of defence lawyers to attend
      interrogations 1062, 1078
legal aid:
  costs 296
  police station advice 1061–2
legal guilt, actual guilt and 1052
legal profession:
  attitudes and practices, shaping of 1078
  growing authority of 75
  guilty pleas and 1078
  see also defence lawyers; legal advice
legalism, welfarism and 663
Lehman, P. M. 154
Lehtinen, M. 293
Leitner, M. 932
Lemert, E. 234, 242, 454–5, 459, 483, 816
Leng, R. 1063–4, 1066
Leo, R. 1067
Leonard, E. 517, 775
Lesieur, H. R. 154
Lesson, G. T. 268–9
Letkemann, P. 817, 820
Levi, K. 818
Levi, M. 154, 181, 983
Levine, Dennis 288
Levine, S. 544
Lewis, Derek 1163, 1186
Liberal Democratic Party
  law and order policies 96, 99
liberal feminism 512
Liberal Party
  law and order policies 89, 91, 95
Liberal/SDP Alliance
  law and order manifesto 1987, 95
Liberty (pressure group) 114
life imprisonment:
  discretionary sentences 1099
  mandatory sentences 1099
lifestyles:
  fear of crime, effect of 589–90
  lifestyle theory 966–7
Light, R. 180
Linebaugh, Peter 60
Lipsey, M. 1222
Little, D. 767
Livingstone, Sonia 193, 205, 206, 213–14,
    217
Lloyd, C. 1077, 1218, 1219
lobby groups *see* pressure groups
local crime surveys 583–6
location of offences:
  explanation of 316–30
    Wikström's tentative model 327–30
  multiple victimization 327
  offenders' use of space 323–6
  opportunity theory and routine activities
    theory 320–3

location of offender residence
  explanation of 330–2
    detailed studies of particular areas
      333–6; socialization processes and area
      offender rate differences 336–8;
      statistical studies of offender-rate
      distribution 332–3
Locke, John 26, 1053
Loeber, R. 365, 369, 387
Lofaso, A. J. 370
Lombrosian project 13–14, 20, 30–4, 36, 38,
  46, 515
Lombroso, C. 15, 16, 25, 27, 30–1, 32, 33, 34,
  36, 763, 777, 949
London, history of policing of 65, 66–7
London School of Economics 38, 49
London Stock Exchange, deregulation of 832
London University 38, 41
Longford, Lord 277
Longford Committee 90
Losel, F. 1223
Lowdham Grange Borstal 81
Luckenbill, D. 256, 817
Lukes, S. 238
Lunacy Acts 27
Lupsha, P. A. 825
Lurigio, A. J. 591
Luttwak, Edward 287

Mac an Ghaill, M. 552
McBain, Ed 204
McBarnet, D. 1009, 1010, 1077
McBride, D. 945
McCardie, H. A. 72
McConville, M. 1056, 1057, 1061, 1062, 1065,
  1066, 1069, 1070, 1072, 1073, 1074
McCord, J. 371, 387, 389
McCoy, C. 945
McCrudden, C. 706
McDermott, K. 1182
McDonald, Ross 205
machismo 866
McIntosh, Mary 254, 483–4
McIvor, G. 1210
Mack, J. 816–17, 820
McKay, H. 307–12, 331, 334, 338, 339, 619,
  804
Mackay, R. D. 682, 683
MacKeith, J. 1064
McLaren, Malcolm 622
McLennan, Gregor 418
McLeod, E. 776
McLynn, F. 767
Macmillan, Harold 109
McMurran, M. 949
Macpherson, C. B. 99
McRobbie, A. 621–2, 810–811
McWilliams, B. 1204
McWilliams, W. 1198, 1216, 1226
Mafia 826, 827, 830, 843, 898

magistrates 76; *see also* magistrates' courts
Magistrates' Association 47, 115, 642, 1128
  Sentencing Guidelines 1107, 1116, 1120,
    1122
magistrates' courts 1104–5
  combination orders 1214
  court bail 1076–7
  expenditure on 296
Magnusson, D. 377
Maguire, M. 146, 180, 591, 594, 596, 817,
  1064, 1065, 1081, 1082
Maguire, P. 810
Maguire Seven 125
Maher, L. 776
Maier-Katkin, D. 680
Mair, G. 1077
Major, John 111, 130
Malcolm X 552
male crime:
  female crime and 764–7
  nature of male offending 629–31
  peak age of offending 627
  see also masculinity
Malinosky-Rummell, R. 388
Malleson, K. 1083
Maltz, Michael 1218
Manchester Group *see* Quantitative
    Criminology Group at Manchester
    University
mandatory prosecution:
  Italy, in 565–71
mandatory sentences 1118–19
  life sentences 1154
Mannet, David 546 n.
Mannheim, H. 1, 14, 24, 38, 43, 45, 46, 47,
  50, 311, 896
Manning, P. 144
manslaughter:
  diminished responsibility, defence of
    685–6
  see also homicide
Marcus, M. 564, 568
marginalization, female crime and 787–8
Mark, Robert 98
market forces 481
market society 297–300
Markus, C. L. 970
marriage rate 623
Marshall, Geoffrey 1032
Marshall, I. H. 367, 369
Marshall, P. 722
Martens, Peter 337
Martinson, R. 1098, 1200, 1216, 1219
Marx, Gary 257
Marx, Karl 1, 266, 787
Marxism 414, 503
  state theory 503–5
  theories of crime 252
  white-collar crime 906
Marxist feminism 512

masculinity:
  crime and 535–57; *see also* male crime
    machismo 866; 'normal' masculine
    personality 536–8; power and multiple
    masculinities 538–9; psycho-analytic
    break with orthodoxy 539–40; sexual
    violence 541–9; violent crime 865–6,
    868; youth crime 549–53
  culture of 868–9
mass manufacturing, demise of 280–8
Massachusetts scheme 1199
Masters, B. 843
Mathieson, T. 1179
Matza, D. 23 n., 241–2, 258, 484, 485, 620,
    806, 807
Maudsley, Henry 30, 34, 35, 36
Maudsley Clinic 39
Mawby, R. I. 315
maximum-security prisons 1178–9
maximum sentences 1105–6
Maxwell, Sir Alexander 47
Maxwell, Robert 139
May, Sir John 128
May Committee 123, 1146–7, 1149, 1172
Mayhew, Henry 26, 62, 64, 104, 272, 305, 803
Mays, J. B. 807
Mead, G. H. 254, 483, 543
media representations of crime 189–31
  apocalyptic approaches 190
  causes of 219–25
    crime news as cultural conflict 222–4;
    elements of 'newsworthiness' 221;
    political ideology of the press 220–1;
    structural determinants of news-making
    221–2
  child sex abuse 202
  consequences of 210–19
    absence of controls 213; fear of crime
    217–19; labelling 211–12; means to
    commit crime 212; motive 212;
    opportunity 213; research evidence
    213–17
  content of:
    deviant news 194–6; extent of crime in
    the news 196–9; fact/fiction boundary
    194; problems of content analysis
    192–4; results of content analysis 194;
    ultra-realism 194
  crime fiction:
    cinema 205, 206; content of 203–4;
    pattern of 204–9
  criminological theory and 211–13
  pattern of crime news 199–203
    offenders and victims, portrayal of 201;
    variations between different media 202
  political conflict 202, 220, 221
  sex crimes 202
  summary 209–10
mediation 602–3
medical reports 1109

Medical Research Council 39
Medico-Legal and Criminological Review 38
medico-legal criminology 38, 42–3
Mellor, David 112
Melly, G. 618
Melossi, D. 456–8, 505
Mendelsohn, B. 578
Mental Health Act Commission 663
Mental Health Review Tribunals 663
mentally disordered offenders 661–701
  categories of 668–9
  community care 671
  court assessment and diversion schemes
    673–4
  definition, problem of 666–9
  homicide inquiries 662
  hospital bed shortage 676
  hospital order with restrictions 667–8
  identification 672–3
  interim hospital orders 668
  mental disorder and offending behaviour,
    relationship between 687–8
  minority group, whether 669–79
  numbers 670–1
  penal disposal 670
  policy 670
  prison populations 675–7
  protective sentencing:
    procedural safeguards *v.* treatment 692–6
  remand population 675
  remand to hospital for reports 668
  remand to hospital for treatment 668
  repeat offenders 671
  special provision 664–5
  supervision registers 671
  therapeutic disposals 667–8
    distrust to 662
  transfer to hospital 668, 677–9
  treatment 686–92
    prison 690–2; psychopathic disorder 686,
    688–90
  trial 679–86
    diminished responsibility 685–6;
    infanticide 684; M' Naghten Rules
    683; not guilty by reason of insanity
    683–4
    psychiatric reasoning 680–1; statutory
    reform 681; unfitness to plead 682
  welfarism and legalism 663
mentally ill:
  deinstitutionalization 460, 461, 462–3
  defence of 664–5, 683
Merighi, J. R. 552
Merry, S. 594
Merseyside Crime Survey 584
Merton, R. 212, 237, 266, 274–6, 277, 289,
    414, 482, 484, 561, 619, 620, 805, 806,
    903, 906
Messerschmidt, James 542–3, 544
Messina family 64

Messner, S. 852
meta-analysis, community penalties and 1223
Metropolitan Police 65, 68, 70, 73, 1029
    creation of 67–8
Metropolitan Police Committee 1029
Mexico 240
Military Corrective Training Centre 650
Milken, Michael 288, 893
Millbank prison 78, 79, 80
Miller, E. 45, 776
Miller, J. C. 1006
Miller, M. 877
Miller, P. 931
Miller, W. B. 808, 813
Mills, C. Wright 415, 416, 418, 429, 505, 893
Ministry of Defence Police 149
minor offences 154
Mirrlees-Black, C. 167, 633, 768, 852
Mirza, H. 933
miscarriages of justice 1052, 1060, 1084
    coercion and false confessions 1065
    review mechanisms 1080–4; *see also*
        reviewing mechanisms
mitigation 1115–16
M' Naghten Rules 683
Mobilization for Youth (United States) 277–8
modern criminology 11–12, 18–21
modernity 480–2
mods and rockers 211, 618, 809
Moffitt, T. E. 372, 386, 387
Molony Committee 639
Monahan, J. 687, 880
money laundering 288–9
money markets 287
    international finance market crimes 288–90
Moodie, S. 1075
Mooney, J. 854
Moore, J. W. 808, 813
Moore, R. 332
Moors Murders 122
moral decline 588
moral panic 140, 211, 478, 620–1, 632, 845
    Bulger case 648–9
moral unease 618
morality crimes 196
Morash, M. 389
More, Thomas 22, 272
Morel 30
Morgan, J. 181
Morgan, Patricia 299
Morgan, R. 1095, 1146, 1147, 1185
Morgan Report 981
Morison Committee 1200
Morris, A. 511, 517, 519–20, 643, 774, 779,
    1107
Morris, N. 45, 877, 1177 n.
Morris, P. 1177 n.
Morris, T. 312, 1177 n.
Morrison, W. 454
Morrison, William Douglas 34

Moston, S. 1064, 1065, 1066
motives 212, 381–2, 394–5
    anomie theory 212
    media and 212
motor vehicles *see* autocrime
Mott, J. 633, 944
Mountbatten, Lord 1165, 1166
Mountbatten Report (1966) 123
Mouzelis, N. 417, 418, 424
Moxon, D. 1107, 1115
Mueller, G. O. W. 984
mugging 140
multiple murderers 864
multiple victimization 172, 327, 592
Muncer, S. 865
murder:
    explanations for violence 864
    families of victims, trauma of 593
    fiction, portrayal in 208
    multiple murders, typology of 864
    risk of 849–50
    serial killers 544, 864
    see also homicide; violent crime
Murphy, D. 986
Murray, C. 282–4, 299, 392
Muslim groups 709, 711; *see also* ethnic
    minorities

NACRO *see* National Association for the
    Care and Resettlement of Offenders
Naffine, N. 515, 522, 524–5, 528
Nagin, D. S. 372
Napoleonic wars 78
Nashville Footstomper 842
Nathan, G. 741–2
National Academy of Sciences 1098
National Association for Mental Health 47–8
National Association for the Care and
    Resettlement of Offenders (NACRO)
    113, 114, 115, 117, 297, 1147–8
National Association of Probation Officers
    1199
National Campaign for the Abolition of the
    Death Penalty (1955) 114
National Council for Morals 189
National Criminal Intelligence Service 951
National Deviancy Conference 51
National Drugs Intelligence Unit 941
National Front 92 n., 98
National Prison Survey 174
National Reporting Centre 121
National Society for the Prevention of Cruelty
    to Children 769
National Standards:
    combination orders 1213, 1214
    community penalties 1202
    community service 1210
    probation orders 1124, 1196
National Survey of Health and Development
    391

National Union of Mineworkers 91, 103
National Union of Police and Prison Officers 72
Nazism 45
  Holocaust 844
Neave, Airey 98
Needham, D. 35
Needle, J. A. 813
neighbourhood change 344–9
Neighbourhood Watch 95, 110 n., 129, 589, 986
Nelken, D. 467
neoclassical economics 292–7
neo-Marxists 254
New Approaches to Juvenile Crime 113–14
New Chicagoans 338–342, 349
New Criminology 143–8, 515
New Labour 104, 105, 129, 130
New Right 104, 109
New York Times 197
Newburn, T. 594, 1033
Newcastle Thousand Family Study 388
Newman, Oscar 248, 249, 312, 973
news *see* crime news
News of the World 197
Newson, J. 391
newspapers 197; *see also* media representations of crime
Newton hearings 1108, 1111
NFA (no further action) 1069–70, 1073
Nicolson, D. 35, 685
Nilsen, Dennis 850
Nixon, Richard (US President) 940
no further action (NFA) 1069–70, 1073
Nobles, R. 1083–4
Nolan Report 112
non-custodial sentencing 1120–7; *see also* community sentences; fines; probation service
normalization 459
Norman, Conolly 36
Normandeau, A. 154
Norris, C. 735, 1064, 1065
Northern Ireland:
  no-jury-single-judge courts 127
  political violence 126–7
not guilty by reason of insanity 683–4
Nothing Works 491, 1216, 1219, 1221, 1224, 1226
Notting Hill Carnival 753
Notting Hill Race Riots (1958) 711
Nottinghamshire crime rates 156
Nuffield studies 96, 97
Nurco, D. 946
Nye, F. I. 176, 390
Nye, Robert 17

obscene telephone calls 842
occupational injuries 593, 842
occupational risks 857–9

offences:
  categories of 58, 1104
  location of *see* location of offences
offenders 61–5, 172–9
  age 367–9
    peak age of offending 398, 627, 638
  anti-social behaviour 363–4
  chronic offenders 374–6
  co-offending and motives 381–2
  compensation to victims 605–6, 1100, 1101, 1102
  corporate crime 178
  counselling 1100
  crime fiction, portrayal in 209
  desistance from offending 373–4
  detention in police station *see* police custody
  development of offending 367–82
  ethnic minorities 720–49, 750; *see also* ethnic minorities
  Family Group Conferences 1100
  gender differences 177–8
  individual offending frequency 369–71
  information about, for sentencing purposes 1108–9
  interrogation *see* police interrogation
  location of:
    explanation of 330–2; *see also* location of offender residence
  media portrayal 201
  mentally disordered *see* mentally disordered offenders
  perceptions of 137
  remand in custody *see* remand in custody
  reoffending, probability of 373
  social class 176–7, 178
  specialization and escalation 380
  versatility 363
  victim-offender mediation 1100
  see also criminal careers; imprisonment
official inquiry, forms of 127–8
Ohlin, L. E. 237, 276–8, 395, 483, 619–20, 806, 807
Okihiro, N. 146
Old Bailey 75
Olweus, D. 379
O'Malley, P. 466
'One Stop Shop' initiative (OSS) 600
OPEC embargo (1974) 286–7
opportunist crimes 324
opportunity theory of crime patterns 320
Oregon Youth Study 380
organized crime 822–30
  alien conspiracy 826–8
  enterprise 828–30
  ethnic succession 824–6
  ethnicity and 828
  globalization 829, 830
  Kefauver Commission 826
  Mafia 826, 827, 830

organized crime (*cont.*):
  pirates and gangsters 823–824
  transnational 829
  white-collar crime and 898, 910
Oswald, P. 933
Ouston, J. 391
Oxford Handbook:
  aims of 3
  second edition 5–6
  theoretical and methodological considerations 3–5
Oz 621

PACE (Police and Criminal Evidence Act) 93, 94, 1025–6, 1056, 1058, 1068, 1069, 1085
  Codes of Practice 1026
    detention and questioning 1063
    stop-and-search powers 1054
  detention in police station 1060–1
    access to legal advice 1061
  impact on policing 1067–8
  record-keeping requirements 1026, 1061
  stop-and-search powers 1054
Packer, H. 1051, 1053, 1079
Paglia, C. 546
Pailthorpe, Grace 39
Painter, K. 171, 322, 854
Palmer, C. 672
Palmerston, Lord 69
parents:
  child-rearing behaviour 387, 398
  conflict 387; *see also* domestic violence
  convicted parents 389–390
  separation and divorce 388
  socialization 336–7
  supervision 623
  youth sub-culture and 807–9
parish constables 65–6, 67
parish watches 66
parish watchmen 67
Park, R. 308, 1004
Parker, H. 620, 633–4, 807, 929, 930
Parker, Robert 205
Parkhurst Prison 121, 124
Parkin, Frank 99
parole 1117, 1200
Parole Board 1154
Parsons, Talcott 537
Parssinen, T. 938
participant observation studies 179
Parton, N. 778
Pasquino, E. B. 452
Paternoster, R. 785
Paterson, Alexander 47
patriarchy 785–7, 865
Patrick, J. 620, 808
Patten, John 119
Patterson, G. R. 380
Pavarini, M. 456–8

PCA (Police Complaints Authority) 1028
PCB (Police Complaints Board) 1027–8
Peach, Blair 92
peak age of offending 398, 627, 638
Pearce, F. 254, 845, 914–15, 916–17
Pearson, G. 180, 189, 614, 616, 625, 671, 673, 803, 934
Pearson, Karl 41
Pearson, Y. 946
Pease, K. 156, 731, 843–4, 977, 978, 1210, 1212
Peay, Jill 6
Peck, D. 934
Peel, Sir Robert 67–8, 79, 1034
Pelat, Roger Patrice 288
Penal Affairs Consortium 114
'penal crisis' 1201
penal reform *see* prisons
Penal Reform League 113
penal servitude 80
Pentonville Prison 79, 80, 1141
Pepinsky, H. 161, 162, 167
Percival, John 189
Perks Committee 150
permissive revolution 618
permissive society 109
Peru:
  cocoa crop 291
Petersilia, J. 382
Pettit, P. 875, 1101, 1102
Pfohl, Stephen 429
Philips, David 59
Phillips, Melanie 191
Phillipson, Mike 259–60
phrenology 26–7, 29
physical disorder 345
physiognomy 26–7
Pick, Daniel 17
Piliavin, I. 294
Piore, M. 286–7, 290
Piper Alpha oil rig 893
pirates 823
Pittsburgh Youth Study 363, 364, 366, 385
Pizzey, Erin 596
Plant, M. 931, 934
Platt, Anthony 478, 1198
Player, E. 691, 779
plea bargaining 1078, 1079, 1086
police 65–73; *see also* police culture; police custody; policing
  accountability *see* police accountability
  active policing 869–70
  aggressive policing 869
  attitudes to young people 635
  British police ideology 1007
  cautioning 1071–2, 1086
  charging 1072–3
  civil actions against 1025, 1082–3
  Codes of Practice 1026
  complaints and discipline procedure 1027–8, 1081–2, 1085

corruption 240
crime clear-up rates 1037–8
decision-making 1054–60; bias, patterns of, 1056–8; discretion 1054–6; incongruity 1058; suspiciousness 1057–8; working rules 1057–8, 1084
development of 65–73
    county police 69–71; efficiency, 72–3; Home Office links 70–2; image of British bobby 73; London 66–8; parish constables 65–6; provinces 68–9; Scotland 70; superintending constables 69; trading justices 66
distinctiveness of 1007–8
ethnic groups and:
    Afro-Caribbeans, relations with 710–11; behaviour towards 736–7; stop and search powers 731–7; victims of crime 717–18
future of 1034–9
governance 1028–30
    centralizing trends 1030, 1032–3; structural reforms 1030–2, 1036, 1037
government confrontation with 1036
growing demands on 1036–7
information to victims 600
interrogation *see* police interrogation
litigation against 1082–3
malpractice 1036
    review mechanisms 1080–4; *see also* reviewing mechanisms
peace-keeping role 1001
'policing' and 1003–8
prosecutions against 1082
public satisfaction with 599
record-keeping 1026, 1061, 1062, 1064
risk of violence against 858–9
secret service 71
stop-and-search *see* stop-and-search powers
study of criminology and 997–9
victims' satisfaction with 599–600
    ethnic minorities 717–18; sexual assault victims 599
violence against 868–71
police accountability:
    individual accountability:
        complaints process 1027–8; legal accountability 1025–7; reform proposals 1032–3
    policy accountability 1028–34
Police and Criminal Evidence Act *see* PACE
police antecedents statement 1109
police authorities 1029, 1030
    structural reforms 1030–2
police bail, 1075–1076 1079
Police Complaints Authority (PCA) 1028, 1081
Police Complaints Board (PCB) 1027–8, 1081
police culture 1016–18, 1055
    conservatism 1017

cultural variations between forces 1020–2
    legalistic style 1021; rural/urban difference 1021–2; service style 1021; watchman style 1021
cultural variations within forces 1018–20
    alienated cynics 1020; law-enforcers 1020; managerial professionals 1020; peace-keepers 1020; 'street' and 'management' cops 1018–19; uniform and detective branches, rivalry between 1019
internal solidarity 1016–17
social isolation 1016–17
structural explanations 1022–4
suspiciousness 1016, 1057–8
police custody 1060–8
access to legal advice 1061–2
detention without charge 1060–1
'helping with inquiries' 1060, 1061
independent custody officers 1060, 1061
police interrogation 1062–5
records 1061, 1062, 1064
rules and constraints (PACE) 1060, 1084
    impact of 1067–8
silence, right to 1065–7
police discretion 1008–34
constabulary independence 1024
control of 1024
explanation of 1015
    cultural explanations 1016–18; individualistic explanations 1015–16
gender and policing 1012–13
Italy 567, 568
operation of 1010–11
racial discrimination 1011–12
rule of law and 1013–14
police diversion 1070–2
Police Federation 72, 115, 1017, 1018
Police Foundation 1003
police interrogation 1062–5, 1084–5
bail offers 1076
Code of Practice 1063
coercion 1064
due process 1063, 1065
failure of defence lawyers to attend 1078
false confessions 1064–5
impact of PACE 1067–8, 1084
informal 1063–4, 1076
new interview styles 1065
right of silence 1065–7
police personality 1015
police research 998
development of 999–1003
    United Kingdom 1000–3; United States 999–1000
Police Research Group 979
policing
bias in 1056–8, 1072
costs 296
crisis in British policing 1035

policing (*cont.*):
detective policing 72
future of 1034–9
gender and 1012–13
goals 1055
impact of PACE on 1067–8, 1084
legal control 1025
meaning of 1004, 1008
'police' and 1003–8
policy 120–121, 125–6
    Golden Age of policing 125
politicization of 1002, 1029
private policing firms 1005–6
problem-oriented policing (POP) 968
rationalization 72
'real' policing 1018
Scotland 70
sex discrimination 1012–13
social control 1004
specialized policing 1006
technology 1006
volunteer bodies 1006
women and 769–72
political conflict:
media portrayal of 202, 220, 221
political deviance 196
political economy of crime 265–303
business cycle and crime 266–72
costs of crime:
    neoclassical economics 292–7
free market policies 284, 287–8
free market society 297–300
inequality and crime 272–92
    demise of mass manufacturing 280–8;
    post-war youthful unemployment
    278–9; underclass 282–3; upward and
    downward options 279–80
international drug trade 290–2
international finance market crimes
    288–90
political ideology of the press 220–1
political violence:
Northern Ireland 126–7
politics, sentencing and 1095–6
Polk, K. 881
poll tax 107 n.
riots (1989–90) 108
Pollak, O. 764, 768, 777
Pollock-Byrne, J. 783, 790
Polsky, N. 254, 820
Pompidou Group 940
Pontell, H. 913, 918
POP (problem-oriented policing) 968
populist punitiveness, rise of 646–51, 652–3
pornography 109
Porter, R. 27
Portillo, Michael 650
Portman Clinic 39
positivist criminology 16, 51, 143–4, 586, 997,
    998

Posner, R. 1098
possessive individualism 99
post-modern feminism 513–514
post-modernism 349
post-modernity 1038–9
post-traumatic stress disorder 592
Potts, W. A. 38, 39
poverty 284, 392, 397, 476, 488; *see also*
    unemployment
crime and 272–92
Powell, Enoch 97
Power, M. J. 392
Poyner, B. 970
pre-charge procedures, formalization of 1060,
    1067
pre-sentence reports 1109, 1124, 1216
pre-trial processes 1075–80
prosecution discretion:
    mandatory rule of prosecution in Italy
    565–71
Preble, E. 945
Prescott-Clarke, P. 709
Presidential Commission on Law Enforcement
    (USA) 999–1000
pressure groups 112–21
victim movement 595–7
prevalence of offending 398
Princeton Prison 78
Prins, H. 687
Prior Committee 127
Prison Department 1163
prison officers 1179–80
women 1180
Prison Officers' Association 115
Prison Reform International (PRI) 117
Prison Reform Trust 113, 114, 115
Prison Rules 1145, 1146, 1164
Prison Service 1163, 1164, 1185
annual report 1164
Corporate Plan 1164
Statement of Purpose 1149, 1150
Prison Service Agency 1163
prisoners 1137, 1151–62; *see also* imprison-
    ment; prisons
ageing population 1158–9
Category A prisoners 1166
complaints system 1172–3
conditions in prison *see* prisons
dangerous prisoners 1175, 1185
difficult prisoners 1159–60, 1182
disruptive prisoners 1175
escapes 123, 124, 1183, 1185
ethnic characteristics 720–9, 1156–7
    disproportionate numbers 476
families and 1187
foreign 1157
growth in prison population 475, 1137–8,
    1151–5, 1184
intractable prisoners 1159–60
judicial review 1171

long-term prisoners:
　growth in 1151–3
mental disorders 675–7
mental health 1162
mentally disordered 1184
nationality 1157
prison officers 1183
prisoner culture 1180
responses to custody 1179
security classification 1165–6
social characteristics:
　National Prison Survey 174
socio-economic character 1161
solidarity 1177, 1179
special prisoner status 1175
suicide 676
　prevention of 1183
time spent in custody 1139, 1151–2
visits 1187
women prisoners 780–1, 1184
growth in number of 1155–6
young prisoners 1158–9
Prisoners' Handbook 1164
prisoners of war 78–9
prisonization 1180
prisons 33; *see also* imprisonment; prisoners
administration 1163, 1164
boards of visitors 1171–12
building programme 1137–8, 1167, 1168
centralization 80
closed and open institutions 1165
community prisons 1166
complaints system 1172–3
conditions 81, 1165, 1167–8
　improvements in 1183–4; overcrowding
　　1167, 1168, 1183, 1201; standards
　　1168–71; Woolf Inquiry 1169–71
contracting out 1173–5
crisis 1183, 1201
decarceration 460–4
deprivations of prison life 1177, 1178
development of 77–80
disturbances 1139, 1160, 1163, 1181–2,
　1183
drugs in 1139
escapes from prison 123, 124, 1183, 1185
expenditure on 296, 1163
future prospects 1183–7
gendered 1155–6
governance 1163
government policy, u-turns 1186–7
growth of 77–8
historical use 1142
industrial disputes 1139
inspection 1171–2
inspectorate 1172
local prisons 1166, 1167
maximum-security prisons 1178–9
modern prison, emergence of 1141–4
Ombudsman 1173

prison culture 1177, 1178
prison policy 123–5
privatization 1163, 1173–5
reform 78–9, 80, 1142, 1143
　pressure-groups 113–21
security measures 1139
security quotient 1186
social character of prison life 1139
sociology of 1176–83
special units 1175–6
suicide prevention 1183
training prisons 1165, 1167
treatment and training 1146–8, 1167, 1187
types of 1165
uniforms 81
vulnerable prisoner units 1140
women's prisons 781–2, 1155, 1166
young offender institutions 1165, 1167
Prisons Board 1163
Prisons Ombudsman 1173
private asylums 27
privatization of prisons 1173–5
Proal, L. 34
probation centres 1207
Probation Inspectorate:
　Quality and Effectiveness inspections
　　1218
probation officers 1199
training 1203
probation orders 1124, 1204–9; *see also*
　　probation service
additional requirements 1207
age factors 1208–9
gender factors 1208
purpose 1217
specified activities 1207–8
statistics 1205–7
summary offences 1206
probation service 638, 1195–7; *see also*
　　probation orders
after-care responsibilities 1200
budgetary constraints 1225
development of 81
effectiveness 1217–8
　reconviction rates 1216, 1218–20
groupwork 1203
history of 1198–1204
rehabilitative ideal 1200
religious missionary ideal 1198–9
responsibilities 1217
scientific diagnostic ideal 1199–1200
Statement of National Objectives and
　　Priorities (Green Paper, 1984) 1202
statistics 1218
superstructural changes 1204
Three-Year Plan for the Probation Service
　　(1996–9) 1217
problem-oriented policing (POP) 968
professional crime 815–22
drugs trade 820–1

professional crime (*cont.*):
    ethics 818–19
    hedonism 819–20
prohibition (United States) 824
Project Metropolitan (Stockholm) 369, 371, 374
property crime, in 208–9
property offences 152
proportionality 1097
prosecution 74–6, 1069
    agencies 1069
    case construction 1073
    criminal prosecutions 75
    Crown Prosecution Service 1073–5
    decision to prosecute, ethnic minorities and 739–42, 750
    discretion to prosecute
        mandatory prosecution rule in Italy 565–71
    due process protections 1052
    exclusionary processes 1086
    historical development 74–6
    no further action (NFA) 1069–70, 1073
    police charging 1072–3
    police diversion 1071–2
    police involvement 74–5
prostitution 771, 776, 847
Protecting the Public (White Paper, 1996) 1096, 1137
provocation 844
    defence of 685
Pryce, K. 811, 933
pseudo-reconvictions 1219
psychiatry 27, 29, 39, 40
    defences 684, 685
psychoanalysis 39–40
    masculinity 545
    psychoanalytical feminism 513
    violence, explanations of 863–4
psychological consequences of crime 591–2
psychological disorders, youth and 624
psychological medicine 26
psychopathy 39
    psychopathic disorder 666, 667, 688–90
pub brawls 155
public opinion 121
public protection sentences 1099
public space, dilapidation of 345
Puffer, J. A. 803
Pulkkinen, L. 374
punishment 603; *see also* sentencing
    desert theory 1096–7
    deterrence theories 1097–8
    discipline 457–8
    historians of 456–7
    historical development 76–82
    labour market theory 457
    other modes of control and 459
    retributive theories 1096–7
    theorists of 456–8

transportation 77, 78
uniformity of 80–1
punk 622

Quantitative Criminology Group at Manchester University 327
questioning *see* police interrogation
Quetelet, Adolphe 26, 266, 267, 305–6, 482

race:
    crime and 551
    sentencing and 745–9
    see also ethnic minorities; racial discrimination
race riots 711
racial anthropology 30
racial attacks 140
racial discrimination 706, 708, 710, 711
    anti-discrimination law 706, 708
    criminal justice system 749–53
    indirect discrimination 706
    personal experiences of 708–9
    police discretion 1011–12
racial harassment 588, 711, 718–20, 842
    impact of 592
    lifestyle and mobility, effect on 590
racial minorities *see* ethnic minorities
racially-motivated crime 718–20
    trends 719
    vulnerability to 582
racism 283
Radford, J. 171, 544, 585
Radical Alternatives to Prison 113
radical criminology 250–2
radio *see* broadcasting
Radzinowicz, L. 1, 14, 24, 25, 40, 43, 45, 46, 47, 48, 49, 1166
Rafter, Hahn N. 781, 790
Rafter, N. H. 517–18, 526
ram-raiding 95 n.
Ramsay, M. 949
Ramsbotham, Sir David 1186
rape 445–6, 541–546
    date-rape 546, 867
    explanations for 543–4, 861, 864, 866–8
    fiction, portrayal in 208
    Greek definition 562
    impact on victims 591
    planned rape 867
    rapists' experiences 544
    rates of 853–4
    reoffending rates 877–8
    reporting of 586
    victims
        precipitation by 579; treatment of 1013; witnesses, as 600
rape crisis centres 597, 777
Rastafarianism 622, 811, 933
rational choice theory 243–245, 260, 293–4, 295, 453, 967

rave movement 625
Rawlinson, P. 829–30
Rawson, W. 25
Raynor, P. 1224
RCCP *see* Royal Commission on Criminal
    Procedure
Reach, Angus Bethune 62
Reagan, Ronald (US President) 269, 940
Reaganomics 288, 294
realism 485; *see also* left realism
recidivists 143
reckless behaviour 841–2
reconviction rates 1219–21
    key correlates 1220
    probation, following 1216, 1218–20
    pseudo-reconvictions 1219 n.
record-keeping 1026, 1061, 1062
    custody records 1061, 1062, 1064
Reed Committee 665
Reed Report 668, 673 n., 674, 696
Reeves, Helen 595
Reformation of Juvenile Offenders 79
reformatories 639
reggae 622
rehabilitative sentencing 1098–9, 1101
Reichman, N. 898
Reiman, Jeffrey 254, 268 n.
Reiner, R. 25, 125
Reiss, A. 344, 586, 802, 999
remand centres 1165
    crowding 1167
remand homes 639, 640
remand in custody 1077
    ethnic minorities, rates for 743–4
    juveniles 1158
remand prisoners:
    time in custody 1152
remarriages 623
remission of sentence 1117
Rendell, Ruth 205
Rengert, G. 324–6, 977
reoffending:
    homicide 878–9
    probability of 373
    rape 877–8
reparative justice 602–7
reparative theories 1100
repeat offending 875
repeat victimization, prevention of 974–6
Reports of the Medical Commissioner of
    Prisons 37
Reppetto, T. A. 977–8
republicanism 1101
residential burglary:
    distribution of offences 319
restitution 603, 1083
restorative theories 1100
retributism 874–5
retributive theories of punishment 1096–7
Reuter, P. 843

reviewing mechanisms 1080–4
    civil actions 1082
    complaints and discipline procedure 1081–2
    juries 1080
    prosecution of the police 1082
    restitution 1083
Revolutionary wars 78
Rex, J. 332
Rice, M. 526
Riis, J. A. 803
Riley, D. 387
risk 382–4, 395
    analyses 971–2
    of crime 490
        media over-emphasis on 199
    social theory and 424–6
    victimization, of *see* victimization
    of violence 848–59; *see also* violence
road deaths 841–2
robbery 155
Robertson, G. 674, 691
Robertson, R. 830
Robins, D. 811
Robins, L. N. 387, 389
Robinson, W. S. 316
Robocop 125
Rock, P. 5, 14, 117, 584
rock'n'roll 618
Roiphe, K. 546
Rolleston Committee 937–9
Romilly, Sir Samuel 15, 79
Rose, Nikolas 18, 466
Roshier, B. 197
Ross, E. A. 451–2, 917
Ross, Nick 971
Ross, Robert 1222
Roth, M. 689
Rothman, D. 462, 1198
routine activities theory 245, 320–3, 394, 966
Rowan, Colonel Charles 69
Rowett, C. 858
Rowntree, John and Margaret 278
Royal College of Psychiatrists 926
Royal Commission on a Rural Constabulary
    68–9
Royal Commission on Criminal Justice
    125–6, 127, 128, 598, 1027, 1060, 1104
Royal Commission on Criminal Procedure
    1025
    pre-charge procedures 1060, 1067
Royal Commission on the Penal System 89
Royal Medico-Psychological Association 48
Rubenstein, H. 973
Rubin, D. 661
Rucker, L. 389
Ruggiero, V. 830, 897–8, 946, 950–1
Ruggles-Brise, Sir Evelyn 33, 39, 81
rule of law 568, 704, 1053, 1085
    police discretion and 1013–14
    undermining of 1059, 1068

Runciman, W. G. 417
rural crime surveys 584
rural violence 846
Rusche, G. 267–269, 279, 456–7, 1142–3
Rush, Benjamin 25
Ruskin, John 272
Russell, D. E. H. 544
Russell, K. 1081
Russell, Whitworth 79, 267
Russian Revolution 71
Rutherford, A. 123
Rutter, M. 391, 393, 624
Rwanda 844

Sabel, C. 286–7, 290
sado-masochism 844
Safer Cities initiative 110 n., 129, 982
St Paul 272
SAMM (Support After Murder and
    Manslaughter) 597
Sampson, A. 974
Sampson, R. 340–1, 374
Sanders, A. 1053, 1061–2, 1062, 1068, 1071,
    1072, 1074, 1076, 1078
Sanders, C. 255
Sanghvi, R. 685
Sargent, Tom 113
Satterfield, J. H. 385
Saunders, S. 171, 585
Sayers, Dorothy 204
Scargill, Arthur 103
Scarman, Lord 127, 202, 711, 1010, 1020,
    1034
schizophrenia 668, 683
school, offending and 392–393
Schuerman, L. 344–5, 348
Schwartz, R. D. 1006
science of criminology, emergence of 30–44
science of man 26
Scientific Group for the Discussion of
    Delinquency Problems 46
Scotland:
    police 70
    prisons, development of 80
Scott, Robert 254
Scott Report 112
Scottish Crime Surveys 580
Scottish Enlightenment 26
Scraton, Phil 463
Scull andrew 268 n., 460, 461, 463
Scully, D. 544 n., 867
Scuola Positiva 24, 31
secondary victimization 593, 599, 604
secret service 71
secure training centres 649
Securities and Exchange Commission (USA)
    288, 913, 920
security bubbles 351
self-policing 322
self-reported offending 366–7

ethnic minorities 729–30
Selke, W. 161, 167
Sellin, T. 143, 307
Sellin-Wolfgang index 154
Seneviratne, M. 733
Sennett, R. 32
sentences:
    appeals against 1110
    mandatory sentences 1118–19
    maximum sentences 1105–6
    normal 1111
    remission 1117
sentencing 32, 1095–135; *see also* punishment;
        sentences
    appeals 1110
    attendance centre orders 1125, 1198, 1200,
        1214–15
    available sentences, range of 1106
    combination orders 1124, 1203, 1213–14
    community sentences 1123–5, 1195,
        1196–7, 1204–24; *see also* community
        sentences; effectiveness of 1216–24
    community service orders 1209–12
    compensation orders 1123
    consistency in 1131
    Crown Court 1104–5
    curfew orders 1124–5, 1198, 1203, 1214–16
    custodial 1111–20; *see also* imprisonment
    discharges 1120–1
    discretion in sentencing 1106–1108
    diversion from custody 1200–1, 1223
    drugs offences 943–4, 951
    English sentencing procedures 1111
    ethnic minorities 745–9, 750
    fines 1121–3, 1197
    guideline judgments 1114
    guidelines to magistrates 1120
    historical development 77–8
    information about the offence 1108
    information about the offender 1108–9
    judicial independence 1127
    life imprisonment 1099
    magistrates' courts 1104–5
    maximum sentences 1105–6
    mechanics of 1102–11
    ministerial decisions 1154
    non-custodial 1120–7
        review of policy and practice 1125–7
    politics and 1095–6
    pre-sentence reports 1109, 1124, 1216
    proportionality and Court of Appeal
        1114–15
    public protection sentences 1099
    rationales for 1096–1102
        appraising the rationales 1101–2;
            deterrence theories 1097–8; incapacita-
            tive sentencing 1099; rehabilitative
            sentencing 1098–9; restorative and
            reparative theories 1100; retributive
            theories 1096–7; social theories 1100–1

reform 1127–31
  further reform in England and Wales
    1129–31; international patterns 1128–9
  representations on sentence 1109–10
  selection of cases for sentence 1103–4
  sentence discounts 1078, 1079
  socio-political basis 1101
  structuring discretion 1128
  suspended sentences 1125
  'tariff' 1111–12, 1184
  training of sentencers 1127–8
  women and 772–3
Sereny, Gitta 547, 548
serial killers 544, 864
Serious Fraud Office 154
sex discrimination 706, 779, 780
  anti-discrimination law 706
  indirect discrimination 706
  policing 1012–13
sex offenders:
  treatment in prison 690
  treatment programmes 876
sexual abuse 181
  children *see* child abuse
  impact on victims 591
sexual crime 74, 152, 171–2; *see also* rape;
    sexual violence
  media reporting of 202
  reporting rates 768
  against women 585–6
sexual harassment 842
sexual violence 171, 842
  explanations for rape 543–4, 866–8
  feminist theorizing 541, 546
  local crime surveys 585
  masculinity and 541–9
  risk factors 850–3, 853–4
  sex-murderers 544–5
  victims:
    impact on 591; satisfaction with police
      response 599; treatment for 876
Shacklady Smith, L. 517
Shah, R. 731
Shapiro, M. 561–2
Shapiro, S. 899–900, 902, 913, 916
Shapland, J. 249, 594, 599, 677, 775, 1057
Shaw, Clifford 307–12, 331, 334, 338, 339
Shaw, C. R. 552, 619, 804
Shaw, M. 387, 980
Shaw, Stephen 1223
Shaw-Lefevre, Charles 69
Shearing, Clifford 250
Sheehy Committee 128
Sheehy Inquiry into Police Responsibilities
    and Rewards 1032, 1033
Sherman, L. 248, 319, 873
shoplifting trends 637–8
shopping centres 353
Short, Clare 109, 110
Short, J. F. 176, 390, 808

Shover, N. 374, 816
Shrewsbury Three 108
Sicilian Mafia 830
signification 255–9
  culture and subculture 257–9
  labelling theory 255–7
silence, right to 127, 1027, 1065–7, 1068
  adverse inferences 1066–7
  silence rates 1066
Silva, P. A. 386
Simenon, Georges 205
Simon, F. 972
Simon, J. 430, 466
Simon, Rita 766
Simon, R. J. 784
Simon, Roger 205
Simpson, O. J. 194, 844 n., 860
Singh, S. 1086
single-parent families 282, 283, 284, 623
situational crime prevention theory 312
skinheads 619, 809–10
Skogan, W. 172, 345–7, 592, 733, 734
Skolnick, J. 144, 1016, 1017
Sky News 200
Smart, C. 260, 412, 511, 517, 520, 522, 766,
    774, 775, 785, 786, 790
Smile, Samuel 72
Smith, Adam 265, 998
Smith, D. 547, 626, 785, 873, 1056
Smith, D. C. 829
Smith, D. J. 624, 706, 735, 736, 897
Smith, J. 103, 545, 546, 547
Smith, L. J. F. 778, 970
Smith, Maurice Hamblin 37–8, 38, 39, 43
Smith, Roger 18
Smith, R. S. 384
Snider, L. 919
SNOP (*Statement of National Objectives
    and Priorities*, Green Paper, 1984)
    1202
Snyder, H. N. 369
social censure 499–509
  hegemonic character of 501–2
  idea of the State 503–5
social class:
  crime and 176–7, 178
  drug use and 931–4
  risk of violence and 856–7
  see also underclass
social construction of crime 144
social context of crime:
  left realism and 486
social control 451–72, 1004–5
  criminology and the control of crime 452–3
  decarceration 460–4
  definition 451–2
  deviance and control, sociology of 453–60
  policing 1004
  post-social control 465–7
  prison to community 460–4

social control (*cont.*):
  re-emergence 465–6
  women and 464–5
Social Darwinism 63–4
social democracy 299
social deprivation:
  drug use and 934–5
social deviance 195–6
social disorder 345
social disorganization 310–11, 341, 342, 619,
  980
  anomie and 238–40
social exclusion 281
social justice 493
social psychological explanations of violence
  864–6
social security offenders 297
social theory:
  action, developments in the theory of
    421–4
  globalization and the problem of 'place'
    426–8
  risk and 424–6
  sentencing theories 1100–1
  study of crime and punishment and
    409–35
socialist feminism 512–13
Society for the Improvement of Prison
  Discipline 79
socio-economic deprivation 390
Socio-Legal Studies Association 2
sociocultural explanations of violence
  864–866
Sociological Review 38
sociological theories of crime 233–64; *see also*
  anomie theory
  control and space 246–50
    Chicago School 246–7; defensible space
    248–9
  control theory 240–3
  functionalist criminology 253–5
  labelling theory 255–7
  radical criminology 250–2
  rational choice theory 243–5, 293–4, 295
  routine activities theory 245
  signification 255–9
  social disorganization 310–11
  subcultural theory 257–9
sociology of deviance 453–60, 566
Solomka, B. 694
Solomos, J. 811
Soothill, K. 877–8
South, N. 946, 950–1, 951
South Asians:
  education 709
  proportion of population 707
  racial discrimination, personal experiences
    of 708–9
  see also ethnic minorities
Southall Riot 98

space 305 n.
  control and 246–50
  defensible space 248–9, 312, 973
  dilapidation of public space 345
  spatial dimension of crime 487
Sparks, R. 175, 580, 590, 846, 1183
Spear, B. 928, 952
specialization 380
specialized policing 1006
Speirits, K. 929
Spencer, John 45
Spillane, Mickey 205
Spitzer, S. 268 n.
Spurzheim, J. C. 26
squeegee merchants 105, 140 n.
Stander, J. 380
Stanko, E. A. 583, 588
Stanley, L. 521
Stapleton, W. V. 813
Star 200
state dependency 299
state-funded compensation 603–5
state theory 503
  advances in 505–7
  Marxist 503–5
Statistical Society of London 25
statistics *see* crime statistics
Stattin, H. 371, 377
Steadman, H. 687, 880
Steele, D. 937
Steer, J. 1069, 1071
Steffensmeier, D. J. 271–2, 764, 780, 817
Stenning, Philip 250
Stenzel, W. W. 978
Stephenson, G. 1064
stereotyping 1058–9
Stern, J. 270, 270 n.
Stern, V. 117, 1147, 1165
Stevenson, S. 112, 122
stock exchanges 287
Stones, R. 411, 418
stop-and-search powers 1054
  absence of controls on 1059
  bias, patterns of 1056–8
  Code of Practice 1054, 1058
  ethnic groups, exercise against 731–7
  increased use of 1059
  police discretion 1054–5
  reasonable suspicion 1026, 1054
  recording of reasons 1061, 1062
  undermining of rule of law 1059
Stouthamer-Loeber, M. 387
Strangeways Prison riot (1990) 121, 123, 1148
Straus, M. 851
Straw, Jack 105, 106
street brawls 155
Strengthening Punishment in the Community
  (Green Paper, 1995) 1196
Strodbeck, F. 808
Strong, S. 866

sub-cultures 489, 490
  criminal 276, 310 n.
  masculinity 869
  police sub-culture 869
  violence 864–6
  youth *see* youth sub-culture
sub-cultural theory 257–9, 483, 517, 561,
  618–22, 805
substance abuse, violent crime and 873–4; *see
  also* drugs
Suez Crisis, 1956 107
suffragettes 771
suicide, prisoners 676
Sullivan, W. C. 42, 43
summary-only offences 1104
Sumner, C. 467, 516
Sun 109–10, 197, 200
Superintendents' Association 1018
supervision orders 1125, 1205
surveillance 248, 249, 250
suspects:
  access to legal advice 1061–62
  confessions 1063–5
  detention without charge 1060–1
  due process protections 1052
  ethnic minorities as 720–49; *see also* ethnic
    minorities
  interrogation by police 1062–1065
  right of silence 1065–7
  stereotyping 1058–9
suspended sentences 1125
  attachment of compensation orders to 606
Sutcliffe, Peter 544, 545, 546, 548
Sutherland, E. 620
Sutherland, Edwin 307–8
Sutherland, E. H. 290, 816, 818, 895–901,
  902, 914, 917
Sutton, M. 982
Sutton, Willie 979
Suzy Lamplugh Trust 597
Sweden:
  sentencing reforms 1129
Switzerland 159 n.
Sykes, G. 782, 806, 807, 1177
symbolic interactionism 482, 483, 484
systematic theory of neighbourhood organiza-
  tion 339

target attractiveness 320
target-hardening 148, 968, 970, 986
Tarling, R. 372, 1107
Taub, Richard 347–8
Tavistock Clinic 39
tax evasion, prosecutions 297
tax havens 289
Taylor, A. 929
Taylor, I. 145, 810
Taylor, Lord 1113, 1114, 1119–20, 1127
Tchaikovsky, C. 1156
teaching of criminology 45, 47, 50

Tebbit, Norman 109
Teds 618
television *see* broadcasting; media representa-
  tions of crime
Templewood, Viscount 47
temporal aspect of crime, left realism and
  486–7
terrorist trials 127
Teske, R. 780
Tham, Henrik 299
Thatcher, Margaret 92, 100, 109, 130, 281, 940
Thatcherism 88, 288, 642–3
Theoretical Criminology 2
theory *see* social theory; sociological theories
  of crime
theory of action 421–4
Theret, Max 288
Theweleit, K. 548–9
thief sub-culture 1178
thief-takers 66
Thomas, David 1112
Thomson, J. Bruce 30, 34, 35
Thrasher, F. 619, 803–4, 812, 813, 814, 824
Tilley, N. 985
The Times 200
tobacco-related deaths 927
Toch, H. 868, 870, 871–2
Tolan, P. H. 372
Tombs, J. 914–15, 916–17, 1075
Tombs, S. 845
Tong, Rosemarie 512–13
Tonry, M. 399, 1156
trade unions:
  Labour Party law and order policies and
    102–4
trading justices 66
traditional representations of crime 21–3
traffic cases:
  fixed penalty notices 1105
training:
  sentencers 1127–8
  treatment and 1146–8, 1167, 1187
training prisons 1165, 1167
Transactions of the Medico-Legal Association
  38
transportation 77, 78, 79–80
Trasler, G. B. 394, 395
treatment and training 1146–8, 1167, 1187
Triads 898
trial:
  Crown Court 1104–5
  magistrates' courts 1104–5
  mentally disordered offenders 679–86
Tribune group 102
True Crimes 194
Tuke, H. 35
Tumim, Judge Stephen 123
Turkus, B. 827
Turnbull, C. 239
Tversky, A. 849

underclass 104–7, 282–3, 352, 454, 813–14
  crime, involvement in 282–4, 299
unemployment 281, 283
  crime and 267–81, 488–9
  free market experiment 284
  polarization of labour market 279–80
  youth unemployment 276–9, 623
unfitness to plead 668, 682
Uniform Crime Reports (FBI) 207
United Kingdom:
  Atomic Energy Authority Police 149
  costs of crime 296
  police research in 1000–3
United Nations:
  Declaration of the Basic Principles of
      Justice for Victims of Crime and Abuse
      of Power 599
  European Seminar on Crime 48
  Single Convention on Narcotic Drugs 939
United States:
  costs of crime 296
  crime surveys 162
  drug control 937
  drug trade 290–1
  imprisonment, rise in 477–8
  inequality and crime 284–5
  legal rights of victims 601
  moral panic about crime 478
  organized crime 823–8
  police research in 999–1000
  political corruption 824
  Presidential Commission on Law
      Enforcement 999–1000
  Prohibition 824
  sentencing reforms 1128
  victim impact statements 601
  youth gangs 813–14
  youth unemployment 276–9
    Mobilization for Youth programme
      277–8
University Grants Council 1
unlawfully obtained evidence
  exclusion of 1080–1
unmarried mothers 282, 283, 284
urban crime 306
Urry, John 285–6

Vagg, J. 249, 1057
Valachi, Joseph 827
Valin, Jonathan 205
Van Creveld, Martin 239–40
Van Dijk, J. 597
Vass, A. A. 1210
Venables, Jon 648
Verhulst, F. C. 379
victim-feminism 546
victim impact statements 601, 1100
victim movement 595–7
  rape crisis centres 597
  women's refuges 596, 597

victim-proneness 578
Victim Support 140, 595–6, 597, 603, 604
  financial backing 598
  Witness Service 600–1
victimization:
  differential patterns of 584–5
  impact of 590–3
  local surveys 583–6
  mass surveys 580–3
  risk of 581–2, 584, 587
    ethnic minorities 582, 584, 713, 749; fear
      of crime and 587–8; young people 635
  sexual 585–6
  social content 584
victims 145–7, 577–611
  blaming of 578, 579
  Council of Europe Convention 599
  crime fiction, portrayal in 209
  criminal justice and 602–7
  criminal justice system, role in 597–602
  ethnic minorities 711–20
    police, satisfaction with 717–18; racially-
      motivated crime 718–20; rates of
      victimization 712–17
  fear of crime 586–8
  impact of crime on 590–3
    differential impact 592; emotional effects
      591; isolated people 592; psychological
      effects 591–2; racial harassment 592;
      violent crime 591; vulnerability 592
  indirect 593
  information to 600
    One Stop Shop initiative (OSS) 600
  lifestyles 589–90
  media portrayal 201
  mediation schemes 602–3
  mobility 589–90
  multiple victimization 327, 592
  needs of 594–5
  outreach 596
  police response, satisfaction with 599–600
    ethnic minorities 717–18
  political concern 598, 607
  precipitation by 578, 579
  rights of 598–9
  secondary 593
  sexual offences, of 585–6
  statements 601–2
  statements of opinion 601
  surveys 586
    local surveys 583–6; national surveys
      580–3
  UN Declaration 599
  victim-offender mediation 1100
  victim-proneness 578
  victimology 577
    classical studies in 578–9
  witnesses, as 600–1
  women 585–6
  young people 634–5

Victim's Charter 598, 1100
Victim's Helpline 598
video films 648
Vietnam War 107
violence:
  attitudes to 843–7
  domestic *see* domestic violence
  explanations of 859–74
    biology 861–3; culture of masculinity
    868–9; genetic factors 862; individual-
    level violence 871–3; psychoanalytical
    and child psychology approaches
    863–4; rape 866–8; situational factors
    873–4; sociocultural and social
    psychological explanations 864–6;
    violence involving the police 869–71
  fear of 842
  mental disorder and 687
  risk of 848–59
    age factors 857; comparative data
    854–6; gender factors 850–3;
    occupation and 857–9; sexual violence
    853–4; social class 856–7
violent crime 136, 581–2, 841–89; *see also*
  homicide
  categories 841–2
  collective violence 843
  comparative data on violence rates 854–6
  dealing with 874–80
    homicide 878–80; incapacitation 876–7,
    879–80; rape 877–8; repeat offending
    875; violence against women 876
  drug-related crime 944
  effects on victims 591
  explanations of violence 859–74; *see also*
    violence
  gender factors 850–3, 865–6
  genocide 844–5
  instrumental violence 842–3
  juvenile offenders 630–1
  measuring violence 847
  moral panic 845
  police and 869–71
  reckless behaviour 841–2
  risk of violence *see* violence
  rural violence 846
  sexual violence *see* sexual violence
  violence against the person 152, 153,
    155
  women:
    violence against 850–3, 856; *see also*
    sexual violence; violence by 631
violent offender 876–7
violent video films 648
Vogler, R. 506
Vold, G. 16, 49, 265–6, 270–1
Von Hentig, H. 146, 578
Von Mayr, George 267, 270–1
vulnerability 592
vulnerable witnesses 600–1

Wadsworth, M. E. J. 391
Walker, Alan 283
Walker, M. A. 733, 734, 736, 738, 741,
  744
Walker, N. 693
Walker, Patrick Gordon 96
Wall Street Crash 619
Wallace, Edgar 205
Wallace, M. 551, 552
Waller, I. 146
Walsh, D. 821
Walsh, M. 817
Walsh, M. E. 817
Walton, P. 145 n.
Wambaugh, Joseph 204
war criminals 844
Ward Jouve, N. 545–6, 547
Wasilchick, J. 324–6
weapons-control policies 846
Webb, B. 970
Weber, M. 323 n., 417, 458, 741
Wedgewood, Josiah 1141
Weisburd, D. 897, 903, 916
welfare fraud 297
welfare programmes 282, 283
welfarism, legalism and 663
Wells, C. 845
Werner, E. E. 384
Wertham, Frederick 578
West, D. 548
West, Fred and Rosemary 850, 860
West Midlands Police Serious Crime Squad
  investigation 1052, 1064
Westwood, Vivienne 622
Wheeler, S. 916
White, J. L. 385
white-collar crime 181, 288–90, 299–300,
  891–923, 1086
  ambiguities 895–921
  ambivalent response to 911–21
  causes 895
    capitalism 905–7, explanation of 901–11
  contested concept 896–901
  definition 895
    contested concept 896–901
  distinctiveness of 907–9
  economic justifications 918
  handling of 895–6, 911–20
    difficulties of controlling 913; enforce-
    ment difficulties 913–14; prosecution
    912, 913
  organized crime and 898, 910
  ostensible legality, cover of 909
  public attitudes to 919
  regulation and self-regulation 916
Whitehouse, Mary 109
Whitelaw, William 642
Whitemoor Prison 121, 124
Whyte, W. F. 805
Widom, C. S. 388

Wiener, M. 17, 33
Wiers, Paul 270
Wikström, P.-O. H. 317–19, 332–3, 369, 372, 374
  tentative model for explaining location of offences 327–30
Wilczynski, A. 680
Wilde, Oscar 1165
Wiles, P. 144–45, 349, 624, 965, 980
Wilkins, L. 50, 234
Williams, Shirley 108
Williamson, T. 1066
Willis, C. 1056
Willis, Paul 549, 810, 811
Wilson, H. 387, 389
Wilson, Harold 90
Wilson, Harriet 242
Wilson, J. 862
Wilson, James Q. 299, 345, 346, 386, 395, 454, 981, 1020, 1021
Wilson, M. 863
Wilson, Sheena 980
Wilson, William Julius 239, 283, 341, 474, 475, 477
Windlesham, Lord 640, 642
Winner, Michael 194
Winter of Discontent (1978–9) 92, 98, 103
Wise, S. 521
Witness Service 600–1
witnesses:
  victims as 600–1
  vulnerable witnesses 600–1
Wolds Prison 1163
Wolfenstein, E. V. 552
Wolfgang, M. 146, 374, 375, 578, 863
Wolfson Foundation 47
women:
  community service 1212
  crime, involvement in 242–3, 517–18, 764–7, 775–6
    agency 776–7; control and conformity 788–90; double deviance 779–80; early studies of 762–4; female offenders 177–8, 777; feminist sceptics 790; gender gap 784–5; gender theories 785; marginalization 787–8; nature of female offending 629–31; patriarchy 785–7; peak age of offending 627; rediscovery of iniquity 777–8; routes to crime 776–7; theories 784–70; violent offences 631
  criminal behaviour 680
  delinquency 621–2, 811
  drugs trade and 821
  fear of crime 588
    lifestyle and mobility, effect on 590
  female-headed households 282, 283, 284
  female sub-culture 621–2
  feminism and criminology *see* feminist criminology

gangs, participation in 812
homicide by:
  diminished responsibility, defence of 685; infanticide 684
police officers, discrimination against female 1013
policing and 769–72
prison officers 1180
prisoners 1184
  growth in number of 1155–6
psychiatric defences 684, 685–6
sentencing and 772–3
social control and 464–5
victimization 770, 786
victims 252, 585
  sexual crime 585–6
violence against *see* sexual violence
women's prisons 781–2, 1166
women's refuges 596, 597, 777
Wood, D. 1099
Woodcock Report 1185
Woodhead, Sir Peter 1173
Woolf, Lord 121
Woolf Inquiry 96, 114, 116, 117, 123–124, 127, 690, 691, 696, 1077, 1149–51, 1166, 1169–71, 1172–3, 1182, 1186
Wootton Committee 940
work and leisure, changes in 480–1
working class communities 809
workplace:
  health and safety regulations, breaches of 842
  occupational injuries 593, 842
Worrall, A. 464, 779, 789
Wright, R. T. 180, 323, 326, 817
wrongful convictions 1079, 1080
  appeals 1083
  overturning of 1083
  preventive mechanisms 1080
  review mechanisms 1080–4
Wymott Prison 1183

Yablonsky, L. 804–5, 808
Yeager, P. 898, 904–5
Yorkshire Ripper 544, 545
Young, A. 412, 523–4, 787
Young, Ian 252
Young, J. 145 n., 170, 212, 234, 252, 281, 465, 515–16, 777
Young, M. 771
Young, R. 1053, 1061, 1062, 1068, 1076, 1078
young offender institutions 1165, 1167
young offenders *see* juvenile offenders
youth:
  adolescence, discovery of 614–17
  crime *see* juvenile crime
  delinquency *see* delinquency
  deviance and 613, 614–38, 805
  drug use 624–5, 632–4
  fin de siècle, at 623–5

gangs *see* youth gangs
police, attitudes to 635
post-war Britain 617–22
prisoners 1158–9
psychological disorders 624
sub-culture *see* youth sub-culture
unemployment 623
    crime and 276–9; Mobilization for Youth
      programme (USA) 277–8
victims 634–5
youth court 645 *see* juvenile court
youth crime *see* juvenile crime
youth culture 143
Youth Custody Centres 643
youth gangs 802, 803–5, 808, 831
    contemporary American research 813–14
    drugs trade and 814
    females in gangs 812
youth justice *see* juvenile justice

youth sub-culture 618, 805–6
    acid house 625
    black youth culture 811–12
    British studies 806–15
    dissociation 807–8
    mods and rockers 618, 809
    parent culture and 807–9
    punks 622
    skinheads 619, 809–10
    style 809–11
    Teds 618

Zedlewski, Edwin 295–6
Zedner, L. 181, 763, 767, 777, 781, 787,
    1085
Zeman, Thomas 26
zero tolerance 100, 106, 454, 981
Zito Trust 597
Zizek, S. 506